Air-Britain

Civil Aircraft Registers of the United Kingdom, Republic of Ireland and the Isle of Man 2009

© Air-Britain (Historians) Ltd 2009

Published by:

Air-Britain (Historians) Limited

Sales Department:

41 Penshurst Road, Leigh, Tonbridge, Kent TN11 8HL
e-mail: sales@air-britain.co.uk

Membership Enquiries:

1 Rose Cottages, 179 Penn Road,
Hazlemere, Bucks HP15 7NE
e-mail: membership@air-britain.co.uk

Web-site:

http://www.air-britain.com

ISBN 978-0-85130-415-1

Printed by Bell & Bain Ltd,
Thornliebank, Glasgow G46 7UQ

COVER PHOTOGRAPHS:

Front: Immaculate Skystar Kitfox 5 G-LESZ on a visit to Westfield Farm, Hailsham on 29.6.08. (Dave Partington)

Rear: Eurocopter EC.155B-1 of Bristow Helicopters seen on contract at Rotterdam 14.9.08. (Henk Wadman)

CZAW Sportcruiser G-VIIZ, an attractive all-metal contender for the Light Sport market. (Roger Birchall)

Most UK gliders and now registered under EASA requirements, including this LS4 G-SVNC which has had a number of previous identities and was noted resident at Nympsfield on 29.3.09. (Dave Partington)

CIVIL AIRCRAFT REGISTERS OF THE UNITED KINGDOM, REPUBLIC OF IRELAND AND THE ISLE OF MAN 2009

45th Year of Publication – Collated and Edited by Tony Pither

©Air-Britain (Historians)Ltd 2009

ISBN 978-0-85130-415-1   ISSN 0264-5270

Air-Britain supports the fight against terrorism and the efforts of the Police and other Authorities in protecting airports and airfields from criminal activity.

If you see anything suspicious do not hesitate to call the
Anti-Terrorist Hotline 0800 789321
or alert a Police Officer.

INTRODUCTION AND EDITORIAL

Welcome to the 45th Air-Britain United Kingdom and Ireland Civil Aircraft and Glider Register including the Isle of Man Civil Aircraft Register. My main rôle has been to maintain the basic details of the UK Register listed in SECTION 1. Generally, this is as provided by the Civil Aviation Authority (CAA) from their G-INFO database. This is now achieved with the unfailing support of Alan Johnson, Bernard Martin and Graham Slack with regular updates from the database provided by Dave Reid. The Irish data in SECTION 2 and Isle of Man data in SECTION 3 is updated by myself. The other important members of the team are Paul Hewins who maintains responsibility for updating details of Overseas civil registered aircraft located in the UK & Ireland (SECTION 5) and Richard Cawsey who oversees the British Gliding Association registration details (SECTION 6). SECTION 4 focuses on the thriving UK preservation scene and specifically concentrates on the historical aspects of those aircraft which have been listed on the UK & Irish civil aircraft registers over many years and are still extant worldwide – this section is still maintained by Barrie Womersley. Most of these are de-registered but they can still be located albeit, some-times, with different identities. The main proviso is that it is possible to view them in Museums around the world and in easily accessible private collections – we hope that this is maintained following the major financial crisis affecting most of the world. One change in SECTION 6 is the addition of a cross reference of former BGA numbers to the new CAA registrations. Finally, SECTION 7 consists of a series of Indices designed to help the reader track down specific aircraft.

A fair percentage of the UK Register is devoted to amateur kit-built aircraft, microlights or hot air balloons. This is the area where the CAA devolves some regulatory tasks to other bodies although overall responsibility for safety regulation remains with them. This devolved segment is a broad one and covers four large groups involved in recreational aviation. These are the British Balloon and Airship Club (BBAC) which governs balloon and airship activity, the Light Aircraft Association (LAA), which regulates amateur-built aircraft and the British Microlight Aircraft Association (BMAA) which regulates microlight activity, The fourth body, which is outside this ambit of this book, is the British Parachute Association (BPA) which controls parachuting. As the majority of balloons and airships are produced commercially we are more concerned with the role of the BMAA and LAA. The BMAA is responsible for regulating those microlights which meet certain criteria. They must either have a wing that is flexible, and can move relative to the main body of the aircraft, or a fixed wing that is rigidly attached to the aircraft's body. The total number of microlight aircraft under BMAA regulations on the current register is over 400. They all operate on a Permit to Fly rather than a CofA. The LAA is responsible for the supervision of aircraft that are amateur-built by individuals, as opposed to commercial manufacturers. They, also, operate on a Permit to Fly (PtoF) rather than a Certificate of Airworthiness (CofA). In addition the LAA regulates a significant number of microlight aircraft, and vintage and classic aircraft, mainly types which do not qualify for an International Civil Aviation Organisation (ICAO) compliant CofA because of the demise of the manufacturer or other design authority.

Many amateur-built aircraft and microlights are now assembled by owners from kits of components supplied by commercial manufacturers to aid construction (the key is that 51% of the work is performed by the 'builder'). To keep within the regulations it is important to avoid iden-tifyng an aircraft as a factory built specimen as this would exclude it from the BMAA and LAA Permit system and require it to hold an ICAO compliant CofA. Thereby, both the BMAAand LAA have introduced their own dedicated plans numbering system designed to identify, specif-ically, those aircraft falling under their devolved regulatory powers. It is this BMAA and LAA reference which is used when a builder-owner seeks to register his aircraft with the CAA and it is this reference which is shown on the CAA's G-INFO database. Unfortunately for the aviation historian, this methodology has the effect of obscuring the real commercial construction (kit) number of the aircraft. Our thanks are due to those devoted members, notably Bernard Martin and Barry Taylor, who for a number of years have set out to establish and record the missing details by either developing commercial contacts or by physical examination of such aircraft. Elsewhere, some kit data has also been unearthed from web-sites, notably those of Europa and Jabiru. A look at SECTION 1 shows that there are still many new aircraft where little prime identity data is recorded other than BMAA and LAA project details. So, it is important to hunt out and record this information before it disappears!

I am grateful to all the following contributors this year. My thanks go to, Pete Bish, Jim Brazier, Peter Budden, Nigel Burch, Phil Butler, Ian Burnett, Mike Cain, Ian Callier, Richard Cawsey, Terry Dann, Phil Dunnington, Kevin Dupuy, Colin Frost, Peter Gerhardt, Paul Hewins, Nigel Hitchman, Alan Johnson, Nigel and Phil Kemp, Bob Kent, Bernard Martin, Dave Partington, Nigel Ponsford, Dave Reid, Bob Sauvary, Rod Simpson, Graham Slack, Andy Smith, Terry Smith, Tony Smith, Martyn Steggalls, Barry V Taylor, D Theobald, John Tietjen, Barrie Towey, Pete Webber and Barrie Womersley, and to all those members who supply regular updates either direct or via ABIX and, or, the A-B Sightings web-site. Once again I am indebted to Dave Partington for his work in completing the book. A final very special thanks goes to Carolyn for her patience.

As mentioned by Barrie last year the UK Register of Civil Aircraft exceeded 20,000 currently registered aircraft for the first time in early 2008 and at the beginning of 2009 it had grown by a further 1441 aircraft during 2008. The rapid growth in numbers on the UK Register, is primar-ily due to the addition of gliders as part of the transition to EASA requirements – these account for over 1100 of the 2008 changes. Elsewhere you can find the CAA's summary of UK registered aircraft from 1st January 1984 to 1st January 2008 and further statistical data is available on their web-site. All official UK aircraft registration and ownership information shown is published by the CAA and this includes the issue and status of each Certificate of Airworthiness. The CAA registration and British Gliding Association data is correct to the first week of February 2009. The Irish Aviation Authority data is correct to the end of January 2009.

Tony Pither   15th February 2009
65, Dacombe Drive
Upton,
Poole,
Dorset, BH16 5JJ

email: tonypither@talktalk.net

A BRIEF HISTORICAL LOOK AT THE UK's CIVIL AIRCRAFT REGULATIONS

BACKGROUND

The Air Board was formed in May 1916 and established the Civil Aerial Transport Committee (CATC) a year later. The CATC's primary brief was to report on the measures necessary to develop aviation for civil and commercial purposes. Meantime the Air Force Bill received the Royal Assent in November 1917 leading to the creation of the Air Council and the Air Ministry. Although the Armistice was negotiated in November 1918 official restrictions on civil flying were not lifted as, technically, a state of war continued until the signing of the Peace Treaty in July 1919.

During the ensuing years, and largely instigated by de Havillands, there was considerable pressure on the Air Ministry to relax control of private aviation. In July 1933 the Secretary of State, Marquess of Londonderry appointed an independent committee under Lord Gorrell, chairman of the Royal Aeronautical Society. The Committee was charged "To examine the requirements of the present air navigation regulations, with particular reference to those governing private flying in such matters as certificates of airworthiness; to consider whether, and in what respects, the present system of control by the Air Ministry should be modified by way of devolution or otherwise; to make recommendations in regard to these and any cognate questions which might remitted to them by the Secretary of State". Initial investigations seemed to be directed towards opposing proposals for the UK to relinquish control to an international authority as discussed at a League of Nation's Disarmament Conference held at Geneva earlier that year. The UK Government had no desire to follow such thinking: although the country was in depression private flying continued to progress. In fact the early 1930s saw an expansion of private flying with an increase in licensed civil aerodromes including several new municipal airfields and, in addition, there was a steady growth in international and internal air services. But there was little increase in privately owned aeroplanes: in 1933 there were just 1055 aircraft on the Register of Aircraft of which only 400 were so defined.

The report of the Gorrell Committee on "Control of Private Flying" was issued in July 1934. The Committee was not unanimous in its findings: one member wanted control to remain with the Air Ministry whilst two others recommended immediate divorce in every aspect of civil aviation. Broadly the Committee agreed that airworthiness regulations and the system of checking design and construction should be handed to an independent body to be named "The Air Registration Board". The Air Ministry duly agreed that the new body would control the system of approved firms, airworthiness requirements, modification procedure, renewal of Certificates of Airworthiness, inspection certificates and supervision of competency of ground engineers. It was also agreed in principle that foreign C of As should have validity on a reciprocal basis. Although required for club aircraft the Air Council was prepared to make them optional for private flying and aerial work. Third party insurance became mandatory. Interestingly, gliders came under these general provisions.

In 1936 the Air Navigation Bill became law and provided for the formation of an Air Registration Board (ARB) based on the Gorrell Report proposal that the Certification of Airworthiness of civil aircraft should devolve upon a "statutory autonomous board"formed from the the the British Corporation Register and Lloyds Register. The constituent groups were drawn from the Society of British Aircraft Constructors (SBAC), the two Insurance registers, commercial operators, and the Royal Aeronautical Society. The board was registered as a company on 26th February 1937. By 1939 the ARB's responsibilites had grown. The Register of Aircraft now contained 1,725 machines and some 75% were airworthy whilst several prototypes were flying under "B" Conditions procedures, see Section 7 Part 3.

Despite the title the ARB had little to do with the issue ofCertificates of Registration for civil aircraft. This was left to the Ministry of Civil Aviation which was created in 1944. In the mid 1950s this department merged with the Ministry of Transport to become the Ministry of Transport and Civil Aviation (MTCA). Responsibility passed through a series of departments before the CAAwas born. In 1967 the Government set up a committee under the chairmanship of Sir Ronald Edwards to inquire into Britain's civil air transport. The committee's findings were published in 1969 and included a recommendation to establish a civil aviation authority. The Civil Aviation Act of 1971 created the new authority, as a public corporation, and it assumed full responsibilities on 1 April 1972. Thus, the Air Registration Board was embodied into the new CAA. Originally the CAA was established as an independent specialist aviation regulator and provider of air traffic services but following the separation of National Air Traffic Services from the CAA in 2001, the CAA now functions solely in the former role with all civil aviation regulatory functions (economic regulation, airspace policy, safety regulation and consumer protection) integrated within a single specialist body. It should be noted that the UK Government requires that the CAA's costs are met entirely from the charges on those whom it regulates. Unlike many other countries there is no direct Government funding of the CAA's work.

REGISTRATION OF AIRCRAFT

There were no international regulations controlling the registration of civil aircraft within the United Kingdom at the end of the First World War. Consequently the Air Ministry's Civil Air Department specified a system of temporary registration marks in May 1919 but this practice prevailed only until July of that year. Two temporary registers were established for (i) military aircraft sold for civil purposes and already bearing Service serials - existing aircraft would be allocated their serials as registration marks with the Service ring markings obliterated and (ii) new aircraft and those built from spares - they were allocated marks in a special Service sequence commencing at K100. Subsequently, a number of these aircraft were re-allocated registrations in the first permanent register which replaced the two temporary registers. This was inaugurated on 31st July 1919 and ran until 29th July 1928 when the registration G-EBZZ had been issued - see Section 1 Part 1. Meantime, the civil use of Airships and Balloons came under the supplementary air traffic regulations of the Air Navigation Act 1911-1919. and a separate lighter-than-air register series, G-FAAA to G-FAAZ, was established until the end of 1928.

With the growth of international civil aviation the Director-General of Civil Aviation decided to terminate the first series and he authorised a new sequence of registration marks commencing at G-AAAA including airships and balloons. This second permanent register was introduced retrospectively from 30th July 1928 and, in effect, continues today - see Section 1 Part 2. Registrations were usually allocated in alphabetical sequence until the late 1970s although there have been numerous sporadic exceptions to this rule throughout this time. The G-AAAA to G-AZZZ series was allocated by July 1972 and a new series G-BAAA onwards was used in the same month: this series became exhausted in June 2001. Notwithstanding this, and commencing in 1974, many registrations were issued ahead of the natural alphabetical sequence and came from all of the forthcoming G-Bxxx to G-Zxxx series, examples being Accountant G-ATEL (August 1957), Concorde G-BSST (May 1968) and Harrier G-VSTO (June 1971). The advance G-Bxxx registrations were eventually subsumed within the proper sequence and we moved on to the G-Cxxx series which has been in regular use since June 2001 and G-Dxxx was populated by a lot of gliders from 2007.

Small parts of an original G-Cxxx series were allocated to Canadian civilian aircraft from 20th April 1920 until 31st December 1928 commencing with G-CAAA. Registration G-CAWI was the last to be issued although G-CAXP had been formally allocated earlier in May 1928 being ex G-EBXP. On 1st January 1929 Canada adopted the nationality marks CF, followed by a hyphen, and three registration marks running from AAA to ZZZ. Those aircraft registered previously with G-CAxxx markings continued to display them until they were retired from service. At least two aircraft were still known to carry the old series markings in 2005, namely Fairchild FC-2W2, G-CART and DH.60X Moth G-CAUA. In addition, two separate series of quasi-military markings were created for aircraft operated on Canadian Government Air Operations by the Royal Canadian Air Force (RCAF). Series G-CYAA to G-CYHD was used from 18th June 1920 to 11th June 1926 and G-CYUR to G-CYZZ, but not sequentially, from 15th March 1927 to 18th July 1931. The batch from G-CYHE to G-CYUQ were not allotted as the RCAF were using a numerical series for registration marks on aircraft in their use by this time and marks were being displayed in an abbreviated form, that is the last two letters only. Aircraft still wearing these marks were absorbed into the existent RCAF numerical series by 1939. Consequently, the Civil Aviation Authority has not allocated any further registrations from the G-CAxx range although nine advance registrations were issued between December 1977 and March 1999 and remain extant. These were not allocated previously although two were reserved in 1928.

In addition, two special registrations series have been used as shown below:

i)   During 1979 and 1980 specific alpha-numeric registrations G-N81AC and G-N94AA to G-N94AE which were used for British Airways' Concordes,

ii) From 1981 until 1998 registration batches G-MBAA to G-MBZZ, G-MGAA to G-MGZZ, G-MJAA to G-MJZZ, G-MMAA to G-MNZZ, G-MTAA to G-MTZZ and G-MYAA to G-MZZZ which were allocated originally for microlight aircraft use. Subsequently, other aircraft can now be found within these batches.

A third series was established in January 1982 when registration blocks G-FYAA to G-FYZZ were confined to Minimum Lift Balloons. G-FYAA was allocated on 4th January 1982 and G-FYNC, the latest, was allocated on 4th August 1986. This series is still in existence.

The CAA web-site explains the Availability and Reservation of UK Registration Marks and is recommended reading.

USER GUIDE

There are a number of purposes to this annual volume. The primary one is to list all aircraft on the current civil aircraft registers, giving full details of types and previous identities, registered ownership and/or operator, probable home base and certification of airworthiness status. This information reproduces, expands upon and amplifies the official country registers. However, we go well beyond that; included are all other known, but no longer currently registered, UK and Irish aircraft noted in a reasonably identifiable condition and which are displayed or on/for rebuild. Some of these are held for instructional, fire or spares use. The majority of these are in located in the UK and Ireland but a few are resident abroad. In addition we detail the extensive numbers of foreign registered aircraft now located in both the UK and Ireland, some of which may aspire to G-, M- or EI- registrations in due course. Finally, we include a comprehensive listing of all gliders in use throughout the area in order to present an all-inclusive guide of the civil aviation scene.

Secondly, on a more technical level, we cater for the aviation specialist and historian who wishes to know more about a particular aircraft by providing detailed information such as the reasons for that aircraft's non-airworthy state where known and if applicable. Also, it has been our policy for many years to record engine details in the text, for example the modification of an airframe to receive a non standard engine has to be approved by the CAA and is then recorded in their Register. When the first microlights appeared in 1981 there was little standardisation and, consequently, we recorded all engine information. Now the majority are produced commercially, either in whole or kit form, engine fitment is standard to type in many cases. Accordingly, a default fit is shown in the Index at Section 7 Part 10 whilst variations remain identified in Section 1. A similar situation exists for LAA and BMAA approved, and other miscellaneous imported, home-build types.

A guide to the main text is as follows:

Registration   Current UK registrations are set out in alphabetic order in Section1, Parts 1 and 2. Aircraft no longer currently registered shown in Part 3. Those aircraft allocated and cancelled in the period since the last register are shown in Part 4. A few aircraft, either real or static reproductions are identified in fictitious UK civil marks for display purposes and are identified in Section 7. Those marks which have been re-issued or re-allotted, particularly either if the first holder or allottee did not use the marks or they were not allocated at the time, are shown with a suffix, for example (2) after the registration.

Type   We adopt the official type description as set down by the manufacturer or designer. Where there is doubt, reference is made to the relevant editions of "Jane's All the World Aircraft", "Airlife's World Aircraft", "The General Aviation Handbook" and the "World Directory of Leisure Aviation". Indication is given if the manufacturer is a successor company or a licence builder - although not always if it is merely a sub-contractor. Under this column, we show engine types in parenthesis if the engine is non-standard for all LAA and BMAA approved and other home-build types and for those vintage and classic aircraft where engines do vary. Standard fit engines for most LAA and BMAA approved types are shown in the respective Indices in Section 7. In addition, and especially for the aforementioned types, we show the manufacturer. Final explanatory notes comment on the airframe's identity and the true position where it is at variance with official records. Numbers quoted in brackets for certain BMAA homebuilt types and their engines refer to detailed variants listed in their Homebuild Aircraft Data Sheets. These can be accessed at www.bmaa.org/techinfo.asp from which the HADS option can be selected and for each type listed the numbered variants can be displayed in full.

Construction Number   Also often referred to as the "Manufacturer's Serial Number (MSN)" the construction number (c/n) is quoted in all official registers. The c/n should be a constant traceable reference throughout an airframe's life by means of a unique identification plate or stamp contained somewhere on the airframe. Homebuilt and kit build examples may have a home-builder's personal reference number as well. Some aircraft have more than one build number, for example LAA and BMAA approved types. Both Associations use dedicated project number (pr.no.) series for their approved designs and these are often accepted as "construction numbers" in the absence of a more specific reference. The CAA records these as their prime identifier. However, most LAA and BMAA examples will have Manufacturers' Plans or Kit numbers and we quote these as our prime reference where known. In these cases the LAA and BMAA pr.nos. are shown with the individual builder details. In the case of self-assembly often main components carry adhesive labels with individual kit numbers when packed by manufacturers but during build these are often discarded and, without any visible identity on a particular airframe, traceability is lost, unfortunately.

The Irish equivalent of the LAA is the Society of Amateur Aircraft Constructors (SAAC), and various aircraft use a SAAC allocation as their construction number.

Production of early weightshift microlights were identfied with two separate construction numbers covering the Trike unit and the Sailwing respectively. As a rule the CAA only records the latter number although we record both numbers where known. Nonetheless, manufacturers Hornet, Mainair and Medway issue a composite construction number comprising of both units and this is generally adopted by the CAA. For example, Mainair Rapier G-BYBV is officially registered as c/n 1183-1198-7-W986 but only the first nine digits form the trike c/n.

Previous Identities   These are set out in reverse order with the most recent identity first. Some of these may have been issued several times and are noted with a suffix as stated above. Registrations shown in parenthesis have been allotted but were never officially used to the best of our knowledge. The nationality of foreign military serials is indicated only where it may not be apparent. Manufacturers' test marks, also known as "B Conditions" identities, are given where known.

Registration Date   This is the date of the original registration for those particular marks even where subsequently removed and restored.

Owner (Operator)   This is the registered owner for current aircraft as recorded in CAA records. Where the operator is known to be different this is shown in parenthesis. Included under this column are details of the latest reported status, for example if the C of A is not current or the aircraft is known to be under repair plus details of any names and, in particular, any military colour schemes and marks worn. Some aircraft are shown as temporary un-registered ("Temp unregd"); this is where the CAA has not received an application from a new owner following a sale. Usually the CAA gives a period of discretion and if no response is received the Certificate is cancelled and the aircraft is not permitted to fly. Such action usually stimulates the new owner to produce the relevant documentation.

(Unconfirmed) Base The information in this column is not guaranteed: there is no official information. Reports by members and other readers who visit airfields and strips are perused to compile this column. Aircraft change base frequently. Balloons are generally shown as being based at their owners' registered address unless we have further information. Bases for active flexwing aircraft can present a problem as trikes are often stored at owners' homes after flying whilst corresponding sailwings are pegged out at base airfields. When the location is uncertain the owner's hometown is shown in parenthesis.

Readers are reminded that the identification of a base, particularly if it is a private strip, is not an invitation to visit and in a number of cases visiting is actively discouraged because of previous abuses. We recognise the need for privacy in this area and consequently not all information held is published. Readers are also directed to the AB-IX Bases database which has current details of airfields and listings of occupants. This is updated frequently.

CERTIFICATES OF AIRWORTHINESS (CofA) STATUS

The formation of the European Aviation Safety Agency (EASA) and the implementation of the associated European legislation has changed the responsibilities and procedures for the regulation of continuing airworthiness. Consistent with these developments, substantial changes have been made to CAA mandatory airworthiness information. I am extremely grateful to Bill Taylor for his time, patience and input in providing a full explanation of the current situation, and I hope he does not mind me using some of his words verbatim.

The law giving effect to the EASA rules came into effect on 30 September 2003 and required full implementation by September 2008; as a result the CAA decided that those aircraft renewing their national CoA up to September 2005 would be granted a full three-year full CofA. Those due renewal two years before September 2008 got a two-year national CofA and those that renewed in the last year were granted one year – as a result all UK-registered aircraft classified as an EASA type would have its national CofA expire in the 12 months 1st October 2008 to 30th September 2009. These new EASA CofAs are now non-expiring, but they have to be accompanied by an ARC (Airworthiness Review Certificate) which has meant headaches for maintenance organisations, but all EASA types will no longer have a CofA expiry date. The ARC date will change each year, and this will be shown in future editions of this register – if this date is not tracked it will be difficult to identify if an aircraft is temporarily withdrawn or undergoing repair etc.

As a direct result of the European legislation UK-registered aircraft were divided into two groups:
- *"EASA aircraft"*; that is, aircraft subject to regulation by EASA; and
- *"Non-EASA aircraft"*; that is ,aircraft that remain subject to regulation by the CAA.

The specific aircraft are detailed in CAP747.

CofA Validity: Information is taken from information published by the CAA. The date indicates the currency of the aircraft's certificate and details of the coding suffix letters applied are set out below [as mentioned above the EASA dates relate to the expiry of the ARC]. In Section 1 the codings shown after the date of expiry indicate the CofA Certification category. The absence of a code letter means an aircraft holds a Private category CofA of either one or three year's duration. Where a CofA has expired or lapsed and an aircraft has been reported since that date further details are shown. Hopefully further information will be provided next year as the situation becomes clearer.

Codes used are as follows:-

      E: EASA Standard CofA – in future this shows the expiry of the ARC [EASA CofAs are non-expiring];

      R: Restricted CofA – this now covers 'orphan' aircraft where the original design authority no longer exists but still come under EASA control;

      S: Standard - national legislation;

      T: Transport – were issued to any Passenger aircraft operated for hire or reward, usually for either one or three years duration. No longer issued and only a few existing aircraft remain in this category;

      P: Permit to Fly - originally introduced in December 1935, but then lapsed during the Second World War, this system was reactivated in 1950. It covers homebuilder, vintage and microlight aircraft. The major criterion set out by the LAA is that the aircraft must be amateur built by it's owner in the UK. A homebuilder must spend at least 500 hours in completing the project for it to qualify under the Permit scheme as homebuilt. Permits are issued by the CAA on the recommendation of the LAA. It is the "prime document" and legalises flight of a Permit aircraft. The Permit is issued for the life of the aircraft but is only valid when certain conditions are fulfilled. The most fundamental of these is the Certificate of Validity (CofV) which is issued by the LAA following a satisfactory report concerning the annual inspection and test flying of the aircraft. A second 'P' now applies to aircraft operating under an EASA Permit to Fly;

      A: Aerial Work - this category normally indicates aerial advertising, mainly by hot air balloons, and a few banner towing aircraft but again is no longer available and hot-air balloons, in particular, now have EASA CofAs;

      X: Non-expiring Exemptions were issued originally to early microlights and hot air balloons. As at early 2008 only a few remained. However, a number of aircraft have now been declared to the BMAA as withdrawing from (or not requiring) the permit to fly scheme and they are now operating under the "Sub-115" exemption granted by the CAA whereby the aircraft effectively becomes "self-certified" by the pilot (type as listed by BMAA)

x

UK REGISTERED AIRCRAFT AS AT 1ST JANUARY EACH YEAR

Aircraft Class	MTOW kg	1985	1986	1987	1988	1989	1990	1991	1992	1993	1994	1995	1996	1997	1998	1999	2000	2001	2002	2003	2004	2005	2006	2007	2008	2009	change since 2008
AIRSHIP (GAS-FILLED)	1 - 750 kg	2	2	3	2	3	5	5	5	5	4	4	4	4	3	3	3	3	0	0	0	0	0	0	0	2	2
AIRSHIP (GAS-FILLED)	751 - 5700 kg	3	3	3	4	4	7	7	7	7	6	6	3	0	3	3	3	0	4	5	5	5	5	3	3	3	0
AIRSHIP (GAS-FILLED)	5701 - 15000 kg	6	6	6	7	6	3	7	4	5	2	1	1	1	0	0	0	0	0	0	0	0	0	0	0	0	0
AIRSHIP (HOT AIR)	1 - 750 kg	17	21	20	23	29	31	28	28	29	27	27	26	21	19	16	18	14	10	11	10	10	9	8	8	8	0
AIRSHIP (HOT AIR)	751 - 5700 kg	4	3	2	2	2	7	7	9	11	9	9	10	13	15	18	18	18	14	15	15	13	13	13	13	11	-2
BALLOON (GAS-FILLED)	Not known	0	0	0	0	0	0	0	0	0	0	0	0	0	0	0	0	0	0	0	0	0	0	0	6	0	-6
BALLOON (GAS-FILLED)	1 - 750 kg	0	0	0	0	0	0	0	0	0	0	0	0	0	0	0	0	0	0	0	0	0	0	0	0	6	6
BALLOON (GAS-FILLED)	751 - 5700 kg	1	0	0	0	1	0	0	0	0	0	0	0	0	0	0	0	0	0	0	0	0	0	0	0	6	6
BALLOON (GAS/HOT AIR)	Not known	0	0	0	0	1	0	0	2	2	0	0	0	1	2	0	2	2	3	0	0	3	0	0	0	3	3
BALLOON (GAS/HOT AIR)	1 - 750 kg	0	0	0	0	1	0	2	2	2	2	3	2	1	2	2	2	2	2	2	5	5	0	0	0	1	0
BALLOON (GAS/HOT AIR)	751 - 5700 kg	1	0	0	0	1	0	0	0	0	0	0	0	1	2	2	2	2	5	6	5	5	5	4	4	4	0
BALLOON (HOT AIR)	Not known	99	114	118	134	147	159	167	162	168	156	158	157	154	148	134	138	142	116	114	107	108	105	102	102	87	-15
BALLOON (HOT AIR)	1 - 750 kg	315	354	402	443	502	584	636	662	659	635	660	674	684	673	663	680	699	624	612	626	636	641	652	657	677	20
BALLOON (HOT AIR)	751 - 5700 kg	109	133	175	237	310	396	606	660	705	756	801	869	881	912	912	955	936	955	961	1000	1043	1056	1090	1103	13
BALLOON (HOT AIR)	5701 - 15000 kg	4	6	7	8	9	8	8	7	6	6	6	6	5	4	4	4	4	4	4	4	4	4	4	4	0	0
BALLOON (MINIMUM LIFT)	Not known	506	500	504	497	246	245	243	245	245	163	172	171	168	169	150	150	150	118	99	99	99	99	100	100	100	0
FIXED-WING AMPHIBIAN	1 - 750 kg	4	4	4	4	6	5	5	5	5	6	6	7	7	7	7	7	6	6	6	7	7	7	7	7	8	0
FIXED-WING AMPHIBIAN	751 - 5700 kg	2	2	3	3	6	5	6	7	9	8	8	8	9	8	10	10	9	9	8	9	9	10	11	12	12	0
FIXED-WING AMPHIBIAN	5701 - 15000 kg	1	1	1	1	2	0	1	2	2	2	2	0	1	1	1	1	0	0	0	0	0	0	0	0	0	0
FIXED-WING LANDPLANE	1 - 750 kg	1766	1845	1855	1879	1969	2143	2295	2289	2385	2507	2593	2657	2712	2758	2827	2813	2824	2832	2859	2914	2994	3022	3077	3153	3186	33
FIXED-WING LANDPLANE	751 - 5700 kg	4019	4219	4291	4459	4807	5003	5176	5228	5187	5130	5075	5043	5111	5190	5292	5347	5429	5442	5461	5556	5647	5711	5822	5887	6000	113
FIXED-WING LANDPLANE	5701 - 15000 kg	175	185	191	204	221	236	256	292	288	278	279	285	257	257	254	254	262	276	267	254	254	253	257	258	270	12
FIXED-WING LANDPLANE	15001 - 50000 kg	200	196	200	218	243	251	273	274	261	263	261	241	246	251	280	289	288	296	307	264	271	256	272	257	270	13
FIXED-WING LANDPLANE	>50000 kg	229	233	231	254	284	324	336	358	380	388	396	401	406	439	499	541	592	624	645	644	662	679	712	760	760	0
FIXED-WING SEAPLANE	1 - 750 kg	0	0	0	0	0	0	0	0	0	0	0	0	0	0	0	0	0	0	0	0	0	0	0	0	0	0
FIXED-WING SEAPLANE	751 - 5700 kg	0	0	0	0	1	1	1	2	2	3	3	2	2	2	2	2	2	2	2	3	3	0	2	2	3	1
FIXED-WING SEAPLANE	15001 - 50000 kg	0	0	0	0	1	0	0	0	0	0	0	0	0	0	0	0	0	0	0	0	0	0	0	0	0	0
FIXED-WING SELF-LAUNCHING MOTOR GLIDER	751 - 5700 kg	111	121	126	131	143	145	157	162	184	186	193	193	196	199	201	202	203	203	199	204	204	204	206	206	209	3
FIXED-WING SELF-LAUNCHING MOTOR GLIDER	1 - 750 kg	25	35	52	52	52	51	52	52	54	48	46	46	49	56	62	66	70	70	70	71	73	76	76	80	86	6
GLIDER	1 - 750 kg	0	0	0	0	0	0	0	0	0	0	0	0	0	0	0	0	0	0	0	0	0	43	147	1094	2241	1147
GLIDER	751 - 5700 kg	13	14	13	14	7	6	6	9	9	9	8	9	8	7	7	7	7	1	0	1	2	2	2	13	17	4
GYROPLANE	1 - 750 kg	115	120	129	132	160	200	226	209	217	227	243	254	258	258	263	242	233	242	244	247	250	248	259	277	305	28
GYROPLANE	751 - 5700 kg	1	1	1	2	1	2	2	1	1	2	3	3	3	3	0	2	0	0	0	0	0	1	1	1	1	0
HANG GLIDER	1 - 750 kg	0	0	0	0	0	0	0	0	0	0	0	0	0	0	0	0	7	10	11	12	12	13	13	13	13	0
HELICOPTER	1 - 750 kg	17	27	43	66	124	188	231	245	254	244	235	228	231	242	262	270	275	267	273	277	291	293	288	289	279	-10
HELICOPTER	751 - 5700 kg	413	448	448	446	491	573	595	574	541	507	515	532	552	561	642	673	715	755	794	814	882	952	1026	1120	1136	16
HELICOPTER	5701 - 15000 kg	93	92	92	85	85	81	86	83	81	81	78	78	76	73	76	70	67	68	67	68	65	69	72	81	80	-1
HELICOPTER	15001 - 50000 kg	4	4	4	4	3	0	0	0	0	0	0	0	0	0	0	0	0	0	0	0	0	0	0	0	0	0
MICROLIGHT	1 - 750 kg	1580	1901	2300	2629	3012	3298	3050	3194	3347	3337	3266	3207	3231	3314	3450	3548	3478	3531	3618	3828	4070	4118	4254	4392	4447	55
TOTAL		9836	10594	11225	11934	12872	13958	14350	14710	15017	14941	15015	15059	15303	15594	16013	16293	16473	16474	16663	17013	17588	17894	18445	18890	21331	1441

Aircraft Class	Weight group	1985	1986	1987	1988	1989	1990	1991	1992	1993	1994	1995	1996	1997	1998	1999	2000	2001	2002	2003	2004	2005	2006	2007	2008	2009	change since 2008
AIRSHIP	All weights	32	35	34	38	46	53	50	51	54	47	47	44	40	40	40	42	33	28	31	30	29	27	24	24	24	0
BALLOON	All weights	529	608	702	821	966	1146	1302	1437	1499	1505	1586	1650	1730	1727	1693	1757	1829	1694	1700	1713	1763	1806	1822	1862	1883	21
BALLOON (MINIMUM LIFT)	All weights	506	500	504	497	246	245	243	245	245	163	172	171	168	169	150	150	150	118	99	99	99	99	100	100	100	0
FIXED WING	All weights	6397	6688	6777	7024	7538	7970	8350	8448	8531	8585	8623	8645	8761	8915	9165	9263	9412	9487	9555	9650	9848	9943	10157	10338	10510	172
FIXED WING SLMG	All weights	136	156	178	183	193	196	209	214	238	234	239	239	245	255	263	268	273	273	270	274	276	280	280	286	295	9
GLIDER	All weights	13	14	13	14	7	6	6	9	9	9	8	9	8	7	7	7	7	1	1	1	2	45	149	1107	2258	1151
GYROPLANE	All weights	116	121	130	134	161	202	228	210	218	229	246	257	261	261	265	244	233	242	244	247	251	249	260	278	306	28
HANG GLIDER	All weights	0	0	0	0	0	0	0	0	0	0	0	0	0	0	0	0	7	10	11	12	12	13	13	13	13	0
HELICOPTER	All weights	527	571	587	601	703	842	912	902	876	832	828	838	859	906	980	1013	1057	1090	1134	1159	1238	1314	1386	1490	1495	5
MICROLIGHT	All weights	1580	1901	2300	2629	3012	3298	3050	3194	3347	3337	3266	3207	3231	3314	3450	3548	3478	3531	3618	3828	4070	4118	4254	4392	4447	55
TOTAL		9836	10594	11225	11934	12872	13958	14350	14710	15017	14941	15015	15059	15303	15594	16013	16293	16473	16474	16663	17013	17588	17894	18445	18890	21331	1441

Data produced on 02/01/2009 by the CAA Aircraft Registration Section, 45-59 Kingsway, London WC2B 6TE. Tel 020 7453 6666, E-mail aircraft.reg@caa.co.uk

GLOSSARY of TERMS and ABBREVIATIONS

AA	Automobile Association		ETPS	Empire Test Pilots' School
AAC	Army Air Corps			
AAIB	Air Accidents Investigation Branch		FAA	Fleet Air Arm
AB	Aktiebolaget (1)		FAAM	Facility for Airborne Atmospheric
ABAC	Assocation of British Aero Clubs and			Measurements
	Centres		FLPH	Foot Launched Propelled Hang-glider
AC	Awaiting Certification		FTS	Flying Training School
AERONCA	Aeronautical Corporation of America		f/f	First flight
AESL	Aero Engine Services Ltd		fsm	Full Scale Model
AIA	Atelier Industriel de l'Aéronautique d'Alger			
AIRCO	Aircraft Manufacturing Co		GAF	Government Aircraft Factory
ALAT	Aviation Légère de l'Armée de Terre		GC	Gliding Club
AMD-BA	Avions Marcel Dassault-Breguet and		GmbH	Gesellschaft mit beschränkter Haftung (4)
	Aviation			
ANEC	Air Navigation and Engineering Co		IAA	Irish Aviation Authority
ANG	Air National Guard		IAC	Integrated Avation Consortium
ApS	Anpartsselskab (2)		IAC	Irish Air Corps
APSS	Aviation Preservation Society of Scotland		IAR	Industria Aeronautica Romania
ASS	Air Signallers School		IAV	Intreprinderea de Avioane
AVIA	Azionara Vercellese Ind.Areo		ICA	Intreprinderea de Constructii
A/c	Aircraft			Aeronautice-Brasov
Aka	also known as		ICAO	International Civil Aviation Organisation
Assn	Association		IDF/AF	Israel Defence Force/Air Force
			III	Iniziative Industriali Italiene
BA	British Aircraft Manufacturing Co Ltd		IMCO	Intermountain Manufacturing Co
BAC	British Aircraft Company		IMES	Irish Marine Emergency Services
BAC	British Aircraft Corporation		IPTN	Industri Pesawat Terbang Nusantara
BAT	British Aerial Transport Co Ltd		IWM	Imperial War Museum
BoBMF	Battle of Britain Memorial Flight		Intl	International
BMAA	British Microlight Aircraft Association			
BV	Besloten Vennootschap (3)		JAA	Joint Aviation Authority
			JAR	Joint Aviation Regulations
CAARP	Coopérative des Ateliers Aéronautiques			
	de la Région Parisienne		KG	Kommanditgesellschaft (5)
CAB	Constructions Aéronautiques de Béarn		KK	Kabushiki Kaisha (6)
CAB	Constructions Aéronautiques de			
	Bourgogne		LAA	Light Aircraft Association
CAF	Canadian Air Force		LAK	Litovskaya Aviatsyonnaya Konstruktsiya
CASA	Construcciones Aeronáuticas SA		LET	Letecky Narodny Podnik
CC	County Council		LLC	Limited Liability Corporation (7)
CCF	Canadian Car and Foundry		LLP	Limited Liability Partnership (8)
CDG	Charles de Gaulle		LVG	Luft-Verkehrs Gesellschaft
CEA	Centre Est Aviation		Lda	Limitada (9)
Cobelavia	Compagnie Belge d'Aviation		Lsg	Leasing
CSS	Centralne Studium Samolotów		Ltd	Limited (10)
CZAL	Ceskoslovenske Zavody Automobilove a			
	Letecke		MBA	Micro Biplane Aviation
Corp	Corporation		MBB	Messerschmitt-Bölkow-Blohm
c	circa		MPA	Man Powered Aircraft
C of A	Certificate of Airworthiness			
C of R	Certificate of Registration		NV	Naamloze Vennootschap (11)
c/s	Colour scheme		NK	Not known
			Ntu	Not taken up
DBF	Destroyed by fire		n/w	nose-wheel
DEFRA	Department for Environment, Food and			
	Rural Affairs		OGMA	Oficinas Gerais de Material Aeronautico
DEFTS	Defence Elementary Flying Training School		Op	Operated by
DF	Defence Force			
DOSAAF	Dobrovol'noe Obshchestvo Sodeistviya		PAP	Propulsion Auxiliare Parapente
	Armii, Aviasii i Flotu		PFA	Popular Flying Association
			PIK	Polytecknikkojen Ilmailukerho
EASA	European Aviation Safety Agency		PLC	Public Limited Company (12)
EKW	Eidgenössische Konstruktions Werkstätte		pr.no.	Project Number
EMBRAER	Empresa Brasileira de Aeronautica SA		PRC	Peoples' Republic of China
EoN	Elliotts of Newbury Ltd		PS	Plane Set
ERCO	Engineering and Research Corporation		PT	Pesawat Terbang (13)

PWFU	Permanently Withdrawn from Use		SNCAN	Société Nationale de Constructions
PZL	Panstwowe Zaklady Lotnicze (State			Aéronautiques du Nord
	Aviation Works)		SOCATA	Société de Construction d'Avions de
				Tourisme et d'Affaires
qv	Which see		SoS	Secretary of State
			SpA	Società per Azioni (18)
R	Reservation		SPP	Strojirny Prvni Petilesky
RAF	Royal Aircraft Factory		SRCM	Société de Recherches et de Constructions
RAF	Royal Air Force			Mécaniques
RAFC	RAF College		Srl	Società a Responsabilità Limata (19)
RAFGSA	RAF Gliding and Soaring Association		Srs.	Series
RCAF	Royal Canadian Air Force		SS	Special Shape (Balloon)
Rep	Reproduction		SZD	Szybcowcowy Zaklad Dowswiadczalny
RFC	Royal Flying Corps		s/n	Serial Number
RJAF	Royal Jordanian Air Force			
RN	Royal Navy		TAD	Technical Aid and Demonstrator
RNAS	Royal Naval Air Service		TBA	To be advised
RSAF	Royal Saudi Air Force		TEAM	Tennessee Engineering and Manufacturing
RTS	Reduced to spares		TWU	Tactical Weapons Unit
			t/a	Trading as
SA	Société Anonyme (14)		tr	Trustee of
SA	Sociedad Anónima (15)		t/w	tail-wheel
SA	Spoika Akeyjna (16)			
SAAC	Society of Amateur Aircraft Constructors		UAS	University Air Squadron
SA(AF)	South Arabian Federation (South Yemen)		ULM	Ultra-Léger Motorisé
SAI	Skandinavsk Aero Industri		USAAC	United States Army Air Corps
SAN	Société Aéronautique Normande			
SAR	Search and Rescue		VTC	Vazduhoplovno Tehnicki Centar
SAS	Société par Actions Simplifiées (17)		VW	Volkswagen
SE	Scouting Experimental			
SEAE	School of Electrical and		WACO	Weaver Aircraft Corp
	Aeronautical Engineering		WFU	Withdrawn from Use
SIPA	Société Industrielle pour l'Aéronautique		WSK	Wytwornia Sprzetu Komunikacy Jnego
SMA	Société de Motorisations Aeronautiques			Okecie
SMD	Southern Microlight Developments			
SNCAC	Société Nationale de Constructions		ZRiPS	Zaklad Remontów i Produkcji Sprzetu
	Aéronautiques du Centre			Lotniczego

Company Constitution Notes

(1)	Sweden	Joint Stock		(11)	Belgian and Netherlands	
(2)	Denmark	Limited Liability		(12)	UK	Public Limited
(3)	Netherlands	Private		(13)	Indonesia	
(4)	Germany	Private Limited		(14)	France and Romania	Public Limited
(5)	Germany	Limited Partnership		(15)	Spain	Public Limited
(6)	Japan			(16)	Poland	
(7)	USA	Limited Partnership		(17)	France	Joint Stock
(8)	UK	Limited Partnership		(18)	Italy	Limited Liability
(9)	Portugal	Private Limited		(19)	Italy	Joint Stock
(10)	UK	Private Limited				

SECTION 1 - UNITED KINGDOM

PART 1 - FIRST PERMANENT REGISTER (1919 to 1928)

Registration	Type	Construction No	Previous Identity	Reg.date	Registered Owner (Operator)	(Unconfirmed) Base	CofA Validity

G-EAAA - G-EAZZ

| G-EASD | Avro 504L (Clerget 130hp) | E 5 | S-AHAA S-AAP, G-EASD, (RAF) | 26. 3.20 | G M New (Under restoration for Avro Heritage Centre 3.04) | Woodford | |

G-EBAA - G-EBZZ

G-EBHX	de Havilland DH.53 Humming Bird (ABC Scorpion II)	98	No.8* (*Lympne 1923 trials)	22. 9.23	Richard Shuttleworth Trustees "L'Oiseau-Mouche" (Noted 10.08)	Old Warden	21. 8.04P
G-EBIA	Royal Aircraft Factory SE.5a (Built Wolseley Motors Ltd) (Wolseley Viper)	654/2404	F904 "D7000", G-EBIA, F904	26. 9.23	Richard Shuttleworth Trustees (As "F904" in RFC 56 Sqdn c/s) Old Warden	13. 4.09P
G-EBIR	de Havilland DH.51 (AirDisco Renault 120bhp)	102	VP-KAA G-KAA, G-EBIR	22. 1.24	Richard Shuttleworth Trustees "Miss Kenya" Old Warden	12. 4.09P
G-EBJO	Air Navigation and Engineering ANEC II (ABC Scorpion II)	1	No.7* (*Lympne 1924 trials)	17. 7.24	Richard Shuttleworth Trustees	Old Warden	11. 6.08P
G-EBKY	Sopwith Pup wks order: 3004/14 (Built Sopwith Aviation Co Ltd as "Dove") (Le Rhône 80hp)		"N5180" "N5184", G-EBKY	27. 3.25	Richard Shuttleworth Trustees "Happy" (As "9917" in RFC c/s to represent Beardmore built Pup) Old Warden	12.07.09P
G-EBLV	de Havilland DH.60 Moth (ADC Cirrus III)	188		22. 6.25	BAE Systems (Operations) Ltd Old Warden (On loan to Richard Shuttleworth Trustees)	6. 9.09P
G-EBNV	English Electric S.1 Wren (ABC 398cc)	4	(BAPC.11) G-EBNV	9. 4.26	Richard Shuttleworth Trustees Old Warden (Composite - principally c/n 3 rebuilt 1955/56: as "No.4")	13. 5.09P
G-EBQP	de Havilland DH.53 Humming Bird (Bristol Cherub III) (Fuselage on rebuild 5.04: will use wings ex Martin Monoplane G-AEYY and carry "J7326")	114	J7326	?. 4.27	P L Kirk and T G Pankhurst Salisbury Hall, London Colney	
G-EBWD	de Havilland DH.60X Moth (ADC Hermes 2)	552		2. 3.28	Richard Shuttleworth Trustees	Old Warden	10. 4.08P

PART 2 – SECOND PERMANENT REGISTER (1928 onwards)

G-AAAA - G-AAZZ

G-AADR (2)	American Moth Corporation DH.60GM Moth	138	NC939M	2. 6.86	E V Moffatt Woodlow Farm, Bosbury	16. 3.09P
G-AAEG	de Havilland DH.60G Moth	1027	D-EUPI D-1599, G-AAEG	4. 2.29	I B Grace (Ada, Michigan, US)	
G-AAHI	de Havilland DH.60G Moth ((Original fuselage used in 1953 rebuild of G-AAWO))	1082		25. 5.29	N J W Reid Lee-on-Solent	22. 5.09P
G-AAHY	de Havilland DH.60M Moth	1362	HB-AFI G-AAHY	10. 5.29	D J Elliott (Brooklands Flying Club titles) Longwood Farm, Morestead	15. 8.09P
G-AAIN	Parnall Elf II (ADC Hermes 2)	2 & J 6		11. 6.29	Richard Shuttleworth Trustees Old Warden (Noted 10.06)	16. 7.05P
G-AAJT	de Havilland DH.60G Moth (Composite rebuild)	1084	NC947M G-AAJT	4. 7.29	M R Paul (Shere, Guildford)	
G-AALY	de Havilland DH.60G Moth	1175	F-AJKM G-AALY	9. 9.29	K M Fresson (Storrington)	15. 5.05T
G-AAMY (2)	American Moth Corporation DH.60GMW Moth (Wright Gipsy L320)	86	N585M NC585M	2. 5.80	Totalsure Ltd Seppe-Hoeven, Netherlands	11. 8.04P
G-AANG (2)	Bleriot Type XI (Anzani 25hp) (1910 original)	14	BAPC.3	29.11.81	Richard Shuttleworth Trustees (No external marks) Old Warden	22. 9.07P
G-AANH (2)	Deperdussin Monoplane (Anzani Y 35hp) (Possibly c/n 143)	43	BAPC.4	29.10.81	Richard Shuttleworth Trustees (No external marks) Old Warden	4. 4.09P
G-AANI (2)	Blackburn Single Seat Monoplane (Gnome 50hp no.683)	"9"	BAPC.5 No.9* (*Lympne 1923 trials)	29.10.81	Richard Shuttleworth Trustees (No external marks) Old Warden	18. 6.09P
G-AANL (2)	de Havilland DH.60M Moth (Composite rebuild)	1446	OY-DEH RDAF S-357, S-107	26. 6.87	R A Palmer (National Flying Services titles) White Waltham	2.12.09P
G-AANM (2)	Bristol F 2b Fighter composite (RR Falcon) (Built British and Colonial Aero Co 1917)	"67626"	BAPC.166	16. 7.87	Aero Vintage Ltd Ottawa, Ontario, Canada (To Canada Aviation Museum 12.06 as "D7889")	25. 6.07P
G-AANO (2)	American Moth Corporation DH.60GMW Moth (Composite rebuild 11.91)	165	N590N NC590N	3. 3.88	A W and M E Jenkins (Comberton, Cambridge)	
G-AANV (2)	de Havilland DH.60M Moth (Built Morane Saulnier)	13	HB-OBU CH-349, F-AJNY	8. 3.84	R A Seeley Phoenix Farm, Lower Upham	22. 6.08P
G-AAOK (2)	Curtiss-Wright Travel Air 12Q Travelair (Warner Scarab 125hp)	12Q-2026	N370N NC370N, NC352M	18.11.81	Shipping and Airlines Ltd Biggin Hill	31. 7.09P
G-AAOR (2)	de Havilland DH.60G Moth (C/n uncertain: probably a composite)	1075	EC-AAO	15. 4.85	B R Cox and N J Stagg (Noted 6.06) Grange Farm, Frogland Cross	17.11.05P
G-AAPZ	Desoutter I (ADC Hermes 2)	D 25		1. 1.31	Richard Shuttleworth Trustees Old Warden	21. 4.09P
G-AAUP	Klemm L 25-1a (Salmson AD9)	145		19. 2.30	J I Cooper tr Newbury Aeroplane Co "Clementine" Denford Manor, Hungerford	21.11.84P
G-AAWO	de Havilland DH.60G Moth (1953 rebuild substituted original fuselage of G-AAHI)	1235		2. 5.30	I C Reid Sopley, Hants	29. 4.09P

G-AAYT	de Havilland DH.60G Moth	1233	DR606	?. 5.30	P Groves	Lee-on-Solent	
			G-AAYT		*(Noted 9.04)*		
G-AAYX	Southern Martlet	202		14. 5.30	Richard Shuttleworth Trustees	Old Warden	21. 4.09P
	(AS Genet Major 1A)						
G-AAZG	de Havilland DH.60G Moth	1253	EC-AAE	23. 5.30	C C, J M Lovell and J A Pothecary *(On rebuild 9.04)*		
			EC-MMA, M-CMMA, MW-133, G-AAZG			Chilbolton	
G-AAZP	de Havilland DH.80A Puss Moth	2047	HL537	4. 6.30	R P Williams *"British Heritage"*		
			G-AAZP, SU-AAC, G-AAZP			Denford Manor, Hungerford	17. 6.09S

G-ABAA - G-ABZZ

G-ABAG	de Havilland DH.60G Moth	1259		23. 6.30	A and P A Wood	Audley End	6. 5.09P
G-ABDA	de Havilland DH.60G Moth	1284	N60GD	7.30	R A Palmer	White Waltham	24. 5.08P
			N1284A, G-ABDA, 2595M, DG583, G-ABDA				
	(Tipped onto nose and extensively damaged following a forced landing in a field near Perth due to engine failure after take-off 4. 5.08)						
G-ABDX	de Havilland DH.60G Moth	1294	HB-UAS	22. 8.30	M D Souch	Hill Farm, Durley	13.10.05P
			G-ABDX				
G-ABEV (2)	de Havilland DH.60G Moth	1823	N4203E	10. 3.77	S L G Darch	East Chinnock, Yeovil	15. 5.09P
			G-ABEV (2), HB-OKI, CH-217				
G-ABHE	Aeronca C.2	A100		11.30	N S Chittenden	(Herodsfoot, Liskeard)	
	(Flew as glider 15. 5.37 after engine blew up 7.36 but no BGA Certificate issued)						
G-ABLS	de Havilland DH.80A Puss Moth	2164		7. 5.31	R A Seeley	Turweston	9. 9.09P
G-ABNT	Civilian CAC.1 Coupe	O 2.3		10. 9.31	Shipping and Airlines Ltd	Biggin Hill	25. 5.07P
	(AS Genet Major 1A) *(C/n also quoted as O 3)*						
G-ABNX	Robinson Redwing 2	9		2. 7.31	R J Burgess tr Redwing Syndicate	Redhill	12. 5.03P
	(AS Genet)				*(Noted 4.06)*		
G-ABOX (2)	Sopwith Pup	-	N5195	2. 9.84	C M D and A P St Cyrien	AAC Middle Wallop	22. 4.93P
	(80hp Le Rhône)				*(On loan to Museum of Army Flying as "N5195")*		
G-ABSD	de Havilland DH.60G Moth	1883	A7-96	21.11.31	M E Vaisey tr Chiltern Flying Club		
			VH-UTN, G-ABSD		*(On rebuild)*	(Hemel Hempstead)	
G-ABUS	Comper CLA.7 Swift	S 32/4		27. 2.32	R C F Bailey	(Slapton, Devon)	19.6.79P
	(Pobjoy Niagara 3)				*(Believed extant 2007)*		
G-ABVE	Arrow Active 2	2		19. 3.32	R A Fleming	Breighton	19. 5.09P
	(DH Gipsy III)						
G-ABWP	Spartan Arrow 1	78		?. 4.32	R E Blain	Redhill	3. 1.06P
	(Cirrus Hermes 2)						
G-ABXL	Granger Archaeopteryx	3A		3. 6.32	J R Granger	(Beeston)	22. 9.82P
	(Cherub III)						
G-ABYA	de Havilland DH.60G Moth	1906		?. 7.32	D A Hay and J F Moore	Biggin Hill	24. 4.11S
G-ABZB (2)	de Havilland Moth Major	5011	SE-AEL	11. 9.80	G M Turner and N Child	(Siddington, Cirencester)	7. 9.09P
			OY-DAK				

G-ACAA - G-ACZZ

G-ACCB	de Havilland DH.83 Fox Moth	4042		24. 1.33	E A Gautrey	(Nuneaton)	20. 7.57
					(Crashed off Southport 25. 9.56 and on rebuild 10.95)		
G-ACDA	de Havilland DH.82A Tiger Moth	3175	BB724	6. 2.33	B D Hughes *(de Havilland School of Flying titles)*		
			G-ACDA			RAF Henlow	15. 7.11
G-ACDC	de Havilland DH.82A Tiger Moth	3177	BB726	6. 2.33	The Tiger Club (1990) Ltd	Headcorn	6. 8.11
	(Composite airframe)		G-ACDC				
G-ACDI	de Havilland DH.82A Tiger Moth	3182	BB742	6. 2.33	D J Wood	Old Sarum	5. 6.11
	(Composite rebuild)		G-ACDI				
G-ACEJ	de Havilland DH.83 Fox Moth	4069		21. 4.33	J I Cooper *(Scottish Motor Traction titles)*		
						Boscombe Down	16. 8.10S
G-ACET	de Havilland DH.84 Dragon	6021	2779M	21. 4.33	M D Souch	Hill Farm, Durley	
			AW171, G-ACET		*(On rebuild 5.06, composite based on original wings)*		
G-ACGZ	de Havilland DH.60G III Moth Major	5038	VT-AFW	30. 5.33	N H Lemon	(Cookham, Maidenhead)	
			G-ACGZ		*(On rebuild 2000)*		
G-ACLL	de Havilland DH.85 Leopard Moth	7028	AW165	16. 1.34	D C M and V M Stiles	Jurby, Isle of Man	6.12.95P
			G-ACLL				
G-ACMA	de Havilland DH.85 Leopard Moth	7042	BD148	14. 3.34	S J Filhol Kilcolman Farm, Enniskean, Co Cork		3. 2.94P
			G-ACMA		*(Noted 5.08)*		
G-ACMD (2)	de Havilland DH.82A Tiger Moth	3195	N182DH	20. 1.88	M J Bonnick	Rectory Farm, Abbotsley	7. 8.11
			EC-AGB, Sp AF 33-5				
	(Provenance doubtful: EC-AGB had interim Spanish AF serial 30-104)						
G-ACMN	de Havilland DH.85 Leopard Moth	7050	X9381	1. 4.34	M R and K E Slack	Duxford	25. 7.09S
			G-ACMN				
G-ACNS	de Havilland DH.60G III Moth Major	5068	ZS-???	?. 3.34	R I and D Souch *"I V Cells"*	Hill Farm, Durley	19. 9.08S
			G-ACNS				
G-ACOJ (2)	de Havilland DH.85 Leopard Moth	7035	F-AMXP	5. 6.87	A J Norman tr Norman Aeroplane Trust		
	(Composite with wings from HB-OXO)					Rendcomb	24. 10.10S
G-ACSP	de Havilland DH.88 Comet	1994	CS-AAJ	21. 8.34	T M, M L, D A and P M Jones	Derby	
			G-ACSP, E-1		*(Under restoration 2005)*		
G-ACSS	de Havilland DH.88 Comet	1996	K5084	4. 9.34	Richard Shuttleworth Trustees *"Grosvenor House"/ "34"*		
			G-ACSS		*(Noted 10.08)*	Old Warden	2. 6.94P
	(In addition, four replicas exist as "G-ACSS" - (1) at Mount Waverley, Victoria, Australia, (2) BAPC.216, (3) BAPC.257 - details in						
	SECTION 5, Part 2,.and (4) N88XD [T7] built by Repeat Aircraft, Riverside CA, US in 1993 for T J Wathen)						
G-ACTF	Comper CLA.7 Swift	S 32/9	VT-ADO	24. 5.34	Richard Shuttleworth Trustees	Old Warden	24. 4.07P
	(Pobjoy Niagara 2)						
G-ACUS (2)	de Havilland DH.85 Leopard Moth	7082	HB-OXA	17.11.77	R A and V A Gammons	RAF Henlow	18.12.11
	(Composite including parts ex HB-OXO c/n 7045)		(G-ACUS)				
G-ACXB (2)	de Havilland DH.60G III Moth Major	5098	EC-ABY	24. 1.89	D F Hodgkinson	(Gravesend)	
			EC-BAX, Sp AF 30-53, EC-YAY			*(On rebuild 2000)*	

G-ACXE   British Klemm L 25c1 Swallow   21   29.10.34   J G Wakeford   Bexhill-on-Sea   7. 4.40
          (On rebuild using components to re-draw plans and produce a substantially "new-build" airframe: progress continuing 2006 at Newbury)
G-ACZE   de Havilland DH.89A Dragon Rapide   6264   G-AJGS   20.11.34   Chewton Glen Aviation Ltd
                                                          G-ACZE, Z7266, G-ACZE
                                                                                                                        Bembridge   2. 7.10S

G-ADAA - G-ADZZ

G-ADEV (2) Avro 504K   R3/LE/61400 G-ACNB   18. 4.84   Richard Shuttleworth Trustees *(As "H5199" in RAF c/s)*
            (110 hp Le Rhône)   "E3404"   Old Warden   21. 4.09P
            (P/i not confirmed but, if correct, full p/i is 3118M, BK892, G-ADEV, H5199)
G-ADGP   Miles M.2L Hawk Speed Six   160   20. 5.35   R A Mills *"8"*   Lasham   17. 6.09P
G-ADGT   de Havilland DH.82A Tiger Moth   3338   BB697   23. 5.35   The Tiger Club 1990 Ltd *(Also carries "BB697")*
                                                          G-ADGT   Headcorn   4. 5.09S
G-ADGV   de Havilland DH.82A Tiger Moth   3340   (D-E...)   23. 5.35   K J and P J Whitehead
                                                          G-ADGV, (G-BACW), BB694, G-ADGV   (Whitchurch Hill, Reading) 1.10.09S
G-ADHD (2) de Havilland DH.60G III Moth Major   5105   EC-...   17. 2.88   M E Vaisey   RAF Henlow
            (Rebuild of ex Spanish components from US) Spanish AF 34-5, EC-W32   *(Noted 7.02)*
G-ADIA   de Havilland DH.82A Tiger Moth   3368   BB747   13. 8.35   S J Beaty   Wold Lodge, Finedon   5. 5.11S
                                                          G-ADIA
G-ADJJ   de Havilland DH.82A Tiger Moth   3386   BB819   29. 8.35   J M Preston   Watchford Farm, Yarcombe   14.12.11
                                                          G-ADJJ
G-ADKC   de Havilland DH.87B Hornet Moth   8064   X9445   27. 3.36   A J Davy   White Waltham   5. 5.11S
                                                          G-ADKC
G-ADKK   de Havilland DH.87B Hornet Moth   8033   W5749   9.11.35   R M and D R Lee   Oaksey Park   18. 4.10
                                                          G-ADKK
G-ADKL   de Havilland DH.87B Hornet Moth   8035   F-BCJO   ?.11.35   P R and M J F Gould
                                                          G-ADKL, W5750, G-ADKL   Coulommiers, Seine-et-Marne, France   8. 7.08
G-ADKM   de Havilland DH.87B Hornet Moth   8037   W5751   12.11.35   S G Collyer   Farley Farm, Romsey   14. 8.11
                                                          G-ADKM
G-ADLY   de Havilland DH.87B Hornet Moth   8020   W9388   5.10.35   Totalsure Ltd *"Leicestershire Foxhound II"*
                                                          G-ADLY   Seppe-Hoeven, Netherlands   1. 1.11
G-ADMT   de Havilland DH.87B Hornet Moth   8093   8. 5.36   D C Reid *"Curlew"*   (Norwich)   30. 7.10
G-ADND   de Havilland DH.87B Hornet Moth   8097   W9385   4. 8.36   D M and S M Weston   Hullavington   22. 3.08P
                                                          G-ADND   *(As "W9385:YG-L" and "3" in RAF 502 Sqdn c/s)*
G-ADNE   de Havilland DH.87B Hornet Moth   8089   X9325   10. 3.36   R Felix tr G-ADNE Group *"Ariadne"*
                                                          G-ADNE   Oaksey Park   16. 5.09P
G-ADNL   Miles M.5 Sparrowhawk   239   12. 8.35   A P Pearson   (Ramsbottom, Bury)   13. 5.58S
            (Reconstructed c1953 as M 77 Sparrowjet)   *(On rebuild in Bristol area 4.04)*
G-ADNZ (2) de Havilland DH.82A Tiger Moth   85614   6948M   10.10.74   D C Wall *(As "DE673" in RAF c/s)*
                                                          DE673   Tibenham   12. 8.09S
G-ADPC   de Havilland DH.82A Tiger Moth   3393   BB852   24. 9.35   D J Marshall   Charity Farm, Baxterley   2. 8.06
                                                          G-ADPC
G-ADPJ   BAC Drone 2   7   21. 8.35   N H Ponsford   (Selby)   17. 5.55
            (Bristol Cherub 3)   *(Crashed Leicester 3. 4.55: on rebuild using parts from G-AEJR c/n 22)*
G-ADPS   BA L.25c Swallow II   410   4. 9.35   J F Hopkins   Watchford Farm, Yarcombe   29. 4.09P
            (Pobjoy Niagara III)
G-ADRA (2) Pietenpol AirCamper   PFA 1514   10. 4.78   A J Mason *"Edna May"*   Bicester   19. 4.09P
            (Built A J Mason) (Continental A65-8F)
G-ADRH (2) de Havilland DH.87B Hornet Moth   8038   G-ADRH   6. 8.82   R G Grocott   Mandeville, Gore, New Zealand
                                                          F-AQBY, HB-OBE   *(On rebuild 2000 - reserved as ZK-ANR)*
            (Originally regd with c/n IMC/8164, amended 20.5.85)
G-ADRR (2) Aeronca C.3   A.734   N17423   6. 9.88   S J Rudkin   (Oakham)
                                                          NC17423   *(On rebuild 2007: wings noted at Skycraft, Spalding 11.01)*
G-ADUR   de Havilland DH.87B Hornet Moth   8085   N9026Y   10. 3.36   W A Gerdes   Swanborough Farm, Lewes   5. 8.11
                                                          G-ADUR
G-ADWJ   de Havilland DH.82A Tiger Moth   3450   BB803   9.12.35   C Adams   (Madley)
                                                          G-ADWJ   *(Under restoration 3.97)*
G-ADWT   Miles M.2W Hawk Trainer   215   CF-NXT   18.11.35   R Earl and B Morris   Landmead Farm, Garford   19.10.09P
                                                          G-ADWT, NF750, G-ADWT
G-ADXT   de Havilland DH.82A Tiger Moth   3436   9.12.35   Plane Heritage Ltd   Goodwood   15. 6.09S
            (Mainly rebuild of components)
G-ADYS   Aeronca C.3   A.600   1. 1.36   J I Cooper *(London Air Park Flying Club titles)*
            (Aeronca E113C)   Grange Farm, Frogland Cross   6. 5.04P

G-AEAA - G-AEZZ

G-AEBB   Mignet HM.14 Pou-Du-Ciel   KWO.1   24. 1.36   Richard Shuttleworth Trustees   Old Warden   31. 5.39
            (Built K W Owen)   *(Noted 8.08)*
G-AEBJ   Blackburn B 2   6300/8   4. 2.36   BAE Systems (Operations) Ltd   Old Warden   31. 7.09P
                                                                                   (On loan to Richard Shuttleworth Trustees)
G-AEDB   BAC Drone 2   13   BGA2731   18. 3.36   P L Kirk and R E Nerou   Hucknall   26. 5.87P
            (Bristol Cherub III)   G-AEDB   *(Composite with wings of G-AEJH and tail of G-AEEN) (Noted 6.07)*
G-AEDU (2) de Havilland DH.90A Dragonfly   7526   N190DH   4. 6.79   A J Norman tr Norman Aeroplane Trust Rendcomb   11. 8.11
                                                          G-AEDU, ZS-CTR, CR-AAB
G-AEEG   Miles M.3A Falcon Major   216   SE-AFN   14. 3.36   P R Holloway   Old Warden   12. 7.10S
                                                          Fv913, SE-AFN, G-AEEG, U-20
G-AEFT   Aeronca C.3   A.610   17. 4.36   N C Chittenden   (Herodsfoot, Liskeard)   8. 5.04P
            (JAP J-99) *(Rebuilt 1976 with major parts of G-AETG (qv))*
G-AELO   de Havilland DH.87B Hornet Moth   8105   AW118   30. 7.36   M J Miller   Audley End   16. 8.10S
                                                          G-AELO
G-AEML   de Havilland DH.89 Dragon Rapide   6337   X9450   1. 9.36   Fundacion Infante de Orleans
                                                          G-AEML   Cuatro Vientos, Spain   4. 7.11S

G-AENP (2)	Hawker Afghan Hind	41H/81902	(BAPC.78)	29.10.81	Richard Shuttleworth Trustees		
	(RR Kestrel V)		R Afghan AF ??		(As "K5414:XV"in RAF 15 Sqdn c/s)	Old Warden	6. 6.09P
G-AEOA	de Havilland DH.80A Puss Moth	2184	ES921	1.10.36	A and P A Wood	(Audley End)	27. 6.95P
			G-AEOA, YU-PAX, UN-PAX				
G-AEOF (2)	Rearwin 8500 Sportster	462	N15863	1.12.81	Shipping and Airlines Ltd	Biggin Hill	5.10.01P
	(Le Blond 5DF 85hp)		NC15863				
G-AEPH	Bristol F 2b Fighter	7575	D8096	13.11.36	Richard Shuttleworth Trustees (As "D8096:D" in RAF c/s)		
	(RR Falcon 3)		G-AEPH, D8096			Old Warden	24. 4.09P
	(Original c/n 3746 and rebuilt C 1931)						
G-AERV	Miles M.11A Whitney Straight	307	EM999	30.12.36	R A Seeley	Turweston	9. 4.66
	(Built Phillips & Powis Aircraft Ltd)		G-AERV		(Flew 17. 9.08 after restoration)		
G-AESB (2)	Aeronca C.3	A.638	N15742	5. 8.88	R J M Turnbull Rydinghurst Farm, Cranleigh		
			NC15742		(On rebuild 6.06)		
G-AESE	de Havilland DH.87B Hornet Moth	8108	W5775	13. 1.37	J G Green "Sheena" Grange Farm, Frogland Cross		10. 8.09S
			G-AESE				
G-AESZ	Chilton DW.1	DW.1/1		?. 1.37	R E Nerou	Old Warden	16. 8.09P
	(Carden Ford 32 hp)						
G-AETG	Aeronca 100	AB.110		?. 2.37	J J Teague tr J Teague and Partners		
					New Barn Farm. Barton Ashes, Crawley		
	(Crashed on take-off Booker 7. 4.69 : cancelled 29. 2.72 as destroyed: major parts to G-AEFT in 1976 - on rebuild with parts from G-AEWV 1996)						
G-AEUJ	Miles M.11A Whitney Straight	313		19. 2.37	R E Mitchell (Stored 11.06)	Sleap	4. 6.70
	(Built Phillips & Powis Aircraft)						
G-AEVS	Aeronca 100	AB.114		3.37	R A Fleming "Jeeves"	Brighton	1. 7.09P
	(JAP J-99) (Composite including parts of original G-AEXD)						
G-AEXD	Aeronca 100	AB.124		1. 4.37	M A and R W Mills	Sywell	20. 4.70P
	(JAP J-99) (Mainly comprises parts of G-AESP after rebuild in 1958)				(On rebuild 10.07)		
G-AEXF	Percival Type E Mew Gull	E 22	ZS-AHM	18. 5.37	R A Fleming	Brighton	17. 6.08P
	(Rebuilt as pr.no.PFA 013-10020)						
G-AEXT	Dart Kitten II	123		?. 4.37	A J Hartfield	Marsh Hill Farm, Aylesbury	2. 7.09P
	(JAP J-99)						
G-AEXZ	Piper J-2 Cub	997		5. 2.38	J R and M Dowson	(Leicester)	2.11.78S
	(Built Taylor Aircraft Co Inc) (Continental A75-9)				(On rebuild: by 3.00 wings only and remainder with owner at home)		
G-AEZJ	Percival Type K Vega Gull	K 65	SE-ALA	2. 7.37	D P H Hulme	Biggin Hill	5. 8.10S
			D-IXWD, PH-ATH, G-AEZJ				

G-AFAA - G-AFZZ

G-AFCL	BA L 25c Swallow II	462		3.11.37	C P Bloxham	Shotteswell	16. 8.04P
	(Pobjoy Niagara 3)						
G-AFDO (2)	Piper J-3C-65 Cub	2593	N21697	7. 6.88	R Wald "Butter Cub"	Hill Farm, Durley	27. 7.99P
	(Frame No.2633)		NC21697		(On rebuild 12.02)		
G-AFEL (2)	Monocoupe 90A	A 782	N19432	7. 6.82	M Rieser	Little Staughton	22.12.05P
	(Lambert R-266)		NC194323		(On rebuild 2007)		
G-AFFD	Percival Type Q Six	Q.21	(G-AIEY)	12. 2.38	B D Greenwood	(Castletown, IoM)	31. 8.56
			X9407, G-AFFD		(On rebuild 2007)		
G-AFFH	Piper J-2 Cub	1166	EC-ALA	26. 3.38	M J Honeychurch	(Charlton, Pewsey)	29. 8.53
	(Built Taylor Aircraft Co Inc) (Continental A40)		G-AFFH		(On restoration at owner's home 10.01)		
G-AFGC	BA L 25c Swallow II	467	BK893	4. 4.38	G E Arden Thorns Cross Farm, Chudleigh		20. 3.51
	(Pobjoy Niagara 3)		G-AFGC		(Stored 1.98)		
G-AFGE	BA L 25c Swallow II	470	BK894	4. 4.38	C W N and A A M Huke	Boscombe Down	15. 5.09P
	(Pobjoy Niagara 2)		G-AFGE				
G-AFGH	Chilton DW.1	DW.1/2		20. 3.38	M L and G L Joseph Denford Manor, Hungerford		7. 7.83P
	(Lycoming O-145-A2) (To be re-engined with Carden-Ford)				(On rebuild 2006)		
G-AFGI	Chilton DW.1	DW.1/3		30. 3.38	K A A McDonald	White Waltham	15. 8.07P
	(Walter Mikron 2)						
G-AFGM (2)	Piper J-4A Cub Coupé	4-943	N26895	30.12.81	P H Wilkinson	Falgunzeon	9.10.06P
	(Continental A65-8)		NC26895				
G-AFGZ	de Havilland DH.82A Tiger Moth	3700	G-AMHI	9. 5.38	M R Paul	Lee-on-Solent	16. 5.09S
			BB759, G-AFGZ				
G-AFHA (2)	Moss MA.1	MA.1/2		27. 2.67	C V Butler	(Allesley, Coventry)	
					(Small components only stored)		
G-AFIN	Chrislea LC.1 Airguard	LC.1	BAPC.203	7. 7.38	N H Wright Queach Farm, Bury St Edmunds		
					(Stored 2.06)		
G-AFIR	Luton LA-4 Minor	JSS.2		7. 7.38	A J Mason	(Aylesbury)	30. 7.71
	(Built J S Squires) (JAP J-99)				(Damaged near Cobham 14. 3.71 and on rebuild 5.05)		
G-AFJA	Taylor-Watkinson Dingbat	DB.100		2. 8.38	A T Christian Walkeridge Farm, Overton		23. 6.75S
	(Built Taylor Watkinson Aircraft Co) (Carden-Ford 32hp)				(Damaged Headcorn 19. 5.75 and partially rebuilt)		
G-AFJB	Foster-Wikner GM.1 Wicko	5	DR613	15. 8.38	J Dible	Hill Farm, Durley	16. 7.08P
	(DH Gipsy Major 1)		G-AFJB				
G-AFJU	Miles M.17 Monarch	789	X9306	25. 8.38	P W Bishop	Oaksey Park	18. 5.64
	(Built Phillips and Powis Aircraft Ltd)		G-AFJU		(Noted for rebuild 11.07)		
G-AFJV (2)	Moss MA.2	MA.2/2		27. 2.67	C V Butler	(Allesley, Coventry)	
					(Small components only stored)		
G-AFNG	de Havilland DH.94 Moth Minor	94014	AW112	2. 5.39	D Saunders tr The Gullwing Trust		
	(Cabin)		G-AFNG		(Stored 10.05) (Galway, County Galway)		21.10.98P
G-AFNI	de Havilland DH.94 Moth Minor	94035	W7972	11. 5.39	J Jennings	Fenland	26. 5.67
			G-AFNI				
G-AFOB	de Havilland DH.94 Moth Minor	94018	X5117	16. 5.39	K Cantwell	(Royston)	11. 5.93P
			G-AFOB				
G-AFOJ	de Havilland DH.94 Moth Minor	9407	E-1	21. 7.39	R M Long "Bugs 2" Salisbury Hall, London Colney		27. 8.69P
	(Cabin)		E-0236, G-AFOJ		(On loan to de Havilland Heritage Museum)		
G-AFPN	de Havilland DH.94 Moth Minor	94044	X9297	23. 5.39	A A A Maitland and R S Jones	Welshpool	2. 6.11
	(Now regd with c/n 94016)		G-AFPN				

Reg	Type	C/n	Prev id	Date	Owner	Location	Date
G-AFRZ	Miles M.17 Monarch	793	G-AIDE W6463, G-AFRZ	24. 3.39	R E Mitchell *(Noted 10.06)*	Sleap	29. 6.70
G-AFSC	Tipsy Trainer 1 (Walter Mikron 2)	11		15. 7.39	D M Forshaw	Panshanger	9. 2.08P
G-AFSV	Chilton DW.1A (Walter Mikron 2)	DW.1A/1		5. 4.39	R E Nerou *(On restoration 2006)*	(Coventry)	12. 7.72
G-AFTA	Hawker Tomtit (AS Mongoose 3C)	30380	K1786 G-AFTA, K1786	26. 4.39	Richard Shuttleworth Trustees *(As "K1786" in RAF c/s)*	Old Warden	21. 4.09P
G-AFUP (2)	Luscombe 8A Silvaire (Continental A65-1)	1246	N25370 NC25370	7. 6.88	R Dispain	(Fordingbridge)	12. 3.97P
G-AFVE (2)	de Havilland DH.82A Tiger Moth *(Built Morris Motors Ltd)*	83720	T7230	1. 2.78	J Mainka *(As "T-7230" in RAF c/s)* (Warsaw, Poland)		30. 4.10T
G-AFWH (2)	Piper J-4A Cub Coupé (Continental A65-8)	4-1341	N33093 NC33093	14. 1.82	C W Stearn and R D W Norton *(Stored 4.04)*	(Ely)	2. 7.01P
G-AFWI	de Havilland DH.82A Tiger Moth	82187	BB814 G-AFWI	19. 7.39	E Newbury Brown Shutters Farm, Norton St Philips, Somerset		28. 2.10
G-AFWT	Tipsy Trainer 1 (Walter Mikron 2)	13		1. 8.39	N Parkhouse	Old Warden	20. 5.08P
G-AFYD (2)	Luscombe 8F Silvaire (Continental C90-14F)	1044	N25120 NC25120	29. 7.75	J D Iliffe	Haw Farm, Hampstead Norrey's	4.11.10
G-AFYO (2)	Stinson HW-75 Voyager (Continental C90-12F)	7039	F-BGQP NC22586	25. 4.77	M Lodge Westfield Farm, Hailsham *(Probably ex French.Military with identity "22586")*		21. 5.07P
G-AFZA (2)	Piper J-4A Cub Coupé (Continental A65-8)	4-873	N26198 NC26198	27. 6.84	R A Benson (Exeter) *(Wings noted at Trenchard Farm, Eggesford 9.05)*		2.12.02P
G-AFZK (2)	Luscombe 8A Silvaire (Continental A65-8)	1042	N25118 NC25118	24.10.88	M G Byrnes	Haverfordwest	15. 6.09P
G-AFZL (2)	Porterfield CP-50 (Continental A50-5 [modified])	581	N25401 NC25401	18. 3.82	P G Lucus and S H Sharpe	White Waltham	21. 7.09P
G-AFZN (2)	Luscombe 8A Silvaire (Continental A65-8)	1186	N25279 NC25279	5.10.81	R J Griffin and J L Truscott Ranston Farm, Iwerne Courtney		25. 7.09P

G-AGAA - G-AGZZ

Reg	Type	C/n	Prev id	Date	Owner	Location	Date
G-AGAT (2)	Piper J-3F-50 Cub (Franklin 4AC-150 Series 50)	4062	N26126 NC26126	17. 7.87	A S Bathgate	Gorebridge	28. 8.09P
G-AGEG (2)	de Havilland DH.82A Tiger Moth (DH Gipsy Major IC)	82710	N9146 D-EDIL, R Neth AF A-32, PH-UFK, A-32, R4769	16. 8.82	A J Norman tr Norman Aeroplane Trust Rendcomb		15. 5.10S
G-AGFT (2)	Avia FL.3 (C.N.A. D4S)	176	I-TOLB MM....	21. 8.84	D Giorgetti *(As "8110" in Croatian Air Force c/s)* (Pisa, Italy)		4. 3.09P
G-AGHY (2)	de Havilland DH.82A Tiger Moth	82292	N9181	17. 2.88	P Groves tr G-AGHY Group	Lee-on-Solent	29. 4.10
G-AGIV (2)	Piper J-3C-65 Cub (L-4J-PI) *(Frame No.12506)* (Continental A65-8)	12676	OO-AFI OO-GBA, 44-80380	13. 8.82	T Welsh tr J3 Cub Group	Compton Abbas	17. 3.09P
G-AGJG	de Havilland DH.89A Dragon Rapide	6517	X7344	25.10.43	M J and D J T Miller *(Camouflage colours with Scottish Airways titles)* Duxford		9.10.10S
G-AGLK	Taylorcraft J Auster 5D (modified)	1137	RT475	25. 8.44	C R Harris	Rochester	10. 6.10S
G-AGMI (2)	Luscombe 8E Silvaire Deluxe (Continental C85-12F)	1569	N28827 NC28827	15.11.88	P J Laycock and J R Pike tr Oscar Flying Group Twineham, West Sussex		16. 4.09P
G-AGNJ	de Havilland DH.82A (Aust) Tiger Moth *(Built de Havilland Aircraft Pty Ltd)*	660	VP-YOJ ZS-BGF, SAAF 2366	21. 2.89	A J, B P and P J Borsberry *(On rebuild 6.95)* (Kidmore End, Reading)		
G-AGPK (2)	de Havilland DH.82A Tiger Moth	86566	N657DH F-BGDN, French AF, PG657	27.10.88	M G and L J Collins	Sywell	23. 4.08E
	(Fitted with wings, tailplane, fin and rudder ex G-ANLH 2002)						
G-AGSH	de Havilland DH.89A Dragon Rapide 6 *(Built Brush Coachworks Ltd)*	6884	EI-AJO G-AGSH, NR808	25. 7.45	Techair London Ltd *"Jemma Meeson"* (BEA titles) Bournemouth		12.11.10
G-AGTM	de Havilland DH.89A Dragon Rapide 6 *(Built Brush Coachworks Ltd)*	6746	JY-ACL D-ABP, G-AGTM, NF875	19. 9.45	Aviation Heritage Ltd	Coventry	31. 5.10S
G-AGTO	Auster V J/1 Autocrat	1822		2.10.45	M J Barnett and D J T Miller	Duxford	9. 3.09S
G-AGTT	Auster V J/1 Autocrat	1826		2.10.45	R Farrer *(Stored 12.97)*	(Bromham, Bedford)	11. 2.93
G-AGVG	Auster V J/1 Autocrat *(Modified tail surfaces)*	1858		7.12.45	P J Benest	Hamstead Marshall	13. 7.09S
G-AGVN	Auster V J/1 Autocrat	1873	EI-CKC G-AGVN	18. 1.46	B C Hogan	Trevet, Dublin	24. 8.09
G-AGVV (2)	Piper J-3C-65 Cub (L-4H-PI) (Continental A65-8)	11163	F-BCZK French AF, 43-29872	19. 2.81	M Molina-Ruano	(Malaga, Spain)	2. 9.04P
G-AGXN	Auster J/1N Alpha	1963		22. 1.46	J J Teagle tr Gentleman's Aerial Touring Carriage Group *(Stored minus wings, noted 9.08)* New Barn Farm, Barton Ashes, Crawley		19. 6.08
G-AGXU	Auster J/1N Alpha	1969		24. 1.46	B H Austen	Oaksey Park	13. 8.06
G-AGXV	Auster V J/1 Autocrat	1970		1. 2.46	B S Dowsett and I M Oliver *"Pamela IV"* Little Gransden		2.11.09S
G-AGYD	Auster J/1N Alpha	1985		4. 2.46	P R Hodson Little Gransden *(Damaged near Felthorpe 25.11.90: on rebuild 4.94)*		24.11.90
G-AGYH	Auster J/1N Alpha *(Built Taylor Aeroplanes)*	1989		4. 2.46	I M Staves	(Northallerton)	10.10.72
G-AGYK	Auster V J/1 Autocrat	2002		4. 2.46	M C Hayes tr Autocraft Syndicate	Shobdon	17. 8.07
G-AGYT	Auster V J/1 Autocrat	1862		18. 1.46	P J Barrett *(On overhaul 6.94)*	(Lightwater)	27. 2.91
G-AGYU	de Havilland DH.82A Tiger Moth *(Built Morris Motors Ltd)*	85265	DE208	10. 1.46	P L Jones *(As "DE-208" in RAF c/s* Tuam, Galway, County Galway		14. 9.10S
G-AGYY (2)	Ryan ST3KR (PT-21-RY) (Gladden Products Kinner R56)	1167	N56792 41-1967	15. 6.83	H de Vries *(As "27" in USAAC c/s)* Hoogeveen, Netherlands		3. 7.09P
G-AGZZ (2)	de Havilland DH.82A (Aust) Tiger Moth *(Built de Havilland Aircraft Pty Ltd)* T256 & 926		N3862 VH-BTU, VH-RNM, VH-BMY, A17-503	14. 5.82	M C Jordan	Eaglescott	9. 9.10

G-AHAA - G-AHZZ

G-AHAG	de Havilland DH.89A Dragon Rapide *(Built Brush Coachworks Ltd)*	6926	RL944	31. 1.46	S G Jones	Membury	15. 7.73
G-AHAL	Auster J/1N Alpha *(Built Taylor Aeroplanes)*	1870		31. 1.46	J W Frecklington and R Merwood tr Wickenby Aviation	Wickenby	4. 5.10S
G-AHAM	Auster V J/1 Autocrat	1885		21. 1.46	C P L Jenkins	Rush Green	11. 5.08S
G-AHAN (2)	de Havilland DH.82A Tiger Moth *(Built Morris Motors Ltd)*	86553	N90406 F-BGDG, French AF, PG644	31. 5.85	Tiger Associates Ltd	Bicester	26. 7.10S
G-AHAP	Auster V J/1 Autocrat *(Rover V-8)*	1887		8. 2.46	W D Hill *(Noted 10.08)*	Fenland	20. 2.91P
G-AHAU	Auster V J/1-160 Autocrat *(Built-up fin/fuselage fillet)*	1850	(HB-EOL)	11. 2.46	A C Webber tr Andreas Auster Group	Andreas, Isle of Man	21. 4.09S
G-AHBL	de Havilland DH.87B Hornet Moth	8135	P6786 CF-BFN	6. 2.46	H D Labouchere	Langham	10. 8.09S
G-AHBM	de Havilland DH.87B Hornet Moth	8126	P6785 CF-BFJ, (CF-BFO), CF-BFJ	6. 2.46	E P and P A Gliddon	Northfield Farm, Mavis Enderby	1.10.11
G-AHCL	Auster J/1N Alpha *(Originally regd as J/1 Autocrat)*	1977	G-OJVC G-AHCL	13. 5.46	D Frankland	RAF Mona	22.10.10S
G-AHCN	Auster J/1N Alpha *(Originally regd as J/1 Autocrat)*	1980	OY-AVM G-AHCN, OY-AVM, G-AHCN	25. 3.46	C L Towell and E Martinsen	Bakersfield	6.10.09P
G-AHCR	Gould-Taylorcraft Plus D Special *(Continental C90-14F)*	211	LB352	15. 4.46	D R Shepherd and D E H Balmford	Dunkeswell	7. 9.07P
G-AHEC (2)	Luscombe 8A Silvaire *(Continental A65-8)*	3428	N72001 NC72001	28.10.88	P G Baxter *(Noted 2.06)*	Hill Farm, Nayland	14. 7.05P
G-AHGD	de Havilland DH.89A Dragon Rapide *(Built Brush Coachworks Ltd)*	6862	NR786	1. 4.46	S G Jones	Membury	20. 9.92
G-AHGW	Taylorcraft Plus D	222	LB375	2. 9.46	C V Butler *(Operated Military Auster Flight as "LB375")*	Shenington	3. 5.96P
G-AHGZ	Taylorcraft Plus D	214	LB367	24. 4.46	M Pocock *(As "LB367" in RAF c/s)*	Henstridge	13.10.05
G-AHHH	Auster J/1N Alpha	2011	F-BAVR G-AHHH	11. 5.46	H A Jones	Swanton Abbot, Norwich	18. 6.08P
G-AHHT	Auster J/1N Alpha	2022		11. 5.46	A C Barber and N J Hudson tr Southdowns Auster Group	Durleighmarsh Farm, Rogate	1.12.07
G-AHIP (2)	Piper J-3C-65 Cub (L-4H-PI) *(Frame No.11950)* *(Officially regd with c/n 12008: see G-AJAD)*	12122	OO-GEJ OO-ALY, 44-79826	3. 7.85	R J Williamson	Crowfield	13.10.09P
G-AHIZ	de Havilland DH.82A Tiger Moth *(Built Morris Motors Ltd) (Regd with fuselage no.4610)*	86533	PG624	23. 4.46	CFG Flying Ltd	Cambridge	4. 6.09S
G-AHKX	Avro 19 Series 2	1333		18. 5.46	BAE Systems (Operations) Ltd *(On loan to Richard Shuttleworth Trustees)*	Old Warden	21. 8.09P
G-AHLK	Taylorcraft E Auster III	700	NJ889	1. 5.46	J H Powell-Tuck *(As "NJ889" in RAF c/s)*	Gloucestershire	27.11.09P
G-AHLT	de Havilland DH.82A Tiger Moth	82247	N9128	2. 5.46	M P Waring	White Waltham	13 8.09S
G-AHNR (2)	Taylorcraft BC-12D	7204	N43545 NC43545	15.11.88	M J Whitwell	Kemble	2. 6.09P
G-AHOO (2)	de Havilland DH.82A Tiger Moth *(Built Morris Motors Ltd)* *(Regd with c/n 86149)*	86150	6940M EM967	6. 6.85	J T and A D Milsom	Little Farm, Hamstead Marshall	14. 8.09S
G-AHPZ	de Havilland DH.82A Tiger Moth	83794	EI-AFJ G-AHPZ, T7280	22. 5.46	N J Wareing	Lee-on-Solent	21.11.10S
G-AHSA	Avro 621 Tutor *(AS Lynx IVM)*	-	K3215 G-AHSA, K3215	21. 6.46	Richard Shuttleworth Trustees *(As "K3241" in RAF Central Flying School 1930s c/s)*	Old Warden	30. 8.09P
G-AHSD	Taylorcraft Plus D	182	LB323	1. 7.46	A L Hall-Carpenter *(Restored and noted 8.06)*	Old Buckenham	10. 9.62
G-AHSO	Auster J/1N Alpha	2123		8. 8.46	W P Miller Northfield Farm, Mavis Enderby *(On rebuild 9.05)*		6. 4.95T
G-AHSP	Auster V J/1 Autocrat	2134	F-BGRO G-AHSP	8. 8.46	R M Weeks	Earls Colne	15. 1.10P
G-AHSS	Auster J/1N Alpha	2136		8. 8.46	A M Roche "Sunday Sierra"	Great Massingham	23. 7.09S
G-AHTE	Percival P.44 Proctor V	Ae58		26. 6.46	D K Tregilgas *(Stored 8.08 awaiting rebuild)*	Great Oakley	10. 8.61
G-AHUF (2)	de Havilland DH.82A Tiger Moth *(Built Morris Motors Ltd)*	86221	A2123 NL750	26. 2.85	Dream Ventures Ltd *(As "T-7997" in RAF c/s)*	Full Sutton	12. 7.09S
G-AHUG	Taylorcraft Plus D	153	LB282	5. 6.46	D Nieman	(Thame)	12. 7.70
G-AHUN (2)	Globe GC-1B Swift *(Lycoming IO-360-A1D)*	3536/766	EC-AJK OO-KAY, NC77764	24. 7.86	R J Hamlet *(On rebuild 1.09)*	North Weald	4. 8.95P
G-AHUV	de Havilland DH.82A Tiger Moth	3894	N6593	24. 6.46	A D Gordon	Blair Athol	27. 7.09S
G-AHVU	de Havilland DH.82A Tiger Moth	84728	T6313	14. 8.46	J B Steel *(As "T6313" in RAF c/s)*	Langham	29.12.11
G-AHVV	de Havilland DH.82A Tiger Moth *(Built Morris Motors Ltd)*	86123	EM929	24. 6.46	Ace Flight Training LLP	Dunkeswell	5. 3.10T
	(Substantially damaged following forced landing in a field near Dunkeswell 14. 9.08 due to loss of engine power and left wing struck a cow)						
G-AHWJ	Taylorcraft Plus D	165	LB294	20. 6.46	M Pocock *(New owner 1.03)*	Kemble	30. 6.71
G-AHXE	Taylorcraft Plus D	171	LB312	9. 7.46	J M C Pothecary *(As "LB312" in RAF c/s)*	AAC Netheravon	16. 7.08P

G-AIAA - G-AIZZ

G-AIBH	Auster J/1N Alpha	2113		19. 8.46	M J Bonnick	Standalone Farm, Meppershall	5. 9 10S
G-AIBM	Auster V J/1 Autocrat	2148		2. 9.46	R Greatrex	Colthrop Manor, Thatcham	21.11.10
G-AIBR	Auster J/1N Alpha	2151		2. 9.46	P R Hodson	Felthorpe	26.10.09S
G-AIBW	Auster J/1N Alpha	2158		2. 9.46	C R Sunter	Breighton	12. 7.09S

G-AIBX	Auster V J/1 Autocrat	2159		2. 9.46	B H Beeston tr The Wasp Flying Group		
						Little Gransden	5.12.08S
G-AIBY	Auster V J/1 Autocrat	2160		2. 9.46	D Morris (Stored 6.97)	Sherburn-in-Elmet	13. 4.81
G-AICX (2)	Luscombe 8A Silvaire	2568	N71141	27. 1.88	C C and J M Lovell *"Easy Grace"*	Chilbolton	23. 9.09P
	(Continental A65-8F)		NC71141				
G-AIDL	de Havilland DH.89A Dragon Rapide 6	6968	TX310	23. 8.46	Air Atlantique Ltd (As *"TX310"* in RAF c/s)	Coventry	29. 8.11
	(Built Brush Coachworks Ltd)						
G-AIDN	Vickers Supermarine VS.502 Spitfire Tr.VII		(N818MT)	22. 8.46	P M Andrews tr The G2 Trust (On rebuild 2008)		
		6S/729058	N58JE , G-AIDN, N32, MT818			Kemble	
G-AIDS	de Havilland DH.82A Tiger Moth	84546	T6055	22. 8.46	K D Pogmore and T Dann *"The Sorcerer"*		
						Benson's Farm, Laindon	11. 8.09S
G-AIEK	Miles M.38 Messenger 2A	6339	U-9	27. 8.46	G B E Pearce (As *"RG333"* in RAF 2 TAF Comm Sqdn c/s)		
						Washington, Suusex	26. 7.10
G-AIFZ	Auster J/1N Alpha	2182		2.11.46	M D Anstey (Noted 2004)		
						Rushett Farm, Chessington	20. 8.01
G-AIGD	Auster V J/1 Autocrat	2186		2.11.46	R B Webber (Noted 8.07)		
						Trenchard Farm, Eggesford	3. 5.07P
G-AIGF	Auster J/1N Alpha	2188		5.11.46	A R C Mathie	Carlisle	2.11.09P
G-AIGT	Auster J/1N Alpha	2176		12.10.46	R R Harris	(Crowfield)	22.10.76
G-AIIH	Piper J-3C-65 Cub (L-4H-PI)	11945	44-79649	14. 9.46	M S Pettit	Oxford	19.12.06P
G-AIJM	Auster V J/4 Archer	2069	EI-BEU	13.11.46	N Huxtable *"Priscilla"*	Cheddington	28. 3.97
			G-AIJM		(Damaged near Tring 5. 1.97: stored pending overhaul and /repairs)		
G-AIJT	Auster V J/4 Series 100 Archer	2075		13.11.46	J L Thorogood tr The Aberdeen Auster Flying Group		
						Pittrichie Farm, Whiterashes	10.11.08S
G-AIKE	Taylorcraft J Auster 5	1097	NJ728	15.11.46	C J Baker	Carr Farm, Thorney, Newark	3. 2.66
	(Built Taylorcraft Aeroplanes Ltd) (Frame No.TAY 2450)				(Crashed Luton 1. 9.65: dismantled 1.05)		
G-AIPR	Auster V J/4 Archer	2084		9. 1.47	R W and M A Mills tr The MPM Flying Group		
						Popham	27. 9.07P
G-AIPV	Auster V J/1 Autocrat	2203		9. 1.47	W P Miller *"Buttercup"*		
						Northfield Farm, Mavis Enderby	7. 2.05
G-AIRC	Auster V J/1 Autocrat	2215		13. 1.47	Z J Rockey	Trenchard Farm, Eggesford	2. 8.07
G-AIRK	de Havilland DH.82A Tiger Moth	82336	N9241	22.10.46	J S and P R Johnson		
						(Bradfield St Clare, Bury St Edmunds)	1. 8.07
G-AISA	Tipsy Trainer 1	17		24. 4.47	S Slater	Bicester	19. 4.08P
	(Walter Mikron 2)						
G-AISC	Tipsy Trainer 1	19		24. 4.47	D R Shepherd tr Wagtail Flying Group	(Prestwick)	23. 5.79P
	(Walter Mikron 2)				(Stored 5.02)		
G-AISS (2)	Piper J-3C-65 Cub (L-4H-PI)	12077	D-ECAV	3. 9.85	K W Wood and F Watson	Insch	25. 6.97P
	(Frame No.11904)		SL-AAA, 44-79781		(Fuselage noted 9.07 hanging from hangar roof unmarked)		
G-AIST	Vickers Supermarine 300 Spitfire IA		AR213	25.10.46	Sheringham Aviation UK Ltd	Wycombe Air Park	09.03.09P
		WASP/20/2			(As *"AR213: JZ-E"* in 57 OTU, RAF c/s)		
	(Built Westland Aircraft Ltd) (Also Heston Aircraft Company c/n HA1 6S/5 139)						
G-AISX	Piper J-3C-65 Cub (L-4H-PI)	11663	43-303722	8.10.46	N P Wedi tr Cubfly (As *"33072"* in USAAF c/s)		
	(Frame No.11489, Rebuilt with ex Spanish airframe, possibly EC-AQZ) (Continental C85-12)					Wycombe Air Park	21. 5.07P
G-AIUA	Miles M.14A Hawk Trainer 3	2035	T9768	11.11.46	D S Hunt	(Cobham)	13. 7.67P
	(Wings fitted 1960s from G-ANWO: crashed Roborough 26.9.65 and original centre section used to rebuild G-AKPF: fuselage stored)						
G-AIXJ	de Havilland DH.82A Tiger Moth	85434	DE426	28.11.46	D Green	(Pulborough)	13. 8.09S
	(Built Morris Motors Ltd) (Probably rebuilt with composite airframe by Newbury Aeroplane Company c 1991)						
G-AIXN	Automobilove Zavody Mraz M 1C Sokol	112	OK-BHA	22. 4.47	A J Wood	Breighton	10. 7.09P
	(Walter Mikron 4-3)						
G-AIYG (2)	SNCAN Stampe SV-4B	21	OO-CKZ	31. 8.89	J E Henny	Shoten, Belgium	17. 4.11S
	(DH Gipsy Major 10 Mk 2)		F-BCKZ, French AF				
G-AIYR	de Havilland DH.89A Dragon Rapide	6676	HG691	11.12.46	Spectrum Leisure Ltd (As *"HG691"* in RAF c/s)		
	(Built Brush Coachworks Ltd)				(Operated Classic Wings)	Duxford	1. 5..08T
G-AIYS	de Havilland DH.85 Leopard Moth	7089	YI-ABI	16.12.46	R A and V A Gammons	RAF Henlow	3. 6.10S
			SU-ABM				
G-AIZU	Auster V J/1 Autocrat	2228		31. 1.47	C J and J G B Morley	Popham	26. 5.09P
G-AIZY	Auster V J/1 Autocrat	2233		31. 1.47	B J Richards	(City of Bristol College, Bristol)	20. 9.78
					(Damaged Portskewett, Caldicot 8.89: on rebuild)		

G-AJAA - G-AJZZ

G-AJAD (2)	Piper J-3C-65 Cub (L-4H-PI)	12008	OO-GEJ (1)	26. 6.84	C R Shipley	Kemble	18. 6.09P
	(Frame No.11835) (Regd with c/n 11700)		44-79712				
	(Airframe has original fuselage of OO-GEJ discarded in a rebuild in 1970s; OO-GEJ rebuilt with Frame No.11950 (c/n 12122) ex						
	OO-ALY/44-79826 and now G-AHIP: OO-ALY rebuilt from c/n 11700 ex OO-TON (ex 43-30409))						
G-AJAE	Auster J/1N Alpha	2237		4. 2.47	J Cooke tr Lichfield Auster Group		
						Streethay Farm, Lichfield	7. 9.09S
G-AJAJ	Auster J/1N Alpha	2243		4. 2.47	R B Lawrence	Watchford Farm, Yarcombe	1. 4.07
G-AJAM	Auster V J/2 Arrow	2371		8. 2.47	D A Porter	Griffins Farm, Temple Bruer	23. 7.09P
G-AJAP (2)	Luscombe 8A Silvaire	2305	N45778	26. 1.89	M Flint	Fenland	8. 7.09P
	(Continental A65-8)		NC45778				
G-AJAS	Auster J/1N Alpha	2319		14. 3.47	C J Baker (Noted complete 1.05)		
						Carr Farm, Thorney, Newark	11. 4.90
G-AJCP (2)	Druine D 31 Turbulent	PFA 512		9. 2.59	B R Pearson tr Turbulent Group	Eaglescott	4. 9.78S
	(Built Rollason Aircraft and Engines) (Ardem 4C02)				(Stored 10.95)		
G-AJEE	Auster V J/1 Autocrat	2309		14. 3.47	P Bate and A C Whitehead	Barton	10. 4.09P
G-AJEH	Auster J/1N Alpha	2312		14. 3.47	J Powell-Tuck	(Mamhilad, Pontypool)	28. 5.90
G-AJEI	Auster J/1N Alpha	2313		14. 3.47	J Siddall	North Moor, Scunthorpe	23. 6.09P
	(Originally regd as Auster J/1 Autocrat) (DH Gipsy Major I) (Composite rebuild 1976 with fuselage of F-BFUT c/n 3357)						
G-AJEM	Auster V J/1 Autocrat	2317	F-BFPB	14. 3.47	C D Wilkinson	Rosemarket	17. 5.10
			G-AJEM				
G-AJES (2)	Piper J-3C-65 Cub (L-4H-PI)	11776	OO-ACB	21. 9.84	G W Jarvis (As *"330485:C-44"* in USAAC c/s)		
	(Frame No.11602)		43-30485			Mill Farm, Shifnal	14. 9.07P

G-AJGJ	Taylorcraft J Auster 5	1147	RT486	31. 1.47	D Gotts and E J Downing tr Auster RT486 Flying Group
					(As "RT486:PF-A" in RAF c/s) Lee-on-Solent 4. 6.10S
G-AJHS	de Havilland DH.82A Tiger Moth	82121	N6866	12. 2.47	J M Voeten and H van Der Paauw tr Flying Wires
					(Operated Vliegend Museum)
					Seppe-Hoeven, Netherlands 22. 7.09S
G-AJIH	Auster V J/1 Autocrat	2318		2. 4.47	D G Curran Newtownards 10. 4.09P
G-AJIS	Auster J/1N Alpha	2336		30. 4.47	J D Smith and J M Hodgson tr Husthwaite Auster Group
					Baxby Manor, Husthwaite 3. 7.09S
G-AJIT	Auster V J/1 Kingsland	2337		30. 4.47	J W Cudby and A P Barrett tr G-AJIT Group
					Netherthorpe 8. 7.09P
G-AJIU	Auster V J/1 Autocrat	2338		30. 4.47	M D Greenhalgh Netherthorpe 20. 6.03
G-AJIW	Auster J/1N Alpha	2340		30. 4.47	W C Walters Spanhoe 22. 8.04
G-AJJS (2)	Cessna 120	13047	8R-GBO	7. 1.87	R W Marchant and S C Parsons tr Robhurst Flying Group
	(Rebuilt 1994 with new airframe?)		VP-GBO		Little Engeham Farm, Woodchurch 20. 5.09P
			VP-TBO, N1106M, YV-T-CTA, NC2786N		
G-AJJT (2)	Cessna 120	12881	N2621N	27. 1.88	J S Robson Franklyn's Field, Chewton Mendip 6. 2.09P
	(Continental C85-12F)		NC2621N		(Believed to have departed during 2008)
G-AJJU (2)	Luscombe 8E Silvaire Deluxe	2295	N45768	10. 1.89	S C Weston and R J Hopcraft "Juliet Uniform"
	(Continental C85-12F)		NC45768		Enstone 7. 9.09P
G-AJKB (2)	Luscombe 8E Silvaire Deluxe	3058	N71631	4. 1.89	L Jump and T Carter (Liverpool) 4.12.09P
	(Continental C85-12F)		NC71631		
G-AJOE	Miles M.38 Messenger 2A	6367		28. 4.47	P W Bishop (Reading) 18.12.07
	(On rebuild 2007 after forced landing in Holland in 2006? which tore off starboard wing)				
G-AJON (2)	Aeronca 7AC Champion	7AC-2633	OO-TWH	3. 1.86	J M Gale Dunkeswell 10. 6.08P
G-AJPI	Fairchild 24R-46A Argus III (UC-61A-FA)	851	HB614	26. 4.47	R Sijben (As "314887" in USAAF c/s)
			43-14887		(Heel, Netherlands) 27. 6.10S
G-AJRB	Auster V J/1 Autocrat	2350		12. 5.47	P D Hamilton-Box Trenchard Farm, Eggesford 10. 4.09P
G-AJRE	Auster V J/1 Autocrat	2603		12. 5.47	P Slater tr Air Tech Spares
					Wellesbourne Mountford 17. 5.10S
G-AJRS	Miles M.14A Hawk Trainer 3	1750	P6382	30. 4.47	Richard Shuttleworth Trustees Old Warden 11. 4.09P
	(Composite a/c, flew as "G-AJDR" 1.54/3.71)		G-AJDR, G-AJRS, P6382		(As "P6382:C" in RAF 16 EFTS c/s)
G-AJTW	de Havilland DH.82A Tiger Moth	82203	N6965	21. 5.47	J A Barker (As "N6965:FL-J") Tibenham 9. 9.00
	(Crashed landing Raydon near Ipswich 7. 6.99 and extensively damaged: wreck noted 7.02)				
G-AJUE	Auster V J/1 Autocrat	2616		5. 6.47	P H B Cole Craysmarsh Farm, Melksham 22. 6.06
G-AJUL	Auster J/1N Alpha	2624		18. 6.47	M J Crees (On rebuild 12.90) Halstead, Essex 11. 9.81
G-AJVE	de Havilland DH.82A Tiger Moth	85814	DE943	28. 5.47	R A Gammons RAF Henlow 10. 6.09S
	(Composite rebuild 1981 including substantial parts of G-APGL c/n 86460 ex NM140)				
G-AJWB	Miles M.38 Messenger 2A	6699		17. 6.47	P W Bishop (Woodley, Reading) 8. 5.11
G-AJXC	Taylorcraft J Auster 5	1409	TJ343	11. 6.47	R D Helliar-Symons, K A and S E W Williams
					Bourne Park, Hurstbourne Tarrant 2. 8.82
G-AJXV	Taylorcraft G Auster 4	1065	F-BEEJ	8. 9.47	B A Farries (As "NJ695" in RAF c/s) "Little Lulu"
			G-AJXV, NJ695		Carr Farm, Thorney, Newark 13. 7.09S
G-AJXY	Taylorcraft G Auster 4	792	MT243	4. 5.48	A G Barrell tr X-Ray Yankee Group
					(Woodbridge) 10.11.70
G-AJYB	Auster J/1N Alpha	847	MS974	3. 2.49	P J Shotbolt Ingthorpe Farm, Great Casterton 3. 8.09P

G-AKAA - G-AKZZ

G-AKAT	Miles M.14A Hawk Trainer 3	2005	F-AZOR	2. 7.47	R A Fleming (As "T9738" in RAF c/s) Breighton 28. 9.09P
			G-AKAT, T9738		
G-AKAZ (2)	Piper J-3C-65 Cub (L-4A-PI)	AN.1 & 8499	F-BFYL	19. 4.82	Frazerblades Ltd (As "G-57" in 83rd FS/78th FG USAAC c/s)
	(Frame No.8616)		French AF, 42-36375		Duxford 12. 4.09P
G-AKDN	de Havilland DHC-1A Chipmunk 10	11		14. 8.47	P S Derry Saskatoon, Canada 31. 5.07
G-AKDW	de Havilland DH.89A Dragon Rapide	6897	F-BCDB	25. 8.47	de Havilland Aircraft Museum Trust Ltd "City of Winchester"
	(Built Brush Coachworks Ltd)		G-AKDW, YI-ABD, NR833		Salisbury Hall, London Colney 8. 5.59
G-AKEN	Miles M.65 Gemini 1A	6486	VH-GBB	8. 9.47	C W P Turner (Snitterfield, Stratford-upon-Avon) 7.10.54
			VH-BTP (1), G-AKEN		
G-AKEX	Percival P.34 Proctor III	H 549	SE-BTR	26. 8.47	M Biddulph (For rebuild 10.08) Great Oakley
	(Built F Hills and Sons Ltd)		G-AKEX, LZ791		
G-AKHP	Miles M.65 Gemini 1A	6519		3.10.47	M Hales Little Staughton 11. 6.09S
G-AKHU	Miles M.65 Gemini 1A	6522	VH-BOB (2)	18.10.47	C W P Turner (Snitterfield, Stratford-upon-Avon) 28. 2.49
			(VH-DFP), VH-WEK, VH-WEJ, VH-BMV, G-AKHU		
G-AKIB (2)	Piper J-3C-90 Cub (L-4H-PI)	12311	OO-RAY	18. 4.84	M C Bennett (As "480015:M-44" in USAAC c/s)
	(Frame No.12139)		44-80015		Perranporth 19. 8.06P
	(Caught by gust of wind and overturned beside runway.Perranporth 2. 7.06 with substantial damage: on rebuild 2007)				
G-AKIF	de Havilland DH.89A Dragon Rapide	6838	LN-BEZ	24. 9.47	Airborne Taxi Services Ltd
			G-AKIF, NR750		Duxford and Wycombe Air Park 5. 7.10S
G-AKIN	Miles M.38 Messenger 2A	6728		19. 9.47	D L Sentance tr Sywell Messenger Group Sywell 11. 7.09S
G-AKIU	Percival Proctor V	Ae129		20. 2.48	Air Atlantique Ltd Seaton Ross 24. 1.65
					(Under restoration by Hornet Aviation 2.04)
G-AKKB	Miles M.65 Gemini 1A	6537		28.10.47	J Buckingham (Air Total c/s) New Farm, Felton 19. 5.08
G-AKKH	Miles M.65 Gemini 1A	6479	OO-CDO	23. 7.48	J S Allison Bicester 5.10.09S
G-AKPF	Miles M.14A Hawk Trainer 3	2228	V1075	27. 1.48	P R Holloway (As "N3788" in RAF c/s) Old Warden 10. 4.09P
	(Rebuilt 1955 as composite with centre-section from G-AIUA, fuselage from G-ANLT, wings from G-AHYL: rebuilt 1970/80 with				
	about 10% of fuselage from G-AKPF: tail unit also from G-ANLT)				
G-AKRA (2)	Piper J-3C-65 Cub (L-4H-PI)	11255	I-FIVI	15. 6.84	W R Savin (On rebuild 5.05) (Cambridge)
	(Frame No.11080)		43-29964		
G-AKRP	de Havilland DH.89A Dragon Rapide 4	6940	CN-TTO	26. 1.48	B R Pearson tr Eaglescott Dominie Group
			(F-DAFS), G-AKRP, RL958		"Northamptonshire Rose" Eaglescott 6. 1.08S
G-AKSY	Taylorcraft J Auster 5	1567	F-BGOO	10. 2.48	A Brier (As "TJ534" in AAC c/s) Breighton 17. 5.10S
			G-AKSY, TJ534		
G-AKSZ	Taylorcraft J Auster 5C	1503	F-BGPQ	10. 2.48	P W Yates and R G Darbyshire
	(Large fin and rudder)		G-AKSZ, TJ457		(Adlington, Chorley) 9. 5.02

G-AKTH (2)	Piper J-3C-65 Cub *(L-4J-PI)*	13211	OO-AGL	14. 7.86	G J Harry, The Viscount Goschen		
	(Frame No.13041)		PH-UCR, 45-4471			Bradleys Lawn, Heathfield	19. 5.09P
	(Regd with incorrect c/n 13047)						
G-AKTI (2)	Luscombe 8A Silvaire	4101	N1374K	27. 5.87	J D May	White Waltham	13. 5.09P
			NC1374K				
G-AKTN (2)	Luscombe 8A Silvaire	3540	N77813	22. 7.88	P C Hignett and PG Ward	(Harwich)	1. 6.04P
			NC77813				
G-AKTO (2)	Aeronca 7BCM Champion	7AC-940	N8515X	19. 5.88	R M Davies	(Amersham)	25. 4.09P
	(Modified ex 7AC standard 1950)		N82311, NC82311				
G-AKTP (2)	Piper PA-17 Vagabond	17-82	N4683H	24. 6.88	P J B Lewis tr Golf Tango Papa Group	Swansea	5. 8.03P
			NC4683H				
G-AKTR (2)	Aeronca 7AC Champion	7AC-3017	N58312	19. 6.89	R Tarplee *"Eddie"*	(Gilfachrheda)	26.10.09P
			NC58312				
G-AKTS (2)	Cessna 120	11875	N77434	26. 5.88	M Isterling	Insch	4.11.09P
			NC77434				
G-AKTT (2)	Luscombe 8A Silvaire	3279	N71852	21. 7.88	S J Charters *(Crashed 6. 7.91: stored)*		
			NC71852			(Eddsfield, Octon Lodge Farm, Thwing)	23. 6.92P
G-AKUE (2)	de Havilland DH.82A Tiger Moth	P 68	ZS-FZL	12. 2.86	D F Hodgkinson	Maypole Farm, Chislet	6.11.10S
	(Built OGMA)		CR-AGM, Portuguese AF FAP ????				
G-AKUF (2)	Luscombe 8F Silvaire	4794	N2067K	1. 8.88	M O Loxton	Parsonage Farm, Eastchurch	7. 8.03P
	(Continental C90-12F)		NC2067K				
G-AKUH (2)	Luscombe 8E Silvaire Deluxe	4644	N1917K	24.10.88	E J Lloyd	Cardington	27. 7.09P
	(Continental O-200-A)		NC1917K				
G-AKUJ (2)	Luscombe 8E Silvaire Deluxe	5282	N2555K	4. 8.88	R C Green	Coventry	31. 7.07P
	(Continental C85-12F)		NC2555K				
G-AKUK (2)	Luscombe 8A Silvaire	5793	N1166B	28.10.88	O R Watts	Roughay Farm, Bishops Waltham	17. 9.09P
	(Continental A65-8F)		NC1166B				
G-AKUL (2)	Luscombe 8A Silvaire	4189	N1462K	9. 2.89	E A Taylor *(Open store 2.09)*	Southend	21. 5.90P
	(Continental A65-8F)		NC1462K				
G-AKUM (2)	Luscombe 8F Silvaire	6452	N2025B	17. 2.88	D A Young	North Weald	20. 5.09P
	(Continental C90-12F)						
G-AKUN (2)	Piper J-3C-85 Cub	6914	N38304	13. 1.89	W R Savin	Coldharbour Farm, Willingham	31. 5.08P
			NC38304				
G-AKUO (2)	Aeronca 11AC Chief	11AC-1376	N9730E	16. 1.89	L W Richardson		
			NC9730E			Ventfield Farm, Horton-cum-Studley,Oxford	11.10.08P
G-AKUP (2)	Luscombe 8E Silvaire Deluxe	5501	N2774K	9. 5.89	D A Young *(Dismantled awaiting rebuild 1.09)*		
			NC2774K			North Weald	
G-AKUR (2)	Cessna 140	13819	N1647V	26. 1.89	J Greenaway and C A Davis *(Noted 10.07 on slow rebuild)*		
			NC1647V			Phoenix Farm, Lower Upham	21. 9.95
G-AKUW	Chrislea CH.3 Series 2 Super Ace	105		8. 3.48	J and S Rickett	North Coates	25. 3.09P
G-AKVF	Chrislea CH.3 Series 2 Super Ace	114	AP-ADT	8. 3.48	B Metters	Little Rissington	15. 4.09P
			G-AKVF				
G-AKVM (2)	Cessna 120	13431	N3173N	10. 1.89	N and S Wise	Croft Farm, Croft-on-Tees	12. 8.09P
			NC3173N				
G-AKVN (2)	Aeronca 11AC Chief	11AC-469	N3742B	13. 1.89	P A Jackson *(Carries "3742B" on fin)*		
			N86047, NC86047			Priory Farm, Tibenham	28. 2.09P
G-AKVO (2)	Taylorcraft BC-12D	9845	N44045	10. 1.89	A Weir	(Cranwell Village, Sleaford)	4. 7.07P
			NC44045				
G-AKVP (2)	Luscombe 8A Silvaire	5549	N2822K	21. 7.48	J M Edis	Charity Farm, Baxterley	2. 7.09P
	(Continental A65-8)		NC2822K				
G-AKVR	Chrislea CH.3 Series 4 Skyjeep	125	VH-OLD	8. 3.48	R B Webber	Trenchard Farm, Eggesford	7. 9.07P
			VH-RCD, VH-BRP, G-AKVR				
G-AKVZ	Miles M.38 Messenger 4B	6352	RH427	25. 6.48	Shipping and Airlines Ltd	Biggin Hill	11. 3.10S
G-AKWS	Auster 5A-160	1237	RT610	1. 4.48	A J Collins tr Interesting Aircraft Company		
					(As "RT610" in AAC c/s)	Long Marston	19. 9.09S
G-AKXP	Taylorcraft J Auster 5	1017	NJ633	13. 4.48	A D Pearce	Eastbach Farm, Coleford	19.12.70
					(Crashed St Mary's, Isles of Scilly 4. 70: noted as "NJ633" 8.07)		
G-AKXS	de Havilland DH.82A Tiger Moth	83512	T7105	13. 4.48	J and G J Eagles	Oaksey Park	21. 3.03T
					(Spun into ground White Waltham 21. 7.02 and badly damaged)		

G-ALAA - G-ALZZ

G-ALBD	de Havilland DH.82A Tiger Moth	84130	T7748	27. 5.48	C H Schoonbeek	Midden Zeeland, Netherlands	31.10.81
			(Damaged Leopoldsburg, Belgium 24. 5.81: noted 10.05 with Gyrocopter Aviation being rebuilt for static display)				
G-ALBJ	Taylorcraft J Auster 5	1831	TW501	3. 6.48	P N Elkington	Cottage Farm, Bloxholm	23. 8.07
G-ALBK	Taylorcraft J Auster 5	1273	RT644	3. 6.48	K Wheatcroft	(Wigston)	29. 6.09S
G-ALEH (2)	Piper PA-17 Vagabond	17-87	N4689H	17. 8.81	A D Pearce	White Waltham	28. 3.09P
			NC4689H				
G-ALFA	Taylorcraft J Auster 5	1236	RT607	20.10.48	G M Rundle	RAF Shawbury	6.12.10
			(P/i uncertain as c/n 1236 considered sold as HB-EOC 4.48: reported as c/n 826 (MS958) but doubtful)				
G-ALGA (2)	Piper PA-15 Vagabond	15-348	N4575H	3.12.86	S T Gilbert	Enstone	17. 9.09P
			NC4575H				
G-ALGT	Vickers Supermarine 379 Spitfire F XIVc	RM689	9. 2.49	Rolls-Royce PLC	Filton	31 .7.92P
		6S/432263	"RM619", G-ALGT, RM689				
			(Destroyed in crash Woodford 27. 6.92: on restoration Sandown 8.04)				
G-ALIJ (2)	Piper PA-17 Vagabond	17-166	N4866H	13. 2.87	A S Cowan tr Popham Flying Group G-ALIJ		
						Popham	18. 3.09P
G-ALIW (2)	de Havilland DH.82A Tiger Moth	82901	N27WB	17. 8.81	F R Curry *(Operated Delta Aviation)*	Sibson	16. 9.09S
			ZK-ATI, NZ899, R5006				
G-ALJF	Percival Proctor III	K 427	Z7252	3. 3.49	J F Moore	Biggin Hill	12. 9.10S
G-ALJL	de Havilland DH.82A Tiger Moth	84726	T6311	7. 3.49	D E and R I Souch	Hill Farm, Durley	28. 9.50
	(Built Morris Motors Ltd)				*(On long term rebuild from components 8.00)*		
G-ALJR	Abbott-Baynes Scud III	2	BGA283-ACF	16. 3.49	L P Woodage	Dunstable	4. 3.06
			G-ALJR, BGA283-ACF				

G-ALLF	Slingsby T 30A Kirby Prefect	548	BGA599	29. 3.49	J F Hopkins and K M Fresson "ARK"		
			PH-1, BGA599, G-ALLF, BGA599			RNAS Yeovilton	
G-ALNA	de Havilland DH.82A Tiger Moth	85061	T6774	11. 4.49	R J Doughton (Brooklands Aviation titles)		
						Vendee Air Park, France	6. 6.10S
G-ALND	de Havilland DH.82A Tiger Moth	82308	N9191	12. 4.49	J Powell-Tuck	(Mamhilad, Pontypool)	11. 4.82
					(Crashed Panshanger 8. 3.81 and on rebuild 3.96)		
G-ALOD (2)	Cessna 140	14691	N2440V	14.10.83	J R Stainer	Whitehall Farm, Benington	11. 1.08E
G-ALRI	de Havilland DH.82A Tiger Moth	83350	ZK-BAB	2. 5.51	T W Smallwood (As "T5672" in RAF c/s)		
	(Built Morris Motors Ltd)		G-ALRI, T5672			(Woodstock)	22. 6.07
G-ALTO (2)	Cessna 140	14253	N2040V	19. 1.82	T M, P M and M L Jones	Derby	30. 6.11S
G-ALUC	de Havilland DH.82A Tiger Moth	83094	R5219	28. 6.49	D R and M Wood Fowle Hall Farm, Paddock Wood		30. 5.11
G-ALWB	de Havilland DHC-1 Chipmunk 22A	C1/0100	OE-ABC	28.12.49	D J Neville and P A D Neville	Little Gransden	13.10.11
			G-ALWB				
G-ALWS	de Havilland DH.82A Tiger Moth	82415	N9328	24. 1.50	A P Beynon (On rebuild 8.00)	Trehelig, Welshpool	
	(Officially regd with c/n 82413)						
G-ALWW	de Havilland DH.82A Tiger Moth	86366	NL923	24. 1.50	D E Findon tr Stratford-upon-Avon Tiger Moth Group		
	(Built Morris Motors Ltd)					Bidford	11. 3.09
G-ALXZ	Taylorcraft J Auster 5-150	1082	D-EGOF	1. 2.50	D J Langrick tr G-ALXZ Syndicate	Sywell	14. 9.09S
	(Frame No.TAY24070)		PH-NER, G-ALXZ, NJ689				
G-ALYG	Taylorcraft J Auster 5D	835	MS968?	14. 3.50	A L Young	Henstridge	19. 1.70
	(Officially regd with incorrect identity MT968)				(Frame stored 8.02: for possible rebuild as Auster 5)		

G-AMAA - G-AMZZ

G-AMAW	Luton LA-4 Minor	JRC.01		29. 4.50	The Real Aeroplane Company Ltd	Breighton	6. 8.88P
	(Built J R Coates) (Aka Swalesong SA.I with c/n SA.I) (Bristol Cherub 3)				(Noted dismantled 12.07)		
G-AMBB	de Havilland DH.82A Tiger Moth	85070	T6801	1. 5.50	J Eagles (On rebuild 6.95)	Oaksey Park	
	(Composite rebuild - parts to "G-MAZY" ? - details in SECTION 6, Part 4)						
G-AMCK	de Havilland DH.82A Tiger Moth	84641	N65N	15. 6.50	Liverpool Flying School Ltd Liverpool-John Lennon		7. 5.10S
			C-GBBF, SLN-05, D-EGXY, HB-UAC, G-AMCK, T6193				
G-AMCM	de Havilland DH.82A Tiger Moth	85295	DE249	14.12.50	A K and J I Cooper	Denford Manor, Hungerford	28. 5.56
	(Regd with c/n "89259")		(Crashed near Somerton 25. 9.55: rear fuselage frame on restoration 10.01 but not original G-AMCM)				
G-AMEN (2)	Piper PA-18 Super Cub 95(L-18C-PI)	18-1998	(G-BJTR)	29.12.81	A Lovejoy and W Cook tr The G-AMEN Flying Group		
	(Frame No.18-1963)		MM52-2398 "EI.71", I-EIAM, MM52-2398, 52-2398			Popham	26. 7.03P
	(Italian rebuild c/n OMA.71-08)						
G-AMHF	de Havilland DH.82A Tiger Moth	83026	R5144	6. 2.51	Wavendon Social Housing Ltd	Sywell	4. 9.11
	(Rebuilt with components from G-BABA c/n 86584 ex F-BGDT/PG687						
G-AMIV	de Havilland DH.82A Tiger Moth	83105	R5246	9. 4.51	K F Crumplin (Noted 8.07) (As "R5246 in RAF c/s)		
						(Croscombe, Wells)	12.11.65
G-AMKU	Auster V J/1B Aiglet	2721	ST-ABD	10. 7.51	P G Lipman	Romney Street Farm, Sevenoaks	11. 7.09S
			SN-ABD, G-AMKU				
G-AMMS	Auster J/5K Aiglet Trainer	2745		11.10.51	R B Webber	Trenchard Farm, Eggesford	21.12.09P
G-AMNN	de Havilland DH.82A Tiger Moth	86457	NM137	24.12.51	I J Perry	Shoreham	23. 3.09S
	(Composite rebuild with unidentified airframe: original G-AMNN posssibly absorbed into G-BPAJ qv)						
G-AMPG (2)	Piper PA-12 Super Cruiser	12-985	N2647M	25. 3.85	A G and S M Measey	Leicester	22.10.09P
	(Hoerner wing-tips)		NC2647				
G-AMPI (2)	SNCAN Stampe SV-4C	213	N6RA	13. 2.84	T W Harris	Wycombe Air Park	20.11.10P
	(Renault 4PO3)		F-BCFX				
G-AMPY	Douglas C-47B-15-DK Dakota 3	15124/26569		8. 3.52	Air Atlantique Ltd (As "KK116" in RAF c/s) Coventry		4. 7.11S
			G-AMPY, N15751, G-AMPY, TF-FIO, G-AMPY, JY-ABE, G-AMPY, KK116, 43-49308				
G-AMRA	Douglas C-47B-15-DK Dakota 6	15290/26735	XE280	8. 3.52	RVL Aviation Ltd (ClassicFlight.com titles)		
			G-AMRA, KK151, 43-49474			Coventry	13. 7.09S
G-AMRF	Auster J/5F Aiglet Trainer	2716	VT-DHA	20. 3.52	D A Hill	Fenland	31. 3.07
			G-AMRF				
G-AMRK	Gloster Gladiator I	?	L8032	16. 5.52	Richard Shuttleworth Trustees (As "K7985 "in 73 Sqdn RAF c/s)		
	(Bristol Mercury 30)		"K8032", G-AMRK, L8032			Old Warden	17. 4.08P
G-AMSG	SIPA 903	77	OO-VBL	25.11.81	S W Markham	Valentine Farm, Odiham	13. 7.08P
			F-BGHB				
G-AMTA	Auster J/5F Aiglet Trainer	2780		24. 5.52	J D Manson	Little Snoring	24.10.09S
G-AMTF	de Havilland DH.82A Tiger Moth	84207	OO-TMW	11. 6.52	H A D Monro (As "T-7842" in RAF c/s)	Headcorn	11.12.09
			G-AMTF, ZK-AVE, G-AMTF, T7842				
G-AMTK	de Havilland DH.82A Tiger Moth	3982	N6709	18. 6.52	M E Vaisey tr Chiltern Flying Club and S W McKay		
					(Stored)	(Berkhamsted)	27. 5.66
G-AMTM	Auster V J/1 Autocrat	3101	G-AJUJ	3. 7.52	R J Stobo	Oaklands Farm, Stonesfield, Witney	5. 7.06P
	(Auster rebuild - originally c/n 2622)		(Struck telegraph pole laid across end of runway landing Oaklands 22. 4.06 and substantially damaged)				
G-AMTV	de Havilland DH.82A Tiger Moth	3858	OO-SOE	5. 8.52	M G and L J Collins (Noted 10.07)	Sywell	4. 3.07
			G-AMTV, N6545				
G-AMUF	de Havilland DHC-1 Chipmunk 21	C1/0832		2. 9.52	Redhill Tailwheel Flying Club Ltd	Dunsfold	6. 3.11P
G-AMUI	Auster J/5F Aiglet Trainer	2790		29. 8.52	R B Webber (Noted 9.08)		
						Trenchard Farm, Eggesford	15. 2.66T
G-AMVD	Taylorcraft J Auster 5	1565	F-BGTF	6.10.52	M Hammond	Airfield Farm, Hardwick	5. 6.09P
			G-AMVD, TJ565		(As "TJ565" in RAF camouflage & D-Day stripes c/s: 652 Sqdn crest)		
G-AMVP	Tipsy Junior	J 111	OO-ULA	23.10.52	A R Wershat	Sandown	21. 4.09P
	(Walter Mikron 2)						
G-AMVS	de Havilland DH.82A Tiger Moth	82784	OO-SOJ	12.11.52	J Powell-Tuck (On rebuild 8.92)		
			G-AMVS, R4852			(Mamhilad, Pontypool)	21.12.53
G-AMYD	Auster J/5L Aiglet Trainer	2773		13. 2.53	R D Thomasson	(Romford)	3. 9.04
G-AMZI	Auster J/5F Aiglet Trainer	3104		4. 5.53	J F Moore	Rexden, Rye	16. 2.07
G-AMZT	Auster J/5F Aiglet Trainer	3107		28. 5.53	D Hyde, J W Saull, and J C Hutchinson		
						Wycombe Air Park	18. 4.10S
G-AMZU	Auster J/5F Aiglet Trainer	3108		28. 5.53	J A Longworth, A R M and C B A Eagle tr Flying Flicks		
						White Waltham	5.10.08S

G-ANAA - G-ANZZ

G-ANAF	Douglas C-47B-35-DK Dakota 3	16688/33436	N170GP	17. 6.53	Air Atlantique Ltd	Coventry	9. 4.10S
			G-ANAF, KP220, 44-77104		*(Thales titles - special radar fit under nose)*		
G-ANCS	de Havilland DH.82A Tiger Moth	82824	R4907	12. 9.53	C E Edwards and E A Higgins		
						(Welling and Chatham)	23. 7.09
G-ANCX	de Havilland DH.82A Tiger Moth	83719	T7229	15. 9.53	D R Wood	Fowle Hall Farm, Paddock Wood	28. 7.02
	(Built Morris Motors Ltd)						
G-ANDE	de Havilland DH.82A Tiger Moth	85957	G-YVFS	21. 6.06	D A Nisbet	Sywell	29. 3.10S
	(Built Morris Motors Ltd)		G-ANDE, EM726				
	(Severe damage to wings following force landing at Homefield Farm, near Redhill 14. 9.07 and collision with a hay bale)						
G-ANDM	de Havilland DH.82A Tiger Moth	3946	EI-AGP	23. 9.53	N J Stagg	Frogland Cross	13. 3.11
			G-ANDM, EI-AGP, G-ANDM, (G-ANDI), N6642				
G-ANDP	de Havilland DH.82A Tiger Moth	82868	D-EBEC	22. 9.53	A H Diver	Newtownards	10.12.11
			N9920F, G-ANDP, R4960				
G-ANEH	de Havilland DH.82A Tiger Moth	82067	N6797	29. 9.53	G J Wells *(As "N-6797" in RAF training c/s)*		
						Wycombe Air Park	18. 7.10
G-ANEL	de Havilland DH.82A Tiger Moth	82333	N9238	1.10.53	Totalsure Ltd	Langham	29. 1.12
G-ANEM	de Havilland DH.82A Tiger Moth	82943	EI-AGN	1.10.53	P J Benest	Hamstead Marshall	19. 7.11S
			G-ANEM, R5042				
G-ANEN	de Havilland DH.82A Tiger Moth	85418	OO-ACG	2.10.53	A J D Douglas-Hamilton	Goodwood	9. 5.11S
			G-ANEN, DE410				
G-ANEW	de Havilland DH.82A Tiger Moth	86458	NM138	6.10.53	K F Crumplin *(Noted 4.07)*	Henstridge	18. 6.62T
	(Built Morris Motors Ltd)						
G-ANEZ	de Havilland DH.82A Tiger Moth	84218	T7849	20.10.53	C D J Bland	Sandown	9. 7.08
G-ANFC	de Havilland DH.82A Tiger Moth	85385	DE363	13.10.53	J E Pierce *(Noted 5.05)*	Ley Farm, Chirk	9.10.03T
	(Built Morris Motors Ltd)						
G-ANFI	de Havilland DH.82A Tiger Moth	85577	DE623	16.10.53	G P Graham *(As "DE623" in RAF c/s)*	Cardiff	4. 6.09
	(Built Morris Motors Ltd)						
	(Note Tiger Moth D-EDON is displayed at Auto und Technik Museum, Sinsheim, Germany also as "DE623")						
G-ANFL	de Havilland DH.82A Tiger Moth	84617	T6169	22.10.53	Felthorpe Tiger Group Ltd	Felthorpe	5. 7.10S
	(Built Morris Motors Ltd)						
G-ANFM	de Havilland DH.82A Tiger Moth	83604	T5888	22.10.53	A J Coker, L S Mitton and N H Lemon tr Reading Flying Group		
	(Built Morris Motors Ltd)					White Waltham	8. 3.11S
G-ANFP	de Havilland DH.82A Tiger Moth	82530	N9503	28.10.53	G D Horn *(Frame only 1.00)*	(Fordingbridge)	1. 7.63
G-ANFV	de Havilland DH.82A Tiger Moth	85904	DF155	1.12.53	R A L Falconer *(As "DF155" in RAF c/s)*		
	(Built Morris Motors Ltd)					Shempston Farm, Lossiemouth	2.10.09S
	(Heavy landing at Shempston Farm strip 21. 6.08 causing fuselage damage)						
G-ANGK (2)	Cessna 140A	15396	N9675A	10. 3.89	I J F MacDonald tr Shempston Cessna Group		
						Longside, Peterhead	12. 8.07
G-ANHK	de Havilland DH.82A Tiger Moth	82442	F-BHIM	4.12.53	J D Iliffe	Haw Farm, Hampstead Norrey's	14. 7.10
			G-ANHK, N9372				
G-ANHR	Taylorcraft J Auster 5	759	MT192	5.12.53	H L Swallow *(Stored 6.04)*	Hibaldstow	20. 7.86
G-ANHS	Taylorcraft G Auster 4	737	MT197	5.12.53	M Stewart and C Tyers tr Mike Tango Group		
					(As "MT197" in RAF c/s)	Spanhoe	21. 9.09P
G-ANHU	Taylorcraft G Auster 4	799	EC-AXR	5.12.53	D J Baker	Carr Farm, Thorney, Newark	22.10.66
			G-ANHU, MT255		*(Noted dismantled, camouflaged 1.05)*		
G-ANHX	Taylorcraft J Auster 5D	2064	TW519	5.12.53	D J Baker	Carr Farm, Thorney, Newark	2.11.73
					(Crashed 28. 3.70: noted dismantled 1.05)		
G-ANIE	Taylorcraft J Auster 5	1809	TW467	5.12.53	R T Ingram *(As "TW467" in AAC c/s)*	Great Oakley	17.11.09P
G-ANIJ	Taylorcraft J Auster 5D	1680	TJ672	5.12.53	B R Whitehead *(On rebuild 2007 as "TJ672: DT-S")*		
						AAC Netheravon	5. 5.71
G-ANJD	de Havilland DH.82A Tiger Moth	84652	T6226	8.12.53	D O Lewis	Wellesbourne Mountford	8. 7.09S
	(Built Morris Motors Ltd)						
G-ANKK	de Havilland DH.82A Tiger Moth	83590	T5854	24.12.53	P A Cambridge tr Halfpenny Green Tiger Group		
					(As "T-5854" in RAF c/s)	Charity Farm, Baxterley	16.12.11
G-ANKT	de Havilland DH.82A Tiger Moth	85087	T6818	24.12.53	Richard Shuttleworth Trustees *(As "K-2585" in RAF CFS c/s)*		
						Old Warden	22. 8.09P
G-ANKZ	de Havilland DH.82A Tiger Moth	3803	(N)	30.12.53	D W Graham *(As "N-6466" in RAF c/s)*		
			F-BHIO, G-ANKZ, N6466			Bossington	24. 7.09S
G-ANLD	de Havilland DH.82A Tiger Moth	85990	OO-DPA	30.12.53	K Peters	White Waltham	17.12.08S
			G-ANLD, EM773				
G-ANLS	de Havilland DH.82A Tiger Moth	85862	DF113	7. 1.54	P A Gliddon	Great Fryup, Egton, Whitby	30. 7.09
	(Built Morris Motors Ltd)						
G-ANMO	de Havilland DH.82A Tiger Moth	3255	F-BHIU	22. 1.54	M G and L J Collins *(As "K-4259:71" in RAF c/s)*		
			G-ANMO, K4259			Sywell	26. 8.09S
G-ANMY	de Havilland DH.82A Tiger Moth	85466	OO-SOL	22. 1.54	Dog Easy Ltd	Landmead Farm, Garford	14. 4.11
			'OO-SOC', G-ANMY, DE470				
G-ANNB	de Havilland DH.82A Tiger Moth	84233	N6037	22. 1.54	G C Bates	(Hemingford Grey)	12. 6.58
			D-EGYN, G-ANNB, T6037				
G-ANNE (2)	de Havilland DH.82A Tiger Moth	"83814"		15. 4.94	C R Hardiman *(On rebuild 9.02)*	Shobdon	30. 5.58
	(Composite airframe)						
G-ANNG	de Havilland DH.82A Tiger Moth	85504	DE524	22. 1.54	P F Walter	Shobdon	5. 3.11
	(Built Morris Motors Ltd)						
G-ANNI	de Havilland DH.82A Tiger Moth	85162	T6953	22. 1.54	C E, O C and M E Ponsford *(As "T-6953" in RAF c/s)*		
						Shoreham	13. 9.09S
G-ANNK	de Havilland DH.82A Tiger Moth	83804	F-BFDO	22. 1.54	D R Wilcox	Sywell	25. 9.87
	(Built Morris Motors Ltd)		G-ANNK, T7290		*(Wings only noted Spanhoe 4.03)*		
G-ANOH	de Havilland DH.82A Tiger Moth	86040	EM838	22. 2.54	N Parkhouse	Redhill	25. 1.09
	(Built Morris Motors Ltd)						
G-ANOM	de Havilland DH.82A Tiger Moth	82086	N6837	2. 3.54	T G I Dark	(Chedworth, Cheltenham)	3. 5.62T
					(Crashed Fairoaks 17.12.61: on rebuild 6.00)		
G-ANON	de Havilland DH.82A Tiger Moth	84270	T7909	4. 3.54	M Kelly *(As "T7909" in RAF c/s)*		
	(Built Morris Motors Ltd)					Sherburn-in-Elmet	12. 7.09S

G-ANOO	de Havilland DH.82A Tiger Moth	85409	DE401	11. 3.54	R K Packman	Little Staughton	17. 4.10
	(Built Morris Motors Ltd)						
G-ANPE	de Havilland DH.82A Tiger Moth	83738	G-IESH	27. 3.54	I E S Hudleston	Duxford	9. 8.09S
	(Built Morris Motors Ltd)		G-ANPE, F-BHAT, G-ANPE, T7397				
G-ANRF	de Havilland DH.82A Tiger Moth	83748	T5850	24. 5.54	C D Cyster	Glenrothes	28. 8.10S
	(Built Morris Motors Ltd)						
G-ANRM	de Havilland DH.82A Tiger Moth	85861	DF112	8. 6.54	Spectrum Leisure Ltd *(As "DF112" in RAF c/s)*		
	(Built Morris Motors Ltd)				*(Operated Classic Wings)*	Duxford	31. 7.10S
G-ANRN	de Havilland DH.82A Tiger Moth	83133	T5368	24. 5.54	J J V Elwes	Old Sarum	19. 5.07
G-ANRP	Taylorcraft J Auster 5	1789	TW439	21. 5.54	P R and J S Johnson *(As "TW439" in RAF c/s)*		
						Lavenham	4. 5.08S
G-ANSM	de Havilland DH.82A Tiger Moth	82909	R5014	3. 6.54	Modi Aviation Ltd	Sibson	28. 8.09T
	(Built Morris Motors Ltd)						
G-ANTE	de Havilland DH.82A Tiger Moth	84891	T6562	20. 9.54	M G and L J Collins	Sywell	15. 9.11
	(Built Morris Motors Ltd)						
G-ANWB	de Havilland DHC-1 Chipmunk 21	C1/0987	G-5-17	15. 2.55	G Briggs	Blackpool	19. 5.11S
G-ANWO	Miles M.14A Hawk Trainer 3	718	L8262	31.12.58	A G Dunkerley	(Bristol)	18. 4.63
	(Dbr Kirton-in-Lindsey 21. 4.62 and cancelled as damaged: restored 24. 6.87 but unlikely little residue: wings to G-AIUA in 1960s and						
	fuselage remnants slight of substance: for possible incorporation into rebuild of G-ADNL (qv))						
G-ANXC	Auster J/5R Alpine	3135	5Y-UBD	4.12.54	R B Webber tr Alpine Group *(Noted 9.08)*		
			VP-UBD, G-ANXC, (AP-AHG), G-ANXC			Trenchard Farm, Eggesford	15. 1.10P
G-ANXR	Percival P.31C Proctor IV	H 803	RM221	14.12.54	N H T Cottrell *(As "RM221" in RAF c/s)*	Biggin Hill	24. 5.10S
	(Built F Hills and Sons Ltd)						
G-ANZT	Thruxton Jackaroo	84176	T7798	4. 3.55	D J and P A D Neville *(As "T7798" in RAF colours)*		
						RAF Henlow	14. 8.08
G-ANZU	de Havilland DH.82A Tiger Moth	3583	L6938	9. 3.55	M I Lodge)	Walton Wood	17. 3.91
G-ANZZ	de Havilland DH.82A Tiger Moth	85834	DE974	14. 3.55	J I B Bennett and P P Amershi	(Hatfield)	28. 2.69T
	(Built Morris Motors Ltd)						

G-AOAA - G-AOZZ

G-AOAA	de Havilland DH.82A Tiger Moth	85908	DF159	14. 3.55	R C P Brookhouse	Thruxton	8.12.91T
	(Built Morris Motors Ltd)				*(Damaged Redhill 4. 6.89: under restoration 2002)*		
G-AOBG	Somers-Kendall SK-1	1		30. 3.55	P W Bishop *(Stored 2007)*	(Woodley, Reading)	26. 6.58
G-AOBH	de Havilland DH.82A Tiger Moth	84350	T7997	31. 3.55	P Nutley *(As "NL750" in RAF c/s)*		
	(Built Morris Motors Ltd) (Officially regd with c/n 83818 ex T7439)					Higherlands Farm, Branscombe	2.12.09
G-AOBU	Hunting Percival P 84 Jet Provost T 1	P84/6	XM129	2. 5.55	T J Manna tr Kennet Aviation *(As "XD693:Z-Q" in RAF 2 FTS c/s)*		
			G-AOBU, G-42-1		*(Noted 1.09) (to move to RAF Cosford)*	North Weald	13. 3.07P
G-AOBX	de Havilland DH.82A Tiger Moth	83653	T7187	26. 4.55	S Bohill-Smith tr David Ross Flying Group		
	(Built Morris Motors Ltd)					White Waltham	27. 6.09
G-AOCR (2)	Taylorcraft J Auster 5D	1060	EI-AJS	25. 5.56	T Taylor *(As "NJ673" in RAF c/s)*	(Boston)	1. 3.09S
			G-AOCR, NJ673				
G-AOCU (2)	Taylorcraft J Auster 5	986	MT349	8. 6.56	S J Ball	Leicester	4. 4.10
G-AODR	de Havilland DH.82A Tiger Moth	86251	G-ISIS	4. 8.55	T Groves tr G-AODR Group	Lee-on-Solent	29. 3.62
	(Built Morris Motors Ltd)		G-AODR, NL779				
G-AODT	de Havilland DH.82A Tiger Moth	83109	R5250	4. 8.55	R A Harrowven	Tibenham	15. 4.10S
G-AOEH	Aeronca 7AC Champion	7AC-2144	N79854	8. 9.55	A Gregori	Nethershields Farm, Chapelton	20. 6.07P
			OO-TWF				
G-AOEI	de Havilland DH.82A Tiger Moth	82196	N6946	14. 9.55	CFG Flying Ltd	Cambridge	16.10.11
	(Regd with fuselage no.MCO/DH3409 which should correspond to ex DE298 [85332]: a/c is probably composite airframe)						
G-AOES	de Havilland DH.82A Tiger Moth	84547	T6056	6.10.55	K A and A J Broomfield	Charity Farm, Baxterley	15. 6.02
	(Built Morris Motors Ltd)				*(Dismantled 10.05)*		
G-AOET	de Havilland DH.82A Tiger Moth	85650	DE720	7.10.55	Techair London Ltd	Bossington	22. 4.10
	(Built Morris Motors Ltd)						
G-AOEX	Thruxton Jackaroo	86483	NM175	10.10.55	A T Christian	Walkeridge Farm, Overton	3. 2.68T
	(Built de Havilland Aircraft Ltd)				*(Rebuild nearing completion 4.05)*		
G-AOFE	de Havilland DHC-1 Chipmunk 22A	C1/0150	WB702	13. 9.56	W J Quinn *(As "WB702" in RAF c/s)*	Dunsfold	21.12.07
G-AOFJ (2)	Auster Alpha 5	3401		3.10.56	L J Kingscott Carnmore, Galway, County Galway		9.12.10S
G-AOFS	Auster J/5L Aiglet Trainer	3143	EI-ALN	28.10.55	P N A Whitehead	Leicester	29. 5.10S
			G-AOFS				
G-AOGI	de Havilland DH.82A Tiger Moth	85922	(N)	14.12.55	W J Taylor *(Stored 10.92)*	(Friskney, Boston)	23. 8.91
	(Built Morris Motors Ltd)		OO-SOA, G-AOGI, DF186				
G-AOGR	de Havilland DH.82A Tiger Moth	84566	XL714	20. 1.56	R J S G Clark *(As "XL714": in RAF c/s)*		
	(Built Morris Motors Ltd)		G-AOGR, T6099			(Cranwell Village, Sleaford)	5. 1.12
G-AOGV	Auster J/5R Alpine	3302		2. 2.56	R E Heading *(Stored 12.97)*		
						Walnut Tree Farm, Thorney, Whittlesey	17. 7.72
G-AOHY	de Havilland DH.82A Tiger Moth	3850	N6537	23. 2.56	R H and J A Cooper	Wickenby	29.10.11
G-AOHZ	Auster J/5P Autocar	3252		28. 2.56	A D Hodgkinson *(Stored 10.07)*		
						Farley Farm, Romsey	25. 9.03
G-AOIL	de Havilland DH.82A Tiger Moth	83673	XL716	20. 8.56	C D Davidson *(As "XL716" in RN c/s)*		
	(Built Morris Motors Ltd)		G-AOIL, T7363			Compton Abbas	17. 9.11
G-AOIM	de Havilland DH.82A Tiger Moth	83536	T7109	27. 8.56	C R Hardiman	Shobdon	19. 8.11
	(Built Morris Motors Ltd)						
G-AOIR	Thruxton Jackaroo	82882	R4972	13. 1.56	K A and A J Broomfield	Charity Farm, Baxterley	10.11.11
	(Built de Havilland Aircaft)						
G-AOIS	de Havilland DH.82A Tiger Moth	83034	R5172	13. 1.56	J K Ellwood *(As "R5172:FIJE" in RAF c/s)*		
						Breighton	26.10.11
G-AOIY	Auster J/5V Series 160 Autocar	3199		1. 3.56	R A Benson Trenchard Farm, Eggesford		14. 5.10
G-AOJH	de Havilland DH.83C Fox Moth	FM.42	AP-ABO	29. 3.56	Connect Properties Ltd	Rendcomb	1. 3.09S
	(Built de Havilland Canada)						
G-AOJJ	de Havilland DH.82A Tiger Moth	85877	DF128	5. 4.56	E and K M Lay *(As "DF128:RCO-U" in RAF c/s)*		
	(Built Morris Motors Ltd)					White Waltham	27. 3.09
G-AOJK	de Havilland DH.82A Tiger Moth	82813	R4896	5. 4.56	R J Willies	Sywell	3. 8.11

G-AOJR	de Havilland DHC-1 Chipmunk 22	C1/0205	SE-BBS	9. 4.56	G J G-H Caubergs and N Marien	Spa, Belgium	31. 7.11
			OY-DFB, D-EGIM, G-AOJR, D-EGIM, G-AOJR, WB756				
G-AOKL	Percival P 40 Prentice 1	PAC-208	VS610	13. 4.56	Richard Shuttleworth Trustees	Old Warden	20. 9.96
					(Under restoration 8.06)		
G-AOLK	Percival P 40 Prentice 1	PAC-225	VS618	25. 4.56	A Hilton	Southend	17. 9.10S
G-AOLU	Percival P 40 Prentice 1	B3/1A/PAC/283	EI-ASP	25. 4.56	N J Butler (As "VS356" in RAF c/s)	(Montrose)	8. 5.76
	(Regd c/n 5830/3)		EI-AOLU, VS356		(Noted 4.02 but status uncertain)		
G-AORB (2)	Cessna 170B	20767	OO-SIZ	13. 2.84	A R Thompson tr Hawley Farm Group	Englefield	9. 4.11S
			N2615D				
G-AORG	de Havilland DH.114 Heron	214101	XR441	1. 5.56	Duchess of Brittany (Jersey) Ltd "Duchess of Brittany"		
	(Built as Sea Heron C 1)		G-AORG, G-5-16		(Jersey Airlines titles) (on overhaul)	Coventry	26. 6.07S
G-AORW	de Havilland DHC-1 Chipmunk 22A	C1/0130	WB682	28. 5.56	Skylark Aviation Ltd	Prestwick	29. 1.09S
G-AOSF	de Havilland DHC-1 Chipmunk 22	C1/0023	D-EIIZ	25. 6.56	T S Olsen (As "WB571:34" in RAF c/s)		
			G-AOSF, HB-TUA, G-AOSF, WB571		(Trier, Germany)		6. 4.06
G-AOSK	de Havilland DHC-1 Chipmunk 22A	C1/0178	WB726	26. 6.56	L J Irvine (As "WB726:E" in RAF Cambridge UAS c/s)		
						RAF Halton	30. 3.09
G-AOSY	de Havilland DHC-1 Chipmunk 22	C1/0037	WB585	29. 6.56	I A Davies tr WFG Chipmunk Group	Seething	26. 6.11S
					(As "WB585:M in RAF red and white c/s)		
G-AOTD	de Havilland DHC-1 Chipmunk 22	C1/0040	WB588	30. 6.56	S Piech (As "WB588:D" in RAF Oxford UAS c/s)		
						Old Sarum	5.11.09
G-AOTF	de Havilland DHC-1 Chipmunk 23	C1/0015	WB563	2. 7.56	T M Holloway tr RAF Gliding and Soaring Association		
	(Lycoming O-360-A4A)				(Operated Cleveland Gliding Club)	AAC Dishforth	21. 7.11
G-AOTK	Druine D 53 Turbi	1		1.11.56	T J Adams	White Fen Farm, Benwick	10.10.09P
	(Built TK Flying Group - pr.no.PFA 230) (Walter Mikron 3)						
G-AOTR	de Havilland DHC-1 Chipmunk 22	C1/0045	HB-TUH	12. 7.56	Ace Leasing Ltd	Duxford	12. 6.06
			D-EGOG, G-AOTR, WB604				
G-AOTY	de Havilland DHC-1 Chipmunk 22	C1/0522	WG472	12. 7.56	A A Hodgson tr Bryn Gwyn Bach Chipmunk Group		
					(As "WG472" in RAF c/s)	Bryn Gwyn Bach	5. 4.10S
G-AOUO	de Havilland DHC-1 Chipmunk 23	C1/0179	WB730	10. 8.56	T M Holloway tr RAF Gliding and Soaring Association		
	(Lycoming O-360-A4A)				(Operated Wrekin Gliding Club)	RAF Cosford	16. 3.08
G-AOUP	de Havilland DHC-1 Chipmunk 22	C1/0180	WB731	10. 8.56	A R Harding	East Winch	3. 8.06
G-AOVW	Taylorcraft J Auster 5	894	MT119	16.11.59	B Marriott	Wilsford, Grantham	15.11.09
G-AOXN	de Havilland DH.82A Tiger Moth	85958	EM727	31.10.56	S L G Darch	(East Chinnock, Yeovil)	21.12.01
	(Built Morris Motors Ltd)						
G-AOZH	de Havilland DH.82A Tiger Moth	86449	NM129	18. 1.57	M H Blois-Brooke (As "K2572" in RAF c/s)		
	(Built Morris Motors Ltd)					Lotmead Farm, Wanborough	10. 6.11T
G-AOZL	Auster J/5Q Alpine	3202		5. 2.57	R M Weeks (On rebuild 8.06)	Earls Colne	28. 5.88
G-AOZP	de Havilland DHC-1 Chipmunk 22A	C1/0183	WB734	14. 2.57	S J Davies	Sandtoft	9. 6.11S

G-APAA - G-APZZ

G-APAF	Auster Alpha 5	3404	G-CMAL	25. 3.57	J J J Mostyn (As "TW511" in AAC c/s)		
			G-APAF			Draycott Farm, Chiseldon	2. 9.09P
G-APAH	Auster Alpha 5	3402		29. 3.57	T J Goodwin (Noted 9.08)	Great Oakley	5. 4.04
G-APAJ	Thruxton Jackaroo	83314	VH-KRK	3. 4.57	J T H and S J Page (Noted 6.07)		
	(Built de Havilland Aircraft Ltd)		G-APAJ, T5616		New Barn Farm, Barton Ashes, Crawley		
G-APAL	de Havilland DH.82A Tiger Moth	82102	N6847	3. 4.57	P J Shotbolt (As "N6847" in RAF c/s)		
					Ingthorpe Farm, Great Casterton		9. 7.06T
G-APAM	de Havilland DH.82A Tiger Moth	3874	N6580	3. 4.57	R P Williams tr Myth Group "Myth"		
					Denford Manor, Hungerford		1.10.10S
G-APAO	de Havilland DH.82A Tiger Moth	82845	R4922	3. 4.57	H J Maguire (As "R4922" in RAF c/s)		
					(Operated Classic Wings)	Duxford	23. 4.09S
G-APAP	de Havilland DH.82A Tiger Moth	83018	R5136	3. 4.57	J C Wright (As "R-5136" in RAF c/s)		
						RAF Henlow	17. 7.09S
G-APBE	Auster Alpha 5	3403		7. 5.57	R B Woods	Haw Farm, Hampstead Norrey's	8. 6.09P
G-APBI	de Havilland DH.82A Tiger Moth	86097	EM903	16. 5.57	C J Zeal	(Twyford, Reading)	19. 4.82
	(Built Morris Motors Ltd)				(Damaged Audley End 7. 7.80: on rebuild 12.90)		
G-APBO	Druine D 53 Turbi	PFA 229		3. 6.57	R C Hibberd	Lower Upham Farm, Chiseldon	12. 7.09P
	(Built F Roche) (Continental C75-12)						
G-APBW	Auster Alpha 5A	3405		23. 5.57	C R W Brown	(Cornillon-Confoux, France)	1. 6.09
G-APCB	Auster J/5Q Alpine	3204		5. 6.57	A A Beswick	Thruxton	15. 4.11S
G-APCC	de Havilland DH.82A Tiger Moth	86549	PG640	11. 6.57	L J Rice	Quebec Farm, Knook, Warminster	15.11.09
G-APFA	Druine D 52 Turbi	PFA 232		5. 2.57	F J Keitch	(Smiths Farm, Brixham)	22. 9.92P
	(Built Britten-Norman Ltd) (Continental A65-3)						
G-APFU	de Havilland DH.82A Tiger Moth	86081	EM879	28. 8.57	Leisure Assets Ltd	Goodwood	11. 4.09S
G-APFV (1)	Piper PA-23-160 Apache	23-1686	G-MOLY	11.12.59	J L Thorogood	Pittrichie Farm, Whiterashes	25. 4.11E
			EI-BAW, G-APFV, EI-ALK, N10F				
G-APGL	de Havilland DH.82A Tiger Moth	86460	NM140	6. 9.57	K A Broomfield		
	(Built Morris Motors Ltd) (Substantial parts used in rebuild of G-AJVE)				(Charity Farm, Baxterley, Atherstone)		
G-APIE	Tipsy Belfair	535	(OO-TIE)	22.10.57	D Beale	White Fen Farm, Benwick	15. 4.09P
	(Walter Mikron 2)						
G-APIH	de Havilland DH.82A Tiger Moth	82981	N111DH	25.10.57	K Stewering	Borken-Gemen, Germany	3. 5.09S
			OY-DGJ, D-EMEX, G-APIH, R5086				
G-APIK	Auster J/1N Alpha	3375		11.11.57	J H Powell-Tuck	Gloucestershire	7. 3.09
G-APIZ	Druine D 31 Turbulent	PFA 478		22.11.57	G M Rundle	RAF Shawbury	6. 2.08P
	(Built Rollason Aircraft and Engines) (Volkswagen 1600)						
G-APJB	Percival P 40 Prentice 1	PAC-086	VR259	28.11.57	Air Atlantique Ltd (As "VR259:M" in RAF 2 ASS c/s)		
						Coventry	24. 7.08T
G-APJZ	Auster J/1N Alpha	3382	5N-ACY	3. 1.58	P G Lipman	Romney Street Farm, Sevenoaks	15. 7.77
			(VR-NDR), G-APJZ		(Damaged Thornicombe 10.11.75: on rebuild 12.97)		
G-APKN	Auster J/1N Alpha	3387		27. 1.58	P R Hodson	Felthorpe	8. 9.05
					(Badly damaged in arson attack Felthorpe 8. 2.03)		
G-APLO	de Havilland DHC-1 Chipmunk 22	C1/0144	EI-AHU	1. 5.58	Lindholme Aircraft Ltd	Coventry	2.11.09S
			WB696		(As "WD379:K" in RAF Cambridge UAS c/s)		

G-APLU	de Havilland DH.82A Tiger Moth	85094	VR-AAY	2. 4.58	R A Bishop and M E Vaisey	Rush Green	22. 7.11
	(Built Morris Motors Ltd)		F-OBKK, G-APLU, T6825				
G-APMH	Auster J/1U Workmaster	3502	F-OBOA	15. 4.58	J L Thorogood	Insch	2. 6.10S
			G-APMH				
G-APMX	de Havilland DH.82A Tiger Moth	85645	DE715	9. 5.58	T A P Hubbard tr Foley Farm Flying Group		
	(Built Morris Motors Ltd)					Redwood Cottage, Meon	17. 7.10S
G-APNT	Currie Wot	P 6399		18. 6.58	B J Dunford *"Airymouse"*		
	(Built Hampshire Aero Club - c/n HAC-3) (Continental PC60)					Longwood Farm, Morestead	29. 6.09P
G-APNZ	Druine D 31 Turbulent	PFA 482		17. 4.58	J Knight	(Hailsham)	13.12.95P
	(Built Rollason Aircraft and Engines) (Ardem 4C02)				*(Damaged River Rother near Iden 3. 9.95: on rebuild)*		
G-APOI	Saunders-Roe Skeeter Series 8	S2/5081		29. 7.58	B Chamberlain *(Noted 8.08)* AAC Middle Wallop		2. 8.00
G-APPA	de Havilland DHC-1 Chipmunk 22	C1/0792	N5073E	11. 9.58	D M Squires	(Wellesbourne Mountford)	14. 7.85
			G-APPA, WP917		*(On slow rebuild 1.03)*		
G-APPL	Percival P 40 Prentice 1	PAC-013	VR189	7.10.58	S J Saggers	Biggin Hill	10. 9.10S
G-APPM	de Havilland DHC-1 Chipmunk 22	C1/0159	WB711	14.10.58	S D Wilch *(As "WB711" in RAF c/s)*	Sywell	7. 9.08
G-APRR	SPP Super Aero 45 Series 04	04-014	OK-KFQ	5. 1.59	M J O'Donnell	Elsted, Midhurst	14. 7.11
G-APRS	Scottish Aviation Twin Pioneer 3	561	G-BCWF	9. 1.59	Aviation Heritage Ltd *"Primrose"*	Coventry	15. 7.08T
			XT610, G-APRS, (PI-C430)		*(Raspberry ripple c/s with ETPS titles)*		
G-APRT	Taylor JT.1 Monoplane	PFA 537		15. 1.59	R A Keech	Guy Lane Farm, Waverton	26. 5.09P
	(Built J Taylor) (Ardem 4C02)						
G-APSA	Douglas DC-6A	45497	4W-ABQ	12. 2.59	Air Atlantique Ltd *(British Eagle colours)* Coventry		23. 5.09T
			HZ-ADA, G-APSA, CF-MC				
G-APSR	Auster J/1U Workmaster	3499	OO-HXA	22. 4.59	D and K Aero Services Ltd *(Operated P De Liens)*		
			G-APSR, VP-JCD, G-APSR, (F-OBHR)			Namur-Temploux, Belgium	22.11.08S
G-APTR	Auster J/1N Alpha	3392		15. 4.59	C J and D J Baker Carr Farm, Thorney, Newark		11. 4.87
					(Noted complete 1.05)		
G-APTU	Auster Alpha 5	3413		20. 4.59	A J and J M Davis tr G-APTU Flying Group		
					(On rebuild 3.00)	Leicester	8. 6.98
G-APTY	Beech G35 Bonanza	D-4789	EI-AJG	4. 6.59	G E Brennand *(Noted 10.07)*	Blackpool	11. 6.06
G-APTZ	Druine D 31 Turbulent	PFA 508		18. 3.59	Tiger Club (1990) Ltd	Headcorn	18. 6.07P
	(Built Rollason Aircraft and Engines) (Volkswagen 1600)						
	(During display practice the aircraft entered disturbed air at Headcorn 15. 3.08 and struck the ground; both wings detached and destroyed)						
G-APUE	Orlican L-40 Meta-Sokol	150708	OK-NMB	2. 6.59	S E and M J Aherne	Top Farm, Croydon	20. 5.09
G-APUR	Piper PA-22-160 Tri-Pacer	22-6711		3. 7.59	S T A Hutchinson		
						Gransha, Rathfriland, County Down	11.11.10S
G-APUW	Auster J/5V Series 160 Autocar	3273		23. 6.59	E A J Hibbard	Hill Farm, Nayland	22. 7.09P
G-APUY	Druine D 31 Turbulent	PFA 509		24. 6.59	C Jones	Barton	10. 6.86P
	(Built K F W Turner) (Volkswagen 1300)				*(On slow rebuild, noted 6.08)*		
G-APVF	Putzer Elster B	006	D-EEQX	29.12.83	C J Riley and M J Forman *(As "97+04" in Luftwaffe c/s)*		
			97+04, D-EJUH			Wickenby	5. 7.08P
G-APVG	Auster J/5L Aiglet Trainer	3306	(ZK-BQW)	10. 7.59	R Farrer	Cranfield	20. 3.00
G-APVL	Saunders-Roe P531-2	S2/5311	XP166	23. 7.59	C J Marsden	Thruxton	10.12.09P
	(Blackburn Nimbus)		G-APVL				
G-APVN	Druine D 31 Turbulent	PFA 511		24. 7.59	R Sherwin *(Stored 6.04)*		
	(Built J P Knight) (Volkswagen 1600)					Swanborough Farm, Lewes	24. 6.94P
G-APVS	Cessna 170B	26156	N2512C	7. 8.59	N Simpson *"Stormin' Norman"*	East Kirkby	6. 7.11S
G-APVU	Orlican L-40 Meta-Sokol	150706	OK-NMI	21. 8.59	S A and M J Aherne	(Smallford, St Albans)	27. 6.79
					(Damaged Manchester 12. 9.78: on rebuild 1993)		
G-APVZ	Druine D 31 Turbulent	PFA 545		23. 7.59	The Tiger Club 1990 Ltd	Headcorn	3.12.08P
	(Built Rollason Aircraft and Engines) (Ardem 4C02)						
G-APWL	EoN AP.10 460 Standard Series 1A		BGA1172 -BRK	2. 9.59	D G Andrew *(Noted 2000)*	Eaglescott	26. 4.00
		EoN/S/001	G-APWL, RAFGSA.268, G-APWL				
G-APWP	Druine D 31 Turbulent	PFA 497		14. 9.59	C F Rogers	(Wheathampstead, St Albans)	27. 6.67
	(Built C F Rogers)						
G-APXJ	Piper PA-24-250 Comanche	24-291	VR-NDA	11.12.59	T Wildsmith	Gamston	4. 2.09E
			N10F				
G-APXR	Piper PA-22-160 Tri-Pacer	22-7172	N10F	29. 1.60	A Troughton	Belfast International	31. 3.11
G-APXT	Piper PA-22-150 Tri-Pacer	22-3854	N4545A	16. 2.60	A E Cuttler	Oaksey Park	15. 6.11S
	(Rebuilt to PA-20 Pacer configuration)						
G-APXU	Piper PA-22 Tri-Pacer	22-474	N1723A	10. 2.60	The Scottish Aero Club Ltd *"The Cloth Bomber" (Noted 12.08)*		
						Perth	20. 2.85
G-APXY	Cessna 150	17711	N7911E	15. 1.60	D A Waghorn *(stored dismantled, noted 11.08)*		
						Compton Abbas	1. 4.08E
G-APYB	Tipsy Nipper T 66 Series 3	T66/39		28. 1.60	B O Smith *(On rebuild)*	Yearby	12. 6.96P
	(Built Avions Fairey SA) (Volkswagen 1834)						
G-APYG	de Havilland DHC-1 Chipmunk 22	C1/0060	OH-HCB	11.11.60	P A and J M Doyle	Little Gransden	27. 8.10
			WB619				
G-APYI	Piper PA-22-135 Tri-Pacer	22-2218	N8031C	8. 2.60	R E Dagless Holly Hill Farm, Guist, Dereham		27. 5.11S
	(Modified to PA-20 Pacer configuration)						
G-APYN	Piper PA-22-160 Tri-Pacer	22-6797	N2804Z	24. 2.60	U Beumling	Rhede, Germany	24. 7.10S
G-APYT	Champion 7FC Tri-Traveler	387		9. 5.60	B J Anning	Watchford Farm, Yarcombe	29. 6.06P
G-APZJ	Piper PA-18-150 Super Cub	18-7233	N10F	29. 1.60	R Jones t/a Southern Sailplanes	Membury	24. 7.11
			(Rebuilt 1986 after accident 12. 6.83 using fuselage frame believed ex G-ATRH (18-7830))				
G-APZL	Piper PA-22-160 Tri-Pacer	22-7054	EI-ALF	27. 1.60	B Robins *(on rebuild)*	Haverfordwest	14. 5.99
			N10F				
G-APZX	Piper PA-22-150 Tri-Pacer	22-5181	N7420D	28. 4.60	V A Holliday	Tatenhill	11. 6.11S
	(Modified to PA-20 Pacer configuration)						

G-ARAA - G-ARZZ

G-ARAI	Piper PA-22-160 Tri-Pacer	22-7421	N10F	17. 5.60	P McCabe	Newtownards	3. 7.11S
	(Fitted witn wings from G-ARSX in 2005/6)						
G-ARAM	Piper PA-18-150 Super Cub	18-7312	N10F	17. 5.60	Skymax (Aviation) Ltd *(Noted on rebuild 9.06)*		
						Sywell	22. 6.02T

G-ARAN	Piper PA-18-150 Super Cub	18-7307	N10F	28. 4.60	A P Docherty	Redhill	8. 6.10S
G-ARAO	Piper PA-18 Super Cub 95	18-7327	N10F	17. 5.60	R G Manton	Manor Farm, Haddenham	12. 8.11
G-ARAS	Champion 7FC Tri-Traveler	7FC-396		12. 9.60	G J Taylor tr Alpha Sierra Flying Group *(Noted 8.07)*		
						Yeatsall Farm, Abbots Bromley	22. 6.01P
G-ARAT	Cessna 180C	50827	N9327T	18. 5.60	S D Pryke and J Graham	Felthorpe	23. 7.09E
G-ARAW	Cessna 182C Skylane	52843	N8943T	18. 5.60	R P Beck, G and R L McLean t/a Ximango UK		
						Rufforth	15. 4.09E
G-ARAX	Piper PA-22-150 Caribbean	22-3830	N4523A	22. 4.60	J W Iliffe	Derby	3.10.11
G-ARAZ	de Havilland DH.82A Tiger Moth	82867	R4959	25. 3.60	D A Porter	Griffins Farm, Temple Bruer	4. 6.10S
G-ARBE	de Havilland DH.104 Dove 8	04517		6. 5.60	M Whale and M W A Lunn *(Noted 1.08)*		
						Little Rissington	3.10.02
G-ARBG	Tipsy Nipper T 66 Series 2	ABAC.1		11. 5.60	D Shrimpton *(On rebuild 2006)*	(Oakhill, Bath)	17. 8.84P
	(Originally built Avions Fairey SA as c/n T66.57) (Volkswagen 1834 Acro)						
G-ARBO	Piper PA-24-250 Comanche	24-2117	N10F	15. 6.60	Tatenhill Aviation Ltd	Tatenhill	27. 5.84
G-ARBS	Piper PA-22-160 Tri-Pacer	22-6858	N2868Z	24. 8.60	S D Rowell *"Greta"*	Valley Farm, Winwick	20. 4.11
	(Modified to PA-20 Pacer configuration)						
G-ARBV	Piper PA-22-160 Tri-Pacer	22-5836	N8633D	29. 6.60	L M Williams		
	(Rebuilt 1983/84 using fuselage of G-ARDP ex N7004B [22-4254])					New Barn Farm, Barton Ashes, Crawley	3. 7.06
G-ARBZ	Druine D 31 Turbulent	PFA 553		6. 5.60	G Richards	Headcorn	12. 5.09P
	(Built Rollason Aircraft and Engines) (Ardem 4C02)						
G-ARCF	Piper PA-22-150 Caribbean	22-4563	N5902D	28. 6.60	M J Speakman	North Coates	24. 5.11
G-ARCS	Auster D 6 Series 180	3703		4. 7.60	R J Fray	Furze Farm, Haddon, Peterborough	10. 4.09P
G-ARCV	Cessna 175A Skylark	17556757	N8057T	7.11.60	R Francis and C Campbell *(Noted damaged 9.07)*		
						Church Farm, Askern	3. 9.05
G-ARCW	Piper PA-23 Apache	23-796	N2187P	7. 7.60	F W Ellis	Cranfield	24. 8.07T
	(Modified to PA-23-160 standard)						
G-ARDB	Piper PA-24-250 Comanche	24-2166	PH-RON	15. 8.60	P Crook	Kemble	9. 7.09E
			G-ARDB, N7019P				
G-ARDD	Scintex CP.301-C1 Emeraude	549		4. 7.60	N C Grayson	Boscombe Down	15. 8.08P
	(Rebuilt EMK Aeroplanes Ltd- c/n EMK.004)						
G-ARDJ	Auster D 6 Series 180	3704		15. 7.60	R E Neal t/a RN Aviation (Leicester Airport)		
				(Damaged near Leicester 30. 5.86: noted 10.07)		Leicester	7. 7.88T
G-ARDO	Jodel D 112J	146	F-PBTE	22. 8.60	W R Prescott		
	(Built Etablissement Couesnon)		F-BBTE, F-WBTE			Ballymageough, Kilkeel, County Down	30. 5.07P
	(Composite with fuselage of G-AYEO ex F-BIGG [684] c 1974)						
G-ARDS	Piper PA-22-150 Caribbean	22-7154	N3214Z	4. 9.60	N P McGowan	Newtownards	20. 7.11
G-ARDV	Piper PA-22-160 Tri-Pacer	22-7487	EI-APA	28. 7.60	M D N Fisher	(Deeping St James)	18. 4.08
			G-ARDV, N10F				
G-ARDY	Tipsy Nipper T 66 Series 2	T66/55		10. 8.60	J K Davies	Green Farm, Chester	12.12.00P
	(Built Avions Fairey SA) (Martlet Volkswagen)						
G-AREH	de Havilland DH.82A Tiger Moth	85287	(G-APYV)	4. 7.60	C D Cyster and A J Hastings	Glenrothes	19. 4.66T
	(Built Morris Motors Ltd)		6746M, DE241				
G-AREI	Taylorcraft E Auster III	518	9M-ALB	14.12.60	R B Webber *(As "MT438" in SEAC c/s) "Akyab"*		
			VR-RBM, VR-SCJ, MT438			Trenchard Farm, Eggesford	18. 4.10
G-AREL	Piper PA-22-150 Caribbean	22-7284	N3344Z	14. 9.60	R Gibson tr The Caribbean Flying Club		
						White Waltham	12. 5.11
G-AREO	Piper PA-18-150 Super Cub	18-7407	N10F	24. 8.60	E P Parkin	Derby	17. 9.07
G-ARET	Piper PA-22-160 Tri-Pacer	22-7590	N10F	2. 9.60	I S Runnalls *(Frame noted hangared 3.07)*		
						Enstone	20. 5.83T
G-AREV	Piper PA-22-160 Tri-Pacer	22-6540	N9628D	25.10.60	D J Ash *"Smart Cat"*	Barton	29. 1.08
G-AREX	Aeronca 15AC Sedan	15AC-61	CF-FNM	12. 9.60	R J M Turnbull	Rydinghurst Farm, Cranleigh	12.10.10S
G-ARFB	Piper PA-22-150 Caribbean	22-7518	N3625Z	8. 9.60	S Young tr The Tripacer Group	Derby	19. 6.11E
G-ARFD	Piper PA-22-160 Tri-Pacer	22-7565	N3667Z	8. 9.60	J R Dunnett	Priory Farm, Tibenham	8. 6.11S
G-ARFG	Cessna 175A Skylark	56505	N7005E	15.11.60	G C Rogers	(Dartford)	4.11.07E
G-ARFI	Cessna 150A	15059100	N41836	1. 2.61	A R Abrey	Filton	30. 9.09E
			G-ARFI, N7000X				
G-ARFO	Cessna 150A	15059174	N7074X	23. 3.61	A P Amor	Phoenix Farm, Lower Upham	26. 9.09E
G-ARFT	SAN Jodel DR.1050 Ambassadeur	170		27.10.60	R Shaw	(Sowerby Bridge)	13.10.84
					(Damaged Prestwick 15. 6.84)		
G-ARFV	Tipsy Nipper T 66 Series 2	T66/44		5.10.60	K Taylor	Eddsfield Octon Lodge Farm, Thwing	29. 9.09P
	(Built Avions Fairey SA) (Volkswagen 1834)						
G-ARGG	de Havilland DHC-1 Chipmunk 22	C1/0247	WD305	19.10.60	D Curtis	Prestwick	27. 2.10S
G-ARGO	Piper PA-22-108 Colt	22-8034		18. 1.61	D R Smith	Wolverhampton	6. 8.11
G-ARGV	Piper PA-18-150 Super Cub	18-7559	N10F	20.12.60	Wolds Gliding Club Ltd	Pocklington	20. 7.09
G-ARGY	Piper PA-22-160 Tri-Pacer	22-7620	G-JEST	20.12.60	D H and R T Tanner	Wellesbourne Mountford	18. 4.09E
	(Modified to PA-20 configuration)		G-ARGY, N10F				
G-ARGZ	Druine D 31 Turbulent	PFA 562		7.11.60	The Tiger Club (1990) Ltd	Headcorn	18.12.09P
	(Built Rollason Aircraft and Engines) (Volkswagen 1600)						
G-ARHB	Forney F-1A Aircoupe	5733		17. 4.61	K J Peacock and S F Turner	Earls Colne	15. 7.11
G-ARHC	Forney F-1A Aircoupe	5734		26. 5.61	A P Gardner	Little Gransden	13.12.10S
G-ARHI	Piper PA-24 Comanche	24-2260	N7299P	20.12.60	D D Smith	Hardwick	8. 8.09E
			N10F				
G-ARHM	Auster 6A	2515	VF557	5. 1.61	R C P Brookhouse *(Noted 3.05)* Wycombe Air Park		9.12.01
G-ARHN	Piper PA-22-150 Caribbean	22-7514	N3622Z	10. 1.61	I S Hodge and S Haughton	Field Farm, Hillington	5. 3.07
	(Rebuilt with parts of G-ATXB which was damaged beyond repair 26.8.74) (Noted 5.07)						
G-ARHP	Piper PA-22-160 Tri-Pacer	22-7549	N3652Z	10. 1.61	A S Cowan tr Popham Flying Group G-ARHP		
						Popham	22. 5.10
	(Crashed into trees on a hillside in the Loire Valley, France 7. 6.08 in bad visibility and believed beyond economic repair)						
G-ARHR	Piper PA-22-150 Caribbean	22-7576	N3707Z	10. 1.61	A R Wyatt	Cottered, Hertford	2. 2.08E
G-ARHW	de Havilland DH.104 Dove 8	04512		10. 1.61	Aviation Heritage Ltd	Coventry	19. 5.06T
G-ARHZ	Druine D 62A Condor	PFA 247		13.12.60	E Shouler	Beeches Farm, South Scarle	7. 1.10P
	(Built Rollason Aircraft and Engines with c/n RAE 602)						
G-ARID	Cessna 172B Skyhawk	48209	N7709X	2. 2.61	L M Edwards	Sleap	3. 8.08E

G-ARIF	Ord-Hume O-H 7 Minor Coupe	PAL 1401		22. 8.60	N H Ponsford *(Stored incomplete 3.96)* (Leeds)
	(Built A W J G Ord-Hume - c/n O-H 7) (Modified Luton LA-4C Minor)				
G-ARIH	Auster 6A	2463	TW591	23. 1.61	M C Jordan *(As "TW591" in RAF 664 (AOP) Sqdn c/s)*
					Eaglescott 27. 4.10S
G-ARIK	Piper PA-22-150 Caribbean	22-7570	N3701Z	26. 1.61	A Taylor Manor Farm, Binham 5. 6.06
G-ARIL	Piper PA-22-150 Caribbean	22-7574	N3705Z	26. 1.61	AJW Construction Ltd. (Hordle, Lymington) 23.10.10
G-ARIM	Druine D 31 Turbulent	PFA 510		27. 2.61	J G McTaggart Archerfield Estate, Direlton
	(Built A Schima)				
G-ARJB	de Havilland DH.104 Dove 8	04518		29. 9.60	M Whale and M W A Lunn Little Rissington 10.12.73T
					"Exporter" (JCB titles: noted 1.08)
G-ARJE	Piper PA-22-108 Colt	22-8184		29. 3.61	C I Fray (Disley) 29. 4.73
G-ARJF	Piper PA-22-108 Colt	22-8199		23. 3.61	Tandycel Co Ltd Glebe Farm, Stockton 16. 3.07
G-ARJH	Piper PA-22-108 Colt	22-8249		29. 3.61	F Vogels Le Plessis-Bellville, France 8.10.06
G-ARJS	Piper PA-23-160 Apache G	23-1977	N10F	3. 3.61	Bencray Ltd *(Operated Blackpool and Fylde Aero Club)*
					Blackpool 16.11.11
G-ARJT	Piper PA-23-160 Apache G	23-1981	N10F	3. 3.61	J A Cole Netherthorpe 18. 8.07T
G-ARJU	Piper PA-23-160 Apache G	23-1984	N10F	3. 3.61	G R Manley Biggin Hill 13. 7.11
G-ARKG	Auster J/5G Cirrus Autocar	3061	AP-AHJ	22. 2.61	R H and J A Cooper Wickenby 19. 6.10S
			VP-KKN		
G-ARKJ	Beech N35 Bonanza	D-6736		5. 5.61	P D and J L Jenkins Goodwood 20. 1.08E
G-ARKK	Piper PA-22-108 Colt	22-8290		12. 4.61	R D Welfare Rochester 20. 1.08E
G-ARKM	Piper PA-22-108 Colt	22-8313		12. 4.61	G Cannon Perranporth 28. 7.11S
G-ARKN	Piper PA-22-108 Colt	22-8327		9. 5.61	R Redfern Derby 29. 1.11S
G-ARKP	Piper PA-22-108 Colt	22-8364		19. 5.61	J P A Freeman and Shenley Farms (Aviation) Ltd
					Headcorn 12.12.07E
G-ARKS	Piper PA-22-108 Colt (modified)	22-8422		7. 6.61	R A Nesbitt-Dufort Bradleys Lawn, Heathfield 28.11.11S
G-ARLB	Piper PA-24-250 Comanche	24-2352	G-BUTL	21. 3.61	D Heater Blackbushe 29. 9.09E
			G-ARLB, N10F		
G-ARLG	Auster D 4/108	3606		4. 4.61	R D Helliar-Symons tr Auster D4 Group
					Bourne Park, Hurstbourne Tarrant 12. 6.09P
G-ARLK	Piper PA-24-250 Comanche	24-2433	EI-ALW	25. 5.61	R P Jackson (Harpenden) 21. 8.09E
			G-ARLK, N10F		
G-ARLP (2)	Beagle A 61 Terrier 1	3724 (1)	VX123	11. 4.61	D R Whitby tr Gemini Flying Group (Fakenham) 31.10.91
	(C/n officially quoted as 2573 (VF631) which became G-ARLM (2) then G-ASDK) (Damaged Truleigh Farm, Edburton 4. 8.91; on rebuild 2000)				
G-ARLR	Beagle A 61 Terrier 2	3721 & B 601	VW996	11. 4.61	M Palfreman *(Noted 2.08)* Bagby 9. 9.01
G-ARLX	SAN Jodel D 140B Mousquetaire II	66		12. 4.61	J S and S V Shaw Perranporth 12. 9.10
G-ARLZ	Druine D 31A Turbulent	RAE 578		7. 4.61	C R Greenaway (Stratford-upon-Avon) 28. 4.09P
	(Built Rollason Aircraft and Engines) (Ardem 4C02)				
G-ARMA	Piper PA-23-160 Apache G	23-1967	N4448P	8. 5.61	C J Hopewell *(Stored 10.01)* Sibson 22. 7.77
G-ARMC	de Havilland DHC-1 Chipmunk 22A	C1/0151	WB703	26. 4.61	J T H Henderson tr John Henderson Childrens Trust
					(As "WB703" in RAF c/s) Wycombe Air Park 26. 4.10S
G-ARMD	de Havilland DHC-1 Chipmunk 22A	C1/0237	WD297	26. 4.61	D M Squires *(Stored 2.04)* (Redditch) 5. 6.76
G-ARMF	de Havilland DHC-1 Chipmunk 22A	C1/0394	WG322	26. 4.61	D M Squires *(As "WZ868:H" in RAF c/s)* (Redditch) 12.10.98
					(Damaged 1996: wings stored Husbands Bosworth 10.07)
G-ARML	Cessna 175B Skylark	17556995	N8295T	12. 7.61	G A Copeland Popham 30.10.08T
G-ARMN	Cessna 175B Skylark (modified)	17556994	N8294T	18. 8.61	B R Nash Lower Wasing Farm, Brimpton 20. 8.09E
G-ARMO	Cessna 172B Skyhawk	17248560	N8060X	12. 6.61	P Bullen RAF Wyton 19. 5.09E
	(Incorrectly shown by CAA as ex N8066X)				
G-ARMR	Cessna 172B Skyhawk	17248566	N8066X	12. 6.61	Sunsaver Ltd Barton 25. 9.09E
G-ARMZ	Druine D 31 Turbulent	PFA 565		2. 5.61	The Tiger Club 1990 Ltd Headcorn Headcorn 28. 8.09P
	(Built Rollason Aircraft and Engines) (Volkswagen 1500)				
G-ARNB	Auster J/5G Cirrus Autocar	3169	AP-AHL	18. 5.61	R F Tolhurst Payden St Farm, Lenham, Maidstone 19. 2.77
	(Blackburn Cirrus Major III)		VP-KNL		*(Possibly on rebuild)*
G-ARND	Piper PA-22-108 Colt	22-8484		6. 6.61	C D Hardwick Perranporth 15.11.10S
G-ARNE	Piper PA-22-108 Colt	22-8502		15. 6.61	R Carter tr The Shiny Colt Group Knettishall 11. 7.10S
G-ARNG	Piper PA-22-108 Colt (modified)	22-8547		26. 6.61	F B Rothera *"Awful Red"*
					Stoneacre Farm, Farthing Corner 27.1.11S
G-ARNJ	Piper PA-22-108 Colt	22-8587		3. 8.61	R A Keech Liverpool-John Lennon 29. 1.11E
G-ARNK	Piper PA-22-108 Colt	22-8622		5. 9.61	I P Burnett Landmead Farm, Garford 6. 2.11S
	(Tail-wheel conversion)				
G-ARNL	Piper PA-22-108 Colt	22-8625		3. 8.61	J A Dodsworth White Waltham 26. 6.11S
G-ARNN	Globe GC-1B Swift	1272	VP-YMJ	11. 5.61	K E Sword *(Crashed Hucknall 1. 9.73)* (Leicester) 11. 7.74
			VP-RDA, ZS-BMX, NC3279K		
G-ARNO	Beagle A 61 Terrier 1	3722	VX113	8. 5.61	R Webber *(As "VX113:36" in AAC c/s)*
	(Official p/i shown as VX115)				Trenchard Farm, Eggesford 26. 2.09S
G-ARNP	Beagle A 109 Airedale	B 503		10. 5.61	S T and M Isbister North Weald 27. 4.09S
	(Originally regd with c/n A109-P1)				
G-ARNY	SAN Jodel D 117	595	F-BHXQ	13. 6.61	P Jenkins tr G-ARNY Flying Group Inverness 12. 4.09P
G-ARNZ	Druine D 31 Turbulent	PFA 579		28. 6.61	The Tiger Club (1990) Ltd Headcorn 27. 4.09P
	(Built Rollason Aircraft and Engines) (Volkswagen 1600)				
G-AROA	Cessna 172B Skyhawk	48628	N8128X	19. 9.61	D E Partridge tr The D and P Group
	(Lycoming O-360)				Rayne Hall Farm, Braintree 28.10.09E
G-AROC	Cessna 175BX Skylark	17556997	G-OTOW	2.10.61	A J Symms High Ham, Langport 9. 6.09E
	(Modified to 172 configuration)		G-AROC, N8297T		
G-ARON	Piper PA-22-108 Colt	22-8822		23.11.61	R Gibson tr The G-ARON Flying Group
					White Waltham 5. 7.01
G-AROO	Forney F-1A Aircoupe	5750	N25B	3.11.61	W J McMeekan Newtownards 11. 7.11
G-AROW	SAN Jodel D 140B Mousquetaire II	71		13. 9.61	A R Crome Great Oakley 17. 6.09P
G-AROY	Boeing Stearman A75N1 (PT-17) Kaydet				
		75-4775	N56418	6. 6.61	I T Whitaker-Bethel and J Mann Spanhoe 10. 3.11S
G-ARRD	SAN Jodel DR.1051 Ambassadeur	274		20. 7.61	D J Taylor and J P Brady RAF Benson 24.10.07P
	(Potez 4E20)				
G-ARRE	SAN Jodel DR.1050 Ambassadeur	275		20. 7.61	W H Greenwood (Swanborough Farm, Lewes) 27.11.09P
G-ARRI	Cessna 175B Skylark	17557001	N8301T	5.10.61	M V Eckley tr G-ARRI Partnership Pembrey 24. 6.09E

Reg	Type	c/n	Prev id	Date	Owner	Location	Date
G-ARRL	Auster J/1N Alpha	2115	VP-KFK	13. 6.61	A C Ladd	Romney Street Farm, Sevenoaks	3. 8.09P
			VP-KPF, VP-KFK, VP-UAK				
G-ARRO	Beagle A 109 Airedale	B 507	EI-AYL (2)	16. 6.61	M and S W Isbister *(Stored for spares as "EI-AYL" 10.07)*		
	(Originally regd with c/n A 109-P5)		G-ARRO, (EI-AVP), G-ARRO			Spanhoe	17. 1.74
G-ARRS	Menavia Piel CP.301A Emeraude	226	F-BIMA	29. 6.61	J F Sully	RAF Scampton	31. 7.09P
G-ARRT	Wallis WA-116/Mc	2		28. 6.61	K H Wallis *(Noted 8.01)*	Reymerston Hall, Norfolk	24. 5.83P
	(Originally regd as a Wallis Gyroplane then became WA-116/Mc) (McCulloch 4318A)						
G-ARRU	Druine D 31 Turbulent	PFA 502		28. 6.61	D G Huck	(Harborough Magna, Rugby)	27. 2.97P
	(Built J O'Connor) (Volkswagen 1600)						
G-ARRX	Auster 6A	2281	VF512	4. 7.61	J E D Mackie *"Peggy Too"*	Popham	22. 6.09
					(As "VF512:PF-M" in RAF 43 OTU c/s)		
G-ARRY	SAN Jodel D 140B Mousquetaire II	72		13. 9.61	C Thomas	Bodmin	5. 3.11S
G-ARRZ	Druine D 31 Turbulent	PFA 580		21. 8.61	T A Stambach	(Hemel Hempstead)	21.12.90P
	(Built Rollason Aircraft and Engines) (Ardem 4C02)				*(Damaged Horley, Surrey 21. 7.90: rear fuselage Priory Farm, Tibenham 6.04)*		
G-ARSG	Avro Triplane Type IV replica	TRI-1	(BAPC.1)	29.10.81	Richard Shuttleworth Trustees	Old Warden	8. 9.09P
	(Built Hampshire Aero Club) (ADC Cirrus III)				*(Built for "Those Magnificent Men in Their Flying Machines" film, as "12")*		
G-ARSL	Beagle A 61 Terrier 2	2539	VF581	13. 7.61	D J Colclough *(As "VF581" in AAC c/s)*		
						Trenchard Farm, Eggesford	1. 5.10S
G-ARSU	Piper PA-22-108 Colt	22-8835	EI-AMI	23.11.61	D Hawkins tr Sierra Uniform Flying Group		
			G-ARSU			Enstone	26. 9.11
G-ARTH	Piper PA-12 Super Cruiser	12-3278	EI-ADO	22. 9.61	R I Souch and B J Dunford *(On rebuild 3.07)*		
						Hill Farm, Durley	21. 4.95P
G-ARTL	de Havilland DH.82A Tiger Moth	"T7281"		22. 9.61	F G Clacherty *(As "T7281" in RAF c/s)*		
	(P/i is doubtful - if correct the c/n is 83795)					Longwood Farm, Morestead	9. 6.09S
G-ARTZ (2)	McCandless M 4 Gyroplane	M4/1		24.10.61	W R Partridge	St Merryn	13.10.69P
	(Volkswagen 1500)				*(Noted 5.03)*		
G-ARUG	Auster J/5G Cirrus Autocar	3272		2. 1.62	D P H Hulme	(Croydon)	18. 4.03
G-ARUH	SAN Jodel DR.1050 Ambassadeur	284		5.12.61	P R Bentley	Roughay Farm, Bishops Waltham	4. 7.88
G-ARUI	Beagle A 61 Terrier 1	2529	VF571	9. 3.62	T W J Dann	Southend	27. 4.09P
G-ARUL	LeVier Cosmic Wind	103	N22C	28.11.61	P G Kynsey *"Ballerina"*	Duxford	4. 7.08P
	(Built Tony LeVier Associates Inc: rebuilt 1973 as pr.no.PFA 1511 but original fuselage, wings and data plate held elsewhere)						
G-ARUV	Piel CP.301 Emeraude Series 1	PFA 700		2. 2.62	P O'Fee *"Emma"*	RAF Keevil	1. 5.09P
	(Built M N Harrison)						
G-ARUY	Auster J/1N Alpha	3394		2. 2.62	D Burnham *(Being restored 10.08)*	Andrewsfield	27.11.05
G-ARUZ	Cessna 175C Skylark	17557080	N8380T	23. 2.62	M Lowe and L E Brown tr Cardiff Skylark Group		
					(Noted 10.08)	Bodmin	18. 5.06
G-ARVO	Piper PA-18 Super Cub 95	18-7252	D-ENFI	18. 1.83	D S Brown and R M Kimbrell tr Victor Oscar Group		
			N3376Z			Sibson	16.12.10
G-ARVT	Piper PA-28-160 Cherokee	28-379		21. 3.62	Red Rose Aviation Ltd	Liverpool-John Lennon	15. 3.09E
G-ARVU	Piper PA-28-160 Cherokee	28-410	PH-ONY	30. 3.62	Barton Mudwing Ltd	Barton	13. 8.09E
			G-ARVU				
G-ARVV	Piper PA-28-160 Cherokee	28-451		11. 7.62	G E Hopkins	Shobdon	17. 3.09E
G-ARVZ	Druine D 62B Condor	RAE 606		6.12.61	A A M Huke	Manor Farm, Dinton	15. 5.09P
	(Built Rollason Aircraft and Engines)						
G-ARWB	de Havilland DHC-1 Chipmunk 22A	C1/0621	WK611	2. 1.62	P S Oglesby tr Thruxton Chipmunk Flying Group		
					(As "WK611" in RAF c/s)	Thruxton	26.11.11
G-ARWO	Cessna 172C Skyhawk	49187	N1487Y	10. 4.62	D Bentley	(Nenagh, County Tipperary)	2. 7.08
G-ARWR	Cessna 172C Skyhawk	49172	N1472Y	13. 4.62	M McCann tr Devanha Flying Group	Insch	13. 3.09E
G-ARWS	Cessna 175C Skylark	17557102	N8502X	12. 4.62	M D Fage	Derby	19.12.09E
G-ARXB	Beagle A 109 Airedale	B 509	EI-BBK	5. 2.62	M Isbister	Spanhoe	9. 9.76
	(Originally regd with c/n A 109-2)		G-ARXB, EI-ATE, G-ARXB		*(Stored for spares as EI-BBK 10.07)*		
G-ARXD	Beagle A 109 Airedale	B 511		19. 4.62	D Howden *(Under restoration 6.00)*		
	(Originally regd with c/n A 109-4)					Tullochvenus Farm, Lumphanan, Banchory	13. 6.86
G-ARXG	Piper PA-24-250 Comanche	24-3154	N10F	21. 2.62	R F Corstin t/a Fairoaks Comanche	Dunsfold	8. 9.09E
G-ARXH	Bell 47	G 40	N120B	13. 2.62	A B Searle *(Noted 8.06)*	Cranfield	6. 7.90
			NC120B				
G-ARXP	Phoenix Luton LA-4A Minor	PAL 1119		23. 2.62	E Evans *(Stored 1.08)*	Benson's Farm, Laindon	17.10.95P
	(Built W C Hymas - pr.no.PFA 816) (Walter Mikron 3)						
G-ARXT	SAN Jodel DR.1050 Ambassadeur	355		14. 3.62	M F Coy tr CJM Flying Group		
						Wellesbourne Mountford	26.11.09P
G-ARXU	Auster 6A (modified)	2295	VF526	5. 3.62	A B Taylor-Roberts and E M Le Gresley		
					(As "VF526:T" in AAC c/s)	AAC Netheravon	8.11.09P
G-ARXW	Morane Saulnier MS.885 Super Rallye	100		30. 3.62	M J Kirk *(Noted 5.05)*	Haverfordwest	4. 5.04
G-ARYH	Piper PA-22-160 Tri-Pacer	22-7039	N3102Z	9. 3.62	C Watt	Crosland Moor	8. 7.09E
G-ARYI	Cessna 172C	49260	N1560Y	13. 7.62	J Rhodes *(stored, noted 10.08)*	Blackbushe	8. 5.09E
G-ARYK	Cessna 172C	49288	N1588Y	13. 7.62	A Winnicott	Lydd	8. 5.09E
G-ARYR	Piper PA-28-160 Cherokee B	28-770		12. 7.62	R P Synge and C S Wilkinson tr GARYR Flying Group		
						Turweston	22. 3.09E
G-ARYS	Cessna 172C Skyhawk	49291	N1591Y	13. 7.62	G Cockerton tr Lucon Chasnais Flying Amis		
						Coventry	16. 1.09E
G-ARYV	Piper PA-24-250 Comanche	24-2516	N7337P	17. 4.62	D C Hanss	Elstree	18. 1.10E
	(incorrectly shown by CAA as ex N1591Y)						
G-ARYZ	Beagle A 109 Airedale	B 512		9. 4.62	C W Tomkins *(Noted 10.07)*	Spanhoe	26. 2.01
G-ARZB	Wallis WA-116 Series 1 Agile	B 203	XR943	18. 4.62	K H Wallis *"Little Nellie"*	Reymerston Hall, Norfolk	29. 6.93P
	(Built Beagle-Miles Aircraft Ltd)		G-ARZB			(McCulloch 4318A)	
	(Flown as "XR943" for evaluation 1962 but remained on UK Register; used in 1966 for James Bond film "You Only Live Twice") *(Noted 8.01)*						
G-ARZN	Beech N35 Bonanza	D-6795	N215DM	23. 5.62	S R Cleary	Perth	2. 3.09E
G-ARZS	Beagle A 109 Airedale	B 515	EI-BAL	11. 5.62	M and S W Isbister	Spanhoe	23. 5.75
			G-ARZS		*(Fuselage noted 10.07)*		
G-ARZW	Phoenix Currie Wot	1		25. 5.62	B R Pearson	Eaglescott	7. 1.89P
	(Built J H B Urmston) (Walter Mikron 3)				*(Damaged near Headcorn 12. 2.88: on rebuild 10.99 as Pfalz D VII scale replica)*		

G-ASAA - G-ASZZ

G-ASAA	Phoenix Luton LA-4A Minor	O-H/4		19. 4.62	M J Aubrey (Noted 2002)		
	(Built P D Lea and Partners) (JAP J-99)				Upper Yield, Floodgates, Kington, Hereford	7. 6.01P
G-ASAI	Beagle A 109 Airedale	B 516		26. 6.62	K R Howden (On rebuild 6.00)	Lumphanan	20. 5.77S
G-ASAJ	Beagle A 61 Terrier 2	B 605	WE569	26. 6.62	T A Collins (As "WE569" (Auster T 7) in AAC c/s)	
	(Initially allocated c/n 3732)				RAF Benson 29.11..09E
G-ASAL (2)	Scottish Aviation Bulldog Series 100/101		(G-BBHF)	5. 9.73	Pioneer Flying Company Ltd	Prestwick	18. 3.09P
		BH120/239	G-31-17			
G-ASAT	Morane Saulnier MS.880B Rallye Club	178		21. 6.62	M Cutovic	Croft Farm, Defford	2. 8.08E
G-ASAU	Morane Saulnier MS.880B Rallye Club	179		21. 6.62	M S Lonsdale	Full Sutton	30. 7.09E
G-ASAX	Beagle A 61 Terrier 2	B 609	TW533	12. 6.62	A D Hodgkinson	(Luton)	1. 9.96
	(Converted from Auster 6 c/n 1911)					
G-ASAZ	Hiller UH-12E-4	2070	N5372V	18. 6.62	R C Hields t/a Hields Aviation (As "XS165:37" in RAF c/s)	
					Sherburn-in-Elmet	27. 4.09E
G-ASBA	Phoenix Currie Wot	AE.1		16. 8.62	J C Lister	Valley Farm, Winwick	9. 5.09P
	(Built A Etherbridge - pr.no.PFA 3005)					
G-ASBH	Beagle A 109 Airedale	B 519		26. 6.62	D T Smollett	Bratton Clovelly, Okehampton	19. 2.99
G-ASBY	Beagle A 109 Airedale	B 523		23. 7.62	F A Forster	Lydd	22. 3.80
G-ASCC	Beagle E 3 Mk.11	B 701	(G-25-12)	23. 7.62	T A Collins (As "XP254" in 'AAC c/s)	
			XP254		South Lodge Farm, Widmerpool	11. 8.07P
	(Struck tree during go-around Filkins near Lechlade 29. 7.07 and fell into field incurring substantial damage)					
G-ASCM	Isaacs Fury II	1		1. 8.62	E C and P King (As "K2050" in pre-war RAF c/s)	
	(Built J O Isaacs - pr.no.PFA 2002/1B - builder's membership no.)				Eastbach Farm, Coleford	24.10.02P
G-ASCZ	Menavia Piel CP.301A Emeraude	233	F-BIMG	1.10.62	P Johnson (In pseudo military marks)	Goodwood	1. 7.09P
G-ASDK	Beagle A 61 Terrier 2	B 702	G-ARLM (2)	26.10.62	J Swallow	Hibaldstow	26.10.09S
	(Converted from Auster AOP.6 c/n 2573)		G-ARLP(1), VF631			
G-ASDY	Beagle-Wallis WA-116/F	B 205	XR944	9.11.62	K H Wallis (Noted 8.01)	Reymerston Hall, Norfolk	28.10.97P
	(Franklin 2A-120-B)		(G-ARZC (1))			
	(Regd with c/n B 204 as Beagle-Wallis WA.116 Srs 1 and powered by McCulloch 4318A: fitted with 990cc Hillman Imp engine 1965					
	and re-styled WA.119: re-engined 1971 with 60hp 2-cylinder Franklin 2A-120-A and re-designated)					
G-ASEA	Phoenix Luton LA-4A Minor	PAL 1154		14.11.62	D Underwood	(Totternhoe, Dunstable)	16. 8.89P
	(Built G P Smith and M Fawkes - pr.no.PFA 1154) (JAP J-99)					
G-ASEB	Phoenix Luton LA-4A Minor	PAL 1149		26.11.62	S R P Harper	Walkeridge Farm, Overton	13. 1.10P
	(Built J A Anning)					
G-ASEO	Piper PA-24-250 Comanche	24-3367	(G-ASDX)	23. 1.63	M Scott tr Pixies Day Nursery	Bournemouth	19. 6.09E
			N10F			
G-ASEP	Piper PA-23-235 Aztec	27-541		28. 1.63	Air Warren Ltd "Miss Max Power" (Maxim titles)	
					Denham	21. 7.09E
G-ASEU	Druine D 62A Condor	RAE 607		12. 2.63	W M Grant	Inverness	14. 5.09P
	(Built Rollason Aircraft and Engines) (Continental C90-8F)					
G-ASFD	SPP Morava L-200A	170808	OK-PHH	26. 2.63	M Emery	(Redhill)	12. 7.84T
G-ASFK	Auster J/5G Cirrus Autocar	3276		7. 3.63	T D G Lancaster	Landmead Farm, Garford	1. 6.09P
G-ASFL	Piper PA-28-180 Cherokee B	28-1170		7. 3.63	M R O Thompson and S M R Hickman	
					Lee-on-Solent	27. 5.09E
G-ASFR	Bölkow BÖ.208C Junior	522	D-EGMO	12. 3.63	S T Dauncey (Stored 2.08)	Yearby	29. 3.90P
G-ASFX	Druine D 31 Turbulent	PFA 513		18. 3.63	E F Clapham and W B S Dobie	
	(Built E F Clapham) (Volkswagen 1600)				Oldbury-on-Severn	11. 6.09P
G-ASHH	Piper PA-23-250 Aztec	27-63	N455SL	25. 3.63	C Fordham and L Barr	(Leicester)	29. 8.03
			N4557P		(Reportedly destroyed by fire on ground c 2005 and removed)	
G-ASHS	SNCAN Stampe SV-4C(G)	265	F-BCFN	23. 4.63	D G Girling	(Liverpool)	17. 3.11S
	(Original fuselage for rebuild of G-AWEF 1980: rebuilt 1984 with fuselage of G-AZIR c/n 452 ex F-BCXR)					
G-ASHT	Druine D 31 Turbulent	PFA 1610		23. 4.63	C W N Huke	Manor Farm, Dinton	2.10.09P
	(Built Rollason Aircraft and Engines) (Volkswagen 1600)					
G-ASHU	Piper PA-15 Vagabond	15-46	N4164H	1. 5.63	T J Ventham tr The Calybe Flying Group "Calybe"	
	(Rotax 912-UL)		NC4164H		Farley Farm, Romsey	21.10.08P
G-ASHX	Piper PA-28-180 Cherokee B	28-1266	N7382W	3. 5.63	Powertheme Ltd	Barton	10. 5.09E
G-ASIB	Cessna F172D Skyhawk	F172-0006	F-WLIR	9. 5.63	A Jones tr G-ASIB Flying Group	Hawarden	29.10.09E
	(Built Reims Aviation SA) (Wichita c/n 17250091)					
G-ASII	Piper PA-28-180 Cherokee B	28-1264		21. 5.63	T R Hart and R W S Matthews	Exeter	25. 5.09E
G-ASIJ	Piper PA-28-180 Cherokee B	28-1333	N7445W	21. 5.63	L O Webb tr G-ASIJ Group	Andrewsfield	11. 6.09E
G-ASIL	Piper PA-28-180 Cherokee B	28-1350	N7461W	21. 5.63	C D Powell	Leicester	8. 8.08E
G-ASIS	Wassmer Jodel D 112	1166	EI-CKX	24. 2.81	W R Prescott	Derryogue, Kilkeel, County Down	20. 8.08P
			G-ASIS, F-BKNR			
G-ASIT	Cessna 180	32567	N7670A	24. 5.63	R A Seeley	Turweston	22. 6.09E
G-ASIY	Piper PA-25-235 Pawnee	25-2446		30. 5.63	T M Holloway tr RAF Gliding and Soaring Association	
					(Operated Chilterns Glidng Centre)	RAF Halton	4. 3.10E
G-ASJL	Beech H35 Bonanza	D-5132	N5582D	14. 6.63	A J Orchard and R L Dargue	Fairoaks	24. 7.08E
G-ASJV	Vickers Supermarine 361 Spitfire LF.IXb		OO-ARA	3. 7.63	Merlin Aviation Ltd	Duxford	1. 6.09P
		CBAF.IX.552			Belgian AF SM-41, Fokker B-13, R Neth AF H-68, H-105, MH434	
					(Operated The Old Flying Machine Company as "MH434:ZD-B" in RAF 316 Sqdn c/s)	
G-ASJY	Sud-Aviation Gardan GY-80-160 Horizon	13		9. 7.63	L W Quigley tr No. 6 Group (Noted 2.08)	Bagby	14.11.07E
G-ASJZ	SAN Jodel D.117A	826	F-BITD	5. 7.63	M A Watts	Farley Farm, Romsey	1. 9.09E
G-ASKL	SAN Jodel D 150 Mascaret	27		18. 7.63	J M Graty	Nuthampstead	27. 2.09P
G-ASKP	de Havilland DH.82A Tiger Moth	3889	N6588	22. 7.63	The Tiger Club (1990) Ltd	Headcorn	14. 3.09S
G-ASKT	Piper PA-28-180 Cherokee B	28-1410	N7497W	24. 7.63	T J Herbert	Biggin Hill	23. 6.09E
G-ASLH	Cessna 182F Skylane	18254905	N3505U	19. 8.63	A L Brown and A L Butcher	Bourn	27. 4.09E
G-ASLV	Piper PA-28-235 Cherokee Pathfinder			11. 9.63	I L Harding tr Sackville Flying Group	
		28-10048			Sackville Lodge, Riseley	26. 3.09E
G-ASLX	Menavia Piel CP.301A Emeraude	292	F-BISV	12. 9.63	J J Reilly	(Thurles, County Tipperary)	4. 3.09P
G-ASMA	Piper PA-30 Twin Comanche	30-143	N10F	17. 9.63	K Cooper (Stored 10.07)	Farley Farm, Romsey	5. 1.03
	(Modified to PA-39 C/R status)					
G-ASME	Bensen B 8M	12		24. 9.63	R M Harris (In container on field)	North Coates	19. 8.08P
	(Rotax 582)					

G-ASMF	Beech D95A TravelAir	TD-565		26. 9.63	M J A Hornblower	White Waltham	11. 8.08T
G-ASMJ	Cessna F172E	F172-0029		25.10.63	Aeroscene Ltd	Sherburn-in-Elmet	11. 6.09E
	(Built Reims Aviation SA) (Wichita c/n 17250584)						
G-ASML	Phoenix Luton LA-4A Minor	PAL 1148		28.10.63	R W Vince	(Stansted, Sevenoaks)	21. 8.09P
	(Built R M Kirby - pr.no.PFA 802) (Volkswagen 1600)						
G-ASMM	Druine D 31 Turbulent	PFA 1611		31.10.63	W J Browning "Mouche Miel"	Redhill	19.10.09P
	(Built Rollason Aircraft and Engines) (Ardem 4C02)						
G-ASMS	Cessna 150A	15059204	N7104X	18.11.63	M Smith	Full Sutton	30.12.09E
G-ASMT	Fairtravel Linnet 2	004		20.11.63	P Harrison	Swanborough Farm, Lewes	17. 7.08P
	(Continental O-200A)						
G-ASMV	Scintex CP.1310-C3 Super Emeraude	919		22.11.63	P F D Waltham	(Thurlton, Norwich)	7.11.94
G-ASMW	Cessna 150D	15060247	N4247U	26.11.63	C Brown	Netherthorpe	27. 9.09E
G-ASMY	Piper PA-23-160 Apache H	23-2032	N4309Y	3.12.63	R D Forster (Noted 11.08)	Ellough, Beccles	25.11.95T
G-ASMZ	Beagle A 61 Terrier 2	B 629	G-35-11	4.12.63	B Andrews (As "VF516" in RAF c/s)		
	(Conversion of Auster AOP.10 c/n 2285)		VF516			Trenchard Farm, Eggesford	11. 5.09
G-ASNC	Beagle D 5/180 Husky	3678		9.12.63	Peterborough and Spalding Gliding Club Ltd		
						Crowland	4. 4.10S
G-ASNI	Scintex CP.1310-C3 Super Emeraude	925		20.12.63	D Chapman	Wickenby	5. 9.08E
G-ASNK	Cessna 205	205-0400	N8400Z	27.12.63	Justgold Ltd (Operated Blackpool Air Centre) (Noted 10.07)		
						Blackpool	26. 6.06T
G-ASNW	Cessna F172E	F172-0031		13. 1.64	W G Brooks tr G-ASNW Group		
	(Built Reims Aviation SA) (Wichita c/n 17250613)					Draycott Farm, Chiseldon	14.10.09E
G-ASOC	Auster 6A Tugmaster	2544	VF603	21. 1.64	M J Kirk	Haverfordwest	18. 5.02
G-ASOH	Beech 95-B55A Baron	TC-656		31. 1.64	G Davis and C Middlemiss	Biggin Hill	29. 5.09E
G-ASOI	Beagle A 61 Terrier 2	B 627	G-35-11	31. 1.64	G D B Delmege	Kemble	12. 8.11
			WJ404				
G-ASOK	Cessna F172E	F172-0057		31. 1.64	D W Disney	Derby	13.10.09E
	(Built Reims Aviation SA) (Continental O-300D)						
G-ASOM	Beagle A 61 Terrier 2	B 622	G-JETS	3. 2.64	D Humphries and W Parsons tr GASOM.org		
	(DH Gipsy Major 10 Mk 1)		G-ASOM, G-35-11, VF505			Spanhoe	5. 7.09S
G-ASOX	Cessna 205A	205-0556	N4856U	3. 2.64	S M C Harvey	Hinton-in-the-Hedges	1. 8.92
G-ASPF	Wassmer Jodel D 120 Paris-Nice	02	F-BFNP	26. 2.64	T J Bates	Dairy House Farm, Worleston	19. 6.09P
G-ASPP	Bristol Boxkite replica	BOX.1 & BM.7279	(BAPC.2)	29.10.81	Richard Shuttleworth Trustees	Old Warden	31. 7.09P
	(Built F G Miles Ltd) (Continental O-200-B)				(Built for "Those Magnificent Men in Their Flying Machines" film, as No."12A")		
G-ASPS	Piper J-3C-65 Cub Special	22809	N3571N	2. 3.64	A J Chalkley	Rhoshirwaun, Pwllheli	27. 5.09P
	(Frame No.21971)		NC3571N				
G-ASPV (2)	de Havilland DH.82A Tiger Moth	84167	T7794	5. 3.64	Z J Rockey	Higherlands Farm, Branscombe	31. 8.97
	(Built Morris Motors Ltd) (P/i obscure - original G-ASPV sold Norway 7.75 and rebuilt as LN-MAX) (On rebuild 2007)						
G-ASRB	Druine D 62B Condor	RAE 608		11. 3.64	B J Douglas	(Killiney, Dublin)	4. 7.08P
	(Built Rollason Aircraft and Engines)						
G-ASRC	Druine D 62C Condor	RAE 609		11. 3.64	C R Isbell	(Felstead, Dunmow)	22.11.08P
	(Built Rollason Aircraft and Engines)						
G-ASRK	Beagle A 109 Airedale	B 538		26. 3.64	Bio Pathica Ltd	Lydd	27. 6.10S
G-ASRO	Piper PA-30 Twin Comanche	30-395	N10F	31. 3.64	D W Blake tr Five Star Flying Group		
						Gloucestershire	18. 8.09E
G-ASRT	SAN Jodel D 150 Mascaret	45		6. 4.64	P Turton (Stored 6.94)	(Holmes Chapel, Crewe)	3. 6.94P
G-ASRW	Piper PA-28-180 Cherokee B	28-1606	N11C	21. 4.64	G N Smith	Thorpe Abbots, Diss	15. 6.09E
G-ASSF	Cessna 182G Skylane	18255593	N2493R	5. 5.64	P S Grellier		
						New Barn Farm, Barton Ashes, Crawley	10. 4.08E
	(Yawed to the left and left wing dropped on take-off at Eddsfield 26.12.07, contacted the ground and came to rest inverted)						
G-ASSP	Piper PA-30 Twin Comanche	30-458	N10F	7. 5.64	P H Tavener	(Rochester)	22.12.07E
G-ASSS	Cessna 172E	17251467	N5567T	7. 5.64	P R March and P Turner	Filton	26. 5.09E
G-ASST	Cessna 150D	15060630	N5930T	7. 5.64	F R H Parker		
						Pear Tree Farm, Marsh Gibbon, Bicester	26. 9.09E
G-ASSV	Kensinger KF	2	N23S	11. 5.64	C I Jefferson	Priory Farm, Tibenham	30. 7.69P
	(Built N Kensinger - pr.no.PFA168-13923) (Continental C85)				(Noted 8.05)		
G-ASSW	Piper PA-28-140 Cherokee	28-20055	N11C	11. 5.64	D K Roberts	Biggin Hill	5. 9.09E
G-ASSY	Druine D 31 Turbulent	PFA 586		12. 5.64	R C Bailey	(Milcombe, Banbury)	20. 4.84P
	(Built F J Parker) (Volkswagen 1500)						
G-ASTA	Druine D 31 Turbulent	152	F-PJGH	12. 5.64	P A Cooke (Fuselage noted 11.06 on lorry at Lechlade)		
	(Built M Barboni) (Ardem 4C02)				(Chippenham)		13.11.97P
G-ASTG	Nord 1002 Pingouin II	183	F-BGKI	21. 5.64	L M Walton (On rebuild, unmarked 4.03)	Duxford	26.10.73S
			French AF 183				
G-ASTI	Auster 6A Tugmaster	3745	WJ359	27. 5.64	S J Partridge	Enstone	9. 1.10S
G-ASUB	Mooney M 20E Super 21	397	N7158U	24. 6.64	S C Coulbeck	North Coates	18. 9.09E
G-ASUD	Piper PA-28-180 Cherokee B	28-1654	N7673W	29. 6.64	P J Wilkinson and A J Rogers tr G-ASUD Flying Group		
						Andrewsfield	17. 3.09E
G-ASUE	Cessna 150D	15060718	N6018T	30. 6.64	D Huckle (Stored 6.94)	(Ware)	1. 8.90
G-ASUI	Beagle A 61 Terrier 2	B 641	VF628	6. 7.64	R J Bentley		
	(Conversion of Auster AOP.10 c/n 2570)				Pallas West, Toomyvara, County Tipperary		11. 1.10
G-ASUP	Cessna F172E	F172-0071		22. 7.64	P T and L.E Trivett tr Gasup Air	Cardiff	24. 5.09E
	(Built Reims Aviation SA)						
G-ASUR	Dornier Do.28A-1	3051	D-IBOM	28. 7.64	N J Taafe	Old Warden	17. 8.09E
G-ASUS	Jurca MJ.2E Tempête	PFA 2001		28. 7.64	R Targonski	Wolverhampton	6. 5.09P
	(Built D G Jones)						
G-ASVG	Rousseau Piel CP.301B Emeraude	109	F-BILV	7. 8.64	K R H Wingate "Emma II" (Also carries "F-BILV")		
						Halwell	31. 5.08P
G-ASVM	Cessna F172E Skyhawk	F172-0077		11. 8.64	R H Bennett	Popham	29.12.09E
	(Built Reims Aviation SA)						
G-ASVN	Cessna 206 Super Skywagon	206-0275	N5275U	12. 8.64	Skydive Brid Ltd	East Leys Farm, Grindale	22. 5.09E
	(Destroyed in hangar fire during 2008)						
G-ASVP	Piper PA-25-235 Pawnee	25-2978	N10F	17. 8.64	Banbury Gliding Club Ltd	Hinton-in-the-Hedges	28. 9.09E
G-ASVZ	Piper PA-28-140 Cherokee	28-20357	N11C	24. 8.64	J S Garvey	Sleap	23. 3.09E

Reg	Type	C/n	Prev ID	Date	Owner	Location	Status
G-ASWL	Cessna F172F	F172-0087		10. 9.64	Ensiform Aviation Ltd	Elstree	28. 9.09E
	(Built Reims Aviation SA)						
G-ASWN	Bensen B 8M	14		15. 9.64	D R Shepherd (Components stored 2003)		
	(Built D R Shepherd)					(Prestwick)	
G-ASWW	Piper PA-30 Twin Comanche	30-556	N7531Y	1.10.64	N C Scanlan tr G-WW Group	RAF Waddington	6.11.07
			N10F				
G-ASWX	Piper PA-28-180 Cherokee C	28-1932	N11C	1.10.64	Gasworks Flying Group Ltd	Little Staughton	16. 4.09E
G-ASXC	SIPA 903	8	G-DWEL	6.10.64	B L Procter	Dunkeswell	
	(Continental C90)		G-ASXC, F-BEYK		(Wide-track sprung-steel undercarriage)		
G-ASXD	Brantly B 2B	435		7.10.64	Lousada PLC		
						Crawley Park, Husborne Crawley, Bedford	2. 7.05
G-ASXI	Tipsy Nipper T 66 Series 3	T66/56	VH-CGH	13.10.64	P G Blenkinsopp		
	(Built Avions Fairey SA) (Jabiru 2200A)		OO-KOC, (VH-CGC)			New Barn Farm, Barton Ashes, Crawley	27. 7.09P
G-ASXJ	Phoenix Luton LA-4A Minor	PFA 801		14.10.64	C R Greenaway	Long Marston	17.12.08P
	(Built P D Lea and E A Linguard) (Lycoming O-145)						
G-ASXR	Cessna 210	57532	5Y-KPW	16.10.64	A Schofield (Noted dismantled 11.04)	Barton	3. 1.93
			VP-KPW, N6532X				
G-ASXS	SAN Jodel DR.1050 Ambassadeur	133	F-BJNG	19.10.64	R A Hunter	Finmere	17.12.06
G-ASXU	Wassmer Jodel D 120A Paris-Nice	196	F-BKAG	19.10.64	M Ferio tr G-ASXU Group		
						Stoneacre Farm, Farthing Corner	2. 5.09P
G-ASXY	SAN Jodel D 117A	914	F-BIVA	27.10.64	A P Davies and D G Claxton tr Pegasus Flying Group		
						Cardiff	27. 3.09P
G-ASXZ	Cessna 182G Skylane	18255738	N3238S	28.10.64	Last Refuge Ltd		
						Gedney Marsh Farm, Gedney, Wells	20.12.09E
G-ASYG	Beagle A 61 Terrier 2	B 637	VX927	3.11.64	T K Rumble tr Terrane Auster Group (As "VX927" in AAC c/s)		
	(Rebuilt to T 7 standard)					Wickenby	7. 6.09S
G-ASYJ	Beech D95A TravelAir	TD-595	N8675Q	6.11.64	Crosby Aviation (Jersey) Ltd	Jersey	12.11.08E
G-ASYP	Cessna 150E	15060794	N6094T	23.11.64	A C Melmore tr Henlow Flying Group RAF Henlow		25.11.08E
G-ASZB	Cessna 150E	15061113	N3013J	16.12.64	R J Scott	Ashleigh Farm, Bracknell	3.10.08E
G-ASZD	Bölkow BÖ.208A-2 Junior	563	D-ENKI	16.12.64	M J Ayres	Full Sutton	23. 6.03P
G-ASZE	Beagle A 61 Terrier 2	B 636	VF552	17.12.64	D R Ockleton	RNAS Yeovilton	2. 7.09S
	(Conversion of Auster 6 c/n 2510)						
G-ASZR	Fairtravel Linnet 2	005		5. 1.65	R Hodgson	Swanborough Farm, Lewes	28. 6.08P
G-ASZS	Sud-Aviation Gardan GY-80-160 Horizon	70		6. 1.65	L R Burton tr ZS Group Wellesbourne Mountford		22. 1.09E
G-ASZU	Cessna 150E	15061152	N3052J	13. 1.65	L J Baker and S L Bassett	Cranfield	29. 8.09E
G-ASZV	Tipsy Nipper T 66 Series 2	T66/45	5N-ADE	14. 1.65	D H Greenwood	Barton	23. 5.90P
	(Built Avions Fairey SA) (Volkswagen 1835)		5N-ADY, VR-NDD		(New owner 5.06)		
G-ASZX	Beagle A 61 Terrier 1	3742	(SE-ELO)	18. 1.65	R B Webber (As "WJ368" in AAC c/s)		
			WJ368			Trenchard Farm, Eggesford	18. 7.10S

G-ATAA - G-ATZZ

Reg	Type	C/n	Prev ID	Date	Owner	Location	Status
G-ATAF	Cessna F172F	F172-0135		25. 1.65	Summit Media Ltd	(Norwich)	15. 8.08E
	(Built Reims Aviation SA)						
G-ATAG	CEA Jodel DR.1050 Ambassadeur	226	F-BKGG	25. 1.65	T M Dawes-Gamble (Noted 8.06)		
						Wishanger Farm, Frensham	4.10.02
G-ATAS	Piper PA-28-180 Cherokee C	28-2137	N11C	4. 2.65	R Osborn tr ATAS Group	Andrewsfield	21. 9.09E
G-ATAU	Druine D 62B Condor	RAE 610		10. 2.65	W J Forrest		
	(Built Rollason Aircraft and Engines)					Ventfield Farm, Horton-cum-Studley, Oxford	29.12.08P
G-ATAV	Druine D 62C Condor	RAE 611		10. 2.65	V A Holliday	Streethay Farm, Lichfield	11. 9.09P
	(Built Rollason Aircraft and Engines)						
G-ATBG	Nord 1002 Pingouin II	121	F-BGVX	24. 2.65	T W Harris (As "NJ+C11" in Luftwaffe c/s)		
			F-OTAN-5, Fr.Military			Audley End	25. 3.09P
	(Made a wheels-up forced landing in a field near Headcorn 15. 8.08 during attempted go-around after a flight from Audley End)						
G-ATBH	SPP Aero 145	20-015		24. 2.65	P D Aviram (On rebuild 1.06)	Redhill	26.10.81
G-ATBI	Beech A23 Musketeer II	M-696		26. 2.65	A C Dent tr Three Musketeers Flying Group Oxford		13. 2.09E
G-ATBJ	Sikorsky S-61N	61-269	N10043?	12. 3.65	British International Helicopter Services Ltd t/a British		
						International (stored 4.08) Plymouth	2. 6.07E
G-ATBL	de Havilland DH.60G Moth	1917	HB-OBA	2. 3.65	J M Greenland Blackacre Farm, Holt, Trowbridge		23. 7.08P
			CH-353				
G-ATBP	Fournier RF3	59		11. 3.65	D McNicholl	Inverness	22. 8.09S
G-ATBS	Druine D 31 Turbulent	PFA 1620		16. 3.65	J A Lear "Fly Baby Fly"		
	(Built C R Shilling) (Volkswagen 1500)					Pittichie Farm, Whiterashes	29.11.08P
G-ATBU	Beagle A 61 Terrier 2	B 635	VF611	17. 3.65	T Jarvis	Shenington	20. 3.09P
	(Conversion of Auster 6 c/n 2552)						
G-ATBW	Tipsy Nipper T 66 Series 2	T66/52	OO-MAG	19. 3.65	S Bloomfield and C Firth tr Stapleford Nipper Group		
	(Built Cobelavia SA) (Volkswagen 1834 Acro)					Stapleford	7. 4.09P
G-ATBX	Piper PA-20-135 Pacer	20-904	VP-KRX	19. 3.65	G D and P M Thomson		
			VR-TCH, VP-KKE			Standalone Farm, Meppershall	29. 6.08E
G-ATCC	Beagle A 109 Airedale	B 542		25. 3.65	J R Bowden	Headcorn	13. 4.09P
G-ATCD	Beagle D 5/180 Husky	3683		25. 3.65	D J O'Gorman	Enstone	4. 4.09S
G-ATCE	Cessna U206 Super Skywagon	U2060380	N2180F	25. 3.65	C Armstrong	East Leys Farm, Grindale	2. 8.08E
G-ATCJ	Phoenix Luton LA-4A Minor	PAL1163		5. 4.65	T D Boyle	Errol	15. 9.09P
	(Built R M Sharphouse - pr.no.PFA 812) (Volkswagen 1600)						
G-ATCL	Victa Airtourer 100	93		5. 4.65	A D Goodall (Noted 8.06)	Oaksey Park	25. 7.05
G-ATCX	Cessna 182H Skylane	18255848	N3448S	26. 4.65	Softnotes Ltd	Turweston	15. 1.09P
					(Note fuselage of cancelled G-OLSC is also marked as "G-ATCX")		
G-ATDA	Piper PA-28-160 Cherokee	28-206	EI-AME	27. 4.65	Portway Aviation Ltd	Shobdon	28. 1.10E
			(G-ARUV)				
G-ATDB	SNCAN 1101 Noralpha	186	F-OTAN-6	27. 4.65	J W Hardie (Partially dismantled 10.07) Prestwick		22.11.78S
			French.Military				
G-ATDN	Beagle A 61 Terrier 2	B 638	TW641	7. 5.65	S J Saggers (As "TW641" in AAC c/s)	Biggin Hill	5. 8.10S
	(Conversion of Auster 6 c/n 2499)						
G-ATDO	Bölkow BÖ.208C Junior	576	D-EGZU	10. 5.65	P Thompson	Crosland Moor	24. 1.08P

Reg	Type	C/n	Prev id	Date	Owner/operator	Location	Status
G-ATEF	Cessna 150E	15061378	N3978U	25. 5.65	A J White and B M Scott t/a Swans Aviation		
						Blackbushe	12.12.09E
G-ATEM	Piper PA-28-180 Cherokee C	28-2329	N11C	26. 5.65	G D Wyles	Bovingdon	25. 6.09E
G-ATEV	CEA Jodel DR.1050 Ambassadeur	18	F-BJHL	31. 5.65	J C Carter and J L Altrip	(Cambridge)	13. 8.71
					(On rebuild 9.00)		
G-ATEW	Piper PA-30 Twin Comanche	30-719	N7640Y	3. 6.65	Air Northumbria (Woolsington) Ltd	Newcastle	20. 1.09E
G-ATEX	Victa Airtourer 100	110	(VH-MTU)	3. 6.65	D R Henson tr Halton Victa Group "Matilda"		
						RAF Halton	29. 9.06P
G-ATEZ	Piper PA-28-140 Cherokee	28-21044	N11C	8. 6.65	EFI Aviation Ltd	Norwich	5. 6.09E
G-ATFD	CEA Jodel DR.1050 Ambassadeur	311	F-BKIM	14. 6.65	K D Hills tr G-ATFD Group	Lee-on-Solent	8.10.09E
G-ATFF	Piper PA-23-250 Aztec C	27-2898	N5769Y	16. 6.65	T J Wassell "53" (Noted 10.07 engineless)		
						Wolverhampton	15. 5.05
G-ATFM	Sikorsky S-61N Mk.II	61-270	CF-OKY	21. 6.65	British International Ltd	Falkland Islands	1.10.09E
			N10052	(US p/i not confirmed)			
G-ATFR	Piper PA-25 Pawnee	25-135	OY-ADJ	28. 6.65	Borders (Milfield) Gliding Club Ltd	Milfield	4. 9.09E
			N10F				
G-ATFW	Phoenix Luton LA-4A Minor	PFA 811		2. 7.65	P A Rose	Walney Island	2.12.97P
	(Built G W Shield)						
G-ATFY	Cessna F172G	F172-0199		8. 7.65	J M Vinall	Kemble	6. 4.09E
	(Built Reims Aviation SA)						
G-ATGE	SAN Jodel DR.1050 Ambassadeur	114	F-BJJF	9. 7.65	H A McKnight	Ballymageough, Kilkeel	8. 3.08E
G-ATGY	Sud-Aviation Gardan GY-80-160 Horizon	121		20. 7.65	D Cowen	Henstridge	1. 7.09E
G-ATGZ	Griffiths GH-4 Gyroplane	G 1		20. 7.65	R W J Cripps (Stored 7.91)	(Shardlow, Derby)	
	(Built G Griffiths)						
G-ATHD	de Havilland DHC-1 Chipmunk 22	C1/0837	WP971	26. 7.65	O L Cubitt and P G Lucas tr Spartan Flying Group		
			G-ATHD, WP971		(As "WP971" in RAF c/s)	Denham	30. 6.09
G-ATHK	Aeronca 7AC Champion	7AC-971	N82339	2. 8.65	D A G Fraser tr The Chase Flying Group		
			NC82339			Compton Abbas	9. 9.09P
G-ATHM	Wallis WA-116/F	402 & 211	4R-ACK	3. 8.65	Wallis Autogyros Ltd (Noted 8.01)		
	(Originally McCulloch, later 60hp Franklin)		G-ATHM			Reymerston Hall, Norfolk	23. 5.93P
G-ATHR	Piper PA-28-180 Cherokee C	28-2343	EI-AOT	11. 8.65	Thomson Airways Ltd	Cranfield	8. 8.09E
			N11C				
G-ATHT	Victa Airtourer 115	120		16. 8.65	D A Beese tr Cotswold Flying Group	Badminton	5.10.09S
G-ATHU	Beagle A 61 Terrier 1	AUS/127/FM	7435M	16. 8.65	J A L Irwin	Park Farm, Eaton Bray	27.11.09P
			WE539				
G-ATHV	Cessna 150F	15062019	N8719S	16. 8.65	S Greenwood tr Cessna Hotel Victor Group		
						Sherburn-in-Elmet	27. 3.09E
G-ATHZ	Cessna 150F	15061586	(EI-AOP)	20. 8.65	R D Forster (Noted 10.08)	Ellough, Beccles	27. 3.98T
			N6286R				
G-ATIC	CEA Jodel DR.1050 Ambassadeur	6	F-BJCJ	23. 8.65	T A Major	Porthtowan	21. 9.09P
G-ATIN	SAN Jodel D 117	437	F-BHNV	8. 9.65	A Ayre	(St Andrews)	18. 4.96P
G-ATIR	AIA Stampe SV-4C	1047	F-BNMC	9. 9.65	Austin Trueman Ltd	Little Gransden	19. 5.08
			G-ATIR, F-BMKQ, Aéronavale 1047, F-BCDM, Aéronavale 1047				
G-ATIS	Piper PA-28-160 Cherokee C	28-2713	N11C	9. 9.65	M J Barton	Lee-on-Solent	26. 3.09E
G-ATIZ	SAN Jodel D 117	636	F-BIBR	15. 9.65	R A Smith	Tower Farm, Wollaston	15. 6.09P
G-ATJA	SAN Jodel DR.1050 Ambassadeur	378	F-BKHL	15. 9.65	A Twigg and D A Head tr Bicester Flying Group		
						Bicester	21.10.09P
G-ATJC	Victa Airtourer 100	125		16. 9.65	Aviation West Ltd	Kirknewton	22. 2.10S
G-ATJG	Piper PA-28-140 Cherokee	28-21299		20. 9.65	C A McGee and L K G Manning	Biggin Hilll	29. 1.09E
G-ATJL	Piper PA-24-260 Comanche	24-4203	N8752P	23. 9.65	C G Sims tr Juliet Lima Flying Group	Enstone	22. 7.09E
			N10F				
G-ATJM	Fokker Dr.1 Triplane replica	002	N78001	23. 9.65	R J Lamplough	Manor Farm, East Garston	3. 7.07P
	(Built Bitz Flugzeugbau GmbH)		EI-APY, G-ATJM		(As "152/17"in German Army Air Service c/s)		
	(Siemens SH-14A-165)						
G-ATJN	Jodel D 119	863	F-PINZ	23. 9.65	J Upex	Rufforth	28. 5.09P
	(Built Etablissement Dormois)						
G-ATJT	Sud-Aviation Gardan GY-80-160 Horizon	108		4.10.65	N R Tench	RAF Halton	15. 6.09P
G-ATJV	Piper PA-32-260 Cherokee Six	32-103	TF-GOS	7.10.65	Wingglider Ltd	Hibaldstow	23. 8.09E
			G-ATJV, N11C				
G-ATKF	Cessna 150F	15062386	N3586L	20.10.65	P Asbridge	Sleap	27.4.06T
G-ATKH	Phoenix Luton LA-4A Minor	PFA 809		25.10.65	H E Jenner	Brenchley, Kent	27. 8.06P
	(Built E B W Woodhall) (Lycoming O-145)						
G-ATKI	Piper J-3C-65 Cub	17545	N70536	25.10.65	B Ryan	Lower Wasing Farm, Brimpton	28. 4.09P
	(Continental A75)		NC70536				
G-ATKT	Cessna F172G	F172-0206		9.11.65	J R Waterman tr KT Group	Shipdham	21. 6.09E
	(Built Reims Aviation SA)						
G-ATKX	SAN Jodel D 140C Mousquetaire III	163		19.11.65	I V Sharman tr Kilo Xray Syndicate	Redhill	6.10.09P
G-ATLA	Cessna 182J Skylane	18256923	N2823F	24.11.65	J W and J T Whicher	Full Sutton	17. 2 09E
G-ATLB	SAN Jodel DR.1050M Excellence	78	F-BIVG	29.11.65	D J Gibson tr Le Syndicate du Petit Oiseau		
						Great Oakley	15.11.10E
G-ATLM	Cessna F172G	F172-0252		6.12.65	Airfotos Ltd	Newcastle	19. 5.09E
	(Built Reims Aviation SA)						
G-ATLP	Bensen B 8M	17		9.12.65	R F G Moyle (Noted 3.07)	St Merryn	19. 5.97P
	(Built C D Julian) (McCulloch Motors 4318F)						
G-ATLT	Cessna U206A Super Skywagon	U2060523	N4823F	13.12.65	Skydive UK Ltd	Dunkeswell	8. 4.09E
G-ATLV	Wassmer Jodel D 120 Paris-Nice	224	F-BKNQ	15.12.65	L S Thorne	Shenstone Hall Farm, Shenstone	8. 7.07P
G-ATMC	Cessna F150F	F150-0020		28.12.65	G H Farrah and D Cunnane		
	(Built Reims Aviation SA) (Wichita c/n 15062849)					Abbeyshrule, County Longford	4. 9.09E
G-ATMH	Beagle D 5/180 Husky	3684		3. 1.66	Dorset Gliding Club Ltd	Eyres Field	16. 7.09S
G-ATMJ	Hawker Siddeley HS.748 Series 2A/225	1593	VP-LAJ	4. 1.66	PTB (Emerald) Proprietary Ltd (Stored 11.08)		
			G-ATMJ, 6Y-JFJ, G-ATMJ			Blackpool	7. 9.06T
G-ATML	Cessna F150F	F150-0014		6. 1.66	G I Smith	Eddsfield, Octon Lodge Farm, Thwing	28.11.09E
	(Built Reims Aviation SA) (Wichita c/n 15062722)						

G-ATMM	Cessna F150F	F150-0016	(N)		6. 1.66	R Marshall	Gamston	9. 7.09E
	(Built Reims Aviation SA) (Wichita c/n 15062775) G-ATMM							
G-ATMT	Piper PA-30 Twin Comanche	30-439	XW938		10. 1.66	Montagu-Smith and Company Ltd	Turweston	7. 9.09E
			G-ATMT, N7385Y					
G-ATMY	Cessna 150F	15062642	SE-ETD		13. 1.66	A Salerno	Weston, Dublin	22. 7.09E
			N8542G					
G-ATNB	Piper PA-28-180 Cherokee C	28-3057	N11C		20. 1.66	K N Macdonald tr Ken Macdonald and Co		
							Stornoway	31. 7.09E
G-ATNE	Cessna F150F	F150-0042			20. 1.66	A D Revill	Tatenhill	8. 4.09E
	(Built Reims Aviation SA) (Wichita c/n 15063252)							
G-ATNL	Cessna F150F	F150-0066			25. 1.66	D F Ranger	Popham	20.12.09E
	(Built Reims Aviation SA) (Wichita c/n 15063652)							
G-ATNV	Piper PA-24-260 Comanche	24-4350	N8896P		28. 1.66	A Heydn and K Powell	King's Farm, Thurrock	23. 1.09E
G-ATOD	Cessna F150F	F150-0003			1. 2.66	D Lugg	RNAS Culdrose	21.12.09E
	(Built Reims Aviation SA) (Wichita c/n 15062342)							
G-ATOH	Druine D 62B Condor	RAE 612			3. 2.66	J Cooke tr Three Spires Flying Group		
	(Built Rollason Aircraft and Engines)						Streethay Farm, Lichfield	28.10.09P
G-ATOI	Piper PA-28-140 Cherokee	28-21556	N11C		3. 2.66	R Ronaldson	RAF Brize Norton	7. 6.08E
G-ATOJ	Piper PA-28-140 Cherokee	28-21584	N11C		3. 2.66	A Flight Aviation Ltd *(Operated Prestwick Flying Club)*		
							Prestwick	3.12.08E
G-ATOK	Piper PA-28-140 Cherokee	28-21612	N11C		3. 2.66	G T S Done and P R Harrison tr ILC Flying Group		
							White Waltham	14. 4.09E
G-ATOL	Piper PA-28-140 Cherokee	28-21626	N11C		3. 2.66	L J and G Nation tr G-ATOL Flying Group		
							(Pontypridd)	23. 1.98
G-ATOM	Piper PA-28-140 Cherokee	28-21640	N11C		3. 2.66	A Flight Aviation Ltd *(Operated Prestwick Flying Club)*		
							Prestwick	25. 9.09E
G-ATON	Piper PA-28-140 Cherokee	28-21654	N11C		3. 2.66	R G Walters tr Stirling Flying Syndicate	Shobdon	3.12.09E
G-ATOO	Piper PA-28-140 Cherokee	28-21668	N11C		3. 2.66	I P Fenny	(Hartlepool)	22.12.09E
G-ATOP	Piper PA-28-140 Cherokee	28-21682	N11C		3. 2.66	P R Coombs tr The Aero 80 Flying Group	Popham	16. 6.09E
G-ATOR	Piper PA-28-140 Cherokee	28-21696	N11C		3. 2.66	D Palmer tr Aligator Group	Shobdon	22. 6.09E
G-ATOT	Piper PA-28-180 Cherokee C	28-3061	N11C		3. 2.66	Totair Ltd *"Totty"*	Shipdham	22. 9.09E
G-ATOU	Mooney M 20E Super 21	961	N5946Q		3. 2.66	Classic Flight Training Services Ltd		
							Wellesbourne Mountford	11. 9.09E
G-ATOZ	Bensen B 8M	18			7. 2.66	N C White *(noted 5.08)*	Sorbie Farm, Kingsmuir	9.12.05P
	(Built J D M Wilson) (Rotax 503) (Substantially rebuilt in 1986, original airframe stored Wimborne: noted 12.07 unmarked)							
G-ATPN	Piper PA-28-140 Cherokee	28-21899	N11C		18. 2.66	R W Harris, M F Hatt, P E Preston and A Jahanfar		
						(Operated Southend Flying Club)	Southend	14. 4.09E
G-ATPT	Cessna 182J Skylane	18257056	N2956F		22. 2.66	C Beer tr Papa Tango Group	Elstree	16. 8.09E
G-ATPV	Gardan GY-20 Minicab	JB-01	F-PJKA		22. 2.66	J K Davies	(Newtownards)	25. 8.09P
	(Continental C90) (Rebuild of GY-20 F-PHUC c/n A 155 by J Barritault-Bauge as JB.01 Minicab)							
G-ATRB	LET L-13 Blanik	173305	BGA1326-BXW	23. 2.66	R A Chapman	Bidford	
			RAFGSA 337, BGA1326-BXW, G-ATRB					
G-ATRG	Piper PA-18-150 Super Cub	18-7764	5B-CAB		1. 3.66	Lasham Gliding Society Ltd	Lasham	6. 6.10S
	(Lycoming O-360-A4)		N4985Z					
G-ATRI	Bölkow BÖ.208C Junior	602	D-ECGY		3. 3.66	S S A Withams tr Kingsmuir Group		
							Sorbie Farm, Kingsmuir	26. 9.09E
G-ATRK	Cessna F150F	F150-0049	(G-ATNC)		4. 3.66	Falcon Aviation Ltd		
	(Built Reims Aviation SA) (Wichita c/n 15063381)						Bourne Park, Hurstbourne Tarrant	7. 8.06T
G-ATRM	Cessna F150F	F150-0053	(G-ATNJ)		4. 3.66	J Redfearn	Durham Tees Valley	14. 7.07T
	(Built Reims Aviation SA) (Wichita c/n 15063454)							
G-ATRO	Piper PA-28-140 Cherokee	28-21871	N11C		4. 3.66	G M Malpass	Exeter	24. 8.09E
G-ATRR	Piper PA-28-140 Cherokee	28-21892	N11C		4. 3.66	Keen Leasing (IOM) Ltd *(Operated Manx Flyers Aero Club)*		
							Ronaldsway	11. 7.09E
G-ATRW	Piper PA-32-260 Cherokee Six	32-360	N11C		8. 3.66	J Pringle tr Pringle Brandon Architects and Moxley Architects		
							Biggin Hill	20.10.07E
G-ATRX	Piper PA-32-260 Cherokee Six	32-390	N11C		8. 3.66	A M, A C M and M R Harrhy	Shoreham	16. 6.09E
G-ATSI	Bölkow BÖ.208C Junior	605	D-EFNU		14. 3.66	N C Ravine	Shenstone	10. 7.09E
G-ATSL	Cessna F172G	F172-0260			16. 3.66	G F Robinson tr Alpha Aviation	Enniskillen	14. 9.09E
	(Built Reims Aviation SA)							
G-ATSR	Beech M35 Bonanza	D-6236	EI-ALL		29. 3.66	C B Linton	Gloucestershire	12. 4.09E
G-ATSX	Bölkow BÖ.208C Junior	608	D-EJUC		7. 4.66	Little Bear Ltd *(Noted 12.05)*	Exeter	1. 7.02
G-ATSY	Wassmer WA.41 Super Baladou IV	117			12. 4.66	R L and K P McLean tr McLean Aviation		
						(Spares use for G-ATZS 5.01)	Rufforth	23.11.91
G-ATSZ	Piper PA-30 Twin Comanche B	30-1002	EI-BPS		13. 4.66	Sierra Zulu Aviation Ltd	Little Staughton	19. 7.09E
			G-ATSZ, (AN-...), G-ATSZ, (EI-BBS), G-ATSZ, N7912Y					
G-ATTB	Wallis WA-116/F	214			19. 4.66	D A Wallis *(As "XR944" in RAF c/s)*		
	(Built Beagle-Wallis Ltd) (Franklin 2A)						Reymerston Hall, Norfolk	27. 5.06P
	(Originally regd as Wallis WA.116 Srs 1 (McCulloch) being rebuild of WA-116 G-ARZC (2) ex XR944 c/n 205)							
	(Made heavy landing Swanton Morley 18. 5.06 with substantial damage)							
G-ATTD	Cessna 182J Skylane	18257229	(EC-)		19. 4.66	Atlantalia Eurobusiness SL		
			G-ATTD, N3129F				Las Palmas, Gran Canaria	11. 5.08
G-ATTI	Piper PA-28-140 Cherokee	28-21951	N11C		24. 4.66	T Marsh tr G-ATTI Flying Group	Bristol	13.12.09E
G-ATTK	Piper PA-28-140 Cherokee	28-21959	N11C		25. 4.66	D J E Fairburn tr G-ATTK Flying Group	Southend	3. 6.09E
G-ATTM	CEA Jodel DR.250/160 Capitaine	65			26. 4.66	C P Tomkinson	(Holmes Chapel)	2. 3.08E
G-ATTR	Bölkow BÖ.208C Junior	612	D-EHEH		28. 4.66	S Luck	Audley End	26. 2.09E
G-ATTV	Piper PA-28-140 Cherokee	28-21991	N11C		2. 5.66	N E Leech tr G-ATTV Group	Andrewsfield	7. 3.09E
G-ATTX	Piper PA-28-180 Cherokee C	28-3390	PH-VDP		2. 5.66	IPAC Aviation Ltd	Earls Colne	14. 2.09E
			(G-ATTX), N11C					
G-ATUB	Piper PA-28-140 Cherokee	28-21971	N11C		2. 5.66	J S Bown	(Worksop)	7. 4.09E
G-ATUD	Piper PA-28-140 Cherokee	28-21979	N11C		2. 5.66	J J Ferguson	Belle Vue Farm, Yarnscombe	20.11.09E
G-ATUF	Cessna F150F	F150-0040			4. 5.66	D P Williams *"Honeysuckle"*	Hill Farm, Nayland	16. 5.08E
	(Built Reims Aviation SA) (Wichita c/n 15063229)							
G-ATUG	Druine D 62B Condor	RAE 614			4. 5.66	C Gill	AAC Netheravon	31. 8.08P
	(Built Rollason Aircraft and Engines)							

G-ATUH	Tipsy Nipper T 66 Series 1	T66/6	OO-NIF	4. 5.66	M D Barnard and C Voelger Glebe Farm, Southam	10. 7.09P
	(Built Avions Fairey SA) (Volkswagen 1600)					
G-ATUI	Bölkow BÖ.208C Junior	611	D-EHEF	4. 5.66	M J Grundy Stapleford	26.11.05
G-ATUL	Piper PA-28-180 Cherokee C	28-3033	N9007J	6. 5.66	Barry Fielding Aviation Ltd Ronaldsway	21. 6.09E
G-ATVF	de Havilland DHC-1 Chipmunk 22	C1/0265	WD327	25. 5.66	T M Holloway tr RAF Gliding and Soaring Association	
	(Lycoming AEIO-360)				(As "WD327" in RAF c/s) RAF Halton	8. 7.10S
G-ATVK	Piper PA-28-140 Cherokee	28-22006	N11C	27. 5.66	R Czornowol (Skipton)	15. 5.09E
G-ATVO	Piper PA-28-140 Cherokee	28-22020	N11C	27. 5.66	G R Bright Little Gransden	5. 8.09E
G-ATVS	Piper PA-28-180 Cherokee C	28-3041	N9014J	1. 6.66	T A Buckley Sandown	3. 1.10E
G-ATVW	Druine D 62B Condor	RAE 615		7. 6.66	G G Roberts Rayne Hall Farm, Braintree	19. 6.08P
	(Built Rollason Aircraft and Engines)					
G-ATVX	Bölkow BÖ.208C Junior	615	D-EHER	9. 6.66	A M Witt RAF Benson	2. 4.08P
G-ATWA	SAN Jodel DR.1050 Ambassadeur	296	F-BKHA	10. 6.66	C R Elliott tr One Twenty Group	
					Nottingham City-Tollerton	23.11.09P
G-ATWB	SAN Jodel D 117	423	F-BHNH	10. 6.66	D P Ash tr Andrewsfield Whisky Bravo Group	
					Andrewsfield	23. 4.08P
G-ATWJ	Cessna F172F	F172-0095	EI-ANS	21. 6.66	Shenley Farm (Aviation) and J P A Freeman	
	(Built Reims Aviation SA)				Headcorn	31. 7.09E
G-ATXA	Piper PA-22-150 Tri-Pacer	22-3730	N4403A	8. 7.66	S Hildrop Top Farm, Croydon, Royston	17. 5.09S
	(Modified to PA-20 Super Pacer configuration)					
G-ATXD	Piper PA-30 Twin Comanche B	30-1166	N8053Y	12. 7.66	P A Brook Shoreham	21. 8.09E
G-ATXN	Mitchell-Procter Kittiwake I	1		19. 7.66	R G Day Biggin Hill	11. 5.09P
	(Built R Procter - pr.no.PFA 1306) (Lycoming O-290)					
G-ATXO	SIPA 903	41	F-BGAP	19. 7.66	C H Morris Kittyhawk Farm, Deanland	27. 6.09P
G-ATXZ	Bölkow BÖ.208C Junior	624	D-ELNE	28. 7.66	M R Kaye tr G-ATXZ Group Tatenhill	12. 7.08P
G-ATYM	Cessna F150G	F150-0074		15. 8.66	B G de Wert (Wick)	12. 2.09E
	(Built Reims Aviation SA)					
G-ATYS	Piper PA-28-180 Cherokee C	28-3296	N9226J	19. 8.66	D G Baverstock Wycombe Air Park	24. 5.09E
G-ATZK	Piper PA-28-180 Cherokee C	28-3128	N9090J	21. 9.66	I A Eddy tr G-ZK Group Oaksey Park	8. 6.09E
			(D-EFUN), N9090J			
G-ATZM	Piper J-3C-90 Cub Special	20868	N2092M	26. 9.66	N D Marshall RAF Halton	6. 2.09P
	(Frame No.21310)		NC2092M			
G-ATZS	Wassmer WA 41 Super Baladou IV	128		30. 9.66	C J Cauwood tr G-ATZS Flying Group Spanhoe	12.12.09E
G-ATZY	Cessna F150G	F150-0135		14.10.66	Aircraft Engineers Ltd Prestwick	12. 1.10E
	(Built Reims Aviation SA)					

G-AVAA - G-AVZZ

G-AVAR	Cessna F150G	F150-0122		27.10.66	J A Rees Haverfordwest	21.12.09E
	(Built Reims Aviation SA)					
G-AVAW	Druine D 62C Condor	RAE 617		10.11.66	S Banyard tr Condor Aircraft Group Tibenham	21. 7.08P
	(Built Rollason Aircraft and Engines) (Continental O-240-A)					
G-AVAX	Piper PA-28-180 Cherokee C	28-3798	N11C	11.11.66	J J Parkes Wolverhampton	12. 6.09E
G-AVBG	Piper PA-28-180 Cherokee C	28-3801	N11C	11.11.66	M C Plomer-Roberts Wellesbourne Mountford	19. 4.09E
G-AVBH	Piper PA-28-180 Cherokee C	28-3802	N11C	11.11.66	T R Smith (Agricultural Machinery) Ltd	
					New Lane Farm, North Elmham	18. 5.09E
G-AVBS	Piper PA-28-180 Cherokee C	28-3938	N11C	14.11.66	A G Arthur Perranporth	5. 7.09E
G-AVBT	Piper PA-28-180 Cherokee C	28-3945	N11C	14.11.66	J F Mitchell Shoreham	24. 7.09E
G-AVCM	Piper PA-24-260 Comanche B	24-4520	N9054P	5.12.66	R F Smith Stapleford	11. 8.09E
G-AVCN	Britten-Norman BN-2A-8 Islander	3	N290VL	6.12.66	Britten-Norman Aircraft Preservation Society	
	(Originally regd as BN-2)		F-OGHG, G-AVCN		(For possible restoration) Bembridge	5.11.76T
G-AVCV	Cessna 182J Skylane	18257492	N3492F	15.12.66	University of Manchester, School of Earth, Atmospheric and	
					Environmental Sciences Liverpool	29. 4.09E
G-AVDA	Cessna 182K Skylane	18257959	N2759Q	16.12.66	F W Ellis Water Leisure Park, Skegness	16. 7.08E
G-AVDG	Wallis WA-116 Series 1 Agile	215		28.12.66	K H Wallis (Stored 8.01) Reymerston Hall, Norfolk	23. 5.92P
	(Variously powered by McCulloch: Fuji 440, Norton twin-rotor Wankel and Rotax 532)					
G-AVDT	Aeronca 7AC Champion	7AC-6932	N3594E	5. 1.67	D Cheney and G Moore (Gransha, Rathfriland)	16.11.09P
			NC3594E			
G-AVDV	Piper PA-22-150 Tri-Pacer	22-3752	N44231	5. 1.67	R Burgun Tattenhill	23.10.03
G-AVDY	Phoenix Luton LA-4A Minor	PAL 1183		10. 1.67	R Targonski (Coventry)	9. 8.00P
	(Built M E Pendlebury - pr.no.PFA 808) (Lycoming O-145)				(Damaged landing Stapleford 18.12.99: on rebuild 2006)	
G-AVEB	Morane Saulnier MS.230Et2	1076	N230EB	13. 1.67	T McG Leaver (As "No.157-01" in French AF c/s)	
	(Built Societé Levasseur)		G-AVEB, F-BGJT, French AF		Meluish Farm, North Moreton	17. 1.08P
G-AVEC	Cessna F172H	F172-0405		13. 1.67	S M Furner Earls Colne	20. 5.09E
	(Built Reims Aviation SA)					
G-AVEF	SAN Jodel D 150 Mascaret	16	F-BLDK	19. 1.67	Prop-Air Corporation Ltd Headcorn	5.11.10E
G-AVEH	SIAI-Marchetti S 205-20R	346		20. 1.67	K Fear tr EH Aviation Crowland	30. 9.09E
G-AVEM	Cessna F150G	F150-0198		23. 1.67	A W J McPheat Headcorn	6. 5.09E
	(Built Reims Aviation SA)					
G-AVEN	Cessna F150G	F150-0202		23. 1.67	R A Lambert Bourn	8.12.09E
	(Built Reims Aviation SA)					
G-AVEO	Cessna F150G	F150-0204	G-DENA	23. 1.67	M Howells Barton	24. 9.09E
	(Built Reims Aviation SA)		G-AVEO, EI-BOI, G-AVEO			
G-AVER	Cessna F150G	F150-0206		23. 1.67	Upperstack Ltd t/a LAC Flying School Barton	28. 1.09E
	(Built Reims Aviation SA)				(Operated Lancashire Aero Club)	
G-AVEU	Wassmer WA.41 Super Baladou IV	136		27. 1.67	H and S Roberts Oaksey Park	21.12.09E
G-AVEX	Druine D 62B Condor	RAE 616		31. 1.67	C A Macleod Hinton-in-the-Hedges	18. 8.09P
	(Built Rollason Aircraft and Engines)					
G-AVEY	Phoenix Currie Super Wot	SE.100		31. 1.67	C K Farley (Also as "2-B-7" in pseudo-WW2 early US Navy c/s)	
	(Built K Sedgwick - pr.no.PFA 3006) (Pobjoy "R")				(Noted 10.07) Watchford Farm, Yarcombe	3. 7.07P
G-AVFR	Piper PA-28-140 Cherokee	28-22747	N11C	1. 2.67	R R Orr Newtownards	21. 8.08P
G-AVFU	Piper PA-32-300 Cherokee Six	32-40182	N11C	1. 2.67	Tri-Star Farms Ltd Andreas, Isle of Man	11. 4.09E
G-AVFX	Piper PA-28-140 Cherokee	28-22757	N11C	1. 2.67	J Watson Strathaven	17.12.09E

G-AVFZ	Piper PA-28-140 Cherokee	28-22767	N11C	1. 2.67	C M Toyne tr G-AVFZ Flying Group	Yeovil 23.12.09E
G-AVGA	Piper PA-24-260 Comanche B	24-4489	N9027P	31. 1.67	G McD.Moir	Derby 7. 9.09E
G-AVGC	Piper PA-28-140 Cherokee	28-22777	N11C	31. 1.67	D Matthews	Gloucestershire 30. 7.09E
G-AVGD	Piper PA-28-140 Cherokee	28-22782	N11C	31. 1.67	T Akeroyd tr Falconer Flying Group	Cranfield 10. 2.08E
	(Force landed in field NE of Deanland 16. 9.07 due to engine failure on approach: both wings torn off)					
G-AVGE	Piper PA-28-140 Cherokee (modified)		N11C	31. 1.67	J D C Lea	Tenerife North, Spain 25. 4.09E
	(Type amended 12. 5.08)	28-22787				
G-AVGI	Piper PA-28-140 Cherokee	28-22822	N11C	31. 1.67	R D A Gilchrist tr GI Group	Barton 23. 1.09E
G-AVGK	Piper PA-28-180 Cherokee C	28-3639	N9516J	2. 2.67	M A Bush	Andrewsfield 7. 9.08E
G-AVGU	Cessna F150G	F150-0199		8. 2.67	Coulson Flying Services Ltd	Cranfield 30. 3.09E
	(Built Reims Aviation SA)					
G-AVGY	Cessna 182K Skylane	18258112	N3112Q	17. 2.67	R M C Sears	East Winch 8.10.09E
G-AVGZ	CEA Jodel DR.1050 Sicile	341	F-BKPR	14. 2.67	D C Webb *(Stored 2.08)*	Bagby 13. 7.97
G-AVHH	Cessna F172H	F172-0337		20. 2.67	Business Brokers Ltd t/a HMC Funding	Bristol 8.11.09E
	(Built Reims Aviation SA)					
G-AVHL	SAN Jodel DR.105A Ambassadeur	90	F-BIVY	23. 2.67	I A Davies tr Seething Jodel Group	Seething 15. 7.09P
G-AVHM	Cessna F150G	F150-0181		24. 2.67	W D Hill	Fenland 20. 8.09E
	(Built Reims Aviation SA) (Rebuilt 1997 with wings from G-ATRL qv)					
G-AVHT	Beagle E 3	Not known	WZ711	1. 3.67	C W Tomkins Ltd *(As "WZ711" in AAC c/s)* Spanhoe 26. 9.10S	
	(Built Auster Aircraft Ltd as Auster AOP.9M) (Lycoming O-360)					
G-AVHY	Fournier RF4D	4009		10. 3.67	I K G Mitchell	Dunkeswell 16.10.07P
G-AVIA	Cessna F150G	F150-0184		10. 3.67	S Lynn t/a American Airplane Breakers	Sibson 5. 5.08E
	(Built Reims Aviation SA)					
G-AVIB	Cessna F150G	F150-0180		10. 3.67	Far North Aviation	Wick 4.12.08E
	(Built Reims Aviation SA)					
G-AVIC	Cessna F172H	F172-0320	N17011	10. 3.67	Leeside Flying Ltd	Cork, County Cork 31. 8.09E
	(Built Reims Aviation SA)					
G-AVID	Cessna 182K	18257734	N2534Q	10. 3.67	Jaguar Aviation Ltd *(Operated Fife Parachute Centre)*	
					(Noted dismantled 9.07)	Erroll 18. 4.06
G-AVII	Agusta-Bell 206B-2 JetRanger II	8011		10. 3.67	Bristow Helicopters Ltd *"Brighton Belle"*	Norwich 25. 3.09E
G-AVIL	Alon A-2	A 5	N5471E	14. 3.67	G D J Wilson *(As "VX147" in RAF c/s)*	Eaglescott 19. 6.11S
G-AVIN	SOCATA MS.880B Rallye Club	884		14. 3.67	R Bunce	Compton Abbas 25. 9.09E
G-AVIP	Brantly B 2B	471		14. 3.67	M Richardson t/a Ilkeston Contractors	Ilkeston 3. 4.08E
G-AVIS	Cessna F172H	F172-0413		14. 3.67	J P A Freeman	Headcorn 22. 2.08E
	(Built Reims Aviation SA)					
G-AVIT	Cessna F150G	F150-0217		14. 3.67	P Cottrell	Wellesbourne Mountford 10.12.09E
	(Built Reims Aviation SA)					
G-AVIZ	Scheibe SF25A Motorfalke	4552	(D-KOFY)	21. 3.67	T J Wiltshire tr Splisby Soaring Trust	
	(Hirth F10A)					(Great Steeping, Spilsby) 19. 9.91
G-AVJF	Cessna F172H	F172-0393		31. 3.67	J A and G M Rees c/o Haverfordwest Air Charter	
	(Built Reims Aviation SA)					Haverfordwest 16. 4.09E
G-AVJJ	Piper PA-30 Twin Comanche B	30-1420	N8285Y	7. 4.67	A H Manser	Gloucestershire 17.12.09E
G-AVJK	SAN Jodel DR.1050M Excellence	453	F-BLJH	7. 4.67	D A Sutton tr Juliet Kilo Syndicate	
	(Originally built as DR.1051)					Sackville Lodge, Riseley 15. 7.09P
G-AVJO	Fokker E III replica	PPS/REP/6		12. 4.67	Bianchi Aviation Film Services Ltd	
	(Built Personal Plane Services Ltd - c/n PPS/FOK/6) (Continental C85)				*(As "E III 422/15" in German Army Air Service c/s)*	
						Wycombe Air Park 5. 4.04P
G-AVJV	Wallis WA-117 Series 1	K/402/X		12. 4.67	K H Wallis *(Stored 8.01)* Reymerston Hall, Norfolk 21. 4.89P	
	(RR Continental O-200-B) (Used major parts of G-ATCV c/n 301)					
G-AVJW	Wallis WA-118/M Meteorite	K/502/X		12. 4.67	K H Wallis *(Stored 8.01)* Reymerston Hall, Norfolk 21. 4.83P	
	(Meteor Alfa 1) (Originally regd as Wallis WA.118 Srs 2: used major components of G-ATPW c/n 401)					
G-AVKB	Brochet MB.50 Pipistrelle	02	F-PFAL	17. 4.67	M G Rummey	(Binderton, West Sussex) 30.10.96P
	(Walter Mikron 3)					*(On long term rebuild 4.06)*
G-AVKD	Fournier RF4D	4024		19. 4.67	R E Cross tr Lasham RF4 Group	Lasham 17. 7.08P
G-AVKG	Cessna F172H	F172-0345		21. 4.67	P R Brown-John	RAF Brize Norton 25. 9.09
	(Built Reims Aviation SA) (Rebuilt with fuselage of G-AVDC c/n F172-0382 in 1986)					
G-AVKI	Nipper T 66 RA.45 Series 3	S 102		24. 4.67	E R Newall	(Riccall, York) 7. 8.91P
	(Ardem Mk.10) (Originally built using Avions Fairey SA c/n T66/31 then rebuilt Slingsby Sailplanes Ltd as c/n 1586 for Nipper Aircraft Ltd)					
G-AVKK	Nipper T 66 RA.45 Series 3	S 104	EI-BJH	24. 4.67	C Watson	Newtownards 6. 4.08P
	(Ardem 4C02)		G-AVKK			
	(Originally built using Avions Fairey SA c/n T66/74 then re-built Slingsby Sailplanes Ltd as c/n 1588 for Nipper Aircraft Ltd)					
G-AVKN	Cessna 401	401-0082	(N3282Q)	26. 4.67	Law Leasing Ltd	Rochester 2. 8.08E
G-AVKP	Beagle A 109 Airedale	B 540	SE-EGA	26. 4.67	D R Williams *(Stored 8.08)*	Peplow 26. 9.03
G-AVKR	Bölkow BÖ.208C Junior	648	D-EGRA	28. 4.67	L Hawkins	Kirdford 3. 9.09E
G-AVLB	Piper PA-28-140 Cherokee	28-23158	N11C	8. 5.67	M Wilson	Sywell 24.10.09E
G-AVLC	Piper PA-28-140 Cherokee	28-23178	N11C	8. 5.67	C Gunn and H Blunt tr Lima Charlie Flying Group	
						Spanhoe 13. 3.10E
G-AVLE	Piper PA-28-140 Cherokee	28-23223	N11C	8. 5.67	G E Wright t/a Video Security Services	
						South Lodge Farm, Widmerpool 23.12.09E
G-AVLF	Piper PA-28-140 Cherokee	28-23268	N11C	8. 5.67	D Kimpton tr Woodbine Group	White Waltham 1. 4.09E
G-AVLG	Piper PA-28-140 Cherokee	28-23358	N11C	8. 5.67	R J Everett	Sproughton 28. 9.09E
G-AVLI	Piper PA-28-140 Cherokee	28-23388	N11C	8. 5.67	I R Richmond and N Arnold tr Lima India Aviation Group	
						Southend 31. 3.09E
G-AVLJ	Piper PA-28-140 Cherokee	28-23393	9H-AAZ	8. 5.67	Cherokee Aviation Holdings Jersey Ltd	Jersey 5. 8.09E
			G-AVLJ, N11C			
G-AVLM	Beagle B 121 Pup Series 2	B121-003		8. 5.67	T M and D A Jones *(On slow restoration 1.03)*	
						Derby 29. 4.69S
G-AVLN	Beagle B 121 Pup Series 2	B121-004		8. 5.67	A Swietocjowska tr Dogs Flying Group	Sywell 17. 5.09E
G-AVLO	Bölkow BÖ.208C Junior	650	D-EGUC	8. 5.67	P J Swain	Sandford Hall, Knockin 8. 6.09P
G-AVLT	Piper PA-28-140 Cherokee	28-23328	G-KELC	9. 5.67	Transcourt Ltd and Turweston Flying School Ltd	
			G-AVLT, N11C			Turweston 14.12.09E
G-AVLY	Wassmer Jodel D 120A Paris-Nice	331		11. 5.67	M E Wills and N V de Candole	
						Stancombe Farm, Askerwell 4. 5.09P
G-AVMA	Sud-Aviation Gardan GY-80-180 Horizon	196		12. 5.67	Z R Hildick	Shenstone Hall Farm, Shenstone 28. 9.09R

Reg	Type	C/n	Prev id	Date	Owner/Operator	Base	Expiry
G-AVMB	Druine D 62B Condor	RAE 621		12. 5.67	L J Dray *"Spirit of Silver City"*		
	(Built Rollason Aircraft and Engines) (Continental C90-14F)					Watchford Farm, Yarcombe	25. 4.08P
G-AVMD	Cessna 150G	15065504	N2404J	16. 5.67	T A White t/a Bagby Aviation	Bagby	8. 5.09E
G-AVMF	Cessna F150G	F150-0203		17. 5.67	J F Marsh	Newton Farm, Sudbury	29.10.09E
	(Built Reims Aviation SA)						
G-AVNC	Cessna F150G	F150-0200		18. 5.67	J Turner *(Noted 9.08)*	Popham	24. 5.04
	(Built Reims Aviation SA)						
G-AVNN	Piper PA-28-180 Cherokee C	28-4049	N11C	26. 5.67	J Acres tr G-AVNN Flying Group	Eaglescott	7. 4.09E
G-AVNO	Piper PA-28-180 Cherokee C	28-4105	N11C	26. 5.67	A F Cornell tr November Oscar Flying Group		
						Southend	14.10.09E
G-AVNS	Piper PA-28-180 Cherokee C	28-4129	N11C	26. 5.67	R J Sharpe	North Weald	27. 7.09E
G-AVNU	Piper PA-28-180 Cherokee C	28-4153	N11C	26. 5.67	O Durrani	Lydd	24. 4.09E
G-AVNW	Piper PA-28-180 Cherokee C	28-4210	N11C	26. 5.67	Len Smith's (Aviation) Ltd	RAF Benson	16. 6.09E
G-AVNZ	Fournier RF4D	4030		26. 5.67	C D Pidler	Watchford Farm, Yarcombe	1.10.09E
G-AVOA	SAN Jodel DR.1050 Ambassadeur	195	F-BJYY	31. 5.67	D A Willies	Anwick	27. 6.08P
G-AVOC	CEA Jodel DR.221 Dauphin	67		2. 6.67	J P Coulter and J Chidley tr Alpha One Flying Group		
						Nuthampstead	25. 5.09E
G-AVOH	Druine D 62B Condor	RAE 622		6. 6.67	Transcourt Ltd	Hinton-in-the-Hedges	16. 5.08T
	(Built Rollason Aircraft and Engines)						
G-AVOM	CEA Jodel DR.221 Dauphin	65		6. 6.67	C J S Drewett tr Avon Flying Group	Bidford	26. 3.09E
G-AVOO	Piper PA-18-150 Super Cub	18-8511	N10F	7. 6.67	Dublin Gliding Club Ltd		
	(Lycoming O-360-A4)					Gowran Grange, Punchestown, County Kildare	14. 5.11
G-AVOZ	Piper PA-28-180 Cherokee C	28-3711	N9574J	13. 6.67	P Hoskins and R Flavell tr Oscar Zulu Flying Group		
						Wycombe Air Park	5. 6.09E
G-AVPD	Jodel D 9 Bébé	MAC.1		15. 6.67	S W McKay *(Stored 12.99)*	(Berkhamsted)	6. 6.75S
	(Built S W McKay using Jodel c/n 521 as-pr.no.PFA 927) (Volkswagen 1500)						
G-AVPI	Cessna F172H	F172-0409		20. 6.67	D R Larder t/a Air-Tech		
	(Built Reims Aviation SA)				*(On rebuild using fuselage and parts ex EI-AOK 4.04)* Water Leisure Park, Skegness		30. 5.03
G-AVPJ	de Havilland DH.82A Tiger Moth	86326	NL879	20. 6.67	C C Silk		
	(Built Morris Motors Ltd)					Bericote Farm, Blackdown, Leamington Spa	5. 9.10S
G-AVPM	SAN Jodel D 117	593	F-BHXO	20. 6.67	L B Clark and J C Haynes	Breighton	9.10.09P
G-AVPO	Hindustan HAL-26 Pushpak	PK-127	9M-AOZ	31. 3.83	M B Johns	Green Farm, Combrook	27.11.08P
	(Continental C90)		VT-DWL				
G-AVPV	Piper PA-28-180 Cherokee C	28-2705	9J-RBP	27. 6.67	K A Passmore *(Noted 10.08)*		
			N11C			Rayne Hall Farm, Braintree	8. 3.03
G-AVPY	Piper PA-25-235 Pawnee C	25-4330	N4636Y	7. 7.67	Southdown Gliding Club Ltd	Parham Park	7. 5.09E
			N10F				
G-AVRK	Piper PA-28-180 Cherokee C	28-4041	N11C	11. 7.67	N D Wyndow tr Sir W G Armstrong-Whitworth Flying Group		
						Coventry	4. 6.09E
G-AVRS	Sud-Aviation Gardan GY-80-180 Horizon	224		14. 7.67	N M Robbins	Sleap	19. 7.09E
G-AVRU	Piper PA-28-180 Cherokee C	28-4025	N11C	17. 7.67	D M Barnett t/a Lanpro	Elstree	7. 1.10E
G-AVRW	Gardan GY-20 Minicab	OH-1549		18. 7.67	D J Smith tr Kestrel Flying Group	Hucknall	2. 9.09P
	(Built R Hart - pr.no.PFA 1800 to JB.01 Minicab standard) (Continental C90)						
G-AVRZ	Piper PA-28-180 Cherokee C	28-4137	N11C	24. 7.67	Mantavia Group Ltd	Guernsey	28. 1.10E
G-AVSA	Piper PA-28-180 Cherokee C	28-4184	N11C	24. 7.67	P A Wells	Ronaldsway	22. 6.09E
G-AVSB	Piper PA-28-180 Cherokee C	28-4191	N11C	24. 7.67	D L Macdonald	Denham	18. 5.09E
G-AVSC	Piper PA-28-180 Cherokee C	28-4193	N11C	24. 7.67	P M Tucker tr G-AVSC Syndicate	Dunkeswell	10. 8.09E
G-AVSD	Piper PA-28-180 Cherokee C	28-4195	N11C	24. 7.67	C B D Owen	Haverfordwest	27. 4.09E
G-AVSE	Piper PA-28-180 Cherokee C	28-4196	N11C	24. 7.67	F Glendon *(Noted 5.06)*	Kilrush, County Kildare	30. 4.00T
G-AVSF	Piper PA-28-180 Cherokee C	28-4197	N11C	24. 7.67	S E Pick and D A Rham tr Monday Club		
						Blackbushe	13. 9.09E
G-AVSI	Piper PA-28-140 Cherokee	28-23148	N11C	24. 7.67	C M Royle tr G-AVSI Flying Group White Waltham		8. 5.09E
G-AVSP	Piper PA-28-180 Cherokee C	28-3952	N11C	8. 8.67	Airways Flight Training (Exeter) Ltd		
			(PJ-ACT)			RNAS Yeovilton	3. 2.09E
G-AVSR	Beagle D 5/180 Husky	3689		8. 8.67	G R Greenfield and S D J Holwill	Dunkeswell	3. 5.09A
G-AVSZ	Agusta-Bell 206B-2 JetRanger II	8032	VH-BEQ	8. 8.67	R H Ryan	(Clendon, Sunderland)	16. 6.99T
			PK-HBZ, VR-BCR, PK-HBD, VR-BCR, G-AVSZ				
G-AVTC	Nipper T 66 RA.45 Series 3	S 106		9. 8.67	R J Cook	Thornhill	30 9.08P
	(Built Slingsby Aircraft Co Ltd as c/n 1583 for Nipper Aircraft Ltd) (Ardem Mk.10)						
G-AVTP	Cessna F172H	F172-0458		17. 8.67	K Bartholomew and M J Green tr Tango Papa Group		
	(Built Reims Aviation SA)					White Waltham	23. 9.09E
G-AVTV	SOCATA MS.893A Rallye Commodore 180	10725		24. 8.67	P Storey	Husbands Bosworth	6. 8.06
G-AVUG	Cessna F150H	F150-0234		11. 9.67	N J Gensler and V J Larkin tr Skyways Flying Group		
	(Built Reims Aviation SA)				(Nuthall, Nottingham and Sheffield)		16. 6.09E
G-AVUH	Cessna F150H	F150-0244		11. 9.67	A G Mclaren	Strubby	1. 1.09E
	(Built Reims Aviation SA)						
G-AVUO	Phoenix Luton LA-4A Minor	PAL 1313		21. 9.67	M E Vaisey	(Hemel Hempstead)	
	(Built C P Butterfield)				*(Initially not completed: parts used in construction of G-AXKH - possible long-term build project)*		
G-AVUS	Piper PA-28-140 Cherokee	28-24065	(G-AVUT)	25. 9.67	D J Hunter	Shipdham	18. 4.08E
			N11C				
G-AVUT	Piper PA-28-140 Cherokee	28-24085	(G-AVUU)	25. 9.67	Bencray Ltd *(Operated Blackpool and Fylde Aero Club)*		
			N11C			Blackpool	21. 8.09E
G-AVUU	Piper PA-28-140 Cherokee	28-24100	(G-AVUS)	25. 9.67	R W Harris, A Jahanfar, P E Preston and M F Hatt		
			N11C			*(Operated Southend Flying Club)*	Southend	11. 5.09E
G-AVUZ	Piper PA-32-300 Cherokee Six	32-40302	N11C	29. 9.67	Ceesix Ltd	Jersey	1. 4.09E
G-AVVC	Cessna F172H	F172-0443		29. 9.67	C W Wilson tr Babs Flying Group		
	(Built Reims Aviation SA)					Durham Tees Valley	17. 6.09E
G-AVVJ	SOCATA MS.893A Rallye Commodore 180	10752		6.10.67	M Powell	Felthorpe	21. 5.09E
G-AVWA	Piper PA-28-140 Cherokee	28-23660	N11C	19.10.67	SFG Ltd	Norwich	24. 4.09E
G-AVWD	Piper PA-28-140 Cherokee	28-23700	N11C	19.10.67	C Bentley and B Marlowe t/a Evelyn Air		
						Leeds-Bradford	28. 4.09E

G-AVWG	Piper PA-28-140 Cherokee	28-23760		19.10.67	Bencray Ltd	Blackpool 11. 8.91T
	(Badly damaged in forced landing Tal-y-Fan, Conwy, Gwynedd 11.12.88: major components used to rebuild G-BBEF 1998 - wings only 4.06)					
G-AVWI	Piper PA-28-140 Cherokee	28-23800	N11C	19.10.67	L M Middleton	Cranfield 17. 3.09E
G-AVWJ	Piper PA-28-140 Cherokee	28-23940	N11C	19.10.67	A C M Harrhy	Sandown 27. 7.08E
G-AVWL	Piper PA-28-140 Cherokee	28-24000	N11C	19.10.67	S H and C L Maynard	Durham Tees Valley 14.10 08E
G-AVWM	Piper PA-28-140 Cherokee	28-24005		19.10.67	A Jahanfar, P E Preston, M F Hatt and R W Harris	
					(Operated Southend Flying Club)	Southend 6. 8.09E
G-AVWN	Piper PA-28R-180 Cherokee Arrow		N11C	19.10.67	Vawn Air Ltd	Jersey 10. 4.09E
		28R-30170			*(Crashed 30. 8.08 and written off)*	
G-AVWO	Piper PA-28R-180 Cherokee Arrow		N11C	19.10.67	I P Scobell	Biggin Hill 19.12.08E
		28R-30205				
G-AVWR	Piper PA-28R-180 Cherokee Arrow		N11C	19.10.67	R W Scarr tr G-AVWR Flying Group	Dunkeswell 17. 6.09E
		28R-30242				
G-AVWT	Piper PA-28R-180 Cherokee Arrow		N11C	19.10.67	F Brecha	Perranporth 4. 6.09E
		28R-30362				
G-AVWU	Piper PA-28R-180 Cherokee Arrow		N11C	19.10.67	A M Alam	Elstree 11. 8.09E
		28R-30380				
G-AVWV	Piper PA-28R-180 Cherokee Arrow		N11C	19.10.67	R V Thornton and R Barron tr Strathtay Flying Group	
		28R-30404				Perth 23. 6.09E
G-AVWY	Fournier RF4D	4031		26.10.67	P Turner	Halesland 10.10.08P
G-AVXA	Piper PA-25-235 Pawnee C	25-4244	N4576Y	26.10.67	South Wales Gliding Club Ltd	Usk 21. 5.09E
	(Re-built using new frame - c/n unknown)					
G-AVXD	Nipper T 66 RA.45 Series 3	S 109		26.10.67	J A Brompton *(Noted 6.07)*	Dundee 19.12.03P
	(Built Slingsby Aircraft Co Ltd as c/n 1606 for Nipper Aircraft Ltd) *(Volkswagen 1834 Acro)*					
G-AVXF	Piper PA-28R-180 Cherokee Arrow		N11C	26.10.67	A D C McNeile tr GAVXF Group	North Weald 9. 7.09E
		28R-30044				
G-AVXW	Druine D 62B Condor	RAE 625		3.11.67	C Willmott	(Somerton) 25. 6.09P
	(Built Rollason Aircraft and Engines)					
G-AVXY	Auster AOP.9	xxxx	XK417	7.11.67	G J Siddall South Lodge Farm, Widmerpool	9. 7.00P
	(Officially regd with Frame no.AUS/120 - believed to be AUS.10/92)					
G-AVYK	Beagle A 61 Terrier 3	B 642	WJ357	20.11.67	R Burgun	Derby 28. 8.93
G-AVYL	Piper PA-28-180 Cherokee D	28-4622	N11C	24.11.67	A C Hogben tr G-AVYL Flying Group	Full Sutton 16. 6.09E
G-AVYM	Piper PA-28-180 Cherokee D	8-4638	N11C	24.11.67	Carlisle Aviation (1985) Ltd	Carlisle 14. 8.09E
G-AVYR	Piper PA-28-140 Cherokee	28-24226	N11C	24.11.67	R M Weeks	Earls Colne 21. 8.09E
G-AVYS	Piper PA-28R-180 Cherokee Arrow		N11C	24.11.67	Musicbank Ltd	Ludham 13. 3.09E
		28R-30456				
G-AVYT	Piper PA-28R-180 Cherokee Arrow		N11C	24.11.67	G N Smith	Gamston 6. 4.09E
		28R-30472				
G-AVYV	Wassmer Jodel D 120A Paris-Nice	252	F-BMAM	27.11.67	A J Sephton	Old Warden 24. 8.09P
G-AVZI	Bölkow BÖ.208C Junior	673	D-EGZF	19.12.67	C F Rogers *(Stored 10.00)* (Wheathampstead)	24. 7.76
G-AVZN	Beagle B 121 Pup Series 1	B121-006		19.12.67	B L Elvy tr Shipdham Aviators Flying Group	
						Shipdham 21. 5.09E
G-AVZP	Beagle B 121 Pup Series 1	B121-008		19.12.67	T A White	Bagby 8. 5.09E
G-AVZR	Piper PA-28-180 Cherokee C	28-4114	N4779L	19.12.67	Lincoln Aero Club Ltd	Sturgate 3. 7.09E
G-AVZU	Cessna F150H	F150-0283		29.12.67	R D Forster *(Rain Air, Beccles titles on tail)*	
	(Built Reims Aviation SA)					Ellough, Beccles 13. 3.09E
G-AVZV	Cessna F172H	F172-0511		29.12.67	E L King and D S Lightbown	Crosland Moor 30. 6.09E
	(Built Reims Aviation SA)					
G-AVZW	EAA Biplane Model P	PFA 1314		29.12.67	R G Maidment and G R Edmondson	
	(Built R G Maidment) *(Lycoming O-290)*					Lower Wasing Farm, Brimpton 4. 7.08P

G-AWAA - G-AWZZ

G-AWAC	Sud-Aviation Gardan GY-80-180 Horizon	234		29.12.67	P B Hodgson *"Le Fantome"*	Enstone 11. 6.04
					(Force landed wheels-up Semley, Wiltshire 22. 7.03: on rebuild 3.07)	
G-AWAJ	Beech D55 Baron	TE-536		1. 1.68	Aflex Hose Ltd	Blackpool 13. 2.09E
G-AWAT	Druine D 62B Condor	RAE 627		8. 1.68	M D Burns	Cumbernauld 16. 4.09P
	(Built Rollason Aircraft and Engines)					
G-AWAX	Cessna 150D	15060153	OY-TRJ	5. 1.68	P L Lovegrove	Bournemouth 18.12.09E
	(Tail-wheel conversion)		N4153U			
G-AWAZ	Piper PA-28R-180 Cherokee Arrow		N11C	8. 1.68	P J Manders tr G-AWAZ Flying Group	
		28R-30512				Poplar Hall Farm, Elmsett 1. 6.09E
G-AWBA	Piper PA-28R-180 Cherokee Arrow		N11C	8. 1.68	A Taplin and G A Dunster tr March Flying Group	
		28R-30528				Stapleford 20. 2.09E
G-AWBB	Piper PA-28R-180 Cherokee Arrow		N11C	8. 1.68	P J Young	Ringstead, Hunstanton 31.12.09E
		28R-30552				
G-AWBC	Piper PA-28R-180 Cherokee Arrow		N11C	8. 1.68	Anglo Aviation (UK) Ltd	Bournemouth 28.12.09E
		28R-30572				
G-AWBE	Piper PA-28-140 Cherokee	28-24266	N11C	8. 1.68	B E Boyle	Shenington 21. 5.09E
G-AWBG	Piper PA-28-140 Cherokee	28-24286	N11C	8. 1.68	B Patrick	Enstone 17. 5.08E
G-AWBH	Piper PA-28-140 Cherokee	28-24306	N11C	8. 1.68	Proofgolden Ltd t/a Mainstreet Aviation	Newcastle 30.12.04T
					(Stored for spares 3.06)	
G-AWBJ	Fournier RF4D	4055		12. 1.68	N J Arthur	Bicester 25. 4.08P
G-AWBM	Druine D 31A Turbulent	PFA 1647		17. 1.68	A D Pratt	(Welwyn Garden City) 20. 7.95P
	(Built J R D Bygrave) *(Volkswagen 1700)*					
G-AWBN	Piper PA-30 Twin Comanche B	30-1472	N8517Y	18. 1.68	Stourfield Investments Ltd	Jersey 19.12.09E
G-AWBS	Piper PA-28-140 Cherokee	28-24331	N11C	22. 1.68	T M Brown	East Winch 23. 9.09E
G-AWBU	Morane Saulnier Type N Rep	PPS/REP/7		22. 1.68	Bianchi Aviation Film Services Ltd	
	(Built D E Bianchi) *(Continental C90-8F)*				*(As "MS824" in French AF c/s)*	Wycombe Air Park 28. 4.04P
G-AWBX	Cessna F150H	F150-0286		22. 1.68	G G L James	Sleap 15. 9.09E
	(Built Reims Aviation SA)					
G-AWCN	Reims FR172E Rocket	FR17200020		25. 1.68	B and C Stobart-Hook	Sandown 12. 8.09S
G-AWCP	Cessna F150H	F150-0354		29. 1.68	C E Mason	Shobdon 19. 2.09E
	(Built Reims Aviation SA) *(Tail-wheel conversion)*					

G-AWDA	Nipper T 66 RA.45 Series 3	S 117		7. 2.68	J A Cheesbrough	Ottringham	27. 5.09P
	(Built Slingsby Aircraft Co Ltd as c/n 1624 for Nipper Aircraft Ltd) (Volkswagen Acro 1834)						
G-AWDO	Druine D 31 Turbulent	PFA 1649		21. 2.68	R N Crosland	Kittyhawk Farm, Deanland	18. 5.09P
	(Built R Watling-Greenwood) (Volkswagen 1600)						
G-AWDP	Piper PA-28-180 Cherokee D	28-4870	N11C	21. 2.68	B H and P M Illston (Operated Norwich School of Flying)		
						Norwich	29. 6.08E
G-AWDR	Reims FR172E Rocket	FR17200004		21. 2.68	B A Wallace	Nuthampstead	21. 4.09E
G-AWDU	Brantly B 2B	481		23. 2.68	B M Freeman	(Stourport-on-Severn)	4.12.09E
G-AWDW	Campbell-Bensen CB.8MS	DS.1330		26. 2.68	M R Langton (Stored 12.00)	(Taplow)	7.10.71P
	(Built D J C Summerfield) (McCulloch.Motors 4318C)						
G-AWEF	SNCAN Stampe SV-4C(G)	549	F-BDCT	29. 3.68	R A F Buchanan	Headcorn	29. 1.11S
G-AWEI	Druine D 62B Condor	RAE 628		6. 3.68	A M Noble (On long term rebuild 2.06)		
	(Built Rollason Aircraft and Engines)					Roughay Farm, Bishops Waltham	10.11.98T
G-AWEK	Fournier RF4D	4071		6. 3.68	M P J Hill	(Macclesfield)	23 .8. 74
G-AWEL	Fournier RF4D	4077		7. 3.68	A B Clymo	Wolverhampton	11. 9.09P
G-AWEM	Fournier RF4D	4078		7. 3.68	B J Griffin	Saltby	20. 6.08P
G-AWEP	Gardan GY-20 Minicab	PFA 1801		12. 3.68	D A Porter	Griffins Farm, Temple Bruer	4. 9.09P
	(Built F S Jackson 1969 to JB.01 Minicab standard) (Continental C90)						
G-AWES	Cessna 150H	15068626	N22933	20. 3.68	D W Vincent	Redhill	21. 9.09E
G-AWEV	Piper PA-28-140 Cherokee	28-24460	N11C	21. 3.68	Norflight Ltd	Ludham	1.10.10E
G-AWEX	Piper PA-28-140 Cherokee	28-24472	N11C	21. 3.68	Reconnaissance Ventures Ltd	Coventry	4. 6.09E
G-AWEZ	Piper PA-28R-180 Cherokee Arrow		N11C	21. 3.68	T R Leighton, R G E Simpson and D A C Clissett		
		28R-30592				Stapleford	15. 1.09E
G-AWFB	Piper PA-28R-180 Cherokee Arrow		N11C	21. 3.68	J C Luke	Filton	18. 8.09E
		28R-30689					
G-AWFC	Piper PA-28R-180 Cherokee Arrow		N11C	21. 3.68	D G and E P Phillips	(Market Drayton)	15.10.09E
		28R-30670					
G-AWFD	Piper PA-28R-180 Cherokee Arrow		N11C	21. 3.68	D J Hill	Moorlands Farm, Farway Common	14. 8.09E
		28R-30669					
G-AWFF	Cessna F150H	F150-0280		25. 3.68	R J Colver	Shobdon	31.10.09E
	(Built Reims Aviation SA)						
G-AWFJ	Piper PA-28R-180 Cherokee Arrow		N11C	26. 3.68	Parplon Ltd	Liverpool	26. 3.09E
		28R-30688					
G-AWFN	Druine D 62B Condor	RAE 629		27. 3.68	J James	Shennington	14. 7.09P
	(Built Rollason Aircraft and Engines)						
G-AWFO	Druine D 62B Condor	RAE 630		27. 3.68	R E and T A Major	Porthtowan, Truro	7.11.09P
	(Built Rollason Aircraft and Engines)						
G-AWFP	Druine D 62B Condor	RAE 631		27. 3.68	D J Taylor tr Blackbushe Flying Club		
	(Built Rollason Aircraft and Engines)					White Waltham	1. 7.09P
G-AWFT	Jodel D 9 Bébé	PFA 932		29. 3.68	W H Cole (Noted 3.07)		
	(Built W H Cole) (Volkswagen 1200)					Spilstead Farm, Sedlescombe	22. 7.69
G-AWFW	SAN Jodel D 117	599	PH-VRE	2. 4.68	C J Rodwell	Hawksbridge Farm, Oxenhope	30. 8.09P
			F-BHXU				
G-AWFZ	Beech 19A Musketeer Sport	MB-323	N2811B	3. 4.68	Bob Crowe Aircraft Sales Ltd	Cranfield	15. 1.10E
G-AWGD	Cessna F172H	F172-0503		5. 4.68	R P Vincent	Shoreham	18. 7.09E
	(Built Reims Aviation SA)						
G-AWGK	Cessna F150H	F150-0347		8. 4.68	G E Allen	(Saxilby, Lincoln)	1. 5.09E
	(Built Reims Aviation SA)						
G-AWGN	Fournier RF4D	4084		9. 4.68	R J Grimstead	(Tillington, Petworth)	17. 6.09P
G-AWGZ	Taylor JT.1 Monoplane	M 1		17. 4.68	R L Sambell	Stoke Golding	15.12.09P
	(Built J Morris - pr.no.PFA 1406) (Ardem 4C02)						
G-AWHE	Hispano HA.1112-MIL Buchon	67	N109ME	14. 5.68	Magnificent Obsessions Ltd	Duxford	
	(Originally regd with incorrect c/n 64)		G-AWHE, C4K-31 Spanish AF				
G-AWHX	Rollason Beta B 2	RAE 04	(G-ATEE)	17. 4.68	S G Jones "Vertigo" (On rebuild 5.05)	Membury	14. 6.87P
G-AWHY	Falconar F-11-3	PFA 1322	G-BDPB	17. 4.68	D Holroyd tr Why Fly Group	Leicester	10. 4.09P
	(Built A E Pritchard and A E Riley-Gale)		(G-AWHY)				
	(Continental C90)						
G-AWIF	Brookland Mosquito	LC-1 & 3		17. 4.68	C A Reeves (Noted 10.03)	Henstridge	7. 1.82P
	(Built Brooklands Aero Ltd)						
G-AWII	Vickers Supermarine 349 Spitfire LF.Vc	AR501		25. 4.68	Richard Shuttleworth Trustees	Old Warden	20. 5.06P
	(Built Westland Aircraft Ltd)	WASP/20/223			(As "AR501:NN-A" in RAF 310 Sqdn c/s) (Noted 8.06)		
G-AWIP	Phoenix Luton LA-4A Minor	PAL 1308		30. 4.68	J Houghton	(North Ferriby)	8. 5.89P
	(Built T Reagan - pr.no.PFA 830) (Continental A65)				(Damaged near Holme-on-Spalding Moor 20.7.88: stored 2000)		
G-AWIR	Bushby-Long Midget Mustang	PFA 1315		30. 4.68	J M Keane	Kittyhawk Farm, Deanland	6. 3.90P
	(Built A F Jarman and Co Ltd) (Continental O-200-A)						
G-AWIT	Piper PA-28-180 Cherokee D	28-4987	N11C	30. 4.68	G-AWIT Ltd	Andreas, Isle of Man	12. 4.09E
G-AWIV	Storey TSR.3	PFA 1325		30. 4.68	P K Jenkins	Long Marston	18. 6.08P
	(Built J M Storey) (Continental PC60) (Officially regd as c/n "1325")						
G-AWIW	SNCAN Stampe SV-4B	532	F-BDCC	2. 5.68	R E Mitchell (Noted 10.06)	Sleap	6. 5.73
G-AWJE	Nipper T 66 RA.45 Series 3	S 121		8. 5.68	K G G Howe	Breighton	11. 6.09P
	(Built Slingsby Aircraft Co Ltd as c/n 1628 for Nipper Aircraft Ltd) (Volkswagen 1834)						
G-AWJX	Moravan Zlin Z-526 Trener Master	1049		22. 5.68	P A Colman	Luxter's Farm, Hambledon	29. 5.85A
G-AWJY	Moravan Zlin Z-526 Trener Master	1050		22. 5.68	M Gainza (Noted dismantled 9.07)		
						Freiburg, Germany	26. 4.03
G-AWKD	Piper PA-17 Vagabond	17-192	F-BFMZ	27. 5.68	A T and M R Dowie	Scotland Farm, Hook	15. 7.09P
	(Continental A65)		N4892H				
G-AWKO	Beagle B 121 Pup Series 1	B121-019		11. 6.68	J Martin	Stapleford	21. 1.09E
G-AWKT	SOCATA MS.880B Rallye Club	1235		17. 6.68	A Ringland and P Keating	Enniskillen	22. 5.08E
G-AWLA	Cessna F150H	F150-0269	N13175	27. 6.68	T A White t/a Bagby Aviation	Bagby	1. 9.09E
	(Built Reims Aviation SA)						
G-AWLF	Cessna F172H	F172-0536		27. 6.68	H Sharp and A Mackey tr Gannet Aviation		
	(Built Reims Aviation SA)					Mullaghmore, Coleraine	5. 1.07
G-AWLG	SIPA 903	82	F-BGHG	27. 6.68	S W Markham (Stored 1997)		
						Valentine Farm, Odiham	22. 8.79P

G-AWLI	Piper PA-22-150 Caribbean	22-5083	N7256D	1. 7.68	J S Lewery "Little Peach"	Shoreham	19.10.11
G-AWLO	Boeing Stearman E75 (PT-13D) Kaydet	75-5563	5Y-KRR VP-KRR, 42-17400	9. 7.68	N D Pickard (Operated Sky High Advertising Ltd)	Panshanger	14.10.11
	(Pratt and Whitney R985)						
G-AWLP	Mooney M 20F Executive	680200		9. 7.68	I C Lomax (Noted 1.05)	Gamston	7. 7.00
G-AWLR	Nipper T 66 RA.45 Series 3	S 125		9. 7.68	T D Reid	Newtownards	16. 5.05P
	(Built Slingsby Aircraft Co Ltd as c/n 1662 for Nipper Aircraft Ltd) (Ardem 4C02)						
G-AWLS	Nipper T 66 RA.45 Series 3	S 126		9. 7.68	G A Dunster and B Gallagher	(Loughton, Essex)	25. 3.88P
	(Built Slingsby Aircraft Co Ltd as c/n 1663 for Nipper Aircraft Ltd) (Ardem Mk.10)				(Damaged Stapleford 14. 1.88)		
G-AWLX	Auster 5 J/2 Arrow	2378	F-BGJQ OO-ABZ	10. 7.68	W J Taylor	(Friskney, Boston)	23. 4.70P
G-AWLZ	Fournier RF4D	4099		12. 7.68	J H Taylor tr Nympsfield RF4 Group	Nympsfield	27. 5.09P
G-AWMD	Jodel D 11	PFA 904		19. 7.68	D L King and J R Cooper	Rhigos	10. 7.09P
	(Built F H French) (Continental C90)						
G-AWMF	Piper PA-18-150 Super Cub	18-8674	N4356Z	23. 7.68	Booker Gliding Club Ltd	Wycombe Air Park	3. 3.11S
	(Lycoming O-360-A4)						
G-AWMI	AESL Airtourer T2 (115)	505		24. 7.68	M Furse	Cardiff	8. 5.08
	(Built Glos Air Ltd)						
G-AWMN	Phoenix Luton LA-4A Minor	PFA 827		30. 7.68	S Penfold	(Halstead)	15. 8.07P
	(Built R Wilks) (Volkswagen 1800)						
G-AWMP	Cessna F172H	F172-0488		31. 7.68	R J D Blois	Yoxford, Saxmundham	2. 2.10E
	(Built Reims Aviation SA)						
G-AWMR	Druine D 31 Turbulent	43		1. 8.68	J R D Bygraves "Demelza"	Little Gransden	12. 5.09P
	(Built S J Hargreaves- pr.no.PFA 1661) (Volkswagen 1390)						
G-AWMT	Cessna F150H	F150-0360		1. 8.68	Strategic Syngernies Ltd	Insch	20. 1.10E
	(Built Reims Aviation SA)						
G-AWNT	Britten-Norman BN-2A Islander	32		2. 8.68	Precision Terrain Surveys Ltd	Southend	18. 9.09E
G-AWOA	SOCATA MS.880B Rallye Club	1258		2. 8.68	A F Walters	Elstree	22. 8.09E
G-AWOE	Aero Commander 680E	680E-753-41	N3844C	5. 8.68	J M Houlder t/a Elstree Flying Club	Elstree	22. 6.09E
G-AWOF	Piper PA-15 Vagabond	15-227	F-BETF	6. 8.68	C M Hicks	Barton	7. 8.08P
	(Continental C90) (Officially registered as "PA-17")						
G-AWOH	Piper PA-17 Vagabond	17-191	F-BFMY N4891H	6. 8.68	A Lovejoy and K Downes	(Basingstoke)	24. 7.03P
	(Continental C90)						
G-AWOT	Cessna F150H	F150-0389		14. 8.68	M J Willoughby	Cranfield	5. 2.09E
	(Built Reims Aviation SA)						
G-AWOU	Cessna 170B	25829	VQ-ZJA ZS-CKY, CR-ADU, N3185A	16. 8.68	S Billington	Ashcroft Farm, Winsford	12. 7.11S
G-AWPH	Percival P 56 Provost T 1	PAC/F/003	WV420	6. 9.68	J A D Bradshaw	Three Mile Cross, Reading	29. 8.09P
G-AWPJ	Cessna F150H	F150-0376		9. 9.68	W J Greenfield (Operated Humberside Flying Club)	Humberside	22. 5.09E
	(Built Reims Aviation SA)						
G-AWPN	Shield Xyla	2		13. 9.68	P N Stacey	Sandown	26. 6.09P
	(Built G W Shield - pr.no.PFA 1320) (Continental A65)						
G-AWPS	Piper PA-28-140 Cherokee	28-20196	5N-AEK	16. 9.68	A R Matthews	Sittles Farm, Alrewas	17. 3.09E
	(Destroyed in an accident at Colwich Junction, Stafford 2. 1.09 when it struck power cables)						
G-AWPU	Cessna F150J	F150-0411		18. 9.68	Upperstack Ltd t/a LAC Flying School	Barton	15. 3.09E
	(Built Reims Aviation SA)				(Operated Lancashire Aero Club)		
G-AWPW	Piper PA-12 Super Cruiser	12-3947	N78572 NC78572	23. 9.68	AK Leasing (Jersey) Ltd	Jersey	1. 6.11S
G-AWPY	Bensen B 8M	CA-314		20. 9.68	J Jordan	(Melrose Farm, Melbourne)	
	(Built Campbell Aircraft Ltd)						
G-AWPZ	Andreasson BA-4B	1	SE-XBS	24. 9.68	J M Vening (On rebuild since early 2007)	Duxford	5.11.03P
	(Built B Andreasson) (Continental O-200A)			(Malmö Flygindustri (MFI) c/n plate on rear fuselage (port) shows c/n as 01)			
G-AWRK	Cessna F150J	F150-0410		8.10.68	Systemroute Ltd (Operated Southern Strut Flying Group)		
	(Built Reims Aviation SA)					Shoreham	31. 7.09E
G-AWRY	Hunting Percival P 56 Provost T 1	PAC/F/339	XF836 8043M	29.10.81	A J House (As "XF836" in RAF c/s)	Lower Wasing Farm, Brimpton	22. 8.88P
G-AWSH	Moravan Zlin Z-526 Trener Master	1052	OK-XRH G-AWSH	23.11.68	Avia Special Ltd	White Waltham	23.12.04T
G-AWSL	Piper PA-28-180 Cherokee D	28-4907	N11C	30.10.68	Fascia Services Ltd	King's Farm, Thurrock	19.12.09E
G-AWSM	Piper PA-28-235 Cherokee Pathfinder	28-11125	N11C	30.10.68	N A Wright tr Aviation Projects	Shoreham	21. 5.09E
G-AWSN	Druine D 62B Condor	RAE 632		31.10.68	M K A Blyth	Little Gransden	12. 5.09P
	(Built Rollason Aircraft and Engines)						
G-AWSP	Druine D 62B Condor	RAE 634		31.10.68	R Q and A S Bond (Noted 5.08)	Enstone	23. 1.95
	(Built Rollason Aircraft and Engines)						
G-AWSS	Druine D 62B Condor	RAE 636		31.10.68	N J and D Butler (Stored at owner's home? 3.98)		
	(Built Rollason Aircraft and Engines)					(Laurencekirk)	19.10.94P
G-AWST	Druine D 62B Condor	RAE 637		31.10.68	T P Lowe	White Fen Farm, Benwick	3. 6.09P
	(Built Rollason Aircraft and Engines)						
G-AWSW	Beagle D 5/180 Husky	3690	XW635 G-AWSW	4.11.68	C Tyers tr Windmill Aviation (As "XW635" in RAF c/s)		
						Spanhoe	6.10.09P
G-AWTJ	Cessna F150J	F150-0419		8.11.68	P L Jameson	Elstree	8.12.04T
	(Built Reims Aviation SA)						
G-AWTL	Piper PA-28-180 Cherokee D	28-5068	N11C	12.11.68	G Lloyd and M Day	King's Farm, Thurrock	28. 7.09E
G-AWTP	Schleicher Ka 6E	4123	BGA 3426-FPV N29JG, G-AWTP, RAFGSA 29	12.11.68	A I McLean and N K Watts	Bembridge	
G-AWTS	Beech 19A Musketeer Sport	MB-412	OO-BGN G-AWTS, N2763B	14.11.68	J G Edwards	Swansea	20.11.09E
G-AWTV	Beech 19A Musketeer Sport	MB-424	N2770B	14.11.68	J Whittaker	Trehelig, Welshpool	30.10.08E
G-AWTX	Cessna F150J	F150-0404		18.11.68	R D Forster	Ellough, Beccles	12. 3.09E
	(Built Reims Aviation SA)						
G-AWUB	Gardan GY-201 Minicab	A 205	F-PERX	22.11.68	R A Hand	Black Spring Farm, Castle Bytham	5. 4.09P
	(Built Aéronautique Havraise) (Continental A65)						
G-AWUE	SAN Jodel DR.1050 Ambassadeur	299	F-BKHE	22.11.68	K W and F M Wood (On rebuild 6.08)	Insch	17.10.87

Reg	Type	c/n	Prev id	Date	Owner	Location	Expiry
G-AWUG	Cessna F150H	F150-0299		25.11.68	Aircraft Engineers Ltd	Prestwick	21. 5.08E
	(Built Reims Aviation SA)						
G-AWUJ	Cessna F150H	F150-0332		25.11.68	S R Hughes	Netherthorpe	30.11.09E
	(Built Reims Aviation SA)						
G-AWUL	Cessna F150H	F150-0346		25.11.68	A J Baron		
	(Built Reims Aviation SA)					Ventfield Farm, Horton-cum-Studley,Oxford	27. 4.09E
G-AWUN	Cessna F150H	F150-0377		25.11.68	S G Brown tr G-AWUN Group		
	(Built Reims Aviation SA)					Eddsfield, Octon Lodge Farm, Thwing	4. 6.09E
G-AWUO	Cessna F150H	F150-0380		25.11.68	K A O'Neill	Plaistows Farm, St Albans	22. 7.09E
	(Built Reims Aviation SA)						
G-AWUT	Cessna F150J	F150-0405		25.11.68	R C Larder	Strubby	22.12.09E
	(Built Reims Aviation SA)						
G-AWUU	Cessna F150J	F150-0408	EI-BRA	25.11.68	W J Hockenhull tr G-AWUU Flying Group		
	(Built Reims Aviation SA)		G-AWUU			East Winch	20. 8.09E
G-AWUX	Cessna F172H	F172-0577		25.11.68	B J Portch tr G-AWUX Group	St Just	24. 5.09E
	(Built Reims Aviation SA)						
G-AWUZ	Cessna F172H	F172-0587		25.11.68	I R Judge tr Five Per Cent Flying Group	Shoreham	19. 6.09E
	(Built Reims Aviation SA)						
G-AWVA	Cessna F172H	F172-0597		25.11.68	Barton Air Ltd	Barton	6.11.09E
	(Built Reims Aviation SA)						
G-AWVB	SAN Jodel D 117	604	F-BIBA	26.11.68	H Davies	Haverfordwest	31. 5.09P
G-AWVC	Beagle B 121 Pup Series 1	B121-026	(OE-CUP)	27.11.68	J J West	Sturgate	23.10.09R
G-AWVE	CEA Jodel DR.1050/M1 Sicile Record	612	F-BMPQ	27.11.68	E A Taylor (For rebuild) Bensons Farm, Laindon		18. 5.00
G-AWVF	Hunting Percival P 56 Provost T 1	PAC/F/375	XF877	28.11.68	A J House (As "XF877:JX" in RAF c/s)		
						Lower Wasing Farm, Brimpton	13. 8.09P
G-AWVG	AESL Airtourer T2 (115)	513	OO-WIC	29.11.68	C J Scholfield	Top Farm, Croydon, Royston	25. 9.10S
	(Built Glos Air Ltd)		G-AWVG				
G-AWVN	Aeronca 7AC Champion	7AC-6005	N2426E	4.12.68	P K Brown tr Champ Flying Group	Rush Green	25. 4.09P
			NC2426E				
G-AWVZ	Jodel D 112	898	F-PKVL	12.12.68	D C Stokes	Dunkeswell	1. 8.09P
	(Built J Coupe)						
G-AWWE	Beagle B 121 Pup Series 2	B121-032	G-35-032	12.12.68	A Bleetman	Coventry	24. 6.09E
G-AWWI	SAN Jodel D 117	728	F-BIDU	13.12.68	W J Evans	Rhigos	13. 6.04P
G-AWWM	Gardan GY-201 Minicab	A 195	F-BFOQ	1. 1.69	P J Brayshaw		
	(Built M Heron) (Continental A65)				(Haddock Stone Farm, Markington, Harrogate)		10.12.92P
G-AWWN	SAN Jodel DR.1050 Sicile	398	F-BLJA	8. 1.69	S Burchfield	(Bar Hill, Cambridge)	21.10.09P
G-AWWP	Aerosport Woody Pusher Mk.3	WA/163		7. 1.69	M S and R D Bird (Stored 6.93)		
	(Built Woods Aeroplanes - pr.no.PFA 1323)					Pepperbox, Salisbury	
G-AWWU	Reims FR172F Rocket	FR17200111		15. 1.69	Westward Airways (Lands End) Ltd	St Just	4.12.08E
G-AWXR	Piper PA-28-180 Cherokee D	28-5171	N11C	24. 1.69	Aero Club of Portugal	(Lisbon, Portugal)	18. 7.09E
G-AWXS	Piper PA-28-180 Cherokee D	28-5283	N11C	24. 1.69	C R and S A Hardiman,	Haverfordwest	19. 3.09E
G-AWXX	Westland Wessex 60 Srs 1	WA694	VH-BHX	29. 1.69	D Brem-Wilson	Joydens Farm, Westerham	29.10.08
			G-AWXX, G-17-6				
G-AWXZ	SNCAN Stampe SV-4C	360	F-BHMZ	30. 1.69	Bianchi Aviation Film Services Ltd		
			French.Army, F-BCOI			Wycombe Air Park	22. 7.11
G-AWYB	Reims FR172F Rocket	FR17200075		30. 1.69	R Windley	Tattershall	4.10.09E
G-AWYI	Royal Aircraft Factory BE.2c replica	001	N1914B	5. 2.69	M C Boddington and S Slater (On rebuild 10.07)		
	(Built C Boddington)		G-AWYI			Sywell	
G-AWYJ	Beagle B 121 Pup Series 2	B121-038	G-35-038	10. 2.69	H C Taylor	Popham	22. 9.09E
G-AWYL	CEA Jodel DR.253B Régent	143		11. 2.69	K Gillam	Radley Farm, Hungerford	30. 5.09E
G-AWYO	Beagle B 121 Pup Series 1	B121-041	G-35-041	11. 2.69	B R C Wild	Popham	21.12.09E
G-AWYX	SOCATA MS.880B Rallye Club	1311		11. 2.69	M J Edwards (Noted 8.03)	St Just	27. 6.86

G-AXAA - G-AXZZ

Reg	Type	c/n	Prev id	Date	Owner	Location	Expiry
G-AXAB	Piper PA-28-140 Cherokee	28-20238	EI-AOA	17. 2.69	Bencray Ltd (Operated Blackpool and Fylde Aero Club)		
			N6206W			Blackpool	22. 9.09E
G-AXAN	de Havilland DH.82A Tiger Moth	85951	F-BDMM	21. 2.69	D and S A Firth (As "EM720" in RAF c/s)		
			French AF, EM720			Old Warden	27. 8.09T
	(Veered off the grass runway on landing at Sandtoft 1. 6.08, went into long grass and overturned)						
G-AXAS	Wallis WA-116-T/Mc	217		25. 2.69	K H Wallis	Reymerston Hall, Norfolk	22. 5.07P
	(72hp McCulloch 4318A) (Originally registered as Wallis WA-116-T two-seater tandem version: used major components from G-AVDH c/n 216)						
G-AXAT	SAN Jodel D 117A	836	F-BITJ	26. 2.69	P S Wilkinson	Garton, Insch	29. 4.09P
G-AXBF	Beagle D 5/180 Husky	3691	OE-DEW	17.10.84	M C R Wills	Southend	20. 9.10S
G-AXBG	Bensen B 8M	RC.1		12. 3.69	G Mowil	(Llanrug, Caernafon)	
	(Built R Curtis)						
G-AXBH	Cessna F172H	F172-0571		12. 3.69	D F Ranger	Popham	18. 5.09E
	(Built Reims Aviation SA)						
G-AXBJ	Cessna F172H	F172-0573		12. 3.69	S E Goodman tr BJ Flying Group	Leicester	9. 4.09E
	(Built Reims Aviation SA)						
G-AXBW	de Havilland DH.82A Tiger Moth	83595	6854M	12. 3.69	G-AXBW Ltd (As "T-5879:RUC-W" in RAF c/s)		
			T5879			Wilshanger Farm, Frensham	24. 4.10S
G-AXBZ	de Havilland DH.82A Tiger Moth	86552	F-BGDF	14. 3.69	W J de Jong Cleyndert	(Dereham)	4.12.11
	(Built Morris Motors Ltd)		French AF, PG643				
G-AXCA	Piper PA-28R-200 Cherokee Arrow II		N11C	18. 3.69	W H Nelson	Southend	20. 3.09E
		28R-35053					
G-AXCG	SAN Jodel D 117	510	PH-VRA	19. 3.69	C A White tr The Charlie Golf Group	Andrewsfield	21. 5.08P
			F-BHXI				
G-AXCM	SOCATA MS.880B Rallye Club	1322		25. 3.69	D C Maniford	Bidford	18. 6.09E
G-AXCX	Beagle B 121 Pup Series 2	B121-046	G-35-046	31. 3.69	L A Pink (On rebuild 9.06)	Glebe Farm, Stockton	10. 7.94
G-AXCY	SAN Jodel D 117A	499	F-BHXB	31. 3.69	S Marom "La Dame en Rouge"		
						Whitehall Farm, Benington	22. 6.09P

Reg	Type	C/n	Prev id	Date	Owner/Operator	Location	Date
G-AXCZ	SNCAN Stampe SV-4C	186	ZS-VFW	31. 3.69	J Price *(Fuselage noted 2.06)*		
			G-AXCZ, F-BCFG			Trenchard Farm, Eggesford	10. 7.83
G-AXDC	Piper PA-23-250 Aztec D	27-4169	N6829Y	8. 4.69	N J Lilley *(Noted 3.07)*	Bodmin	24. 8.98
G-AXDI	Cessna F172H	F172-0574		14. 4.69	M F and J R Leusby t/a Jeanair		
	(Built Reims Aviation SA)					Maypole Farm, Chislet	23. 4.09E
G-AXDK	CEA Jodel DR.315 Petit Prince	378		16. 4.69	M R Weatherhead and J C Lowe tr Delta Kilo Flying Group		
						Sywell	31. 1.10E
G-AXDV	Beagle B 121 Pup Series 1	B121-049		18. 4.69	T A White	Bagby	17. 9.09R
G-AXDW	Beagle B 121 Pup Series 1	B121-053		18. 4.69	I Beaty, P J Abbott and A M Chester tr Cranfield Delta		
					Whiskey Group	Cranfield	31. 3.09E
G-AXED	Piper PA-25-235 Pawnee B	25-3586	OH-PIM	24. 4.69	Wolds Gliding Club Ltd	Pocklington	18. 5.09E
			OH-CPY, N7540Z				
G-AXEO	Scheibe SF25B Falke	4645	D-KEBC	1. 5.69	The Borders (Milfield) Gliding Club Ltd	Milfield	28. 6.07
	(Stark-Stamo MS1500)						
G-AXEV	Beagle B 121 Pup Series 2	B121-070		6. 5.69	G Benson and D S Russell	Gloucestershire	6. 8.09
G-AXFN	Jodel D 119	980	F-PHBU	19. 5.69	M W Olliver	Farley Farm, Romsey	25. 3.09P
	(Built M Ganu)						
G-AXGE	SOCATA MS.880B Rallye Club	1353		23. 5.69	R P Loxton	(Bridport)	8. 2.08E
G-AXGG	Cessna F150J	F150-0440		28. 5.69	A J Simpson and I Coughlan		
	(Built Reims Aviation SA)					Kilrush, County Kildare	7. 1.10E
G-AXGP	Piper J-3C-90 Cub (L-4J-PI)	12544	F-BGPS	2. 6.69	L J Brinkley	Standalone Farm, Meppershall	31. 5.09P
	(Frame No.12374)		F-BDTM, 44-80248				
	(Reported as c/n 9542 ex 43-28251)						
G-AXGR	Phoenix Luton LA-4A Minor	PAL 1125		2. 6.69	B A Schlussler	(Hanthorpe, Bourne)	23. 9.06P
	(Built R Spall) (JAP J 99)						
G-AXGS	Druine D 62B Condor	RAE 638		3. 6.69	P J Huxley tr SAS Flying Group	Compton Abbas	15. 8.09P
	(Built Rollason Aircraft and Engines)						
G-AXGV	Druine D 62B Condor	RAE 641		3. 6.69	S B Robson	Watchford Farm, Yarcombe	6.11.09P
	(Built Rollason Aircraft and Engines)						
G-AXGZ	Druine D 62B Condor	RAE 643		3. 6.69	R M Schweitzer	(Amsterdam, Netherlands)	6. 7.09P
	(Built Rollason Aircraft and Engines)						
G-AXHA	Cessna 337A Super Skymaster	3370484	(EI-ATH)	5. 6.69	I M Latiff *(Noted 9.05)*	Little Staughton	30. 8.02
			N5384S				
G-AXHC	SNCAN Stampe SV-4C	293	F-BCFU	6. 6.69	D L Webley	Wickenby	9. 7.09S
G-AXHO	Beagle B 121 Pup Series 2	B121-077		9. 6.69	L H Grundy	King's Farm, Thurrock	5. 8.09R
G-AXHP	Piper J-3C-65 Cub (L-4J-PI)	12932	F-BETT	9. 6.69	Witham (Specialist) Vehicles Ltd		
	(Frame No.12762)		NC74121, 44-80636		*(As "480636:A-58" in USAAC c/s)*	Spanhoe	25. 9.09P
	(Regd with c/n "AF36506" which is USAAC contract no)						
G-AXHR	Piper J-3C-65 Cub (L-4H-PI)	10892	F-BETI	9. 6.69	K B Raven and E Cundy tr G-AXHR Cub Group		
			43-29601		*(As "329601:D-44" in USAAC c/s)*		
						Hill Farm, Nayland	20. 8.09P
G-AXHS	SOCATA MS.880B Rallye Club	1357		9. 6.69	W B and A Swales *(Noted 2.08)*	Bagby	14. 7.06
G-AXHT	SOCATA MS.880B Rallye Club	1358		9. 6.69	P M Murray *(Noted 2.08)*	Bagby	19. 4.07
G-AXHV	SAN Jodel D 117A	695	F-BIDF	9. 6.69	J S Ponsford tr Derwent Flying Group	Hucknall	22. 9.09P
G-AXIA	Beagle B 121 Pup Series 1	B121-078		17. 6.69	C K Parsons	Kemble	6.12.09R
G-AXIE	Beagle B 121 Pup Series 2	B121-087		17. 6.69	J P Thomas	Elstree	31. 8.09R
G-AXIF	Beagle B 121 Pup Series 2	B121-088	(SE-FGV)	17. 6.69	J R Faulkner	Derby	16.10.09R
G-AXIG	Scottish Aviation Bulldog Series 100/104	BH120/002		24. 6.69	A A Douglas-Hamilton	Cumbernauld	12.11.11
G-AXIO	Piper PA-28-140 Cherokee B	28-25764	N11C	26. 6.69	T Akeroyd	Cranfield	30. 3.09E
G-AXIR	Piper PA-28-140 Cherokee B	28-25795	N11C	26. 6.69	R W Howard	Lasham	8. 9.09E
G-AXIW	Scheibe SF25B Falke	4657	(D-KABJ)	3. 7.69	M Pedley	Nympsfield	13. 8.09E
	(Stark-Stamo MS1500)						
G-AXIX	AESL Airtourer T4 (150)	A 527		3. 7.69	J C Wood	Shobdon	13 .6.10
	(Built Glos Air Ltd)						
G-AXJB	Omega 84 Balloon (Hot Air)	04		9. 7.69	Semajan Ltd tr Southern Balloon Group *"Jester"*		
	(Initially flown as G-AXDT)					Romsey	20. 8.73S
G-AXJH	Beagle B 121 Pup Series 2	B121-089		11. 7.69	D Collings tr The Henry Flying Group	Popham	2. 5.10S
G-AXJI	Beagle B 121 Pup Series 2	B121-090		11. 7.69	J J Sanders	Derby	4. 6.09E
G-AXJJ	Beagle B 121 Pup Series 2	B121-091		11. 7.69	M L, T M, D A and P M Jones	Derby	13.12.09S
G-AXJO	Beagle B 121 Pup Series 2	B121-094		11. 7.69	J A D Bradshaw *"Joey"* Three Mile Cross, Reading		20. 8.09S
G-AXJR	Scheibe SF25B Falke	4652	D-KICD	4. 7.69	R I Hey tr The Falke Syndicate	Nympsfield	14. 8.08E
	(Stark-Stamo MS1500)						
G-AXJV	Piper PA-28-140 Cherokee B	28-25572	N11C	14. 7.69	R Hawkes tr DR Flyers	Tatenhill	7. 6.09E
G-AXJX	Piper PA-28-140 Cherokee B	28-25990	N11C	14. 7.69	C W Hall	Compton Abbas	17. 6.09E
G-AXKH	Phoenix Luton LA-4A Minor	PAL 1316		21. 7.69	M E Vaisey tr Chiltern Flying Club		
	(Built M E Vaisey - pr.no.PFA 823) (Volkswagen 1600)					(Hemel Hempstead)	18. 4.84P
G-AXKJ	Jodel D 9 Bébé	SAS.002		22. 7.69	J M Alexander	Streethay Farm, Lichfield	16. 8.07P
	(Built Southdown Aero Services Ltd - pr.no.PFA 941: also originally PFA 928B) (Volkswagen 1600)						
G-AXKO	Westland-Bell 47G-4A	WA/720	G-17-5	22. 7.69	M Gallagher	(Ballinamore, County Leitrim)	23. 4.10S
G-AXKX	Westland-Bell 47G-4A	WA/728	G-17-13	22. 7.69	A J E Smith	Breighton	4.12.10S
G-AXKY	Westland-Bell 47G-4A	WA/729	G-17-14	22. 7.69	C P Golborne	(Whittlesey, Peterborough)	15. 5.06
G-AXLG	Cessna 310K	310K0204	N3804X	25. 7.69	C Koscso	(King's Lynn)	26.10 07E
G-AXLI	Nipper T 66 RA.45 Series 3	S 131		25. 7.69	D and M Shrimpton		
	(Built Slingsby Aircraft Co Ltd as c/n 1701 for Nipper Aircraft Ltd) (Ardem Mk.10)					Franklyn's Field, Chewton Mendip	2. 7.08P
G-AXLS	SAN Jodel DR.105A Ambassadeur	86	F-BIVR	31. 7.69	J J Boon tr Axle Flying Club	Popham	9. 6.09P
G-AXLZ	Piper PA-18 Super Cub 95	18-2052	PH-NLB	31. 7.69	R J Quantrell	(Low Farm, South Walsham)	23. 4.00
	(L-18C-PI) (Frame No.18-2065)		R Neth.AF R-45, 8A-45, 52-2452 *(Damaged Low Farm 14. 8.97)*				
G-AXMA	Piper PA-24 Comanche	24-3467	N8214P	5. 8.69	P S Grellier		
						New Barn Farm, Barton Ashes, Crawley	26. 5.08
G-AXMN	Auster J/5B Autocar	2962	F-BGPN	14. 8.69	C D Wilkinson	Trenchard Farm, Eggesford	15. 4.04
G-AXMT	Bücker Bü.133C Jungmeister	46	N133SJ	19. 8.69	R A Fleming *(As "U-99" in Swiss AF c/s)*		
	(Built AG Fur Dornier-Flugzeuge)		G-AXMT, HB-MIY, Swiss AF U-99			Breighton	13. 5.09P
G-AXMW	Beagle B 121 Pup Series 1	B121-101		19. 8.69	DJP Engineering (Knebworth) Ltd	Cambridge	17.10.09R

G-AXMX	Beagle B 121 Pup Series 2	B121-103	VH-UPT G-AXMX, G-35-103	19. 8.69	S A Jones	Derby/Cannes, France	8.10.09
G-AXNJ	Wassmer Jodel D 120 Paris-Nice	52	F-BHYO	29. 8.69	D I Vernon tr Clive Flying Group	Sleap	15.10.08P
G-AXNN	Beagle B 121 Pup Series 2	B121-104		3. 9.69	Gabrielle Aviation Ltd *"Gabrielle"*	Shoreham	17. 9.09R
G-AXNP	Beagle B 121 Pup Series 2	B121-106		3. 9.69	J W Ellis and R J Hemmings	Hawarden	30. 6.09E
G-AXNR	Beagle B 121 Pup Series 2	B121-108		3. 9.69	M Brown tr November Romeo Group	Raby's Farm, Great Stukeley	14. 4.09
G-AXNS	Beagle B 121 Pup Series 2	B121-110		3. 9.69	D Beckwith and D Long tr Derwent Aero Group	Gamston	6. 6.09S
G-AXNW	SNCAN Stampe SV-4C	381	F-BFZX French AF	11. 9.69	Carolyn S Grace Blooms Farm, Sible Hedingham		12. 6.09S
G-AXNX	Cessna 182M	18259322	N70606	16. 9.69	H A Harper	Biggin Hill	21.10.09E
G-AXNZ	Pitts S-1C	EB.1		16. 9.69	C D Baglin	(Gamlingay, Sandy)	30. 8.91P
	(Built W Berry and B Etheridge - pr.no.PFA 1383: official c/n shown as EBX2)						
G-AXOH	SOCATA MS.894A Rallye Minerva 220	11062	D-EAGU	17. 9.69	T A D Crook	White Waltham	19.12.08E
G-AXOJ	Beagle B 121 Pup Series 2	B121-109	G-35-109	24. 9.69	T J Martin tr Pup Flying Group	Rochester	9. 7.09E
G-AXOS	SOCATA MS.894A Rallye Minerva 220	11079		3.10.69	R S M Fendt	Shipdham	5. 5.09E
G-AXOT	SOCATA MS.893A Rallye Commodore 180	11433		3.10.69	P Evans	Dalscote, Northampton	26. 3.09E
G-AXOZ	Beagle B 121 Pup Series 1	B121-115	N70290 G-AXOZ, G-35-115	7.10.69	R J Ogborn	Hawarden	20. 7.09R
G-AXPA	Beagle B 121 Pup Series 1	B121-116	D-EATL G-AXPA, G-35-116	7.10.69	A J C Hawks and D Griffiths tr Papa-Alpha Group Draycott Farm, Chiseldon		21.11.09R
G-AXPB	Beagle B 121 Pup Series 1	B121-117	G-35-117	7.10.69	M J K Seary and R T Austin tr Beagle Flying Group	Leicester	12. 3.09E
G-AXPC	Beagle B 121 Pup Series 1	B121-119	PH-VRS G-AXPC	7.10.69	T A White	Bagby	21.11.08E
G-AXPF	Reims Cessna F150K	F15000543		14.10.69	D R Marks *(Stored 9.08)*	Enstone	22. 4.02
G-AXPG	Mignet HM.293	PFA 1333		14.10.69	W H Cole Spilstead Farm, Sedlescombe		20. 1.77P
	(Built W H Cole) (Volkswagen 1300)				*(Noted 3.07)*		
G-AXPM	Beagle B 121 Pup Series 1	B121-122	G-35-122	20.10.69	S C Stanton	Panshanger	10. 9.09R
G-AXPN	Beagle B 121 Pup Series 2	B121-123	G-35-123	20.10.69	A Richardson	Derby	4. 6.09E
G-AXPZ	Campbell Cricket	CA-320		3.11.69	W R Partridge	St Merryn	24. 7.09P
	(Rotax 582)						
G-AXRC	Campbell Cricket	CA-323		3.11.69	L R Morris	(Newry, County Armagh)	18. 5.78S
	(Volkswagen 1600)				*(Damaged Wittering 22.10.77: stored Tattershall Thorpe 7.91)*		
G-AXRP	SNCAN Stampe SV-4C	554	G-BLOL G-AXRP, F-BDCZ	7.11.69	C C Manning	Rotary Farm, Hatch	20.11.06
					(See entry for G-BLOL)		
G-AXRR	Auster AOP.9	B5/10/178	XR241 G-AXRR, XR241	7.11.69	R B Webber (As *"XR241"* in AAC c/s) (Noted 9.08)		
	(Frame no.AUS/178)					Trenchard Farm, Eggesford	11. 5.07P
G-AXRT	Reims Cessna FA150K Aerobat	FA1500018		12.11.69	C C Walley	Elstree	27. 8.09E
	(Tail-wheel conversion)						
G-AXSC	Beagle B 121 Pup Series 1	B121-138	G-35-138	13.11.69	R J MacCarthy	White Waltham	28. 4.07
G-AXSD	Beagle B 121 Pup Series 1	B121-139	G-35-139	13.11.69	AURS Aviation Ltd	Prestwick	10. 5.08T
G-AXSF	Nash Petrel	P 003		17.11.69	Nash Aircraft Ltd *(Stored 10.95)*	Lasham	?. 4.94P
	(Built Nash Aircraft Ltd - pr.no.PFA 1516) (Lycoming O-360)						
G-AXSG	Piper PA-28-180 Cherokee E	28-5605	N11C	17.11.69	The Tago Island Company Ltd	(London SW1Y)	29.11 08E
G-AXSI	Reims Cessna F172H	F17200687	G-SNIP G-AXSI	19.11.69	R Collins	North Coates	17. 9.09E
G-AXSM	CEA Jodel DR.1051 Sicile	512	F-BLRH	20.11.69	T R G and M S Barnby	Headcorn	14. 6.08E
G-AXSW	Reims Cessna FA150K Aerobat	FA1500003		25.11.69	R J Whyham	Blackpool	2. 4.08E
G-AXSZ	Piper PA-28-140 Cherokee B	28-26188	N11C	26.11.69	B J Collins tr The White Wings Flying Group	White Waltham	24. 4.09E
G-AXTA	Piper PA-28-140 Cherokee B	28-26301	N11C	26.11.69	P J Farrell tr G-AXTA Aircraft Group	Shoreham	28. 5.09E
G-AXTC	Piper PA-28-140 Cherokee B	28-26265	N11C	26.11.69	W J Knott tr G-AXTC Group	North Coates	25. 2.10E
G-AXTJ	Piper PA-28-140 Cherokee B	28-26241	N11C	26.11.69	K Patel	Elstree	26. 3.09E
G-AXTL	Piper PA-28-140 Cherokee B	28-26247	N11C	26.11.69	S F Pickering tr Pegasus Aviation Midlands	Tatenhill	20.12.09E
G-AXTO	Piper PA-24-260 Comanche C	24-4900	N9449P N9705N	28.11.69	J L Richardson *"Betsy Baby"*	Conington	4. 8.09E
G-AXTP	Piper PA-28-180 Cherokee C	28-3791	OH-PID	1.12.69	M Whyte Carnmore, Galway, County Galway		6. 2.09E
G-AXUA	Beagle B 121 Pup Series 1	B121-150	G-35-150	4.12.69	P Wood	Audley End	5. 6.08
G-AXUB	Britten-Norman BN-2A Islander	121	5N-AIJ G-AXUB, N859JA, G-51-47	4.12.69	Headcorn Parachute Club Ltd	Headcorn	20. 5.09E
G-AXUC	Piper PA-12 Super Cruiser	12-621	5Y-KFR VP-KFR, ZS-BIN	5.12.69	J J Bunton	Clipgate Farm, Denton	18. 7.08E
G-AXUF	Reims Cessna FA150K Aerobat	FA1500043		9.12.69	B T Walsh	Newtownards	26.11.09E
G-AXUJ	Auster V J/1 Autocrat	1957	G-OSTA G-AXUJ, PH-OTO	11.12.69	P Gill	Yeatsall Farm, Abbots Bromley	1. 6.09P
G-AXUK	SAN Jodel DR.1050 Ambassadeur	292	F-BJYU	11.12.69	G J Keegan tr Downland Flying Group (2KI) Kittyhawk Farm, Deanland		18. 8.09P
G-AXVB	Reims Cessna F172H	F17200703		22.12.69	R and J Turner	Charlton Park, Malmesbury	5. 7.09E
G-AXVK	Campbell Cricket	CA-327		1. 1.70	B Jones	Melrose Farm, Melbourne	16. 4.07P
	(Volkswagen 1600)						
G-AXVM	Campbell Cricket	CA-329		1. 1.70	D M Organ	Gloucestershire	10. 3.09P
	(Volkswagen 1834)						
G-AXVN	McCandless M 4	M4/6		5. 1.70	W R Partridge *(Stored, noted 10.08)* St Merryn		
	(Volkswagen 1700)						
G-AXWA	Auster AOP.9	B5/10/133	XN437	13. 1.70	C M Edwards *(On rebuild 6.07)*	North Weald	
G-AXWT	Jodel D 11	PFA 911		26. 1.70	R C Owen	(Danehill, Haywards Heath)	2. 6.00P
	(Built C King and R C Owen) (Continental C90)						
G-AXWV	CEA Jodel DR.253 Régent	104	F-OCKL	2. 2.70	R Friedlander and D C Ray Manor Farm, Grateley, Andover		11. 5.09E

G-AXWZ	Piper PA-28R-200 Cherokee Arrow II		N11C	3. 2.70	R Silcock tr Whisky Zulu Group	Andrewsfield	4. 1.10E
		28R-35605					
G-AXXC	Rousseau Piel CP.301B Emeraude	117	F-BJAT	4. 2.70	R S C Andrews tr Emy Group		
						Green Farm, Combrook	9. 1.10P
G-AXXV	de Havilland DH.82A Tiger Moth	85852	F-BGJI	24. 2.70	C N Wookey	Membury	1. 7.07
	(Built Morris Motors Ltd)		French AF, DE992		*(As "DE992" in RAF c/s)*		
			(Caught by gust of wind landing Membury 19. 6.07, swung to right and tipped on to nose incurring damage)				
G-AXXW	SAN Jodel D 117	632	F-BIBN	26. 2.70	D F Chamberlain and M A Hughes	Haverfordwest	9. 9.09P
G-AXYK	Taylor JT.1 Monoplane	PFA 1409		2. 3.70	K P Rusling	(Biggleswade)	30. 4.08P
	(Built C Oakins) (Volkswagen 1600)						
G-AXYU	Jodel D 9 Bébé	547	EI-BVE	5. 3.70	P Turton and H C Peake-Jones		
	(Volkswagen 1600)		G-AXYU			(Ashcroft Farm, Winsford)	13. 9.01P
G-AXZD	Piper PA-28-180 Cherokee E	28-5609	N11C	12. 3.70	G M Whitmore	High Cross, Ware	14. 2.09E
G-AXZF	Piper PA-28-180 Cherokee E	28-5688	N11C	12. 3.70	Haimoss Ltd *(Operated Old Sarum Flying Club)*		
						Old Sarum	6. 8.09E
G-AXZH	Glasflügel H201B Standard Libelle	82	BGA2247-DNL	12. 3.70	M C Gregorie	Gransden Lodge	6. 6.08
			RAFGSA 742, RAFGSA 16, G-AXZH				
G-AXZK	Britten-Norman BN-2A-26 Islander	153	V2-LAD	12. 3.70	B-N Group Ltd	Bembridge	16. 4.06
			VP-LAD, G-AXZK, G-51-153				
G-AXZM	Nipper T 66 RA.45 Series 3A	S 133		16. 3.70	G R Harlow	Newcastle	24. 8.89P
	(Re-built S J Booth and A Young - pr.no.PFA 1378) (Volkswagen 1600)				*(Damaged near Eshott 21. 8.89)*		
	(Originally built as c/n 1709 Slingsby Aircraft Co Ltd for Nipper Aircraft Ltd)						
G-AXZO	Cessna 180	31137	N3639C	17. 3.70	J C King tr Bourne Park Flyers		
						Bourne Park, Hurstbourne Tarrant	20.11.09E
G-AXZP	Piper PA-E23-250 Aztec D	27-4464	N13819	17. 3.70	D M Harbottle	Fairoaks	28.11.08E
G-AXZT	SAN Jodel D 117A	607	F-BIBD	17. 3.70	P Guest	(Leeds)	22.11.08P
G-AXZU	Cessna 182N Skylane	18260104	N92233	19. 3.70	W Gollan	Errol	13. 8.09E

G-AYAA - G-AYZZ

G-AYAB	Piper PA-28-180 Cherokee E	28-5804	N11C	24. 3.70	J R Green	Turweston	21. 8.09E
G-AYAC	Piper PA-28R-200 Cherokee Arrow III		N11C	24. 3.70	R I Willcox tr Fersfield Flying Group	Knettishall	24. 3.09E
		28R-35606					
G-AYAN	Slingsby Cadet III Motor Glider	003	BGA1224	6. 4.70	D C Pattison *"Thermal Hopper"*	Brunton	23. 7.07P
	(Volkswagen 1600)		RAFGSA.223				
	(Re-built P J Martin and D R Wilkinson - pr.no.PFA 1385 from Slingsby T 31B [Frame no.SSK/FF776])						
G-AYAR	Piper PA-28-180 Cherokee E	28-5797	N11C	8. 4.70	A Jahanfar *(Operated Seawing Flying Club)*		
						Southend	9. 3 09E
G-AYAT	Piper PA-28-180 Cherokee E	28-5801	N11C	8. 4.70	A Goodchild tr G-AYAT Flying Group	Seething	31. 3.09E
G-AYAW	Piper PA-28-180 Cherokee E	28-5805	N11C	14. 4.70	N S Nixon and R S Scott tr GAYAW Group		
						Denham	15. 9.09E
G-AYBD	Reims Cessna F150K	F15000583		7. 4.70	Apollo Aviation Advisory Ltd *(Operated Ace Aviation)*		
						Shoreham	23.11.09E
G-AYBG	Scheibe SF25B Falke	4696	(D-KECJ)	13. 4.70	H H T Wolf	Eyres Field	4. 4.97
	(Volswagen Danum 1600/1)						
G-AYBO	Piper PA-23-250 Aztec D	27-4510	N13874	15. 4.70	A G Gutknecht	(Langenwang, Austria)	7. 5.06
G-AYBP	Jodel D 112	1131	F-PMEK	16. 4.70	G J Langston	Bidford	19.11.09P
	(Built Aero Club du Rousillon)						
G-AYBR	Wassmer Jodel D 112	1259	F-BMIG	16. 4.70	I S Parker	Damyn's Hall, Upminster	14. 6.09P
G-AYCC	Campbell Cricket	CA-336		20. 4.70	D J M Charity	Hinton-in-the-Hedges	16. 5.07P
	(Rotax 582)						
G-AYCE	Scintex CP.301-C1 Emeraude	530	F-BJFH	20. 4.70	S D Glover	Charterhall	24.10.08P
G-AYCF	Reims Cessna FA150K Aerobat	FA1500055		22. 4.70	E J Atkins	Popham	30. 6.09E
G-AYCG	SNCAN Stampe SV-4C	59	F-BOHF	24. 4.70	N Bignall	White Waltham	4. 7.10
			F-BBAE, French AF				
G-AYCJ	Cessna TP206D Turbo Super Skylane		N8752Z	27. 4.70	White Knuckle Airways Ltd	Leeds-Bradford	15. 7.09E
	(Regd with c/n T206-0552)	P206-0552					
G-AYCK	AIA Stampe SV-4C(G)	1139	G-BUNT	28. 4.70	The Real Flying Company Ltd	Shoreham	23. 4.11T
	(Officially regd as built SNCAN)		G-AYCK, F-BANE, Aeronavale 1139				
G-AYCN	Piper J-3C-65 Cub	"13365"	F-BCPO	28. 4.70	W R and B M Young *(Stored 4.91)*		
	(Frame No.not known: c/n quoted became PH-UCM in 11.46 and p/i is doubtful)				Furze Hill Farm, Rosemarket, Milford Haven		27. 1.89P
G-AYCO	CEA Jodel DR.360 Chevalier	362	F-BRFI	29. 4.70	P L Buckley tr Charlie Oscar Club		
						Hill Farm, Nayland	15.4.09E
G-AYCP	SAN Jodel D 112	67	F-BGKO	30. 4.70	L A Dalglish tr Charlie Papa Group	Cranfield	28. 6.09P
G-AYCT	Reims Cessna F172H	F17200724		1. 5.70	P A and J Rose	Full Sutton	23.12.09E
G-AYDI	de Havilland DH.82A Tiger Moth	85910	F-BDOE	7. 5.70	R B and E W Woods and J D M Barr		
			French AF, DF174			Haw Farm, Hampstead Norrey's	15. 6.09S
G-AYDR	SNCAN Stampe SV-4C	307	F-BCLG	13. 5.70	A J McLuskie (Quebec Farm, Knook, Warminster)		27. 3.75
					(Damaged 16. 6.73 and on rebuild 8.93)		
G-AYDV	Coates Swalesong SA.II Series 1	PFA 1353		18. 5.70	D F Coates *(Noted 12.07)*	Breighton	8. 8.07P
	(Built J R Coates)						
G-AYDX	Beagle A 61 Terrier 2	B 647	VX121	20. 5.70	R A Kirby	Spanhoe	28. 8.09S
G-AYDY	Phoenix Luton LA-4A Minor	PAL 1302		21. 5.70	J Dible	(Sandyford, Dublin)	15. 8.97P
	(Built L J E Goldfinch - pr.no.PFA 817) (Volkswagen 1600)						
G-AYDZ	CEA Jodel DR.200	01	F-BLKV	21. 5.70	D Nickson tr Zero One Group	Enstone	19. 7.11
	(Lycoming O-235)		F-WLKV				
G-AYEB	Wassmer Jodel D 112	586	F-BIQR	26. 5.70	P Goring	Sturgate	18. 6.09P
G-AYEC	Menavia Piel CP.301A Emeraude	249	F-BIMV	26. 5.70	J J Shepherd tr Red Wing Flying Group *"Antoinette"*		
						Netherthorpe	26. 7.09P
G-AYEE	Piper PA-28-180 Cherokee E	28-5813	N11C	28. 5.70	Demero Ltd	Hinton-in-the-Hedges	9. 7.09E
G-AYEF	Piper PA-28-180 Cherokee E	28-5815	N11C	28. 5.70	P A Coleman and P Konnanov tr Pegasus Flying Group		
						Barton	28. 2.09E

G-AYEG	Falconar F-9	PFA 1321		29. 5.70	A L Smith	Sackville Lodge, Riseley	25. 6.09P
	(Built G R Gladstone) (Volkswagen 1600)						
G-AYEH	SAN Jodel DR.1050 Ambassadeur	455	F-BLJB	8. 6.70	H L M Williams *"Jemima"*	(Coventry)	23.11.09P
G-AYEJ	SAN Jodel DR.1050 Ambassadeur	253	F-BJYG	1. 6.70	J M Newbold	Enstone	27. 4.09
G-AYEN	Piper J-3C-65 Cub (L-4H-PI)	12184	F-BGQD	4. 6.70	P J Warde and C F Morris	Old Warden	7. 4.09P
	(Frame No.12012)		(F-BGQA), French AF, 44-79888				
	(Official identity is c/n 9696/43-835 but fuselages probably exchanged with F-BGQA on conversion in 1952/53)						
G-AYEV	SAN Jodel DR.1050 Ambassadeur	179	F-BERH	10. 6.70	L G Evans tr Echo Victor Group	Redhill	17. 4.11
			F-OBTH, F-OBRH				
G-AYEW	CEA Jodel DR.1050 Sicile	443	F-BLMJ	11. 6.70	J M Gale and J R Hope	Dunkeswell	2. 9.09P
G-AYFC	Druine D 62B Condor	RAE 644		19. 6.70	A R Chadwick	Breighton	11.12.08P
	(Built Rollason Aircraft and Engines)						
G-AYFD	Druine D 62B Condor	RAE 645		19. 6.70	B G Manning *(Hourds Travel titles) '94'*		
	(Built Rollason Aircraft and Engines)					Little Down Farm, Milson	24. 7.09P
G-AYFE	Druine D 62B Condor	RAE 646		19. 6.70	M Soulsby	(Morpeth)	6.12.01
	(Built Rollason Aircraft and Engines)						
G-AYFF	Druine D 62B Condor	RAE 647		19. 6.70	A W Maycock and I Macleod		
	(Built Rollason Aircraft and Engines)					Lower Upham Farm, Chiseldon	19. 8.08P
G-AYFG	Druine D 62C Condor	RAE 648		19. 6.70	C Jobling and A J Mackay	RAF Waddington	31. 3 09P
	(Built Rollason Aircraft and Engines) (Continental O-240-A)						
G-AYFV	Andreasson BA-4B	002		26. 6.70	A R C Mathie	(Burgate, Diss)	16.11.09P
	(Built Crosby Aviation Ltd - pr.no.PFA 1359) (Lycoming IO-320)						
G-AYGA	SAN Jodel D 117	436	F-BHNU	30. 6.70	J W Bowes	Hawksbridge Farm, Oxenhope	13. 4.09P
G-AYGC	Reims Cessna F150K	F15000556		2. 7.70	S R Cooper tr Alpha Aviation Group	Barton	3. 8.09E
G-AYGD	CEA Jodel DR.1050 Sicile	515	F-BLRE	3. 7.70	J F M Bartlett and J P Liber	Oaksey Park	24. 6.09P
G-AYGE	SNCAN Stampe SV-4C	242	F-BCGM	6. 7.70	I, L J and S Proudfoot	Duxford	13. 4.11
G-AYGG	Wassmer Jodel D 120 Paris-Nice	184	F-BJPH	10. 7.70	J M Dean	Stoneacre Farm, Farthing Corner	24. 3.09P
G-AYGX	Reims FR172G Rocket	FR17200208		15. 7.70	D Waterhouse tr Reims Rocket Group	Barton	28. 1.09E
G-AYHA	American AA-1A Trainer	AA1-0396	N6196L	21. 7.70	S J Carr	(St Andrews)	8. 5.09E
G-AYHX	SAN Jodel D 117A	903	F-BIVE	23. 7.70	G P Harrington tr Jodel Flying Group	Old Sarum	9. 4.08P
G-AYIA	Hughes 369HS *(Hughes 500)*	99-0120S		29. 7.70	G D E Bilton	Sywell	16. 7.88
	(Badly damaged in heavy landing S of France 1. 6.88; to March Helicopters - stored for spares use 8.97)						
G-AYIG	Piper PA-28-140 Cherokee C	28-26878	N11C	31. 7.70	R W Hinton	(Woolpit, Bury St Edmunds)	14. 5.09E
G-AYII	Piper PA-28R-200 Cherokee Arrow II		N11C	4. 8.70	P W J Gove tr Double India Group	Exeter	23. 4.09E
		28R-35736					
G-AYIJ	SNCAN Stampe SV-4B	376	F-BCOM	4. 8.70	D Savage	Headcorn	23. 6.09S
G-AYIM	Hawker Siddeley HS.748 Series 2A/270	1687	G-11-687	11. 8.70	Janes Aviation Ltd	Liverpool-John Lennon	21.12.08E
			CS-TAG/G-AYIM, G-11-5				
G-AYJA	SAN Jodel DR.1050 Ambassadeur	150	F-BJJJ	8. 9.70	G Connell	Weston, Leixlip, County Kildare	27. 7.09P
G-AYJB	SNCAN Stampe SV-4C(G)	560	F-BDDF	8. 9.70	F J M and J P Esson *"Odette"*Bere Farm, Warnford		24. 9.10
G-AYJD	Fournier RF3	11	F-BLXA	8. 9.70	I O Bull tr Juliet Delta Group	Ringmer	8. 9.09P
G-AYJP	Piper PA-28-140 Cherokee C	28-26403	N11C	15. 9.70	Transcourt Ltd and Demero Ltd		
						Hinton-in-the-Hedges	14. 9.09E
G-AYJR	Piper PA-28-140 Cherokee C	28-26694	N11C	15. 9.70	Transcourt Ltd and Turweston Flying School Ltd		
						Turweston	25. 2.09E
G-AYJY	Isaacs Fury II	PFA 1373		23. 9.70	M S Pettit tr The G-AYJY Group *(As "K2046" in RAF c/s)*		
	(Built A V Francis) (RR Continental C90)					Little Rissington	9. 4.09P
G-AYKD	SAN Jodel DR.1050 Ambassadeur	351	F-BKHR	30. 9.70	I M D L Weston *"Isis"*	Popham	2. 9.09P
G-AYKJ	SAN Jodel D 117A	730	F-BIDX	6.10.70	R J Hughes	(Hepworth, Diss)	20. 6.09P
G-AYKK	SAN Jodel D 117	378	F-BHGM	6.10.70	J M Whitham	(Delves Farm, Delves, Huddersfield)	22. 5.85S
G-AYKS	Leopoldoff L 7 Colibri	125	F-PCZX	8.10.70	W B Cooper	Walkeridge Farm, Overton	11.11.08P
	(Continental A65)		F-APZQ				
G-AYKT	SAN Jodel D 117	507	F-BGYY	9.10.70	D I Walker	Popham	15. 4.09P
			F-OAYY				
G-AYKW	Piper PA-28-140 Cherokee C	28-26931	N11C	12.10.70	S P Rooney and D Griffiths	(Brentwood)	12. 5.09E
G-AYKZ	SAI Kramme KZ-VIII	202	HB-EPB	13.10.70	R E Mitchell *(Stored 11.06)*	Sleap	17. 7.81P
	(DH Gipsy Major 7)		OY-ACB				
G-AYLA	AESL Airtourer T2 (115)	524		12.10.70	D S P Disney	Bristol	28. 6.09
	(Built Glos Air Ltd)						
G-AYLC	CEA Jodel DR.1051 Sicile	536	F-BLZG	12.10.70	E W B Trollope	Wing Farm, Longbridge Deverill	30. 4.09P
G-AYLF	CEA Jodel DR.1051 Sicile	547	F-BLZQ	14.10.70	R Twigg	Rectory Farm, Abbotsley	18. 8.09E
G-AYLL	CEA Jodel DR.1050 Ambassadeur	11	F-BJHK	27.10.70	C Joly	Lee-on-Solent	9. 2.10S
G-AYLP	American AA-1 Yankee	AA1-0445	EI-AVV	21.10.70	D Nairn *(Noted 9.08)*	Haverfordwest	10. 2.02
			G-AYLP				
G-AYLV	Wassmer Jodel D 120 Paris-Nice	300	F-BNCG	27.10.70	M R Henham *(Noted 11.06)*		
						Stancombe Farm, Askerswell	13. 9.83P
G-AYLZ	SPP Super Aero 45 Series 04	06-014	9M-AOF	2.11.70	M J Cobb *(Damaged Andrewsfield 2. 1.76: stored 7.05)*		
			F-BILP			(Charlwood)	11. 6.76
G-AYME	Fournier RF5	5089		6.11.70	R D Goodger	Fowle Hall Farm, Laddingford	3. 9.08P
G-AYMO	Piper PA-23-250 Aztec C	27-2995	5Y-ACX	18.11.70	J A D Richardson	Wellesbourne Mountford	1. 8.09E
			N5845Y, (N5844Y)				
G-AYMP	Phoenix Currie Wot Special	PFA 3014		8.11.70	R C Hibberd	(Chiseldon, Swindon)	4.10.94P
	(Built E H Gould)						
G-AYMR	Lederlin 380L Ladybug	EAA/55189		19.11.70	P Brayshaw *(Last reported under construction 1992)*		
	(Built J S Brayshaw - pr.no.PFA 1513) (Continental C90)					(Harrogate)	
G-AYMU	Wassmer Jodel D 112	1015	F-BJPB	23.11.70	M R Baker	(Eastbourne)	5. 6.92P
						(Damaged Hailsham, East Sussex 7.1.92: on rebuild 2004)	
G-AYMV	Western 20 Balloon (Hot Air)	002		23.11.70	R G Turnbull *"Tinkerbelle"* *(Active 10.05)*		
						Clyro, Hereford	
G-AYNA	Phoenix Currie Wot	PFA 3016		25.11.70	D R Partridge	(East Molesey)	9.12.09P
	(Built R W Hart) (Continental A65)						
G-AYND	Cessna 310Q	310Q0110	N7610Q	2.12.70	Source Group Ltd *(stored, noted 12.08)*		
						Bournemouth	12. 4.08

Reg	Type	c/n	Prev id	Date	Owner/Operator	Location	Expiry
G-AYNF	Piper PA-28-140 Cherokee C	28-26778	N11C (PT-DPV)	3.12.70	BW Aviation Ltd	Wellesbourne Mountford	26. 8.09E
G-AYNJ	Piper PA-28-140 Cherokee C	28-26810	N11C	3.12.70	P C Bird tr Cherry Tree Group	Haverfordwest	27. 3.09E
G-AYNN	Cessna 185B Skywagon	185-0518	8R-GCC, VP-GCC, N2518Z	11.12.70	Bencray Ltd	Blackpool	31 5.08T
			(Operated Blackpool and Fylde Aero Club)				
G-AYOW	Cessna 182N Skylane	18260481	N8941G	6. 1.71	D W and S E Suttill	Full Sutton	3. 7.09E
G-AYOY	Sikorsky S-61N	61-476		7. 1.71	British International Ltd *(stored 4.08)*	Plymouth	21. 4.08E
G-AYOZ	Reims Cessna FA150L Aerobat	FA1500085		7. 1.71	P D Stell	Fenland	15. 3.09E
G-AYPE	MBB BÖ.209 Monsun 160RV	123	D-EFJA	11. 1.71	Papa Echo Ltd *"Buswells Spirit"*	Biggin Hill	23.12.09E
G-AYPG	Reims Cessna F177RG Cardinal RG	F177RG0007		11. 1.71	D P McDermott	Haverfordwest	17. 3.09E
	(Wichita c/n 17700102)						
G-AYPH	Reims Cessna F177RG Cardinal RG	F177RG0018		11. 1.71	M R and K E Slack	Cambridge	27. 5.07
	(Wichita c/n 17700146)						
G-AYPJ	Piper PA-28-180 Cherokee E	28-5821	N11C	12. 1.71	R B Petrie *(Noted 3.07)*	Caernarfon	1.10.04T
G-AYPM	Piper PA-18 Super Cub 95	18-1373	French Army 18-1373, 51-15373	13. 1.71	R Horner *(As "115373-A-373" in US Army c/s)*	Trenchard Farm, Eggesford	1. 9.09P
	(Frame No.18-1282) (L-18C-PI)						
G-AYPO	Piper PA-18 Super Cub 95	18-1615	French Army 18-1615, 51-15615	13. 1.71	A W Knowles	Plymouth	25. 7.11
	(RR Continental O-200-A) (L-18C-PI)						
	(Rebuilt 1984 using OO-TSJ c/n 18-1398 (Frame No.18-1325) and ex LN-TSJ, OO-HMH, 51-15398)						
G-AYPS	Piper PA-18 Super Cub 95	18-2092	French Army 18-2092, 52-2492	13. 1.71	B C Hockley, R J Hamlett, D G and L G Callow	North Weald	12. 5.09P
	(L-18C-PI)						
G-AYPT	Piper PA-18 Super Cub 95	18-1533	(D-EALX) French Army 18-1533, 51-15533	13. 1.71	R G Brooks and T F Lyddon	Dunkeswell	24. 7.11
	(RR Continental O-200-A) (L-18C-PI) *(Frame No.18-1508)*						
G-AYPU	Piper PA-28R-200 Cherokee Arrow II	28R-7135005	N11C	13. 1.71	Monalto Investments Ltd	Jersey	20. 4.09E
G-AYPV	Piper PA-28-140 Cherokee D	28-7125039	N11C	13. 1.71	The Ashley Gardner Flying Club Ltd	Ronaldsway	6. 9.09E
G-AYPZ	Campbell Cricket	CA-343		13. 1.71	A Melody	Henstridge	21. 4.04P
	(Volkswagen 1600)						
G-AYRF	Reims Cessna F150L	F15000665		14. 1.71	D T A Rees	Haverfordwest	25.11.00T
	(Crashed Upper Welson Farm, Haverfordwest 13. 3.99)						
G-AYRG	Reims Cessna F172K	F17200761		14. 1.71	I G Harrison	Derby	8.12.07E
G-AYRH	GEMS MS.892A Rallye Commodore 150	10558	F-BNBX	14. 1.71	S O'Ceallaigh and J Barry *(Noted 9.08)*	Haverfordwest	13. 1.03
G-AYRI	Piper PA-28R-200 Cherokee Arrow II	28R-7135004	N11C	15. 1.71	A E Thompson and J C Houdret	White Waltham	16.12.09E
G-AYRM	Piper PA-28-140 Cherokee D	28-7125049	N11C	19. 1.71	M J Saggers	Biggin Hill	15.10.07E
G-AYRO	Reims Cessna FA150L Aerobat	FA15000102		21. 1.71	S M C Harvey tr Fat Boys Flying Club	Hinton-in-the-Hedges	27.10.09E
G-AYRS	Wassmer Jodel D 120A Paris-Nice	255	F-BMAV	22. 1.71	L R H D'Eath	Knettishall	8. 5.09P
G-AYRT	Reims Cessna F172K	F17200777		22. 1.71	P E Crees	Rhosgoch	7. 5.09E
G-AYRU	Britten-Norman BN-2A-6 Islander	181	G-51-181, OH-BNA, G-51-181	22. 1.71	Saywell International Ltd	Shoreham	16. 6.09E
G-AYSB	Piper PA-30 Twin Comanche C	30-1916	N8760Y	1. 2.71	M J Abbott	(Cereste, France)	24.10.09E
G-AYSD	Slingsby T 61A Falke	1726		4. 2.71	P W Hextall *(Stored 1.95)*	Tatenhill	29. 4.94
G-AYSH	Taylor JT.1 Monoplane	PFA 1413		10. 2.71	C J Lodge	Retreat Farm, Little Baddow	21. 5.09P
	(Built C J Lodge)						
G-AYSK	Phoenix Luton LA-4A Minor	PFA 832		17. 2.71	B A Schlussler and S J Rudkin	(Bourne)	24. 5.05P
	(Built L Plant)						
G-AYSX	Reims Cessna F177RG Cardinal RG	F177RG0024		17. 2.71	A P R Dean	Liverpool	16. 5.09E
	(Wichita c/n 17700175)						
G-AYSY	Reims Cessna F177RG Cardinal RG	F177RG0026		17. 2.71	S A Tuer	Waterstones Farm, Newby Wiske	10. 1.10E
	(Wichita c/n 17700180)						
G-AYTR	Menavia Piel CP.301A Emeraude	229	F-BIMD	3. 3.71	D N P Pcik tr Croft Farm Flying Group	Croft Farm, Defford	17.10.09P
G-AYTT	Phoenix PM-3 Duet	PFA 841		4. 3.71	R B Webber and J K Houlgrave	Trenchard Farm, Eggesford	2.10.09P
	(Built A J Knowles) (Officially regd as "Luton Minor III Duet") (Continental C90)						
G-AYTV	Jurca MJ.2D Tempête	PFA 2002		10. 3.71	C W Kirk tr Shoestring Flying Group	Swanborough Farm, Lewes	4. 9.08P
	(Built A Baggallay) (Continental C90)						
G-AYUA	Auster AOP.9	B5/10/119	7855M, XK416	12. 3.71	P T Bolton	(Widmerpool. Keyworth, Nottingham)	
G-AYUB	CEA Jodel DR.253B Régent	185		15. 3.71	D S Brown and V H R Gray tr Rothwell Group	Rothwell Lodge Farm, Kettering	15.11.08E
G-AYUH	Piper PA-28-180 Cherokee F	28-7105042	N11C	17. 3.71	Broadland Flying Group Ltd	Old Buckenham	7. 5.09E
G-AYUJ	Evans VP-1 Series 2	PFA 1538		17. 3.71	T N Howard *"Unforgettable Juliet"*	New Barn Farm, Barton Ashes, Crawley	6. 8.08P
	(Built J A Wills) (Volkswagen 1776)						
G-AYUM	Slingsby T 61A Falke	1730		19. 3.71	N A Stone and M H Simms	Shipdham	10. 6.02
	(Unmarked and dismantled 6.08)						
G-AYUN	Slingsby T 61A Falke	1731		19. 3.71	R J Watts tr G-AYUN Group	Rattlesden	15. 6.08E
G-AYUP	Slingsby T 61A Falke	1735	XW983, G-AYUP	19. 3.71	P R Williams *(Stored 2.97)*	Bicester	15. 7.96
G-AYUR	Slingsby T 61A Falke	1736		19. 3.71	R Hannigan and R Lingard tr Falke G-AYUR Flying Group	Strubby	6. 8.09E
G-AYUS	Taylor JT.1 Monoplane	PFA 1412		19. 3.71	S P Collins *(Noted 2.06)*	Hill Farm, Nayland	5. 8.05P
	(Built D G J Barker)						
G-AYUT	SAN Jodel DR.1050 Ambassadeur	479	F-BLJZ	22. 3.71	M L Robinson *"Roland"*	Kirkbride	22. 7.09P
G-AYUV	Reims Cessna F172H	F17200752		26. 3.71	Justgold Ltd	Blackpool	16.11.09E
G-AYVO	Wallis WA-120 Series 1	K/602/X		6. 4.71	K H Wallis *(Stored 8.01)*	Reymerston Hall, Norfolk	31.12.75P
	(130hp RR Continental O-240-B)						
G-AYVP	Aerosport Woody Pusher	181		6. 4.71	J R Wraight*(Stored incomplete)*	(Chatham)	
	(Built J R Wraight - pr.no.PFA 1344)						
G-AYWD	Cessna 182N Skylane	18260468	N8928G	15. 4.71	S I Zorb tr Wild Dreams Group	Leicester	15. 1.09
G-AYWE	Piper PA-28-140 Cherokee C	28-26826	N5910U	16. 4.71	Intelcomm (UK) Ltd	Andrewsfield	30. 5.05
	(Had accident Denham 2004/5?: dismantled and to local scrap yard 11.05: wings noted 1.06 - remains on CAA UK Register)						

Reg	Type	c/n	Prev id	Date	Owner	Location	Date
G-AYWH	SAN Jodel D 117A	844	F-BIVO	16. 4.71	D Kynaston	Coldharbour Farm, Willingham	16. 7.08P
G-AYWM	AESL Airtourer T5 (Super 150)	A 534		16. 4.71	J E Gittins tr Star Flying Group	Gloucestershire	8. 7.09
G-AYWT	AIA Stampe SV-4C(G)	1111	F-BLEY F-BAGL	21. 4.71	R A Palmer	(Weybridge)	20. 3.06T
G-AYXP	SAN Jodel D 117A	693	F-BIDD	27. 4.71	G N Davies	Shobdon	30. 9.09P
G-AYXS	SIAI-Marchetti S 205-18R	4-165	OY-DNG	28. 4.71	P J Bloore and J M Biles	Wellesbourne Mountford	26. 6.09E
G-AYXU	Champion 7KCAB Citabria	232-70	N7587F	28. 4.71	A G Hatton	Shobdon	22. 4.11
G-AYYL	Slingsby T 61A Falke	1738		10. 5.71	C Wood	(Aston Clinton, Aylesbury)	2. 6.83
					(Suffered gale damage Manston 15.12.82: on rebuild 7.90)		
G-AYYO	CEA Jodel DR.1050/M1 Sicile Record	622	EI-BAI G-AYYO, F-BMPZ	11. 5.71	D J M White tr Bustard Jodel Group	Boscombe Down	21.10.09P
G-AYYT	CEA Jodel DR.1050/M1 Sicile Record	587	F-BMGU	13. 5.71	W R Prescott tr Yankee Tango Group *(Dismantled 7.07)*	Ballymageough, Kilkeel	7. 9.06E
G-AYYU	Beech C23 Musketeer Custom	M-1353		14. 5.71	D M Powell tr G-AYYU Group	Sturgate	24. 6.09E
G-AYYX	SOCATA MS.880B Rallye Club	1812		18. 5.71	J G MacDonald	Morgansfield, Fishburn	9.11.09E
G-AYZE	Piper PA-39 Twin Comanche C/R	39-92		20. 5.71	J E Balmer	Gloucestershire	18. 9.09E
G-AYZH	Taylor JT.2 Titch	PFA 060-1316	N8934Y	21. 5.71	T D Gardner	Wolverhampton	4. 6.09P
					(Built T D Gardner) (Original regd to K Munro as pr.no. PFA 1316)		
G-AYZI	SNCAN Stampe SV-4C	15	(EI- . . .) G-AYZI, F-BBAA, French AF	24. 5.71	D M and P A Fenton	West End, Seaton Ross	13.11.0
G-AYZK	CEA Jodel DR.1050/M1 Sicile Record	590	F-BMGY	24. 5.71	D G Hesketh	Streethay Farm, Lichfield	8.10.06
G-AYZS	Druine D 62B Condor	RAE 650		4. 6.71	M N Thrush	Manor Farm, Inglesham	11. 3.09P
					(Built Rollason Aircraft and Engines)		
G-AYZU	Slingsby T 61A Falke	1740		4. 6.71	A J Harpley *(Dismantled 2.08)*	Waterstones Farm, Newby Wiske	10. 6.07
G-AYZW	Slingsby T 61A Falke	1743		4. 6.71	I D Walton tr G-ZW Group	Long Mynd	16. 9.09E

G-AZAA - G-AZZZ

Reg	Type	c/n	Prev id	Date	Owner	Location	Date
G-AZAB	Piper PA-30 Twin Comanche B	30-1475	5H-MNM 5Y-AGB	8. 6.71	Bickertons Aerodromes Ltd	Denham	7.10.09E
G-AZAJ	Piper PA-28R-200 Cherokee Arrow II	28R-7135116	N11C	18. 6.71	J C McHugh and P Woulfe	Stapleford	13. 7.09E
G-AZAW	Sud-Aviation Gardan GY-80-160 Horizon	104	F-BMUL	24. 6.71	J W Foley tr G-AZAW Group	Inverness	30.11.09R
G-AZBB	MBB BÖ.209 Monsun 160FV	137	D-EFJO	1. 7.71	J A Webb	Farley Farm, Romsey	3. 5.08
G-AZBE	AESL Airtourer T5 (Super 150)	A 535		5. 7.71	R G Vincent tr BE Flying Group	Gloucestershire	8. 3.09
G-AZBI	SAN Jodel D 150 Mascaret	43	F-BMFB	12. 7.71	F M Ward	AAC Dishforth	12. 3.09P
G-AZBL	Jodel D 9 Bébé	PFA 938		12. 7.71	J Hill *(On rebuild 1993 ?)*	(Dudley)	15.10.85P
					(Built D S Morgans) (Volkswagen 1500)		
G-AZBN	Noorduyn AT-16-ND Harvard IIB	14A-1431	PH-HON R Neth.AF B-97, FT391, 43-13132	13. 7.71	Swaygate Ltd *(As "FT391" in RAF c/s)*	Goodwood	4. 8.09P
G-AZBU	Auster AOP.9	xxxx	7862M XR246	15. 7.71	K Brooks tr Auster Nine Group *(As "XR246" in RAE c/s)*	Nottingham City-Tollerton	19. 5.09P
					(Officially regd with Frame no.AUS/183)		
G-AZCB	SNCAN Stampe SV-4C	140	F-BBCR	21. 7.71	M L Martin	Shoreham	11. 9.10S
G-AZCE	Pitts S-1C	373.H		26. 7.71	R J Oulton	(Tutshill, Chepstow)	18. 6.76S
					(Built R J Oulton - pr.no.PFA 1527) (Lycoming O-235) *(Crashed Eastbach Farm, Coleford 2. 9.75)*		
G-AZCK	Beagle B 121 Pup Series 2	B121-153		30. 7.71	I J Ross	(Onchan, IoM)	29. 8.09R
G-AZCL	Beagle B 121 Pup Series 2	B121-154		30. 7.71	J J Watts and D Fletcher *(Operated Bournemouth Flying Club)*	Bournemouth	27. 7.09E
G-AZCN	Beagle B 121 Pup Series 2	B121-156	HB-NAY G-AZCN	30. 7.71	D M Callaghan, E J Spencer and G Wildgoose	Derby	5. 7.09E
G-AZCP	Beagle B 121 Pup Series 1	B121-158	(D-EKWA) G-AZCP	30. 7.71	T A White	Bagby	17. 9.09R
G-AZCT	Beagle B 121 Pup Series 1	B121-161		30. 7.71	J Coleman	Sibson	7. 8.09E
G-AZCU	Beagle B 121 Pup Series 1	B121-162		30. 7.71	A A Harris	Shobdon	17. 9.09R
G-AZCV	Beagle B 121 Pup Series 2	B121-163	HB-NAR G-AZCV	30. 7.71	N R W Long *(Great Circle Design titles)*	Henstridge	15. 9.09E
G-AZCZ	Beagle B 121 Pup Series 2	B121-167		30. 7.71	L and J M Northover	Cardiff	13.10.09R
G-AZDA	Beagle B 121 Pup Series 1	B121-168		30. 7.71	B D Deubelbeiss	Elstree	23. 7.09
G-AZDD	MBB BÖ.209 Monsun 150FF	143	D-EBJC	3. 8.71	J D Hall and D Lawrence tr Double Delta Flying Group	Rochester	28. 3.09E
G-AZDE	Piper PA-28R-200 Cherokee Arrow II	28R-7135141	N11C	3. 8.71	Metair Ltd	Elstree	20. 4.08E
G-AZDG	Beagle B 121 Pup Series 2	B121-145	(G-BLYM) HB-NAM, (VH-EPT), G-35-145	17. 6.85	J R Heaps *(DHL titles)*	Elstree	5. 8.09R
G-AZDJ	Piper PA-32-300 Cherokee Six D	32-7140068	OY-AJK G-AZDJ, N5273S	23. 8.71	Delta Juliet Ltd	Cardiff	16. 4.09E
G-AZDX	Piper PA-28-180 Cherokee F	28-7105186	N11C	25. 8.71	M Cowan	Brickwall Farm, Hundon	3. 4.09E
G-AZDY	de Havilland DH.82A Tiger Moth	86559	F-BGDJ French AF, PG650	25. 8.71	J B Mills	(Sawbridgeworth)	18. 8.97
					(Built Morris Motors Ltd)		
G-AZEE	Morane Saulnier MS.880B Rallye Club	74	F-BKKA	1. 9.71	J Shelton *(Noted 4.04)*	Water Leisure Park, Skegness	27. 9.98
					(Composite including fuselage of G-AZNJ c/n 5375 in 1980)		
G-AZEF	Wassmer Jodel D 120 Paris-Nice	321	F-BNZS	1. 9.71	P R Sears	Shenstone Hall Farm, Shenstone	29. 5.08P
G-AZEG	Piper PA-28-140 Cherokee D	28-7125530	N11C	1. 9.71	The Ashley Gardner Flying Club Ltd	Ronaldsway	3. 7.09E
G-AZEV	Beagle B 121 Pup Series 2	B121-131	VH-EPM G-35-131	15. 9.71	C J Partridge	Popham	23. 8.09E
G-AZEW	Beagle B 121 Pup Series 2	B121-132	VH-EPN G-35-132	15. 9.71	D and M Bonsall t/a Dukeries Aviation	Netherthorpe	24. 3.10S
G-AZEY	Beagle B 121 Pup Series 2	B121-136	HB-NAK G-AZEY, VH-EPP, G-35-136	15. 9.71	M E Reynolds	(Iping, Midhurst)	8. 7.08
G-AZFA	Beagle B 121 Pup Series 2	B121-143	VH-EPR G-35-143	15. 9.71	J Smith	Sandown	6.10.09R

Reg	Type	c/n	Prev id	Date	Owner/Operator	Location	Status
G-AZFC	Piper PA-28-140 Cherokee D	28-7125486	N11C	16. 9.71	P Hennessy tr WLS Flying Group	White Waltham	22.12.09E
G-AZFF	Wassmer Jodel D 112	1175	F-BLFI	17. 9.71	J Bolger (Bennetts Bridge, County Kilkenny)		26. 1.08P
G-AZFI	Piper PA-28R-200 Cherokee Arrow II		N11C	21. 9.71	GAZFI Ltd	Sherburn-in-Elmet	6. 4.09E
		28R-7135160					
G-AZFM	Piper PA-28R-200 Cherokee Arrow II		N11C	24. 9.71	P J Jenness	Compton Abbas	18.10.09E
		28R-7135218					
G-AZFR	Cessna 401B	401B0121	N7981Q	30. 9.71	R E Wragg (St Andrew, Guernsey)		10. 2.09E
G-AZGA	Wassmer Jodel D 120 Paris-Nice	144	F-BIXV	30. 9.71	A R Neal and S A Lowe	RAF Halton	11. 4.09P
G-AZGE	SNCAN Stampe SV-4C	576	F-BDDV	6.10.71	M R L Astor (Stored 3.97) (East Hatley, Tadlow)		15. 8.94
G-AZGF	Beagle B 121 Pup Series 2	B121-076	PH-KUF	6.10.71	K Singh (Noted 7.08)	Barton	2. 5.98
			G-35-076				
G-AZGL	SOCATA MS.894A Rallye Minerva 220	11929		7.10.71	The Cambridge Aero Club Ltd	Cambridge	20.12.09E
G-AZGY	Rousseau Piel CP.301B Emeraude	122	F-BRAA	12.10.71	R H Braithwaite	RAF Henlow	8. 7.09P
G-AZGZ	de Havilland DH.82A Tiger Moth	86489	F-BGCF	13.10.71	R J King (As "NM181" in RAF c/s)	Rush Green	19. 9.08S
	(Built Morris Motors Ltd)		French AF, NM181				
G-AZHB	Robin HR.100-200B Royal	118		14.10.71	P Fenwick	Headcorn	4. 7.09E
G-AZHC	Wassmer Jodel D 112	585	F-BIQQ	18.10.71	T N Appleyard tr Aerodel Flying Group		
						Netherthorpe	2. 9.09P
G-AZHD	Slingsby T 61A Falke	1753		18.10.71	R J Shallcrass	Challock	4. 9.09
G-AZHH	K & S SA 102.5 Cavalier	PFA 1393		20.10.71	D W Buckle Morton Carr Farm, Nunthorpe		20. 1.00P
	(Built D Buckle) (Lycoming O-290)						
G-AZHI	AESL Airtourer T5 (Super 150)	A 540		20.10.71	Flying Grasshoppers Ltd	Rochester	23. 4.09S
G-AZHK	Robin HR.100-200B Royal	113	G-ILEG	22.10.71	G I Applin	Fairoaks	6. 6.09E
			G-AZHK				
G-AZHR	Piccard Ax6 Balloon (Hot Air)	617	N17US	27.10.71	C Fisher tr Halcyon Balloon Group "Happiness"		
						Aston, Sheffield	
G-AZHT	AESL Airtourer 115	525		29.10.71	Aviation West Ltd (Glasgow)		29. 1.89T
	(Continental O-240)						
G-AZHU	Phoenix Luton LA-4A Minor	PFA 839		1.11.71	W Cawrey	Netherthorpe	20.11.09P
	(Built A E Morris) (Volkswagen 1834)						
G-AZIB	SOCATA ST-10 Diplomate	141		4.11.71	W B Bateson (Noted 10.07)	Blackpool	17. 2.07
G-AZID	Reims Cessna FA150L Aerobat	FA1500083	N9447	8.11.71	P J Griffiths and M S Hill	Wolverhampton	1. 5.09E
G-AZII	SAN Jodel D 117	A 848	F-BNDO	12.11.71	P J Brayshaw Haddock Stone Farm, Markington		11. 4.01P
			F-OBFO				
G-AZIJ	Robin DR.360 Chevalier	634		15.11.71	F M Carter	Fenland	5. 8.09E
G-AZIL	Slingsby T.61A Falke	1756		16.11.71	D W Savage	Arbroath	27. 4.09E
G-AZIP	Cameron O-65 Balloon (Hot Air)	29		24.11.71	P G Dunnington tr Dante Balloon Group "Dante"		
					(Non-airworthy - inflated 9.05) Hungerford		5. 5.81A
G-AZJC	Fournier RF5	5108		30.11.71	W S V Stoney (Impruneta (FI), Italy)		17.10.08P
G-AZJE	Gardan GY-20 Minicab	JBE.1		1.12.71	J B Evans (Stored 1.98) Ventnor, Isle of Wight		7. 7.82P
	(Built J B Evans - pr.no.PFA 1806 to JB.01 Minicab standard) (Continental C90)						
G-AZJN	Robin DR.300-140 Major	642		6.12.71	J F Wright Cherry Tree Farm, Monewden		19. 9.09E
G-AZJV	Reims Cessna F172L	F17200810		8.12.71	M W Smith tr GAZJV Flying Group	Exeter	23. 3.09E
G-AZJY	Reims Cessna FRA150L Aerobat			8.12.71	P J McCartney	White Waltham	30. 9.09E
		FRA1500126					
G-AZKC	SOCATA MS.880B Rallye Club	1914		8.12.71	L J Martin	Sandown	3. 9.09E
G-AZKE	SOCATA MS.880B Rallye Club	1950	(LX-SDT)	8.12.71	J D Headlam tr Kayee Flyers	Southend	11. 4.09E
G-AZKK	Cameron O-56 Balloon (Hot Air)	32		13.12.71	P J Green and C Bosley tr Gemini Balloon Group "Gemini"		
					(Inflated 4.06) Oakley, Basingstoke		23.12.82A
G-AZKO	Reims Cessna F337F Super Skymaster			20.12.71	G James "Bird Dog"	Sleap	30. 8.08E
	(Wichita c/n 33701380)	F33700041					
G-AZKP	SAN Jodel D 117	419	F-BHND	20.12.71	A M and J L Moar	Wick	23. 6.09P
G-AZKR	Piper PA-24 Comanche	24-2192	N7044P	23.12.71	J van der Kwast	Rochester	19. 6.08E
G-AZKS	American AA-1A Trainer	0334	N6134L	23.12.71	P Burrows, K Harrison and P Howlett	Coventry	18. 2.09E
G-AZKW	Reims Cessna F172L	F17200836		23.12.71	J C C Wright	Hinton-in-the-Hedges	10. 7.09E
G-AZKZ	Reims Cessna F172L	F17200814		23.12.71	R D Forster	Ellough, Beccles	21.12.09E
G-AZLE	Boeing Stearman E75 (N2S-5) Kaydet		CF-XRD	29.12.71	A E Poulsom Manor Farm, Tongham		31. 5.10
	(Continental W670)	75-8543	N5619N, Bu43449		(As "1102:102" in US Navy c/s)		
G-AZLF	Wassmer Jodel D 120 Paris-Nice	230	F-BLFL	30.12.71	M S C Ball Garston Farm, Marshfield		25. 6.09P
G-AZLH	Reims Cessna F150L	F15000757		31.12.71	L Papatheocharis and I Buck (Noted 1.07)		
						Cranfield	30.11.03T
G-AZLN	Piper PA-28-180 Cherokee F	28-7105210	N11C	3. 1.72	Liteflite Ltd	Oxford	5. 3.09E
G-AZLV	Cessna 172K	17257908	4X-ALM	10. 1.72	M N Baker tr G-AZLV Flying Group		
			N79138			RAF Waddington	27. 5.09E
G-AZLY	Reims Cessna F150L	F15000771		10. 1.72	S Roberts	Spanhoe	12. 3.10E
G-AZMC	Slingsby T 61A Falke	1757		12. 1.72	P J R White (Sunbury)		21. 8.09
G-AZMD	Slingsby T 61C Falke	1758		12. 1.72	R A Rice Wellesbourne Mountford		24. 6.09E
G-AZMJ	American AA-5 Traveler	0019		27. 1.72	W R Partridge	St Merryn	18. 6.09E
G-AZMZ	SOCATA MS.893A Rallye Commodore 180			8. 2.72	J Palethorpe Blakedown, Kidderminster		31. 8.09E
		11927					
G-AZNK	SNCAN Stampe SV-4A	290	F-BKXF	15. 2.72	R A G Lucas tr November Kilo Group "Globird"		
			F-BCGZ			Redhill	2. 9.10S
G-AZNL	Piper PA-28R-200 Cherokee Arrow II		N11C	16. 2.72	B P Liversidge Poplar Hall Farm, Elmsett		15. 4.09E
		28R-7235006					
G-AZNO	Cessna 182P Skylane	18261005	N7365Q	18. 2.72	A I Bird	Guernsey	4. 4.09E
G-AZNT	Cameron O-84 Balloon (Hot Air)	34		21. 2.72	N Tasker "Oberon"	Bristol	5. 6.85
G-AZOA	MBB BÖ.209 Monsun 150FF	183	D-EAAY	21. 2.72	M W Hurst	Seighford	23. 7.09E
G-AZOB	MBB BÖ.209 Monsun 150FF	184	D-EAAZ	21. 2.72	J A Webb Farley Farm, Romsey		9. 7.84
					(Crashed Droitwich 21. 8.83: stored for spares use 8.92)		
G-AZOE	AESL Airtourer T2 (115)	528		21. 2.72	B J Edmondson and J K Smithson tr G-AZOE 607 Group		
						Shotton Colliery, Peterlee	1.11.09S
G-AZOF	AESL Airtourer T5 (Super 150)	A 549		21. 2.72	C Goldsmith and R C Thursby	Cardiff	3. 5.08
G-AZOG	Piper PA-28R-200 Cherokee Arrow II		N11C	21. 2.72	Atromin Ltd t/a Southend Flying Club	Southend	15.10.09E
		28R-7235009					

Reg	Type	c/n	Prev id	Date	Owner/Operator	Location	Expiry
G-AZOL	Piper PA-34-200 Seneca	34-7250075	N4348T	28. 2.72	Stapleford Flying Club Ltd	Stapleford	3. 9.09E
G-AZOO	Western O-65 Balloon (Hot Air)	015		1. 3.72	Semajan Ltd "Carousel" (Inflated 4.06)	Newbury	6. 6.77S
					(On loan to British Balloon Museum and Library)		
G-AZOT	Piper PA-34-200 Seneca	34-7250073	N4340T	3. 3.72	M Soojeri	Prestwick	13. 9.09E
G-AZOU	SAN Jodel DR.1050 Sicile	354	F-BJYX	7. 3.72	D Elliott and D Holl tr Horsham Flying Group		
						Wellcross Grange, Slinfold	15. 7.09P
G-AZOZ	Reims Cessna FRA150L Aerobat			7. 3.72	Seawing Flying Club Ltd "The Wizard of Oz"		
		FRA1500136				Southend	27. 8.09E
G-AZPA	Piper PA-25-235 Pawnee C	25-5223	N8797L N9749N	7. 3.72	Black Mountains Gliding Club Ltd	Talgarth	17. 2.10E
G-AZPC	Slingsby T.61C Falke	1767		7. 3.72	D Heslop and J R Kimberley	(Colchester)	31. 7.09E
G-AZPF	Fournier RF5	5001	D-KOLT	10. 3.72	R Pye	(Barton, Preston)	30. 8.09P
G-AZPV	Phoenix Luton LA-4A Minor	PFA 833		14. 3.72	J R Faulkner (Noted 3.07)	(Derby)	18. 9.97P
	(Built J Scott) (Lycoming O-145)						
G-AZPX	Western O-31 Balloon (Hot Air)	011		20. 3.72	B L King tr Eugena Rex Balloon Group "Eugena Rex"		
					(Inflated 4.06)	Coulsdon	
G-AZRA	MBB BÖ.209 Monsun 150FF	192	D-EAIH	21. 3.72	Alpha Flying Ltd	Wycombe Air Park	6. 4.09
G-AZRD	Cessna 401B	401B0218	N7999Q	22. 3.72	G Hatton tr Romeo Delta Group (Noted 8.08)		
						Blackpool	6. 4.06T
G-AZRH	Piper PA-28-140 Cherokee D	28-7125585	N11C	23. 3.72	H B Carter tr Trust Flying Group	Jersey	28.10.09E
G-AZRI	Payne Free Balloon (Hot Air) (56,500 cu.ft)			21. 3.72	C A Butter and J J T Cooke t/a Aardvark Balloon Company		
	(Built G F Payne)	GFP.1			"Shoestring"	Newbury and Southall	
G-AZRK	Fournier RF5	5112		23. 3.72	J F Rogers and A B Clymo	Shenington	14. 8.09E
G-AZRL	Piper PA-18 Super Cub 95 (L-18C-PI)	18-1331	OO-SBR	23. 3.72	Group North Ltd, M G Fountain and I H Searson		
	(Frame No.18-1213)		OO-HML, French Army 18-1331, 51-15331			Leicester	13. 2.11
G-AZRM	Fournier RF5	5111		24. 3.72	R Speer and M Millar tr Romeo Mike Group		
	(Volkswagen 1834)					Ringmer	7. 5.09P
G-AZRN	Cameron O-84 Balloon (Hot Air)	28		28. 3.72	C J Desmet	Brussels, Belgium	4. 7.81A
G-AZRP	AESL Airtourer T2 (115)	529		28. 3.72	B F Strawford	Shobdon	28. 1.11
G-AZRS	Piper PA-22-150 Caribbean	22-5141	XT-AAH	28. 3.72	R H Hulls "Sandpiper"	Oaksey Park	30. 7.08E
			F-OCGZ, French Army 22-5141, "FMKAC", N10F				
G-AZRZ	Cessna U206F Stationair	U20601803	N9603G	4. 4.72	Hinton Skydiving Centre Ltd	Perranporth	10. 7.09E
G-AZSA	Stampe et Renard Stampe SV-4B	1203	Belgian AF V-61	5. 4.72	M R Dolman	(Cliddesden, Basingstoke)	2.12.10S
	(Officially regd with c/n 64)						
G-AZSC	Noorduyn AT-16-ND Harvard IIB	14A-1363	PH-SKK	7. 4.72	Goodwood Road Racing Company Ltd		
			R Neth AF B-19, FT323, 43-13064		(As "43:SC" in USAAF c/s)	Goodwood	5. 9.08S
G-AZSF	Piper PA-28R-200 Cherokee Arrow II		N11C	10. 4.72	Plane Talking Ltd	Elstree	5. 9.09E
		28R-7235048					
G-AZSW	Beagle B 121 Pup Series 1	B121-140	PH-VRT	24. 4.72	T A White (Hulk only 2.08)	Bagby	15. 6.09
			G-35-140				
G-AZTA	MBB BÖ.209 Monsun 150FF	190	D-EAIF	25. 4.72	A J Court	Franklyn's Field, Chewton Mendip	9.11.09E
G-AZTF	Reims Cessna F177RG Cardinal RG			28. 4.72	R Burgun	Derby	15. 8.08E
		F177RG0054					
G-AZTK	Cessna F172F	F17200116	PH-CON	27. 4.72	S O'Ceallaigh (Wings noted 9.08 unmarked)		
	(Built Reims Aviation SA)		OO-SIR			Haverfordwest	20.10.00
G-AZTM	AESL Airtourer T2 (115)	A.530		28. 4.72	B J Edmondson tr Victa Restoration Group		
						East Boldon	
G-AZTS	Reims Cessna F172L	F17200866		28. 4.72	R Murray and A Bagley-Murray	Humberside	1. 5.09E
G-AZTV	Stolp SA.500 Starlet	SSM.2		19. 5.72	G G Rowland	Old Sarum	19.11.92
	(Built S S Miles - pr.no.PFA 1584) (Continental C90)				(Damaged Manor Farm, Grateley, Hampshire 4.7.92: on rebuild 1.08)		
G-AZTW	Reims Cessna F177RG Cardinal RG			28. 4.72	I M Richmond	Panshanger	11.12.08E
		F177RG0043					
G-AZUM	Reims Cessna F172L	F17200863		11. 5.72	M S Hills tr Fowlmere Flyers	Fowlmere	15. 4.09E
G-AZUP	Cameron O-65 Balloon (Hot Air)	36		11. 5.72	R S Bailey and A B Simpson "Eight of Hearts"		
						Aylesbury	23.10.77S
G-AZUT	SOCATA MS.893A Rallye Commodore 180		VH-TCH	12. 5.72	J Palethorpe tr Rallye Flying Group		
		10963				Blakedown, Kidderminster	13. 3.08E
G-AZUY	Cessna 310L	310L0012	SE-FEC	15. 5.72	W B Bateson (Noted 11.07)	Blackpool	5.11.05T
			LN-LMH, N2212F				
G-AZUZ	Reims Cessna FRA150L Aerobat			16. 5.72	D J Parker	Netherthorpe	18. 3.09E
		FRA1500146					
G-AZVA	MBB BÖ.209 Monsun 150FF	177	(D-EAAQ)	16. 5.72	C Elder	New Farm, Felton	28. 9.09E
G-AZVB	MBB BÖ.209 Monsun 150FF	178	(D-EAAS)	16. 5.72	E and P M L Cliffe	Tibenham	23. 7.09E
G-AZVF	SOCATA MS.894A Rallye Minerva 220	11999	(F-OCSR)	16. 5.72	J R Hepburn tr Minerva Flying Group		
						Upfield Farm, Usk	6. 4.08E
G-AZVG	American AA-5 Traveler	AA5-0075		16. 5.72	K M Whelan tr G-AZVG Group	Cranfield	21.11.09E
G-AZVH	SOCATA MS.894A Rallye Minerva 220	12017		16. 5.72	P L Jubb	Suton, Norwich	22. 7.09E
G-AZVI	SOCATA MS.892A Rallye Commodore 150			6. 5.72	G C Jarvis	Henstridge	3. 6.09E
		12039					
G-AZVL	Jodel D 119	794	F-BILB	19. 5.72	S P Collins (Noted 9.07)	Hill Farm, Nayland	31. 8.07P
	(Built Etablissement Valladeau)						
G-AZVP	Reims Cessna F177RG Cardinal RG			22. 5.72	C R Brown	Oxford	13.12.08E
		F177RG0057					
G-AZWB	Piper PA-28-140 Cherokee E	28-7225244	N11C	5. 6.72	J A Tyndall tr G-AZWB Flying Group	Oaksey Park	2. 3.10E
G-AZWD	Piper PA-28-140 Cherokee E	28-7225298	N11C	6. 6.72	Whisky Delta Ltd	Redhill	18. 5.09E
G-AZWF	SAN Jodel DR.1050 Ambassadeur	130	F-BJJT	7. 6.72	J A D Reedie tr Cawdor Flying Group	(Dingwall)	17. 2.08
	(Composite including fuselage of DR.1050M F-BLJX c/n 492)						
G-AZWS	Piper PA-28R-180 Cherokee Arrow		N4993J	8. 6.72	G S Blair tr Arrow 88 Flying Group	Eshott	8. 9.08E
		28R-30749					
G-AZWT	Westland Lysander IIIA	Y1536	RCAF 1582	9. 6.72	Richard Shuttleworth Trustees	Old Warden	24. 4.09P
			V9552		(As "V9367:MA-B" in RAF 161 Sqdn c/s)		
G-AZWY	Piper PA-24-260 Comanche C	24-4806	N9310P	16. 6.72	Keymer, Son and Company Ltd	Biggin Hill	15. 6.09E
G-AZXB	Cameron O-65 Balloon (Hot Air)	48		20. 6.72	R J Mitchener and P F Smart t/a Balloon Collection		
					"London Pride II"	Andover	6. 5.81A

G-AZXD	Reims Cessna F172L	F17200878			20. 6.72	R J R Williams and D Palmer	Shobdon	17. 3.09E
G-AZYA	Sud-Aviation Gardan GY-80-160 Horizon	57	F-BLPT		7. 7.72	R G Whyte	(Rugby)	4. 6.08E
						(Departed Sywell for long-term rubdown and repaint)		
G-AZYD	GEMS MS.893A Rallye Commodore 180		F-BNSE		30. 6.72	Staffordshire Gliding Club Ltd	Seighford	13.11.09E
		10645						
G-AZYF	Piper PA-28-180 Cherokee D	28-5227	N7813M		23. 6.72	A R A Grindley tr AZYF Group	Leicester	20. 5.09E
			G-AZYF, 5Y-AJK, N7813N					
G-AZYS	Scintex CP.301-C1 Emeraude	568	F-BJAY		7. 7.72	C G Ferguson and D Drew Jericho Farm, Lambley	10. 5.09P
G-AZYU	Piper PA-23-250 Aztec E	27-4601	N13983		13. 7.72	L J Martin	Bembridge	2. 1.10E
G-AZYY	Slingsby T 61A Falke	1770			12. 7.72	J A Towers	Yearby	21. 8.08P
G-AZYZ	Wassmer WA.51A Pacific	30	F-OCSE		14. 7.72	C R Buxton	(Gourvillette, France)	8. 7.10
G-AZZH	Practavia Pilot Sprite 115	PFA 1532			13. 7.72	A Moore	(Hutton, Brentwood)	
	(Built K G Stewart)							
G-AZZR	Reims Cessna F150L	F15000690	LN-LJX		24. 7.72	E B Atalay	Kimbolton	3. 9.09E
G-AZZV	Reims Cessna F172L	F15000883			18. 7.72	Zentelligence Ltd	Rochester	7. 7.09E
G-AZZZ	de Havilland DH.82A Tiger Moth	86311	F-BGJE		27. 7.72	S W McKay	RAF Henlow	30. 1.11
	(Built Morris Motors Ltd)		French AF, NL864					

G-BAAA - G-BAZZ

G-BAAD	Evans VP-1	PFA 1540			27. 7.72	K Wigglesworth tr Breighton VP-1 Group		
	(Built R W Husband) (Volkswagen 1600)						Breighton	11. 6.09P
G-BAAF	Manning-Flanders MF.1 replica	PPS/REP/8			27. 7.72	Bianchi Aviation Film Services Ltd *(No external marks)*		
	(Built Personal Plane Services Ltd) (Continental C75)						Wycombe Air Park	6. 8.96P
G-BAAI	SOCATA MS.893A Rallye Commodore 180		F-BOVG		31. 7.72	R D Taylor *(Noted 12.08)*	Thruxton	11. 9.00
		10705						
G-BAAT	Cessna 182P Skylane	18260835	N399JF		10. 8.72	T E Earl	Bourne Park, Hurstbourne Tarrant	8. 9.09E
			G-BAAT, N9295G					
G-BAAW	Jodel D 119	366	F-BHMY		11. 8.72	P J Newson tr Alpha Whiskey Flying Group		
	(Built Etablissement Valladeau) (Continental O-200-A)						Cherry Tree Farm, Monewden	21. 7.09P
G-BABC	Reims Cessna F150L	F15000831			15. 8.72	B B Singh	(Hitchin)	30. 8.09E
G-BABD	Reims Cessna FRA150L Aerobat				3. 8.72	K F Mason and D Featherby t/a Anglia Flight		
		FRA1500153					Norwich	30. 7.09E
G-BABE	Taylor JT.2 Titch	PEB/01			3. 8.72	M Bonsall	Netherthorpe	3. 2.05P
	(Built P E Barker, pr.no.PFA 1394)			*(Overturned Elmton 15. 5.04, serious damage to fuselage, starboard wing and engine)*				
	(Continental O-200-A)							
G-BABG	Piper PA-28-180 Cherokee C	28-2031	PH-APU		15. 8.72	C E Dodge tr Mendip Flying Group	Bristol	16.12.09E
			N7978W					
G-BABK	Piper PA-34-200 Seneca	34-7250219	PH-DMN		18. 8.72	D F J Flashman	Biggin Hill	6. 4.09E
			G-BABK, N5203T					
G-BACB	Piper PA-34-200 Seneca	34-7250251	N5354T		25. 8.72	A R Braybrooke t/a Milbrooke Motors	Southend	23.11.09E
G-BACE	Sportavia-Pützer Fournier RF5	5102	(PT-DVZ)		25. 8.72	N P Harrison tr G-BACE Fournier Group		
			D-KCID				Dunkeswell	11. 2.09E
G-BACJ	Wassmer Jodel D 120 Paris-Nice	315	F-BNZC		1. 9.72	J M Allan tr Wearside Flying Association	Eshott	8. 5.09P
G-BACL	SAN Jodel D 150 Mascaret	31	F-BSTY		4. 9.72	D F Micklethwait	Breighton	7. 7.11
			CN-TYY					
G-BACN	Reims Cessna FRA150L Aerobat				4. 9.72	F Bundy	Bodmin	7. 3.09E
		FRA1500161						
G-BACO	Reims Cessna FRA150L Aerobat				4. 9.72	A J Hobbs	Bridge Farm, Acle, Norwich	18. 3.09E
		FRA1500163						
G-BACP	Reims Cessna F150L Aerobat	FRA1500164			4. 9.72	M Markwick tr Aim High Flying Group	Shoreham	3. 6.09E
	(Built originally as FRA150L)							
G-BADC	Rollason Beta B 2A	PFA 002-10140			7. 9.72	D H Greenwood	Barton	31. 1.85P
	(Built H M Mackenzie) (Originally.regd to J J Feely as c/ns JJF.1 and PFA 1384 - then adopted c/n of Beta G-BETA when that was cancelled							
	3. 2.87 by CAA as "not completed": probably incorporated into final build) (Noted 1.07)							
G-BADH	Slingsby T 61A Falke	1774			6. 9.72	A P Askwith	Rhosgoch	30. 3.09E
G-BADJ	Piper PA-E23-250 Aztec E	27-4841	N14279		11. 9.72	C Papadakis	Cranfield	2. 8.08E
G-BADM	Druine D 62B Condor	RAE 653			8. 9.72	D J Wilson	Compton Abbas	16. 7.07P
	(Built K Worksworth and M Harris - pr.no.PFA 049-11442 using uncompleted Rollason build frame)							
G-BADV	Brochet MB.50 Pipistrelle	78	F-PBRJ		13. 9.72	W B Cooper	Walkeridge Farm, Overton	9. 5.79P
	(Built A Bouriquat)							
G-BADW	Pitts S-2A	2035			21. 9.72	R E Mitchell *(Noted 10.06)*	Sleap	16. 9.95T
	(Built Aerotek Inc)							
G-BAEB	Robin DR.400-160 Knight	733			19. 9.72	R Hatton	Andreas, Isle of Man	22. 4.09E
G-BAEE	CEA Jodel DR.1050/M1 Sicile Record	579	F-BMGN		29. 9.72	R Little	Jackrell's Farm, Southwater	14. 6.09P
G-BAEM	Robin DR.400-120 Petit Prince	728			25. 9.72	M A Webb	Denham	2. 6.09E
G-BAEN	Robin DR.400-180 Régent	736			25. 9.72	R H and C R Partington	Milfield	23. 9.09E
G-BAEO	Reims Cessna F172M	F17200911			14. 9.72	L W Scattergood	Sandtoft	6. 2.09E
	(Re-built with original fuselage and remains of G-YTWO)							
G-BAEP	Reims Cessna F150L Aerobat	FRA1500170			14. 9.72	A M Lynn t/a Busy Bee *(Operated RAF Marham Flying Club)*		
	(Built originally as FRA150L)						RAF Marham	12. 5.09E
G-BAER	LeVier Cosmic Wind	106			14. 9.72	A G Truman	Lasham	18. 9.06P
	(Built R S Voice - pr.no.PFA 1571) (Continental O-200-A)							
G-BAET	Piper J-3C-65 Cub (L-4H)	11605	OO-AJI		26. 9.72	C J Rees	Valley Farm, Winwick	10.11.05P
	(Frame No.11430)		43-30314					
G-BAEU	Reims Cessna F150L	F15000873			26. 9.72	L W Scattergood	Full Sutton	1. 7.07T
	(Landed nosewheel first at Full Sutton 4. 6.08, while attempting to avoid a glider landing in the opposite direction, and nosegear collapsed)							
G-BAEV	Reims Cessna FRA150L Aerobat				27. 9.72	B Doyle	(Kilmaley, Ennis, County Clare)	15. 4.09E
		FRA1500173						
G-BAEY	Reims Cessna F172M	F17200915			28. 9.72	Skytrax Aviation Ltd	Derby	19. 4.09E
G-BAEZ	Reims Cessna FRA150L Aerobat				28. 9.72	Donair Flying Club Ltd	Nottingham-East Midlands	27. 3.09E
		FRA1500169						
G-BAFA	American AA-5 Traveler	AA5-0201	N6136A		6.10.72	C F Mackley *(Noted 8.04)*	Sleap	31. 8.01

G-BAFG de Havilland DH.82A Tiger Moth 85995 F-BGEL 13.10.72 Meinl Capital Markets Ltd Boones Farm, Braintree 10.10.10S
(Built Morris Motors Ltd) French.AF, EM778
G-BAFL Cessna 182P Skylane 18261469 N21180 15. 8.72 M Langhammer Old Sarum 24. 3.09E
G-BAFP Robin DR.400-160 Knight 735 19.10.72 M Hoffmann and M W Bodger
Yeatsall Farm, Abbots Bromley 22. 5.09E
G-BAFT Piper PA-18-150 Super Cub 18-5340 (D-E…) 3. 8.72 C A M Neidt (Roosendaal, Netherlands) 2. 5.09S
French Army 18-5340, N10F
G-BAFU Piper PA-28-140 Cherokee 28-20759 PH-NLS 11.10.72 B Higgins (Baldock) 20. 6.09E
G-BAFV Piper PA-18 Super Cub 95 18-2045 PH-WJK 24.10.72 T F and S J Thorpe Kirk Michael 22.11.10S
(L-18C-PI) (Frame No.18-2055) R Neth AF R-40, 8A-40, 52-2445
G-BAFW Piper PA-28-140 Cherokee 28-21050 PH-NLT 24.10.72 A J Peters Derby 15. 5.09E
G-BAFX Robin DR.400-140 Earl 739 30.10.72 R Foster Enstone 14. 5.09E
G-BAGB SIAI-Marchetti SF.260 1-07 LN-BIV 20.10.72 British Midland Airways Ltd
Nottingham-East Midlands 4. 7.09E
G-BAGC Robin DR.400-140 Earl 737 13.10.72 O C Baars (Westbury) 31. 1.10E
G-BAGF Jodel D 92 Bébé 59 F-PHFC 13.11.72 E Evans (Stored 5.08, for sale)
(Built Aero Club Basse-Moselle) Benson's Farm, Laindon
G-BAGG (2)Piper PA-32-300 Cherokee Six 32-7340186 N9562N 7.12.73 Channel Islands Aero Club (Jersey)Ltd Jersey 19.11.09E
G-BAGN Reims Cessna F177RG Cardinal RG 24.10.72 R W J Andrews Wolverhampton 14. 5.09E
F177RG0068
G-BAGR Robin DR.400-140 Petit Prince 753 30.10.72 J D Last Caernarfon 6. 6.09E
G-BAGS Robin DR.400-100 2+2 760 30.10.72 M Whale and M W A Lunn (On rebuild 2.08)
Little Rissington 16. 1.03T
G-BAGT Helio H 295 Super Courier 1288 CR-LJG 31. 7.72 D C Hanss Elstree 30.12.09E
G-BAGV Cessna U206F Stationair U20601867 N9667G 31.10.72 K Brady tr The Scottish Parachute Club Strathallan 14. 5.04
(Badly damaged 5. 5.02: fuselage used for parachute training 1.05)
G-BAGX Piper PA-28-140 Cherokee 28-23633 N3574K 30.10.72 S A King tr The Golf X-Ray Group Conington 5. 3.10E
G-BAGY Cameron O-84 Balloon (Hot Air) 54 17.10.72 P G Dunnington tr Dante Balloon Group "Beatrice"
(Stored 5.07) Hungerford 16. 6.81A
G-BAHD Cessna 182P Skylane 18261501 N21228 25.10.72 J W Hardy tr Lambley Flying Group
Jericho Farm, Lambley 2. 8.09E
G-BAHE Piper PA-28-140 Cherokee C 28-26494 N5696U 30.10.72 A O Jones and M W Kilvert Trehelig, Welshpool 8. 6.95
(Noted heading north from Rhayader on trailer 5.06, stored dismantled)
G-BAHF Piper PA-28-140 Fliteliner 28-7125215 N431FL 30.10.72 BJ Services (Midlands) Ltd Coventry 25. 7.09E
G-BAHH Wallis WA-121/Mc K/701/X 7.11.72 K H Wallis (Noted 8.01) Reymerston Hall, Norfolk 27. 5.98P
(Wallis modified McCulloch)
G-BAHI Cessna F150H F150-0330 PH-EHA 6.11.72 M Player t/a MJP Aviation and Sales
(Built Reims Aviation SA) Little Staughton 14.12.07E
G-BAHJ Piper PA-24-250 Comanche 24-1863 PH-RED 6.11.72 K Cooper Wolverhampton 4. 6.09E
N6735P
G-BAHL Robin DR.400-160 Knight 704 F-OCSR 8.11.72 J B McVeighty Breighton 4. 6.09E
G-BAHO Beech C23 Sundowner M-1456 7.11.72 S C Carty Old Sarum 18. 6.09E
G-BAHP Volmer VJ.22 Sportsman PFA 1313 9.11.72 G K Holloway tr Seaplane Group Aboyne 18.10.93P
(Built J P Crawford) (Continental C90) (Noted 4.07 on restoration)
G-BAHS Piper PA-28R-200 Cherokee Arrow II N15147 9.11.72 A R N Morris Shobdon 16. 9.09E
28R-7335017
G-BAHX Cessna 182P Skylane 18261588 N21363 16.11.72 A P Stone tr Dupost Group
Blackpool 27. 8.09E
G-BAIG Piper PA-34-200 Seneca 34-7250243 OY-BSU 21.11.72 Mid-Anglia Flying Centre Ltd t/a Mid-Anglia School of Flying
G-BAIG, N5257T Cambridge 23. 4.09E
G-BAIH Piper PA-28R-200 Cherokee Arrow II N11C 21.11.72 M G West King's Farm, Thurrock 24. 3.09E
28R-7335011
G-BAII Reims Cessna FRA150L Aerobat 22.11.72 Cornwall Flying Club Ltd Plymouth 14. 6.03T
FRA1500178 (Force landed Hendra Farm, Bodmin 9.9.01 and severely damaged) (Wreck noted 4.02)
G-BAIK Reims Cessna F150L F15000903 22.11.72 M Sollitt (Sheffield) 9. 4.09E
G-BAIP Reims Cessna F150L F15000898 13.11.72 G and S A Jones (Linley Hill, Leven) 28. 9.97T
(Damaged Linley Hill 30. 5.95)
G-BAIS Reims Cessna F177RG Cardinal RG 13.11.72 R M Graham and E P Howard tr Cardinal Syndicate
F177RG0069 Seething 15. 2.09E
G-BAIW Reims Cessna F172M F17200928 14.11.72 W J Greenfield Humberside 22. 1.09E
G-BAIX Reims Cessna F172M F17200931 14.11.72 I S Mcleod and J L Yourell Cranfield 11.11.08E
G-BAIZ Slingsby T 61A Falke 1776 27.11.72 R G Sangster and J J Doswell tr Falke Syndicate
Hinton-in-the-Hedges 20.11.09E
G-BAJA Reims Cessna F177RG Cardinal RG 29.11.72 D W Ward Biggin Hill 1. 9.09E
F177RG0078
G-BAJB Reims Cessna F177RG Cardinal RG 29.11.72 J D Loveridge Guernsey 19. 9.09E
F177RG0080
G-BAJC Evans VP-1 Series 2 PFA 1548 30.11.72 S J Greer (Noted stored 5.08) Shenington 10. 6.04P
(Built J R Clements) (Volkswagen 1834)
G-BAJE Cessna 177 Cardinal 17700812 N29322 30.11.72 R D Bennett tr Juliet Echo Group Blackpool 16. 6.09E
G-BAJN American AA-5 Traveler AA5-0259 29.11.72 J M Cuddy Blackpool 15. 6.09E
G-BAJO American AA-5 Traveler AA5-0260 29.11.72 Montgomery Aviation Ltd Blackpool 3.11.09E
G-BAJR Piper PA-28-180 Cherokee Challenger N11C 1.12.72 J Mahon and J Phelan tr Spectrum Bravo Flying Group
28-7305008 Belfast International 1. 7.09E
G-BAJZ Robin DR.400-2+2 759 4.12.72 Weald Air Services Ltd Headcorn 19. 9.08E
G-BAKD Piper PA-34-200 Seneca 34-7350013 N1378T 28.11.72 Andrews Professional Colour Laboratories Ltd
(Operated Foto Flite) Lydd 30.12.07E
G-BAKH Piper PA-28-140 Cherokee F 28-7325014 N11C 12.12.72 Keen Leasing (IOM) Ltd (Operated Ulster Flying Club)
Belfast International 4.12.08E
G-BAKJ Piper PA-30 Twin Comanche B 30-1232 TJ-AAI 13.12.72 G D Colover, R Jones and N O'Connor Biggin Hill 19. 2.10E
TJ-ADH, N8122Y
G-BAKM Robin DR.400-140 Earl 755 15.12.72 D V Pieri Carlisle 1. 6.09E
G-BAKN SNCAN Stampe SV-4C 348 F-BCOY 15.12.72 M Holloway Watchford Farm, Yarcombe 12.10.11

Reg	Type	C/n	Prev id	Date	Owner/Operator	Location	Status
G-BAKR	SAN Jodel D 117	814	F-BIOV	27.12.72	R W Brown	Stoneacre Farm, Farthing Corner	18. 9.08P
G-BAKV	Piper PA-18-150 Super Cub	18-8993	N9744N	22.12.72	W J Murray	Thruxton	17. 8.07T
G-BAKW	Beagle B 121 Pup Series 2	B121-175		15.12.72	R A Swetman and M J Evans tr Cunning Stunts Flying Group	Redhill	21. 8.09S
G-BAKY	Slingsby T 61C Falke	1777		20.12.72	T J Wiltshire *(Noted 2.08)*	Saltby	7. 8.98
G-BALD	Cameron O-84 Balloon (Hot Air)	58		2. 1.73	C A Gould *"Puffin"*	Ipswich	7. 6.06S
G-BALF	Robin DR.400-140 Earl	772		5. 1.73	G and D A Wasey	Oaksey Park	16. 7.09E
G-BALG	Robin DR.400-180 Régent	771		5. 1.73	R Jones t/a Southern Sailplanes	Membury	24. 5.09E
G-BALH	Robin DR.400-140B Earl	766		5. 1.73	C Johnson tr G-BALH Flying Group	Fenland	10. 4.09E
G-BALI	Robin DR.400 2+2	764		5. 1.73	A Brinkley *(On rebuild 3.96)*	Standalone Farm, Meppershall	3. 9.88
G-BALJ	Robin DR.400-180 Régent	767		5. 1.73	D A Batt and D de Lacey-Rowe	Fridd Farm, Bethersden	10. 7.09E
G-BALN	Cessna T310Q	310Q0684	N7980Q	8. 1.73	O'Brien Properties Ltd	Shoreham	24. 5.09E
G-BALY	Practavia Pilot Sprite 150	"OS-10009"		10. 1.73	A L Young tr Aly Aviation	(Henstridge)	
	(Built A L Young - pr.no.PFA 005-10009)				*(Believed not commenced)*		
G-BALZ	Bell 212	30542	EC-IPD	10. 1.73	Bristow Helicopters Ltd	Mauritania	26. 7.09E
				G-BALZ, EC-GCR, EC-931, G-BALZ, 9Y-TIL, G-BALZ, VR-BIB, N99040, G-BALZ, EI-AWK, G-BALZ, VR-BEK, N2961W				
G-BAMB	Slingsby T 61C Falke	1778		9. 1.73	N J Clemens tr Flying Group G-BAMB	Eaglescott	24. 9.09E
G-BAMC	Reims Cessna F150L	F15000892		12. 1.73	K Evans	Welshpool	27. 8.09E
G-BAMJ	Cessna 182P	18261650	N21469	10. 1.73	A E Kedros	Bournemouth	26. 4.08E
G-BAMR	Piper PA-16 Clipper	16-392	F-BFMS CU-P339	12. 1.73	H Royce	Bradleys Lawn, Heathfield	29. 9.07E
	(Lycoming O-290)						
G-BAMS	Robin DR.400-160 Knight	774		15. 1.73	G-BAMS Ltd	Biggin Hill	8. 4.09E
G-BAMT	Robin DR.400-160 Knight	775		15. 1.73	S G Jones	(Membury)	15. 5.79
			(Crashed Cudham 8.1.78: cancelled 24.4.78 as WFU: wreck stored 1.92 and restored 14. 1.05)					
G-BAMU	Robin DR.400-160 Knight	778		15. 1.73	N P Tyne tr Alternative Flying Group	Sywell	6. 5.09E
G-BAMV	Robin DR.400-180 Régent	777		15. 1.73	K Jones and E A Anderson	Wycombe Air Park	8. 5.09E
G-BAMY	Piper PA-28R-200 Cherokee Arrow II	28R-7335015	N11C	9. 1.73	S R Pool	Lydd	10. 6.09E
G-BANA	CEA Jodel DR.221 Dauphin	73	F-BOZR	22. 1.73	G T Pryor	Tibenham	27. 9.09E
G-BANB	Robin DR.400-180 Régent	776		22. 1.73	A M Quayle	(Ramsgate)	28. 4.09T
G-BANC	Gardan GY-201 Minicab	A 203	F-PCZV F-BCZV	22. 1.73	C R Shipley	Grange Farm, Frogland Cross	31. 5.02P
	(Built M Ducreuzet) (Continental C90)						
G-BANF	Phoenix Luton LA-4A Minor	PFA 838		22. 1.73	W J McCollum	Coagh, County Londonderry	5. 6.92P
	(Built D W Bosworth) (Continental A65)				*(Damaged Mullaghmore, Coleraine 27.6.92: noted 11.01)*		
G-BANU	Wassmer Jodel D 120 Paris-Nice	247	F-BLNZ	31. 1.73	W M and C H Kilner	Shacklewell Farm, Empingham	26. 7.07P
G-BANV	Phoenix Currie Wot	PFA 3010		25. 1.73	K Knight	(Malvern)	26. 6.84P
	(Built C Turner) (Lycoming O-290)				*(Damaged near Leek, Staffs 15. 9.83)*		
G-BANW	CAARP CP.1330 Super Emeraude	941	PH-VRF	30. 1.73	P S Milner	Popham	12. 7.07P
	(Lycoming 0-235-C1)						
G-BANX	Reims Cessna F172M	F17200941		31. 1.73	Oakfleet 2000 Ltd	Biggin Hill	13. 7.09E
G-BAOB	Reims Cessna F172M	F17200949		2. 2.73	R H Taylor and S O Smith	Andrewsfield	12. 5.07T
G-BAOH	SOCATA MS.880B Rallye Club	2250		6. 2.73	A P Swain *(Noted in bare metal 6.05)*	Haverfordwest	28. 7.01
G-BAOJ	SOCATA MS.880B Rallye Club	2252		6. 2.73	R E Jones	Caernarfon	24. 5.08E
G-BAOP	Reims Cessna FRA150L Aerobat	FRA1500190		5. 2.73	R D Forster *(Fuselage noted 10.08)*	Ellough, Beccles	11. 4.02
G-BAOS	Reims Cessna F172M	F17200946		6. 2.73	Wingtask 1995 Ltd	Spanhoe	19. 7.08E
			(Overturned after landing on soft ground in crop field at Seething 30. 5.06 with substantial damage)					
G-BAOU	Grumman AA-5 Traveler	AA5-0298		8. 2.73	R C Mark	Shobdon	27. 2.09E
G-BAPB	de Havilland DHC-1 Chipmunk 22A	C1/0001	WB549	26. 2.73	G V Bunyan	(Bidford)	31. 5.98
G-BAPI	Reims Cessna FRA150L Aerobat	FRA1500195		8. 2.73	Marketing Management Services Ltd	Glasgow	14. 7.09E
G-BAPJ	Reims Cessna FRA150L Aerobat	FRA1500196		8. 2.73	M D Page	Manston	10. 6.09E
G-BAPL	Piper PA-23-250 Aztec E	27-7304966	N14377	12. 2.73	Donington Aviation Ltd	Nottingham-East Midlands	7.10.07E
G-BAPP	Evans VP-1 Coupe	PFA 1580		13. 2.73	A Sharp *(Noted 8.07)*	Sleap	27. 5.98P
	(Built M J Drybanski and M Crow) (Volkswagen 1834)						
G-BAPR	Jodel D 11	295		14. 2.73	J P Liber and J F M Bartlett	Oaksey Park	17. 4.06P
	(Built Crantech Flying Group - pr.no.PFA 914) (Continental PC60)						
G-BAPV	Robin DR.400-160 Knight	742	F-OCSR	19. 2.73	J D and M Millne	(Bedlington)	22. 8.03
G-BAPW	Piper PA-28R-180 Cherokee Arrow	28R-30697	5Y-AIR N4951J	21. 2.73	A G Bourne and M W Freeman	Hinton-in-the-Hedges	22. 1.08E
G-BAPX	Robin DR.400-160 Knight	789		21. 2.73	D Whitton tr G-BAPX Group	Sywell	11. 3.09E
G-BAPY	Robin HR.100-210 Safari II	153		21. 2.73	D M J Williams tr G-BAPY Group	Fairoaks	4. 8.09E
G-BARC	Reims FR172J Rocket	FR17200356	(D-EEDK)	5. 3.73	C H Porter tr Severn Valley Aviation Group	Croft Farm, Defford	24. 4.09E
G-BARF	Wassmer Jodel D 112	1019	F-BJPF	5. 3.73	J J Penney	Rhigos	14.10.08P
G-BARG	Cessna E310Q	310Q0712	N8237Q	2. 3.73	IT Factor Ltd	Oxford	31. 3.06T
G-BARH	Beech C23 Sundowner	M-1473		2. 3.73	G Moorby and J Hinchcliffe	Sherburn-in-Elmet	2. 5.09E
G-BARN	Taylor JT.2 Titch	PFA 060-11136		5. 3.73	R G W Newton	Westfield Farm, Hailsham	25. 9.09P
	(Built R G W Newton) (Continental C90)						
G-BARP	Bell 206B-2 JetRanger II	967	N18092	5. 3.73	Western Power Distribution (South West) PLC	Bristol	17. 5.09E
G-BARS	de Havilland DHC-1 Chipmunk 22	C1/0557	WK520	26. 2.73	J Beattie *(As "1377" in Portuguese AF c/s)*	RNAS Yeovilton	11. 8.11
G-BARV	Cessna 310Q	310Q-0774		7. 3.73	Old England Watches Ltd	Elstree	18. 8.09E
G-BARZ	Scheibe SF28A Tandem Falke	5724	(D-KAUK)	8. 3.73	K Kiely	AAC Dishforth	21. 9.09E
G-BASH	Grumman AA-5 Traveler	AA5-0319	EI-AWV G-BASH, N5419L	12. 3.73	G Jenkins tr BASH Flying Group	Popham	19.11.09E
G-BASJ	Piper PA-28-180 Cherokee Challenger	28-7305136	N11C	13. 3.73	Bristol Aero Club	Filton	20. 2.09E

Reg	Type	c/n	Prev id	Date	Owner/Operator	Base/Date
G-BASL	Piper PA-28-140 Cherokee F	28-7325195	N11C	13. 3.73	P N Clynes	Turweston 14. 6.09E
G-BASM	Piper PA-34-200 Seneca	34-7350120	N16272	13. 3.73	M Gipps	Denham 10. 7.09E
G-BASN	Beech C23 Sundowner	M-1476		13. 3.73	O M O'Neill	(Leigh Woods, Bristol) 24. 2.09E
G-BASO	Lake LA-4-180 Amphibian	358	N2025L	16. 3.73	C J A Macaulay *(Stored 9.07)*	City of Derry 19. 6.06
	(Built Consolidated Aeronautics Inc)					
G-BASP	Beagle B 121 Pup Series 1	B121-149	SE-FOC	14. 3.73	B J Coutts	Sibson 17. 9.09R
			G-35-149			
G-BATC	MBB BÖ.105DB	S 45	D-HDAW	9. 3.73	Bond Air Services *(Operated North Wales Air Ambulance)*	
	(Originally registered as BÖ.105D: rebuilt using new MBB pod 1989 c/n unknown)					Stromness 22. 6.09E
G-BATJ	Jodel D 119	287	F-PIIQ	21. 3.73	M G Davis	Maypole Farm, Chislet 14. 8.09P
	(Built Ecole Technique Aéronautique de Ville) (Continental C90)					
G-BATN	Piper PA-23-250 Aztec E	27-7304987	N14391	26. 3.73	Marshall of Cambridge Aerospace Ltd t/a Marshall Aerospace	
						Cambridge 26. 2.09E
G-BATR	Piper PA-34-200 Seneca	34-7250290	9H-ABH	23. 3.73	A S Bamrah t/a Falcon Flying Services	Biggin Hill 24. 4.05
			G-BATR, LN-BDT	*(Overran landing Woodchurch 4.8.02: struck hedge and badly damaged)*		
G-BATV	Piper PA-28-180 Cherokee F	28-7105022	N5168S	26. 3.73	J N Rudsdale tr The Scoreby Flying Group	
						Full Sutton 28. 1.09E
G-BATW	Piper PA-28-140 Cherokee Fliteliner	N742FL	26. 3.73	C D Sainsbury	Swansea 13. 8.09E
		28-7225587				
G-BAUC	Piper PA-25-235 Pawnee C	25-5243	N8761L	26. 3.73	Southdown Gliding Club Ltd	Parham Park 22. 6.09E
G-BAUH	Dormois Jodel D 112	870	F-BILO	29. 3.73	G A and D Shepherd tr G-BAUH Flying Group	
						Seething 5. 2.08P
G-BAVB	Reims Cessna F172M	F17200965		10. 4.73	T S Sheridan-McGinnitty	Wolverhampton 20. 5.09E
G-BAVH	de Havilland DHC-1 Chipmunk 22	C1/0841	WP975	10. 4.73	D C Murray tr Portsmouth Naval Gliding Club	
	(Lycoming O-360)					Lee-on-Solent 27. 3.09S
G-BAVL	Piper PA-23-250 Aztec E	27-4671	N14063	10. 4.73	S P and A V Chilcott	Durham Tees Valley 11. 8.09E
G-BAVO	Boeing Stearman A75N1 Kaydet	?	4X-AIH	13. 4.73	M Shaw *(As "26" in US Army c/s)*	Old Buckenham 11. 7.10S
	(Continental W670) (Registered with c/n "3250-1405" which is part number: original identity unknown)					
G-BAVR	Grumman AA-5 Traveler	AA5-0348		12. 4.73	G E Murray	Swansea 29. 5.09E
G-BAWG	Piper PA-28R-200 Cherokee Arrow II	N11C	18. 4.73	Solent Air Ltd	Goodwood 19. 3.09E
		28R-7335133				
G-BAWK	Piper PA-28-140 Cherokee Cruiser	28-7325243		24. 4.73	J Stanley	(South Shields) 18.12.09E
G-BAWR	Robin HR.100-210 Safari II	156		27. 4.73	T Taylor *(Noted 3.05)*	Oxford 8. 6.00
G-BAXE	Hughes 269A-1 *(Hughes 300)*	113-0313	N8931F	2. 5.73	Reeve Newfields Ltd	Sywell 21.12.93S
				(Frame only noted 11.01)		
G-BAXS	Bell 47G-5	7908	5B-CFB	11. 5.73	R M Kemp tr RK Helicopters	Fairoaks 5. 6.09S
			G-BAXS, N4098G			
G-BAXU	Reims Cessna F150L	F15000959		14. 5.73	M W Sheppardson	Sibson 21. 7.09E
G-BAXV	Reims Cessna F150L	F15000966		14. 5.73	CBM Associates Consulting Ltd	Linley Hill, Leven 9. 7.09E
G-BAXY	Reims Cessna F172M	F17200905	N10636	15. 5.73	Eaglesoar Ltd	Humberside 14.11.09E
G-BAXZ	Piper PA-28-140 Cherokee C	28-26760	PH-NLX	15. 5.73	C Kearsley and D England tr G-BAXZ (87) Syndicate	
			N11C			Turweston 18. 4.09E
G-BAYO	Cessna 150L	15074435	N19471	18. 5.73	J A, G M, D T A and J A Rees	
					t/a Messrs Rees of Poyston West	Haverfordwest 18. 8.09E
G-BAYP	Cessna 150L	15074017	N18651	18. 5.73	D I Thomas tr Yankee Papa Flying Group	Popham 2. 6.09E
G-BAYR	Robin HR.100-210 Safari II	164		18. 5.73	P D Harries	Pembrey 2. 9.09E
G-BAZC	Robin DR.400-160 Knight	824		29. 5.73	R Jones tr Southern Sailplanes	Membury 24. 6.88
				(Damaged Crosland Moor 21.5.88: stored 10.01)		
G-BAZM	Jodel D 11	PAL 1416		31. 5.73	A F Simpson *"L'oiseau jaune"*	
	(Built Bingley Flying Group - pr.no.PFA 915 and identified as "D 113") (Continental O-200-A)			Watchford Farm, Yarcombe 4. 2.09P		
G-BAZS	Reims Cessna F150L	F15000954		1. 6.73	L W Scattergood *(Operated Sheffield City Flying School)*	
						Sandtoft 14. 1.09E
G-BAZT	Reims Cessna F172M	F17200996		1. 6.73	Exeter Flying Club Ltd	Exeter 16. 7.09E

G-BBAA - G-BBZZ

Reg	Type	c/n	Prev id	Date	Owner/Operator	Base/Date
G-BBAW	Robin HR.100-210 Safari II	167		12. 6.73	F A Purvis *(Noted 2.08)*	Bagby 19. 5.09E
G-BBAX	Robin DR.400-140 Earl	835		12. 6.73	G J Bissex and P H Garbutt	New Farm, Felton 31. 5.09E
G-BBAY	Robin DR.400-140 Earl	841		12. 6.73	J C Stubbs	Sibson 25. 5.09E
G-BBBB	Taylor JT.1 Monoplane	SAM/01		4. 6.73	P J Burgess	(Navenby, Lincoln)
	(Built S A MacConnacher - pr.no.PFA 1422)					
G-BBBC	Reims Cessna F150L	F15000864	N10635	14. 6.73	W J Greenfield	Humberside 24. 1.10E
G-BBBI	Grumman AA-5 Traveler	AA5-0392		15. 6.73	W Haddow tr Go Baby Aviation Group	Prestwick 2. 4.09E
G-BBBN	Piper PA-28-180 Cherokee Challenger	N11C	20. 6.73	Estuary Aviation Ltd	Southend 26.12.09E
		28-7305365				
G-BBBO	SIPA 903	67	F-BGBQ	16. 1.74	G E Morris	Bolt Head, Salcombe 9. 9.09P
G-BBBW	Clutton FRED Series II	DLW.1		26. 6.73	M Palfreman	Waterstones Farm, Newby Wiske 19. 6.08P
	(Built D Webster - pr.no.PFA 1551)					
G-BBBY	Piper PA-28-140 Cherokee Cruiser	N9501N	28. 6.73	W R and R Davies	RAF Mona 29. 7.09E
		28-7325533				
G-BBCA	Bell 206B-2 JetRanger II	1101	N18091	29. 6.73	Heliflight (UK) Ltd	Gloucestershire 23.10.09E
G-BBCB	Western O-65 Balloon (Hot Air)	018		29. 6.73	G M Bulmer *"Cee Bee"*	Credenhill, Hereford 19. 5.76S
G-BBCH	Robin DR.400 2+2	850		4. 7.73	S M Braithwaite and C R Thomas tr Oilburners (2006)	
					Flying Association	Bicester 31. 5.09E
G-BBCI	Cessna 150H	15069282	N50409	4. 7.73	A L and Farideh Alam	Cranfield 9. 8.08E
G-BBCN	Robin HR.100-210	168		11. 7.73	J C King	Bourne Park, Hurstbourne Tarrant 22. 9.06
G-BBCS	Robin DR.400-140B Earl	851		12. 7.73	B N Stevens	(Goole) 31. 5.09E
G-BBCY	Phoenix Luton LA-4A Minor	PFA 825		17. 7.73	J Angiolini and T D Boyle	Errol 15. 4.09P
	(Built C H Difford) (Volkswagen 1600)					
G-BBCZ	Grumman AA-5 Traveler	AA5-0382		18. 7.73	No.1 Investments Ltd	Thurrock 19.12.09E
G-BBDC	Piper PA-28-140 Cherokee Cruiser	N11C	18. 7.73	A Ball and P Grace tr G-BBDC Group	
		28-7325437				Earls Colne 26. 6.09E

Reg	Type	C/n	Prev id	Date	Owner/Operator	Base	CofA
G-BBDE	Piper PA-28R-200 Cherokee Arrow II	28R-7335250	(EI-...) G-BBDE, N11C	18. 7.73	R L Coleman, A Holt and A Crozier	Panshanger	31.10.09E
G-BBDH	Reims Cessna F172M	F17200990		19. 7.73	J D Woodward Franklyn's Field, Chewton Mendip		7. 8.09E
G-BBDJ	Thunder Ax6-56 Balloon (Hot Air)	006		20. 7.73	A D Kent tr Balloon Preservation Flying Group *Jack Tar*	Petworth	5. 8.82A
G-BBDL	Grumman AA-5 Traveler	AA5-0406		18. 7.73	P F Robertshaw tr Delta Lima Flying Group	Durham Tees Valley	3. 1.10E
G-BBDM	Grumman AA-5 Traveler	AA5-0407		18. 7.73	J Rees tr Jackeroo Aviation Group	Thruxton	24.11.09E
G-BBDO	Piper PA-23-250 Aztec E	27-7305120	N40361	24. 7.73	J W Anstee tr G-BBDO Flying Group	Filton	15. 9.09E
G-BBDP	Robin DR.400-160 Major	853		25. 7.73	Robin Lance Aviation Associates Ltd	Rochester	19.12.08E
G-BBDS	Piper PA-31 Turbo Navajo B	31-7300956	N97RJ G-SKKB, G-BBDS, N7565L	26. 7.73	Air Jota Ltd *(Operated Trans Euro Air)*	Southend Southend	17. 4.09E 17. 4.08E
G-BBDT	Cessna 150H	15068839	N23272	26. 7.73	J G N Wilson tr Delta Tango Group	Full Sutton	31. 7.09E
G-BBDV	SIPA 903	7/21	F-BEYY	30. 7.73	W McAndrew	Cardington	20. 6.08P
	(Continental C90) *(Originally ex F-BEYJ c/n 7 but rebuilt in 1978 from F-BEYY c/n 21)*						
G-BBEA	Phoenix Luton LA-4A Minor	PFA 843		30. 7.73	M Howland tr Echo Alpha Syndicate	Wickenby	17. 2.09P
	(Built G J Hewitt) (Volkswagen 1600)						
G-BBEB	Piper PA-28R-200 Cherokee Arrow II	28R-7335292	N9514N	31. 7.73	F J Stimpson and M J Potter	Old Sarum	18. 4.09E
G-BBEC	Piper PA-28-180 Cherokee Challenger	28-7305478	N11C	30. 7.73	A L Gardner	Ronaldsway	30. 5.09E
G-BBED	SOCATA MS.894A Rallye Minerva 220	12097		30. 7.73	C A Shelley t/a Vista Products *(Noted 7.05)* The Mill Industrial Estate, Alcester		13. 9.87T
G-BBEF	Piper PA-28-140 Cherokee Cruiser	28-7325527	N9500N	31. 7.73	CC Helicopters Ltd	Blackpool	7. 9.08E
	(Rebuilt using major components from damaged G-AVWG by 4.99)						
G-BBEN	Bellanca 7GCBC Citabria	496-73	(D-EAUT) N36416	7. 8.73	C A G Schofield Harpsden Court, Henley-on-Thames		10. 5.02
G-BBEX	Cessna 185A Skywagon	185-0491	EI-CMC G-BBEX, 4X-ALD, N99992, N1691Z	7. 8.73	F Byrne and V McCarthy tr Falcon Parachute Centre Hackettstown, County Carlow		27. 2.08E
G-BBFD	Piper PA-28R-200 Cherokee Arrow II	28R-7335342	N9517N	8. 8.73	C H Rose and A R Annable	White Waltham	3. 7.09E
G-BBFL	Gardan GY-201 Minicab	21	F-BHCQ	17. 8.73	R Smith	Roughay Farm, Bishops Waltham	1. 1.08P
	(Built SRCM) (Continental A65)						
G-BBFV	Piper PA-32-260 Cherokee Six	32-778	5Y-ADF	13. 8.73	D T Wright tr G-BBFV Syndicate	Wickenby	20. 7.09E
G-BBGC	SOCATA MS.893E Rallye 180GT	12215	F-BUCV	16. 8.73	P M Nolan	Kilkenny, County Kilkenny	26. 8.09E
G-BBGI	Fuji FA.200-160 Aero Subaru	FA200-228		21. 8.73	P and A West	Henstridge	31. 3.09E
G-BBGL	Oldfield Baby Lakes	7223-B412-B		22. 8.73	F J Ball	Jubilee Farm, Wisbech St Mary	21. 3.02P
	(Built D S Morgan - pr.no.PFA 1593) (Continental C90)						
G-BBGZ	Cambridge Hot Air Balloon Assn CHABA 42 Balloon	CHABA 42		31. 8.73	J L Hinton, G Laslett and R A Laslett *"Phlogiston"* (Inflated 4.02) Bishopston, Bristol		
G-BBHF	Piper PA-23-250 Aztec E	27-7305166	N40453	5. 9.73	G J Williams	Sherburn-in-Elmet	12. 8.09E
G-BBHI	Cessna 177RG Cardinal RG	177RG0225	5Y-ANX N1825Q	7. 9.73	T G W Bunce	Newtownards	20.12.08E
G-BBHJ	Piper J-3C-85 Cub	16378	OO-GEC	7. 9.73	P Dyer tr Wellcross Flying Group		4. 6.07P
	(Frame No.16037)				New Barn Farm, Barton Ashes, Crawley		
G-BBHK	Noorduyn AT-16-ND Harvard IIB	14-787	PH-PPS (PH-HTC), R Neth AF B-158, FH153, 42-12540	7. 9.73	Sheringham Aviation UK Ltd *(As "FH153: 58" in 8SFTS c/s)* Wycombe Air Park		5. 7.09P
G-BBHY	Piper PA-28-180 Cherokee Challenger	28-7305474	EI-BBS G-BBHY, N9508N	7. 9.73	Air Operations Ltd	Guernsey	6. 7.09E
G-BBIF	Piper PA-23-250 Aztec E	27-7305234	N9736N	10. 9.73	D M Davies *"Flying Miss Daisie"*	Tatenhill	5.12.08E
G-BBIH	Enstrom F-28A-UK	026	N4875	12. 9.73	Freibe France Aeronautique SARL Cannes la Bocca, France		28. 6.02T
G-BBII	Fiat G 46-3B	44	I-AEHU MM52801	13. 9.73	G-BBII Ltd	Wycombe Air Park	14. 9.09P
	(As "44mm52801:"97" [black]-"4" [red] in Italian AF c/s)						
G-BBIL	Piper PA-28-140 Cherokee	28-22567	SE-FAR N4219J	13. 9.73	B W Hewison tr Saxondale Group	North Weald	18. 7.09E
G-BBIO	Robin HR.100-210 Safari II	178		14. 9.73	R P Caley Eddsfield, Octon Lodge Farm, Thwing		5.12.08E
G-BBIX	Piper PA-28-140 Cherokee E	28-7225442	LN-AEN	17. 9.73	F A Griffiths and R A Lee tr Sterling Aviation White Waltham		21. 2.10E
G-BBJI	Isaacs Spitfire	2		18. 9.73	R F Cresswell	Shipdham	26. 6.07P
	(Built J O Isaacs - pr.no.PFA 027-10055) (Continental O-200-A)						
	(Collided with hangar during propeller swing Gamston mid 2006 and substantially damaged: wings only noted Shipdham 6.08)						
G-BBJU	Robin DR.400-140 Earl	874		19. 9.73	J C Lister tr Victor Sierra Aero Club Valley Farm, Winwick		13. 6.09E
G-BBJV	Reims Cessna F177RG Cardinal RG	F177RG0098		20. 9.73	P R Powell	Shobdon	2. 4.09E
G-BBJX	Reims Cessna F150L	F15001017		20. 9.73	L W Scattergood *(Operated Sheffield City Flying School)* Sandtoft		4.12.09E
G-BBJY	Reims Cessna F172M Skyhawk II	F17201075		20. 9.73	Cardinal Sin Ltd t/a Staverton Flying School Gloucestershire		30. 6.09E
G-BBJZ	Reims Cessna F172M Skyhawk II	F17201035		20. 9.73	J K and J A Green	Gamston	28.2.09E
G-BBKA	Reims Cessna F150L	F15001029		20. 9.73	W M Wilson	North Moor, Scunthorpe	13. 3.09E
G-BBKB	Reims Cessna F150L	F15001030		20. 9.73	Justgold Ltd *(Operated Blackpool Air Centre)* Blackpool		7. 5.09E
G-BBKE	Reims Cessna F150L	F15001026		20. 9.73	Xpedite (UK) Ltd	Cranfield	3.10.08E
G-BBKG	Reims FR172J Rocket	FR17200465		20. 9.73	R Wright	Coventry	3. 4.09E
G-BBKI	Reims Cessna F172M Skyhawk II	F17201069		20. 9.73	C W and S A Burman *(Dismantled 1.07)* East Winch		16. 3.09E
G-BBKL	Menavia Piel CP.301A Emeraude	237	F-BIMK	21. 9.73	R K Griggs tr Piel G-BBKL	Perth	13. 6.03P
	(Substantially damaged in heavy landing Perth 3. 5.03: noted 12.08)						
G-BBKX	Piper PA-28-180 Cherokee Challenger	28-7305581	N9550N	26. 9.73	RAE Aero Club Ltd	Farnborough	25.11.09E
G-BBKY	Reims Cessna F150L	F15000991		26. 9.73	F W Astbury	Barton	12. 3.09E
G-BBKZ	Cessna 172M Skyhawk	17261495	N20694	27. 9.73	R S Thomson tr KZ Flying Group	Dunkeswell	13. 5.09T

Reg	Type	c/n	Prev ID	Date	Owner/Operator	Base	Fate
G-BBLH	Piper J-3C-65 Cub (L-4B-PI)	10006	F-BFQY	24. 9.73	Shipping and Airlines Ltd	Biggin Hill	29. 6.11S
	(Frame No.9838) (Regd with c/n 10549)		French.Military, 43-1145		*(As "31145:G-26" in 183rd Field Battalion US Army c/s)*		
G-BBLM	SOCATA Rallye 100S	2392		3.10.73	J R Rodgers	Wolverhampton	8. 5.08E
G-BBLS	Grumman AA-5 Traveler	AA5-0440	EI-AYM	8.10.73	A Grant	Perth	15. 8.09E
			G-BBLS				
G-BBLU	Piper PA-34-200 Seneca	34-7350271	N55984	8.10.73	R H R Rue	Turweston	15. 7.09E
G-BBMB	Robin DR.400-180 Régent	848	5Y-ASB	27. 9.73	I James tr Régent Flying Group		
						King's Farm, Thurrock	5. 5.09E
G-BBMH	EAA Biplane Sport Model P1	PFA 1348		11.10.73	M V Batin tr G-BBMH Flying Group	RAF Benson	24. 4.09P
	(Built K Dawson) (Continental C90-14F)						
G-BBMJ	Piper PA-23-250 Aztec E	27-7305150	N40387	12.10.73	Nationwide Caravan Rental Services Ltd		
						Hawarden	24. 3.09E
G-BBMN	de Havilland DHC-1 Chipmunk 22	C1/0300	WD359	12.10.73	R Steiner "3"	North Weald	22. 7.11
G-BBMO	de Havilland DHC-1 Chipmunk 22	C1/0550	WK514	12.10.73	D Squires tr Mike Oscar Group *(As "WK514" in RAF c/s)*		
						Wellesbourne Mountford	10. 6.10
G-BBMR	de Havilland DHC-1 Chipmunk 22	C1/0213	WB763	12.10.73	P J Wood *(Noted 6.08 on rebuild)*	Bodmin	
G-BBMT	de Havilland DHC-1 Chipmunk 22	C1/0712	WP831	12.10.73	J Evans and D Withers tr MT Group		
						Graveley Hall Farm, Graveley	27. 6.10S
G-BBMV	de Havilland DHC-1 Chipmunk 22	C1/0432	WG348	12.10.73	S G Howell and S P Tilling *(As "WG348" in RAF c/s)*		
						Biggin Hill	28. 4.09
G-BBMW	de Havilland DHC-1 Chipmunk 22	C1/0641	WK628	12.10.73	G Fielder and A Wilson *(As "WK628" in RAF c/s)*		
						Goodwood	24. 9.11
G-BBMX	de Havilland DHC-1 Chipmunk 22	C1/0800	WP924	12.10.73	M I Koch	Sonderberg, Denmark	24. 8.08S
G-BBMZ	de Havilland DHC-1 Chipmunk 22	C1/0563	WK548	12.10.73	W N Gibson tr G-BBMZ Chipmunk Symdicate		
						Wycombe Air Park	28. 2.10
G-BBNA	de Havilland DHC-1 Chipmunk 22	C1/0491	WG417	12.10.73	Coventry Gliding Club Ltd	Husbands Bosworth	20. 7.09
	(Lycoming O-360)						
G-BBND	de Havilland DHC-1 Chipmunk 22	C1/0225	WD286	12.10.73	W Norton and D Fradley tr Bernoulli Syndicate		
					(As "WD286" in RAF silver with yellow bands c/s) Little Gransden		18. 5.07S
G-BBNH	Piper PA-34-200 Seneca	34-7350339	N56492	16.10.73	A L Howell, A P Barrow and M G D Baverstock		
						Bournemouth	22. 4.09E
G-BBNI	Piper PA-34-200 Seneca	34-7350312	N56286	16.10.73	M P Grimshaw	North Weald	5. 2.09E
G-BBNJ	Reims Cessna F150L	F15001038		16.10.73	Sherburn Aero Club Ltd	Sherburn-in-Elmet	16.12.09E
G-BBNT	Piper PA-31-350 Navajo Chieftain		EI-CNM	22.10.73	M P Goss	Belfast City	23. 1.10E
		31-7305107	N1201H, G-BBNT, N74958				
G-BBNZ	Reims Cessna F172M Skyhawk II	F17201054		23.10.73	R E Nunn	Clipgate Farm, Denton	31. 7.09E
G-BBOA	Reims Cessna F172M Skyhawk II	F17201066		23.10.73	J D and A M Black	Lodge Farm, St Osyth	3. 8.09E
G-BBOC	Cameron O-77 Balloon (Hot Air)	86		24.10.73	J A B Gray *"Bacchus"*	Daglingworth, Cirencester	6. 1.90A
G-BBOD	Thunder O-5 Balloon (Hot Air)	013		24.10.73	B R and M.Boyle *"Little Titch"*	Budbrooke, Warwick	
G-BBOE	Robin HR.200-100 Club	26		24.10.73	R J Powell	(Wickham, Hampshire)	7. 7.02
	(Badly damaged striking hedge and concrete post landing Wells Cross Farm, Horsham 24.6.01: dismantled)						
G-BBOH	Craft-Pitts S-1S	AJEP-P-S1-S-1		25.10.73	Techair London Ltd *(Noted 5.07)*		
	(Built Pitts Aviation Enterprises Inc - pr.no.PFA 1570)					Rotary Farm, Hatch	8. 9.97P
G-BBOL	Piper PA-18-150 Super Cub	18-7561	D-EMFE	26.10.73	N Artt	Aston Down	18. 7.10
			N3821Z				
G-BBOO	Thunder Ax6-56 Balloon (Hot Air)	012		4.10.73	K Meehan *"Tiger Jack"*	Much Wenlock	31. 5.03A
G-BBOR	Bell 206B-2 JetRanger II	1197	(SE-)	30.10.73	M J Easey	Town Farm, Hoxne, Eye	29. 7.09E
			G-BBOR				
G-BBOX	Thunder Ax7-77 Balloon (Hot Air)	011		24.10.73	The British Balloon Museum and Library Ltd *"Rocinante"*		
					(Inflated 4.06)	Newbury	23.12.82A
G-BBPN	Enstrom F-28A-UK	166		30.10.73	D W C Holmes	Ormonde Fields, Codnor	31. 5.08E
	(Crashed into trees near Ormonde Fields Golf Course, Codnor, Derbyshire 12. 6.07 and substantially damaged)						
G-BBPO	Enstrom F-28A	176		30.10.73	Henfield Lodge Aviation Ltd	Shoreham	1. 4.09E
G-BBPP	Piper PA-28-180 Cherokee Archer		G-WACP	5. 4.89	Big Red Kite Ltd	RAF Benson	30. 7.09E
		28-7405007	G-BBPP, N9559N				
G-BBPS	SAN Jodel D 117	597	F-BHXS	30.10.73	A Appleby	Westfield Farm, Hailsham	29. 4.09P
G-BBPX	Piper PA-34-200 Seneca	34-7250262	N1202T	7.11.73	M Corbett tr The G-BBPX Flying Group		
						Blackbushe	15. 4.09E
G-BBPY	Piper PA-28-180 Cherokee Challenger		N9554N	8.11.73	Sunsaver Ltd	Barton	4. 9.09E
		28-7305590					
G-BBRA	Piper PA-23-250 Aztec E	27-7305197	N40479	12.11.73	R C Lough	Stapleford	23. 7.09E
G-BBRB	de Havilland DH.82A Tiger Moth	85934	OO-EVB	21.11.73	R Barham *(Damaged Biggin Hill 16. 1.87)*		
			Belgian AF T-8, ETA-8, DF198			(West Wickham)	
G-BBRC	Fuji FA.200-180 Aero Subaru	FA200-235		8.11.73	G-BBRC Ltd	Blackbushe	25. 6.09E
G-BBRI	Bell 47G-5A	25158	N18092	8.11.73	Alan Mann Helicopters Ltd	(Fairoaks)	28. 7.02T
	(Composite following several major rebuilds)						
G-BBRN	Mitchell-Procter Kittiwake I	02	XW784	20.11.73	H M Price *(As "XW784:VL" in RN c/s) (Noted 3.06)*		
	(Built Air Engineering, HMS Daedalus - pr.no.PFA 1352)					RNAS Yeovilton	8. 9.05P
	(Continental O-200-A)						
G-BBRV	de Havilland DHC-1 Chipmunk 22	C1/0284	WD347	13.11.73	R L Emeleus	Spanhoe	7. 8.09S
					(As "WD347" in RAF grey and orange dayglo stripes)		
G-BBRX	SIAI-Marchetti S 205-18F	342	LN-VYH	13.11.73	C T Findon and J B Owens	Errol	27. 4.09E
			OO-HAQ				
G-BBRZ	Grumman AA-5 Traveler	AA5-0471	(EI-AYV)	15.11.73	B McIntyre	(Movenis)	2.10.09E
			G-BBRZ				
G-BBSA	Grumman AA-5 Traveler	AA5-0472		15.11.73	Usworth 84 Flying Associates Ltd		
						Durham Tees Valley	16. 4.09E
G-BBSB	Beech C23 Sundowner 180	M-1516		15.11.73	L J Welsh	Perth	2. 8.08E
G-BBSM	Piper PA-32-300 Cherokee Six	32-7440005	N9577N	14.11.73	G C Collings	Hardwick	5. 9.09E
G-BBSS	de Havilland DHC-1 Chipmunk 22	C1/0520	WG470	21.11.73	Coventry Gliding Club Ltd	Husbands Bosworth	21. 5.10S
	(Lycoming O-360)						
G-BBSW	Pietenpol AirCamper	PFA 1506		21.11.73	J K S Wills	(London SE3)	
	(Built J K S Wills)						

G-BBTB	Reims Cessna FRA150L Aerobat			26.11.73	Global Engineering and Maintenance Ltd		
		FRA1500224				Bournemouth	31. 7.09E
G-BBTG	Reims Cessna F172M Skyhawk II	F17201097		26.11.73	L W Huson tr Triple X Flying Group	Biggin Hill	27. 5.09E
G-BBTH	Reims Cessna F172M Skyhawk II	F17201089		26.11.73	Tayside Aviation Ltd	Glenrothes	20. 9.09E
G-BBTJ	Piper PA-23-250 Aztec E	27-7305131	N40369	27.11.73	Cooper Aerial Surveys Ltd	Wickenby	16. 4.09E
G-BBTS	Beech V35B Bonanza	D-9551	N3051W	29.11.73	S Wenham t/a Eastern Air		
						Cannes-Mandelieu, Monaco	5. 6.03
G-BBTY	Beech C23 Sundowner 180	M-1525		29.11.73	A W Roderick and W Price tr TY Group	Cardiff	18. 9.09E
G-BBUE	Grumman AA-5 Traveler	0479		6.12.73	O Balland and T Shotton	Tatenhill	30. 1.09E
G-BBUF	Grumman AA-5 Traveler	0480		6.12.73	G S McNaughton	Prestwick	23. 1.09E
G-BBUG	Piper PA-16 Clipper	16-29	F-BFMC	6.12.73	J Dolan	Enniskillen	28. 8.08E
G-BBUT	Western O-65 Balloon (Hot Air)	020		11.12.73	R G Turnbull "Christabelle II"	Clyro, Hereford	5. 6.06A
G-BBUU	Piper J-3C-75 Cub (L-4A-PI)	10529	F-BBSQ	14. 1.74	C Stokes	Hulcote Farm, Milton Keynes	11. 5.09P
	(Frame No.10354)		F-OAEZ, French AF, 43-29238				
G-BBVO	Isaacs Fury II	PFA 011-10091		20.12.73	R W Hinton	(Woolpit, Bury St Edmunds)	19. 6.09P
	(Built D Silsbury) (Lycoming O-320)				(As "S1579:571" [Hawker Nimrod] of RN FAA 408 Flight, HMS Glorious)		
G-BBWZ	Grumman AA-1B Trainer	AA1B-0334		4. 1.74	A C Jacobs		
						East Winch/Muchiamel, Alicante, Spain	20. 8.09E
G-BBXB	Reims Cessna FRA150L Aerobat			16. 1.74	C and M Laycock	Full Sutton	25.11.09E
		FRA1500236					
G-BBXK	Piper PA-34-200 Seneca	34-7450056	N54366	21. 1.74	J A Rees (Operated Haverfordwest Flight Centre)		
						Haverfordwest	7. 4.08E
G-BBXL	Cessna 310Q II	310Q1076	EI-CLX	21. 1.74	D H Madden and J Phelan tr MD Aviation Group		
			G-BBXL, (N1223G)			(Craigavon and Lisburn)	19. 9.08E
G-BBXS	Piper J-3C-65 Cub (L-4H-PI)	12214	N9865F	25. 1.74	M J Butler (Noted 11.01)	Spanhoe	14. 9.00P
	(Continental C90) (Frame No.12042)		G-ALMA, 44-79918				
	(Officially regd as c/n "9865")						
G-BBXW	Piper PA-28-151 Cherokee Warrior		PH-CPL	21. 1.74	Bristol Aero Club	Filton	20.11.09E
		28-7415050	G-BBXW, N9599N				
G-BBXY	Bellanca 7GCBC Citabria	614-74	N57639	1. 2.74	R R L Windus	Truleigh Manor Farm, Edburton	12. 3.08E
G-BBXZ	Evans VP-1	PFA 1562		31. 1.74	R W Burrows	Swanton Morley	8. 3.96P
	(Built G D Price) (Volkswagen 1600)				(Noted wingless 4.02)		
G-BBYB	Piper PA-18 Super Cub 95 (L-18C-PI) 18-1627		PH-TMA	4. 2.74	The Tiger Club (1990) Ltd	Headcorn	26. 7.07T
	(Frame No.18-1628)		(D-ENCH), French Army 18-1627, 51-15627				
					(Nosed over on take-off Headcorn 17. 3.07: damage to wings and tail)		
G-BBYH	Cessna 182P	18262814	N52744	6. 2.74	Ramco (UK) Ltd	Poplar Farm, Croft, Skegness	18. 5.09E
G-BBYP	Piper PA-28-140 Cherokee F	28-7425158	N9620N	19. 2.74	E Williams	(Abergele)	9.12.09E
G-BBYS	Cessna 182P Skylane	18261520	5Y-ATE	14. 2.74	I M Jones	Gamston	14. 7.09E
			N21256				
G-BBZF	Piper PA-28-140 Cherokee F	28-7425195	N9501N	19. 2.74	C Higgins, C Harte and I O'Brien		
						Waterford, County Waterford	25. 9.08E
G-BBZH	Piper PA-28R-200 Cherokee Arrow II		N9608N	22. 2.74	S I Tugwell	Stapleford	10. 6.09E
		28R-7435102					
G-BBZN	Fuji FA.200-180 Aero Subaru	FA200-230		26. 2.74	D Kynaston, J S V Westwood and P D Wedd		
						Cambridge	18. 3.09E
G-BBZV	Piper PA-28R-200 Cherokee Arrow II		N9609N	11. 3.74	P B Mellor	Standalone Farm, Meppershall	29. 1.10E
		28R-7435105					

G-BCAA - G-BCZZ

G-BCAH	de Havilland DHC-1 Chipmunk 22	C1/0372	WG316	6. 5.74	A W Eldridge (As "WG316" in RAF c/s)	Leicester	25. 6.11
G-BCAZ	Piper PA-12 Super Cruiser	12-2312	5Y-KGK	12. 3.74	A D Williams	Rhos-y-Gilwen Farm, Rhos Hill	5.11.11
			VP-KGK, ZS-BYJ, ZS-BPH				
G-BCBG	Piper PA-23-250 Aztec E	27-7305224	VP-BBN	13. 3.74	M J L Batt	Wycombe Air Park	3. 2.10E
			VR-BBN, (VR-BDM), G-BCBG, N40494				
G-BCBH	Fairchild 24R-46A Argus III	975	(VH-AAQ)	13. 3.74	Dreamticket Promotions Ltd	Spanhoe	28. 6.09S
	(UC-61K-FA)		G-BCBH, ZS-AXH, HB737, 43-15011				
G-BCBJ	Piper PA-25-235 Pawnee C	25-2380/R		18. 3.74	Deeside Gliding Club (Aberdeenshire) Ltd	Aboyne	2. 9.09E
	(Rebuild of G-ASLA { 25-2380))						
G-BCBL	Fairchild 24R-46A Argus III	989	OO-EKE	19. 3.74	F J Cox	Gorrel Farm, Woolsery, Bideford	31. 3.96
	(UC-61K-FA)		D-EKEQ, HB-AEC, HB751, 43-15025				
G-BCBR	Wittman W.8 Tailwind	TW3-380		20. 3.74	D P Jones	Top Farm, Croydon, Royston	2. 8.09P
	(Built AJEP Developments)						
G-BCBX	Reims Cessna F150L	F15001001	F-BUEO	25. 3.74	Merseyflight Ltd	Liverpool	15. 4.08E
G-BCBZ	Cessna 337C Super Skymaster	3370942	SE-FKB	28. 3.74	J Haden	Jersey	30. 5.08E
	(Robertson STOL conversion)		N2642S				
G-BCCC	Reims Cessna F150L	F15001041		8. 4.74	A Mitchell tr Treble Charlie Flying Group	Cranfield	25. 4.09E
G-BCCE	Piper PA-23-250 Aztec E	27-7405282	N40544	3. 4.74	Golf Charlie Echo Ltd (Operated The Flying Hut)		
						Shoreham	28. 2.09E
G-BCCF	Piper PA-28-180 Cherokee Archer		N9632N	3. 4.74	Top Cat Aviation Ltd (Operated Manchester School of Flying)		
		28-7405069				Sleap	5. 8.09E
G-BCCG	Thunder Ax7-65 Balloon (Hot Air)	020		4. 4.74	N H Ponsford t/a Rango Balloon and Kite Company		
					"Zephyr" (Active 99)	Leeds	7.11.83A
G-BCCJ	Grumman AA-5 Traveler	AA5-0546		8. 4.74	T Needham	Exeter	26. 4.08
G-BCCK	Grumman AA-5 Traveler	AA5-0547		8. 4.74	Prospect Air Ltd (Operated Manchester School of Flying)		
						Manchester	19. 9.09E
G-BCCR	Piel CP.301A Emeraude	PFA 712		8. 4.74	J H and C J Waterman		
	(Built Korist Flying Group) (Continental O-200-A)					Armshold Farm, Kingston, Cambridge	23. 2.09P
G-BCCX	de Havilland DHC-1 Chipmunk 22	C1/0531	WG481	17. 4.74	T M Holloway tr RAF Gliding and Soaring Association		
	(Lycoming O-360)				(Operated Cleveland Gliding Club)	AAC Dishforth	11. 5.09S
G-BCCY	Robin HR.200-100 Club	37		18. 4.74	M E Hicks	St Mary's, Isles of Scilly	27. 4.09E
G-BCDJ	Piper PA-28-140 Cherokee	28-24276	PH-NLV	29. 4.74	T J Addison (Operated Air Navigation and Trading)		
			N1841J				Blackpool	6. 3.09E

Reg	Type	C/n	Prev id	Date	Owner/Operator	Location	
G-BCDK (2)	Partenavia P68B	32	A6-ALN	4. 7.75	Mach 014 SAS Di Albertaion Michele and Co		
			G-BCDK			Aqui Terme, Italy	11. 9.08
G-BCDL	Cameron O-42 Balloon (Hot Air)	115		24. 4.74	D P and B O Turner *"Chums"*		
						Leigh upon Mendip, Radstock	13. 7.83A
G-BCDY	Reims Cessna FRA150L Aerobat			7. 5.74	R L Nunn and T R Edwards King's Farm, Thurrock		20. 8.09E
		FRA1500237					
G-BCEA	Sikorsky S-61N Mk.II	61-721		7. 6.74	British International Ltd	Falkland Islands	13. 7.09E
G-BCEB	Sikorsky S-61NM Mk.II	61-454	N4023S	2.10.74	Bitish International Helicopter Services Ltd t/a British		
					International *"The Isles of Scilly"* Penzance Heliport		16.12.08E
G-BCEE	Grumman AA-5 Traveler	AA5-0571		7. 5.74	P J Marchant	RAF Henlow	17.12.09E
G-BCEF	Grumman AA-5 Traveler	AA5-0572		7. 5.74	D G Price tr G-BCEF Group	Enstone	9. 6.09E
G-BCEN	Fairey Britten-Norman BN-2A-26 Islander	403	4X-AYG	6. 5.74	Reconnaissance Ventures Ltd	Manston	7.11.09E
			SX-BFB, 4X-AYG, N90JA, G-BCEN *(Operated Marine and Coastguard Agency)*				
G-BCEP	Grumman AA-5 Traveler	AA5-0576		7. 5.74	Orchard Motor Co Ltd	Southend	25.11.09E
G-BCER	Gardan GY-201 Minicab	8	F-BGJP	8. 5.74	D Beaumont	West Freugh	21. 5.08P
	(Built Con. Aéronautique de Bearn) (Continental A65)						
G-BCEU	Cameron O-42 Balloon (Hot Air)	111		9. 5.74	P Glydon	Knowle, Bristol	31. 5.85A
G-BCEX	Piper PA-23-250 Aztec E	27-7305024	N40225	13. 5.74	I Kazi Stoneacre Farm, Farthing Corner		27. 5.09E
G-BCEY	de Havilland DHC-1 Chipmunk 22	C1/0515	WG465	14. 5.74	T C B Dehn and C A Robey tr Gopher Flying Group		
					(As "WG465" in RAF c/s)	White Waltham	2.10.08S
G-BCFF	Fuji FA.200-160 Aero Subaru	FA200-237		21. 5.74	S A Cole	Exeter	13. 5.09E
G-BCFN	Cameron O-65 Balloon (Hot Air)	109		23. 5.74	W G Johnston and H M Savage *"Fireball" (Noted 6.00)*		
						Edinburgh	15. 5.77S
G-BCFO	Piper PA-18-150 Super Cub	18-5335	(D-EIOZ)	29. 5.74	D C Murray tr Portsmouth Naval Gliding Club		
			French Army 18-5335, N10F			Lee-on-the-Solent	13. 5.07
G-BCFR	Reims Cessna FRA150L Aerobat			30. 5.74	M Garrard tr Foxtrot Romeo Group,	Earls Colne	2. 2.10E
		FRA1500244					
G-BCFW	SAAB 91D Safir	91-437	PH-RLZ	29. 5.74	D R Williams *(Stored 8.08)*	Peplow	24. 7.06
G-BCFY	Phoenix Luton LA-4A Minor	PAL 1301		29. 5.74	G Capes *(Stored 8.92)*	(Welton, Brough)	17. 1 92P
	(Built G F M Garner - pr.no.PFA 824) (Ardem Mk.6)						
G-BCGB	Bensen B 8	PCL-14		3. 6.74	J W Birkett	Little Rissington	19. 8.08P
	(Built P C Lovegrove) (Rotax 503)						
G-BCGC	de Havilland DHC-1 Chipmunk 22	C1/0776	WP903	13. 3.74	J C Wright tr Henlow Chipmunk Group		
					(As "WP903" in Queen's Flight c/s)	RAF Henlow	2. 8.10S
G-BCGH	SNCAN NC.854S	122	F-BAFG	10. 6.74	T J N H Palmer tr Nord Flying Group		
						Hill Farm, Nayland	28. 5.09P
G-BCGI	Piper PA-28-140 Cherokee Cruiser		N9573N	10. 6.74	G Hurst	Barton	30. 9.09E
		28-7425283					
G-BCGJ	Piper PA-28-140 Cherokee Cruiser		N9574N	10. 6.74	Demero Ltd and Transcourt Ltd		
		28-7425286				Hinton-in-the-Hedges	4.11.09E
G-BCGM	Wassmer Jodel D 120 Paris-Nice	50	F-BHQM	15. 7.74	N J Orchard-Armitage	Rochester	22. 7.09P
			F-BHYM				
G-BCGN	Piper PA-28-140 Cherokee F	28-7425323	N9595N	10. 6.74	Golf November Ltd	Oxford	9.10.09E
G-BCGS	Piper PA-28R-200 Cherokee Arrow II		N4893T	13. 6.74	S Rayne tr Arrow Aviation Group	Little Gransden	1. 9.09E
		28R-7235133					
G-BCGW	Jodel D 11	CC.001		14. 6.74	G H and M D Chittenden	(London NW7)	30. 1.85P
	(Built G H and M D Chittenden - pr.no.PFA 912 & EAA/61554) (Lycoming O-290)						
G-BCHK	Reims Cessna F172H	F17200716	9H-AAD	19. 6.74	D Darby *(Noted 7.04)*	Haverfordwest	23.11.03T
G-BCHL	de Havilland DHC-1 Chipmunk 22A	C1/0680	WP788	20. 6.74	Shropshire Soaring Ltd *(As "WP788" in RAF c/s)*		
						Sleap	2. 2.10S
G-BCHP	Scintex CP.1310-C3 Super Emeraude	902	G-JOSI	24. 6.74	G and A G Hughes	Earls Colne	2. 7.09P
			G-BCHP, F-BJVQ				
G-BCHT	Schleicher ASK 16	16021	BGA1996	25. 6.74	D E Cadisch tr Dunstable K16 Group	Dunstable	2. 7.09E
			D-KAMY				
G-BCHV	de Havilland DHC-1 Chipmunk 22	C1/0703	WP807	27. 6.74	K I Sutherland	(Stevington, Bedford)	20. 6.98
G-BCID	Piper PA-34-200 Seneca	34-7250303	N1381T	3. 7.74	Shenley Farms (Aviation) Ltd	Headcorn	9.11.09E
G-BCIH	de Havilland DHC-1 Chipmunk 22	C1/0304	WD363	3. 7.74	J M Hosey *(As "WD363" in RAF c/s)*	Audley End	12. 6.09S
G-BCIJ	Grumman AA-5 Traveler	AA5-0603	N6143A	3. 7.74	D G Page tr Arrow Association	Elstree	11. 7.09E
G-BCIN	Thunder Ax7-77 Balloon (Hot Air)	030		5. 7.74	R A, P M G and N T M Vale *(Tethered 9.05)*		
						Hurcott, Kidderminster	5. 5.84A
G-BCIR	Piper PA-28-151 Cherokee Warrior		N9587N	9. 7.74	R W Harris *(Operated Willowair Flying Club)*		
		28-7415401				Southend	21.12.09E
G-BCJM	Piper PA-28-140 Cherokee F	28-7425321	N9592N	17. 7.74	APB Leasing Ltd	Swansea	5. 3.09E
G-BCJN	Piper PA-28-140 Cherokee Cruiser		N9618N	17. 7.74	Top Cat Aviation Ltd *(Operated Manchester School of Flying)*		
		28-7425350				Manchester	8. 9.08E
G-BCJO	Piper PA-28R-200 Cherokee Arrow II		N9640N	17. 7.74	R Ross	Inverness	4. 9.09E
		28R-7435272					
G-BCJP	Piper PA-28-140 Cherokee	28-24187	N1766J	15. 8.74	J Wilson	Newtownards	19. 5.09E
G-BCKN	de Havilland DHC-1 Chipmunk 22	C1/0707	WP811	5. 8.74	T M Holloway tr RAF Gliding and Soaring Association		
	(Lycoming O-360)				*(Operated Cranwell Gliding Club)*	RAF Cranwell	20. 2.10S
G-BCKS	Fuji FA.200-180AO Aero Subaru	FA200-250		2. 8.74	S Hyland	Dunkeswell	14. 6.09E
G-BCKT	Fuji FA.200-180 Aero Subaru	FA200-251		2. 8.74	A G Dobson	(Rallt)	20. 7.09E
G-BCKU	Reims Cessna FRA150L Aerobat			1. 8.74	Stapleford Flying Club Ltd	Stapleford	9.11.09E
		FRA1500256					
G-BCKV	Reims Cessna FRA150L Aerobat			1. 8.74	Blastaway Leasing Ltd	Full Sutton	8. 8.09E
		FRA1500251					
G-BCLD	Sikorsky S-61N Mk.II	61-739	9M-BED	4. 2.75	Bristow Helicopters Ltd	Humberside	7. 8.09E
			G-BCLD				
G-BCLI	Grumman AA-5 Traveler	AA5-0643		12. 8.74	W D Smith	Lee-on-Solent	6. 2.09E
G-BCLL	Piper PA-28-180 Cherokee C	28-2400	SE-EON	13. 8.74	J Nash tr G-BCLL Group	Popham	14.11.07E
G-BCLS	Cessna 170B	20946	N8094A	23. 8.74	N Simpson	(Chapel Hill, Lincoln)	6. 7.11S
G-BCLT	SOCATA MS.894A Rallye Minerva 220	12003	EI-BBW	1. 8.74	K M Bowen *(stored 9.08)* Upfield Farm, Whitson		17. 7.05
			G-BCLT, F-BTRL				
G-BCLU	SAN Jodel D 117	506	F-BHXG	28. 8.74	J B Dovey	Crowfield	29. 5.09P

Reg	Type	C/n	Prev id	Date	Owner / Notes	Base / Date
G-BCLW	Grumman AA-1B Trainer	AA1B-0463		29. 8.74	C R White	Conington 20.12.09E
G-BCMD	Piper PA-18 Super Cub 95	18-2055	OO-SPF	4. 9.74	P Stephenson	Great Oakley 5. 7.11S
	(L-18C-PI) (Frame No.18-2071)		R Neth AF R-70, 52-2455			
G-BCMJ	K & S SA.102.5 Cavalier	MJ.1		9. 9.74	N F Andrews	(Oakham) 8. 8.85P
	(Built M Johnson - pr.no.PFA 001-1546) (Tailwheel u/c)					
G-BCMT	Isaacs Fury II	PFA 1522		9. 9.74	R W Burrows	Priory Farm, Tibenham
	(Built M H Turner) (Continental O-200-A)					
G-BCNC	Gardan GY-201 Minicab	A 202	F-BICF	9. 9.74	J R Wraight	(Chatham)
	(Built Nouvelle Soc Cometal)					
G-BCNP	Cameron O-77 Balloon (Hot Air)	117		16. 9.74	P Spellward *"Blue Fret"*	Bristol 28. 7.00A
G-BCNX	Piper J-3C-65 Cub *(L-4H-PI)*	11168	F-BEGM	17. 9.74	K J Lord tr The Grasshopper Flying Group	
	(Frame No.10993)		French AF, 43-29877			Cherry Tree Farm, Monewden 20. 4.09P
G-BCNZ	Fuji FA.200-160 Aero Subaru	FA200-257		16. 9.74	W Dougan	Prestwick 23. 2.08E
G-BCOB	Piper J-3C-65 Cub *(L-4H-PI)*	10696	F-BCPV	19. 9.74	J W Marjoram *(As "329405:A-23" in USAAC c/s)*	
	(Frame No.10521)		43-29405			Low Farm, South Walsham 2. 7.09P
G-BCOI	de Havilland DHC-1 Chipmunk 22	C1/0759	WP870	24. 9.74	M J Diggins *(As "WP870:12" in RAF grey c/s)*	
						Rayne Hall Farm, Braintree 21. 5.11E
G-BCOJ	Cameron O-56 Balloon (Hot Air)	124		25. 9.74	T J Knott and M J Webber tr Phoenix Balloon Group	
					"Red Squirrel"	Rickmansworth 12. 7.87A
G-BCOL	Reims Cessna F172M Skyhawk II	F17201233		25. 9.74	M Power tr November Charlie Flying Group	
						Gamston 15. 7.09E
G-BCOM	Piper J-3C-90 Cub (L-4A-PI)	10478	F-BDTP	27. 9.74	S L McKinnon tr Dougal Flying Group *"Dougal"*	
	(Frame No.10303)		F-BFQP, OO-ADI, 43-29187 *(On rebuild 8.03)*			Butlers Gyhll, Southwater 8. 7.02P
	(Officially regd as c/n 12040 which is correct identity of G-BGPD: fuselages probably exchanged in France)					
G-BCOO	de Havilland DHC-1 Chipmunk 22	C1/0209	WB760	10.10.74	T G Fielding and M S Morton	Hawarden 1. 6.08
G-BCOR	SOCATA Rallye 100ST	2544	F-OCZK	7. 1.75	J A Levey	Andrewsfield 14. 8.09E
G-BCOU	de Havilland DHC-1 Chipmunk 22	C1/0559	WK522	10.10.74	P J Loweth *"Thunderbird 5" (As "WK522" in RAF c/s)*	
					(Noted 1.07)	Duxford 30. 3.95
G-BCOY	de Havilland DHC-1 Chipmunk 22	C1/0212	WB762	10.10.74	Coventry Gliding Club Ltd	Husbands Bosworth 24. 1.09S
	(Lycoming O-360)					
G-BCPD	Gardan GY-201 Minicab	18	F-BGKN	24.10.74	P R Cozens	Hinton-in-the-Hedges 2. 8.09P
	(Built Con. Aéronautique de Bearn) (Continental A65)					
G-BCPG	Piper PA-28R-200 Cherokee Arrow II	28R-35705	N4985S	16.10.74	A G Antoniades tr Roses Flying Group	Barton 30.11.09E
G-BCPH	Piper J-3C-65 Cub (L-4H-PI)	11225	F-BCZA	13.12.74	M J Janaway Siege Cross Farm, Thatcham 6. 5.09P	
	(Frame No.11050)		French AF, 43-29934		*(As "329934:B-72" in 25th AOP French Armoured Divn of US 3rd Army c/s)*	
G-BCPJ	Piper J-3C-65 Cub (L-4J-PI)	13206	F-BDTJ	5.11.74	S Hollingsworth tr Piper Cub Group	Popham 17. 4.09P
	(Frame No.13036)					
G-BCPK	Reims Cessna F172M Skyhawk II	F17201194	(D-ELOB)	21.10.74	D C C Handley *(Noted 4.07)*	Little Staughton 12. 1.01T
G-BCPN	Grumman AA-5 Traveler	AA5-0665	N6155A	21.10.74	J R Walker tr G-BCPN Group	Gamston 10. 4.09E
G-BCPU	de Havilland DHC-1 Chipmunk 22	C1/0839	WP973	24.10.74	P Waller	Wycombe Air Park 3.10.08S
G-BCRB	Reims Cessna F172M Skyhawk II	F17201259		29.10.74	Wingtask 1995 Ltd	Seething 8. 5.09E
G-BCRI	Cameron O-65 Balloon (Hot Air)	135		5.11.74	V J Thorne *"Joseph"*	Nailsea, Bristol 26. 8.81A
G-BCRK	K & S SA 102.5 Cavalier	PFA 001-10049		5.11.74	P G R Brown *(In external store 11.06)*	
	(Built R Y Kendal) (Lycoming O-235)					Trenchard Farm, Eggesford 14. 7.00P
G-BCRL	Piper PA-28-151 Cherokee Warrior	28-7415689	N9564N	5.11.74	BCRL Ltd *(Operated Soloflight)*	Humberside 17. 8.09E
G-BCRR	Grumman AA-5B Tiger	AA5B-0006		7.11.74	P A Rutherford tr Tiger Group	Popham 6. 2.09E
G-BCRT	Reims Cessna F150M	F15001164		18.11.74	Almat Flying Club Ltd	Coventry 11. 6.09E
G-BCRX	de Havilland DHC-1 Chipmunk 22	C1/0232	WD292	22.11.74	M I Robinson and P J Tuplin *(As "WD292" in RAF c/s)*	
						White Waltham 4. 9.09S
G-BCSA	de Havilland DHC-1 Chipmunk 22	C1/0691	WP799	25.11.74	T M Holloway tr RAF Gliding and Soaring Association	
	(Lycoming O-360)				*(Operated Fulmar Gliding Club)*	Easterton 6. 4.09S
G-BCSL	de Havilland DHC-1 Chipmunk 22	C1/0524	WG474	26.11.74	Chipmunk Flyers Ltd	Liverpool 26. 3.11T
G-BCSX	Thunder Ax7-77 Balloon (Hot Air)	031		2.12.74	C Wolstenholme *"Woophski" (Tethered 9.05)*	
						Macclesfield 5. 7.86A
G-BCTF	Piper PA-28-151 Cherokee Warrior	28-7515033	N9585N	11.12.74	E Reed t/a St George Flight Training	
			(Rebuilt 1989/90 using major components from G-BFXZ)			Durham Tees Valley 31. 1.10E
G-BCTI	Schleicher ASK 16	16029	D-KIWA	23.12.74	J G Batch tr Tango India Syndicate	
						Hinton-in-the-Hedges 22.10.09E
G-BCTK	Reims Cessna FR.172J Rocket	FR17200546		23.12.74	J R Gore	(Llanishen) 3. 6.09E
G-BCTT	Evans VP-1	PFA 1543		24.12.74	E R G Ludlow	(Harleston, Norfolk) 25. 3.05P
	(Built B J Boughton) (Volkswagen 1600)				*(Crashed Priory Farm, Tibenham: wreck stored 7.05)*	
G-BCUB	Piper J-3C-65 Cub (L-4J-PI)	13370	F-BFBU	13.12.74	A L Brown *(Noted 10.05)*	Bourn 13. 6.01P
	(Lippert Reed conversion)		45-4630			
	(Officially regd with c/n 13186 which is G-BDOL (qv): airframes switched during conversion in UK)					
G-BCUF	Reims Cessna F172M Skyhawk II	F17201279		3. 1.75	R N Howell t/a Howell Plant Hire and Construction	
						Water Leisure Park, Skegness 28. 9.09E
G-BCUH	Reims Cessna F150M	F15001195		7. 1.75	M G Montgomerie tr G-BCUH Group	Elstree 8. 4.09E
G-BCUJ	Reims Cessna F150M	F15001176		9. 1.75	J Oleksyn and G Astle	Kemble 8. 6.09E
G-BCUO	Scottish Aviation Bulldog Series 120/122	BH120/371	Ghana AF, G-107, G-BCUO	9. 1.75	Cranfield University	Cranfield 10. 5.10S
G-BCUS	Scottish Aviation Bulldog Series 120/122	BH120/373	Ghana AF, G-109, G-BCUS	9. 1.75	R G Hayes tr Falcon Group	Kemble 22. 6.11S
G-BCUV	Scottish Aviation Bulldog Series 120/122	BH120/376	Ghana AF, G-112, G-BCUV	9. 1.75	Dolphin Property (Management) Ltd *(As "XX704" in RAF c/s)*	
						Old Sarum 15. 6.09T
G-BCUY	Reims Cessna FRA150M Aerobat	FRA1500269		14. 1.75	J C Carpenter	Clipgate Farm, Denton 24. 3.09E
G-BCVB	Piper PA-17 Vagabond	17-190	F-BFMT	22. 1.75	A T Nowak	Popham 16. 7.09P
	(Continental A65)		N4890H			
G-BCVC	SOCATA Rallye 100ST	2548	F-OCZO	16. 1.75	W Haddow	Prestwick 8. 6.09E
G-BCVF	Practavia Pilot Sprite 115	GBC.1		27. 1.75	D G Hammersley	Tatenhill 5. 9.08P
	(Built G B Castle - pr.no.PFA 1362) (Continental C125)					

G-BCVG	Reims Cessna FRA150L Aerobat		(I-AFAD)	16. 1.75	I G Cooper tr G-BCVG Flying Group		
		FRA1500245				Compton Abbas	18. 1.09E
G-BCVH	Reims Cessna FRA150L Aerobat			16. 1.75	M A James	Perth	23. 1.09E
		FRA1500258					
G-BCVJ	Reims Cessna F172M Skyhawk II	F17201305		16. 1.75	Rothland Ltd	RAF Woodvale	1. 5.09E
G-BCVY	Piper PA-34-200T Seneca II	34-7570022	N32447	28. 1.75	Oxford Aviation Academy (Oxford) Ltd	Oxford	9. 8.09E
G-BCWB	Cessna 182P Skylane II	18263566	N5848J	29. 1.75	M F Oliver and A J Mew	White Waltham	17. 2.09E
G-BCWH	Practavia Pilot Sprite 115	PFA 1366		3. 2.75	R Tasker	Blackpool	12. 6.08P
	(Built K B Parkinson and R Tasker) (Continental O-240-A)						
G-BCWK	Fournier RF3	24	F-BMDD	7. 2.75	T J Hartwell	Thurleigh	13. 8.02P
G-BCXB	SOCATA Rallye 100ST	2546	F-OCZM	7. 2.75	T Gillespie tr The Rallye Group	Bagby	17. 6.09E
G-BCXE	Robin DR.400 2+2	1015		19. 2.75	Weald Air Services Ltd	Headcorn	18. 9.09E
G-BCXJ	Piper J-3C-65 Cub (L-4J-PI)	13048	F-BFFH	21. 2.75	W Readman *(As "480752:E-39" in USAAC c/s)*		
	(Frame No.12878)		OO-SWA, 44-80752			Old Sarum	9. 9.09P
G-BCXN	de Havilland DHC-1 Chipmunk 22	C1/0692	WP800	7. 3.75	G M Turner *(As "WP800:2" in RAF Southampton UAS c/s)*		
						RAF Halton	29. 5.09S
G-BCYH	Slingsby Cadet III Motor Glider	2	BGA1158	10. 3.75	R O Johnson tr G-BCYH Group		
	(Re-built D C Pattison - pr.no.PFA 1568)		RAFGSA.264, XA297			Stoneacre Farm, Farthing Corner	5 10.07P
	(Formerly Slingsby T 31B c/n 839 now officially regd as Cadet III Motor Glider) (Volkswagen 1600)						
G-BCYM	de Havilland DHC-1 Chipmunk 22	C1/0598	WK577	13. 3.75	J B Ince tr G-BCYM Group *(As "WK577" in RAF c/s)*		
						Little Rissington	29.11.09S
G-BCYR	Reims Cessna F172M Skyhawk II	F17201288		20. 3.75	Highland Flying School Ltd	Inverness	10. 2.09E
G-BCZM	Reims Cessna F172M Skyhawk II	F17201350		3. 4.75	Cornwall Flying Club Ltd	Bodmin	9. 4.09E
G-BCZO	Cameron O-77 Balloon (Hot Air)	158		27. 3.75	W O T Holmes *"Leo" (Inflated 6.02)*	Shrewsbury	11.10.86A

G-BDAA - G-BDZZ

G-BDAD	Taylor JT.1 Monoplane	PFA 1453		2. 4.75	J N Hanson	Breighton	5. 6.09P
	(Built J F Bakewell) (Volkswagen 1700)						
G-BDAG	Taylor JT.1 Monoplane	PFA 1430		1. 4.75	N R Osborne	Longside, Peterhead	20. 2.09P
	(Built R S Basinger)						
G-BDAI	Reims Cessna FRA150M Aerobat			21. 4.75	D F Ranger	Popham	25. 7.09E
		FRA1500266					
G-BDAK	Rockwell Commander 112A	252	N1252J	10. 4.75	M C Wilson	Top Farm, Croydon, Royston	29. 4.09E
G-BDAO	SIPA S91	2	F-BEPT	10. 4.75	S B Churchill	Eastbach Farm, Coleford	15.10.09P
	(Continental C85)						
G-BDAP	Wittman W.8 Tailwind	0387		9. 4.75	J Whiting	Bagby	28. 2.06P
	(Built J and A Whiting - pr.no.PFA 3507)						
G-BDAR	Evans VP-1 Series 2	PFA 062-10461		10. 4.75	R F Powell	(Llanrwst)	20. 7.84P
	(Built S C Foggin and M J Dunmore - pr.no.PFA 1537) (Volkswagen 1600)						
G-BDAY	Thunder Ax5-42A Balloon (Hot Air)	042		8. 4.75	T M Donnelly *"Meconium"* Sprotbrough, Doncaster		16. 1.93A
G-BDBD	Wittman W.8 Tailwind	133	N1198S	25. 4.75	W S Siebert and B Ohrman tr Tailwind Group		
	(Built Hamilton Tool Company)					Wellesbourne Mountford	22. 2.09P
G-BDBF	Clutton FRED Series II	PFA 1528		15. 4.75	G E and R E Collins	Derby	18. 3.98P
	(Built W T Morrell) (Volkswagen 1600)						
G-BDBH	Bellanca 7GCBC Citabria	758-74	OE-AOL	15. 4.75	C J Gray	Finmere	26. 9.10S
G-BDBI	Cameron O-77 Balloon (Hot Air)	162		15. 4.75	C Jones *"Funny Money"*		
						Sonning Common, Reading	11. 7.87A
G-BDBJ	Cessna 182P Skylane II	18263646	N4644K	18. 4.75	T Ward and M Dodsworth	Ellough, Beccles	8. 5.09E
G-BDBU	Reims Cessna F150M	F15001174		30. 4.75	E Veitch	(Glasgow)	26. 8.08E
G-BDBV	Aero Jodel D 11	V 3	D-EGIB	23. 4.75	S Pavey tr Seething Jodel Group	Seething	28. 2.09P
	(Buillt Schwabach W Wolfrum) (Continental C90)						
G-BDCD	Piper J-3C-65 Cub *(L-4J-PI)*	12429	OO-AVS	28. 4.75	S Willard tr Cubby Cub Group	Shoreham	9.10.09P
	(Continental C90) *(Frame No.12257)*		44-80133		*(As "480133:B-44" in US Army c/s)*		
G-BDCI	Menavia Piel CP.301C Emeraude	503	F-BIRC	25. 4.75	D L Sentance	Rothwell Lodge Farm, Kettering	9. 2.09P
G-BDCO	Beagle B 121 Pup Series 1	B121-171		6. 5.75	R J Page and M H Simms		
					(Bolney, Haywards Heath and Shipdham, Thetford)		28. 7.97
G-BDDD	de Havilland DHC-1 Chipmunk 22	C1/0326	WD387	16. 5.75	RAE Aero Club Ltd	Farnborough	27. 6.10T
G-BDDF	Wassmer Jodel D 120 Paris-Nice	97	F-BIKZ	20. 5.75	J V Thompson	Breighton	10.11.03P
G-BDDG	Dormois Jodel D 112	855	F-BLNE	20. 5.75	D G Palme *(Noted 6.05)*	Sturgate	28. 7.04P
G-BDDS	Piper PA-25-260 Pawnee C	25-4757	CS-AIU	22. 5.75	T J Price tr Vale of Neath Gliding Club	Rhigos	21. 7.08E
			N10F				
G-BDDZ	Menavia Piel CP.301A Emeraude	253	F-BIMZ	30. 5.75	E C Mort	(Winwick, Warrington)	20. 6.84P
					(Damaged Cranwell North 3.6.84: on rebuild 1.01)		
G-BDEC	SOCATA Rallye 100ST	2552	F-OCZS	28. 5.75	J Fingleton	Kilkenny, Co Kilkenny	19.12.09E
G-BDEH	Wassmer Jodel D 120A Paris-Nice	239	F-BLNE	2. 6.75	A J Warman tr EH Group	Oaksey Park	27. 8.08P
G-BDEI	Jodel D 9 Bébé	585		2. 6.75	R Q.T Newns tr The Noddy Group *"Noddy"*		
	(Built L T Dix - pr.no.PFA 936) (Volkswagen 1600)					White Waltham	20.10.08P
G-BDEU	de Havilland DHC-1 Chipmunk 22	C1/0704	WP808	17. 6.75	Skylark Aviation Ltd *(As "WP808" in RAF c/s)*		
						Prestwick	17.12.09
G-BDEX	Reims Cessna FRA150M Aerobat			12. 6.75	A P F Tucker	Belle Vue Farm, Yarnscombe	30. 7.06T
		FRA1500279					
G-BDEY	Piper J-3C-65 Cub (L-4J-PI)	12538	OO-AAT	17. 6.75	W J and J.Morecraft tr Ducksworth Flying Club		
	(Frame No.12366)		OO-GAC, 44-80242			Highfield Farm, Empingham	17. 5.08P
G-BDEZ	Piper J-3C-65 Cub (L-4J-PI)	12383	OO-SOC	17. 6.75	R J M Turnbull	Rydinghurst Farm, Cranleigh	17. 8.09P
	(Frame No.12211)		OO-EPI, 44-80087				
G-BDFB	Phoenix Currie Wot	PFA 3008		20. 6.75	J Jennings	Little Gransden	12.10.07P
	(Built D F Faulkner-Bryant and J Jennings) (Walter Mikron III)						
G-BDFH	Auster AOP.9	B5/10/176	XR240	24. 6.75	R B Webber *(As "XR240" in AAC c/s)*		
	(Officially regd with Frame No.AUS/177)					RNAS Yeovilton	23. 7.09P
G-BDFJ	Reims Cessna F150M	F15001182		25. 6.75	C J Hopewell	Sibson	13. 7.02T
G-BDFR	Fuji FA.200-160 Aero Subaru	FA200-262		7. 7.75	M S Bird *(Noted 9.06)*	Glebe Farm, Stockton	1.11.04
G-BDFW	Rockwell Commander 112A	308	N1308J	18. 6.75	M E and E G Reynolds	Blackbushe	22.11.08E

G-BDFX	Taylorcraft J Auster 5	2060	F-BGXG TW517	9. 7.75	J Eagles	Oaksey Park	3. 6.94T
	(Damaged Oaksey Park 10.10.93: on rebuild 4.02)						
G-BDFY	Grumman AA-5 Traveler	AA5-0806		10. 7.75	G Robertson tr The Grumman Group	Edinburgh	17. 6.09E
	(Operated Edinburgh Flying Club)						
G-BDFZ	Reims Cessna F150M	F15001184	(D-EIWB) (F-BXIH)	14. 7.75	L W Scattergood	Full Sutton	29. 6.09E
G-BDGB	Gardan GY-20 Minicab	PFA 1819		23. 6.75	D G Burden Armshold Farm, Kingston, Cambridge		12. 6.01P
	(Built D G Burden to JB.01 Minicab standard) (Continental PC-60)						
G-BDGH	Thunder Ax7-77 Balloon (Hot Air)	049		16. 7.75	R J Mitchener and P F Smart t/a Balloon Collection		
					"London Pride III "	Andover	30. 8.83A
G-BDGM	Piper PA-28-151 Cherokee Warrior	28-7415165	N41307	30. 7.75	R Murgatroyd tr FlyBPL.com	Breighton	1.12.09E
G-BDHK	Piper J-3C-65 Cub *(L-4A-PI)*	8969	F-PHFZ 42-38400	24. 7.75	S Pritchard tr Knight Flying Group *(As "329417" in USAAC c/s)*		
	(Frame No.9068)					Eastbach Farm, Coleford	27.10.09P
	(Official c/n quoted as "261" with p/i 42-36414 but this corresponds to c/n 8538/N75366)						
G-BDIE	Rockwell Commander 112A	342	N1342J	14. 8.75	R J Adams	RAF Brize Norton	13.12.09E
G-BDIG	Cessna 182P Skylane II	18263938	N9877E	26. 8.75	P B Barrett and A R Bruce tr Air Group 6 Gamston		22. 9.09E
	(Reims-assembled with c/n F18200020)						
G-BDIH	SAN Jodel D 117	812	F-BIOT	22. 8.75	N D H Stokes	Garston Farm, Marshfield	7. 8.09P
G-BDIJ	Sikorsky S-61N Mk.II	61-751	9M-AYF G-BDIJ	3.10.75	Bristow Helicopters Ltd *"Crathes"*	Aberdeen	31. 5.09E
	(SAR conversion)						
G-BDJD	Jodel D 112	PFA 910		3. 9.75	J E Preston *"Marianne"*	Linley Hill, Leven	29. 5.09P
	(Built J V Derrick) (Continental A65)						
G-BDJG	Phoenix Luton LA-4A Minor	PFA 828		3. 9.75	S K Rose tr Very Slow Flying Club	(Ringwood)	1. 7.04P
	(Built D J Gaskin) (Volkswagen 1835)						
G-BDJP	Piper J-3C-65 Cub Special	22992	OO-SKZ PH-NCV, NC3908K	11.12.75	S T Gilbert	Enstone	18. 5.03T
	(Continental C90) *(Frame No.21017)*						
G-BDJR	SNCAC NC.858	2	F-BFIY	30. 9.75	R F M Marson *(On rebuild 9.00)*	(Fleet)	23. 5.92P
G-BDJV	Britten-Norman BN-2A-27 Islander	476	Belgian Army B-03, G-BDJV	29. 9.75	Cormack (Aircraft Services) Ltd *(Noted 9.06)*		
	(Was BN-2A-26, amended 22.10.08)					Cumbernauld	
G-BDKC	Cessna A185F Skywagon	185-02569	N1854R	30. 9.75	Bridge of Tilt Company Ltd	Blair Atholl	23. 4.09E
G-BDKD	Enstrom F-28A	319		30. 9.75	P J Price	(Warrington)	12. 2.09E
G-BDKH	Menavia Piel CP.301A Emeraude	241	F-BIMN	15.10.75	C Lobban tr G-BDKH Group	Perth	10. 8.09P
G-BDKJ	K & S SA.102.5 Cavalier	72207		14.10.75	D A Garner	Rhigos	5. 6.95P
	(Built H B Yardley - pr.no.PFA 1589) (Continental O-240-A)				*(Damaged Gloucestershire 14. 9.97, on rebuild 9.08)*		
G-BDKM	SIPA 903	98	F-BGHX	17.11.75	S W Markham	Valentine Farm, Odiham	17. 7.09P
G-BDKW	Rockwell Commander 112A	106	N1277J ZS-MIB, N1106J	3.11.75	J T Klaschka	Poplar Hall Farm, Elmsett	13.11.09E
G-BDLO	Grumman AA-5A Cheetah	AA5A-0026	N6154A	3.11.75	S and J Dolan	Elstree	7.10.08E
G-BDLT	Rockwell Commander 112A	363	N1363J	4.11.75	D L Churchward	Exeter	12. 6.09E
G-BDLY	K & S SA 102.5 Cavalier	PFA 001-10011		14.11.75	P R Stevens	Thruxton	2. 6.04P
	(Built B S Reeve) (Lycoming O-290)						
G-BDMS	Piper J-3C-65 Cub (L-4J-PI)	13049	F-BEGZ 44-80753	4.11.75	A T H Martin *(As "FR886" in RAF c/s)*		
						Old Sarum	2. 8.08P
G-BDMW	SAN Jodel DR.100A Ambassadeur	79	F-BIVM	2.12.75	P R H Moore tr G-Mike Whisky Group	(Tarporley)	7. 8.08E
G-BDNC	Taylor JT.1 Monoplane	PFA 1454		8.12.75	D W Mathie	(Diss)	23. 9.09P
	(Built N J Cole) (Walter Mikron III)						
G-BDNG	Taylor JT.1 Monoplane	PFA 1405		12.12.75	W Long	Shobdon	14. 7.06P
	(Built D J Phillips) (Volkswagen 1834)						
G-BDNO	Taylor JT.1 Monoplane	PFA 1431		15.12.75	R Wilkinson	(Lifton, Plymouth)	8.10.09P
	(Built A J Gray)						
G-BDNT	Jodel D 92 Bébé	397	F-PINL	2. 1.76	R J Stobo Oaklands Farm, Stonesfield, Witney		24. 9.09P
	(Built J Siry) (Volkswagen 1600)						
G-BDNU	Reims Cessna F172M Skyhawk II	F17201405		2. 1.76	J and K G McVicar	Elstree	21. 8.09E
G-BDNW	Grumman AA-1B Trainer	AA1B-0588		8. 1.76	A Turnbull	(Bedlington)	22.12.09E
G-BDNX	Grumman AA-1B Trainer	AA1B-0590		8. 1.76	D M and P A Fenton	Sherburn-in-Elmet	7. 9.09E
G-BDOC	Sikorsky S-61N Mk.II	61-765		20. 3.76	Bristow Helicopters Ltd *"Tolquhoun"*		
	(SAR conversion)					Den Helder, Netherlands	27.12.09E
G-BDOD	Reims Cessna F150M	F15001266		20. 1.76	P R Green tr OD Group	RAF Benson	2. 7.09E
G-BDOE	Reims FR172J Rocket	FR17200559		20. 1.76	D Sansome	Little Chase Farm, Kenilworth	5. 5.09E
G-BDOG	Scottish Aviation Bulldog Series 200	BH200/381		18.12.75	D C Bonsall *(Phoenix Flying Group titles)*		
						Netherthorpe	13. 5.09P
G-BDOL	Piper J-3C-65 Cub (L-4J-PI)	13186	F-BCPC 45-4446	18.12.75	L R Balthazor	Lee-on-Solent	10. 9.08P
	(Officially regd as c/n 13370: holds c/n & USAAC plates which relate to correct 13370 - G-BCUB, as airframes switched during UK conversion)						
G-BDOT	Fairey Britten-Norman BN-2A Mk.III-2 Trislander	1025	ZK-SFF N900TA, N903GD, N3850K, VH-BPB, G-BDOT	21. 1.76	Lyddair Ltd	Lydd	3. 3.09E
G-BDOW	Reims Cessna FRA150M Aerobat	FRA1500296		26. 1.76	Joystick Aviation Ltd	Cranfield	15. 4.09E
G-BDPA	Piper PA-28-151 Cherokee Warrior	28-7615033	N9630N	26. 1.76	Aircraft Engineers Ltd	Prestwick	16.12.08E
G-BDPJ	Piper PA-25-235 Pawnee B	25-3665	(PH-VBF) G-BDPJ, SE-EPZ	2. 2.76	T M Holloway tr RAF Gliding and Soaring Association		
	(Lycoming O-540A1B5)					RAF Halton	23. 1.10E
G-BDPK	Cameron O-56 Balloon (Hot Air)	191		4. 2.76	K J and G R Ibbotson	Abbeydale, Gloucester	29.12.88A
G-BDPN	Britten-Norman BN-2A-21 Islander	498	Belgian Army B-04, G-BDPN	5. 2.76	Fly BN Ltd	Bembridge	2. 6.09E
G-BDRD	Reims Cessna FRA150M Aerobat	FRA1500289		9. 2.76	Aircraft Engineers Ltd	Prestwick	15. 4.09E
G-BDRG	Taylor JT.2 Titch	PFA 060-10295		19.12.78	D R Gray	(Wilmslow)	
	(Built D R Gray)						
G-BDRJ	de Havilland DHC-1 Chipmunk 22	C1/0742	WP857	19. 2.76	D MacDonald and D Friel tr WP857 Aircraft Trust		
					(As "WP857:24" in RAF c/s)	Prestwick	8.12.08E
G-BDRK	Cameron O-65 Balloon (Hot Air)	205		12. 2.76	R J Mitchener and P F Smart *"Smirk" (Tethered 9.05)*		
						Andover and Oakley, Basingstoke	20. 6.86A

Reg	Type	C/n	Prev id	Date	Owner/Operator	Location	Status
G-BDSB	Piper PA-28-181 Cherokee Archer II	28-7690107	N8221C	23. 2.76	Testfair Ltd	Fairoaks	2. 5.09E
G-BDSE	Cameron O-77 Balloon (Hot Air)	210		27. 2.76	British Airways PLC "Concorde" (Tethered 9.05) Worplesdon		31. 3.90A
G-BDSF	Cameron O-56 Balloon (Hot Air)	209		1. 3.76	J H Greensides "Itzuma"	Burton Pidsea, Hull	29.11.09E
G-BDSH	Piper PA-28-140 Cherokee Cruiser	28-7625063	N9638N	1. 3.76	D Jones tr The Wright Brothers Flying Group	Nottingham City-Tollerton	30. 8.09E
G-BDSK	Cameron O-65 Balloon (Hot Air)	166		3. 3.76	Semajan Ltd tr Southern Balloon Group "Carousel II"	France	15. 9.09E
G-BDSL	Reims Cessna F150M	F15001306		5. 3.76	M Howells	Willey Park Farm, Caterham	24. 6.04E
	(Lost power on take-off Netherthorpe 16. 2.04 and substantially damaged: to Nalson Aviation Ltd for spares recovery and noted 3.06)						
G-BDSM	Slingsby T.31 Motor Cadet III	2464/3B		5. 3.76	F C J Wevers	(Amersfoort, Netherlands)	22. 5.02P
	(Re-built D W Savage - pr.no.PFA 042-10507)						
G-BDTB	Evans VP-1 Series 2	PFA 7009		15. 3.76	P F Moffatt (Noted 12.07)	Breighton	29.10.04P
	(Built T E Boyes) (Volkswagen 1834)						
G-BDTL	Evans VP-1	PFA 7012		17. 3.76	A K Lang	(Ilton, Ilminster)	5. 9.85P
	(Built A K Lang) (Volkswagen 1600)						
G-BDTN	Fairey Britten-Norman BN-2A Mk.III-2 Trislander	1026	S7-AAN VQ-SAN, G-BDTN	16. 3.76	Aurigny Air Services Ltd (Stored 3.03)	Guernsey	10. 6.98T
G-BDTO	Fairey Britten-Norman BN-2A Mk.III-2 Trislander	1027	G-RBSI G-OTSB, G-BDTO, 8P-ASC, G-BDTO, (C-GYOX), G-BDTO	16. 3.76	Aurigny Air Services Ltd	Guernsey	31. 3.09E
G-BDTU	Van Den Bemden Omega III Gas Balloon (20,000 cu.ft)	VDB-35		16. 3.76	R G Turnbull "Omega III"	Clyro, Hereford	4. 8.99A
	(Abingdon Free Balloon c/n AFB.4)						
G-BDTV	Mooney M 20F Executive	22-1307	N6934V	16. 3.76	S Redfearn	Gamston	11. 8.09E
G-BDTX	Reims Cessna F150M	F15001275		19. 3.76	F W Ellis	Water Leisure Park, Skegness	6.11.09E
G-BDUI	Cameron V-56 Balloon (Hot Air)	218		19. 3.76	D C Johnson "True Brit"	Farnham	6. 7.91A
G-BDUL	Evans VP-1	PFA 1557		25. 3.76	J C Lindsay	(Inworth, Colchester)	17. 3.07P
	(Built C Goodman) (Volkswagen 1834)						
G-BDUM	Reims Cessna F150M	F15001301	F-BXZB	29. 3.76	P B Millington and D Grant	Earls Colne	8. 5.09E
G-BDUN	Piper PA-34-200T Seneca II	34-7570163	(EI-BLR) G-BDUN, SE-GIA	29. 3.76	R Paris	Oxford	14. 4.09E
G-BDUO	Reims Cessna F150M Commuter	F15001304		29. 3.76	D W Locke	Popham	18.11.09E
G-BDUY	Robin DR.400-140B Major	1120		5. 4.76	J G Anderson	Hatton, Peterhead	13. 4.09E
G-BDUZ	Cameron V-56 Balloon (Hot Air)	213		30. 3.76	P J Bish tr Zebedee Balloon Service "Hot Lips"	Newtown, Hungerford	29.11.09E
G-BDVA	Piper PA-17 Vagabond	17-206	CN-TVY F-BFFE	23. 4.76	I M Callier	(Berry Grove Farm, Liss)	13. 8.03P
	(Continental C90)						
G-BDVB	Piper PA-15 Vagabond	15-229	F-BHHE SL-AAY, F-BETG	23. 4.76	B P Gardner	(Calcot, Reading)	5. 6.09P
	(Continental C90) (Regd as "PA-17")						
G-BDVC	Piper PA-17 Vagabond	17-140	F-BFBL	29. 9.76	A R Caveen	Sandford Hall, Knockin	21. 8.09P
	(Continental C90)						
G-BDWA	SOCATA Rallye 150ST	2695		20. 4.76	J T Wilson (Noted 8.07)	Derrytrasna Glen, Bannfoot	7. 6.01
G-BDWE	Flaglor Sky Scooter	DWE-01		12. 4.76	P King	Eastbach Farm, Coleford	27. 6.05P
	(Built D W Evernden - pr.no.PFA 1332 & KF-S-66) (Volkswagen 1600)						
G-BDWH	SOCATA Rallye 150ST	2697		20. 4.76	M A Jones	Upper Harford Farm, Bourton-on-the-Water	21. 2.09E
G-BDWJ	Replica Plans SE.5a	PFA 020-10034	"C1904" "F8010"	27. 4.76	D W Linney (As "F8010/Z" in RFC c/s)	(Langport)	15. 8.08P
	(Built M L Beach) (Continental C90)						
G-BDWM	Bonsall DB-1 Mustang	PFA 073-10200		3. 5.76	D C Bonsall (As "FB226:MT-A" in RAF c/s: on rebuild 5.04)	Netherthorpe	15. 6.98P
	(Built D C Bonsall) (Lycoming IO-360)						
G-BDWO	Howes Ax6 Balloon (Hot Air)	RBH.2		5. 5.76	R B and C Howes "Griffin"	Keysoe	
	(Built R B and C Howes)						
G-BDWP	Piper PA-32R-300 Cherokee Lance	32R-7680176	N8784E	7. 5.76	A Belcastro and I Bardelloni	Rome, Italy	27. 3.09E
G-BDWX	Wassmer Jodel D 120A Paris-Nice	311	F-BNHT	13. 5.76	R P Rochester	Wombleton	24. 4.09P
G-BDWY	Piper PA-28-140 Cherokee E	28-7225378	PH-NSC N11C	14. 5.76	A Boorman and D Bishop	Oxford	11. 8.09E
G-BDWZ	Slingsby T.59J Kestrel 22	1867	BGA.2470-DXU	17. 5.76	T J Wilkinson	Sackville Lodge, Riseley	29. 4.08
	(Converted from T.59H 1979)						
G-BDXJ	Boeing 747-236B	21831	N1792B	2.5.80	Aces High Ltd (Open storage, for use as classroom)	Dunsfold	18.11.07E
G-BDXX	SNCAN NC.858S	110	F-BEZO	17. 5.76	K M Davis (On rebuild 5.04)	North Weald	3. 7.96P
G-BDYD	Rockwell Commander 114	14014	N1914J	21. 5.76	J R Pybus	Sherburn-in-Elmet	16.12.08E
G-BDYH	Cameron V-56 Balloon (Hot Air)	233		24. 5.76	B J Godding "Novocastrian" (Inflated 6.08)	Didcot	25.11.90A
G-BDZA	Scheibe SF25E Super Falke	4320	(D-KECW)	1. 6.76	G Pybus tr Hereward Flying Group	Crowland	23. 4.09E
	(Limbach SL-1700)						
G-BDZC	Reims Cessna F150M	F15001316		1. 6.76	A M Lynn	Sibson	10. 7.09E
G-BDZD	Reims Cessna F172M Skyhawk II	F17201478		1. 6.76	Skydive Aircraft Ltd	AAC Netheravon	7. 8.09E
G-BDZG	Slingsby T.59H Kestrel 22	1868	BGA2481-DYG G-BDZG	3. 6.76	R E Gretton "592"	Crowland	19. 4.08
G-BDZI	Britten-Norman BN-2A-21 Islander	531	Belgian Army B-08, G-BDZI	9. 6.76	Fly BN Ltd	Bembridge	27. 7.09E

G-BEAA - G-BEZZ

Reg	Type	C/n	Prev id	Date	Owner/Operator	Location	Status
G-BEAB	CEA Jodel DR.1051 Sicile	228	F-BKGH	18. 8.76	R C Hibberd	(Chiseldon, Swindon)	13. 7.07
G-BEAC	Piper PA-28-140 Cherokee	28-21963	4X-AND	4. 6.76	R Murray and A Bagley-Murray	Humberside	10. 7.09E
G-BEAG	Piper PA-34-200T Seneca II	34-7670204	N9395K	18. 6.76	Oxford Aviation Academy (Oxford) Ltd	Oxford	22.10.09E
G-BEAH	Auster V J/2 Arrow	2366	F-BFUV F-BFVV, OO-ABS	28. 6.76	J G Parish tr Bedwell Hey Flying Group "Llewellyn" Bedwell Hey Farm, Little Thetford, Ely		26. 4.09P
	(Continental C85)						
G-BEBE	Grumman AA-5A Cheetah	AA5A-0154		28. 6.76	Bills Aviation Ltd	Biggin Hill	11. 6.09E
G-BEBG	PZL-Bielsko SZD-45A Ogar	B-655		29. 6.76	D W Coultrip tr The Ogar Syndicate	Hinton-in-the-Hedges	30.10.09E

Reg	Type	c/n	Prev id	Date	Owner/Operator	Location	Expiry
G-BEBN	Cessna 177B Cardinal	17701631	4X-CEW N34084	1. 7.76	R Turrell and P Mason	King's Farm, Thurrock	16. 4.09E
G-BEBR	Gardan GY-201 Minicab	PFA 1824		5. 7.76	P G Kavanagh	Warrington	6.11.08P
	(Built A S Jones) (Originally officially regd with c/n PFA 1670)						
G-BEBS	Andreasson BA-4B	HA/01		7. 7.76	N J W Reid	Lee-on-Solent	22. 5.09P
	(Built D M Fenton [tr Hornet Aviation] - pr.no.PFA 038-10157) (Continental O-200-A)						
G-BEBU	Rockwell Commander 112A	272	N1272J	8. 7.76	Aeros Engineering Ltd *(Noted 1.06)*	Gloucestershire	19. 6.04T
G-BEBZ	Piper PA-28-151 Cherokee Warrior	28-7615328	N6193J	14. 7.76	Airways Flight Training (Exeter) Ltd	Exeter	27. 4.09E
G-BECA	SOCATA Rallye 100ST	2751		14. 7.76	A C Stamp	Redhill	4.11.09E
G-BECB	SOCATA Rallye 100ST	2783		14. 7.76	D H Tonkin	Bugle, St Austell	7. 9.09E
G-BECF	Scheibe SF25A Motorfalke (Hirth F23A)	4555	OO-WIZ (D-KARA)	14. 7.76	North County Ltd *(Fuselage noted 5.05)*	Barton	1. 3.94P
G-BECK	Cameron V-56 Balloon (Hot Air)	136		27. 7.76	A M and N H Ponsford	Leeds	9. 5.06A
G-BECN	Piper J-3C-65 Cub (L-4J-PI)	12776	F-BCPS HB-OCI (1), 44-80480	27. 7.76	G Denney *"Miss Monica" (As "480480:E-44" in USAAC c/s)*	Audley End	8.12.11
G-BECS	Thunder Ax6-56A Balloon (Hot Air)	074		4. 8.76	A Sieger	Munster, Germany	5. 6.08A
G-BECT	CASA 1-131E Jungmann	"3974"	Spanish AF E3B-338	3. 8.76	G M S Scott tr Alpha 57 Group *(As "A-57" in Swiss AF c/s)*	(London SW18)	19. 2.07P
G-BECW	CASA 1-131E Jungmann	2037	Spanish AF E3B-423	3. 8.76	C M Rampton *(As "A-10" in Swiss AF c/s)*	(Lyminge, Folkestone)	4.11.06P
	(Incorporating parts of G-BECY ex E3B-459)						
G-BECZ	Mudry CAP.10B	68	F-BXHK	26. 7.76	Avia Special Ltd	Little Gransden	2. 6.07T
G-BEDD	SAN Jodel D 117A	915	F-BITY	3. 8.76	M D Howlett tr Dubious Group	Shrove Furlong Farm, Ilmer	29. 7.09P
G-BEDF	Boeing B-17G-105-VE Fortress	8693	N17TE F-BGSR, 44-85784	5. 8.76	B-17 Preservation Ltd *(As "124485:DF-A" in USAAC c/s) "Sally B" (port)/"Memphis Belle" (std)*	Duxford	22. 5.09P
G-BEDG	Rockwell Commander 112A	482	N1219J	5. 8.76	G-BEDG Ltd	Blackbushe	29. 6.09E
G-BEDJ	Piper J-3C-65 Cub (L-4J-PI)	12890	F-BDTC 44-80594	5. 8.76	R Earl *(Stored frame 2.07)*	White Waltham	8.10.96P
	(Frame No.12720)						
G-BEDP	Fairey Britten-Norman BN-2A Mk.III-2 Trislander	1039	ZK-SFG N902TA, N1FY, N401JA, G-BEDP	17. 8.76	Blue Islands Ltd t/a Blue Islands	Alderney	28. 5.09E
G-BEDW	Britten-Norman BN-2A-20 Islander	541	Belgian Army B-10, G-BEDW	25. 8.76	Fly BN Ltd	Bembridge	30.10.09E
G-BEEG	Fairey Britten-Norman BN-2A-26 Islander	550	(C-GYUH) G-BEEG	25. 8.76	M D Carruthers and S F Morris t/a North West Parachute Centre	Cark-in-Cartmel	5. 4.05T
G-BEEH	Cameron V-56 Balloon (Hot Air)	250		24. 8.76	Sade Balloons Ltd *"Tywi"*	Coulsdon	16.11.09E
G-BEEI	Cameron N-77 Balloon (Hot-Air)			24. 8.76	Zebedee Balloon Service Ltd	Hungerford	11. 3.90A
G-BEER	Isaacs Fury II	PFA 1588		31. 8.76	R S C Andrews *(As "K2075" in RAF c/s)*	Bidford	13. 6.09P
	(Built M J Clark) (Lycoming O-235)						
G-BEEU	Piper PA-28-140 Cherokee F	28-7325247	PH-NSE N11C	9. 9.76	H and E Merkado	Conington	6. 3.09E
G-BEFA	Piper PA-28-151 Cherokee Warrior	28-7615416	N6978J	8. 9.76	M A Verran t/a Verran Freight	RAF Benson	5. 5.09E
G-BEFF	Piper PA-28-140 Cherokee F	28-7325228	PH-NSF N11C	27. 9.76	H and E Merkado	Panshanger	22. 5.09E
G-BEGG	Scheibe SF25E Super Falke (Limbach SL1700)	4326	(D-KDFB)	15.10.76	H Altmann tr G-BEGG Motorfalke	Hinton-in-the-Hedges	6. 6.09E
G-BEHH	Piper PA-32R-300 Cherokee Lance	32R-7680323	N6172J	29.10.76	K Swallow	Sherburn-in-Elmet	5. 9.09E
G-BEHU	Piper PA-34-200T Seneca II	34-7670265	N6175J	3.11.76	Pirin Aeronautical Ltd	Stapleford	6. 4.09E
G-BEHV	Reims Cessna F172N Skyhawk II	F17201541		3.11.76	Edinburgh Air Centre Ltd	Edinburgh	23.11.09E
G-BEIA	Reims Cessna FRA150M Aerobat	FRA1500317		8.11.76	C J Hopewell	Sibson	27.10.03T
G-BEIF	Cameron O-65 Balloon (Hot Air)	259		17.11.76	C Vening *"Solitaire" (Operated Balloon Preservation Group)*	Petworth	22. 4.07A
G-BEIG	Reims Cessna F150M	F15001361		18.11.76	R D Forster and M S B Thorp	Ellough, Beccles	1. 8.08E
G-BEII	Piper PA-25-235 Pawnee D	25-7656059	N54918	16.11.76	Burn Gliding Club Ltd	Burn	7. 4.09E
G-BEIL	SOCATA Rallye 150T	2653	F-BXDL	1.12.76	J I Oakes and R A Harris tr The Rallye Flying Group	Hill Farm, Nayland	23. 7.09E
G-BEIP	Piper PA-28-181 Cherokee Archer II	28-7790158	N6628F	22.11.76	S Pope	Barton	24. 9.09E
G-BEIS	Evans VP-1	PFA 7029		25.11.76	P J Hunt *(Stored 2.99)*	Thruxton	16. 7.90P
	(Built D J Park) (Volkswagen 1600)						
G-BEJD	Avro 748 Series 1/105	1543	LV-HHE LV-PUF	17.12.76	PTB (Emerald) Proprietary Ltd *(Stored 11.08)*	Blackpool	29. 3.06E
G-BEJK	Cameron S-31 Balloon (Hot Air)	256		1.12.76	A M and N H Ponsford t/a Rango Balloon and Kite Company *"L'Essence"*	Leeds	16. 2.92A
G-BEJV	Piper PA-34-200T Seneca II	34-7770062	N7657F	31.12.76	Oxford Aviation Academy (Oxford) Ltd	Oxford	19. 9.09E
G-BEKL	Bede BD-4E-150	151 & BD4E/2	(G-AYKB)	11. 1.77	F E Tofield	(Farnborough)	14.10.80P
	(Built Brookmoor Bede Aircraft) (Lycoming O-320)						
G-BEKM	Evans VP-1	PFA 7025		12. 1.77	G J McDill	Westmoor Farm, Thirsk	23. 3.95P
	(Built G J McDill) (Volkswagen 1834)				*(Stored 7.98)*		
G-BEKO	Reims Cessna F182Q Skylane II	F18200037		12. 1.77	G J and F J Leese	Sherburn-in-Elmet	21. 4.09E
G-BELT	Cessna F150J	F150-0409X		26. 1.77	A Kumar	Blackpool	22. 9.09E
	(Built Reims Aviation SA) (Mainly rebuild of G-AWUV and parts of G-ATND)						
G-BEMB	Reims Cessna F172M Skyhawk II	F17201487		27. 1.77	Stocklaunch Ltd	Goodwood	23. 4.09E
G-BEMM	Slingsby Cadet III Motor Glider	1247	BGA942 RAFGSA 289, BGA942	27. 1.77	E and P McEvoy	Kilrush, County Kildare	10.10.06P
	(Re-built M N Martin from Slingsby T 31B) (Volkswagen 1600)						
G-BEMU	Thunder Ax5-42 Balloon (Hot Air)	097		9. 2.77	M A Hall *"Chrysophylax"*	Stoneleigh	16. 1.99A
G-BEMW	Piper PA-28-181 Cherokee Archer II	28-7790243	N9566N	9. 2.77	Touch and Go Ltd	White Waltham	30.12.09E

Reg	Type	c/n	Prev id	Date	Owner/Operator	Location	
G-BEMY	Reims Cessna FRA150M Aerobat	FRA1500315		9. 2.77	J R Power	Kilrush, County Kildare	13.12.09E
G-BEND	Cameron V-56 Balloon (Hot Air)	260		14. 2.77	P J Bish tr Dante Balloon Group "Le Billet" (Tethered 9.05)	Newtown, Hungerford	1. 1.94A
G-BENJ	Rockwell Commander 112B	522	N1391J	7. 3.77	D J Gibney tr BENJ Flying Group	Top Farm, Croydon, Royston	4. 9.09E
G-BENK	Reims Cessna F172M Skyhawk II	F17201509		2. 3.77	Bulldog Aviation Ltd	Earls Colne	23. 6.09E
G-BENN	Cameron V-56 Balloon (Hot Air)	278		4. 3.77	S J Hollingsworth and M K Bellamy "English Rose" (Inflated 4.06)	Bleasby, Nottingham	15. 3.87A
G-BEOD	Cessna 180	32092	OO-SPZ D-EDAH, SL-AAT, N3294D	14. 3.77	I Addy (Noted stored 9.08)	Spanhoe	6. 9.91
G-BEOE	Reims Cessna FRA150M Aerobat	FRA1500322		21. 3.77	W J Henderson tr Air Images	Kilbride	9. 9.09E
G-BEOH	Piper PA-28R-201T Turbo Arrow III	28R-7703038	N1905H	11. 3.77	K G Harper tr Gloucestershire Flying Club	Gloucestershire	23. 6.09E
G-BEOI	Piper PA-18-150 Super Cub (Lycoming O-360-A4)	18-7709028	N54976	11. 3.77	Southdown Gliding Club Ltd	Parham Park	9. 3.11
G-BEOK	Reims Cessna F150M	F15001366		14. 3.77	KPOW Ltd	Gamston	18. 5.09E
G-BEOL	Short SC.7 Skyvan 3 Variant 100	SH1954	ZS-OIO JA8803 (2), G-BEOL, G-14-122	16. 3.77	Invicta Aviation Ltd	Hibaldstow	23. 4.09E
G-BEOY	Reims Cessna FRA150L Aerobat	FRA1500150	F-BTFS	30. 3.77	J H Ponsford	(Chichester)	28. 7.09E
G-BEPC	SNCAN Stampe SV-4C	64	F-BFUM F-BFZM, French.Military	17.10.77	M J Parr	White Waltham	7.11.09S
G-BEPF	SNCAN Stampe SV-4C	424	F-BCVD	30. 3.77	C C Rollings and F J Hodson	Gloucestershire	
G-BEPV	Fokker S 11.1 Instructor	6274	PH-ANK Dutch Navy 174, Dutch AF E-31	13. 4.77	S W, M Isbister and C Tyers (As "174:K:" in Royal Netherlands Navy c/s)	Spanhoe	13. 2.08P
G-BEPY	Rockwell Commander 112B	524	N1399J	20. 4.77	T L Rippon	Blackbushe	17. 1.10E
G-BERA	SOCATA Rallye 150ST	2821	F-ODEX	13. 4.77	A L Hall-Carpenter	Old Buckenham	3.12.07E
G-BERC	SOCATA Rallye 150ST	2858		13. 4.77	R S Jones tr The Severn Valley Aero Group	Welshpool	20. 4.09E
G-BERD	Thunder Ax6-56A Balloon (Hot Air)	106		25. 4.77	P M Gaines "Goldfinger"	Stockton-on-Tees	14. 5.04A
G-BERI	Rockwell Commander 114	14234	N4909W	6. 5.77	K B Harper	Blackbushe	21. 5.09E
G-BERN	Saffery S 330 Balloon (Minimum Lift)	4		19. 4.77	B Martin "Beeze I" (Extant 5.07)	Somersham, Huntingdon	
G-BERT	Cameron V-56 Balloon (Hot Air)	273		19. 4.77	Semajan Ltd tr Southern Balloon Group "Bert"	(France)	15. 9.09E
G-BERY	Grumman AA-1B Trainer	0193	N9693L	27.10.77	R H J Levi "79"	Stapleford	2. 8.09E
G-BETD	Robin HR.200-100 Club	20	PH-SRL	28. 4.77	C L Wilsher	Sywell	24. 1.08
G-BETE	Rollason Beta B 2A (Built T Jones) (Incorporates parts from PFA 1304)	PFA 002-10169		26. 4.77	T M Jones (Under construction 4.04)	Derby	
G-BETG	Cessna 180K Skywagon	180-52873	N64146	17. 5.77	W Flood	(Mullingar, Ireland)	13. 3.09E
G-BETI	Pitts S-1D (Built B Bray - pr.no.PFA 009-10156) (Lycoming O-320)	7-0314	G-PIII G-BETI	28. 4.77	D R Puleston tr On A Roll Aerobatics Group	Leicester	17. 3.09P
G-BETL	Piper PA-25-235 Pawnee D	25-7656016	N54874	27. 5.77	Cambridge Gliding Club Ltd	Gransden Lodge	23. 1.10E
G-BETM	Piper PA-25-235 Pawnee D	25-7656066	N54927	5. 5.77	Yorkshire Gliding Club (Proprietary) Ltd	Sutton Bank	1. 5.09E
G-BEUA	Piper PA-18-150 Super Cub (Lycoming O-360-A4)	18-8212	D-ECSY N4146Z	21. 6.77	London Gliding Club Proprietary Ltd	Dunstable	29. 1.11
G-BEUD	Robin HR.100-285 Tiara	534	F-BXRC	8. 6.77	E A and L M C Payton	Cranfield	11. 8.09E
G-BEUI	Piper J-3C-65 Cub (L-4H-PI) (Frame No.12002) (Regd as ex 43-29245 which is actually G-KIRK)	12174	F-BFEC F-OAJF, French AF, 44-79878	19. 5.77	M C Jordan	Eaglescott	5. 3.08P
G-BEUM	Taylor JT.1 Monoplane (Built Speedwell Sailplanes) (Volkswagen 1700)	PFA 1438		8. 6.77	J M Burgess (Noted under restoration 4.07)	(Helston)	28. 7.04P
G-BEUP	Robin DR.400-180 Régent	1228		19. 5.77	Legal Week Ltd t/a Samuels Aviation	Biggin Hill	18. 8.09E
G-BEUU	Piper PA-18 Super Cub 95 (L-18C-PI) (Frame No.should be 18-1523)	18-1551	F-BOUU French Army 18-1551, 51-15551	27. 6.77	F Sharples	Sandown	20. 5.09P
G-BEUX	Reims Cessna F172N Skyhawk II	F17201596		30. 5.77	Multiflight Ltd	Hawarden	19. 3.09E
G-BEUY	Cameron N-31 Balloon (Hot Air)	283		31. 5.77	Zebedee Balloon Service Ltd (Typhoo Tea titles)	Woodcote, Reading	25. 6.09E
G-BEVB	SOCATA Rallye 150ST	2860		2. 6.77	M Smullen (Lullymore, Rathangan, County Kildare)		23. 6.09E
G-BEVC	SOCATA Rallye 150ST	2861		2. 6.77	I R Chaplin	Andrewsfield	10. 8.08E
G-BEVG	Piper PA-34-200T Seneca II	34-7570060	VQ-SAM N32854	31. 5.77	Direct Aviation Management Ltd	Humberside	26. 3.09E
	(Nose undercarriage collapsed on landing at Sibson 12.12.07, both propellers and nose damaged; noted engineless Sibson 9.08)						
G-BEVO	Fournier RF5	5107	5N-AIX D-KAAZ	27. 6.77	M Hill	(Stratford-upon-Avon)	24. 8.08P
G-BEVS	Taylor JT.1 Monoplane (Built D Hunter) (Volkswagen 1835)	PFA 1429		8. 6.77	D Hunter	Orange Grove, Chavenage, Tetbury	17. 4.08P
G-BEVT	Fairey Britten-Norman BN-2A Mk.III-2 Trislander	1057		10. 6.77	Aurigny Air Services Ltd	Guernsey	13. 7.09E
G-BEVW	SOCATA Rallye 150ST	2928		2. 6.77	S W Brown	Fenland	29. 5.09E
G-BEWN	de Havilland DH.82A (Aust) Tiger Moth (Built de Havilland Aircraft Pty Ltd - rebuild as official c/n T305)	952	VH-WAL RAAF A17-529	16. 6.77	H D Labouchere	Langham	22. 7.09S
G-BEWO	Moravan Zlin Z-326 Trener Master	915	CS-ALU	23.11.77	P A Colman	Luxter's Farm, Hambledon	2. 7.03
G-BEWR	Reims Cessna F172N Skyhawk II	F17201613		13. 6.77	R C Baker	Liverpool	15. 12.09E
G-BEWX	Piper PA-28R-201 Cherokee Arrow III	28R-7737070	N5723V	23. 6.77	P J Collins and T M Freeman tr Three Greens Arrow Group	Headcorn	23. 5.09E
G-BEWY	Bell 206B-2 JetRanger II	348	G-CULL EI-BXQ, G-BEWY, 9Y-TDF	27. 6.77	Polo Aviation Ltd	Bristol	13. 5.09E
G-BEXN	Grumman AA-1C Lynx	AA1C-0045	N6147A	7. 9.77	H Sykes and M Holliday "0045"	North Weald	27. 4.09E

Reg	Type	c/n	Prev id	Date	Owner/Operator	Location	Code
G-BEXW	Piper PA-28-181 Cherokee Archer II	28-7790521	N38122	11. 7.77	J O'Keefe	Waterford, County Waterford	10. 9.08E
G-BEXX	Cameron V-56 Balloon (Hot Air)	274		29. 6.77	K A Schlussler *"Rupert of Rutland"* Bourne, Lincoln		2. 7.86A
G-BEXZ	Cameron N-56 Balloon (Hot Air)	294		7. 7.77	D C Eager and G C Clark *"Valor"*		
						Bracknell and Worcester	20. 2.09E
G-BEYA	Enstrom 280C Shark	1104		15. 8.77	Hovercam Ltd	Staddon Heights, Plymouth	11. 7.08E
G-BEYL	Piper PA-28-180 Cherokee Archer	28-7405098	PH-SDW N9518N	6. 9.77	D W Gerrard tr Yankee Lima Group	Compton Abbas	2. 4.09E
G-BEYT	Piper PA-28-140 Cherokee	28-20330	D-EBWO N6280W	19. 7.77	R M Dene	Oxford	4. 6.09E
G-BEYV	Cessna T210M Turbo Centurion II	21061583	N732KX	19. 7.77	Castleridge Ltd	Bagby	22.12.09E
G-BEYW	Taylor JT.1 Monoplane	RJS.100		22. 7.77	R A Abrahams *"Red Hot"*	Barton	5. 6.07P
	(Built R A Abrahams - pr.no.PFA 055-10279) (Volkswagen 1834)						
G-BEYZ	CEA Jodel DR.1050/M1 Sicile Record	588	F-BMGV	22. 7.77	M L Balding	Biggin Hill	15. 7.09P
G-BEZC	Grumman AA-5 Traveler	AA5-0493	F-BUYN (N7193L)	29. 7.77	C M O'Connell	Southend	27. 8.09E
G-BEZE	Rutan VariEze	PFA 074-10207		26. 7.77	S K Cockburn	(Stanford-Le-Hope)	2. 6.04P
	(Built J Berry) (Continental O-200-A)				*(Force-landed 5ms from Rayleigh 17.12.03 and badly damaged)*		
G-BEZF	Grumman AA-5 Traveler	AA5-0538	F-BVJP	29. 7.77	J E Kearney tr The ZF Group	Conington	27. 1.10E
G-BEZG	Grumman AA-5 Traveler	AA5-0561	F-BVRJ	29. 7.77	M D R Harling	Shobdon	31. 5.09E
G-BEZH	Grumman AA-5 Traveler	AA5-0566	F-BVRK N9566L	29. 7.77	L and S M Sims	Fenland	11. 6.09E
G-BEZI	Grumman AA-5 Traveler	AA5-0567	F-BVRL N9567L	29. 7.77	H Matthews tr The BEZI Flying Group	Cranfield	27. 9.09E
G-BEZK (2)	Cessna F172H	F172-0462	D-EBUD D-ENHC, SLN-07, N20462	17. 8.77	S Jones	Ellough, Beccles	13.10.09E
	(Built Reims Aviation SA)						
G-BEZL	Piper PA-31 Navajo C	31-7712054	SE-GPA	1. 8.77	A Jahanfar *(Operated Flywatch Ltd)*	Southend	20. 7.09E
G-BEZO	Reims Cessna F172M Skyhawk II	F17201392		24. 8.77	Cardinal Sin Ltd t/a Staverton Flying School		
						Gloucestershire	9. 4.09E
G-BEZP	Piper PA-32-300 Cherokee Six	32-7740087	N38572	19. 8.77	T P McCormack and J K Zealley	White Waltham	2. 6.09S
G-BEZR	Reims Cessna F172M Skyhawk II	F17201395		24. 8.77	Kirmington Aviation Ltd	Thruxton	8. 5.09E
G-BEZV	Reims Cessna F172M Skyhawk II	F17201474	(I-CCAY)	24. 8.77	A T Wilson tr Insch Flying Group	Insch	28. 4.09E
G-BEZY	Rutan VariEze	1167		26. 7.77	I J Pountney	(Malvern)	18. 5.96P
	(Built R J Jones - pr.no.PFA 074-10225) (Continental PC60)						
G-BEZZ	Jodel D 112	397	F-BHMC	12. 8.77	K R Nestor tr G-BEZZ Group	Barton	1.12.09P
	(Built Passot Aviation)						

G-BFAA - G-BFZZ

Reg	Type	c/n	Prev id	Date	Owner/Operator	Location	Code
G-BFAA	Sud-Aviation Gardan GY-80-160 Horizon	78	F-BLVY	20.10.77	G R Williams	(Biddulph, Stoke-on-Trent)	18.11.90
G-BFAF	Aeronca 7BCM Champion (L-16A-AE)	7BCM-11	N797US N2552B, 47-797	15. 8.77	D C W Harper *(As "7797" in US Army c/s)* Finmere *(Noted 8.06)*		30. 8.01P
G-BFAH	Phoenix Currie Wot	PFA 058-11376		22. 8.77	R W Clarke	(Cheadle)	
	(Built N Hamilton-Wright)						
	(Initially allocated as c/n PFA 3017: on build as Replica SE.5a, project probably confused with PFA 101-11376, a Sopwith Pup replica)						
G-BFAI	Rockwell Commander 114	14304	N4984W	17. 8.77	A J Procter tr BFAI Flying Group		
						Sherburn-in-Elmet	28. 1.09E
G-BFAK	GEMS MS.892A Rallye Commodore 150	10595	F-BNNJ	9. 8.77	J M Hedges *"54"* Lower Upham Farm, Chiseldon		31. 5.09E
G-BFAP	SIAI-Marchetti S 205-20R	4-213	I-ALEN	1. 9.77	A O'Broin	Raby's Farm, Great Stukeley	14.12.09E
G-BFAS	Evans VP-1 Series 2	PFA 7033		15. 8.77	A I Sutherland	Fearn	17. 7.09P
	(Built A I Sutherland) (Volkswagen 1834)						
G-BFAW	de Havilland DHC-1 Chipmunk 22	C1/0733	8342M WP848	31. 8.77	R V Bowles	Husbands Bosworth	6. 6.08S
G-BFAX	de Havilland DHC-1 Chipmunk 22	C1/0496	8394M WG422	31. 8.77	N Rushton *(As "WG422:16" in RAF c/s) (Noted 9.08)* Trenchard Farm, Eggesford		23. 6.05
G-BFBA	SAN Jodel DR.100A Ambassadeur	88	F-BIVU	12. 9.77	W H Sherlock Manor Farm, Drayton St Leonard		5. 2.11
G-BFBB	Piper PA-23-250 Aztec E	27-7405294	SE-GBI	1. 9.77	D Byrne	Elstree	5. 6.09E
G-BFBC	Taylor JT.1 Monoplane	PFA 055-10280		5. 9.77	G Heins	(Rochdale)	
	(Built A Brooks)						
G-BFBE	Robin HR.200-100 Club	12	PH-SRK	9. 9.77	A C Pearson	Rochester	16. 4.09E
G-BFBM	Saffery S 330 Balloon (Minimum Lift)	7		1. 9.77	B Martin *"Beeze II"* (Extant 5.07)		
						Somersham, Huntingdon	
G-BFBR	Piper PA-28-161 Cherokee Warrior II	28-7716277	N38845	15. 9.77	Moore Flying Ltd	Fairoaks	14. 5.09E
G-BFBU	Partenavia P68B	24		25. 1.78	Geminair Services Ltd	Thruxton	24. 4.09E
G-BFBY	Piper J-3C-65 Cub (L-4H-PI)	10998	SE-FTM F-BDTG 43-29707	29. 9.77	M Shaw	Old Buckenham	30. 8.07P
G-BFCT	Cessna TU206F Turbo Stationair II	U20603202	(LN-TVF) N8341Q	15. 9.77	D I Schellingerhout Mount Airey Farm, South Cave		21. 5.09E
G-BFDC	de Havilland DHC-1 Chipmunk 22	C1/0525	7989M WG475	15.11.77	N F O'Neill	Newtownards	29.10.09S
G-BFDF	SOCATA Rallye 235E	12834	F-GAKT	6.10.77	M A Wratten Bourne Park, Hurstbourne Tarrant		20. 5.09E
G-BFDI	Piper PA-28-181 Cherokee Archer II	28-7790382	N2205Q	5.10.77	Truman Aviation Ltd Nottingham City-Tollerton		28.10.09E
G-BFDK	Piper PA-28-161 Cherokee Warrior II	28-7816010	N40061	23. 9.77	S T Gilbert	Enstone	21. 6.09E
G-BFDL	Piper J-3C-65 Cub (L-4J-PI)	13277	HB-OIF 45-4537	30.11.77	B A Nicholson and P J Lochhead *(As "454537:J-04" in US Army c/s)*		
	(Continental O-200-A) (Frame No.13107)				Shempston Farm, Lossiemouth		20. 5.08P
G-BFDO	Piper PA-28R-201T Turbo Arrow III	28R-7703212	N38396	3.10.77	J Blackburn and J Driver	Elstree	27. 2.09E
G-BFEB	SAN Jodel D 150 Mascaret	34	F-BMJR OO-LDY, F-BLDX	14.10.77	A W Russell tr Jodel Syndicate	Portmoak	10. 3.09P

Reg	Type	C/n	Prev ID	Date	Owner/Operator	Location	Date
G-BFEF	Agusta-Bell 47G-3B1	1541	XT132	11.10.77	I F Vaughan	Guernsey	25. 8.11
G-BFEH	SAN Jodel D 117A	828	F-BITG	5.10.77	J A Crabb	Dunkeswell	19.11.09P
G-BFEK	Reims Cessna F152 II	F15201442		11.10.77	Cardinal Sin Ltd t/a Staverton Flying School		
						Gloucestershire	27. 2.10E
G-BFEV	Piper PA-25-235 Pawnee D	25-7756060	N82547	20.10.77	Trent Valley Aerotowing Club Ltd	Kirton-in-Lindsey	4. 6.09E
G-BFFC	Reims Cessna F152 II	F15201451		27.10.77	Multiflight Ltd	Leeds-Bradford	4. 1.10E
G-BFFE	Reims Cessna F152 II	F15201454		27.10.77	A J Hastings	Prestwick	4. 7.08E
G-BFFJ	Sikorsky S-61N Mk.II	61-777	N6231	17. 1.78	British International Helicopter Services Ltd t/a British		
					International *"Tresco"* (stored 6.08)	Plymouth	22. 3.09E
G-BFFP	Piper PA-18-150 Super Cub	18-8187	PH-OTC	9.11.77	East Sussex Gliding Club Ltd	Ringmer	14. 6.11S
	(Lycoming O-360-A4) *(Frame No.18-8402)*		N10F				
G-BFFT	Cameron V-56 Balloon (Hot Air)	360		7.11.77	R I McKean Kerr and D C Boxall tr The Red Section		
					Balloon Group *"Red Leader"*	Bristol	16. 2.03A
G-BFFW	Reims Cessna F152 II	F15201447		14.11.77	Aircraft Engineers Ltd	Prestwick	31. 7.09E
G-BFGD	Reims Cessna F172N Skyhawk II	F17201545	F-WZDT	14.11.77	J T Armstrong	Fairoaks	4.12.09E
G-BFGG	Reims Cessna FRA150M Aerobat	FRA1500321	F-WZDS	14.11.77	J M Machin	Netherthorpe	16. 4.09E
G-BFGH	Reims Cessna F337G Super Skymaster			14.11.77	T Perkins	Bagby	22. 5.09E
	(Wichita c/n 33701754)	F33700081					
G-BFGK	SAN Jodel D 117	644	F-BIBT	27. 6.78	B F J Hope	Stoneacre Farm, Farthing Corner	7. 7.09P
G-BFGL	Reims Cessna FA152 Aerobat	FA1520339		14.11.77	E-Plane Ltd	Fenland	3. 8.09E
G-BFGO	Fuji FA.200-160 Aero Subaru	FA200-219	PH-KDB	25.11.77	R J Everett	(Sproughton, Ipswich)	23. 8.92
					(Damaged taxying Rush Green 18. 8.93)		
G-BFGS	SOCATA MS.893E Rallye 180GT	12571	F-BXYK	31. 8.76	Chiltern Flyers Ltd		
			French AF 12571 FSCAZ, "41-AZ"			Park Farm, Eaton Bray/Turweston	8.11.09E
G-BFGX	Reims Cessna FRA150M Aerobat		F-BUDX	28.11.77	Aircraft Engineers Ltd *(Noted 10.07)*	Prestwick	20.11.08E
		FRA1500328					
G-BFGZ	Reims Cessna FRA150M Aerobat			28.11.77	C M Barnes	Garden Piece, Basingstoke	4. 4.08T
		FRA1500329					
	(Bounced on landing at Popham 10. 2.08 and nose undercarriage collapsed damaging nose and propeller)						
G-BFHH	de Havilland DH.82A Tiger Moth	85933	F-BDOH	25.11.77	P Harrison and M J Gambrell		
	(Built Morris Motors Ltd)		French AF, DF197			Swanborough Farm, Lewes	26. 5.07
G-BFHI	Piper J-3C-65 Cub (L-4J-PI)	12532	F-BFBT	25.11.77	N Glass and A J Richardson *(Noted 8.07)*		
			44-80236			Derrytrasna Glen, Bannfoot	28. 5.04P
G-BFHP	Champion 7GCAA Citabria	114	HB-UAX	8.12.77	R Bell and I Walton tr Citabriation Group	Barton	10.10.10S
G-BFHR	CEA Jodel DR.220 2+2	30	F-BOCX	1.12.77	J E Sweetman	(Kingston, Sturminster Newton)	29. 7.09E
G-BFHU	Reims Cessna F152 II	F15201461		7.12.77	D J Cooke and Company Ltd	Liverpool	16. 1.09E
					(Operated Cheshire Air Training Services Ltd)		
G-BFHV	Reims Cessna F152 II	F15201470		21.12.77	A S Bamrah t/a Falcon Flying Services	Biggin Hill	10. 1.10E
G-BFIB	Piper PA-31 Turbo Navajo	31-684	LN-NPE	21.12.77	Richard Hannon Ltd	Thruxton	10. 4.09E
			OY-DVH, LN-RTJ				
G-BFID	Taylor JT.2 Titch	PFA 060-10311		13.12.77	R W Kilham	(Langtoft, Peterborough)	23. 8.99P
	(Built W F Adams) (Continental O-200-A)				*(Damaged Breighton 31. 5.99)*		
G-BFIE	Reims Cessna FRA150M Aerobat			12. 1.78	J P A Freeman	Headcorn	27. 3.09E
		FRA1500331					
G-BFIG	Reims FR172K Hawk XP	FR17200615		12. 1.78	Tenair Ltd	Barton	26. 3.09E
G-BFIJ	Grumman AA-5A Cheetah	AA5A-0486	N6160A	1. 3.78	T H and M G Weetman	Prestwick	7. 5.09E
G-BFIN	Grumman AA-5A Cheetah	AA5A-0520	N6145A	22. 3.78	Aircraft Engineers Ltd	Prestwick	31. 7.09E
G-BFIT	Thunder Ax6-56Z Balloon (Hot Air)	136		20.12.77	J A G Tyson *"Folly"*	Torphins, Banchory	3. 5.91
G-BFIU	Reims FR172K Hawk XP	FR17200591	N96098	12. 1.78	B M Jobling tr The G-BFIU Flying Group		
						Hinton-in-the-Hedges	20.10.09E
G-BFIV	Reims Cessna F177RG Cardinal RG		N96106	12. 1.78	C Fisher	Blackbushe	25. 5.09E
		F177RG0161					
G-BFIX	Thunder Ax7-77A Balloon (Hot Air)	133		9.12.77	R Owen *"Animal Magic"*	Standish, Wigan	23. 1.79
G-BFIY	Reims Cessna F150M	F15001381	OE-CMT	11. 1.78	R J Scott	Ashleigh Farm, Bracknell	25. 9.08E
G-BFJJ	Evans VP-1	PFA 062-10273		30.12.77	M A Watts	Farley Farm, Romsey	23. 6.96P
	(Built P R Pykett) (Volkswagen 1800)				*(Crashed in a field near Farley Mount 20.4.08)*		
G-BFJR	Reims Cessna F337G Super Skymaster		N46297	4. 1.78	Columbus Systems Ltd	(Laxey, Isle of Man)	22.10.09E
	(Wichita c/n 33701761)	F33700082	(N53658)				
G-BFJZ	Robin DR.400-140B Major	1290		20. 1.78	Weald Air Services Ltd	Headcorn	26. 8.07T
G-BFKB	Reims Cessna F172N Skyhawk II	F17201601	PH-AXO	16. 1.78	R L Clarke and D Tench tr Shropshire Flying Group		
						Sleap	31. 3.09E
G-BFKF	Reims Cessna FA152 Aerobat	FA1520337		26. 1.78	Aerolease Ltd	Conington	5. 6.09E
G-BFKL	Cameron N-56 Balloon (Hot Air)	369		23. 1.78	Merrythought Ltd	Telford	17. 7.92A
G-BFLH	Piper PA-34-200T Seneca II	34-7870065	N2126M	16. 2.78	Air Medical Ltd	Oxford	8. 6.06T
G-BFLU	Reims Cessna F152 II	F15201433		15. 2.78	Atlantic Flight Training Ltd	Coventry	24. 6.09E
G-BFLX	Grumman AA-5A Cheetah	AA5A-0524	N6147A	14. 3.78	A M Verdon	Blackbushe	27. 7.08E
G-BFLZ	Beech 95-A55 Baron	TC-220	PH-ILE	16. 3.78	K A Graham t/a Caterite Food Service	Carlisle	27. 8.09E
			HB-GOV				
G-BFMF	Cassutt Racer IIIM	PFA 034-10147		17. 2.78	M C R Sims	(Chichester)	24. 5.91P
	(Built P H Lewis) (Continental C90)						
G-BFMG	Piper PA-28-161 Cherokee Warrior II		N3506Q	11. 5.78	Stardial Ltd	Fairoaks	29.10.09E
		28-7716160					
G-BFMH	Cessna 177B Cardinal	17702034	N34836	18. 4.78	Aerofoil Aviation Ltd	Leeds-Bradford	10. 7.09E
G-BFMK	Reims Cessna FA152 Aerobat	FA1520344		6. 3.78	The Leicestershire Aero Club Ltd	Leicester	15. 4.09E
G-BFMR	Piper PA-20 Pacer 125	20-130	N7025K	20. 2.78	J Knight	Headcorn	6. 3.06
G-BFMX	Reims Cessna F172N Skyhawk II	F17201732		24. 8.78	A2Z Wholesale Fashion Jewellery Ltd		
						Wolverhampton	15. 5.09E
G-BFMZ	Payne Ax7-62 Balloon (Hot Air)	GFP.2		1. 3.78	E G Woolnough *(Inflated 4.06)* Halesworth, Suffolk		
	(Built G F Payne)						
G-BFNG	Wassmer Jodel D 112	1321	F-BNHI	6. 3.78	M Cooke and P H Jeffcote	Leicester	29. 5.09P
G-BFNI	Piper PA-28-161 Cherokee Warrior II		N9505N	8. 3.78	P R J Welch t/a Lion Services	Hawarden	28. 7.09E
		28-7816215					

Reg	Type	C/n	Prev id	Date	Owner/Operator	Base	Expiry
G-BFNK	Piper PA-28-161 Cherokee Warrior II	N9527N		8. 3.78	Oxford Aviation Training Ltd	Oxford	13. 3.09E
		28-7816282					
G-BFNM	Globe GC-1B Swift	2205	N78205	15. 6.78	M J Butler	Spanhoe	25.10.08P
			NC78205				
G-BFOE	Reims Cessna F152 II	F15201475		23. 3.78	Redhill Air Services Ltd	Redhill	24. 1.10E
G-BFOF	Reims Cessna F152 II	F15201448		9. 3.78	Cardinal Sin Ltd tr Staverton Flying School		
						Gloucestershire	21. 6.09E
G-BFOG	Cessna 150M	15076223	N66706	13. 3.78	C L Day	Haverfordwest	13. 5.09E
G-BFOJ	American AA-1 Yankee	AA1-0395	OH-AYB	4. 4.78	N W Thomas	Bournemouth	20.11.09E
			(LN-KAJ), (N6195L)				
G-BFOP	Wassmer Jodel D 120 Paris-Nice	32	F-BHTX	23. 3.78	R J Wesley and G D Western "Jean"	Nayland	12. 6.04P
G-BFOU	Taylor JT.1 Monoplane	PFA 055-10333		17. 3.78	G Bee	(Stockton-on-Tees)	
	(Built I N M Cameron)						
G-BFOV	Reims Cessna F172N Skyhawk II	F17201675		18. 5.78	D J Walker	Shoreham	18.10.09E
G-BFPA	Scheibe SF25B Falke	46179	D-KAGM	29. 3.78	R Gibson and R Hamilton	Portmoak	17. 1.10E
	(Volkswagen Danum 1600/1)						
G-BFPH	Reims Cessna F172K	F17200802	PH-VHN	23. 3.78	T Marriott tr Linc-Air Flying Group	Gamston	18. 8.09E
G-BFPO	Rockwell Commander 112B	530	N1412J	10. 5.78	J G Hale Ltd	Shoreham	4. 2.09E
G-BFPP	Bell 47J-2 Ranger	2851	F-BJAN	23. 5.78	M R Masters Phoenix Farm, Lower Upham		11.11.99
			TR-LKD, F-OCBU		(Noted 11.08)		
G-BFPR	Piper PA-25-235 Pawnee D	25-7856007	SE-KGY	4. 4.78	The Windrushers Gliding Club Ltd	Bicester	18. 3.09E
			I-TOZU, G-BFPR, N82591				
G-BFPS	Piper PA-25-235 Pawnee D	25-7856013	N82598	4. 4.78	Kent Gliding Club Ltd	Challock	30. 6.09E
G-BFPZ	Reims Cessna F177RG Cardinal RG	N56PZ	3. 4.78	O C Baars	(Heywood, Westbury)	11.12.09E
		F177RG0079	G-BFPZ, PH-AUK, D-EGBM, (OO-DVE), G-BFPZ				
G-BFRD	Bowers Fly Baby 1A	PFA 016-10300		27. 1.78	R A Phillips	(Elgin)	
	(Built F R Donaldson and R A Phillips)				(Under construction 6.00)		
G-BFRI	Sikorsky S-61N Mk.II	61-809		26. 5.78	British International Helicopter Services Ltd t/a British		
					International	Plymouth	16. 1.09E
G-BFRR	Reims Cessna FRA150M Aerobat	LN-ALO	19. 4.78	S Cosgrove tr Romeo Romeo Flying Group		
		FRA1500326				Tatenhill	7.10.09E
G-BFRS	Reims Cessna F172N Skyhawk II	F17201555	LN-ALP	19. 4.78	Aerocomm Ltd	King's Farm, Thurrock	6. 6.09E
G-BFRV	Reims Cessna FA152 Aerobat	FA1520345		17. 4.78	Solo Services Ltd	Shoreham	3.10.09E
G-BFRY	Piper PA-25-260 Pawnee D	25-7405789	SE-GIB	23. 5.78	Yorkshire Gliding Club (Proprietary) Ltd		
						Sutton Bank	9. 7.09E
G-BFSA	Reims Cessna F182Q Skylane II	F18200074	F-WZDG	17. 4.78	Ensiform Aviation Ltd	Cranfield	13.12.08E
G-BFSC	Piper PA-25-235 Pawnee D	25-7656068	N82302	2. 6.78	Essex Gliding Club Ltd	Ridgewell	23. 1.10E
G-BFSD	Piper PA-25-235 Pawnee D	25-7656084	N82338	2. 6.78	Deeside Gliding Club (Aberdeenshire) Ltd Aboyne		1. 5.09E
G-BFSR	Cessna F150J	F150-0504	OH-CBN	7. 7.78	W Ali	Cranfield	17. 7.09E
	(Built Reims Aviation SA)						
G-BFSS	Reims FR172G Rocket	FR17200167	OH-CDY	7. 7.78	Albedale Farms Ltd		
					Manor Farm, Grateley, Andover		1. 6.09E
G-BFSY	Piper PA-28-181 Cherokee Archer II	N9503N	19. 4.78	A S Domone t/a Downland Aviation	Goodwood	53. 2.10E
		28-7890200					
G-BFTA	Piper PA-28-161 Warrior II	28-7816553	A6-EFU	19. 4.78	D A G Roseblade	(Dubai, UAE)	
			A6-AFC, G-BFTA, N9577N				
G-BFTC	Piper PA-28R-201T Turbo Arrow III	N3868M	19. 4.78	D Petty tr Top Cat Flying Group Sherburn-in-Elmet		22.12.09E
		28R-7803197					
G-BFTF	Grumman AA-5B Tiger	AA5B-0879		7. 9.78	F C Burrow Ltd	Sherburn-in-Elmet	7. 8.09E
G-BFTG	Grumman AA-5B Tiger	AA5B-0777		15. 5.78	D Hepburn and G R Montgomery	Perth	4.11.09E
G-BFTH	Reims Cessna F172N Skyhawk II	F17201671		3. 5.78	T W Oakley	Bagby	15. 9.09E
G-BFTT	Cessna 421C Golden Eagle	421C-0462	N6789C	3. 5.78	M A Ward	Goodwood	11. 7.09E
G-BFTX	Reims Cessna F172N Skyhawk II	F17201715		2. 5.78	F P Hall tr Tri Society	Clipgate Farm, Denton	6. 5.06
	(Abandoned take-off Clipgate Farm, Denton 15.7.04 resulting in extensive damage: cancelled 30.12.04 as destroyed: noted wrecked 4.6.05						
	but restored 7.6.05).						
G-BFUB	Piper PA-32RT-300 Lance II	32R-7885052	N9509C	18. 5.78	Jolida Holdings Ltd	Jersey	18. 5.09E
G-BFUD	Scheibe SF25E Super Falke	4313	D-KLDC	19. 5.78	J S Halford tr SF25E Syndicate	Eyres Field	6. 8.09E
	(Limbach SL1700)						
G-BFUZ	Cameron V-77 Balloon (Hot Air)	398		24. 5.78	A W Macdonald tr Servowarm Balloon Syndicate		
					(Servowarm titles)	Leigh-on-Sea	3. 4.09E
G-BFVG	Piper PA-28-181 Cherokee Archer II	N31746	1. 6.78	P Anderson	Blackpool	1. 7.09E
		28-7890408	N9558N				
G-BFVH	AirCo DH.2 Replica	WA/4		1. 6.78	R H and J A Cooper (As "5964") Wickenby		6. 8.09P
	(Built Westward Airways (Lands End) Ltd) (125 hp Kinner B54)				(BAPC.112 also marked as "5964")		
G-BFVS	Grumman AA-5B Tiger	0784	N28736	11. 8.78	T R Chapman and M R Place tr G-BFVS Flying Group		
						Denham	1. 3.09E
G-BFVU	Cessna 150L Commuter	15074684	N75189	10. 8.78	Aviation South West Ltd	Exeter	2. 8.09E
G-BFWB	Piper PA-28-161 Cherokee Warrior II	N31752	22. 6.78	Mid-Anglia Flight Centre Ltd t/a Mid-Anglia School of Flying		
		28-7816584				Cambridge	24. 7.09E
G-BFWD	Phoenix Currie Wot	PFA 3009		22. 6.78	D Silsbury and B Proctor	Dunkeswell	6.10.96P
	(Built F E Nuthall) (Walter Mikron 3)				(On restoration 12.05 as "C3009/B" in RFC c/s)		
G-BFXF	Andreasson BA-4B	AAB-001		10. 7.78	P N Birch	Ludham	30. 8.07P
	(Built A Brown - pr.no.PFA 038-10351) (Lycoming O-290-G)						
G-BFXG	Druine D 31 Turbulent	PFA 1663		10. 7.78	E J I Musty and M J Whatley (Partially complete 6.07)		
	(Built S Griffin)				(White Waltham)		
G-BFXK	Piper PA-28-140 Cherokee F	28-7325387	PH-NSK	1. 8.78	D M Wheeler	Rochester	22. 6.09E
G-BFXR	Wassmer Jodel D 112	247	F-BFTM	27. 7.78	M R Coreth	Henstridge	27. 8.09P
G-BFXS	Rockwell Commander 114	14271	N4949W	3. 8.78	Romeo Whiskey Ltd	Old Buckenham	16. 7.09E
G-BFXW	Gulfstream AA-5B Tiger	AA5B-0940		21. 2.79	Campsol Ltd	Leeds-Bradford	23. 6.09E
G-BFXX	Gulfstream AA-5B Tiger	AA5B-0917		3.10.78	W R Gibson	North Weald	6. 2.10E
G-BFYA	MBB BÖ.105DB	S 321	D-HJET	31.10.78	Sterling Helicopters Ltd (Operated Norfolk Police)		
						Norwich	25. 5.09E
G-BFYC	Piper PA-32RT-300 Lance II	32R-7885200	N36645	31. 7.78	A A Barnes tr Cyril Silver and Partners	Biggin Hill	12. 1.10E
G-BFYI	Westland-Bell 47G-3B1	WA/326	XT167	24. 1.79	K P Mayes	Hawarden	11.11.11

G-BFYK	Cameron V-77 Balloon (Hot Air)	433	EI-BAY G-BFYK	16. 8.78	L E Jones	Worcester	21. 9.09E
G-BFYL	Evans VP-2	PFA 063-10146		15. 8.78	W C Brown	(Camberley)	17.12.98P
	(Built A G Wilford) (Volkswagen 1834)						
G-BFYM	Piper PA-28-161 Cherokee Warrior II	28-7816586	N812E N480X, G-BFYM, N31813	14. 8.78	Sheffield City Flying School Ltd	Sandtoft	29. 5.09E
G-BFYW	Slingsby T.65A Vega	1888	BGA2592-EDA G-BFYW	1. 9.78	S A Whitaker	Parham Park	
G-BFZA	Fournier RF3	5	F-BLEL	14. 9.78	T J Hartwell	(Sackville Lodge, Riseley)	
G-BFZB	Piper J-3C-65 Cub (L-4J-PI)	13019	D-ECEL HB-OSP, 44-80723	21. 9.78	M S Pettit *(As "480723:E5" and "J" in USAF c/s)*	Bidford	18. 2.09P
	(Continental C85) (Frame No.12849)						
G-BFZD	Reims Cessna FR182 Skylane RG II	FR18200010		9.10.78	R B Lewis tr R B Lewis and Company	Sleap	7. 2.09E
G-BFZH	Piper PA-28R-200 Cherokee Arrow II	28R-35307	OY-BDB	25.10.78	A Mason t/a Mason Aviation	Prestwick	25. 9.08E
G-BFZM	Rockwell Commander 112TC-A	13191	N4661W	9.10.78	J A Hart and R J Lamplough	Filton	21. 8.09E
G-BFZN	Reims Cessna FA152 Aerobat	FA1520348		20.10.78	A S Bamrah t/a Falcon Flying Services	Biggin Hill	29.11.81T
	(Crashed Narborough, Leicestershire 4.10.80: on rebuilld 2.95)						
G-BFZO	Gulfstream AA-5A Cheetah	AA5A-0697		1.11.78	J W Cross and A E Kempson	Elstree	16. 8.09E
G-BFZU	Reims Cessna FA152 Aerobat	FA1520355		29. 6.79	BJ Aviation Ltd	Welshpool	30. 4.09E
G-BFZV	Reims Cessna F172M	F17201093	SE-FZR	2.11.78	The Royal Artillery Aero Club Ltd tr The Army Flying Association	AAC Middle Wallop	16. 3.09T

G-BGAA - G-BGZZ

G-BGAA	Cessna 152 II	15281894	N67529	18. 7.78	PJC (Leasing) Ltd	Stapleford	24. 6.09E
G-BGAB	Reims Cessna F152 II	F15201531		13.10.78	TG Aviation Ltd *(Operated Thanet Flying Club)*	Manston	26. 6.09E
G-BGAE	Reims Cessna F152 II	F15201540		8.11.78	Aerolease Ltd	Conington	19. 6.09E
G-BGAF	Reims Cessna FA152 Aerobat	FA1520349		13.10.78	P E Preston tr G-BGAF Group *(Operated Southend Flying Club)*	Southend	18. 6.09E
G-BGAG	Reims Cessna F172N Skyhawk II	F17201754	"G-KING"	13.10.78	R Clarke	Tatenhill	25. 5.07T
G-BGAJ	Reims Cessna F182Q Skylane II	F18200096		13.10.78	Ground Airport Services Ltd	Guernsey	27.11.09E
G-BGAX	Piper PA-28-140 Cherokee F	28-7325409	PH-NSH	20.10.78	B L Newbold tr G-BGAX Group	Breighton	5. 3.09E
G-BGAZ	Cameron V-77 Balloon (Hot Air)	439		20.10.78	C.J Madigan and D H McGibbon *(Cameron Balloons titles)*	Bristol	14. 7.09E
	(Rebuilt envelope)						
G-BGBA	Robin R2100A Club	133	F-OCBJ	2. 5.78	Cotswold Aviation Services Ltd	Gloucestershire	23.10.09E
G-BGBE	SAN Jodel DR.1050 Ambassadeur	260	F-BJYT	29.11.78	J A and B.Mawby	Graveley Hall Farm, Graveley	20. 4.08E
G-BGBF	Druine D.31A Turbulent	PFA 1658		24.10.78	T A Stambach	RAF Henlow	25. 3.04P
	(Built L Davis)						
G-BGBG	Piper PA-28-181 Archer II	28-7990012	N39730	2.11.78	Harlow Printing Ltd	Carlisle	13. 7.09E
G-BGBI	Reims Cessna F150L	F15000688	PH-LUA	28.11.78	C P Tapp	Bourn	5.12.09E
G-BGBK	Piper PA-38-112 Tomahawk	38-78A0433	N9738N	2.11.78	Truman Aviation Ltd	Nottingham City-Tollerton	25. 7.09E
G-BGBN	Piper PA-38-112 Tomahawk	38-78A0511	N9657N	29.11.78	Bonus Aviation Ltd	Cranfield	8.10.09E
G-BGBR	Reims Cessna F172N Skyhawk II	F17201772		8.11.78	S Papi *(Operated Willowair Flying Club)*	Southend	2. 5.09E
G-BGBV	Slingsby T.65A Vega 17L	1890	BGA2800/EMS G-BGBV	1. 2.08	M P Day tr Vega Syndicate BGA2800	Tibenham	8.11.81
G-BGBW	Piper PA-38-112 Tomahawk	38-78A0670	N9710N	8.11.78	Truman Aviation Ltd	Nottingham City-Tollerton	18. 7.09E
G-BGBZ	Rockwell Commander 114	14423	N5878N	9.10.78	G W Dimmer	Old Sarum	9. 7.09E
G-BGCB	Slingsby T.65A Vega	1892	BGA2794-EML G-BGCB	20.11.78	P W Williams *"EML"*	Bidford	30.10.08
G-BGCM	Gulfstream AA-5A Cheetah	AA5A-0835		23. 3.79	G and S A Jones	Linley Hill, Leven	17.10.09E
G-BGCO	Piper PA-44-180 Seminole	44-7995128	N2103D	20.12.78	BAE Systems (Operations) Ltd	Warton	11.1.10E
G-BGCU	Slingsby T.65A Vega 17L	1893	BGA2611-EDV G-BGCU	28.11.78	K Challinor	Long Mynd	
G-BGCY	Taylor JT.1 Monoplane	PFA 055-10370		23.11.78	A T Lane	Fenland	19. 7.08P
	(Built M T Taylor)						
G-BGEH	Monnett Sonerai II	209		1.12.78	D and Vivienne T Hubbard	(Basingstoke)	16. 8.96P
	(Built R E Finlay- p/no PFA 015-10254) (Volkswagen 2234)						
G-BGEI	Oldfield Baby Lakes	PFA 010-10016		1.12.78	M T Taylor	Griffins Farm, Temple Bruer	11. 5.09P
	(Built D H Greenwood) (Fuselage of PFA 1576 incorporated during construction) (Continental A65)						
G-BGEW	SNCAN NC.854S	63	F-BFSJ	13.12.78	S A Francis	Bourne Park, Hurstbourne Tarrant	5. 6.09P
	(Continental A65)						
G-BGFC	Evans VP-2	V2-1278		15.12.78	S W C Hollins	(Shavington, Crewe)	29. 9.93P
	(Built J A Jones - pr.no.PFA 063-10441) (Volkswagen 1834)						
G-BGFF	Clutton FRED Series II	PFA 029-10261		18.12.78	I Pearson and P C Appleton	Bodmin	4. 3.09P
	(Built G R G Smith) (Volkswagen 1834)						
G-BGFG	Gulfstream AA-5A Cheetah	AA5A-0687	N6158A	25. 1.79	R C Willis-Fleming tr Cheetah Flying Group	Exeter	30. 5.09E
G-BGFI	Gulfstream AA-5A Cheetah	AA5A-0733	N6142A	5. 3.79	I J Hay and A Nayyar tr GFI Group	Biggin Hill	23. 4.09E
G-BGFJ	Jodel D 9 Bébé	PFA 1324		11.12.78	O G Jones	Watchford Farm, Yarcombe	28.10.08P
	(Built C M Fitton) (Volkswagen 1600)						
G-BGFT	Piper PA-34-200T Seneca II	34-7870218	N9714C	17. 1.79	Oxford Aviation Academy (Oxford) Ltd	Oxford	14. 9.09E
G-BGFX	Reims Cessna F152 II	F15201555		28.12.78	A J Gomes	Fairoaks	29.11.09E
G-BGGA	Bellanca 7GCBC Citabria 150S	1104-79		5. 2.79	L A King	Wickenby	8. 6.11S
G-BGGB	Bellanca 7GCBC Citabria 150S	1105-79		7. 2.79	R S Kiddy tr Citabria Syndicate	Rattlesden	14.4.11S
G-BGGC	Bellanca 7GCBC Citabria 150S	1106-79		5. 2.79	R P Ashfield and J M Stone tr G-BGGC Flying Group	Stancombe Farm, Askerswell	19.10.07E
G-BGGD	Bellanca 8GCBC Scout	284-78		5. 2.79	The Bristol Gliding Club Proprietary Ltd	Nympsfield	17.12.09E
G-BGGE	Piper PA-38-112 Tomahawk	38-79A0161	N9673N	10. 1.79	Truman Aviation Ltd	Nottingham City-Tollerton	25. 6.09E
G-BGGG	Piper PA-38-112 Tomahawk	38-79A0163	N9675N	10. 1.79	M Temple and J Bell tr GGG Group	Bagby	28. 6.04T
G-BGGI	Piper PA-38-112 Tomahawk	38-79A0165	N9675N	10. 1.79	Truman Aviation Ltd	Nottingham City-Tollerton	8. 5.09E
G-BGGL	Piper PA-38-112 Tomahawk	38-79A0169	N9696N	10. 1.79	Grunwick Processing Laboratories Ltd *(Operated Bonus Aviation)*	Cranfield	31. 7.09E

Reg	Type	c/n	Prev id	Date	Owner/Operator	Base	Expiry
G-BGGM	Piper PA-38-112 Tomahawk	38-79A0170	N9698N	10. 1.79	Grunwick Processing Laboratories Ltd *(Operated Bonus Aviation)*	Cranfield	18.12.09E
G-BGGN	Piper PA-38-112 Tomahawk	38-79A0171	N9706N	10. 1.79	Bell Aviation Ltd	Cranfield	8. 9.09E
G-BGGO	Reims Cessna F152 II	F15201569		8. 3.79	East Midlands Flying School Ltd	Nottingham-East Midlands	31. 7.09E
G-BGGP	Reims Cessna F152 II	F15201580		8. 3.79	East Midlands Flying School Ltd	Nottingham-East Midlands	7. 1.10E
G-BGGU	Wallis WA-116 RR (Subaru EA61)	702		28.12.78	K H Wallis *(Noted 8.01)*	Reymerston Hall, Norfolk	
G-BGGV	Wallis WA-120 Series 2	703		28.12.78	K H Wallis *(Not completed)*	Reymerston Hall, Norfolk	
G-BGGW	Wallis WA-122 RR (RR Continental O-240-A)	704		28.12.78	K H Wallis	Reymerston Hall, Norfolk	30. 5.08P
G-BGHI	Reims Cessna F152 II	F15201560		15. 1.79	V R McCready	Shoreham	4. 6.09E
G-BGHJ	Reims Cessna F172N Skyhawk II	F17201777	EI-BVF G-BGHJ	15. 1.79	Airplane Ltd	Humberside	18. 8.09E
G-BGHM	Robin R1180T Aiglon	227		19. 2.79	H Price	Blackpool	13. 5.09E
G-BGHP	Beech 76 Duchess	ME-190	N60132	16. 1.79	Magenta Ltd *(Operated Airways Flight Training)*	Exeter	6. 8.09E
G-BGHS	Cameron N-31 Balloon (Hot Air)	501		15. 1.79	W R Teasdale *"Baby Champion"* *(On loan to British Balloon Museum and Library)*	Newbury	29.11.09E
G-BGHT	Falconar F-12 (Built T K Baillie) (Lycoming O-290)	PFA 022-10040		17. 1.79	C R Coates	(Sneaton Thorpe, Whitby)	
G-BGHU	North American T-6G-NF Texan	182-729	FAP1707 French AF 115042, 51-15042	22. 1.79	C E Bellhouse *(As "115042:TR-042" in USAF c/s) "Carly"*	Headcorn	30. 5.08P
G-BGHY	Taylor JT.1 Monoplane (Built J Prowse)	PFA 1455		12. 1.79	G W Hancox	Priory Farm, Tibenham	2. 9.09P
G-BGHZ	Clutton FRED Series II (Built A G Edwards)	PFA 029-10445		12. 1.79	A J Perry	(Bognor Regis)	
G-BGIB	Cessna 152 II	15282161	N68169	3. 7.79	Redhill Air Services Ltd	Redhill	12.12.09E
G-BGIG	Piper PA-38-112 Tomahawk	38-78A0773	N2607A	23. 1.79	Air Claire Ltd *(Operated Glasgow Flying Club)*	Glasgow	14. 4.09E
G-BGIU	Cessna F172H (Built Reims Aviation SA)	F172-0620	PH-VIT	26. 2.79	A G Arthur	Perranporth	10. 8.09E
G-BGIX	Helio H 295 Super Courier	1467	(G-BGAO) N68861	17.10.79	C M Lee	Fanners Farm, Great Waltham	14. 5.09E
G-BGIY	Reims Cessna F172N Skyhawk II	F17201824		31. 1.79	Air Claire Ltd *(Operated Glasgow Flying Club)*	Glasgow	23.11.09E
G-BGJU	Cameron V-65 Balloon (Hot Air)	499		5. 2.79	J A Folkes *"Spoils"*	Loughborough	4. 4.93A
G-BGKC	SOCATA Rallye 110ST	3262		25. 4.79	J H Cranmer *(Dumped 4.07)*	Bidford	8. 9.99
G-BGKO	Gardan GY-20 Minicab (Built R B Webber)	PFA 1827		14. 2.79	M N King *(On long term rebuild 8.06)*	Higherlands Farm, Branscombe	
G-BGKS	Piper PA-28-161 Warrior II	28-7916221	N9562N	12. 2.79	Mid America (UK) Ltd	Inverness	4. 6.09E
G-BGKT	Auster AOP.9 (Officially regd with Frame no.AUS/137)	B5/10/137	XN441	28.12.78	G T Gimblett tr Kilo Tango Group *(As "XN441" in AAC c/s) (Noted 9.08)*	Trenchard Farm, Eggesford	11. 5.07P
G-BGKU	Piper PA-28R-201 Arrow III	28R-7837237	N31585	8. 3.79	Aerolease Ltd	Conington	13. 3.09E
G-BGKV	Piper PA-28R-201 Cherokee Arrow III	28R-7737156	N44985	21. 5.79	R Haverson and A K Lake	Little Snoring	12. 5.09E
G-BGKY	Piper PA-38-112 Tomahawk	38-78A0737	N9732N	2. 3.79	APB Leasing Ltd	(Edgerley, Oswestry)	26. 9.08E
G-BGKZ	Auster J/5F Aiglet Trainer	2776	F-BGKZ	15.12.78	R B Webber *(Noted 2.06)*	Trenchard Farm, Eggesford	25. 2.95
G-BGLA	Piper PA-38-112 Tomahawk	38-78A0741	N9699N	9. 3.79	B H and P M Illston t/a Norwich School of Flying	Norwich	23. 4.09E
G-BGLF	Evans VP-1 Series 2 (Built R A Abrahams) (Volkswagen 1834)	PFA 062-10388		28. 2.79	B A Schlussler Black Spring Farm, Castle Bytham		2. 5.09P
G-BGLG	Cessna 152 II	15282092	N67909	11. 4.79	L W Scattergood *(Operated Sheffield City Flying School)*	Sandtoft	7. 8.09E
G-BGLK	Monnett Sonerai IIL (Built G L Kemp) (Volkswagen 1783)	PFA 015-10304		24. 2.78	J Bradley *(Noted 10.08)*	City of Derry	1. 6.05P
G-BGLN	Reims Cessna FA152 Aerobat	FA1520354		8. 3.79	Bflying Ltd *(Forced landed Ingleby Cross, Northallerton 27. 7.04 and substantially damaged: wreck stored 1.07)*	Bournemouth	18. 9.06T
G-BGLO	Reims Cessna F172N Skyhawk II	F17201900		8. 3.79	J R Isabel	Southend	29. 1.09E
G-BGLS	Oldfield Baby Lakes (Built D S Morgan) (Lycoming O-235)	PFA 010-10237		11.12.78	J F Dowe *(Stored dismantled 1.08)*	Queach Farm, Bury St Edmunds	18. 6.88P
G-BGLZ	Stits SA-3A Playboy (Built D J Stadler) (Continental C90)	71-100	N9996	19. 6.79	P C Sheard	Strubby	15. 5.07P
G-BGME	SIPA 903	96	G-BCML "G-BCHU", F-BGHU	1. 1.81	M Emery	Redhill	17. 6.94P
G-BGMJ	Gardan GY-201 Minicab (Built Con. Aéronautique de Bearn) (Continental A65)	12	F-BGMJ	19. 6.78	A W Wakefield tr G-BGMJ Group	Sibson	9.12.09P
G-BGMP	Cessna F172G (Built Reims Aviation SA)	F172-0240	PH-BNV	26. 3.79	B M O'Brien	Headcorn	10. 9.09E
G-BGMR	Gardan GY-20 Minicab (Built A B Holloway to JB.01 Minicab standard) (Continental C90)	PFA 056-10153		12. 3.79	R A M Smith tr Mike Romeo Flying Group *(Noted 6.06)*	White Waltham	29. 9.04P
G-BGMS	Taylor JT.2 Titch (Built M A J Spice - pr.no.PFA 060-10400)	MS.1		20.10.78	M A J Spice	(Middlewich, Cheshire)	
G-BGMT	SOCATA Rallye 235E	13126		14. 9.78	C G Wheeler	Morgansfield, Fishburn	17. 2.10E
G-BGMV	Scheibe SF25B Falke (Stark-Stamo MS1500)	4648	D-KEBG	15. 5.79	C A Bloom and A P Twort *(Stored 2004)*	Kittyhawk Farm, Deanland	16.11.01
G-BGND	Reims Cessna F172N Skyhawk II	F17201576	PH-AYI (F-GAQA)	3. 3.78	A J M Freeman	Andrewsfield	27.11.09E
G-BGNT	Reims Cessna F152 II	F15201644		23.10.79	Aerolease Ltd	Conington	10. 4.09E
G-BGNV	Gulfstream GA-7 Cougar	GA7-0078	N790GA	20. 4.79	G J Bissex	Norton Malreward	12. 5.09E

Reg	Type	c/n	Prev id	Date	Owner/Operator	Location	Date
G-BGOD	Colt 77A Balloon (Hot Air)	040		4. 4.79	C and M D Steuer *"Harvey Wallbanger"*		
						London NW1	18. 6.97A
G-BGOG	Piper PA-28-161 Warrior II	28-7916350	N9639N	8. 6.79	W D Moore	Cranfield	26. 6.09E
G-BGOI	Cameron O-56 Balloon (Hot Air)	526		4. 4.79	M J Streat *(Teachers Assurance titles)*	Bristol	21. 5.08A
G-BGOJ	Reims Cessna F150L	F15000931	G-MABI	19. 4.79	D J Hockings	(Hailsham)	21. 7.97
			G-BGOJ, PH-KDA				
G-BGOL	Piper PA-28R-201T Turbo Arrow III		N36705	11. 4.79	R G Jackson	Bournemouth	5. 3.09E
		28R-7803335					
G-BGON	Gulfstream GA-7 Cougar	GA7-0095	N9527Z	24. 4.79	J P E Walsh t/a Walsh Aviation *(Operated Cabair)*		
						Elstree	30. 8.08E
G-BGOR	North American AT-6D-NT Harvard III		FAP1508	28. 3.79	P Meyrick *(As "14863" in USAAF c/s)*		
	(Reported as c/n 88-14880)	88-14863	SAAF 7504, EX935, 41-33908			Rednal	5. 9.09P
G-BGPA	Cessna 182Q Skylane II	18266538	C-GYBW	11. 7.79	Hydestile Business Systems Ltd	Dunsfold	27. 4.09E
			(N94935)				
G-BGPB	CCF Harvard 4 (T-6J-CCF Texan)	CCF4-538	FAP1747	4. 4.79	1959 Ltd *(As "1747" in Portuguese AF c/s)*		
			WGAF BF+050, WGAF AA+050, 53-4619			Duxford	11. 4.09P
G-BGPD	Piper J-3C-65 Cub (L-4H-PI)	12040	F-BFQP	18. 4.79	P R Whiteman	Marsh Hill Farm, Aylesbury	20. 6.07P
	(Frame No.11867)		F-BDTP, 44-79744		*(As "479744:49-M" in 92nd Armoured FA Btn, US 9th Army c/s)*		
	(Officially c/n 10478 which is ex 43-29187/OO-ADI/F-BFQP: G-BGPD is ex 44-79744/F-BDTP: fuselages exchanged in France - see G-BCOM)						
G-BGPH	Gulfstream AA-5B Tiger	AA5B-1248	(G-BGRU)	14. 8.79	Shipping and Airlines Ltd	Biggin Hill	17. 3.09E
G-BGPI	Plumb BGP-1 Biplane	PFA 083-10359		26. 6.78	B G Plumb	Hinton-in-the-Hedges	2. 4.09P
	(Built B G Plumb) (Continental O-200A)						
G-BGPJ	Piper PA-28-161 Warrior II	28-7916288	N9602N	24. 4.79	West Lancs Warrior Co Ltd	RAF Woodvale	23. 4.09E
G-BGPL	Piper PA-28-161 Warrior II	28-7916289	N9603N	20. 4.79	Montash Properties Ltd	Manston	9. 9.09E
G-BGPM	Evans VP-2	PFA 063-10335		17. 4.79	E Stinton tr Cheap as Chips Group		
	(Built T Painter)					Gloucestershire	29. 4.86P
G-BGPN	Piper PA-18-150 Super Cub	18-7909044	N9750N	12. 4.79	D McHugh and A R Darke	Wycombe Air Park	5. 2.11S
G-BGRC	Piper PA-28-140 Cherokee B	28-26208	SE-FHF	12. 6.79	Tecair Aviation Ltd and G F Haigh	Shipdham	26.10.97T
			N5501U		*(Stored and dismantled 8.05)*		
G-BGRE	Beech 200 Super King Air	BB-568		8. 5.79	Martin-Baker (Engineering) Ltd	Chalgrove	16.10.09E
G-BGRG	Beech 76 Duchess	ME-233		8. 5.79	S J Skilton t/a Aviation Rentals	Bournemouth	10. 4.09E
					(Operated Professional Air Training)		
G-BGRH	Robin DR.400 2+2	1411		21. 5.79	A P and P Hatton	(Newark)	5. 4.09E
G-BGRI	CEA Jodel DR.1050 Sicile	540	F-BLZJ	27. 4.79	R G Hallam	Netherthorpe	5. 3.11S
G-BGRM	Piper PA-38-112 Tomahawk	38-79A1067	N9673N	1. 8.79	I W Goodger t/a Classair	Biggin Hill	22. 6.09E
G-BGRO	Reims Cessna F172M Skyhawk II	F17201129	PH-KAB	4. 5.79	A N Pirie t/a Cammo Aviation	Kirknewton	14. 1.10E
G-BGRR	Piper PA-38-112 Tomahawk	38-78A0336	OO-FLT	8. 5.79	Pure Air Aviation Ltd	Gloucestershire	27. 3.09E
			N9685N				
G-BGRS	Thunder Ax7-77Z Balloon (Hot Air)	203		21. 5.79	P M Gaines	Stockton-on-Tees	26. 4.03A
G-BGRT	Steen Skybolt	RCT.001		12. 9.78	O Meier	St Johann In Tirol, Austria	8. 1.09P
	(Built R C Teverson - pr.no.PFA 064-10171)						
G-BGRX	Piper PA-38-112 Tomahawk	38-79A0609	N9662N	11. 5.79	Bonus Aviation Ltd	Cranfield	16.11.09E
G-BGSA	SOCATA MS.892E Rallye 150GT	12838	F-GAKC	29. 5.79	D H Tonkin	Perranporth	28. 8.09E
G-BGSH	Piper PA-38-112 Tomahawk	38-79A0562	N9719N	11. 5.79	S Padidar-Nazar	Carlisle	11.12.09E
G-BGSJ	Piper J-3C-65 Cub (L-4A-PI)	8781	F-BGXJ	21. 5.79	A J Higgins *(As "236657:D-72" in USAAC c/s)*		
	(Frame No.8917)		French AF, 42-36657			Dunkeswell	3. 3.09P
G-BGSV	Reims Cessna F172N Skyhawk II	F17201830		1. 8.79	Southwell Air Services Ltd	Linley Hill, Leven	18. 3.09E
G-BGSW	Beech F33 Bonanza	CD-1253	OH-BDD	30. 5.79	C Wood	Wellesbourne Mountford	11. 9.09E
G-BGSY	Gulfstream GA-7 Cougar	GA7-0096		4. 6.79	N D Anderson	Old Sarum	21.12.09E
G-BGTC	Auster AOP.9	xxxx	XP282	12.10.79	T K Rumble tr Terranne Auster Group *(noted 8.08)*		
	(Officially regd with Frame no.AUS/168)					RAF Scampton	9. 6.97P
G-BGTF	Piper PA-44-180 Seminole	44-7995287	N2131Y	20. 6.79	Shemburn Ltd	Weston, Dublin	18.12.09E
G-BGTG	Piper PA-23-250 Aztec F	27-7954061	N2454M	23. 5.79	ASG Leasing Ltd	Guernsey	13. 2.09E
G-BGTI	Piper J-3C-65 Cub (L-4J-PI)	12940	F-BFFL	17. 5.79	A P Broad	Brandy Wharf, Waddingham	30.10.09P
	(Rotax 582) (Frame No.12770)		44-80644				
G-BGTJ	Piper PA-28-180 Cherokee Archer		OY-BIO	3. 7.79	Serendipity Aviation Ltd	Gloucestershire	20.12.08E
		28-7405083	SE-GAH		*(Missing on a flight from Gloucestershire to Kilrush*		
	25.10.08; wreck located near the summit of Corriebracks Mountain, County Wicklow. All four occupants killed and aircraft destroyed)						
G-BGTT	Cessna 310R II	310R1641	N1AN	13. 7.79	Capital Air Charter Ltd	Exeter	14. 6.09E
			(N2635D)				
G-BGTX	SAN Jodel D 117	698	F-BIDI	22. 6.79	C Adams and H F Young tr Madley Flying Group (Cisavia)		
						Shobdon	26. 8.09P
G-BGUB (2)	Piper PA-32-300 Six	32-7940252	N2387U	29.11.79	A J Diplock	Biggin Hill	14. 7.09E
G-BGVB	CEA Jodel DR.315 Petit Prince	308	F-BPOP	20. 7.79	P J Leggo	Leicester	18. 5.09E
G-BGVE	Scintex CP.1310-C3 Super Emeraude	931	F-BMJE	8. 6.79	R Whitwell	(Doncaster)	14. 7.06P
G-BGVH	Beech 76 Duchess	ME-260		8. 6.79	W J and J.C M Golden t/a Valco Marketing		
						Bowerchalke, Salisbury	6. 9.09E
G-BGVK	Piper PA-28-161 Cherokee Warrior II		PH-WPT	13. 6.79	Aviation South West Ltd	Exeter	29. 5.09E
		28-7816400	G-BGVK, N6244C				
G-BGVN	Piper PA-28RT-201 Arrow IV	28R-7918168	N2846U	22. 6.79	John Wailing Ltd	Fairoaks	3.12.08E
G-BGVS	Reims Cessna F172M	F17200992	PH-HVS	3. 5.79	J W Tulloch tr Kirkwall Flying Club	Kirkwall	22.12.09E
			(PH-LUK)				
G-BGVV	Gulfstream AA-5A Cheetah	AA5A-0750		27. 6.79	W A Davidson	Prestwick	22. 5.09E
G-BGVY	Gulfstream AA-5B Tiger	AA5B-1080	(G-BGVU)	21. 8.79	R J C Neal-Smith	Compton Abbas	3.12.09E
			(F-GBOO)				
G-BGVZ	Piper PA-28-181 Archer II	28-7990528	N2886A	12. 7.79	W Walsh and S R Mitchell	RAF Woodvale	16. 7.09E
G-BGWC	Robin DR.400-180 Régent	1420		26. 6.79	M A Newman	Thruxton	12. 7.09E
G-BGWH	Piper PA-18-150 Super Cub	18-7605	ST-ABR	18. 6.79	Richard Shuttleworth Trustees	Old Warden	7.10.11
			G-ARSR, N10F				
G-BGWK	Sikorsky S-61N Mk.II	61-820	N1346C	10. 9.79	Bristow Helicopters Ltd *"Dun Robin"*	Aberdeen	28.11.09E
			G-BGWK				
G-BGWM	Piper PA-28-181 Archer II	28-7990458	N2817Y	29. 6.79	Thames Valley Flying Club Ltd	Wycombe Air Park	23. 5.09E
G-BGWN	Piper PA-38-112 Tomahawk	38-79A0918	N9693N	2. 7.79	J R Davison	Woodhall Spa	17. 7.08E

G-BGWO	Jodel D 112	227	F-BHGQ	22. 6.79	R C Williams tr G-BGWO Group	Breighton	5. 5.09P
	(Built Etablissement Valladeau)						
G-BGWR	Cessna U206A Super Skywagon	U2060653	G-DISC	6. 7.79	Airkix Aircraft Ltd	Sibson	29. 1.09E
			G-BGWR, PH-OTD, N4953F				
G-BGWV	Aeronca 7AC Champion	7AC-4082	OO-GRI	23. 8.79	J A Webb tr RFC Flying Group	(Alton)	10.10.86P
			OO-TWR		*(Damaged Popham 8. 6.86)*		
G-BGXA	Piper J-3C-65 Cub (L-4H-PI)	10762	F-BGXA	1. 3.78	P King *(As "329471:F-44" in USAAC c/s)*		
	(Frame No.10587 - regd with c/n 11170)		French AF, 43-29471			Eastbach Farm, Coleford	24. 4.07P
G-BGXB	Piper PA-38-112 Tomahawk	38-79A1007	N9728N	2. 7.79	Signtest Ltd *(Noted Museum site 4.08)*		
						East Fortune	16. 8.04T
G-BGXC	SOCATA TB-10 Tobago	35		19.10.79	D H Courtley	Alderney	19. 8.08E
G-BGXD	SOCATA TB-10 Tobago	39		19.10.79	D F P Finan	Durham Tees Valley	10. 8.09E
G-BGXO	Piper PA-38-112 Tomahawk	38-79A0982	N9703N	5. 7.79	Goodwood Road Racing Company Ltd	Goodwood	12. 2.09E
					(Operated Goodwood Flying Club)		
G-BGXR	Robin HR.200-100 Club	53	F-BVYH	1.10.79	J R Cross	Derby	16. 4.09E
G-BGXS	Piper PA-28-236 Dakota	28-7911198	N2836Z	12. 7.79	M Holland tr G-BGXS Group	Gamston	24. 4.09E
G-BGXT	SOCATA TB-10 Tobago	40		3.10.79	J L Alexander	Haverfordwest	27.11.08E
G-BGYH	Piper PA-28-161 Warrior II	28-7916313	N209LG	17. 7.79	Paper Space Ltd	Full Sutton	19. 8.09E
			N580X, G-BGYH, N9619N				
	(Landed short of the runway at Full Sutton 3. 5.08 and right main undercarriage detached causing substantial damage)						
G-BGYN	Piper PA-18-150 Super Cub	18-7709137	N62747	19. 7.79	B J Dunford	Longwood Farm, Morestead	21.11.10
G-BGZF	Piper PA-38-112 Tomahawk	38-79A1015	N9700N	26. 7.79	APB Leasing Ltd	Hawarden	2.12.07E

G-BHAA - G-BHZZ

G-BHAA	Cessna 152 II	15281330	N49809	12. 2.79	Herefordshire Aero Club Ltd	Shobdon	18. 6.09E
G-BHAD	Cessna A152 Aerobat	A1520807	N7390L	12. 2.79	Shropshire Aero Club Ltd	Sleap	20. 5.09E
G-BHAI	Reims Cessna F152 II	F15201625	(D-EJAY)	14. 8.79	S Fyfe t/a Scottish Aircraft Sales	Perth	4. 3.09E
G-BHAJ	Robin DR.400-160 Major 80	1430		22. 8.79	Rowantask Ltd	Biggin Hill	25. 3.09E
G-BHAR	Westland-Bell 47G-3B1	WA/353	XT194	7. 8.79	T J Wright	(Mullingar, County Westmeath)	8. 7.09E
G-BHAV	Reims Cessna F152 II	F15201633		15. 8.79	T M and M L Jones *(Operated Derby Aero Club)*		
						Derby	17. 3.08E
G-BHAW	Reims Cessna F172N Skyhawk II	F17201858		15. 8.79	J Smith	Breighton	28. 6.09E
G-BHAX	Enstrom F-28C-2-UK	486-2	N5689N	22.10.79	J L Ferguson	Barton	21.11.08E
G-BHAY	Piper PA-28RT-201 Arrow IV	28R-7918213	N2910N	17. 8.79	Alpha Yankee Ltd	Newcastle	25. 6.09E
G-BHBA	Campbell Cricket	SMI-1		15. 8.79	S N McGovern	Little Rissington	27.11.09P
	(Built S M Irwin) Rotax 503)						
G-BHBE	Westland-Bell 47G-3B1	WA/422	XT510	29.10.79	T R Smith (Agricultural Machinery) Ltd *(Stored 6.05)*		
	(Soloy conversion)				New Lane Farm, North Elmham		21.12.01
G-BHBF	Sikorsky S-76A II Plus	760022	N4247S	9.11.79	Bristow Helicopters Ltd "Spirit of Paris"	Aberdeen	21. 7.09E
G-BHBG	Piper PA-32R-300 Lance	32R-7780515	N408RC	18. 9.79	D E Gee	Blackbushe	4.10.09E
			N9590N				
G-BHBT	Marquart MA.5 Charger	PFA 068-10190		3. 9.79	R G and C J Maidment	Goodwood	4.12.09P
	(Built R G Maidment) (Lycoming O-320)						
G-BHBZ	Partenavia P68B	191		10. 9.79	Geminair Services Ltd	Thruxton	27. 3.09E
G-BHCC	Cessna 172M Skyhawk II	17266711	(G-BGLY)	26.10.79	D Wood-Jenkins	Shobdon	7. 8.08E
			N80713				
G-BHCE	SAN Jodel D 117A	381	F-BHME	1.10.79	D G Jones	Pool Quay, Breidden	16. 2.08P
	(Originally built as D 112A and converted during rebuild between 1985 and 2004)						
G-BHCM	Cessna F172H	F172-0468	SE-FBD	25. 9.79	J Dominic	Denham	10. 4.09E
	(Built Reims Aviation SA)						
G-BHCP	Reims Cessna F152 II	F15201640		31.10.79	Eastern Air Executive Ltd	Sturgate	19. 5.09E
G-BHCZ	Piper PA-38-112 Tomahawk	38-78A0321	N214MD	26. 9.79	J E Abbott	(Storrington, Pulborough)	8.11.09E
G-BHDD	Vickers 668 Varsity T 1	?	WL626	18.10.79	G Vale *(Noted Aeropark museum as "WL626:P" 3.06)*		
						Nottingham-East Midlands	
G-BHDE	SOCATA TB-10 Tobago	58		2. 1.80	Alpha-Alpha Ltd	Liverpool	7. 3.09E
G-BHDM	Reims Cessna F152 II	F15201684		15.10.79	Big Red Kite Ltd	RAF Benson	19. 4.09E
G-BHDP	Reims Cessna F182Q Skylane II	F18200131		15.10.79	Zone Travel Ltd	Wycombe Air Park	4. 7.09E
G-BHDR	Reims Cessna F152 II	F15201680		15.10.79	Heron-Air Ltd	(Glasgow)	29. 7.07T
	(Rebuilt 2003/4 using parts from G-BPGM)				*(Incurred accident 1. 8.06: removed from Cumbernauld 2.07)*		
G-BHDS	Reims Cessna F152 II	F15201682		15.10.79	Tayside Aviation Ltd	Glenrothes	14. 7.09E
G-BHDV	Cameron V-77 Balloon (Hot Air)	585		1. 2.80	P Glydon "Dorm Ouse"	Barnt Green, Birmingham	25. 4.09E
G-BHDW	Reims Cessna F152 II	F15201652		15.10.79	Aircraft Engineers Ltd	Prestwick	13. 7.09E
G-BHDX	Reims Cessna F172N Skyhawk II	F17201889		5.10.79	GDX Ltd	Cranfield	22. 7.09E
G-BHDZ	Reims Cessna F172N Skyhawk II	F17201911		3.12.79	Abbey Security Services Ltd		
					Great Ashfield, Bury St Edmunds		31. 5.09E
G-BHEC	Reims Cessna F152 II	F15201676		3.12.79	Stapleford Flying Club Ltd	Stapleford	22. 7.09E
G-BHED	Reims Cessna FA152 Aerobat	FA1520359		3.12.79	TG Aviation Ltd *(Operated Thanet Flying Club)*		
						Manston	3. 7.09E
G-BHEG	SAN Jodel D 150 Mascaret	46	PH-ULS	3. 7.80	D M Griffiths	RAF Mona	25. 6.0P
			OO-SET				
G-BHEK	Scintex CP.1315-C3 Super Emeraude	923	F-BJMU	11.10.79	D B Winstanley	Barton	4.12.08P
G-BHEL	SAN Jodel D 117	735	F-BIOA	8.10.79	N Wright	Priory Farm, Tibenham	22.10.08P
G-BHEM	Bensen B 8MV	EK.14		8.10.79	G C Kerr *(Noted 7.08)*	Kirkbride	5.10.00P
	(Built E Kenny - pr.no.PFA G/01-1016) (Rotax 503)						
G-BHEN	Reims Cessna FA152 Aerobat	FA1520363		3. 1.80	The Leicestershire Aero Club Ltd	Leicester	1. 4.09E
G-BHEU	Thunder Ax7-65 Series 1 Balloon (Hot Air)	238		16.10.79	J Edwards "Polomoche"	Northampton	7. 4.09E
G-BHEV	Piper PA-28R-200 Cherokee Arrow II		PH-BOY	23.10.79	P Hardy tr 7-Up Group	Gamston	16. 4.09E
		28R-7435159	N41244				
G-BHEX	Colt 56A Balloon (Hot Air)	056		15.10.79	A S Dear, R B Green and W S Templeton tr Hale Hot		
					Air Balloon Group "Superwasp"	Fordingbridge	30. 8.09E
G-BHEZ	SAN Jodel D 150 Mascaret	22	F-BLDO	31. 1.80	A Shorter tr Air Yorkshire Group	Sherburn-in-Elmet	7. 1.10P
G-BHFC	Reims Cessna F152 II	F15201436		7. 4.78	Premier Flight Training Ltd	Old Buckenham	22. 9.09E

Reg	Type	C/n	Prev ID	Date	Owner/Operator	Location	Date
G-BHFE	Piper PA-44-180 Seminole	44-7995324	Abu Dhabi AF 2 005, G-BHFE, N2383U	2.10.79	Grunwick Processing Laboratories Ltd *(Operated Bonus Aviation)*	Cranfield	9. 2.10E
G-BHFF	Dormois Jodel D 112	322	F-BEKJ	19.10.79	G H Gilmour-White	(Thorverton, Exeter)	28. 3.02P
	(Force landed in field 4 nm W of Marlborough 1.9.01: damage to port u/c, port wing and engine: wing donated to G-BIVB 2003)						
G-BHFG	SNCAN Stampe SV-4C	45	F-BJDN Aeronavale 45, Fr.AF	31.10.79	C C Rollings and T F J Hodson tr Tiger Airways	Gloucestershire	17. 4.08T
G-BHFH	Piper PA-34-200T Seneca II	34-7970482	N8075Q	23.10.79	Oxford Aviation Academy (Oxford) Ltd	Oxford	22. 4.09E
G-BHFI	Reims Cessna F152 II	F15201685		22.10.79	C A Carnell and R D Turner tr BAE (Warton) Flying Club	Blackpool	10. 6.09E
G-BHFJ	Piper PA-28RT-201T Turbo Arrow IV	28R-7931298	N8072R	22.10.79	A D R Northeast and S A Cook	White Waltham	26.10.07E
G-BHFK	Piper PA-28-151 Cherokee Warrior	28-7615088	N8325C	12.12.79	Ilkeston Car Sales Ltd	Jericho Farm, Lambley	24. 3.09E
G-BHGC	Piper PA-18-150 Super Cub	18-8793	PH-NKH N4447Z	3. 4.79	Vectis Gliding Club Ltd	Bembridge	29. 2.08E
G-BHGF	Cameron V-56 Balloon (Hot Air)	574		5.11.79	P Spellward *"Biggles"*	Bristol	27. 7.09E
G-BHGJ	Wassmer Jodel D 120 Paris-Nice	336	F-BOYB	15. 1.80	Q.M B Oswell	RAF Halton	12. 4.09P
G-BHGO	Piper PA-32-260 Cherokee Six	32-7800007	PH-BGP N9656C	16.11.79	L C Myall	(Maidenhead)	14.12.09E
G-BHGY	Piper PA-28R-200 Cherokee Arrow II	28R-7435086	PH-NSL N57365	23.11.79	Truman Aviation Ltd	Nottingham City-Tollerton	8. 8.09E
G-BHHB	Cameron V-77 Balloon (Hot Air)	170		26.11.79	R M Powell *"Pax"*	Stockbridge	27. 2.09E
G-BHHE	CEA Jodel DR.1051/M1 Sicile Record	628	F-BMZC	26. 4.80	P Bridges and P C Matthews	Fowle Hall Farm, Laddingford	4. 8.09P
G-BHHG	Reims Cessna F152 II	F15201725		4. 3.80	TG Aviation Ltd *(Operated Thanet Flying Club)*	Manston	15. 3.09E
G-BHHH	Thunder Ax7-65 Bolt Balloon (Hot Air)	245		5.12.79	C A Hendley (Essex) Ltd *"Christmas"* *(Inflated 4.06)*	Oakwood Hill, Loughton	27. 9.87A
G-BHHK	Cameron N-77 Balloon (Hot Air)	547		5.12.79	I S Bridge *"Shadowfax II"* *(On loan to British Balloon Museum and Library)*	Newbury	7.12.87A
G-BHHN	Cameron V-77 Balloon (Hot Air)	549		29.11.79	P Gooch tr The Itchen Valley Balloon Group *"Valley Crusader"*	Alresford	27. 5.09E
G-BHHX	Jodel D 112 *(Built Etablissement Valladeau)*	223	F-BFAJ	19. 2.80	M J Wells tr G-BHHX Group	Watchford Farm, Yarcombe	26. 8.09P
G-BHIB	Reims Cessna F182Q Skylane II	F18200134		18.12.79	S N Chater and B Payne	Sherburn-in-Elmet	30. 4.09E
G-BHIG	Colt 31A Air Chair Balloon (Hot Air)	060	SE-... G-BHIG	12.12.79	P A Lindstrand *(Operated S Ericsson)*	Upplands Vasby, Sweden	3. 3.00A
G-BHII	Cameron V-77 Balloon (Hot Air)	548		10.12.79	R V Brown *"Tosca"*	Maidenhead	2. 9.96A
G-BHIJ	Eiriavion PIK-20E	20241		9. 1.80	P M Yeoman	(Scalford, Melton Mowbray)	2. 4.09E
G-BHIK	Adam RA.14 Loisir *(Continental A65)*	11-bis	F-PHLK	6. 2.80	L Lewis *(Damaged near Lancaster 17.4.85: stored 1.02)*	(Redcar)	20. 8.85P
G-BHIN	Reims Cessna F152 II	F15201715		28. 1.80	Sussex Flying Club Ltd	Shoreham	18.11.09E
G-BHIS	Thunder Ax7-65 Bolt Balloon (Hot Air)	254		26.11.79	J R Wilson tr The Hedgehoppers Balloon Group *"Yo-Yo"*	Didcot	30.10.09E
G-BHIT	SOCATA TB-9 Tampico	63		7.12.79	C J P Webster *(Reported at Mahon, Menorca 6.03 apparently abandoned)*	Biggin Hill	31. 1.01T
G-BHIY	Cessna F150K	F15000627	F-BRXR	18.12.79	G J Ball	Old Sarum	18. 4.09E
G-BHJF	SOCATA TB-10 Tobago	83		2. 1.80	D J Saunders tr Flying Fox Group	Fairoaks	19.12.08E
G-BHJI	Mooney M 20J Mooney 201	24-0925	N3753H	11. 2.80	Hearing Centre Aarhus	Exeter	2. 4.09E
G-BHJK	Maule M-5-235C Lunar Rocket	7296C	N56359	25. 2.80	P J Kelsey	Glenrothes	23. 6.08E
G-BHJN	Fournier RF4D	4021	F-BORH	3. 1.80	R F Wondrak tr RF4 Flying Group	Enstone	30. 3.09E
G-BHJO	Piper PA-28-161 Cherokee Warrior II	28-7816213	OO-FLD N9507N, N6034H	4. 1.80	A Sangster, I Young and T R Whittome tr Brackla Flying Group	Inverness	16. 5.09E
G-BHJS	Partenavia P68B	172	I-KLUB	28.12.79	J J Watts and D Fletcher	Bournemouth	15. 7.09E
G-BHJU	Robin DR.400 2+2	1288	D-ECDK	9. 1.80	J Barlow and P Crow tr Ageless Aeronauts	Lydd	29. 5.09E
G-BHKH	Cameron O-65 Balloon (Hot Air)	592		7. 1.80	P Donkin *"Daisey"*	Caerwent, Caldicot	6. 2.08A
G-BHKJ	Cessna 421C Golden Eagle *(Robertson STOL conversion)*	421C0848	(N26596)	25. 1.80	Totaljet Ltd	Hawarden	6.10.08E
G-BHLE	Robin DR.400-180 Régent	1466		25. 1.80	B D Greenwood	Ronaldsway	17. 4.09E
G-BHLH	Robin DR.400-180 Régent	1320	F-GBIG	11. 2.80	A Hegner tr G-BHLH Group	Wycombe Air Park	22. 4.09E
G-BHLJ	Saffery-Rigg S 200 Skyliner Balloon (Minimum Lift) *(Built C Saffery)*	IAR/01		23. 1.80	I A Rigg *"Skyliner"*	Pendlebury, Swinton	
G-BHLT	de Havilland DH.82A Tiger Moth *(Built Morris Motors Ltd)*	84997	ZS-DGA SAAF 2272, T6697	9. 6.80	Skymax (Aviation) Ltd	Damyn's Hall, Upminster	26. 2.90
G-BHLU	Fournier RF3	79	F-BMTN	14. 4.80	G Sabatino	(Uxbridge)	19. 4.08P
G-BHLW	Cessna 120 *(Continental C85)*	10210	N73005 NC73005	24. 3.80	L W Scattergood *"Sky Ranger"*	Sherburn-in-Elmet	24. 9.08P
G-BHLX	Grumman AA-5B Tiger	AA5B-0573	OY-GAR	1. 2.80	M D McPherson	Cranfield	11. 8.09E
G-BHMA	SIPA 903	61	OO-FAE F-BGBK	13. 3.80	H J Taggart	Ballymoney, County Antrim	8. 7.09P
G-BHMG	Reims Cessna FA152 Aerobat	FA1520368		10. 6.80	R D Smith	Popham	16. 7.09E
G-BHMI	Reims Cessna F172N Skyhawk II	F17202036	G-WADE G-BHMI	6. 8.80	GMI Aviation Ltd	(Ormskirk)	27. 3.09E
G-BHMJ	Avenger T 200-2112 Balloon (Minimum Lift) *(Built R Light)*	002		29. 1.80	R Light *"Lord Anthony I"*	Stockport	
G-BHMK	Avenger T 200-2112 Balloon (Minimum Lift) *(Built P Kinder)*	003		29. 1.80	P Kinder *"Lord Anthony II"*	Stockport	
G-BHMR	Stinson 108-3 Voyager *(Built Consolidated Vultee Aircraft)*	108-4352	F-BABO F-DABO, NC6352M	12. 2.80	G Cormack	Cumbernauld	23.11.90
G-BHMT	Evans VP-1 *(Built P E J Sturgeon) (Volkswagen 1834)*	PFA 062-10473		18. 2.80	R T Callow	(Aslackby Decoy Farm, Sleaford)	14.10.09P
G-BHNA	Cessna F152 II	F15201683		12. 2.80	Eastern Air Executive Ltd	Sturgate	19. 2.07E
G-BHNC	Cameron O-65 Balloon (Hot Air)	588		7. 2.80	D Bareford and C Charley *"Hot N'Cold"*	Cookley, Kidderminster and Wymeswold, Loughborough	13. 7.09E

Reg	Type	c/n	Prev id	Date	Owner/Operator	Location	Date
G-BHND	Cameron N-65 Balloon (Hot Air)	582		7. 2.80	S M Wellband	Little Keyford, Frome	24. 6.89A
G-BHNK	Wassmer Jodel D 120A Paris-Nice	243	F-BLNK	26. 3.80	K R Daly	Le Saint, Brittany, France	20. 4.09P
G-BHNL	Wassmer Jodel D 112	1206	F-BLNL	30. 1.80	M D Mold tr HNL Group		
						Watchford Farm, Yarcombe	21.10.09P
G-BHNO	Piper PA-28-181 Archer II	28-8090211	N81413	7. 2.80	B J Richardson	RAF Cosford	8. 9.09E
G-BHNP	Eiriavion PIK-20E	20253		29. 2.80	D A Sutton "NP"	Sackville Lodge, Riseley	26. 5.09E
G-BHNV	Westland-Bell 47G-3B1	WA/700	F-GHNM	11. 3.80	Leyline Helicopters Ltd (Noted 10.02)	(Penrith)	28. 5.89T
			G-BHNV, XW180				
G-BHNX	SAN Jodel D 117	493	F-BHNX	7. 9.78	M J A Trudgill	RAF Henlow	12. 1.87P
G-BHOA	Robin DR.400-160 Major 80	1478		27. 1.80	Goudhurst Service Station Ltd	Goudhurst	11. 9.09E
G-BHOG	Sikorsky S-61N Mk.II	61-825	PT-YEK	25. 3.80	British International Helicopter Services Ltd t/a British		
			G-BHOG,		International (Stored 4.08)	Plymouth	
			(LN-ONK), G-BHOG				
G-BHOJ	Colt 12A Cloudhopper Balloon (Hot Air)	080		27. 2.80	J A Folkes (Inflated 4.06)	Bulcote, Nottingham	
	(Originally registered as Colt 14A)						
G-BHOL	CEA Jodel DR.1050 Ambassadeur	35	F-BJQL	6. 2.80	S P Tilling	Old Hay, Paddock Wood	9. 3.11S
G-BHOM	Piper PA-18 Super Cub 95	18-1391	OO-PIU	7. 3.80	P Myers tr Oscar Mike Flying Group		
	(L-18C-PI) (Frame No.18-1272)		OO-HMT, French Army 51-15391			Whitehall Farm, Benington	2. 5.08P
G-BHOO	Yorkshire Air Balloon A66 Balloon (Hot Air)	001		26. 2.80	D Livesey and J M Purves "Scraps"		
	(Built D Livesey and J M Purves)					Brampton and York	
G-BHOR	Piper PA-28-161 Warrior II	28-8016331	N82162	12. 6.80	A J Harewood tr Oscar Romeo Flying Group		
						Biggin Hill	15. 8.09E
G-BHOT	Cameron V-65 Balloon (Hot Air)	777		15. 9.81	J A Baker tr The Dante Balloon Group "Le Billet Doux"		
						Hungerford	8. 8.99A
G-BHOZ	SOCATA TB-9 Tampico	84		11. 3.80	G-BHOZ Management Ltd	Kemble	21.12.09E
G-BHPK	Piper J-3C-65 Cub (L-4A-PI)	8979	F-BEPK	26. 2.80	L B Smith tr L4 Group (As "238410:A-44" in USAAF c/s)		
	(Frame No.9098: official c/n 12161)		French Military, 42-38410			Priory Farm, Tibenham	7. 4.09P
G-BHPL	CASA 1-131E Jungmann	1058	Spanish AF	17. 7.80	A Burroughes (As "E3B-350:05 97" in Spanish AF c/s)		
			E3B-350			Compton Abbas	18. 7.08P
G-BHPS	Wassmer Jodel D 120A Paris-Nice	148	F-BIXI	11. 6.80	T J Price	Rhigos	16. 7.08P
G-BHPY	Cessna 152 II	15282983	N46009	26. 3.80	TGD Leasing Ltd	Wellesbourne Mountford	17.12.09E
G-BHPZ	Cessna 172N Skyhawk II	17272017	N6411E	26. 3.80	O'Brien Properties Ltd	Shoreham	22. 4.09E
G-BHRB	Reims Cessna F152 II	F15201707		20. 3.80	Upperstack Ltd t/a LAC Flying School	Barton	26. 3.09E
					(Operated Lancashire Aero Club)		
G-BHRC	Piper PA-28-161 Warrior II	28-7916430	N9527N	3. 4.80	The Sherwood Flying Club Ltd		
						Nottingham City-Tollerton	9. 3.09E
G-BHRH	Reims Cessna FA150K Aerobat	FA1500056	PH-ECB	24. 3.80	Merlin Flying Club Ltd	Hucknall	25. 6.09E
			D-ECBL, (D-EKKW)				
G-BHRN	Reims Cessna F152 II	F15201728	F-GCHV	8. 4.80	S R Mendes (Operated Flying Time)	Shoreham	5. 9.09E
G-BHRO	Rockwell Commander 112A	364	N1364J	20. 3.80	R A Blackwell	North Weald	22. 9.09E
G-BHRR	Menavia Piel CP.301A Emeraude	270	F-BISK	28. 3.80	T W Offen (Noted 8.07)	Maypole Farm, Chislet	28. 5.87P
G-BHRW	CEA Jodel DR.221 Dauphin	93	F-BPCP	10. 7.80	D H Williams and I Bell tr Dauphin Flying Group		
						Oaksey Park	1.6.09E
G-BHSB	Cessna 172N Skyhawk II	17272977	(N1225F)	25. 6.80	JW Cope and M P Wimsey	Strubby	5. 2.09E
G-BHSD	Scheibe SF25E Super Falke	4357	D-KDGG	21. 7.80	L Barber tr Upwood Motorglider Group	Upwood	25. 7.09E
	(Limbach SL1700)						
G-BHSE	Rockwell Commander 114	14161	N4831W	15. 5.80	604 Squadron Flying Group Ltd Wycombe Air Park	16. 5.09E	
			AN-BRL, (N4831W)				
G-BHSN	Cameron N-56 Balloon (Hot Air)	595		10. 4.80	I Bentley	Bath	9. 7.05A
G-BHSP	Thunder Ax7-77Z Balloon (Hot Air)	272		15. 4.80	G A Fisher tr Out-of-the Blue "Chicago" (Inflated 4.06)		
	(Originally built as D-TRIER c/n 221)					Guildford	23. 2.94A
G-BHSS	Pitts S-1S	C 1461M	N1704	19. 9.80	C W Burkett	Little Gransden	3. 3.09P
	(Built C H McClendon) (Lycoming O-320)						
G-BHSY	CEA Jodel DR.1050 Sicile	546	F-BLZO	6. 5.80	T R Allebone	Easton Maudit	23. 2.08
G-BHTA	Piper PA-28-236 Dakota	28-8011102	N8197H	22. 4.80	Dakota Ltd	Jersey	8.10.09E
G-BHTC	CEA Jodel DR.1051/M1 Sicile Record	581	F-BMGR	1. 5.80	A H Macaskill and G Clark	Oaksey Park	24. 6.09P
G-BHTG	Thunder Ax6-56 Bolt Balloon (Hot Air)	273		18. 4.80	F R and S.H MacDonald "Halcyon"		
						Newdigate, Dorking	18.12.91A
G-BHUE	SAN Jodel DR.1050 Ambassadeur	185	F-BERM	21. 4.80	M J Harris	(Lower Broadheath, Worcester)	19.10.92
			F-OBRM				
G-BHUG	Cessna 172N Skyhawk II	17272985	N1283F	24. 6.80	F G Baulch t/a FGT Aircraft Hire	Dunkeswell	29. 3.09E
G-BHUI	Cessna 152 II	15283144	N46932	27. 5.80	Galair International Ltd	Wellesbourne Mountford	11. 3.09E
G-BHUJ	Cessna 172N Skyhawk II	17271932	N5752E	27. 5.80	K B Dupuy tr Uniform Juliet Group	Southend	20. 7.09E
G-BHUM	de Havilland DH.82A Tiger Moth	85453	VT-DGA	9. 6.80	S G Towers	Beckwithshaw, Harrogate	10. 7.09S
			VT-DDN, RIAF, SAAF 4622, DE457				
G-BHUR	Thunder Ax3 Mini Sky Chariot Balloon (Hot Air)			9. 5.80	B F G Ribbans "Ben Hur"	Newbury	6. 6.06A
		277			(On loan to British Balloon Museum and Library)		
G-BHUU	Piper PA-25-235 Pawnee D	25-8056035	N2440Q	28. 5.80	Booker Gliding Club Ltd	Wycombe Air Park	24. 4.09E
	(Modified to PA-25-260 standard)						
G-BHVB	Piper PA-28-161 Warrior II	28-8016260	N9638N	16. 5.80	P J Clarke	Wolverhampton	9. 9.07E
G-BHVF	SAN Jodel D 150A Mascaret	11	F-BLDF	28.10.80	R V Smith	(Fleet)	8. 1.10P
G-BHVP	Cessna 182Q Skylane II	18267071	N97374	15.12.80	R J W Wood	Gregory Farm, Mirfield	18.12.09E
G-BHVR	Cessna 172N Skyhawk II	17270196	N738SG	27. 5.80	C Vincent tr Victor Romeo Group	Elstree	9. 7.09E
G-BHVV	Piper J-3C-65 Cub (L-4A-PI)	8953	F-BGXF	27. 6.80	C A Ward and C A Cash (As "31430" in USAAF c/s)		
	(Frame No.9048)		French Military, 42-38384			Perranporth	26. 5.09P
	(Regd with c/n 10291/43-1430 ex F-BEGF: frames probably exchanged in 1953 rebuild)						
G-BHWA	Reims Cessna F152 II	F15201775		28. 3.80	Lincoln Enterprises Ltd	Wickenby	12. 7.09E
G-BHWB	Reims Cessna F152 II	F15201776	(G-BHWA)	14. 4.80	Lincoln Enterprises Ltd	Wickenby	22.11.09E
G-BHWH	Weedhopper JC-24A	0074		23. 4.80	G A Clephane	Basingstoke	X
	(Fuji-Robin EC-34-PM) (Modified to JC-24C)				(As "Bu.126603" in US Navy c/s) "Dream Machine"		
G-BHWK	SOCATA MS.880B Rallye Club	870	F-BONK	27. 8.80	D Spencer	Shotton Colliery, Peterlee	31. 8.09E
G-BHWY	Piper PA-28R-200 Cherokee Arrow II		N56904	17. 6.80	I C Rogers and R B Cheek tr Kilo Foxtrot Flying Group		
		28R-7435059				Sandown	10. 6.09E

G-BHWZ	Piper PA-28-181 Cherokee Archer II	N3379M	8. 4.80	M A Abbott	Fairoaks	6.10.09E
		28-7890299				
G-BHXA	Scottish Aviation Bulldog Series 120/1210	Botswana DF OD19. 6.80		Air Plan Flight Equipment Ltd (Deltair Aviation titles)		
		BH120/407	G-BHXA		Derby	10. 8.09S
G-BHXD	Wassmer Jodel D 120 Paris-Nice	258	F-BMIA	3. 7.80	D A Garner	Rhigos	20.10.09P
G-BHXK	Piper PA-28-140 Cherokee	28-21106	VR-HGB	14. 7.80	J Moreland tr GXK Flying Group	Thruxton	7. 5.09E
			9V-BAJ, (9M-AOM)				
G-BHXS	Wassmer Jodel D 120 Paris-Nice	133	F-BIXS	27. 8.80	R I Walker tr Plymouth Jodel Group	Plymouth	19. 7.09P
G-BHXY	Piper J-3C-65 Cub (L-4H-PI)	11905	D-EAXY	1. 7.80	F W Rogers (As "44-79609:S-44 in USAAF c/s)		
	(Frame No.11733)		F-BFQX, 44-79609			Bealbury, Plymouth	29. 5.09P
G-BHYA	Cessna R182 Skylane RG II	R18200532	N1717R	10. 7.80	B Davies	Withybush	27. 3.09E
G-BHYC	Cessna 172RG Cutlass II	172RG0404	(N4868V)	24. 6.80	IB Aeroplanes Ltd	City of Derry	31. 3.09E
G-BHYD	Cessna R172K Hawk XP	R1722734	N736RS	11.12.80	Sylmar Aviation and Services Ltd		
					Lower Wasing Farm, Brimpton	11. 5.09E
G-BHYG	Piper PA-34-200T Seneca II	34-8070235	N8225X	30. 6.80	Oxford Aviation Academy (Oxford) Ltd	Oxford	21.11.08E
G-BHYI	SNCAN Stampe SV-4A	18	F-BAAF	11. 7.80	D Hicklin	(Brightlingsea, Colchester)	25. 7.07
			French AF				
G-BHYP	Reims Cessna F172M Skyhawk II	F17201108	OY-BFR	30. 6.80	Avior Ltd	Oxford	16. 6.09E
G-BHYR	Reims Cessna F172M	F17200922	OY-DZH	30. 6.80	R G Forster tr G-BHYR Group	Stapleford	10. 7.09E
			SE-FZH, (OH-CFQ)				
G-BHYV	Evans VP-1	LC.2		2. 7.80	L Chiappi	White Waltham	
	(Built L Chiappi - pr.no.PFA 1569) (Volkswagen 1600)			(Noted 6.07 dumped outside less engine - far side black hangar)		
G-BHYX	Cessna 152 II	15281832	N67434	4. 7.80	Stapleford Flying Club Ltd	Stapleford	10. 4.09E
G-BHZE	Piper PA-28-181 Cherokee Archer II		OO-FLR	4.11.80	Zegruppe Ltd	White Waltham	5. 2.09T
		28-7890291	(OO-HCM), N3053M				
G-BHZH	Reims Cessna F152 II	F15201786		25. 7.80	Plymouth Flying School Ltd	Plymouth	27. 9.09E
G-BHZK	Grumman AA-5B Tiger	AA5B-0743	N28670	8. 9.80	R G Seth-Smith tr Zulu Kilo Group	Elstree	29. 5.09E
G-BHZO	Gulfstream AA-5A Cheetah	AA5A-0692	N26750	21. 7.80	P Middleton tr PG Air	Headcorn	25. 3.09E
G-BHZR	Scottish Aviation Bulldog Series 120/1210	Botswana DF	23. 7.80	White Knuckle Air Ltd "Winston"	Haverfordwest	9. 7.09S
		BH120/410	OD4, G-BHZR				
G-BHZS	Scottish Aviation Bulldog Series 120/1210	Botswana DF	23. 7.80	Air Plan Flight Equipment Ltd	Derby	20. 2.06T
		BH120/411	OD5, G-BHZS				
G-BHZT	Scottish Aviation Bulldog Series 120/1210	Botswana DF	23. 7.80	D M Curties	Kemble	14. 4.11T
		BH120/412	OD6, G-BHZT				
G-BHZU	Piper J-3C-65 Cub (L-4B-PI)	9775	F-BETO	17. 7.80	J K Tomkinson	Brook Farm, Boylestone	16. 7.07P
	(Continental O-200-A)		(F-BFKH), 43-914				
	(Regd with Frame No.9606 fitted to F-BETO in 1961 rebuild replacing c/n 13164 ex 45-4424)						
G-BHZV	Wassmer Jodel D 120A Paris-Nice	278	F-BMON	23. 7.80	J Gunson tr G-BHZV Group	Brook Farm, Pilling	24. 6.09P
G-BHZX	Thunder Ax7-69A Balloon (Hot Air)	288		25. 7.80	R J and H.M Beattie "After Eight"		
						Wendover, Aylesbury	10. 6.94A

G-BIAA - G-BIZZ

G-BIAC	SOCATA Rallye 235E Gabier	13323		17. 7.80	D R Watson and A J Haigh tr G-BIAC Flying Group		
						Maypole Farm, Chislet	14. 7.09E
G-BIAH	Wassmer Jodel D 112	1218	F-BMAH	20. 8.80	P A Gange	Thruxton	22. 7.08P
G-BIAI	Wallingford WMB.2 Windtracker Balloon (Minimum Lift)		1. 7.80	I Chadwick tr Unicorn Group "Amanda I"		
		008				Partridge Green, Horsham	
G-BIAP	Piper PA-16 Clipper	16-732	F-BBGM	25. 6.80	P J Bish	Draycott Farm, Chiseldon	14. 4.11S
	(Frame No.16-733)		F-OAGS				
G-BIAR	Rigg Skyliner II Balloon (Minimum Lift) AKC-59		9. 7.80	I A Rigg	Pendlebury, Swinton	
	(Built I A Rigg - c/n IAR/02)						
G-BIAX	Taylor JT.2 Titch	GFR-1		30. 7.80	D M Bland	(Malvern)	11. 5.04P
	(Built J T Everest and G F Rowley - pr.no.PFA 3228) (Continental O-200)						
G-BIAY	Grumman AA-5 Traveler	AA5-0423	OY-GAD	26. 8.80	P Moderate tr Group AY	Headcorn	30. 7.09E
			N7123L				
G-BIBA	SOCATA TB-9 Tampico	149		17. 7.80	TB Aviation Ltd	Denham	1. 5.09E
G-BIBB	Mooney M 20C Mark 21	2803	OH-MOD	22. 7.80	Lefay Engineering Ltd	Popham	23. 6.08E
G-BIBG	Sikorsky S-76A II Plus	760083	5N-BCE	18. 8.80	Bristow Helicopters Ltd "Loch Seaforth"	Aberdeen	18. 8.09E
			G-BIBG				
G-BIBJ	Enstrom 280C-UK-2 Shark	1187		13. 8.80	C J Swift	Little Snoring	24. 3.09E
G-BIBN	Reims Cessna FA150K Aerobat	FA1500078	F-BSHN	29.10.80	B V Mayo	Maypole Farm, Chislet	8. 5.09E
G-BIBO	Cameron V-65 Balloon (Hot Air)	667		7. 8.80	D M Hoddinott	Bristol	13. 8.09E
G-BIBS	Cameron P-20 Balloon (Hot Air)	671		14. 8.80	Cameron Balloons Ltd (Stored 2006)	Bristol	
G-BIBT	Gulfstream AA-5B Tiger	AA5B-1047	N4518V	8. 9.80	Horizon Aviation Ltd	Swansea	18.11.08E
G-BIBW	Reims Cessna F172N Skyhawk II	F17201756		13.10.78	Shields Estates Ltd	Lydd	19. 4.09E
G-BIBX	Wallingford WMB.2 Windtracker Balloon (Minimum Lift)		18. 8.80	I A Rigg "Bumble"	Pendlebury, Swinton	
		9					
G-BICD	Taylorcraft J Auster 5	735	F-BFXH	20. 8.80	T R Parsons (Carries "MT166")		
			MT166			Beeches Farm, South Scarle	30. 4.09P
G-BICE	North American AT-6C-1-NT Harvard IIA	FAP1545	3. 9.80	C M L Edwards (As "41-33275:CE" in USAAF c/s)		
		88-9755	SAAF 7084, EX302, 41-33275			Great Oakley	14. 1.09P
G-BICG	Reims Cessna F152 II	F15201796		3. 9.80	A S Bamrah t/a Falcon Flying Services	Biggin Hill	12. 4.09E
G-BICJ	Monnett Sonerai II	726		22. 8.80	P Daukas	Conington	24. 1.06P
	(Built J R Heaton - pr.no.PFA 015-10531) (Volkswagen 1834)						
G-BICM	Colt 56A Balloon (Hot Air)	095		1. 9.80	W S Templeton and R B Green tr The Avon Advertiser		
					Balloon Club "Ladybird"	Fordingbridge	30. 8.09E
G-BICP	Robin DR.360 Chevalier	610	F-BSPH	2.10.80	J B McVeighty (On rebuild 08)	(Huntingdon, York)	28. 7.08E
G-BICR	Wassmer Jodel D 120A Paris-Nice	135	F-BIXR	5. 9.80	G L Perry tr Beehive Flying Group	White Waltham	21.12.08P
G-BICS	Robin R2100A Club	128	F-GBAC	4.12.80	I Young	Sandown	18. 7.09E
G-BICU	Cameron V-56 Balloon (Hot Air)	680		9. 9.80	G A Chadwick t/a Black Pearl Balloons		
						Partridge Green, Horsham	12. 2.09E
G-BICW	Piper PA-28-161 Warrior II	28-7916309	N2091U	8.10.80	S Morley tr Charlie Whisky Flying Group		
						Blackbushe	27. 2.09E

Reg	Type	C/n	Prev ID	Date	Owner/Operator	Base	Exp
-BICX	Maule M-5-235C Lunar Rocket	7287C	(G-MAUL (1)) N56352	2. 2.81	A T Jeans and J F Clarkson Compton Chamberlayne, Salisbury		22. 5.09E
G-BIDD	Evans VP-1	PFA 062-10974		27.10.78	J Hodgkinson *(Reported 7.05)* (Hill Farm, Nayland)		2.12.00P
	(Built J Wedgebury and regd initially as c/n PFA 062-10167 but combined project) (Volkswagen 1600)						
G-BIDF	Reims Cessna F172P Skyhawk II	F17202045	(PH-JPO)	18. 9.80	C J Chaplin and N J C Howard	Redhill	3. 4.10E
G-BIDG	SAN Jodel D 150A Mascaret	08	F-BLDG	11. 9.80	D R Gray	Barton	17. 9.08P
G-BIDH	Cessna 152 II	15280546	G-DONA G-BIDH, N25234	12. 9.80	Hull Aero Club Ltd	Linley Hill, Leven	5. 8.09E
G-BIDI	Piper PA-28R-201 Arrow III	28R-7837135	N3759M	11.11.80	A Lidster and T A N Brierley (East Cowton, Northallerton and York)		20. 5.09E
G-BIDJ	Piper PA-18A-150 Super Cub	18-6007	PH-MAY N7798D	22. 9.80	Flight Solutions Ltd	Panshanger	29. 7.11
	(Frame No.18-6089)						
G-BIDK	Piper PA-18-150 Super Cub (L-21A-PI)	"18-6591"	PH-MAI R Neth AF R-211, 51-15679, N7194K	22. 9.80	J and M.A McCullough Ivyville Farm, Newtownards		19. 8.11
	(Composite of PH-MAI originally Frame No.18-6714 [c/n 18-6591] ex LN-TVB/N9285D rebuilt 1976 with Frame No.18-503 [c/n 18-565] ex R Neth AF R-211)						
G-BIDO	Piel CP.301A Emeraude	327	F-POIO	25. 3.81	A R Plumb	Hill Farm, Nayland	2. 8.08P
G-BIDX	Dormois Jodel D 112	876	F-BIQY	19. 9.80	P Turton and H C Peake-Jones *(Noted 11.07)* Ash Farm, Winsford		5. 9.05P
G-BIEF	Cameron V-77 Balloon (Hot Air)	679		25. 9.80	Zebedee Balloon Services Ltd *"Daedalus"* Hungerford		1. 1.10E
G-BIEJ	Sikorsky S-76A II Plus	760097		21.10.80	Bristow Helicopters Ltd *"Glen Lossie"*	Norwich	21. 2.09E
G-BIEN	Wassmer Jodel D 120A Paris-Nice	218	F-BKNK	3. 6.81	C Newton	(Tilhouse, France)	19. 5.06P
G-BIEO	Wassmer Jodel D 112	1296	F-BMOK	19. 3.82	S C Solley tr Clipgate Flyers Clipgate Farm, Denton		15. 8.08P
G-BIES	Maule M-5-235C Lunar Rocket	7334C	N56394	24. 7.81	W Procter t/a William Procter Farms Stowe Farm, Tillingham		23. 5.09E
G-BIET	Cameron O-77 Balloon (Hot Air)	674		30. 9.80	G M Westley *"Archimedes"*	Petworth	11. 1.02A
G-BIEY	Piper PA-28-151 Cherokee Warrior	28-7715213	PH-KDH OO-HCB, N9540N	10.11.80	2020 Aviation Ltd	Fairoaks	13. 2.09E
G-BIFA	Cessna 310R II	310R1606	N36868	29. 1.81	J S Lee	Wycombe Air Park	18.12.09E
G-BIFB	Piper PA-28-150 Cherokee C	28-1968	4X-AEC	6.10.80	P Coombs	Sturgate	29. 5.09E
G-BIFO	Evans VP-1	PFA 062-10411		29. 9.80	R Broadhead Eddsfield, Octon Lodge Farm, Thwing		21. 5.09P
	(Built P Raggett) (Volkswagen 1834)						
G-BIFY	Reims Cessna F150L	F15000829	PH-CEZ	9.10.80	Bonus Aviation Ltd	Cranfield	12.11.09E
G-BIGJ	Reims Cessna F172M	F17200936	PH-SKT	2.12.80	Cirrus Aviation Ltd	Clacton	9. 6.09E
G-BIGK	Taylorcraft BC-12D	8302	N96002 NC96002	29.10.80	N P St J Ramsay *(Also carries "NC96002")* Sackville Lodge, Riseley		6. 6.08P
	(Continental A65)						
G-BIGL	Cameron O-65 Balloon (Hot Air)	690		22.10.80	P L and S V Mossman *"Biggles"* Llanishen, Chepstow		25. 4.09E
G-BIGR	Avenger T 200-2122 Balloon (Minimum Lift)	004		6.10.80	R Light	Stockport	
	(Built R Light)						
G-BIGZ	Scheibe SF25B Falke	46142	D-KCAI	22.12.80	C N Jones tr Big-Z Owners Group	RAF Henlow	18.11.09E
	(Stark-Stamo MS1500)						
G-BIHD	Robin DR.400-160 Major 80	1510		29.10.80	G I J Thomson and R A Hawkins	East Winch	26. 3.09E
G-BIHF	Replica Plans SE.5a	079275		27.10.80	S H O'Connell *(As "F-943" in RFC 92 Sqdn c/s) "Lady Di"* White Waltham		13.11.08P
	(Built K J Garrett - pr.no.PFA 020-10548) (Continental O-200-A)						
G-BIHI	Cessna 172M Skyhawk II	17266854	(G-BIHA) N1125U	18.11.80	E-Plane Ltd	Fenland	26.11.09E
G-BIHO	de Havilland DHC-6-310 Twin Otter	738	A6-ADB G-BIHO	9. 1.81	Isles of Scilly Skybus Ltd	St Just	18. 4.09E
G-BIHP (2)	Van Den Bemden 1000m3 Gas Balloon	VDB-38	OO-VBA	19.12.80	J J Harris *"Belgica"*	London SW6	3. 5.01
	(C/n quoted as "18" by Belgian owner: believed rebuilt with 600m3 canopy c/n VDB-47)						
G-BIHT	Piper PA-17 Vagabond	17-41	N138N N8N, N4626H, NC4626H	9. 1.81	B Carter	Old Sarum	31. 7.09P
	(Continental A65)						
G-BIHU	Saffery S 200 Balloon (Minimum Lift)	25		5.11.80	B L King	Coulsdon	
	(Built Cupro Sapphire Ltd)						
G-BIHX	Bensen B 8MR	PFA G/01-1003		12.11.00	P P Willmott	North Coates	30. 7.08P
	(Built P P Willmott) (Rotax 503)						
G-BIIA	Fournier RF3	51	F-BMTA	14.11.80	J D Webb and J D Bally	Rhosgoch	26. 4.08P
G-BIIB	Reims Cessna F172M Skyhawk II	F17201110	PH-GRE	18.11.80	Civil Service Flying Club (Biggin Hill) Ltd	Rochester	26. 4.09E
G-BIID	Piper PA-18 Super Cub 95 (L-18C-PI)	18-1606	OO-LPA OO-HMK, French Army 18-1606, 51-15606	5. 1.81	D A Lacey	Cumbernauld	29. 7.09P
	(Frame No.18-1558)						
G-BIIE	Reims Cessna F172P Skyhawk II	F17202051		31.12.80	Sterling Helicopters Ltd	Norwich	12. 3.09E
G-BIIK	SOCATA MS.883 Rallye 115	1552	F-BSAP	28.11.80	N J Garbett	Fenland	8. 9.08E
G-BIIL	Thunder Ax6-56 Bolt Balloon (Hot Air)	306		12.11.80	R Powell	Craswall, Hereford	14. 3.06A
G-BIIT	Piper PA-28-161 Warrior II	28-8116052	N82744	1.12.80	Highland Flying School Ltd	Inverness	30. 3.09E
G-BIIV	Piper PA-28-181 Archer II	28-7990028	N20875	19.12.80	J Thuret	(Montpellier, France)	21. 8.09E
G-BIIZ	Great Lakes 2T-1A	57	N603K NC603K	1. 4.81	Circa 42 Ltd (Great Horkesley, Colchester) *(Damaged Upper Harford, Gloucestershire 8. 8.98)*		4. 2.99P
G-BIJB	Piper PA-18-150 Super Cub	18-8009001	N23923 N2573H	18. 8.80	James Aero Ltd	Stapleford	9. 8.11
G-BIJD	Bölkow BÖ.208C Junior	636	PH-KAE (PH-DYM), OO-SIS, (D-EGFA)	9.12.80	P Singh tr Sikh Syndicate	Leicester	7. 4.09E
G-BIJE	Piper J-3C-65 Cub (L-4A-PI)	8367	F-BIGN French Military, 42-15248	5. 5.81	R L Hayward and A G Scott *(On rebuild 4.91)* (Cardiff and Usk)		
	(Frame No.8504)						
G-BIJS	Phoenix Luton LA-4A Minor	PAL 1348		18. 5.78	I J Smith	(Brook Farm, Boylestone)	14.11.95P
	(Built I J Smith - pr.no.PFA 835) (Volkswagen 1600)						
G-BIJU	Menavia Piel CP.301A Emeraude	221	G-BHTX F-BIJU	10. 6.80	J R Large tr Eastern Taildraggers Flying Club	Stapleford	18. 7.09P
G-BIJV	Reims Cessna F152 II	F15201813		22.12.80	A S Bamrah t/a Falcon Flying Services	Lydd	21. 3.09E
G-BIJW	Reims Cessna F152 II	F15201820		22.12.80	A S Bamrah t/a Falcon Flying Services	Rochester	26. 2.09E
G-BIKC	Boeing 757-236	22174		31. 1.83	DHL Air Ltd	Brussels, Belgium	9. 2.10E

Reg	Type	C/n	Prev ID	Date	Owner/Operator	Location	Date
G-BIKE	Piper PA-28R-200 Cherokee Arrow II	28R-7335173	OY-DVT N55047	18. 4.80	R Monette	(Sheffield)	4. 1.10E
G-BIKF (2)	Boeing 757-236	22177	(G-BIKG)	28. 4.83	DHL Air Ltd	Brussels, Belgium	14. 9.09E
G-BIKG (2)	Boeing 757-236	22178	(G-BIKH)	26. 8.83	DHL Air Ltd	Brussels, Belgium	26. 8.09E
G-BIKI (2)	Boeing 757-236	22180	OO-DLO G-BIKI (2)	30.11.83	DHL Air Ltd	Brussels, Belgium	23. 6.09E
G-BIKJ (2)	Boeing 757-236	22181	(G-BIKK)	9. 1.84	DHL Air Ltd	Brussels, Belgium	11. 1.10E
G-BIKK (2)	Boeing 757-236	22182	(G-BIKL)	1. 2.84	DHL Air Ltd	Brussels, Belgium	1. 2.10E
G-BIKM (2)	Boeing 757-236	22184	N8293V (G-BIKN)	21. 3.84	DHL Air Ltd	Brussels, Belgium	22. 3.09E
G-BIKN (2)	Boeing 757-236	22186	(G-BIKP)	23. 1.85	DHL Air Ltd	Brussels, Belgium	22. 9.09E
G-BIKO (2)	Boeing 757-236	22187	(G-BIKR)	14. 2.85	DHL Air Ltd	Brussels, Belgium	18. 2.09E
G-BIKP (2)	Boeing 757-236	22188	(G-BIKS)	11. 3.85	DHL Air Ltd	Brussels, Belgium	14. 3.09E
G-BIKS (2)	Boeing 757-236	22190	(G-BIKU)	31. 5.85	DHL Air Ltd	Brussels, Belgium	2. 6.09E
G-BIKU (2)	Boeing 757-236	23399		7.11.85	DHL Air Ltd	Brussels, Belgium	7.11.09E
G-BIKV	Boeing 757-236	23400		9.12.85	DHL Air Ltd	Brussels, Belgium	11.12.09E
G-BIKZ	Boeing 757-236	23532		15. 5.86	DHL Air Ltd	Brussels, Belgium	30. 9.09E
G-BILB	Wallingford WMB.2 Windtracker Balloon (Minimum Lift) 14			22. 1.81	B L King	Coulsdon	
G-BILE	Morris Scruggs BL-2B Balloon (Minimum Lift) 81231			13. 3.81	P D Ridout	Eastleigh	
G-BILG	Morris Scruggs BL-2B Balloon (Minimum Lift) 81232			13. 3.81	P D Ridout	Eastleigh	
G-BILH	Slingsby T.65C Sport Vega	1942	BGA2700-EHN G-BILH, BGA2700-EHN	27. 5.08	M M MacDonald	(Cupar)	
G-BILI	Piper J-3C-65 Cub (L-4J-PI) *(Frame No.13044)*	13207	F-BDTB 45-4467	14. 1.81	S C Wilson and J A Goodridge tr G-BILI Flying Group *(As "454467:J-44" in US Army c/s)* White Waltham		27 7.08P
G-BILL	Piper PA-25-235 Pawnee D *(260hp Lycoming O-540-G2A5)*	25-7856028	N9174T	3. 1.79	A E and W J Taylor t/a Pawnee Aviation	East Winch	27. 7.08A
G-BILR	Cessna 152 II	15284822	N4822P	19. 3.81	Shropshire Aero Club Ltd	Sleap	8. 5.09E
G-BILS	Cessna 152 II	15284857	N4954P	3. 6.81	Mona Aviation Ltd t/a Mona Flying Club RAF Mona		7. 9.09E
G-BILU	Cessna 172RG Cutlass II	172RG0564	N5540V	29. 1.81	Full Sutton Flying Centre Ltd	Full Sutton	23. 7.09E
G-BILZ	Taylor JT.1 Monoplane *(Built G Beaumont and regd officially as c/n PFA 055-10124)*	PFA 055-10244		15.12.80	A Petherbridge *(Damaged Ingoldmells 10. 6.90: stored 8.00)*	(Sibsey)	29. 2.91P
G-BIMK	Baron Tiger T 200 Series 1 Balloon (Minimum Lift) *(Built M K Baron)* 7/MKB-01			22.12.80	M K Baron	Woodley, Stockport	
G-BIMM	Piper PA-18-150 Super Cub *(L-21B-PI)(Frame No.18-3881)*	18-3868	PH-VHO R Neth AF R-178, 54-2468	8. 1.81	Spectrum Leisure Ltd	Clacton	15.11.10S
G-BIMN	Steen Skybolt *(Built C R Williamson)*	PFA 064-10329		31.12.80	R J Thomas	(Ashford)	3. 4.08P
G-BIMO	SNCAN Stampe SV-4C	394	F-BADG French AF	5. 3.81	E L P A Dupont *(As "394" in French AF c/s)* Wellcross Farm, Slinfold		3. 5.10S
G-BIMT	Cessna FA152 Aerobat *(Built Reims Aviation SA)*	FA1520361	N8062L	9. 1.81	Cardinal Sin Ltd t/a Staverton Flying School	Gloucestershire	26. 5.09E
G-BIMU	Sikorsky S-61N Mk.II *(SAR conversion)*	61-752	N8511Z VH-CRU, N4042S	9. 1.81	Bristow Helicopters Ltd "Stac Pollaidh"	Den Holder, Netherlands	23.10.09E
G-BIMX	Rutan VariEze *(Built A S Knowles)* (Continental O-200-A)	PFA 074-10544		6. 1.81	D G Crew	Biggin Hill	9. 9.08P
G-BIMZ	Beech 76 Duchess	ME-169	N6021K	20. 3.81	R P Smith	Gloucestershire	5. 7.08T
G-BINL	Morris Scruggs BL-2B Balloon (Minimum Lift) 81231		5. 2.81	P D Ridout	Eastleigh	
G-BINM	Morris Scruggs BL-2B Balloon (Minimum Lift) 81217			5. 2.81	P D Ridout	Eastleigh	
G-BINR	Unicorn UE-1A Balloon (Minimum Lift) 81004			20. 1.81	I Chadwick tr Unicorn Group "Lady Diana" (Extant 5.07) Partridge Green, Horsham		
G-BINS	Unicorn UE-2A Balloon (Minimum Lift) 80002			22.12.80	I Chadwick tr Unicorn Group "Caroline" (Extant 5.07) Partridge Green, Horsham		
G-BINT	Unicorn UE-1A Balloon (Minimum Lift) 80001			22.12.80	D E Bint	Downham Market	
G-BINX	Morris Scruggs BL-2B Balloon (Minimum Lift) 81219			5. 2.81	P D Ridout	Eastleigh	
G-BINY	Morton Oriental Air-Bag Balloon (Minimum Lift) *(Built J L Morton)* OAB-001			22. 1.81	J L Morton	Wokingham	
G-BIOA	Hughes 369D *(Hughes 500)*	120-0880D	OO-HFS LX-HLE, OO-HFS, G-BIOA	9. 2.81	AH Helicopter Services Ltd	Dunkeswell	25. 7.09E
G-BIOB	Reims Cessna F172P Skyhawk II	F17202042		23. 1.81	Flight Images LLP	Fairoaks	27. 5.09E
G-BIOC	Reims Cessna F150L	F15000848	F-BUEC	3. 2.81	R M A Robinson	(Hornsea)	3.11.09E
G-BIOI	SAN Jodel DR.1050M Excellence	477	F-BLJQ	21. 1.81	A A Alderdice	(Kilkeel, Newry)	21. 4.09P
G-BIOJ	Rockwell Commander 112TC-A	13192	N4662W	22. 1.82	A T Dalby *(Noted 9.08)*	Sibson	13.12.02
G-BIOK	Reims Cessna F152 II	F15201810		2. 2.81	A D H MacDonald	Glenrothes	28. 4.09E
G-BIOU	SAN Jodel D 117A	813	F-BIOU	9. 8.78	M R Routh and T de Salis tr Jemalk Group *(Noted 10.08)* Wycombe Air Park		2. 9.09P
G-BIOW	Slingsby T 67A	1988		26. 2.81	A B Slinger tr Slingsby T.67A Group Sherburn-in-Elmet		29. 9.09E
G-BIPA	Grumman AA-5B Tiger	AA5B-0200	OY-GAM	24. 3.81	Tri-Star Developments Ltd Andreas, Isle of Man		14. 8.09E
G-BIPH	Morris Scruggs BL-2B Balloon (Minimum Lift) 81224			10. 2.81	C M Dewsnap	(Owlsmoor, Sandhurst)	
G-BIPI	Everett Gyroplane *(Volkswagen 1834)*	001		30. 4.81	C A Reeves *(Noted 5.03)* Apperley, Gloucestershire		19. 6.01P
G-BIPN	Fournier RF3	35	F-BMDN	26. 2.81	J C R Rogers tr G-BIPN Group RAF Cranwell		16. 9.08P
G-BIPO	Mudry CAP.20 LS 200	03	F-GAUB	5. 3.81	A McClean tr The CAP 20 Group White Waltham		8. 5.05S
G-BIPT	Wassmer Jodel D 112	1254	F-BMIB	11. 3.81	C R Davies	Allensmore, Hereford	30. 9.09P
G-BIPV	Gulfstream AA-5B Tiger	AA5B-0981	N28266	10. 3.81	Echo Echo Ltd	Bournemouth	14. 6.09E
G-BIPW	Avenger T 200-2112 Balloon (Minimum Lift) 10 *(Built R Light)*			24. 2.81	B L King	Coulsdon	

G-BIPY	Montgomerie-Bensen B 8MR	AJW.01		25. 2.81	P A Clare	North Connel, Oban 23. 6.09P
	(Built A J Wood - pr.no.PFA G/01-1007) (Rotax 532)					
G-BIRD	Pitts S-1D	707-H		3.11.77	N E Smith	(Horsham) 25. 3.09P
	(Built R N York – pr.no. PFA 1596)					
G-BIRE	Colt Bottle 56 SS Balloon (Hot Air)	323		4. 3.81	D J Stagg	Spixworth, Norwich 24. 5.08A
	(Satzenbrau Bottle)					
G-BIRH	Piper PA-18-150 Super Cub	18-3853	PH-LET	19. 3.81	Banbury Gliding Club Ltd (As 54-2453:R-163" in R Neth AF c/s)	
	(L-21B-PI) (Lycoming O-360-A4)		R Neth AF R-163, 54-2453			Hinton-on-the-Hedges 3. 5.09S
	(Frame No.18-3857)					
G-BIRI	CASA 1-131E Jungmann	1074	Spanish AF	14. 4.81	D Watt	Sibson 25. 4.08P
			E3B-113			
G-BIRL	Avenger T 200-2112 Balloon (Minimum Lift)			10. 3.81	R Light	Stockport
	(Built R Light)	008				
G-BIRP	Ridout Arena Mk.17 Skyship Balloon (Minimum Lift)			13. 3.81	A S Ridout	Eastleigh
		01				
G-BIRT	Robin R1180TD Aiglon	276		25. 3.81	W D'A Hall	White Waltham 21.12.08E
G-BISG	Clutton FRED Series III	RAC 01-224		13. 3.81	T Littlefair "Fuzz Bee"	Lymington 29.10.86P
	(Built R A Coombe - pr.no.PFA 029-10675) (Volkswagen 1600)					
G-BISH	Cameron V-65 Balloon (Hot Air)	707		16. 3.81	P J Bish "Tsaritsa"	Newtown, Hungerford 8. 4.09E
G-BISL	Morris Scruggs BL-2B Balloon (Minimum Lift)			13. 3.81	P D Ridout	Eastleigh
		81233				
G-BISM	Morris Scruggs BL-2B Balloon (Minimum Lift)			13. 3.81	P D Ridout	Eastleigh
		81234				
G-BISS	Morris Scruggs BL-2C Balloon (Minimum Lift)			13. 3.81	P D Ridout	Eastleigh
		81235				
G-BIST	Morris Scruggs BL-2C Balloon (Minimum Lift)			13. 3.81	P D Ridout	Eastleigh
		81236				
G-BISX	Colt 56A Balloon (Hot Air)	324		18. 3.81	C D Steel (Active 7.05)	St Boswells 18. 8.99A
G-BISZ	Sikorsky S-76A II Plus	760156		19. 3.81	Bristow Helicopters Ltd	Redhill 6.11.09E
G-BITA	Piper PA-18-150 Super Cub	18-8109037	N82585	24. 3.81	D J Gilmour	North Weald 5. 6.11
G-BITE	SOCATA TB-10 Tobago	193		7. 5.81	M A Smith	Eshott 23. 4.09E
G-BITF	Reims Cessna F152 II	F15201822		27. 3.81	J Parker tr G-BITF Owners	Glenrothes 30. 8.09E
G-BITH	Reims Cessna F152 II	F15201825	G-TFSA	27. 3.81	J R Hyde	Derby 2.10.09E
			G-BITH			
G-BITK	Clutton FRED Series II	PFA 029-10369		23. 3.81	D J Wood	(Eythorne, Dover)
	(Built B J Miles) (Volkswagen 1500)					
G-BITM	Reims Cessna F172P Skyhawk II	F17202046		13. 4.81	Dreamtrade Ltd	Barton 15.12.09E
G-BITO	Wassmer Jodel D 112D	1200	F-BIUO	20. 3.81	A Dunbar (Noted 7.04)	Barton 5. 9.02P
G-BITS	Drayton B-56 Balloon (Hot Air)	MJB-01/81		16. 3.81	M J Betts "Hedger"	Drayton, Norwich
	(Operated Eastern Region, British Balloon and Airship Club)					
G-BITY	Bell FD.31T Flying Dodo Balloon (Minimum Lift)			25. 3.81	A J Bell	Luton
		2604				
G-BIUM	Reims Cessna F152 II	F15201807		3. 4.81	Sheffield Aero Club Ltd	Netherthorpe 16. 1.09E
G-BIUP	SNCAN NC.854S	54	(G-AMPE)	4. 6.81	J Greenaway and T D Cooper tr BIUP Flying Group	
			G-BIUP, F-BFSC			New Barn Farm, Barton Ashes, Crawley 10. 7.07P
G-BIUV	Hawker Siddeley HS.748 Series 2A/275LFD		5W-FAN	11. 5.81	PTB (Emerald) Proprietary Ltd (Stored 11.08)	
		1701	G-AYYH, G-11-8			Blackpool 23. 2.09P
G-BIUW	Piper PA-28-161 Warrior II	28-8116128	N9506N	14. 4.81	D R Staley	Gamston 27. 6.09E
G-BIUY	Piper PA-28-181 Archer II	28-8190133	N8318X	3. 4.81	J S Develin and Z Islam	Shoreham 16. 4.09E
G-BIVA	Robin R2112	137	F-GBAZ	6. 5.81	I G McDonald tr Seahawk Flying Group	
						RNAS Culdrose 21.12.09E
G-BIVB	Wassmer Jodel D 112	1009	(G-BIVC)	18. 9.81	N M Harwood Roughay Farm, Bishops Waltham 20.11.09P	
	(Continental A65)		F-BJII			
G-BIVC	Wassmer Jodel D 112	1219	F-BMAI	1. 6.81	M J Barnby Grange Farm, Frogland Cross 13. 7.00P	
	(Continental A65)					
G-BIVF	Scintex CP.301-C3 Emeraude	594	F-BJVN	4.11.81	R J Moore "Emma"	Sywell 11.12.08P
G-BIVK	Bensen B 8MV	PFA G/01-1008		10. 4.81	M J Atyeo "Skyrider"	(Bognor Regis) 19.11.03P
	(Built J G Toy) (Registered as B 8M) (Volkswagen 1834)					
G-BIWA	Ridout Stevendon Skyreacher Balloon (Minimum Lift)			8. 6.81	S D Barnes	Eastleigh
		102				
G-BIWB	Morris Scruggs RS.5000 Balloon (Minimum Lift)			8. 6.81	P D Ridout	Eastleigh
		81541				
G-BIWC	Morris Scruggs RS.5000 Balloon (Minimum Lift)			26. 6.81	P D Ridout "Waterloo"	Eastleigh
		81546				
G-BIWF	Ridout Warren Windcatcher Balloon (Minimum Lift)			3. 7.81	P D Ridout	Eastleigh
		WW.013				
G-BIWG	Ridout Zelenski Mk.2 Balloon (Minimum Lift)			3. 7.81	P D Ridout	Eastleigh
	(Officially regd with c/n 2401)	Z 401				
G-BIWJ	Unicorn UE-1A Balloon (Minimum Lift)	81014		14. 7.81	B L King	Coulsdon
G-BIWK	Cameron V-65 Balloon (Hot Air)	719		22. 4.81	I R Williams and R G Bickerdike "Double Fantasy"	
						Bedford and Huntingdon 27. 3.09E
G-BIWN	Wassmer Jodel D 112	1314	F-BNCN	5. 6.81	C R Coates Eddsfield, Octon Lodge Farm, Thwing 8.10.09P	
G-BIWR	Mooney M 20F Executive	22-1339	N6972V	1. 6.81	M Broady	(Middlewich) 15. 7.09E
G-BIWU	Cameron V-65 Balloon (Hot Air)	717		15. 5.81	J Tyrrell and W Rousell Wollaston, Wellingborough 12.11.05A	
G-BIWW	American AA-5 Traveler	AA5-0263	OY-AYV	2. 6.81	L S Morrice	(London SW6) 15. 6.09E
G-BIXA	SOCATA TB-9 Tampico	205		7. 5.81	W Maxwell	Perth 11.12.08E
G-BIXB	SOCATA TB-9 Tampico	208		7. 5.81	B G Adams	Shobdon 3. 4.09E
G-BIXH	Reims Cessna F152 II	F15201840		30. 4.81	Cleveland Flying School Ltd Durham Tees Valley 13. 4.09E	
G-BIXL	North American P-51D-20-NA Mustang		Israel DFAF 2343	3. 7.81	R J Lamplough "Miss Helen"	
		122-38675	Swedish AF Fv.26116, 44-72216			Manor Farm, East Garston 26. 6.09P
	(As "472216:HO-M" in 487th Fighter Sqdn/352nd Fighter Group USAF c/s)					
G-BIXN	Boeing Stearman A75N1 (PT-17-BW) Kaydet		N51132	15. 6.81	V S E Norman	Rendcomb 3. 8.96
	(Continental W670)	75-2248	41-8689			
G-BIXV	Bell 212	30870	N16931	27. 5.81	Bristow Helicopters Ltd	Kazakhstan 22. 7.09E

G-BIXW	Colt 56B Balloon (Hot Air)	348		18. 5.81	N A P Bates *"Spam"*	Tunbridge Wells	17. 8.97A
G-BIXX	Pearson Series 2 Balloon (Minimum Lift)	00327		8. 5.81	D Pearson	Solihull	
G-BIXZ	Grob G109	6019	D-KGRO	14. 5.81	D L Nind and I Allum	Enstone	2. 4.09E
G-BIYI	Cameron V-65 Balloon (Hot Air)	722		21. 5.81	P F Smart tr The Sarnia Balloon Group *"Penny"*	Oakley, Basingstoke	9. 7.09E
G-BIYJ	Piper PA-18 Super Cub 95 (L-18C-PI)	18-1000	MM51-15303 I-EIST, MM51-15303, 51-15303	5. 6.81	S Russell	Pilmuir Farm, Lundin Links	17. 3.09P
G-BIYK	Isaacs Fury II *(Built R S Martins)* (Continental C90)	PFA 011-10418		20. 5.81	S M Roberts	(Guernsey)	4. 7.07P
G-BIYP	Piper PA-20 Pacer 125	20-802	CN-TYP F-DACJ, OO-ADP	25. 5.83	A W Hoy and S W M Johnson tr G-BIYP Flying Group	Berry Grove Farm, Liss	3. 6.08E
G-BIYR	Piper PA-18-150 Super Cub (L-21B-PI) *(Frame No. 18-3843)*	18-3841	(G-BIYB) PH-GER, R Neth AF R-151, 5G-96, 54-2441	26. 5.81	B H and M J Fairclough tr The Delta Foxtrot Flying Group *(As "R-151" in R Neth AF c/s)*	Watchford Farm, Yarcombe	30. 8.10S
G-BIYT	Colt 17A Cloudhopper Balloon (Hot Air)	344		13. 7.81	J-M Francois	Salles-Courbatiers, France	18. 1.05A
G-BIYU	Fokker S 11.1 Instructor	6206	(PH-HOM) R Neth AF E-15	13. 5.81	A Eckersley tr Fokker Syndicate *(As "E-15" in R Neth AF c/s)*	Bagby	29. 9.09P
G-BIYW	Wassmer Jodel D 112	1209	F-BLNR	26. 5.81	K Balaam tr Pollard/Balaam/Bye Flying Group	Great Oakley	7. 1.10P
G-BIYX	Piper PA-28-140 Cherokee Cruiser	28-7625064	OY-BLD	19. 6.81	W B Bateson	Blackpool	1. 4.09E
G-BIYY	Piper PA-18 Super Cub 95 (L-18C-PI) 18-1979 *(Frame No.18-1914)*		MM52-2379 I-EIGA, MM52-2379, 52-2379	2. 6.81	A E and W J Taylor	East Winch	21.10.11
G-BIZE	SOCATA TB-9 Tampico	209	9H-ABJ G-BIZE	15. 6.81	J R Burch tr Gloster Aero Group	Gloucestershire	3. 7.08E
	(Ran out of fuel and force-landed in a field near Gloucestershire 4. 5.08 while on local flight with damage to tailplane and undercarriage)						
G-BIZF	Reims Cessna F172P Skyhawk II	F17202070		16. 6.81	R S Bentley	Bourn	18.09.09E
G-BIZG	Reims Cessna F152 II	F15201873		16. 6.81	M A Judge tr Aero Group 78	Netherthorpe	2. 8.09E
G-BIZI	Robin DR.400 2+2	1543		29. 5.81	BIZI Club Ltd	RAF Benson	10. 5.09E
G-BIZK	Nord 3202B1	78	N2255E French Army	22.11.85	A I Milne *(As "78" in all-yellow French AF c/s)*	Little Snoring	29. 1.10P
G-BIZM	Nord 3202B	91	N2256K French Army	22.11.85	Global Aviation Ltd	Humberside	30. 4.09P
G-BIZO	Piper PA-28R-200 Cherokee Arrow II	28R-7535339	OY-DLH N1578X	16. 6.81	P J Mason and J F Leather tr Lemas Air	Bristol	4. 4.09E
G-BIZR	SOCATA TB-9 Tampico	210	G-BSEC G-BIZR	15. 6.81	E S Murphy and G Ward tr Fenland Flying Group	Fenland	23. 8.08E
G-BIZV	Piper PA-18 Super Cub 95 (L-18C-PI)	18-2001	EI-74 I-EIDE, MM52-2401, 52-2401	12. 6.81	S P McCormick *(As "18-2001" in US Army c/s)*	Dunlaoghaira, Ireland	11.10.08P
G-BIZW	Champion 7GCBC Citabria	0157	D-EGPD	16. 7.81	J C Read tr G Read and Sons	North Reston	30. 8.04
G-BIZY	Wassmer Jodel D 112	1120	F-BKJL	13. 7.81	W Tunley t/a Wayland Tunley and Associates	Hinton-in-the-Hedges	25. 5.09P

G-BJAA - G-BJZZ

G-BJAD	Clutton FRED Series II *(Built C Allison - pr.no..PFA 29-10586)*	CA.1		11. 6.81	Newark (Nottinghamshire and Linclonshire) Air Museum Ltd	Newark	
G-BJAE	Starck AS.80 Holiday *(Built J R Lavadoux)* (Continental A65)	04	F-PGGA F-WGGA	17. 6.81	D J and S.A E Phillips *(Damaged Woburn 17. 8.91)*	(Leamington Spa)	8. 8.92P
G-BJAF	Piper J-3C-65 Cub (L-4A-PI) *(Frame No.8540)*	8437	D-EJAF HB-OAD, 42-15318	23. 6.81	P J Cottle	Craysmarsh Farm, Melksham	18. 2.08P
G-BJAG	Piper PA-28-181 Archer II	28-7990353	PH-LDB (PH-BEG), (OO-FLM), N2244W	23. 6.81	C R Chubb	Manston	18. 9.09E
G-BJAJ	Gulfstream AA-5B Tiger	AA5B-1177	N4532V	2. 7.81	A J Byrne tr Draycott Tiger Club	Draycott Farm, Chiseldon	17.9.09E
G-BJAL	CASA 1-131E Jungmann *(Spanish AF serial no. conflicts with G-BUCC)*	1028	Spanish AF E3B-114	11. 9.78	I C Underwood and S B J Chandler tr G-BJAL Group	Breighton	1. 8.08P
G-BJAO	Montgomerie-Bensen B 8MR *(Built A Gault - pr.no.PFA G/01-1001: officially regd as c/n GL5-01)* (Rotax 582)	GLS-01		28. 8.81	A P Lay	Henstridge	2. 4.01P
G-BJAP	de Havilland DH.82A Tiger Moth *(Built J A Pothecary - pr.no.PFA 157-12897)* (Composite rebuild)	0482		15. 6.81	K Knight *(As "K2587" in pre-war RAF 32 Sqdn/CFS c/s)*	Shobdon	9. 9.08P
G-BJAS	Rango NA-9 Balloon (Minimum Lift)	TL-19		22. 6.81	A Lindsay	Twickenham	
G-BJAV	Sud-Aviation Gardan GY-80-160 Horizon	28	OO-AJP F-BLVB	8. 9.81	W R Maloney	Popham	18.12.09E
G-BJAW	Cameron V-65 Balloon (Hot Air)	745		19. 6.81	G A McCarthy *"Breezin"*	Shepton Mallet	16. 4.86A
G-BJAY	Piper J-3C-65 Cub (L-4H-PI) *(Frame No.11914)*	12086	F-BFBN OO-EAC, 44-79790	1.11.78	D W Finlay (Lamourache Nord, Aquitaine, France)		12. 6.06P
G-BJBK	Piper PA-18 Super Cub 95 (L-18C-PI) 18-1431 (Continental O-200-A) *(Frame No.18-1370)*		F-BOME French Army 51-15431	21. 8.81	M S Bird	Pepperbox, Salisbury	9. 7.09P
G-BJBM	Monnett Sonerai I *(Built Lyster Aviation Ltd - pr.no.PFA 015-10022)* (Volkswagen 2074)	MEA-117		2. 7.81	N J Cowley *"The Answer"* (Noted 8.06)	Popham	9. 1.97P
G-BJBO	CEA Jodel DR.250/160 Capitaine	40	F-BNJG	24. 8.81	J A Hobby tr Wiltshire Flying Group	Oaksey Park	30. 3.09E
G-BJBW	Piper PA-28-161 Warrior II	28-8116280	N2913Z	22. 7.81	T G Phillips and C Greenland tr 152 Group	Popham	23. 1.09E
G-BJBX	Piper PA-28-161 Warrior II	28-8116269	N8414H	17. 7.81	Haimoss Ltd *(Operated Old Sarum Flying Group)*	Compton Abbas	23. 5.09E
G-BJCA	Piper PA-28-161 Warrior II	28-7916473	N2846D	30. 7.81	Plane Sailing (South West) Ltd	Plymouth	21. 2.09E
G-BJCF	Scintex CP.1310-C3 Super Emeraude	936	F-BMJH	19.11.81	K M Hodson and C G H Gurney	Little Snoring	18.11.09P
G-BJCI	Piper PA-18-150 Super Cub *(Lycoming O-360-A4)*	18-6658	N9388D	10. 9.81	The Borders (Milfield) Gliding Club Ltd	Milfield	10. 7.11E
G-BJCW	Piper PA-32R-301 Saratoga II SP	32R-8113094	N2866U	6. 8.81	Golf Charlie Whisky Ltd	Fairoaks	11. 5.09E

G-BJDE	Reims Cessna F172M	F17200984	OO-MSS D-EGBR	25. 8.81	J K P Amor	Sandown	10. 7.09E
G-BJDF	SOCATA MS.880B Rallye 100T	3000	F-GAKP	21. 9.81	A J Wilkinson tr G-BJDF Group		
						Coldharbour Farm,Willingham	20. 3.09E
G-BJDK	Ridout European E 157 Balloon (Minimum Lift)			17. 8.81	E Osborn tr Aeroprint Tours	Eastleigh	
		S 2					
G-BJDW	Reims Cessna F172M Skyhawk II	F17201417	PH-JBE	10. 8.81	J Rae	Earls Colne	13. 2.09E
G-BJEE	Pilatus Britten-Norman BN-2T Turbine Islander		C9-TAH	28. 7.81	Cormack (Aircraft Services) Ltd	Cumbernauld	
	(Originally regd as a BN-2B)	2120	G-BJEE				
G-BJEF	Pilatus Britten-Norman BN-2T Turbine Islander		C9-TAK	28. 7.81	Cormack (Aircraft Services) Ltd	Cumbernauld	
	(Originally regd as a BN-2B)	2121	G-BJEF				
G-BJEI	Piper PA-18 Super Cub 95	18-1988	EI-66	27. 7.81	H J Cox	Westover Farm, Sheepwash	30. 3.09P
	(L-18C-PI) (Frame No.18-1938)		I-EILO, MM52-2388, 52-2388				
G-BJEJ	Pilatus Britten-Norman BN-2T Turbine Islander		C9-TAJ	28. 7.81	Cormack (Aircraft Services) Ltd	Cumbernauld	
	(Originally regd as a BN-2B)	2124	G-BJEJ				
G-BJEL	SNCAN NC.854S	113	F-BEZT	7. 8.81	C A James *"Jessie"*	Doynton	30. 6.09P
G-BJEV	Aeronca 11AC Chief	11AC-270	N85897	12. 8.81	R F Willcox (As *"897:E"* in US Navy c/s)		
			NC85897			Eastbach Farm, Coleford	7. 4.09P
G-BJEX	Bölkow BÖ.208C Junior	690	F-BRHY D-EEAM	27. 8.81	G D H Crawford	(Henley-on-Thames)	28. 1.88
G-BJFC	Ridout European E 8 Balloon (Minimum Lift)			17. 8.81	P D Ridout *(Extant 5.07)*	Eastleigh	
		S 1					
G-BJFE	Piper PA-18 Super Cub 95	18-2022	EI-91	17. 8.81	P H Wilmot-Allistone	Watchford Farm, Yarcombe	22. 8.07P
	(L-18C-PI)		I-EISU, MM52-2422, 52-2422				
G-BJFL	Sikorsky S-76A II Plus	760056	EZ-S704	28. 8.81	Bristow Helicopters Ltd	Aberdeen	8.10.09E
			G-BJFL, N160BH, N1546T, (G-BHRK)				
G-BJFM	Wassmer Jodel D 120 Paris-Nice	227	F-BLFM	8.10.81	J V George and P A Smith	Popham	11.10.08P
G-BJGK	Cameron V-77 Balloon (Hot Air)	696		3. 9.81	M E Orchard	Bristol	5. 9.09E
G-BJGM	Unicorn UE-1A Balloon (Minimum Lift)	81015		21. 8.81	D Eaves and P D Ridout *"Capricorn" (Extant 5.07)*		
						Southampton and Eastleigh	
G-BJGX	Sikorsky S-76A II Plus	760026	N103BH N4251S	4. 9.81	Bristow Helicopters Ltd *"Glen Elgin"*	Norwich	8.10.09E
G-BJGY	Reims Cessna F172P Skyhawk II	F17202128		13.10.81	K and S Martin	Gunton Park, Somerton	22. 4.09E
G-BJHB	Mooney M 20J Mooney 201	24-1190	N1145G	23.12.81	Zitair Flying Club Ltd	Wycombe Air Park	23. 5.09E
G-BJHK	EAA Acrosport	PFA 072-10470		20. 3.80	M R Holden	Stoneacre Farm, Farthing Corner	31. 8.04P
	(Built J H Kimber) (Lycoming IO-360)						
G-BJIA	Allport Hot Air Free Balloon (Minimum Lift)	1		2. 9.81	D J Allport	Bourne	
G-BJIC	Eaves Dodo 1A Balloon (Minimum Lift)	DD.3		4. 9.81	P D Ridout *(Extant 5.07)*	Eastleigh	
G-BJID	Chown Osprey Lizzieliner Mk-1B Balloon (Minimum Lift)			4. 9.81	P D Ridout	Eastleigh	
		28					
G-BJIG	Slingsby T 67A	1992		16. 9.81	A D Hodgkinson	(Luton)	15. 4.04
G-BJIV	Piper PA-18-150 Super Cub	18-8262	N5972Z	17. 9.81	Yorkshire Gliding Club (Proprietary) Ltd		
	(Lycoming O-360-A4)					Sutton Bank	5. 4.09
G-BJKF	SOCATA TB-9 Tampico	240		30. 9.81	C J Archer tr G-BJKF Group	Headcorn	17. 7.09E
G-BJKW	Wills Aera 2	A3JKW		1. 3.78	J K S Wills	(London SE3)	
	(Built J K S Wills)						
G-BJKY	Reims Cessna F152 II	F15201886		22. 9.81	Manx Aero Marine Management Ltd	Blackpool	28. 2.09E
					(Operated Westair Flying Services)		
G-BJLB	SNCAN NC.854S	58	(OO-MVM) F-BFSG	5.11.81	M J Barmby	(Llanishen, Cardiff)	30. 6.83T
					(Crashed near Newport,Gwent 29. 7.84: stored 8.90)		
G-BJLC	Monnett Sonerai IIL	942L		18. 9.81	P D Yeo *(Noted 1.08)*	AAC Netheravon	11. 5.98T
	(Built J P Whitham - pr.no.PFA 015-10634) (Volkswagen 1835)						
G-BJLF	Unicorn UE-1C Balloon (Minimum Lift)	81018		21. 9.81	I Chadwick tr Unicorn Group *(Extant 5.07)*		
						Partridge Green, Horsham	
G-BJLG	Unicorn UE-1B Balloon (Minimum Lift)	81017		21. 9.81	I Chadwick tr Unicorn Group		
						Partridge Green, Horsham	
G-BJLX	Cremer Cracker Balloon (Minimum Lift)	711		24. 9.81	P W May	Wilmslow	
G-BJLY	Cremer Cracker Balloon (Minimum Lift)	709		24. 9.81	P Cannon *(Extant 5.07)*	Luton	
G-BJML	Cessna 120	10766	N76349 NC76349	5.10.81	R A Smith	Great Yeldham Hall, Halstead	28. 6.09P
G-BJMO	Taylor JT.1 Monoplane	PFA 055-10612		30. 9.81	R C Mark	(Orelton, Ludlow)	
	(Built R C Mark)						
G-BJMR	Cessna 310R II	310R1624	N2631Z	16. 7.79	J H Sandham t/a Sandham Aviation	Carlisle	21. 9.09E
G-BJMW	Thunder Ax8-105 Series 2 Balloon (Hot Air)			14.10.81	G M Westley	Petworth	11. 1.02A
		369					
G-BJMX	Ridout Jarre JR-3 Balloon (Minimum Lift)			6.10.81	P D Ridout	Eastleigh	
		81601					
G-BJMZ	Ridout European EA-8A Balloon (Minimum Lift)			6.10.81	P D Ridout *(Extant 5.07)*	Eastleigh	
		S 5					
G-BJNA	Ridout Arena Mk.117P Balloon (Minimum Lift)			6.10.81	P D Ridout *(Extant 5.07)*	Eastleigh	
		202					
G-BJND	Chown Osprey Mk.1E Balloon (Minimum Lift)			7.10.81	A Billington and D Whitmore	Liverpool	
		AKC.53					
G-BJNF	Reims Cessna F152 II	F15201882		21.10.81	D M and B Cloke	Dunkeswell	26. 2.09E
G-BJNG	Slingsby T 67AM	1993		16.10.81	D F Hodgkinson *(Noted dismantled 5.08)*		
						Dunkeswell	23. 7.01T
G-BJNH	Chown Osprey Mk.1E Balloon (Minimum Lift)			8.10.81	D A Kirk	Manchester	
		AKC.57					
G-BJNN	Piper PA-38-112 Tomahawk	38-80A0064	N9684N	15.10.81	S Padidar-Nazar	Carlisle	17. 8.09E
G-BJNY	Aeronca 11CC Super Chief	11CC-264	CN-TYZ F-OAEE	28.10.81	P I and D M Morgans *(Stored 4.91)*		
						Furze Hill Farm, Rosemarket, Milford Haven	9. 8.90P
G-BJNZ	Piper PA-23-250 Aztec F	27-7954099	G-FANZ N6905A, C-GTJG	5.10.81	Bonus Aviation Ltd	Cranfield	10. 8.09E

G-BJOB	SAN Jodel D 140C Mousquetaire III	118	F-BMBD	2.11.81	T W M Beck and M J Smith	
						Southwater Farm, Horsham 29. 6.09P
G-BJOE	Wassmer Jodel D 120A Paris-Nice	177	F-BJIU	12.11.81	J F Govan tr Forth Flying Group	East Fortune 31. 7.08P
G-BJOP	Pilatus Britten-Norman BN-2B-26 Islander			29.10.81	Loganair Ltd	Kirkwall 5. 9.08E
		2132				
G-BJOT	SAN Jodel D 117	688	F-BJCO	12.11.81	R A Kilbride	Full Sutton 19.12.08P
			CN-TVH, F-DABU			
G-BJOV	Reims Cessna F150K F15000558		PH-VSD	4. 2.82	T H Lee tr G-BJOV FlyingGroup	
	(Incorrectly shown by CAA as ex D-KEBD)					Baker Street Farm, Maidstone 20.10.09E
G-BJPI	Bede BD-5G	1		30.10.81	M D McQueen	(Beckenham)
	(Built M D McQueen - pr.no.PFA 014-10218) (Hirth 230R)					
G-BJPL	Chown Osprey Mk.4A Balloon (Minimum Lift)			13.10.81	M Vincent	St Helier, Jersey
	AKC-39					
G-BJRA	Chown Osprey Mk.4B Balloon (Minimum Lift)			23.10.81	E Osborn t/a Aeroprint Tours	Eastleigh
	AKC.87					
G-BJRG	Chown Osprey Mk.4B Balloon (Minimum Lift)			26.10.81	A de Gruchy	St Brelade, Jersey
	AKC.95					
G-BJRH	Rango NA-36 Ax3 Balloon (Minimum Lift)			4.11.81	N H Ponsford t/a Rango Balloon and Kite Company	
	NHP-23					Leeds
G-BJRP	Cremer Cracker Balloon (Minimum Lift)			29.10.81	M D Williams *(Extant 5.07)*	Houghton Regis
	15.712 PAC					
G-BJRR	Cremer Cracker Balloon (Minimum Lift)			29.10.81	M D Williams *(Extant 5.07)*	Houghton Regis
	15.715 PAC					
G-BJRV	Cremer Cracker Balloon (Minimum Lift)			29.10.81	M D Williams *(Extant 5.07)*	Houghton Regis
	15.713 PAC					
G-BJSS	Allport Hot Air Free Balloon (Minimum Lift)	2		9.11.81	D J Allport	Bourne
G-BJST	CCF Harvard 4 (T-6J-CCF Texan)	CCF4-...	MM53795	21.12.81	P J Tuplin (and estate of P W Portelli) *(As "KF729" in RAF c/s)*	
			SC-66			White Waltham 29. 7.09P
G-BJSV	Piper PA-28-161 Warrior II	28-8016229	PH-VZL	25.11.81	Airways Flight Training (Exeter) Ltd	Exeter 28.10.09E
			(OO-HLM), N35787			
G-BJSW	Thunder Ax7-65Z Balloon (Hot Air)	378		16.11.81	J Edwards	Northampton 27. 9.09E
G-BJSZ	Piper J-3C-65 Cub *(L-4H-PI)*	12047	D-EHID	20.11.81	H Gilbert	Enstone 22. 6.08P
	(Regd with c/n 11874)		(D-ECAX), (D-EKAB), PH-NBP, 44-79751			
G-BJTB	Cessna A150M Aerobat	A1500627	(G-BIVN)	28.10.82	Cirrus Aviation Ltd	Clacton 27.11.07E
			N9818J			
G-BJTF	Kirk Skyrider Mk.1 Balloon (Minimum Lift)			18.11.81	D A Kirk	Manchester
	KSR-01					
G-BJTN	Solent Osprey Mk.4B Balloon (Minimum Lift)			23.11.81	M Vincent	St Helier, Jersey
	ASC-112					
G-BJTP	Piper PA-18 Super Cub 95	18-999	EI-51	26.11.81	J T Parkins	Croft Farm, Defford 28.10.09P
	(L-18C-PI)		I-EICO, MM51-15302, 51-15302		*(As "115302:TP" in VMO-6 Sqdn, US Marines c/s) "Sittin' Duck"*	
G-BJTY	Solent Osprey Mk.4B Balloon (Minimum Lift)			23.11.81	A E de Gruchy	St Brelade, Jersey
	ASC-115					
G-BJUB	Wild BVS Special 01 Balloon (Minimum Lift)			25.11.81	P G Wild	Linley Hill, Leven
	VS/PW01					
G-BJUC	Robinson R22	0228		13. 1.82	B C Seedle t/a Brian Seddle Helicopters Blackpool	6. 1.10E
G-BJUD	Robin DR.400-180R Remorqueur	870	PH-SRM	27.11.81	Lasham Gliding Society Ltd	Lasham 31. 1.09E
	(Rebuilt using new fuselage: original scrapped Membury 11.88)					
G-BJUE	Solent Osprey Mk.4B Balloon (Minimum Lift)			23.11.81	M Vincent	St Helier, Jersey
	ASC-114					
G-BJUR	Piper PA-38-112 Tomahawk	38-79A0915	N9722N	5. 2.82	Truman Aviation Ltd *(Operated Nottingham School of Flying)*	
						Nottingham City-Tollerton 27.11.09E
G-BJUS	Piper PA-38-112 Tomahawk	38-80A0065	N9690N	10.12.81	J D Wiliams	High Cross, Ware 14. 2.09E
G-BJUU	Solent Osprey Mk.4B Balloon (Minimum Lift)			23.11.81	M Vincent	St Helier, Jersey
	ASC-113					
G-BJUV	Cameron V-20 Balloon (Hot Air)	792		9.12.81	P Spellward *"Busy Bee"*	Bristol
G-BJVC	Evans VP-2	PFA 063-10599		17. 2.82	S J Greer and S E Clarke *(Fuselage noted 5.08)*	
	(Built R G Fenn) (Volkswagen 1911)					Shenington 19. 6.91P
G-BJVH	Reims Cessna F182Q Skylane II F18200106		D-EJMO	21.12.81	R J D Cuming	Salcombe 11.12.09E
			PH-AXU (2)			
G-BJVJ	Reims Cessna F152 II	F15201906		6. 1.82	Wilkins and Wilkins (Special Auctions) Ltd t/a	
					Henlow Flying Club	RAF Henlow 5. 8.09E
G-BJVK	Grob G109	6074		11. 3.82	B A Kimberley	(Hook Norton, Banbury) 22. 5.92
G-BJVM	Cessna 172N Skyhawk II	17269374	N737FA	29. 1.85	R D and M S B Forster	Ellough, Beccles 13.10.09E
G-BJVS	Scintex CP.1310-C3 Super Emeraude	903	F-BJVS	5. 1.79	N F Harris	(Sutton) 9.11.09P
G-BJVT	Reims Cessna F152 II	F15201904		12. 1.82	Cleveland Flying School Ltd Durham Tees Valley 25. 3.09E	
G-BJVU	Thunder Ax6-56 Bolt Balloon (Hot Air)	397		31.12.81	G V Beckwith *"Cooper"*	Xanten, Germany 26. 4.91A
G-BJVV	Robin R1180TD Aiglon II	79		5.11.81	P Hawkins	Cardiff 16. 7.09E
G-BJWH	Reims Cessna F152 II	F15201919		7. 5.82	J D Baines	Elstree 27. 9.09E
G-BJWI	Reims Cessna F172P Skyhawk II F17202172			14. 5.82	Bflying Ltd *(Operated Bournemouth Flying Club)*	
						Bournemouth 2. 9.09E
G-BJWJ	Cameron V-65 Balloon (Hot Air)	802		25. 1.82	R G Turnbull and S G Farse *"Gawain"*	
						Glasbury, Hereford 9. 8.09E
G-BJWO	Fairey Britten-Norman BN-2A-26 Islander 334		4X-AYR	16. 2.82	Metachem Diagnostics Ltd	Turweston 30. 5.09A
			SX-BBX, 4X-AYR, G-BAXC			
G-BJWT	Wittman W.10 Tailwind PFA 031-10688			5. 1.82	J F Bakewell tr Tailwind Group	Hucknall 8. 2.08P
	(Built J F Bakewell) (Lycoming O-290-G)					
G-BJWV	Colt 17A Cloudhopper Balloon (Hot Air)	391		22. 1.82	D T Meyes *(Bryant Homes titles)* Leamington Spa 26. 3.97A	
G-BJWW	Reims Cessna F172P Skyhawk II F17202148		(D-EFTV)	1. 2.82	Manx Aero Marine Management Ltd	Blackpool 19.11.08E
					(Operated Westair Flying Services)	
G-BJWX	Piper PA-18 Super Cub 95 (modified) 18-1985		EI-64	23. 2.82	R A G Lucas tr G-BJWX Syndicate	Redhill 11. 6.09P
	(L-18C-PI) (Continental O-200-A)		I-EIME, MM52-2385, 52-2385			

G-BJWZ   Piper PA-18 Super Cub 95   18-1361   OO-HMO   18. 1.82   R C Dean tr G-BJWZ Syndicate   Redhill 24. 5.08P
          (L-18C-PI) (Frame No.18-1262)   French Army 18-1361, 51-15361
          (Extensively damaged after left tyre detached on landing at Eshott 8. 6.08, it veered to the right and tipped on its nose)
G-BJXB   Slingsby T 67A   1995   8. 2.82   XRay Bravo Ltd   Barton 20.12.09E
G-BJXK   Fournier RF5   5054   D-KINB   3. 2.82   S J Jenkins tr RF5 Syndicate   Usk 20.10.09E
G-BJXP   Colt 56B Balloon (Hot Air)   393   29. 3.82   H J Anderson *"Bart"*   Oswestry   9. 9.00A
G-BJXR   Auster AOP.9   xxxx   XR267   2. 2.82   I Churm and J Hanson
          (Officially regd with Frame no.AUS/184)   (Mickleover, Derby and Duffield, Belper)
G-BJXX   Piper PA-23-250 Aztec E   27-4692   F-BTCM   7. 4.82   V Bojovic *(Noted 3.04)*   Padinska Skela, Serbia 23. 6.01
                                                         N14094
G-BJXZ   Cessna 172N Skyhawk II   17273039   PH-CAA   24. 3.82   T M Jones *(Operated Derby Aero Club)*   Derby   2.12.09E
                                                         N1949F
G-BJYD   Reims Cessna F152 II   F15201915   25. 3.82   N J James   Welshpool 24. 3.09E
G-BJYF   Colt 56A Balloon (Hot Air)   401   1. 3.82   A J Moore *"Fanta"*   Northwood, Middx 30. 9.09E
G-BJYK   Wassmer Jodel D 120A Paris-Nice   185   (G-BJWK)   11. 5.82   M R Baker   Westfield Farm, Hailsham   5. 7.09P
                                                         F-BJPK
G-BJYN   Piper PA-38-112 Tomahawk   38-79A1076   G-BJTE   12. 3.82   Panshanger School of Flying Ltd High Cross, Ware   6. 3.00T
                                                         N24310, N9671N
G-BJZA   Cameron N-65 Balloon (Hot Air)   820   4. 3.82   N D Hepworth   Stockport   3. 6.97A
G-BJZB   Evans VP-2   PFA 063-10633   10. 3.82   R B McComish   Bow, Totnes 15. 1.03P
          (Built A Graham) (Volkswagen 1834)
          (Was believed scrapped 2002/3 - fuselage noted 4.03; wings and engine fitted to a new VP-2 on site believed to be G-CCEI)
G-BJZF   de Havilland DH.82A Tiger Moth   NAS-100   8. 3.82   M I Lodge   Lavenham   6. 6.08P
          (Built Norfolk Aerial Spraying Ltd from spares and officially redesignated "NAS Tiger Moth")
G-BJZN   Slingsby T 67A   1997   31. 3.82   P B Rice   Brighton 16. 9.09E
G-BJZR   Colt 42A Balloon (Hot Air)   402   18. 3.82   A F Selby tr Selfish Balloon Group *"Selfish"*
                                                                                                             Loughborough 27. 9.09E

G-BKAA - G-BKZZ

G-BKAE   Wassmer Jodel D 120 Paris-Nice   200   F-BKCE   5. 5.82   S J Harris   Sleap 11. 5.09P
G-BKAF   Clutton FRED Series II   PFA 029-10337   23. 3.82   J M Robinson   (Achill Island, Co Mayo) 30. 5.97P
          (Built L G Millen) (Volkswagen 1835)
G-BKAM   Slingsby T 67M-160 Firefly   1999   26. 4.82   R C P Brookhouse   Maypole Farm, Chislet 13. 7.09E
G-BKAO   Wassmer Jodel D 112   249   F-BFTO   22. 3.82   R Broadhead
                                                                                                  Eddsfield, Octon Lodge Farm, Thwing 29. 5.08P
G-BKAS   Piper PA-38-112 Tomahawk   38-79A1075   N24291   16. 4.82   E Reed t/a St George Flight Training
                                                         N9670N   Durham Tees Valley 17. 8.09E
G-BKAY   Rockwell Commander 114   14411   SE-GSN   28. 9.81   D L Bunning   Dunkeswell   5. 6.09E
G-BKAZ   Cessna 152 II   15282832   N89705   27. 4.82   L W Scattergood *(Operated Sheffield City Flying School)*
                                                                                                            Sandtoft 12. 6.09E
G-BKBB   Hawker Fury replica   WA/6   OO-HFU   2. 4.82   Brandish Holdings Ltd *(As "K1930" in RAF 43 Sqdn c/s)*
          (Built Westward Airways (Lands End) Ltd)   OO-XFU, G-BKBB *(Noted 11.05)*   Kortrijk-Wevelgem, Belgium   3. 6.04P
          (RR Kestrel 5)
G-BKBD   Thunder Ax3 Maxi Sky Chariot Balloon (Hot Air)   5. 4.82   M J Casson   Lyth, Kendal
                                                 418
G-BKBF   SOCATA MS.894A Rallye Minerva 220 11622   F-BSKZ   8. 9.82   K A Hale and L C Clark   Draycott Farm, Chiseldon 15. 9.09E
G-BKBN   SOCATA TB-10 Tobago   287   4. 6.82   F L Hunter   Sturgate   8. 5.09E
G-BKBO   Colt 17A Cloudhopper Balloon (Hot Air) 342   1. 9.82   J Armstrong, M A Ashworth and H Davey
                                                                                "Captain Courageous"   Newquay 19. 2.04A
G-BKBP   Bellanca 7GCBC Citabria   465-73   N8693   1. 6.82   M G and J R Jefferies t/a H G Jefferies and Son
                                                                                                       Little Gransden   1.12.06T
G-BKBS   Bensen B 8MV   PFA G/01-1027   14. 4.82   L Harrison   (Southend-on-Sea) 10. 8.09P
          (Built G Dawe) (Rotax 532)
G-BKBV   SOCATA TB-10 Tobago   288   F-BNGO   4. 6.82   T C H Wright   (Harborne, Birmingham) 24. 3.09E
G-BKBW   SOCATA TB-10 Tobago   289   4. 6.82   P J Bramhall and D F Woodhouse tr Merlin Aviation
                                                                                                            Bristol 26. 5.09E
G-BKCC   Piper PA-28-180 Cherokee Archer   OY-BGY   13. 5.82   DR Flying Club Ltd   Gloucestershire   2.11.09E
                                   28-7405099
G-BKCE   Reims Cessna F172P Skyhawk II F17202135   N9687R   26. 4.82   The Leicestershire Aero Club Ltd   Leicester 27. 6.09E
G-BKCI   Brügger MB.2 Colibri   PFA 043-10692   22. 4.82   M R Walters *(Noted 11.06)*   Leicester
          (Built E R Newall) (Volkswagen 1600)
G-BKCN   Phoenix Currie Wot   PFA 3018   27. 4.82   N A A Pogmore   Benson's Farm, Laindon 22.11.08P
          (Built S E O Tomlinson) (Continental A65)
G-BKCR   SOCATA TB-9 Tampico   297   6. 5.82   P A Little *(Noted 11.05)*   Haverfordwest   3. 8.98T
G-BKCV   EAA Acrosport II   430   5. 5.82   R J Bower   (Sittingbourne) 14. 4.09P
          (Built M J Clark) - pr.no.PFA 072A-10776) (Lycoming 0-360)
G-BKCW   Wassmer Jodel D 120A Paris-Nice   285   (G-BKCP)   1. 6.82   I C Waddell tr Dundee Flying Group   Perth 12.12.08P
                                                         F-BMYF
G-BKCX   Mudry CAP.10B   149   28. 7.82   G P Gorvett   Rhosgoch   9.10.09E
G-BKCZ   Wassmer Jodel D 120A Paris-Nice   207   F-BKCZ   23. 4.82   I K Ratcliffe   (Eastbourne)   5. 3.09P
G-BKDC   Monnett Sonerai IIL   876   2. 7.82   K J Towell *(Damaged Breighton 7. 8.90)* (Guildford) 18. 6.90P
          (Built J Boobyer - pr.no.PFA 15-10597) (Volkswagen 1834)
G-BKDH   Robin DR.400-120 Dauphin 80   1582   PH-CAB   25. 5.82   Dauphin Flying Group Ltd
                                                                                              Draycott Farm, Chiseldon 24.11.09E
G-BKDI   Robin DR.400-120 Dauphin 80   1583   PH-CAD   25. 5.82   Mistral Aviation Ltd   Dunsfold 19. 7.08E
G-BKDJ   Robin DR.400-120 Dauphin 80   1584   PH-CAC   25. 5.82   I C Colwell and S Pritchard   Gloucestershire 26. 5.07
G-BKDK   Thunder Ax7-77Z Balloon (Hot Air)   428   21. 6.82   A J Byrne *"Cider Riser"*   Thatcham 17. 9.95A
          (Had EASA CofA dated 23.11.09 issued but details reverted to previous issue on 24. 1.09)
G-BKDP   Clutton FRED Series III   PFA 029-10650   24. 5.82   M Whittaker   (Wolverhampton)
          (Built M Whittaker)
G-BKDR   Pitts S-1S   PFA 009-10654   14. 6.82   J H Milne and T H Bishop   (Norwich) 21. 5.08P
          (Built Maypole Engineering Ltd)

Reg	Type	c/n	Prev ID	Date	Owner	Location	Date
G-BKDS	Colt 14A Cloudhopper Balloon (Hot Air)	340	SE-ZBZ	1. 6.82	D M and K R Sandford (Tethered 10.06)		
			G-BKDS			Knutsford and Northwich	
G-BKDX	SAN Jodel DR.1050 Ambassadeur	55	F-BITX	1. 6.82	H D Colliver	Landmead Farm, Garford	23.11.09P
G-BKEP	Reims Cessna F172M Skyhawk II	F17201095	OY-BFJ	8. 7.82	R M Dalley	Perth	29. 5.09E
	(Thielert TAE 125-01)						
G-BKER	Replica Plans SE.5a	PFA 020-10641		15. 6.82	N K Geddes (As "F5447:N" in RAF c/s)		
	(Built N K Geddes) (Continental O-200A)					South Barnbeth Farm, Bridge of Weir	30. 6.09P
G-BKET	Piper PA-18 Super Cub 95	18-1990	EI-67	17. 6.82	H M MacKenzie	Inverness	27. 5.09P
	(L-18C-PI)		I-EIBI, MM52-2390, 52-2390				
G-BKEU	Taylor JT.1 Monoplane	PFA 055-10553		18. 6.82	A J Moore	(Turweston, Brackley)	20. 7.95P
	(Built R J Whybrow and J M Springham)						
G-BKEV	Reims Cessna F172M Skyhawk II	F17201443	PH-WLH	8. 7.82	G Henn tr Derby Arrows	Derby	19. 4.09E
			OO-CNE				
G-BKEW	Bell 206B-3 JetRanger III	3010	D-HDAD	8. 7.82	N R Foster t/a Foster Associates	Biggin Hill	14. 8.09E
G-BKEY	Clutton FRED Series III	PFA 029-10208		27. 5.82	G S Taylor	(Rock, Kidderminster)	
	(Built G S Taylor) (Volkswagen 1600)						
G-BKFA	Monnett Sonerai IIL	PFA 015-10524		21. 6.82	S J N Robbie (On long term rebuild 2.06)		
	(Built R F Bridge)					Roughay Farm, Bishops Waltham	
G-BKFC	Reims Cessna F152 II	F15201443	OO-AWB	1. 9.82	C Walton Ltd tr Sulby Aerial Surveys		
						Bruntingthorpe	5. 3.09E
G-BKFI	Evans VP-1 Series 2	PFA 062-10491		24. 6.82	P L Naylor	Morgansfield, Fishburn	4. 6.09P
	(Built R F A Lavergne) (Volkswagen 1834)						
G-BKFL	Aerosport Scamp	PFA 117-10814		17. 8.82	J Sherwood	(Royston, Barnsley)	
	(Built I D Daniels)						
G-BKFM	QAC Quickie 1	PFA 094-10570		28. 6.82	G E Meakin	(Ruddington)	29. 6.98P
	(Built R I Davidson and P Cheney) (Rotax 503)				(Damaged on take off Cranfield 4.7.98)		
G-BKFR	Scintex CP.301-C Emeraude	519	F-BUUR	30. 6.82	D G Burgess tr Devonshire Flying Group		
			F-BJFF			Trenchard Farm, Eggesford	18. 7.08P
G-BKFW	Percival P 56 Provost T 1	PAC/F/303	XF597	21. 9.82	Sylmar Aviation and Services Ltd		
					(As "XF597:AH in RAF College c/s)		
						Lower Wasing Farm, Brimpton	27. 7.07P
G-BKGA	SOCATA MS.892E Rallye 150GT	13287	F-GBXJ	15. 7.82	C J Spradbery	Coventry	1.10.09E
G-BKGB	Wassmer Jodel D 120 Paris-Nice	267	F-BMOB	21. 6.82	B A Ridgway	Rhigos	20. 3.09P
G-BKGC	Maule M-6-235C Super Rocket	7413C	N56465	23. 7.82	The Vale of the White Horse Gliding Centre Ltd		
						Sandhill Farm, Shrivenham	26.11.09P
G-BKGL	Beech D18S (3TM)	CA-164	CF-QPD	14. 7.82	A T J Darrah (As "1164" in USAAC c/s)	Duxford	30. 3.08
	(Beech c/n A-764)		RCAF 5193, 1564				
G-BKGM	Beech 3NM (D18S)	CA-203	N5063N	14. 7.82	Skyblue Aviation Ltd (As "HB275" in RAF SEAC c/s)		
	(Beech c/n A-853)		G-BKGM, CF-SUQ, RCAF 2324			Exeter	17. 9.09S
G-BKGR	Cameron O-65 Balloon (Hot Air)	864		6. 8.82	K Kidner and L E More	Newton Abbot	8. 5.93P
G-BKGT	SOCATA Rallye 110ST Galopin	3361		23. 7.82	P F Platt tr Long Marston Flying Group		
						Long Marston	14. 2.09E
G-BKGW	Reims Cessna F152 II	F15201878	N9071N	11. 8.82	The Leicestershire Aero Club Ltd	Leicester	15. 5.09E
G-BKHD	Oldfield Baby Lakes	8133-F-802B		5. 8.82	P J Tanulak	(Myddle, Shrewsbury)	11. 4.96P
	(Built P J Tanulak - pr.no.PFA 010-107182) (Continental O-200-A)				(Damaged Shrewsbury 22.10.95)		
G-BKHG	Piper J-3C-65 Cub (L-4H-PI)	12062	F-BCPT	13. 9.82	H C Cox "Puddle Jumper" (As "479766:63-D" in HQ 9th Army,		
			NC79807, 44-79766		USAAC c/s)	Grange Farm, Frogland Cross	29. 8.08P
G-BKHJ	Cessna 182P Skylane II	18264129	PH-CAT	25. 8.82	Sameiet LN MTW	Bodo, Norway	18. 7.09E
	(Reims c/n F18200040)		D-EATV, N6223F				
G-BKHW	Stoddard-Hamilton Glasair RG	357		27.8.82	P J Mansfield	(Newark)	19.11.09P
	(Built N Clayton - pr.no.PFA 149-11312) (Lycoming O-320)						
G-BKHY	Taylor JT.1 Monoplane	PFA 1416		8. 9.82	B C J O'Neill	Benson's Farm, Laindon	29.10.08P
	(Built J Hall)						
G-BKIB	SOCATA TB-9 Tampico	323		25. 8.82	G A Vickers	Hawarden	12. 6.09E
G-BKIF	Fournier RF6-100	3	F-GADR	8.10.82	C C Rollings and F J Hodgson t/a Tiger Airways		
						Gloucestershire	31. 1.10E
G-BKII	Reims Cessna F172M Skyhawk II	F17201370	PH-PLO	8.10.82	Sealand Aerial Photography Ltd	Goodwood	6. 3.09E
			(D-EGIA)				
G-BKIJ	Reims Cessna F172M	F17200920	PH-TGZ	15.10.82	Cirrus Aviation Ltd	Clacton	8. 8.08E
G-BKIR	SAN Jodel D 117	737	F-BIOC	30. 9.82	D M Hardaker (On rebuild 3.96)		
						Bird's Edge, Penistone	28. 8.92P
G-BKIS	SOCATA TB-10 Tobago	329		22. 9.82	R J Burrows and S M Cuthill, tr Wessex Flyers		
						Thruxton	7. 7.09E
G-BKIT	SOCATA TB-9 Tampico	330		22. 9.82	Cavendish Aviation UK Ltd	Earls Colne	30. 6.09E
G-BKIU	Colt 17A Cloudhopper Balloon (Hot Air)	420		29. 9.82	S R J Pooley	Elstree	30. 8.09E
G-BKIZ	Cameron V-31 Air Chair Balloon (Hot-Air)	842		1. 2.83	A P S Cox	Basingstoke	10. 9.09E
G-BKJB	Piper PA-18-135 Super Cub	18-574	PH-GAI	1. 8.83	W S Stanley	Gloucestershire	6.11.10
	(L-21A-PI) (Frame No.18-522)		R Neth AF R-204, 51-15657, N1003A				
G-BKJF	SOCATA MS.880B Rallye 100T	2300	F-BULF	16.12.82	R Neeson	Weston, Dublin	3.10.08E
G-BKJS	Wassmer Jodel D 120A Paris-Nice	191	F-BJPS	4.10.82	B F Baldock and T J Nicholson		
						Clipgate Farm, Denton	8. 1.09P
G-BKJW	Piper PA-23-250 Aztec E	27-4716	N14153	3.11.78	Alan Williams Entertainments Ltd	Southend	17.12.09E
G-BKKN	Cessna 182R Skylane II	18267801	N6218N	30.11.82	R A Marven t/a Marvagraphic		
						Coleman Green, Hertfordshire	23. 5.09E
G-BKKO	Cessna 182R Skylane II	18267852	N4907H	30.11.82	E L King and D S Lightbown	Crosland Moor	1. 6.09E
G-BKKZ	Pitts S-1S	PFA 009-10525	(G-BIVW)	10.11.82	G M Huffen	Sherburn-in-Elmet	2. 9.09P
	(Built J A Coutts)						
G-BKLO	Reims Cessna F172M Skyhawk II	F17201380	PH-BET	22. 3.83	Stapleford Flying Club Ltd	Stapleford	11. 6.09E
			D-EFMS				
G-BKMA	Mooney M 20J Mooney 201	24-1316	N1170N	13.12.82	C A White tr Foxtrot Whisky Aviation	Cambridge	5. 8.09E
G-BKMB	Mooney M 20J Mooney 201	24-1307	N1168P	15.12.82	W A Cook tr G-BKMBFlying Group		
						Sherburn-in-Elmet	21. 1.09E
G-BKMG	Handley Page 0/400 replica	TPG-1		8.12.82	M G King tr The Paralyser Group		
	(Built The Paralyser Group)					(Wroxham, Norwich)	

Reg	Type	c/n	Prev id	Date	Owner / Notes / Location	Expiry
G-BKMI	Vickers Supermarine 359 Spitfire HF.VIIIc	6S/583793	A58-671 MV154	23.12.82	R J Lamplough *(As "MT928:ZX-M" in RAF 145 Sqdn c/s)* Filton	27. 6.09P
G-BKMT	Piper PA-32R-301 Saratoga II SP	32R-8213013	N8005Z	4. 2.83	P Squires Blackpool	23. 4.09E
G-BKMX	Short SD.3-60 Variant 100	SH3608	G-14-3608	13.12.82	ACL Aircraft Trading Ltd *"City of Bristol"* Inverness	31. 7.09E
G-BKNI	Sud-Aviation Gardan GY-80-160D Horizon	249	F-BRJN	28. 1.83	A Hartigan tr Blue Horizon Flying Group *"Blue Lady"* *(Stored 10.05)* Bourn	13. 5.02
G-BKNO	Monnett Sonerai IIL	792		11. 3.83	S Hardy (Northchurch, Hemel Hempstead)	15. 6.99P
	(Built S Tattersfield and K Bailey - pr.no.PFA 015-10528) (Volkswagen 1834)					
G-BKNP	Cameron V-77 Balloon (Hot Air)	874		22.12.82	K Jakobsson Goteborg, Sweden	16. 2.09E
G-BKNZ	Menavia Piel CP.301A Emeraude	296	F-BISZ	21. 1.83	J A Thomas Lydd	12.11.09P
G-BKOA	SOCATA MS.893E Rallye 180GT	12432	F-BOFB F-ODAT, F-BVAT	2. 3.83	M Jarrett (Yaxley, Peterborough)	31.10.05
G-BKOB	Moravan Zlin Z-326 Trener Master	757	F-BKOB	28. 9.81	A L Rae Luxter's Farm, Hambledon	30. 5.09E
G-BKOK	Pilatus Britten-Norman BN-2B-26 Islander	2174	OY-CFV G-BKOK	27. 1.83	Cormack (Aircraft Services) Ltd Cumbernauld	
	(Type amended to BN-2B-26 16. 8.08)					
G-BKOT	Wassmer WA.81 Piranha	813	F-GAIP	17. 2.87	B N Rolfe *(Noted 10.05)* Bourn	
G-BKOU	Hunting Percival P 84 Jet Provost T 3	PAC/W/13901	XN637	17. 2.83	G-BKOU/2 Ltd *"Where Eagles Share"* North Weald	31. 8.08P
G-BKPA	Hoffmann H 36 Dimona	3522		16. 6.83	M A V Gatehouse, S J Clark and R Matthews North Hill	4. 9.09E
G-BKPB	Aerosport Scamp	PFA 117-10736		23. 2.83	B R Thompson Hucknall	8. 8.07P
	(Built R Scroby) (Volkswagen 1834)					
G-BKPC	Cessna A185F AgCarryall	185-03809	N4599E	10. 7.80	The Black Knights Parachute Centre Ltd Bank End Farm, Cockerham	10.11.07E
G-BKPD	Viking Dragonfly	302		11. 3.83	E P Browne and G J Sargent (Cambridge)	20. 1.00P
	(Built P E J Sturgeon - pr.no.PFA 139-10897) (Revmaster 2100D) *(Damaged Cambridge 17. 7.99)*					
G-BKPE	CEA Jodel DR.250/160 Capitaine	35	F-BNJD	18. 3.83	J S and J D Lewer Dunkeswell	16.12.04
G-BKPN	Cameron N-77 Balloon (Hot Air)	923		9. 3.83	R H Sanderson *"Do It All"* Nuneaton	21. 5.87A
	(Donated to Balloon Preservation Group 1.03)					
G-BKPS	Grumman AA-5B Tiger	AA5B-0007	OO-SAS OO-HAO, (OO-WAY), N1507R	7. 3.83	A E T Clarke Rochester	19. 5.09E
G-BKPX	Wassmer Jodel D 120A Paris-Nice	240	F-BLNG	19. 1.84	D M Garrett and C A Jones Defford	9. 7.09P
G-BKPZ	Pitts S-1T	PFA 009-10852		4. 3.83	P R Rutterford Redhill	10. 7.09P
	(Built G C Masterton)					
G-BKRA	North American T-6G-NH Texan	188-90	MM53-664 RM-9, 51-15227	19. 8.83	First Air Ltd *(As "115227 in US Navy c/s)* Shoreham	21. 3.10S
G-BKRF	Piper PA-18 Super Cub 95 (L-18C-PI)	18-1525	F-BOUI French Army, 51-15525	7.11.83	K M Bishop Croft Farm, Defford	20. 5.08P
	(Frame No.18-1502)					
G-BKRH	Brügger MB.2 Colibri	142		15. 3.83	M R Benwell Bodmin	9. 9.09P
	(Built M R Benwell - pr no.PFA 043-10150) (Volkswagen 1835)					
G-BKRK	SNCAN Stampe SV-4C	57	Aeronavale 57	30. 3.83	J R Bisset tr Strathgadie Stampe Group (Aboyne)	28. 6.98
G-BKRN	Beech D18S	A-675	CF-DTN RCAF A675, RCAF 1500	14. 4.83	A A Marshall and P L Turland *(Under restoration 3.02)* Bruntingthorpe	26. 6.83P
	(Official c/n CA-75 suggests Canadian rebuild)					
G-BKRS	Cameron V-56 Balloon (Hot Air)	908		23. 3.83	D N and L J Close *"Bonkers"* Chute Forest, Andover	25. 9.09E
G-BKRZ	Dragon 77 Balloon (Hot Air)	001		11. 4.83	J R Barber *"Rupert"* Newbury	5. 3.94A
	(On loan to British Balloon Museum and Library)					
G-BKSD	Colt 56A Balloon (Hot Air)	361		11. 4.83	M J Casson *"Entwhistle Green"* Kendal	11. 2.09E
G-BKSE	QAC Quickie 1	PFA 094-10748		6. 4.83	M D Burns (Kirkintilloch, Glasgow)	8. 5.89P
	(Built Taylor, M D Burns and Ibbott and officially regd with c/n PFA 094-10784) (Onan B48M) (Stored 6.00)					
G-BKSP	Schleicher ASK 14	14028	D-KOMO	25. 5.83	J H Bryson Bellarena	11. 9.09E
G-BKST	Rutan VariEze	12718-001		20. 4.83	R Towle (Barrasford, Hexham)	
	(Built R Towle)					
G-BKSX	SNCAN Stampe SV-4C	61	F-BBAF French AF	16. 5.83	C A Bailey and J A Carr *(Stored 11.02)* (Eggesford)	15. 6.89
G-BKTA	Piper PA-18 Super Cub 95	18-3223	OO-HBA Belg AF OL-L49, L-149, 53-4823	10. 5.83	M J Dyson Roddige	10. 8.05P
	(L-18C-PI) (Frame No.18-3246)					
G-BKTH	Hawker Sea Hurricane IB	CCF/41H/4013	Z7015	24. 5.83	Richard Shuttleworth Trustees Old Warden	10. 5.09P
	(Built Canadian Car and Foundry Co)				*(As "Z7015:7-L" in RN 880 Sqdn c/s)*	
G-BKTM	PZL-Bielsko SZD-45A Ogar	B-656		31. 5.83	J T Pajdak Challock	13.10.09E
G-BKTR	Cameron V-77 Balloon (Hot Air)	951		6. 6.83	C M Morley and C Williamson Upchurch, Sittingbourne and Goudhurst, Cranbrook	25. 9.09E
G-BKTV	Reims Cessna F152 II	F15201450	OY-BJK	8. 8.83	ACS Aviation Ltd Perth	10. 9.09E
G-BKTZ	Slingsby T 67M Firefly	2004	G-SFTV	26. 8.83	P R Elvidge Eddsfield, Octon Lodge Farm, Thwing	24. 1.09E
	(Fuselage marked as "G-BKTZ" noted 10.07)					
G-BKUE	SOCATA TB-9 Tampico	369	F-BNGX	31. 5.83	R N Swinney tr Fife TB9ers Glenrothes	28. 3.09E
G-BKUI	Druine D.31 Turbulent	PFA 038-10789		28. 6.83	E Shouler Beeches Farm, South Scarle	
G-BKUR	Menavia Piel CP.301A Emeraude	280	(G-BKBX) F-BMLX, F-OBLY	19.10.83	T Harvey Sorbie Farm, Kingsmuir	25. 6.09P
G-BKUU	Thunder Ax7-77 Series 1 Balloon (Hot Air)	522		3. 8.83	M A Mould *"Tanglefoot"* Winchester	12. 4.03A
G-BKVA	SOCATA Rallye 180T Galerien	3274	SE-GFS F-GBXA	30. 6.83	Buckminster Gliding Club Ltd Saltby	20. 7.09E
G-BKVB	SOCATA Rallye 110ST Galopin	3258	OO-PIP	22. 6.83	A and K Bishop Haverfordwest	11.12.05
	(While parked at Haverfordwest, with CofA expired 11.12.05, was blown over by high winds there on 10. 3.08)					
G-BKVC	SOCATA TB-9 Tampico	372	F-BNGQ	4. 7.83	D M Hook Bicester	20. 5.09E
G-BKVF	Clutton FRED Series III	PFA 029-10791		29. 7.83	G E and R E Collins Derby	
	(Built N E Johnson)					
G-BKVG	Scheibe SF25E Super Falke	4362	(D-KNAE)	25. 8.83	G-BKVG Ltd North Hill	4. 6.09E
	(Limbach SL1700)					
G-BKVK	Auster AOP.9	xxxx	WZ662	8. 8.83	J K Houlgrave *(As "WZ662" in AAC c/s)* Trenchard Farm, Eggesford	23. 7.09P
	(Officially regd with Frame no.AUS/10/2)					
G-BKVL	Robin DR.400-160 Major	1625		26. 7.83	Tatenhill Aviation Ltd t/a Tatenhill Aviation Tatenhill	3. 4.09E

G-BKVM	Piper PA-18-150 Super Cub	18-849	PH-KAZ	26. 8.83	D G Caffrey (As "115684:VM" in US Army c/s)		
	(L-21A-PI) (Frame No.18-824)		R Neth AF R-214, 51-15684		"Spirit of Goxhill"	Strubby	12.11.11
G-BKVO	Pietenpol AirCamper	PFA 047-10799		8. 8.83	M C Hayes	Woonton, Nr Almley	16. 4.09P
	(Built M J Honeychurch) (Continental A65)						
G-BKVP	Pitts S-1D	002		19. 8.83	S W Doyle	Popham	26. 7.07P
	(Built P J Leggo - pr.no.PFA 009-10800)						
G-BKVS	Campbell Cricket	PFA G/01-1047		11. 8.83	K Hughes	(Amlwch, Gwynedd)	10. 8.05P
	(Built V Scott) (Volkswagen 1834)						
G-BKVT	Piper PA-23-250 Aztec F	27-7754002	G-HARV	6. 2.84	BKS Surveys Ltd	Belfast International	3. 4.09E
			N62760				
G-BKVW	Airtour AH-56 Balloon (Hot Air)	AH.003		27. 6.84	L D and H Vaughan "Lunardi"	Wilstone, Tring	
G-BKVX	Airtour AH-56C Balloon (Hot Air)	AH.002		27. 6.84	P Aldridge "Featherspin" or "Liebling"		
						Halesworth, Suffolk	
G-BKWD	Taylor JT.2 Titch	PFA 060-10232		17. 8.83	J F Sully	Sturgate	26. 6.09P
	(Built E H Booker and originally regd as c/n PFA 060-10143 - presumed absorbed into this project on build) (Continental PC60)						
G-BKWR	Cameron V-65 Balloon (Hot Air)	970		26. 8.83	Window on the World Ltd	London SW4	18. 1.07A
G-BKWW	Cameron V-77 Balloon (Hot Air)	984		13. 9.83	A M Marten "Kouros"	Woking	18. 1.89A
G-BKWY	Reims Cessna F152	F15201940		22. 9.83	Cleveland Flying School Ltd	Durham Tees Valley	20. 2.09E
G-BKXA	Robin R2100	114	F-GAOS	24.11.83	M Wilson	Little Gransden	22.10.99
G-BKXD	Aérospatiale SA.365N Dauphin 2	6088	F-WMHD	7. 9.83	CHC Scotia Ltd	Blackpool	18.12.09E
G-BKXF	Piper PA-28R-200 Cherokee Arrow II		OY-DZN	10.11.83	P L Brunton	Welshpool	25.9.09E
		28R-7335351	N56092				
G-BKXM	Colt 17A Cloudhopper Balloon (Hot Air)	531		3.10.83	R G Turnbull	Glasbury, Hereford	19. 8.09E
G-BKXN	ICA IS-28M2A	48		24.10.83	J Pool	Sturgate	2. 8.08E
G-BKXO	Rutan LongEz	PFA 074A-10580		24.10.83	M G Parsons	RAF Kinloss	13. 5.09P
	(Built P Wareham) (Continental O-200-A)						
G-BKXP	Auster AOP.6	2830	A-14	12.10.83	B J Ellis (On rebuild 7.91)	Thruxton	
	(Frame No.TAY841BJ)		Belg AF, VT987				
G-BKXR	Druine D 31A Turbulent	303	OY-AMW	1.11.83	M B Hill	Draycott Farm, Chiseldon	15. 9.09P
	(Built H Husted) (Volkswagen 1700)						
G-BKZB	Cameron V-77 Balloon (Hot Air)	995		11.11.83	K B Chapple		
					Montastruc, Hautes-Pyrenees, France		6. 7.01A
G-BKZE	Aérospatiale AS.332L Super Puma	2102	F-WKQE	30. 9.83	CHC Scotia Ltd	Aberdeen	25. 9.09E
G-BKZF	Cameron V-56 Balloon (Hot Air)	246	F-BXUK	14.11.83	C F Sanger-Davies	Eldersfield, Gloucester	18. 3.97A
G-BKZG	Aérospatiale AS.332L Super Puma	2106	HB-ZBT	30. 9.83	CHC Scotia Ltd	Aberdeen	25. 8.09E
			G-BKZG				
G-BKZI	Bell 206A JetRanger	118	(5B-CGC or 'CGD)7.12.83		Bucklefields Business Developments Ltd		
			G-BKZI, N6238N		(Ogbourne St George, Marlborough)		19. 9.09E
G-BKZM	Isaacs Fury	PFA 011-10742		27. 9.83	E McNeill and P O'Reilly	Naas, County Kildare	1.10.90P
	(Built R J Smith and J Evans)						
G-BKZT	Clutton FRED Series II	PFA 029-10715		20.10.83	U Chakravorty (Noted 6.05) Clipgate Farm, Denton		2. 7.02P
	(Built A E Morris) (Volkswagen 1834)						
G-BKZV	Bede BD-4	380	ZS-UAB	31. 8.84	T S Smith	(Rugby)	28.10.05P
	(Built A L Bergamasgo) (Lycoming O-320)						

G-BLAA - G-BLZZ

G-BLAC	Reims Cessna FA152 Aerobat	FA1520370		25. 3.80	D C C Handley	Little Staughton	30. 5.08E
G-BLAF	Stolp SA.900 V-Star	PFA 106-10651		13. 9.83	P R Skeels	Yew Tree Farm, Lymm Dam	15. 4.08P
	(Built J E Malloy) (Continental O-200-A)						
G-BLAG	Pitts S-1D	PFA 009-10195		1.12.83	R S Grace	Bentwaters	19. 5.09P
	(Built B Bray)						
G-BLAH	Thunder Ax7-77 Series 1 Balloon (Hot Air) 526			3.10.83	T M Donnelly "Blah"	Sprotbrough, Doncaster	19. 8.01A
					(Active Albuquerque , New Mexico 10.03)		
G-BLAI	Monnett Sonerai IIL	PFA 015-10583		6.12.83	T Simpson (Noted 12.01)	(Kirkcaldy)	12. 1.99P
	(Built T Simpson and officially regd with c/n PFA 15-10584)						
G-BLAM	CEA Jodel DR.360 Chevalier	345	F-BRCM	6. 2.84	D J Durell	Rochester	18. 8.09E
G-BLAT	SAN Jodel D 150 Mascaret	56	F-BNID	30. 1.84	N T Coote and I R Willis tr G-BLAT Flying Group		
						Glenrothes	28.11.07P
G-BLAX	Reims Cessna FA152 Aerobat	FA1520385		11.10.83	N C and M L Scanlan	RAF Waddington	28. 5.09E
G-BLCC	Thunder Ax7-77Z Balloon (Hot Air)	532		7.12.83	W J Treacy and P Murphy	(Trim, County Meath)	27. 9.06A
G-BLCG	SOCATA TB-10 Tobago	61	G-BHES	17. 3.80	R Deery and D Tunks tr Charlie Golf Flying Group		
						Shoreham	10. 8.09E
G-BLCH	Colt 65D Balloon (Hot Air)	392	G-BJHT (1)	14.11.83	Balloon Flights Club Ltd "Geronimo"		
						Kings Norton, Leicester	
G-BLCI	EAA Acrosport P	P-10A	N6AS	29. 2.84	M R Holden "Bluebottle" (Damaged Farthing Corner 1996)		
					(Stoneacre Farm, Farthing Corner)		16. 6.97P
G-BLCM	SOCATA TB-9 Tampico	194	OO-TCT	2.12.83	K J Steele and D J Hewitt		
			(OO-TBC)		(Kynnersley, Telford and Himley, Dudley)		22. 7.09E
G-BLCT	CEA Jodel DR.220 2+2	23	F-BOCQ	22.12.83	J Paulson	Hawarden	10. 8.09E
G-BLCU	Scheibe SF25B Falke	4699	D-KECC	30.12.83	J D Johnson tr Charlie Uniform Syndicate	Rufforth	21. 1.10E
	(Stark-Stamo MS1500)						
G-BLCV	Hoffmann H 36 Dimona	36113	EI-CJO	21. 3.84	R and M Weaver	Usk	20. 7.09E
			G-BLCV				
G-BLCW	Evans VP-1	PFA 062-10835		19.12.83	G R Cotterill "Le Plank"	Fincham, King's Lynn	15. 6.09P
	(Built K D Pearce) (Volkswagen 1600)						
G-BLCY	Thunder Ax7-65Z Balloon (Hot Air)	487		13. 1.84	C M George "Warsteiner" (Active Germany 2005)		
						Newton Ferrers, Plymouth	26. 2.99A
G-BLDB	Taylor JT.1 Monoplane	PFA 055-10506		28.12.83	C J Bush	Great Oakley	12. 5.09P
	(Built C J Bush)						
G-BLDD	Wag-Aero CUBy AcroTrainer	PFA 108-10653		29.12.83	A F Stafford	Combrook	4.10.06P
	(Built C A Lacock) (Lycoming O-320)						
G-BLDG	Piper PA-25-235 Pawnee C	25-4501	SE-FLB	9. 1.84	York Gliding Centre Ltd	Rufforth	25. 6.09E
	(Modified to PA-25-260 standard)		LN-VYM				

Reg	Type	C/n	Prev id	Date	Owner/Operator	Location	Status
G-BLDK	Robinson R22	0139	C-GSGU	17. 1.84	Flight Academy (Gyrocopters) Ltd	Barton	29. 8.09E
G-BLDN	Rand Robinson KR-2 PFA 129-10913			12. 1.84	P R Diffey	Top Farm, Croydon, Royston	16. 4.09P
	(Built R Y Kendal) (Volkswagen 1834)						
G-BLDV	Pilatus Britten-Norman BN-2B-26 Islander	2179	D-INEY	13. 1.84	Loganair Ltd (Highland Park titles)	Glasgow	19. 7.09E
			G-BLDV				
G-BLEB	Colt 69A Balloon (Hot Air)	537		20. 1.84	I R M Jacobs	Padworth Common, Reading	30. 3.85A
G-BLEP	Cameron V-65 Balloon (Hot Air)	102		27. 2.84	D Chapman tr The Ground Hogs "Manor Marquees"		
						Maidstone	10. 9.96A
G-BLES	Stolp SA.750 Acroduster Too	197		8.12.83	C J Kingswood	RAF Church Fenton	31. 7.09P
	(Built W G Hosie - pr.no.PFA 089-10428) (Lycoming O-360)						
G-BLET	Thunder Ax7-77 Series 1 Balloon (Hot Air)	539		16. 2.84	Servatruc Ltd "Servatruc"	Nottingham	15. 8.97A
G-BLEZ	Aérospatiale SA.365N Dauphin 2	6131		24. 1.84	CHC Scotia Ltd	Blackpool	27. 8.09E
G-BLFI	Piper PA-28-181 Archer II	28-8490034	N4333Z	22. 2.84	Bonus Aviation Ltd	Cranfield	11. 8.09E
G-BLFW	Grumman AA-5 Traveler	AA5-0786	OO-GLW	22. 2.84	D C A Milne tr Grumman Club		
						Bournemouth	11.10.07E
G-BLFY	Cameron V-77 Balloon (Hot Air)	1030		16. 3.84	A N F Pertwee "Groupie"	Frinton-on-Sea	5. 4.92A
G-BLFZ	Piper PA-31 Navajo C	31-7912106	PH-RWS	21. 3.84	London Executive Aviation Ltd	Stapleford	14.11.09E
			(PH-ASV), N3538W				
G-BLGH	Robin DR.300-180R Remorqueur	570	D-EAFL	10. 4.84	Booker Gliding Club Ltd	Wycombe Air Park	2. 6.09E
G-BLGS	SOCATA Rallye 180T	3206		7. 7.78	A Waters t/a London Light Aircraft	Dunstable	21. 5.99
					(Gutted fuselage noted 6.08)		
G-BLGV	Bell 206B-2 JetRanger II	982	5B-JSB	2. 5.84	Heliflight (UK) Ltd	Gloucestershire	22. 5.09E
			C-FDYL, CF-DYL				
G-BLHH	CEA Jodel DR.315 Petit Prince	324	F-BPRH	3. 7.84	S J Luck	Tower Farm, Wollaston	24. 7.09E
G-BLHI	Colt 17A Cloudhopper Balloon (Hot Air)	506		8. 9.86	J A Folkes "Hopping Mad"	Loughborough	24.11.01A
G-BLHJ	Reims Cessna F172P Skyhawk II	F17202182		26. 3.84	J H Sandman t/a Sandman Aviation	Carlisle	18.6.09E
G-BLHM (2)	Piper PA-18 Super Cub 95	18-3120	LX-AIM	23. 7.84	A G Edwards	(Llandegla)	8. 8.09P
	(L-18C-PI) (Lycoming O-320)		D-EOAB, Belgian AF OL-L46, L-46, 53-4720				
G-BLHN	Robin HR.100-285 Tiara	539	F-GABF	20. 2.78	E A and L M C Payton	Spanhoe	.12.06
					(Fuselage on trailer, wings stacked 10.07)		
G-BLHR	Gulfstream GA-7 Cougar	GA7-0109	OO-RTI	12. 4.84	W B Orde-Powlett	Full Sutton	13. 4.09E
			(OO-HRC), N751G				
G-BLHS	Bellanca 7ECA Citabria 115	1342-80	OO-RTQ	12. 4.84	N J F Campbell and D J Lockett tr Hotel Sierra Group		
						Inverness	10. 6.09E
G-BLHW	Varga 2150A Kachina	VAC161-80		17. 7.84	J R Surbey tr Wilburton Flying Group		
						Blockmoor Farm, Soham, Ely	23. 9.09E
G-BLID	de Havilland DH.112 Venom FB.50 (FB.1)	815	Swiss AF J-1605	13. 7.84	P G Vallance Ltd	Charlwood, Surrey	
	(Built F + W)				(In Gatwick Aviation Museum: as "J-1605" in Swiss AF c/s)		
G-BLIK	Wallis WA-116/F/S	K-218X		30. 4.84	K H Wallis	Reymerston Hall, Norfolk	31 5.07P
	(Franklin 2A-120)						
G-BLIT	Thorp T-18CW PFA 076-10550			24. 4.84	A P Tyrwhitt-Drake	Ellough, Beccles	15. 8.09P
	(Built A J Waller) (Lycoming O-320)						
G-BLIW	Percival P 56 Provost T 51	PAC/F/125	IAC.177	12. 6.85	A D Mand K B Edie (As "177" in IAC c/s) (Noted 11.05)		
						Shoreham	16. 5.05P
G-BLIX	Saro Skeeter AOP.12	S2/5094	PH-HOF	3. 5.84	K M Scholes (As "XL809" in AAC c/s)		
			(PH-SRE), XL809			(Clapham, Bedford)	2. 6.06
G-BLIY	SOCATA MS.892A Rallye Commodore 150	11639	F-BSCX	9. 5.84	A J Brasher	Landmead Farm, Garford	26. 9.09E
G-BLJH	Cameron N-77 Balloon (Hot Air)	1047		14. 5.84	D Glenis and D J Phillips t/a Phillair "Daydream"		
						Dosthill, Tamworth	27. 6.89A
G-BLJM	Beech 95-B55 Baron	TC-1997	SE-GRT	3. 3.78	A Nitsche	(Bensheim, Germany)	29.12.09E
G-BLJO	Reims Cessna F152 II	F15201627	OY-BNB	21. 6.84	J S Develin and Z Islam	Blackbushe	14. 1.10E
G-BLKM	CEA Jodel DR.1051 Sicile (modified)	519	F-BLRO	26. 6.84	F H Lissimore tr Kilo Mike Group	Biggin Hill	18. 8.09E
G-BLKY	Beech 58 Baron	TH-1440		22. 8.84	R A Perrot	Guernsey	5. 8.09E
G-BLLA	Bensen B 8M PFA G/01-1055			27. 6.84	K T Donaghey	Henstridge	21. 5.07P
	(Built K T Donaghey) (Volkswagen 1834)						
G-BLLB	Bensen B 8MR PFA G/01A-1059			4. 9.84	D H Moss (Noted 12.02)	Henstridge	14. 6.01P
	(Built D H Moss) (Rotax 532)						
G-BLLD	Cameron O-77 Balloon (Hot Air)	1060		16. 7.84	G Birchall	Ormskirk	24. 8.07A
G-BLLH	CEA Jodel DR.220A/B 2+2	131		17. 7.84	M D Hughes	Tower Farm, Wollaston	22. 8.09E
G-BLLN	Piper PA-18 Super Cub 95 (L-18C-PI)	18-3447	D-ECLN	27. 6.84	P L Pilch and C G Fisher	Rochester	13. 1.11S
	(Continental O-200A) (Frame No.18-3380)		96+23, PY+901, QZ+011, AC+508, AS+507, 54-747				
G-BLLO	Piper PA-18 Super Cub 95 (L-18C-PI)	18-3099	D-EAUB	11. 7.84	D G Margetts	Vaynor Farm, Llanidloes	1.12.09P
	(Frame No 18-3058)		Belgian AF OL-L25, L-25, 53-4699				
G-BLLP	Slingsby T 67B Firefly	2008		19. 7.84	Air Navigation and Trading Company Ltd (On rebuild 11.06)		
						Blackpool	4.12.00T
G-BLLR	Slingsby T 67C Firefly	2011		19. 7.84	R L Brinklow	Exeter	17. 3.08E
	(Lycoming O-320) (Regd as "T 67B (mod)")						
G-BLLS	Slingsby T 67B Firefly	2013		19. 7.84	Freedom Aviation Ltd	RAF Lyneham	12. 7.09E
G-BLLW	Colt 56B Balloon (Hot Air)	578		11. 9.84	G Fordyce, R Wickens and S A Sawyer "Angel Clare"		
						Olney	30. 4.09E
G-BLLZ	Rutan LongEz PFA 074A-10830			16. 7.84	R S Stoddart-Stones	(Woldingham, Caterham)	22. 6.94P
	(Built G E Relf, D G Machin and E F Braddon) (Lycoming O-235)						
G-BLMA	Moravan Zlin Z-526 Trener Master	922	F-BORS	23. 7.84	G P Northcott	Redhill	30. 3.09E
G-BLME	Robinson R22HP	0032	N90261	16. 4.85	Heli Air Ltd	Denham	22. 1.10E
G-BLMG	Grob G109B	6322		27. 9.84	R W Littledale tr Mike Golf Syndicate	Enstone	16.11.09E
G-BLMI	Piper PA-18 Super Cub 95 (L-18C-PI)	18-2066	D-ENWI	5. 6.84	I Mackinnon tr G-BLMI Flying Group		
	(Frame No.18-2086)		R Neth AF R-55, 52-2466		(As "52-2466:R-55" in R Neth AF c/s)		
						White Waltham	12.10.09P
G-BLMN	Rutan LongEz PFA 074A-10643			3. 7.84	S E Bowers tr G-BLMN Flying Group	Blackbushe	16.11.09P
	(Built Farrington and Farrington and officially regd as c/n PFA 074A-10648) (Lycoming O-235)						
G-BLMP	Piper PA-17 Vagabond	17-193	F-BFMR	15. 5.84	D and M Shrimpton		
	(Continental C90)		N4893H			Phoenix Farm, Lower Upham	29. 6.09P

G-BLMR	Piper PA-18-150 Super Cub (L-18C-PI) (Lycoming O-320) (Frame No.18-2070)	18-2057	PH-NLD R Neth AF R-72, 52-2457	29. 5.84	Limadelta Aviation Ltd	Phoenix Farm, Lower Upham	8.10.11
G-BLMT	Piper PA-18-135 Super Cub (Frame No.18-2724)	18-2706	D-ELGH N8558C	12. 9.84	I S Runnalls	Enstone	14.11.10
G-BLMW	Nipper T 66 Series 3 (Built S L Millar) (Ardem 10)	PFA 025-11020		31. 8.84	S L Millar	Crowland	8. 4.09P
G-BLMZ	Colt 105A Balloon (Hot Air)	404		24. 9.84	M D Dickinson "Zulu"	Bristol	28. 3.97A
G-BLNJ	Pilatus Britten-Norman BN-2B-26 Islander	2189		3. 9.84	Panhispanica Digital SL	(Madrid, Spain)	3.12.07E
G-BLNO	Clutton FRED Series III (Built L W Smith)	PFA 029-10559		17.10.84	L W Smith	(Sale, Cheshire)	
G-BLOL	SNCAN Stampe SV-4A (Officialy regd for rebuild of G-AXRP but restored as such)	SS-SV-R1		12. 2.85	T Moore t/a Skysport Engineering	Rotary Farm, Hatch	
G-BLOR	Piper PA-30 Twin Comanche	30-59	HB-LAE N7097Y, N10F	19. 7.85	R L C Appleton	Westover Farm, Sheepwash	21. 5.09E
G-BLOS	Cessna 185A Skywagon	185-0359	LN-BDS N4159Y	17. 9.84	D C Minshaw	Old Warden	20. 6.09E
G-BLOT	Colt 56B Balloon (Hot Air)	424		11. 9.84	H J Anderson "Pathfinder"	Oswestry	17. 7.96A
G-BLOV	Thunder Ax5-42 Series 1 Balloon (Hot Air)	590		11. 9.84	A G R Calder "Puff The Magic Dragon"	(California, US)	29.11.02A
G-BLPA	Piper J-3C-65 Cub (L-4H-PI) (Frame No.11152)	11327	OO-AJL OO-JOE, 43-30036	27. 9.84	A C Frost	Rectory Farm, Abbotsley	26. 8.08P
G-BLPB	Turner TSW Hot Two Wot (Built J R Woolford and K M Thomas) (Lycoming O-320-A)	PFA 046-10606		19.10.84	J M Fforde	Lane Farm, Clyro, Hereford	18. 8.09P
G-BLPE	Piper PA-18 Super Cub 95 (L-18C-PI) 18-3084 (Continental O-200-A) (Also quoted as 18-3083)	18-3084	D-ECBE Belgian Army L-10, 53-4684	28. 9.84	A A Haig-Thomas	Thorpe-le-Soken	11. 7.08P
G-BLPF	Reims FR172G Rocket	FR17200187	N4594Q D-EEFL	29. 1.85	S Culpin	Fenland	5. 5.09E
G-BLPG	Auster J/1N Alpha	3395	G-AZIH	21. 5.82	P J Gill t/a Annic Marketing (As "16693:693" in RCAF c/s)	Whaley Bridge	8. 9.09P
G-BLPH	Cessna FRA.150L Aerobat (Built Reims Aviation SA)	FRA1500239	EI-BHH PH-ASH	19. 9.84	J D Baines	Elstree	2. 4.09E
G-BLPI	Slingsby T 67B Firefly	2016		24. 9.84	The Pathfinder Flying Club Ltd	RAF Wyton	25. 3.09E
G-BLPP	Cameron V-77 Balloon (Hot Air)	432		19. 9.78	R J Gooch	Alresford	27. 5.09E
G-BLRA	British Aerospace BAe 146 Series 100	E1017	N117TR N462AP, CP-2249, N462AP, G-BLRA, G-5-02	3.10.84	BAE Systems (Operations) Ltd	Warton	15.10.09E
G-BLRC	Piper PA-18-135 Super Cub (L-21B-PI) 18-3602 (Frame No.18-3790)	18-3602	OO-DKC PH-DKC, R NethAF R-112, 54-2402	27.11.84	S Hornung tr Supercub Group	Seething	11. 3.10S
	(Original fuselage (Frame No: 18-3790) reported removed and used in 1984 rebuild of OO-POU (c/n 18-7860 ex-D-EHRY). If so then OO-DKC has no connection with the original aircraft or the fuselage frame was not used in the rebuild of OO-POU)						
G-BLRF	Slingsby T 67C Firefly	2014		30.11.84	R C Nicholls	Wellesbourne Mountford	30. 7.09E
G-BLRL	Scintex CP.301-C1 Emeraude	552	(G-BLNP) F-BJFT	5.11.84	J A Macleod and I M Macleod	Stornoway	21. 7.09P
G-BLRM	Glaser-Dirks DG-400	4-107		5. 2.85	J A and W S Y Stephen "400"	Aboyne	21. 5.09E
G-BLTA	Colt 77A Coil Balloon (Hot Air)	525		8. 6.84	K A Schlussler "James Sadler"	Bourne, Lincoln	7. 8.91A
G-BLTC	Druine D 31A Turbulent (Built G P Smith and A W Burton) (Volkswagen 1600)	PFA 048-10964		18.12.84	S J Butler	RAF Henlow	15. 5.09P
G-BLTF	Robinson R22 Alpha	0428	N8526A	10. 1.85	Brian Seedle Helicopters Ltd (Noted 10.07)	Blackpool	5. 4.04T
G-BLTK	Rockwell Commander 112TC-A	13106	SE-GSD	11.12.84	T A Stoate and I M Mackay tr Commander TC Group	Blackbushe	6. 6.08E
G-BLTM	Robin HR.200-100 Club Club	96	F-GAEC	21.11.84	J S Swale tr Barton Robin Group	Barton	25.1.09E
G-BLTN	Thunder Ax7-65 Balloon (Hot Air)	621		4. 1.85	A H Symonds	Little Leighs, Chelmsford	16. 4.09E
G-BLTR	Scheibe SF25B Falke (Built Sportavia-Pützer) (Stark-Stamo MS1500)	4823	D-KHEC	23. 1.85	V Mallon	(Kleve-Wisseler Dünen, Germany)	1. 4.94
G-BLTS	Rutan LongEz (Built R W Cutler)	PFA 074A-10741		14. 1.85	R W Cutler	(Thorverton, Exeter)	
G-BLTW	Slingsby T 67B Firefly	2026		16. 1.85	R L Brinklow	Hinton-in-the-Hedges	15. 9.06T
G-BLTY	Westland WG.30 Series 160	019	VT-EKG G-17-9, G-BLTY, G-17-19	14. 1.85	D Brem-Wilson	(Joydens Farm, Westerham)	
G-BLUI	Thunder Ax7-65 Balloon (Hot Air)	553		22. 2.85	S Jones "Rhubarb and Custard"	Thornton-Cleveleys	31. 7.00A
G-BLUM	Aérospatiale SA.365N Dauphin 2	6101		21. 1.85	CHC Scotia Ltd	Blackpool	14. 4.09E
G-BLUV	Grob G109B	6336		1. 2.85	S K D'Urso and J Bailey tr The 109 Flying Group	North Weald	6.12.09E
G-BLUX	Slingsby T 67M-200 Firefly	2027	G-7-145 G-BLUX, G-7-113	31. 1.85	R L Brinklow tr Richard Brinklow Aviation	Rochester	27. 4.07T
G-BLUZ	de Havilland DH.82B Queen Bee	1435 & SAL.150	LF858	9. 4.85	C I Knowles and J Flynn tr The Bee Keepers Group (As "LF858" in RAF c/s)	RAF Henlow	18. 3.09P
G-BLVA	Airtour AH-31 Balloon (Hot Air)	AH.004		12. 2.86	A van Wyk (Active 11.02)	Caxton, Cambridge	
G-BLVB	Airtour AH-56 Balloon (Hot Air)	AH.005		12. 2.86	J J Daly Halfway House, County Waterford		
G-BLVI	Slingsby T 67M Firefly II	2017	(PH-KIF) G-BLVI	1. 2.85	Brooke Park Ltd (Operated Sheffield City Flying School)	Sandtoft	13. 5.09E
G-BLVK	Mudry CAP.10B	141	JY-GSR	11. 3.85	E K Coventry	Childerditch	17. 5.09E
G-BLVL	Piper PA-28-161 Warrior II	28-8416109	N43677	11. 2.85	TG Aviation Ltd	Manston	18. 1.10E
G-BLVS	Cessna 150M Commuter	15076869	EI-BLS N45356	19. 2.85	R Collier	Fenland	14.12.07E
G-BLVW	Cessna F172H (Built Reims Aviation SA)	F172-0422	D-ENQU	16. 5.85	R and D Holloway (Theydon Mount Nursery) Ltd	Stapleford Tawney	10. 7.00
G-BLWD	Piper PA-34-200T Seneca II	34-8070334	ZS-KKV ZS-XAT, N8253E	14. 3.85	Bencray Ltd (Noted 10.07)	Blackpool	7. 5.05T
G-BLWF	Robin HR.100-210 Safari II	183	F-BUSR	8. 3.85	Starguide Ltd	North Weald	28. 2.09E

Reg	Type	c/n	Prev id	Date	Owner/Operator	Location	Date
G-BLWH	Fournier RF6-100	7	F-GADF	3. 4.85	I R March	Wycombe Air Park	5. 9.03
					(Noted on slow restoration 6.08)		
G-BLWP	Piper PA-38-112 Tomahawk	38-78A0367	OY-BTW	7. 6.85	J E Rowley	Hawarden	23.10.07T
					(Heavy landing at Hawarden 11.10.07)		
G-BLWT	Evans VP-1 Series 2	PFA 062-10639		27. 3.85	N Clark	(New Milton)	8. 1.10P
	(Built G B O'Neill) (Volkswagen 1834)						
G-BLWV	Reims Cessna F152 II	F15201843	EI-BIN	25. 2.85	J S Develin and Z Islam	Blackbushe	8. 7.09E
G-BLWY	Robin R2160	176	F-GCUV	15. 4.85	Charlie Yankee Ltd	Filton	23. 1.10E
			SE-GXE				
G-BLXA	SOCATA TB-20 Trinidad	284	SE-IMO	11. 4.85	Trinidad Flyers Ltd	Blackbushe	9.12.09E
			F-ODOH				
G-BLXG	Colt 21A Cloudhopper Balloon (Hot Air)	605		2. 5.85	A Walker *"Britannia Park"*	Richmond, Surrey	6. 5.98A
G-BLXH	Fournier RF3	39	F-BMDQ	25. 3.85	J E Dallison	Enstone	24.10.08P
G-BLXI (2)	Scintex CP.1310-C3 Super Emeraude	937	F-BMJI	1. 4.85	R Howard Grove Moor Farm, Treswell, Retford		11. 4.09P
G-BLXO	SAN Jodel D 150 Mascaret	10	F-BLDB	9. 5.85	P R Powell	Shobdon	23.11.09P
G-BLXP	Piper PA-28R-200 Cherokee Arrow II		N5226T	29. 7.85	M B Hamlett	Le Plessis-Belleville, France	6.11.09E
		28R-7235200					
G-BLXR	Aérospatiale AS.332L Super Puma	2154		14. 5.85	Bristow Helicopters Ltd *"Cromarty"*	Aberdeen	1. 7.09E
G-BLYD	SOCATA TB-20 Trinidad	518		1. 5.85	Yankee Delta Corporation Ltd	Biggin Hilll	20. 4.09E
G-BLYE	SOCATA TB-10 Tobago	521		1. 5.85	Silverstar Aviation Ltd	Blackpool	8.10.08E
G-BLYK	Piper PA-34-220T Seneca III	34-8433083	N4371J	30. 5.85	Fly (CI) Ltd *(Operated Trans Euro Air)*	Alderney	6. 1.10E
G-BLYP	Robin R3000/120	109		15. 5.85	Weald Air Services Ltd *(Noted dismantled 8.05)*		
						Headcorn	5. 5.01T
G-BLYT	Airtour AH-77 Balloon (Hot Air)	AH.008		7. 7.87	I J Taylor and R C Kincaid *"Signal 2"*	Bristol	9. 8.03A
G-BLZA	Scheibe SF25B Falke	4684	D-KBAJ	22. 5.85	G W L Howarth tr Zulu Alpha Syndicate		
	(Sauer S1800S)					RAF Halton	18.12.08E
G-BLZE	Reims Cessna F152 II	F15201579	G-CSSC	3. 5.85	Redhill Aviation Ltd *(Operated Redhill Flying Club)*		
			PH-AYF (2)			Redhill	8. 7.09E
G-BLZF	Thunder Ax7-77 Balloon (Hot Air)	660		3. 6.85	H M Savage *"Hector"*	Edinburgh	10. 9.03A
G-BLZH	Reims Cessna F152 II	F15201965		21. 6.85	P D'Costa	Rochester	17.12.09E
G-BLZN	Bell 206B-2 JetRanger II	314	ZS-HMV	12. 7.85	E Miles	Manston	26.10.09E
			C-GWDH, N1408W				
G-BLZP	Reims Cessna F152 II	F15201959		10. 7.85	Nottingham Flying School Ltd		
						Nottingham-East Midlands	4. 2.10E
G-BLZS	Cameron O-77 Balloon (Hot Air)	479		22. 5.85	C D Steel	St Boswells, Melrose	26.11.04A

G-BMAA - G-BMZZ

Reg	Type	c/n	Prev id	Date	Owner/Operator	Location	Date
G-BMAD	Cameron V-77 Balloon (Hot Air)	1166		10. 6.85	M A Stelling *"Nautilus"*	Barton-le-Clay, Bedford	29. 9.99A
					(Inflated 4.06)		
G-BMAL	Sikorsky S-76A II Plus	760120	F-WZSA	27.11.80	CHC Scotia Ltd	North Denes	9. 5.09E
			G-BMAL				
G-BMAO	Taylor JT.1 Monoplane	PFA 1411		29. 7.85	S J Alston	Hinton-in-the-Hedges	11. 3.09P
	(Built V A Wordsworth)						
G-BMAX	Clutton FRED Series II	PFA 029-10322		20.12.78	D A Arkley	(Little Green, Chelmsford)	24. 8.99P
	(Built P Cawkwell and D A Arkley) (Volkswagen 1834)						
G-BMAY	Piper PA-18-135 Super Cub(L-21B-PI)18-3925		OO-LWB	3. 7.85	R W Davies Little Engeham Farm, Woodchurch		3. 6.11S
	(Frame No.18-3961)		"EI-229", I-EIJZ, MM54-2525, 54-2525				
G-BMBB	Reims Cessna F150L	F15001136	OO-LWM	2. 8.85	G.P.Robinson	Netherthorpe	29. 1.09E
			PH-GAA				
G-BMBJ	Schempp-Hirth Janus CM	20/209	(G-BLZL)	9. 9.85	M Critchlow tr BJ Flying Group *"BJ"*	RAF Keevil	30. 6.09E
G-BMBS	Colt 105A Balloon (Hot Air)	704		18. 7.85	H G Davies	Cheltenham	27. 8.91A
G-BMBW	Bensen B 8MR	MV-001		27. 8.85	M E Vahdat-Hagh	(Uxbridge)	30. 6.93P
	(Built M E Vahdat-Hagh - pr.no.PFA G/01-1064) (Rotax 503)						
G-BMBZ	Scheibe SF25E Super Falke	4322	D-KEFQ	17. 7.85	K E Ballington	Yeatsall Farm, Abbots Bromley	26. 9.08E
	(Limbach SL1700)						
G-BMCC	Thunder Ax7-77 Balloon (Hot Air)	705		12. 7.85	A K and C.M Russell *"Charlie Charlie"*		
						Wheaton Aston, Stafford	23. 2.99A
G-BMCD	Cameron V-65 Balloon (Hot Air)	1234		26. 6.85	R Lillyman	Irchester, Wellingborough	8. 9.09E
G-BMCG	Grob G109B	6362	(EAF673)	25. 7.85	Lagerholm Finnimport Ltd	Wycombe Air Park	15. 6.09E
G-BMCI	Reims Cessna F172H	F17200683	OO-WID	19. 8.85	A B Davis *(Operated Edinburgh Flying Club)*		
						Edinburgh	4. 3.09E
G-BMCN	Reims Cessna F152 II	F15201471	D-ELDM	7. 8.85	M C R Wills	Doncaster-Sheffield	9. 3.07T
	(Noted with Marshall Aerospace Engineering College 11.07 as Instructional airframe)						
G-BMCS	Piper PA-22-135 Tri-Pacer	22-1969	5Y-KMH	6. 9.85	T A Hodges	(Brynteg)	23. 1.11S
			VP-KMH, ZS-DJI				
G-BMCV	Reims Cessna F152 II	F15201963		2.10.85	The Leicestershire Aero Club Ltd	Leicester	15. 6.09E
G-BMCW	Aérospatiale AS.332L Super Puma	2161	F-WYMG	4.10.85	Bristow Helicopters Ltd *"Monifieth"*	Aberdeen	7.11.09E
			G-BMCW				
G-BMCX	Aérospatiale AS.332L Super Puma	2164		7.10.85	Bristow Southeast Asia Ltd	Redhill	14.11.08E
G-BMDB	Replica Plans SE.5a	PFA 020-10931		12. 8.85	D Biggs *(As "F235:B" in RFC c/s)*	Lee-on-Solent	22. 5.09P
	(Built D Biggs) (Continental O-200-A)						
G-BMDE	Pietenpol AirCamper	PFA 047-10989		12. 8.85	P B Childs	New Farm, Felton	18. 8.03P
	(Built D Silsbury) (Continental O-200-A)						
G-BMDJ	Price Ax7-77S Balloon (Hot Air)	003		1. 8.85	R A Benham *"Wings of Phoenix"*	Burton-on-Trent	
	(Built T P Price - c/n TPB.1) (Regd as Price TPB.1)						
G-BMDK	Piper PA-34-220T Seneca III	34-8133155	ZS-LOS	16. 9.85	Air Medical Fleet Ltd	Oxford	17. 1.10E
			N84209, N9553N				
G-BMDP	Partenavia P64B Oscar 200	08	HB-EPQ	20. 8.85	S T G Lloyd	Cardiff	21. 7.08S
G-BMDS	Wassmer Jodel D 120 Paris-Nice	281	F-BMOS	12. 8.85	N Lynch	Red Moor Farm, North Duffield	6. 4.09P
G-BMEA	Piper PA-18 Super Cub 95	18-3204	(D-ECZF)	27. 8.85	M J Butler	Spanhoe	3.12.09P
	(L-18C-PI)		Belg AF OL-L07, L-130, 53-4804				
	(Frame No. reported as 18-3206 [c/n 18-3194 ex OL-L20/L-120/53-4794]: c/n 18-3204 has Frame No.18-3216)						
G-BMEE	Cameron O-105 Balloon (Hot Air)	1189		4. 9.85	A G R Calder	Los Angeles, CA, US	8.10.89A

G-BMEH	Jodel D 150 Special Super Mascaret			15. 8.85	R J and C J Lewis *"Noir Coupar"*		
		PFA 151-11047				Garston Farm, Marshfield	21. 5.08P
	(Built E J Horsfall as rebuild of incomplete SAN Jodel D 150 Mascaret c/n 62) (Lycoming O-235)						
G-BMET	Taylor JT.1 Monoplane	PFA 1465		4. 9.85	M K A Blyth	Little Gransden	14. 7.09P
	(Built M Blythe)						
G-BMEU	Isaacs Fury II	PFA 011-10179		11. 9.85	I G Harrison *(90% complete 6.99)*	Derby	
	(Built G R G Smith) (Salmson 90hp)						
G-BMEX	Cessna A150K Aerobat	A1500169	N8469M	18. 9.85	R Barry	Shoreham	16. 6.09E
G-BMFD	Piper PA-23-250 Aztec F	27-7954080	G-BGYY	6. 9.79	Giles Aviation Ltd		
			N6834A, N9741N			Little Engeham Farm, Woodchurch	14. 4.09E
G-BMFG	Dornier Do.27A-1	27-1003-342	FAP 3460	23. 9.85	R F Warner *(On rebuild 5.08)*		
			AC+955			Grange Farm, Boughton South	
G-BMFI	PZL-Bielsko SZD-45A Ogar	B-657		23. 9.85	S L Morrey	Andreas, Isle of Man	30. 5.08E
G-BMFP	Piper PA-28-161 Warrior II	28-7916243	N3032L	1.11.85	T J Froggatt and C A Lennard tr Bravo Mike Fox Papa Group		
						Blackbushe	8. 8.09E
G-BMFU	Cameron N-90 Balloon (Hot Air)	628		1.10.85	J J Rudoni	Great Haywood, Stafford	19. 5.03T
G-BMFY	Grob G109B	6401		8.10.85	P J Shearer	Kirkwall	23. 9.09E
G-BMFZ	Reims Cessna F152 II	F15201953		3.12.85	Cornwall Flying Club Ltd	Bodmin	13. 4.09E
G-BMGB	Piper PA-28R-200 Cherokee Arrow II		N15864	8.11.85	A L Ings tr Malmesbury Specialist Cars	Kemble	27.10.09E
		28R-7335099					
G-BMGG	Cessna 152 II	15279592	OO-ADB	10.10.85	A S Bamrah t/a Falcon Flying Services	Biggin Hill	22.1.09E
			PH-ADB, D-EHUG, F-GBLM, N757AT				
G-BMGR	Grob G109B	6396		27.11.85	M Clarke tr BMGR Group	Lasham	27. 4.09E
G-BMHA	Rutan LongEz	PFA 074A-10973		18.10.85	S F Elvins	(Staple Hill, Bristol)	
	(Built S F Elvins)						
G-BMHC	Cessna U206F Stationair II	U20603427	N10TB	17.11.76	T J Morley t/a H and R Morley	Leeds-Bradford	19. 2.07T
			G-BMHC, N8571Q				
G-BMHJ	Thunder Ax7-65 Series 1 Balloon (Hot Air) 743			2. 1.86	M G Robinson *"Kittylog"*	Great Milton, Oxford	19. 5.92A
G-BMHL	Wittman W.8 Tailwind	PFA 031-10503		28.11.85	O M Nash New Barn Farm, Barton Ashes, Crawley		28. 5.09P
	(Built T G Hoult)						
G-BMHS	Reims Cessna F172M	F17200964	PH-WAB	7. 4.86	R A Hall tr Tango Xray Flying Group		
						Rayne Hall Farm, Braintree	21. 7.08E
G-BMHT	Piper PA-28RT-201T Turbo Arrow IV		ZS-LCJ	18.11.85	G Lungley and P A Lamming tr G-BMHT Flying Group		
		28R-8231010	N8462Y			Sherburn-in-Elmet	17. 7.09E
G-BMID	Wassmer Jodel D 120 Paris-Nice	259	F-BMID	18. 8.81	T W Nichols tr G-BMID Flying Group		
						RAF Shawbury	13. 4.09P
G-BMIG	Cessna 172N Skyhawk II	17272376	ZS-KGI	13. 5.86	R B Singleton-McGuire tr BMIG Group	Elstree	16. 1.09E
			(N48630)				
G-BMIM	Rutan LongEz	8102/160	OY-CMT	12.12.85	R M Smith	Biggin Hill	13. 2.08P
	(Built K A I Christensen) (Lycoming O-235)		OY-8102				
G-BMIO	Stoddard-Hamilton Glasair RG PFA 149-11016			25.11.85	P Bint and L McMahon	Kemble	8. 7.08P
	(Buillt A H Carrington) (Lycoming O-360)						
G-BMIP	Wassmer Jodel D 112	1264	F-BMIP	7.12.78	F J E Brownsill	(Fairford)	24. 3.09P
G-BMIS	Monnett Sonerai II	755	VR-HIS	26. 2.87	S R Edwards	Kemble	24. 9.08P
	(Built B A Bower - pr.no.PFA 015A-10813) (Revmaster R2100DQ)						
G-BMIV	Piper PA-28R-201T Turbo Arrow III		ZS-JZW	7. 1.86	Firmbeam Ltd	Wycombe Air Park	12. 7.09E
		28R-7703154	N5816V				
G-BMIW	Piper PA-28-181 Archer II	28-8190093	ZS-KTJ	6.12.85	Oldbus Ltd	Shoreham	30. 4.09E
			N8301J				
G-BMIX	SOCATA TB-20 Trinidad	579	EI-BSV	5.12.85	Air Touring Ltd *(Noted stored 12.08)*	Biggin Hill	
			G-BMIX				
G-BMIY	Oldfield Baby Lakes	PFA 010-10194	G-NOME	3.12.85	J B Scott	(Thornton-Cleveleys)	27. 8.87P
	(Built J B Scott, Parkinson and Brown) (Continental O-200-A)						
G-BMIZ	Robinson R22 Beta	0505	OO-VCE	11.11.85	Castlehill Aviation Ltd	Glenrothes	21. 5.09E
			OO-XCE, G-BMIZ, N2270B				
G-BMJA	Piper PA-32R-301 Saratoga II SP		ZS-KTH	23.12.85	H Merkado	Panshanger	6.11.08E
		32R-8113019	N8309E				
G-BMJB	Cessna 152	15280030	N757VD		A J Gomes	(Croydon)	
G-BMJC	Cessna 152 II	15284989	N623AP	3. 2.86	Cleveland Flying School Ltd Durham Tees Valley		22. 8.09E
G-BMJD	Cessna 152 II	15279755	N757HP	21.11.85	Donair Flying Club Ltd Nottingham-East Midlands		19. 8.09E
G-BMJL	Rockwell Commander 114	14006	A2-JRI	8. 1.86	D J and S M Hawkins	(Woking)	20. 8.09E
			ZS-JRI, N1906J				
G-BMJM	Evans VP-1	PFA 062-10763		21.11.85	S E Clarke *(Fuselage noted stored 5.08)*		
	(Built J A Mawby) (Volkswagen 1834)					Shenington	1. 9.05P
G-BMJN	Cameron O-65 Balloon (Hot Air)	1212		6.12.85	P M Traviss *"F'red"*	Yarm	11. 5.08A
G-BMJO	Piper PA-34-220T Seneca III	34-8533036	N6919K	5.12.85	Deep Cleavage Ltd	Exeter	27. 3.09E
			N9565N				
G-BMJR	Cessna T337H Super Skymaster	33701895	G-NOVA	10. 7.84	Eastcote Services Ltd	Sturgate	22.11.08E
			N1259S				
G-BMJX	Wallis WA-116/X Series 1	K/219/X		31.12.85	K H Wallis	Reymerston Hall, Norfolk	1. 4.89P
	(Limbach L-2000)				*(Stored 8.01)*		
G-BMJY	SPP Yakovlev Yak C-18A	?	(France)	21. 1.86	R J Lamplough *(As "07" (yellow) in Russian AF c/s)*		
			Egypt AF 627			Manor Farm, East Garston	27.11.01P
G-BMJZ	Cameron N-90 Balloon (Hot Air)	1219		16.12.85	P Spellward tr Bristol University Hot Air Ballooning Society		
					"Uvistat" (Inflated 7.06)	Bristol	31. 3.94A
G-BMKB	Piper PA-18-135 Super Cub	18-3817	OO-DKB	11.12.85	Cubair Flight Training Ltd	Redhill	3. 7.06T
	(L-21B-PI) (Frame No.18-3818)		PH-DKB, (PH-GRP), R Neth AF R-127, 54-2417				
G-BMKC	Piper J-3C-65 Cub *(L-4H-PI)*	11145	F-BFBA	2. 1.86	E P Parkin *"Little Rockette Jnr"*	Derby	6.11.09P
	(Continental C90) (Frame No.10970)		43-29854		*(As "329854:R-44" in USAAC 533rd BS/381st Bomb Group c/s)*		
G-BMKD	Beech C90A King Air	LJ-1069	N223CG	30.12.85	A E Bristow	Fairoaks	13. 4.09E
			N67516				
G-BMKF	CEA Jodel DR.221 Dauphin	96	F-BPCS	3. 2.86	S T and L J Gilbert	Enstone	22. 3.09E
G-BMKG	Piper PA-38-112 Tomahawk II	38-82A0050	ZS-LGC	3. 2.86	Glasgow Aviation Ltd	Glasgow	15. 1.10E
			N91544				

Reg	Type	C/n	Prev id	Date	Owner/Operator	Location	Expiry
G-BMKI	Colt 21A Cloudhopper Balloon (Hot Air)	753		30.12.85	A C Booth	Bristol	31.12.04A
G-BMKJ	Cameron V-77 Balloon (Hot Air)	1235		2. 1.86	R C Thursby	Barry	10. 5.09E
G-BMKK	Piper PA-28R-200 Cherokee Arrow II	28R-7535265	ZS-JNY N9537N	16. 1.86	P M Murray	Bagby	9.11.09E
G-BMKP	Cameron V-77 Balloon (Hot Air)	724	(G-BMFX)	10. 1.86	R Bayly *"And Baby Makes 10" (Noted 8.02)*	Clutton, Bristol	7. 8.93A
G-BMKR	Piper PA-28-161 Warrior II	28-7916220	G-BGKR N9561N	14. 6.84	D R Shrosbee tr Field Flying Group	Goodwood	5. 6.09E
G-BMKW	Cameron V-77 Balloon (Hot-Air)	608			S A Townley	Ellesmore Port	27. 9.09E
G-BMKY	Cameron O-65 Balloon (Hot Air)	1246		4. 3.86	A R Rich *"Orion"*	Hyde	2. 5.09E
G-BMLB	Wassmer Jodel D 120A Paris-Nice	295	F-BNCI	20. 1.86	C A Croucher	Fowle Hall Farm, Laddingford	20.10.09P
G-BMLJ	Cameron N-77 Balloon (Hot Air)	1263		7. 3.86	C J Dunkley tr Wendover Trailers *"Mr Funshine"*	Aylesbury	28. 3.08A
G-BMLK	Grob G109B	6424		24. 2.86	J J Mawson tr Brams Syndicate	Rufforth	11. 6.09E
G-BMLL	Grob G109B	6420		13. 3.86	J M Dougans tr G-BMLL Flying Group	Dunstable	1. 9.09E
G-BMLM	Beech 95-58 Baron	TH-405	N111LM G-BMLM, F-GEPV, 3D-ADF, ZS-LOZ, G-BMLM, G-BBJF	20. 1.86	Atlantic Bridge Aviation Ltd	Lydd	22. 5.08E
G-BMLS	Piper PA-28R-201 Cherokee Arrow III	28R-7737167	N47496	11. 2.86	R M Shorter	Wycombe Air Park	24. 4.09E
G-BMLT	Pietenpol AirCamper (Built R A and F Hawke) (Continental C90)	PFA 047-10949		28. 1.86	W E R Jenkins	Waits Farm, Belchamp Walter	18. 9.09P
G-BMLW	Cameron O-77 Balloon (Hot Air)	813		6. 2.86	M L and L P Willoughby *"Stelrad"*	Woodcote, Reading	7. 8.95A
G-BMLX	Reims Cessna F150L	F15000700	PH-VOV	21. 3.86	J P A Freeman	Headcorn	26. 2.09E
G-BMMF	Clutton FRED Series II (Built J M Jones) (Volkswagen 1834)	PFA 029-10296		20. 2.86	R C Thomas	(Llantwit Major)	18. 7.03P
G-BMMI	Pazmany PL-4A (Built M L Martin) (Continental PC 60)	PFA 017-10149		6. 2.86	P I Morgans *(Noted 11.05)*	Haverfordwest	18. 7.03P
G-BMMK	Cessna 182P Skylane II (Reims-assembled c/n F18200038)	18264117	OO-AVU N6129F	24. 3.86	G G Weston	Denham	17.10.09E
G-BMMM	Cessna 152 II	15284793	N4652P	10. 9.86	Falcon Flying Services Ltd	Fairoaks	12.12.08E
G-BMMP	Grob G109B	6432		27. 6.86	E W Reynolds tr G-BMMP Syndicate	Tatenhill	9. 6.09E
G-BMMV	ICA IS-28M2A	57		10. 3.86	C D King	Shobdon	15. 7.09E
G-BMMW	Thunder Ax7-77 Balloon (Hot Air)	782		10. 3.86	P A George *"Ethos"*	Princes Risborough	3. 6.96A
G-BMNL	Piper PA-28R-200 Cherokee Arrow II	28R-7535040	N32280 (N18MW), N32280	17. 9.86	Elston Ltd t/a Arrow Flying Group	Elstree	30. 5.09E
G-BMNV	SNCAN Stampe SV-4C	108	F-BBNI	14. 3.86	Wessex Aviation and Transport Ltd *(Noted 5.05)*	Haverfordwest	29. 8.03P
G-BMOE	Piper PA-28R-200 Cherokee Arrow II	28R-7635226	PH-PCB OO-HAS, N9221K	20. 5.86	Piper Leasing Ltd	Exeter	1.12.09E
G-BMOF	Cessna U206G Stationair 6	U20603658	N7427N	17. 4.86	D M Penny t/a Wild Geese Skydiving Centre	Coleraine, Co Londonderry	26. 3.09E
G-BMOG	Thunder Ax7-77 Balloon (Hot Air)	793		2. 4.86	R M Boswell	Bawburgh, Norwich	28. 8.95A
G-BMOH	Cameron N-77 Balloon (Hot Air)	1270		2. 4.86	P J Marshall and M A Clarke *"Ellen Gee"*	Rye and Wokingham	9.7.09E
G-BMOI	Partenavia P68B	103	I-EEVA	4. 4.86	Simmette Ltd	Exeter	4. 7.09E
G-BMOK	ARV Aviation ARV-1 Super 2	011		14. 4.86	R E Griffiths	Stoke, Isle of Grain	9. 9.10P
G-BMOM	ICA IS-28M2A (Rebuilt 2001 with forward fuselage of G-BKAB)	50		30. 6.86	J Pool	Sandtoft	2. 4.09E
G-BMOT	Bensen B 8M (Built R S W Jones) (Volkswagen 1834)	PFA G/01-1066		17. 4.86	A J Thomas	(Sutton Coldfield)	13. 8.01P
G-BMOV	Cameron O-105 Balloon (Hot Air)	1307		11. 4.86	C Gillott *"Up and Down"*	Stroud	1. 7.99A
G-BMPC	Piper PA-28-181 Cherokee Archer II	28-7790436	LN-NAT	23. 4.86	C J and R J Barnes	Nottingham-East Midlands	16. 3.09E
G-BMPD	Cameron V-65 Balloon (Hot Air)	1200		4. 6.86	D Triggs	Alresford	30. 7.09E
G-BMPL	Optica OA.7 Optica	016		14. 4.86	J K Edgley	Thruxton	2. 8.97T
G-BMPP	Cameron N-77 Balloon (Hot Air)	1303		15. 4.86	P F Smart tr The Sarnia Balloon Group *"Tuppence"* (Inflated 4.06)	Oakley, Basingstoke	14. 5.93A
G-BMPR	Piper PA-28R-201 Arrow III	28R-7837175	ZS-LMF N417GH	22. 4.86	T J Brammer and D T Colley	Biggin Hill	30. 7.09E
G-BMPS	Strojnik S-2A (Built T J Gardiner)	045		18. 4.86	G J Green	(Darley Bridge, Matlock)	
G-BMPY	de Havilland DH.82A Tiger Moth	"82619"	ZS-CNR SAAF??	25. 4.86	N M Eisenstein	Sandford Hall, Knockin	15. 6.11S
G-BMRA	Boeing 757-236	23710		2. 3.87	DHL Air Ltd	Brussels, Belgium	2. 8.09E
G-BMRB	Boeing 757-236	23975		25. 9.87	DHL Air Ltd	Brussels, Belgium	29. 9.09E
G-BMRC	Boeing 757-236	24072	(N....)	2.12.87	DHL Air Ltd	Brussels, Belgium	26. 1.10E
G-BMRD	Boeing 757-236	24073	(N....) G-BMRD	2.12.87	DHL Air Ltd	Brussels, Belgium	3. 3.09E
G-BMRE	Boeing 757-236	24074	(N)	2.12.87	DHL Air Ltd	Brussels, Belgium	28. 4.09E
G-BMRF	Boeing 757-236	24101		13. 5.88	DHLAir Ltd	Brussels, Belgium	17. 5.09E
G-BMRH	Boeing 757-236	24266		21. 2.89	DHL Air Ltd	Brussels, Belgium	28. 2.09E
G-BMRJ	Boeing 757-236	24268		6. 3.89	DHL Air Ltd	Brussels, Belgium	13. 3.09E
G-BMSA	Stinson HW-75 Voyager	7040	G-BCUM F-BGQO, NC21189	26. 3.86	M A Thomas tr The Stinson Group *"Iron Eagle"* (On major overhaul 1.07)	Barton	9. 9.05P
G-BMSB	Vickers Supermarine 509 Spitfire Tr.9	CBAF.7722	G-ASOZ IAC158, G-15-171, MJ627	3. 5.78	M S Bayliss (As *"MJ627:9G-P"* in RAF 441 Sqdn c/s)	RAF Coningsby	21. 4.09P
G-BMSC	Evans VP-2 (Built Youth Opportunity Project -pr.no.PFA 063-10785) (Volkswagen 1834)	V2-482MSC		25. 8.82	L G Hunt *(Noted 4.06)*	Sittles Farm, Alrewas	29. 4.05P
G-BMSD	Piper PA-28-181 Cherokee Archer II	28-7690070	EC-CVH N9646N	2. 7.86	H Merkado	Panshanger	21. 9.09E
G-BMSE	Valentin Taifun 17E	1082	D-KHVA(17)	20. 5.86	A Wiseman	Gers, France	4. 6.09E
G-BMSF	Piper PA-38-112 Tomahawk	38-78A0524	N4277E	9. 2.79	B Catlow	Haverfordwest	13. 6.09E

Reg	Type	C/n	Prev id	Date	Owner/Operator	Location	
G-BMSG	SAAB 32A Lansen	32028	Swedish AF Fv32028	22. 7.86	J E Wilkie *(Open store in bare-metal finish.1.06)* Cranfield		
G-BMSL	Clutton FRED Series III *(Built A C Coombe)*	PFA 029-11142		19. 5.86	S Slater	Bicester	9. 6.09P
G-BMSU	Cessna 152 II	15279421	N714TN	29. 8.86	S Waite tr LBA Flying Group *(Operated Sheffield City Flying School)*	Sandtoft	17. 8.09E
G-BMTA	Cessna 152 II	15282864	N89776	27. 8.86	ACS Aviation Ltd	Perth	2. 8.09E
G-BMTB	Cessna 152 II	15280672	N25457	19. 8.86	Sky Leisure Aviation (Charters) Ltd	Blackbushe	18. 9.09E
G-BMTC	Aérospatiale AS.355F1 Ecureuil 2	5302	G-EPOL G-SASU, G-BSSM, G-BMTC, G-BKUK	9.12.83	Sterling Helicopters Ltd	Norwich	12.11.10E
G-BMTJ	Cessna 152 II	15285010	N6389P	19. 6.86	The Pilot Centre Ltd	Denham	17. 6.09E
G-BMTN	Cameron O-77 Balloon (Hot Air)	1305		4. 6.86	Industrial Services (Material Handling) Ltd t/a Flete Rental *"Fletie"* Westbury-on-Trym, Bristol		1. 6.97A
G-BMTO	Piper PA-38-112 Tomahawk II	38-81A0051	N25679	28.11.86	A S Bamrah t/a Falcon Flying Services	Biggin Hill	13. 8.09E
G-BMTR	Piper PA-28-161 Warrior II	28-8116119	N83179	19. 6.86	Aeros Leasing Ltd	Gloucestershire	14. 5.09E
G-BMTU	Pitts S-1E *(Built O R Howe)*	PFA 009-10801		4. 6.86	C Lambropoulos	Sherburn-in-Elmet	25.11.08P
G-BMTX	Cameron V-77 Balloon (Hot Air)	733		19. 6.86	J A Langley *"Boondoggle" (Buses for Bristol titles)* Stroud		7. 9.09E
G-BMUD	Cessna 182P Skylane	18261786	OY-DVS N78847	6.11.81	Mescal E Taylor	RAF Waddington	14. 5.09E
G-BMUG	Rutan LongEz *(Built P Richardson) (Lycoming O-235)*	PFA 074A-10987		17. 6.86	A G Sayers *(Noted 3.06)*	RAF Kinloss	12. 1.06P
G-BMUO	Cessna A152 Aerobat	A1520788	4X-ALJ N7328L	4. 6.86	Sky Leisure Aviation (Charters) Ltd	Shoreham	14. 9.07T
G-BMUT	Piper PA-34-200T Seneca II	34-7570320	EC-CUH N3935X	23. 1.87	G-DAD Air Ltd	Cranfield	22.12.09E
G-BMUU	Thunder Ax7-77 Balloon (Hot Air)	827		1. 8.86	A R Hill *"Fiesta" (Noted 05)* Rolvenden, Cranbrook		29.10.98A
G-BMUZ	Piper PA-28-161 Warrior II	28-8016329	EC-DMA N9559N	24. 7.86	Northumbria Flying School Ltd	Newcastle	5. 4.08E
G-BMVA	Scheibe SF25B Falke *(Limbach SL1700)*	46223	RAFGGA.512 D-KAEN	28. 7.86	M L Jackson	Challock	5. 6.08
G-BMVB	Reims Cessna F152 II	F15201974		10. 9.86	M P Barnard	Enstone	27. 3.10E
G-BMVG	QAC Quickie Q.1 *(Built P M Wright) (Rotax 503)*	PFA 094-10749		11. 6.86	P M Wright	Cambridge	1. 1.02P
G-BMVL	Piper PA-38-112 Tomahawk	38-79A0033	N2391B	5. 9.86	T Akeroyd	Cranfield	20.12.09E
G-BMVM	Piper PA-38-112 Tomahawk	38-79A0025	N2359B	5. 9.86	R Davitt and C J Wheeler tr Brimpton Flying Group Lower Wasing Farm, Brimpton		13. 8.09E
G-BMVS	Cameron Benihana 70 SS Balloon (Hot Air) *(Aka Chef's Hat)*	1252		27.10.86	Benihana (UK) Ltd	London W1	9. 2.07A
G-BMVT	Thunder Ax7-77A Balloon (Hot Air)	102	SE-ZYY	15. 7.86	M L and L P Willoughby *"Trygg Hansa"* Woolcote, Reading		
G-BMVU	Monnett Moni *(Built S R Lee) (KEF-107)*	PFA 142-10948		14. 8.86	D Prentice	(Sheffield)	20. 9.99P
G-BMVW	Cameron O-65 Balloon (Hot Air)	1331		27. 6.86	S P Richards *"Olau Ferries"*	Cranbrook	15. 8.91A
G-BMWA	Hughes 269C *(Hughes 300)*	14-0271	N8998F	1. 7.86	D G Lewendon (Chantrigne, Mayenne, France)		10. 1.09E
G-BMWF	ARV Aviation ARV-1 Super 2	013		1. 7.86	G E Collard	(Frensham)	2. 4.90T
G-BMWR	Rockwell Commander 112A	365	N1365J	23. 9.86	M and J Edwards	Blackbushe	30. 1.09E
G-BMWU	Cameron N-42 Balloon (Hot Air)	1346		22.12.88	I Chadwick tr Balloon Preservation Group *(Helix Motor Oil titles)* Partridge Green, Horsham		27. 4.09E
G-BMWV	Putzer Elster B	024	D-EEKB 97+14, D-EBGI	5. 8.86	E A J Hibbard tr Magpie Group Hill Farm, Nayland		27.10,06P
G-BMXA	Cessna 152 II	15280125	N757ZC	14. 7.86	ACS Aviation Ltd *(Operated Leading Edge)*	Perth	13.11.09E
G-BMXB	Cessna 152 II	15280996	N48840	14. 7.86	C I J Young	Leicester	20. 1.09E
G-BMXC	Cessna 152 II	15280416	N24858	14. 7.86	MK Aero Support Ltd	Andrewsfield	2. 6.09E
G-BMXJ	Reims Cessna F150L	F15000853	F-BUBA	18. 7.86	R Harman tr Arrow Aircraft Group	Tatenhill	20. 6.03
G-BMXM	Colt 180A Balloon (Hot Air)	838	(C-) G-BMXM	28. 7.86	D A Michaud *(Noted 05)* Edmonton, Alberta, Canada		20.12.04A
G-BMXX	Cessna 152 II	15284953	N5469P	10. 9.86	Evensport Ltd *(Noted 10.07)*	Wolverhampton	1. 9.02T
G-BMYC	SOCATA TB-10 Tobago	696		1. 9.86	E A Grady	Old Buckenham	9. 5.09E
G-BMYD	Beech A36 Bonanza	E-2350		28.11.86	Seabeam Partners Ltd	Wellesbourne Mountford	21. 3.09E
G-BMYF	Bensen B 8M *(Built P Entwistle)*	PE-01		18. 8.86	G Callaghan	Rich Hill, County Armagh	
G-BMYG	Cessna FA152 Aerobat *(Built Reims Aviation SA)*	FA1520365	OO-JCA (OO-JCC), PH-AXG	23.10.86	Greer Aviation Ltd	Prestwick	14. 6.09E
G-BMYI	Grumman AA-5 Traveler	AA5-0568	EI-BJF F-BVRM, N9568L	1. 9.86	W C and S C Westran	Shoreham	16.10.08E
G-BMYJ	Cameron V-65 Balloon (Hot Air)	726		8. 9.86	S P Harrowing *"Skylark II"*	Port Talbot	23. 3.08A
G-BMYN	Colt 77A Balloon (Hot Air)	873		2. 9.86	J E Wetters and M H Read Timperley, Altrincham		24. 3.07A
G-BMYS	Thunder Ax7-77Z Balloon (Hot Air)	887		3.11.86	J E Weidema *(Operated Pinkel Balloons)* Baambrugge, Netherlands		1. 6.01A
G-BMYU	Wassmer Jodel D 120 Paris-Nice	289	F-BMYU	23. 6.78	A J L Gordon	Bicester	18. 6.09P
G-BMZB	Cameron N-77 Balloon (Hot Air)	1370		30.10.86	D C Eager *"Dreamland"*	Bracknell	30. 4.95A
G-BMZN	Everett Gyroplane Series 1 *(Volkswagen 1835)*	008		13.11.86	K Ashford	(Walsall)	2.12.02P
G-BMZS	Everett Gyroplane Series 1 *(Volkswagen 1835)*	012		13.11.86	L W Cload	St Merryn	6.11.06P
G-BMZW	Bensen B 8MR *(Built P D Widdicombe) (Rotax 532)*	PFA G/01-1021		16.10.86	P D Widdicombe	Huntington, York	25. 8.99P
G-BMZX	Wolf W-11 Boredom Fighter *(Built J J Penney)*	PFA 146-11042		31.10.86	A D Bales	Stoke Holy Cross	

G-BNAA - G-BNZZ

G-BNAG	Colt 105A Balloon (Hot Air)	906		31.10.86	R W Batchelor	Thame	19.12.89A
G-BNAI	Wolf W-11 Boredom Fighter PFA 146-11083			31.10.86	C M Bunn (As "5:146-11083" in USAAC c/s)		
	(Built PJ Gronow to represent Spad replica) (Continental A65)					Haverfordwest	12. 4.09P
	(Left landing gear collapsed on landing at RNAS Yeovilton 9. 6.08 and ground loop; damage to left main undercarriage leg and wing)						
G-BNAJ	Cessna 152 II	15282527	C-GZWF	3.11.86	Galair Ltd (Operated Surrey and Kent Flying Club)		
			(N69173)			Biggin Hill	11. 3.10E
G-BNAN	Cameron V-65 Balloon (Hot Air)	1333		28.10.86	A M and N H Ponsford t/a Rango Balloon and Kite Company		
					"Actually"	Leeds	7. 7.01A
G-BNAU	Cameron V-65 Balloon (Hot Air)	1395		13.11.86	T J Ellenrieder tr 4-Flight Group	Bristol	4.11.05E
G-BNAW	Cameron V-65 Balloon (Hot Air)	1366		24.10.86	A and P A Walker (HMS Recruitment titles) "Hippo-Thermia"		
						Richmond, Surrey	24. 8.08A
G-BNBL	Thunder Ax7-77 Balloon (Hot Air)	910		7. 1.87	F W Ewer "K2" (inflated 10.08)		
						Lighthorne Heath, Leamington Spa	4.10.06A
G-BNBW	Thunder Ax7-77 Balloon (Hot Air)	914		11.12.86	IS and S W Watthews "Mutley"		
						Grange-over-Sands	9. 9.99A
G-BNBY	Beech 95-B55A Baron	TC-1347	G-AXXR	14. 2.83	J Butler	(Lisle Sur Tarn, France)	19. 7.09E
G-BNCB	Cameron V-77 Balloon (Hot Air)	1401		2.12.86	C W Brown "Phoenix Tyres"	Melton Mowbray	9. 7.09E
G-BNCC	Thunder Ax7-77 Balloon (Hot Air)	924		11.12.86	C J Burnhope "Charlie"	(US)	9.10.99A
G-BNCJ	Cameron V-77 Balloon (Hot Air)	815		16.12.86	D Johnson	Bromley	17.10.05A
G-BNCO	Piper PA-38-112 Tomahawk	38-79A0472	N2482F	8. 1.87	D K Walker	Gamston	3. 6.09E
G-BNCR	Piper PA-28-161 Warrior II	28-8016111	G-PDMT	10.12.86	Airways Aero Associations Ltd Wycombe Air Park		19. 5.09E
			ZS-LGW, N8103D		(Operated British Airways Flying Club)		
G-BNCS	Cessna 180	30022	OO-SPA	7. 1.87	C Elwell Transport (Repairs) Ltd	Tatenhill	17. 2.95
			D-ENUX, N2822A				
G-BNCU	Thunder Ax7-77 Balloon (Hot Air)	928		7. 1.87	W De Bock	Peterborough	14. 7.00A
G-BNDE	Piper PA-38-112 Tomahawk	38-79A0363	EI-BUR	13. 1.87	M Magrabi	Bournemouth	24. 4.09E
			G-BNDE, N2541D				
G-BNDG	Wallis WA-201/R Series 1	K/220/X		22. 1.87	K H Wallis (Stored 8.01) Reymerston Hall, Norfolk		3. 3.88P
	(Rotax 64hp x 2)						
G-BNDN	Cameron V-77 Balloon (Hot Air)	1443		8. 1.87	A Hornshaw	Ugborough, Ivybridge	30. 8.09E
G-BNDO	Cessna 152 II	15284574	N5387M	11. 2.87	Simair Ltd	Andrewsfield	6.10.07E
			(Crashed Wick Farm, Layer Marney, Colchester 11. 7.06 and badly damaged: wreck noted 9.07)				
G-BNDP	Brügger MB.2 Colibri PFA 043-10956			8. 1.87	A C Barber	(Newmarket)	15. 9.09P
	(Built M Black) (Volkswagen 1834)						
G-BNDR	SOCATA TB-10 Tobago	740		12. 2.87	Delta Fire Ltd	Norwich	25. 3.09E
G-BNDT	Brügger MB.2 Colibri PFA 043-10981			8. 1.87	H Haigh tr Colibri Flying Group	Bagby	14. 7.09P
	(Built A Szep) (Volkswagen 1834)						
G-BNDV	Cameron N-77 Balloon (Hot Air)	1427		25. 2.87	R E Jones (English Lake Hotels titles)		
						Lytham St Annes	9. 5.93A
G-BNDW	de Havilland DH.82A Tiger Moth	3942	N6638	10.12.86	C R Hardiman (Noted 5.03)	Caernarfon	29.10.08P
G-BNEE	Piper PA-28R-201 Arrow III	28R-7837084	N630DJ	28. 1.87	J W Reid tr Britannic Management Aviation		
			N9518N			Turweston	22.12.09E
G-BNEK	Piper PA-38-112 Tomahawk II	38-82A0081	N9096A	28. 1.87	APB Leasing Ltd	Trehelig, Welshpool	17. 5.00T
G-BNEL	Piper PA-28-161 Warrior II	28-7916314	N2246U	27. 4.87	S C Westran	Shoreham	23.11.09E
G-BNEN	Piper PA-34-200T Seneca II	34-8070262	N8232V	18. 2.87	CE Ventures Ltd Nottingham-East Midlands		21. 7.09E
G-BNEO	Cameron V-77 Balloon (Hot Air)	1408		9. 2.87	J G O'Connell "Rowtate"	Braintree	2.11.00
G-BNEV	Viking Dragonfly PFA 139-10935			28.11.86	N W Eyre	(Kirkbymoorside, York)	
	(Built N W Eyre) (Volkswagen 1834)						
G-BNFG	Cameron O-77 Balloon (Hot Air)	1416		5. 3.87	Capital Balloon Club Ltd "Dolores"	London NW1	13. 1.94A
G-BNFI	Cessna 150J	15069417	N50588	8. 1.87	A Waters	Enstone	21.11.09E
G-BNFM	Colt 21A Cloudhopper Balloon (Hot Air)	668		5. 3.87	M E Dworski	Vermenton, France	24. 7.01A
G-BNFN	Cameron N-105 Balloon (Hot Air)	1442		13. 3.87	P Glydon	Barnt Green, Birmingham	17. 6.97T
G-BNFO	Cameron V-77 Balloon (Hot Air)	816		5. 3.87	M B Young	Bristol	12. 4.09E
G-BNFP	Cameron O-84 Balloon (Hot Air)	1474		29. 4.87	M Clarke	Egham	1. 7.09E
G-BNFR	Cessna 152 II	15282035	N67817	8. 4.87	A Jahanfar (Operated Seawing Flying Club)		
						Southend	29. 4.09E
G-BNFS	Cessna 152 II	15283899	N5545B	10. 4.87	P J Clarke	Tatenhill	14. 7.08E
G-BNFV	Robin DR.400-120 Dauphin 80	1767		4. 3.87	J P A Freeman	Headcorn	4. 2.09E
G-BNGE	Auster AOP.6	1925	7704M	18. 3.87	M Pocock (As "TW536:T-SV" in RAF 657 Sqdn c/s)		
			TW536		(Operated Military Auster Flight) AAC Netheravon		3. 9.09P
G-BNGJ	Cameron V-77 Balloon (Hot Air)	1487		18. 3.87	P O Atkins "Latham Timber"	High Wycombe	3.12.09E
G-BNGN	Cameron N-77 Balloon (Hot Air)	817		3. 4.87	N Dykes "Falcon"	Tostock, Bury St Edmunds	27. 4.09E
G-BNGO	Thunder Ax7-77 Balloon (Hot Air)	971		26. 3.87	J S Finlan tr The G-BNGO Group "Thunderbird" (Philips titles)		
						Hamilton, New Zealand	16. 4.06A
G-BNGT	Piper PA-28-181 Archer II	28-8590036	N149AV	29. 4.87	Edinburgh Flying Club Ltd	Edinburgh	18. 5.09E
			N9559N				
G-BNGV	ARV Aviation ARV-1 Super 2	021		4. 6.87	N A Onions (Noted 8.07) (North End, Dunmow)		28. 4.06
G-BNGW	ARV Aviation ARV-1 Super 2	022		4. 6.87	Southern Gas Turbines Ltd	Goodwood	8. 7.90T
G-BNGY	ARV Aviation ARV-1 Super 2	019	(G-BMWL)	9. 6.87	S C Smith	Shobdon	25. 3.08P
G-BNHB	ARV Aviation ARV-1 Super 2	026		13. 7.87	C J Challener	Barton	23.11.06E
G-BNHG	Piper PA-38-112 Tomahawk II	38-82A0030	N91435	23. 3.87	Highland Flying School Ltd	Inverness	8. 6.09E
G-BNHJ	Cessna 152 II	15281249	N49418	4. 6.87	The Pilot Centre Ltd	Denham	19.12.08E
G-BNHK	Cessna 152 II	15285355	N80161	30. 3.87	N Houghton tr Wayfarers Flying Group	Derby	1. 8.09E
G-BNHT	Fournier RF3	80	(D-KITX)	13. 4.87	D G Hey tr G-BNHT Group	Little Gransden	27. 2.08P
			G-BNHT, F-BMT				
G-BNID	Cessna 152 II	15284931	N5378P	24. 4.87	MK Aero Support Ltd	Andrewsfield	5. 7.09E
G-BNII	Cameron N-90 Balloon (Hot Air)	1497		15. 4.87	S M Ratcliffe tr Topless Balloon Group		
						Lower Bourne, Farnham	13. 3.05
G-BNIK	Robin HR.200-120 Club	43	LX-AIK	15. 4.87	P A Guest tr G-BNIK Group	Leicester	8. 6.09E
			LX-PAA				
G-BNIM	Piper PA-38-112 Tomahawk	38-78A0148	N9631T	18. 6.87	Air Claire Ltd (Operated Glasgow Flying Club)		
						Glasgow	2. 4.09E

Reg	Type	C/n	Prev id	Date	Owner/Operator	Base	
G-BNIN	Cameron V-77 Balloon (Hot Air)	1079	G-RRSG (1) (G-BLRO)	15. 4.87	MJ.L Hilditch t/a Cloud Nine Balloon Group *"Cloud Nine"* Southwick, Brighton	18. 5.09E	
G-BNIO	Luscombe 8A Silvaire (Continental A75)	2120	N45593 NC45593	15. 4.87	R C Dyer	Landmead Farm, Enstone	17. 9.09P
G-BNIP	Luscombe 8A Silvaire (Continental A65)	3547	N77820 NC77820	15. 4.87	M J Diggins	White Waltham	6. 2.09P
G-BNIU	Cameron O-77 Balloon (Hot Air)	1499		28. 4.87	MC VH SA	Brussels, Belgium	22. 9.08A
G-BNIW	Boeing Stearman A75N1 (PT-17) Kaydet (Pratt and Whitney R985)	75-1526	N49291 41-7967	22. 4.87	R C Goold	East Winch	17. 7.10S
G-BNJB	Cessna 152 II	15284865	N4970P	27. 4.87	Aerolease Ltd	Conington	16.09.09E
G-BNJC	Cessna 152 II	15283588	N4705B	27. 4.87	Stapleford Flying Club Ltd	Stapleford	26. 8.09E
G-BNJD	Cessna 152 II	15282044	N67833	27. 4.87	M Howells	Barton	6. 5.06T
G-BNJG	Cameron O-77 Balloon (Hot Air)	1502		9. 5.89	A M Figiel	High Wycombe	4. 4.97
G-BNJH	Cessna 152 II	15285401	C-GORA (N93101)	21. 7.87	ACS Aviation Ltd *(Operated Leading Edge)*	Perth	24. 9.09E
G-BNJL	Bensen B 8MR *(Built C G Ponsford)* (Rotax 532)	PFA G/01-1020		30. 4.87	S Ram	(Lowestoft)	29. 3.03P
G-BNJO	QAC Quickie Q.2 (Revmaster 2100D)	2217	N17LM	6.10.87	J D McKay	(Exeter Street, North Tawton)	14. 5.93P
G-BNJR	Piper PA-28RT-201T Turbo Arrow IV	28R-8031104	N8212U	8. 5.87	D Crocker	Blackbushe	20.10.09E
G-BNJT	Piper PA-28-161 Warrior II	28-8116184	N8360T	11. 6.87	M Jones tr Hawarden Flying Group	Hawarden	13. 2.10E
G-BNJZ	Cassutt Racer IIIM *(Built Miller Aerial Spraying)*	PFA 034-11228		14. 5.87	J Cull	Popham	17. 5.08P
G-BNKC	Cessna 152 II	15281036	N48894	26. 5.87	Herefordshire Aero Club Ltd	Shobdon	14.12.09E
G-BNKD	Cessna 172N Skyhawk II	17272329	N4681D	19. 5.87	Barnes Olson Aero Leasing Ltd *(Operated Bristol Flying Centre)*	Bristol	22. 4.09E
G-BNKE	Cessna 172N Skyhawk II	17273886	N6534J	20. 5.87	T Jackson tr Kilo Echo Flying Group	Barton	14. 7.09E
G-BNKH	Piper PA-38-112 Tomahawk II	38-81A0078	N25874	14. 5.87	Goodwood Road Racing Company Ltd *(Operated Goodwood Flying Club)*	Goodwood	10. 8.09E
G-BNKI	Cessna 152 II	15281765	N67337	19. 5.87	Royal Air Force Halton Aeroplane Club Ltd	RAF Halton	16. 7.09E
G-BNKP	Cessna 152 II	15281286	N49460	18. 5.87	Spectrum Leisure Ltd	Clacton	6. 4.09E
G-BNKR	Cessna 152 II	15281284	N49458	18. 5.87	Keen Leasing (IoM) Ltd *(Operated Ulster Flying Club)*	Newtownards	20. 2.09E
G-BNKS	Cessna 152 II	15283186	N47202	18. 5.87	Shropshire Aero Club Ltd	Sleap	22. 5.09E
G-BNKT	Cameron O-77 Balloon (Hot Air)	1356		13. 2.87	A A Brown *"Katie II"*	Guildford	5. 9.09E
G-BNKV	Cessna 152 II	15283079	N46604	18. 5.87	S C Westran	Shoreham	6. 1.10E
G-BNLA	Boeing 747-436	23908	N60665	30. 6.89	British Airways PLC	London Heathrow	29. 6.09E
G-BNLB	Boeing 747-436	23909		31. 7.89	British Airways PLC *(stored Cardiff-Wales 3.11.08)*	London Heathrow	13. 3.09E
G-BNLC	Boeing 747-436	23910		21. 7.89	British Airways PLC *(stored Cardiff-Wales 29.10.08)*	London Heathrow	26. 7.09E
G-BNLD	Boeing 747-436	23911	N6018N	5. 9.89	British Airways PLC	London Heathrow	5. 9.09E
G-BNLE	Boeing 747-436	24047		14.11.89	British Airways PLC	London Heathrow	16.11.00E
G-BNLF	Boeing 747-436	24048		23. 2.90	British Airways PLC	London Heathrow	11.10.09E
G-BNLG	Boeing 747-436	24049		23. 2.90	British Airways PLC	London Heathrow	1.10.08E
G-BNLH	Boeing 747-436	24050	VH-NLH G-BNLH	28. 3.90	British Airways PLC	London Heathrow	13. 5.09E
G-BNLI	Boeing 747-436	24051		19. 4.90	British Airways PLC	London Heathrow	20. 4.09E
G-BNLJ	Boeing 747-436	24052	N60668	23. 5.90	British Airways PLC	London Heathrow	24. 5.09E
G-BNLK	Boeing 747-436	24053	N6009F	25. 5.90	British Airways PLC	London Heathrow	28. 5.09E
G-BNLL	Boeing 747-436	24054		13. 6.90	British Airways PLC	London Heathrow	13. 6.09E
G-BNLM	Boeing 747-436	24055	N6009F	28. 6.90	British Airways PLC	London Heathrow	27. 6.09E
G-BNLN	Boeing 747-436	24056		26. 7.90	British Airways PLC	London Heathrow	26. 7.09E
G-BNLO	Boeing 747-436	24057		25.10.90	British Airways PLC	London Heathrow	24.10.09E
G-BNLP	Boeing 747-436	24058		17.12.90	British Airways PLC	London Heathrow	10. 9.09E
G-BNLR	Boeing 747-436	24447	N6005C	15. 1.91	British Airways PLC	London Heathrow	16. 1.10E
G-BNLS	Boeing 747-436	24629		13. 3.91	British Airways PLC	London Heathrow	12. 3.09E
G-BNLT	Boeing 747-436	24630		19. 3.91	British Airways PLC	London Heathrow	14.11.09E
G-BNLU	Boeing 747-436	25406		28. 1.92	British Airways PLC	London Heathrow	27. 1.10E
G-BNLV	Boeing 747-436	25427		20. 2.92	British Airways PLC	London Heathrow	19. 2.10E
G-BNLW	Boeing 747-436	25432		4. 3.92	British Airways PLC	London Heathrow	4. 3.09E
G-BNLX (2)	Boeing 747-436	25435		1. 4.92	British Airways PLC	London Heathrow	2. 4.09E
G-BNLY (2)	Boeing 747-436	27090	N60659	10. 2.93	British Airways PLC	London Heathrow	9. 1.10E
G-BNLZ (3)	Boeing 747-436	27091		4. 3.93	British Airways PLC	London Heathrow	3. 3.09E
G-BNMA	Cameron O-77 Balloon (Hot Air)	830		15.12.87	A Wilkes and N Woodham *"Finian"* Temple Cloud, Bristol and Fawley, Southampton		7.12.09E
G-BNMB	Piper PA-28-151 Cherokee Warrior	28-7615369	N6826J	6.10.87	Thomson Airways Ltd *(Operated Thomson Airways Flying Club)*	Liverpool	11.12.09E
G-BNMD	Cessna 152 II	15283786	N5170B	28. 5.87	T M Jones *(Stored 9.02)*	Derby	28. 7.01T
G-BNME	Cessna 152 II	15284888	N5159P	25. 9.87	A R Jury	Mnaor Farm, Inglesham	22.12.09E
G-BNMF	Cessna 152T	15285563	N93858	21. 7.87	Central Aircraft Leasing Ltd *(Operated Midland Flight Centre)* Wolverhampton		20. 5.09E
G-BNMG	Cameron O-77 Balloon (Hot Air)	1500		27. 5.87	J H Turner	Bridgnorth	4. 4.03A
G-BNMH	Pietenpol AirCamper *(Built N M Hitchman)*	NH-1-001		2. 6.87	N M Hitchman	Hinton-in-the-Hedges	
G-BNML	Rand Robinson KR-2 *(Built R J Smyth)* (Volkswagen 1834)	PFA 129-11240		23. 6.87	PJ Brookman	(Shepshed, Loughborough)	17. 8.00P
G-BNMO	Cessna R182 Skylane RG II	R18200956	N738RK	3. 7.87	Kenrye Developments Ltd	Movenis, Coleraine	10. 7.06
G-BNMX	Thunder Ax7-77 Balloon (Hot Air)	1003		15. 6.87	S A D Beard	Cheltenham	20. 6.06A
G-BNNA	Stolp SA.300 Starduster Too *(Built T C Maxwell)* (Lycoming O-360)	1462	N8SD	29. 6.87	M A Neeves tr Banana Group	Leicester	5. 6.09P
G-BNNE	Cameron N-77 Balloon (Hot Air)	1413		15. 6.87	J A Hibberd	Rotterdam, Netherlands	12. 8.09E

Reg	Type	c/n	Prev id	Date	Owner/Operator	Base	Date
G-BNNO	Piper PA-28-161 Cherokee Warrior II	28-8116099	N8307X	15. 6.87	I A Anderson	Little Snoring	5. 8.09E
G-BNNR	Cessna 152 II	15285146	N40SX N40SU, N6121Q	15. 6.87	J H Sandham t/a J H Sandham Aviation (Operated Argyll Aero Club)	North Connel, Oban	15.11.08E
G-BNNS	Piper PA-28-161 Warrior II	28-8116061	N8283C	26. 6.87	S J French	Turweston	23. 6.09E
G-BNNT	Piper PA-28-151 Cherokee Warrior	28-7615056	N7624C	12. 6.87	S T Gilbert and D J Kirkwood	Kemble	26. 7.09E
G-BNNU	Piper PA-38-112 Tomahawk II	38-81A0037	N25650	12. 6.87	Edinburgh Flying Club Ltd	Edinburgh	18. 1.10E
G-BNNX	Piper PA-28R-201T Turbo Arrow III	28R-7703009	N9005F	14. 7.87	Bristol Flying Centre Ltd	Bristol	13. 2.09E
G-BNNY	Piper PA-28-161 Warrior II	28-8016084	N8092M	1. 9.87	A S Bamrah t/a Falcon Flying Services	Biggin Hill	14.12.09E
G-BNNZ	Piper PA-28-161 Warrior II	28-8016177	N8135Y	24. 7.87	R West	(Shorne, Gravesend)	19. 2.09E
G-BNOB	Wittman W.8 Tailwind	258/DH1		13. 7.87	M Robson-Robinson "Imogen"	(Abbots Bromley)	14. 5.02P
	(Built D G Hammersley - pr.no.PFA 3502) (Continental.PC60)						
G-BNOE	Piper PA-28-161 Warrior II	2816013	N9121X N9568N	26. 6.87	Sherburn Aero Club Ltd	Sherburn-in-Elmet	6. 3.09E
G-BNOF	Piper PA-28-161 Warrior II	2816014	N9122B	26. 6.87	Tayside Aviation Ltd	Dundee	31. 3.09E
G-BNOH	Piper PA-28-161 Warrior II	2816016	N9122L	26. 6.87	Sherburn Aero Club Ltd	Sherburn-in-Elmet	6. 2.09E
G-BNOJ	Piper PA-28-161 Warrior II	2816018	N9122R	26. 6.87	R D Turner and W M Brown tr BAE (Warton) Flying Club	Blackpool	13. 8.09E
G-BNOM	Piper PA-28-161 Warrior II	2816024		26. 6.87	Air Navigation and Trading Company Ltd	Blackpool	4. 6.09E
G-BNON	Piper PA-28-161 Warrior II	2816025		26. 6.87	Tayside Aviation Ltd	Dundee	13. 3.09E
G-BNOP	Piper PA-28-161 Warrior II	2816027		26. 6.87	R D Turner and F J Smith tr BAE (Warton) Flying Club	Blackpool	16. 9.09E
G-BNOZ	Cessna 152 II	15281625	EI-CCP G-BNOZ, N65570	22. 6.87	R J Whyham	Blackpool	12. 5.09E
G-BNPE	Cameron N-77 Balloon (Hot Air)	1519	(G-BNPX)	25. 8.87	R N Simpkins "Skint Garden Denters"	Barrs Court, Bristol	30. 7.09E
G-BNPF	Slingsby Cadet III Motor Glider (Stark Stamo MS.1400A)	826	XA284	3.11.87	S Luck, P Norman and D R Winder "Noddy"	Audley End	10. 8.00P
	(Re-built S Luck and Partners - pr.no.PFA 042-11122 from Slingsby T 31M: with wings from XE791 which became OO-ZDQ)						
G-BNPH	Percival P 66 Pembroke C 1 (Offiicially regd with c/n "PAC66/027")	P66/41	WV740	30. 6.87	A and G A Gainsford Dixon (As "WV740" in RAF 60 Sqdn c/s)	Bournemouth	19. 5.09P
G-BNPM	Piper PA-38-112 Tomahawk	38-79A0374	N2561D	28. 7.87	D and L K Britten t/a Papa Mike Aviation	Cranfield	19. 5.09E
G-BNPO	Piper PA-28-181 Cherokee Archer II	28-7890123	N47720	28. 7.87	Bonus Aviation Ltd	Cranfield	26. 6.09E
G-BNPV	Bowers Fly Baby 1A (Built J G Day)	PFA 016-11120		2. 7.87	J G Day (As "C L 1.1801/18" in German Army Air Service c/s to represent Junkers CL1)	Rushett Farm, Chessington	3. 3.09P
G-BNPY	Cessna 152 II	15280249	N24388	30. 6.87	Traffic Management Services Ltd	Gamston	1. 5.09E
G-BNRA	SOCATA TB-10 Tobago	772		15. 7.87	S N Kingan tr Double D Airgroup "Triple One"	Nottingham City-Tollerton	27. 2.09E
G-BNRG	Piper PA-28-161 Warrior II	28-8116217	N83810	7. 7.87	RAF Brize Norton Flying Club Ltd	RAF Brize Norton	14. 9.09E
G-BNRL	Cessna 152 II	15284250	N5084L	13. 7.87	Bulldog Aviation Ltd	Earls Colne	19. 6.09E
G-BNRP	Piper PA-28-181 Cherokee Archer II	28-7790528	N984BT	25.11.87	Bonus Aviation Ltd	Cranfield	19. 6.09E
G-BNRR	Cessna 172P Skyhawk II	17274013	N5213K	13. 7.87	P H Archard t/a PHA Aviation	Elstree	22. 5.09E
G-BNRX	Piper PA-34-200T Seneca II	34-7970336	N2898A	25.11.87	Truman Aviation Ltd	Nottingham City-Tollerton	3. 5.09E
G-BNRY	Cessna 182Q Skylane II	18265629	N735RR	20. 7.87	K F and S J Farey	Wycombe Air Park	6. 6.09E
G-BNSG	Piper PA-28R-201 Arrow III	28R-7837205	N9516C	30. 7.87	W R Ronnie	Birmingham	7. 1.10E
G-BNSI	Cessna 152 II	15284853	N4945P	6. 8.87	Sky Leisure Aviation (Charters) Ltd	Shoreham	20. 4.09E
G-BNSL	Piper PA-38-112 Tomahawk II	38-81A0086	N25956	21. 7.87	Lomac Aviators Ltd	Liverpool	9. 7.09E
G-BNSM	Cessna 152 II	15285342	N68948	23. 7.87	Cornwall Flying Club Ltd	Bodmin	26. 7.09E
G-BNSN	Cessna 152 II	15285776	N94738	21. 7.87	The Pilot Centre Ltd	Denham	19. 3.09E
G-BNSO	Slingsby T 67M Firefly II	2021		20. 8.87	R M Rennoldson	Full Sutton	19. 5.09E
G-BNSP	Slingsby T 67M Firefly II	2044		20. 8.87	M S Roadhouse tr Slingsby Group	Netherthorpe	9. 1.09E
G-BNSR	Slingsby T 67M Firefly II	2047		20. 8.87	E Whitehead tr Slingsby SR Group	Redhill	26. 6.09E
G-BNST	Cessna 172N Skyhawk II	17273661	N4670J	21. 9.87	J Revill tr CSG Bodyshop	Netherthorpe	1. 5.09E
G-BNSU	Cessna 152 II	15281245	N49410	2.12.87	A L Brown t/a Channel Aviation (Operated Rural Flying Corps)	Bourn	13.10.07E
G-BNSV	Cessna 152 II	15284531	N5322M	4.12.87	A L Brown t/a Channel Aviation (Fuselage noted 10.05)	Bourn	12. 7.97T
G-BNSY	Piper PA-28-161 Warrior II	28-8016017	N4512M	18. 8.87	Light Aircraft Leasing Ltd	Cardiff	6.11.09E
G-BNSZ	Piper PA-28-161 Warrior II	28-8116315	N8433B	20. 8.87	Haimoss Ltd	Old Sarum	7. 1.09E
G-BNTC	Piper PA-28RT-201T Turbo Arrow IV	28R-8131081	N83428	4.11.87	Central Aircraft Leasing Ltd (Operated Halfpenny Green Flight Centre)	Wolverhampton	7. 7.08E
G-BNTD	Piper PA-28-161 Cherokee Warrior II	28-7716235	N38490 N9539N	5. 8.87	A M and F.Alam	Elstree	29.11.08E
G-BNTP	Cessna 172N Skyhawk II	17272030	N6531E	4. 9.87	Westnet Ltd	Barton	7. 4.09E
G-BNTT	Beech 76 Duchess	ME-228	N54SB	8.10.87	Plane Talking Ltd (Operated Cabair)	Bournemouth	18. 6.09E
G-BNTW	Cameron V-77 Balloon (Hot Air)	1574		13. 8.87	P Goss "Cecilia"	Alton	6.11.99A
G-BNTZ	Cameron N-77 Balloon (Hot Air)	1518		27. 8.87	P M Watkins tr Balloon Team	Chippenham	26. 8.02A
G-BNUC	Cameron O-77 Balloon (Hot Air)	1575		18. 8.87	T J Bucknall "Bridges Van Hire II"	Hawarden	
G-BNUL	Cessna 152 II	15284486	N4852M	2.10.87	Big Red Kite Ltd (RAF Benson Flying Club titles)	RAF Benson	4. 5.09E
G-BNUN	Beech 58PA Baron	TJ-256	N6732Y	19. 8.87	British Midland Airways Ltd	Nottingham-East Midlands	8. 5.09E
G-BNUO	Beech 76 Duchess	ME-250	N6635Y	29. 9.87	Pace Projects Ltd and Professional Flight Simulation Ltd	Bournemouth	31. 5.09E
G-BNUS	Cessna 152 II	15282166	N68179	26. 8.87	Stapleford Flying Club Ltd	Stapleford	10. 7.09E
G-BNUT	Cessna 152 II	15279458	N714VC	26. 8.87	Stapleford Flying Club Ltd	Stapleford	5. 6.09E
G-BNUV	Piper PA-23-250 Aztec F	27-7854038	N97BB N63894	2.10.87	L J Martin	Sandown	3. 2.09E
G-BNUX	Hoffmann H 36 Dimona	36236		26. 8.87	G Hill tr Buckminster Dimona Syndicate	Saltby	3.11.09E

G-BNUY	Piper PA-38-112 Tomahawk II	38-81A0093	N26006	10. 9.87	D C Storey (Noted 10.07)	Bodmin	17. 8.03T
G-BNVB	Grumman AA-5A Cheetah	AA5A-0758	N26843	28. 8.87	V R Coultan tr Grumman Group	Turweston	9. 4.09E
	(Regd as such but plate indicates Gulfstream American production)						
G-BNVD	Piper PA-38-112 Tomahawk	38-79A0055	N2421B	16.11.87	D Sharp	Bagby	1. 5.09E
G-BNVE	Piper PA-28-181 Archer II	28-8490046	N4338D	28. 8.87	Solent Flight Ltd	Lee-on-Solent	13.12.07E
G-BNVT	Piper PA-28R-201T Turbo Arrow III	28R-7703157	N5863V	26. 1.88	T Yeung tr Victor Tango Group	Prestwick	27. 3.09E
G-BNWA	Boeing 767-336	24333	N6009F	19. 4.90	British Airways PLC	London Heathrow	24. 4.09E
G-BNWB	Boeing 767-336	24334	N6046P	2. 2.90	British Airways PLC	London Heathrow	12. 2.10E
G-BNWC	Boeing 767-336	24335		2. 2.90	British Airways PLC	London Heathrow	25. 4.09E
G-BNWD	Boeing 767-336	24336	N6018N	2. 2.90	British Airways PLC	London Heathrow	31. 8.09E
G-BNWH	Boeing 767-336	24340	N6005C	31.10.90	British Airways PLC	London Heathrow	30.10.09E
G-BNWI	Boeing 767-336	24341		18.12.90	British Airways PLC	London Heathrow	17.12.09E
G-BNWM	Boeing 767-336	25204		24. 6.91	British Airways PLC	London Heathrow	24. 6.09E
G-BNWN	Boeing 767-336	25444		30.10.91	British Airways PLC	London Heathrow	29.10.09E
G-BNWO	Boeing 767-336	25442		2. 3.92	British Airways PLC	London Heathrow	1. 3.09E
G-BNWR	Boeing 767-336	25732		20. 3.92	British Airways PLC	London Heathrow	19. 3.09E
G-BNWS	Boeing 767-336	25826	N6018N	19. 2.93	British Airways PLC	London Heathrow	18. 2.10E
G-BNWT	Boeing 767-336	25828		8. 2.93	British Airways PLC	London Heathrow	29.11.09E
G-BNWU	Boeing 767-336	25829		16. 3.93	British Airways PLC	London Heathrow	15. 3.09E
G-BNWV	Boeing 767-336	27140		29. 4.93	British Airways PLC	London Heathrow	28. 4.09E
G-BNWW	Boeing 767-336	25831		3. 2.94	British Airways PLC	London Heathrow	18. 3.09E
G-BNWX	Boeing 767-336	25832		1. 3.94	British Airways PLC	London Heathrow	28. 2.09E
G-BNWY	Boeing 767-336	25834	N5005C	22. 4.96	British Airways PLC	London Heathrow	21. 4.09E
G-BNWZ	Boeing 767-336	25733		25. 2.97	British Airways PLC	London Heathrow	24. 2.10E
G-BNXD	Cessna 172N Skyhawk II	17272692	N6285D	25. 9.87	M and N Jahanfar (Operated The FlightCentre) Southend		2. 7.09E
G-BNXE	Piper PA-28-161 Warrior II	28-8116034	N8262D	24. 9.87	M S Brown	Leicester	26. 1.09E
G-BNXK	Nott-Cameron NCA ULD/3 Balloon (Hot Air)	7 & 1110	(G-BLJN)	23. 9.87	J R P Nott Twain-Harte, California and Bristol		
	(Built Airship Industries (UK) Ltd)			(Hot air envelope stored Twain-Harte 7.03 - helium inner envelope stored Bristol 1995)			
G-BNXL	Glaser-Dirks DG-400	4-216		2.10.87	C I Cowley tr G-BNXL Syndicate		
						Husbands Bosworth	2. 5.09E
G-BNXM	Piper PA-18 Super Cub 95 (L-21B-PI) (Continental O-200-A)	18-4019	MM54-2619 EI-276, I-EIVC, MM54-2619, 54-2619	23.11.87	C J Gowthorpe	(Dunnington, York)	7. 5.09P
	(Italian Frame rebuild No.0006)						
G-BNXR	Cameron O-84 Balloon (Hot Air)	1515		23. 9.87	J A B Gray "Bacchus II" (Noted 8.06)		
						Daglingworth, Cirencester	9.12.04T
G-BNXT	Piper PA-28-161 Cherokee Warrior II	28-7716168	N4047Q	23. 9.87	A S Bamrah t/a Falcon Flying Services (Operated Euroflyers)		
						Biggin Hill	30.11.09E
G-BNXU	Piper PA-28-161 Warrior II	28-7916129	N2082C	23. 9.87	R E Woolsey tr Friendly Warrior Group		
						Newtownards	31. 5.09E
G-BNXV	Piper PA-38-112 Tomahawk	38-79A0826	N2399N	10.12.87	W B Bateson	Blackpool	6.10.09E
G-BNXX	SOCATA TB-20 Trinidad	664	N20GZ	15. 9.87	Air Touring Ltd	Biggin Hill	4. 7.08E
G-BNXZ	Thunder Ax7-77 Balloon (Hot Air)	1105		13.10.87	W S Templeton, R B Green and A S Dear tr Hale Hot Air Balloon Group "Dragonfly"	Fordingbridge	30. 8.09E
G-BNYB	Piper PA-28-201T Turbo Dakota	28-7921040	N2856A N9533N	27. 1.88	Rosetta Sourcing Ltd	Wycombe Air Park	10. 9.09E
G-BNYD	Bell 206B-2 JetRanger II	1911	N3254P C-GTWM, N49712	1.10.87	Fast Helicopters Ltd	Hawarden	12.11.07E
G-BNYK	Piper PA-38-112 Tomahawk II	38-82A0059	N2376V	23.10.87	Lomac Aviators Ltd	Liverpool-John Lennon	16. 6.09E
G-BNYL	Cessna 152 II	15280671	N5454	6.10.87	V J Freeman	Headcorn	12.12.08E
G-BNYM	Cessna 172N Skyhawk II	17273854	N6089J	13.11.87	D J Skinner tr Kestrel Syndicate	AAC Netheravon	24. 4.09E
G-BNYO	Beech 76 Duchess	ME-78	N2010P	28.10.87	Multiflight Ltd	Leeds-Bradford	26. 4.09E
G-BNYP	Piper PA-28-181 Archer II	28-8490027	N4330K	19.10.87	R D Cooper (Operated Sandra's Flying Group)		
						Turweston	13. 3.09E
G-BNYX	Denney Kitfox Model 1	PFA 172-11285		28.10.87	W J Husband	Blackbrook Farm, Sheffield	20. 2.08P
	(Built R W Husband) (Rotax 532)						
G-BNYZ	SNCAN Stampe SV-4E	200	F-BFZR Aeronavale 200	10.12.87	Bianchi Aviation Film Services Ltd	Wycombe Air Park	13. 3.10S
	(Also reported as ex N180SV(?) with c/n "200-53" but may be ex Belgian V-53 c/n 1195)						
	(Lower right wing and undercarriage struck the perimeter fence at Weybourne/Mucklebury 26.7.08 after abandoning original approach on wrong runway. The aircraft then landed but overturned and was extensively damaged – subsequent change of ownership)						
G-BNZB	Piper PA-28-161 Warrior II	28-7916521	N2900U	18.11.87	Falcon Flying Services Ltd	Lydd	31. 1.10E
G-BNZC	de Havilland DHC-1 Chipmunk 22	C1/0778	G-ROYS 7438M, WP905	11.11.87	Richard Shuttleworth Trustees (As "RCAF 671" in RCAF c/s)	Old Warden	12. 4.10
G-BNZK	Thunder Ax7-77 Balloon (Hot Air)	1104		10.11.87	T D Marsden "Shropshire Lass" Limber, Grimsby		28. 5.97A
G-BNZL	RotorWay Scorpion 133	2839		2.11.87	J R Wraight (Complete and stored 5.95)		
	(Built J Evans)					Stoneacre Farm, Farthing Corner	
G-BNZM	Cessna T210N Turbo Centurion II	21063640	N4828C	9.11.87	A J M Freeman	North Weald	9. 4.09E
G-BNZN	Cameron N-56 Balloon (Hot Air)	1471	SE-ZFA G-BNZN	9.11.87	Balloon Sports HB	Partille, Sweden	13. 4.09E
G-BNZO	RotorWay Executive (modified)	3535/5186		9.11.87	J S David (Noted 9.08) (RotorWay RW162)	Street Farm, Takeley	7. 9.07P
	(Built M J Wiltshire) (Originally regd with c/n RW152/3535, amended 8. 3.08)						
G-BNZR	Clutton FRED Series II	PFA 029-10727		10.11.87	R M Waugh	(Belfast)	25. 5.99P
	(Built R M Waugh)						
G-BNZV	Piper PA-25-235 Pawnee D	25-7405649	C-GSKU N9548P	22. 2.88	Aeroklub Alpski Letalski Center Lesce	Lesce-Bled, Slovenia	11. 6.09E
G-BNZZ	Piper PA-28-161 Warrior II	28-8216184	N8253Z	17.11.87	Providence Aviation Ltd	Wellesbourne Mountford	8. 3.09E

G-BOAA - G-BOZZ

G-BOAH	Piper PA-28-161 Warrior II	28-8416030	N43401 N9554N	21. 1.88	Aircraft Engineers Ltd	Prestwick	4. 3.09E

Reg	Type	C/n	Prev id	Date	Owner/Operator	Base	Expiry
G-BOAI	Cessna 152 II	15279830	C-GSJH N757LS	8. 1.88	Aviation Spirit Ltd	Shobdon	12. 1.10E
G-BOAL	Cameron V-65 Balloon (Hot Air)	1600		5.11.87	A M and N H Ponsford *"Nameless"*	Leeds	7. 2.02A
G-BOAS	Air Command 503 Commander	0388		3.12.87	R Robinson	(Leighton Buzzard)	
	(Built R Robinson - pr.no.PFA G/04-1094)						
G-BOAU	Cameron V-77 Balloon (Hot Air)	1606		10.12.87	G T Barstow *"Flying Colours/Duster I"*		
						Llandrindod Wells	21.10.09E
G-BOBA	Piper PA-28R-201 Arrow III	28R-7837232	N31249	4. 1.88	GT Ventures Ltd	Coventry	13. 7.09E
G-BOBH	Airtour AH-77B Balloon (Hot Air)	009		2.12.87	J and K Francis *"Gloworm"* (Noted 8.06)		
						Dibden Purlieu, Southampton	29. 6.02A
G-BOBR	Cameron N-77 Balloon (Hot Air)	1623		10.12.87	Trigger Concepts Ltd	Swallowfield, Reading	24. 4.06A
G-BOBT	Stolp SA.300 Starduster Too	CJ-01	N690CM	15.12.87	S C Lever tr G-BOBT Group	White Waltham	20. 2.09P
	(Built C J Anderson) (Lycoming O-360)						
G-BOBV	Cessna F150M	F15001415	EI-BCV	14.12.87	Sheffield Aero Club Ltd	Netherthorpe	14. 5.09E
	(Built Reims Aviation SA)						
G-BOBY	Monnett Sonerai II	PFA 015-10223		26.10.78	R G Hallam	(Netherthorpe)	8.11.82P
	(Built R G Hallam) (Volkswagen 2233)				*(Damaged near Barton 31.10.82: stored 9.96)*		
G-BOCG	Piper PA-34-200T Seneca II	34-7870359	N36759	30.12.87	Oxford Aviation Academy (Oxford) Ltd	Oxford	26. 2.09E
G-BOCI	Cessna 140A	15497	N5366C	17.11.87	J B Bonnell *"Whitey"*	Thruxton	12. 1.08
	(Continental C90)						
G-BOCK	Sopwith Triplane replica	NAW-1		26. 1.88	Richard Shuttleworth Trustees	Old Warden	31. 7.09P
	(Built Northern Aeroplane Workshops) (Sopwith c/n 153) (130hp Clerget Rotary 9B) *(As "N6290" in RNAS 8 Sqdn c/s)* "Dixie II"						
G-BOCL	Slingsby T 67C Firefly	2035		5. 1.88	Richard Brinklow Aviation Ltd *(Operated The Flying Hut)*		
						Shoreham	26. 2.07T
G-BOCM	Slingsby T 67C Firefly	2036		5. 1.88	Richard Brinklow Aviation Ltd	RAF Benson	12. 5.09E
G-BOCN	Robinson R22 Beta	0726	N... G-BOCN	8. 1.88	Aga Property Development Ltd		
						(Brideswell, Athlone, County Westmeath)	2. 4.08E
G-BODB	Piper PA-28-161 Warrior II	2816042	N9606N	23. 2.88	Sherburn Aero Club Ltd	Sherburn-in-Elmet	13. 2.08E
G-BODC	Piper PA-28-161 Warrior II	2816041	N9605N	23. 2.88	Sherburn Aero Club Ltd	Sherburn-in-Elmet	12. 7.08E
G-BODD	Piper PA-28-161 Warrior II	2816040	N9604N	23. 2.88	L W Scattergood *(Operated Sheffield City Flying School)*		
						Sandtoft	29.10.09E
G-BODE	Piper PA-28-161 Warrior II	2816039	N9603N	23. 2.88	Sherburn Aero Club Ltd	Sherburn-in-Elmet	9. 9.09E
G-BODI	Stoddard-Hamilton Glasair III SH-3R	(HB-...)		14. 4.89	R R Arias	(Soto del Real, Madrid, Spain)	18. 5.09P
	(Built Jackson Barr Ltd) EMK .030 & 3088	G-BODI					
	(Lycoming O-360)						
G-BODM	Piper PA-28-180 Cherokee Challenger	N56016		2. 2.88	R Emery	Clutton Hill Farm, Clutton	12.11.08E
	28-7305519						
G-BODO	Cessna 152 II	15282404	N68923	29. 1.88	M and D C Brooks	Bidford	9.10.09E
G-BODP	Piper PA-38-112 Tomahawk II	38-81A0010	N25616	5. 1.88	Bethan Petrie	Hawarden	13. 3.09E
G-BODR	Piper PA-28-161 Warrior II	28-8116318	N8436B	5. 1.88	Airways Aero Associations Ltd	Wycombe Air Park	23. 1.10E
					(Operated British Airways Flying Club)		
G-BODS	Piper PA-38-112 Tomahawk	38-79A0410	N2379F	3. 2.88	Coulson Flying Services Ltd	Cranfield	25. 8.09E
G-BODT	Jodel D 18	173		14. 1.88	L D McPhillips tr Jodel G-BODT Syndicate		
	(Built R A Jarvis - pr.no.PFA 169-11290) (Rotax 912-UL)					Portmoak	29. 5.09P
G-BODU	Scheibe SF25C-2000 Falke	44434	D-KIAA	19. 1.88	Hertfordshire County Scout Council		
	(Limbach L2000)					Gransden Lodge	11. 5.09E
G-BODX	Beech 76 Duchess	ME-309	N67094	26. 2.88	S J Skilton t/a Aviation Rentals	Bournemouth	3. 9.09E
					(Operated Professional Air Training)		
G-BODY	Cessna 310R II	310R1503	N4897A	17.12.87	Reconnaissance Ventures Ltd	Coventry	23. 2.09E
					(Atlantic Flight Training on tip tanks)		
G-BODZ	Robinson R22 Beta	0729		8. 1.88	Langley Aviation Ltd	Gamston	25. 4.10E
G-BOEE	Piper PA-28-181 Cherokee Archer II	N6168J		20. 1.88	H A Barrs	Blackbushe	13. 6.09E
	28-7690359						
G-BOEG	Short SD.3-60 Variant 100	SH3733	CS-TLS	27. 1.88	ACL Aircraft Trading Ltd *(stored less std engine in BAC colours)*		
			G-BOEG, D-CFXE, N163DD, N133PC, G-BOEG, G-14-3733			Southend	5. 3.09E
G-BOEH	Robin DR.340 Major	434	F-BRVN	4. 1.88	G Bowles tr Piper Flyers Group		
						Bradleys Lawn, Heathfield	24. 5.09E
G-BOEK	Cameron V-77 Balloon (Hot Air)	1658		25. 1.88	R I M Kerr, R S McLean and P McCheyne	Bristol	14. 4.09E
					"Secret Leader" (Cameron Balloons colours)		
G-BOEM	Pitts S-2A (Built Aerotek Inc)	2255	N31525	17. 2.88	M Murphy	Spanhoe	29.10.08E
G-BOEN	Cessna 172M Skyhawk	17261325	N20482	12. 2.88	C Barlow	Standalone Farm, Meppershall	16. 4.09E
G-BOER	Piper PA-28-161 Warrior II	28-8116094	N83030	21. 1.88	M and W Fraser-Urquhart	Blackpool	18. 5.09E
G-BOET	Piper PA-28RT-201 Arrow IV	28R-8018020	G-IBEC G-BOET, N8116V	28. 1.88	B C Chambers	Jersey	28. 9.09E
G-BOFC	Beech 76 Duchess	ME-217	N6628M	28. 1.88	Magenta Ltd *(Operated Airways Flight Training)*		
						Exeter	8. 4.09E
G-BOFD	Cessna U206G Stationair 6	U20604181	N756LS	27. 1.88	Baulip Sports	(Tallard, France)	24. 8.09E
G-BOFE	Piper PA-34-200T Seneca II	34-7870381	N39493	22. 2.88	Nauku I Technik SP z.o.o	Rzeszow, Poland	7. 6.09E
G-BOFF	Cameron N-77 Balloon (Hot Air)	1666		26. 1.88	R S McKibbin (Systems 80 titles)	Thornbury, Bristol	9. 8.09E
G-BOFL	Cessna 152 II	15284101	N5457H	28. 1.88	Gem Rewinds Ltd	Coventry	12. 8.09E
G-BOFM	Cessna 152 II	15284301	N6445M	28. 1.88	Gem Rewinds Ltd	Wolverhampton	2. 9.09E
G-BOFW	Cessna A150M Aerobat	A1500612	N9803J	15. 2.88	D F Donovan	Elstree	23. 1.09E
G-BOFY	Piper PA-28-140 Cherokee Cruiser	N43521		3. 2.88	Light Aircraft Leasing Ltd	Cardiff	29. 7.09E
	28-7425374						
G-BOFZ	Piper PA-28-161 Cherokee Warrior II	N2189M		10. 2.88	R W Harris *(Operated The FlightCentre)* Southend		3. 2.09E
	28-7816255						
G-BOGI	Robin DR.400-180 Régent	1821		15. 2.88	A L M Shepherd	Rochester	4. 7.09E
G-BOGK	ARV Aviation ARV-1	K 006		10. 2.88	M K Field	Sleap	23. 7.08P
	(Built Monewden Flying Group - pr.no.PFA 152-11138)						
G-BOGM	Piper PA-28RT-201T Turbo Arrow IV	N8173C		10. 2.88	R J Pearce t/a RJP Aviation *(Operated RJP Flying School)*		
	28R-8031077					Wolverhampton	24. 4.09E
G-BOGO	Piper PA-32R-301T Turbo Saratoga II SP	N8165W		6. 4.88	A S Doman	Fairoaks	28. 7.09E
	32R-8029064						

G-BOGP	Cameron V-77 Balloon (Hot Air)	896		30. 3.88	T Gunn tr Wealden Balloon Group "Dire Straits"		
						Crowborough	10. 7.00A
G-BOGV	Air Command 532 Elite	0399		10. 3.88	G M Hobman	Heworth, York	10. 1.91P
	(Built Deandell Products Ltd - pr.no.PFA G/04-1102)						
G-BOGY	Cameron V-77 Balloon (Hot Air)	1650		15. 2.88	P Spellward and A Reimann		
						Bristol and Merrenberg, Germany	18. 4.09E
G-BOHA	Piper PA-28-161 Cherokee Warrior II		N3526M	16. 3.88	Flying at Lee-on-Solent Ltd t/a Phoenix Aviation		
		28-7816352				Lee-on-Solent	13. 6.09E
G-BOHD	Colt 77A Balloon (Hot Air)	1214		4. 3.88	D B Court "Bluebird"	Ormskirk	5. 8.02A
G-BOHF	Thunder Ax8-84 Balloon (Hot Air)	1197		8. 4.88	J A Harris	Stalbridge, Sturminster Newton	1. 9.05A
G-BOHH	Cessna 172N Skyhawk II	17273906	N131FR	19. 2.88	M H Anderson tr G-BOHH Group	Swansea	7. 5.09E
			N7333J				
G-BOHI	Cessna 152 II	15281241	N49406	29. 2.88	Cirrus Aviation Ltd	Clacton	5. 6.09E
G-BOHJ	Cessna 152 II	15280558	N25259	29. 2.88	A G Knight tr Airlaunch	Tibenham	22. 3.09E
G-BOHL	Cameron A-120 Balloon (Hot Air)	1701		11. 3.88	T J Bucknall "Son of City of Bath"	Colwyn Bay	12.10.02
G-BOHM	Piper PA-28-180 Cherokee Challenger		N55000	18. 2.88	B F Keogh and R A Scott		
		28-7305287				Lockmead Farm, South Marston	8. 5.09E
G-BOHO	Piper PA-28-161 Warrior II	28-8016196	N747RH	25. 2.88	H M Sherriff and D G Buchanan tr Egressus Flying Group		
			N9560N				Duxford	17. 1.09E
G-BOHR	Piper PA-28-151 Cherokee Warrior		C-GNFE	29. 2.88	R M E Garforth	Southend	20. 4.09E
		28-7515245					
G-BOHS	Piper PA-38-112 Tomahawk	38-79A0988	N2418P	26. 2.88	A S Bamrah t/a Falcon Flying Services Earls Colne		15. 4.07T
G-BOHT	Piper PA-38-112 Tomahawk	38-79A1079	N25304	14. 4.88	E Reed t/a St George Flight Training		
			C-GAYW, N24052				Durham Tees Valley	30.10.09E
G-BOHU	Piper PA-38-112 Tomahawk	38-80A0031	N25093	26. 2.88	D A Whitmore	Swansea	20. 5.09E
G-BOHV	Wittman W 8.Tailwind	621		3. 3.88	R A Povall	Yearby	10. 9.09P
	(Built R A Povall - pr.no.PFA 031-11151)						
G-BOHW	Van's RV-4	PFA 181-11309		16. 6.88	P J Robins	Deenethorpe	22. 8.09P
	(Built R W H Cole) (Lycoming O-320)						
G-BOIA	Cessna 180K Skywagon II	18053121	N2895K	3. 3.88	R E, P E R, J E R and R J W Styles tr Old Warden Flying		
					and Parachute Group	Rush Green	26. 7.09E
G-BOIB	Wittman W.10 Tailwind	PFA 031-10551		3. 3.88	R F Bradshaw	Valley Farm, Winwick	17. 4.09P
	(Built P H Lewis) (Continental O-300-D)						
G-BOIC	Piper PA-28R-201T Turbo Arrow III		N2336M	7. 4.88	M J Pearson	Stapleford	17. 6.09E
		28R-7803123					
G-BOID	Bellanca 7ECA Citabria	1092-75	N8676V	3. 3.88	D Mallinson	Birds Edge, Penistone	11. 6.08E
G-BOIG	Piper PA-28-161 Warrior II	28-8516027	N4390B	1. 3.88	D Vallance-Pell	Gamston	11. 8.09E
			N9519N				
G-BOIJ	Thunder Ax7-77 Series 1 Balloon (Hot Air) 964			11. 3.88	K Dodman	Stowmarket	6. 7.07A
G-BOIK	Air Command 503 Commander	0420		8. 3.88	F G Shepherd	Alston, Cumbria	22. 1.90P
	(Built G R Horner - pr.no.PFA G/04-1090)						
G-BOIL	Cessna 172N Skyhawk II	17271301	N23FL	2. 3.88	Upperstack Ltd	Barton	10. 8.09E
			N23ER, (N2494E)				
G-BOIO	Cessna 152 II	15280260	N24445	7. 3.88	J H Sandham t/a J H Sandham Aviation	Carlisle	27. 9.09E
G-BOIR	Cessna 152 II	15283272	N48041	7. 3.88	Shropshire Aero Club Ltd	Sleap	13. 6.09E
G-BOIT	SOCATA TB-10 Tobago	810		10. 3.88	M J Ryan t/a G-BOIT Flying Group (Fly Navy titles)		
						RNAS Yeovilton	6. 4.09E
G-BOIV	Cessna 150M Commuter	15078620	N704HH	30. 3.88	M J Page tr India Victor Group	Seething	13.12.08E
G-BOIX	Cessna 172N Skyhawk II	17271206	C-GMMX	9. 3.88	JR Flying Ltd	Bournemouth	28. 2.09E
			N2253E				
G-BOIY	Cessna 172N Skyhawk II	17267738	N73901	9. 3.88	L W Scattergood (Operated Sheffield City Flying School)		
						Sandtoft	4.12.09E
G-BOIZ	Piper PA-34-200T Seneca II	34-8070014	N81081	25. 2.88	R W Tebby t/a S F Tebby and Son	Bristol	15.10.09E
					(Operated Bristol Flying Centre)		
G-BOJB	Cameron V-77 Balloon (Hot Air)	1615		11. 3.88	I M and S D Warner	(Luton)	3. 4.09E
G-BOJI	Piper PA-28RT-201 Arrow IV	28R-7918221	N2919X	31. 3.88	K B Frost and M J Berry tr Arrow Two Group		
						Blackbushe	4. 6.09E
G-BOJK	Piper PA-34-220T Seneca III	3433020	G-BRUF	11. 3.88	Redhill Aviation Ltd (Operated Redhill Flying Club)		
			N9113D				Redhill	22.10.09E
G-BOJM	Piper PA-28-181 Archer II	28-8090244	N8155L	21. 3.88	R P Emms	Gamston	12. 5.09E
G-BOJR	Cessna 172P Skyhawk II	17275574	N64539	22. 4.88	Exeter Flying Club Ltd	Exeter	14. 6.09E
G-BOJS	Cessna 172P Skyhawk II	17274582	N52699	29. 3.88	B A Paul	Denham	29.11.09E
G-BOJU	Cameron N-77 Balloon (Hot Air)	1718		21. 3.88	M A Scholes "GB Transport"	London SE25	7. 9.97A
G-BOJW	Piper PA-28-161 Cherokee Warrior II		N1668H	28. 3.88	Brewhamfield Farm Ltd	Enstone	3. 8.09E
		28-7716038					
G-BOJZ	Piper PA-28-161 Warrior II	28-7916223	N2113J	28. 3.88	A S Bamrah t/a Falcon Flying Services	Rochester	31. 3.09E
G-BOKA	Piper PA-28-201T Turbo Dakota	28-7921076	N2860S	15. 3.88	CBG Aviation Ltd	Fairoaks	14. 5.09E
G-BOKB	Piper PA-28-161 Warrior II	28-8216077	N8013Y	29. 3.88	Apollo Aviation Advisory Ltd	Shoreham	20. 8.09E
G-BOKF	Air Command 532 Elite	0404		28. 3.88	J K Padden	(Leeds)	22. 9.99P
	(Built N J Brunskill - pr.no.PFA G/04-1101)						
G-BOKH	Whittaker MW7	PFA 171-11281	(G-MTWT)	21. 3.88	G J Chater	Landmead Farm, Garford	6. 6.09E
	(Built M Whittaker and officially regd as PFA 171-11231)						
G-BOKW	Bölkow BÖ.208C Junior	689	G-BITT	6. 1.88	G C Patel	Popham	11 11.08P
			F-BRHX, (D-EEAL)				
G-BOKX	Piper PA-28-161 Cherokee Warrior II		N39709	28. 3.88	Shenley Farms (Aviation) Ltd	Headcorn	21. 8.09E
		28-7816680					
G-BOKY	Cessna 152 II	15285298	N67409	6. 4.88	D F F and J E Poore	Bournemouth	1. 7.09E
G-BOLB	Taylorcraft BC-12-65	3165	N36211	17. 5.88	C E Tudor	Leicester	15. 4.09P
	(Continental A65)		NC36211				
G-BOLC	Fournier RF6-100	1	F-BVKS	28. 3.88	J D Cohen	Dunkeswell	13.10.09E
G-BOLD	Piper PA-38-112 Tomahawk	38-78A0180	N9740T	8. 7.88	B R Pearson tr BOLD Group	Eaglescott	16. 3.09E
G-BOLE	Piper PA-38-112 Tomahawk	38-78A0475	N2506E	13. 7.88	J and G Stevenson tr Double S Group		
						Nottingham City-Tollerton	28. 5.09E

G-BOLF	Piper PA-38-112 Tomahawk	38-79A0375	N583P	13. 7.88	P W Carlton	Durham Tees Valley	5. 5.09E
			YV-583P, YV-133E, YV-1696P, N9666N				
				(Ditched in Robin Hood Bay, off Whitby 17.10.08 and destroyed)			
G-BOLG	Bellanca 7KCAB Citabria	517-75	N8706V	25.11.88	B R Pearson tr Aerotug	Eaglescott	21. 5.08E
G-BOLI	Cessna 172P Skyhawk II	17275484	N63794	30. 3.88	W White tr BOLI Flying Club	Denham	8. 8.09E
G-BOLL	Lake LA-4-200 Skimmer	295	(F-GRMX)	4. 5.88	M C Holmes *(stored 10.08)*	City of Derry	3. 5.08
			G-BOLL, EI-ANR, N1133L				
G-BOLN	Colt 21A Cloudhopper Balloon (Hot Air)	1226		4. 5.88	G Everett	Maidstone	26. 9 09E
G-BOLO	Bell 206B-2 JetRanger II	1522	N59409	2.11.87	Hargreaves Leasing Ltd *(Operated Blades Helicopters)*		
						(Rustington, Littlehampton)	16. 3.09E
G-BOLP	Colt 21A Cloudhopper Balloon (Hot Air)	1227		4. 5.88	J E Rose	Abingdon	11.10.09E
G-BOLR	Colt 21A Cloudhopper Balloon (Hot Air)	1228		3. 5.88	C J Sanger-Davies	Hawarden	23. 8.09E
G-BOLS	Clutton FRED Series II	PFA 029-10676		6. 4.88	I F Vaughan *"The Ruptured Uck"*		
	(Built R J Goodburn)					(St Martin, Guernsey)	
G-BOLT	Rockwell Commander 114	14428	N5883N	16.10.78	I R Harnett	Elstree	9. 7.09E
G-BOLU	Robin R3000/120	106	F-GFAO	14. 4.88	M A Hogbin	Biggin Hill	3. 8.09E
			SE-IMS				
G-BOLV	Cessna 152 II	15280492	N24983	8. 4.88	Synergy Aircraft Leasing Ltd	Fairoaks	15. 6.09E
G-BOLW	Cessna 152 II	15280589	N25316	9. 6.88	A Jahanfar *(Operated Seawing Flying Club)*		
						Southend	30. 8.09E
G-BOLY	Cessna 172N Skyhawk II	17269004	N734PJ	31. 3.88	Simair Ltd	Biggin Hill	20. 6.09E
G-BOMB	Cassutt Racer IIIM	PFA 034-10386		18.12.78	R S Grace *"Blind Panic"* and *"3"*	Bentwaters	23. 5.08P
	(Built D Ford)						
G-BOMN	Cessna 150F	15063089	N6489F	25. 4.89	P A Chamberlaine tr Auburn Flying Group		
						Movenis, Coleraine	11. 4.09E
G-BOMO	Piper PA-38-112 Tomahawk II	38-81A0161	N91324	8. 4.88	APB Leasing Ltd	Swansea	12. 8.09E
G-BOMP	Piper PA-28-181 Cherokee Archer II	28-7790249	N8482F	8. 4.88	D Carter	Little Gransden	23. 4.09E
G-BOMS	Cessna 172N Skyhawk II	17269448	N737JG	11. 4.88	Almat Flying Club Ltd and Penchant Ltd	Coventry	28.10.09E
G-BOMU	Piper PA-28-181 Cherokee Archer II	28-7790318	N1631H	8. 4.88	J Sawyer	Blackbushe	29.12.09E
G-BOMY	Piper PA-28-161 Warrior II	28-8216049	N8457S	28. 6.88	D A Cobham tr BOMY Group	Headcorn	16. 2.09E
G-BOMZ	Piper PA-38-112 Tomahawk	38-78A0635	N2315A	30. 6.88	I C Barlow and I Cummins tr BOMZ Aviation		
						Wycombe Air Park	19. 3.09E
G-BONC	Piper PA-28RT-201 Arrow IV	28R-7918007	C-GXYX	13. 5.88	Finglow Ltd	Fowlmere	7.10.09E
			N3069K				
G-BONG	Enstrom F-28A-UK	154	N9604	22. 4.88	J D Beeson	Barton	21. 9.09E
G-BONP	CFM Streak Shadow	108		4. 5.88	R Lawes	Old Sarum	18. 5.09P
	(Built CFM Metal-Fax as c/n SS-01P and pr.no.PFA 161A-11344) (Rotax 582)						
G-BONR	Cessna 172N Skyhawk II	17268164	C-GYGK	18. 4.88	D I Claik	Biggin Hill	21. 7.09E
			(N733BH)				
G-BONS	Cessna 172N Skyhawk II	17268345	C-GIUF	18. 4.88	M G Montgomerie tr G-BONS Group	Elstree	17. 9.09E
G-BONT	Slingsby T 67M Firefly II	2054		3. 5.88	Babcock Support Services Ltd t/a Babcock Defence Services		
						AAC Middle Wallop	10. 2.09E
G-BONU	Slingsby T 67B Firefly	2037		3. 5.88	R L Brinklow *(Noted 5.06)*	Hinton-in-the-Hedges	29. 6.00T
G-BONW	Cessna 152 II	15280401	OY-CPL	15. 4.88	Lincoln Aero Club Ltd	Sturgate	22. 8.09E
			N24825				
G-BONY	Denney Kitfox Model 1	166		11. 5.88	R Dunn and P F Hill	Old Sarum	3.10.08P
	(Built J S Penny - pr.no.PFA 172-11351) (Rotax 532) *(Inscribed as "Mk.2")*						
G-BONZ	Beech V35B Bonanza	D-10282	N6661D	6. 4.88	P M Coulten	Boughton, Norfolk	16. 2.07
G-BOOB	Cameron N-65 Balloon (Hot Air)	515		12.11.79	P J Hooper	Southville, Bristol	24. 8.09E
G-BOOC	Piper PA-18-150 Super Cub	18-8279	SE-EPC	29. 4.88	S A C Whitcombe	Redwood Cottage, Meon	1. 1.09E
G-BOOD	Slingsby T.31	PFA 042-11264		4. 5.88	K A Hale	Lotmead Farm, Wanborough	10. 1.08P
	(Built P J Titherington with wings ex XE810 c/n 923) (Fuji-Robin EC-44-2PM)						
G-BOOE	Gulfstream GA-7 Cougar	GA7-0093	N718G	7. 6.88	R J Moller	(Leeds)	6. 8.08E
G-BOOF	Piper PA-28-181 Cherokee Archer II	28-7890084	N47510	16. 6.88	H Merkado	Panshanger	13.11.09E
G-BOOG	Piper PA-28RT-201T Turbo Arrow IV	28R-8331036	N4303K	6. 5.88	Simair Ltd	Earls Colne	17. 6.09E
G-BOOH	Jodel D 112	481	F-BHVK	16. 5.88	R M MacCormac	Tibenham	9. 8.09P
	(Built Etablissement Valladeau)						
G-BOOI	Cessna 152 II	15280751	N25590	22. 8.88	Stapleford Flying Club Ltd	Stapleford	19. 5.09E
G-BOOL	Cessna 172N Skyhawk II	17272486	C-GJSY	27. 4.88	J R Payne	Biggin Hill	21.12.08E
			N5271D				
G-BOOW	Aerosport Scamp	PFA 117-10709		10. 5.88	D A Weldon	Kilrush, County Kildare	7. 9.09P
	(Built C Tyers) (Volkswagen 1834)						
G-BOOX	Rutan LongEz	PFA 074A-10844		3. 5.88	I R Wilde	Deenethorpe	23. 5.09P
	(Built I R Thomas and I R Wilde) (Lycoming O-235)						
G-BOOZ	Cameron N-77 Balloon (Hot Air)	904	(G-BKSJ)	21. 6.83	J E F Kettley *"Bluebell"*		
	(New home built envelope c 6.98)					Littleton Drew, Chippenham	25. 4.09E
G-BOPA	Piper PA-28-181 Archer II	28-8490024	N43299	28. 4.88	Flyco Ltd	Denham	5. 9.09E
G-BOPC	Piper PA-28-161 Warrior II	28-8216006	N2124X	6. 5.88	Aeros Leasing Ltd	Gloucestershire	10. 9.09E
G-BOPD	Bede BD-4	632	N632DH	25. 5.88	S T Dauncey	Yearby	17. 6.09P
	(Built D E Hewes) (Lycoming O-320)						
G-BOPH	Cessna TR182 Turbo Skylane RG II	R18201031	N756BJ	11. 5.88	J M Mitchell	Derby	12. 5.09E
G-BOPO	FLS Aerospace OA.7 Optica Series 301	021	EC-FVM	17. 5.88	J K Edgley	Thruxton	5. 6.09R
			EC-435, G-BOPO				
G-BOPR	FLS Aerospace OA.7 Optica Series 301	023		17. 5.88	Aeroelvira Ltd	Thruxton	
G-BOPT	Grob G115	8046		10. 5.88	Upperstack Ltd t/a LAC Flying School	Barton	21. 1.09E
					(Operated Lancashire Aero Club)		
G-BOPU	Grob G115	8059		10. 5.88	Upperstack Ltd t/a LAC Flying School	Barton	27. 2.09E
					(Operated Lancashire Aero Club)		
G-BOPX	Cessna A152 Aerobat	A1520932	N761BK	11. 5.88	A J Gomes *(Noted dismantled 10.07)*	Rochester	24. 1.98T

G-BORB	Cameron V-77 Balloon (Hot Air)		1348		24. 8.88	M H Wolff	Liskeard	9. 7.02A
G-BORD	Thunder Ax7-77 Balloon (Hot Air)		1164		26. 5.88	D D Owen *"Marvin"*	Wotton-under-Edge	11.12.99A
G-BORE	Colt 77A Balloon (Hot Air)		642		24. 5.88	J D Medcalf and C Wilson tr Little Secret Hot Air		
						Balloon Group *"My Little Secret"*	Enfield	4. 1.10E
G-BORG	Campbell Cricket	PFA G/03-1085			8. 6.88	R L Gilmore	(Cressage, Shrewsbury)	25. 4.05P
	(Built N G Bailey) (Rotax 503)							
G-BORH	Piper PA-34-200T Seneca II		34-8070352	N8261V	7. 6.88	The Construction Workers Guild Ltd	Elstree	25. 3.08E
G-BORK	Piper PA-28-161 Warrior II		28-8116095	G-IIIC		T W Eagles tr Warrior Group *(Orange Communications titles)*		
				G-BORK, N83036			Turweston	17. 1.09E
G-BORL	Piper PA-28-161 Cherokee Warrior II			N2190M	28. 9.88	Westair Flying School Ltd	Blackpool	18. 2.09E
			28-7816256					
G-BORN	Cameron N-77 Balloon (Hot Air)		1777		13. 5.88	I Chadwick *"Ian"*	Partridge Green, Bolney	2.10.09E
G-BORR	Thunder AX8-90 Balloon (Hot Air)		1256		13. 6.88	W J Harris	Schwarzhofen, Germany	10. 9.05A
G-BORS	Piper PA-28-181 Archer II		28-8090156	N8127C	31. 5.88	Silverstar Aviation Ltd	Blackpool	29. 6.06T
G-BORT	Colt 77A Balloon (Hot Air)		1255		7. 6.88	J Triquet	St Gemmes-Le-Robert, France	10. 9.01A
G-BORW	Cessna 172P Skyhawk II		17274301	N51357	23. 8.88	Briter Aviation Ltd	Coventry	24.10.09E
G-BORY	Cessna 150L		15072292	N6792G	27. 5.88	C J Twelves t/a Alexander Aviation	Fenland	21. 7.09E
G-BOSB	Thunder Ax7-77 Balloon (Hot Air)		1199		7. 6.88	M Gallagher	Consett	5. 4.09E
	(Regd as c/n 581 but built as above)							
G-BOSD	Piper PA-34-200T Seneca II		34-7570085	N33086	7. 6.88	Bristol Flying Centre Ltd	Bristol	16. 8.09E
G-BOSE	Piper PA-28-181 Archer II		28-8590007	N143AV	17. 5.88	J Lemon and R Pawsey tr G-BOSE Group		
							White Waltham	4. 6.09E
G-BOSJ	Nord 3400		124	N9048P	26. 5.88	A I Milne	Etthornes Farm, Swaffham	1.11.94P
	French Army *"MOO"* (As *"124"* in French AF c/s) (Damaged Fenland 12.6.94: stored 9.02)							
G-BOSM	CEA Jodel DR.253B Régent		168	F-BSBH	24. 5.88	A G Stevens	Full Sutton	26. 2.09E
G-BOSN	Aérospatiale AS.355F1 Ecureuil 2		5266	N2109L	22. 8.88	L L F Smith t/a Helicopter Services		
				5N-AYL, G-BOSN, 5N-AYL			Wycombe Air Park	10. 3.09E
G-BOSO	Cessna A152 Aerobat		A1520975	N761PD	25. 5.88	J S Develin and Z Islam	Redhill	12.10.09E
G-BOSR	Piper PA-28-140 Cherokee		28-22092	N7464R	26. 5.88	C R Guggenheim tr Sierra-Romeo Group		
							Old Sarum	20.11.08E
G-BOTD	Cameron O-105 Balloon (Hot Air)		1611		6. 6.88	P J Beglan	Marminiac, France	14. 2.09E
G-BOTF	Piper PA-28-151 Cherokee Warrior			C-GGIF	8. 6.88	P E Preston tr G-BOTF Group *(Operated Southend Flying Club)*		
			28-7515436				Southend	29.10.09E
G-BOTG	Cessna 152 II		15283035	N46343	9. 6.88	Donington Aviation Ltd Nottingham-East Midlands		23.11.09E
G-BOTH	Cessna 182Q Skylane II		18267558	N202PS	9. 6.88	P E Gethin	(Great Yarmouth)	13. 6.09E
				N114SP, N5172N				
G-BOTI	Piper PA-28-151 Warrior		28-7515251	C-GNFF	9. 6.88	A J Bamrah t/a Falcon Flying Services	Biggin Hill	31. 8.09E
	(Converted to PA-28-161 model)							
G-BOTK	Cameron O-105 Balloon (Hot Air)		1765		9. 6.88	N Woodham	Fawley, Southampton	7.12.09E
G-BOTN	Piper PA-28-161 Warrior II		28-7916261	N2173N	9. 6.88	Apollo Aviation Advisory Ltd	Shoreham	23. 9.09E
G-BOTO	Bellanca 7ECA Citabria		939-73	N57398	9. 6.88	A K Hulme tr G-BOTO Group		
							Rayne Hall Farm, Braintree	21.12.07E
G-BOTP	Cessna 150J		15070736	N61017	2. 8.88	R F Finnis and C P Williams	Thruxton	2. 6.09E
G-BOTU	Piper J-3C-65 Cub		19045	N98803	8. 7.88	T L Giles	Browns Farm, Hitcham	15. 4.08P
	(Continental A75)			NC98803				
G-BOTV	Piper PA-32RT-300 Lance II		32R-7885153	N36039	7. 6.88	Robin Lance Aviation Associates Ltd	Rochester	12. 5.09E
G-BOTW	Cameron V-77 Balloon (Hot Air)		1761		14. 6.88	M R Jeynes *(Inflated 4.06)*	Redditch	17. 6.03A
G-BOUE	Cessna 172N Skyhawk II		17273235	N6535F	8. 8.88	P Gray and G N R Bradley	Gamston	17. 4.09E
G-BOUF	Cessna 172N Skyhawk II		17271900	N5605E	24. 6.88	B P and M I Sneap	Ripley, Derbyshire	11. 9.09E
G-BOUJ	Cessna 150M Commuter		15076373	N3058V	25. 8.88	R D Billins tr UJ Flying Group	Cranfield	5. 2.09E
G-BOUK	Piper PA-34-200T Seneca II		34-7570124	N33476	31. 8.88	C J and R J Barnes Nottingham-East Midlands		24.10.08E
G-BOUL	Piper PA-34-200T Seneca II		34-7670157	N8936C	26. 8.88	Oxford Aviation Academy (Oxford) Ltd	Oxford	18. 4.09E
G-BOUM	Piper PA-34-200T Seneca II		34-7670136	N8401C	3. 8.88	Oxford Aviation Academy (Oxford) Ltd	Oxford	7. 4.09E
G-BOUN	Rand Robinson KR-2	PFA 129-10945			23. 6.88	P J Brookman	Knapthorpe Lodge, Caunton	30.11.07P
	(Propeller blade detached after touch-and-go Horse Leys Farm, Burton-on-the-Wolds 28. 3.07: forced landed, overturned & substantially damaged)							
G-BOUP	Piper PA-28-161 Warrior II		2816059	N9139X	12. 7.88	Aeros Holdings Ltd	Gloucestershire	19. 3.09E
G-BOUT	Colomban MC-12 Cri-Cri		12-0135	N120JN	14. 6.88	C K Farley	(Wolverhampton)	
	(Built J A Nelson)							
G-BOUV	Montgomerie-Bensen B 8MR	PFA G/01-1092			23. 6.88	L R Phillips	(Shafton, Barnsley)	13. 6.03P
	(Built P Wilkinson) (Rotax 532)							
G-BOUZ	Cessna 150G		15065606	N2606J	15. 6.88	Atlantic Bridge Aviation Ltd	Lydd	19. 1.08E
G-BOVB	Piper PA-15 Vagabond		15-180	N4396H	23. 6.88	J R Kimberley	(Lawford, Manningtree)	18. 5.05P
	(Lycoming O-145)			NC4396H				
	(Failed to gain height on take-off Whitefields Farm, South Molton, Devon 16.10.04 and suffered major damage)							
G-BOVK	Piper PA-28-161 Warrior II		28-8516061	N69168	7. 9.88	Multiflight Ltd	Leeds-Bradford	3. 6.09E
G-BOVT	Cessna 150M Commuter		15078032	N8962U	1.12.88	C J Hopewell	Sibson	13. 4.07T
G-BOVU	Stoddard-Hamilton Glasair III		3090		16. 9.88	B R Chaplin	Deenethorpe	19. 6.09P
	(Buillt A H Carrington) (Lycoming IO-540)							
G-BOVV	Cameron V-77 Balloon (Hot Air)		1724		26. 9.88	P Glydon *"Debs Delight"*	Knowle, Bristol	18. 3.09E
G-BOVW	Colt 69A Balloon (Hot Air)		1286		13. 7.88	V Hyland *"Enderby-Hyland Painting"*		
							Turnditch, Derby	6. 4.94A
G-BOVX	Hughes 269C *(Hughes 300)*		38-0673	N58170	12. 7.88	P E Tornberg	Hannington, Rushden	11. 2.09E
G-BOWB	Cameron V-77 Balloon (Hot Air)		1767		13. 7.88	R A Benham	Chellaston, Derby	9. 7.09E
G-BOWE	Piper PA-34-200T Seneca II		34-7870405	N39668	14. 7.88	Oxford Aviation Academy (Oxford) Ltd	Oxford	25. 2.09E
G-BOWL	Cameron V-77 Balloon (Hot Air)		1780		26. 7.88	P G and G R Hall *"Matrix"*	Meanwood, Chard	12. 5.00A
G-BOWM	Cameron V-56 Balloon (Hot Air)		1781		26. 7.88	C G Caldecott and Georgina Pitt	Woore, Crewe	27. 5.09E
G-BOWN	Piper PA-12 Super Cruiser		12-1912	N3661N	26. 7.88	T L Giles	Brown Farm, Hitcham, Ipswich	1.11.10S
	(Lycoming O-235)			NC3661N				
G-BOWO	Cessna R182 Skylane RG II		R18200146	(G-BOTR)	20. 7.88	D A H Morris	Wolverhampton	23.12.09E
				N2301C				
G-BOWP	Wassmer Jodel D 120A Paris-Nice		319	F-BNZM	26. 7.88	J M Pearson	Bird's Edge, Penistone	19. 3.09P
	(Continental O-200-A)							
G-BOWU	Cameron O-84 Balloon (Hot Air)		1779		1. 8.88	C F Pooley and D C Ball tr St Elmos Fire Syndicate		
						"Elmo"	Barnwood, Gloucester	7. 8.01A

Reg	Type	C/n	Prev id	Date	Owner/Operator	Location	Date
G-BOWV	Cameron V-65 Balloon (Hot Air)	1800		24. 8.88	R A Harris *"Sigmund"*	Axminster	31. 5.09E
G-BOWY	Piper PA-28RT-201T Turbo Arrow IV		N404EL	8. 8.88	J S Develin and Z Islam	Blackbushe	24.11.09E
		28R-8131114	N83648				
G-BOWZ	Bensen B.80V	PFA G/01-1060		4. 7.08	W W Heslop	Little Rissington	29.10.08P
	(Built W M Day)						
G-BOXA	Piper PA-28-161 Warrior II	2816075	N9149Q	1.11.88	Channel Islands Aero Club (Jersey) Ltd	Jersey	8. 1.10E
G-BOXC	Piper PA-28-161 Warrior II	2816063	N9142D	12. 8.88	Channel Islands Aero Club (Jersey) Ltd	Jersey	10. 6.09E
G-BOXG	Cameron O-77 Balloon (Hot Air)	1792		26. 8.88	R A Wicks	Norwich	22. 3.09E
G-BOXH	Pitts S-1S Special	MP4	N8LA	29. 7.88	G R Cotterell	(Kings Lynn)	16. 5.07P
	(Built S Halstock and J Mills)						
G-BOXJ	Piper J-3C-90 Cub (L-4H-PI)	12193	OO-ADJ	1. 8.88	A Bendkowski *(As "479897:JD" in USAF c/s)*		
	(Continental C90) (Frame No.12021)		44-79897			Kittyhawk Farm, Deanland	4. 8.07P
G-BOXR	Grumman American GA-7 Cougar	GA7-0059	N772GA	19.10.88	Plane Talking Ltd *(Operated Cabair)*	Biggin Hill	11. 9.09E
	(C/n plate shows manufacturer as Gulfstream American)						
G-BOXT	Hughes 269C *(Hughes 300)*	104-0367	SE-HMR	1. 8.88	Jetscape Leisure Ltd	Gloucestershire	28. 4.09E
			PH-JOH, D-HBOL				
G-BOXU	Grumman AA-5B Tiger	AA5B-0026	N1526R	28. 7.88	M Hamer tr Marcher Aviation Group	Welshpool	19. 5.09E
G-BOXV	Pitts S-1S	7-0433	N27822	8. 8.88	C Waddington	Shobdon	6.11.08P
	(Built J R Castrillo)						
G-BOXW	Cassutt Racer IIIM	PFA 034-11317		11. 8.88	D I Johnson	(Leigh-on-Sea)	
	(Built D I Johnson)						
G-BOYB	Cessna A152 Aerobat	A1520928	N761AW	29. 7.88	Modi Aviation Ltd	Sibson	27. 9.09E
G-BOYC	Robinson R22 Beta	0837		22. 8.88	M D Thorpe t/a Yorkshire Helicopters		
						Coney Park, Leeds	9. 6.09E
G-BOYF	Sikorsky S-76B	760343		15. 9.88	Darley Stud Management Company Ltd *(Operated Air Hanson)*		
						Cambridge	24.11.09E
G-BOYH	Piper PA-28-151 Cherokee Warrior		N8795F	8. 8.88	D Wood-Jenkins, Skytime Flight Training Ltd and D A Keen		
	(Converted to PA-28-161 model)	28-7715290				Shobdon	27. 3.09E
G-BOYI	Piper PA-28-161 Cherokee Warrior II		N9032K	8. 8.88	R E Grimster and D R L Hughes tr G-BOYI Group		
		28-7816183				Sleap	11. 6.09E
G-BOYL	Cessna 152 II	15284379	N6232L	11. 8.88	Redhill Air Services Ltd *(Operated Flying Time)*		
						Shoreham	11. 3.09E
G-BOYM	Cameron O-84 Balloon (Hot Air)	1796		25. 8.88	M P Ryan *"Frontline"*	Newbury	21. 9.09E
G-BOYO	Cameron V-20 Balloon (Hot Air)	1843		27. 9.88	J M Willard	Burgess Hill	
G-BOYP	Cessna 172N Skyhawk II	17270349	N738YU	22. 8.88	I D and D Brierley	North Weald	19. 5.09E
G-BOYR	Reims Cessna F337G Super Skymaster		RA-04147	9. 9.88	Tri-Star Farms Ltd	Andreas, Isle of Man	30. 4.09E
	(Wichita c/n 33701589)	F33700070	G-BOYR, PH-RPE				
G-BOYS	Cameron N-77 Balloon (Hot Air)	1759		16. 6.88	Julie King	Chippenham	8. 3.05T
G-BOYU	Cessna A150L Aerobat	A1500497	N8121L	31. 8.88	Upperstack Ltd	Barton	14.11.07E
G-BOYV	Piper PA-28R-201T Turbo Arrow III		N1143H	1. 9.88	S and S Aviation Ltd	(Sheffield)	1. 8.09E
		28R-7703014					
G-BOYX	Robinson R22 Beta	0862	N90813	25. 8.88	R Towle	(Barrasford, Hexham)	28. 9.91T
	(Damaged Teesside 18. 7.90)						
G-BOZI	Piper PA-28-161 Warrior II	28-8116120	(G-BOSZ)	14. 7.88	Aerolease Ltd	Conington	20.12.09E
			N8318A				
G-BOZN	Cameron N-77 Balloon (Hot Air)	1807		1. 9.88	Calarel Developments Ltd *"Calarel Developments"*		
						Chipping Campden	10. 5.06A
G-BOZO	Gulfstream AA-5B Tiger	AA5B-1282	N4536Q	12. 8.88	Caslon Ltd	Biggin Hill	27. 2.09E
G-BOZR	Cessna 152 II	15284614	N6083M	7. 9.88	Gem Rewinds Ltd	Coventry	5. 5.09E
G-BOZS	Pitts S-1C	221-H	N10EZ	31. 8.88	T A S Rayner	(Edinburgh)	2. 9.09P
	(Built W A Orr) (Lycoming O-320-A2B)						
G-BOZU	Aero Dynamics Sparrow Hawk Mk II			12.12.88	R V Phillimore	(Bexhill-on-Sea)	
	(Built R V Phillimore)	PFA 184-11371					
G-BOZV	Robin DR.340 Major	416	F-BRTS	9. 8.88	C J Turner and S D Kent Garston Farm, Marshfield		30.11.09E
G-BOZW	Bensen B 8MR	PFA G/01-1096		1. 9.88	M E Wills	Lytchett Matravers	20. 7.09P
	(Built M E Wills) (Rotax 532)						
G-BOZY	Cameron RTW-120 Balloon (Hot Air)	1770		1. 9.88	Magical Adventures Ltd		
						West Bloomfield, Michigan, US	21. 4.97A
G-BOZZ	Gulfstream AA-5B Tiger	AA5B-1155	N4530N	22. 8.88	A W Matthews tr Solent Tiger Group	Popham	10. 3.09E

G-BPAA - G-BPZZ

Reg	Type	C/n	Prev id	Date	Owner/Operator	Location	Date
G-BPAA	Acro Advanced	AA-001		26. 8.88	B O and F A Smith	Yearby	7. 8.08P
	(Built B O Smith - pr.no.PFA 200-11528) (Volkswagen Acro 2100)						
G-BPAB	Cessna 150M Commuter	15077244	N63335	21. 9.88	M J Diggins	Rayne Hall Farm, Braintree	18. 9.09E
G-BPAF	Piper PA-28-161 Cherokee Warrior II		N3199Q	6. 9.88	S T and T W Gilbert	RAF Brize Norton	23. 9.09E
		28-7716142					
G-BPAJ	de Havilland DH.82A Tiger Moth	83472	G-AOIX	5.11.80	P A Jackson	Raby's Farm, Great Stukeley	11. 7.09S
	(Built Morris Motors Ltd)		T7084		*(May be composite rebuild from original G-AMNN qv)*		
G-BPAL	de Havilland DHC-1 Chipmunk 22	C1/0437	G-BCYE	29.10.86	K F and Phyllis Tomsett *(As "WG350" in RAF c/s)*		
			WG350			(Carvoeiro, Portigal)	12. 9.09
G-BPAW	Cessna 150M Commuter	15077923	N8348U	5. 9.88	P D Sims tr G-BPAW Group		
						Lower Wasing Farm, Brimpton	18.11.09E
G-BPAX	Cessna 150M Commuter	15077401	N63571	5. 9.88	M K Casely and S Boyes tr The Dirty Dozen		
						Shoreham	23. 9.09E
G-BPAY	Piper PA-28-181 Archer II	28-8090191	N3568X	12. 9.98	D A C Smith	Conington	13. 5.07T
G-BPBB	Evans VP-2	PFA 063-11261		2. 9.88	A Bleese	Hill Farm, Nayland	9. 6.97P
	(Built J S Penny)				*(Noted 5.03)*		
G-BPBJ	Cessna 152 II	15283639	N4793B		W Shaw and P G Haines		
						Whaley Farm, New York, Lincoln	4. 5.09E
G-BPBK	Cessna 152 II	15283417	N49095	9. 9.88	Atlantic Flight Training Ltd	Coventry	26. 8.09E
G-BPBM	Piper PA-28-161 Warrior II	28-7916272	N3050N	12. 9.88	Redhill Air Services Ltd	Rochester	21. 2.10E
G-BPBO	Piper PA-28RT-201T Turbo Arrow IV		N8431H	28. 9.88	Tile Holdings Ltd	Sandtoft	29. 7.09E
		28R-8131195					

G-BPBP	Brügger MB.2 Colibri Mk.II	PFA 043-10246		6. 2.78	D A Preston	(Ulverston)	16. 9.08P
	(Built B Perkins) (Volkswagen 1600)						
G-BPBV	Cameron V-77 Balloon (Hot Air)	1821		21. 9.88	S J Farrant *"Sugar Plumb"*	Hydestile, Godalming	10. 6.05A
					(Noted 8.06)		
G-BPBW	Cameron O-105 Balloon (Hot Air)	1841		14.10.88	R J Mansfield *"October Gold"*		
						Bowness-on-Windermere	22. 2.09E
G-BPBY	Cameron V-77 Balloon (Hot Air)	1818	(G-BPCS)	9.12.88	C Kunert	Wokingham	1. 7.09E
G-BPCA	Pilatus Britten-Norman BN-2B-26 Islander		G-BLNX	28. 1.88	Loganair Ltd *(Highland Park titles)*	Kirkwall	16. 2.09E
		2198					
G-BPCF	Piper J-3C-65 Cub	4532	N140DC	12. 5.89	J S Evans	Wycombe Air Park	1. 9.09P
	(Continental O-200-A)		N28033, NC28033		*(Lippert Reed clipped-wing conversion - s/n SA811SW)*		
G-BPCG	Colt AS-80 Mk.II Airship (Hot Air)	1300		14.10.88	N Charbonnier *"Greensport"* and *"Napapijri"*		
						Aosta, Italy	10.10.96A
G-BPCI	Cessna R172K Hawk XP	R1722360	N9976V	3. 1.89	N A Bairsto	Great Oakley	11. 4.09E
G-BPCK	Piper PA-28-161 Warrior II	28-8016279	N8529N	26. 9.88	Compton Abbas Airfield Ltd	Compton Abbas	22.10.09E
			C-GMEI, N9519N				
G-BPCL	Scottish Aviation Bulldog Series 120/128		HKG-6	20. 9.88	Isohigh Ltd tr 121 Group	North Weald	6. 9.10S
		BH120/393	G-31-19		*(As "HKG-6" in Royal Hong Kong AAF c/s)*		
G-BPCM	RotorWay Executive	E 3293	N979WP	21. 9.88	D Rigby	(Barnsley)	25.11.91P
	(Built W Petrie) (RotorWay RW152)						
G-BPCR	Mooney M 20K Mooney 231	25-0532	N98433	23. 9.88	T and R Harris *"Over The Moony"*	Biggin Hill	23.10.09E
G-BPCV	Montgomerie-Bensen B 8MR	PFA G/01-1088		11.10.88	M A Hayward	(Liskeard)	25. 7.91P
	(Built J Fisher) (Rotax 532)						
G-BPCX	Piper PA-28-236 Dakota	28-8211004	N8441S	25.10.88	Blue Yonder Aviation Ltd	Earls Colne	17. 9.08E
G-BPDG	Cameron V-77 Balloon (Hot Air)	1839		21.10.88	F R Battersby *"Pretty Damn Good"*		
						Worsley, Manchester	5.11.09E
G-BPDJ	Chris Tena Mini Coupe	275	N13877	4.10.88	J J Morrissey	(Teddington)	
	(Volkswagen 1835)				*(Wings only noted Durham Tees Valley 4.05)*		
G-BPDM	CASA 1-131E Jungmann	2058	Spanish AF	24.10.88	J D Haslam *(As "E3B-369:781-32" in Spanish AF c/s)*		
			E3B-369			(Northallerton)	22. 6.96P
G-BPDT	Piper PA-28-161 Warrior II	28-8416004	N4317Z	22.12.88	Channel Islands Aero Club (Jersey) Ltd	Jersey	19.12.09E
G-BPDV	Pitts S-1S	27P	N330VE	15. 9.88	J Vize	Leicester	13. 1.09P
	(Built C H Pitts)						
G-BPEC	Boeing 757-236	24882		6.11.90	British Airways PLC	London Heathrow	12.11.09E
G-BPED	Boeing 757-236	25059		30. 4.91	British Airways PLC	London Heathrow	29. 4.09E
G-BPEE	Boeing 757-236	25060		3. 5.91	British Airways PLC	London Heathrow	2. 5.09E
G-BPEI	Boeing 757-236	25806	(G-BMRK)	9. 3.94	British Airways PLC	London Heathrow	8.12.09E
G-BPEJ	Boeing 757-236	25807	(G-BMRL)	22. 4.94	British Airways PLC *(Operated Open Skies 6.08)*		
					"Penny"	Paris-Orly, France	24. 4.09E
G-BPEK	Boeing 757-236	25808	(G-BMRM)	17. 3.95	British Airways PLC *(Operated Open Skies 7.08)*		
						Paris-Orly, France	16. 3.09E
G-BPEM	Cessna 150K	15071707	N6207G	24.10.88	C G Rice	Henstridge	24. 2.09E
G-BPEO	Cessna 152 II	15283775	C-GQVO	10.10.88	JHP Aviation Ltd	Coventry	17. 7.09E
			(N5147B)				
G-BPES	Piper PA-38-112 Tomahawk II	38-81A0064	N25728	2.11.88	The Sherwood Flying Club Ltd		
						Nottingham City-Tollerton	30. 1.10E
G-BPEZ	Colt 77A Balloon (Hot Air)	1324		14.10.88	J W Adkins *"T&C Demo"*	Market Harborough	13. 7.09E
G-BPFB	Colt 77A Balloon (Hot Air)	1334		26.10.88	S Ingram	Oldham	1. 7.09E
G-BPFC	Mooney M 20C Mark 21	20-1243	N3606H	21.10.88	D P Wring	Dunkeswell	14. 5.09E
G-BPFD	Jodel D 112	312	F-PHJT	3.11.88	B W Webb tr Kitchener Flying Group		
	(Built Aero Club de L`Orne)					Clipgate Farm, Denton	26. 4.09P
G-BPFF	Cameron DP-70 Airship (Hot Air)	1831		24.10.88	John Aimo Balloons SAS	Mondovi, Italy	22. 5.09E
G-BPFH	Piper PA-28-161 Warrior II	28-8116201	N83723	3.11.88	M H Kleiser *(Operated Edinburgh Flying Club)*		
						Edinburgh	11. 3.09E
G-BPFI	Piper PA-28-181 Archer II	28-8090113	N8103G	5. 1.89	F Teagle	Bodmin	18. 7.09E
G-BPFL	Davis DA-2A	051	N72RJ	27.10.88	B W Griffiths	Coventry	11. 1.09P
	(Built A Tribling) (Continental O-200-A)						
G-BPFM	Aeronca 7AC Champion	7AC-4751	N1193E	13.10.88	D Boyce	Bodmin	7. 8.08P
			NC1193E				
G-BPFZ	Cessna 152 II	15285741	N94594	27.10.88	Devon and Somerset Flight Training Ltd		
						Dunkeswell	21. 2.09E
G-BPGC	Speich Air Command Gyroplane	0440		11.10.88	A G W Davis	Little Rissington	30.10.09P
	(Built G A Speich - pr.no.PFA G/04-1108 as modified Air Command 532 Elite)						
G-BPGD	Cameron V-65 Balloon (Hot Air)	2000		9. 9.88	Gone With The Wind Ltd *"Silver Lining"*		
	(Rebuilt with new envelope c/n 4969 c 8.01)					Schwieberdingen, Germany	28. 1.10E
G-BPGE	Cessna U206C Super Skywagon	U2061013	N29017	7.11.88	K Brady tr The Scottish Parachute Club		
						Strathallan	6. 4.09E
G-BPGF	Thunder Ax7-77 Balloon (Hot Air)	1355		22.11.88	M Schiavo *"Dovetail"*	Manchester	25. 8.95A
G-BPGH	EAA Acrosport II	422	N12JE	14.11.88	M F Humphries	Exeter	22.10.09P
	(Built J Ellenbaas) (Continental IO-346)						
G-BPGK	Aeronca 7AC Champion	7AC-7187	N4409E	7. 2.89	D A Crompton and G C Holmes		
	(Continental A65)					Yeatsall Farm, Abbots Bromley	15. 6.09P
G-BPGT	Colt AS-80 Mk.II Airship (Hot Air)	1248	(I -. . . .)	14.11.88	P Porati	Milan, Italy	20. 7.00A
			G-BPGT				
G-BPGU	Piper PA-28-181 Archer II	28-8490025	N4330B	26.10.88	G Underwood	Nottingham City-Tollerton	1. 4.09E
G-BPGV	Robinson R22 Beta	0887		3.11.88	G Gazza	(Monte Carlo, Monaco)	24. 5.06T
G-BPGZ	Cessna 150G	15064912	N3612J	14.11.88	J B Scott	Blackpool	20. 5.09E
G-BPHD	Cameron N-42 Balloon (Hot Air)	1863		21. 2.89	P J Marshall and M A Clarke *"Ellen Gee II"*	Ruislip	9. 6.02A
G-BPHG	Robin DR.400-180 Régent	1887		29.11.88	A B Brock	Sywell	7. 7.09E
G-BPHH	Cameron V-77 Balloon (Hot Air)	1840		2.12.88	C D Aindow *"Office Angels"*	Tonbridge	5. 9.09E
G-BPHI	Piper PA-38-112 Tomahawk	38-79A0002	N2535T	22.11.88	J S Develin and Z Islam	Shoreham	24.11.09E
G-BPHJ	Cameron V-77 Balloon (Hot Air)	1881		23.11.88	C W Brown *"Twiggy"*	Nottingham	14. 4.06A
G-BPHK	Whittaker MW7	PFA 171-11389		24.11.88	J S Shufflebottom	Over Farm, Gloucester	23. 6.04P
	(Built J G Beesley)						

G-BPHL	Piper PA-28-161 Warrior II	28-7916315	N555PY	2.12.88	J D Swales *(Noted 3.05)*	Bagby	19. 7.04T
			N2247U				
G-BPHO	Taylorcraft BC-12D	8497	N96197	10. 1.89	B J Swanton *"Spirit of Missouri" (Noted 7.07)*		
			NC96197			Ballymageough, Kilkeel, County Down	31. 5.07P
G-BPHP	Taylorcraft BC-12-65	2799	N33948	12.12.88	J S Jackson	Derby	2.11.99P
	(Continental A65)		NC33948				
G-BPHR	de Havilland DH.82A (Aust) Tiger Moth (mod)	N48DH		3. 1.89	N Parry tr A17-48 Group *(As "A17-48" in RAAF c/s)*		
	(Built de Havilland Aircraft Pty Ltd)	45	VH-BLX, A17-48			Lotmead Farm, Wanborough	15. 5.09
G-BPHT	Cessna 152 II	15282401	N961LP	5.12.88	I A Anderson	Norwich	22. 8.09E
G-BPHU	Thunder Ax7-77 Balloon (Hot Air)	1365		19.12.88	R P Waite	St Helens	15. 5.09E
G-BPHW	Cessna 140	11035	N76595	13. 1.89	L J A Bell	White Waltham	18. 6.08E
	(Continental C85)		NC76595				
G-BPHX	Cessna 140	12488	N2252N	2.12.88	M McChesney	(Enniskillen)	23. 5.93
	(Continental C85)		NC2252N				
G-BPHZ	Morane Saulnier MS.505 Criquet	53/7	F-BJQC	17. 4.89	Aero Vintage Ltd *(As "DM+BK" in I/JG54 Luftwaffe c/s)*		
			French Military			Audley End	29. 4.09P
G-BPIF	Bensen-Parsons Two-Place Gyroplane	UK-01		19.12.88	B J L P and W J A L de Saar *(Noted 8.06)*		
	(Built W Parsons) (Rotax 532)					Shipdham	28. 3.96P
G-BPII	Denney Kitfox Model 1	213		15.12.88	P Etherington tr G-BPII Group		
	(Built R Derbyshire - pr.no.PFA 172-11496) (IAME KFM 112)					North Moor, Scunthorpe	17. 9.08P
G-BPIJ	Brantly B 2B	465	N2293U	23. 3.89	I Davies tr Seething Brantly Group	Seething	3. 4.09E
G-BPIK	Piper PA-38-112 Tomahawk II	38-82A0028	N3947M	2.12.88	Fly Me Ltd	Gwernaffield, Mold	2. 3.09E
			ZP-EAP, N91423				
G-BPIL	Cessna 310B	35620	N620GS	16.11.89	A L Brown *"Fast Lady" (On slow rebuild 10.05)*		
			OO-SEF, N5420A			Bourn	28. 4.00T
G-BPIN	Glaser-Dirks DG-400	4-242		14.12.88	C E Griffiths and J N Stevenson	Lasham	11. 4.10E
G-BPIP	Slingsby T.31 Motor Cadet III	PFA 042-10771		14.11.88	V K Meers	Pendeford, Wolverhampton	27. 9.96P
	(Re-built J H Beard) (Volkswagen 1600)						
G-BPIR	Scheibe SF25E Super Falke	4332	N25SF	15.12.88	A P Askwith	Rhosgoch	17. 4.09E
	(Limbach SL1700)		(D-KDFX)				
G-BPIT	Robinson R22 Beta	0907	N80011	22.12.88	NA Air Ltd	Blacklaw Farm, Aberbothrie	16.10.09E
G-BPIU	Piper PA-28-161 Warrior II	28-7916303	N3028T	28.12.88	T S Rafter tr Golf India Uniform Group	Fairoaks	14. 4.09E
G-BPIV	Bristol 149 Blenheim IV	?	"Z5722"	152.89	Blenheim (Duxford) Ltd *(On rebuild 12.08)* Duxford		19. 6.04P
	(Built Fairchild Aircraft Ltd as Bollingbroke IVT)		RCAF 10201		*(As "R3821:UX-N"in RAF c/s) "Spirit of Britain First"*		
G-BPIZ	Gulfstream AA-5B Tiger	AA5B-1154	N4530L	14. 2.89	N R F McNally	Shoreham	21. 8.09E
G-BPJB	Schweizer 269C *(Schweizer 300)*	S 1331	N75065	7.11.88	Elborne Holdings Ltd	Cascais, Portugal	19 .3.09E
G-BPJD	SOCATA Rallye 110ST	3253	OY-CAV	22.12.88	L P Claydon	(Gedding, Bury St Edmunds)	30. 9.09E
G-BPJE	Cameron A-105 Balloon (Hot Air)	1864		8.11.88	A Parsons tr Loughborough Students Hot Air Balloon Club		
						Loughborough	11. 5.09E
G-BPJG	Piper PA-18-150 Super Cub	18-8350	SE-EZG	4. 1.89	M W Stein	Oaksey Park	12. 9.10
			N4172Z				
G-BPJH	Piper PA-18 Super Cub 95	18-1980	EI-59	24. 5.83	P J Heron	Blackhill, Draperstown	18. 8.09P
	(L-18C-PI)		I-EICA, MM52-2380, 52-2380				
G-BPJO	Piper PA-28-161 Cadet	2841014	N9153Z	15.12.88	Plane Talking Ltd	Elstree	3. 4.09E
G-BPJP	Piper PA-28-161 Cadet	2841015	N9154K	22.12.88	S J Skilton t/a Aviation Rentals *(Operated Solent Flight)*		
	(Thielert TAE 125)					Bournemouth	28. 6.09E
G-BPJR	Piper PA-28-161 Cadet	2841024	N9154X	17. 1.89	Plane Talking Ltd	Denham	22.12.09E
G-BPJS	Piper PA-28-161 Cadet	2841025	EC-IBG	12. 1.89	Abraxas Aviation Ltd	Denham	18.12.09E
			G-BPJS, N9154Z				
G-BPJU	Piper PA-28-161 Cadet	2841032	N9156Z	11. 1.89	S J Skilton t/a Aviation Rentals	Lee-on-Solent	15. 4.09E
					(Operated Bookajet Operations Ltd)		
G-BPJV	Taylorcraft F-21	F-1005	N2004L	12. 1.89	P Glennon tr TC Flying Group	Enstone	9. 9.05P
			(Crashed in field near Corn Dean Lane, Winchcombe 28.11.05 and substantially damaged)				
G-BPJW	Cessna A150K Aerobat	A1500127	C-FAJX	4. 1.89	G Duck	Bagby	20.12.10E
			CF-AJX, N8427M				
G-BPKF	Grob G115	8075		3. 1.89	Swiftair Maintenance Ltd	Leicester	27. 1.10E
G-BPKK	Denney Kitfox Model 1	264		19.12.88	D Moffat	Lochview House, Limerigg	11.10.02P
	(Built R W Holmes - pr.no.PFA 172-11411) (Originally laid down as Model 2) (Rotax 532)						
G-BPKM	Piper PA-28-161 Warrior II	28-7916341	PH-CKO	6. 1.89	R Cass	Durham Tees Valley	17. 8.09E
			N2140X, N9630N				
G-BPKO	Cessna 140	8936	N89891	12. 1.89	M G Rummey	(Binderton, West Sussex)	18. 12.11
			NC89891				
G-BPKR	Piper PA-28-151 Cherokee Warrior		N4341X	13. 3.89	Aeros Leasing Ltd	Gloucestershire	4. 6.09E
		28-7515446					
G-BPLH	CEA Jodel DR.1051 Sicile	401	F-BLAE	27. 2.89	C K Farley	Wolverhampton	29. 1.08E
	(Potez 4E20A)						
G-BPLM	AIA Stampe SV-4C	1004	F-BHET	8. 2.89	C J Jesson	Phoenix Farm, Lower Upham	30. 1.09S
	(Officially regd as built by SNCAN)		French Army, F-BDKC				
G-BPLV	Cameron V-77 Balloon (Hot Air)	1822		23. 1.89	MC VH SA	Brussels, Belgium	22. 9.08A
	(Rebuilt1998)						
G-BPLY	Pitts S-2B	5149		25. 1.89	P A Greenhalgh	Spilstead Farm, Sedlescombe	26. 8.09E
	(Built Christen Industries Inc) (Lycoming AEIO-540)						
G-BPLZ	Hughes 369HS *(Hughes 500)*	91-0342S	N126CM	15. 2.89	M A and R J Fawcett	(Leeds)	22.11.08E
G-BPMB	Maule M-5-235C Lunar Rocket	7284C	N5635T	13. 8.79	J P Morley ta Maule Flying Group	Crosland Moor	1. 6.09E
G-BPME	Cessna 152 II	15285585	N94021	24. 1.89	A Jahanfar *(Operated FlightCentre)*		
						Southend	24. 3.09T
G-BPMF	Piper PA-28-151 Cherokee Warrior (mod)		C-GOXL	2. 2.89	A Hill and P A Lewis tr Mike Foxtrot Group		
	(Type amended 1. 5.08)	28-7515050				(Harrogate and Barrow-in-Furness)	13. 5.09E
G-BPML	Cessna 172M Skyhawk II	17267102	N1435U	17.11.89	N A Bilton	Priory Farm, Tibenham	1. 1.10E
G-BPMM	Champion 7ECA Citabria	498	N5132T	22. 3.89	H J Taggart	(Enfield, Ireland)	25. 2.99P
G-BPMR	Piper PA-28-161 Warrior II	28-8416119	N4373S	25. 1.89	Aeros Holdings Ltd	Gloucestershire	7. 8.09E
			N9620N				
G-BPMU	Nord 3202B	70	(G-BIZJ)	26. 1.89	A I Milne *"AIX" (Stored owner's workshop 2007)*		
			N22546, French Army			(Swanton Morley)	19.10.90P

Reg	Type	C/n	Prev ID	Date	Owner/Operator	Location	Date
G-BPMW	QAC Quickie Q.2 *(Built R Davidson-Outbridge)* (Revmaster R2100DQ)	PFA 094A-10790	G-OICI G-OGKN	13. 3.89	P M Wright *(Damaged near Basingstoke 16. 2.91: on repair 9.00)*	(Waldringfield, Woodbridge)	17. 8.91P
G-BPMX	ARV Aviation ARV-1 Super 2 *(Built B Houghton - pr.no.PFA 152-11128)*	K 005		30. 1.89	R A Collins	Kemble	22. 9.06P
G-BPNA	Cessna 150L	15073042	N1742Q	10. 2.89	M P Whitley and G W Todd tr Wolds Flyers Syndicate	Eddsfield, Octon Lodge Farm, Thwing	17. 6.09E
G-BPNI	Robinson R22 Beta	0948		6. 2.89	Heliflight (UK) Ltd	Gloucestershire	13. 4.09E
G-BPNJ	Hawker Siddeley HS.748 Series 2A/263	1680	ZS-ODJ F-GHKA, G-BPNJ, 9J-ABW, G-11-4	3. 2.89	PTB (Emerald) Proprietary.Ltd *(On fire dump as "ZS-ODJ" 6.06)*	Blackpool	
G-BPNN	Montgomerie-Bensen B 8MR *(Built M E Vahdat-Hagh)*	MV-003		3. 2.89	M E Vahdat-Hagh	(Uxbridge)	
G-BPNO	Moravan Zlin Z-526 Trener Master	930	F-BPNO	18. 2.86	J A S Baldry and S T Logan	RAF Cranwell	21. 6.08E
G-BPNT	British Aerospace BAe 146 Series 300QT	E3126		4. 1.89	BAe Systems	Bucharest	31. 5.08E
G-BPNU	Thunder Ax7-77 Balloon (Hot Air)	1011		9. 2.89	M J Barnes *"Firefly"*	Ivybridge	16. 8.02T
G-BPOB	Sopwith Camel F 1 replica *(Built Tallmantz Aviation Inc)* (Warner Scarab 165)	TM-10	N8997	14. 3.89	Bianchi Aviation Film Services Ltd *(As "B2458:R" in RFC c/s)*	Wycombe Air Park	24. 7.05P
G-BPOM	Piper PA-28-161 Warrior II	28-8416118	N4373Q N9619N	15. 2.89	C Dale tr POM Flying Group *(Operated Soloflight)*	Humberside	25. 4.09E
G-BPON	Piper PA-34-200T Seneca II	34-7570040	N675ES N32644	13. 2.89	Aeros Leasing Ltd	Gloucestershire	13. 8.09E
G-BPOO	Montgomerie-Bensen B 8MR *(Built M E Vahdat-Hagh - pr.no.PFA G/01A-1109)*	MV-002		3. 2.89	M E Vahdat-Hagh *(Believed not constructed)*	(Uxbridge)	
G-BPOS	Cessna 150M	15075905	N66187	21. 2.89	Brooke Park Ltd	Durham Tees Valley	17. 3.09E
G-BPOT	Piper PA-28-181 Cherokee Archer II	28-7790267	N8807F	7. 2.89	Icarus Flyers Ltd	Rochester	21. 1.10E
G-BPOU	Luscombe 8A Silvaire (Continental A65)	4159	N1432K NC1432K	14. 2.89	J L Grayer	(Danehill, Haywards Heath)	4.11.02P
G-BPPA	Cameron O-65 Balloon (Hot Air)	1930		15. 2.89	Rix Petroleum Ltd *"Rix Petroleum"*	Hull	9. 2.09E
G-BPPE	Piper PA-38-112 Tomahawk	38-79A0189	N2445C	15. 2.89	First Air Ltd *(Rebuilt with parts of G-BNPL to provide a single flyer)*	Haverfordwest	30. 4.09E
G-BPPF	Piper PA-38-112 Tomahawk	38-79A0578	N2329K	15. 2.89	D J Bellamy tr Bristol Strut Flying Group	Bristol	31. 1.09E
G-BPPK	Piper PA-28-151 Cherokee Warrior	28-7615054	N7592C	10. 3.89	Idfit Ltd	Biggin Hill	15. 7.09E
G-BPPO	Luscombe 8A Silvaire (Continental A65)	2541	N3519M N71114, NC71114	15. 2.89	M G Rummey	Goodwood	18. 9.09P
G-BPPP	Cameron V-77 Balloon (Hot Air)	1700		29. 2.88	P F Smart tr The Sarnia Balloon Group *"Thruppence"* *(Inflated 4.06)*	Oakley, Basingstoke	28. 6.97A
G-BPPS	Mudry CAP.21	09	F-GDTD	3. 5.85	L van Vuuren	Durham Tees Valley	27. 9.07E
G-BPPU	Air Command 532 Elite *(Built J Hough - pr.no.PFA G/04-1120)*	0438		22. 2.89	J Hough	Alresford	18.10.91P
G-BPPY	Hughes 269B *(Hughes 300)*	20-0448	N9554F	10. 3.89	M D Lenney	(Patrington, Hull)	11. 5.08E
G-BPPZ	Taylorcraft BC-12D (Continental C85)	7988	N28286 NC28286	22. 3.89	I R Henderson	Mosside Farm, Carluke	31. 5.09P
G-BPRA	Aeronca 11AC Chief	11AC-1344	N9702E NC9702E	22. 3.89	P L Clements	Beeches Farm, South Scarle	13. 5.09P
G-BPRC	Cameron Elephant 77 SS Balloon (Hot Air)	1871		21. 2.89	A Schneider *"Elefant Benjamin"*	Borken, Germany	27. 3.08A
G-BPRD	Pitts S-1C *(Built P C Serkland)*	ZZ.1	N10ZZ	21. 2.89	P Rhodes and R Trickey tr Parrot Aerobatic Group	Pittrichie Farm, Whiterashes	17. 7.06P
G-BPRI	Aérospatiale AS.355F1 Ecureuil 2	5181	G-TVPA G-BPRI, N364E	22. 2.89	MW Helicopters Ltd	Stapleford	14. 11.09E
G-BPRJ	Aérospatiale AS.355F1 Ecureuil 2	5201	N368E	22. 2.89	PLM Dollar Group Ltd	Cumbernauld	6.12.09E
G-BPRL	Aérospatiale AS.355F1 Ecureuil 2	5154	N362E	22. 2.89	MW Helicopters Ltd	Stapleford	26.10.09E
G-BPRM	Reims Cessna F172L	F17200825	G-AZKG	20. 4.88	BJ Aviation Ltd	Welshpool	30. 1.09E
G-BPRN	Piper PA-28-161 Warrior II	28-8116109	N83112	6. 3.89	Air Navigation and Trading Company Ltd	Blackpool	2. 6.08E
G-BPRR	Rand Robinson KR-2 *(Built M W Albery)*	PFA 129-11105		1. 3.89	P E Taylor	(Ferndown)	
G-BPRX	Aeronca 11AC Chief (Continental A75)	11AC-94	N86288 NC86288	3. 3.89	J E S Turner	(Thatcham)	23. 8.99P
G-BPRY	Piper PA-28-161 Warrior II	28-8416120	N4373Y N9621N	2. 3.89	R C White tr White Wings Aviation *"17"*	Nottingham-East Midlands	30. 6.09E
G-BPSH	Cameron V-77 Balloon (Hot Air)	1837		21. 2.89	P G Hossack *"Coconut Ice"*	Pewsey	5. 4.97T
G-BPSJ	Thunder Ax6-56 Balloon (Hot Air)	1479		13. 3.89	V Hyland	(Turnditch, Derby)	15. 5.09E
G-BPSK	Montgomerie-Bensen B 8M *(Built P Harrison)* (Rotax 532)	PFA G/01-1100		15. 3.89	P T Ambrozik	(Great Orton)	25.11.99P
G-BPSL	Cessna 177 Cardinal	17701138		3. 3.89	K S Herbert	Elstree	9.12.08E
G-BPSO	Cameron N-90 Balloon (Hot Air)	1959		10. 3.89	J Oberprieler	Mauern, Germany	21. 9.09E
G-BPSR	Cameron V-77 Balloon (Hot Air)	1962		10. 3.89	K J A Maxwell *"Norma Jean" (Noted 5.07)*	Haywards Heath	11. 5.05T
G-BPSS	Cameron A-120 Balloon (Hot Air)	1947		27. 2.89	Anglian Countryside Balloons Ltd	Burnham-on-Crouch	17. 3.06E
G-BPTA	Stinson 108-2 Voyager *(Built Consolidated Vultee Aircraft)*	108-3429	N429C NC429C	22. 3.89	M L Ryan	Garston Farm, Marshfield	29.10.10
G-BPTD	Cameron V-77 Balloon (Hot Air)	2001		14. 3.89	J Lippett *"Visions 2001"*	South Petherton	31. 5.04A
G-BPTE	Piper PA-28-181 Cherokee Archer II	28-7690178	N8553E	9. 3.89	J S Develin and Z Islam	Blackbushe	24.11.09E
G-BPTG	Rockwell Commander 112TC	13067	N4577W	31. 3.89	B Ogunyemi	Perth	9. 9.09E
G-BPTI	SOCATA TB-20 Trinidad	414	N41BM	21. 4.89	N Davis	Blackbushe	3. 7.09E
G-BPTL	Cessna 172N Skyhawk II	17268652	N733YJ	22. 3.89	L Stanton tr Tin Lizzie Group	Little Snoring	10. 8.09E
G-BPTS	CASA 1-131E Jungmann	?	Spanish AF E3B-153 "781-75"	23. 5.89	Aerobatic Displays Ltd *(Operated The Old Flying Machine Co)* *(As "E3B-153:781-75" in Spanish AF c/s)*	Duxford	16. 3.07P

Reg	Type	C/n	Prev id	Date	Owner/Operator	Location	Expiry
G-BPTU	Cessna 152 II	15282955	N45946	22. 3.89	A M Alam (Stored dismantled 1.09)	North Weald	21.10.06T
G-BPTV	Bensen B 8	PFA G/01-1058		30. 3.89	C Munro	(Trawden, Colne)	
	(Built L Chiappi)						
G-BPTX	Cameron O-120 Balloon (Hot Air)	1972		29. 3.89	S J Colin t/a Skybus Ballooning	Cranbrook	2. 6.05T
G-BPTZ	Robinson R22 Beta	0958		22. 3.89	Aero Maintenance Ltd	Gamston	3. 2.10E
G-BPUA	EAA Biplane Sport	xxxx	EI-BBF	30. 3.89	J F Heath and R Hatton	Kirkbride	5. 9.08P
	(Built B B Feeley - pr.no.SAAC-02) (Lycoming O-235)						
G-BPUB	Cameron V-31 Air Chair Balloon (Hot Air)	1114		15. 3.89	M T Evans	Peasedown St John, Bath	3. 6.94A
G-BPUE	Air Command 532 Elite	0441		29. 3.89	J K Padden	(Longhirst, Morpeth)	11. 9.91P
	(Built R A Fazerkerley - pr.no.PFA G/04-1136)						
G-BPUF	Thunder Ax6-56Z Balloon (Hot Air)	270	(G-BHRL)	30. 4.80	R C and M A Trimble "Buf Puf"	Henley-on-Thames	10. 2.90A
G-BPUG	Air Command 532 Elite	0401		29. 3.89	T A Holmes	(Melrose Farm, Melbourne)	18. 4.91P
	(Built C Slater - pr.no.PFA G/04-1157)				(Possibly moved to Spain by 2000)		
G-BPUL	Piper PA-18A-150 Super Cub	18-2517	OO-LUL	12. 4.89	C D Duthy-James	Chauvigny, France	15. 7.11
	(L-18C-PI) (Frame no. may be in 18-25xx series)		PH-NEV				
G-BPUM	Cessna R182 Skylane RG II	R18200915	N738DZ	2. 5.89	R C Chapman	Marley Hall, Ledbury	30. 4.09E
G-BPUP	Whittaker MW7	PFA 171-11473		2. 8.89	J H Beard	(Buckfastleigh, Devon)	
	(Built J H Beard)						
G-BPUR	Piper J-3L-65 Cub	4708	N30228	14. 6.89	H A D Monro (As "VM286" in RAF c/s)		
	(Frame No.4764)		NC30228			(Westfield, Hastings)	
G-BPUS	Rans S-9 Chaos	PFA 196-11487		7. 4.89	C R Buckle	(Helpringham, Sleaford)	5. 1.10P
	(Built P M Shipman)						
G-BPUU	Cessna 140	13722	N4251N	31. 3.89	D R Speight	Full Sutton	16. 1.08E
			NC4251N				
G-BPUW	Colt 90A Balloon (Hot Air)	1436		12. 4.89	Gefa-Flug GmbH	Aachen, Germany	28.10.09E
G-BPVA	Cessna 172F Skyhawk	17252286	N8386U	13. 4.89	P Makin and J Knott tr South Lancashire Flyers Group		
						Barton	3. 9.09E
G-BPVC	Cameron V-77 Balloon (Hot Air)	1302		7. 4.89	B D Pettitt (Active 5.07)		
						Barningham, Bury St Edmunds	16. 8.05A
G-BPVE	Bleriot Type XI 1909 replica	1	N1197	20. 6.89	Bianchi Aviation Film Services Ltd (As "01")		
	(Built R D Henry, Texas, 1967)					Wycombe Air Park	29. 6.01P
G-BPVH	Piper Cub J-3 Prospector	178C	CF-DRY	7. 4.89	D E Cooper-Maguire (Incurred damage 17. 7.05)		
	(Continental C85)					Washington, Sussex	28.10.08P
G-BPVI	Piper PA-32R-301 Saratoga II SP	3213021	N91685	24. 4.89	M T Coppen	Goodwood	23. 8.09E
G-BPVK	Varga 2150A Kachina	VAC-85-77	N4626V	4. 5.89	H W Hall	Southend	12.12.07P
G-BPVM	Cameron V-77 Balloon (Hot Air)	1970		4. 4.89	J Dyer	Farnborough	22..4.05A
G-BPVN	Piper PA-32R-301T Turbo Saratoga		N8178W	14. 4.89	R Weston	North Weald	8.12.09E
		32R-8029073					
G-BPVO	Cassutt Racer IIIM	DG.1	N19DD	13. 4.89	R S Grace "VooDoo" and "2"	Bentwaters	26. 6.09P
	(Built D Giorgi)						
G-BPVW	CASA 1-131E Jungmann	2133	Spanish AF	17. 5.89	C and J-W Labeij	Goodwood	18. 6.09P
			E3B-559				
G-BPVY	Cessna 172D Skyhawk	17250568	N2968U	20. 4.89	S J Davies	Sandtoft	14. 7.09E
G-BPVZ	Luscombe 8E Silvaire Deluxe	5565	N2838K	9. 5.89	W E Gillham and P Ryman		
	(Continental C85)		NC2838K			Croft Farm, Croft-on-Tees	18. 8.09P
G-BPWB	Sikorsky S-61N Mk.II	61-822	EI-BHO	4. 5.89	Bristow Helicopters Ltd "Portland Castle" (stored)		
			G-BPWB, EI-BHO			Sumburgh	10. 7.09E
G-BPWC	Cameron V-77 Balloon (Hot Air)	1986		12. 4.89	H B Roberts "Hot Flush"	Failand, Bristol	10. 8.08T
G-BPWD	Cessna 120	10026	N72839	14. 4.89	L L Bee tr Peregrine Flying Group	Hucknall	19.10.09P
	(Continental O-240-E)		NC72839				
G-BPWE	Piper PA-28-161 Warrior II	28-8116143	N8330P	2. 5.89	RPR Associates Ltd	Haverfordwest	2. 7.09E
G-BPWG	Cessna 150M	15076707	(G-BPTK)	10. 4.89	W Spicer tr G-B Pilots Wilsford Group		
			N45029			Hanbeck Farm, Wilsford, Grantham	20. 9.09E
G-BPWI	Bell 206B-3 JetRanger III	3087	9M-BSR	14. 4.89	M J Coates t/a Warren Aviation	Goodwood	10.10.08E
			VH-HXZ, ZK-HXX, XC-PFH				
G-BPWK	Sportavia-Pützer RF5B Sperber	51036	N56JM	17. 4.89	S L Reed and J J Sorrell tr G-BPWK Flying Group		
			(D-KEAR)				Usk	3. 12.07P
G-BPWL	Piper PA-25-235 Pawnee	25-2304	N6690Z	14. 4.89	Tecair Aviation Ltd	Shipdham	17. 5.09E
			G-BPWL, N6690Z				
G-BPWM	Cessna 150L	15072820	N1520Q	17. 4.89	P D Button	Old Sarum	18.12.09E
G-BPWN	Cessna 150L	15074325	N19308	17. 4.89	A J and N J Bissex	Norton Malreward, Pensfold	12. 5.09E
G-BPWP	Rutan LongEz	PFA 074A-11132		17. 4.89	D A Field	Biggin Hill	29. 6.09P
	(Built J F O'Hara and A J Voyle) (Continental O-240)						
G-BPWR	Cessna R172K Hawk XP	R1722953	N758AZ	21. 4.89	J A, D T A, J and G M Rees t/a Messrs Rees		
						Haverfordwest	22.11.09E
G-BPWS	Cessna 172P Skyhawk II	17274306	N51387	21. 4.89	Chartstone Ltd	Redhill	1. 1.10E
G-BPXA	Piper PA-28-181 Archer II	28-8390064	N4305T	12. 5.89	D Howdle and D L Heighington tr Cherokee Flying Group		
						Netherthorpe	4. 6.09E
G-BPXB	Glaser-Dirks DG-400	4-248		2. 5.89	V A S de Brederode	(Queluz, Portugal)	25. 7.09E
G-BPXE	Enstrom 280C Shark	1089	N379KH	21. 4.89	A Healy		
			C-GMLH, N660H			Hampden Manor, Little Hampden, Great Missenden	25. 7.09E
G-BPXF	Cameron V-65 Balloon (Hot Air)	2003		21. 4.89	D Pascall (Noted 2003)	Croydon	
G-BPXG	Colt 42A Balloon (Hot Air)	1445		25. 4.89	Zebedee Balloon Service Ltd		
						Newtown, Hungerford	18. 9.09E
G-BPXH	Colt 17A Cloudhopper Balloon (Hot Air)	667	OO-BWG	21. 4.89	Sport Promotion SRL (Active 5.07)	Belbo, Italy	8. 9.00A
G-BPXJ	Piper PA-28RT-201 Turbo Arrow IV		N8061U	21. 4.89	J France and M Holubecki	Bagby	8.12.08E
		28R-8231023					
G-BPXX	Piper PA-34-200T Seneca II	34-7970069	N923SM	21. 4.89	Yorkshire Aviation Ltd	Sherburn-in-Elmet	10. 9.09E
			N9556N				
G-BPXY	Aeronca 11AC Chief	11AC-S-50	N3842E	10. 4.89	P L Turner	Morgansfield, Fishburn	6.11.09P
G-BPYJ	Wittman W.8 Tailwind	PFA 031-11028		12. 5.89	Y Tutt and J P Mills	Barton	8.12.09P
	(Built J Dixon) (Continental PC60)						
G-BPYL	Hughes 369D (Hughes 500)	100-0796D	N65AM	10. 5.89	Morcorp (BVI) Ltd	Fairoaks	2.12.09E
			G-BPYL, HB-XKT				

G-BPYN	Piper J-3C-65 Cub *(L-4H-PI)*	11422	F-BFYN	14. 3.79	D W Stubbs tr The Aquila Group	White Waltham	5. 9.09P
			HB-OFN, 43-30131				
G-BPYO	Piper PA-28-181 Archer II	2890114	SE-KIH	22. 5.89	Sherburn Aero Club Ltd	Sherburn-in-Elmet	25. 9.09E
G-BPYR	Piper PA-31 Navajo C	31-7812032	G-ECMA	15. 5.89	Synergy Aircraft Leasing Ltd	Fairoaks	13. 5.09E
			N27493				
G-BPYS	Cameron O-77 Balloon (Hot Air)	2008		9. 5.89	D J Goldsmith *"Aqualisa II"*	Edenbridge	3. 1.10E
G-BPYT	Cameron V-77 Balloon (Hot Air)	1984		9. 5.89	M H Redman	Stalbridge, Sturminster Newton	
G-BPYV	Cameron V-77 Balloon (Hot Air)	1992		17. 5.89	R J Shortall *(Spa Vehicle Electrics titles)*		
						Peasedown St John, Bath	9. 4.09E
G-BPYZ	Thunder Ax7-77 Balloon (Hot Air)	1521		11. 5.89	J E Bayly *"Axis" (Stolen Crewkerne, Somerset 23.10.97)*		
						(Clutton, Bristol)	7. 7.96A
G-BPZA	Luscombe 8A Silvaire	4326	N1599K	18. 4.89	M J Wright	St Junien, Haute-Vienne, France	2.10.08P
	(Continental A65)		NC1599K				
G-BPZB	Cessna 120	8898	N89853	25. 5.89	J F Corkin tr Cessna 120 Group	White Waltham	14. 9.09P
	(Continental C90)		NC89853				
G-BPZC	Luscombe 8A Silvaire	4322	N1595K	6. 6.89	C C and J M Lovell	(Ropley, Alresford)	5. 7.90P
	(Continental A65)		NC1595K		*(Damaged by gales Cranfield 25.1.90: used for spares 10.96)*		
G-BPZD	SNCAN NC.858S	97	F-BEZD	26. 1.79	G Richards tr Zula Delta Syndicate	Headcorn	26. 6.07P
	(Continental C90) *(Built as NC.854S with Continental C65)*						
	(Right hand main landing gear collapsed due to heavy landing London City 1.7.06 with substantial damage)						
G-BPZE	Luscombe 8E Silvaire Deluxe	3904	N1177K	6. 6.89	A V Harmer	(Hardwick)	2. 5.08P
	(Continental C85)		NC1177K		*(Failed to get airborne Hardwick 8. 7.07, struck crops and overturned)*		
G-BPZK	Cameron O-120 Balloon (Hot Air)	1982		7. 4.89	D L Smith *"Hot Stuff"*	Newbury	12. 5.97T
G-BPZM	Piper PA-28RT-201 Arrow IV	28R-7918238	G-ROYW	12. 5.89	Airways Flight Training (Exeter) Ltd	Exeter	27.10.09E
			G-CRTI, SE-ICY				
G-BPZP	Robin DR.400-180R Remorqueur	1471	D-EFZP	4. 5.89	S G Jones	Membury	23. 5.07
G-BPZS	Colt 105A Balloon (Hot Air)	1312		25. 5.89	L E Giles *(Carousel Carpets titles)*		
						Westbury-on-Trym, Bristol	27. 5.09E
G-BPZU	Scheibe SF25C-2000 Falke	44471	D-KIAV	21. 7.89	Southdown Gliding Club Ltd	Parham Park	25. 8.09E
	(Limbach L2000)						
G-BPZY	Pitts S-1C	RN-1	N1159	15. 5.89	J S Mitchell	White Waltham	28. 2.10P
	(Built R N Newbauer) (Lycoming O-320)						
G-BPZZ	Thunder Ax8-105 Balloon (Hot Air)	1441		25. 5.89	Capricorn Balloons Ltd	Loughborough	27. 9.09E

G-BRAA - G-BRZZ

G-BRAA (2)	Pitts S-1C	101-GM	N14T	12. 5.89	G Hunter	(Direlton, North Berwick)	26. 4.91P
	(Built G R Miller)						
G-BRAK	Cessna 172N Skyhawk II	17273795	C-GBPN	23. 6.88	The Burnett Group Ltd *(Noted 9.08)*	Kemble	11. 3.07T
			(N5438J)				
G-BRAR	Aeronca 7AC Champion	7AC-6564	N2978E	14. 6.89	R B Armitage	Maypole Farm, Chislet	18.10.09P
			NC2978E				
G-BRAX	Payne Knight Twister KT-85B	203	N979	4. 5.89	R Earl *(Fuselage noted 4.05)*		
	(Built M Anderson and C Sunderland) (Continental O-200-A)					Landmead Farm, Garford	29. 9.93P
G-BRBA	Piper PA-28-161 Warrior II	28-7916109	N2090B	25. 5.89	B Willis	Full Sutton	23.12.09E
G-BRBB	Piper PA-28-161 Warrior II	28-8116030	N8260W	28. 6.89	M A and A J Bell	Gloucestershire	17.12.09E
G-BRBC	North American T-6G-NH Texan	182-156	Italian AF	4. 9.92	A P Murphy *(Under rebuild 2008)*	Audley End	
			MM54-099, 51-14470				
G-BRBD	Piper PA-28-151 Cherokee Warrior		N41702	28. 6.89	Compton Abbas Airfield Ltd *"Shaftesbury Belle"*		
		28-7415315				Compton Abbas	10. 4.09E
G-BRBE	Piper PA-28-161 Warrior II	28-7916437	N2815D	13. 6.89	Solo Services Ltd *(Operated Sussex Flying Club)*		
						Shoreham	20. 1.10E
G-BRBG	Piper PA-28-180 Cherokee Archer		N3927X	12. 6.89	B J Millington	Fenland	6. 9.09E
		28-7505248					
G-BRBH	Cessna 150H	15069283	N50410	13. 6.89	J Maffia	Panshanger	8. 8.09E
G-BRBI	Cessna 172N Skyhawk II	17269613	N737RJ	7. 7.89	N A J Robinson tr Skyhawk Flying Group	Popham	12. 9.09E
G-BRBJ	Cessna 172M Skyhawk II	17267492	N73476	26. 5.89	W J Howe	Carlisle	12. 1.02
G-BRBK	Robin DR.400-180 Régent	1915		31. 5.89	R Kemp	Thruxton	30.11.09E
G-BRBL	Robin DR.400-180 Régent	1920		5. 7.89	C A Marren	Trenchard Lines, Upavon	6. 3.09E
G-BRBM	Robin DR.400-180 Régent	1921		5. 7.89	R W Davies	Little Engeham Farm, Woodchurch	5. 7.08E
G-BRBN	Pitts S-1S	G 3	N81BG	14. 7.89	D R Evans	Gloucestershire	5. 7.08P
	(Built W L Garner)						
G-BRBO	Cameron V-77 Balloon (Hot Air)	1877		30. 5.89	M B Murby *"Patches"*	Cheltenham	28. 5.09E
G-BRBP	Cessna 152 II	15284915	N5324P	14. 6.89	Cardinal Sin Ltd t/a Staverton Flying School		
						Gloucestershire	24. 7.09E
G-BRBS	Bensen B 8M	PFA G/01-1039		30. 5.89	K T MacFarlane *(Under construction 6.00)*		
	(Built J Simpson) (Rotax 503)					(Kilmacolm)	
G-BRBT	Trotter Ax3-20 Balloon (Hot Air)	RMT-001		13. 6.89	R M Trotter	Chew Magna, Bristol	
	(Built R M Trotter)						
G-BRBV	Piper J-4A Cub Coupé	4-1080	N27860	13. 6.89	P Clarke	(Drefach, Llanybydder)	30. 8.08P
G-BRBW	Piper PA-28-140 Cherokee Cruiser		N40737	3. 7.89	Air Navigation and Trading Company Ltd		
		28-7425153				Blackpool	1.11.04
G-BRBX	Piper PA-28-181 Cherokee Archer II		N8674E	20. 7.89	C M Oldham and R Perks tr Trent 199 Flying Group		
		28-7690185				Tatenhill	27. 4.09E
G-BRBY	Robinson R22 Beta	1027		15. 6.89	Helijet Ltd	Glenrothes	14. 8.09E
G-BRCA	Jodel D 112	1203	F-BLIU	11. 7.89	R C Jordan	Marsh Hill Farm, Aylesbury	10.11.09P
	(Built Etablissement Valladeau)						
G-BRCE	Pitts S-1C	1001	N4611G	22. 6.89	M P and S T Barnard *(Stored, noted 7.08)*		
	(Built Davis and Blake) (Lycoming O-290)					Hulcote Farm, Salford, Bedford	25.11.97P
G-BRCF	Montgomerie-Bensen B 8MR	PFA G/01A-1131		12. 6.89	J S Walton	(Nannerch, Mold)	31.10.08P
	(Built B E Trinder) (Rotax 532)						
G-BRCJ	Cameron H-20 Balloon (Hot Air)	2028	(OO-BXV)	13. 6.89	P A Sweatman	Birmingham	22. 7.09E
			G-BRCJ				
G-BRCM	Cessna 172L Skyhawk	17259960	N3860Q	19. 6.89	S G E Plessis and D C C Handley	Little Staughton	17. 9.08E

G-BRCO	Cameron H-20 Balloon (Hot Air)	2030		19. 6.89	P Lawman	Northampton	10. 1.03A
G-BRCT	Denney Kitfox Model 2	396		23. 6.89	M L Roberts	Bodmin	16. 4.09P
	(Built M L Roberts - pr.no.PFA 172-11521)						
G-BRCV	Aeronca 7AC Champion	7AC-282	N81661	19. 9.89	P I and D M Morgans	Haverdfordwest	24.10.08P
	(Continental A65)		NC81661				
G-BRCW	Aeronca 11BC Chief	11AC-386	N85964	16.10.89	S J Waddy	Bodmin	20.11.09P
	(Continental C85)		NC85964				
	(Officially regd with incorrect c/n 11AC-366)						
G-BRDB	Zenair CH.701 STOL	7-1300		11. 7.89	D L Bowtell and N C Pettengell	Benington	24.10.09P
	(Built D L Bowtell - pr.no.PFA 187-11412)						
G-BRDD	Mudry CAP.10B	224		3. 8.88	R D Dickson	Gamston	30.12.09E
G-BRDE	Thunder Ax7-77 Balloon (Hot Air)	1538		22. 6.89	D J Keys	Bailieborough, County Cavan	20. 8.09E
G-BRDF	Piper PA-28-161 Cherokee Warrior II		N1139Q	26. 6.89	White Waltham Airfield Ltd	White Waltham	17. 8.09E
		28-7716085			*(Operated West London Aero Services)*		
G-BRDG	Piper PA-28-161 Cherokee Warrior II		N44934	26. 6.89	A S Bamrah t/a Falcon Flying Services	Biggin Hill	18. 5.09E
		28-7816047					
G-BRDJ	Luscombe 8A Silvaire	3411	N71984	28. 6.89	P G Stewart	Popham	4. 3.09P
	(Continental A65)		NC71984				
	(Officially regd as Luscombe 8F with Contintental C90)						
G-BRDM	Piper PA-28-161 Cherokee Warrior II		N8464F	26. 6.89	White Waltham Airfield Ltd	White Waltham	11. 2.09E
		28-7716004			*(Operated West London Aero Services)*		
G-BRDN	SOCATA MS.880B Rallye Club	1212	OY-DTV	14. 7.89	A J Gomes *(Noted dismantled 6.06)*	Sandown	27. 4.02
G-BRDO	Cessna 177B Cardinal	17702166	N35030	13. 7.89	C R Granton and I S Jane tr Cardinal Aviation		
						Durham Tees Valley	13. 3.09E
G-BRDT	Cameron DP-70 Airship (Hot Air)	2029		3. 7.89	Tim Balloon Promotion Airships Ltd Nailsea, Bristol		7. 6.07A
	(Konig SD 570)						
G-BRDW	Piper PA-24 Comanche	24-1733	N6612P	12. 3.90	I P Gibson	Sion, Switzerland	1.10.07E
G-BREB	Piper J-3C-65 Cub	7705	N41094	3. 7.89	J R Wraight	Pent Farm, Postling	8.12.09P
			NC41094				
G-BREE	Whittaker MW7	PFA 171-11497		22. 6.89	D A Couchman	Lower Upham Farm, Chiseldon	28. 7.09P
	(Built M J Hayman) (Rotax 503)						
G-BREH	Cameron V-65 Balloon (Hot Air)	2049		7. 7.89	S E and V D Hurst *"Promise"*	Mansfield	6. 9.09E
G-BREP	Piper PA-28RT-201 Arrow IV	28R-7918119	EC-HZN	19. 6.90	B W Gomez	Wolverhampton	22. 5.09E
			G-BREP, N2230Z				
G-BRER	Aeronca 7AC Champion	7AC-6758	N3157E	12. 7.89	I Sinnett tr Rabbit Flight *(Noted 4.08)*	Bodmin	9. 6.06P
	(Continental A65)		NC3157E				
G-BREU	Montgomerie-Bensen B 8MR PFA G/01A-1137			20. 7.89	J S Firth	Sherburn-in-Elmet	16. 5.08P
	(Built M Hayward) (Rotax 582)						
G-BREX	Cameron O-84 Balloon (Hot Air)	2019		14. 7.89	P Hegarty	Magherafelt, Belfast	13. 7.09E
G-BREY	Taylorcraft BC-12D	7299	N43640	14. 7.89	R J Pitts tr BREY Group	Leicester	18. 5.09P
			NC43640				
G-BREZ	Cessna 172M Skyhawk	17266742	EI-CHS	14. 7.89	L A Mills	Duxford	19. 3.09E
			G-BREZ, N80775				
G-BRFB	Rutan LongEz	PFA 074A-10646		14. 7.89	A R Oliver	Duxford	15. 5.09P
	(Built R A Gardiner) (Lycoming O-290)						
G-BRFC	Percival P 57 Sea Prince T 1	P57/71	N7SY	10. 9.80	A and G A Gainsford Dixon *(On overhaul 11.08)*		
			G-BRFC, WP321			Bournemouth	
G-BRFE	Cameron V-77 Balloon (Hot Air)	1835		20. 7.89	D L C Nelmes tr Ezmerelda Balloon Syndicate *"Ezmerelda"*		
						Abbots Leigh, Bristol	21. 4.06A
G-BRFI	Aeronca 7DC Champion	7AC-4609	N1058E	1. 8.89	A C Lines *(Damaged 1990: on rebuild 4.96)*		
	(Continental C85)		NC1058E			Leicester	19. 2.91P
G-BRFJ	Aeronca 11AC Chief	11AC-796	N9163E	28. 7.89	J M Mooney *(Stored 2.03)*		
	(Continental A65)		NC9163E			Lochview House, Limerigg	11. 9.02P
G-BRFL	Piper PA-38-112 Tomahawk	38-79A0431	N2416F	17. 8.89	D P Chowen	Shoreham	17. 6.09E
G-BRFM	Piper PA-28-161 Warrior II	28-7916279	N2234P	17.10.89	British Disabled Flying Association	Lasham	25. 1.10E
G-BRFO	Cameron V-77 Balloon (Hot Air)	2025		6. 7.89	N J Bland tr Hedgehoppers Balloon Group *"Lurcher"*		
					(Inflated 6.08)	Oxford	31. 7.00A
G-BRFW	Montgomerie-Bensen B 8 Two-Seat			20. 7.89	A J Barker	Sorbie Farm, Kingsmuir	7. 9.06P
	(Built J M Montgomerie) PFA G/01-1073						
	(Rotax 582)						
G-BRFX	Pazmany PL-4A	PFA 017-10079		14. 7.89	D E Hills	(Ipswich)	
	(Built D E Hills) (Volkswagen 1700)						
G-BRGD	Cameron O-84 Balloon (Hot Air)	2043		20. 7.89	R G Russell	Henllys, Cwmbran	25. 4.09E
G-BRGF	Luscombe 8E Silvaire Deluxe	5475	N23FP	20. 7.89	N Surman tr Luscombe Flying Group		
	(Continental C85)		N944BL, N2748K, NC2748K			Hinton-in-the-Hedges	1. 11.08P
G-BRGG	Luscombe 8A Silvaire	3795	N1068K	20. 7.89	M A Lamprell	Popham	6.10.05P
	(Continental A65)		NC1068K				
G-BRGI	Piper PA-28-180 Cherokee E	28-5827	N77VG	24. 7.89	R A Buckfield	Rochester	4. 7.09E
			NlIVG				
G-BRGO	Air Command 532 Elite	0615		7. 8.89	A McCredie	Sorbie Farm, Kingsmuir	13. 2.91P
	(Built D A Wood - pr.no.PFA G/04-1149)				*(Frame noted 5.05)*		
G-BRGT	Piper PA-32-260 Cherokee Six	32-658	N3744W	7.11.89	D A Hitchcock		
					(St Germain de Longue Chaume, France)		21. 2.09E
G-BRGW	Gardan GY-20 Minicab	PFA 1823		13.11.78	R G White	Bossington	17. 7.09P
	(Built R G White to JB.01 Minicab standard) (Continental O-200-A)						
G-BRHA	Piper PA-32RT-300 Lance II	32R-7985076	N2093P	27. 7.89	D J Chatterton and P MacKinnon tr Lance G-BRHA Group		
						Earls Colne	8.12.09E
G-BRHG	Colt 90A Balloon (Hot Air)	1568		11. 9.89	R D Allen *(Badgerline titles)*	Stockley, Calne	17. 8.04A
G-BRHL	Montgomerie-Bensen B 8MR PFA G/01A-1123			7. 8.89	T M Jones and B Moore *(Noted 7.08)*	Kirkbride	26. 8.03P
	(Built N D Marshall) (Rotax 503)						
G-BRHO	Piper PA-34-200 Seneca	34-7350037	N15222	20. 9.89	Andrews Professional Colour Laboratories Ltd		
						Biggin Hill	26. 3.09P
G-BRHP	Aeronca O-58B Grasshopper	058B-8533	N58JR	2. 8.89	C J Willis *(As "3-1923" in US Army c/s)* Dunkeswell		22. 2.01P
	(Continental A65)		N46536, 43-1923		*(If US Army serial is correct, type should be L-3C-AE)*		

G-BRHR	Piper PA-38-112 Tomahawk	38-79A0969	N2377P	21. 8.89	Bell Investments Ltd	Elstree	9.11.07E
G-BRHW	de Havilland DH.82A Tiger Moth	85612	7Q-YMY	26. 7.89	P J and A J Borsberry		
	(Built Morris Motors Ltd)		VP-YMY, ZS-DLB, SAAF 4606, DE671		*(Sonning Common, Reading)*		
G-BRHX	Luscombe 8E Silvaire Deluxe	5114	N176M	8. 8.89	J Lakin	Eaglescott	12. 8.09P
	(Continental C90)		N2387K, NC2387K				
G-BRHY	Luscombe 8E Silvaire Deluxe	5138	N2411K	8. 8.89	A R W Taylor	Sleap	29. 4.09P
	(Continental C85)		NC2411K				
G-BRIA	Cessna 310L	310L0010	N2210F	4. 8.89	B J Tucker	Cardiff	29. 6.08E
G-BRIE	Cameron N-77 Balloon (Hot Air)	2076		8. 8.89	S F Redman	Stalbridge, Sturminster Newton	12. 7.06A
G-BRIH	Taylorcraft BC-12D	7421	N43762	24. 8.89	A D Duke tr IH Flying Group	Leicester	17. 4.08P
	(Continental A75)		NC43762				
G-BRII	Zenair CH.600 Zodiac	PFA 162-11392		18. 8.89	A C Bowdrey *(Under build 2000)*		
	(Built A C Bowdrey)					*(Hemel Hempstead)*	
G-BRIJ	Taylorcraft F-19	F-119	N3863T	23. 8.89	M W Olliver	Farley Farm, Romsey	12. 6.01P
G-BRIK	Nipper T 66S Series 3	PFA 025-10174		26. 4.77	P R Bentley	Roughay Farm, Bishops Waltham	17. 5.08P
	(Built C W R Piper as rebuild of G-AVKH) (Volkswagen 1834)						
G-BRIL	Piper J-5A Cub Cruiser	5-572	N35183	2. 8.89	P L Jobes and D J Bone		
	(Continental A75)		NC35183			Spite Hall Farm, Pinchinthorpe	26.11.09P
G-BRIO	Turner Super T-40A	PFA 104-10636		7. 8.89	S Bidwell	*(Brighton)*	8. 9.06P
	(Built D McIntyre and officially regd incorrectly as c/n PFA 104-10736)) (Continental O-200-A)						
G-BRIR	Cameron V-56 Balloon (Hot Air)	2056		17. 8.89	H G Davies and C Dowd *"Spirit of Century"*		
					(Skyviews Windows titles)	Cheltenham	6. 9.97A
G-BRIS	Steen Skybolt	01	N870MC	30. 8.89	M R Jones	*(Windsor)*	4. 3.04P
	(Built M.K.Callen)						
G-BRIV	SOCATA TB-9 Tampico Club	939		24. 8.89	S J Taft	RAF Scampton	17. 4.09E
G-BRIY	Taylorcraft DF-65	6183	N59687	1. 2.90	S R Potts	Stanton, Morpeth	10. 7.98P
	(Continental A65) (Built as TG-6 glider)		NC59687, 42-58678		*(As "42-58678:IY" in L-2A USAAC c/s: noted on rebuild 8.07)*		
G-BRJA	Luscombe 8A Silvaire	3744	N1017K	12. 9.89	A D Keen	Halwell	2.10.09P
	(Continental A65)		NC1017K				
G-BRJC	Cessna 120	12077	N1833N	21. 8.89	A L Hall-Carpenter	Shipdham	21. 3.04P
	(Continental C85)		NC1833N				
G-BRJK	Luscombe 8A Silvaire	4205	N1478K	21. 8.89	C J L Peat and M Richardson	Chilbolton	19.12.08P
	(Continental A65)		NC1478K				
G-BRJL	Piper PA-15 Vagabond	15-157	N4370H	21. 8.89	A R Williams	Garston Farm, Marshfield	14.10.09P
	(Continental C85)		NC4370H				
G-BRJN	Pitts S-1C	1-MA	N6A	23. 8.89	W Chapel	Sherburn-in-Elmet	20. 5.04P
	(Built M G Acker) (Lycoming O-320)						
G-BRJT	Cessna 150H	15068426	N44SS	31. 8.89	M R Winter tr Romeo Tango Group	Welshpool	9.12.09E
G-BRJV	Piper PA-28-161 Cadet	2841167	N9185G	24. 8.89	Northumbria Flying School Ltd	Carlisle	25. 3.09E
G-BRJX	Rand Robinson KR-2	PFA 129-11386		22. 8.89	J R Bell	*(Parcllyn, Cardigan)*	15. 4.97P
	(Built C Willcocks)						
G-BRJY	Rand Robinson KR-2	PFA 129-11308		22. 8.89	R E Taylor *(Under restoration 6.00)* *(Bonar Bridge)*		23. 5.96P
	(Built J M Scott) (Revmaster 2100D)						
G-BRKC	Auster V J/1 Autocrat	2749	F-BFYT	31. 8.89	J W Conlon	Bury Farm, High Easter	16. 3.09P
G-BRKH	Piper PA-28-236 Dakota	28-7911003	N21444	30. 8.89	A P H and E Hay	Popham	22. 2.09E
G-BRKR	Cessna 182R Skylane II	18268468	N9896E	2. 6.89	A R D Brooker	Springfield Farm, Ettington	15. 7.09E
G-BRKW	Cameron V-77 Balloon (Hot Air)	2093		1. 9.89	T J Parker	Burnham-on-Crouch	11.12.09E
G-BRKY	Viking Dragonfly Mk II	PFA 139-11117		7. 9.89	G D Price *(Stored less engine 6.04)*		
	(Built G D Price) (Volkswagen 2180)					Kittyhawk Farm, Deanland	8. 6.94P
G-BRLB	Air Command 532 Elite	0622		4. 9.89	F G Shepherd	*(Great Orton)*	
	(Built H R Bethune)						
G-BRLF	Campbell Cricket replica	PFA G/03-1077		6. 9.89	J L G McLane	*(Gilling East, York)*	7. 9.09P
	(Built D Wood) (Rotax 503)						
G-BRLG	Piper PA-28RT-201T Turbo Arrow IV		N4379P	12. 9.89	P Lodge and J G McVey	Liverpool-John Lennon	27. 2.10E
		28R-8431027	N9600N				
G-BRLI	Piper J-5A Cub Cruiser	5-822	N35951	23. 8.89	Little Bear Ltd	Exeter	11. 9.09P
	(Lycoming O-290)		NC35951				
G-BRLL	Cameron A-105 Balloon (Hot Air)	2032		7. 9.89	P A Sweatman *(Extant 5.07)*	Coventry	4. 4.06T
G-BRLO	Piper PA-38-112 Tomahawk	38-78A0621	N2397K	26.10.89	E Reed t/a St George Flight Training		
			N9680N			Durham Tees Valley	26. 3.09E
G-BRLP	Piper PA-38-112 Tomahawk	38-78A0011	N9301T	4.10.89	P D Brooks	Inverness	10. 4.09E
G-BRLR	Cessna 150G	15064822	N4772X	4.10.89	Blue Skys Aviation (NE) Ltd		
						(Ponteland, Newcastle)	8. 9.09E
G-BRLS	Thunder Ax7-77 Balloon (Hot Air)	1603		29. 9.89	E C Meek	Oswestry	27. 9.09E
G-BRLT	Colt 77A Balloon (Hot Air)	1588		12. 9.89	D Bareford *"Pro-Sport"*	Kidderminster	28. 5.09E
G-BRLV	CCF Harvard 4 (T-6J-CCF Texan)	CCF4-194	N90448	14. 9.89	Extraviation Ltd *"Texan Belle"*	North Weald	10.9.08P
			RCAF 20403		*(As "93542:LTA-542" in USAF 6148th TCS c/s)*		
G-BRME	Piper PA-28-181 Cherokee Archer II		OY-BTA	14. 9.89	Keen Leasing Ltd	Belfast International	17. 7.09E
		28-7790105					
G-BRMI	Cameron V-65 Balloon (Hot Air)	2104		14. 9.89	M Davies *"Sapphire"*	Callington, Plymouth	25. 8.01A
G-BRMT	Cameron V-31 Air Chair Balloon (Hot Air) 2038			31. 8.89	B M Reed	Paizay le Sec, France	
G-BRMU	Cameron V-77 Balloon (Hot Air)	2109		19. 9.89	K J and G R Ibbotson *"Hyperion"*	Gloucester	9. 6.09E
G-BRMV	Cameron O-77 Balloon (Hot Air)	2103		25. 9.89	P D Griffiths *"Viscount"*	Southampton	1. 7.09E
G-BRMW	Whittaker MW7	PFA 171-11395		25. 9.89	G S Parsons	*(Coventry)*	21. 4.03P
	(Built M Grunwell)						
G-BRNC	Cessna 150M Commuter	15078833	N704SG	29. 9.89	Penny Hydraulics Ltd *(Operated Sheffield City Flying School)*		
						Sandtoft	30. 6.09E
G-BRND	Cessna 152 II	15283776	N5148B	7.11.89	T M and M L Jones *(Operated Derby Aero Club)*		
						Derby	27. 7.09E
G-BRNE	Cessna 152 II	15284248	N5082L	4.10.89	Redhill Air Services Ltd	Fairoaks	15. 2.10E
G-BRNK	Cessna 152 II	15280479	N24969	22. 9.89	D C and M Bonsall	Netherthorpe	17. 4.09E
G-BRNN	Cessna 152 II	15284735	N6452M	22. 9.89	Sheffield Aero Club Ltd	Netherthorpe	25. 2.09E
G-BRNT	Robin DR.400-180 Régent	1935		3.10.89	C E, O C and M E Ponsford *(Operated Cega Aviation)*		
						Shoreham	23. 3.09E

Reg	Type	C/n	Prev id	Regd	Owner/Operator	Location	Expiry
G-BRNU	Robin DR.400-180 Régent	1937		31.10.89	November Uniform Travel Syndicate Ltd	White Waltham	10. 6.09E
G-BRNV	Piper PA-28-181 Cherokee Archer II	28-7790402	N2537Q	7.12.89	N S Lyndhurst	Goodwood	10. 3.09E
G-BRNW	Cameron V-77 Balloon (Hot Air)	2138		2.10.89	G Smith and N Robertson *"Mr Blue Sky"* (Inflated 8.08) Alveston, Bristol and Walton-on-Thames		4. 8.06A
G-BRNX	Piper PA-22-150 Caribbean	22-2945	N2610P	3.10.89	S N Askey	Draycott Farm, Chiseldon	10. 2.11
G-BRNZ	Piper PA-32-300 Cherokee Six B	32-40594	N4229R	7. 2.90	W Anderson tr Longfellow Flying Group	Headcorn	20. 6.08E

(Substantially damaged in gales Fenland 1.07: wreck noted 4.07)

Reg	Type	C/n	Prev id	Regd	Owner/Operator	Location	Expiry
G-BROE	Cameron N-65 Balloon (Hot Air)	2098		5.10.89	A I Attwood *"Lancia"*	(Inverness)	5. 9.09E
G-BROG	Cameron V-65 Balloon (Hot Air)	2121		6. 9.89	R Kunert *"The Dodger"*	Finchampstead, Wokingham	18. 9.09E
G-BROI	CFM Streak Shadow	K 115-SA		16.11.89	A Collinson	Brook Farm, Pilling	13. 6.09P

(Built G W Rowbotham - pr.no.PFA 161-11586) (Rotax 532)

Reg	Type	C/n	Prev id	Regd	Owner/Operator	Location	Expiry
G-BROJ	Colt 31A Balloon (Hot Air)	1468		6.10.89	N J Langley	Clapton in Gordano, Bristol	26. 6.09E

(Fly Virgin, Pocara Sweat and Nature Mate titles)

Reg	Type	C/n	Prev id	Regd	Owner/Operator	Location	Expiry
G-BROO	Luscombe 8E Silvaire Deluxe (Continental O-200-A)	6154	N75297, N1527B, NC1527B	28. 9.89	P R Bush	(Milford Haven)	1. 5.09P
G-BROR	Piper J-3C-65 Cub (*L-4H-PI*)	10885	F-BHMQ, 43-29594	7.12.89	J H Bailey and A P J Wiseman tr White Hart Flying Group	Sturgate	30. 7.09P
G-BROX	Robinson R22 Beta	1127	N8061V	13.10.89	J G Burgess	(Waldron, Heathfield)	29. 8.09E
G-BROY	Cameron O-90 Balloon (Hot Air)	2173		6. 9.89	T G S Dixon *(Dixon Furnace Division tiles)*	Bromsgrove	10. 9.09E
G-BROZ	Piper PA-18-150 Super Cub	18-6754	HB-ORC, N9572D	20. 9.89	P G Kynsey	Headcorn	9. 2.11E
G-BRPE	Cessna 120 (Continental C85)	13326	N3068N, NC3068N	11.10.89	W B Bateson *(Noted 10.07)*	Blackpool	7. 7.05P
G-BRPF	Cessna 120 (Continental C85)	9902	N72723, NC72723	11.10.89	A L Hall-Carpenter	Shipdham	15. 5.05P
G-BRPG	Cessna 120 (Continental C85)	9882	N72703, NC72703	11.10.89	I C Lomax	(Thirtlebury, Hull)	29. 8.94P
G-BRPH	Cessna 120 (Continental C85)	12137	N1893N, NC1893N	11.10.89	J A Cook	Pent Farm, Postling	31. 5.09P
G-BRPJ	Cameron N-90 Balloon (Hot Air)	2071		11. 9.89	P Johnson t/a Cloud Nine Balloon Company *"Presto"*	Ebchetser, Consett	10. 3.99T
G-BRPK	Piper PA-28-140 Cherokee Cruiser	28-7325070	N15449	17.11.89	G R Bright tr G-BRPK Group	Little Gransden	17. 7.09E
G-BRPL	Piper PA-28-140 Cherokee Cruiser	28-7325160	N15771	13.10.89	Silverstar Aviation Ltd	Blackpool	6.11.05T
G-BRPM	Nipper T 66 Series 3B	PFA 025-11038		4. 3.85	T C Horner *(Under construction 6.00)*	(Barrhead)	

(Built R Morris)

Reg	Type	C/n	Prev id	Regd	Owner/Operator	Location	Expiry
G-BRPP	Gyroflight Brookland Hornet (Volkswagen 1776)	DC-1		16.10.89	B J L P and W J A L de Saar *(For rebuild 2000)*	(Great Yarmouth)	23. 8.93E
G-BRPR	Aeronca O-58B Grasshopper (Continental A65)	058B-8823	N49880, 43-1952	17.10.89	C S Tolchard *(As "31952" in USAAC c/s)*	Waits Farm, Belchamp Walter	30. 5.09P

(If US Army serial is correct, type should be L-3C-AE)

Reg	Type	C/n	Prev id	Regd	Owner/Operator	Location	Expiry
G-BRPS	Cessna 177B Cardinal	17702101	N34935	23.10.89	R C Tebbett	Shobdon	16. 6.08E
G-BRPT	Rans S-10 Sakota	0589.052		18.10.89	A R Hawes	Mendlesham	5. 5.09P

(Built J G Beesley - pr.no.PFA 194-11554)

Reg	Type	C/n	Prev id	Regd	Owner/Operator	Location	Expiry
G-BRPU	Beech 76 Duchess	ME-140	N6007Z	17.10.89	Plane Talking Ltd *(Operated Cabair)*	Bournemouth	18.10.09E
G-BRPV	Cessna 152 II	15285228	N6311Q	6.11.89	Eastern Air Executive Ltd	Sturgate	6. 4.09E
G-BRPX	Taylorcraft BC-12D (Continental A65)	6462	N39208, NC39208	12.12.89	R Chapman tr The BRPX Group	Leicester	25. 9.09P
G-BRPY	Piper PA-15 Vagabond (Continental C85)	15-141	N4356H, NC4356H	23.10.89	J and V Hobday	Barton	26. 4.09P
G-BRPZ	Luscombe 8A Silvaire (Continental A65)	911	N22089, NC22089	13.12.89	P Dixon tr Bumble Bee Group	Shacklewell Farm, Empingham	8.12.09P
G-BRRB	Luscombe 8E Silvaire Deluxe (Continental C85)	2611	N71184, NC71184	23.10.89	J Nicholls	(Bishops Waltham)	14. 5.00P
G-BRRD	Scheibe SF25B Falke	4811	D-KBAT	30.10.89	P J Gill tr G-BRRD Group	Seighford	18. 6.09E

(Built Sportavia-Pützer) (Stark-Stamo MS1500)

Reg	Type	C/n	Prev id	Regd	Owner/Operator	Location	Expiry
G-BRRF	Cameron O-77 Balloon (Hot Air)	2101		24.10.89	K P and G J Storey	Sawbridgeworth	19. 8.09E
G-BRRG	Glaser-Dirks DG-500M	5E7-M5		7.11.89	P J Fincham tr G-BRRG Syndicate (Milton Keynes)		6. 4.10E
G-BRRK	Cessna 182Q Skylane II	18266160	N759PW	30.10.89	Werewolf Aviation Ltd	Elstree	27. 2.09E
G-BRRL	Piper PA-18 Super Cub 95 (*L-18C-PI*)	18-1615	G-AYPO (1), French Army 18-1615, 51-15615	17. 9.90	A J White tr Acebell G-BRRL Syndicate	(Redhill)	

(Regd using paperwork of wrecked D-EMKE [18-2050])

Reg	Type	C/n	Prev id	Regd	Owner/Operator	Location	Expiry
G-BRRR	Cameron V-77 Balloon (Hot Air)	2070		13.10.89	K P and G J Storey *"Breezy"*	Sawbridgeworth	19. 8.09E
G-BRRU	Colt 90A Balloon (Hot Air)	1591		1.11.89	Reach For The Sky Ltd	Guildford	31. 7.09E
G-BRRY	Robinson R22 Beta	1193		14.11.89	Fast Helicopters Ltd	Shoreham	9. 1.10E
G-BRSA (2)	Cameron N-56 Balloon (Hot Air)	2113		8.11.89	C Wilkinson	Newcastle	5. 4.09E
G-BRSD (2)	Cameron V-77 Balloon (Hot Air)	2174		8.11.89	M E Granger	Little Bytham, Grantham	24. 4.09E
G-BRSE (2)	Piper PA-28-161 Warrior II	28-8016276	N8163R	5.12.89	Falcon Flying Services Ltd	Biggin Hill	12. 7.09E
G-BRSF (2)	Vickers Supermarine 361 Spitfire HF.IXc	56322	SAAF 5632, RR232	2.11.89	M B Phillips *(As "RR232" in RAF c/s) (Noted 2007)*	Newton St Cyres, Exeter	

(Composite including tail and parts ex Mk.VIII, JF629 from Western Australia and wings ex Mk.XIV, R Thai AF U14-6/93, RAF RM873)

Reg	Type	C/n	Prev id	Regd	Owner/Operator	Location	Expiry
G-BRSJ (2)	Piper PA-38-112 Tomahawk II	38-81A0044	N25664	29.12.89	APB Leasing Ltd	Swansea	10. 4.09E
G-BRSN	Rand Robinson KR-2	PFA 129-11178		10.11.89	K W Darby	(Teignmouth)	

(Built K W Darby) (Volkswagen 1834)

Reg	Type	C/n	Prev id	Regd	Owner/Operator	Location	Expiry
G-BRSO	CFM Streak Shadow	K 133-SA		16.11.89	B C Norris *(Noted 8.07)*	Trenchard Farm, Eggesford	14.11.03P

(Built P H Slade - pr.no.PFA 161A-11601) (Rotax 618)

Reg	Type	C/n	Prev id	Regd	Owner/Operator	Location	Expiry
G-BRSP	MODAC (Air Command) 503	0626		13.11.89	G M Hobman	Melrose Farm, Melbourne	27. 5.09P

(Built D R G Griffith - pr.no.PFA G04-1158)

G-BRSW	Luscombe 8A Silvaire	3249	N71822	15.11.89	P H Needham tr Bloody Mary Aviation "Bloody Mary"
	(Continental A75)		NC71822		Fenland 24. 4.09P
G-BRSX	Piper PA-15 Vagabond	15-117	N4334H	27.10.89	M R Holden (Hagworthingham, Spilsby) 3. 8.06P
	(Continental A65)		NC4334H		
G-BRSY	Hatz CB-1	6	N2257J	15.11.89	W Senior Breighton 21. 1.08P
	(Built M Ondrus) (Lycoming O-290-D)				
G-BRTD	Cessna 152 II	15280023	N757UW	11. 1.90	R G Prince, T G Phillips and C Greenland tr 152 Group
					Popham 21. 6.09E
G-BRTJ	Cessna 150F	15061749	N8149S	22.11.89	Avon Aviation Ltd Bristol 18. 8.09E
G-BRTL	Hughes 369E (Hughes 500)	0356E	(F-GHLF)	5. 1.90	Crewhall Ltd Sywell 23. 7.09E
G-BRTP	Cessna 152 II	15281275	N49448	28.11.89	R Lee Mount Airey Farm, South Cave 5.10.09E
G-BRTT	Schweizer 269C (Schweizer 300)	S 1411		29.11.89	Technical Exponents Ltd Denham 3.10.09E
G-BRTV	Cameron O-77 Balloon (Hot Air)	2182		1.12.89	R J Clements Lower Weston, Bath 15.12.09E
G-BRTW	Glaser-Dirks DG-400	4-259		22.12.89	I J Carruthers (Great Orton) 17. 8.09E
G-BRTX	Piper PA-28-151 Cherokee Warrior		N8307C	27.12.89	J Phelan and J Mahon tr Spectrum Alpha Flying Group
		28-7615085			Belfast International 16. 5.09E
G-BRUB	Piper PA-28-161 Warrior II	28-8116177	N8351Y	27.12.89	Flytrek Ltd Compton Abbas 19. 2.09E
G-BRUD	Piper PA-28-181 Archer II	28-8390010	N8300S	9. 2.90	Wilkins and Wilkins (Special Auctions) Ltd
					t/a Henlow Flying Club RAF Henlow 18. 3.09E
G-BRUG	Luscombe 8E Silvaire Deluxe	4462	N1735K	15.12.89	N W Barratt Ranston Farm, Iwerne Courtney 21. 3.09P
	(Continental C85)		NC1735K		
G-BRUH	Colt 105A Balloon (Hot Air)	1650		15.12.89	D C Chipping Grantham 29. 7.93T
G-BRUI	Piper PA-44-180 Seminole	44-7995150	N2230E	15.12.89	D Engmann Biggin Hill 12.11.09E
			G-BRUI, N2230E		
G-BRUJ	Boeing Stearman A75N1 (PT-17) Kaydet		N55557	6. 4.90	R M Hughes (As "16136:205" in USN c/s)
	(Continental R670)	75-4299	42-16136		Liverpool-John Lennon 25. 7.10S
G-BRUM	Cessna A152 Aerobat	A1520870	N4693A	12. 3.86	Central Aircraft Leasing Ltd Kemble 15. 8.08E
G-BRUN	Cessna 120	9294	G-BRDH	29. 8.89	O C Brun Great Massingham 23. 4.09P
	(Continental C85)		N72127, NC72127		
G-BRUO	Taylor JT.1 Monoplane PFA 055-10859			15.12.89	R Hatton Kirkbride 17. 1.08P
	(Built P C Cardno)				
G-BRUV	Cameron V-77 Balloon (Hot Air)	2100		16. 8.89	T W and R F Benbrook "biG-BRUVver" Romford 3. 4.09E
G-BRUX	Piper PA-44-180 Seminole	44-7995151	N2245E	8. 3.79	C J Thomas Tatenhill 23. 1.10E
G-BRVB	Stolp SA.300 Starduster Too	409	N33MH	21.12.89	M N Petchey tr G-VB Group Andrewsfield 23.10.09P
	(Built M Hoover) (Lycoming O-360)				
G-BRVE	Beech D17S Traveller Mk.1 (UC-43-BH)	6701	N1193V	12. 3.90	Patina Ltd (Operated The Fighter Collection)
			NC1193V, Bu.32874, FT475, 44-67724, (Bu.23689)		Duxford 29. 6.11S
G-BRVF	Colt 77A Balloon (Hot Air)	1651		19.12.89	J Adkins "NAPS" titles Market Harborough 25. 6.09E
G-BRVG	North American SNJ-7C Texan	88-17676	N830X	24. 1.90	D J Gilmour (As "90678:27" in USN VS-932 Sqdn c/s)
			N4134A, Bu.90678, (42-85895)		North Weald 4. 9.10S
G-BRVI	Robinson R22 Beta	1240		27.12.89	M D Thorpe t/a Yorkshire Helicopters
					Coney Park, Leeds 4.12.09E
G-BRVJ	Slingsby Cadet III Motor Glider	701	BGA3360	24. 1.90	B Outhwaite Yearby 18.11.09P
	(Volkswagen 1600)		WT906		
	(Re-built D F Micklethwaite and J R Paskins - pr.no.PFA 042-11382 and modified ex T 31B)				
G-BRVL	Pitts S-1C	559H	N2NW	10. 1.90	M F Pocock RAF Leeming 9. 4.08P
	(Built N Williams) (Lycoming IO-320)				
G-BRVN	Thunder Ax7-77 Balloon (Hot Air)	1614		28.12.89	D L Beckwith Kislingbury, Northampton 9. 8.09E
G-BRVO	Aérospatiale AS.350B Ecureuil	2315		3. 1.90	Rotorhire LLP (Allington, Maidstone) 25.10.08E
G-BRVR	Barnett Rotorcraft J4B-2	216-2		20. 2.90	M Richardson t/a Ilkeston Contractors Ilkeston
G-BRVS	Barnett Rotorcraft J4B-2	210-2		20. 2.90	M Richardson t/a Ilkeston Contractors Ilkeston
	(Built M Richardson)				
G-BRVU	Colt 77A Balloon (Hot Air)	1652		4. 1.90	J K Woods "Concorde Watches" Chatham 25. 6.02A
G-BRVY	Thunder Ax8-90 Balloon (Hot Air)	1676		9. 1.90	G E and J V Morris "Golden Gem" Cheltenham 6. 5.04A
G-BRVZ	SAN Jodel D 117	433	F-BHNR	22.12.89	L Holland (Nottingham) 29. 5.09P
G-BRWA	Aeronca 7AC Champion	7AC-351	N81730	20. 3.90	D D Smith and J R Edwards Scotland Farm, Hook 24. 4.09P
			NC81730		
G-BRWD	Robinson R22 Beta	1231	N8064U	15. 1.90	Just Plane Trading Ltd
					Top Farm, Croydon, Royston 5. 6.09E
G-BRWO	Piper PA-28-140 Cherokee Cruiser		N55985	11. 1.90	B and C Taylor Humberside 7. 9.09E
		28-7325548			
G-BRWP	CFM Streak Shadow	K 122		17. 1.90	R Biffin Kirknewton 24. 7.07P
	(Built D F Gaughan - pr.no.PFA 161A-11596) (Rotax 532)				
G-BRWR	Aeronca 11AC Chief	11AC-1319	N9676E	17. 1.90	A W Crutcher Cardiff 2. 7.09P
	(Continental A65)				
G-BRWT	Scheibe SF25C-2000 Falke	44480	D-KIAY	11. 1.90	Booker Gliding Club Ltd Wycombe Air Park 1. 5.09E
	(Limbach L2000)				
G-BRWU	Phoenix Luton LA-4A Minor	PAL 1141		18. 1.90	R B Webber Trenchard Farm, Eggesford 9.10.09P
	(Built R B Webber and P K Pike - pr.no.PFA 1141) (JAP J 99)				
G-BRWV	Brügger MB.2 Colibri	PFA 043-11027		18. 1.90	M P Wakem Barton 15.10.09P
	(Built S J McCollom) (Volkswagen 1834)				
G-BRWX	Cessna 172P Skyhawk II	17274729	N53363	17. 1.90	R A Brown and A C Dove (Chesterfield) 28. 6.09E
	(Thielert TAE 125-01)				
G-BRWZ	Cameron Macaw 90 SS Balloon (Hot Air) 2206			29. 1.90	Forbes Global Inc "Capitalist Tool"
					Balleroy, Calvados, France 10. 6.09E
G-BRXA	Cameron O-120 Balloon (Hot Air)	2217		19. 1.90	R J Mansfield Bowness-on-Windermere 22. 2.09E
G-BRXB	Thunder Ax7-77 Balloon (Hot Air)	1631		18. 1.90	H Peel Petworth 22. 7.02A
	(Donated to Balloon Preservation Group 2004)				
G-BRXD	Piper PA-28-181 Archer II	28-8290126	D-EHWN	19. 2.90	D D Stone Wellesbourne Mountford 15. 4.09E
			N9690N, N8203E		
G-BRXE	Taylorcraft BC-12D	9459	N95059	25. 1.90	B T Morgan and W J Durrad "Flying Fishes"
	(Continental A65)		NC95059		Eastbach Farm, Coleford 23. 4.09P
G-BRXF	Aeronca 11AC Chief	11AC-1033	N9396E	25. 1.90	C G Nice tr Aeronca Flying Group Andrewsfield 16. 4.09P
	(Continental A65)		NC9396E		

G-BRXG	Aeronca 7AC Champion	7AC-3910	N85178	1. 3.90	J D Webb tr X-Ray Golf Flying Group		
	(Continental A65)		NC85178			Hill Farm, Nayland	18. 9.09P
G-BRXH	Cessna 120	10462	N76068	25. 1.90	A C Garside tr BRXH Group	Headcorn	18. 6.09P
			NC76068				
G-BRXL	Aeronca 11AC Chief	11AC-1629	N3254E	31. 1.90	P L Green (As "42-78044" in US Army AC L-3F c/s)		
	(Continental A65)		NC3254E			Great Oakley	14. 9.09P
G-BRXN	Montgomerie-Bensen B 8MR	PFA G/01-1160		31. 1.90	C M Frerk	Spanhoe	14. 9.07P
	(Built J C Aitken) (Rotax 532)						
G-BRXP	SNCAN Stampe SV-4C	678	N33528	2. 2.90	T Brown ("SFASA Saint-Yan" titles)		
			F-BGGU, French AF 678, (F-BDNX)			Maypole Farm, Chislet	5. 9.10S
G-BRXS	Howard Special T-Minus	REC-1	N2278C	14. 2.90	F A Bakir	Barton	12. 4.08P
	(Built C Howard) (Lycoming O-290) (Modified Taylorcraft BC)						
G-BRXV	Robinson R22 Beta	1246		7. 2.90	Heliflight (UK) Ltd	Gloucestershire	4.12.09E
G-BRXW	Piper PA-24-260 Comanche	24-4069	N8621P	16. 2.90	P A Jenkins tr Oak Group	Farley Farm, Romsey	11. 2.06
G-BRXY	Pietenpol AirCamper	PFA 047-11416		7. 2.90	P S Ganczakowski	Great Eversden	3.12.09P
	(Built A E Morris) (Continental C90)						
G-BRZA	Cameron O-77 Balloon (Hot Air)	2231		7. 2.90	L and R J Mold "Breezy"	High Wycombe	13. 3.09E
	(Originally regd with c/n 2237 - see G-BSCA)				(Phil Dunson and Wycombe Insurance titles)		
G-BRZD	HAPI Cygnet SF-2A	PFA 182-11443		8. 2.90	C I Coghill	(Farnham)	7.10.04P
	(Built L G Millen) (Volkswagen 2078)						
G-BRZE	Thunder Ax7-77 Balloon (Hot Air)	1633		8. 2.90	G V Beckwith and F Schoeder "Jenlain"		
					Zanten and Mulheim Ruhr, Germany	31. 8.97A
G-BRZG	Enstrom F-28A	169	N9053	8. 2.90	P J Price	(Preston)	3. 9.08E
G-BRZI	Cameron N-180 Balloon (Hot Air)	2215		8. 2.90	C E Wood t/a Eastern Balloon Rides	Witham	24. 2.00T
G-BRZK	Stinson 108-2 Voyager	108-2846	N9846K	17. 4.90	P C G Wyld tr Voyager G-BRZK Syndicate		
	(Built Consolidated Vultee Aircraft)		NC9846K			Wycombe Air Park	1. 1.10
G-BRZL	Pitts S-1D	01	N899RN	26. 2.90	T R G Barnby (Noted on rebuild 5.00)	Headcorn	2. 8.96P
	(Built R C Nelson)						
G-BRZS	Cessna 172P Skyhawk II	17275004	N54585	2.10.90	M H Seville and P F Hughes tr YP Flying Group		
						Blackpool	12. 3.09E
G-BRZT	Cameron V-77 Balloon (Hot Air)	2241		21. 2.90	B Drawbridge "Hoopla"	Cranbrook	19. 2.01A
G-BRZW	Rans S-10 Sakota	0789.058		21. 2.90	D L Davies (Noted 8.07)	Greenlands, Rhuallt	6. 8.98P
	(Built D L Davies - pr.no.PFA 194-11932)						
G-BRZX	Pitts S-1S	711-H	N272H	22. 2.90	J S Dawson	Sherburn-in-Elmet	15. 5.09P
	(Built M M Lotero) (Lycoming O-320)						
G-BRZZ	CFM Streak Shadow	K 135		22. 2.90	J A Weston	Sumburgh	13. 5.08P
	(Built P R Oakes - pr.no.PFA 161A-11628) (Rotax 532)						

G-BSAA - G-BSZZ

G-BSAI	Stoddard-Hamilton Glasair III	3102		31. 1.90	K J and P.J Whitehead	Wycombe Air Park	6.10.09P
	(Buillt K J Whitehead) (Lycoming IO-540)						
G-BSAJ	CASA 1-131E Jungmann	2209	Spanish AF	23. 1.90	P G Kynsey	Headcorn	15. 7.09P
			E3B-209				
G-BSAK	Colt 21A Sky Chariot Balloon (Hot Air)	1696		26. 2.90	G A Chadwick t/a Black Pearl Balloons		
						Partridge Green, Horsham	8. 9.09E
G-BSAS	Cameron V-65 Balloon (Hot Air)	2191		27. 2.90	P Donkin	Ulverston	11. 9.09E
G-BSAV	Thunder Ax7-77 Balloon (Hot Air)	1555		26. 2.90	I G Lloyd "Burnt Savings"	Derby	22. 6.03A
G-BSAW	Piper PA-28-161 Warrior II	28-8216152	N8203C	27. 2.90	Haimoss Ltd	Old Sarum	10. 8.09E
			YV-2265P, N8203C				
G-BSAZ	Denney Kitfox Model 2	602	(G-BRVW)	5. 3.90	A J Lloyd, D M Garrett and J T Lane	Shobdon	26. 6.97P
	(Built P E Hinkley - pr.no.PFA 172-11664)						
G-BSBA	Piper PA-28-161 Warrior II	28-8016041	N2574U	1. 3.90	Falcon Flying Services Ltd	Fairoaks	27. 5.09E
G-BSBG	CCF Harvard 4 (T-6J-CCF Texan)	CCF4-483	Moz.PLAF 1753	5. 3.90	A P St John (As "20310:310" in RCAF c/s)		
			FAP 1753,WGAF BF+053, WGAF AA+053, 52-8562			Tatenhill	21.10.09P
G-BSBI	Cameron O-77 Balloon (Hot Air)	2245		6. 3.90	D M Billing "Calibre"	Uckfield	22. 8.09E
G-BSBR	Cameron V-77 Balloon (Hot Air)	2247		26. 2.90	R P Wade "Honey"	Wigan	4. 5.09E
G-BSBT	Piper J-3C-65 Cub	17712	N70694	9. 3.90	N C Stone	Stanton, Morpeth	17. 5.07P
			NC70694				
G-BSBV	Rans S-10 Sakota	1089.064		9. 3.90	P M Harrison	Wickenby	17.12.09P
	(Built J Whiting - pr.no.PFA 194-11769)						
G-BSBW	Bell 206B-3 JetRanger III	3664	N43EA	12. 3.90	D T Sharpe	Shoreham	31. 1.09E
			N6498V, 9Y-THC				
G-BSBX	Montgomerie-Bensen B 8MR PFA G/01A-1135			12. 3.90	W Toulmin and R J Roan	(Peterborough)	26. 5.93P
	(Built B Ibbott) (Rotax 503)						
G-BSBZ	Cessna 150M	15077093	N63086	29. 3.90	D T Given t/a DTG Aviation	Newtownards	15. 9.09E
G-BSCA	Cameron N-90 Balloon (Hot Air)	2237	(9M-)	12. 3.90	J Steiner	Kuala Lumpur, Malaysia	21. 5.05A
	(Originally regd with c/n 2239 - also see G-BRZA)		G-BSCA				
G-BSCC	Colt 105A Balloon (Hot Air)	1006		15. 3.90	Capricorn Balloons Ltd	Loughborough	9. 8.09E
G-BSCE	Robinson R22 Beta	1245		15. 3.90	H.Sugden (Operated Soloflight)	Humberside	17. 3.09E
G-BSCF	Thunder Ax7-77 Balloon (Hot Air)	1537		14. 3.90	V P Gardiner "Charlie Farley"	Stoke-on-Trent	22.11.02A
G-BSCG	Denney Kitfox Model 2	PFA 172-11620		23. 4.90	A Levitt	(Hebden Bridge)	17. 9.08P
	(Built A C and T G Pinkstone)						
G-BSCH	Denney Kitfox Model 2	510		16. 3.90	J D Cheeseman	(Poole)	30.10.08P
	(Built Baldoon Leisure Flying Co Ltd - pr.no.PFA 172-11621)						
G-BSCI	Colt 77A Balloon (Hot Air)	1683		16. 3.90	J L and S Wrigglesworth "Brody"	Ilminster	27. 9.09E
G-BSCK	Cameron H-24 Balloon (Hot Air)	2263		16. 3.90	J D Shapland "Monacle"	Wadebridge	11. 6.95A
G-BSCN	SOCATA TB-20 Trinidad	1070	D-EGTC	27. 3.90	B W Dye (Noted 6.05)	Biggin Hill	1. 6.02
			G-BSCN				
G-BSCO	Thunder Ax7-77 Balloon (Hot Air)	1635		6. 3.90	F J Whalley "Bluebell"	Cleish	21. 9.09E
G-BSCP	Cessna 152 II	15283289	N48135	20. 3.90	Moray Flying Club (1990) Ltd	RAF Kinloss	21.10.09E
G-BSCS	Piper PA-28-181 Cherokee Archer II		N47392	3. 4.90	Wingtask 1995 Ltd	Seething	16. 5.09E
		28-7890064					

Reg	Type	c/n	Prev id	Date	Owner/Operator	Location	Date
G-BSCV	Piper PA-28-161 Cherokee Warrior II	28-7816135	C-GQXW	22.3.90	R J L Beynon tr Southwood Flying Group	Earls Colne	31. 1.09E
G-BSCW	Taylorcraft BC-65	1798	N24461 NC24461	22. 3.90	S Leach (Carries "C24461" on fin)	Plymouth	15. 6.09P
G-BSCX	Thunder Ax8-105 Balloon (Hot Air)	1748		21. 3.90	Balloon Flights Club Ltd "Balloon Flights"	Leicester	14. 7.99T
G-BSCY	Piper PA-28-151 Cherokee Warrior (Converted to PA-28-161 model)	28-7515046	C-GOBE	22. 3.90	Take Flight Aviation Ltd	Wellesbourne Mountford	20. 4.09E
G-BSCZ	Cessna 152 II	15282199	N68226	22. 3.90	The Royal Air Force Halton Aeroplane Club Ltd	RAF Halton	7. 9.09E
G-BSDA	Taylorcraft BC-12D (Continental A75)	7316	N43657 NC43657	15.11.90	D G Edwards	Ellens Green, West Sussex	9. 9.09P
G-BSDD	Denney Kitfox Model 2 (Built M Richardson and J Cook - pr.no.PFA 172-11797)	639		28. 3.90	D C Crawley	(Calverton, Nottingham)	10. 5.08P
G-BSDH	Robin DR.400-180 Régent	1980		18. 4.90	R L Brucciani	Leicester	10. 5.09E
G-BSDI	Corben Junior Ace Model E (Built Oliver and Clark)	3961	N91706	28. 3.90	J R Ravenhill	Chavenage, Tetbury	12. 1.07P
G-BSDJ	Piper J-4E Cub Coupé (Continental C85)	4-1456	N35975 NC35975	13. 2.91	W J Siertsema	Bicester	14. 9.09P
G-BSDK	Piper J-5A Cub Cruiser (Continental A75)	5-175	N30337 NC30337	28. 3.90	J E Mead	Oaksey Park	1.10.09P
G-BSDL	SOCATA TB-10 Tobago	156		7.10.80	P Middleton and G Corbin tr Delta Lima Group	Sherburn-in-Elmet	13. 7.09E
G-BSDN	Piper PA-34-200T Seneca II	34-7970335	N2893A	2. 4.90	Aircraft Asset Management Ltd	Cardiff	15. 6.08E
G-BSDO	Cessna 152 II	15281657	N65894	23. 5.90	L W Scattergood (Operated Sheffield City Flying School)	Sandtoft	7. 8.09E
G-BSDP	Cessna 152 II	15280268	N24468	11. 6.90	B A Paul	Denham	3. 4.09E
G-BSDS	Boeing Stearman E75 (PT-13A) Kaydet (Continental W670)	75-118 38-470	N57852	6. 4.90	A Basso (As "118" in US Army c/s)	Biel-Kappelen, Switzerland	16. 5.08E
G-BSDV	Colt 31A Balloon (Hot Air)	1722		30. 3.90	S J Roake	Frimley, Camberley	5. 9.09E
G-BSDW	Cessna 182P Skylane II	18264688	N9125M	9. 4.90	Parker Diving Ltd	St Just	21. 8.09E
G-BSDX	Cameron V-77 Balloon (Hot Air) (Officially regd with c/n 2050)	541	(G-BGWA) G-SNOW (1)	30. 3.90	G P and S J Allen	Abingdon	16.10.09E
G-BSDZ	Enstrom 280FX	2051	OO-MHV (OO-JMH), G-ODSC, G-BSDZ	3. 4.90	Avalon Group Ltd (Noted 2007)	Botany Bay, Chorley	25. 7.05
G-BSED	Piper PA-22-160 Tri-Pacer (Hoerner wing-tips: tail-wheel conversion)	22-6377	N9404D	7. 6.90	Tayflite Ltd (Had accident Stonehaven 21. 6.02 - wreck stored 12.08)	Perth	5. 9.03
G-BSEE	Rans S-9 (Built P M Semler) (Rotax 532)	PFA 196-11635		2. 3.90	R P Hothersall	St Michaels	26.11.01P
G-BSEF	Piper PA-28-180 Cherokee C	28-1846	N7831W	18. 4.90	I D Wakeling Franklyn's Field, Chewton Mendip		2.11.06
G-BSEG	Ken Brock KB-2 (Built H Bancroft-Wilson)	PFA G/06-1106		3. 4.90	S J M Ledingham	Carlisle	2. 7.02P
G-BSEJ	Cessna 150M Commuter	15076261	N66767	4. 5.90	D J Dimmer and B Robins	High Ham, Langport	22. 8.09E
G-BSEK	Robinson R22	0027	N45AD N90193	10. 4.90	S J Strange	Blackpool	12. 5.09E
G-BSEL	Slingsby T 61G Super Falke	1986		31. 3.80	D G Holley	RAF Keevil	29. 8.08E
G-BSEP	Cessna 172	46555	N6455E	12. 4.90	R J Watts tr EP Aviation	Redhill	15. 3.09E
G-BSER	Piper PA-28-160 Cherokee B	28-790	N5665W	19. 4.90	Yorkair Ltd	Leeds-Bradford	26.11.09E
G-BSEU	Piper PA-28-181 Cherokee Archer II	28-7890108	N47639	1. 5.90	Euro Aviation 91 Ltd	Blackbushe	25. 5.09E
G-BSEV	Cameron O-77 Balloon (Hot Air)	2271		20. 4.90	P B Kenington (Donor Card titles)	Devauden, Chepstow	25. 4.09E
G-BSEY	Beech A36 Bonanza	E-1873	N1809F	17. 5.90	P Malam-Wilson	Coventry	30.10.08E
G-BSFA	Aero Designs Pulsar (Built S A Gill - pr.no.PFA 202-11754) (Tri-cycle u/c)	176		18. 4.90	P F Lorriman	Rochester	8. 6.06P
G-BSFB	CASA 1-131E Jungmann Series 2000	2053	Spanish AF E3B-449	27. 4.90	M L J Goff (As "S5+B06" in Luftwaffe c/s)	Old Buckenham	4. 3.09P
G-BSFD	Piper J-3C-65 Cub	16037	N88419 NC88419	25. 5.90	P E S Latham (As "16037" in US Army training c/s)	Sleap	9. 7.09P
G-BSFE	Piper PA-38-112 Tomahawk II	38-82A0033	N91452	26. 4.90	D J Campbell	Perth	10. 6.07T
G-BSFF	Robin DR.400-180R Remorqueur	1295	D-ELMM	20. 4.90	Lasham Gliding Society Ltd	Lasham	4. 7.09E
G-BSFP	Cessna 152T	15285548	N93764	9. 5.90	The Pilot Centre Ltd	Denham	18. 8.09E
G-BSFR	Cessna 152 II	15282268	N68341	9. 5.90	Galair Ltd	Biggin Hill	21. 4.10E
G-BSFV	Woods Woody Pusher (Built P E Hall) (Continental C85)	201	N16WP	30. 4.90	M G Parsons	RAF Kinloss	17. 7.09P
G-BSFW	Piper PA-15 Vagabond (Continental A65)	15-273	N4484H NC4484H	26. 4.90	J R Kimberley (Noted 11.06)	Bounds Farm, Ardleigh	21.12.05P
G-BSFX	Denney Kitfox Model 2 (Built D A McFadyean - pr.no.PFA 172-11723)	506		23. 4.90	M W Hanley	Perranporth	30. 7.09P
G-BSFY	Denney Kitfox Model 2 (Built J R Howard - PFA pr.no. duplicates Kitfox G-MWCH)	PFA 172-11632		16. 3.90	C I Bates	Long Marston	8. 6.04P
G-BSGB	Gaertner Ax4 Skyranger Balloon (Hot Air) (Built B Gaertner)	SR.0001		30. 3.90	B Gaertner	Biddenden, Ashford	
G-BSGD	Piper PA-28-180 Cherokee E	28-5691	N3463R	4. 5.90	R J Cleverley	Draycott Farm, Chiseldon	6. 6.09P
G-BSGF	Robinson R22 Beta	1383		1. 5.90	L B Clark	Breighton	28. 6.09E
G-BSGG	Denney Kitfox Model 2 (Built C G Richardson) (Jabiru 2200A)	PFA 172-11666		1. 5.90	C G Richardson	Fulbeck, Lincoln	16. 6.07P
G-BSGH	Airtour AH-56B Balloon (Hot Air)	014		1. 5.90	A R Hardwick "Battle of Britain"	Shefford	
G-BSGJ	Monnett Sonerai II (Built W Hossink) (Volkswagen 1835)	300	N34WH	1. 5.90	J L Loweth (Noted 5.06)	Duxford	6. 9.91P
G-BSGK	Piper PA-34-200T Seneca II	34-7870331	N36450	22. 5.90	Aeros Holdings Ltd	Gloucestershire	18.11.09E
G-BSGL	Piper PA-28-161 Warrior II	28-8116041	N82690	10. 5.90	Keywest Air Charter Ltd "Liverbird V" (Operated Cheshire Air Training Services Ltd)	Liverpool-John Lennon	5. 2.10E
G-BSGP	Cameron N-65 Balloon (Hot Air)	2293		1. 5.90	R Leslie	Ennistymon, Ireland	17. 6.09E

Reg	Type	C/n	Prev id	Date	Owner/Operator	Base	
G-BSGS	Rans S-10 Sakota	1289.076		9. 5.90	M R Parr	Kirkbride	4. 3.09P
	(Built R Handley - pr.no.PFA 194-11724)						
G-BSGT	Cessna 210N Turbo Centurion II	21063361	LX-ATL	21. 5.90	E A T Brenninkmeyer	Biggin Hill	14. 1.09E
	(Reims-assembled c/n F2100020)		D-EOGB, N5308A				
G-BSHA	Piper PA-34-200T Seneca II	34-7670216	N9707K	2. 5.90	Justgold Ltd	Blackpool	19.12.09E
G-BSHC	Colt 69A Balloon (Hot Air)	1668		8. 5.90	Magical Adventures Ltd		
						West Bloomfield, Michigan, US	29. 9.09E
G-BSHD	Colt 69A Balloon (Hot Air)	1736		8. 5.90	F W Ewer	Lighthorne Heath, Leamington Spa	11.12.09E
G-BSHH	Luscombe 8E Silvaire Deluxe	3981	N1254K	11. 5.90	S L Lewis	Lower Upham Farm, Chiseldon	17. 3.09P
	(Continental C85)		NC1254K				
G-BSHI	Luscombe 8F Silvaire	1821	N39060	11. 5.90	P R Bush	(Mastlebridge, Milford Haven)	14. 8.01P
	(Continental C90)		NC39060				
G-BSHK	Denney Kitfox Model 2	449		11. 5.90	D Doyle and C Aherne	Kilrush, County Kildare	29. 8.08P
	(Built A C Cree - pr.no.PFA 172-11752) (Rotax 532)						
G-BSHO	Cameron V-77 Balloon (Hot Air)	2313		16. 5.90	C Stewart and D J Duckworth		
						London E7 and Bellingdon, Chesham	21. 9.07A
G-BSHP	Piper PA-28-161 Warrior II	28-8616002	N190X	31. 5.90	S J Skilton t/a Aviation Rentals	Bournemouth	5.12.09E
	(Thielert TAE 125)		G-BSHP, N9107Y				
G-BSHS	Colt 105A Balloon (Hot Air)	1674	(D-OCAT)	16. 5.90	I Novosad	Planegg, Germany	9. 9.01A
			G-BSHS				
G-BSHV	Piper PA-18-135 Super Cub	18-3123	OO-GDG	5. 7.90	G T Fisher	North Side, Thorney	20. 5.04
	(L-18C-PI)		Belgian Army L-49, 53-4723				
G-BSHY	EAA Acrosport	PFA 072-10928		17. 4.90	R J Hodder	Eastfield Farm, Manby	20.12.05P
	(Built T Butterworth and R J Hodder) (Lycoming O-290)				*(Landed long Keal Coates, Lincoln 2.5.05 and substantially damaged)*		
G-BSIC	Cameron V-77 Balloon (Hot Air)	2322		17. 5.90	T R Tillson	Ilkeston	29.11.09E
G-BSIF	Denney Kitfox Model 2	563		5. 7.90	R J Humphries	Walkeridge Farm, Overton	6.10.09P
	(Built R M Kimbell and M H Wylde - pr.no.PFA 172-11889)						
G-BSIG	Colt 21A Cloudhopper Balloon (Hot-Air)	1322		18. 5.90	C J Dunkley	Wendover	
G-BSIH	Rutan LongEz	1200-1		31. 5.90	W S Allen	(Cheltenham)	
	(Built W S Allen - pr.no.PFA 074A-11492)						
G-BSII	Piper PA-34-200T Seneca II	34-8070336	N8253N	16. 5.90	T Belso	Fowlmere	15. 7.09E
G-BSIJ	Cameron V-77 Balloon (Hot Air)	2164		23. 5.90	G B Davies	Thorney, Peterborough	16. 7.09E
G-BSIK	Denney Kitfox Model 1	51		5. 6.90	M Bromage	(Stonehouse)	26. 6.06P
	(Built R L Cunliffe) (Rotax 503)						
G-BSIM	Piper PA-28-181 Archer II	28-8690017	N9092Y	22. 5.90	Central Aircraft Leasing Ltd	Wolverhampton	7. 9.08E
G-BSIO	Cameron Furness House 56 SS Balloon (Hot Air)	2310		25. 5.90	R E Jones *"Pinkie"*	Lytham St Annes	29.11.09E
G-BSIU	Colt 90A Balloon (Hot Air)	1774		25. 5.90	S Travaglia	Firenze, Italy	12. 7.04A
G-BSIY	Schleicher ASK 14	14005	5Y-AID	4. 6.90	P W Andrews	Husbands Bosworth	20.11.09E
			D-KOIC				
G-BSIZ	Piper PA-28-181 Archer II	28-7990377	N2162Y	25. 5.90	P J Gerrard and M J Cunnliffe		
						Liverpool-John Lennon	21. 6.09E
G-BSJB	Bensen B 8	PFA G/01-1080		5. 6.90	J W Limbrick	(Bewdley)	
	(Built J W Limbrick)						
G-BSJU	Cessna 150M	15076430	N3230V	14. 6.90	A C Williamson *(Operated Crowfield Flying Club)*		
						Crowfield	14. 3.09E
G-BSJX	Piper PA-28-161 Warrior II	28-8216084	N8036N	30. 5.90	MK Aero Supprt Ltd	Andrewsfield	23. 7.09E
G-BSJZ	Cessna 150J	15070485	N60661	7. 5.91	M H Campbell	Kemble	20.11.09E
G-BSKA	Cessna 150M	15076137	N66588	31. 7.90	R J Cushing	Ellough, Beccles	1. 9.09E
G-BSKD	Cameron V-77 Balloon (Hot Air)	2336		4. 6.90	M J Gunston *"Skulduggery"*		
						Blackwater, Camberley	4. 8.06A
G-BSKE	Cameron O-84 Balloon (Hot Air)	1604	ZS-HYD	4. 6.90	S F Redman	Stalbridge, Sturminster Newton	19. 8.03A
	(Incorrectly listed by CAA as ex ZS-HYJ)		G-BSKE				
G-BSKG	Maule MX-7-180 Super Rocket	11072C		7. 6.90	J R Surbey	East Winch	10. 2.06
					(On rebuild East Winch 10.08 following accident at Top Farm 20.11.05)		
G-BSKL	Piper PA-38-112 Tomahawk	38-78A0509	N4252E	11. 6.90	A S Bamrah t/a Falcon Flying Services	Biggin Hill	22.11.08E
G-BSKU	Cameron O-84 Balloon (Hot Air)	2330		8. 6.90	Alfred Bagnall and Sons (West) Ltd *"Bagnalls II"*		
						Bristol	7. 6.02A
G-BSKW	Piper PA-28-181 Archer II	2890138	N91940	1. 6.90	Shropshire Aero Club Ltd	Sleap	9. 4.09E
G-BSLA	Robin DR.400-180 Régent	1997		22. 6.90	A B McCoig tr Robin Lima Alpha Group	Rochester	19. 3.09E
G-BSLH	CASA 1-131E Jungmann Series 2000	2222	Spanish AF	27. 7.90	P Warden	Biel-Kappelen, Switzerland	12. 8.08P
	(Officially quoted c/n and p/i incorrect)		E3B-622				
	(Built new Bücker Prado SL, Albacete, Spain)						
G-BSLI	Cameron V-77 Balloon (Hot Air)	2115		15. 6.90	R S McKibbin	Thornbury, Bristol	11. 8.09E
G-BSLK	Piper PA-28-161 Warrior II	28-7916018	N20849	15. 6.90	R A Rose	Wellesbourne Mountford	1. 7.09E
G-BSLM	Piper PA-28-160 Cherokee	28-308	N5262W	22. 6.90	R Fulton	Popham	25. 4.08
G-BSLT	Piper PA-28-161 Warrior II	28-8016303	N81817	19. 6.90	L W Scattergood *(Operated Sheffield City Flying School)*		
						Sandtoft	4. 2.09E
G-BSLU	Piper PA-28-140 Cherokee	28-24733	OY-PJL	19. 6.90	W E Lewis	Shobdon	6. 2.09E
			OH-PJL, SE-FFA				
G-BSLV	Enstrom 280FX	2054	D-HHAS	26. 6.90	T Carroll	Barton	20. 5.09E
			G-BSLV				
G-BSLW	Champion 7ECA Citabria	431-66	N9696S	16. 7.90	D W Mann tr Shoreham Citabria Group	Shoreham	6. 9.03
	(Officially regd as "Bellanca 7ECA Citabria")						
G-BSLX	WAR Focke-Wulf FW190 replica	24	N698WW	19. 6.90	D Featherby tr FW190 Gruppe *(As "1+4" in Luftwaffe c/s)*		
	(Built W Wilson)					Norwich	2. 8.02P
G-BSMD	SNCAN 1101 Noralpha	139	F-GDPQ	26. 6.90	J W Hardie *(As "+14" in Luftwaffe c/s)*	Prestwick	16. 6.09P
			F-YEEE, F-YCZK, CAN-11, French Military				
G-BSME	Bölkow BÖ.208C Junior	596	D-ECGA	25. 6.90	D J Hampson	(Rotterdam)	12. 3.10E
G-BSMG	Montgomerie-Bensen B 8M	PFA G/01-1170		22. 6.90	A C Timperley	(Dull, Aberfeldy)	16. 7.97P
	(Built A C Timperley) (Rotax 532)						
G-BSMK	Cameron O-84 Balloon (Hot Air)	2328		26. 6.90	D F Maine and D M Newton tr G-BSMK Shareholders		
						Redditch	9. 7.09E

Reg	Type	C/n	Prev id	Date	Owner	Location	Exp
G-BSML	Schweizer 269C *(Schweizer 300)*	S 1462	PH-HUH N134DM	10.10.90	K P Foster and B I Winsor t/a Moorgoods Helicopters	Liskeard Heliport	9. 5.09E
G-BSMM	Colt 31A Sky Chariot Balloon (Hot Air)	1779		27. 6.90	D V Fowler	Cranbrook	14. 7.09E
G-BSMN	CFM Streak Shadow	K 137-SA		26. 6.90	P J Porter *"Cute with Attitude"*	Henstridge	29. 8.08P
	(Built K Daniels - pr.no.PFA 161A-11656) (Rotax 582)						
G-BSMS	Cameron V-77 Balloon (Hot Air)	2356		26. 6.90	R Ashford	Petworth	30. 6.07A
G-BSMT	Rans S-10 Sakota	1289.077		29. 6.90	S J Kidd	Chilsford Farm, Kirdford	8. 6.05P
	(Built N Woodworth - pr.no.PFA 194-11793)						
G-BSMU	Rans S-6-116N Coyote II	1089.090	G-MWJE	27. 6.90	A Wright *(Active 6.08)*	Church Farm, Askern	30. 6.07P
	(Built W D Walker - pr.no.PFA 204-11732)						
G-BSMV	Piper PA-17 Vagabond	17-94	N4696H NC4696H	29. 6.90	A Cheriton *"Sophie" (Carries 'N4696H' on tail)*	Wellesbourne Mountford	11. 2.09P
	(Continental C85)						
G-BSMX	Bensen B 8MR	PFA G/01-1171		3. 7.90	J S E R McGregor	(Birmingham)	
	(Built J S E R McGregor)						
G-BSND	Air Command 532 Elite	PFA G/04-1180		16. 7.90	T A Holmes	(Leeds)	
	(Built B J Castle)						
G-BSNE	Luscombe 8E Silvaire Deluxe	5757	N1130B NC1130B	2.11.90	C B Buscombe, R Goldsworthy and G Vitta	Bodmin	13.11.09P
	(Continental C85)						
G-BSNF	Piper J-3C-65 Cub	3070	N23317 NC23317	17. 8.90	D A Hammant *(Lippert Reed conversion)*	Bere Farm, Warnford	17. 9.09P
	(Continental O-200-A) *(Frame No.3116)*						
G-BSNG	Cessna 172N Skyhawk II	17270192	N738SB	19. 7.90	A J and P C MacDonald	Edinburgh	26. 2.09E
G-BSNJ	Cameron N-90 Balloon (Hot Air)	2335		6. 7.90	D P H Smith	Ilkley	8. 6.04A
G-BSNL	Bensen B 8MR	PFA G/01-1181		16. 7.90	A C Breane	(Ballybofey, County Donegal)	20. 7.97P
	(Built T R Grief) (Rotax 532)						
G-BSNP	Piper PA-28R-201T Turbo Arrow III	28R-7703236	N38537	18. 7.90	D F K Singleton	(Teck, Germany)	7.10.09E
G-BSNT	Luscombe 8A Silvaire	1679	N37018 NC37018	16. 7.90	P K Jordan tr Luscombe Quartet	Stoneacre Farm, Farthing Corner	1. 4.08P
	(Continental A65) *(Built as Model 8C)*						
G-BSNU	Colt 105A Balloon (Hot Air)	1811		23. 7.90	M P Rich tr Gone Ballooning *"Sun Rise"*	Warmley, Bristol	12. 4.09E
G-BSNX	Piper PA-28-181 Archer II	28-7990311	N3028S	19. 7.90	Central Aircraft Leasing Ltd	Wolverhampton	25. 8.09E
G-BSNY	Bensen B 8M	PFA G/01-1176		16. 7.90	H McCartney	(Stockport)	6. 9.01P
	(Built A S Deakin) (Arrow GT500R)						
G-BSNZ	Cameron O-105 Balloon (Hot Air)	2364		16. 7.90	J Francis *"Firefly"*	Dibden Purlieu, Southampton	28. 8.09E
G-BSOE	Luscombe 8A Silvaire	4331	N1604K NC1604K	22. 8.90	S B Marsden *(Stored dismantled as "N1604K" 8.05)*	Sturgate	
	(C/n would indicate Model 8E)						
G-BSOF	Colt 25A Sky Chariot Mk.II Balloon (Hot Air)	1820		27. 7.90	J M Bailey	Pill, Bristol	18. 5.09E
G-BSOG	Cessna 172M Skyhawk II	17263636	N1508V	16. 7.90	S Eustace	Crowfield	17. 2.09E
G-BSOJ	Thunder Ax7-77 Balloon (Hot Air)	1818	JA-... G-BSOJ	31. 7.90	R J S Jones	Stourbridge	13. 7.09E
G-BSOK	Piper PA-28-161 Cherokee Warrior II	28-7816191	N9749K	19. 7.90	Aeros Leasing Ltd	Gloucestershire	5. 2.09E
G-BSOM	Glaser-Dirks DG-400	4-126	LN-GMC D-KGDG	12. 7.90	M J Watson tr G-BSOM Group *"403"*	Sutton Bank	29. 5.09E
G-BSON	Green S-25 Balloon (Hot Air)	001		7. 6.90	J J Green *(Inflated 1.09)*	Newbury	
	(Built J J Green)						
G-BSOO	Cessna 172F	17252431	N8531U	19. 7.90	P W Lawrence tr Double Oscar Flying Group	Seething	5.12.08E
G-BSOR	CFM Streak Shadow	K 131-SA		23.10.89	A Parr	(Lewes, Sussex)	11. 6.09P
	(Built J P Sorensen - pr.no.PFA 161A-11602) (Rotax 532)						
G-BSOT	Piper PA-38-112 Tomahawk II	38-81A0053	N25682	23. 7.90	APB Leasing Ltd	Sleap	29.12.09E
G-BSOU	Piper PA-38-112 Tomahawk II	38-81A0130	N23373	23. 7.90	D J Campbell	Perth	22. 2.08E
G-BSOX	Luscombe 8AE Silvaire	2318	N45791 NC45791	7. 8.90	R S Lanary *"Bobby Sox"*	Sixpenny Handley, Dorset	15. 6.09P
	(Continental O-200-A)						
G-BSOZ	Piper PA-28-161 Warrior II	28-7916080	N30220	14. 8.90	Highland Asset Management Ltd	Stapleford	22. 1.09E
G-BSPA	QAC Quickie Q.2	2227	N227T	16. 8.90	G V Mckirdy and B K Glover	Enstone	25. 5.06P
	(Built C C and MA Wilde) (Revmaster R2100DQ)						
G-BSPB	Thunder Ax8-84 Balloon (Hot Air)	1803		24. 7.90	A N F Pertwee	Great Holland, Frinton-on-Sea	22. 9.00T
G-BSPE	Reims Cessna F172P Skyhawk II	F17202073		31.12.80	T W Williamson	Hinkle Grange Farm, Barton	21. 7.09E
G-BSPG	Piper PA-34-200T Seneca II	34-8070168	N8176S	8. 8.90	Andrews Professional Colour Laboratories Ltd	Headcorn	12. 8.09E
G-BSPI	Piper PA-28-161 Warrior II	28-8116025	N8258V	26. 7.90	TGD Leasing Ltd	Wellesbourne Mountford	30. 4.09E
G-BSPJ	Campell Cricket replica	PFA G/01-1061		3. 8.90	D Ross	(Londonderry)	8. 1.04P
	(Built P Barlow ,A Scott and C Jones)						
G-BSPK	Cessna 195A	7691	N1079D	14. 8.90	A G and D L Bompas	Biggin Hill	22. 5.11S
	(Jacobs R-755-9)						
G-BSPL	CFM Streak Shadow	K 140-SA		26. 7.90	G L Turner	Pittrichie Farm, Whiterashes	15. 7.09P
	(Built CFM Metal-Fax) (Rotax 582)						
G-BSPM	Piper PA-28-161 Warrior II	28-8116046	N82679	27. 7.90	S J Skilton tr Aviation Rentals *(Operated West London Aero Services)*	White Waltham	23. 1.10E
	(Thielert TAE 125)						
G-BSPN	Piper PA-28R-201T Turbo Arrow III	28R-7703171	N5965V	31. 7.90	V E H Taylor	Haverfordwest	27. 3.09E
G-BSPT	Pilatus Britten-Norman BN-2B-20 Islander	2240	TF-VEG N52WA, OY-PHY, JA5316, G-BSPT	3. 8.90	Hebridean Air Services Ltd	Cumbernauld	29. 3.09E
	(Originally regd as BN-2B-26)						
G-BSPW	Avid Speed Wing	PFA 189-11840		17. 7.90	M J Sewell	(Haydock, St Helens)	4. 9.04P
	(Built P D Wheatland)						
G-BSRD	Cameron N-105 Balloon (Hot Air)	1568	D-ORSD G-BSRD	3. 8.90	A Ockelmann t/a Ballon Reisen	Buchholz, Germany	4. 9.04A
G-BSRH	Pitts S-1C	LS-2	N4111	7. 8.90	C D Swift *(Carries "N4111" on rudder)*	Redhill	20.10.09P
	(Built L Smith)						
G-BSRI	Neico Lancair 235	PFA 191-11467		9. 8.90	G Lewis	Liverpool-John Lennon	7. 8.09P
	(Built G Lewis) (Lycoming O-235) *(Tri-cycle u/c)*						
G-BSRK	ARV Aviation ARV-1 Super 2	K 007	ZK-FSQ	8. 8.90	D M Blair	RAF Mona	19. 6.08P

G-BSRL	Campbell Cricket Mk.4 replica PFA G/03-1325			8. 8.90	S L Kennett	Little Rissington	4. 2.09P
	(Built I Rosewall from Everett Gyroplane Series 2 c/n 0022)						
G-BSRP	RotorWay Executive	3824		15. 8.90	R J Baker	Hawarden	1. 5.08P
	(Built J P Dennison) (RotorWay RW 152)						
G-BSRR	Cessna 182Q Skylane II	18266915	N96961	25. 7.90	C M Moore		
					Thornborough Grounds, Buckingham/Turweston		1. 4.09E
G-BSRT	Denney Kitfox Model 2	742		9. 8.90	A Rooker	(Histon, Cambridge)	12. 5.09P
	(Built L R James - pr.no.PFA 172-11873)						
G-BSRX	CFM Streak Shadow	K 148-SA		15. 8.90	W Southcott	Old Sarum	15.12.09P
	(Built C Penman - pr.no.PFA 206-11870) (Rotax 618)						
G-BSSA	Luscombe 8E Silvaire Deluxe	4176	N1449K	15. 8.90	K R Old tr Luscombe Flying Group	White Waltham	24.10.08P
	(Continental C85)		NC1449K				
G-BSSB	Cessna 150L Commuter	15074147	N19076	15. 8.90	D T A Rees *(Operated Haverfordwest Air Charter Services)*		
						Haverfordwest	29. 6.09E
G-BSSC	Piper PA-28-161 Warrior II	28-8216176	N81993	15. 8.90	G-BSSC Ltd	Norwich	25. 3.09E
			N9529N, N8234B				
G-BSSE	Piper PA-28-140 Cherokee Cruiser		N33440	22.10.90	D Hoyle	Blackpool	14.11.07E
		28-7525192					
G-BSSF	Denney Kitfox Model 2	738		15. 8.90	A M Smith	(Broughton, Brigg)	9.10.08P
	(Built D M Orrock - pr.no.PFA 172-11796)						
	(Engine failed during a practice forced landing near Humberside 30. 6.08; aircraft overturned in a field of standing crops)						
G-BSSI	Rans S-6-116N Coyote II	0190.112	(G-MWJA)	17. 8.90	J Currell *(Believed stored)*		
	(Built D A Farnwroth - pr.no.PFA 204-11782)					(Bangor, Co Down)	16.11.99P
G-BSSK	QAC Quickie Q.200 PFA 094A-11354			5. 9.90	D G Greatrex	(Crookham, Thatcham)	23. 9.99P
	(Built D G Greatrex) (Continental O-200-A)						
G-BSSP	Robin DR.400-180R Remorqueur	2015		24. 9.90	Soaring (Oxford) Ltd *(Operated Air Cadets Gliding School)*		
						RAF Syerston	5. 2.10E
G-BSSV	CFM Streak Shadow	K 129-SA		21. 8.90	R W Payne	(Langtoft, Peterborough)	5. 5.98P
	(Built A M Green - pr.no.PFA 206-11657) (Rotax 532)						
G-BSSW	Piper PA-28-161 Cherokee Warrior II						
		28-7816143	N47850	29. 8.90	D J Skidmore and E F Rowland	Filton	5. 9.08E
G-BSTC	Aeronca 11AC Chief	11AC-1660	N3289E	15.10.90	J Armstrong and D Lamb	(Crook)	26. 6.93P
	(Continental A65)		NC3289E		*(Damaged Henstridge 18.4.93: on rebuild 12.95)*		
G-BSTE	Aérospatiale AS.355F2 Ecureuil 2	5453		29. 8.90	Oscar Mayer Ltd	Redhill	21.12.09E
G-BSTH	Piper PA-25-235 Pawnee C	25-5009	N8599L	25. 9.90	Scottish Gliding Union Ltd	Portmoak	1. 5.09E
G-BSTI	Piper J-3C-65 Cub	19144	N6007H	31. 8.90	J A Scott Chesnut Farm, Tipsend, Welney		13. 7.09P
	(Frame No.19073) (Continental C85)		NC6007H				
G-BSTK	Thunder Ax8-90 Balloon (Hot Air)	1838		17. 9.90	M Williams	Wadhurst, East Sussex	28. 1.08A
G-BSTL	Rand Robinson KR-2 PFA 129-11863			6. 9.90	C S Hales and N Brauns	Shenington	30. 6.05P
	(Built C S Hales)						
G-BSTM	Cessna 172L Skyhawk	17260143	N4243Q	25. 9.90	A C G Brown tr G-BSTM Group	Duxford	18. 3.09P
G-BSTO	Cessna 152 II	15282133	N68005	4. 9.90	Plymouth Flying School Ltd	Plymouth	20. 1.10E
G-BSTP	Cessna 152 II	15282021	N89953	4. 9.90	Cobham Leasing Ltd	Bournemouth	18. 3.10E
G-BSTR	Grumman AA-5 Traveler	AA5-0688	OO-ALR	8.10.90	B D Jones	Wellesbourne Mountford	1. 3.09E
			OO-HAN, (OO-WAZ)				
G-BSTT	Rans S-6 Coyote II	0190.115		5. 9.90	D G Palmer	Mintlaw, Peterhead	2.12.02P
	(Built M W Holmes - pr.no.PFA 204-11880) (Rotax 582)						
G-BSTV	Piper PA-32-300 Cherokee Six	32-40378	N4069R	13. 9.90	B C Hudson *(In open store 9.08)*	Popham	
G-BSTX	Luscombe 8A Silvaire	3301	EI-CDZ	10. 9.90	C Chambers	(Kilkeel, Newry)	22. 5.09P
	(Continental A65)		G-BSTX, N71874, NC71874				
G-BSTY	Thunder Ax8-90 Balloon (Hot Air)	394		12. 9.90	High On Adventure Balloons Ltd		
						Storrington, Pulborough	15. 4.09E
G-BSTZ	Piper PA-28-140 Cherokee Cruiser		N1674H	10.10.90	Air Navigation and Trading Company Ltd		
		28-7725153				Blackpool	15. 7.09E
G-BSUA	Rans S-6 Coyote II	0190.109		29.10.90	A J Todd	Abbey Warren Farm, Bucknall	1. 2.08P
	(Built P S Dopson - pr.no.PFA 204-11910) (Rotax 582)						
G-BSUB	Colt 77A Balloon (Hot Air)	1801		30.10.90	M P Hill and J M Foster *"Bristol Blue"*		
						Flax Bourton, Bristol	3. 5.09E
G-BSUD	Luscombe 8A Silvaire	1745	N37084	14. 9.90	I G Harrison	Derby	16. 9.08P
	(Continental A65)		NC37084				
G-BSUE	Cessna U206G Stationair 6	U20604334	N756TB	6. 9.90	I C Austin, G S Chapman and J Dyer		
						Little Gransden	22. 6.09E
G-BSUF	Piper PA-32RT-300 Lance II	32R-7885240	N32PL	17. 9.90	S A Fell and J Gibbs	Guernsey	21. 2.09E
			ZP-PJQ, N9641N				
G-BSUK	Colt 77A Balloon (Hot Air)	1374		21. 9.90	A J Moore	Northwood, Harrow	22. 7.09E
G-BSUO	Scheibe SF25C-2000 Falke	44501	D-KIOK	6.12.90	J G Smith and J L Riley tr Portmoak Falke Syndicate		
	(Limbach L2000)					Portmoak	20. 8.09E
G-BSUV	Cameron O-77 Balloon (Hot Air)	2407		26. 9.90	J F Trehern	Edinburgh	3. 8.09E
G-BSUW	Piper PA-34-200T Seneca II	34-7870081	N2360M	26. 9.90	NPD Direct Ltd	Fenland	26. 2.09E
G-BSUX	Carlson Sparrow II PFA 209-11794			5.10.90	J Stephenson	Wombleton	17. 6.06P
	(Built J Stephnson) (Rotax 532)						
G-BSUZ	Denney Kitfox Model 3	745		10. 9.90	P C Avery	Fenland	30. 7.09P
	(Built E T Wicks - pr.no.PFA 172-11875) (Converted from Model 2)						
G-BSVB	Piper PA-28-181 Archer II	2890098	N9155S	10. 9.90	K A Boost	High Cross, Ware	5. 2.10E
G-BSVE	Binder CP.301S Smaragd	113	HB-SED	27. 9.90	R E Perry tr Smaragd Flying Group		
						Smalls Farm, Charterhouse	27. 4.09P
G-BSVG	Piper PA-28-161 Warrior II	28-8516013	C-GZAV	2.10.90	Airways Aero Associations Ltd Wycombe Air Park		22.12.09E
					(Operated British Airways Flying Club)		
G-BSVH	Piper J-3C-65 Cub	15360	N87702	2.10.90	C R and K A Maher	RAF Woodvale	18. 7.08P
	(Continental A75) *(Frame No.15003)*		NC87702				
G-BSVI	Piper PA-16 Clipper	16-186	N5379H	7.11.90	J Watkins and S Northway tr Clipper Aviation		
						Wadswick Manor Farm , Corsham	19.12.10
G-BSVK	Denney Kitfox Model 2 PFA 172-11731			2.10.90	C Cox	Jackrell's Farm, Southwater	5. 4.94P
	(Built K P Wordsworth)						

Reg	Type	C/n	Prev id	Date	Owner/Operator	Base	Date2
G-BSVM	Piper PA-28-161 Warrior II	28-8116173	N8351N	7.11.90	EFG Flying Services Ltd	Biggin Hill	10. 2.09E
G-BSVN	Thorp T-18	107	N4881	17. 9.90	D Prentice	(Sheffield)	8. 7.05P
	(Built M R Miller) (Lycoming O-290)						
G-BSVP	Piper PA-23-250 Aztec F	27-7754115	N959JB	9. 2.78	S G Spier	Elstree	1. 5.09E
			G-BSVP, N63787				
G-BSVR	Schweizer 269C (Schweizer 300)	S 1236	OO-JWW	14.11.90	M K E Askham	(Low Catton, York)	30. 9.09E
			D-HLEB				
G-BSVS	Robin DR.400-100 Cadet	2017		22.10.90	D M Chalmers		
					Upper Harford Farm, Bourton-on-the-Water		23. 3.09E
G-BSWB	Rans S-10 Sakota	0489.046		8.10.90	F A Hewitt	Garston Farm, Marshfield	11.12.09P
	(Built F A Hewitt - pr.no.PFA 194-11560)						
G-BSWC	Boeing Stearman E75 (PT-13D) Kaydet	75-5560	N17112	16.11.90	Richard Thwaites Aviation Ltd (As "112" in US Army c/s)		
	(Lycoming R-680)		N5021V, 42-17397			Gloucestershire	22. 6.08E
G-BSWF	Piper PA-16 Clipper (modified)	16-475	N5865H	12.10.90	P E Bates tr Durham Clipper Group		
	(Lycoming O-320)				High Flatts Farm, Chester le Street		27. 4.11
G-BSWG	Piper PA-17 Vagabond	15-99	N4316H	8.10.90	P E J Sturgeon Queach Farm, Bury St Edmunds		31.10.09P
	(Continental A65-8)		NC4316H				
G-BSWH	Cessna 152 II	15281365	N49861	15.10.90	Airspeed Aviation Ltd	Derby	14. 3.02T
G-BSWL	Slingsby T 61F Venture T 2	1974	EI-CCQ	15.10.90	Bidford Gliding Ltd	Bidford	14. 7.09E
			G-BSWL, ZA655				
G-BSWM	Slingsby T 61F Venture T 2	1965	ZA629	12.10.90	P S Holmes tr Venture Gliding Group	Bellamena	10. 7.09
G-BSWR	Pilatus Britten-Norman BN-2T Islander	2245		22.10.90	Police Service of Northern Ireland		
						Belfast International	2. 3.10S
G-BSWV	Cameron N-77 Balloon (Hot Air)	2369		22.10.90	S Charlist "Leicester Mercury"	Leicester	30. 9.09E
G-BSWX	Cameron V-90 Balloon (Hot Air)	2401		22.10.90	B J Burrows "Beeswax"	Bristol	27. 7.09E
G-BSWY	Cameron N-77 Balloon (Hot Air)	2428		12.10.90	A S Davidson tr Nottingham Hot Air Balloon Club		
						Woodville, Swadlincote	5. 7.05A
G-BSXA	Piper PA-28-161 Warrior II	28-8416121	N4373Z	11.12.90	A S Bamrah t/a Falcon Flying Services	Biggin Hill	3. 8.09E
			N9622N				
G-BSXB	Piper PA-28-161 Warrior II	28-8416125	N4374D	4.12.90	Aeros Leasing Ltd	Gloucestershire	10. 5.08E
			N9626N				
G-BSXC	Piper PA-28-161 Warrior II	28-8416126	N4374F	4.12.90	L T Halpin	Cameley, Somerset	5.10.07E
			N9627N				
G-BSXD	Soko P-2 Kraguj	030	Yugoslav AF	22.10.90	S M Johnstone (As "146" in Yugoslav Air Force c/s)		
			30146			RAF Linton-on-Ouse	16. 4.08P
G-BSXI	Mooney M 20E Super 21	700056	N6766V	31.10.90	A N Pain	Earls Colne	8. 6.09E
G-BSXM	Cameron V-77 Balloon (Hot Air)	2446		5.11.90	C A Oxby "Oxby"	Doncaster	31. 8.05A
G-BSXS	Piper PA-28-181 Archer II	28-7990151	N3055C	26.11.90	J K Milner	Kemble	10. 8.09E
G-BSXT	Piper J-5A Cub Cruiser	5-498	N33409	8.11.90	L Jobes Spite Hall Farm, Pinchinthorpe		26. 7.03P
	(Continental C85)		NC33409				
G-BSXX	Whittaker MW7	PFA 171-11469		16.10.90	H J Stanley	(Abingdon)	
	(Built H J Stanley)						
G-BSYA	Jodel D 18	PFA 169-11316		7.11.90	K Wright	Andreas, Isle of Man	1.10.07P
	(Built S Harrison) (Volkswagen 1834)						
G-BSYB	Cameron N-120 Balloon (Hot Air)	2406		7.11.90	M Buono (Cameron Balloon titles) Mondovi, Italy		24. 7.03A
G-BSYF	Luscombe 8A Silvaire	3455	N72028	12.11.90	Atlantic Connexions Ltd t/a Atlantic Aviation		
	(Continetnal C85)		NC72028			Old Warden	12. 3.09P
G-BSYG	Piper PA-12 Super Cruiser	12-2106	N3228M	12.11.90	E R Newall tr Fat Cub Group	Breighton	9. 8.07P
	(Lycoming O-235)		NC3228M				
G-BSYH	Luscombe 8A Silvaire	2842	N71415	13.11.90	N R Osborne	Insch	15. 5.09P
	(Continental A65)		NC71415				
G-BSYI	Aérospatiale AS.355F1 Ecureuil 2	5197	M-MJI	14.11.90	Sky Charter UK Ltd	Manston	28.11.09E
G-BSYO	Piper J-3C-65 Cub (L-4B-PI)	12809	(G-BSMJ)	19. 2.91	C R Reynolds and J D Fuller Pent Farm, Postling		17. 5.08P
	(Continental O-200-A) (Frame No.12639)		(G-BRHE), EC-AIY, HB-ODO, HB-OUA, 44-80513				
	(Officially regd as c/n 10244 which is HB-OVG ex 43-1383/F-BFYF)						
G-BSYU	Robin DR.400-180 Régent	2027		26.11.90	P D Smoothy	Hinton-in-the-Hedges	22. 4.09E
G-BSYV	Cessna 150M	15078371	N9423U	16.11.90	E-Plane Ltd	Fenland	15. 4.09E
G-BSYW	Cessna 150M	15078446	N9498U	16.11.90	Cada Vliegtuilgen BV (The Hague, Netherlands)		27.11.09E
G-BSYY	Piper PA-28-161 Warrior II	2816009	N440X	26.11.90	S J Skilton t/a Aviation Rentals (Operated Solent Flight)		
	(Thielert TAE 125)		G-BSYY, N9100X			Compton Abbas	6. 2.09E
G-BSYZ	Piper PA-28-161 Warrior II	28-8516051	N6908H	22.11.90	S W Cowie tr Yankee Zulu Group	Glasgow	5.11.09E
					(Operated Glasgow Flying Club)		
G-BSZB	Stolp SA.300 Starduster Too	545	N5495M	3.12.90	D T Gethin	Swansea	3. 6.09P
	(Built J W Matthews) (Lycoming O-360)						
G-BSZC	Beech C-45H-BH Expeditor	AF-258	N9541Z	14.12.90	Weston Ltd (As "51-11701A:AF258/"in USAF c/s)		
			51-11701		"Southern Comfort" Weston, Leixlip, County Kildare		4. 6.06
	(Built as AT-7 42-2490 [4166]: re-manufactured 4.52)						
G-BSZD	Robin DR.400-180 Régent	2029		21.11.90	M Rowland	Draycott Farm, Chiseldon	24. 4.09E
G-BSZF	CEA Jodel DR.250/160 Capitaine	32	F-BNJB	29.11.90	J B Randle	Biggin Hill	15. 7.09E
G-BSZG	Stolp SA.100 Starduster	101	N70P	27.11.90	D F Chapman (Noted 6.05)	Headcorn	4. 7.00P
	(Built L Stolp and G Adams) (Lycoming O-320)						
G-BSZH	Thunder Ax7-77 Balloon (Hot Air)	1848		27.11.90	T J Wilkinson	Sackville Lodge, Riseley	13. 7.09E
G-BSZI	Cessna 152 II	15285856	N95139	17.12.90	Eglinton Flying Club Ltd	City of Derry	21. 4.09E
G-BSZJ	Piper PA-28-181 Archer II	28-8190216	N8373Z	6.12.90	R D Fuller and M L A Pudney "21"		
					West Newlands Farm, St Lawrence, Bradwell-on-Sea		3. 5.09E
G-BSZM	Montgomerie-Bensen B 8MR	PFA G/01-1193		30.11.90	A McCredie (Noted 7.08)	Kirkbride	13. 8.07P
	(Built J H H Turner) (Rotax 582)						
G-BSZO	Cessna 152 II	15280221	N24334	30.11.90	M and N Jahanafar (Operated The Flight Centre)		
						Southend	18. 1.10E
G-BSZT	Piper PA-28-161 Warrior II	28-8116027	N8260D	31.12.90	Golf Charlie Echo Ltd (Operated The Flying Hut)		
						Shoreham	26. 4.09E
G-BSZU	Cessna 150F Commuter	15063481	N6881F	3.12.90	C Partington	Ronaldsway	23. 1.09E
G-BSZV	Cessna 150F	15062304	N3504L	3.12.90	C A Davis	Sandown	15.11.09E

| G-BSZW | Cessna 152 II | 15281072 | N48958 | 3.12.90 | Haimoss Ltd (Operated Old Sarum Flying Club) | | |
| | | | | | | Old Sarum | 14. 2.09E |

G-BTAA - G-BTZZ

G-BTAG	Cameron O-77 Balloon (Hot Air)	2454		12.11.90	R A Shapland "Tag-Along"	Petworth	21. 9.09E
G-BTAK	EAA Acrosport II	1468	N440X	27.12.90	S E Ford	Mitchells Farm, Wilburton	22. 4.09P
	(Built A P Savage) (Lycoming O-320)						
G-BTAL	Reims Cessna F152 II	F15201444		7. 4.78	Herefordshire Aero Club Ltd	Shobdon	16. 3.09E
G-BTAM	Piper PA-28-181 Archer II	2890093	RA-01765	10. 1.91	Tri-Star Farms Ltd	Glenforsa, Isle of Mull	6. 1.09E
			G-BTAM, N9153D				
G-BTAN	Thunder Ax7-65Z Balloon (Hot Air)	517		4. 5.83	A S Newnham	Southampton	23. 8.06A
G-BTAS	Piper PA-38-112 Tomahawk	38-79A0545	F-GTAS	21. 2.91	Ravenair Aircraft Ltd	Ronaldsway	17. 6.09E
			G-BTAS, N2492G				
G-BTAT	Denney Kitfox Model 2	689		6.11.90	M Lawton	Otherton, Cannock	22. 7.09E
	(Built D G Marwick - pr.no.PFA 172-11832)						
G-BTAU	Thunder Ax7-77 Balloon (Hot Air)	1429		13.12.90	S and G Gebauer	Lippstadt, Germany	10. 9.09E
G-BTAW	Piper PA-28-161 Warrior II	28-8616031	N9259T	14.12.90	T J Parish tr Piper Flying Group	Newcastle	27. 6.09E
G-BTAZ	Evans VP-2	PFA 063-11474		13.12.90	G S Poulter (Noted complete 10.05)	Norwich	
	(Built G S Poulter)						
G-BTBA	Robinson R22 Beta	1717		18. 3.91	Heliflight (UK) Ltd	Gloucestershire	30. 4.09E
G-BTBB	Thunder Ax8-105 Series 2 Balloon (Hot Air)			23.11.90	G J Boulden	Ash, Aldershot	30. 8.09E
		1871					
G-BTBC	Piper PA-28-161 Warrior II	28-7916414	N28755	19.12.90	Synergy Aircraft Leasing Ltd	Fairoaks	11. 5.09E
G-BTBF	Fisher Super Koala	SK.067	(G-MWOZ)	24.12.90	E A Taylor (Construction suspended 1.09)		
	(Built E A Taylor - pr.no.PFA 158-11954)					(Southend-on-Sea)	
G-BTBG	Denney Kitfox Model 2	PFA 172-11845		18.12.90	R Noble (Noted 10.08)	Shobdon	31. 5.06P
	(Built J Catley)						
G-BTBH	Ryan ST3KR (PT-22-RY)	2063	N854	18. 2.91	P R Holloway (As "854" in US Army Air Corp c/s)		
	(Kinner R56)		N50993, 41-20854			Old Warden	12. 5.09P
G-BTBJ	Cessna 190 (modified)	16046	F-AZRE	2.10.91	R H Reeves	Rednal	
			G-BTBJ, N4461C				
G-BTBL	Montgomerie-Bensen B 8MR PFA G/01A-1183			21.12.90	N H Collins tr AES Radionic Surveillance Systems (Noted 4.04)		
	(Built J M Montgomerie) (Rotax 532)					Melrose Farm, Melbourne	2. 9.01P
G-BTBP	Cameron N-90 Balloon (Hot Air)	2464		21.12.90	M Catalani	Pistoia, Italy	16. 4.09E
G-BTBU	Piper PA-18-150 Super Cub	18-7509010	N9665P	3. 1.91	A J White tr G-BTBU Syndicate	Redhill	2. 7.11S
G-BTBW	Cessna 120	14220	N2009V	24. 1.91	M J Willies "40"	Sywell	19. 8.10S
	(Continental C90)		NC2009V				
G-BTBX	Piper J-3C-65 Cub	6334	N35367	29. 1.91	J B Hargrave and P Simms tr Henlow Taildraggers		
			NC35367			RAF Henlow	6.12.09
G-BTBY	Piper PA-17 Vagabond	17-195	N4894H	4. 1.91	G W Miller	Jenkin's Farm, Navestock	21. 4.08P
	(Continental C85)						
G-BTCA	Piper PA-32R-300 Lance	32R-7780381	N5941V	10. 1.91	R Page tr Lance Group	Sleap	11. 6.09E
G-BTCB	Air Command 582 Sport	0634		9. 1.91	G Scurrah	(Duddon Bridge, Millom)	
	(Built G Scurrah - pr.no.PFA G/04-1198)						
G-BTCC	Grumman F6F-5K Hellcat	A-11286	(N10CN)	31.12.90	Patina Ltd (As "40467:19" in VF-6 Sqdn:US Navy c/s)		
			N100T, FN80142, Bu.80141		(Operated The Fighter Collection)	Duxford	6. 7.09P
	(Composite with centre section ex Bu.08831 [A-218] ex F6F-3)						
G-BTCD	North American P-51D-25-NA Mustang		N51JJ	11. 1.91	Pelham Ltd (As "413704:B7-H" in 374th FG:USAAF c/s)		
		122-39608	N6340T, RCAF 9568, 44-73149		"Ferocious Frankie"	Duxford	19. 5.09P
					(Operated The Old Flying Machine Company)		
G-BTCE	Cessna 152 II	15281376	N49876	10. 1.91	S T Gilbert	Enstone	15.12.09E
	(Tail-wheel conversion)						
G-BTCH	Luscombe 8E Silvaire Deluxe	6403	N1976B	11. 2.91	J Grewcock and R C Carroll tr G-BTCH Flying Group		
	(Continental C85)		NC1976B			Popham	14.10.09P
G-BTCI	Piper PA-17 Vagabond	17-136	N4839H	11. 1.91	T R Whittome	Inverness	9. 8.05P
	(Continental A65)		NC4839H				
G-BTCJ	Luscombe 8AE Silvaire	1869	N41908	16. 1.91	J M Lovell	Chilbolton	9. 6.08P
	(Continental O-200A)		NC41908				
G-BTCM	Cameron N-90 Balloon (Hot Air)	1306	(G-BMPW)	8. 5.86	G Everett	Maidstone	16. 4.06A
G-BTCR	Rans S-10 Sakota	0290.091		11. 1.91	B J Hewitt	Newtownards	6. 2.08P
	(Built S H Barr - pr.no.PFA 194-11877)						
G-BTCS	Colt 90A Balloon (Hot Air)	1895		11. 1.91	L A Watts "Variety Club" titles	Pangbourne	17. 6.09E
G-BTCZ	Cameron Chateau-84 SS Balloon (Hot Air)						
	(Forbes Chateau de Balleroy shape)	2246		18. 1.91	Forbes Global Inc "Chateau II"	London SW11	14.11.09E
G-BTDA	Slingsby T 61F Venture T 2	1870	XZ550	17. 4.91	T M Holloway tr RAF Gliding and Soaring Association		
					(Operated Anglia Gliding Club)	AAC Wattisham	23. 5.08E
G-BTDC	Denney Kitfox Model 2	405		11. 1.91	D M Smith	Halwell	26. 6.07P
	(Built D Collinson and O Smith - pr.no.PFA 172-11483)						
G-BTDD	CFM Streak Shadow	K 127-SA		14. 1.91	S H Merrony	(Egham)	12.10.06P
	(Built S J Evans - pr.no.PFA 161A-11622) (Rotax 582)						
G-BTDE	Cessna C-165 Airmaster	551	N21911	18. 1.91	R H Screen	Liverpool-John Lennon	24. 4.10
			NC21911				
G-BTDF	Luscombe 8A Silvaire	2205	N45678	17. 4.91	D M Watts	(Eastleigh)	19 .8.93P
			NC45678				
G-BTDI	Robinson R-22 Beta	1670	PH-HTA	29. 1.91	S Klinge	Kilmarnock	29. 3.09E
			G-BTDI				
G-BTDN	Denney Kitfox Model 2	688		22. 1.91	S D Arnold tr Foxy Flyers Group		
	(Built A B Butler - pr.no.PFA 172-11826)					Wellesbourne Mountford	29. 6.05P
G-BTDR	Aero Designs Pulsar	PFA 202-11962		24. 1.91	R A Blackwell	North Weald	4. 1.08P
	(Built R M Hughes and T Packe)						
G-BTDS	Colt 77A Balloon (Hot Air)	1897		29. 1.91	C P Witter Ltd "Witters II"	Chester	31. 5.09E
G-BTDT	CASA 1-131E Jungmann Series 2000	2131	Spanish AF	5. 2.91	T A Reed	Headcorn	24. 5.09P
			E3B-505				

G-BTDV	Piper PA-28-161 Cherokee Warrior II	N3548M	25. 2.91	Falcon Flying Services Ltd	Biggin Hill	5. 3.09E
	28-7816355					
G-BTDW	Cessna 152 II	15279864	N757NC	25. 2.91	Border Air Training Ltd	Carlisle	20. 1.09E
G-BTDZ	CASA 1-131E Jungmann Series 2000	2104	Spanish AF	5. 2.91	M and R J Pickin	Headcorn	29.11.08P
			E3B-524		('Fliegerschule Luxeuil' - silver with Nazi tail flash)		
G-BTEA	Cameron N-105 Balloon (Hot Air)	284		31. 5.77	M W A Shemilt "Big Red"	Henley-on-Thames	8. 5.99A
G-BTEE	Cameron O-120 Balloon (Hot Air)	2499		24. 1.91	W H and J P Morgan "Y Ddraig Goch" and "The Red Dragon"		
						Swansea	4. 8.09E
G-BTEF	Pitts S-1	515H	N88PR	19. 2.91	C Davidson (Noted 10.07)	Blackpool	28.10.97P
	(Built D R Brewer)						
G-BTEL	CFM Streak Shadow	K 125-SA		31. 1.91	J E Eatwell	Boscombe Down	19.11.08P
	(Built J E Eatwell - pr.no.PFA 206-11667) (Rotax 618)						
G-BTES	Cessna 150H	15068371	N22575	29. 4.91	R A Forward	Biggin Hill	9.10.09E
G-BTET	Piper J-3C-65 Cub	18296	N98141	5. 2.91	K Handley	Higher Barn Farm, Houghton	12. 5.09P
			NC98141				
G-BTEU	Aérospatiale AS.365N2 Dauphin 2	6392		11. 2.91	CHC Scotia Ltd	Humberside	1. 4.09E
G-BTEW	Cessna 120	10238	CF-ELE	29. 4.91	J H Milne and T H Bishop	Felthorpe	29. 6.10S
	(Continental C90)						
G-BTEX	Piper PA-28-140 Cherokee	28-23773	CF-XXL	24. 4.91	E Latimer	Little Snoring	11. 2.10E
			N3907K				
G-BTFC	Reims Cessna F152 II	F15201668		23. 5.79	Aircraft Engineers Ltd	Prestwick	16. 8.09E
G-BTFE	Parsons Gyroplane Model 1	38		13. 2.91	J R Goldspink	Haverfordwest	27.10.01P
	(Built I Brewster) (Rotax 582) (Tandem Trainer)						
G-BTFG	Boeing Stearman A75N1 (N2S-4) Kaydet	N4467N	20. 2.91	TG Aviation Ltd (As "441" in USN c/s)	Manston	2. 7.11S
	(Continental W670)	75-3441	Bu.30010				
G-BTFJ	Piper PA-15 Vagabond	15-159	N4373H	13. 2.91	C W Thirtle	Old Sarum	17. 3.09P
	(Continental C 90)		NC4373H				
G-BTFK	Taylorcraft BC-12D	10540	N599SB	13. 2.91	A O'Rourke		
	(Continental A65)		N5240M			Pallas West, Toomyvara, County Tipperary	10. 6.09P
G-BTFL	Aeronca 11AC Chief	11AC-1727	N3403E	18. 2.91	J G Vaughan tr BTFL Group		
			NC3403E			Eastbach Farm, Coleford	8.12.09P
G-BTFM	Cameron O-105 Balloon (Hot Air)	2623		12. 8.91	P Forster and J Trehern tr Edinburgh University		
					Hot Air Balloon Club	Edinburgh	22.12.07A
G-BTFO	Piper PA-28-161 Cherokee Warrior II	N31728	12. 3.91	Flyfar Ltd	RAF Woodvale	27. 5.09E
	28-7816580						
G-BTFT	Beech 58 Baron	TH-979	N2036W	14. 3.91	Fastwing Air Charter Ltd	Thruxton	13.12.08E
G-BTFU	Cameron N-90 Balloon (Hot Air)	2391		28. 2.91	J J Rudoni and A C K Rawson t/a Wickers World		
					Hot Air Balloon Company "Maltesers II"	Stafford	26. 3.05A
G-BTFV	Whittaker MW7	PFA 171-11722		8. 2.91	S J Luck	Tower Farm, Wollaston	12.12.05P
	(Built S J Luck)						
G-BTFW	Montgomerie-Bensen B 8MR PFA G/01A-1141		20. 2.91	C G Ponsford	Willingale	14. 6.06P
	(Built A Mansfield) (Rotax 532)						
G-BTFX	Bell 206B-2 JetRanger II	1648	N400MH	20. 2.91	Action Vehicles Ltd	Redhill	16. 6.09E
			N90219				
G-BTGD	Rand Robinson KR-2	PFA 129-11150		22. 2.91	B M Neary	(Coventry)	2. 8.08P
	(Built D W Mullin) (Volkswagen 1915)						
G-BTGG	Rans S-10 Sakota	0790.113		20. 2.91	C A James	Doynton	22. 6.96P
	(Built A R Cameron - pr.no.PFA 194-11944)						
G-BTGH	Cessna 152 II	15281048	N48919	2. 4.91	P J Clarke	Wolverhampton	25. 4.07T
G-BTGI	Rearwin 175 Skyranger	1517	N32308	26. 2.91	J M Fforde	Lane Farm, Clyro, Hereford	6.11.07P
	(Continental A75)		NC32308				
G-BTGJ	Smith DSA-1 Miniplane	NM.II	N1471	25. 3.91	G J Knowles	Goodwood	23. 4.09P
	(Built S J Malovic) (Continental C90)						
G-BTGL	Avid Speed Wing	PFA 189-11885		27. 2.91	I Kazi (Noted 1.07)		
	(Built A J Maxwell)					Stoneacre Farm, Farthing Corner	4. 9.03P
G-BTGM	Aeronca 7AC Champion	7AC-3665	N84943	11. 3.91	G P Gregg	Shacklewell Farm, Empingham	18. 7.08P
	(Continental A65)		NC84943				
G-BTGO	Piper PA-28-140 Cherokee D	28-7125613	N1998T	20. 2.91	Demero Ltd and Transcourt Ltd	Oxford	14. 9.09E
G-BTGP	Cessna 150M Commuter	15078921	N704WA	28. 2.91	Billins Air Services Ltd	Bournemouth	30. 5.08E
G-BTGR	Cessna 152 II	15284447	N6581L	28. 2.91	A J Gomes	Shoreham	25. 7.00T
					(Crashed Mile Oak, Portslade, Sussex 7.10.99:)		
G-BTGS (2)	Stolp SA.300 Starduster Too	EAA/50553	G-AYMA	30. 9.87	G N Elliott tr G N Elliott and Partners	Shoreham	9. 9.09P
	(Build initiated T G Solomon - pr.no.PFA 035-10076: completed P G Leggo)(Lycoming O-320)						
G-BTGT	CFM Streak Shadow	K 164-SA	(G-MWPY)	1. 3.91	G J Sargent	Bourn	29.11.07P
	(Built M Allison - pr.no.PFA 206-11964) (Rotax 582)						
G-BTGV	Piper PA-34-200T Seneca II	34-7970077	N3004H	26. 3.91	Oxford Aviation Academy (Oxford) Ltd	Oxford	16. 8.09E
G-BTGW	Cessna 152 II	15279812	N757KY	5. 3.91	Stapleford Flying Club Ltd	Stapleford	13. 8.09E
G-BTGX	Cessna 152 II	15284950	N5462P	5. 3.91	Stapleford Flying Club Ltd	Stapleford	24. 8.09E
G-BTGY	Piper PA-28-161 Warrior II	28-8216199	N9574N	5. 3.91	Stapleford Flying Club Ltd	Stapleford	23. 6.09E
			N9574N				
G-BTGZ	Piper PA-28-181 Cherokee Archer II	N47956	8. 4.91	Allzones Ltd	Biggin Hill	19.12.09E
	28-7890160						
G-BTHE	Cessna 150L	15075340	N11348	7. 3.91	M S Williams	Mount Airey Farm, South Cave	17. 9.09E
G-BTHF	Cameron V-90 Balloon (Hot Air)	2543		7. 3.91	N J and S J Langley	Bristol	26. 6.09E
G-BTHH	CEA Jodel DR.100A Ambassadeur	5	F-BJCH	28. 2.91	H R Leefe	Bourg-en-Bresse, France	20.12.10E
G-BTHI	Robinson R22 Beta	1732		26. 3.91	Summerline Aviation Ltd	Coventry	25. 4.09E
G-BTHJ	Evans VP-2	PFA 063-10901		14. 3.91	C J Moseley (Under construction 8.92)		
	(Built C J Moseley)					Bournemouth	
G-BTHK	Thunder Ax7-77 Balloon (Hot Air)	1906		11. 3.91	M S Trend	Maidstone	25. 6.06A
G-BTHM	Thunder Ax8-105 Balloon (Hot Air)	1925		11. 3.91	F Bonsergent	La Poveze, France	25. 9.09E
G-BTHN	Murphy Renegade 912	384		12. 3.91	D Baker	(Enfield, County Meath)	8. 8.06P
	(Built Meridian Ultralights Ltd - pr.no.PFA 188-12005)						
G-BTHP	Thorp T-211	101		13. 6.91	M J Newton	Barton	30. 4.09E

G-BTHV	MBB BÖ.105DBS-4	S 855	D-HMBV	20. 3.91	Bond Air Services Ltd *(Operated County Air Ambulance)*	
			G-BTHV, D-HFHM			Welshpool	22. 5.09E
G-BTHW	Beech F33C Bonanza	CJ-130	PH-BNA	18. 3.91	Robin Lance Aviation Associates Ltd	Rochester	25. 9.06
			N23787				
G-BTHX	Colt 105A Balloon (Hot Air)	1939		18. 3.91	PSH Skypower Ltd	Pewsey	10. 3.09E
G-BTHY	Bell 206B-3 JetRanger III	2290	N6606M	20. 3.91	Suffolk Helicopters Ltd	(Ipswich)	11. 6.09E
			VH-BIQ, ZK-HBQ, DQ-FEN, ZK-HLU				
G-BTHZ	Cameron V-56 Balloon (Hot Air)	486	OO-BBC	20. 3.91	(C N Marshall)	(Staplehurst)	
					(UK registration believed not taken up and remains as "OO-BBC" 2008)		
G-BTID	Piper PA-28-161 Warrior II	28-8116036	N82647	25. 6.91	Aviation South West Ltd	Exeter	6. 4.09E
G-BTIE	SOCATA TB-10 Tobago	187		30. 3.81	Aviation Spirit Ltd	Shobdon	11.11.09E
G-BTIF	Denney Kitfox Model 3	684		27. 2.91	M Lally	(Chorley)	10. 8.01P
	(Built C R Thompson and J Scott - pr.no.PFA 172-11862) (Converted from Model 2)						
G-BTII	Gulfstream AA-5B Tiger	AA5B-1256	N4560S	5. 6.91	S A Niechial and P W Gillott tr BTII Group		
						Biggin Hill	13. 5.08E
G-BTIJ	Luscombe 8E Silvaire Deluxe	5194	N2467K	3. 4.91	S J Hornsby	Ranston Farm, Iwerne Courtney	9. 1.08P
	(Continental C85)		NC2467K				
G-BTIK	Cessna 152 II	15282993	N46068	26. 3.91	K O'Connor	Weston, Leixlip, County Kildare	15. 6.09E
G-BTIL	Piper PA-38-112 Tomahawk	38-80A0004	N24730	26. 3.91	B J Pearson *(Noted as "N24730" dismantled 7.05)*		
						Eaglescott	
G-BTIM	Piper PA-28-161 Cadet	2841159	N9185D	24. 8.89	Plane Talking Ltd	Elstree	5.12.09E
			(SE-KIO)				
G-BTIO	SNCAN Stampe SV-4C	303	N73NS	28. 3.91	M D and C F Garratt	RNAS Yeovilton	9.10.11
			F-BCLC				
G-BTIR	Denney Kitfox Model 2	PFA 172-11952		26. 3.91	R B Wilson	(Levens, Kendal)	25.10.09P
	(Built J N C Shields and D J Millar) (Hewland AE75)						
G-BTIU	SOCATA MS.892A Rallye Commodore 150		F-BPQS	7. 5.91	Cole Aviation Ltd *(Noted Nalson Aviation 3.06)*		
		10914				Willey Park Farm, Caterham	16. 6.05
G-BTIV	Piper PA-28-161 Warrior II	28-8116044	N82697	10. 5.91	B R Pearson tr Warrior Group *(Noted 8.07)*		
						Eaglescott	24. 7.06T
G-BTIZ	Cameron A-105 Balloon (Hot-Air)	2546	VT-WOW	11. 3.91	Gone With The Wind Ltd	Bristol	10. 7.08A
			G-BTIZ				
G-BTJA	Luscombe 8E Silvaire Deluxe	5037	N2310K	4. 4.91	M W Rudkin	(Holmes Chapel, Crewe)	15. 6.09P
	(Continental O-200A)		NC2310K				
G-BTJB	Luscombe 8E Silvaire Deluxe	6194	N1567B	4. 4.91	M Loxton	Parsonage Farm, Eastchurch	20. 7.09P
	(Continental C85)		NC1567B				
G-BTJC	Luscombe 8F Silvaire	6589	N2162B	4. 4.91	A M Noble	Chilbolton	18.10.99P
	(Lycoming O-290D2)				*(Damged Glebe Farm, Stockton, Warminster 31. 7.99: noted 7.04)*		
G-BTJD	Thunder Ax8-90 Series 2 Balloon (Hot Air) 1865			28. 3.91	R E Vinten *"Beez Neez"*	Wellingborough	17. 6.09E
G-BTJH	Cameron O-77 Balloon (Hot Air)	2559		3. 4.91	H Stringer *"Oriel"*	Scarborough	9. 9.09E
G-BTJK	Piper PA-38-112 Tomahawk	38-79A0838	N2427N	3. 4.91	Ravenair Aircraft Ltd	Liverpool-John Lennon	14.12.09E
G-BTJL	Piper PA-38-112 Tomahawk	38-79A0863	N2477N	3. 4.91	J S Develin and Z Islam	Shoreham	26. 3.09E
G-BTJN	Montgomerie-Bensen B 8MR	PFA G/01-1194		3. 4.91	A Hamilton	Strathaven	9.12.00P
	(Built A Hamilton) (Rotax 532)						
G-BTJO	Thunder Ax9-140 Balloon (Hot Air)	1948		3. 4.91	G P Lane *(Pacific Flyer titles) (Stored 5.07)*	USA	28. 4.92A
G-BTJS	Montgomerie-Bensen B 8MR	PFA G/01-1083		8. 4.91	T A Holmes	(Leeds)	13. 3.09P
	(Built J M P Annand) (Rotax 532)						
G-BTJU	Cameron V-90 Balloon (Hot Air)	2554		8. 4.91	Flambe Balloons Ltd *"C W Jones Carpets"*		
						Shipham, Winscombe	27. 9.09E
G-BTJX	Rans S-10 Sakota	0790.114		9. 4.91	P C Avery	Lower Mountpleasant Farm, Chatteris	15. 9.04P
	(Built M Goacher - pr.no.PFA 194-12014) (Rotax 582)						
G-BTKA	Piper J-5A Cub Cruiser	5-954	N38403	11. 4.91	J M Lister	Valley Farm, Winwick	9. 5.09P
			NC38403				
G-BTKB	Murphy Renegade 912	376		11. 4.91	P and J Calvert	Rufforth	27. 9.08P
	(Built G S Blundell - pr.no.PFA 188-11876)						
G-BTKD	Denney Kitfox Model 4	853		15. 4.91	R A Hills	Dunkeswell	30. 9.09P
	(Built J F White - pr.no.PFA 172-11941) (Denny kit no.indicates Model 3 and conflicts with N653CP)						
G-BTKG	Avid Flyer	PFA 189-12037		16. 4.91	J Dennedy tr Avid Group (Blanchardstown, Dublin)		4.10.06P
	(Built P R Snowden)						
G-BTKL	MBB BÖ.105DB-4	S 422	D-HDMU	2. 5.91	Gryphon Aviation LLP	Cardiff Heliport	2. 3.09E
			Swedish Army 09076, D-HDMU				
G-BTKN	Cameron O-120 Balloon (Hot Air)	2579	OO-BQQ	24. 4.91	R H Etherington	Siena, Italy	16. 4.03A
G-BTKP	CFM Streak Shadow	K 174		24. 4.91	C D Creasey and C A Sargent		
	(Built K S Woodward - pr.no.PFA 206-12036) (Rotax 582)					Wickambrook, Newmarket	14. 7.09P
G-BTKT	Piper PA-28-161 Warrior II	28-8216218	N429FT	9. 5.91	Biggin Hill Flying Club Ltd	Thruxton	16. 4.09E
			N9606N				
G-BTKV	Piper PA-22-160 Tri-Pacer	22-7157	N3216Z	25. 4.91	R A Moore	Gransha, Rathfriland, County Down	23. 9.10S
G-BTKW	Cameron O-105 Balloon (Hot Air)	2566		25. 4.91	P Spellward tr Bristol University Hot Air Ballooning Society		
					(Inflated 5.06)	Bristol	9. 3.01A
G-BTKX	Piper PA-28-181 Cherokee Archer II		N47866	14. 5.91	R M Pannell	Eaglescott	3. 6.09E
		28-7890146					
G-BTKZ	Cameron V-77 Balloon (Hot Air)	2573		26. 4.91	S P Richards *"Lancaster Jaguar"*	Tonbridge	7. 6.97T
G-BTLB	Wassmer WA.52 Europa	42	F-BTLB	17. 4.89	A S Cowan tr Popham Flying Group G-BTLB		
						Popham	12.11.08E
G-BTLG	Piper PA-28R-200 Cherokee Arrow II		N5045S	29. 4.91	P J Moore	Lee-on-Solent	18. 3.09E
		28R-35811					
G-BTLM	Piper PA-22-160	22-6162	N9025D	16. 5.91	A C and M D N Fisher	Leicester	13. 8.11S
	(Tail-wheel conversion)						
G-BTLP	Grumman AA-1C Lynx	AA1C-0109	N9732U	13. 5.91	Partlease Ltd *"28" (Operated Stapleford Flying Club)*		
						Stapleford	2. 2.09E
G-BTMA	Cessna 172N Skyhawk II	17273711	N5136J	2. 5.91	East of England Flying Group Ltd	North Weald	1.12.09E
G-BTMK	Cessna R172K Hawk XP	R1722787	N736TZ	10. 6.91	K E Halford	Upfield Farm, Whitson	25. 3.09E
G-BTMN	Thunder Ax9-120 Series 2 Balloon (Hot Air)			17. 5.91	M E White *(Inflated 6.08)*	Dublin	8. 3 99T
		2003					

G-BTMO	Colt 69A Balloon (Hot Air)	2004		20. 5.91	Cameron Balloons Ltd t/a Thunder and Colt Bristol	
G-BTMP	Everett Campbell Cricket	024		20. 5.91	P W McLaughlin	Little Rissington 30. 5.08P
	(Built D GHill - pr.no.PFA G/03-1226) (Rotax 532)					
G-BTMR	Cessna 172M Skyhawk II	17264985	N64047	20. 5.91	Linley Aviation Ltd	Linley Hill, Leven 23. 7.09E
G-BTMS	Avid Speed Wing	908	(CS-)	24. 4.91	J Makonnen	
			G-BTMS		New Barn Farm, Barton Ashes, Crawley	9. 4.09P
	(Built D L Docking and M J Kay - pr.no.PFA 189-12023)					
G-BTMT	Denney Kitfox Model 1	66		10. 5.91	L G Horne	(Ashford, Kent) 5.11.04P
	(Built J Lindzalone) (Rotax 532)					
G-BTMV	Everett Gyroplane Series 2	025		21. 5.91	L Armes	(Pitsea, Basildon)
G-BTMW	Zenair CH.701 STOL	PFA 187-11808		21. 5.91	L Lewis *(Stored 2.08)*	Yearby 9. 4.96P
	(Built L Lewis) (Rotax 582)					
G-BTMY	Cameron Train 80 SS Balloon (Hot Air)	2561	(SE-...)	22. 5.91	Balloon Sports HB	Partille, Sweden 9. 2.97A
			G-BTMY			
G-BTNA	Robinson R22 Beta	1800	N40820	23. 5.91	Helicopter Training and Hire Ltd	Newtownards 6. 6.09E
G-BTNC	Aérospatiale AS.365N2 Dauphin 2	6409		21. 6.91	CHC Scotia Ltd	Humberside 29. 5.09E
G-BTND	Piper PA-38-112 Tomahawk	38-78A0155	N9671T	23. 5.91	Ravenair Aircraft Ltd	Biggin Hill 2. 9.09E
G-BTNE	Piper PA-28-161 Warrior II	28-8116212	N8379H	22. 7.91	Fly Welle Ltd	Wellesbourne Mountford 18. 7.09E
G-BTNH	Piper PA-28-161 Warrior II	28-8216202	G-DENH	28. 5.91	A S Bamrah t/a Falcon Flying Services	Fairoaks 9.10.09E
			G-BTNH, N253FT, N9577N			
G-BTNO	Aeronca 7AC Champion	7AC-3132	N84441	31. 5.91	B J and G B Robe	(Hexham and Riding Mill) 13. 8.08P
			NC84441			
G-BTNR	Denney Kitfox Model 3	921		31. 5.91	J Beirne tr High Notions Flying Group	
	(Built J W G Ellis - pr.no.PFA 172-12035)				Kilrush, County Kildare	14. 9.09P
G-BTNT	Piper PA-28-151 Cherokee Warrior		N6929J	31. 5.91	Thompson Airways Ltd	Cranfield 15.11.09E
		28-7615401			*(Operated Thomson Airways Flying Club)*	
G-BTNV	Piper PA-28-161 Cherokee Warrior II		N31878	20. 6.91	G M Bauer and A M Davies	Wickenby 18. 8.09E
		28-7816590				
G-BTNW	Rans S-6-ESA Coyote II	0391.174		3. 6.91	R H Hughes *(Noted 8.07)*	Greenlands, Rhuallt 8. 8.06P
	(Built A Barbone - pr.no.PFA 204-12077) (Rotax 582)					
G-BTOC	Robinson R22 Beta	1801	N23004	10. 6.91	Summerline Aviation Ltd Damyn's Hall, Upminster	20. 9.09E
G-BTOG	de Havilland DH.82A Tiger Moth	86500	F-BGCJ	5. 9.91	S W Barratt tr TOG Group	(Silsoe, Bedford)
	(Built Morris Motors Ltd)		French AF, NM192			
G-BTOL	Denney Kitfox Model 3	919		26. 6.91	P J Gibbs	Woodlands Barton Farm, Roche 28. 7.09P
	(Built C R Phillips - pr.no.PFA 172-12052)					
G-BTON	Piper PA-28-140 Cherokee Cruiser		N43193	15. 7.91	G R Read tr Group G-BTON	Crowfield 4.12.09E
		28-7425343				
G-BTOO	Pitts S-1C	5215-24A	N37H	12. 6.91	G H Matthews	(Fareham)
	(Built E Lawrence)					
G-BTOP	Cameron V-77 Balloon (Hot Air)	2484		14. 6.91	J J Winter *"Big Top"* Michaelston-y-Fedw, Cardiff	
G-BTOT	Piper PA-15 Vagabond	15-60	N4176H	22. 5.91	S J Raw tr Vagabond Flying Group	
	(Continental O-200)		NC4176H		Morgansfield, Fishburn	26. 5.09P
G-BTOU	Cameron O-120 Balloon (Hot Air)	2606		2. 7.91	J J Daly	Halfway House, County Waterford 16.10.08E
G-BTOW	SOCATA Rallye 180T Galerien	3360	F-BNGZ	9.11.82	M Jarrett	(Yaxley, Peterborough) 16. 4.09E
G-BTOZ	Thunder Ax9-120 Series 2 Balloon (Hot Air)			28. 6.91	H G Davies	(Cheltenham) 13. 5.09E
		2008				
G-BTPA	British Aerospace ATP	2007	EC-HGC	19. 8.88	Atlantic Airlines Ltd	Coventry 5.10.09E
			G-BTPA, EC-GYE, G-BTPA, (N377AE)			
G-BTPE	British Aerospace ATP	2012	EC-HGE	1. 9.88	Atlantic Airlines Ltd	Coventry 28. 2.09E
			G-BTPE, EC-GZH, G-BTPE, (N382AE)			
G-BTPF	British Aerospace ATP	2013	EC-HCY	2. 9.88	Atlantic Airlines Ltd	Coventry 8.11.09E
			G-BTPF, G-11-013, G-BTPF, (N383AE)			
G-BTPG	British Aerospace ATP	2014	EC-HEH	2. 9.88	Capital Bank Leasing 5 Ltd *(Noted 9.08)* Coventry	22. 5.99T
			G-BTPG, (N384AE)			
G-BTPH	British Aerospace ATP	2015	(G-JEMF)	2. 9.88	Atlantic Airlines Ltd	Coventry 23. 7.09E
			EC-HFM, G-BTPH, (N385AE)			
G-BTPJ	British Aerospace ATP	2016	EC-HFR	2. 9.88	Capital Bank Leasing 7 Ltd *(Noted 9.08)* Coventry	9. 7.99T
			G-BTPJ, (N386AE)			
G-BTPL	British Aerospace ATP	2042	EC-HES	3.10.91	Trident Aviation Leasing Services (Jersey) Ltd	
			G-BTPL, (PH-MJK), EC-GLH, G-BTPL, G-11-042		Coventry	1. 6.08E
			(Stored 8.07 less engines in Magic Bird livery - PH-MGB reserved since 9.06)			
G-BTPT	Cameron N-77 Balloon (Hot Air)	2575		10. 6.91	H J Andrews *"Hi Society"*	Selborne, Alton 1. 7.09E
G-BTPV	Colt 90A Balloon (Hot Air)	1956		14. 6.91	R S Kent tr Balloon Preservation Flying Group	
					(Mondial Assistance titles)	Petworth 14. 4.09E
G-BTPX	Thunder Ax8-90 Balloon (Hot-Air)	1873		18. 6.91	B J Ross	Fareham
G-BTRB	Colt Mickey Mouse SS Balloon (Hot Air)	1959		4. 7.91	Stratos Ballooning Gmbh and Co KG *"Calibre"*	
					Ennigerloh, Germany	18. 3.05A
G-BTRC	Avid Speed Wing	913		2. 7.91	Grangecote Ltd	Chilsford Farm, Kirdford 11. 8.07P
	(Built A A Craig - pr.no.PFA 189-12076) (BMW R100)					
G-BTRF	Aero Designs Pulsar	PFA 202-12051		4. 7.91	C Smith	Spilstead Farm, Sedlescombe 19.10.09P
	(Built C Smith) (Tri-cycle u/c)					
G-BTRG	Aeronca 65C Super Chief	C4149	N22466	4. 7.91	A Welburn	Mount Airey Farm, South Cave 14. 9.06P
	(Continental A65)		NC22466			
G-BTRI	Aeronca 11CC Super Chief	11CC-246	N4540E	4. 7.91	P A Wensak *(Noted 7.08)* Bounds Farm, Ardleigh	16. 7.06P
	(Continental C85)		NC4540E			
G-BTRK	Piper PA-28-161 Warrior II	28-8216206	N297FT	8. 7.91	Stapleford Flying Club Ltd	Stapleford 26.10.09E
			N9594N			
G-BTRL	Cameron N-105 Balloon (Hot Air)	2622		5. 7.91	J Lippett *"Harrods"* South Petherton, Somerset	24. 8.02A
G-BTRN	Thunder Ax9-120 Series 2 Balloon (Hot Air)			11. 7.91	A R Hardwick	Shefford 6. 9.09E
		1983				
G-BTRO	Thunder Ax8-90 Balloon (Hot Air)	1872		11. 7.91	Capital Balloon Club Ltd	Hounslow 29. 7.07A
G-BTRP	Hughes 369E *(Hughes 500)*	0475E	N1607D	11. 7.91	P C Shann and P C Shann Management and Research Ltd	
					Fulford, York	25. 3.05
G-BTRR	Thunder Ax7-77 Balloon (Hot Air)	1905		12. 7.91	P J Wentworth	Stanford in the Vale, Faringdon 27. 5.09E

G-BTRS	Piper PA-28-161 Warrior II	28-8116004	N8248V	12. 7.91	K D Taylor and T Bailey tr Airwise Flying Group		
						Barton	12. 3.09E
G-BTRT	Piper PA-28R-200 Cherokee Arrow II		N1189X	24. 7.91	C D Barden and D G Smith tr Romeo Tango Group		
		28R-7535270				Barton	24. 3.09E
G-BTRU	Robin DR.400-180 Régent	2089		12. 7.91	R H Mackay		
G-BTRW	Slingsby T 61F Venture T 2	1968	ZA632	5. 7.91	G B Monslow tr The Falke Syndicate Long Marston		3.12.09E
G-BTRY	Piper PA-28-161 Warrior II	28-8116190	N8363L	18. 7.91	Oxford Aviation Academy (Oxford) Ltd	Oxford	4. 4.09E
G-BTRZ	Jodel D 18	148		16. 7.91	A P Aspinall	Little Gransden	31. 5.07P
	(Built R Collin - pr.no.PFA 169-11271) (Volkswagen 1834)						
G-BTSB	Corben Baby Ace D	JC-1	N3599	16. 7.91	M R Overall (Camouflage scheme with RFC roundels)		
	(Built J Cole) (Continental A65)					Whitehill Farm, Wethersfield	17. 9.09P
G-BTSJ	Piper PA-28-161 Cherokee Warrior II		N9417C	23. 7.91	Plymouth School of Flying Ltd	Plymouth	21. 1.09E
		28-7816473					
G-BTSN	Cessna 150G	15065106	N3806J	30. 8.91	M L F Langrick	Haverfordwest	26. 5.09E
G-BTSP	Piper J-3C-65 Cub	7647	N41013	30. 8.91	J A Walshe and A Corcoran		
			NC41013			Strandhill, Sligo, County Sligo	2. 7.09P
G-BTSR	Aeronca 11AC Chief	11AC-785	N9152E	30. 8.91	S M McBride	(Stirling)	7. 2.09P
	(Continental A65)		NC9152E				
G-BTSV	Denney Kitfox Model 3	PFA 172-11920		24. 7.91	R J Folwell	Wishanger Farm, Frensham	6. 7.07P
	(Built D J Sharland)						
G-BTSW	Colt AS-105 GD Airship (Hot Air)	1999		24. 7.91	Gefa-Flug GmbH (Adler Modemarkt titles)		
						Aachen, Germany	10. 4.09E
G-BTSX	Thunder Ax7-77 Balloon (Hot Air)	2027		24. 7.91	C Moris-Gallimore Sao Bras de Alportel, Portugal		18. 9.94
G-BTSZ	Cessna 177A Cardinal	17701198	N30332	30. 7.91	T Akeroyd	(Sandy)	17. 5.09P
G-BTTB	Cameron V-90 Balloon (Hot Air)	2624		22. 7.91	D C Mitchell tr Royal Engineers Balloon Club "Sapper IV"		
						Codford, Warminster	22. 7.09E
G-BTTD	Montgomerie-Bensen B 8MR	PFA G/01-1204		31. 7.91	A J P Herculson (Noted 5.08)	Little Snoring	28. 4.05P
	(Built K J Parker) (Rotax 582)						
G-BTTE	Cessna 150L	15075558	N11602	31. 7.91	C A Wilson and W B Murray "The Sky's the Limit"		
						Hill Farm, Nayland	8. 1.09E
G-BTTL	Cameron V-90 Balloon (Hot Air)	2649		12. 8.91	A J Baird "Hyde Farm Dairy"	Cheltenham	24. 4.09E
G-BTTO	British Aerospace ATP	2033	EC-HNA	16. 8.91	Atlantic Airlines Ltd	Coventry	7.12.09E
			EC-GJU, G-BTTO, G-OEDE, G-BTTO, TC-THV, G-BTTO, S2-ACZ, G-11-033				
G-BTTR	Pitts S-2A	2208	N38MP	16. 8.91	Yellowbird Adventures Ltd	Kemble	27. 6.09E
	(Built Aerotek Inc) (Lycoming AEI0-360)						
G-BTTS	Colt 77A Balloon (Hot Air)	1861		16. 8.91	J A Lomas tr Rutland Balloon Club		
						Melton Mowbray	4. 5.08A
G-BTTW	Thunder Ax7-77 Balloon (Hot Air)	2016		27. 8.91	J Kenny	Athlone, Co Roscommon	1. 7.09E
G-BTTY	Denney Kitfox Model 2	PFA 172-11823		29. 7.91	G T Leedham	Grangewood	10.11.09P
	(Built K J Fleming)						
G-BTTZ	Slingsby T 61F Venture T 2	1961	ZA625	30. 7.91	M W Olliver	Halesland	3. 9.03
G-BTUA	Slingsby T 61F Venture T 2	1985	ZA666	20. 8.91	Shenington Gliding Club	Shenington	21.10.09E
G-BTUB	LET Yakovlev C-11	172623	(France)	29. 8.91	M G and J R Jefferies (Soviet AF c/s without serial)		
	(Identity of 039 quoted)		Egyptian AF 543			Little Gransden	4. 1.08P
G-BTUE	British Aerospace ATP	2039	VT-FFB	5. 9.91	Aircraft Maintenance Services Ltd	Blackpool	
	G-BTUE, EC-GSF, EC-GKI, G-OEDH, G-OGVA, G-OEDH, G-BTUE, TC-THT, G-BTUE, TC-THT, G-11-039, G-BTUE, G-11-039						
G-BTUG	SOCATA Rallye 180T	3208		10. 7.78	Herefordshire Gliding Club Ltd	Shobdon	14. 2.09E
G-BTUH	Cameron N-65 Balloon (Hot Air)	1452		28. 8.91	J S Russon "Zanussi" Cheadle Hulme, Cheadle		14. 4.09E
G-BTUK	Pitts S-2A	2260	N5300J	2. 9.91	S H Elkington	Wickenby	1.11.09E
	(Built Aerotek Inc)						
G-BTUL	Pitts S-2A	2200	N900RS	2. 9.91	J M Adams	RAF Syerston	15. 5.09E
	(Built Aerotek Inc)						
G-BTUM	Piper J-3C-65 Cub	19516	N6335H	6. 9.91	I M Mackay tr G-BTUM Syndicate		
	(Continental C85) (Frame No.19586)		NC6335H			North Weald	6. 8.09P
G-BTUR	Piper PA-18 Super Cub 95 (L-18C-PI) 18-3205		OO-LVM	11. 9.91	N T Oakman	Andrewsfield	9. 9.11
	(Continental C90) (Frame No.18-3218)		Belgian AF OL-L08, L-131, 53-4805				
G-BTUS	Whittaker MW7	PFA 171-11999		5. 9.91	C T Bailey	Croft Farm, Defford	27. 6.05P
	(Built J F Bakewell) (Rotax 503)						
G-BTUV	Aeronca 65TAC Defender	C 1661TA	N36816	12. 9.91	S Hudson, P McLoughlin and F McMorrow		
			NC36816		(As "C1661:TR" in USAF c/s)	Dublin, Ireland	27. 7.08P
G-BTUW	Piper PA-28-151 Cherokee Warrior		N54458	12. 9.91	T S Kemp	Enstone	14.10.09E
		28-7415066					
G-BTUX	Aérospatiale AS.365N2 Dauphin 2	6424	LN-OLL	12. 9.91	CHC Scotia Ltd	Aberdeen	
			G-BTUX				
G-BTUZ	American General AG-5B Tiger	10075	N11939	3.10.91	R V Grocott	Sleap	26. 2.09E
G-BTVA	Thunder Ax7-77 Balloon (Hot Air)	2009		16. 9.91	C M Waters	Holbeach, Spalding	9. 7.09E
G-BTVB	Everett Gyroplane Series 3	026		24. 9.91	J P Whitter	(Leigh)	5. 5.06P
	(Rotax 532)						
G-BTVC	Denney Kitfox Model 2	PFA 172-11784		23. 9.91	M J Downes	Pool Quay, Breidden	23. 9.09P
	(Built R Swinden)						
G-BTVE	Hawker Demon I	?	2292M	18. 9.91	Demon Displays Ltd (As "K8203" in RAF 64 Sqdn c/s)		
	(Built Boulton Paul Aircraft Ltd) (RR Kestrel V)		K8203		(On final rebuild 4.05)	Rotary Farm, Hatch	
G-BTVV	Reims Cessna F337G Super Skymaster		PH-RPD	25. 9.91	C Keane Weston, Leixlip, County Kildare		12. 1.03T
	(Wichita c/n 33701476)	F33700058	N1876M		(Noted 5.06)		
G-BTVW	Cessna 152 II	15279631	N757CK	23. 9.91	TGD Leasing Ltd	Wellesbourne Mountford	20. 2.09E
G-BTVX	Cessna 152 II	15283375	N48786	23. 9.91	Traffic Management Services Ltd	Gamston	19.10.09E
G-BTWB	Denney Kitfox Model 3	920	(G-BTTM)	21. 8.91	J and O Houlihan	(Holywood, Ireland)	16. 8.09P
	(Built J E Toothill - pr.no.PFA 172-12278)						
G-BTWC	Slingsby T 61F Venture T 2	1975	ZA656	23. 9.91	T M Holloway tr RAF Gliding and Soaring Association		
						Trenchard Lines, Upavon	22. 6.09S
					(Operated Wyvern (Army) Gliding Club)		
G-BTWD	Slingsby T 61F Venture T 2	1976	ZA657	23. 9.91	York Gliding Centre Ltd t/a York Gliding Centre		
						Rufforth	10. 4.09E

G-BTWE	Slingsby T 61F Venture T 2	1980	ZA661	23. 9.91	J L Clegg tr Aston Down G-BTWE Syndicate	
						Aston Down 25. 6.09E
G-BTWF	de Havilland DHC-1 Chipmunk 22	C1/0564	WK549	30. 9.91	J A and V G Simms *(As "WK549" in RAF c/s)*	
						Breighton 31. 5.10S
G-BTWI	EAA Acrosport	230	N10JW	2.10.91	S Alexander and W M Coffee	Long Marston 18.12.09P
	(Built J N Wharton) (Lycoming O-290)					
G-BTWJ	Cameron V-77 Balloon (Hot Air)	2670		3.10.91	C Gingell and M Holden-Wadsworth	
						Nailsea, Bristol 2. 8.09E
G-BTWL	Wag-Aero CUBy Sport Trainer			3.10.91	F Horan	*(Derrylvskin Fethard, Ireland)* 19.10.09P
	(Built Penair) (Lycoming O-235)PFA 108-10893					
G-BTWM	Cameron V-77 Balloon (Hot Air)	2163		4.10.91	R C Franklin *"Aerolus"*	Chesham 27. 9.09E
G-BTWV	Cameron O-90 Balloon (Hot Air)	2675		10.10.91	A J Timmis tr The Cybele Flying Group	
						Princes Risborough 4. 1.10E
G-BTWX	SOCATA TB-9 Tampico Club	1401		14.10.91	Archer Two Ltd	Lydd 2. 3.09E
G-BTWY	Aero Designs Pulsar	PFA 202-12040		15.10.91	R Bishop	Headcorn 12.11.08P
	(Built J J Pridal and A K Pirie) (Tail-wheel u/c)					
G-BTWZ	Rans S-10 Sakota	0990.117		15.10.91	P C Avery Lower Mountpleasant Farm, Chatteris 10. 4.09P
	(Built D G Hey - pr.no.PFA 194-12117) (Rotax 912 - officially regd with Rotax 582)					
G-BTXD (2)	Rans S-6-ESA Coyote II	0591.191		22.10.91	A I Sutherland	Fearn 25. 7.08P
	(Built M Isterling - pr.no.PFA 204-12104) (Rotax 582) *(Tail-wheel u/c)*					
G-BTXF	Cameron V-90 Balloon (Hot Air)	2692		2.10.91	G Thompson	Ambleside 3. 3.03
G-BTXG	British Aerospace Jetstream Series 3102	719	SE-FVP	23.10.91	Highland Airways Ltd	Inverness 9. 7.09E
	G-BTXG, OK-REJ, G-BTXG, OY-EEC, G-BTXG, N418MX, G-31-719					
G-BTXH	Colt AS-56 Airship (Hot Air)	2078		23.10.91	L Kiefer	March-Flugstetten, Germany 26. 3.93A
G-BTXI	Noorduyn AT-16-ND Harvard IIB	14-429	Swedish AF	25.10.91	Patina Ltd *(As "FE695:94" in RAF c/s)*	
	Fv16105, RCAF FE695, FE695, 42-892				*(Operated The Fighter Collection)*	Duxford 11. 4.09P
G-BTXK	Thunder Ax7-65 Balloon (Hot Air)	1910	ZS-HYP	28.10.91	A F Selby Woodhouse Eaves , Loughborough 1. 7.09E
			G-BTXK			
G-BTXM	Colt 21A Cloudhopper Balloon (Hot Air)	2082		29.10.91	H J Andrews	Selborne, Alton 30. 8.09E
G-BTXS	Cameron O-120 Balloon (Hot Air)	2141		16.10.91	Semajan Ltd tr Southern Balloon Group	*(France)* 16. 9.09E
G-BTXT	Maule MXT-7-180 Super Rocket	14027C		7.10.91	E A Gibson tr G-BTXT Group	
						Morgansfield, Fishburn 10. 6.09E
G-BTXW	Cameron V-77 Balloon (Hot Air)	2717		31.10.91	P C Waterhouse *"Scott's Whisky"*	
						Wadhurst, East Sussex 19. 9.07A
G-BTXX	Bellanca 8KCAB Decathlon	595-80	OY-CYC	1.10.91	Tatenhill Aviation Ltd	Tatenhill 20. 5.09E
			SE-IEP, N5063G			
G-BTXZ	Zenair CH.250	PFA 113-12170		24.10.91	J Glendinning tr G-BTXZ Group	
	(Built B F Arnall) (Lycoming O-290)					Hinton-in-the-Hedges 27. 2.09P
G-BTYC	Cessna 150L	15075767	N66002	4.11.91	Polestar Aviation Ltd	Jersey 10. 4.09E
G-BTYE	Cameron A-180 Balloon (Hot Air)	2704		5.11.91	K J A Maxwell and D S Messmer *"Rolling Rock"* (Active 5.07)	
						Uckfield 26. 3.00T
G-BTYF	Thunder Ax10-180 Series 2 Balloon (Hot Air)			7.11.91	I Bentley *(Operated Innovation Balloons)* Bath 6.10.08T
		2086				
G-BTYH	Pottier P 80S	PFA 160-11121		11.11.91	G E Livings	RAF Halton 7. 1.08P
	(Built R Pickett) (Volkswagen 1834)					
G-BTYI	Piper PA-28-181 Archer II	28-8190078	N8287T	15.11.91	G B Jeffery	Fenland 23. 3.09E
G-BTYT	Cessna 152 II	15280455	N24931	25.11.91	Cristal Air Ltd	Shoreham 21. 9.09E
G-BTYW	Cessna 120	11725	N77283	27.11.91	A R Dix and R Nisbet	
	(Continental C85)		NC77283			Shacklewell Farm, Empingham 27.11.10S
G-BTYX	Cessna 140	11004	N76568	2. 5.08	R F Richards	*(Uckfield)*
			NC76568			
G-BTYY	Curtiss Robertson C-2 Robin	475	N348K	8.10.91	R R L Windus *(Noted 7.04)*	
	(Continental W-670)		NC348K			Truleigh Manor Farm, Edburton 1. 9.97P
G-BTZA	Beech F33A Bonanza	CE-957	PH-BNT	22.11.91	H Mendelssohn tr G-BTZA Group	Kirknewton 29. 6.09E
G-BTZB	Yakovlev Yak-50	801810	DOSAAF 77	27.11.91	D H Boardman *(As "10" in DOSAAF c/s)*	
						Lee-on-Solent 29. 9.09P
G-BTZD	Yakovlev Yak-1 Series 1	8188	1342	10.12.91	Historic Aircraft Collection Ltd	
	(C/n stamped on engine bearers)		(Soviet AF)			*(Westfield, Hastings)*
	(Salvaged from lake in N Russia mid 1991 after forced landing c.1942: for completion by 2009)					
G-BTZE	LET Yakovlev C-11	171312	(France)	11. 2.92	M V Rijkse	Gyor-Per, Hungary
	(C/n noted on plate as 172503)		Egypt AF, OK-JIK			
G-BTZG	British Aerospace ATP	2046	PK-MTV	11.12.91	Trident Aviation Leasing Services (Jersey) Ltd	
			(PK-MAA), G-BTZG		*(Stored as "PK-MTV" 3.06, b/u by 8.08)* Woodford	
G-BTZO	SOCATA TB-20 Trinidad	1409		18.12.91	A P Howells	Cardiff 11. 6.09E
G-BTZP	SOCATA TB-9 Tampico Club	1421		18.12.91	M W Orr	Oxford 18. 6.08E
G-BTZS	Colt 77B Balloon (Hot Air)	2088		18.12.91	P T R Ollivere *"Petal"*	Sutton 27. 5.04A
G-BTZU	Cameron Concept 60 Balloon (Hot Air)	2734		20.12.91	S A Simington	Eccles, Norwich 2. 4.09E
G-BTZV	Cameron V-77 Balloon (Hot Air)	2410		20.12.91	D J and H M Brown *"Vulcan"*	Redditch 1. 7.09E
G-BTZX	Piper J-3C-65 Cub	18871	N98648	27. 2.92	D A Woodhams and J T Coulthard tr ZX Cub Group	
			NC98648			Bidford 6. 8.11
G-BTZY	Colt 56A Balloon (Hot Air)	2084		17.10.91	S J Wardle	Kettering 21. 9.05A
G-BTZZ	CFM Streak Shadow	K 169-SA		23.12.91	D R Stennett	Mendlesham 6.11.07P
	(Built D R Stennett - pr.no.PFA 206-12155) (Rotax 582)					

G-BUAA - G-BUZZ

G-BUAA	Corben Baby Ace D	561	N516DH	19.11.91	S Burchfield	*(Bar Hill, Cambridge)* 20.11.08P
	(Built D E Hale) (Continental A65)					
G-BUAB	Aeronca 11AC Chief	11AC-1759	N3458E	17. 1.92	J Reed	Craysmarsh Farm, Melksham 10. 9.09P
	(Continental A65)		NC3458E			
G-BUAC	Slingsby T.31 Motor Cadet III PFA 042-12059		(??)	17. 1.92	D A Wilson and C R Partington *(Noted 1.04)*	
	(Re-built D C Pattison) (Volkswagen 1200) *(P/i unknown, rebuilt after crash near Kingussie with minor modification)* Milfield 4.10.94P					
G-BUAF	Cameron N-77 Balloon (Hot Air)	2746		2. 1.92	Zebedee Balloon Service Ltd Szekszárd, Hungary 17. 8.09E
	(Rebuilt from 5N-ATT)					

G-BUAG   Jodel D 18   PFA 169-11651   3. 1.92   A L Silcox   Bodmin   1. 7.03P
         (Built A L Silcox) (Volkswagen 1834)
G-BUAI   Everett Gyroplane Series 3   030   6. 1.92   D Bateson   (Haslemere)   9. 4.04P
         (Rotax 532)
G-BUAJ   Cameron N-90 Balloon (Hot Air)   2735   7. 1.92   Skyview Ballooning Ltd t/a Kent Ballooning
                                                                                                                   Stanford, Ashford   3. 1.10E
G-BUAM   Cameron V-77 Balloon (Hot Air)   2470   10. 1.92   N Florence "J and E Page Flowers"   London SW11   3. 5.06A
G-BUAO   Luscombe 8A Silvaire   4089   N1362K   15. 1.92   K E Ballington   Yeatsall Farm, Abbots Bromley 11. 8.04P
         (Continental A65)   NC1362K
G-BUAT   Thunder Ax9-120 Balloon (Hot Air)   2093   24. 1.92   J Fenton "Calor"   Preston   17. 3.00T
G-BUAV   Cameron O-105 Balloon (Hot Air)   2767   27. 1.92   O and T Dorrell   Manchester 19.10.09E
G-BUAX   Rans S-10 Sakota   0390.095   28. 1.92   A W McKee   White Waltham 10. 8.07P
         (Built J W Topham - pr.no.PFA 194-11848) (Rotax 582)
G-BUBN   Pilatus Britten-Norman BN-2B-26 Islander   14. 2.92   Isles of Scilly Skybus Ltd   St Just 18. 2.09E
                                                    2270
G-BUBS   Lindstrand LBL 77B Balloon (Hot Air)   144 (2)   10.10.94   B J Bower "Bubbles Balloon"   Perugia, Italy   27. 3.09E
G-BUBT   Stoddard-Hamilton Glasair IIS RG   2026   6. 2.92   DOC Tiles Ltd   (Watford)   3. 6.09P
         (Builltt M D Evans - pr.no.PFA 149-11633) (Lycoming IO-320)
G-BUBU   Piper PA-34-220T Seneca III   34-8233060   N8043B   9. 7.87   Brinor (Holdings) Ltd   Poplar Hall Farm, Elmsett 13. 8.09E
G-BUBW   Robinson R22 Beta   2048   7. 2.92   Plane Talking Ltd   Elstree   18. 5.09E
G-BUBY   Thunder Ax8-105 Series 2 Balloon (Hot Air)   3. 2.92   T M Donnelly   "Jorvik Viking Centre"
                                                    2115   Sprotbrough, Doncaster 17. 6.09E
G-BUCA   Cessna A150K Aerobat   A1500220   N5920J   14. 6.89   D Featherby tr BUCA Group   Norwich   4. 5.09E
G-BUCB   Cameron H-34 Balloon (Hot Air)   2777   11. 2.92   A S Jones   Wolverhampton 30. 6.07A
G-BUCC   CASA 1-131E Jungmann   1109   G-BUEM   11. 9.78   P L Gaze (As "BU+CC: w/no.1109" in Luftwaffe c/s)
         (Spanish AF serial conflicts with G-BJAL)   G-BUCC, Spanish AF E3B-114   Goodwood   4. 6.08P
G-BUCG   Schleicher ASW 20L TOP   20396   BGA3140   19. 2.92   W B Andrews "344"   Davidstow Moor   3. 8.09E
         (Konig SD430)   I-FEEL
G-BUCH   Stinson V-77 (AT-19) Reliant   77-381   N9570H   21. 2.92   Gullwing Trading Ltd   White Waltham   8. 8.09
                                                            FB531 (RN)
G-BUCK   CASA 1-131E Jungmann Series 1000   1113   Spanish AF   11. 9.78   A G Truman tr Jungmann Flying Group
                                                            E3B-322   (As "BU+CK" in Luftwaffe c/s)   White Waltham 27. 4.07P
G-BUCM   Hawker Sea Fury FB.11   -   VX653   26. 2.92   Patina Ltd (Operated The Fighter Collection)
                                                                                     (On rebuild 10.08)   Duxford
G-BUCO   Pietenpol AirCamper   PFA 047-11829   10. 2.92   A James   Siege Cross Farm, Thatcham 10. 9.08P
         (Built A James) (Continental C90)
G-BUCS   Cessna 150F   15062368   N3568L   25. 8.89   London Ashford Airport Ltd   Lydd   1. 4.04T
G-BUCT   Cessna 150L   15075326   N11320   14. 6.89   Aircraft Engineers Ltd   Prestwick   9. 5.09E
G-BUDA   Slingsby T 61F Venture T 2   1963   ZA627   18. 2.92   T M Holloway tr RAF Gliding and Soaring Association
                                                                                                                   RAF Cranwell   8. 1.10E
G-BUDB   Slingsby T 61F Venture T 2   1964   ZA628   18. 2.92   T M Holloway tr RAF Gliding and Soaring Association
                                                                                     (Operated Fenland Gliding Club)   RAF Marham 15.12.09E
G-BUDC   Slingsby T 61F Venture T 2   1971   ZA652   18. 2.92   I P Litchfield tr T 61 Group (As "ZA652" in RAF c/s)
                                                                                                                       Enstone   28. 7.09
G-BUDE   Piper PA-22-135 Tri-Pacer   22-980   N1144C   9. 4.92   P Robinson
                                                                                           Upper Harford Farm, Bourton-on-the-Water 20.11.10
G-BUDF   Rand Robinson KR-2   PFA 129-11155   26. 2.92   M Stott   (Bedford) 3.12.03P
         (Built J B McNab) (HAPI Magnum 75)
G-BUDI   Aero Designs Pulsar   PFA 202-12185   25. 2.92   R W L Oliver   Popham   7. 8.07P
         (Built R W L Oliver)
G-BUDK   Thunder Ax7-77 Balloon (Hot Air)   2076   2. 3.92   W Evans   Wrexham   9. 9.09E
G-BUDL   Taylorcraft E Auster III   458   PH-POL   5. 3.92   K B Owen (As "NX534" in RAF c/s)   Spanhoe   8.10.09P
         (Regd with Frame No.TAY 5810)   8A-2, R Neth AF R-17, NX534
G-BUDN   Cameron Shoe 90 SS Balloon (Hot Air)   2761   6. 3.92   Magical Adventures Ltd "Converse Allstar Boot"
         (Converse Allstar Trainers shape)   West Bloomfield, Mi, USA 29. 9.09E
G-BUDO   PZL-110 Koliber 150   03900045   (D-EIVT)   12. 3.92   A S Vine (stored, noted 9.08)   Haverfordwest 27. 7.06
G-BUDR   Denney Kitfox Model 3   1066   16. 3.92   N J P Mayled   Dunkeswell 26.11.08P
         (Built D Silsbury - pr.no.PFA 172-12107)
G-BUDS   Rand Robinson KR-2   PFA 129-10937   31.12.85   D W Munday (Stored, noted 9.08)   Popham
         (Built D W Munday)
G-BUDT   Slingsby T 61F Venture T 2   1883   XZ563   30. 3.92   D S Puttock tr G-BUDT Group
                                                                                                 Belle Vue Farm, Yarnscombe   4. 1.10E
G-BUDU   Cameron V-77 Balloon (Hot Air)   2447   16. 3.92   T M G Amery   Llandeilo 18. 9.03A
G-BUDW   Brügger MB.2 Colibri   PFA 043-10644   G-GODS   19. 3.92   S P Barrett   (Irby-in-the-Marsh, Skegness) 30. 7.09P
         (Built J M Hoblyn) (Volkswagen 1600)
G-BUEC   Van's RV-6   21015   17. 3.92   A H Harper   High Ham, Langport 29. 3.09P
         (Built D W Richardson and R D Harper - pr.no.PFA 181C-11884) (Lycoming O-360)
G-BUED   Slingsby T 61F Venture T 2   1979   ZA660   12. 3.92   F B Rutterford tr 617 VGS Flying Group
                                                                                                            Waldershare Park   9. 9.09
G-BUEF   Cessna 152 II   15280862   N25928   17. 3.92   A L Brown tr Channel Aviation   Bourn   7. 9.09E
G-BUEG   Cessna 152 II   15280407   N24736   17. 3.92   Aviation South West Ltd   Exeter   1.10.09E
G-BUEI   Thunder Ax8-105 Balloon (Hot Air)   2172   23. 3.92   K P Barnes   Bristol 20. 8.09E
G-BUEK   Slingsby T 61F Venture T 2   1879   XZ559   30. 3.92   G E Draycott and B L Owen tr G-BUEK Group
                                                                                                                    Shipdham 11. 3.09E
G-BUEN   Magni M-14 Scout   VPM14-UK101   19. 3.92   J L G McLane   (Gilling East, York) 14. 8.09P
         (Arrow GT1000R)
G-BUEP   Maule MXT-7-180 Super Rocket   14023C   24. 3.92   N J B Bennett   Henstridge 23. 6.09E
G-BUEV   Cameron O-77 Balloon (Hot Air)   2810   EI-CFW   31. 3.92   K C Tanner "BONI"   Thame   17. 6.09E
                                                            G-BUEV
G-BUEW   Rans S-6 Coyote II   0190-111 G-MWYF   1. 4.92   J D Clabon   Shobdon 18. 8.09P
         (Built D J O'Gorman - pr.no.PFA 204-12021)   (EI-CEL)
         (Rotax 582) (Tri-cycle u/c)
G-BUFA   Cameron R-77 Gas/Balloon (Hot Air)   2712   19. 3.92   Noble Adventures Ltd (Stored 1996) (Netherlands) 10. 6.93A
G-BUFC   Cameron R-77 Gas/Balloon (Hot Air)   2823   19. 3.92   Noble Adventures Ltd (Stored 1996) (Netherlands) 23. 6.93A

Reg	Type	C/n	Prev ID	Date	Owner/Operator	Location	Expiry
G-BUFE	Cameron R-77 Gas/Balloon (Hot Air)	2825		19. 3.92	Noble Adventures Ltd (Stored 1996) (Netherlands)		21. 6.93A
G-BUFG	Slingsby T 61F Venture T 2	1977	ZA658	3. 4.92	Transcourt Ltd	Hinton-in-the-Hedges	3.10.08E
G-BUFH	Piper PA-28-161 Warrior II	28-8416076	N43520	15. 4.92	R J Gibson	Bournemouth	13. 7.09E
G-BUFJ	Cameron V-90 Balloon (Hot Air)	2809		7. 4.92	S P Richards	Tonbridge	7. 7.06T
G-BUFN	Slingsby T 61F Venture T 2	1967	ZA631	8. 4.92	S C Foggin tr BUFN Group		
						Sandhill Farm, Shrivenham	16.12.09E
G-BUFR	Slingsby T 61F Venture T 2 (Rollason RS Mk.2)	1880	XZ560	9. 4.92	East Sussex Gliding Club Ltd	Ringmer	16.12.08E
G-BUFT	Cameron O-120 Balloon (Hot Air)	2814		9. 4.92	D Bron	St Barthelemy, France	19. 2.09E
G-BUFV	Avid Speed Wing Mk.4 (Built S C Ord) (BMW R100)	PFA 189-12192		15. 4.92	M and B Gribbin	(Antrim, Co Antrim)	16. 9.05P
					(Lost power on take-off Toomebridge and ditched in Lough Neagh 10. 6.05)		
G-BUFW	Aérospatiale AS.355F1 Ecureuil 2	5112	5N-BAK G-BUFW, N57904	21. 4.92	RCR Aviation Ltd	Thruxton	31. 5.92A
G-BUFY	Piper PA-28-161 Warrior II	28-8016211	N130CT N8TS, N3571K	14. 4.92	Bickertons Aerodromes Ltd (Operated The Pilots Centre)		
						Denham	1. 7.09E
G-BUGB	Stolp SA.750 Acroduster Too (Built D Burnham) (Lycoming O-360)	PFA 089-11942		22. 4.92	R M Chaplin	Rochester	31. 3.09P
G-BUGD	Cameron V-77 Balloon (Hot Air)	2195		23. 4.92	P Haslett	Arcy sur Cure, France	11. 9.04A
G-BUGE	Bellanca 7GCAA Citabria	339-77	N4165Y	23. 4.92	V Vaughan and N O'Brien		
					Kilkenny, County Kilkenny and Mullinahone, County Tyrone		14.10.10S
G-BUGG	Cessna 150F	15062479	N8379G	24. 3.92	C P J Taylor and D M Forshaw	Panshanger	21.11.08E
G-BUGI	Evans VP-1 (Built D Silsbury)	PFA 7201		16. 4.92	D E Wood (Pseudo German WW1 markings)		
						Hill Farm, Nayland	27. 8.09P
G-BUGJ	Robin DR.400-180 Régent	2137		28. 4.92	W E R Jenkins	Little Gransden	26. 3.09E
G-BUGL	Slingsby T 61F Venture T 2	1966	ZA630	29. 4.92	S Bradford and M Bean tr VMG Group	Tibenham	27. 1.09E
					(Also carries "ZA630" on tail)		
G-BUGM	CFM Streak Shadow (Built W J de Gier - pr.no.PFA 206-12069) (Rotax 582)	K 176-SA		29. 4.92	S J Welch and W D Berry tr The Shadow Group		
						Sywell	24.10.09P
G-BUGP	Cameron V-77 Balloon (Hot Air)	2278	OO-BEE	10. 3.92	R Churcher	Canterbury	16. 7.09E
G-BUGS	Cameron V-77 Balloon (Hot Air)	2482		14. 4.92	S J Dymond "Bugs Bunny"	Tidworth	14. 9.01T
G-BUGT	Slingsby T 61F Venture T 2	1871	XZ551	22. 4.92	R W Hornsey tr Bambi Aircraft Group	Rufforth	3. 8.09E
G-BUGV	Slingsby T 61F Venture T 2	1884	XZ564	28. 4.92	Oxfordshire Sportflying Ltd	Enstone	28. 6.09E
G-BUGW	Slingsby T 61F Venture T 2	1962	ZA626	22. 4.92	Transcourt Ltd	Hinton-in-the-Hedges	1. 5.09E
G-BUGY	Cameron V-90 Balloon (Hot Air)	2800		9. 4.92	I J Culley tr Dante Balloon Group "Florence"		
						Hungerford	4.10.09E
G-BUGZ	Slingsby T 61F Venture T 2	1981	ZA662	22. 4.92	R W Spiller tr Dishforth Flying Group		
						AAC Dishforth	13. 6.09E
G-BUHA	Slingsby T 61F Venture T 2	1970	ZA634	29. 4.92	Buckminster Gliding Club Ltd (As "ZA634:C" in RAF c/s)		
						Saltby	18.12.09E
G-BUHM	Cameron V-77 Balloon (Hot Air)	2481		7. 5.92	J Skinner "Blue Horizon"	Chart Sutton, Maidstone	9. 8.09E
G-BUHO	Cessna 140 (Continental C90)	14402	N2173V	1. 5.92	W B Bateson	Blackpool	6.10.11
G-BUHR	Slingsby T 61F Venture T 2	1874	XZ554	8. 5.92	W G Miller tr Connel Motor Glider Group		
						North Connel, Oban	11.11.09E
G-BUHS	Stoddard-Hamilton Glasair SH TD-1 (Built F L Binder) (Lycoming O-360)	149	C-GYMB	8. 5.92	T F Horrocks	Wick	6. 2.09E
G-BUHU	Cameron N-105 Balloon (Hot Air)	2785		13. 5.92	Unipart Group Ltd tr Unipart Balloon Club		
						Cowley, Oxford	21.11.96A
G-BUHZ	Cessna 120	14950	N3676V	1. 5.92	M R Houseman tr C140 Group	RAF Henlow	18. 5.09P
G-BUIE	Cameron N-90 Balloon (Hot Air)	2863		22. 5.92	B Conway	Wheatley, Oxford	24. 1.01A
G-BUIF	Piper PA-28-161 Warrior II	28-7916406	N28375	29. 5.92	Northumbria Flying School Ltd	Newcastle	14. 7.09E
G-BUIG	Campbell Cricket (Built T A Holmes) (Rotax 532)	PFA G/03-1173		27. 5.92	J A English (Noted 7.08)	Kirkbride	27. 4.05P
G-BUIH	Slingsby T 61F Venture T 2	1876	XZ556	29. 5.92	L E Ingram tr Falcon Gliding Group		
						Wellesbourne Mountford	5. 7.09E
G-BUIJ	Piper PA-28-161 Warrior II	28-8116210	N83784	3. 6.92	P F Wells t/a OPS Aero Support Services		
						Okehampton	25. 8.09E
G-BUIK	Piper PA-28-161 Warrior II	28-7916469	N2845P	2. 6.92	A S Bamrah t/a Falcon Flying Services	Biggin Hill	5.11.09E
G-BUIL	CFM Streak Shadow (Built P N Bevan and L M Poor - pr.no.PFA 206-12121) (Rotax 582)	K 182-SA		8. 5.92	J A McKie	Stoke, Isle of Grain	11. 2.09P
G-BUIN	Thunder Ax7-77 Balloon (Hot Air)	1882		5. 6.92	P C Johnson	Gloucester	5. 7.09E
G-BUIP	Denney Kitfox Model 2 (Built G D Lean - pr.no.PFA 172-11874)	710		8. 6.92	Avcomm Developments Ltd	Enstone	7. 8.08P
G-BUIR	Avid Speed Wing Mk.4 (Buillt K N Pollard)	PFA 189-12213		9. 6.92	M J Cook	Plaistows Farm, St Albans	27. 2.09P
G-BUIU	Cameron V-90 Balloon (Hot Air)	2641		11. 6.92	H Micketeit	Bielefeld, Germany	18. 4.03A
G-BUIZ	Cameron N-90 Balloon (Hot Air) (Telecoms Shape)	2850		12. 6.92	R S Kent tr Balloon Preservation Flying Group "Hutchinson"	Petworth	1. 7.09E
G-BUJA	Slingsby T 61F Venture T 2	1972	ZA653	22. 5.92	T M Holloway tr RAF Gliding and Soaring Association (Operated Wrekin Gliding Club)	RAF Cosford	28. 3.09E
G-BUJB	Slingsby T 61F Venture T 2	1978	ZA659	21. 5.92	O F Vaughan and D A Fall tr Falke Syndicate		
						Shobdon	14. 7.09
G-BUJE	Cessna 177B Cardinal	17701920	N34646	10. 6.92	J Flux tr FG93 Group	Old Sarum	6. 4.09E
G-BUJH	Colt 77B Balloon (Hot Air)	2207		23. 6.92	R P Cross and R Stanley	Luton and Harpenden	27. 4.09E
G-BUJI	Slingsby T 61F Venture T 2	1882	XZ562	22. 5.92	Solent Venture Syndicate Ltd	Lee-on-Solent	19. 5.09E
G-BUJJ	Avid Speed Wing (Built M Cox)	213	N614JD	20.10.92	R A Dawson	Shenstone Hall Farm, Shenstone	13. 9.06P
G-BUJK	Montgomerie-Bensen B 8MR (Built J M Montgomerie) (Rotax 582)	PFA G/01-1211		25. 6.92	P C W Raine	Walkeridge Farm, Overton	7. 8.08P
G-BUJL	Aero Designs Pulsar (Built J J Lynch)	PFA 202-11892		16. 6.92	J J Lynch	(Dunstable)	
G-BUJM	Cessna 120 (Continental C85)	11784	N77343 NC77343	19. 6.92	D H Mackay tr Cessna 120 Flying Group	RNAS Yeovilton	7. 5.11S
G-BUJN	Cessna 172N Skyhawk II	17272713	N6315D	19. 6.92	M Djukic and J Benfell	(Newcastle, Staffordshire)	17. 3.09E

G-BUJO	Piper PA-28-161 Cherokee Warrior II	N1014Q	19. 6.92	A S Bamrah t/a Falcon Flying Services	Biggin Hill	4. 8.09E
	28-7716077					
G-BUJP	Piper PA-28-161 Warrior II	28-7916047	N21624	19. 6.92	J M C Manson *(Operated Ace Aviation)*	Shoreham	15.12.09E
G-BUJR	Cameron A-180 Balloon (Hot Air)	2821		22. 6.92	Dragon Balloon Company Ltd		
						Castleton, Hope Valley	16.10.00T
G-BUJV	Avid Speed Wing Mk.4	PFA 189-12250		3. 7.92	C Thomas	Shenstone Hall Farm, Shenstone	28. 7.94P
	(Built D N Anderson)				*(Damaged 13. 8.93 Caernarfon - remnants dumped 8.06, noted 11.08)*		
G-BUJW	Thunder Ax8-90 Series 2 Balloon (Hot Air)			6. 7.92	G J Grimes	Farnham	26.12.08E
	2208						
G-BUJX	Slingsby T 61F Venture T 2	1873	XZ553	7. 7.92	K E Ballington	Saltby	6.11.09E
G-BUJZ	RotorWay Executive 90	5119/6973		9. 7.92	M P Swoboda	Street Farm, Takeley	7. 9.07P
	(Built T W Aisthorpe and R J D Crick) (RotorWay RI 162)			*(Landed in field near Willingdale 27. 6.07 and substantially damaged: noted 9.08)*			
	(Originally regd as c/n 5119: rebuilt 2004/5 after accident 6.03 with new official c/n 5119/6973 although c/n plate states "5218/6973")						
G-BUKB	Rans S-10 Sakota	0790.112		13. 7.92	M K Blatch	RAF Brize Norton	18. 4.07P
	(Built M K Blatch - pr.no.PFA 194-12078) (Rotax 582)						
G-BUKF	Denney Kitfox Model 4	PFA 172A-12247		2. 6.92	A G V McClintock tr Kilo Foxtrot Group		
	(Built M R Crosland)					East Fortune	16. 7.08P
G-BUKH	Druine D 31 Turbulent	PFA 048-11419		14. 8.92	J G Wilkins	Headcorn	16.10.08P
	(Built J S Smith) (Volkswagen 1600)						
G-BUKI	Thunder Ax7-77 Balloon (Hot Air)	2239		8. 7.92	Airxcite Ltd t/a Virgin Balloon Flights	Wembley	1.10.09E
G-BUKJ	British Aerospace ATP	2052	(PH-MGC)	5. 8.92	Trident Aviation Leasing Services (Jersey) Ltd		
	G-BUKJ, EC-HCO, G-BUKJ, (PH-MJL), EC-GLD, G-OEDF, G-BUKJ, TC-THZ, G-BUKJ					Bucharest, Romania	15. 4.08E
G-BUKK	Bücker Bü.133D Jungmeister	27	N44DD	15.11.89	E J F McEntee *(As "U-80" in Swiss AF c/s)*		
	(Built Dornier-Werke AG)		HB-MKG, Swiss AF U-80			Iron Pear Tree Farm, Kirdford	11. 5.09P
G-BUKN	Piper PA-15 Vagabond	15-215	N4427H	15. 7.92	M A Goddard	(Southampton)	
			NC4427H				
G-BUKO	Cessna 120	13089	N2828N	15. 7.92	S Warrener	Fenland	12. 5.09P
			NC2828N		*(Rebuilt using components ex G-GAWA)*		
G-BUKP	Denney Kitfox Model 2	PFA 172-12301		22. 7.92	FAA Europe Ltd	(King's Lynn)	11. 2.09P
	(Built T D Reid)						
G-BUKR	SOCATA MS.880B Rallye 100T	2923	LN-BIY	27. 7.92	G R Russell tr G-BUKR Flying Group		
						Middle Pymore Farm, Bridport	27. 2.09E
G-BUKS	Colt 77B Balloon (Hot Air)	2241		6. 7.92	R and M Bairstow	Middlewich, Cheshire	22. 6.08A
G-BUKU	Luscombe 8E Silvaire Deluxe	4720	N1993K	30. 7.92	D J Warren tr Silvaire Flying Group	Rochester	17. 6.09P
	(Continental C85)		NC1993K				
G-BUKX	Piper PA-28-161 Cherokee Warrior II	N231PA	5. 8.92	LNP Ltd		Dunkeswell	22.12.09E
	28-7816674						
G-BUKY	CCF Harvard 4 (T-6J-CCF Texan)	CCF4-464	N455V	13. 7.92	R A Fleming *(As "52-8543-'66" in US Navy c/s)*		
			G-BUKY, FAP 1766 , WGAF BF-063 , WGAF AA-063, 52-8543			Breighton	21.12.09P
G-BUKZ	Evans VP-2	PFA 063-10761		5. 8.92	P R Farnell *(Noted 7.02)*	Wombleton	
	(Built P R Farnell)						
G-BULB	Thunder Ax7-77 Balloon (Hot Air)	1968		3. 7.92	G B Davies	Thorney, Peterborough	15. 2.09E
G-BULC	Avid Flyer Mk.4	PFA 189-12202		6. 7.92	C Nice	Popham	1. 4.09P
	(Built C Nice)						
G-BULD	Cameron N-105 Balloon (Hot Air)	2136		6. 8.92	R J Collins	Hurtmore, Godalming	26. 1.09E
G-BULF	Colt 77A Balloon (Hot Air)	2043		10. 8.92	P Goss and T C Davies *"Nursery"*	Christchurch	17. 6.09E
G-BULG	Van's RV-4	JRV4-1	C-FELJ	28. 7.92	V D Long	Wymondham	16. 7.08P
	(Built L Johnson) (Lycoming O-320)						
G-BULH	Cessna 172N Skyhawk II	17269869	N738CJ	2. 7.92	R Murgatroyd t/a FlyBPL.com	Blackpool	16. 1.06T
G-BULJ	CFM Streak Shadow	K 191-SA		10. 8.92	C C Brown	Wellesbourne Mountford	4.11.09P
	(Built C C Brown - pr.no.PFA 206-12199) (Rotax 582)						
G-BULK	Thunder Ax9-120 Series 2 Balloon (Hot Air)			3. 7.92	S J Colin tr Skybus Ballooning	Cranbrook	11.10.04T
	2237						
G-BULL	Scottish Aviation Bulldog Series 120/128	HKG-5	20. 9.88	N V Sills *(As "HKG-5" in Royal Hong Kong AAF c/s)*			
	BH120/392	G-31-18				Kemble	17.10.10S
G-BULN	Colt 210A Balloon (Hot Air)	2265		13. 8.92	H G Davies	Woodmancote, Cheltenham	9. 8.09E
G-BULO	Luscombe 8F Silvaire	4216	N1489K	13. 8.92	B W Foulds	(Weston-on-Trent)	12. 7.09P
	(Continental O-200A)		NC1489K				
G-BULR	Piper PA-28-140 Cherokee B	28-25230	HB-OHP	8. 7.92	G R Bright	Little Gransden	4. 7.08E
			N7320F				
G-BULT	Everett Gyroplane Series 1	PFA G/03A-1213		20. 8.92	A T Pocklington	(Bishops Stortford)	26. 5.05P
	(Built A T Pocklington)						
G-BULY	Avid Flyer	PFA 189-12309		12. 8.92	J Angiolini	Cumbernauld	23. 7.06P
	(Built M O Breen)						
G-BULZ	Denney Kitfox Model 2	PFA 172-11546		31. 7.92	T G F Trenchard		
	(Built D J Dumulo)				Newton Peverill Farm, Sturminster Marshall		22.11.05P
G-BUMP	Piper PA-28-181 Cherokee Archer II	PH-MVA	17. 1.79	A J Keen *(Operated Ulster Flying Club)*			
	28-7790437	OO-HCH, N3105Q				Newtownards	13. 9.09E
G-BUNB	Slingsby T 61F Venture T 2	1969	ZA633	25. 8.92	T M Holloway tr RAF Gliding and Soaring Association		
						Lee-on-Solent	23. 7.09E
G-BUNC	PZL-104 Wilga 35A	129444	SP-TWP	2. 9.92	R F Goodman	Husbands Bosworth	6. 7.09E
G-BUND	Piper PA-28RT-201T Turbo Arrow IV	N8219V	18. 7.88	L J Martin		Sandown	29.11.09E
	28R-8031107						
G-BUNG	Cameron N-77 Balloon (Hot Air)	2905		2. 9.92	A Kaye tr The Bungle Balloon Group *"Bungle"*		
					(Aspen titles)	Wellingborough	17. 6.09E
G-BUNH	Piper PA-28RT-201T Turbo Arrow IV	N8255H	26. 8.92	J H Sandham t/a J H Sandham Aviation	Carlisle	25. 3.09E	
	28R-8031166						
G-BUNJ	K & S SA 102.5 Cavalier	PFA 001-10058		10. 9.92	J A Smith	Great Massingham	
	(Built J S Smith)				*(On build 9.97)*		
G-BUNM	Denney Kitfox Model 3	PFA 172-12111		15. 9.92	P N Akass	(Beauly)	5. 5.04P
	(Built P J Carter) (Floatplane)						
G-BUNO	Neico Lancair 320	PFA 191-12332		11. 9.92	J Softley *(On build 2000)*	(Newbury)	
	(Built J Softley)						

Reg	Type	C/n	Prev id	Date	Owner/Operator	Base	CofA
G-BUNV	Thunder Ax7-77 Balloon (Hot Air)	1967		23. 9.92	R Stone and R M Garnett		
					(Romsey and Bursledon, Southampton)		22. 7.09E
G-BUNZ	Thunder Ax10-180 Series 2 Balloon (Hot Air)			7. 9.92	M A Scholes (WFU and dismembered 2006)		
		2271				Haywards Heath	27. 2.06T
G-BUOA	Whittaker MW6-S Fatboy Flyer Series A			25. 9.92	H N Graham	(Lisbellaw, Enniskillen)	30.10.06P
	(Built D A Izod) (Rotax 582) PFA 164-11959						
G-BUOB	CFM Streak Shadow	K 186-SA		29. 9.92	W J White	Insch	7. 1.10P
	(Built A M Simmons - pr.no.PFA 206-12156) (Rotax 582)						
G-BUOD	Replica Plans SE.5a PFA 020-10474			5.10.92	M D Waldron (As "B595:W" in RFC 56 Sqdn c/s)		
	(Built M D Waldron) (Continental C90)					Croft Farm, Defford	16.11.09P
G-BUOE	Cameron V-90 Balloon (Hot Air)	2938		6.10.92	B and Joy Smallwood "Flying Colours 2"		
	(New envelope 7.05 - c/n not known)					Marshfield	26. 8.09E
G-BUOF	Druine D 62B Condor PFA 049-11236			6.10.92	R P Loxton	Wyke Farm, Sherbourne	7. 1.10P
	(Built K Jones)						
G-BUOI	Piper PA-20-135 Pacer	20-571	OY-ALS	18. 9.92	T A P Hubbard tr Foley Farm Flying Group		
	(Lycoming O-320) (Hoerner wing-tips)		D-EHEN, N7750K			Redwood Cottage, Meon	21. 5.11
G-BUOK	Rans S-6-116 Coyote II	0692.314		9.10.92	M Morris Fieldhead Farm, Denholme, Bradford		18. 6.09P
	(Built M Morris - pr.no.PFA 204A-12317) (Rotax 912-UL)						
G-BUOL	Denney Kitfox Model 3 PFA 172-12142			12.10.92	L A James Wharf Farm, Market Bosworth		22. 6.09P
	(Built J G D Barbour)						
G-BUON	Avid Aerobat PFA 189-12160			13.10.92	S R Winder	(Bolton)	6.11.01P
	(Built I A J Lappin)						
G-BUOR	CASA 1-131E Jungmann Series 2000	2134	N89542	21.10.92	M I M Schermer Voest (Flies in Hungarian Air Force colours)		
			EC-336, Spanish AF E3B-508			De Kooy, Netherlands	15. 6.09P
G-BUOS	Vickers Supermarine 394 Spitfire FR.XVIIIe		Indian AF	19.10.92	Historic Flying Ltd (As "SM845:GZ-J" in RAF c/s)		
		6S/672224	HS687, SM845		(Operated Aircraft Restoration Company) Duxford		21. 8.09P
G-BUOW	Aero Designs Pulsar XP PFA 202-12206			22.10.92	T J Hartwell Sackville Lodge, Riseley		8. 6.95P
	(Built D F Gaughan)						
G-BUOZ	Thunder Ax10-180 Balloon (Hot Air)	1962	(SX-)	29.10.92	S J Colin t/a Skybus Ballooning	Headcorn	3.11.09E
			G-BUOZ				
G-BUPA	Rutan LongEz	750	N72SD	22. 9.92	N G Henry	(Gloucester)	27. 4.06P
	(Built D Moore) (Lycoming O-235)						
G-BUPB	Stolp SA.300 Starduster Too	RH.100	N8035E	3.11.92	J R Edwards tr Starduster PB Group	Popham	16. 4.08P
	(Built R Harte) (Lycoming IO-360)						
G-BUPC	Rollason Beta B 2 PFA 002-12369			29.10.92	C A Rolph	Liverpool-John Lennon	3. 6.03P
	(Built C A Rolph) (Continental C90)				(Veered off runway Clutton Hill Farm, Clutton and overturned 12. 9.02)		
G-BUPF	Bensen B 8MR PFA G/01-1209			5.11.92	P W Hewitt-Dean	(Wootton Bassett)	1. 8.02P
	(Built G M Hobman) (Rotax 532)						
G-BUPG	Cessna 180K Skywagon	18052490	N52086	15.10.92	T P A Norman	Langham	1.12.09E
G-BUPH	Colt 25A Balloon (Hot Air)	2023		10.11.92	BAB-Ballonwerbung GmbH Hanover, Germany		11. 2.05A
G-BUPI	Cameron V-77 Balloon (Hot Air)	1778	G-BOUC	28. 7.88	H W R Stewart Burslecombe, Tiverton		6. 9.09E
G-BUPJ	Fournier RF4D	4119	N7752	10.11.92	M R Shelton	Tatenhill	
G-BUPM	Magni M-16 Tandem Trainer VPM16-UK-102			16.10.92	A Kitson	RAF Mona	18. 7.08P
	(Rotax 914)						
G-BUPP	Cameron V-42 Balloon (Hot Air)	2789		21. 7.92	L J Schoeman	Basildon	13. 5.04A
G-BUPR	Jodel D 18 PFA 169-11289			23.11.92	R W Burrows Priory Farm, Tibenham		15. 5.08P
	(Built R W Burrows) (Limbach L2000)						
G-BUPU	Thunder Ax7-77 Balloon (Hot Air)	2305		25.11.92	R C Barkworth and D G Maguire "Puzzle"		
						Pulborough	26. 3.01A
G-BUPV	Great Lakes 2T-1A	126	N865K	26.11.92	R J Fray	Sibson	18. 6.09P
	(Gladden Kinner R55)		NC865K				
G-BUPW	Denney Kitfox Model 3 PFA 172-12281			22.10.92	G M Park tr Forfoxake Flyers Kense Farm, Beith		1. 8.08P
	(Built D Sweet) (Rotax 912)						
G-BURD	Reims Cessna F172N Skyhawk II F17201677		PH-AXI	26. 4.78	Tayside Aviation Ltd	Glenrothes	17.12.09E
G-BURE	Jodel D 9 Bébé PFA 944			30.11.92	N P StJ Ramsay	(Milton Keynes)	
	(Built P B Shilling and C R Kingsford)				(Noted 7.08, moved to owners home for completion)		
G-BURG	Colt 77A Balloon (Hot Air)	2042		12. 1.93	S T Humphreys "Lily"	Great Missenden	13. 7.09E
G-BURH	Cessna 150E	15061225	EI-AOO	2.12.92	C A Davis	Sandown	30.10.09E
			G-BURH, EI-AOO, N2125J				
G-BURI	Enstrom F-28C	433	N51743	11.12.92	R L Heath tr India Helicopters Group Headcorn		5. 6.09E
G-BURJ	Hawker Siddeley HS.748 Series 2A/256	1667	9N-ACP	14.12.92	Clewer Aviation Ltd	Blackpool	
G-BURL	Colt 105A Balloon (Hot Air)	2297		18.11.92	J E Rose "Isis"	Abingdon	9. 6.06T
G-BURN	Cameron O-120 Balloon (Hot Air)	2793		18. 2.92	Innovation Ballooning Ltd "Innovations"	Bath	17. 9.05T
G-BURP	RotorWay Executive 90	5116		8.10.92	N K Newman (Stored 7.99)	(Buckingham)	13. 9.96P
	(Built A GAEdwards) (RotorWay RI 162)						
G-BURR	Auster AOP.9	-	7851M	28. 9.92	P J Gill t/a Annic Aviation	Whaley Bridge	
			WZ706				
G-BURS	Sikorsky S-76A II Plus	760040	(HP-)	4. 5.89	Premiair Aviation Services Ltd	Denham	25.10.09E
			G-BURS, G-OHTL				
G-BURT	Piper PA-28-161 Cherokee Warrior II		N2459Q	10. 6.81	B A Paul	Denham	3. 5.09E
		28-7716105					
G-BURX	Cameron N-105 Balloon (Hot Air)	2959	G-NPNP	8. 1.93	R S Kent tr Balloon Preservation Flying Group		
			G-BURX			"National Power III"	Petworth	16. 7.09E
G-BURZ	Hawker Nimrod II	41H-59890	K3661	22.12.91	Historic Aircraft Collection Ltd	Duxford	26. 3.09P
					(As "K3661:562" in RAF 802 Sqdn c/s)		
G-BUSG	Airbus A320-211	0039	F-WWDM	30. 5.89	British Airways PLC	London Heathrow	30. 5.09E
G-BUSH	Airbus A320-211	0042	F-WWDT	19. 6.89	British Airways PLC	London Heathrow	18. 6.09E
G-BUSI	Airbus A320-211	0103	F-WWDB	23. 3.90	British Airways PLC	London Heathrow	21. 3.09E
G-BUSJ	Airbus A320-211	0109	F-WWIC	6. 8.90	British Airways PLC	London Heathrow	5. 8.09E
G-BUSK	Airbus A320-211	0120	F-WWIN	12.10.90	British Airways PLC	London Heathrow	11.10.09E
G-BUSN	RotorWay Executive 90	5141		6. 1.93	J A McGinley	Street Farm, Takeley	7. 1.09P
G-BUSR	Aero Designs Pulsar PFA 202-12356			15.12.92	S S Bateman and R A Watts	Cheddington	21. 6.09P
	(Built S S Bateman and R A Watts) (Tail-wheel u/c)						

Reg	Type	c/n	Prev id	Date	Owner/Operator	Location	Date
G-BUSS	Cameron Bus 90 SS Balloon (Hot Air)	1685		11. 3.88	Magical Adventures Ltd *(National Express tiles)*		
						West Bloomfield, Michigan, USA	31. 1.96A
G-BUSV	Colt 105A Balloon (Hot Air)	2324		12. 1.93	M N J Kirby	Northwich	10. 9.09E
G-BUSW	Rockwell Commander 114	14079	N4749W	18. 1.93	J M J Palmer	Biggin Hill	17.11.09E
G-BUTB	CFM Streak Shadow	K 190		20. 1.93	H O Maclean and S MacKechnie		
	(Built F A H Ashmead - pr.no.PFA 206-12243) (Hirth 2706 R05)					North Connel, Oban	21. 7.09P
G-BUTD	Van's RV-6	PFA 181-12152		21. 1.93	N W Beadle	Airfield Farm, Hardwick	29. 1.10P
	(Built N Reddish) (Lycoming O-320)						
G-BUTE	Anderson EA-1 Kingfisher Amphibian		G-BRCK	15. 8.91	T Crawford	Cumbernauld	15.10.99P
	(Built T Crawford)	PFA 132-10798	(Lycoming O-235)				
G-BUTF	Aeronca 11AC Chief	11AC-1578	N3231E	21. 1.93	D Horne tr Fox Flying Group		
			NC3231E			Bury Farm, High Easter	28. 5.09P
G-BUTG	Zenair CH.601HD Zodiac	PFA 162-12225		22. 1.93	I J McNally	Bourn	7. 5.09P
	(Built J M Scott) (Continental C90-14F)						
G-BUTH	CEA Jodel DR.220 2+2	6	F-BNVK	10. 2.93	P J Gristwood tr Phoenix Flying Group	Dunkeswell	28. 6.09E
G-BUTJ	Cameron O-77 Balloon (Hot Air)	2991		25. 1.93	D Hoddinott	Nottingham	13. 2.09E
G-BUTK	Murphy Rebel	PFA 232-12091		25. 1.93	G S Claybourn	Walton Wood	27. 6.08P
	(Built D Webb) (Rotax 912-UL)						
G-BUTM	Rans S-6-116 Coyote II	0792.323		22. 1.93	A B King	Ellough, Beccles	2. 7.07P
	(Built M Rudd - pr.no.PFA 204A-12414) (Rotax 912-UL) *(Tailwheel u/c)*						
	(Made a heavy landing at the Grove Farm strip, near Gamston 7. 5.08, veered to the left and went into standing crops, damaging the fuselage)						
G-BUTT	Reims Cessna FA150K Aerobat	FA1500029	G-AXSJ	18. 8.86	Global Engineering and Maintenance Ltd		
					(stored 12.08)	Bournemouth	24.10.99T
G-BUTX	Bücker Bü.133C Jungmeister	1010?	Spanish AF E1-4 3. 2.93		J G Brander tr Bücker Flying Group		
	(Warner Super Scarab) *(Possibly CASA 1.133L?)* Spanish AF ES.1-4, 35-4					White Waltham	9. 2.07P
G-BUTY	Brügger MB.2 Colibri	PFA 043-12387		30.11.92	R M Lawday	(Milford, Derby)	
	(Built R M Lawday)						
G-BUTZ	Piper PA-28-180 Cherokee C	28-3107	G-DARL	23. 4.93	M H Canning	Leicester	9. 8.09E
			4R-ARL, 4R-ONE, SE-EYD				
G-BUUA	Slingsby T 67M Firefly II	2111		17. 3.93	Babcock Support Services Ltd t/a Babcock Defence Services		
						AAC Middle Wallop	12. 7.09E
G-BUUB	Slingsby T 67M Firefly II	2112		17. 3.93	Babcock Support Services Ltd t/a Babcock Defence Services		
						AAC Middle Wallop	25. 7.09E
G-BUUC	Slingsby T 67M Firefly II	2113		17. 3.93	Babcock Support Services Ltd t/a Babcock Defence Services		
						AAC Middle Wallop	10.11.09E
G-BUUE	Slingsby T 67M Firefly II	2115		17. 3.93	J R Bratty	Nottingham City-Tollerton	27.10.09E
G-BUUF	Slingsby T 67M Firefly II	2116		17. 3.93	C C Rollings and F J Hodson t/a Tiger Airways		
						Gloucestershire	9.12.09E
G-BUUI	Slingsby T 67M Firefly II	2119		17. 3.93	Bustard Flying Club Ltd	Boscombe Down	14. 2.09E
G-BUUJ	Slingsby T 67M Firefly II	2120		17. 3.93	A C Lees	Bagby	13. 8.09E
G-BUUK	Slingsby T 67M Firefly II	2121		17. 3.93	Babcock Support Services Ltd t/a Babcock Defence Services		
						AAC Middle Wallop	17. 3.09E
G-BUUM	Piper PA-28RT-201 Arrow IV	28R-7918090	N2145X	14. 1.93	CCHM Aviation Ltd	Enniskillen	3. 4.09E
G-BUUO	Cameron N-90 Balloon (Hot Air)	2994		9. 2.93	M P Rich tr Gone Ballooning Group	Bristol	19. 6.03A
G-BUUP	British Aerospace ATP	2008	G-MANU	18. 2.93	Atlantic Airlines Ltd	Coventry	26. 5.09T
			G-BUUP, CS-TGA, G-11-8, (N378AE)				
G-BUUR	British Aerospace ATP	2024	EC-GUX	18. 2.93	Atlantic Airlines	Coventry	28. 9.09E
			G-OEDJ, G-BUUR, CS-TGC, G-BUUR, CS-TGC, G-11-024				
G-BUUT	Interavia 70TA Balloon (Hot Air)	04509-92		21. 1.93	Aero Vintage Ltd	(Northiam, Rye)	
G-BUUX	Piper PA-28-180 Cherokee D	28-5128	OY-BCW	17. 2.93	M A Judge tr Aero Group 78	Netherthorpe	7. 1.09E
G-BUVA	Piper PA-22-135 Tri-Pacer (modified)	22-1301	N8626C	12. 2.93	K W Thomas tr Oaksey VA Group	Oaksey Park	28. 9.11
G-BUVE	Colt 77B Balloon (Hot Air)	2376		8. 3.93	G D Philpot *"Trident"*	Hemel Hempstead	27. 7.09E
G-BUVL	Fisher Super Koala	PFA 228-11399		3. 3.93	A D Malcolm *"Spirit of Throwley"*		
	(Built A D Malcolm) (Jabiru 2200A)					Park Farm, Throwley, Faversham	30. 9.04P
G-BUVM	CEA Jodel DR.250/160 Capitaine	54	OO-NJR	11. 3.93	M Lodge tr G-BUVM Group	Crosland Moor	1.12.09P
			F-BNJR				
G-BUVN	CASA 1-131E Jungmann Series 2000	2092	Spanish AF	12. 3.93	W van Egmond *(As "BI:005" in R Neth AF c/s)*		
			EC-333, Spanish AF E3B-487			Hoogeveen, Netherlands	1. 7.09P
G-BUVO	Reims Cessna F182P Skylane II	F18200022	G-WTFA	10. 3.93	P N Stapleton tr Romeo Mike Flying Group		
			PH-VDH, D-EJCL				Plymouth	20. 6.09E
G-BUVR	Christen A-1 Husky	1162		12. 3.93	A E Poulsom	Manor Farm, Tongham	3. 7.09E
G-BUVS	Colt 77A Balloon (Hot Air)	2381		12. 3.93	J Pelling	Cranleigh	27. 3.09E
G-BUVT	Colt 77A Balloon (Hot Air)	2382		12. 3.93	N A Carr	Leicester	26. 4.09E
G-BUVW	Cameron N-90 Balloon (Hot Air)	3020		19. 3.93	P Spellward	Bristol	27. 9.09E
G-BUVX	CFM Streak Shadow SA	K 214-SA		22. 3.93	T J Shaw	North Coates	7. 4.09P
	(Built G K R Linney -pr.no.PFA 206-12410) (Rotax 582)						
G-BUVZ	Thunder Ax10-180 Series 2 Balloon (Hot Air)			24. 3.93	A van Wyk	Caxton	4. 9.04T
		2380					
G-BUWE	Replica Plans SE.5a	PFA 020-11816		25. 3.93	Airpark Flight Centre Ltd *(As "C9533:M" in RFC c/s)*		
	(Built D Biggs) (Continental C90)					Coventry	9.12.09P
G-BUWF	Cameron N-105 Balloon (Hot Air)	3036		26. 3.93	R E Jones *"British Aerospace II"*	Lytham St Annes	22. 2.09E
G-BUWH	Parsons Two-Place Gyroplane	PFA G/08-1215		1. 4.93	R V Brunskill	Melrose Farm, Melbourne	22. 8.95P
	(Built R V Brunskill) (Rotax 532)						
G-BUWI	Lindstrand LBL 77A Balloon (Hot Air)	023		5. 4.93	Capital Balloon Club Ltd *"Throw Up"*	London NW1	11. 9.09E
G-BUWJ	Pitts S-1C	2002	N110R	25. 3.93	R V Barber	Audley End	8. 5.09P
	(Built J T Griffins)						
G-BUWK	Rans S-6-116N Coyote II	1292.410		7. 4.93	R Warriner	Maypole Farm, Chislet	3. 6.09P
	(Built R Warriner - pr.no.PFA 204A-12448) (Rotax 912)						
G-BUWL	Piper J-4A Cub Coupé	4-1047	N27828	8. 4.93	M L Ryan	Garston Farm, Marshfield	
			NC27828				
G-BUWR	CFM Streak Shadow	K 177-SA		26. 4.93	T Harvey	Grove Farm, Raveningham	24. 4.07P
	(Built T Harvey - pr.no.PFA 206-12068) (Rotax 582)						
G-BUWS	Denney Kitfox Model 2	PFA 172-11831		26. 4.93	J E Brewis	(Castletown, Isle of Man)	
	(Built J E Brewis)						

G-BUWT	Rand Robinson KR-2	PFA 129-10952		5. 4.93	C M Coombe	(Ruislip)	
	(Built C M Coombe)						
G-BUWU	Cameron V-77 Balloon (Hot Air)	3053		27. 4.93	T R Dews	Hill Deverill, Warminster	25. 6.08A
G-BUXC	CFM Streak Shadow	K 188		20. 4.93	J P Mimnagh	Guy Lane Farm, Waverton	22.12.09P
	(Built T Hosier - pr.no.PFA 206-12177) (Rotax 582)						
G-BUXD	Maule MXT-7-160 Super Rocket	17001C	N9231R	4. 5.93	S Baigent	East Winch	19.10.07E
	(Tri-cycle u/c)						
G-BUXI	Steen Skybolt	PFA 064-10755		16. 3.93	D Tucker	Little Rissington	16. 8.08P
	(Built M Frankland)						
G-BUXK	Pietenpol AirCamper	PFA 047-11901		12. 5.93	B M D Nelson	Finmere	31. 8.07P
	(Built G R G Smith) (Continental C90)						
G-BUXL	Taylor JT.1 Monoplane	PFA 055-11819		12. 5.93	P J Hebdon *(Noted stored 5.08)*	Shenington	12. 5.07P
	(Built M W Elliott)						
G-BUXN	Beech C23 Sundowner 180	M-1752	N9256S	13. 5.93	D G Tudor tr Private Pilots Syndicate Bournemouth		17. 1.09E
G-BUXO	Pober P-9 Pixie	PFA 105-10647		17. 5.93	J Mangiapane tr P-9 Flying Group	(Matlock)	
	(Built T Moore)				*(Nearing completion 2000)*		
G-BUXS	MBB BÖ.105DBS-4	S 913	G-PASA	19. 5.93	Bond Air Services *"Im Bru" (Operated Northern Lighthouse)*		
	(Originally c/n S 41: rebuilt 1993)		G-BGWP, F-ODMZ, G-BGWP, HB-XFD, N153BB, D-HDAS				Aberdeen	25. 5.09E
G-BUXV	Piper PA-22-160 Tri-Pacer	22-6685	N9769D	20. 5.93	J Mathews tr Romeo Delta Juliet Group		
	(Super Pacer Tail-wheel conversion)			*(Noted 5.06 damaged and stored)*	Weston, Leixlip, County Kildare		18.10.03
G-BUXW	Thunder Ax8-90 Series 2 Balloon (Hot Air) 2405			25. 5.93	A S Davidson tr Nottingham Hot Air Balloon Club		
					"Silver Lady"	Woodville, Swadlincote	26.11.09E
G-BUXX	Piper PA-17 Vagabond	17-28	N4611H	31. 3.93	R H Hunt	Old Sarum	12. 7.08P
	(Continental A75)		NC4611H				
G-BUXY	Piper PA-25-235 Pawnee	25-2705	C-GZCR	18. 3.93	Bath, Wilts and North Dorset Gliding Club Ltd		
			N6959Z			Kingston Deverill	17.12.09E
G-BUYB	Aero Designs Pulsar	PFA 202-12193		28. 5.93	A P Fenn	Shobdon	14. 5.07P
	(Built A P Fenn) (Tail-wheel u/c)						
G-BUYC	Cameron Concept 80 Balloon (Hot Air)	3095		28. 5.93	R P Cross *(Windrush titles)*	Luton	4.12.09E
G-BUYD	Thunder Ax8-90 Balloon (Hot Air)	2422		28. 5.93	S and S McGuigan	Draperstown, Magherafelt	9. 7.09E
G-BUYF	American Aircraft Falcon XP	600179	N512AA	13. 5.93	M J Hadland	Tarn Farm, Cockerham	21. 5.04P
	(Built R W Harris) (Rotax 503)						
G-BUYJ	Lindstrand LBL 105A Balloon (Hot Air)	039		1. 6.93	G Fordyce	Olney	28. 2.09E
G-BUYK	Denney Kitfox Model 4	PFA 172A-12214		1. 6.93	M S Shelton	Hill Farm, Nayland	25. 4.08P
	(Built R D L Mayes) (Rotax 912-UL)						
G-BUYL	Rotary Air Force RAF 2000	H2-92-361	C-FPFN	2. 6.93	Newtonair Gyroplanes Ltd		
	(Built D A Lafleur: rebuilt by Newtonair using parts from G-TXSE)					Watchford Farm, Yarcombe	6. 9.06P
G-BUYO	Colt 77A Balloon (Hot Air)	2398		4. 6.93	S F Burden	Noordwijk, Netherlands	11. 8.09E
G-BUYS	Robin DR.400-180 Régent	2197		21. 6.93	P R Currer tr G-BUYS Flying Group Nuthampstead		7. 4.09E
G-BUYU	Bowers Fly Baby 1A	PFA 016-12222		7. 6.93	R Metcalfe	Rushett Farm, Chessington	15. 4.09P
	(Built J A Nugent) (Continental A65)			*(As "C L 1.1803/18" in German Army Air Service c/s to represent Junkers CL1)*			
G-BUYY	Piper PA-28-180 Cherokee B	28-1028	C-FXDP	18. 3.93	A J Hedges and C E Yates tr G-BUYY Group		
			CF-XDP, N7214W			Bristol	20.11.09E
G-BUZA	Denney Kitfox Model 3	1178		10. 6.93	A O'Brien	Abbeyshrule, County Longford	4. 4.09P
	(Built R Hill - pr.no.PFA 172-12547)						
G-BUZB	Aero Designs Pulsar XP	PFA 202-12312		14. 6.93	S M Lancashire	(Timperley, Altrincham)	15. 9.09P
	(Built M J Whatley) (Tail-wheel u/c)						
G-BUZC	Everett Gyroplane Series 3A	034		14. 7.93	M P Lhermette	(Sproughton, Ipswich)	
					(Damaged 7.94: stored 12.95)		
G-BUZD	Aérospatiale AS.332L Super Puma	2069	C-GSLJ	11. 2.93	CHC Scotia Ltd	Aberdeen	13. 1.10E
			N189EH, C-GSLJ, HC-BNB, C-GSLJ, PT-HRN, C-GSLJ				
G-BUZE	Avid Speed Wing	PFA 189-12047		16. 6.93	P B Harrison	(Wirral)	7. 9.06P
	(Built N L E Nupee)						
G-BUZG	Zenair CH.601HD Zodiac	PFA 162-12457		17. 6.93	P G Morris	Insch	10. 6.08P
	(Built N C White) (Continental O-200-A)						
G-BUZH	Star-Lite SL-1	119	N4HC	17. 6.93	C A McDowall	(Blackfield, Southampton)	8. 9.00P
	(Built H M Cottle) (Rotax 447)			*(Damaged Farley Farm, Romsey 10. 8.00: in container 9.00 - fuselage only)*			
G-BUZJ	Lindstrand LBL 105A Balloon (Hot Air)	038		17. 6.93	A M Holly	Breadstone, Berkeley	30. 7.09E
G-BUZK	Cameron V-77 Balloon (Hot Air)	2962		17. 6.93	J T Wilkinson	Blackland, Calne	15. 6.09E
G-BUZL	VPM M16 Tandem Trainer	VPM16UK105		18. 6.93	P Robinson	Kirkbride	22 4.08P
G-BUZM	Avid Speed Wing Mk.3	PFA 189-12179		30. 4.93	R McLuckie and O G Jones	RAF Mona	14. 5.07P
	(Built R McLuckie and O G Jones) (Jabiru 2200) *(Officially regd with Rotax 582)*						
G-BUZN	Cessna 172H	17256056	N2856L	24. 6.93	H D Jones	Barton	1. 2.10P
G-BUZO	Pietenpol AirCamper	PFA 047-12408		28. 6.93	D A Jones	(Maidenhead)	
	(Built D A Jones) (Salmson AD9)						
G-BUZR	Lindstrand LBL 77A Balloon (Hot Air)	044		29. 6.93	Lindstrand Technologies Ltd	Oswestry	17.12.08E
G-BUZS	Colt Flying Pig SS Balloon (Hot Air)	2415		2. 7.93	Banco Bilbao Vizcaya	Bilbao, Spain	20. 5.96A
G-BUZT	Kolb Twinstar Mk.IIIA	K0009-0193		1. 7.93	J A G Robb	Caim, County Wexford	3. 7.07P
	(Built A C Goadby - pr.no.PFA 205-12367)						
	(Force landed at Killoughrum, nr Enniscorthy, Co Wexford 4. 6.07 due to engine failure and severely damaged)						
G-BUZV	Ken Brock KB-2	PFA G/06-1152		1. 7.93	K Hughes	(Amlwch, Gwynedd)	
	(Built K Hughes)						
G-BUZZ	Agusta-Bell 206B-2 JetRanger II	8178	F-GAMS	13. 4.78	Rivermead Aviation Ltd *(Operated Rise Helicopters)*		
			HB-XGI, OE-DXF			Gloucestershire	2. 3.09E

G-BVAA - G-BVZZ

G-BVAB	Zenair CH.601HDS Zodiac	PFA 162-12475		26. 5.93	B N Rides	Garston Farm, Marshfield	27. 6.09P
	(Built A R Bender)						
G-BVAC	Zenair CH.601HD Zodiac	PFA 162-12504		1. 6.93	J A Tyndall and S Wisedale	Oaksey Park	8. 9.09P
	(Built A G Cozens)						
G-BVAF	Piper J-3C-65 Cub	4645	OO-UBU	14. 6.93	N M Hitchman	Garston Farm, Marshfield	19. 6.09P
	(Continental C85)		N28199, NC28199				

G-BVAH	Denney Kitfox Model 3	PFA 172-12031		22.10.91	S Allinson	Shobdon	7. 8.08P
	(Built V A Hutchinson) (Rotax 912)						
G-BVAI	PZL-110 Koliber 150	03900040	OY-CYJ	7. 7.93	C P Ware and A R Williams		
						Garston Farm, Marshfield	10. 1.10E
G-BVAM	Evans VP-1	PFA 062-12132		7. 7.93	R F Selby	(East Preston, Littlehampton)	
	(Built R F Selby)						
G-BVAO	Colt 25A Balloon (Hot Air)	2024		9. 7.93	M E Dworski	Vermenton, France	5. 5.06A
G-BVAW	Staaken Z-1 Flitzer	PFA 223-12058		12. 7.93	L R Williams t/a Flitzer Sportflugverein *(As "D692")*		
	(Built L R Williams and D J Evans) (Volkswagen 1834)					Rhigos	19. 6.09P
G-BVAX	Colt 77A Balloon (Hot Air)	1213		30. 3.88	P H Porter *"Vax"*	Tenbury Wells	5. 8.95A
G-BVAY	Rutan VariEze	RS.8673/345	N5MS	3. 9.93	D A Young	(Sunderland)	11.11.02P
	(Built R N Saunders)						
G-BVAZ	Montgomerie-Bensen B 8MR	PFA G/01-1190		12. 7.93	N Steele	Newtownards	22. 7.04P
	(Built R Patrick) (Rotax 582)				*(Suffered engine failure on take off Newtownards 30. 8.03, rolled over to right damaging rotors)*		
G-BVBR	Avid Speed Wing	PFA 189-12085		3. 8.93	P D Thomas	(Whitchurch)	25.11.08P
	(Built H R Rowley)						
G-BVBS	Cameron N-77 Balloon (Hot Air)	3128		4. 8.93	S M Gabb t/a Heart of England Balloons		
						Haselor, Alcester	20. 2.09E
G-BVBU	Cameron V-77 Balloon (Hot Air)	3076	(OO-BYS)	5. 8.93	J Manclark *(Operated Alba Ballooning)* Haddington		15. 3.04A
G-BVBV	Avid Speed Wing	PFA 189-12187		4. 8.93	L W M Summers	Popham	3. 7.09E
	(Built D A Jarvis)						
G-BVCA	Cameron N-105 Balloon (Hot Air)	3129		11. 8.93	Unipart Group Ltd tr Unipart Balloon Club	Cowley	25. 6.00A
G-BVCC	Monnett Sonerai IILT	PFA 015-10547		12. 8.93	J Eggleston	(Ainderby Steeple, Northallerton)	
	(Built J Eggleston)						
G-BVCG	Van's RV-6	PFA 181-11783		17. 8.93	P C J Stone and K Dennison	Warton	26. 1.10P
	(Built G J Newby and E M Farquharson) (Lycoming O-320)						
G-BVCL	Rans S-6-116 Coyote II	0493.486		25. 8.93	J Powell	Roughay Farm, Bishops Waltham	8. 8.08P
	(Built W E Willetts - pr.no.PFA 204A-12551) (Rotax 912-UL) *(Tri-cycle u/c)*						
G-BVCM	Cessna 525 CitationJet	525-0022	N1329N	2. 5.94	Kenmore Aviation Ltd and BLP 2003-19 Ltd tr The Aircraft Trust		
					(stored Perth for winter 08/09)	Edinburgh	22. 5.09E
G-BVCN	Colt 56A Balloon (Hot Air)	2445		25. 8.93	J A W Dyer	Farnborough	3. 8.09E
G-BVCO	Clutton FRED Series II	PFA 029-10947		25. 8.93	I W Bremner	(Dornoch, Sutherland)	21. 6.06P
	(Built I W Bremner)						
G-BVCP	Piper CP.1 Metisse	PFA 253-12512		24. 6.93	B M Diggins	RAF Mona	15. 7.09P
	(Built C W R Piper) (Revmaster 2200)						
G-BVCS	Aeronca 7AC Champion	7AC-1346	N69BD	1. 9.93	A C Lines	Leicester	4. 6.08P
	(Continental A65)		N82702, NC82702				
G-BVCT	Denney Kitfox Model 4-1200	1761		27. 8.93	A F Reid	Comber, County Down	7. 9.07P
	(Built A F Reid - pr.no.PFA 172A-12456) (Rotax 912-UL)						
G-BVCX	Sikorsky S-76A	760183	OY-HIW	21. 9.93	CHC Scotia Ltd	North Denes	21. 4.08E
			G-BVCX, N951L, N5450M				
G-BVCY	Cameron H-24 Balloon (Hot Air)	3136		3. 9.93	A C K Rawson and J J Rudoni t/a Wickers World Hot Air		
					Balloon Company *(Bryant Homes titles)*	Stafford	14. 1.09E
G-BVDB	Thunder Ax7-77 Balloon (Hot Air)	2364	G-ORDY	6. 9.93	S J Hollingsworth and M K Bellamy		
						Ironville, Notts	6. 9.09E
G-BVDC	Van's RV-3	PFA 099-12218		12. 7.93	R J Hodder	Eastfield Farm, Manby	1. 1.09P
	(Buit D Calibritto) (Lycoming O-235)						
G-BVDH	Piper PA-28RT-201 Arrow IV	28R-7918030	N2176L	13. 9.93	Dazzz Aviation Ltd	Elstree	28. 5.09E
G-BVDI	Van's RV-4	2058	N55GJ	13. 9.93	J Glen-Davis Gorman	Headcorn	10. 4.09P
	(Built G P Larson) (Lycoming O-320)						
G-BVDJ	Campbell Cricket replica	PFA G/03-1189		13. 9.93	S Jennings	St Merryn	4. 3.09P
	(Built C D Julian and S Jennings) (Rotax 582)						
G-BVDM	Cameron Concept 60 Balloon (Hot Air)	3141		15. 9.93	M P Young	Dover	24. 4.09E
G-BVDO	Lindstrand LBL 105A Balloon (Hot Air)	055		16. 9.93	A E Still	Edgcott, Aylesbury	6. 9.09E
G-BVDP	Sequoia F 8L Falco	PFA 100-10879		17. 9.93	N M Turner	Wellcross Farm, Slinfold	11. 6.09P
	(Built T G Painter)						
G-BVDR	Cameron O-77 Balloon (Hot Air)	2452		21. 9.93	N J Logue	Pembroke Dock	12. 5.09E
G-BVDS	Lindstrand LBL 69A Balloon (Hot Air)	102		23. 9.93	Lindstrand Hot Air Balloons Ltd	Oswestry	26. 6.01A
G-BVDT	CFM Streak Shadow SA-I	K 223		23. 9.93	H J Bennet	North Connel, Oban	27. 1.10P
	(Built H J Bennet - pr.no.PFA 206-12462) (Rotax 582)						
G-BVDW	Thunder Ax8-90 Balloon (Hot Air)	2507		30. 9.93	S C Vora *"Cosmic"*	Oadby	14. 8.07
G-BVDX	Cameron V-90 Balloon (Hot Air)	3159	OO-BMY	30. 9.93	R K Scott *"Merlin"*	North Perrott, Crewkerne	25. 9.05A
			G-BVDX				
G-BVDY	Cameron Concept 60 Balloon (Hot Air)	3167		30. 9.93	P Baker	Abbeyview, Trim, County Meath	1.12.09E
G-BVDZ	Taylorcraft BC-12D	9043	N96743	21. 1.94	P N W England	(Hove)	
			NC96743				
G-BVEA	Nostalgair N 3 Pup	01-GB	G-MWEA	7. 6.93	D Pike	(Waddington)	30. 8.09P
	(Built B D Godden - pr.no.PFA 212-11837) and officially regd as *"Mosler Motors N-3 Pup")* (Mosler MM-CB35)						
G-BVEH	Wassmer Jodel D 112		F-BMOH	29.10.93	M L Copland	Breighton	23 .8.09P
G-BVEL	Evans VP-1 Series 2	PFA 062-11983		6.10.93	M J and S J Quinn	(Scholes, Holmfirth)	
	(Built M J Quinn)						
G-BVEN	Cameron Concept 80 Balloon (Hot Air)	3164		6.10.93	R M Powell	Broughton, Stockbridge	27. 2.09E
G-BVEP	Luscombe 8A Silvaire	1468	N28707	8.10.93	B H Austen	Oaksey Park	21.10.09S
	(Continental A-65)		NC28707				
G-BVER	de Havilland DHC-2 Beaver 1	1648	G-BTDM	13. 8.91	Seaflite Ltd *(As "XV268" in AAC c/s)* Cumbernauld		23. 4.95T
			XV268		*(Fuselage stored 1.05)*		
G-BVES	Cessna 340A II	340A0077	N1378G	8. 9.93	K P Gibbin and I M Worthington		
						Nottingham-East Midlands	24. 6.09E
G-BVEV	Piper PA-34-200 Seneca	34-7250316	N1428T	8.10.93	R W Harris, D Quick, A Jahanfar and Atromin Ltd		
			HB-LLN, D-GHSG, N1428T		*(Operated Southend Flying Club)*	Southend	9. 8.09E
G-BVEW	Lindstrand LBL 150A Balloon (Hot Air)	057		14.10.93	A van Wyk	Cambridge	15. 8.02T
G-BVEY	Denney Kitfox Model 4-1200	PFA 172A-12527		14.10.93	J H H Turner	(Houston)	7. 7.09P
	(Built J S Penny)						

G-BVEZ	Hunting Percival P 84 Jet Provost T 3A	XM479	13.10.93	N T McCarthy tr Newcastle Jet Provost Group		
	PAC/W/9287			(As "XM479:54" in RAF c/s)	Newcastle	5. 9.09P
G-BVFA	Rans S-10 Sakota	1090.116	7. 9.93	D S Wilkinson (Noted 9.08)	Kemble	27. 3.03P
	(Built D Allam and D Parkinson - pr.no.PFA 194-12298) (Rotax 582)					
G-BVFB	Cameron N-31 Balloon (Hot Air)	3175	20.10.93	P Lawman	Northampton	13.10.07A
G-BVFF	Cameron V-77 Balloon (Hot Air)	3161	26.10.93	R J Kerr and G P Allen	Abingdon	16.10.09E
G-BVFM	Rans S-6-116 Coyote II	0793.522	2.11.93	F D C de Beer	Wishanger Farm, Frensham	14. 7.09P
	(Built P G Walton - pr.no.PFA 204A-12579) (Rotax 912-UL) (Tri-cycle u/c)					
G-BVFO	Avid Speed Wing	PFA 189-12053	9. 9.93	G E MacCuish tr G-BVFO Flying Group		
	(Built P Chisman)				North Connel, Oban	20. 4.07P
G-BVFP	Cameron V-90 Balloon (Hot Air)	3179	2.11.93	D E and J M Hartland	Hognaston, Ashbourne	9. 9.09E
G-BVFR	CFM Streak Shadow	K 237-SA	3.11.93	S C Reeve	Headon Farm, Retford	15. 5.09P
	(Built M G B Stebbing - pr.no.PFA 206-12567) (Rotax 582)					
G-BVFS	Slingsby T.31M Cadet III	PFA 042-11387	ex RAF?	3.11.93	S R Williams (Stored dismantled 1.09)	Southend	
	(Re-built M Gagffney and R Jones to Motor Tutor standard)					
G-BVFT	Maule M-5-235C Lunar Rocket	7183C	N6180M	5.11.93	S R Clark tr Newnham Joint Flying Syndicate		
					Newnham, Baldock	6. 6.09E
G-BVFU	Cameron Sphere 105 SS Balloon (Hot Air)		18.11.93	Stichting Phoenix (Greenpeace titles)		
		3137		Amsterdam, Netherlands	12. 8.09E
G-BVFZ	Maule M-5-180C Lunar Rocket	8082C	N5664D	21. 2.94	R C Robinson	(Bury St Edmunds)	20. 4.09E
G-BVGA	Bell 206B-3 JetRanger III	2922	N54AJ	11.11.93	J L Leonard t/a Findon Air Services	(Brentwood)	31. 1.10E
			VH-SBC				
G-BVGB	Thunder Ax8-105 Series 2 Balloon (Hot Air)		11.11.93	E K Read "Scouts"	Timperley, Altrincham	15. 1.09E
		2408				
G-BVGE	Westland WS-55 Whirlwind HAR.10	WA/100	8732M	18.11.93	J F Kelly (As "XJ729" in RAF Rescue c/s)		
			XJ729		Cloghan, Mullingar, County Westmeath	17 6.08P
G-BVGF	Europa Aviation Europa	034	18.11.93	A Graham and G G Beal	Morgansfield, Fishburn	23.10.08P
	(Built A Graham - pr.no.PFA 247-12565) (Tri-gear u/c)					
G-BVGG	Lindstrand LBL 69A Balloon (Hot Air)	011	30.11.93	L P Hooper	St George, Bristol	9. 7.09E
G-BVGH	Hawker Hunter T 7	HABL 004328	XL573	26.11.93	Global Aviation Services Ltd (As "XL573" in RAF c/s)		
	(Centre fuselage no.is HABL 003360)				Exeter	19.11.08P
G-BVGI	Pereira Osprey 2	PFA 070-10536	29.11.93	A A Knight	North Connel, Oban	25.11.03P
	(Built B Weare) (Lycoming O-320)					
G-BVGJ	Cameron Concept 80 Balloon (Hot Air)	3099	7.12.93	J M J and V F Roberts "Pizza Express"	Epping	3. 4.09E
G-BVGK	Lindstrand LBL Newspaper SS Balloon (Hot Air)	SE-ZHC	3.12.93	H Holmqvist	Lund, Sweden	9.10.09E
		059	G-BVGK				
G-BVGO	Denney Kitfox Model 4-1200 PFA 172A-12362		15.11.93	G Edwards	Walkeridge Farm, Overton	30. 7.09P
	(Built R K Dunford)					
G-BVGP	Bücker Bü.133C Jungmeister	42	F-AZMN	3.12.93	M V Rijkse (As "U-95" Swiss AF c/s)		
	(Built Dornier-Werke AG)	G-BVGP F-AZFQ, N15696, HB-MIE, D-EIII, HB-MIE, Swiss AF U-95			Wycombe Air Park	4.11.09P
G-BVGT	Crofton Auster V J/1A Special	PFA 000-220	19.11.93	K D and C S Rhodes	Henstridge	20. 6.09P
	(Built L A Groves from unknown J/1 Autocrat frame used as engine test rig) (Blackburn Cirrus 2)					
G-BVGW	Luscombe 8A Silvaire	4823	N2096K	18.11.93	J Smith	Yeatsall Farm, Abbots Bromley	7. 9.09P
	(Continental A65)		NC2096K				
G-BVGY	Luscombe 8E Silvaire Deluxe	4754	N2027K	18.11.93	M C Burlock	Lower Wasing Farm, Brimpton	18. 6.09P
	(Continental C85)		NC2027K				
G-BVGZ	Fokker Dr.1 Triplane replica	VHB-10	20.12.93	R A Fleming	Breighton	12. 8.09P
	(Built V H Bellamy - pr.no.PFA 238-12654) (Lycoming AIO-360)		(As "450/17" in German Army Air Service c/s)			
G-BVHC	Grob G115D-2 Heron	82005	D-EARG	14.12.93	Tayside Aviation Ltd	Dundee	6. 6.09E
G-BVHD	Grob G115D-2 Heron	82006	D-EARJ	14.12.93	Tayside Aviation Ltd	Glenrothes	8. 6.09E
G-BVHE	Grob G115D-2 Heron	82008	D-EASR	14.12.93	Tayside Aviation Ltd	Glenrothes	25. 1.10E
			G-BVHE, D-EARQ				
G-BVHF	Grob G115D-2 Heron	82011	D-EARV	14.12.93	Tayside Aviation Ltd	Dundee	3. 3.09E
G-BVHG	Grob G115D-2 Heron	82012	D-EARX	14.12.93	Tayside Aviation Ltd	Dundee	25. 5.09E
G-BVHI	Rans S-10 Sakota	0990.119	20.12.93	J D Amos	Redlands, Swindon	24. 6.09P
	(Built P D Rowley - pr.no.PFA 194-12608) (Rotax 582)					
G-BVHK	Cameron V-77 Balloon (Hot Air)	3209	23.12.93	A R Rich "Intel Inside"	Hyde	2. 5.09E
G-BVHL	Nicollier HN.700 Ménestrel II PFA 217-12614		24.12.93	M W Bodger	Yeatsall Farm, Abbots Bromley	
	(Built I H R Walker and C Herbert)					
G-BVHM	Piper PA-38-112 Tomahawk	38-79A0313	G-DCAN	14.11.91	A J Gomes (Operated Sky Leisure Aviation)		
			N2490D			Shoreham	17.10.09E
G-BVHO	Cameron V-90 Balloon (Hot Air)	3158	29.12.93	N W B Bews	Tenbury Wells	18. 7.03
G-BVHR	Cameron V-90 Balloon (Hot Air)	3174	5. 1.94	G P Walton	Bagshot	9. 8.09E
G-BVHS	Murphy Rebel	050	5. 1.94	S T Raby	Grange Farm, Woodwalton	16. 8.08P
	(Built J Brown, B Godden and M Hanley - pr.no.PFA 232-12180)					
G-BVHT	Avid Speed Wing Mk.4	PFA 189-12226	28.10.93	H B S Stephens		
	(Built R S Holt)				Lausanne-La Blecherette, Switzerland	4. 6.07P
G-BVHV	Cameron N-105 Balloon (Hot Air)	3215	6. 1.94	Wye Valley Aviation Ltd "Rover"	Ross-on-Wye	25. 9.07T
G-BVIA	Rand Robinson KR-2	PFA 129-11004	14. 1.94	K Atkinson	(Ulverston)	2. 3.08P
	(Built K Atkinson)					
G-BVIE	Piper PA-18 Super Cub 95 (L-18C-PI) 18-1549	G-CLIK	26. 1.94	J C Best tr C'est La Vie Group "C'est La Vie"		
	(Continental O-200-A) (Frame No.18-1521)	(G-BLMB), D-EDRB, French Army 18-1549, 51-15549			Andrewsfield	13. 5.09P
G-BVIF	Montgomerie-Bensen B 8MR PFA G/01A-1228		26. 1.94	R M and D Mann (Last noted 4.00)	(Brodick, Arran)	21. 8.95P
	(Built R M Mann) (Rotax 582)					
G-BVIK	Maule MXT-7-180 Super Rocket	14056C	31. 1.94	D S Simpson tr Graveley Flying Group		
					Graveley Hall Farm, Graveley	25.10.09E
G-BVIL	Maule MXT-7-180 Super Rocket	14059C	31. 1.94	K and S C Knight	Shobdon	5. 2.09E
G-BVIN	Rans S-6-ESA Coyote II	1292.406	25.10.93	J R and J M Bartlett	(Henley-on-Thames)	27. 9.06P
	(Built K J Vincent - pr.no.PFA 204-12533) (Tail-wheel u/c)					
G-BVIR	Lindstrand LBL 69A Balloon (Hot Air)	079	2. 2.94	Aerial Promotions Ltd (Vauxhall titles)	Cannock	25. 5.01A
G-BVIS	Brügger MB.2 Colibri	PFA 043-10666	2. 2.94	B H Shaw	Spanhoe	24. 1.10P
	(Built B H Shaw) (Volkswagen 1600)					
G-BVIT	Campbell Cricket replica	PFA G/03-1229	4. 2.94	D R Owen (Noted 7.08)	Kirkbride	24. 7.97P
	(Built A N Nesbit) (Rotax 582)					

G-BVIV	Avid Speed Wing	PFA 189-12034		25.10.93	S Styles	(Bromsgrove)	17. 5.08P
	(Built V and J Hobday - rebuilt R C Holmes)						
G-BVIW	Piper PA-18-150 Super Cub	18-8277	SE-EPD	4. 2.94	I H Logan	Popham	29. 6.11S
G-BVIZ	Europa Aviation Europa	052		24. 1.94	T J Punter and P G Jeffers tr The Europa Group		
	(Built T J Punter and P G Jeffers - pr.no.PFA 247-12601) (Tri-gear u/c)					Wycombe Air Park	1. 5.09P
G-BVJF	Montgomerie-Bensen B 8MR	PFA G/01-1082		18. 2.94	D M F Harvey	(Yate, Bristol)	
	(Built D M F Harvey)						
G-BVJG	Cyclone AX3K/582	C 3123187	G-69-14	15. 2.94	T D Reid	Newtownards	23. 4.07P
	(Built T D Reid - pr.no.PFA 245-12663)		(G-MYOP)				
G-BVJK	Glaser-Dirks DG-800A	8-24-A21		30. 3.94	J S Forster	Ringmer	2. 4.09E
G-BVJN	Europa Aviation Europa	066		2. 3.94	P Gibson tr JN Europa Group	Cumbernauld	30. 6.09P
	(Built N Adam - pr.no.PFA 247-12666) (Tri-gear u/c)						
G-BVJT	Reims Cessna F406 Caravan II	F406-0073		2. 2.94	M Evans and A Jay t/a Nor Leasing Farnborough		29. 3.09E
G-BVJU	Evans VP-1	PFA 062-10691		10. 3.94	B A Schlussler	(Hanthorpe, Bourne)	
	(Built R Waring and B A Schlussler)						
G-BVJX	Marquart MA.5 Charger	PFA 068-11239		12. 1.94	A E Cox	Morgansfield, Fishburn	11. 6.09E
	(Built M L Martin) (Lycoming O-360)						
G-BVJZ	Piper PA-28-161 Cherokee Warrior II		N2088M	22. 3.94	J Brown *(Operated Sheffield City Flying School)*		
		28-7816248				Sandtoft	29.10.09E
G-BVKB	Boeing 737-59D	27268	SE-DNM	24. 3.94	British Midland Airways Ltd *(Operated bmiBaby)*		
					"foxy baby"	Nottingham-East Midlands	11. 4.09E
G-BVKD	Boeing 737-59D	26421	SE-DNK	25.11.94	British Midland Airways Ltd *(Operated bmiBaby)*		
					"ice ice baby"	Nottingham-East Midlands	15.12.09E
G-BVKF	Europa Aviation Europa	050		11. 3.94	T R Sinclair	Lamb Holm Farm, Orkney	18. 5.09P
	(Built T R Sinclair - pr.no.PFA 247-12638) (Tri-gear u/c)						
G-BVKH	Thunder Ax8-90 Balloon (Hot Air)	2574		15. 3.94	L Ashill *"Pisces"*	Combe Down, Bath	4. 4.07
G-BVKK	Slingsby T 61F Venture T 2	1984	ZA665	22. 2.94	Buckminster Gliding Club Ltd	Saltby	30. 5.09E
G-BVKL	Cameron A-180 Balloon (Hot Air)	3255		17. 3.94	Dragon Balloon Company Ltd		
						Castleton, Hope Valley	23. 6.09E
G-BVKM	Rutan VariEze	1933	N7137G	5. 4.94	J P G Lindquist	Neuchatel, Switzerland	25.10.06P
	(Built K H Duncan) (Continental O-200-A)		N14KM				
G-BVKU	Slingsby T 61F Venture T 2	1877	XZ557	22. 3.94	N R Bowers tr G-BVKU Syndicate		
						Kingston Deverill	18.12.09E
G-BVKZ	Thunder Ax9-120 Balloon (Hot Air)	2547		23. 3.94	D J Head	Newbury	25. 7.00T
G-BVLA	Neico Lancair 320	PFA 191-11751		29. 3.94	T K Pullen tr Eaglescott Lancair Group		
	(Built A R Welstead and T K Pullen)					Eaglescott	
G-BVLD	Campbell Cricket	PFA G/01A-1163		29. 3.94	C Berry	Bruntingthorpe	15.10.08P
	(Built C Berry) (Arrow GT500)						
G-BVLE	McCandless M 4	PFA G/10-1232		29. 3.94	H Walls *(Stored 2006)*		
	(Built H Walls)					(Stonewalls , Victoria Bridge, Strabane)	
G-BVLF	CFM Starstreak Shadow SS-D	K 250-SSD		4. 3.94	R W Chatterton	Griffins Farm, Temple Bruer	18. 6.09P
	(Built B R Johnson- pr.no.PFA 206-12662)						
G-BVLG	Aérospatiale AS.355F1 Ecureuil 2	5011	N57745	31. 3.94	PLM Dollar Group Ltd	Cumbernauld	6. 4.09E
G-BVLL	Lindstrand LBL 210A Balloon (Hot Air)	101		9. 3.94	Airborne Balloon Flights Ltd		
						Paddock Wood, Tonbridge	19. 8.09E
G-BVLN	Aero Designs Pulsar XP	PFA 202-12530		6. 4.94	D A Campbell	(Cheadle, Stoke-on-Trent)	
	(Built D A Campbell)						
G-BVLP	Piper PA-38-112 Tomahawk II	38-82A0002	N91355	8. 4.94	M Housley	Derby	26. 5.09E
G-BVLR	Van's RV-4	PFA 181-12306		13. 4.94	S D Arnold and S J Moody tr RV4 Group		
	(Built M Weaver and S D Arnold) (Lycoming 0320-E2A)					(Leamington Spa and Coventry)	
G-BVLT	Bellanca 7GCBC Citabria 150S	1103-79	SE-GHV	6. 4.94	A G Craig	Easterton, Devizes)	2.12.10S
G-BVLU	Druine D 31 Turbulent	PFA 1604		18. 4.94	C D Bancroft	Litlte Down Farm,Milson	17.11.08P
	(Built C D Bancroft) (Jabiru 2200A)						
G-BVLV	Europa Aviation Europa	039		10. 3.94	J T Naylor tr Euro 39 Group	Bidford	13.10.09P
	(Built J T Naylor - pr.no.PFA 247-12585) (Monowheel u/c)						
G-BVLW	Avid Hauler Mk.4	PFA 189-12577		24. 3.94	J P Chappell (Newbiggin-on-Lune, Kirkby Stephen)		20.10.07P
	(Built D M Johnstone) (Hirth F30)						
G-BVLX	Slingsby T 61F Venture T 2	1973	ZA654	19. 4.94	T M Holloway tr RAF Gliding and Soaring Association		
					(Operated Fulmar Gliding Club)	Easterton	2. 5.09E
G-BVLZ	Lindstrand LBL 120A Balloon (Hot Air)	063		4. 3.94	Balloon Flights Club Ltd Kings Norton, Leicester		17.11.09E
G-BVMA	Beech 200 Super King Air	BB-797	G-VPLC	22. 7.93	Dragonfly Aviation Services LLP	Cardiff	26.10.09E
			N84B				
G-BVMH	Wag-Aero CUBy Sport Trainer PFA 108-12647			28. 4.94	J Mathews *(As "624:D-39" in US Army c/s)*		
	(Built D M Jagger) (Continental C90-8)					(Trim, County Meath)	13. 6.09P
G-BVMI	Piper PA-18-150 Super Cub	18-4649	D-EIAC	6. 4.94	S Sampson	Morgansfield, Fishburn	3. 4.08E
	(Frame No.18-4613)		(PH-WDP), D-EIAC, D-EKAF, N10F				
	(Officially regd with c/n 18-8482 ex OH-PIN/N4262Z but rebuilt from D-EIAC [18-4649] after crash 15. 8.95)						
G-BVMJ	Cameron Eagle 95 SS Balloon (Hot Air)	3262		28. 4.94	R D Sargeant	Wollerau, Switzerland	23. 8.05A
G-BVML	Lindstrand LBL 210A Balloon (Hot Air)	094		29. 4.94	Ballooning Adventures Ltd	Hexham	25. 3.03T
G-BVMM	Robin HR.200-100 Club	41	F-BVMM	18. 8.80	J J Burch tr Gloster Aero Group Gloucestershire		19.10.09E
G-BVMN	Ken Brock KB-2	PFA G/06-1218		29. 4.94	S A Scally	Kirkbride	7. 5.08P
	(Built S McCullagh)						
G-BVMR	Cameron V-90 Balloon (Hot Air)	3269		28. 3.94	I R Comley *"Midnight Rainbow"*		
						Churchdown, Gloucester	1. 7.09E
G-BVMU	Aerostar Yakovlev Yak-52	9411809	YR-013	11. 5.94	Ascendances SPRL *(As "09" in DOSAAF c/s)*		
						Sint-Truiden, Belgium	16. 4.09P
G-BVNG	de Havilland Moth Major	?	EC-AFK	17. 5.94	P and T.Groves *(On rebuild 4.03)*		
			EE1-81, 30-81			Lee-on-Solent	
G-BVNI	Taylor JT.2 Titch	PFA 060-11107		20. 5.94	T V Adamson *(Noted 8.06)*	Rufforth	
	(Built T V Adamson)						
G-BVNR	Cameron N-105 Balloon (Hot Air)	3288		24. 5.94	Liquigas SpA	Milan, Italy	1.12.09E
	(New envelope c/n 4994 in 2001)						
G-BVNS	Piper PA-28-181 Cherokee Archer II		N6163J	13. 4.94	Scottish Airways Flyers (Prestwick) Ltd Prestwick		27.11.09E
		28-7690358					

G-BVNU FLS Aerospace Sprint Club   004   25. 5.94 M D R Elmes   Earls Colne 30.11.09P

G-BVNY Rans S-7 Courier   0290.072   24. 5.94 D M Byers-Jones   Popham 24. 7.09P

(Built J Whiting - pr.no.PFA 218-11951) (Rotax 532)

G-BVOB Fokker F 27 Friendship 500   10366   PH-FMN   5. 7.94 ACL Aircraft Trading Ltd   Southend 6.10.06T

                                     PT-LZM, F-BPNA, PH-FMN *(In open store 2.09 less engines)*

G-BVOC Cameron V-90 Balloon (Hot Air)   3291   8. 6.94 H W R Stewart *"Western Daily Post"*

                                                                   Exton, Oakham 6. 9.09E

G-BVOH Campbell Cricket replica   PFA G/03-1220   14. 6.94 G A Kitson   RAF Mona 14. 8.08P

(Built B F Pearson) (Rotax 532)

G-BVOI Rans S-6-116 Coyote II   0893.524   14. 6.94 C R Buckle   Bucknall 23. 6.07P

(Built A P Bacon - pr.no.PFA 204A-12712) (Rotax 582) (Tail-wheel u/c)

(Caught by gust of wind on take-off at Dairy House Farm, nr Nantwich 17. 4.07. The aircraft became airborne but the left main undercarriage detached as it struck a drainage ditch. It then made a successful forced-landing in an adjoining field)

G-BVOK Aerostar Yakovlev Yak-52   9111505 RA-9111505 14. 6.94 Trans Holdings Ltd *(As "55" in DOSAAF c/s)*

                                        DOSAAF55   Shoreham 11. 9.09P

G-BVON Lindstrand LBL 105A Balloon (Hot Air) 001 N532LB   16. 6.94 D J Farrar   Tadcaster 5. 3.06

                                        G-BVON

G-BVOP Cameron N-90 Balloon (Hot Air)   3317   21. 6.94 October Gold Ballooning Ltd   Windermere 22. 2.09E

G-BVOR CFM Streak Shadow   K 238-SA   31. 3.94 J M Chandler   Field Farm, Oakley 22.11.08P

(Built J Lord -pr.no.PFA 206-12695) (Rotax 582)

G-BVOS Europa Aviation Europa   003   11. 4.94 D A Young tr Durham Europa Group

(Built D Collinson and D A Young- pr.no.PFA 247-12562) (Mid-West AE100R) (Monowheel u/c)   Shotton Colliery, Peterlee 13. 3.09P

G-BVOU Hawker Siddeley HS.748 Series 2A/270 1721 CS-TAH   21. 6.94 PTB (Emerald) Proprietary Ltd *(Stored 11.08)*

                                          G-11-6   Blackpool 30. 7.07T

G-BVOV Hawker Siddeley HS.748 Series 2A/372 1777 CS-TAO   21. 6.94 PTB (Emerald) Proprietary Ltd *(Stored 11.08)*

                                          G-11-4   Blackpool 11. 5.07T

G-BVOW Europa Aviation Europa   084   27. 6.94 H P Brooks   Wellcross Grange, Slinfold 5. 2.09P

(Built M W Cater - pr.no.PFA 247-12679) (Monowheel u/c)

G-BVOX Taylorcraft F-22   2208 N221UK   20. 5.94 R K Jordan   Leicester 30. 8.09E

G-BVOY RotorWay Executive 90   5238   17. 6.94 Southern Helicopters Ltd *(Stored 9.08)*

(Built N J Bethell) (RotorWay RI 162)   Street Farm, Takeley

G-BVOZ Colt 56A Balloon (Hot Air)   2595   21. 6.94 Balloon School (International) Ltd t/a British School of

                                        Ballooning   Colhook Common, Petworth 14. 7.09E

G-BVPA Thunder Ax8-105 Series 2 Balloon (Hot Air)   24. 6.94 J Fenton t/a Firefly Balloon Promotions   Preston 4. 5.09E

                                     2600

G-BVPD CASA 1-131E Jungmann   2086 F-AZNG   12. 7.94 D Bruton   Abbeyshrule, County Longford 13. 3.07P

                                      Spanish AF E3B-482

G-BVPK Cameron O-90 Balloon (Hot Air)   3313   1. 7.94 D V Fowler   Cranbrook 10. 6.07T

G-BVPM Evans VP-2   V2-1016   6.11.78 P Marigold *(Stored 7.95)*

(Built P Marigold - pr.no.PFA 7205) (Continental A65-8)   (Locking, Weston-super-Mare) 31. 5.94P

G-BVPN Piper J-3C-65 Cub   6917 G-TAFY   6. 7.94 K I Munro   Plymouth 11. 9.08P

                                      N31073, N38207, N38307, NC38307

(Officially regd with c/n 5298 but has Frame No.7002 which was N38207: probably used in rebuild of N31073 in early 1970s)

G-BVPP Folland Gnat T 1   FL.536 8620M   22. 4.94 Red Gnat Ltd *(As "XR993" in RAF Red Arrows c/s 6.07)*

                              XP534   North Weald 14. 1.05P

G-BVPR Robinson R22 Beta   1612 G-KNIT   17. 6.94 Helicentre Blackpool Ltd   Blackpool 3. 2.10E

G-BVPS Jodel D 11   1403   6. 7.94 P J Sharp   Rush Green 25.10.08P

(Built P J Sharp - pr.no.PFA 917) (Continental A65)

G-BVPV Lindstrand LBL 77B Balloon (Hot Air) 119   13. 7.94 A R Greensides *"Reverend Leonard"*

                                                    Burton Pidsea, Hull 8. 8.09E

G-BVPW Rans S-6-116 Coyote II   0294.587   12. 7.94 T B Woolley   (Narborough, Leicester) 17. 3.05P

(Built J G Beesley - pr.no.PFA 204-12737) (Rotax 582) (Tri-cycle u/c)

G-BVPX Bensen B 8 Tyro Gyro Mk.II   PCL125   13. 7.94 A W Harvey   Henstridge 19. 9.08P

(Built P C Lovegrove - pr.no.PFA G/11-1237)

G-BVPY CFM Streak Shadow   K 204   14. 6.94 R J Mitchell

(Built R J Mitchell - pr.no.PFA 206-12375) (Rotax 582)   *(Operates from Tingwall)* (Scalloway, Shetland) 24. 5.08P

G-BVRA Europa Aviation Europa   008   25. 7.94 N E Stokes *"Hummingbird"*   Sleap 10. 4.09P

(Built E J J Pels - pr.no.PFA 247-12635) (Monowheel u/c)

G-BVRH Taylorcraft BL-65   1657 N23929   15. 7.94 M J Kirk   New Barn Farm, Barton Ashes, Crawley 23. 9.06

                                      G-BVRH, N24322, NC24322

G-BVRL Lindstrand LBL 21A Balloon (Hot Air) 130   3. 8.94 M J Axtell   Todmorden 28. 5.09E

G-BVRR Lindstrand LBL 77A Balloon (Hot Air) 133   9. 8.94 M Icam   Carquefou, France 11. 7.04A

G-BVRU Lindstrand LBL 105A Balloon (Hot Air) 131   15. 8.94 C M Duggan   Selby 5. 4.08E

G-BVRV Van's RV-4   793 N144TH   23. 6.94 A Troughton   Armagh Field, Woodview 9. 5.07P

(Built C Thomas Hahn) (Lycoming AEIO-320)

G-BVRZ Piper PA-18 Super Cub 95 18-3442 SE-ITP   22.11.94 R W Davison   Rhedyn Coch Farm, Rhuallt 13. 9.10S

(Regd with Frame No.18-3381)   LN-LJG, D-EDCM, 96+19, QW+901, QZ+001, AC+507, AS+506, 54-752

G-BVSB TEAM Mini-MAX 91A   PFA 186-12241   1. 7.94 D G Palmer   Fetterangus 20.12.07P

(Built C Nice) (Rotax 503)

G-BVSD Sud-Aviation SE.3130 Alouette II   1897 Swiss AF V-54 8. 9.94 M J Cuttell *(As "V-54" in Swiss AF c/s)*

                                                  Gloucestershire 5.11.11

G-BVSF Aero Designs Pulsar   PFA 202-12071   1. 7.94 R J and J A Freestone Kittyhawk Farm, Deanland 21.10.08P

(Built S N and R J Freestone) (Tri-cycle u/c)

G-BVSM Rotary Air Force RAF 2000 EW-42   24. 8.94 S Ram   (Lowestoft) 24. 1.97P

(Built K Quigley and T M Truesdale) (Subaru EA82)

G-BVSN Avid Speed Wing   PFA 189-12088   24. 8.94 R C Bowley   (Kerswell Green, Worcester) 26.10.06P

(Built D J Park)

G-BVSO Cameron A-120 Balloon (Hot Air)   3339   25. 8.94 A Kaye tr Khaos Ballooning *(Cameron Balloons titles)*

                                                  Wellingborough 1. 7.09E

G-BVSP Hunting Percival P 84 Jet Provost T 3A XM370   31. 8.94 H G Hodges and Son Ltd *(Noted 1.07)* Hawarden 10. 6.04P

                                  PAC/W/6327

G-BVSS Jodel D 150 Mascaret   118   22. 8.94 A P Burns   RAF Woodvale 14. 1.10P

(Built A P Burns - pr.no.PFA 151-11878) (Continental O-200-A)

G-BVST	Jodel D 150 Mascaret	130		11. 8.94	A Shipp	Full Sutton	9. 1.08P
	(Built A Shipp - pr.no.PFA 235-12198) (Continental O-200-A)						
G-BVSX	TEAM Mini-MAX 91A	PFA 186-12463		9. 9.94	J A Clark	Orchard Farm, Sittingbourne	18. 7.03P
	(Built G N Smith) (Mosler MM CB-35)						
G-BVSZ	Pitts S-1E	PFA 009-11235		9. 9.94	H J Morton	(L'Huisserie, France)	24.10.09P
	(Built K Garrett and R P Millinship)						
G-BVTA	Tri-R KIS	PFA 239-12450		26. 8.94	P J Webb	Dunkeswell	2. 8.08P
	(Built P J Webb) (Continental O-240-E)						
G-BVTC	British Aircraft Corporation BAC 145 Jet Provost T 5A			7. 9.94	Global Aviation Ltd (As "XW333" in RAF c/s)		
		EEP/JP/997	XW333			Humberside	27. 8.09P
G-BVTD	CFM Streak Shadow	K 159-SA		14. 9.94	M Walton	Old Sarum	29. 8.07P
	(Built M Walton - pr.no.PFA 206-11972) (Rotax 582)						
G-BVTL	Colt 31A Air Chair Balloon (Hot Air)	2572		5. 7.94	A Lindsay	Twickenham	15. 5.97
G-BVTM	Reims Cessna F152 II	F15201827	G-WACS	31. 8.94	Royal Air Force Halton Aeroplane Club Ltd		
			D-EFGZ			RAF Halton	19. 9.09E
G-BVTN	Cameron N-90 Balloon (Hot Air)	3361		16. 9.94	P Zulehner	Peterskirchen, Austria	17. 7.08A
G-BVTV	RotorWay Executive 90	5243/6599		16. 9.94	D W J Lee	(Northiam, Rye)	30.11.09P
	(Built J J Bull) (RotorWay RI 162)						
G-BVTW	Aero Designs Pulsar	PFA 202-12172		14. 9.94	R J Panther	(Stoke Golding, Nuneaton)	25. 1.10P
	(Built J D Webb)						
G-BVTX	de Havilland DHC-1 Chipmunk 22A	C1/0705	WP809	2. 8.94	P W Skinner tr TX Flying Group (As "WP809:78" in RN c/s)		
						Husbands Bosworth	15. 4.11S
G-BVUA	Cameron O-105 Balloon (Hot Air)	3369		27. 9.94	D C Eager	Bracknell	28. 5.00A
G-BVUC	Colt 56A Balloon (Hot Air)	2608	G-639	30. 9.94	J F Till (Corks and Cans Norton titles)		
	("B" Conditions markings carried 9.94 as shown)					Welburn, York	2. 4.09E
G-BVUG	Betts TB.1	PFA 265-12770		3.10.94	H F Fekete	(Melsomvik, Norway)	23. 5.07P
	(Built T A Betts from modified AIA Stampe SV.4C c/n 1045 ex G-BEUS) (Tigre G IV-A2 120hp)						
G-BVUH	Thunder Ax7-65B Balloon (Hot Air)	243	JA-A0075	3.10.94	K B Chapple		
						Montastruc, Hautes-Pyrenees, France	23. 4.09E
G-BVUI	Lindstrand LBL 25A Cloudhopper Balloon (Hot Air)			5.10.94	J W Hole	Mondovi, Italy.	3. 8.08A
		148					
G-BVUK	Cameron V-77 Balloon (Hot Air)	3372		11.10.94	H G Griffiths and W A Steel	Reading	6. 9.09E
G-BVUM	Rans S-6-116 Coyote II	0893.528		11.10.94	M A Abbott	Glenrothes	22.12.09P
	(Built J L Donaldson - pr.no.PFA 204A-12685) (Rotax 582)						
G-BVUN	Van's RV-4	3363UK		11.10.94	D J Harvey	(Bedale)	6. 3.09P
	(Built I G Glenn - pr.no.PFA 181-12488) (Lycoming O-360)						
G-BVUT	Evans VP-1 Series 2	PFA 062-12092		24.10.94	M J Barnett	Shobdon	29. 9.99P
	(Built P J Weston) (Volkswagen 1600)				(Damaged on take off Pepperbox, Wiltshire 13. 3.99: on restoration 10.08)		
G-BVUU	Cameron C-80 Balloon (Hot Air)	3383		11.10.94	T M C McCoy "Ascent" Peasedown St John, Bath		15. 6.05T
G-BVUV	Europa Aviation Europa	141		23. 9.94	R J Mills	Gamston	8. 8.08P
	(Built R J Mills - pr.no.PFA 247-12762) (Monowheel u/c)						
G-BVUZ	Cessna 120	11334	Z-YGH	20. 9.94	M J Medland	Spanhoe	4. 9.09P
			VP-YGH, VP-NAM, VP-YGH				
G-BVVA	IAV-Bacau Yakovlev Yak-52	877610	LY-ANN	24.10.94	S T G Lloyd	Swansea	10. 4.09P
			DOSAAF 52				
G-BVVB	Carlson Sparrow II	PFA 209-11809		26. 9.94	L M McCullen	(North Ballachulish, Onich)	1. 8.06P
	(Built L M McCullen) (Rotax 532)				(Noted 5.07)		
G-BVVE	Wassmer Jodel D 112	1070	F-BKAJ	28.10.94	G D Gunby	Crowfield	14. 7.09P
G-BVVG	Nanchang CJ-6A	2751219	(F-.....)	10.10.94	R Davy tr Nanchang CJ6A Group (As "68" in Chinese AF c/s)		
	(Yak 18)		G-BVVG, Chinese PLAAF			White Waltham	2.10.09P
G-BVVH	Europa Aviation Europa	014		31.10.94	T G Hoult	Octon Grange Farm, Foxholes	15.10.09P
	(Built T G Hoult and M P Whitley - pr.no.PFA 247-12505) (Monowheel u/c)						
G-BVVI	Hawker Audax I	?	2015M	3.11.94	Aero Vintage Ltd (On rebuild 8.95) (Northiam, Rye)		
	(Built Avro Aircraft Ltd)		K5600				
G-BVVK	de Havilland DHC-6-310 Twin Otter	666	LN-BEZ	21.12.94	Loganair Ltd	Glasgow	15. 1.10E
G-BVVL	EAA Acrosport II	PFA 072A-10887		11.11.94	G A Breen	Portimão, Faro, Portugal	1.10.09P
	(Built D Park, A J Maxwell and P Price) (Lycoming O-360)						
G-BVVM	Zenair CH.601HD Zodiac	PFA 162-12539		3.10.94	D Macdonald	Popham	12. 5.09P
	(Buillt J G Small)						
G-BVVN	Brügger MB.2 Colibri	PFA 043-10979		12.10.94	T C Darters	Valley Farm, Winwick	11. 6.09P
	(Built N F Andrews) (Volkswagen 1834)						
G-BVVP	Europa Aviation Europa	088		20. 9.94	I Mansfeld	Kemble	14.10.09P
	(Built J S Melville - pr.no.PFA 247-12697) (Monowheel u/c)						
G-BVVR	Stits SA-3A Playboy	P-736	N4620S	14.11.94	D Dean	Breighton	23.11.08P
	(Built S Goins) (Continental A65)						
G-BVVS	Van's RV-4	PFA 181-12324		15.11.94	E C and N S C English	North Weald/Turweston	17. 9.09P
	(Built E C English) (Lycoming O-320)						
G-BVVU	Lindstrand LBL Four SS Balloon (Hot Air)	155	HB-QAP	18.11.94	Magical Adventures Ltd		
			G-BVVU			West Bloomfield, Michigan, US	30. 9.09E
G-BVVW	IAV-Bacau Yakovlev Yak-52	844605	RA-01361	16.11.94	M Blackman	Cherry Tree Farm, Monewden	30.10.09P
	(Official c/n suspect as plate shows 833519)		DOSAAF 15, DOSAAF 95				
G-BVVZ	Corby CJ-1 Starlet	PFA 134-12293		9.11.94	P V Flack	Lasham	27. 1.04P
	(Built A E Morris) (Volkswagen 1834)						
G-BVWB	Thunder Ax8-90 Series 2 Balloon (Hot Air)			2.12.94	M A Stelling, K C and K Tanner "Starship"		
		3000				Barton-Le-Clay, Thame and Sutton	13. 7.09E
G-BVWC	English Electric Canberra B 2	71399	WK163	2.12.94	Classic Aviation Projects Ltd	Coventry	29. 6.08P
	(Built Avro Aircraft Ltd) Regd as B 6 but c/n relates to nose section originally fitted to XH568) (As "WK163" in RAF 617 Sqdn c/s)						
G-BVWI	Cameron Light Bulb 65 SS Balloon (Hot Air)			8.12.94	A D Kent tr Balloon Preservation Flying Group		
		3405			"Phillips Energy Saver"	Petworth	2. 6.97A
G-BVWM	Europa Aviation Europa	070		14.12.94	A Aubeelack tr Europa Syndicate	White Waltham	13. 3.07P
	(Built A Aubeelack and C J Hadley - pr.no.PFA 247-12620) (Monowheel u/c)						
G-BVWW	Lindstrand LBL 90A Balloon (Hot Air)	169		28.12.94	Drawflight Ltd "Double Whiskey"	Hastings	1. 7.09E
G-BVWY	Porterfield CP-65	720	N27223	23.11.94	R L Earl and B Morris	Landmead Farm, Garford	22. 5.09P
	(Continental A65)		NC27223				

G-BVWZ	Piper PA-32-301 Saratoga	3206055	I-TASP N9184N	3. 1.95	M A Kesteven tr The Saratoga (WZ) Group		
						Newcastle	16. 4.09E
G-BVXA	Cameron N-105 Balloon (Hot Air)	3441		4. 1.95	R E Jones *(Ribby Hall titles)*	Lytham St Annes	19. 3.05T
G-BVXB	Cameron V-77 Balloon (Hot Air)	3442		4. 1.95	J A Lawton *"Pat McLean"*	Godalming	8. 1.09E
G-BVXD	Cameron O-84 Balloon (Hot Air)	3432		5. 1.95	J R Wilson tr Hedge Hoppers Balloon Group		
						Oxford	9. 8.09E
G-BVXE	Steen Skybolt	PFA 064-11123	G-LISA	5. 1.95	J Buglass *"Billie"*	Sleap	18. 9.09P
	(Built T C Humphreys and T J Reeve)						
G-BVXF	Cameron O-120 Balloon (Hot Air)	3400		21. 9.94	Off The Ground Balloon Co Ltd	Lyth, Kendal	11. 2.09E
G-BVXJ	Bücker Bü.133 Jungmeister	?	Spanish AF E1-9	11. 1.95	A C Mercer *(Also carries "ES-9" in Spanish Air Force c/s)*		
	(Built CASA) (Official c/n is "E1-9")		Spanish AF ES1-9, 35-9		*(Noted 12.07)*	Breighton	22. 5.06P
G-BVXK	Aerostar Yakovlev Yak-52	9111306	RA-44508 (1)	12. 1.95	E G Gavazzi *(As "26" in DOSAAF c/s)*		
			DOSAAF 26			Zuoz, Switzerland	4. 6.09E
G-BVXM	Aérospatiale AS.350B Ecureuil	2013	I-AUDI	10. 1.95	The Berkeley Leisure Group Ltd	Sparkford	5. 3.09E
			I-CIOC				
G-BVXR	de Havilland DH.104 Devon C 2	04436	XA880	13. 1.95	M Whale and M W A Lunn *(Stored as "XA880" in RAE c/s)*		
						Little Rissington	
G-BVXS	Taylorcraft BC-12D	9284	N96984	27. 1.95	M Hickin and R I Biddles tr XRay Sierra Group		
	(Continental A65)		NC96984			Leicester	6. 5.09P
G-BVYF	Piper PA-31-350 Navajo Chieftain		G-SAVE	8. 2.95	J A, G M, D T A and J A Rees t/a Messrs Rees of		
		31-7952102	N3518T		Poynston West	Haverfordwest	22. 1.10E
G-BVYG	Robin DR.300-180R Remorqueur	611	F-BSQB	9. 1.95	Ulster Gliding Club Ltd	Bellarena	27. 4.09E
			F-BSPI				
G-BVYK	TEAM Mini-MAX 91A	PFA 186-12598		13. 2.95	A G Ward	Longacre Farm, Sandy	26. 1.10P
	(Built S B Churchill) (DAF) (Officially regd with Rotax 447)						
G-BVYM	Robin DR.300-180R Remorqueur	656	F-BTBL	9.12.94	London Gliding Club Proprietary Ltd	Dunstable	19. 7.09E
G-BVYO	Robin R2160	288		11. 1.95	D J S McClean	City of Derry	30. 4.09E
G-BVYP	Piper PA-25-235 Pawnee B	25-3481	N7475D	13. 2.95	Bidford Gliding Ltd	Bidford	2. 6.09E
			OY-CLT, N7475Z				
G-BVYU	Cameron A-140 Balloon (Hot Air)	3544		17. 2.95	Balloon Flights Club Ltd	Leicester	30. 9.09E
G-BVYX	Avid Speed Wing Mk.4	PFA 189-12370		16. 2.95	K N Cobb	Weston Zoyland	6. 5.09P
	(Built G J Keen)						
G-BVYY	Pietenpol AirCamper	PFA 047-12559		20. 2.95	T F Harrison tr Pietenpol G-BVYY Group		
	(Built J R Orchard)					(Perton, Wolverhampton)	
G-BVYZ	Stemme S 10-V	14-011	D-KGDD	6. 3.95	A D Gubbay	Bicester	1. 5.09E
G-BVZD	Tri-R KIS	PFA 239-12416		21. 2.95	G A Haines	Carlisle	24. 7.09P
	(Built R T Clegg) (Canadian Air Motive CAM.100) (Tri-cycle u/c)						
G-BVZE	Boeing 737-59D	26422	SE-DNL	7. 3.95	British Midland Airways Ltd *(Operated bmiBaby)*		
					"little costa baby"	Nottingham-East Midlands	22. 3.09E
G-BVZJ	Rand Robinson KR-2	PFA 129-11049		21. 2.95	P D'Arcy Button	AAC Netheravon	19. 3.09P
	(Built J P McConnell-Wood) (Revmaster)		*(Damaged 15. 7.98 and rebuilt with KR2 fuselage pr.no.PFA 129-11174 c 2004-5)*				
G-BVZN	Cameron C-80 Balloon (Hot Air)	3546		28. 2.95	S J Clarke	Watford	11.10.09E
G-BVZO	Rans S-6-116 Coyote II	0494.606		1. 3.95	P J Brion New Barn Farm, Barton Ashes, Crawley		18. 5.09P
	(Built P Atkinson pr.no.PFA 204A-12710) (Rotax 582) (Tri-cycle u/c)						
G-BVZR	Zenair CH.601HD Zodiac	PFA 162-12417		2. 3.95	R A Perkins	Holmbeck Farm, Leighton Buzzard	10. 9.08P
	(Built J D White) (Tri-cycle u/c)						
G-BVZT	Lindstrand LBL 90A Balloon (Hot Air)	183		9. 3.95	J Edwards *"Molly Mae" (Pork Farms/Bowyers titles)*		
						Northampton	22. 7.09E
G-BVZV	Rans S-6-116N Coyote II	1294.708		16. 2.95	A R White *(Active 7.08)*	Popham	13. 6.05P
	(Built J Fothergill - pr.no.PFA 204A-12832: kit no.reported also as 0195.719 and possibly repaired with kit no.0493.471) (Rotax 582)						
G-BVZX	Cameron H-34 Balloon (Hot Air)	3564		15. 3.95	J B Turnau tr Chianti Balloon Club	Siena, Italy	16. 6.08A
G-BVZZ	de Havilland DHC-1 Chipmunk 22	C1/0687	WP795	5. 1.95	D C Murray tr Portsmouth Naval Gliding Club		
					(As "WP795:901" in RN c/s) Husbands Bosworth		14. 6.04

G-BWAA - G-BWZZ

G-BWAA	Cameron N-133 Balloon (Hot Air)	3471		9. 3.95	C and J M Bailey t/a Bailey Balloons *(Brunel Ford titles)*		
						Bristol	14.11.04T
G-BWAB	Jodel D 140 Mousquetaire	PFA 251-12469		25. 1.95	W A Braim	(Driffield)	25.11.08P
	(Built W A Braim) (Lycoming O-360)						
G-BWAC	Waco YKS-7	4693	N50RA	19. 8.92	D N Peters	Little Gransden	9. 9.11
	(Jacobs R-755)		N2896D, NC50				
G-BWAD	Rotary Air Force RAF 2000	147		27. 2.95	Newtonair (Gyroplanes) Ltd *(Operated A Melody)*		
	(Built J R Legge - pr.no.PFA G/13-1254) (Subaru EA82)					Little Rissington	22.11.08P
G-BWAF	Hawker Hunter F 6A	S4/U/3393	8831M	24. 2.95	RV Aviation Ltd *(As "XG160:U" in CFS Black Arrows c/s)*		
	(Built Armstrong-Whitworth Aircraft)		XG160			Bournemouth	
G-BWAG	Cameron O-120 Balloon (Hot Air)	3478		3. 2.95	P M Skinner *"Joker"* Chart Sutton, Maidstone		9. 8.09E
G-BWAH	Montgomerie-Bensen B 8MR	PFA G/01-1208		16. 3.95	J B Allan	Little Rissington	13. 6.07P
	(Built S J O Tinn) (Rotax 582)				*"The Flying Sealander" and "The Flying Scotsman"*		
G-BWAI	CFM Streak Shadow SA	K 235-SA		21. 3.95	C M James	Old Sarum	15. 7.04P
	(Built J M Heath - pr.no.PFA 206-12556 but originally allocated as pr.no.BMAA HB/052 C 1990) (Rotax 582)						
G-BWAJ	Cameron V-77 Balloon (Hot Air)	3579		22. 3.95	K Graham	Spennymoor	19. 8.09E
G-BWAN	Cameron N-77 Balloon (Hot Air)	3499		24. 3.95	I Chadwick tr Balloon Preservation Flying Group		
					(BPG tiltes) Partridge Green, Horsham		3.10.09E
G-BWAO	Cameron C-80 Balloon (Hot Air)	3436		24. 3.95	S Mitchell and M D Freeston	Hertford	25. 6.09E
G-BWAP	Clutton FRED Series III	PFA 029-10959		24. 3.95	G A Shepherd	(Mutford, Beccles)	
	(Built R J Smyth)						
G-BWAR	Denney Kitfox Model 3	PFA 172-12432		16. 3.95	I Wightman	(Berwick-upon-Tweed)	10. 9.08P
	(Built C E Brookes)						
G-BWAT	Pietenpol AirCamper	PFA 047-11594		15. 3.95	P W Aitchison	Enstone	9. 9.09P
	(Built D R Waters) (Continental C90)						
G-BWAU	Cameron V-90 Balloon (Hot Air)	3569		27. 3.95	A M and K M Hall	London N10	28. 5.09E
G-BWAV	Schweizer 269C *(Schweizer 300)*	S 1204	SE-JAY	28. 2.95	B Maggs tr Helihire	Shere, Guildford	20.12.09E
			LN-OTS, OY-HDW, N41S				

G-BWAW	Lindstrand LBL 77A Balloon (Hot Air)	207		28. 3.95	D Bareford *(Seton Healthcare titles)* Kidderminster	13. 7.09E
G-BWBA	Cameron V-65 Balloon (Hot Air)	3456		27. 2.95	P G Dunnington tr Dante Balloon Group		
					(British Airways titles) Newtown, Hungerford	7. 2.10E
G-BWBB	Lindstrand LBL 14A Balloon (Hot Air) (Gas filled)			3. 4.95	Oxford Promotions (UK) Ltd *(Operated F Prell)*	
		222			Kentucky, USA	
G-BWBE	Colt Flying Ice Cream Cone SS Balloon (Hot Air)			3. 4.95	Stratos Ballooning Gmbh and Co KG	
		3560			Ennigerloh, Germany	5. 5.05A
G-BWBF	Colt Flying Ice Cream Cone SS Balloon (Hot Air)			3. 4.95	Stratos Ballooning Gmbh and Co KG	
		3561			Ennigerloh, Germany	17. 4.03A
G-BWBI	Taylorcraft F-22A	2207	N22UK	3. 4.95	R T G Preston Little Rissington	9.10.11E
G-BWBO	Lindstrand LBL 77A Balloon (Hot Air)	157		10. 4.95	T J Orchard, N J Glover and S R Godfrey	
					Aylesbury	29. 8.09E
G-BWBT	Lindstrand LBL 90A Balloon (Hot Air)	184		3. 4.95	British Telecommunications PLC *"Beattie"*	
					Newbury	9. 4.05A
G-BWBY	Schleicher ASH 26E	26076		30. 8.95	J S Wand *"WBY"* Bidford	31. 1.10E
G-BWBZ	ARV Aviation ARV-1 Super 2 PFA 152-12802			10. 3.95	J A Straw *(Noted 6.07)* Langar	23. 4.07P
	(Built J N C Shields and officially regd as "ARV K1 Super 2") (Mid-West AE.100R)					
G-BWCA	CFM Streak Shadow	K 160		19. 4.95	I C Pearson (Horsham)	11. 7.07P
	(Built R Thompson - pr.no.PFA 206-11985) (Rotax 582)					
G-BWCC	Van Den Bemden 460m3 (Gas) Free Balloon	PH-BOX		5. 4.95	R W Batchelor tr Piccard Balloon Group Thame	
		"022"		*"Prof A Piccard"*		
	(C/n may be a corruption of Netherlands owner 622) (Netherlands records indicate some parts from OO-BGX which itself became G-BBFS)					
G-BWCG	Lindstrand LBL 42A Balloon (Hot Air)	223		25. 4.95	Oxford Promotions (UK) Ltd *(Operated F Prell)*	
					(Kentucky, US)	10. 1.97A
G-BWCK	Everett Gyroplane Series 3	036		26. 4.95	B F Pearson (Eakring, Newark)	28. 3.08P
	(Rotax 582)					
G-BWCS	British Aircraft Corporation BAC 145 Jet Provost T 5A			28. 4.95	J H Ashcroft *(As "XW293:Z" in RAF c/s)*	
		EEP/JP/957	XW293		*(stored, noted 1.09)* Bournemouth	3. 2.09P
G-BWCT	Tipsy Nipper T 66 Series 1	T66/11	"OO-NIC"	27. 4.95	J S Hemmings and C R Steer	
	(Built Avions Fairey SA)		PH-MEC, D-EMEC, OO-NIC		(Heathfield and Bexhill-on-Sea)	
G-BWCV	Europa Aviation Europa	041		4. 5.95	G V McKirdy Enstone	13. 7.07P
	(Built M P Chetwynd-Talbot - pr.no.PFA 247-12591) (NSI EA-81/100) *(Monowheel u/c)*					
					(Struck hedge landing Portbury 16.7.06 and substantially damaged)	
G-BWCY	Murphy Rebel	058R		15. 5.95	S Burrow (Wentbridge, Pontefract)	11. 7.09P
	(Built A Jones, R Hallam and A Koneczek - pr.no.PFA 232-12135)					
G-BWDA	Aérospatiale-Alenia ATR 72-202	444	F-WQNG	29. 6.95	Aurigny Air Services Ltd Guernsey	28. 8.09E
			G-BWDA, (9M-AMB), G-BWDA, F-WWEQ			
G-BWDB	Aérospatiale-Alenia ATR 72-202	449	F-WQNI	14. 6.95	Aurigny Air Services Ltd Guernsey	16. 9.09E
			G-BWDB, (9M-AMA) G-BWDB, F-WWEE			
G-BWDF	PZL-104 Wilga 35A	21950955		17. 5.95	Sky Banners Ltd Dunsfold	3. 6.09A
G-BWDH	Cameron N-105 Balloon (Hot Air)	3549		22. 5.95	Bridges Van Hire Ltd Awsworth, Nottingham	26. 9.09E
G-BWDM	Lindstrand LBL 120A Balloon (Hot Air)	263	(F-GYDM)	26. 5.95	A N F Pertwee Frinton-on-Sea	14. 2.02T
			(F-GUMP), G-BWDM			
G-BWDP	Europa Aviation Europa	062		7. 6.95	S Attubato Bodmin	23. 8.07P
	(Built I Valentine - pr.no.PFA 247-12637) *(Monowheel u/c)*					
G-BWDR	Hunting Percival P 84 Jet Provost T 3A	XM376		6. 6.95	Global Aviation Ltd Humberside	24.10.02P
		PAC/W/6603				
G-BWDS	Hunting Percival P 84 Jet Provost T 3A	XM424		6. 6.95	Aviation Heritage Ltd *(As "XM424" in RAF c/s)*	
	(Correct c/n PAC/W/9231?)	"PAC/W/932"	(N77506?), XM424		Coventry	11. 2.09P
G-BWDT	Piper PA-34-220T Seneca III	34-8233045	PH-TWI	21. 9.88	H R Chambers Blackbushe	19.11.06T
			G-BKHS, N8472H			
G-BWDU	Cameron V-90 Balloon (Hot Air)	3143		19. 6.95	D M Roberts Llandeilo	1. 2.08A
G-BWDV	Schweizer 269C *(Schweizer 300)*	S 1712	N86G	16. 6.95	Flightframe Ltd (Pontardawe, Swansea)	5.11.09E
G-BWDX	Europa Aviation Europa	056		13. 6.95	J Robson RAF Benson	6. 8.07P
	(Built J B Crane - pr.no.PFA 247-12603) *(Monowheel u/c)*					
G-BWDZ	Sky 105-24 Balloon (Hot Air)	002		13. 6.95	Westcountry Ballooning Ltd Queen Camel, Yeovil	9. 4.09E
G-BWEA	Lindstrand LBL 120A Balloon (Hot Air)	252		14. 6.95	S R Seager *(Parrott and Coales titles)* Aylesbury	8. 7.00T
G-BWEB	British Aircraft Corporation BAC 145 Jet Provost T 5A			19. 6.95	S Patrick tr XW422 Group *(As "XW422" in RAF c/s)*	
		EEP/JP/1044	XW422		Kemble	22. 7.09P
G-BWEE	Cameron V-42 Balloon (Hot Air)	3480		8. 3.95	A J Davey Hosbach-Rottenberg, Germany	14.10.09E
G-BWEF	SNCAN Stampe SV-4C(G)	208	G-BOVL	13. 5.93	D A Smith tr Acebell BWEF Syndicate Redhill	4. 6.10S
			N20SV, F-BHES, F-BBLC			
G-BWEG	Europa Aviation Europa	053		4. 4.95	R J Marsh Exeter	19. 4.09P
	(Built B A Selmes and R J Marsh - pr.no.PFA 247-12600) *(Conventional u/c)*					
G-BWEM	Vickers Supermarine 358 Seafire L III	?	IAC.157	28. 6.95	Mark One Partners LLC *(Noted 10.08)* Duxford	
	(Build Westland Aircraft Ltd)		RX168			
G-BWEN	Macair Merlin GT	050194		20. 6.95	D A Hill (Terrington St Clement, King's Lynn)	7.12.95P
	(Built B W Davies - pr.no.PFA 208A-12859) (Subaru EA81)					
G-BWEU	Reims Cessna F152 II	F15201894	EI-BNC	15. 6.95	Affair Aircraft Leasing LLP	
			N9079Y		*(Operated Sheffield City Flying School)* Sandtoft	28.10.09E
G-BWEV	Cessna 152 II	15283182	EI-BVU	28. 6.95	MK Aero Support Ltd Andrewsfield	6.12.08E
			N47184			
	(Landed long at Full Sutton 13. 4.08, went off the runway onto soft ground and overturned)					
G-BWEW	Cameron N-105 Balloon (Hot Air)	3637		30. 6.95	Unipart Group Ltd tr Unipart Balloon Club *(Unipart titles)*	
					Cowley	3. 3.06A
G-BWEY	Bensen B 8	PFA G/01-1197		3. 7.95	F G Shepherd (Leadgate, Alston)	
	(Built F G Shepherd)					
G-BWEZ	Piper J-3C-85 Cub	6021	N29050	3. 7.95	J G McTaggart *(As "436021" in USAAF c/s)*	
			NC29050		Archerfield Estate, Dirleton	9. 5.09P
G-BWFG	Robin HR.200-120B	293		20. 7.95	RVL Aviation Ltd Coventry	19. 3.10P
	(Type amended from HR.200-120 18.11.08)					
G-BWFH	Europa Aviation Europa	201		14. 7.95	B L Wratten Kittyhawk Farm, Deanland	18. 8.09P
	(B L Wratten and R W Baylie - pr.no.PFA 247-12842) *(Monowheel u/c)*					
G-BWFI	HOAC DV.20 Katana	20128		17. 7.95	Air Aqua Ltd RAF Benson	22. 8.09E

G-BWFJ Evans VP-1   PFA 062-10349   1. 9.78   P A West *(Stored 5.94)* (Middle Spillmans, Stroud) 27. 1.93P
        (Built W E Jones) (Volkswagen 1600)

G-BWFK Lindstrand LBL 77A Balloon (Hot Air)   289   17. 7.95   R S Kent tr Balloon Preservation Flying Group *"Mr Orange"*
                                                                                                                                    Petworth 27. 5.09E

G-BWFM Yakovlev Yak-50   781208   NX5224R   19. 7.95   J Hurrell tr Fox Mike Group *(Noted 10.07)*
                                                        DDR-WQX, DM-WQX   Blackpool 6.10.06P

G-BWFN HAPI Cygnet SF-2A   PFA 182-11335   19. 7.95   K Shelton and G J Green tr G-BWFN Group
        (Built T Crawford) (HAPI 60)   Derby 16.11.09P

G-BWFO Colomban MC-15 Cri-Cri   PFA 133-11253   19. 7.95   K D and C S Rhodest *(Stored, noted 1.08)*
        (Built O G Jones) (JPX PUL-212)   Bourne Park, Hurstbourne Tarrant

G-BWFP IAV-Bacau Yakovlev Yak-52   855503   RA-44501 (1) 20. 7.95   M C Lee   Spanhoe 5.11.09P
                                                        DOSAAF 43, DOSAAF 61 (blue)
        (Official c/n suspect as plate shows 855606- possible composite?)

G-BWFT Hawker Hunter T 8M   41H-695332 XL602   24. 7.95   Global Aviation Services Ltd *(As "XL602": on rebuild 9.08)*
                                                                                                                                   Exeter 23. 7.99P

G-BWFX Europa Aviation Europa   038   26. 7.95   A D Stewart   Rayne Hall Farm, Braintree . 3.08P
        (Built A D Stewart - pr.no.PFA 247-12586) (Monowheel u/c)

G-BWFZ Murphy Rebel   PFA 232-12536 G-SAVS   19. 7.95   S Beresford   Willow Farm, Gringley-on-the-Hill 10. 7.09P
        (Built I E Spencer)

G-BWGA Lindstrand LBL 105A Balloon (Hot Air)   295   2. 8.95   R Thompson   Berry Grove Farm, Liss 6. 9.09E

G-BWGF British Aircraft Corporation BAC 145 Jet Provost T 5A   10. 8.95   Viper Jet Provost Group Ltd *(As "XW325:E" in RAF c/s)*
                                           EEP/JP/989 XW325   Hawarden 30. 9.09P

G-BWGG Max Holste MH.1521C1 Broussard   20   F-GGKG   10. 7.95   M J Burnett Jnr and R B Maalouf   Kemble 16. 9.06
                                                        F-WGKG, French Military   *(As "20:315-SQ" in French Army c/s)*

G-BWGJ Chilton DW.1A   PFA 225-12615   11. 8.95   T J Harrison *(Complete 5.00)*
        (Built T J Harrison) (Lycoming O-145-A2)   Phoenix Farm, Lower Upham

G-BWGK Hawker Hunter GA.11   HABL-003032 XE689   15. 8.95   B R Pearson tr GA11 Group *(Stored as "XE689:864-VL" 8.06)*
        (Centre fuselage no.is 41HR HABL 003032)   Kemble 11. 7.01P

G-BWGL Hawker Hunter T 8C   HABL-003086 XF357   15. 8.95   Stichting Dutch Hawker Hunter Foundation
        (Officially regd with c/n 41H-695946)   Leeuwarden, Netherlands 12. 3.09P
                                                                                       (As "N-321" in R Netherlands AF c/s)

G-BWGM Hawker Hunter T 8C   HABL-003008 XE665   15. 8.95   B J Pearson tr The Admirals Barge   Kemble 24. 6.98P
        (Officially regd with c/n 41H-695940)   *(Noted 9.08 as "XE665:876:VL")*

G-BWGN Hawker Hunter T 8C   41H-670689   WT722   15. 8.95   B J Pearson tr T8C Group   Kemble 3. 9.97P
                                                                                       (In open store as "WT722:878:VL")

G-BWGO Slingsby T 67M-200 Firefly   2048   SE-LBC   15. 8.95   R Gray   Denham 23. 7.09E

G-BWGP Cameron C-80 Balloon (Hot Air)   3631   17. 8.95   Zebedee Balloon Service Ltd
                                                                                                                        Newtown, Hungerford 27. 9.09E

G-BWGS British Aircraft Corporation BAC 145 Jet Provost T 5A   18. 8.95   G-BWGS Ltd *"Where Eagles Share"* North Weald 2. 9.08P
                                           EEP/JP/974 XW310

G-BWGT Hunting Percival P 84 Jet Provost T 4   8991M   XR679   21. 8.95   G M Snow   (Wigan) 20 7.06P
        (Reported as c/n PAC/W/19992) PAC/W/21624

G-BWGY HOAC DV.20 Katana   20134   22. 8.95   Stars Fly Ltd   Elstree 6.12.08E
G-BWHD Lindstrand LBL 31A Balloon (Hot Air)   292   29. 8.95   Directorate Army Aviation   Middle Wallop 4. 1.10E
G-BWHF Piper PA-31-325 Navajo C/R   31-7612076 F-GECA   7. 9.95   Awyr Cymru Cyf   Welshpool 1.11.09E
                                                        D-IBIS, N59862

G-BWHG Cameron N-65 Balloon (Hot Air)   3619   7. 9.95   M Stefanini and F B Alaoui   Firenze, Italy 31. 3.07A
G-BWHI de Havilland DHC-1 Chipmunk 22   C1/0637   WK624   8. 9.95   N E M Clare *(As "WK624:M" in RAF c/s)* Blackpool 2. 3.08T
        (Hulk of WK624/M may have been used in rebuild of G-AOSY c1998/99)

G-BWHK Rans S-6-116 Coyote II   0695.834   15. 9.95   S J Wakeling   (Tamworth) 12. 5.07P
        (Built N D White - pr.no.PFA 204A-12908) (Rotax 582) (Tri-cycle u/c)

G-BWHP CASA 1-131E Jungmann   2109   Spanish AF 18. 8.95   J F Hopkins *(As "S4+A07" in Luftwaffe c/s)*
                                                        E3B-513   Watchford Farm, Yarcombe 19. 6.08P

G-BWHR Tipsy Nipper T 66 Series 1   PFA 025-12843 (OO-KAM) 19. 9.95   L R Marnef   (Koningshooikt, Belgium)
        (Built L R Marnef)   OO-69   *(Composite homebuild of original Fairey build c/ns 29 and 711)*

G-BWHS Rotary Air Force RAF 2000   PFA G/13-1253   25. 9.95   A W Findlay and B J Payne   (Aberdeen) 28. 9.07P
        (Built V G Freke) (Subaru EA82)

G-BWHU Westland Scout AH.1   F9517   XR595   27. 9.95   N J F Boston *(As "XR595:M" in AAC c/s)*
                                                                                                                            North Weald 11. 7.09P

G-BWHY Robinson R22   0098   N90366   24. 3.87   P Boal   Nutts Corner, Crumlin 30. 8.08E
G-BWIA Rans S-10 Sakota   xxxx.xxx   15. 9.95   I D Worthington   (Raskell, York) 24. 7.07P
        (Built P A Beck - pr.no.PFA 194-12044) (Rotax 582) (Engine failed during touch and go Kingsnorth, Kent 7. 4.07 and substantially damaged)

G-BWIB Scottish Aviation Bulldog Series 120/122   Ghana AF   10.10.95   B I Robertson *(As "XX514" in RAF c/s)*
                                           BH120/227   G-103   (Pontiac, Michigan, US) 16. 6.08T
G-BWID Druine D 31 Turbulent   201   F-PHFR   16.10.95   A M Turney   Cheddington 21. 7.05P
        (Built R Druine and H Gindre) (Volkswagen 1200)

G-BWII Cessna 150G   15065308   N4008J   22. 9.95   J D G Hicks   Sturgate 30. 1.09E
                                                        (G-BSKB), N4008J

G-BWIJ Europa Aviation Europa   006   19.10.95   R Lloyd   Kemble
        (Built R Lloyd - pr.no.PFA 247-12513)   (Landed with u/c in fully retracted position Kemble 23. 5.07 and substantially damaged)

G-BWIK de Havilland DH.82A Tiger Moth   86417   7015M   20.10.95   B J Ellis *(On rebuild as "NL985")*   Little Gransden
                                                        NL985

G-BWIL Rans S-10 Sakota   1089.065   G-WIEN   4.10.95   S H Leahy   Lower Mountpleasant Farm, Chatteris 12. 4.07P
        (Built J C Longmore - pr.no.PFA 194-11770) (Rotax 582)

G-BWIP Cameron N-90 Balloon (Hot Air)   3668   20.10.95   S H Fell   Carlisle 27.10.96A
G-BWIR Dornier 328-100   3023   D-CDXF   18.10.95   Suckling Airways (Cambridge) Ltd t/a Scot Airways
                                                        N328DA, D-CDHH   London City 19.10.09E

G-BWIV Europa Aviation Europa   210   27.10.95   T G Ledbury   (Holyport, Maidenhead) 9. 9.99P
        (Built J R Lockwood-Goose - pr.no.PFA 247-12871) (Rotax 912) (Monowheel u/c)

G-BWIW Sky 180-24 Balloon (Hot Air)   008   1.11.95   T M Donnelly   Sprotborough, Doncaster 21. 4.09E
G-BWIX Sky 120-24 Balloon (Hot Air)   009   31.10.95   J M Percival *"Mayfly III"*
                                                                                               Bourton-on-the-Wolds, Loughborough 7. 1.09E

G-BWIZ QAC Quickie Tri-Q 200   PFA 094-12330   21. 8.95   M C Davies *(Noted dismantled 1.09)*   Turweston 23. 6.98P
        (Built B Cain) (Continental O-200)

G-BWJG	Mooney M 20J Model 201	24-3319	N1083P	7.11.95	S Nahum	Elstree	18. 6.09E
G-BWJH	Europa Aviation Europa	007		10.11.95	T P Cripps	Haverfordwest	9.10.09P
	(Built D, J and A R D Hood - pr.no.PFA 247-12643) (Tri-gear u/c)						
G-BWJI	Cameron V-90 Balloon (Hot Air)	3727		13.11.95	Calarel Developments Ltd (*"Calarel" titles*)		
						Chipping Camden	12. 5.09E
G-BWJM	Bristol 20 M 1C replica	NAW-2		23.11.95	Richard Shuttleworth Trustees	Old Warden	13. 4.09P
	(Built Northern Aeroplane Workshops)				*(As "C4918" in RFC 72 Sqdn c/s)*		
G-BWJN	Montgomerie-Bensen B 8MR PFA G/01-1262			16.11.95	C R Gordon	Kirkbride	3. 7.09P
	(Built M G Mee) (Rotax 582)						
G-BWJW	Westland Scout AH.1	F9705	XV130	29.11.95	S Dadak and G Sobell (*As "XV130:R" in RAF 666 Sqdn c/s*)		
						Thruxton	25. 1.06P
G-BWJY	de Havilland DHC-1 Chipmunk 22	C1/0519	WG469	5.12.95	K J Thompson (*As "WG469:72" in RAF c/s*)		
						Strandhill, Sligo, County Sligo	7. 8.09S
G-BWKD	Cameron O-120 Balloon (Hot Air)	3773		8.12.95	L J and M Schoeman	Basildon	7. 3.03T
G-BWKE	Cameron AS-105GD Airship (Hot Air)	3685		8.12.95	W Arnold	Kassel, Germany	4. 2.09E
G-BWKF	Cameron N-105 Balloon (Hot Air)	3736		8.12.95	R M M Botti	Grosseto, Italy	30. 3.08A
G-BWKJ	Rans S-7 Courier	xxxx.xxx		14.12.95	B Tierney tr Three Point Aviation		
	(Built J P Kovacs - pr.no.PFA 218-12918) (Verner SVS1400) (Officially recorded as Rotax 582)					Kilrush, County Kildare	4.11.04P
G-BWKK	Auster AOP.9	B5/10/165	XP279	30. 7.79	C A Davis and D R White (*As "XP279" in AAC c/s*)		
	(Officially regd with Frame no.AUS/166)					(Winchester)	1. 8.96P
G-BWKR	Sky 90-24 Balloon (Hot Air)	014		18.12.95	B Drawbridge	Cranbrook	16. 3.03T
G-BWKT	Laser Lazer Z200	PFA 123-11421		19.12.95	P D Begley	Deenethorpe	27. 4.09P
	(Built P D Begley) (Lycoming IO-360)						
G-BWKU	Cameron A-250 Balloon (Hot Air)	3730		21.12.95	Balloon School (International) Ltd t/a British Club of		
					Ballooning	Colhook Common, Petworth	27. 5.09E
G-BWKV	Cameron V-77 Balloon (Hot Air)	3780		27.12.95	C A Bryant	Yatton, Bristol	21.10.09E
G-BWKW	Thunder Ax8-90 Balloon (Hot Air)	3770		28.12.95	Venice Simplon-Orient Express Ltd *"Road to Mandalay"*		
						Bristol	1. 9.09E
G-BWKX	Cameron A-250 Balloon (Hot Air)	3731		2. 1.96	Balloon School (International) Ltd t/a Hot Airlines		
					(Hot Airlines titles)	Colhook Common, Petworth	4. 7.06T
G-BWKZ	Lindstrand LBL 77A Balloon (Hot Air)	340		21.12.95	J H Dobson	Reading	4. 2.07T
G-BWLA	Lindstrand LBL 69A Balloon (Hot Air)	339		3. 1.96	I Chadwick tr Balloon Preservation Flying Group		
					"Virgin Atlantic"	Partridge Green, Horsham	22. 7.09E
G-BWLD	Cameron O-120 Balloon (Hot Air)	3774	(I-. . . .)	16. 1.96	D, P Pedri and C Nicolodi		
						Villa Lagarina, Rovereto, Italy	25. 1.09E
G-BWLF	Cessna 404 Titan	404-0414	G-BNXS	26.10.94	Blom Aerofilms Ltd	Cranfield	3.12.08E
			HKG-4, (N8799K)				
G-BWLJ	Taylorcraft DCO-65	O-4331	C-GUSA	16. 1.96	C Evans (*As "42-35870:129" in USNavy c/s*) *"Grasshopper"*		
			?, 42-35870			Great Oakley	4.10.07P
G-BWLL	Murphy Rebel	PFA 232-12499		22. 1.96	F W Parker	Richmond, North Yorkshire	28. 7.09P
	(Built F W Parker)						
G-BWLR	Max Holste MH.1521C1 Broussard	185	F-GGKJ	25. 1.96	Chicory Crops Ltd (*As "185:44-CA" in French AF c/s*)		
			F-WGKJ, French AF			Gloucestershire	20. 9.09S
G-BWLY	RotorWay Executive	5142		11. 1.93	P W and I P Bewley	Ley Farm, Chirk	1. 5.08P
	(Built P W and I P Bewley) (RotorWay RI 162)						
G-BWLZ	Wombat Gyrocopter	PFA G/09-1255		28.12.95	M R Harrisson *(Stored 3.98)* (Brecqhou, Guernsey)		
	(Built J M Shippen)						
G-BWMA	Colt 105A Balloon (Hot Air)	1853		31.10.90	L Lacroix		
						St Paul en Chablais, Haute-Savoie, France	24. 4.06A
G-BWMB	Wassmer Jodel D 119	77-1492	F-BGMA	17. 2.78	C Hughes	Finmere	22. 5.09P
	(Orig F-BGMA [77] became F-PHQH and rebuilt as Larrieu JL.2: presumed a rebuild using some components of c/n 77 and new build c/n 1492)						
G-BWMC	Cessna 182P Skylane II	18263117	N5462J	30. 1.96	P F N Burrow and E N Skinner tr Eggesford Eagles		
	G-BWMC, OO-RGM, (OO-RAN), F-BVOU, N7333N				Flying Group	Trenchard Farm, Eggesford	11. 9.09E
G-BWMF	Gloster Meteor T 7	G5/356460	7917M	15.12.95	Aviation Heritage Ltd	Coventry	
			WA591				
G-BWMH	Lindstrand LBL 77B Balloon (Hot Air)	152		7. 2.96	J W Hole	Much Wenlock	8. 9.09E
G-BWMI	Piper PA-28RT-201T Turbo Arrow IV		F-GCTG	31. 1.96	O Cowley	Fairoaks	27. 2.09E
		28R-8031131	N82482, N9571N				
G-BWMJ	Nieuport Scout 17/23 replica PFA 121-12351			8. 2.96	R Gauld-Galliers and L J Day (*As "N1977:8" in French AF c/s*)		
	(Built R Gauld-Galliers and L J Day) (Warner Scarab 165)					Popham	27. 7.09P
G-BWMK	de Havilland DH.82A Tiger Moth	84483	T8191	9. 2.96	APB Leasing Ltd	Trehelig, Welshpool	
	(Built Morris Motors Ltd)						
G-BWML	Cameron A-275 Balloon (Hot Air)	3725		12. 2.96	A J Street *(Exeter Balloons titles)*	Exeter	17. 8.01T
G-BWMN	Rans S-7 Courier	0193.104		14. 2.96	G J Knee	Turweston	10. 4.09P
	(Built T M Turnbull - pr.no.PFA 218-12446) (Rotax 912-UL)						
G-BWMO	Oldfield Baby Lakes	JAL.3	G-CIII	14. 2.96	D Maddocks	Sleap	12. 3.08P
	(Built J A List) (Continental C85)		N11JL				
G-BWMS	de Havilland DH.82A Tiger Moth	82712	OO-EVJ	14. 2.96	Foundation Early Birds (Nederhorst, Netherlands)		
			T-29, R4771				
G-BWMU	Cameron Monster Truck 105 SS Balloon (Hot Air)			20. 2.96	Magical Adventures Ltd *"Skycrusher"*		
		3607				West Bloomfield, Mi, USA	29. 9.09E
G-BWMV	Colt AS-105 Mk.II Airship (Hot Air)	3775		22. 2.96	D Stuber	Schwabenheim, Germany	1. 7.09E
G-BWMX	de Havilland DHC-1 Chipmunk 22	C1/0481	WG407	19. 2.96	K S Kelso tr 407th Flying Group (*As "WG407:67" in RAF c/s*)		
						Fen End Farm, Smithy Fen, Cottenham	23. 9.11
G-BWMY	Cameron Bradford and Bingley 90 SS Balloon (Hot Air)			23. 2.96	Magical Adventures Ltd *(Bradford and Bingley titles)*		
	(Bowler Hat special shape)	3808				West Bloomfield, Michigan, USA	29. 9.09E
G-BWNB	Cessna 152 II	15280051	N757WA	23. 8.96	Galair International Ltd	Wellesbourne Mountford	2. 6.09E
G-BWNC	Cessna 152 II	15284415	N6487L	23. 8.96	Galair International Ltd	Wellesbourne Mountford	10.10.09E
G-BWND	Cessna 152 II	15285905	N95493	23. 8.96	Galair International Ltd and G Davies		
						Wellesbourne Mountford	29. 7.09E
G-BWNI	Piper PA-24 Comanche	24-136	N5123P	15. 2.96	W A Stewart	North Connel, Oban	24.11.09E
G-BWNJ	Hughes 269C *(Hughes 300)*	86-0528	N42LW	29. 2.96	L R Fenwick Long Fosse House, Beelsby, Grimsby	12. 6.09E
			N27RD, N7458F				

G-BWNK	de Havilland DHC-1 Chipmunk 22	C1/0317	WD390	4. 3.96	S Smith tr WD390 Group (As "WD390:68" in RAF c/s)
					(Wragby, Market Rasen)	1. 8.09S
G-BWNM	Piper PA-28R-180 Cherokee Arrow		N934BD	5. 3.96	M and Rosa C Ramnial	Gloucestershire	12.11.09E
		28R-30435				
G-BWNO	Cameron O-90 Balloon (Hot Air)	3716		5. 3.96	T Knight (Action Research titles)
					Ightfield, Whitchurch	31. 8.09E
G-BWNP	Cameron Club-90 SS Balloon (Hot Air)	1717	EI-BVQ	6. 3.96	L P Hooper anf A R Hardwivk "Club Orange"
	(Club Orange Soft Drink Can shape)				Bristol/ Shefford	5. 9.09E
G-BWNS	Cameron O-90 Balloon (Hot Air)	3842		6. 3.96	Smithair Ltd "Hector" (Self Assessment Tax titles)
					Billingshurst	21. 4.09E
G-BWNT	de Havilland DHC-1 Chipmunk 22	C1/0772	WP901	7. 3.96	P G D Bell and R A Stafford (As "WP901:B" in RAF c/s)
					Nottingham-East Midlands	28. 5.09S
G-BWNU	Piper PA-38-112 Tomahawk	38-78A0334	N9294T	8. 3.96	Kemble Aero Club Ltd	Kemble	9. 1.09E
G-BWNY	Aeromot AMT-200 Super Ximango	200055		11. 6.96	Powell-Brett Associates Ltd	(Leamington Spa)	2.10.09E
				(Landed at RAF Syerston 25. 6.08 with undercarriage retracted after a local flight)
G-BWNZ	Agusta A109C	7654		3. 4.96	Anglo Beef Processors Ltd	(Ardlee, Co Louth)	23. 4.09E
G-BWOA	Sky 105-24 Balloon (Hot Air)	027		13. 3.96	Akhter Group PLC	(Harlow)	11. 7.02A
G-BWOB	Luscombe 8F Silvaire	6179	N1552B	14. 3.96	P J Tanulak and H T Lawc(Noted 8.07)	Sleap
			NC1552B			
G-BWOD	IAV-Bacau Yakovlev Yak-52	833810	LY-ALY	14. 3.96	Insurefast Ltd (As "139" in DOSAAF c/s)
			DOSAAF 139			Whitland	31. 7.09P
G-BWOF	British Aircraft Corporation BAC 145 Jet Provost T 5			18. 3.96	Techair London Ltd	Bournemouth	18. 2.08P
		EEP/JP/955	XW291			
G-BWOH	Piper PA-28-161 Cadet	2841061	EC-IBH	18. 3.96	Abraxas Aviation Ltd	Elstree	11.12.09E
			G-BWOH, D-ENXG, N9142S			
G-BWOI	Piper PA-28-161 Cadet	2841307	N270X	18. 3.96	S J Skilton t/a Aviation Rentals	Kemble	4.10.09E
			G-BWOI, D-EJTM, N9264N, N9208P			
G-BWOJ	Piper PA-28-161 Cadet	2841331	N630X	18. 3.96	S J Skilton t/a Aviation Rentals	Wolverhampton	26. 8.09E
	(Thielert TAE 125-01)		G-BWOJ, D-ESTM, N92242, (N123ND), N92242			
G-BWOK	Lindstrand LBL 105G Balloon (Hot-Air)	370		19. 3.96	Lindstrand Hot Air Balloons Ltd	Oswestry
G-BWON	Europa Aviation Europa	112		29. 1.96	MZ Beheer BV	(Lemelerveld, Netherlands)	16.11.09P
	(Built G T Birks - pr.no.PFA 247-12720) (Conventional u/c)
G-BWOR	Piper PA-18-135 Super Cub (L-18C)	18-2547	OO-WIS	21. 3.96	C D Baird	(Lower Froyle, Alton)	26. 8.11
			OO-HMF, French Army, 52-6229			
G-BWOT	Hunting Percival P 84 Jet Provost T 3A		XN459	25. 3.96	M Soor (As "XN459" in RAF Red Pelicans c/s)
	(Reported as PAC/W/949267)	PAC/W/10138				North Weald	27. 3.09P
G-BWOV	Enstrom F-28A	222	N690BR	26. 3.96	P A Goss	Draycott Farm, Chiseldon	25. 7.09E
			G-BWOV, F-BVRG			
G-BWOW	Cameron N-105 Balloon (Hot Air)	3805		31. 1.96	S J Colin t/a Skybus Ballooning "Skybus"
					Cranbrook	7. 5.09E
G-BWOX	de Havilland DHC-1 Chipmunk 22	C1/0728	WP844	27. 3.96	J St Clair-Quentin (As "WP844" in RAF c/s)
					Spanhoe	10. 7.00
G-BWOY	Sky 31-24 Balloon (Hot Air)	029		28. 3.96	C Wolstenholme	Bristol	9.10.09E
G-BWOZ	CFM Streak Shadow SA	K 154--SA		1. 4.96	J A Lord	Stapleford	11. 2.09P
	(Built H Witt - pr.no.PFA 206-12988) (Rotax 582)
G-BWPC	Cameron V-77 Balloon (Hot Air)	3867		1. 4.96	H Vaughan (Cancer Research UK titles)	Tring	14. 2.09E
G-BWPE	Murphy Renegade 912	PFA 188-12791		2. 4.96	J Hatswell	Clipgate Farm, Denton	23. 5.09P
	(Built G Wilson)				(Also wears "83-EB" under starboard wing)
G-BWPF	Sky 120-24 Balloon (Hot Air)	028		3. 4.96	Zebedee Balloon Service Ltd "Whisper"
					Newtown, Hungerford	6. 9.09E
G-BWPH	Piper PA-28-181 Cherokee Archer II		N1408H	4. 4.96	H and E Merkado	Panshanger	4. 5.09E
		28-7790311				
G-BWPJ	Steen Skybolt	PFA 064-12854		9. 4.96	D Houghton	Croft Farm, Defford	23. 1.08P
	(Built W R Penaluna) (Continental IO-346)
G-BWPP	Sky 105-24 Balloon (Hot Air)	031		9. 4.96	P F Smart tr The Sarnia Balloon Group (nice day titles)
					Oakley, Basingstoke	9. 7.09E
G-BWPS	CFM Streak Shadow SA	K 275-SA		9. 2.96	P J Mogg	Stour Row, Sturminster Newton	11. 6.09P
	(Built P G A Sumner - pr.no.PFA 206-12954) (Rotax 618)
G-BWPT	Cameron N-90 Balloon (Hot Air)	3838		5. 3.96	G Everet	Sandway, Maidstone	9. 9.09E
G-BWPZ	Cameron N-105 Balloon (Hot Air)	3889		19. 4.96	D M Moffat "Jaguar"	Bristol	12. 8.09E
G-BWRA	Sopwith LC-1T Triplane replica		G-PENY	19. 4.96	S M Truscott and J M Hoblyn (As "N500" in RAF c/s)
	(Built J S Penny)	PFA 021-10035	(Warner Scarab 165)			RNAS Yeovilton	28. 4.09P
	(Made a forced landing near Rendcomb 12. 7.08 and overturned in a field of standing crops after engine cowling started to separate)
G-BWRC	Avid Hauler Mk.4	PFA 189-12979		22. 2.96	M J E Walsh	Stancombe Farm, Askerswell	22. 7.08P
	(Built B Williams) (Hirth F30)
G-BWRM	Colt 105A Balloon (Hot Air)	3734		23. 4.96	N Charbonnier (Espace Mont Blanc titles)
					Aosta, Italy	16. 1.10E
G-BWRO	Europa Aviation Europa	196		22. 4.96	J G Murphy tr G-BWRO Group
	(Built E C Clark - pr.no.PFA 247-12849) (Monowheel u/c)					Morgansfield, Fishburn	8. 3.09P
G-BWRR	Cessna 182Q Skylane II	18266660	N95861	29. 3.94	D Ridley	Bagby	30. 7.09E
G-BWRS	SNCAN Stampe SV-4C	437	(N . . .)	24. 4.96	G P J M Valvekens (Stored 2006)	(Diest, Belgium)
			F-BCVQ			
G-BWRT	Cameron Concept 60 Balloon (Hot Air)	3078	EI-BYP	22.10.96	W R Teasdale	Maidenhead	9.11.09E
G-BWRY	Cameron N-105 Balloon (Hot Air)	3817		24. 4.96	G Aimo "Ferodo"	Mondovi, Italy	6. 5.06A
G-BWRZ	Lindstrand LBL 105A Balloon (Hot Air)	383		26. 4.96	D J Palmer	Bury St Edmunds	24. 4.09E
G-BWSB	Lindstrand LBL 105A Balloon (Hot Air)	384		26. 4.96	R Calvert-Fisher	Abingdon	9. 8.09E
G-BWSC	Piper PA-38-112 Tomahawk II	38-81A0125	N23203	29. 4.96	J C Field	Shipdham	22. 9.09E
G-BWSD	Campbell Cricket	PFA G/03-1216		3. 5.96	R F G Moyle	(Penryn)
	(Built R F G Moyle)
G-BWSG	British Aircraft Corporation BAC 145 Jet Provost T 5			13. 5.96	J Bell (As "XW324:K" in RAF 6FTS c/s)
		EEP/JP/988	XW324			(Nottingham)	20. 5.09P
G-BWSH	Hunting Percival P 84 Jet Provost T 3A		XN498	13. 5.96	Global Aviation Ltd (Noted 12.05)	Humberside	8. 7.03P
		PAC/W/10159				

G-BWSI	K & S SA.102.5 Cavalier PFA 001-10624		18. 4.84	B W Shaw	Wathstones Farm, Newby Wiske	19. 4.08P
	(Built B W Shaw) (Lycoming O-235)					
G-BWSJ	Denney Kitfox Model 3 PFA 172-12204		15. 5.96	J M Miller	Great Oakley	23. 7.09P
	(Built J M Miller)					
G-BWSL	Sky 77-24 Balloon (Hot Air) 004		16. 5.96	D Baggley	Stoke-on-Trent	19. 3.09E
G-BWSN	Denney Kitfox Model 3 PFA 172-12141		16. 5.96	M J Laundy	(London W5)	19. 3.08P
	(Built W J Forrest)					
G-BWSO	Cameron Apple 90 Balloon (Hot Air) 3915		17. 5.96	Flying Pictures Ltd *"Sainsbury's Apple"* Chilbolton		11. 6.02A
G-BWSP	Cameron Carrots 80 Balloon (Hot Air) 3914		17. 5.96	Flying Pictures Ltd *"Sainsbury's Carrots"* Chilbolton		5. 7.02A
G-BWST	Sky 200-24 Balloon (Hot Air) 036		20. 5.96	S A Townley t/a Sky High Leisure	Wrexham	28. 4.06T
G-BWSU	Cameron N-105 Balloon (Hot Air) 3848		20. 5.96	A M Marten *"Wonder Bra"*	Guildford	19.12.08E
G-BWSV	IAV-Bacau Yakovlev Yak-52 877601	DOSAAF 43	20. 5.96	M W Fitch	North Weald	19. 3.09P
G-BWSZ	Montgomerie-Bensen B 8MR PFA G/01-1268		14. 5.96	D Cawkwell	Goole	6. 1.98P
	(Built D Cawkwell) (Rotax 582)					
G-BWTB	Lindstrand LBL 105A Balloon (Hot Air) 374		29. 5.96	Servatruc Ltd	Nottingham	12. 8.09E
G-BWTC	Moravan Zlin Z-242L 0697		2. 8.96	S W Turley	Wickenby	7. 5.09E
G-BWTD	Moravan Zlin Z-242L 0698		2. 8.96	Oxford Aviation Academy (Oxford) Ltd	Oxford	19.11.09E
G-BWTE	Cameron O-140 Balloon (Hot Air) 3885		30. 5.96	T G Chuch t/a Pendle Balloon Co		
					Clayton le Dale, Blackburn	22. 2.09E
G-BWTG	de Havilland DHC-1 Chipmunk 22 C1/0119	WB671	4. 6.96	P M M de Graaf tr Chipmunk 4 Ever Foundation		
				(As "WB671:910" in RN c/s) Teuge, Netherlands		24. 9.06
G-BWTH	Robinson R22 Beta 1767	HB-XYD	5. 6.96	L L F Smith t/a Helicopter Services		
		N4052R			Wycombe Air Park	17. 7.09E
G-BWTJ	Cameron V-77 Balloon (Hot Air) 3917		7. 6.96	A J Montgomery	Yeovil	12. 6.07A
G-BWTK	Rotary Air Force RAF 2000 GTX-SE					
	(Built M P Lehermette) PFA G/13-1264		7. 6.96	M Love	Blackbushe	4. 6.09P
G-BWTN	Lindstrand LBL 90A Balloon (Hot Air) 357		12. 6.96	Clarks Drainage Ltd *(Clark's Drainage and Polypipe titles)*		
					Oakham	25. 6.09E
G-BWTO	de Havilland DHC-1 Chipmunk 22 C1/0852	WP984	5. 6.96	Skycraft Services Ltd *(As "WP984:H" in RAF c/s)*		
					Little Gransden	20.11.11
G-BWTR	Slingsby T 61F Venture T 2 1881	XZ561	12. 6.96	P R Williams	(Stow on the Wold)	
G-BWTW	Mooney M 20C Mark 21 20-1188	EI-CHI	5. 6.96	T J Berry	Kemble	17. 7.09E
		N6955V				
G-BWUA	Campbell Cricket replica PFA G/03-1248		17. 6.96	N J Orchard	(Portishead, Bristol)	31.10.07P
	(Built R T Lancaster)					
G-BWUB	Piper PA-18S-135 Super Cub *(L-21C)* 18-3986	N786CS	13. 6.96	Caledonian Seaplanes Ltd St Fillans, Loch Earn		12. 5.08T
	(Floatplane) (Regd with c/n 18-3786)	G-BWUB, SX-AHB, EI-263, I-EIUO, MM54-2586, 54-2586				
G-BWUE	Hispano HA.1112-MIL Buchon 223	N9938	14. 6.96	Spitfire Ltd *(As "1" [Red] in Luftwaffe c/s)* Duxford		21. 6.09P
	(Reported as c/n 172: C4K-154 was c/n 223)	G-AWHK, C4K-102				
	(Rebuilt Airframe Assemblies; at some stage fuselage of C4K-154 believed used in rebuild of N9938 c/n 172)					
G-BWUH	Piper PA-28-181 Archer III 2843048	N9272E	30. 8.96	Just Plane Trading Ltd		
		(G-BWUH)			Top Farm, Croydon, Royston	7.11.08E
G-BWUJ	RotorWay Executive 162F 6153		2. 7.96	Southern Helicopters Ltd Street Farm, Takeley		10. 8.09P
	(Built Southern Helicopters Ltd) (RotorWay RI 162F)					
G-BWUK	Sky 160-24 Balloon (Hot Air) 043		2. 7.96	Cameron Flights Southern Ltd		
					Woodborough, Pewsey	1. 3.09E
G-BWUL	Noorduyn AT-16 Harvard IIB 14A-1415	N16NA	4. 7.96	P Fama and F Scichilone *(As "FT375" in RAF c/s)*		
		G-BWUL, FT375, 43-13116			(Rome, Italy)	30. 6.09P
G-BWUN	de Havilland DHC-1 Chipmunk 22 C1/0253	WD310	5. 7.96	T Henderson *(As "WD310:B" in RAF c/s)*		
					Kittyhawk Farm, Deanland	6. 6.09
G-BWUP	Europa Aviation Europa 104		3. 7.96	G W Grant	Inverness	22. 6.07P
	(Built T J Harrison - pr.no.PFA 247-12703) (NSI EA-81/100) (Conventional u/c) (Stored 9.07)					
G-BWUS	Sky 65-24 Balloon (Hot Air) 040		16. 7.96	N A P Bates *"Sky Demo"*	Tunbridge Wells	17. 6.09E
G-BWUT	de Havilland DHC-1 Chipmunk 22 C1/0918	WZ879	4. 6.96	Aero Vintage Ltd *(As "WZ879:X" in RAF c/s)*		
					Duxford	15. 6.09S
G-BWUU	Cameron N-90 Balloon (Hot Air) 3954		17. 7.96	Bailey Balloons Ltd *"Discovery Channel"*		
					Pill, Bristol	5. 9.09E
G-BWUV	de Havilland DHC-1 Chipmunk 22A C1/0655	WK640	18. 7.90	P Ray *(As "WK640:C" in RAF c/s)*	Bagby	24. 2.11S
G-BWUZ	Campbell Cricket replica PFA G/03-1267		24. 6.96	K A Touhey	Little Rissington	22.10.08P
	(Built M A Concannon) (Rotax 582)					
G-BWVB	Pietenpol AirCamper PFA 047-11777		24. 7.96	M R Badminton	Baxby Manor, Husthwaite	11. 7.07P
	(Built M J Whatley) (Continental O-200-A)					
G-BWVC	Jodel D 18 PFA 169-11331		29. 7.96	R W J Cripps	(Spondon, Derby)	
	(Built R W J Cripps)					
G-BWVF	Pietenpol AirCamper PFA 047-11936		5. 8.96	N Clark	(New Milton)	
	(Built R M Sharphouse)					
G-BWVH	Robinson R44 Astro 0072	SX-HDE	10. 9.96	Bingley Aviation Ltd	Denham	17. 1.10E
		(D-HBBT)				
G-BWVI	Stern ST 80 Balade PFA 166-11190		7. 8.96	I M Godfrey-Davies		
	(Built P E Parker) (Volkswagen 1834)				Bourne Park, Hurstbourne Tarrant	11. 8.06P
G-BWVN	Whittaker MW7 PFA 171-11839		19. 8.96	L C Coyne	(Bishop's Stortford)	
	(Built J W May)					
G-BWVP	Sky 16-24 Balloon (Hot Air) 044		21. 8.96	JK (England) Ltd	London W1	7. 5.06
G-BWVR	IAV-Bacau Yakovlev Yak-52 878202	LY-AKQ	27. 8.96	I Parkinson *"52"*	Eshott	7.12.06P
		DOSAAF 134				
G-BWVS	Europa Aviation Europa 085		28. 8.96	D R Bishop	Popham	26. 6.09P
	(Built D R Bishop - pr.no.PFA 247-12686) (Monowheel u/c)					
G-BWVT	de Havilland DH.82A (Aust) Tiger Moth 1039	N71350	27. 8.96	R Jewitt	Fowle Hall Farm, Laddingford	7. 8.11
	(Built de Havilland Aircraft Pty Ltd)	VH-SNZ, A17-604, VH-AIN, A17-604				
G-BWVU	Cameron O-90 Balloon (Hot Air) 3204		28. 8.96	J Atkinson	Dorchester	3. 9.09E
G-BWVV	Jodel D 18 PFA 169-12699		29. 8.96	D S Howarth	Hawksbridge Farm, Oxenhope	20. 8.08P
	(Built P Cooper) (Volkswagen 1834)					
G-BWVY	de Havilland DHC-1 Chipmunk 22 C1/0766	WP896	3. 9.96	N Gardner *(As "WP896" in RAF c/s)*	(Harpenden)	6. 1.11

G-BWVZ	de Havilland DHC-1 Chipmunk 22	C1/0614	WK590	16. 7.96	D Campion (As "WK590:69" in RAF c/s)
					Grimbergen, Belgium 15. 4.11S
G-BWWA	Ultravia Pelican Club GS PFA 165-12242			6. 9.96	J S Aplin	Tirley, Gloucestershire 22. 5.08P
	(Built E F Clapham) (Rotax 912-UL)				
G-BWWB	Europa Aviation Europa	080		9. 9.96	S M O'Reilly	Redhill 21. 2.09P
	(Built M G Dolphin- pr.no.PFA 247-12670) (Monowheel u/c)				
G-BWWC	de Havilland DH.104 Dove 7	04498	XM223	14. 6.96	Air Atlantique Ltd (As "XM223" in RAF c/s) (Stored 6.02)
	(Wings from G-APSO fitted early 2000)				(Coventry)
G-BWWE	Lindstrand LBL 90A Balloon (Hot Air)	410		11. 9.96	B J Newman	Rushden, Northampton 17. 6.09E
G-BWWF	Cessna 185A Skywagon	185-0240	N4893K	13. 9.96	F Byrne and V M McCarthy
			G-BWWF, 9J-MCK, 5Y-BBG, ET-ACI, N4040Y		Hackettstown,
					County Carlow 12. 6.09E
G-BWWG	SOCATA Rallye 235E Gabier	13121	EI-BIF	23.10.96	J J Frew	City of Derry 28. 7.06
			HB-EYT, N344RA		
G-BWWI	Aérospatiale AS.332L Super Puma	2040	OY-HMF	11. 9.96	Bristow Helicopters Ltd "Johnshaven"	Aberdeen 8.11.09E
			(G-TIGT)		
G-BWWK	Hawker Nimrod I	41H-43617	S1581	13. 9.96	Patina Ltd (As "S1581:573" in RN 802 Sqdn c/s)
	(RR Kestrel)				Duxford 25. 6.09P
G-BWWL	Colt Flying Egg SS Balloon (Hot Air)	1813	JA-AC513	19. 9.96	Magical Adventures Ltd
					West Bloomfield, Michigan, US 2. 8.01A
G-BWWN	Isaacs Fury II PFA 011-10957			23. 9.96	F J Ball (As "K8303:D" in RAF c/s)
	(Built D H Pattison) (Lycoming O-235-H2C)				Jubilee Farm, Wisbech St Mary 13. 6.09P
G-BWWP	Rans S-6-116 Coyote II	1293.570		2.10.96	P Lewis	Park Farm, Eaton Bray 14. 9.09P
	(Built S A Beddus - pr.no.PFA 204A-12648) (Rotax 582) (Tailwheel u/c)				
G-BWWS	RAF 2000 GTX-SE PFA G/13-1277		U-P29	7.10.96	T D Grieve	Little Rissington 16. 8.09P
			G-BWWS		
G-BWWT	Dornier 328-100	3022	D-CDXO	12.11.96	Suckling Airways (Cambridge) Ltd t/a Scot Airways
			VT-VIG, D-CDHG		London City 8.11.09E
G-BWWU	Piper PA-22-150 Caribbean	22-5002	N7139D	9.10.96	K M Bowen	Upfield Farm, Whitson 17. 5.08
	(Hoerner wing-tips: tail-wheel conversion)				
G-BWWW	British Aerospace Jetstream Series 3102	614	G-31-614	8. 7.83	BAE Systems (Operations) Ltd (BAe Flying Test Bed)
					Cranfield 11. 6.11S
G-BWWX	Yakovlev Yak-50	853003	LY-AOI	11.10.96	D P McCoy	Weston, Leixlip, County Kildare 11. 6.09P
			DOSAAF		
G-BWWY	Lindstrand LBL 105A Balloon (Hot Air)	411		14.10.96	M J Smith (Corks and Cans Norton titles)
					Westow, York 10. 5.09E
G-BWXA	Slingsby T 67M-260 Firefly	2236		19. 3.96	Babcock Support Services Ltd t/a Babcock Defence Services
					RAF Barkston Heath 16.10.09E
G-BWXB	Slingsby T 67M-260 Firefly	2237		19. 3.96	Babcock Support Services Ltd t/a Babcock Defence Services
					RAF Barkston Heath 12.10.09E
G-BWXC	Slingsby T 67M-260 Firefly	2238		19. 3.96	Babcock Support Services Ltd t/a Babcock Defence Services
					(Operated DEFTS) RAF Barkston Heath 28. 9.09E
G-BWXD	Slingsby T 67M-260 Firefly	2239		19. 3.96	Babcock Support Services Ltd t/a Babcock Defence Services
					(Operated DEFTS) RAF Barkston Heath 14. 2.09E
G-BWXE	Slingsby T 67M-260 Firefly	2240		19. 3.96	Babcock Support Services Ltd t/a Babcock Defence Services
					RAF Barkston Heath 21. 7.09E
G-BWXF	Slingsby T 67M-260 Firefly	2241		19. 3.96	Babcock Support Services Ltd t/a Babcock Defence Services
					(Operated DEFTS) RAF Barkston Heath 18. 1.10E
G-BWXG	Slingsby T 67M-260 Firefly	2242		19. 3.96	Babcock Support Services Ltd t/a Babcock Defence Services
					(Operated DEFTS) RAF Barkston Heath 3. 7.09E
G-BWXH	Slingsby T 67M-260 Firefly	2243		19. 3.96	Babcock Support Services Ltd t/a Babcock Defence Services
					AAC Middle Wallop 20.10.09E
G-BWXI	Slingsby T 67M-260 Firefly	2244		19. 3.96	Babcock Support Services Ltd t/a Babcock Defence Services
					(Operated DEFTS) RAF Barkston Heath 28.11.09E
G-BWXJ	Slingsby T 67M-260 Firefly	2245		19. 3.96	Babcock Support Services Ltd t/a Babcock Defence Services
					(Operated DEFTS) RAF Barkston Heath 18. 1.10E
G-BWXK	Slingsby T 67M-260 Firefly	2246		19. 3.96	Babcock Support Services Ltd t/a Babcock Defence Services
					RAF Barkston Heath 3. 7.09E
G-BWXL	Slingsby T 67M-260 Firefly	2247		19. 3.96	Babcock Support Services Ltd t/a Babcock Defence Services
					RAF Barkston Heath 31. 1.10E
G-BWXM	Slingsby T 67M-260 Firefly	2248		19. 3.96	Babcock Support Services Ltd t/a Babcock Defence Services
					RAF Barkston Heath 1. 5.09E
G-BWXN	Slingsby T 67M-260 Firefly	2249		19. 3.96	Babcock Support Services Ltd t/a Babcock Defence Services
					RAF Barkston Heath 11. 3.09E
G-BWXO	Slingsby T 67M-260 Firefly	2250		19. 3.96	Babcock Support Services Ltd t/a Babcock Defence Services
					(Operated DEFTS) RAF Barkston Heath 21. 2.09E
G-BWXP	Slingsby T 67M-260 Firefly	2251		19. 3.96	D S McGregor	Rayne Hall Farm, Braintree 14. 3.09E
G-BWXR	Slingsby T 67M-260 Firefly	2252		19. 3.96	Babcock Support Services Ltd t/a Babcock Defence Services
					(Operated DEFTS) RAF Barkston Heath 6. 2.09E
G-BWXS	Slingsby T 67M-260 Firefly	2253		19. 3.96	Babcock Support Services Ltd t/a Babcock Defence Services
					(Operated DEFTS) "6" RAF Barkston Heath 10. 4.09E
G-BWXT	Slingsby T 67M-260 Firefly	2254		19. 3.96	Babcock Support Services Ltd t/a Babcock Defence Services
					(Operated DEFTS) RAF Barkston Heath 24. 4.09E
G-BWXU	Slingsby T 67M-260 Firefly	2255		19. 3.96	Babcock Support Services Ltd t/a Babcock Defence Services
					RAF Barkston Heath 9. 4.09E
G-BWXV	Slingsby T 67M-260 Firefly	2256		19. 3.96	Babcock Support Services Ltd t/a Babcock Defence Services
					RAF Barkston Heath 1. 7.09E
G-BWXW	Slingsby T 67M-260 Firefly	2257		19. 3.96	Babcock Support Services Ltd t/a Babcock Defence Services
					RAF Barkston Heath 6. 1.09E
G-BWXX	Slingsby T 67M-260 Firefly	2258		19. 3.96	Babcock Support Services Ltd t/a Babcock Defence Services
					RAF Barkston Heath 28. 2.09E
G-BWXY	Slingsby T 67M-260 Firefly	2259		19. 3.96	Babcock Support Services Ltd t/a Babcock Defence Services
					(Operated DEFTS) RAF Barkston Heath 30. 4.09E

G-BWXZ	Slingsby T 67M-260 Firefly	2260		19. 3.96	Babcock Support Services Ltd t/a Babcock Defence Services	
						RAF Barkston Heath 21. 8.09E
G-BWYB	Piper PA-28-160 Cherokee	28-263	N6374A	16. 9.96	I M Latiff	Little Staughton 21. 7.08E
			G-BWYB, 6Y-JLO, 6Y-JCH, VP-JCH			
G-BWYD	Europa Aviation Europa	072		28. 8.96	F H Mycroft	Kirknewton 3. 4.08P
	(Built H J Bendiksen - pr.no.PFA 247-12621) (Monowheel u/c)					
G-BWYE	Cessna 310R II	310R1654	F-GBPE	6. 9.96	ACS Contracts Ltd (stored 12.08)	Perth 10. 9.09E
			(N26369)			
G-BWYG	Cessna 310R II	310R1580	F-GBMY	28.10.96	R F Jones tr Kissair Aviation	Biggin Hill 28. 9.09E
			(N1820E)			
G-BWYI	Denney Kitfox Model 3	PFA 172-12143		30.10.96	M J Blanchard	Old Sarum 24. 7.08P
	(Built J Adamson) (Rotax 912)					
G-BWYK	Yakovlev Yak-50	812004	RA-01386	9. 8.96	R A L Hubbard tr Foley Farm Flying Group	
			DOSAAF 51			Redwood Cottage, Meon 22. 1.09P
G-BWYN	Cameron O-77 Balloon (Hot Air)	1162	G-ODER	13.11.96	W H Morgan "Hobo"	Swansea 4. 8.09E
G-BWYO	Sequoia F 8L Falco	PFA 100-10920		7.11.96	M C R Sims	Goodwood 16.10.09P
	(Built S Harper) (Lycoming O-320-E2A)					
G-BWYP	Sky 56-24 Balloon (Hot Air)	053		8.11.96	S A Townley t/a Sky High Leisure	Wrexham 9.11.01A
G-BWYR	Rans S-6-116 Coyote II	1294-700		8.11.96	E A Pearson	Weston Zoyland 18.10.07P
	(Built S Palmer - pr.no.PFA 204A-13058) (Rotax 912-UL) (Tailwheel u/c)					
G-BWYS	Cameron O-120 Balloon (Hot Air)	3997		30. 9.96	J M Stables t/a Aire Valley Balloons	
						Arkendale, Knaresborough 3. 4.09E
G-BWYU	Sky 120-24 Balloon (Hot Air)	052		13.11.96	Aerosaurus Balloons Ltd	Whimple, Exeter 15. 4.09E
G-BWZA	Europa Aviation Europa	063		1.11.96	T G Cowlishaw	Full Sutton 31.10.09P
	(Built M C Costin - pr.no.PFA 247-12626) (Monowheel u/c)					
G-BWZG	Robin R2160	311	F-WZZZ	6.11.96	Sherburn Aero Club Ltd	Sherburn-in-Elmet 17.10.08E
G-BWZJ	Cameron A-250 Balloon (Hot Air)	4021		2.12.96	Balloon School (International) Ltd t/a Balloon Club of	
					Great Britain	Colhook Common, Petworth 8. 5.09E
G-BWZU	Lindstrand LBL 90B Balloon (Hot Air)	418		12.12.96	K D Pierce	Cranbrook 21. 9.09E
G-BWZX	Aérospatiale AS.332L Super Puma	2120	F-WQDX	12.12.96	Bristow Helicopters Ltd "Muchalls"	Aberdeen 5. 5.09E
			G-BWZX, F-WQDX, 5V-MCD, 5V-TAH, LN-OLE			
G-BWZY	Hughes 269A (Hughes 300)	95-0378	G-FSDT	4.12.96	Reeve Newfields Ltd	Sywell 6. 3.09E
			N269CH, N1336D, 64-18066			

G-BXAA - G-BXZZ

G-BXAB	Piper PA-28-161 Warrior II	28-8416054	G-BTGK	7.10.96	TG Aviation Ltd	Manston 5.11.09E
			N4344C			
G-BXAC	Rotary Air Force RAF 2000 GTX-SE					
	(Built D C Fairbrass)	PFA G/13-1279		21.11.96	J A Robinson	Eaglescott 13. 6.08P
G-BXAD	Thunder Ax11-225 Series 2 Balloon (Hot Air)					
		4052		18.12.96	M E White	Trim, County Meath 24. 7.04T
G-BXAF	Pitts S-1D	PFA 009-12258		6.12.96	N J Watson	Sandown 23. 5.09P
	(Built F Sharples)					
G-BXAH	Piel CP.301A Emeraude	AB.422	D-EBAH	29.10.96	A P Goodwin	(Christchurch) 18. 8.09P
	(Built Fliegerclub Eichstatt EV) (Continental C90)					
G-BXAJ	Lindstrand LBL 14A Balloon (Gas-Filled)	425		23.12.96	Oscair Project AB	Täby, Sweden
G-BXAK	IAV-Bacau Yakovlev Yak-52	811508	LY-ASC	23.12.96	J Calverley	Tatenhill 20. 8.09P
			DOSAAF			
G-BXAL	Cameron Bertie Bassett 90 SS Balloon (Hot Air)			13. 1.97	Trebor Bassett Ltd "Bertie Bassett"	
		4034			(Operated Balloon Preservation Group) Petworth 27. 1.02A	
G-BXAM	Cameron N-90 Balloon (Hot Air)	4035		13. 1.97	Trebor Bassett Ltd "Bertie Junior" (Bassett's titles)	
						Shoreham 22. 4.04A
G-BXAN	Scheibe SF25C Falke	44299	D-KDGQ	13. 1.97	J P Harrison tr C Falke Syndicate	Darlton 23. 4.09E
	(Limbach SL1700)					
G-BXAO	Avtech Jabiru SK	0099		14. 1.97	P J Thompson	(Llanddaniel, Gaerwen) 23. 4.99P
	(Built I M Donnelly - pr.no.PFA 274-13066)				(Damaged Ledicot near Shobdon 3. 5.98)	
G-BXAR	British Aerospace Avro 146-RJ100	E3298	G-6-298	27. 3.97	BA Cityflyer Ltd	London City 29. 3.09E
G-BXAS	British Aerospace Avro 146-RJ100	E3301	G-6-301	23. 4.97	BA Cityflyer Ltd	Manchester 29. 4.09E
G-BXAU	Pitts S-1	GHG.9	N9GG	22. 1.97	L Westnage	
	(Built G Goodrich) (Lycoming O-320)					Little Rissington 3. 1.08P
	(Lower left wing struck the runway after landing at Kemble 16. 7.08; aircraft ground looped damaging undercarriage and fuselage)					
G-BXAV	Aerostar Yakovlev Yak-52	9111608	RA-01325	24. 1.97	RA 293 Group Ltd	Tatenhill 22. 7.09P
			DOSAAF 73			
G-BXAY	Bell 206B-3 JetRanger III	3946	N85EA	24. 1.97	Viewdart Ltd	Conington 22. 9.08E
			N521RC, N3210D			
G-BXBA	Cameron A-210 Balloon (Hot Air)	4072		10. 1.97	Reach For The Sky Ltd	Guildford 31. 7.09E
G-BXBC	Anderson EA-1 Kingfisher Amphibian			28. 1.97	S Bichan (Noted 12.05) Lamb Holm Farm, Orkney	
	(Built S Bichan)	PFA 132-11302				
G-BXBK	Mudry CAP.10B	17	N170RC	30. 1.97	S Skipworth	White Waltham 8. 5.09E
			French AF "307-SO"			
G-BXBL	Lindstrand LBL 240A Balloon (Hot Air)	317		31. 1.97	J Fenton t/a Firefly Balloon Promotions Preston 4. 5.09E	
G-BXBM	Cameron O-105 Balloon (Hot Air)	3990		31. 1.97	P Spellward tr Bristol University Hot Air Ballooning Society	
						Bristol 10. 2.07A
G-BXBP	Denney Kitfox Model 2	PFA 172-12149		3. 2.97	N J Kerr tr Flying Spanners Group	Shoreham 18.11.06P
	(Built G S Adams)					
G-BXBR	Cameron A-120 Balloon (Hot Air)	1983	SE-ZDY	4. 2.97	M G Barlow (Active 5.07))	Carelton, Skipton
G-BXBU	Mudry CAP.10B	103	N173RC	11. 2.97	J F Cosgrave and H R Pearson	
			French AF			Luxter's Farm, Hambledon 31. 7.09E
G-BXBY	Cameron A-105 Balloon (Hot Air)	4077		13. 2.97	D J Littlewood (Roman Baths titles)	Bath 9. 4.09E
G-BXBZ	PZL-104 Wilga 80	CF21930941	EC-GDA	13. 2.97	J H Sandham t/a J H Sandham Aviation	Carlisle 2. 7.09E
			ZK-PZQ			
G-BXCA	Hapi Cygnet SF-2A	PFA 182-12921		22. 1.97	J D C Henslow "Fighting Cygnets"	(Midhurst) 5. 9.09E
	(Built G E Collard) (Rotax 912-UL)					

Reg	Type	C/n	Prev id	Date	Owner/Operator	Base	Status
G-BXCC	Piper PA-28-201T Turbo Dakota	28-7921068	D-EKBM N2855A	19. 2.97	Greer Aviation Ltd	(Prestwick)	15. 1.10E
G-BXCD	TEAM Mini-MAX 91A (Built R Davies) (Rotax 503)	PFA 186-12393		18. 2.97	R Davies	RAF Halton	19. 3.09P
G-BXCG	Jodel DR.250 (Built J M Scott - pr.no.PFA 299-13146)	060	D-EHGG	22. 5.97	J C Carter tr CG Group	Cambridge	26. 8.09P
G-BXCH	Europa Aviation Europa (Built D M Stevens - pr.no.PFA 247-12980) (Monowheel u/c)	186		19. 2.97	R E T Hatton	Enstone	18. 6.07P
G-BXCJ	Campbell Cricket replica (Built R A Friend) (Rotax 532)	PFA G/03-1177		24. 2.97	A G Peel	Little Rissington	28. 4.09P
G-BXCL	Montgomerie-Bensen B 8MR (Built A V Francis) (Rotax 582)	PFA G/01-1287		26. 2.97	M L L Temple	Eddsfield	2. 8.09P
G-BXCM	Lindstrand LBL 150A Balloon (Hot Air)	443		26. 2.97	Aerosaurus Balloons Ltd	Whimple, Exeter	4. 7.07E
G-BXCN	Sky 105-24 Balloon (Hot Air) "Rainbow"	047	(PH-RTH)	27. 2.97	A S Davidson tr Nottingham Hot Air Balloon Club	Woodville, Swadlincote	12. 8.09E
G-BXCO	Colt 120A Balloon (Hot Air)	4086		3. 3.97	J R Lawson (Super Golf Invicta titles)	High Easter, Chelmsford	20.10.09E
G-BXCP	de Havilland DHC-1 Chipmunk 22	C1/0744	WP859	27. 2.97	Propshop Ltd (As "WP859:E" in RAF c/s)	Duxford	9.10.11
G-BXCT	de Havilland DHC-1 Chipmunk 22	C1/0145	WB697	3. 3.97	J W Frecklington and R Merewood tr Wickenby Aviation (As "WB697:95" in RAF c/s)	Wickenby	2. 5.09S
G-BXCU	Rans S-6-116 Coyote II (Built M R McNeil - pr.no.PFA 204A-13105) (Rotax 912-UL) (Tri-cycle u/c)	1096.1044		6. 3.97	R S Gent	Leicester	11. 5.09P
G-BXCV	de Havilland DHC-1 Chipmunk 22	C1/0807	WP929	3. 3.97	Ardmore Aviation Services Ltd (As "WP929" in RAF c/s)	Duxford	18. 2.10S
G-BXCW	Denney Kitfox Model 3 (Built M J Blanchard)	PFA 172-12619		6. 3.97	M J Blanchard	Old Sarum	7.11.06P
G-BXDA	de Havilland DHC-1 Chipmunk 22	C1/0747	WP860	7. 3.97	S R Cleary and D Mowat (As "WP860:6" in RAF c/s)	Kirknewton	17. 8.09S
G-BXDB	Cessna U206F Stationair	U20602233	G-BMNZ F-BVJT, N1519U	18.12.96	D A Howard	Colonsay, Isle of Colonsay	2. 9.08E
G-BXDD	Rotary Air Force RAF 2000 GTX-SE (Built R M Savage)	PFA G/13-1284		9. 1.97	R M Harris	(Nottingham)	
G-BXDE	Rotary Air Force RAF 2000 GTX-SE (Built A McCredie)	PFA G/13-1280		14. 1.97	B Jones	(Grimsby)	9. 6.09P
G-BXDF	Beech 95-B55 Baron	TC-2011	SE-IXG OY-ASB	7. 3.97	Chesh-Air Ltd	Liverpool-John Lennon	6. 2.10E
G-BXDG	de Havilland DHC-1 Chipmunk 22	C1/0644	WK630	7. 3.97	Felthorpe Flying Group Ltd (As "WK630" in RAF c/s)	Felthorpe	4. 11.10S
G-BXDH	de Havilland DHC-1 Chipmunk 22	C1/0270	WD331	10. 3.97	D F Ranger (As "WD331" in RAF c/s)	Popham	26. 5.08
G-BXDI	de Havilland DHC-1 Chipmunk 22	C1/0312	WD373	10. 3.97	Propshop Ltd (As "WD373:12" in RAF c/s)	Duxford	22.10.09S
G-BXDM	de Havilland DHC-1 Chipmunk 22	C1/0723	WP840	28. 2.97	Ace Leasing Ltd (As "WP840:9" in RAF c/s)	Conington	12. 4.09S
G-BXDN	de Havilland DHC-1 Chipmunk 22	C1/0618	WK609	18. 3.97	W D Lowe and L A Edwards (As "WK609:93" in RAF c/s)	Wycombe Air Park	15. 2.10
G-BXDO	Rutan Cozy (Built C R Blackburn) (Lycoming O-235) (Force landed near Junction 12 on M5 10. 7.04 and substantially damaged: on rebuild 2008 from remnants of LongEz G-BLZH)	PFA 159-12032		21. 3.97	J Foreman	Lydd	4. 7.05P
G-BXDP	de Havilland DHC-1 Chipmunk 22	C1/0659	WK642	27. 2.97	T A McBennet and J Kelly (As "WK642" in RAF c/s)	Kilrush, County Kildare	7.10.06
G-BXDR	Lindstrand LBL 77A Balloon (Hot Air)	441		25. 3.97	British Telecommunications PLC "Bright Future"	Thatcham	6. 9.09E
G-BXDT	Robin HR.200-120B	315		25. 3.97	Multiflight Ltd	Leeds-Bradford	8. 6.09E
G-BXDU	Aero Designs Pulsar (Built M P Board) (Tri-cycle u/c)	PFA 202-11991		25. 3.97	M P Board	Damyn's Hall, Upminster	18. 6.09P
G-BXDV	Sky 105-24 Balloon (Hot Air)	049		26. 3.97	A Parsons tr Loughborough Students Union Hot Air Balloon Club	Loughborough	1. 5.09E
G-BXDY	Europa Aviation Europa (Built D G Watts - pr.no.PFA 247-12914: sequence no.conflicts with G-MYZP) (Monowheel u/c)	229		27. 3.97	D G and S.Watts "The Rocketeer"	Fowle Hall Farm, Laddingford	15. 5.09P
G-BXDZ	Lindstrand LBL 105A Balloon (Hot Air)	437		4. 4.97	D J and A D Sutcliffe "Akito/Yes"	Harrogate	27. 9.09E
G-BXEA	Rotary Air Force RAF 2000 GTX-SE (Built R Firth)	PFA G/13-1270		2. 4.97	R Firth	Netherthorpe	23. 5.06P
G-BXEC	de Havilland DHC-1 Chipmunk 22	C1/0647	WK633	3. 4.97	D S Hunt (As "WK633:B" in RAF c/s)	Redhill	28. 6.07
G-BXEJ	Magni M-16 Tandem Trainer (Arrow GT 1000)	D-9302	D-MIFF	8. 4.97	N H Collins t/a AES Radionic Surveillance Systems	Cork Farm, Streethay	9. 6.09P
G-BXEN	Cameron N-105 Balloon (Hot Air) (New envelope c/n 10288, 3.03)	4090		11. 4.97	G Aimo "Liquigas"	Mondovi, Piedmont, Italy	11.12.09E
G-BXES	Hunting Percival P 66 Pembroke C 1 (Regd with c/n PAC/W/3032)	P66/101	N4234C 9042M, XL954	14. 4.97	Air Atlantique Ltd (As "XL954" in RAF 60 Sqdn c/s)	Coventry	9. 5.07P
G-BXET	Piper PA-38-112 Tomahawk	38-80A0028	N25089	14. 4.97	Highland Flying School Ltd	Inverness	5. 5.09E
G-BXEX	Piper PA-28-181 Cherokee Archer II	28-7790463	N3562Q	16. 4.97	R Mayle	Redhill	23. 8.09E
G-BXEY	Colt AS-105 GD Airship (Hot Air)	3936		15. 4.97	D Mayer "Luftwerbung"	Felsberg, Germany	23. 3.09P
G-BXEZ	Cessna 182P Skylane II (Reims assembled c/n F18200054)	18264344	OH-CHJ N1479M	16. 4.97	Forhawk Ltd	Perranporth	3. 6.09E
G-BXFB	Pitts S-1 (Built B J Dziuba)	9543	N77ZZ	16. 4.97	O P Sparrow tr Foxtrot Bravo Flying Group	Redhill	29. 4.09P
G-BXFC	Jodel D 18 (Builllt B S Godbold) (Revmaster 2100D)	PFA 169-11322		17. 4.97	B S Godbold	Little Gransden	28. 7.09P
G-BXFE	Mudry CAP 10B	135	N175RC French AF	18. 4.97	Avion Aerobatic Ltd	White Waltham	8. 4.09E
G-BXFG	Europa Aviation Europa (Built A Rawicz-Szczerbo - pr.no.PFA 247-12500) (Monowheel u/c)	018		21. 4.97	A Rawicz-Szczerbo	Eaglescott	11. 7.09P

G-BXFI	Hawker Hunter T 7	41H-670815	WV372	24. 4.97	Fox-One Ltd *(As "WV372:R" in RAF 2 Sqdn c/s)*
					Kemble　7. 8.09P
G-BXFK	CFM Streak Shadow	K 206		24. 4.97	W J Bernasinski　(Crawley Down, Crawley)　30. 8.09P
	(Built D Adcock - pr.no.PFA 206-12329) (Rotax 582)				
G-BXFN	Cameron Colt 77A Balloon (Hot Air)	4145		25. 4.97	Charter Ballooning Ltd　Liphook　27. 4.09E
G-BXGA	Eurocopter AS.350B2 Ecureuil	2493	OO-RCH	30. 4.97	PLM Dollar Group Ltd　(Cumbernauld)　27. 8.09E
			OO-XCH, F-WZFX		
G-BXGD	Sky 90-24 Balloon (Hot Air)	067		6. 5.97	Servo and Electronic Sales Ltd
					(Operated Cameron Flights Southern) Woodborough, Pewsey　10. 3.09E
G-BXGG	Europa Aviation Europa	178		29. 4.97	C J H and P A J Richardson
	(Built B W Faulkner - pr.no.PFA 247-12803) (Monowheel u/c)				Bremridge Farm, Shillingford　15. 6.09P
G-BXGH	Diamond DA.20-A1 Katana	10151		20. 5.97	M Dorrian　(Glasgow)　16. 7.09E
G-BXGL	de Havilland DHC-1 Chipmunk 22	C1/0924	WZ884	12. 5.97	Airways Aero Associations Ltd　Wycombe Air Park　30. 1.10S
					(Operated British Airways Flying Club)
G-BXGM	de Havilland DHC-1 Chipmunk 22	C1/0806	WP928	9. 5.97	D Parkinson tr Chipmunk G-BXGM Group
					(As "WP928:D" in AAC c/s)　Shoreham　17.11.09S
G-BXGO	de Havilland DHC-1 Chipmunk 22	C1/0097	WB654	13. 5.97	I C Barlow and T J Orchard tr Trees Group
					(As "WB654:U" in AAC c/s)　Wycombe Air Park　26.10.09
G-BXGP	de Havilland DHC-1 Chipmunk 22	C1/0927	WZ882	12. 5.97	T K Pullen tr Eaglescott Chipmunk Group
					(As "WZ882:K" in AAC c/s)　Eaglescott　20. 8.07T
G-BXGS	Rotary Air Force RAF 2000	PFA G/13-1290		14. 5.97	C R Gordon　(Cupar)　4.12.08P
	(Built N C White)				
G-BXGT	III Sky Arrow 650 T	PFA 298-13085		7. 5.97	J S C Goodale　Popham　15. 8.08P
	(Built Sky Arrow (Kits) UK Ltd)				
G-BXGV	Cessna 172R Skyhawk	17280240	N9300F	7. 1.98	P Cooke tr Skyhawk Group　White Waltham　18. 2.09E
G-BXGW	Robin HR.200-120B	317		16. 5.97	Multiflight Ltd *(Operated Multiflight Club)*
					Leeds-Bradford　1.12.09E
G-BXGX	de Havilland DHC-1 Chipmunk 22	C1/0609	WK586	19. 5.97	Interflight (Air Charter) Ltd) *(As "WK586:V" in AAC c/s)*
					Duxford　6. 8.10S
G-BXGY	Cameron V-65 Balloon (Hot Air)	4125		18. 4.97	R J Plume tr Dante Balloon Group　Northwood　26. 3.09E
G-BXGZ	Stemme S 10-V	14-023	D-KSTE	18. 8.97	D Tucker and K Lloyd "S10"　Aston Down　2. 4.09E
			EC-GGD, D-KGDF		
G-BXHA	de Havilland DHC-1 Chipmunk 22	C1/0801	WP925	20. 5.97	F A de Munck and C S Huijers *(As "WP925:C" in AAC c/s)*
					Seppe-Hoeven, Netherlands　27.11.11
G-BXHD	Beech 76 Duchess	ME-284	OY-ARM	22. 5.97	Plane Talking Ltd *(Operated Cabair)* Bournemouth　10. 9.09E
			N223JC		
G-BXHE	Lindstrand LBL 105A Balloon (Hot Air)	459		23. 5.97	L H Ellis　Burcott, Leighton Buzzard　4. 9.09E
G-BXHF	de Havilland DHC-1 Chipmunk 22	C1/0808	WP930	28. 5.97	R A Wallis tr Hotel Fox Sydicate　*(As "WP930:J" in AAC c/s)*
					Redhill　13. 5.10
G-BXHH	Grumman AA-5A Cheetah	AA5A-0105	N9705U	3. 6.97	M G Greenslade tr Oaklands Flying　Biggin Hill　12. 6.09E
G-BXHJ	Hapi Cygnet SF-2A	PFA 182-12159		29. 5.97	I J Smith　Brook Farm, Boylestone
	(Built I J Smith) (Volkswagen 1835)				
G-BXHL	Sky 77-24 Balloon (Hot Air)	055		29. 5.97	R K Gyselynck "Harlequin"　Port Erin, Isle of Man　9. 8.09E
G-BXHN	Lindstrand LBL Pop Can SS Balloon (Hot Air)			30. 5.97	R S Kent t/a Ornithological Desires Balloon Group
		465			Petworth　29. 5.06A
G-BXHO	Lindstrand Telewest Sphere SS Balloon (Hot Air)			30. 5.97	Magical Adventures Ltd *(Telewest titles)*
		474			West Bloomfield, Mi, USA　30. 9.09E
G-BXHR	Stemme S 10-V	14-030	D-KSTE	23. 7.97	J H Rutherford　Sleap　21. 2.09E
G-BXHT	Bushby-Long Midget Mustang	PFA 168-13077		3. 6.97	P P Chapman　Headcorn　16. 4.09P
	(Built P P Chapman)				
G-BXHU	Campbell Cricket Mk.6	PFA G/16-1293		3. 6.97	P J Began　Henstridge　18. 8.06P
	(Built P C Lovegrove) (Rotax 503)				
G-BXHY	Europa Aviation Europa	022		6. 6.97	A L Thorne and B Lewis tr Jupiter Flying Group
	(Built A L Thorne - pr.no.PFA 247-12514) (Monowheel u/c)				White Waltham　12. 3.09P
G-BXIA	de Havilland DHC-1 Chipmunk 22	C1/0056	WB615	9. 6.97	W Askew and C Duckett tr Dales Aviation
					(As "WB615:E" in AAC c/s)　Blackpool　12. 6.09S
G-BXIC	Cameron A-275 Balloon (Hot Air)	4162		9. 6.97	Aerosaurus Balloons Ltd　Whimple, Exeter　10. 9.09E
G-BXIE	Cameron Colt 77B Balloon (Hot Air)	4181		11. 6.97	L C Sanders　Marden, Hereford　17. 6.09E
G-BXIF	Piper PA-28-181 Cherokee Archer II		PH-SWM	12. 6.97	Piper Flight Ltd　Cardiff　12. 8.09E
		28-7690404	OO-HAY, N6827J		
G-BXIG	Zenair CH.701 STOL	PFA 187-12065		16. 6.97	A J Perry　Marsh Farm, Bracklesham　23. 9.09P
	(Built A J Perry)				
G-BXIH	Sky 200-24 Balloon (Hot Air)	076		16. 6.97	Skyview Ballooning Ltd t/a Kent Ballooning Ashford　5.12.08E
G-BXII	Europa Aviation Europa	175		30. 4.97	D A McFadyean　Long Marston　11. 9.09P
	(Built D A McFadyean - pr.no.PFA 247-12812) (Tailwheel u/c)				
G-BXIJ	Europa Aviation Europa	076		16. 6.97	R James　Shobdon　27. 4.09P
	(Built D G and E A Bligh - pr.no.PFA 247-12698) (Monowheel u/c)				
G-BXIM	de Havilland DHC-1 Chipmunk 22	C1/0548	WK512	13. 5.97	P R Joshua and A B Ascroft *(As "WK512:A" in AAC c/s)*
					RAF Brize Norton　5. 7.09
G-BXIO	SAN Jodel DR.1050M Excellence	493	F-BNIO	16. 5.97	R S Palmer　Sandown　2. 9.09P
G-BXIT	Zebedee V-31 Balloon (Hot Air)	Z1/3999		8. 5.97	P J Bish *(Active 10.06)*　Newtown, Hungerford
	(Built Zebedee Balloon Service)				
G-BXIW	Sky 105-24 Balloon (Hot Air)	073		24. 6.97	Idea Balloon SAS Di Stefano Travaglia and Co
					Firenze, Italy　9. 7.09E
G-BXIX	Magni M-16 Tandem Trainer	PFA G/12-1292		13. 6.97	D Beevers　Melrose Farm, Melbourne　20. 8.09P
	(Built D Beevers) (Arrow GT1000R)				
G-BXIY	Blake Bluetit	01	BAPC.37	26. 6.97	J Bryant *(Noted 1.09)*　North Weald
	(Built W H C Blake) (Gnat 32hp) (Pre-war composite from Spartans G-AAGN, G-AAJB and Avro 504K)				
G-BXIZ	Lindstrand LBL 31A Balloon (Hot Air)	476		3. 7.97	I Chadwick tr Balloon Preservation Flying Group
					Partridge Green, Horsham　9.11.09E
G-BXJA	Cessna 402B	402B0356	N5753M	17. 7.97	Reconnaissance Ventures Ltd　Coventry　17.10.07T
			XA-RFK, N5753M		
G-BXJB	IAV-Bacau Yakovlev Yak-52	877403	LY-ABR	30. 6.97	D Leggett tr Bumbles Angels "15"　Earls Colne　22. 1.09P
			DOSAAF 15		

Reg	Type	C/n	Prev ID	Date	Owner/Operator	Location	Expiry
G-BXJC	Cameron A-210 Balloon (Hot Air)	419		12. 7.97	Balloon School (International) Ltd t/a British School of Ballooning	Colhook Common, Petworth	7. 5.09E
G-BXJD	Piper PA-28-180 Cherokee C	28-4215	OY-BBZ	27. 6.97	M A Powell	Shobdon	17. 3.09E
G-BXJG	Lindstrand LBL 105B Balloon (Hot Air)	478		11. 7.97	C E Wood	Witham	1. 7.09E
G-BXJH	Cameron N-42 Balloon (Hot Air)	4194		15. 7.97	B Conway	Wheatley, Oxford	22. 9.01A
G-BXJJ	Piper PA-28-161 Cadet	2841200	EC-IGN, G-BXJJ, G-GFCC, N9189N	26. 6.97	Plane Talking Ltd *(Operated Cabair)*	Elstree	8.12.09E
G-BXJM	Cessna 152 II	15282380	OO-HOQ, F-GHOQ, N68797	15. 7.97	ACS Aviation Ltd *(Operated Leading Edge)*	Perth	19.11.09E
G-BXJO	Cameron O-90 Balloon (Hot Air)	4190		16. 7.97	Dragon Balloon Company Ltd	Castleton, Hope Valley	18. 2.09E
G-BXJP	Cameron C-80 Balloon (Hot Air)	4171		17. 7.97	AR Cobaleno Pasta Fresca SRL *(Arco Baleno titles)*	Basta Umbria, Perugia, Italy	1. 4.06A
G-BXJS	Schempp-Hirth Janus CM	35/265	OH-819	7. 7.97	R A Hall tr Janus Syndicate	Enstone	3. 2.10E
G-BXJT	Sky 90-24 Balloon (Hot Air)	072		18. 7.97	J G O'Connell	(Braintree)	18.11.07A
G-BXJV	Diamond DA.20-A1 Katana	10152		23. 7.97	Enniskillen Flying School Ltd	Enniskillen	7. 8.09E
G-BXJW	Diamond DA.20-A1 Katana	10211	(OE- VPX), N811CH, C-FDVA	23. 7.97	Enniskillen Flying School Ltd	Enniskillen	26. 8.09E
G-BXJY	Van's RV-6 *(Built D J Sharland) (Lycoming O-320-D3G)*	PFA 181-12447		23. 7.97	D J Sharland	Popham	10. 5.09P
G-BXJZ	Cameron C-60 Balloon (Hot Air)	4168		23. 7.97	R S Mohr	Ditteridge, Box, Chippenham	12. 8.09E
G-BXKF	Hawker Hunter T 7 *(Regd with c/n 41H-003315)*	HABL-003314	8676M, XL577	28. 7.97	R F Harvey *(As "XL577/V" in colours of RAF 92 Sqdn "Blue Diamonds" aerobatic team)*	Kemble	9.10.09P
G-BXKL	Bell 206B-3 JetRanger III	3006	N5735Y	8.10.97	Swattons Aviation Ltd	Thruxton	18.11.09E
G-BXKM	Rotary Air Force RAF 2000 GTX-SE *(Built J R Huggins)*	PFA G/13-1291		5. 8.97	P J Houtman	Little Rissington	9. 9.09P
G-BXKO	Sky 65-24 Balloon (Hot Air)	083		11. 8.97	J-M Reck	Evette-Salbert, France	20. 2.09E
G-BXKU	Colt AS-120 Mk.II Airship (Hot Air)	4165		15. 8.97	D C Chipping	Grantham	19. 4.01A
G-BXKW	Slingsby T 67M-200 Firefly	2061	VR-HZS, HKG-13, G-7-129	15. 8.97	N A and LM Whatling *(As "HKG-13" in Royal Hong Kong AAF c/s)*	Spanhoe	17. 6.09E
G-BXKX	Taylorcraft J Auster 5	803	D-EMXA, HB-EOK, MS938	19. 8.97	J A Clark	Orchard Farm, Sittingbourne	5. 6.08
G-BXLC	Sky 120-24 Balloon (Hot Air)	085		20. 8.97	Dragon Balloon Company Ltd	Mexico City, Mexico	23. 3.08A
G-BXLF	Lindstrand LBL 90A Balloon (Hot Air)	487		3. 9.97	J Tyrrell and W Rousell *(Variohm Components titles)*	Wollaston, Wellingborough	30. 8.09E
G-BXLG	Cameron C-80 Balloon (Hot Air)	4250		5. 3.98	S M Anthony	Northam, Bideford	27. 5.07A
G-BXLK	Europa Aviation Europa *(Built R G Fairall - pr.no.PFA 247-12613) (Monowheel u/c)*	074		11. 9.97	R G Fairall	Redhill	12. 8.09E
G-BXLN	Fournier RF4D	4022	F-BORK	15. 9.97	P W Cooper	(Eaton, Congleton)	26. 5.09E
G-BXLO	Hunting Percival P 84 Jet Provost T 4	PAC/W/19986	9032M, XR673	14. 8.97	S J Davies and S Eagle *(As "XR673" in RAF c/s)*	(Rotherham and Doncaster)	19. 9.09P
G-BXLP	Sky 90-24 Balloon (Hot Air)	084		18. 9.97	G B Lescott *"Heart of Gold"*	Oxford	3.12.09E
G-BXLR	PZL-110 Koliber 160A	04980077	SP-WGF (2), (SP-WGF (1)), (N150CD)	10. 6.98	I Foster tr Sligo Koliber Group	Strandhill, Sligo, County Sligo	18. 3.09E
G-BXLS	PZL-110 Koliber 160A	04980078	SP-WGG (2), SP-PEB (2), (SP-WGG (1) (N150CP)	23. 6.98	D C Bayes	Gamston	20. 9.09E
G-BXLT	SOCATA TB-200 Tobago XL	1457	F-GRBB, EC-FNX, EC-234, F-GLFP	28. 4.97	R M Shears	Fairoaks	18. 6.09E
G-BXLW	Enstrom F-28F	734	N279SA, G-BXLW, Thai Government/KASET 1712	11. 9.97	I Martin	Barton	14.10.07E
G-BXLY	Piper PA-28-151 Cherokee Warrior (modified) *(Type amended 28. 2.08)*	28-7715220	G-WATZ, N7641F	19. 9.97	Multiflight Ltd	Leeds-Bradford	13. 5.09E
G-BXMF	Cassutt Racer IIIM *(Built J F Bakewell)*	PFA 034-13003		19. 9.97	P R Fabish	Cambridge	30. 7.09P
G-BXMG	Rotary Air Force RAF 2000 *(Built G Hansen)*	H2-92-3-59	PH-TEN	18. 8.97	J S Wright	(Huddersfield)	17.12.03P
G-BXMK	Lindstrand LBL 240A Balloon (Hot-Air)	324	PH-GPJ, G-BXMK	25. 9.97	M E White	Trim, Ireland	12.10.09E
G-BXML	Mooney M 20A	1594	OY-AIZ	26. 9.97	G Kay	Crosland Moor	28. 7.08E
G-BXMM	Cameron A-180 Balloon (Hot Air)	4252		28.10.97	B Conway	Wheatley, Oxford	3.11.00A
G-BXMV	Scheibe SF25C Falke *(Limbach SL1700)*	44223	D-KDFV	7. 8.97	K E Ballington	Yeatsall Farm, Abbots Bromley	24. 7.09E
G-BXMX	Phoenix Currie Wot *(Built M J Hayman)*	PFA 058-13055		23. 9.97	M R Coreth	Compton Abbas	18. 6.09P
G-BXMY	Hughes 269C *(Hughes 300)*	74-0328	N9599F	20.10.97	R J Scott	Ashleigh Farm, Bracknell	28. 8.09E
G-BXMZ	Diamond DA.20-A1 Katana	10236	C-GDMB	4.12.97	Lombard North Central PLC	Gamston	5.11.09E
G-BXNA	Avid Flyer *(Built L Pickett) (Rotax 503)*	118	N5531J	10.10.97	A P Daines	(Great Yeldham, Halstead)	14.10.08P
G-BXNC	Europa Aviation Europa *(Built J K Cantwell - pr.no.PFA 247-12970)*	122		13.10.97	J K Cantwell	(Ashton-under-Lyne)	
G-BXNN	de Havilland DHC-1 Chipmunk 22	C1/0849	WP983	4. 8.97	J N Robinson *(As "WP983:B" in AAC c/s)*	Trenchard Farm, Eggesford	24. 4.08
G-BXNS	Bell 206B-3 JetRanger III	2385	N16822	3.11.97	Sterling Helicopters Ltd	Norwich	21.12.09E
G-BXNT	Bell 206B-3 JetRanger III	2398	N94CA, N123AL	11.11.97	Sterling Helicopters Ltd	Hawarden	6.11.09E
G-BXNV	Colt AS-105 GD Airship (Hot Air)	4231		19. 2.98	The Sleeping Society	Edegem, Belgium	24. 7.04A
G-BXNX	Lindstrand LBL 210A Balloon (Hot Air)	318		3.11.97	Balloon School (International) Ltd	Colhook Common, Petworth	24. 3.05T
G-BXOA	Robinson R22 Beta	1614	N41132, JA7832	10.11.97	MG Group Ltd	Sywell	12. 3.09E
G-BXOC	Evans VP-2 *(Built H J Cox)*	PFA 063-10305		29. 9.97	H J and E M Cox	(Bideford)	29. 4.08P
G-BXOF	Diamond DA.20-A1 Katana	10256	C-FDVP	4.12.97	M Dorrian	(Glasgow)	5. 2.09E
G-BXOI	Cessna 172R Skyhawk	17280145	N9990F	17.11.97	E J Watts	Bodmin	25. 1.10E

Reg	Type	C/n	Prev id	Date	Owner/Operator	Location	CofA
G-BXOJ	Piper PA-28-161 Warrior III	2842010	N9265G	15.12.97	Craigard Property Trading Ltd	Coventry	5. 3.09E
G-BXOM	Isaacs Spitfire	PFA 027-12768		25.11.97	J H Betton	(Betws, Ammanford)	
	(Built J H Betton)						
G-BXON	Auster AOP.9	xxxx	WZ729	1.12.97	C J and D J Baker *(On rebuild 1.05)*		
	(Officially regd with Frame no.AUS/10/60)					Carr Farm, Thorney, Newark	
G-BXOR	Robin HR.200-120B	321		1.12.97	Multiflight Ltd	Leeds-Bradford	23. 4.09E
G-BXOS	Cameron A-200 Balloon (Hot Air)	4286		19. 2.98	Airborne Balloon Management Ltd		
						Paddock Wood, Tonbridge	22. 5.04T
G-BXOT	Cameron C-70 Balloon (Hot Air)	4200		21.10.97	R J Plume tr Dante Balloon Group	Hungerford	9. 7.09E
G-BXOU	CEA Jodel DR.360 Chevalier	312	F-BPOU	6.10.97	J A Lofthouse	Blackpool	20. 5.09E
G-BXOW	Cameron Colt 105A Balloon (Hot Air)	4228		9. 1.98	M E White	Dublin	13. 7.09E
G-BXOX	Grumman American AA-5A Cheetah		F-GBDS	27. 2.98	R L Carter and P J Large	Turweston	16. 4.09E
		AA5A-0694					
G-BXOY	QAC Quickie Q.235	PFA 094-12183		17.11.97	C C Clapham *(Noted 9.08)*	Enstone	3. 9.04P
	(Built C C Clapham) (Lycoming O-235)						
G-BXOZ	Piper PA-28-181 Cherokee Archer II		N6927F	14.10.97	Oz Air Ltd	Panshanger	14. 5.09T
		28-7790173					
G-BXPC	Diamond DA.20-A1 Katana	10258	C-GKAN	4.12.97	Cubair Flight Training Ltd	Redhill	2. 4.10E
G-BXPD	Diamond DA.20-A1 Katana	10259	C-GDMU	4.12.97	Cubair Flight Training Ltd	Redhill	2. 4.10E
G-BXPI	Van's RV-4	PFA 181-12426		2. 1.98	S T G Lloyd	Swansea	26. 6.08P
	(Built E M Marsh) (Lycoming O-360-A1A)						
G-BXPK	Cameron A-250 Balloon (Hot Air)	4226		2. 2.98	Alba Ballooning Ltd	Edinburgh	27. 3.08T
G-BXPL	Piper PA-28-140 Cherokee	28-24560	N7224J	10.12.97	P J Meakin	Rednal	10. 6.09T
G-BXPM	Beech 58 Baron	TH-1677	N207ZM	10.10.97	Foyle Flyers Ltd	City of Derry	17. 5.09E
G-BXPP	Sky 90-24 Balloon (Hot Air)	092		17.12.97	S J Farrant	Hydestile, Godalming	9. 3.09E
G-BXPR	Cameron Colt Can 110 SS Balloon (Hot Air)			2. 2.98	P O Wagner	Blankenhagen, Germany	10. 9.09E
		4218					
G-BXPT	UltraMagic H-77 Balloon (Hot Air)	77/140		22.12.97	G D O Bartram	Ordino, Andorra	25. 6.09E
G-BXRA	Mudry CAP.10B	03	Fr AF 03	12.12.97	J W Scott	Croft Farm, Defford	15. 9.09E
	(P/i F-TFVR also quoted but this may be c/n 3)						
G-BXRB	Mudry CAP.10B	100	FrAF 100	12.12.97	T T Duhig	Spilstead Farm, Sedlescombe	29. 7.09E
G-BXRC	Mudry CAP.10B	134	FrAF 134	12.12.97	I F Scott tr Group Alpha	Fenland	9. 4.09E
G-BXRD	Enstrom 280FX	2012	PH-JVM	22.12.97	K Payne and M A Stephenson		
			N213M			(Maxey, Peterborough)	3. 6.09E
G-BXRF	Scintex CP.1310-C3 Super Emeraude	935	OO-NSF	9. 1.98	D T Gethin	Swansea	4. 8.09P
			F-BMJG				
G-BXRG	Piper PA-28-181 Archer II	28-7990036	PH-LEC	29. 1.98	Alderney Flying Training Ltd	Alderney	16. 3.09E
			N21173				
G-BXRH	Cessna 185A Skywagon	185-0413	HB-CRX	10.12.97	R E M Holmes	Ronaldsway	7. 6.09E
	(Hoerner wing-tips)		N1613Z				
G-BXRM	Cameron A-210 Balloon (Hot Air)	4237		23. 4.98	Dragon Balloon Company Ltd		
						Castleton, Hope Valley	9. 4.09E
G-BXRO	Cessna U206G Stationair II	U20604217	OH-ULK	9. 2.98	M Penny	Movenis, Coleraine	17. 4.09E
			N756NE				
G-BXRP	Schweizer 269C *(Schweizer 300)*	S 1334	OH-HSP	27. 1.98	AH Helicopter Services Ltd	Dunkeswell	4. 6.09E
			N7506U				
G-BXRR	Westland Scout AH.1	F9740	XW612	28. 1.98	M Soor	(Farnham Common)	12.10.09P
G-BXRS	Westland Scout AH.1	F9741	XW613	28. 1.98	B-N Group Ltd *(As "XW613" in AAC c/s)*		
						Bembridge	15. 5.08P
G-BXRT	Robin DR.400-180 Régent	2382		23. 2.98	R A Ford	White Waltham	15. 7.09E
G-BXRV	Van's RV-4	PFA 181-12482		12. 1.98	B J Oke tr Cleeve Flying Group	Gloucestershire	9. 6.09P
	(Built B J Oke) (Lycoming O-320)						
G-BXRY	Bell 206B-2 JetRanger II	208	N4054G	19. 3.98	Corbett Holdings Ltd	Hawarden	23. 9.09E
G-BXRZ	Rans S-6-116 Coyote II	0897.1146		12. 3.98	M P Hallam	Jackrells Farm	18. 6.09P
	(Built C M White - pr.no.PFA 204A-13195) (Rotax 912-UL) (Tailwheel u/c)						
G-BXSC	Cameron C-80 Balloon (Hot Air)	4251		12.12.97	N A Apsey	Hazlemere, High Wycombe	27. 7.09E
G-BXSD	Cessna 172R Skyhawk	17280310	N431ES	12. 3.98	R Paston	Wellesbourne Mountford	6. 3.09E
G-BXSE	Cessna 172R Skyhawk	17280352	N9321F	19. 5.98	MK Aero Support Ltd	Andrewsfield	15. 7.09E
G-BXSG	Robinson R22 Beta II	2789		3. 2.98	Rivermead Aviation Ltd *(Operated Rise Helicopters)*		
						Gloucestershire	14. 4.09E
G-BXSH	DG Flugzeugbau DG-800B	8-121B50		5. 2.98	R O'Conor *"SH"*	Sutton Bank	12.12.09E
G-BXSI	Avtech Jabiru SK	0139		5. 2.98	P F Gandy	(Heathfield)	11. 7.09P
	(Built V R Leggott pr.no.PFA 274-13204)						
G-BXSJ	Cameron C-80 Balloon (Hot Air)	4330		24. 3.98	Balloon School (International) Ltd t/a British School of		
					Ballooning	Colhook Common, Petworth	26. 7.05T
G-BXSP	Grob G109B	6335	D-KNEA	25. 3.98	J R Dransfield tr Deeside Grob Group	Aboyne	25.10.09E
G-BXSR	Reims Cessna F172N Skyhawk II	F17202003	PH-SPY	6. 2.98	N C K G Copeman	Fowlmere	30. 4.09E
			D-EITH				
G-BXST	Piper PA-25-235 Pawnee C	25-4952	PH-BAT	9. 2.98	The Northumbria Gliding Club Ltd	Currock Hill	28. 9.09E
	(Frame No.25-4971)		N8532L				
G-BXSU	TEAM Mini-MAX 91A	PFA 186-12357	G-MYGL	20. 2.98	M R Overall	Whitehall Farm, Wethersfield	30. 7.08P
	(Built A R Carr) (Rotax 503)						
G-BXSV	SNCAN Stampe SV-4C	556	N21PM	10.10.02	B A Bower *(Noted 2.06 for rebuild)*		
			F-BDDB				New Barn Farm, Barton Ashes, Crawley	
G-BXSX	Cameron V-77 Balloon (Hot Air)	4329		6. 4.98	D R Medcalf *"All Tech"*	Bromsgrove	28. 5.09E
G-BXSY	Robinson R22 Beta II	2778		27. 1.98	N M G Pearson	Bristol	5. 2.09E
G-BXTB	Cessna 152 II	15282516	OH-CMS	25. 2.98	Northumbria Flying School Ltd	Newcastle	17 .9.09E
			N69151				
G-BXTD	Europa Aviation Europa	155		26. 2.98	P R Anderson	Hucknall	3. 6.09P
	(Built P R Anderson - pr.no.PFA 247-12772) (Monowheel u/c)						
G-BXTF	Cameron N-105 Balloon (Hot Air)	4304		2. 4.98	Flying Pictures Ltd *"Sainsbury's Strawberry"*		
						Chilbolton	30. 6.06A
G-BXTG	Cameron N-42 Balloon (Hot Air)	4305		2. 4.98	P M Watkins and S M M Carden	Chippenham	25. 4.09E
G-BXTH	Westland SA.341D Gazelle HT.3	WA1120	XW866	13. 3.98	Armstrong Aviation Ltd *"E"*	Kirkbride	3. 8.09P

Reg	Type	C/n	Prev id	Date	Owner/Operator	Base	C of A
G-BXTI	Pitts S-1S *(Built N J Pesch)*	NP-1	ZS-VZX N96MM	9. 3.98	A B Theherne-Pollock tr BXTI Group	White Waltham	25. 7.09P
G-BXTJ	Cameron N-77 Balloon (Hot Air)	4332		6. 4.98	J M Albury *(Chubb titles)*	Cirencester	27. 9.09E
G-BXTN	Aérospatiale-Alenia ATR 72-202	483	F-WQNR G-BXTN, F-WWEV	24.10.97	Aurigny Air Services Ltd	Guernsey	19. 2.09E
G-BXTO	Hindustan HAL-26 Pushpak *(Continental C90-8F)*	PK-128	9V-BAI VT-DWM	12. 2.98	P Q Benn	Draycott Farm, Chiseldon	22. 5.09P
G-BXTS	Diamond DA.20-A1 Katana	10308	N638DA C-GKAC	10. 3.98	I M Armitage	Bristol	28. 5.09E
G-BXTT	Grumman AA-5B Tiger	AA5B-0749	F-GBDH	27. 2.98	M N Stevens	Popham	16. 4.09E
G-BXTV	Cope Bug	BUG.2		12. 3.98	B R Cope	(Bewdley)	
G-BXTW	Piper PA-28-181 Archer III	2843137	N41279 (G-BXTW), N41279	26. 5.98	J N Davison t/a Davison Plant Hire	Compton Abbas	28. 6.09E
G-BXTY	Piper PA-28-161 Cadet	2841179	PH-LED	11. 3.98	Bflying Ltd *(Operated Bournemouth Flying Club)*	Bournemouth	27. 6.09E
G-BXTZ	Piper PA-28-161 Cadet	2841181	PH-LEE	11. 3.98	Bflying Ltd *(Operated Bournemouth Flying Club)*	Bournemouth	17. 4.09E
G-BXUA	Campbell Cricket Mk.5 *(Built P C Lovegrrove)* (Rotax 582)	PFA G/03-1272		12. 3.98	R N Bodley	Henstridge	2. 9.09P
G-BXUC	Robinson R22 Beta	0908	OY-HFB	17. 3.98	Rivermead Aviation Ltd *(Operated Rise Helicopters)*	Goodwood	29. 4.09E
G-BXUE	Sky 240-24 Balloon (Hot Air)	098		30. 4.98	G M Houston t/a Scotair Balloons *"Scotair Balloons"*	Lesmahagow	8. 5.09E
G-BXUF	Agusta-Bell 206B-2 JetRanger II	8633	EC-DUS	12. 5.98	SJ Contracting Services Ltd	Beckley, Oxford	13. 8.09E
G-BXUG	Lindstrand Baby Bel SS Balloon (Hot Air)	512		14. 5.98	Karl-Heinz Gruenauer *"Baby Bel"*	Schwaebisch Hall, Germany	28. 4.09E
G-BXUH	Lindstrand LBL 31A Balloon (Hot Air)	513		2. 6.98	A D Kent tr Balloon Preservation Flying Group	Petworth	18. 5.09E
G-BXUI	DG Flugzeugbau DG-800B	8-105B39	BGA4382 D-KKLC	12. 5.98	J Le Coyte	Sandhill Farm, Shrivenham	22. 3.09E
G-BXUM	Europa Aviation Europa *(Built D Bosomworth - pr.no.PFA 247-12611) (Monowheel u/c)*	067		19. 3.98	D Bosomworth *"The Doghouse"* *(Transported from home for flying)*	Popham	8. 5.07P
G-BXUO	Lindstrand LBL 105A Balloon (Hot Air)	520		27. 3.98	Lindstrand Technologies Ltd	Oswestry	14. 7.09E
G-BXUS	Sky 65-24 Balloon (Hot Air)	111		6. 4.98	PSH Skypower Ltd *"Sky Demo"*	Woodborough, Pewsey	2. 3.09E
G-BXUU	Cameron V-65 Balloon (Hot Air)	4362		23. 4.98	M D Freeston and S Mitchell	Hertford	25. 6.09E
G-BXUW	Cameron Colt 90A Balloon (Hot Air)	4317		23. 4.98	Zycomm Electronics Ltd	Ripley	17. 6.09E
G-BXUX	Brandli BX-2 Cherry *(Built M F Fountain)* (Continental C90-12F)	PFA 179-12571		4. 4.98	M F Fountain	Clipgate Farm, Denton	26.11.08P
G-BXUY	Cessna 310Q	310Q0231	N137SA D-IHMT, N7731Q	16. 4.98	Massair Ltd	Liverpool-John Lennon	20. 8.09E
G-BXVA	SOCATA TB-200 Tobago XL	1325	F-GJXL F-WJXL	15. 4.98	H R Palser	Cardiff	10. 8.09E
G-BXVB	Cessna 152 II	15282584	N69250	15. 4.98	PJC (Leasing) Ltd	Stapleford	25. 9.09E
G-BXVD	CFM Streak Shadow SA *(Built CFM Aircraft Ltd - pr.no..PFA 206-13304) (Rotax 912)*	K 301-SA		1. 4.98	I J C Burman	(Westbury-sub-Mendip, Wells)	9. 2.10P
G-BXVG	Sky 77-24 Balloon (Hot Air)	99		28. 5.98	M Wolf	Wallingford	30. 9.09E
G-BXVJ	Cameron O-120 Balloon (Hot Air)	2201	PH-VVJ G-IMAX	12. 3.98	Aerosaurus Balloons Ltd	Whimple, Exeter	4. 4.06T
G-BXVK	Robin HR.200-120B	326		1. 7.98	Modi Aviation Ltd	Sibson	8. 1.10E
G-BXVL	Sky 180-24 Balloon (Hot Air)	113		16. 6.98	A W Talbott	Birmingham	24. 7.05T
G-BXVM	Van's RV-6A *(Built J G Small)* (Lycoming O-320)	PFA 181-13103		26. 2.98	J C Lomax	Andreas, Isle of Man	22. 5.08P
G-BXVO	Van's RV-6A *(Built P J Hynes)* (Lycoming O-320-D1A)	PFA 181-12575		28. 4.98	M E and P J Hynes	Sleap	24. 8.09P
G-BXVP	Sky 31-24 Balloon (Hot Air)	056		28. 4.98	T Dudman *(Sky Balloon titles)*	Cleeve, Bristol	1. 7.09E
G-BXVR	Sky 90-24 Balloon (Hot Air)	061		20. 7.98	P Hegarty	Magherafelt, Co Londonderry	13. 7.09E
G-BXVS	Brügger MB.2 Colibri *(Built G T Snoddon)* (Volkswagen 1834)	PFA 043-11948		5. 5.98	G T Snoddon	Newtownards	19. 5.03P
G-BXVT	Cameron A-77 Balloon (Hot Air)	1444	PH-MKB	30. 7.98	R P Wade	Shevington, Wigan	
G-BXVU	Piper PA-28-161 Cherokee Warrior II	28-7816063	N47372	5. 5.98	Jet Connections Ltd	Enstone	24. 8.09E
G-BXVV	Cameron V-90 Balloon (Hot Air)	4369		5. 5.98	Floating Sensations Ltd	Thatcham	8. 8.09E
G-BXVW	Colt Piggy Bank SS Balloon (Hot Air)	4366		2. 7.98	G Binder	Sonnennbuhl, Germany	2. 8.03A
G-BXVX	Rutan Cozy Classic *(Built G E Murray)* (Lycoming O-320)	PFA 159-12680		6. 5.98	G E Murray	Swansea	21.10.03P
G-BXVY	Cessna 152	15279808	N757KU	11. 5.98	Stapleford Flying Club Ltd	Stapleford	20.11.09E
G-BXVZ	WSK-PZL Mielec TS-11 Iskra	3H-1625	SP-DOF	27. 3.98	J Ziubrzynski *(Noted 7.05)*	Manston	
G-BXWA	Beech 76 Duchess	ME-232	OY-CYM (SE-IUY), D-GBTD	8. 4.98	Aviation South West Ltd	Exeter	18. 7.09E
G-BXWB	Robin HR.100-200B Royal	08	HB-EMT	29. 4.98	W A Brunwin	Oaksey Park	19.12.09E
G-BXWC	Cessna 152	15283640	N4794B	11. 5.98	PJC (Leasing) Ltd	Stapleford	12. 7.07T
	(Bounced on landing during circuits at Stapleford 24. 5.07; the nose undercarriage collapsed also damaging the propeller)						
G-BXWG	Sky 120-24 Balloon (Hot Air)	114		28. 5.98	M E White	Trim, County Meath	20. 5.09E
G-BXWH	Denney Kitfox Model 4-1200 Speedster *(Built B J Finch)*	PFA 172A-12343		4. 3.98	M G Porter and H Hedley-Lewis *"Bumble 2"*	Croft Farm, Melksham	11. 6.09P
G-BXWK	Rans S-6-ESA Coyote II *(Built J Whiting - pr.no.PFA 204-13317) (Rotax 582) (Tri-cycle u/c)*	0298.1020		19. 5.98	G P Gibson	(Llanfairpwllgwyngyll)	15. 5.09P
G-BXWL	Sky 90-24 Balloon (Hot Air)	117		20. 7.98	D J Baggley	Stoke-on-Trent	19. 3.09E
G-BXWO	Piper PA-28-181 Archer II	28-8190311	D-ENHA (2) N8431C	22. 5.98	J S Develin and Z Islam	Redhill	15. 6.09E
G-BXWP	Piper PA-32-300 Cherokee Six	32-7340088	N8143D G-BXWP, OE-DRR, N16452	26. 5.98	J M Hill and I Jones tr Alliance Aviation	Barton	11. 2.09E

G-BXWR	CFM Streak Shadow SA	K 289-SA	G-MZMI	22. 5.98	M A Hayward	Bodmin	6. 1.10P
	(Built M Hayward - pr.no.PFA 206-13205) (Rotax 912)						
G-BXWT	Van's RV-6	PFA 181-12639		19. 7.96	R C Owen	Danehill	11.10.08P
	(Built R C Owen) (Lycoming O-360						
G-BXWU	FLS Aerospace Sprint 160	003	G-70-503	5. 6.98	Eurojet Aircraft Leasing 3 Ltd	(Bexhill-on-Sea)	
G-BXWV	FLS Aerospace Sprint 160	005	G-70-505	5. 6.98	Eurojet Aircraft Leasing 3 Ltd	(Bexhill-on-Sea)	
G-BXWX	Sky 25-16 Balloon (Hot Air)	082		29. 5.98	C O'Neill and G Davis		
						Crosserlough, Co Cavan	8. 8.09E
G-BXXG	Cameron N-105 Balloon (Hot Air)	3662		19. 6.98	Allen Owen Ltd	Wotton-under-Edge	2. 4.02A
G-BXXH	Hatz CB-1	PFA 143-12445		9. 6.98	R F Shingler	Forest Farm, Welshpool	18. 6.09P
	(Built R F Shingler)						
G-BXXI	Grob G109B	6400	F-CAQR	9. 6.98	M N Martin	Saltby	16.12.08E
			F-WAQR				
G-BXXJ	Colt Flying Yacht SS Balloon (Hot Air)	1797	JA-A0515	10. 6.98	Magical Adventures Ltd		
						West Bloomfield, Michigan, US	29. 9.09E
G-BXXK	Reims Cessna F172N Skyhawk II	F17201806	D-EOPP	15. 6.98	J A Havers and R A Blackwell	North Weald	10. 9.09E
G-BXXL	Cameron N-105 Balloon (Hot Air)	4408		16. 7.98	Flying Pictures Ltd (Blue Peter titles)	Chilbolton	11. 9.05A
G-BXXN	Robinson R22 Beta	0720	N720HH	16. 6.98	L L F Smith t/a Helicopter Services		
						Wycombe Air Park	2.11.09E
G-BXXO	Lindstrand LBL 90B Balloon (Hot Air)	534		6. 7.98	K Temple	Tivetshall St Margaret, Norwich	7. 8.07A
G-BXXP	Sky 77-24 Balloon (Hot Air)	124		20. 7.98	T R Wood	London SW18	5. 9.09E
G-BXXR	Lovegrove AV-8 Gyroplane	PFA G/15-1263		29. 6.98	P C Lovegrove	(Didcot)	
	(Built P C Lovegrove and officially regd. as "Lovegrove BGL Four Runner" with c/n PFA G/15-1273)						
G-BXXS	Sky 105-24 Balloon (Hot Air)	116		30. 7.98	L D and H Vaughan "Skylark"	Tring	9. 7.09E
G-BXXT	Beech 76 Duchess	ME-212	(N212BE)	17. 7.98	Pridenote Ltd	Sturgate	16.12.09E
			F-GBOZ				
G-BXXU	Colt 31A Balloon (Hot Air)	4427		21. 8.98	Sade Balloons Ltd	Coulsdon	24. 4.09E
G-BXXW	Enstrom F-28F	771	G-SCOX	2. 7.98	Fast Helicopters Ltd	Shoreham	23.11.09E
			N330SA, G-BXXW, JA7823				
G-BXYD	Eurocopter EC.120B Colibri	1006		7. 7.98	Aero Maintenance Ltd	Walton Wood	23.12.09E
G-BXYE	Scintex CP.301-C1 Emeraude	559	F-BTEO	8. 7.98	D T Gethin	Swansea	
			F-PTEO, F-WTEO, F-BJFV				
G-BXYF	Colt AS-105 GD Airship (Hot Air)	4433		7. 8.98	LN Flying Ltd	(Germany)	19.11.08E
G-BXYG	Cessna 310D	39089	HB-LSF	14. 8.98	Equitus SARL	Merville-Calonne, France	18. 9.09E
			F-GEJT, 3A-MCA, F-BBOT, F-OBOT, (N6789T)				
G-BXYH	Cameron N-105 Balloon (Hot Air)	4441		7. 8.98	N J Langley	Clapton in Gordano, Bristol	10. 5.06A
G-BXYI	Cameron H-34 Balloon (Hot Air)	4442		7. 8.98	S P Harrowing	Margam, Port Talbot	4. 5.09E
G-BXYJ	SAN Jodel DR.1050 Ambassadeur	143	F-BJNA	28. 7.98	C Brooke tr G-BXYJ Group	Netherthorpe	25. 1.10P
G-BXYK	Robinson R22 Beta	1579	N4037B	27. 7.98	D N Whittlestone	(Oxenhope)	10. 2.09E
G-BXYM	Piper PA-28-235 Cherokee Pathfinder	28-10858	SE-FAM	18. 8.98	Redfly Aviation Ltd	Shoreham	22.12.09E
G-BXYO	Piper PA-28RT-201 Arrow IV	28R-8018046	PH-SDD	18. 8.98	Airways Flight Training (Exeter) Ltd	Exeter	5. 1.10E
			N8164M				
G-BXYP	Piper PA-28RT-201 Arrow IV	28R-8018050	PH-SBO	18. 8.98	G I Cooper	(Raydon, Ipswich)	27.11.09E
			N8168H				
G-BXYR	Piper PA-28RT-201 Arrow IV	28R-8018101	PH-SDA	3. 8.98	A Dayani	Exeter	29. 3.09E
			N8251B				
G-BXYT	Piper PA-28RT-201 Arrow IV	28R-7918198	PH-SBN	3. 8.98	Hitachi Capital (UK) PLC	(Hounslow)	13.11.08E
			(PH-SBM), OO-HLA, N2878W				
G-BXYX	Van's RV-6	22293	N2399C	31. 7.98	A G Palmer	Wellesbourne Mountford	30. 3.09P
	(Built A G Palmer) (Lycoming O-320-E2D)						
G-BXZA	Piper PA-38-112 Tomahawk	38-78A0864	N2480N	6. 8.98	P D Brooks	Inverness	29.11.08E
G-BXZB	Nanchang CJ-6A	2632019	Chinese AF	18. 9.98	Wingglider Ltd (As "2632019")	Hibaldstow	31. 5.02P
G-BXZF	Lindstrand LBL 90A Balloon (Hot Air)	575		8. 1.99	R G Carrell	Havant	17. 3.09E
G-BXZI	Lindstrand LBL 90A Balloon (Hot Air)	543		14. 8.98	J A Viner	Caterham	6. 5.09E
G-BXZK	MD Helicopters MD.900 Explorer	900-00057	N9238T	27. 8.98	Dorset Police Air Support Unit	Winfrith Newburgh	17. 2.08E
			G-76-057				
G-BXZM	Cessna 182S Skylane	18280310	N2683L	8.10.98	AB Integro Aviation Ltd	White Waltham	4.12.09E
G-BXZO	Pietenpol AirCamper	PFA 047-12818		10. 7.98	P J Cooke	Westfield Farm, Hailsham	14. 7.08P
	(Built P J Cooke) (Continental A65)						
G-BXZT	Morane Saulnier MS.880B Rallye Club	1733	OO-EDG	2. 9.98	C O'Connor tr Naas Flying Group		
			D-EBDG, F-BSVL			(Naas, County Kildare)	11. 3.10E
G-BXZU	Micro Aviation B 22S Bantam	98-015	ZK-JJL	21. 9.98	M E Whapham and R W Hollamby		
						Corn Wood Farm, Adversane	11. 7.08P
G-BXZY	CFM Shadow Series DD	296-DD		21. 9.98	P A James t/a Cloudbase Aviation G-BXZY Redhill		16.12.07P

G-BYAA - G-BYZZ

G-BYAD	Boeing 757-204ER	26963		6. 5.92	Thomson Airways Ltd	Luton	17.12.09E
G-BYAE	Boeing 757-204ER	26964		12. 5.92	Thomson Airways Ltd	Luton	17.12.09E
G-BYAH	Boeing 757-204	26966		5. 2.93	Thomson Airways Ltd	Luton	10.2.10E
G-BYAI	Boeing 757-204	26967		1. 3.93	Thomson Airways Ltd	Luton	4. 3.09E
G-BYAK	Boeing 757-204	26267		6. 4.93	Thomson Airways Ltd	Luton	13. 4.09E
G-BYAL	Boeing 757-204	25626		13. 5.93	Thomson Airways Ltd	Luton	18. 5.09E
G-BYAO	Boeing 757-204	27235		3. 2.94	Thomson Airways Ltd "Eric Morecambe OBE"	Luton	2. 2.10E
G-BYAP	Boeing 757-204	27236		15. 2.94	Thomson Airways Ltd "John Lennon"	Luton	14. 2.10E
G-BYAS	Boeing 757-204	27238		9. 3.94	Thomson Airways Ltd "Gordon Hill"	Luton	31. 1.10E
G-BYAT	Boeing 757-204	27208		21. 3.94	Thomson Airways Ltd	Luton	24. 3.09E
G-BYAU	Boeing 757-204	27220		18. 5.94	Thomson Airways Ltd	Luton	17. 5.09E
G-BYAV	Taylor JT.1 Monoplane	PFA 055-11010		27. 8.98	J S Marten-Hale	RAF Henlow	1. 5.09P
	(Built C J Pidler)						
G-BYAW	Boeing 757-204	27234		3. 4.95	Thomson Airways Ltd "Phil Stanley"	Luton	2. 4.09E

Reg	Type	C/n	Prev Id	Date	Owner / Operator	Location	Expiry
G-BYAX	Boeing 757-204	28834		24. 2.99	Thomson Airways Ltd	Luton	28. 2.09E
G-BYAY	Boeing 757-204	28836	N1786B	13. 4.99	Thomson Airways Ltd	Luton	18.12.09E
G-BYAZ	CFM Streak Shadow SA	K 244		1. 9.98	A G Wright	Old Sarum	15. 8.09P
	(Built A G Wright - pr.no.PFA 206-12656) (Rotax 582)						
G-BYBC	Agusta-Bell 206B-2 JetRanger II	8567	G-BTWW EI-BJV, G-BTWW	31. 3.98	Sky Charter UK Ltd	Hawarden	21.11.07E
G-BYBD	Cessna F172H	F172-0487	G-OBHX G-AWMU	6. 7.98	D G Bell and J Cartmell	Derby	29. 6.09E
	(Built Reims Aviation SA)						
G-BYBE	Wassmer Jodel D 120A Paris-Nice	269	OO-FDP	24. 7.98	P G Wiggett and O Downes	Shipdham	29. 5.09E
G-BYBF	Robin R2160i	329 (2)		1.10.98	D J R Lloyd-Evans	Bournemouth	25. 5.08E
	(Airframe replaced after collision with Kitfox G-LEED 9.02 but c/n retained)						
G-BYBH	Piper PA-34-200T Seneca II	34-8070078	N119SA (G-BYBH), N4023K, N3567B	9. 6.00	Goldspear (UK) Ltd	(Holyport, Maidenhead)	7. 6.07
G-BYBI	Bell 206B-3 JetRanger III	3668	ZS-RGP N5757M	19.10.98	Winkburn Air Ltd	Elstree	3. 4.09E
G-BYBJ	Medway Hybred 44XLR-C	MR156/135-C		22. 1.99	M Gardner	Rochester	25. 4.01P
	(Rotax 503)						
G-BYBK	Murphy Rebel	260R	N95LD	19. 8.98	M J Whiteman-Haywood	Pound Green, Buttonoak, Bewdley	13. 4.06P
	(Built L A Dyer)						
G-BYBL	Sud-Aviation Gardan GY-80-160D Horizon	127	F-BMUY	25. 9.98	M J Sutton	(Walsall)	16. 9.09R
G-BYBM	Avtech Jabiru SK	0201		18. 9.98	P J Hatton	(Bridestowe, Okehampton)	30.10.08P
	(Built M Rudd - pr.no.PFA 274-13377)						
G-BYBN	Cameron N-77 Balloon (Hot Air)	3082	N6004M	30. 9.98	M G Howard	Dubai, UAE	14. 4.09E
G-BYBO	Medway Eclipse R	155/134		14. 9.98	C Bayliss	Ince Blundell	16.12.07P
	(Jabiru 2200A)						
G-BYBP	Cessna A185F	185-03804	OO-DCD F-GDCD, F-ODIA, N4593E	15.10.98	G M S Scott	Bradley's Lawn, Heathfield	2. 3 09E
G-BYBR	Rans S-6-116 Coyote II	0996.1042		10. 7.98	S and A F Williams	Exeter	5.11.07P
	(Built J B Robinson - pr.no.PFA 204A-13081) (Rotax 912-UL) (Tri-cycle u/c)						
G-BYBS	Sky 80-16 Balloon (Hot Air)	136		27.10.98	B K Rippon	Upton, Didcot	17. 6.09E
G-BYBU	Murphy Renegade Spirit UK	PFA 188-13229		12.10.98	R L Williams	Cottage Farm, Norton Juxta	14. 9.08P
	(Built K R Anderson)						
G-BYBV	Mainair Rapier	1183-1198-7-W986		20.10.98	M W Robson	(Market Weighton, York)	1.11.02P
G-BYBX	Slingsby T 67M-260 Firefly	2261		21.10.98	Slingsby Advanced Composites Ltd	Kirkbymoorside	
G-BYBY	Thorp T-18C Tiger	492	N77KK	17. 7.98	P G Mair	Perth	24. 7.08P
	(Built K K Knowles)						
G-BYBZ	Avtech Jabiru SK	0162		7. 9.98	Stenor Environmental Services Ltd	Swansea	19. 5.09P
	(Built A W Harris - pr.no.PFA 274-13290)						
G-BYCA	Piper PA-28-140 Cherokee D	28-7125223	PH-VRZ N11C	24. 9.98	A Reay	Caernarfon	10. 4.09E
G-BYCB	Sky 21-16 Balloon (Hot Air)	142		28.10.98	S J Colin *(Active 5.07)*	Headcorn, Ashford	
G-BYCD	Cessna 140	13744	N4273N NC4273N	28. 9.98	G P James	(Oak Farm, Cowbit)	30. 6.11S
	(Continental O-200-A)						
G-BYCE	Robinson R44 Astro	0520		12.10.98	C A Rosenberg	(Groesfaen, Pontyclun)	24.11.09E
G-BYCF	Robinson R22 Beta II	2866		12.10.98	R F McLachlan	(Rodsley, Ashbourne)	27. 1.10E
G-BYCJ	CFM Shadow Series DD	K 294-DD		14.10.98	P I Hodgson	(Ilford)	19. 7.08P
	(Built J W E Pearson - pr.no.PFA 161-13258)						
G-BYCM	Rans S-6-ES Coyote II	0298.1204		15. 9.98	E W McMullan	(Dunnyvadden, Co Antrim)	7.11.00P
	(Built E W McMullan - pr.no.PFA 204-13315)						
G-BYCN	Rans S-6-ES Coyote II	0298.1205		15. 9.98	T J Croskery	City of Derry	14. 8.09P
	(Built J K and R L Dunseath - pr.no.PFA 204-13314) (Rotax 582)						
G-BYCP	Beech B200 Super King Air	BB-966	F-GDCS	15.10.98	London Executive Aviation Ltd	Stapleford	11. 2.09E
G-BYCS	CEA Jodel DR.1051 Sicile	201	F-BJUJ	28.10.98	M C Bennett	Perranporth	22.10.09P
G-BYCT	Aero L-29A Delfin	395142	ES-YLH Estonian AF, Soviet AF	29.10.98	Propeller BVBA *(Noted 1.09)*	North Weald	2. 6.04P
G-BYCV	Murphy Maverick	PFA 259-12925		24. 9.98	M Martin	Fenland	19. 8.08P
	(Built P C Vallance) (Rotax 503)						
G-BYCW	Mainair Blade	1185-1198-7-W988		5.11.98	P C Watson	St Michaels	14. 6.08P
G-BYCX	Westland Wasp HAS.1	F9754 & WA-B-Z3	ZK-HOX South African Navy 92	9.11.98	BN Helicopters Ltd *(As "92" in South African Navy c/s)* *(Noted 1.08)*	Thruxton	12. 7.06P
G-BYCY	III Sky Arrow 650 T	PFA 298-13332		10.11.98	K A Daniels	Upfield Farm, Whitson	7. 8.08P
	(Built A S Spriglings)						
G-BYCZ	Avtech Jabiru SK	xxxx		16.10.98	R Scroby	Leicester	12.9.09P
	(Built C Hewer - pr.no.PFA 274-13388)						
G-BYDB	Grob G115B	8025	VH-JVL D-EFCG	26. 3.99	J B Baker	Tatenhill	28. 4.09E
G-BYDE	Vickers Supermarine 361 Spitfire IX	CBAF IX.2922	Soviet AF PT879	11.11.98	P A Teichman *(Parts for restoration, noted 1.09)*	North Weald	
G-BYDF	Sikorsky S-76A	760364	JA6615	9. 1.98	Brecqhou Development Ltd	Guernsey	12. 7.09E
G-BYDG	Beech C24R Sierra	MC-627	OY-AZL	9.11.98	Professional Flight Simulation Ltd	Bournemouth	14. 6.09E
G-BYDJ	Colt 120A Balloon (Hot Air)	3527		17.11.98	D K Hempleman-Adams	Corsham	8. 8.09E
G-BYDK	SNCAN Stampe SV-4C	55	F-BCXY French AF	20.11.98	Bianchi Aviation Film Services Ltd *(Stored in rafters in hangar)*	Wycombe Air Park	
	(Official p/i quoted as F-BCXV which is c/n 298)						
G-BYDL	Hawker Hurricane IIB	?	Soviet AF Z5207	17.11.98	P J Lawton	Thruxton	
G-BYDT	Cameron N-90 Balloon (Hot Air)	4499		28. 1.99	N J Langley *"Tesco"*	Clapton in Gordano, Bristol	10. 5.06A
G-BYDU	Cameron Cart SS Balloon (Hot Air)	4500		28. 1.99	N J Langley *"Tesco"*	Clapton in Gordano, Bristol	3. 4.04A
G-BYDV	Van's RV-6	PFA 181-13264		3.12.98	R G Andrews	King's Farm, Thurrock	8. 6.08P
	(Built G L Carpenter) (Lycoming O-320)						
G-BYDY	Beech 58 Baron	TH-1852	C-GBWF	10.11.98	Pilot Services Flying Group Ltd	Fairoaks	6. 2.09E
G-BYDZ	Cyclone Airsports Pegasus Quantum 15-912	7493		22.12.98	P Newson	Sutton Meadows	30. 4 09E

G-BYEA	Cessna 172P Skyhawk	17275464	PH-ILL N63661	7.10.98	Falcon Flying Services Ltd	Biggin Hill	20. 9.09E
G-BYEC	DG Flugzeugbau DG-800B	8-102B36	D-KSDG	13.11.98	P R Redshaw *"23"*	Walney Island	30. 3.09E
G-BYEE	Mooney M 20K Mooney 231	25-0282	N231JZ	20. 7.88	R J Baker and W Woods tr Double Echo Flying Group		
						Coventry	23.11.09E
G-BYEH	CEA Jodel DR.250/160 Capitaine	15	OO-SOL F-BMZL	6.10.98	Nicholson Decommissioning Ltd	Derryogue	17. 4.09E
G-BYEJ	Scheibe SF28A Tandem Falke	5713	OE-9070 (D-KDAM)	18.12.98	D Shrimpton	RAF Keevil	1. 5.09E
G-BYEK	Stoddard-Hamilton GlaStar PFA 295-13087		ZK-NEW	14. 9.98	G M New *(Tailwheel u/c)*	Bagby	14. 4.09P
	(Built G M New) (Continental IO-240)		G-BYEK				
G-BYEL	Van's RV-6 PFA 181-12568			7. 1.99	D Millar	Bidford	19. 8.09P
	(Built D T Smith) (Lycoming O-320)						
G-BYEM	Cessna R182 Skylane RG II	R18200822	N494 D-ELVI, N737FT	8. 1.99	Wycombe Air Centre Ltd	Wycombe Air Park	30. 1.10E
G-BYEO	Zenair CH.601HDS Zodiac PFA 162-13345			11. 1.99	B S Carpenter	Strubby	20. 7.08P
	(Built B S Carpenter, M W Elliott and M J Diggins) (Tail-wheel u/c)						
G-BYER	Cameron C-80 Balloon (Hot Air)	4513		19.11.98	J M Langley	Ebley, Stroud	7. 9.09E
G-BYES	Cessna 172P Skyhawk	17274514	PH-ILN N172TP, N52424	7.10.98	Redhill Air Services Ltd	Redhill	1.12.09E
G-BYEW	Cyclone Airsports Pegasus Quantum 15-912 7499			15. 1.99	D Martin *"Attitude not Altitude"*	Perth	30. 6.08P
G-BYEX	Sky 120-24 Balloon (Hot Air)	135		21. 1.99	Ballongflyg Upp and Ner AB	Stockholm, Sweden	5. 3.08A
G-BYEY	Lindstrand LBL 21 Silver Dream Balloon (Hot Air) 577			15. 1.99	Oscair Project Ltd	Täby, Sweden	
G-BYEZ	Dyn'Aéro MCR-01 Club	47		25.11.98	J P Davies	Leicester	14. 9.09P
	(Built J P Davies - pr.no.PFA 301-13185)						
G-BYFA	Reims Cessna F152 II	F15201968	G-WACA	19.11.98	A J Gomes	Fairoaks	16. 3.09E
G-BYFC	Avtech Jabiru SK	0209		5. 2.99	M Flint	(Wisbech)	10. 5.09P
	(Built A C N Freeman - pr.no.PFA 274-13344)						
	(Misidentified strip 1 mie W of Tibenham 26. 7.08 and struck the ground near High Fields, The Heywood, Diss and substantially damaged)						
G-BYFD	Grob G115A	8100	EI-CCN G-BSGE	15. 1.99	S Kumpen and H Joosten		
					(Beringen, Belgium/Eindhoven, Netherelands)		25. 9.09E
G-BYFF	Cyclone Airsports Pegasus Quantum 15-912 7500			1. 2.99	D Young tr Kemble Flying Club	Kemble	2. 4.08P
G-BYFG	Europa Aviation Europa XS	396		22. 1.99	R Hawkes tr BDR Flying Group	Tatenhill	2.12.07P
	(Built P R Brodie - pr.no.PFA 247-13407) (Jabiru 3300) (Tri-gear u/c) *(Wings only noted at Morgansfield, Fishburn 6.08)*						
	(Bounced on landing at Tatenhill 13. 2.08 and nosewheel detached, made a go-arounf and then landed on mainwheels).						
G-BYFI	CFM Starstreak Shadow SA-II	xxx		11. 2.99	J A Cook	(Aldringham, Leiston)	3. 9.08P
	(Built D G Cook - pr.no.PFA 206-13300)						
G-BYFJ	Cameron N-105 Balloon (Hot Air)	4545		4. 3.99	R J Mercer	Belfast	3. 8.09E
G-BYFL	Diamond HK 36 TTS Super Dimona	36.623		5. 2.99	J G Kosak tr Seahawk Gliding Club		
						RNAS Culdrose	26. 7.09E
G-BYFM	Jodel DR.1050-M1 Sicile Record PFA 304-13237			26. 2.99	A J Roxburgh	Barton	5. 6.09P
	(Built P M Standen and A J Roxburgh) (Continental O-200-A)						
G-BYFR	Piper PA-32R-301 Saratoga IIHP	3246133	N4135P G-BYFR, N9515N	13. 4.99	Buckleton Ltd	Fairoaks	12. 7.09E
G-BYFT	Pietenpol AirCamper PFA 047-13057			22.12.98	G Everett	Headcorn	10.11.09P
	(Built M W Elliott) (Subaru EA81)						
G-BYFU	Lindstrand LBL 105B Balloon (Hot Air)	594		9. 3.99	ULM Decouverte	Pizay, France	20. 7.09E
G-BYFV	TEAM Mini-MAX 91 PFA 186-13431			5. 2.99	W E Gillham	Croft Farm, Croft-on-Tees	16. 7.08P
	(Built W E Gillham)						
G-BYFX	Colt 77A Balloon (Hot Air)	4547		4. 3.99	Wye Valley Aviation Ltd	Bridstowe, Ross-on-Wye	5. 5.05A
G-BYFY	Mudry CAP.10B	263	F-GKKD	9. 3.99	R N Crosland	Kittyhawk Farm, Deanland	1. 8.09E
G-BYGA	Boeing 747-436	28855		15.12.98	British Airways PLC	London Heathrow	13.12.09E
G-BYGB	Boeing 747-436	28856		17. 1.99	British Airways PLC	London Heathrow	3. 7.09E
G-BYGC	Boeing 747-436	25823		19. 1.99	British Airways PLC	London Heathrow	23.10.09E
G-BYGD	Boeing 747-436	28857		26. 1.99	British Airways PLC	London Heathrow	23.10.09E
G-BYGE	Boeing 747-436	28858		5. 2.99	British Airways PLC	London Heathrow	4. 2.10E
G-BYGF	Boeing 747-436	25824		17. 2.99	British Airways PLC	London Heathrow	16. 2.10E
G-BYGG	Boeing 747-436	28859		29. 4.99	British Airways PLC	London Heathrow	28. 4.09E
G-BYGC	Cameron Z-90 Balloon (Hot Air)	4555		16. 3.99	S M Sherwin *(Darlows titles)*	Morton, Bourne	14. 2.09E
G-BYHE	Robinson R22 Beta	2023	N82128 LV-VAB	14. 1.99	Helicopter Services Ltd	Wycombe Air Park	3. 3.09E
G-BYHG	Dornier 328-100	3098	D-CDAE D-CDXZ	7. 4.99	Suckling Aviation (Cambridge) Ltd t/a Scot Airways *(Operated Blue Islands)*	Jersey	6. 4.09E
G-BYHH	Piper PA-28-161 Warrior III	2842050	N4126Z G-BYHH, N9527N	15. 6.99	Stapleford Flying Club Ltd	Stapleford	19. 6.09E
G-BYHI	Piper PA-28-161 Warrior II	28-8116084	SE-IDP	4. 1.99	Haimoss Ltd *(Operated Old Sarum Flying Club)*	Old Sarum	13. 4.09E
G-BYHJ	Piper PA-28R-201 Arrow	2844020	N41675 G-BYHJ, N41675	25. 2.00	Bflying Ltd *(Operated Bournemouth Flying Club)*	Bournemouth	4. 5.09E
G-BYHK	Piper PA-28-181 Archer II	2843240	N4128V (G-BYHK), N9519N	20. 5.99	T-Air Services Ltd	Ronaldsway	25. 4.09E
G-BYHL	de Havilland DHC-1 Chipmunk 22	C1/0361	WG308	15. 3.99	M R and I D Higgins *(As "WG308:8" in RAF c/s)*	RAF Cranwell	15.11.09
G-BYHM	British Aerospace BAe 125 Series 800B		VP-BTM	12. 2.99	MAZAG	Biggin Hill	18. 6.09E
	(Build Corporate Jets Ltd) 258233		VR-BTM, (VR-BQH), F-WQCD, D-CAVW, G-5-770				
G-BYHN	Mainair Blade 912	1191-0399-7-W994		9. 4.99	R Stone	(Stoke-on-Trent)	24.11.06P
G-BYHO	Mainair Blade 912	1197-0599-7-W1000		16. 3.99	K Bailey	St Michaels	30. 3.08P
G-BYHP	CEA Jodel DR.253B Régent	161	OO-CSK	29. 3.99	S D Atherton tr HP Flying Group	Sywell	15.10.09E
G-BYHR	Cyclone Airsports Pegasus Quantum 15-912 7518			6. 4.99	I D Chantler	Longacre Farm, Sandy	1.11.08P

Reg	Type	C/n	Prev ID	Date	Owner/Operator	Location	Date
G-BYHS	Mainair Blade 912	1187-0299-7-W990		11. 3.99	T J Grange, R Beard and K Meechan	(Telford)	26. 4.09P
G-BYHT	Robin DR.400-180R Remorqueur	811	HB-EUU	9. 4.99	R C Wilson tr Deeside Robin Group	Aboyne	1. 9.09E
G-BYHU	Cameron N-105 Balloon (Hot Air)	4567		30. 4.99	ABC Flights Ltd	Clapton in Gordano, Bristol	26. 6.09E
G-BYHV	Raj Hamsa X'Air 582(6)	381		25. 3.99	M G Adams	Knapthorpe Lodge, Caunton	27. 6.09P
	(Built J Bowditch - pr.no.BMAA HB/090)						
G-BYHX	Cameron A-250 Balloon (Hot Air)	4565		16. 4.99	Balloon School (International) Ltd	Colhook Common, Petworth	9. 9.05T
G-BYHY	Cameron V-77 Balloon (Hot Air)	4493		22. 3.99	P Spellward "Biggles"	Bristol	17. 4.09E
G-BYIA	Avtech Jabiru SK	0237		10. 2.99	J Hume tr Teesside Aviators Group	Morgansfield, Fishburn	17. 3.09P
	(Built M F Cottam - pr.no.PFA 274-13436)						
G-BYIB	Rans S-6-ESA Coyote II	0498 1222		26. 3.99	W Anderson	Linlithgow	6. 1.10P
	(Built G A Clayton - pr.no.PFA 204-13387) (Rotax 582) (Tail-wheel u/c)						
G-BYID	Rans S-6-ES Coyote II	0498.1218		11. 5.99	J A E Bowen	Davidstow Moor	16. 1.08P
	(Built D J Brotherhood - pr.no.PFA 204-13348) (Rotax 582) (Tri-cycle u/c)						
G-BYIE	Robinson R22 Beta II	2933		22. 4.99	G Givens t/a Givens Aviation	(Ewenny, Bridgend)	6. 6.09E
G-BYII	TEAM Mini-MAX 91	PFA 186-11820		22. 1.99	R W L Breckell tr Golf Delta Group	Ince Blundell	20. 3.09P
	(Built J S R Moodie)						
G-BYIJ	CASA 1-131E Jungmann	2110	Spanish AF E3B-514	16. 7.90	P R Teager and R N Crosland	Deanland	18. 6.09P
G-BYIK	Europa Aviation Europa	154		2. 2.99	P M Davis	Oxford	5.10.09P
	(Built P M Davis - pr.no.PFA 247-12771) (Monowheel u/c)						
G-BYIL	Cameron N-105 Balloon (Hot Air)	4591		29. 4.99	Oakfield Farm Products Ltd "Oakfield"	Broadway	30. 4.09E
G-BYIM	Avtech Jabiru UL	PFA 274A-13397		22.12.98	A and J McVey	Ince Blundell	27. 3.08P
	(Built W J Dale and R F Hinton)						
G-BYIN	Rotary Air Force RAF 2000 GTX-SE			19. 1.99	J R Legge	(Rossendale)	21. 2.09P
	(Built J R Legge)	PFA G/13-1305					
G-BYIO	Colt 105A Balloon (Hot Air)	4601		30. 4.99	N Charbonnier (Lindt titles)	Aosta, Italy	16. 1.10E
G-BYIP	Pitts S-2A	2244	N109WA TC-ECN	23. 2.99	D P Heather-Hayes	Perth	29. 709E
	(Built Aerotek Inc)						
G-BYIR	Pitts S-1S	1-0063	N103WA TC-ECP	23. 2.99	M Henschen	Hamburg, Germany	26. 9.09E
	(Built Aerotek Inc)						
G-BYIS	Cyclone Airsports Pegasus Quantum 15-912	7508		25. 2.99	L M Tidman	Linley Hill, Leven	3. 7.09P
G-BYIT	Robin DR.500-200i Président	0010		27. 1.99	D Quirke	Rochester	26. 5.09E
	(Officially regd as DR.400-500)						
G-BYIU	Cameron V-90 Balloon (Hot Air)	4552		6. 4.99	H Micketeit	Bielefeld, Germany	8. 9.09E
G-BYIV	Cameron PM-80 Balloon (Hot Air)	4595		14. 5.99	A Schneider	Borken, Germany	30. 8.09E
	(Coca Cola bottle)						
G-BYIX	Cameron PM-80 Balloon (Hot Air)	4597		14. 5.99	A Schneider	Borken, Germany	8.11.09E
	(Coca Cola bottle)						
G-BYIY	Lindstrand LBL 56B Balloon (Hot Air)	601		26. 3.99	J H Dobson	Streatley, Reading	9. 7.09E
G-BYIZ	Cyclone Airsports Pegasus Quantum 15-912	7504		8. 2.99	J D Gray	Eshott	28. 5.08P
G-BYJA	Rotary Air Force RAF 2000 GTX-SE			6. 4.99	B Errington-Weddle	Henstridge	18. 7.02P
	(Built B Errington-Weddle)	PFA G/13-1297					
G-BYJB	Mainair Blade 912	1192-0499-7-W995		6. 4.99	M Atkinson	Arclid Green, Sandbach	6. 5.09P
G-BYJC	Cameron N-90 Balloon (Hot Air)	4562		30. 4.99	A G Merry (Bentleys of Knaresborough titles)	Alresford	27. 5.09E
G-BYJD	Avtech Jabiru UL	0172		16. 4.99	M W Knights	Blue Tile Farm, Hindolveston	21. 5.09P
	(Built G Wallis and M W Knights - pr.no.PFA 274-13376 although type prefix should be "274A")						
G-BYJE	TEAM Mini-MAX 91	PFA 186-12327		6. 4.99	A D Bales	Priory Farm, Tibenham	25. 8.09P
	(Built A W Austin and M F Cottam)						
G-BYJF	Thorp T-211	107	N2545C	20. 5.99	AD Aviation Ltd	Liverpool-John Lennon	22. 5.09E
	(Built Venture Light Aircraft Resources)						
G-BYJG	Lindstrand LBL 77A Balloon (Hot Air)	600		16. 4.99	Lindstrand Hot Air Balloons Ltd	Oswestry	20.12.08E
G-BYJH	Grob G109B	6512	D-KFRI	19. 5.99	A J Buchanan	Parham Park	26. 6.09E
G-BYJI	Europa Aviation Europa	F0004	G-ODTI	19. 4.99	P S Jones	Wolverhampton	20. 6.08P
	(Built Europa Aviation Ltd - pr.no.PFA 247-13010) (Monowheel u/c)						
G-BYJJ	Cameron C-80 Balloon (Hot Air)	4436	SX-MAX	20. 4.99	Proxim SPA (RF/Max titles)	Agrate Brianza, Milan, Italy	30. 3.08A
G-BYJK	Cyclone Airsports Pegasus Quantum 15-912	7524		7. 5.99	B S Smy	East Fortune	2. 6.09P
G-BYJL	Aero Designs Pulsar 3	PFA 202-13311		20. 4.99	F A H Ashmead	Woodcock Lane, Hordle	4. 7.09P
	(Built F A H Ashmead) (Tricycle u/c)						
G-BYJM	Cyclone AX2000	7523		25. 5.99	A M Smith tr Caunton Ax2000 Syndicate	Knapthorpe Lodge, Caunton	30. 5.09P
G-BYJN	Lindstrand LBL 105A Balloon (Hot Air)	605		30. 4.99	B Meeson	Pwllheli	29. 4.00A
G-BYJO	Rans S-6-ES Coyote II	0498.1217		4. 3.99	G Ferguson	Blue Tile Farm, Hindolveston	18. 9.08P
	(Built G Ferguson - pr.no.PFA 204-13338) (Rotax 582) (Tail-wheel u/c)						
G-BYJP	Pitts S-1S	1-0064	N105WA TC-ECR, Turkish AF?	16. 3.99	T Riddle tr Eaglescott Pitts Group	Eaglescott	18. 4.09
	(Built Aerotek Inc)						
G-BYJR	Lindstrand LBL 77B Balloon (Hot Air)	608		30. 4.99	B M Reed	Antigny, France	17. 2.09P
G-BYJS	SOCATA TB-20 Trinidad	1875	F-OIGE	15. 1.99	A P Bedford tr Juliet Sierra Group	Oxford	30. 5.09E
G-BYJT	Zenair CH.601HDS Zodiac	PFA 162-13130		4. 5.99	J D T Tannock	Nottingham City-Tollerton	4. 6.09P
	(Built J D T Tannock) (Tri-cycle u/c)						
G-BYJU	Raj Hamsa X'Air 582(1)	429		6. 5.99	G P Morling	Andreas, Isle of Man	22. 8.08P
	(Built C W Payne - pr.no.BMAA HB/098)						
G-BYJW	Cameron Sphere 105 SS Balloon (Hot Air)	4585		15. 6.99	Forbes Global Inc	Far Hills, New Jersey, US	23.11.09E
G-BYJX	Cameron C-70 Balloon (Hot Air)	4580		30. 4.99	B Perona	Torino, Italy	21. 5.08A
G-BJYZ	Linstrand LBL 105A Balloon (Hot-Air)	609		27. 5.99	C J Dunkley (Gulf Air titles)	Wendover	26. 7.02A
G-BYKA	Lindstrand LBL 69A Balloon (Hot Air)	612		7. 5.99	B Meeson (Vauxhall titles)	Rhiw, Pwllheli	21. 6.07A
G-BYKB	Rockwell Commander 114	14121	SE-GSM N4801W	18. 5.99	A Walton	Conington	21. 7.09P

Reg	Type	C/n	Prev id	Date	Owner	Location	Date
G-BYKC	Mainair Blade 912	1196-0599-7-W999		7. 5.99	A Voyce	(Hallow, Worcs)	6. 9.08P
G-BYKD	Mainair Blade 912	1198-0599-7-W1001		7. 5.99	D C Boyle	(Chorley)	11. 4.08P
G-BYKF	Enstrom F-28F	725	JA7684	19. 5.99	G T Williams and S C Severeyns		
					(Newcastle Emlyn and Llandysul))		7. 1.10E
G-BYKG	Pietenpol AirCamper	PFA 047-12827		17. 3.99	K B Hodge	(Mynydd Isa, Mold)	
	(Built K B Hodge)				(Last known nearing completion 2000!)		
G-BYKI	Cameron N-105 Balloon (Hot Air)	4635		4. 6.99	J A Leahy	Navan, County Meath	20. 8.09E
G-BYKJ	Westland Scout AH.1	F9696	XV121	6. 8.99	B H Austen t/a Austen Associates	Glenrothes	4. 1.10P
G-BYKK	Robinson R44 Astro	0572		4. 3.99	M N Cowley t/a Dragonfly Aviation		
						Red House Farm, Preston Capes	16. 4.09E
G-BYKL	Piper PA-28-181 Archer II	28-8090162	HB-PFB	15. 7.99	Transport Command Ltd	Shoreham	26.10.09E
			N8129Y				
G-BYKP	Piper PA-28RT-201T Turbo Arrow IV		HB-PDB	22. 6.99	D L Grimes and D W Knox	Bristol	8.11.09E
		28R-7931029	N3010G				
G-BYKS	Leopoldoff L 6 Colibri	129	N10LC	19. 4.99	I M Callier (Nearing completion 7.08)	(Hungerford)	
	(Continental C90)		F-BGIT, F-WGIT				
G-BYKT	Cyclone Airsports Pegasus Quantum 15-912			28. 5.99	D A Bannister and N J Howarth		
		7529				Sackville Farm, Riseley	7. 6.08P
G-BYKU	BFC Challenger II	PFA 177A-13252		25. 5.99	K W Seedhouse	Otherton, Cannock	7. 8.08P
	(Built K W Seedhouse)						
G-BYKW	Lindstrand LBL 77B Balloon (Hot Air)	620		22. 6.99	K Allemand	Plassal, France	2. 5.09E
G-BYKX	Cameron N-90 Balloon (Hot-Air)	4657		10. 8.99	G Davis	Crosserlough, Ireland	16.11.09E
G-BYKZ	Sky 140-24 Balloon (Hot Air)	147		25. 2.99	D J Head	Newbury	6. 8.05T
G-BYLB	de Havilland DH.82A Tiger Moth	83286	T5595	24. 5.99	P A Layzell (Noted 5.08)	Old Buckenham	
G-BYLC	Cyclone Airsports Pegasus Quantum 15-912			25. 6.99	A Cordes	Deenethorpe	22. 8.09P
		7528					
G-BYLD	Pietenpol AirCamper	PFA 047-13392		27. 4.99	S Bryan	(Chipping Warden, Banbury)	
	(Built S Bryan)						
G-BYLF	Zenair CH.601HDS Zodiac	PFA 162-13179		3. 6.99	G Waters	Swansea	21.10.08P
	(Built M and J S Thomas and G Waters) (Tricycle u/c)						
G-BYLH	Robin HR.200-120B	335		9. 7.99	Multiflight Ltd	Leeds-Bradford	5.11.09E
G-BYLI	Nova Vertex 22	14319		9. 4.99	M Hay	(Dundee)	
G-BYLJ	Letov LK-2M Sluka	PFA 263-13464		9. 6.99	W J McCarroll	Mullaghmore, Coleraine	
	(Built N E Stokes) (Rotax 447)						
G-BYLL	Sequoia F 8L Falco	PFA 100-10843		6.12.85	N J Langrick	Breighton	6. 3.09P
	(Built N J Langrick) (Lycoming O-320-A3C)						
G-BYLO	Tipsy Nipper T 66 Series 1	T66/04	OO-NIA	27. 4.99	M J A Trudgill	RAF Henlow	24. 6.04P
	(Built Avions Fairey SA) (Volkswagen 1600)						
G-BYLP	Rand Robinson KR-2	PFA 129-11431		19. 4.99	C S Hales (Under construction 5.08)	Shenington	
	(Built C S Hales)						
G-BYLS	Bede BD-4	PFA 037-11288		13.12.90	G H Bayliss	Welshpool	12.10.09P
	(Built G H Bayliss) (Lycoming O-320-E2F)						
G-BYLT	Raj Hamsa X'Air 582(1)	411		8. 6.99	T W Phipps	Craysmarsh Farm, Melksham	23. 9.05P
	(Built R J Turner - pr.no.BMAA HB/095)						
G-BYLV	Thunder Ax8-105 Series 2 Balloon (Hot Air)			6. 7.99	KB Voli de Chiozzi Bartolomeo EC SAS		
		4061				Cappella Cantone, Italy	1. 8.09E
G-BYLW	Lindstrand LBL 77A Balloon (Hot Air)	615		11. 6.99	Associazione Gran Premio Italiano	Perugia, Italy	10. 6.00A
G-BYLX	Lindstrand LBL 105A Balloon (Hot Air)	614		11. 6.99	Italiana Aeronavi	Cervignano, Italy	17. 8.09E
G-BYLY	Cameron V-77 Balloon (Hot Air)	3375	G-ULIA (2)	16. 7.97	R Bayly	Clutton, Bristol	30. 7.09E
G-BYLZ	Rutan Cozy Mk.4	PFA 159-12464		21. 5.99	E R Allen	Dunsfold	18.11.08P
	(Built E R Allen)						
G-BYMB	Diamond DA.20-C1 Katana	C0051	C-GDMB	9. 7.99	S C Brown t/a Enstone Flying Club	Enstone	19. 3.09E
G-BYMC	Piper PA-38-112 Tomahawk II	38-82A0034	N91457	18. 6.99	Central Aircraft Leasing Ltd	Wolverhampton	2. 7.06T
G-BYMD	Piper PA-38-112 Tomahawk II	38-82A0009	N91342	18. 6.99	M A Petrie	Hawarden	23. 8.08E
G-BYME	Sud-Aviation Gardan GY-80-180 Horizon	207	F-BPAA	24. 5.99	R M Osborne tr Air Venturas Group	Bagby	13. 3.09E
G-BYMF	Cyclone Airsports Pegasus Quantum 15-912			9. 7.99	G R Stockdale	Rufforth	9. 5.09P
		7540					
G-BYMG	Cameron A-210 Balloon (Hot Air)	4631		17. 9.99	P Johnson t/a Cloud Nine Balloon Company		
						Ebchester, Consett	28. 2.09E
G-BYMH	Cessna 152	15284980	N6127P	15. 7.99	PJC (Leasing) Ltd	Stapleford	21. 7.09E
G-BYMI	Cyclone Airsports Pegasus Quantum 15	7533		9. 7.99	N C Grayson	Knapthorpe Lodge, Caunton	18. 7.08P
	(Rotax 503)						
G-BYMJ	Cessna 152	15285564	N93865	16. 7.99	Stapleford Flying Club Ltd	Stapleford	26.11.09E
G-BYMK	Dornier 328-100	3062	LN-ASK	9. 6.99	Suckling Aviation (Cambridge) Ltd t/a Scot Airways		
			D-CDXE			London City	8. 6.09E
G-BYML	Dornier 328-100	3069	D-CDUL	27. 7.99	Suckling Aviation (Cambridge) Ltd t/a Scot Airways		
			LN-ASL, D-CDXT (2)		(CityJet titles)	London City	14. 8.09E
G-BYMN	Rans S-6-ESA Coyote II	0199.1292		16. 6.99	R L Barker	Chase Farm, Little Bursted	19. 2.09P
	(Built H Smith - pr.no.PFA 204-13477) (Jabiru 2200) (Tri-cycle u/c)						
G-BYMO	Campbell Cricket	PFA G/03-1266		16. 7.99	P G Rawson	(Huddersfield)	23. 5.06P
	(Built D G Hill) (Rotax 532)						
G-BYMP	Campbell Cricket Mk.1	PFA G/03-1265		16. 6.99	J J Fitzgerald	(Newtownards)	
	(Built J J Fitzgerald)						
G-BYMR	Raj Hamsa X'Air R100(3)	434		18. 6.99	W Drury (Noted 7.07)		
	(Built W M McMinn - pr.no.BMAA HB/094)					Slieve Croob, Slievanamoney, Castlewellen	26.12.06P
G-BYMT	Cyclone Airsports Pegasus Quantum 15-912			16. 7.99	C M Mackinnon	Strathaven	30. 7.09P
		7549					
G-BYMU	Rans S-6-ESN Coyote II	0498.1219		25. 6.99	I R Russell and S Palmer	Swinford, Rugby	23. 6.09P
	(Built I R Russell - pr.no.PFA 204-13424) (Verner VM133)						
G-BYMV	Rans S-6-ESN Coyote II	0998.1265		25. 6.99	P Rayson	Cottage Farm, Norton Juxta, Twycross	25. 7.09P
	(Built G A Squires - pr.no.PFA 204-13444) (Rotax 582) (Tri-cycle u/c)						
G-BYMW	Boland 52-12 Balloon (Hot Air)	001		25. 6.99	C Jones (Noted active 1.09)		
	(Built C Jones)					Sonning Common, Reading	

G-BYMX	Cameron A-105 Balloon (Hot Air)	4629			16. 7.99	H Reis	Aachen, Germany	9. 3.09E
					(ZENTIS titles and "Einfach traumhaft gut" lettering =Simply Fantastically Good)			
G-BYMY	Cameron N-90 Balloon (Hot Air)	4653			19. 7.99	A Cakss	Segny, France	17. 8.09E
G-BYNA	Cessna F172H	F172-0626	OO-VDW		15. 1.99	D M White	Popham	8. 5.09E
	(Built Reims Aviation SA)		PH-VDW, (G-AWTH), F-WLIT					
G-BYND	Cyclone Airsports Pegasus Quantum 15	7546			16. 7.99	D G Baker	(East Meon. Petersfield)	3.11.09P
	(Rotax 582)							
G-BYNE	Pilatus PC-6/B2-H4 Turbo Porter	631	HB-FLW		10. 8.99	D M Penny	Le Luc, Cennes, France	3.10.09E
			C-FRAV, N631SA, N62148, HS-..., N62148, XW-PFC, XW-PDK, HB-FCR					
G-BYNF	North American NA-64 Yale I	64-2171	N55904		10. 1.00	R S van Dijk (As "3349" in RCAF c/s)	Duxford	4. 3.08P
			RCAF 3349					
G-BYNH	RotorWay Executive 162F	6323			5. 7.99	R C Mackenzie	(Clavering, Saffron Walden)	
	(Built R Mackenzie) (RotorWay RI 162F)							
G-BYNI	RotorWay Executive 90	5216			16. 7.99	M Bunn	(Wacton, Norwich)	30.11.09E
	(Built M Bunn) (RotorWay RI 162)							
G-BYNJ	Cameron N-77 Balloon (Hot Air)	4661			26. 7.99	G Aimo *(Primagaz titles)*	Mondovi, Italy	28. 5.05A
G-BYNK	Robin HR.200-160	338			28. 7.99	R J Stainer and D A Healey tr Penguin Flight Group	Bodmin	5.10.09E
G-BYNM	Mainair Blade 912	1204-0799-7-W1007			20. 7.99	J P Hanlon and A C McAllister	Ince Blundell	4. 8.07P
G-BYNN	Cameron V-90 Balloon (Hot Air)	4643			16. 7.99	J L Hilditch t/a Cloud Nine Balloon Group *"Cloud Nine"*	Southwick, Brighton	1. 5.09E
G-BYNP	Rans S-6-ES Coyote II	1098.1269			22. 7.99	R J Lines	Sandtoft	17. 8.09P
	(Built R J Lines - pr.no.PFA 204-13414) (Rotax 582)							
G-BYNR	Avtech Jabiru UL	0129	EI-MAT		23. 7.99	M P Maughan *(Noted 10.07)*	Rufforth	14. 7.07P
	(Built A Parker - pr.no.SAAC 66 and also UL series no.UL0001)							
G-BYNS	Avtech Jabiru SK	0159			23. 7.99	D K Lawry *(Noted 6.08)*	Tibenham	10. 8.05P
	(Built D K Lawry - pr.no.PFA 274-13235)							
G-BYNT	Raj Hamsa X'Air V2(1)	457			20. 7.99	A Evans	Longside, Peterhead	14. 7.08P
	(Built G R Wallis - pr.no.BMAA HB/107)							
G-BYNU	Thunder AX7-77 Balloon (Hot Air)	3520			29. 7.99	P M Gaines *"Soup Dragon"*	Sedgefield, Stockton-on-Tees	27. 9.09E
G-BYNV	Sky 105-24 Balloon (Hot Air)	165			11. 8.99	Par Rovelli Construzioni SRL	Mazzini, Italy	10. 9.09E
G-BYNW	Cameron H-34 Balloon (Hot Air)	4666			27. 7.99	I M Ashpole *(Energis titles)*	Bridstow, Ross-on-Wye	13. 9.08A
G-BYNX	Cameron RX-105 Balloon (Hot Air)	4656			26. 7.99	Cameron Balloons Ltd	Bristol	1.11.00A
G-BYNY	Beech 76 Duchess	ME-247	N247ME		4. 8.99	Magenta Ltd *(Operated European Flight Training)*	Exeter	7.11.09E
			OE-FES, N6635H					
G-BYOB	Slingsby T 67M-260 Firefly	2263			8. 6.99	Stapleford Flying Club Ltd	Stapleford	23.10.09E
G-BYOD	Slingsby T 67C Firefly	2265			13. 6.00	TDR Aviation Ltd	Newtownards	4. 2.09E
G-BYOG	Cyclone Airsports Pegasus Quantum 15-912	7555			15. 9.99	M D Hinge	Old Sarum	14. 4.08P
G-BYOH	Raj Hamsa X'Air 582(2)	443			23. 7.99	P H J Kent	Belle Vue Farm, Yarnscombe	3. 5.08P
	(Built G A J Salter - pr.no.BMAA HB/101)							
G-BYOI	Sky 80-16 Balloon (Hot Air)	163			5. 8.99	I S and S W Watthews	Cark-in-Cartmel	7. 6.09E
G-BYOJ	Raj Hamsa X'Air 582(1)	458			23. 7.99	C G Thompson	Wing Farm, Longbridge Deverill)	11. 8.08P
	(Built R R Hadley - pr.no.BMAA HB/108)							
G-BYOK	Cameron V-90 Balloon (Hot Air)	3726			9. 8.99	D S Wilson	Norwich	5. 3.09E
G-BYOM	Sikorsky S-76C	760464	G-IJCB		25. 8.99	Starspeed Ltd	Blackbushe	30. 3.09E
G-BYON	Mainair Blade	1199-0599-7-W1002			4. 8.99	P G Mallon	Wing Farm, Longbridge Deverill	17. 6.09P
	(Rotax 503)							
G-BYOO	CFM Streak Shadow SA	K 270			6. 8.99	G R Eastwood	Full Sutton	10. 8.09P
	(Built C I Chegwen - pr.no.PFA 206-12806) (Rotax 912-UL)							
G-BYOR	Raj Hamsa X'Air 582(2)	478			11. 8.99	R V Horlock	(Grayshott, Hindhead)	23. 7.07P
	(Built A R Walker - pr.no.BMAA HB/117)							
G-BYOT	Rans S-6-ES Coyote II	0498.1221			29. 7.99	G Shaw	Lower Mountpleasant Farm, Chatteris	7. 5.08P
	(Built H F Blakeman - pr.no.PFA 204-13363) (Tri-cycle u/c)						Arclid Green, Sandbach	7. 5.08P
G-BYOU	Rans S-6-ES Coyote II	1298.1288			1. 6.99	P G Bright and P L Parker	(South Cave, Brough)	30.10.09P
	(Built Light Flight Ltd and R Germany - pr.no.PFA 204-13460) (Rotax 582) *(Tri-cycle u/c)*							
G-BYOW	Mainair Blade	1207-0899-7-W1010			9. 8.99	T H Ferguson	East Fortune	23. 3.08P
	(Rotax 582)							
G-BYOX	Cameron Z-90 Balloon (Hot Air)	4672			31. 8.99	D G Such *(Virgin Atlantic titles)*	Barkway, Royston	27. 2.09E
G-BYOZ	Mainair Rapier	1208-0899-7-W1011			12. 8.99	D P Harvey	Arclid Green, Sandbach	2. 8.08P
G-BYPA	Aérospatiale AS.355F2 Ecureuil 2	5348	G-NWPI		20. 8.99	P and J Carter	Redhill	28. 3.08E
			F-GMAO *(Crashed in woods Wansford near Peterborough 2. 5.07 & substantially damaged)*					
G-BYPB	Cyclone Airsports Pegasus Quantum 15-912	7566			3. 9.99	S Graham	Redlands, Swindon	23. 9.06P
G-BYPD	Cameron A-105 Balloon (Hot Air)	4680			6. 1.00	Headland Hotel Company Ltd *(Headland Hotel titles)*	Newquay	28. 2.09E
G-BYPE	Sud-Aviation Gardan GY-80-160 Horizon	180	F-BNYD		10. 8.99	P B Hodgson	Gloucestershire	28. 5.09E
G-BYPF	Thruster T 600N Sprint	9089-T600N-034			17. 8.99	R J Oakley tr Canary Syndicate	Shobdon	26. 1.10P
	(Rotax 582UL)							
G-BYPG	Thruster T 600N Sprint	9089-T600N-035			17. 8.99	N S Dell tr G-BYPG Syndicate	Dunkeswell	21. 5.09P
	(Rotax 582UL)							
G-BYPH	Thruster T 600N	9089-T600N-036			17. 8.99	D M Canham	Leicester	30. 4.08P
	(Rotax 582UL) *(Officially regd with incorrect c/n as 9099-T600N-036)*							
G-BYPJ	Cyclone Airsports Pegasus Quantum 15-912	7565			17. 9.99	M Watson	(Oakington)	10.12.07P
G-BYPL	Cyclone Airsports Pegasus Quantum 15-912	7558			9. 9.99	I T Carlse	(Fowlmere)	26. 9.08P
G-BYPM	Europa Aviation Europa XS	404			16.12.98	P Mileham	Dunkeswell	30. 7.08P
	(Built P Mileham - pr.no.PFA 247-13418) (Tri-gear u/c)							
G-BYPN	SOCATA MS.880B Rallye Club	2043	F-BTPN		23. 7.99	R and T C Edwards, S A and D Bell	Sturgate	5.11.09E
G-BYPO	Raj Hamsa X'Air 582(1)	439			25. 8.99	D W Willis tr X'Air Group	Brook Farm, Pilling	10.12.09P
	(Built N G Woodhall and A S Leach - pr.no.BMAA HB/111)							

G-BYPP	Medway Rebel SS	168/146		25.10.99	J L Gowens	(Leeds, Maidstone)	17. 3.01P
	(2 Stroke International 690L70)						
G-BYPR	Zenair CH.601HD Zodiac	PFA 162-12816		25. 8.99	S C Ord	(Chester)	20. 8.09P
	(Built D Clark) (Lycoming O-235-C2C)						
G-BYPT	Rans S-6-ESN Coyote II	0499.1316		27. 8.99	M A Sims	Redlands, Swindon	11. 6.09P
	(Built G R Pritchard - pr.no.PFA 204-13508) (Jabiru 2200A) (Tri-cycle u/c)						
G-BYPU	Piper PA-32R-301 Saratoga IIHP	3246150	N4160K	2.12.99	AM Blatch Electrical Contractors Ltd	East Winch	24. 1.10E
			G-BYPU, N9518N				
G-BYPW	Raj Hamsa X'Air 582(3)	441		1. 9.99	K J Kimpton	(Gravesend)	22.12.08P
	(Built P A Mercer - pr.no.BMAA HB/113)						
G-BYPY	Ryan ST3KR	1001	F-AZEV	5.10.99	T Curtis-Taylor (As "001" in US Army c/s)		
			N18926			Old Warden	28. 8.09P
G-BYPZ	Rans S-6-S-116 Super Six	0299.1304		14. 7.99	R A Blackbourn	Perth	26. 3.09P
	(Built P G Hayward - pr.no.PFA 204A-13448) (Rotax 912-UL) (Tri-cycle u/c)						
G-BYRC	Westland Wessex HC.Mk.2	WA539	XT671	23. 9.99	D Brem-Wilson	Joydens Farm, Westerham	
G-BYRG	Rans S-6-ES Coyote II	1298.1289		9. 9.99	S J Macmillan	Easter Poldar Farm, Thornhill	14.10.09P
	(Built J Whiting - pr.no.PFA 204-13518) (Rotax 582) (Tri-cycle u/c)						
G-BYRH	Medway Hybred 44XLR	MR165/143		25.10.99	G R Puffett (Noted 2.06)	Landmead Farm, Garford	5. 9.05P
	(Rotax 503)						
G-BYRJ	Cyclone Airsports Pegasus Quantum 15-912			24. 9.99	A L Brown	Long Marston	3. 7.09P
		7548					
G-BYRK	Cameron V-42 Balloon (Hot Air)	4662		14. 7.99	R Kunert	Finchamstead, Wokingham	30. 7.09E
G-BYRO	Mainair Blade	1210-0899-7-W1013		20. 8.99	P W F Coleman	Corn Wood Farm, Adversane	2. 6.07P
	(Rotax 582)x						
G-BYRP	Mainair Blade 912	1075-1295-7-W877		15. 9.99	J T and A C Swannick	Ince Blundell	17. 4.07P
	(C/n amended to 1075-0999-7-W877 by Mainair)						
G-BYRR	Mainair Blade 912	1211-0999-7-W1015		17. 8.99	G R Sharples	(Harrow)	18. 6.04P
	(C/n amended to 1222-0999-7-W1015 by Mainair)						
G-BYRS	Rans S-6-ES Coyote II	0998.1266		17. 9.99	A E Turner	Longacre Farm, Sandy	23.10.09P
	(Built R Beniston - pr.no.PFA 204-13425) (Rotax 582) (Tri-cycle u/c)						
G-BYRU	Cyclone Airsports Pegasus Quantum 15-912			24. 9.99	V R March tr The Sarum QTM912 Group		
		7574				Old Sarum	28. 9.08P
G-BYRV	Raj Hamsa X'Air 582(2)	387		10. 9.99	A D Russell		
	(Built A Hipkin - pr.no.BMAA HB/106)					(Coolboy, Letterkenny, County Donegal)	22. 7.09P
G-BYRX	Westland Scout AH.1	F9640	XT634	5.10.99	Historic Helicopters Ltd (As "XT634" in AAC c/s)		
						Thruxton	2.11.09P
G-BYRY	Slingsby T 67M-200 Firefly	2042	B-HZQ	28. 9.99	T R Pearson (As "HKG-11" in Royal Hong Kong AAF c/s)		
			VR-HZQ, HKG-11			Inverness	23. 9.09E
G-BYRZ	Lindstrand LBL 77M Balloon (Hot Air)	643		28. 9.99	Challenge Transatlantique "Conseil Régional de Lorraine"		
	(Reported to be rebuild of G-BXDX)					Metz, France	5.12.00A
G-BYSA	Europa Aviation Europa XS	360		23. 8.99	R L Hitchcock "Sadie"	Bentley Farm, Coal Aston	31. 5.09P
	(Built B Allsop - pr.no.PFA 247-13199) (Monowheel u/c)						
G-BYSE	Agusta-Bell 206B-2 JetRanger II	8553	G-BFND	3.11.81	Alspath Properties Ltd	Coventry	26.10.09E
G-BYSF	Avtech Jabiru UL	0195		5.10.99	M W Sayers	Sittles Farm, Alrewas	17.11.09P
	(Built M M Smith - pr.no.PFA 274A-13356)						
G-BYSG	Robin HR.200-120B	339		22.11.99	Modi Aviation Ltd	Sibson	18.12.09E
G-BYSI	PZL-110 Koliber 160A	04990081	SP-WGI	21. 1.00	J and Dawn F Evans	Gamston	29. 3.09E
G-BYSJ	de Havilland DHC-1 Chipmunk 22	C1/0021	SE-BON	12.10.99	C H Green (As "WB569:R" in RAF c/s)	Kemble	2. 1.10S
			WB569				
G-BYSK	Cameron A-275 Balloon (Hot Air)	4699		23. 2.00	Balloon School (International) Ltd (British School of		
					Ballooning titles) Colhook Common, Petworth		8. 5.09E
G-BYSM	Cameron A-210 Balloon (Hot Air)	4698		12. 4.00	Balloon School (International) Ltd "Bath Heritage"		
					(Operated Heritage Balloons)	Bath	27. 5.09E
G-BYSN	Rans S-6-ES Coyote II	1098.1270		19.10.99	A L and A R Roberts (Llantwit Major and Lincoln)		3.12.07P
	(Built A L Roberts - pr.no.PFA 204-13459) (Rotax 582) (Tri-cycle u/c)						
G-BYSP	Piper PA-28-181 Archer II	28-8590047	D-EAUL	12.10.99	Take Flight Aviation Ltd	Wellesbourne Mountford	10.12.09E
			N6909D				
G-BYSS	Medway EclipseR	167/145		25.10.99	D W Allen	Popham	7.12.09E
G-BYSV	Cameron N-120 Balloon (Hot Air)	4704		15.10.99	S Simmington	Eccles, Norwich	8. 2.09E
G-BYSW	Enstrom 280FX Shark	2026	I-LUST	19. 9.00	D A Marks	(Milbrook, Bedford)	19. 3.09E
			N88CV				
	(Made a precautionary landing at Hay Tor, Dartmoor 30. 8.08 due to bad weather; landed in gorse bushes and rolled to the left damaging the rotor blades and left side of the fuselage)						
G-BYSX	Cyclone Airsports Pegasus Quantum 15-912			23.11.99	D W Ormond	Deenethorpe	1. 2.09P
		7586					
G-BYSY	Raj Hamsa X'Air 582(2)	448		21.10.99	J M Davidson		
	(Built J M Davidson - pr.no.BMAA HB/109)					Oxleaze Grange, Hawling, Cheltenham	8. 5.09P
G-BYTA	Kolb Twinstar Mk.III (mod)	PFA 205-13240		2. 9.99	L R Morris	Ballymageough, Kilkeel	14. 2.08P
	(Built R E Gray) (Collided with a hedgerow and barbed wire fence during an attempted forced landing in a field at Kilkeel, NI 16.11.07 due to engine failure. Damaged beyond repair).						
G-BYTB	SOCATA TB-20 Trinidad	2002	F-OILE	18. 5.00	Watchman Aircraft Ltd	Jersey	5.10.09E
G-BYTC	Cyclone Airsports Pegasus Quantum Q.2 Sport 15-912			25.10.99	R J Marriott	Headon Farm, Retford	22.11.06P
		7571					
G-BYTG	Glaser-Dirks DG-400	4-211	D-KBBP	18.11.99	P R Williams and B Sebestik		
						Cheltenham and Porto, Portugal	18. 4.09E
G-BYTH	Airbus A320-231	0429	C-GTDM	21. 1.00	Thomas Cook Airlines Ltd	Manchester	12. 1.10E
	G-BYTH, C-GTDM, G-BYTH, C-GTDM, G-BYTH, D-ASSR, (D-AUKT), G-BYTH, EI-TLE, D-AORX, N429RX, F-WWIZ						
G-BYTI	Piper PA-24-250 Comanche	24-3489	D-ELOP	9.11.99	M Carruthers and G Auchterlonie	Gamston	6.11.09E
			N8297P, N10F				
G-BYTJ	Cameron Concept 80 Balloon (Hot Air)	4703		19.11.99	M White (Rapido titles)	Cirencester	10. 9.09E
G-BYTK	Avtech Jabiru SPL-450	0265		8.11.99	P J Reilly	(Salisbury)	25. 8.09P
	(Built K A Fagan and S R Pike - pr.no.PFA 274A-13465)						
G-BYTL	Mainair Blade 912	1224-0999-7-W1017		19.10.99	P B Spencer	(Barton, Preston)	17.10.08P

G-BYTM	Dyn'Aéro MCR-01 Club	83		1.10.99	I Lang	Shobdon	12. 8.09P

(Built I Lang - pr.no.PFA 301-13440)

| G-BYTN | de Havilland DH.82A Tiger Moth | 3993 | 7014M
N6720 | 18.11.99 | J W Freckington and R Merewood *(As "N6720:VX" in RAF c/s)*
Wickenby | | 2. 9.10S |

| G-BYTR | Raj Hamsa X'Air 582(1) | 460 | | 5.10.99 | D R Western and J F Northey | Weston Zoyland | 26. 9.08P |

(Built A P Roberts and R Dunn - pr.no.BMAA HB/105)

| G-BYTS | Montgomerie-Bensen B 8MR | MGM-2 | | 22. 9.99 | M G Mee | Kirkbride | 18. 7.08P |

(Built M G Mee) (Rotax 912)

| G-BYTU | Mainair Blade 912 | 1225-1099-7-W1018 | | 26.11.99 | J E Morgan | Caernarfon | 3. 5.09P |
| G-BYTV | Avtech Jabiru UL-450 | 0264 | | 3.11.99 | M G Speers | Andreas, Isle of Man | 7.10.09P |

(Built E Bentley - pr.no.PFA 274A-13454)

| G-BYTW | Cameron O-90 Balloon (Hot Air) | 4747 | | 11. 4.00 | Sade Balloons Ltd | London EC2 | 24. 4.09E |
| G-BYTX | Whittaker MW6-S Fatboy Flyer | | | | | | |

(Built J K Ewing) (Rotax 532) PFA 164-12819

| | | | | 2.12.99 | J K Ewing | Mapperton Farm, Newton Peverill | 15. 8.06P |
| G-BYTZ | Raj Hamsa X'Air 582(6) | 472 | | 26.10.99 | R Armstrong | (Dungannon) | 3. 7.09P |

(Built A B Wilson and K C Millar - pr.no.BMAA HB/120)

| G-BYUA | Grob G115E Tutor | 82086E | D-EUKB | 22. 7.99 | VT Aerospace Ltd | RAF Wyton | 5. 8.09E |

(Operated Cambridge UAS [5 AEF] and University of London AS)

| G-BYUB | Grob G115E Tutor | 82087E | | 22. 7.99 | VT Aerospace Ltd | RAF Cranwell | 5. 8.09E |

(Operated East Midlands UAS [7 AEF])

| G-BYUC | Grob G115E Tutor | 82088E | | 22. 7.99 | VT Aerospace Ltd | RAF Cranwell | 5. 8.09E |

(Operated -East Midlands UAS [7 AEF])

| G-BYUD | Grob G115E Tutor | 82089E | | 22. 7.99 | VT Aerospace Ltd | Glasgow | 5. 8.09E |

(Operated Universities of Glasgow and Strathclyde AS [4 AEF]

| G-BYUE | Grob G115E Tutor | 82090E | | 12. 8.99 | VT Aerospace Ltd | RAF Cranwell | 30. 8.09E |

(Operated East Midlands UAS [7 AEF])

| G-BYUF | Grob G115E Tutor | 82091E | | 12. 8.99 | VT Aerospace Ltd | RAF Cosford | 30. 8.09E |

(Operated University of Birmingham AS [8 AEF])

| G-BYUG | Grob G115E Tutor | 82092E | | 22. 9.99 | VT Aerospace Ltd | RAF Wyton | 27. 9.09E |

(Operated Cambridge UAS [5 AEF] and University of London AS)

| G-BYUH | Grob G115E Tutor | 82093E | | 22. 9.99 | VT Aerospace Ltd | Colerne | 27. 9.09E |

(Operated Bristol UAS [3 AEF])

| G-BYUI | Grob G115E Tutor | 82094E | | 24. 9.99 | VT Aerospace Ltd | RAF Woodvale | 27. 9.09E |

(Operated Liverpool UAS and Manchester and Salford Universities AS [10 AEF])

| G-BYUJ | Grob G115E Tutor | 82095E | | 24. 9.99 | VT Aerospace Ltd | RAF Church Fenton | 27. 9.09E |

(Operated Yorkshire Universities AS [9 AEF])

| G-BYUK | Grob G115E Tutor | 82096E | | 18.10.99 | VT Aerospace Ltd | RAF Woodvale | 28.10.09E |

(Operated Liverpool UAS and Manchester and Salford Universities AS [10 AEF])

| G-BYUL | Grob G115E Tutor | 82097E | | 18.10.99 | VT Aerospace Ltd | Boscombe Down | 27.10.09E |

(Operated Southampton UAS [2 AEF])

| G-BYUM | Grob G115E Tutor | 82098E | | 18.10.99 | VT Aerospace Ltd | RAF Leuchars | 28.10.09E |

(Operated East of Scotland UAS [12 AEF])

| G-BYUN | Grob G115E Tutor | 82099E | | 18.10.99 | VT Aerospace Ltd | RAF Leuchars | 28.10.09E |

(Operated East of Scotland UAS [12 AEF])

| G-BYUO | Grob G115E Tutor | 82100E | | 19.11.99 | VT Aerospace Ltd | RAF Wyton | 28.11.09E |

(Operated Cambridge UAS [5 AEF] and University of London AS)

| G-BYUP | Grob G115E Tutor | 82101E | | 19.11.99 | VT Aerospace Ltd | RAF Cranwell | 28.11.09E |

(Operated CFS Tutor Sqdn)

| G-BYUR | Grob G115E Tutor | 82102E | | 19.11.99 | VT Aerospace Ltd | RAF Leuchars | 28.11.09E |

(Operated East of Scotland UAS [12 AEF])

| G-BYUS | Grob G115E Tutor | 82103E | | 19.11.99 | VT Aerospace Ltd | RAF Church Fenton | 28.11.09E |

(Operated Yorkshire Universities AS [9 AEF])

| G-BYUT | Grob G115E Tutor | 82104E | | 7.12.99 | VT Aerospace Ltd | RAF St Athan | 13.12.09E |

(Mid-air collision with G-BYVN 11.2.09 near Porthcawl, Wales)   *(Operated University of Wales AS [1 AEF])*

| G-BYUU | Grob G115E Tutor | 82105E | | 7.12.99 | VT Aerospace Ltd | RAF Leuchars | 14.12.09E |

(Operated East of Scotland UAS [12 AEF])

| G-BYUV | Grob G115E Tutor | 82106E | | 7.12.99 | VT Aerospace Ltd | RAF Benson | 14.12.09E |

(Operated Oxford University AS [6 AEF])

| G-BYUW | Grob G115E Tutor | 82107E | | 7.12.99 | VT Aerospace Ltd | RAF Wyton | 16.12.08E |

(Operated Cambridge UAS [5 AEF] and University of London AS)

| G-BYUX | Grob G115E Tutor | 82108E | | 18. 1.00 | VT Aerospace Ltd | RAF Leuchars | 31. 1.10E |

(Operated East of Scotland UAS [12 AEF])

| G-BYUY | Grob G115E Tutor | 82109E | | 18. 1.00 | VT Aerospace Ltd | RAF Leuchars | 31. 1.10E |

(Operated East of Scotland UAS [12 AEF])

| G-BYUZ | Grob G115E Tutor | 82110E | | 18. 1.00 | VT Aerospace Ltd | RAF Woodvale | 31. 1.10E |

(Operated Liverpool UAS and Manchester and Salford Universities AS [10 AEF])

| G-BYVA | Grob G115E Tutor | 82111E | | 18. 1.00 | VT Aerospace Ltd | RAF Cranwell | 31. 1.10E |

(Operated East Midlands UAS [7 AEF])

| G-BYVB | Grob G115E Tutor | 82112E | | 17. 2.00 | VT Aerospace Ltd | RAF Woodvale | 28. 2.09E |

(Operated Liverpool UAS and Manchester and Salford Universities AS [10 AEF])

| G-BYVC | Grob G115E Tutor | 82113E | | 17. 2.00 | VT Aerospace Ltd | RAF Wyton | 2. 3.09E |

(Operated Cambridge UAS [5 AEF] and University of London AS)

| G-BYVD | Grob G115E Tutor | 82114E | | 17. 2.00 | VT Aerospace Ltd | RAF Leuchars | 2. 4.09E |

(Operated East of Scotland UAS [12AEF])

| G-BYVE | Grob G115E Tutor | 82115E | | 17. 2.00 | VT Aerospace Ltd | RAF Wyton | 8. 4.09E |

(Operated Cambridge UAS [5 AEF] and University of London AS)

| G-BYVF | Grob G115E Tutor | 82116E | | 22. 2.00 | VT Aerospace Ltd | RNAS Yeovilton | 28. 2.09E |

(Operated 727 Sqdn)

| G-BYVG | Grob G115E Tutor | 82117E | | 22. 3.00 | VT Aerospace Ltd | RAF Church Fenton | 2. 4.09E |

(Operated Yorkshire Universities AS [9 AEF])

| G-BYVH | Grob G115E Tutor | 82118E | | 22. 3.00 | VT Aerospace Ltd | RAF Woodvale | 4. 4.09E |

(Operated Liverpool UAS and Manchester and Salford Universities AS [10 AEF])

| G-BYVI | Grob G115E Tutor | 82119E | | 22. 3.00 | VT Aerospace Ltd | RAF Wyton | 4. 4.09E |

(Operated Cambridge UAS [5 AEF] and University of London AS)

G-BYVJ	Grob G115E Tutor	82120E	14. 4.00	VT Aerospace Ltd	RAF Church Fenton	25. 4.09E
				(Operated Yorkshire Universities AS [9 AEF])		
G-BYVK	Grob G115E Tutor	82121E	14. 4.00	VT Aerospace Ltd	RNAS Yeovilton	25. 4.09E
				(Operated 727 Sqdn)		
G-BYVL	Grob G115E Tutor	82122E	14. 4.00	VT Aerospace Ltd	RAF Benson	26. 4.09E
				(Operated Oxford University AS [6 AEF])		
G-BYVM	Grob G115E Tutor	82123E	14. 4.00	VT Aerospace Ltd	RAF Wyton	26. 4.09E
				(Operated Cambridge UAS [5 AEF] and University of London AS)		
G-BYVN	Grob G115E Tutor	82124E	18. 5.00	VT Aerospace Ltd	RAF St Athan	31. 5.09E
	(Mid-air collision with G-BYUT 11.2.09 near Porthcawl, Wales)			(Operated University of Wales AS [1 AEF])		
G-BYVO	Grob G115E Tutor	82125E	18. 5.00	VT Aerospace Ltd	RAF Leuchars	31. 5.09E
				(Operated East of Scotland UAS [12AEF])		
G-BYVP	Grob G115E Tutor	82126E	18. 5.00	VT Aerospace Ltd	RAF Benson	31. 5.09E
				(Operated Oxford University AS [6 AEF])		
G-BYVR	Grob G115E Tutor	82127E	18. 5.00	VT Aerospace Ltd	RAF Cranwell	31. 5.09E
				(Operated CFS Tutor Sqdn)		
G-BYVS	Grob G115E Tutor	82128E	20. 6.00	VT Aerospace Ltd	RAF Cranwell	29. 6.09E
				(Operated CFS Tutor Sqdn)		
G-BYVT	Grob G115E Tutor	82129E	20. 6.00	VT Aerospace Ltd	RAF Wyton	29. 6.09E
				(Operated Cambridge UAS [5 AEF] and University of London AS)		
G-BYVU	Grob G115E Tutor	82130E	20. 6.00	VT Aerospace Ltd	RAF Benson	29. 6.09E
				(Operated Oxford University AS [6 AEF])		
G-BYVV	Grob G115E Tutor	82131E	20. 6.00	VT Aerospace Ltd	RAF Leeming	29. 6.09E
				(Operated Northumbrian Universities AS [11 AEF])		
G-BYVW	Grob G115E Tutor	82132E	21. 7.00	VT Aerospace Ltd	RAF St Athan	6. 8.09E
				(Operated University of Wales AS [1 AEF])		
G-BYVX	Grob G115E Tutor	82133E	21. 7.00	VT Aerospace Ltd	RAF Church Fenton	6. 8.09E
				(Operated Yorkshire Universities AS [9 AEF])		
G-BYVY	Grob G115E Tutor	82134E	21. 7.00	VT Aerospace Ltd	RAF Cosford	6. 8.09E
				(Operated University of Birmingham AS [8 AEF])		
G-BYVZ	Grob G115E Tutor	82135E	21. 7.00	VT Aerospace Ltd	RAF Church Fenton	6. 8.09E
				(Operated Yorkshire Universities AS [9 AEF])		
G-BYWA	Grob G115E Tutor	82136E	21. 8.00	VT Aerospace Ltd	RAF Benson	30. 8.09E
				(Operated Oxford University AS [6 AEF])		
G-BYWB	Grob G115E Tutor	82137E	21. 8.00	VT Aerospace Ltd	RAF Cranwell	30. 8.09E
				(Operated CFS Tutor Sqdn)		
G-BYWC	Grob G115E Tutor	82138E	18. 9.00	VT Aerospace Ltd	RAF Benson	27. 9.09E
				(Operated Oxford University AS [6 AEF])		
G-BYWD	Grob G115E Tutor	82139E	18. 9.00	VT Aerospace Ltd	RAF Wyton	27. 9.09E
				(Operated Cambridge UAS [5 AEF] and University of London AS)		
G-BYWE	Grob G115E Tutor	82140E	18. 9.00	VT Aerospace Ltd	Colerne	23.10.09E
				(Operated Bristol UAS [3 AEF])		
G-BYWF	Grob G115E Tutor	82141E	18. 9.00	VT Aerospace Ltd	RAF Cranwell	27. 9.09E
				(Operated East Midlands UAS [7 AEF])		
G-BYWG	Grob G115E Tutor	82142E	13.10.00	VT Aerospace Ltd	RAF Cranwell	29.10.09E
				(Operated CFS Tutor Sqdn)		
G-BYWH	Grob G115E Tutor	82143E	13.10.00	VT Aerospace Ltd	RAF Leeming	29.10.09E
				(Operated Northumbrian Universities AS [11 AEF])		
G-BYWI	Grob G115E Tutor	82144E	13.10.00	VT Aerospace Ltd	RAF Woodvale	29.10.09E
				(Operated Liverpool UAS and Manchester and Salford Universities AS [10 AEF])		
G-BYWJ	Grob G115E Tutor	82145E	13.10.00	VT Aerospace Ltd	RAF Woodvale	29.10.09E
				(Operated Liverpool UAS and Manchester and Salford Universities AS [10 AEF])		
G-BYWK	Grob G115E Tutor	82146E	17.11.00	VT Aerospace Ltd	Boscombe Down	28.11.09E
				(Operated Southampton UAS [2 AEF])		
G-BYWL	Grob G115E Tutor	82147E	17.11.00	VT Aerospace Ltd	RAF Cranwell	28.11.09E
				(Operated CFS Tutor Sqdn)		
G-BYWM	Grob G115E Tutor	82148E	17.11.00	VT Aerospace Ltd	RNAS Yeovilton	28.11.09E
				(Operated 727 Sqdn)		
G-BYWN	Grob G115E Tutor	82149E	17.11.00	VT Aerospace Ltd	RAF Woodvale	28.11.09E
				(Operated Liverpool UAS and Manchester and Salford Universities AS [10 AEF])		
G-BYWO	Grob G115E Tutor	82150E	7.12.00	VT Aerospace Ltd	RAF Wyton	13. 1.10E
				(Operated Cambridge UAS [5 AEF] and University of London AS)		
G-BYWP	Grob G115E Tutor	82151E	7.12.00	VT Aerospace Ltd	RAF Church Fenton	14. 1.09E
				(Operated Yorkshire Universities AS [9 AEF])		
G-BYWR	Grob G115E Tutor	82152E	18. 5.00	VT Aerospace Ltd	RAF Wyton	5. 2.10E
				(Operated Cambridge UAS [5 AEF] and University of London AS)		
G-BYWS	Grob G115E Tutor	82153E	7.12.00	VT Aerospace Ltd	RAF Wyton	15. 1.10E
				(Operated Cambridge UAS [5 AEF] and University of London AS)		
G-BYWT	Grob G115E Tutor	82154E	12.12.00	VT Aerospace Ltd	RAF Leeming	16. 1.09E
				(Operated Northumbrian Universities AS [11 AEF])		
G-BYWU	Grob G115E Tutor	82155E	19. 1.01	VT Aerospace Ltd	RAF Wyton	28. 1.10E
				(Operated Cambridge UAS [5 AEF] and University of London AS)		
G-BYWV	Grob G115E Tutor	82156E	19. 1.01	VT Aerospace Ltd	RAF Church Fenton	27. 1.10E
				(Operated Yorkshire Universities AS [9 AEF])		
G-BYWW	Grob G115E Tutor	82157E	19. 1.01	VT Aerospace Ltd	Boscombe Down	28. 1.10E
				(Operated Southampton UAS [2 AEF])		
G-BYWX	Grob G115E Tutor	82158E	14. 2.01	VT Aerospace Ltd	RAF Wyton	25. 2.09E
				(Operated Cambridge UAS [5 AEF] and University of London AS)		
G-BYWY	Grob G115E Tutor	82159E	14. 2.01	VT Aerospace Ltd	RAF Cranwell	25. 2.09E
				(Operated East Midlands UAS [7 AEF])		
G-BYWZ	Grob G115E Tutor	82160E	14. 2.01	VT Aerospace Ltd	RAF Cranwell	4. 3.09E
				(Operated East Midlands UAS [7 AEF])		
G-BYXA	Grob G115E Tutor	82161E	14. 2.01	VT Aerospace Ltd	RAF Benson	4. 3.09E
				(Operated Oxford University AS [6 AEF])		

G-BYXB	Grob G115E Tutor	82162E		19. 3.01	VT Aerospace Ltd	Boscombe Down	1. 4.09E
					(Operated Southampton UAS [2 AEF])		
G-BYXC	Grob G115E Tutor	82163E		19. 3.01	VT Aerospace Ltd	RAF Benson	1. 4.09E
					(Operated Oxford University AS [6 AEF])		
G-BYXD	Grob G115E Tutor	82164E		19. 3.01	VT Aerospace Ltd	Boscombe Down	1. 4.09E
					(Operated Southampton UAS [2 AEF])		
G-BYXE	Grob G115E Tutor	82165E		19. 3.01	VT Aerospace Ltd)	RAF Church Fenton	1. 4.09E
					(Operated Yorkshire Universities AS [9 AEF])		
G-BYXF	Grob G115E Tutor	82166E		12. 4.01	VT Aerospace Ltd	RAF Cosford	25. 4.09E
					(Operated University of Birmingham AS [8 AEF])		
G-BYXG	Grob G115E Tutor	82167E		12. 4.01	VT Aerospace Ltd)	RAF Cosford	25. 4.09E
					(Operated University of Birmingham AS [8 AEF])		
G-BYXH	Grob G115E Tutor	82168E		12. 4.01	VT Aerospace Ltd	Colerne	29. 4.09E
					(Operated Bristol UAS [3 AEF])		
G-BYXI	Grob G115E Tutor	82169E		12. 4.01	VT Aerospace Ltd	RAF Woodvale	29. 4.09E
					(Operated Liverpool UAS and Manchester and Salford Universities AS [10 AEF])		
G-BYXJ	Grob G115E Tutor	82170E		16. 5.01	VT Aerospace Ltd	Boscombe Down	28. 5.09E
					(Operated Southampton UAS [2 AEF])		
G-BYXK	Grob G115E Tutor	82171E		16. 5.01	VT Aerospace Ltd	RNAS Yeovilton	28. 5.09E
					(Operated 727 Sqdn)		
G-BYXL	Grob G115E Tutor	82172E		16. 5.01	VT Aerospace Ltd	RAF Cosford	28. 5.09E
					(Operated University of Birmingham AS [8 AEF])		
G-BYXM	Grob G115E Tutor	82173E		16. 5.01	VT Aerospace Ltd	RAF Cranwell	28. 5.09E
					(Operated CFS Tutor Sqdn)		
G-BYXN	Grob G115E Tutor	82174E		8. 6.01	VT Aerospace Ltd	RAF Cranwell	11. 6.09E
					(Operated East Midlands UAS [7 AEF]) "XN"		
G-BYXO	Grob G115E Tutor	82175E		8. 6.01	VT Aerospace Ltd	RAF Cosford	11. 6.09E
					(Operated University of Birmingham AS [8 AEF])		
G-BYXP	Grob G115E Tutor	82176E		8. 6.01	VT Aerospace Ltd	RAF Wyton	11. 6.09E
					(Operated Cambridge UAS [5 AEF] and University of London AS)		
G-BYXR	Grob G115E Tutor	82177E		8. 6.01	VT Aerospace Ltd	RAF Benson	11. 6.09E
					(Operated Oxford University AS [6 AEF])		
G-BYXS	Grob G115E Tutor	82178E		18. 7.01	VT Aerospace Ltd	RNAS Yeovilton	29. 7.09E
					(Operated 727 Sqdn)		
G-BYXT	Grob G115E Tutor	82179E		18. 7.01	VT Aerospace Ltd	RAF Wyton	1.11.09E
					(Operated Cambridge UAS [5 AEF] and University of London AS)		
G-BYXV	Medway EclipseR	162/140		25.10.99	K A Christie	Nether Balgillo Farm, Finavon	10. 5.04P
G-BYXW	Medway EclipseR	166/147		25.10.99	G A Hazell	Lower Upham Farm, Chiseldon	25. 5.08P
	(Officially registered as c/n 166/144)						
G-BYXX	Grob G115E Tutor	82180E		18. 7.01	VT Aerospace Ltd	RAF Woodvale	1.11.09E
					(Operated Liverpool UAS and Manchester and Salford Universities AS [10 AEF])		
G-BYXY	Grob G115E Tutor	82181E		18. 7.01	VT Aerospace Ltd	RAF Wyton	30. 9.09E
					(Operated Cambridge UAS [5 AEF] and University of London AS)		
G-BYXZ	Grob G115E Tutor	82182E		15. 8.01	VT Aerospace Ltd	RAF Cranwell	17. 9.09E
					(Operated CFS Tutor Sqdn)		
G-BYYA	Grob G115E Tutor	82183E		15. 8.01	VT Aerospace Ltd	RAF Leeming	23. 9.08E
					(Operated Northumbrian Universities AS [11 AEF])		
G-BYYB	Grob G115E Tutor	82184E		15. 8.01	VT Aerospace Ltd	RAF Woodvale	17. 9.09E
					(Operated Liverpool UAS and Manchester and Salford Universities AS [10 AEF])		
G-BYYC	Hapi Cygnet SF-2A	PFA 182-12311		25.11.99	G H Smith	Shenstone Hall Farm, Shenstone	18. 6.08P
	(Built C D Hughes and G H Smith) (Volkswagen 2180)						
G-BYYD	Cameron A-250 Balloon (Hot Air)	4712		31. 3.00	C and J.M Bailey	Bristol	1. 7.09E
G-BYYE	Lindstrand LBL 77A Balloon (Hot Air)	151		25.11.99	C G Dobson	Streatley, Reading	9. 7.09E
G-BYYG	Slingsby T 67C Firefly	2101	PH-SGI	30.11.99	The Pathfinder Flying Club Ltd	RAF Wyton	9. 4.09E
G-BYYJ	Lindstrand LBL 25A Cloudhopper Balloon (Hot Air)	651		10.12.99	A M Barton	Coulsdon	14. 8.07A
G-BYYL	Avtech Jabiru UL-450	xxxx		10.12.99	K C Lye	Edington Hill, Keevil	16. 7.09P
	(Built C Jackson - pr.no.PFA 274A-13480)						
G-BYYM	Raj Hamsa X'Air 582(1)	476		21.10.99	S M S Smith	(Malborough, Kingsbridge)	11.11.09P
	(Built J J Cozens - pr.no.BMAA HB/119)						
G-BYYN	Cyclone Airsports Pegasus Quantum 15-912	7601		6. 1.00	R K Johnson	Tarn Farm Cockerham	14. 6.08P
G-BYYO	Piper PA-28R-201 Arrow	2837061	(N182ND) N9249C, G-BYYO, N9249C	11. 2.00	Stapleford Flying Club Ltd	Stapleford	26. 4.09E
G-BYYP	Cyclone Airsports Pegasus Quantum 15	7603		11. 2.00	D A Linsey-Bloom	(Long Ashton, Bristol)	9. 5.09P
	(Rotax 582)						
G-BYYR	Raj Hamsa X'Air 582(4)	453		23.12.99	T D Bawden	Weston Zoyland	11. 5.04P
	(Built T D Bawden - pr.no.BMAA HB/115)						
G-BYYT	Avtech Jabiru UL-450	0259		18.11.99	A J Young and A C Gale	Marley Hall, Ledbury	4. 9.08P
	(Built T D Saveker - pr.no.PFA 274A-13452)						
G-BYYX	TEAM Mini-MAX 91	PFA 186-13410		6. 1.00	J Batchelor	Gerpins Farm, Upminster	30. 7.09P
	(Built P L Turner)						
G-BYYY	Cyclone Airsports Pegasus Quantum 15-912	7564		8.12.99	Clearprop Microlight School Ltd Redlands, Swindon		8. 2.09P
G-BYYZ	Staaken Z-21A Flitzer	PFA 223-13324		12.11.99	T White	Headcorn	26. 3.08P
	(Built A E Morris) (Volkswagen 1834)						
G-BYZA	Aérospatiale AS.355F2 Ecureuil 2	5518	JA6784 F-OHNK	20.12.99	MMAir Ltd	Redhill	17. 4.09E
G-BYZB	Mainair Blade	1229-1299-7-W1022		14. 1.00	A M Thornley	(Acthorp Top, Louth)	29. 9.08P
G-BYZF	Raj Hamsa X'Air 582(1)	461		7. 1.00	R P Davies	(Eccleston, Chorley)	
	(Built S W Grainger - pr.no.BMAA HB/110)				*(Crashed during test-flying Brook Farm, Pilling: stored dismantled 6.07)*		
G-BYZG	Cameron A-275 Balloon (Hot Air)	4706		23. 2.00	Cameron Flights Southern Ltd *"Horizon Balloons"* Woodborough, Pewsey		6. 4.09E

G-BYZJ	Boeing 737-3Q8	24962	G-COLE PP-VOX	11. 1.00	British Midland Airways Ltd *(Operated bmiBaby)* *"pudsey baby"*	Nottingham-East Midlands	20.11.09E
G-BYZL	Cameron GP-65 Balloon (Hot Air)	4494		6. 4.00	P Thibo	Junglinster, Luxembourg	28.10.09E
G-BYZO	Rans S-6-ES Coyote II	1298.1287		14. 1.00	B E J Badger and J E Storer	Long Marston	22. 9.09P
	(Built S C Jackson - pr.no.PFA 204-13560) (Rotax 582) (Tri-cycle u/c)						
G-BYZP	Robinson R22 Beta II	3018		9.12.99	Propwash Investments Ltd	Swansea	4. 2.10E
G-BYZR	III Sky Arrow 650 TC	C001	D-ENGF I-TREI	24. 1.00	J O Harkness and R Moncrieff tr G-BYZR Flying Group	Gamston	14. 8.08P
	(Built Iniziative Industriali Italian)						
G-BYZS	Avtech Jabiru UL-450	xxxx		25. 1.00	N Fielding	Ince Blundell	17. 7.09P
	(Built N Fielding - pr.no.PFA 274A-13489)						
G-BYZT	Nova Vertex 26	13345		21. 1.00	M Hay	(Dundee)	
G-BYZU	Cyclone Airsports Pegasus Quantum 15-	7613		15. 2.00	N I Clifton	East Fortune	25. 4.09P
	(Rotax 582)						
G-BYZV	Sky 90-24 Balloon (Hot Air)	174		15. 8.00	P Farmer	Wadhurst	19. 1.01
G-BYZW	Raj Hamsa X'Air 582(1)	499		19. 1.00	J Magill	(Braystones, Beckermet)	7. 8.09P
	(Built P A Gilford - pr.no.BMAA HB/129)						
G-BYZX	Cameron R-90 Balloon (Hot Air)	4751		31. 3.00	D K Hempleman-Adams *"Britannic Challenge"*	Corsham	22. 3.05A
	(Rebuilt with envelope c/n 10369)						
G-BYZY	Pietenpol AirCamper	PFA 047-12190		2.12.99	D N Hanchet	Siege Cross Farm, Thatcham	31. 1.09P
	(Built D N Hanchet)						
G-BYZZ	Robinson R22 Beta II	3000		1.12.99	Casdron Enterprises Ltd	Kemble	8.11.09E

G-BZAA - G-BZZZ

G-BZAA	Mainair Blade 912	1142-0198-7-W945		22.11.99	G P Spittles	(Brackley)	4. 4.08P
	(Rotax 462) (Trike c/n amended to 1142-1299-7 by Mainair Sports Ltd)						
G-BZAB	Mainair Rapier	1228-1299-7-W1021		23.12.99	B Myers	(Wisbech)	11. 4.08P
G-BZAE	Cessna 152	15281300	N49480	22. 3.00	APB Leasing Ltd	Sleap	5. 6.09E
G-BZAF	Raj Hamsa X'Air 582(1)	503		18. 1.00	Y A Evans	Rufforth	26. 1.09P
	(Built P Hassett - pr.no.BMAA HB/130)						
G-BZAG	Lindstrand LBL 105A Balloon (Hot Air)	542		29..2.00	A M Figiel	High Wycombe	17. 6.09E
G-BZAH	Cessna 208B Grand Caravan	208B0811	N5196U	28. 2.00	R Durie tr Army Parachute Association	AAC Netheravon	13. 4.09E
G-BZAI	Cyclone Airsports Pegasus Quantum 15	7614		9. 2.00	S I Close	Deenethrope	3. 5.09P
	(Rotax 503)						
G-BZAK	Raj Hamsa X'Air 582(9)	477		20. 1.00	R J Ripley	Field Farm, Oakley	25. 5.09P
	(Built B W Austen - pr.no.BMAA HB/114)						
G-BZAL	Mainair Blade 912	1205-0799-7-W1008		27. 1.00	J Potts	Tarn Farm, Cockerham	27. 7.07P
G-BZAM	Europa Aviation Europa	265		6.12.99	D Corbett	Shobdon	1. 6.09P
	(Built D U Corbett - pr.no.PFA 247-12969) (Monowheel u/c)						
G-BZAO	Rans S-12XL Airaile	PFA 307-13394		1. 2.00	M L Robinson	Kirkbride	11. 7.08P
	(Built M L Robinson) (Rotax 582)						
G-BZAP	Avtech Jabiru UL-450	0280		13.12.99	D R Griffiths and I J Grindley	Top Farm, Croydon, Royston	30. 6.08P
	(Built S Derwin - pr.no.PFA 274A-13479)						
G-BZAR	Denney Kitfox Model 4-1200 Speedster		G-LEZJ	17. 2.00	C E Brookes "Ol' Red"	Little Battleflats Farm, Ellistown, Coalville	19. 6.08P
	(Built L A James)	PFA 172B-12529					
	(Rotax 912-UL)						
G-BZAS	Isaacs Fury II	PFA 011-10837		10. 2.00	A W Maycock *(As "K5673" in RAF c/s) "Spirit of Dunsfold"*	Little Rissington	17. 9.09P
	(Built H A Brunt and H Frick) (Canadian Air Motive CAM100)						
G-BZAT	British Aerospace Avro 146-RJ100	E3320	G-6-320	18.11.97	BA Cityflyer Ltd	Birmingham	8. 1.10E
G-BZAU	British Aerospace Avro 146-RJ100	E3328	G-6-328	25. 4.98	BA Cityflyer Ltd	Birmingham	11. 6.09E
G-BZAV	British Aerospace Avro 146-RJ100	E3331	G-6-331	19. 5.98	BA Cityflyer Ltd	Birmingham	23. 7.09E
G-BZAW	British Aerospace Avro 146-RJ100	E3354	G-6-354	11. 6.99	BA Cityflyer Ltd	Manchester	15. 7.09E
G-BZAX	British Aerospace Avro 146-RJ100	E3356	G-6-356	9. 7.99	BA Cityflyer Ltd	Manchester	16. 8.09E
G-BZAY	British Aerospace Avro 146-RJ100	E3368	G-5-368	15. 2.00	BA Cityflyer Ltd	Manchester	27. 3.09E
G-BZAZ	British Aerospace Avro 146-RJ100	E3369	G-5-369	15. 2.00	BA Cityflyer Ltd	Manchester	13. 4.09E
G-BZBC	Rans S-6-ES Coyote II	0499.1314		2. 2.00	A J Baldwin	Derby	29. 8.08P
	(Built A J Baldwin - pr.no.PFA 204-13525) (Rotax 582) (Tri-cycle u/c)						
G-BZBE	Cameron A-210 Balloon (Hot Air)	4708		9. 5.00	Dragon Balloon Company Ltd	Castleton, Hope Valley	23. 6.09E
G-BZBF	Cessna 172M	17262258	N126SA G-BZBF, 9H-ACV, N12785	20.12.99	L W Scattergood	Sandtoft	30. 9.09E
	(Lycoming O-360)						
G-BZBH	Thunder Ax7-65 Bolt Balloon (Hot Air)	173		28.11.78	P J Hebdon and Charlotte A Fraser *"Serendipity II"*	Milton, Banbury	27. 3.09E
G-BZBI	Cameron V-77 Balloon (Hot Air)	4740		4. 4.00	C and A I Gibson *"Flying Colours"*	Stockport	8. 6.09E
G-BZBJ	Lindstrand LBL 77A Balloon (Hot Air)	646		29. 2.00	P T R Ollivere	Eastbourne	22. 7.09E
G-BZBL	Lindstrand LBL 120A Balloon (Hot Air)	676		23. 2.00	East Coast Balloons Ltd	York	31. 3.09E
G-BZBO	Stoddard-Hamilton Glasair III	3032		21. 2.00	M B Hamlett	(Lagny le Sec, France)	
	(Built M B Hamlett)						
G-BZBP	Raj Hamsa X'Air 582(5)	470		29. 2.00	D P Sudworth	Maypole Farm, Chislet	27. 8.08P
	(Built D F Hughes - pr.no.BMAA HB/131)						
G-BZBR	Cyclone Airsports Pegasus Quantum 15	7631		26. 5.00	A Asslanian	Hunsdon	15. 8.09P
	(Rotax 503)						
G-BZBS	Piper PA-28-161 Warrior III	2842080	N4180H G-BZBS, N9529N	10. 5.00	S J Skilton t/a Aviation Rentals	White Waltham	21. 5.09E
G-BZBT	Cameron Hopper H-34 Balloon (Hot Air)	4730		18. 5.00	British Telecommunications PLC	Thatcham	9. 4.05A
G-BZBU	Robinson R22	0131	OH-HLB SE-HOH	23. 5.00	I C Macdonald *(Noted 10.07)*	Blackpool	21. 4.09T
G-BZBW	RotorWay Executive 162F	6415		23. 2.00	Southern Helicopters Ltd	Street Farm, Takeley	28.11.08P
	(Built M Gardiner) (RotorWay RI 162F)						
G-BZBX	Rans S-6-ES Coyote II	0499.1317		26. 1.00	P E De-Ville and M W Shepherd	Otherton, Cannock	6. 7.07P
	(Built R Johnstone - pr.no.PFA 204-13501) (Rotax 582) (Tri-cycle u/c)						
G-BZBZ	Jodel D 9 Bébé	519	OO-48	29. 2.00	S Marom	Whitehall Farm, Benington	28. 7.06P
	(Built Etienne de Schrevel, Gent 1970-77) (Volkswagen 1600)						

Reg	Type	C/n	Prev id	Date	Owner/Operator	Base	Date2
G-BZDA	Piper PA-28-161 Warrior III	2842087	N41814 G-BZDA, N41814	29. 6.00	S J Skilton t/a Aviation Rentals	White Waltham	5. 7.09E
G-BZDB	Thruster T 600T Sprint 450 Jab	0030-T600T-041		7. 3.00	R M Raikes	Clench Common	7. 7.08P
G-BZDC	Mainair Blade (Rotax 462)	1232-0100-7-W1025		13. 3.00	E J Wells and P J Smith	Over Farm, Gloucester	8. 5.09P
G-BZDD	Mainair Blade 912	1238-0200-7-W1031		21. 1.00	A S Facey tr Barton Blade Group	Barton	13. 4.09P
G-BZDE	Lindstrand LBL 210A Balloon (Hot Air)	665		6. 3.00	Toucan Travel Ltd *(Toucan Travel titles)*	Basingstoke	2. 4.09E
G-BZDF	CFM Streak Shadow SA *(Built J W Beckett - pr.no.PFA 206-12609)* *(Rotax 582)*	K 241	(EI-) G-BZDF	7. 3.00	W M Moylan	Glencorrig, Shinrone Birr, County Offaly	11. 7.09P
G-BZDH	Piper PA-28R-200 Cherokee Arrow II	28R-7235028	5B-CJU G-BZDH, HB-OHH, N4390T	8. 3.00	G-BZDH Ltd	Maypole Farm, Chislet	10. 7.09E
G-BZDI	Aero L-39C Albatros	031822	ES-ZLB Soviet AF	7. 6.00	C C Butt	Hawarden	12. 2.10P
G-BZDJ	Cameron Z-105 Balloon (Hot Air)	4832		27. 6.00	BWS Security Systems Ltd *"BWS"*	Corston, Bath	1. 5.09E
G-BZDK	Raj Hamsa X'Air 582(2) *(Built B Park and R Barnes - pr.no.BMAA HB/124)*	447		8. 2.00	B Park *(Operates from Truro and noted 10.06)*	(Lanner Moor, Redruth)	20. 1.06P
G-BZDL	Cyclone Airsports Pegasus Quantum 15-912	7629		18. 4.00	D M Merritt-Colman	Ince Blundell	16. 6.09P
G-BZDM	Stoddard-Hamilton GlaStar *(Built F G Miskelly)*	PFA 295-13283		13. 3.00	F G Miskelly	(London SW6)	26. 7.09P
G-BZDN	Cameron N-105 Balloon (Hot Air)	2840	D-OABB D-Saxonia (2)	26. 4.00	I R Warrington and P A Foot *"Wir Geben Gas" and "Erdgas" titles*	Stamford	17. 2.09E
G-BZDP	Scottish Aviation Bulldog Series 120/121	BH120/244	XX551	31. 3.00	D J Rae (As "XX551:E" in RAF c/s)	Colerne	8. 7.10S
G-BZDR	Tri-R KIS *(Built B S Neilson) (Continental IO-240)*	9403		8. 3.00	J A and J M Jackson	Sleap	28. 6.08P
G-BZDS	Cyclone Airsports Pegasus Quantum 15-912	7633		17. 4.00	K C Yeates	(Bitteswell, Luterworth)	11. 2.09P
G-BZDU	de Havilland DHC-1 Chipmunk 22	C1/0714	WP833	31. 3.00	M R Clark (As "WP833" in RAF c/s)	Newcastle	6. 7.09S
G-BZDV	Westland SA.341C Gazelle HT.2	1150	3D-HXL G-BZDV, XW884	31. 3.00	A Murphy t/a European Plant and Machinery Sales	(Hayling Island)	8. 5.08P
G-BZDX	Cameron Colt Sugarbox 90 SS Balloon (Hot Air)	4814		17. 5.00	Stratos Ballooning GmbH and Co KG	Ennigerloh, Germany	6. 5.04A
G-BZDY	Cameron Colt Sugarbox 90 SS Balloon (Hot Air)	4815		22. 5.00	Stratos Ballooning GmbH and Co KG	Ennigerloh, Germany	7. 4.04A
G-BZDZ	Avtech Jabiru SP-430 *(Built R M Whiteside)*	0232	ZU-BVB	14. 5.01	C O'Donnell tr DZ Group	Rathcoole, Ireland	1. 5.09P
G-BZEA	Cessna A152	A1520824	N7606L	13. 3.00	Sky Leisure Aviation (Charters) Ltd	Blackbushe	29. 7.09E
G-BZEB	Cessna 152	15282772	N89532	31. 1.00	Sky Leisure Aviation (Charters) Ltd *(Noted 9.07)*	Redhill	24. 9.03T
G-BZEC	Cessna 152	15284475	N4655M	21. 1.00	Sky Leisure Aviation (Charters) Ltd	Shoreham	28. 8.09E
G-BZED	Cyclone Airsports Pegasus Quantum 15-912	7600		17. 3.00	D Crozier	Shotton Colliery, Peterlee	9. 6.08P
G-BZEE	Agusta-Bell 206B-2 JetRanger II	8554	G-OJCB	22 .2.00	Atlantic Aviation 2007 Ltd	(Hook)	17. 4.09E
G-BZEG	Mainair Blade (Rotax 912-UL)	1239-0200-7-W1032		3. 3.00	R P Cookson	Ince Blundell	3. 7.09P
G-BZEH	Piper PA-28-235 Cherokee Pathfinder	28-10838	9M-ARW RP-C704, PI-C704, N9182W	31. 3.00	G-BZEH Aviation Ltd	Elstree	8. 6.09E
G-BZEI	Agusta A.109E Power	11056	N449J G-RCMS, G-BZEI	8. 6.00	FB Leasing Ltd	(Basingstoke)	11. 6.06E
G-BZEJ	Raj Hamsa X'Air 582(7) *(Built H Hall - pr.no.BMAA HB/134)*	500		31. 3.00	C Ricketts tr H-Flight X'Air Flying Group	Otherton, Cannock	4.12.09P
G-BZEK	Cameron C-70 Balloon (Hot Air)	4860		30. 5.00	Ballooning 50 Degrees Nord SARL	Fouhren, Luxembourg	2. 4.09E
G-BZEL	Mainair Blade (Rotax 582)	1245-0300-7-W1038		27. 3.00	M W Bush	Belle Vue Farm, Yarnscombe	17. 4.09P
G-BZEN	Avtech Jabiru UL *(Built B W Stockil - pr.no.PFA 274-13272)*	0161		4. 4.00	B W Stockil	Bagby	23. 9.09P
G-BZEP	Scottish Aviation Bulldog Series 120/121	BH120/257	XX561	4. 4.00	A J Amato (As "XX561:7" in RAF c/s)	Biggin Hill	25. 5.05T
G-BZER	Raj Hamsa X'Air R100(1) *(Built N P Lloyd and H Lloyd-Hughes - pr.no.BMAA HB/133)*	526		22. 3.00	N P Lloyd and H Lloyd-Hughes	Greenlands, Rhuallt	4. 3.09P
G-BZES	RotorWay Executive 90 *(Built D C Luffingham)*	6191	G-LUFF	25. 4.00	Southern Helicopters Ltd *(Noted 10.08)*	(Street Farm, Takeley)	
G-BZET	Robin HR.200-120B	345	F-GTZG	9. 5.00	Bulldog Aviation Ltd	Earls Colne	22. 5.09E
G-BZEU	Raj Hamsa X'Air 582(8) *(Built J C Harris - pr.no.BMAA HB/140)*	518		20. 4.00	D E Foster	(Atherstone)	2. 2.08P
G-BZEV	Vahdat-Hagh Semicopter 1 *(Built M E Vahdat-Hagh)*	002		10.10.00	M E Vahdat-Hagh	(Uxbridge)	
G-BZEW	Rans S-6-ES Coyote II *(Built D Kingslake - pr.no.PFA 204-13450) (Rotax 582) (Tri-cycle u/c) (Rebuilt and redated after accident ? as kit no.0998.1268.0199)*	0998.1268		5. 4.00	M J Wooldridge	(Siege Cross Farm, Thatcham)	24. 6.09P
G-BZEX	Raj Hamsa X'Air R100(2) *(Built J M McCullough and R T Henry - pr.no.BMAA HB/135)*	530		5. 4.00	R Johnston	Newtownards	20. 4.09P
G-BZEY	Cameron N-90 Balloon (Hot Air)	4829		15. 5.00	Northants Auto Parts and Service Ltd *(NAPS titles)*	Northampton	23. 8.09E
G-BZEZ	CFM Streak Shadow SA *(Built M F Cottam - pr.no.PFA 206-13503) (Rotax 582)*	K 332		1 .2.00	G J Pearce	Jackrells Farm, Southwater	10. 5.09P
G-BZFB	Robin R2112A Alpha	175	EI-BIU	7. 4.00	T F Wells	Sackville Lodge, Riseley	12. 7.09E
G-BZFC	Cyclone Airsports Pegasus Quantum 15	7640		14. 4.00	G Addison	East Fortune	6 9.08P
G-BZFD	Cameron N-90 Balloon (Hot Air)	2725	OO-BFD	24. 5.00	David Hathaway Holdings Ltd *("David Hathaway Transport" titles)*	Yate, Bristol	24. 3.09E

Reg	Type	c/n	Prev id	Date	Owner	Location	Date
G-BZFH	Cyclone Airsports Pegasus Quantum 15-912	7660		15. 5.00	D W Adams	(Horsham)	6. 7.09P
G-BZFI	Avtech Jabiru UL-450	0271		27. 3.00	A W J Findlay tr Group Family	Wolvey	10. 7.09P
	(Built A W J and A I Findlay - pr.no.PFA 274A-13497)						
G-BZFK	TEAM Mini-MAX 88	PFA 186-12060		17. 4.00	D W Tewson	(Dorchester)	9. 9.08P
	(Built C Vandenberghe)						
G-BZFN	Scottish Aviation Bulldog Series 120/121	BH120/325	XX667	18. 4.00	Risk Logical Ltd *(As "XX667:16 in RAF c/s)* Ronaldsway		11. 3.11S
G-BZFO	Mainair Blade	1235-0100-7-W1028		29. 3.00	G S McCombie	Balado Bridge	5.12.08P
	(Rotax 503)						
G-BZFP	de Havilland DHC-6-310 Twin Otter	696	C-GGNF N712PV, N696WJ, F-ODUH, TR-LZN, C-GKIQ	11. 8.00	Loganair Ltd	Glasgow	13. 8.09E
G-BZFR	Extra EA.300/L	203		26. 6.00	T C Beadle	North Weald	1. 9.09E
	(Official c/n outside normal EA300L c/n batch: possibly ex D-EDGE [03?])						
G-BZFS	Mainair Blade 912	1243-0300-7-W1036		23. 3.00	A Sorah and D G Barnes	(Glossop and Hyde)	4. 5.09P
G-BZFT	Murphy Rebel	PFA 232-13224		7. 4.00	N A Evans	Higherlands Farm, Branscombe	12. 6.09P
	(Built N A Evans) (Lycoming O-320)						
G-BZFU	Lindstrand LBL HS-110 Airship (Hot Air)	671		25. 4.00	Lindstrand Hot Air Balloons Ltd	Oswestry	19.10.09E
G-BZFV	Zenair CH.601UL Zodiac	PFA 162A-13547		14. 4.00	M E Caton	Sibson	14. 5.09P
	(Built I M Donnelly)						
G-BZGA	de Havilland DHC-1 Chipmunk 22	C1/0608	WK585	31. 3.00	The Real Flying Company Ltd *(As "WK585" in RAF c/s)* Shoreham		30. 4.10S
G-BZGB	de Havilland DHC-1 Chipmunk 22	C1/0905	WZ872	31. 3.00	Silverstar Aviation Ltd *(As "WZ872:E" in RAF c/s)* *(Noted 10.07)*	Blackpool	18. 8.06
G-BZGF	Rans S-6-ES Coyote II	0199 1297		25. 4.00	C A Purvis	London Colney	31. 8.09P
	(Built D F Castle - pr.no.PFA 204-13594) (Rotax 582) (Original kit no.was 0899.1334 but changed - possibly after accident 22. 7.01)						
G-BZGG	Sud-Aviation SE.313B Alouette II	1430	G-POSE G-BZGG, EI-CTH, F-GKML, French Army	22. 2.00	G A Wheeler	(Fraserburgh)	23. 4.09E
G-BZGH	Reims Cessna F172N Skyhawk II	F17201789	EI-BGH	1.12.98	D Behan tr Golf Hotel Group Weston, Leixlip, County Kildare		23. 4.09E
G-BZGI	UltraMagic M-145 Balloon (Hot Air)	145/12		9. 6.00	European Balloon Company Ltd Great Missenden		9. 8.09E
G-BZGJ	Thunder Ax10-180 Series 2 Balloon (Hot Air)	3956	LN-CBT	8. 5.00	M Wady t/a Merlin Balloons	Hamstreet	27. 9.09E
G-BZGK	North American OV-10B Bronco	338-17	Luftwaffe 9932 D-9561, Bu 158308	9. 6.00	Invicta Aviation Ltd *(Operated Aircraft Restoration Company as "99+32")*	Duxford	11.11.09P
G-BZGL	North American OV-10B Bronco	338-11	Luftwaffe 9926 D-9555, Bu 158302	9. 6.00	Invicta Aviation Ltd *(Operated Aircraft Restoration Company noted 10.08)*	Duxford	
G-BZGM	Mainair Blade 912	1247-0400-7-W1040		14. 4.00	D Young	North Coates	8. 7.09P
G-BZGN	Raj Hamsa X'Air 582(2)	445		3. 5.00	D I Hall	North Coates	20. 8.06P
	(Built B G M Chapman - pr.no.BMAA HB/128)						
G-BZGO	Robinson R44 Astro	0757		14. 4.00	Flight Academy (Gyrocopters) Ltd	Barton	17. 5.09E
G-BZGR	Rans S-6-ES Coyote II	0999.1338		3. 5.00	J M Benton	Long Marston	28. 7.09P
	(Built J M Benton and G R Pritchard - pr.no.PFA 204-13595) (Jabiru 2200A) (Tri-cycle u/c) (Carries "J M Benton" in script on nose)						
G-BZGS	Mainair Blade 912	1242-0300-7-W1035		10. 5.00	R J Coppin	Broadmeadow Farm, Hereford	28. 4.09P
G-BZGT	Avtech Jabiru UL-450	0291		4. 5.00	J White	(Burnham-on-Sea)	16. 7.08P
	(Built P H Ronfel - pr.no.PFA 274A-13539)						
G-BZGU	Raj Hamsa X'Air 582(4)	512		4. 5.00	W Bracken Limetree, Portarlington, County Laois *(Noted 10.05)*		8.10.05P
	(Built C Kiernan - pr.no.BMAA HB/138)						
G-BZGV	Lindstrand LBL 77A Balloon (Hot Air)	695		9. 5.00	J H Dryden "Skylark"	Okehampton	13. 4.09E
G-BZGW	Mainair Blade	1246-0400-7-W1039		5. 5.00	C S M Hallam	Barton	15 8.08P
G-BZGX	Raj Hamsa X'Air 582(6)	400		2. 6.00	A Crowe	Newtownards	14. 6.09P
	(Built A Crowe - pr.no.BMAA HB/099)						
G-BZGY	Dyn'Aéro CR100C	21	F-TGCI	7. 6.00	B Appleby	Wolverhampton	10. 4.09P
G-BZGZ	Cyclone Airsports Pegasus Quantum 15-912	7674		7. 6.00	D W Beech	Ince Blundell	8. 2.09P
G-BZHA	Boeing 767-336	29230	N60668	22. 5.98	British Airways PLC	London Heathrow	21. 5.09E
G-BZHB	Boeing 767-336	29231		30. 5.98	British Airways PLC	London Heathrow	29. 5.09E
G-BZHC	Boeing 767-336	29232		29. 6.98	British Airways PLC	London Heathrow	28. 6.09E
G-BZHE	Cessna 152	15281303	D-EAOC N49484	20. 4.00	Simair Ltd	Andrewsfield	24. 7.09E
G-BZHF	Cessna 152	15283986	D-EMJA N4858H	20. 4.00	Modi Aviation Ltd	Earls Colne	24. 7.09E
G-BZHG	Tecnam P92-EM Echo	PFA 318-13606		24. 5.00	R W F Boarder	Field Farm, Oakley	24. 3.09P
	(Built M Rudd)						
G-BZHI	Enstrom F-28A-UK	281	G-BPOZ N246Q	14.12.99	Tindon Engineering Ltd	Little Snoring	10. 8.09E
G-BZHJ	Raj Hamsa X'Air 582(7)	482		10. 5.00	P J Smith	Otherton, Cannock	1. 6.08P
	(Built A P Harvey and B Baker - pr.no.BMAA HB/126)						
G-BZHK	Piper PA-28-181 Archer III	2843347	N41647 N9519N	14. 7.00	J Middlemass	Duxford	15. 8.09E
G-BZHL	North American AT-16 Harvard IIB	14A-1158	FT118 43-12859	6. 6.00	R H Cooper and S Swallow Hemswell *(Officially quoted USAF p/i is "43-12959") (Stored 1.02)*		
G-BZHN	Cyclone Airsports Pegasus Quantum 15-912	7677		20. 6.00	A M Sirant Mokewsell Farm, Horrabridge		17. 6.09P
G-BZHO	Cyclone Airsports Pegasus Quantum 15- 7658			19. 5.00	N D Major Cottage Farm, Norton Juxta, Twycross		23. 7.09P
	(Rotax 582)						
G-BZHP	Quad City Challenger II	CH2-0995-CW-1398		11. 5.00	J Morris	Clench Common	20. 7.09P
	(Built F Payne - pr.no.PFA 177-13153) (Rotax 582)						
G-BZHR	Avtech Jabiru UL-450	0267		16. 5.00	G W Rowbotham	(Loughborough)	14. 9.09P
	(Built G W Rowbotham - pr.no.PFA 274A-13493)						
G-BZHS	Europa Aviation Europa	207		16. 5.00	P Waugh	(Caudeval, France)	25. 8.07P
	(Built P Waugh - pr.no.PFA 247-12865) (Monowheel u/c)						
G-BZHT	Piper PA-18A-150 Super Cub	18-5886	ZK-BTF	25. 5.00	The Furness Gliding Club Proprietary Ltd tr Lakes Gliding Club Walney Island		24. 1.09

Reg	Type	C/n	Prev id	Date	Owner/Operator	Base	Expiry
G-BZHU	Wag-Aero CUBy Sport Trainer *(Built D C Hoffman)*	AACA/351	ZK-MPH	25. 5.00	S D Clark tr Teddy Boys Flying Group	Gloucestershire	26.11.07P
G-BZHV	Piper PA-28-181 Archer III	2843382	N41848 G-BZHV, N41848	17.10.00	R M and T A Limb	Bournemouth	4.12.09E
G-BZHX	Thunder Ax11-250 S2 Balloon (Hot-Air)	4880		21. 6.00	Wizzard Balloons Ltd	Bury St Edmunds	13. 9.08E
G-BZIA	Raj Hamsa X'Air 700(1) *(Built A U I Hudson - pr.no.BMAA HB/116)*	475		1. 6.00	J L Pritchett	(Gloucester)	9. 5.09P
G-BZIC	Lindstrand LBL Sun SS Balloon (Hot Air)	702		8. 6.00	Ballongaventyr I Skane AB	Lund, Sweden	1.10.09E
G-BZID	Montgomerie-Bensen B 8MR *(Built A Gault from cannibalised Air Command Elite G-BOGW)*	PFA G/01-1315		31. 5.00	S C Gillies	(Buckie)	
G-BZIG	Thruster T 600N Sprint *(Rotax 582 UL)*	0400-T600N-042		25. 4.00	Ultra Air Ltd	Leicester	8. 5.09P
G-BZIH	Lindstrand LBL 31A Balloon (Hot Air)	700		7. 6.00	R S Kent t/a Skyart Balloons *"Budweiser"*	Lancing	8. 1.09E
G-BZII	Extra EA.300/L	119		13. 9.00	R J Verrall Luxter's Farm, Hambledon		30. 9.09E
G-BZIJ	Robin DR.500-200i Président *(Officially regd as DR.400-500)*	0023		9. 3.00	Rob Airways Ltd	Guernsey	13. 4.09E
G-BZIK	Cameron A-250 Balloon (Hot Air)	4890		27. 6.00	Breckland Balloons Ltd	Dereham	1. 4.09E
G-BZIL	Cameron Colt 120A Balloon (Hot Air)	4876		7. 7.00	S R Seager tr Champagne Flights *(Parrott and Coles Solicitors titles)*	Aylesbury	17. 6.09E
G-BZIM	Cyclone Airsports Pegasus Quantum 15-912	7678		20. 6.00	A Cuthbertson	Swansea	20. 5.09P
G-BZIO	Piper PA-28-161 Warrior III	2842085	EC-IBJ G-BZIO, N41796, (VH-PWF), N41796	29.06.00	S J Skilton t/a Aviation Rentals	White Waltham	1. 1.10E
G-BZIP	Montgomerie-Bensen B 8MR PFA G/01A-1319 *(Built S J Boxall) (Rotax 582)*			11. 5.00	S J Boxall	Church Farm, Askern	12. 6.07P
G-BZIS	Raj Hamsa X'Air 582(2) *(Built J Way and R Bonnett - pr.no.BMAA HB/142)*	520		12. 6.00	M D Bell	Ince Blundell	8. 3.09P
G-BZIT	Beech 95-B55 Baron	TC-564	HB-GBS I-ALGE, HB-GBS, N6845Q	12. 6.00	Propellorhead Aviation Ltd	Turweston	17.10.09E
G-BZIV	Avtech Jabiru SPL-450 *(Built V R Leggott - pr.no.PFA 274A-13587)*	0341		20. 6.00	V R Leggott Coldharbour Farm, Willingham		7. 9.09P
G-BZIW	Cyclone Airsports Pegasus Quantum 15-912	7681		17. 7.00	J M Hodgson Baxby Manor, Husthwaite		20. 1.09P
G-BZIX	Cameron N-90 Balloon (Hot Air)	4867		3. 8.00	M Stefanini and P Marmugi *"Info Strada"*	Florence, Italy	22. 5.07A
G-BZIY	Raj Hamsa X'Air 582(5) *(Built I K Hogg - pr.no.BMAA HB/141)*	488		19. 6.00	A L A Gill Bedlands Gate, Little Strickland		10. 1.09P
G-BZIZ	UltraMagic H-31 Balloon (Hot Air)	31/02		12. 6.00	G D O Bartram Andorra la Vella, Spain		12.10.09E
G-BZJA	Cameron Fire 90 SS Balloon (Hot Air) *(Chubb Fire Extinguisher shape)*	4757		5. 5.00	Chubb Fire Ltd *"Chubb"*	Sunbury-on-Thames	27. 9.09E
G-BZJB	IAV Bacau Yakovlev Yak-52	811601	ZU-YAK ZS-YAK, RA-01356, DOSAAF	18. 9.00	Matristar Ltd	Elstree	14. 8.09P
G-BZJC	Thruster T 600N Sprint	0070-T600N-044		21. 6.00	M H Moulai	Sandtoft	12. 6.08P
G-BZJD	Thruster T 600T 450 Jab	0070-T600T-045		21. 6.00	P G Valentine	(Rochechouart, France)	28. 5.05P
G-BZJH	Cameron Z-90 Balloon (Hot Air)	4920		10. 7.00	Cameron Balloons Ltd *"Greeco"*	(Italy)	2.11.04A
G-BZJI	Nova X-Large 37	18946		28. 6.00	M Hay	(Dundee)	
G-BZJJ	Robinson R22 Beta II	3081		12. 6.00	M J Burgess	(Caernarfon)	29. 6.09E
G-BZJL	Mainair Blade 912S	1252-0600-7-W1046		4. 7.00	D N Powell	Ince Blundell	20. 2.04P
G-BZJM	Magni M-16 Tandem Trainer PFA G/12-1301 *(Built J Musil)*			19. 6.00	D Wood	(Holbeach, Spalding)	26. 9.07P
G-BZJN	Mainair Blade 912	1254-0600-7-W1048		13. 7.00	L Campbell and M A Haughey	Newtownards	10. 8.08P
G-BZJO	Cyclone Airsports Pegasus Quantum 15 7699 *(Rotax 503)*			6. 9.00	J D Doran Shinglis, Ballymore, County Westmeath		29. 9.05P
G-BZJP	Zenair CH.701UL STOL PFA 187-13579 *(Built D Jerwood) (Verner SVS1400)*			30. 6.00	J A Ware	Haverfordwest	17.12.07P
G-BZJU	Cameron A-200 Balloon (Hot Air)	4810		30. 6.00	Leeds Castle Enterprises Ltd *(Leeds Castle titles)*	Leeds Castle, Maidstone	23. 5.05T
G-BZJV	CASA 1-131E Jungmann Series 1000	1075	Spanish AF E3B-367	31. 7.00	J A Sykes	Stretton	20.12.07P
G-BZJW	Cessna 150F	15062054	OO-WIH OO-SIH, N8754S	27. 6.01	P Ligertwood Ventfield Farm, Horton-cum-Studley, Oxford		20. 4.09E
G-BZJX	UltraMagic N-250 Balloon (Hot Air)	250/12		4. 7.00	Hot Air Balloons Ltd *(e-homes titles)*	Henley-on-Thames	8. 6.09E
G-BZJZ	Cyclone Airsports Pegasus Quantum 15 7697 *(Rotax 503)*			2. 8.00	S Baker	Long Marston	6. 5.09E
G-BZKC	Raj Hamsa X'Air 582(2) *(Built P J Cheyney and M C Reed - pr.no.BMAA HB/144)*	502		12. 7.00	N Flint	(London SW19)	31. 7.08P
G-BZKD	Stolp SA.300 Starduster Too *(Built R D Merritt) (Lycoming IO-360)*	1	N70DM	3. 7.00	P and C Edmunds	Enstone	26. 7.07P
G-BZKE	Lindstrand LBL 77B Balloon (Hot Air)	708		17. 7.00	D B Green	Llantysilio, Llangollen	1.11.09E
G-BZKF	Rans S-6-ES Coyote II *(Built A W Hodder - pr.no.PFA 204-13610) (Rotax 582) (Tri-cycle u/c)*	0499.1315		17. 7.00	A W Lowrie	Eshott	28. 2.09P
G-BZKG	Extreme/Silex	E761 01A		17. 7.00	R M Hardy	(Radwell, Baldock)	
G-BZKH	Flylight Doodle Bug-Target	DB023		17. 7.00	B Tempest	(Halifax)	
G-BZKI	Flylight Doodle Bug-Target	DB063		17. 7.00	S Bond	(Golcar, Huddersfield)	
G-BZKJ	Flylight Doodle Bug-Target	DB067		17. 7.00	Flylight Airsports Ltd	Sywell	
G-BZKK	Cameron V-56 Balloon (Hot Air)	396		2. 8.78	P J Green and C Bosley tr Gemini Balloon Group *"Gemini II"*	Oakley, Basingstoke	13. 8.96A
G-BZKL	Piper PA-28R-201 Cherokee Arrow III	28R-7737152	D-EFFZ N40000	20. 7.00	S Empson	Denham	25. 9.09E
G-BZKN	Campbell Cricket Mk.4 PFA G/03-1304 *(Built C G Hooghkirk)*			20. 7.00	C G Ponsford *(Noted 8.07)*	Willingale	
G-BZKO	Rans S-6ES Coyote II *(Built J A R Hartley)*	0199.1293		30. 5.08	J R Moore	(Barnard Castle)	28. 5.08P

G-BZKU	Cameron Z-105 Balloon (Hot Air)	4931		21. 7.00	N A Fishlock *"Wyevale Garden Centres"*	
						Welland, Malvern 31. 5.09E
G-BZKV	Cameron Sky 90-24 Balloon (Hot Air)	4857		5. 9.00	Omega Selection Services Ltd *"Omega"*	
						Stonehouse 9. 6.08A
G-BZKW	UltraMagic M-77 Balloon (Hot Air)	77/179		25. 7.00	T G Church *"Pendle"* Clayton le Dale, Blackburn 1. 7.09E
G-BZKX	Cameron V-90 Balloon (Hot Air)	4505		19. 7.00	Cameron Balloons Ltd Dalien, PRC 26. 7.01A
G-BZLC	PZL-110 Koliber 160A	04980084	SP-WGL	13. 9.00	G F Smith Turweston 19. 6.09E
G-BZLE	Rans S-6-ES Coyote II	0499.1311		12. 7.00	J C Rose Manor Farm, Haddenham 13. 4.09P
	(Built W S Long - pr.no.PFA 204-13608) (Jabiru 2200A) (Tri-cycle u/c)					
G-BZLF	CFM Shadow Series CD	K 236		31. 7.00	D W Stacey *(Possibly not completed)* (St Albans)
	(Built D W Stacey - pr.no.BMAA HB/053)					
G-BZLG	Robin HR.200-120B	353		7. 7.00	M C Turner (Campbeltown) 19. 3.09E
G-BZLH	Piper PA-28-161 Warrior II	28-8316075	N43069	23. 8.00	S J Skilton t/a Aviation Rentals Lasham 21. 9.09E
	(Thielert TAE 125)				*(Operated British Disabled Flying Association)*
G-BZLI	SOCATA TB-21 Trinidad TC	500	F-GENI	29. 9.00	K B Hallam Fairoaks 31. 1.09E
G-BZLK	Slingsby Cadet III Motor Glider	683	BGA2976	2. 8.00	G Smith (Walton-on-Thames) 15. 8.08P
	(Re-built I P Manley - pr.no.PFA 042-13629 ex Slingsby T 31B WT873) (Volkswagen 1834)					
G-BZLL	Cyclone Airsports Pegasus Quantum 15-912			9. 8.00	D W Logue Strathaven 22.11.09P
		7693				
G-BZLP	Robinson R44 Raven	0814		17. 7.00	R C Hayward and J H Garrioch t/a Polar Helicopters
						Manston 11. 9.09E
G-BZLS	Cameron Sky 77-24 Balloon (Hot Air)	4858		17. 8.00	D W Young Stenhousemuir 14. 7.09E
G-BZLT	Raj Hamsa X'Air 582(1)	486		10. 8.00	G S Millar Moygashel, County Tyrone 7. 8.08P
	(Built G S Millar - pr.no.BMAA HB/125)					
G-BZLU	Lindstrand LBL 90A Balloon (Hot Air)	719		9. 8.00	A E Lusty *"Tetris 1"* (Morton, Bourne) 12. 4.09E
G-BZLV	Avtech Jabiru UL-450	xxxx		15. 8.00	G Dalton Dunkeswell 6. 8.09P
	(Built G Dalton - pr.no.PFA 274A-13537)					
G-BZLX	Cyclone Airsports Pegasus Quantum 15-912			30. 8.00	D McCabe Eshott 19. 5.09P
		7714				
G-BZLY	Grob G109B	6242	D-KLMG	24. 8.00	A Baker (Brough) 1.12.09E
			G-BZLY, OE-9230			
G-BZLZ	Cyclone Airsports Pegasus Quantum 15-912			13. 9.00	A S Martin Eaglescott 8. 5.09P
		7721				
G-BZMB	Piper PA-28R-201 Arrow III	28R-7837144	HB-PBY	20. 4.00	S J White tr Thurrock Arrow Group
			N3963M			King's Farm, Thurrock 4. 6.09E
G-BZMC	Avtech Jabiru UL-450	PFA 274A-13593		18. 8.00	D Maddison Headon Farm, Retford 29. 8.08P
	(Built J R Banks)					
G-BZMD	Scottish Aviation Bulldog Series 120/121		XX554	18. 8.00	D Ridley tr Mad Dog Flying Group *(As "XX554:09" in RAF c/s)*
		BH120/247				Shoreham 20. 5.11S
G-BZME	Scottish Aviation Bulldog Series 120/121		XX698	18. 8.00	S J Whitworth *(As "XX698:9" in RAF c/s)* Brighton 2.12.10S
		BH120/347				
G-BZMF	Rutan LongEz	PFA 074-10698		30. 8.00	R A Gardiner Cumbernauld 13. 6.09P
	(Built A McCaughlin)					
G-BZMG	Robinson R44 Raven	0815		16. 8.00	MX Aviation Ltd (Chacombe, Banbury) 14. 9.09E
G-BZMH	Scottish Aviation Bulldog Series 120/121		XX692	21. 8.00	M E J Hingley and Co Ltd *(As "XX692:A" in RAF c/s)*
		BH120/341				Wellesbourne Mountford 29. 1.11S
G-BZMI	Cyclone Airsports Pegasus Quantum 15-912			22. 9.00	P L Jarvis (Ruislip) 28.12.09P
		7716				
G-BZMJ	Rans S-6-ES Coyote II	0899.1337ES		31. 8.00	E Foster and J H Peet Brook Farm, Pilling 30. 7.09P
	(Built J Seddon, F J Lloyd and T I Bull - pr.no.PFA 204-13631) (Jabiru 2200A) (Tri-cycle u/c)					
G-BZML	Scottish Aviation Bulldog Series 120/121		XX693	1. 9.00	I D Anderson *(As "XX693:07" in RAF c/s)*
		BH120/342				Poplar Hall Farm, Elmsett 9. 6.11S
G-BZMM	Robin DR.400-180R Remorqueur	918	OE-KIR	17. 7.00	N A C Norman Feshiebridge 21. 9.09E
			D-EAWR			
G-BZMO	Robinson R22 Beta	1219	N24282	31. 7.00	Heli Charter Ltd Manston 4. 1.10E
			JA7814, N8056H			
G-BZMR	Raj Hamsa X'Air 582(2)	480		11. 9.00	M Grime Brook Farm, Pilling 4. 6.08P
	(Built M Grime - pr.no.BMAA HB/149)					
G-BZMS	Mainair Blade	1256-0700-7-W1050		2. 8.00	T R Villa Priory Farm, Tibenham 3.11.07P
	(Rotax 582)					
G-BZMT	Piper PA-28-161 Warrior III	2842107	N4147D	29.11.00	S J Skilton t/a Aviation Rentals White Waltham 5.12.09E
			G-BZMT, N9519N, N4147D			
G-BZMV	Cameron Concept 80 Balloon (Hot Air)	4930		26. 9.00	KB Voli di Chiozzi Bartolomeo EC SAS
						Cappela Cantone, Italy 1. 8.08A
G-BZMW	Cyclone Airsports Pegasus Quantum 15-912			26. 9.00	G C Kemp Stoke, Isle of Grain 31. 5.08P
		7720				
G-BZMY	SPP Yakovlev Yak C-11	171314	F-AZSF	4.10.00	Classic Displays Ltd *(As "1" in Soviet AF c/s)*
			Egyptian AF			North Weald/Alscot 15. 8.06P
G-BZMZ	CFM Streak Shadow	K 265-CD		13. 9.00	J F F Fouche Old Sarum 11.12.08P
	(Built J F F Fouche - original pr.no.BMAA HB/051 but completed as pr.no. PFA 206-13848) (Rotax 582)					
G-BZNB	Cyclone Airsports Pegasus Quantum 15	7739		10.11.00	M P and R A Wells Croft Farm, Defford 5. 5.09P
	(Rotax 503)					
G-BZNC	Cyclone Airsports Pegasus Quantum 15-912			25.10.00	D E Wall Long Marston 11. 8.08P
		7736				
G-BZND	Sopwith Pup replica	PFA 101-11815		27. 9.00	M A Goddard *(As "N5199" in RNAS c/s)*
	(Built B F Goddard)					Watchford Farm, Yarcombe 29. 7.09P
G-BZNE	Beech B300 Super King Air	FL-286	N4486V	17.10.00	Skyhopper LLP Fairoaks 16.11.09E
G-BZNF	Cameron Colt 120A Balloon (Hot Air)	4866		13.11.00	N Charbonnier *(Grand St Bernard - Le Tunnel titles)*
						Aosta, Italy 16. 1.10E
G-BZNG	Raj Hamsa X'Air Jabiru(2)	571		4.10.00	J Walshe Newtownards 10. 8.06P
	(Built G L Craig - pr.no.BMAA HB/147)					
G-BZNH	Rans S-6-ES Coyote II	0899.1333		18.10.00	J R Parker Headcorn 21. 8.09P
	(Built V Whiting - pr.no.PFA 204-13660) (Rotax 582) (Tri-cycle u/c)					

Reg	Type	C/n	Prev id	Date	Owner/Operator	Base	Date2
G-BZNI	Bell 206B-2 JetRanger II	2142	G-ODIG G-NEEP, N777FW, N3CR	4.10.00	Heliscan AS	Stjordal, Norway	18. 6.09E
G-BZNJ	Rans S-6-ES Coyote II (Built S P Read - pr.no.PFA 204-13640) (Rotax 582) (Tailwheel u/c)	0700.1382		23.10.00	R A McKee	(Newry)	5. 6.09P
G-BZNK	Morane Saulnier MS.315E D2	354	F-BCNY French AF	2.11.00	R H Cooper and S Swallow (Wickenby) (Dismantled, in advanced stage of restoration 1.05)		
G-BZNM	Cyclone Airsports Pegasus Quantum 15 (Rotax 582)	7754		20.11.00	M Tomlinson	(Burton-on-Trent)	25. 7.09P
G-BZNN	Beech 76 Duchess	ME-343	N6133P F-GHSU, N6722L	25.10.00	S J Skilton t/a Aviation Rentals Bournemouth (Operated Bournemouth Flying Club)		14.12.09E
G-BZNP	Thruster T 600N 450 (Rotax 582)	0100-T600N-047		27.10.00	J D Gibbons	Derryogue	9. 2.09P
G-BZNS	Mainair Blade (Rotax 582)	1263-1000-7-W1057		23.11.00	A G Laycock	Arclid Green, Sandbach	1. 4.09P
G-BZNU	Cameron A-300 Balloon (Hot Air) (New envelope reported fitted as c/n 4960 (2))	4960		29.11.00	Balloon School (International) Ltd Colhook Common, Petworth		27. 5.09E
G-BZNV	Lindstrand LBL 31A Balloon (Hot Air)	741		12.12.00	G R Down	Gillingham	1. 7.09E
G-BZNW	Isaacs Fury II (Built J E D Rogerson)	PFA 011-13402		10.11.00	J E D Rogerson (As "K2048" in RAF c/s) RAF Linton-on-Ouse		19. 6.08P
G-BZNX	SOCATA MS.880B Rallye Club	2113	F-BTVX	17.11.00	P C Avery	Fenland	25. 2.09E
G-BZNY	Europa Aviation Europa XS (Built A K Middlemas - pr.no.PFA 247-13355) (Tri-gear u/c)	401		14.11.00	W J Harrison	Cambridge	8. 6.09P
G-BZNZ	Lindstrand LBL Cake SS Balloon (Hot Air)	747		21.12.00	Oxford Promotions (UK) Ltd (Operated F Prell) Kentucky, USA		6. 8.09E
G-BZOB	Slepcev Storch (Built J E Ashby)	PFA 316-13592		21.11.00	B J Chester-Master (As "6G+ED" in Luftwaffe c/s) Shobdon		27. 1.10P
G-BZOD	Cyclone Airsports Pegasus Quantum 15-912	7763		18.12.00	V J Vaughan	(Mullinahone, Ireland)	2. 9.08P
G-BZOE	Cyclone Airsports Pegasus Quantum 15 (Rotax 582)	7723		14. 9.00	C Gane and G Barrell	(Horley & Redhill)	27. 4.09P
G-BZOF	Montgomerie-Bensen B 8MR MGM3 & SJML1 (Built M G Mee and S J M Ledingham) (Rotax 912-UL)			7.11.00	S J M Ledingham	Carlisle	24. 8.08P
G-BZOG	Dornier 328-100	3088	D-CDXN (5) F-GNPR	19.12.00	Suckling Airways (Cambridge) Ltd t/a Scot Airways London City		18.11.09E
G-BZOI	Nicollier HN.700 Ménestrel II (Built S J McCollum - pr.no.PFA 217-12604) (Volkswagen 2180)	122		27.10.00	S J McCollum	Newtownards	22. 5.09P
G-BZOL	Robin R3000/140	124	F-GEKZ	20.12.00	S D Baker	Exeter	24. 7.09E
G-BZOM	RotorWay Executive 162F (Built G and S Waugh)	6243	N767SG	27. 3.01	R L Cole	(Haverfordwest)	6. 6.08P
G-BZON	Scottish Aviation Bulldog Series 120/121	XX528 BH120/214		19.12.00	D J Critchley (As "XX528:D" in RAF c/s) Earls Colne		18. 4.10S
G-BZOO	Cyclone Airsports Pegasus Quantum 15-912	7702		15. 8.00	T A Dobbins	Ince Blundell	3. 9.08P
G-BZOP	Robinson R44	0958		11. 1.01	C N Joinery and Building Services LLP (Ballynahinch)		27. 2.09E
G-BZOR	TEAM Mini-MAX 91 (Built A Watt)	PFA 186-13312		9. 8.00	J F Govan	(East Linton, Edinburgh)	13. 5.07P
G-BZOU	Cyclone Airsports Pegasus Quantum 15-912	7768		22. 3.01	M J Canty (Raheen, Limerick, County Limerick		12. 4.08P
G-BZOV	Cyclone Airsports Pegasus Quantum 15-912	7769		22. 3.01	D Turner	(Bicester)	29. 5.03P
G-BZOW	Whittaker MW7 (Built G W Peacock)	PFA 171-13118		15.12.00	G W Peacock	(Kirk Sandall, Doncaster)	
G-BZOX	Cameron Colt 90B Balloon (Hot Air)	10000		8. 2.01	D J Head	Newbury	21. 3.07A
G-BZOY	Beech 76 Duchess	ME-144	EC-ICJ G-BZOY, F-GFFH, 5T-AOH, F-ODJQ, F-GBLO	3.1.01	S J Skilton t/a Aviation Rentals (Operated CTC Aviation) Bournemouth		4. 8.09E
G-BZOZ	Van's RV-6 (Built V Edmundson)	PFA 181A-12455		14. 9.00	M and S Sheppard	Cambridge	31. 1.09P
G-BZPA	Mainair Blade 912S	1264-1100-7-W1058		13.12.00	J McGoldrick Slieve Croob, Slievenamoney, Castlewellen		3. 5.08P
G-BZPB	Hawker Hunter GA.11	41H-670758	WV256	15. 1.01	B R Pearson	Kemble	17. 7.03P
					(Noted as "WB188" Hunter prototype in duck-egg green c/s 5.07)		
G-BZPC	Hawker Hunter GA.11	HABL-003061	XF300	15. 1.01	B R Pearson	Kemble	
					(Noted as "WB188" Hunter prototype in all-red c/s 9.08)		
G-BZPD	Cameron V-65 Balloon (Hot Air)	4700		10.11.00	P Spellward "Buzbee"	Heidelburg, Germany	30. 7.09E
G-BZPE	Lindstrand LBL 310A Balloon (Hot Air)	746		16. 2.01	Aerosaurus Balloons Ltd	Whimple, Exeter	10. 9.09E
G-BZPF	Scheibe SF24B Motorspatz I	4028	D-KROA PH-971, OE-9005, (D-KECO)	19. 1.01	J S Gorrett	(Skenfrith, Abergavenny)	24. 8.08E
G-BZPG	Beech C24R Sierra	MC-556	N23840	27. 3.01	Wycombe Air Centre Ltd	Wycombe Air Park	18. 6.09E
G-BZPH	Van's RV-4 (Built A G Truman) (Lycoming O-360)	PFA 181-12867		6. 9.00	A G Truman tr G-BZPH RV-4 Group	Lasham	7. 2.09P
G-BZPI	SOCATA TB-20 Trinidad	1814	SX-ATT	20.12.00	K M Brennan	Leicester	24. 5.09E
G-BZPJ	Beech 76 Duchess	ME-227	N6630Z	2. 3.01	S J Skilton tr Aviation Rentals Bournemouth (Operated Bournemouth Flying Club)		29. 3.09E
G-BZPK	Cameron C-80 Balloon (Hot Air)	4183		23. 2.01	Horizon Ballooning Ltd	Alton	6.12.07T
G-BZPL	Robinson R44 Clipper	0948		10. 1.01	M K Shaw	San Bonet, Majorca, Spain	6. 2.09E
G-BZPM	Cessna 172S Skyhawk SP	172S8561	N72760	11. 1.01	R Carey	Weston, Lucan, County Dublin	27. 3.09E
G-BZPN	Mainair Blade 912S	1268-0101-7-W1062		25. 1.01	G R Barker	(Epping)	14. 9.08P
G-BZPP	Westland Wasp HAS.1	F9675	XT793	15. 1.01	C J Marsden (As "XT793:456" in RN c/s) RNAS Yeovilton		21. 8.08P
G-BZPR	UltraMagic N-210 Balloon (Hot Air)	210/14		16. 1.01	European Balloon Display Company Ltd (MIX 96 titles) Great Missenden		17. 6.09E
G-BZPS	Scottish Aviation Bulldog Series 120/121	XX658 BH120/316		8. 1.01	A J Robinson and M J Miller (As "XX658:03" in RAF c/s 1.03) Audley End		

G-BZPT	UltraMagic N-210 Balloon (Hot Air)	210/15		16. 1.01	European Balloon Company Ltd *(Bucks Free Press titles)*		
						Great Missenden	10. 4.09E
G-BZPV	Lindstrand LBL 90B Balloon (Hot Air)	727		17. 1.01	D P Hopkins *(Lakeside Lodge Golf Centre titles)*		
						Pidley, Huntingdon	11.10.09E
G-BZPW	Cameron V-77 Balloon (Hot Air)	6245	N4463V	2. 2.01	J Vonka	New Malden	12. 8.08A
G-BZPX	UltraMagic S-105 Balloon (Hot Air)	105/78		12. 2.01	G M Houston t/a Scotair Balloons *"Remax" titles*		
						Biggar	8. 5.09E
G-BZPY	UltraMagic H-31 Balloon (Hot Air)	31/03		12. 2.01	G M Houston t/a Scotair Balloons	Biggar	18. 5.09E
G-BZPZ	Mainair Blade	1265-1200-7-W1059		23. 1.01	K Lynn	Sywell	14. 6.08P
	(Rotax 582)						
G-BZRA	Rans S-6-ES Coyote II	0600-1376		16. 1.01	K J Warburton		
	(Built A W Fish - pr.no.PFA 204-13683) (Rotax 912-UL)				Cottage Farm, Norton Juxta, Twycross		9. 3.09P
G-BZRB	Mainair Blade	1270-0201-7-W1064		7. 3.01	J-B Weber	Mill Farm, Shifnal	3.11.08P
	(Rotax 582)						
G-BZRG	Hunt Avon 582(3)/Hunt Wing	0009090		16. 1.01	W G Reynolds	(Overstrand, Cromer)	12. 6.08P
	(Built W G Reynolds - pr.no.BMAA HB/154)						
G-BZRJ	Cyclone Airsports Pegasus Quantum 15-912			5. 2.01	P J Fletcher tr G-BZRJ Group		
	7783				Longacre Farm, Sandy		14. 4.09P
G-BZRO	Piper PA-30 Twin Comanche C	30-1923	SE-IYL	2. 3.01	Comanche Hire Ltd	Gloucestershire	13.10.09E
			D-GATI, I-KATI, N8767Y				
G-BZRP	Cyclone Airsports Pegasus Quantum 15-912			24. 1.01	T P Williams	(Penmaenmawr)	14. 6.09P
	7758						
G-BZRR	Cyclone Airsports Pegasus Quantum 15-912			4.10.00	S E Garner	(Stone)	29.10.08P
	7727						
G-BZRS	Eurocopter EC.135 T2	0166		22. 3.01	Bond Air Services Ltd	Aberdeen	8. 4.09E
G-BZRT	Beech 76 Duchess	ME-89	EC-HYO	21. 3.01	S J Skilton t/a Aviation Rentals	Bournemouth	29. 1.10E
			G-BZRT, F-GHBL, N2074G				
G-BZRU	Cameron V-90 Balloon (Hot Air)	10053		1. 5.01	R Trombetti tr Aerostatica Monte	Villanteto, Italy	22. 9.09E
G-BZRV	Van's RV-6	PFA 181A-13573		12.10.00	N M Hitchman	Leicester	11. 8.08P
	(Built E Hicks, P Hicks and N M Hitchman) (Lycoming O-320)						
G-BZRW	Mainair Blade 912S	1266-0101-7-W1060		6. 2.01	G J E Alcorn	(Carrickfergus, NI)	26. 3.09P
G-BZRX	UltraMagic M-105 Balloon (Hot Air)	105/80		3. 5.01	P A Foot and I R Warrington	Stamford	17. 2.09E
G-BZRY	Rans S-6-ES Coyote II	0600-1375		1. 2.01	A G Smith	Longacre Farm, Sandy	5.10.08P
	(Built S Forman - pr.no.PFA 204-13666) (Rotax 582)						
G-BZRZ	Thunder Ax11-250 Series 2 Balloon (Hot Air)			11.10.01	A C K Rawson and J J Rudoni *"Kinetic"*	Stafford	11.10.08E
	10013						
G-BZSA	Cyclone Airsports Pegasus Quantum 15 7784			25. 1.01	M Skrinar	(Feltham)	21. 7.08P
	(Rotax 503)						
G-BZSB	Pitts S-1S	PFA 009-13697		2. 2.01	A D Ingold *(On build 2004)*	(Harlow)	
	(Built A D Ingold)						
G-BZSC	Sopwith Camel F 1 replica	NAW-3		15. 1.01	Richard Shuttleworth Trustees	Batley	
	(Built Northern Aeroplane Workshops)				*(On display Yorkshire Motor Museum)*		
G-BZSE	Hawker Hunter T 8C	41H-670788	9096M	6. 2.01	Towerdrive 2000 Ltd *(As "WV322:Y" in RAF c/s)*		
			WV322			Exeter	19.11.09P
	(Officially.regd as T 8B (c/n 41H-670792) see G-FFOX)						
G-BZSG	Cyclone Airsports Pegasus Quantum 15-912			22. 2.01	S Andrews	Newtownards	26. 4.09P
	7766						
G-BZSH	UltraMagic H-77 Balloon (Hot Air)	77/191		12. 4.01	P M G Vale	Hurcote, Kidderminster	10. 8.09E
G-BZSI	Cyclone Airsports Pegasus Quantum 15 7787			12. 3.01	M O O'Brien	Rufforth	4. 5.08P
	(Rotax 582)						
G-BZSL	Sky 25-16 Balloon (Hot Air)	138		31. 1.01	A E Austin	Naseby	29.11.09E
G-BZSM	Cyclone Airsports Pegasus Quantum 15 7788			23. 2.01	C A Brock	Deenethorpe	5.11.09P
	(Rotax 503)						
G-BZSO	UltraMagic M-77C Balloon (Hot Air)	77/190		22. 3.02	C C Duppa-Miller	Warwick	19. 8.09E
G-BZSP	Stemme S 10-V	10-14	HB-2217	10. 5.01	A Flewelling and L Bleaken *"626"*	Aston Down	11.11.09E
	(Limbach L2400)		D-KDNE				
	(Officially regd as S-10 but converted to S-10-V when HB-2217: in theory c/n should now be 14-014M)						
G-BZSS	Cyclone Airsports Pegasus Quantum 15-912			6. 2.01	T R Marsh		
	7770				Brown Shutters Farm, Norton St Philips, Somerset		9. 6.08P
G-BZST	Avtech Jabiru UL-450	0400		13. 2.01	D J and L Rhys	Perranporth	18. 9.09P
	(Built G Hammond - pr.no.PFA 274A-13616)						
G-BZSU	Cameron A-315 Balloon (Hot Air)	10009		13. 6.01	Ballooning Network Ltd *(Bath Building Society titles)*		
						Bristol	16. 7.09E
G-BZSV	Aherne Barracuda	631		20. 2.01	M J Aherne	(St Albans)	
	(Built M J Aherne)						
G-BZSX	Cyclone Airsports Pegasus Quantum 15-912			23. 2.01	G L Hall	Rufforth	22. 7.09P
	7789						
G-BZSY	SAN Stampe SV-4A	677	N12426	12. 3.01	G P J M Valvekens *(Stored 2006)* Diest, Belgium		
			F-BGGT, French AF, (F-BDNV)				
G-BZSZ	Avtech Jabiru UL-450	0220		16. 2.01	M P Gurr and D R Burridge Clipgate Farm, Denton		9. 9.09P
	(Built R Riley and F Overall - pr.no.PFA 274A-13432)						
G-BZTA	Robinson R44 Raven	0968		20. 2.01	Jarretts Motors Ltd	Redhill	26. 3 09E
G-BZTC	TEAM Mini-MAX 91	PFA 186-13336		23. 1.01	G G Clayton Woodlands Barton Farm, Roche		24. 6.09P
	(Built G G Clayton)						
G-BZTD	Thruster T 600T 450 Jab	0021-T600T-049		22. 2.01	B O and B C McCartan		
						Drumnahare, Banbridge, County Down	18. 7.08P
G-BZTF	IAV-Bacau Yakovlev Yak-52	866703	LY-AKE	28. 2.01	A C Pledger tr KY Flying Group	Duxford	20.11.09P
			DOSAAF				
G-BZTG	Piper PA-34-220T Seneca V	3449126	EC-HGK	4. 4.01	Mainstreet Aviation Ltd	Newcastle	2. 7.09E
			N4141N				
G-BZTH	Europa Aviation Europa	010		21.12.00	T J Houlihan	Croft Farm, Defford	27. 4.09P
	(Built T J Houlihan - pr.no.PFA 247-12494) (Monowheel u/c)						
G-BZTI	Europa Aviation Europa XS	124		30. 3.01	D E Puttock	Perranporth	27. 5.09P
	(Built W Hoolachan - pr.no.PFA 247-13172) (Rotax 914-UL) *(Tri-gear u/c)*						

G-BZTJ Bücker Bü.133C Jungmeister   41   Spanish AF   7. 3.01   R A Seeley *(As "17+TF" in Luftwaffe c/s)*
    ES1-41   Turweston 7.10.09P
(Officially recorded as built by CASA but c/n dubious and believed to be Bücker built)

G-BZTK Cameron V-90 Balloon (Hot Air)   10083   6. 3.01   E Appollodorus   London W12 27. 9.09E

G-BZTM Mainair Blade   1273-0201-7-W1068   16. 3.01   B A Richards   Watnall 16. 8.09P

G-BZTN Europa Aviation Europa XS   504   16. 3.01   M K McGreavey and S A Smith   Perth 6. 8.08P
(Built W Pringle and J Dewberry - pr.no.PFA 247-13715) (Tri-gear u/c)

G-BZTR Mainair Blade   1276-0301-7-W1071   8. 3.01   A Raithby and N McCusker   Rufforth 25. 4.09P

G-BZTS Cameron Bertie Bassett 90 SS Balloon (Hot Air)   3. 5.01   Trebor Bassett Ltd *"Bertie II"*   Shoreham 16. 7.09E
    10050

G-BZTT Cameron A-275 Balloon (Hot Air)   4953   28. 8.01   Cameron Flights Southern Ltd
    Woodborough, Pewsey 28. 5.09E

G-BZTU Mainair Blade 912   1272-0201-7-W1066   2. 4.01   C T Halliday   Ince Blundell 31.10.09P

G-BZTV Mainair Blade 912S   1278-0301-7-W1073   2. 4.01   R D McManus (Bignall End, Stoke-on-Trent) 30. 5.09P

G-BZTW Hunt Avon 582(1)/Huntwing   9906092   17. 1.01   T S Walker (Sandbach) 23. 6.09P
(Built T S Walker- pr.no.BMAA HB/136)

G-BZTX Mainair Blade 912   1267-0101-7-W1061   9. 2.01   K A Ingham *(Noted 8.05)*   Shipdham 20. 7.05P

G-BZTY Avtech Jabiru UL-450   0288   1. 3.01   R P Lewis White House Farm, Southery 18. 8.09P
(Built R P Lewis - pr.no.PFA 274A-13533)

G-BZUB Mainair Blade   1274-0201-7-W1069   27. 3.01   J Campbell and T Scott
    (Immingham and Hemswell, Gainsborough) 22. 5.09P

G-BZUC Cyclone Airsports Pegasus Quantum 15-912   10. 4.01   G A Breen Portimão, Faro, Portugal 28. 4 09P
    7796

G-BZUD Lindstrand LBL 105A Balloon (Hot Air)   780   27. 3.01   A Nimmo *(HSBC titiles)*   Dubai, UAE 22.12.09E

G-BZUE Cyclone Airsports Pegasus Quantum 15 7800   23. 4.01   S J Bunce   Shobdon 28. 5.09P
    (Rotax 503)

G-BZUF Mainair Rapier   1277-0301-7-W1072   27. 3.01   C A Denver   St Michaels 24. 3.08P

G-BZUG TLAC RL7A XP Sherwood Ranger   23. 3.01   J G Boxall *(In pseudo RAF c/s as false serial "SR-XP020")*
(Built S P Sharp) (Rotax 618) PFA 237-13040   Pittrichie Farm, Whiterashes 23. 9.09P

G-BZUH Rans S-6-ES Coyote II   0600.1371   26. 3.01   J D Sinclair-Day *(Noted 9.07)*   Eshott 13. 7.07P
(Built G M Prowling - pr.no.PFA 204-13716) (Tri-cycle u/c) (Jabiru 2200A)

G-BZUI Cyclone Airsports Pegasus Quantum 15-912   8. 5.01   A P Slade Field Farm, Oakley 21. 4.09P
    7798

G-BZUK Lindstrand LBL 31A Balloon (Hot Air)   776   7. 3.01   G R J Luckett Fort Collins, Colorado, US 30. 8.09P

G-BZUL Avtech Jabiru UL-450   PFA 274A-13678   28. 3.01   A M Hemmings North Moor, Scunthorpe 31. 8.09P
(Built P Hawkins)

G-BZUN Mainair Blade 912   1279-0301-7-W1074   18. 4.01   A D Jones   Ince Blundell 2. 6.05P

G-BZUO Cameron A-340HL Balloon (Hot Air)   4952   18. 5.01   Anglian Countryside Balloons Ltd
    Burnham-on-Crouch 22. 3.09E

G-BZUU Cameron O-90 Balloon (Hot Air)   10058   14. 6.01   D C Ball and C F Pooley *"Elmo II"*
    Tring and Barnwood, Gloucester 17. 8.09E

G-BZUV Cameron H-24 Balloon (Hot Air)   2665   LX-JLW   27. 4.01   J N Race *"The Gerkin"*   Lewes 27. 9.09E

G-BZUX Cyclone Airsports Pegasus Quantum 15- 7819   22. 5.01   K M MacRae, J D and C A Capewell Dunfermline 23. 6.08P
    (Rotax 582)

G-BZUY Van's RV-6   PFA 181A-13471   23. 5.01   T W Wielkooloski tr Uniform Yankee Group
(Built D M Gale and K F Crumplin) (Lycoming O-320)   Dunkeswell 2. 8.09P

G-BZUZ Hunt Avon-Blade R100(1)   BMAA HB/162   9. 2.01   C Hershaw   Doynton 22. 7.09P
(Built J A Hunt) (Uses Mainair Sailwing c/n W1067) (BMW R100)

G-BZVA Zenair CH.701UL STOL   PFA 187-13635   21. 3.01   M W Taylor   Insch 21. 4.09P
(Built M W Taylor)

G-BZVB Reims FR172H Rocket   FR17200327   G-BLMX   29. 8.00   K G Worcester tr Victor Bravo Group
    PH-RPC   Wing Farm, Longbridge Deverill 22. 1.09E

G-BZVC Mickleburgh L107 Sparrow   PFA 256-12549   21. 3.01   D R Mickleburgh   Fenland 27. 2.09P
(Built D R Mickleburgh)

G-BZVD Cameron Colt Forklift 105 SS Balloon (Hot Air)   15. 6.01   Stratos Ballooning GmbH and Co KG *"JungHeinrich"*
    10084   Ennigerloh, Germany 19. 4.07A

G-BZVE Cameron N-133 Balloon (Hot Air)   10092   20. 6.01   I M Ashpole *"American Chopper"*
    Bridstow, Ross-on-Wye 22. 7.09E

G-BZVH Raj Hamsa X'Air 582(1)   561   20. 4.01   M Smullen (Lullymore, Rathangan, County Klldare) 13.10.07P
(Built B and D Bergin - pr.no.BMAA HB/160)

G-BZVI Nova Vertex 24   13379   24. 5.01   M Hay   (Dundee)

G-BZVJ Cyclone Airsports Pegasus Quantum 15 7821   12. 6.01   O P Gall   (Lerwick, Shetland) 1. 7.08P
    (Rotax 582)

G-BZVK Raj Hamsa X'Air 582(11)   592   22. 2.01   P F Berry and P G Wilcox   (Berkeley) 12. 1.09P
(Built K P Taylor - pr.no.BMAA HB/152)

G-BZVM Rans S-6-ES Coyote II   1000.1394ES   1. 3.01   N N Ducker   Tatenhill 20. 7.09P
(Built N N Ducker - pr.no.PFA 204-13705) (Rotax 912-UL)

G-BZVN Van's RV-6   PFA 181-13188   25. 4.01   J A Booth (Todwick, Sheffield) 30. 7.09P
(Built J A Booth) (Lycoming O-360)

G-BZVO Cessna TR182 Turbo Skylane RG II   D-EPOL   3. 4.01   Swiftair Ltd   Elstree 11.12.09E
    R18200990   N739CX

G-BZVR Raj Hamsa X'Air 582(4)   566   13. 3.01   P Travis tr Hummingbird Club Davidstow Moor 25. 4.09P
(Built R P, D Sims, E Bowen and P and E Travis - pr.no.BMAA HB/146) (Originally regd as 582 (8), amended 16. 5.08)

G-BZVT III Sky Arrow 650 T   PFA 298-13333   23. 3.01   D J Goldsmith   Headcorn 22. 8.09P
(Built R N W Wright)

G-BZVU Cameron Z-105 Balloon (Hot Air)   10078   9. 8.01   The Mall Balloon Team Ltd   Bristol 25. 4.09E
    (The Mall and Cribbs Causeway titles)

G-BZVV Cyclone Airsports Pegasus Quantum 15-912   12. 3.01   C J Shorter   (Fareham) 2. 6.08P
    7793

G-BZVW Ilyushin Il-2 Stormovik   1870710   Soviet AF   16. 5.01   S Swallow and R H Cooper *(Noted 10.06)*
    1870710   Wickenby

G-BZVX Ilyushin Il-2 Stormovik   1878576   Soviet AF   16. 5.01   S Swallow and R H Cooper *(Noted 10.06)*
    1878576   Wickenby

G-BZWB Mainair Blade 912   1284-0507-7-W1079   26. 4.01   L Parker   Newtownards 6. 9.09P

Reg	Type	C/n	Prev ID	Date	Owner/Operator	Location	Notes
G-BZWC	Raj Hamsa X'Air Falcon 912(1)	587		9. 5.01	C McAfee	Nether Glastry, Dunblane	21. 8.06P
	(Built G A J Salter - pr.no.BMAA HB/157)						
G-BZWG	Piper PA-28-140 Cherokee Cruiser	28-7625188	N9656K	17. 5.01	H and E Merkado	Panshanger	12. 7.09E
G-BZWH	Cessna 152	15281339	N49819	17. 5.01	J and H Aviation Services Ltd	Panshanger	19. 8.09E
G-BZWI	Medway EclipseR	170/148		3. 5.01	R A Keene	Over Farm, Gloucester	28. 3.05P
G-BZWJ	CFM Streak Shadow SA	K 338		8. 5.01	T A Morgan "Harmony Angel"	Popham	18. 8.09P
	(Built T A Morgan - pr.no.PFA 206-13553) (Rotax 582)						
G-BZWK	Avtech Jabiru SK	xxxx		8. 5.01	G M R Abrey	East Winch	29. 9.09P
	(Built R Thompson - pr.no.PFA 274-13292)						
G-BZWM	Cyclone Airsports Pegasus XL-Q	7792		18. 5.01	D T Evans (Noted 11.07)		
	(Built using Trike SW-TE-0136 from G-MVKM)					Broadmeadow Farm, Hereford	24. 6.04P
G-BZWN	Van's RV-8	PFA 303-13692		14. 5.01	A J Symms and R D Harper	High Ham, Langport	13. 5.09P
	(Built A J Symms and R D Harper) (Lycoming IO-360)						
G-BZWS	Cyclone Airsports Pegasus Quantum 15-912	7813		26. 4.01	G B Smith tr G-BZWS Syndicate	Knapthorpe Lodge, Caunton	9. 5.09P
G-BZWT	Tecnam P92-EA Echo	PFA 318-13681		17. 5.01	R F Cooper	Field Farm, Oakley	17. 3.09P
	(Built R F Cooper) (Marked as "P92S")						
G-BZWU	Cyclone Airsports Pegasus Quantum 15-912	7831		19. 7.01	A Rothin	Roddige	23. 6.08P
G-BZWV	Steen Skybolt	PFA 064-10751		30. 5.01	P D and K Begley	Sywell	27. 4.09P
	(Built P D Begley)						
G-BZWX	Whittaker MW5-D Sorcerer	PFA 163-13599		1. 6.01	B J Syson	Landmead Farm, Garford	24. 7.08P
	(Built P G Depper)						
G-BZWY	CFM Streak Shadow SA	xxxx		31. 5.01	B Cartwright	The Polo Field, Lurgan	10. 9.09P
	(Built B Cartwright - pr.no.PFA 206-13601)						
G-BZWZ	Van's RV-6	PFA 181A-13419		26. 4.01	A P Mardlin	(Tring)	9. 4.09P
	(Built J Shanley) (Lycoming O-320)						
G-BZXA	Raj Hamsa X'Air V2(2)	560		31. 5.01	D W Mullin	Ash Farm, Winsford	3. 9.08P
	(Built D W Mullin - pr.no.BMAA HB/148)						
G-BZXB	Van's RV-6	PFA 181A-13625		4. 6.01	B J King-Smith and D J Akerman	Goodwood	6. 3.09P
	(Built B J King-Smith and D J Akerman) (Lycoming O-360)						
G-BZXD	RotorWay Executive 162F	6494		5. 6.01	P G King (Noted 10.08)	Street Farm, Takeley	27. 4.06P
	(Built P G King) (RotorWay RI 162F)						
G-BZXF	Cameron A-210 Balloon (Hot Air)	4999		5. 2.02	Off The Ground Balloon Company Ltd	Lyth, Kendal	11. 2.09E
G-BZXG	Dyn'Aéro MCR-01 ULC	156		26.10.01	J L Ker	Longframlington	19. 2.08P
	(Built J M Scott and G J Sargent - pr.no.PFA 301B-13815)						
G-BZXI	Nova Philou 26	11207		16. 5.01	M Hay	(Dundee)	
G-BZXJ	Schweizer 269C-1 (Schweizer 300)	0128		20. 6.01	Helicentre Liverpool Ltd	Liverpool-John Lennon	15. 8.08E
G-BZXK	Robin HR.200-120B	286	F-GNNV	12. 6.01	Helicopter One Ltd	Bournemouth	20.11.09E
G-BZXL	Whittaker MW5-D Sorcerer	PFA 163-13738		7. 6.01	R Hatton	Kirkbride	2. 7.04P
	(Built K Wright and C Gale) (Rotax 503)						
G-BZXM	Mainair Blade 912	1283-0501-7-W1078		20. 4.01	M E Fowler	Steeple Claydon, Buckingham	1. 8 09P
G-BZXN	Avtech Jabiru UL-450	PFA 274A-13747		7. 6.01	D A Hall and V G J Davies	Lee-on-Solent	27. 5.09P
	(Built A R Silvester)						
G-BZXO	Cameron Z-105 Balloon (Hot Air)	10125		27. 6.01	D K Jones and K D Thomas	(Alton and Epsom)	24. 8.09E
G-BZXP	Air Création 582(1)/Kiss 400	FL001		14. 6.01	A Fairbrother	Sywell	20. 4.09P
	(Built P M Dewhurst - pr.no.BMAA HB/169 for Flylight kit comprising Trike s/n T00100 and Wing s/n A00056-0054)						
G-BZXR	Cameron N-90 Balloon (Hot Air)	10124		3. 9.01	H J Andrews	Selborne, Alton	1. 7.09P
G-BZXS	Scottish Aviation Bulldog Series 120/121	BH120/296	XX631	21. 6.01	K J Thompson (As "XX631:W" in RAF c/s)	Strandhill, Sligo, County Sligo	7. 5.10S
G-BZXT	Mainair Blade 912	1286-0501-7-W1081		25. 5.01	S R Vinsun tr Barton 912 Flyers	Barton	4. 5.09P
G-BZXV	Cyclone Airsports Pegasus Quantum 15-912	7828		28. 6.01	P I Oliver	Rufforth	21. 7.08P
G-BZXW	Magni M-16 Tandem Trainer	PFA G/12-1249	G-NANA	30. 4.01	P J Troy-Davis	(Fleetwood)	31. 8.00P
	(Built J W P Lewis) (Rotax 912S)						
G-BZXX	Cyclone Airsports Pegasus Quantum 15-912	7812		20. 4.01	C S Povey tr G-BZXX Group	Tarn Farm, Cockerham	8. 5.09P
G-BZXY	Robinson R44 Raven	1027		12. 6.01	Helicopter Services Ltd	Wycombe Air Park	16. 7.09E
G-BZXZ	Scottish Aviation Bulldog Series 120/121	BH120/294	XX629	1. 6.01	R I Kelly and E J Burford (As "XX629:V" in RAF c/s)	Wellesbourne Mountford	5.12.10S
G-BZYA	Rans S-6-ES Coyote II	0499.1313		12. 6.01	M R Osbourn	Long Marston	21. 4.09P
	(Built D J Clack - pr.no.PFA 204-13529) (Rotax 582) (Tri-cycle u/c)						
G-BZYD	Westland SA.341B Gazelle AH.1	1648	XZ329	14. 6.01	Aerocars Ltd (As "XZ329" in AAC c/s)	Filton	15. 6.09P
		(C/n 1652 quoted also)					
G-BZYE	Robinson R22 Beta II	3231		15. 6.01	Plane Talking Ltd	Blackbushe	11. 7.09E
G-BZYG	DG Flugzeugbau DG-500MB	(5E220B15)		25. 9.01	R C Bromwich "94"	Aboyne	16.12.09E
G-BZYI	Nova Phocus 123	9748		8. 6.01	M Hay	(Dundee)	
G-BZYK	Avtech Jabiru UL-450	0140		21. 6.01	P A James tr Cloudbase Aviation G-BZYK	Redhill	12.11.09P
	(Built A S Forbes - pr.no.PFA 274A-13227)						
G-BZYL	Rans S-6-ES Coyote II	1000.1395ES		22. 6.01	C B Heslop	Lower Wasing Farm, Brimpton	20. 7.09P
	(Build J D Harris - pr.no.PFA 204-13718) (Jabiru 2200A) (Tri-cycle u/c)						
G-BZYM	Raj Hamsa X'Air 133(1)	649		21. 6.01	D R Sutton	Brook Farm, Pilling	14. 7.09P
	(Built G Fleck - pr.no.BMAA HB/172) (Verner VM133)						
G-BZYN	Cyclone Airsports Pegasus Quantum 15-912	7835		15. 8.01	J Cannon	Graveley Hall Farm, Graveley	26.10.09P
G-BZYO	Colt 210A Balloon (Hot Air)	3523	D-OSPM	19. 7.01	P M Forster (Operated Alba Ballooning)	Edinburgh	17. 3.04T
			(Understood stripped for spares with envelope to Art College for non aviation use 2006)				
G-BZYR	Cameron N-31 Balloon (Hot Air)	10137		6. 8.01	C J Sanger-Davies	Hawarden	30. 8.09E
G-BZYS	Micro Aviation B 22S Bantam	94-001	ZK-JDO	12. 7.01	D L Howell (Noted 10.05)	Stoke, Isle of Grain	12. 9.02P
G-BZYT	Interavia 80TA Balloon (Hot Air)	04309-92		6. 7.01	J King	Leighton Buzzard	
G-BZYU	Whittaker MW6 Merlin	PFA 164-13647		2. 7.01	K J Cole	Over Farm, Gloucester	8. 7.04P
	(Built K J Cole) (Rotax 582)						

G-BZYV	Noble Hardman Snowbird Mk.V 582(1)			5. 7.01	M A Oakley	Kemble	
	(Built S Jones)	BMAA HB/175					
G-BZYW	Cameron N-90 Balloon (Hot Air)	10134		6. 8.01	C and J M Bailey t/a Bailey Balloons (Bass titles)		
						Pill, Bristol	31. 8.09E
G-BZYX	Raj Hamsa X'Air 700(1A)	653		15. 6.01	A M Sutton	Otherton, Cannock	25. 8.08P
	(Built A G Marsh - pr.no.BMAA HB/173)						
G-BZYY	Cameron N-90 Balloon (Hot Air)	10130		30. 8.01	Mason Zimbler Ltd "Up Down"	Bristol	27. 9.09E
G-BZZD	Reims Cessna F172M Skyhawk II	F17201436	G-BDPF	14. 4.98	R H M Richardson-Bunbury	Bodmin	3. 8.09E

G-CAAA - G-CAZZ

G-CAHA	Piper PA-34-200T Seneca II	34-7770010	N23PL	7. 7.98	Aeros Holdings Ltd	Gloucestershire	10. 6.09E
			SE-GPY, (D-IIIC), SE-GPY				
G-CALL	Piper PA-23-250 Aztec F	27-7754061	N62826	21.12.77	J D Moon	Belfast International	22. 6.09E
G-CAMB	Aérospatiale AS.355F2 Ecureuil 2	5416	N813LP	17.12.96	Tiger Helicopters Ltd	Shobdon	31. 5.09E
G-CAMM	Hawker Cygnet replica	PFA 077-10245	(G-ERDB)	30. 5.91	R W Cashmore (As "6":and carries "G-CAMM" on wings only)		
	(Built D M Cashmore) (Mosler MM-CB35)				(On loan to Richard Shuttleworth Trustees) Old Warden		27. 7.09P
G-CAMP	Cameron N-105 Balloon (Hot Air)	4546		24. 3.99	R D Parry (Operated Hong Kong Balloon and Airship Club)		
						Hong Kong, PRC	1. 7.09E
G-CAMR	BFC Challenger II	xxxxx		26. 3.99	P R A Walker	Old Sarum	
	(Built P R A Walker - pr.no.PFA 177-12569 - should be 177A type prefix)						
G-CAPI	Mudry CAP.10B	76	G-BEXR	16. 3.99	C Wills tr PI Group	Orchard House, Littleport	27.11.06T
G-CAPX	Akrotech Europe CAP.10B	280		21. 9.98	H J Pessall	Leicester	8. 5.09E

G-CBAA - G-CBZZ

G-CBAB	Scottish Aviation Bulldog Series 120/121	XX543		14. 6.01	J N R Davison, L C T George and P J R Hill		
		BH120/235			(As "XX543:F" in RAF c/s)	Duxford	26. 7.11
G-CBAD	Mainair Blade 912	1287-0601-7-W1082		8. 6.01	J Stocking	Wolverhampton	7. 7.09P
G-CBAF	Neico Lancair 320	PFA 191-13567		11. 6.01	L N and M van Cleef	Lydd	17. 7.05P
	(Built R W Fairless) (Lycoming IO-320)		(Nose undercarriage collapsed landing Lydd 11.6.05: propeller struck ground shock loading engine)				
G-CBAH	Raj Hamsa X'Air 133(1)	640		4. 7.01	D N B Hearn		
	(Built D N B Hearn - pr.no.BMAA HB/174)					Little Heathfield Farm, Atherfield, Ventnor	27. 4.07P
G-CBAI	Flight Design CT2K	01-02-04-07	G-69-52	4. 7.01	J R Hughes tr Newtownards Microlight Group		
	(Assembled Pegasus Aviation - no Pegasus c/n issued)					Newtownards	21. 7.09P
G-CBAK	Robinson R44 Clipper	1089		2. 8.01	CEL Electrical Logistics Ltd	(Tadcaster)	27. 8.09E
G-CBAL	Piper PA-28-161 Warrior II	28-8116087	LN-MAD	25. 3.94	Thomson Airways Ltd	Cranfield	13. 4.09E
			N83007				
G-CBAN	Scottish Aviation Bulldog Series 120/121	XX668		26. 7.01	C Hilliker (As "XX668:I" in RAF c/s)	Colerne	21. 5.10S
		BH120/326					
G-CBAP	Zenair CH.601UL Zodiac	PFA 162A-13656		12. 7.01	A G Marsh	Inverkip	13. 3.09P
	(Built L J Lowry)						
G-CBAR	Stoddard-Hamilton GlaStar	PFA 295-13133		18. 5.01	C M Barnes	Garden Piece, Basingstoke	4. 6.09P
	(Built C M Barnes) (Tri-cycle u/c)						
G-CBAS	Rans S-6-ES Coyote II	1100.1399ES		4. 7.01	S Stockill	RAF Halton	11. 4.09P
	(Built S R Green - pr.no.PFA 204-13688) (Rotax 912-UL) (Tailwheel u/c)						
G-CBAT	Cameron Z-90 Balloon (Hot Air)	10099		1. 6.01	British Telecommunications PLC	Thatcham	6. 9.09E
G-CBAU	Rand Robinson KR-2	PFA 129-12789		11. 7.01	B Normington	(Leamington Spa)	
	(Built B Normington)						
G-CBAV	Raj Hamsa X'Air V2(2)	399		7. 9.01	D W Stamp and G J Lampitt		
	(Built D W Stamp and G J Lampitt - pr.no.BMAA HB/127)				Pound Green, Buttonoak, Bewdley		15. 9.08P
G-CBAW	Cameron A-300 Balloon (Hot Air)	10148		16. 4.02	D K Hempleman-Adams	Corsham	
G-CBAX	Tecnam P92-EM Echo	PFA 318-13698		26. 6.01	R P Reeves	Dunkeswell	1.12.08P
	(Built R P Reeves)						
G-CBAZ	Rans S-6-ES Coyote II	0998.1267		12. 7.01	J G J McDill	(Westmoor Farm,, Thirsk)	5. 1.06P
	(Built G V Willder - pr.no.PFA 204-13596) (Rotax 582)						
G-CBBA	Robin DR.400-180 Régent	2505		27. 7.01	Whitby Seafoods Ltd	Durham Tees Valley	15. 8.09E
G-CBBB	Cyclone Airsports Pegasus Quantum 15-912			22. 6.01	D Workman	(Brierley Hill)	21. 6.09P
		7827					
G-CBBC	Scottish Aviation Bulldog Series 120/121	XX515		8. 6.01	Bulldog Flyers Ltd (As "XX515:4" in RAF c/s)		
		BH120/201				Blackbushe	4. 1.11S
G-CBBF	Beech 76 Duchess	ME-352	OY-BED	23. 7.01	Bflying Ltd (Operated Bournemouth Flying Club)		
			EI-BHS			Bournemouth	6.11.09E
G-CBBG	Mainair Blade	1291-0601-7-W1086		23. 7.01	S L Cogger	Willingale	19. 4.09P
G-CBBH	Raj Hamsa X'Air V2(2)	435		19. 7.01	S P Macdonald	Sackville Lodge, Riseley	13. 8.07P
	(Built W G Colyer - pr.no.BMAA HB/143)						
G-CBBK	Robinson R22 Beta	3233	EI-CWP	26. 7.01	R J Everett	(Sproughton, Ipswich)	14. 8.09E
			G-CBBK				
G-CBBL	Scottish Aviation Bulldog Series 120/121	XX550		8. 8.01	A Cunningham	Abbeyshrule, County Longford	30. 3.11
		BH120/243					
G-CBBM	ICP MXP-740 Savannah Jabiru(1)			10. 8.01	C E Passmore	East Barling, Essex	10. 7.09P
	(Built P J Wilson & S Whittaker) 01-03-51-062				(Project.no.BMAA HB/176)		
G-CBBN	Cyclone Airsports Pegasus Quantum 15-912			9. 8.01	P R Rowe tr G-CBBN Group	Dunkeswell	31. 8.08P
		7844					
G-CBBO	Whittaker MW5-D Sorcerer	PFA 163-13443		23. 7.01	P J Gripton	Baxby Manor, Husthwaite	11. 6.09P
	(Built P J Gripton)						
G-CBBP	Cyclone Airsports Pegasus Quantum 15-912			31. 7.01	C Thompson	(Wombourne, Wolverhampton)	30. 7.09P
		7843					
G-CBBR	Scottish Aviation Bulldog Series 120/121	XX625		8. 8.01	G V Crowe and D L Thompson (As "XX625:01" in RAF c/s)		
		BH120/290				Norwich	
G-CBBS	Scottish Aviation Bulldog Series 120/121	XX694		8. 8.01	Newcastle Aerobatic Academy Ltd (As "XX694:E" in RAF c/s)		
		BH120/343				Newcastle	6. 7.09S

G-CBBT	Scottish Aviation Bulldog Series 120/121	XX695	8. 8.01	Newcastle Bulldog Group Ltd (As "XX695:3" in RAF c/s)
	BH120/344			Morgansfield, Fishburn 7. 3.10T
G-CBBU	Scottish Aviation Bulldog Series 120/121	XX711	6. 8.01	Newcastle Bulldog Group Ltd (Noted 6.06) Derby
	BH120/360			
G-CBBW	Scottish Aviation Bulldog Series 120/121	XX619	1. 8.01	S E Robottom-Scott (As "XX619:T" in RAF c/s)
	BH120/277			Coventry 27. 8.03T
G-CBBX	Lindstrand LBL 69A Balloon (Hot Air) 805		2. 8.01	J L F Garcia Guadalajara, Spain 5. 8.02A
G-CBCB	Scottish Aviation Bulldog Series 120/121	XX537	25. 9.01	The General Aviation Trading Company Ltd
	BH120/223			(As "XX537:C" in RAF c/s) North Weald 12. 5.11S
G-CBCD	Cyclone Airsports Pegasus Quantum 15 7845		6. 8.01	I A Lumley (Penrith) 5. 6.08P
	(Rotax 582)			
G-CBCF	Cyclone Airsports Pegasus Quantum 15-912		23. 8.01	S Speake tr G-CBCF Group
	7846			(Newton Bank, Daresbury) 17.12.07P
G-CBCH	Zenair CH.701UL STOL PFA 187-13568		8. 8.01	L G Millen (Sittingbourne)
	(Built L G Millen)			
G-CBCI	Raj Hamsa X'Air 582(11) 659		9. 8.01	C P Lincoln Stoke, Isle of Grain 14. 4.09P
	(Built P A Gilford - pr.no.BMAA HB/180)			
G-CBCJ	Rotary Air Force RAF 2000 GTX-SE		13. 8.01	B Errington-Weddle Henstridge 9.10.08P
	(Built J P Comerford) PFA G/13-1331			
G-CBCK	Nipper T 66 Series 3 T66/30	G-TEDZ	14. 8.01	N M Bloom Abbots Hill Farm, Hemel Hempstead 14.12.06P
	(Jabiru 2200A)			
	(Originally built Avions Fairey SA: rebuilt C Edwards C 1998 as G-TEDZ - pr.no.PFA 25-11051: later rebuilt N Bloom c 2001 and re-regd)			
G-CBCL	Stoddard-Hamilton GlaStar PFA 295-13089		5. 9.97	M I Weaver Streethay Farm, Lichfield 27. 5.09P
	(Built C J Norman) (Tri-cycle u/c)			
G-CBCM	Raj Hamsa X'Air 700(1A) 656		23. 7.01	M Ellis North Moor, Scunthorpe 21. 8.06P
	(Built A Hipkin - pr.no.BMAA HB/177)		(Undercarriage damaged following precautionary landing nr Yablethorpe 20. 9.08)
G-CBCN	Schweizer 269C-1 (Schweizer 300) 0129	EI-CWS	17. 9.01	Helicentre Liverpool Ltd Liverpool-John Lennon 29. 6.09E
		G-CBCN		
G-CBCP	Van's RV-6A PFA 181A-13643		6. 8.01	A M Smith tr G-CBCP Group Crowfield 27. 5.09P
	(Built AM Smith)			
G-CBCR	Scottish Aviation Bulldog Series 120/121	XX702	5. 9.01	D Wells (As "XX702" in RAF c/s) Derby 16.11.11
	BH120/351			
G-CBCV	Scottish Aviation Bulldog Series 120/121	XX699	30. 8.01	C A Patter (As "XX699:F" in RAF c/s) North Coates 24. 8.08S
	BH120/348			
G-CBCX	Cyclone Airsports Pegasus Quantum 15 7848		10. 9.01	T J Heaton (Sleaford) 9. 9.08P
	(Rotax 582)			
G-CBCY	Beech C24R Sierra MC-491	N881RS	26. 9.01	Wycombe Air Centre Ltd Wycombe Air Park 25. 3.09E
		PH-HLA		
G-CBCZ	CFM Streak Shadow SLA K 340-SLA		13. 9.01	J O'Malley Kane "Alana Rose"
	(Built J A Hambleton - pr.no.PFA 206-13586) (Rotax 582)			Great Yeldham Hall, Halstead 12. 8.09P
G-CBDC	Thruster T 600N 450 Jabiru Sprint		12. 7.01	L J Greenhough (Carraghoe, Ireland) 3. 8.09P
	0071-T600N-054			
G-CBDD	Mainair Blade 1293-0701-7-W1088		1. 8.01	M Turner (Nantwich) 31. 8.08P
G-CBDG	Zenair CH.601HD Zodiac PFA 162-13375		3. 9.01	R E Lasnier Sleap 15. 6.08P
	(Built R E Lasnier)			
G-CBDH	Flight Design CT2K 01-07-02-17		4.10.01	K Tuck (Horningtoft, Dereham) 27. 4.09P
	(Assembled Pegasus Aviation with c/n 7849)			
G-CBDI	Denney Kitfox Model 2 PFA 172-11888		4. 9.01	J G D Barbour Sherriff Hall Estate, Balgone 12. 6.09P
	(Built J G D Barbour)			
G-CBDJ	Flight Design CT2K 01-07-01-17		11.10.01	P J Walker Griffins Farm, Temple Bruer 25.10.08P
	(Assembled Pegasus Aviation with c/n 7850)			
G-CBDK	Scottish Aviation Bulldog Series 120/121	XX611	26. 9.01	J N Randle (As "XX611:7" in RAF c/s) Coventry 9. 4.08S
	BH120/259			
G-CBDL	Mainair Blade 1292-0701-7-W1087		1. 8.01	D Lightwood (Macclesfield) 14.11.03P
G-CBDM	Tecnam P92-EM Echo PFA 318-13756		11. 7.01	J J Cozens RNAS Yeovilton 19. 6.09P
	(Built J J Cozens and C J Willy)			
G-CBDN	Mainair Blade 1297-0801-7-W1092		20. 9.01	T Peckham (Graveney, Faversham) 16.11.08P
C-CBDO	Raj Hamsa X'Air 582(1) 583		12.11.01	A Campbell Newtownards 22.10.07P
	(Built R T Henry - pr.no.BMAA HB/170)			
G-CBDP	Mainair Blade 912 1295-0801-7-W1090		17. 8.01	D S Parker Carlisle 16. 8.09P
G-CBDS	Scottish Aviation Bulldog Series 120/121	XX707	27. 7.01	J R Parry (As "XX707:4" in RAF c/s) Caernarfon 27. 5.11S
	BH120/356			
G-CBDT	Zenair CH.601HD Zodiac PFA 162-12474		17. 9.01	D G Watt Cark-in-Cartmell 31. 7.09P
	(Built D G Watt)			
G-CBDU	Quad City Challenger II PFA 177-13000		14. 9.01	Hiscox Cases Ltd (Noted 8.05)
	(Built B A Hiscox)			Otherton, Cannock
G-CBDV	Raj Hamsa X'Air 582(6) 616		6. 8.01	T S Davis Davidstow Moor 7. 7.08P
	(Built R J Brown and D J Prothero - pr.no.BMAA HB/161)			
G-CBDW	Raj Hamsa X'Air Jabiru(1) 575		18. 9.01	B H Emery (Rugeley) 5.10.07P
	(Built P R Reynolds - pr.no.BMAA HB/150)			
G-CBDX	Cyclone Airsports Pegasus Quantum 15 7857		11.10.01	P Sinkler Shobdon 14.12.09P
	(Rotax 582)			
G-CBDY	Raj Hamsa X'Air V2(2) 588		26. 9.01	K McNaughton Doncaster 29. 5.08P
	(Built D Mahajan - pr.no.BMAA HB/155)			
G-CBDZ	Cyclone Airsports Pegasus Quantum 15-912		11. 9.01	J J Brutnell Hunsdon 6.10.08P
	7852			
G-CBEB	Air Création 582(1)/Kiss 400 FL003/135		3.10.01	M Harris Redlands, Swindon 27. 5.08P
	(Built P J A Bradshaw.and A R R Williams - pr.no.BMAA HB/184 for Flylight kit)			
G-CBEC	Cameron Z-105 Balloon (Hot Air) 10105		16.10.01	A L Ballarino Piedimonte Matese, Italy 3. 8.08A
G-CBED	Cameron Z-90 Balloon (Hot Air) 10121		15.10.01	John Aimo Balloons SAS (Citta di Mondovi titles)
				Mondovi, Italy 9. 6.09E
G-CBEE	Piper PA-28R-200 Cherokee Arrow II	N4479X	5.10.01	IHC Ltd Biggin Hill 5. 2.10E
	28R-7635055			

G-CBEF	Scottish Aviation Bulldog Series 120/121	XX621	3.10.01	J A Ingram (As "XX621:H" in RAF c/s)	Leicester	15. 2.08
		BH120/286					
G-CBEH	Scottish Aviation Bulldog Series 120/121	XX521	28. 9.01	J E Lewis (As "XX521:H" in RAF c/s)	Enstone	3.12.11
		BH120/207					
G-CBEI	Piper PA-22-108 Colt	22-9136	SE-CZR	5. 6.02	D Sharp	Breighton	9. 1.11S
G-CBEJ	Colt 120A Balloon (Hot Air)	10181		11.10.01	J A B Gray	Daglingworth, Cirencester	26. 2.09E
G-CBEK	Scottish Aviation Bulldog Series 120/121	XX700	26. 9.01	B P Robinson (As "XX700:17" in RAF c/s)	
		BH120/349				Blackbushe	5. 2.11S
G-CBEL	Hawker Iraqi Fury FB.11	37579	N36SF	6. 8.01	J A D Bradshaw (Also carries "361 Navy")	
			Iraqi AF 315			Bournemouth	30.10.09P
G-CBEM	Mainair Blade	1294-0801-7-W1089		17. 8.01	M Earp	Calton Moor Farm, Ashbourne	14.11.09P
G-CBEN	Cyclone Airsports Pegasus Quantum 15-912		8.10.01	S Clarke	Swinford, Rugby	12. 3.08P
		7855					
G-CBES	Europa Aviation Europa	061	27. 9.01	M R Hexley	(Penmaenmawr)	7. 5.07P
	(Built M R Hexley - pr.no.PFA 247-12691) (Monowheel u/c)					
G-CBET	Mainair Blade 912S	1296-0801-7-W1091	6. 9.01	D F Kenny	Finmere	26. 1.08P
G-CBEU	Cyclone Airsports Pegasus Quantum 15-912		16.10.01	S D Cox	(Northiam, Rye)	23. 1.09P
		7869					
G-CBEV	Cyclone Airsports Pegasus Quantum 15-912		16.10.01	K R W Barton tr G-CBEV Group	
		7854				Longacre Farm, Sandy	13. 2.09P
G-CBEW	Flight Design CT2K	01-08-02-23	19.10.01	A J Webb tr Shy Talk Group	Oxford	23.12.07P
	(Assembled Pegasus Aviation with c/n 7868)					
G-CBEX	Flight Design CT2K	01-08-01-23	29.10.01	A G Quinn	Knapthorpe Lodge, Caunton	13. 4.09P
	(Assembled Pegasus Aviation with c/n 7867)					
G-CBEY	Cameron C-80 Balloon (Hot Air)	10190	31.10.01	D V Fowler	Cranbrook	7. 1.09E
G-CBEZ	Robin DR.400-180 Régent	2511	26. 2.02	K V Field	Turweston	8. 4.10E
G-CBFA	Diamond DA.40 Star	40063	25.10.01	Lyrastar Ltd	Redhill	2. 4.10E
G-CBFE	Raj Hamsa X'Air 582(1)	636	19.10.01	M L Powell	Brook Farm, Pilling	14. 7.09P
	(Built S Whittle - pr.no.BMAA HB/186)					
G-CBFF	Cameron O-120 Balloon (Hot Air)	10167	20.11.01	T M C McCoy (Operated Ascent Balloons)	
				(Ascent titles)	Peasedown St John, Bath	31. 5.09E
G-CBFH	Thunder AX8-105 Series 2 Balloon (Hot Air)		13.11.01	D V Fowler and A N F Pertwee	
		10188			Cranbrook and Frinton-on-Sea	10.11.06A
G-CBFJ	Robinson R44 Raven	1131	7.11.01	Safedem Ltd	(Doune)	8.11.08E
G-CBFK	Murphy Rebel	PFA 232-13340	13. 9.01	P J Gibbs	Truro	13.10.03P
	(Built D Webb)					
G-CBFM	SOCATA TB-21 Trinidad GT	710	PH-BLM	2. 1.02	Execflight Ltd	Southend	20. 5.09E
			D-EFAK (4)				
G-CBFN	Robin HR.100-200B Royal	112	F-BTBP	1. 3.02	T H A Alington tr Foxtrot November Group	
				(Noted 1.08)	Bourne Park, Hurstbourne Tarrant	11. 6.05T
G-CBFO	Cessna 172S Skyhawk SP	172S8929	N3520A	22.10.01	P Gray	Gamston	25.11.09E
G-CBFP	Scottish Aviation Bulldog Series 120/121	XX636	29. 10.01	R Nisbet and A R Dix (As "XX636:Y" in RAF c/s)	
		BH120/306				Shacklewell Farm, Empingham	12. 6.11
G-CBFU	Scottish Aviation Bulldog Series 120/121	XX628	12.11.01	J R and S J Huggins (As "XX628:9" in RAF c/s)	
		BH120/293				Chalksole Green Farm, Alkham	4. 6.11S
G-CBFV	Comco Ikarus C42 FB UK	PFA 322-13774	5.11.01	A W Leadley	
	(Built P A D Chubb)			(Lismonaghan, Letterkenny, County Donegal)	28. 4.08P
G-CBFW	Montgomerie-Bensen B 8MR	PFA G/01-1312	6.11.01	I Mclean	Little Rissington	21.12.07P
	(Built B F Pearson)					
G-CBFX	Rans S-6-ESN Coyote II	1000.1392	8.11.01	J R Lowman Lower Mountpleasant Farm, Chatteris	9. 9.09P
	(Built J Whiting - pr.no.PFA 204-13820) (Rotax 582) (Tri-cycle u/c)				
G-CBFY	Cameron Z-250 Balloon (Hot Air)	10023	9.11.01	M L Gabb	Haselor, Alcester	20. 2.09E
G-CBFZ	Avtech Jabiru SPL-450	0353	8.11.01	A H King	(Orpington)	26. 5.07P
	(Built A H King - pr.no.PFA 274A-13617) (Originally designated with addtional UL series c/n "UL0103")				
G-CBGA	PZL-110 Koliber 160A	04010086	SP-WGM	14.11.01	STG Fabrications Ltd	Old Sarum	14. 2.09E
G-CBGB	Zenair CH.601UL Zodiac	PFA 162A-13819	12.11.01	J F Woodham	Hollow Hill Farm, Granborough	28. 4.09P
	(Built R Germany) (Tri-cycle u/c)					
G-CBGC	SOCATA TB-10 Tobago	1584	VH-YHB	21. 9.01	Tobago Aviation Ltd	Blackbushe	27. 2.09E
G-CBGD	Zenair CH.701UL STOL	PFA 187-13785	13.11.01	I S Walsh	Dunkeswell	3. 9.09P
	(Built I S Walsh)					
G-CBGE	Tecnam P92-EM Echo	PFA 318-13680	9.11.01	I D Rutherford	(Calvert, Buckingham)	31. 8.09P
	(Built T C Robson)					
G-CBGG	Cyclone Airsports Pegasus Quantum 15	7874	27.11.01	T E Davies	Headon Farm, Retford	6. 4.09P
	(Rotax 503)					
G-CBGH	Teverson Bisport	PFA 267-12784	7.11.01	R C Teverson	Waits Farm, Belchamp Walter	14. 3.09P
	(Built R C Teverson)					
G-CBGJ	Aeroprakt A22 Foxbat	PFA 317-13803	14.11.01	M McCall "002"	(Moira, Craigavon)	29. 8.08P
	(Built W R Davis-Smith)					
G-CBGL	Max Holste MH.1521M Broussard	19	F-BMJO	3.12.01	A I Milne tr Broussard Flying Group	(Horsford)
			F-BNEN, French AF		(Stored awaiting rebuild 4.06)	
G-CBGO	Murphy Maverick 430	PFA 259-13470	24.10.01	C R Ellis and E A Wrathall	(Chapel-en-le-Frith)	16.10.09P
	(Built C R Ellis) (Jabiru 2200A)					
G-CBGP	Comco Ikarus C42 FB UK	PFA 322-13741	22.11.01	G F Welby	Bakersfield	20. 5.09P
	(Built A R Lloyd)					
G-CBGR	Avtech Jabiru UL-450	xxxx	21.11.01	R G Kirkland	RAF Henlow	10..4.09P
	(Built K R Emery - pr.no.PFA 274A-13682)					
G-CBGS	Cyclone AX2000 HKS	7866	8. 3.02	K P Puckey	Enstone	3. 7.07P
G-CBGU	Thruster T 600N 450	0121-T600N-055	21.11.01	B R Cardosi	Wick	2.12.07P
G-CBGV	Thruster T 600N 450 Sprint	0121-T600N-056	21.11.01	J R Nutter	(Shanklin)	1. 4.08P
G-CBGW	Thruster T 600N 450 Sprint	0121-T600N-058	21.11.01	M C Arnold and A R Pluck	
					Damyn's Hall, Upminster	22. 5.09P
G-CBGX	Scottish Aviation Bulldog Series 120/121	XX622	26.11.01	Henfield Lodge Aviation Ltd (As "XX622:B" in RAF c/s)	
		BH120/287				Shoreham	15.12.11
G-CBGZ	Westland SA.341C Gazelle HT.2	1923	ZB646	30.10.01	D Weatherhead Ltd	Cambridge	19. 9.09P

G-CBHA	SOCATA TB-10 Tobago	1583	VH-YHA	6.11.01	Oscar Romeo Aviation Ltd	Redhill	8. 6.09E
G-CBHB	Raj Hamsa X'Air 582(5)	611		22.11.01	R A J Graham	Kirkbride	27. 2.09P
	(Built R A J Graham - pr.no.BMAA HB/189)						
G-CBHC	Rotary Air Force RAF 2000 GTX-SE			22.11.01	A J Thomas	(Sutton Coldfield)	30. 9.09P
	(Built A J Thomas)	PFA G/13-1326					
G-CBHD	Cameron Z-160 Balloon (Hot Air)	10225		1. 3.02	Ballooning 50 Degrees Nord SARL *"Nichobetzen Founzen"*		
						Fouhren, Luxembourg	2. 4.09E
G-CBHG	Mainair Blade 912S	1298-1001-7-W1093		12.12.01	B S Hope	(Marsh Gibbon, Bicester)	9. 7.08P
G-CBHI	Europa Aviation Europa XS	373		31.10.01	B Price tr Hotel India Group	(Southampton)	15. 6.09P
	(Built B Price - pr.no.PFA 247-13245) (Monowheel u/c)						
G-CBHJ	Mainair Blade 912	1305-1201-7-W1100		28. 1.02	B C Jones	(Altrincham)	29. 7.09P
G-CBHK	Cyclone Airsports Pegasus Quantum 15	7871		6.12.01	B Dossett	Plaistows Farm, St Albans	5. 4.08P
	(HKS 700E)						
G-CBHM	Mainair Blade 912	1301-1100-7-W1096		3.12.01	F J Thorne	Ince Blundell	24. 5.09P
G-CBHN	Cyclone Airsports Pegasus Quantum 15-912			6.12.01	G G Cook	Clench Common	28. 1.10P
		7872					
G-CBHO	Gloster Gladiator II	?	N5719 (?)	11.12.01	Retro Track and Air (UK) Ltd	(Dursley)	
G-CBHP	Corby CJ-1 Starlet	PFA 134-12498		12.12.01	R F Creswell	Turweston	28. 8.09P
	(Built J D Muldowney and D H Barker)						
G-CBHR	Laser Lazer Z200	Q056	VH-IAC	31.12.01	P F Brice	White Waltham	22. 6.09P
	(Built H Selvey)						
G-CBHT	Dassault Falcon 900EX	48	G-GPWH	3. 1.02	TAG Aviation (UK) Ltd	Farnborough	23.11.09E
			F-WWFP				
G-CBHU	TLAC RL5B XP Sherwood Ranger	xxxx		12.12.01	A J Glading tr G-CBHU Group	(Leafield, Witney)	2.10.07P
	(Built M J Gooch - pr.no. PFA 237-12477) (Jabiru 2200A)						
G-CBHW	Cameron Z-105 Balloon (Hot Air)	10217		16. 1.02	Bristol Chamber of Commerce, Industry and Shipping *"Bridg-it"*		
					(Crea8ive and Business West titles)	Bristol	3. 4.09E
G-CBHX	Cameron V-77 Balloon (Hot Air)	3950		19.12.01	N A Apsey *"Irene"*	Hazlemere, High Wycombe	27. 7.09E
G-CBHY	Cyclone Airsports Pegasus Quantum 15-912			7. 1.02	A Hope	Stoke, Isle of Grain	6. 3.08P
		7859					
G-CBHZ	Rotary Air Force RAF 2000 GTX-SE			2. 1.02	M P Donnelly	(Thurso)	
	(Built M P Donnelly)	PFA G/13-1321					
G-CBIB	Flight Design CT2K	01-08-06-23		21. 1.02	J A Moss	Grove Farm, Needham	12. 4.09P
	(Assembled Pegasus Aviation with c/n 7878)						
G-CBIC	Raj Hamsa X'Air V2(2)	608		2. 1.02	J T Blackburn and D R Sutton	Brook Farm, Pilling	17. 4.07P
	(Built J T Blackburn and D R Sutton - pr.no.BMAA HB/156)						
G-CBID	Scottish Aviation Bulldog Series 120/121	XX549		14.12.01	D A Steven tr Red Dog Group *(As "XX549:6" in RAF c/s)*		
		BH120/242				White Waltham	25. 1.10S
G-CBIE	Flight Design CT2K	01-09-01-23		10. 1.02	S R McKiernan	Ince Blundell	3. 5.09P
	(Assembled Pegasus Aviation with c/n 7879)						
G-CBIF	Avtech Jabiru SPL-450	xxxx		3. 1.02	S N J Huxtable	Weston Zoyland	12. 7.09P
	(Built J A Iszard - pr.no.PFA 274A-13789)						
G-CBIH	Cameron Z-31 Balloon (Hot Air)	10243		4. 1.02	Gone With The Wind Ltd	Bristol	13.10.09E
G-CBIJ	Comco Ikarus C42 FB UK	0102-6319		3. 1.02	J A Smith	Octon Lodge Farm, Thwing	16. 6.08P
	(Built A Jones - pr.no.PFA 322-13720) (Kit no. not confirmed)						
G-CBIK	RotorWay Executive 162F	6112		9. 1.02	J Hodson *(Noted 10.08)*	Street Farm, Takeley	
	(Built J Hodson) (RotorWay RI 162F)						
G-CBIL	Cessna 182K Skylane	18257804	(G-BFZZ)	9.10.78	E Bannister and J R C Spooner		
			D-ENGO, N2604Q			Nottingham-East Midlands	27. 6.09E
G-CBIM	Lindstrand LBL 90A Balloon (Hot Air)	817		28. 1.02	R K Parsons	Bishop's Caundle, Sherborne	6. 3.09E
G-CBIN	TEAM Mini-MAX 91	PFA 186-13111		7. 1.02	A R Mikolaczyk	Chuch Farm, Askern	26. 3.09P
	(Built D E Steade) (Rotax 503) (Enclosed cockpit)						
G-CBIO	Thruster T 600N 450 Jab	0022-T600N-062		7. 1.02	J Kenyon tr Sandown Microlights	Sandown	22. 7.09P
G-CBIP	Thruster T 600N 450	0022-T600N-060		7. 1.02	K D Mitchell tr G-CBIP Group		
						Kittyhawk Farm, Deanland	15. 6.09P
G-CBIR	Thruster T 600N 450	0022-T600N-061		7. 1.02	E G White	Landmead Farm, Garford	18.10.09P
G-CBIS	Raj Hamsa X'Air 582(2)	708		15. 1.02	P T W T Derges	Long Marston	17. 4.08P
	(Built P T W T Derges - pr.no.BMAA HB/199)						
G-CBIT	Rotary Air Force RAF 2000 GTX-SE			27.11.01	Terrafirma Services Ltd		
	(Built M P Lehermette)	PFA G/13-1340				Lamberhurst Farm, Faversham	
G-CBIU	Cameron Flame 95 SS Balloon (Hot Air)	10222		6. 2.02	PSH Skypower Ltd *(British Gas-Think Energy titles)*		
						Woodborough, Pewsey	17. 6.09E
G-CBIV	Best Off Sky Ranger 912(1)	SKRxxxxxxx		25. 1.02	K Brown	Bakersfield	4.10.08P
	(Built P M Dewhurst - pr.no.BMAA HB/201)						
G-CBIW	Lindstrand LBL 310A Balloon (Hot Air)	821		24. 1.02	C E Wood	Witham	9. 3.09E
G-CBIX	Zenair CH.601UL Zodiac	PFA 162A-13765		24.12.01	R A and B M Roberts	Griffins Farm, Temple Bruer	3. 9.09P
	(Built M F Cottam)						
G-CBIY	Evektor EV-97 Eurostar	PFA 315-13846		23. 1.02	R Soltysik	Otherton, Cannock	22. 3.09P
	(Built E M Middleton)						
G-CBIZ	Cyclone Airsports Pegasus Quantum 15-912			6.12.01	M P Duckett	Rufforth	25. 4.09P
		7870					
G-CBJD	Stoddard-Hamilton GlaStar	PFA 295-13853		23. 1.02	K F Farey	(Bourne End)	
	(Built K F Farey)						
G-CBJE	Rotary Air Force RAF 2000 GTX-SE			23. 1.02	V G Freke	Little Rissington	13. 5.09P
	(Built K F Farey)	PFA G/13-1342					
G-CBJG	de Havilland DHC-1 Chipmunk 22	63	CS-AZT	8. 2.02	C J Rees *(As "1373" in Portuguese AF c/s)*		
	(Built OGMA)		Portuguese AF FAP 1373			Dalkeith Farm, Winwick	29. 4.10S
G-CBJH	Aeroprakt A22 Foxbat	PFA 317-13847		30. 1.02	H Smith	Morgansfield, Fishburn	9.12.09P
	(Built H Smith)						
G-CBJJ	Scottish Aviation Bulldog Series 120/121	XX525		3.12.01	G V Crowe and D L Thompson *(As "XX525:8" in RAF c/s)*		
		BH120/211				Norwich	4. 4.09S
G-CBJL	Air Création 582(1)/Kiss 400	FL005		8. 2.02	R E Morris	(Kidwelly, Dyfed)	30. 7.04P
	(Built R E Morris - pr.no.BMAA HB/205 for Flylight kit comprising Trike s/n T01099 and s/n Wing A01158-1164)						

G-CBJM	Avtech Jabiru SP-470	xxxx		11.12.01	G R T Elliott	Newtownards	22. 5.09P
	(Built A T Moyce - pr.no.PFA 274B-13769)						
G-CBJN	Rotary Air Force RAF 2000 GTX-SE			30. 1.02	R Hall	(Truro)	
	(Built R Hall)	PFA G/13-1335					
G-CBJO	Cyclone Airsports Pegasus Quantum 15-912			10.12.01	P A Martland	Arclid Green, Sandbach	14.11.09P
		7861					
G-CBJP	Zenair CH.601UL Zodiac	PFA 162A-13590		31. 1.02	R E Peirse	Armshold Farm, Kingston, Cambridge	31. 8.08P
	(Built R E Peirse) (Tri-cycle u/c)						
G-CBJR	Evektor EV-97 Eurostar	PFA 315-13845		31. 1.02	R B Skinner	Belle Vue Farm, Yarnscombe	22. 3.09P
	(Buillt B J Crockett)						
G-CBJS	Cameron C-60 Balloon (Hot Air)	10253		17. 4.02	N Ivison	Barton Seagrave, Kettering	16. 2.09E
G-CBJT	Mainair Blade	1302-1101-7-W1097		12.12.01	D Maddison	Headon Farm, Retford	3.10.08P
G-CBJU	Van's RV-7A	PFA 323-13868		1. 2.02	T W Waltham	(Teffont Evias, Salisbury)	
	(Built T W Waltham)						
G-CBJV	RotorWay Executive 162F	6589		13. 2.02	R J Green	Street Farm, Takeley	6.11.09P
	(Built Southern Helicopters Ltd) (RotorWay RI 162F)						
G-CBJW	Comco Ikarus C42 FB UK	PFA 322-13811		13. 2.02	J A Robinson	Tarn Farm, Cockerham	14. 5.07P
	(Built T J Cale)						
G-CBJX	Raj Hamsa X'Air Falcon Jabiru(1)	622		13. 2.02	P M and M Stoney	Willingale	3.11.08P
	(Built M R Coreth - pr.no.BMAA HB/181)						
G-CBJY	Avtech Jabiru UL-450	401		14. 2.02	D L H Person	Great Ashfield, Suffolk	30. 9.09P
	(Built D L H Person - pr.no.PFA 274A-13613)						
G-CBJZ	Westland SA.341G Gazelle HT.3	1734	3D-HGW XZ932	13. 2.02	K G Theurer	Sion, Switzerland	10. 4.09P
G-CBKA	Westland SA.341G Gazelle HT.3	1746	XZ937	20. 2.02	J Windmill	(Ilkeston)	14.12.09P
G-CBKB	Bücker Bü.181C Bestmann	121	F-PCRL F-BCRU	28. 1.02	W R and G D Snadden	(Alexandria)	
G-CBKC	Westland SA.341D Gazelle HT.3	1104	XW862	20. 2.02	C R Onslow	(Heyton, Royston)	9. 4.09P
G-CBKD	Westland SA.341C Gazelle HT.2	1130	XW868	20. 2.02	Flying Scout Ltd	Welshpool	25. 4.09P
G-CBKE	Air Création 582(1)/Kiss 400	FL010		18. 2.02	P Blackbourn	Headon Farm, Retford	22. 6.09P
	(Built R J Howell - pr.no.BMAA HB/206 for Flylight kit comprising Trike s/n T02011 and s/n Wing A02014-2007)						
G-CBKF	Reality Easy Raider J2.2(2)	0003		24. 1.02	R R Armstrong	Headcorn	24. 4.09P
	(Built R J Creasey - pr.no.BMAA HB/202)						
G-CBKG	Thruster T 600N 450	0022-T600N-059		1. 3.02	A R Hughes tr Silver Shadow Group	Yatesbury	8. 4.09P
G-CBKI	Cameron Z-90 Balloon (Hot Air)	10236		22. 3.02	Wheatfields Park Ltd (Roundtrees Garden Centres titles)		
						Churchill, Winscombe	31. 5.09E
G-CBKJ	Cameron Z-90 Balloon (Hot Air)	10251		6. 3.02	Invista (UK) Holdings Ltd	Brockworth, Gloucester	26. 5.09E
G-CBKK	UltraMagic S-130 Balloon (Hot Air)	130/32		19. 3.02	Airborne Adventures Ltd (co.uk titles)		
						Rylestone, Skipton	26. 5.09E
G-CBKL	Raj Hamsa X'Air 582(12)	682		18. 2.02	S Smith tr Caithness X-Air Group	Wick	8. 3.09P
	(Built J Garcia - pr.no.BMAA HB/203)						
G-CBKM	Mainair Blade 912	1310-0102-7-W1105		21. 1.02	N Purdy	Headon Farm, Retford	25. 4.09P
G-CBKN	Mainair Blade 912	1316-0302-7-W1111		11. 3.02	D S Clews	Headon Farm, Retford	19. 4.09P
G-CBKO	Mainair Blade 912S	1311-0102-7-W1106		11. 2.02	P W Jordan	(Bradford)	26. 3.08P
G-CBKR	Piper PA-28-161 Warrior III	2842143	N5334N	15. 3.02	Devon and Somerset Flight Training Ltd		
						Dunkeswell	30. 3.09E
G-CBKS	Air Création 582(1)/Kiss 400	FL007		28. 1.02	S Kilpin	Manor Farm, Haddenham	6.10.08P
	(Built S Kilpin - pr.no.BMAA HB/197 for Flylight kit comprising.Trike s/n T01113 and Wing s/n A01193-1203)						
G-CBKU	Comco Ikarus C42 FB UK	0112-6431	(EI-)	4. 3.02	C Blackburn	Carnowen, County Donegal	4. 6.09P
	(Built R G Q Clarke and P Walton - pr.noPFA 322-13862)						
G-CBKV	Cameron Z-77 Balloon (Hot Air)	4946		15. 3.02	J F Till	Welburn, York	9. 5.09E
G-CBKW	Cyclone Airsports Pegasus Quantum 15-912			25. 3.02	W G Coulter	Strathaven	25. 6.09P
		7892					
G-CBKY	Avtech Jabiru SP-470	xxxx		6. 3.02	P R Sistern	City of Derry	22.10.09P
	(Built P R Sistern - pr.no.PFA 274B-13764)						
G-CBLA	Aero Designs Pulsar XP	367	N367JR	15. 2.02	J P Kynaston	Holmbeck Farm, Leighton Buzzard	20. 1.10P
	(Built J L Reeves)						
G-CBLB	Tecnam P92-EM Echo	PFA 318-13770		12. 3.02	F G Walker	(Lleweni Parc)	17. 8.09P
	(Built M A Lomas)						
G-CBLD	Mainair Blade 912S	1306-1201-7-W1101		21. 3.02	N E King	St Michaels	17. 4.09P
G-CBLE	Robin R2120U Alpha 120T	364		16. 4.02	Cardiff Academy of Aviation Ltd	Cardiff	29.12.09E
G-CBLF	Raj Hamsa X'Air 582(11)	696		18. 3.02	B J Harper and P J Soukup	Eaglescott	7. 6.09P
	(Built E G Bishop and E N Dunn - pr.no.BMAA HB/194)						
G-CBLH	Raj Hamsa X'Air 582(11)	673		18. 3.02	P Sykes	Mapperton Farm, Newton Peverill	6. 7.09P
	(Built S Rance - pr.no.BMAA HB/182)						
G-CBLJ	IAV-Bacau Yakovlev Yak-52	888615	RA-44472 LY-AHF, DOSAAF 57 (yellow)	19. 4.02	A R Richards (As "61" (black))	Shoreham	28.1.09P
G-CBLK	Hawker Hind	41H-82971	R Afghan AF L718120. 3.02 Aero Vintage Ltd (Noted unmarked 10.08) Duxford				
G-CBLL	Cyclone Airsports Pegasus Quantum 15-912			22. 3.02	P R Jones	Felthorpe	16. 6.08P
		7891					
G-CBLM	Mainair Blade 912	1308-0102-7-W1103		12. 2.02	A S Saunders	(Crewe)	26. 4.09P
G-CBLN	Cameron Z-31 Balloon (Hot Air)	10285		26. 4.02	P M Oggioni	Sant'Albano Stura, Italy	17. 8.09E
G-CBLO	Lindstrand LBL 42A Balloon (Hot Air)	854		3. 4.02	N K and R H Calvert	Bradley Stoke, Bristol	22. 6.09E
G-CBLP	Raj Hamsa X'Air 582(11)	646		26. 3.02	A C Parsons (Noted 8.07)	Dunkeswell	17. 5.06P
	(Built M J Kaye and S Litchfield - pr.no.BMAA HB/213)						
G-CBLS	Fiat CR.42 Falco	920	Swedish AF 2542	20. 7.05	Patina Ltd (Operated The Fighter Collection) (Stored 10.08)		
						Duxford	
G-CBLT	Mainair Blade 912	1315-0202-7-W1110		25. 4.02	B J Bader	Dunkeswell	25. 5.09P
G-CBLU	Cameron C-90 Balloon (Hot Air)	10128		30. 4.02	A G Martin "Harlequin"	Bristol	23. 8.09E
G-CBLV	Flight Design CT2K	02-01-04-04		11. 4.02	A K Pickering	(Villefollett, Deux-Sèvres, France)	31. 3.06P
	(Assembled Pegasus Aviation with c/n 7886)						
G-CBLW	Raj Hamsa X'Air Falcon V2(1)	641		13. 3.02	R G Halliwell	Ince Blundell	30.10.08P
	(Built R R Hadley - pr.no.BMAA HB/209)						

G-CBLX	Air Création 582(1)/Kiss 400	FL008		3. 4.02	B J Curtis	(Todmorden)	30.10.08P

(Built J H Hayday - pr.no.BMAA HB/208 being Flylight kit comprising Trike s/n T02010 and Wing s/n A02013-2003)

G-CBLY	Grob G109B	6403	D-KITZ (2)	12. 3.02	D A Smith tr G-CBLY Syndicate		
			(F-WAQS)			Wing Farm, Longbridge Deverill	23. 5.09E
G-CBLZ	Rutan LongEz	1046	F-PYYV	5. 6.02	S K Cockburn	Southend	22.11.08P

(Built N W Ruston) (Lycoming O-235)

G-CBMA	Raj Hamsa X'Air 582(10)	739		14. 2.02	A J Baker	Stoke, Isle of Grain	24.11.09P

(Built K Angel - pr.no.BMAA HB/204)

G-CBMB	Cyclone AX2000 HKS	7894		18. 6.02	York Microlight Centre Ltd	Rufforth	6. 8.09P
G-CBMC	Cameron Z-105 Balloon (Hot Air)	10274		30. 4.02	B R Whatley *(Edward Ware Homes titles)*	Bristol	1. 8.09E
G-CBMD	IAV-Bacau Yakovlev Yak-52	822710	RA-44460	4.11.02	R J Hunter	Headcorn	9. 1.09P
			LY-AHE, DOSAAF 100 (yellow)				
G-CBME	Reims Cessna F172M	F17201060	TF-FTV	28. 2.02	Skytrax Aviation Ltd	Derby	27. 4.08E
			TF-POP, SE-FZP				
G-CBMI	IAV-Bacau Yakovlev Yak-52	855907	LY-AOZ	24. 7.02	D P Holland *(Empire Test Pilots' School c/s)*	Tatenhill	16. 5.08P
			RA-02050, DOSAAF 107 (blue)				
G-CBMK	Cameron Z-120 Balloon (Hot Air)	10293		11. 4.02	G Davies	Thorney, Peterborough	12. 4.09E
G-CBML	de Havilland DHC-6-310 Twin Otter	695	C-FZSP	5. 6.02	Isles of Scilly Skybus Ltd	St Just	4. 6.09E
			HB-LSN, C-FZSP, TR-LZO, C-GJZK				
G-CBMM	Mainair Blade 912	1312-0202-7-W1107		9. 9.02	L E Donaldson *(Noted 2.08)* Headon Farm, Retford		14.10.07P
G-CBMO	Piper PA-28-180 Cherokee D	28-4806	ZS-ONK	16. 5.02	C Woodliffe	Bagby	14. 7.09E
			9J-RHN, N6391J				
G-CBMP	Cessna R182 Skylane RG II	R18201325	ZS-MWT	9. 4.02	Orman (Carrolls Farm) Ltd	Great Massingham	26. 9.09E
			N38MH, YV-2034P, N2286S				
G-CBMR	Medway EclipseR	172/150		27. 3.02	D S Blofeld	Stoke, Isle of Grain	30. 6.08P
G-CBMS	Medway EclipseR	173/151		27. 3.02	R R Bagge *(Noted 1.06)*	Field Farm, Oakley	31.10.05P
G-CBMT	Robin DR.400-180 Régent	2538		3. 5.02	A C Williamson	Crowfield	13. 7.09E
G-CBMU	Whittaker MW6-S Fatboy Flyer	PFA 164-13339		30. 4.02	F J Brown	Sackville Farm, Riseley	21.12.09P

(Built F J Brown)

G-CBMV	Cyclone Airsports Pegasus Quantum 15	7893		3. 5.02	M J D J Long	Stoke, Isle of Grain	13.10.09P
	(Rotax 582)						
G-CBMW	Zenair CH.701UL STOL	PFA 187-13788		9. 4.02	I Park	(Gretna)	5. 9.08P

(Built C Long) (Jabiru 2200A)

G-CBMX	Air Création 582(1)/Kiss 400	FL009		28. 3.02	D L Turner	(Sidcup)	7. 9.08P

(Built D L Turner - pr.no.BMAA HB/207 being Flylight kit comprising Trike s/n T02009 and Wing s/n A02012-2004)

G-CBMZ	Evektor EV-97 Eurostar	PFA 315-13890		12. 4.02	J C O'Donnell	Church Farm, Shotteswell	29. 7.09P

(Built P Grenet and J C O'Donnell)

G-CBNA	Flight Design CT2K	02-01-06-04		31. 5.02	D M Wood	Hook Norton	16. 6.09P

(Assembled Pegasus Aviation with c/n 7887)

G-CBNB	Eurocopter EC.120B Colibri	1040		8. 6.99	Arenberg Consultadoria e Servicos LDA		
						(Madeira, Portugal)	26. 6.09E
G-CBNC	Mainair Blade 912	1319-0402-7-W1114		17. 4.02	A C Rowlands	Dalscote, Northamptonshire	13. 6.09P
G-CBNF	Rans S-7 Courier	xxxx		12. 4.02	M Henderson	(Aberdeen)	

(Built T R Grief - pr.no.PFA 218-13762

G-CBNG	Robin R2112 Alpha	180	PH-ROL	20. 5.02	B Scott and D J Wilson tr Solway Flyers Group		
			F-GCAF			Carlisle	18. 8.09E
G-CBNI	Lindstrand LBL 90A Balloon (Hot Air)	857		16. 4.02	Cancer Research UK *(Cancer Research UK titles)*		
						Bath	27. 3.09E
G-CBNJ	Raj Hamsa X'Air 912(1)	680		23. 4.02	M G Lynes	(East Woodhay, Newbury)	24. 7.09P

(Built M K Slaughter, J L Francis and M Hunt - pr.no.BMAA HB/187)

G-CBNL	Dyn'Aéro MCR-01 Club	PFA 301A-13805		12. 4.02	D H Wilson	Coal Aston	20. 9.08P

(Built D H Wilson)

G-CBNO	CFM Streak Shadow	xxxx		8. 3.02	D J Goldsmith	(Crockham Hill, Edenbridge)	9.10.04P

(Built D J Goldsmith - pr.no.PFA 206-13809)

G-CBNT	Cyclone Airsports Pegasus Quantum 15-912	7860		14. 5.02	B H Goldsmith	Clench Common	13. 7.09P
G-CBNU	Vickers Supermarine 361 Spitfire LF.IX	Turkish AF	27. 8.02	M Aldridge	(Ashford)		
		CBAF IX 2115	ML411				
G-CBNV	Rans S-6-ES Coyote II	1000 1393 ES		23. 4.02	F H Cook	Chilbolton	5. 1.10P

(Built C W J Davis - pr.no.PFA 204-13817) (Rotax 582) (Tri-cycle u/c)

G-CBNW	Cameron N-105 Balloon (Hot Air)	10283		16. 5.02	C and J M Bailey t/a Bailey Balloons *(Bristol and West titles)*		
						Pill, Bristol	1. 7.09E
G-CBNX	Montgomerie-Bensen B 8MR PFA G/01A-1345		26. 4.02	A C S M Hart	Farley Farm, Romsey		25. 4.09P

(Built C Hewer) (Rotax 912-UL)

G-CBNY	Air Création 582(1)/Kiss 400	FL013		30. 4.02	R Redman	(Grantham)	10. 6.09P

(Built R Redman - pr.no.BMAA HB/218 being Flylight kit comprising Trike s/n T02035 and Wing A02051-2047)

G-CBNZ	TEAM Hi-MAX 1700R	PFA 272-13624		30. 4.02	A P S John	(Conderton, Tewkesbury)	15.11.08P

(Built J J Penny)

G-CBOA	Auster B 8 Agricola Series 1	AIRP/860	ZK-BXO	22. 4.02	C J Baker	Carr Farm, Thorney, Newark	
			ZK-BMN			*(Outer wings removed 1.05)*	

(Built Airepair, New Zealand 1966 from spares using parts of ZK-BMN c/n B 106)

G-CBOC	Raj Hamsa X'Air 582(5)	623		1. 5.02	A J McAleer	(Dungannon)	3. 4.06P

(Built A J McAleer - pr.no.BMAA HB/166) (Undercarriage struck trees Crocknagaran, Pomeroy 22. 6.05 and damaged)

G-CBOE	Hawker Hurricane IIB	R30040	RCAF 5487	24. 5.02	P J Tuplin (and P W Portelli) *(on rebuild)*	Thruxton	

(Built Canadian Car and Foundry Co)

G-CBOF	Europa Aviation Europa XS	431		1. 5.02	I W Ligertwood	Sleap	12. 2.08P

(Built I W Ligertwood - pr.no.PFA 247-13462)

G-CBOG	Mainair Blade 912S	1309-0102-7-W1104		26. 3.02	J S Littler	(Standish)	9. 5 07P
G-CBOK	Rans S-6-ES Coyote II	1201.1426		19. 4.02	I Johnson	Great Oakley	30.10.09P

(Built C J Arthur - pr.no.PFA 204-13864) (Rotax 912-UL)

G-CBOM	Mainair Blade 912	1314-0202-7-W1109		30. 4.02	G Suckling	Graveley Hall Farm, Graveley	22. 5.09P
G-CBON	Cameron Bull-110 SS Balloon (Hot Air)	10261		14. 6.02	Stratos Ballooning GmbH and Co KG		
						Ennigerloh, Germany	26. 5.05A

Reg	Type	C/n	Prev ID	Date	Owner	Location	Date
G-CBOO	Mainair Blade 912S	1317-0302-7-W1112		4. 4.02	N J Holt	Weston Zoyland	15. 8.09P
G-CBOP	Avtech Jabiru UL-450	0355		2. 5.02	D W Batchelor	Sandtoft	14. 2.09P
	(Built D W Batchelor - pr.no.PFA 274A-13611)						
G-CBOR	Reims Cessna F172N Skyhawk II	F17201656	PH-BOR PH-AXG (1)	28. 5.87	P Seville	Barton	24. 5.09E
G-CBOS	Rans S-6-ES Coyote II	1201.1428		8. 5.02	W Gillam	(Henstridge)	18. 6.07P
	(Built R Skene - pr.no.PFA 204-13859) (Jabiru 2200A) (Tri-cycle u/c)						
G-CBOT	Robinson R44 Raven	1194		11. 4.02	Helicopter One Ltd	Bournemouth	10. 5.09E
G-CBOU	Bensen-Parsons Two-Place Gyroplane			8. 5.02	R Collin and M S Sparkes	Kirkbride	6.11.08P
	(Built R Collin)	PFA G/8-1311					
G-CBOW	Cameron Z-120 Balloon (Hot Air)	10302		7. 8.02	Associated Technologies Ltd *(Torex titles)*	Hook Norton	27. 9.09E
G-CBOY	Cyclone Airsports Pegasus Quantum 15-912	7898		17. 4.02	I W Barlow Park Hall Farm, Mapperley, Ilkeston		16. 4.09P
G-CBOZ	IAV-Bacau Yakovlev Yak-52	811308	LY-AOC DOSAAF 30	15.11.02	T M Boxall	Headcorn	10.11.08P
G-CBPC	Sportavia-Pützer RF5B Sperber	51013	OY-XKC	27. 6.02	J Bennett tr Lee RF5B Group	Lee-on-Solent	22. 1.09E
G-CBPD	Comco Ikarus C42 FB UK	0112-6444		14. 5.02	A Haslam tr Waxwing Group	Kirkbride	10. 4.09P
	(Built M L Robinson - pr.no.PFA 322-13863)						
G-CBPE	SOCATA TB-10 Tobago	129	HB-EZR	13. 6.02	A F Welch	(Cambridge)	24. 6.09E
G-CBPG	The Balloon Works Firefly 7 Balloon (Hot Air)	FS7-001	N9045C	14. 6.02	I Chadwick tr Balloon Preservation Flying Group Partridge Green, Horsham		
G-CBPH	Lindstrand LBL 105A Balloon (Hot Air)	850		29. 5.02	Vastano Ivan	Firenze, Italy	18. 8.05A
G-CBPI	Piper PA-28R-201 Arrow	2844073	N53496	23. 5.02	Atsi Aviation Ltd	Denham	23. 7.09E
G-CBPL	TEAM Mini-MAX 93	PFA 186-13100		24. 5.02	K M Moores	(Boston)	
	(Built K M Moores)						
G-CBPM	Yakovlev Yak-50	812101	LY-ASG DOSAAF 58 ?	10. 7.02	P W Ansell (As *"50" (black)*)	North Weald	16. 7.09P
G-CBPN	Thruster T 600N 450	0052-T600N-065		23. 5.02	J S Webb	Old Sarum	17.10.09P
G-CBPP	Avtech Jabiru UL-450	0354		23. 4.02	D G Bennett	Headon Farm, Retford	1. 8.08P
	(Built J N Pearson - pr.no.PFA 274A-13607)						
G-CBPR	Avtech Jabiru UL-450	xxxx		16. 5.02	F B Hall	Bodmin	12. 4.06P
	(Built P L Riley and F B Hall - pr.no.PFA 274A-13492)						
G-CBPU	Raj Hamsa X'Air R100(3)	442		27. 5.02	A D Bales	Priory Farm, Tibenham	29.10.09P
	(Built M S McCrudden and W P Byrne - pr.no.BMAA HB/123)						
G-CBPV	Zenair CH.601UL Zodiac	PFA 162A-13689		28. 5.02	R D Barnard	Calton Moor Farm, Ashbourne	16. 9.09P
	(Built R D Barnard)						
G-CBPW	Lindstrand LBL 105A Balloon (Hot Air)	863		12. 6.02	Flying Pictures Ltd *(Samsung titles)*	Chilbolton	2. 7.04A
G-CBPZ	UltraMagic N-300 Balloon (Hot Air)	300/04		25. 6.02	Skyview Ballooning Ltd t/a Kent Ballooning Ashford		28. 5.08T
G-CBRB	UltraMagic S-105 Balloon (Hot Air)	105/103		19. 6.02	I S Bridge	Shrewsbury	8. 4.09E
G-CBRC	Jodel D 18	PFA 169-11408		31. 5.02	B W Shaw Wathstones Farm, Newby Wiske		
	(Built B W Shaw)				*(Noted 2.08)*		
G-CBRD	Jodel D 18	PFA 169-11484		31. 5.02	J D Haslam Wathstones Farm, Newby Wiske		29. 8.09P
	(Built J D Haslam)						
G-CBRE	Mainair Blade 912	1330-0602-7-W1125		19. 6.02	R G McCron	Broadmeadow Farm. Hereford	13. 6.08P
G-CBRF	Comco Ikarus C42 FB100 VLA	0202-6454		7. 6.02	T W Gale	Trim, County Meath	14.11.08P
	(Built T W Gale - pr.no.PFA 322-13900)						
G-CBRG	Cessna 560XL Citation Excel	560-5266	N5245D	13. 8.02	Queensway Aviation Ltd	Belfast International	14. 8.09E
G-CBRH	IAV-Bacau Yakovlev Yak-52	844815	LY-ALO DOSAAF 135	6. 9.02	B M Gwynnett	Haverfordwest	29. 2.08P
G-CBRJ	Mainair Blade 912	1321-0502-7-W1116		24. 4.02	R W Janion	Humberside	30. 5.08P
	(Rotax 582-2V)						
G-CBRK	UltraMagic M-77 Balloon (Hot Air)	77/212		8. 7.02	R T Revel *"UltraMagic"*	Great Missenden	22. 7.09E
G-CBRM	Mainair Blade	1326-0502-7-W1121		19. 6.02	M H Levy	(Northwich)	25.10.08P
G-CBRO	Robinson R44 Raven	1221		17. 6.02	R D Jordan	Cranfield	8. 7.09E
G-CBRP	IAV-Bacau Yakovlev Yak-52	822603	RA-02041 LY-AID, DOSAAF 105	22. 9.04	R J Pinnock	Gloucestershire	18. 1.07P
G-CBRR	Evektor EV-97 Eurostar	PFA 315-13919		18. 6.02	T O Powley	(Bungay)	25.10.09P
	(Built C M Theakstone)						
G-CBRT	Murphy Elite	PFA 232-13461		19. 6.02	R W Baylie	(Hailsham)	
	(Built R W Baylie) (Wilksch WAM-120)				*(Flying 11.07)*		
G-CBRU	IAV-Bacau Yakovlev Yak-52	888911	RA-02042 DOSAAF 98 (yellow)	21. 1.03	R Rawicz-Szczerbo (As *"42" (red)* in Soviet Air Force c/s) Bicester		18.12.09P
G-CBRV	Cameron C-90 Balloon (Hot Air)	10323		31. 7.02	C J Teall	Salford, Chipping Norton	3.12.09E
G-CBRW	Aerostar Yakovlev Yak-52	9111415	RA-44464 DOSAAF 50	4. 2.03	M A Gainza (As *"50"* in DOSAAF c/s) White Waltham		27. 5.09P
G-CBRX	Zenair CH.601UL Zodiac	PFA 162A-13833		21. 6.02	J B Marshall		
	(Built J B Marshall)					Eddsfield, Octon Lodge Farm, Thwing	9. 5.09P
G-CBRY	Cyclone Airsports Pegasus Quik	7902		24. 6.02	Cyclone Airsports t/a Pegasus Aviation (Elm Tree Farm, Manton)		
G-CBRZ	Air Création 582(1)/Kiss 400	FL015	(EI-) G-CBRZ	21. 6.02	J J Ryan Ardenagh Great, Taghmon, County Wexford		23. 7.09P
	(Built B Chantry - pr.no.BMAA HB/226 being Flylight kit comprising Trike s/n T02052 and s/n Wing A02086-2080)						
G-CBSD	Westland SA.341C Gazelle HT.2	1045	XW854	6. 6.02	Mexsky Ltd (As *"XW854"* in RN c/s)	Earls Colne	2. 3.09P
G-CBSF	Westland SA.341C Gazelle HT.2	1924	ZB647	6. 6.02	Falcon Aviation Ltd (As *"ZB647:40"*)		
						(Tileshurst, Reading)	
G-CBSH	Westland SA.341G Gazelle HT.3	1344	XX406	28.10.02	Alltask Ltd (As *"XX406:P"* in RAF c/s)	Rochester	17. 4.09P
G-CBSI	Westland SA.341G Gazelle HT.3	1736	XZ934	6. 6.02	P S Unwin (As *"XZ934:U"* in RAF c/s)		
						Bourne Park, Hurstbourne Tarrant	24. 7.09P
G-CBSK	Westland SA.341G Gazelle HT.3	1914	ZB627	6. 6.02	P J Whitaker and B W Stuart tr Falcon Flying Group (As *"ZB627:A"* in RAF c/s)		
						Bourne Park, Hurstbourne Tarrant	11.12.09P
G-CBSL	IAV-Bacau Yakovlev Yak-52	822013	RA-44534	13. 1.03	N and A D Barton	Leicester	20. 8.09P
G-CBSM	Mainair Blade 912	1331-0602-7-W1126		10. 5.02	Mainair Sports Ltd	Rochdale	

G-CBSO	Piper PA-28-181 Cherokee Archer II	28-7690376	D-EOFL N9595N	18. 7.02	Archer One Ltd	Lydd	12. 8.09E
G-CBSP	Cyclone Airsports Pegasus Quantum 15-912	7903		9. 7.02	D S Carstairs	Dundee	7. 7.08P
G-CBSR	IAV-Bacau Yakovlev Yak-52	877913	LY-AQB	10. 7.02	Grovinvest Srl	Jibou, Romania	20. 8.09P
	Ukraine AF 10 (yellow), DOSAAF 100 (yellow?)						
G-CBSS	IAV-Bacau Yakovlev Yak-52	833707	RA-44475	19. 2.03	E J F Verhellen	Namur-Temploux, Belgium	3. 4.09P
	LY-AIJ, DOSAAF 121?						
G-CBSU	Avtech Jabiru UL-450	xxxx		15. 7.02	P K Sutton *(Noted engineless 6.05)*	Coventry	23. 6.05P
	(Built P K Sutton - pr.no.PFA 274A-13812)						
G-CBSV	Montgomerie-Bensen B 8MR PFA G/01A-1344			1. 7.02	J A McGill	Damyn's Hall, Upminster	17. 2.09P
	(Built J A McGill) (Rotax912-UL)						
G-CBSX	Air Création Clipper/Kiss	FL014		3. 7.02	R A Atkinson	(Hull)	4. 4.09P
	(Built N Hartley - pr.no.BMAA HB/225 being Flylight kit comprisong Trike s/n T02051 and Wing s/n A02085-2079)						
G-CBSZ	Mainair Blade 912S	1334-0602-7-W1129		6. 8.02	W Gray	(Leven)	21. 4.09P
G-CBTB	III Sky Arrow 650 T	PFA 298-13832		25. 6.02	D A and J A S T Hood	Seething	12.11.08P
	(Built D A .and J A S T Hood)						
G-CBTD	Cyclone Airsports Pegasus Quantum 15-912	7904		9. 7.02	D Baillie	Glassonby	19. 7.09P
G-CBTE	Mainair Blade 912S	1328-0602-7-W1123		10. 7.02	K J Miles	St Michaels	10. 8.08P
G-CBTG	Comco Ikarus C42 FB UK	PFA 322-13849		25. 6.02	R McLaughlin	(Letterkenny, County Donegal)	11. 5.09P
	(Built J A Way and R Bonnett)						
G-CBTK	Raj Hamsa X'Air 582(5)	589		9. 7.02	A R Cook	Lower Upham Farm, Chiseldon	18.11.08P
	(Built C D Wood - pr.no.BMAA HB/168)						
G-CBTL	Monnett Moni	PFA 142-11558		8. 7.02	G Dawes *(Fuselage noted 3.08)*		
	(Built G Dawes)					Clipgate Farm, Denton	
G-CBTM	Mainair Blade	1322-0502-7-W1117		2. 7.02	D A A Hewitt	Headon Farm, Retford	14. 8.08P
	(Rotax 582)						
G-CBTN	Piper PA-31 Navajo C	31-7812073	OO-VLH N27636	7. 8.02	Durban Aviation Services Ltd	Biggin Hill	6. 3.09E
G-CBTO	Rans S-6-ES Coyote II	1201.1427		16. 7.02	C G Deeley	Sittles Farm, Alrewas	8.11.08P
	(Built B J Mould and M Walsh - pr.no.PFA 204-13910) (Rotax 912-UL) (Tri-cycle u/c)						
G-CBTR	Lindstrand LBL 120A Balloon (Hot Air)	733		22. 7.02	R H Etherington	Siena, Italy	13. 8.05A
G-CBTS	Gloster Gamecock replica	GA 97		17. 7.02	Retro Track and Air (UK) Ltd	(Dursley)	
	(Built Retro Track and Air (UK) Ltd)						
G-CBTT	Piper PA-28-181 Cherokee Archer II	28-7890127	G-BFMM N47735	22. 7.02	Citicourt Aviation Ltd	Denham	17.11.09E
G-CBTW	Mainair Blade 912	1329-0602-7-W1124		20. 6.02	D Hyatt	Stoke, Isle of Grain	1. 8.09P
G-CBTX	Denney Kitfox Model 2	PFA 172-11721		19. 7.02	G I Doake	(Craigavon, County Armagh)	
	(Built W M Farrell and G I Doake)						
G-CBTZ	Cyclone Airsports Pegasus Quantum 15-912	7909		29. 7.02	A J Craven	(Stapenhill, Burton-on-Trent)	15.10.08P
G-CBUA	Extra EA.230	009	N230KR N286PA	5. 9.02	J Murfitt and S P R Madle	White Waltham	31. 3.09P
					(Damaged 17.10.08 at White Waltham)		
G-CBUC	Raj Hamsa X'Air 582(5)	779		22. 7.02	M N Watson	Sackville Lodge, Riseley	7. 4.08P
	(Built A P Fenn and D R Lewis - pr.no.BMAA HB/228)						
G-CBUD	Cyclone Airsports Pegasus Quantum 15-912	7906		30. 7.02	G N S Farrant	Chase Farm, Little Burstead	21. 6.09P
G-CBUE	UltraMagic N-250 Balloon (Hot Air)	250/25		5.12.02	Elinore French Ltd t/a Imagination Balloon Flights		
						Longframlington	25. 3.09E
G-CBUF	Flight Design CT2K	02-04-04-18		26. 7.02	J T James	Sutton Meadows	13.11.06P
	(Assembled Pegasus Aviation with c/n 7901)				*(Engine failure at High Wych 10.6.06 with major damage)*		
G-CBUG	Tecnam P92-EM Echo	PFA 318-13662		20. 6.01	J J Bodnarec	Hawksbridge Farm, Oxenhope	15. 5.08P
	(Built R C Mincik) (Rotax 912-ULS) (Marked as "P92S")						
	(Directional control lost landing Oxenhope 1. 9.07, struck earth bank and substantially damaged)						
G-CBUH	Westland Scout AH.1	F9475	XP849	5. 8.02	C J Marsden *(Wears old Raspberry Ripple scheme)*		
						(Thruxton)	5. 9.09P
G-CDUI	Westland Wasp HAS.1	F9590	XT420	5. 8.02	The Helicopter Squadron Ltd *(As "XT420:606" in RN c/s)*		
						Bembridge	2. 3.09P
G-CBUJ	Raj Hamsa X'Air 582(10)	651		1. 8.02	J T Laity tr G-CBUJ Flying Group	Kemble	11. 2.09P
	(Built J T Laity - pr.no.BMAA HB/212)						
G-CBUK	Van's RV-6A	PFA 181A-13614		25. 7.02	P G Greenslade	Wellcross Farm, Slinfold	9.12.09P
	(Built P G Greenslade)						
G-CBUN	Barker Charade	PFA 166-13520		31. 7.02	T Coldwell and D R Wilkinson		
	(Built P E Barker) (Jabiru 2200A)					Sackville Lodge, Riseley	7. 9.09P
G-CBUO	Cameron O-90 Balloon (Hot Air)	3353	CC-PMH	15. 8.02	W J Treacy and P M Smith	Trim, County Meath	12. 8.09E
G-CBUP	Magni M-16 Tandem Trainer	SA-M16-10M	ZU-AIH	28. 8.02	J S Firth	Burn	12. 6.08P
	(Built R W Husband - pr.no.PFA G/12-1346)						
G-CBUR	Zenair CH.601UL Zodiac	PFA 162A-13891		19. 7.02	N A Jack *(Noted 6.08)*	Insch	18. 9.03P
	(Built R J Kelly)						
G-CBUS	Cyclone Airsports Pegasus Quantum 15	7916		29. 8.02	J Liddiard	Yatesbury	9.12.09P
	(Rotax 582)						
G-CBUU	Cyclone Airsports Pegasus Quantum 15-912	7917		27. 8.02	J R Elcocks	(Stourbridge)	27. 8.07P
G-CBUW	Cameron Z-133 Balloon (Hot Air)	10322		29. 8.02	Balloon School (International) Ltd *"British School of Ballooning" titles*	Colhook Common, Petworth	3. 8.09E
G-CBUX	Cyclone AX2000	7918		2.10.02	R Thompson	(Sawbridgeworth)	27. 8.08P
	(Rotax 582)						
G-CBUY	Rans S-6-ES Coyote II	0302.1436		13. 8.02	K R Crawley	Rufforth	3. 3.09P
	(Built S C Jackson - pr.no.PFA 204-13954) (Rotax 582) (Tri-cycle u/c)						
G-CBUZ	Cyclone Airsports Pegasus Quantum 15	7907		31. 7.02	D G Seymour	Craysmarsh Farm, Melksham	22. 8.08P
	(Rotax 503)						
G-CBVA	Thruster T 600N 450	0082-T600N-068		14. 8.02	D J Clingan *(Noted 2.08)*	Derryogue	6.12.05P
G-CBVB	Robin R2120U	365		26. 7.02	Cardiff Academy of Aviation Ltd	Cardiff	12. 6.09E

Reg	Type	C/n	Prev id	Date	Owner/Operator	Location	Status
G-CBVC	Raj Hamsa X'Air 582(5)	792		15. 8.02	K J Underwood	(Amberley, Arundel)	15.12.07P
	(Built M J Male - pr.no.BMAA HB/230)						
G-CBVD	Cameron C-60 Balloon (Hot Air)	10338		31.10.02	Phoenix Balloons Ltd "Popeye"	Bristol	22. 4.09E
G-CBVE	Raj Hamsa X'Air Falcon 912(1)	766		19. 8.02	T A England	Dowsby, Bourne	15. 3.09P
	(Built D F Hughes - pr.no.BMAA HB/229)						
G-CBVF	Murphy Maverick	PFA 259-12876		19. 8.02	H A Leek	(Scalford, Melton Mowbray)	
	(Built J Hopkinson)						
G-CBVG	Mainair Blade 912S	1338-0802-7-W1133		27. 8.02	A M Buchanan	Kirkbride	1. 3.09P
G-CBVH	Lindstrand LBL 120A Balloon (Hot Air)	870		2. 9.02	Line Packaging and Display Ltd	Gillingham, Kent	1. 7.09E
G-CBVI	Robinson R44 Raven	1259		21. 8.02	G Erskine	Newtownards	15. 9.09E
G-CBVK	Schroeder Fire Balloons G Balloon (Hot Air)	408	D-OVHS	30. 9.02	S Travaglia t/a Idea Balloon	Fiorentino, Italy	
G-CBVL	Robinson R22 Beta II	3353	N71650	23. 8.02	Helicopter Training and Hire Ltd	Newtownards	26. 9.09E
G-CBVM	Evektor EV-97 Eurostar	PFA 315-13932		8. 8.02	R J Butler	Guy Lane Farm, Waverton	17.11.09P
	(Built J Cunliffe and A Costello)						
G-CBVN	Mainair Sports Pegasus Quik	7919		27. 8.02	C Kearney	Ince Blundell	20.12.09P
G-CBVO	Raj Hamsa X'Air 582(5)	627		27. 8.02	C J Burley	Sackville Lodge, Riseley	5. 6.08P
	(Built W E Richards - pr.no.BMAA HB/227)						
G-CBVR	Best Off Sky Ranger 912(2)	SKRxxxx209		6. 9.02	S H Lunney	Ince Blundell	18. 5.09P
	(Built R H J Jenkins - pr.no.BMAA HB/231)						
G-CBVS	Best Off Sky Ranger 912(2)	SKR0207215		19. 8.02	S C Cornock	Shenstone Hall Farm, Shenstone	17. 7.09P
	(Built S C Cornock - pr.no.BMAA HB/234)						
G-CBVT	IAV-Bacau Yakovlev Yak-52	9010305	LY-AGR	19. 9.02	Lancair Espana SL	(Alicante, Spain)	14. 2.08P
			Ukraine AF 02 (yellow), DOSAAF 02 (yellow)				
G-CBVU	Piper PA-28R-200 Cherokee Arrow	28R-7135007	ZS-RER N11C	12. 9.02	E W Guess (Holdings) Ltd	Spanhoe	20. 1.09E
G-CBVV	Cameron N-120 Balloon (Hot Air)	10331		13. 9.02	John Aimo Balloons SAS (Warsteiner titles)	Mondovi, Italy	9. 6.09E
G-CBVX	Cessna 182P Skylane	18263419	ZS-IYZ N9653G	16.12.02	P and A de Weerdt	Old Sarum	26. 6.09E
G-CBVY	Comco Ikarus C42 FB UK	0112-6436		4. 9.02	M J Hendra and R Gossage	Brook Farm, Pilling	29. 4.09P
	(Built M J Hendra and R Gossage - pr.no.PFA 322-13835)						
G-CBVZ	Flight Design CT2K	02-05-06-04		19. 9.02	A N D Arthur	Denham	29. 7.08P
	(Assembled Pegasus Aviation Ltd with c/n "9714" - this should be "7914")						
G-CBWA	Flight Design CT2K	02-06-01-04		11.10.02	C A Hasell and D J Collier tr G-CBWA Group		22. 2.09P
	(Assembled Pegasus AviationLtd with c/n "7921")					Lower Mountpleasant Farm, Chatteris	
G-CBWB	Piper PA-34-200T Seneca II	34-7770188	N2495Q	31.10.02	Fairoaks Airport Ltd	Fairoaks	7. 2 09E
G-CBWD	Piper PA-28-161 Warrior III	2842160	N5357G	1.10.02	Fleetwash Ltd	Blackbushe	16.10.09E
G-CBWE	Evektor EV-97 Eurostar	PFA 315-13958		16. 9.02	J and C W Hood	Longframlington	7. 1.10P
	(Built E Clarke)						
G-CBWG	Evektor EV-97A Eurostar	03-1162		17. 9.02	A B Cameron and B Waterson tr Southside Flyers		14.11.09P
	(Built M Rhodes - pr.no.PFA 315-13918)					Prestwick	
G-CBWI	Thruster T 600N 450	0102-T600N-071		20. 9.02	P L Jarvis	Stoke, Isle of Grain	17.10.08P
G-CBWJ	Thruster T 600N 450 Sprint	0092-T600N-069		20. 9.02	D Cioffi tr Voliamo Group	Broad Farm, Eastbourne	26.11.09P
G-CBWK	UltraMagic H-77 Balloon (Hot Air)	77/218		4.11.02	H C Peel	Worcester	17.12.09E
G-CBWM	Mainair Blade 912	1339-0802-7-W1134		22. 8.02	G Homan	Appleton, Warrington	12. 7.09P
	(Rotax 503) (Built with major components of G-BZUM)						
G-CBWN	Campbell Cricket Mk.6	PFA G/16-1328		24. 9.02	P G Rawson	Crosland Moor	9. 6.09P
	(Built G J Layzell) (Marked as "Layzell AV-18A")						
G-CBWO	RotorWay Executive 162F	6597		24. 9.02	Handyvalue Ltd	Street Farm, Takeley	14. 2.09P
	(Built S P Tetley) (RotorWay RI 162F)						
G-CBWP	Europa Aviation Europa	233		1.10.02	T W Greaves ("Flying Yorkshireman" on fin)		2. 9.09P
	(Built T W Greaves - pr.no.PFA 247-12930) (Monowheel u/c)					(Gardon Field, Hull)	
G-CBWS	Whittaker MW6 Merlin	PFA 164-12863		7.10.02	D W McCormack	(Atherstone)	
	(Built D W McCormack)						
G-CBWU	RotorWay Executive 162F	6416		4.10.02	F A Cavaciuti t/a Usk Valley Trout Farm		17.12.08P
	(Built F A Cavaciuti) (RotorWay RI 162F)					Street Farm, Takeley	
G-CBWV	Falconar F-12A Cruiser	PFA 22-13904		7.10.02	A Ackland	(Reading)	
	(Built A Ackland)						
G-CBWW	Best Off Sky Ranger 912(2)	SKRxxxx210		30. 8.02	N S Wells	Dumbarton	9.11.08P
	(Built R L and S H Tosswill - pr.no.BMAA HB/232)						
G-CBWY	Raj Hamsa X'Air 582(6)	775		17.10.02	J C Rose	Eastbach Farm, Coleford	9. 4.08P
	(Built T Collins - pr.no.BMAA HB/244)						
G-CBWZ	Robinson R22 Beta II	3101	N141DC	23.10.02	Plane Talking Ltd	Blackbushe	27.11.09E
G-CBXA	Raj Hamsa X'Air 582(5)	790		18.10.02	A J Sharratt	Sackville Lodge, Riseley	4. 3.09P
	(Built N Stevenson-Guy - pr.no.BMAA HB/245)						
G-CBXC	Comco Ikarus C42 FB UK	PFA 322-13955		23.10.02	B J Mould	Wolverhampton	7. 4.09P
	(Built A R Lloyd)						
G-CBXD	Bell 206L-3 LongRanger III	51328	D-HAUA N21AH, N21830	22.10.02	GBN Charters Ltd	Stapleford	7. 4.09E
G-CBXE	Reality Easy Raider J2.2(2)	0006		22. 8.02	A Appleby	Westfield Farm, Hailsham	
	(Built A Appleby - pr.no.BMAA HB/198)				(Stored after damage in transit to the strip)		
G-CBXF	Reality Easy Raider J2.2(2)	0001		19.11.02	F Colman	Eshott	18. 1.10P
	(Built F Colman - pr.no.BMAA HB/196)						
G-CBXG	Thruster T 600N 450 Sprint	0112-T600N-073		29.10.02	J R Hughes tr Newtownards Microlight Group		6. 8.08P
						Newtownards	
G-CBXJ	Cessna 172S Skyhawk SP	172S8125	N2391J	30.10.02	Steptoe and Sons Properties Ltd	Caernarfon	11. 2.10E
G-CBXK	Robinson R22 Mariner	2302M	N3052P LQ-BLD, N80524	4.11.02	Helicentre Liverpool Ltd	Liverpool-John Lennon	17. 4.09E
G-CBXM	Mainair Blade	1335-0802-7-W1130		19. 8.02	B A Coombe	(Billingshurst)	21. 9.09P
G-CBXN	Robinson R22 Beta II	3385		11.11.02	N M Pearson	Bristol	11.12.09E
G-CBXR	Raj Hamsa X'Air Falcon 582(1)	612		11.11.02	A R Rhodes	Kirkbride	2.10.08P
	(Built J F Heath - pr.no..BMAA HB/224)						

G-CBXS	Best Off Sky Ranger J2.2(1)	SKRxxxx246		13.11.02	C J Erith (Noted 5.07 less wings)	
	(Built C J Erith - pr.no.BMAA HB/248)					Lower Wasing Farm, Brimpton
G-CBXU	TEAM Mini-MAX 91A	PFA 186-13037		13.11.02	C D Hatcher	Bakersfield 27. 8.09P
	(Built T J Shaw)					
G-CBXV	Mainair Blade	1343-1002-7-W1138		4.10.02	S E Harper	Priory Farm, Tibenham 8. 2.09P
G-CBXW	Europa Aviation Europa XS	494		18.11.02	R G Fairall	Redhill
	(Built R G Fairall - pr.no.PFA 247-13674) (Monowheel u/c)					
G-CBXZ	Rans S-6-ESN Coyote II	0302.1438		20.11.02	D Tole (Noted 4.06)	Long Marston 12. 4.05P
	(Built D Tole - pr.no.PFA 204-13988) (Rotax 582)					
G-CBYB	RotorWay Executive 162F	6623		20.11.02	T Clark t/a Clark Contracting	(Amersham)
	(Built T Clark) (RotorWay RI 162F)					
G-CBYC	Cameron Z-275 Balloon (Hot Air)	10342		20. 3.03	P Baker (Park Furnishers titles)	
						Trim, County Meath 9. 8.09E
G-CBYD	Rans S-6-ESA Coyote II	1201.1429		21.11.02	R Burland	Strathaven 17. 3.09P
	(Built R Burland - pr.no.PFA 204-13871) (Rotax 912)					
G-CBYE	Cyclone Airsports Pegasus Quik	7933		27. 1.03	C E Morris	Enstone 23. 2.09P
G-CBYF	Mainair Blade	1349-1202-7-W1144		2. 1.03	J Ayre	Cottage Farm, Norton Juxta, Twycross 7. 6.08P
G-CBYH	Aeroprakt A22 Foxbat	PFA 317-13902		2.12.02	G C Moore tr G-CBYH Foxbat Group	
	(Built G C Moore, G R Reynolds, M W Shepherd and P C de-Ville)					Otherton, Cannock 1. 5.09P
G-CBYI	Cyclone Airsports Pegasus Quantum 15	7931		2. 1.03	J M Hardy	Deenethorpe 9. 2.09P
	(Rotax 503)					
G-CBYJ	Steen Skybolt	PFA 064-13354		2.12.02	F G Morris	Newtownards 26. 7.09P
	(Built F G Morris)					
G-CBYM	Mainair Blade	1323-0502-7-W1118		13. 9.02	P E Hudson	(Birchwood, Warrington) 27. 4.07P
	(Rotax 582)					
G-CBYN	Europa Aviation Europa XS	518		5.12.02	G M Tagg	Compton Abbas 10. 9.09P
	(Built A B Milne - pr.no.PFA 247-13751) (Tri-gear u/c)					
G-CBYO	Cyclone Airsports Pegasus Quik	7928		5.12.02	P F Mayo and C J Roper	East Fortune 2.12.07P
G-CBYP	Whittaker MW6-S LW Fatboy Flyer					
	(Built R J Grainger)	PFA 164-13131		6.12.02	R J Grainger	(Sywell) 10. 8.09P
G-CBYS	Lindstrand LBL 21A Balloon (Hot Air)	156		17.12.02	B M Reed	Paizay Le Sec, France 17. 2.10E
G-CBYT	Thruster T 600N 450	0102-T600N-072		10.10.02	B E Smith	Eshott 8.11.09P
G-CBYU	Piper PA-28-161 Warrior III	2842173	N53606	12. 2.03	Stapleford Flying Club Ltd	Stapleford 19. 2.09E
G-CBYV	Cyclone Airsports Pegasus Quantum 15-912			19. 9.02	A R Vincent	Chiltern Park, Wallingford 3.11.09P
		7920				
G-CBYW	Hatz CB-1	PFA 143-13710		16. 1.03	T A Hinton	Doynton 26. 8.09P
	(Built T A Hinton)					
G-CBYX	Bell 206B-3 JetRanger III	480	HB-ZBX	5. 3.03	Sky Charter UK Ltd	Biggin Hill 28. 7.09E
			N203WB, C-GRGP, N2502M			
G-CBYY	Robinson R44 Raven	1250	N71837	11. 9.02	Helicopter Training and Hire Ltd	Newtownards 18.11.08E
G-CBYZ	Tecnam P92-EA Echo-Super					
	(Built M Rudd)	PFA 318A-13984		17.12.02	B Weaver	(Osmington, Weymouth) 12. 8.08P
G-CBZA	Mainair Blade	1344-1002-7-W1139		28.10.02	D Wilkinson	(Northwich) 14. 4.09P
G-CBZB	Mainair Blade	1346-1102-7-W1141		6.12.02	A Bennion	Arclid Green, Sandbach 7. 2.08P
G-CBZD	Mainair Blade	1348-1102-7-W1143		12.12.02	G F Jones	Mill Farm, Shifnal 24. 7.09P
G-CBZE	Robinson R44 Clipper	1276		12.12.02	Alps (Scotland) Ltd	(Kilwinning) 14. 2.09E
G-CBZF	Robinson R22 Beta II	3393	N71878	6.12.02	J Drake	Rush Green 4. 5.09E
G-CBZG	Rans S-6-ES Coyote II	1201.1430		9. 1.03	S Bayes	Bagby 21. 5.09P
	(Built N McKenzie - pr.no.PFA 204-13894) (Jabiru 2200) (Tri-cycle u/c)					
G-CBZH	Cyclone Airsports Pegasus Quik	7934		30. 1.03	M Bond	Marshfield 3. 9.08P
G-CBZI	RotorWay Executive 162F	6718		3. 1.03	T D Stock	Street Farm, Takeley
	(Built T Stock) (RotorWay RI 162F)				(Noted 10.08)	
G-CBZJ	Lindstrand LBL 25A Cloudhopper Balloon (Hot Air)			9. 1.03	J L and T J Hilditch t/a Pegasus Ballooning	
		892			(Lindstrand Balloons titles)	Southwick, Brighton 18. 5.09E
G-CBZK	Robin DR.400-180 Régent	2543		12. 2.03	R A Fleming	Breighton 17. 4.09E
G-CBZL	Westland SA.341D Gazelle HT.3	WA2010	ZB629	17. 1.03	Armstrong Aviation Ltd (As "ZB629" in RAF c/s)
	(Struck power cables landing Mouswald near Dumfries 22.11.03 and substantially damaged)					Kirkbride 25. 8.04P
G-CBZM	Avtech Jabiru SPL-450	xxxx		2. 1.03	M E Ledward	Old Sarum 27.11.08P
	(Built M E Ledward - pr.no.PFA 274A-13827)					
G-CBZN	Rans S-6-ES Coyote II	0600.1374		6. 1.03	A James	Otherton, Cannock 12. 6.07P
	(Built A James - pr.no.PFA 204-13652) (Rotax 582) (Tri-cycle u/c)					
G-CBZP	Hawker Fury 1	41H-67550	SAAF??	2. 4.03	Historic Aircraft Collection Ltd (On rebuild 2008)	
						(Duxford)
G-CBZR	Piper PA-28R-201 Arrow	2837029	EC-IJX	13. 1.03	Plane Talking Ltd (Operated Cabair) Bournemouth 9. 3.09E
			N175ND			
G-CBZS	Lynden Aurora	PFA 313-13534		13. 1.03	J Lynden	Brook Farm, Pilling 10. 4.09P
	(Built J Lynden)					
G-CBZT	Cyclone Airsports Pegasus Quik	7936		6. 1.03	A P Portsmouth	(Gateshead) 17. 3.09P
G-CBZU	Lindstrand LBL 180A Balloon (Hot Air)	877		13. 1.03	European Balloon Co Ltd	Great Missenden 17. 4.09E
G-CBZV	UltraMagic S-130 Balloon (Hot Air)	130/36		5. 3.03	P Goldschmidt	San Casciano, Italy 17. 8.09E
G-CBZW	Zenair CH.701UL STOL	PFA 187-13731		13. 1.03	T M Stiles	(Heathfield) 20.11.09P
	(Built T M Stiles)					
G-CBZX	Dyn'Aéro MCR-01 ULC	221		15. 1.03	A C N Freeman and M P Wilson	Bournemouth 28. 4.09P
	(Built S L Morris - pr.no.PFA 301B-13957)					
G-CBZY	Flylight Doodle Bug-Target	DB022		22.11.02	A I Calderhead-Lea	(Basildon)
G-CBZZ	Cameron Z-275 Balloon (Hot Air)	10346		12. 2.03	A C K Rawson and J J Rudoni t/a Wickers World	
					Hot Air Balloon Company	Stafford 19. 3.09E

G-CCAA - G-CCZZ

G-CCAB	Mainair Blade	1345-1002-7-W1140		28. 1.03	A J Morris	Sutton Meadows 3. 3.09P
G-CCAC	Evektor EV-97A Eurostar	PFA 315-13979		26.11.02	J S Holden "Slightly Dangerous"	
	(Built P J Ladd and J S Holden)					Wadswick Manor Farm, Corsham 14. 3.09P
G-CCAD	Cyclone Airsports Pegasus Quik	7924		3.12.02	J C Price	New Duston, Northants 22. 4.09P

Reg	Type	C/n	Prev id	Date	Owner	Location	Review
G-CCAE	Avtech Jabiru UL-450	xxxx		17. 1.03	M P and R A Wells	Croft Farm, Defford	23. 7.08P
	(Built C E Daniels - pr.no.PFA 274A-13938)						
G-CCAF	Best Off Sky Ranger 912(1)	SKRxxxx212		28.11.02	D W and M.L Squire	(Hewas Water, St Austell)	
	(Built D W Squire - pr.no.BMAA HB/235)						
G-CCAG	Mainair Blade 912	1350-1202-7-W1145		22.11.02	W Cope	(Warslow, Buxton)	26. 1.07P
G-CCAH	Magni M-16C Tandem Trainer	16-06-3494		19. 6.06	Magni Gyro Ltd	(Waddington, Clitheroe)	
	(Rotax 914)					(Noted NEC Birmingham 11.07)	
G-CCAK	Zenair CH.601HD Zodiac	PFA 162-13469		11.12.02	A Kinmond	Perth	
	(Built A Kinmond)						
G-CCAL	Tecnam P92-EM Echo	PFA 318-13842		6.12.02	S Clegg	Maypole Farm, Chislet	6. 1.10P
	(Built D Cassidy)						
G-CCAM	Mainair Blade	1347-1102-7-W1142		6.12.02	M D Peacock	Cottage Farm, Norton Juxta	1. 8.09P
G-CCAN	Cessna 182P Skylane	18264069	SE-LON	16. 1.03	D J Hunter	Priory Farm, Tibenham	12. 5.09E
			OH-COZ, C-GWXC, (N6052F)				
G-CCAP	Robinson R22 Beta II	3413		11. 2.03	S G Simpson t/a HJS Helicopters		
						Lower Baads Farm, Peterculter	22. 3.09E
G-CCAR	Cameron N-77 Balloon (Hot Air)	464		5.12.78	D P Turner	Leigh-on-Mendip	2. 6.05A
	(Rebuilt with envelope c/n 670 8.80: with c/n 2108 in 1989 and with c/n 2658 in 1992) (Mitsubishi Cars titles)						
G-CCAS	Cyclone Airsports Pegasus Quik	7935		11. 2.03	J L Pollard tr Caunton Alpha		
						Knapthorpe Lodge, Caunton	3. 4.09P
G-CCAT	Gulfstream AA-5A Cheetah	AA5A-0893	G-OAJH	16. 1.92	A Ohringer	Blackbushe	31.10.09E
			G-KILT, G-BJFA, N27169				
G-CCAU	Eurocopter EC.135 T1	0040	G-79-01	30. 6.98	West Mercia Constabulary (Operated Central Counties Police)		
						Wolverhampton	21. 7.10S
G-CCAV	Piper PA-28-181 Archer II	28-8090353	D-EXRT	31. 3.03	S Turner tr Alpha Victor Group	Southend	12. 5.09E
			N8233A				
G-CCAW	Mainair Blade 912	1351-0103-7-W1146		5. 2.03	S D Morris	(Llay, Wrexham)	21. 5.08P
G-CCAY	Cameron Z-42 Balloon (Hot Air)	10373		27. 2.03	P Stern	Deggendorf, Germany	23. 1.09E
G-CCAZ	Cyclone Airsports Pegasus Quik	7927		3.12.02	J P Floyd	Sywell	26. 4.09P
G-CCBA	Best Off Sky Ranger R100(1)	SKR0211277		23. 1.03	R M Bremner tr Fourstrokes Group		
	(Built R M Bremner - pr.no.BMAA HB/256)					New Barn Farm, Barton Ashes, Crawley	23.10.08P
G-CCBB	Cameron N-90 Balloon (Hot Air)	10085	G-TEEZ (2)	11. 2.03	L E and S C A Craze "Fresh Air"	Berkhamsted	6. 9.09E
	(Note: G-TEEZ (1) stolen and cut up)						
G-CCBC	Thruster T 600N 450	0013-T600N-077		23. 1.03	E J Girling and J A E Bowen	Davidstow Moor	25. 4.09P
G-CCBF	Maule M-5-235C Lunar Rocket	7276C	G-NHVH	29.11.02	R Windley	Northfield Farm, Mavis Enderby	27. 3.05
			N5634N		(Damaged Leicester 15. 5.03: noted 7.06)		
G-CCBG	Best Off Sky Ranger 912(2)	SKR0207214		28. 1.03	P R Mailer	Longacre Farm, Sandy	23.12.09P
	(Built G R Wallis - pr.no.BMAA HB/240)						
G-CCBH	Piper PA-28-235 Cherokee Pathfinder		PH-ABL	29. 1.03	J R Hunt and S M Packer	Thruxton	23. 9.09E
		28-10648	F-BNFY, N9054W				
G-CCBJ	Best Off Sky Ranger 912(2)	SKRxxxx285		4. 2.03	A T Hayward	Mill Farm, Hughley, Much Wenlock	4. 8.09P
	(Built A T Hayward - pr.no.BMAA HB/262)						
G-CCBK	Evektor EV-97 Eurostar	03-1198(?)		5. 2.03	B S Waycott	Eastbach Farm, Coleford	3. 4.09P
	(Built J A and G R Pritchard - pr.no.PFA 315-14025)						
G-CCBL	Agusta-Bell 206B-2 JetRanger II	8732	OO-VCI	5. 3.03	Wilson Aviation Ltd	Southend	17. 6.09E
			PH-VCP, OO-VCI, (OO-XCI)				
G-CCBM	Evektor EV-97 Eurostar	PFA 315-14023		5. 2.03	W Graves	Sackville Lodge, Riseley	8. 5.09P
	(Built W Graves)						
G-CCBN	Replica Plans SE.5a	077246	PH-WWI	2. 4.03	V C Lockwood (As "80105:19" in US Air Service c/s)		
	(Built B Barra)		N8010S			(Boscombe Down)	14.11.08P
G-CCBP	Lindstrand LBL 60X Balloon (Hot Air)	908		12. 2.03	D Strasmann	Mulheim ad Ruhr, Germany	22. 6.09E
G-CCBR	Wassmer Jodel D 120 Paris-Nice	59	OO-JAL	18. 2.03	A Dunne and M Munnelly	Kilrush, County Kildare	29. 5.09P
			(OO-CMF), F-BHYP				
G-CCBT	Cameron Z-90 Balloon (Hot Air)	10340		24. 3.03	I J Sharpe	Caterham	1. 7.09E
G-CCBU	Hamsa X'Air 582(9)	756		19. 2.03	J S Rakkar	Stoke, Isle of Grain	22. 6.07P
	(Built M L Newton, completed J S Rakkar - pr.no.BMAA HB/237)						
G-CCBV	Cameron Z-225 Balloon (Hot Air)	10365		10. 4.03	Compagnie Aéronautique du Grand-Duché de Luxembourg		
						Junglister, Luxembourg	2. 4.09E
G-CCBW	TLAC RL5A LW Sherwood Ranger	xxxx		18. 2.03	P H Wiltshire		
	(Built P H Wiltshire - pr.no.PFA 237-13002) (Rotax 582)					New Barn Farm, Barton Ashes, Crawley	21.11.08P
G-CCBX	Raj Hamsa X'Air 133(2)	745		28. 5.03	A D'Amico	Longacre Farm, Sandy	10. 4.08P
	(Built A D'Amico - pr.no.BMAA HB/286)						
G-CCBY	Avtech Jabiru UL-450	xxxx		. 2.03	M Goodman	Baxby Manor, Husthwaite	3. 7.07P
	(Built D M Goodman - PFA 274A-13528)					(Noted 9.07)		
G-CCBZ	Aero Designs Pulsar	1936	N4075X	17. 2.03	J M Keane	(Brighton)	18. 1.06P
	(Built R N Wasserman) (Tri-cycle u/c)				(Force-landed in field near Deanland 2.7.05 and substantially damaged)		
G-CCCA	Vickers Supermarine 509 Spitfire Tr.IX		G-TRIX	18. 2.03	Historic Flying Ltd (As "H-98" in R Netherlands AF c/s)		
		CBAF.9590	(G-BHGH), IAC 161, G-15-174, PV202			Duxford	17. 3.09P
G-CCCB	Thruster T 600N 450 Sprint	0033-T600N-078		24. 2.03	J Williams (Noted 10.07)	Leicester	2. 9.06P
G-CCCD	Cyclone Airsports Pegasus Quantum 15	7929		12. 6.03	R N Gamble	Plaistows Farm, St Albans	17. 6.08P
	(Rotax 582)						
G-CCCE	Aeroprakt A22 Foxbat	PFA 317-14002		16. 1.03	C V Ellingworth	Henstridge	10. 3.09P
	(Built C V Ellingworth)						
G-CCCF	Thruster T 600N 450 Sprint	0033-T600N-081		24. 2.03	G A Fowler (Noted 10.07)	Leicester	24. 3.07P
G-CCCG	Mainair Sports Pegasus Quik	7946		16. 4.03	S I Lawrence	Hunsdon	21. 4.09P
G-CCCI	Medway EclipseR	174/152		11. 2.03	V Grayson	Stoke, Isle of Grain	25. 3.09P
G-CCCJ	Nicollier HN.700 Ménestrel II	PFA 217-13707		26. 2.03	G A Rodmell	Linley Hall, Leven	30. 3.09P
	(Built R Y Kendall)						
G-CCCK	Best Off Sky Ranger 912(2)	SKRxxxx289		26. 2.03	P L Braniff	Newtownards	1. 8.08P
	(Built J S Liming - pr.no.BMAA HB/265)						
G-CCCM	Best Off Sky Ranger 912(2)	SKRxxxx292		3. 3.03	I A Forrest and C K Richardson	(East Fortune)	23. 9.08P
	(Built J R Moore - pr.no.BMAA HB/263)						
G-CCCN	Robin R3000/160	167	OE-KOM	5. 3.03	R W Denny	Crowfield	8. 6.09E

G-CCCO	Evektor EV-97 Eurostar	03-1181		11. 3.03	D R G Whitelaw	North Connel, Oban	11. 5.09P
	(Built Connel Flying Club Eurostar Group - pr.no.PFA 315-14006)						
G-CCCP	IAV-Bacau Yakovlev Yak-52	899404	LY-AKV	30.11.93	A H Soper	Jenkin's Farm, Navestock	12.10.09P
			DOSAAF16 (yellow)				
G-CCCR	Best Off Sky Ranger 912(2)	SKRxxxx---		19. 3.03	A L S Routledge	Baxby Manor, Husthwaite	6. 5.09P
	(Built T C Viner, pr. no BMAA HB/163)						
G-CCCT	Comco Ikarus C42 FB UK	0211-6504		19. 3.03	J Kilpatrick	(Convoy, Lifford, County Donegal)	25. 9.09P
	(Built G A Pentelow - pr.no.PFA 322-13975)						
G-CCCU	Thruster T 600N 450	0034-T600N-084		29. 4.03	A F Cashin	Stoke, Isle of Grain	13. 5.08P
	(Official c/n incorrect - date of manufacture [April 2003] indicates correct version should be 0043-T 600N-084)						
G-CCCV	Raj Hamsa X'Air Falcon 133(1)	614		20. 3.03	G J Boyer	Weston Zoyland	15. 9.05P
	(Built G A J Salter - pr.no.BMAA HB/252)				*(New owner 1.08)*		
G-CCCW	Pereira Osprey 2	PFA 070-13408		10. 4.03	D J Southward	Kirkbride	29. 5.09P
	(Built D J Southward)						
G-CCCY	Best Off Sky Ranger 912(2)	SKR0211278		25. 3.03	A Watson	Redlands, Swindon	16. 9.08P
	(Built D M Cottingham - pr.no.BMAA HB/260)						
G-CCDB	Mainair Sports Pegasus Quik	7948		8. 4.03	C J van Dyke	Maypole Farm, Chislet	10. 4.09P
G-CCDC	Rans S-6-ES Coyote II	0302.1439		28. 1.03	A S Luketa	Stoke, Isle of Grain	11. 6.07P
	(Built G N Smith - pr.no.PFA 204-13992) (Rotax 582) (Tri-cycle u/c)						
G-CCDD	Mainair Sports Pegasus Quik	7951		31. 3.03	M P Hadden and M H Rollins	Long Marston	4. 6.09P
G-CCDE	Robinson R22 Beta II	3400	N71906	2. 4.03	J K Mavis, A J, C and C A Houldcroft		
					t/a J K and M Houldcroft and Sons	Hawarden	15. 5.09E
G-CCDF	Mainair Sports Pegasus Quik	7949		23. 4.03	R P McGann	Headon Farm, Retford	24. 4.09P
G-CCDG	Best Off Sky Ranger 912(1)	SKR0302294		1. 4.03	T H Filmer	Newtownards	26. 9.08P
	(Built W P Byrne - pr.no.BMAA HB/271)						
G-CCDH	Best Off Sky Ranger 912(2)	SKRxxxx211		5. 2.03	P K Goff	(Letchworth)	8.12.09P
	(Built D M Hepworth - pr.no.BMAA HB/233)						
G-CCDJ	Raj Hamsa X'Air Falcon 582(2)	692		18. 2.03	J M Spitz	Longacre Farm, Sandy	24. 4.09P
	(Built J M Spitz - pr.no.BMAA HB/214)						
G-CCDK	Cyclone Airsports Pegasus Quantum 15	7947		19. 3.03	S Brock	Bourn	15. 6.08P
G-CCDL	Raj Hamsa X'Air Falcon 582(2)	819		1. 4.03	G M Brown	Craysmarsh Farm, Melksham	3. 8.08P
	(Built H Burroughs - pr.no.BMAA HB/274)						
G-CCDM	Mainair Blade	1352-0203-7-W1147		21. 3.03	P R G Morley	Newnham, Baldock	5. 5.08P
G-CCDO	Mainair Sports Pegasus Quik	7944		19. 3.03	M S Brewster	(Connah's Quay)	26. 4.09P
G-CCDP	Raj Hamsa X'Air 582(14)	847		10. 4.03	F J McGuigan	Stoke, Isle of Grain	16. 3.09P
	(Built J A McKie - pr.no.BMAA HB/276)						
G-CCDR	Raj Hamsa X'Air Falcon Jabiru(3)	787		16. 4.03	P D Sibbons	Duxford	22. 6.08P
	(Built P D Sibbons - pr.no.BMAA HB/253)						
G-CCDS	Nicollier HN.700 Ménestrel II	PFA 217-13915		13. 3.03	B W Gowland	(Rhoshirwaun, Pwllheli)	
	(Built B W Gowland)						
G-CCDU	Tecnam P92-EM Echo	PFA 318-13721		23. 4.03	B N Thresher	Dunkeswell	30. 9.09P
	(Built M J Barrett)						
G-CCDV	Thruster T 600N 450 Sprint	0034-T600N-082		24. 4.03	D J Whysall	(Ripley)	6. 6.09P
	(Official c/n incorrect - manufactured April 2003 and should be 0043-T600N-082)						
G-CCDW	Best Off Sky Ranger 582(1)	SKR0302309		27. 3.03	P Reed tr Debts R Us Family Group	Graveley	1.12.09P
	(Built P Reed - pr.no.BMAA HB/268)						
G-CCDX	Evektor EV-97 Eurostar	PFA 315-14013		18. 2.03	J M Swash	Sittles Farm, Alrewas	22. 1.10P
	(Built H F Breakwell and R A Morris)						
G-CCDY	Best Off Sky Ranger 912(2)	SKRxxxx310		10. 4.03	N H Copperthwaite	(Baildon, Shipley)	30.11.07P
	(Built A V Dunne and G S Gee-Carter - pr.no.BMAA HB/275)						
G-CCDZ	Mainair Sports Pegasus Quantum 15	7952		24. 4.03	K D Baldwin	Graveley Hall Farm, Graveley	27. 4.09P
G-CCEA	Mainair Sports Pegasus Quik	7950		8. 4.03	G D Ritchie	East Fortune	25. 4.09P
G-CCEB	Thruster T 600N 450 Sprint	0035-T600N-085		24. 4.03	V Goddard	Craysmarsh Farm, Melksham	15. 6.08P
	(Official c/n incorrect - manufactured May 2003 and should be 0053-T600N-085)						
G-CCED	Zenair CH.601UL Zodiac	PFA 162A-13946		4. 4.03	R P Reynolds	Hall Farm, Shenstone	9.12.09P
	(Built R P Reynolds)						
G-CCEE	Piper PA-15 Vagabond	15-248	G-VAGA	31. 3.03	I M Callier	Berry Grove Farm, Liss	11. 1.08P
	(Continental C-90)		N4458H, NC4458H				
G-CCEF	Europa Aviation Europa	302		24. 4.03	C P Garner	Eaglescott	10. 9.09P
	(Built C P Garner - pr.no.PFA 247-13038) (Monowheel u/c)						
G-CCEG	Rans S-6-ES Coyote II	1000.1391		24. 4.03	W F Whitfield	Eshott	13. 5.09P
	(Built E O Bartle - pr.no.PFA 204-13831) (Rotax 582) (Tri-cycle u/c)						
G-CCEH	Best Off Sky Ranger 912(2)	SKRxxxx291		28. 4.03	A Eastham tr ZC Owners	Brook Farm, Pilling	4.11.09P
	(Built A Eastham - pr.no.BMAA HB/267)						
G-CCEI	Evans VP-2	PFA 063-11377		16. 4.03	P L Duguay	(Portsmouth)	
	(Built I P Manley and J Pearce) (Volkswagen 1834)						
	(Incorporates wings and engine from G-BJZB [PFA 063-10633] which was scrapped 2002: new fuselage noted 4.03)						
G-CCEJ	Evektor EV-97 Eurostar	PFA 315-14011		1. 5.03	K R Haskell and N A Quintin	Henstridge	6. 5.09P
	(Built C R Ashley)						
G-CCEK	Air Création 582(1)/Kiss 400	BMAA HB/272		2. 5.03	G S Sage	RAF Scampton	17.12.07P
	(Built G S Sage)						
G-CCEL	Avtech Jabiru UL-450	PFA 247A-13976		12. 2.03	S K Armstrong	(Dundrum, Newcastle)	2. 5.09P
	(Built R Pyper)						
G-CCEM	Evektor EV-97A Eurostar	03-1148		19. 2.03	L Wademan tr Oxenhope Flying Group		
	(Built E Atherden - pr.no.PFA 315-13987)					Hawksbridge Farm, Oxenhope	10. 8.08P
G-CCEN	Cameron Z-120 Balloon (Hot Air)	10399		9. 5.03	R Hunt *"J C Balls"*	Ripley	21. 9.09E
G-CCEO	Thunder Ax10-180 Series 2 Balloon (Hot Air)		OE-RZH	10. 6.03	P Heitzeneder	Desselbrunn, Austria	30. 7.09E
		4634			t/a 1 Oberösterreichischer and t/a Ballonfahrerverein		
G-CCEP	Raj Hamsa X'Air Falcon Jabiru(4)	716		6. 5.03	K Angel	Stoke, Isle of Grain	14. 9.06P
	(Built A McIvor - pr.no.BMAA HB/264)						
G-CCES	Raj Hamsa X'Air 2706(2)	401		8. 5.03	G V McCloskey	Blackhill, Draperstown	
	(Built G V McCloskey - pr.no.BMAA HB/104)				*(Noted 2007)*		
G-CCET	Nova Vertex 28	14296		25. 3.03	M Hay	Dundee	

Registration	Type	c/n	Prev id	Date	Owner/Operator	Location	Expiry
G-CCEU	Rotary Air Force RAF 2000 GTX-SE	001	N97ZP	24. 6.03	N G Dovaston	Morgansfield, Fishburn	30. 9.08P
	(Built J L Rollins)						
G-CCEW	Mainair Sports Pegasus Quik	7966		17. 6.03	N F Mackenzie	Strathaven	10. 7.08P
G-CCEY	Raj Hamsa X'Air 582(11)	833		12. 5.03	P J F Spedding	(Ashford)	8. 5.09P
	(Built P J F Spedding - pr.no.BMAA HB/258)						
G-CCEZ	Reality Easy Raider J2.2(2)	0010		7. 5.03	P J Clegg	Tarn Farm, Cockerham	31. 1.09P
	(Built S A Chambers - pr.no.BMAA HB/220)				(CAA quote M Peters as builder)		
G-CCFA	Air Création 582(1)/Kiss 400	xxxxx		16. 5.03	N Hewitt	Sywell	12. 3.08P
	(Built N Hewitt - pr.no.BMAA HB/282)						
G-CCFB	Mainair Sports Pegasus Quik	7955		16. 6.03	P Bailey	Longside, Peterhead	5. 3.09P
G-CCFC	Robinson R44 Raven II	10151		16. 9.03	The Winning Zone Ltd	White Waltham	11.11.09E
G-CCFD	Quad City Challenger II	CH-0597-UK-1617		20. 5.03	W Oswald (On build 4.07)	Longside, Peterhead	
	(Built W Oswald - pr.no.PFA 177-13180)						
G-CCFE	Tipsy Nipper T 66 Series 2	T66/37	OO-PLG	12. 6.03	D R Smith tr G-CCFE Group	RNAS Yeovilton	12. 3.09P
	(Built Avions Fairey SA)						
G-CCFG	Dyn'Aéro MCR-01 Club	PFA 301A-14047		8. 4.03	A Jones	Headon Farm, Retford	5.10.09P
	(Built M P Sargent)						
G-CCFI	Piper PA-32-260 Cherokee Six	32-7400002	OO-PCT N56630	30. 6.03	McManus Truck and Trailer Spares Ltd	Trim, County Meath	22. 8.09E
G-CCFJ	Kolb Twinstar Mk.III Xtra	PFA 205-14014		29. 5.03	D Travers	(Ealand, Scunthorpe)	30. 7.08P
	(Built M H Moulai)						
G-CCFK	Europa Aviation Europa	502		29. 5.03	C R Knapton	Eddsfield	21. 1.10P
	(Built C R Knapton - pr.no.PFA 247-13744)						
G-CCFL	Mainair Sports Pegasus Quik	7960		16. 6.03	J C Higham	Otherton, Cannock	15. 6.08P
G-CCFN	Cameron N-105 Balloon (Hot Air)	10442		5. 8.03	ABC Flights Ltd "Clairol"	Clapton in Gordano, Bristol	25. 6.09E
G-CCFO	Pitts S-1S	001	C-FYXO	28. 5.03	R J Anderson	Priory Farm, Tibenham	8.11.08P
	(Built R B Innes)						
G-CCFR	Diamond DA.40D Star	D4.032		3. 9.03	B Wronski	Oxford	8.10.09E
G-CCFS	Diamond DA.40D Star	D4.034		3. 9.03	R H Butterfield (Operated Sheffield City Flying School)	Sandtoft	29. 1.09E
G-CCFT	Mainair Sports Pegasus Quantum 15-912	7961		17. 6.03	D J Gardner	Dunkeswell	8. 8.08P
G-CCFU	Diamond DA.40D Star	D4.035		3. 9.03	Egnatia Aviation Ltd	Kavala International, Greece	6. 3.09E
G-CCFV	Lindstrand LBL 77A Balloon (Hot Air)	934		23. 6.03	Alton Aviation Ltd	Oswestry	23. 8.09E
G-CCFW	WAR Focke-Wulf FW190 replica	PFA 081-12729		27. 5.03	D B Conway (As "- + 9" in Luftwaffe c/s)	Little Rissington	1. 6.09P
	(Built D B Conway)						
G-CCFX	EAA Acrosport II	PFA 072-11221		23. 6.03	C D Ward	(Leyburn)	
	(Built C D Ward)						
G-CCFY	RotorWay Executive 162F	6719		27. 6.03	Southern Helicopters Ltd	Street Farm, Takeley	
	(Built M Hawley)				(Noted 10.08)		
G-CCFZ	Comco Ikarus C42 FB UK	PFA 322-14040		2. 5.03	B W Drake	Over Farm, Gloucester	28. 4.09P
	(Built B W Drake)						
G-CCGB	TEAM Mini-MAX 91	PFA 186-13767		4. 6.03	A D Pentland	Baxby Manor, Husthwaite	22. 9.09P
	(Built A D Pentland)						
G-CCGC	Mainair Sports Pegasus Quik	7958		27. 5.03	R W Street	(Edinburgh)	1. 6.09P
G-CCGE	Robinson R22 Beta II	3453		25. 6.03	Heli Aitch Be Ltd	Redhill	9. 7.09E
G-CCGF	Robinson R22 Beta II	3454		25. 6.03	PLM Dollar Group Ltd t/a PDG Helicopters	Kintore Heliport	13. 7.08E
	(Tail rotor struck ground during hover taxi Skinstown, County Kilkenny 10. 4.07 incurring substantial damage: noted 12.08)						
G-CCGG	Avtech Jabiru J400	0xxx		16. 6.03	G E Hall	Dunkeswell	28. 4.09P
	(Built K D Pearce - pr.no.PFA 325-14055)						
G-CCGH	Super Marine Spitfire Mk.26	021		17. 6.03	K D Pearce (As "AB196" in RAF c/s)	Shoreham	16. 4.08P
	(Built K D Pearce - pr.no.PFA 324-14054) (Jabiru 5100)						
G-CCGI	Mainair Sports Pegasus Quik	7967		7. 7.03	M C Kerr	Clench Common	7. 9.08P
G-CCGK	Mainair Blade	1355-0603-7-W1150		18. 7.03	C M Babiy and M Hurn	Graveley Hall Farm, Graveley	19. 7.08P
G-CCGL	SOCATA TB-20 Trinidad	2187	F-OIMN	28. 5.03	Pembroke Motor Services Ltd	Cardiff	24. 6.09E
G-CCGM	Air Création 582(2)/Kiss 450	xxxxx		23. 5.03	A I Lea	Benson's Farm, Laindon	23. 6.08P
	(Built G P Masters - pr.no.BMAA HB/277 being Flylight kit comprising Trike s/n T03026 and Wing s/n A2049-2044)						
G-CCGO	Medway AV8R	176/154		11. 4.03	C J Draper tr Medway Microlights	Stoke, Isle of Grain	
	(Rotax 582 - no. 5589987)						
G-CCGP	Holman Bristol Type 2000	PFA 270-12858		1. 7.03	R G Holman (On build 1.04)	Kemble	
	(Built R G Holman)						
G-CCGR	Raj Hamsa X'Air 133(1)	865		12. 6.03	C M Wilkes	New Barn Farm, Barton Ashes, Crawley	24. 6.09p
	(Built J M Weston - pr.no.BMAA HB/284)						
G-CCGS	Dornier 328-100	3101	D-CPRX D-CDXR	18. 3.04	Suckling Airways (Cambridge) Ltd t/a Scot Airways	London City	17. 3.09E
G-CCGT	Cameron Z-425 Balloon (Hot Air)	10398		16. 6.03	A A Brown	Guildford	17. 6.09E
G-CCGU	Van's RV-9A	PFA 320-13798		10. 7.03	B J Main, C W Hague and A Strachan	Henstridge	20. 5.09P
	(Built B J Main)						
G-CCGW	Europa Aviation Europa	026		8. 7.03	G C Smith	Bourn	17. 6.05P
	(Built G C Smith - pr.no.PFA 247-12548)						
G-CCGY	Cameron Z-105 Balloon (Hot Air)	10422		8. 7.03	Cameron Balloons Ltd (Cameron Balloons titles)	Bristol	9. 8.09E
G-CCGZ	Cameron Z-250 Balloon (Hot Air)	10438		4. 9.03	Ballooning Adventures Ltd	Hexham	19. 8.09E
G-CCHA	Diamond DA.40D Star	D4.046		14. 7.03	Diamond Hire UK Ltd	Gamston	5.11.09E
G-CCHC	Diamond DA.40D Star	D4.050		26. 8.03	Diamond Aircraft UK Ltd	Gamston	24. 9.08E
G-CCHD	Diamond DA.40D Star	D4.051		3. 9.03	Diamond Aircraft UK Ltd	Southend	8.10.09E
G-CCHF	Diamond DA.40D Star	D4.055		3. 9.03	Diamond Aircraft UK Ltd	Gamston	24. 9.08E
G-CCHG	Diamond DA.40D Star	D4.058		3. 9.03	Diamond Aircraft UK Ltd	Shoreham	9.10.08E
G-CCHH	Mainair Sports Pegasus Quik	7963		24. 6.03	C A Green	(Shalford, Guildford)	27. 8.08P
G-CCHI	Mainair Sports Pegasus Quik	7971		29. 7.03	M R Starling	(Swafield, North Walsham)	16. 9.08P
G-CCHJ	Air Création 582(1)/Kiss 400	FL016		28. 4.03	H C Jones	(Wolvey)	15. 6.09P
	(Built H C Jones - pr.no.BMAA HB/257 being Flylight kit comprising, Trike s/n T02117 and Wing s/n A02184-02179)						

G-CCHK	Diamond DA.40D Star	D4.059		3. 9.03	Diamond Aircraft UK Ltd	Gamston 24. 9.08E
G-CCHL	Piper PA-28-181 Archer III	2843176	OY-JAA N9501N	4. 8.03	Archer Three Ltd	Lydd 23. 8.09E
G-CCHM	Air Création 582(1)/Kiss 450	FL022		15. 7.03	M J Jessup	(Edenbridge) 10. 6.09P
	(Built W G Colyer - pr.no.BMAA HB/292 being Flylight kit comprising Trike s/n T03057 and Wing s/n A03099-3016)					
G-CCHN	Corby CJ-1 Starlet	PFA 134-12848		15. 7.03	D C Mayle	(Woodcote, Reading)
	(Built D C Mayle)					
G-CCHO	Mainair Sports Pegasus Quik	7968		9. 7.03	M Allan	Latch Farm 16. 7.09P
G-CCHP	Cameron Z-31 Balloon (Hot Air)	10443		20. 8.03	M H Redman	Stalbridge, Sturminster Newton 9. 9.08P
G-CCHR	Reality Easy Raider 503(1)	0008		24. 6.03	R B M Etherington	Halwell
	(Built R B Hawkins - pr.no.BMAA HB/223)					
G-CCHS	Raj Hamsa X'Air 582(10)	840		4. 7.03	M Howes tr HS Flying Group	
	(Built I Lonsdale - pr.no.BMAA HB/291)					Tarn Farm, Cockerham 16. 8.09P
G-CCHT	Cessna 152	15285176	9H-ACW N6159Q	17. 7.03	J S Devlin and Z Islam	Blackbushe 11. 2.09E
G-CCHV	Mainair Rapier	1353-0403-7-W1148		15. 9.03	K M Hughes	(Spilsby) 10. 2.07P
G-CCHW	Cameron Z-77 Balloon (Hot Air)	10426		26. 6.03	A Murphy	Dunshaughlin, County West Meath 19. 8.09E
G-CCHX	Scheibe SF25C Falke	44694	D-KBCI	25. 9.03	Lasham Gliding Society Ltd	Lasham 6.11.09E
	(Rotax 912S)					
G-CCHY	Bücker Bü.131 Jungmann	21	I-CABI	12.11.03	M V Rijkse *(As "A-12" in Swiss AF c/s)*	
	(Built Dornier-Werke AG)		HB-UTZ, Swiss AF A-12			Wycombe Air Park 16. 7.08P
G-CCID	Avtech Jabiru J400	0xxx		25. 7.03	J Bailey	Crowfield 4. 3.09P
	(Built J Bailey - pr.no.PFA 325-14059)					
G-CCIE	Colt 315A Balloon (Hot Air)	10176		25. 7.03	T M Donnelly	Sprotbrough, Doncaster 14. 7.09E
G-CCIF	Mainair Blade	1356-0703-7-W1151		28. 7.03	S P Moores	(Biddulph, Stoke-on-Trent) 11. 2.09P
G-CCIG	Aero Designs Pulsar	PFA 202-12133		15. 7.03	P Maguire	(Accrington)
	(Built P Maguire)					
G-CCIH	Mainair Sports Pegasus Quantum 15	7973		31. 7.03	T Smith	Challock 12. 8.08P
	(Rotax 582)					
G-CCII	ICP MXP-740 Savannah Jabiru(4)			6. 6.03	J R Livett and D Chaloner	Enstone 15.10.08P
		01-04-51-063				
	(Built M J Kaye - pr.no.BMAA HB/285)					
G-CCIJ	Piper PA-28R-180 Cherokee Arrow		SE-FDZ	14. 7.03	S A Hughes	Andrewsfield 14. 9.09E
		28R-30873				
G-CCIK	Best Off Sky Ranger 912(2)	SKR0212279		30. 7.03	M D Kirby	Chase Farm, Little Bursted 24. 2.09P
	(Built L E Cowling and A P Chapman - pr.no.BMAA HB/278)					
G-CCIO	Best Off Sky Ranger 912(2)	SKR0212284		4. 8.03	B Berry	Crosland Moor 2. 4.07P
	(Built B Berry - pr.no.BMAA HB/261)					
G-CCIR	Van's RV-8	PFA 303-13732		7. 8.03	G Johnson	North Weald 16. 3.09P
	(Built D Marsh)					
G-CCIS	Scheibe SF28A Tandem Falke	5791	OE-9154 (D-KDFZ)	15.10.03	P T Ross	St Merryn 15.12.09E
G-CCIT	Zenair CH.701UL STOL	PFA 187-13911		30. 6.03	I M Sinclair	Glenrothes 16.10.09P
	(Built I M Sinclair) (Jabiru 2200A)					
G-CCIU	Cameron N-105 Balloon (Hot Air)	10485		18. 8.03	W W Leitlein	Wolpertshangen, Germany 11.12.09E
G-CCIV	Mainair Sports Pegasus Quik	7977		13. 8.03	F Omaraie-Hamdanie	Hunsdon 2. 9.08P
G-CCIW	Raj Hamsa X'Air 582(5)	838		11. 8.03	N Watts	Otherton, Cannock 14. 5.06P
	(Built G Wilkinson - pr.no.BMAA HB/281)					
G-CCIY	Best Off Sky Ranger 912(2)	SKR0210244		14. 8.03	L F Tanner	Sywell 14. 4.09P
	(Built L F Tanner -pr.no.BMAA HB/250)					
G-CCIZ	PZL-110 Koliber 160A	04010087	SP-WGN (2)	21. 8.03	Horizon Aviation Ltd	Swansea 3. 2.09E
G-CCJA	Best Off Sky Ranger 912(2)	SKR0307364		6. 8.03	C Day	(Salisbury) 22. 5.09P
	(Built T R Southall - pr.no.BMAA HB/299)					
G-CCJB	Zenair CH.701 STOL	7-3659		24. 6.03	E G Brown	(Luton)
	(Built E G Brown - pr.no.PFA 187-13270)					
G-CCJC	British Aerospace BAe 146 Series 200	E2060	EI-DDE	12 .9.03	BAE Systems (Operations) Ltd *(stored)*	Exeter
	G-CCJC, D-AZUR, N352BA, CP-2260, N352BA, XA-RMO, N402XV, G-5-060					
G-CCJD	Mainair Sports Pegasus Quantum 15	7974		3. 9.03	P Clark	Yatesbury 5. 8.08P
	(Rotax 582)					
G-CCJF	Cameron C-90 Balloon (Hot Air)	10483		14.10.03	Balloon School (International) Ltd	
						Colhook Common, Petworth 20. 9.08P
G-CCJG	Cameron A-200 Balloon (Hot Air)	10484		12. 2.04	J M Stables t/a Aire Valley Balloons	
						Knaresborough 3. 4.09P
G-CCJH	Lindstrand LBL 90A Balloon (Hot Air)	906		5. 8.03	J R Hoare	Plymouth 23. 8.09E
G-CCJI	Van's RV-6	PFA 181A-13572		4. 7.03	N A Thomas *"jadeair.co.uk"*.	Hunsdon 18. 9.09P
	(Built E M Marsh)					
G-CCJJ	Medway SLA 80 Executive	18803		20. 8.03	P K Bennett	Stoke, Isle of Grain 9. 1.10P
	(Originally regd as Medway Piranah until 10.03)					
G-CCJK	Aerostar Yakovlev Yak-52	9612001	RA-02622 LY-AFH	3. 3.04	S R Thomas tr G-CCJK Group	White Waltham 26. 6.09P
G-CCJL	Super Marine Spitfire Mk.26	PFA 324-14053		22. 8.03	M W Hanley and P M Whitaker *(As "PV303:ON-B" in RAF c/s)*	
	(Built P M Whitaker and M Hanley)					Perranporth 30. 8.08P
G-CCJM	Mainair Sports Pegasus Quik	7970		24. 7.03	P Crosby	Ince Blundell 26. 7.09P
G-CCJN	Rans S-6-ES Coyote II	0899.1336		28. 8.03	M G A Wood	Church Farm, Askern 20. 7.09P
	(Built M G A Wood - pr.no.PFA 204-13575) (Rotax 582) (Tri-cycle u/c)					
G-CCJO	ICP MXP-740 Savannah Jabiru(4)			28. 8.03	R and I Fletcher	Sandtoft 25. 8.08P
		03-05-01-213				
	(Built R and I Fletcher - pr.no.BMAA HB/295)					
G-CCJP	British Aerospace BAe 146 Series 200	E2066	I-TERK	17.10.03	BAE Systems (Operations) Ltd *(Stored 9.08)*	
	G-CCJP D-ALOA, N356BA, C-FHNX, N356BA, XA-RTI, N405XV, C-FHNX, N405XV, G-5-066, N405XV					Kemble
G-CCJT	Best Off Sky Ranger 912(2)	SKRxxxx366		30. 7.03	M S R Burak tr Juliet Tango Group	
	(Built J W Taylor - pr.no.BMAA HB/300)					Over Farm, Gloucester 13. 8.09P

Reg	Type	C/n	Prev id	Date	Owner/Operator	Base	
G-CCJU	ICP MXP-740 Savannah Jabiru(4)			3. 9.03	K R Wootton and A Colverson		
		03-05-01-214				Hollym, Withernsea	15.11.08P
	(Built K R Wootton and A Colverson - pr.no.BMAA HB/294)						
G-CCJV	Aeroprakt A22 Foxbat	PFA 317-14082		3. 9.03	J C Forrester tr Foxbat UK015 Syndicate		
	(Built M J Barrett, A Dace, S McRoberts and J C Forrester)					Otherton, Cannock	20. 7.09P
G-CCJW	Best Off Sky Ranger 912(2)	SKRxxxx366		3. 9.03	J R Walter	Hunterston Farm, Stair	8. 6.09P
	(Built J R Walter - pr.no.BMAA HB/303)						
G-CCJX	Europa Aviation Europa XS	509		9. 9.03	J S Baranski	Wycombe Air Park	12. 6.09P
	(Built J S Baranski - pr.no.PFA 247-13727)						
G-CCJY	Cameron Z-42 Balloon (Hot Air)	10465		12. 9.03	D J Griffin *(Cameron Balloons titles)*		
						Bowerhill, Melksham	3. 1.10E
G-CCKF	Best Off Sky Ranger 912(2)	SKRxxxx314		4. 9.03	T P M Turnbull	Eshott	10. 6.09P
	(Built S A Owen - pr.no.BMAA HB/289)						
G-CCKG	Best Off Sky Ranger 912(2)	SKR03077375		26. 8.03	J Hannibal	Otherton, Cannock	27. 7.09P
	(Built J Hannibal - pr.no.BMAA HB/302)						
G-CCKH	Diamond DA.40D Star	D4.039		23.10.03	Flying Time Ltd	Shoreham	21. 2.09E
G-CCKI	Diamond DA.40D Star	D4.038		23.10.03	S C Horwood	North Weald	15. 1.09E
G-CCKJ	Raj Hamsa X'Air 582(5)	855		2.10.03	D Robertson	Higher Barn Farm, Hoghton	14. 8.09P
	(Built S Thompson - pr.no.BMAA HB/306)						
G-CCKL	Evektor EV-97A Eurostar	PFA 315-14117		15. 9.03	K Stewart tr G-CCKL Group	Plymouth	18.11.09P
	(Built J S Liming and A U I Hudson) (Type modified to EV-97A 8. 1.09)						
G-CCKM	Mainair Sports Pegasus Quik	7985		22. 9.03	C I Poole and W T Milburn	(Southport)	13. 2.09P
G-CCKN	Nicollier HN.700 Ménestrel II	PFA 217-13943		23. 9.03	C R Partington	Stanton, Morpeth	6. 3.09P
	(Built C R Partington)						
G-CCKO	Mainair Sports Pegasus Quik	7982		27. 8.03	M J Mawle, C R Bunce and C D Waldron		
						Redlands, Swindon	31. 8.09P
G-CCKP	Robin DR.400-120 Dauphin 2+2	2044	F-GKQD	15. 9.04	B A Mills t/a Duxford Flying Group	Duxford	
G-CCKR	Pietenpol Aircamper	PFA 047-12295		22. 8.03	T J Wilson	Bodmin	16. 8.08P
	(Built T J Wilson) (Continental O-200-A)						
G-CCKT	HAPI Cygnet SF-2A	PFA 182-13366		15. 7.03	P W Abraham	Upfield Farm, Whitson	13. 5.08P
	(Built P W Abraham)						
G-CCKU	Canadian Home Rotors Safari	S2113		7.10.03	J C Collingwood	(Cranbrook)	
	(Built J C Collingwood) (Verner VM133)						
G-CCKV	Isaacs Fury II	PFA 011-13695		10.10.03	S T G Ingram *(As "K7271" in RAF c/s, noted 4.08)*		
	(Built S T G Ingram)					St Just	
G-CCKW	Piper PA-18-135 Super Cub	18-3535	G-GDAM	16. 9.03	G T Fisher	(Northside, Thorney)	11. 8.91
	(Frame No.18-3648) (L-21B-PI)		PH-PVW, (PH-DKE), R Neth AF R-107, 54-2335 *(Also see G-CUBI)*				
G-CCKX	Lindstrand LBL 210A Balloon (Hot Air)	931		23. 1.04	Alba Ballooning Ltd	Edinburgh	5.12.09E
G-CCKY	Lindstrand LBL 240A Balloon (Hot Air)	943		21.11.03	Cameron Flights Southern Ltd		
						Woodborough, Pewsey	9.10.09E
G-CCKZ	Customcraft A25 Balloon (Hot Air)	CC005		10.10.03	A van Wyk *(Noted 2004)*		
						Higham, Bury St Edmunds	
G-CCLB	Diamond DA.40D Star	D4.074		19. 1.04	Diamond Finance Services GmbH	Rochester	17. 5.08E
G-CCLC	Diamond DA.40D Star	D4.073		22. 1.04	Diamond Aircraft UK Ltd	Gamston	7. 8.09E
	(Marked as DA40TDi)						
G-CCLF	Best Off Sky Ranger 912(2)	SKRxxxx380		16.10.03	J Bannister and N J Sutherland	Perth	22. 9.08P
	(Built G K R Linney - pr.no.BMAA HB/311)						
G-CCLH	Rans S-6-ES Coyote II	0600.1372		24.10.03	K R Browne	Sackville Lodge, Riseley	23. 4.09P
	(Built K R Browne - pr.no.PFA 204-13658) (Tri-cycle u/c)						
G-CCLJ	Piper PA-28-140 Cherokee Cruiser		OY-TOJ	1. 9.03	A M George	North Weald	2. 8.08E
		28-7525049					
G-CCLL	Zenair CH.601XL Zodiac	PFA 162B-14081		4. 9.03	L Lewis	Yearby	
	(Built L Lewis)						
G-CCLM	Mainair Sports Pegasus Quik	7986		7.10.03	D J Shippen and C C Colclough		
						Newton Bank Farm, Daresbury	30.10.09P
G-CCLO	UltraMagic H-77 Balloon (Hot Air)	77/244		19. 2.04	J P Moore	Great Missenden	9. 8.09E
G-CCLP	ICP MXP-740 Savannah Jabiru(4)	xxx		31.10.03	S Woolmington	Earls Colne	13. 7.08P
	(Built M J Kaye, pr. no BMAA HB/314)						
G-CCLR	Schleicher ASH 26E	26209		26.11.03	M T Burton and S Edwards *"26E"*	Dunstable	17.12.09E
G-CCLS	Comco Ikarus C42 FB UK	0302-6534		19. 9.03	SLS Computing Services Ltd	Swinford, Rugby	31. 3.09P
	(Built J Spinks and T Greenhill - pr.no.PFA 322-14050) (Kit no.not confirmed)						
G-CCLU	Best Off Sky Ranger 912(2)	SKR0309379		11.11.03	C M Babiy	Park Farm, Eaton Bray	6. 3.09P
	(Built L Stanton - pr.no.BMAA HB/316)						
G-CCLV	Diamond DA.40D Star	D4.052		22.12.03	D J Watson	Blackpool	28. 6.09E
G-CCLW	Diamond DA.40D Star	D4.068		19.12.03	Diamond Aircraft UK Ltd	Gamston	16.12.09E
G-CCLX	Mainair Sports Pegasus Quik	7996		13.11.03	S D Pain	Rayne Hall Farm, Braintree	12. 4.09P
G-CCMC	Avtech Jabiru UL-450	xxxx		9. 9.03	J Johnston	(Knocklong, County Limerick)	28. 6.09P
	(Built J T McCormack - pr.no.PFA 274A-13775)						
G-CCMD	Mainair Sports Pegasus Quik	7991		23.10.03	J T McCormack	Broomhill Farm, West Calder	16. 2.09P
G-CCME	Mainair Sports Pegasus Quik	7995		7.11.03	J L Merriman tr Caunton Graphites		
						Knapthorpe Lodge, Caunton	22. 4.08P
G-CCMF	Diamond DA.40D Star	D4.075		19.12.03	Diamond Aircraft UK Ltd	Gamston	23. 3.07T
G-CCMH	Miles M.2H Hawk Major	172	EC-ABI	20.10.03	J A Pothecary	(Newton Tony, Salisbury)	
			EC-CAS, EC-DDB, EC-W44				
G-CCMI	Scottish Aviation Bulldog Series 120/121		G-KKKK	20.11.03	H R M Tyrrell *(As "XX513:10" in RAF c/s)*	Sleap	7. 5.11S
		BH120/199	XX513				
G-CCMJ	Reality Easy Raider Jab22	0009		13.11.03	G F Clews	Roddige	
	(Built G F Clews - pr. no BMAA HB/254)						
G-CCMK	Raj Hamsa X'Air Falcon Jabiru(3)	827		17.11.03	G J Digby	(Southend)	26. 5.09P
	(Built M A Beadman - pr.no.BMAA HB/301)						
G-CCML	Mainair Sports Pegasus Quik	7992		14.10.03	G G Wood	(Melrose)	28.10.09P
G-CCMM	Dyn'Aéro MCR-01 ULC	131		8. 9.03	J D Harris	Garston Farm, Marshfield	11. 6.09P
	(Built J P Davis - pr.no.PFA 301B-13945)						
G-CCMN	Cameron C-90 Balloon (Hot Air)	10519		27. 1.04	A E Austin	Sibbertoft, Market Harborough	16. 2.09E

G-CCMO	Evektor EV-97A Eurostar	PFA 315-14155		11.11.03	E M and P M Woods	Lydney-St Briavels	15. 3.09P
	(Built E M Woods)						
G-CCMP	Evektor EV-97A Eurostar	PFA 315-14127		23.10.03	E K McAlinden	Derryogue	5. 3.09P
	(Built W K Wilkie)						
G-CCMR	Robinson R22 Beta II	3497	N75273	9. 1.04	G F Smith	Cranfield	13. 1.10E
G-CCMS	Mainair Sports Pegasus Quik	7997		1.12.03	A J Roche	Elm Farm, Wickford	21. 4.09P
G-CCMT	Thruster T 600N 450	1031-T600N-092		14.11.03	S P McCaffrey	(Abingdon)	27. 6.08P
G-CCMU	Rotorway Executive 162F	6720		20.11.03	D J Fravigar and J Smith		
						Clough Farm, Croft, Skegness	28. 8.07P
G-CCMW	CFM Shadow Series DD	K 348		2. 9.03	M Wilkinson	Enstone	31. 8.09P
	(Built M Wilkinson - pr.no.PFA 161-13869) (Rotax 582)						
G-CCMX	Best Off Sky Ranger 912(2)	SKR0210243		25.11.03	K J Cole	Over Farm, Gloucester	27. 3.08P
	(Built K J Cole - pr.no.BMAA HB/255)						
G-CCMZ	Best Off Sky Ranger 912(2)	SKR0304316		23.10.03	D D Appleford	Draycott Farm, Chiseldon	13. 6.09P
	(Built D D Appleford - pr.no.BMAA HB/288)						
G-CCNA	Jodel DR.100A replica	PFA 304-13519		21.11.03	W R Davis-Smith and R Everitt (Noted 6.07)		
	(Built R Everitt -reported as rebuild of G-ATHX)					Ley Farm, Chirk	
G-CCNB	Rans S-6-ES Coyote II	1202.1469		2. 9.03	M S Lawrence	Mill Farm, Shifnal	7. 6.05P
	(Built D Bedford - pr.no.PFA 204-14027)			(Stalled and crashed Weston Park, Shifnal 28.3.05 and substantially damaged)			
G-CCNC	Cameron Z-275 Balloon (Hot Air)	10504		16. 4.04	Ladybird Balloons Ltd	Bingham, Nottingham	9. 6.09E
G-CCND	Van's RV-9A	PFA 320-14142		10.12.03	K S Woodard	Airfield Farm, Hardwick	18.11.09P
	(Built K S Woodard)						
G-CCNE	Cyclone Airsports Pegasus Quantum 15	7093	T2-2795	11.12.03	P R Hanman	Over Farm, Gloucester	21. 4.08P
	(Rotax 582)						
G-CCNF	Raj Hamsa X'Air Falcon 133(1)	644		9.12.03	M F Eddington	Henstridge	13.11.08P
	(Built M F Eddington - pr.no.BMAA HB/211)						
G-CCNG	Flight Design CT2K	03-06-02-27		5. 1.04	David Goode Sculpture Ltd	Enstone	13.12.07P
	(Assembled Mainair Sports Ltd with c/n 8004)						
G-CCNH	Rans S-6-ES Coyote II	0503.1498		11. 9.03	N C Harper tr Coyote Group		
	(Built N C Harper - pr.no.PFA 204-14114) (Rotax 912)					Grove Farm, Needham	12.12.09P
G-CCNJ	Best Off Sky Ranger 912(2)	SKR0310392		17.12.03	J D Buchanan	Coldharbour Farm, Willingham	18.11.09P
	(Built J D Buchanan - pr.no..BMAA HB/330)						
G-CCNM	Mainair Sports Pegasus Quik	8002		2.12.03	H M N and N M Corr	Enniskillen	10.12.08P
G-CCNN	Cameron Z-90 Balloon (Hot Air)	10512		8. 1.04	J H Turner (Gottex titles)	Broad Chalke, Salisbury	11.12.07A
G-CCNP	Flight Design CT2K	03.07.03.34		22. 1.04	M J Hawkins	Bagber Farm, Dorchester	20. 4.08P
	(Assembled Mainair Sports Ltd with (official) c/n 8005: now reported by P&M Aviation as c/n 8104 but inspection shows c/n 8124)						
	(Veered to the left on take-off at Bagber Farm 23. 5.08 and went into a field of wheat; nose undercarriage collapsed and aircraft overturned)						
G-CCNR	Best Off Sky Ranger 912(2)	SKR0309381		4.12.03	A J Lewis	(Lydney)	18. 5.09P
	(Built S J Huxtable - pr.no.BMAA HB/315)						
G-CCNS	Best Off Sky Ranger 912(2)	SKR0401434		24. 2.04	G G Rowley and M Liptrot	Glassonby	6. 6.09P
	(Built G G Rowley and M Liptrot - pr.no.BMAA HB/356)						
G-CCNT	Comco Ikarus C42 FB80	0311-6585		19.12.03	D J Collier tr Sunfun Group		
	(Rotax 912-UL)					Lower Mountpleasant Farm, Chatteris	25. 1.10P
G-CCNU	Best Off Sky Ranger J2.2(2)	SKRxxxx319		9. 1.04	P D Priestley	Sturgate	27.11.07P
	(Built D P Toulson and R L Nyman - pr.no.BMAA HB/297)						
G-CCNV	Cameron Z-210 Balloon (Hot Air)	10505		22. 4.04	J A Cooper	Ugborough, Ivybridge	8. 4.09E
G-CCNW	Mainair Sports Pegasus Quantum 15	8010		28. 1.04	J Childs	Deenethorpe	15.11.09P
	(Rotax 582)						
G-CCNX	CAB CAP.10B	311		6. 1.04	Arc Input Ltd	Great Oakley	31. 3.09E
	(Marked as "CAP.10C")						
G-CCNY	Robinson R44 Raven	1349		18.11.03	C M Evans and J W Blaylock	(Kirton, Boston)	22. 1.10E
G-CCNZ	Raj Hamsa X'Air 133(1)	888		5.11.03	J Anderson	Dunkeswell	17.10.08P
	(Built K J Foxall - pr.no.BMAA HB/308)						
G-CCOB	Aero C 104	247	N2348	21. 1.04	William Tomkins Ltd	Spanhoe	17. 7.08P
	(Bücker Bü.131 Jungmann)		LN-BNG, OK-AXV, Czech AF				
G-CCOC	Mainair Sports Pegasus Quantum 15	7999		16.12.03	S I P Hardman	Tarn Farm, Cockerham	9. 2.08P
	(Rotax 582)						
G-CCOF	Rans S-6-ESA Coyote II	1202.1472		8. 1.04	A J Wright and M Govan		
	(Built A J Wright and M Govan - pr.no.PFA 204-14037, tailwheel variant)					Yeatsall Farm, Abbots Bromley	2. 7.09P
G-CCOG	Mainair Sports Pegasus Quik	8001		16.12.03	A O Sutherland	Latch Farm, Kirknewton	17. 5.09P
G-CCOH	Raj Hamsa X'Air Falcon 133(1)	831		13. 1.04	M O Roach	Otherton, Cannock	4.10.05P
	(Built A R Emerson - pr.no.BMAA HB/338)						
G-CCOK	Mainair Sports Pegasus Quik	8000		5. 1.04	R Cotterrell	(Kenilworth)	28. 6.08P
G-CCOM	Westland Lysander IIIA	Y1363	N3093K	10.12.03	Propshop Ltd (Noted for restoration 10.08) Duxford		
			RCAF V9312				
G-CCOO	Raj Hamsa X'Air 133(1)	754		12.11.03	A Hipkin	Droppingwell Farm, Bewdley	11.11.09P
	(Built A Hipkin - pr.no.BMAA HB/320)						
G-CCOP	UltraMagic M-105 Balloon (Hot Air)	105/113		19. 1.04	G Holtam "Holtams Kitchens"	Heage, Belper	7. 5.09P
G-CCOR	Sequoia F 8L Falco	PFA 100-10588		9.12.03	D J and K S Thomas	White Fen Farm, Benwick	17. 6.09P
	(Built D J Thomas)						
G-CCOS	Cameron Z-350 Balloon (Hot Air)	10513		8. 3.04	M L Gabb	Haselor, Alcester	20. 2.09E
G-CCOT	Cameron Z-105 Balloon (Hot Air)	10517		14. 1.04	Airborne Adventures Ltd (Invista titles)	Skipton	26. 5.09E
G-CCOU	Mainair Sports Pegasus Quik	8012		21. 1.04	D E J McVicker	(Toombebridge)	4. 4.09P
G-CCOV	Europa Aviation Europa XS	543		19. 1.04	G N Drake	Fowle Hall Farm, Laddingford	14.10.09P
	(Built G N Drake - pr.no.PFA 247-13998)						
G-CCOW	Mainair Sports Pegasus Quik	8008		28. 1.04	R F Dye and G S B Airth	Perth	27. 2.09P
G-CCOX	Piper J-3C-65 Cub	7278	EI-CCH	21. 1.04	R P Marks (On rebuild 9.06)	(Honiton)	
			N38801, NC38801				
G-CCOY	North American AT-6D Harvard II	88-14555	Portuguese AF	22. 3.04	Classic Aero Services Ltd	Mendlesham	
			1513, SAAF 7426, EX884, 41-33857 (Parts noted 8.06, cockpit on rebuild Bruntingthorpe)				
G-CCOZ	Monnett Sonerai II	0197		31. 5.78	P R Cozens (Noted 10.07)		
	(Built P R Cozens - pr.no.PFA 015-10107) (Volkswagen 1900)					Spilstead Farm, Sedlescombe	26. 3.04P
G-CCPA	Air Création 582(1)/Kiss 400	FL023		13. 1.04	C P Astridge	Sywell	17. 8.08P
	(Built C P Astridge - pr.no.BMAA HB/334 being Flylight kit comprising Trike s/n T03102 and Wing s/n A03183-3172)						

G-CCPC (2)	Mainair Sports Pegasus Quik		7994		26.11.03	P M Coppola	East Fortune 14.12.07P
G-CCPD	Campbell Cricket Mk.4	PFA G/03-1333			27. 1.04	N C Smith	(Newport, Isle of Wight)
	(Built N C Smith)						
G-CCPE	Steen Skybolt	PFA 064-12830			10.12.03	C Moore	Kirkbride 22. 6.09P
	(Built C Moore)						
G-CCPF	Best Off Sky Ranger 912(2)	SKR0311396			26. 1.04	A R Tomlinson	(Norwich) 15. 7.09P
	(Built T A Willcox - pr.no.BMAA HB/340)						
G-CCPG	Mainair Sports Pegasus Quik		8016		13. 5.04	A W Lowrie	Eshott 12. 5.09P
G-CCPH	Evektor EV-97 teamEurostar UK		1814		9. 1.04	A H Woolley	(Hucknall) 17. 4.09P
G-CCPJ	Evektor EV-97 teamEurostar UK		1909		13. 2.04	S D Austen	(Torpoint, Devon) 12. 2.09P
G-CCPK	Murphy Rebel		274R	N2283B	20. 1.04	B A Bridgewater and D Webb	Shobdon 27. 4.09P
	(Built M C Sentall)						
G-CCPL	Best Off Sky Ranger 912(2)	SKR0310385			29. 1.04	John Charles Turner tr G-CCPL Group	
							Tarn Farm, Cockerham 29.12.09P
	(Built P Openshaw, B Hartley, T Seed, P and J Turner - pr.no.BMAA HB/342)						
G-CCPM	Mainair Blade 912	1360-1203-7-W1155			12. 1.04	T D Thompson	(Knutsford) 11. 1.10P
G-CCPN	Dyn'Aéro MCR-01 Club		271		28.11.03	M Sibson	Boylestone, Ashbourne 7. 7.08P
	(Built P H Nelson - pr.no.PFA 301A-14133)						
G-CCPO	Cameron N-77 Balloon (Hot Air)		3217	(ZS-HPR)	4. 2.04	M J Woodcock and A C Woodcock "Mitsubishi Motors"	
				G-MITS			East Grinstead and Bristol 16. 7.09E
	(Originally built as c/n 1115 and regd G-MITS, re-built with unknown new envelope c 1994 and then third envelope c/n 3217 and re-registered)						
G-CCPP	Cameron Concept-70 Balloon (Hot Air) 10515				16. 3.04	P F Smart tr The Sarnia Balloon Group	
							Oakley, Basingstoke 9. 7.09E
G-CCPS	Comco Ikarus C42 FB100 VLA	0310-6584			5. 2.04	H Cullens	Charterhall 12. 8.09P
	(Built H Cullens -pr.no.PFA 322-14138)						
G-CCPT	Cameron Z-90 Balloon (Hot Air)		10534		14. 4.04	Charter Ballooning Ltd (Castlepoint titles)	Liphook 17. 4.09E
G-CCPV	Avtech Jabiru J400	0xxx			12. 2.04	J R Lawrence	Nether Huntlywood, Gordon 19.12.08P
	(Built J R Lawrence - pr.no.PFA 325-14058)						
G-CCPW	British Aerospace Jetstream Series 3102 785			SE-LDI	23. 4.04	Highland Airways Ltd "www.jetstreamexpress.com"	
				C-FHOE, G-31-785			Inverness 1.10.09E
G-CCPX	Diamond DA.40D Star		D4.092		18. 3.04	R T Dickinson (Operated Sheffield City Flying School)	
							Sandtoft 10. 3.09E
G-CCPY	Hughes 369D (Hughes 500)		20-0674D	N622WA	22. 3.04	Hughes Helicopter Co Ltd t/a Biggin Hill Helicopters	
				N833RW, N58381			Biggin Hill
G-CCPZ	Cameron Z-225 Balloon (Hot Air)		10506		11. 3.04	Cameron Flights Southern Ltd "Horizon Balloons"	
							Woodborough, Pewsey 11. 3.09E
G-CCRA	DG Flugzeugbau DG-800B	8-308B208			19. 1.04	R Arkle "RA"	Aboyne 23. 4.09E
G-CCRB	Kolb Twinstar Mk.III (mod)	PFA 205-13993			9.12.03	R W Burge	(Ilfracombe) 7. 6.09P
	(Built R W Burge)						
G-CCRC	Cessna TU206G Turbo Stationair 6			9A-DLC	24. 2.04	D M Penny	(Movenis, Coleraine) 25. 9.09E
		U20607001		YU-DLC, N9960R			
G-CCRF	Mainair Sports Pegasus Quantum 15	8009			3. 3.04	D W Pearce	Redlands, Swindon 24. 4.09P
	(Rotax 582)						
G-CCRG	UltraMagic M-77 Balloon (Hot Air)	77/249			19. 4.04	Aerial Promotions Ltd	Cannock 30. 6.07A
G-CCRH	Cameron Z-315 Balloon (Hot Air)	10489			19. 3.04	Ballooning Network Ltd (Bath Building Society titles)	
							Bristol 30. 7.09E
G-CCRI	Raj Hamsa X'Air 582(5)		891		26. 2.04	B M Tibenham	Longside, Peterhead 3. 6.08P
	(Built R A Wright - pr.no.BMAA HB/354)						
G-CCRJ	Europa Aviation Europa		259		27. 2.04	J F Cliff	(Binfield, Bracknell)
	(Built J F Cliff -pr.no.PFA 247-12966)						
G-CCRK	Luscombe 8A Silvaire		3186	N71759	16. 2.04	J R Kimberley	(Bounds Farm, Ardleigh) 12. 5.09P
	(Continental A65)			NC71759			
G-CCRN	Thruster T 600N 450 Sprint	1031-T600N-096			25. 2.04	R A Wright	(Hundleby, Spilsby) 5. 9.08P
G-CCRP	Thruster T.600N 450 Sprint	0043-T600N-099		G-ULLY	17. 3.04	M R Jones	Wing Farm, Longbridge Deverill 7.10.09P
	(Rotax 582)			G-CCRP			Wing Farm, Longbridge Deverill/South Wraxall 7.10.09P
G-CCRR	Best Off Sky Ranger 912(1)	SKR0310393			16. 1.04	M Cheetham	Plaistows Farm, St Albans 9. 6.09P
	(Built J A Hunt - pr.no.BMAA HB/329)						
G-CCRS	Lindstrand LBL 210A Balloon (Hot Air)	981			4. 3.04	Aerosaurus Balloons Ltd	Whimple, Exeter 28. 9.09E
G-CCRT	Mainair Sports Pegasus Quantum 15	8014			3. 2.04	C R Whitton	East Fortune 1. 6.09P
	(Rotax 582)						
G-CCRV	Best Off Sky Ranger 912(2)	SKR0304315			20. 2.04	A C Thomson	Parkhill Farm, Ilkeston 15. 9.09P
	(Built M R Mosley - pr.no.BMAA HB/283)						
G-CCRW	Mainair Sports Pegasus Quik		8003		16. 3.04	S D Hutchinson	St Michaels 15. 3.07P
G-CCRX	Avtech Jabiru UL-450		xxxx		3. 3.04	M Everest	Cottage Farm, Norton Juxta 23. 5.09P
	(Built M Everest - pr.no.PFA 274A-14032)						
G-CCSA	Cameron Z-350 Balloon (Hot Air)	10490			19. 3.04	Ballooning Network Ltd (Bristol Balloons titles)	
							Southville, Bristol 30. 7.09E
G-CCSD	Mainair Sports Pegasus Quik		8023		19. 3.04	N S Lomax	(St Columb, Cornwall) 10. 3.08P
G-CCSF	Mainair Sports Pegasus Quik		8030		1. 4.04	J S Walton	(Mold) 31. 3.08P
G-CCSG	Cameron Z-275 Balloon (Hot Air)	10518			2. 4.04	M L Gabb	Haselor, Alcester 20. 2.09E
G-CCSH	Mainair Sports Pegasus Quik		8020		1. 3.04	D G Adley	Weston Zoyland 14. 3.09P
G-CCSI	Cameron Z-42 Balloon (Hot Air)	10563			30. 3.04	Ikea Ltd "Ikea"	Eastgate, Bristol 22. 4.09E
G-CCSJ	Cameron A-275 Balloon (Hot Air)	10510			7. 5.04	Dragon Balloon Company Ltd	
							Castleton, Hope Valley 9. 4.09E
G-CCSL	Mainair Sports Pegasus Quik		8029		26. 4.04	A J Harper	Croughton 29. 4.09P
G-CCSM	Lindstrand LBL 105A Balloon (Hot Air)	991			18. 3.04	M A Webb (Gulf Air c/s)	Oswestry 30. 8.09E
G-CCSN	Cessna U206G Stationair 6	U20604224		F-GECP	26. 3.04	K Brady (Operated Strathallan Parachute Club)	
				D-EKAX, (OY-ASG), N756NM			Strathallan 14. 5.09P
G-CCSO	Raj Hamsa X'Air Falcon VM133(1)	921			15. 3.04	K N Rigley and D Thorpe	
							(Carlton-le-Moorland, Lincoln and Grantham) 5.12.09P
	(Built P Richardson - pr.no.BMAA HB/364)						
G-CCSP	Cameron N-77 Balloon (Hot Air)	2882	SE-ZFV		17. 3.04	Ballongforeningen Oscair I Goteborg	
							Giteborg, Karlstad, Sweden 10. 4.09E
G-CCSR	Evektor EV-97A Eurostar	PFA 315-14174			18. 3.04	A Galante tr Sierra Romeo Group	Netherthorpe 20. 6.08P
	(Built M Lang)						
G-CCSS	Lindstrand LBL 90A Balloon (Hot Air)	973			11. 2.04	British Telecommunications PLC "BT"	Thatcham 15. 4.09E

G-CCST	Piper PA-32R-301 Saratoga IIHP	3246182	N4180T	14. 2.01	G R Balls		Biggin Hill	30. 3.09E
G-CCSU	IAV-Bacau Yakovlev Yak-52	888712	LY-APO	26. 4.04	S Ullrich	Bad Worishofen, Germany	15. 5.09P
			DOSAAF 69 (yellow)					
G-CCSV	ICP MXP-740 Savannah Jabiru(4)			18. 3.04	R D Wood		Rochester	12. 3.08P
	03-12-51-261							
	(Built R D Wood - pr.no.BMAA HB/362)							
G-CCSW	Nott PA Balloon (Hot Air)	9		24. 3.04	J R P Nott		London NW3	
G-CCSX	Best Off Sky Ranger 912(2)	SKR0401425		24. 3.04	T Jackson	The Chase, Wickwar	5.10.08P
	(Built T Jackson - pr.no.BMAA HB/366)							
G-CCSY	Mainair Sports Pegasus Quik	8022		27. 2.04	C H Henderson		Perth	14. 8.08P
G-CCTA	Zenair CH.601UL Zodiac	6-9207		4. 2.04	R E Gray and G T Harris		(Oxted)	17.10.09P
	(Built R E Gray and G T Harris, pr no PFA162A-13725)							
G-CCTC	Mainair Sports Pegasus Quik	8021		23. 2.04	D R Purslow	(Cleobury Mortimer, Kidderminster)	9. 7.08P
G-CCTD	Mainair Sports Pegasus Quik	8040		16. 3.04	R N S Taylor	Headon Farm, Retford	9. 6.08P
G-CCTE	Dyn'Aéro MCR-01 Club	61		22 .3.04	P G Mackintosh and J T M McNie tr Kinloss Flying Group			
	(Built G J Slater - pr.no.PFA 301-13268)						RAF Kinloss	23.6.09P
G-CCTF	Pitts S-2A	2146	N51ST	26. 3.04	M S Hill		Crosland Moor	9.12.09E
	(Built Aerotek Inc)							
G-CCTG	Van's RV-3B	PFA 099-10518		9. 3.04	A Donald		Netherthorpe	12. 6.09P
	(Built I G Glenn) (PFA pr.no.identical to Van's RV-3 G-BHXN [c/n EAA 105098] builder P Hing which was cancelled 2. 9.91 by CAA)							
G-CCTH	Evektor EV-97 teamEurostar UK	2005		12. 3.04	P R Whitmore and S J Downing			
						Upfield Farm, Whitson	17. 3.09P
G-CCTI	Evektor EV-97 teamEurostar UK	2009		6. 4.04	Flylight Airsports Ltd		Swell	26. 4.09P
G-CCTL	Robinson R44 Raven II	10309		30. 3.04	Aerocorp Ltd	Liverpool-John Lennon	30. 4.09E
G-CCTM	Mainair Blade	1363-0504-7-W1158		5. 4.04	J N Hanson	Tarn Farm, Cockerham	4. 6.09P
G-CCTN	UltraMagic T-180 Balloon (Hot Air)	180/48		5. 7.04	A Derbyshire *"Trentham"*	Woodseaves, Stafford	15. 2.09E
G-CCTO	Evektor EV-97 Eurostar	PFA 315-14136		17. 3.04	A J Boulton	Sittles Farm, Alrewas	25. 8.09P
	(Built A J Boulton)							
G-CCTP	Evektor EV-97 Eurostar	PFA 315-14185		18. 2.04	P E Rose		Ince Blundell	30. 5.09P
	(Built G M Yule)							
G-CCTR	Best Off Sky Ranger 912(2)	SKR0401410		2. 3.04	A H Trapp		(Kidderminster)	21. 3.08P
	(Built A H Trapp - pr.no.BMAA HB/350)							
G-CCTS	Cameron Z-120 Balloon (Hot Air)	10570		22. 6.04	F R Hart *(Snap Survey titles)* Bishop Sutton, Bristol			13. 2.09E
G-CCTT	Cessna 172SP Skyhawk	172S8157	N957SP	12. 2.04	A Reay		Caernarfon	10. 4.09E
G-CCTU	Mainair Sports Pegasus Quik	8024		21. 4.04	R S Swift		(Milton Keynes)	6. 5.09P
G-CCTV	Rans S-6-ES Coyote II	0302.1437		19. 6.03	G and S Simons	Grove Farm, Needham	19.12.09P
	(Built R M Broom - pr.no.PFA 204-14069) (Tri-cycle u/c)							
G-CCTW	Cessna 152	15279882	N757NW	26. 4.04	R J Dempsey		Bournemouth	8. 8.09E
G-CCTX	Rans S-6-ES Coyote II	1003.1524		19. 2.04	D A Tibbals		Rufforth	26. 6.09P
	(Built L M Leachman - pr.no.PFA 204-14143) (Tri-cycle u/c)							
G-CCTZ	Mainair Sports Pegasus Quik	8031		13. 4.04	S Baker		Long Marston	10. 5.09P
G-CCUA	Mainair Sports Pegasus Quik	8032		27. 4.04	B Hornsey	Damyn's Hall, Upminster	28. 4.08P
G-CCUB	Piper J-3C-65 Cub	2362A	N33528	2. 4.81	Cormack (Aircraft Services) Ltd *(On rebuild 2001)*			
			NC33528, NX33528				Rothesay	
G-CCUD	Best Off Sky Ranger J2.2(1)	SKRxxxx454		13. 4.04	A D Haughey	Newtownards	24.11.09P
	(Built J Johnston - pr.no.BMAA HB/374)							
G-CCUE	UltraMagic T-180 Balloon (Hot Air)	180/45		10. 5.04	Espiritu Balloon Flights Ltd Minsterley, Shrewsbury			11.12.09E
G-CCUF	Best Off Sky Ranger 912(2)	SKRxxxx459		15. 4.04	R E Parker		Hunsdon	15.10.08P
	(Built C D Hogbourne and D J Parrish - pr.no.BMAA HB/375)							
G-CCUH	Rotary Air Force RAF 2000 GTX-SE			16. 4.04	J H Haverhals	(Graffham, Petworth)	3. 7.08P
	(Built D R Lazenby)	PFA G/13-1356						
				(Substantially damaged on landing at Wellcross Farm, Slinfold 22. 7.08)				
G-CCUI	Dyn'Aéro MCR-01	236		1. 4.04	J T Morgan		Sywell	9. 8.09P
	(Built J T Morgan - pr.no.PFA 301-13963)							
G-CCUJ	Cameron C-90 Balloon (Hot Air)	10576		5. 7.04	R D Jones t/a Rudgleigh Inn *(The Rudgleigh Inn titles)*			
						Easton-in-Gordano, Bristol	27. 5.05A
G-CCUK	Agusta A109A II	7263	RP-C109	5. 4.04	Churchgate Aviation LLP (Battlesbridge, Wickford)			4.10.07E
			I-SEIE, N109AE					
G-CCUL	Europa Aviation Europa XS	336		20. 4.04	I P Dole tr Europa 6	Rayne Hall Farm, Braintree	25. 4.09P
	(Built I Dole - pr.no.PFA 247-13119) (Monowheel u/c)							
G-CCUO	Hughes 369D *(Hughes 500)*	40-0711D	N655WA	30. 4.04	M and K Pinfold t/a Claremont Air Services			
			C-GKHI				Wolverhampton	27. 8.09E
G-CCUP	Westland Wessex HC.Mk.2	WA/127	XR502	12.11.04	D Brem-Wilson and J Buswell			
	(Built Avions Fairey SA)				*(Joydens Farm, Westerham and Sevenoaks)*			
G-CCUR	Mainair Sports Pegasus Quantum 15-912							
		8034		30. 4.04	D W Power and D James		Swansea	22. 5.08P
G-CCUS	Diamond DA.40D Star	D4.082		29. 4.04	Diamond Finance Services GmbH	Rochester	29. 8.08E
G-CCUT	Evektor EV-97 Eurostar	PFA 315-14191		9. 3.04	C C Pagett tr Doctor and the Medics			
	(Built C K Jones)						Croft Farm, Defford	17. 8.08P
G-CCUU	Vahdat-Hagh Shiraz	MV-009		15. 3.04	M E Vahdat-Hagh		(Uxbridge)	
	(Built M E Vahdat-Hagh)							
G-CCUV	Piper PA-25-260 Pawnee C	25-5201	VT-EBH	31. 1.05	D B Almey	(Weston Hills, Spalding)	
			N8745L					
G-CCUY	Europa Aviation Europa	xxx		14. 4.04	N Evans	Old Buckenham	27.11.06P
	(Built N Evans pr.no.PFA 247-13189)				*(Noted 9.07)*			
G-CCUZ	Thruster T 600N 450 Sprint	0044-T600N-102		29. 4.04	Fly 365 Ltd		Wickenby	14. 6.09P
G-CCVA	Evektor EV-97 Eurostar	PFA 315-14226		21. 4.04	D A Palmer	Wolverhampton	29. 8.09P
	(Built T A Jones)							
G-CCVB	Mainair Sports Pegasus Quik	8033		6. 5.04	L Chesworth		(Malpas)	17. 5.09P
G-CCVD	Cameron Z-105 Balloon (Hot Air)	10583		25. 5.04	Associazione Sportiva Sorvolare *(Casanova titles)*			
						Crevalcore, Italy	17. 8.09E
G-CCVF	Lindstrand LBL 105A Balloon (Hot Air)	953		6. 5.04	S Villiers and A W Patterson tr Alan Patterson Design			
						Bangor	13. 7.09E

Reg	Type	C/n	Prev Id	Date	Owner	Base & CofA
G-CCVH	Curtiss H75A-1	12881	NX80FR G-CCVH, French AF 82	25.5.04 5.5.04	Patina Ltd (As French AF "82" coded X881) (Operated The Fighter Collection)	Duxford 12.6.09P
G-CCVI	Zenair CH.701SP STOL (Built C R Hoveman)	PFA 187-14181		5.5.04	M Miles tr The 701 Group	Old Sarum 30.5.08P
G-CCVJ	Raj Hamsa X'Air Falcon 133(1) (Built G A J Salter - pr.no.BMAA HB/381)	916		7.5.04	F J Rodrigues	Rhedyn Coch Farm, Rhuallt 8.3.08P
G-CCVK	Evektor EV-97 teamEurostar UK	2016		19.5.04	S A Kirk tr Kent Eurostar Group	Rochester 4.6.08P
G-CCVL	Zenair CH.601XL Zodiac (Built A Y-T Leung and G Constantine) (Tri-cycle u/c)	PFA 162B-14204		22.4.04	A Y-T Leung and G Constantine	Beccles 5.4.09P
G-CCVM	Van's RV-7A (Built J G Small)	PFA 323-14213		12.3.04	J G Small	(Southport) 28.10.08P
G-CCVN	Avtech Jabiru SP-470 (Built J C Collingwood - pr.no.PFA 274B-13677)	xxxx		10.5.04	J C Collingwood	Wittersham, Tenterden 6.6.07P
G-CCVO	Bell 206B-3 JetRanger III	4326	N471M JA6150, N20334, C-GLZU	22.6.04	Bell Trailers (Rental) Ltd	(Nelson) 5.8.09E
G-CCVP	Beech 58 Baron	TH-1948	PH-ZEM N80VS	13.5.04	Richard Nash Cars Ltd	Norwich 15.7.09E
G-CCVR	Best Off Sky Ranger 912(2) (Built M J Batchelor - pr.no.BMAA HB/353)	SKR0311407		29.4.04	M J Batchelor	The Chase, Wickwar 14.9.08P
G-CCVS	Van's RV-6A (Built J Edgeworth)	PFA 181A-13413	G-CCVC	29.3.04	J Edgeworth	Morgansfield, Fishburn
G-CCVT	Zenair CH.601UL Zodiac (Built D McCormack) (Tri-cycle u/c)	PFA 162A-14160		2.4.04	P Millar	Kirknewton 19.6.08P
G-CCVU	Robinson R22 Beta II	3600		11.5.04	London Helicopter Centres Ltd	Redhill 5.6.09E
G-CCVW	Nicollier HN.700 Ménestrel II (Built B F Enock)	PFA 217-11950		13.5.04	B F Enock	Shenington
G-CCVX	Mainair Tri Flyer 250/Flexiform Striker	AS-001		18.5.04	J A Shufflebotham	(Macclesfield)
G-CCVZ	Cameron O-120 Balloon (Hot Air)	10586		27.7.04	T M C McCoy (Operated Ascent Balloons)	Peasedown St John, Bath 11.6.09E
G-CCWB	Aero L-39ZA Albatros	132036	N404ZA Romanian AF 136	4.6.04	Freespirit Charters Ltd (Noted 10.08)	Duxford
G-CCWC	Best Off Sky Ranger 912(2) (Built C Hewer - pr.no.BMAA HB/367)	SKRxxxx422		4.5.04	R M Nutt, E B Maxwell and M J Richardson tr Carlisle Sky Rangers	Carlisle 21.9.08P
G-CCWD	Robinson R44 Raven	1296		10.3.03	Mulroy Car Sales (Letterkenny) Ltd	County of Derry/Eglinton 3.4.09E
G-CCWE	Lindstrand LBL 330A Balloon (Hot Air)	984		22.4.04	Adventure Balloons Ltd	Hartley Wintney, Hook 2.4.09E
G-CCWF	Raj Hamsa X'Air 133(1) (Built G A J Salter - pr.no.BMAA HB/331)	675		19.5.04	F Loughran	(Kildarky, County Meath) 6.10.05P
G-CCWG	Whittaker MW6 Merlin (Built D E Williams)	PFA 164-11998		8.4.04	D E Williams	(Llangynwyd, Maesteg)
G-CCWH	Dyn'Aéro MCR-01 Club (Built M G Rasch - pr.no.PFA 301-13949)	233		20.4.04	B J Mills and N J Mines	Wadswick Manor Farm, Corsham 8.5.09P
G-CCWJ	Robinson R44 Clipper II (Officially regd as "Raven II")	10363		16.6.04	Saxon Logistics Ltd	Denham 17.11.09E
G-CCWK	Aérospatiale AS.355F2 Ecureuil 2	5439	N8066G LN-OES, F-GGRS	10.9.04	RCR Aviation Ltd	Thruxton 13.9.07T
G-CCWL	Mainair Blade	1364-0504-7-W1159		19.5.04	T J Burrow	St Michaels 23.5.09P
G-CCWM	Robin DR.400-180 Régent	2457	F-GTZM	3.6.04	M R Clark	Newcastle 19.10.09E
G-CCWN	Mainair Sports Pegasus Quantum 15-912	8045		11.6.04	D M Broom	Sutton Meadows 16.8.08P
	(Landed very heavily at Sutton Meadows 16.9.08 and tumbled several times)					
G-CCWO	Mainair Sports Pegasus Quantum 15-912	8042		16.6.04	R Fitzgerald	(London N10) 16.6.08P
	(Drifted to the left on landing at Plaistows Farm14.10.07 and went into a ploughed field. Damage to pod, nose gear and sailwing spar)					
G-CCWP	Evektor EV-97 teamEurostar UK (Built Cosmik Aviation)	2010		9.6.04	N P de G Lambert	White Waltham 13.4.09P
G-CCWR	Mainair Sports Pegasus Quik	8053		1.6.04	C J Meadows	Chewton Mendip 5.7.08P
G-CCWT	Balony Kubicek BB20GP Balloon (Hot Air)	298	OK-0298	18.5.04	H C J and S L G Williams "Little Roo"	Langford, Bristol 10.9.08E
G-CCWU	Best Off Sky Ranger 912(2) (Built D M Lane - pr.no.BMAA HB/386)	SKR0403461		1.6.04	W J Byrd	Long Marston 28.5.08P
G-CCWV	Mainair Sports Pegasus Quik	8043		1.6.04	W J Dawson	Baxby Manor, Husthwaite 6.6.07P
G-CCWW	Mainair Sports Pegasus Quantum 15-912	8035		4.5.04	Virginia G Concannon tr Double Whisky Syndicate	Knapthorpe Lodge, Caunton 3.5.08P
G-CCWZ	Raj Hamsa X'Air Falcon 133(1) (Built M A Evans - pr.no.BMAA HB/380)	925		4.5.04	M A Evans	Weston Zoyland 6.11.09P
G-CCXA	Boeing Stearman A75N1 Kaydet (N2S-4 Kaydet)	75-3616	N75TL N5148N, Bu.37869	1.6.04	Skymax (Aviation) Ltd (As "669" in USAAC c/s)	Damyns Hall, Upminster 9.8.11S
G-CCXB	Boeing Stearman B75N1 Kaydet (N2S-3 Kaydet)	75-7854	N1363M Bu.38233	26.7.05	Skymax (Aviation) Ltd (As "699" in USAAC c/s)	Damyns Hall, Upminster 3.10.08S
G-CCXC	Mudry CAP.10B	165	N4247M Mexican AF EPC-162	26.5.04	Skymax (Aviation) Ltd	Damyns Hall, Upminster 16.10.09E
G-CCXD	Lindstrand LBL 105B Balloon (Hot Air)	996		14.6.04	J H Dobson "Rainbow Blue"	Streatley, Reading 9.7.09E
G-CCXE	Cameron Z-120 Balloon (Hot Air)	10596		3.6.04	Hans-Juergen Haas-Wittmuess	Gmund-St Quirin, Germany 9.9.09E
G-CCXF	Cameron Z-90 Balloon (Hot Air)	10593		3.8.04	R G March and T J Maycock "Unison"	Market Harborough 9.7.09E
G-CCXG	Replica Plans SE.5a (Built C Morris)	PFA 020-11785		11.6.04	C Morris (As "C5430:V" in RFC c/s)	Gresford, Wrexham 10.9.08P
G-CCXH	Best Off Sky Ranger J2.2(1)	SKR0403458		4.6.04	M J O'Connor	(Carshalton) 2.8.09P
	(Built P Welsh - pr.no.BMAA HB/377, built Sky Ranger UK Ltd according to CAA who were original owner)					
G-CCXI	Thorp T-211 (Built S G R and J Gilroy)	PFA 305-13504		22.9.03	J Gilroy	(Worth, Crawley)
G-CCXJ	Cessna 340A	340A0912	N25PJ HB-LNM, LN-TEA, N27026	13.7.04	Kilo Aviation Ltd	Liverpool-John Lennon 25.7.08E

G-CCXK	Pitts S-1S	AACA/1061	ZK-ECO	14. 6.04	P G Bond	Shipdham	21. 1.10P
	(Built E C Roberts)						
G-CCXL	Best Off Sky Ranger 912(2)	SKRxxxx411		18. 6.04	F W McCann	Strathaven	5. 6.08P
	(Built R G Cameron - pr.no.BMAA HB/335)						
G-CCXM	Best Off Sky Ranger 912(2)	SKR0311394		16. 6.04	C J Finnigan	Enstone	14.12.09P
	(Built C J Finnigan - pr.no.BMAA HB/337)						
G-CCXN	Best Off Sky Ranger 912(2)	SKRxxxx833		4. 6.04	P D Brisco and G P Martin		
						Mill Farm, Hughley, Much Wenlock	25. 8.08P
	(Built C I Chegwen - pr.no.BMAA HB/323)						
G-CCXO	Corby CJ-1 Starlet	PFA 134-13267		21. 6.04	I W L Aikman	Lower Wasing Farm, Brimpton	16. 9.09P
	(Built I W L Aikman)						
G-CCXP	ICP MXP-740 Savannah Jabiru(4)			30. 4.04	B J Harper	Eaglescott	8. 4.09P
		03-09-51-231					
	(Built B J Harper - pr.no.BMAA HB/318)						
G-CCXR	Mainair Blade	1367-0604-7-W1162		5. 7.04	J McErlain	(Tralee, County Kerry)	10. 8.09P
G-CCXS	Montgomerie-Bensen B 8MR PFA G/01A-1350			26. 5.04	S A Sharp *(Noted 7.08)*	Kirkbride	
	(Built S A Sharp)						
G-CCXT	Mainair Sports Pegasus Quik	8046		18. 6.04	C Turner	Priory Farm, Tibenham	23. 6.09P
G-CCXU	Diamond DA.40D Star	D4.037	ZK-SFH	28. 6.04	R J and L Hole	(Norwich)	21. 8.09E
G-CCXV	Thruster T 600N 450	0045-T600N-103		18. 6.04	W G Dunn	Dowland, Winkleigh	12. 7.09P
G-CCXW	Thruster T 600N 450	0045-T600N-104		15. 7.04	J Walsh *(Operated Saxon Microlights)*		
						Jenkin's Farm, Navestock	14. 7.09P
G-CCXX	American General AG-5B Tiger	10160	PH-MLG	19. 4.04	N R Dick and D O'Donnell tr Osprey Flying Group		
			YL-CAH			Aberdeen	21. 7.09E
G-CCXZ	Mainair Sports Pegasus Quik	8038		24. 5.04	K J Sene	Barton	21. 5.08P
G-CCYA	Avtech Jabiru J430	0xxx		22. 6.04	D J Royce	Ludham	20. 6.09P
	(Built D J Royce - pr.no.PFA 336-14060)						
G-CCYB	Reality Escapade 912(1)	JAESC 0034		24. 6.04	B E and S M Renehan	Lasham	5. 7.09P
	(Built B E Renehan - pr.no.BMAA HB/391)						
G-CCYC	Robinson R44 Raven II	10388		24. 6.04	Derg Developments Ltd		
						Ballyvally, Killaloe, County Clare	16. 7.09E
G-CCYE	Mainair Sports Pegasus Quik	8050		30. 7.04	J Lane	Lower Upham Farm, Chiseldon	29. 7.09P
G-CCYF	Aerophile 5500 Tethered Balloon (Gas-filled) 6		F-GPRS	30. 6.04	High Point Balloons Ltd *(GWR titles)*		
						Alveston, Bristol	27. 5.06T
G-CCYG	Robinson R44 Raven II	10424		9. 7.04	P Durkin t/a Moorland Windows	Blackpool	8. 8.09E
G-CCYI	Cameron O-105 Balloon (Hot Air)	10604		30. 7.04	Media Balloons	Policoro, Italy	17. 8.09E
G-CCYJ	Mainair Sports Pegasus Quik	8054		2. 8.04	A Blair-Smart tr YJ Syndicate	Balado Bridge	21.11.09P
G-CCYL	Mainair Sports Pegasus Quantum 15	8055		26. 7.04	M J L Morris	Swansea	4.11.08P
	(Rotax 582)						
G-CCYM	Best Off Sky Ranger 912(2)	SKR0401412		16. 7.04	I Pilton	Brook Farm, Pilling	18. 3.09P
	(Built D McDonagh - pr.no.BMAA HB/390)						
G-CCYO	Christen Eagle II	HAYNER 0001	N56RJ	13. 9.04	P C Woolley	Cadwell Park, Louth	20.11.07P
	(Built R Hayner)						
G-CCYP	Colt 56A Balloon (Hot Air)	302	SE-ZXG	23. 7.04	Magical Adventures Ltd	Oswestry	27. 9.09E
	(Special Shape Beefburger)						
G-CCYR	Comco Ikarus C42 FB80	0408-6612		20. 9.04	Airbourne Aviation Ltd	Popham	20 .9.08P
G-CCYS	Reims Cessna F182Q Skylane	F18200126	OY-BNG	31. 8.04	S Dyson	Netherthorpe	16. 7.09E
G-CCYT	Robinson R44 Raven II	10443		28. 7.04	B E Llewellyn t/a Bell Commercials	Swansea	17.10.09E
G-CCYU	UltraMagic S-90 Balloon (Hot Air)	90/70		17. 8.04	A R Craze	St Leonards-on-Sea	20. 5.09E
G-CCYX	Bell 412	34001	PK-HMI	2. 8.04	RCR Aviation Ltd	Thruxton	
	(Built Ndustri Pesawat Terbang Nusantara)						
G-CCYY	Piper PA-28-161 Warrior II	2816094	HB-PML	17. 6.04	Flightcontrol Ltd	Fairoaks	26. 8.09E
G-CCYZ	Dornier EKW C-3605	338	N31624	30. 9.04	William Tomkins Ltd *(Noted 10.06)*	Wickenby	
	(Built Federal Aircraft Factory)		Swiss AF C-558				
G-CCZA	SOCATA MS.894A Rallye Minerva 220 12094		D-EBWL	14. 7.05	R N Aylett	(Bromsgrove)	5. 6.09E
			F-BUVI				
G-CCZB	Mainair Sports Pegasus Quantum 15	8052		21. 7.04	A Johnson	Deenethorpe	15. 3.08P
	(Rotax 582)						
G-CCZD	Van's RV-7	PFA 323-14087		28. 5.04	D Powell	Hall Farm, Shenstone	20. 1.10P
	(Built R T Clegg)						
G-CCZH	Robinson R44 Raven	1423		6. 9.04	Newtown Aviation Ltd (Enfield, County Meath)	18.10.08E	
G-CCZI	Cameron A-275 Balloon (Hot Air)	10626		4. 4.05	Balloon School (International) Ltd		
						Colhook Common, Petworth	27. 5.09E
G-CCZJ	Raj Hamsa X'Air Falcon 582(2)	xxx		5. 8.04	P A Linford	(Huddersfield)	27.10.09P
	(Built A B Gridley - pr.no.BMAA HB/401)						
G-CCZK	Zenair CH.601UL Zodiac	PFA 162A-14270		11. 8.04	R J Hopkins	Popham	7. 5.09P
	(Built R J Hopkins)						
G-CCZL	Comco Ikarus C42 FB80	0410-6620		29.11.04	D Stokes	(The Gambia)	28.11.05P
G-CCZM	Best Off Sky Ranger 912S(1)	SKRxxxx455		1. 7.04	D Woodward	(Marple, Stockport)	2. 2.08P
	(Built D M Hepworth - pr.no.BMAA HB/372)						
G-CCZN	Rans S-6-ES Coyote II	0404 1561 ES		9. 8.04	R D Proctor	RAF Wyton	12. 2.09P
	(Built M Taylor - pr.no.PFA 204-14275)						
G-CCZO	Mainair Sports Pegasus Quik	8066		2. 9.04	J V Clewer Harringe Court, Sellindge, Folkestone	7. 9.08P	
G-CCZP	Super Marine Spitfire Mk.26	25		10. 6.04	J W E Pearson *(As "JF343:JW-P" in RAF c/s)*		
	(Built J W E Pearson and H Luck - pr.no.PFA 324-14062)					Panshanger	21. 1.10P
G-CCZR	Medway EclipseR	177/155		15. 7.04	K A Sutton	(Dartford)	12.12.08P
G-CCZS	Raj Hamsa X'Air Falcon 582(2)	xxxx		16. 8.04	A T Kilpatrick (Convoy, Lifford, Co Donegal)	9.10.08P	
	(Built P J Sheehy - pr.no.BMAA HB/403)						
G-CCZT	Van's RV-9A	PFA 320-13777		10. 8.04	N A Henderson	Bicester	23. 4.08P
	(Built N A Henderson)						
G-CCZU	Diamond DA.40D Star	D4.125	OE-VPU	24. 8.04	Diamond Finance Services GmbH	Gamston	1. 4.09E
G-CCZV	Piper PA-28-151 Cherokee Warrior		OY-CHR	7. 7.04	P D P Deal	Elstree	8. 9.09E
		28-7715089	SE-GNY				
G-CCZW	Mainair Blade	1368-0904-7-W1163		21.10.04	C J Wright	(Penrith)	27.11.09P
G-CCZX	Robin DR.400-180 Régent	2127	F-GLKY	15. 9.04	M Conrad	North Weald	10. 5.09E

Reg	Type	c/n	Prev id	Date	Owner/Operator	Location	Expiry
G-CCZY	Van's RV-9A	PFA 320-14154		23. 8.04	G Williams tr Mona RV-9 Group	RAF Mona	7. 7.09P
	(Built G Williams and Partners)						
G-CCZZ	Evektor EV-97 Eurostar	PFA 315-14158		28. 5.04	B M Starck and J P Aitken	Bourn	5. 8.09P
	(Built B M Starck and R Bastin)						

G-CDAA – G-CDZZ

Reg	Type	c/n	Prev id	Date	Owner/Operator	Location	Expiry
G-CDAA	Mainair Sports Pegasus Quantum 15-912	8069		27. 8.04	I A Macadam	Damyn's Hall, Upminster	26. 8.08P
G-CDAB	Stoddard-Hamilton Glasair IIS RG			7. 7.04	W L Hitchins (On build 11.06)		
	(Built W L Hitchins)	PFA 149-13231				Landmead Farm, Garford	
G-CDAC	Evektor EV-97 teamEurostar UK	2116		30. 9.04	Nene Valley Microlights Ltd	Conington	29. 9.08P
G-CDAD	Lindstrand LBL 25A Cloudhopper Balloon (Hot Air)	1003		21. 9.04	G J Madelin	Farnham	6.11.09E
G-CDAE	Van's RV-6A	PFA 181A-13018		5. 8.04	K J Fleming	RAF Woodvale	8. 2.09P
	(Built K J Fleming)						
G-CDAF	Bell 412	33105	PK-HMS	2. 8.04	RCR Aviation Ltd	Thruxton	
G-CDAG	Mainair Blade	1325-0502-7-W1120		10. 9.04	D K May	Tarn Farm, Cockerham	26. 4.09P
G-CDAI	Robin DR.400-140B	2574	D-EEAQ G-CDAI	13.12.04	D Hardy and J Sambrook	Derby	23.11.09E
G-CDAK	Zenair CH.601UL Zodiac	PFA 162A-14210		21. 7.04	K Kerr	Sleap	12. 2.09P
	(Built K Kerr) (Tri-cycle u/c)						
G-CDAL	Zenair CH.601UL Zodiac	PFA 162A-14195		7. 6.04	R J Howell	Weston Zoyland	18. 9.09P
	(Built D Cassidy) (Tri-cycle u/c)						
G-CDAO	Mainair Sports Pegasus Quantum 15-912	8061		17. 8.04	J C Duncan	(High Askomil, Campbeltown)	12. 9.07P
G-CDAP	Evektor EV-97 teamEurostar UK	2114		28. 7.04	R W Caress	Fenland	27. 7.09P
G-CDAR	Mainair Sports Pegasus Quik	8060		17. 8.04	A R Pitcher	(Rye)	16. 8.09P
G-CDAT	ICP MXP-740 Savannah Jabiru(4)	03-05-51-211	(Built R Simpson – pr. no.BMAA HB/327)	7. 7.04	R Simpson	Eshott	23. 5.09P
G-CDAW	Robinson R22 Beta	3703		11.10.04	Airtask Group PLC	Stapleford	26.11.09E
G-CDAX	Mainair Sports Pegasus Quik	8068		8. 9.04	I D Nuttall	Over Farm, Gloucester	12. 1.10P
G-CDAY	Best Off Sky Ranger 912(2)	SKR0404473		7. 7.04	D A Perkins tr G-CDAY Group		
	(Built M E Furniss - pr.no.BMAA HB/394)					Tarn Farm, Cockerham	4.12.09P
G-CDAZ	Evektor EV-97 Eurostar	2004 21.10		13. 8.04	M C J Ludlow		
	(Built M C J Ludlow - pr.no.PFA 315-14268)					Harringe Court, Sellindge, Folkestone	29.10.09P
G-CDBA	Best Off Sky Ranger 912(2)	SKR0404484		21.10.04	P J Brennan	Ashcroft Fam, Winsford	2. 6.08P
	(Built P J Brennan - pr.no.BMAA HB/406)						
G-CDBB	Mainair Sports Pegasus Quik	8062		16. 8.04	D W Watson	Eshott	29.10.09P
G-CDBC	Aviation Enterprises Magnum	001	G-61-2	27. 8.04	Aviation Enterprises Ltd	Membury	
G-CDBD	Avtech Jabiru J400	0xxx		16. 8.04	E Bentley	Morgansfield, Fishburn	12. 4.09P
	(Built S Derwin and E Bentley - pr.no.PFA 325-14077)						
G-CDBE	Montgomerie-Bensen B 8M	PFA G/01-1360		7. 9.04	P Harwood	Kirkbride	8. 8.07P
	(Built P Harwood)						
G-CDBG	Robinson R22 Beta II	3682		11.10.04	CC Helicopters Ltd	Blackpool	5.11.09E
G-CDBJ	Yakovlev Yak-3	02-03	RA-44553	1.11.07	C E Bellhouse	Pent Farm, Folkestone	12. 5.09P
	(Official p/i and c/n appear incorrect - thought, as new-build, to be 0470203)				(Noted 8.07 as "21" (white) in Russian AF c/s)		
	(Overran the runway after landing at Pent Farm, Folkestone 5. 7.08 and left main undercarriage detached)						
G-CDBK	Rotorway Executive 162F	6834		20. 9.04	Car Builder Solutions Ltd	(Staplehurst, Tonbridge)	13. 8.08P
	(Built N and M Foreman)						
G-CDBM	CAB Robin DR.400-180 Régent	2573		16.11.04	C M Simmonds	St Just	18.12.09E
G-CDBO	Best Off Sky Ranger 912(2)	SKRxxxx424		13. 8.04	A C Turnbull	Perth	14.11.09P
	(Built A M Dalgetty - pr.no.BMAA HB/370)						
G-CDBR	Stolp SA.300 Starduster Too	PFA 035-13036		15. 9.04	R J Warren	(West Drayton)	
	(Built R J Warren)				(Fuselage noted 4.06 heading West Drayton to M4)		
G-CDBS	MBB BÖ.105DBS-4	S 738	D-HDRZ VH-MBK, N970MB, D-HDRZ	29. 9.89	Bond Air Services Ltd	Glasgow City Heliport	8.11.09E
G-CDBU	Comco Ikarus C42 FB100	0411-6632		26. 1.05	S E Meehan and J K Agarwala	Ince Blundell	25 4.09P
G-CDBV	Best Off Sky Ranger 912S(1)	SKR0406499		23. 9.04	K Hall	Harringe Court, Sellindge, Folkestone	24. 4.09P
	(Built K Hall - pr.no.BMAA HB/409)						
G-CDBX	Europa Aviation Europa XS	568		16. 9.04	R Marston	Hall Farm, Shenstone	17. 2.09P
	(Built R Marston - pr.no.PFA 247-13971)						
G-CDBY	Dyn'Aéro MCR-01 ULC	288		23. 8.04	R Clark	Sherburn-in-Elmet	18. 1.08P
	(Built R Germany- pr.no.PFA 301B-14269)						
G-CDBZ	Thruster T 600N 450	0047-T600N-106		24. 9.04	J A Lynch	Sandown	29. 9.08P
G-CDCB	Robinson R44 Raven II	10532		8.11.04	Microwave Sales and Services Ltd	Enniskillen	17. 2.09P
G-CDCC	Evektor EV-97A Eurostar	PFA 315A-14262		11. 8.04	R E and N G Nicholson "The Dream"		
	(Built R E and N G Nicholson)					Bodmin	15. 4.09P
G-CDCD	Van's RV-9A	PFA 320-13925		20. 1.04	M Weaver and S D Arnold tr RV9ers	(Coleshill)	
	(Built M Weaver and S D Arnold)				(Exhibited incomplete Kemble 7.05)		
G-CDCE	Mudry CAP.10B	39	F-BNDC CN-TBW, F-BUDG	3.11.04	The Tiger Club 1990 Ltd	Headcorn	11. 5.09E
G-CDCF	Mainair Sports Pegasus Quik	8076		8.11.04	T J Gayton-Polley	(Billingshurst)	17.11.09P
G-CDCG	Comco Ikarus C42 FB UK	0408-6625		16. 8.04	N E Ashton and R H J Jenkins	Ince Blundell	27. 6.08P
	(Built N E Ashton and R H J Jenkins - pr.no.PFA 322-14281)						
G-CDCH	Best Off Sky Ranger 912(2)	SKR0401436		28. 9.04	K Laud	Nottage Farm, Swadlincote	17. 8.09P
	(Built K Laud - pr.no.BMAA HB/384)						
G-CDCI	Mainair Sports Pegasus Quik	8077		14. 1.05	S G Murray	Fowle Hall Farm, Laddingford	5. 5.08P
G-CDCK	Mainair Sports Pegasus Quik	8078		22.10.04	S G Ward	Elm Tree Farm, Manton	9.11.07P
	(Original trike fitted to G-CEVP 10.07 qv)						
G-CDCM	Comco Ikarus C42 FB UK	0408-6624		26.10.04	S T Allen	Craysmarsh Farm, Melksham	7. 4.09P
	(Built S T Allen as pr.no.PFA 322-14280) (Carries "Icarus C42B" titles)						
G-CDCO	Comco Ikarus C42 FB UK	PFA 322-14315		7.10.04	Churchill Trading Ltd	Plaistows Farm, St Albans	27.11.09P
	(Built G G Bevis)						

G-CDCP	Avtech Jabiru J400	0xxx		7.10.04	M W T Wilson	Morgansfield, Fishburn	1. 5.09P
	(Built M W T Wilson - pr.no.PFA 325-14094)						
G-CDCR	ICP MXP-740 Savannah Jabiru(4)			14. 1.05	T Davidson and G McKinstry		
		04-06-51-291				Slieve Croob, Slievenamoney, Castlewellen	21. 9.08P
	(Built T Davidson and G McKinstry, pr.no.BMAA HB/405)						
G-CDCS	Piper PA-12 Super Cruiser	12-2907	N854CC	29. 9.04	D Todorovic	Spanhoe	8. 8.11E
			CS-ACC				
G-CDCT	Evektor EV-97 teamEurostar UK	2117		15. 9.04	R W Skelton	Mullahead, Tandragee	17.10.09P
G-CDCU	Mainair Blade	1369-1004-7-W1164		19.10.04	W S Clare	(Stratford-upon-Avon)	4. 4.09P
G-CDCV	Robinson R44 Clipper II	10536		28.10.04	Central Chiswick Developments Ltd	Denham	12.12.09E
G-CDCW	Reality Escapade 912(1)	JAESC 0050		4.10.04	P Nicholls	(Ludlow)	24. 4.09P
	(Built P Nicholls - pr.no.BMAA HB/413)						
G-CDCX	Cessna 750 Citation X	750-0194	N194CX	26. 6.03	P W Harris t/a Pendley Farm	Luton	25. 6.09E
			N5192E				
G-CDCY	Mainair Sports Pegasus Quantum 15	8065		29.10.04	H Kearns	(Sallins, County Kildare)	23.10.07P
	(Rotax 582)						
G-CDDA	SOCATA TB-20 Trinidad	1860	PH-SXE	22.10.04	Oxford Aviation Academy (Oxford) Ltd	Oxford	17. 1.10E
			F-OIGL				
G-CDDB	Standard Cirrus	577G	BGA5102-KHJ	13.10.04	K D Barker *"KM"* (St Nicholas de la Grave, France)		5. 2.08
	(Built Burkhart Grob Flugzeugbau)		F-CEMG				
G-CDDC	Cameron Z-275 Balloon (Hot Air)	10656		19. 7.05	Airborne Balloon Management Ltd	Paddock Wood	4. 9.09E
G-CDDD	Robinson R22 Beta II	3658		24. 8.04	TDR Aviation Ltd	(Mullahead, Tandragee)	17.10.09E
G-CDDE	PZL-110 Koliber 160A	04020088	SP-WGO	26.10.04	J Staszak	Oblaczkowo, Poland	26. 3.09E
G-CDDF	Mainair Sports Pegasus Quantum 15-912						
		8079		8.11.04	B C Blackburn and J L Dalgetty	Balado Bridge	14.11.09P
G-CDDG	Piper PA-28-161 Warrior II	2816065	HB-PLU	4.10.04	A Oxenham	Hinton-in-the-Hedges	5.12.09E
G-CDDH	Raj Hamsa X'Air Falcon Jabiru(3)	944		26.10.04	B and Lorna Stanbridge	Wickenby	18. 9.08P
	(Built B Stanbridge - pr.no.BMAA HB/419)						
G-CDDI	Thruster T 600N 450	1040-T600N-109		26.10.04	R Nayak	North Coates	28.11.08P
	(Hit power lines on approach to strip at Usselby, Market Rasen 16. 9.08 and substantially damaged)						
G-CDDK	Cessna 172M Skyhawk	17265258	TF-SIX	1.12.04	M H and P R Kevern	Shoreham	14. 4.09E
			N64478				
G-CDDL	Cameron Z-350 Balloon (Hot Air)	10632		24. 5.05	Balloon School (International) Ltd *"British School of*		
					Ballooning" titles	Colhook Common, Petworth	27. 5.09E
G-CDDM	Lindstrand LBL 90A Balloon (Hot Air)	902	ZS-HAI	14. 1.05	A M Holly	Breadstone, Berkeley	4. 3.09E
G-CDDN	Lindstrand LBL 90A Balloon (Hot Air)	903	ZS-HAK	14. 1.05	I J Martin and D J Groombridge t/a Flying Enterprises		
					(Fishtank.com titles)	Bristol	23. 7.09E
G-CDDO	Raj Hamsa X'Air 133(2)	941		2.11.04	N C Marciano	Ince Blundell	10. 2.09P
	(Built R N Tarrant - pr.no.BMAA HB/407)						
G-CDDP	Laser Lazer Z230	001	N230RT	16.11.04	A Smith	Bagby	14. 8.09P
	(Built F L Thomson)						
G-CDDR	Best Off Sky Ranger 582(1)	SKR0406502		26.10.04	M J Saywell	Kimbolton	9. 6.08P
	(Built R J Milward - pr.no.BMAA HB/418)						
G-CDDS	Zenair CH.601HD Zodiac	PFA 162-14223		8.10.04	S Foreman	Tibenham	20. 6.09P
	(Built S Foreman)						
G-CDDT	SOCATA TB-20 Trinidad	1858	PH-SXC	24.11.04	Oxford Aviation Academy (Oxford) Ltd	Oxford	30. 6.09E
			F-OIGJ				
G-CDDU	Best Off Sky Ranger 912(2)	SKR0404506		10.11.04	A Rastall	Darley Moor, Ashbourne	16. 4.09P
	(Built R C Reynolds - pr.no.BMAA HB/422)						
G-CDDV	Cameron Z-250 Balloon (Hot Air)	10625		22. 3.05	Off The Ground Balloon Co Ltd t/a High Adventure		
						Lyth, Kendal	11. 2.09E
G-CDDW	Aeroprakt A22 Foxbat	PFA 317-14261		8. 9.04	M Raflewski Dungannon, Kilmaddy, County Tyrone		8. 5.09P
	(Built D A A Wineberg)						
G-CDDX	Thruster T 600N 450	0049-T600N-107		11.11.04	P A G Harper	Priory Farm, Tibenham	26. 1.09P
G-CDDY	Van's RV-8	80912	N701CZ	24.11.04	C A Foss tr The AV8ors	Shoreham	22. 5.09P
	(Built C S Ziekle)						
G-CDEA	SAAB-Scania 2000	2000-009	SE-LOX	20. 1.05	Air Kilroe Ltd t/a Eastern Airways	Aberdeen	19. 1.10E
			HB-IZF, (D-ADIC), SF-009				
G-CDEB	SAAB-Scania 2000	2000-036	SE-036	30.11.04	Air Kilroe Ltd t/a Eastern Airways	Aberdeen	29.11.09E
			HZ-IZT, SE-036				
G-CDEC	Mainair Sports Pegasus Quik	8081		27. 1.05	S Bradie and A Huyton *(Noted 11.06)*		
						Broomhill Farm, West Calder	26. 1.06P
G-CDED	Robinson R22 Beta II	3747	N74365	19. 1.05	Flight Solutions Ltd	Panshanger	13. 2.09E
G-CDEF	Piper PA-28-161 Cadet	2841341	D-ESTD	12.11.04	Western Air (Thruxton) Ltd	Thruxton	12.12.09E
			N9184X, N621FT, (OH-PFB)				
G-CDEG	Boeing 737-8BK/W	33022		21. 3.05	Globespan Airways Ltd t/a Flyglobespan.com		
						Edinburgh	20. 3.09E
G-CDEH	ICP MXP-740 Savannah LS(1)	03-03-51-200		18.11.04	A J Webb	Manor Farm, Drayton St Leonard	1.11.09P
	(Built S Whittaker and P J Wilson - pr.no.BMAA HB/349) (Suzuki LS1000)						
G-CDEJ	Diamond DA.40D Star	D4.142	OE-VPU	1.12.04	Diamond Aircraft UK Ltd	Cumbernauld	23. 2.09E
G-CDEK	Diamond DA.40D Star	D4.143	OE-VPW	1.12.04	A D and C Realff t/a ADR Aviation	Shoreham	23. 2.09E
G-CDEL	Diamond DA.40D Star	D4.144	OE-VPW	1.12.04	Diamond Aircraft UK Ltd	Gamston	23. 2.09E
G-CDEM	Raj Hamsa X'Air 133(1)	939		17.11.04	R J Froud Little Atherfield Farm, Chale, IoW		
	(Built R J Froud - pr.no.BMAA HB/421)						
G-CDEN	Mainair Sports Pegasus Quantum 15-912						
		8087		30.11.04	J D J Spragg	Roddige	11.12.09P
G-CDEO	Piper PA-28-180 Cherokee Archer		HB-OQE	17. 2.05	G G Hammond	Biggin Hill	29. 6.09E
		28-7405011	N9568N				
G-CDEP	Evektor EV-97 teamEurostar UK	2128		6.12.04	N Morrison and P S Rose tr Echo Papa Group		
						Wycombe Air Park	6.12.09P
G-CDER	Piper PA-28-161 Warrior II	28-8116222	HB-PHL	18. 2.05	Archer Five Ltd	Lydd	20. 3.09E
			D-EBKC, N9537N, N8383S				
G-CDET	Culver LCA Cadet	129	N29261	10.11.86	J Gregson	Durham Tees Valley	2. 9.08P
	(Continental O-200-A)		NC29261				

G-CDEU	Lindstrand LBL 90B Balloon (Hot Air)	1015		7. 2.05	N Florence and P J Marshall	Ruislip	9. 7.09E
G-CDEV	Reality Escapade 912(1)	JAESC 0024		26.10.04	M B Devenport	Popham	20. 9.08P
	(Built M B Devenport - pr.no.BMAA HB/360)						
G-CDEW	Mainair Sports Pegasus Quik	8083		13. 1.05	K M Sullivan	Newtownards	14. 3.09P
G-CDEX	Europa Aviation Europa	012		21.10.04	J M Carter	Morgansfield, Fishburn	31.10.08P
	(Built S Collins - pr.no.PFA 247-12507) (Tri-Gear u/c)						
G-CDFA	Kolb Twinstar Mk.III Xtra	M3X-04-7-00057		25.11.04	S Soar and W A Douthwaite		
	(Built M H Moulai - pr.no.PFA 205-14274)					Tarn Farm, Cockerham	16. 8.08P
G-CDFC	UltraMagic S-160 Balloon (Hot Air)	160/39		30. 3.05	Over The Rainbow Balloon Flights Ltd		
						Forest Town, Mansfield	28. 4.09E
G-CDFD	Scheibe SF25C Falke	44705	D-KEOQ	1.12.04	T M Holloway tr RAF Gliding and Soaring Association		
	(Rotax 912S)				(Operated Bannerdown Gliding Club)	RAF Keevil	3. 2.09E
G-CDFE	IAV-Bacau Yakovlev Yak-52	855712	LY-APU	29.11.04	D P Curtis	(Ayr)	27. 4.09P
			G-CDFE, N151PA, Kyrgyz AF, DOSAAF 82 (blue)?				
G-CDFF	Aérospatiale-Alenia ATR 42-300	331	LN-FAI (5)	30. 3.04	NAC Nordic Aviation Contractor A/S	Guernsey	1. 4.09E
			G-BVEF, (F-GKNF), F-WWLP				
G-CDFG	Mainair Sports Pegasus Quik	8082		21.12.04	D Gabbott	Ince Blundell	22.12.09P
G-CDFI	Cameron Colt 31A Balloon (Hot Air)	10655		6.12.04	A M Holly tr Exclusive Ballooning (Sloggi titles)		
						Berkeley	9. 6.09E
G-CDFJ	Best Off Sky Ranger 912(2)	SKR0404490		6.12.04	A Worthington tr Heskin Flyers Group		
	(Built W C Yates - pr.no.BMAA HB/424)					Tarn Farm, Cockerham	19. 9.08P
G-CDFK	Avtech Jabiru SPL-450	xxxx		2.12.04	H J Bradley	Shobdon	10. 9.09P
	(Built H J Bradley - pr.no.PFA 274A-14144)						
G-CDFL	Zenair CH.601UL Zodiac	PFA 162A-14309		30.11.04	F G Green tr Caunton Zodiac Group		
	(Built F G Green, R Welch and V Causey) (Tri-cycle u/c)					Knapthorpe Lodge, Caunton	11. 3.09P
G-CDFM	Raj Hamsa X'Air 582(5)	920		2.12.04	W A Keel-Stocker	Norton, Gloucestershire	3. 4.08P
	(Built J Griffiths - pr.no.BMAA HB/417)						
G-CDFN	Thunder Ax7-77 Balloon (Hot Air)	3697	I-FMCL (2)	22. 2.06	E Rullo	Caulonia Marina (RC), Italy	
G-CDFO	Mainair Sports Pegasus Quik	8080		17. 1.05	C J Gordon	Ince Blundell	23. 4.09P
G-CDFP	Best Off Sky Ranger 912(2)	SKR0409522		10.12.04	J M Gammidge	Sywell	4. 9.08P
	(Built J M Gammidge - pr.no.BMAA HB/431)						
G-CDFR	Cyclone Airsports Pegasus Quantum 15	6943	CS-UGX	8. 3.05	A Jopp	(Pill, Bristol)	18. 4.09P
	(Rotax 582)						
G-CDFU	Rans S-6-ES Coyote II	0304.1560		3.11.04	P W Taylor	Priory Farm, Tibenham	31. 5.08P
	(Built P W Taylor - pr.no.PFA 204-14232) (Tri-cycle u/c)						
G-CDFW	Sheffy Gyroplane	PFA G/19-1366		5. 9.05	P C Lovegrove	(Didcot)	
	(Built P C Lovegrove)						
G-CDFY	Beech B200 Super King Air	BB-1715	N607TA	4. 2.05	BAE Systems Marine Ltd	Walney Island	3. 2.10E
G-CDGA	Taylor JT.1 Monoplane	6020/1		28.12.78	R M Larimore	(Spondon, Derby)	
	(Built D G Anderson - pr.no.PFA 055-10382)						
G-CDGB	Rans S-6-116 Coyote II	0696.1006		21.12.04	S Penoyre	(Windlesham)	15.10.08P
	(Built S Penoyre - pr.no.PFA 204A-13047)						
G-CDGC	Mainair Sports Pegasus Quik	8090		26. 1.05	A T K Crozier	Kirknewton	4. 5.09P
G-CDGD	Mainair Sports Pegasus Quik	8086		11.11.04	I D and V A Milne (Noted 5.07)	St Michaels	12.12.06P
G-CDGE	AirBorne XT912-B-Streak III-B	XT912-028	T2-2253	22.12.04	M R Leyshon	(Brierley Hill)	30. 5.09P
	(Wing s/n S3B-009)						
G-CDGF	UltraMagic S-105 Balloon (Hot Air)	105/127		9. 3.05	D and Karin Bareford	Cookley, Kidderminster	28. 5.09E
G-CDGG	Dyn'Aéro MCR-01 Club	291		26.10.04	N Rollins	Hawksbridge Farm, Oxenhope	15. 6.09P
	(Built P Simpson and P A B Morgan - pr.no.PFA 301A-14267)						
G-CDGH	Rans S-6-ES Coyote II	1203.1537 ES		22.12.04	K T Vinning tr G-CDGH Group	Long Marston	2. 4.09P
	(Built K T Vinning -pr.no.PFA 204-14209) (Tri-cycle u/c)						
	(Stalled on take-off Broadmeadow 25. 8.07 and substantially damaged in collision with Quiks G-CCJM and G-CDFG)						
G-CDGI	Thruster T 600N 450 Sprint	1041-T600N-108		5. 1.05	R North	(Spilsby)	19. 7.09P
G-CDGN	Cameron C-90 Balloon (Hot Air)	10641		24. 2.05	M C Gibbons "Betty"	Bristol	14. 4.09E
G-CDGO	Mainair Sports Pegasus Quik	8084		11.11.04	Mainair Sports Ltd	(Rochdale)	10. 5.09P
G-CDGP	Zenair CH.601XL Zodiac	PFA 162B-14313		6. 1.05	T J Bax	Henstridge	29. 7.08P
	(Built T J Bax) (Tailwheel u/c)						
G-CDGR	Zenair CH.701UL STOL	PFA 187-14327		6. 1.05	I A R Sim	(Elsworth, Cambridge)	24. 7.09P
	(Built M Morris)						
G-CDGS	American General AG-5B Tiger	10097	PH-BMA	7. 2.05	K Hennessy tr Premier Flying Group		
			N1195Q			Waterford, County Waterford	6. 3.09E
G-CDGT	Montgomerie-Parsons Two-Place Gyroplane			10. 1.05	J B Allan	Little Rissington	30. 8.08P
	(Built A A Craig)	PFA G/08-1361					
G-CDGU	Vickers Supermarine 300 Spitfire I	6S-75156	X4276	7. 1.05	A J E Smith	(Gateforth, Selby)	
G-CDGW	Piper PA-28-181 Archer II	28-7990402	HB-PDZ	13. 1.05	B F Millet and D L Jones tr Rutland Flying Group		
			N2156Z			(Stamford)	22. 6.09E
G-CDGX	Mainair Sports Pegasus Quantum 15-912	8096		28. 1.05	S R Green	(Bishops Itchington, Southam)	22. 4.09P
G-CDGY	Vickers Supermarine 349 Spitfire Vc	WWA3832	ZK-MKV	19. 1.05	Aero Vintage Ltd	(Northiam, Rye)	
	(Built Westland Aircraft Ltd)		A58-149, EF545				
G-CDHA	Best Off Sky Ranger 912S(1)	SKR0407508		18. 1.05	A T Cameron	City of Derry	12. 8.08P
	(Built K J Gay - pr.no.BMAA HB/428)						
G-CDHB	British Aircraft Corporation 167 Strikemaster Mk.80A	EEP/JP/4096	R Saudi AF 1130, G-27-296	31. 1.05	S J Davies	(South Grove, Rotherham)	29. 7.09P
G-CDHC	Slingsby T 67C Firefly	2081	PH-SGC	20. 1.05	N J Morgan	Tatenhill	28. 4.09E
			(PH-SBC), G-7-138				
G-CDHD	Balony Kubicek BB22 Balloon (Hot Air)	342	OK-0342	22. 2.05	R C Franklin	Aylesbury	27. 9.09E
G-CDHE	Best Off Sky Ranger 912(2)	SKRxxxx500		26. 1.05	E Clayton tr Barton Syndicate	Barton	5. 7.08P
	(Built S Owen - pr.no.BMAA HB/412)			(Overturned on landing at Crosland Moor 3. 5.08 causing extensive damage)				
G-CDHF	Piper PA-30 Twin Comanche B	30-1111	LX-AML	17. 2.05	Raid International (Guernsey) Ltd		
			F-BJCC, N8005Y			Le Plessis-Bellville, France	19. 6.09E
G-CDHG	Mainair Sports Pegasus Quik	8092		21. 2.05	T W Pelan	Balgrummo Steading, Bonnybank	13. 5.08P
G-CDHH	Robinson R44 Raven II	10660		4. 3.05	Forest Fencing Ltd t/a Abwood Homes		
						(Newcastle, County Wicklow)	28. 5.09E

G-CDHK	Lindstrand LBL 330A Balloon (Hot Air)	1022		9. 2.05	Skyview Ballooning tr Kent Ballooning *"Norfolk Jumbo"*
					Ashford 27. 1.09E
G-CDHL	Lindstrand LBL 330A Balloon (Hot Air)	1028		9. 2.05	Richard Nash Cars Ltd *"Richard Nash"* Norwich 27. 1.10E
G-CDHN	Lindstrand LBL 317A Balloon (Hot Air)	1027		6. 4.05	Aerosaurus Balloons Ltd *(Aerosaurus Balloons titles)*
					Exeter 10. 9.09E
G-CDHO	Raj Hamsa X'Air 133(1)	902		8. 2.05	J D Aitchison and J Jore Damyn's Hall, Upminster 22.11.06P
	(Built W E Corps - pr.no.BMAA HB/408)				
G-CDHP	Lindstrand LBL 150A Balloon (Hot Air)	754	G-OHRH	11. 2.05	Floating Sensations Ltd Llandeilo 1. 6.09E
G-CDHR	Comco Ikarus C42 FB80	0502-6652		21. 2.05	Airbourne Aviation Ltd Popham 18. 2.09P
G-CDHS	Cameron N-90 Balloon (Hot Air)	4367	LX-BIS	10. 3.05	C Moulin Neville le Liene, France 16. 2.09E
G-CDHU	Best Off Sky Ranger 912(2)	SKRxxxx546		22. 2.05	G V Rodgers and A R Parker
	(Built S J Smith - pr.no.BMAA HB/444)				Upfield Farm, Whitson 6.10.08P
G-CDHX	Aeroprakt A22 Foxbat	PFA 317-14297		28. 2.05	N E Stokes and B N Searle
	(Built N E Stokes and B N Searle)				Haughton Farm, Haughton, Ellesmere 22.10.09E
G-CDHY	Cameron Z-90 Balloon (Hot Air)	10675		6. 7.05	D M Roberts Ffairfach, Llanelli 4. 3.09E
G-CDHZ	Nicollier HN.700 Ménestrel II	PFA 217-14163		1. 3.05	G E Whittaker (Formby, Liverpool)
	(Built G E Whittaker)				
G-CDIA	Thruster T 600N 450 Sprint	0051-T600N-111		8. 3.05	A D Tomlins Andreas, Isle of Man 2 12.09P
G-CDIB	Cameron Z-350 Balloon (Hot Air)	10622		11.5.05	Ballooning Network Ltd Southville, Bristol 30. 7.09E
G-CDIF	CAB CAP.10B	302	N126SM	21. 6.05	J D Gordon Shobdon 18. 7.09E
			F-GYKD		
G-CDIG	Evektor EV-97 Eurostar	2004-2208		22. 2.05	M Sanders Ince Blundell 15. 5.09P
	(Built J Cunliffe and A Costello - pr.no.PFA 315-14353)				
G-CDIH	Cameron Z-275 Balloon (Hot Air)	10613		6. 4.05	Bailey Balloons Ltd *(Bailey Balloons titles)*
					Pill, Bristol 30. 8.09E
G-CDIJ	Best Off Sky Ranger 912(2)	SKR0501553		3. 3.05	E B Toulson Baxby Manor, Husthwaite 1. 9.08P
	(Built E B Toulson - pr.no.BMAA HB/445)				
G-CDIK	Cameron Z-120 Balloon (Hot Air)	10698		8. 3.05	Cameron Balloons Ltd *(Cameron Balloons titles)*
					Bristol 2. 1.10E
G-CDIL	Mainair Sports Pegasus Quantum 15-912			21.12.04	G W Hillidge Dunkeswell 12. 2.10P
		8093			
G-CDIM	Robin DR.400-180 Régent	2584		6. 4.05	L R Marks Lasham 29. 4.09E
G-CDIO	Cameron Z-90 Balloon (Hot Air)	10695		28. 4.05	P Oggioni Fossano, Italy 17. 8.09E
G-CDIP	Best Off Sky Ranger 912S(1)	SKR0407507		11. 1.05	M S McCrudden Newtownards 17. 8.09P
	(Built M S McCrudden - pr.no.BMAA HB/429)				
G-CDIR	Mainair Sports Pegasus Quantum 15-912			8. 3.05	A S Turner Dunkeswell 11.11.09P
		8108			
G-CDIS	Cessna 150F	15062718	SE-ETR	23. 5.05	S P Fox *(Operated RAF Marham Flying Club)*
			N11B, N8618G		East Winch 29. 6.09E
G-CDIT	Cameron Z-105 Balloon (Hot Air)	10702		6. 4.05	Bailey Balloons Ltd *(EDF Energy titles)* Pill, Bristol 31. 8.09E
G-CDIU	Best Off Sky Ranger 912S(1)	SKR0401405		15. 3.05	C P Dawes and J English Darley Moor, Ashbourne 4. 9.08P
	(Built C P Dawes and R A Budd - pr.no.BMAA HB/376)				
G-CDIV	Lindstrand LBL 90A Balloon (Hot Air)	1021		18. 3.05	The Packhouse Ltd *"Packhouse Antiques"*
					Tongham 2. 9.09E
G-CDIX	Comco Ikarus C42 FB100	0504-6669		20. 4.05	Assured Quality Catering Mangement Services Ltd
					Stoke Golding 6. 5.09P
G-CDIY	Evektor EV-97A Eurostar	2004.21.27		30.12.04	J M Grunwell and G M Laurence (Barnstable) 26. 3.09P
	(Built G R Pritchard - pr.no.PFA 315-14345)				
G-CDIZ	Reality Escapade 912(1)	JAESC 0033		7. 1.05	E G Bishop and E N Dunn
	(Built E G Bishop and E N Dunn - pr.no.BMAA HB/393)				Dunkery, Wootton Courtenay, Minehead 9. 6.09P
G-CDJB	Van's RV-4	1270	N21RP	21. 1.05	W D Garlick and R J Napp Brock Farm, Billericay 18. 2.09P
	(Built T A Rudisill and R G Pettyjohn)				
G-CDJC	Best Off Sky Ranger 912(2)	SKRxxxx540		16. 3.05	J L A Campbell Dunkeswell
	(Built J L A Campbell - pr.no.BMAA HB/440)				*(Noted 10.08)*
G-CDJD	ICP MXP-740 Savannah Jabiru(1)	03-05-51-209		22. 3.05	D W Mullin Hawarden
	(Built D W Mullin)				*(Pr.no.BMAA HB/321)*
G-CDJE	Thruster T 600N 450 Sprint	0053-T600N-112		24. 3.05	K R Ford Wickenby 14. 4.09P
G-CDJF	Flight Design CT2K	03-07-04-35		8. 7.05	P A James Redhill 7. 7.08P
	(Assembled Mainair Sports Ltd with (official) c/n 8104: now reported by P&M Aviation as c/n 8005)				
G-CDJG	Zenair CH.601UL Zodiac	PFA 162A-14374		9. 3.05	D Garcia Moscow, Galston 29. 2.08P
	(Built J Garcia)				
G-CDJI	UltraMagic M-120 Balloon (Hot Air)	120/12		17. 5.05	The Ballooning Business Ltd *(Zirtec titles)*
					Walcote, Alcester 20. 2.09E
G-CDJJ	IAV Bacau Yakovlev Yak-52	899912	LY-AQI	26. 5.05	J J Miles *"JM"* Shoreham 9. 7.09P
			HA-HUY, LY-AFR, 99 (yellow) DOSAAF		
G-CDJK	Comco Ikarus C42 FB80	0504-6666		26. 4.05	Cornish Aviation Ltd Davidstow Moor 25. 4.09P
G-CDJL	Avtech Jabiru J400	0xxx		4. 2.05	J Gardiner and R Holden-White (Aberdeen) 21. 1.10P
	(Built T R Sinclair - pr.no.PFA 325-14215)				
G-CDJM	Zenair CH.601XL Zodiac	6-9593		30.12.04	S A Rennison (Boroughbridge) 26. 4.09P
	(Built T J Adams-Lewis, pr. no PFA 162B-14303)				
G-CDJN	Rotary Air Force RAF 2000 GTX-SE			11. 3.05	D J North (Andover) 15. 8.08P
	(Built D J North)	PFA G/13-1363			
G-CDJO	de Havilland DH.82A (Aust) Tiger Moth	915	VH-BGH (2)	11. 4.05	D Dal Bon *(Noted 8.06)*
	(Built de Havilland Aircraft Pty Ltd)		VH-BGA, A17-492		Ventfield Farm, Horton-cum-Studley,Oxford
G-CDJP	Best Off Sky Ranger 912(2)	SKRxxxx501		18. 1.05	J S Potts Hunterston Farm, Stair 3. 9.08P
	(Built J S Potts - pr.no.BMAA HB/435) (Tailwheel u/c)				
G-CDJR	Evektor EV-97 teamEurostar UK	2318		24. 3.05	P G Gale t/a W J Gale and Son
					Edington Hill, Keevil 15. 3.09P
G-CDJT	Aérospatiale SA.341G Gazelle 1	1509	N401S	19. 8.05	Simlot Ltd Oxton, Nottingham 30.10.09E
G-CDJU	CASA 1-131E Jungmann Series 1000	1078	OO-OLE	25. 8.05	B Roemer *(As "OO-OLE" and "E3B-379")*
			EC-DKV, Spanish AF E3B-379		Strandhill, Sligo, County Sligo 19.12.07P
G-CDJV	Beech A36 Bonanza	E-951	HB-EJP	27. 4.05	Atlantic Bridge Aviation Ltd Lydd 1. 7.09E
			D-EICH, N4296S		

Reg	Type	C/n	Prev id	Date	Owner/Operator	Location	Date
G-CDJW	Van's RV-7	PFA 323-14045		17. 3.05	J B Shaw	Full Sutton	3.10.09P
	(Built D J Williams)						
G-CDJX	Cameron N-56 Balloon (Hot Air)	10715		6. 4.05	Cameron Balloons Ltd *(Cameron Balloons titles)*	Bristol	30. 9.09E
G-CDJY	Cameron C-80 Balloon (Hot Air)	10677		16. 5.05	British Airways PLC	West Drayton	28. 5.09E
G-CDKA	SAAB-Scania 2000	2000-006	SE-006 HB-IZC, SE-006	10. 3.05	Air Kilroe Ltd t/a Eastern Airways	Norwich	9. 3.09E
	(Aberdeen City and Shire titles and artwork)						
G-CDKB	SAAB-Scania 2000	2000-032	SE-032 LY-SBG, HB-IZQ, SE-032	22. 4.05	Air Kilroe Ltd t/a Eastern Airways	Humberside	21. 4.09E
G-CDKC	Raj Hamsa X'Air 582(3)	531		14. 4.05	F G Walker	(Hawarden)	3 .4.09P
	(Built G Walker - pr.no.BMAA HB/159)						
G-CDKE	Rans S-6-ES Coyote II	0603.1506		9. 5.05	J E Holloway	(Saltash)	4.12.09P
	(Built J E Holloway - pr.no.PFA 204-14119)						
G-CDKF	Reality Escapade 912(1)	JAESC 0035		15. 2.05	N Forman	Barton	22. 1.08P
	(Built P J Little - pr.no.BMAA HB/389)						
G-CDKH	Best Off Sky Ranger 912S(1)	SKRxxxxx545		14. 4.05	C Lenaghan	Crossmaglen, NI	17. 8.09P
	(Built W P Byrne - pr.no.BMAA HB/448)						
G-CDKI	Best Off Sky Ranger 912S(1)	SKR0209242		15. 4.05	J M Hucker	Broadmeadow Farm, Hereford	6.12.09P
	(Built J M Hucker - pr.no.BMAA HB/434)						
G-CDKJ	Silence Twister	PFA 329-14336		5. 5.05	European Land Solutions Ltd	Radley Farm, Hungerford	29. 8.08P
	(Built A Stansfield)						
G-CDKK	Mainair Sports Pegasus Quik	8097		4. 3.05	P M Knight	Elm Farm, Wickford	23. 4.09P
G-CDKL	Reality Escapade 912(1)	JAESC 0023		21. 4.05	D Harker	Morgansfield, Fishburn	
	(Built D Harker - pr.no.BMAA HB/359) (Change of Type 9.07)						
G-CDKM	Mainair Sports Pegasus Quik	8091		28. 1.05	P Lister	Ince Blundell	26. 4.09P
G-CDKN	ICP MXP-740 Savannah Jabiru(4)	04-05-51-293		7. 4.05	N R Benson	Biggar	12.10.08P
	(Built F McGuigan - pr.no.BMAA HB/397)						
G-CDKO	ICP MXP-740 Savannah Jabiru(4)	04-01-51-274		25. 4.05	C Jones and B Hunter	Barton	5. 9.08P
	(Built C Jones and B Hunter - pr.no.BMAA HB/402).						
G-CDKP	Avtech Jabiru UL-D Calypso	0636		18. 2.05	Rochester Microlights Ltd Damyn's Hall, Upminster		27. 3.09P
G-CDKR	Diamond DA.42 Twin Star	42.029	(D-GAAA)	28. 6.05	R H Butterfield and A M Dyson t/a Principle Aircraft		17. 8.09P
	(Operated Sheffield City Flying School)					Sandtoft	
G-CDKT	Boeing 737-683	28303	SE-DNU N1786B	18. 5.05	Globespan Airways Ltd t/a Flyglobespan.com	Edinburgh	18. 5.09E
G-CDKX	Best Off Sky Ranger J2.2(1)	SKR0404474		23. 5.05	M S Ashby	(Kingsbridge)	2. 4.09P
	(Built M S Ashby - pr.no.BMAA HB/395)						
G-CDKY	Robinson R44 Raven	1470		11. 3.05	Bernard Hunter Ltd Gilmerton Helipad, Edinburgh		7. 4.09E
G-CDKZ	Thunder Ax10-160 Series 2 Balloon (Hot Air)	10648		13. 4.05	D J Head	Newbury	24. 4.09E
G-CDLA	Mainair Sports Pegasus Quik	8102		4. 4.05	C R Stevens	(Egerton, Ashford)	24. 4.08P
G-CDLB	Cameron Z-120 Balloon (Hot Air)	10672		8. 6.05	Interbrew UK Ltd *(Bass titles)*	Luton	31. 8.09E
G-CDLC	CASA 1-131E Jungmann Series 2000	2095	N46923 Spanish AF E3B-494	10. 6.05	R D and M Loder *(As "E3B-494:81-47" in Spanish AF c/s)* Lower Upham Farm, Chiseldon		8. 8.07P
	(C/n 2095 is quoted also for Jungmann D-EEGN ex-Spanish AF E3B-351)						
G-CDLD	Mainair Sports Pegasus Quik	8106		16. 3.05	W Williams	Headon Farm, Retford	24. 3.08P
G-CDLE	Reality Escapade 912(1)	JAESC 0005		12. 5.05	R A J Paddock	Eastbach Farm, Coleford	16.12.09P
	(Built R A J Paddock - pr.no.BMAA HB/317)						
G-CDLG	Best Off Sky Ranger 912(2)	SKRxxxxx457		19. 5.05	D J Saunders	(Ashdon, Saffron Walden)	7. 6.09P
	(Built D J Saunders - pr.no.BMAA HB/387)						
G-CDLI	Airco DH.9	1414	E8894	31. 5.05	Aero Vintage Ltd *(On rebuild as "E8894" 2007)*	(Northiam, Rye)	
	(Built Aircraft Maufacturing Co Ltd 1918) (Siddeley Puma)						
G-CDLJ	Mainair Sports Pegasus Quik	8111		9. 5.05	M L Johnston	Graveley Hall Farm, Graveley	8. 5.09P
G-CDLK	Best Off Sky Ranger 912S(1)	SKRxxxx570		11. 7.05	L E Cowling and A P Chapman	Hawksbridge Farm, Oxenhope	13.12.09P
	(Built L E Cowling and A P Chapman - pr.no.BMAA HB/452)						
G-CDLL	Dyn'Aéro MCR-01 ULC	PFA 301B-14348		23. 3.05	D Cassidy	(Canterbury)	24. 6.09P
	(Built D Cassidy)						
G-CDLR	ICP MXP-740 Savannah Jabiru(4)	04-06-51-292		9. 5.05	R Locke *(Noted 8.05)*	Headon Farm, Retford	
	(Built R Locke - pr.no.BMAA HB/399)						
G-CDLS	Avtech Jabiru J400	Jxxxx		9. 3.05	G M Geary	Morgansfield, Fishburn	9.10.09P
	(Built G M Geary - pr.no.PFA 325-14319)						
G-CDLT	Raytheon Hawker 800XP	258710	N37010	27. 5.05	Gama Aviation Ltd	Farnborough	26. 5.09E
G-CDLV	Lindstrand LBL 105A Balloon (Hot Air)	1050		1. 7.05	Smartfusion SV Ltd *(Nokia titles)*	London SW8	26. 6.09E
G-CDLW	Zenair CH.601UL Zodiac	PFA 162-13944		23. 6.05	W A Stephen	Popham	21.12.07P
	(Built W A Stephen)						
G-CDLY	Cirrus SR20	1519	N54212	10. 6.05	Partside Aviation Ltd	Shobdon	14. 6.09E
G-CDLZ	Mainair Sports Pegasus Quantum 15-912	8113		19. 4.05	C M Jeffrey and J L Dalgetty	Insch	18. 4.09P
G-CDMA	Piper PA-28-151 Cherokee Warrior	28-7415650	OY-TFL SE-GBV	3. 5.05	A Cabre	(Hainford, Norwich)	3. 9.09E
G-CDMC	Cameron Z-105 Balloon (Hot Air)	10671		14. 3.05	The Balloon Company Ltd t/a First Flight *(A-Gas titles)* Langford, Bristol		1. 4.09E
G-CDMD	Robin DR.500-200i Président	42		14.10.05	P R Liddle	Rochester	13.11.09E
	(Officially regd as DR.400-500)						
G-CDME	Van's RV-7	PFA 323-14151		13. 5.05	M W Elliott	Shenstone	8. 8.09P
	(Built M W Elliott)						
G-CDMF	Van's RV-9A	PFA 320-14157		29. 6.05	S R Neale and T R Donovan	Oaksey Park	11. 4.09P
	(Built J Shanley)						
G-CDMG	Robinson R22 Beta	1874	N2305J	7. 4.05	Heli Aitch Be Ltd	Redhill	1. 8.08E
G-CDMH	Cessna P210N Pressurized Centurion	P21000131	LX-ACP N33CP, C-GRAT, N4901P	25. 7.05	J G Hinley	Wellesbourne Mountford	11.12.09E
G-CDMJ	Mainair Sports Pegasus Quik	8107		17. 3.05	J Rodgers	Barton	28. 4.09P

Reg	Type	C/n	Prev id	Date	Owner	Location	Expiry
G-CDMK	Montgomerie-Bensen B 8MR						
	(Built P Rentell)	PFA G/01A-1358		8. 7.05	P Rentell	(St Clement, Truro)	
G-CDML	P&M Pegasus Quik	8127		15. 7.05	H T Beattie	Perth	18. 8.08P
G-CDMM	Cessna 172P Skyhawk	17275124	N55161	8. 7.05	Cristal Air Ltd	North Weald	13. 2.09E
G-CDMN	Van's RV-9	PFA 320-14108		8. 6.05	G J Smith	(Manton)	29. 5.09P
	(Built G J Smith)						
G-CDMO	Cameron S Can-100 Balloon (Hot Air)	2178	OE-ZCU	22. 7.05	A Schneider	Borken, Germany	28.10.09E
			OE-CZU				
G-CDMP	Best Off Sky Ranger 912S(1)	SKRxxxxx600		8. 7.05	J A Charlton	(Ashbourne)	24. 4.09P
	(Built J A Charlton - pr.no.BMAA HB/457)						
G-CDMS	Comco Ikarus C42 FB80	0506-6689		19. 7.05	Airbourne Aviation Ltd	Popham	18. 7.09P
G-CDMT	Zenair CH.601XL Zodiac	PFA 162B-14359		17. 6.05	L Hogan	Glenrothes	16. 4.09P
	(Built D McCormack) (Tri-cycle u/c)						
G-CDMU	P&M Pegasus Quik	8121		19. 8.05	T M Bolton and S D Jones	Barton	6. 9.08P
G-CDMV	Best Off Sky Ranger 912S(1)	SKRxxxxx575		28. 7.05	D O'Keeffe and K E Rutter	London Colney	21.11.09P
	(Built D O'Keeffe, K E Rutter and A J Clarke - pr.no.BMAA HB/455)						
G-CDMX	Piper PA-28-161 Warrior II	28-7916006	PH-SBY	4. 8.05	S Collins	(Barnsley)	13. 9.09E
			N39746				
G-CDMY	Piper PA-28-161 Warrior II	28-7916007	PH-SBZ	25. 8.05	J S Develin and Z Islam	Shoreham	2.12.09E
			N30768				
G-CDMZ	P&M Pegasus Quik	8116		3. 8.05	R Solomons	(Pembury, Tunbridge Wells)	7. 8.09P
G-CDNA	Grob G109B	6324	D-KEOJ	28. 7.05	J W Sage tr Army Gliding Association	Trenchard Lines, Upavon	4. 9.09E
G-CDND	Gulfstream American GA-7 Cougar GA7-0057		(OY-GAV)	19. 7.05	C J Chaplin	Redhill	13. 3.10E
			G-CDND, OY-GAV, (OY-SVO), LN-ALY, OY-GAV, N770GA				
G-CDNE	Best Off Sky Ranger 912S(1)	SKRxxxxx574		28. 7.05	J A Kentzer	(Sheffield)	14. 9.08P
	(Built G S Gee-Carter and A Dunne - pr.no.BMAA HB/454)						
G-CDNF	Aero Designs Pulsar 3	PFA 202-13253		28. 4.05	D Ringer	Perth	29. 6.09P
	(Built D Ringer)						
G-CDNG	Evektor EV-97 teamEurostar UK	2319		18. 5.05	S M Hillyer-Jones	Shobdon	6. 6.09P
	(Built Cosmik Aviation)						
G-CDNH	P&M Pegasus Quik	8126		2. 8.05	C D Andrews	Swinford, Rugby	16. 9.08P
G-CDNI	Evektor EV-97 teamEurostar UK	2321		11. 7.05	D Parsons tr G-CDNI Group	(Didcot)	6. 8.09P
G-CDNJ	Colomban MC-15 Cri-Cri	69	F-PEAH	16. 6.05	J Johnston tr Cri Cri Group	(Knocklong, Ireland)	
	(Built E Ahlrichs)						
G-CDNK	Learjet Model 45	45-280	N40079	17.10.05	Air Partner Private Jets Ltd	Biggin Hill	16.10.09E
G-CDNM	Evektor EV-97 teamEurostar UK	2407		5. 8.05	H C Lowther	(Penrith)	24. 8.08P
G-CDNO	Westland SA.341B Gazelle AH.1	1385	XX432	23. 9.05	Falcon Aviation Ltd (As "XX432")	Deer Park Farm, Babcary	
G-CDNP	Evektor EV-97 teamEurostar UK	2320		13. 6.05	B R Pearson tr Eaglescott Eurostar Group	Eaglescott	27. 6.08P
G-CDNR	Comco Ikarus C42 FB100	0507-6696		12. 8.05	M T Sheelan	(Carlingford, Ireland)	11. 8.08P
G-CDNS	Westland SA.341B Gazelle AH.1	1614	XZ321	23. 9.05	Falcon Aviation Ltd	Bourne Park, Hurstbourne Tarrant	
G-CDNT	Zenair CH.601XL Zodiac	PFA 162B-14360		17. 6.05	W McCormack	Glenrothes	14. 8.08P
	(Built W McCormack)						
G-CDNW	Comco Ikarus C42 FB UK	PFA 322-14426		6. 7.05	W Gabbott	Barton	10. 4.09P
	(Built W Gabbott)						
G-CDNY	Avtech Jabiru SP-470	xxxx		4. 8.05	G Lucey	Popham	13. 1.10P
	(Built G Lucey - pr.no.PFA 274B-14020)						
G-CDNZ	UltraMagic M-120 Balloon (Hot Air)	120/08	D-OHFJ	12. 8.05	R H Etherington	Montisi, Siena, Italy	17. 8.09E
G-CDOA	Evektor EV-97 teamEurostar UK	2506		12. 9.05	T K Duffy	Ellough, Beccles	11. 9.08P
G-CDOB	Cameron C-90 Balloon (Hot Air)	10756		10. 8.05	G D and S M Philpot	Hemel Hempstead	27. 7.09E
G-CDOC	P&M Aviation Quik GT450	8123		20.10.05	D M Broom	Sutton Meadows	1. 3.08P
G-CDOD	Aviat A-1B Husky	2292	(D-E)	30. 8.05	K Anspach	Kempten, Germany	16.11.09E
			G-CDOD, N322PA				
G-CDOG	Lindstrand LBL Dog SS Balloon (Hot Air)	938		7. 1.04	ABC Flights Ltd "Churchill"	Clapton-in-Gordano, Bristol	21.10.09E
G-CDOI	Cameron Z-90 Balloon (Hot Air)	10765		12. 8.05	Cameron Balloons Ltd (Cameron Balloons titles)	Bristol	18.12.09E
G-CDOJ	Schweizer 269C-1 (Schweizer 300)	0218	N86G	1.11.05	Sterling Helicopters Ltd	Norwich	19.11.09E
G-CDOK	Comco Ikarus C42 FB100	0509-6757		4.10.05	M Aviation Ltd	Old Sarum	11.10.08P
G-CDOM	Mainair Sports Pegasus Quik	8118		20. 5.05	J A Dearn tr G-CDOM Flying Group	Barton	4. 8.09P
G-CDON	Piper PA-28-161 Warrior II	28-8216185	N8254D	24. 5.88	A Logan and A Martin tr G-CDON Group	Nottingham-East Midlands	1. 6.09E
G-CDOO	P&M Pegasus Quantum 15-912	8130		2. 8.05	O C Harding Park Hall Farm, Mapperley, Ilkeston		10. 9.08P
G-CDOP	P&M Pegasus Quik	8129		16. 8.05	H A Duthie and R C Tadman	Perth	31. 5.08P
G-CDOR	Mainair Blade	1372-0805-7-W1167		8. 9.05	J D Otter	Wyberton	4.10.06P
G-CDOT	Comco Ikarus C42 FB100	0505-6678		24. 6.05	A C Anderson	Dunkeswell	24. 6.08P
G-CDOV	Best Off Sky Ranger 912(2)	SKRxxxx606		5. 9.05	B Richardson	Eshott	3. 4.08P
	(Built B Richardson - pr.no.BMAA HB/459)						
G-CDOY	Robin DR.400-180R Remorqueur	1206	D-EGRY	25.10.05	Lasham Gliding Society Ltd	Lasham	14. 1.10E
			SE-GRY				
G-CDOZ	Evektor EV-97 Eurostar	2005.25.07		2. 9.05	J P McCall	Jenkin's Farm, Navestock	2. 7.09P
	(Built J P McCall - pr.no.PFA 315-14437)						
G-CDPA	Alpi Pioneer 300	17		26. 8.05	N D White and N G Dowding	(Northampton and Towcester)	11.11.08P
	(Built A R Lloyd - pr.no.PFA 330-14415)						
G-CDPB	Best Off Sky Ranger 582(1)	SKRxxxxx423		24.10.05	N S Bishop	Manor Farm, Fencott	7. 7.08P
	(Built N S Bishop - pr.no.BMAA HB/385)						
G-CDPC	Cameron C-90 Balloon (Hot Air)	10754		14. 3.07	Cameron Balloons Ltd	Bristol	
G-CDPD	Mainair Sports Pegasus Quik	8051		5. 8.04	P C Davis	Weston Zoyland	15. 8.09P
G-CDPE	Best Off Sky Ranger 912(2)	SKRxxxxx382		13. 9.05	P A Mercer	Tarn Farm, Cockerham	17. 5.09P
	(Built P A Mercer - pr.no.BMAA HB/432)						

G-CDPG	Crofton Auster V J/1A	PFA 000-325		11. 8.05	P and T Groves	(Lee-on-Solent)	
	(Built P Groves aka Crofton Aeroplane Service)						
G-CDPH	TLAC RL5A LW Sherwood Ranger ST			23. 9.05	K F Crumplin	Henstridge	20. 5.09P
	(Built K F Crumplin)	PFA 237-12920					
G-CDPI	Zenair CH.601UL Zodiac	PFA 162A-14406		24. 6.05	M J Kaye	(Swinton, Mexborough)	
	(Built M J Kaye)						
G-CDPJ	Van's RV-8	80661		5. 5.05	P Johnson	Morgansfield, Fishburn	2.11.08P
	(Built P Johnson - pr.no.PFA 303-13295)						
G-CDPL	Evektor EV-97 teamEurostar UK	2207		13. 1.05	C D H Garrison	Sutton Meadows	12. 1.10P
G-CDPM	Jurca MJ.100 Spitfire	PFA 130-12007		22. 9.05	J E D Rogerson *(As "X4683 EB-N" 41 Sqdn)*		
	(Built J E D Rogerson) (80% scale replica Spitfire) (Walter Lom 6-cylinder 250hp inline) (Substantially complete 5.07)						
						(East Howle, Ferryhill)	
G-CDPN	UltraMagic S-105 Balloon (Hot Air)	105/135		3. 1.06	D J MacInnes	Britford, Salisbury	3. 1.10E
G-CDPP	Comco Ikarus C42 FB100 VLA			22. 9.05	H M Owen	(Foelgastell, Llanelli)	21. 7.09P
	(Built H M Owen)	PFA 322-14423					
G-CDPR	Piper PA-18 Super Cub 95	18-3202	OY-AVT	17.11.05	J P Hibble	(St Peter Port, Guernsey)	12. 3.11S
		D-ELFT, OL-L05 Belgian Army, L-128, 53-4802					
G-CDPS	Raj Hamsa X'Air Falcon 133(1)	919		31. 8.05	P R Smith *(Noted 11.06)*	(Eccleston, Chorley)	
	(Built P R Smith - pr.no.BMAA HB/332)						
G-CDPT	Boeing 767-319ER	29388	ZK-NCN	6. 4.06	Globespan Airways Ltd t/a Flyglobespan.com		
						Edinburgh	16. 4.09E
G-CDPV	Piper PA-34-200T Seneca II	34-8070086	PH-MRM	14.10.05	Partside Aviation Ltd *(Operated Willowair Flying Club)*		
		D-GIGF, N99GN, C-FJRN, N35717				Southend	19.12.09E
G-CDPW	P&M Pegasus Quantum 15-912	8138		14.10.05	T P R Wright		
						Ilkeston	20.10.08P
G-CDPX	Schleicher ASH 25Mi	25256		5. 1.06	P Pozerskis and M C Costin *"260"*		
	(Officially regd as ASH 25M) (Diamond IAE50R-AA)					Husbands Bosworth	6. 4.09E
G-CDPY	Europa Aviation Europa	303		8. 3.00	A Burrill	(Calcot, Reading)	
	(Built A Burrill - pr.no.PFA 247-13029) (Monowheel u/c)						
G-CDPZ	Flight Design CT2K	03-06-03-28		23. 6.05	M E Henwick	Popham	22. 6.09P
	(Assembled Mainair Sports Ltd with (official) c/n 8124 but thought to be c/n 8104)						
G-CDRC	Cessna 182Q Skylane	18267085	N97418	2. 9.05	A G Hill t/a R S Hill and Sons	Bournemouth	31. 1.09E
G-CDRD	AirBorne XT912-B-Streak III-B	XT912-096		24.10.05	Fly NI Ltd	Tarsan Lane, Portadown	17.10.07P
	(Wing s/n SB3-80)						
G-CDRF	Cameron Z-90 Balloon (Hot-Air)	10763		20. 1.06	Chalmers Ballong Corps	Goteborg, Sweden	3. 4.09E
G-CDRG	P&M Pegasus Quik	8137		19.10.05	R J Gabriel	Yatesbury	20.10.08P
G-CDRH	Thruster T 600N	0056-T600N-114		30. 6.05	A Cope and G L Pritt	Carlisle	12. 7.09P
G-CDRI	Cameron O-105 Balloon (Hot Air)	10794		22.12.05	R J Fuller tr Snapdragon Balloon Group		
						Godalming	27. 2.09E
G-CDRJ	Air Création Tanarg 912S/iXess 15	FLT003		23.11.05	J H Hayday	Plaistows Farm, St Albans	4. 6.09P
	(Built J H Hayday - pr.no.BMAA HB/464 being Flylight kit comprising Trike s/n T05071 and Wing s/n A05148-5135)						
G-CDRM	Van's RV-7A	PFA 323-14203		26. 7.05	R A Morris	Hall Farm, Shenstone	22.10.07P
	(Built R A Morris)	*(Nose gear dug in after landing Croft Farm, north of Gloucester 9. 6.07: overturned causing substantial damage)*						
G-CDRN	Cameron Z-225 Balloon (Hot-Air)	10750		25. 4.06	Balloon School (International) Ltd		
						Colhook Common, Petworth	8. 5.09E
G-CDRO	Comco Ikarus C42 FB80	0507-6750		17. 8.05	Airbourne Aviation Ltd	Popham	16. 8.09P
G-CDRP	Comco Ikarus C42 FB80	0509-6762		26.10.05	D S Parker	Carlisle	26.10.08P
G-CDRR	P&M Pegasus Quantum 15-912	8134		12. 9.05	A W Buchan	Knapthorpe Lodge, Caunton	13. 9.08P
G-CDRS	Rotorway Executive 162F	6956		30. 8.05	R C Swann	(Blofield, Norwich)	
	(Built R C Swann)						
G-CDRT	P&M Pegasus Quik	8131		22.11.05	R Tetlow	(Uppermill, Oldham)	7. 5.08P
G-CDRU	CASA 1-131E Jungmann	2321	EC-DRU	19. 1.90	P Cunniff *"Yen a Bon"*	White Waltham	19. 5.09P
			Spanish AF E3B-530				
G-CDRV	Van's RV-9A	PFA 320-14186		29. 6.05	R J Woodford	(Danbury, Chelmsford)	
	(Built R J Woodford)						
G-CDRW	P&M Pegasus Quik	8141		21. 9.05	G Fearon	Oxton, Nottingham	28. 1.09P
G-CDRX	Cameron Z-275 Balloon (Hot Air)	10773		25. 4.06	Balloon School (International) Ltd *"British School of Ballooning"*		
						Colhook Common, Petworth	27. 5.09E
G-CDRY	Comco Ikarus C42 FB100 VLA			26. 9.05	R J Mitchell	Tingwall	
	(Built R J Mitchell)	PFA 322-14448					
G-CDRZ	Balony Kubicek BB22 Balloon (Hot Air)	395		6. 3.06	Club Amatori Del Volo In Mongolfiera		
						Macherio, Italy	10. 9.09E
G-CDSA	P&M Pegasus Quik	8144		9.11.05	D J Cornelius	Lee-on-Solent	24.11.09P
G-CDSB	Alpi Pioneer 200	PFA334-14443		4.11.04	T A and P M Pugh	Shobdon	12. 3.09P
	(Built T W Skinner)						
G-CDSC	Scheibe SF25C Falke	44643	D-KIEX	2.12.05	I K G Mitchell tr Devon & Somerset Motorglider Group		
	(Rotax 912-S)					North Hill	9. 3.09E
G-CDSD	Alpi Pioneer 300	PFA 330-14439		3.11.05	J A R Blick	Upper Greenhill Farm, Coalville	5. 2.09P
	(Built F A Cavaciuti)						
G-CDSF	Diamond DA.40D Star	D4.190	OE-VPU	24. 2.06	Flying Time Ltd	Shoreham	13. 4.09E
	(Thierlert TAE 125, marked as "DA40TDi")						
G-CDSG	Sud-Aviation SA.316B Alouette III	14	Romanian AF 0711.11.05		G Snook	(Leeds)	
	(Built ICA-Brasov as type IAR.316B)						
G-CDSH	ICP MXP-740 Savannah Jabiru(5)			9.11.05	J P Bell	Eshott	25. 9.08P
		05-07-51-413					
	(Built S Whittaker and P J Wilson, pr.no.BMAA HB/463)						
G-CDSI	Avtech Jabiru J400	0xxx		17.11.05	G H Gilmour-White	(Thorverton, Exeter)	9. 4.09P
	(Built G H Gilmour-White - pr.no.PFA 325-14183)						
G-CDSJ	Sud-Aviation SA.316B Alouette III	20	Rom AF12	17.11.05	S Atherton *(Noted 6.07)*	(Tadcaster)	
	(Built ICA-Brasov as "IAR.316B")						
G-CDSK	Reality Escapade Jabiru(3)	UKESC 0004		15.11.05	R H Sear	(Lincoln)	27. 2.08P
	(Built R H Sear - pr.no.BMAA HB/469)						
G-CDSM	P&M Aviation Quik GT450	8146		20.10.05	A Munro	Willingale	18.12.07P

Reg	Type	C/n	Prev id	Date	Owner/Operator	Location	Expiry
G-CDSN	Raj Hamsa X'Air Jabiru(3)	1042		16.11.05	S P Heard	(Cheshunt)	17.10.09P
	(Built G W Cole - pr.no.BMAA HB/472)						
G-CDSO	Thruster T 600N 450	1051-T600N-115		9.12.05	W G Reynolds	(Overstrand, Cromer)	2. 7.09P
G-CDSR	Learjet Model 45	45-286	N50126	30. 1.06	Air Partner Private Jets Ltd	Biggin Hill	30. 1.10E
G-CDSS	P&M Pegasus Quik	8142		16.11 05	P A Bass	(Marsden, Huddersfield)	31. 5.09P
G-CDST	UltraMagic N-250 Balloon (Hot Air)	250/37		27. 7.05	S A Towney t/a Sky High Leisure	Ellesmere Port	26. 6.09E
G-CDSU	Robinson R22 Beta	3464	EI-MUR	15.12.05	C Poundes	Brook Farm, Hulcote	17. 1.09E
G-CDSV	Aérospatiale AS.332L Super Puma	2058	N171EH	1.12.05	CHC Helicopters International Inc (Noted 12.05)		
			C-GSLA, PT-HRM, C-GSLA			Aberdeen	
G-CDSW	Comco Ikarus C42 FB80	0511-6772		23.11.05	P J Barton	Longacre Farm, Sandy	14. 2.09P
G-CDSX	English Electric Canberra T Mk.4	71367	WJ874	27. 3.06	Aviation Heritage Ltd	Coventry	10. 2.09P
	(As "VN799" to represent the A1 Canberra prototype)						
G-CDSY	Robinson R44 Raven	1534		3. 1.06	E Meegan		
						Bloomfield , Castle Blayney, County Monaghan	10. 2.09E
G-CDSZ	Diamond DA.42 Twin Star	42.084		1. 3.06	Aviation Services Ltd	Ronaldsway	23. 3.09E
G-CDTA	Evektor EV-97 teamEurostar UK	2509		19.10.05	R D Stein	Redlands, Swindon	22.10.08P
G-CDTB	P&M Pegasus Quantum 15-912	8136		6.10.05	D W Corbett		
						Cottage Farm, Norton Juxta	4.10.08P
G-CDTC	P&M Pegasus Quantum 15-912	8135		12.10.05	C W J Davis	(Swadlincote)	4.10.08P
G-CDTD	Eurocopter AS.350B2 Ecureuil	9072	F-GUAZ	20. 2.06	Aviamax GmbH	Hannover, Germany	12. 3.09E
			F-WQED,F-WW..				
G-CDTE	Tecnam P2002-JF Sierra	029		23. 1.06	Tecnam Gen. Aviation Ltd	Clench Common	18. 3.09E
G-CDTG	Diamond DA.42 Twin Star	42.083		6. 2.06	Twinstar Ltd	Liverpool-John Lennon	9. 3.09E
G-CDTH	Schempp-Hirth Nimbus 4DM	65		7. 7.06	M A V Gatehouse	North Hill	28. 7.09E
G-CDTI	Messerschmitt Bf109E-1	4034		12.12.05	Rare Aero Ltd	(Jersey)	
	(Built Focke-Wulf at Bremen 1939?)						
G-CDTJ	Reality Escapade Jabiru(1)	UKESC 0003		13.12.05	P Anning	Davidstow Moor	30.12.09P
	(Built D Little - pr.no.BMAA HB/461)						
G-CDTL	Avtech Jabiru J400	0xxx		13.12.05	M I Sistern	Sleap	9.11.09P
	(Built M I Sistern - pr.no.PFA 325-14386)						
G-CDTM	Westland Seafire XVII	-	A2054	21.12.05	Seafire Displays Ltd	North Weald	
			A646, SX300				
	(Fuselage off-site, wings under restoration/rebuild and may be incorporated into rebuild of LA564)						
G-CDTO	P&M Aviation Quik GT450	8149		11. 1.06	J R Houston	Balado Bridge	30. 1.08P
G-CDTP	Best Off Sky Ranger 912S(1)	SKRxxxxx617		21.12.05	P M Whittaker	Hawksbridge Farm, Oxenhope	27. 7.08P
	(Built J R S Heaton - pr.no.BMAA HB/475)						
G-CDTR	P&M Aviation Quik GT450	8153		20.12.05	D J Collier t/a Sunfun Group		
						Lower Mountpleasant Farm, Chatteris	2. 1.08P
G-CDTT	ICP MXP-740 Savannah Jabiru(4)			29. 9.05	M J Day	Oak Farm, Woodton	29.10.07P
		04-01-51-273					
	(Built M P Middleton - pr.no.BMAA HB/383)						
G-CDTU	Evektor EV-97 teamEurostar UK	2522		5.1.06	I Shaw tr G-CDTU Group	Arclid Farm, Sandbach	22.12.08P
G-CDTV	Tecnam P2002-EA Sierra	PFA 333-14501		19.1.06	S A Noble	Rayne Hall Farm, Braintree	13. 6.08P
	(Built M Rudd)						
G-CDTX	Reims Cessna F152	F15201662	D-EERU	22.12.05	Z Islam and J S Develin	Blackbushe	15. 6.09E
			N1659C				
G-CDTY	ICP MXP-740 Savannah Jabiru(5)			5. 1.06	D McCormack and Senga Bradie		
		05-09-51-414				Broomhill Farm, West Calder	26. 6.08P
	(Built J N Anyan - pr.no.BMAA HB/467)						
G-CDTZ	Aeroprakt A22 Foxbat	PFA 317-14433		21.12.05	P C Piggott and M E Hughes	Husbands Bosworth	31. 5.08P
	(Built P C Piggott and M E Hughes)						
G-CDUE	Robinson R44 Raven	1549		24. 1.06	Scotia Helicopters Ltd	Cumbernauld	11. 2.09E
G-CDUH	P&M Aviation Quik GT450	8167		14. 2.06	R W Thornborough	Ince Blundell	28. 2.09P
G-CDUJ	Lindstrand LBL 31A Balloon (Hot Air)	1080		27. 1.06	J M Frazer	Holystone, Morpeth	14. 4.09E
G-CDUK	Comco Ikarus C42 FB80	0511-6770		21.11.05	D M Lane	Long Marston	14.12.09P
G-CDUL	Best Off Sky Ranger 912(2)	SKR0506615		23. 1.06	T W Thiele and C D Hogbourne	Radwell	19. 5.09P
	(Built T W Thiele - pr.no.BMAA HB/471)						
G-CDUS	Best Off Sky Ranger 912S(1)	SKR0508643		26. 1.06	C S Robinson	Newtownards	11. 9.08P
	(Built W P Byrne - pr.no.BMAA HB/490)						
G-CDUT	Avtech Jabiru J400	0xxx		2. 2.06	T W and A Pullin	(Barrow-in-Furness)	11. 7.09P
	(Built T W and A Pullin - pr.no.PFA 325-14352)						
G-CDUU	P&M Aviation Quik GT450	8165		16. 3.06	A Rose tr Caunton Charlie Delta Group		
						Knapthorpe Lodge, Caunton	7. 5.09P
G-CDUV	ICP MXP-740 Savannah Jabiru(5)			5. 1. 06	D M Blackman	Rochester	26. 6.08P
		05-09-51-415					
	(Built M Leachman – pr.no.BMAA HB/465)						
G-CDUW	Aeronca C 3	A 517	(F-AZKE)	20. 2.06	N K Geddes South Barnbeth Farm, Bridge of Weir		
			N64765, NC14631				
G-CDUX	Piper PA-32-300 Cherokee Six	32-7340074	EC-DUX	31. 7.02	D J Mason	Ronaldsway	5. 2.10E
			F-BSGY, 5T-TJR, N11C				
G-CDUY	Colt 77A Balloon (Hot Air)	600	D-HIPPO	9. 2.06	G D D Jones tr De Hippo Balloon Group		
			D-WESTFALEN (2)				Tarleton, Preston	21.10.09E
G-CDVA	Best Off Sky Ranger 912(2)	SKR0211247		21.12.05	D C Mole	Enniskillen	27. 7.09P
	(Built R J Hoare - pr.no.BMAA HB/269)						
G-CDVD	Evektor EV-97 Eurostar	PFA 315-14485		6. 1.06	P Ritchie	Glenrothes	6. 3.09P
	(Built G R Pritchard)						
G-CDVF	Rans S-6-ES Coyote II	PFA 204-14464		2. 2.06	S G Beeson	(Stoke-on-Trent)	21. 9.08P
	(Built G P Jones)						
G-CDVG	P&M Pegasus Quik	8152		24. 1.06	C M Lewis	Longacre Farm, Sandy	27. 1.09P
G-CDVH	P&M Pegasus Quantum 15	8166		20. 2.06	M J Hyde	Deenethorpe	21. 8.08P
G-CDVI	Comco Ikarus C42 FB80	0602-6794		13. 3.06	Airbourne Aviation Ltd	Popham	1. 5.09P
G-CDVJ	Montgomerie-Bensen B 8MR PFA G/01A-1355			17. 1.06	D J Martin	Little Rissington	
	(Built D J Martin)						

G-CDVK	ICP MXP-740 Savannah Jabiru(5)			24. 1.06	M Peters	Wing Farm, Longbridge Deverill 25. 9.08P
		05-02-51-372	*(Built M Peters - pr.no.BMAA HB/449)*			
G-CDVL	Alpi Pioneer 300	xxx		27. 1.06	TC Robson and A N Pascoe	Great Massingham 7. 8.08P
	(Built TC Robson and A N Pascoe - pr.no.PFA 330-14379)					
G-CDVN	P&M Aviation Quik GT450	8176		11. 4.06	R E J Pattenden	Rochester 24. 4.09P
G-CDVO	P&M Pegasus Quik	8147		9.12.05	M C Shortman	Broadmeadow Farm, Hereford 12.12.06P
G-CDVR	P&M Aviation Quik GT450	8160		27. 1.06	N H McCorquodale	East Fortune 12. 2.09P
G-CDVS	Europa Aviation Europa XS	364		20. 2.06	J F Lawn	(Holy Cross, Norwich) 21.11.07P
	(Built J F Lawn - pr.no.PFA 247-13217)					
G-CDVT	Van's RV-6	20206	N391DS	7. 2.06	P D Wood	(Leigh, Worcester) 31. 5.09P
	(Built D W Sorrels)					
G-CDVU	Evektor EV-97 teamEurostar UK	2525		13. 3.06	W D Kyle and T J Dowling	Newtownards 1. 4.09P
	(Built Cosmik Aviation)					
G-CDVV	Scottish Aviation Bulldog Series 120/121		9290M	27. 1.06	D M Squires *(As "XX626: 02" and "9290M")*	
		BH120/291	XX626			Wellesbourne Mountford 13. 7.09S
G-CDVX	Republic TP-47G-10-CU Thunderbolt	21953	N47DG	20. 2.06	Patina Ltd *"Little Demon" (As "28476:YJ-X")*.	
	(Built Curtiss-Wright Corporation)		N42354, 42-25068			Duxford
G-CDVZ	P&M Aviation Quik GT450	8151		30. 1.06	A K Burden	Colliers Elm, Churcham 2. 5.09P
	(Rolled to the left just before landing at Mount Airey, Huddersfield 10. 6.08, aircraft bounced back into the air but landed nose first and bounced					
	again. On the third touchdown the aircraft veered to the right and left wing tip dug in; damage to wing, trike and undercarriage)					
G-CDWA	Balony Kubicek BB37 Balloon (Hot Air)	424		2. 3.06	Fly In Balloons SRL	Salmour, Italy 16. 4.09E
G-CDWB	Best Off Sky Ranger 912(2)	SKRxxxx627		19. 1.06	V J Morris	Forest Farm, Redruth 12. 7.09P
	(Built V J Morris - pr.no.BMAA HB/477)					
G-CDWD	Cameron Z-105 Balloon (Hot Air)	10827		3. 5.06	P Spellward t/a Bristol University Ballooning Society	
					"Eric" ("Bristol University" titles)	Bristol 15. 2.09E
G-CDWE	Nord NC.856 Norvigie	01	F-WFKF	10. 3.06	R H and J A Cooper	Wickenby
			F-BFKF			
G-CDWG	Dyn'Aéro MCR-01 Club	PFA 301A-14132		10. 2.06	S E Gribble	Hulcote Farm, Salford 17. 5.09P
	(Built S E Gribble)					
G-CDWH	Curtiss P-40B	16073	N80FR	27. 1.06	Patina Ltd *(As "284 18P" in USAAF c/s)*	Duxford 10. 7.09P
	(Built Curtiss-Wright Corporation)		G-CDWH, 41-13297		*(Operated.The Fighter Collection)*	
	(Restored c 1990 using parts ex 39-285 and 39-287)					
G-CDWI	Comco Ikarus C42 FB80	0601-6783		9. 1.06	E Wright	Wickenby 12. 3.08P
G-CDWJ	Flight Design CTSW	05.11.16		9. 3.06	B W T Rood	Sywell 27. 6.09P
	(Assembled P&M Aviation Ltd with c/n 8157)					
G-CDWK	Robinson R44 Raven II	11116		3. 4.06	J O'Connor t/a Speedyparts Direct	
					(Mullingar, County Westmeath)	29. 4.09E
G-CDWL	Raj Hamsa X'Air 582(5)	xxxx		30. 1.06	I Bennett tr The CDWL Flying Group	
	(Built C Lenaghan - pr.no.BMAA HB/484)				(Dublin, Ireland)	14. 9.08P
G-CDWM	Best Off Sky Ranger 912S(1)	SKRxxxx616		15.12.05	W H McMinn	
	(Buillt W H McMinn- pr.no.BMAA HB/470)				Slieve Croob, Slievenamoney, Castlewellen	4. 6.09P
G-CDWN	UltraMagic N-210 Balloon (Hot Air)	210/33		22. 5.06	S R Seager *"Sky Personnel" titles*	
						Weedon, Aylesbury 17. 6.09E
G-CDWO	P&M Aviation Quik GT450	8175		3. 4.06	M D Harris	(Earls Barton, Northampton) 6. 4.09P
G-CDWP	P&M Aviation Quik GT450	8173		16. 3.06	S M Hall	Headon Farm, Retford 3. 4.08E
G-CDWR	P&M Aviation Quik GT450	8181		10. 4.06	D P Creedy	(Haslington, Crewe) 26. 4.09E
G-CDWS	P&M Aviation Quik GT450	8178		26. 4.06	H N Barrott	East Fortune 4. 5.09P
G-CDWT	Flight Design CTSW	05.12.10		9. 3.06	R Scammell	Sywell 2. 7.08P
	(Assembled P&M Aviation Ltd with c/n 8162)					
G-CDWU	Zenair CH.601UL Zodiac	PFA 162A-14332		16. 3.06	A D Worrall	Tarn Farm, Cockerham 4.11.09P
	(Built A D Worrall)					
G-CDWV	Lindstrand LBL House SS Balloon (Hot Air)			13. 3.06	LSB Public Relations Ltd	Abergavenny 15. 1.09E
		1089			*(Stroud and Swindon Building Society titles)*	
G-CDWW	P&M Aviation Quik GT450	8156		6. 1.06	J H Bradbury	Arclid Green, Sandbach 30.11.09P
G-CDWX	Lindstrand LBL 77A Balloon (Hot Air)	1088		13. 3.06	LSB Public Relations Ltd	Abergavenny 15. 1.09E
					(Stroud and Swindon Building Society titles)	
G-CDWY	Agusta A109S Grand	22011		15. 6.06	Sportsdirect.com Retail Ltd	Sywell 14. 6.09E
G-CDWZ	P&M Aviation Quik GT450	8154		2. 2.06	B J Holloway	Bicester 5. 2.09P
G-CDXA	Robinson R44 Raven	1584		31. 3.06	R A J Graham t/a J and D Graham	
					(Operated Northumbrian Helicopters)	Newcastle 27. 4.09E
G-CDXB	Robinson R44 Raven	1578		31. 3.06	HJS Helicopters Ltd	
					Lower Baads Farm, Peterculter	4. 5.09E
G-CDXD	Medway SLA 100 Executive	070306		8. 3.06	K J Draper *"Lilac Lil"*	Stoke, Isle of Grain 23.11.07P
G-CDXE	Westland Gazelle AH.Mk.1	1524	XZ299	29. 3.06	S Atherton *(On rebuild 2008, as "XZ299")*	
					Deer Park Farm, Babcary	
G-CDXF	Lindstrand LBL 31A Balloon (Hot Air)	1076		7. 4.06	Roman Trading Ltd	Box, Corsham 12. 8.09E
G-CDXG	P&M Pegasus Quantum 15-912	8180		28. 4.06	E H Gatehouse Pound Green, Buttonoak, Bewdley	19. 5.09P
G-CDXH	British Aerospace Avro 146-RJ100	E3237	TC-THD	21. 4.06	Trident Jet Leasing (Ireland) Ltd *(Stored 9.08)*	
			G-6-237			Kemble
G-CDXI	Cessna 182P Skylane	18263554	SE-GXY	2. 3.06	B G McBeath	Lydd 11. 9.09E
			OY-ANT, N5820J			
G-CDXJ	Avtech Jabiru J400	0xxx		27. 3.06	J C Collingwood	Wittersham, Tenterden 7. 5.09P
	(Built J C Collingwood - pr.no.PFA 325-14356)					
G-CDXK	Diamond DA.42 Twin Star	42.136		6. 6.06	A M Healy	Cranfield 7. 7.09E
G-CDXL	Flight Design CTSW	06.05.17		4. 7.06	A K Paterson	(Pointon, Sleaford) 9. 7.08P
	(Assembled P&M Aviation Ltd with c/n 8191)					
G-CDXM	P&M Pegasus Quik	8159		8. 2.06	Mainair Microlight Centre Ltd	Barton 10. 2.08P
	(Believed rebuilt with Trike c/n 8197 in 4.06 taking original build no)					
G-CDXN	P&M Aviation Quik GT450	8171		15. 5.06	Microflight Aviation Ltd	Headon Farm, Retford 22. 5.09P
G-CDXO	Zenair CH.601UL Zodiac	PFA 162A-14524		6. 4.06	D P W Smith	(Barrow-in-Furness) 15. 9.09P
	(Built R O Lewthwaite and R E Welche)					
G-CDXP	Evektor EV-97 Eurostar	2005.26.26		6. 4.06	B J Crockett	Broadmeadow Farm, Hereford 16 .5.09P
	(Built B J Crockett, pr. no PFA 315-14530)					

Reg	Type	c/n	Prev id	Date	Owner/Operator	Location	Date
G-CDXR	Fokker Dr.1 Triplane replica	PFA 238-14043		13. 4.06	J G Day (As "403/17" in German Army Air Service c/s)		
	(Built J G Day)					Rushett Farm, Chessington	26. 7.08P
G-CDXS	Evektor EV-97 teamEurostar UK	2005.26.27		22. 2.06	R T P Harris	Manor Farm, Haddenham	3. 4.08P
	(Officially regd with c/n 2627)						
G-CDXT	Van's RV-9	PFA 320-14376		11. 4.06	T M Storey	Newells Farm, Lower Beeding	10. 8.09P
	(Built T M Storey)						
G-CDXU	Chilton DW.1A	PFA 225-12038		19. 4.06	M Gibbs	(London SW11)	
	(Built R W Burrows)						
G-CDXV	Campbell Cricket Mk.6A	PGA G/16-1339		19. 4.06	W G Spencer	Little Rissington	
	(Built W G Spencer) (Marked as "Layzell AV-18A").						
G-CDXW	Cameron Orange 120 SS Balloon (Hot Air)		HB-BXL	22. 5.06	A Biasioli	Padova, Veneto, Italy	
		2947					
G-CDXX	Robinson R44 Raven II	10624		31. 1.05	Emsway Developments Ltd	(Cannock)	3. 4.09P
G-CDXY	Skystar Kitfox Mk.7	PFA 172D-14112		24. 2.06	D E Steade	Croft Farm, Defford	3. 4.09P
	(Built D E Steade)						
G-CDYA	Gippsland GA-8 Airvan	GA8-05-090	VH-IMI	7. 4.06	P Marsden	Redlands, Swindon	4. 5.09E
G-CDYB	Rans S-6-ES Coyote II	PFA 204-14416		28. 3.06	D Sykes and J M Hardstaff	Rufforth	15. 6.08P
	(Built D Sykes)						
G-CDYC	Piper PA-28RT-201 Arrow IV	28R-7918164	N2835D	26. 4.06	Arrowflight Ltd	Swansea	22. 7.09E
G-CDYD	Comco Ikarus C42 FB80	0604-6812		9. 6.06	F A Stephens tr C42 Group		
						Baxby Manor, Husthwaite	19. 6.08P
G-CDYF	Rotorsport UK MT-03	RSUK/MT-03/003		21. 8.06	A J P Herculson	Little Snoring	30. 8.07P
G-CDYG	Cameron Z-105 Balloon (Hot Air)	10870		10. 5.06	A Service Di Tartaglini Emanuela (Vodaphone titles)		
						Recanati, Marche, Italy	29.11.09E
G-CDYI	British Aerospace Jetstream Series 4100		N305UE	8. 6.06	Air Kilroe Ltd t/a Eastern Airways	Humberside	
	(Built Jetstream Aircraft Ltd)	41019	G-4-019				
G-CDYJ	Best Off Sky Ranger 912(1)	SKRxxxx681		16. 5.06	D S Taylor	(Leeds, Maidstone)	
	(Built D S Taylor - pr.no.BMAA HB/498)						
G-CDYL	Lindstrand LBL 77A Balloon (Hot Air)	1098		20. 6.06	J H Dobson (Lambert Smith Hampton titles)		
						Streatley, Reading	23. 6.09E
G-CDYM	Murphy Maverick 430	PFA 259-12981		20. 3.06	M R Cann	Woodlands Barton Farm, Rochel	4.12.07P
	(Built G T Leedham)						
G-CDYO	Comco Ikarus C42 FB80	0604-6810		10.10.06	B Goodridge	Dunkeswell	16.12.09P
G-CDYP	Evektor EV-97 teamEurostar UK	2628		1. 6.06	R V Buxton and R Cranborne	(Wymondham)	25. 5.09P
G-CDYR	Bell 206L-3 LongRanger III	51237	N341AJ	20. 9.07	M D Thorpe t/a Yorkshire Helicopters		
			5Y-BFL			Coney Park, Leeds	24. 9.08E
G-CDYT	Comco Ikarus C42 FB80	0603-6798		4. 5.06	J W D Blythe	Swansea	3. 5.09P
G-CDYU	Zenair CH.701UL STOL	PFA 187-14489		8. 5.06	A Gannon	Wick	12.12.07P
	(Built M Henderson)						
G-CDYW	Schweizer 269C-1 (Schweizer 300)	0247	N86G	20. 6.06	C R and S E Hewgill t/a CSL Industrial	Doncaster	7. 9.08E
G-CDYX	Lindstrand LBL 77B Balloon (Hot Air)	1094		6. 7.06	H M Savage	Edinburgh	21. 9.09E
G-CDYY	Alpi Pioneer 300	PFA 330-14323		14. 2.06	B Williams	Shobdon	28.10.09P
	(Built B Williams)						
G-CDYZ	Van's RV-7	PFA 323-14276		1. 2.06	Holden Group Ltd	Crowfield	26. 4.09P
	(Built G A Martin and W D Garlick) (Tailwheel u/c)						
G-CDZA	Alpi Pioneer 300	xxx		15. 3.06	J F Dowe	Parham	18. 9.08P
	(Built J Dowe - pr.no.PFA 330-14329)						
G-CDZB	Zenair CH.601UL Zodiac	PFA 162A-14431		10. 5.06	L J Dutch	Tarn Farm, Cockerham	3.11.07P
	(Built L J Dutch)						
G-CDZD	Van's RV-9A	PFA 320-13966	G-DUGS	24. 1.06	R D Masters	Standalone Farm. Meppershall	1. 5.09P
	(initially built D M Provost and completed R T Clegg) (Wilksch WAM120)						
G-CDZG	Comco Ikarus C42 FB80	0604-6808		20. 4.06	Mainair Microlight School Ltd	Barton	1. 5.08P
G-CDZH	Boeing 737-804	28227	SE-DZH	19. 5.06	Thomson Airways Ltd	Luton	18. 5.09E
			N1786B				
G-CDZI	Boeing 737-804	28229	SE-DZI	24. 5.06	Thomson Airways Ltd	Luton	23. 5.09E
G-CDZJ	Tecnam P92-JS	050		15. 6.06	Tecnam General Aviation Ltd	Clench Common	24. 7.08E
G-CDZK	Tecnam P92-JS	052		7. 8.06	Tecnam General Aviation Ltd	Clench Common	21. 9.08E
G-CDZL	Boeing 737-804	30465	D-ATUA	28. 4.06	Thomson Airways Ltd	Luton	18.12.09E
			SE-DZL, PH-AAV, G-BYNC, N1786B, (SE-DZK)				
G-CDZM	Boeing 737-804	30466	D-ATUB	23.11.05	Thomson Airways Ltd	Luton	22.11.09E
			SE-DZM, PH-ABE, G-BYNB, N1786B				
G-CDZO	Lindstrand LBL 60X Balloon (Hot Air)	1104		7. 7.06	R D Parry (Chelsea Financial Services titles)		
						Chalford, Stroud	5. 9.09E
G-CDZR	Nicollier HN.700 Menestrel II	PFA 217-13773		17. 5.06	P Berkin	Turweston	2. 6.09P
	(Built T M Williams)						
G-CDZS	Kolb Twinstar Mk.III Xtra	PFA 205-14278		23. 5.06	P W Heywood	Trewince Manor, Portscatho	
	(Built P W Heywood)						
G-CDZT	Beech B200 Super King Air	BB-1619	N240AJ	3. 7.06	BAE Systems Marine Ltd	Walney Island	2. 7.09E
			N719TA				
G-CDZU	ICP MXP-740 Savannah Jabiru(5)			17. 5.06	P J Cheyney	Bird's Edge, Penistone	9. 8.09P
		04-06-51-295					
	(Built P J Cheyney -pr.no.BMAA HB/398)						
G-CDZW	Cameron N-105 Balloon (Hot Air)	2204	SE-ZEK	23. 5.06	K Abrahamsson	Arsta, Sweden	16. 2.10E
G-CDZY	Medway SLA 80 Executive	180406		19. 4.06	K J Draper t/a Medway Microlights		
						Stoke, Isle of Grain	5. 5.09P
G-CDZZ	Rotorsport UK MT-03	RSUK/MT-03/002	G-94-1	4. 8.06	S J Boxall	Church Farm, Askern	8. 8.09P

G-CEAA - G-CEZZ

Reg	Type	c/n	Prev id	Date	Owner/Operator	Location	Date
G-CEAE	Boeing 737-229	20912	OO-SDF	25. 1.00	European Skybus Ltd (stored 11.08)		
						Marana, Arizona	28. 2.09E
G-CEAF	Boeing 737-229	20910	G-BYRI	13. 1.00	European Skybus Ltd (stored 1.09)		
			OO-SDD, EC-EEG, OO-SDD			Bournemouth	3. 4.09E

Reg	Type	c/n	Prev id	Date	Owner/operator	Location	Status
G-CEAH	Boeing 737-229	21135	OO-SDG	1. 8.00	European Aviation Air Charter Ltd (stored 1.09)		
						Bournemouth	14.11.09E
G-CEAK	Comco Ikarus C42 FB80	0606-6826		20. 7.06	M J Rhodes tr Barton Heritage Flying Group		
						Barton	13. 8.09P
G-CEAM	Evektor EV-97 teamEurostar UK	2729		13. 6.06	Flylight Airsports Ltd	Sywell	15. 6.09P
G-CEAN	Comco Ikarus C42 FB80	0606-6825		20. 6.06	Airbourne Aviation Ltd	Popham	31. 7.09P
G-CEAO	Jurca MJ.5 Sirocco	PFA 2209		23. 5.06	P S Watts	Kemble	5. 1.10P
	(Built P S Watts)						
G-CEAR	Alpi Pioneer 300	xxx		25. 5.06	A Parker "SW-1"	Rufforth	26. 2.08P
	(Built A Parker - pr.no.PFA 330-14511)						
G-CEAT	Zenair CH.601HDS Zodiac	PFA 162-13930		11. 5.06	T B Smith	Henstridge	10. 4.09P
	(Built T B Smith)						
G-CEAU	Robinson R44 Clipper II	11311		22. 6.06	Mullahead Property Company Ltd		
						Mullahead, Tandragee	20. 7.09E
G-CEAV	UltraMagic M-105 Balloon (Hot Air)	105/140		24. 5.06	G Everett (Saga Insurance titles)		
						Sandway, Maidstone	26. 9.09E
G-CEAW	Schweizer 269C-1 (Schweizer 300)	0241	N15120	24. 5.06	Aerocorp Ltd	Birkenhead	22. 7.09E
			N86G				
G-CEAX	UltraMagic S-130 Balloon (Hot Air)	130/49		14. 7.06	Anglian Countryside Balloons Ltd		
						Burnham-on-Crouch	3. 1.10E
G-CEAY	UltraMagic H-42 Balloon (Hot Air)	42/13		24. 7.06	J D A Shields	Hastings	25. 7.07E
G-CEBA	Zenair CH.601XL Zodiac	PFA 162B-13426		21. 4.06	I J M Donnelly	Perth	16. 4.09P
	(Built I J M Donnelly)						
G-CEBC	ICP MXP-740 Savannah Jabiru(5)			25. 5.06	E W Chapman	North Moor, Scunthorpe	14. 3.09P
	(Built E W Chapman)	BMAA HB/503					
G-CEBD	P&M Aviation Quik GT450	8193		22. 5.06	E J Douglas	East Fortune	21. 5.09P
G-CEBE	Schweizer 269C-1 (Schweizer 300)	0253	N86G	19. 6.06	Milburn World Travel Services Ltd	Edinburgh	10. 9.09E
G-CEBF	Evektor EV-97A Eurostar	2005.24.05		6. 6.06	M Lang	Netherthorpe	2.11.09P
	(Built M Lang, pr. no PFA 315A-14525)						
G-CEBG	Balony Kubicek BB26 Balloon (Hot Air)	442		26. 6.06	P M Smith (Beechwood Lodge titles)		
						Trim, County Meath	12. 8.09P
G-CEBH	Air Création Tanarg 912S/iXess 15	FLT.xxx		14. 6.06	D A Chamberlain	Roddige	27. 2.09P
	(Built D A Chamberlain - pr.no.BMAA HB/481 being Flylight kit comprising Trike s/n T05098 and Wing s/n A05186-5193)						
G-CEBI	Kolb Twinstar Mk III Extra	PFA 205-14361		6. 6.06	R W Livingstone	(Lisnaskea, Enniskillen)	29. 7.09E
	(Built R W Livingstone) (Jabiru 2200A)						
G-CEBK	Piper PA-31-350 Navajo Chieftain		PH-SAV	31. 8.06	De Jong Management BV	Norwich	16.10.08E
		31-7652056	N59818				
G-CEBL	Balony Kubicek BB20GP Balloon (Hot Air)	456		23. 8.06	Associazione Sportiva Aerostatica Lombada		
					(X Bianci Group titles)	Milan, Italy	10. 9.09E
G-CEBM	P&M Aviation Quik GT450	8197		23. 5.06	R A Keene	Over Farm, Gloucester	8. 8.09P
G-CEBN	British Aerospace Avro 146-RJ100	E3238	TC-THE	20. 7.06	Trident Jet Leasing (Ireland) Ltd (Stored all-white 2.09)		
			G-6-238			Southend	
G-CEBO	UltraMagic M-65C Balloon (Hot Air)	65/77	D-OWBZ	26. 6.06	M J Woodstock "Warsteiner"	East Grinstead	16. 7.09E
G-CEBP	Evektor EV-97 teamEurostar UK	2825		3. 7.06	T R Southall "Lady Jean"	Shobdon	29. 6.09P
G-CEBT	P&M Aviation Quik GT450	8199		22. 6.06	A J Ridell	Henstridge	29. 6.09P
G-CEBV	Europa Aviation Europa XS	573		28. 6.06	S Vestuti	Swansea	20. 5.09P
	(Built S Vestuti - pr.no.PFA 247-14007)						
G-CEBW	North American P-51D-20-NA Mustang		44-72181	5. 7.06	Dental Insurance Solutions Ltd	(Bayfield, Holt)	
		122-38640					
G-CEBY	Air Création Tanarg 912S(2)/iXess 15	FLT.xxx		30. 6.06	P S Bewley	Weston Zoyland	18.10.08P
	(Built P S Bewley - pr.no.BMAA HB/504 being Flylight kit comprising Trike s/n xxxx and Wing s/n xxxx)						
G-CEBZ	Zenair CH.601UL Zodiac	PFA 162A-13942		12. 5.06	I M Ross and A Watt	Insch	16.12.09P
	(Built I M Ross and A Watt)						
G-CECA	P&M Aviation Quik GT450	8185		16. 8.06	A Weatherall	St Michaels	21. 8.08P
G-CECB	ELA Aviacion ELA 07S	11050710722		14. 7.06	A D Gordon	Blair Atholl	
G-CECC	Comco Ikarus C42 FB80	0607-6832		14. 6.06	K D Mitchell tr G-CECC Group		
						Kittyhawk Farm, Deanland	3. 9.09P
G-CECD	Cameron C-90 Balloon (Hot Air)	10898		7. 8.06	S P Harrowing (Adez titles)	Port Talbot	13. 5.09E
G-CECE	Avtech Jabiru UL-D	656		8. 6.06	ST Aviation Ltd		
						Oaklands Farm, Horsham and Southery	1. 8.08P
G-CECF	Reality Escapade Jabiru(3)	UKESC 0007		8. 6.06	M M Bayle	Over Farm, Gloucester	9.10.08P
	(Built T F Francis - pr.no.BMAA HB/496) (Tailwheel u/c)						
G-CECG	Avtech Jabiru UL-D	661		18. 7.06	R K Watson "Pauline"	Damyn's Hall, Upminster	21. 8.08P
G-CECH	Jodel D 150	174		19. 7.06	W R Prescott	Ballymageough, Kilkeel	5.12.08P
	(Built D Kennedy - pr.no.PFA 235-13889)						
G-CECI	Pilatus PC-6/B2-H4 Turbo Porter	936	N2TS	3. 3.06	D M Penny	(Movenis, Coleraine)	22. 3.09E
			N424PS, HB-FMD				
G-CECJ	Aeromot AMT-200S Super Ximango	200168	PR-AMU	14.11.06	C J and S C Partridge	Lasham	27. 4.09E
G-CECK	ICP MXP-740 Savannah Jabiru(5)06-01-51-453			11. 7.06	K W Eskins	Weston Zoyland	24. 4.08P
	(Built K W Eskins - pr.no.BMAA HB/495)						
G-CECL	Comco Ikarus C42 FB80	0607-6834		4. 7.06	C Lee	Longacre Farm, Sandy	11.10.08P
G-CECM	P&M Aviation Quik GT450	8195		4. 9.06	C S Mackenzie	Balado Bridge	4. 9.08P
G-CECO	Hughes 269C (Hughes 300)	114-0377	D-HAEK	14. 9.06	P A Leverton	(Kirkby-in-Ashfield, Nottingham)	23.10.09E
			JA7574				
G-CECP	Best Off Sky Ranger 912(2)	SKR0508639		13. 7.06	A Assiansian	Hunsdon	20. 5.09P
	(Built D C Davies - pr.no.BMAA HB/483) (C/n possibly SKR0509639)						
G-CECR	Bilsam Sky Cruiser	S-CR-7B-XHP-2006		16.11.06	J C Collingwood	Wittersham, Tenterden	
G-CECS	Lindstrand LBL 105A Balloon (Hot Air)	1121		25. 7.06	Beam Global Distribution (UK) Ltd	Telford	16. 7.09E
					(Harvey's Orange titles)		
G-CECU	Boeing 767-222	21864	N603UA	2. 1.07	UK International Airlines Ltd		
					(Airline suspended operations 2008 and stored)		
G-CECV	Van's RV-7	PFA 323-14338		30. 5.06	D M Stevens	Haverfordwest	28.10.09P
	(Built D M Stevens)						
G-CECW	Robinson R44 Raven II	11446		9.10.06	VHE Construction Ltd	(Rethmines, Dublin)	5.11.09E

G-CECX	Robinson R44 Raven II	11390		6. 9.06	Dolphin Property (Management) Ltd	Thruxton	2.10.09E
G-CECY	Evektor EV-97 Eurostar	2006.28.28		21. 7.06	M R M Welch	Goodwood	4. 9.09P
	(Built M R M Welch, pr. no PFA 315-14551)						
G-CECZ	Zenair CH.601XL Zodiac	PFA 162B-14458		17. 7.06	G M Johnson	Fen Drayton	11.12.08P
	(Built G M Johnson) (Tail-wheel u/c)						
G-CEDA	Cameron Z-105 Balloon (Hot Air)	10910		9. 8.06	N Charbonnier *(Sanpaulo Leasint titles)* Aosta, Italy		16. 1.10E
G-CEDB	Reality Escapade Jabiru(3)	UKESC.0002		12. 4.06	P Travis	Davidstow Moor	
	(Built D Bedford - pr.no.BMAA HB/456)						
G-CEDC	Comco Ikarus C42 FB100	0607-6831		14. 8.06	P D Ashley	Dunkeswell	31. 8.08P
G-CEDD	Piper PA-28RT-201 Arrow IV	28R-8018100	N82507	16. 6.06	R Hammond	Southend	11. 6.08E
G-CEDE	Flight Design CTSW	06.06.14		16. 8.06	F Williams and J A R Hartley		
	(Assembled P&M Aviation Ltd with c/n 8212)					Combrooke, Stratford-upon-Avon	8. .409P
G-CEDF	Cameron N-105 Balloon (Hot Air)	10884		31. 7.06	Bailey Balloons Ltd *(EDF Energy titles)*	Bristol	16. 7.09E
G-CEDG	Robinson R44 Raven	11639		31. 8.06	Wiksy Charter Ltd	Fairoaks	14. 9.09E
G-CEDI	Best Off Sky Ranger 912(2)	SKRxxxx700		10..8.06	P B Davey	(Wittersham, Tenterden)	6. 7.09P
	(Built P B Davey - pr.no.BMAA HB/513)						
G-CEDJ	Aero Designs Pulsar XP	207	N383B	21.12.06	P F Lorriman	Rochester	15.11.08P
	(Built W Becker)						
G-CEDK	Cessna 750 Citation X	750-0252	N252CX	20. 3.07	The Duke of Westminster	Hawarden	19. 3.09E
			N5000R				
G-CEDL	TEAM Mini-MAX 91	PFA 186-12546		18. 7.06	J W Taylor	Over Farm, Gloucester	18.11.09P
	(Built J W Taylor)						
G-CEDM	Flight Design CTSW	06.06.14		17. 8.06	A P Sellars	North Coates	17. 8.07P
	(Assembled P&M Aviation Ltd with c/n 8214)						
G-CEDN	P&M Pegasus Quik	8206		15. 8.06	N J Hargreaves	(Southport)	19. 9.09P
G-CEDO	Raj Hamsa X'Air Falcon 133(1)	xxxxx		3. 8.06	A P Lambert and J Lane		
	(Built A P Lambert and J Lane - pr.no.BMAA HB/511) (Change of Type 10.06)			*(Noted 3.07)*	Lower Upham Farm, Chiseldon		
G-CEDR	Comco Ikarus C42 FB80	0606-6833		1. 8.06	R S O'Carroll	Mullahead, Tandragee	3. 8.09P
G-CEDT	Air Création Tanarg 912S/iXess 15	FLT.xxx		14. 7.06	R A Taylor	RAF Wyton	20. 5.08P
	(Built R A Taylor - pr.no.BMAAHB/510 being Flylight kit comprising Trike s/n T06033 and Wing s/n xxxx)						
G-CEDV	Evektor EV-97 teamEurostar UK	2826		29. 9.06	Airbourne Aviation Ltd	Popham	5.10.08P
	(Built Cosmik Aviation)						
G-CEDW	TEAM Mini-MAX 91	PFA 186-12472		22. 6.06	A T Peatman	(Dursley)	
	(Built A T Peatman)					*(Noted unmarked and unfinished PFA Kemble 8.06)*		
G-CEDX	Evektor EV-97 teamEurostar UK	2827		6. 9.06	M W Houghton	Bakersfield	3. 9.09P
G-CEDZ	Best Off Sky Ranger 912(2)	SKRxxxx685		28. 7.06	I Bell and J E Walendowski	Sandtoft	
	(Built J E Walendowski - pr.no.BMAA HB/505)(BMAA claim I Bell as builder but he was not original owner)						
G-CEEA	ELA Aviacion ELA 07R	04040430712		30. 8.06	S J Tyler	Kirkbride	
G-CEEB	Cameron C-80 Balloon (Hot Air)	10923		18. 8.06	Cameron Balloons Ltd	Bristol	27. 9.09E
G-CEEC	Raj Hamsa X'Air Hawk	1096		23. 8.06	B G King	Dunkeswell	26. 7.08P
	(Built G A J Salter - pr.no.PFA 340-14559)						
G-CEED	ICP MXP-740 Savannah Jabiru(5)06-03-51-470			24. 8.06	A U I Hudson	Bracon Ash	1. 4.08P
	(Built A U I Hudson - pr.no.BMAA HB/500)						
G-CEEE	Robinson R44 Raven II	10005		26.11.02	Caswell Environmental Services Ltd	(Stevenage)	14. 1.09E
G-CEEF	ELA Aviacion ELA 07R	06040440712		8. 9.06	G Millward	(Calow, Chesterfield)	
G-CEEG	Alpi Pioneer 300	26		31. 8.06	D McCormack	Kirknewton	9.11.07P
	(Built D McCormack - pr.no.PFA 330-14556)						
G-CEEI	P&M Aviation Quik GT450	8218		16.10.06	R A Hill	Enstone	30.10.08P
G-CEEJ	Rans S-7S Courier	0105-392		31. 8.06	J G J McDill	Felixkirk	10. 4.09P
	(Built J G J McDill - pr.no.PFA 218-14557)						
G-CEEK	Cameron Z-105 Balloon (Hot Air)	10909		9.11.06	PSH Skypower Ltd *(Thomson Local titles)*		
						Woodborough, Pewsey	9.10.09E
G-CEEL	UltraMagic S-90 Balloon (Hot Air)	90/89		12. 9.06	Impresa San Paolo SRL*(Impresa S Paolo titles)*		
						Reggio Emilia, Italy	17. 8.09E
G-CEEM	P&M Aviation Quik GT450	8216		29. 9.06	T Griffiths	Haverfordwest	6. 2.09P
G-CEEN	Piper PA-28-161 Cadet	2841293	EC-IHA	22. 9.06	Plane Talking Ltd	Denham	10.10.09E
			N9202N				
G-CEEO	Flight Design CTSW	06.08.12		29. 9.06	E McCallum	Longframlington	19.12.09P
	(Assembled P&M Aviation Ltd with c/n 8225)						
G-CEEP	Van's RV-9A	90062	N966AM	7.09.06	J M Ghosh and M P Wiseman		
	(Built R A Jones)					Mount Airey Farm, South Cave	20. 1.10P
G-CEER	ELA Aviacion ELA 07R	04040420712		8. 9.06	F G Shepherd	Kirkbride	
G-CEES	Cameron C-90 Balloon (Hot Air)	11916		11.10.06	P C May	Poling, Arundel	11.10.09E
G-CEEU	Piper PA-28-161 Cadet	2841038	N224FT	8. 2.07	Plane Talking Ltd	Elstree	27. 2.10E
			EC-IIF, N9158J				
G-CEEV	Piper PA-28-161 Warrior III	2842162	N5352X	11.12.06	Plane Talking Ltd	Elstree	14. 2.09E
	(Thielart TAE 125)						
G-CEEW	Comco Ikarus C42 FB100	0609-6847		18. 9.06	Autocom Products Ltd	Long Marston	7. 2.09P
G-CEEX	ICP MXP-740 Savannah Jabiru(5) xx-xx-xx-xxx			21. 8.06	M A Jones	(Bracebridge Heath, Lincoln)	8. 2.09P
	(Built T Brumpton and M Hicks - pr.no.BMAA HB/508)						
G-CEEY	Piper PA-28-161 Warrior III	2842168	N53583	11.12.06	Plane Talking Ltd	Elstree	19. 4.09E
	(Thielart TAE 125)						
G-CEEZ	Piper PA-28-161 Warrior III	2842161	N53513	11.12.06	Plane Talking Ltd	Elstree	6. 3.09E
	(Thielert TAE 125)						
G-CEFA	Comco Ikarus C42 FB UK	0609-6851		7.11.06	J Morrisroe	Frenchpark, County Roscannon	30. 5.08P
	(Built J Little - pr.no.PFA 322-14570)						
G-CEFB	UltraMagic H-31 Balloon (Hot Air)	31/06		30.10.06	P Dickinson	St Martins, Oswestry	1. 7.09E
G-CEFC	Super Marine Spitfire Mk.26	PFA 324-14417		21. 9.06	D R Bishop *(As "RB412:DW-B" in RAF c/s)*		
	(Built D R Bishop)					Kemble	
G-CEFG	Boeing 767-319ER	26264	ZK-NCH	27.10.06	Globespan Airways Ltd t/a Flyglobespan.com		
						Edinburgh	1.11.09E
G-CEFJ	Sonex Aircraft Sonex	FF05-4-00048		9.10.06	M H Moulai	Sandtoft	11.11.08P
	(Built M H Moulai - pr.no.PFA 337-14518) (Hirth F33)						
G-CEFK	Evektor EV-97 teamEurostar UK	2823		13.11.06	P Morgan	Ince Blundell	12.11.08P

G-CEFM	Cessna 152	15284357	N6102L	19.10.06	Cristal Air Ltd	Kittyhawk Farm, Deanland	14.10.09E
G-CEFP	Avtech Jabiru J430	0xxx		23.10.06	G Hammond	Headcorn	8. 8.09P
	(Built G Hammond - pr.no.PFA 336-14452)						
G-CEFS	Cameron C-100 Balloon (Hot Air)	11000		2. 1.07	Gone With The Wind Ltd *"Stairway to Heaven"*		
						Bristol	1. 9.09E
G-CEFT	Whittaker MW5-D Sorcerer	PFA 163-14335		20.10.06	W Bruce	(Immingham)	
	(Built W Bruce)						
G-CEFV	Cessna 182T Skylane	18281538	N66167	2.11.06	D H, P M, A H and R H Smith t/a G H Smith and Son		
						Bagby	4.12.08E
G-CEFY	ICP MXP-740 Savannah Jabiru(4)			17.11.06	B Hartley	Brook Farm, Pilling	4. 7.08P
		04-07-51-316					
	(Built B Hartley - pr.no.BMAA HB/453)						
G-CEFZ	Evektor EV-97 teamEurostar UK	2824		9.11.06	G Robertson and D Young tr Robo Flying Group		
						Kemble	21.11.09P
G-CEGC	Cameron Z-105 Balloon (Hot Air)	10930		2.11.06	The Balloon Company Ltd t/a First Flight		
					(Humberts titles)	Langford, Bristol	10.10.09E
C-CEGD	Robin HR100/210 Safari	159	CS-ARI		Unknown	Cranfield	
			F-BUHW		*(Arrived early 2008 but export paperwork problems, stored)*		
G-CEGE	Swearingen SA.226TC Metro II	TC-258	OY-NPA	14. 3.07	Blue City Aviation Ltd	Coventry	18. 9.09E
			(SP-MRB), OY-NPA, C-GBDF, 4X-CSA, N5463M				
G-CEGG	Lindstrand LBL 25A Cloudhopper Balloon (Hot Air)			20. 7.06	C G Dobson	Streatley, Reading	17. 9.09E
		1120					
G-CEGH	Van's RV-9A	PFA 320-14468		5. 9.06	M E Creasey	Crowfield	18.12.08P
	(Built M E Creasey)						
G-CEGI	Van's RV-8	81480	N747RF	10.10.06	W H Greenwood	Swanborough Farm, Lewes	28. 4.09P
	(Built R Faller)				*(Also carries "N747RF")*		
G-CEGJ	P&M Aviation Quik GT450	8234		5. 1.07	Flylight Airsports Ltd	Sywell	4. 1.10P
G-CEGK	ICP MXP-740 Savannah VG Jabiru(1)			9.11.06	S Whittaker and P J Wilson t/a Sandtoft Ultralights Partnership		
		06-03-51-474				*(Noted NEC Birmingham 11.08)*	Sandtoft 24.10.08P
	(Built S Whittaker and P J Wilson - pr.no.BMAA HB/515)				*(Damaged on landing at Church Inn Field, Chichester 3. 5.08)*		
G-CEGL	Comco Ikarus C42 FB80	0609-6848		21. 9.06	FES Autogas Ltd	Caernarfon	11.12.09P
G-CEGO	Evektor EV-97A Eurostar	PFA 315A-14552		25. 8.06	N J Keeling, R F McLachlan and J A Charlton		
						Ashbourne	18.10.09P
G-CEGP	Beech 200 Super King Air	BB-726	G-BXMA	14. 5.01	Cega Air Ambulance Ltd	Bournemouth	7. 8.09E
			(N58AJ), G-BXMA, N622JA, N522JA, N222JD				
G-CEGR	Beech 200 Super King Air	BB-351	N68CP	23. 7.97	Henfield Lodge Aviation Ltd *(Operated Cega Aviation)*		
			N351FW, N6666C, N6666K			Shoreham	18. 8.09E
G-CEGS	Piper PA-28-161 Warrior II	28-7816418	N6391C	20.11.06	S J Skilton t/a Aviation Rentals	Wolverhampton	18.10.09E
	(Thielert TAE 125)						
G-CEGT	P&M Aviation Quik GT450	8208		15. 8.06	J Plenderleith	Inverness	3. 9.08P
G-CEGU	Piper PA-28-151 Cherokee Warrior (modified)		N575DM	20.11.06	S J Skilton t/a Aviation Rentals	Wolverhampton	30.11.09E
	(Thielert TAE 125)	28-7715165	N5990F				
G-CEGV	P&M Aviation Quik GT450	8203		18. 8.06	G Shaw	Winspurs Farm, Northrepps	31. 8.08P
G-CEGW	P&M Aviation Quik GT450	8223		2.11.06	P Barrow	Arclid Green, Sandbach	1.11.07P
G-CEGY	ELA Aviacion ELA 07R	02050570712		21.11.06	A Buchanan *(Noted 7.08)*	Kirkbride	
G-CEGZ	Comco Ikarus C42 FB80	0609-6852		14.12.06	G E Spark tr Ikarus Flying Group	Barton	26. 1.09E
G-CEHC	P&M Aviation Quik GT450	8231		4.12.06	G H Sharwood-Smith	(Edinburgh)	13.12.09P
G-CEHD	Best Off Sky Ranger 912(2)	SKR0604716		17.11.06	A A Howland	(Battle)	14. 6.08P
	(Built A A Howland - pr.no.BMAA HB/520)						
G-CEHE	Medway SLA 100 Executive	171106		11. 2.08	R P Stoner	Stoke, Isle of Grain	
G-CEHG	Comco Ikarus C42 FB100	0612-6861		17.11.06	G E Cole	Over Farm, Gloucester	2. 5.09P
G-CEHH	AirBorne XT912-B-Streak III-B	XT912-065	5B-HAZ	15.11.06	J Madhvani and K Bolton		
						Plaistows Farm, St Albans	16. 1.08P
	(Struck a tree and crashed at Blunts Lane, Potters Crouch, St Albans 28. 3.07 on approach to Plaistows Farm while performing engine-off approach. The aircraft was substantially damaged)						
G-CEHI	P&M Aviation Quik GT450	8229		14.12.06	A Costello	Brook Farm, Pilling	15.12.09P
G-CEHJ	Short S312 Tucano T Mk.1	S 116 & T87	ZF373	14. 2.07	C C Butt	Hawarden	
	(Officially regd as T166)						
G-CEHK	Robinson R44 Raven II	11513		11.12.06	C Gallagher and Rathcoole Construction Ltd		
						(Ennis, County Clare and Dublin)	20.12.09E
G-CEHL	Evektor EV-97 teamEurostar UK	2928		16. 1.07	B P Connally	Gloucestershire	26. 1.09P
	(Built Cosmik Aviation, plate showing 2006.29.28 also on G-ZZAC)						
G-CEHM	Rotorsport UK MT-03	RSUK/MT-03/004	G-94-1	18.10.06	K O Maurer	Stoke, Isle of Grain	23.11.09P
G-CEHN	Rotorsport UK MT-03	RSUK/MT-03/008		8.12.06	P A Harwood	Rufforth	19.12.09P
G-CEHO	ELA Aviacion ELA 07R	06040480712		6. 2.07	C Gilholm	(Selkirk)	
G-CEHR	Auster AOP.9	B5/10/149	XP241	7.12.06	J Cooke and R B Webber *(Noted 9.08)*		
						Trenchard Farm, Eggesford	
G-CEHS	CAB CAP.10B	304	HS-BCS	8. 3.07	Cole Aviation Ltd *(Noted 11.07 as "HS-BCS")*		
						Spilstead Farm, Sedlescombe	
G-CEHT	Rand Robinson KR-2	PFA 129-14288		7.12.06	P P Geoghegan	Redhill	19. 8.09P
	(Built P P Geoghegan)						
G-CEHU	Cameron Z-105 Balloon (Hot Air)	10973		8.12.06	M G Howard *(Dubailand titles)*	Dubai, UAE	22.12.09E
G-CEHV	Comco Ikarus C42 FB80	0610-6854		14.12.06	Mainair Microlight School Ltd	Barton	13.12.09P
G-CEHW	P&M Aviation Quik GT450	8241		8.12.06	Exodus Airsports Ltd	Plaistows Farm, St Albans	17.12.09P
	(Sailwing used as demonstrator with G-CERW trike: frequently interchanges with sailwing from G-CERW (standard Quik) on G-CEHW trike)						
G-CEHX	Lindstrand LBL 9A Balloon (Hot Air)	1147		19.12.06	P Baker	Abbeyview, Trim, County Meath	5.12.08E
G-CEHZ	AirBorne XT912-B-Streak III-B	XT912-144		14.12.06	J Horan	Tarsan Lane, Portadown	21. 1.08P
G-CEIA	Rotorsport UK MT-03	RSUK/MT-03/009		12.12.06	M P Chetwynd-Talbot	(Coxwold, York)	19.12.08P
G-CEIB	Yakovlev Yak-18A	1160403	RA-3336K	23. 5.07	G M Bauer	Wickenby	12. 6.09P
G-CEID	Van's RV-7	PFA 323-14403		29.11.06	A Moyce	Newtownards	2. 4.09P
	(Built A Moyce)						
G-CEIE	Flight Design CTSW	06.10.01		14.12.06	D K Ross	Sittles Farm, Alrewas	15.10.08P
	(Assembled P&M Aviation Ltd with c/n 8243)						

Reg	Type	C/n	Prev id	Date	Owner	Location	Status
G-CEIG	Van's RV-7 *(Built W K Wilkie)*	PFA 323-14402		5.12.06	W K Wilkie	Newtownards	2. 4.09P
G-CEIH	British Aerospace Avro 146-RJ100	E3232	TC-THA G-6-232	23. 2.07	Trident Jet Leasing (Ireland) Ltd *(Noted 2.08)* Bacau, Romania		
G-CEII	Medway SLA 80 Executive	010107		27. 7.07	F J Clarehugh	Eshott	11. 7.08P
G-CEIK	UltraMagic M-90 Balloon (Hot Air)	90/92		19. 2.07	Elinore Frence Ltd t/a Imagination Balloon Flights Morpeth		25. 3.09E
G-CEIL	Reality Escapade 912(2) *(Built D E Bassett - pr.no.BMAA HB/506)*	JAESC xxxx		5.12.06	D E Bassett	St Michaels	
G-CEIM	Robinson R44 Raven II	11583		29. 1.07	K and J Aviation Ltd	Leicester	8. 2.10E
G-CEIN	Cameron Z-105 Balloon (Hot Air)	10989		18.12.06	M G Howard	Dubai, UAE	22.12.09E
G-CEIR	Britten-Norman BN-2T-4S Islander	4017		20.12.06	Britten-Norman Aircraft Ltd	Bembridge	
G-CEIS	SAN Jodel DR.1050 Ambassadeur	469	F-BLJL	9. 1.07	M Hales	North Coates	18. 8.09P
G-CEIT	Van's RV-7 *(Built S S Gould)*	PFA 323-13696		21.12.06	S S Gould	(Bedford)	4. 9.09P
G-CEIV	Air Création Tanarg 912S/iXess 15 *(Built G Brown - pr.no.BMAA HB/516 being Flylight kit comprising Trike s/n T06079 and Wing s/n A06121-6106)*	FLT.xxx		17.10.06	Focus Property Services Ltd	Long Marston	
G-CEIW	Europa Aviation Europa *(Built R Scanlan - pr.no.PFA 247-12707)*	xxxx		6.11.06	R Scanlan	Trenchard Farm, Eggesford	
G-CEIX	Alpi Pioneer 300 *(Built R F Bond - pr.no.PFA 330-14656)*	xxx		10. 4.07	R F Bond	Garston Farm, Marshfield	31. 8.09P
G-CEIY	UltraMagic M-120 Balloon (Hot Air)	120/23		20. 3.07	Societa Cooperativa Sociale Il Paraticchio Barletta, Italy		27. 9.09E
G-CEIZ	Piper PA-28-161 Warrior II	28-8116076	D-EIAL N8291D	21. 2.07	Altus Aviation Ltd	Blackbushe	10. 3.09E
G-CEJA	Cameron V-77 Balloon (Hot Air)	2469	G-BTOF	17. 6.91	L and C Gray	Farnborough	14. 7.09E
G-CEJB	PIper PA-46-500TP Malibu Meridian	4697240	OY-PHO N31278, N9512N	12. 1.07	Crestron (UK) Ltd	Fairoaks	24. 1.08E
G-CEJC	Cameron N-77 Balloon (Hot Air)	4164	G-VODA (2)	12. 1.07	Zebedee Balloon Service Ltd *(Also see G-VODA (1))* Newtown, Hungerford		8. 4.09E
G-CEJD	Piper PA-28-161 Warrior III	2842244	D-EGVY N31044	5. 2.07	Western Air (Thruxton) Ltd	Thruxton	27. 2.09E
G-CEJE	Wittman W.10 Tailwind *(Built R A Povall)*	PFA 031-14003		15..1.07	R A Povall	Yearby	4. 9.09P
G-CEJF	Piper PA-28-161 Cadet *(Thielart TAE 125)*	2841224	N230FT N134ND	14.11.07	S J Skilton t/a Aviation Rentals	Bournemouth	19. 6.09E
G-CEJG	UltraMagic M-56 Balloon (Hot Air)	56/37		2. 8.07	M J Warne	Tavistock	26. 9.09E
G-CEJI	Lindstrand LBL 105A Balloon (Hot Air)	1144		29. 1.07	Richard Nash Cars Ltd	Norwich	27. 1.10E
G-CEJJ	P&M Aviation Quik GT450	8236		2. 1.07	I M Bracegirdle tr Juliet Juilet Group (Knapthorpe Lodge, Caunton)		3. 2.09P
G-CEJK	Lindstrand LBL 260A Balloon (Hot Air)	1141		26. 3.07	T G Church t/a Pendle Balloon Company *(Bowker titles)* Clayton-le-Dale, Blackburn		5. 5.09E
G-CEJL	UltraMagic H-31 Balloon (Hot Air)	31/08		4. 6.07	Robert Wiseman Dairies PLC *(Fresh n'lo milk titles)* Skirling, Biggar		6. 6.09E
G-CEJM	Boeing 757-28A	26276	TF-FIK	23. 3.07	Globespan Airways Ltd t/a Flyglobespan.com Edinburgh		23. 3.09E
G-CEJN	Mooney M 20F Executive	670216	N237MM F-BOJP, N9639M	12. 2.07	I Watson tr Mooney M 20F Club	Bournemouth	27. 4.09E
G-CEJO	Boeing 737-8BK	29643		27. 6.07	Globespan Airways Ltd t/a Flyglobespan.com Edinburgh		27. 6.09E
G-CEJP	Boeing 737-8BK	29646		8. 6.07	Globespan Airways Ltd t/a Flyglobespan.com Edinburgh		10. 6.09E
G-CEJR	Cameron Z-90 Balloon (Hot Air)	10967		29. 1.07	KB Voli di Chiozzi Bartolomeo EC SAS Cappela Cantone, Italy		19. 8.09E
G-CEJT	Cameron Z-31 Balloon (Hot Air)	10972		29. 1.07	Cameron Balloons Ltd	Bristol	27. 9.08E
G-CEJU	Bell P-39Q-6-BE Airacobra	26E-397	N793QG (N139DP), 42-19993	21. 2.07	Patina Ltd *"Brooklyn Bum-2nd"* *(Operated The Fighter Collection as "219993" in USAAF c/s)*	Duxford	1. 7.09E
G-CEJV	Piper PA-28-161 Cadet	2841225	N144ND	1. 2.07	S J Skilton t/a Aviation Rentals	Wolverhampton	12. 3.09E
G-CEJW	Comco Ikarus C42 FB80	0612-6860		4. 1.07	M I Deeley	Otherton, Cannock	8. 1.10P
G-CEJX	P&M Aviation Quik GT450	8249		13. 3.07	P Stewart and A J Huntly	Easter Poldar Farm, Thornhill	19. 3.09P
G-CEJY	Aerospool WT9 UK Dynamic *(Official c/n is "DY165")"*	DY165/2007		9. 3.07	R G Bennett	Manor Farm, Drayton St Leonard	8. 1.10P
G-CEJZ	Cameron C-90 Balloon (Hot Air)	10970		20. 4.07	A M Holly *(AMO Complete titles)* Breadstone, Berkeley		29. 3.09E
G-CEKA	Robinson R44 Raven II	11639		5. 3.07	M Virdee t/a Heligift.com	(Plaistow, Billingshurst)	2. 4.09E
G-CEKB	Taylor JT.1 Monoplane *(Built C J Bush) (Volkswagen 1834)*	PFA 055-12113		14. 2.07	C J Bush	Great Oakley	23.10.09P
G-CEKC	Medway SLA 100 Executive	70207		11. 3.08	B W Webb	Sackville Lodge, Riseley	10. 3.09P
G-CEKD	Flight Design CTSW *(Assembled P&M Aviation Ltd with c/n 8255)*	06.11.05		28. 3.07	M K Arora	Long Marston	8. 4.09P
G-CEKE	Robin DR.400-180 Régent	943	HB-EXG	12. 4.07	M F Cuming	Shenington	2. 5.09E
G-CEKF	Robinson R44 Raven II	11650		18. 4.07	Aughakilmore Developments Ltd Ballinalee, County Longford		2. 9.09E
G-CEKG	P&M Aviation Quik GT450	8261		16. 4.07	J Sneddon tr G-CEKG Flying Group *(Permit revoked 6. 9.08)*	East Fortune	10. 4.09P
G-CEKH	UltraMagic M-105 Balloon (Hot Air)	105/149		3. 5.07	A Derbyshire	Woodseaves, Stafford	22. 3.09E
G-CEKI	Cessna 172P Skyhawk	17274356	N51829	19. 4.07	Zentelligence Ltd	Maypole Farm, Chislet	7. 6.09E
G-CEKJ	Evektor EV-97A Eurostar *(Built C W J Vershoyle-Greene)*	PFA 315A-14584		20.11.06	C W J Vershoyle-Greene	Kilrush, County Kildare	25. 2.09P
G-CEKK	Best Off Sky Ranger Swift 912S(1) *(Built J A Hunt - pr.no.BMAA HB/522)*	SKR0610744		15. 2.07	J A Hunt	(Clydach, Abergavenny)	29. 4.09P

G-CEKL	Replica Plans SE.5a	PFA 020-13793		28. 2.07	B P North(As "C6468:A" in RFC c/s) RAF Halton
	(Built B P North)				
G-CEKM	Avtech Jabiru UL-450	PFA 274A-14436		15. 2.07	D R Morton and R H Bain Headon Farm, Retford 22. 9.09P
	(Built D R Morton and R H Bain)				
G-CEKO	Robin DR.400-100 Cadet	1932	PH-VSU	30. 3.07	R J Hopkins Exeter 3. 4.09E
			OO-KPF, PH-VSU		
G-CEKS	Cameron Z-105 Balloon (Hot Air)	11003		13. 6.07	Phoenix Balloons Ltd "Champagne Taittinger"
					Bristol 22. 4.09E
G-CEKT	Flight Design CTSW	07.02.14		5. 4.07	G Lund tr Charlie Tango Group Wycombe Air Park 4. 4.08P
	(Assembled P&M Aviation Ltd with c/n 8272)				
G-CEKV	Europa Aviation Europa	PFA 247-12493		19. 3. 07	K Atkinson (Greenodd, Ulverston)
	(Built K Atkinson)				
G-CEKW	Avtech Jabiru J430	PFA 336-14340		12. 1.07	J G Culley tr J430 Syndicate
	(Buit J G Culley and 3 partners)				Hall Farm, Lillingstone Lovell, Buckingham 13. 6.09P
G-CEKX	Robinson R44 Raven II	11680		17. 4.07	Heli Air Ltd
					Wellesbourne Mountford/Wycombe Air Park 28. 4.09E
G-CELA	Boeing 737-377QC	23663	VH-CZK	15. 8.03	Dart Group PLC (Operated.Jet2.com) "jet 2 Newcastle"
					Leeds-Bradford 20. 1.10E
G-CELB	Boeing 737-377	23664	VH-CZL	3. 7.03	Dart Group PLC (Operated.Jet2.com) "jet 2Yorkshire"
					Leeds-Bradford 10. 5.09E
G-CELC	Boeing 737-33A	23831	N190FH	4. 7.03	Dart Group PLC (Operated.Jet2.com) "jet2 Prague"
			VH-CZV, G-OBMA		Leeds-Bradford 12.10.09E
G-CELD	Boeing 737-33A	23832	N191FH	4. 7.03	Dart Group PLC (Operated.Jet2.com) "jet2 Espana"
			VH-CZW, G-OBMB		Leeds-Bradford 1. 2.10E
G-CELE	Boeing 737-33A	24029	VH-CZX	11. 7.03	Dart Group PLC (Operated.Jet2.com) "jet2 Belfast"
			G-MONN		Leeds-Bradford 18. 8.09E
G-CELF	Boeing 737-377	24302	S7-ABB	5.10.04	Dart Group PLC (Operated.Jet2.com) "jet2 Valencia"
			VH-CZM, N113AW, VH-CZM		Leeds-Bradford 7.11.09E
G-CELG	Boeing 737-377	24303	S7-ABD	26.10.04	Dart Group PLC (Operated.Jet2.com) "jet2 London"
			VH-CZN		Leeds-Bradford 19.12.09E
G-CELH	Boeing 737-330	23525	D-ABXD	23. 8.04	Dart Group PLC (Operated.Jet2.com) "jet2 Faro"
			(PR-GLB), D-ABXD, TF-ABL, D-ABXD		Leeds-Bradford 24. 9.09E
G-CELI	Boeing 737-330	23526	D-ABXE	21. 9.04	Dart Group PLC (Operated.Jet2.com) "jet2 Manchester)
			(PR-GLC), D-ABXE		Leeds-Bradford 17.11.09E
G-CELJ	Boeing 737-330	23529	LZ-BOG	23.12.04	Dart Group PLC (Operated.Jet2.com) "jet 2 Italia"
			(PR-GLF), (D-ABXI), LZ-BOG, D-ABXI		Leeds-Bradford 12. 2.09E
G-CELK	Boeing 737-330	23530	LZ-BOH	11. 2.05	Dart Group PLC (Operated.Jet2.com) "jet 2 Edinburgh"
			(PR-GLJ), (D-ABXK), LZ-BOH, D-ABXK		Leeds-Bradford 9. 3.09E
G-CELM	Cameron C-80 Balloon (Hot Air)	10931		10. 5.07	L Greaves Doulting, Shepton Mallet 9. 7.09E
G-CELN	UltraMagic S-105 Balloon (Hot Air)	105/155		15. 6.07	B S Smith Congleton 17. 6.08E
G-CELO	Boeing 737-33A(QC)	24028	TF-ELO	17. 2.06	Dart Group PLC (Operated.Jet2.com)
			G-CELO, TF-ELO, F-GIXK, G-MONP		Leeds-Bradford 22. 1.10E
G-CELP	Boeing 737-330	23522	TF-ELP	27.10.03	Dart Group PLC (Operated.Jet2.com)
			D-ABXA, N1786B		Leeds-Bradford 26.10.09E
G-CELR	Boeing 737-330	23523	TF-ELR	4.11.03	Dart Group PLC (Operated.Jet2.com)
			D-ABXB		Leeds-Bradford 3.11.09E
G-CELS	Boeing 737-377	23660	VH-CZH	17. 5.02	Dart Group PLC (Operated.Jet2.com) "jet2 Leeds Bradford"
					Leeds-Bradford 19. 6.09E
G-CELU	Boeing 737-377	23657	VH-CZE	13. 6.02	Dart Group PLC (Operated.Jet2.com) "jet2 Barcelona"
					Leeds-Bradford 30. 7.09E
G-CELV	Boeing 737-377	23661	VH-CZI	2.10.02	Dart Group PLC (Operated.Jet2.com) "jet2 Amsterdam"
					Leeds-Bradford 10. 2.09E
G-CELW	Boeing 737-377	23659	N659DG	4. 7.02	Dart Group PLC (Operated.Jet2.com)
			G-CELW, VH-CZG		Leeds-Bradford 14.10.08E
G-CELX	Boeing 737-377	23654	VH-CZB	5. 3.03	Dart Group PLC (Operated.Jet2.com) "jet2 Malaga"
			N5573B		Leeds-Bradford 15. 4.09E
G-CELY	Boeing 737-377	23662	N662DG	29. 4.03	Dart Group PLC (Operated.Jet2.com) "jet2 Ireland"
			G-CELY, VH-CZJ		Leeds-Bradford 22. 4.09E
G-CELZ	Boeing 737-377	23658	VH-CZF	22. 9.03	Dart Group PLC (Operated.Jet2.com) "jet2 Paris"
					Leeds-Bradford 2. 8.09E
G-CEMA	Alpi Pioneer 200	PFA 334-14569		5. 3.07	D M Bracken Shobdon 7. 5.09P
	(Built D M Bracken)				
G-CEMB	P&M Aviation Quik GT450	8262		13. 4.07	M E Howard tr RAF Microlight Flying Association
					RAF Halton 12. 4.08P
G-CEMC	Robinson R44 Raven II	11620		26. 2.07	Aerocorp Ltd Liverpool-John Lennon 14. 3.09E
G-CEMD	Piper PA-28-161 Warrior II	2842263	D-EVCC	10. 4.07	Caernarfon Airworld Ltd Caernarfon 18. 4.09E
			N31367		
G-CEME	Evektor EV-97 Eurostar	PFA 315-14632		20. 2.07	M P and E J Hill Milton, Cleobury Mortimer 20. 3.09P
	(Built G R Pritchard)				
G-CEMF	Cameron C-80 Balloon (Hot Air)	10892		22. 6.07	Linear Communications Consultants Ltd (Linear
					Communications titles) Devauden, Chepstow 25. 4.09E
G-CEMG	UltraMagic M-105 Balloon (Hot Air)	105/153		16. 4.07	Comunicazione In Volo SRL Carpineti, Italy 17. 8.09E
G-CEMH	Cessna 172S Skyhawk	172S10420	N12067	16. 4.07	S Viner Blackpool 13. 5.09E
G-CEMI	Europa Aviation Europa XS	PFA 247-13989		2. 4.07	B D A Morris (Cheltenham)
	(Built B D A Morris)				
G-CEMK	Boeing 767-222	21865	N604UA	23. 2.07	UK International Airlines Ltd
					(Airline suspended operations and not delivered)
G-CEML	P&M Pegasus Quik	8260		5. 4.07	C J Kew Longacre Farm, Sandy 13. 4.08P
G-CEMM	P&M Aviation Quik GT450	8253		23. 4.07	M A Rhodes (Congleton) 22. 4.09P
G-CEMN	UltraMagic S-130 Balloon (Hot Air)	130/56		9. 5.07	Associazione Sportiva Sorvoolare
					Crevalcore, Italy 23.10.09E
G-CEMO	P&M Aviation Quik GT450	8265		8. 5.07	L E Craig (Welling) 29. 5.08E
G-CEMP	BB Ultralight BB-03 UK Trya 503(1)	xxx		14. 3.07	P Robshaw (Trike noted SPLASH, NEC 11.08)
	(Built P Robshaw - pr.no. BMAA HB/527)				Rufforth

G-CEMR	Mainair Blade 912	1066-0196-7-W868	I-4651	13. 4.07	D A Valentine	(Hargrave, Wellingborough)	13. 4.09P
G-CEMS	MD Helicopters MD.900 Explorer	900-00089	PK-OCR N70089	30. 3.07	Yorkshire Air Ambulance Ltd	Leeds-Bradford	15. 8.09E
G-CEMT	P&M Aviation Quik GT450	8251		22. 2.07	A Dixon	Tarn Farm, Cockerham	8. 5.09P
G-CEMU	Cameron C-80 Balloon (Hot Air)	11029		13. 7.07	J G O'Connell	Pattiswick, Braintree	12. 8.09E
G-CEMV	Lindstrand LBL 105A Balloon (Hot Air)	1164		22. 6.07	R G Turnbull	Glasbury, Hereford	19. 8.09E
G-CEMW	Lindstrand LBL Bananas SS Balloon (Hot Air) 388		G-OCAW	23. 4.07	T G Read t/a Top Banana Balloon Team	Mobberley, Knutsford	1. 7.09E
G-CEMX	P&M Aviation Quik	8281		30. 8.07	S J Meehan	(Liss)	29. 8.08P
G-CEMY	Alpi Pioneer 300	PFA 330-14440		24. 4.07	J C A Garland and P F Salter	Kemble	21. 8.08P
	(Built J C A Garland, P F and C M Salter)						
G-CEMZ	P&M Pegasus Quik	8280		31. 5.07	D Jessop	Abbey Warren Farm, Bucknall	30. 5.09P
G-CENA	Dyn'Aéro MCR-01 ULC Banbi	PFA 301B-14640		25. 5.07	R Germany	Knapthorpe Lodge, Caunton	28. 8.08P
	(Built R Germany)						
	(Veered to the left after landing at Caunton 21. 4.08 and went into a ditch, causing substantial damage)						
G-CENB	Evektor EV-97 teamEurostar UK	2913		16. 4.07	G Suckling and S J Joseph	Graveley Hall Farm, Graveley	15. 4.09P
G-CENC	Christen Eagle II	PFA 138-14627		20. 4.07	J R Pearce	Compton Abbas	11. 5.09P
	(Built J R Pearce)						
G-CEND	Evektor EV-97 teamEurostar UK	2916		10. 5.07	Flylight Airsports Ltd	Sywell	9. 5.09P
G-CENE	Flight Design CTSW	07.03.20		1. 5.07	G K Kenealey tr CT Flying Group	Barton	30. 4.09P
	(Assembled P&M Aviation Ltd with c/n 8273)						
G-CENF	ELA Aviacion ELA 07S	01071220722		3. 9.07	D G Hill	(Blackpool)	
G-CENG	Best Off Sky Ranger 912(2)	SKR0603701		1. 5.07	R A Knight	Chilbolton	7. 7.09P
	(Built R A Knight - pr.no.BMAA HB/518)						
G-CENH	Tecnam P2002-EA Sierra	PFA 333-14564		3. 5.07	M W Taylor	Insch	14.11.08P
	(Built M W Taylor and J P Kovacs)						
G-CENI	Super Marine Spitfire Mk.26	PFA 324-14102		24. 4.07	D B Smith	Aboyne	
	(Built D B Smith)						
G-CENJ	Medway SLA 100 Executive	240407		2. 5.07	M Ingleton *"Hot Lips"*	Stoke, Isle of Grain	1. 5.09P
	(Originally registered as Medway SLA 951, amended 2 .6.08)						
G-CENK	Schempp-Hirth Nimbus 4DT	9/40	BGA4482-JFQ	4. 5.07	B C Morris tr November Kilo Syndicate *"651"*	Lasham	16. 9.09
G-CENL	P&M Aviation Quik GT450	8267		26. 5.07	S Baker and P von Sydow	Long Marston	25. 5.08P
G-CENM	Evektor EV-97 Eurostar	2003.20.07		20. 3.07	N D Meer	Tamworth	31. 5.08E
	(Built N D Meer, pr. no PFA 315-14247; kit no conflicts with G-IHOT)						
G-CENN	Cameron C-60 Balloon (Hot Air)	11013		15. 3.07	Stonebee Ltd	Chedworth, Cheltenham	30. 7.09E
G-CENO	Aerospool WT9 UK Dynamic	DY188/2007		8. 5.07	R O Lewthwaite	Caunton	15. 1.10P
	(Official c/n is "DY188")						
G-CENP	Ace Magic Laser	AA00126	G-93-1	19. 6.07	P & M Aviation Ltd	(Trike noted 12.08) Rochdale	
	(Solo 35 fitted to another trike without serial number and pi on dash-panel; AA00126 is possibly wing number)						
G-CENR	ELA Aviacion ELA 07S	03061030722		2.11.07	M S Gough	(Trottiscliffe, West Malling)	
G-CENS	Best Off Sky Ranger Swift 912S(1)			9. 5.07	N D and M Stannard	RAF Halton	16. 3.09P
	(Built N D Stannard)	SKR0701769	*(Pr.no.BMAA HB/536)*				
G-CENU	ICP MXP-740 Savannah Jabiru(5)	04-11-51-344		15. 5.07	N Farrell	(Tarmonbarry, County Roscommon)	
	(Built N Farrell - pr.no.BMAA HB/534)						
G-CENV	P&M Aviation Quik GT450	8275		4. 6.07	M E Howard tr RAF Microlight Flying Association (NV)	RAF Wyton	3. 8.08P
G-CENW	Evektor EV-97 Eurostar	PFA 315-14612		14. 3.07	W S Long	Mayfield Farm, Stevenston	1. 7.09P
	(Built W S Long)						
G-CENX	Lindstrand LBL 360A Balloon (Hot-Air)	1160		4. 6.07	Richard Nash Cars Ltd *(Job 24/ Drive 24 titles)*	Norwich	27. 1.10E
G-CENZ	Aeros Discus-Alizé	014.07/001		19. 7.07	J D Buchanan	Coldharbour Farm, Wilingham	
	(Discus wing and DTA Alizé trike)						
G-CEOB	Pitts S-1S Special	DIH-1	N8036J C-FQEZ	30. 5.07	P A Moslin and I Gallacher	RAF Halton	5. 2.09E
	(Built D I Heaps)			*(Originally regd as S-1, amended 17.3.08)*			
G-CEOC	Tecnam P2002-EA Sierra	PFA 333-14604		31. 5.07	M A Lomas	Leicester	14 1.09P
	(Built M A Lomas)						
G-CEOD	Boeing 767-319ER	30586	ZK-NCO	6. 9.07	Globespan Airways Ltd t/a Flyglobespan.com	Edinburgh	27. 9.09E
G-CEOE	American Champion 8KCAB Super Decathlon	803-97	N748PH	27. 4.07	R Boucher	Griffins Farm, Temple Bruer	16. 7.09E
G-CEOF	Piper PA-28R-201 Arrow III	2837008	N805ND	4. 6.07	J H Sandham t/a J H Sandham Aviation	Carlisle	8. 6.09E
G-CEOG	Piper PA-28R-201 Arrow III	2837025	N173ND	4. 6.07	A J Gardiner	Stapleford	11.12.09E
G-CEOH	Raj Hamsa X'Air Falcon ULP(1)	666		13. 6.07	Miles Blackburn Ltd *(Noted 7.08)*	(Sedburgh)	
	(Built J C Miles - pr.no.BMAA HB/525) (UL250i)						
G-CEOI	Cameron C-60 Balloon (Hot Air)	10977		27. 6.07	M E White	Abbeyview, Trim, County Meath	9. 7.09E
G-CEOJ	Eurocopter EC.155B	6575	C-FORE	1. 8.07	Starspeed Ltd	Blackbushe	4. 9.09E
G-CEOK	Cessna 150M	15077928	N8375U	12. 6.07	G Johnson	North Weald	27. 4.09E
G-CEOL	Flylight Lightfly-Discus	001		12. 6.07	R M Ellis	(Bredons Norton, Tewkesbury)	X
	(Ukraine built Aeros Discus T sailwing on basic trike unit and marketed as "Flight Dragonfly Discus")						
G-CEOM	Avtech Jabiru UL-450	PFA 27A-14455		12. 6.07	J R Caylow	Headon Farm, Retford	22. 9.09P
	(Built J R Caylow)						
G-CEON	Raj Hamsa X'Air Hawk	PFA 340-14673		15. 6.07	K S Campbell	(Erskine)	11. 5.09P
	(Built A Anderson)						
G-CEOO	P&M Aviation Quik GT450	8257		30. 3.07	S Moran	(Werrington, Stoke-on-Trent)	7. 4.09P
G-CEOP	Aeroprakt A22-L Foxbat	PFA 317A-14671		15. 6.07	P M Ford	(South Weald, Brentwood)	1. 9.09P
	(Built P M Ford)						
G-CEOS	Cameron C-90 Balloon (Hot Air)	11047		4. 9.07	Balloon School (International) Ltd t/a British School of Ballooning	Colhook Common, Petworth	4. 8.09E
G-CEOT	Bailey Quattro 175-Dudek reAction Sport	P 02908		30. 5.07	J Kelly	Longstanton, Cambridgeshore	X
G-CEOU	Lindstrand LBL 31A Balloon (Hot Air)	1157		15. 6.07	Lindstrand Hot Air Balloons Ltd *"LBL"*	Oswestry	5. 9.09E

Reg	Type	C/n	Prev id	Date	Owner/Operator	Location	Expiry
G-CEOV	Lindstrand LBL 120A Balloon (Hot Air)	1158		18. 7.07	Lindstrand Hot Air Balloons Ltd "LBL"	Oswestry	29. 7.09E
G-CEOW	Europa Aviation Europa XS	xxx		4. 6.07	R W Wood	(Little Cowarne, Bromyard)	
	(Built R W Wood - pr.no.PFA 247-13877)						
G-CEOX	Rotorsport UK MT-03	RSUK/MT-03/014		27. 6.07	L C Griffiths	(Temple Guiting, Cheltenham)	9.10.09P
G-CEOY	Schweizer 269C-1 (Schweizer 300)	0234	EI-DOJ	2. 7.07	C R and S E Hewgill t/a CBL Industrial (Operated Bournemouth Helicopters)	Bournemouth	28. 6.09E
G-CEOZ	Passion'Ailes Chariot Z-Paramania Action GT26	1006148		21. 6.07	A M Shepherd	(Silverstone, Towcester)	
	(Powered paraglider (PPG) consisting of Paramania Action GT26 sailwing and Passion'Ailes (PAP = Propulsion Auxiliare Parapente) Chariot Z)						
G-CEPA	McDonnell Douglas MD-82	49425	B-2104 N1005T	10. 5.07	PL Aviation Ltd (Noted as "B-2104 "10.07)	Bucharest, Romania	
G-CEPB	McDonnell Douglas MD-82	49428	B-2105 N1005U	17. 5.07	PL Aviation Ltd (Noted as "B-2105" 10.07)	Bucharest, Romania	
G-CEPC	McDonnell Douglas MD-82	49502	B-2108	22. 3.07	PL Aviation Ltd (Noted as "B-2108" 10.07)	Bucharest, Romania	
G-CEPD	McDonnell Douglas MD-82	49505	B-2121	17. 5.07	PL Aviation Ltd (Noted as "B-2121" 10.07)	Bucharest, Romania	
G-CEPE	McDonnell Douglas MD-82	49506	B-2122	10. 5.07	PL Aviation Ltd (Noted as "B-2122" 10.07)	Bucharest, Romania	
G-CEPI	McDonnell Douglas MD-82	53169	B-2148 N838AU	8. 6.07	PL Aviation Ltd (Noted as "B-2148" 10.07)	Bucharest, Romania	
G-CEPJ	McDonnell Douglas MD-82	53170	B-2149 N839AU	8. 6.07	PL Aviation Ltd (Noted as "B-2149" 10.07)	Bucharest, Romania	
G-CEPK	McDonnell Douglas MD-82	53171	B-2150 N840AU	8. 6.07	PL Aviation Ltd (Noted as "B-2150" 10.07)	Bucharest, Romania	
G-CEPL	Super Marine Spitfire Mk.26	PFA 324-14507		19. 6.07	S R Marsh	(Grays)	
	(Built S R Marsh)						
G-CEPM	Avtech Jabiru J430	PFA 336-14517		1. 5.07	T R Sinclair	Lamb Holm Farm, Orkney	9. 6.09P
	(Built T R Sinclair)						
G-CEPN	New Kolb Firefly	FF05.4.00048		20 06.07	P A Brigstock tr Papa November Group	Shacklewood Farm, Empingham	
	(Built M H Moulai)						
G-CEPP	P&M Aviation Quik GT450	8266		10. 5.07	W M Studley	Middle Pymore Farm, Bridport	9. 5.09P
G-CEPR	Cameron Z-90 Balloon (Hot Air)	11057		4. 9.07	Sport Promotion SRL "Pan di Stelle"	La Morra, Italy	30. 8.09E
G-CEPS	TL Ultralight TL-2000 Sting	PFA 347-14705		2. 7.07	P A Saunders	Otherton, Cannock	
	(Built P A Saunders)						
G-CEPT	SOCATA TB-20 Trinidad	1240	G-BTEK	27. 8.04	P J Caiger	Biggin Hill	20.11.09E
G-CEPU	Cameron Z-77 Balloon (Hot Air)	11030		31. 8.07	Liquigas SpA "Liquigas"	Mondovi, Italy	9. 7.09E
G-CEPV	Cameron Z-77 Balloon (Hot Air)	11031		31. 8.07	Liquigas SpA "Liquigas"	Mondovi, Italy	9. 7.09E
G-CEPW	Alpi Pioneer 300	xxx		27. 6.07	N K Spedding	(Hatton Green)	
	(Built N K Spedding - pr.no.PFA 330-14293)						
G-CEPX	Cessna 152	15285792	N94808	13. 6.07	Cristal Air Ltd	Shoreham	13. 9.09E
G-CEPY	Comco Ikarus C42 FB80	0707-6900		6. 8.07	L Lay	Clench Common	5. 8.09P
G-CEPZ	Dan Rihn DR.107 One Design	0038	N107TH	14. 5.07	P J Pengilly	(Church Crookham, Fleet)	
	(Built J J Tomlinson)						
G-CERA	Flight Design CTSW	07.04.05		4. 6.07	Mainair Microlight School Ltd	Barton	6. 6.09P
	(Assembled P&M Aviation Ltd with c/n 8287)						
G-CERB	Best Off Sky Ranger Swift 912S(1)			31. 5.07	J J Littler		
	(Built J J Littler)	SKRxxxx772				(Limmer Pond, Aldingbourne, Chichester)	
	(Pr.no.BMAA HB/537)						
G-CERC	Cameron Z-350 Balloon (Hot Air)	11028		20.12.07	Ballooning Network Ltd "Bath Building Society"	Southville, Bristol	8.10.09E
G-CERD	de Havilland DHC-1 Chipmunk 22	7	CS-AZM Portuguese AF 1317	25. 7.07	A C Darby	(Aylesbury)	
	(Built OGMA)						
G-CERE	Evektor EV-97 teamEurostar UK	2931		4. 7.07	Airbourne Aviation Ltd (Damaged at Newton Peverill 9.9.08)	Popham	3. 7.09P
	(Built Cosmik Aviation)						
G-CERF	Rotorsport UK MT-03	RSUK/MT-03/017		24. 7.07	P J Robinson	Kirkbride	22. 9.09P
G-CERG	Magni M16C Tandem Trainer	892851		10. 8.07	D C Fairbrass	Willingale	
	(Officially regd as c/n 16-07-4344)						
G-CERH	Cameron C-90 Balloon (Hot Air)	10941		17. 7.07	J Tyrell and W Rousell	Wellingborough	30. 9.09E
G-CERI	Europa Aviation Europa XS	511		20. 8.03	S J M Shepherd	(Bodelwyddan, Rhyl)	
	(Built S J M Shepherd - pr.no.PFA 247-13970)						
G-CERK	Van's RV-9A	PFA 320-14049		2. 7.07	P E Brown	Swansea	4. 9.09P
	(Built P E Brown)						
G-CERL	UltraMagic M-77 Balloon (Hot Air)	77/309		17. 9.07	A M Holly "The Book People"	Breadstone, Berkeley	28.10.08E
G-CERM	Kubicek BB-22Z Balloon (Hot Air)	528		25. 7.07	A M Holly (AMO Blink Eye Drops titles)	Breadstone, Berkeley	29. 3.09E
G-CERN	P&M Aviation Quik GT450	8299		26. 7.07	N D Leak	Clench Common	30. 7.09P
G-CERO	Agusta A109C	7627	G-OBEK G-CDDJ, RP-C2877, TC-HCM, D-HAAV, JA9999	31. 5.07	Castle Air Charters Ltd (Operated Agusta Westland)	Yeovil	4. 8.08E
G-CERP	P&M Aviation Quik GT450	8285		12. 7.07	A Morrison	East Fortune	11. 7.08P
G-CERS	Robinson R44 Raven II	11840		23. 7.07	P J Egan tr Egan Helicopters	Ellough, Beccles	23. 8.09E
G-CERT	Mooney M 20K Mooney 231	25-1134		5.10.87	J A Nisbet	Fowlmere	13. 6.09E
G-CERV	P&M Aviation Quik GT450	8300		31. 7.07	J MacDonald tr East Fortune Flyers	East Fortune	30. 7.09P
G-CERW	P&M Pegasus Quik	8294		3. 5.07	J I Smith	St Michaels	29. 1.10P
G-CERX	Raytheon Hawker 850XP	258810	OE-GJA	21 8.07	Hangar 8 Ltd	Oxford	6. 9.09E
G-CERY	SAAB-Scania 2000	2000-008	SE-008, HB-!ZE, (D-ADIB), SE-008	21 9.07	Air Kilroe Ltd t/a Eastern Airways	Humberside	20. 9.09E
G-CERZ	SAAB-Scania 2000	2000-042	SE-LSA	24. 8.07	Air Kilroe Ltd t/a Eastern Airways	Humberside	22. 8.09E
G-CESA	Jodel DR.1050M-1 Excellence replica	PFA 304-13753		9. 7.07	P D Thomas and T J Bates	Dairy House Farm, Worleston	
	(Built P D Thomas and T J Bates)						
G-CESB	Robinson R44 Raven I	1369	OO-FXS	5. 6.07	MFH Helicopters Ltd	Conington	26. 6.09E
G-CESC	Cameron Z-105 Balloon (Hot Air)	11055		30. 7.07	Klober Ltd (Permo Air titles)	Pill, Bristol	19. 8.09E

G-CESD	Best Off Sky Ranger Swift 912S(1)			15. 5.07	S E Dancaster	Newton Bank Farm, Daresbury	19.12.09P
	(Built S E Dancaster)	SKR0701770	*(Project no.BMAA HB/535)*				
G-CESF	Evektor EV-97 teamEurostar UK	3008		4. 3.08	W Goldsmith	(Boldon Colliery)	13. 8.08P
	(Built Cosmik Aviation Ltd)						
G-CESG	P&M Aviation Quik GT450	8211	I-8211	19. 7.07	L Greco	Centallo, Italy	
G-CESH	Cameron Z-90 Balloon (Hot Air)	11061		30. 7.07	The Balloon Company Ltd t/a First Flight *"Cabot Circus"*		
						Langford, Bristol	19. 8.09E
G-CESI	Aeroprakt A22-L Foxbat	PFA 317A-14643		25. 7.07	D J Ashley	(Llandrindod Wells)	12.12.08P
	(Built D J Ashley)						
G-CESJ	Raj Hamsa X'Air Hawk	1124		8. 8.07	J Bolton and R Shewan		
	(Built B K Harrison and R G Cameron, pr. no PFA 340-14677)					Pittrichie Farm, Whiterashes	17. 6.09P
G-CESL	Fresh Breeze Muller & Werner Flyke-Silex L-Monster			1. 6.07	T J Gayton-Polley	(Billingshurst)	X
	F1073, 19609 and M0114						
G-CESM	TL 2000 Sting Carbon	LAA 347-14801		15. 9.08	E Stephenson	(South Shields)	
	(Built E Stephenson)						
G-CESN	Robinson R-22 Beta	4176	N30667	27. 9.07	Helieagle Ltd	Coventry	11.10.09E
G-CESO	Robinson R44 Raven II	11859		3. 8.07	Heliverne	(La Vilie Aux Dames, France)	1.10.09P
G-CESP	Rutan Cozy Mk.4	PFA 159A-13860		29. 6.07	T N Craigie	(Kirkcaldy)	
	(Built T N Craigie)						
G-CESR	P&M Aviation Quik GT450	8304		20. 8.07	G Kerr	East Fortune	19. 8.08P
G-CESS	Cessna F172G	F172-0181	G-ATGO	23. 7.07	Liverpool Flying School Ltd	Liverpool-John Lennon	26.11.09E
	(Built Reims Aviation SA)						
G-CEST	Robinson R44 Raven	1424	D-HALZ	19. 7.07	Roofline Scotland Ltd	Lower Baads, Peterculter	24. 8.09E
G-CESU	Robinson R22 Beta	4139	N30804	4. 9.07	Alcock and Brown Aviation Ltd	County of Derry	23.10.08E
G-CESV	Evektor EV-97 teamEurostar UK	3011		17. 9.07	N Jones	Willingale	15. 9.09P
G-CESW	Flight Design CTSW	07.06.04		20. 6.07	J Cunliffe and A Costello	St Michaels	7. 7.09P
	(Assembled P&M Aviation Ltd with c/n 8296)						
G-CESX	Cameron Z-31 Balloon (Hot Air)	11074		6. 9.07	Wye Valley Aviation Ltd	Ross-on-Wye	8. 9.08E
G-CESY	Cameron Z-31 Balloon (Hot Air)	11075		6. 9.07	Wye Valley Aviation Ltd	Ross-on-Wye	8. 9.08E
G-CESZ	CZAW Sportcruiser	PFA 338-14652		8. 8.07	J A and J M Iszard	Great Oakley	2. 4.09P
	(Built J A Iszard)						
G-CETB	Robin DR.400-180 Régent	1369	D-EFQR	31. 7.07	M W Cater tr QR Flying Club	Husbands Bosworth	29. 9.09E
G-CETD	Piper PA-28-161 Warrior III	2842152	N5351Y	17. 7.07	Plane Talking Ltd	Elstree	19.12.09E
G-CETE	Piper PA-28-161 Warrior III	2842079	N120FT	17. 7.07	Plane Talking Ltd	Elstree	30.10.09E
	(Thielert TAE 125)						
G-CETF	Flight Design CTSW	07.06.05		24. 8.07	P&M Aviation Ltd	Rochdale	23. 8.09P
	(Assembled P&M Aviation Ltd with c/n 8318)						
G-CETG	Alpha Aviation Alpha R2160i	160Ai-0008		01. 2.08	D J Lawrence	Poplar Hall Farm, Elmsett	18. 2.09E
	(Marked as "Alpha 160 Ai")						
G-CETH	Flight Design CTSW	07.07.17		29. 8.07	R A Morris	Shenstone	28. 8.08P
	(Assembled P&M Aviation Ltd with c/n 8317)						
G-CETI	Van's RV-8	PFA 303-14466		11. 7.07	Cavendish Aviation Ltd	Gamston	
	(Built E M Marsh)						
G-CETJ	Slingsby T 59D Kestrel 19	1863	BGA1988-DBQ	17. 8.07	S M Sanderson	Sutton Bank	10.10.07
G-CETK	Cameron Z-145 Balloon (Hot Air)	4770	OO-BWN	12. 9.07	R H Etherington	Siena, Italy	9.11.09E
G-CETL	P&M Aviation Quik GT450	8307		13. 8.07	J I Greenshields	Dunkeswell	12. 8.09P
G-CETM	P&M Aviation Quik GT450	8298		31. 7.07	I Burnside	East Fortune	30. 7.09P
G-CETN	Haseldine Hummelbird	PFA 127-13044		31. 8.07	A A Haseldine	(Craswell, Hereford)	
	(Built A A Haseldine)						
G-CETO	Best Off Sky Ranger Swift 912S(1)			13. 7.07	B and J Hudson	(Gosport)	29. 1.09P
	(Built P J Shergold)	SKRxxxxxx	*(Project no.BMAA HB/541)*				
G-CETP	Van's RV-9A	PFA 320-14012		3. 9.07	D Boxall and S Hill	(Bath)	
	(Built D Boxall and S Hill)						
G-CETR	Comco Ikarus C42 FB100	0706-6898		2. 8.07	A E Lacy-Hulbert	Redlands, Swindon	12. 8.09P
	(Built Aerosport Ltd)						
G-CETS	Van's RV-7	70529	N557WM	23. 8.07	J A Crew tr TS Group	Swanborough Farm, Lewes	15. 1.09P
	(Built M R Wyatt)						
G-CETT	Evektor EV-97 teamEurostar UK	3006		24. 7.07	S R Pike	Wycombe Air Park	17. 7.09P
G-CETU	Best Off Sky Ranger Swift 912S(1)			12. 9.07	M A Sweet	Brook Farm, Pilling	26. 6.09P
	(Built M A Sweet)	SKRxxxx803	*(Project no.BMAA HB/551)*				
G-CETV	Best Off Sky Ranger Swift 912S(1)			22. 6.07	K J Gay	Newtownards	22. 8.08P
	(Built K J Gay)	SKRxxxx759	*(Project no.BMAA HB/532)*				
G-CETX	Alpi Pioneer 300	PFA 330-14573		23. 7.07	M C Ellis	(Medstead, Alton)	
	(Built M C Ellis)						
G-CETY	Rans S-6-ES Coyote II	PFA 204-14654		17. 7.07	J North	(Felmersham, Bedford)	
	(Built J North)						
G-CETZ	Comco Ikarus C42 Cyclone FB100	0706-6899		8.11.07	Airways Airsports Ltd	Darley Moor, Ashbourne	7.11.08P
G-CEUB	Britten-Norman BN-2B-26 Islander	2306		27. 7.07	Britten-Norman Aircraft Ltd	Bembridge	
	(Originally regd as BN-2B-20, type amended 18.12.08)						
G-CEUC	Britten-Norman BN-2B-20 Islander	2307		27. 7.07	Britten-Norman Aircraft Ltd	Bembridge	
G-CEUD	Britten-Norman BN-2B-20 Islander	2309		27. 7.07	Britten-Norman Aircraft Ltd	Bembridge	
G-CEUE	Britten-Norman BN-2B-20 Islander	2310		27. 7.07	Britten-Norman Aircraft Ltd	Bembridge	
G-CEUF	P&M Aviation Quik GT450	8325		12.10.07	G T Snoddon	Newtownards	11.10.08P
G-CEUG	Schleicher ASW 27	27114	BGA4696-JQM	13. 9.07	R J Smith	Wycombe Air Park	29.11.07
G-CEUH	P&M Aviation Quik GT450	8316		25.10.07	North West Turf Ltd	(Ormskirk)	28.10.08P
G-CEUJ	Best Off Sky Ranger Swift 912S(1)			14.12.07	J P Batty and J R C Brightman		
		SKRxxxx802				Sackville Lodge, Riseley	6. 7.09P
	(Built J P Batty and J R C Brightman - pr.no.BMAA HB/548)						
G-CEUL	UltraMagic M-105 Balloon (Hot Air)	105/157		4. 1.08	R A Vale	Hurcott, Kidderminster	20. 1.09E
G-CEUM	UltraMagic M-120 Balloon (Hot Air)	120/30		28.11.07	Bridges Van Hire Ltd	Awsworth, Nottingham	25.11.09E
G-CEUN	Schempp-Hirth Discus CS	075CS	BGA4694-JQK	8.10.07	J G Arnold tr RAF Gliding and Soaring Association		
			RAFGGA 501		*(Operated Chilterns Gliding Centre)*	RAF Halton	15. 1.08
G-CEUO	Cessna 550 Citation II	550-0033	LX-GDL	26.11.07	Unique Air International Ltd	Newcastle	30. 9.09E
			LX-JET, LX-GDL, F-WPLT, F-GPLT, N46DA, N755CM, N59MJ, TR-LYE, (N3252M)				

Reg	Type	C/n	Prev id	Date	Owner/Operator	Location	Date
G-CEUP	PZL-Swidnik PW-5 Smyk	17.04.010	BGA4988-KCQ OY-XYE	27. 9.07	P H Young	Chipping	27. 3.08
G-CEUR	Schempp-Hirth Ventus 2cxT	109/303	BGA5060-KFQ D-KKAO	26. 9.07	P R Hamblin *"P6"*	Lasham	6. 9.08
G-CEUS	Cessna 152	15281906	N67548	17. 1.08	R Germany	Norwich	
G-CEUT	Hoffman H 36 Dimona	36270	LY-GDW F-CGAX	5.10.07	P Pozerskis	Husbands Bosworth	9. 4.09E
G-CEUU	Robinson R44 Raven II	11949		12.10.07	A Stafford-Jones	(Churt, Farnham)	13.11.09E
G-CEUV	Cameron C-90 Balloon (Hot Air)	11078		18.12.07	A M Holly *"Silverline"*	Breadstone, Berkeley	16. 1.09E
G-CEUW	Zenair CH.601XL Zodiac (Built M Taylor)	PFA 162B-14554		4.10.07	M Taylor	(Hollym, Withernsea)	10. 3.09P
G-CEUX	Robinson R44 Raven II	11864		12.10.07	O'Reilly Aviation Ltd	(Wicklow, County Wicklow)	23.10.08E
G-CEUZ	P&M Aviation Quik GT450	8321		25.10.07	M Gallagher	Charterhall	24.10.08P
	(Damaged on landing at Charterhall 6. 5.08)						
G-CEVA	Comco Ikarus C42 FB80 (Built Aerosport Ltd)	0709-6915		25.10.07	Sport Aviation Training Ltd	(Nunnington, York)	28.10.09P
G-CEVB	P&M Aviation Quik GT450	8315		3.10.07	J L Guy and N Hartley	Baxby Manor, Husthwaite	2.10.08P
G-CEVC	Van's RV-4 (Built K W Pabo)	2726	N2063Z	21. 9.07	P A Brook	Shoreham	15. 1.10P
G-CEVD	Rolladen-Schneider LS3	3024	BGA2979-EVD N63LS, D-7914	21.12.07	C H Appleyard	Lasham	14. 2.08
G-CEVE	Centrair 101A Pégase	101A0141	BGA2980-EVE	17. 9.07	J W North and T Newham *"49"*	Lasham	29. 9.09
G-CEVG	P&M Pegasus Quik	8319		25.10.07	R Higton tr Barton Quik Group	Barton	24.10.09P
G-CEVH	Cameron V-65 Balloon (Hot Air)	2765	OO-BGG	12.10.07	J A Atkinson	Dorchester	3.12.09E
G-CEVI	Robinson R44 Raven II	11993		12.11.07	Redwood Properties Ltd	Weston, Leixlip, County Kildare	11.12.09E
G-CEVJ	Alpi Pioneer 200 (Built B W Bartlett)	PFA 334-14710		16.10.07	B W Bartlett	North Wootton, Shepton Mallet)	15. 1.10P
	(Stalled and crashed on final approach to Franklyn's Field, Wells 14. 6.08)						
G-CEVK	Schleicher Ka 6CR	6541	BGA2870-EQQ AGA 24, BGA1353-BYZ	11.10.07	C R Reese tr K6 Syndicate *"451"*	Challock	24. 2.10
G-CEVL	Fairchild M-62A-4 Cornell	T43-4361	N9606H FJ662, 42-15491	22.11.07	T K Rumble tr UK Cornell Group *(On rebuild 2008)* (Planned as "FJ662" in 33 EFTS c/s)	Wickenby	
G-CEVM	Tecnam P2002-EA Sierra (Built R C Mincik)	PFA 333-14709		27. 7.07	R C Mincik	Bournemouth	12. 5.09P
G-CEVN	Rolladen-Schneider LS7	7029	BGA3438-FQH D-1316	25.10.07	B C Toon and N Gaunt	Sutton Bank	28. 9.08
G-CEVO	Grob G-109B	6237	D-KGLM	14. 3.08	T J Wilkinson	Sackville Lodge, Riseley	10. 4.09E
G-CEVP	P&M Aviation Quik	8329		30.10.07	S G Ward	(Chatham)	29.10.09P
	(Fitted with trike ex G-CDCK qv, has GT 450 wing but reuses older trike and is badged as a Quik)						
G-CEVS	Evektor EV-97 team Eurostar UK	3102		16.11.07	R Joy tr Eurostar Group	Leicester	15.11.08P
G-CEVT	Bailey Quattro 175-Dudek Reaction 27P	03193		3. 8.07	J Kelly	Longstanton, Cambridgeshire	
G-CEVU	ICP MXP-740 Savannah VG Jabiru(1) (Built B L Cook)	07-05-51-600		2.11.07	B L Cook	Sandtoft	24. 9.09P
	(Pr.no.BMAA HB/552)						
G-CEVV	Rolladen-Schneider LS3	3035	BGA2251-DNQ	25.10.07	M C Cooper tr LS3 307 Syndicate	Challock	8. 3.08
G-CEVW	P&M Aviation Quik GT450	8314		25. 9.07	R W Sutherland	Balado Bridge	20. 9.08P
G-CEVX	Aeriane Swift'Light PAS	111		19.10.07	J S Firth	Sherburn-in-Elmet	
G-CEVY	Rotorsport UK MT-03	RSUK/MT-03/025		20.12.07	P Robinson	Willingale	21 1.10P
G-CEVZ	Centrair ASW 20FL	20184	BGA2726-EJQ	1.10.07	J R Rayner and J R Matthews	Parham Park	4. 4.08
G-CEWC	Schleicher ASK 21	21157	BGA2871-EQR	2.11.07	London Gliding Club Proprietary Ltd *"EQR"*	Dunstable	10. 1.10
G-CEWD	P&M Aviation Quik GT450	8330		15.11.07	J Murphy	Eshott	14.11.09P
G-CEWE	Schempp-Hirth Nimbus 2	4	BGA1725-CQP	29.10.07	D Caunt *"918"*	Wycombe Air Park	8. 1.08
G-CEWF	Jacobs V35 Airchair Balloon (Hot Air) (Built E J Jacobs)	EJ-194	ZS-HYU	28. 1.08	D J Farrar	Tadcaster	
G-CEWG	Aerola Alatus-M	AS 01-011		17.12.07	Flylight Airsports Ltd	Sywell	X
G-CEWH	Mainair Pegasus Quik	8324		5.11.07	B W Hunter	East Fortune	4.11.08P
G-CEWI	Schleicher ASW 19B	19086	BGA4410-JCQ PH-562	31.10.07	K Steele and S R Edwards	Hinton-in-the-Hedges	22. 2.08
G-CEWK	Cessna 172S Skyhawk	172S8294	N397SP	29. 4.08	G Price t/a Skytrek Aviation Services	Rochester	30. 4.09E
G-CEWL	Alpi Pioneer 200 (Built M A Hogg)	PFA 334-14712		29.10.07	M A Hogg	(Finchampstead, Wokingham)	
G-CEWM	de Havilland DHC-6-300 Twin Otter	656	N70551	7. 4.08	Isles of Scilly Skybus Ltd	St Just	13. 4.09E
G-CEWN	Diamond DA.42 Twin Star	42.32		11. 1.08	Airedale Mechanical and Electrical Ltd	Gamston	30. 1.09E
G-CEWO	Schleicher Ka 6CR	1065	BGA2301-DQS D-5144	10. 8.07	J M Robinson tr DQS Group *"DQS"*	North Hill	9. 2.08
G-CEWP	Grob G102 Astir CS	1258	BGA2155-DJQ	8.11.07	R D Slater	Usk	18. 3.10
G-CEWR	Aeroprakt A22-L Foxbat (Built C S Bourne and G P Wiley)	PFA 317A-14736		22.11.07	C S Bourne and G P Wiley	Otherton ,Cannock	16. 3.09P
G-CEWS	Zenair CH.701SP STOL (Built I J M Donnelly)	PFA 187A-14692		13.11.07	G E MacCuish	North Connel	27. 3.09P
G-CEWT	Flight Design CTSW	07.10.10		21.11.07	A and R W Osborne	Priory Farm, Tibenham	20.11.09P
	(Assembled P&M Aviation Ltd with c/n 8333)						
G-CEWU	UltraMagic H-77 Balloon (Hot-Air)	77/316		18. 4.08	P C Waterhouse	Wadhurst	21. 4.09E
G-CEWV	Robinson R44 Raven II	12008		4.12.07	Sibelle Industrie	Monte Carlo Heliport, Monaco	7. 1.10E
G-CEWW	Grob G102 Astir CS77	1758	BGA2442-DWQ	25.10.07	M R Woodiwiss *"DWQ"*	Sleap	14. 4.08
G-CEWX	Cameron Z-350 Balloon (Hot-Air)	11092		25. 3.08	Original Bristol FM Ltd *(Original 106.5 Bristol titles)*	Bristol	30. 3.09E
G-CEWY	Murphy Quicksilver GT500 (Built W Murphy)	PFA 348-14707		21.11.07	W Murphy	(Twyford, Reading)	
G-CEWZ	Schempp-Hirth Discus bT	128/490	BGA4032-HLQ	17. 8.07	J F Goudie *"381"*	Portmoak	17.11.07
G-CEXL	Comco Ikarus C42 FB80 (Built Aerosport Ltd)	0711-6927		23.11.07	R S O'Carroll tr Syndicate C42-1	Mullahead, Tandragee	15. 1.10P
G-CEXM	Best Off Sky Ranger Swift 912S(1)SKRxxxx812 (Built A F Batchelor - pr.no.BMAA HB/556)			1.11.07	A F Batchelor	Rayne Hall Farm, Braintree	

G-CEXN	Cameron A-120 Balloon (Hot Air)	11089		3. 1.08	Dragon Balloon Company Ltd		
						Castleton, Hope Valley	16. 1.09E
G-CEXO	Piper PA-28-161 Warrior III	2842041	N250ND	28.11.07	Plane Talking Ltd	Denham	19.12.09E
G-CEXR	Piper PA-28-161 Warrior III	2842076	N70FT	28.11.07	Plane Talking Ltd (Operated Cabair)	Biggin Hill	18. 2.09E
G-CEXX	Rotorsport UK MT-03	RSUK/MT-03/022		12.11.07	D B Roberts	(Kinoulton, Nottingham)	12. 1.10P
G-CEXY	Schleicher ASW 19B	19265	BGA2862-EQG	16.10.07	B A Tansley tr ASW 239 Syndicate	Challock	7. 2.10
			PH-665				
G-CEYA	Robinson R44 Clipper II	11892		2.11.07	Fast Helicopters Ltd	Shoreham	11. 5.09E
G-CEYC	DG Flugzeugbau DG-505 Elan Orion		BGA4690-JQF	27.11.07	Scottish Gliding Union Ltd	Portmoak	28. 2.10
		5E194X38	S5-7516				
G-CEYD	Cameron N-31 Balloon (Hot Air)	3558	G-LLYD	22. 6.07	G A Chadwick t/a Black Pearl Balloons		
						Partridge Green	17. 7.08E
G-CEYE	Piper PA-32R-300 Cherokee Lance		SE-KCD	24.10.02	D L Claydon	Brickwall Farm, Hundon	31. 1.09E
		32R-7780533	OH-PAS				
G-CEYF	Euocopter EC.135 T1	0115	P4-XTC	13. 3.08	Starspeed Ltd	Blackbushe	24. 3.09E
			P4-LGB, G-HARP, VP-CAF, D-HEGG				
G-CEYG	Cessna 152	15280287	N24495	14. 4.08	Air Atlantique Ltd	Bodmin	
G-CEHH	Cessna 152	15282689	N89253	14. 4.08	Blackburn Aeroplane Co Ltd	Bodmin	26. 8.09E
G-CEYI	Cessna 152	15283208	N47281	14. 4.08	Blackburn Aeroplane Co Ltd	Bodmin	
G-CEYK	Europa Aviation Europa XS	PFA 247-14476		10.12.07	A B Milne	Lower Wasing Farm, Brimpton	30. 6.09P
	(Built A B Milne)						
G-CEYL	Bombardier BD-700-1A10 Global Express		VP-CRC	10.10.08	Aravco Ltd	Luton	9.10.09E
		9196	C-FEBQ				
G-CEYM	Van's RV-6	PFA 181A-14595		12.12.07	H Gordon-Roe	(Cambridge)	17. 8.09P
	(Built H Gordon-Roe)						
G-CEYN	Grob G109B	6256	D-KGFY	12.12.07	Lasham Gliding Society Ltd	Lasham	23. 1.09E
G-CEYO	Aérospatiale AS.350B2 Ecureuil	2312	EC-EVM	29. 7.08	FB Leasing Ltd	RAF Shawbury	
	(Under conversion to Squirrel HT.1 for DHFS as ZK200)						
G-CEYP	North Wing Design Stratus-ATF	7642		21.12.07	J S James	(Petersfield)	
	(MZ34 engine)						
G-CEYR	Rotorsport UK MT-03	RSUK/MT-03/032		14. 2.08	N Wright	Little Rissington	20. 2.09P
G-CEYU	Aérospatiale SA.365N1 Dauphin	6298	N97SV	9. 9.08	Total Asset Ltd	Leeds-Bradford	28.10.09E
			N365SB, N365SC, N60132				
G-CEYX	Rotorsport UK MT-03	RSUK/MT-03/038		10. 4.08	A Reay	Kirkbride	20. 4.09P
G-CEYY	Evektor EV-97 teamEurostar UK	3123		7. 1.08	N J James	Welshpool	6. 1.09P
G-CEYZ	Sikorsky S-76C	760669	N4514R	10. 1.08	Bristow Helicopters Ltd	Norwich	13. 3.09E
G-CEZA	Comco Ikarus C42 Cyclone FB80	0711-6923		13.11.07	P Harper and P J Morton	St Michaels	16.12.08P
	(Built Aerosport Ltd)						
G-CEZB	ICP MXP-740 Savannah VG Jabiru(1)			14.12.07	J N Anyan	Glentham Grange, Market Rasen	13. 7.09P
		07-05-51-599					
	(Built J N Anyan - pr.no.BMAA HB/549)						
G-CEZD	Evektor EV-97 teamEurostar UK	3107		22.12.07	G P Jones	(Stoke-on-Trent)	21.12.09P
G-CEZE	Best Off Sky Ranger Swift 912S(1)			9.11.07	L Robinson , N McAllister and R N Tarrant		
	(Built N McAllister)	SKRxxxx811	(Pr.no.BMAA HB/555)			Sackville Lodge, Riseley	7. 7.09P
G-CEZF	Evektor EV-97 teamEurostar UK	3205		18. 2.08	D J Dick	Broadmeadow Farm, Hereford	17. 2.09P
G-CEZG	Diamond DA.42 Twin Star	42.330		4. 3.08	Diamond Aircraft UK Ltd	Gamston	11. 3.09P
G-CEZH	Aerochute Dual	321		14. 1.08	A Kay	(Croston, Leyland)	
	(C/n refers to trike unit – wing c/n 1288 and engine s/n 6478655) (Rotax 503)						
G-CEZI	Piper PA-28-161 Cadet II	2841228	N131ND	4. 1.08	Plane Talking Ltd	Blackbushe	13. 4.09E
G-CEZK	Stolp SA.750 Acroduster Too	PFA 089-13726		24. 1.08	R I M Hague	Full Sutton	13. 4.09P
	(Built R I M Hague)						
G-CEZL	Piper PA-28-161 Cadet II	2841247	OO-JAG	14. 1.08	Plane Talking Ltd	Denham	2. 4.09E
			N9192Z				
G-CEZM	Cessna 152	152-85179	N6167Q	7. 1.08	Cristal Air Ltd	Lydd	5. 3.09E
G-CEZN	Pacific Airwave Pulse 2-Skycycle			30. 1.08	G W Cameron	(Edinburgh)	
		IR008-10157-11					
G-CEZO	Piper PA-28-161 Cadet II	2841226	N145ND	4. 1.08	Plane Talking Ltd	Elstree	4. 3.09E
G-CEZP	Diamond DA.40D Star	D4.342		2. 4.08	Diamond Aircraft UK Ltd (Operated Flying Time)		
						Shoreham	8. 4.09E
G-CEZR	Diamond DA.40D Star	D4.343	OE-VPT	2. 4.08	Diamond Aircraft UK Ltd	Shoreham	8. 4.09E
G-CEZS	Zenair CH.601HDS Zodiac	PFA 162-14030		1. 2.08	R Wyness	Bicester	31. 8.09P
	(Built R Wyness)						
G-CEZT	P&M Aviation Quik GT450	8349		22. 2.08	B C Blackburn	Balado Bridge	21. 2.09P
G-CEZU	CFM Streak Shadow SA	K337		5. 2.08	M R Foreman	(Priorslees, Telford)	
	(Built M R Foreman - pr no.PFA 206-13597)						
G-CEZV	Zenair CH.601HDS Zodiac	PFA 162-13748		4. 2.08	G Waters	Swansea	8.10.09P
	(Built G Waters)						
G-CEZW	Jodel D.150 Mascaret	PFA 235-13866		5. 2.08	N J Kilford	(New Barn Farm, Whitchurch)	
	(Built N J Kilford)						
G-CEZX	P&M Aviation Quik GT450	8360		7. 3.08	P K Morley	Redlands, Swindon	6. 3.09P
G-CEZZ	Flight Design CTSW	07.08.05		20. 9.07	S Emery	Damyn's Hall, Upminster	18. 9.08P
	(Assembled P&M Aviation Ltd with c/n 8326)						

G-CFAA - G-CFZZ

G-CFAA	British Aerospace Avro 146-RJ100	E3373		9. 5.00	BA Cityflyer Ltd	Manchester	15. 6.09E
G-CFAG	Rotorsport UK MT-03	RSUK/MT-03/034		5. 3.08	M D Cole	Morgansfield, Fishburn	16. 3.09P
G-CFAI	Rotorsport UK MT-03	RSUK/MT-03/027		23. 1.08	Airbourne Aviation Ltd	Popham	30. 1.09P
G-CFAJ	DG Flugzeugbau DG-300 Elan	3E50	BGA3103-FAJ	7. 1.08	B A Brown	Milfield	11. 3.08
G-CFAK	Rotorsport UK MT-03	RSUK/MT-03/030		14. 2.08	Capallini LLP	Kirkbride	21. 2.09P
G-CFAM	Schempp-Hirth Nimbus 3/24.5	79	BGA3106-FAM	19.10.07	K J Hartley tr Nimbus III Syndicate J15 "J15"		
						Bicester	11. 6.08
G-CFAN	Robinson R44 Clipper	0689	N829PM	4. 6.07	A M Payne	Barton	25.10.09E
G-CFAO	Rolladen-Schneider LS4	4465	BGA3109-FAQ	5.11.07	C A Meir	Seighford	9. 3.08

G-CFAP	Interplane ZJ-Viera	VIERAA5-08M		14. 2.08	Flylight Airsports Ltd	Sywell	
	(27hp Fly 200) (F/f 18. 2.08)						
G-CFAR	Rotorsport UK MT-03	RSUK/MT-03/026		20.12.07	P M Twose	Kirkbride	8. 1.09P
G-CFAS	Reality Escapade Jabiru(3)	xxxxx		7. 1.08	C G N Boyd	(Malahide, County Dublin)	
	(Built C G N Boyd - pr.no.BMAA HB/473)						
G-CFAT	P&M Pegasus Quik GT450	8355		28. 2.08	T A Jackson	Compton Abbas	27. 2.09P
G-CFAU	Cameron Z-105 Balloon (Hot-Air)	11136		15. 4.08	High on Adventure Balloons Ltd	Guildford	16. 4.09E
G-CFAV	Comco Ikarus C42 FB80	0802-6939		20. 3.08	D T J Smith	Northrepps	10. 4.09P
	(Built Aerosport Ltd)						
G-CFAW	Lindstrand LBL 35A Cloudhopper Balloon (Hot-Air)			16. 4.08	A Walker	Crediton	
		899	HB-QIV				
G-CFAX	Comco Ikarus C42 FB80	0712-6933		5. 3.08	R E Parker and B Cook	(Hoddesdon and Harlow)	13. 3.09P
	(Built Aerosport Ltd)						
G-CFAY	Sky 120-24 Balloon (Hot Air)	74	OE-ZAY	8. 1.08	G B Lescott	Oxford	2. 1.10E
G-CFAZ	Flight Design CTSW	07.10.17		3.12.07	L K Wright tr CT Aviation Group	Barton	2.12.08P
	(Assembled P&M Aviation Ltd with c/n 8347)				(Crashed Saddleworth Moor 8.10.08, permit suspended)		
G-CFBA	Schleicher ASW 20BL	20665	BGA3119-FBA	21. 1.08	A.Docherty	(Newcastle-upon-Tyne)	31. 3.08
G-CFBB	Schempp-Hirth Standard Cirrus	327G	BGA3120-FBB	25. 9.07	R Andrewartha and B F R Smyth "822" Nympsfield		26. 8.08
			RAFGGA 312				
G-CFBC	Schleicher ASW 15B	15356	BGA3121-FBC	10.12.07	C Knock and J J A Myrdal		
			OH-439			Sandhill Farm, Shrivenham	26. 8.08
G-CFBE	Comco Ikarus C42 FB80	0804-6958		27. 6.08	GS Aviation (Europe) Ltd	Clench Common	13. 7.09P
	(Built Aerosport Ltd)						
G-CFBF	Lindstrand LBL 203T Balloon (Gas Filled)			13. 2.08	S and D Leisure (Europe) Ltd	Bournemouth	25. 3.09E
		HF010			"Wave 105 Bournemouth Eye"		
G-CFBH	Glaser-Dirks DG-100G Elan	E156G123	BGA3126-FBH	22.11.07	N Riggott "177"	Lasham	22. 3.08
G-CFBI	Colt 56A Balloon (Hot Air)	570		11. 7.84	G A Fisher tr Out-of-the-Blue "Air O"	Petworth	24. 7.91A
					(Operated Balloon Preservation Group)		
G-CFBJ	Rotorsport UK MT-03	RSUK/MT-03/042		4. 3.08	A D Lysser	Kirkbride	16. 3.09P
G-CFBK	British Aircraft Corporation 167 Strikemaster Mk.80A			12. 2.08	Trans Holdings Ltd (As "636" in Kuwait AF c/s)		
		EEP/JP/4091	R Saudi AF 1125, G-27-291	(Stored dismantled)		North Weald	
G-CFBL	Best Off Sky Ranger Swift 912S(1)			14. 2.08	S R Isaac	Hunsdon	30.11.09P
	(Built S R Isaac)	SKRxxxx824		(Pr.no.BMAA HB/558)			
G-CFBM	P&M Pegasus Quantum 15-912	8352		14. 2.08	F W and N A Milne	Sutton Meadows	13. 2.09P
G-CFBN	Glasflügel H303 Mosquito B	167	BGA3131-FBN	5. 9.07	S R and J Nash	Sandhill Farm, Shrivenham	28. 9.08
			D-6364				
G-CFBO	Reality Escapade Jabiru(3)	UK ESC 0011		14. 2.08	J F Thornton	Old Sarum	
	(Built J F Thornton - pr.no.BMAA HB/538)						
G-CFBP	Hawker Siddeley HS.125 Series 700A	257105	N560SB	14. 5.08	Hawker 700 Ltd	Biggin Hill	8. 6.09E
			HB-VLL, N700DE, N44BB, N125T, N125BA, G-5-11				
G-CFBS	Best Off Sky Ranger Swift 912S(1)			21. 2.08	A J Tyler	(Blackboys, Uckfield)	
		SKRxxxxxxx					
	(Built A J Tyler - pr.no.BMAA HB/563)						
G-CFBT	Schempp-Hirth Ventus bT	35/218	BGA3136-FBT	6.12.07	S H Gibson tr 488 (Gransden) Group		
						Gransden Lodge	18.12.07
G-CFBV	Schleicher ASK 21	21223	BGA3138-FBV	8. 1.08	London Gliding Club Proprietary Ltd	Dunstable	8. 3.08
G-CFBW	Glaser-Dirks DG-100G Elan	E174G140	BGA3139-FBW	12.12.07	G N Phillips tr G-CFBW Syndicate "395"	Lasham	9. 2.08
G-CFBX	Beech C90GTi King Air	LJ-1890	N3400H	22. 9.08	Eastern Airways (UK) Ltd	Humberside	24. 9.09E
G-CFBY	Best Off Sky Ranger Swift 912S(1)			26. 2.08	J A Armin	(Morpeth)	
	(Built J A Armin)	SKRxxxxxxx		(Pr.no BMAA HB/562)			
G-CFBZ	Schleicher Ka 6CR	6016	BGA3142-FBZ	4.12.07	R E Branch	Wycombe Air Park	10. 2.08
			D-4667, D-KIMN, D-4667				
G-CFCA	Schempp-Hirth Discus b	336	BGA4117-HQJ	7. 2.08	M R Hayden	Dunstable	23. 3.07
			D-1762				
G-CFCB	Centrair 101 Pégase	10100178	BGA3144-FCB	11. 9.07	M Forster and N Stratton	Portmoak	7. 2.08
			F-CGEA				
G-CFCC	Cameron Z-275 Balloon (Hot Air)	11103		27. 2.08	The Balloon Company Ltd t/a First Flight		
					(Park Furnishers titles)	Langford, Bristol	27. 2.09E
G-CFCD	Best Off Sky Ranger Swift 912S(1)			18.12.07	R J Gilbert	Dunnyvadden	
	(Built R J Gilbert)	SKRxxxx801		(Pr.no,BMAA HB/554)			
G-CFCE	Raj Hamsa X'Air Hawk	xxx		20. 2.08	P C Bishop	(Chard)	
	(Built P C Bishop -pr.no.PFA 340-14751)						
G-CFCF	Aerochute Dual	327		2. 6.08	C J Kendal and S G Smith	(Stockport)	
G-CFCG	Rotorsport UK MT-03	RSUK/MT-03/035		10. 4.08	The Gyrocopter UK Co Ltd	Rufforth	20. 4.09P
G-CFCH	Campbell Cricket Mk.4	PFA G/03-1347		28. 2.08	E J Barton	(Bramley, Tadley)	
	(Built E J Barton)						
G-CFCI	Reims Cessna 172N Skyhawk	F17202995	SE-IFB	19. 4.08	J Blacklock	Derby	15. 7.09E
G-CFCJ	Grob G102 Astir CS	1231	BGA3151-FCJ	13.11.07	R M and B T Green	(Bodmin)	28. 9.08
			D-4205				
G-CFCK	Best Off Sky Ranger Swift 912S(1)			28. 2.08	C M Sperring	Weston Zoyland	24. 9.09P
	(Built C M Sperring)	SKRxxxxxxx		(Pr.no,BMAA HB/565)			
G-CFCL	Rotorsport UK MT-03	RSUK/MT-03/043		12. 5.08	A Parker	(Bingley)	21. 5.09P
	(Originally registered 29.2.08 but removed for paperwork issues, used for Sky Watch, a charitable service and carries SEARCH on pod)						
G-CFCM	Robinson R44 Raven	1635	OO-PMD	10. 4.08	A J Brough	(Preston)	14. 5.09E
G-CFCN	Schempp-Hirth Standard Cirrus	131	BGA3155-FCN	22.10.07	S M Robinson	Nympsfield	3. 3.08
			D-0191				
G-CFCO	UltraMagic M-130 Balloon (Hot-Air)	130/61		31. 3.08	I Vastano	Montemurlo, Italy	3. 6.09E
G-CFCP	Rolladen-Schneider LS6-a	6030	BGA3156-FCP	8. 1.08	R E Robertson	Dunstable	1. 4.08
G-CFCR	Schleicher Ka 6 E	4223	BGA3158-FCR	7.11.07	R F Whittaker	Lasham	27. 2.08
			OH-375, OH-REC				
G-CFCS	Schempp-Hirth HS.5 Nimbus 2C	233	BGA3159-FCS	7.11.07	J Luck and P Dolling	Hinton-in-the-Hedges	13.12.07
G-CFCT	Evektor EV-97 teamEurostar UK	3208		25. 3.08	T J A Geering tr Sutton Eurostar Group		
	(Built Cosmik Aviation Ltd)					Sutton Meadows	

G-CFCU	Lindstrand LBL 203T Balloon (Gas)	HF045		12. 3.08	Lindstrand Aeroplatforms Ltd "The English Riviera" Torquay		18. 5.09E
G-CFCV	Schleicher ASW 20	20075	BGA3162-FCV RAFGSA R24	13. 3.08	M J Davis	RAF Cosford	
G-CFCW	Rotorsport UK MT-03	RSUK/MT-03/036		6. 3.08	W C Walters	(Stamford)	16. 3.09P
G-CFCX	Rans S-6-ES Coyote II	0407.1803		5. 3.08	D Morrison and S Fortune	(Melrose)	
	(Built D Morrison, pr.no PFA/204-14699)						
G-CFCY	Best Off Sky Ranger Swift 912S (1)	SKRxxxx793		10. 3.08	M E and T E Simpson	(Hucclecote)	
	(Built ME Simpson - pr.no BMAA HB/545)						
G-CFCZ	P&M Aviation Quik GT450	8359		9. 4.08	P K Dale	Bagby	
G-CFDA	Schleicher ASW 15	15050	BGA3167-FDA D-0511	12.10.07	N I Newton tr 7 Delta Group	Wycombe Air Park	13.11.07
G-CFDC	P&M Aviation Quik GT450	8357		5. 3.08	P R Davies	(St Maur, Indre, France)	4. 3.09
G-CFDD	Fokker F.28-0100	11491	EC-JRV HB-JVB, N1465K, PH-EZV	4. 8.08	Eskglen Shipping Co Ltd	(London EC 1)	
G-CFDE	Schempp-Hirth Ventus bT	53/256	BGA3171-FDE	6. 9.07	P Clay	Sutton Bank	27. 3.08
G-CFDF	UltraMagic S-90 Balloon (Hot-Air)	90/101		9. 6.08	A A Leggate and H M Savage tr Edinburgh University Hot Air Balloon Club "Edinburgh University"	Edinburgh	10. 6.09E
G-CFDG	Schleicher Ka 6CR	6235	BGA3441-FQL HB-772	18. 3.08	P R Alderson tr Delta-Golf Group	Lasham	
G-CFDH	British Aerospace 146 Series 200	E2108	EC-CWD EC-KKY, EI-CWD, SE-DRK, N295UE, G-5-108	30. 6.08	BAE Systems (Operations) Ltd (stored all-white 2.09)	Southend	
G-CFDI	Van's RV-6	23116	N76GC	13. 3.08	M D Challoner	(Sturminster Newton)	
	(Built G M Chancey)						
G-CFDJ	Evektor EV-97 teamEurostar UK	3209		30. 4.08	J D J Spragg and M Jones	(Tamworth)	21. 4.09P
	(Built Cosmik Aviation Ltd)						
G-CFDK	Rans S-6-SE Coyote II	0507.1805		25. 3.08	Conair Sports Ltd	Deppers Bridge, Southam	
	(Built C Beal, pr no LAA 204-24767, nosewheel variant)						
G-CFDL	P&M Aviation QuikR	8370		30. 4.08	P&M Aviation Ltd	Clench Common	2. 9.09P
G-CFDM	Schempp-Hirth Discus b	87	BGA3185-FDM	1.10.07	J L and T G M Whiting "H20"	Shenington	28. 3.08
G-CFDN	Best Off Sky Ranger Swift 912S(1)	SKRxxxx842		9. 4.08	D A Perkins	Tarn Farm, Cockerham	
	(Built DA Perkins - pr.no. BMAA HB/564)						
G-CFDO	Flight Design CTSW	07.12.09		10. 4.08	A Vaughan	Eshott	9. 4.09P
	(Assembled P&M Aviation Ltd with c/n 8366)						
G-CFDP	Flight Design CTSW	8367		8. 4.08	N Forsythe and G Roberts	(Craigavon, NI)	9. 4.09P
	(Assembled P&M Aviation Ltd)						
G-CFDR	Schleicher Ka 6CR	6119	BGA3182-FDR D-8456	25. 1.08	Dartmoor Gliding Society Ltd	Brentor	1. 8.08
G-CFDS	TL 2000 Sting Carbon	LAA 347-14785		8. 4.08	P H Ronfell tr TL Sting G-CFDS Group	Tarn Farm, Cockerham	
	(Built PH Ronfell)						
G-CFDT	Aerola Alatus-M	AS 01-014		28. 4.08	M Pedley	Bembridge	
G-CFDU	BB Microlights BB03 Trya / BB103	080101005DR2NF		9. 4.08	N J Sutherland	Perth	
G-CFDV	Sikorsky S-76C	760666	N45140	26. 2.08	Bristow Helicopters Ltd	Norwich	20. 5.09E
G-CFDX	PZL-Bielsko SZD-48-1 Jantar Standard 2	B-1251	BGA3188-FDX (BGA2916-ESN)	3. 3.08	RJ Simpson tr The Jantar Syndicate	Upper Broyle Farm, Ringmer	
G-CFDY	P&M Aviation Quik GT450	8373		9. 4.08	C N Thornton	Eshott	8. 4.09P
G-CFDZ	Flight Design Exxtacy/ Alize	980501002		4. 4.08	N C O Watney	Rochester	
G-CFEA	Cameron C-90 Balloon (Hot-Air)	11158		8. 5.08	A M Holly "Barclays"	Broadstone, Berkeley	6. 8.09E
G-CFEB	Cameron C-90 Balloon (Hot-air)	11174		6. 5.08	A M Holly "Robert Hitchins"	Broadstone, Berkeley	16. 6.09E
G-CFED	Van's RV-9	PFA 320-14414		9. 4.08	E Taylor and P Robinson	(Bluntisham, Cambs)	
	(Built E Taylor and P Robinson)						
G-CFEE	Evektor EV-97 Eurostar	2008.32.21		21. 2.08	S K Ackerley tr G-CFEE Flying Group	(Croydon)	2. 4.09P
	(Built G R Pritchard, pr. no LAA 315-14778)						
G-CFEF	Grob G102 Astir CS	1164	BGA3196-FEF OY-XGC	8. 2.08	M Bacic tr Oxford University Gliding Club	Bicester	4. 3.08
G-CFEG	Schempp-Hirth Ventus b/16.6	279	BGA3197-FEG	23.11.07	K F Moorhouse and R W Partridge	Lasham	27. 3.08
G-CFEH	Centrair 101A Pégase	101A0268	BGA3198-FEH	13.12.07	Booker Gliding Club Ltd "318"	Wycombe Air Park	9. 4.09
	(Rebuilt with new fuselage c/n 01304: original fuselage rebuilt as BGA3560)						
G-CFEI	RAF 2000 GTX-SE	PFA G/13-1369		10. 4.08	A M Wells	(Milton Keynes)	
	(Built A M Wells)						
G-CFEJ	Schempp-Hirth Discus b	76	BGA3199-FEJ	17.12.07	L Coles	Wycombe Air Park	4. 2.08
G-CFEK	Cameron Z-105 Balloon (Hot-Air)	11176		30. 6.08	R M Penny (Plant Hire and Demolition) Ltd (Penny Plant Hire titles)	Radstock	30. 6.09E
G-CFEL	Evektor EV-97 Eurostar	PFA/315-14740		14. 3.08	S R Green	Over Farm, Gloucester	19. 6.09P
G-CFEM	P&M Aviation Quik GT450	8388		2. 6.08	H Cooke	Chester-le-Street	1. 6.09P
G-CFEN	PZL-Bielsko SZD-50-3 Puchacz	B-1326	BGA3203-FEN	17. 1.08	The Northumbria Gliding Club Ltd	Currock Hill	23. 9.08
G-CFEO	Evektor EV-97 Eurostar	PFA 315-14737		15. 4.08	J B Binks	Baxby Manor, Husthwaite	10.11.09P
	(Built J B Binks)						
G-CFER	Schempp-Hirth Discus b	75	BGA3206-FER	25. 3.08	S R Westlake	Aston Down	
G-CFES	Schempp-Hirth Discus b	88	BGA3207-FES	22.11.07	P W Berridge "564"	Sandhill Farm, Shrivenham	2. 2.08
G-CFET	Van's RV-7	70686	LY-ASJ	18. 7.08	J Astor	Denham	23. 7.09P
	(Built A Jonusas)						
G-CFEV	P&M Aviation Quik	8375		30. 4.08	W T Davis	Balado Bridge	29. 4.09P
G-CFEW	Lindstrand LBL 240A Balloon (Hot-Air)	197	SE-ZGK	19. 3.08	M E White	Trim, Ireland	9.11.09E
G-CFEX	P&M Aviation Quik GT450	8362		20. 5.08	C Lamb	(Rye)	19. 5.09P
G-CFEY	Aerola Alatus-M	AS 01-017		30. 5.08	P D Harvey	(Southampton)	10.11.09P
G-CFEZ	CZAW Sportcruiser	PFA 338-14675		14. 2.08	J F Barber and J R Large	Stapleford	10.11.09P
	(Built J F Barbe and J R Large)						
G-CFFA	UltraMagic M-90 Balloon (Hot-Air)	90/59	HB-QKA	15. 5.08	Proxim SPA	Milan, Italy	4.12.09E

Reg	Type	c/n	Prev ids / Date	Owner	Location	Date
G-CFFB	Grob G102 Astir CS	1123	BGA3216-FFB 8.10.07 RAFGSA R9, RAFGSA R97, BGA3216-FFB, D-6977	J G Arnold tr RAF Gliding and Soaring Association *(Operated Chilterns Gliding Centre)*	RAF Halton	28. 9.08
G-CFFC	Centrair 101A Pégase	101A0255	BGA3217-FFC 21.12.07	B Douglas	Rufforth	16. 4.08
G-CFFD	Robinson R44 Raven I	1866	25. 4.08	Andrew Dunne (Aviation) Ltd	Leeds-Bradford	3. 6.09E
G-CFFE	Evektor EV-97 teamEurostar UK *(Built Cosmik Aviation)*	3211	13. 5.08	C Hewer and D Lowe	Carlisle	12. 5.09P
G-CFFF	Pitts S-1S Special	LAA 009-14779	18. 3.08	N N Bentley	(Orkney)	
G-CFFG	Aerochute Dual	320	8. 5.08	R S McFayden	(Tamworth)	
G-CFFH	Aeros Discus 15T/Dragonfly	00908/002	16. 5.08	D Wilson	(Oakham)	
G-CFFJ	Flight Design CTSW *(Built P&M Aviation Ltd with c/n 8391)*	07.12.10	15. 5.08	R Germany	Knapthorpe Lodge, Caunton	14. 5.09P
G-CFFK	Schempp-Hirth Nimbus 3/24.5	87	BGA3224-FFK 21.12.07	I Ashdown "128"	Parham Park	29. 9.09
G-CFFL	Lindstrand LBL 317A Balloon (Hot-Air)	1205	13. 6.08	Aerosauras Balloons Ltd	Exeter	17. 6.09E
G-CFFM	Bell 206-2 JetRanger II	1246	N83RH 6.11.08 N704SD, N37467, XC-GII	Apple International Inc Ltd	Southend	
G-CFFN	P&M Aviation Quik GT450	8380	19. 6.08	Kent County Scout Council	(Gillingham)	18. 6.09P
G-CFFO	P&M Aviation Quik GT450	8361	30. 4.08	D E McGauley	Ince Blundell	29. 4.09P
G-CFFP	Eurocopter EC.120B Colibri	1558	10. 7.08	Eurocopter UK Ltd	Oxford	
G-CFFS	Centrair 101A Pégase	101A0265	BGA3231-FFS 9.11.07	W Murray	Gransden Lodge	3. 4.08
G-CFFT	Schempp-Hirth Discus b	110	BGA3232-FFT 28.11.07	R Maskell	Gransden Lodge	4. 4.08
G-CFFU	Glaser-Dirks DG-100G Elan	E200G166	BGA3233-FFU 17.10.07	K T Tutthill tr FFU Group	Chipping	31. 3.08
G-CFFV	PZL-Bielsko SZD-51-1 Junior	B-1616	BGA3234-FFV 12. 2.08 F-WGJA	Herefordshire Gliding Club Ltd	Shobdon	5. 4.08
G-CFFW	Eurocopter AS.365N3 Dauphin 2	6823	7. 8.08	Eurocopter UK Ltd	Oxford	
G-CFFX	Schempp-Hirth Discus b	109	BGA3236-FFX 10.12.07	P J Tiller	Husbands Bosworth	5. 4.08
G-CFFY	PZL-Bielsko SZD-51-1 Junior	W-938	BGA3237-FFY 17. 1.08	Scottish Gliding Union Ltd	Portmoak	2. 4.08
G-CFGA	Vickers Supermarine 502 Spitfire Tr.VII *(Built as LF.VIIc)*		JG668 5. 1.09 A58-441	The Pembrokeshire Spitfire Aeroplane Co Ltd	Haverfordwest	
G-CFGB	Cessna 680 Citation Sovereign	680-0234	N5057F 22. 9.08	Keepflying LLP	Leeds-Bradford	21. 9.09E
G-CFGC	Demoiselle *(Built R B Hewing)*	15	4. 6.08	R B Hewing	(London SE24)	
G-CFGD	P&M Aviation Quik GT450	8374	24. 4.08	J Lawrance	Audley End	
G-CFGE	Stinson 108-1 Voyager	108-1127	ZS-BHW 7.10.08 NC97127	R H and J A Cooper	Wickenby	
G-CFGF	Schempp-Hirth Nimbus 3T	25/91	BGA3244-FGF 5.10.07	R E Cross	Lasham	14. 1.08
G-CFGG	Rotorsport UK MT-03	RSUK/MT-03/049	19. 6.08	C M Jones	Kirkbride	14. 7.09P
G-CFGH	Jabiru J160 *(Built D F Sargant)*	PFA 346-14693	6. 5.08	D F Sargant and D J Royce	Ludham	
G-CFGI	Vickers-Supermarine 358 Seafire F.IIc	6S-239292	MB293 13. 8.08	Mark One Partners LLC *(Noted 10.08)*	Duxford	
G-CFGJ	Vickers-Supermarine 300 Spitfire I	-	N3200 11.8.08	Mark One Partners LLC *(Noted 10.08)*	Duxford	
G-CFGK	Grob G102 Astir CS	1323	BGA3248-FGK, 20.12.07 RAFGSA R61, RAFGSA 316	P Allingham	Eyres Field	15. 4.08
G-CFGM	Comco Ikarus C42 *(Built Aerosport Ltd)*	0804-6969	12. 5.08	R S O'Carroll	Tandragee	21. 5.09P
G-CFGN	Vickers Supermarine 300 Spitfire IA	6S-30564	P9373 10. 9.08	Mark One Partners LLC *(noted 10.08)*	Duxford	
G-CFGO	Best Off Sky Ranger Swift 912S(1) *(Built S J Smith)*	SKRxxxx869	4. 6.08 *(Pr. no BMAA HB/574)*	S J Smith	Chase Farm, Chipping Sodbury	14.12.09P
G-CFGP	Schleicher ASW 19	19121	BGA3252-FGP 3.12.07 C-GJXG	A E Prime tr Foxtrot Golf Alpha Group	Tibenham	20. 3.08
G-CFGR	Schleicher ASK 13 *(Built Jubi GmbH Sportflugzeugbau)*	13655AB	BGA3254-FGR 6. 2.08	T World tr Portsmouth Naval Gliding Centre "N29"	Lee-on-Solent	10. 8.07
G-CFGT	P&M Aviation Quik GT450	8384	23. 5.08	G I Taylor	Dunstable	26. 5.09P
G-CFGU	Schempp-Hirth Standard Cirrus	147	BGA3257-FGU 16. 3.08	D Higginbottom	Snitterfield	
G-CFGV	P&M Aviation Quik GT450	8387	26. 6.08	R Bennett	(Canterbury)	29. 6.09P
G-CFGW	Centrair 101A Pégase	101A0275	BGA3259-FGW 2.11.07	L P Smith	Kingston Deverill	18. 3.08
G-CFGX	Evektor EV-97 teamEurostar UK *(Built Cosmik Aviation)*	3212	9. 7.08	I P Seurre tr Golf XRay Group	Wycombe Air Park	8. 7.09P
G-CFGY	Rotorsport UK MT-03	RSUK/MT-03/039	10. 4.08	G J Slater and N D Leak	Clench Common	20. 4.09P
G-CFGZ	Flight Design CTSW *(Built P&M Aviation Ltd with c/n 8390)*	08.05.23	19. 6.08	B Gorvett	Haverfordwest	23. 6.09P
G-CFHB	Micro Aviation B.22J Bantam	08-321	ZK-LNZ 4. 7.08	K T Bettington tr Micro Aviation (UK and Ireland) Ltd	(Brierley Hill)	
G-CFHC	Micro Aviation B.22J Bantam	08-322	ZK-VNZ 4. 7.08	K T Bettington tr Micro Aviation (UK and Ireland) Ltd	(Brierley Hill)	
G-CFHD	Schleicher ASW 20BL	20694	BGA3266-FHD 18.12.07 RAFGGA ???	D P Smith tr 196 Syndicate	Bicester	30. 4.08
G-CFHF	PZL-Bielsko SZD-51-1 Junior	W-952	BGA3268-FHF 1.12.07	Black Mountains Gliding Club	Talgarth	30. 4.08
G-CFHG	Schempp-Hirth Mini Nimbus C	140	BGA3269-FHG 12.10.07 (BGA3213-FEY), ZS-GNI	R W and M P Weaver	Usk	21.12.06
G-CFHI	Van's RV-9 *(Built M Stewart)*	PFA 320-14603	9. 4.08	M Stewart	Spanhoe	
G-CFHJ	Centrair 101A Pegase	101A0278	BGA3271-FHJ 17. 3.08	Booker Gliding Club Ltd	Wycombe Air Park	
G-CFHK	Aeroprakt A22 Foxbat *(Built R and J Bellew)*	LAA 317A-14834	16. 7.08	R Bellew	(Collon, Ireland)	16.11.09P
G-CFHL	Rolladen-Schneider LS4	4633	BGA3273-FHL 28.11.07	I P Hicks "136"	Dunstable	19. 2.08
G-CFHM	Schleicher ASK 13	13662AB	BGA3274-FHM 16.11.07	Lasham Gliding Society Ltd "P"	Lasham	13.12.07
G-CFHN	Schleicher K 8B	8797	BGA3275-FHN 15. 4.08 RAFGSA R85, RAFGSA 385, RAF 360	The Nene Valley Gliding Club	Upwood	
G-CFHO	Grob G103 Twin Astir II	3566	BGA5275-KPI 19. 4.07 F-CFHO	The Surrey Hills Gliding Club Ltd "KPI"	Kenley	27. 4.08

Reg	Type	C/n	Prev id	Date	Owner/Operator	Location	Date
G-CFHP	Comco Icarus C42 FB80	0805-6972		23. 7.08	Airbourne Aviation Ltd	Popham	20. 8.09P
	(Built Aerosport Ltd)						
G-CFHR	Schempp-Hirth Discus b	152	BGA3278-FHR	7. 2.08	J Jervis, M Fursedon and T Turner	Shenington	8. 2.08
G-CFHS	Tchemma T01/77 Balloon (Hot-Air)	T01/77		24. 6.08	J A Hibberd	Ijsser, Netherlands	
	(Built J A Hibberd)						
G-CFHT	Grob G102 Astir CS	1234	BGA3280-FHT	18. 1.08	E K Sharp	Bicester	9. 5.08
			D-4208				
G-CFHU	Robinson R22 Beta	3809	EI-EMG	23. 6.08	J Smith	(Blairgowrie)	31. 7.09E
G-CFHV	PZL-Bielsko SZD-48-1 Jantar Standard 2		BGA3282-FHV	17. 9.07	R A Williams tr Jantar FHV Syndicate	Long Mynd	10. 5.08
		B-1036	D-4516				
G-CFHW	Grob G102 Astir CS	1087	BGA3283-FHW	7.12.07	P Haliday tr Astir 698 Group	Lasham	18. 2.08
			D-6987				
G-CFHX	Schroeder Fire Balloons G22/24 Balloon (Hot-Air)						
		928	LX-BEO	27. 6.08	T J Ellenreider	Bristol	
G-CFHY	Fokker Dr.1 Triplane Replica PFA 238-14408			19. 6.08	P G Bond	(Norwich)	
	(Built P G Bond)						
G-CFHZ	Schleicher Ka 6CR	949	BGA3286-FKT	4. 3.08	G D Leatherland	Husbands Bosworth	
G-CFIA	Best Off Sky Ranger Swift 912S(1)			16. 5.08	W Lofts	North Coates	30.11.09P
		SKRxxxx825					
	(Built W Loft - pr. no BMAA HB/561)						
G-CFIB	Aerianne Swift Light PAS	88		2. 9.08	D J Blackman	(Brighton)	
G-CFIC	CEA Jodel DR.1050/M1 Sicile Record	432	OO-LME	18. 6.08	J H and P I Kempton	Dunkeswell	18. 8.09P
	(Originally DR.1051/M1, amended 10.10.08)		F-BLME				
G-CFID	Air Création Tanarg 912S/iXess 15 FLT.xxx			25. 6.08	D Smith	(Garstang)	
	(Built D Smith - pr.no.BMAA HB/507being Flylight kit comprising Trike s/n Txxxxx and Wing s/n A06070-6047)						
G-CFIE	Rotorsport UK MT-03	RSUK/MT-03/048		25. 7.08	A McCredie	Carlisle	12. 8.09P
G-CFIF	Christen Eagle II	BEERS-0001	N171CB	6. 6.08	A Corcoran	Strandhill, Sligo, County Sligo	4. 9.09P
	(Built C Beers)						
G-CFIG	P&M Aviation Quik GT450	8382		23. 5.08	J Whitfield	East Fortune	22. 5.09P
G-CFIH	Piel CP.1320	PFA 170-11266		1. 7.08	I W L Aikman	Lower Wasing Farm, Brimpton	
	(Built I W L Aikman)						
G-CFII	de Havilland DH82A Tiger Moth	85584	N90277	20. 5.08	Motair LLP	(Charing, Kent)	
	(Built Morris Motors)		VT-DKN, HU726 indian AF, SAAF 4613, DE630				
G-CFIJ	Christen Eagle II	PERNER-001	N161RJ	29. 7.08	S J Perkins	Little Staughton	14. 8.09P
	(Built C Perner)						
G-CFIK	Lindstrand LBL 60X Balloon (Hot-Air)	1220		30.6.08	A M Holly "Avenue Q"	Breadstone, Berkeley	2. 7.09E
G-CFIL	P&M Aviation Quik GT450	8394		11. 7.08	S N Catchpole	Thurton	20. 7.09E
G-CFIM	P&M Aviation Quik GT450	8395		30. 5.08	K G Grayson	Tideswell, Buxton	
G-CFIO	Cessna 172S Skyhawk II	172S9079	N5104Y	17. 7.08	G Price t/a Skytrek Air Services	Rochester	14. 8.09E
G-CFIP	Raj Hamsa X'Air Falcon 700(1)	918		20. 5.08	M Skinner	(Hatfield)	
	(Built M Skinner, pr no BMAA HB/540)						
G-CFIS	Jabiru UL-D	668		24. 7.08	O Matthews	(Blackrock, Dublin)	22. 9.09P
G-CFIT	Comco Ikarus C42 FB100	0804-6966		16. 7.08	N Hammerton	(Oxted)	
	(Built Aerosport Ltd)						
G-CFIU	CZAW Sportcruiser	LAA 338-14822		4. 7.08	G Everett and D Smith	(Maidstone)	
	(Built G Everett and D Smith)						
G-CFIW	Balony Kubicek BB20XR Balloon (Hot-Air)	615		4. 8.08	H C J Williams"Kubicek"	Bristol	3. 8.09E
G-CFIY	Comco Ikarus C42A FB100	0804-6954		17. 6.08	Aerosport Training Ltd	Mill Farm, Shifnal	16. 6.09P
	(Built Aerosport Ltd)						
G-CFIZ	Best Off Sky Ranger Swift 912S(1)			20. 5.08	J R Hartshorne	(Newbridge-on-Wye)	
	(Built J R Hartshorne)	SKRxxxx732	(Pr. no BMAA HB/530)				
G-CFJA	Embraer EMB.135BJ Legacy	14501045	EC-KOK	1. 8.08	TAG Aviation (UK) Ltd	Farnborough	16. 9.09E
			PT-SEC				
G-CFJB	Rotorsport UK MT-03	RSUK/MT-03/052		29. 9.08	N J Hargreaves	(Southport)	
G-CFJC	Sikorsky S-76C	760708	N415Y	13. 8.08	Bristow Helicopters Ltd	Aberdeen	1.10.09E
			G-CFJC, N415Y				
G-CFJD	Campbell Cricket Mk.6A	LAA G/16-1370		14. 7.08	C Seaman	(Selby)	
	(Built C Seaman)						
G-CFJE	Schleicher ASW 20BL	20953	BGA3291-FJE	25.10.07	A Groves	Lasham	28. 9.08
G-CFJF	Schempp-Hirth SHK-1	58	BGA3646-FZC	18. 6.08	J F Mills	RAF Cranwell	
			OH-357, OH-SHA				
G-CFJG	Best Off Sky Ranger Swift 912S(1)			7. 0.08	G J Crago	Bodmin	8. 1.10P
	(Built G J Crago)	SKRxxxx794	(Pr. no BMAA HB/546)				
G-CFJH	Grob G102 Astir CS77	1763	BGA3294-FJH	13. 6.08	Shalbourne Soaring Society Ltd	Rivar Hill	
			AGA 7				
G-CFJI	UltraMagic M-105 Balloon (Hot-Air)	105/168		16.10.08	Communicazione In Volo Sri	Carpineti, Italy	6.11.09E
G-CFJJ	Best Off Sky Ranger Swift 912S (1)			11. 6.08	J J Ewing	Tarsan Lane, Portadown	
	(Built J J Ewing)	SKRxxxx865	(Pr. no BMAA HB/571)				
G-CFJK	Centrair 101A Pégase	101070	BGA3296-FJK	4.12.07	A W McKee and T J Parker	Hinton-in-the-Hedges	26. 4.08
			N4429W				
G-CFJL	Raj Hamsa X'Air Hawk	1087		25. 7.08	G L Craig	Newtownards	
	(Built G L Craig, pr. no PFA 340-14702)						
G-CFJM	Rolladen-Schneider LS4-a	4665	BGA3298-FJM	21.12.07	K Woods and S Hill "143"	Dunstable	22. 6.08
			D-1431				
G-CFJN	Diamond DA.40D Star	D4.295	JY-EEE	14.10.08	Atlantic Flight Training Ltd	Coventry	17.12.09E
			OE-UHK, OE-VPU				
G-CFJO	Diamond DA.40D Star	D4.296	JY-FFF	14.10.08	Atlantic Flight Training Ltd	Coventry	3.11.09E
			OE-UDV, OE-VPU				
G-CFJP	Cameron N-56 Balloon (Hot-Air)	3674	HB-QBQ	19. 6.08	K-H Gruenauer	Schwaebisch Hall, Germany	22. 9.09E
G-CFJR	DG Flugzeugbau DG-300 Club Elan	3E270C2	BGA3302-FJR	17. 1.08	H Smith and W.J.Palmer	Lasham	11. 3.08
G-CFJS	DG Flugzeugbau DG-300 Club Elan	3E271C3	BGA3303-FJS	7.11.07	K L Goldsmith	Rattlesden	9. 4.08
G-CFJU	Raj Hamsa X'Air Hawk	1128		27. 6.08	R J Minns and H M Wooldridge	(Burnley)	
	(Built RJ Minns, pr. no PFA 40-14731)						

Reg	Type	C/n	Prev ID	Date	Owner	Location	Date
G-CFJV	Schleicher ASW 15	15109	BGA3306-FJV D-0710	17. 7.08	R Abercrombie	Milfield	
G-CFJW	Schleicher K 7 Rhönadler	980	BGA3307-FJW OH-241, OH-KKF	1. 2.08	A J Pettitt tr K7 Group	Rivar Hill	9. 6.08
G-CFJX	DG Flugzeugbau DG-300 Elan	3E261	BGA3308-FJX	10.12.07	Crown Service Gliding Club	Lasham	4. 2.08
G-CFJZ	Schempp-Hirth SHK-1	14	BGA3310-FJZ D-9330	13.11.07	B S Irwin and R H Hanna	Bellarena	24. 6.08
G-CFKA	Rotorsport UK MT-03	RSUK/MT-03/051		18. 8.08	Moles Co Ltd	(Bath)	
G-CFKB	CZAW Sportcruiser	4018		2. 7.08	B S Williams	(Leatherhead)	
	(Built B S Wiliams, pr. no LAA 338-14766)						
G-CFKC	Robinson R44 Clipper II	12484		30. 9.08	Angel Events APS	Fredericia, Denmark	24.11.09E
G-CFKD	Raj Hamsa X'Air Falcon Jabiru (4)	995		6. 6.08	A M Fawthrop	Rufforth	
	(Built A M Fawthrop, pr. no BMAA HB/550)						
G-CFKE	Raj Hamsa X'Air Hawk	1120		22. 7.08	S Rance	Mapperton Farm, Newtown Peverill	
	(Built S Rance, pr. no PFA/340-14752)						
G-CFKF	Cameron Z-210 Balloon (Hot-Air)	11177		23. 7.08	The Balloon Company Ltd t/a First Flight "House of Fraser"	Bristol	23. 7.09P
G-CFKG	Rolladen-Schneider LS4-a	4673	BGA3317-FKG	27.11.07	D A Smith	Kingston Deverill	16. 3.08
G-CFKH	Zenair CH.601XL Zodiac	PFA 162B-14566		6. 8.08	M A Baker	Southminster	
G-CFKI	Cameron Z-120 Balloon (Hot-Air)	11201		29. 8.08	KB Voli di Chiozzi Bartolemo EC SAS	Cappella Cantone, Italy	14. 9.09E
G-CFKJ	P&M Aviation Quik GT450	8405		22. 8.08	B Geary	(Tralee, Ireland)	21. 8.09P
G-CFKK	Flylight Dragonfly	007		31. 7.08	P B J Everleigh	(Ipswich)	
G-CFKL	Schleicher ASW 20BL	20954	BGA3321-FKL	19.12.07	J Ley	Wormingford	18.12.07
G-CFKM	Schempp-Hirth Discus b	212	BGA3322-FKM	13. 5.08	North Downs Gliding Trust Ltd "SH3"	Lasham	
G-CFKN	Lindstrand GA-22 Mk II Airship (Helium)	GA014-01		11. 8.08	Lindstrand Technologies Ltd	Oswestry	
G-CFKO	P&M Aviation Quik GT450	8401		7. 7.08	P Millership	Tarn Farm, Cockerham	28. 7.09P
G-CFKP	Performance Designs Barnstormer/Voyager	UK1		26. 8.08	Wessex Aviation and Transport Ltd	Chalmington Manor	28. 7.09P
G-CFKR	P&M Aviation Quik	8403		12. 8.08	R D Ballard	(Bexhill)	18. 8.09P
G-CFKS	Flight Design CTSW	08 05 22		10. 9.08	D J M Williams	Guernsey	
	(Built P&M Aviation with c/n 8396)						
G-CFKT	Schleicher K 8B	8382	BGA3328-FKT D-5366	4. 3.08	A R Bushnell tr FKT Group	Lyveden	
G-CFKU	P&M Aviation Quik GT450	8404		18. 8.08	D J Collier tr Sunfun Group	Lower Mountpleasant Farm, Chatteris	17. 8.09P
G-CFKV	ICP MXP-740 Savannah VG Jabairu (I)	08-04-51-712		22. 8.08	D Thorpe and K N Rigley	(Grantham)	
	(Built D Thorpe and K N Rigley)		(Pr. no BMAA HB/579)				
G-CFKW	Alpi Pioneer 200-M	LAA 344-14828		16. 7.08	P Rayson	Cottage Farm, Norton Juxta	15.12.09P
	(Built F A Cavaciuti) (Originally regd as Pioneer 200, amended 1.09)						
G-CFKX	Cameron Z-160 Balloon (Hot-Air)	11163		20.10.08	Tiger Aspect Promotions Ltd	London W1	21.10.09E
G-CFKY	Schleicher Ka 6CR	822	BGA3329-FKU D-0025	12. 2.08	J A Timmis	Camphill	25. 6.08
G-CFKZ	Europa Aviation Europa XS	PFA 247-14178		5. 5.08	N P Davis	(Guildford)	
	(Built N P Davis)						
G-CFLA	P&M Aviation Quik GT450	8393		4. 8.08	D Blake	Dundrum, County Tipperary	3. 8.09P
G-CFLB	Paratoys 28/Lowboy 313	705617		15. 9.08	P R Nation	(Warrington)	
	(Compact Radial Engines 313)						
G-CFLC	DG Flugzeugbau DG-300 Elan	3E310	BGA3337-FLC	12.11.07	J L Hey	Rufforth	19. 3.08
G-CFLD	Comco Ikarus C42 FB80	0807-6982		9. 9.08	L McWilliams	(Harrogate)	1.10.09E
	(Built Aerosport Ltd)						
G-CFLE	Schempp-Hirth Discus b	207	BGA3339-FLE	15.10.07	Booker Gliding Club Ltd	Wycombe Air Park	29. 9.09
G-CFLF	Rolladen-Schneider LS4-a	4694	BGA3340-FLF	19. 3.08	D Lamb	Wycombe Air Park	
G-CLFG	CZAW Sportcruiser	LAA 338-14771		16. 7.08	D A Buttress	Charity Farm, Baxterley	
	(Built D A Buttress)						
G-CFLH	Schleicher K 8B	22	BGA3342-FLH OH-361, OH-RTW	25. 1.08	The South Wales Gliding Club Ltd	Usk	14. 4.08
G-CFLI	Europa Aviation Europa	PFA 247-13144		24. 7.08	A and E Bennett	(Parbold, Wigan)	
	(Built A Bennett)						
G-CFLK	Cameron C-90 Balloon (Hot-Air)	11207		18.11.08	A M Holly	Breadstone, Berkeley	
G-CFLL	Evektor EV-97 Eurostar	LAA 315-14825		15. 7.08	D R Lewis	(Hereford)	31. 8.09P
	(Built D R Lewis)						
G-CFLM	P&M Aviation Pegasus Quik	8399		29. 7.08	G J Wharmby tr JAG Flyers	Ince Blundell	28. 7.09P
G-CFLN	Best Off Sky Ranger Swift 912S(1)	SKRxxxx886		25. 9.08	D Bletcher	(Kenilworth)	
	(Built D Bletcher - pr no. BMAA/HB/577)						
G-CFLO	Rotorsport UK MT-03	RSUK/MT-03/053		18. 8.08	R G Mulford	(Chatham)	
G-CFLP	Druine D.31 Turbulent	PFA 048-13170		11. 8.08	T K Pullen tr Eaglescott Turbulent Group	Eaglescott	
	(Built T K Pullen and F Blick)						
G-CFLR	P&M Aviation Quik GT450	8409		21.10.08	G Shaw	Lower Mountpleasant Farm, Chatteris	20.10.09P
G-CFLS	Schleicher Ka 6CR	6180	BGA3351-FLS D-4001	2. 7.08	J Wellman tr University College London Union	RAF Halton	
G-CFLU	SAAB-Scania 2000	2000-055	SE-LSG OH-SAX, SE-LSG, SE-055	17.12.08	Air Kilroe Ltd t/a Eastern Airways	Humberside	31. 8.09E
G-CFLV	SAAB-Scania 2000	2000-023	SE-023 LY-SBD, F-GTSD, D-ADSD, SE-023	3. 2.09	Air Kilroe Ltd t/a Eastern Airways	Humberside	19.11.09E
G-CFLW	Schempp-Hirth Standard Cirrus 75	656	BGA3355-FLW F-CEMT	4.10.07	J Pack "51"	Lasham	28. 9.08
G-CFLX	DG Flugzeugbau DG-300 Club Elan	3E304C19	BGA3356-FLX	4.12.07	R Emms tr Felix Flying Group	Upwood	16. 3.08
G-CFLZ	Scheibe SF 27A Zügvogel V	6061	BGA3358-FLZ D-5378	21. 7.08	M F Frost tr SF Group	Ridgewell	

Reg	Type	C/n	Prev ID	Date	Owner/Operator	Location	
G-CFMA	BB Ultralight BB-03 UK Trya 503(1)			8. 7.08	D Sykes	Rufforth	
		081006005DRDS			*(Wing fitted to Solo Flight Solo trike at SPLASH, NEC 12.08)*		
G-CFMB	P&M Aviation Quik GT450	8408		5. 9.08	P&M Aviation Ltd	Rochdale	
G-CFMC	Van's RV-9A	PFA 320-14575		25. 9.08	G Griffith	(Penmaenmawr)	
	(Built G Griffith)						
G-CFMD	P&M Aviation Quik GT450	8417		6.11.08	Wilson G Jamieson Ltd	(Galashiels)	4.11.09P
G-CFME	SOCATA TB-10 Tobago	1795	F-GNHU	15. 4.98	Charles Funke Associates Ltd	Goodwood	23. 7.09E
G-CFMF	Lindstrand LBL 203T Balloon (Gas)	HF046		1. 10.08	Hiflyer Polska SP.z.o.o	Krakow, Poland	4.12.09E
G-CFMH	Schleicher ASK 13	13673AB	BGA3366-FMH	31.10.07	Lasham Gliding Society Ltd *"B"*	Lasham	28. 9.08
G-CFMI	Best Off Sky Ranger 912(1)	SKRxxxx897		3.10.08	P Shelton	St Michaels on Wyre	
	(Built P Shelton - pr no BMAA/HB/580)						
G-CFMK	Centrair 101 Pégase Club	10100293	BGA3368-FMK	11.12.07	D Hatch	Nympsfield	28. 1.08
G-CFML	Schleicher ASW 15B	15294	BGA3369-FML	13. 9.07	D A Senior tr STJ Syndicate	Camphill	6. 1.08
			F-CEGR				
G-CFMM	Cessna 172S Skyhawk	172S8242	N216MM	16. 5.08	Cristal Air Ltd	Shoreham	30. 7.09E
			XB-HQZ				
G-CFMN	Schempp-Hirth Ventus cT	123/397	BGA3371-FMN	15. 2.08	R E Matthews tr FMN Glider Syndicate *"FMN"*		
						Lasham	1. 2.08
G-CFMO	Schempp-Hirth Discus b	243	BGA3373-FMQ	28.11.07	P D Bagnall	Nympsfield	5. 4.08
G-CFMP	Europa Aviation Europa XS	PFA 247-13505		3.10.08	M P Gamble	(Camberley)	
	(Built M P Gamble)						
G-CFMR	UltraMagic V-14 Balloon (Hot-Air)	14/001		20.11.08	M W A Shemilt	Hemley-on-Thames	
G-CFMS	Schleicher ASW 15	15061	BGA3375-FMS	15. 2.08	A F Brind and W Orson	Rivar Hill	22. 6.08
			N111SP				
G-CFMT	Schempp-Hirth Standard Cirrus	249	BGA3376-FMT	30. 1.08	J M Brooke	(Burgess Hill)	20. 6.08
			N2HM				
G-CFMU	Schempp-Hirth Standard Cirrus	236	BGA3377-FMU	31.10.07	A Harrison and J Gammage	Aston Down	16. 2.08
			N3LB				
G-CFMV	Aerola Alatus-M	AS 01-019		26.11.08	M G Lynes	(East Woodhay, Newbury)	
G-CFMW	Scheibe SF25C Falke 2000	44378	D-KNIB	8.12.08	The Windrushers Gliding Club Ltd	Bicester	
G-CFMX	Piper PA-28-161 Warrior II	28-8316073	N4306Z	3.11.08	Stapleford Flying Club Ltd	Stapleford	16.12.09E
G-CFMY	Rolladen-Schneider LS7	7004	BGA3381-FMY	16. 1.08	N J Howes tr G-CFMY Group	Camphill	17. 4.08
			D-1256				
G-CFMZ	Agusta A109E Power	11744		28. 1.09	Irish and European Properties Ltd	Dublin, Ireland	27. 1.10E
G-CFNB	Cameron TR-70 Balloon (Hot-Air)	11140		13.10.08	Cameron Balloons Ltd	Bristol	
G-CFNC	Flylight Dragonfly	004		3. 9.08	W G Minns	(Norwich)	
G-CFND	Schleicher Ka 6E	4069	BGA3386-FND	20. 9.07	T Barton	Talgarth	12. 2.08
			PH-366				
G-CFNE	PZL-Bielsko SZD-38A Jantar 1	B-612	BGA3387-FNE	14. 5.08	T Robson, J Murray and I Gordon	Rivar Hill	
			HB-1215				
G-CFNF	Robinson R44 Raven II	12496		5.12.08	Sloane Helicopters Ltd	Sywell	
G-CFNG	Schleicher ASW 24	24015	BGA3389-FNG	17. 9.07	P H Pickett	Snitterfield	28. 9.08
G-CFNH	Schleicher ASW 19	19194	BGA3390-FNH	10.12.07	S N and P E S Longland	Gransden Lodge	8. 4.08
			D-7969				
G-CFNI	AirBorne XT912-B-Streak III-B	XT912-258		11. 9.08	Fly NI Ltd	Tarsan Lane, Portadown	
	(Built AirBorne Windsports, wing serial no S3-526)						
G-CFNJ	Cameron Z-120 Balloon (Hot-Air)	11230		19.11.08	M G Howard	Dubai, United Arab Emirates	
G-CFNK	Slingsby T.65A Vega	1897	BGA3392-FNK	24. 4.08	I P Goldstraw and V Luscombe-Mahoney *"FNK"*		
			N9023H			Dunstable	
G-CFNL	Schempp-Hirth Discus b	253	BGA3393-FNL	3.12.07	A S Ramsay and P P Musto *"705"*	Long Mynd	31. 1.08
G-CFNM	Centrair 101B Pegase	101B0289	BGA3394-FNM	25.10.07	D T Hartley	Husbands Bosworth	28. 9.08
			F-CGSE				
G-CFNN	Schempp-Hirth Ventus cT	130	BGA3395-FNN	27.11.07	D G Every	Eyres Field	6.12.07
G-CFNO	Best Off Sky Ranger Swift 912S(1)			16. 9.08	J W Taylor	(Ross-on-Wye)	
	(Built J W Taylor)	BMAA/HB/566					
G-CFNP	Schleicher Ka 6CR	567	BGA3396-FNP	29. 7.08	P Pollard-Wilkins	Ringmer	
			D-4657				
G-CFNR	Schempp-Hirth Discus b	255	BGA3398-FNR	22.10.07	R A Amor	Nympsfield	13. 4.08
G-CFNS	DG Flugzeugbau DG-300 Club Elan		BGA3399-FNS	14. 1.08	J M Price, K F Byrne and P.E.Williams	Portmoak	2. 7.08
		3E314C23					
G-CFNT	Glaser-Dirks DG-600	6-12	BGA3400-FNT	21. 9.07	M R Johnson tr G-CFNT Group	Sutton Bank	29. 3.08
G-CFNU	Rolladen-Schneider LS4-a	4732	BGA3401-FNU	23. 8.07	R J Simpson	Nympsfield	6. 1.08
			D-1376				
G-CFNV	CZAW Sportscruiser	LAA 338-14844		10.10.08	Sprite Aviation Services Ltd		
	(Built G Smith)					Inglenook Farm, Maydensole	
G-CFNW	Evektor EV-97 teamEurostar UK	3317		5. 1.09	The Scottish Aero Club Ltd	Balado Bridge	
	(Built Cosmik Aviation)						
G-CFNX	Air Création Tanarg 912S/iXess 13	FLT.xxx		20.10.08	Flylight Airposrts Ltd	Sywell	
	(Originally regd with iXess 15 wing but type amended 13.11.08)						
	(Built Flylight Airsports Ltd - pr.no.BMAA HB/569, official wing number A07162-7186 but noted 12.08 as A07162-7198)						
G-CFNY	Flylight Dragonfly	009		29.10.08	G S Ungless	Sutton, Ely	
G-CFNZ	AirBorne XT912-B-Streak III-B	XT912-290		27.10.08	R G Mason	(Aston Clinton)	15.12.09P
	(Rotax 912 UL)						
G-CFOA	Eurocopter EC.130B4	4597		3.11.08	Eurocopter UK Ltd	Oxford	
G-CFOB	Schleicher ASW 15B	15340	BGA3432-FQB	1. 2.08	A Maitland	Drumshade	16. 3.08
			D-2345				
G-CFOC	Glaser-Dirks DG-200/17	2-178CCL19	BGA3433-FQC	5. 3.08	R and C Nunn	Wormingfod	
			HB-1645				
G-CFOE	Cameron Z-210 Balloon (Hot-Air)	11220		9.12.08	I Charbonnier	Aosta, Italy	8.12.09E
G-CFOF	Scheibe SF27A Zugvögel V	6025	BGA3436-FQF	5. 2.08	S Maddex	Darlton	6. 5.08
			D-0009				
G-CFOG	Comco Ikarus C42 FB UK	0511-6773		19. 4.06	P D Coppin	Lee-on-Solent	17. 9.09P
	(Built P D Coppin - pr.no.PFA 322-14482)						

Reg	Type	C/n	Prev ID	Date	Owner	Location	Date
G-CFOH	Gulfstream Aerospace Gulfstream IV	1202	HB-ITF N369XL, JY-RAY, V8-009, V8-MSB, N432GA	21.11.08	Gama Aviation Ltd	Farnborough	
G-CFOI	Cessna 172N Skyhawk II	17269315	N737CN	14.11.08	P Fearon	(Romsey)	
G-CFOK	Grob G103C Twin III Acro	34123	BGA3440-FOK	16.10.07	York Gliding Centre Ltd	Rufforth	29. 3.08
G-CFOL	UltraMagic M-90 Balloon (Hot-Air)	90/93					
G-CFOM	Scheibe SF27A	6098	BGA3442-FQM D-9421	3. 3.08	R D Noon and D Foster	Darlton	
G-CFON	Wittman W.8 Tailwind (Built C F O'Neill)	PFA 031-11789		7.11.07	C F O'Neill	Newtownards	
G-CFOO	P&M Aviation QuikR	8413		26.11.08	Terratrip (UK) Ltd t/a Microavionics (Horsley, Derby)		1.12.09P
G-CFOP	Cameron Shopping Bag 120 SS Balloon (Hot-Air)	3642	HB-QAO	18.11.08	M G Howard	Dubai, United Arab Emirates	
G-CFOR	Schleicher K 8B	8537	BGA3446-FQR PH-349	22. 4.08	Dorset Gliding Club Ltd	Eyres Field	
G-CFOS	Flylight Dragonfly	017		18.11.08	S N Bond	Sywell	
G-CFOT	PZL Bielsko SZD-48-3 Jantar Standard 3	B-1891	BGA3448-FQT (BGA3409-FPC)	29. 2.08	T H Greenwood	Rivar Hill	18. 5.08
G-CFOU	Schleicher K 7 Rhönadler	1139	BGA3449-FQU D-8614, HB-709	20.11.07	Channel Gliding Club Ltd	Waldershare Park	3. 3.08
G-CFOV	CZAW Sportcruiser (Built J G Murphy, J Holt, R Morey and S Whitehead)	LAA 338-14832		18.11.08	J G Murphy t/a G-CFOV Group Morgansfield, Fishburn		
G-CFOW	Best Off Sky Ranger Swift 912S(1) (Built A Chappell)	BMAA HB/583		19.11.08	A Chappell	(Dollar)	
G-CFOX	Marganski MDM-1 Fox	224	BGA4566-JKC	26. 9.07	M Newman tr Fox Glider Syndicate	Saltby	23. 1.09E
G-CFOY	Schempp-Hirth Discus b	274	BGA3453-FQY	21. 9.07	B W Mills and J W Slater	Dunstable	28. 9.08
G-CFOZ	Rolladen-Schneider LS1-f	391	BGA3454-FQZ F-CEKH	12. 2.08	A G Wallace tr L51 Group	Bidford	26. 2.08
G-CFPA	CZAW Sportcruiser (Built K D Taylor and S Lowe)	LAA 338-14869		20.11.08	K D Taylor	(Wigsley, Newark)	
G-CFPB	Schleicher ASW 15B	15243	BGA3408-FPB D-2068	23. 4.08	R C Tatlow tr G-CFPB Syndicate	Darlton	
G-CFPC	Gulfstream AA-5B Tiger	AA5B-1187	G-JENN N4533T	25.11.08	Airtime Aviation France Ltd	Bournemouth	28. 3.08E
G-CFPD	Rolladen-Schneider LS7	7033	BGA3410-FPD D-5178	11. 3.08	S Wilson and M White "973"	Dunstable	
G-CFPE	Schempp-Hirth Ventus cT	131/408	BGA3411-FPE	28. 2.08	R Palmer	Bidford	5. 4.08
G-CFPF	Scheibe L-Spatz 55	720	BGA3412-FPF RAFGGA 537, D-8376	9. 9.08	N C Stone	(Morpeth)	
	(Officially registered with c/n 2720 but above believed correct, dating from 1961; the previous identities are confirmed by the owner)						
G-CFPH	Centrair ASW 20F	20132	BGA3414-FPH F-CFFX	4.12.07	R Wardell-Yerburgh tr GB2 Syndicate Kingston Deverill		11. 3.08
G-CFPI	P&M Aviation Quik GT450	8422		1.12.08	E J Douglas	East Fortune	1.12.09P
G-CFPJ	CZAW Sportcruiser (Built S R Winter)	LAA 338-14858		31.10.08	S R Winter	Willingdale	
G-CFPL	Schempp-Hirth Ventus c	409	BGA3417-FPL	23. 8.07	R V Barrett	Nympsfield	28. 9.08
G-CFPM	PZL-Bielsko SZD-51-1 Junior	B-1788	BGA3418-FPM	29.10.07	Kent Gliding Club Ltd "FPM"	Challock	28. 9.08
G-CFPN	Schleicher ASW 20	20376	BGA3419-FPN RAFGGA 545, D-8780	15. 2.08	M Rayner	Lasham	19. 8.08
G-CFPO	Aero L-39C Albatross	232207	ZU-RUN 207 Ukraine AF, 207 Soviet AF	2.12.08	G P Williams	Swansea	
G-CFPP	Schempp-Hirth Nimbus 2B	142	BGA3420-FPP D-6779, D-2111	21. 4.08	R Jones and R Murfitt	Walney island	
G-CFPR	P&M Aviation QuikR (Trike marked as Quik)	8415		6.11.08	P&M Aviation Ltd	Rochdale	1.12.09P
G-CFPS	Sky 25-16 Balloon (Hot-Air)	075		1.12.08	Zebedee Balloon Service Ltd	Hungerford	
G-CFPT	Schleicher ASW 20	20007	BGA3424-FPT D-7574	27. 3.08	L Hornsey tr L Hornsey & L Weeks Syndicate "574" RAF Halton		
G-CFPU	Sikorsky S-76C-2	760732	N25740	22. 1.09	Bristow Helicopters (International) Ltd	Redhill	
G-CFPW	Glaser-Dirks DG-600	6-17	BGA3427-FPW	27. 3.08	P B Gray	Camp Hill	
G-CFPX	Schleicher ASK 13	13325	BGA3428-FPX F-CDYR	3. 1.08	R B Witter	Lleweni Parc	17. 8.07
G-CFPY	Sikorsky S-76C	760735	N20380	19. 1.09	Bristow Helicopters (International) Ltd	Redhill	
G-CFRB	Schempp-Hirth Ventus c	404	BGA3456-FRB	19. 9.07	C J Ratcliffe	Seighford	14. 3.08
G-CFRC	Schempp-Hirth Nimbus 2B	151	BGS 3457-FRC D-4980	6. 3.08	T J Lean tr Tim and Martin Nimbus 2B Group Lasham		
G-CFRE	Schleicher Ka 6E	4349	BGA3459-FRE F-CDTL	13. 3.08	D J Stewart tr K6-FRE Syndicate	Parham Park	
G-CFRF	Lindstrand LBL 31A Balloon (Hot-Air)	1232		19.12.08	A I Attwood tr RAF Halton Hot Air Balloon Club RAF Halton		4. 1.10E
G-CFRH	Schleicher ASW 20CL	20740	BGA3462-FRH D-9229	13. 3.08	J N Wilton "634"	Husbands Bosworth	
G-CFRJ	Schempp-Hirth Standard Cirrus	103	BGA3463-FRJ HB-1041	3. 9.08	C J Lawrence	Tibenham	
G-CFRK	Schleicher ASW 15 B	15214	BGA3464-FRK	29.11.07	M Hill	Shenington	21.10.07
G-CFRL	Grob G102 Astir CS	1373	BGA3465-FRL D-7402	25. 1.08	The South Wales Gliding Club Ltd	Usk	13. 4.08
G-CFRM	Best Off Sky Ranger Swift 912S(1) (Built R K and T A Willcox - pr.no BMAA/HB/578)	SKRxxxx885		4.12.08	R K and T A Willcox Chase Farm, Chipping Sodbury		
G-CFRP	Centrair 101A Pégase	101A0311	BGA3458-FRP EI-162, BGA3458	8. 7.08	C Bessent tr Bessent and Prentice Group Rivar Hill		
G-CFRR	Centrair 101A Pégase	101034	BGA3470-FRR (BGA3451-FQW), F-CFQA	27.11.07	P A Lewis	Walney Island	4. 6.08

G-CFRS	Scheibe Zugvögel IIIB	1097	BGA3471-FRS D-2171, HB-749	29. 1.08	S W Vallei and R C Theobald	Rivar Hill	26. 4.08
G-CFRT	Evektor EV-97 teamEurostar UK (Built Cosmik Aviation Ltd)	3224		3. 9.08	Cosmik Aviation Ltd	Deppers Bridge, Southam	
G-CFRV	Centrair 101A Pégase	101A0325	BGA3474-FRV	2.11.07	P J Britten	Wycombe Air Park	15. 1.08
G-CFRW	Schleicher ASW 20L	20202	BGA3475-FRW D-5981	11. 1.08	S R Jarvis "268"	Lasham	4. 3.08
G-CFRX	Centrair 101A Pégase	101A0315	BGA3476-FRX	10. 1.08	S Woolrich	(Auchtermuchty, Cupar)	13. 2.08
G-CFRY	Zenair CH.601UL Zodiac (Built C K Fry)	PFA 162A-14302		5. 1.05	C K Fry	(Lytchett Minster, Poole)	
G-CFRZ	Schempp-Hirth Standard Cirrus (Built Burkhart Grob-Flugzeugbau)	348G	BGA3478-FRZ HB-1194, D-2172	16. 7.08	SG Lapworth and N E Smith	Lasham	
G-CFSA	Piper PA-44-180 Seminole	4496170	N492AF G-CCDA, N53487	27. 9.06	Northern Aviation Ltd	Durham Tees Valley	30.10.08E
G-CFSB	Tecnam P2002-RG Sierra (Built P G Gale)	LAA 333A-14864		20 .1.09	P G Gale t/a W J Gale and Son	Edington Hill, Keevil	
G-CFSC	Bombardier CL600-2B16 (Challenegr 605)	5744	N744JC C-FQQS	14. 1.09	Gama Aviation Ltd	Farnborough	
G-CFSD	Schleicher ASK 13	13367	BGA3482-FSD D-0863	29. 1.08	T World tr Portsmouth Naval Gliding Centre	Lee-on-Solent	16. 8.08
G-CFSF	P&M Aviation QuikR	8421		7. 1.09	A M Dalgetty	Balado Bridge	6. 1.10P
G-CFSH	Grob G102 Astir CS Jeans	2090	BGA3486-FSH D-7532	23. 1.08	Buckminster Gliding Club Ltd	Saltby	7. 7.08
G-CFSI	Aerola Alatus-M	AS 01-020		9. 2.09	T J Birkbeck	Rufforth	
G-CFSJ	Jabiru J160 (Built M Flint)	LAA 346-14838		22. 1.09	M Flint	Fenland	
G-CFSK	Dyn'Aero MCR-01 VLA Sportster (Built S Collins, pr. no PFA 301-14704)	365		16. 1.09	S Collins	(Wem, Shrewsbury)	
G-CFSM	Cessna 172Q Cutlass	17275933	N918AT N918ER (N65959)	5. 1.09	Cristal Air Ltd	Shoreham	
G-CFSN	Aerola Alatus M	AS 01-021		6. 2.09	A G Phillips	(Doune)	
G-CFSO	Flylight Dragonfly	025		28. 1.09	C J Haste	(Lochearnhead)	
G-CFSR	DG Flugzeugbau DG-300 Elan	3E343	BGA3494-FSR	18.12.07	A P Montague and J E May	Nympsfield	22. 1.08
G-CFSS	Schleicher Ka 6E	4019	BGA3495-FSS D-5260	30. 7.08	P R Robey tr FSS Syndicate	Lasham	
G-CFST	Schleicher ASH 25E	25073	BGA3496-FST (BGA3530)	30. 8.07	D Tucker and K H Lloyd	Aston Down	18. 3.08
G-CFSV	Piper PA-18 Super Cub	18-6038	VH-JVL ZS-JVX, TR-LPC, TN-ABK, F-OBKU	26. 1.09	Aviad Europe Ltd	(Biggleswade)	
G-CFSU	Scheibe Zügvogel IIIA	1060	BGA 3497-FSU D-9055	22. 8.08	F F Dodds "55"	Bellarena	
G-CFSW	Best Off Sky Ranger Swift 912S (1) (Built S B Williams)	BMAA HB/587		8. 1.09	S B and L S Williams	Headcorn	
G-CFSX	ICP MXP-740 Savannah VG Jabiru (1) (Built J P Swadling)	BMAA HB/581		26. 1.09	J P Swadling	(Waterlooville)	
G-CFSY	Lindstrand LBL 120A Balloon (Hot-Air)	527	OH-BKK	27. 1.09	R Trombetti	Villanterio, Italy	
G-CFSZ	Grob G102 Astir CS77	1841	BGA3502-FSZ D-2908	16.11.07	N Greenwood	Aston Down	17. 3.08
G-CFTA	Ace Magic Laser (Assembled P&M Aviation) (Trike believed to be AA MT 00111)	AA00138		23. 1.09	N Ragg	(London N10)	
G-CFTB	Schleicher Ka 6CR	019	BGA3504-FTB D-8900	31.10.07	P J F Blair	Bidford	24. 1.08
G-CFTC	PZL-Bielsko SZD-51-1 Junior	B-1860	BGA3505-FTC	07.02.08	J G Kosak tr Seahawk Gliding Club	RNAS Culdrose	20. 3.08
G-CFTD	Schleicher ASW 15B	15191	BGA3506-FTD D-0872	11. 1.08	E Stephenson	Milfield	29. 4.08
G-CFTE	P&M Aviation QuikR	8426		16. 1.09	R J Erlam	Ince Blundell	
G-CFTG	P&M Aviation QuikR	8414		5. 1.09	A V Cosser	East Fortune	4. 1.10P
G-CFTH	PZL-Bielsko SZD-50-3 Puchacz	B-1881	BGA3510-FTH	24.10.07	Buckminster Gliding Club Ltd (Noted 2.08)	Saltby	17.12.07
G-CFTI	Evektor EV-97Eurostar	xxx		16. 1.09	G R Pritchard	Hardwicke, Hay-on-Wye	
	(Built G R Pritchard, originally EV-97A, pr.no PFA 315-14878 – type amended to EV-97 21. 1.09)						
G-CFTJ	Evektor EV-97A Eurostar (Built C B Flood, pr. no PFA 315-14504)	2005.26.25		13. 2.06	C B Flood	Ince Blundell	9. 8.08P
G-CFTK	Grob G102 Astir CS Jeans	2059	BGA3512-FTK OE-5152	5.10.07	Ulster Gliding Club Ltd	Bellarena	8. 9.07
G-CFTL	Schleicher ASW 20CL	20751	BGA3513-FTL	9.10.07	J S and S V Shaw	Perranporth	22. 4.08
G-CFTM	Cameron C-80 Balloon (Hot-Air)	11121		20. 1.09	P A Meecham	Chipping Norton	
G-CFTN	Schleicher K 8B	996	BGA3515-FTN D-8539, D-KAEL, D-8539	11. 9.08	Mendip Gliding Club Ltd	Halesland	
G-CFTO	Comco Ikarus C42 FB UK (Built Aerosport Ltd)	0809-7007		22.10.08	Fly Hire Ltd	Rufforth	28.10.09P
G-CFTP	Schleicher ASW 20CL	20733	BGA3516-FTP D-3640	14. 2.08	D J Pengilley and M S Hawkins "332"	Kingston Deverill	31. 5.08
G-CFTR	Grob G102 Astir CS77	1606	BGA3518-FTR D-4807	5.12.07	The Furness Gliding Club Proprietary Ltd tr Lakes Gliding Club	Walney Island	9. 3.08
G-CFTS	DG Flugzeugbau DG-300 Club Elan	3E349C38	BGA3519-FTS	15. 1.08	A J E Taylor	Parham Park	23. 5.08
G-CFTT	Van's RV-7	72230		12. 1.09	R I and D J Blain	Newtownards	
G-CFTV	Rolladen-Schneider LS7-WL (Built R I and D J Blain, pr no LAA 323-14405)	7073	BGA3522-FTV	6.12.07	D Hilton	Wycombe Air Park	6. 3.08
G-CFTW	Schempp-Hirth Discus b	292/1	BGA3523-FTW	17. 9.07	P A Startup "230"	North Hill	29. 9.09
	(Rebuilt with new fuselage after accident 21. 6.91; original fuselage rebuilt as BGA3879; originally registered as 292 but amended 8.10.08)						

Reg	Type	C/n	BGA/other	Date	Owner/Operator	Base	Date2
G-CFTX	Jabiru J160	LAA 346-14829		2. 9.08	R K Creasey	(Ashford)	
	(Built R K Creasey)						
G-CFTY	Rolladen-Schneider LS7-WL	7075	BGA3525-FTY	14. 1.08	A Burgess and J D Thomson "753"	Easterton	4. 4.08
G-CFTZ	Evektor EV-97 Eurostar	xxx		14. 1.09	G G Bevis	Old Sarum	
	(Built G G Bevis, pr.no. LAA 315-14857)						
G-CFUB	Schleicher Ka 6CR	6007	BGA3528/FUB	24. 6.08	D E Hooper	Brent Tor	
			D-8573				
G-CFUD	Best Off Sky Ranger Swift 912S(1)			2. 1.09	V D Carmichael	Tarsan Lane, Portadown	
		SKRxxxx912	(Built V D Carmichael –pr.no BMAA HB/584)				
G-CFUG	Grob G109B	6314	D-KEOP	12. 1.09	D A Smith	Wing Farm, Longbridge Deverill	
G-CFUH	Schempp-Hirth Ventus c	438	BGA3533-FUH	6. 9.07	C G T Huck	Cirencester	28. 9.08
G-CFUJ	DG Flugzeugbau DG-300 Elan	3E353	BGA3534-FUJ	7.11.07	V A Leitch tr Foxtrot Uniform Juliet Grp	Portmoak	4. 3.08
G-CFUL	Schempp-Hirth Discus b	293	BGA3535-FUL	1.12.07	J Greenwood tr Discus 803 Syndicate	Dunstable	22. 2.08
G-CFUN	Schleicher ASW 20CL	20813	BGA3537-FUN	5.11.07	S Economu and W H Parker	Wycombe Air Park	6. 3.08
			D-3432				
G-CFUP	Schempp-Hirth Discus b	291	BGA3538-FUP	13. 5.08	North Downs Gliding Trust Ltd	Lasham	
G-CFUR	Schempp-Hirth Ventus cT	145/446	BGA3540-FUR	5. 3.08	K Martin and D Townson	Shobdon	
G-CFUS	PZL-Bielsko SZD-51-1 Junior	B-1912	BGA3541-FUS	2.11.07	Scottish Gliding Union Ltd	Portmoak	28. 9.08
G-CFUT	Glaser-Dirks DG-300 Club Elan	3E350C39	BGA3542-FUT	18. 6.08	M J Barnett and A C Ellis	Gransden Lodge	
G-CFUU	DG Flugzeugbau DG-300 Club Elan		BGA3543-FUU	6. 9.07	D S Penny	Perranporth	28. 9.08
		3E360C45					
G-CFUV	Rolladen-Schneider LS7-WL	7068	BGA3544-FUV	9.11.07	E Alston	North Hill	13. 1.10
G-CFUY	PZL-Bielsko SZD-50-3 Puchacz	B-1983	BGA3546-FUY	19. 2.08	The Bath, Wilts and North Dorset Gliding Club Ltd		
						Kingston Deverill	6. 5.08
G-CFUZ	CZAW Sportcruiser	PFA 338-14664		11.12.08	M W Bush	Belle Vue Farm, Yarncombe	
	(Built M W Bush)						
G-CFVC	Schleicher ASK 13	13682AB	BGA3550-FVC	22.12.07	Mendip Gliding Club Ltd	Halesland	25. 1.08
G-CFVE	Schempp-Hirth Nimbus 2C	202	BGA3553-FVF-	28.11.07	L Mitchell	Chipping	19. 6.08
G-CFVH	Rolladen-Schneider LS7	7067	BGA3555-FVH	18. 1.08	B.R.Forrest	Wycombe Air Park	11. 4.08
			(BGA3527-FUA)				
G-CFVJ	Cvjetkovic CA-65 Skyfly	PFA 233-14129		21. 1.09	D Hunter	Orange Grove, Chavenage, Tetbury	
	(Built D Hunter and P Gheysens)						
G-CFVK	Best Off Sky Ranger HKS	SKR0511662		6. 2.09	B Barrass	Sywel	
	(Built B Barrass, pr.no BMAA HB/497)						
G-CFVL	Scheibe Zügvogel 111B	1082	BGA2558-FVL	28. 4.08	T G Homan and M Balogh	Darlton	
			D-5224				
G-CFVM	Centrair 101A Pégase	101A0345	BGA3559-FVM	10.12.07	S H North	Kingston Deverill	11. 4.08
G-CFVN	Centrair 101A Pégase	101A0268/2	BGA3560-FVN	6. 2.08	G G Butler	Snitterfield	1. 2.08
G-CFVP	Centrair 101A Pégase	101A0350	BGA3561-FVP	27. 9.07	J R Parry tr Foxtrot Victor Papa Group	Long Mynd	8. 3.08
G-CFVS	Schempp-Hirth Standard Cirrus	359G	BGA3564-FVS	29.10.07	P A Clark	Lasham	24. 1.08
			D-2168				
G-CFVT	Schempp-Hirth Nimbus 2	18	BGA3565-FVT	26. 9.08	I Dunkley	Camphill	
			N795				
G-CFVU	Schleicher ASK 13	13062	BGA3566-FVU	1.11.07	The Vale of the White Horse Gliding Centre Ltd		
			D-1348			Sandhill Farm, Shrivenham	28. 9.08
G-CFVV	Centrair 101A Pégase	101A0353	BGA3567-FVV	29. 2.08	Cambridge Gliding Club Ltd	Gransden Lodge	1. 7.08
G-CFVW	Schempp-Hirth Ventus bT	51-252	BGA3568-FVW	4.12.07	I C Champness and R F Barber	Lasham	28. 9.08
			D-KORN				
G-CFVZ	Schleicher Ka 6E	4007	BGA3571-FVZ	12.12.07	R C Fisher	Kingston Deverill	21. 6.08
			D-4104				
G-CFWA	Schleicher Ka 6CR	6227	BGA3572-FWA	10. 9.07	C C Walley	(Bushey)	5.10.07
			D-1062				
G-CFWB	Schleicher ASK 13	13224	BGA3573-FWB	21. 1.08	Cotswold Gliding Club	Aston Down	19. 1.08
			HB-989				
G-CFWC	Grob G103C Twin III Acro	34154	BGA3574-FWC	25. 1.08	The South Wales Gliding Club Ltd	Usk	17. 3.08
G-CFWE	PZL-Bielsko SZD-50-3 Puchacz	B-1984	BGA3576-FWE	25.10.07	Deeside Gliding Club (Aberdeenshire) Ltd	Aboyne	28. 9.08
			(BGA3547-FUZ)				
G-CFWF	Rolladen-Schneider LS7	7097	BGA3577-FWF	14. 8.08	G P Hibberd "LS7"	Husbands Bosworth	
G-CFWH	Scheibe SF27A	6024	BGA3579-FWH	15. 9.08	M D Smith	Aston Down	
			D-4733				
G-CFWK	Schempp-Hirth Nimbus 3DT	32	BGA3581-FWK	7. 1.08	A J Dibdin tr 29 Syndicate	Gransden Lodge	27. 3.08
G-CFWL	Schleicher K 8B	106-58	BGA3582-FWL	11. 2.08	M Staniscia	(Kettering)	3. 8.08
			D-7151				
G-CFWM	DG Flugzeugbau DG-300 Club Elan	3E373C50	BGA3583-FWM	26.10.07	S A Gunn-Russell tr FWM Group	Long Mynd	28. 9.08
G-CFWP	Schleicher ASW 19B	19262	BGA3585-FWP	3. 1.08	B Spriggs "980"	Dunstable	17. 3.08
			D-5980				
G-CFWR	Best Off Sky Ranger 912(2)	SKRxxxx525		2.12.04	A M Wood and J Mills		
	(Built R W Clarke - pr.no.BMAA HB/426)					Longacre Farm, Sandy	19. 3.08P
G-CFWS	Schleicher ASW 20C	20765	BGA3588-FWS	10.12.07	R Hawtree tr 662 Syndicate	Ridgewell	3. 4.08
			D-6623				
G-CFWT	PZL-Bielsko SZD-50-3 Puchacz	B-1988	BGA3589-FWT	3.10.07	Coventry Gliding Club Ltd tr The Gliding Centre		
					"FWT"	Husbands Bosworth	11. 1.08
G-CFWU	Rolladen-Schneider LS7-WL	7080	BGA3590-FWU	21.12.07	G E Thomas	Husbands Bosworth	29. 3.08
G-CFWW	Schleicher ASH 25E	25093	BGA3592-FWW	24. 3.06	A T Farmer tr FWW Syndicate	Bicester	28. 2.08
G-CFWY	Centrair 101A Pégase	101071	BGA3594-FWY	17. 1.08	R Johnson tr Foxtrot Whiskey Yankee	Lasham	5. 4.08
			F-CFRZ				
G-CFWZ	Schleicher ASW 19B	19342	BGA3595-FWZ	21. 2.08	C M Worrall tr G-CFWZ Flying Group	Camphill	15.12.07
			D-2603				
G-CFXA	Grob G104 Speed Astir IIB	4083	BGA3596-FXA	16. 8.07	C M Hawkes and D C White	Ringmer	29.11.07
			D-2671				
G-CFXB	Schleicher K 8B	8193/A	BGA3597/FXB	3. 7.08	R Morris and R Sansom	Brent Tor	
			D-5597				
G-CFXC	Schleicher Ka 6E	4268	BGA3598-FXC	15. 4.08	A K Bailey and G Pook	Kingston Deverill	
			D-0150				

Reg	Type	C/n	BGA/ID	Date	Owner	Base	Date
G-CFXD	Centrair 101A Pégase	101A0346	BGA3599-FXD (BGA3563-FVR)	2.10.07	D G England and R Banks	Husbands Bosworth	27.12.07
G-CFXH	Schleicher K 7 Rhönadler	353	BGA3603-FXH D-4040	11. 1.08	T J Price tr Vale of Neath Gliding Club	Rhigos	6. 9.08
G-CFXJ	Schleicher ASW 24	24086	BGA3604-FXJ	21. 8.07	A K Laylee "247"	Lasham	28. 5.08
G-CFXM	Schempp-Hirth Discus bT	16/301	BGA3607-FXM D-KHIA	18. 8.08	R Bottomley "173"	Pocklington	
G-CFXO	PZL-Bielsko SZD-50-3 Puchacz	B-2024	BGA3658-FXQ (BGA3637-FYT)	3.10.07	Coventry Gliding Club Ltd tr The Gliding Centre "FXQ"	Husbands Bosworth	28. 9.08
G-CFXS	Schleicher Ka 6E	4228	BGA3612-FXS D-0073	3. 9.08	B C F Wade and R B Woodhouse	Tibenham	
G-CFXU	Schleicher Ka 6E	4071	BGA3614-FXU OH-343, OH-RSY	4. 1.08	T Ward	Lasham	14. 3.08
G-CFXW	Schleicher K 8B	8651	BGA3616-FXW D-7203, D-KOLA, D-7203	25. 1.08	The South Wales Gliding Club Ltd	Usk	24. 3.07
G-CFXY	Schleicher ASW 15B	15348	BGA3618-FXY F-CEJL	5. 3.08	E L Armstrong	Husbands Bosworth	
G-CFYA	PZL-Bielsko SZD-50-3 Puchacz	B-2022	BGA3620-FYA	8.11.07	W R Longstaff tr Cairngorm Gliding Club	Feshie Bridge	25. 3.08
G-CFYB	Rolladen-Schneider LS7	7102	BGA3621-FYB	6. 9.07	A T Macdonald and V P Haley	Wormingford	13. 2.10
G-CFYC	Schempp-Hirth Ventus b	83	BGA3622-FYC F-CEDR, F-WEDR	8. 1.08	K Fear	Crowland	20. 4.08
G-CFYE	Scheibe Zügvogel IIIB (Original identies not confirmed)	1067	BGA3624-FYE OY-MHX, SE-TCE, OY-EFX, D-1814	17. 6.08	R Staines	Brent Tor	
G-CFYF	Schleicher ASK 21	21470	BGA3625-FYF	22. 5.08	London Gliidng Club (Proprietary) Ltd	Dunstable	
G-CFYG	Glasflügel Club Libelle 205	22	BGA3626-FYG OH-545, D-9476?	14. 8.08	P R Thomas tr FYG Syndicate "FYG"	Talgarth	
G-CFYH	Rolladen-Schneider LS4-a	4804	BGA3627-FYH	21. 8.08	G W and C A Craig "224"	RAF Weston-on-the-Green	
G-CFYJ	Schempp-Hirth Standard Cirrus	581G	BGA3628-FYJ D-8931	16.11.07	S A Gibson tr FYJ Syndicate	Pocklington	29.12.07
G-CFYK	Rolladen-Schneider LS7-WL	7108	BGA3629-FYK	19.11.07	R R Ward	Gransden Lodge	26. 1.08
G-CFYL	PZL-Bielsko SZD-50-3 Puchasz	B-1990	BGA3630-FYL	16.11.07	Deeside Gliding Club (Aberdeenshire) Ltd	Aboyne	29. 9.09
G-CFYM	Schempp-Hirth Discus bT	31	BGA3631-FYM	5.10.07	B F Laverick-Smith	Challock	28. 9.08
G-CFYN	Schempp-Hirth Discus b	179	BGA3632-FYN N75J	12.11.07	N White and P R Foulger	Wormingford	21. 3.08
G-CFYR	LET L-23 Super Blanik	917816	BGA3635-FYR	28. 3.08	T Newby tr G-CFYR Group	(Bingley)	
G-CFYU	Glaser-Dirks DG-100 Elan	E111	BGA3638-FYU OY-XMR, SE-TYO	14. 2.08	I M and C Shepherd "DG"	RAF Weston-on-the-Green	5. 7.08
G-CFYV	Schleicher ASK 21	21468	BGA3639-FYV	6.11.07	The Bristol Gliding Club Proprietary Ltd	Nympsfield	28. 9.08
G-CFYW	Rolladen-Schneider LS7	7111	BGA3640-FYW	10.12.07	D S Lodge "KC"	Pocklington	19. 1.08
G-CFYX	Schempp-Hirth Discus b	32/333	BGA3641-FYX	31. 3.08	D A Salmon tr Discus FYX Group	Camp Hill	
G-CFYY	Schleicher ASK 13	13685AB	BGA3642-FYY	12. 3.08	Lasham Gliding Society Ltd "S"	Lasham	
G-CFYZ	Schleicher ASH 25	25097	BGA3643-FYZ	4. 6.08	M G Thick "171"	Lasham	
G-CFZA	PZL-Bielsko SZD-51-1 Junior	B-1913	BGA3644-FZA	13.12.07	Booker Gliding Club Ltd "FZA"	Wycombe Air Park	29. 1.08
G-CFZB	Glasflügel H201B Standard Libelle	669	BGA3645-FZB OH-388, OH-GLA	3. 1.08	J C Meyer "669"	Nympsfield	2. 1.08
G-CFZF	PZL-Bielsko SZD-51-1 Junior	B-1861	BGA3649-FZF	30.11.07	Devon & Somerset Gliding Club Ltd	North Hill	28. 9.08
G-CFZH	Schempp-Hirth Ventus c	455	BGA3651-FZH	12.11.07	G D Clack tr FZH Group	Lasham	22. 1.08
G-CFZK	Schempp-Hirth Standard Cirrus	81	BGA3653-FZK HB-967	9. 6.08	S Lucas and R Burgoyne	Aston Down	
G-CFZL	Schleicher ASW 20CL	20764	BGA3654-FZL D-5937	25. 9.07	A L and R M Housden	Aboyne	8.11.07
G-CFZN	Schleicher ASK 13	13045	BGA3656-FZN D-5759	1.12.07	Black Mountains Gliding Club	Talgarth	16. 5.08
G-CFZO	Schempp-Hirth Numbus-3DT	31	BGA3610-FXQ	17.11.07	D Tanner "954"	Lasham	28. 9.08
G-CFZP	PZL-Bielsko SZD-51-1 Junior	B-1926	BGA3657-FZP	28. 1.08	T World tr Portsmouth Naval Gliding Centre	Lee-on-Solent	19. 6.08
G-CFZR	Schleicher Ka 6CR	6136	BGA3659-FZR D-8459	24.11.08	M H Simms	Shipdham	
G-CFZV	Rolladen-Schneider LS7	7116	BGA3663-FZV	18. 1.08	R N Boddy	Wycombe Air Park	8. 3.08
G-CFZW	DG Flugzeugbau DG-300 Club Elan	3E378C53	BGA3664-FZW	16. 1.08	D O'Flanagan, G Rogers and G Stilgoe	Parham Park	7. 3.08
G-CFZZ	LET L-33 Solo	940220	BGA3667-FZZ	25. 3.08	D A R Wiseman	Andreas, IoM	

G-CGAA - G-CGZZ

Reg	Type	C/n	BGA/ID	Date	Owner	Base	Date
G-CGAB	AB Sportine LAK-12 Lietuva	6170	BGA3669-GAB	10. 4.08	M J Wilshere	RAF Halton	
G-CGAD	Rolladen-Schneider LS3	3032	BGA3671-GAD HB-1363	16. 7.08	P B Turner "L5"	Challock	
G-CGAF	Schleicher ASK 21	21152	BGA3673-GAF ZD652, BGA2892-ERO	16. 1.08	Lasham Gliding Society Ltd "778"	Lasham	15. 3.08
G-CGAG	Schleicher ASK 21	21143	BGA3674-GAG ZD645, BGA2885-ERF	24. 9.07	Stratford on Avon Gliding Club Ltd	Snitterfield	31. 1.10
G-CGAH	Schempp-Hirth Standard Cirrus	572	BGA3675-GAH HB-1240	19.12.07	J W Williams	Nympsfield	30. 3.08
G-CGAM	Schleicher ASK 21	21144	BGA3679-GAM ZD646, BGA2886-ERG	8. 2.08	M Bacic tr Oxford University Gliding Club	Bicester	24. 2.08
G-CGAN	Glasflügel H-301 Libelle	8	BGA3680-GAN D-4111	1.10.08	S and C A Noujam "83"	Nympsfield	
G-CGAP	Schempp-Hirth Ventus bT	14/150	BGA3681-GAP OH-774, N416DP	12. 8.08	J R Greenwell	Milfield	
G-CGAR	Rolladen-Schneider LS6-C	6205	BGA3683-GAR	26. 6.08	A Warbrick	Feshiebridge	

Reg	Type	Serial	BGA/ID	Date	Owner	Location	Date
G-CGAS	Schempp-Hirth Ventus cT	157/509	BGA3684-GAS	3.10.07	M W Edwards	Kingston Deverill	28. 9.09
G-GGAT	Grob G102 Astir CS	1130	BGA3685-GAT	9. 5.08	N J Hooper and C Smales	Cross Hayes	
			D-4176				
G-CGAU	Glasflügel H201B Standard Libelle	498	BGA3686-GAU	31. 3.08	M J Frawley tr G-CGAU Group	Dunstable	
			F-CELA				
G-CGAV	Scheibe SF27A Zugvögel V	6073	BGA3687-GAV	8. 2.08	R A Kempton tr GAV Syndicate	Darlton	1. 9.08
			D-5287				
G-CGAW	Beech 200 Super King Air	BB-700	N440WA	24. 5.07	G A Warburton	Guernsey	26. 7.09E
			N200PY, N101TS, N101SK				
G-CGAX	PZL-BielskoSZD-55-1 Promyk	551190008	BGA3689-GAX	2 .6.08	I D Macro and P Gold	Rougham	
G-CGBA	Schleicher ASK 13	13417	BGA3692-GBA	9. 5.08	The Burn Gliding Club Ltd	Burn	
			D-2114				
G-CGBB	Schleicher ASK 21	21073	BGA3693-GBB	25. 2.08	I R McTernan tr Edinburgh University Gliding Club		
			D-3239			Portmoak	17. 3.08
G-CGBD	PZL-Bielsko SZD-50-3 Puchacz	B-2028	BGA3695-GBD	3. 1.08	The Northumbria Gliding Club Ltd	Currock Hill	17. 6.08
G-CGBF	Schleicher ASK 21	21142	BGA3697-GBF	4.12.07	R E Neal tr BBC (London) Club	Lasham	30. 1.10
			ZD644, BGA2883-ERD				
G-CGBG	Rolladen-Schneider LS6-c	6214	BGA3698-GBG	6.12.07	C M and M A Greaves	Rufforth	7. 2.08
			D-3482				
G-CGBJ	Grob G102 Astir CS	1107	BGA3700-GBJ	6.11.07	Banbury Gliding Club Ltd	Hinton-in-the-Hedges	16. 4.08
			D-4167				
G-CGBK	Grob G102 Astir CS	1461	BGA3701-GBK	29.11.07	B J Griffiths	Saltby	28. 9.08
G-CGBL	Rolladen-Schneider LS7-WL	7119	BGA3702-GBL	14. 1.08	M J Aldridge	Rougham	2. 3.08
G-CGBN	Schleicher ASK 21	21141	BGA3704-GBN	13.12.07	Essex & Suffolk Gliding Club Ltd	Wormingford	21. 3.10
			ZD643, BGA2884-ERE				
G-CGBO	Rolladen-Schneider LS6	6082	BGA3706-GBQ	6 2.08	G D Sutherland tr C30 Group	Wycombe Air Park	17. 3.08
			D-3725				
G-CGBR	Rolladen-Schneider LS6-c	6196	BGA3707-GBR	7.12.07	V L Brown "167"	Snitterfield	12. 9.08
G-CGBS	Glaser-Dirks DG-300 Club Orion	3E389C58	BGA3708-GBS	27. 5.08	I W Paterson	Portmoak	
G-CGBU	Centrair 101A Pegase 90	101A0394	BGA3710-GBU	1. 2.08	A D Wood, P S Tickner and S I Ross	Parham Park	15. 2.08
G-CGBV	Schleicher ASK 21	21149	BGA3711-GBV	10.10.07	Wolds Gliding Club Ltd	Pocklington	27. 3.08
			ZD649, BGA 2889-ERK				
G-CGBX	Schleicher ASW 22	22029	BGA3713-GBX	21.12.07	D A Ashby	Sutton Bank	26. 2.08
			D-4325				
G-CGBY	Rolladen-Schneider LS7	7121	BGA3714-GBY	13. 3.08	W J and S E Morecraft	Nympsfield	
G-CGBZ	DG Flugzeugbau DG-500 Elan Trainer		BGA3715-GBZ	23.11.07	Needwood Forest Gliding Club Ltd	Cross Hayes	11. 5.08
		5E34T10					
G-CGCA	Schleicher ASW 19B	19281	BGA3716-GCA	21.12.07	Deeside Gliding Club (Aberdeenshire) Ltd	Aboyne	30. 1.08
			D-3179				
G-CGCC	PZL-Bielsko SZD-51-1 Junior	B-1928	BGA3718-GCC	2.10.07	Coventry Gliding Club Ltd t/a The Gliding Centre		
						Husbands Bosworth	31. 3.08
G-CGCD	Schempp-Hirth Standard Cirrus	476	BGA3719-GCD	17. 6.08	W G Anderson tr Cirrus Syndicate	Feshiebridge	
			PH-507				
G-CGCF	Schleicher ASK 23	23010	BGA3721-GCF	20.11.07	Needwood Forest Gliding Club Ltd	Cross Hayes	18. 2.08
			AGA 9				
G-CGCK	PZL-Bielsko SZD-50-3 Puchaz	B-2025	BGA3725-GCK	5 .6.08	Kent Gliding Club Ltd "GCK"	Challock	
			G-BTJV, BGA3725-GCK				
G-CGCL	Grob G .102 Astir CS	1194	BGA3726-GCL	17. 8.07	J A Williams	Parham Park	23. 6.07
			D-7311				
G-CGCM	Rolladen-Schneider LS6-c	6216	BGA3727-GCM	12.10.07	G R Glazebrook "347"	Dunstable	28. 9.08
G-CGCO	Schempp-Hirth Cirrus VTC	135Y	BGA3730-GCQ	11. 9.08	Dumfries and District Gliding Club	Falgunzeon	
			D-2945				
G-CGCP	Schleicher Ka 6CR	6416	BGA3729-GCP	23. 1.08	B Clarke and D Clarke	Burn	28. 5.08
			D-6369				
G-CGCR	Schleicher ASW 15B	15447	BGA3731-GCR	10. 1.08	R C Page "748"	Nympsfield	17. 3.08
			D-6887				
G-CGCT	Schempp-Hirth Discus b	360	BGA3733-GCT	14. 2.08	D A White	Talgarth	17. 2.08
G-CGCU	PZL-Bielsko SZD-50-3 Puchacz	B-2023	BGA3734-GCU	23. 1.08	Buckminster Gliding Club Ltd	Saltby	27. 2.08
			(BGA3619-FXZ)				
G-CGCX	Schleicher ASW 15	15034	BGA3726-GCX	18. 3.08	P T Collier	Snitterfield	
			D-0420				
G-CGCY	Centrair 101A Pegase	101A0392	BGA3727-GCY	18. 6.08	M S W Meagher	Shenington	
G-CGDA	Rolladen-Schneider LS3-17	3448	BGA3739-GDA	15.10.07	A R Fish	Saltby	1. 2.08
			RAFGGA 546				
G-CGDB	Schleicher K 8B	8152	BGA3740-GDB	11.12.07	The Welland Gliding Club Ltd	Lyveden	7. 8.08
			HB-738				
G-CGDD	Bölkow Phoebus C	836	BGA3742-GDD	6. 8.08	G C Kench	Crowland	
			D-0060				
G-CGDE	Schleicher Ka 6CR	6570SI	BGA3743-GDE	29. 8.07	P D Rowlands tr K6 Syndicate	North Hill	7.10.07
			D-5306				
G-CGDF	Schleicher Ka 6BR	389	BGA3744-GDF	16. 9.08	J B Clarke	RAF Wittering	28. 9.09
			D-8544				
G-CGDJ	Piper PA-28-161 Warrior II	28-8116256	G-ETDA	12. 9.06	C G D Jones	Blackbushe	14. 4.09E
			N84051				
G-CGDK	Schleicher K 8B	8240	BGA3748-GDK	23. 1.08	T J Price tr Vale of Neath Gliding Club	Rhigos	24. 7.08
			D-5381, D-KANU, D-5381				
G-CGDO	Grob G102 Astir CS	1145	BGA3753-GDQ	16.11.07	P Lowe and R Bostock	Seighford	28. 9.08
			D-7229				
G-CGDR	Schempp-Hirth Discus CS	016CS	BGA3754-GDR	31. 3.08	N Tarbox tr GDR Group	Husbands Bosworth	
G-CGDS	Schleicher ASW 15B	15205	BGA3755-GDS	9. 1.08	B Birk and P A Crouch	Ringmer	17. 2.08
			D-0902				
G-CGDT	Schleicher ASW 24	24120	BGA3756-GDT	19. 2.08	R D Mcvean tr Tango 54 Syndicate	Chipping	4. 4.08
G-CGDU	Schleicher ASW 24	24118	BGA3757-GDU	21. 9.07	G J Moore	Dunstable	31. 1.10

G-CGDX	Schempp-Hirth Discus CS	023CS	BGA3760-GDX 3.10.07	Coventry Gliding Club Ltd tr The Gliding Centre "HB2"		
					Husbands Bosworth	28. 9.08
G-CGDY	Schleicher ASW 15B	15220	BGA3761-GDY 13.12.07	G A Stewart tr Cloud Nine Syndicate	Bidford	20. 2.08
			D-0947			
G-CGDZ	Schleicher ASW 24	24116	BGA3762-GDZ 5.12.07	J M Norman tr 24 Group "524"	Pocklington	1. 4.08
G-CGEB	Grob G102 Astir CS77	1628	BGA3764-GEB 9. 9.08	T R Dews	Kingston Deverill	
			PH-576			
G-CGEE	Glasflügel H201B Standard Libelle	94	BGA3767-GEE 7. 3.08	C Metcalfe and J Kelsey	Kirton-in-Lindsay	
			D-0928			
G-CGEG	Schleicher K 8B	689	BGA3769-GEG 25. 6.08	Darlton Gliding Club Ltd	Darlton	
			HB-639			
G-CGEH	Schleicher ASW 15B	15276	BGA3770-GEH 4. 6.08	C J Ireland tr C Ireland and Partners	Challock	
			D-2124			
G-CGEL	PZL-Bielsko SZD-50-3 Puchacz	B-20308	BGA3772-GEL 3. 1.08	The Northumbria Gliding Club Ltd	Currock Hill	7. 5.08
G-CGEM	Schleicher Ka 6CR	6249	BGA3773-GEM 2. 4.08	M A Clark tr GEM Syndicate	Thame	
			D-8466			
G-CGEP	Schempp-Hirth Standard Cirrus	205G	BGA3775-GEP 14.12.07	D J Bundock	Wycombe Air Park	30. 3.08
	(Built Burkhart Grob-Flugzeugbau)		D-0917			
G-CGGG	Robinson R44 Astro	0626	G-SJDI 24. 8.07	R D Masters	Standalone Farm, Meppershall	31. 7.09E
G-CGHM	Piper PA-28-140 Cruiser	28-7425143	PH-NSM 25. 4.79	A Reay	Caernarfon	10. 2.07T
			N9614N			
G-CGIJ	Agusta AW139	31203	27. 2.08	CHC Scotia Ltd (Operated Marine and Coastguard Agency)		
					Lee-on-Solent	3. 3.09E
G-CGMU	Sikorsky S-92A	920034	N8010S 5. 6.07	CHC Scotia Ltd (Operated Marine and Coastguard Agency)		
					Stornoway	14. 6.09E
G-CGOC	Sikorsky S-92A	920051	N45165 30.11.07	CHC Scotia Ltd	Aberdeen	2.12.09E
G-CGOD	Cameron N-77 Balloon (Hot Air)	2647	5. 9.91	G P Lane "Neptune"	Waltham Abbey	9. 7.09E
G-CGRD	Cirrus SR22	2234	N613SR 16. 2.07	Craigard Property Trading Ltd	Goodwood	13. 3.09E
G-CGRI	Agusta A109S Grand	22003	I-RAID 3. 8.05	C G Roach	Liskeard Heliport	26. 7.09E
G-CGWB	Agusta AW139	31209	24. 4.08	CHC Scotia Ltd (Operated Marine and Coastguard Agency)		
					Portland	29. 4.09E
G-CGWD	Robinson R44 Raven	1695	23. 3.07	J M Henderson	(Newtownards)	11. 4.09E

G-CHAA - G-CHZZ

G-CHAB	Schleicher Ka 6CR	6596	BGA3778-HAB 12.10.07	P Saunders	Usk	18. 1.08
			D-1596			
G-CHAC	PZL-Bielsko SZD-50-3 Puchacz	B-2035	BGA3779-HAC 16. 4.08	Peterborough and Spalding Gliding Club Ltd		
					Crowland	
G-CHAD	Aeroprakt A22 Foxbat	PFA 317-13909	30. 4.02	R A Neal tr DJB Foxbat	Otherton, Cannock	19. 7.09P
	(Built D Winsper)					
G-CHAF	PZL-Bielsko SZD-50-3 Puchacz	B-2031	BGA3782-HAF 29.11.07	J G Kosak tr Seahawk Gliding Club		
					RNAS Culdrose	13. 3.08
G-CHAH	Europa Aviation Europa XS	252	14. 6.04	T Higgins	Welshpool	26. 3.09P
	(Built T Higgins - pr.no.PFA 247-12949)					
G-CHAI	Bombardier CL-600-2B16	5152	G-FBFI 9.10.07	Hangar 8 Ltd	Oxford	19. 1.10E
	(CL-601-3R Challenger)	N601FB, G-FBFI, N388PG, (N933PG), N18RF, N605BA, VP-COJ, VR-COJ, N777XX, C-GLWX				
G-CHAM	Cameron Pot 90 SS Balloon (Hot Air)	2912	29. 9.92	T G Church t/a Pendle Balloon Co "Yogpot"		
	(Chambourcy Pot shape)				Clayton-le-Dale, Blackburn	29.11.09E
G-CHAN	Robinson R22 Beta	3794	16. 3.05	Artall Air LLP	Panshanger	17. 4.09E
G-CHAO	Rolladen-Schneider LS 6b	6150	BGA3791-HAQ 30.11.07	A R J Hughes	Wycombe Air Park	13. 4.08
			D-8079			
G-CHAP	Robinson R44 Astro	0326	9. 4.97	Brierley Lifting Tackle Company Ltd		
					Wolverhampton	16. 9.09E
G-CHAR	Grob G109B	6435	21. 5.86	T M Holloway tr RAF Gliding and Soaring Association		
				(Operated RAFGSA Chilterns Centre)	RAF Halton	7. 5.09E
G-CHAS	Piper PA-28-181 Archer II	28-8090325	N82228 18. 3.91	C H Elliott	Stapleford	10. 7.09E
G-CHAX	Schempp Hirth Standard Cirrus	2	DGA3798-HAX 21.11.07	C Keating and R Jarvis	Rivar Hill	28. 4.08
			ZS-GHZ, ZS-TIM, ZS-GGR, D-0302			
G-CHAY	Rolladen-Schneider LS7	7154	BGA3799-HAY 28. 2.08	N J Leaton	Gransden Lodge	19. 3.08
G-CHBA	Rolladen-Schneider LS7	7156	BGA3801-HBA 29.10.07	P O'Donald tr LS7 729 Group	Gransden Lodge	28. 9.08
			D-6041			
G-CHBB	Schleicher ASW 24	24132	BGA3802-HBB 3.12.07	London Gliding Club Proprietary Ltd	Dunstable	28. 9.08
G-CHBC	Rolladen-Schneider LS6-c	6209	BGA3803-HBC 20.10.07	R Crowden	Talgarth	28. 9.08
			D-xxxx			
G-CHBD	Glaser-Dirks DG-200	2-12	BGA3804-HBD 29. 8.07	D A Clempson	Portmoak	28. 9.08
			HB-1384			
G-CHBE	DG Flugzeugbau DG-300 Elan	3E237	BGA3805-HBE 12.11.07	G Dixon and M J Weston tr DG 356 Group "356"		
			SE-UFB		Aston Down	28. 9.08
G-CHBF	Schempp-Hirth Nimbus 2C	191	BGA3806-HBF 22. 5.08	K Richards and J Clark "HBF"	Talgarth	
			D-3369			
G-CHBG	Schleicher ASW 24	24133	BGA3807-HBG 14. 2.08	Imperial College of Science, Technology and Medicine		
				"96"	Lasham	25. 3.08
G-CHBH	Grob G103C Twin III Acro	36006	BGA3808-HBH 14. 2.08	Imperial College of Science, Technology and Medicine		
				"496"	Lasham	3. 3.08
G-CHBK	Grob G103 Twin Astir Trainer	3254-T-31	BGA3810-HBK 3. 3.08	S Naylor	Burn	
	(Type amended to Twin Astir Trainer 27.11.08)					
G-CHBL	Grob G102 Astir CS77	1626	BGA3811-HBL 18. 3.08	Bidford Gliding Ltd	Bidford	
			RAFGSA R78, RAFGSA 778			
G-CHBM	Grob G102 Astit CS77	1633	BGA3812-HBM 2. 4.08	P W Brown and J D M Sharp	AAC Wattisham	
			RAFGSA R65, RAFGSA R66, RAFGSA 546			
G-CHBO	Schleicher Ka 6CR	6611	BGA3815-HBQ 12. 3.08	M I Perrier and H Southworth	(Garforth)	
			D-5616			
G-CHBP	Glaser-Dirks DG-500/22 Elan	5E36S8	BGA3814-HBP 9. 6.08	A Taverna	Borgo San Lorenzo, Italy	

Reg	Type	c/n	Prev ID	Date	Owner	Location	Expiry
G-CHBS	PZL-Bielsko SZD-41A Jantar Standard	B-852/Z	BGA3817-HBS D-4160	16. 6.08	P J Chaisty and D Hendry	Usk	
G-CHBT	Grob G102 Astir CS Jeans	2235	BGA3819-HBT PH-675	20.12.07	M D Evans tr Astir Syndicate	Darlton	23. 3.08
G-CHBU	Centrair ASW 20F	20527	BGA3820-HBU F-CFSI	2.11.07	M Staljan, S Brogger and C Behrendt	Finnentrop, Germany	
G-CHBV	Schempp-Hirth Nimbus 2B	143	BGA3821-HBV D-7850	22. 2.08	G J Evison, J Lynas and R Strerup	Sutton Bank	11. 4.08
G-CHCD	Sikorsky S-76A II Plus	760101	OY-HEZ G-CHCD, G-CBJB, N288SP, C-GIMN, YV-326C	16. 1.98	CHC Scotia Ltd	North Denes Heliport	28.11.09E
G-CHCF	Eurocopter AS.332L2 Super Puma	2567		30.11.01	CHC Scotia Ltd	Aberdeen	15. 1.10E
G-CHCG	Eurocopter AS.332L2 Super Puma	2592		1. 7.03	CHC Scotia Ltd	Aberdeen	23. 7.09E
G-CHCH	Eurocopter AS.332L2 Super Puma	2601		16.12.03	CHC Scotia Ltd	Aberdeen	26. 1.10E
G-CHCI	Eurocopter AS.332L2 Super Puma	2395	LN-OHD F-WQDN	30. 9.05	CHC Scotia Ltd	Aberdeen	8.10.09E
G-CHCK	Sikorsky S-92A	920030	N8001N	28. 2.06	CHC Scotia Ltd	Aberdeen	30. 3.09E
G-CHCL	Eurocopter EC.225LP Super Puma	2674	F-WWOS	14.11.07	CHC Scotia Ltd	Aberdeen	14.12.09E
G-CHCM	Eurocopter EC.225LP Super Puma	2675	F-WWOV	21.12.07	CHC Scotia Ltd	Aberdeen	7. 1.10E
G-CHCN	Eurocopter EC.225LP Super Puma	2679	F-WWON	5. 3.08	CHC Scotia Ltd	Aberdeen	6. 3.09E
G-CHCO	Aérospatiale AS.365N2 Dauphin 2	6358	LN-ODB G-NTWO	15. 4.08	CHC Scotia Ltd	Aberdeen	5. 6.09E
G-CHCP	Agusta AW139	31046	PH-IEH	12. 9.06	CHC Scotia Ltd	North Denes	12. 9.09E
G-CHCR	Aérospatiale AS.365N2 Dauphin 2	6423	LN-OMN F-GHXG, F-WYMS	1. 4.08	CHC Scotia Ltd	Aberdeen	
G-CHCT	Agusta AW139	31042	PH-TRH	13. 7.06	CHC Scotia Ltd	Aberdeen	13. 7.09E
G-CHCV	Agusta AW139	41005	N106AW	17. 1.08	CHC Scotia Ltd	North Denes	30. 1.10E
G-CHDA	Pilatus B4-PC11AF	17	BGA3851-HDA D-0964	13. 2.08	F P and C M E Bois	Saltby	5. 6.08
G-CHDB	PZL-Bielsko SZD-51-1 Junior	B-1997	BGA3852-HDB	24. 9.07	Stratford on Avon Gliding Club Ltd	Snitterfield	12. 1.08
G-CHDC	Schleicher ASK 13	13308	BGA3853-HDC D-0750	15. 4.08	Derbyshire and Lancashire Gliding Club Ltd	Camphill	
G-CHDD	Centrair 101B Pégase 90	101B0425	BGA3854-HDD	30.10.07	P M Weston tr 591 Glider Syndicate	Gransden Lodge	28. 9.08
G-CHDE	Pilatus B4-PC11AF	223	BGA3855-HDE VH-XDZ, VH-WQP	25. 1.08	A A Jenkins	Wycombe Air Park	5. 5.08
G-CHDJ	Schleicher ASW 20CL	20828	BGA3859-HDJ D-8442	6. 2.08	G E G Lambert and L M M Sebreights	Weelde, Belgium	30. 4.08
G-CHDL	Schleicher ASW 20	20082	BGA3861-HDL D-1617, OH-495	14. 2.08	C R Faulkner tr 137 Syndicate	Currock Hill	21. 5.08
G-CHDN	Schleicher K 8B	2	BGA3863-HDN D-8017	14. 2.08	Upward Bound Trust	Thame	28. 4.08
G-CHDP	PZL-Bielsko SZD-50-3 Puchacz	B-2050	BGA3864-HDP	23. 1.08	D J Marpole tr Heron Gliding Club	RNAS Yeovilton	30. 3.08
G-CHDR	DG Flugzeugbau DG-300 Elan	3E95	BGA3866-HDR RAFGSA R30	7. 1.08	R Robins	Pocklington	22. 1.08
G-CHDU	PZL-Bielsko SZD-51-1 Junior	B-1996	BGA3869-HDU	18.10.07	Cambridge Gliding Club Ltd	Gransden Lodge	9.12.09
G-CHDV	Schleicher ASW 19B	19345	BGA3870-HDV D-2876	19. 3.08	D C Jones tr ASW Aviation	Long Mynd	
G-CHDX	Rolladen-Schneider LS7-WL	7161	BGA3872-HDX	23. 1.08	D Holborn and R T Halliburton	Pocklington	15. 3.08
G-CHDY	Schleicher K 8B	8277	BGA3873-HDY D-4094	7. 2.08	V Mallon	Kleve-Wisseler Dünen, Germany	13. 4.08
G-CHEB	Europa Aviation Europa	263		16. 9.96	P Whittingham	Sittles Farm, Alrewas	20. 7.09P
	(Built C H P Bell - pr.no.PFA 247-12967) (NSI EA-81/100)						
G-CHEC	PZL-Bielsko SZD-55-1 Promyk	551191019	BGA3877-HEC	1.11.07	D Pye	Challock	24. 4.08
G-CHEE	Schempp-Hirth Discus b	292	BGA3879-HEE	26. 9.08	A Henderson	Bicester	
	(Rebuilt with fuselage of BGA3523 (c/n 292) which had been rebuilt with a new fuselage but retained the c/n and registered as G-CFTW; later amended to 292/1 to avoid both having the same c/n)						
G-CHEF	DG Flugzeugbau DG-500 Elan Trainer	5E53T20	BGA3880-HEF	17. 1.08	Yorkshire Gliding Club (Proprietary) Ltd	Sutton Bank	20. 3.08
G-CHEG	AB Sportine Aviacija LAK-12 Lietuva	6206	BGA3881-HEG	7. 3.08	R Hannigan, Z Kmita and S Grant	Kirton-in-Lindsey	
G-CHEH	Rolladen-Schneider LS7-WL	7163	BGA3882-HEH D-6078	17. 9.07	P Candler "795"	Dunstable	30. 1.08
G-CHEJ	Schleicher ASW 15B	15441	BGA3883-HEJ D-6871	20.11.07	A F F Webb	Wycombe Air Park	11. 1.08
G-CHEK	PZL-Bielsko SZD-51-1 Junior	B-2009	BGA3884-HEK BGA3893-HEU, (BGA3884-HEK)	11.12.07	Cambridge Gliding Club Ltd	Gransden Lodge	16. 3.08
G-CHEL	Colt 77B Balloon (Hot Air)	4823		18. 5.00	Chelsea Financial Services PLC	Chalford, Stroud	7. 7.09E
					(Chelsea Financial Service titles)		
G-CHEM	Piper PA-34-200T Seneca II	34-8170032	N8292Y	26. 8.87	London Executive Aviation Ltd	Stapleford	4. 3.09E
G-CHEN	Schempp-Hirth Discus b	422	BGA3887-HEN	22.12.07	M D Kerley tr G-CHEN Group	Challock	8. 3.08
G-CHEO	Schleicher ASW 20	20410	BGA3889-HEQ D-6747	4.12.07	P Morrison tr The Eleven Group	North Hill	27. 2.08
G-CHEP	PZL-Bielsko SZD-50-3 Puchacz	B-2057	BGA3888- HEP	28. 2.08	Peterborough & Spalding Gliding Club Ltd	Crowland	5. 4.08
G-CHER	Piper PA-38-112 Tomahawk II	38-82A0004	G-BVBL N91339	19.12.00	C R and S A Hardiman	(Blaenannerch, Cadigan)	9.12.09E
G-CHET	Europa Aviation Europa XS	376		12. 2.98	H H R Lagache	Leicester	19. 4.08P
	(Built C R Arkle - pr.no.PFA 247-13277) (Rotax 914-UL) (Tri-gear u/c)						
G-CHEW	Rolladen-Schneider LS6-c18	6250B	BGA4952-KBC BGA3985-HEW	12. 3.08	H Stone tr 486 Group "486"	RAF Weston-on-the-Green	19. 5.09
G-CHEY	Piper PA-31T2 Cheyenne IIXL	31T-8166033	N67PD N42NE, N42ND, N59WA, N9092Y	27. 7.05	Air Medical Fleet Ltd	Oxford	16.10.08E

Reg	Type	C/n					
G-CHEZ	Pilatus Britten-Norman BN-2B-20 Islander	2234	9M-TAM	30. 4.01	The Cheshire Police Authority	Hawarden	11. 8.11
G-CHFA	Schempp-Hirth Ventus b/16.6	251	G-BSAG BGA3899-HFA	23. 7.08	A K Lincoln "65"	Lasham	
G-CHFB	Schleicher Ka 6CR	6344SI	RAFGSA R24 BGA3900-HFB	12.11.07	P J Galloway	Rhigos	25. 9.07
G-CHFF	Schempp-Hirth Standard Cirrus	539	D-5825 BGA3904-HFF	2.11.07	R S Morrisroe tr Foxtrot 2 Group	Upwood	4. 4.08
G-CHFH	PZL-Bielsko SZD-50-3 Puchacz	B-2059	D-8916 BGA3906-HFH	18.12.07	Trent Valley Aerotowing Club Ltd	Kirton-in-Lindsey	6. 3.08
G-CHFV	Schempp-Hirth Ventus b-16.6	204	BGA3918-HFV	5.12.07	A Cliffe and B Pearson	Seighford	4. 4.08
G-CHFW	Schleicher K 8B	8108	D-5235 BGA3919-HFW	12. 9.08	Oxford Gliding Co Ltd RAF Weston-on-the-Green		
G-CHFX	Schempp-Hirth Nimbus 4T	12	HB-705 BGA3920-HFX	7.11.07	R Jones "82"	Lasham	26. 3.08
G-CHFY	Schempp-Hirth Ventus cT	168	BGA3921-HFY	21.12.07	D J Ellis and M Day	Lasham	28. 9.08
G-CHGB	Grob G102 Astir CS	1356	(BGA3916-HFT), (BGA3867-HDS) BGA3924-HGB	13. 2.08	A A M Wahlberg, G Clark and P Hollamby		
			D-7386			Lee-on-Solent	11. 9.08
	(Rebuilt with wings and components from RAFGGA 507)						
G-CHGF	Schleicher ASW 15B	15264	BGA2928-HGF	15. 3.08	P Mylett tr HGF Flying Group	Camphill	
G-CHGG	Schempp-Hirth Standard Cirrus	362	D-2128 BGA3929-HGG	28. 1.08	N P Holifield	(Bicester)	21. 3.08
G-CHGK	Schempp-Hirth Discus bT	96/435	HB-1172 BGA3932-HGK	29.10.07	C C Redrup tr HGK Syndicate	Lasham	18. 3.10
G-CHGL	Bell 206B-2 JetRanger II	1669	EI-WSN	29. 4.98	Vantage Aviation Ltd	(Salisbury)	14.10.09E
G-CHGO	AB Sportine Aviacija LAK-12	6208	G-CHGL, G-BPNG, G-ORTC, G-BPNG, N20EA, C-GHVB BGA3937-HGO	27. 5.08	P Raymond and J-M Peuffier		
						Pujaut, Salon de Provence, France	
G-CHGP	Rolladen-Schneider LS6-c	6270	BGA3936-HGP	17. 3.08	D R Elrington	Camphill	
G-CHGR	Sportline Aviacija LAK-12 Lietuva	6186	BGA3938-HGR	21. 9.07	F R and R G Stevens	Husbands Bosworth	28. 9.08
G-CHGS	Schempp-Hirth Discus b	439	BGA3939-HGS	8.10.07	M J Armes tr G-CHGS Syndicate	Lasham	28. 9.08
G-CHGT	FFA Diamant 16.5	40	BGA3940-HGT	15. 1.08	E Gibson and R.W.Collins	Burn	30. 4.08
G-CHGV	DG Flugzeugbau DG-500/22 Elan	5E70S11	HB-929 BGA3942-HGV	12.11.07	A J Hulme tr Hotel Golf Victor Syndicate		
						Gransden Lodge	14. 1.08
G-CHGW	Centrair ASW 20F	20102	BGA3943-HGW	23. 8.07	S C Moss	Nympsfield	3.11.07
G-CHGX	AB Sportine LAK-12 Lietuva	6201	F-CFFB BGA3944-HGX	7. 4.08	M Jenks	Kingston Deverill	
G-CHGZ	Schempp-Hirth Discus bT	95-434	BGA3946-HGZ	23. 1.08	S H Baker tr HUA Syndicate "502"	Lasham	6. 3.08
G-CHHH	Rolladen-Schneider LS6-c	6289	BGA3954-HHH	18.10.07	P H Rackham "963"	Dunstable	28. 9.08
G-CHHK	Schleicher ASW 19B	19384	BGA3956-HHK	29.11.07	M Walker	Burn	11. 5.07
G-CHHM	Sportline Aviacija LAK-12 Lietuva	6195	ZD661, BGA2897-ERT BGA3958-HHM	24.10.07	D Martin	(Bordeaux, France)	17. 1.08
G-CHHN	Schempp-Hirth Ventus b/16.6	205	BGA3959-HHN	3. 4.08	N A C Norman and R K Forrest	Feshiebridge	
G-CHHO	Schempp-Hirth Discus bT	106/453	RAFGSA R27 BGA3961-HHO	30.10.07	P J Tratt and M Davis tr 97Z Syndicate		
						Parham Park	27. 3.08
G-CHHP	Schempp-Hirth Discus b	399	BGA3960-HHP	3. 7.08	F R Knowles "KL"	Easterton	
G-CHHR	PZL-Bielsko SZD-55-1 Promyk	551191020	SE-UKL BGA3962-HHR	27. 9.07	R T and G Starling "100"	Nympsfield	28. 9.08
G-CHHS	Schleicher ASW 20	20008	BGA3963-HHS	8. 2.08	D Britt and P J Rocks	Kirton-in-Lindsey	1. 4.08
G-CHHT	Rolladen-Schneider LS6-c	6292	SE-TTU BGA3964-HHT	13.11.07	G O Humphries	Kingston Deverill	1. 3.08
G-CHHU	Rolladen-Schneider LS6-c	6296	BGA3965-HHU	17. 8.07	J S Weston	Bellarena	28. 9.08
G-CHHW	Sportline Aviacija LAK-12 Lietuva	6212	BGA3967-HHW	8.12.07	A J Dibdin	Dunstable	4. 3.08
G-CHHX	Wassmer WA.26P Squale	014	BGA3968-HHX	24. 7.08	M H Gagg	(Halesowen)	
G-CHIK	Reims Cessna F152 II	F15201628	F-CDQJ G-BHAZ	19.10.81	Stapleford Flying Club Ltd	Stapleford	7.12.09E
G-CHIP	Piper PA-28-181 Archer II	28-8290095	(D-EHLE) N81337	22. 2.82	J A Divis	Shoreham	15. 4.09E
G-CHIS	Robinson R22 Beta	1740		5. 4.91	Staffordshire Helicopters Ltd	Tatenhill	1. 4.09E
G-CHIX	Robin DR.500-200i Président	0036	F-GXGD	29.11.01	P A and R Stephens Moor Farm, West Haslerton		13. 3.09E
	(Officially regd as DR.400-500)		F-WQPN				
G-CHJA	VFW-Fokker FK-3	0008	BGA3971-HJA	14.12.07	M A Johnson	Sackville Lodge, Riseley	17. 3.08
G-CHJC	Rolladen-Schneider LS6-c	6290	D-0409 BGA3973-HJC	25.10.07	F J Davies and I C Woodhouse "25"		
						Husbands Bosworth	28. 9.08
G-CHJE	Schleicher K 8B	8259	BGA3975-HJE	23. 7.08	J J Sconce "505"	Camphill	
G-CHJF	Rolladen-Schneider LS6-c	6291	(BGA3926-HGD), RAFGGA 505, RAFGGA 971 BGA3976-HJF	17.10.07	J L Bridge	Gransden Lodge	28. 9.08
G-CHJH	Schempp-Hirth Discus bT	65	BGA3978-HJH	29. 1.08	J C Leonard tr Hotel Juliet Hotel Group		
						Bembridge	25. 4.08
G-CHJL	Schempp-Hirth Discus bT	105/451	N224WT BGA3981-HJL	16.10.07	M J Huddart	Saltby	28. 9.08
G-CHJP	Schleicher Ka 6CR	616	BGA3985-HJP	4.1.08	D M Cornelius	Dunstable	5. 5.08
G-CHJR	Glasflügel H201B Standard Libelle	102	OH-210, OH-RSB BGA3986-HJR	14. 2.08	B O Marcham and B Magnani "B9"	Tibenham	29. 5.08
G-CHJT	Centrair ASW 20F	20115	SE-TIO BGA3988-HJT	30. 4.08	M O Breen	Wycombe Air Park	
G-CHJV	Grob G102 Astir CS	1007	F-CFFL BGA3990-HJV	6. 6.08	Costwold Gliding Club	Aston Down	
G-CHJX	Rolladen-Schneider LS6-c	6271	D-7000 BGA3991-HJX	4. 9.08	R S Hatwell and M R Haynes	Wormingford	
G-CHJY	Schempp-Hirth Standard Cirrus	459	BGA3992-HJY	19. 2.08	J M Hogbin tr The Cirrus Group	Currock Hill	28. 7.08
			HB-1207				

G-CHKA	Schempp-Hirth Discus CS	120CS	BGA3994-HKA 12.10.07	R W and M P Weaver	Usk	13.12.07
G-CHKB	Grob G102 Astir CS77	1658	BGA3995-HKB 19. 2.08 D-7491	R Peach tr G-CHKB Group	RAF Keevil	5. 4.08
G-CHKC	Schempp-Hirth Standard Cirrus	520G	BGA3996-HKC 11.12.07 D-3268	S Foster	Long Mynd	1. 5.08
G-CHKD	Schempp-Hirth Standard Cirrus	576G	BGA3997-HKD 12.11.07 F-CEMF	M Tomlinson	Talgarth	24. 4.08
G-CHKK	Schleicher K 8 B	8886	BGA4003-HKK 7.12.07 D-0866	W Rossmann tr HKK Syndicate	Drumshade	3. 4.08
G-CHKM	Grob G102 Astir CS Jeans	2108	BGA4005-HKM 20. 6.08 D-7636	Essex and Suffolk Gliding Club Ltd	Wormingford	
G-CHKN	Air Création 582(1)/Kiss 400	FL002/134	18. 9.01	P J Higgins		
	(Built I Tomkins - pr.no.BMAA HB/183 being Flylight kit comprising Trike s/n xxxxx and Wing s/n xxxx)					
				Red House Farm, Gedney Dyke, Spalding		26. 4.09P
G-CHKR	Jastreb Standard Cirrus G/81	276	BGA4009-HKR 22. 1.08 OH-663	N White and S Crozier	Crowland	30. 5.08
G-CHKS	Jastreb Standard Cirrus G/81	361	BGA4010-HKS 6. 2.08 SE-TZS	G G Butler	Snitterfield	1. 4.08
G-CHKU	Schempp-Hirth Standard Cirrus	513G	BGA4012-HKU 8. 5.08 F-CEMA	T J Wheeler and T M O'Sullivan "C29"		
					Hinton-in-the-Hedges	
G-CHKV	Scheibe Zugvögel IIIA	1034	BGA4013-HKV 31. 1.08 D-8294	Dartmoor Gliding Society	Brentor	11. 9.08
	(Type amended to Zugvögel IIIA 1.12.08)					
G-CHKX	Rolladen-Schneider LS4-b	4933	BGA4015-HKX 3.10.07	D J Hughes tr HKX Group	Long Mynd	19. 2.08
G-CHKY	Schempp-Hirth Discus b	461	BGA4016-HKY 30.11.07	C V Hill and O J Anderson	Bellarena	3. 4.08
G-CHKZ	CARMAM JP 15-36AR Aiglon	31	BGA4017-HKZ 19. 9.08 F-CFGA	T A and A J Hollings	Rufforth	
G-CHLB	Rolladen-Schneider LS4-b	4935	BGA4019-HLB 5. 3.08	E G Leach and K F Rogers	Wormingford	
G-CHLC	Pilatus B4-PC11AF	177	BGA4020-HLC 25. 2.08 SE-UFX, OH-455	E A Lockhart	Lasham	2. 5.08
G-CHLH	Schleicher K 8B	8637	BGA4025-HLH 5. 8.08 RAFGGA 569, D-5691	Shenington Gliding Club	Shenington	
G-CHLK	Glasflügel H301 Libelle	85	BGA4027-HLK 11. 6.08 SE-TFS	G L J Barrett and H Fletcher		
					RAF Weston-on-the-Green	
G-CHLL	Lindstrand LBL 90A Balloon (Hot Air)	941	7. 1.04	P J Hollingsworth (www.churchill.com titles)		
					Grappenhall, Warrington	22. 9.08E
G-CHLM	Schleicher ASW 19B	19269	BGA4029-HLM 14. 2.08 OH-538	R A Colbeck	Dunstable	24. 5.05
G-CHLN	Schempp-Hirth Discus CS	143CS	BGA4030-HLN 28. 1.08	T World tr Portsmouth Naval Gliding Centre		
					Lee-on-Solent	6. 4.07
G-CHLP	Schleicher ASK 21	21597	BGA4031-HLP 9.11.07	Southdown Gliding Club Ltd	Parham Park	25. 3.08
G-CHLS	Schempp-Hirth Discus b	114	BGA4034-HLS 7. 9.07 RAFGSA R11	R A Lennard	Dunstable	8. 1.08
G-CHLV	Schleicher ASW 19B	19325	BGA4038-HLV 18.12.07 D-8799	P J Belcher and R I Brickwood	Gransden Lodge	15. 1.08
G-CHLX	Schleicher ASH 25	25124	BGA4039-HLX 21.12.07 D-3988	P Armstrong tr HLX Group	Husbands Bosworth	9. 3.08
G-CHLY	Schempp-Hirth Discus CS	161CS	BGA4040-HLY 17. 1.08	S J Pearce	(Solihull)	14. 4.08
G-CHMA	PZL-Bielsko SZD-51-1 Junior	B-2132	BGA4042-HMA 2.10.07	The Welland Gliding Club Ltd	Lyveden	15. 1.08
G-CHMB	DG Flugzeugbau DG-300 Elan	3E105	BGA4043-HMB 15.11.07 D-4676	A D and P Langlands	Shenington	31. 1.08
G-CHMG	ICA IS-28B2	353	BGA4044-HMG 4. 3.08	A Sutton, R Wood and AJ Palfreyman	Snitterfield	
G-CHMK	Rolladen-Schneider LS6-18W	6324	BGA4046-HMK 16.10.07 D-1245	A S Decloux	Gransden Lodge	11. 3.08
G-CHML	Schempp-Hirth Discus CS	114CS	BGA4047-HML 22. 8.08 OO-ZTU	I D Bateman "38"	Parham	
G-CHMM	Jastreb Glasflügel 304B	322	BGA4048-HMM 3.12.07 SE-UGZ, D-1005	A P Cullen tr Delta 19 Group	Husbands Bosworth	20.12.07
G-CHMO	Schempp-Hirth Discus CS	099CS	BGA4051-HMO 23.10.07 D-7160	S Barter "364"	Ringmer	28. 9.08
G-CHMS	Glaser-Dirks DG-100	40	BGA4053-HMS 16. 4.08 D-2579	D A Fall	Shobdon	
G-CHMT	Glasflügel H303 Mosquito B	153	BGA4054-HMT 29.10.07 F-CEDY	J Taberham	North Hill	28. 9.08
G-CHMU	CARMAM JP-15/36AR Aiglon	22	BGA4055-HMU 20.11.07 F-CETT	J R Holmes tr HMU Syndicate	Kingston Deverill	9. 3.08
G-CHMV	Schleicher ASK 13	13177	BGA4056-HMV 18. 4.08 D-0268	The Windrusher's Gliding Club Ltd	Bicester	
G-CHMX	Rolladen-Schneider LS4-a	4230	BGA4058-HMX 15. 1.08 OO-ZNN, F-CEIO	I M Evans	(Ledbury)	
G-CHMY	Schempp-Hirth Standard Cirrus	121	BGA4059-HMY 20. 2.08 HB-1034	D Nisbet tr HMY Syndicate		
					RAF Weston-on-the-Green	2. 5.08
G-CHMZ	Federov ME7 Mechta	M004	BGA4060-HMZ 3. 9.08	R Andrews	Long Mynd	
G-CHNA	DG Flugzeugbau DG-500/20 Elan	5E128W3	BGA4061-HNA 30.11.07	M S Armstrong tr G-CHNA Group	Camphill	28. 9.08
G-CHNC	Schleicher ASW 19B	19297	BGA4063-HNC 9.11.07 OH-515	T J Highton	Tibenham	4. 4.08
G-CHNE	Schempp-Hirth Nimbus 2B	91	BGA4065-HNE 18. 3.08 D-2786	P J Uden	Saltby	
G-CHNF	Schempp-Hirth Duo Discus	11	BGA4066-HNF 15.10.07	Booker Gliding Club Ltd "315"	Wycombe Air Park	28. 9.08
G-CHNG	Schleicher K 8B	132/59	BGA4067-HNG 16. 9.08 D-8378	Bidford Gliding Ltd	Bidford	
G-CHNH	Schempp-Hirth HS.5 Nimbus 2C	187	BGA4068-HNH 27.11.07 D-2830	R J Hart	Tibenham	6. 2.08
G-CHNK	PZL-Bielsko SZD-51-1 Junior	B-1496	BGA4070-HNK 15.10.07 SP-3299, (SP-3290)	Booker Gliding Club Ltd "HNK"	Wycombe Air Park	28. 9.08

G-CHNM	Jastreb Standard Cirrus G-81	360	BGA4072-HNM 30.11.07 SE-TZT	S E Cooper tr Windrushers Gliding Club Bicester Husbands Bosworth	9. 4.08
G-CHNN	Schempp-Hirth Duo Discus	21	BGA4073-HNN 27 .8.08	B T Spreckley Ontur, Spain	
G-CHNT	Schleicher ASW 15	15167	BGA4078-HNT 9. 6.08 F-CEAQ	S J Lintott and I Dawkins Waldershare Park	
G-CHNU	Schempp-Hirth Nimbus 4DT	3/5	BGA4079-HNU 20. 9.07 D-KHIA	D E Findon "48" Bidford	28. 9.08
G-CHNV	Rolladen-Schneider LS4-b	4960	BGA4080-HNV 2.11.07	P H Dixon and S K Armstrong "692" Kirton-in-Lindsey	2. 5.08
G-CHNW	Schempp-Hirth Duo Discus	25	BGA4081-HNW 23.10.07	W J Head tr G-CHNW Group "220" Gransden Lodge	21. 3.08
G-CHNY	Centrair 101A Pégase	101020	BGA4083-HNY 26. 9.08 F-CFRP	M O Breen Wycombe Air Park	
G-CHNZ	Centrair 101A Pégase	101032	BGA4084-HNZ 26.10.07 F-CFRY	R H Partington Milfield	19. 2.08
G-CHOD	Schleicher ASW 20	20288	BGA4112-HQD 24. 6.08 SE-ULA, OH-548	S E Archer-Jones "A20" Bicester	
G-CHOF	CARMAM M.100S Mesange	26	BGA4114-HQF 11. 9.08 F-CCSO	M A Farrelly Long Mynd	
G-CHOM	Schempp-Hirth Discus b	44	BGA4120-HQM 25.10.07	Cambridge Gliding Club Ltd Gransden Lodge	28. 9.08
G-CHOP	Westland-Bell 47G-3B1	WA/380	XT221 19.12.78	Classic Flight Training Services Ltd Wellesbourne Mountford	2. 4.11
G-CHOR	Schempp-Hirth Discus b	531	BGA4123-HQR 25. 2.08	A Twigg and L Brandt "T19" Bicester	31. 3.08
G-CHOS	Grob G103 Twin Astir	3155	BGA4124-HQS 5. 9.08 OO-ZEG	Essex and Suffolk Gliding Club Ltd Wormingfold	
G-CHOV	PZL-Bielsko SZD-51-1 Junior	B-2139	BGA4127-HQV 5.10.07	Coventry Gliding Club Ltd tr The Gliding Centre "HQV" Husbands Bosworth	28. 9.08
G-CHOW	Schempp-Hirth Discus b	538	BGA4128-HQW 29. 8.07	M H Hardwick "MH" Wycombe Air Park	13.11.07
G-CHOX	Europa Aviation Europa XS (Built P Field - pr.no.PFA 247-13974)	566	2. 4.03	Chocks Away Ltd (Chertsey)	
G-CHOY	Schempp-Hirth Mini Nimbus C	113	BGA4130-HQY 18.10.07 D-3364	A H Sparrow Rivar Hill	26. 2.08
G-CHOZ	Rolladen-Schneider LS6-18W	6353	BGA4131-HQZ 18. 1.08 D-1486	R E Scott (Henfield)	21. 1.08
G-CHPA	Robinson R22 Beta	3442	EI-EHC 18. 4.07 N71850	Rivermead Aviation Ltd (Operated Rise Helicopters) Gloucestershire	14. 9.09E
G-CHPD	Rolladen-Schneider LS6-c18	6331	BGA4088-HPD 29.10.07 D-1054	C J and K A Teagle Sutton Bank	28. 9.08
G-CHPE	Schleicher ASK 13	13510	BGA4089-HPE 23. 1.08 D-3992	Dumfries and District Gliding Club Falgunzeon	13. 7.08
G-CHPH	Schempp-Hirth Discus CS	174CS	BGA4092-HPH 26.11.07	A D Johnson and J E Kelk Wormingfold	8. 5.08
G-CHPK	Van's RV-8 (Started M R Tingle, built A C Andover, pr no PFA 303-14535)	82530	G-JILS 26. 9.08	Vicount A C Andover Charlton Park, Malmesbury	
G-CHPL	Rolladen-Schneider LS4-b	4959	BGA4095-HPL 9.11.07 (BGA4071-HNL)	Southdown Gliding Club Ltd Parham Park	30. 1.08
G-CHPO	Schleicher Ka 6 CR	6200	BGA4099-HPQ 26.11.07 D-1933	N Robinson Crowland	23. 3.08
G-CHPR	Robinson R22 Beta	3854	25. 5.05	O Oberhofer (München, Germany)	7. 7.09E
G-CHPT	Fedorov Me7 Mechta	M006	BGA4102-HPT 8. 2.08	A E Griffiths Long Mynd	4. 4.08
G-CHPV	Schleicher ASK 21	21608	BGA4104-HPV 27.11.07	Scottish Gliding Union Ltd Portmoak	28. 9.08
G-CHPW	Schleicher ASK 21	21609	BGA4105-HPW 2.11.07	Scottish Gliding Union Ltd Portmoak	28. 9.08
G-CHPX	Schempp-Hirth Discus CS	177CS	BGA4106-HPX 14.11.07	M A Whitehead tr G-CHPX Group Gransden Lodge	28. 9.08
G-CHPY	de Havilland DHC-1 Chipmunk 22	C1/0093	WB652 7. 3.97	Devonair Executive Business Transport Ltd Little Rissington	6. 7.08T
G-CHRA	Grob G102 Astir CS	1109	BGA4132-HRA 29. 1.08 D-4169	T World tr Portsmouth Naval Gliding Centre Lee-on-Solent	29. 3.08
G-CI IRB	Sportline Aviacija LAK-12 Lietuva	6223	BCA4133-HRB 15.10.07	J E Nevill Aboyne	28. 9.08
G-CHRC	DG Flugzeugbau DG-500/20 Elan (Type amended 25. 2.08)	5E136W5	BGA4134-HRC 10.10.07	D Rhys-Jones tr DG500-390 Syndicate Parham Park	24. 4.08
G-CHRG	PZL-Bielsko SZD-51-1 Junior	B-2013	BGA4138-HRG 17. 1.08 B-2013	Scottish Gliding Union Ltd Portmoak	3. 6.08
G-CHRH	Schempp-Hirth Discus 2cT	74	BGA5323-KSG 3. 7.08	C Hyett Lasham	30. 6.09
G-CHRJ	Schleciher K 8B	8093Ei	BGA4139-HRJ 8. 8.08 D-5048	Shenington Gliding Club Shenington	
G-CHRK	Centrair 101 Pegase	101048	BGA4140-HRK 27. 3.08 F-CFQJ	P T Bushill and M Morris Dunstable	
G-CHRL	Schempp-Hirth Standard Cirrus	525	BGA4141-HRL 19. 3.08 D-3099	A Smurthwaiteand M Harbour Camphill	
G-CHRN	Schleicher ASK 18	18026	BGA4143-HRN 3.10.07 HB-1308	Stratford on Avon Gliding Club Ltd Snitterfield	9. 3.08
G-CHRS	Schempp-Hirth Discus CS	100CS	BGA4147-HRS 25.10.07 D-5100	F E P Vandenheede Rixensart, Belgium	14. 3.08
G-CHRW	Schempp-Hirth Duo Discus	43	BGA4151-HRW 17. 9.07 (BGA4160), BGA4151-HRW	A J Davis tr 802 Syndicate "802" Nympsfield	28. 9.08
G-CHRX	Schempp-Hirth Discus a	545	BGA4152-HRX 21. 1.08	G S Bird & N Worrell Lasham	15. 2.08
G-CHSA	Rolladen-Schneider LS6-18W	6361	BGA4155-HSA 11.10.07	D A Benton Snitterfield	11.10.07
G-CHSB	Glaser-Dirks DG-303 Elan	3E641	BGA4156-HSB 23. 7.08	A R Kerwin-Nye Ringmer	
G-CHSD	Schempp-Hirth Discus b	258/1	BGA4158-HSD 1.11.07 (BGA4142-HRM)	J R Reed tr G-CHSD Group Dunstable	27. 3.08
G-CHSE	Grob G102 Astir CS77	1635	BGA4159-HSE 15. 1.08 RAFGSA R68, RAFGSA 548	A Mutch Portmoak	8. 3.08
G-CHSG	Scheibe SF27A Zugvögel V (Originally c/n 1705/E, amended 22. 7.08)	6103	BGA4161-HSG 3. 3.08 D-7827, OE-0827	C T Oliver tr HSG Syndicate Lyveden	

G-CHSK	Schleicher ASW 20CL	20827	BGA4164-HSK	19. 3.08	A J Watson and C C Ramshorn	Gransden Lodge	
			D-3499				
G-CHSM	Schleicher ASK 13	13145	BGA4166-HSM-	24. 9.07	Stratford on Avon Gliding Club Ltd	Snitterfield	2. 3.08
			D-0168				
G-CHSN	Schleicher Ka 6CR	6218	BGA4167-HSN	20.11.07	Needwood Forest Gliding Club Ltd	Cross Hayes	16. 2.08
			OO-ZZF, D-8546				
G-CHSO	Schempp-Hirth Discus b	99	BGA4169-HSQ	10.12.07	Midland Gliding Club Ltd "493"	Long Mynd	28. 9.08
			D2943				
G-CHSU	Eurocopter EC.135 T1	0079		4. 2.99	Thames Valley Police Authority	RAF Benson	12. 4.11S
					(Operated Chiltern Air Support Unit)		
G-CHSX	Scheibe SF27A Zugvögel V	6031	BGA4176-HSX	6.11.07	C Downes and G M Wright	Wormingford	7. 2.08
			SE-TDT				
G-CHSZ	Rolladen-Schneider LS8-a	8030	BGA4178-HSZ	7. 3.08	I G Garden	Wycombe Air Park	
G-CHTA	Grumman AA-5A Cheetah	AA5A-0631	G-BFRC	3. 3.86	T Hale	Biggin Hill	9. 4.09E
G-CHTB	Schempp-Hirth Janus	7	BGA4180-HTB	20. 2.08	J B Maddison tr Janus G-CHTB Syndicate		
			D-3114			Kirton-in-Lindsey	1. 5.08
G-CHTC	Schleicher ASW 15B	15188	BGA4181-HTC	20. 5.08	C Knapp tr HTC Syndicate	Camphill	
			OE-0930				
G-CHTD	Grob G102 Astir CS	1012	BGA4182-HTD	7. 1.08	C R Little and T Hatton tr Tango Delta Group		
			D-6508			Halesland	8. 3.08
G-CHTE	Grob G102 Astir CS77	1716	BGA4183-HTE	20.11.07	S Maxwell tr HTE Group	Challock	9. 4.08
			RAFGSA R82, RAFGSA 882				
G-CHTF	Sportline Aviacija LAK-12 Lietuva	6180	BGA4184-HTF	19.12.07	N C Harrison and S Pozerskis Husbands Bosworth		30. 4.08
G-CHTJ	Schleicher ASK 13	13125	BGA4185-HTJ	8.10.08	Queen's University Gliding Club "HTJ"	Bellarena	
			D-0648, PL62, Belgian Air Cadets				
G-CHTM	Rolladen-Schneider LS8-18	8036	BGA4190-HTM	5.10.07	M J Chapman	Seighford	28. 9.08
G-CHTN	Schleicher ASW 22	22013	BGA4191-HTN	17. 8.07	R C Hodge	Dunstable	23.10.07
			ZS-GLN				
G-CHTR	Grob G102 Astir CS	1190	BGA4194-HTR	25.10.07	I P and D M Wright	Kingston Deverill	11. 3.08
			D-7307				
G-CHTS	Rolladen-Schneider LS8-18	8040	BGA4195-HTS	23.10.07	A R Head and P Rowden "H8"	Gransden Lodge	27. 3.08
G-CHTU	Schempp-Hirth Cirrus	88	BGA4197-HTU	19. 2.08	G V Higgins tr Open Cirrus Group	Burn	12. 4.08
			D-0478				
G-CHTV	Schleicher ASK 21	21624	BGA4198-HTV	1. 2.08	Cambridge Gliding Club Ltd	Gransden Lodge	20. 3.08
			D-8355				
G-CHTY	LET L-13 Blanik	026318	BGA4201-HTY	26.11.07	T Taberham tr North Devon Gliding Club Blanik Syndicate		
			LY-GDT, DOSAAF			Eaglescott	8. 6.08
G-CHUA	Schleicher ASW 19B	19091	BGA4203-HUA	16. 1.08	G D Vaughan	East Hardwick, Pontefract	5. 5.07
			D-3840				
G-CHUD	Schleicher ASK 13	13018	BGA4206-HUD	12.10.07	London Gliding Club Proprietary Ltd	Dunstable	28. 9.08
			D-9203				
G-CHUE	Schleicher ASW 27	27022	BGA4207-HUF	22, 8.08	M J Smith "N5"	Dunstable	
G-CHUF	Schleicher ASK 13	13109	BGA4208-HUF	11.12.07	The Welland Gliding Club Ltd	Lyveden	25. 3.08
			OO-ZWE				
G-CHUG	Europa Aviation Europa	260		29. 7.96	C M Washington	Sleap	31. 3.09P
	(Built C M Washington - pr.no.PFA 247-12960) (Monowheel u/c)						
G-CHUH	Schempp-Hirth Janus	15	BGA4210-HUH	18. 1.08	R A Gardiner tr Janus D31 Syndicate		
			D-3116			(Uppingham, Oakham)	14. 7.08
G-CHUJ	Centrair ASW 20F	20170	BGA4211-HUJ	3.10.07	D M Cornish tr HUJ Group	Rattlesden	30. 5.08
			F-CFLY				
G-CHUK	Cameron O-77 Balloon (Hot Air)	2773		6. 3.92	R Ashford	Petworth	10. 7.09E
G-CHUL	Schempp-Hirth Cirrus	V3	BGA4213-HUM	21. 8.08	I Ashton "624"	Chipping	
			HB-900				
G-CHUM	Robinson R44 Raven	0839		2. 8.00	Just Plane Trading Ltd		
						Top Farm, Croydon, Royston	20. 9.09E
G-CHUN	Grob G102 Astir CS Jeans	2089	BGA4215-HUN	3. 1.08	Staffordshire Gliding Club Ltd	Seighford	12. 3.08
			D-7531				
G-CHUO	Fedorov Me7 Mechta	M007	BGA4217-HUQ	10. 1.08	E A Hull "DP"	Dunstable	9. 4.08
G-CHUR	Schempp-Hirth HS.2 Cirrus	12	BGA4218-HUR	30.11.07	M Rossiter and A G Thomas	Talgarth	23. 4.08
			HB-927				
G-CHUS	Scheibe SF27A Zügvogel V	6010	BGA4219-HUS	2. 4.08	P J Duffy tr SF27 HUS Syndicate	Shenington	
G-CHUT	Centrair ASW 20F	20187	BGA4220-HUT	6. 9.07	G Macfadyen	Nympsfield	28. 9.08
			F-CEUQ				
G-CHUU	Schleicher ASK 13	AB13527	BGA4221-HUU	12.12.07	Upward Bound Trust	Thame	21. 9.08
			D-7506, D-8945				
G-CHUW	Rolladen-Schneider LS8-a	8058	BGA4223-HUW	12.12.07	S E Bort tr S8 Group "S8"	Challock	17. 3.08
G-CHUY	Schempp-Hirth Ventus cT	84/329	BGA4225-HUY	30 8.07	M H and M N Challans	Lasham	28. 9.08
			D-KILZ				
G-CHUZ	Schempp-Hirth Discus bT	158/559	BGA4226-HUZ	30.11.07	P A Gelsthorpe "200" (Blackwater, Camberley)		1. 3.08
G-CHVE	Schempp-Hirth Ventus 2cT	8/19	BGA4231-HVE	17. 8.07	T Vestergaard and D Fjord (Silkeborg, Denmark)		28. 9.08
			D-KHIA				
G-CHVF	Rolladen-Schneider LS8-18	8059	BGA4232-HVF	23. 8.07	J Haigh and R B Coote	Parham Park	28. 9.08
			D-1683				
G-CHVG	Schleicher ASK 21	21062	BGA4233-HVG	10. 4.08	Rattlesden Gliding Club Ltd "RP1"	Rattlesden	
			D-2606				
G-CHVH	Pilatus B4-PC11	067	BGA4234-HVH	19. 6.08	London Gliding Club Proprietary Ltd	Dunstable	
			D-2156				
G-CHVK	Grob G102 Astir CS	1161	BGA4236-HVK	10. 1.08	P G Goulding	Crowland	7. 5.08
			D-4182				
G-CHVL	Rolladen-Schneider LS8-18	8060	BGA4237-HVL	19.10.07	M W Durham tr Cumulus Gliding Syndicate "LS8"		
						Bicester	30. 3.08
G-CHVM	Glaser-Dirks DG-300 Elan	3E177	BGA4238-HVM	24. 4.08	North Downs Gliding Trust Ltd "393"	Lasham	
			D-4314				

G-CHVO	Schleicher ASK 13	13251	BGA4241-HVQ D-0605	6. 8.08	R B Brown	Bidford	
G-CHVP	Schleicher ASW 20	20374	BGA4240-HVP D-1961	7. 1.08	E J P Smallbone tr 930 Syndicate "930"	Lasham	13. 2.08
G-CHVR	Schempp-Hirth Discus b	560	BGA4242-HVR	13. 3.08	Yorkshire Gliding Club (Proprietary) Ltd	Sutton Bank	
G-CHVT	Schempp-Hirth Ventus 2b	37	BGA4244-HVT	12.11.07	G Alison tr Victor Tango Group "A9"	Wycombe Air Park	28. 9.08
G-CHVU	Rolladen-Schneider LS8-a	8066	BGA4245-HVU	14. 1.08	B T Spreckley (Operated European Soaring Club)	(France)	20. 3.08
G-CHVV	Rolladen-Schneider LS4-b	41009	BGA4246-HVV	6.11.07	A J Bardgett	Milfield	28. 9.08
G-CHVW	Schleicher ASK 13	13431	BGA4247-HVW D-2140	31. 1.08	Rattlesden Gliding Club Ltd	Rattlesden	17.12.07
G-CHVX	Centrair ASW 20F	20528	BGA4248-HVX F-CFSJ	1.12.07	J A Castle	Hinton-in-the-Hedges	8. 4.08
G-CHVZ	Schempp-Hirth Standard Cirrus	567G	BGA4250-HVZ HB-1269	27.11.07	P H V Alexander tr ABC Soaring	(Glossop)	6. 4.08
G-CHWA	Schempp-Hirth Ventus 2C	8	BGA4251-HWA	27. 5.08	C Garton "31"	Lasham	
G-CHWB	Schempp-Hirth Duo Discus	84	BGA4252-HWB	17. 7.08	Lasham Gliding Society Ltd "775"	Lasham	
G-CHWC	Glasflugel H201B Standard Libelle	310	BGA4253-HWC HB-1076	12.12.07	J C R Rogers tr Whiskey Charlie Group	RAF Cranwell	24. 8.08
G-CHWF	Jastreb Standard Cirrus G/81	281	BGA4256-HWF SE-TZC	12. 3.08	D P Mansbridge and M D Langford	Talgarth	
G-CHWH	Schempp-Hirth Ventus cT	182/599	BGA4258-HWH RAFGGA 506	20. 8.07	H R Browning	Lasham	28. 9.08
G-CHWL	Rolladen-Schneider LS8-a	8076	BGA4261-HWL	18. 1.08	W M Coffee	Snitterfield	9. 2.08
G-CHWP	Glaser-Dirks DG-100G Elan (Type amended to DG-100G 14.1.09)	E24G13	BGA4264-HWP D-3772	23. 6.08	D Procter	Pocklington	
G-CHWS	Rolladen-Schneider LS8-18	8080	BGA4267-HWS	15.11.07	G A and H B Chalmers	Easterton	15. 2.08
G-CHWW	Grob G103A Twin II Acro	3658-K-27	BGA4271-HWW OE-5285	10.12.07	Crown Service Gliding Club	Lasham	27. 3.08
G-CHWX	PZL-Bielsko SZD-59 Acro	B-2170	BGA4272-HWX	16. 1.08	D W F Gosden	Talgarth	10. 8.08
G-CHXA	Scheibe Zügvogel IIIB	1107	BGA4275-HXA D-2005	29.10.08	P Kent "Z33"	Saltby	
G-CHXB	Grob G102 Astir CS77	1819	BGA4276-HXB D-6755	12. 9.08	T S Miller	Lyveden	
G-CHXC	Rolladen-Schneider LS8-18	8094	BGA4278-HXC	17.10.07	S M Smith "M8"	Gransden Lodge	28. 9.08
G-CHXD	Schleicher ASW 27	27030	BGA4279-HXD	3.12.07	J Quartermaine and M Jerman	Wormingford	28. 9.08
G-CHXE	Schleicher ASW 19B	19053	BGA4280-HXE D-6699	6.11.07	M Hargreaves and V Bettle	Wormingford	29. 5.08
G-CHXH	Schempp-Hirth Discus b	573	BGA4283-HXH BGA4375-JBD, (BGA4283-HXH)	16.11.07	Deeside Gliding Club (Aberdeenshire) Ltd	Aboyne	28. 9.08
G-CHXJ	Schleicher ASK 13	13216	BGA4284-HXJ D-0417	23.10.07	Cotswold Gliding Club	Aston Down	28. 9.08
G-CHXM	Grob G102 Astir CS	1272	BGA 4287-HXM D-7367	13. 6.08	M D Rogers tr Bristol University Gliding Club	Nympsfield	
G-CHXO	Schleicher ASH 25B	25187	BGA4290-HXQ OH-874	4.12.07	P Morrison tr The Eleven Group	North Hill	13. 3.08
G-CHXP	Schleicher ASK 13	13023	BGA4289-HXP D-3656	28.11.07	The Vale of the White Horse Gliding Centre Ltd	Sandhill Farm, Shrivenham	7. 3.08
G-CHXR	Schempp-Hirth Ventus cT	88/333	BGA4291-HXR D-KESH	19.10.07	J W a'Court and M Benson	Lasham	28. 9.08
G-CHXT	Rolladen-Schneider LS 4a	4325	BGA4293-HXT ZS-GNV	3.12.07	B T Spreckley (Operated European Soaring Club)	Ontur, Spain	5. 4.08
G-CHXU	Schleicher ASW 19B	19359	BGA4294-HXU SE-TXN	1. 2.08	D P Binney	Pocklingtonn	7. 9.08
G-CHXV	Schleicher ASK 13	13080	BGA4295-HXV D-5462	17.10.07	Banbury Gliding Club Ltd	Hinton-in-the-Hedges	20. 1.08
G-CHXW	Rolladen-Schneider LS8-18	8097	BGA4296-HXW	19.12.07	W Aspland "325"	Wycombe Air Park	23. 3.08
G-CHXX	Schempp-Hirth Standard Cirrus	154G	BGA4297-HXX D-0363	2. 4.08	D K Bwye tr G-CHXX Group	Lasham	
G-CHXY	Grob G102 Astir CS77 (Type amended 27.11.08)	1781	BGA4298-HXY D-7689	8. 1.08	G W Powell	Shenington	25. 3.08
G-CHXZ	Rolladen-Schneider LS4	4249	BGA4299-HXZ SE-TXF	1. 2.08	E J Foggin, G N Turner and J D Huband	Sandhill Farm, Shrivenham	8. 2.08
G-CHYA	Rolladen-Schneider LS6c-18	6349	BGA4300-HYA D-2162	5.11.07	R H Dixon	(Mere, Warminster)	2. 3.08
G-CHYD	Schleicher ASW 24	24039	BGA4303-HYD OE-5460	20.11.07	E B Adlard	Long Mynd	5. 2.08
G-CHYE	DG Flugzeugbau DG-500 Elan Orion	5E167X22	BGA4304-HYE	12. 9.07	The Bristol Gliding Club Proprietary Ltd "913"	Nympsfield	9. 4.08
G-CHYF	Rolladen-Schneider LS8-18	8106	BGA4305-HYF	26.10.07	R E Francis "660"	Nympsfield	28. 9.08
G-CHYH	Rolladen-Schneider LS3-17	3186	BGA4307-HYH D-6650	15. 5.08	B Sike	Bellarena	
G-CHYJ	Schleicher ASK 21	21066	BGA4308-HYJ D-2724	5. 3.08	Highland Gliding Club Ltd	Easterton	
G-CHYK	Centrair ASW 20FL	20176	BGA4309-HYK F-CEUN	21. 5.08	K B Ellis tr Yankee Kilo Group	Rufforth	
G-CHYL	Robinson R22 Beta	1197		28.11.89	C M Gough-Cooper	(Macclesfield)	28. 4.09E
G-CHYP	PZL-Bielsko SZD-50-3 Puchacz	B-2082	BGA4313-HYP	11. 3.08	Rattlesden Gliding Club Ltd	Rattlesden	
G-CHYR	Schleicher ASW 27	27013	BGA4315-HYR	20.11.07	A P Brown and A R Hutchings	Dunstable	21. 2.07
G-CHYS	Schleicher ASK 21	21519	BGA4316-HYS RAFGSA 514	1. 5.08	P Fanning tr Army Gliding Assocaition "A14" (Operated Anglia Gliding Club)	AAC Wattisham	

G-CHYT	Schleicher ASK 21	21568	BGA4317-HYT 29. 1.08 AGA20	J W Sage tr Army Gliding Association	Trenchard Lines, Upavon	7. 2.08
G-CHYU	Schempp-Hirth Discus CS	192CS	BGA4318-HYU 1. 5.08 AGA ??, RAFGGA 561	P Fanning tr Army Gliding Association	AAC Wattisham	
G-CHYW	Schleicher K 8B	8163A	BGA4320-HYW 29. 2.08 D-5316, D-3202	Lincolnshire Gliding Club Ltd	Strubby	5. 4.08
G-CHYX	Schleicher K 8B	686	BGA4321-HYX 8. 2.08 D-5742	M Bacic tr Oxford University Gliding Club	Bicester	2. 2.08
G-CHYY	Schempp-Hirth Nimbus 3dT	21	BGA4322-HYY 6.11.07 RAFGSA R26, D-KAFA	M Ellis tr G-CHYY Syndicate	(Dewsbury)	28. 9.08
G-CHZA	Schempp-Hirth Nimbus 3/24.5	94	BGA4324-HZA 16.10.07 SE-UFO	P J Kite tr 374 Syndicate "374"	Lasham	13.12.07
G-CHZB	PZL-Swidnik PW-5 Smyk	17.06.021	BGA4325-HZB 9. 5.08	The Burn Gliding Club Ltd	Burn	
G-CHZD	Schleicher ASW 15B	15327	BGA4327-HZD 4.12.07 D-2191	C P Ellison and W C Davis	Rivar Hill	13. 4.08
G-CHZE	Schempp-Hirth Discus CS	121CS	BGA4328-HZE 27. 7.07 D-6946	S B Marshall tr HZE Glider Syndicate	Portmoak	28. 9.08
G-CHZG	Rolladen-Schneider LS8-18	8118	BGA4330-HZG 15.11.07	M J and T J Webb "X8"	RAF Halton	22. 3.08
G-CHZH	Schleicher Ka 6CR	6461	BGA4331-HZH 6. 1.09 HB-836	M E de Torre	Darlton	
G-CHZJ	Schempp-Hirth Standard Cirrus	23	BGA4332-HZJ 27.11.07 HB-981	P Fletcher and R H D Adams	Shenington	28. 3.08
G-CHZM	Rolladen-Schneider LS4-a	4762	BGA4335-HZM 15.11.07 D-1394	B Toulson and J M Bevan "UI" Husbands Bosworth		17. 3.08
G-CHZN	Robinson R22 Beta	0884	G-GHZM 9. 4.99 G-FENI	Cloudbase Ltd	(Rugby)	9. 4.09E
G-CHZO	Schleicher ASW 27	27018	BGA4338-HZQ 23. 1.08 D-4499	A A Gilmore "LZ"	Husbands Bosworth	6. 4.08
G-CHZR	Schleicher ASK 21	21079	BGA4339-HZR 17.12.07 D-4491	D J Brookman tr K21 HZR Group	Aston Down	29. 3.08
G-CHZU	Schempp-Hirth Standard Cirrus	366	BGA4342-HZU 28.11.07 HB-1258, N71KW	N S Murning	Eyres Field	31. 1.08
G-CHZV	Schempp-Hirth Standard Cirrus	305	BGA4343-HZV 6 .6.08 VH-GFZ, BGA4343-HZV, HB-1457, D-2061	S M Sheard "P61"	Pocklington	
G-CHZX	Schleicher K 8B	8257	BGA4345-HZX 19. 4.08 D-8476	T I Naylor-Peach	Upwood	
G-CHZY	Rolladen-Schneider LS4	4479	BGA4346-HZY 7.11.07 D-3458	N P Wedi	Wycombe Air Park	28. 9.08
G-CHZZ	Schleicher ASW 20L	20353	BGA4347-HZZ 6.11.07 HB-1691, D-1153, N20EE	C M Davey tr LD Syndicate "LD"	RAF Wittering	31. 5.08

G-CIAA - G-CIZZ

G-CIAO	III Sky Arrow 650 T (Built J Hosier)	PFA 298-13095		23. 7.97	G Arscott	Popham 12.11.09P
G-CIAS	Pilatus Britten-Norman BN-2B-21 Islander	2162	HC-BNS G-BKJM	1. 5.91	Channel Island Air Search Ltd	Guernsey 11. 3.09E
G-CIBO	Cessna 180K Skywagon	18053177	VH-JNS N19029	23. 7.04	CIBO Ops Ltd	Rush Green 14. 1.09E
G-CICI	Cameron R-15 Gas/Hot Air Balloon	673	(N) G-CICI, (G-BIHP)	11.11.80	Noble Adventures Ltd	Bristol 5. 6.91P
G-CIDA	Robinson R44 Raven II	11611		19. 2.07	A Dallinger	Wels, Austria 8. 3.09E
G-CIDD	Bellanca 7ECA Citabria	1002-74	N86577	29.11.00	S Wells	Belle Vue Farm, Yarnscombe 4.11.10S
G-CIEL	Cessna 560XL Citation Excel	560-5247	N57RL N7RL, N51038	29. 4.05	Enerway Ltd (Operated London Executive Aviation)	London Stansted 9. 5.09E
G-CIGY	Westland-Bell 47G-3B1	WA/350	G-BGXP XT191	26.10.98	Heli-Highland Ltd	Glastullich Farm, Tain 28.10.11E
G-CIRI	Cirrus SR20 GTS	1791	N473SR	15. 5.07	C D Palfreyman tr Cirrus Flyers Group	Turweston 16. 5.09E
G-CIRS	Cirrus SR20	1911	N191PG	29. 4.08	Cumulus Aircraft Rentals Ltd	Fairoaks
G-CITJ	Cessna 525 CitationJet	525-0084	D-ITSV (N5092D)	23. 2.07	Centreline Air Charter Ltd	Bristol 1. 3.09E
G-CITR	Cameron Z-105 Balloon (Hot Air)	10278		22. 2.02	Flying Pictures Ltd (Citroën C3 titles)	Chilbolton 19. 5.04A
G-CITY	Piper PA-31-350 Navajo Chieftain	31-7852136	N27741	12. 9.78	Woodgate Aviation (IoM) Ltd	Ronaldsway 18.12.09E
G-CIVA	Boeing 747-436	27092		19. 3.93	British Airways PLC	London Heathrow 18. 3.09E
G-CIVB	Boeing 747-436	25811	(G-BNLY)	15. 2.94	British Airways PLC	London Heathrow 14. 2.10E
G-CIVC	Boeing 747-436	25812	(G-BNLZ)	26. 2.94	British Airways PLC	London Heathrow 25. 2.09E
G-CIVD	Boeing 747-436	27349		14.12.94	British Airways PLC	London Heathrow 3. 8.09E
G-CIVE	Boeing 747-436	27350		20.12.94	British Airways PLC	London Heathrow 22. 8.09E
G-CIVF	Boeing 747-436	25434	(G-BNLY)	29. 3.95	British Airways PLC	London Heathrow 20. 9.09E
G-CIVG	Boeing 747-436	25813	N6009F	20. 4.95	British Airways PLC	London Heathrow 18. 4.09E
G-CIVH	Boeing 747-436	25809		23. 4.96	British Airways PLC	London Heathrow 22. 4.09E
G-CIVI	Boeing 747-436	25814		2. 5.96	British Airways PLC	London Heathrow 1. 5.09E
G-CIVJ	Boeing 747-436	25817		11. 2.97	British Airways PLC	London Heathrow 10. 9.09E
G-CIVK	Boeing 747-436	25818		28. 2.97	British Airways PLC	London Heathrow 30. 8.09E
G-CIVL	Boeing 747-436	27478		28. 3.97	British Airways PLC	London Heathrow 26.11.09E
G-CIVM	Boeing 747-436	28700		5. 6.97	British Airways PLC	London Heathrow 4. 6.09E
G-CIVN	Boeing 747-436	28848		29. 9.97	British Airways PLC	London Heathrow 28. 9.09E
G-CIVO	Boeing 747-436	28849	N6046P	5.12.97	British Airways PLC	London Heathrow 4.12.09E
G-CIVP	Boeing 747-436	25850		17. 2.98	British Airways PLC	London Heathrow 16. 2.10E
G-CIVR	Boeing 747-436	25820		2. 3.98	British Airways PLC	London Heathrow 21. 2.10E
G-CIVS	Boeing 747-436	28851		13. 3.98	British Airways PLC	London Heathrow 12. 3.09E
G-CIVT	Boeing 747-436	25821	(G-CIVN)	20. 3.98	British Airways PLC	London Heathrow 9.11.09E

G-CIVU	Boeing 747-436	25810	(G-CIVO)	24. 4.98	British Airways PLC	London Heathrow	23. 4.09E
G-CIVV	Boeing 747-436	25819	N6009F	23. 5.98	British Airways PLC	London Heathrow	10. 4.09E
			(G-CIVP)				
G-CIVW	Boeing 747-436	25822	(G-CIVR)	15. 5.98	British Airways PLC	London Heathrow	14. 5.09E
G-CIVX	Boeing 747-436	28852		3. 9.98	British Airways PLC	London Heathrow	2. 9.09E
G-CIVY	Boeing 747-436	28853		29. 9.98	British Airways PLC	London Heathrow	28. 9.09E
G-CIVZ	Boeing 747-436	28854		31.10.98	British Airways PLC	London Heathrow	30.10.09E
G-CIZZ	Beech 58 Baron	TH-2041	N5000S	16. 1.08	Bonanza Flying Club Ltd	Wycombe Air Park	17. 1.09E

G-CJAA - G-CJZZ

G-CJAB	Dornier 328-300	3200	OE-HAA	16. 9.05	Corporate Jet Realisations Ltd *(stored)*	Biggin Hill	19. 9.09E
			D-BDXN, (G-CJAB), D-BDXN, N328BC, D-BDMO, D-BDXN, (V5-NMC), (D-BMAH)				
G-CJAD	Cessna 525 CitationJet	525-0435	N525AD	28. 6.02	A B Davis tr Davis Aircraft Operations	Edinburgh	27. 6.09E
			N5244F				
G-CJAG	Raytheon RB390 Premier 1	RB-122	N3722Z	20.12.05	Xclusive Jet Charter Ltd	Southampton	8. 1.08E
G-CJAI	P&M Aviation Quik GT450	8198		19.10.07	J C Kitchen	Hunsdon	4.12.09P
	(Possibly fitted with trike c/n 7979 ex G-CJAY qv)						
G-CJAL	Schleicher Ka 6E	4380	BGA4358-JAL	1. 5.08	J Stewart tr JAL Syndicate	Lee-on-Solent	
			F-CDTX				
G-CJAO	Schempp-Hirth Discus b	190	BGA4362-JAQ	11. 1.08	A Lyth and J Weddell	Ringmer	18. 3.08
G-CJAR	Schempp-Hirth Discus bT	83/417	BGA4363-JAR	19. 3.08	D G Maddicks and S P Withey	Nympsfield	
			D-KHEI				
G-CJAS	Glasflügel H201 Standard Libelle	109	BGA4364-JAS	1.12.07	M J Collett *"7Q"*	Wycombe Air Park	21.12.07
			SE-TIS				
G-CJAT	Schleicher K 8B	8150	BGA4365-JAT	10.10.07	Wolds Gliding Club Ltd	Pocklington	19. 7.07
			D-4390				
G-CJAV	Schleicher ASK 21	21662	BGA4367-JAV	10.10.07	Wolds Gliding Club Ltd	Pocklington	1. 2.08
G-CJAW	Glaser-Dirks DG-200-17	2-180-1759	BGA4368-JAW	19.12.07	J P Kirby and T McKinley	Bembridge	21. 3.08
			D-5618				
G-CJAX	Schleicher ASK 21	21665	BGA4369-JAX	10.10.07	Wolds Gliding Club Ltd	Pocklington	28. 9.08
G-CJAY	P&M Aviation Quik 450	7979		18. 8.03	J C Kitchen	Stoke, Isle of Grain	1.10.07P
	(Originally built by Mainair as Sports Pegasus Quik: new Sailwing (c/n 8198) fitted 6.06 and re-registered as Quik GT450: subsequently reverted to Quik status c.2007 and believed trike donated to G-CJAI qv)			*(Noted 2.08)*			
G-CJAZ	Grob G102 Astir CS Jeans	2073	BGA4371-JAZ	11. 9.08	The Bath, Wilts and North Dorset Gliding Club Ltd		
			D-7586			Longbridge Deverill	
G-CJBB	Rolladen-Schneider LS8-a	8003	BGA4373-JBB	2. 4.08	C Bruce	Parham Park	
			D-8023				
G-CJBC	Piper PA-28-180 Cherokee D	28-5470	OY-BDE	28.11.80	J B Cave	Wolverhampton	30. 9.09E
G-CJBF	Glasflügel H201B Standard Libelle	246	BGA4377-JBF	2. 4.08	S Carmichael	Dunstable	
			F-CDPV				
G-CJBH	Eiriavion PIK-20D	20621	BGA4379-JBH	14.11.07	S R Domoney tr 537 Syndicate	Parham Park	13. 2.09R
			OH-529				
G-CJBJ	Schempp-Hirth Standard Cirrus	280	BGA4380-JBJ	6.11.08	S T Dutton	Lasham	
			SE-TZD				
G-CJBK	Schleicher ASW 19B	19204	BGA4381-JBK	7.11.07	D Caielli and P Sharpe	Dunstable	9. 1.08
			D-4099, PH-602				
G-CJBM	Schleicher ASK 21	21089	BGA4383-JBM	10.12.07	Midland Gliding Club Ltd	Long Mynd	5. 6.08
			D-6391				
G-CJBO	Rolladen-Schneider LS8-18	8148	BGA4386-JBQ	15. 8.08	C G Watt tr L7 Syndicate *"L7"*	Dunstable	
G-CJBR	Schempp-Hirth Discus b	90	BGA4387-JBR	8. 2.08	M R C Corrance, M Pointon and R Fitch	Kenley	20. 9.08
			F-CGGD, F-WGGD				
G-CJBS	Sportline Aviacija LAK-12 Lietuva	6115	BGA4388-JBS	8. 2.08	N G Davies tr Bravo Sierra Bigwigs Flying Group		
						(Seaford)	14. 3.08
G-CJBT	Schleicher ASW 19B	19075	BGA4389-JBT	14.11.07	C H Braithwaite	Kingston Deverill	29. 7.08
			D4477				
G-CJBW	Schempp-Hirth Discus bT	34/337	BGA4392-JBW	17.10.07	N Pringle tr G-CJBW Syndicate	Lasham	23. 1.08
			D-KBJR				
G-CJBX	Rolladen-Schneider LS4	4293	BGA4393-JBX	21. 3.07	P W Lee and P A Ivens *"JBX"*	Nympsfield	27. 3.07
			D-9111				
G-CJBY	Sportline Aviacija LAK-12 Lietuva	6185	BGA4394-JBY	26. 2.08	N Clarke and P G Steggles	Rattlesden	25. 7.08
G-CJCA	Schleicher ASW 15B	15202	BGA4396-JCA	21. 4.08	S Briggs	Currock Hill	
			(BGA4049-HMN), OH-410				
G-CJCC	Cessna 680 Citation Sovereign	680-0189	N5245D	31. 3.08	Viking Airways Ltd	Belfast International	31. 3.09E
G-CJCD	Schleicher ASW 24	24101	BGA4399-JCD	24. 9.07	M D Evershed *"HS"*	Gransden Lodge	1. 3.08
			D-6091				
G-CJCF	Grob G102 Astir CS77	1705	BGA4401-JCF	3. 1.08	The Northumbria Gliding Club Ltd	Currock Hill	2. 6.08
			PH-1012, D-7634				
G-CJCG	PZL-Swidnik PW-5 Smyk	17.09.003	BGA4402-JCG	3. 9.07	J Lavery	Bellarena	20.12.07
G-CJCJ	Schempp-Hirth Standard Cirrus	434G	BGA4404-JCJ	23.10.07	R Johnson and R Carter *"C3"*	Husbands Bosworth	18. 4.08
			SE-TNC				
G-CJCK	Schempp-Hirth Discus bT	92/430	BGA4405-JCK	29. 8.07	D C Coppin	Lasham	28.10.07
			D-KIDE				
G-CJCM	Schleicher ASW 27	27064	BGA4407-JCM	8. 1.08	J R Klunder and K E Singer	Camphill	4. 5.08
G-CJCN	Schempp-Hirth Standard Cirrus 75	646	BGA4408-JCN	8.12.07	S C J Barker *"JA9"*	Pocklington	28. 9.08
			D-7247				
G-CJCP	Rolladen-Schneider LS8-18	8146	BGA4409-JCP	16. 8.07	Associazione Equipe Volo Alpino		
						Pieve di Cadena, Italy	28. 9.08
G-CJCT	Schempp-Hirth Nimbus 4T	21	BGA4413-JCT	22. 1.08	D S Innes *"176"*	Lasham	8. 5.08
			D-KKKL				
G-CJCU	Schempp-Hirth Standard Cirrus B	688	BGA4414-JCU	21.11.07	R A Davenport	Aston Down	13. 3.08
			D-6604				
G-CJCV	Schleicher ASW 25E	25069	BGA4415-JCV	28. 4.08	R C Verdier tr ASH Group	Gransden Lodge	
			D-KAIM				

G-CJCW	Grob G102 Astir CS77	1612	BGA4416-JCW PH-573	7. 4.08	N G Smith	Nympsfield	
G-CJCX	Schempp-Hirth Discus bT	93/432	BGA4417-JCX D-KJOB	8. 1.08	A J Cox	Bidford	27. 3.08
G-CJCY	Rolladen-Schneider LS8-18	8171	BGA4418-JCY	11. 6.08	R Zaccour	Alzate Brianza, Italy	
G-CJCZ	Schleicher Ka 6CR	6108	BGA4418-JCZ D-7152	30. 4.08	N Barnes	Eyres Field	
G-CJDB	Cessna 525 CitationJet	525-0648		8. 8.07	Breed Aircraft Ltd.	Jersey	8. 8.09E
G-CJDC	Schleicher ASW 27	27010	BGA4422-JDC D-6209	17.10.07	J J Marshall	Dunstable	28. 9.08
G-CJDD	Glaser-Dirks DG-200/17	2-17CL17	BGA4423-JDD PH-717	20. 5.08	D A Littler tr Juliet Delta Delta Group *"R3"* RAF Keevil		
G-CJDE	Rolladen-Schneider LS8-18	8151	BGA4424-JDE	29.10.07	B Kerby and M Davies	Snitterfield	16. 4.08
G-CJDF	Schleicher ASH 25E	25150	BGA4425-JDF D-KPAS	2. 5.08	R Dell tra 522 Syndicate	Pocklington	
G-CJDG	Rolladen-Schneider LS6-b	6145	BGA4426-JDG D-5675	5.10.07	A and R H Moss *"KW"*	Nympsfield	2. 3.08
G-CJDJ	Rolladen-Schneider LS3	3010	BGA4428-JCJ D-7729	16.10.07	J C Burdett	Walney Island	10. 2.08
G-CJDK	Rolladen-Schneider LS8-18	8153	BGA4429-JDK	1.10.07	S M Tilling	Long Mynd	28. 9.08
G-CJDM	Schleicher ASW 15B	15280	BGA4431-JDM F-CEGL	19. 2.08	W Ellis *"WE"*	Wormingford	20. 4.08
G-CJDP	Glaser-Dirks DG-202/17	2-134/1732	BGA4433-JDP D-6545	4.12.07	M Downie and R Fielding tr The Owners of JDP Camphill		28. 9.08
G-CJDR	Schleicher ASW 15	15053	BGA4434-JDR D-6910	20.11.07	M J Waters *"Rocinante"*	Waldershare Park	2. 4.08
G-CJDS	Schempp-Hirth Standard Cirrus 75	638	BGA4436-JDS D-4057, OY-XCZ	13. 9.07	S Holland	Rivar Hill	16. 3.08
G-CJDT	Rolladen-Schneider LS8-a	8172	BGA4437-JDT	28. 2.08	H A Rebbeck	Dunstable	14. 5.08
G-CJDU	LET L-13 Blanik	026303	BGA4438-JDU D-8919	19.10.07	Herefordshire Gliding Club Ltd	Shobdon	14. 7.07
G-CJDV	DG Flugzeugbau DG-300 Elan Acro	3E481A24	BGA4439-JDV	24.10.07	S C Williams tr G-CJDV Group	Wycombe Air Park	6.12.07
G-CJDX	Wassmer WA-28F Espadon	101	BGA4441-JDX F-CDZU	11. 1.08	K J Woods	(Impington, Cambridge)	10. 5.08
G-CJDY	Rolladen-Schneider LS8-18	8173	BGA4442-JDY	7. 4.08	P O R Paterson *"P2"*	Lasham	
G-CJDZ	Schempp-Hirth Nimbus-4T	18	BGA4443-JDZ D-KOLF	29. 9.08	P J Harvey	Dunstable	
G-CJEA	Rolladen-Schneider LS8-18	8159	BGA4444-JEA D-2411	26.10.07	D J Westwood and R I Davidson *"D4"* Husbands Bosworth		25. 4.08
G-CJEB	Schleicher ASW 24	24172	BGA4445-JEB D-9344	16.11.07	M A Taylor and S L Barnes	Rattlesden	28. 2.08
G-CJEC	PZL-Bielsko SZD-50-3 Puchacz	B-2197	BGA4446-JEC	16.10.07	Cambridge Gliding Club Ltd	Gransden Lodge	28. 9.08
G-CJED	Schempp-Hirth Nimbus 3/24.5	37	BGA4822-JVT D-3176	26. 2.08	J R Edyvean	Bicester	23. 5.08
G-CJEE	Schleicher ASW 20L	20073	BGA4448-JEE (BGA4456-JEQ)	1.11.07	J C Baldock	Nympsfield	28. 9.08
G-CJEH	Glasflügel H303 Mosquito B	172	BGA4451-JEH	19.12.07	M J Vickery *"KE"*	Lasham	22. 3.08
G-CJEL	Schleicher ASW 24	24044	BGA4454-JEL PH-866	8. 2.08	D Robson	Milfield	12. 5.08
G-CJEM	Schempp-Hirth Duo Discus	146	BGA4455-JEM	22.11.07	D W Briggs tr Duo Discus 572 Flying Group Aston Down		28. 9.08
G-CJEP	Rolladen-Schneider LS4-b	41021	BGA4457-JEP	22.11.07	C F Carter and N Backes	Long Mynd	16. 4.08
G-CJER	Schempp-Hirth Standard Cirrus 75	654	BGA4459-JER D-6475, OO-ZBM	20.11.07	S R Brown tr Cirrus Group	Snitterfield	7. 4.08
G-CJEU	Glasflügel H201 Standard Libelle	55	BGA4462-JEU SE-TIC	21.11.07	D B Johns	Aston Down	30. 3.08
G-CJEV	Schempp-Hirth Standard Cirrus B	650	BGA4463-JEV OE-5072	25. 9.07	G F King and E Perrin	North Hill	22. 1.08
G-CJEW	Schleicher Ka 6CR	6493	BGA4464-JEW D-4116	14. 1.08	S Blundell	(Birmingham)	1. 3.08
G-CJEX	Schempp-Hirth Ventus 2a	64	BGA4465-JEX	3.10.07	D S Watt *"DW"*	Bicester	21. 2.08
G-CJEZ	Glaser-Dirks DG-100	03	BGA4467-JEZ PH-792, D-3721	16. 1.09	G Prior	Wycombe Air Park	
G-CJFA	Schempp-Hirth Standard Cirrus	225	BGA4468-JFA D-0974	14. 1.08	P.M.Sheahan	Lasham	21. 3.08
G-CJFC	Schempp-Hirth Discus CS	054CS	BGA4470-JFC RAFGSA R55	9. 5.07	T M Holloway tr RAF Gliding and Soaring Association *"R55"* *(Operated Fenland Gliding Club)* RAF Marham		28.10.07
G-CJFE	Schempp-Hirth Janus Ce	(21)/299	BGA4472-JFE- RAFGSA R16	26. 9.07	J G Arnold tr RAF Gliding and Soaring Association *(Operated Bannerdown Gliding Club)* RAF Keevil		30.10.07
G-CJFF	Schempp-Hirth Duo Discus	131	BGA4473-JFF RAFGSA R26	17.10.07	P Armstrong tr JFF Group	(Welford)	28. 9.08
G-CJFH	Schempp-Hirth Duo Discus	118	BGA4475-JFH RAFGSA R1	27. 2.08	J G Arnold tr RAF Gliding and Soaring Association *(Operated Fulmar Gliding Club)* Easterton		4. 4.08
G-CJFJ	Schleicher ASW 20 CL	20830	BGA4476-JFJ D-8307, F-CGCS	29. 1.08	R J Stirk	Burn	1. 4.08
G-CJFK	Schleicher ASW 20L	20201	BGA4477-JFK D-5979	19. 4.07	D Holt *"JFK"*	Llantisilio	16. 5.08
G-CJFM	Schleicher ASK 13	13222	BGA4479-JFM D-0396	25. 6.08	Darlton Gliding Club Ltd	Darlton	
G-CJFR	Schemmp-Hirth Ventus cT	170/560	BGA4483-JFR RAFGSA R24	24.10.07	J G Allen *"221"*	Bicester	9. 1.08
G-CJFT	Schleicher K 8B	8451	BGA4485-JFT D-1883	15.11.07	The Surrey Hills Gliding Club Ltd	Kenley	31. 8.06

Reg	Type	c/n	Previous id	Owner/Operator	Location	Date
G-CJFU	Schleicher ASW 19 B	19038	BGA4486-JFU 28. 1.08 D-4531	M T Stanley	Sutton Bank	9. 3.08
G-CJFX	Rolladen-Schneider LS8-a	8174	BGA4489-JFX 16.10.07	P E Baker "144"	Gransden Lodge	28. 9.08
G-CJFY	Federov Me7 Mechta	8	BGA4490-JFY 5. 3.08	Shalbourne Soaring Society Ltd	Rivar Hill	
G-CJFZ	Fedorov Me7b Mechta	M009	BGA4491-JFZ 26. 8.08	R J Colbourne	(Farnham)	
G-CJGB	Schleicher K 8B (Amateur build)	AB.02	BGA4493-JGB 28. 3.08 D-8868	P O'Donald tr Cambridge University Gliding Club	Gransden Lodge	
G-CJGD	Schleicher K 8B (Officially regd as c/n 8214)	8214A-SH	BGA4495-JGD 30. 1.08 D-....	C A McLay and R E Pettifer	Chipping	21. 4.08
G-CJGE	Schleicher ASK 21	21068	BGA4496-JGE 6. 3.08 RAFGSA R21	M R Wall	Bidford	
G-CJGF	Schempp-Hirth Ventus c	517	BGA3785-HAJ 24. 4.08	J G Fisher	(Taporley)	
G-CJGG	P&M Aviation Quik GT450	8305	30. 8.07	J M Pearce	(Sandbank, Dunoon)	17.10.08P
G-CJGH	Schempp-Hirth Nimbus 2C	188	BGA4499-JGH 5. 6.08 OO-ZZM, D-2624	J Swannack tr G-CJGH Syndicate	Darlton	
G-CJGJ	Schleicher ASK 21	21039	BGA4500-JGJ 10.12.07 RAFGSA R22	Midland Gliding Club Ltd	Long Mynd	28. 9.08
G-CJGK	Eiriavion PIK-20D	20571	BGA4501-JGK 22.10.07 OO-ZDL, D-6707	R Cassidy and W Stephen	Milfield	20. 4.08
G-CJGL	Schempp-Hirth Discus CS	148CS	BGA4502-JGL 14. 1.08 RAFGSA R27	J G Arnold tr RAF Gliding and Soaring Association (Operated Chilterns Gliding Centre) RAF Halton		28. 9.08
G-CJGM	Schempp-Hirth Discus CS	036CS	BGA4503-JGM 27. 2.08 RAFGSA R53	J G Arnold tr RAF Gliding and Soaring Association (Operated Fulmar Gliding Club)	Easterton	6. 5.08
G-CJGN	Schempp-Hirth Standard Cirrus	554	BGA4504-JCN 29. 1.08 D-8674	P A Shuttleworth	Long Mynd	21. 5.08
G-CJGR	Schempp-Hirth Discus bT	10/275	BGA4507-JGR 3. 1.08 D-KGPS, D-5461	D A Sinclair	Lasham	19. 3.08
G-CJGS	Rolladen-Schneider LS8-18	8180	BGA4508-JGS 16.10.07	M D Allan "L2"	Shobdon	28. 9.08
G-CJGU	Schempp-Hirth Mini Numbus B	69	BGA4510-JGU 6. 8.08 HB-1427	N D Ashton	Darlton	
G-CJGW	Schleicher ASK 13	13146	BGA4512-JGW 11. 1.08 D-0169	Darlton Gliding Club Ltd	Darlton	3. 2.08
G-CJGX	Schleicher K 8B	753	BGA4513-JGX 25. 3.08 D-1878	D Smith tr Andreas K8 Group	Andreas, Isle of Man	
G-CJGY	Schempp-Hirth Standard Cirrus	333	BGA4514-JGY 14. 4.08 SE-TMU	P J Shout "C3"	Husbands Bosworth	
G-CJGZ	Glasflügel H201B Standard Libelle	193	BGA4515-JGZ 9 .1.09	C J Davison	Saltby	
G-CJHD	Schleicher Ka 6E	4307	BGA4519-JHD 30. 8.07 OY-XGS, D-0272	M A King	Lyveden	25. 3.08
G-CJHG	Grob G102 Astir CS	1084	BGA4522-JHG 2. 9.08 D-6984	P L E Zelazowski	Shenington	
G-CJHJ	Glasflügel H201B Standard Libelle	495	BGA4524-JHJ 18.10.07 HB-1187	M E Hahnefeld tr G-CJHU Group	Parham Park	9. 2.08
G-CJHK	Schleicher K 8B	558	BGA4525-JHK 3.10.07 AGA 21, (BGA4319-HYV), RAFGGA 558	Stratford on Avon Gliding Club Ltd	Snitterfield	12. 4.08
G-CJHL	Schleicher Ka 6E	4073	BGA4526-JHL 20. 2.08 SE-TFB	J R Gilbert and M R Doran	Wormingford	4. 4.08
G-CJHM	Schempp-Hirth Discus b	373	BGA4527-JHM 5. 2.08 OO-ZGZ	J C Thwaites	Sutton Bank	13. 3.08
G-CJHN	Grob G102 Astir CS Jeans	2110	BGA4528-JHN 20. 5.08 D-7638	A M Percival and J C Hume	Kingston Deverill	
G-CJHO	Schleicher ASK 18	18021	BGA4530-JHQ 23. 1.08 RAFGSA R43, RAFGSA 713, RAFGSA 113	J G Arnold tr RAF Gliding and Soaring Association (Operated Wrekin Gliding Club) RAF Cosford		5. 3.08
G-CJHP	Flight Design CTSW (Assembled P&M Aviation Ltd with c/n 8327)	07.08.06	2.11.07	J Prentice	Perth	11.11.09P
G-CJHR	Centrair SNC-34C Alliance	34026	BGA4531-JHR 25. 2.08	The Borders (Milfield) Gliding Club Ltd	Milfield	21. 6.08
G-CJHS	Scheicher ASW 19B	19047	BGA4532-JHS 9. 7.08 D-6716	B Crow tr JHS Syndicate	Usk	
G-CJHU	Rolladen-Schneider LS8-18	8197	BGA4534-JHU 23. 4.08	S P Hall	Pocklington	
G-CJHW	Glaser-Dirks DG-200	2-19	BGA4536-JHW 27.10.08 HB-1400	A W Thornhill and S Webster "JHW"	Burn	
G-CJHX	Bölkow Phoebus C	930	BGA4537-JHX 12. 3.08 OO-ZYN, F-CDON	J Hewitt	Shipdham	
G-CJHY	Rolladen-Schneider LS8-18	8181	BGA4538-JHY 21. 9.07 D-9988	L E N Tanner and N Wall	Nympsfield	10. 2.08
G-CJHZ	Schleicher ASW 20	20313	BGA4539-JHZ 6. 9.07 D-6532	T J Stanley	Sutton Bank	28. 9.08
G-CJJB	Rolladen-Schneider LS4	4542	BGA4541-JJB 9. 1.08 D-2397	M Tomlinson "615"	Talgarth	3. 4.08
G-CJJD	Schempp-Hirth Discus bT	5/262	BGA4543-JJD 12. 3.08	P D Turner and D Wilson	Burn	
G-CJJE	Schempp-Hirth Discus a	379	BGA4544-JJE 12. 8.08 OE-5530, VH-XQT	A Soffici "JO1"	Firenze, Italy	
G-CJJF	Schleicher ASW 27	27086	BGA4545-JJF 12.10.07	G F Read "JJF"	Wycombe Air Park	28. 9.08
G-CJJH	DG Flugzeugbau DG-800S	8-137S30	BGA4547-JJH 29. 1.08	W R Brown "899"	Husbands Bosworth	15. 5.08
G-CJJJ	Schempp-Hirth Standard Cirrus	284	BGA4548-JJJ 21. 9.07 D-2946	F R and R G Stevens (Also carries "2946") Husbands Bosworth		28. 9.08
G-CJJK	Rolladen-Schneider LS 8-18	8199	BGA4549-JJK 26.11.07	J White	Dunstable	28. 9.08
G-CJJL	Schleicher ASW 19B	19302	BGA4550-JJL 3. 3.08 D-4227	M Bacic tr G-CJJL Group	Bicester	
G-CJJP	Schempp-Hirth Duo Discus	180	BGA4553-JJP 25. 9.07	N Clements "494"	Long Mynd	28. 9.08
G-CJJR	Schleicher ASK 21	21054	BGA4555-JJR 8.10.07 RAFGSA R73, RAFGGA 513	J G Arnold tr RAF Gliding and Soaring Association "R73" (Operated Chilterns Gliding Centre) RAF Halton		9.11.07
G-CJJT	Schleicher ASW 27	27070	BGA4557-JJT 6. 2.08 D-6209	T World tr Portsmouth Naval Gliding Centre "933" Lee-on-Solent		5. 5.08

G-CJJX	Schleicher ASW 15B	15323	BGA4561-JJX D-2312	31.10.07	M D Brooks	Saltby	26. 3.08
G-CJJZ	Schempp-Hirth Discus bT	156/556	BGA4563-JJZ OO-ZQX	27. 9.07	S J C Parker *"15"*	Nympsfield	28. 9.08
G-CJKA	Schleicher ASK 21	21059	BGA4564-JKA D-8835	18. 1.08	East Sussex Gliding Club Ltd	Ringmer	14. 6.08
G-CJKB	PZL-Swidnik PW-5 Smyk	17.10.008	BGA4565-JKB	25. 3.08	J C Gibson	Chipping	
G-CJKD	Rolladen-Schneider LS8-18	8215	BGA4567-JKD	14.11.07	D Abbey and G Glover *"P1"*	Husbands Bosworth	29. 4.08
C-GJKE	PZL-Swidnik PW-5 Smyk	17.11.025	BGA4568-JKE	30. 5.08	The Burn Gliding Club Ltd	Burn	
G-CJKF	Glaser-Dirks DG-200	2-35	BGA4569-JKF D-6069	2. 4.08	J M Barrett and R L Wakem	North Hill	
G-CJKG	Schleicher ASK 18	18036	BGA4570-JKG RAFGSA R48, RAFGSA 448	17.10.07	J G Arnold tr RAF Gliding and Soaring Association *(Operated Chilterns Gliding Centre)* RAF Halton		10.12.07
G-CJKJ	Schleicher ASK 21	21679	BGA4572-JKJ (RAFGSA R21)	17.10.07	J G Arnold tr RAF Gliding and Soaring Association *"R 21"* *(Operated Chilterns Gliding Centre)* RAF Halton		7. 1.08
G-CJKK	Schleicher ASK 21	21182	BGA4573-JKK AGA 11	1. 5.08	P Fanning tr Army Gliding Association *"A7"* *(Operated Anglia Gliding Club)* AAC Wattisham		
G-CJKM	Glaser-Dirks DG-200/17	2-148/1746	BGA4575-JKM D-4155	8. 1.08	E W Russell *"Z10"*	Portmoak	28. 9.08
G-CJKN	Rolladen-Schneider LS8-18	8214	BGA4576-JKN	2.11.07	D A Booth *"790"*	Husbands Bosworth	28. 9.08
G-CJKO	Schleicher ASK 21	21098	BGA4578-JKQ RAFGSA R20	18. 1.08	J G Arnold tr RAF Gliding and Soaring Association *"R20"* RAF Wittering *(Operated Four Counties Gliding Club)*		20. 7.07
G-CJKP	Rolladen-Schneider LS4-b	41000	BGA4577-JKP PH-1089	17.10.07	D M Hope	Wycombe Air Park	18. 2.08
G-CJKR	Schempp-Hirth Discus b	151	BGA4579-JKR	21.12.07	T Wright	Husbands Bosworth	4. 3.08
G-CJKS	Schleicher ASW 19B	19362	BGA4580-JKS D-1273	18. 1.08	R J P Lancaster and P D F Adshead	Dunstable	19. 6.08
G-CJKT	Schleicher ASK 13	13615	BGA4581-JKT RAFGSA R7	4. 4.08	J G Arnold tr RAF Gliding and Soaring Association *(Operated Cleveland Gliding Club)* AAC Dishforth		
G-CJKU	Schleicher ASK 18	18022	BGA4582-JKU, RAFGSA R33, RAFGSA 223	19.12.07	J G Arnold tr RAF Gliding and Soaring Association *(Operated Cleveland Gliding Club)* AAC Dishforth		28. 9.08
G-CJKV	Grob G103A Twin II Acro	34042-K-273	BGA4583-JKV RAFGSA R52	11.12.07	The Welland Gliding Club Ltd	Lyveden	13. 6.08
G-CJKW	Grob G102 Astir CS77	1666	BGA4584-JKW RAFGSA R60, RAFGSA 560	22.12.07	The Bath, Wilts and North Dorset Gliding Club Ltd Kingston Deverill		24. 6.08
G-CJKX	Schempp-Hirth Discus b	247	BGA4585-JKX RAFGSA R17	10. 7.07	A R Armstrong	RAF Keevil	13. 4.08
G-CJKY	Schempp-Hirth Ventus cT	181/597	BGA4586-JKY RAFGSA R24, RAFGGA 557	29.10.07	M P Osborn and G V Matthews	RAF Cosford	13. 1.08
G-CJKZ	Schleicher ASK 21	21123	BGA4587-JKZ RAFGSA R25	17.10.07	J G Arnold tr RAF Gliding and Soaring Association *"R 25"* *(Operated Chilterns Gliding Centre)* RAF Halton		19. 2.08
G-CJLA	Schempp-Hirth Ventus 2cT	26/94	BGA4588-JLA PH-1129	28. 2.08	E C and P M Neighbour	Camphill	19. 9.08
G-CJLC	Schempp-Hirth Discus CS	193CS	BGA4590-JLC RAFGSA R10	5. 2.08	J G Arnold tr RAF Gliding and Soaring Association *"R10"* RAF Syerston		25. 3.08
G-CJLG	PZL-Bielsko SZD-51-1 Junior	B-1933	BGA4594-JLG AGA 5, (BGA3699-GBH)	18. 2.08	J W Sage tr Army Gliding Association *"JLG"* Trenchard Lines, Upavon *(Operated Wyvern Gliding Club)*		17. 2.08
G-CJLH	Rolladen-Schneider LS4	4256	BGA4595-JLH AGA 1	1.11.07	C A Sorace tr JLH Syndicate *"JLH"*	Dunstable	19. 4.08
G-CJLJ	Rolladen-Schneider LS4-B	4997	BGA4596-JLJ AGA 2	29. 1.08	J W Sage tr Army Gliding Association *"A8"* Trenchard Lines, Upavon *(Operated Wyvern Gliding Club)*		9. 5.08
G-CJLK	Rolladen-Schneider LS7	7112	BGA4597-JLK AGA 3	9. 1.08	D N Munro and S G Hamilton	Rougham	5. 5.08
G-CJLL	Robinson R44 Raven II	11588		29. 1.07	AT and P Rentals Ltd	Durham Tees Valley	27. 2.09E
G-CJLN	Rolladen-Schneider LS8-18	8169	BGA4600-JLN RAFGSA R4	25.10.07	J G Arnold tr RAF Gliding and Soaring Association *"R4"* RAF Syerston		28. 9.08
G-CJLO	Schleicher ASK 13	13608	BGA4602-JLQ RAFGSA R40, RAFGSA R4	20. 9.07	Bowland Forest Gliding Club Ltd	Chipping	28. 9.08
G-CJLP	Schempp-Hirth Discus CS	034CS	BGA4601-JLP RAFGSA R39	1. 2.08	J G Arnold tr RAF Gliding and Soaring Association *(Operated Cranwell Gliding Club)* RAF Cranwell		7. 2.08
G-CJLR	Grob G102 Astir CS	1509	BGA4603-JLR RAFGSA R57, RAFGSA 507	17.12.07	J G Arnold tr RAF Gliding and Soaring Association *(Operated Cranwell Gliding Club)* RAF Cranwell		28. 9.08
G-CJLS	Schleicher K 8B	8950	BGA4604-JLS RAFGSA R75, RAFGSA 285	9. 1.08	J G Arnold tr RAF Gliding and Soaring Association *"R75"* *(Operated Crusaders Gliding Club)* Kingsfield, Dhekelia, Cyprus		1.12.07
G-CJLV	Schleicher Ka 6E	4192	BGA4607-JLV OY-XEU, D-4424	4. 8.08	J C and J M Cooper	Lyveden	
G-CJLW	Schempp-Hirth Discus CS	033CS	BGA4608-JLW RAFGSA R87	11. 2.08	J G Arnold tr RAF Gliding and Soaring Association *(Operated Wrekin Gliding Club)* RAF Cosford		17. 3.08
G-CJLY	Schleicher ASW 27	27111	BGA4610-JLY	26.11.07	L M Astle and P C Piggott	Husbands Bosworth	16. 5.08
G-CJLZ	Grob G103A Twin II Acro	3633-K-15	BGA4611-JLZ D-7912	2.11.07	A C Arthurs tr 21 Syndicate *"21"*	Lasham	28. 3.08
G-CJMA	Schleciher ASK 18	18038	BGA4612-JMA RAFGSA R36, RAFGSA 236	20. 8.8	J G Arnold tr RAF Gliding and Soaring Association *"R36"* RAF Wittering *(Operated Four Counties Gliding Club)*		
G-CJMB	Bombardier CL-600-2B19 *(CL-600 Regional Jet)*	8055	N850RJ	21. 8.07	Corporate Jet Management Ltd	Farnborough	23. 8.09E
G-CJMD	Embraer EMB-135BJ Legacy	14500994	P4-SAO PT-SKN	2.11.07	Corporate Jet Management Ltd	Farnborough	4.11.09E
G-CJMG	PZL-Bielsko SZD-51-1 Junior	B-2192	BGA4618-JMG	8. 4.08	Kent Gliding Club Ltd	Challock	

G-CJMH	Schempp-Hirth Standard Cirrus	571	BGA4619-JMH 19. 2.08 HB-1263	J G Walker	Pocklington 28. 4.08
G-CJMJ	Schleicher ASK 13	13616	BGA4620-JMJ 25. 9.08 RAFGSA R46, RAFGSA R16 *(Operated Fenland Gliding Club)*	J G Arnold tr RAF Gliding and Soaring Association RAF Marham	
G-CJMK	Schleicher ASK 18	18023	BGA4621-JMK 9. 1.08 RAFGSA R49, RAFGSA 318 *(Operated Crusaders Gliding Club)*	J G Arnold tr RAF Gliding and Soaring Association *"R49"* Kingsfield, Dhekelia, Cyprus	2. 8.07
G-CJML	Grob G102 Astir CS77	1718	BGA4622-JML 17. 9.08 RAFGSA R63, RAFGSA 883	J G Arnold tr RAF Gliding and Soaring Association RAF Odiham	
G-CJMN	Schempp-Hirth Nimbus 2	38	BGA4624-JMN 26. 9.07 D-1129, HB-1159	R.A.Holroyd	Pocklington 28. 9.08
G-CJMO	Rolladen-Schneider LS8-18	8225	BGA4625-JMO 12.11.07	D J Langrick *"781"*	Husbands Bosworth 20. 4.08
G-CJMP	Schleicher ASK 13	13436	BGA4626-JMP 18. 1.08 D-2984	East Sussex Gliding Club Ltd	Ringmer 11. 3.08
G-CJMR	Rolladen-Schneider LS8-18	8198	BGA4628-JMR 5. 3.08 D-0280	J N Rebbeck	Dunstable
G-CJMS	Schleicher ASK 21	21212	BGA4629-JMS 9. 7.08 RAFGSA 521	J G Arnold tr RAF Gliding and Soaring Association *"R23"* RAF Odiham	
G-CJMT	Rolladen-Schneider LS8-18	8223	BGA4630-JMT 1.11.07	D P and K M Draper *"301"*	Lasham 28. 9.08
G-CJMU	Rolladen-Schneider LS8-18	8246	BGA4631-JMU 15. 1.08	J G Guy	Portmoak 27. 2.08
G-CJMV	Schempp-Hirth Nimbus 2C	179	BGA4632-JMV 4. 1.08 D-6738	G Tucker	Lee-on-Solent 10. 3.08
G-CJMW	Schleicher ASK 13	13688AB	BGA4633-JMW 11.10.07 RAFGSA R61, RAFGGA 567	J G Arnold tr RAF Gliding and Soaring Association *"R61"* *(Operated Bannerdown Gliding Club)* RAF Keevil	11. 4.08
G-CJMX	Schleicher ASK 13	13107	BGA4634-JMX 5. 3.08 RAFGSA R86, RAFGSA 386	Shalbourne Soaring Club ltd	Rivar Hill
G-CJMY	PZL-Bielsko SZD-51-1 Junior	W-959	BGA4635-JMY 11. 2.08 OO-ZRH	Highland Gliding Club Ltd	Easterton 27. 8.08
G-CJMZ	Schleicher ASK 13	13099	BGA4636-JMZ 9. 1.08 RAFGSA R37, RAFGGA 378 *(Operated Crusaders Gliding Club))*	J G Arnold tr RAF Gliding and Soaring Association *"R37"* Kingsfield, Dhekelia,Cyprus	27. 4.08
G-CJNA	Grob G102 Astir CS Jeans	2160	BGA4637-JNA 11. 6.08 D-4556	Shenington Gliding Club	Shenington
G-CJNB	Rolladen-Schneider LS8-18	8227	BGA4638-JNB 10. 4.08	Tatenhill Aviation Ltd *"D1"*	Tatenhill
G-CJNE	Schempp-Hirth Discus 2a	18	BGA4641-JNE 4.12.07 D-4499	R Priest	Wycombe Air Park 19. 4.08
G-CJNF	Schempp-Hirth Discus 2a	12	BGA4642-JNF 17. 3.08	H Hay	Eyres Field
G-CJNG	Glasflügel H201B Standard Libelle	006	BGA4643-JNG 1.10.07 SE-TFU	C A Willson	Rivar Hill 17. 8.08
G-CJNJ	Rolladen-Schneider LS8-18	8226	BGA4645-JNJ 12.11.07	A B Laws	Crowland 15. 3.08
G-CJNK	Rolladen-Schneider LS8-18	8244	BGA4646-JNK 24. 4.08	J W Sage tr Army Gliding Association *"676"* Trenchard Lines, Upavon	
G-CJNM	Rolladen-Schneider LS8-18	8232	BGA4648-JNM 23. 4.08	M H Patel and P Onn *"P4"*	Dunstable
G-CJNN	Schleicher K 8B	8744	BGA4649-JNN 23. 1.08 D-8583	Buckminster Gliding Club Ltd	Saltby 3. 6.08
G-CJNO	DG Flugzeugbau DG-300 Elan	3E341	BGA4651-JNQ 15. 1.08 SE-UHO	R Friend	Husbands Bosworth 24. 4.08
G-CJNP	Rolladen-Schneider LS6-b	6109	BGA4650-JNP 31.10.07 D-5853	P.S.Fink	Lasham 21. 4.08
G-CJNR	Glasflügel H303 Mosquito B	159	BGA4652-JNR 12.11.07 D-5908	B R Smith and I H Agutter	Wormingford 2. 3.08
G-CJNT	Schleicher ASW 19B	19371	BGA4654-JNT 20.12.07 D-2233	M D Borrowdale	Lasham 18. 3.08
G-CJNX	LET L-13 Blanik	827408	BGA4658-JNX 27.11.07 OK-2712	Vectis Gliding Club Ltd	Bembridge 28. 9.08
G-CJNZ	Glaser-Dirks DG-100	70	BGA4660-JNZ 13. 2.08 (D-7324), HB-1324	R Jones and T Tordoff	Rufforth 4. 8.08
G-CJOA	Schempp-Hirth Discus b	265	BGA4685-JQA 4.10.07 BGA 4535, RAFGGA 547, RAFGGA 500	J G Arnold tr RAF Gliding and Soaring Association *(Operated Bannerdown Gliding Club)* RAF Keevil	28. 9.08
G-CJOB	Schleicher K 8B	8880	BGA4686-JQB 6. 3.08 RAFGSA R98, RAFGSA 398	T R Edwards tr JQB Syndicate	Shenington
G-CJOC	Schempp-Hirth Discus bT	127/488	BGA4687-JQC 16.11.07 D-KITT	D Cooper tr 287 Syndicate	Wycombe Air Park 2. 4.09
G-CJOD	Rolladen-Schneider LS8-18	8224	BGA4688-JQD 20. 9.07	J G Arnold tr RAF Gliding and Soaring Association *(Operated Bannerdown Gliding Club)* RAF Keevil	28. 9.08
G-CJOE	Schempp-Hirth Standard Cirrus	25	BGA4689-JQE 7. 3.08 OO-ZRS, D-0483	P T Johnson	Wormingford
G-CJOG	Grob G103A Twin II Acro	33964-K-197	BGA4691-JQG 19.12.07 RAFGSA R50	R G J Tait tr Acro Syndicate	Easterton 25. 5.08
G-CJOH	AB Sportine LAK-12 Lieyuva	6188	BGA4692-JQH 1. 5.08	J and D Lee	Pocklington
G-CJOJ	Schleicher K 8B	8795	BGA4693-JQJ 15. 1.08 RAFGSA R47, BGA1564	P W Burgess	Seighford 27. 5.08
G-CJON	Grob G102 Astir CS 77	1634	BGA4697-JQN 18. 8.08 RAFGSA R67, RAFGSA 547	J G Arnold tr RAF Gliding and Soaring Association *"R67"* Easterton	
G-CJOO	Schempp-Hirth Duo Discus	227	BGA4699-JQQ 24. 1.08	K G Reid tr 185 Syndicate	Rivar Hill 10. 3.08
G-CJOP	Centrair 101A Pegase	101066	BGA4698-JOP 31. 3.08 F-CFQY	R H Moss, A Moss and R Garang	Nympsfield
G-CJOR	Schempp-Hirth Ventus 2cT	49/152	BGA4700-JQR 17. 9.07	A M George and N A MacLean	Lasham 28. 9.08
G-CJOS	Schempp-Hirth Standard Cirrus	251G	BGA4701-JOS 20. 2.08 D-1147	R K Arkley tr G-CJOS Group	Milfield 7. 7.08
G-CJOU	AB Sportine Aviacija LAK-17A	102	BGA4703-JQU 5.10.07	B Dorozko	Osowice, Poland 18. 1.08
G-CJOV	Schleicher ASW 27	27112	BGA4704-JQV 23. 9.08	J W White	Wycombe Air Park

Reg	Type	C/N	BGA & prev id	Date	Owner/Operator	Location	Date
G-CJOW	Schempp-Hirth Cirrus (Type amended 27.11.08)	47	BGA4705-JQW D-0186	1. 2.08	North Wales Gliding Club Ltd	Llantysilio	19. 1.08
G-CJOX	Schleicher ASK 21	21702	BGA4706-JQX	11. 9.07	Southdown Gliding Club Ltd	Parham Park	28. 9.08
G-CJOZ	Schleicher K 8B	8854	BGA4708-JQZ RAFGSA R42, RAFGSA 323	1. 5.08	Derbyshire and Lancashire Gliding Club Ltd	Camphill	
G-CJPA	Schempp-Hirth Duo Discus	201	BGA4661-JPA	3.10.07	Coventry Gliding Club Ltd tr The Gliding Centre *"HB1"*	Husbands Bosworth	20. 3.08
G-CJPC	Schleicher ASK 13	13256	BGA4663-JPC RAFGSA R51	13. 6.08	Shalbourne Soaring Society Ltd	Rivar Hill	
G-CJPF	Glaser- Dirks DG-100	22	BGA4666-JPF D-3735	17. 4.08	D C W Sanders	Parham Park	
G-CJPH	Rolladen-Schneider LS8-18	8259	BGA4668-JPH	31.10.07	J P Ben-David	Lasham	6. 4.08
G-CJPJ	Grob G104 Speed Astir IIB	4089	BGA4669-JPJ OE-5352	2. 5.08	R J L Maisonpierre	Rougham	
G-CJPL	Rolladen-Schneider LS8-18	8249	BGA4671-JPL D-2562	12.10.07	I A Reekie	Dunstable	8. 3.08
G-CJPM	Grob G102 Astir CS Jeans	2209	BGA4672-JPM D-3825	1. 4.08	J Thorpe tr The Four Aces	Camphill	
G-CJPO	Schleicher ASK 18	18002	BGA4675-JPQ RAFGSA R32, RAFGSA 213, D-3978	5.10.07	J G Arnold tr RAF Gliding and Soaring Association *"32"* (Operated Bannerdown Gliding Club)	RAF Keevil	16. 3.08
G-CJPP	Schempp-Hirth Discus b	206	BGA4674-JPP AGA 4	23. 8.07	Scottish Gliding Union Ltd	Portmoak	28. 9.08
G-CJPR	Rolladen-Schneider LS 8-18	8245	BGA4676-JPR	28.11.07	D M Byass and J A McCoshim *"161"*	Wycombe Air Park	5. 4.08
G-CJPS	Schleicher ASW 27	27108	BGA4677-JPS	23.11.07	E W and P T Healy *"CL"*	Lasham	22. 1.08
G-CJPT	Schleicher ASW 27	27113	BGA4678-JPT	20. 2.08	R C Willis-Fleming	North Hill	16. 4.08
G-CJPV	Schleicher ASK 13	13312	BGA4680-JPV RAFGSA R88, RAFGSA 186	9. 1.08	J G Arnold tr RAF Gliding and Soaring Association *"R88"* (Operated Crusaders Gliding Club)	Kingsfield, Dhekelia, Cyprus	5. 6.08
G-CJPW	Glaser-Dirks DG-200	2-48	BGA4681-JPW D-2201	18. 8.08	J R Parr	Bun	
G-CJPX	Schleicher ASW 15	15160	BGA4682-JPX D-0823	21. 1.08	P Daly and R Hayden	Upwood	14. 4.08
G-CJPY	Schleicher ASK 13	13653AB	BGA4683-JPY RAFGGA 509	22.12.07	J G Arnold tr RAF Gliding and Soaring Association (Operated Cranwell Gliding Club)	RAF Cranwell	5. 1.08
G-CJPZ	Schleicher ASK 18	18027	BGA4684-JPZ RAFGSA R65, RAFGGA 563	17.12.07	J G Arnold tr RAF Gliding and Soaring Association (Operated Cranwell Gliding Club)	RAF Cranwell	19. 1.08
G-CJRA	Rolladen-Schneider LS8-18	8263	BGA4709-JRA	30.10.07	J Williams *"253"*	Kirton-in-Lindsey	28. 9.08
G-CJRB	Schleicher ASW 19B	19227	BGA4710-JRB D-2713	5. 2.08	J W Baxter tr S33 Syndicate *"S33"*	Long Mynd	12. 3.07
G-CJRC	DG Flugzeugbau DG-300 Elan	3E20	BGA4711-JRC HB-1718	18. 1.08	P.J.Sillett	Tibenham	3.11.07
G-CJRD	Grob G102 Astir CS	1487	BGA4712-JRD RAFGSA R18, RAFGSA 540, D-4791	28. 8.08	A J Hadwin and S J Kape	(Reading)	
G-CJRE	Schleicher ASW 15	15048	BGA4713-JRE LN-GGL, D-391, OH-RWA	5. 9.07	R A Starling *"RS"*	Darlton	28. 9.08
G-CJRF	PZL-Bielsko SZD-50-3 Puchacz	B-1395	BGA4714-JRF OO-ZTX, D-8213, SP-3285	10.10.07	Wolds Gliding Club Ltd	Pocklington	11. 8.08
G-CJRG	Schempp-Hirth HS.4 Standard Cirrus	146	BGA4715-JRG D-0297	5.11.07	D P and K M Draper	Lasham	28. 9.08
G-CJRH	Schleicher ASW 27	27118	BGA4716-JRH	23. 8.07	C Jackson and P C Jarvis	Lasham	28. 9.08
G-CJRJ	PZL-Bielsko SZD-50-3 Puchacz	503199327	BGA4717-JRJ	11. 2.08	Bidford Gliding Ltd	Bidford	18. 7.08
G-CJRL	Glaser-Dirks DG-101G Elan	E185G151	BGA4719-JRL D-1246	29.10.07	P Lazenby	Aston Down	20. 2.08
G-CJRR	Schempp-Hirth Discus bT	50/367	BGA4724-JRR PH-1087, D-KBHM	15.10.07	J P Walker and M W Cater *"LA"*	Husbands Bosworth	17. 5.08
G-CJRT	Schempp-Hirth Standard Cirrus	99	BGA4726-JRT D-0734	29. 8.07	J A Tipler tr JRT Syndicate	Husbands Bosworth	28. 9.08
G-CJRU	Schleicher ASW 24	24168	BGA4727-JRU D-7085	2.11.07	S A Kerby	Snitterfield	28. 9.08
G-CJRV	Schleciher ASW 19B	19233	BGA4728-JRV D-2644	26. 6.08	M Roome	Lasham	
G-CJRX	Schleicher ASK 13	13375	BGA4730-JRX RAFGSA R41, RAFGSA 241	28. 4.08	J G Arnold tr RAF Gliding and Soaring Association (Operated Chilterns Gliding Centre)	RAF Halton	
G-CJSD	Grob G102 Astir CS	1133	BGA4736-JSD RAFGSA R77, D-4177	24. 1.08	J G Arnold tr RAF Gliding and Soaring Association (Operated Fenland Gliding Club)	RAF Marham	16. 2.08
G-CJSE	Schempp-Hirth Discus b	365	BGA4737-JSE PH-918	14. 2.08	Imperial College of Science, Technology and Medicine	Lasham	9. 3.08
G-CJSG	Schleicher Ka 6E	4248	BGA4739-JSG D-0090	4.10.07	A J Emck	Lasham	17. 1.07
G-CJSH	Grob G102 Club Astir IIIB	5504CB	BGA4740-JSH D-6470	13. 5.08	North Downs Gliding Trust Ltd *"SH9"*	Lasham	
G-CJSJ	Rolladen-Schneider LS7-WL	7058	BGA4741-JSJ D-5774	6.11.07	S P Woolcock *"7X"*	Gransden Lodge	24. 2.08
G-CJSK	Grob G102 Astir CS	1521	BGA4742-JSK D-7455	22.12.07	J D Hanton and P T Pearce	Brent Tor	28. 9.08
G-CJSL	Schempp-Hirth Ventus cT	121/395	BGA4743-JSL D-KIFL	7.11.07	D Latimer	Sutton Bank	30.12.07
G-CJSN	Schleicher K 8B	8916	BGA4745-JSN RAFGSA R45, RAFGSA 245	6. 6.08	Cotswold Gliding Club	Aston Down	
G-CJSS	Schleicher ASW 27	27121	BGA4749-JSS	4. 2.08	G K and S R Drury	Challock	28. 2.08

G-CJST	Rolladen-Schneider LS1-c	86	BGA4750-JST	7. 1.08	M W Hands	Saltby	5. 4.08
			OO-ZPA, D-0766				
G-CJSU	Rolladen-Schneider LS8-18	8297	BGA4751-JSU	22. 1.08	J G Bell	Parham Park	17. 1.08
			D-0543				
G-CJSV	Schleicher ASK 13	13127	BGA4752-JSV	26. 9.08	RAF Gliding and Soaring Association	RAF Odiham	
			RAFGSA R80, BGA1509-CFN				
G-CJSW	Rolladen-Schneider LS4-a	4262	BGA4753-JSW	22.11.07	B T Spreckley *(Operated European Soaring Club)*		
			ZS-GOP			Ontur, Spain	28. 9.08
G-CJSX	AMS-Flight DG-500 Elan Orion	5E200X44	BGA4754-JSX	10. 6.08	Oxford Gliding Co Ltd RAF Weston-on-the-Green		
G-CJSZ	Schleicher ASK 18	18012	BGA4756-JSZ	27. 2.08	C J N Weston	Challock	1. 5.08
			D-6878				
G-CJTB	Schleicher ASW 24	24017	BGA4758-JTB	2.10.07	M E Knell tr V17 Syndicate *"V17"*	RAF Keevil	28. 9.08
			D-3465				
G-CJTF	Schleicher ASW 27	27125	BGA4762-JTF	4. 3.08	T J Scott *"Z3"*	Wycombe Air Park	
G-CJTH	Schleicher ASW 24	24218	BGA4764-JTH	13. 2.08	R J and J E Lodge	Dunstable	9. 4.08
			D-7681				
G-CJTJ	Schempp-Hirth Mini-Nimbus B	73	BGA4765-JTJ	15. 1.08	A Richards	(Gweek, Helston)	6. 4.08
			D-7620				
G-CJTK	DG Flugzeugbau DG-303 Elan Acro		BGA4766-JTK	22. 1.08	A Jorgensen	Wycombe Air Park	6. 3.08
		3E487A28					
G-CJTL	Rolladen-Schneider LS8-18	8317	BGA4766-JTL	24. 4.08	L S, J M and R S Hood *"352"*	Lasham	
G-CJTM	Rolladen-Schneider LS8-18	8268	BGA4768-JTM	7. 1.08	A D Holmes *"418"*	Nympsfield	26. 2.08
G-CJTN	DG Flugzeugbau DG-300 Elan	3E19	BGA4769-JTN	11. 1.08	I P McKavney *"E5"*	Nympsfield	24. 2.08
			HB-1717				
G-CJTO	Glasflügel H303A Mosquito	88	BGA4771-JTQ	17. 1.08	I Hamilton tr Tango Oscar Group	Chipping	20. 4.08
			OO-ZYL				
G-CJTP	Schleicher ASW 20L	20569	BGA4770-JTP	12. 2.08	C A Sheldon	Pocklington	4. 5.08
			D-4688				
G-CJTR	Rolladen-Schneider LS7-WL	7104	BGA4772-JTR	8.11.07	G W L Howarth tr D53 Syndicate *"D53"*		
			D-5309			RAF Halton	14. 1.08
G-CJTS	Schempp-Hirth Cirrus VTC	108	BGA4773-JTS	4. 9.08	S and P Skinner	Kenley	
			S5-3059, SL-3059, YU-4200				
G-CJTU	Schempp-Hirth Duo Discus T	4/234	BGA4775-JTU	28 .2.08	M J Philpott tr G-CJTU Syndicate	(Ruislip)	30. 3.08
G-CJTW	Glasflügel Mosquito B	199	BGA4777-JTW	28. 7.08	M Wright *"AV8"*	Tibenham	
			F-CELX				
G-CJTY	Rolladen-Schneider LS 8a	8102	BGA4779-JTY	30.11.07	R E Neal tr BBC (London) Club	Wycombe Air Park	28. 9.08
			SE-USA				
G-CJUB	Schempp-Hirth Discus CS	268CS	BGA4782-JUB	1. 8.08	Coventry Gliding Club Ltd t/a The Gliding Centre *"894"*		
						Husbands Bosworth	
G-CJUD	Denney Kitfox Model 3	847		17. 1.91	P J and B-J Chandler	(Bristol)	13.11.08P
	(Built C W Judge - pr.no.PFA 172-11939)						
G-CJUE	Rolladen-Schneider LS8-18	8295	BGA4785-JUE	30. 8.07	G Goudie and S Waterfall *"X15"*	Gransden Lodge	28. 9.08
G-CJUF	Schempp-Hirth Ventus 2cT	53/174	BGA4786-JUF	4. 2.09	M H B Pope	Bidford	
G-CJUG	Issoire E78B Silene	09	BGA4787-JUG	11. 6.08	J M Sanders	Ringmer	
			F-CFED				
G-CJUH	Schleicher ASW 27	27129	BGA4788-JUH	30. 4.08	R A Johnson *"J1"*	Husbands Bosworth	
G-CJUJ	Schleicher ASW 27	27127	BGA4789-JUJ	17. 9.08	P M Wells	Wycombe Air Park	
G-CJUK	Grob G102 Astir CS	1430	BGA4790-JUK	18. 3.08	P Freer and S J Calvert	Wycombe Air Park	
			PH-552				
G-CJUM	Schempp-Hirth Duo Discus T	243	BGA4792-JUM	10.10.07	B A Bateson tr 2 UP Group *"2UP"*	Parham Park	25. 3.08
G-CJUN	Schleicher ASW 19B	19096	BGA4793-JUN	21. 7.08	M P S Roberts *"M19"*	Gransden Lodge	
			D-3844				
G-CJUP	Schempp-Hirth Discus-2b	60	BGA4794-JUP	6. 2.08	N Parkin and O Ward *"183"*	Aston Down	29. 3.08
G-CJUR	Valentin Mistral C	MC042/81	BGA4796-JUR	12. 5.08	Essex Gliding Club Ltd	Ridgewell	
			HB-1596				
G-CJUS	Grob G102 Astir CS	1403	BGA4797-JUS	18. 1.08	East Sussex Gliding Club Ltd	Ringmer	25. 5.08
			(BGA4774), D-4269				
G-CJUU	Schempp-Hirth Standard Cirrus	450	BGA4799-JUU	1.12.07	H R Fraser	Milfield	14. 5.08
			PH-500				
G-CJUV	Schempp-Hirth Discus b	551	BGA4800-JUV	22. 1.08	North Downs Gliding Trust Ltd *"SH2"*	Lasham	29. 3.08
			D-8257				
G-CJUW	Schleicher ASW 19B	19074	BGA4801-JUW	15. 5.08	B Worley tr G-CJUW Group	RAF Keevil	
			D-4476				
G-CJUX	Aviastroitel AC-4C	051	BGA4802-JUX	10.12.08	R J Walton	Saltby	
G-CJUZ	Schleicher ASW 19B	19146	BGA4804-JUZ	6. 9.07	D Heaton	Seighford	28. 9.08
			D-7932				
G-CJVA	Schempp-Hirth Ventus 2cT	66/203	BGA4805-JVA	15.10.07	M S Armstrong	Camphill	28. 9.08
G-CJVB	Schempp-Hirth Discus bT	111/462	BGA4806-JVB	11.10.07	C J Edwards *"DF"*	Nympsfield	28. 9.08
			D-KUNK				
G-CJVC	PZL-Bielsko SZD-51-1 Junior	B-1799	BGA4807-JVC	29.10.07	York Gliding Centre Ltd	Rufforth	28. 9.08
			SP-3434				
G-CJVE	Eiriavion PIK-20D	20631	BGA4809-JVE	18.12.07	S R Wilkinson *"X15"*	Kirton-in-Lindsey	1. 5.08
			OY-XJC				
G-CJVF	Schempp-Hirth Discus CS	271CS	BGA4810-JVF	27. 5.08	J Hodgson	(Guildford)	
G-CJVG	Schempp-Hirth Discus bT	121/477	BGA4811-JVG	31. 3.08	S J Bryan and P J Bramley	Lasham	
			D-KSOP				
G-CJVJ	AB Sportine Aviacija LAK-17A	108	BGA4813-JVJ	14. 1.08	J.A.Sutton	Milfield	6. 3.08
G-CJVL	DG Flugzeugbau DG-300 Elan	3E158	BGA4815-JVL	4.12.07	A T Vidion and A Griffiths	Tibenham	11. 1.08
			HB-1833				
G-CJVM	Schleicher ASW 27B	27138	BGA4816-JVM	18.12.07	G K Payne *"GP"*	Dunstable	28. 9.08
G-CJVP	Glaser-Dirks DG-200	2-1	BGA4818-JVP	9. 1.08	M S Howey and S Leadbeater *"D8"*	Burn	1. 4.08
			D-8200				
G-CJVS	Schleicher ASW 28	28003	BGA4821-JVS	11. 9.07	Zulu Glasstek Ltd Baileys Farm, Long Crendon		28. 9.08
			D-4008				

G-CJVU	Schempp-Hirth Standard Cirrus CS 11-75L	28	BGA4823-JVU	7. 1.08	H C Yorke tr Cirrus 75 Syndicate	Snitterfield	14. 1.08

G-CJVU Schempp-Hirth Standard Cirrus CS 11-75L 28 BGA4823-JVU 7. 1.08 H C Yorke tr Cirrus 75 Syndicate Snitterfield 14. 1.08
F-CEVT

G-CJVV Schempp-Hirth Janus C 176 BGA4824-JVV 2. 5.08 G Jenkins and G Smith Lasham
D-4150

G-CJVW Schleicher ASW 15 15042 BGA4825-JVW 10. 9.07 C F McGinn and E Hawke (Herne Bay) 12.10.07
HB-992

G-CJVX Schempp-Hirth Discus CS 087CS BGA4826-JVX 23.11.07 M P Kemp tr G-CJVX Syndicate (West Malling) 26. 3.08
D-0263

G-CJVZ Schleicher ASK 21 21721 BGA4828-JVZ 6.11.07 Yorkshire Gliding Club (Proprietary) Ltd "Sharpe's Classique"
Sutton Bank 28. 9.08

G-CJWA Schleicher ASW 28 28005 BGA4829- JWA 21. 8.07 M J Taylor and P R Porter Lyveden 28. 9.08
G-CJWB Schleicher ASK 13 13671AB BGA4830-JWB 18. 1.08 East Sussex Gliding Club Ltd Ringmer 8. 5.08
(Built Jubi GmbH Sportflugzeugbau) D-1066

G-CJWD Schleicher ASK 21 21724 BGA4832-JWD 8. 1.08 London Gliding Club Proprietary Ltd "JWD"
Dunstable 27. 3.08

G-CJWF Schleicher ASW 27 27144 BGA4834-JWF 10 .9.08 B A Fairston and A Stotter Husbands Bosworth
G-CJWG Schempp-Hirth Nimbus 3DT 11 BGA4835-JWG 15.11.07 P G Kynsey tr 880 Group Lasham 5.11.07
D-KMGD

G-CJWJ Schleicher ASK 13 13599 BGA4837-JWJ 11. 1.08 J G Arnold tr RAF Gliding and Soaring Association
RAFGSA R38, RAFGSA R3 (Operated Wrekin Gliding Club) RAF Cosford 13. 1.08

G-CJWK Schempp-Hirth Discus bT 453/1 BGA4838-JWK 14. 2.08 R Thompson tr 722 Syndicate "722" Nympsfield 2. 4.09
(Officially regd as c/n "122" - correct c/n 122 was BGA4021 w/o Parham 7. 5.95; plate still shows 127 from donor fuselage))
(Composite airframe built up from BGA4687 (127/488) (fuselage) and BGA3961 (106/453) (left wing) and right wing ex New Zealand. The c/n
plate shows 127. (BGA4838) was originally registered with BGA as c/n 106 but changed to "453/1" when BGA noted a duplicate c/n 106)

G-CJWM Grob G103 Twin Astir II 3536 BGA4840-JWM 15. 2.08 Norfolk Gliding Club Ltd Tibenham 17. 4.08
D-8730

G-CJWP Bolkow Phoebus B1 875 BGA4842-JWP 11. 9.08 A Fidler Crowland
D-0128

G-CJWR Grob G102 Astir CS 1271 BGA4844-JWR 18.12.07 G J Hunter tr Astir JWR Portmoak 20. 1.08
D-7366

G-CJWT Glaser-Dirks DG-200 2-42 BGA4846-JWT 12.11.07 K R Nash Kingston Deverill 28. 9.08
D-6560

G-CJWU Schempp-Hirth Ventus bT 19/159 BGA4847-JWU 31. 7.08 G Tabbner "GA" Wycombe Air Park
ZS-GOW

G-CJWV Glasflügel H201B Standard Libelle 411 BGA4848-JWV 12.10.07 A Beatty (Welwyn Garden City) 28. 9.08
OY-XBG

G-CJWX Schempp-Hirth Ventus 2cT 63/198 BGA4850-JWX 31.10.07 S.G.Olender Santo Tome de Puerto, Spain 28. 9.08
G-CJXA Schempp-Hirth Nimbus 3dT 9 BGA4853-JXA 2.11.07 J B Maddison tr Y4 Syndicate Lasham 17. 2.08
D-KKYY, D-4444

G-CJXB Centrair 201B Marianne 201015 BGA4854-JXB 12. 2.08 C A Sheldon tr Marianne Syndicate Pocklington 27. 3.08
F-CGMN

G-CJXC Wassmer WA-28 Espadon 102 BGA4855-JXC 22.12.07 A P Montague Nympsfield 5. 6.08
F-CDZV

G-CJXG Eiriavion PIK-20D 20660 BGA4859-JXG 19.12.07 D Ingledew Lee-on-Solent 21. 4.08
PH-670

G-CJXL Schempp-Hirth Discus CS 278CS BGA4863-JXL 1.12.07 J Hall and M J Hasluck Parham Park 23. 1.08
G-CJXM Schleicher ASK 13 13542 BGA4864-JXM 7. 2.08 The Windrushers Gliding Club Ltd Bicester 23. 3.08
RAFGSA R34, F-CERF

G-CJXN Centrair 201B Marianne 201B035 BGA4865-JXN 13.12.07 J D Trussell (Ilkeston)
F-CBLI

G-CJXP Glaser-Dirks DG-100 18 BGA4866-JXP 13. 2.08 R M Wootten Eyres Field 19. 3.08
PH-520

G-CJXR Schempp-Hirth Discus b 540 BGA4868-JXR 29. 2.08 Cambridge Gliding Club Ltd "DM" Gransden Lodge 25. 3.08
D-9152

G-CJXT Schleicher ASW 24B 24233 BGA4870-JXT 11.10.07 P McAuley Snitterfield 10.12.07
D-6706

G-CJXW Schempp-Hirth Duo Discus T 7/250 BGA4873-JXW 16.11.07 C Bainbridge Wormingford 7. 6.08
D-KOZX

G-CJXX Pilatus B4-PC11AF 13 BGA4874-JXX 21.12.07 N H Buckenham Rattlesden 6. 6.08
HB-1112

G-CJXY Neukom Elfe S4A 68 BGA4875-JXY 17. 9.08 D V Wilson Ringmer
HB-1267

G-CJYC Grob G102 Astir CS 1429 BGA4880-JYC 14. 8.07 R A Christie Easterton 4.11.07
RAFGSA R19, RAFGGA 742, D-7425

G-CJYD Schleicher ASW 27 27155 BGA4881-JYD 1.11.07 J E Gatfield Wycombe Air Park 17.10.07
G-CJYE Schleicher ASK 13 13191 BGA4882-JYE 23. 1.08 North Wales Gliding Club Ltd Llantisilio 15. 5.08
D-0347

G-CJYF Schempp-Hirth Discus CS 281CS BGA4883-JYF 4.12.07 R D Stroud Wycombe Air Park 17. 3.08
G-CJYL Sportine Aviacija LAK-12 Lietuva 6197 BGA4888-JYL 11. 6.08 A Camerotto Udine, Italy
G-CJYN Schempp-Hirth Discus 2b 94 BGA4890-JYN 7. 1.08 R Brigliadori Alzate Brianza, Italy 27. 6.08
G-CJYP Grob G102 Astir CS 5018C BGA4891-JYP 7. 2.08 Norfolk Gliding Club Ltd "B12" Tibenham 25. 9.08
D-8743

G-CJYR Schempp-Hirth Duo Discus T 16/267 BGA4893-JYR 14. 3.08 R Starmer "B20" Bidford
D-KOZX

G-CJYS Schempp-Hirth Mini-Nimbus C 106 BGA4894-JYS 9. 1.08 A Jenkins Shobdon 5. 7.08
HB-1437

G-CJYU Schempp-Hirth Ventus 2cT 70/216 BGA4896-JYU 8.10.07 J G Arnold tr RAF Gliding and Soaring Association "R11"
(Operated Chilterns Gliding Centre) RAF Halton 3. 4.08

G-CJYX Rolladen-Schneider LS3-17 3289 BGA4899-JYX 21. 4.08 D Meyer-Beeck and V G Diaz Ontur, Spain
D-3517

G-CJZB DG Flugzeugbau DG-500 Elan Orion BGA4903-JZB 7. 1.08 P N Cadle tr Bicester JZB Syndicate "Jezabel"
5E223X61 Bicester 28. 9.08

G-CJZE Schleicher ASK 13 13423 BGA4906-JZE 20.11.07 Needwood Forest Gliding Club Ltd Cross Hayes 16. 3.08
OY-XPJ, D-2125

G-CJZG	Schempp-Hirth Discus bT	9/272	BGA4908-JZG D-KISM	7. 9.07	R H C Acreman	Nympsfield	2. 5.08
G-CJZH	Schleicher ASW 20CL	20754	BGA4909-JZH D-5932	11. 9.07	C P Gibson and C A Hunt	Lasham	28. 9.08
G-CJZK	DG Flugzeugbau DG-500 Elan Orion	5E225X63	BGA4911-JZK	18.12.07	Devon & Somerset Gliding Club Ltd	North Hill	29. 7.08
G-CJZL	Schempp-Hirth Mini Nimbus B	92	BGA4912-JZL HB-1453	2.11.07	S J Aldridge	Saltby	16. 5.08
G-CJZM	Schempp-Hirth Ventus 2a	117	BGA4913-JZM	7. 1.08	S Crabb *"C64"*	Lyveden	28. 9.08
G-CJZN	Schleicher ASW 28	28038	BGA4914-JZN	19.10.07	P J Coward *"JZN"*	Husbands Bosworth	8.12.07
G-CJZX	Schleicher ASW 27B	27166	BGA4923-JZX	18.10.07	D M Jones and P R Barley *"P10"*	RAF Halton	28. 9.08
G-CJZY	Grob G102 Standard Astir III	5600S	BGA4924-JZY D-6951	13. 3.08	North Downs Gliding Trust Ltd *"SH7"*	Lasham	
G-CJZZ	Rolladen-Schneider LS7-WL	7128	BGA4925-JZZ SE-UIU	8.12.07	J H Tucker *"ZZ"*	Gransden Lodge	22. 3.08

G-CKAA - G-CKZZ

G-CKAC	Glaser-Dirks DG-200	2-159	BGA4928-KAC HB-1611	10. 9.08	C Morton-Fincham	Saltby	
G-CKAE	Centrair 101A Pegase	101A0152	BGA4930-KAE F-CGBN	25. 3.08	Rattlesden Gliding Club Ltd	Rattlesden	
G-CKAH	Schempp-Hirth Discus bT	112-464	BGA4933-KAH D-KNZZ	10.12.07	P Brown tr The Discus Syndicate	Bidford	28. 9.08
G-CKAJ	Schempp-Hirth Ventus 2cT	86/...	BGA4934-KAJ	08.11.07	A N Redington	RNAS Culdrose	23. 4.08
G-CKAK	Schleicher ASW 28	28032	BGA4935-KAK	4. 3.08	S J Kelman *"S1"*	Gransden Lodge	
G-CKAL	Schleicher ASW 28	28031	BGA4936-KAL	30.10.07	P A Ivens and D A Smith *"A28"*	Nympsfield	16. 2.08
G-CKAM	Glasflügel H205 Club Libelle	83	BGA4937-KAM D-8928	14. 9.07	P A Cronk and R C Tallowin	Lyveden	9.12.07
G-CKAN	PZL-Bielsko SZD-50-3 Puchacz	B-2106	BGA4938-KAN PH-1104	26.11.07	The Bath, Wilts and North Dorset Gliding Club Ltd Kingston Deverill		28. 2.08
G-CKAP	Schempp-Hirth Discus CS	290CS	BGA4939-KAP	5.10.07	A A Stewart tr KAP Syndicate	Portmoak	28. 9.08
G-CKAR	Schempp-Hirth Duo Discus T	35/309	BGA4941-KAR	6. 3.08	J Giacopazzi tr 977 Syndicate *"977"*	Portmoak	
G-CKAS	Schempp-Hirth Ventus 2cT	93-271	BGA4942-KAS (BGA4995-KCX), (BGA4942-KAS)	24. 1.08	R E Fletcher tr KAS Club (Finchampstead, Wokingham)		29. 8.08
G-CKAU	AMS Flight DG-303 Elan Acro	3E500A35	BGA4994-KAU	22. 4.08	G Earle	Talgarth	
G-CKAV	Rolladen-Schneider LS4-a	4696	BGA4945-KAV D-1055	17.11.07	A J Cockerell *"535"*	Aston Down	28. 9.08
G-CKAW	DG Flugzeugbau DG-500 Elan Orion	5E228X66	BGA4946-KAW	30. 8.07	Midland Gliding Club Ltd	Long Mynd	16. 9.09
G-CKAX	DG Flugzeugbau DG-500 Elan Orion	5E229X67	BGA4947-KAX	29.11.07	York Gliding Centre Ltd	Rufforth	7. 5.08
G-CKAY	Grob G102 Astir CS	1452	BGA4948-KAY D-7433	18. 1.08	D Ryder and P Carrington	Strubby	17. 2.08
G-CKBA	Centrair 101A Pégase 90	101A0435	BGA4950-KBA HB-3096	27. 2.08	C Weston tr KBA Pégase 101A Syndicate	Challock	18. 4.08
G-CKBC	Rollason-Schneider LS6-c *(Rebuilt using original fuselage and wings of BGA3895)*	6250-1	BGA4952-KBC	22. 9.08	B A Fairston tr G-CKBC Group	Husbands Bosworth	
G-CKBD	Grob G102 Astir CS	1217	BGA4953-KBD D-7290	29.10.07	R A Morriss	Crowland	3. 3.07
G-CKBF	AMS Flight DG-300 Elan *(Originally regd as DG-303 Elan, amended 20. 3.08)*	3E498	BGA4955-KBF	21. 9.07	A L Garfield	Dunstable	28. 9.08
G-CKBG	Schempp-Hirth Ventus 2cT	83-250	BGA4956-KBG	14. 2.08	J F d'Arcy tr 71 Syndicate	Lasham	7. 4.08
G-CKBH	Rolladen-Schneider LS6	6072	BGA4957-KBH D-7798	24.10.07	F C Ballard anf P Walker	Nympsfield	5. 5.07
G-CKBK	Schempp-Hirth Ventus 2cT	79/244	BGA4959-KBK	9.10.07	D Rhys-Jones	Parham Park	4. 3.08
G-CKBL	Grob G102 Astir CS	1464	BGA4960-KBL D-7436	15. 2.08	Norfolk Gliding Club Ltd *"N12"*	Tibenham	9. 2.08
G-CKBM	Schleicher ASW 28	28046	BGA4961-KBM D-0001	2.11.07	M E Newland-Smith and M Poole *"73"*	Dunstable	28. 9.08
G-CKBN	PZL-Bielsko SZD-55-1 Promyk	551190004	BGA4962-KBN SE-ULV	1.10.07	N D Pearson	Ringmer	15. 3.08
G-CKBS	Glaser-Dirks DG-600	6-42	BGA4966-KBS OO-YPH, D-4882	20. 8.07	M S Szymkowicz	Bicester	21. 2.08
G-CKBT	Schempp-Hirth Standard Cirrus	561G	BGA4967-KBT D-4755	28. 3.08	P R Johnson	Wormingford	
G-CKBU	Schleicher ASW 28	28040	BGA4968-KBU	15.10.07	G C Metcalfe *"104"*	Lasham	28. 9.08
G-CKBV	Schleicher ASW 28	28045	BGA4969-KBV	2.11.07	P Whipp *"H4"*	Dunstable	6. 9.08
G-CKBX	Schleicher ASW 27	27092	BGA4917-KBX PH-1146	5. 3.08	M Wright and T J Davies	Tibenham	
G-CKCB	Rolladen-Schneider LS4-a	4776	BGA4975-KCB PH-887, D-1597	26. 9.07	The Bristol Gliding Club Proprietary Ltd *"MY"* Nympsfield		28. 9.08
G-CKCD	Schempp-Hirth Ventus 2cT	91/267	BGA4977-KCD	11. 9.08	R S Jobar and S G Jones	Lasham	
G-CKCE	Schempp-Hirth Ventus 2cT	85/256	BGA4978-KCE	5. 3.08	J G Arnold tr RAF Gliding and Soaring Association *"24"* Dishforth		
G-CKCH	Schempp-Hirth Ventus 2cT	56/186	BGA4981-KCH PH-1191	12.11.07	J J Pridal and L R Marks *"EA"*	Lasham	24. 4.08
G-CKCJ	Schleicher ASW 28	28051	BGA4982-KCJ	9. 1.08	S L Withall	Dunstable	
G-CKCK	Enstrom 280FX Shark	2071	OO-PVL	5. 5.95	Rhoburt Ltd	(Styal, Wilmslow)	27. 2.09E
G-CKCM	Glasflügel H201B Standard Libelle	104	BGA4985-KCM HB-968	9. 7.08	G A Cox *"CM"*	Eyres Field	
G-CKCN	Schleicher ASW 27	27188	BGA4986-KCN D-0001	23.10.07	A Walford and W J Head *"700"*	Gransden Lodge	28. 9.08

Reg	Type	C/n	Prev id	Date	Owner/Operator	Base	
G-CKCP	Grob G102 Astir CS	104	BGA4987-KCP OY-XDB	15. 7.08	Norfolk Gliding Club Ltd *"NG1"*	Tibenham	
G-CKCR	AB Sportine Aviacija LAK-17A	132	BGA4989-KCR	26. 2.08	L Bertoncini	Alzate Brianza, Italy	29. 6.08
G-CKCT	Schleicher ASK 21	21751	BGA4991-KCT	31. 8.07	Kent Gliding Club Aircraft Ltd *"KCT"*	Challock	28. 9.08
G-CKCV	Schempp-Hirth Duo Discus T	54/339	BGA4993-KCV D-KOZZ	20. 9.07	A J Buchanan tr WE4 Group	Parham Park	28. 9.08
G-CKCW	Glaser-Dirks DG-200/17	2-137/1735	BGA4994-KCW D-0153	11. 3.08	R W Adamson and K A B Morgan	Portmoak	
G-CKCY	Schleicher ASW 20	20068	BGA4996-KCY PH-597, (OY-XTM), PH-597	12. 2.08	A J Wilson and S R Tromans *"AV"*	Nympsfield	3. 3.08
G-CKCZ	Schleicher ASK 21	21749	BGA4997-KCZ	25. 1.08	Booker Gliding Club Ltd	Wycombe Air Park	21. 3.08
G-CKDA	Schemmp-Hirth Ventus 2B	138	BGA4998-KDA (BGA5008-KDL), D-4999	19.10.07	D J Eade	Lasham	25. 2.08
G-CKDB	Schleicher Ka 6CR	6431	BGA4999-KDB HB-805	17.10.07	Banbury Gliding Club Ltd	Hinton-in-the-Hedges	20. 1.08
G-CKDC	Centrair ASW 20F	20524	BGA5000-KDC F-CFSF	11. 9.07	M Staljan, S Brogger and C Behrendt	(Finnetrop, Germany)	
G-CKDF	Schleicher ASK 21	21006	BGA5003-KDF D-6539	29. 1.08	T World tr Portsmouth Naval Gliding Centre *"E7"*	Lee-on-Solent	30. 3.08
G-CKDH	Schleicher K 8B	E4	BGA5005-KDH D-8428	20.12.07	Midland Gliding Club Ltd	Long Mynd	29. 9.08
G-CKDK	Rolladen-Schneider LS4-a	4352	BGA5007-KDK	21.12.07	M C Ridger	Long Mynd	13. 4.08
G-CKDN	Schleicher ASW 27	27208	BGA5010-KDN-	17. 8.07	J S McCullagh	Lasham	28. 9.08
G-CKDO	Schempp-Hirth Ventus 2cT	97/..	BGA5012-KDQ	27. 9.07	A R Milne	Kingston Deverill	6.12.07
G-CKDP	Schleicher ASK 21	21760	BGA5011-KDP	17. 4.08	Kent Gliding Club Aircraft Ltd *"KDP"*	Challock	
G-CKDS	Schleicher ASW 27	27202	BGA5014-KDS	31.10.07	A W Gillett and G D Morris	Nympsfield	28. 9.08
G-CKDU	Glaser-Dirks DG-200/17	2-161/1752	BGA5016-KDU D-6000	8. 1.08	P G Noonan	Bicester	28. 3.08
G-CKDV	Schempp-Hirth Ventus b/16.6	224	BGA5017-KDV HB-1770	21. 9.07	M A Codd	Talgarth	28. 9.08
G-CKDW	Schleicher ASW 27	27196	BGA5018-KDW	21.11.07	C Colton	Gransden Lodge	16. 3.08
G-CKDX	Glaser-Dirks DG-200	2-11	BGA5019-KDX D-7218	26. 2.08	A M Bailey	Aston Down	21. 3.08
G-CKDY	Glaser-Dirks DG-100	78	BGA5020-KDY D-2591	2.11.07	P T Claiden tr 503 Group *"503"*	Dunstable	27.11.07
G-CKDZ	Schempp-Hirth Standard Cirrus 75	696	BGA5021-KDZ OO-ZKF	30. 9.08	H E Williams tr Charlie 75	RAF Cranwell	
G-CKEA	Schempp-Hirth Cirrus 18	11	BGA5022-KEA D-8807, HB-911	9.11.07	C M Reed	Rattlesden	5. 1.08
G-CKEB	Schempp-Hirth Standard Cirrus	436G	BGA5023-KEB F-CEFN	22. 2.08	A J Mugleston	(Cullompton)	27. 3.08
G-CKEC	Rolladen-Schneider LS4-a	4469	BGA5024-KEC D-5170	22.11.07	B T Spreckley *(Operated European Soaring Club)*	Ontur, Spain	28. 9.08
G-CKED	Schleicher ASW 27B	27203	BGA5025-KED D-0001	6.11.07	M H Bull *"MB"*	Crowland	28. 9.08
G-CKEE	Grob G102 Astir CS	1135	BGA5026-KEE D-4179	13.12.07	Essex & Suffolk Gliding Club Ltd	Wormingford	17. 1.08
G-CKEJ	Schleicher ASK 21	21765	BGA5030-KEJ	16. 4.08	London Gliding Club Proprietary Ltd	Dunstable	
G-CKEK	Schleicher ASK 21	21767	BGA5031-KEK	12.11.07	Devon & Somerset Gliding Club Ltd	North Hill	28. 9.08
G-CKEL	Rolladen-Schneider LS8-18	8454	BGA5032-KEL	8. 2.08	C W Nicolson and P Kaye	Gransden Lodge	16. 4.08
G-CKEM	Robinson R44 Clipper II	11375		24. 8.06	True Course Helicopter Ltd	Gibraltar	30. 9.09E
G-CKEP	Rolladen-Schneider LS6-b	6168	BGA5035-KEP F-CGUI, F-WGUI, D-5017	30. 5.08	T W M Beck	Parham Park	
G-CKER	Schleicher ASW 19B	19224	BGA5037-KER OY-XJI	6.11.07	B Van Woerden tr G-CKER Syndicate Feshiebridge		15. 4.08
G-CKES	Schempp-Hirth Cirrus 18	46	BGA5038-KES D-6955, HB-955	28.11.07	D Judd	RAF Cosford	30. 5.08
G-CKET	Rolladen-Schneider LS8-8	8459	BGA5039-KET	30. 6.08	J C Taylor and M B Jefferyes *"456"*	Dunstable	
G-CKEV	Schempp-Hirth Duo Discus	368	BGA5041-KEV	25.10.07	J G Arnold tr RAF Gliding and Soaring Association *"R2"*	RAF Syerston	28. 9.08
G-CKEX	Schleicher ASW 19B	19115	BGA5043-KEX I-IUUH, D-7551	6.12.07	E D Johnson	Lyveden	28. 9.08
G-CKEY	Piper PA-28-161 Warrior II	28-7916061	N510PU N22166	4. 1.07	B W Gomez	Wolverhampton	19. 6.09E
G-CKEZ	DG Flugzeugbau LS8-t	8464	BGA5045-KEZ D-KSAB	25.10.07	D A Jesty	Brentor	19. 6.08
G-CKFA	Schempp-Hirth Standard Cirrus 75	644	BGA5046-KFA D-2124, F-CEMQ	8. 2.08	C F Jordan *"S75"*	Aboyne	23. 5.08
G-CKFB	Schempp-Hirth Discus 2T	30-179	BGA5047-KFB D-KOZZ	12.12.07	P L and P A G Holland	Kirton-in-Lindsey	23. 9.08
G-CKFC	Schempp-Hirth Ventus 2cT	105	BGA5048-KFC D-KOZZ	3.10.07	P Lecci	(Chaton, France)	28. 9.08
G-CKFD	Schleicher ASW 27	27211	BGA5049-KFD	30. 1.08	W T Craig *"906"*	Dunstable	14. 2.08
G-CKFE	Eiriavion PIK 20D	20520	BGA5050-KFE D-8103, OE-5103	11. 1.08	M J McSorley	Bellarena	24. 8.07
G-CKFG	Grob G103A Twin II Acro	3771-K-57	BGA5052-KFG D-1339	6. 2.08	The Surrey Hills Gliding Club Ltd	Kenley	23. 6.08
G-CKFH	Schempp-Hirth HS-7 Mini Nimbus	15	BGA5053-KFH D-4819	26.11.07	D Nichols	Aston Down	16. 4.07
G-CKFJ	Schleicher ASK 13	13136	BGA5054-KFJ PH-383	29.11.07	York Gliding Centre Ltd	Rufforth	11. 3.08
G-CKFK	VTC Standard Cirrus	203	BGA5055-KFK S5-3058, SL-3058, YU-4295	29.10.07	P R Wilkinson	Tibenham	29. 3.08

G-CKFL	Rolladen-Schneider LS4	4080	BGA5056-KFL HB-1619	17. 1.08	D R Taylor and D A O'Brien	Tibenham	23. 2.08
G-CKFM	Rolladen-Schneider LS8-18	8475	BGA5057-KFM D-9502	13. 9.07	A J H Smith *"149"*	Tibenham	13. 7.08
G-CKFN	DG Flugzeugbau DG-1000S	10-29S28	BGA5058-KFN	5.12.07	Yorkshire Gliding Club (Proprietary) Ltd	Sutton Bank	22.12.07
G-CKFP	Schempp-Hirth Ventus 2cT	110/304	BGA5059-KFP D-KKAH	9.11.07	C R Sutton *"124"*	Saltby	25. 1.08
G-CKFR	Schleicher ASK 13	13433	BGA5061-KFR D-3536, RAFGSA 535, D-3535	23. 4.08	Club Acrupacion de Pilotos del Sureste	Albacete, Spain	
G-CKFT	Schempp-Hirth Duo Discus T	77/383	BGA5063-KFT D-KIIH	12. 2.08	L R Merritt tr Duo Discus Syndicate	Saltby	4. 4.08
G-CKFV	DG Flugzeugbau LS8-t	8476	BGA5065-KFV D-KOBP	11. 1.08	G A Rowden and K I Arkley	Sutton Bank	16. 4.08
G-CKFY	Schleicher ASK 21	21776	BGA5068-KFN	23. 1.06	Cambridge Gliding Club Ltd	Gransden Lodge	28 .9.08
G-CKGA	Schempp-Hirth Ventus 2cxT	115/312	BGA5070-KGA D-KIBL	24. 4.06	D R Campbell *"370"*	Wycombe Air Park	28. 9.08
G-CKGB	Schempp-Hirth Ventus 2CT	117	BGA5071-KGB	3. 1.06	D R Irving *"T3"*	Portmoak	28. 9.08
G-CKGC	Schempp-Hirth Ventus 2cxT	118/317	BGA5072-KGC D-KMAF	7.10.05	C P A Jeffery *"64"*	Gransden Lodge	28. 9.08
G-CKGD	Schempp-Hirth Ventus 2cT	119/318	BGA5073-KGD D-KEAD	7.10.05	C Morris *"V9"*	Bidford	28. 9.08
G-CKGF	Schempp-Hirth Duo Discus T	84/397	BGA5075-KGF	17.10.05	P O'Donald tr Duo 233 Group *"233"*	Gransden Lodge	7.12.07
G-CKGH	Grob G102 Club Astir II	5057C	BGA5077-KGH OO-ZVS	6. 9.06	I M Gavan	Kenley	22.11.07
G-CKGK	Schleicher ASK 21	21766	BGA5079-KGK	21.12.05	T M Holloway tr RAF Gliding and Soaring Association *"R28"* *(Operated Cleveland Gliding Club)* AAC Dishforth		28. 9.08
G-CKGL	Schempp-Hirth Ventus 2cT	88/263	BGA5080-KGL EI-152	13. 2.06	S H Baker tr Kilo Gulf Lima Syndicate	Lasham	26. 4.08
G-CKGM	Centrair 101A Pegase	101055	BGA5081-KGM F-CFQR	3. 9.08	S France	Usk	
G-CKGN	Schleicher ASW 28-18	28505	BGA5082-KGN D-3063, D-0001	15. 3.06	M Jerman	Sutton Bank	17. 3.07
G-CKGT	Standard Cirrus 75-VTC *(Built Jastreb Fabrika Aviona I Jedrilica)*	294	BGA5087-KGT HA-4283	4.10.06	D M Raffello *"41"*	Enemonzo, Italy	1. 7.08
G-CKGU	Schleicher ASW 19B	19208	BGA5088-KGU Belgian Air Cadets PL68	21. 4.06	D M Ruttle *"690"*	Strubby	22. 4.07
G-CKGV	Schleicher ASW 28-18	28512	BGA5089-KGV D-7062	4.10.05	A H Reynolds	Long Mynd	30. 3.08
G-CKGX	Scheicher ASK 21	21782	BGA5091-KGX	9. 5.06	Coventry Gliding Club Ltd *"KGX"*	Husbands Bosworth	4. 5.08
G-CKGY	Scheibe Bergfalke IV	5839	BGA5092-KGY SE-TLL	17. 1.06	B R Pearson tr North Devon Gliding Club	Eaglescott	23. 6.07
G-CKHA	PZL-Bielsko SZD-51-1 Junior	B-1918	BGA5094-KHA (SP-3691), D-2843, DDR-2803	1.12.05	Devon & Somerset Gliding Club Ltd	North Hill	28. 9.08
G-CKHB	Rolladen-Schneider LS3	3316	BGA5095-KHB D-2635	28. 3.06	P A Dunthorne	Nympsfield	13. 4.08
G-CKHC	DG Flugzeugbau DG-500/20 Elan	5E178W11	BGA5096-KHC D-6401	12.12.05	G M Brightman and J Donovan tr G-CKHC Group	Lyveden	23. 3.08
G-CKHD	Schleicher ASW 27	27222	BGA5097-KHD	1.12.05	N D Tillett *"T4"*	Dunstable	28. 9.08
G-CKHE	AB Sportine Aviacija LAK-17AT	122	BGA5098-KHE OM-0118	17. 1.07	A J Garrity and N J Gough *"X17"*	RAF Wittering	25. 5.08
G-CKHF	Schleicher ASW 20	20229	BGA5099-KHF D-3162	21. 9.05	C H Brown *"XD2"*	AAC Dishforth	14. 5.08
G-CKHG	Schleicher ASW 27	27223	BGA5100-KHG	28.11.05	R A F King *"K5"*	Dunstable	7. 2.08
G-CKHH	Schleicher ASK 13	13171	BGA5101-KHH LN-GAX	15. 3.06	Lincolnshire Gliding Club Ltd	Strubby	6. 3.08
G-CKHK	Schempp-Hirth Duo Discus T	100/426	BGA5103-KHK	29. 6.06	I Ashton tr Duo Discus Syndicate	Chipping	23. 6.08
G-CKHM	Centrair 101A Pégase 90	101A0359	BGA5105-KHM F-CHDE	23.11.05	A Bland tr G-CKHM Group	Lasham	4. 4.08
G-CKHN	PZL-Bielsko SZD-51-1 Junior	B-2142	BGA5106-KHN OE-5614, SP-3612	17. 3.06	The Nene Valley Gliding Club Ltd	Upwood	10. 6.07
G-CKHP	Rolladen-Schneider LS8-18	8337	BGA5107-KHP N818FD	28. 3.06	A D May *"70"*	Dunstable	2. 5.08
G-CKHR	PZL-Bielsko SZD-51-1 Junior	B-1775	BGA5109-KHR HB-1928	15.11.06	Wolds Gliding Club Ltd	Pocklington	19. 3.08
G-CKHS	Rolladen-Schneider LS7-WL	7043	BGA5110-KHS PH-862, D-5157	20.12.05	G F Coles tr Kilo Oscar Group *"KO"*	Wormingford	15. 3.08
G-CKHT	Standard Cirrus *(Built Burkhart Grob Flugzeugbau)*	259G	BGA5111-KHT D-1139	31. 8.06	M Holden *"424"*	Lasham	8. 3.08
G-CKHV	Glaser-Dirks DG-100	77	BGA5112-KHV HB-1331	8. 2.08	M E Laxaback and M J Brown	Chipping	29. 7.08
G-CKHW	PZL-Bielsko SZD-50-3 Puchacz	503.A 004.001	BGA5113-KHW	14. 8.07	Derbyshire and Lancashire Gliding Club Ltd	Camphill	16. 8.06
G-CKJA	Schleicher ASW 28-18	28712	BGA5117-KJA D-6051	27. 1.06	J Vella-Grech *"28E"*	(Shrewsbury)	7. 2.08
G-CKJB	Schempp-Hirth Ventus bT	26/191	BGA5118-KJB D-KBST	9. 3.06	J D Sorrell *"LW"*	Usk	16. 7.07
G-CKJC	Schempp-Hirth Nimbus 3T	6/57	BGA5119-KJC D-KUPA, OY-KHX, D-KHXB	16. 1.06	A C Wright *"617"*	Sutton Bank	9. 2.08
G-CKJD	Schempp-Hirth Standard Cirrus 75-VTC *(Built Vazduhoplovno Tehnicki Centar)*	241	BGA5120-KJD F-CDOZ	30. 3.07	L Rebbeck *"KJD"*	Wycombe Air Park	4. 5.08
G-CKJE	DG Flugzeugbau LS8-18	8498	BGA5121-KJE	6. 9.06	M D Wells *"321"*	Bidford	28. 9.08

G-CKJF	Schempp-Hirth Standard Cirrus	414G	BGA5122-KJF	16. 1.06	J G Wilson tr G-CKJF Group *"GW"*	Bicester	23. 3.08
			OY-XGW, D-9247				
G-CKJG	Schempp-Hirth Cirrus	153Y	BGA5123-KJG	11.10.05	S J Wright *"901"*	Rattlesden	23. 3.08
			EC-CKO				
G-CKJH	DG Flugzeugbau DG-300 Elan	3E506	BGA5124-KJH	9.12.05	Yorkshire Gliding Club (Proprietary) Ltd		
	(Type amended 1.12.07)					Sutton Bank	28. 9.08
G-CKJJ	DG Flugzeugbau DG-500 Elan Orion		BGA5125-KJJ	29. 3.06	Ulster Gliding Club Ltd	Bellarena	28. 9.08
		5E249X79	S5-AMS01				
G-CKJL	Schleicher ASK 13	13468	BGA5127-KJL	18. 9.06	Lincolnshire Gliding Club Ltd	Strubby	22. 9.07
			D-2338				
G-CKJM	Schempp-Hirth Ventus cT	120/394	BGA5128-KJM	10.11.05	K R Merritt tr G-CKJM Group	Halesland	28. 9.08
	(Officially regd with c/n 120)		D-KAHE, OH-781				
G-CKJN	Schleicher ASW 20	20052	BGA5129-KJN	22.12.05	R Logan *"9E"*	Bellarena	17.11.07
			D-7964				
G-CKJP	Schleicher ASK 21	21783	BGA5130-KJP	17. 1.06	T M Holloway tr RAF Gliding and Soaring Association *"R12"*		
			D-0001		*(Operated Bannerdown Gliding Club)*	RAF Keevil	24.11.07
G-CKJS	Schleicher ASW 28-18E	28713	BGA5132-KJS	9. 3.06	D J Tagg tr G-CKJS Syndicate	Wycombe Air Park	15. 3.08
			D-KHJW				
G-CKJV	Schleicher ASW 28-18E	28725	BGA5145-KJV	25. 1.06	A C Price *"AP"*	Nympsfield	19. 3.08
			D-KFAP, D-KOAB				
G-CKJZ	Schempp-Hirth Discus bT	75/403	BGA5149-KJZ	28.11.05	A I Mawer tr G-CKJZ Group *"E17"*		
			OE-9367			Kirton-in-Lindsey	13. 2.08
G-CKKB	Centrair 101A Pégase	101A0209	BGA5151-KKB	8. 3.06	D M Rushton	Lyveden	9. 6.08
			SE-TZU				
G-CKKC	DG Flugzeugbau DG-303 Elan Acro	3E509A41	BGA5152-KKC	8. 5.06	M P Ellis tr Charlie Kilo Kilo Charlie Syndicate	Burn	14. 5.08
G-CKKD	Schleicher ASW 28-18E	28734	BGA5153-KKD	28. 4.06	A Palmer *"AP1"*	Dunstable	29. 3.08
G-CKKE	Schempp-Hirth Duo Discus T	103/429	BGA5154-KKE	30. 1.06	C Morris tr Foxtrot Group	Bidford	29. 3.08
			D-KOZZ				
G-CKKF	Schempp-Hirth Ventus 2cT	139/364	BGA5155-KKF	23. 9.05	A R MacGregor *"306"*	Kingston Deverill	28. 9.08
G-CKKH	Schleicher ASW 27	27231	BGA5157-KKH	20.10.05	P L Hurd *"218"*	Wycombe Air Park	28. 9.08
			D-0001				
G-CKKK	AB Sportine Aviacija LAK-17A	161	BGA5159-KKK	12. 9.06	C J Nicolas *"960"*	Ridgewell	13. 4.08
			LY-GGF				
G-CKKN	Schempp-Hirth Duo Discus	165	BGA5162-KKN	10. 3.06	M Jordy tr Golf Bravo One *"GB1"*		
			D-8215			Husbands Bosworth	22. 2.08
G-CKKP	Schleicher ASK 21	21795	BGA5163-KKP	24. 4.06	Bowland Forest Gliding Club Ltd *"BF1"*	Chipping	23. 6.08
G-CKKR	Schleicher ASK 13	13065	BGA5164-KKR	5.12.05	Banbury Gliding Club Ltd	Hinton-in-the-Hedges	26. 4.08
			PH-391				
G-CKKV	DG Flugzeugbau DG-1000S	10-57T2	BGA5167-KKV	10. 2.06	Lasham Gliding Society Ltd *"776"*	Lasham	14. 5.08
G-CKKX	Rolladen-Schneider LS4-a	4827	BGA5169-KKX	19. 1.06	B W Svenson tr 449 Syndicate *"449"*		
			PH-928, D-3529			Pocklington	2. 2.08
G-CKKY	Schempp-Hirth Duo Discus T	124/...	BGA5170-KKY	19. 1.06	P D Duffin tr G-CKKY Group *"D6"*	Wormingford	29. 3.08
G-CKLA	Schleicher ASK 13	13363	BGA5172-KLA	16. 6.06	Booker Gliding Club Ltd *"KLA"*		
			PH-1084, D-0857			Wycombe Air Park	14. 6.07
G-CKLB	Schleicher ASW 27	27234	BGA5173-KLB	19.10.05	N Kries	Saarbrucken, Germany	28. 9.08
G-CKLC	Glasflügel H206 Hornet	39	BGA5174-KLC	16. 2.06	P R Thomas	Dunstable	9. 6.08
			SE-TPL				
G-CKLD	Schempp-Hirth Discus 2cT	1	BGA5175-KLD	27.10.05	J P Galloway *"797"*	Portmoak	22.10.08E
			D-KDCC				
G-CKLF	Schempp-Hirth Janus	59	BGA5177-KLF	15. 9.06	T J Edmunds *"08"*	RAF Marham	21. 9.08
			D-2170, I-ANUS				
G-CKLG	Rolladen-Schneider LS 4	4264	BGA5178	7. 8.06	P M Scheiwiller, P S Graham and J P Heath		
			F-CAEQ, D-5530			Sandhill Farm, Shrivenham	29. 8.08
G-CKLN	Rolladen-Schneider LS4-a	4791	BGA5183-KLN	12. 6.06	K E Jenkinson *"M11"*	Husbands Bosworth	5. 7.08
			D-2823				
G-CKLP	Schleicher ASW 28-18E	28737	BGA5184-KLP	16. 3.06	J T Birch *"205"*	Gransden Lodge	29. 8.08
			D-KOAB				
G-CKLR	PZL-Bielsko SZD-55-1 Promyk	551193056	G-CKLM-KLR	25. 1.06	D T King and A Gibson tr Zulu Five Gliding Group *"Z55"*		
			BGA5185, F-CHSP, F-WHSP			Trenchard Lines, Upavon	22. 4.08
G-CKLS	Rolladen-Schneider LS4	4637	BGA5186-KLS	29. 6.06	Wolds Gliding Club Ltd	Pocklington	16. 6.08
			D-6786				
G-CKLT	Schempp-Hirth Nimbus 3/24.5	1	BGA5187-KLT	22. 5.06	G N Thomas *"GT"*	AAC Wattisham	5. 4.08
			D-5052, EC-EBP, D-2111				
G-CKLV	Schempp-Hirth Discus 2cT	20/27	BGA5188-KLV	8. 2.06	J Iglehart	Lasham	15. 3.08
			D-KKFC				
G-CKLW	Schleicher ASK 21	21799	BGA5189-KLW	9.12.05	Yorkshire Gliding Club (Proprietary) Ltd		
						Sutton Bank	29. 8.08
G-CKLY	DG Flugzeugbau DG-1000T	10-66T6	BGA5191-KLY	3.10.05	R J Large tr G-CKLY Group *"440" and "D6"*		
			D-KAAD			Husbands Bosworth	8. 5.08
G-CKMA	DG Flugzeugbau LS8-T	8510	BGA5192-KMA	5.12.05	G Rizk *"GR8"*	Saltby	30.11.06
G-CKMB	AB Sportine Aviacija LAK-19T	018	BGA5193-KMB	7. 3.07	D J McKenzie *"KMB"*	Camphill	14. 3.08
			LY-GJE				
G-CKMC	Grob G102 Astir CS77	1625	BGA5194-KMC	20. 9.05	L J Gregoire *"207"*	Lasham	8.11.07
			LN-GBA, D-4799				
G-CKMD	Schempp-Hirth Standard Cirrus	31	BGA5195-KMD	8.11.05	C I Roberts *"V12"*	Snitterfield	13. 3.08
			SE-TIX, D-0528				
G-CKME	DG Flugzeugbau LS8-T	8504	BGA5196-KME	22.12.05	D Bradley *"DB"*	Sutton Bank	16. 2.08
G-CKMF	Centrair 101A Pégase	101038	BGA5197-KMF	8. 5.06	D L M Jamin	Dunstable	29. 4.08
			F-CFQE				
G-CKMG	Glaser-Dirks DG-100G Elan	E159G126	BGA5198-KMG	27. 9.06	A W Roberts *"AD"*	Dunstable	4. 4.08
			HB-1733				
G-CKMI	Schleicher K 8C	81006	BGA5200-KMI	6. 9.06	V Mallon	Kleve-Wisseler Dünen, Germany	28. 8.08
			RAFGGA 562				

G-CKMJ	Schleicher Ka 6CR	6109	BGA5201-KMJ 15. 8.06 RAFGGA 555. D-8455	V Mallon	Kleve-Wisseler Dünen, Germany	27. 9.06
G-CKML	Schempp-Hirth Duo Discus T	52/336	BGA5203-KML 12. 4.06 PH-1256	J J Pridal tr KML Group *"KA"*	Lasham	12. 4.08
G-CKMM	Schleicher ASW 28-18E	28742	BGA5204-KMM 23. 1.06	R G Munro *"RM"*	Wycombe Air Park	18.12.07
G-CKMO	Rolladen-Schneider LS7-WL	7007	BGA5206-KMO 15.12.05 PH-861, D-1264	G E M Turpin *"L7"*	RAF Keevll	5. 4.08
G-CKMP	AB Sportine Aviacija LAK-17A	173	BGA5207-KMP 17. 1.06 LY-GMZ	J L Mciver	Portmoak	29. 8.08
G-CKMR	Letov LF-107 Lunak	54	BGA5208-KMR 6.12.05 OK-0838	W Seitz	Pohlheim, Germany	10. 4.08
G-CKMT	Grob G103C Twin III Acro	34157	BGA5210-KMT 3. 1.06 PH-1151, D-0659	The Borders (Milfield) Gliding Club Ltd	Milfield	14. 1.08
G-CKMV	Rolladen-Schneider LS3-17	3329	BGA5212-KMV 8.11.05 D-6931	F Roles	Husbands Bosworth	29. 8.08
G-CKMW	Schleicher ASK 21	21798	BGA5213-KMW 9.12.05	T M Holloway tr RAF Gliding and Soaring Association *"R18"*		29. 8.08
				(Operated Cranwell Gliding Club)	RAF Cranwell	
G-CKMY	Schleicher ASW20L	20392	BGA5215-KMY 17. 1.06 PH-803, D-8833	C M Davey tr WR Soaring Group *"W81"*	RAF Wittering	18. 4.08
G-CKMZ	Schleicher ASW 28-18	28716	BGA5216-KMZ 6. 1.06 D-KBJM	J R Martindale *"J5"*	Walney Island	7. 2.08
G-CKNB	Schempp-Hirth Standard Cirrus	222	BGA5218-KNB 17. 3.06 S5-3056, SL-3056, YU-4209	A Booker *"505"*	Lasham	16. 4.08
G-CKNC	Caproni Vizzola Calif A-21S	240	BGA5219-KNC 8. 2. 06 F-CEUE	J J and M E Pritchard *"NC"*	Lasham	19. 5.08
G-CKND	DG Flugzeugbau DG-1000T	10-76T15	BGA5220-KND 12. 6.06	S Heaton tr KND Group	Sutton Bank	11. 6.08
G-CKNE	Schempp-Hirth Standard Cirrus 75-VTC	199	BGA5221-KNE 27. 7.06	G D E Macdonald	Lasham	
	(Built Vzaduhoplovno Tehnicki Centar)		S5-3057, SL-3057, YU-4293			
G-CKNF	DG Flugzeugbau DG-1000T	10-81T20	BGA5222-KNF 12. 7.06	R Johnson tr Six November Fox	Lasham	9. 7.08
G-CKNG	Schleicher ASW 28-18E	28747	BGA5223-KNG 16. 8.06	M P Brockington	Talgarth	6. 8.07
G-CKNI	Glasflügel H205 Club Libelle	150	BGA5225-KNI 3.08R F-CEQG	K Sleigh *"W9"*	Rattlesden	
G-CKNJ	Schempp-Hirth Duo Discus xT	142/...	BGA5224-KNJ 6. 6.06	P Hurd tr Duo D11 Flying Group *"D11"*	Dunstable	28. 9.08
G-CKNK	DG Flugzeugbau DG-500 Elan Trainer		BGA5226-KNK 27. 3.06	Cotswold Gliding Club	Aston Down	1. 5.08
		5E116T48	D-5661			
G-CKNL	Schleicher ASK 21	21811	BGA5228-KNL 15. 5.06	Buckminster Gliding Club Ltd *"KNL"*	Saltby	29. 4.08
G-CKNM	Schleicher ASK 18	18037	BGA5229-KNM 4. 7.06 PH-908, D-4539	I L Pattingale *"K18"*	RAF Odiham	28. 9.08
G-CKNN	Slingsby T 21B Sedbergh	MHL.012	BGA5230-KNN 21. 4.06	R Wassermann	Donxdorf, Germany	26. 4.08
	(Built Martin Hearn Ltd)		OY-XSI, SE-SMA, WB985			
G-CKNO	Schempp-Hirth Ventus 2cxT	179/429	BGA5231-KNO 4. 9.06	C McEwen	Aston Down	28. 9.08
G-CKNR	Schempp-Hirth Ventus 2cxT	181/...	BGA5233-KNR 27. 7.06	R J Nicholls	Husbands Bosworth	23. 7.07
G-CKNS	Rolladen-Schneider LS4-a	4398	BGA5234-KNS 5. 6.06 SE-UEP, OH-714	I R Willows	Husbands Bosworth	6. 6.08
G-CKNU	Schleicher ASW 27-18E	29501	BGA5236-KNU 19. 3.08 D-KPRC, D-2529	R A Cheetham *"E1"*	Husbands Bosworth	16. 3.09
G-CKNV	Schleicher ASW 28-18E	28749	BGA5237-KNV 24. 7.06	D G Brain	Dunstable	28. 9.08
G-CKOD	Schempp-Hirth Discus bT	11/282	BGA5245-KOD 1.12.06 HB-2157, D-KCCE	A L Harris and M W Talbot	Nympsfield	28. 9.08
G-CKOE	Schleicher ASG 29	29024	BGA5246-KOE 3.08R D-9729	D Strange and R C Bromwich *"290"*	RAF Keevil	25.10.09
G-CKOH	DG Flugzeugbau DG-1000T	10-87T25	BGA5249-KOH 20.11.06	Lasham Gliding Society Ltd *"45"*	Lasham	22.11.07
G-CKOI	AB Sportine Aviacija LAK-17AT	183	BGA5250-KOI 6.12.06 LY-GQF	C G Corbett *"170"*	Dunstable	28. 9.08
G-CKOJ	Schempp-Hirth Duo Discus	188	BGA5251-KOJ 21.11.06 OE-5583	M R Dawson	Saintes, France	28. 9.08
G-CKOK	Schempp-Hirth Discus 2cT	50	BGA5252-KOK 17. 4.07	B D Scougall *"KOK" and "X9"*	Portmoak	12. 4.08
G-CKOL	Schempp-Hirth Duo Discus T	164	BGA5253-KOL 24. 4.07	P M Harmer tr Oscar Lima Syndicate *"KOL"*		
					North Hill	22. 4.08
G-CKOM	Schleicher ASW 27-18	29023	BGA5254-KOM 11. 1.08 D-9529, D-0001	M D Wells *"LE"*	Nympsfield	28. 9.08
G-CKON	Schleicher ASG 29E	29512	BGA5255-KON 1. 5.08 D-KBJG	J P Gorringe *"XE"*	Lasham	29. 4.09
G-CKOO	Schleicher ASG 29E	29519	BGA5256-KOO 3.08R D-KAAD	A Darlington, J P Lewis and C T P Williams *"7"*	Lasham	26. 4.09
G-CKOR	DG Flugzeugbau DG-300 Elan	3E110	BGA5258-KOR 20.12.06 PH-768	C D Prescott and J A Sparrow	Gransden Lodge	15.12.07
G-CKOT	Schleicher ASK 21	21818	BGA5260-KOT 17. 5.07	Ulster Gliding Club Ltd *"KOT"*	Bellarena	29. 5.08
G-CKOU	AB Sportine Aviacija LAK-19T	027	BGA5261-KOU 25. 5.07 LY-GNP	D Le Roux, R Walker and A Challoner *"KOU" & "1UP"*		4. 6.08
				(Operated Southdown Gliding Club)	Parham Park	
G-CKOV	Issoire E-78B Silene	05	BGA5262-KOV 16. 3.07 F-CFEB	I P Stork *"KOV"*	(Alviazere, Portugal)	26. 4.08
G-CKOW	DG Flugzeugbau DG-500 Elan Orion		BGA5263-KOW 16. 5.07	Southdown Gliding Club Ltd *"KOW"*	Parham Park	15. 5.08
		5E260X89				
G-CKOX	DG Flugzeugbau DG-500 Elan Orion		BGA5264-KOX 4. 9.07	M Blowers tr Seahawk Gliding Club		
		5E258X87			RNAS Culdrose	1. 9.08
G-CKOY	Schleicher ASG 29E	29510	BGA5265-KOY 13. 5.08 D-KNZG	N P Woods tr G-CKOY Group *"S9"*	(Collingtree)	9. 5.09
G-CKOZ	Schleicher ASG 29E	29513	BGA5266-KOZ 9. 4.08 D-KEEJ	E W Johnston *"G9"*	Dunstable	
G-CKPA	AB Sportine Aviacija LAK-19T	020	BGA5267-KPA 14. 2.07 (BGA5214), LY-GMV	Baltic Sailplanes Ltd *"KPA" and "L19"*		
					Husbands Bosworth	28. 9.08
G-CKPE	Schempp-Hirth Duo Discus	56	BGA5271-KPE 27. 4.07 HB-3088	M F Cuming *"KPE"*	Shenington	9. 4.08

G-CKPG	Schempp-Hirth Discus 2cT	59	BGA5273-KPG	25. 7.07	G Knight and R Baker	Gransden Lodge	26. 7.08
G-CKPJ	Neukom S-4D Elfe	411AB	BGA5276-KPJ	26. 3.07	J Szladowski *"KPJ"*	Camphill	
	(Built Jubi GmbH)		D-4598				
G-CKPK	Schempp-Hirth Ventus 2cxT	197	BGA5277-KPK	19. 7.07	I C Lees	Pocklington	17. 7.08
G-CKPL	Schempp-Hirth Standard Cirrus 75	649	BGA5278-KPL	2. 4.07	L B Roberts *"KPL"*	Nympsfield	28. 9.08
			F-CEMS		*(To OM-4742 and canx from BGA 27.10.07)*		
G-CKPM	DG Flugzeugbau LS8-st	8517	BGA5279-KPM	1. 6.07	J Bayford tr 8T Soaring *"8T"*	Gransden Lodge	19. 5.08
G-CKPN	PZL-Bielsko SZD-51-1 Junior	B-1927	BGA5280-KPN	1. 2.08	Rattlesden Gliding Club Ltd	Rattlesden	12. 9.08
			HB-3036				
G-CKPO	Schempp-Hirth Duo Discus xT	171	BGA5281-KPO	19. 7.07	B F Walker *"KPO"*	Nympsfield	15. 7.08
			(D-KDWF)				
G-CKPP	Schleicher ASK 21	21824	BGA5282-KPP	25. 7.07	Coventry Gliding Club Ltd tr The Gliding Centre		
						Husbands Bosworth	19. 7.08
G-CKPU	Schleicher ASW 27-18E	29531	BGA5286-KPU	18. 3.08	A J Kellerman *"293"*	Gransden Lodge	
G-CKPV	Schempp-Hirth HS.7 Mini-Nimbus B	63	BGA5287-KPV	20. 6.07	C J Pollard *"KPV"*	Rougham	
			PH-607, (PH-606)				
G-CKPX	PZL-Swidnik PW-6U	78.04.03		25. 9.07	J C Gibson tr KPX Syndicate	Chipping	
G-CKPY	Schempp-Hirth Duo Discus xT	174	BGA5290-KPY	30.11.07	C A Marren tr Duo-Discus Syndicate *"P7"*		
						Trenchard Lines, Upavon	3.12.09E
G-CKPZ	Schleicher ASW 20	20360	BGA5291-KPZ	5. 9.07	T Davies	RAF Cranwell	7. 9.08
			D-4090				
G-CKRB	Schleicher ASK 13	13292	BGA5293-KRB	13. 9.07	Derbyshire and Lancashire Gliding Club Ltd		
			D-0220			Camp Hill	12. 9.08
G-CKRC	Schleicher ASW 28-18 E	28735	BGA5294-KRC	19.10.07	M Woodcock	(Mickle Trafford, Chester)	26. 9.08
			D-KUPC				
G-CKRD	Schleicher ASW 27-18E	29537	BGA5295-KRD	31. 3.08	R F Thirkell *"B3"*	Lasham	
G-CKRF	DG Flugzeugbau DG-300 Elan	3E392	BGA5297-KRF	5.12.07	G A King *"KRF"*	Talgarth	13. 2.09E
			PH-923				
G-CKRH	Grob G103 Twin Astir II	3596	BGA5299-KRH	22.11.07	Staffordshire Gliding Club Ltd	Seighford	
			F-CFYJ, D-3963				
G-CKRI	Schleicher ASK 21	21835	BGA5300-KRI	14. 5.08	Kent Gliding Club Aircraft Ltd *"KRI"*	Challock	
G-CKRJ	Scheicher ASW 27-18E	29544	BGA5301-KRJ	30. 5.08	J C Thompson	Dunstable	
G-CKRM	Schleicher ASW 27	27174	BGA5304-KRM,	14. 2.08	C Luton *"GO"*	Husbands Bosworth	
			EI-GMA, EI-151				
G-CKRN	Grob G102 Astir CS	1261	BGA5305-KRN	31. 1.08	P Sallis *"PS1"*	(Brixworth, Northampton)	
			D-7356				
G-CKRO	Schempp-Hirth Duo Discus XLT	185	(BGA5306-KRQ)	15. 8.08	B C Morris tr Duo Discus Syndicate KRO		
						Wycombe Air Park	
G-CKRR	Schleicher ASW 15B	15393	BGA5308-KRR	26. 2.08	S A Day	Camphill	6. 6.09
			D-9288				
G-CKRS	FFA Diamant 16.5	038	(BGA5309-KRS)	8. 8.08	K J Burns tr G-CKRS Syndicate	Shenington	5. 8.09
			OO-ZII, BGA1471				
G-CKRT	Schleicher ASW 27-18E (ASG-29E)	29549	BGA5310-KRT	3. 7.08	J D Spencer *"601"*	Dunstable	1. 7.09
G-CKRU	Zaklad Szybowcowy Jezow PW-6U	78.04.07	BGA5311-KRU	21. 5.08	Cotswold Gliding Club	Aston Down	
G-CKRV	Schleicher ASW 27-18E (ASG-29E)	29555	(BGA5312-KRV)	22. 8.08	J Cruttenden and J Taylor	Lasham	18. 8.09
G-CKRW	Schleicher ASK 21	21337	BGA5313-KRW	22. 5.08	J G Arnold tr RAF Gliding and Soaring Association		
			D-4833			RAF Halton	28. 4.09
G-CKRX	Zaklad Szybowcowy Jezow PW-6U	78.04.08	BGA5314-KRX	25. 6.08	Cotswold Gliding Club	Aston Down	
G-CKSD	Rolladen-Schneider LS8-a	8096	N901T	2. 5.08	C Emson *"131"*	Bicester	6. 8.09
G-CKSH	PZL-Bielsko SZD-30 Pirat	B-544	BGA5324-KSH	31. 7.08	J K Hoffman	(Alloa)	
			D-1989, DDR-1849, DM-1849				
G-CKSK	Pilatus B4-PC11AF	004	BGA5327-KSK	21. 7.08	I H Keyser	(Dover)	13. 7.09
			HB-1103				
C-CKSL	Schleicher ASW 15B	15285	BGA5328-KSL	4. 9.08	A P B Long tr Sierra Lima Group	Camphill	20. 8.09
			D-2987				
G-CKSM	Schempp-Hirth Duo Discus T	191	BGA5329-KSM	16.10.08	J H May and S P Ball	Sutton Bank	11.11.09E
G-CKSO	Pilatus P4-BC11AF	064	(BGA5331-KSO)	27. 8.08	I H Keyser	(Dover)	13. 7.09
			HB-1125				
G-CKSY	Rolladen-Schneider LS7-WL	7110	BGA5340-KSY	2.12.08	C M Lewis	(Ely)	
			PH-902, D-1509				

G-CLAA - G-CLZZ

G-CLAC	Piper PA-28-161 Warrior II	28-8116241	N8396U	18. 5.87	J M Holley tr G-CLAC Group	Blackbushe	7. 3.09E
G-CLAS	Short SD.3-60 Variant 200	SH3635	EI-BEK	28. 7.93	BAC Group Ltd	Edinburgh	11. 9.09E
			G-BLED, G-14-3635				
G-CLAV	Europa Aviation Europa	060		11.10.02	C Laverty	Glenforsa, Isle of Mull	30. 7.09P
	(Built C Laverty - pr.no.PFA 247-12641) (Monowheel u/c)						
G-CLAX	Jurca MJ.5 Sirocco	PFA 2204	G-AWKB	22. 4.99	G D Claxton	(Talbot Green, Pontyclun)	
	(Built G D Claxton)						
G-CLAY	Bell 206B-3 JetRanger III	4409	G-DENN	16. 9.02	Claygate Distribution Ltd		
			N75486, C-GFNO			Paynetts Farm, Goudhurst	7. 8.09E
G-CLDS	Rotorsport UK Calidus	RSUK/CALS/001		19.11.08	Rotorsport UK Ltd		
					Poplar Farm, Prolly Moor, Wentnor Bishops Castle		
G-CLEA	Piper PA-28-161 Warrior II	28-7916081	N30296	28. 8.80	R J Harrison and A R Carpenter	Oaksey Park	19. 8.09E
G-CLEE	Rans S-6-ES Coyote II	0600.1373 ES		29. 6.01	R Holt	Mill Farm, Shifnal	30. 9.09P
	(Built R Holt - pr.no.PFA 204-13670) (Jabiru 2200A) (Tri-cycle u/c)						
G-CLEG	Flight Design CTSW	07.02.13		12. 4.07	P J Clegg	Barton	11. 4.08P
	(Assembled P&M Aviation Ltd with c/n 8269)						
G-CLEM	Bölkow BÖ.208A-2 Junior	561	G-ASWE	22. 9.81	J J Donely and K Herbert tr Bölkow Group		
			D-EFHE			Coventry	25. 9.08P
G-CLEO	Zenair CH.601HD Zodiac	PFA 162-13500		9. 8.99	K M Bowen	(Whitson, Newport)	
	(Built K M Bowen)						
G-CLFC	Mainair Blade	1324-0502-7-W1119		11. 6.02	G N Cliffe and G Marshall	(Winsford)	20. 6.09P

G-CLGC	Schempp-Hirth Duo Discus	173	BGA4511-JGV D-4020	1. 5.08	London Gliding Club (Proprietary) Ltd	Dunstable	
G-CLIC	Cameron A-105 Balloon (Hot Air)	2557		18. 4.91	R S Mohr *(Clic Trust titles)*	Box, Corsham	12. 8.09E
	(Second envelope fitted as c/n 3395, 4.95: third envelope fitted as c/n 10514, 4.04)						
G-CLIF	Comco Ikarus C42 FB UK PFA 322-14377			14. 3.05	C Sims	Old Sarum	11. 8.08P
	(Built C Sims)			*(Struck trees on go-around at Newton Peveril 6. 6.08 and force landed in adjacent field)*			
G-CLIN	Comco Ikarus C42 FB100	0712-6943		19. 3.08	G C Linley	(English Bicknor)	18. 3.09P
	(Built Aerosport Ltd)						
G-CLOE	Sky 90-24 Balloon (Hot Air)	019		11. 3.96	J Skinner	Chart Sutton, Maidstone	9. 8.09E
G-CLOP	Piper PA-32R-301T Saratoga TC	3257257	OY-PHW SX-ACV, N5346S	12.12.06	D Sander	Lydd	23. 1.10E
G-CLOS	Piper PA-34-200T Seneca II	34-7870361	HB-LKE N36783	17. 6.86	P S Kirby	Coventry	24. 6.09E
G-CLOT	Robinson R44 Raven	1912		25. 9.08	Tracey Plant Ltd	Donegal	25. 9.09E
G-CLOW	Beech 200 Super King Air	BB-821	N821RC TC-DBY, N144TM, F-GDCB	2.11.99	Clowes Estates Ltd	Nottingham-East Midlands	29.11.09E
G-CLRK	Sky 77-24 Balloon (Hot Air)	101		3. 3.98	William Clark and Son (Parkgate) Ltd *"Clark"*	Dumfries	10. 9.09E
G-CLUB	Reims Cessna FRA150N Aerobat	FRA1500347	OO-AWZ F-WZAZ, (F-WZDZ)	10. 2.83	J H and C M Cooper	Great Oakley	1. 9.09E
G-CLUE	Piper PA-34-200T Seneca II	34-7970502	N8089Z	15. 9.92	K Sutcliffe	(Clevedon, Bristol)	8. 7.09E
G-CLUX	Reims Cessna F172N Skyhawk II	F17201996	PH-AYG (3)	1. 5.80	J G Jackman and K M Drewitt	Hawarden	20. 8.09E
G-CLWN	Cameron Clown SS Balloon (Hot Air)	2857	SE-ZGU G-UBBE		Magical Adventures Ltd	Oswestry	27. 9.09E

G-CMAA - G-CMZZ

G-CMAF	Embraer EMB-135BJ Legacy	14501011	PT-SVE	18.10.07	TAG Aviation (UK) Ltd	Marseilles/Marignane, France	17.10.09E
G-CMBL	Bombardier CL-600-2B19	8067	C-FLKA C-FMMN	23. 1.08	TAG Aviation (UK) Ltd	Farnborough	23. 1.10E
	(CL-600 Regional Jet)						
G-CMBR	Cessna 172S Skyhawk	172S8144	N948SP	18. 4.08	C M B Reid	Rochester	14. 7.09E
G-CMBS	MD Helicopters MD.900 Explorer	900-00111	N70124 N7011V, (PH-PXG)	24. 4.06	Cambridgeshire Constabulary	RAF Wyton	16. 5.09S
G-CMCC	Robinson R44 Raven II	11837		2. 8.07	C McCann	(Lanark)	7. 9.09E
G-CMED	SOCATA TB-9 Tampico Club	1867	F-GSZK	19. 3.01	S C Brown t/a Enstone Flying Club	Enstone	20. 4.09E
G-CMGC	Piper PA-25-235 Pawnee D	25-7756042	G-BFEX N82525	19.11.91	Midland Gliding Club Ltd	Long Mynd	14. 7.09E
G-CMLS	Cirrus SR20	1315	N1298C	24. 4.07	Cumulus Aircraft Rentals Ltd	Shoreham	18. 6.09E
G-CMOR	Best Off Sky Ranger 912(2)	SKR0412542		25. 2.05	P Moore	Bakersfield	22. 8.07P
	(Built C Moore - pr.no.BMAA HB/441)						
G-CMOS	Cessna T303 Crusader	T30300222	D-IPMG N121JH, N9858C	15.12.06	C J Moss	Goodwood	28. 2.09E
G-CMSN	Robinson R22 Beta	1669	G-MGEE G-PHEL, G-RUMP, N2405T	29. 6.04	S Meadows	Gamston	22. 4.09E
G-CMWK	Grob G-102 Astir CS	1518	(BGA5330) PH-820, D-7454	8.8.08	S Saunders	RAF Marham	25. 8.09
G-CMXX	Robinson R44 Raven II	10661		9. 3.05	Northern Excavators Ltd	Ballinderry	14. 4.09E

G-CNAA - G-CNZZ

G-CNAB	Avtech Jabiru UL-450	xxxx		27. 9.00	W A Brighouse	Eddsfield, Octon Lodge Farm, Thwing	17.12.07P
	(Built W A Brighouse - pr.no.PFA 274-13651 although type prefix should be "274A")						
G-CNCN	Rockwell Commander 112TC-A	13151	HB-NCN N4620W	1. 6.05	R A and P A Symmonds	Southend	21. 7.08E

G-COAA - G-COZZ

G-COAI	Cranfield A 1-400 Eagle	001	G-BCIT	1. 6.98	Cranfield University *(Noted 1.07)*	Cranfield	
	(Built Cranfield Institute of Technology)						
G-COCO	Reims Cessna F172M Skyhawk II	F17201373	PH-SMO OO-ADI	27.10.80	P C Sheard and R C Larder	Strubby	14. 4.09E
G-CODY	Kolb Twinstar Mk.III Xtra M3X05-2-00070			8. 2.06	J W Codd	(Broughton, Brigg)	17. 6.08P
	(Built J W Codd - pr.no.PFA 205-14456)						
G-COIN	Bell 206B-2 JetRanger II	897	EI-AWA	11. 3.85	J P Niehorster, S Pool and J Woodward (Buntingford, Ramsey, Isle of Man and Stevenage)		10. 4.09E
G-COLA	Beech F33C Bonanza	CJ-137	G-BUAZ PH-BNH	31. 3.92	J R C Spooner and P M Scarratt	Nottingham-East Midlands	20.11.09E
G-COLH	Piper PA-28-140 Cherokee	28-23143	G-AVRT N11C	13.10.00	Full Sutton Flying Centre Ltd	Full Sutton	7. 4.09E
G-COLI	Rotorsport UK MT-03	RSUK/MT-03/037		10. 4.08	G Gilholm	(Selkirk)	20. 4.09P
G-COLL	Enstrom 280C-UK-2 Shark	1223		17. 8.81	D M Astall	Ramsey, Isle of Man	7. 1.10E
G-COLS	Van's RV-7A	PFA 323-14312		6.10.04	C Terry	(Grampound. Truro)	
	(Built C Terry)						
G-COMB	Piper PA-30 Twin Comanche B	30-1362	G-AVBL N8236Y	14. 9.84	M R Booker	Full Sutton	7. 3.08E
G-COML	Eurocopter EC.120B Colibri	1326	PH-VIS F-WQDL	20. 1.09	Combilift	(Gallinagh, Ireland)	
G-COMU	Flight Design CT2K	03-03-01-08		16. 6.03	Comunica Industries International Ltd	Roughay Farm, Bishops Waltham	29. 1.08P
	(Assembled Mainair Sports Ltd with c/n 7965)						
G-CONB	Robin DR.400-180 Régent	2176	G-BUPX	14. 4.93	M D Souster	Redhill	4. 3.09E
G-CONC	Cameron N-90 Balloon (Hot Air)	2139		13.11.89	A A Brown *"Concorde"*	Guildford	4. 9.09E
G-CONL	SOCATA TB-10 Tobago	173	F-GCOR	22.12.98	J M Huntington	Full Sutton	1. 6.09E
G-CONR	Champion 7GCBC Citabria	280-70	YU-CAB	15. 5.06	N O'Brien	Glountha, Kilkenny, County Down	11. 8.08

G-COOT	Aerocar Taylor Coot A	EE-1A		16. 9.81	P M Napp *(Noted stored 8.07)*	Stanton, Morpeth	
	(Built D A Hood)						
G-COPS	Piper J-3C-65 Cub (L-4H-PI)	11911	F-BFYC	17. 7.79	R W Sproat	Lenox Plunton Farm, Borgue	12. 5.09P
	(Frame No.11739)		French AF, 44-79615				
	(Officially regd with c/n 36-817 which is USAAC contract no)						
G-COPZ	Van's RV-7	71605		8.12.03	R S Horan	(Melrose)	
	(Built R S Horan - pr.no.PFA 323-14150)						
G-CORA	Europa Aviation Europa XS	467	G-ILUM	30. 5.06	A P Gardner	Little Gransden	
	(Built A R Haynes - pr.no.PFA 247-13565) (Tri-gear u/c)						
G-CORB	SOCATA TB-20 Trinidad	1178	F-GKUX	12. 4.99	G D Corbin	Flamstone Park, Bishopstone	27. 4.09E
G-CORD	Nipper T 66 RA.45 Series 3	S 129	G-AVTB	21. 3.88	A V Lamprell	Charity Farm, Baxterley	3. 7.04P
	(Built Slingsby Sailplanes Ltd as c/n 1565 (G-AVTB) for Nipper Aircraft Ltd with c/n S 105 then rebuilt as c/n 1676 (G-CORD) with Nipper c/n S 129)						
G-CORL	Eurocopter AS.350B3 Ecureuil	4454	SE-HJI	1. 8.08	Abbeyflight Ltd	Redhill	21. 8.09E
G-COSY	Lindstrand LBL 56A Balloon (Hot Air)	017		18. 2.93	D D Owen	Wotton-under-Edge	2. 4.03A
G-COTT	Cameron Flying Cottage 60 SS Balloon (Hot Air)	"G-HOUS"		13. 2.81	Dragon Balloon Company Ltd *"Nottingham Building Society"*		
		687				Castleton, Hope Valley	21. 9.09E
G-COUP	Ercoupe 415C	1903	N99280	27. 5.93	S M Gerrard *"Jenny Lin"*	Goodwood	. 3.10S
	(Continental C75)		NC99280				
G-COUZ	Raj Hamsa X'Air 582(2)	444		2. 1.09	D J Couzens	(Sleaford)	
	(Built D J Couzens, pr no BMAA HB/153)						
G-COVA	Piper PA-28-161 Warrior III	2842217	G-CDCL	18. 2.05	Coventry (Civil) Aviation Ltd	Coventry	12.12.09E
			N3072G				
G-COVB	Piper PA-28-161 Warrior III	2842234	N3094S	13. 6.05	Coventry (Civil) Aviation Ltd	Coventry	21. 6.09E
G-COVE	Avtech Jabiru UL	0214		23. 7.99	A A Rowson	Emlyn's Field, Rhuallt	14. 9.07P
	(Built A A Rowson - pr.no.PFA 274A-13409)						
G-COXS	Aeroprakt A22 Foxbat	PFA 317-14168		9. 3.04	S Cox	(Hinckley)	30. 6.09P
	(Built S Cox)						
G-COXY	Air Création 582(1)/Kiss 400	FL.025		11. 3.04	B G Cox	Hunsdon	30. 6.07P
	(Built B G Cox - pr.no.BMAA HB/351 being Flylight kit comprising Trike s/n T03107 and s/n Wing A03186-3184)						
G-COZI	Rutan Cozy	PFA 159-12162		19. 7.93	R Machin	Ronaldsway	9. 4.09P
	(Built D G Machin) (Lycoming O-320)						

G-CPAA - G-CPZZ

G-CPCD	CEA Jodel DR.221 Dauphin	81	F-BPCD	11.12.90	D J Taylor	Enstone	12. 7.08
G-CPDW	Mudry CAP.10B	195	N502DW	23.04.07	Hilfa Ltd	Rochester and Sywell	22. 7.09E
G-CPEL	Boeing 757-236	24398	N602DF	24. 8.92	British Airways PLC	London Heathrow	26.10.09E
			EC-EOL, EC-597, G-BRJE, EC-EOL, EC-278, G-BRJE				
G-CPEM	Boeing 757-236	28665		28. 3.97	British Airways PLC	London Heathrow	27. 3.09E
G-CPEN	Boeing 757-236	28666		23. 4.97	British Airways PLC	London Heathrow	22. 4.09E
G-CPEO	Boeing 757-236	28667		11. 7.97	British Airways PLC	London Heathrow	10. 7.09E
G-CPEP	Boeing 757-2Y0	25268	C-GTSU	16. 4.97	Thomson Airways Ltd	Manchester	9. 7.09E
			EI-CLP, N400KL, XA-TAE				
G-CPER	Boeing 757-236	29113		29.12.97	British Airways PLC	London Gatwick	28.12.09E
G-CPES	Boeing 757-236	29114		17. 3.98	British Airways PLC	London Heathrow	16. 3.09E
G-CPET	Boeing 757-236	29115		12. 5.98	British Airways PLC	London Heathrow	11. 5.09E
G-CPFC	Reims Cessna F152 II	F15201430		1.12.77	Falcon Flying Services Ltd	Biggin Hill	20. 7.09E
G-CPHA	Robinson R44 Raven II	12641		27. 1.09	Heli Air Ltd		
					Wellesbourne Mountford/Wycombe Air Park		
G-CPMK	de Havilland DHC-1 Chipmunk 22	C1/0866	WZ847	28. 6.96	P A Walley *(As "WZ847:F" in RAF c/s)*	Elstree	12. 1.09S
G-CPMS	SOCATA TB-20 Trinidad	1607	F-GNHA	7. 4.98	Charlotte Park Management Services Ltd		
						Goodwood	13. 6.09E
G-CPOL	Aérospatiale AS.355F1 Ecureuil 2	5007	N5775T	30.11.95	MW Helicopters Ltd	Stapleford	17. 6.09E
			C-GJJB, N5775T				
G-CPPM	North American Harvard II	81-4013	RCAF 3019	2. 3.07	S D Wilch	Bruntingthorpe	
G-CPRI	Learjet 45	45-037	OE-GDI	18. 6.08	TAG Aviation (UK) Ltd	Farnborough	24. 7.09E
			N50145				
G-CPSF	Cameron N-90 Balloon (Hot Air)	3747	G-OISK	21. 4.99	S A Simington and J D Rigden	Norwich	1. 5.04A
G-CPSH	Eurocopter EC.135 T1	0209	D-HECJ	8. 4.02	Thames Valley Police Authority	Benson	20. 6.11E
G-CPTM	Piper PA-28-151 Cherokee Warrior		G-BTOE	9. 7.91	C and T J Mackay	(Wettenhall, Winsford)	12. 3.09E
		28-7715012	N4264F				
G-CPTS	Agusta-Bell 206B-2 JetRanger II	8556		1. 6.78	A R B Aspinall	(Skipton)	3.10.09E
G-CPXC	CAB CAP.10C	301		11.12.01	J M Wicks	Boones Farm, Braintree	31. 7.09E

G-CRAA - G-CRZZ

G-CRAB	Best Off Sky Ranger 912(1)	SKR0210245		1.11.02	R A Weller	Priory Farm, Tibenham	16. 9.08P
	(Built R A Bell - pr.no.BMAA HB/246)						
G-CRAR	CZAW Sportcruiser	LAA 338-14841		4. 9.08	R B Armitage	Maypole Farm, Chislet	
	(Built R B Armitage)						
G-CRAY	Robinson R22 Beta	0919		12. 1.89	Heli Air Ltd		
					Wellesbourne Mountford/Wycombe Air Park		10. 7.09E
G-CRBV	Balony Kubicek BB26 Balloon (Hot Air)	373	OK-0373	22. 7.05	Charter Ballooning Ltd *(Reading Business Venue titles)*		
						Liphook	17.4 .09E
G-CRDY	Agusta-Bell 206A JetRanger	8112	G-WHAZ	22.12.03	Loughbeigh Properties Ltd	(Craughwell, Ireland)	28. 1.09E
			OH-HRE, G-WHAZ, OH-HRE				
G-CRES	Denney Kitfox Model 2	PFA 172-11574		7. 6.90	J McGoldrick	Newtownards	14. 6.07P
	(Built R J Cresswell) (Rotax 912)						
G-CREY	Progressive Aerodyne Searey Amphibian			2. 1.07	A F Reid and P J Gallagher		
		PFA 343-14619				(Newtownards and Bangor)	
	(Built A F Reid & P J Gallagher)						
G-CRIB	Robinson R44 Raven	0980	G-JJWL	28. 3.03	D G Williams tr Cribarth Helicopters	Bulith Wells	11. 4.09E

G-CRIC	Colomban MC-15 Cri-Cri	PFA 133-10915		22. 7.83	R S Stoddart-Stones	(Woldingham, Caterham)	5. 5.99P
	(Built A J Maxwell) (JPX PUL.212)						
G-CRIK	Colomban MC-15 Cri-Cri	PFA 133-13289		10.11.04	A R Robinson	(Prestbury, Macclesfield)	
	(Built A R Robinson)						
G-CRIL	Rockwell Commander 112B	521	N1388J	22. 6.79	J W Reynolds tr Rockwell Aviation Group	Cardiff	14.12.09E
G-CRIS	Taylor JT.1 Monoplane	PFA 055-10318		5. 6.79	C R Steer	(Spilstead Farm, Sedlescombe)	
	(Built C J Bragg)				*(Bare fuselage noted 5.01)*		
G-CRJW	Schleicher ASW 27-18	29568	BGA5333-KSR	22.12.08	R J Welford	Gransden Lodge	
G-CROB	Europa Aviation Europa XS	442		25. 4.02	R G Hallam	Sleap	21. 2.08P
	(Built R G Hallam - pr.no.PFA 247-13510) (Jabiru 3300) (Tri-Gear u/c)						
G-CROL	Maule MXT-7-180 Super Rocket	14032C	N9232F	24.11.93	W E Willets	(Bewdley)	4. 3.04
G-CROO	Cessna 525A CitationJet CJ2	525A0388	N5267T	7. 3.08	Rooney Air Ltd	Biggin Hill	6. 3.09E
G-CROP	Cameron Z-105 Balloon (Hot-Air)	11157		20. 5.08	PSH Skypower Ltd *"New Holland Agriculture"*		
						Pewsey	4. 6.09E
G-CROW	Robinson R44 Raven	0754		19. 4.00	Longmoore Ltd *(Operated FAST Helicopters Ltd)*		
						Shoreham	2.12.09E
G-CROY	Europa Aviation Europa	101		7. 2.97	M T Austin	Kirkwall	29. 6.09P
	(Built A T Croy - pr.no.PFA 247-12896) (Monowheel u/c)						
G-CRPH	Airbus A320-231	0424	F-WQBB	10. 4.95	Thomas Cook Airlines Ltd	Manchester	14.4.09E
			F-WWIV				
G-CRUI	CZAW Sportcruiser	PFA 338-14723		1. 5.08	J Massey	Wellcross Grange, Slinfold	1. 7.09P
	(Built J Massey)						
G-CRUM	Westland Scout AH.1	F9712	XV137	17. 3.98	D O Sears tr G-CRUM Group *(As "XV137" in AAC c/s)*		
						Draycott Farm, Chiseldon	30. 1.09P
G-CRUZ	Cessna T303 Crusader	T30300004	N9336T	7.12.90	Bank Farm Ltd	Bank Farm, Benwick	10. 7.09E
G-CRWZ	CZAW Sportcruiser	PFA 338-14648		23. 4.08	P B Lowry	Dealand	
	(Built P B Lowry)						
G-CRZA	CZAW Sportcruiser	PFA 338-14657		17. 4.08	A J Radford	Tatenhill	
	(Built A J Radford)						

G-CSAA - G-CSZZ

G-CSAM	Van's RV-9A	PFA 320-14384		1. 3.07	B G Murray	(Teignmouth)	
	(Built B G Murray)						
G-CSAV	Thruster T 600N 450	0032-T600N-064		14. 3.02	R C Best	Wickenby	12. 8.08P
G-CSAW	CZAW Sportcruiser	PFA/338-14649		11. 3.08	B C Fitzgerald-O'Connor	(London E13)	
	(Built B C M Fitzgerald-O'Connor)						
G-CSBD	Piper PA-28-236 Dakota	28-8211019	G-CSBO	18. 7.05	S B and S-J Dunnett	Upfield Farm, Whitson	15. 8.09E
			N8471Y				
G-CSBM	Reims Cessna F150M	F15201359	PH-AYC	24. 5.78	Transcourt Ltd	Hinton-in-the-Hedges	5. 2.09E
G-CSCS	Reims Cessna F172N Skyhawk II	F17201707	PH-MEM	28.11.86	C Sullivan	Stapleford	10. 6.09E
			(PH-WEB), N9899A				
G-CSDJ	Avtech Jabiru UL	0201		23. 3.99	D W and J Johnston, C D and S Slater		
	(Built D W Johnston and C D Slater - pr.no.PFA 274A-13337)					Redlands, Swindon	22. 5.09P
G-CSDR	Corvus CA22 Crusader	CA22-010		28. 7.08	J B Mills	Duxford	
	(Officially registered with type 56-01 on c/n plate and various other data-plates)						
G-CSFC	Cessna 150L	15075360	(G-BFLX)	21. 3.78	S J Williams tr Foxtrot Charlie Flying Group		
			N11370			RNAS Culdrose	3. 4.09E
G-CSFD	UltraMagic M-90 Balloon (Hot Air)	90/56		12.12.02	L A Watts *(Chelmsford titles)*		
						Pangbourne, Reading	27. 9.09E
G-CSGT	Piper PA-28-161 Warrior II	2816069	G-BPHB	31. 1.06	M J Wade	Turweston	20. 4.09E
			N9148G				
G-CSIX	Piper PA-32-300 Cherokee Six	32-7840030	ZS-OMX	15. 6.01	A J Hodge	Hinton-in-the-Hedges	14. 9.08E
			Z-WJM, VP-WJM, HB-PCX, ZS-KBR, N9857K				
G-CSMK	Evektor EV-97 Eurostar	PFA 315-13813		4.12.01	R Frey	Derby	4. 4.09P
	(Built N R Beale)						
G-CSPR	Van's RV-6A	25584	N9004F	16. 5.07	P J Pengilly	(Church Crookham, Fleet)	22. 7.09P
	(Built D L Reed)						
G-CSUE	ICP MXP-740 Savannah Jabiru(5)			26.10.06	J R Stratton	Bodmin	3. 9.08P
		06-07-51-505					
	(Built J R Stratton - pr.no.BMAA HB/517)						
G-CSWH	Piper PA-28R-180 Cherokee Arrow		N4647J	5. 4.02	J F Gould	Yoxall, Burton-on-Trent	18. 2.09E
		28R-30541	G-CSWH, N4647J				
G-CSWL	Bell 206L-1 LongRanger	45565	G-VOLK	6. 5.97	Milford Garage Ltd t/a Milford Aviation	Cranfield	1.11.08E
			G-GBAY, G-CSWL, G-SIRI, G-CSWL, F-GDAD				
G-CSZM	Zenair CH.601XL Zodiac	PFA 162B-14367		9.12.05	C Budd	(Tairgwaith, Ammanford)	
	(Built C Budd)						

G-CTAA - G-CTZZ

G-CTAA	Schempp-Hirth Janus	16	BGA5133-KJT	9.11.05	D Catt tr AA Group *"AA"*	Bicester	27. 1.08
			N2AA				
G-CTAG	Rolladen-Schneider LS8-18	8150	BGA4450-JEG	11. 9.07	C D R Tagg *"C1"*	Pocklington	15.11.07
G-CTAV	Evektor EV-97 teamEurostar UK	2129		25.11.04	P Simpson	Bourn	3.12.09P
G-CTCD	Diamond DA.42 Twin Star	42.079	OE-VPI	8. 2.06	CTC Aviation Group PLC	Bournemouth	17. 3.09E
G-CTCE	Diamond DA.42 Twin Star	42.043	OE-VPI	25. 8.05	CTC Aviation Group PLC	Bournemouth	21. 9.09E
G-CTCF	Diamond DA.42 Twin Star	42.045	OE-VPY	25. 8.05	CTC Aviation Group PLC	Bournemouth	21. 9.09E
G-CTCH	Diamond DA.42 Twin Star	42.238	(ZK-CTP)	4. 5.07	CTC Aviation Group PLC	Bournemouth	22. 5.09E
			OE-VPY				
G-CTCL	SOCATA TB-10 Tobago	1107	G-BSIV	16. 7.90	Gift Aviation Ltd	Gamston	26.10.09E
G-CTDH	Flight Design CT2K	02-08-01-31		1. 5.03	A D Thelwall	Baxby Manor, Husthwaite	25. 5.09P
	(Assembled Mainair Sports Ltd with c/n 7939)						

G-CTDW	Flight Design CTSW		07.05.05		22. 6.07	B S Keene	Compton Abbas 21. 6.08P
	(Assembled P&M Aviation Ltd with c/n 8295)						
G-CTEC	Stoddard-Hamilton GlaStar	PFA 295-13260			9.11.99	B N C Mogg	(Bibberne Farm, Stalbridge)
	(Built A J Clarry)						
G-CTED	Van's RV-7A	PFA 323-14631			24. 5.07	E W Lyon	(Gattonside, Melrose)
	(Built E W Lyon)						
G-CTEL	Cameron N-90 Balloon (Hot Air)		3933		27. 8.96	M R Noyce *(Gabletop titles)*	Hatherden, Andover 28. 5.09E
G-CTEN	Cessna 750 Citation X		750-0281	N50639	13. 3.08	Pendley Aviation LLP	Luton 12. 3.09E
G-CTGR	Cameron N-77 Balloon (Hot Air)		1775	G-CCDI	28. 8.97	T G Read *(Charles Church titles)*	Knutsford 13. 9.03T
G-CTIO	SOCATA TB-20 Trinidad GT		2174	F-OIMH	7.11.02	I R Hunt	Biggin Hill 1.12.09E
G-CTIX	Vickers Supermarine 509 Spitfire Tr.9		xxx	N462JC	9. 4.85	A A Hodgson *(As "PT462:SW-A" in RAF c/s)*	
	(Major rebuild from parts pre 1994)			G-CTIX, IDF/AF 2067, 0607, MM4100, PT462			Bryn Gwyn Bach 20. 5.09P
G-CTKL	Noorduyn AT-16 Harvard IIB		07-30	(G-BKWZ)	22.11.83	M R Simpson *(As "FE788" in RAF c/s)*	Rochester 22. 5.09P
	(C/n also quoted as "76-80")			MM54-137, RCAF3064			
G-CTLS	Flight Design CTLS		F08-09-12		19. 1.09	P&M Aviation Ltd	Rochdale
G-CTOY	Denney Kitfox Model 3		1176		14.10.91	B McNeilly	(Newtownards) 10. 5.93P
	(Built G S Cass and G C Brooke - pr.no.PFA 172-12150)						
G-CTRL	Robinson R22 Beta II		3601		13. 5.04	Central Helicopters Ltd	Nottingham City-Tollerton 12. 6.09E
G-CTSW	Flight Design CTSW		05.11.15		7.12.05	C J Powell tr Dragon Syndicate	
	(Assembled P&M Aviation Ltd with c/n 8158)						Upfield Farm, Whitson 20. 8.07P
G-CTUG	Piper PA-25-235 Pawnee C		25-4448	N4713Y	13. 9.04	The Borders (Milfield) Gliding Club Ltd	Milfield 4. 1.10E
G-CTWO	Schempp-Hirth Standard Cirrus		256	BGA4836-JWH	11. 7.07	R J Griffin	Shenington 26. 1.08
				SE-TMZ			
G-CTWW	Piper PA-34-200T Seneca II		34-7970191	G-ROYZ	21. 7.93	Fly (CI) Ltd *(Operated Trans Euro Air)*	Southend 13. 4.09E
				G-GALE, N3052X			
G-CTZO	SOCATA TB-20 Trinidad GT		2166	F-OIME	7.10.02	M R Munn	Turweston 13.10.09E

G-CUAA - G-CUZZ

G-CUBB	Piper PA-18-150 Super Cub *(L-18C-PI)*		18-3111	PH-WAM	5.12.78	Bidford Gliding Ltd	Bidford 18. 4.11
	(Lycoming O-360-C2) (Frame No.18-3009)			Belgian AF OL-L37, 53-4711			
G-CUBE	Best Off Sky Ranger 912(2)		SKR0311409		13. 1.04	T R Villa	Priory Farm, Tibenham 6. 7.09P
	(Built T R Villa - pr.no.BMAA HB/336)						
G-CUBI	Piper PA-18-125 Super Cub		18-3181	PH-GAV	26. 2.79	G T Fisher	(Northside, Thorney) 4.11.94T
	(L-18C-PI)			PH-VCV, R Neth AF L-107, 53-4781			
	(Official c/n 18-559 related to PH-GAV prior to 1970 rebuild when it incorporated Frame No.18-3170 from PH-VCV: possible link to G-CCKW qv)						
G-CUBJ	Piper PA-18-150 Super Cub		18-2036	PH-MBF	15.12.82	A L Grisay	Old Warden 9.11.07E
	(L-18C-PI) (Frame No.18-2035)			PH-NLF, R Neth AF R-43, 8A-43, 52-2436 *(As "18-5395:CDG" in French Army c/s)*			
	(Regd with c/n 18-5395 after 1974 rebuild of PH-NLF: acquired data plate from, and took identity of, PH-MBF - note G-SUPA also carries this c/n)						
G-CUBN	Piper PA-18-150 Super Cub		18-7902	SE-ECN	17.11.05	N J R Minchin	Hill Top Farm, Hambledon 4. 3.11S
G-CUBP	Piper PA-18-150 Super Cub		18-8482	N1136Z	8. 8.96	D W Berger	Trenchard Farm, Eggesford 22. 5.11
	(Frame No.18-8725)			G-BVMI, OH-PIN, N4262Z			
	(Regd with c/n 18-8823 the "official" identity of N1136Z/D-EIAC: rebuilt 1984/85 with Frame No.18-4613 ex D-EKAF: this frame fitted to G-BVMI following accident on 15.8.95: repaired frame of G-BVMI has now become G-CUBP)						
G-CUBS	Piper J-3C-65 Cub		"17792"	G-BHPT	26.10.01	S M Rolfe tr Sunbeam Aviation	
	(Frame No.17792)			F-BSGQ, LX-AIH, N70688, NC70688			Willington, Bedford 13. 7.05P
	(Official p/i is frame no. - possibly c/n 18105 ex NC71076, N71076)						
G-CUBW	Wag-Aero AcroTrainer	PFA 108-13581			26.11.02	B G, N D Plumb and A G Bourne	
	(Built B G, N D Plumb and A G Bourne)						Hinton-in-the-Hedges 17. 3.09P
G-CUBY	Piper J-3C-65 Cub		16317	G-BTZW	2. 3.95	C A Bloom	Shoreham 11. 7.09P
	(Rebuilt with new fuselage 1996/97)			N88689, NC88689			
G-CUCU	Colt 180A Balloon (Hot Air)		3869		22. 4.96	S R Seager	Aylesbury 28. 5.06T
G-CUDY	Enstrom 480B		5087	G-REAN	4. 2.09	Toure International Ltd	Oxford 27. 3.09E
G-CUIK	QAC Quickie Q.200	PFA 094A-11204			15.12.04	C S Rayner	Enstone 6. 1.10P
	(Built C S Rayner)						
G-CULF	Robinson R44 Raven II		11770		8. 6.07	I Nicoll	Southend 28. 6.09E
G-CUMU	Schempp-Hirth Discus b		259	BGA3397-FNQ	25. 9.08	C E Fernando	Aston Down
G-CUPP	Pitts S-2A		2166	N42XX	27. 3.07	Avmarine Ltd	Rusper, Horsham 12. 6.09E
	(Built Aerotek Inc)			N86PS			
G-CUPS	IAV Bacau Yakovlev Yak-52		9010312	LY-AMD	13. 6.03	L R Haunch tr Fenland Flying School	Fenland 30.10.09P
				Ukraine AF 09 (yellow), DOSAAF 09 (yellow)			
G-CURV	Avid Speed Wing	PFA 189-12169			28. 3.00	K S Kelso Fen End Farm, Smithy Fen, Cottenham	
	(Built K S Kelso)					*(On build 3.06)*	
G-CUTE	Dyn'Aéro MCR-01 Club		132		7. 9.99	E G Shimmin	Shobdon 16. 5.09P
	(Built E G Shimmin - pr.no.PFA 301-13511)						
G-CUTY	Europa Aviation Europa		224		20. 8.96	D J and M Watson	
	(Built D J and M Watson - pr.no.PFA 247-12910) (Tri-gear u/c)						(San Miguel de Salinas, Alicante, Spain)

G-CVAA - G-CVZZ

G-CVAL	Comco Ikarus C42 FB100		0608-6836		15. 8.06	J I Greenshields tr G-CVAL Group	Dunkeswell 3.10.08P
G-CVBF	Cameron A-210 Balloon (Hot Air)		3588		2. 6.95	Airxcite Ltd t/a Virgin Balloon Flights	Wembley 15. 8.01T
G-CVII	Dan Rihn DR.107 One Design				9. 3.06	R M Davies tr One Design Group	
		PFA 264-14478					(Melton Mowbray)
G-CVIX	de Havilland DH.110 Sea Vixen D 3		10125	XP924	26. 2.96	Drilling Systems Ltd *(As "XP524:134/E" in RN c/s)*	
	(Regd as FAW.2 with c/n 10132)						Bournemouth 26. 6.09P
G-CVLH	Piper PA-34-200T Seneca II		34-8070332	F-GCPK	5. 9.02	Atlantic Aviation Ltd	St Brieuc, France 12. 9.05T
				N8252D, N8250H		*(stored in poor condition)*	
G-CVMI	Piper PA-18-150 Super Cub		18-5700	SE-CEE	23. 5.05	D Heslop and T P Spurge	Great Oakley 20. 7.11S
G-CVPM	Magni M-16 Tandem Trainer	VPM16-UK-110			26. 3.98	P J Troy-Davies	(Fleetwood) 29. 6.09P
	(Built C S Teuber) (Arrow GT1000R)						
G-CVST	Jodel D 140 Mousquetaire	PFA 251-13384			21. 5.03	A Shipp *(Noted 8.08)*	Full Sutton
	(Built A Shipp)						

G-CVXN	Reims Cessna F406 Caravan II	F406-0064	G-SFPA	3.12.08	Caledonian Airborne Systems Ltd	Aberdeen	25. 2.09E

G-CWAA - G-CWZZ

G-CWAG	Sequoia F 8L Falco	PFA 100-10895		11. 5.92	D R Austin	Standalone Farm, Meppershall	22.10.09P
	(Built C C Wagner) (Lycoming O-320)						
G-CWAL	Raj Hamsa X'Air 133(1)	777		27. 4.04	L R Morris	Ballymegeough, Ireland	31.10.09P
	(Built C Walsh - pr.no.BMAA HB/339)						
G-CWAY	Comco Ikarus C42 FB100	0707-6907		6. 9.07	M Conway	(Cookstown, Belfast)	18.10.08P
G-CWBM	Phoenix Currie Wot	PFA 3020	G-BTVP	28. 3.94	M J Bond	(Wellingore, Lincs)	3.10.09P
	(Built B V Mayo) (Continental C85)						
G-CWEB	P&M Aviation Quik GT450	8343		20. 2.08	K A and M Forsyth	(Lempitlaw, Kelso)	19. 2.09P
G-CWFA	Piper PA-38-112 Tomahawk	38-78A0120	G-BTGC N9507T	17. 8.99	V Henning	Hawarden	26. 6.09E
G-CWFB	Piper PA-38-112 Tomahawk	38-78A0623	G-OAAL N4471E	13. 1.00	P M Moyle (Noted 10.07)	Bodmin	8. 2.07T
G-CWIC	Mainair Sports Pegasus Quik	8067		21. 9.04	A Battersby tr G-CWIC Group	Barton	29.12.09P
G-CWIK	Mainair Sports Pegasus Quik	8018		23. 4.04	C D Jackson	Easter Poldar Farm, Thornhill	15 .5.09P
G-CWLC	Schleicher ASH 25	25105	BGA3720-GCE	9. 1.08	C.L.Withall	Dunstable	1. 4.08
G-CWMC	P&M Aviation Quik GT450	8201		26. 8.06	A R Hughes	Yatesbury	9. 4.09P
G-CWMT	Dyn'Aéro MCR-01	PFA 301-14347		7. 9.05	J Jones	(Pontardawe. Swansea)	22.10.08P
	(Built J Jones)						
G-CWOT	Phoenix Currie Wot	PFA 3019		31. 1.78	D Doyle and Helena Duggan (Noted 5.06)		
	(Built D A Lord) (Walter Mikron 2)					Kilrush, County Kildare	19. 1.04P
G-CWTD	Aeroprakt A22 Foxbat	PFA 317-14131		21.10.03	J V Harris	Ley Farm, Chirk	11. 4.09P
	(Built J V Harris)						
G-CWVY	Mainair Sports Pegasus Quik	7984		29. 9.03	R K Jenkins	Swansea	26. 3.09P

G-CXAA - G-CXZZ

G-CXCX	Cameron N-90 Balloon (Hot Air)	1242		14. 3.86	Cathay Pacific Airways (London) Ltd "Cathay Pacific IV"		
	(Replacement envelope c/n 3332, replaced itself in 4.08 by new unidentified envelope)					Swindon	27. 9.09E
G-CXDZ	Cassutt Speed Two	PFA 034-13816		27.12.02	J A H Chadwick (Noted 4.07)	Little Staughton	
	(Build R Whinsper, J A H Chadwick and S Thompson)						
G-CXHK	Cameron N-77 Balloon (Hot Air)	4978		22. 2.01	Cathay Pacific Airways (London) Ltd	London SW1	27.12.07A
G-CXIP	Thruster T 600N Jab Sprint	1031-T600N-095		17.11.03	R J Howells tr India Papa Syndicate		
						Upfield Farm, Whitson	25.10.08P
G-CXSM	Cessna 172R Skyhawk II	17280320	G-BXSM N432ES	1. 2.07	Airtime Aviation France Ltd	Compton Abbas	25. 4.09E

G-CYAA - G-CYZZ

G-CYLL	Sequoia F 8L Falco	PFA 100-14572		30.10.06	N J Langrick and A J Newall	Breighton	
	(Built N J Langrick and A J Newall)						
G-CYLS	Cessna T303 Crusader	T30300005	N20736	20.12.90	Hangar 8 Ltd	Oxford	18. 5.08E
			G-BKXI, N303CC, (N9355T) (Stored after nose wheel failure at Guernsey 12.07)				
G-CYMA	Gulfstream GA-7 Cougar	GA7-0083	G-BKOM N794GA	15. 8.83	Cyma Petroleum (UK) Ltd	Elstree	27. 8.09E
G-CYOT	Rans S-6S ES Coyote II	0507.1810		12. 0.08	J E Midder tr Yatesbury Coyote Pack	Yatesbury	
	(Built JE Midda, pr.no LAA 204-14770)						
G-CYPM	Cirrus SR22	3185	N270CP	4.11.08	R M Stevens	Turweston	12.11.09E
G-CYRA	Kolb Twinstar Mk.III (mod)	PFA 205-12434	G-MYRA	30. 1.03	S J Fox	Popham	19.10.09P
	(Built S J Fox and A P Pickford) (Rotax 503)						
G-CYRS	Bell 206L LongRanger	45030	OH-HOH	16. 6.06	Sky Charter UK Ltd	Manston	20. 8.09E
			C-GIIP, N221AM, N66BH, N66LJ, N49770				

G-CZAA - G-CZZZ

G-CZAC	Zenair CH.601XL Zodiac	6-9112		26. 3.04	D Pitt	Roughay Farm, Bishops Waltham	26. 2.09P
	(Built D Pitt - pr.no.PFA 162B-14113) (Tri-cycle u/c)						
G-CZAF	Vickers Supermarine 361 Spitfire FR.IXe	N94141	10. 8.07	Historic Flying Ltd	Duxford	
	(Built as LF.IXb))	CBAF IX.571	Burma AF UB425, (Burma AF UB425), Israel DF 2042, Czech AF JT-10, SL633				
G-CZAG	Sky 90-24 Balloon (Hot Air)	171		5.10.99	S McCarthy	Rothersthorpe, Northampton	17. 6.09E
G-CZAW	CZAW Sportcruiser	PFA 338-14542		19. 6.06	Sprite Aviation Services Ltd		
	(Built G Smith)					Inglenook Farm, Maydensole	10. 4.09P
G-CZCZ	Mudry CAP.10B	54	OE-AYY	28. 7.94	M Farmer	Garston Farm, Marshfield	16.11.09P
			F-WZCG, HB-SAK, F-BUDT				
G-CZMI	Best Off Sky Ranger 912(2)	SKR0308377		18.11.03	L M Bassett	Longacre Farm, Sandy	22. 1.09P
	(Built T W Thiele - pr.no.BMAA HB/307)						
G-CZNE	Pilatus Britten-Norman BN-2B-20 Islander	G-BWZF	27. 7.04	Skyhopper LLP	Gloucestershire	26. 6.09E
		2301					
G-CZSC	CZAW Sportcruiser	LAA 338-14814		23. 6.08	A K Lynn	Priory Farm, Tibenham	
	(Built A K Lynn)						

G-DAAA - G-DAZZ

G-DAAH	Piper PA-28RT-201T Turbo Arrow IV	N3026U	27. 4.79	D A H Morris	Wolverhampton	9. 7.09E
		28R-7931104					
G-DAAM	Robinson R22 Beta	2043		3. 6.92	J N Plange	(Scunthorpe)	20. 7.09E
G-DAAT	Eurocopter EC.135 T2	0312		4. 5.04	Bond Air Services Ltd (Operated Devon Air Ambulance)		
						Eaglescott	13. 7.09E

Reg	Type	C/n	Prev id	Date	Owner/Operator	Location	Status
G-DAAZ	Piper PA-28RT-201T Turbo Arrow IV	28R-7931247	N2896B	17. 1.03	Calais Ltd	Guernsey	11.12.09E
G-DABS	Robinson R22 Beta II	3083		15. 5.00	BI6 Ltd	Culter Helipad	1. 6.09E
G-DACA	Percival P 57 Sea Prince T 1	P57/12	WF118	6. 5.80	P G Vallance Ltd	Charlwood, Surrey	17. 7.81P
					(In Gatwick Aviation Museum 2007 as "WF118")		
G-DACC	Cessna 401B	401B-0112	N77GR	1. 9.86	Niglon Ltd	Wellesbourne Mountford	13.10.07E
			N4488A, G-AYOU, N7972Q				
G-DACF	Cessna 152 II	15281724	G-BURY	13. 6.97	T M and M L Jones *(Operated Derby Aero Club)*		
			N67285			Derby	22. 1.09E
G-DADA	Rotorsport UK MT-03	RSUK/MT-03/040		12. 5.08	A D Watson	*(Prestwick)*	21. 5.09P
G-DADG	Piper PA-18-150 Super Cub	18-5237	N45498	13.10.04	F J Cox	Trnchard Farm, Eggesford	7. 5.11S
			IDF/AF 069				
G-DADJ	Glaser-Dirks DG-200	2-43	BGA2394-DUQ	29. 2.08	T Forsey	Wormingford	25. 5.08
G-DADZ	CZAW Sportcruiser	LAA 338-14792		7. 4.08	D A Rose tr Meon Flying Group	*(Swanmore)*	
	(Built D A Rose)						
G-DAFY	Beech 58 Baron	TH-1591	N5684C	6.10.93	P R Earp	Gloucestershire	17. 1.09E
G-DAGJ	Zenair CH.601XL Zodiac	PFA 162B-14317		28.10.05	D A G Johnson	(Stanford in the Vale, Faringdon)	
	(Built D A G Johnson)						
G-DAIR	Luscombe 8A Silvaire	1474	G-BURK	3.10.97	D F Soul	Emberton, Olney	19.10.99P
	(Continental A65)		N28713, NC28713		*(Noted fitted with Diesel Air 100hp 7.03)*		
G-DAIV	UltraMagic H-77 Balloon (Hot Air)	77/184		2.11.00	D Harrison-Morris	Ellesmere	14. 1.10E
G-DAJB	Boeing 757-2T7	23770		26. 2.87	Monarch Airlines Ltd	Luton	13. 5.09E
G-DAJC	Boeing 767-31K	27206	C-GJJC	15. 4.94	Thomas Cook Airlines Ltd	Manchester	20. 5.09E
			G-DAJC				
G-DAKI	Pilatus PC-12/47	885	HB-FQR	12. 3.08	Aquarelle Investments Ltd	Bournemouth	11. 3.09E
G-DAKK	Douglas C-47A-35-DL Dakota	9798	(G-OFON)	26. 7.94	General Technics Ltd *(To Aviodrome Museum 10.06)*		
			F-GEOM, French Navy 36, OK-WZB, OK-WDU, 42-23936			Lelystad, Netherlands	23. 5.03T
G-DAKM	Diamond DA.40D Star	D4.222	OE-VPT	21. 9.06	K MacDonald	Blackpool	15.10.09E
			OE-VPU				
G-DAKO	Piper PA-28-236 Dakota	28-7911187	PH-ARW	29. 7.99	Methods Consulting Ltd	Denham	2. 1.10E
			(PH-MFB), D-EECG, PH-ARW, OO-HCX, N29718				
G-DAMY	Europa Aviation Europa	105		21.10.94	R J Kelly and U A Schliessler	Wycombe Air Park	11. 9.09P
	(Built Hart Aviation Ltd - pr.no.PFA 247-12781) (Tri-gear u/c)						
G-DANA	Replica Jodel DR200	PFA 304-13351	G-DAST	2.12.02	F A Bakir tr Cheshire Eagles		
	(Built F A Bakir)					Yew Tree Farm, Lymm Dam	
				(On rebuild 9.05 reportedly a composite of an unknown fuselage and wings)			
G-DAND	SOCATA TB-10 Tobago	72		5.12.79	Portway Aviation Ltd	Shobdon	2. 1.10E
G-DANT	Rockwell Commander 114	14298	N4978W	9. 7.96	J Terreaux	St Brieuc, France	31. 3.09E
G-DANY	Avtech Jabiru UL	0340		28.12.00	D A Crosbie	*(Sudbury)*	
	(Built D A Crosbie - pr.no.PFA 274A-13588)						
G-DANZ	Eurocopter AS.355N Ecureuil 2	5658		14. 9.98	Melesey Ltd	Denham	9. 2.10E
G-DAPH	Cessna 180K Skywagon II	18053016	N2620K	29. 1.92	M R L Astor	East Hatley, Tadlow	18. 2.09E
G-DARK	CFM Shadow Series DD	K 295		13. 7.00	M W Fitch	North Weald	2. 9.09E
	(Built P M Dewhurst - pr.no.PFA 161-13308) (Rotax 582)						
G-DASH	Rockwell Commander 112A	237	G-BDAJ	31. 3.87	Gee Dash Ltd	Andrewsfield	2. 4.09E
			N1237J				
G-DASS	Comco Ikarus C42 FB100	0509-6758		30. 9.05	D Sempers tr DAS Services	Wickenby	5.10.08P
G-DASY	Hughes 369E *(Hughes 500)*	0574E	N574PP	1. 2.08	R A Roberts tr Puddleduck Plane Partnership		
						Dunsfold	1. 4.09E
G-DATG	Reims Cessna F182P Skylane II	F18200013	D-EATG	8.11.01	Oxford Aeroplane Company Ltd	Oxford	21. 4.09E
G-DAUF	Aérospatiale AS.365N2 Dauphin 2	6407	N31EH	3. 1.06	Gama Leasing Ltd	Farnborough	22. 3.09E
			XA-SWT, N488FA, JA6676				
G-DAVD	Reims FR172K Hawk XP		D-EFJT	23.12.99	D M Driver and S Copeland	Spanhoe	6. 4.09E
		FR17200632	(PH-ADL), PH-AXO				
G-DAVE	Jodel D 112	667	F-BICH	16. 8.78	N W Cawley tr Temple Flying Group		
	(Built Etablissement Valladeau)					Griffins Farm, Temple Bruer	23. 8.08P
G-DAVG	Robinson R44 Raven II	10038	G-WOWW	28. 4.03	AG Aviation Ltd	Naas, County Kildare	11. 2.09E
G-DAVO	Gulfstream AA-5B Tiger	AA5B-1226	G-GAGA	5. 1.96	Douglas Head Consulting Ltd	Elstree	12. 2.09E
			G-BGPG, (G-BGRW)				
G-DAVS	AB Sportine Aviacija LAK-17AT	158	BGA5171-KKZ	12. 6.06	D Peters tr G-DAVS Syndicate	Burn	18. 5.08
			LY-GIW				
G-DAVV	Robinson R44 Raven II	11079		16. 2.06	B D Keith	Kintore	31. 3.09E
G-DAVZ	Cessna 182T Skylane	18281958	N2461C	19.11.07	D Edmondson	Cambridge	30.11.09E
G-DAWG	Scottish Aviation Bulldog Series 120/121	BH120/208	XX522	13. 3.02	R H Goldstone *(As "XX522:06" in RAF c/s)* Barton		2.10.06
G-DAWZ	Glasflügel 304 CZ	33	BGA5232-KNP	5. 5.06	D A Whitley *"DA"*	Parham Park	14. 4.07
	(Built HPH SPOL. Sro)		D-8304				
G-DAYS	Europa Aviation Europa	177		9. 5.95	D A Gittins	Sleap	9. 7.09P
	(Built SD, A and A J Hall - pr.no.PFA 247-12810) (Monowheel u/c)						
G-DAYZ	Pietenpol AirCamper	PFA 047-12342		22. 6.01	J G Cronk	*(Earnley, Chichester)*	
	(Built J G Cronk)						
G-DAZY	Piper PA-34-200T Seneca II	34-7770335	N953A	4. 2.03	Fly (CI) Ltd *(Operated Trans Euro Air)*	Southend	4. 4.09E
			PH-DLM, OE-FGG, N38727				
G-DAZZ	Van's RV-8	PFA 303-14245		20.10.04	D M Hartfree-Bright tr Wishanger RV8		
	(Built D M Hartfree-Bright)					Wishanger Farm, Frensham	14. 2.09P

G-DBAA - G-DBZZ

Reg	Type	C/n	Prev id	Date	Owner/Operator	Location	Status
G-DBAT	Lindstrand LBL 56A Balloon (Hot Air)	1001		9. 6.04	G R J Luckett	Fort Collins, Colorado, US	30. 8.09E
G-DBCA	Airbus A319-131	2098	D-AVYV	23. 2.04	British Midland Airways Ltd	London Heathrow	22. 2.09E
G-DBCB	Airbus A319-131	2188	D-AVYA	23. 4.04	British Midland Airways Ltd	London Heathrow	22. 4.09E
G-DBCC	Airbus A319-131	2194	D-AVYT	14. 5.04	British Midland Airways Ltd	London Heathrow	13. 5.09E
G-DBCD	Airbus A319-131	2389	D-AVYJ	9. 2.05	British Midland Airways Ltd	London Heathrow	8. 2.10E
G-DBCE	Airbus A319-131	2429	D-AVWG	31. 3.05	British Midland Airways Ltd	London Heathrow	30. 3.09E

G-DBCF	Airbus A319-131	2466	D-AVYA	26. 5.05	British Midland Airways Ltd	London Heathrow	25. 5.09E
G-DBCG	Airbus A319-132	2694	D-AVXD	21. 2.06	British Midland Airways Ltd	London Heathrow	20. 2.09E
G-DBCH	Airbus A319-132	2697	D-AVXE	23. 2.06	British Midland Airways Ltd	London Heathrow	22. 2.09E
G-DBCI	Airbus A319-131	2720	D-AVWC	5. 5.06	British Midland Airways Ltd	London Heathrow	4. 5.09E
G-DBCJ	Airbus A319-131	2981	D-AVXG	9. 1.07	British Midland Airways Ltd	London Heathrow	8. 1.10E
G-DBCK	Airbus A319-131	3049	D-AVYG	2. 3.07	British Midland Airways Ltd	London Heathrow	1. 3.09E
G-DBDB	Magni M-16 Tandem Trainer PFA G/12-1239		G-IROW	19.10.99	D R Bolsover	RAF Lossiemouth	28. 5.09P
	(Built D R Bolsover) (Rotax 914-UL)		G-DBDB				
G-DBIN	Medway SLA 80 Executive	070707		22. 4.08	D Binnington	Stoke, Isle of Grain	
G-DBJD	PZL-Bielsko SZD-9bis Bocian 1D	P-391	BGA998-BJD	8. 2.08	A D Popple tr Bertie the Bocian Glider Syndicate		
						Lasham	20. 3.08
G-DBLA	Boeing 767-35EER	26063	B-16603	23. 6.06	Thomson Airways Ltd	Manchester	11.10.09E
G-DBLX	Aviat A-1B Husky	2438	N117AA	28. 8.08	R A Roberts tr Puddleduck Plane Partnerships		
						Dunsfold	12. 3.09E
G-DBND	Schleicher Ka 6CR	1157	BGA1094-BND	18. 4.08	E Richards and A H Hall	Strubby	
G-DBNH	Schleicher Ka 6CR	6115	BGA1098-BNH	14. 7.08	The Bath, Wilts and North Dorset Gliding Club Ltd		
						Kingston Deverill	
G-DBOK	Aérospatiale AS355F2 Ecureuil 2	5463	N620LH	24.10.07	Venturi Capital Ltd	Elstree	30.10.09E
			N158BC, XU-018, N158BC, D-HKEV, N620LH				
G-DBOL	Schleicher Ka 6CR	725	BGA1149-BQL	10. 6.08	A C Thorne	Brent Tor	
			D-7117				
G-DBRY	Slingsby T.51 Dart	1434	BGA1185-BRY	6. 2.08	D J Knights	Kirton-in-Lindsey	18. 6.08
G-DBSA	Slingsby T.51 Dart 15	1405	BGA1187-BSA	22.10.07	G Burton	Seighford	15. 4.09R
G-DBSL	Slingsby T.51 Dart 17	1445	BGA1197-BSL	8. 9.08	J C G Owles tr G-DBSL Group	Tibenham	
G-DBSR	Balony Kubicek BB26Z Balloon (Hot Air)	514		20. 8.07	G J Bell	Petersfield	30. 8.09E
G-DBTJ	Schleicher Ka 6CR	6367	BGA1219-BTJ	18. 4.08	S Xiao Ju Xie	Kingston Deverill	
G-DBUF	Slingsby T.51 Dart 17R	1469	BGA1240-BUF	23.11.07	K W Clarke and N G Harrison	Chipping	10. 4.09R
G-DBUG	Robinson R44 Clipper	1256	G-OBHI	4. 3.04	Dio (Aviation) Ltd	Welshpool	2.12.09E
G-DBUZ	Schleicher Ka 6CR	6418	BGA1257-BUZ	4. 1.08	J J Leacroft	Lyveden	24. 5.08
G-DBVB	Schleicher K 7 Rhönadler	7230	BGA1259-BVB	25. 1.08	Dartmoor Gliding Society Ltd	Brent Tor	30. 4.08
	(Modified to ASK 13 standard)						
G-DBVH	Slingsby T.51 Dart 17R	1485	BGA1265-BVH	29. 2.08	P G Addy	(Pudsey)	2. 4.08
G-DBVR	Schleicher Ka 6CR	6441	BGA1273-BVR	1.11.07	R C Beecroft tr K6CR-BVR Syndicate	Lasham	8. 4.08
G-DBVX	Schleicher Ka 6CR	6439	BGA1279-BVX	1. 5.08	R Lynch	Kingston Deverill	
G-DBVY	LET L-13 Blanik	173121	BGA1280-BVY	14. 3.08	D G Goats tr Victor Yankee Group	Portmoak	
G-DBVZ	Schleicher Ka 6CR	6446	BGA1281-BVZ	12.11.07	L Blair tr G-DBVZ Group	Bellarena	11.11.07
G-DBWC	Schleicher Ka 6CR	6449	BGA1284-BWC	26. 3.08	R Maksymowicz tr K6CR BWC Syndicate		
						Snitterfield	
G-DBWJ	Slingsby T.51 Dart 17R	1495	BGA1290-BWJ	14. 2.08	M F Defendi	Wormingford	29. 3.09
G-DBWM	Slingsby T.51 Dart 17R	1500	BGA1293-BWM	13. 5.08	P L Poole	Kenley	13. 5.09R
G-DBWO	Slingsby T.51 Dart	1505	BGA1296-BWQ	21. 2.08	G Winch	Wormingford	14. 8.09R
G-DBWP	Slingsby T.51 Dart 17R	1501	BGA1295-BWP	7. 1.08	R.Johnson	Talgarth	13. 5.09R
G-DBWS	Slingsby T.51 Dart 17R	1502	BGA1298-BWS	4.12.07	R D Broome	Hinton-in-the-Hedges	17. 6.09R
G-DBXE	Slingsby T.51 Dart 15R	1509	BGA1310-BXE	4. 7.08	S R Campbell tr Group G-DBXE	Currock Hill	
G-DBXG	Slingsby T.51 Dart 17R	1512	BGA1312-BXG	31. 7.08	J M Whelan "686"	Saltby	
G-DBXH	Slingsby T.51 Dart 17R	1516	BGA1313-BXH	14. 2.08	C Rodwell	Husbands Bosworth	15. 5.09R
G-DBYC	Slingsby T.51 Dart 17R	1526	BGA1332-BYC	11. 3.08	N A Jaffray	Snitterfield	
G-DBYL	Schleicher Ka 6CR	6517	BGA1340-BYL	20.11.07	Channel Gliding Club Ltd	Waldershare Park	2. 2.08
G-DBYM	Schleicher Ka 6CR	6518	BGA1341-BYM	17.10.07	K S Smith "558"	Rattlesden	2. 4.08
			RAFGSA 381, BGA1341-BYM				
G-DBYU	Schleicher Ka 6CR	6525	BGA1348-BYU	11. 1.08	G B Sutton	Seighford	28. 3.08
			XW640, BGA1348-BYU				
G-DBYX	Schleicher Ka 6E	4055	BGA1351-BYX	19.12.07	J R Dent	Chipping	9. 4.08
G-DBZF	Slingsby T.51 Dart 17R	1570	BGA1359-BZF	18. 3.08	S Rhenius and D Charles	Ridgewell	
G-DBZX	Schleicher Ka 6CR	6571	BGA1375-BZX	27. 6.08	M T Woodhouse tr Leeds University Union Gliding Society		
						AAC Dishforth	
G-DBZZ	PZL-Bielsko SZD-24-4A Foka 4	W-308	BGA1377-BZZ	23. 8.07	A P Benbow	Portmoak	1. 6.08

G-DCAA - G-DCZZ

G-DCAE	Schleicher Ka 6E	4076	BGA1381-CAE	9.11.07	N Rolfe	Seighford	20. 3.08
G-DCAG	Schleicher Ka 6E	4080	BGA1383-CAG	28.11.07	S A Farmer tr 715 Syndicate		
						(Hall Green, Birmingham)	30. 4.08
G-DCAO	Schempp-Hirth SHK-1	37	BGA1391-CAQ	4. 7.08	M G Entwistle and A K Bartlett "812"	Talgarth	
G-DCAS	Schleicher Ka 6E	4029	BGA1393-CAS	4.10.07	R F Tindall	Gransden Lodge	22. 8.02
			RAFGSA 372				
G-DCAZ	Slingsby T.51 Dart 17R	1611	BGA1400-CAZ	4. 6.08	D A Bullock and M L Chow	Bicester	19. 6.09R
G-DCBA	Slingsby T.51 Dart 17R	1612	BGA1401-CBA	1. 2.08	M Parsons	Snitterfield	4. 3.09R
G-DCBI	Schweizer 269C-1 (Schweizer 300)	0295	N86G	10. 7.07	Heli North West Ltd	Barton	11.11.09E
G-DCBW	Schleicher ASK 13	13034	BGA1421-CBW	24. 9.07	Stratford on Avon Gliding Club Ltd	Snitterfield	28. 9.08
G-DCBY	Schleicher Ka 6CR	960	BGA1423-CBY	3. 3.08	G Martin tr Talgarth 475	Talgarth	
			RAFGSA 322, D-3222				
G-DCCA	Schleicher Ka 6E	4126	BGA1425-CCA	16. 5.08	R K Forrest	Feshiebridge	
G-DCCB	Schempp-Hirth SHK-1	52	BGA1426-CCB	12. 9.07	R M Johnson tr CCB Syndicate	Milfield	17. 9.08
G-DCCE	Schleicher ASK 13	13047	BGA1429-CCE	25. 2.08	Oxford Gliding Company Ltd		
						RAF Weston-on-the-Green	3. 3.08
G-DCCF	Schleicher ASK 13	13042	BGA1430-CCF	7. 2.08	Norfolk Gliding Club Ltd	Tibenham	17. 3.08
G-DCCG	Schleicher Ka 6E	4125	BGA1431-CCG	24. 6.08	R J Playle	Shenington	
G-DCCJ	Schleicher Ka 6CR	6145	BGA1433-CCJ	29. 9.08	S Badby	Shenington	
			RAFGSA 323				
G-DCCL	Schleicher Ka 6E	4129	BGA1435-CCL	14. 2.08	J Tayler tr G-DCCL Group	Sutton Bank	30. 3.08
G-DCCM	Schleicher ASK 13	13053	BGA1436-CCM	9. 5.08	The Burn Gliding Club Ltd	Burn	
G-DCCP	Schleicher ASK 13	13052	BGA1438-CCP	4. 2.08	G D Pullen tr Lima 99 Syndicate "661"	Lasham	12. 3.08
G-DCCR	Schleicher Ka 6E	4149	BGA1440-CCR	16.11.07	A Shaw	Bicester	1. 4.08

G-DCCT	Schleicher ASK 13	13057	BGA1442-CCT	24. 9.07	Stratford on Avon Gliding Club Ltd	Snitterfield	15. 2.08
G-DCCU	Schleicher Ka 6E	4122	BGA1443-CCU	5.10.07	J L Hasker	RAF Keevil	11. 4.08
G-DCCV	Schleicher Ka 6E	4160	BGA1444-CCV	28. 1.08	T M Bell and C H Page	Lasham	17. 8.08
G-DCCW	Schleicher ASK 13	13051	BGA1445-CCW	20.11.07	Needwood Forest Gliding Club Ltd	Cross Hayes	17. 2.08
G-DCCX	Schleicher ASK 13	13054	BGA1446-CCX	23. 1.08	Trent Valley Gliding Club Ltd	Kirton-in-Lindsey	30. 5.08
G-DCCY	Schleicher ASK 13	13050	BGA1447-CCY	30.11.07	Devon & Somerset Gliding Club Ltd	North Hill	29. 3.08
G-DCCZ	Schleicher ASK 13	13070	BGA1448-CCZ	11. 9.08	The Windrushers Gliding Club Ltd	Bicester	
G-DCDA	Schleicher Ka 6E	4136	BGA1449-CDA	26. 6.08	F Bick tr CDA Group	Aboyne	
G-DCDC	Lange E1 Antares	25	D-KJWI	15.11.07	J D Williams "Z7"	Portmoak	14.11.09E
G-DCDF	Schleicher Ka 6E	4162	BGA1454-CDF	5. 2.08	K G Reid tr CDF Syndicate	Rivar Hill	3. 7.08
G-DCDG	FFA Diamant 18	35	BGA1455-CDG	2. 4.08	J Cashin and D McCarty	Kilkenny, Ireland	
G-DCDH	Schempp-Hirth HS.2 Cirrus	10	BGA1456-CDH	6.12.07	A K Moore "619"	Shenington	25. 3.08
G-DCDW	FFA Diamant 18	033	BGA1469-CDW	3. 8.07	D R Chapman	Llantisilio	28. 8.08
G-DCDZ	Schleicher Ka 6E	4177	BGA1472-CDZ	19. 4.08	J R J Minns	Wormingford	
G-DCEB	PZL-Bielsko SZD-9bis Bocian 1E	P-433	BGA1474-CEB	5. 2.08	The Bath, Wilts and North Dorset Gliding Club Ltd		
						Kingston Deverill	1. 8.08
G-DCEC	Schempp-Hirth Cirrus	22	BGA1475-CEC	17. 3.08	C R Ellis tr Cirrus 18 Group	Long Mynd	
G-DCEL	Schleicher Ka 6E	4174	BGA1483-CEL	12. 9.08	Essex and Suffolk Gliding Club Ltd "JD"		
						Wormingford	
G-DCEM	Schleicher Ka 6E	4212	BGA1484-CEM	23. 1.08	E W Black	(Newmarket)	23. 3.08
G-DCEO	Schleicher Ka 6E	4230	BGA1487-CEQ	27. 6.08	C L Lagden and J C Green	Wormingford	
G-DCEW	Schleicher Ka 6E	4209	BGA1493/CEW	5. 3.08	J W Richardson tr JW Richardson and Partners Group		
						Shrewsbury	
G-DCEX	Schleicher ASK 13	13108	BGA1494-CEX	19. 2.08	Carlton Moor Gliding Club	Carlton Moor	26. 5.08
G-DCEY	Schleicher Ka 6E	4222	BGA1495-CEY	12.11.07	R Saunders	Walney Island	11. 2.08
G-DCFA	Schleicher ASK 13	13113	BGA1497-CFA	21. 2.08	G P Saw	Wycombe Air Park	22. 5.08
G-DCFE	Schleicher ASK 13	13112	BGA1501-CFE	30. 7.08	J D Morris tr Loughborough Students Union Gliding Club		
			EI-143, BGA1501-CFE			RAF Wittering	
G-DCFF	Schleicher K 8B	8765	BGA1502-CFF	22. 8.08	Derbyshire and LancashireGliding Club Ltd		
						Camphill	
G-DCFG	Schleicher ASK 13	13115	BGA1503-CFG	27. 2.08	The Nene Valley Gliding Club Ltd	Upwood	9. 3.08
G-DCFK	Schempp-Hirth Cirrus	38	BGA1506-CFK	18.10.07	M P Webb	(Stoke-on-Trent)	28. 9.08
G-DCFL	Schleicher Ka 6E	4215	BGA1507-CFL	9. 9.08	L M Causer	Long Mynd	
G-DCFS	Glasflügel H201B Standard Libelle	83	BGA1513-CFS	9. 9.08	P J Flack	Shipdham	
G-DCFW	Glasflügel H201B Standard Libelle	275	BGA1517-CFW	11. 6.08	T J Price and D J Edwardes	Rhigos	
G-DCFX	Glasflügel H201B Standard Libelle	274	BGA1518-CFX	17. 9.07	K D Fishenden	Dunstable	28. 9.08
G-DCFY	Glasflügel H201B Standard Libelle	270	BGA1519-CFY	8. 8.08	C W Stevens "862"	Pocklington	
G-DCGB	Schleicher Ka 6E	4247	BGA1522-CGB	16.11.07	P M Turner and S C Male	Long Mynd	31.10.07
G-DCGD	Schleicher Ka 6E	4202	BGA1524-CGD	19. 7.08	I N McRae tr Charlie Golf Delta Group	Camphill	
G-DCGE	SchleicherKa 6E	4246	BGA1525-CGE	22.11.07	C V Hill and P C Hazlehurst	Bellarena	26. 1.08
G-DCGH	Schleicher K 8B	8772	BGA1528-CGH	6. 2.08	T G B Hobbis tr K7 (1971) Syndicate	Lasham	24. 5.08
G-DCGM	FFA Diamant 18	53	BGA1532-CGM	10. 9.08	J G Batch	Hinton-in-the-Hedges	
G-DCGO	Schleicher ASK 13	13153	BGA1535-CGQ	18.12.07	Oxford Gliding Company Ltd		
						RAF Weston-on-the-Green	4. 1.08
G-DCGS	FFA Diamant 18	055	BGA1537-CGS	28.11.07	P K Hayward	Parham Park	3. 7.08
G-DCGT	Schempp-Hirth SHK-1	38	BGA1538-CGT	23. 1.08	A J Fardoe	Husbands Bosworth	13. 4.08
			D-1966				
G-DCGY	Schempp-Hirth Cirrus	51	BGA1543-CGY	28. 1.08	R A J Jones and G Nevisky	Eaglescott	14. 3.08
G-DCHB	Schleicher Ka 6E	4235	BGA1546-CHB	15. 4.08	D L Jones	RAF Weston-on-the-Green	
G-DCHC	Bölkow Phoebus C	858	BGA1547-CHC	7. 3.08	D A Gardner and D C Ephraim	Rhigos	
G-DCHJ	Bölkow Phoebus C	879	BGA1553-CHJ	19. 9.08	D C Austin	Sutton Bank	
G-DCHL	PZL-Bielsko SZD-30 Pirat	B-295	BGA1555-CHL	0. 8.08	A P P Scorer and A Stocks	Rufforth	
G-DCHO	Aquila AT01	AT01-177		18. 2.08	D R and C A Ho	Lower Grounds Farm, Shirlowe	26. 2.09E
G-DCHT	Schleicher ASW 15	15013	BGA1562-CHT	1. 2.08	J N Kelly and L Walker "846"		
						Hinton-in-the-Hedges	15. 3.08
G-DCHU	Schleicher K 8B	8794	BGA1563-CHU	10 .7.08	H B Chalmers tr Highland Gliding Club K8 Syndicate		
						Easterton	
G-DCHW	Schleicher ASK 13	13187	BGA1565-CHW	23.12.08	Dorset Gliding Club Ltd	Eyres Field	
G-DCHZ	Schleicher Ka 6E	4153	BGA1568-CHZ	12. 5.08	V Harrington "857"	Ridgewell	
			N6916				
G-DCJB	Bölkow Phoebus C	919	BGA1570-CJB	25.10.07	D Clarke and R Idle	Burn	28. 9.08
G-DCJK	Schempp-Hirth SHK-1	35	BGA1578-CJK	7. 5.08	R H Short	Lyveden	
			RAFGSA 25				
G-DCJN	Schempp-Hirth SHK-1	55	BGA1581-CJN	15. 8.08	R J Makin	Camphill	
G-DCJR	Schempp-Hirth Cirrus	87	BGA1584-CJR	22.12.07	A Rhodes tr CJR Syndicate	AAC Dishforth	5. 4.08
G-DCJY	Schleicher Ka 6CR	555	BGA1591-CJY	4. 4.08	K J Hartley tr CJY Syndicate	Bicester	
			(RAFGSA)				
G-DCKD	PZL-Bielsko SZD-30 Pirat	B-327	BGA1596-CKD	25. 2.08	The Borders (Milfield) Gliding Club Ltd	Milfield	3. 9.08
G-DCKK	Reims Cessna F172N Skyhawk II	F17201589	PH-GRT	19. 5.80	J Maffia	North Weald	25. 8.09E
			PH-AXA				
G-DCKL	Schleicher Ka 6E	4336	BGA1603-CKL	2. 6.08	D I Lowes tr BGA1603 Owners Syndicate	Milfield	
G-DCKN	PZL-Bielsko SZD-9bis Bocian 1E	P-496	BGA1605-CKN	13. 5.08	L I Rigby tr Bocian Syndicate	Crowland	
G-DCKP	Schleicher ASW 15	15058	BGA1606-CKP	3.10.08	M G Shaw tr ASW 15-BGA1606 Partnership "CKP"		
						Portmoak	
G-DCKR	Schleicher ASK 13	13247	BGA1608-CKR	7. 8.08	Essex Gliding Club Ltd	Ridgewell	
G-DCKU	Schleicher ASK 13	13243	BGA1611-CKU	29. 9.08	Essex Gliding Club Ltd "CKU"	Ridgewell	
G-DCKV	Schleicher ASK 13	13253	BGA1612-CKV	1.12.07	Black Mountains Gliding Club	Talgarth	16. 7.08
G-DCKY	Glasflügel H201B Standard Libelle	139	BGA1615-CKY	18. 6.08	G Herbert	Shenington	
G-DCKZ	Schempp-Hirth Standard Cirrus	52	BGA1616-CKZ	4.12.07	G I Bustin	Saltby	9. 5.08
			RAFGSA, BGA1616-CKZ				
G-DCLA	Schempp-Hirth Standard Cirrus	63	BGA1617-CLA	3.10.07	C Hughes and D J Dye	Nympsfield	28. 9.08
G-DCLM	Glasflügel H201B Standard Libelle	178	BGA1628-CLM	20. 6.08	C J Heide and J H Newberry	North Hill	
G-DCLO	Schempp-Hirth Cirrus	99	BGA1631-CLQ	19. 6.08	J F Beringer tr Bravo Delta Group	Shipdham	
G-DCLP	Glasflügel H201B Standard Libelle	176	BGA1630-CLP	1.10.07	M Schlotter "948"	Kingston Deverill	28. 9.08

Reg	Type	C/n	Prev ID	Date	Owner	Base	Date
G-DCLT	Schleicher K 7 Rhönadler *(Partly modified to ASK 13 standard)*	251	BGA1634-CLT D-5529	15. 2.08	A H Watkins and K W Gardner	Rhigos	2. 9.08
G-DCLV	Glasflügel H201B Standard Libelle	180	BGA1636-CLV	20. 8.07	P Ottomaniello	(Valeggio Sul Mincio, Italy)	29.11.07
G-DCLZ	Schleicher Ka 6E	4056	BGA1640-CLZ AGA 2	1. 2.08	R M King and T D Fielder	Kenley	29. 8.08
G-DCMF	PZL-Bielsko SZD-32A Foka 5	W-534	BGA1646-CMF	17. 1.08	P R Teager	Upper Broyle Farm, Ringmer	21. 6.08
G-DCMG	Schleicher K 7 Rhönadler	462	BGA1647-CMG D-8116	6. 2.08	T G B Hobbis tr K7 (1971) Syndicate "Fledermaus Zero Five"	Lasham	5. 5.08
G-DCMH	Glasflügel H201B Standard Libelle	224	BGA1648-CMH	20. 2.08	D Williams "165"	North Hill	20. 1.08
G-DCMI	Mainair Sports Pegasus Quik	7972		7. 8.03	S J E Smith	Eshott	16. 8.09P
G-DCMK	Schleicher ASK 13	13305	BGA1650-CMK	25. 1.08	The South Wales Gliding Club Ltd	Usk	24. 3.08
G-DCMN	Schleicher K 8B	8870	BGA1653-CMN	21. 4.08	The Bristol Gliding Club Proprietary Ltd	Nympsfield	
G-DCMO	Glasflügel H201B Standard Libelle	233	BGA1655-CMQ	17. 1.08	E V Todd and L C Wood	Wycombe Air Park	13. 5.08
G-DCMR	Glasflügel H201B Standard Libelle	225	BGA1656-CMR	18. 3.08	S F Scougall	Portmoak	
G-DCMS	Glasflügel H201B Standard Libelle	234	BGA1657-CMS	28. 1.08	R J Shallcross tr Libelle 602 Syndicate	Challock	17. 6.08
G-DCMV	Glasflügel H201B Standard Libelle	235	BGA1660-CMV (BGA1517-CFV)	17. 9.07	E P Lambert "184"	Aston Down	28. 9.08
G-DCMW	Glasflügel H201B Standard Libelle	242	BGA1661/CMW	23. 4.08	T Rose	Wycombe Air Park	
G-DCNC	Schempp-Hirth Standard Cirrus	167	BGA1667-CNC	28.11.07	J H Fox tr Cirrus 273 Syndicate	Portmoak	14. 6.08
G-DCND	PZL-Bielsko SZD-9bis Bocian 1E	P-428	BGA1668-CND RAFGSA 392	28. 4.08	Angus Gliding Club Ltd	Drumshade	
G-DCNE	Glasflügel H201B Standard Libelle	266	BGA1669-CNE	8. 7.08	E T Melville tr 25 Syndicate "525"	Portmoak	
G-DCNF	Glasflügel H201B Standard Libelle	271	BGA1670-CNF	23. 5.08	T J Mottershead	Pocklington	
G-DCNG	Glasflügel H201B Standard Libelle	265	BGA1671-CNG	5. 9.07	J Mitcheson	Nympsfield	28. 9.08
G-DCNJ	Glasflügel H201B Standard Libelle	272	BGA1673-CNJ	21.11.07	R Thornley	Crowland	8. 3.08
G-DCNM	PZL-Bielsko SZD-9bis Bocian 1E	P-551	BGA1676-CNM	13. 5.08	L I Rigby tr Bocian Syndicate	Crowland	
G-DCNP	Glasflügel H201B Standard Libelle	264	BGA1678-CNP	8. 9.08	I G Carrick and I R Thompson	Camphill	
G-DCNS	Slingsby T.59A Kestrel	1724	BGA1681/CNS	16. 6.08	J R Greenwell	Carlton Moor	
G-DCNW	Slingsby T.59F Kestrel 19	1791	BGA1684-CNW	26.10.07	S R Watson	Seighford	13. 3.09R
G-DCNX	Slingsby T.59F Kestrel 19	1792	BGA1685-CNX	28. 3.08	M Boxall	Rufforth	30. 6.09R
G-DCNY	Glasflügel H201B Standard Libelle	322	BGA1686-CNY	29.11.07	A D Stevenson tr Libelle 151 Syndicate	Portmoak	14. 4.08
G-DCOJ	Slingsby T.59A Kestrel 17	1727	BGA1720-CQJ	6.12.07	T W Treadaway	Husbands Bosworth	9. 4.08
G-DCON	Robinson R44 Raven	1646		25. 9.06	D Connelly	Enniskillen	11.11.09E
G-DCOR	Schempp-Hirth Standard Cirrus	220G	BGA1727-CQR	4. 2.08	S Brown	Wycombe Air Park	30. 5.08
G-DCOY	Schempp-Hirth Standard Cirrus	214	BGA1734-CQY	12. 9.07	A D Walsh	Husbands Bosworth	14. 6.08
G-DCPA	Eurocopter MBB BK-117C-1C	7511	D-HECU D-HXXL, G-LFBA, D-HECU, D-HMBF	16.12.97	Devon and Cornwall Constabulary	Exeter	16. 6.11
G-DCPD	Schleicher ASW 17	17026	BGA1691-CPD	21. 2.08	A J Hewitt	Tibenham	18. 8.08
G-DCPJ	Schleicher Ka 6E	4059	BGA1696-CPJ OO-ZDA	24. 4.07	E Lown "CPJ"	Shenington	24. 5.08
G-DCPM	Glasflügel H201B Standard Libelle	179	BGA1699-CPM	5. 2.08	K Marsden and P E Jessop	Trenchard Lines, Upavon	4. 5.08
G-DCPU	Schempp-Hirth Standard Cirrus	194	BGA1706-CPU	15. 8.08	P J Ketelaar "761"	Feshiebridge	
G-DCPV	PZL-Bielsko SZD-30 Pirat	B-470	BGA1707-CPV	19. 5.08	G Francis tr CPV Group	Portmoak	
G-DCRB	Glasflügel H201B Standard Libelle	243	BGA1737-CRB	13. 2.08	A I Mawer	Kirton-in-Lindsey	25. 6.08
G-DCRH	Schempp-Hirth Standard Cirrus	233G	BGA1743-CRH	7. 2.08	P E Thelwall "DV8"	Gransden Lodge	25. 4.08
G-DCRN	Schempp-Hirth Standard Cirrus	234G	BGA1748-CRN	13. 3.08	S McLaughlin and J Craig "566"	Dunstable	
G-DCRO	Glasflügel H201B Standard Libelle	326	BGA1750-CRO	24.10.07	K G Counsell tr G-DCRO Group	Usk	19. 2.08
G-DCRS	Glasflügel H201B Standard Libelle	325	BGA1752-CRS	28. 3.08	J R Hiley	(Billingshurst)	
G-DCRT	Schleicher ASK 13	13396	BGA1753-CRT	20. 9.07	Bowland Forest Gliding Club Ltd	Chipping	3. 3.08
G-DCRV	Glasflügel H201B Standard Libelle	329	BGA1755-CRV	18. 1.08	S.Cervantes	Portmoak	23. 5.08
G-DCRW	Glasflügel H201B Standard Libelle	324	BGA1756-CRW	10.12.07	A Billingham tr 417 Syndicate	Nympsfield	6. 4.08
G-DCSD	Slingsby T.59D Kestrel 19	1800	BGA1763-CSD	14.11.07	R J Toon	Sutton Bank	9. 5.09R
G-DCSE	Robinson R44 Astro	0659		23. 9.99	Heli Air Ltd	Wellesbourne Mountford/Wycombe Air Park	23.10.09E
G-DCSF	Slingsby T.59F Kestrel 19	1802	BGA1765-CSF	15. 1.08	R Birch "34Z"	Aston Down	31. 3.09R
G-DCSG	Robinson R44 Raven	0960	G-TRYG	27. 7.05	Voute Sales Ltd	Wellesbourne Mountford	5. 3.09E
G-DCSJ	Glasflügel H201B Standard Libelle	372	BGA1768-CSJ	4. 6.08	P J Gill	Seighford	
G-DCSK	Slingsby T.59D Kestrel 20	1806	BGA1769-CSK	1.11.07	H A Torode tr Kestrel CSK Group	Lasham	24. 3.09R
G-DCSN	Pilatus B4-PC11AF	21	BGA1772-CSN	21. 2.08	J S Firth	(Huddersfield)	14. 5.08
G-DCSP	Pilatus B4 PC-11	027	BGA1773-CSP	28. 8.08	A S Huggon tr G-DCSP Group	Chipping	
G-DCSR	Glasflügel H201B Standard Libelle	368	BGA1775-CSR	12.11.07	J Eagleton tr Glasgow and West	Portmoak	28. 9.08
G-DCTA	British Aerospace BAe 125 Series 800B	258130	G-OSPG D-CPAS, G-ETOM, G-BVFC, G-TPHK, G-FDSL, G-5-620	15. 1.07	Direct Air Executive Ltd	Oxford	15. 2.09E
G-DCTB	Schempp-Hirth Standard Cirrus *(Built Burkhart Grob-Flugzeugbau)*	264G	BGA1785-CTB	19.11.07	I M Young and S McCurdy "579"	RAF Weston-on-the-Green	22. 2.08
G-DCTE	Schleicher ASW 17	17012	BGA1788-CTE	14. 1.08	T Linee	Eyres Field	8. 4.08
G-DCTJ	Slingsby T.59D Kestrel 19	1810	BGA1792-CTJ	20. 2.08	H B Walrond	(Cockfield, Bury St Edmunds)	10. 9.08
G-DCTL	Slingsby T.59D Kestrel 19	1812	BGA1794-CTL	3. 4.08	E S E Hibbard	Wormingford	28. 6.09R
G-DCTM	Slingsby T.59D Kestrel 19	1813	BGA1795-CTM	20.11.07	C Roney	Gransden Lodge	31. 5.09R
G-DCTO	Slingsby T.59D Kestrel 19	1816	BGA1798-CTQ	9. 1.08	K A Moules	Trenchard Lines, Upavon	21. 4.08
G-DCTP	Slingsby T.59D Kestrel 19	1815	BGA1797-CTP	6. 3.08	D C Austin	Sutton Bank	2. 7.09R
G-DCTR	Slingsby T.59D Kestrel 19	1817	BGA1799-CTR	6. 6.08	D J Marpole	RNAS Yeovilton	
G-DCTT	Schempp-Hirth Standard Cirrus	277G	BGA1801-CTT	1. 4.08	E Sparrow "873"	Lasham	
G-DCTU	Glasflügel H201B Standard Libelle	371	BGA1802-CTU	20. 2.08	F K Hutchinson and P M Davies	Husbands Bosworth	14. 5.08
G-DCTV	PZL-Bielsko SZD-30	B-528	BGA1803-CTV	14. 3.08	D L King and B J Fantham	Rhigos	
G-DCTX	PZL-Bielsko SZD-30	B-527	BGA1805-CTX	19. 6.08	P G Goulding	Crowland	
G-DCUB	Pilatus B4-PC-11	047	BGA1809-CUB	7. 9.07	G S Sanderson	Gransden Lodge	22. 2.08
G-DCUC	Pilatus B4-PC-11	003	BGA1810-CUC HB-1102	3. 3.08	R Burghall, T G Taverner and H M Pantin	Dishforth	
G-DCUD	Yorkshire Sailplanes YS53 Sovereign *(Mispainted as G-DUCD on fuselage and wings, noted 9.08)*	02	BGA1811-CUD	9. 7.08	T J Wilkinson	Sackville Lodge, Riseley	

Reg	Type	C/n	BGA	Date	Owner	Location	Date
G-DCUJ	Glasflügel H201B Standard Libelle	370	BGA1816-CUJ	13.11.07	T G B Hobbis	Lasham	2. 5.08
G-DCUL	Schempp-Hirth Standard Cirrus	265G	BGA1818-CUL	15. 1.09	B Berendsen	(Delft, Netherlands)	
G-DCUS	Schempp-Hirth Cirrus VTC	126Y	BGA1822-CUS	19. 3.08	G Wearing tr G Wearing and Partners	Chipping	
G-DCUO	Pilatus B4-PC11	40	BGA1821-CUQ	6. 6.08	Cotswold Gliding Club	Aston Down	
G-DCUT	Pilatus B4 PC-11AF	041	BGA1823-CUT	1. 6.07	A L Walker "B4"	Lasham	19. 8.08
G-DCVA	LET L-13 Blanik	025418	BGA1830-CVA	25. 3.08	Andreas Gliding Club Ltd	Andreas, IoM	
G-DCVB	LET L-13 Blanik	025419	BGA1831-CVB	22. 2.08	K S Wells and M A Prickett tr Blanik Syndicate	Lyveden	13. 4.08
G-DCVE	Schempp-Hirth HS.2 Cirrus VTC	127Y	BGA1834-CVE	13.11.07	H Whybrow	Dunstable	26. 3.08
G-DCVG	Pilatus B4-PC11AF	045	BGA1836-CVG	29. 1.08	I H Keyser	(Germany)	31. 3.08
G-DCVK	Pilatus B4-PC11AF	048	BGA1839-CVK	15.10.07	J P Marriott	Bicester	9. 1.08
G-DCVL	GlasflÜGEL H201B Standard Libelle	369	BGA1840-CVL	11. 4.08	J Williams	Kirton-in-Lindsey	
G-DCVM	Pilatus B4 PC-11AF	036	BGA1841-CVM	31. 7.07	J A Mace	Rivar Hill	28. 9.08
G-DCVS	PZL-Bielsko SZD-36A Cobra 15	W-610	BGA1846-CVS	11. 1.08	I A Burgin tr CVS Group	Darlton	14. 4.08
G-DCVV	Pilatus B4-PC-11AF	028	BGA1849-CVV	17. 9.07	F R Wolff tr Syndicate CVV	North Hill	3. 3.08
G-DCVW	Slingsby T.59D Kestrel 19	1818	BGA1850-CVW	28. 5.08	P J R Hogarth and M A Longhurst	Halesland	
G-DCVY	Slingsby T.59D Kestrel 19	1821	BGA1852-CVY	20. 2.08	D F Catherwood	Chipping	18. 3.07
G-DCWA	Slingsby T.59D Kestrel 19	1825	BGA1854-CWA	25. 1.08	D J Jeffries	Usk	9. 5.09R
G-DCWB	Slingsby T.59D Kestrel 19	1833	BGA1855-CWB	28.11.07	D J Deacon tr Kestrel 677 Syndicate	Saltby	9. 5.09R
G-DCWD	Slinsgby T.59D Kestrel 19	1835	BGA1857-CWD	11. 6.08	J R Dransfield tr Deeside Kestrel Group	Aboyne	
G-DCWE	Glasflügel H201B Standard Libelle	482	BGA1858-CWE	22.11.07	T W J Stoker	Rufforth	3. 4.08
G-DCWF	Slingsby T.59D Kestrel 19	1838	BGA1859-CWF	18.10.07	P F Nicholson	Hinton-In-the-Hedges	29. 4.09R
G-DCWG	Glasflügel H201B Standard Libelle	391	BGA1860-CWG	28.11.07	G Mitcheson tr Libelle 322 Group	Milfield	10. 7.08
G-DCWH	Schleicher ASK 13	13424	BGA1861-CWH	16.10.07	York Gliding Centre Ltd	Rufforth	28. 9.08
G-DCWJ	Schleicher K7	630	BGA1862-CWJ D-6057, D-5273	30. 4.08	W Rossman tr Angus Gliding Club K7 Syndicate	Drumshade	
G-DCWR	Schempp-Hirth Cirrus	133Y	BGA1869-CWR	14.12.07	P J Concannon tr CWR Group	Thame	23. 6.08
G-DCWS	Schempp-Hirth Cirrus VTC	129Y	BGA1870-CWS	14. 7.08	K Ruxton, R Cassells, D Fairbank and B A Hutchins	Ridgewell	
G-DCWT	Glasflügel H201B Standard Libelle	384	BGA1871-CWT	20. 6.08	S W Swan	Parham Park	
G-DCWX	Glasflügel H201B Standard Libelle	36	BGA1875-CWX RAFGSA 132	11. 1.08	C A Weyman	Eyres Field	21. 4.08
G-DCWY	Glasflügel H201B Standard Libelle	387	BGA1876-CWY	24. 9.08	S J Taylor	Long Mynd	
G-DCWZ	Glasflügel H201B Standard Libelle	392	BGA1877-CWZ	1. 4.08	F C F Van der Linden	(Nieuw-Namen, Netherlands)	
G-DCXK	Glasflügel H201B Standard Libelle	383	BGA1887-CXK	17. 3.08	C A Turner	Cross Hayes	
G-DCXL	SAN Jodel D 140C Mousquetaire III	101	F-BKSM		A C D Norris	(Caluire et Cuire, France)	26. 6.09P
G-DCXM	Slingsby T.59D Kestrel 19	1820	BGA1889-CXM	6.12.07	R P Beck and T Potter	AAC Dishforth	15. 4.09R
G-DCXV	Yorkshire Sailplanes YS-53 Sovereign	03	BGA1897-CXV	27. 5.08	P G Myers tr T53 Syndicate	Chipping	
G-DCYA	Pilatus B4-PC-11	072	BGA1902-CYA	8.11.07	E J Bromwell tr B4-072 Group	North Hill	2. 2.08
G-DCYD	PZL-Bielsko SZD-30 Pirat	B-559	BGA1905-CYD	8. 9.08	I Johnston	Milfield	
G-DCYG	Glasflügel H201B Standard Libelle	441	BGA1908-CYG	22.12.07	D Cooke and R Barsby	Husbands Bosworth	14. 1.08
G-DCYM	Schempp-Hirth Standard Cirrus	48	BGA1913-CYM RAFGSA, D-0578	26. 9.07	K M Fisher	Husbands Bosworth	28. 9.08
G-DCYO	Schempp-Hirth Standard Cirrus	364	BGA1916-CYQ	18. 3.08	M Woolner tr G-DCYO Group	North Hill	
G-DCYT	Schempp-Hirth Standard Cirrus	357G	BGA1919-CYT	25. 9.07	G Royle	Llantisilio	23. 4.08
G-DCYZ	Schleicher K 8B	8882	BGA1925-CYZ	8. 4.08	Oxford Gliding Co Ltd RAF Weston-on-the-Green		
G-DCZD	Pilatus B4-PC-11	081	BGA1929-CZD	8. 8.07	S E Marples	Milfield	5. 8.08
G-DCZE	PZL-Bielsko SZD-30 Pirat	S-01.14	BGA1930-CZE	10.12.07	M R Biddle tr G-DCZE Group	Snitterfield	29. 4.08
G-DCZG	PZL-Bielsko SZD-30 Pirat	S-01.16	BGA1932-CZG	2. 9.08	J T Pajdak	Kenley	
G-DCZJ	PZL-Bielsko SZD-30 Pirat	S-01.15	BGA1934-CZJ	21. 1.08	C L Groves tr Pirat CZJ Group	Husbands Bosworth	5. 4.08
G-DCZN	Schleicher ASW 15B	15329	BGA1938-CZN	6. 6.08	P C Tuppen tr G-DCZN Group	Bembridge	
G-DCZO	Slingsby T.59D Kestrel 19	1840	BGA1940-CZQ	4. 8.08	P W Schartau "K19"	Bicester	
G-DCZR	Slingsby T.59D Kestrel 19	1842	BGA1941-CZR	6.11.07	R P Brisbourne	Rufforth	14. 4.09R
G-DCZU	Slingsby T.59D Kestrel 19	1849	BGA1944-CZU	9. 7.08	M P Edwards	(Wyberton, Boston)	
G-DCZZ	Slingsby T.59D Kestrel 19	1739	BGA1949-CZZ	18. 3.08	C J Lowrie	Parham Park	

G-DDAA - G-DDZZ

Reg	Type	C/n	BGA	Date	Owner	Location	Date
G-DDAC	PZL-Bielsko SZD-36A Cobra 15	W-656	BGA1952-DAC	4 .1.08	R J A Colenso	Husbands Bosworth	6. 5.08
G-DDAJ	Schempp-Hirth Nimbus 2	50	BGA1958-DAJ	17. 8.07	J D Jones "14"	Nympsfield	28. 9.08
G-DDAK	Schleicher K 7 Rhönadler	893	BGA1959-DAK D-8851	11. 1.08	T J Price tr Vale of Neath Gliding Club	Rhigos	7. 9.08
G-DDAN	PZL-Bielsko SZD-30 Pirat	S-01.45	BGA1962-DAN	29. 1.08	J M A Shannon	(Cambridge)	22.11.07
G-DDAP	PZL-Bielsko SZD-30 Pirat	S-01.47	BGA1963-DAP	13. 2.08	T D Younger tr Delta Alpha Papa Group	Currock Hill	19. 5.08
G-DDAS	Schempp-Hirth Standard Cirrus	378	BGA1966-DAS (BGA1925)	21.11.07	G Goodenough	Burn	2. 4.08
G-DDAU	PZL-Bielsko SZD-30 Pirat	S-01.50	BGA1968-DAU	26. 9.08	J Sentence tr G-DDAU Flying Group	Saltby	
G-DDAV	Robinson R44 Raven II	12124		7. 3.08	D A Gold	(London NW8)	29. 4.09E
G-DDAW	Schleicher Ka 6CR	951	BGA1970-DAW RAFGSA, D-2025	20. 2.08	P S Holmes and R G Charlesson	Bellarena	14. 9.08
G-DDAY	Piper PA-28R-201T Turbo Arrow III	28R-7703112	G-BPDO N3496Q	24.11.88	W G Thompson tr G-DDAY Group	Tatenhill	22. 6.09E
G-DDBC	Pilatus B4-PC11	135	BGA1976-DBC	12. 5.08	J H France and G R Harris	Shobdon	
G-DDBD	Europa Aviation Europa XS (Built B Davies - pr.no.PFA 247-13569)	454		11. 2.03	B Davies	Dunsfold	22. 8.09P
G-DDBG	ICA IS-29D	31	BGA1980-DBG	11. 6.08	P S Whitehead	Walney Island	
G-DDBK	Slingsby T.59D Kestrel 19	1861	BGA1983-DBK	8.10.08	G A Adams tr 523 Syndicate "523"	North Hill	
G-DDBN	Slingsby T.59D Kestrel 19	1857	BGA1986-DBN	11. 1.08	J D Westwood	Nympsfield	4. 5.08
G-DDBP	Glasflügel H205 Standard Club Libelle	51	BGA1987-DBP	17.10.07	J P Beach	Wormingford	28. 9.08
G-DDBS	Slingsby T.59D Kestrel 19	1864	BGA1990-DBS	23. 7.08	G M Barratt	Darlton	
G-DDBV	PZL-Bielsko SZD-30 Pirat	S-02.27	BGA1993-DBV	19. 2.08	A Rasul	Usk	19. 5.08

Reg	Type	c/n	Identity / date	Owner	Base	Date
G-DDBX	PZL-Bielsko SZD-9bis Bocian 1E	P-642	BGA1995-DBX 13. 2.08	A Veitch tr Highland Bocian Syndicate	Easterton	28. 4.08
G-DDCA	PZL-Bielsko SZD-36A Cobra 15	W-686	BGA1998-DCA 28.11.07	J R Aylesbury	Upwood	10. 6.07
G-DDCC	Glasflügel H201B Standard Libelle	585	BGA2000-DCC 15.10.07	K Maryin tr G-DDCC Syndicate	Shobdon	7. 3.08
G-DDCW	Schleicher Ka 6CR	1076	BGA2018-DCW 1.10.08 D-5228	B W Rendall "DCW"	Strubby	
G-DDDA	Schempp-Hirth Standard Cirrus	532G	BGA2022-DDA 17. 9.07	A J Davis and C G Wrigley	Nympsfield	4. 3.08
G-DDDB	Schleicher ASK 13	13493	BGA2023-DDB 9. 6.08	Shenington Gliding Club	Shenington	
G-DDDD	Evektor EV-97 teamEurostar UK	2907	13. 3.07	S Sebastian	East Barling, Essex	12. 3.09E
G-DDDE	PZL-Bielsko SZD-38A Jantar 1	B-641	BGA2026-DDE 28. 2.08	D W F Gosden tr Jantar One Syndicate	Talgarth	18. 3.08
G-DDDL	Schleicher K 8B	218/61	BGA2032-DDL 16. 4.08 D-5156	Yorkshire Gliding Centre Ltd	Rufforth	
G-DDDM	Schempp-Hirth Cirrus	164Y	BGA2033-DDM 11. 1.08	G J W Booth tr DDM Syndicate	Ridgewell	5. 5.08
G-DDDN	PZL-Bielsko SZD-9bis Bocian 1E	P-429	BGA2034-DDN 1. 5.08 RAFGSA 393	The Bath, Wilts and North Dorset Gliding Club Ltd	Longbridge Deverill	
G-DDDR	Schempp-Hirth Standard Cirrus	531G	BGA2037-DDR 16.10.07	J D Ewence "680"	Pocklington	28. 9.08
G-DDDW	PZL-Bielsko SZD-30	S-04.33	BGA2042-DDW 23. 4.08	R M Golding, D Gear and S B Butcher	Parham Park	
G-DDDY	P&M Aviation Quik GT450	8308	23. 8.07	J W Dodson	Leicester	29. 8.08P
G-DDEA	Slingsby T.59D Kestrel 19	1865	BGA2046-DEA 15. 9.08	A Pickles	Lasham	
G-DDEG	ICA IS-28B2	48	BGA2051-DEG 7. 9.07	P S Whitehead	Skelling Farm, Penrith	16.11.07
G-DDEO	Glasflügel H205 Club Libelle	97	BGA2059-DEQ 18.12.07	N J Mitchell	Kingston Deverill	24. 3.08
G-DDEV	Schleicher Ka 6CR	6453	BGA2064-DEV 7. 1.08 RAFGSA 354	A N and L M Morley	Rattlesden	22. 3.08
G-DDEW	ICA IS-29D	40	BGA2065-DEW 30.11.07	G V Prater	(Lower Earley, Reading)	4. 7.07
G-DDEX	LET L-13 Blanik	026348	BGA2066-DEX 11. 9.07 RAFGSA R4, BGA2066-DEX	B A Hutchins tr Blanik DEX Group	Talgarth	24.10.07
G-DDFC	Schempp-Hirth Standard Cirrus	592G	BGA2071-DFC 7. 3.08	C E and I Helme	Usk	
G-DDFE	Molino PIK-20B	20052	BGA2073-DFE 7. 7.08	M A Rolf-Jarrett	Lasham	
G-DDFK	Molino PIK-20	20039	BGA2078-DFK 31.10.07 OH-500	B H and M J Fairclough	North Hill	17. 3.09P
G-DDFL	SZD-38A Jantar-1	B-682	BGA2079-DFL 9.10.07	P Bellham	Kirton-in-Lindsey	6. 5.08
G-DDFN	Glaser-Dirks DG-100	30	BGA2081-DFN 2. 5.08	D J Clarke and J Melling	Wormingford	
G-DDFR	Grob G102 Astir CS	1038	BGA2084-DFR 10. 3.08	The Windrushers Gliding Club	Bicester	
G-DDFV	PZL- Bielsko SZD-38A Jantar 1	B-684	BGA2088-DFV 21. 8.08	G Bambrook and J M Sherman	Horsham and Wokingham	
G-DDFW	PZL-Bielsko SZD-30 Pirat	S-05.45	BGA2089-DFW 22. 2.08	R G Skerry tr Cloud Nine Syndicate	Strubby	29. 8.07
G-DDFX	PZL-Bielsko SZD-41A Jantar Standard 1	B-691	BGA2090-DFX 6. 8.08	J C Tait tr Jantar Syndicate	Easterton	
G-DDGA	Schleicher K 8B	8587	BGA2093-DGA 11.12.07 RAFGSA 334, BGA1926-CZA, RAFGSA 334	The Welland Gliding Club Ltd	Lyveden	1. 5.08
G-DDGE	Schempp-Hirth Standard Cirrus	606	BGA2097-DGE 9. 1.08	M Bond	Bury	4. 5.08
G-DDGG	Schleicher Ka 6E	4061	BGA2099-DGG 1. 8.08 RAFGSA 263	N F Holmes and F D Platt	Long Mynd	
G-DDGJ	American Champion 8KCAB Super Decathlon	1049-2007	17. 8.07	PHI Projects Ltd	Old Sarum	18.12.09E
G-DDGK	Schleicher Ka 6CR	6287	BGA2102-DGK 22.11.07	N Riggott "Betty Blue"	Lasham	9. 5.08
G-DDGX	Schempp-Hirth Standard Cirrus 75	619	BGA2114-DGX 24. 4.08 AGA 3, BGA2114-DGX	G Seaman	Lasham	
G-DDGY	Schempp-Hirth Nimbus 2	105	BGA2115-DGY 31.10.07	J.H.Taylor "195"	Nympsfield	15. 1.08
G-DDHA	Schleicher K8	3	BGA2117-DHA 30. 4.08 D-8848, D-5148	Shalbourne Soaring Society Ltd	Rivar Hill	
G-DDHC	PZL-Bielsko SZD-41A Jantar Standard 1	B-710	BGA2119-DHC 7. 1.08 (BGA2109)	M C Burlock and P J Kelly	Rivar Hill	29. 3.08
G-DDHE	Slingsby T.53B	1718	BGA2132-DHE 13.11.07	J Mattocks tr Aviation Preservation Society of Scotland (APSS)	Portmoak	31. 3.09R
G-DDHG	Schleicher Ka 6CR	1131	BGA2123-DHG 28. 4.08 D-5170	Angus Gliding Club Ltd	Drumshade	
G-DDHH	Eiriavion PIK-20B	20124	BGA2124-DHH 16. 7.08	D M Steed "116"	Sackville Lodge, Riseley	
G-DDHJ	Glaser-Dirks DG-100	48	BGA2125-DHJ 13.12.07	G E McLaughlin	Bellarena	25. 6.08
G-DDHK	Glaser-Dirks DG-100	50	BGA2126-DHK 30. 8.07	B J Griffin	Kirton in Lindsey	28. 9.08
G-DDHL	Glaser-Dirks DG-100	52	BGA2127-DHL 25.10.07	T L Webster tr DHL Syndicate	Challock	24. 2.08
G-DDHM	Schleicher Ka 6E	4124	BGA2128-DHM 19.10.07 RAFGSA 26	J G Heard	Seighford	7. 3.08
G-DDHN	Eiriavion PIK-20B	20082	BGA2129-DHN 15.10.08	G J Bass tr G Bass and Partners "824"	Challock	
G-DDHT	Schleicher Ka 6E	4065	BGA2134-DHT 11.12.07 D-7202	S Foster	Long Mynd	20. 2.08
G-DDHV	Eiriavion PIK 20B	20111	BGA2136-DHV 22. 4.08	M R Parker	Nympsfield	
G-DDHW	Schempp-Hirth Nimbus 2	106	BGA2137-DHW 20. 8.08	M J Carruthers and D Thompson "951"	Portmoak	
G-DDHX	Schempp-Hirth Standard Cirrus B (Rebuilt using airframe from D-3264, c/n 533G)	'635'	BGA2138-DHX 27. 5.08	J Franke	Lasham	
G-DDHZ	PZL-Bielsko SZD-30	S-06	BGA2140-DHZ 20. 6.08	Peterborough and Spalding Gliding Club	Crowland	
G-DDIG	Rockwell Commander 114	14397	G-CCDT 11. 7.06 D-EKGD, OE-KGD, D-EIBC	D Millard tr Daedalus Flying Group	Lee-on-Solent	16. 5.08E
G-DDJB	Schleicher K 8B	8879	BGA2142-DJB 29. 1.08 AGA17	T World tr Portsmouth Naval Gliding Centre	Lee-on-Solent	16. 2.08
G-DDJD	Grob G102 Astir CS	1226	BGA2144-DJD 16.10.07	P E Gascoigne	Kingston Deverill	28. 9.08
G-DDJE	Schleicher Ka 6CR	6412	BGA2145/DJE, 13.12.07 D-3682	E W Russell tr The Friday Syndicate	Wormingford	28. 9.08
G-DDJF	Schempp-Hirth Duo Discus T	121/...	BGA5182-KLM 21. 4.06	R J H Fack "JF"	Long Mynd	14. 5.08
G-DDJK	Scheichler ASK 18	18030	BGA2150-DJK 30. 4.08	Booker Gliding Club Ltd	Wycombe Air Park	
G-DDJL	PZL-Bielsko SZD-41A Jantar Standard 1	B-714	BGA2151-DJL 14. 9.07	A M Cooper	Llantisilio	28. 9.08
G-DDJM	PZL-Bielsko SZD-41A Jantar Standard	B-715	BGA2152-DJM 31. 7.08	G Dennis, P Moorehead and T Davies	Halesland	

Reg	Type	C/n	BGA/Prev	Date	Owner/Operator	Base	Date2
G-DDJN	Eiriavion PIK-20B	20140C	BGA2153-DJN	20.11.07	M Ireland and S Lambourne	Kingston Deverill	16. 3.09R
G-DDJR	Schleicher Ka 6CR	680	BGA2156-DJR D-8423	27. 8.08	A S Hillman tr Syndicate K6	Perranporth	
G-DDJX	Grob G102 Astir CS	1259	BGA2162-DJX	4. 1.08	P Barnwell	Crowland	13. 4.08
G-DDKC	Schleicher K 8B	8261	BGA2167-DKC D-1431	22. 4.08	Yorkshire Gling Club (Proprietary) Ltd	Sutton Bank	
G-DDKD	Glasflügel H206 Hornet	67	BGA2168-DKD (BGA2165-DKA)	3. 1.08	B J W Thomas	Eyres Field	28. 4.08
G-DDKE	Schleicher ASK 13	13548	BGA2169-DKE	25. 1.08	The South Wales Gliding Club Ltd	Usk	13. 4.08
G-DDKG	Schleicher Ka 6CR	6233	BGA2171-DKG D-4327	10. 3.08	R T Brooker ta Kilo Golf Group	Wormingford	
G-DDKL	Schempp-Hirth Nimbus-2	86	BGA2175-DKL D-2111	1. 2.08	G J Croll *"444"*	Rattlesden	20. 4.08
G-DDKM	Glasflügel H206 Hornet	49	BGA2176-DKM (BGA2213), BGA2176, D-7816	11. 4.08	R S Lee	Rattlesden	
G-DDKN	Schleicher Ka 6CR	6456	BGA2177-DKN D-9358	17. 1.08	A Ciccone	Upwood	2. 4.08
G-DDKR	Grob G102 Astir CS	1327	BGA2180-DKR	27. 5.08	Oxford Gliding Co Ltd	RAF Weston-on-the-Green	
G-DDKS	Grob G102 Astir CS	1530	BGA2181-DKS	1. 7.08	C K Lewis *"788"*	Lasham	
G-DDKT	Eiriavion PIK-20B	20155C	BGA2182-DKT	29. 2.08	F P Wilson	Pocklington	23. 4.08
G-DDKU	Grob G102 Astir CS	1326	BGA2183-DKU	12. 9.07	P N Stapleton tr Delta Kilo Uniform Syndicate	North Hill	28. 9.08
G-DDKW	Grob G102 Astir CS	1329	BGA2185-DKW	8. 2.08	J Friend and R Robertson	Lleweni Parc	30. 3.08
G-DDKX	Grob G102 Astir CS	1331	BGA2186-DKX	23. 1.08	L R Bennett	Usk	30. 4.08
G-DDLA	Pilatus B4-PC11	149	BGA2189-DLA RAFGSA	17. 8.07	P R Seddon	Walney Island	3. 6.08
G-DDLB	Schleicher ASK 18	18040	BGA2190-DLB	28.11.07	The Vale of the White Horse Gliding Centre Ltd	Sandhill Farm, Shrivenham	9. 2.08
G-DDLC	Schleicher ASK 13	13549	BGA2191-DLC	22. 4.08	Lasham Gliding Society Ltd *"C"*	Lasham	
G-DDLE	Schleicher Ka 6E	4074	BGA2193-DLE AGA 8, RAFGSA	1. 5.08	D C Unwin tr 433 Syndicate	Darlton	
G-DDLH	Grob G102 Astir CS77	1646	BGA2196-DLH	28. 1.08	M D and M E Saunders	Lasham	19. 4.08
G-DDLJ	Eiriavion Pik 20B	20157	BGA2197-DLJ	9. 5.08	M S Parkes	Milfield	
G-DDLM	Grob G102 Astir CS	1260	BGA2200-DLM (BGA2163-DJY)	6. 8.08	I A Davison *"226"*	North Hill	
G-DDLP	Schleicher Ka 6CR	6519	BGA2202-DLP RAFGSA 355	18. 1.08	J.R Crosse	Crowland	24. 4.08
G-DDLS	Schleicher K 8B	8650	BGA2205-DLS D-5718	2. 9.08	B R Pearson tr North Devon Gliding Club	Eaglescott	
G-DDLT	ICA IS-28B2	32	BGA2206-DLT	8. 2.08	M H Simms	Shipdham	3. 7.03
G-DDLY	Eiriavion PIK-20B	20509	BGA2211-DLY	13.12.07	M Conrad	Bidford	23. 5.08
G-DDMB	Schleicher K 8B	8209	BGA2214-DMB D-4331	27. 9.07	Crown Service Gliding Club *"831"*	Lasham	3. 2.08
G-DDMD	Glaser-Dirks DG-100	75	BGA2216-DMD	12.12.07	N M Hill *"251"*	RAF Weston-on-the-Green	24. 2.08
G-DDMG	Schleicher K 8B	8763	BGA2219-DMG RAFGSA 382	6.11.07	Dorset Gliding Club Ltd	Eyres Field	28. 9.08
G-DDMH	Grob G102 Astir CS	1511	BGA2220-DMH	8. 7.08	Oxford Gliding Club Ltd RAF Weston-on-the-Green		
G-DDMK	Schempp-Hirth SHK-1	25	BGA2222-DMK D-5401	6. 6.08	D Breeze	Aston Down	
G-DDML	Schleicher K 7 Rhönadler	929	BGA2223-DML D-6194, D-5005	12.12.07	Dumfries and District Gliding Club	Falgunzeon	11. 2.07
G-DDMM	Schempp-Hirth Nimbus 2	125	BGA2224-DMM	14. 1.08	T.E.Linee	Eyres Field	22. 4.08
G-DDMO	Schleicher Ka 6E	4062	BGA2227-DMQ RAFGSA 264	23. 1.08	Trent Valley Gliding Club Ltd	Kirton-in-Lindsey	18. 6.08
G-DDMP	Grob G102 Astir CS	1239	BGA2226-DMP ZS-GKF	6. 6.08	P Miles tr Kingswood Syndicate	Dunstable	
G-DDMR	Grob G102 Astir CS	1435	BGA2228-DMR	22.12.07	Mendip Gliding Club Ltd *"511"*	Halesland	16. 2.08
G-DDMS	Glasflügel H201B Standard Libelle	385	BGA2229-DMS RNGSA 259	1.12.07	K C Springate tr G-DDMS Group	(Goole)	12. 4.08
G-DDMU	Eiriavion PIK-20D	20524	BGA2231-DMU	6. 8.08	J Mjels *"392"*	Sutton Bank	
G-DDMV	North American T-6G-NF Texan	168-313	N3240N Haitian AF 3209, 49-3209	30. 4.90	C Dabin (As *"493209:ANG"* in USAAF *"CALIF ANG"* yellow c/s)	Sywell	6. 4.09T
G-DDMX	Schleicher ASK 13	13567	BGA2234-DMX	25. 1.08	Dartmoor Gliding Society Ltd	Brent Tor	1. 8.08
G-DDNC	Grob G102 Astir CS	1428	BGA2239-DNC	18.10.07	K S Wells and R A Lovegrove	Lyveden	27. 6.99
G-DDND	Pilatus B4-PC11AF	136	BGA2240-DND	7. 2.08	R J Happs tr DND Group	Lasham	21. 4.08
G-DDNE	Grob G102 Astir CS77	1631	BGA2241-DNE	22.12.07	J Green and M A Wintle tr 621 Astir Syndicate	Halesland	26. 3.08
G-DDNF	PZL-Bielsko SZD-9bis Bocian 1D	P-354	BGA2242-DNF	7. 4.08	M G Shaw tr Portmoak Bocian (DNF) Group	Portmoak	
G-DDNG	Schempp-Hirth Nimbus 2	265	BGA2243-DNG	9.10.07	B H Penfold tr Nimbus 265 Syndicate *"265"*	Trenchard Lines, Upavon	5. 3.08
G-DDNJ	Schleicher ASK 18	18042	BGA2245-DNJ	17. 1.08	Derbyshire & Lancashire Gliding Club	Camphill	18. 1.08
G-DDNK	Grob G102 Astir CS	1434	BGA2246-DNK	5.10.07	A Page tr G-DDNK Group *"745"*	Rattlesden	1. 3.08
G-DDNT	PZL-Bielsko SZD-30 Pirat	S-07.12	BGA2254-DNT	13.12.07	R A Lashly	Drumshade	27. 4.08
G-DDNU	PZL-Bielsko SZD-42-1 Jantar 2	B-783	BGA2255-DNU	19. 4.08	C D Rowland and D Chalmers-Brown	Wycombe Air Park	
G-DDNV	Schleicher ASK 13	13568	BGA2256-DNV	24. 6.08	Channel Gliding Cub Ltd	Waldershare Park	
G-DDNW	Schleicher Ka 6CR	829	BGA2257-DNW	21.11.07	K Marchant and P Carey	Shenington	23. 4.08
G-DDNX	Schleicher Ka 6CR	6094SI	BGA2258-DNX D-5107	1.12.07	Black Mountains Gliding Club	Talgarth	28. 9.08
G-DDNZ	Schleicher K 8B	8095	BGA2260-DNZ D-1711	1. 9.08	L J Gregoire tr Southampton University Gliding Club	Lasham	
G-DDOA	Schleicher ASK 13	13582	BGA2285-DQA	12.11.07	Essex & Suffolk Gliding Club Ltd	Wormingford	28. 9.08
G-DDOB	Grob G102 Astir CS77	1653	BGA2286-DQB	6.12.07	C E Hutson	Kirton-in-Lindsey	1. 4.08

G-DDOC	Schleicher Ka 6CR	6373SI	BGA2269-DQC 20. 6.08 D-5725	W St G V Stoney	(Impruneta, Italy)	
G-DDOE	Grob G102 Astir CS77	1636	BGA2289-DQE 26. 6.08 RNGSA N34	D J Marpole tr Heron Gliding Club	RNAS Yeovilton	
G-DDOF	Schleicher Ka 6CR	6417	BGA2290-DQF 6. 2.08 D-5827	A Graham	Portmoak	24. 4.08
G-DDOG	Scottish Aviation Bulldog Series 120/121	BH120/210	XX524 18. 6.01	Deltaero Ltd (As "XX524:04" in RAF c/s)	Malaga, Spain	12. 2.09S
G-DDOK	Schleicher Ka 6E	4341	BGA2294-DQK 13. 2.08 D-0541	R S Hawley and S Y Duxbury	Long Mynd	7. 4.08
G-DDOR	Grob G102 Astir CS77	1667	BGA2300-DQR 25.10.07	V A Watt	Kingston Deverill	28. 9.08
G-DDOU	Eiriavion PIK 20D	20579	BGA2303-DQU 21. 4.08	J Mattocks tr DQU Syndicate	Portmoak	
G-DDOX	Schleicher K 7 Rhönadler	743	BGA2306-DQX 4. 1.08 D-9127	The Nene Valley Gliding Club Ltd	Upwood	31. 3.08
	(Regd as K 7 but believed modified earlier to ASK 13 standard with fuselage from ASK 13 BGA1833 and wings from BGA3331)					
G-DDOY	Schleicher K 8B	647	BGA2307-DQY 22.12.07 D-4375	Mendip Gliding Club Ltd	Halesland	18. 8.08
G-DDPA	Schleicher ASK 18	18044	BGA2261-DPA 11. 1.08	Rangetour Ltd	Bembridge	4. 3.08
G-DDPH	Schempp-Hirth Mini-Nimbus 8	09	BGA2268-DPH 25. 4.08	J W Murdoch	Portmoak	
G-DPPK	Glasflügel H303A Mosquito	27	BGA2270-DPK 25. 3.08	G Lawley	Cross Hayes	
G-DDPL	Eiriavion PIK-20D	20549	BGA2271-DPL 25. 2.08	H A Schuricht tr 437 Syndicate	Dunstable	22. 1.08
G-DDPO	Grob G102 Astir CS77	1632	BGA2275-DPQ 9. 1.08	Dorset Gliding Club Ltd	Eyres Field	14. 4.08
G-DDPY	Grob G102 Astir CS77	1652	BGA2283-DPY 30.10.07	D S Burton	Shenington	27. 5.08
G-DDRA	Schleicher Ka 6CR	1118	BGA2309-DRA 18. 8.08 D-9011	D S Edwards tr K 6CR Group Shobdon "904"	Shobdon	
G-DDRB	Glaser-Dirks DG-100	31	BGA2310-DRB 1. 8.08 PH-532	J D Peck tr DRB Syndicate "86"	Bicester	
G-DDRD	Schleicher Ka 6CR	6377SI	BGA2312-DRD 4.10.07 D-9080	Essex & Suffolk Gliding Club Ltd	Wormingford	28. 9.08
G-DDRE	Schleicher Ka 6CR	6197	BGA2313-DRE 28. 8.08 D-8558	J H Howett and I D King	North Hill	
G-DDRJ	Schleicher ASK 13	13583	BGA2317-DRJ 22. 4.08	Lasham Gliding Society Ltd "D"	Lasham	
G-DDRL	Scheibe SF 26A	5040	BGA2319-DRL 21. 1.09 D-7073	D G King	Strubby	
G-DDRM	Schleicher K 7 Rhönadler	7017	BGA2320-DRM 31.10.07 D-4666	L.G.Cross tr K7 DRM Glider Syndicate	Dunstable	3.10.07
G-DDRN	Glasflügel H303A Mosquito	82	BGA2321-DRN 19. 3.08	A and V R Roberts	Cross Hayes	
G-DDRO	Grob G103 Twin Astir	3027	BGA2323-DRQ 3. 4.08	J Catmur tr Astir 258 Syndicate	Sleap	
G-DDRP	Pilatus B4-PC-11	080	BGA2322-DRP 17. 3.08 RAFGSA, BGA1927	M Moxon tr DRP Syndicate	RAF Weston-on-the-Green	
G-DDRT	Eiriavion PIK-20D	20587	BGA2326-DRT 20.11.07	P F C Fowler tr 688 Syndicate	Long Mynd	4. 4.08
G-DDRU	Grob G102 Astir CS77	1685	BGA2327-DRU 4.10.07	G Rybak "334"	Lasham	26. 2.08
G-DDRV	Schleicher K 8B	8026	BGA2328-DRV 26. 9.08 D-6169	P Clayton tr DRV Syndicate	Portmoak	
G-DDRW	Grob G102 Astir CS	1081	BGA2329-DRW 1. 2.08 D-3311	P A Brooks tr 798 Syndicate	Lasham	1. 5.08
G-DDRY	Schleicher Ka 6CR	370	BGA2331-DRY 23. 4.08 D-5553	S Urry	Tibenham	
G-DDRZ	Schleicher K 8B	668	BGA2332-DRZ 18. 1.08 D-4622, D-KANB, D-4622	East Sussex Gliding Club	Ringmer	31. 7.08
G-DDSB	Schleicher Ka 6E	4300	BGA2334-DSB 12.12.07 D-0263	G B Griffiths	Rattlesden	6. 3.08
G-DDSF	Schleicher K 8B	8220	BGA2338-DSF 10. 1.08 D-7114	I A McTernan tr Edinburgh University Gliding Club "Snoopy"	Portmoak	28. 9.08
G-DDSH	Grob G102 Astir CS77	1696	BGA2340-DSH 21. 1.08	R B Petrie tr Astir 648 Syndicate	Portmoak	7. 6.08
G-DDSJ	Grob G103 Twin Astir	3050	BGA2341-DSJ 11. 8.08	Herefordshire Gliding Club Ltd	Shobdon	
G-DDSL	Grob G103 Twin Astir	3041	BGA2343-DSL 11. 9.08	R A Jones tr DSL Syndicate	Brent Tor	
G-DDSP	Schempp-Hirth Mini-Nimbus B	33	BGA2346-DSP 25. 3.08	R I Hey tr 270 Syndicate	Nympsfield	
G-DDST	Schleicher ASW 20L	20059	BGA2350-DST 17. 9.07	D J Miller	Dunstable	22. 2.08
G-DDSU	Grob G102 Astir CS77	1663	BGA2351-DSU 21. 1.08	Bowland Forest Gliding Club Ltd	Chipping	28. 9.08
G-DDSV	Pilatus B4-PC11AF	134	BGA2352-DSV 21. 1.08 RAFGSA 718, RAFGSA 518	G M Drinkell and S J Brunton	Wormingford	1. 6.08
G-DDSX	Schleicher ASW 19B	19188	BGA2354-DSX 18.10.07	B Ashbourn and G Kamp	Kingston Deverill	28. 9.08
G-DDSY	Schleicher Ka 6CR	561	BGA2355-DSY 4. 1.08 D-5702	D A Senior "Daisy"	Camphill	14. 3.08
G-DDTA	Glaser-Dirks DG-200	2-27	BGA2357-DTA 13.12.07	M D Bowman	Rufforth	17. 7.08
G-DDTC	Schempp-Hirth Janus B	63	BGA2359-DTC 22. 5.08 RAFGSA R9, RAFGSA 16, BGA2359	Darlton Gliding Club Ltd	Darlton	
G-DDTE	Schleicher ASW 19B	19185	BGA2361-DTE 7. 2.08	A and G R Purcell	Shenington	4.12.07
G-DDTG	Schempp-Hirth SHK-1	12	BGA2363-DTG 6. 6.08 D-2034	D B Smith	(Gourock)	
G-DDTK	Glasflügel H303 Mosquito B	109	BGA2366-DTK 4.12.07	P France	Usk	28. 9.08
G-DDTM	Glaser-Dirks DG-200	2-34	BGA2368-DTM 18.12.07	R S Skinner	Wormingford	12. 3.08
G-DDTN	Schleicher K 8B	117/58	BGA2369-DTN 7.10.08	C G and G N Thomas "DTN"	Wattisham	
G-DDTP	Schleicher ASW 20	20078	BGA2370-DTP 27. 9.07	T S and S M Hills	Lasham	28. 9.08
G-DDTS	CARMAM M-100S Mesange	31	BGA2373-DTS 10. 3.08	R C Holmes	Lleweni Parc	
G-DDTU	Schempp-Hirth Nimbus 2B	167	BGA2375-DTU 14. 8.07	R E Wooller tr Nimbus Syndicate	Chipping	12. 4.08
G-DDTV	Glasflügel H303 Mosquito B	110	BGA2376-DTV 4.12.07	S R Evans	Aston Down	14. 9.08
G-DDTW	PZL-Bielsko SZD-30 Pirat	S-07.11	BGA2377-DTW 25. 4.08	C Kaminsk tr NDGC Pirat Syndicate	Eaglescott	
G-DDTX	Glasflügel H303 Mosquito B	111	BGA2378-DTX 4. 1.08	P T S Nash	Crowland	23. 1.02
G-DDTY	Glasflügel H303 Mosquito B	112	BGA2379-DTY 6. 2.08	W H L Bullimore "766"	Gransden Lodge	2.11.07
G-DDUB	Glasflügel H303 Mosquito B	113	BGA2382-DUB 11. 3.08	F B Reilly tr Mosquito Group	Portmoak	
G-DDUE	Schleicher ASK 13	13591	BGA2385-DUE 1. 5.08 AGA 15, BGA2385-DUE	P Fanning tr Army Gliding Association	AAC Wattisham	

G-DDUF	Schleicher K 8B	8296A	BGA2386-DUF 24.10.07	M Staljan	Nympsfield	6. 7.08
			D-5294			
G-DDUH	Scheibe L-Spatz 55	760	BGA2388-DUH 29. 9.08	R J Aylesbury and J Young	Upwood	
G-DDUK	Schleicher K 8B	752	BGA2390-DUK 29. 1.08	The Bristol Gliding Club Proprietary Ltd	Nympsfield	13. 3.08
			D-4048			
G-DDUL	Grob G102 Astir CS77	1720	BGA2391-DUL 3. 1.08	G R Davey	Kirton-in-Lindsey	2. 4.08
G-DDUR	Schleicher Ka 6CR	6273	BGA2395-DUR 12.11.07	B N Bromley and M Whitthread	Strubby	8.12.07
			OY-DLX			
G-DDUT	Schleicher ASW 20	20089	BGA2397-DUT 14. 4.08	M E Doig and E T J Murphy	Portmoak	
G-DDUX	Grob G102 Astir CS Jeans	2140	BGA2401-DUX 22.11.07	B T Spreckley (Operated European Soaring Club)		
					Ontur, Spain	28. 9.08
G-DDVB	Schleicher ASK 13	13596	BGA2405-DVB 12.11.07	Essex & Suffolk Gliding Club Ltd	Wormingford	2. 2.08
	(Components including c/n plate donated to BGA3493)					
G-DDVC	Schleicher ASK 13	13597	BGA2406-DVC 18. 8.08	Staffordshire Gliding Club Ltd	Seighford	
G-DDVD	LET L-13 Blanik	027021	BGA2417-DVD 27.11.07	Vectis Gliding Club Ltd	Bembridge	27.12.08
			(RNGSA N22)			
G-DDVG	Schleicher Ka 6CR	3	BGA2410-DVG 21.12.07	G Tilley tr G-DDVG Banana Group	Ringmer	20. 2.08
G-DDVH	Schleicher Ka 6E	4117	BGA2411-DVH 3. 9.08	M A K Cropper	Brent Tor	
			RAFGSA 315			
G-DDVK	PZL-Bielsko SZD-48 Jantar Standard	W-868	BGA2413-DVK 25. 6.08	G P Nuttall	Wycombe Air Park	
G-DDVL	Schleicher ASW 19	19222	BGA2414-DVL 17.11.07	A C M Phillips "X96"	Lasham	30. 3.08
G-DDVM	Glasflügel H205 Club Libelle	52	BGA2415-DVM 22. 2.08	M A Field	Wormingford	4. 4.08
			RAFGGA 581			
G-DDVN	Eiriavion PIK-20D	20641	BGA2416-DVN 28. 1.08	T P Bassett and A D Butler	Burn	2. 6.09R
G-DDVP	Schleicher ASW 19B	19220	BGA2417-DVP 17. 1.08	P O R Cumming tr VP Syndicate		
					Wycombe Air Park	29. 1.08
G-DDVS	Schempp-Hirth Standard Cirrus	380	BGA2420-DVS 24.10.07	J C and T J Milner "VS"	Rufforth	23. 3.08
			RAFGSA 824			
G-DDVV	Schleicher ASW 20L	20100	BGA2423-DVV 12. 8.08	A M Hooper "810"	Usk	
G-DDVX	Schleicher AS-K 13	13598	BGA2425-DVX 5. 8.08	Shenington Gliding Club "S13"	Shenington	
	(Type amended to AS-K 13 on 1.12.08)					
G-DDVY	Schempp-Hirth Cirrus	52	BGA2426-DVY 12. 2.08	G Martin and M G Ashton	Talgarth	27. 7.08
			OO-ZIR			
G-DDVZ	Glasflügel H303 Mosquito B	133	BGA2427-DVZ 23. 6.08	B H Shaw and R Spreckley	Husbands Bosworth	
G-DDWB	Glasflügel H303 Mosquito B	135	BGA2429-DWB 19. 3.08	D T Edwards	Skirwith	
G-DDWC	Schleicher Ka 6E	4111	BGA2430-DWC 6.11.07	D E Jones	Ridgewell	12. 4.08
			AGA 11			
G-DDWG	Schleicher K 8B	165-60	BGA2434-DWG 31. 1.08	Dartmoor Gliding Society	Brentor	12.12.07
			D-5750			
G-DDWJ	Glaser-Dirks DG-200	2-59	BGA2436-DWJ 7. 3.08	A P Kamp and P R Desmond "191"	Chipping	
G-DDWL	Glasflügel H303 Mosquito B	141	BGA2438-DWL 1.11.07	H A Stanford	Husbands Bosworth	3. 4.08
G-DDWN	Schleicher K 7 Rhönadler	7101	BGA2440-DWN 12. 2.08	L R and J E Merritt	Saltby	27. 5.08
			D-5360			
G-DDWR	Glasflügel H303 Mosquito B	134	BGA2443-DWR 16.10.07	C D Lovell	Lasham	11. 3.08
			(BGA2428-DWA)			
G-DDWS	Eiriavion PIK 20D	20652	BGA2444-DWS 9. 4.08	D G Slocombe	Burn	
G-DDWT	Slingsby T.65C Vega	1898	BGA2445-DWT 11.10.07	A P Grimley	(Alderley Edge)	28. 9.08
G-DDWU	Grob G102 Astir CS	1201	BGA2446-DWU 25.10.07	D Evans and I B Cronyn	Dunstable	20.12.07
			D-7269			
G-DDWW	Slingsby T.65A Vega	1896	BGA2448-DWW 28. 3.08	G Robertson tr G-DDWW Flying Group	Usk	
G-DDXA	Glasflügel H303 Mosquito B	137	BGA2452-DXA 6. 3.08	A Walker tr G-DDXA Group	Gransden Lodge	
G-DDXB	Schleicher ASW 20	20142	BGA2453-DXB 25.10.07	J A Timpany tr 81 Syndicate "81"	Nympsfield	28. 9.08
G-DDXD	Slingsby T.65A Vega	1901	BGA2455-DXD 26 .2.08	R M King tr G-DDXD Flying Group	Kenley	21. 9.08
G-DDXE	Slingsby T.65C Vega	1902	BGA2456-DXE 16.11.07	H K Rattray	Usk	18. 1.08
G-DDXF	Slingsby T.65A Vega	1903	BGA2457-DXF 26. 3.08	B A Walker	Crowland	
G-DDXG	Slingsby T.65A Vega	1906	BGA2458-DXG 13. 3.08	A D Morrison ta DXG Group	Feshiebridge	
G-DDXH	Schleicher Ka 6E	4198	BGA2459-DXH 25. 1.08	B Hughes tr DXH Syndicate	Bicester	22. 3.08
			RAFGSA 489, D-4093			
G-DDXJ	Grob G102 Astir CS77	1762	BGA2460-DXJ 6.12.07	M T Stickland	Portmoak	10. 3.08
G-DDXK	Centrair ASW 20F	20108	BGA2461-DXK 2. 6.08	E and A Townsend	Nympsfield	
G-DDXL	Schempp-Hirth Standard Cirrus	203G	BGA2462-DXL 17.11.07	C J Button	Aston Down	30. 3.08
			AGA 1			
G-DDXN	Glaser-Dirks DG-200	2-63	BGA2464-DXN 9. 1.08	J.A.Johnston	Gransden Lodge	16. 3.08
G-DDXT	Schempp-Hirth Mini-Nimbus C	97	BGA2469-DXT 10.12.07	H Altmann tr G-DDXT Mini-Nimbus		
					Wycombe Air Park	4. 3.08
G-DDXW	Glasflügel H303 Mosquito B	142	BGA2472-DXW 6.12.07	P Newmark	Burn	16. 2.08
G-DDXX	Schleicher ASW 19B	19245	BGA2473-DXX 14.12.07	B C P Crook	Challock	28. 9.08
G-DDYC	Schleicher Ka 6CR	6390	BGA2478-DYC 24. 1.08	S S Ryan	Walney Island	22. 4.08
			D-1545			
G-DDYE	Schleicher ASW 20L	20143	BGA2479-DYE 5. 9.07	T A Sage tr 828 Syndicate "828"	Dunstable	28. 9.08
G-DDYF	Grob G102 Astir CS77	1805	BGA2480-DYF 29.10.07	York Gliding Centre Ltd	Rufforth	28. 9.08
G-DDYH	Glaser-Dirks DG-200	2-75	BGA2482-DYH 27. 5.08	P Johnson	Milfield	
G-DDYJ	Schleicher Ka 6CR	6583	BGA2483-DYJ 19. 2.08	Upward Bound Trust	Thame	14. 7.08
			D-5838			
G-DDYL	CARMAN JP 15-36AR	37	BGA2485-DYL 23. 4.08	P A Pickering	Crowland	
G-DDYR	Schleicher K7 Rhonadler	766	BGA2489-DYR 12. 5.08	K Tomlinson tr University of the West of England Gliding Club		
			D-5220		Aston Down	
G-DDYU	Schempp-Hirth Nimbus 2C	181	BGA2491-DYU 12.12.07	K Richards	(Talgarth)	31. 3.05
G-DDYX	Schleicher ASW 20	20125	BGA2494-DYX 3. 6.08	J L Bugbee "M5"	North Hill	
G-DDZA	Slingsby T.65A Vega 17L	1907	BGA2496-DZA 21. 9.07	K H Kuntze	Dunstable	2. 3.08
G-DDZB	Slingsby T.65A Vega	1908	BGA2497-DZB 6. 3.08	A A Black	Drumshade	
G-DDZF	Schempp-Hirth Standard Cirrus	421G	BGA2501-DZF 24. 4.08	L S, J M and R S Hood "152"	Lasham	
			RAFGSA 27			
G-DDZG	Schleicher ASW 19B	19267	BGA2502-DZG 27.11.07	S P Wareham	Kingston Deverill	18. 2.08

Reg	Type	c/n	Identity	Date	Owner/Operator	Base	Date
G-DDZJ	Grob G102 Astir CS Jeans	2230	BGA2504-DZJ	29. 5.08	D W Bassett tr Mendip Astir Syndicate	Halesland	
G-DDZM	Slingsby T.65A Vega	1909	BGA2507-DZM	17. 3.08	C I R Harris tr Vega Syndicate	Long Mynd	
G-DDZP	Slingsby T.65A Vega	1911	BGA2509-DZP	14. 2.08	M T Crews	Milfield	25. 6.08
G-DDZR	ICA IS-28B2	87	BGA2511-DZR	5.12.07	The Furness Gliding Club Proprietary Ltd tr Lakes Gliding Club	Walney Island	9. 5.08
G-DDZT	Eiriavion PIK-20D	20661	BGA2513-DZT	31.10.07	A C Garside tr PIK20D 106 Group	Challock	1. 3.09R
G-DDZU	Grob G102 Astir CS	1076	BGA2514-DZU D-3308	19. 4.08	P Clarke	Wycombe Air Park	
G-DDZY	Schleicher ASW 19B	19275	BGA2518-DZY	13. 9.07	M C Fairman	Dunstable	29. 1.08

G-DEAA - G-DEZZ

Reg	Type	c/n	Identity	Date	Owner/Operator	Base	Date
G-DEAE	Schleicher ASW 20L	20224	BGA2524-EAE	1. 5.08	R Burghall	(Rotherham)	
G-DEAF	Grob G102 Astir CS77	1830	BGA2525-EAF	25. 2.08	The Borders (Milfield) Gliding Club Ltd	Milfield	29. 9.08
G-DEAG	Slingsby T.65A Vega	1913	BGA2526-EAG	19. 3.08	D L King	Rhigos	
G-DEAH	Schleicher Ka 6E	4085	BGA2527-EAH D-7542, D-7142	5. 2.08	M Lodge	Lasham	14. 6.08
G-DEAJ	Schempp-Hirth HS.5 Nimbus 2	7	BGA2528-EAJ D-0699	12.11.07	D R Piercey and N Hanney	Eyres Field	31. 3.08
G-DEAK	Glasflügel H303 Mosquito B	155	BGA2529-EAK	14. 2.08	T A L Barnes	Aston Down	9. 6.08
G-DEAM	Schempp-Hirth Nimbus 2B	93	BGA2531-KAM D-2787	30.10.07	J Davies tr Alpha Mike Syndicate	Chipping	28. 9.08
G-DEAN	Solar Wings Pegasus XL-Q *(Trike c/n SW-TE-0117)*	SW-WQ-0123	G-MVJV	30.11.98	Y G Richardson *(Noted 1.08)* Damyn's Hall, Upminster		17. 8.05P
G-DEAR	Eiriavion PIK-20D	20550	BGA2535-EAR RAFGSA 16	21. 9.07	D Irwin and R Penman	(Yeovil and Bridport)	15. 2.09R
G-DEAT	Eiriavion PIK-20D-78	20664	BGA2537-EAT	25. 7.08	A Spencer and D Bieniasz "786"	Kirton-in-Lindsey	
G-DEAW	Grob G102 Astir CS77	1831	BGA2540-EAW	7.11.07	J Cooke tr EAW Syndicate	Camphill	15.11.07
G-DEBR	Europa Aviation Europa *(Built A J Calvert and C T Smallwood - pr.no.PFA 247-12922) (Tri-gear u/c)*	232		31. 1.01	P Curley	Tatenhill	4. 6.09P
G-DEBT	Alpi Pioneer 300 *(Built N J T Tonks - pr.no.PFA 330-14291)*	8		5.10.04	N J T Tonks	Shobdon	12. 6.08P
G-DEBX	Schleicher ASW 20	20058	BGA2565-EBX D-7973	12.11.07	C F Cownden and J P Davies "644" Gransden Lodge		15. 2.08
G-DECC	Schleicher Ka 6CR	60/01	BGA2570-ECC D-5080	28. 2.08	G V Higgins tr Redwing	Burn	18. 4.08
G-DECF	Schleicher Ka 6CR	856	BGA2573-ECF D-5808	23.10.07	S J Daniel tr ECF Group	Aston Down	15. 4.08
G-DECG	Schempp-Hirth SHK-1	19	BGA2574-ECG D-5259, D-1329	31. 3.08	J L Williams and M F Hardy Trenchard Lines, Upavon		
G-DECH	Glasflügel H303 Mosquito B	173	BGA2575-ECH	6. 3.08	A and R Walker	Rattlesden	
	(Overshot field landing and crashed in a stream, West Head Farm, Thirlmere 25.4.08)						
G-DECJ	Slingsby T.65A Vega	1916	BGA2576-ECJ	4. 4.08	J Hart	Sutton Bank	
G-DECK	Cessna T210N Turbo Centurion II	21064017	N958MK D-ERDK, N4834Y	29. 2.00	C E Wright	Fenland	24. 4.09E
G-DECL	Slingsby T.65A Vega 17L	1918	BGA2578-ECL	8.12.07	J Strzebrakowski	Lyveden	19. 6.08
G-DECM	Slingsby T.65A Vega	1919	BGA2579-ECM	26. 9.08	F Wilson	Aston Down	
G-DECO	Dyn'Aéro MCR-01 Club *(Built A W Bishop and G Castelli - pr.no.PFA 301A-14246)*	285		15. 9.04	A W Bishop and G Castelli tr G-DECO Flying Group Cambridge		31. 7.09P
G-DECP	Rolladen-Schneider LS3-17	3426	BGA2581-ECP	8.10.07	D Crowhurst and M Ewer	Crowland	17. 3.08
G-DECS	Glasflügel Mosquito B	166	BGA2584-ECS	5. 8.08	K L Fixter and A C Cummins "955"	Llantisilio	
G-DECW	Schleicher ASK 21	21008	BGA2588-ECW	15. 7.08	Norfolk Gliding Club Ltd	Tibenham	
G-DECX	P&M Aviation Quik GT450	8263		26. 4.07	D V Lawrence	(Stourbridge)	25. 4.09P
G-DECZ	Schleicher ASK 21	21009	BGA2591-ECZ	15.10.07	Booker Gliding Club Ltd "ECZ"	Wycombe Air Park	28. 9.08
G-DEDB	CARMAM JP-15/36AR Aiglon	40	BGA2593-EDB	17. 1.08	R A Putt tr Carmam EDB Group Husbands Bosworth		29. 3.08
G-DEDG	Schleicher Ka 6CR	6512	BGA2598-EDG RAFGSA 541(?)	5. 9.08	S J Wood	RAF Cranwell	
G-DEDJ	Glasflügel H303 Mosquito B	185	BGA2600-EDJ	24. 1.08	D Martin and R Bollow	Camphill	26. 2.08
G-DEDK	Schleicher K 7 Rhönadler *(Partly modified to ASK 13 standard)*	791	BGA2601-EDK D-1633	23. 1.08	North Wales Gliding Club Ltd	Llantisilio	18. 4.08
G-DEDM	Glaser-Dirks DG-200	2-98	BGA2603-EDM	17. 9.07	A H G St Pierre	Sutton Bank	29. 3.08
G-DEDN	Glaser-Dirks DG-100G Elan	E12G6	BGA2604-EDN	12. 3.08	S J Gooch tr DG 280 Syndicate	Currock Hill	
G-DEDU	Schleicher ASK 13	13613	BGA2610-EDU	10. 1.08	Channel Gliding Club Ltd	Waldershare Park	28. 2.08
G-DEDX	Slingsby T.59D Vega	1928	BGA2613-EDX	1. 7.08	G Kirkham	Camphill	
G-DEDY	Slingsby T.65D Vega	1929	BGA2614-EDY	29.11.07	S J Steadman tr Steadman and Partners Husbands Bosworth		27. 3.08
G-DEDZ	Slingsby T.65C Sport Vega	1931	BGA2615-EDZ	7. 4.08	R C R Copley tr Echo Delta Zulu Group Walney Island		
G-DEEA	Slingsby T.65C Sport Vega	1932	BGA2616-EEA	24. 4.08	G M Lawrie tr Borders Sport Vega Syndicate (337) Milfield		
G-DEEC	Schleicher ASW 20L	20311	BGA2618-EEC (G-BSTS), BGA2618-EEC	19.10.07	D M Cushway	Challock	5. 3.08
G-DEEF	Rolladen-Schneider LS3-17	3441	BGA2621-KEF	27. 9.07	P Morgan tr Echo Echo Foxtrot Group	Rivar Hill	28. 9.08
G-DEEG	Slingsby T.65C Sport Vega	1922	BGA2622-EEG EI-129, BGA2622-EEG	21.11.07	G Harris tr Vega Syndicate	Rufforth	2. 5.08
G-DEEH	Schleicher ASW 19	19042	BGA2623-EEH RAFGGA 166	30. 6.08	K Kiely	AAC Dishforth	
G-DEEJ	Schleicher ASW 20L	20314	BGA2624-EEJ	11. 8.08	M C Rupasinha	Dunstable	
G-DEEK	Schempp-Hirth HS.5 Nimbus 2C	201	BGA2625-EEK	6.11.07	M N Erlund	Saltby	28. 9.08
G-DEEM	Schleicher K 8B	8688AB	BGA2627-EEM D-0254	25. 1.08	The South Wales Gliding Club Ltd	Usk	28. 5.08
G-DEEN	Schempp-Hirth Standard Cirrus 75	621	BGA2628-EEN (BGA2609-EDT), RAFGSA 87	22. 2.08	J Hanlon tr G-DEEN Flying Group RAF Weston-on-the-Green		20. 4.08

G-DEEO	Grob G102 Club Astir Ii	50155	BGA2630-EEO (RNGSA N12)	11. 3.08	P A Jewell	Lleweni Parc
G-DEEP	Wassmer WA.26P Squale	36	BGA2629-EEP F-CDSX	15. 2.08	B J Key	Aston Down 15. 4.08
G-DEER	Robinson R22 Beta II	2827		17. 7.98	S R Baber (Groesfaen, Pontyclun)	7. 8.09E
G-DEES	Rolladen-Schneider LS3-17	3248	BGA2632	17. 7.98	J Illidge	Camphill 28. 9.08
G-DEEW	Schleicher Ka 6 CR	6188	BGA2636-EEW RAFGGA, D-6151	29.11.07	S M Dodds	Saltby 31. 7.08
G-DEEX	Rolladen-Schneider LS3-17	3442	BGA2637-EEX	22. 2.08	M A M Pirie	Aston Down 31. 3.08
G-DEFA	Schleicher ASW 20L	20326	BGA2640-EFA	20. 5.08	R G Cooper tr Eight Eighties Syndicate "470"	Dunstable
G-DEFB	Schempp-Hirth Nimbus 2C	216	BGA2641-EFB	30. 7.08	N Revell	Saltby
G-DEFE	Centrair ASW 20F	20139	BGA2644-EFE	1. 2.08	D A Mackenzie and W A Horne	Aston Down 5. 4.08
G-DEFF	Schempp-Hirth HS.5 Nimbus 2C	208	BGA2645-EFF	30.11.07	P J D Smith and J W L Clarke	Rivar Hill 23. 4.08
G-DEFG	Schleicher K 8B	8284	BGA2645-EFG RAFGSA	12. 5.08	Essex Gliding Club Ltd	Ridgewell
G-DEFM	British Aerospace BAe 146 Series 200	E2016	G-DEBM C-FHAZ, N605AW	22.10.99	Flightline Ltd (Stored all-white 2.09) (Ceased operations 3.12.08)	Southend 13. 9.09E
G-DEFT	Flight Design CTSW (Assembled P&M Aviation Ltd with c/n 8313)	07 07 16		4. 9.07	D Arnold	Damyn's Hall, Upminster 3. 9.08P
G-DEFV	Schleicher ASW 20	20041	BGA2659-EFV OE-5162	22. 1.08	A R McKillen	Bellarena 13. 5.08
G-DEFW	Slingsby T.65C Sport Vega	1938	BGA2660-EFW	20. 2.08	Darlton Gliding Club Ltd	Darlton 22. 9.08
G-DEFY	Robinson R22 Beta II	3633	N73750	5. 7.04	P M M P Silveira	Cascais-Tires, Portugal 1. 9.09E
G-DEFZ	Rolladen-Schneider LS3-a	3273	BGA2663-EFZ	18. 3.08	D H Gardner tr EFZ Syndicate	Aston Down
G-DEGD	Schleicher ASW 17	17028	BGA2667-EGD D-2343	21. 4.08	C J Teagle	Sutton Bank
G-DEGE	Rolladen-Schneider LS3-a	3465	BGA2668-EGE	29.10.07	G Szabo-Toth tr EGE Glider Syndicate	Nympsfield 28. 9.08
G-DEGH	Slingsby T.65C Sport Vega	1943	BGA2671-EGH	26.11.07	K Dykes, M J Davies and R A Starling	Darlton 29. 4.08
G-DEGJ	Slingsby T.65C Sport Vega	1944	BGA2672-EGJ	4.12.07	M J Heneghan tr 672 Syndicate "672"	Lee-on-Solent 7. 3.08
G-DEGK	Schempp-Hirth Standard Cirrus (Built Burkhart Grob-Flugzeugbau)	542G	BGA2673-EGK RAFGSA 569, RAFGSA R2	31.10.07	P H Robinson	Eyres Field 28. 9.08
G-DEGN	Grob G103 Twin Astir II	3542	BGA2676-EGN	2. 9.08	Staffordshire Gliding Club Ltd	Seighford
G-DEGR	Breguet 905SA Fauvette	18	BGA2679-EGR F-CCGT	11. 9.08	P Parker	Dunstable
G-DEGS	Schempp-Hirth Nimbus 2CS	192	BGA2680-EGS D-2111	29. 1.08	R C Nichols	Pocklington 22. 3.08
G-DEGT	Slingsby T.65C Sport Vega	1933	BGA2681-EGT	8. 4.08	D M Bradley tr Vega Syndicate EGT	Sleap
G-DEGW	Schempp-Hirth Mini-Nimbus C	078	BGA2684-EGW HB-1447	8. 9.08	A Brook tr I F Barnes and partners	Ridgewell
G-DEGX	Slingsby T.65C Sport Vega	1937	BGA2685-EGX RAFGSA R23, BGA2685-EGX	14. 2.08	C P Raine tr Haddenham Vega Syndicate	Thame 2. 5.07
G-DEGZ	Schleicher ASK 21	21030	BGA2687-EGZ	1.12.07	Black Mountains Gliding Club	Talgarth 10. 3.08
G-DEHG	Slingsby T.65C Sport Vega	1940	BGA2694-EHG	27. 2.08	A E Smith tr Vega Syndicate	Lasham 19. 1.05
G-DEHH	Shempp-Hirth Ventus a	07	BGA2695-EHH	23. 7.08	J A White "V7"	Lasham
G-DEHK	Rolladen-Schneider LS4	4068	BGA2697-EHK	27. 9.07	S Eyles and D Puttock "490"	Nympsfield 28. 9.08
G-DEHL	Rolladen-Schneider LS4	4024	BGA2698-EHL	25. 9.07	R Theil	Crowland 28. 9.08
G-DEHM	Schleicher Ka 6E	4118	BGA2699-EHM RAFGSA 318	3. 3.08	J B Symonds	Kingston Deverill
G-DEHO	Schleicher ASK 21	21035	BGA2702-EHQ	18. 1.08	Lasham Gliding Society Ltd "431"	Lasham 20. 2.08
G-DEHP	Schempp-Hirth HS.5 Nimbus 2C	234	BGA2701-EHP	27.11.07	D J King	Rattlesden 11. 3.08
G-DEHT	Schempp-Hirth Nimbus 2C	235	BGA2705-EHT	14. 1.08	S.D.Codd	Shenington 21. 3.08
G-DEHU	Glasflügel 304	209	BGA2706-EHU	25.10.07	F Townsend	Bidford 28. 9.08
G-DEHV	Schleicher ASW 20 L	20385	BGA2707-EHV	19. 9.07	M A and B A Roberts "481"	Wormingford 24. 2.08
G-DEHW	ICA IS-28B2	86	BGA2708-EHW	27. 2.08	P V P V Besouw tr Y6 Group (Dorst, Netherlands)	14. 4.08
G-DEHY	Slingsby T.65D Vega	1941	BGA2710-EHY	19. 5.08	B Skilton tr Vega Syndicate	Upton Broyle Farm, Ringmer
G-DEHZ	Schleicher ASW 20L	20388	BGA2711-EHZ	29.10.07	D Crimmins	Challock 19. 2.08
G-DEJA	ICA IS-28B2	88	BGA2712-EJA	1. 2.08	M H Simms	Shipdham 19. 4.07
G-DEJB	Slingsby T.65C Sport Vega	1945	BGA2713-EJB	28. 3.08	D Tait and I G Walker	Cross Hayes
G-DEJC	Slingsby T.65C Sport Vega	1946	BGA2714-EJC	10. 1.08	D Redfearn and I Powis	Darlton 14. 4.08
G-DEJE	Slingsby T.65C Sport Vega	1947	BGA2716-EJE	10.12.07	Crown Service Gliding Club	Lasham 24. 2.08
G-DEJF	Schleicher K 8B	8966	BGA2717-EJF D-2328	19. 9.08	Cotswold Gliding Club	Aston Down
G-DEJH	Eichelsdörfer SB-5E	5041A	BGA2719-EJH D-5430, D-0087	7. 2.08	B J Dawson and S E Richardson	Pocklington 24. 7.08
G-DEJR	Schleicher ASW 19B	19334	BGA2727-EJR	1.11.07	M D Thompson tr 193 Syndicate "193"	Nympsfield 28. 9.08
G-DEJZ	Scheibe SF26A Standard	5020	BGA2735-EJZ D-8473	1. 7.08	J M Collin	Shipdham
G-DEKA	Cameron Z-90 Balloon (Hot Air)	10665		16.12.04	Sport Promotion SRL (Dekalb titles)	La Morra, Piedmont, Italy 17. 8.09E
G-DEKC	Schleicher Ka 6E	4079	BGA2738-EKC OO-ZDV, OE-0813	14. 2.08	S L Benn	RAF Cranwell 23. 3.08
G-DEKD	Schleicher ASK 13	13539	BGA2739-EKD OH-494	10.12.07	Midland Gliding Club Ltd	Long Mynd 19. 4.08
G-DEKF	Grob G102 Club Astir III (Originally regd as G102 Astir III, type amended 5.12.08)	5519C	BGA2741-EKF	17. 4.08	The Bristol Gliding Club Proprietary Ltd	Nympsfield
G-DEKG	Schleicher ASK 21	21067	BGA2742-EKG AGA 8, BGA2742-EKG	19.11.07	J W Sage tr Army Gliding Association (Operated Wyvern Gliding Club)	Trenchard Lines, Upavon 28. 9.08
G-DEKJ	Schempp-Hirth Ventus b	36	BGA2744-EKJ	22.10.07	I J Metcalfe	Nympsfield 28. 9.08
G-DEKS	Scheibe SF27A Zugvögel V	6096	BGA2752-EKS D-8166	31. 1.08	J C Johnson	Parham Park 5. 3.08

Reg	Type	c/n	Prev id	Date	Owner	Base	Expiry
G-DEKT	Wassmer WA.30 Bijave	241	BGA2753-EKT	7. 7.08	D C Reynolds	AAC Dishforth	
			F-CDML				
G-DEKU	Schleicher ASW 20L	20384	BGA2754-EKU	6.11.07	A J Gillson	Sleap	28. 4.08
G-DEKV	Rolladen-Schneider LS4	4102	BGA2755-EKV	16.11.07	S L Helstrip	Lasham	29. 3.08
G-DEKW	Schempp-Hirth Nimbus-2B	111	BGA2756-EKW	31. 3.08	R S Jobar	Lasham	
			D-7245				
G-DELA	Schleicher ASW 19B	19346	BGA2760-ELA	3.12.07	A Stark tr ELA Syndicate	Aboyne	28. 9.08
G-DELD	Slingsby T.65C Sport Vega	1950	BGA2763-ELD	5. 9.07	N R Skelding tr ELD Syndicate	Snitterfield	21. 2.08
G-DELF	Aero L-29A Delfin	194555	ES-YLM	28. 8.97	B R Green	Manston	26. 9.01P
			Soviet AF 12 (Red)				
G-DELG	Schempp-Hirth Ventus b/16.6	46	BGA2766-ELG	14.11.07	A G Machin	Burn	17. 4.08
G-DELN	Grob G102 Astir CS Jeans	2024	BGA2772-ELN	26. 2.08	Bowland Forest Gliding Club Ltd	Chipping	14. 5.08
G-DELO	Slingsby T.65D Vega	1934	BGA2774-ELQ	25. 3.08	I Sim	Milfield	
G-DELR	Schempp-Hirth Ventus b	45	BGA2775-ELR	16.10.07	I D Smith	Nympsfield	28. 9.08
G-DELX	Schleicher K 7 Rhönadler	928	BGA2781-ELX	9. 1.08	The Nene Valley Gliding Club	Upwood	16. 5.08
			D-4023				
G-DELZ	Schleicher ASW 20L	20310	BGA2783-ELZ	15.10.07	D A Fogden	Wycombe Air Park	28. 9.08
			RAFGGA 569				
G-DEMB	Rolladen-Schneider LS4	4185	BGA2785-EMB	7. 2.08	R A Hine "RH"	Wycombe Air Park	29. 1.08
	(Hit tree on field landing near Andoversfield 22. 8.08)						
G-DEME	Glaser-Dirks DG-200/17	2-176CL18	BGA2788-EME	16. 1.08	E.D.Casagrande	Usk	19. 3.08
G-DEMF	Rolladen-Schneider LS4	4187	BGA2789-EMF	18. 1.08	M C Oggelsby and R N Johnston	Hinton-in-the-Hedges	15. 3.08
G-DEMG	Rolladen-Schneider LS4	4242	BGA2790-EMG	7.11.07	R C Bowsfield	Aston Down	5. 3.08
G-DEMH	Reims Cessna F172M Skyhawk II	F17201137	G-BFLO	18.11.91	M Hammond	Airfield Farm, Hardwick	15. 6.09E
	(Lycoming O-360)		PH-DMF, (EI-AYO)				
G-DEMJ	Slingsby T.65C Sport Vega	1951	BGA2792-EMJ	17. 9.07	D J Miles	Seighford	28. 4.08
G-DEMM	Eurocopter AS.350B2 Ecureuil	3741		6.10.03	Three Counties Helicopter Co Ltd	Stapleford	17. 2.09E
G-DEMN	Slingsby T.65D Vega	1935	BGA2796-EMN	13.12.07	C D Sword	Milfield	23. 7.08
G-DEMP	Slingsby T.65C Sport Vega	1952	BGA2797-EMP	15.11.07	The Surrey Hills Gliding Club Ltd	Kenley	7. 2.08
G-DEMR	Slingsby T.65C Sport Vega	1954	BGA2799-EMR	5. 9.08	D A Woodforth	Strubby	
G-DEMT	Rolladen-Schneider LS 4	4243	BGA2801-EMT	28.11.07	M R Fox "MF"	Husbands Bosworth	17. 4.08
G-DEMU	Glaser-Dirks DG-200	2-162-1753	BGA2802-EMU	11.10.07	A Butterfield and N Swinton	RAF Weston-on-the-Green	28. 9.08
G-DEMZ	Slingsby T.65A Vega	1891	BGA2807-EMZ	7. 9.07	F S Smith tr Vega Syndicate	Portmoak	25. 4.08
			G-BGCA				
G-DENB	Cessna F150G	F150-0136	G-ATZZ	14.12.95	M W Sheppardson	Sibson	7. 7.09E
	(Built Reims Aviation SA)						
G-DENC	Cessna F150G	F150-0107	G-AVAP	14.12.95	T C Aldrich tr G-DENC Cessna Group	Popham	11. 5.09E
	(Built Reims Aviation SA)						
G-DEND	Reims Cessna F150M	F15001201	G-WAFC	6. 6.97	R N Tate	Bagby	9.11.09E
			G-BDFI, (OH-CGD)				
G-DENE	Piper PA-28-140 Cherokee	28-21710	G-ATOS	5. 2.98	D V Magee	Dunkeswell	11.12.09E
			N11C				
G-DENI	Piper PA-32-300 Cherokee Six	32-7340006	G-BAIA	7.12.95	A Bendkowski	Rochester	2.11.09E
			N11C				
G-DENJ	Schempp-Hirth Ventus b/16.6	62	BGA2816-ENJ	26. 9.08	S Boyden	Lasham	
G-DENO	Glasflügel H201B Standard Libelle	232	BGA1662-CMX	14.11.07	D M Bland	Burn	6. 3.08
G-DENS	Binder CP.301S Smaragd	121	D-ENSA	20.11.85	I S Leader tr Garston Smaragd Group	Garston Farm, Marshfield	2.12.08P
	(Also carries c/n AB.429 denoting completion as Amateur Build)						
G-DENT	Cameron N-145 Balloon (Hot Air)	4135		8. 4.97	P D Claridge	Treyford, Midhurst	17.12.08E
G-DENU	Glaser-Dirks DG-100G Elan	E108G78	BGA2826-ENU	28. 3.08	R Johnson tr 435 Syndicate	Long Mynd	
G-DENV	Schleicher ASW 20L	20554	BGA2827-ENV	2.11.07	R D Hone	Wycombe Air Park	9. 5.08
G-DENX	PZL-Bielsko SZD-48 Jantar Standard 2	W-857	BGA2829-ENX	3. 3.08	J M Hire	Currock Hill	
			(BGA2746-EKL)				
G-DENZ	Piper PA-44-180 Seminole	44-7995327	G-INDE	3. 7.97	Stella Aviation Charter BV	Teuge, Netherlands	21. 9.09E
			G-BHNM, N8077X				
G-DEOA	Rolladen-Schneider LS4	4259	BGA2856-EQA	10. 1.08	A A Jenkins and R.L.Smith	Wycombe Air Park	15. 4.08
G-DEOB	PZL-Bielsko SZD-30 Pirat	S-06.48	BGA2857-EQB	16. 5.08	R A Firmin	Rattlesden	
			D-2702				
G-DEOD	Grob G102 Astir CS77	1614	BGA2869-EQD	3. 6.08	D S Fenton	Usk	
			PH-570				
G-DEOE	Schleicher ASK 13	13627AB	BGA2860-EQE	1. 5.08	Essex Gliding Club Ltd	Ridgewell	
G-DEOF	Schleicher ASK 13	13626AB	BGA2861-EQF	1. 5.06	Essex Gliding Club Ltd	Ridgewell	
G-DEOJ	Centrair ASW 20FL	20512	BGA2864-EQJ	15. 2.08	J Sanders and R Grey "968"	Nympsfield	24. 5.08
G-DEON	Schempp-Hirth Nimbus 3-25.5	31	BGA2868-EQN	8.12.07	R A Lovegrove tr N3 Group "117"	Lyveden	4. 3.08
G-DEOT	Grob G-103A Twin II Acro	3787-K-65	BGA2873-EQT	14. 4.08	R Tyrrell	Shenington	
			RAFGSA R58, BGA2873-EQT				
G-DEOU	Pilatus B4-PC11	201	BGA2874-EQU	26. 2.08	H R E Stott	Chipping	3. 5.08
			PH-535				
G-DEOV	Schempp-Hirth Janus C	169	BGA2875-EQV	14.12.07	Burn Gliding Club Ltd	Burn	14. 3.08
			ZD974, BGA2875-EQV				
G-DEOW	Schempp-Hirth Janus C	171	BGA2876-EOW	8.2.08	C C Pike tr 383 Syndicate	Rivar Hill	11. 4.08
			ZD975, BGA2876-EQW				
G-DEOZ	Schleicher K 8B	8113A	BGA2879-EQZ	10. 6.08	Cotswold Gliding Club	Aston Down	
			D-8763				
G-DEPD	Schleicher ASK 21	21119	BGA2835-EPD	3. 3.08	R Banks tr EPD Glider Syndicate	Dunstable	
G-DEPE	Schleicher ASW 19B	19335	BGA2836-EPE	22.11.07	P A Goulding "PG"	Crowland	15.12.07
			RAFGSA R18, BGA2836-EPE, RAFGSA R18				
G-DEPF	Centrair ASW 20FL	20515	BGA2837-EPF	23.11.07	D J E Howse tr 323 Syndicate	Gransden Lodge	6. 4.08
G-DEPP	Schleicher ASK 13	1609	BGA2845-EPP	22.12.07	Mendip Gliding Club Ltd	Halesland	12. 4.08
G-DEPS	Schleicher ASW 20 L	20245	BGA2848-EPS	1.10.07	C Beveridge	Sandhill Farm, Shrivenham	22. 3.08
			RAFGSA 87				

Reg	Type	c/n	BGA/prev id	Owner/Operator	Base	Date
G-DEPT	Schleicher K 8B	146/59	BGA2849-EPT 21.12.07 RAFGGA 504, D-5004	P H Emerton	Lasham	5. 3.08
G-DEPU	Glaser-Dirks DG-101G Elan	E116G85	BGA2850-EPU 2. 7.07 (BGA2833)	J F Rogers	Wycombe Air Park	3. 8.08
G-DEPX	Schempp-Hirth Ventus b/16.6	107	BGA2853-EPX 22.10.07	M E S Thomas	(Llanelli)	28. 9.08
G-DERA	Centrair ASW 20FL	20526	BGA2880-ERA 14.12.07	R J Lockett "283"	Wormingford	19. 4.08
G-DERB	Robinson R22 Beta	1005	G-BPYH 28. 6.95	Heli Air Ltd	Denham	10. 7.09E
G-DERH	Schleicher ASK 21	21147	BGA2887-ERH 4. 1.08 ZD647, BGA2887-ERH	Burn Gliding Club Ltd	Burn	5. 5.08
G-DERI	Piper PA-46-500TP Malibu Meridian	4697078	G-PCAR 9.11.03 N51151	Intesa Leasing SpA	(Milan, Lombardy, Italy)	6. 8.09E
G-DERJ	Schleicher ASK 21	21148	BGA2888-ERJ 9.4.08 RAFGSA R35, ZD648, BGA2888	J G Arnold tr RAF Gliding and Soaring Association"R35" RAF Wittering		
G-DERK	Piper PA-46-500TP Malibu Meridian	4697152	N165MA 3. 4.03	D Priestley	Dunkeswell	14. 5.09E
G-DERP	Schleicher ASW 19B	19348	BGA2893-ERP 23. 1.08 ZD657, BGA2893-ERP, BGA2773-ELO	M K Lavender "ML"	Bicester	22. 2.08
G-DERR	Schleicher ASW 19B	19382	BGA2895-ERR 21. 8.08 ZD659, BGA2895	D M Hook	Dunstable	
G-DERS	Schleicher ASW 19B	19383	BGA2896-ERS 9. 1.08 ZD660, BGA2896-ERS	J C and C C Marshall	Eyres Field	30. 4.08
G-DERV	Cameron Truck 56 SS Balloon (Hot Air)	1719	21. 3.88	J M Percival Bourton-on-the-Wolds, Loughborough "Shell UK Truck" (Inflated 8.08)		22. 2.00A
G-DESB	Schleicher ASK 21	21176	BGA2905-ESB 23.10.07	A L Garfield tr The Old Boys	Dunstable	8. 3.08
G-DESC	Rolladen-Schneider LS4	4261	BGA2906-ESC 28. 3.08	J Crawford and J M Staley "379"	Bicester	
G-DESH	Centrair 101A Pégase	101069	BGA2911-ESH 9.11.07	J E Moore	Wycombe Air Park	28. 1.08
G-DESJ	Schleicher K 8B	8730	BGA2912-ESJ 4. 9.07 D-5010	Bowland Forest Gliding Club Ltd	Chipping	16.12.07
G-DESO	DG Flugzeugbau DG-300 Elan	3E10	BGA2918-ESQ 1. 2.08	G R P Brown	Sandhill Farm, Shrivenham	31. 3.08
G-DEST	Mooney M 20J Mooney 201	24-3429	6.11.98	Allegro Aviation Ltd	Guernsey	9. 3.09E
G-DESU	Schleicher ASK 21	21180	BGA2922-ESU 6.11.07 RAFGSA R40, BGA2922-ESU	Banbury Gliding Club Ltd	Hinton-in-the-Hedges	25. 5.08
G-DESW	Centrair 101A Pégase	101068	BGA2924-ESW 23. 1.08	D A Brown	(Hove)	1. 4.08
G-DETA	Schleicher ASK 21	21181	BGA2928-ETA 25. 3.08	P Hawkins	RAF Weston-on-the-Green	
G-DETD	Schleicher K 8B	8918	BGA2931-ETD 11. 6.08 RAFGSA R44, BGA2931-ETD, RAFGSA 244	Cotswold Gliding Club	Aston Down	
G-DETG	Rolladen-Schneider LS4	4349	BGA2934-ETG 12. 9.07	N P Woods "NW"	Gransden Lodge	28. 9.08
G-DETJ	Centrair 101A Pégase	101A0110	BGA2936-ETJ 14. 1.08	S C Phillips	(Potton, Sandy)	23. 3.08
G-DETK	PZL-Bielsko SZD-48 Jantar Standard 2	W-876	BGA2937-ETK 13. 3.08 OK-XJO	D G Coats tr Tango Kilo Group "215"	Portmoak	
G-DETM	Centrair 101A Pégase	101A0111	BGA2939-ETM 8.11.07	B J Darton and J Bone	Wormingford	15. 3.08
G-DETS	Schleicher ASK 13	13635AB	BGA2944-ETS 12.12.07	Upward Bound Trust	Bicester	14. 4.08
G-DETV	Rolladen-Schneider LS4	4314	BGA2947-ETV 23. 6.08 (BGA2919-ESR)	T A Meaker	Lasham	
G-DETY	Rolladen-Schneider LS4	4368	BGA2950-ETY 23. 8.07 (Carries "BGA2350" on fin)	D T Staff	Wycombe Air Park	7.11.07
G-DETZ	Schleicher ASW 2O CL	20730	BGA2951-ETZ 28. 1.08	N L Clowes tr The 20 Syndicate	Tibenham	23. 2.08
G-DEUC	Schleicher ASK 13	13104	BGA2954-EUC 28. 4.08 AGA 12	The Bristol Gliding Club Proprietary Ltd	Nympsfield	
G-DEUD	Schleicher ASW 20C	20734	BGA2955-EUD 23.10.07	R Tietema "RT"	Husbands Bosworth	15. 2.08
G-DEUF	PZL-Bielsko SZD-50-3 Puchacz	B-1090	BGA2957-EUF 23. 1.08	A J Pettitt tr uchacz Group	Rivar Hill	26. 8.08
G-DEUH	Rolladen-Schneider LS4	4382	BGA2959-EUH 4.10.07	A R Turner and F J Parkinson "446"	Nympsfield	13. 4.08
G-DEUJ	Schempp-Hirth Ventus b-16.6	162	BGA2960-EUJ 13.12.07	S C Renfrew	(Bratton, Westbury)	18.11.08
G-DEUK	Centrair ASW 20FL	20530	BGA2961-KUK 26. 9.07	D S Kershaw "992"	Lasham	26. 2.08
G-DEUS	Schempp-Hirth Ventus b-16.6	192	BGA2968-EUS 4.10.07	R J Whitaker	Lasham	26. 8.08
G-DEUV	PZL-Bielsko SZD-42 Jantar 2	B-934	BGA2969-EUV 16.10.08	G V McKirdy	Shenington	
G-DEUX	Aérospatiale AS.355F Ecureuil 2	5027	F-GIBI 30. 9.05 D-HAST, F-ODNS	Elmridge Ltd	Kintore	19.11.09E
G-DEUY	Schleicher ASW 20BL	20645	BGA2974-EUY 16.10.07	D G Roberts tr ASW 20BL - G-DEUY Group "88"	Aston Down	28.12.07
G-DEVF	Schempp-Hirth Nimbus 3T	15/76	BGA2981-EVF 19.10.07 D-KHIJ	A G Leach	Bembridge	20. 2.08
G-DEVH	Schleicher K 10A	10008	BGA2983-EVH 6. 8.08 HB-791	C W And K T Matten	Brent Tor	
G-DEVJ	Schleicher ASK 13	13637AB	BGA2984-EVJ 24. 9.08	Lasham Gliding Society Ltd	Lasham	
G-DEVK	Grob G102 Astir CS	1397	BGA2985-EVK 2. 4.08 PH-546	Peterborough and Spalding Gliding Club Ltd	Crowland	
G-DEVL	Eurocopter EC.120B Colibri	1273	7. 6.02	Saxon Logistics Ltd	Elstree	30. 7.09E
G-DEVM	Centrair 101A Pégase	101A0157	BGA2987-EVM 29.11.07	J G Kosak tr Seahawk Gliding Club	RNAS Culdrose	28. 4.08
G-DEVO	Centrair 101A Pégase	101A0149	BGA2990-EVQ 24. 6.08	P G Scott	Gransden Lodge	
G-DEVP	Schleicher ASK 13	13638AB	BGA2993-EVP 29. 9.08	Lasham Gliding Society Ltd	Lasham	
G-DEVS	Piper PA-28-180 Cherokee B	28-830	G-BGVJ 5. 3.85 D-ENPI, N7066W	B J Hoptroff and J M Whiteley tr 180 Group	Thruxton	19. 5.09E
G-DEVV	Schleicher ASK 23	23004	BGA2995-EVV 10.12.07	Midland Gliding Club Ltd	Long Mynd	26. 8.08
G-DEVW	Schleicher ASK 23	23006	BGA2996-EVW 8. 2.08	London Gliding Club Proprietary Ltd	Dunstable	2. 5.08
G-DEVX	Schleicher ASK 23	23007	BGA2997-EVX 8. 2.08	London Gliding Club Proprietary Ltd	Dunstable	12. 4.08
G-DEVY	Schleicher ASK 23	23008	BGA2998-EVY 8. 2.08	London Gliding Club Proprietary Ltd	Dunstable	12. 7.08
G-DEWA	Flight Design CTSW	07.10.18	17.12.07	R Eve	Damyns Hall, Upminster	16.12.08P
	(Assembled P&M Aviation Ltd with c/n 8348) (P&M show 07.10.07 but believed incorrect)					
G-DEWE	Flight Design CTSW		13. 1.09	W D Dewey	Wishanger Farm, Frensham	22. 1.10P
	(Assembled P&m Aviation Ltd with c/n 8435)					
G-DEWG	Grob G103A Twin II Acro	33885-K-123	BGA3006-EWG 20. 5.08 ZE501, BGA3006-EWG	J P Ryan	Lyveden	

G-DEWP	Grob G103A Twin II Acro	33892-K-130	BGA3013-EWP 11.12.07	Cambridge Gliding Club Ltd	Gransden Lodge	22. 2.08
			ZE523, BGA3013-EWP			
G-DEWR	Grob G103A Twin II Acro	33894-K-132	BGA3015-EWR 8.12.07	The Bristol Gliding Club (Proprietary) Ltd *"P70"*		
			RAFGSA R70, ZE525, BGA3015-EWR		Nympsfield	26. 8.08
G-DEWZ	Grob G103A Twin II Acro	33981-K-214	BGA3076-EZE 9. 9.08	T R Dews	Kingston Deverill	
			ZE634, BGA3076-EZE			
G-DEXA	Grob G103A Twin II Acro	33908-K-143	BGA3024-EXA 23. 1.08	Trent Valley Aerotowing Club Ltd	Kirton-in-Lindsey	27. 6.08
			ZE534, BGA3024-EXA			
G-DEXP	ARV Aviation ARV-1 Super 2	003	24. 4.85	M Davies	(Rotherham)	28. 4.09P
	(Built ARV Aviation - pr.no.PFA 152-11154)					
G-DEYS	Grob G103A Twin II Acro	33961-K-194	BGA3064-EYS 10. 4.08	J G Arnold tr RAF Gliding and Soaring Association		
			RAFGSA R71, ZE612, BGA3064		RAF Marham	

G-DFAA - G-DFZZ

G-DFAF	Schleicher ASW 20L	20214	BGA3101-FAF 22.11.07	A S Miller	RAF Keevil	21. 4.08
			RAFGSA 271, RAFGSA R27			
G-DFAR	Glasflügel H205 Club Libelle	58	BGA3110-FAR 28. 2.08	G Gair	Ringmer	24. 4.08
			HB-1262			
G-DFAT	Schleicher ASK 13	13528	BGA3112-FAT 9. 1.08	Dorset Gliding Club Ltd	Eyres Field	22. 4.08
			PH-456			
G-DFAV	ICA IS-32A	5	BGA3114-FAV 8. 5.08	J A Horley tr Ibis 32 Syndicate	Talgarth	
G-DFAW	Schempp-Hirth Ventus b/16.6	26	BGA3115-FAW 25. 2.08	P R Stafford-Allen	RAF Marham	29. 3.08
			D-6768			
G-DFBD	Schleicher ASW 15B	15407	BGA3122-FBD 12. 3.08	D A Wilson	Milfield	
			OH-445			
G-DFBE	Rolladen-Schneider LS6	6028	BGA3123-FBE 27. 5.08	J B Van Woerden	Feshiebridge	
			D-9384			
G-DFBJ	Schleicher K 8B	8221	BGA3127-FBJ 16. 9.08	Bidford Gliding Ltd	Bidford	
			D-6340			
G-DFBM	Schempp-Hirth Nimbus 3/24.5	73	BGA3130-FBM 22. 9.08	D Gardiner	Portmoak	
G-DFBO	Schleicher ASW 20BL	20669	BGA3133-FBQ 10. 3.08	R A Robertson tr 464 Syndiacte	Talgarth	
G-DFBY	Schempp-Hirth Discus b	20	BGA3141-FBY 15. 7.08	D Latimer *"780"*	Sutton Bank	
G-DFCD	Centrair 101A Pégase	101A0207	BGA3146-FCD 23. 6.08	G J Bass	Challock	
G-DFCM	Glaser-Dirks DG-300 Elan	3E+94	BGA3154-FCM 11. 3.08	A Davis and I D Roberts	Cross Hayes	
G-DCFW	Schleicher ASK 13	13642AB	BGA3163-FCW 22. 8.08	Lasham Gliding Society Ltd *"L"*	Lasham	
G-DFCY	Schleicher ASW 15	15122	BGA3165-FCY 16. 4.08	M R Shaw	Ridgewell	
			D-0748			
G-DFDK	Slingsby T.59D Kestrel 19	1832	BGA3176-FDK 23. 6.08	T Holzhauser	Speyer, Germany	
			(BGA4927-KAB, BGA3176-KAB, G-BBVC			
G-DFDP	ICA IS-30	08	BGA3180-FDP 19. 6.08	J Hewitt	Shipdham	
G-DFEA	Grob G103 Twin Astir	3151	BGA3191-FEA 17. 4.08	A J Pellatt tr FEA Twin Astir Syndicate	Llantisilio	
			RAFGSA R83, RAFGSA 833			
G-DFEB	Grob G102 Club Astir III	5643C	BGA3192-FEB 13. 5.08	North Downs Gliding Trust Ltd *"SH8"*	Lasham	
G-DFEO	Schleicher ASK 13	13650AB	BGA3205-FEQ 22. 4.08	Lasham Gliding Society Ltd	Lasham	
G-DFEX	Grob G102 Astir CS 77	1660	BGA3212-FEX 22. 8.08	J Taylor	Saltby	
			D-7492			
G-DFFP	Schleicher ASW 19B	19317	BGA3228-FFP 27. 6.08	J M Hutchinson *"93"*	Wycombe Air Park	
			RAFGSA R19			
G-DFGJ	Schleicher Ka 6CR	6634	BGA3247-FGJ 17. 9.08	F A Spaargaren tr K6 Syndicate	Llantysilio	
			D-1041			
G-DFGT	Glaser-Dirks DG-300 Elan	3E217	BGA3256-FGT 27. 5.08	T J Gray	Bellarena	
G-DFHS	Schempp-Hirth Ventus cT	82/326	BGA3279-FHS 10. 9.08	R Andrews tr 154 Group	Long Mynd	
G-DFKB	Glaser-Dirks DG-600	6-8	BGA3312-FKB 12. 8.08	J A Watt	Long Mynd	
G-DFKH	Schleicher Ka 6CR	6343	BGA3318-FKH 8. 9.08	I A Megarry	Bellarena	
			EI-109, IGA 106			
G-DFKI	Westland SA.341C Gazelle HT.2	1216	G-BZOT 12. 2.02	Foremans Aviation Ltd	Full Sutton	2. 4.09P
			XW907			
G-DFLY	Piper PA-38-112 Tomahawk	38-79A0450	N9655N 15. 2.79	Ravenair Aircraft Ltd	Liverpool-John Lennon	30. 7.09E
G-DFMG	Schempp-Hirth Discus b	242	BGA3365-FMG 6. 3.08	M T Davis	Dunstable	
G-DFOG	Rolladen-Schneider LS 7	7050	BGA3437-FQG 29.11.07	D W Smith *"952"*	Sutton Bank	27. 4.08
			D-1712			
G-DFOX	Aérospatiale AS.355F1 Ecureuil 2	5203	G-NAAS 8. 1.07	Venturi Capital Ltd	Redhill	17. 7.09E
			G-BPRG, G-NWPA, G-NAAS, G-BPRG, N370E			
G-DFRA	Rolladen-Schneider LS6-b	6151	BGA3455-FRA 5.10.07	M Randle tr 79 Syndicate	Aston Down	28. 9.08
			D-8081			
G-DFSA	Grob G102 Astir CS	1277	BGA3479-FSA 28. 7.08	J R Carpenter tr Astir 498 Syndicate *"498"*	Lasham	
			D-7371			
G-DFTJ	PZL Bielsko SZD-48 Jantar Standard 2	W-889	BGA3511-FTJ 23.11.07	P Nock	Kirton-in-Lindsey	6. 3.08
			HB-1472			
G-DFUN	Van's RV-6	PFA 181A-13191	21. 8.06	P R Turner tr G-DFUN Flying Group	(Hook)	
	(Built P R Turner and S Hollingsworth)					

G-DGAA - G-DGZZ

G-DGAW	Schleicher Ka 6CR	61-08	BGA3688-GAW 21. 1.08	D Searle & H C Yorke	Snitterfield	13. 3.08
			D-6320			
G-DGCL	DG Flugzeugbau DG-800B	8-185B109	27. 3.00	C J Lowrie *"102"*	Parham Park	18. 4.10E
G-DGDJ	Rolladen-Schneider LS4-a	4832	BGA3747-GDJ 9. 7.08	A Clark tr 450 Syndicate *"450"*	Lee-on-Solent	
G-DGET	Bombardier CL-600-2B19	5608	C-FDWU 21. 2.06	TAG Aviation (UK) Ltd	Farnborough	21. 2.09E
	(CL-604 Challenger)		C-GLXQ			
G-DGHI	Dyn'Aéro MCR-01 Club	275	11.12.03	D G Hall	Fridd Farm, Bethersden	25. 9.09P
	(Built D G Hall - pr.no.PFA 301A-14128)					

G-DGIK	DG Flugzeugbau DG-1000S	10-72T11	BGA5211-KMU D-3800	5.12.05	R P Davis *"460"*	(West Mersea, Colchester)	1. 2.08
G-DGIO	Glaser-Dirks DG-100G Elan	E19G7	BGA2605-EDP	1.10.07	P Smith tr EDP Group	North Hill	28. 9.08
G-DGIV	DG Flugzeugbau DG-800B	8-145B69		27.11.98	R Parkin	Kirton-in-Lindsey	7. 2.09E
G-DGOD	Robinson R22 Beta II	3889		28.10.05	Casdron Enterprises Ltd		
						Phoenix Farm, Lower Upham	19.12.09E
G-DGSM	Glaser-Dirks DG-400-17	4-164	D-KCHH	4. 8.08	T E Snoddy and L J McKelvie	Bellarena	21. 8.09E
G-DGWW	Rand Robinson KR-2	PFA 129-11044		7. 3.91	W Wilson	Liverpool-John Lennon	30. 9.08P
	(Built W Wilson) (Hapi Magnum 75)						

G-DHAA - G-DHZZ

G-DHAA	Glasflügel H201B Standard Libelle	356	BGA3777-HAA HB-1090	18.12.07	D J Jones and R N Turner	Gransden Lodge	11.12.07
G-DHAD	Glasflügel H201B Standard Libelle	3	BGA3780-HAD D-8914	13. 2.08	A Presland	Lasham	24. 5.08
G-DHAH	Aeronca 7BCM Champion (Continental C85)	7AC-4185	G-JTYE N85445, NC85445	12. 7.05	G D Horn	(Mappowder, Sturminster Newton)	23. 7.09P
	(Modified ex 7AC standard, type amended to 7BCM (modified) 11.12.08)						
G-DHAL	Schleicher ASK 13	13690AB	BGA3787-HAL	19.10.07	The Windrushers Gliding Club Ltd	Bicester	28. 9.08
G-DHAP	Schleicher Ka 6E	4335	BGA3790-HAP HB-985	22. 2.08	M Fursedon and T Turner	Shenington	6.10.07
G-DHAT	Glaser-Dirks DG-200/17	2-93/1709	BGA3794-HAT D-6843	5. 3.08	G K Holloway tr G-DHAT Group	Aboyne	
G-DHCA	Grob G103A Twin Astir	3289	BGA3826-HCA D-0094, OO-ZOH, D-3063	9. 9.08	A Jordan and P Burton	Rougham	
G-DHCC	de Havilland DHC-1 Chipmunk 22	C1/0393	WG321	28. 5.97	Eureka Aviation BVBA (As *"WG321:G"* in AAC c/s)		
						Antwerp, Belgium	7. 5.10S
G-DHCE	Schleicher ASW 19B	19305	BGA3831-HCE D-6527	3.10.07	R T Halliburton	Pocklington	28. 9.08
G-DHCF	PZL-Bielsko SZD-50-3 Puchacz	B-2047	BGA3832-HCF	17. 1.08	Shalbourne Soaring Society Ltd	Rivar Hill	27. 4.08
G-DHCH	Centrair ASW 20F	20178	BGA3834-HCH F-CEUL	1.11.07	A C Turk *"355"*	Bidford	15. 3.08
G-DHCJ	Grob G103A Twin II	3709	BGA3855-HCJ D-2611	16. 5.08	Peterborough and Spalding Gliding Club Ltd		
	(Originally regd as Twin II Acro, amended 2.6.08)					Crowland	
G-DHCL	Schempp-Hirth Discus B	136	BGA3837-HCL D-4682	4.12.07	C E Broom and L Chilcot	Usk	7. 3.08
G-DHCO	Glasflügel H201B Standard Libelle	197	BGA3841-HCQ HB-999	16.11.07	M J Birch	Dunstable	16. 3.08
G-DHCR	PZL-Bielsko SZD-51-1 Junior	B-2003	BGA3842-HCR	18. 1.08	East Sussex Gliding Club Ltd *"394"*	Ringmer	16. 3.08
G-DHCU	DG Flugzeugbau DG-300 Club Elan	3E407C66	BGA3845-HCU	19.12.07	J C A Garland and M S Smith	Kingston Deverill	18. 3.08
G-DHCV	Schleicher ASW 19B	19084	BGA3846-HCV D-4486	4. 1.08	Novak Consultancy Ltd	Tibenham	4. 5.08
G-DHCW	PZL-Bielsko SZD-51-1 Junior	B-2002	BGA3847-HCW (BGA3844-HCT)	21.12.07	Deeside Gliding Club (Aberdeenshire) Ltd Aboyne		6. 1.08
G-DHCX	Schleicher ASK 21	21541	BGA3848-HCX	6.11.07	Devon & Somerset Gliding Club Ltd	North Hill	28. 9.08
G-DHCZ	de Havilland DHC-2 Beaver AL.Mk.1	1442	G-BUCJ XP772	2. 3.06	Propshop Ltd (As *"XP772"* in AAC c/s) (On rebuild 1.07)		
						Duxford	
G-DHDH	Glaser-Dirks DG-200	2-197	BGA3858-HDH	26. 2.08	A R Winton	Wormingford	11. 5.09E
G-DHDV	de Havilland DH.104 Dove 8	04205	VP981	26.10.98	Air Atlantique Ltd	Coventry	19. 9.10S
					(As "VP981" in 'Royal Air Force Transport Command' titles)		
G-DHEB	Schleicher Ka 6CR	6289	BGA2876-HEB HB-773	17.11.08	J Burrow	North Hill	
G-DHEM	Schempp-Hirth Discus CS	073CS	BGA3886-HEM	9. 1.08	G G Lee tr 473 Syndicate	Lasham	28. 9.08
G-DHER	Schleicher ASW 19B	19240	BGA3890-HER F-CERR	11. 2.08	B Meech	Upwood	17. 5.08
G-DHES	Centrair 101A Pégase	101039	BGA3891-HES F-CFQF	29. 1.08	C J Cole and S B Lewis	Usk	8. 3.08
G-DHET	Rolladen-Schneider LS6-c18	6263	BGA3892-HET	22.11.07	M P Brooks *"335"*	Lasham	28. 2.08
G-DHEV	Schempp-Hirth Cirus	41	BGA3894-HEV OO-ZXY, (OO-ZOZ), D-0104	14. 8.08	K Moffat tr HEV Syndicate	Portmoak	
G-DHEZ	Rolladen-Schneider LS6-c	6264	BGA3898-HEZ	17.10.07	J Herman	Wycombe Air Park	22. 4.08
G-DHGL	Schempp-Hirth Discus b	431	BGA3933-HGL	29.10.07	R G Corbin and S E Buckley	Aston Down	16. 3.08
G-DHJH	Airbus A321-211	1238	D-AVZL	7. 6.00	Thomas Cook Airlines Ltd	Manchester	6. 6.09E
G-DHKL	Schempp-Hirth Discus bT	120/476	BGA4004-HKL	17.10.07	M A Thorne *"919"*	Kingston Deverill	24. 2.08
G-DHLE	Boeing 767-3JHF	37805		.09R	DHL Air Ltd	Nottingham-East Midlands	
G-DHLF	Boeing 767-3JHF	37806		.09R	DHL Air Ltd	Nottingham-East Midlands	
G-DHLG	Boeing 767-3JHF	37807		.09R	DHL Air Ltd	Nottingham-East Midlands	
G-DHLI	Colt World 90 SS Balloon (Hot Air)	2603		2. 6.94	A D Kent tr Balloon Preservation Flying Group *"DHL World"*		
						Petworth	17.12.98A
G-DHMP	Schempp-Hirth Discus b	497	BGA4050-HMP	1. 2.08	P Charatan tr HMP Discus Syndicate	Challock	31. 5.08
G-DHNX	Rolladen-Schneider LS 4b	4937	BGA4082-HNX	28.11.07	C S Crocker and K J Screen	Long Mynd	3. 4.08
G-DHOK	Schleicher ASW 20CL	20854	BGA4118-HQK D-3366	28.11.07	S D Minson	North Hill	1. 4.08
G-DHOP	Van's RV-9A	PFA 320-14173		11. 6.08	A S Orme	(Castletown, IoM)	
	(Built A S Orme)						
G-DHOX	Schleicher ASW 15B	15326	BGA4129-HQX D-2315	21.11.07	P Ridgill	Upwood	14. 4.08
G-DHPA	Issoire E78 Silene	04	BGA4085-HPA F-CFEA	21. 8.08	P Woodcock	Burn	
G-DHPM	de Havilland DHC-1 Chipmunk 22	55	CS-AZS Portuguese AF FAP1365	28. 3.02	P Meyrick (As *"1365"* in Portuguese AF c/s) Sywell		11.10.11
	(Built OGMA)						
G-DHPR	Schempp-Hirth Discus b	532	BGA4100-HPR	23. 8.07	G J Bowser *"K9"*	Nympsfield	18.10.07

G-DHRR	Schleicher ASK 21	21033	BGA4146-HRR	5.12.07	The Furness Gliding Club Proprietary Ltd t/a Lakes Gliding Club		
			D-7083			Walney Island	30. 1.08
G-DHSJ	Schempp-Hirth Discus b	546	BGA4163-HSJ	9. 1.08	A.A.Jenkins *"D54"*	Bicester	3. 3.08
G-DHSL	Schempp-Hirth Ventus 2c	1/2	BGA4165-HSL	29.10.07	H G Woodsend	Aston Down	15. 3.08
	(Incomplete airframe assembled Southern Sailplanes)		(BGA4154)				
G-DHSR	Sportline Aviacija LAK-12 Lietuva	6178	BGA4170-HSR	1. 2.08	G Forster	Milfield	7. 6.08
G-DHSS	de Havilland DH.112 Venom FB.50 (FB.1) 836		Swiss AF J-1626	26. 3.99	Aviation and Computer Consultancy Ltd *(Stored 1.09)*		
	(Built F + W)				*(As "WR360" in white RAF c/s)*	Bournemouth	22. 4.03P
G-DHTG	Grob G102 Astir CS	1510	BGA4185-HTG	23. 1.08	Trent Valley Gliding Club Ltd	Kirton-in-Lindsey	19. 9.08
			RAFGSA R59, RAFGSA R69, RAFGSA 519				
G-DHTM	DH.82A Tiger Moth (replica)						
	(Type amended 6. 3.08)	PFA 157-11095		6. 1.86	C R Hardiman	Shobdon	
	(Built L Causer and E G Waite-Roberts, amended to C Hardiman 3. 3.08)				*(Believed parts consumed within rebuild of G-APPN qv)*		
G-DHTT	de Havilland DH.112 Venom FB.50 (FB.1) 821		(G-BMOC)	17.10.96	Aviation and Computer Consultancy Ltd		
	(Built F + W)		Swiss AF J-1611		*(As "WR421": stored 1.09)*	Bournemouth	17. 7.99P
G-DHUB	PZL-Bielsko SZD-48 Jantar 3	B-1527	BGA4204-HUB	2. 4.08	C J M Chatburn	Portmoak	
			DOSAAF				
G-DHUK	Schleicher Ka 6CR	6385	BGA4212-HUK	2. 9.08	T Donovan and B Hucker	Shenington	
			SE-TCN				
G-DHUU	de Havilland DH.112 Venom FB.50 (FB.1) 749		(G-BMOD)	26. 2.96	Aviation and Computer Consultancy Ltd *(Noted 1.09)410" in*		
	(Built F + W)		Swiss AF J-1539		*(As "WR410" in RAF 6 Sqdn c/s)*	(Bournemouth)	24. 5.02P
G-DHVM	de Havilland DH.112 Venom FB.50 (FB.1) 752		G-GONE	26.11.03	Aviation Heritage Ltd	Coventry	9. 3.09P
	(Built F + W)		Swiss AF J-1542		*(As "WR470" in RAF 208 Sqdn c/s)*		
G-DHVV	de Havilland DH.115 Vampire T 55	55092	Swiss AF U-1214	5. 9.91	Aviation and Computer Consultancy Ltd *(Noted 1.09)*		
	(Built F + W) (Reported as built with c/n 974)				*(As "XE897"in RAF 54 Sqdn c/s)*	(Bournemouth)	5. 6.03P
G-DHWW	de Havilland DH.115 Vampire T 55	979	Swiss AF U-1219	5. 9.91	Aviation and Computer Consultancy Ltd *(Noted 1.00)*		
	(Built F + W) (Reported as built with c/n 974)				*(As "XG775" in RN FOFT c/s)*	(Bournemouth)	23. 4.03P
G-DHXX	de Havilland DH.100 Vampire FB.6	682	Swiss AF J-1173	5. 9.91	Aviation and Computer Consultancy Ltd *(Noted 1.09)*		
	(Built F + W)				*(As "VT871" in RAF 54 Sqdn c/s)*	(Bournemouth)	14. 8.02P
G-DHYL	Schempp-Hirth Ventus 2a	44	BGA4310-HYL	6.11.07	Leinster Gliders Ltd	(London W2)	31.10.07
G-DHZF	de Havilland DH.82A Tiger Moth	82309	G-BSTJ	7. 7.99	C A Parker and M R Johnson *(As "N-9192:RCO-N" in RAF c/s)*		
			OO-MEH, OO-GEB, OO-MOR, RNethAF A-13, PH-UFB, A-13, N9192			Sywell	17. 5.09S

G-DIAA - G-DIZZ

G-DIAL	Cameron N-90 Balloon (Hot Air)	1851		7.11.88	A J Street *"London" (Inflated 8.06)* Whimple, Exeter		11. 5.00A
G-DIAM	Diamond DA.40D Star	D4.204		23. 5.06	A Overton	Sywell	28. 6.09E
G-DIAT	Piper PA-28-140 Cherokee Cruiser	28-7425322	G-BCGK	19. 7.89	D J Skidmore	Bristol	21. 9.09E
			N9594N				
G-DICK	Thunder Ax6-56Z Balloon (Hot Air)	159		6. 7.78	R D Sargeant *"Bandag"*	Altendorf, Switzerland	10. 9.09E
G-DIDG	Van's RV-7	LAA 323-14764		15. 2.08	E T and D K Steele	(Sittingbourne)	
	(Built E T Steele)						
G-DIDY	Thruster T600T 450	1052-T600T-116		30. 1.06	D R Sims	Halwell	2. 4.09P
G-DIGG	Robinson R44 Raven II	11904		21. 9.07	Thames Materials Ltd	Denham	15.10.09E
G-DIGI	Piper PA-32-300 Six	32-7940224	D-EIES	13.10.98	D Stokes tr Security UN Ltd Group	Stapleford	9.12.09E
			N2947M				
G-DIGN	Robin DR.400-180 Régent	2651		14. 7.08	D M Green	Wolverhampton	11. 8.09E
G-DIKY	Murphy Rebel	PFA 232-13182		13. 2.98	R J P Herivel	Alderney	15. 6.09P
	(Built R J P Herivel)						
G-DIMB	Boeing 767-31K	28865		28. 4.97	Monarch Airlines Ltd	Luton	27. 4.09E
G-DIME	Rockwell Commander 114	14123	N49829	9. 3.88	H B Richardson	Badminton	11. 4.09E
G-DINA	Gulfstream AA-5B Tiger	AA5B-1218	N4555Y	27. 2.81	Portway Aviation Ltd	Shobdon	6. 8.09E
G-DING	Colt 77A Balloon (Hot Air)	1862		28. 6.91	G J Bell *"Dingbat"*	Petersfield	8. 4.09E
G-DINO	Cyclone Airsports Pegasus Quantum 15	7225	G-MGMT	15.12.98	P W Day	(Blidworth, Mansfield)	25. 4.09P
	(Rotax 582)						
G-DINT	Bristol 156 Beaufighter IF	STAN B1 184604	3858M	17. 6.91	T E Moore	Rotary Farm, Hatch	
			X7688		*(On rebuild from various ex Australian components 10.99)*		
G-DIPI	Cameron Tub 80 SS Balloon (Hot Air)	1745		6. 5.88	C G Dobson *"KP Choc Dips"*	Streatley, Reading	30. 8.09E
G-DIPM	Piper PA-46-350P Malibu Mirage	4636325	N5350V	20. 2.02	Intesa Leasing SpA	(Milan, Italy)	23. 4.09E
G-DIRK	Glaser-Dirks DG-400	4-124	D-KEKT	18. 9.86	D G Clews tr G-DIRK Syndicate *"RK"* Parham Park		27. 4.09E
G-DISA	Scottish Aviation Bulldog Series 100/125		RJordan AF 420	25. 8.04	British Disabled Flying Association	Lasham	21. 7.11S
		BH120/435	RJordan AF 1142, G-31-44				
G-DISK	Piper PA-24-250 Comanche	24-1197	G-APZG	9. 8.89	A M and A C M Harrhy	Bembridge	26. 6.09E
			EI-AKW, N10F				
G-DISO	SAN Jodel D 150 Mascaret	24	9Q-CPK	16.12.86	P F Craven	Wombleton	26. 6.09P
			OO-APK, F-BLDT				
G-DIWY	Piper PA-32-300 Cherokee Six B	32-40731	OY-DLW	26.11.91	IFS Chemicals Ltd	East Winch	8.10.09E
			D-EHMW, N8931N				
G-DIXY	Piper PA-28-181 Archer III	2843195	N41284	10.12.98	M G Bird tr MGB Air	Fowlmere	16.12.08E
			G-DIXY, N41284				
G-DIZI	Reality Escapade 912(1)	JAESC 0012		1. 3.04	N Baumber	(Grantham)	
	(Built N Baumber - pr.no.BMAA HB/355)						
G-DIZO	Wassmer Jodel D 120A Paris-Nice	326	G-EMKM	30. 5.91	D Aldersea	Breighton	7. 5.09P
			F-BOBG				
G-DIZY	Piper PA-28R-201T Turbo Arrow III		N47570	13.10.88	Calverton Flying Group Ltd	Rochester	16.11.09E
		28R-7703401					
G-DIZZ	Hughes 369HE *(Hughes 500)*	89-0105E	N9029F	19. 2.97	R H Kirke	Redhill	29. 5.09E

G-DJAA - G-DJZZ

G-DJAA	Schempp-Hirth Janus B	163	BGA4348-JAA	16. 1.08	C J Hoare tr Janus B Group	Parham Park	30. 1.08
			D-3147				

G-DJAB	DG Flugzeugbau DG-300 Elan	3E320	BGA4349-JAB	16.10.07	I G Johnston	Sutton Bank	28. 9.08
			OY-XTC				
G-DJAC	Schempp-Hirth Duo Discus	128	BGA4350-JAC	28. 8.08	D G Roberts tr G-DJAC Group	Aston Down	
G-DJAD	Schleicher ASK 21	21659	BGA4351-JAD	25 .2.08	The Borders (Milfield) Gliding Club Ltd	Milfield	18. 8.08
G-DJAE	Cessna 500 Citation I	500-0339	G-JEAN	3.11.98	Kenmare Bay Homes Ltd	Dublin	24. 7.09E
			N300EC, N707US, G-JEAN, (N5339J)				
G-DJAH	Schempp-Hirth Discus b	572	BGA4355-JAH	11. 6.08	C F M Smith and K Neave	Nympsfield	
G-DJAN	Schempp-Hirth Discus b	575	BGA4360-JAN	1.10.07	N F Perren "603"	Dunstable	28. 9.08
G-DJAY	Avtech Jabiru UL-450	PFA 274A-13633		8. 8.00	D J Pearce	(Reading)	24. 7.09P
	(Built D J Pearce)						
G-DJBC	Comco Ikarus C42 FB100	0802-6937		5. 2.08	D Meegan	(Newry)	10. 4.09P
G-DJCR	Varga 2150A Kachina	VAC 155-80	EI-CFK	11. 4.96	D J C Robertson	(Clocksbridge, Forfar)	30. 4.99
			G-BLWG, OO-HTD, N8360J				
G-DJED	Schleicher ASW 15B	15427	BGA4447-JED	11. 7.08	J T Leppanen tr Grupo JED	(Perafita, Portugal)	
			D-3976				
G-DJET	Diamond DA.42 Twin Star	42.122	OE-VPW	30. 3.06	Papa Bravo Ltd	Bagby	21. 5.09E
G-DJGG	Schleicher ASW 15B	15332	BGA4498-JGG	5.12.07	A A Cole	(Ringmer)	19. 3.08
			D-2325				
G-DJHP	Valentin Mistral C	MC048/82	BGA4529-JHP	21. 1.08	P B Higgs	(Rossett, Wrexham)	22. 2.08
			D-4948				
G-DJJA	Piper PA-28-181 Archer II	28-8490014	N4326D	14. 9.87	Interactive Aviation Ltd	Denham	7. 1.10E
G-DJLL	Schleicher ASK 13	13144	BGA4598-JLL	29. 1.08	T World tr Portsmouth Naval Gliding Centre		
			HB-952			Lee-on-Solent	16. 2.08
G-DJMC	Schleicher ASK 21	21681	BGA4614-JMC	23. 5.08	J G Arnold tr RAF Gliding and Soaring Association "R22"		
			(RAFGSA R22)			Kenley	
G-DJMD	Schempp-Hirth Discus B	241	BGA4615-JMD	7.12.07	R C Oliver tr Papa 23 Group	Kenley	24. 1.08
			RAFGSA R23				
G-DJMM	Cessna 172S Skyhawk	172S8482	N227ME	10. 3.05	M Manston	Panshanger	12. 3.09E
G-DJNC	ICA Brasov IS-28B2	33	BGA2207-DLU	5. 8.08	J Rigby tr Delta Juliet November Group		
			RAFGSA R93, NEJSGSA 3, EI-141, BGA2207-DLU			(Bury St Edmunds)	
G-DJNH	Denney Kitfox Model 3	772		20. 9.90	B D Hanscomb	Shobdon	22. 8.08P
	(Built D J N Hall - pr.no.PFA 172-11896)						
G-DJST	Air Création Clipper/iXess 912	xxx		12.10.04	D J Stimpson	Sywell	15. 5.09P
	(Buiilt D J Stimpson - pr. no. BMAA HB/416)						
G-DJWS	Schleicher ASW 15B	15098S	BGA4845-JWS	7. 4.08	B Pridgeon	Kirton-in-Lindsey	
			D-4656				

G-DKAA - G-DKZZ

G-DKBA	DKBA AT 0301-0 Balloon (Hot Air)	013.07.93		15. 5.07	I Chadwick (Active 8.08) Patrridge Green, Horsham		
G-DKBW	Valentin Mistral C	MC021/79	BGA4725-JRS	17.12.07	A Towse "JRS"	Rattlesden	9. 4.08
			D-4921				
G-DKDP	Grob G109	6100	(G-BMBD)	9. 7.85	D W and J E Page tr Grob 4	Tibenham	9. 6.09E
			D-KAMS				
G-DKEN	Rolladen-Schneider LS4-a	4172	BGA5034-KEN	15.11.07	K L Sangster and B Lytollis	Kelso	10. 2.08
			OO-ZSM, (OO-ZDG)				
G-DKEY	Piper PA-28-161 Warrior II	28-7716084	N1120Q	4. 1.07	B W Gomez	Wolverhampton	13. 6.08E
G-DKFU	Schempp-Hirth Ventus -2cxT	114/311	G-CKFU	19.11.07	W F Payton	Sutton Bank	23. 3.08
			BGA5064-KFU, D-KOAX				
G-DKMK	Robinson R44 Raven II	11398		18.12.06	Clear Sky Views Ltd		
					(Bishopscourt, Straffan, County Kildare)		4. 2.09E
G-DKNY	Robinson R44 Raven II	11651		1. 3.07	D Watson and J Kennedy Liverpool-John Lennon		22. 3.09E

G-DLAA - G-DLZZ

G-DLCB	Europa Aviation Europa	046		16.11.95	K Richards	Talgarth	26.11.09P
	(Built D J Lockett - pr./no.PFA 247-12652) (Monowheel u/c)						
G-DLCH	Boeing 737-8Q8	30040		22. 4.05	Globespan Airways Ltd t/a Flyglobespan.com		
						Edinburgh	24. 4.09E
G-DLDL	Robinson R22 Beta	1971		2. 1.92	Airtask Group PLC	Conington	2. 5.09E
G-DLEE	SOCATA TB-9 Tampico Club	884	G-BPGX	18. 2.04	D A Lee	Dunkeswell	12. 7.08E
G-DLOM	SOCATA TB-20 Trinidad	1102	N2823Y	13.12.90	J N A Adderley	(Verbier, Switzerland)	13. 7.09E
G-DLTR	Piper PA-28-180 Cherokee E	28-5803	G-AYAV	15. 3.96	Light Aircraft Leasing Ltd	Cardiff	6.11.09E
			N11C				

G-DMAA - G-DMZZ

G-DMAC	Avtech Jabiru SP-430	0184		15.10.98	C J Pratt	Goodwood	8. 9.09P
	(Built B Macfadden - pr.no.PFA 274-13321) (Originally regd as Jabiru UL, amended 1.09)						
G-DMAH	SOCATA TB-20 Trinidad GT	2039	F-OILY	2. 4.01	R C and C G Bell	Little Rissington	9. 4.09E
G-DMCD	Robinson R22 Beta	1201	G-OOLI	14.11.89	Heliair Ltd	Denham	8. 1.10E
			G-DMCD				
G-DMCI	Comco Ikarus C42 FB100	0707-6906		16. 8.07	D McCartan	(Sixmilecross, Omagh)	24.10.09P
G-DMCS	Piper PA-28R-200 Cherokee Arrow II		G-CPAC	29. 5.84	W G Ashton and J Bingley t/a Arrow Associates		
		28R-7635284	PH-SMW, OO-HAU, N75220			Goodwood	19. 4.09E
G-DMCT	Flight Design CT2K	01-04-02-12		10. 7.01	A M Sirant	Monkswell Farm, Horrabridge	10.11.08P
	(Assembled Pegasus Aviation Ltd - no c/n issued)						
G-DMND	Diamond DA.42 Twin Star	42.068		4.11.05	MC Air Ltd	Wellesbourne Mountford	20.12.08E
G-DMRA	Robinson R44 Raven II	11802		8. 6.07	D M Richards	(Rock, Kidderminster)	12. 7.09E
G-DMRS	Robinson R44 Raven II	10513		29.10.04	Nottinghamshire Helicopters (2004) Ltd	Costock	25. 2.09E
G-DMSS	Westland SA.341D Gazelle HT.3	1089	XW858	13. 7.01	Woods of York Ltd (As "XW858:C" in RAF c/s)		
						Murton, York	2. 8.09P

| G-DMWW | CFM Shadow Series DD | 304-DD | | 12.10.98 | Microlight Sport Aviation Ltd | | |
| | | | | | | Damyns Hall, Upminster | 10. 4.08P |

G-DNAA - G-DNZZ

G-DNBH	Raj Hamsa X'Air Hawk	LAA 340-14819		20.10.08	D N B Hearn	Little Heathfield Farm, Ventnor	
	(Built D N B Hearn)						
G-DNGA	Balony Kubicek BB20 Balloon (Hot Air)	235	OK-0235	1. 5.03	G J Bell	Wokingham	9. 7.09E
G-DNGR	Colt 31A Balloon (Hot Air)	10162		18.10.01	G J Bell	Wokingham	30. 8.09E
G-DNKS	Comco Ikarus C42 FB80	0606-6822		15. 6.06	D N K and M A Symon	Eshott	27. 7.09P
G-DNOP	Piper PA-46-350P Malibu Mirage	4636303	N4174A	26. 7.00	Campbell Aviation Ltd	Denham	3. 8.09E

G-DOAA - G-DOZZ

G-DOCA	Boeing 737-436	25267		21.10.91	British Airways PLC	London Gatwick	20.12.08E
G-DOCB	Boeing 737-436	25304		16.10.91	British Airways PLC	London Gatwick	15. 2.10E
G-DOCE	Boeing 737-436	25350		20.11.91	British Airways PLC	London Gatwick	6. 8.09E
G-DOCF	Boeing 737-436	25407		9.12.91	British Airways PLC	London Gatwick	9. 7.09E
G-DOCG	Boeing 737-436	25408		16.12.91	British Airways PLC	London Gatwick	15. 8.09E
G-DOCH	Boeing 737-436	25428		19.12.91	British Airways PLC	London Gatwick	18. 8.09E
G-DOCL	Boeing 737-436	25842		2. 3.92	British Airways PLC	London Gatwick	1. 3.09E
G-DOCN	Boeing 737-436	25848		21.10.92	British Airways PLC	London Gatwick	20.10.09E
G-DOCO	Boeing 737-436	25849		26.10.92	British Airways PLC	London Gatwick	25.10.09E
G-DOCS	Boeing 737-436	25852		1.12.92	British Airways PLC	London Gatwick	30.11.09E
G-DOCT	Boeing 737-436	25853		22.12.92	British Airways PLC	London Gatwick	23.12.08E
G-DOCU	Boeing 737-436	25854		18. 1.93	British Airways PLC	London Gatwick	19. 1.10E
G-DOCV	Boeing 737-436	25855		25. 1.93	British Airways PLC	London Gatwick	24. 1.09E
G-DOCW	Boeing 737-436	25856		2. 2.93	British Airways PLC	London Gatwick	3. 2.10E
G-DOCX	Boeing 737-436	25857		29. 3.93	British Airways PLC	London Gatwick	28. 3.09E
G-DOCY	Boeing 737-436	25844	OO-LTQ	17.10.96	British Airways PLC	London Gatwick	17.10.09E
			G-BVBY, TC-ALS, G-BVBY, (G-DOCY)				
G-DOCZ	Boeing 737-436	25858	EC-FXJ	12.12.94	British Airways PLC	London Gatwick	11. 1.10E
			EC-657, G-BVBZ, (G-DOCZ)				
G-DODB	Robinson R22 Beta	0911	N8005R	3. 5.96	L A and G M Evans t/a Helibern Helicopter Services		
						(Tartwell, Louth)	26. 9.09E
G-DODD	Reims Cessna F172P Skyhawk II	F17202175		5.10.82	K Watts	Moorlands Farm, Farway Common	6. 8.08E
G-DODG	Evektor EV-97A Eurostar	PFA 315-14258		23. 6.04	K L Clarke and R Barton	Keal Cotes, Spilsby	4.10.08P
	(Built R Barton)						
G-DOEA	Gulfstream AA-5A Cheetah	AA5A-0895	G-RJMI	30. 4.96	CJW Holdings Ltd t/a Fairway Flying Services		
			N27170			Sandown	6.10.09E
G-DOFY	Bell 206B-3 JetRanger III	3637	N2283F	26. 8.87	Cinnamond Ltd (Operated Cabair Helicopters)		
						Silver Springs, Denham	13. 2.09E
G-DOGE	Scottish Aviation Bulldog Series 100/101		G-AZHX	5.12.05	W P Cooper	North Weald	14. 3.11S
		BH100/126	SE-LNO, Swedish Army Fv61022, G-AZHX				
G-DOGG	Scottish Aviation Bulldog Series 120/121		XX638	3.10.01	P Sengupta (As "XX638" in RAF c/s)		
		BH120/308				Bourne Park, Hurstbourne Tarrant	26. 3.08T
G-DOGY	Aviat A-1B Husky	2421	N11UK	28. 2.08	Aviat Aircraft (UK) Ltd		
						Lower Grounds Farm, Sherlowe	28. 2.09E
G-DOGZ	Rogerson Horizon 1	PFA 241-13129		10. 8.98	J E D Rogerson	Morgansfield, Fishburn	8. 1.10P
	(Built J E D Rogerson) (Marked as "Fisher Super Koala") (Rotax 912-UL)						
G-DOIG	CZAW Sportcruiser	LAA 338-14859		30.10.08	J H Doyle	(Manchester)	
G-DOIN	Best Off Sky Ranger 912S(1)	SKR0403460		26. 4.04	A G Borer	Stoke, Isle of Grain	16.12.09P
	(Built C D and L J Church - pr.no.BMAA HB/379)						
G-DOIT	Aérospatiale AS.350B2 Ecureuil	1902	F-GMAZ	10.10.01	FBS Ltd	RAF Shawbury	22.11.07T
	(Under conversion to Squirrel HT1)		LN-OTA, SE-JAC, LN-OBD, (F-GHYU), LN-OBD, SE-JAC, HB-XPH				
G-DOLF	Eurocopter AS.365N3 Dauphin 2	6779	F-WWPP	25.10.07	Profred Partners LLP	(London EC4)	25. 2.09E
G-DOLI	Cirrus SR20	2009	N554PG	7. 8.08	Furness Asset Management Ltd	Blackpool	20. 8.09E
G-DOLY	Cessna T303 Crusader	T30300107	N303MK	20. 7.94	KW Aviation Ltd	Biggin Hill	24. 6.09E
			G-BJZK, (N3645C)				
G-DOME	Piper PA-28-161 Warrior III	2842062	N4160V	12. 1.00	Haimoss Ltd (Operated Professional Air Training)		
						Bournemouth	6. 2.09E
G-DOMS	Evektor EV-97A Eurostar	PFA 315-14254		24. 6.04	R K and C A Stewart	Hinton-in-the-Hedges	15. 4.09P
	(Built D J Cross)						
G-DONI	Gulfstream AA-5B Tiger	AA5B-1029	G-BLLT	20. 7.95	W P Moritz	Elstree	23. 1.09E
			OO-RTG, (OO-HRS)				
G-DONS	Piper PA-28RT-201T Turbo Arrow IV		N8336L	22. 4.88	C E Griffiths	Blackbushe	12. 5.09E
		28R-8131077					
G-DONT	Zenair CH.601XL Zodiac	PFA 162B-14172		24. 5.04	A C J Butcher	Whaley Farm, New York, Lincoln	18. 6.07P
	(Built N C Butcher)						
G-DOOM	Cameron Z-105 Balloon (Hot Air)	10660		14. 3.05	The Balloon Company Ltd t/a First Flight (Doom Bar titles)		
						Langford, Bristol	1. 4.09E
G-DORA	Focke-Wulf FW.190-D9	211028	Luftwaffe	21. 5.03	P R Holloway (Completion scheduled for 2009)		
			211028			Old Warden	
G-DORM	Robinson R44 Clipper II	12330		9. 7.08	M McGlone	(Magherafelt)	21. 9.09E
G-DORN	Dornier EKW C-3605	332	HB-RBJ	15. 5.98	R G Gray (As "C-552" in Swiss AF c/s)		
	(Built F + W)		Swiss AF C-552			Bournemouth	15.11.08P
G-DORS	Eurocopter EC.135 T2+	0517		14.12.06	Bond Aviation Leasing Ltd	Henstridge	21. 2.09E
					(Operated Dorset and Somerset Air Ambulance)		
G-DOSC	Diamond DA.42M Twin Star	42M.001	OE-FOG	23.12.08	DO Systems Ltd (For MoD)	Old Sarum	
G-DOTT	CFM Streak Shadow	PFA 206-13582		30.11.04	R J Bell	Movenis, Coleraine	31. 8.09P
	(Built R J Bell)						
G-DOTW	ICP MXP-740 Savannah VG Jabiru (1)			25. 6.08	I S Wright	North Coates	24.11.09P
	(Built I S Wright)	08-03-51-694	(Pr. no BMAA HB/575) (Jabiru 2200A)				

G-DOTY	Ran's RV-7	71966			21.10.08	H A Daines		Ellough, Beccles	
	(Built H A Daines, pr no PFA 323-14387)								
G-DOVE	Cessna 182Q Skylane II	18266724	N96446		26. 6.80	P Seckington tr G-DOVE Group		Popham	28. 7.09E
G-DOVS	Robinson R44 Raven II	11858			8. 8.07	D B Hamilton		(Stonehouse)	29. 8.09E
G-DOWN	Colt 31A Air Chair Balloon (Hot Air)	1570			3. 8.89	M Williams "Up and Down"		Wadhurst, Sussex	8. 6.00A
G-DOZI	Comco Ikarus C42 FB100	0606-6824			22. 5.06	D A Izod		Gerpins Lane, Upminster	7.7.09P
G-DOZZ	Best Off Sky Ranger Swift 912S(1)				16. 5.08	J P Doswell		Bodmin	30.11.09P
	(Built J P Doswell)	SKR 0803866	(Pr. no BMAA HB/573)						

G-DPAA - G-DPZZ

G-DPEP	Aero AT-3 R100	AT3-027			24. 9.07	Cunning Plan Development Ltd			
						(Operated Old Sarum Flying Club)		Old Sarum	1.10.09P
G-DPHN	Aérospatiale SA.365N1 Dauphin 2	6307	HB-ZBY		11. 4.06	Atlantic Air Ltd		Biggin Hill	17. 1.09E
			LX-HGR, JA9902						
G-DPJR	Sikorsky S-76B	760352	G-JCBA		20. 3.07	Blackbird Logistics Ltd		(London, W1)	2. 3.09E
			N95UT, N95LT, N120PP, N120PM						
G-DPPF	Agusta A109E Power	11216			26. 6.03	Dyfed-Powys Police Authority			
								(Llangunnor, Carmarthen)	14.. 3.10T
G-DPYE	Robin DR.500-200i Président	14	F-GPDT		26. 8.06	Pye Consulting Group Ltd		Blackpool	23. 9.09E
	(Officially regd as DR.400-500)								

G-DRAA - G-DRZZ

G-DRAM	Reims FR172F Rocket	FR17200102	OH-CNS		18. 9.98	H R Mitchell and J P Roland tr Clyde River Rats			
	(Floatplane)					"Spirit of Scotland"		Lochearnhead	11. 4.09E
G-DRAT	Slingsby T.51 Dart 17R	1517	BGA1316-BXL		8. 5.08	W R Longstaff		Feshiebridge	
G-DRAW	Colt 77A Balloon (Hot Air)	1830			31. 8.90	A G Odell "Readers Digest"		Macclesfield	22. 9.09E
G-DRAY	Taylor JT.1 Monoplane	PFA 1452			13. 7.78	L J Dray		(Sidmouth)	
	(Built L J Dray)								
G-DRBG	Cessna 172M Skyhawk	17265263	G-MUIL		18. 1.95	Wilkins and Wilkins (Special Auctions) t/a Henlow			
			N64486			Flying Club Ltd		RAF Henlow	17. 5.09E
G-DRCS	Schleicher ASH 25E	25060	BGA4480-JFN		10. 4.08	C R Smithers "M25"		Gransden Lodge	
			D-KCOH						
G-DREG	Cosmik Super Chaser	SCH001W			4. 6.07	N R Beale		Deppers Bridge, Southam	
	(Built N R Beale) (Hirth EC34)					(Noted NEC Birmingham 11.07)			
G-DREX	Cameron Saturn 110 SS Balloon (Hot Air)				28.10.97	LRC Products Ltd		Broxbourne, Hertford	3.11.99A
		217							
G-DRFC	Aérospatiale-Alenia ATR 42-320	007	OY-CIB		1. 6.04	Bravo Aviation Ltd (stored 9.08)		Exeter	9. 8.09E
			F-GFLL, OY-CIB, F-WWEC						
G-DRGN	Cameron N-105 Balloon (Hot Air)	2024			13. 6.91	W I Hooker and C Parker		(Nottingham)	4. 7.01T
G-DRGS	Cessna 182S Skylane	18280375	N2389X		17.11.98	D R G Scott		Edinburgh	3. 3.09E
G-DRID	Reims FR172J Rocket	FR1720434	I-ALGB		19. 9.03	D T J Hoskins, D H Hoskins and G Williams			
								Upfield Farm, Whitson	16. 6.09E
G-DRIV	Robinson R44 Raven II	10126	N75233		19. 9.03	C Reynard		Walton Wood	14.11.09E
			N3624J						
G-DRLH	Eurocopter EC.120B Colibri	1477	F-HFLB		8. 8.07	R L Hartshorn	Hill Top Farm, Parkhead, Matlock		15. 8.09E
G-DRMM	Europa Aviation Europa	362			27. 7.98	T J Harrison		(Bristol)	
	(Built M W Mason - pr.no.PFA 247-13201) (Tri-gear u/c)								
G-DRNT	Sikorsky S-76A II Plus	760201	N93WW		5. 4.90	CHC Scotia Ltd		North Denes	1. 5.09E
			N3WQ, N3WL, N3121G						
G-DROP	Cessna U206C Super Skywagon	U2061230	G-UKNO		7. 8.87	K Brady		Strathallan	24. 4.09E
			G-BAMN, 4X-ALL, N71943						
G-DRPK	Reality Escapade	LAA 345-14824			30. 6.08	P A Kirkham		(Cranleigh)	
	(Built P A Kirkham)								
G-DRSV	Robin DR315X Petit Prince	624	F-ZWRS		7. 6.90	R S Voice		Rushett Farm, Chessington	17. 6.08P
	(Officially regd with pr.no.PFA 210-11765 following major rebuild by R S Voice)								
G-DRYI	Cameron N-77 Balloon (Hot Air)	2046			7. 8.89	C A Butter (Barbour titles)		Marsh Benham	18. 4.09E
G-DRYS	Cameron N-90 Balloon (Hot Air)	3377			1.12.95	C A Butter (Barbour titles)		Marsh Benham	12. 8.09E
G-DRZF	CEA Jodel DR.360 Chevalier	451	F-BRZF		4. 9.91	P K Kaufeler		Earls Colne	20.12.09E

G-DSAA - G-DSZZ

G-DSFT	Piper PA-28R-200 Cherokee Arrow II		G-LFSE		22.11.00	J Jones		Headcorn	12. 5.09T
		28R-7335157	G-BAXT, N11C						
G-DSGC	Piper PA-25-260 Pawnee C	25-4890	OY-BDA		3. 5.95	Devon & Somerset Gliding Club Ltd		North Hill	27. 4.09E
G-DSID	Piper PA-34-220T Seneca IV	3447001			21. 7.95	I S Giilbe		(Leigh Woods, Bristol)	13. 7.09E
G-DSKI	Evektor EV-97 Eurostar	PFA 315-14088			25. 6.04	D R Skill		Eshott	15. 8.09P
	(Built D R Skill)								
G-DSLL	Cyclone Airsports Pegasus Quantum 15-912				5. 7.01	R G Jeffery		(Sandbach)	5. 7.09P
		7836							
G-DSMA	P&M Aviation QuikR	8410			11.08R				
G-DSPI	Robinson R44 Astro	0661			25.10.99	Central Helicopters Ltd	Nottingham City-Tollerton		13.12.09E
	(Marked as "Raven")								
G-DSPK	Cameron Z-140 Balloon (Hot Air)	10640			7. 1.05	Bailey Balloons Ltd (D S Smith Packaging titles)			
								Pill, Bristol	19.12.09E
G-DSPL	Diamond DA.40 Star	40.037			19.11.07	Dynamic Signal Processing Ltd			
								(Kingsclere, Newbury)	13. 2.09E
G-DSPZ	Robinson R44 Raven II	10351			5. 5.04	Focal Point Communications Ltd		(Alresford)	8. 6.09E
G-DSVN	Rolladen-Schneider LS8-18	8079	BGA4262-HWM		3. 1 08	A R Paul "D7"		Dunstable	26. 1.08

G-DTAA - G-DTZZ

G-DTAR	P&M Aviation Quik GT450	8416		3.10.08	D Tarvit	Edinburgh	
G-DTCP	Piper PA-32R-300 Cherokee Lance	32R-7780255	G-TEEM N2604Q	27. 3.92	M G A Hussein	(London N10)	17. 5.07E
G-DTFF	Cessna T182T Turbo Skylane	T18208474	N2196K	25.10.06	Rajair Ltd	Dudleston Heath, Ellesmere	25.10.09E
G-DTOY	Comco Ikarus C42 FB100 (Rotax 912-ULS)	0309-6570		20.10.03	C W Laskey	Upfield Farm, Whitson	23.10.08P
G-DTSM	Evektor EV-97 teamEurostar UK (Built Cosmik Aviation)	3218		1. 8.08	J R Stothart	(Dartmouth)	31. 7.09P
G-DTUG	Wag-Aero Super Sport (Built D A Bullock)	PFA 108-14026		13. 5.04	D A Bullock (Noted 1.07)	Bicester	
G-DTWO	Schempp-Hirth Discus 2A	9	BGA5217-KNA D-2140	18. 1.06	O Walters tr GW-LL Group "LL"	Bicester	6. 3.08

G-DUAA - G-DUZZ

G-DUBI	Lindstrand LBL 120A Balloon (Hot Air)	1123		4.10.06	A Nimmo (HSBC titles) Dubai, United Arab Emirates		22.12.09E
G-DUDE	Van's RV-8 (Built W M Hodgkins)	PFA 303-13246		16. 7.99	W M Hodgkins Crowfield ("Van's Air Force" and "19" on tail)		29. 6.09P
G-DUDZ	Robin DR.400-180 Régent	2367	G-BXNK	3.12.97	D H Pattison	Lower Upham Farm, Chiseldon	26.12.09E
G-DUGE	Comco Ikarus C42 FB UK (Built D Stevenson)	PFA 322-13855		30. 7.02	D Stevenson	Plaistows Farm, St Albans	4. 6.09P
G-DUGI	Lindstrand LBL 90A Balloon (Hot Air)	562		16. 8.99	J A Folkes	Bulcote, Nottingham	17. 5.09E
G-DUKK	Extra EA.300/L	125	D-EXAC	27.11.00	Extra Aviation Ltd	Sherburn-in-Elmet	5. 6.09E
G-DUKY	Robinson R44 Raven	1455		21. 2.05	English Braids Ltd	Gloucestershire	28. 2.09E
G-DUMP	Customcraft A25 Balloon (Hot Air)	CC003		19. 5.04	P C Bailey	Over, Cambridge	
G-DUNK	Reims Cessna F172M Skyhawk	F17201402	N90SA PH-TWS, OY-BUL	2. 5.07	Devon and Somerset Flight Training Ltd Dunkeswell		29. 6.09E
G-DUOD	Bombardier CL-600-2C10 (CL-600 Regional Jet 700)	10048	G-MRSH C-GIAI	22. 9.03	A/S Maersk Aviation Holding Copenhagen, Denmark		16. 4.08E
G-DUOT	Schempp-Hirth Duo Discus T	123/...		3. 8.05	A P Moulang tr G-DUOT Group "666"	Challock	6. 3.07
G-DUOX	Schempp-Hirth Duo Discus	474	BGA5209-KMS D-4498	3. 4.06	British Gliding Association Ltd "98"	Bicester	14.12.07
G-DURO	Europa Aviation Europa (Built R Swinden - pr.no.PFA 247-12554) (Monowheel u/c)	033		15.11.93	W R C Williams-Wynne	Talybont, Gwynedd	21. 7.09P
G-DURX	Colt 77A Balloon (Hot Air)	1522		25. 5.89	R C and M A Trimble (Durex and Avanti titles) (Nuffield, Henley-on-Thames)		26. 6.02A
G-DUSK	de Havilland DH.115 Vampire T 11	15596	XE856	1. 2.99	R M A Robinson and R Horsfield Bournemouth (Stored in Museum 12.08)		
G-DUST	Stolp SA.300 Starduster Too (Built J O Perritt) (Lycoming O-360)	JP-2	N233JP	28. 4.88	N M Robinson	Compton Abbas	26.11.08P
G-DUVL	Reims Cessna F172N Skyhawk II	F17201723	G-BFMU (1)	16. 8.78	I Mackinnon tr G-DUVL Flying Group White Waltham		7. 8.09E

G-DVAA - G-DZZZ

G-DVAA	Eurocopter EC.135 T2+	0656		14. 3.08	Devon Air Ambulance Trading Co Ltd	Exeter	3. 9.09E
G-DVBF	Lindstrand LBL 210A Balloon (Hot Air)	188		6. 3.95	Airxcite Ltd t/a Virgin Balloon Flights	Wembley	1. 6.05T
G-DVON	de Havilland DH.104 Devon C 2/2	04201	(G-BLPD) VP955	26.10.84	C L Thatcher tr The 955 Preservation Group (Stored 1.08) (As "VP955" in RAF c/s)	Little Rissington	29. 5.96
G-DWCE	Robinson R44 Raven II	11511		17.11.06	G Walters (Leasing) Ltd	(Hirwaun, Aberdare)	27.11.09E
G-DWIA	Chilton DW.1A (Built D Elliott)	PFA 225-12256		25. 1.93	D Elliott	(Brooks Green, Horsham)	
G-DWIB	Chilton DW.1B (Built J Jennings)	PFA 225-12374		22.12.93	J Jennings	(Meldreth, Royston)	
G-DWJM	Cessna 550 Citation II	550-0296	G-BJIR N6888C	19. 5.05	MP Aviation LLP	Biggin Hill	3. 2.09E
G-DWMS	Avtech Jabiru UL-450 (Built D H S Williams - pr.no.PFA 274A-13491)	0266		21. 6.00	B J Weighell	(Spalding)	20.10.09P
G-DWPF	Tecnam P92-EM Echo (Built P I Franklin and D J M Williams)	PFA 318-13838		17. 5.02	D J M Williams tr GDWPF Group	Guernsey	28. 9.09P
G-DWPH	UltraMagic M-77 Balloon (Hot Air)	77/109		17. 3.95	UltraMagic SA	Igualada, Spain	19.12.09E
G-DXCC	UltraMagic M-77 Balloon (Hot Air)	77/269		1. 2.06	A Murphy	Dunshaughlin, County Meath	19. 8.09E
G-DYCE	Robinson R44 Raven II	10148		3. 9.03	P Durkin t/a Moorland Windows	Blackpool	29. 9.09E
G-DYKE	Dyke JD-2 Delta (Built P Wilson and M S Bird)	PFA 1331		6. 1.04	M S Bird	Pepperbox, Salisbury	
G-DYMC	Aerospool Dynamic WT9 UK (Official c/n is "DY200")	DY200/2007		6.11.07	D R Stevens	Kemble	29.11.09P
G-DYNA	Aerospool Dynamic WT9 UK (Official c/n is "DY135")	DY135/2006		9. 5.06	Yeoman Light Aircraft Company Ltd Drayton Manor, Drayton St Leonard		1. 3.09P
G-DYNM	Aerospool Dynamic WT9 UK (Official c/n is "DY161")	DY161/2007		30. 5.07	D M Pearson Manor Farm, Drayton St Leonard		29. 5.08P
G-DZDZ	Rolladen-Schneider LS4	4027	BGA3885-HEL (BGA3896-HEX), BGA3885-HEL, D-6431	3. 3.08	I MacArthur "DZ"	Long Mynd	

G-EAAA - G-EZZZ (see SECTION 1, PART 1 for original G-EA.. and G-EB..[1919 to 1928] registrations)

G-EAGA (2)	Sopwith Dove replica (80hp Le Rhône)	"3004/1"	(G-BLOO)	22.11.89	A Wood	Old Warden	16. 5.01P

(On loan to Richard Shuttleworth Trustees)

(Original Dove G-EAGA c/n 3004/1 to Australia and in use as K-157 by 11.12.19: remains of unregistered Dove, thought to have been K-157 and which crashed Essendon, Victoria 9.3.30, brought to UK circa 1987/88, rebuilt as G-BLOO and subsequently re-registered as above)

Reg	Type	c/n	Prev id	Date	Owner/Operator	Base	
G-EAVX (2)	Sopwith Pup	PFA 101-10523	B1807	16. 1.78	K A M Baker *(To be "B1807:A7" in RFC c/s)*		
	(Officially regd with c/n "B1807": claimed as rebuild of original Sopwith Pup)					RNAS Yeovilton	
G-EBJI (2)	Hawker Cygnet replica	PFA 077-10240		9. 8.77	C J Essex *(Under construction 7.99)*		
	(Built C J Essex)					(Coventry)	
G-EBZN (2)	de Havilland DH.60X Moth	608	VP-NAA	28.10.88	J Hodgkinson *(On rebuild from original components)*		
	(Cirrus I)		VP-YAA, ZS-AAP, G-UAAP			(Gravesend)	
G-ECAC	Alpha Aviation R2120U	120T-0001	ZK-SXY	23. 1.08	Bulldog Aviation Ltd	Earls Colne	6. 2.09E
	(Marked as "Alpha 120T")						
G-ECAD	Reims Cessna FA152 Aerobat	FA1520369	G-JEET	10.12.87	Bulldog Aviation Ltd	Earls Colne	7.10.09E
			G-BHMF				
G-ECAN	de Havilland DH.84 Dragon	2048	VH-DHX	11. 1.01	A J Norman tr Norman Aeroplane Trust		
	(Built de Havilland Aircraft Pty Ltd)		VH-AQU, RAAF A34-59		*(Railway Air Services Ltd titles)*	Rendcomb	25. 6.09S
G-ECBH	Reims Cessna F150K	F15000577	D-ECBH	16. 5.85	B Sedgi tr ECBH Flying Group	Cardiff	9. 7.09E
G-ECBI	Schweizer 269C-1 *(Schweizer 300)*	0282	N86G	17. 5.07	Iris Aviation Ltd	Southend	9. 7.09E
G-ECBO	Eurocopter EC.130 B4	4276		5. 7.07	Hawkrise Aviation LLP Minworth, Sutton Coldfield		28.11.09E
G-ECDB	Schleicher Ka 6E	4137	BGA1450-CDB	13. 2.08	C W R Neve	Currock Hill	7. 5.08
G-ECDS	de Havilland DH.82A Tiger Moth	86347	N82DS	6.12.07	N C Wilson	Sywell	6. 7.11
			F-BGFA, NL904				
G-ECDX	de Havilland DH.71 Tiger Moth replica	SP.7		1.11.94	M D Souch and N Parkhouse *(Under build 2.03)*		
	(DH Gipsy I)					Hill Farm, Durley	
G-ECEA	Schempp-Hirth Cirrus	21	BGA1473/CEA	2. 4.08	M Greenwood tr CEA Group	Long Mynd	
			XZ405, BGA1473, D-8437				
G-ECGC	Reims Cessna F172N Skyhawk II	F17201850		10.10.79	Cranfield Aviation Leasing Ltd	Cranfield	3. 3.08E
G-ECGO	Bölkow BÖ.208C Junior	599	D-ECGO	24. 8.89	A Flight Aviation Ltd *(Operated Prestwick Flying Club)*		
						Prestwick	15. 4.09E
G-ECJI	Dassault Falcon 10	161	I-CREM	21.12.05	Fleet International Aviation and Maritime Finance Ltd		
			F-WWZK, I-CREM, N50SL, N30CN, N230FJ, F-WZGM			Farnborough	9. 7.09E
G-ECJM	Piper PA-28R-201T Turbo Arrow III		G-FESL	25. 9.90	Regishire Ltd	Bournemouth	16. 5.08E
		28R-7803178	G-BNRN, N321EC, N3561M				
G-ECKB	Reality Escapade 912	JA ESC 0003		20.12.07	C M and C P Bradford		
	(Built C M Bradford - pr.no:BMAA HB/533)					Wing Farm, Longbridge Deverill	
G-ECLW	Glasflügel H201 Standard Libelle	174	BGA1637-CLW	26.11.07	R G Parker	Kirton-in-Lindsey	17. 4.08
G-ECMK	Piper PA-18-150 Super Cub	18-8209022	N45531	8. 7.08	T W Harris	(Leighton Buzzard)	20. 8.11
			111 Israel DF/AF				
G-ECOA	Bombardier DHC-8-402	4180	C-FMUE	14.12.07	Flybe Ltd	Exeter	18.12.09E
G-ECOD	Bombardier DHC-8-402	4206	C-FPEX	14. 7.08	Flybe Ltd	Exeter	20. 7.09E
			(G-ECOD), C-FPEX				
G-ECOG	Bombardier DHC-8-402	4220	C-FSRQ	17.10.08	Flybe Ltd	Exeter	16.10.09E
G-ECOH	Bombardier DHC-8-402	4221	C-FSRW	24.10.08	Flybe Ltd	Exeter	23.10.09E
G-ECOI	Bombardier DHC-8-402	4224	C-FTIE	7.11.08	Flybe Ltd	Exeter	6.11.09E
G-ECOJ	Bombardier DHC-8-402	4229	C-FTUS	9. 1.09	Flybe Ltd	Exeter	22. 1.10E
G-ECOK	Bombardier DHC-8-402	4230	C-FTUT	23. 1.09	Flybe Ltd	Exeter	
G-ECOL	Schempp-Hirth Nimbus 2	11	BGA1722-CQL	3.12.07	A D F Flintoft and L I Rigby	Crowland	6. 4.08
G-ECOM	Bombardier DHC-8-402	4233	C-FUCR	18.12.08	Flybe Ltd	Exeter	
G-ECON	Cessna 172M Skyhawk	17264490	G-JONE	18. 9.03	S J Skilton t/a Aviation Rentals	Bournemouth	18. 6.09E
	(Thielert TAE 125-01) (3-blade propeller)		N9724V		*(Operated Bournemouth Flying Club)*		
G-ECOO	Bombardier DHC-8-402	4237	C-FUOH	30. 1.09	Flybe Ltd	Exeter	29. 1.10E
G-ECOP	Bombardier DHC-8-402	4242	C-F	.09R	Flybe Ltd	Exeter	
G-ECOR	Bombardier DHC-8-402	4248	C-F	.09R	Flybe Ltd	Exeter	
G-ECOT	Bombardier DHC-8-402	4251	C-F	.09R	Flybe Ltd	Exeter	
G-ECOU	Aérospatiale AS.355F2 Ecureuil 2	5464	N4360N	15. 6.07	Rulegate Ltd	(Hamstead Marshall, Newbury)	9.11.09E
			4X-BJV, N355FT, JA6646				
G-ECOV	Bombardier DHC-8-402	4033	LN-RDM	25. 7.08	Flybe Ltd	Exeter	24. 7.09E
			N481DC, (LN-RDM), C-GFRP				
G-ECOW	Bombardier DHC-8-402	4021	LN-RDF	29. 8.08	Flybe Ltd	Exeter	28. 8.09E
			(OY-KCB, LN-RDF, (SE-LRF), (LN-RDD), C-FDHZ				
G-ECOX	Pietenpol AirCamper GN.1	WLAW.1		5.12.78	H C Cox	(Frogland Cross, Bristol)	
	(Built H C Cox - pr.no..PFA 047-10356)				*(Under construction 2001)*		
G-ECOY	Bombardier DHC-8-402	4022	LN-RDG	30. 9.08	Flybe Ltd	Exeter	30. 9.09E
			(OY-KCC), LN-RDG, C-FGNP, (OY-KCC), (SE-LRG), (SE-LOG)				
G-ECOZ	Bombardier DHC-8-402	4034	LN-RDR	31.10.08	Flybe Ltd	Exeter	
			N482DC, (SE-LRG), C-GFYI				
G-ECPA	Glasflügel H201B Standard Libelle	328	BGA1688-CPA	23. 1.08	M J Witton *"466"*	Long Mynd	6. 4.08
G-ECSW	Pilatus B4-PC11AF	22	BGA1780-CSW	8. 1.08	I.H.Keyser	Waldershare Park	9. 4.08
G-ECTF	Comper CLA.7 Swift replica	PFA 103-13078		12. 4.07	P R Cozens	Hinton-in-the-Hedges	
	(Built P R Cozens)						
G-ECUB	Piper PA-18-150 Super Cub	18-6279	G-CBFI	28.11.03	J K Padden	Breighton	10. 8.11
			SE-FDY, LN-HHA, SE-CTA, N8675D				
G-ECVB	Pietenpol AirCamper	PFA 047-13014		20. 4.00	S E Leach	(Longniddry)	26 .4.09P
	(Built K S Matcham) (Continental O-200-A)						
G-EDAV	Scottish Aviation Bulldog Series 120/121		XX534	8. 8.01	Historic Helicopters Ltd *(As "XX534:B "in RAF c/s)*		
		BH120/220				Nottingham City-Tollerton	10. 8.11
G-EDCJ	Cessna 525 CitationJet	525-0105	N305CJ	23. 1.06	Jetphase Ltd	Blackbushe	13. 2.09E
			(D-IAFD), N52081				
G-EDCK	Cessna 525 CitationJet	525-0510	N971DM	19.10.06	Air Charter Scotland (Holdings) Ltd	Glasgow	8.11.09E
			(N278CA), N971DM, N1DM, N5058J				
G-EDCL	Cessna 525A CitationJet CJ2	525A0083	N975DN	14. 8.07	Air Charter Scotland (Holdings) Ltd	Glasgow	29. 8.09E
G-EDCM	Cessna 525A CitationJet CJ2	525A0213	ES-LUX	17. 3.08	Air Charter Scotland (Holdings) Ltd	Glasgow	17. 3.09E
			N213CJ, (OE-FJR), N5244W				
G-EDCS	Raytheon Hawker 400XP	RK-487	N487XP	26. 9.06	Mountain Aviation Ltd	Edinburgh	9. 1.10E
G-EDDD	Schempp-Hirth Nimbus 2	84	BGA2025	21. 8.08	C A Mansfield *"695"*	(Bracknell)	
			G-BKPM, BGA2025				
G-EDDS	CZAW Sportcruiser	PFA 338-14660		14. 2.08	E H Bishop	(North Duffield, Selby)	
	(Built E H Bishop)						

Reg	Type	c/n	Prev id	Date	Owner/Operator	Base	Date
G-EDDV	PZL-Bielsko SZD-38A Jantar 1	B-664	BGA2041-DDV	16.10.08	G V McKirdy	Shenington	
G-EDEE	Comco Ikarus C42 FB100	0511-6769		15.11.05	Terratrip (UK) Ltd t/a Microavionics		
	(Built Aerosport Ltd)					(Horsley, Derby)	25. 1.08P
	(Landed nosewheel first at Sutton Meadows 9. 4.08, nosegear collapsed and damaged propeller and engine cowling)						
G-EDEN	SOCATA TB-10 Tobago	66		8. 1.80	N G Pistol tr Group Eden	Elstree	7. 6.09E
G-EDES	Robinson R44 Raven II	10480		8. 9.04	A D Russell	Bourn	16.10.09E
G-EDFS	Pietenpol AirCamper	PFA 047-13206		24. 3.98	D F Slaughter	(Redhill)	
	(Built D F Slaughter)						
G-EDGA	Piper PA-28-161 Warrior II	28-8516024	D-EDGA N9512N	30.8.05	The Royal Air Force Halton Aeroplane Club Ltd	RAF Halton	9. 1.10E
G-EDGE	Jodel D 150 Mascaret	111		14. 9.88	A D Edge	RAF Wyton	12. 3.09P
	(Built A D Edge - pr.no.PFA 151-11223) (Continental O-200-A)						
G-EDGI	Piper PA-28-161 Warrior II	28-7916565	D-EBGI N2941R	19. 1.99	R A Forster	Cardiff	3. 8.09E
G-EDGY	Zivko Edge 540	0018	N540JN N540SA	16.10.07	C R A Scrope	Little Gransden	
	(Built S K Andeline)						
G-EDHO	Cirrus SR20-G2	1542	N790BH	20. 2.08	Cumulus Aircraft Rentals Ltd	Bournemouth	26. 2.10E
G-EDLY	AirBorne XT912-B-Streak III-B	XT912-073		27. 4.05	M and P L Eardley	Tarn Farm, Cockerham	26. 4.09P
	(Wing s/n ST3-058)						
G-EDMC	Cyclone Airsports Pegasus Quantum 15-912	7513		11. 3.99	M W Riley *(Noted 9.07)*	Longframlington	13. 4.04P
G-EDMV	Eiriavion PIK-20D	20526	BGA2232-DMV	12.12.07	R Cochrane tr BNA MV	Bellarena	13. 4.08
G-EDNA	Piper PA-38-112 Tomahawk	38-78A0364	OY-BRG	4. 9.84	Top Cat Aviation Ltd	Barton	6. 3.09E
G-EDRE	Lindstrand LBL 90A Balloon (Hot Air)	1081		17. 3.06	Edren Homes Ltd	Gretton, Corby	9. 8.09E
G-EDRV	Van's RV-6A	PFA 181A-13451		20. 8.99	E A Yates	North Weald	15. 6.09P
	(Built E A Yates)						
G-EDTO	Reims FR172F Rocket	FR17200090	D-EDTQ	21. 3.01	N G Hopkinson	Fenland	11. 6.09E
G-EDVL	Piper PA-28R-200 Cherokee Arrow II	28R-7235245	G-BXIN D-EDVL, N1243T	30. 6.97	J S Develin and Z Islam *(Operated Sky Leisure)*	Shoreham	21. 8.09E
G-EDYO	Piper PA-32-260 Cherokee Six	32-415	D-EDYQ (N3529W), N11C	30. 3.07	A L Paton and D Bursey	Guernsey	25. 4.09E
G-EEAD	Slingsby T.65A Vega	1912	BGA2523-EAD	2.11.07	D S Smith	Sutton Bank	
G-EEBA	Slingsby T.65A Vega	1914	BGA2544-EBA	22. 4.08	M W Dickson	Portmoak	
G-EEBB	Sikorsky S-76C	760620	N81027	22. 2.07	Haughey Air Ltd	Belfast City	15. 3.09E
G-EEBD	Scheibe Bergfalke IV	5822	BGA2547-EBD D-1005	7. 1.08	D A Bell tr Mr D A Bell Syndicate	Burn	10. 7.08
G-EEBE	Issoire E-78B Silene	07	BGA2548-EBE	25. 3.08	B Broom tr Silene Group	Husbands Bosworth	
G-EEBF	Schempp-Hirth Mini Nimbus C	138	BGA2549-EBF	23. 8.07	M Pingel	Talgarth	28. 9.08
G-EEBJ	Cessna 525A CitationJet CJ2	525A0202	N719WP N202CJ	14. 9.07	Skyblue Business Services LLP	Farnborough	17. 9.09E
G-EEBK	Schempp-Hirth Mini Nimbus C	139	BGA2553-EBK AGA 2	9.10.07	G Smith and N P Frost	Parham Park	28. 9.08
G-EEBL	Schleicher ASK 13	13610	BGA2554-EBL	10. 4.08	Derbyshire and Lancashire Gliding Club Ltd	Camphill	
G-EEBM	Grob G102 Astir CS77	1843	BGA2555-EBM	17. 1.08	Yorkshire Gliding Club (Proprietary) Ltd	Sutton Bank	30. 1.08
G-EEBN	Centrair ASW 20FL	20118	BGA2556-EBN	9. 7.08	S MacArthur and R Carlisle "37"	Camphill	
G-EEBR	Glaser-Dirks DG-200/17	2-89-1706	BGA2559-EBR D-6893	4. 1.08	S R Carrigan	(Bury St Edmunds)	10. 6.08
G-EEBS	Scheibe Zugvogel IIIA	1054	BGA2560-EBS LX-CAF, D-8363	22. 5.08	I D McLeod	Challock	
G-EEBZ	Schleicher ASK 13	13614	BGA2567-EBZ	13.12.07	Booker Gliding Club Ltd "EBZ"	Wycombe Air Park	28. 9.08
G-EECC	Aerospool Dynamic WT9 UK	DY189/2007		6.11.07	C V Ellingworth	Henstridge	17.12.08P
	(Official c/n recorded as "DY/189")						
G-EECK	Slingsby T.65A Vega	1917	BGA2577-ECK	23.10.07	J P Dunnington	Portmoak	19. 1.08
G-EECO	Lindstrand LBL 25A Cloudhopper Balloon (Hot Air)	668		1. 2.00	P A and A J A Bubb	(Storrington, Pulborough)	2.10.09E
G-EEDE	Centrair ASW 20F	20128	BGA2596-EDE	4. 1.08	G M Cumner	Aston Down	11. 1.08
G-EEEK	Extra EA.300/200	1034	D-EXTT	31. 5.06	A R Willis	Nayland	1. 6.09E
G-EEER	Schempp-Hirth Mini Nimbus C	150	BGA2631-EER	30. 8.07	D J Uren	Culdrose	14. 3.08
G-EEEZ	American Champion 8KCAB Super Decathlon	1034-2007		28. 2.07	Les Wallen Manufacturing Ltd	Rochester	23. 3.09E
G-EEFA	Cameron Z-90 Balloon (Hot Air)	11076		18.12.07	A Murphy	Dunshaughlin, County Meath	31. 1.09E
G-EEFK	Centrair ASW 20FL	20140	BGA2649-EFK F-WFLZ	7.11.07	A P Balkwill and G B Monslow	Snitterfield	21. 2.08
G-EEFT	Schempp-Hirth Nimbus 2B	26	BGA2657-EFT HB-1160	31. 3.08	S A Adlard	Long Mynd	
G-EEGL	Christen Eagle II	AES/01/0353	5Y-EGL	14.12.90	M P Swoboda and S L Nicholson	Andrewsfield	31. 1.09P
	(Lycoming AEIO-360)						
G-EEGU	Piper PA-28-161 Warrior II	28-7916457	D-EEGU N2831A	7. 5.02	B C Barber	Norwich	14. 7.09E
G-EEJE	Piper PA-31 Turbo Navajo B	31-825	OH-PNG	18. 5.01	Geeje Ltd	Full Sutton	6. 8.09E
G-EEKA	Glaser-Dirks DG-200/17	2-128-1730	BGA2736-EKA	4.10.07	M J R Lindsay and P Hayward	Tibenham	5. 3.08
G-EEKY	Piper PA-28-140 Cherokee B	28-25422	OY-DFP LN-BNX, (N8218N)	20. 6.05	W J Hockenhull tr Gauntlet Holdings	RAF Waddington	9. 8.09E
G-EELS	Cessna 208 Grand Caravan	208B0619		3. 3.97	Glass Eels Ltd	Gloucestershire	15. 9.09E
G-EELT	Rolladen-Schneider LS4	4186	BGA2777-ELT	15. 1.08	K J Wood tr ELT Syndicate	Lasham	9. 3.08
G-EELY	Schleicher Ka 6CR	6536	BGA2782-ELY D-5172	6.12.07	D Webster tr K6 ELY Group	Bellarena	12. 5.08
	(BGArecords for BGA2782 including de-registration certificate for D-5172 confirms the c/n as 6485/Si: details for c/n 6536 not known)						
G-EENA	Piper PA-32R-301 Saratoga II SP	32R-8013011	C-GBBU	3.10.97	Gamit Ltd	North Weald	17. 9.08E
G-EENE	Rolladen-Schneider LS4	4271	BGA2812-ENE	9.11.07	A P C Sampson	Talgarth	28. 9.08

Reg	Type	C/n	Prev ID	Date	Owner/Operator	Location	Date
G-EENI	Europa Aviation Europa	199		28. 7.98	M P Grimshaw	Milton Keynes	
	(Built M P Grimshaw - pr.no.PFA 247-12831)						
G-EENK	Schleicher ASK 21	21106	BGA2817-ENK	18.10.07	W T Alden tr ENK Group	Aston Down	12. 4.08
G-EENN	Schempp-Hirth Nimbus 3	9	BGA2820-ENN	14. 8.07	I B Kennedy *"345"*	Usk	23. 2.08
G-EENT	Glasflügel 304	210	BGA2825-ENT	30. 7.08	M Hastings and P D Morrison *"902"*		
						RAF Weston-on-the-Green	
G-EENW	Schleicher ASW 20L	20567	BGA2828-ENW	26.11.07	J T A Hunter	Pocklington	13. 3.08
G-EENY	Gulfstream GA-7 Cougar	GA7-0094	N721G	21. 6.79	Jade Air PLC *(Noted 11.04)*	Thruxton	20. 7.03T
G-EENZ	Schleicher ASW 19B	19366	BGA2831-ENZ	26. 3.08	O L Pugh	Wycombe Air Park	
G-EERH	Ruschmeyer R90-230RG	003	D-EERH	5. 4.01	D Sadler	Aberdeen	2. 5.09E
G-EERV	Van's RV-6	PFA 181-13381	G-NESI	13. 9.01	C B Stirling	Damyn's Hall, Upminster	23. 4.09P
	(Built G Ness, P G Stewart and C B Stirling) (Lycoming O-320)						
G-EERY	Robinson R22 Beta	4128		27. 3.07	EGB (Helicopters) Ltd	Redhill	13. 5.09E
G-EESA	Europa Aviation Europa	025	G-HIIL	9. 4.96	C Deith	(Broadbridge Heath, Horsham)	1. 3.08P
	(Built C B Stirling - pr.no.PFA 247-12535) (NSI EA-81/100) *(Monowheel u/c)*						
G-EESY	Rolladen-Schneider LS4	4334	BGA2926-ESY	19.10.07	D A Parkes	Kingston Deverill	23. 6.08
G-EETG	Cessna 172Q	17275928	N913AT	30. 6.05	R W Simpson tr Tango Golf Flying Group	Redhill	22. 7.09E
			N913ER, (N65939)				
G-EEUP	SNCAN Stampe SV-4C	451	F-BCXQ	1. 9.78	A M Wajih	Redhill	20. 9.10S
G-EEUX	Schleicher ASK 18	18005	BGA2973-EUX	9.11.07	Southdown Gliding Club Ltd	Parham Park	26. 8.08
			D-3988				
G-EEVL	Grob G102 Astir CS77	1638	BGA2986-EVL	29. 4.08	M Dawson tr SA1 Syndicate *"SA 1"*	Lasham	
			PH-575				
G-EEWS	Cessna T210N Turbo Centurion	21064341	D-EBWS	28. 5.08	A N MacDonald and S M Jack	(York)	15. 9.09E
G-EEWZ	Mainair Sports Pegasus Quik	8101		16. 3.05	A Gillett	Willingale	9. 5.09P
G-EEYE	Mainair Blade 912	1313-0202-7-W1108		13. 5.02	B J Egerton	Ince Blundell	2. 6.07P
G-EEZA	Robinson R44 Raven II	10071	N71959	29. 4.03	Teleology Ltd	(Todmorden)	30. 5.09E
G-EEZO	DG Flügzeugbau DG-808C	8-398B297X59		16.10.08	A H Brown tr G-ZO Syndicate	(Scone, Perth)	11.11.09E
G-EEZR	Robinson R44 Raven II	11391		24. 8.06	AC Helicopters Ltd	(Hook)	28. 9.09E
G-EEZS	Cessna 182P Skylane	18261338	D-EEZS	8.11.99	R E Dagless Holly Hill Farm, Guist, Dereham		20. 9.09E
			N63054, D-EEZS, (N20981)				
G-EEZZ	Zenair CH.601XL Zodiac	PFA 162B-14392		4. 8.05	B Fraser	Latch Farm, Kirknewton	18.12.08P
	(Built B Fraser)						
G-EFAM	Cessna 182S Skylane	18280442	D-EFAM	7. 6.05	S P Myers tr G-EFAM Flying Group	Barton	7. 7.09E
			N7269H				
G-EFBP	Reims FR172K Hawk XP	FR1720664	D-EFBP	7. 1.04	A Webster	Manston	19. 6.09E
			PH-AXF				
G-EFCM	Piper PA-28-180 Cherokee D	28-4766	SE-FCM	16.11.07	ATC Trading Ltd	Lasham	20.11.09E
G-EFFI	Rotorway Executive 162F	7006		28. 6.06	P D Annison	(Tillingham, Southminster)	
	(Built P D Annison)						
G-EFGH	Robinson R22 Beta	1487	G-ROGG	3. 5.01	Kingsfield Helicopters Ltd	Perth	3. 8.09E
G-EFIR	Piper PA-28-181 Archer II	28-8090275	D-EFIR	5. 5.99	The Leicestershire Aero Club Ltd	Leicester	4. 8.09E
			N8179R				
G-EFJD	MBB BÖ 209-160FV Monsun	126	D-EFJD	22.10.08	E J Smith	(Truro)	
G-EFLT	Glasflügel H201B Standard Libelle	41	BGA3352-FLT	2. 6.08	J Horwood and S Gilmore Husbands Bosworth		
			D-0211				
G-EFLY	Centrair ASW 20FL	20133	BGA2650-EFL	3. 9.07	I D and J H Atherton	Tibenham	14. 9.08
G-EFOF	Robinson R22 Beta II	3605	N73323	19. 5.04	N T Burton tr NT Burton Aviation	Costock	16. 7.09E
G-EFSM	Slingsby T 67M-260 Firefly	2072	G-BPLK	16. 7.92	The Cambridge Aero Club Ltd	Cambridge	13. 6.09E
G-EFTE	Bölkow BÖ.207	218	D-EFTE	4. 1.90	R L Earl and B Morris		
						Quebec Farm, Knook, Warminster	10. 7.09E
G-EFTF	Aérospatiale AS.350B Ecureuil	1847	G-CWIZ	1. 4.03	T J French	(Cumnock)	28. 5.09E
			CS-HDF, G-DJEM, G-ZBAC, G-SEBI, G-BMCU				
G-EFUN	E-Plane	001		2. 7.08	A W Bishop and G Castelli	Cambridge	
	(Built A W Bishop and G Castelli)						
G-EGAG	SOCATA TB-20 Trinidad	1675	D-EGAG (3)	29. 8.06	D and E Booth	Sherburn-in-Elmet	8. 9.09E
G-EGAL	Christen Eagle II	0042-86	SE-XMU	11. 3.96	J H Penfold tr Eagle Partners	Shoreham	25. 6.09P
	(Lycoming AEIO-360)						
G-EGAN	Enstrom F-28A-UK	103	G-SERA	24. 5.05	Helimove Ltd	Ellough, Beccles	13. 7.09E
			G-BAHU, EI-BDF, G-BAHU				
G-EGBS	Van's RV-9A	90933		13. 4.05	D M Johnstone tr Shobdon RV-9A Group Shobdon		19.8.09P
	(Built D M Johnstone, A and C Price, M Rowland, M Sweeny and J Turner, pr no PFA 320-14234) (Wilksch WAM-120)						
G-EGEE	Cessna 310Q	310Q0040	G-AZVY	14.11.83	R C Devine	Hawarden	22. 3.08E
			SE-FKV, N7540Q				
G-EGEG	Cessna 172R Skyhawk	17280894	N7262H	4. 7.00	C D Lever	Elstree	20.12.09E
G-EGEL	Christen Eagle II	S 308	N388AG	4. 2.91	P Miny tr G-EGEL Flying Group		
	(Built MLP Aviation Ltd) (Lycoming AEIO-360)		G-EGEL			(Riehen, Switzerland)	5. 8.09P
G-EGGI	Comco Ikarus C42 FB UK	0112-6442?		18. 4.02	A G and G J Higgins	Ashby Lane, Bitteswell	22. 1.10P
	(Built A G and G J Higgins - pr.no.PFA 322-13872) (Kit no.not confirmed) (Struck hedge on go-around 6. 5.08 and extensively damaged)						
G-EGGS	Robin DR.400-180 Régent	1443		15.11.79	R Foot	Lasham	12. 7.09E
G-EGHB	Ercoupe 415D	1876	N3414G	1. 9.95	P G Vallance	Rochester	29. 9.09S
	(Continental O-200-A)		N99253, NC99253				
G-EGHH	Hawker Hunter F 58	41H-697450	Swiss AF J-4083	4. 7.95	Heritage Aviation Developments Ltd *(On rebuild 2007)*		
						(Mursley, Milton Keynes)	
G-EGIL	Christen Eagle II	BOYD-0001	N21SB	7.11.07	Smoke On Go Ltd	Shawbury	24. 4.09P
	(Built S F Boyd) (Lycoming AEIO-360)						
G-EGJA	SOCATA TB-20 Trinidad	1101	N2807D	13.12.90	D A Williamson	Elstree	20.12.08E
G-EGKE	SOCATA Rallye 180TS Galérien	3325	D-EGKE	18. 6.08	T Slater tr Suffolk Soaring Tug Group	Rougham	16.10.09E
G-EGLE	Christen Eagle II	F 0053		30. 3.81	D Thorpe tr Eagle Group	North Weald	27. 5.09P
	(Built Airmore Aviation) (Lycoming AEIO-360)						
G-EGLG	Piper PA-31 Turbo Navajo C	31-7812103	N45TY	8. 9.06	H Merkado	Panshanger	29.11.08E
			4X-CCY, N36SG, N27703, G-OATC, G-OJPW, G-BGCC, N27703				
G-EGLL	Piper PA-28-161 Cherokee Warrior II		G-BLEJ	17. 3.06	Airways Aero Associations Ltd Wycombe Air Park		7. 6.09E
		28-7816257	N2194M		*(Operated British Airways Flying Club)*		

G-EGLS	Piper PA-28-181 Archer III	2843348	N4187C	5. 6.00	O Sylvester	(Grantham)	16. 7.09E
G-EGLT	Cessna 310R II	310R1874	G-BHTV	9. 9.93	Reconnaissance Ventures Ltd	Coventry	10. 4.09E
			N1EU, (N3206M)				
G-EGNA	Diamond DA42 Twin Star	42.149		17. 7.06	Egnatia Aviation Ltd Kavala International, Greece		6. 8.09E
G-EGNS	Gulfstream Aerospace Gulfstream V-SP	5167	N967GA	22. 1.08	Pobedy Corporation	Ronaldsway	21. 1.10E
	(Gulfstream 550)						
G-EGPG	Piper PA-18-135 Super Cub	18-3569	N719CS	3. 4.06	G Cormack	Easter Polder Farm, Thornhill	8. 6.11
			G-BWUC, SX-ASM, EI-181, I-EIYB, MM54-2369, 54-2369				
G-EGSJ	Avtech Jabiru J400	PFA 325-14618	G-MGRK	29. 8.07	B Greathead tr Seething Jabiru Group	Seething	12. 5.09P
	(Built M R Tingle) (Builders amended to H Daines, B Greathead, S Hiscox and M Page 12.12.08)						
G-EGTB	Piper PA-28-161 Cherokee Warrior II		G-BPWA	21. 1.04	Airways Aero Association Ltd Wycombe Air Park		24. 6.09E
		28-7816074	N47450		(Operated British Airways Flying Club)		
G-EGTC	Robinson R44 Raven	1357	G-CCNK	14. 3.05	Beds Heli Services Ltd	Sywell	8. 2.09E
G-EGTR	Piper PA-28-161 Cadet	2841281	G-BRSI	25. 4.98	Stars Fly Ltd	Elstree	14. 2.09E
			N92001				
G-EGUL	Christen Eagle II	Argence 0001	G-FRYS	19. 1.93	S Shutt (Noted 9.07)	RAF Coningsby	3. 6.08P
	(Built Argence EA) (Lycoming AEIO-360)		N66EA				
	(Destroyed by fire at Seething after hitting crop-sprayer on approach 29.10.08 with one fatality)						
G-EGUR	SAN Jodel D 140B Mousquetaire II	52	D-EGUR	9. 1.04	S H Williams Hawksbridge Farm, Oxenhope		22. 9.07P
G-EGWN	American Champion 7ECA Citabria Aurora			4.12.07	The Royal Air Force Halton Aeroplane Club Ltd		
		1399-2007				RAF Halton	18.12.09E
G-EHAV	Glasflügel H201B Standard Libelle	40	BGA3796-HAV	12.11.07	A Liran and M Truelove "J34"	Rivar Hill	3. 5.08
			HB-950				
G-EHBJ	CASA 1-131E Jungmann Series 2000	2150	Spanish AF	19. 7.90	E P Howard (Also carries "E 3B-550")		
			E3B-550			Airfield Farm, Hardwick	15. 9.09P
G-EHCB	Schempp-Hirth Nimbus 3DT	47	BGA3827-HCB	28. 2.07	H A Torode tr G-EHCB Group "754"	Lasham	7. 5.08
G-EHCC	PZL-Bielsko SZD-50-3 Puchacz	B-2048	BGA3829-HCC	27. 3.08	DJ Marpole tr Heron Gliding Club RNAS Yeovilton		
G-EHCZ	Schleicher K 8B	8114	BGA3850-HCZ	20. 2.08	The Surrey Hills Gliding Club Ltd	Kenley	4. 9.08
			D-4675				
G-EHDS	CASA 1-131E Jungmann Series 2000	2108	G-DUDS	21. 2.05	C W N and A A M Huke	Manor Farm, Dinton	3. 6.00P
	(Enma Tigre G-1V-B)		D-EHDS, Spanish AF E3B-512				
G-EHGF	Piper PA-28-181 Cherokee Archer II		D-EHGF	23.10.00	G P Robinson	Netherthorpe	15. 7.09E
		28-7790188	N9534N				
G-EHIC	SAN Jodel D 140B Mousquetaire II	53	D-EHIC	20.10.04	M Tolson and D W Smith	RAF Halton	9. 3.11E
G-EHLX	Piper PA-28-181 Archer II	28-8090317	D-EHLX	5.11.99	ASG Leasing Ltd	Guernsey	13. 1.10E
			N8218S				
G-EHMF	Isaacs Fury II	PFA 011-14109		8.10.03	M A Farrelly	(Frodsham)	
	(Built M A Farrelly)						
G-EHMJ	Beech S35 Bonanza	D-7879	D-EHMJ	12. 1.99	A J Daley	Gamston	16. 3.09E
G-EHMM	Robin DR.400-180R Remorqueur	867	D-EHMM (1)	10.12.84	Booker Gliding Club Ltd Wycombe Air Park		20. 5.09E
G-EHMS	MD Helicopters MD.900 Explorer	900-00068	N3212K	12. 7.00	Virgin HEMS (London) Ltd	Denham	20.10.08E
					(All-red Virgin c/s operating London Ambulance Service)		
G-EHTT	Schleicher ASW 20CL	20627	BGA4196-HTT	22. 4.08	M Corcoran tr HTT Syndicate	Camphill	
			D-2410				
G-EHUP	Aérospatiale SA.341G Gazelle 1	1407	F-GIJR	3.10.97	M W Helicopters Ltd	Stapleford	22. 3.07T
			N869GT, N869, N49523				
G-EHXP	Rockwell Commander 112A	227	D-EHXP	27. 1.00	A L Stewart	Wolverhampton	29. 4.09E
			N1227J				
G-EIBM	Robinson R22 Beta	1993	G-BUCL	25. 3.94	HJS Helicopters Ltd Lower Baads, Peterculter		6. 3.09E
G-EICK	Cessna 172S Skyhawk	172S10426	N12173	13. 7.07	Centenary Flying Group Ltd Cork, County Cork		5. 8.09E
G-EIER	Marganski Swift S-1	119	BGA4915-JZP	11. 2.08	C Cain and D Poll	(Austria)	6. 8.08
			F-CIAB				
G-EIGG	British Aerospace Jetstream Series 3102	773	SE-LGH	8. 5.07	Highland Airways Ltd	Inverness	14. 5.09E
			OY-SVO, C-FAMK, G-31-773				
G-EIKY	Europa Aviation Europa	054		27. 9.94	J D Milbank tr Europa G-EIKY Group		
	(Built J D Milbank - pr.no.PFA 247-12634) (Monowheel u/c)					Longside, Peterhead	28. 7.09P
G-EIRE	Cessna T182T Turbo Skylane	T18208049	N3500U	24. 7.01	J Byrne	Englefield	26. 4.09E
G-EISG	Beech A36 Bonanza	E-3212	N2533J	2. 4.07	R J and B Howard	Sherburn-in-Elmet	30. 5.09E
			(G-EISG), N326R				
G-EISO	SOCATA MS.892A Rallye Commodore 150		G-EISO	23. 1.01	T E H Simmons tr G-EISO Group	Sandown	9.10.08E
		10563	F-BNSO				
G-EITE	Luscombe 8F Silvaire	3407	N71980	27. 7.88	S R H Martin	Manor Farm, Haddenham	7 12.09P
	(Continental C90)						
G-EIWT	Reims Cessna FR182 Skylane RG II		D-EIWT	28. 1.86	P P D Howard-Johnston	Glenrothes	19. 4.09E
		FR18200052	OO-BLI				
G-EIZO	Eurocopter EC.120B Colibri	1120	N20GH	31.12.04	R M Bailey	Addiston Mains, Dalmahoy	2. 3.09E
			D-HSUN				
G-EJAE	Glaser-Dirks DG-200	22678	BGA4352-JAE	7. 2.08	D L P H Waller	RAF Keevil	24. 3.08
			HB-1443				
G-EJAR	Airbus A319-111	2412	D-AVYV	7. 3.05	EasyJet Airline Company Ltd London Stansted		3. 8.09E
G-EJEL	Cessna 550 Citation II	550-0643	N747CR	19.12.01	B Elliott	Leeds-Bradford	8. 1.10E
			N643MC, PT-ODW, N13091, (N1259S)				
G-EJGO	Moravan Zlin Z-226T Trener Spezial	199	D-EJGO	7. 8.85	S K T and C M Neofytou	Breighton	3.11.09E
			OK-MHB				
G-EJJB	Airbus A319-111	2380	D-AVWV	1. 2.05	EasyJet Airline Company Ltd London Stansted		5. 8.09E
G-EJMG	Cessna F150H	F150-0301	D-EJMG	27. 4.98	P R Booth	Durham Tees Valley	20.12.09E
	(Built Reims Aviation SA)						
G-EJOC	Aérospatiale AS.350B Ecureuil	1465	G-GEDS	21.12.94	E and S Vandyk t/a Leisure and Retail Helicopters		
			G-HMAN, G-SKIM, G-BIVP			Oxford	8. 7.09E
G-EJRC	Robinson R44 Raven II	11605		29. 1.07	E J R Canvin t/a Perry Farming Company		
						Conington	5. 3.09E
G-EJRS	Piper PA-28-161 Cadet	2841115	D-EJRS	5. 5.04	Carlisle Flight Training Ltd	Carlisle	5. 2.09E
			N9175X				
G-EJTC	Robinson R44 Clipper II	10623		31. 1.05	N Parkhouse Chelwood Gate, Haywards Heath		23. 3.09E

Reg	Type	C/n	Previous identity	Date	Owner/Operator	Location	Expiry
G-EKEY	Schleicher ASW 20CL	20840	BGA5044-KEY D-3171	11. 1.08	K W Payne	Husbands Bosworth	2. 5.08
G-EKIM	Alpi Pioneer 300 *(Built M Langmead and M Elliott)*	PFA 330-14491		11. 5.06	M Langmead and M Elliott	Little Rissington	4. 6.09P
G-EKIR	Piper PA-28-161 Cadet	2841157	SE-KIR (SE-KII)	17. 6.02	Aeros Leasing Ltd *(Operated Aeros Flying Club)* Gloucestershire		11. 8.09E
G-EKKL	Piper PA-28-161 Warrior II	28-8416087	D-EKKL N43588	24. 3.99	Apollo Aviation Advisory Ltd	Shoreham	11. 5.09E
G-EKKO	Robinson R44 Raven	0821		18. 7.00	W A Hawkeswood	(Knowle, Solihull)	11.07.09E
G-EKMN	Moravan Zlin Z-242L	0652	SE-KMN	15. 5.01	R C Poolman	Gloucestershire	23. 9.07T
G-EKOS	Reims Cessna FR182 Skylane RG II	FR18200017	D-EKOS	15. 7.98	S Charlton	Sherburn-in-Elmet	28. 9.09E
G-EKYD	Robinson R44 Raven II	10081		20. 5.03	MDL Air and Leisure Ltd	(Sawston, Cambridge)	12. 6.09E
G-ELAM	Piper PA-30 Twin Comanche B	30-1477	N26PJ 14.10.04 G-BAWU, (G-BAWV), 9J-RFW, ZS-FAM, N8332Y		Hangar 39 Ltd	North Weald	27.11.09E
G-ELDR	Piper PA-32-260 Cherokee Six	32-7400027	SE-GBK	21. 1.03	Elder Aviation Ltd	Oxford	14. 4.09E
G-ELEE	Cameron Z-105 Balloon (Hot Air)	4882		11. 7.00	D Eliot	Aberdeen	9. 8.09E
G-ELEN	Robin DR.400-180 Régent	2363		16. 9.97	N R and E Foster	Biggin Hill	21. 7.09E
G-ELIS	Piper PA-34-200T Seneca II	34-8070265	G-BOPV N82323	11. 9.03	Bristol Flying Centre Ltd	Bristol	19. 8.09E
G-ELIT	Bell 206L LongRanger	45091	SE-HTK N2652	28. 7.99	Simon Wright Homes Ltd	(Aylesford, Maidstone)	18. 8.09E
G-ELIZ	Denney Kitfox Model 2 *(Built A J Ellis - pr.no.PFA 172-11835)*	717		19. 7.90	A J Ellis *(Damaged Brighstone, Isle of Wight 10. 5.93)*	(Ryde, Isle of Wight)	5.11.93P
G-ELKA	Christen Eagle II *(Built R R James c/n JAMES-0001)* *(Lycoming AEIO-360)*	0001	N121DJ 18.10.94 N1DJ, N99DJ		J T Matthews	Old Buckenham	22. 5.09E
G-ELKS	Avid Speed Wing Mk.4 *(Built H S Elkins)* *(Jabiru 2200A)*	PFA 189-13109		6. 1.98	H S Elkins	(Hebron, Whitland)	9. 7.09E
G-ELLA	Piper PA-32R-301 Saratoga IIHP	3246050	N9279Q 13. 8.96 G-ELLA		C C W Hart	Old Buckenham	15. 5.09E
G-ELLE	Cameron N-90 Balloon (Hot Air)	4498		11. 1.99	D J Stagg	Spixworth, Norwich	15. 6.07A
G-ELLI	Bell 206B-3 JetRanger III	4231	D-HMOF	24. 6.97	Italian Clothes Ltd	Hawarden	16. 7.09E
G-ELMH	North American AT-6D-NT Harvard III	88-16336	FAP1662 22. 7.92 EZ341, 42-84555		M Hammond *(As "42-84555:EP-H" in USAAC c/s)* "Fools Rush-In"	Airfield Farm, Hardwick	31. 5.09P
G-ELMO	Robinson R44 Raven II	10509		7.10.04	Locumlink Associates Ltd	(Ballsbridge, Dublin)	11.12.08E
G-ELOA	Cessna 560XL Citation Excel	560-5106	HB-VND 18. 7.07 N506AM, N5221Y		TAG Aviation (UK) Ltd	Farnborough	18. 7.09E
G-ELSE	Diamond DA.42 Twin Star	42.114	OE-VPY	29. 6.06	R Swann	Bournemouth	16. 7.09E
G-ELSI	Air Création Tanarg 912S/iXess 15	FLT.001		19. 1.06	D Daniel	Weston Zoyland	19. 6.08P
	(Built D Daniel - pr.no.BMAA HB/466 being Flylight kit comprising Trike s/n T05069 and Wing s/n A05146-5134)						
G-ELTE	Agusta A109A II	7269	G-BWZI, 13. 2.06 OH-HAD, N109AK		Henfield Lodge Aviation Ltd	Redhill	12. 3.09E
G-ELUN	Robin DR.400-180R Remorqueur	1102	D-ELUN 29. 5.02 I-ALSA		P Harper-Little and I A Lane tr Cotswold DR.400 Syndicate	Kemble	5. 5.09E
G-ELUT	Piper PA-28R-200 Cherokee Arrow II	28R-7435009	D-ELUT 21.11.03 N56514		Green Arrow Europe Ltd	Goodwood	1. 3.09E
G-ELZN	Piper PA-28-161 Warrior II	28-8416078	D-ELZN 20. 7.99 N9579N		M Stott tr ZN Flying Group	Old Buckenham	22. 9.09E
G-ELZY	Piper PA-28-161 Warrior II	28-8616027	D-ELZY 13. 4.99 N9095Z, (N163AV), N9641N		Goodwood Road Racing School Ltd *(Operated Goodwood Flying Club)*	Goodwood	12. 6.09E
G-EMAA	Eurocopter EC.135 T2	0448		17. 1.06	Bond Air Services Ltd *(Operated County Air Ambulance)*	Cosford	26. 3.09E
G-EMAX	Piper PA-31-350 Navajo Chieftain	31-7952029	N276CT 8.12.98 SE-KKP, Swedish Navy 54202, SE-KKP, LN-PAI		Atlantic Bridge Aviation Ltd	Lydd	6. 7.09E
G-EMBC	Embraer EMB-145EU	145024	PT-SYU	1.10.97	Port One Ltd *(Stored 6.08)*	Exeter	8.10.08E
G-EMBI	Embraer EMB-145EU	145126	PT-SDD	23. 4.99	Flybe Ltd	Exeter	22. 4.09E
G-EMBJ	Embraer EMB-145EU	145134	PT-SDL	24. 5.99	Flybe Ltd	Exeter	26. 5.09E
G-EMBK	Embraer EMB-145EU	145167		26. 8.99	Flybe Ltd	Exeter	25. 8.09E
G-EMBL	Embraer EMB-145EU	145177	PT-SEY	4.10.99	Flybe Ltd	Exeter	3.10.10E
G-EMBM	Embraer EMB-145EU	145196	PT-SGL	22.11.99	Flybe Ltd	Exeter	21.11.09E
G-EMBN	Embraer EMB-145EU	145201	PT-SGQ	13. 1.00	British Midland Regional Ltd	Aberdeen	12. 1.10E
G-EMBP	Embraer EMB-145EU	145300	PT-SKR	25. 8.00	Flybe Ltd	Exeter	24. 8.09E
G-EMBU	Embraer EMB-145EU	145458	PT-SVD	22. 6.01	Flybe Ltd	Exeter	21. 6.09E
G-EMBV	Embraer EMB-145EU	145482	PT-SXB	12. 9.01	Flybe Ltd	Exeter	11. 9.09E
G-EMBW	Embraer EMB-145EU	145546	PT-SZJ	19.12.01	Flybe Ltd	Exeter	18.12.09E
G-EMBX	Embraer EMB-145EU	145573	PT-SBJ	21. 3.02	Flybe Ltd	Exeter	20. 3.09E
G-EMBY	Embraer EMB-145EU	145617	PT-SDF	17. 7.02	Flybe Ltd	Exeter	16. 7.09E
G-EMCA	Commander Aircraft Commander 114B	14661	D-EMCA	23. 7.04	S Roberts	Oaksey Park	21. 8.09E
G-EMDM	Diamond DA.40 Diamond Star	40.009	OE-KPO 7.10.02 OE-VPO		D J Munson	Oxford	20.10.09E
G-EMEL	Robinson R44 Raven I	1726		11. 6.07	AGF Aviation Ltd	Welwyn	12. 7.09E
G-EMER	Piper PA-34-200 Seneca	34-7350002	N3081T	29. 7.91	Haimoss Ltd *(Operated Old Sarum Flying Club)*	Old Sarum	27. 2.09E
G-EMHB	Agusta A109E Power	11111	YR-TIA 24. 3.05 HB-ZDL		FB Leasing Ltd	RAF Shawbury	6. 4.09E
G-EMHC	Agusta A109E Power	11721		13. 2.08	Looporder Ltd, t/a East Midlands Helicopters	Costock	12. 2.09E
G-EMHH	Aérospatiale AS.355F2 Ecureuil 2	5169	G-BYKH 3. 8.99 SX-HNP, VR-CCM, N57967		Hancocks Holdings Ltd	Costock	26. 7.09E
G-EMHK	MBB BÖ.209 Monsun 150FV	101	G-BLRD 23. 2.06 D-EBOA, (OE-AHM), D-EBOA		T A Crone	Cranfield	26. 2.10E
G-EMID	Eurocopter EC.135 P2+	0524		20.12.06	East Midlands Air Support Unit	Sibbertoft	29. 7.11

G-EMIN	Europa Aviation Europa	083		1. 3.94	S A Lamb	Rochester	12.11.09P
	(Built G M Clarke and E W Gladstone - pr.no.PFA 247-12673) (Monowheel u/c)						
G-EMJA	CASA 1-131E Jungmann Series 2000	013	(Spanish AF)	2. 9.94	N J Radford	Bicester	13.10.09P
	(Built P J Brand - pr.no.PFA 242-12340) (Enma Tigre G-IV-B) (Composite from Spanish spares imported in 1991)						
G-EMLE	Evektor EV-97 Eurostar	PFA 315-14251		9. 6.04	A R White	Scotland Farm, Hook	21. 7.09P
	(Built A R White)						
G-EMLI	Bombardier Canadair CL-600-2B16	5383	N383DT	8. 5.07	A J Walter (Aviation) Ltd	London Gatwick	8. 5.09E
	(CL-604 Challenger)		C-GLYK				
G-EMLS	Cessna T210L Turbo Centurion	21060094	D-EMLS	11. 5.07	I K F Simcock	Denham	12. 7.09E
			(G-BCJJ), N59107				
G-EMLY	Cyclone Airsports Pegasus Quantum 15-912			30. 6.99	S J Reid	Old Sarum	27. 6.09P
		7531					
G-EMMI	Robinson R44 Clipper II	10075		6. 6.03	Hub Of The Wheel Ltd	(Offham, West Malling)	27. 6.09E
G-EMMM	Diamond DA.40 Star	40.753		12. 4.07	A J Leigh	Gamston	4. 6.09E
G-EMMS	Piper PA-38-112 Tomahawk	38-78A0526	OO-TKT	14. 9.79	Ravenair Aircraft Ltd	Liverpool-John Lennon	18. 3.09E
			N4414E				
G-EMMY	Rutan VariEze	577		21. 8.78	M J Tooze	Biggin Hill	13. 3.09P
	(Built M J Tooze - pr.no.PFA 074-10222) (Lycoming O-235)						
G-EMSB	Piper PA-22-160 Tri-Pacer	22-7602	G-ARHU	13. 8.03	M S Bird	Pepperbox, Salisbury	10.12.98
			N3726Z				
G-EMSI	Europa Aviation Europa	191		24. 1.95	P W L Thomas	(Askham Bryan, York)	
	(Built P W L Thomas - pr.no.PFA 247-12817) (Tri-gear u/c)						
G-EMSL	Piper PA-28-161 Warrior II	28-8216117	G-TSFT	20. 2.02	Falcon Flying Services Ltd	Biggin Hill	7. 3.09E
			G-BLDJ, N9632N				
G-EMSY	de Havilland DH.82A Tiger Moth	83666	G-ASPZ	27. 6.91	B E Micklewright tr G-EMSY Group	Old Sarum	11. 3.10P
	(Built Morris Motors Ltd)		D-EDUM, T7356		(Rebuilt with parts ex OO-MOT)		
G-ENBD	Lindstrand LBL 120A Balloon (Hot Air)	1184		7.11.07	A Nimmo	Dubai, United Arab Emirates	12.11.08E
G-ENCE	Partenavia P68B	141	G-OROY	1. 6.84	J J H and A E Hanna t/a Bicton Aviation	Exeter	24.10.09E
			G-BFSU				
G-ENEE	CFM Streak Shadow	K 280		14. 8.00	N R Beale	Deppers Bridge, Southam	4. 6.04P
	(Built T Green - pr.no.PFA 206-13628) (Rotax 912-UL)						
G-ENES	Bell 206B-3 JetRanger III	4601	C-FFQR	16.10.06	Eastern Atlantic Helicopters Ltd	Shoreham	20.11.09E
G-ENGO	Steen Skybolt	PFA 064-13429		15.11.00	R G Fulton	Lower Wasing Farm, Brimpton	12. 5.09P
	(Built C Docherty and R G Fulton)				(Undercarriage collapsed during circuits at Lower Wasing Farm 31.5.08)		
G-ENGR	Head AX8-105 Balloon (Hot-Air)	380		4. 8.08	D C Mitchell tr Royal Engineers Balloon Club "Sapper"		
						Warminster	23.11.09E
G-ENHP	Enstrom 480B	5084		17. 8.05	H J Pelham	Cleeves Farm, Chilmark, Salisbury	21. 9.09E
G-ENIA	Staaken Z-21 Flitzer	PFA 223-14447		20.10.08	A F Wankowski	(Stowmarket)	
	(Built A F Wankowski)						
G-ENIE	Nipper T 66 Series 3	PFA 025-10214		17. 3.78	R W Chatterton	Griffins Farm, Temple Bruer	18. 6.09P
	(Built A J Waller) (Volkswagen 1800))						
G-ENII	Reims Cessna F172M Skyhawk II	F17201352	PH-WAG	18. 1.79	J Howley	Fenland	23. 4.09E
			(D-EDQM)				
G-ENIO	Pitts S-2C	6083	N31PS	22. 9.08	Advanced Flying (London) Ltd "Scarlett O'Hara"		
	(Built Aviat Aircraft Inc)					Redhill	21.10.09E
G-ENNA	Piper PA-28-161 Warrior II	28-7916060	G-ESFT	1. 5.90	Falcon Flying Services Ltd	Rochester	11. 5.09E
			G-ENNA, N22065				
G-ENNI	Robin R3000/180	128	F-GGJA	5.10.99	I F Doubtfire	Goodwood	24.10.09E
G-ENNK	Cessna 172S Skyhawk SP	172S8538	N72729	15. 9.00	Pooler-LMT Ltd	Lower Grounds Farm, Shirlowe	11.11.09E
G-ENNY	Cameron V-77 Balloon (Hot Air)	1399		1.12.86	J H Dobson	Streatley, Reading	25.10.05A
G-ENOA	Cessna F172F	F172-0138	G-ASZW	2. 9.81	M K Acors	King's Farm, Thurrock	9. 1.10E
	(Built Reims Aviation SA)						
G-ENRE	Avtech Jabiru UL-450	xxxx		28. 6.01	P R Turton	Old Sarum	27.11.09P
	(Built J C Harris - pr.no.PFA 274A-13755)						
G-ENRI	Lindstrand LBL 105A Balloon (Hot Air)	294		4. 8.95	P G Hall (Henry Numatic Vacuum Cleaners titles)		
						Meanwood, Chard	5. 8.04T
G-ENRY	Cameron N-105 Balloon (Hot Air)	2096		26. 9.89	P G and G R Hall "Henry" (To Balloon Preservation Group 2.04)		
						Petworth	7. 7.94T
G-ENST	CZAW Sportcruiser	LAA 338-14769		28. 1.08	L M Radcliffe, C Slater and D G Price		
	(Built L M Radcliffe, C Slater and D G Price)				(Wolverhampton, Milton Keynes and Aylesbury)		
G-ENTS	Van's RV-9A	PFA 320-13917		6. 1.04	L G Johnson	(Washington)	
	(Built L G Johnson)						
G-ENTT	Reims Cessna F152 II	F15201750	G-BHHI	9.11.93	C and A R Hyett	Blackbushe	27. 4.09E
			(PH-CBA)				
G-ENTW	Reims Cessna F152 II	F15201479	G-BFLK	21. 1.93	Firecrest Aviation Ltd	Elstree	10.12.08E
G-ENVO	MBB BÖ.105CBS-4	S.593	SX-HCK	29. 2.08	F C Owen	(Burnley)	16. 4.09E
			D-HDQP, Sweden 73, D-HDQP				
G-ENVY	Mainair Blade	1260-1000-7-W1054		20.12.00	P J Lomax and J A Robinson	St Michaels	15.12.09P
	(Rotax 912-UL)						
G-ENZO	Cameron Z-105 Balloon (Hot Air)	10914		21. 9.06	Garelli VI SpA (IVECO Garelli VI titles)		
						Mondovi, Italy	9. 6.09E
G-EODE	Piper PA-46-350P Malibu Mirage	4636217	N45YM	30. 6.06	H J D S Baioes	Cranfield	25. 7.09E
			G-BYLM				
G-EOFF	Taylor JT.2 Titch	PFA 060-10319		6. 7.78	J R Faulkner	Derby	
	(Built G Wylde)						
G-EOFS	Europa Aviation Europa	296		22. 7.98	A Fletcher and G Plenderleith	(Lowestoft)	24. 9.09P
	(Built G T Leedham - pr.no.PFA 247-13033) (Rotax 914-UL) (Tri-gear u/c)						
G-EOFW	Cyclone Airsports Pegasus Quantum 15-9127582			15.10.99	C D Livingstone tr G-EOFW Microlight Group		
						Enstone	14.10.08P
G-EOHL	Cessna 182L Skylane	18259279	D-EOHL	4. 3.99	G B Dale and M C Terris	(Armagh)	10. 7.09E
			N70505				
G-EOID	Aeroprakt A22-L Foxbat	LAA 317A-14836		3.11.08	M D Northwood	(Chipping Norton)	
	(Built M D Northwood)						

G-EOIN	Zenair CH.701UL STOL	PFA 187-13490			19.11.99	D G Palmer	Mintlaw, Peterhead	8. 1.10P
	(Built I M Donnelly) (Verner SVS1400)							
G-EOLD	Piper PA-28-161 Warrior II	28-8516030	D-EOLD	31. 3.00		Goodwood Road Racing Company Ltd	Goodwood	19. 6.09E
			N4390F, N9531N			*(Operated Goodwood Flying Club)*		
G-EOLX	Cessna 172N Skyhawk II	17269099	G-BOLX	12. 4.06		Westward Airways (Lands End) Ltd	St Just	18.12.09E
			N734TK					
G-EOMA	Airbus A330-243	265	F-WWKU	26. 4.99		Monarch Airlines Ltd	Luton	25. 4.09E
G-EOMK	Robin DR.400-180 Régent	1267	D-EOMK	22.11.07		F Warin	Nympsfield	
G-EORG	Piper PA-38-112 Tomahawk	38-78A0427	N9734N	18. 9.78		P W Carlton and D W Breden	Durham Tees Valley	11. 8.09E
	(Rebuilt with new fuselage: old one stored 9.96)							
G-EORJ	Europa Aviation Europa	347			23. 7.99	P E George	Hall Farm, Shenstone	12. 7.07P
	(Built P E George - pr.no.PFA 247-13139) (Monowheel u/c)							
G-EPAR	Robinson R22 Beta II	2781			26. 2.98	J W Ramsbottom tr Jepar Rotorcraft		
							Higher Barn Farm, Houghton	12. 6.09E
G-EPDI	Cameron N-77 Balloon (Hot Air)	370			25. 1.78	R Moss *"Pegasus"*	Banchory	29. 6.91A
G-EPIC	Avtech Jabiru UL-450	xxxx			4.11.03	T Chadwick	(Market Weighton)	
	(Built T Chadwick - pr.no.PFA 274A-14125)							
G-EPOC	Avtech Jabiru UL-450	0290			9. 6.04	S Cope	(Laceby)	
	(Built S Cope - pr.no.PFA 274A-13531)							
G-EPOX	Aero Designs Pulsar XP	PFA 202-12355			27. 4.94	D R Stansfield	(Horbling, Sleaford)	30. 5.08P
	(Built W A Stewart and K F Farey) (Tri-cycle u/c)							
G-EPSN	UltraMagic M-105 Balloon (Hot Air)	105/159			7. 1.08	G Everett *(Epson titles)*	Sandway, Maidstone	30.1.10E
G-EPTR	Piper PA-28R-200 Cherokee Arrow II		D-EPTR	26. 5.98		ACS Aviation Ltd	Perth	17. 8.09E
		28R-7235090	OH-PTR, (SE-KVF), N4558T					
G-ERBL	Robinson R22 Beta II	2711			26. 6.97	G V Maloney	(Cavan, County Cavan)	6.11.09E
G-ERCO	Ercoupe 415D	3210	N2585H	7. 4.93		A R and M V Tapp	Manston	31. 8.08S
	(Continental C85)		NC2585H					
G-ERDA	Staaken Z-21A Flitzer	PFA 223-13947			15. 1.03	J Cresswell	Woodcock Lane, Hordle	6. 6.09P
	(Built J Cresswell)							
G-ERDS	de Havilland DH.82A Tiger Moth	85028	ZS-BCU	27. 7.94		W A Gerdes	(Florida, US)	11. 7 10
	(Floatplane)		SAAF 2267, T6741					
G-ERFS	Piper PA-28-161 Warrior II	28-8216051	D-EPFS	29.11.02		Cunning Plan Development Ltd	Old Sarum	11. 3.09E
			N84570			*(Operated Old Sarum Flying School)*		
G-ERIC	Rockwell Commander 112TC	13010	SE-GSA	26. 9.78		Atomchoice Ltd	Cranfield	10. 5.09E
G-ERIK	Cameron N-77 Balloon (Hot Air)	1753			18. 5.88	T M Donnelly *"Norsewind"* Sprotbrough, Doncaster		24. 2.00A
G-ERIS	Hughes 369D *(Hughes 500)*	11-0871D	G-PJMD	1. 3.96		R J Howard	Sherburn-in-Elmet	6. 5.09E
	(Modified to 500E standard)		G-BMJV, N1110S					
G-ERIW	Staaken Z-21 Flitzer	PFA 223-13834			9. 1.04	R I Wasey	Calcot	8. 6.07P
	(Built R I Wasey) (Volkswagen 2180)							
G-ERJA	Embraer EMB-145EP	145229			25. 2.00	Flybe Ltd	Exeter	24. 2.09E
G-ERJC	Embraer EMB-145EP	145253	PT-SIN	25. 4.00		Flybe Ltd	Exeter	25. 4.09E
G-ERMO	ARV Aviation ARV-1 Super 2	018	G-BMWK	7. 1.87		S Vince	(Bradfield, North Walsham)	31. 8.06E
G-ERMS	Thunder AS-33 Airship (Hot Air)	A 1			28.11.78	B R and M.Boyle *"Microbe"*	Budbrooke, Warwick	
G-ERNI	Piper PA-28-181 Archer II	28-8090146	G-OSSY	9.10.91		N F P Hopwood and M Lodge tr The G-ERNI Flying Group		
			N81215				Headcorn	18. 3.09E
G-EROL	Westland SA.341G Gazelle 1	1108	G-NONA	18.10.02		The Coin Group Ltd	Wycombe Air Park	11. 9.09E
			G-FDAV, G-RIFA, G-ORGE, G-BBHU					
G-EROM	Robinson R22 Beta II	3383			19.11.02	Airtask Group PLC	Cambridge	22. 3.09E
G-EROS	Cameron H-34 Balloon (Hot Air)	2296			6. 4.90	A A Brown tr Reach For The Sky *(Evening Standard titles)*		
						Perry Hill, Worplesdon, Guildford		20. 8.09E
G-ERRI	Lindstrand LBL 77A Balloon (Hot Air)	811			20. 2.02	K J Baxter	Norton, Worcester	27. 9.09E
G-ERRY	Grumman AA-5B Tiger	AA5B-0725	G-BFMJ	20. 3.84		Haniel Aviation Ltd	Turweston	13.12.08E
G-ERTE	Best Off Sky Ranger 912S(1)	SKRxxxx566			27. 4.05	A P Trumper	(Auborn, Lincoln)	12. 7.08P
	(Built A P Trumper - pr.no.BMAA HB/451)							
G-ERTI	Staaken Z-21A Flitzer	PFA 233-14166			29. 9.06	B S Carpenter	Wycombe Air Park	
	(Built B S Carpenter)							
G-ERYR	P&M Aviation Quik GT450	8381			15. 5.08	Cardiff Backpacker Caerdydd Ltd	Cardiff	
G-ESCA	Reality Escapade Jabiru(1)	JAESC 0002			25. 4.03	W R Davis-Smith	Sleap	17. 9.08P
	(Built T F Francis - pr.no.BMAA HB/280)							
G-ESCC	Reality Escapade 912	JAESC 0032			7.10.04	G and S Simons	Jackrell's Farm, Southwater	11.11.09P
	(Built G Simons - pr.no.BMAA HB/414)							
G-ESCP	Reality Escapade Jabiru(1)	JAESC 0004			19. 1.04	R G Hughes	(Stanford Bridge, Worcester)	3. 6.09P
	(Built R G Hughes - pr.no.BMAA HB/313)							
G-ESEX	Eurocopter EC.135 T2+	0267	D-HECP	9. 4.03		Essex Police Authority	Boreham	18. 6.09S
	(Type amended to T2+ 28. 1.08)							
G-ESGA	Reality Escapade	UK.CKT.010			20. 8.07	I Bamford	(Keysworth, Notts)	13. 4.09P
	(Built T F Francis - pr.no.PFA 345-14706)							
G-ESKA	Reality Escapade 912(1)	JAESC 0006			13. 5.04	J H Beard	Buckfast, Buckfastleigh	25. 4.07P
	(Built T F Francis - pr.no.BMAA HB/371)							
G-ESME	Cessna R182 Skylane RG II	R18201026	G-BNOX	10. 6.03		G C Cherrington	Draycott Farm, Chiseldon	7. 4.09E
			N756AW					
G-ESSL	Cessna 182R Skylane II	18267947	D-EIMP	7.12.06		Euro Seaplane Services Ltd	Blackbushe	14. 8.09E
	(Floatplane)		PH-AXP, N9434H					
G-ESSY	Robinson R44 Raven	1281			17. 1.03	EW Guess (Holdings) Ltd	Sibson	27. 5.09E
G-ESTA	Cessna 550 Citation II	550-0127	G-GAUL	24. 6.98		Executive Aviation Services Ltd	Gloucestershire	25. 8.09E
			N550TJ, (N29TG), N29TC, N2631N					
G-ESTR	Van's RV-6	PFA 181A-13638			11. 9.00	R M Johnson *"Jester"*	Midlem Farm, Midlem	2. 5.09P
	(Built R M Johnson)							
G-ESUS	RotorWay Executive 162F	6169/6724			7.10.96	J Tickner	Street Farm, Takeley	28. 8.0PE
	(Built J Tickner) (RotorWay RI 162F)							
G-ETAT	Cessna 172S Skyhawk	172S8674	N747SP	7. 7.05		A D and C Realff t/a ADR Aviation	Shoreham	7. 7.09E
G-ETBY	Piper PA-32-260 Cherokee Six	32-211	G-AWCY	13. 7.89		K Richards-Green and M B Smithson tr G-ETBY Group		
	(Rebuilt with spare Frame No.32-858S)		N3365W				Sherburn-in-Elmet	19.10.09E

G-ETCW	Stoddard-Hamilton GlaStar (Built T Wright) (Tri-cycle u/c)	5627	D-ETCW	12.12.01	P G Hayward	Little Snoring	16. 1.10P
G-ETDC	Cessna 172P Skyhawk II	17274690	N53133	4. 5.88	The Moray Flying Club (1990)	RAF Kinloss	29. 7.09E
G-ETFF	Robinson R44 Raven	1747	G-HSLJ	26.10.07	Rajair Ltd	Sleap	13. 9.09E
G-ETFL	Cirrus SR22-G3 GTSX	2899	N998CT	13. 3.08	T F Lambert	Denham	
G-ETHY	Cessna 208 Caravan I	20800293	N1295M N-ETHY	19.10.98	N A Moore	Movenis, Coleraine	2. 4.09E
G-ETIM	Eurocopter EC.120B Colibri	1387	VH-NZZ	27. 4.05	T R Smith (Agricultural Machinery) Ltd New Lane Farm, North Elmham		9. 6.09E
G-ETIN	Robinson R22 Beta	0853	N9081D	7. 9.88	J M Lynch	(Birmingham)	24. 9.09E
G-ETIV	Robin DR.400-180 Régent	2454		12. 7.00	J Macgilvray	Goodwood	14. 9.09E
G-ETME	Nord 1002 Pingouin (Lycoming O-540)	274	N108J F-BFRV, French AF 274	18. 4.00	S H O'Connell and J N Pittock tr 108 Flying Group (As "KG+EM" in Luftwaffe North Africa c/s) White Waltham		3. 4.10S
G-ETNT	Robinson R44 Raven	1479		27. 4.05	P Irwin t/a Irwin Plant Hire	Enniskillen	28. 5.09E
G-ETOU	Agusta A109S Grand	22028		19.12.06	P J Ogden	Jetou	16. 1.10E
G-ETPS	Hawker Hunter FGA.9	41H-679959	XE601	15. 9.04	Skyblue Aviation Ltd (As "XE601" in ETPS c/s) Exeter		28. 6.09P
G-EUAB	Europa Aviation Europa XS (Built A D Stephens)	PFA 247-13959		16. 5.07	A D Stephens	(London WC1)	
G-EUAN	Avtech Jabiru UL-D	666		30.11.07	M Wade and M Lusted	Rochester	24. 2.09P
G-EUFO	Rolladen-Schneider LS7-WL	7079	BGA3562-FVQ	10. 1.08	J R Bane and R Hardy	Gransden Lodge	1. 4.08
G-EUJG	Avro 594 Avian IIIA	R3/CN/185	VH-UJG G-AUJG	21. 5.07	R I and D E Souch	Hill Farm, Durley	
G-EUKA	Airbus A320			.08R	British Airways PLC	London Heathrow	
G-EUKB	Airbus A320			.08R	British Airways PLC	London Heathrow	
G-EUKC	Airbus A320			.08R	British Airways PLC	London Heathrow	
G-EUKD	Airbus A320			.08R	British Airways PLC	London Heathrow	
G-EUKE	Airbus A320			.08R	British Airways PLC	London Heathrow	
G-EUKF	Airbus A320			.08R	British Airways PLC	London Heathrow	
G-EUKG	Airbus A320			.08R	British Airways PLC	London Heathrow	
G-EUKH	Airbus A320			.08R	British Airways PLC	London Heathrow	
G-EUKI	Airbus A320			.08R	British Airways PLC	London Heathrow	
G-EUKJ	Airbus A320			.08R	British Airways PLC	London Heathrow	
G-EUKK	Airbus A320			.08R	British Airways PLC	London Heathrow	
G-EUKL	Airbus A320			.08R	British Airways PLC	London Heathrow	
G-EUNA	Airbus A318-121	4007	D-A	.09R	British Airways PLC	London-City	
G-EUNB	Airbus A318-121	4039	D-A	.09R	British Airways PLC	London-City	
G-EUOA	Airbus A319-131	1513	D-AVYE	15. 6.01	British Airways PLC	London Heathrow	14. 6.09E
G-EUOB	Airbus A319-131	1529	D-AVWH	4. 7.01	British Airways PLC	London Heathrow	3. 7.09E
G-EUOC	Airbus A319-131	1537	D-AVYP	16. 7.01	British Airways PLC	London Heathrow	15. 7.09E
G-EUOD	Airbus A319-131	1558	D-AVYJ	16. 8.01	British Airways PLC	London Heathrow	15. 8.09E
G-EUOE	Airbus A319-131	1574	D-AVWF	5. 9.01	British Airways PLC	London Heathrow	4. 9.09E
G-EUOF	Airbus A319-131	1590	D-AVYW	23.10.01	British Airways PLC	London Heathrow	22.10.09E
G-EUOG	Airbus A319-131	1594	D-AVWU	23.10.01	British Airways PLC	London Heathrow	22.10.09E
G-EUOH	Airbus A319-131	1604	D-AVYM	14.12.01	British Airways PLC	London Heathrow	13.12.09E
G-EUOI	Airbus A319-131	1606	D-AVYN	13.11.01	British Airways PLC	London Heathrow	12.11.09E
G-EUPA	Airbus A319-131	1082	D-AVYK	6.10.99	British Airways PLC	London Heathrow	5.10.09E
G-EUPB	Airbus A319-131	1115	D-AVYT	9.11.99	British Airways PLC	London Heathrow	8.11.09E
G-EUPC	Airbus A319-131	1118	D-AVYU	12.11.99	British Airways PLC	London Heathrow	11.11.09E
G-EUPD	Airbus A319-131	1142	D-AVWG	10.12.99	British Airways PLC	London Heathrow	9.12.09E
G-EUPE	Airbus A319-131	1193	D-AVYT	27. 3.00	British Airways PLC	London Heathrow	26. 3.09E
G-EUPF	Airbus A319-131	1197	D-AVWS	30. 3.00	British Airways PLC	London Heathrow	29. 3.09E
G-EUPG	Airbus A319-131	1222	D-AVYG	25. 5.00	British Airways PLC	London Heathrow	24. 5.09E
G-EUPH	Airbus A319-131	1225	D-AVYK	23. 5.00	British Airways PLC	London Heathrow	22. 5.09E
G-EUPJ	Airbus A319-131	1232	D-AVYJ	30. 5.00	British Airways PLC	London Heathrow	29. 5.09E
G-EUPK	Airbus A319-131	1236	D-AVYO	30. 5.00	British Airways PLC	London Heathrow	29. 5.09E
G-EUPL	Airbus A319-131	1239	D-AVYP	8. 6.00	British Airways PLC	London Heathrow	7. 6.09E
G-EUPM	Airbus A319-131	1258	D-AVYR	30. 6.00	British Airways PLC	London Heathrow	29. 6.09E
G-EUPN	Airbus A319-131	1261	D-AVWA	10. 7.00	British Airways PLC	London Heathrow	9. 7.09E
G-EUPO	Airbus A319-131	1279	D-AVYU	1. 8.00	British Airways PLC	London Heathrow	31. 7.09E
G-EUPP	Airbus A319-131	1295	D-AVWU	14. 8.00	British Airways PLC	London Heathrow	13. 8.09E
G-EUPR	Airbus A319-131	1329	D-AVYH	9.10.00	British Airways PLC	London Heathrow	8.10.08E
G-EUPS	Airbus A319-131	1338	D-AVYM	23.10.00	British Airways PLC	London Heathrow	22.10.09E
G-EUPT	Airbus A319-131	1380	D-AVWH	5.12.00	British Airways PLC	London Heathrow	4.12.09E
G-EUPU	Airbus A319-131	1384	D-AVWP	14.12.00	British Airways PLC	London Heathrow	13.12.09E
G-EUPV	Airbus A319-131	1423	D-AVYE	13. 2.01	British Airways PLC	London Heathrow	13. 2.10E
G-EUPW	Airbus A319-131	1440	D-AVYP	6. 3.01	British Airways PLC	London Heathrow	5. 3.09E
G-EUPX	Airbus A319-131	1445	D-AVWB	14.12.01	British Airways PLC	London Heathrow	14.12.09E
G-EUPY	Airbus A319-131	1466	D-AVYK	12. 4.01	British Airways PLC	London Heathrow	11. 4.09E
G-EUPZ	Airbus A319-131	1510	D-AVYY	7. 6.01	British Airways PLC	London Heathrow	6. 6.09E
G-EURT	Eurocopter EC 155 B1	6764	F-WWOO F-WWAT	6. 6.07	William Ewart Properties Ltd	Shawsbridge	30. 5.09E
G-EURX	Europa Aviation Europa XS (Built C C Napier, pr no PFA 247-13661)	482		15.12.00	C C Napier	(Newtownards)	
G-EUSO	Robin DR.400-140 Major	904	F-BUSO	18. 9.03	Weald Air Services Ltd	Headcorn	3.12.07E
G-EUUA	Airbus A320-232	1661	F-WWIH	31. 1.02	British Airways PLC	London Heathrow	30. 1.10E
G-EUUB	Airbus A320-232	1689	F-WWBE	14. 2.02	British Airways PLC	London Heathrow	13. 2.10E
G-EUUC	Airbus A320-232	1696	F-WWIO	28. 2.02	British Airways PLC	London Heathrow	27. 2.10E
G-EUUD	Airbus A320-232	1760	F-WWBN	29. 4.02	British Airways PLC	London Heathrow	28. 4.09E
G-EUUE	Airbus A320-232	1782	F-WWDO	30. 5.02	British Airways PLC	London Heathrow	29. 5 09E
G-EUUF	Airbus A320-232	1814	F-WWIY	29. 7.02	British Airways PLC	London Heathrow	28. 7.09E
G-EUUG	Airbus A320-232	1829	F-WWIU	30. 8.02	British Airways PLC	London Heathrow	29. 8.09E
G-EUUH	Airbus A320-232	1665	F-WWIG	25.10.02	British Airways PLC	London Heathrow	24.10.09E

G-EUUI	Airbus A320-232	1871	F-WWBI	22.11.02	British Airways PLC	London Heathrow	21.11.09E
G-EUUJ	Airbus A320-232	1883	F-WWBQ	25.11.02	British Airways PLC	London Heathrow	24.11.09E
G-EUUK	Airbus A320-232	1899	F-WWDO	20.12.02	British Airways PLC	London Heathrow	19.12.09E
G-EUUL	Airbus A320-232	1708	F-WWIV	20.12.02	British Airways PLC	London Heathrow	19.12.09E
G-EUUM	Airbus A320-232	1907	F-WWDN	23.12.02	British Airways PLC	London Heathrow	22.12.09E
G-EUUN	Airbus A320-232	1910	F-WWDP	31. 1.03	British Airways PLC	London Heathrow	30. 1.10E
G-EUUO	Airbus A320-232	1958	F-WWIT	11. 4.03	British Airways PLC	London Heathrow	10. 4.09E
G-EUUP	Airbus A320-232	2038	F-WWDB	27. 6.03	British Airways PLC	London Heathrow	26. 6.09E
G-EUUR	Airbus A320-232	2040	F-WWID	29. 7.03	British Airways PLC	London Heathrow	28. 7.09E
G-EUUS	Airbus A320-232	3301	F-WWIF	5.12.07	British Airways PLC	London Heathrow	4.12.09E
G-EUUT	Airbus A320-232	3314	F-WWIT	12.12.07	British Airways PLC	London Heathrow	11.12.09E
G-EUUU	Airbus A320-232	3351	F-WWID	7. 3.08	British Airways PLC	London Heathrow	6. 3.09E
G-EUUV	Airbus A320-232	3368	F-WWBD	18. 4.08	British Airways PLC	London Heathrow	17.4.09E
G-EUUW	Airbus A320-232	3499	F-WWIN	2. 6.08	British Airways PLC	London Heathrow	1. 6.09E
G-EUUX	Airbus A320-232	3550	F-WWDM	11. 7.08	British Airways PLC	London Heathrow	10. 7.09E
G-EUUY	Airbus A320-232	3607	F-WWIC	18. 9.08	British Airways PLC	London Heathrow	17. 9.09E
G-EUUZ	Airbus A320-232	3649	F-WW	21.10.08	British Airways PLC	London Heathrow	20.10.09E
G-EUXC	Airbus A321-231	2305	D-AVZE	15.10.04	British Airways PLC	London Heathrow	14.10.09E
G-EUXD	Airbus A321-231	2320	D-AVZO	28.10.04	British Airways PLC	London Heathrow	27.10.09E
G-EUXE	Airbus A321-231	2323	D-AVZP	29.10.04	British Airways PLC	London Heathrow	28.10.09E
G-EUXF	Airbus A321-231	2324	D-AVZQ	4.11.04	British Airways PLC	London Heathrow	3.11.09E
G-EUXG	Airbus A321-231	2351	D-AVZU	2.12.04	British Airways PLC	London Heathrow	1.12.09E
G-EUXH	Airbus A321-231	2363	D-AVZW	17.12.04	British Airways PLC	London Heathrow	16.12.09E
G-EUXI	Airbus A321-231	2536	D-AVZE	5. 8.05	British Airways PLC	London Heathrow	4. 8.09E
G-EUXJ	Airbus A321-231	3081	D-AVZL	17. 4.07	British Airways PLC	London Heathrow	16. 4.09E
G-EUXK	Airbus A321-231	3235	D-AVZI	30. 8.07	British Airways PLC	London Heathrow	29. 8.09E
G-EUXL	Airbus A321-231	3254	D-AVZV	21. 9.07	British Airways PLC	London Heathrow	20. 9.09E
G-EUXM	Airbus A321-231	3290	D-AVZC	21.11.07	British Airways PLC	London Heathrow	23.11.09E
G-EUYA	Airbus A320-232	3697	F-WWBM	24.11.08	British Airways PLC	London Heathrow	23.11.09E
G-EUYB	Airbus A320-232	3703	F-WWBV	27.11.08	British Airways PLC	London Heathrow	26.11.09E
G-EUYC	Airbus A320-232	3721	F-WWBY	12.12.08	British Airways PLC	London Heathrow	11.12.09E
G-EUYD	Airbus A320-232	3726	F-WWDH	16.12.08	British Airways PLC	London Heathrow	15.12.09E
G-EUYE	Airbus A320-232	3912		6.09R	British Airways PLC	London Heathrow	
G-EUYF	Airbus A320-232	4057		.09R	British Airways PLC	London Heathrow	
G-EUYG	Airbus A320-232	4104		.09R	British Airways PLC	London Heathrow	
G-EUYH	Airbus A320-232			.10R	British Airways PLC	London Heathrow	
G-EUYI	Airbus A320-232			.10R	British Airways PLC	London Heathrow	
G-EUYJ	Airbus A320-232			.10R	British Airways PLC	London Heathrow	
G-EUYK	Airbus A320-232			.10R	British Airways PLC	London Heathrow	
G-EUYL	Airbus A320-232			.10R	British Airways PLC	London Heathrow	
G-EUYM	Airbus A320-232			.10R	British Airways PLC	London Heathrow	
G-EVAJ	Best Off Sky Ranger Swift 912S(1)			22. 2.07	A B Gridley	Sackville Lodge, Riseley	19.11.08P
		SKRxxxx760					
	(Built A B Gridley- pr.no.BMAA HB/526)						
G-EVBF	Cameron Z-350 Balloon (Hot Air)	10687		14. 3.05	Airxcite Ltd t/a Virgin Balloon Flights	Wembley	23. 8.09E
G-EVET	Cameron Concept 80 Balloon (Hot Air)	3703		30.10.95	L D and H Vaughan	Wilstone, Tring	9. 7.09E
G-EVEV	Robinson R44 Raven II	10908	G-FAKE	10.12.08	M P Wilkinson	Sandtoft	3.11.08E
G-EVEY	Thruster T 600N 450 Sprint	0121-T600N-057		22.11.01	K J Crompton	Newtownards	16.12.09P
G-EVIE	Piper PA-28-161 Warrior II	28-8316043	G-ZULU	31. 3.04	Tayside Aviation Ltd	Dundee	23.10.09E
			N4292X				
G-EVIG	Evektor EV-97 teamEurostar UK	2930		9. 3.07	A S Mitchell	Shobdon	8. 3.08E
G-EVII	Schempp-Hirth Ventus 2cT	10/41	BGA4292-HXS	31.10.07	Active Aviation Ltd *"V11"*	(Urchfont, Devizes)	18. 3.08
G-EVLE	Rearwin 8125 Cloudster	803	G-BVLK	10. 4.03	M C Hiscock	Popham	20. 4.09P
			N25403, NC25403				
G-EVLN	Gulfstream Aerospace Gulfstream G-IV	1175	N18WF	3. 6.02	Metropix Ltd	Luton	5. 9.09E
			VH-CCA, (N1175B), HB-ITJ, N17588				
G-EVPI	Evans VP-1 Series 2	PFA 062-13136		10. 4.03	C P Martyr	Kittyhawk Farm, Deanland	21. 3.09P
	(Built C P Martyr) (Volkswagen 1834)						
G-EVRD	Beech 390 Premier 1	RB-172	N7102U	25. 4.07	Commercial Aviation Charters Ltd	Farnborough	25. 4.09E
G-EVRO	Evektor EV-97 Eurostar	PFA 315-14137		30. 1.04	J G McMinn	(Lisburn)	9. 1.10P
	(Built R I and D J Blain)						
G-EVTO	Piper PA-28-161 Warrior II	28-8016271	N5012V	12. 7.05	Redhill Air Services Ltd	Redhill	2. 6.09E
			G-EVTO, D-EVTO, N81615				
G-EWAD	Robinson R44 Raven II	12296		5. 6.08	Excel Law Ltd	(Atrincham)	16. 6.09E
G-EWAN	Protech PT-2C-160 Prostar	PFA 249-12425		23. 6.93	C G Shaw	Truleigh Manor Farm, Edburton	17. 4.09P
	(Built C G Shaw) (Lycoming O-320-B2B)						
G-EWAW	Bell 206B-3 JetRanger III	3955	G-DORB	25. 7.03	J Tobias	Barton	9. 4.09E
			SE-HTI, TC-HBN				
G-EWBC	Avtech Jabiru SK	0249		3.11.00	E W B Comber	White Fen Farm, Benwick	3.10.09P
	(Built E W B Comber - pr.no.PFA 274-13457)						
G-EWES	Alpi Pioneer 300	7		24.11.04	D A Ions	Morgansfield, Fishburn	12. 6.09P
	(Built R Y Kendal and D A Ions - pr.no.PFA 330-14322)						
G-EWEW	AB Sportine Aviacija LAK-19T	024	BGA5241-KNZ	22. 5.07	G Paul *"EW2"*	Dunstable	21. 5.08
			LY-GNC				
G-EWHT	Robin R2112 Alpha	371		4. 5.04	Ewan Ltd *(Operated Cotswold Aero Club)*		
						Gloucestershire	4. 6.09E
G-EWIZ	Pitts S-2S	S18	VH-EHQ	12.11.82	G R J Caunter	Popham	13. 3.08P
	(Built H M Shelvey) (Lycoming AEIO-540)						
G-EWME	Piper PA-28-235 Cherokee Pathfinder		D-EECN	24. 9.04	E S Ewen and C J Mewis	Oaksey Park	21.10.09E
		28-7310156	N55766				
G-EWRT	Eurocopter EC.135 T2+	0347	D-HECF	6.12.04	Eurocopter UK Ltd	Oxford	2. 3.09E
G-EWZZ	CZAW Sportcruiser	LAA 338-14815		20. 6.08	D W Bessell	(Bulmer)	
	(Built D W Bessell)						

G-EXAM	Piper PA-28RT-201T Turbo Arrow IV	28R-8431003	N45AW N43230	25. 5.05	H S Urquhart tr Zwetsloot	Inverness 16. 6.09E
G-EXEA	Extra EA.300/L	082		9. 3.99	P J Lawton	Blackbushe 10. 2.09E
G-EXEC	Piper PA-34-200 Seneca	34-7450072	(G-EXXC) OY-BGU	11. 5.78	Sky Air Travel Ltd	Stapleford 21. 8.09E
G-EXES	Europa Aviation Europa XS	578		25. 4.03	D Barraclough	Morgansfield, Fishburn 15. 9.09P
	(Built D Barraclough - pr.no.PFA 247-13574)					
G-EXEX	Cessna 404 Titan	404-0037	SE-GZF (N5418G)	3. 5.79	Reconnaissance Ventures Ltd	Lydd 29. 7.09E
					(Coastguard titles, red and white c/s with MCA logo on tail)	
G-EXGC	Extra EA.300/200	027	D-EXGC	10. 6.08	P J Bull	Andrewsfield 17. 6.09E
G-EXIT	SOCATA MS.893E Rallye 180GT	12979	F-GARX	22. 9.78	M A Baldwin tr G-EXIT Group	
						Maypole Farm, Chislet 1. 7.09E
G-EXLL	Zenair CH.601XL Zodiac PFA 162B-14205			4. 3.04	N Grantham	Bourn 20. 8.08P
	(Built B McFadden, B Gardner and R Fox)(Tri-cycle u/c)					
G-EXON	Piper PA-28-161 Cadet	2841283	G-EGLD N92007	9.12.03	Plane Talking Ltd	Elstree 29. 1.10E
G-EXPD	Stemme S 10-VT	11-063		5. 7.01	Global Gliding Expeditions Ltd	Rhosgoch 27.11.08E
	(Rotax 914)					
G-EXPL	American Champion 7GCBC Explorer 1220-96			9. 5.96	M W Meynell	Morgansfield, Fishburn 15. 6.09E
G-EXPS	Short SD.3-60 Variant 100	SH3661	EI-SMB	11. 5.99	ACL Aircraft Trading Ltd	
	G-EXPS, TC-AOA, G-BLRT, SE-KRV, G-BLRT, G-14-3661					Kassel, Hessen, Germany 28. 2.09E
G-EXRS	Bombardier BD-700-1A10 Global Express	9274	N974TS C-FOAB	14. 1.09	Ocean Sky Aviation Ltd	Manchester
G-EXTR	Extra EA.260	004	D-EDID	10. 8.92	S J Carver	Netherthorpe 28. 3.08P
G-EXXO	Piper PA-28-161 Cadet	2841210	G-CBXP N117ND	22. 1.04	Plane Talking Ltd *(Operated Cabair)*	
						Blackbushe 28. 2.09E
G-EYAK	Yakovlev Yak-50	801804	RA-01193 DOSAAF?	19. 2.03	P N A Whitehead	Leicester 12. 6.09P
G-EYAS	Denney Kitfox Model 2 PFA 172-11858			3. 3.93	R E Hughes	(Lyme Regis) 23. 7.09P
	(Built E J Young)					
G-EYCO	Robin DR.400-180 Régent	1949		12. 3.90	S J York	Bagby 25. 5.09E
G-EYNL	MBB BÖ.105DBS-5	S 382	LN-OTJ	19. 8.96	Sterling Helicopters Ltd	Norwich 10.12.09E
			D-HDLR, EC-DSO, D-HDLR *(Operated East Anglian Air Ambulance)*			
G-EYOR	Van's RV-6 PFA 181A-13259			15.10.99	S I Fraser	Henstridge 28. 2.09P
	(Built S I Fraser) (Lycoming O-320)					
G-EYRE	Bell 206L-1 LongRanger	45229	G-STVI N60MA, N5019K	12.11.90	European Aviation and Technical Services Ltd	
						Malta 18. 10.09E
G-EZAA	Airbus A319-111	2677	D-AVYU	10. 2.06	EasyJet Airline Company Ltd	Luton 2.10.09E
G-EZAB	Airbus A319-111	2681	D-AVYY	6. 2.06	EasyJet Airline Company Ltd	Luton 4.10.09E
G-EZAC	Airbus A319-111	2691	D-AVXB	16. 2.06	EasyJet Airline Company Ltd	Luton 4.11.09E
G-EZAD	Airbus A319-111	2702	D-AVXI	28. 2.06	EasyJet Airline Company Ltd	Luton 4.11.09E
G-EZAE	Airbus A319-111	2709	D-AVYI	9. 3.06	EasyJet Airline Company Ltd	Luton 6.11.09E
G-EZAF	Airbus A319-111	2715	D-AVYT	16. 3.06	EasyJet Airline Company Ltd	Luton 2.12.09E
G-EZAG	Airbus A319-111	2727	D-AVXG	29. 3.06	EasyJet Airline Company Ltd	Luton 2. 2.10E
G-EZAH	Airbus A319-111	2729	D-AVXK	30. 3.06	EasyJet Airline Company Ltd	Luton 4. 2.10E
G-EZAI	Airbus A319-111	2735	D-AVXM.	6. 4.06	EasyJet Airline Company Ltd	Luton 6 .2.10E
G-EZAJ	Airbus A319-111	2742	D-AVXP	13. 4.06	EasyJet Airline Company Ltd	Luton 12. 4.09E
G-EZAK	Airbus A319-111	2744	D-AVXQ	20. 4.06	EasyJet Airline Company Ltd	Luton 5. 3.09E
G-EZAL	Airbus A319-111	2754	D-AVWG	27. 4.06	EasyJet Airline Company Ltd	Luton 7. 3.09E
G-EZAM	Airbus A319-111	2037	HB-JZA G-CCKA, D-AVYS	14. 9.04	EasyJet Airline Company Ltd	Luton 4. 6.09E
G-EZAN	Airbus A319-111	2765	D-AVWL	4.05.06	EasyJet Airline Company Ltd	Luton 9. 3.09E
G-EZAO	Airbus A319-111	2769	D-AVWO	9. 5.06	EasyJet Airline Company Ltd	Luton 3. 4.09E
G-EZAP	Airbus A319-111	2777	D-AVYG	16. 5.06	EasyJet Airline Company Ltd	Luton 5. 4.09E
G-EZAR	Mainair Sports Pegasus Quik	7942		18. 3.03	I B Smith	Deenethorpe 27. 4.09P
G-EZAS	Airbus A319-111	2779	D-AVYH	.24. 5.06	EasyJet Airline Company Ltd	Luton 7. 4.09E
G-EZAT	Airbus A319-111	2782	D-AVYO	1. 6.06	EasyJet Airline Company Ltd	Luton 31. 5.09E
G-EZAU	Airbus A319-111	2795	D-AVWQ	9. 6.06	EasyJet Airline Company Ltd	Luton 3. 5.09E
G-EZAV	Airbus A319-111	2803	D-AVWV	22. 6.06	EasyJet Airline Company Ltd	Luton 5. 5.09E
G-EZAW	Airbus A319-111	2812	D-AVYU	4. 7.06	EasyJet Airline Company Ltd	Luton 2. 7.09E
G-EZAX	Airbus A319-111	2818	D-AVXA	6. 7.06	EasyJet Airline Company Ltd	Luton 4. 7.09E
G-EZAY	Airbus A319-111	2827	D-AVXE	12. 7.06	EasyJet Airline Company Ltd	Luton 10. 7.09E
G-EZAZ	Airbus A319-111	2829	D-AVXF	20. 7.06	EasyJet Airline Company Ltd	Luton 17. 8.09E
G-EZBA	Airbus A319-111	2860	D-AVWB	18. 8.06	EasyJet Airline Company Ltd	Luton 16. 8.09E
G-EZBB	Airbus A319-111	2854	D-AVXM	9. 8.06	EasyJet Airline Company Ltd	Luton 7. 8.09E
G-EZBC	Airbus A319-111	2866	D-AVWD	5. 9.06	EasyJet Airline Company Ltd	Luton 3. 9.09E
G-EZBD	Airbus A319-111	2873	D-AVWK	13. 9.06	EasyJet Airline Company Ltd	Luton 11 .9.09E
G-EZBE	Airbus A319-111	2884	D-AVXO	28.11.06	EasyJet Airline Company Ltd	Luton 6. 6.09E
G-EZBF	Airbus A319-111	2923	D-AVYK	2.11.06	EasyJet Airline Company Ltd	Luton 12. 7.09E
G-EZBG	Airbus A319-111	2946	D-AVXA	24.11.06	EasyJet Airline Company Ltd	Luton 7. 6.09E
G-EZBH	Airbus A319-111	2959	D-AVXH	15.12.06	EasyJet Airline Company Ltd	Luton 6.10.09E
G-EZBI	Airbus A319-111	3003	D-AVYB	6. 2.07	EasyJet Airline Company Ltd	Luton 8.12.09E
G-EZBJ	Airbus A319-111	3036	D-AVWJ	21. 2.07	EasyJet Airline Company Ltd	Luton 9.11.09E
G-EZBK	Airbus A319-111	3041	D-AVWK	22. 2.07	EasyJet Airline Company Ltd	Luton 10.11.09E
G-EZBL	Airbus A319-111	3053	D-AVYJ	14. 3.07	EasyJet Airline Company Ltd	Luton 11. 11.09E
G-EZBM	Airbus A319-111	3059	D-AVWE	22. 3.07	EasyJet Airline Company Ltd	Luton 3. 1.09E
G-EZBN	Airbus A319-111	3061	D-AVWH	23. 3.07	EasyJet Airline Company Ltd	Luton 5. 1.09E
G-EZBO	Airbus A319-111	3082	D-AVYK	4. 4.07	EasyJet Airline Company Ltd	Luton 8. 2.10E
G-EZBP	Airbus A319-111	3084	D-AVYP	11. 4.07	EasyJet Airline Company Ltd	Luton 10. 2.10E
G-EZBR	Airbus A319-111	3088	D-AVYY	26. 4.07	EasyJet Airline Company Ltd	Luton 11. 3.09E
G-EZBT	Airbus A319-111	3090	D-AVWM	27. 4.07	EasyJet Airline Company Ltd	Luton 14. 3.09E
G-EZBU	Airbus A319-111	3118	D-AVWW	14. 5.07	EasyJet Airline Company Ltd	Luton 9. 4.09E
G-EZBV	Airbus A319-111	3122	D-AVWX	23. 5.07	EasyJet Airline Company Ltd	Luton 11. 4.09E
G-EZBW	Airbus A319-111	3134	D-AVXE	5. 6.07	EasyJet Airline Company Ltd	Luton 5. 6.09E

G-EZBX	Airbus A319-111	3137	D-AVXH	15. 6.07	EasyJet Airline Company Ltd	Luton	9. 5.09E
G-EZBY	Airbus A319-111	3176	D-AVXJ	11. 7.07	EasyJet Airline Company Ltd	Luton	9. 6.09E
G-EZBZ	Airbus A319-111	3184	D-AVYF	13. 7.07	EasyJet Airline Company Ltd	Luton	11. 7.09E
G-EZDA	Airbus A319-111	3413	D-AVYH	21. 2.08	EasyJet Airline Company Ltd	Luton	20. 2.09E
G-EZDB	Airbus A319-111	3411	D-AVYF	20. 2.08	EasyJet Airline Company Ltd	Luton	18.1.10E
G-EZDC	Airbus A319-111	2043	HB-JZB	20. 9.04	EasyJet Airline Company Ltd	Luton	11. 6.09E
			G-CCKB, D-AVYU				
G-EZDD	Airbus A319-111	3442	D-AVYL	17. 3.08	EasyJet Airline Company Ltd	Luton	16. 3.09E
G-EZDE	Airbus A319-111	3426	D-AVYP	6. 3.08	EasyJet Airline Company Ltd	Luton	5. 3.09E
G-EZDF	Airbus A319-111	3432	D-AVYG	13. 3.08	EasyJet Airline Company Ltd	Luton	12. 3.09E
G-EZDG	Rutan VariEze	002	G-EZOS	1.11.05	D M Gale	Henstridge	4.11.08P
	(Built O Smith - pr.no.PFA 074-10221) (Continental O-200-A)						
G-EZDH	Airbus A319-111	3466	D-AVWM	14. 4.08	EasyJet Airline Company Ltd	Luton	13. 4.09E
G-EZDI	Airbus A319-111	3537	D-AVWC	29. 5.08	EasyJet Airline Company Ltd	Luton	28. 5.09E
G-EZDJ	Airbus A319-111	3544	D-AVWJ	3. 6.08	EasyJet Airline Company Ltd	Luton	2. 6.09E
G-EZDK	Airbus A319-111	3555	D-AVWP	11. 6.08	EasyJet Airline Company Ltd	Luton	10. 6.09E
G-EZDL	Airbus A319-111	3569	D-AVWT	23. 6.08	EasyJet Airline Company Ltd	Luton	22. 6.09E
G-EZDM	Airbus A319-111	3571	D-AVWU	1. 7.08	EasyJet Airline Company Ltd	Luton	30.6.09E
			(D-AGWM)				
G-EZDN	Airbus A319-111	3608	D-AVWU	8. 8.08	EasyJet Airline Company Ltd	Luton	7. 8.09E
G-EZDO	Airbus A319-111	3634	D-AVYP	4. 9.08	EasyJet Airline Company Ltd	Luton	3. 9.09E
G-EZDP	Airbus A319-111	3675	D-AVYX	8.10.08	EasyJet Airline Company Ltd	Luton	7. 10.09E
G-EZDR	Airbus A319-111	3683	D-AVYZ	21.10.08	EasyJet Airline Company Ltd	Luton	20.10.09E
G-EZDS	Airbus A319-111	3702	D-AVWP	10.11.08	EasyJet Airline Company Ltd	Luton	9.11.09E
G-EZDT	Airbus A319-111	3720	D-AVWR	26.11.08	EasyJet Airline Company Ltd	Luton	25.11.09E
G-EZDU	Airbus A319-111	3735	D-AVWX	9.12.08	EasyJet Airline Company Ltd	Luton	8.12.09E
G-EZDV	Airbus A319-111	3742	D-AVWY	15.12.08	EasyJet Airline Company Ltd	Luton	14.12.09E
G-EZDW	Airbus A319-111	3746	D-AVXA	18.12.08	EasyJet Airline Company Ltd	Luton	17.12.09E
G-EZDX	Airbus A319-111	3754	D-AVXB	12. 1.09	EasyJet Airline Company Ltd	Luton	11. 1.10E
G-EZDY	Airbus A319-111	3763	D-AVXF	14. 1.09	EasyJet Airline Company Ltd	Luton	13. 1.10E
G-EZDZ	Airbus A319-111	3774	D-AVXI	22. 1.09	EasyJet Airline Company Ltd	Luton	21. 1.10E
G-EZEA	Airbus A319-111	2119	D-AVWZ	18. 2.04	EasyJet Airline Company Ltd	Luton	14.11.09E
G-EZEB	Airbus A319-111	2120	D-AVYK	25. 3.04	EasyJet Airline Company Ltd	Luton	12. 2.10E
G-EZEC	Airbus A319-111	2129	D-AVWR	19. 3.04	EasyJet Airline Company Ltd	Luton	6. 1.10E
G-EZED	Airbus A319-111	2170	D-AVWT	7. 4.04	EasyJet Airline Company Ltd	Luton	15. 2.09E
G-EZEF	Airbus A319-111	2176	D-AVYS	19. 3.04	EasyJet Airline Company Ltd	Luton	4.12.09E
G-EZEG	Airbus A319-111	2181	D-AVWF	1. 4.04	EasyJet Airline Company Ltd	Luton	17. 2.09E
G-EZEJ	Airbus A319-111	2214	D-AVYO	5. 5.04	EasyJet Airline Company Ltd	Luton	13. 4.09E
G-EZEK	Airbus A319-111	2224	D-AVYZ	6. 5.04	EasyJet Airline Company Ltd	Luton	15. 4.09E
G-EZEL	Westland SA.341G Gazelle 1	1073	(F-GIVQ)	1.12.00	W R Pitcher/Regal Group UK	Leatherhead	18. 6.09E
			I-ATOM, F-BXPG, G-BAZL				
G-EZEO	Airbus A319-111	2249	D-AVYN	17. 6.04	EasyJet Airline Company Ltd	Luton	11. 5.09E
G-EZEP	Airbus A319-111	2251	D-AVYQ	1. 7.04	EasyJet Airline Company Ltd	Luton	29. 6.09E
G-EZER	Cameron H-34 Balloon (Hot Air)	2366	LX-ROM	31.10.02	D P Tuck	Hinton Charterhouse, Bath	11. 8.06E
G-EZET	Airbus A319-111	2271	D-AVWY	11. 8.04	EasyJet Airline Company Ltd	Luton	15. 6.09E
G-EZEU	Airbus A319-111	2283	D-AVYP	5.10.04	EasyJet Airline Company Ltd	Luton	11. 8.09E
G-EZEV	Airbus A319-111	2289	D-AVYV	9. 9.04	EasyJet Airline Company Ltd	Luton	13. 6.09E
G-EZEW	Airbus A319-111	2300	D-AVWH	15.10.04	EasyJet Airline Company Ltd	Luton	13. 8.09E
G-EZEZ	Airbus A319-111	2360	D-AVWP	9.12.04	EasyJet Airline Company Ltd	Luton	24. 9.09E
G-EZFA	Airbus A319-111	3788	D-AVXK	2. 2.09	EasyJet Airline Company Ltd	Luton	1. 2.10E
G-EZFB	Airbus A319-111	3799	D-AVXN	09R	EasyJet Airline Company Ltd	Luton	
G-EZFC	Airbus A319-111	3808	D-AVYC	09R	EasyJet Airline Company Ltd	Luton	
G-EZFD	Airbus A319-111	3810	D-AVYF	09R	EasyJet Airline Company Ltd	Luton	
G-	Airbus A319-111	3824	D-AVYI	09R	EasyJet Airline Company Ltd	Luton	
G-	Airbus A319-111	3844	D-AVYT	09R	EasyJet Airline Company Ltd	Luton	
G-	Airbus A319-111	3845	D-AVYU	09R	EasyJet Airline Company Ltd	Luton	
G-	Airbus A319-111	3849	D-AVYV	09R	EasyJet Airline Company Ltd	Luton	
G-	Airbus A319-111	3888	D-AV	09R	EasyJet Airline Company Ltd	Luton	
G-	Airbus A319-111	3993	D-AV	09R	EasyJet Airline Company Ltd	Luton	
G-	Airbus A319-111	4000	D-AV	09R	EasyJet Airline Company Ltd	Luton	
G-	Airbus A319-111	4004	D-AV	09R	EasyJet Airline Company Ltd	Luton	
G-	Airbus A319-111	4018	D-AV	09R	EasyJet Airline Company Ltd	Luton	
G-	Airbus A319-111	4024	D-AV	09R	EasyJet Airline Company Ltd	Luton	
G-	Airbus A319-111	4040	D-AV	09R	EasyJet Airline Company Ltd	Luton	
G-	Airbus A319-111	4046	D-AV	09R	EasyJet Airline Company Ltd	Luton	
G-	Airbus A319-111	4054	D-AV	09R	EasyJet Airline Company Ltd	Luton	
G-	Airbus A319-111	4067	D-AV	09R	EasyJet Airline Company Ltd	Luton	
G-	Airbus A319-111	4076	D-AV	09R	EasyJet Airline Company Ltd	Luton	
G-	Airbus A319-111	4082	D-AV	09R	EasyJet Airline Company Ltd	Luton	
G-	Airbus A319-111	4085	D-AV	09R	EasyJet Airline Company Ltd	Luton	
G-	Airbus A319-111	4091	D-AV	09R	EasyJet Airline Company Ltd	Luton	
G-	Airbus A319-111	4099	D-AV	09R	EasyJet Airline Company Ltd	Luton	
G-	Airbus A319-111	4121	D-AV	09R	EasyJet Airline Company Ltd	Luton	
G-	Airbus A319-111	4153	D-AV	09R	EasyJet Airline Company Ltd	Luton	
G-	Airbus A319-111	4157	D-AV	09R	EasyJet Airline Company Ltd	Luton	
G-	Airbus A319-111	4163	D-AV	09R	EasyJet Airline Company Ltd	Luton	
G-EZIA	Airbus A319-111	2420	D-AVYL	18. 3.05	EasyJet Airline Company Ltd	Luton	6.12.09E
G-EZIC	Airbus A319-111	2436	D-AVWC	7. 4.05	EasyJet Airline Company Ltd	Luton	18. 1.10E
G-EZID	Airbus A319-111	2442	D-AVWT	14. 4.05	EasyJet Airline Company Ltd	Luton	15. 3.09E
G-EZIE	Airbus A319-111	2446	D-AVWQ	18. 4.05	EasyJet Airline Company Ltd	Luton	17. 3.09E
G-EZIG	Airbus A319-111	2460	D-AVYM	3. 5.05	EasyJet Airline Company Ltd	Luton	19. 3.09E
G-EZIH	Airbus A319-111	2463	D-AVWV	9. 5.05	EasyJet Airline Company Ltd	Luton	17. 4.09E
G-EZII	Airbus A319-111	2471	D-AVYK	25. 5.05	EasyJet Airline Company Ltd	Luton	20. 4.09E
G-EZIJ	Airbus A319-111	2477	D-AVYU	2. 6.05	EasyJet Airline Company Ltd	Luton	13. 5.09E

G-EZIK	Airbus A319-111	2481	D-AVYV	31. 5.05	EasyJet Airline Company Ltd	Luton	22. 4.09E
G-EZIL	Airbus A319-111	2492	D-AVWM	15. 6.05	EasyJet Airline Company Ltd	Luton	5. 5.09E
G-EZIM	Airbus A319-111	2495	D-AVYO	17. 6.05	EasyJet Airline Company Ltd	Luton	17. 5.09E
G-EZIN	Airbus A319-111	2503	D-AVYZ	28. 6.05	EasyJet Airline Company Ltd	Luton	19. 5.09E
G-EZIO	Airbus A319-111	2512	D-AVWP	7. 7.05	EasyJet Airline Company Ltd	Luton	5. 7.09E
G-EZIP	Airbus A319-111	2514	D-AVWQ	12. 7.05	EasyJet Airline Company Ltd	Luton	10. 7.09E
G-EZIR	Airbus A319-111	2527	D-AVWK	27. 7.05	EasyJet Airline Company Ltd	Luton	25. 7.09E
G-EZIS	Airbus A319-111	2528	D-AVWJ	2. 8.05	EasyJet Airline Company Ltd	Luton	31. 7.09E
G-EZIT	Airbus A319-111	2538	D-AVYN	11. 8.05	EasyJet Airline Company Ltd	Luton	9. 8.09E
G-EZIU	Airbus A319-111	2548	D-AVYF	1. 9.05	EasyJet Airline Company Ltd	Luton	31. 8.09E
G-EZIV	Airbus A319-111	2565	D-AVYY	4.10.05	EasyJet Airline Company Ltd	Luton	19. 9.09E
G-EZIW	Airbus A319-111	2578	D-AVXE	17.10.05	EasyJet Airline Company Ltd	Luton	8. 7.09E
G-EZIX	Airbus A319-111	2605	D-AVXP	17.11.05	EasyJet Airline Company Ltd	Luton	24. 9.09E
G-EZIY	Airbus A319-111	2636	D-AVWH	15.12.05	EasyJet Airline Company Ltd	Luton	10.10.09E
G-EZIZ	Airbus A319-111	2646	D-AVWQ	12. 1.06	EasyJet Airline Company Ltd	Luton	12.10.09E
G-EZJA	Boeing 737-73V	30235		13.10.00	EasyJet Airline Company Ltd	Luton	21. 8.09E
G-EZJB	Boeing 737-73V	30236	N1787B	22.11.00	EasyJet Airline Company Ltd	Luton	18. 9.09E
G-EZJC	Boeing 737-73V	30237		15.12.00	EasyJet Airline Company Ltd	Luton	18.10.09E
G-EZJF	Boeing 737-73V	30243		15. 8.01	EasyJet Airline Company Ltd	Luton	21. 6.09E
G-EZJJ	Boeing 737-73V	30245		30. 1.02	EasyJet Airline Company Ltd (wfs 12.08)	Luton	24.11.09E
G-EZJK	Boeing 737-73V	30246		7. 2.02	EasyJet Airline Company Ltd (wfs 1.12.08)	Luton	20.11.09E
G-EZJL	Boeing 737-73V	30247		12. 2.02	EasyJet Airline Company Ltd (wfs 10.1.09)	Luton	8.12.09E
G-EZJM	Boeing 737-73V	30248		24. 4.02	EasyJet Airline Company Ltd	Luton	21. 2.09E
G-EZJN	Boeing 737-73V	30249		8. 5.02	EasyJet Airline Company Ltd	Luton	21. 3.09E
G-EZJO	Boeing 737-73V	30244		6. 6.02	EasyJet Airline Company Ltd	Luton	23. 4.09E
G-EZJP	Boeing 737-73V	32412		11. 6.02	EasyJet Airline Company Ltd	Luton	25. 4.09E
G-EZJR	Boeing 737-73V	32413		20. 8.02	EasyJet Airline Company Ltd	Luton	14. 7.09E
G-EZJS	Boeing 737-73V	32414		23. 9.02	EasyJet Airline Company Ltd	Luton	19. 9.09E
G-EZJT	Boeing 737-73V	32415		19.12.02	EasyJet Airline Company Ltd	Luton	22.10.09E
G-EZJU	Boeing 737-73V	32416	N6046P	21.12.02	EasyJet Airline Company Ltd	Luton	8. 1.10E
G-EZJV	Boeing 737-73V	32417		3. 3.03	EasyJet Airline Company Ltd	Luton	10. 1.10E
G-EZJW	Boeing 737-73V	32418		28. 3.03	EasyJet Airline Company Ltd	Luton	12. 1.10E
G-EZJX	Boeing 737-73V	32419	N1787B	12. 5.03	EasyJet Airline Company Ltd	Luton	23. 3.09E
G-EZJY	Boeing 737-73V	32420		27. 6.03	EazyJet Airline Company Ltd	Luton	21. 5.09E
G-EZJZ	Boeing 737-73V	32421		31. 7.03	EasyJet Airline Company Ltd	Luton	5. 5.09E
G-EZKA	Boeing 737-73V	32422	(G-ESYA)	12. 8.03	EasyJet Airline Company Ltd	Luton	16. 7.09E
G-EZKB	Boeing 737-73V	32423	(G-ESYB)	21. 1.04	EasyJet Airline Company Ltd	Luton	22.11.09E
G-EZKC	Boeing 737-73V	32424	(G-ESYC)	12. 2.04	EasyJet Airline Company Ltd	Luton	10.12.09E
G-EZKD	Boeing 737-73V	32425	N1787B	13. 2.04	EasyJet Airline Company Ltd	Luton	12.12.09E
G-EZKE	Boeing 737-73V	32426	(G-ESYE)	30. 3.04	EasyJet Airline Company Ltd	Luton	23. 2.09E
G-EZKF	Boeing 737-73V	32427	(G-ESYF)	22. 4.04	EasyJet Airline Company Ltd	Luton	25. 2.09E
G-EZKG	Boeing 737-73V	32428	(G-ESYG)	27. 5.04	EasyJet Airline Company Ltd	Luton	25. 3.09E
G-EZMH	Airbus A319-111	2053	HB-JZD	24. 9.04	EasyJet Airline Company Ltd	Luton	17. 6.09E
			G-CCKD, D-AVYB				
G-EZMS	Airbus A319-111	2378	D-AVWS	21. 1.05	EasyJet Airline Company Ltd	Luton	14.10.09E
G-EZNC	Airbus A319-111	2050	HB-JZC	22. 9.04	EasyJet Airline Company Ltd	Luton	19. 8.09E
			G-CCKC, D-AVWF				
G-EZNM	Airbus A319-111	2402	D-AVWH	1. 3.05	EasyJet Airline Company Ltd	Luton	16.11.09E
G-EZPG	Airbus A319-111	2385	D-AVYD	15. 2.05	EasyJet Airline Company Ltd	Luton	16.10.09E
G-EZSM	Airbus A319-111	2062	HB-JZE	8.10.04	EasyJet Airline Company Ltd	Luton	19. 6.09E
			G-CCKE, D-AVYD				
G-EZTA	Airbus A320-214	3805	D-AVVD	09R	EasyJet Airline Company Ltd	Luton	
G-	Airbus A320-214	3843	D-AV	09R	EasyJet Airline Company Ltd	Luton	
G-	Airbus A320-214	3871	D-AV	09R	EasyJet Airline Company Ltd	Luton	
G-	Airbus A320-214	3909	D-AV	09R	EasyJet Airline Company Ltd	Luton	
G-	Airbus A320-214	3913	D-AV	09R	EasyJet Airline Company Ltd	Luton	
G-	Airbus A320-214	3922	D-AV	09R	EasyJet Airline Company Ltd	Luton	
G-	Airbus A320-214	3946	D-AV	09R	EasyJet Airline Company Ltd	Luton	
G-	Airbus A320-214	3953	D-AV	09R	EasyJet Airline Company Ltd	Luton	
G-	Airbus A320-214	3975	D-AV	09R	EasyJet Airline Company Ltd	Luton	
G-	Airbus A320-214	3979	D-AV	09R	EasyJet Airline Company Ltd	Luton	
G-	Airbus A320-214	3991	D-AV	09R	EasyJet Airline Company Ltd	Luton	
G-	Airbus A320-214	4004	D-AV	09R	EasyJet Airline Company Ltd	Luton	
G-	Airbus A320-214	4034	D-AV	09R	EasyJet Airline Company Ltd	Luton	
G-	Airbus A320-214	4046	D-AV	09R	EasyJet Airline Company Ltd	Luton	
G-	Airbus A321-231	4148	D-AV	09R	EasyJet Airline Company Ltd	Luton	
G-	Airbus A321-231	4155	D-AV	09R	EasyJet Airline Company Ltd	Luton	
G-EZUB	Zenair CH.601HD Zodiac	PFA 162-12765		13. 9.04	R A C Stephens	(Billingshurst)	
	(Built R A C Stephens)						
G-EZVS	Colt 77B Balloon (Hot Air)	063	SE-ZVS	6. 7.04	A J Lovell	Goteborg, Sweden	24. 2.09E
G-EZXO	Colt 56A Balloon (Hot Air)	421	SE-ZXO	6. 7.04	A J Lovell	Goteborg, Sweden	24. 2.09E
G-EZYU	Piper PA-34-200 Seneca	34-7450110	G-BCDB	4. 7.01	G F Strain	Bournemouth	20.11.08E
			N41346		*(Current status uncertain, damaged in Galway 16.2.08)*		
G-EZZA	Europa Aviation Europa XS	537		10. 5.02	J C R Davey	(Bicester)	
	(Built J C R Davey - pr.no.PFA 247-13841) *(Rotax 914)* *(Monowheel u/c)*						
G-EZZY	Evektor EV-97 Eurostar	2006.28.30		1. 8.06	G and P M G Verity		
	(Built G Verity, pr. no PFA315-14533)					Newton Bank Farm, Daresbury	3. 4.09P

G-FAAA - G-FZZZ

G-FABB	Cameron V-77 Balloon (Hot Air)	822	LX-FAB	13.12.89	P Trumper	Whitchurch Canonicorum, Bridport	23.10.09E
G-FABI	Robinson R44 Astro	0325		5. 4.97	R C Hields t/a Hields Aviation	Hawarden	21. 5.09E
G-FABM	Beech 95-B55A Baron	TC-2259	G-JOND	22. 2.91	P E T Price, J E Balmer and F B Miles		
			G-BMVC, N66456			Gloucestershire	10. 9.09E

G-FABS	Thunder Ax9-120 Series 2 Balloon (Hot Air)	2399		8. 6.93	R C Corrall	Cretingham, Woodbridge	19.10.02T
G-FACE	Cessna 172S Skyhawk SP	172S9194	N52733	24.10.02	M O Loxton	Parsonage Farm, Eastchurch	6.11.08E
G-FAIR	SOCATA TB-10 Tobago	241		13.10.81	Fairwings Ltd	Rochester	16. 8.09E
G-FAJC	Alpi Pioneer 300 Hawk	xxx		19. 4.07	F A Cavaciuti	Hardwick, Abergavenny	6. 6.08P
	(Built F A Cavaciuti - PFA 330A-14639)						
G-FAJM	Robinson R44 Raven II	12394		8. 9.08	A McFarlane	Perth	12.11.09E
G-FALC	Aeromere F 8L Falco 3	224	G-AROT	19. 2.81	D M Burbridge	Enstone	19. 6.11S
G-FALO	Sequoia F 8L Falco	1401		10. 5.02	M J and S E Aherne	(Smallford, St Albans)	
G-FAME	CFM Starstreak Shadow SA-II	K 273-SA		23. 5.96	B Hawley	Enstone	14. 1.09P
	(Built T J Palmer - pr.no.PFA 206A-12973) (Jabiru 2200)						
G-FAMH	Zenair CH.701 STOL	PFA 187-13301		26. 6.98	F Omaraie-Hamdanie	Hunsdon	23.11.09P
	(Built A M Harrhy) (Jabiru 2200A)						
G-FANL	Cessna R172K Hawk XP	R1722873	N736XQ	7. 6.79	J A Rees (Operated Haverfordwest Air Charter Services)		
						Haverfordwest	24. 7.09E
G-FARA	British Aerospace Jetstream Series 3102	740	LN-FAM	15. 7.08	Highland Airways Ltd	Inverness	31. 8.09E
			C-GJPO, (N2247R), C-GJPO, (N331QC), G-31-470				
G-FARE	Robinson R44 Raven II	10454		16. 8.04	Toriamos Ltd	(Harolds Cross, Dublin)	7.10.09E
G-FARL	Pitts S-1E	1	N333AB	22.10.03	F L McGee (Carries "N333AB" also)		
	(Built S C Burgess)					Liverpool-John Lennon	12. 4.09P
G-FARO	Star-Lite SL-1	PFA 175-11359		19. 6.89	M K Faro	Henstridge	18.11.08P
	(Built M K Faro) (Rotax 447)						
G-FARR	SAN Jodel D 150 Mascaret	58	F-BNIN	21. 7.81	G H Farr	Dairy House Farm, Worleston	19. 5.09P
G-FARY	QAC Quickie Tri-Q	PFA 094A-10951		2. 4.02	A Bloomfield and A Underwood		
	(Built J C Simpson and F Sayyah) (Limbach L2000)					Headon Farm, Retford	15. 6.08P
G-FATB	Commander Aircraft Commander 114B	14624	N6037Y	3. 7.96	James D Peace and Co	(Kirkwall)	28. 9.09E
G-FATE	Sequoia F.8L Falco	757	N290	8.10.08	D Mottram tr G-FATE Flying Group	(Blackwater)	
	(Built R M Moore)						
G-FAUX	Cessna 182S Skylane	18280190	D-EWEI	4.12.03	R S Faux	Southend	23. 4.09E
G-FAVC	de Havilland DH.80A Puss Moth	DHC.225	CF-AVC	21.11.03	Liddell Aircraft Ltd (Noted 6.07)	Bournemouth	
	(Built de Havilland Canada)						
G-FAVS	Piper PA-32-300 Cherokee Six	32-7540091	G-BKEK OY-TOP	15. 8.08	Favourites Racing Ltd	Turweston	13. 8.09E
G-FBAT	Aeroprakt A22 Foxbat	PFA 317-13591		16. 5.00	J Jordan	Otherton, Cannock	13. 7.09P
	(Built G Faulkner) (Rotax 912-S)						
G-FBEA	Embraer ERJ 190-200 LR	19000029	PT-SGD	1. 9.06	Flybe Ltd "Wings Of The Community"	Exeter	31. 8.09E
	(Embraer 195)						
G-FBEB	Embraer ERJ 190-200 LR	19000057	PT-SII	1.12.06	Flybe Ltd	Exeter	4.12.09E
	(Embraer 195)						
G-FBEC	Embraer ERJ 190-200 LR	19000069	PT-SJI	23. 3.07	Flybe Ltd	Exeter	25. 3.09E
	(Embraer 195)						
G-FBED	Embraer ERJ 190-200 LR	19000084	PT-SNB	4. 6.07	Flybe Ltd	Exeter	5. 6.09E
	(Embraer 195)						
G-FBEE	Embraer ERJ 190-200 LR	19000093	PT-SNN	26. 7.07	Flybe Ltd	Exeter	29. 7.09E
	(Embraer 195)						
G-FBEF	Embraer ERJ 190-200 LR	19000104	PT-SNY	6. 9.07	Flybe Ltd	Exeter	9. 9.09E
	(Embraer 195)						
G-FBEG	Embraer ERJ 190-200 LR	19000120	PT-SQO	1.11.07	Flybe Ltd	Exeter	4.11.09E
	(Embraer 195)						
G-FBEH	Embraer ERJ 190-200 LR	19000128	PT-SQX	23.11.07	Flybe Ltd	Exeter	26.11.09E
	(Embraer 195)						
G-FBEI	Embraer ERJ 190-200 LR	19000143	PT-SYV	10. 1.08	Flybe Ltd	Exeter	14. 1.10E
	(Embraer 195)						
G-FBEJ	Embraer ERJ 190-200 LR	19000155	PT-SAK	6. 3.08	Flybe Ltd	Exeter	
	(Embraer 195)						
G-FBEK	Embraer ERJ 190-200 LR	19000168	PT-SDC	25. 4.08	Flybe Ltd	Exeter	28. 4.09E
	(Embraer 195)						
G-FBEL	Embraer ERJ 190-200 LR	19000184	PT-SDS	23. 6.08	Flybe Ltd	Exeter	26. 6.09E
	(Embraer 195)						
G-FBEM	Embraer ERJ 190-200 LR	19000204	PT-SGN	28. 8.08	Flybe Ltd	Exeter	27. 8.09E
	(Embraer 195)						
G-FBEN	Embraer ERJ 190-200 LR	19000213	PT-	16.10.08	Flybe Ltd	Exeter	15.10.09E
	(Embraer 195)						
G-FBII	Comco Ikarus C42 FB100	0310-6574		18.12.03	F Beeson	(Nantwich)	9. 2.09P
	(Built Aerosport Ltd)						
G-FBLI	Cessna 510 Citation Mustang	510-0130		6.11.08	TAG Aviation (UK) Ltd (Operated Blink Air Taxi Service)		
						Farnborough	5.11.09E
G-FBLK	Cessna 510 Citation Mustang	510-0027	N327CM N4092E	2. 5.08	TAG Aviation (UK) Ltd (Operated Blink Air Taxi Service)		
						Farnborough	1. 5.09E
G-FBMW	Cameron N-90 Balloon (Hot Air)	3019		23. 4.93	K-J Schwer	Erbach-Donaurieden, Germany	10. 9.05A
G-FBNK	Cessna 510 Mustang	510-0067	N967CM	22.12.08	TAG Aviation (UK) Ltd (Operated Blink Air Taxi Service)		
						Farnborough	12. 1.10E
G-FBOY	Skystar Kitfox Mk.7	PFA 172D-14696		12. 9.07	A Bray	(Brinklow, Rugby)	
	(Built A Bray)						
G-FBPI	Air Navigation and Engineering Co ANEC IV Missel Thrush			19. 1.99	R Trickett (On loan to Boulton Paul Heritage Project)		
	(Built R Trickett)	PFA 312-13417				Pendeford, Wolverhampton	
G-FBRN	Piper PA-28-181 Archer II	28-8290166	D-ERBN N82628	3. 8.98	Herefordshire Aero Club Ltd	Shobdon	17.11.09E
G-FBTT	Aeroprakt A22-L Foxbat	PFA 317A-14743		8. 1.08	G C Ellis	RAF Honington	27. 5.09P
	(Built G C Ellis)						
G-FBWH	Piper PA-28R-180 Cherokee Arrow		SE-FCV	23. 8.78	F T Short	Whaley Farm, New York, Lincoln	6. 5.09E
		28R-30368					
G-FCAB	Diamond DA.42 Twin Star	42.060	OE-VPI	25.10.05	Halfpenny Green Flight Centre Ltd		
						Wolverhampton	15.11.08E

Reg	Type	c/n	Prev id	Date	Owner/Operator	Location	Expiry
G-FCAP	Cessna 560XL Citation XLS	560-5793	N5264A	25. 6.08	Direct Air Executive Ltd	Stansted	24. 6.09E
G-FCAV	Schleicher ASK 13	13015	BGA1396-CAV	2. 9.08	M F Cuming	Shenington	
G-FCBI	Schweizer 269C-1 *(Schweizer 300)*	0296	N86G	10. 7.07	CSE Bournemouth Ltd	Bournemouth	29. 4.09E
G-FCCC	Schleicher AS-K 13	13035	BGA1427-CCC	5. 8.08	Shenington Gliding Club Ltd	Shenington	
	(Type amended to AS-K 13 on 1.12.08)		RAFGSA R83, BGA1427				
G-FCDB	Cessna 550 Citation Bravo	550-0985	N5269J	10. 9.01	Eurojet Aviation Ltd	Birmingham	9. 9.09E
G-FCED	Piper PA-31T2 Cheyenne IIXL	31T-8166013	C-FCED	27. 9.04	Air Medical Fleet Ltd	Oxford	8. 2.09E
			N2501Y				
G-FCKD	Eurocopter EC.120B Colibri	1209	PH-ECK	11. 1.06	Pacific Helicopters Ltd	Denham	16. 2.09E
			ZK-HJD, ZK-HVQ				
G-FCLB	Boeing 757-28A	28164	N751NA	25. 3.97	Thomas Cook Airlines Ltd	Manchester	29. 4.09E
G-FCLC	Boeing 757-28A	28166		9. 5.97	Thomas Cook Airlines Ltd	Manchester	8. 5.09E
G-FCLE	Boeing 757-28A	28171		24. 5.98	Thomas Cook Airlines Ltd	Manchester	23. 5.09E
G-FCLF	Boeing 757-28A	28835		24. 3.99	Thomas Cook Airlines Ltd	Manchester	14. 1.10E
G-FCLG	Boeing 757-28A	24367	N701LF	18.12.98	Thomas Cook Airlines Ltd	Manchester	2. 4.09E
			EI-CLM, N381LF, N240LA, C-GTSK, C-GNXI, G-GAWB *(for FedEx as N914FD)*				
G-FCLH	Boeing 757-28A	26274	N751LF	17. 2.99	Thomas Cook Airlines Ltd	Manchester	12. 5.09E
			EI-CLU, N161LF				
G-FCLI	Boeing 757-28A	26275	N651LF	17. 3.99	Thomas Cook Airlines Ltd	Manchester	1. 6.09E
			EI-CLV, N151LF				
G-FCLJ	Boeing 757-2Y0	26160	N160GE	26. 4.99	Thomas Cook Airlines Ltd	Manchester	25. 4.09E
			EI-CJX, N3519M, N1786B, (B-2830)				
G-FCLK	Boeing 757-2Y0	26161	N161GE	6. 4.99	Thomas Cook Airlines Ltd	Manchester	5 4.09E
			EI-CJY, N3521N				
G-FCOM	Slingsby T.59F Kestrel 19	1765	BGA1723-CQM	23. 1.09	P A C Wheatcroft and A Guy	Lasham	
G-FCSL	Piper PA-31-350 Navajo Chieftain		PH-PTC	18. 4.08	Culross Aerospace Ltd	(Chessington)	27. 7.09E
		31-7852052	G-CLAN, N27549				
G-FCSP	Robin DR.400-180 Régent	2022		24.10.90	F C Smith	Biggin Hill	13. 4.09E
G-FCUK	Pitts S-1C	02	OH-XPB	9. 8.02	P J Burgess	RAF Cranwell	27. 2.09P
	(Built A Ronnberg) (Lycoming O-360)						
G-FCUM	Robinson R44 Raven II	11723		28. 4.07	The Grange Country Club Ltd	Neston, Chester	20. 5.09E
G-FDDY	Schleicher Ka 6CR	678	BGA2044-DDY	28. 3.08	D Bowden tr DDY Group	Cross Hayes	
G-FDPS	Pitts S-2C	6066	N130PS	11. 2.05	Flights and Dreams Ltd	Cranfield	10. 3.09E
	(Built Aviat Aircraft Inc) (Lycoming AEIO-540)						
G-FDZA	Boeing 737-8Q5	35134	N1786B	23. 1.07	Thomson Airways Ltd	Luton	22. 1.10E
G-FDZB	Boeing 737-8Q5	35131		19. 4.07	Thomson Airways Ltd	Luton	18. 4.09E
G-FDZD	Boeing 737-8Q5	35132		30. 5.07	Thomson Airways Ltd	Luton	29. 5.09E
G-FDZE	Boeing 737-8K5	35137	N1786B	16. 1.08	Thomson Airways Ltd	Luton	15. 1.10E
G-FDZF	Boeing 737-8K5	35138	N1786B	4. 2.08	Thomson Airways Ltd	Luton	3. 2.09E
G-FDZG	Boeing 737-8K5	35139		10. 3.08	Thomson Airways Ltd	Luton	9. 3.09E
G-FDZJ	Boeing 737-8K5	34690	D-ATUI	30. 4.08	Thomson Airways Ltd	Luton	30. 4.09E
			N1786B				
G-FDZO	Boeing 737-8K5	34691	D-ATUA	3. 6.08	Thomson Airways Ltd	Luton	2. 6.09E
G-FDZP	Boeing 737-8K5	34692	D-ATUB	2. 7.08	Thomson Airways Ltd	Luton	2. 7.09E
			N1786B				
G-FDZR	Boeing 737-8K5	35145		.08R	Thomson Airways Ltd	Luton	
G-FDZS	Boeing 737-8K5	35147		.08R	Thomson Airways Ltd	Luton	
G-FEAB	Piper PA-28-181 Archer III	2843567	N53690	7. 7.04	Feabrex Ltd	Rochester	18. 7.09E
G-FEBB	Grob G104 Speed Astir IIB	4040	BGA2545-EBB	3.12.07	A F Grinter tr The Astir Group	Pocklington	27. 4.08
G-FEBJ	Schleicher ASW 19B	19282	BGA2552-EBJ	2.11.07	J C Armstrong tr G-FEBJ Group	(Huntingdon)	28. 9.08
G-FECO	Grob G102 Astir CS77	1837	BGA2582-ECQ	14.12.07	C Peterson	Tibenham	16. 5.08
G-FEDA	Eurocopter EC.120B Colibri	1129	F-WQOD	2. 8.00	J Henshall	(Cobham)	28. 8.09E
G-FEET	P&M Pegasus Quik	8133		6.10.05	A N Wilkinson	Headon Farm, Retford	17.10.08P
G-FEFE	Scheibe SF25B Falke	46126	EI-BVZ	11. 4.94	M H Simms	Shipdham	8. 6.06
	(Stark-Stamo MS1500)		D-KADB				
G-FELL	Europa Aviation Europa	372		17. 3.98	N J Wakeling tr G-FELL Flying Group	Leicester	7. 2.09P
	(Built J A Fell - pr.no.PFA 247-13208) (Tri-gear u/c)						
G-FELT	Cameron N-77 Balloon (Hot Air)	1174		19. 7.85	Allan Industries Ltd *"Fuzzy Felt"*		
						Aston Rowant, Watlington	9. 7.09E
G-FELX	CZAW Sportcruiser	PFA 338-14661		17. 9.07	T F Smith	Cherry Tree Farm, Monewdon	3. 8.09P
	(Built T F Smith) (Rotax 912ULS)						
G-FERN	Mainair Blade 912	1342-1002-7-W1137		18.10.02	M H Moulai *(Operated Silver Fern Microlights)*		
						Sandtoft	26.11.09P
G-FERV	Rolladen-Schneider LS4	4257	BGA2899-ERV	12. 9.07	R J J Bennett	Long Mynd	20. 9.08
G-FESS	Cyclone Airsports Pegasus Quantum 15-912						
		7840	G-CBBZ	12. 2.08	P M Fessi	Swinford, Rugby	16. 9.08P
G-FEVS	PZL-Bielsko SZD-50-3 Puchacz	B-1091	BGA2992-EVS	14. 8.08	Deeside Gliding Club (Aberdeenshire) Ltd	Aboyne	27. 8.09E
G-FEWG	Fuji FA.200-160 Aero Subaru	FA200-232	G-BBNV	15.10.04	Caseright Ltd	Turweston	27. 8.09E
G-FEZZ	Agusta-Bell 206B-2 JetRanger II	8317	SU-YAD	16. 9.98	R J Myram	Wycombe Air Park	11.11.09E
			YU-HAT				
G-FFAB	Cameron N-105 Balloon (Hot Air)	4067		20. 2.97	B J Hammond *(Forever Friends titles)*	Chelmsford	10. 7.09E
G-FFAF	Reims Cessna F150L	F15001033	I-FFAF	10. 2.06	M Howells	Barton	9. 6.09E
G-FFEN	Reims Cessna F150M	F15001204	PH-VGL	25. 8.78	W Stitt and M Fryer	Cherry Tree Farm, Monewden	23. 4.09E
G-FFFG	Dassault Falcon 900EX	155	N852CA	30.10.08	TAG Aviation (UK) Ltd	Farnborough	12. 1.10E
			LN-AOC, F-GSMT, F-WQBN, N955EX, F-WWFN, (LN-SEH)				
G-FFFT	Lindstrand LBL 31A Balloon (Hot Air)	705		30. 5.00	J Tyrrell and W Rousell *"Financial Times"*		
						Wollaston, Wellingborough	1. 5.09E
G-FFIT	P&M Aviation Quik	8238		15. 1.07	K A Armstrong	South Cave	11. 2.09P
G-FFOX	Hawker Hunter T 7B	41H-670788	WV318	10. 1.96	N Sills tr WV318 Group *(As "WV318:D" in RAF c/s)*		
	(Composite including components of WV322- see G-BZSE)					Kemble	29. 4.09P
G-FFRA	Dassault Falcon 20DC	132	N902FR	28. 5.92	Cobham Leasing Ltd	Durham Tees Valley	20.10.09E
			(N23FR), (N149FE), N2FE, N560L, N4348F, F-WMKG				
G-FFRI	Aérospatiale AS.355F1 Ecureuil 2	5120	G-GLOW	15. 4.93	Sterling Helicopters Ltd	Norwich	23. 5.09E
			G-PAPA, G-CNET, G-MCAH				

G-FFTI	SOCATA TB-20 Trinidad	1065		23. 2.90	R Lenk	Old Buckenham	6. 3.09E
G-FFTT	Lindstrand LBL Newspaper SS Balloon (Hot Air) 673			10. 7.00	P Mason and P Saunders	Brentwood	11.11.06A
G-FFUN	Cyclone Airsports Pegasus Quantum 15 (Rotax 503)	6655	G-MYMD	9. 6.99	J R F Hollingstead	(London NW6)	25. 1.09P
G-FFWD	Cessna 310R II	310R0579	G-TVKE	20. 2.90	T S Courtman	Nottingham-East Midlands	8.12.09E
			G-EURO, N87468				
G-FGAZ	Schleicher Ka 6E	4103	BGA2651-EFM	21. 9.07	G.S.Foster	Parham Park	17. 4.08
			RAFGSA				
G-FGID	Vought FG-1D Corsair (Built Goodyear Aircraft Corporation)	3111	N8297 N9154Z, Bu.88297	1.11.91	Patina Ltd *(As "KD345:130:A" in RN 1850 Sqdn c/s)* *(Operated The Fighter Collection)* Duxford		20.11.09P
G-FGSI	Montgomerie-Bensen B8MR (Built F G Shepherd)	PGA G/01A-1354		19. 4.07	F G Shepherd	(Leadgate, Alston)	
G-FGSK	Cameron Beer Crate-120 SS Balloon (Hot Air) 10417			6. 4.04	Ballon-Sport und Luftwerbung Dresden GmbH Dresden, Germany		28. 5.09E
G-FHAS	Scheibe SF25E Super Falke (Limbach SL1700)	4359	(D-KOOG)	14. 5.81	Burn Gliding Club Ltd	Burn	18. 7.08E
G-FIAT	Piper PA-28-140 Cherokee F	28-7425162	G-BBYW N9622N	19. 7.89	Demero Ltd and Transcourt Ltd	Oxford	19. 8.09E
G-FIBS	Aérospatiale AS.350BA Ecureuil	2074	JA9732	14. 6.94	G Mazza	(Sarnico, Italy)	8. 8.09E
G-FICS	Flight Design CTSW	07.10.18		17.12.07	R Eve	Damyns Hall, Upminster	16.12.08P
	(Assembled P&M Aviation Ltd with c/n 8348) (P&M show 07.10.07 but believed incorrect)						
G-FIFA	Cessna 404 Titan	404-0644	G-TVIP	24. 5.07	Fly (CI) Ltd *(Operated Trans Euro Air)*	Southend	5. 2.10E
			G-KIWI, G-BHNI, LN-LGM, SE-IFV, G-BHNI, (N5302J)				
G-FIFE	Reims Cessna FA152 Aerobat	FA1520351	G-BFYN	15. 2.95	Tayside Aviation Ltd	Dundee	1. 3.09E
G-FIFI	SOCATA TB-20 Trinidad	688	G-BMWS	16. 1.87	F A Saker	Denham	12. 8.09E
G-FIFO	Cessna 152	15285177	G-OAFT	4. 9.08	A Kitts and C Salway	Popham	22. 9.09E
			G-BNKM, N6161Q				
G-FIFT	Comco Ikarus C42 FB100	0409-6623		2. 8.04	A R Jones	Carlisle	17.10.09P
G-FIGA	Cessna 152 II	15284644	N6243M	3. 6.87	Central Aircraft Leasing Ltd	Exeter	31. 8.09E
G-FIGB	Cessna 152 II	15285925	N95561	16.11.87	A J Gomes *(Fuselage noted 3.08)*	Biggin Hill	12. 2.00T
G-FIGP	Boeing 737-2E7	22875	EI-CJI	11. 4.05	European Skybus Ltd	Bournemouth	5. 6.08E
			G-BMDF, (PK-RI.), G-BMDF, 4X-BAB, N4570B *(Stored engineless 1.09)*				
G-FIII	Extra EA.300/L	091	G-RGEE D-ESEW	6.12.04	J S Allison	Andrewsfield	16. 3.09E
G-FIJJ	Reims Cessna F177RG Cardinal RG *(Wichita c/n 17700194)*	F177RG0031	G-AZFP	29. 4.99	D R Vale	Derby	15. 6.09E
G-FIJR	Lockheed L188PF Electra	1138	(EI-HCF)	12. 9.91	Atlantic Airlines Ltd	Coventry	12. 9.09E
			G-FIJR, C-FIJR, CF-IJR, N134US				
G-FIJV	Lockheed L188C Electra	1129	EI-HCE	29. 8.91	Atlantic Airlines Ltd *(noted in open storage 8.08)*		
			G-FIJV, C-FIJV, CF-IJV, N7143C			Coventry	27. 9.07T
G-FILE	Piper PA-34-200T Seneca II	34-8070108	N8140Z	23. 7.87	Bristol Flying Centre Ltd	Bristol	19.12.09E
G-FILL	Piper PA-31 Navajo C	31-7912069	OO-EJM N3521	28. 6.96	P V Naylor-Leyland	Milton, Peterborough	13.10.09E
G-FINA	Reims Cessna F150L	F15000826	G-BIFT PH-CEW	12.10.93	A G Freeman	Turweston	3. 4.09E
G-FIND	Reims Cessna F406 Caravan II	F406-0045	OY-PEU	16. 8.90	Reconnaisance Ventures Ltd *(Operated Ordnance Survey)*		
			5Y-LAN, G-FIND, PH-ALV, F-WZDT			Blackpool	5. 5.09E
G-FINK	British Aerospace BAe 125 Series 1000B (Built Corporate Jets Ltd)	259087	XA-RGG XA-TGK, G-SHEC, G-SCCC, G-5-771	18. 1.07	B T Fink	Southend	11. 2.09E
G-FINT	Piper L-4B Cub	9444	N10491 43-583, (42-59393)	5.12.08	G and H M Picarella *(Painted as "3583:44D" in USAAF c/s)*	(Billingshurst)	
G-FINZ	III Sky Arrow 650 T (Built A G Counsell)	PFA 298-13824		8. 1.03	A G Counsell	Perth	12. 5.09P
G-FIRM	Cessna 550 Citation Bravo	550-0940	N5263S	29. 9.00	Marshall of Cambridge Aerospace Ltd	Cambridge	2.10.09E
G-FIRS	Robinson R22 Beta II	2807		15. 4.98	Multiflight Ltd	Leeds-Bradford	23. 5.09E
G-FIRZ	Murphy Renegade 912 (Built D M Wood and M Hanley)	PFA 188-13494		10.12.99	S Koutsoukos	Perth	12. 5.09P
G-FISH	Cessna 310R II	310R1845	N2740Y	8. 5.81	ACS Contracts Ltd	Perth	28.10.07E
G-FIXX	Van's RV-7 (Built P C Hambilton)	PFA 323-14225		31. 8.06	Hambilton Engineering Ltd (Penwortham, Preston)		
G-FIZU	Lockheed L188CF Electra	2014	EI-CHY	6. 4.93	Atlantic Airlines Ltd	Coventry	3. 1.09E
			G-FIZU, SE-IZU, (N857ST), N857U, PH-LLG				
G-FIZY	Europa Aviation Europa XS	384	G-DDSC	16.12.99	R Eyles	White Ox Mead, Norton St Philip	17. 9.09P
	(Built G N Holland - pr.no.PFA 247-13291) (Jabiru 3300) (Tri-gear u/c)						
G-FIZZ	Piper PA-28-161 Cherokee Warrior II	28-7816301	N2721M	1.12.78	Tecair Aviation Ltd	Shipdham	14. 7.09E
	(Officially registered by CAA with pi N857U)						
G-FJCE	Thruster T 600T (Rotax 532)	9128-T600T-032		25.11.98	F Cameron	(Craigavon, Belfast)	31. 7.04P
G-FJET	Cessna 550 Citation II	550-0419	G-DCFR G-WYLX, VH-JVS, G-JETD, N1217N	7. 7.97	London Executive Aviation Ltd	London City	17. 1.10E
G-FJMS	Partenavia P68B	113	G-SVHA OY-AJH	7. 9.92	J B Randle	Church Farm, Piltdown	27. 8.09E
G-FJTH	Aeroprakt A22 Foxbat (Built F J T Hancock)	PFA 317-13928		16. 7.03	F J T Hancock	(Berrow, Malvern)	5. 3.09P
G-FKNH	Piper PA-15 Vagabond (Continental C85)	15-291	CF-KNH N4517H, NC4517H	19. 3.97	M J Mothershaw	RAF Woodvale	15. 5.11S
G-FKOS	Piper PA-28-181 Archer II	28-7790591	OE-KOS OY-BTL	27. 3.07	M K Johnson	Shoreham	26. 4.09E
G-FLAG	Colt 77A Balloon (Hot Air)	2000		20. 9.90	B A Williams	Maidstone	18.10.06T
G-FLAK	Beech E55 Baron	TE-1128	N4771M	26. 9.89	P W Huntley *"Red Baron"*	(Leatherhead)	29. 7.09E
G-FLAV	Piper PA-28-161 Warrior II	28-8016283	N8171X	7. 4.94	S D E Mills tr The Crew Flying Group Nottingham City-Tollerton		7. 2.10E

Reg	Type	C/n	Prev id	Date	Owner/operator	Location	Date2
G-FLBI	Robinson R44 Raven II	10158		10. 9.03	Freshfield Lane Brickworks Ltd	Shoreham	29.10.09E
G-FLBK	Cessna 510 Citation Mustang	510-0068	N968CM	6.11.08	TAG Aviation (UK) Ltd *(Operated Blink Air Taxi Service)*	Farnborough	10.11.09E
G-FLCA	Fleet 80 Canuck	068	CS-ACQ CF-DQP	18. 7.90	E C Taylor tr Tamyco-Oag *(Noted 1.09)*	Turweston	
G-FLCT	Hallam Fleche	PFA 309-13389		21.10.98	R G Hallam	(Nether Alderley, Macclesfield)	
	(Built R G Hallam)						
G-FLDG	Best Off Sky Ranger 912(2)	SKRxxxx390		21. 4.04	A J Gay	South Wraxall	5. 9.08P
	(Built A J Gay - pr.no.BMAA HB/328)						
G-FLEA	SOCATA TB-10 Tobago	235	PH-TTP G-FLEA	31. 7.81	R Kilburn tr TB Group	Leicester	8. 8.09E
G-FLEE	Interplane ZJ-Viera	VIERA A6/08M		26. 1.09	P C Piggott	Husbands Bosworth	
G-FLEW	Lindstrand LBL 90A Balloon (Hot Air)	586		21. 1.99	A Nimmo *(Lindstrand Balloons titles)*	Dubai, United Arab Emirates	13. 9.09E
G-FLEX	Mainair Sports Pegasus Quik	7953		15. 5.03	J W McCarthy	Ince Blundell	23. 7.09P
G-FLGT	Lindstrand LBL 105A Balloon (Hot Air)	888		5.12.02	Ballongaventyr I Skane AB	Kävlinge, Sweden	1. 4.09E
G-FLIK	Pitts S-1S	PFA 009-10513		7. 1.81	R P Millinship	Leicester	18. 6.09P
	(Built R P Millinship) (Lycoming O-320)						
G-FLIP	Reims Cessna FA152 Aerobat	FA1520375	G-BOES G-FLIP	29.12.80	Cristal Air Ltd	Shoreham	6.10.09E
G-FLIT	RotorWay Executive 162F	6324		22.12.98	R S Snell	Phoenix Farm, Lower Upham	13. 8.09P
	(Built R F Rhodes) (RotorWay RI 162F)						
G-FLIZ	Staaken Z-21 Flitzer	006		24. 3.97	M J Clark *(Also carries "D-694")*	Kittyhawk Farm, Deanland	3. 4.09P
	(Built G L Brown - pr.no.PFA 223-13115)						
	(Touched down left main wheel first in a crosswind at Lossiemouth 22. 8.08 and aircraft overturned causing substantial damage)						
G-FLKE	Scheibe SF25C Falke	44673		5.10.01	T M Holloway tr RAF Gliding and Soaring Association	RAF Halton	5. 2.09E
	(Rotax 912S)						
G-FLKS	Scheibe SF25C Falke	44662	D-KIEQ	16.10.00	London Gliding Club Proprietary Ltd	Dunstable	5. 2.10E
	(Rotax 912S)						
G-FLOA	Cameron O-120 Balloon (Hot Air)	4006		4.10.96	Floating Sensations Ltd	Thatcham	11. 8.08T
G-FLOP	Cessna 152	15282590	N69265	25.11.05	Cloud 9 Aviation (Leasing) Ltd	Full Sutton	20. 2.08E
G-FLOR	Europa Aviation Europa	171		11.11.98	A F C van Eldik	Pent Farm, Postling	1.10.09P
	(Built A F C Van Eldik - pr.no.PFA 247-12793) (Monowheel u/c)						
G-FLOW	Cessna 172S Skyhawk	172S9677	N6127S	19. 8.04	M P Dolan	City of Derry	24. 8.09E
G-FLOX	Europa Aviation Europa	129		28. 6.95	T W Eaton tr DPT Group		
	(Built P S Buchan, T W Eaton & B Lewer - pr.no.PFA 247-12732) (Jabiru 2200A) (Monowheel u/c) Fowle Hall Farm, Laddingford						9.10.09P
G-FLPI	Rockwell Commander 112A	205	SE-FLP (N1205J)	16. 3.79	H J Freeman	Newcastle	15. 4.09E
G-FLSH	IAV Bacau Yakovlev Yak-52	877409	RA-44550 LY-AKF, DOSAAF 21? (yellow)	9. 6.03	M A Wright tr Boogair *"52"*	Little Gransden	14. 9.09P
G-FLTA	British Aerospace BAe 146 Series 200	E2048	N189US N365PS	25. 2.98	Flightline Ltd	Southend	26. 2.09E
					(Ceased operations 3.12.08, stored all-white 2.09)		
G-FLTB	British Aerospace BAe 146 Series 200	E2024	EI-CZO	14. 5.02	Flightline Ltd *(Stored 2.09, BA titles)*	Southend	30. 1.09E
	G-FLTB, G-CLHA, (G-GNTX), G-DEBC, N168US, N348PS *(Ceased operations 3.12.08)*						
G-FLTC	British Aerospace BAe 146 Series 300	E3205	G-JEBH	15.12.04	Flightline Ltd *(Stored 2.09)*	Southend	17.10.09E
	G-BTVO, G-NJID, B-1777, G-BTVO, G-6-205 *(Ceased operations 3.12.08)*						
G-FLTF	British Aerospace BAe 146 Series 200	E2022	EI-DMK	25. 4.08	Flightline Ltd *(Stored, BA titles 2.09)*	Southend	24. 4.09E
	G-DEBE, N163US, N346PS *(Ceased operations 3.12.08)*						
G-FLTG	Cameron A-140 Balloon (Hot Air)	4506		3.11.00	Floating Sensations Ltd	Thatcham	13. 9.06T
G-FLTL	McDonnell Douglas MD-83	49790	OE-LHG EC-FZC, EC-742, EC-ESJ, EC-307	12. 2.07	Flightline Ltd *(Stored 2.09 all-white)*	Southend	4. 3.09E
					(Ceased operations 3.12.08)		
G-FLTZ	Beech 58 Baron	TH-1154	G-PSVS N5824T, YV-266P	21. 9.93	Flightline Ltd	Southend	21.10.08E
					(Ceased operations 3.12.08)		
G-FLUZ	Rolladen-Schneider LS8-18	8267	BGA4718-JRK	30. 4.08	D M King *"618"*	Snitterfield	
G-FLYA	Mooney M 20J Mooney 201	24-3124		8. 6.89	B Willis	Full Sutton	30. 3.09E
G-FLYB	Comco Ikarus C42 FB100	0309-6572		15. 9.03	C D Back tr G-FLYB Group	Old Sarum	20.11.09P
G-FLYC	Comco Ikarus C42 FB100	0503-6656		7. 4.05	Solent Flight Ltd	Lower Upham	6. 4.09P
G-FLYF	Mainair Blade 912	1371-0305-7-W1166		30. 3.05	Cool Water Direct Ltd	Baxby Manor, Husthwaite	2.12.09P
G-FLYG	Slingsby T.67C	2074	PH-SGA (PH-SBA)	23. 8.02	G Laden	Mount Airey Farm, South Cave	13. 7.09E
G-FLYH	Robinson R22 Beta	1932	CS-HEQ G-BXMR, N923FM, N2306E	4.10.02	J R Huggins	Lamberhurst Farm, Faversham	18.12.08E
G-FLYI	Piper PA-34-200 Seneca	34-7250144	G-BHVO SE-FYY	1. 9.81	Falcon Flying Services Ltd	Biggin Hill	10. 8.08E
G-FLYM	Comco Ikarus C42 FB100	0707-6903		30. 7.07	M G McQuillan	Newry	13. 9.08P
G-FLYP	Beagle B 206 Srs 2	B 058	N40CJ N97JH, G-AVHO, VQ-LAY, G-AVHO	15.10.98	Key Publishing (Holdings) Ltd	Cranfield	7.10.10S
G-FLYS	Robinson R44 Astro	0347		5. 6.97	Newmarket Plant Hire Ltd	Cambridge	3. 8.09E
G-FLYT	Europa Aviation Europa	057		15. 5.95	K F and R.Richardson	Wellesbourne Mountford	6. 5.00P
	(Built D W Adams - pr.no.PFA 247-12653) (NSI EA-81/100) (Conventional u/c)					(Noted 11.07)	
G-FLYX	Robinson R44 Raven II	11669		11. 4.07	Sitecrest Aviation LLP	Damyn's Hall, Upminster	19. 4.10E
G-FLYY	British Aircraft Corporation 167 Strikemaster Mk.80A		R Saudi AF 1112, G-27-31	3. 9.01	D T Barber	City of Derry	10. 6.09P
		EEP/JP/163					
G-FLZR	Staaken Z-21 Flitzer	PFA 223-13219		21. 9.01	J F Govan *(Complete 4.07)*	(East Linton)	
	(Built J F Govan)						
G-FMAM	Piper PA-28-151 Cherokee Warrior	28-7415056	G-BBXV N9603N	7. 6.90	P B Anderson tr Lima Tango Flying Group	Southend	15. 3.09E
G-FMGG	Maule M-5-235C Lunar Rocket	7260C	G-RAGG N5632M	30. 4.02	S Bierbaum	Bodmin	29. 5.09E
					(Operated Bodmin Light Aeroplane Services Ltd)		
G-FMKA	Diamond HK 36 TC Super Dimona	36.672		26. 4.00	G P Davis	Kemble	16. 7.09E
G-FMSG	Reims Cessna FA150K Aerobat	FA1500081	G-POTS G-AYUY	4. 1.95	G Owen	Humberside	21. 1.07T
G-FNES	Dassault Falcon 900EX	159	N900SG N900EX, N959EX, F-WWFR	12. 6.07	Matrix Aviation Ltd	Paris Le Bourget	26. 6.09E

G-FNEY	Reims Cessna F177RG Cardinal RG	F177RG0059	F-BTFQ	24. 2.04	F Ney	Nottingham-East Midlands	2.11.09E
G-FNLD	Cessna 172N Skyhawk II	17270596	(G-BOUG) N739KD	3. 8.88	R C Laming and M J Humphrey tr Papa Hotel Flying Group	Fenland	26. 2.09E
G-FNLY	Reims Cessna F172M	F17200910	G-WACX G-BAEX	20. 3.89	Skytrax Aviation Ltd	Manor Farm, Glatton	16. 4.09E
G-FNPT	Piper PA-28-161 Warrior III	2842163	N5346Y	2.10.02	Fleetwash Ltd (Cabair titles)	Elstree	16.10.09E
G-FOFO	Robinson R44 Raven II	10320		6. 4.04	Kuki Helicopter Sales Ltd	Gamston	24. 5.09E
G-FOGG	Cameron N-90 Balloon (Hot Air)	1365		21.11.86	J P E Money-Kyrle "Phileas Fogg"	Chippenham	25. 9.96A
G-FOGI	Europa Aviation Europa XS	385		29.10.04	B Fogg	Sleap	10. 8.09P
	(Built B Fogg -pr.no.PFA 247-13313)						
G-FOGY	Robinson R22 Beta	1020	N62991 F-GGAI	5. 7.99	Aero Maintenance Ltd	Walton Wood	29. 7.09E
G-FOKK	Fokker Dr.1 Triplane replica	PFA 238-14253		18. 1.06	S E and P D Ford (As "477/17" in German military (red) c/s)	Syhwell	20. 7.09P
	(Built P D Ford)						
G-FOLI	Robinson R22 Beta II	2813		25. 4.98	G M Duckworth	Wolverhampton	18. 6.09E
G-FOLY	Pitts S-2A	2213	N31477	26. 7.89	C T Charleston	Great Horkesley, Colchester	19. 3.09E
	(Built Aerotek Inc) (Lycoming AEIO-360)						
G-FONZ	Best Off Sky Ranger 912(2)	SKRxxxx369		15. 9.03	A A Pacitti tr G-FONZ Sky Ranger Group	Strathaven	28. 7.08P
	(Built A A Pacitti - pr.no.BMAA HB/304)						
G-FOPP	Neico Lancair 320	PFA 191-12319		14. 8.92	Airsport (UK) Ltd	Cranfield	30. 4.09P
	(Built M A Fopp) (Lycoming IO-320)						
G-FORA	Schempp-Hirth Ventus cT	126-400	BGA4449-JEF D-KFWH	28.11.07	A D Cook "4A"	RAF Weston-on-the-Green	6.12.07
G-FORC	SNCAN Stampe SV-4C	665	(G-BLTJ) F-BDNJ	6. 6.85	C C Rollings and F J Hodson	Gloucestershire	12. 6.09T
	(Renault 4P03)						
G-FORD	SNCAN Stampe SV-4C(G)	129	F-BBNS	7. 2.78	P H Meeson	Rotary Farm, Hatch	24. 5.10S
	(Gipsy Major 10)						
G-FORR	Piper PA-28-181 Archer III	2843336	N4160Z G-FORR, N4160Z	20. 4.00	A D Hoy	Jersey	23. 4.09E
G-FORZ	Pitts S-1S	PFA 009-13393		3.11.98	N W Parkinson (Noted 11.07)	(High Wycombe)	
	(Built N Parkinson)						
G-FOSY	SOCATA MS.880B Rallye Club	1304	G-AXAK	7.12.00	A G Foster	Humberside	17. 5.04
G-FOWL	Colt 90A Balloon (Hot Air)	1198		11. 3.88	The Packhouse Ltd	Farnham	17. 9.09E
G-FOWS	Cameron N-105 Balloon (Hot Air)	3995		11.12.96	S Hartnell, D L C Nelmes and R Waycott t/a Ezmerelda Balloon Syndicate "Fowlers Motorcycles"	Bristol	28. 5.09E
G-FOXA	Piper PA-28-161 Cadet	2841240	N9192B	17.11.89	The Leicestershire Aero Club Ltd	Leicester	10. 8.09E
G-FOXB	Aeroprakt A22 Foxbat	PFA 317-13878		15. 3.02	G D McCullough	Slieve Croob, Slievenamoney, Castlewellen	27. 9.07P
	(Buillt M Raflewski)						
G-FOXC	Denney Kitfox Model 3	773		8. 1.91	G Hawkins "Foxc Lady"	Newton Peverill Farm, Sturminster Marshall	10. 6.09P
	(Built B W Davis - pr.no.PFA 172-11900)						
G-FOXD	Denney Kitfox Model 2	PFA 172-11618		22.11.89	P P Trangmar	Kittyhawk Farm, Deanland	26.10.09P
	(Built D Hanley)						
G-FOXF	Denney Kitfox Model 4	PFA 172-12399		24. 3.00	M S Goodwin	Bridge of Weir	26. 7.08P
	(Built M S Goodwin) (Rotax 912-UL)						
G-FOXG	Denney Kitfox Model 2	452		15. 8.90	J U McKercher	Errol	13. 6.08P
	(Built S M Jackson - pr.no.PFA 172-11886) (Rotax 532)						
G-FOXI	Denney Kitfox Model 2	PFA 172-11508		21. 9.89	I M Walton	Wellesbourne Mountford	21. 8.04P
	(Built I N Jennison) (Rotax 532)						
G-FOXL	Zenair CH.601XL Zodiac	PFA 162B-14537		11.12.06	M J Lloyd	(Worcester)	
	(Built M J Lloyd)						
G-FOXM	Bell 206B-2 JetRanger II	1514	G-STAK G-BNIS, N35HF, N135VG	5. 2.93	R P Maydon tr Milton Keynes City Air (Operated for Fox FM Radio)	Oxford	11. 6.09E
G-FOXS	Denney Kitfox Model 2	458		15. 8.90	S P Watkins and C C Rea	Sheepcote Farm, Stourbridge	25. 4.07P
	(Built S P Watkins and C C Rea - pr.no.PFA 172-11571)						
G-FOXX	Denney Kitfox	PFA 172-11509		1.11.89	A W Hodder	Higherlands Farm, Branscombe	10. 9.07P
	(Built R O F Harper and P R Skeels) (Struck wire fence on take-off Branscombe 28. 8.07, crashed into line of trees and substantially damaged)						
G-FOXZ	Denney Kitfox	PFA 172-11834		4.12.90	S C Goozee	Mapperton Farm, Newton Peverill	17.12.07P
	(Built M Smalley and J C Whittle)						
G-FOZZ	Beech A36 Bonanza	E-2788	N345SF D-EUWR, N82404	23. 8.05	Go To Air Ltd	Blackpool	22. 9.09E
G-FPIG	Piper PA-28-151 Cherokee Warrior	28-7615001	G-BSSR N1190X	22. 3.00	G F Strain	(Whiteparish, Salisbury)	27. 4.09E
G-FPLB	Beech B200 Super King Air	BB-1048	N739MG N223MD, 9Y-TGY	3.12.97	Cobham Leasing Ltd (Operated Flight Precision)	Durham Tees Valley	11. 1.10E
G-FPLD	Beech B200 Super King Air	BB-1433	N43CE N43AJ, C-GMEV, C-GMEH, N8043K	2.11.01	Cobham Flight Inspection Ltd	Durham Tees Valley	19.11.09E
G-FPLE	Beech B200 Super King Air	BB-1256	N230DC N1847S, N184JS, N2676M	12. 9.05	Cobham Leasing Ltd (Operated Flight Precision)	Durham Tees Valley	19.12.08E
G-FPSA	Piper PA-28-161 Warrior II	28-8616038	G-RSFT G-WARI, N9276Y	28. 2.03	Deep Cleavage Ltd	Exeter	6. 5.09E
G-FRAD	Dassault Falcon 20E	304/511	9M-BDK G-FRAD, G-BCYF, F-WRQP	26.11.86	Cobham Leasing Ltd	Bournemouth	13. 6.09E
G-FRAF	Dassault Falcon 20E	295/500	N911FR I-EDIM, F-WRQQ	1. 9.87	Cobham Leasing Ltd (Operated FR Aviation)	Bournemouth	2. 7.09E
G-FRAG	Piper PA-32-300 Six	32-7940284	N3566L	21. 1.80	T A Houghton	Rochester	24. 5.09E
G-FRAH	Dassault Falcon 20DC	223	G-60-01 N900FR, (N904FR), N22FE, N4407F, F-WPUX	31. 5.90	Cobham Leasing Ltd (Operated FR Aviation)	Bournemouth	7.10.09E
G-FRAI	Dassault Falcon 20E	270	N901FR N37FE, N4435F, F-WPUZ	17.10.90	Cobham Leasing Ltd (Operated FR Aviation)	Bournemouth	3. 6.09E
G-FRAJ	Dassault Falcon 20DC	20	N903FR (N25FR), N5FE, (N146FE), N5FE, N367GA, N367, N842F, F-WMKJ	30. 4.91	Cobham Leasing Ltd (Operated FR Aviation)	Bournemouth	12.12.09E
G-FRAK	Dassault Falcon 20DC	213	N905FR N32FE, N4390F, F-WJMM	9.10.91	Cobham Leasing Ltd (Operated FR Aviation)	Bournemouth	13. 4.09E

SECTION 1 - UK Civil Aircraft Register

Reg	Type	C/n	Prev id	Date	Owner/Operator	Base	Status
G-FRAL	Dassault Falcon 20DC	151	N904FR	17. 3.93	Cobham Leasing Ltd *(Operated FR Aviation)*	Bournemouth	22.12.09E
	(N24FR), N3FE, (N148FE), N3FE, N810PA, N810F, N4360F, F-WMK						
G-FRAN	Piper J-3C-65 Cub *(L-4J-PI)*	12617	G-BIXY	14. 7.86	I Dole tr Essex L-4 Group *(As "480321:H-44" in USAAC c/s)*		
	(Continental C90) *(Frame No.12447)*		F-BDTZ, 44-80321			Rayne Hall Farm, Braintree	25.11.09P
G-FRAO	Dassault Falcon 20DC	214	N906FR	23.10.92	Cobham Leasing Ltd *(Operated FR Aviation)*		
			N33FE, N4400F, F-WNGO			Bournemouth	28. 1.09E
G-FRAP	Dassault Falcon 20DC	207	N908FR	12. 7.93	Cobham Leasing Ltd *(Operated FR Aviation)*		
			N27FE, N4395F, F-WMKF			Bournemouth	19.10.09E
G-FRAR	Dassault Falcon 20DC	209	N909FR	2.12.93	Cobham Leasing Ltd *(Operated FR Aviation)*		
			N28FE, N4396F, F-WLCX			Bournemouth	15. 2.10E
G-FRAS	Dassault Falcon 20C	82/418	CAF117501	31. 7.90	Cobham Leasing Ltd *(Operated FR Aviation)*		
			20501, F-WJMM			Durham Tees Valley	1.12.09E
G-FRAT	Dassault Falcon 20C	87/424	CAF117502	31. 7.90	Cobham Leasing Ltd *(Operated FR Aviation)*		
			20502, F-WJMJ			Bournemouth	21. 2.10E
G-FRAU	Dassault Falcon 20C	97/422	CAF117504	31. 7.90	Cobham Leasing Ltd *(Operated FR Aviation)*		
			20504, F-WJMJ			Bournemouth	15.12.09E
G-FRAW	Dassault Falcon 20C	114/420	CAF117507	31. 7.90	Cobham Leasing Ltd *(Operated FR Aviation)*		
			20507, F-WJMM			Durham Tees Valley	9. 4.09E
G-FRAY	Cassutt Racer IIIM	PFA 034-11211		24.10.90	C I Fray	(Disley, Stockport)	
	(Built C I Fray)						
G-FRBA	Dassault Falcon 20C	178/459	OH-FFA	16. 7.96	Cobham Leasing Ltd *(Operated FR Aviation)*		
			F-WPXF			*"Tornado Trials"* Bournemouth	16. 5.09E
G-FRDY	Aerospool WT9 UK Dynamic	DY239		29. 4.08	P J and F S Dodd t/a Peter Dodd Consultants		
	(Built Yeoman Light Aircraft Co Ltd)					Enstone	28. 4.09P
G-FRGN	Piper PA-28-236 Dakota	2811046	N9244N	8. 2.96	P J Vacher	Meluish Farm, North Moreton	26. 3.09E
G-FRGT	P&M Aviation Quik GT450	8341		21.12.07	P J and F S Dodd t/a Peter Dodd Consultants		
						Enstone	22. 2.09P
G-FRIL	Lindstrand LBL 105A Balloon (Hot Air)	1086		19. 9.06	S Travaglia Tavarnelle Val di Pesa, Florence, Italy		26. 5.09E
G-FRNK	Best Off Sky Ranger 912(2)	SKR xxxx528		26. 1.05	M J Burns		
	(Built F Tumelty - pr.no.BMAA HB/439)					Slieve Croob, Slievenamoney, Castlewellen	26. 7.09P
G-FROM	Comco Ikarus C42 FB100	0309-6554		15. 9.03	D M Pearson tr G-FROM Group		
						Chiltern Park, Wallingford	14.10.08P
G-FROS	Piper PA-28R-201 Arrow III	2844118	D-EGXC	7. 2.07	G and P Frost	Southend	26. 2.09E
			N3117A				
G-FRYI	Beech 200 Super King Air	BB-210	G-OAVX	15. 3.96	London Executive Aviation Ltd	Stapleford	26. 3.09E
			G-IBCA, G-BMCA, N5657N				
G-FRYL	Raytheon RB390 Premier 1	RB-97	N6197F	11. 8.04	Hawk Air Ltd	Farnborough	17. 8.09E
G-FSEU	Beech 200 Super King Air	BB-331	N87LP	9. 8.06	Air Mercia Ltd	Bristol	20. 9.08E
			N111WA, N400WH, N111JW				
G-FSHA	Denney Kitfox Model 2	PFA 172-11906		20. 9.99	P P Trangmar	(Hailsham)	
	(Built S J Alston)						
G-FSZY	SOCATA TB-10 Tobago	1892	F-GSZY	23. 5.08	R G Leonard	Enstone	1. 7.09E
G-FTDF	Airbus A320-231	437	C-FTDF	11. 5.05	Thomas Cook Airlines Ltd	Manchester	4. 4.09E
	G-FTDF, C-FTDF, G-FTDF, C-FTDF, D-AAMS, G-EPFR, C-FTDF, G-EPFR, G-BVJV, N437RX, G-BVJV, C-FWOQ, G-BVJV, N427RX, F-WWDM						
G-FTIL	Robin DR.400-180 Régent	1825		10. 3.88	The Pathfinder Flying Club Ltd	RAF Wyton	18. 8.09E
G-FTIN	Robin DR.400-100 Cadet	1830		6. 5.88	N C G Cutler tr YPF Flying Group	Blackpool	18.12.09E
G-FTSE	Fairey Britten-Norman BN-2A Mk.III-2 Trislander	1053	G-BEPI	23. 5.00	Aurigny Air Services Ltd	Guernsey	18.12.09E
G-FTSL	Bombardier CL-600-2B16	5416	N161MD	8.12.04	Farglobe Transport Services Ltd		
	(CL-604 Challenger)		(G-), N161MN, N161MM, N604MG, C-GLXG			(Hamilton, Bermuda)	8.12.09E
G-FUEL	Robin DR.400-180 Régent	1537		15. 5.81	R Darch	East Chinnock, Yeovil	29. 6.09E
G-FUFU	Agusta A109S Grand	22058		20.11.07	Air Harrods Ltd	London Stansted	21.11.09E
G-FUKM	Westland SA.341B Gazelle AH.1	1799	ZA730	18. 8.03	Falcon Aviation Ltd *(Airframe noted 12.07, as "ZA730")*		
						Deer Park Farm, Babcary	
G-FULL	Piper PA-28R-200 Cherokee Arrow II	28R-7435248	G-HWAY	26.11.84	Stapleford Flying Club Ltd	Stapleford	10.12.09E
			G-JULI, (G-BKDC), OY-POV, CS-AQF, N43128				
G-FULM	Sikorsky S-76C	760583	N7110J	2. 9.05	Air Harrods Ltd	London Stansted	1. 9.09E
G-FUND	Thunder Ax7-65Z Balloon (Hot Air)	376		3.11.81	G Everett	Sandway, Maidstone	8. 9.09E
G-FUNK	Yakovlev Yak-50	852908	RA852908	27. 3.98	Redstar Aero Services Ltd	Tibenham	20.11.09P
			DOSAAF (46 blue ?)				
G-FUNN	Plumb BGP-1 Biplane	PFA 083-12744		16.10.95	J D Anson	(Le Marchais, Fomperron, France)	
	(Built J D Anson)						
G-FUNY	Robinson R44 Raven II	11101		10. 3.06	Concept Group International Ltd	Coventry	16. 4.09E
G-FURI	Isaacs Fury II	PFA 011-14467		7. 2.06	S M Johnston	(Brompton on Swale, Richmond)	
	(Built S M Johnston)						
G-FUSE	Cameron N-105 Balloon (Hot Air)	10639		30.11.04	S A Lacey	Norwich Common, Wymondham	5. 8.09E
G-FUZZ	Piper PA-18 Super Cub 95	18-1016	(OO-HMY)	11. 9.80	G W Cline *(As "51-15319:A-319" in USAAF c/s)*		
	(L-18C-PI) (Frame No.18-1086)		French Army-FMBIT, 51-15319			Gipsy Wood Farm, Warthill	19. 4.09P
G-FVEL	Cameron Z-90 Balloon (Hot Air)	10580		24. 8.04	Fort Vale Engineering Ltd *"Fort Vale"*	Nelson	28. 6.09E
G-FVRY	Colt 105A Balloon (Hot Air)	746	C-FVRY	21. 7.05	R Thompson *(Inflated 1.09)*	(Liss)	12. 9.06E
			N300NN				
G-FWAB	Flug Werk Focke-Wulf FW190-A8 replica	980554		13. 2.08	Spitfire Ltd *(In German AF c/s)*	Duxford	
G-FWAY	Lindstrand LBL 90A Balloon (Hot Air)	967		7. 5.04	Harding and Sons Ltd t/a Fairway Furniture		
						(Fairway Furniture titles) Plymouth	27. 5.09E
G-FWKS	Air Création Tanarg 912S/iXess 15	FLT.xxx	G-SYUT	20.07.07	M A Coffin	(Wrotham, Sevenoaks)	1. 5.09P
	(Built L Cottle - pr.no.BMAA HB/492 being Flylight kit comprising Trike s/n T05100 and Wing s/n A05188-5195)						
G-FWPW	Piper PA-28-236 Dakota	2811028	N9145L	10.10.88	P A and Franziska.C Winters	Weston, Dublin	24. 2.09E
G-FXBT	Aeroprakt A22 Foxbat	PFA 317-13787		7. 2.02	R H Jago	Mapperton Farm, Newton Peverill	14. 2.08P
	(Built R Jago)						
G-FYAN	Williams Westwind Balloon (Minimum Lift)	MDW-1		6. 1.82	M D Williams	Houghton Regis, Dunstable	
G-FYAO	Williams Westwind Balloon (Minimum Lift)	MDW-001		6. 1.82	M D Williams	Houghton Regis, Dunstable	

G-FYAU	Williams Mk.2 Balloon (Minimum Lift) MDW-02			6. 1.82	M D Williams *(Extant 5.07)*	Houghton Regis, Dunstable
G-FYAV	Osprey Mk.4E2 Balloon (Minimum Lift) ASC-247			12. 1.82	C D Egan and C Stiles *(Extant 5.07)*	Hounslow and Feltham
G-FYBD	Osprey Mk.1E Balloon (Minimum Lift) ASC-136			20. 1.82	M Vincent	St Helier, Jersey
G-FYBE	Osprey Mk.4D Balloon (Minimum Lift) ASC-128			20. 1.82	M Vincent	St Helier, Jersey
G-FYBF	Osprey Mk.5 Balloon (Minimum Lift) ASC-218			20. 1.82	M Vincent	St Helier, Jersey
G-FYBG	Osprey Mk.4G2 Balloon (Minimum Lift) ASC-204			20. 1.82	M Vincent	St Helier, Jersey
G-FYBH	Osprey Mk.4G Balloon (Minimum Lift) ASC-214			20. 1.82	M Vincent	St Helier, Jersey
G-FYBI	Osprey Mk.4H Balloon (Minimum Lift) ASC-234			20. 1.82	M Vincent	St Helier, Jersey
G-FYCL	Osprey Mk.4G Balloon (Minimum Lift) ASC-213			9. 2.82	P J Rogers	Banbury
G-FYCV	Osprey Mk.4D Balloon (Minimum Lift) ASK-276			19. 2.82	A L Hunter	Luton
G-FYCZ	Osprey Mk.4D2 Balloon (Minimum Lift) ASC-244			24. 2.82	P Middleton	Colchester
G-FYDF	Osprey Mk.4D Balloon (Minimum Lift) ASK-278			22. 3.82	K A Jones	Thornton Heath
G-FYDI	Williams Westwind Two Balloon (Minimum Lift) MDW-005			29. 3.82	M D Williams	Houghton Regis, Dunstable
G-FYDN	Eaves European 8C Balloon (Minimum Lift) DD34/S 22			5. 4.82	P D Ridout	Eastleigh
G-FYDO	Osprey Mk.4D Balloon (Minimum Lift) ASK-262			15. 4.82	N L Scallan	Hayes
G-FYDP	Williams Westwind Three Balloon (Minimum Lift) MDW-006			29. 3.82	M D Williams *(Extant 5.07)*	Houghton Regis, Dunstable
G-FYDS	Osprey Mk.4D Balloon (Minimum Lift) ASK-261			15. 4.82	M E Scallan	Hayes
G-FYEK	Unicorn UE-1C Balloon (Minimum Lift) 82024			2. 7.82	D and D Eaves *(Extant 5.07)*	Southampton
G-FYEO	Scallan Eagle Mk.1A Balloon (Minimum Lift) 001			20. 7.82	M E Scallan	Hayes
G-FYEV	Osprey Mk.1C Balloon (Minimum Lift) ASK-294			10. 8.82	M E Scallan	Hayes
G-FYEZ	Scallan Firefly Mk.1 Balloon (Minimum Lift) MNS-748			22. 9.82	M E and N L Scallan	Hayes
G-FYFI	Eaves European E 84PS Balloon (Minimum Lift) S 29			1.12.82	M A Stelling *(Extant 5.07)*	Barton-le-Clay, Bedford
G-FYFJ	Williams Westwind Two Balloon (Minimum Lift) MDW-010			14.12.82	M D Williams *(Extant 5.07)*	Houghton Regis, Dunstable
G-FYFN	Osprey Saturn 2 DC3 Balloon (Minimum Lift) ATC-250-MJS-11			17. 2.83	J and M Woods	Bracknell
G-FYFW	Rango NA-55 Balloon (Minimum Lift) NHP-40 *(Radio controlled)*			8.10.84	A M and N H Ponsford t/a Rango Balloon and Kite Company *"Vaughan Williams"*	Leeds
G-FYFY	Rango NA-55RC Balloon (Minimum Lift) *(Radio controlled)* AL-43			28. 2.85	A M Ponsford t/a Rango Balloon and Kite Company *"Fifi"*	Leeds
G-FYGI	Rango NA-55RC Balloon (Minimum Lift) *(Radio controlled)* NHP-54			26. 6.90	D K Fish	Manchester
G-FYGJ	Wells Airspeed-300 Balloon (Minimum Lift) 001			8.10.91	N Wells	Paddock Wood, Tunbridge Wells
G-FYGM	Saffery/Smith Princess Balloon (Minimum Lift) *(Built C Saffery and N Smith)* 551			24.11.97	A and N Smith	Pollington, Goole
G-FZIS	Staaken Z-1S Stummelflitzer xxx *(Built V Long)*			3.08R	V Long *(On build 9.06)*	Not known
G-FZZA	General Avia F22-A 018			13. 8.98	APB Leasing Ltd	Sleap 30.12.09E
G-FZZI	Cameron H-34 Balloon (Hot Air) 2105			30.10.89	Magical Adventures Ltd	
						West Bloomfield, Michigan, US 23.10.09E

G-GAAA - G-GZZZ

G-GABS	Cameron TR-70 Balloon (Hot-Air) 10937			10 3.08	N M Gabriel	Kimberley, Notts 30. 3.09E
G-GACA	Percival P 57 Sea Prince T 1 P57/58	WP308		2. 9.80	P G Vallance Ltd *(In Gatwick Aviation Museum 2007 as "WP308/572")*	Charlwood, Surrey 4.11.80P
G-GACB	Robinson R44 Raven II 10243			9. 1.04	A C Barker	Black Bank Farm, Foxt, Stoke-on-Trent 14. 2.09E
G-GAFA	Piper PA-34-200T Seneca II 34-7970218	D-GAFA N2247Z		12.10.99	Oxford Aviation Academy (Oxford) Ltd	Oxford 23. 1.09E
G-GAFT	Piper PA-44-180 Seminole 4496162	N5324Q		24. 1.03	GT Ventures Ltd	Coventry 13. 2.09E
G-GAII	Hawker Hunter GA.11 HABL-003028 *(Officially regd with c/n 41H-004038)*	XE685		7.12.94	A G Fowles *(As "XE685:861" in RN c/s)*	Exeter 18. 6.09P
G-GAJB	Gulfstream AA-5B Tiger AA5B-1179	G-BHZN N37519		6. 4.87	R Berman and S A Niechcia tr G-GAJB Group	Biggin Hill 19. 2.09E
G-GALA	Piper PA-28-180 Cherokee E 28-5794	G-AYAP N11C		31. 7.89	Flyteam Aviation Ltd	Elstree 10. 5.09E
G-GALB	Piper PA-28-161 Warrior II 28-8616021	D-EHMP N9097E, (N157AV), N9635N		1. 9.00	LB Aviation Ltd	Humberside 25. 7.09E
G-GALL	Piper PA-38-112 Tomahawk 38-78A0025	G-BTEV N9315T		1. 6.00	M Lowe and K Hazelwood	Cardiff 30. 5.09E
G-GALX	Dassault Falcon 900EX 163	F-WWFX		13. 7.06	Charter Air Ltd	Farnborough 16. 7.09E

Reg	Type	C/n	Prev ID	Date	Owner/Operator	Base	Date
G-GAME	Cessna T303 Crusader	T30300098	(F-GDFN) N2693C	25. 2.83	P Heffron	Swansea	17. 9.08E
G-GAND	Agusta-Bell 206B-2 JetRanger II	8073	G-AWMK 9Y-TFC, G-AWMK, (VR-BCV), G-AWMK	11. 1.00	The Henderson Group	Gollanfield, Inverness	1. 7.09E

(Officially regd with c/n 8073 airframe exchanged with 5N-AQJ [8051] in 1999, original 5N-AQJ remained as c/n 8051 and became VH-JEF 1.00)

Reg	Type	C/n	Prev ID	Date	Owner/Operator	Base	Date
G-GANE	Sequoia F 8L Falco	906		25. 9.85	S J Gane	Kemble	15. 6.09P

(Built S J Gane - pr.no.PFA 100-11100) (Lycoming IO-320)

Reg	Type	C/n	Prev ID	Date	Owner/Operator	Base	Date
G-GANG	Bell 206L-4 Long Ranger IV	52352	N70258	6.11.07	The Henderson Group	Gollanfield, Nairn	25.11.08E
G-GAOH	Robin DR.400-2+2 Tri-cycle	1217	F-GAOH	9. 5.05	Exavia Ltd	Exeter	15. 8.09E
G-GAOM	Robin DR.400-2+2 Tri-cycle	1220	F-GAOM	24. 6.05	P M and P A Chapman	Bodmin	1. 9.09E
G-GASP	Piper PA-28-181 Cherokee Archer II	28-7790013	N4328F	15.10.90	M L Robinson tr G-GASP Flying Group	Fairoaks	2. 2.09E
G-GASS	Thunder Ax7-77 Balloon (Hot Air)	1746		19. 4.90	M W Axon tr Servowarm Balloon Syndicate *"Travel Gas III"*	Brentwood	4. 7.03A
G-GATE	Robinson R44 Raven II	10448		28. 7.04	J W Gate	Stainsby Grange Farm, Thornaby	3.10.09E
G-GATT	Robinson R44 Raven II	10531		15.11.04	B W Faulkner	(Petersfield)	3. 1.10E
G-GAZA	Aérospatiale SA.341G Gazelle 1	1187	G-RALE G-SFTG, N87712	19. 6.92	The Auster Aircraft Company Ltd	Melton Mowbray	5. 8.09P
G-GAZN	P&M Aviation Quik GT450	8271		24. 5.07	G Nicholls	Rufforth	23. 5.09P
G-GAZZ	Aérospatiale SA.341G Gazelle 1	1271	F-GFHD YV-242CP, HB-XGA, F-WMHC	14. 3.90	Stratton Motor Company (Norfolk) Ltd *(Operated Cheqair Ltd)* Tharston Industrial Estate, Long Stratton		14. 9.09E
G-GBAB	Piper PA-28-161 Warrior II	28-7816495	HB-PAB D-ELET, N9564N	13.12.06	B A Mills	Duxford	3. 8.09E
G-GBAO	Robin R1180TD Aiglon	277	F-GBAO	9. 9.81	J Toulorge	(Copthorne, Crawley)	14. 2.09E

(Rebuild of R 1180 prototype F-WVKU c/n 01)

Reg	Type	C/n	Prev ID	Date	Owner/Operator	Base	Date
G-GBBB	Schleicher ASH 25	25074	BGA3532-FUG (BGA3526-FTZ)	15.10.07	M J Wells tr ASH 25 BB Glider Syndicate *"BB"*	Lasham	30. 1.08
G-GBBT	UltraMagic M-90 Balloon (Hot-Air)	90/103		13. 8.08	British Telecommunications PLC *"Helping Britain Win"*	Thatcham	18. 8.09E
G-GBEE	Mainair Sports Pegasus Quik	8039		21. 5.04	M G Evans	Finmere	26. 5.09P
G-GBEN	Robinson R44 Raven II	10743	G-CDJZ	20. 6.07	BG(H) Aviation Ltd	(Hednesford, Cannock)	23. 6.09E
G-GBFF	Reims Cessna F172N Skyhawk II	F17201565	F-GBFF	16. 6.99	S J Skilton t/a Aviation Rentals	Bournemouth	14. 9.09E

(Thielert TAE 125-01) (3-blade propeller)   *(Operated Solent School of Flying)*

Reg	Type	C/n	Prev ID	Date	Owner/Operator	Base	Date
G-GBFR	Reims Cessna F177RG Cardinal RG	F177RG0172	F-GBFR	7. 4.04	Airspeed Aviation Ltd	Derby	
G-GBGA	Scheibe SF25C Falke	44683	D-KIEJ	28. 8.02	British Gliding Association Ltd	Bicester	17. 5.09E

(Rotax 912S)

Reg	Type	C/n	Prev ID	Date	Owner/Operator	Base	Date
G-GBGB	UltraMagic M-105 Balloon (Hot Air)	105/126		30.12.04	Universal Car Services Ltd	Aldershot	22. 7.07E
G-GBGF	Cameron Dragon SS Balloon (Hot Air)	3016	C-GBGF G-BUVH	23. 8.07	Magical Adventures Ltd	Oswestry	27. 9.09E
G-GBHI	SOCATA TB-10 Tobago	19	F-GBHI	12.11.97	Robert Purvis Plant Hire Ltd	Glenrothes	21.12.08E
G-GBJP	Mainair Sports Pegasus Quantum 15	8036		16. 8.04	M P Chew	(Buckfastleigh, Devon)	15. 8.09P

(Rotax 582)

Reg	Type	C/n	Prev ID	Date	Owner/Operator	Base	Date
G-GBJS	Robin HR.200-100S Club	73	F-BXJS	4. 5.06	R Bowen	Bodmin	24. 8.08E
G-GBLP	Reims Cessna F172M Skyhawk II	F17201042	G-GWEN G-GBLP, N14496	9.11.84	Aviate Scotland Ltd	Glenrothes	20.11.08E
G-GBLR	Reims Cessna F150L	F15001109	N961L (D-EDJE)	30. 4.85	Almat Flying Club Ltd	Coventry	17.11.09E
G-GBMR	Beech B200 Super King Air	BB-1693	N771SC N773TP	29.03.06	M and R Aviation LLP	(Leicester)	30. 3.09E
G-GBOB	Alpi Pioneer 300 Hawk	PFA 330A-14681		20. 8.07	R E Burgess	(Carmel, Caernarfon)	

(Built R E Burgess)

Reg	Type	C/n	Prev ID	Date	Owner/Operator	Base	Date
G-GBPP	Rolladen-Schneider LS6-c	6230	BGA3809-HBJ	24.10.07	G J Lyons and R Sinden *"949"*	Wycombe Air Park	28. 9.08
G-GBRB	Piper PA-28-180 Cherokee C	28-2583	N8381W	2. 2.00	M S Marsland	Blackbushe	4. 5.09E
G-GBRU	Bell 206B-3 JetRanger III	3997	G-CDGV N217PM, XC-PFS	15. 2.05	R A Fleming Ltd	(Harrogate)	5. 5.09E
G-GBSL	Beech 76 Duchess	ME-265	G-BGVG	27. 3.81	M H Cundey *"Dolly"*	Redhill and Alderney	29. 5.09E
G-GBTA	Boeing 737-436	25859	G-BVHA	7. 2.94	British Airways PLC	London Gatwick	31.10.09E
G-GBTB	Boeing 737-436	25860	OO-LTS G-BVHB, OO-LTS, G-BVHB, (G-GBTB)	23.10.96	British Airways PLC	London Gatwick	28.10.09E
G-GBTL	Cessna 172S Skyhawk	172S10322	N1261M	21.11.06	Bohana Technology Ltd	Wadsick Manor Farm, Corsham	23.11.09E
G-GBUE	Robin DR.400-120A Petit Prince	1354	G-BPXD F-GBUE	11. 5.89	J A Kane	Bagby	22.12.09E
G-GBUN	Cessna 182T Skylane	18281280	N2157P	11.12.03	G M Bunn	Goodwood	4. 2.10E
G-GBVX	Robin DR.400-120A Petit Prince	1419	F-GBVX	2. 3.06	M Patterson	Sorbie Farm, Kingsmuir	6. 6.09E
G-GBXF	Robin HR.200-120 Acrobin	25	HB-EXF	13. 1.06	B A and L A Mills	Cambridge	7. 2.08E
G-GBXS	Europa Aviation Europa XS	F0005	"G-2000"	1. 4.98	P G Wood	West Throstle Nest Farm, Moorsholm	4. 6.08P

(Built Europa Aviation Ltd, pr.no.PFA 247-13196) G-GBXS (Rotax 914-UL) (Monowheel u/c)

Reg	Type	C/n	Prev ID	Date	Owner/Operator	Base	Date
G-GCAC	Europa Aviation Europa XS	559		21. 8.02	J L Gunn	(Hoveton, Norwich)	

(Built G J Cattermole - pr.no.PFA 247-13940) (Tri-gear u/c)

Reg	Type	C/n	Prev ID	Date	Owner/Operator	Base	Date
G-GCAT	Piper PA-28-140 Cherokee B	28-26032	G-BFRH OH-PCA	22.10.81	P F Jude tr Group CAT	Humberside	28. 2.09E
G-GCCL	Beech 76 Duchess	ME-322	(G-BNRF) N6714U	5. 8.87	Aerolease Ltd	Conington	31. 1.09E
G-GCEA	P&M Pegasus Quik	8209		12. 9.06	J D Ash	Wickenby	13. 9.09P
G-GCIY	Robin DR.400-140B Major	1488	F-GCIY	7. 7.08	Exavia Ltd	Exeter	10. 7.09E
G-GCJA	Rolladen-Schneider LS8-18	8354	BGA4871-JXU	14. 5.08	C J Alldis *"646"*	Long Mynd	
G-GCKI	Mooney M 20K Mooney 231	25-0401	N4062H	15. 8.80	B Barr	Seething	5.12.08E
G-GCMW	Grob G102 Astir CS	1112	BGA5040-KEU OY-XDE	6.11.07	E F Weaver	AAC Wattisham	27. 6.07
G-GCUF	Robin DR.400-160 Chevalier	1504	F-GCUF	19. 4.06	S T Bates	Eddsfield, Octon Lodge Farm, Thwing	27. 5.09E
G-GCYC	Reims Cessna F182Q Skylane II	F18200157	F-GCYC	11. 2.00	A G Dodd	Kemble	21 9.09E
G-GDAV	Robinson R44 Raven II	10813		12. 7.05	G H Weston	(Leeds)	15. 9.09E

Reg	Type	C/n	Prev ID	Date	Owner/Operator	Location	Date
G-GDEF	Robin DR.400-120 Petit Prince	1538	F-GDEE	26. 7.07	J M Shackleton	Sherburn-in-Elmet	10. 8.09E
G-GDER	Robin R1180TD Aiglon II	280	F-GDER	15. 5.97	Berkshire Aviation Services Ltd	Fairoaks	26. 7.09E
G-GDJF	Robinson R44 Raven II	11406	G-DEXT	8. 2.07	Berkley Properties Ltd	(Croft, Skegness)	31.10.08E
G-GDKR	Robin DR.400-140B Major	1623	F-GDKR	12. 6.06	L J Milbank	Sibson	13.11.09E
G-GDMW	Beech 76 Duchess	ME-316	D-GDMW	29.10.04	Apollo Aviation Advisory Ltd	Shoreham	14. 1.09E
			LX-DRS, F-GCGB				
G-GDOG	Piper PA-28R-200 Cherokee Arrow II		G-BDXW	17. 4.89	N J Morton tr Mutley Crew Group	Conington	14.12.09E
		28R-7635227	N9235K				
G-GDOV	Robinson R44 Raven	1503		27. 7.05	M K E Hayes	(Clay Cross)	17. 8.09E
G-GDRV	Van's RV-6	21367	C-GDRV	26.11.01	M A Jardim de Queiroz tr G-GDRV Group "Slavka"		
	(Built D Piper) (Lycoming O-320)					Gloucestershire	27.12.09P
G-GDSG	Agusta A109E Power	11656		16.11.05	Pendley Aviation LLP	Pendley Farm, Aldbury	17.11.09E
G-GDTU	Mudry CAP.10B	193	F-GDTU	27. 5.99	A L Farr and D C Cooper	RAF Yeovilton	20.12.09E
			(N.....), F-GDTK, F-WZCI				
G-GEBJ	Cessna 525 CitationJet	525-0528	N528CJ	9. 2.08	EBJ Operations Ltd	London Stansted	11. 2.09E
G-GEDY	Dassault Falcon 2000	208	F-WWVV	6. 5.04	Victoria Aviation Ltd	(Geneva, Switzerland)	11. 4.09E
G-GEEP	Robin R1180TD Aiglon	266		9. 4.80	C Stratford tr The Aiglon Flying Group	North Weald	11. 2.09E
G-GEES	Cameron N-77 Balloon (Hot Air)	357		8.11.77	N A Carr	Leicester	31. 5.00A
G-GEEZ	Cameron N-77 Balloon (Hot Air)	1159		3. 5.85	Charnwood Forest Turf Accountants Ltd "Tic Tac"		
						Leicester	7. 4.96A
G-GEHL	Cessna 172S Skyhawk SP	172S8324	N163RA	18. 6.03	Ebryl Ltd	White Waltham	21. 8.09E
G-GEHP	Piper PA-28RT-201 Arrow IV	28R-8218014	F-GEHP	24. 4.98	Aeros Leasing Ltd	Gloucestershire	7. 8.09E
			N82023				
G-GEMM	Cirrus SR20	1138	N241CD	14.12.05	Cumulus Aircraft Rentals Ltd	Filton	7. 3.09E
G-GEMS	Thunder Ax8-90 Series 2 Balloon (Hot Air)		G-BUNP	6.11.92	B Sevenich, Benedikt, S Harren and C Walter		
		2287				Aachen and Bonn, Germany	25. 6.09E
G-GEMX	P&M Aviation Quik GT450	8344		31. 1.08	J A Gilchrist	Little Snoring	30. 1.09P
G-GENI	Robinson R44 Raven II	11396		13. 9.06	G-GENI LLP	(Hove)	21.10.09E
G-GEOF	Pereira Osprey 2	PFA 070-10384		7. 9.78	G Crossley	(Poulton-le-Fylde)	
	(Built G Crossley)						
G-GEOS	Diamond HK 36 TTC-ECO Super Dimona		N842WS	19.10.05	University Court of the University of Edinburgh		
		36.582	(G-GEOS), N842WS, C-GETC			Glenrothes	13. 3.09E
G-GERS	Robinson R44 Clipper II	12217		17. 4.08	Bang Media London Ltd	Denham	19. 5.09E
G-GERT	Van's RV-7	PFA 323-13836		22. 3.04	M Castle-Smith tr Barnstormers	Compton Abbas	8.12.09P
	(M Castle-Smith, B West and A Burroughs)						
G-GERY	Stoddard-Hamilton GlaStar	PFA 295-13475		6. 7.01	S G Brown Eddsfield, Octon Lodge Farm, Thwing		1. 9.09P
	(Built G E Collard) (Tailwheel u/c)						
G-GEST	Robinson R44 Clipper II	11159		4. 4.06	Gest Air Ltd	Rennes St Jacques, France	12. 5.09E
G-GEVO	Cessna 680 Citation Sovereign	680-0145	OE-GVO	3. 6.08	TAG Aviation (UK) Ltd	Farnborough	2. 6.09E
			N5117U				
G-GEZZ	Bell 206B-2 JetRanger II	1301	N68TJ	16 .2.07	Rivermead Aviation Ltd (Operated Rise Helicopters)		
			N59489			Gloucestershire	14.11.08E
G-GFAA	Slingsby T.67A	1994	G-BJXA	28. 7.08	Aircraft Grouping Ltd	Blackpool	30. 1.10E
G-GFAB	Cameron N-105 Balloon (Hot Air)	2048		4. 8.89	R K Scott	North Perrott, Crewkerne	26. 5.09E
G-GFCA	Piper PA-28-161 Cadet	2841100	N9174X	24. 4.89	Aeros Leasing Ltd	Gloucestershire	12.10.09E
G-GFCB	Piper PA-28-161 Cadet	2841101	N9175X	24. 4.89	A J Warren	Bristol	22. 8.09E
G-GFCD	Piper PA-34-220T Seneca III	34-8133073	G-KIDS	31. 5.90	Stonehurst Aviation Ltd	Blackbushe	28. 4.09E
			N83745				
G-GFDA	Diamond DA.42 Twin Star	42.187	G-CEFX	19. 3.08	Saltair Motor Company	Barton	15. 3.09E
			OE-VPY				
G-GFEA	Cessna 172S Skyhawk II	172S10214	G-CEDY	27. 9.06	Saltaire Motor Company Ltd tr Allan Jefferies		
			N60361			Barton	5.10.09E
G-GFEY	Piper PA-34-200T Seneca II	34-7870343	D-GFEY	13. 5.98	Steptoe and Sons Properties Ltd	Caernarfon	2. 3.09E
			D-IFEY, N36599				
G-GFFD	Boeing 737-59D	26419	LY-BFV	3. 7.00	British Airways PLC (wfs 01.10.08)	Norwich	13. 8.09E
			OY-SEG, G-OBMY, SE-DNI				
G-GFFH	Boeing 737-5H6	27354	VT-JAW	24.10.00	British Airways PLC	London Gatwick	23. 1.10E
			9M-MFG				
G-GFFI	Boeing 737-528	27425	LX-LGS	9.11.00	British Airways PLC	Manchester	18.12.08E
			(F-GJNQ)				
G-GFFJ	Boeing 737-5H6	27355	VT-JAZ	19. 1.01	British Airways PLC	Manchester	12. 3.09E
			9M-MFH				
G-GFIA	Cessna 152	15281685	F-GGLI	18. 9.06	Aircraft Grouping Ltd	Barton	11.11.09E
			N66950				
G-GFIB	Reims Cessna F152 II	F15201556	G-BPIO	14.11.06	Aircraft Grouping Ltd	Blackpool	19.11.09E
			PH-VSO, PH-AXS				
G-GFIC	Cessna 152 II	15281672	G-BORI	12.11.07	Aircraft Grouping Ltd	Blackpool	20.10.09E
			N66936				
G-GFID	Cessna 152 II	15282649	G-BORJ	28.7.08	Silverstar Maintenance Services Ltd	Blackpool	25. 2.10E
			N89148				
G-GFKY	Zenair CH.250	34	C-GFKY	23. 4.93	R G Kelsall	RAF Mona	6. 5.09P
	(Built D Koch) (Lycoming O-235)						
G-GFLY	Reims Cessna F150L	F15000822	PH-CES	28. 8.80	Leagate Ltd	Seething	13. 7.09P
G-GFMT	Cessna 172S Skyhawk	172S8258	C-GFMT	2.11.04	A D Cameron and D Hey tr G-GFMT Flying Group		
			N341SP			Barton	11. 6.09E
G-GFNO	Robin ATL	16	F-GFNO	23. 3.05	D J Watson	Sleap	12. 5.08E
			F-WFNO				
G-GFOX	Aeroprakt A22 Foxbat	PFA 317-14368		25. 5.05	I A Love and G F Elvis	Mill Farm, Shifnal	14.11.09P
	(Build B J Mould)						
G-GFPA	Piper PA-28-181 Archer III	2843010	N115RT	13.11.06	Saltaire Motor Company Ltd t/a Allan Jefferies		
			N9256J			Barton	15. 1.10E
G-GFPB	Piper PA-28-181 Archer III	2843409	G-BZHW	29.10.07	S Viner	Blackpool	12. 3.09E
			N4184D, G-BZHW, N4184D				

Reg	Type	C/n	Prev id	Date	Owner/Operator	Location	Status
G-GFPC	Piper PA-28-181 Archer III	2843328	G-CCWA D-ELEM, PH-AEG, N41776	28. 5.08	Flight Academy Blackpool Ltd	Blackpool	17. 7.09E
G-GFRD	Robin ATL	53	F-GFRD	2. 2.05	C Long	Haverfordwest	12. 2.09E
G-GFRO	Robin ATL	64	F-GFRO	28.11.06	B F Walker	Gloucestershire	13.10.09E
G-GFSA	Cessna 172R Skyhawk	17280221	N410ES	26.10.06	Aircraft Grouping Ltd	Barton	22.12.09E
G-GFTA	Piper PA-28-161 Warrior III	2842047	N4132L G-GFTA, N9525N	1. 4.99	One Zero Three Ltd	Guernsey	21. 4.09E
G-GFTB	Piper PA-28-161 Warrior III	2842048	N4120V G-GFTB, N4120V	7. 5.99	One Zero Three Ltd	Guernsey	6. 5.09E
G-GGCT	Flight Design CT2K (Assembled Pegasus Aviation Ltd with c/n 7938)	02-08-02-31		18. 2.03	G R Graham	Kirkbride	17. 4.09P
G-GGDV	Schleicher Ka 6E	4099	BGA3758-GDV OO-ZWQ, I-NEST, OE-0807	6. 3.08	P Hardman	Dunstable	
G-GGGG	Thunder Ax7-77 Balloon (Hot Air)	162		2. 8.78	T A Gilmour tr Flying G Group "Flying G" (Active 9.05)	Stockbridge	17. 8.99A
G-GGHZ	Robin ATL	123	F-GGHZ	10. 2.05	Modesto's Bakeries Ltd	Barton	18. 5.08E
G-GGJK	Robin DR.400-140B Major 80	1805	F-GGJK	24. 3.05	D Kember tr Headcorn Jodelers	Headcorn	27. 4.09E
G-GGLE	Piper PA-22-108 Colt (Frame No.108-915) (Tail-wheel conversion incorporating parts from G-AROM c/n 22-8805)	22-8914	N5234Z	13. 5.93	K De Dobbelaere	(Wilrijk, Belgium)	10.12.10S
G-GGNG	Robinson R44 Clipper II	11172		25. 5.06	Bburton Helicopters Ltd	(London W1)	25. 6.09E
G-GGOW	Colt 77A Balloon (Hot Air)	1542		19. 6.89	G Everett "Charles Rennie Mackintosh"	Dartford	26. 9.09E
G-GGRR	Scottish Aviation Bulldog Series 120/121	120/121 BH120/272	G-CBAM XX614	11. 7.01	M Litherland (As "XX614:V" in RAF c/s)	Enstone	15.10.08S
G-GGTT	Agusta-Bell 47G-4A	2538	F-GGTT I-ANDO	21. 8.97	Phoenix Aviation Refinishers Ltd	(Earlsheaton, Dewsbury)	5. 7.10S
G-GHEE	Evektor EV-97 Eurostar PFA 315-13840 (Built C J Ball)			14.12.01	C J Ball Oxleaze Grange, Hawling, Cheltenham (Involved in mid-air collision with Cessna 152 G-BNXC near.Moreton-in-Marsh 18.12.05)		2.11.08P
G-GHIA	Cameron N-120 Balloon (Hot Air)	2442		13.11.90	J A Marshall (Active 5.07)	Plaistow, Billingshurst	25. 8.04T
G-GHIN	Thunder Ax7-77 Balloon (Hot Air)	1802		16. 7.90	N T Parry "Pegasus"	Ascot	4. 9.00A
G-GHKX	Piper PA-28-161 Warrior II (Thielert TAE 125-01)	28-8416005	N380X G-GHKX, F-GHKX, N4318X	10. 6.99	S J Skilton t/a Aviation Rentals	Bournemouth	20. 4.09E
G-GHOW	Reims Cessna F182Q Skylane II	F18200151	OO-MCD F-BJCE	20. 2.01	J F Busby	Top Farm, Croydon, Royston	3. 5.09E
G-GHPG	Cessna 550 Citation II	550-0897	N5079V	22. 2.02	Descaro Ltd (Operated by London Executive Aviation)	Biggin Hill	18. 3.09E
G-GHRW	Piper PA-28RT-201 Arrow IV	28R-7918140	G-ONAB G-BHAK, N29555	8.12.83	Bonus Aviation Ltd	Cranfield	23. 1.10E
G-GHZJ	SOCATA TB-9 Tampico	941	F-GHZJ	4. 3.98	P K Hayward	Turweston	2. 9.09E
G-GIBB	Robinson R44 Raven II	11777		13. 6.07	Tingdene Aviation Ltd	Sywell	6. 7.09E
G-GIDY	Europa Aviation Europa XS (Built I N Robson, P Stewart, R Tuckwell and H Carmichael - pr.no.PFA 247-13467)	432		18. 2.04	I N Robson tr Gidy Group	(Repton, Derby)	
G-GIGI	SOCATA MS.893A Rallye Commodore 180	11637	G-AYVX F-BSFJ	28. 9.81	D J Moore (Noted 3.03)	(Aston Down)	13. 4.00
G-GIGZ	Van's RV-8 PFA 303-14577			17.12.08	C D Mitchell	(Faringdon)	
G-GILI	Robinson R44 Raven	1436		5. 1.05	Twylight Management Ltd	(Douglas, Isle of Man)	28. 1.09E
G-GIRY	American General AG-5B Tiger	10146	F-GIRY	5. 2.99	F Neefs tr Romeo Yankee Flying Group	Elstree	9. 5.09E
G-GIWT	Europa Aviation Europa XS (Built A Twigg - pr.no.PFA 247-13623) (Monowheel u/c)	463		29. 3.01	A Twigg (Noted incomplete 7.07)	(Wootton Bassett)	
G-GJCD	Robinson R22 Beta	0966		22. 2.89	J C Lane	Gloucestershire	21.10.09E
G-GKAT	Enstrom 280C Shark	1200	F-GKAT N5694Y	26. 8.97	D Cummaford	(Wilmslow)	9. 8.08E
G-GKFC	TLAC RL5A LW Sherwood Ranger (Built K F Crumplin- pr.no. PFA 237-12947) (Jabiru 2200A)	xxxx	G-MYZI	24.11.98	T R Janaway	Enstone	23. 7.08P
G-GKKI	Avions Mudry CAP 231EX	02	G-GKKI G-BVXL, F-GKKF, F-WGZC	23. 1.07	Acro Laser Company Ltd	Hawarden	10. 5.09E
G-GKUE	SOCATA TB-9 Tampico	1129	F-GKUE	5. 2.07	I Parkinson	Bagby	8. 5.09E
G-GLAD	Gloster Gladiator II (C/n amended 29. 8.08)	G5/75751	N5903	5. 1.95	Patina Ltd (Operated The Fighter Collection as "N5903":in 72 Sqdn RAF c/s)	Duxford	1. 9.09P
G-GLAK	Sportline Aviacija LAK-12 Lietuva	647	BGA3717-GCB	15.11.07	L M Middleton "236"	Easterton	5. 4.08
G-GLAW	Cameron N-90 Balloon (Hot Air)	1808		10.10.88	R A Vale	Hurcott, Kidderminster	15. 2.06A
G-GLED	Cessna 150M	15076673	C-GLED	6. 1.89	Firecrest Aviation Ltd	Elstree	16. 3.09E
G-GLHI	Best Off Sky Ranger 912S(1) (Built G L Higgins - pr.no.BMAA HB/392)	SKR0403468		30. 6.04	S F Winter	Lower Upham Farm, Chiseldon	9. 6.08P
G-GLIB	Robinson R44 Raven	1226		12. 6.02	Helisport UK Ltd	Earls Colne	11. 7.09E
G-GLID	Schleicher ASW 28-18E	28723	BGA5131-KJR D-KEBB, D-KOAB	18. 4.06	S Bovin and Compagnie Belge d'Assurances Aviation	(Leuven, Belgium)	22. 4.08
G-GLII	Great Lakes 2T-1A-2	813	N3613L	8. 8.07	T J Richardson	Popham	
G-GLKE	Robin DR.400-180 Régent	2119	F-GLKE	15. 6.07	Karrek Financial Management Ltd	Bodmin	4 .7.09E
G-GLOC	Extra EA.300/200	1039		30. 3.07	The Cambridge Aero Club Ltd "cambridgeaeroclub.com"	Cambridge	17. 4.09E
G-GLST	Great Lakes 2T-1A Sport Trainer (Built D A Graham) PFA 321-13646			21. 7.03	D A Graham	New Barn Farm, Barton Ashes, Crawley	
G-GLSU	Bücker Bü.181B-1 Bestmann (Built Hagglund and Soner)	25071	D-EDUB Swedish AF Fv25071	21. 7.04	P R Holloway (As "GL+SU":6 1 in pseudo Luftwaffe c/s)	Old Warden	4.10.10S
G-GLTT	Piper PA-31-350 Chieftain	31-8452004	N27JV XA-SVW, XA-SGZ, N606SM, N4115D	19. 9.97	Airtime Aviation France Ltd	Bournemouth	28. 5.09E
G-GLUC	Van's RV-6 (Built L De Sadeleer) (Lycoming O-320)	20153	C-GLUC	15.10.99	Speedfreak Ltd	Crosland Moor	17. 4.09P
G-GLUE	Cameron N-65 Balloon (Hot Air)	390		17. 3.81	L J M Muir and G D Hallett (Mobile Windscreens titles) "Tacky Jack" and "Jack of Herts"	East Molesey	17. 7.90A
G-GMAA	Learjet Model 45	45-167	N5012V	1. 5.02	Gama Aviation Ltd	Farnborough	1. 5.09E
G-GMAB	British Aerospace BAe 125 Series 1000B (Build Corporate Jets Ltd)	259034	N81HH N290H, G-BUWX, G-5-761	21.11.01	Gama Aviation Ltd	Farnborough	11. 3.09E

G-GMAX	SNCAN Stampe SV-4C	141	G-BXNW	19. 6.87	Glidegold Ltd	(Cookham,, Maidenhead)	29. 8.93T
	(Renault 4PE)		F-BBPB		*(Damaged in crash Booker 3. 6.91: on rebuild 5.96)*		
G-GMED	Piper PA-42-720 Cheyenne IIIA	42-5501050	N950TA	27.10.08	Air Medical Fleet Ltd	Oxford	
			JA8873, N92275				
G-GMIB	Robin DR.500-200i Président	0002	F-GMIB	5. 9.08	J D L Richardson	Exeter	15. 9.09E
	(Officially regd as DR.400-500)						
G-GMKD	Robin HR.200-120B	256	F-GMKD	13.11.06	Cardiff Academy of Aviation Ltd	Cardiff	30. 4.09E
G-GMKE	Robin HR.200/120B Club	257	F-GMKE	7.11.07	B A Mills	Duxford	12.12.08E
G-GMPB	Pilatus Britten-Norman BN-2T-4S Defender 4000	G-BWPU	5. 4.02	Greater Manchester Police Authority	Manchester	1. 7.09S
		4011	(9M-TPD), G-BWPU				
G-GMPX	MD Helicopters MD.900 Explorer	900-00122	N9114R	29. 1.08	Greater Manchester Police Authority	Barton	
G-GMSI	SOCATA TB-9 Tampico	145		18. 9.80	M L Rhodes	Wolverhampton	17. 8.09E
G-GNAA	MD Helicopters MD.900 Explorer	900-00079	PH-RVD	15.12.04	Police Aviation Services Ltd	Durham Tees Valley	13.12.09E
			N70279		*(Operated Great North Air Ambulance)*		
G-GNJW	Comco Ikarus C42 FB100 VLA	0106-9356		21. 8.01	I R Westrope	(Steeple Bumpstead, Haverhill)	1. 7.09P
	(Built I R Westrope - pr.no.PFA 322-13717) (Kit no unconfirmed - may be 0106-6326)						
G-GNRV	Van's RV-9A	PFA 320-14344		20. 6.05	N K Beavins	Rayne Hall Farm, Braintree	24. 7.09P
	(Built N K Beavins)						
G-GNTB	SAAB-Scania SF.340A	340A-082	HB-AHL	30. 9.91	Loganair Ltd	Glasgow	13. 3.09E
			SE-E82				
G-GNTF	SAAB-Scania SF.340A	340A-113	SE-F13	27.10.94	Loganair Ltd	Glasgow	6. 9.09E
			G-GNTF, HB-AHO, SE-F13				
G-GNTZ	British Aerospace BAe 146 Series 200	E2036	G-CLHB	31. 3.00	Flybe Ltd *(Stored 9.08)*	Exeter	25.11.07E
			G-GNTZ, HB-IXB, N175US, N355PS				
G-GOAC	Piper PA-34-200T Seneca II	34-7770007	D-GOAC	9.12.03	Oxford Aviation Academy (Oxford) Ltd	Oxford	23.11.09E
			N5329F				
G-GOAL	Lindstrand LBL 105A Balloon (Hot Air)	420		18.11.96	I Chadwick tr Balloon Preservation Flying Group		
					(Benfield Reinsurance titles) Partridge Green, Horsham		23. 8.09E
G-GOBD	Piper PA-32R-301 Saratoga IIHP	3246193	G-OARW	22. 8.05	F and M Graventa	Genoa, Italy	20. 1.10E
			EC-IJT, N5339Z				
G-GOBT	Colt 77A Balloon (Hot Air)	1815		13. 2.91	British Telecommunications PLC *"Sky Piper"*		
						Thatcham	18. 3.00A
G-GOCX	Cameron N-90 Balloon (Hot Air)	2619		7. 8.91	R D Parry	Chalford, Stroud	20. 8.09E
G-GOES	Robinson R44 Raven I	10942	EI-KHL	14. 1.08	J Graver t/a JG Commercials		
						Brooke Manor, Brooke, Norwich	21. 2.09E
G-GOGB	Lindstrand LBL 90A Balloon (Hot Air)	1011	G-CDFX	20. 1.05	J Dyer *(Union Flag colours)*	Farnborough	22. 7.09E
G-GOGS	Piper PA-34-200T Seneca II	34-7570228	N1172X	23. 7.03	A Semple	Old Buckenham	13. 4.09E
G-GOGW	Cameron N-90 Balloon (Hot Air)	3304		31. 8.94	S E Carrol *(Great Western titles)*	Cullompton	27. 9.09E
G-GOLF	SOCATA TB-10 Tobago	250		21.12.81	A C Scamell tr Golf Golf Group	Biggin Hill	1.10.09E
G-GOLY	Cessna 150L	15075261	SE-KCM	13. 8.07	E Al-Kirkhy	Wycombe Air Park	13. 9.08E
G-GOMO	Learjet Model 45	45-055	G-OLDF	2. 6.05	Air Partner Private Jets Ltd	Biggin Hill	23. 1.09E
			G-JRJR, N45LR, N63MJ				
G-GOOD	SOCATA TB-20 Trinidad	1657	F-GNHJ	4.11.94	S H Takanaki	(London W14)	21.10.09E
G-GORE	CFM Streak Shadow	K 138-SA		12. 4.90	M S Clinton	Old Sarum	5. 9.08P
	(Built D N Gore - pr.no.PFA 206-11646) (Rotax 532) (PFA sequence no. duplicates TEAM Mini-MAX G-MWFD)						
G-GORV	Van's RV-8	LAA 303-14847		20. 1.09	A Zymslowski tr G-GORV Group	(Southport)	
	(Built A Zymslowski, M Yates and S Dooley)						
G-GOSL	Robin DR.400-180 Régent	1974	G-BSDG	14. 1.02	R M Gosling	Stones Farm, Wickham St Pauls	23. 5.09E
G-GOTC	Gulfstream GA-7 Cougar	GA7-0074	G-BMDY	25. 6.97	Wakelite Ltd	Denham	22. 3.09E
			OO-LCR, OO-HRA				
G-GOTF	Cessna 208B Grand Caravan	208B1175	N208AZ	11.12.06	Trailfinders (Services) Ltd	Oxford	17.12.08E
			N5117U				
G-GOTH	Piper PA-28-161 Warrior III	2842208	N3088U	21. 6.04	J Gosling tr Goose Aviation Syndicate	Barton	25. 6.09E
G-GOUP	Robinson R22 Beta	1663	G-DIRE	9. 1.01	Heli Air Ltd		
						Wellesbourne Mountford/Wycombe Air Park	29. 8.09E
G-GPAG	Van's RV-6	PFA 181A-13306		18. 5.01	P A Green	Old Sarum	31. 1.09P
	(Built P A Green) (Lycoming O-320)						
G-GPAS	Avtech Jabiru UL-450	xxxx		15. 1.02	G D Allen	Priory Farm, Tibenham	18. 1.10P
	(Built G D Allen - pr.no.PFA 274A-13823)						
G-GPBV	Short SD.3-60 Variant 100	SH3747	G-BPFN	15. 5.08	Alebco Corporation A/S *(Operated Ben-Air)*		
			N747HH, N747SA, G-BPPN, G-14-3747			Stauning, Denmark	21. 1.09E
G-GPEG	Cameron Sky 90-24 Balloon (Hot Air)	4849		31. 5.00	N T Parrry *"Pegasus"*	Bracknell	2.10.09E
G-GPFI	Boeing 737-229	20907	VH-OZQ	31. 7.03	European Skybus Ltd *(stored 1.09)*	Bournemouth	2. 4.09E
			G-GPFI, VH-OZQ, G-GPFI, F-GVAC, OO-SDA, LX-LGN, OO-SDA				
G-GPMW	Piper PA-28RT-201T Turbo Arrow IV		N3576V	3. 7.89	Calverton Flying Group Ltd	White Waltham	14. 5.09E
		28R-8031041					
G-GPPN	Cameron TR-70 Balloon (Hot Air)	10940		25.10.06	P Lesser	Partille, Sweden	14. 4.09E
G-GPSF	Avtech Jabiru J430	0xxx		21. 4.06	P S Furlow	Lodge Farm, East Hanningfield	28.10.09P
	(Built P S Furlow - pr.no.PFA 336-14516)						
G-GREY	Piper PA-46-350P Malibu Mirage	4636155	OY-LAR	28.11.03	S T Day and S C Askham	Gloucestershire	10.12.09E
			N1280K, N4129D				
G-GRIN	Van's RV-6	PFA 181-12409		8. 1.98	A Phillips	Boarhunt Farm, Fareham	28. 6.09P
	(Built A Phillips) (Lycoming O-320)						
G-GRMN	Aerospool Dynamic WT9 UK	DY159/2006		2.10.06	R M North	Kimbolton	1. 5.08P
	(Official c/n is "DY/159")						
G-GRND	Agusta A109S Grand	22009		5. 1.06	DFS Trading Ltd	(Doncaster)	22. 1.10E
G-GROE	Grob G115A	8054	I-GROE	22. 6.04	H and E Merkado	Panshanger	30.10.09E
			(D-EGVV)				
G-GROL	Maule MXT-7-180 Super Rocket	14091C		16. 6.98	D C, C and C Croll *(Noted 1.09)*	Southend	28.11.07E
G-GRPA	Comco Ikarus C42 FB100	0407-6609		26. 8.04	G R Page	(Waterrow, Taunton)	27 .8.08P
G-GRRC	Piper PA-28-161 Warrior II	2816076	G-BXJX	9. 3.98	Goodwood Road Racing Company Ltd	Goodwood	8. 1.09E
			HB-POM, D-EJTB, N9149X		*(Operated Goodwood Flying Club)*		
G-GRRR	Scottish Aviation Bulldog Series 120/122		G-BXGU	19.10.98	Horizons Europe Ltd	Compton Abbas	7. 7.11S
		BH120/229	Ghana AF G-105				

Reg	Type	C/n	Prev id	Date	Owner/Operator	Location	Date
G-GRSR	Schempp-Hirth Discus bT	165/578	BGA4430-JDL	6. 3.08	S Robinson tr SR Group	Chipping	
G-GRVE	Van's RV-6	PFA 181-12566		14. 4.07	R D Carswell	Perranporth	3. 4.09P
	(Built R D Carswell)						
G-GRWL	Lilliput Type 4 Balloon (Minimum Lift) SS Model Bear	L-04		22. 6.06	A E and D E Thomas	Weston, Honiton	
G-GRWW	Robinson R44 Raven II	10382	G-HEEL	6.12.04	G R Williams	Phoenix Farm, Lower Upham	17. 6.09E
G-GRYZ	Beech F33A Bonanza	CE-1668	F-GRYZ	4.10.99	J Kawadri and M Kaveh	Fairoaks	10. 1.09E
			D-ESNE, N80011, (OY-GEN), N80011				
G-GRZZ	Robinson R44 Raven II	12149		6. 3.08	Graegill Aviation Ltd	Liverpool-John Lennon	18. 3.09E
G-GSAL	Grass Strip Aviation Fokker E.III	GS-101		13. 5.08	Grass Strip Aviation Ltd	Aston Down	
					(Noted NEC Birmingham 11.08)		
G-GSCV	Comco Ikarus C42 FB UK	PFA 322-13939		5. 9.02	G Sipson	(Coventry)	25. 6.09P
	(Built G Sipson)						
G-GSGZ	Mudry CAP.232	08	F-GSGZ	22.11.07	J Paulson	Hawarden	13. 1.09E
	(Extensively damaged when it force-landed and overturned in a field at Burton green, near Wrexham 2. 9.08 due to fuel problems)						
G-GSJH	Bell 206B-3 JetRanger III	3958	G-PENT	15. 3.02	TJ Morris Ltd	Blackpool	10. 6.09E
			G-IIRB, N903CA				
G-GSMT	Rotorsport UK MTOsport	RSUK/MTOS/001		11. 6.08	Rotorsport UK Ltd	(Wentor, Bishops Castle)	
	(originally registered as RSUK/MT-03/046; amended type and c.n 27. 1.09)						
G-GSOO	Hughes 369E *(Hughes 500)*	0336E	OE-XHA	6. 9.07	C Springthorpe tr CS Properties		
			D-HABC, F-GGCJ			Nottingham City-Tollerton	12.11.09E
G-GSPG	Hughes 369HS *(Hughes 500)*	45-0738S	G-GEEE	17. 1.03	S P Giddings tr S Giddings Aviation		
			G-BDOY			Gowles Farm, Sherrington, Buckingham	17. 1.09E
G-GSPN	Boeing 737-31S	29267	(G-SPAN)	9. 2.04	Globespan Airways Ltd t/a Flyglobespan.com		
			D-ADBW, N60436, N1787B			Edinburgh	28. 3.09E
G-GSPY	Robinson R44 Raven II	10772		31. 8.05	Percy Wood Leasure Ltd	Sherburn-in-Elmet	21. 9.09E
G-GSRV	Robin DR.500-200i Président	0009	F-GSRV	30.10.07	R G Fairall	Redhill	30.10.09E
	(Officially regd as DR.400-500)						
G-GSSA	Boeing 747-47UF	29256	N495MC	23. 1.02	Global Supply Systems Ltd	London Stansted	27. 1.10E
			(N496MC)				
G-GSSB	Boeing 747-47UF	29252	N491MC	17. 1.03	Global Supply Systems Ltd	London Stansted	4.10.09E
G-GSSC	Boeing 747-47UF	29255	N494MC	27. 8.03	Global Supply Systems Ltd	London Stansted	28. 8.09E
			OO-TJA, N494MC				
G-GSSO	Gulfstream Aerospace Gulfstream V-SP	5019	SE-RDX	15. 8.06	TAG Aviation (UK) Ltd	Farnborough	16. 8.09E
	(Gulfstream 550)		N919GA				
G-GSST	Grob G102 Astir CS77	1649	BGA2291-DQG	8.12.07	A G Veitch tr 770 Group "770"	Easterton	13. 4.08
G-GSYJ	Diamond DA.42 Twin Star	42.135	OE-VPI	11. 5.06	Crosby Aviation (Jersey) Ltd	Jersey	1. 6.09E
G-GSYS	Piper PA-34-220T Seneca V	3449363	N60383	8.10.07	Sys (Scaffolding Contractors) Ltd	Gamston	24.10.09E
G-GTDL	Airbus A320-231	0476	C-GTDL	27. 4.05	Thomas Cook Airlines Ltd	Manchester	2. 4.09E
			G-GTDL, C-GTDL, G-GTDL, C-CDTL, D-AUKT, (D-ASSR), N168GB, EI-TLF, F-WWBR				
G-GTEE	P&M Aviation Quik GT450	8256		26. 3.07	Fly Hire Ltd	Rufforth	22. 3.09P
G-GTFC	P&M Pegasus Quik	8184		20. 6.06	A J Fell	(Great Cambourne, Cambridge)	25. 7.09P
G-GTGT	P&M Aviation Quik GT450	8145		8.12.05	G C Weighell	Enstone	7.12.09P
G-GTHM	Piper PA-38-112 Tomahawk II	38-81A0171	C-GTHM	17.11.86	A B King and T P Powley	Ellough, Beccles	10. 3.09E
			N91338				
G-GTJD	P&M Aviation Quik GT450	8183		1. 6.06	R D McKellar t/a Robert McKellar Aviation		
						North Coates	11. 6.08P
G-GTJM	Eurocopter EC.120B Colibri	1428	F-WQDC	20. 7.06	T J Morris Ltd	Blackpool	9.11.09E
G-GTOM	Alpi Pioneer 300	LAA 330-14795		25. 6.08	T F Freake	(Colwyn Bay)	11. 8.09P
	(Built T F Freake)						
G-GTSO	P&M Aviation Quik GT450	8164		10. 3.06	J R North	Ince Blundell	7. 3.09P
G-GTTP	P&M Aviation Quik GT450	8228		27.11.06	T A H Pollock	Kemble	13.12.08P
G-GTWO	Schleicher ASW 15	15146	BGA3315-FKE	18.12.07	J M G Carlton	Shenington	11. 2.08
			D-0794				
G-GUAY	Enstrom 480	5036	(EC-)		J P Belmonde	Shoreham	12.11.09E
			G-GUAY				
G-GUCK	Beech C23 Sundowner 180	M-2221	G-BPYG	9. 4.92	J T Francis	Biggin Hill	5.12.08E
			N6638R				
G-GUFO	Cameron Saucer 80 SS Balloon (Hot Air)	1641	C-GUFO	10. 6.98	Magical Adventures Ltd		
			G-BOUB			West Bloomfield, Michigan, US	14. 8.05A
G-GULP	III Sky Arrow 650 T	K130		4.12.00	S Marriott	East Kirknewton, Wooler	19. 1.10P
	(Built H R Rotherwick - pr.no.PFA 298-13664) (Rotax 914)						
G-GUMS	Cessna 182P Skylane	18261643	G-CBMN	11.11.02	L W Scattergood *(Operated Sheffield City Flying School)*		
			ZS-KJS, N21458				Sandtoft	6. 4.09E
G-GUNS	Cameron V-77 Balloon (Hot Air)	2221		9. 5.90	J Pithois	St Urbain, France	17. 2.09E
G-GUNZ	Van's RV-8	PFA 303-14475		12. 8.08	R Ellingworth	(Grantham)	
	(Built R Ellingworth)						
G-GURN	Piper PA-31 Navajo C	31-7912117	G-BHGA	20. 6.01	Neric Ltd	Fowlmere	23.11.08E
	(Winglets)		N3539M				
G-GURU	Piper PA-28-161 Warrior II	28-8316018	PH-SVJ	12. 2.02	Fly Guru LLP	Hawarden	15. 5.09E
			N83085				
G-GUSS	Piper PA-28-151 Cherokee Warrior	28-7415497	G-BJRY	16. 8.95	M J Cleaver and J M Newman	Southend	25. 6.09E
			N43453				
G-GUST	Agusta-Bell 206B-2 JetRanger II	8192	G-CBHH	30. 8.96	DNH Helicopters Ltd *(Operated Cranfield Helicopters)*		
			F-GALU, G-AYBE			Cranfield	27. 5.08E
G-GUYS	Piper PA-34-200T Seneca II	34-7870283	G-BMWT	14. 7.87	Jowett Homes Ltd	Gamston	14.11.09E
			N31984				
G-GVPI	Evans VP-1 Series 2	PFA 062-10668		9. 8.02	G Martin	Stoke Golding	13. 6.08P
	(Built P A Schafle and G Martin)						
G-GWIZ	Colt Clown SS Balloon (Hot Air)	1369	(G-BPWU)	25. 4.89	Magical Adventures Ltd		
						West Bloomfield, Michigan, US	29. 9.09E
G-GWYN	Reims Cessna F172M Skyhawk II	F17201217	PH-TWN	5. 3.81	C G Tandy tr Magic Carpet Flying Company		
						Denham	30. 4.09E

G-GYAK	Yakovlev Yak-50	852905	RA-02246	9.12.02	M V Rijske and M W Levy *"46"*	Wycombe Air Park	23.12.08P
			DOSAAF (43 blue ?)				
G-GYAT	Sud-Aviation Gardan GY-80-160 Horizon	136	D-EAZZ	13.12.02	J Luck tr Rochester GYAT Flying Group Club		
			HB-DCL, F-BMUU			Rochester	26. 4.09E
G-GYAV	Cessna 172N Skyhawk II	17271362	C-GYAV	26. 8.87	Southport and Merseyside Aero Club (1979) Ltd		
						Hawarden	15. 5.09E
G-GYBO	Sud-Aviation Gardan GY-80-180 Horizon	228	OY-DTN	4. 8.98	A L Fogg	Wellesbourne Mountford	30. 1.09E
			SE-FGL, OY-DTN				
G-GYMM	Piper PA-28R-200 Cherokee Arrow II		G-AYWW	22. 2.90	MRR Aviation Ltd	Gloucestershire	10.12.08E
		28R-7135049	N11C				
G-GYRO	Campbell Cricket replica	PFA G/03-1046		26. 2.82	J W Pavitt	St Merryn	19. 6.08P
	(Built Howell, Pitcher and J W Pavitt) (Originally registered as Bensen B 8 (c/n 01 and PFA G/01-1046) (Rotax 532)						
G-GYTO	Piper PA-28-161 Warrior III	2842082	N160FT	11. 5.00	Plane Talking Ltd	Elstree	1. 6.09E
			N9511N				
G-GZDO	Cessna 172N Skyhawk II	17271826	C-GZDO	11.10.88	G Cambridge and G W J Hall tr Cambridge Hall Aviation		
			(N5299E)		*(Operated Firecrest Aviation)*	Elstree	27. 8.09E
G-GZIP	Rolladen-Schneider LS8-18	8309	BGA4784-JUD	14.12.07	D S St J Haughton	Long Mynd	4. 3.08
G-GZRP	Piper PA-42-720 Cheyenne IIIA	42-5501011	C-GZRP	10. 1.07	Air Medical Fleet Ltd	Oxford	7. 2.09E
			N100CS, N888FW, N288FA, PT-OLT, N4116W, (N35DG), N4116W				

G-HAAA - G-HZZZ

G-HAAH	Schempp-Hirth Ventus 2cT	52-173	BGA4776-JTV	6.12.07	C R Lewis tr The V66 Group *"V66"*	Lasham	9. 1.08
G-HAAT	MD Helicopters MD.900 Explorer	900-00081	G-GMPS	15. 8.08	Police Aviation Services Ltd	North Weald	31. 8.09E
			N7033K		*(Operated Hertfordshire Air Ambulance)*		
G-HABI	Best Off Sky Ranger Swift 912S(1)			26. 2.07	J Habicht	(Elsworth, Cambridge)	6. 7.09P
		SKRXxxx738					
	(Built J Habicht - pr.no.BMAA HB/524)						
G-HABT	Super Marine Spitfire Mk.26	PFA 324-14487		29. 8.06	B Trumble *(In RAF c/s with code "A-BT" on starboard side)*		
						Full Sutton	19. 6.09P
	(Built B Trumble) (stored 10.08 following substantial damage)						
G-HACE	Van's RV-6A	1951	C-GOLZ	22. 5.06	D C McElroy	Perth	30. 7.08P
	(Built J and S Brennan)						
G-HACK	Piper PA-18-150 Super Cub	18-7168	SE-CSA	20.11.97	S J Harris	East Winch	5.12.10S
			N10F				
G-HAEC	Commonwealth CAC-18 Mustang 22		VR-HIU	1. 5.85	R W Davies *(As "472218:WZ-I" in 78th FG USAAF c/s)*		
		CACM-192-1517	(RP-C651),		*(Operated The Old Flying Machine Company)*		
			PI-C651, VH-FCB, A68-192 *"Big Beautiful Doll"*				
	(Composite rebuilt 1974-76 using major components ex Philippine AF P-51D 44-72917)					Little Engeham Farm, Woodchurch	23. 7.09P
G-HAFG	Cessna 340A	340A1806	JY-AFG	5. 8.04	Goldcrest 2001 Ltd	Jersey	11. 9.09E
			N1230V				
G-HAFT	Diamond DA.42 Twin Star	42.057		13.10.05	Atlantic Flight Training Ltd	Coventry	25.11.09E
G-HAGL	Robinson R44 Raven II	12403		21. 7.08	Devon Helicopters Ltd	Exeter	14. 8.09E
G-HAIB	Aviat A-1B Husky	2255	N53HY	16.11.04	H Brockmueller	Shoreham	9. 3.09E
G-HAIG	Rutan LongEz	1983-L		20. 5.86	C Docherty	RAF Wyton	14. 5.09P
	(Built P N Haig pr.no. PFA 074A-11149) (Lycoming O-235)						
G-HAIR	Robin DR.400-180 Régent	2479		7.12.00	S P Copson	Shotteswell	25. 1.09E
G-HAJJ	Glaser-Dirks DG-400	4-225		15. 2.88	W G Upton and J G Kosak	RNAS Culdrose	21. 6.09E
G-HALC	Piper PA-28R-200 Cherokee Arrow II		N91253	26.11.90	Halcyon Aviation Ltd	Barton	12.10.09E
		28R-7335042	C-FFQO, CF-FQO				
G-HALJ	Cessna 140	8336	N89308	30. 4.96	H A Lloyd-Jennings	Henstridge	5.10.07E
	(Continental C85)		NC89308				
G-HALL	Piper PA-22-160 Tri-Pacer	22-7423	G-ARAH	8.11.79	F P Hall	Clipgate Farm, Denton	27. 3.08E
			N10F				
G-HALP	SOCATA TB-10 Tobago	192	G-BITD	19. 8.81	D Halpern	Wycombe Air Park	25. 9.06T
G-HALT	Mainair Sports Pegasus Quik	8063		1. 9.04	S Dixon	Longframlington	25. 4.09P
G-HAMI	Fuji FA.200-180 Aero Subaru	FA200-188	G-OISF	31. 1.92	K G Cameron and M P Antoniak		
			G-BAPT			Glebe Farm, Stockton	9.12.09E
G-HAMM	Yakovlev Yak-50	832409	LY-ANG	15.10.02	Propeller Studios Ltd	(Hitchin)	10.11.09P
			DOSAAF 81				
G-HAMP	Aeronca 7ACA Champ	30-72	N9173L	8. 8.88	R J Grimstead	(Tillington, Petworth)	17. 9.09P
G-HAMR	Piper PA-28-161 Warrior II	28-8416077	PH-AMR	18. 7.06	Electric Scribe 2000 Ltd	Aberdeen	28.11.09E
			N4353B				
G-HAMS	P&M Pegasus Quik	8224		1.11.06	P C D Hamilton	(Southwell)	31.10.08P
G-HAMY	Van's RV-6	PFA 181-12305		19. 4.05	P W Armstrong	Spanhoe	18. 9.09P
	(Built P W Armstrong)						
G-HANG	Diamond DA.42 Twin Star	42.026		7. 6.05	Atlantic Flight Training Ltd	Coventry	23. 6.09E
G-HANS	Robin DR.400 2+2	1384		2. 3.79	J S Russell	Strathaven	23.1.09E
G-HANY	Agusta-Bell 206B-3 JetRanger III	8598	G-JEKP	5. 1.01	Hirecopter Ltd	Shoreham	17. 9.09E
			D-HMSF, G-ESAL, G-BHXW				
G-HAPI	Lindstrand LBL 105A Balloon (Hot Air)	669		21. 3.00	Adventure Balloons Ltd *"Happy Birthday"*		
						Hartley Wintney, Hook	2. 4.09E
G-HAPY	de Havilland DHC-1 Chipmunk 22	C1/0697	WP803	3. 7.96	Astrojet Ltd *(As "WP803" in RAF c/s)*		
						Wycombe Air Park	9.12.11
G-HARD	Dyn'Aéro MCR-01 ULC	PFA 301B-14427		31. 3.06	N A Burnet	Compton Abbas	29. 7.08P
G-HARE	Cameron N-77 Balloon (Hot Air)	1467		12. 3.87	D H Sheryn and C A Buck		
						London SE16 and Longwick, Princes Risborough	3.12.09E
G-HARI	Raj Hamsa X'Air V2(2)	375?		11. 6.99	S T Welsh	Ince Blundell	12 3.08P
	(Built D Mahajan - pr.no.BMAA HB/103)						
G-HARK	Bombardier CL-600-2B16	5646	N646JC	14. 9.06	Corbridge Ltd	(Guernsey)	14. 9.09E
	(CL-604 Challenger)		C-GLXD				
G-HARN	Piper PA-28-181 Archer II	28-8290108	G-DENK	3. 2.00	K Saxton	Coventry	24. 3.09E
			G-BXRJ, HB-PGO				
G-HARR	Robinson R22 Beta II	3514	N75301	14. 6.04	Unique Helicopters Ltd	Enniskillen	2. 7.09E

Reg	Type	C/n	Previous identity	Date	Owner / Operator	Base	Status
G-HART	Cessna 152 II (Tail-wheel u/c conversion)	15279734	(G-BPBF), N757GS	2. 2.89	RVL Aviation Ltd	Coventry	29. 6.09E
G-HARY	Alon A-2	A 188	G-ATWP	15. 3.93	M B Willis	Bourn	26. 7.10S
G-HASO	Diamond DA.40D Star	D4.070	G-CCLZ	21. 4.04	Diamond Aircraft UK Ltd	Gamston	25. 3.08E
G-HATF	Thorp T-18CW (Built A T Fraser and G Hill)	PFA 076-11481		6.12.01	A T Fraser	(Crowthorne)	
G-HATZ	Hatz CB-1 (Lycoming O-320)	17	N54623	11. 5.89	S P Rollason (Carries 'N54623' on tail)	Long Marston	16.11.07P
G-HAUS	Hughes 369HM (Hughes 500)	52-0214M	G-KBOT, G-RAMM, EI-AVN, N9037F	20. 7.99	J Pulford tr Pulford Aviation	Hannington, Rushden	21. 8.09E
G-HAUT	Schempp-Hirth Mini Nimbus C	149	BGA2597	8.10.07	L J Kaye tr 530 Syndicate	Shobdon	1. 1.08
G-HAZE	Thunder Ax8-90 Balloon (Hot Air)	989		3. 8.88	T G Church (Tethered 9.05)	Blackburn	23. 6.97T
G-HBBC	de Havilland DH.104 Dove 8	04211	G-ALFM, VP961, G-ALFM, VP961	24. 1.96	BBC Air Ltd (Noted 10.08)	Compton Abbas	23. 3.06
G-HBBH	Comco Ikarus C42 FB100 (Built Aerosport Ltd)	0608-6835		5. 7.06	B R W Hay	Kemble	25.10.09E
G-HBEK	Agusta A109C	7633		24. 6.08	Starspeed Ltd	Blackbushe	23. 6.09E
G-HBJT	Eurocopter EC155 B1	6807	G-DATE, G-RNLD, I-ANAG	31. 1.06	HPM Investments Ltd	(Poole)	25. 7.09E
G-HBMW	Robinson R22	0170	G-BOFA, N9068D	7. 7.94	Durham Aviation Ltd	Croft Farm, Croft-on-Tees	18.12.09E
G-HBOB	Eurocopter EC135 T2+	0664		24. 4.08	Bond Air Services Ltd (Operated as Thames Valley Air Ambulance)	RAF Benson	
G-HBOS	Scheibe SF25C Falke (Rotax 912-A)	44574	D-KTIN	26. 7.01	Coventry Gliding Club Ltd	Husbands Bosworth	24.10.09E
G-HBRO	Eurocopter AS.355NP Ecureuil 2	5755	F-HAJE, F-WQDD	7.12.07	Henry Brothers (Magherafelt) Ltd	Redhill	3. 2.09E
G-HBUG	Cameron N-90 Balloon (Hot Ai)	1991	G-BRCN	21. 6.89	R T and Hilary.Revel (Thorn-EMI Computeraid titles)	High Wycombe	14.12.08E
G-HCAC	Schleicher Ka 6E	4054	BGA1380-CAC	1. 2.08	M Burridge	Crowland	16. 3.08
G-HCBI	Schweizer 269C-1 (Schweizer 300)	0259	N86G	11. 8.06	Plane Talking Ltd	Turweston	12.12.09E
G-HCGD	Learjet 45	45-328	F-HCGD, N40081	18. 6.08	TAG Aviation (UK) Ltd	Farnborough	18. 6.09E
G-HCSA	Cessna 525A CitationJet CJ2	525A0334	N52699	20.12.06	Bookajet Aircraft Management Ltd	Farnborough	4. 1.09E
G-HCSL	Piper PA-34-220T Seneca III	34-8133237	N84375	9. 5.91	Fly (CI) Ltd (Operated Trans Euro Air)	Southend	11.12.09E
G-HDAE	de Havilland DHC-1 Chipmunk 22	C1/0280	CS-DAE, Portuguese AF 1304	4. 6.03	Airborne Classics Ltd (As "1304" in Portuguese AF c/s)	Enstone	10. 8.09S
G-HDAV	PZL-Bielsko SZD-38A Jantar 1	B-608	BGA1969-DAV	28. 8.08	S A Lewis tr Jantar 1 DAV "240"	Brent Tor	
G-HDEF	Robinson R44 Raven II	11010	G-LOCO, G-TEMM	11. 8.08	Arena Aviation Ltd	Redhill	3. 2.09E
G-HDEW	Piper PA-32R-301 Saratoga II SP	3213026	G-BRGZ, N91787	4.12.89	G R Williams	Phoenix Farm, Lower Upham	17. 4.09E
G-HDIX	Enstrom 280FX Shark	2076	N506DH, D-HDIX	19. 2.98	Clovetree Ltd	Hawarden	19. 5.09E
G-HDTV	Agusta A109A II	7266	G-BXWD, N565RJ, I-URIA, D-HEMZ, N109BD	16. 9.04	Castle Air Charters Ltd	Liskeard Heliport	6. 7.09E
G-HEAD	Colt Flying Head SS Balloon (Hot-Air) (Compac Computerised Head shape)	304	SE-ZHE, G-HEAD	18. 8.81	Ikeair	Fredericksoord, Netherlands	
G-HEAN	Eurocopter AS.355NP	5747	SE-JJR	29. 8.07	Brookview Developments Ltd	Garvargh	30 .8.08E
G-HEBB	Schleicher ASW 27-18E	29550	BGA5317-KSA	25. 6.08	B A Bateson and E Y Heinonen "HE"	Parham Park	3. 7.09
G-HEBE	Bell 206B-3 JetRanger III	3745	CS-HDN, N3179A	5. 2.97	Helispan Ltd	(Tring)	24. 6.09E
G-HEBJ	Cessna 525 CitationJet	525-0437	N717NA, N5181V	5. 3.08	Air Charter Scotland Ltd	Glasgow	6. 3.09E
G-HEBS	Pilatus Britten-Norman BN-2B-26 Islander	2267	N450PM, OY-PHV, JA5318, G-BUBJ	7.12.07	Hebridean Air Services Ltd	Cumbernauld	4. 3.09E
G-HEBZ	Fairey Britten-Norman BN-2A-26 Islander	823	G-BELF, D-IBRA, G-BELF	21. 3.07	Cormack (Aircraft Services) Ltd (Noted 3.07)	Cumbernauld	12. 3.01
G-HECB	Fuji FA.200-160 Aero Subaru	FA200-238	G-BBZO	16. 5.05	H E W E Bailey	(Samois-sur-Seine, France)	24. 8.08E
G-HEHE	Eurocopter EC.120B Colibri	1480	EC-KCR	20. 6.07	HE Group Ltd	(Rochester)	23. 7.09E
G-HEJB	Cirrus SR22 GTS	2311	N963SR	23.02.07	G A J Bowles	Carlisle	3. 4.09E
G-HEKK	Rotary Air Force RAF 2000 GTX-SE (Built J S Penny)	PFA G/13-1285	G-BXEB	18. 7.07	C J Watkinson	(Great Heck, Goole)	10. 4.04P
G-HEKL	Percival Mew Gull Replica	PFA 013-14759		29. 4.08	Innomech Ltd	(Ely)	
G-HELA	SOCATA TB-10 Tobago	135	F-GCOF	31.12.03	S J Heller tr Group TB-10	Panshanger	19. 7.09E
G-HELE	Bell 206B-3 JetRanger III	3789	G-OJFR, N18095	21. 2.91	B E E Smith	White Waltham	4. 5.09E
G-HELM	Eurocopter AS.350B2 Ecureuil	4303	(SE-HJE)	23. 8.07	Astro Aviation Ltd	(Middlesbrough)	19. 9.09E
G-HELN	Piper PA-18 Super Cub 95 (L-21B-PI) (Frame No.18-3400)	"18-3400"	G-BKDG, MM52-2392, EI-69, EI-141, EI-IWB, MM53-7765, 53-7765	10. 1.86	J J Anziani tr Helen Group	Wycombe Air Park	3. 9.09P
G-HELP	Colt 17A Cloudhopper Balloon (Hot Air)	902		16. 2.87	A D Kent tr Balloon Preservation Flying Group "Mondial Cloudhopper"	Petworth	3.10.06A
G-HELV	de Havilland DH.115 Vampire T 55 (Built F + W)	975	Swiss AF U-1215	17. 9.91	Aviation Heritage Ltd (Operated Air Atlantique as "XJ771" in RAF c/s)	Coventry	12. 6.09P
G-HEMS	Aérospatiale SA.365N Dauphin 2	6009	8P-BHD, G-HEMS, F-WYMJ, G-HEMS, N365AM, N365AH	22. 8.88	PLM Dollar Group Ltd (North Cumbria Air Ambulance)	Carlisle	6.10.09E
G-HENT	SOCATA Rallye 110ST Galopin	3210	OO-MBV	28.11.01	R J Patton	City of Derry	31. 3.09E
G-HENY	Cameron V-77 Balloon (Hot Air)	2486		9. 1.91	R S D'Alton "Henny"	Newbury	16. 6.07A
G-HERB	Piper PA-28R-201 Arrow III	28R-7837118	ZS-LAG, N3504M	5. 6.86	E A Sullivan	Stapleford	2.11.09E
G-HERC	Cessna 172S Skyhawk SP	172S8985	N5113P	10.12.01	The Cambridge Aero Club Ltd	Cambridge	27. 2.09E
G-HERD	Lindstrand LBL 77B Balloon (Hot Air)	707		31. 7.00	S W Herd	Mold	24. 1.09E
G-HEVN	SOCATA TB-200 Tobago XL	2013	D-EVHN	29.10.03	I K Maclean	Enstone	1.12.09E

Reg	Type	c/n	Prev identity	Date	Owner	Location	Date
G-HEWI	Piper J-3C-65 Cub (*L-4J-PI*)	12566	G-BLEN	20. 7.84	R Preston tr Denham Grasshopper Flying Group		
	(Continental C90) (*Frame No.12396*)		D-EBEN, HB-OFZ, 44-80270			Denham	22. 5.09E
G-HEXE	Colt 17A Balloon (Hot Air)	2221		24. 2.04	A Dunnington	Bristol	13. 8.09E
G-HEYY	Cameron Bear 72 SS Balloon (Hot Air)	1244		21. 1.86	Magical Adventures Ltd (*Hofmeister Lager Bear*)		
					"George"	West Bloomfield, Michigan, US	30.11.98A
G-HFBM	Curtiss Robertson C-2 Robin	352	LV-FBM	24. 4.90	D M Forshaw	High Cross, Ware	22. 2.09P
	(Continental W-670)		NC9279				
G-HFCA	Cessna A150L Aerobat	A1500381	N6081J	30. 8.91	T H Scott	Rayne Hall Farm, Braintree	14.12.09E
	(*Texas tail-wheel u/c conversion*)						
G-HFCB	Reims Cessna F150L	F15000798	G-AZVR	10. 2.87	P R Mortimer	Cherry Tree Farm, Monewden	28. 7.09E
G-HFCL	Reims Cessna F152 II	F15201663	G-BGLR	11.10.88	MK Aero Support Ltd	Andrewsfield	16. 7.09E
G-HFCT	Reims Cessna F152 II	F15201861		27. 1.81	Stapleford Flying Club Ltd	Stapleford	17. 6.09E
G-HFLY	Robinson R44 Raven II	11876		19.10.07	Helifly (UK) Ltd	Shoreham	21.10.09E
G-HGPI	SOCATA TB-20 Trinidad	851		4. 8.88	M J Jackson and I R Harwood	Bournemouth	14. 5.09E
G-HGRB	Robinson R44 Raven	0776	G-BZIN	21. 4.06	Hangar 8 Ltd	Oxford	11. 7.09E
G-HGRC	Cessna 525A CitationJet CJ2	525A-0360	N13474	12.10.07	Hangar 8 Ltd	Oxford	11.10.09E
			N52655				
G-HHAA	Hawker Siddeley Buccaneer S 2B	B3-01-73	9225M	6.12.02	Hawker Hunter Aviation Ltd (As "XX885" in RAF c/s)		
	(*C/n officially quoted as B3-R-50-67*)		XX885			RAF Scampton	
G-HHAB	Hawker Hunter F 58	41H-697439	Swiss AF J-4072	13. 1.03	Hawker Hunter Aviation Ltd (*Stored as "J-4072" 5.04*)		
						RAF Scampton	
G-HHAC	Hawker Hunter F 58	41H-691770	G-BWIU	10.12.02	Hawker Hunter Aviation Ltd (As "J-4021" in Swiss AF c/s)		
			Swiss AF J-4021			RAF Scampton	12. 7.09P
G-HHAF	Hawker Hunter F 58	41H-697448	G-BWKB	13. 1.03	Hawker Hunter Aviation Ltd (*Stored as "J-4081" 5.04*)		
			Swiss AF J-4081			RAF Scampton	
G-HHAV	SOCATA MS.894A Rallye Minerva 220	11620	G-AYDG	9.10.02	Moorside Aviation Ltd	Perranporth	12. 8.09E
G-HHDR	Cessna 182T Skylane	18282071	N6322X	23. 9.08	D R and H Howell	Biggin Hill	7.10.09E
G-HHII	Hawker Hurricane IIB	CCF/R20023	G-HRLO	5. 4.07	P Teichman t/a Hangar 11 Collection North Weald		
	(*Built Canadian Car and Foundry Co*)		RCAF 5403		(As "BE403:XP-L" in 135 Sqdn RCAF c/s)		
G-HHOG	Robinson R44 Clipper II	10584		23.12.04	Fast Helicopters Ltd	Shoreham	1. 2.09E
G-HHUK	Robin HR.200-120B	282	SE-KYN	23. 8.07	S P Elsby	Leeds-Bradford	19. 9.08E
G-HIBM	Cameron N-145 Balloon (Hot Air)	3197		8. 2.94	Alba Ballooning Ltd	Edinburgh	14.12.08E
G-HIEL	Robinson R22 Beta	1120		28. 9.89	Naylors Timber Recovery Ltd (Royston, Barnsley)		17. 2.10E
G-HIJK	Cessna 421C Golden Eagle	421C-0218	G-OSAL	25. 2.00	G R Case	Guernsey	30. 8.09E
			G-HIJK, G-OSAL, OY-BEC, SE-GZI, N5471G				
G-HIJN	Comco Ikarus C42 FB100	0403-6597		19. 5.04	J R North	Ince Blundell	18. 5.09P
G-HILO	Rockwell Commander 114	14224	N4894W	6. 2.98	J G Gleeson	(Dover)	6. 5.09E
G-HILS	Reims Cessna F172H	F172-0522	G-AWCH	20.12.88	B F W Lowdon tr Lowdon Aviation Group		
						Blackbushe	30. 4.09E
G-HILT	SOCATA TB-10 Tobago	298	(G-BMYB)	13. 5.82	S Harison	Lee-on-Solent	1. 4.09E
			EI-BOF, G-HILT				
G-HILZ	Van's RV-8	PFA 303-14471		14. 6.06	A G and E A Hill	(Windlesham)	25.11.09P
	(*Built A G and E A Hill*)						
G-HIND	Maule MT-7-235 Super Rocket	18037C		26. 3.98	M A Ashmole	Perth	29. 4.09E
G-HINZ	Avtech Jabiru SK	xxxx		1. 2.00	B Faupel	Little Staughton	1. 8.09P
	(*Built B Faupel - pr.no.PFA 274-13441*)						
G-HIPE	Sorrell SNS-7 Hyperbipe	209	N18RS	6. 4.93	B G Ell	Crowfield	26. 3.09P
	(*Built R Stephen*)						
G-HIPO	Robinson R22 Beta	1719	G-BTGB	11. 9.92	SI Plan Electronics (Research) Ltd	Cranfield	24. 4.09E
G-HIRE	Gulfstream GA-7 Cougar	GA7-0091	G-BGSZ	10.12.81	London Aerial Tours Ltd	Rochester	26. 5.09E
			N704G				
G-HISS	Pitts S-2A	2137	G-BLVU	17. 3.92	F L McGee	Liverpool-John Lennon	14.11.07E
	(*Built Aerotek Inc*)		SE-GTX				
G-HITM	Raj Hamsa X'Air Falcon Jabiru(1)	455		23. 2.00	K J Meyers	RNAS Culdrose	25. 4.09P
	(*Built D J Hickey - pr.no.BMAA HB/112*)						
G-HITT	Hawker Hurricane 1		Soviet AF	19.12.08	H Taylor (*on rebuild Hawker Restorations*)		
	(*Built as Mk 1 but rebuilt as Mk IIA 7.41*)		DR348, P3717			Moat Farm, Milden	
G-HIUP	Cameron A-250 Balloon (Hot Air)	4464		16. 4.99	Ladybird Balloons Ltd	Bingham, Nottingham	29. 9.09E
G-HIVA	Cessna 337A Super Skymaster	33700429	G-BAES	28. 3.88	G J Banfield	Gloucestershire	30. 8.09E
			SE-CWW, N5329S				
G-HIVE	Reims Cessna F150M	F15001186	G-BCXT	19. 4.85	M P Lynn	Humberside	10. 5.09E
G-HIYA	Best Off Sky Ranger 912(2)	SKRxxxx648		30.10.06	R D and C M Parkinson		
	(*Built R D Parkinson - pr.no.BMAA HB/493*)					Lower Mountpleasant Farm, Chatteris	19. 9.08P
G-HIZZ	Robinson R22 Beta II	2677	G-CNDY	2. 8.04	S Gallimore and T Hehir t/a Flyfare	Barton	17. 6.09E
			G-BXEW				
G-HJSM	Schempp-Hirth Nimbus 4DM	22/32	G-ROAM	19. 2.01	S H C Marriott tr 60 Syndicate "60"	Lasham	22. 2.09E
G-HJSS	AIA Stampe SV-4C	1101	G-AZNF	7. 9.92	H J Smith	Shoreham	21. 6.09
			F-BGJM, Aeronavale 1101, French AF				
G-HKAA	Schempp-Hirth Duo Discus T	69/364	BGA5033-KEM	20. 9.07	A Aveling "570"	Lasham	2. 2.08
G-HKCF	Enstrom 280C-UK Shark	1149	G-MHCF	27.11.08	H K, D and K Collier t/a HKC Helicopter Services		
			G-GSML, G-BNNV, SE-HIY			Barton	11. 8.07T
G-HKHM	Hughes 369D (*Hughes 500*)	71-1019D	B-HHM	8. 4.99	Heli Air Ltd		
			VR-HHM, N50605			Wellesbourne Mountford/Wycombe Air Park	12. 6.09E
G-HKSD	Diamond HK 36TC Super Dimona	36.714	N105AM	9. 6.08	D King and N Everett	(Newton Abbott)	
G-HLCF	CFM Starstreak Shadow SA-II	K 256-CD		10. 5.96	F E Tofield	(Farnborough)	22. 6.07P
	(*Built S M E Solomon - pr.no.PFA 206-12796*) (Rotax 618)						
G-HLEE	Best Off Sky Ranger J2.2(1)	SKRxxxx655		6. 3.07	L Harland	Rochester	
	(*Built L Harland - pr.no.BMAA HB/502*)						
G-HMBJ	Commander Aircraft Commander 114B	14636	N6036F	30. 6.97	D W R Best	Guernsey	3. 9.09E
G-HMCB	Best Off Sky Ranger Swift 912S(1)	SKRxxx		2. 1.09	R W Goddin	White Hill Farm, Melbourn	
	(*Built R W Goddin pr. no. BMAA HB/586*)						
G-HMED	Piper PA-28-161 Warrior III	2842020	LX-III	21. 7.97	Eglinton Flying Club Ltd	City of Derry	17. 9.09E
G-HMEI	Dassault Mystere Falcon 900	1	F-HOCI	2. 7.04	Executive Jet Group Ltd	RAF Northolt	15. 7.09E
			F-GIDE, F-WIDE				

Reg	Type	c/n	Prev id	Date	Owner/Operator	Location	Date
G-HMEV	Dassault Mystere Falcon 900	5	N905FJ	21. 6.06	Maughold Ltd	(Douglas, Isle of Man)	20. 6.09E
			PT-WQM, N905TS, F-GGRH, VH-BGF, N404FJ, F-WWFB				
G-HMJB	Piper PA-34-220T Seneca III	34-8133040	N8356R	12. 7.89	Cross Atlantic Ventures Ltd *(External storage 10.07)*		
						Blackpool	10.10.04
G-HMPH	Bell 206B-2 JetRanger II	1232	G-BBUY	20. 6.88	Bubnell Ltd	(Bakewell)	3. 3.09E
			N18090				
G-HMPT	Agusta-Bell 206B-2 JetRanger II	8168	D-HARO	7.11.91	Helicopter Express Ltd		
						Ventfield Farm, Horton-cum-Studley,Oxford	16.10.09E
G-HNGE	Comco Ikarus C42 FB100	0607-6838		21. 8.06	Haimoss Ltd	Compton Abbas	21. 8.07E
G-HNLY	Bell 206L-3 LongRanger III	51048	N209MB	27. 3.08	Henley Aviation Ltd	(Henley-on-Thames)	18. 1.10E
			N906PH, N515KA				
G-HOBO	Denney Kitfox Model 4	PFA 172A-12140		10. 9.92	J P Donovan *"Navy Baby"*		
	(W M Hodgkins)					Holmbeck Farm, Leighton Buzzard	16.11.09P
G-HOCA	Robinson R44 Raven II	12388		17. 7.08	Howcan Air Services Ltd	Dublin	14. 8.09E
G-HOCK	Piper PA-28-180 Cherokee D	28-4395	G-AVSH	15. 5.86	J I Simper tr G-HOCK Flying Group	Goodwood	14.10.09E
			N11C				
G-HOFF	P&M Aviation Quik GT450	8383		19. 5.08	M Holman	(Banbury)	18. 5.09P
G-HOFM	Cameron N-56 Balloon (Hot Air)	1245		21. 1.86	Magical Adventures Ltd	Petworth	29. 9.09E
					(Operated Balloon Preservation Group)		
G-HOGS	Cameron Pig 90 SS Balloon (Hot Air)	4121		7. 4.97	Magical Adventures Ltd *"Britannia Piggy Bank"*		
						West Bloomfield, Michigan, US	27. 9.09E
G-HOGZ	IAV Bacau Yakovlev Yak-52	9010313	ZU-HOG	26.11.08	G P Williams	Swansea	27.11.09P
			10 Ukraine AF, 10 (yellow) DOSAAF				
G-HOJO	Schempp-Hirth Discus 2a	2	BGA4533-JHT	12.11.07	R Jones tr Southern Sailplanes *"6"*	Lasham	10. 4.08
G-HOLI	UltraMagic M-77 Balloon (Hot Air)	77/294		23. 2.07	G Everett *(Holiday Inn titles)*	Sandway, Maidstone	26. 9.09E
G-HOLM	Eurocopter EC.135 T2+	0574		20. 8.07	Oxford Air Services Ltd	Oxford	30. 1.10E
G-HOLY	SOCATA ST-10 Diplomate	108	F-BSCZ	31. 1.90	M K Barsham	Fenland	26. 9.05
G-HOME	Colt 77A Balloon (Hot Air)	032		26. 2.79	G L Barnett tr Anglia Balloons *"Tardis"*	Newbury	27. 5.86A
					(On loan to British Balloon Museum and Library)		
G-HONG	Slingsby T 67M-200 Firefly	2060	VR-HZR	24. 3.94	Jewel Aviation and Technology Ltd	Fairoaks	27. 3.09E
			HKG-12, G-7-128				
G-HONI	Robinson R22 Beta	0871	G-SEGO	27. 1.00	Patriot Aviation Ltd	Cranfield	9. 1.10E
			N9081N				
G-HONK	Cameron O-105 Balloon (Hot Air)	1813		30. 9.88	T G S Dixon	Bromsgrove	10. 9.09E
G-HONY	Lilliput Type 1 Series A Balloon (Minimum Lift)			31. 7.98	A E and D E Thomas	Weston, Honiton	
		L-01					
G-HOOD	SOCATA TB-20 Trinidad GT	2008	F-OILJ	25. 7.00	M J Hoodless	Blackbushe	20. 9.08E
G-HOOV	Cameron N-56 Balloon (Hot Air)	388		2. 3.78	H R Evans *"Hoover"*	Ross-on-Wye	26. 5.89A
G-HOPA	Lindstrand LBL 35A Cloudhopper Balloon (Hot Air)						
		972		16. 1.04	S F Burden	Munich, Germany	25. 4.09E
G-HOPE	Beech F33A Bonanza	CE-805	N2024Z	27. 2.79	Hope Aviation	Bournemouth	24. 5.09E
G-HOPI	Cameron N-42 Balloon (Hot Air)	2724		5.12.91	Ballonverbung Hamburg GmbH	Kiel, Germany	30. 4.05A
G-HOPR	Lindstrand LBL 25A Cloudhopper Balloon (Hot Air)			21. 6.04	K C Tanner	Thame	3.10.09E
		999					
G-HOPY	Van's RV-6A	PFA 181-12742		4.12.95	R C Hopkinson	Landmead Farm, Garford	8. 6.09P
	(Built R C Hopkinson) (Lycoming O-320-B2B)						
G-HORK	Alpi Pioneer 300 Hawk	xxx		8.12.07	R Y Kendal	(Ewesley Farm, Morpeth)	9. 6.09P
	(Built R Y Kendal - pr.no.PFA 330A-14741)						
G-HOSS	Beech F33A Bonanza	CE-1151	OY-BVT	3. 1.06	T D Broadhurst tr Beech Baron Aviation	Sleap	14. 4.09E
G-HOTA	Evektor EV-97 teamEurostar UK	3318		16.12.08	A C Aiken	Plaistows Farm, St Albans	15.12.09P
	(Built Cosmik Aviation Ltd)						
G-HOTB	Eurocopter EC155 B1	6789	G-CEXZ	22. 4.08	Noirmont (EC155) Ltd	Dinan, France	14. 4.09E
			F-WQDF				
G-HOTI	Colt 77A Balloon (Hot Air)	750		13. 7.87	G C Dare	Barrington, Ilminster	10. 6.09E
G-HOTM	Cameron C-80 Balloon (Hot-Air)	11172		11. 6.08	J K Macleod *"Ford"*	Cranleigh	11. 6.09E
G-HOTT	Cameron O-120 Balloon (Hot Air)	2581		30. 4.91	D L Smith *"Floating Sensations"*	Newbury	17. 5.97T
G-HOTZ	Colt 77B Balloon (Hot Air)	2218		16. 6.92	C J and S M Davies	Castleton, Hope Valley	9.10.09E
G-HOUS	Colt 31A Air Chair Balloon (Hot Air)	099		7.10.80	The British Balloon Museum and Library	Newbury	3. 5.90A
					(Barratts titles) "K9" (Inflated 4.06)		
G-HOWE	Thunder Ax7-77 Balloon (Hot Air)	1340		10. 4.89	C Suggitt *"Howie/Howzat"*	Beverley	15. 8.95A
G-HOWL	Rotary Air Force RAF 2000 GTX-SE		N4994U	2. 7.01	C J Watkinson	(Great Heck, Goole)	5.10.07P
	(Built M Urbanczyk)	H2-95-6-164					
G-HOXN	Van's RV-9	PFA 320-14229		26. 9.06	F A L Castleden tr XRay November Flying Club		
	(Built F A L Castleden)					Horham, Eye	16. 4.09P
G-HPAD	Bell 206B-3 JetRanger III	1997	G-CITZ	2. 9.02	Helipad Ltd	(West Bridgford, Nottingham)	22.10.09E
			G-BRTB, N9936K			*(Operated Total Air Management Services (TAMS))*		
G-HPOL	MD Helicopters MD.900 Explorer	900-00082	N70082	24. 1.01	Humberside Police Authority	Humberside	3. 9.10S
G-HPPY	Learjet 40	40-2102	N4003K	15. 7.08	TAG Aviation (UK) Ltd	Farnborough	14. 7.09E
G-HPSB	Commander Aircraft Commander 114B	14678	N6118R	24.10.01	International Employment Services Ltd	Guernsey	5.12.09E
G-HPSF	Commander Aircraft Commander 114B	14590	N6003F	16.11.04	S A James	Guernsey	10. 1.10E
G-HPSL	Commander Aircraft Commander 114B	14682	N115KL	26. 8.04	M B Endean	Guernsey	22.10.09E
G-HPUX	Hawker Hunter T 7	41H-693455	8807M	12. 3.99	Hawker Hunter Aviation Ltd *(Stored 5.04 as "XL587/Z")*		
			XL587			RAF Scampton	
G-HRBS	Robinson R22 Beta II	3537	N75353	11. 3.04	Insight Human Resource and Mangement Consultancy Ltd		
						Goodwood	17. 3.09E
G-HRCC	Robin HR.200-100 Club	18	D-EAWT	1. 2.06	P R and J S Johnson	(Lavenham)	
G-HRDS	Gulfstream Aerospace Gulfstream V-SP	5032	N932GA	14.12.04	Fayair (Jersey) Co Ltd	London Stansted	13.12.09E
	(Gulfstream 550)						
G-HRHE	Robinson R22 Beta	1950	G-BTWP	24. 1.97	P Irwin t/a Irwin Plant Sales	(Holywood, Belfast)	22. 1.09E
G-HRHI	Beagle B 206 Basset CC.1	B 014	XS770	6. 7.89	M D Lewis *(As "XS770" in Queens Flight c/s)*		
					(Noted 1.07)	Cranfield	20.10.06
G-HRHS	Robinson R44 Astro	0323		15. 4.97	Stratus Aviation Ltd	North Weald	16. 4.09E
G-HRIO	Robin HR.100-210 Safari II	149	F-BTZR	22. 1.87	R Mullender	Grimbergen, Belgium	14. 1.10E
G-HRLI	Hawker Hurricane I	41H-136172	V7497	25. 4.02	Hawker Restorations Ltd	Milden	

Reg	Type	C/n	Prev id	Date	Owner	Base	Date
G-HRLK	SAAB 91D/2 Safir	91376	G-BRZY PH-RLK	6. 3.90	Sylmar Aviation and Services Ltd Lower Wasing Farm, Brimpton		15. 8.10
G-HRLM	Brügger MB.2 Colibri (Built R A Harris) (Volkswagen 1834)	PFA 043-10118		28.12.78	D G Reid "Titch"	Morgansfield, Fishburn	13. 7.07P
G-HRND	Cessna 182T Skylane	18281936	N2252X	31. 5.07	Dingle Star Ltd	Denham	19. 6.09E
G-HRNT	Cessna 182S Skylane	18280395	N2369H	29. 1.99	C R Thompson	Driffield	27. 4.09E
G-HROI	Rockwell Commander 112A	326	N1326J	19. 6.89	Intereuropean Aviation Ltd	Jersey	16. 7.09E
G-HRPN	Robinson R44 Raven II	10007		26.11.02	D Gerado and L Maurizio S Georgio Magno / Calcinato, Italy		14. 1.09E
G-HRVD	CCF Harvard 4 (T-6J-CCF Texan) (Possibly a composite with rear fuselage of Moz PLAF/FAP 1780/AA+614/53-4622) (On rebuild 5.05)	CCF4-548	G-BSBC Moz PLAF 1741, FAP 1741, WGAF BF+055, WGAF AA+055, 53-4629	8.12.92	K F Mason and D Featherby t/a Anglia Flight Bruntingthorpe		14. 1.09E
G-HRVS	Van's RV-8 (Built D J Harvey, pr.no PFA 303-14444)	81842		2.10.08	D J Harvey and M S Pettit (Lytham St Annes / Chipping Norton)		
G-HRYZ	Piper PA-28-180 Cherokee Archer	28-7505090	G-WACR, N9517N G-BCZF, N9517N	6. 2.06	Lees Avionics Ltd	Fairoaks	9. 7.09E
G-HSBC	Lindstrand LBL 69X Balloon (Hot Air)	1153		21. 9.07	A Nimmo	Dubai, United Arab Emirates	29.11.09E
G-HSKE	Aviat A-1B Husky	2437	N65HY	11. 6.08	Aviat Aviation (UK) Ltd Lower Grounds Farm, Shirlowe		6.10.09E
G-HSKI	Aviat A-1B Husky	2312		20. 1.06	C J R Flint	Eastwick, Ellesmere	22. 6.09E
G-HSLA	Robinson R22 Beta	1130	G-BRTI EI-CDW, (EI-CFJ), G-BRTI, N8044U	22.11.01	Summerline Aviation Ltd	Coventry	11.11.09E
G-HSOO	Hughes 369HE (Hughes 500)	109-0208E	G-BFYJ F-BRSY	3.11.93	Kuki Helicopter Sales Ltd and S J Nicholls	Gamston	27. 9.03T
G-HSTH	Lindstrand LBL HS-110 Airship (Hot Air)	546		20. 8.98	Ballonsport Helmut Seitz	Kissleg, Germany	26. 5.06A
G-HSXP	Raytheon Hawker 850XP	258827	N7077S	26. 3.07	Fowey Services Ltd	(Cannes, France)	7. 4.09E
G-HTEL	Robinson R44 Raven	1155	N70319	25. 1.02	A G and R S Higgins	Bitteswell	12. 2.09E
G-HTRL	Piper PA-34-220T Seneca III	34-8333061	G-BXXY PH-TLN, N4295X	8. 2.00	Air Medical Fleet Ltd	Oxford	29. 3.09E
G-HTWE	Rans S-6-116 Coyote II (Built H C C Coleridge - pr.no.PFA 204-14698)	0407.1804		8. 1.08	H C C Coleridge (Meysey Hampton, Cirencester)		
G-HUBB	Partenavia P68B	194	OY-BJH SE-GXL	27. 5.83	G-HUBB Ltd	Denham	7.10.09E
G-HUCH	Cameron Carrots 80 SS Balloon (Hot Air)	2258	G-BYPS	13. 3.91	Magical Adventures Ltd "Magic Carrots" West Bloomfield, Michigan, US		27. 9.09E
G-HUES	Hughes 369HS (Hughes 500)	1100270S	G-GASC G-WELD, G-FROG, OO-KAR	1.11.07	A C Richardson (Hulme Walfield, Congleton)		22. 5.09E
G-HUEW	Europa Aviation Europa XS (Built C R Wright - pr.no.PFA 247-14156)	592		22. 7.04	C R Wright	Tatenhill	1. 8.09P
G-HUEY	Bell UH-1H-BF Iroquois (Argentine Army), 73-22077 (Also coded "560" in "US Army" camouflage c/s)	13560	AE-413	23. 7.85	M Grimshaw t/a G-HUEY Partnership North Weald		6. 4.09P
G-HUFF	Cessna 182P Skylane II (Reims-assembled with c/n F18200033)	18264076	PH-CAS N6059F	31.10.78	A E G Cousins	Southend	16. 7.09E
G-HUGO	Colt 260A Balloon (Hot Air)	2559		20. 1.94	P G Hall	Meanwood, Chard	5. 8.04T
G-HUGS	Robinson R22 Beta	1455	G-BYHD N900AB	27. 2.02	C M and E A Addison t/a C M Addison Knapthorpe Lodge, Caunton		21. 4.09E
G-HUKA	Hughes 369E (Hughes 500)	0298E	G-OSOO	12. 2.02	B P Stein	(London WC2)	1. 9.09E
G-HULK	Best Off Sky Ranger 912(2) (Built L C Stockman - pr.no.BAA/HB/238)	SKR0207213		16. 1.07	L C Stockman	Plaistows Farm, St Albans	24. 5.09P
G-HULL	Reims Cessna F150M	F15001255	PH-TGR	19. 1.79	Hull Aero Club Ltd	Linley Hill, Leven	6.11.09E
G-HUMH	Van's RV-9A (Built H A Daines)	PFA 320-14357		15.11.05	H A Daines	Seething	4. 9.09P
G-HUND	Aviat A-1B Husky	2435	N55HY	1. 4.08	U Ladurner	Meran, Italy	14. 5.09E
G-HUNI	Bellanca 7GCBC Citabria	541-73	OO-IME D-EIME	21.10.96	The Pilot Centre Ltd	Denham	15.11.10S
G-HUPW	Hawker Hurricane I (Built Gloster Aircraft Co Ltd)	G5-92301	R4118	21. 8.01	P J and P M A Vacher t/a Minmere Farm Partnership (As "R4118:UP-W") Meluish Farm, North Moreton		24. 3.09P
G-HURI	Hawker Hurricane XIIA (IIB) (Built Canadian Car and Foundry Co) (Composite - probably includes parts from c/n 44019 ex RCAF 5424, RCAF 5625 and RCAF 5547)	72036	RCAF 5711	9. 6.83	Historic Aircraft Collection Ltd (Operated The Fighter Collection) (As "Z5140/HA-C" in RAF 126 Sqdn c/s) Duxford		12. 7.09P
G-HURN	Robinson R22 Beta	1441		18. 7.90	Sloane Helicopters Ltd	Sywell	5. 6.09E
G-HUSK	Aviat A-1B Husky	2214		2. 1.03	P H Yarrow and A T Duke Wisbridge Farm, Reed, Royston		24. 4.09E
G-HUTE	Aerochute Dual (Rotax 503) (Wing serial no. 1305)	342		22. 7.08	R J Watkin and W A Kimberlin (Melton Mowbray)		21. 9.09P
G-HUTT	Denney Kitfox Model 2 (Built M A J Hutt and B Davies - pr.no.PFA 172-11634)	509		24. 1.90	H D Colliver	Landmead Farm, Garford	20. 7.09P
G-HUTY	Van's RV-7 (Built S A Hutt)	PFA 323-14571		26.10.06	S A Hutt	(Angmering, Littlehampton)	
G-HVAN	TLAC RL5A LW Sherwood Ranger (Built H T H van Neck - pr.no.PFA 237-13074) (BMW R100)	xxxx		10.12.98	H T H van Neck (Noted 8.08)	Ince Blundell	
G-HVBF	Lindstrand LBL 210A Balloon (Hot Air)	372		23. 5.96	Airxcite Ltd t/a Virgin Balloon Flights	Wembley	25. 3.07E
G-HVER	Robinson R44 Raven II	11754		29. 5.07	Equation Associates Ltd	Denham	14. 6.09E
G-HVRD	Piper PA-31-350 Navajo Chieftain	31-7305052	G-BEZU SE-GDP, N74920, N9666N	11. 6.87	N Singh	Caernarfon	23. 6.09E
G-HVRZ	Eurocopter EC.120B Colibri	1338	HB-ZEZ	17. 1.07	EDM Helicopters Ltd	Elstree	16. 1.09E
G-HWAA	Eurocopter EC.135 T2	0375		21. 2.05	Bond Air Services Ltd (Operated County Air Ambulance) Strensham		6. 4.09E
G-HXTD	Robin DR.400-180 Régent	2510		24.10.01	Richmond Aviation Ltd	Bodmin	1. 1.09E
G-HYAK	IAV Bacau Yakovlev Yak-52	9011107	LY-ALU DOSAAF 124	27. 8.02	Goodridge (UK) Ltd	Exeter	15.11.09P
G-HYLT	Piper PA-32R-301 Saratoga II SP	32R-8213001	N84588	23. 4.86	T G Gordon	(Castlebar, County Mayo)	12. 3.09E
G-HYST	Enstrom 280FX Shark	2082		9. 7.98	S Patten	Barton	9. 6.08E

G-IAAA - G-IZZZ

Reg	Type	C/n	Prev ID	Date	Owner/Operator	Location	Date
G-IACA	Sikorsky S-92A	920050	N81254	23. 4.07	Bristow Helicopters Ltd	Aberdeen	20. 5.09E
G-IACB	Sikorsky S-92A	920062	N4516G	14.11.07	Bristow Helicopters Ltd	Aberdeen	14.11.09E
G-IACC	Sikorsky S-92A	920063	N45158	15.11.07	Bristow Helicopters Ltd	Aberdeen	21.11.09E
G-IACD	Sikorsky S-92A	920065	N4515G	20.12.07	Bristow Helicopters Ltd	Aberdeen	9. 1.10E
G-IACE	Sikorsky S-92A	920066	N45148	20.12.07	Bristow Helicopters Ltd	Aberdeen	9. 1.10E
G-IACF	Sikorsky S-92A	920068	N4509G	5. 2.08	Bristow Helicopters Ltd	Aberdeen	19. 2.09E
G-IAJJ	Robinson R44 Raven II	11953		13.11.07	Valley and Vale Properties Ltd	(Chelford. Macclesfield)	2. 1.10E
G-IAJS	Comco Ikarus C42 FB UK	0503-6657		27. 7.05	A J Slater	Dairy House Farm, Worrleston	28. 7.09P
	(Built A J Slater - pr.no.PFA 322-14393)						
G-IAMP	Cameron H-34 Balloon (Hot Air)	2541		11. 3.91	R S Kent tr Balloon Preservation Flying Group *(BPG titles)*	Petworth	15. 5.09E
G-IANB	DG Flugzeugbau DG-808B	8-246B159		12. 3.02	I S Bullous	Sutton Bank	12.10.09E
G-IANC	SOCATA TB-10 Tobago	150	G-BIAK	15.12.04	I Corbin and P D Seed	Biggin Hill	15. 2.09E
G-IANH	SOCATA TB-10 Tobago	1843	F-OILI	13. 3.00	XD Flight Management Ltd	Goodwood	12. 4.09E
G-IANI	Europa Aviation Europa XS	505		20. 4.01	I F Rickard and I A Watson	Fairoaks	26 11.09P
	(Built I F Rickard and I A Watson - pr.no.PFA 247-13714) *(Rotax 914)* *(Tri-Gear u/c)*						
G-IANJ	Reims Cessna F150K	F15000548	G-AXVW	19. 5.98	J A, G M, D T A and J A Rees t/a Messrs Rees of Poyston West	Haverfordwest	4.11.09E
G-IANN	Kolb Twinstar Mk.III Xtra	PFA 205-14259		7.10.04	I Newman *(in container on field)*	North Coates	26. 2.08P
	(Built I Newman)						
G-IANV	Diamond DA42 Twin Star	42.150	OE-VPI	21. 7.06	TGD Leasing Ltd	Gloucestershire	14. 8.09E
G-IANW	Eurocopter AS.350B3 Ecureuil	3447	F-WQPU	18. 9.01	Milford Aviation Services Ltd	(Harrow)	20. 1.09E
G-IARC	Stoddard-Hamilton GlaStar	PFA 295-13261		9.11.99	A A Craig	Prestwick	3. 7.08P
	(Built A A Craig) *(Tri-cycle u/c)*						
G-IASL	Beech 60 Duke	P-21	G-SING, D-IDTA, SE-EXT	18. 4.97	Castlelaurie Property Ltd	(Falkirk)	8. 3.09E
G-IATU	Cessna 182P Skylane	18261436	G-BIRS, G-BBBS, N21131	8. 1.03	R J Bird	Bournemouth	21. 4.09E
G-IBAZ	Comco Ikarus C42 FB100	0409-6622		30. 9.04	B R Underwood	Bulkington, Bedworth, Warwickshire	13.10.08P
G-IBBC	Cameron Sphere 105 SS Balloon (Hot Air)	4082		2. 4.97	R S Kent tr Balloon Preservation Group	Shoreham	17. 7.03A
G-IBBS	Europa Aviation Europa	118		8. 9.94	R H Gibbs	Popham	26. 5.09P
	(Built R H Gibbs - pr.no.PFA 247-12745) *(Monowheel u/c)*						
G-IBED	Robinson R22 Alpha	0500	G-BMHN	7. 9.93	B C Seedle tr Brian Seedle Helicopters	(Blackpool)	30. 9.94
G-IBEV	Cameron C-90 Balloon (Hot Air)	10375		10. 4.03	B Drawbridge	Cranbrook	3. 4.09E
G-IBFC	BFC Challenger II Long Wing	CH2-0898-UK-1774		9.11.98	K V Hill	Husbands Bosworth	10. 4.08P
	(Built K N Dickinson)		*(Pr.no.PFA 177B-13369)*				
G-IBFP	Magni M-16 Tandem Trainer	PFA G/12-1240		22. 3.05	B F Pearson	Headon Farm, Retford	4.10.07P
G-IBFW	Piper PA-28R-201 Arrow III	28R-7837235	N31534	22. 1.79	Archer Four Ltd	Lydd	26. 3.09E
G-IBHH	Hughes 269C *(Hughes 300)*	74-0327	G-BSCD, PH-HSH, SE-HFG	20. 8.99	Hughes Helicopter Co Ltd t/a Biggin Hill Helicopters	Biggin Hill	21. 6.07T
G-IBIG	Bell 206B-3 JetRanger III	2202	G-BORV, C-GVTY, N16763	20. 3.02	Big Heli-Charter Ltd	Manston	28. 7.08E
G-IBLU	Cameron Z-90 Balloon (Hot Air)	4913		4. 8.00	John Aimo Balloons SAS *(Blu titles)*	Mondovi, Piedmont, Italy	6. 5.06A
G-IBMS	Robinson R44 Raven II	11287		20. 6.06	Beoley Mill Software Ltd (Astwood Bank, Redditch)		6. 7.08E
G-IBUZ	CZAW Sportcruiser	LAA 338-14835		21.10.08	R C-E Wheeler and D W Bessell	Lorkins Farm, Twinstead, Sudbury	
	(Built R C-E Wheeler and D W Bessell)						
G-IBZS	Cessna 182S Skylane	18280529	N7269A	11.12.99	D C Shepherd	Rochester	5. 1.10E
G-ICAS	Pitts S-2B	5344	N511P	19. 6.97	J C Smith	Full Sutton	12. 7.09E
	(Built Aviat Inc)						
G-ICBI	Schweizer 269C-1 *(Schweizer 300)*	0272	N86G	14. 3.07	Plane Talking Ltd	Turweston	30. 3.09E
G-ICBM	Stoddard-Hamilton Glasair III Turbine	3337		18.12.00	G V Waters and D N Brown	Deenethorpe	7.12.09P
	(Built G V Waters) *(Allison 250-B17B)*						
G-ICCL	Robinson R22 Beta	1608	G-ORZZ	25.11.93	A Jahanfar	Southend	28. 3.09E
G-ICES	Thunder Ax6-56 SP.1 Balloon (Hot Air)	283		3. 7.80	British Balloon Museum and Library Ltd *"Ashfords"*	Newbury	3. 6.94A
	(Ice Cream special shape)						
G-ICKY	Lindstrand LBL 77A Balloon (Hot Air)	029		19. 5.93	C J Sanger-Davies	Hawarden	23. 8.09E
G-ICMT	Evektor EV-97 Eurostar	PFA 315-14598		4.12.06	C M Theakstone	Prospect Farm, Wollaston	17. 1.10P
	(Built C M Theakstone)						
G-ICOI	Lindstrand LBL 105A Balloon (Hot Air)	564	(D-O...), G-ICOI	3.11.98	F Schroeder	Mülheim Ruhr, Germany	20. 3.03A
G-ICOM	Reims Cessna F172M Skyhawk II	F17201212	G-BFXI, PH-ABA, D-EEVC	25. 4.94	C G Elesmore	Headcorn	25. 7.09E
G-ICON	Rutan LongEz	PFA 074A-11104		29.11.00	S J and M A Carradice *(Noted 5.06)*	Gamston	
	(Built S J Carradice)						
G-ICRS	Comco Ikarus C42 FB UK	0202-6458		11. 3.02	Ikarus Flying Group Ltd	RAF Halton	15. 4.09P
	(Built A J Whitlock - pr.no.PFA 322-13873)						
G-ICSG	Aérospatiale AS.355F1 Ecureuil 2	5104	G-PAMI, G-BUSA	6. 4.93	Sky Charter UK Ltd	(Whitstable)	7. 8.08E
G-ICWT	Cyclone Airsports Pegasus Quantum 15-912	7632		7. 4.00	S L Mould	Mill Farm, Shifnal	14. 7.09P
G-IDAB	Cessna 550 Citation Bravo	550-0917	EI-DAB, N5100J	16. 3.04	EASSDA Ireland Ltd	(Templepatrick, Ballyclare)	14. 5.09E
G-IDAY	Skyfox CA-25N Gazelle	CA25N-028	VH-RCR	29. 4.96	G G Johnstone	Sorbie Farm, Kingsmuir	30. 6.09E
	(Rotax 912)						
G-IDDI	Cameron N-77 Balloon (Hot Air)	2383		21. 8.90	PSH Skypower Ltd *(Allen and Harris - Royal Sun Alliance titles)*	Woodborough, Pewsey	
G-IDER	Schempp-Hirth Discus CS	078CS	BGA3874-HDS	15.10.07	A J Preston and D B Keith *"W4"*	Bicester	28. 9.08

Reg	Type	C/n	Prev id	Date	Owner/Operator	Base	
G-IDII	Dan Rihn DR.107 One Design PFA 264 12953			16. 6.99	C Darlow	Shacklewell Farm, Empingham	16. 3.09P
	(Built C Darlow) (Lycoming O-360)						
G-IDOL	Evektor EV-97 Eurostar PFA 315-14549			4. 9.06	K L Manning	(Chelmsford)	29. 3.09P
	(Built T D Baker, J J Lynch and C Moore)						
G-IDSL	Flight Design CT2K	02-06-02-04		28.10.02	W D Dewey	Wishanger Farm, Frensham	27. 4.09P
	(Assembled Pegasus Aviation Ltd with c/n 7922)						
G-IDUP	Enstrom 280C Shark	1163	G-BRZF	11. 5.92	Antique Buildings Ltd		
			N5687D			Huntersworod Farm, Dunsfold	4. 7.09E
G-IDWR	Hughes 369HS (Hughes 500)	69-0101S	G-AXEJ	26. 5.81	M A and M Gradwell	Barton	11. 2.09E
G-IEIO	Piper PA-34-200T Seneca II	34-7670274	EI-EIO	6.12.02	J and D Stadelman	Bournemouth	25. 3.09E
			N6257J				
G-IEJH	SAN Jodel D 150A Mascaret	02	G-BPAM	28. 2.95	A Turner and D Worth	Crowfield	1. 5.09P
			F-BLDA, F-WLDA				
G-IEYE	Robin DR.400-180 Régent	2123		29. 1.92	G Wood	Sherburn-in-Elmet	18. 9.09E
G-IFAB	Reims Cessna F182Q Skylane II	F18200127		6. 1.98	Manda Construction Ltd	Inverness	10. 2.09E
			N61AN				
			G-IFAB, OO-ELM, (OO-HNU)				
G-IFBP	Eurocopter AS.350B2 Ecureuil	9051	F-GTKR	27.10.03	F Bird t/a Frank Bird Aviation	Carlisle	19. 3.09E
			(F-GYBR)				
G-IFDM	Robinson R44 Astro	0707		24. 1.00	MFH Helicopters Ltd	Conington	16. 3.09E
G-IFFR	Piper PA-32-300 Cherokee Six	32-7340123	G-BWVO	1. 4.97	D J D , G D Ritchie and J.C Gilbert	RAF Henlow	18. 2.09E
			OO-JPC, N55520				
G-IFIF	Cameron TR-60 Balloon (Hot Air)	10811		17.11.05	M G Howard "VGL/if"	Dubai, UAE	5.10.09E
G-IFIT	Piper PA-31-350 Chieftain	31-8052078	G-NABI	31.12.85	Dart Group PLC (Operated.Jet2.com)		
			G-MARG, N3580C			Leeds-Bradford	3. 4.09E
G-IFLE	Evektor EV-97 teamEurostar UK	2113		1. 7.04	M R Smith	Otherton, Cannock	10. 7.09P
G-IFLI	Gulfstream AA-5A Cheetah	AA5A-0831	N26948	7. 7.82	C M Petherbridge tr I Fly Group	Linley Hill, Leven	9. 1.10E
G-IFLP	Piper PA-34-200T Seneca II	34-8070029	N81WS	4. 1.88	ACS Aviation Ltd	Perth	28. 8.09E
			N81149				
G-IFRH	Agusta A109C	7619	N637CG	7. 1.08	Helicopter Services Ltd	Wycombe Air Park	21.2.09E
G-IFTE	British Aerospace HS 125 Series 700B		G-BFVI	16. 5.96	Albion Aviation Management Ltd	Biggin Hill	9. 9.09E
		257037	G-5-18				
G-IFTF	British Aerospace BAe 125 Series 800B		G-RCEJ	21. 1.08	Albion Aviation Management Ltd	Biggin Hill	14. 6.09E
		258021	VR-CEJ, G-GEIL, G-5-15				
G-IFTS	Robinson R44 Astro	0366		16. 9.97	G P Jones	Swansea	4. 2.10E
G-IFWD	Schempp-Hirth Ventus cT	148/468	BGA3575-FWD	8.11.07	J C Ferguson and C J Hamilton	(Dunfermline)	1. 4.08
G-IGGL	SOCATA TB-10 Tobago	146	G-BYDC	26. 3.99	G M Richards tr G-IGGL Flying Group		
			F-GCOL			White Waltham	5. 2.09E
G-IGHH	Enstrom 480	5034		1.12.98	Raw Sports Ltd	Gloucestershire	27. 2.09E
G-IGHT	Van's RV-8	82525		25. 7.08	E A Yates	North Weald	
	(Built E A Yates, pr.no PFA 303-14520)						
G-IGIA	Eurocopter AS.350B3 Ecureuil	3243	I-CFVA	21. 3.07	Faloria Ltd	(Wickford)	23. 7.09E
G-IGIE	SIAI-Marchetti SF.260	2-42	D-EHGB	13. 3.02	D Fletcher and J J Watts	Bournemouth	12. 5.09E
G-IGII	Europa Aviation Europa	011		9. 4.02	C D Peacock	Sywell	3. 7.07P
	(Built W C Walters - pr.no.PFA 247-12506) (NSI EA/81-100) (Conventional u/c)						
G-IGJC	Robinson R44 Raven II	12499		2.10.08	G Corbett	(Winsford)	
G-IGLA	Colt 240A Balloon (Hot Air)	2228		3. 7.92	M L and S M Gabb tr Heart of England Balloons		
					(Barclaycard titles)	Haselor, Alcester	29. 8.03T
G-IGLE	Cameron V-90 Balloon (Hot Air)	2609		11. 6.91	A A Laing "Giggle"	Aberdeen	28. 5.09E
G-IGLY	P&M Aviation Quik GT450	8372		9. 4.08	VFR Ltd	Ashcroft Farm, Winsford	8. 4.09P
G-IGLZ	American Champion 8KCAB Super Decathlon			18. 2.03	Woodgate Aviation (IoM) Ltd	Belfast International	18. 2.09E
		914-2003					
G-IGPW	Eurocopter EC.120B Colibri	1027	G-CBRI	31. 7.99	J Havakin	Middleton One Row, Darlington	10. 9.09E
G-IGZZ	Robinson R44 Raven II	12192		3.10.08	Rivermead Aviation Ltd (Operated Rise Helicopters)		
						Gloucestershire	3.12.09E
G-IHDC	Eurocopter AS.350B Ecureuil	4512	SE-JKT	11.11.08	Rockfield Aviation Ltd	(Maynooth, Ireland)	20. 1.10E
G-IHOP	Cameron Z-31 Balloon (Hot Air)	10782		28.11.05	N W Roberts	Cardiff	20.10.09E
G-IHOT	Evektor EV-97 teamEurostar UK	2003.20.07		1. 4.04	Exodus Airsports Ltd	Plaistows Farm, St Albans	31. 3.07P
	(C/n conflicts with G-CENM)						
G-IIAC	Aeronca 11AC Chief	11AC-169	G R Moore	2. 7.91	G R Moore	Black Spring Farm, Castle Bytham	16. 5.09P
	(Continental A65)		N86359, NC86359				
G-IIAI	Mudry CAP.232	7	F-GJGM	22. 1.08	C Butler	(Clowne, Chesterfield)	9.12.09E
G-IIAN	Aero Designs Pulsar PFA 202-12123			10. 9.91	I G Harrison	(Pentrich, Ripley)	
	(Built I G Harrison)						
G-IICI	Pitts S-2C	6017	N113PS	20. 5.02	D G Cowen tr Charlie India Group	Redhill	18.12.09E
	(Built Aviat Inc) (Lycoming AEIO-540)						
G-IICT	Schempp-Hirth Ventus 2cT	72/225	BGA4921-JZV	12. 7.07	P McLean "V2C"	RAF Marham	10. 6.08
G-IICX	Schempp-Hirth Ventus 2cxT	171/...	BGA5199-KMH	3. 4.06	R Jones tr Southern Sailplanes "410"	Lasham	30.11.07
G-IIDI	Extra EA.300/L	047	D-EXJH	5.10.01	Power Aerobatics Ltd (Operated Xtreme Team)		
						Kemble	14. 3.09E
G-IIDY	Pitts S-2B	5000	G-BPVP	11.11.02	R P Millinship tr The S-2B Group	Leicester	8.11.09E
	(Built Aerotek Inc)		N5302M				
G-IIEX	Extra EA.300/L	04	JA300L	25. 5.05	Extreme Aerobatics Ltd	Shoreham	21. 8.08E
			N123EX, D-ETYM, (D-ETYL)				
	(Made a forced landing at Hastingleigh, nr Ashford 26.5.08 due to engine problems)						
G-IIFR	Robinson R22 Beta II	2841		2. 9.98	R C Hields t/a Hields Aviation	Sherburn-in-Elmet	15. 9.09E
G-IIGI	Van's RV-4	381	N44BZ	7. 4.04	A Darlington tr G-IIGI Flying Club	Popham	21. 8.09P
	(Built R F and C Palmer)						
G-IIHI	Extra EA.300/SC	SC008		19.12.08	Yak UK Ltd	Little Gransden	18.12.09E
G-IIID	Dan Rihn DR.107 One Design PFA 264-12766			6. 7.00	D A Kean	Wellcross Farm, Slinfold	28. 8.08P
	(Built M A N and A J Newall)						
G-IIIE	Pitts S-2B	5017	N9WQ	8. 3.04	S Navacerrada	(Seville, Spain)	7.12.09E
	(Built Aerotek Inc)		N9WR				
G-IIIG	Boeing Stearman A75N1 (PT-17) Kaydet		G-BSDR	25. 3.91	O Josse and S Bolyn	(Spa, Belgium)	24. 7.09S
	(Continental W670)	75-4354	N61827, 42-16191				

Reg	Type	c/n	Prev id	Date	Owner/Operator	Base	Status
G-IIII	Pitts S-2B	5010	N5330G	6. 1.89	Four Eyes Aerobatics Ltd	Barton	28. 3.09E
	(Built Christen Industries Inc) (Lycoming AEIO-540)						
G-IIIL	Pitts S-1T	008	OH-XPT G-IIIL, N15JE	15. 2.89	Empyreal Airways Ltd	Leicester	13. 1.10P
	(Built J L Edwardson)						
G-IIIM	Stolp SA.100 Starduster	4258549	N40D	21. 4.06	H Mackintosh	Old Hay	
	(Built Starduster Corporation)						
G-IIIO	Schempp-Hirth Ventus 2cM	41/73	PH-1110 D-KBBF	10. 8.04	S J Clark	(South Brent)	25. 9.09E
G-IIIR	Pitts S-1S	604	N27M	21. 1.93	R O Rogers	Hulcote Farm, Salford, Bedford	9. 7 09P
	(Built Milam)						
G-IIIS	Sukhoi Su-26M2	06-07	RA-01321 N626RM, RA-0607, DOSAAF 55 (black)	7.10.03	Airtime Aerobatics Ltd (Red Bull Matadors titles)	Kemble	9. 7.09P
G-IIIT	Pitts S-2A	2222	N7YT	16. 1.89	Aerobatic Displays Ltd (Breitling Angels c/s)	Wycombe Air Park	8. 6.09E
	(Built Aerotek Inc)						
G-IIIV	Pitts Super Stinker 11-260	PFA 273-13005		4. 2.97	S D Barnard	Leicester	13. 5.09P
	(Built A N R Houghton) (Lycoming IO-540) (Marked as a "Pitts S1.11B")						
G-IIIX	Pitts S-1S	AJT	G-LBAT G-UCCI, G-BIYN, N455T	22. 5.89	D S T Eggleton	Waits Farm, Belchamp Walter	18.11.09P
	(Built J Tarascio)						
G-IIIZ	Sukhoi Su-26M	04-05	RA-44444 DOSAAF 35 (black)	14. 5.03	P M M Bonhomme (Red Bull Matadors titles)	Audley End	9. 7.09P
G-IIJC	Bushby-Long Midget Mustang	XU-5	G-CEKU C-GFPF	28. 7.08	Longacre Aviation Ltd	Enstone	3. 8.09P
	(Built R W Eaves)						
G-IIMI	Extra EA.300/L	141	D-EXLE	2. 5.01	A Birch	(Blackpool)	31. 5.09E
G-IIMT	Bushby-Long Midget Mustang	PFA 168-1327	G-BDGA	13.11.03	P J Hebdon "4"	Shenington	14. 6.08P
	(Built M J A Trudgill - pr.no.formerly PFA 1327)						
G-IINI	Van's RV-9A	PFA 320-13781		6. 8.04	G J Burlington	Oaksey Park	8. 5.09P
	(Built S Sampson)						
G-IIPB	Dan Rihn DR.107 One Design			28.10.08	P D Baisden	Benfleet	
	(Built P D Baisden)	PFA 264-14538					
G-IIPT	Robinson R22 Beta	2506	G-FUSI N83306	10. 5.01	Highmark Aviation Ltd	(Scunthorpe)	23. 9.09E
G-IIRG	Stoddard-Hamilton Glasair IIS RG			29. 6.93	A C Lang	RNAS Yeovilton	20. 8.07P
	(Built D S Watson)	PFA 149-11937			(Lycoming IO-360)		
G-IIRW	Van's RV-8	RV80449	N42KL N70DY	11. 6.08	R Winward	Boscombe Down	
	(Built J M Sturgis)						
G-IIUI	Extra EA.300/S	004	G-CCBD OK-XTA, D-EBEW	26.11.03	C W Burkett , J R and M G Jefferies	Little Gransden	30. 4.09E
G-IIVI	Mudry CAP 232	21	F-GUJM	20. 1.05	Skylane Aviation Ltd	Sherburn-in-Elmet	21. 2.10E
G-IIXF	Van's RV-7	705592		14. 3.07	C A and S Noujaim	Gloucestershire	18. 8.09P
	(Believed project commenced as N11XF, built C A and S Noujaim - pr. no PFA 323-13844)						
G-IIXI	Extra EA.300/L	134	YR-EWG	6. 8.03	B H D H Frere	Higherlands Farm, Branscombe	4.12.09E
G-IIXX	Parsons Two-Place Gyroplane	PFA G/8-1225		13.10.93	J M Montgomerie	Kirkbride	
	(Built J M Montgomerie) (Rotax 912)				(Noted 11.05)		
G-IIYK	Yakovlev Yak-50	842706	LY-AFZ DOSAAF 24	15.10.02	D A Hammant	Bere Farm, Warnford	11. 8.09P
G-IIZI	Extra EA.300	037	JY-RNB D-ETXA	12.12.96	Power Aerobatics Ltd (Operated Extreme Team)	Kemble	12. 2.09E
G-IJAC	Avid Speed Wing Mk.4	PFA 189-12095		31.12.92	I J A Charlton	Chilsford Farm, Kirdford	
	(Built I J A Charlton)						
G-IJAG	Cessna 182T Skylane	18281683	N2284F	7.11.05	R Wicks tr AG Group	Denham	19.12.09E
G-IJBB	Enstrom 480	5010	G-LIVA N900SA, G-PBTT, JA6169	17. 9.99	R P Bateman	Hurley Lodge, Westerham	11.11.09E
G-IJMC	Magni M-16 Tandem Trainer	VPM16-UK-106	G-POSA G-BVJM	10. 6.98	P Adams	(Beaconsfield)	25.11.09P
	(Arrow GT1000R)						
G-IJMI	Extra EA.300/L	1193		16. 2.05	DEP Promotions Ltd	(Dublin)	18. 5.09E
G-IJNK	Robinson R44 Clipper	0780	G-KTOL	28. 9.07	Hi-Range Ltd	(Rough Park, Rugeley)	31. 8.09E
G-IJOE	Piper PA-28RT-201T Turbo Arrow IV	28R-8031178	N8265X N9599N	14. 8.90	J H Bailey tr G-IJOE Group	Sturgate	22. 7.09E
G-IJYS	British Aerospace Jetstream Series 3102	715	G-BTZT N416MX, G-31-715	5.10.92	Avient Ltd	(Amesbury, Salisbury)	18.11.08E
G-IKAH	Slingsby T.51 Dart 17R	1483	BGA1262-BVE	28. 4.08	K A Hale	Sandhill Farm, Shrivenham	
G-IKAP	Cessna T303 Crusader	T30300182	N63SA D-IKAP, N9518C	4. 3.99	T M Beresford (Noted 10.05)	Fowlmere	23. 9.05T
G-IKBP	Piper PA-28-161 Warrior II	28-8216132	N81762	16. 7.90	K B Page	Goodwood	4. 6.09E
G-IKEA	Cameron IKEA 120 SS Balloon (Hot Air)	10562		14. 6.04	IKEA Ltd (IKEA titles)	Bristol	6. 5.09E
G-IKES	Stoddard-Hamilton GlaStar	5763	N8066A	17. 8.05	M Stow	Newcastle	
	(Built J K Tofte)						
G-IKEV	Avtech Jabiru UL-450	xxxx		29. 6.04	D J Turner	Sackville Lodge, Riseley	12. 3.09P
	(Built K J Bream - pr.no.PFA 274A-14075)						
G-IKON	Van's RV-4	PFA 181-14474		22. 2.06	S Sampson	Ladybank House, Kiplin	22. 9.09E
	(Built S Sampson)						
G-IKOS	Cessna 550 Citation Bravo	550-0957	N957PH N51780	27. 5.04	Medox Enterprises Ltd	Biggin Hill	9. 6.09E
G-IKRK	Europa Aviation Europa	202		16. 4.02	K R Kesterton	Andrewsfield	24. 6.09P
	(Built K R Kesterton - pr.no.PFA 247-12903) (Monowheel u/c)						
G-IKRS	Comco Ikarus C42 FB UK	PFA 322-13719		1. 8.01	K J Warburton	Egginton, Derby	29. 6.07P
	(Built P G Walton)						
G-IKUS	Comco Ikarus C42 FB UK	PFA 322-14130		10.10.03	C I Law	Wickenby	1. 5.07P
	(Built C I Law)						
G-ILBO	Rolladen-Schneider LS3-a	3458	BGA2639-EEZ	19. 9.07	J P Gilbert "157"	Wormingford	28. 9.08
G-ILDA	Vickers Supermarine 361 Spitfire T.IX		G-BXHZ	11. 7.02	P W Portelli (deceased) (As "H-99" in R Netherlands AF c/s)	Thruxton	1. 2.10P
	(Rebuilt as Tr.XI)	CBAF.10164	SAAF???, SM520		(First post restoration flight 17.10.08)		
G-ILEE	Colt 56A Duo Chariot Balloon (Hot Air)	2624		29. 7.94	G I Lindsay "Gillie"	Storrington, Pulborough	21. 4.09E
G-ILET	Robinson R44 Raven II	10789		28. 6.05	Lear Group Ltd	(Stourbridge)	11. 8.09E

G-ILIB	PZL-Bielsko SZD-36A	W-667	HB-1213	6. 1.09	I H Keyser	Waldershare Park	
G-ILLE	Boeing Stearman E75 (PT-13D) Kaydet		N68979	7. 3.90	A C Ansalt (Also carries "379" in USAAC c/s)		
	(Continental W670)	75-5028	42-16865, Bu.60906			(Ruggell, Liechtenstein)	4.10.08S
G-ILLG	Robinson R44 Raven II	11416		22. 9.06	C B Ellis	(Preston Patrick, Milnthorpe)	2.11.09E
G-ILLY	Piper PA-28-181 Cherokee Archer II		SE-GND	21. 2.80	R A and G.M Spiers		
		28-7690193				Harpsden Court, Henley-on-Thames	19.12.93
G-ILPY	Cessna 172S Skyhawk	172S8704	N2437B	2. 7.07	D R Turner	Dunkeswell	7. 8.09E
G-ILRS	Comco Ikarus C42 FB UK	PFA 322-13927		19. 6.02	Knitsley Mill Leisure Ltd		
	(Built L R Smith)					Knitsley Mill Airfield, Consett	30. 6.09P
G-ILSE	Corby CJ-1 Starlet	PFA 134-10818		9. 1.84	S Stride	Wolverhampton	17. 4.09P
	(Built S Stride) (HAPI Magnum 75)						
G-ILTS	Piper PA-32-300 Six	32-7940217	G-CVOK	28. 3.90	Foremans Aviation Ltd	Full Sutton	3. 6.09E
			OE-DOH, N2941C				
G-ILUA	Alpha Aviation Alpha R2160i	160Ai-07007	ZK-SXY	22. 5.07	A R Haynes	Duxford	24. 6.09E
G-IMAB	Europa Aviation Europa XS	331		1. 2.00	T J Price	Rhigos	14. 5.09P
	(Built A H Brown - pr.no.PFA 247-13128)						
G-IMAC	Bombardier CL-600-2A12	3065	LX-GDC	6.09.05	Gama Aviation Ltd	Farnborough	22. 9.09E
	(CL-601 Challenger)		N601JP, (N45PA), N601JP, N500PE, (N128PE), N1623, N602CC, C-GLYA				
G-IMAD	Cessna 172P Skyhawk	17275122	G-BYET	9.12.08	H Khalifa	Bournemouth	4.11.09E
			PH-ILP, N55158				
G-IMAN	Colt 31A Sky Chariot Balloon (Hot Air)	2605		23. 6.94	Stratos Ballooning Gmbh and Co KG		
						Ennigerloh, Germany	17. 3.05A
G-IMAR	Agusta A109E Power	11703		14. 5.07	Inishway Properties Ltd	Newtownards	14. 5.09E
G-IMBI	QAC Quickie 1	484	G-BWIT	7.10.02	J D King	Biggin Hill	28. 2.06P
	(Rotax 503)		N4482Z				
G-IMBY	Pietenpol AirCamper	PFA 047-12402		22.12.93	P F Bockh	(Milbourne Port, Sherborne)	
G-IMCD	Van's RV-7	PFA 323-13965		14. 4.04	I G McDowell	Old Buckenham	18. 2.09P
	(Built I G McDowell)						
G-IMEA	Beech 200 Super King Air	BB-302	G-OWAX	1.11.06	Airtime Aviation France Ltd (Operated Airtime Charter)		
			N86Y, N300BW, N600CP			Bournemouth	16. 9.09E
G-IMEC	Piper PA-31 Navajo C	31-7512017	G-BFOM	1.11.06	Airtime Aviation France Ltd (Stored 12.08)		
			(F-GJHV), EI-DMI, G-BFOM, HB-LHH, N59933			Bournemouth	8.12.09E
G-IMEL	Rotary Air Force RAF 2000	LAA G13-1371		30. 1.09	P F Murphy	(Abersoch, Pwllheli)	
G-IMIC	IAV Bacau Yakovlev Yak-52	8910001	RA-02149	21. 8.02	J S and H A Jewell	Seething	6. 8.09E
			DOSAAF 103 (Yellow)				
G-IMLI	Cessna 310Q	310Q0491	G-AZYK	3. 4.86	J McNamara	Haverfordwest	30. 4.09E
			N4182Q				
G-IMME	Zenair CH.701 STOL	PFA 187-14080		29. 8.03	M Spearman	(Greenhithe)	
	(Built M Spearman)						
G-IMMY	Robinson R44 Clipper I	1890		1. 7.08	A J Cain t/a Tony Cain Leisure Services	(Leeds)	20. 8.09E
G-IMNY	Reality Escapade 912(2)	JAESC 0022		25. 5.04	D S Bremner	Higher Barn Farm, Hoghton	23.11.09P
	(Built D S Bremner - pr.no.BMAA HB/358)						
G-IMOK	Hoffman HK 36R Super Dimona	36317	I-NELI	31. 7.97	A L Garfield	Dunstable	30. 8.09E
	(Rotax 912)		OE-9352				
G-IMPX	Rockwell Commander 112B	512	N1304J	25.10.90	P A Day	Old Sarum	18. 5.09E
G-IMPY	Avid Flyer C	PFA 189-11439		10. 4.89	T R C Griffin	Haverfordwest	22.10.08P
	(Built T R C Griffin) (Rotax 532)						
G-IMUP	Air Création Tanarg 912S/iXess 15	FLT.005		8. 2.06	P D Hill	Kemble	30. 7.08P
	(Built P D Hill - pr.no.BMAA HB/478 being Flylight kit comprising;Trike s/n T05082 and Wing s/n A05150-5145)						
G-INCA	Glaser-Dirks DG-400	4-199		22. 1.87	K D Hook "320"	Portmoak	17. 3.09E
G-INCE	Best Off Sky Ranger 912(2)	SKR0302293		12. 3.03	N P Sleigh	Ince Blundell	2. 7.08P
	(Built N P Sleigh - pr.no.BMAA HB/270)						
G-INDC	Cessna T303 Crusader	T30300122	G-BKFH	28. 6.83	J-Ross Developments Ltd	Welshpool	7. 4.09E
			N4766C				
G-INDX	Robinson R44 Clipper II	10491		20.10.04	Kinetic Avionics Ltd	Elstree	8.11.09E
G-INGA	Thunder Ax8-84 Balloon (Hot Air)	2149		16. 6.92	M L J Ritchie	Weybridge	30. 9.94A
G-INGE	Thruster T 600N Sprint	9039-T600N-033		23. 2.99	M Conway tr Thruster 1 Group		
						Mullahead, Tandragee	7.10.08P
G-INGS	American Champion 8KCAB Super Decathlon			7. 3.08	Scotflight Ltd	Cumbernauld	27. 5.09E
		1063-2008					
G-INJA	Comco Ikarus C42 FB100 VLA			24. 4.03	J W G Andrews	Sutton Meadows	3. 3.09P
	(Built J W G Andrews)	PFA 322-14044					
G-INKY	Robinson R22 Beta	1101	G-UDAY	10. 8.05	SIPS Industries Ltd	Hillend, Dunfermline	26. 9.09E
G-INNI	Wassmer Jodel D 112	540	F-BHPU	30. 8.94	S Barry	(Mullinavat, County Kilkenny)	6. 7.08P
G-INNY	Replica Plans SE.5a	PFA 020-10439		18.12.78	M J Speakman (As "F5459:Y" in RFC c/s)		
	(Built R M Ordish) (Continental C90)					North Coates	15. 5.09P
G-INOW	Monnett Moni	223		30. 3.84	W C Brown	(Frimley Green, Camberley)	20. 8.88P
	(Built ARV Aviation Ltd - pr.no.PFA 142-10953) (KEF 107)				(Stored 8.97)		
G-INSR	Cameron N-90 Balloon (Hot Air)	4320		23. 4.98	P J Waller and The Smith and Pinching Group Ltd		
						Wymondham	21. 9.09E
G-INTO	Pilatus PC-12/45	609	HS-SMC	2. 1. 07	A Colin t/a Into Air	Shoreham	28. 1.09E
			N595PB, HB-FRI				
G-INTS	Van's RV-4	1780		17. 5.06	N J F Campbell	Inverness	7. 8.09P
	(Built N J F Campbell - pr.no.PFA 181-13069)						
G-IOCO	Beech 58 Baron	TH-1783		6. 6.96	Arenberg Consultadoria E Servicos LDA		
						(Madeira, Portugal)	20. 6.09E
G-IOFR	Lindstrand LBL 105A Balloon (Hot Air)	1041		1. 3.05	A I Attwood tr RAF Halton Hot Air Balloon Club		
						Halton Camp, Aylesbury	11. 9.09E
G-IOIA	III Sky Arrow 650 T	P/98/024		20. 3.03	P J Lynch, P G Ward and N J C Ray	Old Sarum	6. 5.09P
	(Built P J Lynch, P G Ward and N J C Ray - pr.no.PFA 298-14008)						
G-IONA	Aérospatiale-Alenia ATR 42-300	017	SP-KEE	19.12.02	Bravo Aviation Ltd	Jersey	19.11.07E
			G-IONA, N971NA, F-WWER				
G-IOOI	Robin DR.400-160 Major 80	1700		31. 5.85	N B Mason	Rendcomb	21. 5.09E

Reg	Type	C/n	Prev id	Date	Owner/Operator	Base	Date2
G-IOOP	Christen Eagle II	RUPPERT-0001	N414DE	7. 3.07	A P S Maynard	Shoreham	7. 8.09P
	(Built E J Ruppert)						
G-IOPT	Cessna 182P Skylane	18261731	N182EE	9. 6.98	A J Marks and D Madden tr Indy Oscar Group		
			D-ECVM, N21585			Elstree	23. 5.09E
G-IORG	Robinson R22 Beta	1679	OH-HRU	28. 1.00	Highmark Aviation Ltd	Sandtoft	21. 5.09E
			G-ZAND				
G-IORV	Van's RV-10	PFA 339-14610		26. 3.07	A F S and B L Caldecourt	(Knaphill, Woking)	
	(Built A F S Caldecout)						
G-IOSI	CEA Jodel DR.1050 Sicile	526	F-BLRS	6.10.80	G A Saxby tr Sicile Flying Group		
						Wellesbourne Mountford	24. 7.08E
G-IOSL	Van's RV-9	90121	G-CFIX	22. 1.09	S Leach	Plymouth	21. 9.09P
	(Built S Shannon)		N211TX				
G-IOSO	CEA Jodel DR.1050 Ambassadeur	46	OO-VDV	13. 7.00	A E Jackson	Podington	2.12.06
			F-BJUE				
G-IOWE	Europa Aviation Europa XS	368		30. 7.99	P A Lowe	Wolverhampton	7. 8.09P
	(Built P A Lowe - pr.no.PFA 247-13303) (Tri-gear u/c)						
G-IPAT	Avtech Jabiru SP-470	xxxx		14. 4.04	G Fleck	Kirkbride	7. 5.09P
	(Built M G Thatcher - pr.no.PFA 274B-14227)						
G-IPAX	Cessna 560XL Citation Excel	560-5228	EI-PAX	13. 2.04	Pacific Aviation Ltd	Birmingham	19. 2.09E
G-IPFM	Montgomerie-Bensen B 8MR	PFA G/01-1320	G-BZJR	18.10.05	I P F Meiklejohn	(Forres)	29.11.07P
	(Built N H Collins) (Rotax 582)						
G-IPKA	Alpi Pioneer 300	12		9. 2.05	M E Hughes	(Ewerby, Sleaford)	9. 6.09P
	(Built I P King - pr.no.PFA 330-14355)						
G-IPSI (2)	Grob G109B	6425	G-BMLO	29. 5.86	D G Margetts	Shobdon	12. 6.09E
G-IPSY	Rutan VariEze	1512	(G-IPSI)	19. 6.78	R A Fairclough	Biggin Hill	8. 7.09P
	(Built R A Fairclough - pr.no.PFA 074-10284 (Continental PC60)						
G-IPUP	Beagle B 121 Pup Series 2	B121-036	HB-NAC	17. 7.95	R G Hayes	North Weald & Elstree	28. 1.10R
			G-35-036				
G-IRAF	Rotary Air Force RAF 2000 GTX-SE			17. 6.96	P Robichaud	Henstridge	10. 9.09P
	(Built C D Julian)	PFA G/13-1278					
G-IRAL	Thruster T 600N 450	0035-T600N-083		24. 4.03	J Giraldez	(Burgh Le Marsh, Skegness)	6. 2.10P
	(Official c/n incorrect - date of manufacture [May 2003] indicates correct version should be 0053-T600N-083)						
G-IRAR	Van's RV-9	PFA 320-14106		26. 2.07	J Mapplethorpe	(Compton Martin, Bristol)	
	(Built J Mapplethorpe)						
G-IRHJ	Champion 7ECA Citabria Aurora	1401-2008		19. 4.08	T A Mann	Ballasalla, Isle of Man	
G-IRIS	Gulfstream AA-5B Tiger	AA5B-1184	G-BIXU	14.12.87	C Nichol	Perranporth	23. 7.08E
			N4533N				
G-IRKB	Piper PA-28R-201 Cherokee Arrow III		D-EJDS	7. 3.00	R K Brierley	Earls Colne	8. 6.09E
		28R-7737071	N5814V				
G-IRLE	Schempp-Hirth Ventus cT	172/562	BGA3935-HGN	19. 2.08	D J Scholey	Lasham	21. 3.08
G-IRLY	Colt 90A Balloon (Hot Air)	1620		28.12.89	C E R Smart (Maple Leaf symbols)	Waterlooville	8.11.09E
G-IRLZ	Lindstrand LBL 60X Balloon (Hot Air)	1092		5. 4.06	A M Holly (Sloggi titles)	Breadstone, Berkeley	28. 5.09E
G-IROE	Flight Design CTSW	07.10.11		12.11.07	S Roe	South Hykeham, Lincoln	11.11.09P
	(Assembled P&M Aviation Ltd with c/n 8334)						
G-IRON	Europa Aviation Europa XS	583		4. 5.04	T M Clark	(Guildford)	7. 1.10P
	(Built T M Clark - pr.no.PFA 247-14235)						
G-IRPC	Cessna 182Q Skylane II	18266039	G-BSKM	15. 5.91	R Warner	Cambridge	13. 1.09E
			N559CT, N759JV				
G-IRPW	Europa Aviation Europa XS	PFA 247-14495		4.11.08	R P Wheelwright	(Stainland, Halifax)	
	(Built R P Wheelwright)						
G-IRSH	Embraer EMB-135BJ Legacy	14501048	PT-SEE	3. 6.08	Legemb Ltd	Birmingham	2. 6.09E
G-IRTH	Lindstrand LBL 150A Balloon (Hot Air)	772	G-BZTO	20. 6.02	A M Holly (Cowlin Construction titles)		
						Breadstone, Berkeley	30. 8.09E
G-IRYC	Schweizer 269C-1 (Schweizer 300)	0194	N86G	8. 3.05	CSL Industrial Ltd	Bournemouth	17. 9.09E
G-ISAX	Piper PA-28-181 Archer III	2843453	N5325G	28. 6.01	M S Kontowtt	Barton	7. 9.09E
G-ISAY	British Aerospace Jetstream Srs 4100	41014	G-MAJN	30. 4.08	Highland Airways Ltd	Inverness	8. 9.09E
	(Built Jetstream Aircraft Ltd)		OY-SVS, G-4-014				
G-ISCA	Piper PA-28RT-201 Arrow IV	28R-8118012	N8288Y	12. 2.91	D J and P Pay	Plymouth	19. 6.09E
			N9608N				
G-ISDB	Piper PA-28-161 Warrior II	28-7716074	G-BWET	19. 2.96	Action Air Services Ltd	White Waltham	10. 6.09E
			SX-ALX, D-EFFQ, N9612N				
G-ISDN	Boeing Stearman B75N1 (N2S-3) Kaydet		N4197X	6. 2.95	D R L Jones(As "14" in US Army c/s)	Rendcomb	19.12.11
	(Officially regd as "A75N1")	75-1263	XB-WOV, Bu.3486				
G-ISEH	Cessna 182R Skylane II	18267843	G-BIWS	9.11.90	S J Nash	North Weald	24. 4.09E
			N6601N				
G-ISEL	Best Off Sky Ranger 912(2)	SKRxxxx368		7.11.03	P A Robertson	Sywell	4. 6.09P
	(Built P A Robertson - pr.no.BMAA HB/312)						
G-ISEW	P&M Aviation Quik GT450	8170		20. 4.06	J D Doran	Newtownards	11. 6.09P
G-ISFC	Piper PA-31 Turbo Navajo B	31-7300970	G-BNEF	23. 3.94	I M Latiff	Little Staughton	25. 5.08E
			N7574L				
G-ISHA	Piper PA-28-161 Warrior III	2842211	N3092D	21. 7.04	Upperstack Ltd t/a LAC Flying School	Barton	15. 9.09E
G-ISHK	Cessna 172S Skyhawk	172S9783	N66116	4. 3.05	Matchpage Ltd	Fairoaks	4. 4.09E
G-ISKA	WSK-PZL Mielec TS-11 Iskra	1H1018	Polish AF 1018	11. 5.00	P C Harper (As "1018" in Polish AF c/s)		
					(Noted 3.04)	Bruntingthorpe	
G-ISLB	British Aerospace Jetstream Series 3202	871	N871JX	6. 1.06	Blue Islands Ltd t/a Blue Islands	Jersey	29. 3.09E
			N871AE, G-31-871				
G-ISLC	British Aerospace Jetstream Series 3202	873	N873JX	2. 3.06	Blue Islands Ltd t/a Blue Islands	Jersey	24. 5.09E
			N873AE, G-31-873				
G-ISLD	British Aerospace Jetstream Series 3202	915	N915AE	24. 7.06	Blue Islands Ltd t/a Blue Islands	Jersey	3. 9.09E
			G-31-915				
G-ISMA	Van's RV-7A	PFA 323-13875	G-STAF	7.12.07	S Marriott	East Kirknewton, Wooler	
	(Built A F Stafford)						

G-ISMO	Robinson R22 Beta	0870	OH-HOR	14.10.88	Moy Motorsport Ltd	Sywell	25. 8.09E
			G-ISMO, N8214T				
G-ISPH	Bell 206B-3 JetRanger III	4259	G-OPJM	3. 3.06	Blades Aviation (UK) LLP		
						Nottingham-East Midlands	13. 3.09E
G-ISST	Eurocopter EC.155 B1	6778		13. 6.07	Bristow Helicopters Ltd	Aberdeen	28. 6.09E
G-ISSU	Eurocopter EC.155 B1	6762	F-WWOM	22. 3.07	Bristow Helicopters Ltd	Aberdeen	6. 4.09E
G-ISSV	Eurocopter EC.155 B1	6757	F-WWOG	20.12.06	Bristow Helicopters Ltd	Aberdeen	17. 1.10E
G-ISSW	Eurocopter EC.155 B1	6755	F-WWOD	1.12.06	Bristow Helicopters Ltd	Aberdeen	14.12.08E
G-ISSY	Eurocopter EC.120B Colibri	1236	G-CBCG	11.10.01	D R Williams	Stapleford	9.12.09E
			F-WQPT				
G-ITAF	SIAI-Marchetti SF.260AM	40-013	MM54532	10.12.08	N A Whatling	Leicester	
			Italian AF				
G-ITBT	Alpi Pioneer 300 Hawk	xxx		19. 6.07	F Paolini	(Kingswood, Bristol)	7. 8.08P
	(Built F Paolini - pr.no.PFA 330A-14641)						
G-ITFL	Diamond DA.42 Twin Star	42.246	OE-VPY	30. 7.07	Tyrone Fabrication Ltd	Belfast International	14. 8.09P
G-ITIG	Dassault Falcon 2000EX	102	F-WWMD	1. 3.07	TAG Aviation (UK) Ltd	Farnborough	28. 2.09E
G-ITII	Pitts S-2A	2223	I-VLAT	5. 7.95	Aerobatic Displays Ltd	Wycombe Air Park	31. 1.08E
	(Built Aerotek Inc)						
G-ITOI	Cameron N-90 Balloon (Hot Air)	4785		14. 1.00	A E Lusty	Bourne	12. 4.09E
G-ITPH	Robinson R44 Clipper II	11909		17. 9.07	Island Air Ltd	Bangor Helipad	12.11.08E
G-ITUG	Piper PA-28-180 Cherokee C	28-4121	G-AVNR	14. 8.02	S I Tugwell	Rayne Hall Farm, Braintree	20.1.09E
			N11C				
G-ITVM	Lindstrand LBL 105A Balloon (Hot Air)	1017		8.11.04	I J Wadley tr Elmer Balloon Team (Meridian Tonight titles)		
						Storrington, Pulborough	21. 4.09E
G-ITWB	de Havilland DHC-1 Chipmunk 22	48	CS-AZO	16. 9.04	I T Whitaker-Bethel	Bury St Edmunds	18. 5.09S
	(Built OGMA)		Portuguese AF FAP 1358				
G-IUAN	Cessna 525 CitationJet	525-0324	N5163C	30. 6.99	RF Celada SpA	Milan-Linate, Italy	23. 3.09E
			(N428PC)				
G-IUII	Aerostar Yakovlev Yak-52	9111604	RA-1281K	28.11.06	W Hanekom	Little Gransden	25. 7.09P
			RA-01281, DOSAAF 69 (grey)				
G-IUMB	Schleicher ASW 20L	20386	BGA2691-EHD	16. 5.08	B Lumb	Sutton Bank	
G-IVAC	Airtour AH-77B Balloon (Hot Air)	012		28.11.89	T D Gibbs	Plaistow, Billingshurst	22. 8.08A
G-IVAL	CAB CAP.10B	307		8. 4.03	I Valentine "307"	Kilrush, County Kildare	6. 7.09E
G-IVAN	Shaw Twin-Eze	PFA 074-10502		11. 9.78	A M Aldridge "Mistress" (Noted 2000)		
	(Built I Shaw - c/n 39) (Norton-Wankel)					Ostend, Belgium	5.10.90P
G-IVAR	Yakovlev Yak-50	791504	D-EIVI	24. 2.89	A H Soper	Jenkin's Farm, Navestock	14. 8.09P
			(N5219K), DDR-WQT, DM-WQT				
G-IVDM	Schempp-Hirth Nimbus 4DM	39/55	D-KABV	18.10.02	G W Lynch	Rattlesden	4. 6.09E
G-IVEL	Fournier RF4D	4029	G-AVNY	29. 6.95	V S E Norman	(Rendcomb)	14. 4.01A
G-IVEN	Robinson R44 Raven II	10442		28. 7.04	OKR Group	(Dublin)	13. 9.09E
G-IVER	Europa Aviation Europa XS	486		14. 8.00	I Phillips	Lydd	2. 6.09P
	(Built I Phillips - pr no.PFA 247-13632) (Convertible u/c)						
G-IVET	Europa Aviation Europa	020		23. 5.97	K J Fraser	(Abingdon)	
	(Built K J Fraser - pr.no.PFA 247-12511) (Conventional u/c)						
G-IVII	Van's RV-7	PFA 323-14222		31. 8.04	M A N Newall	Bagby	
	(Built M A N Newall)						
G-IVIV	Robinson R44 Astro	0016	(N803EH)	2. 8.93	D Brown	(Newton Stewart)	19.12.09E
G-IVJM	Agusta A109E Power	11154	G-MOMO	4. 3.08	Air Harrods Ltd	Stansted	30. 4.09E
G-IVOR	Aeronca 11AC Chief	11AC-1035	EI-BKB	18. 6.82	P R White tr South Western Aeronca Group		
			G-IVOR, EI-BKB, N9397E			Bodmin	22. 7.09P
G-IVYS	Parsons Two-Place Gyroplane	PFA G/8-1275		11. 1.00	R M Harris	(Nottingham)	
	(Built R M Harris) (Mazda RX-7)						
G-IWIN	Raj Hamsa X'Air Hawk	xxx		11. 6.07	R Wooldridge (Noted 10.07)	Carlisle	
	(Built R Wooldridge - pr.no.PFA 340-14679)						
G-IWIZ	Flylight Dragonfly	008		3. 9.08	S Wilosn	(Bury St Edmunds)	
G-IWON	Cameron V-90 Balloon (Hot Air)	2504	G-BTCV	17. 2.92	D P P Jenkinson (Cameron - 21 years titles) Tring		16. 7.09E
G-IWRB	Agusta A109A II	7386	G-VIPT	10. 8.06	Fuel The Jet LLP	Liskeard Helicopter	22.10.09E
			N109SM, N109AZ, JA9694, N1ZN				
G-IWRC	Eurocopter EC.135 T2	0241	D-HECA	9. 9.02	Bond Air Services Ltd	Gloucestershire	13.11.07E
G-IXCC	Vickers Supermarine 361 Spitfire IX	????	N644TB	18. 5.88	Spitfire Ltd (As "PL344/TL-B" in RAF c/s)	Duxford	6. 7.09P
			G-IXCC, PL344				
G-IXES	Air Création Clipper/iXess 912	FL.027		3. 3.04	G J Little	Sywell	15. 7.08P
	(Built R Grimwood - pr.no.BMAA HB/357 being Flylight kit comprising Trike s/n T03027 and Wing s/n 04019-4014)						
	(Trike believed ex French 07-JF)						
G-IXII	Christen Eagle II	T0001	G-BPZI	9. 1.03	R P Marks tr Eagle Flying Group	Dunkeswell	29. 4.09P
	(Built J Trent and R Eicher) (Lycoming IO-360)		N48BB				
G-IXXI	Schleicher ASW 27-18E	29543	BGA5318-KSB	15. 4.08	G P Stingemore "XI"	Husbands Bosworth	
G-IYCO	Robin DR.500-200i Président	0031		23. 2.01	Timgee Holdings Ltd	Jersey	1. 4.09E
	(Officially regd as DR.400-500)						
G-IZII	Marganski Swift S-1	110	BGA5240-KNY	9.10.06	G C Westgate	Parham Park	20. 5.09E
			N110LG				
G-IZIT	Rans S-6-116 Coyote II	0695.841		7. 3.96	A J Best and M Watson Baxby Manor, Husthwaite		9. 7.08P
	(Built D A Crompton - pr.no.PFA 204A-12965) (Rotax 912-UL) (Tri-cycle u/c)						
	(New frame fitted 1999 after accident 6.9.98 - kit no not known: original frame 841 rebuilt and used to repair G-MWUN qv)						
G-IZZI	Cessna T182T Turbo Skylane	T18208100	N51197	19. 3.02	D J and E-S Lucey	(Leys Tyning, Frome)	20. 5.09E
G-IZZS	Cessna 172S Skyhawk SP	172S8152	N952SP	1. 7.99	Air Claire Ltd (Operated Glasgow Flying Club)		
						Glasgow	7.11.09E
G-IZZY	Cessna 172R Skyhawk	17280419	G-BXSF	7. 9.99	P A Adams and T S Davies	(Llanelli)	11. 7.09E
			N9967F				
G-IZZZ	American Champion 8KCAB Super Decathlon			29. 1.04	A M Read	Goodwood	8. 2.10E
		939-2003					

G-JAAA - G-JZZZ

Reg	Type	c/n	Prev id	Date	Owner/Operator	Location	Date
G-JAAB	Avtech Jabiru UL-D	655		28. 3.06	R Holt	Mill Farm, Shifnal	26. 4.09P
G-JABA	Avtech Jabiru SK	PFA 274-13297		14.12.99	M Flint	(Wisbech)	19. 6.03P
	(Built A P Gornall)						
G-JABB	Avtech Jabiru UL-450	0328		27. 4.00	D J Abbott	Coldharbour Farm, Willingham	29. 4.09P
	(Built D J Royce - pr.no.PFA 274A-13555)						
G-JABE	Avtech Jabiru UL-D	0657	G-CDZX	9.10.06	H M Manning and P M Jones		
						Damyn's Hall, Upminster	1. 8.08P
G-JABI	Avtech Jabiru J400	PFA 325-14098		3.10.03	R D W Rippingale tr Anvilles Flying Group		
	(Built R A Shaw)					Radey Farm, Hungerford	31.12.09P
G-JABJ	Avtech Jabiru J400	PFA 325-14126		17.11.03	F H Hancock and L B Watkins		
	(Built P G Leonard)					Draycott Farm, Chiseldon	23.12.09P
G-JABS	Avtech Jabiru UL-450	PFA 274A-13704		27. 6.02	P E Todd tr Jabiru Flyer Group	Chilbolton	6. 3.09P
	(Built I R Cook and P E Todd)						
G-JABU	Avtech Jabiru J430	PFA 336-14515		9. 1.06	S D Miller	Bourn	2.11.09P
	(Built R J Chapman)						
G-JABY	Avtech Jabiru SPL-450	PFA 274A-13672		2. 2.01	J T Grant	Little Snoring	11. 9.09P
	(Built J T Grant)						
G-JABZ	Avtech Jabiru UL-450	PFA 274A-14289		3. 5.05	A C Barnes	Eshott	7. 1.10P
	(Built A C Barnes)						
G-JACA	Piper PA-28-161 Warrior III	2842139	N5328Q	28. 2.02	Channel Islands Aero Club (Jersey) Ltd	Jersey	6. 3.10E
G-JACB	Piper PA-28-181 Archer III	2843278	G-PNNI	23. 7.02	Channel Islands Aero Club (Jersey) Ltd	Jersey	3.11.09E
			N41651				
G-JACC	Piper PA-28-181 Archer III	2843222	G-GIFT	23.12.02	Magnum Holdings Ltd	Jersey	20. 1.10E
			G-IMVA, SE-KIH, N9524N, N4166F				
G-JACH	Piper PA-28-181 Archer III	2843585	G-IDPH	19. 1.09	Goldcrest 2001 Ltd	Jersey	28. 2.09E
			N3054D				
G-JACK	Cessna 421C Golden Eagle	421C1411	N421GQ	29. 4.97	JCT 600 Ltd	Leeds-Bradford	3. 5.09E
			N125RS, N12028				
G-JACO	Avtech Jabiru UL	0215		14. 4.99	C D Matthews	Kilrush, County Kildare	26. 6.07P
	(Built S Jackson - pr.no.PFA 274A-13371)						
G-JACS	Piper PA-28-181 Archer III	2843078	N9287J	15. 4.97	Vector Air Ltd	Fowlmere	11. 6.09E
			(G-JACS)				
G-JADJ	Piper PA-28-181 Archer III	2843009	N49TP	27. 7.99	ACS Aviation Ltd	Perth	28. 7.09E
	(Originally intended as c/n 2890240)		N92552				
G-JADW	Comco Ikarus C42 FB80	0810-7013		3.12.08	J W and D A Wilding	(Brierley Hill)	4. 1.10P
	(Built Aerosport Ltd)						
G-JAEE	Van's RV-6A	PFA 181A-13571		16. 9.02	J A E Edser	(Market Rasen)	
	(Built J A E Edser)						
G-JAES	Bell 206B-2 JetRanger II	1513	G-STOX	13. 1.04	Audisio Automobili Cuneo SRL	Cuneo, Italy	7. 8.09E
			G-BNIR, N59615				
G-JAGS	Reims Cessna FRA150L Aerobat		G-BAUY	24.10.01	G Bremer tr RAF Marham Aero Club	RAF Marham	27. 4.09E
		FRA1500167	N10633				
G-JAIR	Mainair Blade	1249-0500-7-W1042		11. 7.00	A J Varga *"Joe Loughran"*	Rufforth	11. 5.06P
	(Rotax 582)						
G-JAJA	Robinson R44 Raven II	11691		18. 4.07	Jara Aviation Ltd	Jaggards House, Weeley Heath	27. 5.09E
G-JAJB	Grumman American AA-5A Cheetah		OY-CJE	30. 4.02	J Bradley	Thruxton	16. 6.09E
		AA5A-0590	N26434				
G-JAJK	Piper PA-31-350 Chieftain	31-8152014	G-OLDB	16.12.99	Keen Leasing (IoM) Ltd	Belfast International	24. 7.09E
			OY-SKY, G-DIXI, N40717		*(Operated Woodgate Executive Air Services)*		
G-JAJP	Avtech Jabiru UL-450	0359		1.12.00	J W E Pearson and J Anderson		
	(Built J W E Pearson - pr.no.PFA 274A-13627)					Plaistows Farm, St Albans	16.11.09P
G-JAKF	Robinson R44 Raven II	10866		23. 9.05	J G Froggatt	(Marple Bridge, Stockport)	28.10.09E
G-JAKI	Mooney M 20R Ovation	29-0030		7. 2.95	J M Moss and D M Abrahamson	Dublin	14. 5.09E
G-JAKS	Piper PA-28-160 Cherokee	28-339	G-ARVS	2. 7.99	K Harper	Stapleford	16. 1.10E
G-JAMA	Schweizer 269C-1 *(Schweizer 300)*	0165		2. 4.04	JWL Helicopters Ltd	Biggin Hill	12. 6.08E
G-JAME	Zenair CH.601UL Zodiac	6-2818	G-CDFZ	14. 1.05	A Batters	Baxby Manor, Husthwaite	26. 6.08P
	(Built J P Harris, B Yoxall, K Yoxall and N Barnes - pr.no.PFA 162A-14279) (Tri-cycle u/c)						
G-JAMP	Piper PA-28-151 Cherokee Warrior		G-BRJU	3. 4.95	Lapwing Flying Group Ltd	Denham	31. 8.09E
		28-7515026	N44762				
G-JAMY	Europa Aviation Europa XS	449		5. 1.01	J P Sharp	Rayne Hall Farm, Braintree	9. 9.08P
	(Built J P Sharp - pr.no.PFA 247-13557)						
G-JANA	Piper PA-28-181 Archer II	28-7990483	N2838X	12. 2.87	S I van Haaren tr Vanair Aviation	Stapleford	3. 6.09E
G-JANI	Robinson R44 Astro	0110	N7027W	21. 7.95	JT Helicopters Ltd	(Thruxton)	1.12.09E
			EI-CUI, G-JANI, D-HIMM (2)				
G-JANN	Piper PA-34-220T Seneca III	3433133	N9154W	23. 6.89	MBC Aviation Ltd	Fairoaks	30. 8.07T
					(Operated Synergy Aviation)		
G-JANO	Piper PA-28RT-201 Arrow IV	28R-7918091	SE-IZR	14. 5.98	Nasaire Ltd	Liverpool-John Lennon	3.12.09E
			N2146X				
G-JANS	Reims FR172J Rocket	FR17200414	PH-GJO	11. 8.78	I G Aizlewood	Rush Green	4. 1.09E
			D-EGJO				
G-JANT	Piper PA-28-181 Archer II	28-8390075	N4297J	23. 2.87	Janair Aviation Ltd	Denham	1. 4.09E
	(Originally built as c/n 28-8290117/N81992/YV-2234P: not delivered and re-manufactured as c/n stated)						
G-JANV	Learjet Model 45	45-124	N124AV	1. 5.07	Jannaire LLP	(Runcorn)	30. 4.09E
			G-OLDL, N4003Q				
G-JARA	Robinson R22 Beta	1837		11. 6.91	Northumbria Helicopters Ltd	Newcastle	14. 9.08E
G-JASE	Piper PA-28-161 Warrior II	28-8216056	N8461R	13. 2.91	Mid-Anglia Flight Centre Ltd tr Mid-Anglia School of Flying		
						Cambridge	23. 8.09E
G-JASS	Beech 200 Super King Air	BB-983	N983AJ	23. 6.08	Platinum Executive Aviation LLP	Lydd	23. 6.09E
			D-ISAZ, N983EB, D-ILTO, N87FE, N6JE, (D-IKFC), N6JE, N6JL				
G-JAST	Mooney M 20J Mooney 201	24-1010	OO-RYL	1.10.04	M J Willis	Elstree	16. 1.09E
			(N4004H)				

Reg	Type	C/n	Prev ID	Date	Owner/Operator	Base	Expiry
G-JATD	Robinson R22 Beta	0534		10. 7.03	Rotormotive Ltd	Little Blakenham	22. 2.08E
G-HUMF			N23743				
G-JAVO	Piper PA-28-161 Warrior II	28-8016130		17. 9.97	Victor Oscar Ltd	Wellesbourne Mountford	23. 7.09E
G-BSXW			N8119S				
G-JAWC	Cyclone Airsports Pegasus Quantum 15-912	7692		21. 7.00	M H Husey	Damyn's Hall, Upminster	18. 7.08P
G-JAWZ	Pitts S-1S	PFA 009-12846		6.11.95	A R Harding	Leicester	27.11.08P
	(Built S Howes)						
G-JAXS	Avtech Jabiru UL-450	xxxx		10.12.99	J P Pullin	Weston Zoyland	20.10.09P
	(Built C A Palmer - pr.no.PFA 274A-13548)						
G-JAYI	Auster V J/1 Autocrat	2030	OY-ALU D-EGYK, OO-ABF	5. 2.93	Aviation Heritage Ltd	Coventry	11. 7.07S
G-JAYS	Best Off Sky Ranger 912S(1)	SKR0408509		14.12.04	R A Green	Lower Wasing Farm, Brimpton	15. 7.09P
	(Built J Williams - pr.no.BMAA HB/433: kit no.not confirmed - may be SKR0407509)						
G-JAYZ	CZAW Sportcruiser	PFA 338-14670		16. 5.08	J Williams	(Mansfield)	
	(Built J Williams)						
G-JBAS	Neico Lancair 200	PFA 191-11465		21.11.03	A Slater	(Douglas, IoM)	
	(Built B A Slater)						
G-JBBZ	Eurocopter AS.350B3 Ecureuil	3580	F-WQDE F-WQPV	13. 1.03	Milford Aviation Services Ltd	(London SW8)	16. 2.09E
G-JBDB	Agusta-Bell 206B-2 JetRanger II	8238	G-OOPS G-BNRD, Oman AF 602	11. 4.96	Dicksons Van World Ltd	Newcastle	29. 6.09E
G-JBDH	Robin DR.400-180 Régent	1901		17. 3.89	W A Clark	Netherthorpe	9. 6.09E
G-JBEN	Mainair Blade 912	1337-0802-7-W1132		13. 9.02	G J Bentley	(Blacon, Chester)	4. 5.07P
G-JBHH	Bell 206B-2 JetRanger II	1129	G-SCOO G-CORC, G-CJHI, G-BBFB, N18094	26. 4.04	D and G Cars Ltd	Biggin Hill	9. 6.09E
G-JBII	Robinson R22 Beta	1368	G-BXLA SE-HVX, N4014G	13. 3.03	Fast Helicopters Ltd	Shoreham	27. 5.09E
G-JBIS	Cessna 550 Citation II	550-0447	HB-VIS (N447CJ), N12482, N1248K	11. 1.07	247 Jet Ltd	Southend	1. 3.09E
G-JBIZ	Cessna 550 Citation II	550-0073	VP-CTJ F-GBTL, N4621G	7.11.05	247 Jet Ltd	Southend	8.12.09E
G-JBJB	Colt 69A Balloon (Hot Air)	1274		26. 7.88	Justerini and Brooks Ltd *"J & B Jeremy"*	London SW1	19. 5.02A
G-JBKA	Robinson R44 Raven	1175		12. 3.02	KG MotorsportLtd	City of Derry	26. 3.09E
G-JBRE	Rotorsport UK MT-03	RSUK/MT-03/016		23. 7.07	J B R Elliot	Ellough, Beccles	9. 8.09P
G-JBRN	Cessna 182S Skylane	18280029	N432V G-RITZ, N9872F	11. 6.99	Parallel Flooring Accessories Ltd	Wickenby	30. 6.09E
G-JBRS	Van's RV-8	81083		6. 2.09	C Jobling	RAF Waddington	
	(Built C Jobling, pr. no PFA 303-14212)						
G-JBSP	Avtech Jabiru SP-470	0289		12.10.99	C R James	Ludham	26. 6.09P
	(Built C R James - pr.no.PFA 274B-13486)						
G-JBTR	Van's RV-8	PFA 303-14562		18. 9.06	R A Ellis	(Haverfordwest)	
	(Built R A Ellis,originally registered as RV-8A, amended 8. 9.08)						
G-JBUZ	Robin DR.400-180R Remorqueur	1158	OE-DNW	2. 6.05	D L Saywell	(Pannal, Harrogate)	31. 7.09E
G-JCAP	Robinson R22 Beta II	3415	EI-EWM	25. 6.04	Fly Executive Ltd	(Emberton, Olney)	8. 7.09E
G-JCAR	Piper PA-46-350P Malibu Mirage	4636223	N4148N	17.12.99	Aquarelle Investments Ltd	Shoreham	20. 2.09E
G-JCAS	Piper PA-28-181 Archer II	28-8690036	N9093N (N170AV), N9648N	12. 6.89	Charlie Alpha Ltd	Jersey	19. 6.09E
G-JCBB	Gulfstream Aerospace Gulfstream V-SP	5186	N286GA	5. 8.08	J C Bamford Excavators Ltd	Nottingham-East Midlands	4. 8.09E
	(Gulfstream 550)						
G-JCBC	Gulfstream Aerospace Gulfstream V-SP	5060	N960GA	3. 8.05	J C Bamford Excavators Ltd	Nottingham-East Midlands	3. 8.09E
	(Gulfstream 550)						
G-JCBJ	Sikorsky S-76C	760502		9. 7.99	J C Bamford Excavators Ltd	Nottingham-East Midlands	3. 8.09E
G-JCJC	Colt Flying Jeans SS Balloon (Hot Air)	1747	SE-ZHS	8. 6.90	Magical Adventures Ltd	Oswestry	27. 9.09E
G-JCKT	Stemme S 10-VT	11-004	D-KSTE	8. 4.98	J C Taylor	Portmoak	15. 5.09E
	(Rotax 914)						
G-JCMW	Rand Robinson KR-2	PFA 129-11064		3. 2.99	M Wildish and J Cook	(Gainsborough and Winterton, Scunthorpe)	7.10.09P
	(Built M Wildish)						
G-JCOP	Eurocopter AS.350B3 Ecureuil	4345		8.12.07	Optimum Ltd	(Ramsey, IoM)	14. 4.09E
G-JCUB	Piper PA-18-135 Super Cub	18-3531	PH-VCH R Neth AF R-103 , 54-2331	21. 1.82	N Cummins and S Bennett	Weston, Leixlip, County Kildare	19.10.11
	(L-21B-PI) (Frame No.18-3630)						
G-JCWM	Robinson R44 Raven II	11860		17. 9.07	M L J Goff	Old Buckenham	3.12.08E
G-JDBC	Piper PA-34-200T Seneca II	34-7570150	G-BDEF N33695	9.10.02	Bowdon Aviation Ltd	Manchester	16.11.09E
G-JDEE	SOCATA TB-20 Trinidad	333	G-BKLA F-BNGX	1. 5.84	M J Wright, M Baker, N Jeffery and E Foers	Leicester	12. 6.09E
G-JDEL	Jodel D 150 Mascaret	112	G-JDLI	19. 9.95	K F and R Richardson	Wellesbourne Mountford	
	(Built K F Richardson - pr.no.PFA 151-11276)				*(Noted 11.07)*		
G-JDIX	Mooney M 20B Mark 21	1866	G-ARTB	28.11.85	A L Hall-Carpenter *(Noted 1.09)*	Old Buckenham	16. 1.00
G-JDJM	Piper PA-28-140 Cherokee C	28-26877	(G-HSJM) G-AYIF, N11C	11.10.00	R Jackson-Moore and D J Street tr The Hare Flying Group	White Waltham	27. 9.09E
G-JDPB	Piper PA-28R-201T Turbo Arrow III	28R-7803024	G-DNCS N47841	22. 9.08	BC Arrow Ltd	(Shrewsbury)	20.10.09E
G-JEAJ	British Aerospace BAe 146 Series 200QT	E2099	(OE-IAA) G-JEAJ, G-OLCA, G-5-099	20. 9.93	Trident Aviation Leasing Services (Jersey) Ltd *(stored 11.08)*	Southend	30. 8.08E
G-JEAM	British Aerospace BAe 146 Series 300	E3128	G-BTJT HS-TBK, G-11-128	24. 5.93	Flybe Ltd *"Pride of Jersey" (stored 9.08)*	Exeter	23. 5.09E
G-JEAO	British Aerospace BAe 146 Series 100	E1010	C-GNVX, N802RW, G-5-512, PT-LEP, G-BKXZ, PT-LEP *(Stored 1.09)*	19. 9.94	Trident Aviation Leasing Services (Jersey) Ltd	Filton	4. 6.05T
G-JEAS	British Aerospace BAe 146 Series 200	E2020	G-OLHB G-BSRV, G-OSUN, C-FEXN, N604AW	13. 2.96	Flybe Ltd *(Stored 9.08)*	Exeter	13. 7.09E

G-JEAX	British Aerospace BAe 146 Series 200	E2136	EI-DNJ,	16. 2.98	BAE Systems (Operations) Ltd	Bacau, Romania	19. 2.07T
			G-JEAX, N136JV, C-FHAP, N136TR, N882DV, (N719TA), N882DV, G-5-136 (Noted 10.07)				
G-JEAY	British Aerospace BAe 146 Series 200	E2138	SE-DRL	27. 3.01	BAE Systems (Operations) Ltd	Bacau, Romania	26. 3.07T
			N138JV, C-FHAA, N138TR, (N719TA), N883DV, G-5-138 (Noted 2.08)				
G-JEBA	British Aerospace BAe 146 Series 300	E3181	HS-TBL	16. 6.98	Flybe Ltd (Stored 10.08)	Exeter	27. 7.09E
			G-6-181, G-BSYR, G-6-181				
G-JEBB	British Aerospace BAe 146 Series 300	E3185	HS-TBK	26. 6.98	Flybe Ltd (Stored 9.08)	Exeter	31.10.09E
			G-6-185				
G-JEBF	British Aerospace BAe 146 Series 300	E3202	G-BTUY	25. 6.04	Bank of Scotland plc (stored 9.08)	Exeter	25. 6.09E
			G-NJIC, B-17811, B-1781, G-BTUY, G-6-202				
G-JEBG	British Aerospace BAe 146 Series 300	E3209	G-BVCE	20. 7.04	Bank of Scotland plc (stored 9.08)	Exeter	13. 7.09E
			G-NJIE, B-1778, G-BVCE, G-6-209				
G-JEBV	British Aerospace Avro 146-RJ100	E3236	G-CDCN	15. 2.05	Trident Jet Leasing (Ireland) Ltd	Kemble	
			TC-THC, G-6-236		(Noted stored 9.08)		
G-JECE	Bombardier DHC-8-402	4094	C-FDHU	26. 8.04	Flybe Ltd	Exeter	2. 9.09E
G-JECF	Bombardier DHC-8-402	4095	C-FDHV	7.10.04	Flybe Ltd	Exeter	12.10.09E
G-JECG	Bombardier DHC-8-402	4098	C-FAQH	7. 1.05	Flybe Ltd	Exeter	13. 1.10E
G-JECH	Bombardier DHC-8-402	4103	C-FCQC	29. 4.05	Flybe Ltd	Exeter	4. 5.09E
G-JECI	Bombardier DHC-8-402	4105	C-FCQI	10. 6.05	Flybe Ltd	Exeter	16. 6.09E
G-JECJ	Bombardier DHC-8-402	4110	C-FCVN	16.12.05	Flybe Ltd	Exeter	20.12.09E
G-JECK	Bombardier DHC-8-402	4113	C-FDRL	27. 1.06	Flybe Ltd	Exeter	31. 1.10E
G-JECL	Bombardier DHC-8-402	4114	C-FDRN	27. 1.06	Flybe Ltd "The George Best"	Exeter	5. 2.10E
G-JECM	Bombardier DHC-8-402	4118	C-FFCE	6. 4.06	Flybe Ltd	Exeter	10. 4.09E
G-JECN	Bombardier DHC-8-402	4120	C-FFCL	27. 4.06	Flybe Ltd	Exeter	2. 5.09E
G-JECO	Bombardier DHC-8-402	4126	C-FFPT	4. 7.06	Flybe Ltd	Exeter	11. 7.09E
G-JECP	Bombardier DHC-8-402	4136	C-FHEL	31.10.06	Flybe Ltd	Exeter	17.10.09E
G-JECR	Bombardier DHC-8-402	4139	C-FHQM	12.12.06	Flybe Ltd	Exeter	17.12.09E
G-JECS	Bombardier DHC-8-402	4142	C-FHQV	10.1.07	Flybe Ltd	Exeter	14. 1.10E
G-JECT	Bombardier DHC-8-402	4144	C-FHQY	30.1.07	Flybe Ltd "Matt Le Tissier"	Exeter	2.10E
G-JECU	Bombardier DHC-8-402	4146	C-FJKY	1. 2.07	Flybe Ltd	Exeter	5. 2.10E
G-JECV	Bombardier DHC-8-402	4148	C-FJLE	19. 4.07	Flybe Ltd	Exeter	23. 4.09E
G-JECW	Bombardier DHC-8-402	4152	C-FJLK	24. 4.07	Flybe Ltd	Exeter	29. 4.09E
G-JECX	Bombardier DHC-8-402	4155	C-FLKO	13. 6.07	Flybe Ltd	Exeter	17. 6.09E
G-JECY	Bombardier DHC-8-402	4157	C-FLKV	22. 6.07	Flybe Ltd	Exeter	27. 6.09E
G-JECZ	Bombardier DHC-8-402	4179	C-FMTY	20.11.07	Flybe Ltd	Exeter	25.11.09E
G-JEDH	Robin DR.400-180 Régent	2343		3. 2.97	J B Hoolahan	Challock	8. 7.09E
G-JEDI	Bombardier DHC-8-402	4052	C-GFOD	25.10.01	Flybe Ltd	Exeter	24.10.09E
G-JEDJ	Bombardier DHC-8-402	4058	C-FDHZ	23. 1.02	Flybe Ltd	Exeter	4. 2.10E
G-JEDK	Bombardier DHC-8-402	4065	C-GEMU	23. 4.02	Flybe Ltd "Vignoble de Bergerac"	Exeter	30. 4.09E
G-JEDL	Bombardier DHC-8-402	4067	C-GEOZ	17. 6.02	Flybe Ltd	Exeter	30. 6.09E
G-JEDM	Bombardier DHC-8-402	4077	C-FGNP	18. 7.03	Flybe Ltd	Exeter	22. 7.09E
G-JEDN	Bombardier DHC-8-402	4078	C-FNGB	31. 7.03	Flybe Ltd	Exeter	7. 8.09E
G-JEDO	Bombardier DHC-8-402	4079	C-GDFT	1. 8.03	Flybe Ltd	Exeter	13. 8.09E
G-JEDP	Bombardier DHC-8-402	4085	C-FDHO	30. 1.04	Flybe Ltd	Exeter	4. 3.09E
G-JEDR	Bombardier DHC-8-402	4087	C-FDHI	5. 3.04	Flybe Ltd	Exeter	15. 3.10E
G-JEDS	Andreasson BA-4B	HA/02	G-BEBT	17.12.02	S B Jedburgh	White Waltham	29. 1.09P
	(Built A Horsfall [Hornet Aviation] - pr.no.PFA 038-10158) (Lycoming O-235-C)						
G-JEDT	Bombardier DHC-8-402	4088	C-FDHP	19. 3.04	Flybe Ltd	Exeter	23. 3.09E
G-JEDU	Bombardier DHC-8-402	4089	C-GEMU	7. 4.04	Flybe Ltd "Pride of Exeter"	Exeter	13. 4.09E
G-JEDV	Bombardier DHC-8-402	4090	C-FDHX	7. 5.04	Flybe Ltd	Exeter	18. 5.09E
G-JEDW	Bombardier DHC-8-402	4093	C-GFBW	27. 7.04	Flybe Ltd	Exeter	2. 8.09E
G-JEEP	Evektor EV-97 Eurostar	PFA 315-13888	G-CBNK	8.08.06	P A Brigstock tr G-JEEP Group		
	(Built M R M Welch)				Shacklewell Farm, Empingham		24. 6.08E
G-JEFA	Robinson R44 Astro	0710		7. 2.00	Simlot Ltd	Denham	15. 6.09E
G-JEJE	Rotary Air Force RAF 2000 GTX-SE			21. 1.03	J W Erswell	(South Brent)	15. 6.09P
	(Built J W Erswell)	PFA G/13-1278					
G-JEJH	CEA Jodel DR.1050 Ambassadeur	301	F-GIGZ	29.10.08	E J Horsfall	Blackpool	
			OO-HGZ, F-BKIG				
G-JELI	Schweizer 269C-1 (Schweizer 300)	0164	G-CCVG	20. 3.08	Jelico Ltd	(Downham Market)	10.12.09E
			N86G				
G-JEMA	British Aerospace ATP	2028	N854AW	24. 2.04	PTB (Emerald) Proprietary Ltd	Blackpool	6. 5.07T
			G-11-028, N5000R)		(Stored internally 2.08)		
G-JEMC	British Aerospace ATP	2032	N856AW	29.12.03	PTB (Emerald) Proprietary Ltd	Blackpool	15. 4.07T
			G-11-032		(Stored externally 2.08)		
G-JEMD	British Aerospace ATP	2026	S2-ACX	3. 2.04	PTB (Emerald) Proprietary Ltd (Stored 9.08)		
	(Freighter conversion)		(SE-LHX), S2-ACX, G-11-026			Kemble	
G-JEME	British Aerospace ATP	2027	S2-ACY	3. 2.04	PTB (Emerald) Proprietary Ltd (Stored 9.08)		
	(Freighter conversion)		(SE-LHY), S2-ACY, G-11-027			Kemble	19.10.09E
G-JEMH	Aérospatiale AS.355F2 Ecureuil 2	5424	G-CDFV	1. 3.06	PJM Helicopters LLP	Costock	25. 9.09E
			RP-C1688, JA9964				
G-JEMI	Lindstrand LBL 90A Balloon (Hot Air)	1189		12.12.07	J A Lawton	Enton, Godalming	4.12.09E
G-JEMX	Short SD.3-60 Variant 100	SH3715	G-SSWX	10. 3.04	BAC Leasing Ltd (Emerald A/W colours)	Southend	2.12.06E
			N711PM, G-BNDL, G-14-3715		(In open store 2.09 less engines)		
G-JENA	Mooney M 20J Mooney 201	24-1304	N1168D	5. 7.82	P Leverkuehn tr Jena Air Force		
						Antwerp-Deurne, Belgium	19. 9.09E
G-JENC	Beech B300C Super King Air	FM-14	N814KA	16.10.07	Raytheon Systems Ltd	Hawarden	14.11.08
	(Planned to become Beech 350C ER Shadow R.1 "ZZ416" for AAC but still flying in RAF c/s but with civilian marks 12.08)						
G-JENI	Cessna R182 Skylane RG II	R18200267	N3284C	17. 9.87	R A Bentley	Stapleford	9. 7.09E
G-JENK	Comco Ikarus C42 FB80	0806-6978		1. 8.08	R K Jenkins	Swansea	20. 8.09P
	(Built Aerosport Ltd)						
G-JENO	Lindstrand LBL 105A Balloon (Hot Air)	916		28. 4.03	S F Redman	Stalbridge, Sturminster Newton	21. 7.09E
G-JERO	Europa Aviation Europa XS	492		13. 6.02	P Jenkinson and N Robshaw	Wombleton	21. 5.07P
	(Built B Robshaw and P Jenkinson - pr.no.PFA 247-13691) (Rotax 914) (Tri-gear u/c)						
G-JERS	Robinson R22 Beta	1610		21.12.90	Sloane Helicopters Ltd	Sywell	6.11.09E

Reg	Type	C/n	Prev id	Date	Owner/Operator	Location	Date
G-JESA	Mainair 582 Gemini/Southdown Raven X 664-688-6 & SN2232/0117		G-MNLB	14. 4.04	A E James	Lower Upham Farm, Chiseldon	4. 8.06P
			(Officially regd as "Southdown Raven X [modified Gemini F2A Trike]")				
G-JESI	Aérospatiale AS.350B Ecureuil	1205	G-JOSS	16.12.03	Staske Construction Ltd	(Hulcote)	25. 2.09E
			F-WQJY, 3A-..., G-WILX, G-RAHM, G-UNIC, G-COLN, G-BHIV				
G-JESS	Piper PA-28R-201T Turbo Arrow III 28R-7803334		G-REIS N36689	18. 9.95	R E Trawicki	Elstree	5. 9.09E
G-JETA	Cessna 550 Citation II	550-0094	G-RDBS G-JETA, (N26630)	3. 9.79	Icon Two Ltd	Kemble	10. 9.08E
G-JETC	Cessna 550 Citation II	550-0282	G-JCFR G-JETC, N68644	28. 5.81	Interceptor Aviation Ltd	Southend	24. 3.09E
G-JETF	Dassault Falcon 2000EX	078	I-JETF (F-GOTF), F-WWGO	9. 1.07	TAG Aviation (UK) Ltd	Farnborough	10. 1.10E
G-JETH	Hawker Sea Hawk FGA.6	AW-6385	"XE364" XE489	10. 8.83	P G Vallance Ltd	Charlwood, Surrey	
	(Builtt Armstrong-Whitworth Aircraft) (Composite with WM983, A2511)				*(In Gatwick Aviation Museum 2007 as "XE489")*		
G-JETJ	Cessna 550 Citation II	550-0154	G-EJET G-DJBE, (N8887N)	9. 2.93	G-JETJ Ltd	Liverpool	26. 8.09E
G-JETM	Gloster Meteor T 7	-	VZ638	10. 8.83	P G Vallance Ltd	Charlwood, Surrey	
					(In Gatwick Aviation Museum 2007 as "VZ638" in RN/FRU c/s)		
G-JETO	Cessna 550 Citation II	550-0441	N80LA G-RVHT, N221GA, HB-VKS, VR-CCE, N56PC, N50LM, N1220J	9. 1.06	Jet Options Ltd	Birmingham	1. 5.09E
G-JETU	Aérospatiale AS.355F2 Ecureuil 2	5450	VR-CET JA6623	18. 4.96	Arena Aviation Ltd	Redhill	22. 5.09E
G-JETX	Bell 206B-3 JetRanger III	3208	N3898L	9. 2.88	S J Shephard	Shoreham	17. 5.09E
G-JETZ	Hughes 369E *(Hughes 500)*	0450E	VR-HJI	26. 3.97	J G Matchett	Sywell	20. 1.10E
G-JEZZ	Best Off Sky Ranger 582(1)	SKR0402456		6. 4.04	A S Ashton	Phoenix Farm, Lower Upham	13. 4.08P
	(Built J W Barwick - pr.no.BMAA HB/368)						
G-JFDI	Aerospool Dynamic WT9 UK	DY192/2007		8. 5.07	M S Gregory	(Chinnor)	1.11.09P
	(Official c/n is "DY192")						
G-JFER	Commander Aircraft Commander 114B	14638	G-HPSE N6038V	26. 8.97	J C and J A Ferguson	Andrewsfield	27. 9.09E
G-JFLO	Aerospool Dynamic WT9 UK	DY197/2007		6.11.07	J Flood	Perth	29.11.08P
	(Official c/n is "DY197")						
G-JFMK	Zenair CH.701SP STOL PFA 187-14264			24. 9.04	J D Pearson	(Uplawmor, Glasgow)	7. 8.08P
	(Built J D Pearson)						
G-JFRV	Van's RV-7A PFA 323-13851			8.10.03	J H Fisher	Haverfordwest	2. 9.09P
	(Built J H Fisher) (Tri-cycle u/c)						
G-JFWI	Reims Cessna F172N Skyhawk II	F17201622	PH-DPA PH-AXY	1. 9.80	Staryear Ltd	Barton	17. 3.09E
G-JGBI	Bell 206L-4 LongRanger IV	52257	N91285 C-GBUP	13. 8.01	Dorbcrest Homes Ltd	Blackpool	12.10.09E
G-JGMN	CASA 1-131E Jungmann Series 2000	2011	Spanish AF E3B-407	17. 4.91	P D Scandrett	Rendcomb	20. 6.09P
	(Officially regd as c/n 2011 but carries c/n plate 2104 in rear cockpit - c/n 2011 is regd as N65522)						
G-JGSI	Cyclone Airsports Pegasus Quantum 15-912 7515			19. 4.99	Airways Airsports Ltd	Darley Moor, Ashbourne	9. 9.09P
G-JHAC	Reims Cessna FRA150L Aerobat FRA1500160		EI-BRX G-BACM, EI-BRX, G-BACM	16. 9.02	J H A Clarke	Oaks Farm, Bromham, Chippenham	27. 8.09E
G-JHEW	Robinson R22 Beta	0672	N23677	20. 7.87	Burbage Farms Ltd	Hinckley	22. 1.09E
G-JHKP	Europa Aviation Europa XS	536		5.11.03	J D Heykoop	(Pulborough)	
	(Built J D Heykoop - pr.no.PFA 247-13828)						
G-JHNY	Cameron A-210 Balloon (Hot Air)	10487		17. 3.04	Floating Sensations Ltd	Llandeilo	28. 5.09E
G-JHPC	Cessna 182T Skylane	18282125	N63108	18. 8.08	JHP Aviation Ltd	Coventry	11. 9.09E
G-JHYS	Europa Aviation Europa	314		6. 3.01	B C Moorhouse	(Castle Cary)	5.12.09P
	(Built J D Boyce and G E Walker - pr.no.PFA 247-13307) (Tri-gear u/c)						
G-JIFI	Schempp-Hirth Duo Discus T	95/420	BGA5115-KHY D-KOZZ	26. 9.05	D K McCarthy *"620"*	Lasham	30.12.07
	(Officially regd with c/n 95)						
G-JIII	Stolp SA.300 Starduster Too	2-3-12	N9043	27. 5.93	J G McTaggart tr VTIO Company		
	(Built C S Johnson) (Lycoming IO-360)					Archerfield Estate, Dirleton	18. 3.09P
G-JILL	Rockwell Commander 112TC-A	13304	(OO-HPB) G-JILL, N8070R, HB-NCW	25. 7.80	D Carlton	Sherburn-in-Elmet	13. 5.09E
G-JILY	Robinson R44 Raven	0959		5. 1.01	R R Orr	(Dromore)	5. 3.09E
G-JIMB	Beagle B 121 Pup Series 1	B121-033	G-AWWF	7. 4.94	P G Fowler	Enstone	23. 7.09R
G-JIMG	Beech B300C Super King Air	FM-17	N817KA	31. 3.08	Raytheon Systems Ltd	Hawarden	
	(Planned to become Beech 350C ER Shadow R.1 "ZZ418" for AAC but still flying in RAF c/s but with civilian marks 12.08)						
G-JIMH	Reims Cessna F152 II	F15201839	G-SHAH OH-IHA, SE-IHA	17. 6.05	S A Edkins and D Howell tr Emmalin Wolverhampton		7. 6.09E
G-JIMM	Europa Aviation Europa XS	579		13. 7.04	J Riley	(Crays Hill, Billericay)	
	(Built J Riley - pr.no.PFA 247-14071)						
G-JIMZ	Van's RV-4	2488	N30GB	28. 7.06	J W Hale	Netherthorpe	2. 6.09P
	(Built J Banks and J Giatrakis 1991)						
G-JINI	Cameron V-77 Balloon (Hot Air)	11025		27. 7.07	I R Warrington	Great Casterton, Stamford	30. 8.09E
G-JIVE	Hughes 369E *(Hughes 500)*	0486E	G-DRAR N101LH, N1608Z	24. 5.01	Sleekform Ltd	(Sowerby Bridge)	27. 2.09E
G-JJAB	Avtech Jabiru J400	0xxx		6. 4.05	Propitious Aviation Ltd	Dunsfold	25. 3.09P
	(Built K Ingebrigtsen - pr.no.PFA 325-14339)						
G-JJAN	Piper PA-28-181 Archer II	2890007	N9105Z	28. 3.88	J S Develin and Z Islam	Blackbushe	25. 5.09E
G-JJDC	Aviat A-1B Husky	2291	N96HY	31. 8.05	Aerographic Ltd	Crowfield	13. 3.09E
G-JJEN	Piper PA-28-181 Archer III	2843370	N4190D	25. 8.00	K M R Jenkins	Jersey	27. 8.09E
G-JJFB	Eurocopter EC.120B Colibri	1506		16. 8.07	P A Winslow	(Courteenhall, Northampton)	30.10.09E
G-JJIL	Extra EA 300/L	1270		8.11.07	S French	(Sandon, Buntingford)	4. 1.09E
G-JJJL	Agusta A109E Power	11159	G-CEJS RP-C2838	12. 4.07	Brookes Air Charter LLP	Fairoaks	28. 1.09E

G-JJSI	British Aerospace BAe 125 Series 800B		G-OMGG	16. 4.04	Gama Leasing Ltd	Farnborough	24.11.09E
		258058	N125JW, G-5-637, N125JW, VH-NMR, ZK-EUI, (ZK-EUR), G-5-510				
G-JKAY	Robinson R44 Raven II	11093		10. 3.06	Jamiroquai Ltd	Wycombe Air Park	6. 4.09E
G-JKMH	Diamond DA.42 Twin Star	42.168		18. 9.06	A D and C Realff t/a ADR Aviation	Shoreham	1.11.09E
G-JKMJ	Diamond DA.42 Twin Star	42.141		23. 6.06	Medox Enterprises Ltd	(Paphos, Cyprus)	16. 7.09E
G-JLAT	Evektor EV-97 Eurostar	PFA 315-14068		14. 5.03	J Latimer	Barton	16. 7.09P
	(Built J Latimer)						
G-JLCA	Piper PA-34-200T Seneca II	34-7870428	G-BOKE	3. 9.97	Tayside Aviation Ltd	Dundee	16. 5.09E
			N21030				
G-JLEE	Agusta-Bell 206B-3 JetRanger III	8588	G-JOKE	10. 2.88	J S Lee	Wycombe Air Park	10.12.09E
			G-CSKY, G-TALY				
G-JLHS	Beech A36 Bonanza	E-2571	N8046U	30.11.90	I G Meredith	Lydd	9. 3.09E
G-JLIN	Piper PA-28-161 Cadet	2841013	D-ENXI	24. 8.05	Westmorland Aviation Ltd	Carlisle	16.10.09E
			N9153X				
G-JLMW	Cameron V-77 Balloon (Hot Air)	1768		23. 6.88	J L M Watkins	Ivybridge	26. 2.99T
G-JLRW	Beech 76 Duchess	ME-165	N60206	4.11.87	Magenta Ltd *(Operated Airways Flight Training)*		
						Exeter	5. 2.10E
G-JMAA	Boeing 757-3CQ	32241		24. 4.01	Thomas Cook Airlines Ltd	Manchester	23. 4.09E
G-JMAB	Boeing 757-3CQ	32242		14. 5.01	Thomas Cook Airlines Ltd	Manchester	13. 5.09E
G-JMAL	Avtech Jabiru UL-D	669		19. 8.08	T J Adams-Lewis	Haverfordwest	11.12.09P
G-JMAN	Mainair Blade 912S	1290-0601-7-W1085		12. 7.01	J Manuel	(Southport)	15. 7.02P
G-JMAX	Raytheon Hawker 800XP	258456	N41762	13.10.04	J Hargreaves t/a J-Max Air Services	Blackpool	13.10.09E
			N800EM				
G-JMCD	Boeing 757-25F	30757	C-FLCD	24. 6.00	Thomas Cook Airlines Ltd	Manchester	29. 4.09E
			G-JMCD, N1795B				
G-JMCE	Boeing 757-25F	30758	XA-JPB	24. 6.00	Thomas Cook Airlines Ltd	Manchester	25. 4.09E
			G-JMCE				
G-JMCF	Boeing 757-28A	24369	C-FMCF	20. 5.00	Thomas Cook Airlines Ltd	Manchester	29. 4.09E
			G-JMCF, C-FOOE				
G-JMCG	Boeing 757-2G5	26278	SX-BLV	27. 4.00	Thomas Cook Airlines Ltd	Manchester	29. 4.09E
			G-JMCG, D-AMUQ				
G-JMCL	Boeing 737-322F	23951	D-AGEA	18.12.08	Atlantic Airlines Ltd	Coventry	
			N319UA		*(Undergoing freight conversion at Dothan, AL)*		
G-JMDI	Schweizer 269C *(Schweizer 300)*	S 1398	G-FLAT	24. 9.91	J J Potter	Sherburn-in-Elmet	24. 4.08E
G-JMDW	Cessna 550 Citation II	550-0183	HB-VGS	16. 2.04	Xclusive Jet Charter Ltd	Southampton	2. 4.09E
			(XC-DUF), N98630				
G-JMJR	Cameron Z-90 Balloon (Hot Air)	10611		17. 1.05	J-M Reck	Evette-Salbert, France	20. 2.09E
	(Lion's Head Shape)						
G-JMKE	Cessna 172S Skyhawk SP	172S9248	N53012	17.12.02	115CR (146) Ltd	Wellesbourne Mountford	23. 6.09E
G-JMMX	Dassault Falcon 900EX	184	F-WWFN	22.10.07	J Hargreaves t/a J-Max Air Services	Blackpool	21.10.09E
G-JMON	Agusta A109A II	7411	G-RFDS	4. 8.06	Jermon Ltd Kilmaddy, Dungannon, County Tyrone		29. 6.09E
			N1YU, VP-CLA, VR-CLA, G-BOLA, VR-CMP, G-BOLA				
G-JMOS	Piper PA-34-220T Seneca V	3449378	N60936	1. 9.08	J W Moss	Barton	9. 9.09E
G-JMMP	Bombardier CL-600-2B16	5528	D-AJAG	15. 2.08	MP Aviation LLP	Biggin Hill	9. 3.09E
	(CL-604 Challenger)		N528DT, C-GLYO				
G-JMRV	Van's RV-7	PFA 323-14591		16. 5.07	J W Marshall	(Haslingbourne, Petworth)	
	(Built J W Marshall)						
G-JMTS	Robin DR.400-180 Régent	2045		29.11.90	P A Mansbridge	White Waltham	13. 7.09E
G-JMXA	Agusta A109E Power Elite	11156		31. 5.02	J Hargreaves t/a J-Max Air Services	Blackpool	30. 5.09E
G-JNAS	Grumman American AA-5A Cheetah		SE-GEI	28.11.00	C J Williams	Farley Farm, Romsey	9. 3.07T
		AA5A-0604	LN-KLE		*(On rebuild 10.07)*		
G-JNNB	Colt 90A Balloon (Hot Air)	2063		20.12.91	N A P Godfrey *(J & B Rare titles)* West Leith, Tring		8. 4.07A
G-JNSC	Schempp-Hirth Janus CT	2-185	BGA4186-HTH	11.12.07	D S Bramwell tr Janus Syndicate	Thame	13. 7.08
			N137DB, D-KHIE				
G-JNUS	Schempp-Hirth Janus C	215	BGA4062-HNB	6. 9.07	C Fox *"563"*	Sleap	27. 3.08
			D-4149				
G-JOAL	Beech B200 Super King Air	BB-1158	N66LM	23. 5.06	South Coast Air Charter LLP	Bournemouth	31. 5.09E
			N419TW, N158EF, N158TJ, N18245, N200KK, (N712PW), N200KK, N200KA				
G-JOBA	P&M Aviation Quik GT450	8174		31. 5.06	M B Smith	Tarn Farm, Cockerham	11. 6.08P
G-JOBS	Cessna T182T Turbo Skylane	T18208009	N737RM	29. 9.07	Nortrax Aviation Ltd	(Chester)	30.10.09E
			G-BZVF, N109LP				
G-JODI	Agusta A109A II	7265	G-BVCJ	27. 2.04	Heli Air (Jersey) Ltd	(St Helier, Jersey)	26.11.08E
			G-CLRL, G-EJCB				
G-JODL	SAN Jodel DR.1050M Excellence	99	F-BJJC	28. 4.86	D Silsbury (Noted 6.04)	Dunkeswell	26.11.99
G-JOEL	Bensen B.8M Gyrocopter	PFA G/01-1300			C Quinn	Little Rissington	6. 7.99P
	(Built G C Young, originally regd as pr.no PFA G/03-1300)						
G-JOEW	Cirrus SR20	1087	N184CD	15.10.08	Styrene Packaging and Insulation Ltd	(Bradford)	
G-JOEY	Fairey Britten-Norman BN-2A Mk.III-2 Trislander		G-BDGG	27.11.81	Aurigny Air Services Ltd	Guernsey	18. 4.09E
		1016	C-GSAA, G-BDGG				
G-JOIE	American Champion 7GCAA Citabria			5.12.05	N Baumber	(Grantham)	8. 4.09E
		502-2005					
G-JOJO	Cameron A-210 Balloon (Hot Air)	2674		20. 9.91	A C Rawson and J J Rudoni t/a Wickers World Hot-Air		
					Balloon Company	Stafford	11. 4.06T
G-JOKR	Extra EA.300/L	1278		28. 2.08	C Vogelgesang and R Hockey	Wycombe Air Park	22. 4.09E
G-JOLY	Cessna 120	13872	OO-ACE	3. 9.81	B V Meade	Garston Farm, Marshfield	13. 6.09P
	(Continental C85)						
G-JONB	Robinson R22 Beta II	2593		29. 4.96	J Bignall	(Naphill, High Wycombe)	27. 5.09E
G-JONG	Rotorway Executive 162F	6168	N630GH	27. 4.04	J V George	Street Farm, Takeley	17.12.08P
	(Built S A Foster)						
G-JONH	Robinson R22 Beta	2170		3. 6.93	J H Garrioch and R C Hayward t/a Polar Helicopters		
						Manston	18. 9.09E
G-JONI	Reims Cessna FA152 Aerobat	FA1520346	G-BFTU	6. 7.84	Flight Academy (Gyrocopters) Ltd	Barton	18. 2.09E
G-JONM	Piper PA-28-181 Archer III	2843614	OY-PHH	15. 1.08	J H Massey	Nottingham-East Midlands	12. 3.09E

G-JONO	Colt 77A Balloon (Hot Air)	1086			22. 6.87	The Sandcliffe Motor Group Ltd *"Sandcliffe Ford"*		
						(On loan to British Balloon Museum and Library) Newbury	17. 9.95A
G-JONW	Agusta A109E Power	11624	EI-JON		12. 9.07	Milford Aviation Services Ltd	Cranfield	19. 9.09E
G-JONY	Cyclone AX2000 HKS	7503			12. 3.99	K R Matheson *(USAF c/s)* Headon Farm, Retford	18. 6.08P
G-JONZ	Cessna 172P Skyhawk II	17276233	N97835		28. 9.89	Truman Aviation Ltd Nottingham City-Tollerton	8. 6.09E
G-JOOL	Mainair Blade 912	1262-1000-7-W1056			8.12.00	J R Gibson	Ince Blundell	16. 2.08P
G-JOON	Cessna 182D	18253067	(N....)		9. 6.81	Go Adventure Ireland Ltd		
			G-JOON, OO-ACD, N9967T			Feathard, County Tipperary	13. 2.09E
G-JOPT	Cessna 560 Citation V	560-0159	D-CLEO		26. 1.07	Jet Options Ltd	Birmingham	1. 2.10E
			N68MA, (N68854)					
G-JORD	Robinson R44 Raven II	11725			14. 5.07	Overby Ltd	(Ascot)	31. 5.09E
G-JOSH	Cameron N-105 Balloon (Hot Air)	1319			13. 8.86	M White	Cirencester	16. 8.96T
G-JOST	Europa Aviation Europa	234			17. 6.98	A V Orchard and J A Austin	RAF Mona	6.12.07P
	(Built J A Austin - pr.no.PFA 247-12916) (Tri-gear u/c)							
G-JOYD	Robinson R22 Beta II	2769	G-SIMN		17. 6.05	RH Property Services Ltd		
						(Burton-upon-Stather, Scunthorpe)	4. 3.09E
G-JOYT	Piper PA-28-181 Archer II	28-7990132	G-BOVO		13. 2.90	John K Cathcart Ltd	Enniskillen	21. 4.09E
			N2239B					
G-JOYZ	Piper PA-28-181 Archer III	2843018	N9262R		19. 1.96	S W and J E Taylor	Biggin Hill	2. 3.09E
			(G-JOYZ)					
G-JPAL	Eurocopter AS.355N Ecureuil II	5692	F-GSJP		9.10.01	JPM Ltd	(Horsham)	6.11.09E
G-JPAT	Robin HR.200-100 Club	76	G-BDJN		13. 9.00	L Girardier and A J McCulloch Sherburn-in-Elmet	11. 9.09E
G-JPJR	Robinson R44 Raven II	11198			4. 5.06	Longstop Investments Ltd (Pettistree, Woodbridge)	14. 5.09E
G-JPMA	Avtech Jabiru UL	xxxx			24. 5.99	J P Metcalfe *"Sheila"*	Lydd	19.11.09P
	(Built J P Metcalfe -pr.no.PFA 274A-13399)							
G-JPOT	Piper PA-32R-301 Saratoga II HP		G-BIYM		1. 8.94	P J Wolstencroft	Duxford	8. 9.08E
		32R-8113065	N8385X					
G-JPRO	British Aircraft Corporation BAC 145 Jet Provost T 5A				10. 8.95	Air Atlantic Ltd *(As "XW433 "in RAF CFS c/s)*		
		EEP/JP/1055	XW433			Coventry	19. 3.08P
G-JPSX	Dassault Falcon 900EX	132	F-WWFJ		17. 2.04	Sorven Aviation Ltd	Gloucestershire	16. 2.09E
G-JPTT	Enstrom 480	5032	G-PPAH		10. 4.02	P G Lawrence	Gloucestershire	5. 3.09E
G-JPTV	British Aircraft Corporation BAC 145 Jet Provost T 5A				2. 5.96	S J Davies *(As "XW354 " in RAF c/s)*	Sandtoft	1. 9.07P
	(C/n '...1002' also reported)	EEP/JP/1005	XW355					
G-JPVA	British Aircraft Corporation BAC 145 Jet Provost T 5A				22. 2.95	H Cooke *(As "XW289:73" in RAF 1FTS c/s)*		
		EEP/JP/953	G-BVXT, XW289			RNAS Yeovilton	8.10.09P
G-JPWM	Best Off Sky Ranger 912(2)	SKR0412541			24. 3.05	R S Waters and M Pittock	(Etchingham)	21. 5.08P
	(Built R S Waters and M Pittock- pr.no.BMAA HB/442)							
G-JRED	Robinson R44 Raven II	11286			5. 7.06	J Reddington Ltd	Denham	17. 8.09E
G-JREE	Maule MX-7-180 Super Rocket	11096C	N99MX		13. 4.01	J M P Ree	(Hampstead Marshall, Newbury)	19. 4.09E
			N30051					
G-JRKD	Jodel D 18	W177	19-3431		7.12.06	R K Davies	Old Sarum	
	(Built J Elari, Australia)							
G-JRME	Jodel D 140E	444			13.11.02	J E and L L Rex	(Eggborough, Goole)	
	(Built J E and L L Rex - pr.no.PFA 251-13155)							
G-JSAK	Robinson R22 Beta II	2959			30. 6.99	J W F and S M Tuke tr Tukair Aircraft Charter		
						Headcorn	14.11.09E
G-JSAR	Eurocopter AS.332L2 Super Puma	2576	F-WQRE		3. 9.02	Bristow Helicopters Ltd Den Helder, Netherlands	18.12.07E
						(Ditched in North Sea 21.11.06 and washed ashore at Texel)	
G-JSAT	Pilatus Britten-Norman BN-2T Islander	2277	G-BVFK		5. 2.98	P Moore tr Rhine Army Parachute Association		
						Sennelager, Germany	2. 3.09E
G-JSON	Cameron N-105 Balloon (Hot Air)	2933			21. 5.92	Up and Away Ballooning Ltd *"Jason"*		
						High Wycombe	7. 9.04A
G-JSPL	Avtech Jabiru SPL-450	0358			27.12.00	A E Stowe	(Harrow)	25. 6.09P
	(Built J A Lord - pr.no.PFA 274A-13604)							
G-JSRV	Van's RV-6	xxxx			23. 8.05	J Stringer Graveley Hall Farm, Graveley	16. 5.09P
	(Built J Stringer – pr.no. PFA 181A-14407)							
G-JTEM	Van's RV-7	xxxx			30. 4.04	J C Bacon	(Gwehelog, Usk)	
	(Built J C Bacon – pr.no. PFA 323-14237)							
G-JTNC	Cessna 500 Citation I	500-0264	G-OEJA		9. 1.04	Eurojet Aviation Ltd	Birmingham	15. 1.09E
			G-BWFL, F-GLJA, N205FM, N5264J					
G-JTPC	Aeromot AMT-200 Super Ximango	200067			28. 5.97	J T Potter and P G Cowling tr G-JTPC Falcon 3 Group		
						Rufforth	1.10.09E
G-JTSA	Robinson R44 Raven II	11659			2. 4.07	JTS Aviation Ltd	Denham	17. 4.09E
G-JTWO	Taylor J-2 Cub	1754	G-BPZR		23.10.89	O D Usherwood *(Carries "NC19554" on tail)*		
	(Built Taylor Aircraft Co Inc) (Continental A65)		N19554, NC19554			(Romney Marsh)	8. 4.09P
G-JUDD	Avtech Jabiru UL-450	0349			9. 8.00	C Judd Lark Engine Farmhouse, Prickwillow, Ely	15. 9.09P
	(Built C Judd- pr.no.PFA 274A-13570)							
G-JUDE	Robin DR.400-100 Régent	1869			14.10.88	Bravo India Flying Group Ltd	RAF Woodvale	15. 2.09E
G-JUDI	North American AT-6D-NT Harvard III		FAP 1502		17.11.78	A A Hodgson *(As "FX301:FD-NQ" in RAF c/s)*		
	(Regd as c/n "EX915-326165")	88-14722	SAAF7439, EX915, 41-33888			Bryn Gwyn Bach	4. 9.08P
G-JUDY	Grumman AA-5A Cheetah	AA5A-0620	(G-BFWM)		31. 8.78	R Gray t/a Gray Hooper Holt LLP	Biggin Hill	27.11.09E
			N26480					
G-JUGE	Evektor EV-97 teamEurostar UK	1709			7.10.03	L J Appleby	Leicester	12.10.08P
G-JUIN	Cessna T303 Crusader	T30300014	OO-PEN		29. 2.88	M J and J M Newman	Denham	14. 5.09E
			N9401T					
G-JULE	P&M Aviation Quik GT450	8219			13.10.06	A J A Fowler Corn Wood Farm, Adversane	17.10.08P
G-JULL	Stemme S 10-VT	11-039			10. 2.00	J P C Fuchs	Rufforth	2. 1.09E
	(Rotax 914)							
G-JULU	Cameron V-90 Balloon (Hot Air)	3611			7. 7.95	N J Appleton	Bristol	4. 4.08A
G-JULZ	Europa Aviation Europa	312			8.10.96	M Parkin	Sandtoft	16. 6.07P
	(Built M Parkin - pr.no.PFA 247-13045) (Rotax 914) (Monowheel u/c)							
G-JUNG	CASA 1-131E Jungmann	1121	Spanish AF		23.11.88	K H Wilson	Compton Abbas	30. 6.09P
			E3B-143					

Reg	Type	C/n	Prev id	Date	Owner/Operator	Location	Review
G-JUPP	Piper PA-32RT-300 Lance II	32R-7885098	N31539	3.10.02	Jupp Air LLP	Wolverhampton	15.10.09E
G-JURA	British Aerospace Jetstream Series 3102	772	SE-LDH OY-SVK, C-FAMJ, G-31-772	21. 5.01	Highland Airways Ltd *"City of Inverness"*	Inverness	11. 7.09E
G-JURG	Rockwell Commander 114A GT *(Laid-down as c/n 14449)*	14516	N4752W	19. 9.79	J A Marsh	(Sutton Coldfield)	4. 5.09E
G-JUST	Beech F33A Bonanza	CE-1165	N334CW	11.10.00	Just Plane Trading Ltd	Elstree	28. 4.09E
G-JVBF	Lindstrand LBL 210A Balloon (Hot Air)	265		6. 6.95	Airxcite Ltd t/a Virgin Balloon Flights	Wembley	19. 6.06E
G-JVBP	Evektor EV-97 teamEurostar UK	2730		31. 5.06	B J Partridge and J A Valentine	Bourn	4. 6.09P
G-JVJK	Alpi Pioneer 300 Hawk	LAA 330A-14861		4. 2.09	D R Vale	(Derby)	
G-JWBI	Agusta-Bell 206B-2 JetRanger II	8435	G-RODS G-NOEL, G-BCWN	3. 4.96	J W Bonser	(Shareshill, Wolverhampton)	26. 9.08E
G-JWCM	Scottish Aviation Bulldog Series 120/1210	BH120/408	G-BHXB Botswana DF OD2, G-BHXB	19.10.99	Goon Aviation Ltd	North Weald	2. 1.10S
G-JWDB	Comco Ikarus C42 FB80	0509-6760		24.10.05	J W D Blythe	Swansea	23.10.08P
G-JWDS	Cessna F150G *(Built Reims Aviation SA)*	F150-0216	G-AVNB	15.12.88	G Sayer	Upfield Farm, Whitson	20. 1.10E
G-JWEB	Robinson R44 Raven	1334		3. 9.03	Mastercraft Helicopter Hire Ltd	Sherburn-in-Elmet	12. 9.09E
G-JWFT	Robinson R22 Beta	0989		16. 3.89	M Fowkes t/a Rotorfun Aviation	(Derby)	19. 4.08E
G-JWIV	CEA Jodel DR.1051 Sicile	431	F-BLMD	6. 9.78	C M Fitton	(Stoke Fleming, Dartmouth)	20. 1.10P
G-JWJW	CASA 1-131E Jungmann Series 2000	419	PH-MRK (PH-MRN), D-EDWC, Spanish AF E3B-419	15. 5.03	J T and J W Whicher	Breighton	25. 2.09P
G-JXTA	British Aerospace Jetstream Series 3103	610	D-CNRY SE-KHC, OY-EDB, SE-KHC, D-CONI (2), G-31-50	3. 1.06	Jetstream Executive Travel Ltd	Inverness	15. 9.09E
G-JXTC	British Aerospace Jetstream Series 3108	690	PH-KJG G-LOGT G-BSFH, PH-KJG, G-31-690 *(Noted as "PH-KJG" 7.07 in open storage)*	21. 6.06	Jetstream Executive Travel Ltd Eindhoven, Netherlands		
G-JYAK	Yakovlev Yak-50	853001	RA-01493 DOSAAF 49 (blue) ?)	26.11.02	J W Stow *(As "R-93" (white))*	North Weald	13. 1.09P
G-JYRO	Rotorsport UK MT-03	RSUK/MT-03/006		18.10.06	A Richards	Kirkbride	7. 1.09P

G-KAAA - G-KZZZ

Reg	Type	C/n	Prev id	Date	Owner/Operator	Location	Review
G-KAAT	MD Helicopters MD.900 Explorer	900-00056	G-PASS N9234P	22. 2.00	Police Aviation Services Ltd *(Operated Kent Air Ambulance)*	Marden	19. 4.09E
G-KAEW	Fairey Gannet AEW.Mk.3 *(Built Westland Aircraft Ltd)*	F9459	XL500 A2701, XL500	9. 1.04	T J Manna *(on extended rebuild)*	Exeter	
G-KAFT	Diamond DA.40D Star	D4.191	OE-VPU	13. 3.06	Atlantic Flight Training Ltd	Coventry	9. 4.09E
G-KAIR	Piper PA-28-181 Archer II	28-7990176	N3075D	28.12.78	Keen Leasing (IoM) Ltd *(Operated Cumbernauld Flying School)*	Cumbernauld	20.12.08E
G-KALS	Bombardier BD-100-1A10 Challenger 300	20106	C-FIDX	12.10.06	Descaro Ltd	London Stansted	12.10.09E
G-KAMP	Piper PA-18-135 Super Cub *(L-18C)*	18-3451	D-EDPM 96+27, NL+104, AC+502, AS+501, 54-751	9. 5.97	J R G Furnell	Perth	26. 8.10
G-KANE	Aérospatiale SA.341G Gazelle 1	1136	G-GAZI G-BKLU, N32PA, N341VH, N90957	5.12.07	MW Helicopters Ltd	Stapleford	1. 7.09E
G-KANZ	Westland Wasp HAS.1	F9664	NZ3909 XT782	21.12.05	T J Manna *(Noted 6.07 in RNZAF c/s, coded "09")*	North Weald	
G-KAOM	Scheibe SF25C Falke *(Limbach SL1700)*	4417	D-KAOM	3. 2.98	W T Barnard, G Mckay and J Murdoch tr Falke G-KAOM Syndicate	Portmoak	25. 6.09E
G-KAOS	Van's RV-7 *(Built A E N Nicholas and D F McGarvey)*	PFA 323-13956		20. 5.03	A E N Nicholas and D F McGarvey	(Sevenoaks)	
G-KAPW	Percival P 56 Provost T 1	PAC/F/311	XF603	22. 9.97	Richard Shuttleworth Trustees *(As "XF603" in RAF c/s)*	Old Warden	29. 5.09P
G-KARA	Brügger MB.2 Colibri *(Built Carlton Flying Group)* (Volkswagen 1834)	PFA 043-10980	G-BMUI	1. 6.95	C L Reddish	Netherthorpe	21. 8.04P
G-KARI	Fuji FA.200-160 Aero Subaru	FA200-236	G-BBRE	19.12.84	C P Rowley	Prestwick	25. 6.09E
G-KARK	Dyn'Aéro MCR-01 Club *(Built R Bailes-Brown)*	PFA 301A-14010		29.12.03	R Bailes-Brown Yeatsall Farm, Abbotss Bromley		1. 5.09P
G-KART	Piper PA-28-161 Warrior II	28-8016088	N8097B	10. 7.91	N Clark	Newcastle	24. 1.04T
G-KASX	Vickers Supermarine 384 Seafire F XVII *(Built Westland Aircraft Ltd)*	FLWA.25488	G-BRMG A2055, SX336	30.10.03	T J Manna *(As "SX336:105:VL" in RN c/s)*	North Weald	31. 5.09P
G-KATG	Bell 206L-1 LongRanger	45783	D-HABB N102RD	23. 3.07	Lothian Helicopters Ltd	(Pathhead)	2. 5.09E
G-KATI	Rans S-7 Courier *(Built S M Hall - pr.no.PFA 218-12917)* (Jabiru 2200)	0795.151		5. 3.96	N Rawlinson Yeatsall Farm, Abbots Bromley *(Noted 8.07)*		10. 4.07P
G-KATS	Piper PA-28-140 Cherokee Cruiser	28-7325022	G-BIRC OY-BGE	26. 8.83	D R A Bott tr G-KATS Group	(Kingston St Mary, Taunton)	8. 6.09E
G-KATT	Cessna 152 II	15285661	G-BMTK N94387	10. 6.93	Central Aircraft Leasing Ltd *(Operated RJP Flying School)*	Wolverhampton	5. 6.09E
G-KAWA	Denney Kitfox Model 2 *(Built T W C Maton)*	PFA 172-11822		11. 3.91	L A James	(Market Bosworth, Nuneaton)	10. 9.07P
G-KAXF	Hawker Hunter F 6A *(Built Armstrong-Whitworth Aircraft)*	S4/U/3361	8830M XF515	20.12.95	Stichting Dutch Hawker Hunter Foundation *(As "N-294" in RNeth AF c/s)* Leeuwarden, Netherlands		2.10.09E
G-KAXT	Westland Wasp HAS.1	F9669	NZ3905 XT787	5. 3.02	T J Manna *(As "XT787" in RN c/s)*	North Weald	7. 6.09P
G-KAYH	Extra EA.300/L	144		9. 4.02	Integrated Management Practices Ltd	Budel, Netherlands	7. 5.09E
G-KAYI	Cameron Z-90 Balloon (Hot Air)	10710		30. 6.05	Snow Business International Ltd *(Snow Business titles)*	Ebley, Stroud	30. 7.09E
G-KAZA	Sikorsky S-76C	760615	N81085	18. 9.06	Bristow Helicopters Ltd	Kazakhstan	25. 2.10E
G-KAZB	Sikorsky S-76C	760614	N8094S	22. 9.06	Bristow Helicopters Ltd	Kazakhstan	15. 1.10E
G-KAZI	P&M Pegasus Quantum 15-912	8120		10. 8.05	Edren Homes Ltd	Deenethorpe	10. 4.08P

Reg	Type	c/n	Prev ID	Date	Owner	Location	Date
G-KBOX	Flight Design CTSW *(Assembled P&M Aviation Ltd with c/n 8365)*	08.02.15		19. 4.08	C R Mason	Alderney	18. 4.09P
G-KBPI	Piper PA-28-161 Cherokee Warrior II	28-7816468	G-BFSZ, N9556N	21. 5.81	Goodwood Road Racing Company Ltd *(Operated Goodwood Flying Club)*	Goodwood	14. 9.09E
G-KCHG	Schempp-Hirth Ventus cT	87/332	BGA5146-KJW, D-KCHG	16. 3.06	J Burrow tr Ventus KJW Syndicate	North Hill	28. 9.08
G-KCIG	Sportavia-Pützer RF5B Sperber	51005	D-KCIG	19. 6.80	J R Bisset tr Deeside Fournier Group	Aboyne	4. 7.06P
G-KCIN	Piper PA-28-161 Cadet	2841102	G-CDOX, HB-PQC, PH-TED, C-FDYA	3.11.05	G Conrad	Denham	10.10.09E
G-KDCC	Europa Aviation Europa XS *(Built K A C Dodd - pr.no.PFA 247-13562)*	452		25. 4.05	K A C Dodd	(Dunmow)	6. 1.10P
G-KDCD	Thruster T 600N	9098-T600N-025	G-MZNW	9.11.05	K J Draper	Stoke, Isle of Grain	13.12.07P
G-KDET	Piper PA-28-161 Cadet	2841158	(SE-KIR), N9184Z	8. 8.89	Rapidspin Ltd	Perranporth	9. 7.09E
G-KDEY	Scheibe SF25E Super Falke *(Limbach SL1700)*	4325	D-KDEY	8. 1.99	D Tucker tr Falke Syndicate	Aston Down	14. 8.09E
G-KDIX	Jodel D 9 Bébé *(Built K Barlow) (Volkswagen 1600)*	PFA 054-10293		23.11.78	P M Bowden	Barton	4. 6.08P
G-KDMA	Cessna 560 Citation Ultra	560-0553	N5145V	4. 4.01	Forest Aviation Ltd	Gamston	26. 4.09E
G-KDOG	Scottish Aviation Bulldog Series 120/121	BH120/289	XX624	18. 6.01	Gamit Ltd (As "XX624:E" in RAF c/s)	North Weald	6. 9.10S
G-KEAM	Schleicher ASH 26E	26116	D-KEAM	3. 3.04	D T Reilly "AM"	North Hill	12. 4.09E
G-KEEF	Commander Aircraft Commander 114B	14610	N828DL, VT-PVA, (F-GSDV), VT-PVA, N6025M	17. 6.04	K D Pearse	Jersey	17. 6.09E
G-KEEN	Stolp SA.300 Starduster Too *(Built R E Ellenbest) (Lycoming IO-540)*	800	PH-HAB, (PH-PET), G-KEEN, N800RE	19. 7.78	H Sharp tr Sharp Aerobatics (Cullybacky, Ballymena, County Antrim) *(Under restoration following accident (?) at City of Derry)*		27. 4.04P
G-KEES	Piper PA-28-180 Cherokee Archer	28-7505025	OO-AJV, OO-HAC, N32102	29. 5.97	C N Ellerbrook	(Morley St Boltolph, Wymondham)	15. 9.09E
G-KEHO	HOAC DV.20 Katana *(Rotax 912)*	20141	G-BWLP, OE-UDV	19. 5.08	R A Kehoe	Andrewsfield	28. 8.09E
G-KEIF	Robinson R44 Raven II	11877	N30675	12.10.07	Flying G Spot Ltd	Shoreham	29.11.09E
G-KEJY	Evektor EV-97 teamEurostar UK	2017		23. 6.04	D Young tr Kemble Eurostar 1	Kemble	22. 6.09P
G-KELI	Robinson R44 Raven II	11040		16. 2.06	KN Network Services (Northern Ireland) Ltd	Dungannon	30. 3.09E
G-KELL	Van's RV-6 *(Built J D Kelsall) (Lycoming O-320)*	PFA 181-12845		16. 5.95	R G Stephens	Kilrush, County Kildare	15. 6.09P
G-KELS	Van's RV-7 *(Built J D Kelsall)*	PFA 323-13801		22. 2.02	R G Stephens	Kilrush, County Kildare	2. 4.09P
G-KELV	Diamond DA.42 Twin Star	42.051	(G-CTCH), OE-VPI	8.11.05	K K Freeman	Plymouth	8.12.08E
G-KELY	Eurocopter AS350B Ecureuil	2668	G-WKRD, G-BUJG, G-HEAR, G-BUJG	21. 2.07	Kelly Sales and Services Donegal Ltd (Mountcharles, County Donegal)		18. 8.09E
G-KELZ	Van's RV-8 *(Built D J Hunt and J D Kelsall)*	PFA 303-13665	G-DJRV	9.11.06	J D Kelsall	Netherthorpe	9. 4.09E
G-KEMC	Grob G109	6024	D-KEMC	19.10.84	Norfolk Gliding Club Ltd	Tibenham	30.10.09E
G-KEMI	Piper PA-28-181 Archer III	2843180	N41493	28.10.98	Modern Air (UK) Ltd	Fowlmere	19.11.08E
G-KEMW	SOCATA TBM-850 *(Officially registered as TBM-700, amended 19. 6.08 and type showm as TBM-700N)*	475		30. 5.08	Ming Wai Lau	Biggin Hill	23. 9.09E
G-KEMY	Cessna 182T Skylane	18281206	N53397	27. 8.03	Allen Aircraft Rental Ltd	Cambridge	16.10.09E
G-KENB	Air Command 503 Commander *(Built K Brogden)*	PFA G/4-1153		7.11.89	K Brogden	(Heywood)	24. 9.93P
G-KENG	Rotorsport UK MT-03	RSUK/MT-03/011		22. 1.07	K A Graham	RAF Benson	27. 2.09P
G-KENI	RotorWay Executive 152 *(Built K Hassall) (RotorWay RW 152)*	3599		14. 3.89	P A Taylor (noted 10.08)	(Fenstanton, Cambs)	28.11.08P
G-KENM	Luscombe 8E Silvaire Deluxe *(Continental C90)*	2908	N21NK, N71481, NC71481	9. 1.91	M G Waters	Ranston Farm, Iwerne Courtney	22.12.09P
G-KENW	Robin DR.500-200i Président *(Officially regd as DR.400-500)*	0039		20. 2.03	K J White	Homefield Farm, Lingfield	28. 5.09E
G-KENZ	Rutan VariEze *(Built T N F Snead) (Continental O-200-A)*	PFA 074-10960		13. 8.04	K M McConnell	Belfast International	9. 5.09P
G-KEPE	Schempp-Hirth Nimbus 3DT	25	BGA5116-KHZ, D-KEPE	14.10.05	T Salter tr Nimbus Syndicate "PE"	Lasham	5. 2.08
G-KEPP	Rans S-6-ES Coyote II *(Built S Munday -pr.no.PFA 204-14308)*	xxxxx		19.10.04	J Carr	(Letterkenny, Ireland)	8. 3.09P
G-KESS	Glaser-Dirks DG-400	4-257	F-CGRH	15. 8.05	T Flude and N H T Cottrell	Ringmer	21. 8.09E
G-KEST	Steen Skybolt *(Built A Todd)*	1	G-BNKG, G-RATS, G-RHFI, N443AT	11. 6.91	B Tempest tr G-KEST Syndicate	Leicester	19.12.08P
G-KESY	Slingsby T.59D Kestrel 19	1839	BGA2902-ERY, EI-125, D-9253	1.11.07	A J Whiteman	Halesland	12. 2.09R
G-KETH	Agusta-Bell 206B-2 JetRanger II	8418	OO-HOP, PH-HAP, SX-HAP, (HB-XEX)	14.10.03	DAC Leasing Ltd	(Mannington, Norwich)	2. 6.09E
G-KEVB	Piper PA-28-181 Archer III	2843098	N9289E	29. 8.97	Palmair Ltd	Elstree	2.12.09E
G-KEVG	Rotorsport UK MT-03	RSUK/MT-03/031		14. 2.08	K J Robinson and R N Bodley	RAF Benson	21. 2.09P
G-KEVI	Avtech Jabiru J400 *(Built K A Allen - pr.no.PFA 325-14321)*	0xxx		19.10.04	K A Allen	Ludham	23. 6.08P
G-KEVS	P&M Aviation Quik GT450	8311		17. 9.07	K Mallin	Pound Green, Buttonoak, Bewdley	16. 9.08P
G-KEWT	UltraMagic M-90 Balloon (Hot Air)	90/66		27. 5.04	Kew Technik Group Ltd (Kew Technik titles)	Basingstoke	22. 7.09E
G-KEYS	Piper PA-23-250 Aztec F	27-7854052	N63909	6.10.78	R E Myson	Hardings Farm, Ingatestone	13.11.09E
G-KEYY	Cameron N-77 Balloon (Hot Air)	1748	G-BORZ	14. 6.88	B N Trowbridge	Allestree, Derby	22. 6.09E
G-KFAN	Scheibe SF25B Falke *(Stark-Stamo MS1500)*	46301	D-KFAN	14. 5.96	R G and J.A Boyes *(Stored 8.07)*	Trenchard Farm, Eggesford	29. 5.99

G-KFLY	Flight Design CTSW	06.11.04	G-LFLY	5. 9.07	K L Chorley tr G-KFLY Group	(Long Crendon)	12. 2.09P
	(Assembled P&M Aviation Ltd with c/n 8244)						
G-KFOX	Denney Kitfox Model 2	298		11.10.88	I R Lawrence and R Hampshire	Eaglescott	25. 6.09P
	(Built J Hannibal - pr.no.PFA 172-11447)						
G-KFRA	Piper PA-32-300 Cherokee Six	32-7840182	G-BGII	9. 9.97	M Drake and W Rankin tr West India Flying Group		
			N20879			Weston, Leixlip, County Kildare	4. 1.10E
G-KFZI	Williams KFZ-1 Tigerfalck	PFA 153-11054		2. 2.89	L R Williams	(Hirwaun, Aberdare)	
	(Built L R Williams - originally laid-down as Kestrel Sport c/n PFA 1530) (Continental C90)						
G-KGAO	Scheibe SF25C-2000 Falke	44386	D-KGAO	30. 7.99	C R Ellis tr Falke 2000 Group	Long Mynd	5. 9.09E
	(Limbach L2000)						
G-KGED	Campbell Cricket Mk.4	PFA G/03-1337		27. 2.04	K G Edwards	(Bridgwater)	
G-KHCC	Schempp-Hirth Ventus bT	34/215	BGA5224-KNH	3. 4.06	J L G McLane "LM"	Sutton Bank	3. 4.08
			D-KHCC				
G-KHEH	Grob G109B	6436	D-KHEH	27. 3.08	N A Tziros	RAF Halton	6. 4.09E
G-KHOM	Aeromot AMT-200S Super Ximango	200.091		5. 5.98	P R Desmond tr Bowland Ximango Group		
	(Rotax 912)					Blackpool	28. 6.09E
G-KHOP	Zenair CH.601HDS Zodiac	PFA 162-13561		14. 9.05	K Hopkins	Sleap	3.10.09P
	(Built K Hopkins) (Rotax 912ULS)						
G-KHRE	SOCATA Rallye 150SV Garnement	2931	F-GAYR	25. 3.82	D M Gale and K F Crumplin	Henstridge	9. 6.09E
G-KICK	Cyclone Airsports Pegasus Quantum 15-912						
		7679		28. 6.00	Graham van der Gaag	March	11. 7.09P
G-KIDD	Avtech Jabiru J430	0xxx	G-CEBB	26.10.06	R L Kidd	Panshanger	30. 8.08P
	(Built K D Pearce - pr.no.PFA 336-14541)						
G-KIDG	Robinson R44 Raven II	11836		23. 7.07	Skylink UK Ltd	Gamston	6. 8.09E
G-KIEV	DKBA AT 0300-0 Balloon (Hot-Air)	03		11. 3.08	P A Sweatman tr The Volga Balloon Team		
	(Built 1991 by Dolgoprudnenskogo Design Bureau of Automation)				"The Volga"	Coventry	
G-KIII	Extra EA.300/L	1246		2.11.06	Extra 200 Ltd	Denham	18.11.09E
G-KIMA	Zenair CH.601XL Zodiac	PFA 162B-14207		21. 3.06	K Martindale	Morgansfield, Fishburn	20. 5.09P
	(Built K Martindale) (Tri-cycle u/c)						
G-KIMB	Robin DR.300-140 Major	470	F-BPXX	23. 3.90	R M Kimbell	Rothwell Lodge Farm, Kettering	2. 6.09E
			F-WPXX				
G-KIMK	Partenavia P68B	27	G-BCPO	23. 2.01	M Konstantinovic	King's Farm, Thurrock	24. 4.09E
G-KIMM	Europa Aviation Europa XS	404		20. 7.99	P A D Clarke	Wadswick Manor Farm, Corsham	20.11.09P
	(Built P A D Clarke - pr.no.PFA 247-13404) (Rotax 912ULS) (Monowheel u/c)						
G-KIMY	Robin DR.400-140B Major	1401	PH-SRX	7. 6.00	S G Jones	Membury	4. 7.03T
G-KINE	Gulfstream AA-5A Cheetah	AA5A-0896	N27173	20. 7.82	Plane Talking Ltd	Blackbushe	27. 7.09E
G-KIPP	Thruster T 600N 450	1031-T600N-094		19.12.03	Compton Abbas Airfield Ltd	Compton Abbas	18.12.07P
G-KIRB	Europa Aviation Europa XS	474	G-OIZI	25.10.06	D E Steade	Croft Farm, Defford	
	(Built K S Duddy - pr.no.PFA 247-13615)						
G-KIRC	Pietenpol AirCamper	1008	G-BSVZ	20. 3.06	M K Kirk (Noted 1.07)		
	(Built H Challis) (Continental C85)		N3265			New Barn Farm, Barton Ashes, Crawley	
	(Regd as Pietenpol/Challis Chaffinch)						
G-KIRK	Piper J-3C-65 Cub	10536	F-BBQC	28. 2.79	M J Kirk	(Barry)	20. 1.09P
	(Regd with Frame No.12490,		French AF, 43-29245		"Liberty Girl"		
	but correct frame actually 10361)		(Ditched in Caribbean 75 miles NW Puerto Plata, Dominican Republic due to engine failure 16. 2.08)				
G-KISS	Rand Robinson KR-2	PFA 129-10899		2. 8.83	E A Rooney	(Whitstable)	
	(Built A C Waller) (Volkswagen 1835)						
G-KITF	Denney Kitfox	1156	N156BH	10. 5.89	T Wright	(Christow, Exeter)	2. 9.08P
	(Built J B Hartline) (Rotax 532)						
G-KITH	Alpi Pioneer 300	xxx		22. 9.06	K G Atkinson	Wombleton	
	(Built K G Atkinson - pr.no.PFA 330-14510)						
G-KITI	Pitts S-2E	002	N36BM	21. 6.90	B R Cornes "Super Turkey II"	Kemble	14. 7.08P
	(Built R Jones) (Lycoming IO-360)						
G-KITS	Europa Aviation Europa XS	468		13. 6.94	J R Evernden	Wellesbourne Mountford	26. 4.07P
	(Built Europa Aviation Ltd - pr.no.PFA 247-12844) (Mid-West AE.100R) (Tri-gear u/c)						
G-KITT	Curtiss TP-40M Kittyhawk	27490	F-AZPJ	4. 3.98	P A Teichman (As "49" in USAAF c/s) "Bengal Tiger"		
	(Officially regd with c/n 31423)		N1009N, N1233N, RCAF 840, 43-5802			North Weald	21. 6.09P
	(C/n 31423 was P-40N 43-23484/RCAF 877/N1009N (1) which was scrapped in 1965 when this identity adopted by RCAF 840)						
G-KITY	Denney Kitfox Model 2	467		18. 8.89	J P Jenkins tr Kitfox KFM Group		
	(Built T Ringshaw - pr.no.PFA 172-11565, officially regd as c/b 456) (IAME KFM 112)				South Lodge Farm, Widmerpool	11. 2.08P
G-KIZZ	Air Création 582(1)/Kiss 450	xxxxx		24. 6.04	J C A Page	(Great Gransden, Sandy)	16. 8.09P
	(Built P David - pr.no.BMAA HB/388 being Flylight kit comprising Trike s/n T04028 and Wing s/n A04068-4969)						
G-KKAM	Schleicher ASW 22BLE	22065	D-KKAM	24. 6.08	D P Taylor	Sutton Bank	16. 7.09E
	(Rotax 505A)		D-KBJL		(Originally regd as 20BLE-50R, amended 29. 7.08)		
G-KKCW	Flight Design CT2K	03-02-04-07		17. 6.03	K C Wigley and Co Ltd	(Shottle, Belper)	9. 5.09P
	(Assembled Mainair Sports Ltd with c/n 7964)						
G-KKER	Avtech Jabiru UL-450	0255		1.10.99	W K Evans	Swansea	28. 5.09P
	(Built K Kerr - pr.no.PFA 274A-13474)						
G-KKEV	de Havilland DHC-8-402	4201	C-FOUU	25. 4.08	Flybe Ltd "Kevin Keegan"	Exeter	
G-KLAS	Robinson R44 Raven II	11308		11. 7.06	Coates Aviation Ltd	(Ballymount, Dublin)	20. 7.09E
G-KLEM	Klemm Kl.35D	1979	N5050	3.08R	P R Holloway (Noted 8.07)	Old Warden	
G-KLNR	Hawker 400A	RK-552	N552EU	27. 1.09	Skydrift Ltd	Norwich	
G-KLNW	Cessna 510 Mustang	510-0157		2. 2.09	Skydrift Ltd	Norwich	
G-KLYE	Best Off Sky Ranger Swift 912S(1)			7. 5.08	D M Hepworth and B A Ritchie	Perth	
		SKRxxxx867					
	(Built D M Hepworth and B A Ritchie, pr. no BMAA HB/572)						
G-KLYN	Beech B200 Super King Air	BB-1931	G-CLCG	3.10.07	Klyne Air Ltd	Norwich	9.11.09E
			N37101				
G-KMCL	Cessna 152	15281565	N65462	17. 9.07	A A McLellan	North Weald	31. 1.09E
G-KMRV	Van's RV-9A	PFA 320-14093		17.11.04	G K Mutch	Hawarden	28. 2.09P
	(Built G K Mutch)						
G-KNAP	Piper PA-28-161 Warrior II	28-8116129	G-BIUX	15. 2.90	Keen Leasing (IoM) Ltd	Belfast International	28. 4.02T
			N9507N				
	(Crashed on take off Stevensons Field, Letterkenny, County Donegal 13. 7.99: wreck stored 2.01)						

Reg	Type	C/n	Prev ID	Date	Owner/Operator	Location	Date
G-KNCG	Piper PA-32-301FT Six 6x	3232017	SX-ARP N3064J, N9519N	5. 3.08	TGD Leasing tr Pilot Flight Training	Gloucestershire	13. 3.09E
G-KNEE	UltraMagic M-77C Balloon (Hot Air)	77/234		20. 6.03	M A Green	Rednal	13. 7.09E
G-KNEK	Grob G109B	6437	D-KNEK	22. 5.00	R A Winley tr Syndicate 109	Currock Hill	13. 6.09E
G-KNIB	Robinson R22 Beta II	3145		30.10.00	C G Knibb	Sywell	22. 1.10E
G-KNIX	Cameron Z-315 Balloon (Hot Air)	10728		11. 8.05	Cameron Flights Southern Ltd	Woodborough, Pewsey	27. 3.09E
G-KNOW	Piper PA-32-300 Cherokee Six	32-7840111	N9694C	21. 9.88	A S Bansal	Stapleford	13. 9.08E
G-KNYT	Robinson R44 Astro	0723		13. 3.00	C W and Keeley A M Bootman tr Aircol	Cranfield	8. 6.09E
G-KOBH	Schempp-Hirth Discus bT	154/549	D-KOBH	23.11.06	C F M Smith and K Neave "920"	Nympsfield	11. 1.08
G-KODA	Cameron O-77 Balloon (Hot Air)	1448		26. 3.87	K Stamurs	Jumprava, Latvia	27. 5.09E
G-KOFM	Glaser-Dirks DG-600/18M	6-66M16	D-KOFM	13. 7.99	A Mossman	Feshiebridge	28. 7.09E
G-KOHF	Schleicher ASK 14	14033	D-KOHF	4. 9.01	J Houlihan	Gowran Grange, Punchestown, County Kildare	24. 6.09E
G-KOKL	Hoffmann H 36 Dimona	36276	D-KOKL	4. 3.98	R Smith and R Stembrowicz	Rufforth	18. 4.09E
G-KOLB	Kolb Twinstar Mk.IIIA PFA 205-12228 (Built P A Akines) (Rotax 912-UL)			30. 6.93	J L Moar (Noted 5.05)	Wick	29. 9.03P
G-KOLI	PZL-110 Koliber 150	03900038		23. 7.90	J R Powell	Turweston	10. 9.09E
G-KONG	Slingsby T 67M-200 Firefly	2041	VR-HZP HKG-10, G-7-119	24. 3.94	R C Morton "293"	North Weald	10. 3.09E
G-KOOL	de Havilland DH.104 Sea Devon C 2/2	04220	"G-DOVE" VP967	12. 1.82	D S Hunt	Redhill	
G-KORN	Cameron Berentzen Bottle 70 SS Balloon (Hot Air)	1655		10. 5.88	A D, R S Kent, I M Martin and I Chadwick tr Balloon Preservation Flying Group "Berentzen"	Petworth	23. 6.00A
G-KOTA	Piper PA-28-236 Dakota	28-8011044	N8130R	23.12.88	D J Fravigar t/a JF Packaging	Clough Farm, Croft, Skegness	14. 4.08E
G-KOYY	Schempp-Hirth Nimbus 4T	9	BGA5205-KMN D-KOYY	28.10.05	R Kalin "Y7"	Rufforth	21. 5.08
G-KPAO	Robinson R44 Astro	0382	G-SSSS	19.11.98	Avonair Ltd	Shobdon	28.11.09E
G-KPEI	Cessna 560XL Citation	560-5785	N5260U	19. 6.08	Queensway Aviation Ltd	Belfast International	18. 6.09E
G-KPLG	Schempp-Hirth Ventus 2cxM	163	BGA5302-KRK D-KPLG	18.12.07	M F Lassan "111"	Talgarth	27. 2.09E
G-KPTT	SOCATA TB-20 Trinidad	1821	F-GRBI	13. 6.01	T C Smith	Southend	27. 8.09E
G-KRES	Stoddard-Hamilton Glasair Super II-SRG xxxx (Built G Kresfelder - pr.no.PFA 149-12984) (Lycoming IO-360)			12. 6.96	A D Murray	Perth	4. 6.09P
G-KRIB	Robinson R44 Raven II	12640		20. 1.09	Heli Air Ltd	Wellesbourne Mountford/Wycombe Air Park	
G-KRII	Rand Robinson KR-2 PFA 129-10934 (Built M R Cleveley)			4. 8.89	M R Cleveley	(All Saints South Elmham, Halesworth)	
G-KRMA	Cessna 425 Corsair	425-0003	D-INGA N98751	21.12.06	Speedstar Holdings Ltd	Wycombe Air Park	14. 4.09E
G-KRNW	Eurocopter EC.135 T2	0175		9. 7.01	Bond Air Services Ltd (Operated Cornwall Air Ambulance)	RAF St Mawgan	11. 7.09E
G-KRUZ	CZAW Sportcruiser LAA 338-14765 (Built A W Shellis and P Whittingham)			22. 5.08	A W Shellis and P Whittingham	(Birmingham)	
G-KSFR	Bombardier BD-100-1A10 Challenger 3000	20189	C-FQOI	30. 4.08	The Lily Partnership Ltd	London Stansted	29. 4.09E
G-KSHI	Beech A36 Bonanza	E-2353	D-EKDN N7241Y	7.11.08	Kashie Inns Ltd	(London N20)	20.11.09E
G-KSIR	Stoddard-Hamilton Glasair IIS RG	2151		15. 4.94	K M Bowen	Upfield Farm, Whitson	10. 6.09P
	(Built R Cayzer - pr.no.PFA 149-12137) (Lycoming IO-360)						
G-KSIX	Schleicher Ka 6E	4165	BGA1452-CDD	23. 6.08	C D Sterritt	Lasham	
G-KSKS	Cameron N-105 Balloon (Hot Air)	4963		21. 3.01	A Kaye t/a Kiss the Sky Ballooning "Kwik Kaye"	Irchester, Wellingborough	17. 9.09E
G-KSKY	Sky 77-24 Balloon (Hot Air)	170		15.10.99	J W Dale	Sinderhope, Hexham	9. 8.09E
G-KSSH	MD Helicopters MD.900 Explorer	900-00062	G-WMID N3063T	21. 9.07	Police Aviation Services Ltd (Operated Surrey Air Ambulance)	Dunstable	24. 9.09E
G-KSVB	Piper PA-24-260 Comanche B	24-4657	G-ENIU G-AVJU, N9199P, N10F	8.11.91	S Juggler	Stapleford	16. 6.09E
G-KSWI	Hughes 369E (Hughes 500)	0204E	G-OOCS G-OTDB, G-BXUR, HA-MSC	19. 4.07	K S Williams	(St Mellion, Saltash)	19. 8.09E
G-KTEE	Cameron V-77 Balloon (Hot Air)	2177		28.12.89	D C and N P Bull tr Katie Group "Katie"	Princes Risborough	8. 2.09E
G-KTKT	Sky 260-24 Balloon (Hot Air)	110		19. 5.98	T M Donnelly "Kit Kat"	Sprotbrough, Doncaster	16. 7.09E
G-KTTY	Denney Kitfox Model 3 PFA 172-12001 (Built L A James)		G-LESJ	28.11.05	S D Morris	(East Dean, Eastbourne)	25. 8.09P
G-KTWO	Cessna 182T Skylane	18281742	N282SS	23.11.06	S J G Mole	(Halesowen)	19.12.09E
G-KUIK	Mainair Sports Pegasus Quik	7990		17.10.03	I A Macadam	Harringe Court, Sellindge, Folkestone	24. 4.09P
G-KUKI	Robinson R22 Beta	1802	G-BTNB N23006	15. 8.02	R O'Grady	Hill Farm, Sproughton	30. 7.08E
G-KULA	Best Off Sky Ranger 912S(1) SKRxxxx353 (Built C R Mason - pr.no..BMAA HB/344)			26. 1.04	J Lane and A P Lambert	Lower Upham Farm, Chiseldon	24. 2.09P
G-KUPP	Flight Design CTSW	06.08.21		24.10.06	S J Peet	(Milton Keynes)	16.12.08P
	(Assembled P&M Aviation with c/n 8227)						
G-KURK	Piper J3C-65 Cub (L-4H-PI)	11527	G-BJTO F-BEGK, OO-AAL, 43-30236	6. 1.09	G V E Kirk	New Barn Farm, Barton Ashes, Crawley	16. 7.09P
	(Frame No.11352)				(To be shipped to USA for continuance of round-the-world trip)		
G-KUTU	QAC Quickie Q.2 PFA 094A-10758 (Built Quick Construction Group) (Limbach L2000)			8. 3.82	J Parkinson and R Nash	Wycombe Air Park	29. 4.86P
					(Damaged Cranfield 18.5.85: stored engineless 6.03)		
G-KUUI	Piper J-3C-65 Cub	17521	N2MD N70515, NC70515	25. 8.05	V S E Norman	Rendcomb	3.10.08E
G-KVBF	Cameron A-340HL Balloon (Hot Air)	4313		6. 4.98	Airxcite Ltd t/a Virgin Balloon Flights	Wembley	7. 4.09E

G-KVIP	Beech 200 Super King Air	BB-487	G-CBFS	17. 5.02	Capital Air Charter Ltd	Exeter	29. 5.09E
			G-PLAT, N8PY, VH-PIL, N198SC, PT-OYR, N40QN, VH-NIC, N40QN, N400N, N243KA				
G-KWAK	Scheibe SF25C Falke	44581	D-KWAK	8. 1.03	Mendip Gliding Club Ltd	Halesland	6. 2.08E
	(Rotax 912-A)						
G-KWAX	Cessna 182E Skylane	18253808	N9902	18. 5.78	D Shaw	Derby	6. 3.09E
			YV-T-PTS, N2808Y				
G-KWIC	Mainair Sports Pegasus Quik	7962		25. 6.03	T Southwell	(Spalding)	21. 5.09P
G-KWIN	Dassault Falcon 2000EX	052	F-WWMA	29. 4.05	Quinn Aviation Ltd	Enniskillen	23. 5.09E
G-KWKI	QAC Quickie Q.200	PFA 094-12158		22.10.91	R Greatrex	Colthrop Manor, Thatcham	28.10.08P
	(Built D G Greatrex and B M Jackson) (Continental O-200-A)						
G-KWKR	P&M Aviation QuikR	8412		7. 1.09	L G White	Finmere	6. 1.10P
G-KWLI	Cessna 421C Golden Eagle	421C0168	G-DARR	13.11.98	Langley Aviation Ltd	Gamston	3. 3.09E
			G-BNEZ, N87386				
G-KXXI	Schleicher ASK 21	21024	SE-TVH	6. 1.09	R C and C G Bell	Enstone	
G-KYAK	SPP Yakovlev Yak C-11	171101	F-AZQI	21.12.78	M Gainza (As "36" (white) in Soviet AF c/s)		
			G-KYAK, F-AZHQ, G-KYAK, IDF/AF, Egyptian AF 590, Czech AF Little Gransden 12. 3.09P				
G-KYLE	Thruster T 600N 450	0053-T600N-113		3. 6.05	C E Walsh tr MKS Syndicate	Newtownards	2. 6.09P
G-KYTE	Piper PA-28-161 Warrior II	28-8216043	G-BRRN	20. 1.06	G Whitlow and I C Barlow	Wycombe Air Park	16. 3.09E
			N84533				

G-LAAA - G-LZZZ

G-LAAC	Cameron C-90 Balloon (Hot Air)	10778		27. 1.06	Directorate Army Aviation	AAC Middle Wallop	9. 6.09E
G-LABS	Europa Aviation Europa	049		1. 3.94	C T H Pattinson	Bicester	21. 9.09P
	(Built C T H Pattinson - pr.no.PFA 247-12595) (Rotax 912-UL) (Monowheel u/c)						
G-LACA	Piper PA-28-161 Cherokee Warrior II	N44883		22. 6.90	Upperstack Ltd t/a LAC Flying School	Barton	11. 4.09E
		28-7816036			(Operated Lancashire Aero Club)		
G-LACB	Piper PA-28-161 Warrior II	28-8216035	N8450A	12. 6.90	Upperstack Ltd t/a LAC Flying School	Barton	15. 6.09E
					(Operated Lancashire Aero Club)		
G-LACD	Piper PA-28-181 Archer III	2843157	G-BYBG	11.11.98	Central Aircraft Leasing Ltd	Wolverhampton	9.12.09E
			N47BK				
G-LACE	Europa Aviation Europa	256		15. 4.96	J H Phillingham	(Benson, Wallingford)	
	(Built J H Phillingham - pr.no.PFA 247-12962) (Monowheel u/c)						
G-LACI	Cessna 172S Skyhawk	172S9978	N2310C	28.11.05	L Endresz	Blackpool	13. 2.09E
G-LACR	Denney Kitfox	PFA 172-11945		4.12.90	C M Rose	(Scone)	
	(Built C M Rose)				(Under construction 2.06)		
G-LADD	Enstrom 480	5037		20. 5.99	R C G Davidson		
						Kilmaddy, Dungannon, County Tyrone	1. 8.08E
G-LADS	Rockwell Commander 114	14314	N4994W	6.12.90	D F Soul	Emberton, Olney	5. 3.09E
			(N114XT), N4994W				
G-LADZ	Enstrom 480	5001	N480E	31.10.05	Falcon Helicopters Ltd	Barton	27. 6.09E
			HB-XUX, N480E				
G-LAFT	Diamond DA.40D Star	D4.193		28. 3.06	Atlantic Flight Training Ltd	Coventry	11. 4.09E
G-LAGR	Cameron N-90 Balloon (Hot Air)	1628		25. 1.88	J R Clifton	Nelson, New Zealand	11.10.03A
G-LAIN	Robinson R22 Beta	1992		7. 2.92	Patriot Aviation Ltd	Cranfield	5. 9.08E
G-LAIR	Stoddard-Hamilton Glasair IIS FT	2106		12. 9.91	A I O'Broin and S T Raby		
	(Built D L Swallow and S T Raby - pr.no.PFA 149-11923)					Grange Farm, Woodwalton	24 .9.08P
G-LAKE	Lake LA-250 Renegade	70	(EI-PJM)	12. 7.88	Educational Programmes International Ltd		
	(Built Aerofab Inc)		G-LAKE, N8415B			Biggin Hill	6. 2.09E
G-LAKI	CEA Jodel DR.1050 Sicile	534	G-JWBB	12.11.79	V Panteli	Clipgate Farm, Denton	15. 7.09E
			G-LAKI, F-BLZD				
G-LAMM	Europa Aviation Europa	244		20.11.95	S A Lamb	(Paddock Wood, Tonbridge)	
	(Built S A Lamb - pr.no.PFA 247-12941) (Monowheel u/c)						
G-LAMP	Cameron Lightbulb 110 SS Balloon (Hot Air)			21. 7.00	S A Lacey	Norwich Common, Wymondham	21. 6.08A
		4899					
G-LAMS	Reims Cessna F152 II	F15201431	N54558	23. 6.88	APB Leasing Ltd	Sleap	2.12.09E
G-LANE	Reims Cessna F172N Skyhawk II	F17201853		27. 6.79	G C Bantin	Sproatley	29. 6.09E
G-LANS	Cessna 182T Skylane	18281910	N11827	30. 5.07	AK Enterprises Ltd "Betty Boop"		
						Wycombe Air Park	27. 6.09E
G-LAOK	IAV Bacau Yakovlev Yak-52	877404	LY-AOK	22. 1.03	I F Vaughan and J P Armitage (As "74-JA" and "62-IV")		
			DOSAAF 16 (yellow)			Nottingham City-Tollerton	20. 9.08P
G-LAOL	Piper PA-28RT-201 Arrow IV	28R-7918211	D-EAOL	6.10.99	Goodwood Road Racing Company Ltd "19"		
			N2903Y			Goodwood	17. 3.09E
G-LAOR	Raytheon Hawker 800XP	258384	N955MC	2. 3.04	Select Plant Hire Company Ltd	Southend	26. 3.09E
			N23455, TC-MDC, N23455				
G-LAPN	Avid Aerobat	PFA 189-12146		4. 3.93	I A P Harper	Croft Farm, Defford	3.10.06P
	(Built R M Shorter) (Jabiru 2200)						
G-LAPS	Lindstrand LTL.203T Balloon (Gas Filled)			13. 4.07	Lindstrand Aeroplatforms Ltd	Leeds Castle	30. 4.09E
		HF042					
G-LARA	Robin DR.400-180 Régent	2050		14. 2.91	K D and C A Brackwell	Goodwood	8. 5.09E
G-LARE	Piper PA-39 Twin Comanche C/R	39-16	N8861Y	20. 2.91	Glareways (Neasden) Ltd	Biggin Hill	26. 4.08E
G-LARK	Helton Lark 95	9517	N5017J	3.12.85	J Fox	Wycombe Air Park	29. 3.09P
	(Continental C90)						
G-LARR	Eurocopter AS.350B3 Ecureuil	4137	F-WWXN	15. 1.07	Larsen Manufacturing Ltd	(Belfast)	28. 3.09E
G-LARY	Robinson R44 Raven II	10255	(EI-)	20. 4.07	E and N Salini LLP	(Ammanford)	7. 7.09E
			G-LARY, G-CCRZ				
G-LASN	Best Off Sky Ranger 912(2)	SKRxxxx479		19. 7.04	L C F Lasne	Derryogue	27. 4.08P
	(Built L C F Lasne - pr.no.BMAA HB/396)						
G-LASR	Stoddard-Hamilton Glasair Super II-SRG	2027		8. 1.90	G Lewis	(Heswall, Wirral)	
	(Built P Taylor and G Lewis)						
G-LASS	Rutan VariEze	PFA 074-10209		20. 9.78	J Mellor	Sleap	14. 6.08P
	(Built Calvert, Foreman and O'Hara) (Continental O-200-A)						
G-LASU	Eurocopter EC.135 T2	0228	D-HTSH	3. 9.02	Lancashire Constabulary Air Support Unit	Warton	15.10.11S

G-LAVE	Cessna 172R Skyhawk	17280663	G-BYEV N2377J, N41297	10. 3.99	M L Roland	Southend	10. 5.09E
G-LAXY	Everett Gyroplane Series 3 (Built Everett Gyroplanes Ltd - pr.no.PFA G/03-1233)	035		17. 2.94	E J Barton	(Bramley, Tadley)	
G-LAZA	Laser Lazer Z200 (Built M Hammond) (Lycoming AEIO-360)	PFA 123-12682		15. 6.95	D G Jenkins	(Stanton, Bury St Edmunds)	9. 2.09P
G-LAZL	Piper PA-28-161 Warrior II	28-8116216	D-EAZL N9536N	9. 6.99	C P Awdry t/a P and J Awdry and Son	Old Sarum	21. 8.09E
G-LAZR	Cameron O-77 Balloon (Hot Air)	2240		6. 3.90	Laser Holdings (UK) Ltd	Worcester	10. 6.97A
G-LAZZ	Stoddard-Hamilton GlaStar (Built G K Brunwin and A N Evans) (Lycoming O-320) (Tri-cycle u/c)	PFA 295-13059		31.10.96	A N Evans	Ashcroft Fam, Winsford	9. 1.10P
G-LBDC	Bell 206B-3 JetRanger III	3806	N206GF (G-), N509KK, JA9448, N206JG, N3186Z	17. 3.06	Freshair (UK) Ltd	Field Farm, Launton, Bicester	30. 3.09E
G-LBLI	Lindstrand LBL 69A Balloon (Hot Air)	010		4.11.92	N M Gabriel	Kimberley, Nottingham	30. 6.07A
G-LBMM	Piper PA-28-161 Cherokee Warrior II	28-7816440	N6940C	28.11.89	Flexi-Soft Ltd	Wellesbourne Mountford	21. 6.09E
G-LBRC	Piper PA-28RT-201 Arrow IV	28R-7918051	N2245P	20. 7.88	D J V Morgan	Wolverhampton	28. 3.09E
G-LBUK	Lindstrand LBL 77A Balloon (Hot Air)	922		15. 5.03	Lindstrand Hot Air Balloons Ltd (Lindstrand titles)	Oswestry	19. 8.09E
G-LBUZ	Evektor EV-97A Eurostar (Built D P Tassart - pr.no.PFA 315-14425)	2004-2312		15. 7.05	D P Tassart	Scotland Farm, Hook	14. 8.09P
G-LCGL	Comper CLA.7 Swift replica (Built J M Greenland) (Pobjoy Niagara 1A)	PFA 103-11089		1.7.92	J M Greenland	Blackacre Farm, Holt, Trowbridge	25. 4.09P
G-LCKY	Flight Design CTSW (Assembled P&M Aviation Ltd with c/n 8274)	07.05.04		9. 7.07	A G A Edwards	Perranporth	23. 7.09P
G-LCMW	TL 2000 Sting Carbon (Built L Chadwick and M J White)	LAA 347-14787		2. 4.08	L Chadwick and M J White	Sleap	
G-LCOC	Britten-Norman BN-2A Mk.III-1 Trislander	366	G-BCCU 4X-CCK, G-BCCU, 9L-LAR, G-BCCU, (LN-VIV)	30. 7.01	AirX Ltd tr Blue Islands	Alderney	6. 1.10E
G-LCPL	Aérospatiale AS.365N2 Dauphin 2	6393	PT-YIF ZS-RAZ, F-WYMI	8. 4.05	Charterstyle Ltd	(Kingswinford)	4. 8.09E
G-LCUB	Piper PA-18 Super Cub 95 (L-18C-PI)	18-1631	G-AYPR French Army 18-1631, 51-15631	9. 2.07	The Tiger Club 1990 Ltd	Headcorn	4. 2.11S
G-LCYA	Dassault Falcon 900EX	105	F-WWFC	5. 8.02	Airport Management and Investment Ltd	London City	4. 8.09E
G-LCYB	British Aerospace Avro 146-RJ85	E2383	OH-SAH	25. 1.08	BA Cityflyer Ltd	London City	7. 4.09E
G-LCYC	British Aerospace Avro 146-RJ85	E2385	OH-SAI G-6-385	24. 4.08	BA Cityflyer Ltd	London City	14. 5.09E
G-LDAH	Best Off Sky Ranger 912(2) (Built A S Haslam and L Dickinson - pr.no.BMAA HB/241)	SKR0209216		8.10.02	P D Brookes and L Dickinson	Long Marston	17. 9.08P
G-LDER	Schleicher ASW 22	22027	BGA3261-FGY D-3527	1. 2.08	D Starer and P Shrosbree "527"	Dunstable	19. 3.08
G-LDFM	Cessna 560XL Citation Excel	560-5242	TC-LMA	17. 2.05	Granard Ltd	Biggin Hill	17. 2.09E
G-LDVO	Europa Aviation Europa XS (Built D J Park, pr. no PFA 247-13254)	371		7. 7.08	D J Park	(Cheadle)	
G-LDWS	SAN Jodel D 150 Mascaret	48	G-BKSS F-BMFC	13. 2.04	D H Wilson-Spratt (Noted 10.06)	Ronaldsway	
G-LDYS	Thunder Ax6-56Z Balloon (Hot Air) (Originally regd as Colt 56A)	347		18. 5.81	M J Myddelton "Gladys"	Bristol	18. 3.09E
G-LEAA	Cessna 510 Citation Mustang	510-0072	N4082U	29. 4.08	London Executive Aviation Ltd	London Stansted	7. 5.09E
G-LEAB	Cessna 510 Citation Mustang	510-0073	N4082Y	29. 4.08	London Executive Aviation Ltd	London Stansted	7. 5.09E
G-LEAC	Cessna 510 Citation Mustang	510-0075	N4048A	4. 6.08	London Executive Aviation Ltd	Biggin Hill	4. 6.09E
G-LEAF	Reims Cessna F406 Caravan II	F406-0018	EI-CKY PH-ALN, OO-TIW, F-WZDX	7. 3.96	Reconnaissance Ventures Ltd	Coventry	20. 5.09E
G-LEAH	Alpi Pioneer 300 (Built J C Ferguson - pr.no.PFA 330-14497) (Rotax 912 ULS)	174		11. 1.06	A Bortolan	North Weald	28. 7.09P
G-LEAI	Cessna 510 Citation Mustang	510-0052		15. 1.08	London Executive Aviation Ltd	Farnborough	21. 1.10E
G-LEAM	Piper PA-28-236 Dakota	28-8011061	G-BHLS N35650	1. 7.80	A Incisa tr G-LEAM Group	Elstree	14. 8.09E
G-LEAP	Pilatus Britten-Norman BN-2T Islander	2183	G-BLND	19. 8.87	Skydive Swansea Ltd	Swansea	24. 4.09E
G-LEAS	Sky 90-24 Balloon (Hot Air)	158		4. 5.99	C I Humphrey(LNG The Leasing Group titles)	Tilehurst, Reading	9. 7.09E
G-LEAU	Cameron N-31 Balloon (Hot Air)	761		5. 8.81	P L Mossman "Perrier"	Trellech, Monmouth	25. 4.09E
G-LEBE	Europa Aviation Europa (Built P Atkinson - pr.no.PFA 247-12927) (Wilksch WAM-120) (Monowheel u/c)	237		17. 5.01	P Atkinson	(Carnforth)	
G-LECA	Aérospatiale AS.355F1 Ecureuil 2	5043	G-BNBK C-GBKH	6. 2.87	Western Power Distribution (South West) PLC	Bristol	24. 7.09E
G-LEDR	Westland SA.341C Gazelle HT.2	1081	G-CBSB XW857	18.12.06	R D Leader	Bourne Park, Hurstbourne Tarrant	3. 4.09P
G-LEED	Denney Kitfox Model 2 (Built G T Leedham - pr.no.PFA 172-11577)	450		24. 4.91	S J Walker	Shobdon	22. 9.09P
G-LEEE	Avtech Jabiru UL-450 (Built L E G Fekete - pr.no.PFA 274A-13516)	0293		18. 1.00	L E G Fekete and J P Mimnagh	(Ellesmere Port and Neston)	14. 7.09P
G-LEEH	UltraMagic M-90 Balloon (Hot Air)	90/79		3. 8.05	Sport Promotion SRL (Lee titles)	La Morra, Piedmont, Italy	17. 8.09E
G-LEEK	Reality Escapade (Built S J Pugh-Jones, W J Jones and P B Bishop)	LAA 345-14843		27.11.08	P B Bishop tr Phoenix Group	(Llanelli)	
G-LEEN	Aero Designs Pulsar XP (Built D F Gaughan)	PFA 202-12147	G-BZMP G-DESI	16. 7.01	R B Hemsworth	Eaglescott	12. 6.07P
G-LEES	Glaser-Dirks DG-400	4-238		4.10.88	J Bradley	Trenchard Lines, Upavon	9. 4.09E
G-LEEZ	Bell 206L-1 LongRanger	45761	G-BPCT D-HDBB, N3175G	22. 1.92	Pennine Helicopters Ltd	Oakdene Farm, Saddleworth	27.1.10E
G-LEGG	Reims Cessna F182Q Skylane II	F18200145	G-GOOS	26. 6.96	W A L Mitchell	Dunsfold	6. 4.09E
G-LEGO	Cameron O-77 Balloon (Hot Air)	1975		14. 4.89	P M Traviss "Jigsaw II"	Yarm	10. 5.09E

Reg	Type	C/n	Prev id	Date	Owner	Location	Code
G-LEGY	Flight Design CTLS	F-08-09-13		13. 1.09	P J Clegg	Tarn Farm, Cockerham	
G-LEIC	Reims Cessna FA152 Aerobat	FA1520416		16. 9.86	The Leicestershire Aero Club Ltd	Leicester	31. 8.09E
G-LELE	Lindstrand LBL 31A Balloon (Hot Air)	806		16. 8.01	S A Lacey	Norwich Common, Wymondham	25. 4.09E
G-LEMM	UltraMagic Z-90 Balloon (Hot-Air)	90/102		20.10.08	M Marangoni	Bagnacavallo, Italy	10.11.09E
G-LEMO	Cessna U206G Stationair 6	U20605407	LN-ALX N6300U	15.11.05	Garden House Properties Ltd	East Winch	27. 1.10E
G-LENF	Mainair Blade 912S	1362-0104-7-W1157		18. 2.04	G D Fuller	North Coates	20. 4.09P
G-LENI	Aérospatiale AS.355F1 Ecureuil 2	5311	G-ZFDB G-BLEV	9. 8.95	Grid Defence Systems Ltd	Wycombe Air Park	21. 4.09E
G-LENN	Cameron V-56 Balloon (Hot Air)	1833		29. 9.88	D J Groombridge	Portishead, Bristol	29. 4.09E
G-LENS	Thunder Ax7-77Z Balloon (Hot Air)	168		3.11.78	R S Breakwell	Bridgnorth	11.10.09E
G-LENX	Cessna 172N Skyhawk II	17272232	G-BMVJ N9347E	15. 2.02	M J Folkard	Cranfield	27. 5.09E
G-LEOD	Pietenpol Aircamper (Built I D McCleod)	PFA 047-13499		23.11.05	I D McLeod "Dame Flora"	(Farthing Corner)	
G-LEOS	Robin DR.400-120 Dauphin 2+2	1884		29.11.88	R J O Walker	Gamston	6. 8.09E
G-LESZ	Skystar Kitfox Model 5 (Built L A James) (Rotec R2800)	PFA 172C-12822		25.10.02	D A Lord	Shoreham	10. 7.09P
G-LEVI	Aeronca 7AC Champion	7AC-4001	N85266 NC85266	17. 4.90	J P A Pumphrey tr G-LEVI Group (Carries "NC85266" on fin)	White Waltham	13. 5.08P
G-LEVO	Robinson R44 Raven II	11444		29. 9.06	Leavesley Aviation Ltd	Tatenhill	23.10.09E
G-LEXI	Cameron N-77 Balloon (Hot Air)	438		26.10.78	T Gilbert (Rolls Royce & Jaguar titles)	Hutton, Weston-super-Mare	9. 8.09E
G-LEXX	Van's RV-8 (Built A A Wordsworth)	PFA 303-13896		11. 4.02	S Emery	Damyn's Hall, Upminster	1.10.08P
G-LEXY	Van's RV-8 (Built A A Wordsworth)	PFA 303-14756		15. 1.08	A A Wordsworth	(Huthwaite, Sutton-in-Ashfield)	
G-LEZE	Rutan Long-EZ (Built K G M Loyal)	PFA 074A-10702		31. 3.82	Bill Allen's Autos Ltd	Gloucestershire	5.11.01P
G-LFIX	Vickers Supermarine 509 Spitfire Tr.9 (C/n is firewall plate no)	CBAF.8463	IAC162 G-15-175, ML407	1. 2.80	C S Grace (As "ML407:OU-V" in RAF 485 Sqdn c/s) "Nicholson Leslie"	Bentwaters	15. 4.09P
G-LFOR	Piper J-3C-65 Cub	11876	G-BHZA F-BBIN, 44-79580	11.12.07	A Hoskins and J A Gowdy	(Storrington, Pulborough)	24. 2.84P
G-LFSA	Piper PA-38-112 Tomahawk	38-78A0430	G-BSFC N9739N	22.10.90	Liverpool Flying School Ltd	Liverpool	8. 5.09E
G-LFSB	Piper PA-38-112 Tomahawk	38-78A0072	G-BLYC D-ELID, N9715N	20.10.94	J D Burford	Swansea	18. 7.09E
G-LFSC	Piper PA-28-140 Cherokee Cruiser	28-7425005	G-BGTR OY-BGO, SE-GDS	4. 9.95	P A Harvie	Mount Airey Farm, South Cave	21. 7.09E
G-LFSD	Piper PA-38-112 Tomahawk II	38-82A0046	G-BNPT G-LFSD, N91522	21.10.96	Liverpool Flying School Ltd	Liverpool	13. 7.08E
G-LFSG	Piper PA-28-180 Cherokee E	28-5799	G-AYAA N11C	19. 6.00	Liverpool Flying School Ltd	Liverpool	26. 2.09E
G-LFSH	Piper PA-38-112 Tomahawk	38-78A0352	G-BOZM N6247A	16. 7.01	Liverpool Flying School Ltd	Liverpool	27. 6.09E
G-LFSI	Piper PA-28-140 Cherokee C	28-26850	G-AYKV N11C	14. 7.89	M J Green	Humberside	8. 6.09E
G-LFSJ	Piper PA-28-161 Warrior II	28-7916536	G-BPHE N2911D	4.11.02	R Murgatroyd t/a FlyBPL.com	Blackpool	28. 9.09E
G-LFSK	Piper PA-28-161 Cherokee Warrior II	28-7816599	SE-IAD	23. 4.04	Cloud 9 Aviation (Leasing) Ltd	(Sheffield City)	6. 9.08E
G-LFSM	Piper PA-38-112 Tomahawk	38-78A0449	G-BWNR N2361E	21. 9.04	Liverpool Flying School Ltd	Liverpool	23. 6.09E
G-LFSN	Piper PA-38-112 Tomahawk	38-78A0073	G-BNYV N9364T	4.12.06	Liverpool Flying School Ltd	Liverpool	17. 9.09E
G-LFVB	Vickers Supermarine 349 Spitfire LF.V	CBAF.2403	8070M 5377M, EP120	9. 5.94	Patina Ltd (As "EP120:AE-A" in 402 Sqdn c/s) "City of Winnipeg" (Operated The Fighter Collection)	Duxford	20. 4.09P
G-LGAR	Bombardier Learjet Model 60	60-286	N262DB (D-CSIS), N4003K	5. 4.06	TAG Aviation (UK) Ltd	Farnborough	4. 4.09E
G-LGCA	Robin DR.400-180R Remorqueur	1686	HB-KAP	17. 2.04	London Gliding Club Proprietary Ltd	Dunstable	3.12.09E
G-LGCB	Robin DR.400-180R Remorqueur	1990	D-EHRA	28. 4.05	London Gliding Club Proprietary Ltd	Dunstable	3.12.09E
G-LGCC	Robin DR.400-180R Remorqueur	1021	G-BNXI SE-FNI	21. 8.07	London Gliding Club Proprietary Ltd	Dunstable	4.12.09E
G-LGEZ	Rutan Long-EZ (Built P C Elliott)	PFA 074A-11361		26. 7.06	P C Elliott	Dunsfold	28 .6.09P
G-LGKO	Bombardier CL-600-2B16 (CL-604 Challenger)	5610	C-FEFW C-GLXU	2.11.05	TAG Aviation (UK) Ltd	Farnborough	3.11.09E
G-LGNA	SAAB-Scania SF.340B	340B-199	N592MA SE-F99	11. 6.99	Loganair Ltd	Glasgow	14. 6.09E
G-LGNB	SAAB-Scania SF.340B	340B-216	N595MA SE-G16	8. 7.99	Loganair Ltd	Glasgow	8. 7.09E
G-LGNC	SAAB-Scania SF.340B	340B-318	SE-KXC F-GTSF, EC-GMI, SE-KXC, F-GMVZ, SE-C18	9. 6.00	Loganair Ltd	Glasgow	18. 6.09E
G-LGND	SAAB-Scania SF.340B	340B-169	G-GNTH N588MA, SE-F69	7. 9.01	Loganair Ltd	Glasgow	4. 2.09E
G-LGNE	SAAB-Scania SF.340B	340B-172	G-GNTI N589MA, SE-F72	31. 8.01	Loganair Ltd	Glasgow	5. 2.10E
G-LGNF	SAAB-Scania SF.340B	340B-192	N192JE G-GNTJ, N591MA, SE-F92	8. 8.02	Loganair Ltd	Glasgow	7. 8.09E
G-LGNG	SAAB-Scania SF.340B	340B-327	SE-C27 VH-CMH, SE-C27	16.12.02	Loganair Ltd	Glasgow	17.12.09E
G-LGNH	SAAB-Scania SF.340B	340B-333	SE-C33 VH-XDA, F-GMVX, SE-C33	28. 5.04	Loganair Ltd	Glasgow	30. 5.09E

Reg	Type	C/n	Prev id	Date	Owner/Operator	Location	Expiry
G-LGNI	SAAB-Scania SF.340B	340B-160	SE-F60	4. 5.05	Loganair Ltd	Glasgow	3. 5.09E
			ER-SGC, HB-AKA, SE-F60				
G-LGNJ	SAAB-Scania SF.340B	340B-173	SE-F73	27. 5.05	Loganair Ltd	Glasgow	26. 5.09E
			F-GPKD, HB-AKD, SE-F73				
G-LGNK	SAAB-Scania SF.340B	340B-185	SE-F85	7. 7.05	Loganair Ltd	Glasgow	10. 7.09E
			D-CDAU, F-GPKG, (YR-VGT), F-GPKG, HB-AKG, SE-F85				
G-LGNL	SAAB-Scania SF.340B	340B-246	SE-G46	2. 1.08	Loganair Ltd	Glasgow	2. 1.09E
			N869DC, XA-TUM, N354BE, SE-G46				
G-LGNM	SAAB-Scania SF.340B	340B-187	SE-F87	18. 3.08	Loganair Ltd	Glasgow	24. 3.09E
			N347BE, XA-TUN, N347BE, SE-F87				
G-LGNN	SAAB-Scania SF.340B	340B-197	SE-F97	30. 4.08	Loganair Ltd	Glasgow	30. 4.09E
			N350BE, XA-ASM, N350BE, SE-F97				
G-LGOC	Aero AT-3 R100	AT3.020	(F-GURG)	9. 3.07	London Transport Flying Club Ltd	Fairoaks	1. 5.09E
G-LGTE	Boeing 737-3Y0	24908	TC-SUP	25. 1.01	British Airways PLC	London Gatwick	26. 3.09E
			TC-IAC, CS-TIE				
G-LGTF	Boeing 737-382	24450	N115GB	7. 3.01	British Airways PLC	London Gatwick	30. 4.09E
G-LGTG	Boeing 737-3Q8	24470	N696BJ	4. 4.01	British Airways PLC	London Gatwick	14. 6.09E
			SX-BFT, N470KB, PK-GWD				
G-LGTH	Boeing 737-3Y0	23924	OO-LTV	4. 4.01	British Airways PLC (wfs 15.12.08)	Glasgow	8. 6.09E
			XA-SEM, G-BNGL				
G-LGTI	Boeing 737-3Y0	23925	OO-LTY	2. 4.01	British Airways PLC (wfs 1.09)	London Gatwick	25. 7.09E
			XA-SEO, G-BNGM				
G-LHCA	Robinson R22 Beta II	2947	N299FA	28.10.02	London Helicopter Centres Ltd	Redhill	6.12.09E
G-LHCB	Robinson R22 Beta II	3241	G-SIVX	14. 6.04	London Helicopter Centres Ltd	Redhill	1. 8.09E
G-LHCC	Eurocopter EC.120B Colibri	1379	RP-C2579	15. 6.06	B Orr and D M McGarrity (Ballynure/Newtonabbey)		27 .7.09E
			F-OISB, F-WWPC				
G-LHCI	Bell 47G-5	2639	G-SOLH	10.12.07	Leamington Hobby Centre Ltd		
			G-AZMB, CF-NJW			Wellesbourne Mountford	26. 5.11S
G-LHEL	Aérospatiale AS.355F2 Ecureuil 2	5462	N42AT	29. 3.04	Beechview Aviation Ltd	Toome	24. 5.09E
			N70PB				
G-LHMS	Eurocopter EC.120B Colibri	1442	N120CL	9. 5.07	Hadley Helicopters Ltd	Elstree	9. 5.09E
G-LHXL	Robinson R44 Raven	1702	N66PH	16. 5.08	Lloyd Helicopters Europe Ltd	Redhill	1. 7.09E
G-LIBB	Cameron V-77 Balloon (Hot Air)	2463		21. 6.91	R J Mercer	Belfast	30. 8.09E
G-LIBL	Glasflügel H201B Standard Libelle	119	BGA3969-HHY	24.10.07	P A Pearson "T"	(Whyteleafe)	18. 3.08
			SE-TIU				
G-LIBS	Hughes 369HS (Hughes 500)	43-0469S	N9147F	20. 8.85	R J H Strong	(Vagg Hill, Yeovil)	28. 6.09E
G-LIBY	Glasflügel H201B Standard Libelle	175	BGA1629-CLN	29.11.07	R P Hardcastle	Rufforth	24. 6.08
G-LICK	Cessna 172N Skyhawk II	17270631	N172AG	17. 7.02	Sky Back Ltd	Cranfield	21.11.08E
			G-LICK, G-BNTR, N739LQ				
G-LIDA	Hoffman HK 36R Super Dimona	36355		15. 4.92	Bidford Airfield Ltd	Bidford	17. 3.09E
G-LIDE	Piper PA-31-350 Navajo Chieftain	31-7852156	(G-VIDE)	26.10.78	Keen Leasing (IoM) Ltd	Ronaldsway	27.10.08E
			N27800				
G-LIDY	Schleicher ASW 27B	27132	BGA4791-JUL	25. 9.07	T Stuart	Nympsfield	13.12.07
G-LIFE	Thunder Ax6-56Z Balloon (Hot Air)	135		11. 1.78	D P Hopkins t/a Lakeside Lodge Golf Centre		
					"Golden Delicious"	Pidley, Huntingdon	24. 8.07A
G-LILA	Bell 206L-1 LongRanger	45548	G-NEUF	22. 3.06	Lothian Helicopters Ltd	(Manston)	11.10.08E
			G-BVVV, D-HUGO, OE-KXT, C-GLMM (Operated Helicharter?)				
G-LILP	Europa Aviation Europa XS	487		22. 5.02	G L Jennings	(Shoreham-by-Sea)	
	(Built G L Jennings - pr.no.PFA 247-13802) (Monowheel u/c)						
G-LILY	Bell 206B-3 JetRanger III	4107	G-NTBI	14. 3.95	T S Brown	Goodwood	16. 6.09E
			C-FIJD				
G-LIMO	Bell 206L-1 LongRanger	45476	N5742H	12. 6.03	Heliplayer Ltd	(Sheffield City)	3. 9.09E
			G-LIMO, N5742H				
G-LIMP	Cameron C-80 Balloon (Hot Air)	10391		4. 6.03	T and B Chamberlain	Melbourne, York	22. 7.09E
G-LINC	Hughes 369HS (Hughes 500)	43-0467S	C-FDUZ	14. 5.87	Wavendon Social Housing Ltd	Sywell	28. 2.07T
			CF-DUZ				
	(Heavy landing Sywell 2. 1.06 and suffered substantial damage: noted wrecked 10.07)						
G-LINE	Eurocopter AS.355N Ecureuil 2	5566		22. 3.94	National Grid Electricity Transmission PLC	Oxford	21. 5.09E
G-LINN	Europa Aviation Europa XS	598		20. 8.04	T Pond	Yeatsall Farm, Abbots Bromley	13. 5.09P
	(Built T Pond - pr.no.PFA 247-14118)						
G-LINX	Schweizer 269C-1 (Schweizer 300)	0239	N86G	5. 4.06	Heli-Lynx Ltd	Blackpool	11. 5.09E
G-LION	Piper PA-18-135 Super Cub	18-3857	PH-KLB	29. 9.80	J G Jones tr JG Jones Haulage "Grin'n Bare It"		25. 6.11S
	(L-21B-PI) (Frame No.18-3841)		(PH-DKG), R Neth AF R-167, 54-2457 (As "R-167" in R Neth AF c/s)			Caernarfon	
G-LIOT	Cameron O-77 Balloon (Hot Air)	2378		7. 8.90	N D Eliot	London SW19	27. 5.05A
G-LIPE	Robinson R22 Beta	1882	G-BTXJ	23. 1.92	HJS Helicopters Ltd		
						Lower Baads Farm, Peterculter	4. 4.09E
G-LIPS	Cameron Lips 90 SS Balloon (Hot Air)	4846	G-BZBV	15.11.00	Reach For The Sky Ltd	Worplesdon, Guildford	14. 7.09E
G-LISO	SIAI-Marchetti SM.1019	045	MM57-237	1. 7.04	C Daliso (Noted 4.06)	Vicenza, Italy	
			Ital. Army				
G-LITE	Rockwell Commander 112A	291	OY-RPP	13. 6.80	B G Rhodes	(Henbury, Macclesfield)	1. 2.08E
G-LITZ	Pitts S-1E	PFA 009-11131		3. 3.92	R P Millinship "Glitz"	Leicester	22. 6.06P
	(Built K Eld and J Hughes) (Lycoming IO-360)						
G-LIVH	Piper J-3C-65 Cub (L-4H-PI)	11529	OO-JAN	31. 3.94	U E Allman (As "330238:A-24" in US Army c/s)		
	(Frame No.11354)		OO-AAT, OO-PAX, 43-30238			Eaglescott	9. 8.09S
G-LIVS	Schleicher ASH 26E	26228		24. 2.05	P O Sturley "261"	RAF Wittering	2. 4.09E
G-LIZA	Cessna 340A II	340A1021	G-BMDM	15. 2.90	Air Charter Scotland Ltd	Glasgow	29. 6.09E
			ZS-KRH, N4620N				
G-LIZI	Piper PA-28-160 Cherokee	28-52	G-ARRP	26. 1.89	N F Andrews and A J Kingston tr G-LIZI Group		
			N5050W			Netherthorpe	27. 4.09E
G-LIZZ	Piper PA-E23-250 Aztec E	27-7405268	G-BBWM	26. 7.93	T J Nathan	Biggin Hill	17. 3.09E
			N40532				
G-LJCC	Murphy Rebel	PFA 232-13335		8. 7.98	P H Hyde	(Newton Longville, Milton Keynes)	
	(Built J Clarke)						

Reg	Type	C/n	Prev id	Date	Owner/Operator	Base	Expiry
G-LJRM	Sikorsky S-76C	760426	D-HBAG, N101MY, N101MM	22. 9.05	Ballymore Management Services Ltd	Dublin	4. 4.09E
G-LKTB	Piper PA-28-181 Archer III	2843496	N5339X	18.12.01	Top Cat Aviation Ltd	Manchester	12. 1.10E
G-LLAN	Grob G109B	6398	OH-747	19.11.04	J D Scott	Shobdon	9. 3.09E
G-LLCH	Cessna 172S Skyhawk	172S8822	G-PLBI, N35368	27. 6.08	N A Smith	Perth	2.10.09E
G-LLEW	Aeromot AMT-200S Super Ximango (Rotax 912 S4)	200126		15.11.00	N J Watt tr Echo Whiskey Ximango Syndicate	Glenrothes	15. 5.09E
G-LLIZ	Robinson R44 Raven II	12140		18. 2.08	W R Harford	(Tring)	6. 3.09E
G-LLLL	Rolladen-Schneider LS8-18	8217	BGA4657-JNW	25. 9.07	P C Fritche "L4"	Parham Park	28. 9.08
G-LLMW	Diamond DA.42 Twin Star	42.167	OE-VPY	21. 9.06	M Wai Lau	Biggin Hill	22.10.09E
G-LLOD	Learjet Model 45	45-236	N66DN, N125GW, N5018G	6.11.07	S R Lloyd	Leeds-Bradford	3. 1.10E
G-LLOY	Alpi Pioneer Hawk (Built A R Lloyd and F Cavaciuti)	PFA 330A-14568		14.11.06	A R Lloyd	Orlingbury Hold Farm, Orlingbury	21. 3.09P
G-LMAX	Sequoia F 8L Falco (Built J Maxwell)	PFA 100-13423		28.10.02	J Maxwell	(Ascot)	
G-LMBO	Robinson R44 Raven	1743		8. 8.07	Jewel Aviation and Technology Ltd	Blackbushe	16. 9.09E
G-LMCG	Robinson R44 Raven II	10370	OO-GOW, D-HALQ	18. 1.07	Glendale Helicopter Services Ltd	Highfield, Strathaven	7. 2.09E
G-LMLV	Dyn'Aéro MCR-01 Club (Built L La Vecchia - pr.no.PFA 301A-13524)	82		25.10.99	L and Maddelena La Vecchia	Cambridge	20. 7.09E
G-LNAA	MD Helicopters MD.900 Explorer	900-00074	G-76-074, G-LNAA, N7030B	26. 9.00	Police Aviation Services Ltd (Operated Lincolnshire and Nottingham Air Ambulance)	RAF Waddington	6.12.09E
G-LNAD	Robinson R44 Raven	1913		16. 7.08	P J Tallis	(Freshford, Ireland)	21. 9.09E
G-LNTY	Aérospatiale AS.355F1 Ecureuil 2	5300	G-ECOS, G-DOLR, G-BPVB, OH-HAJ, D-HEHN	29. 9.03	Sky Select Ltd	Gloucestershire	26. 2.09T
G-LNYS	Reims Cessna F177RG Cardinal RG	F177RG0120	G-BDCM, OY-BIP	30.11.92	D M White	Popham	23. 6.09E
G-LOAD	Dan Rihn DR.107 One Design (Built M J Clark)	PFA 264-13776		7. 6.02	M J Clark	Wellcross Farm, Slinfold	12. 3.09P
G-LOAN	Cameron N-77 Balloon (Hot Air)	1434		9. 1.87	P Lawman (Newbury Building Society titles)	Northampton	10. 9.09E
G-LOBO	Cameron O-120 Balloon (Hot Air)	3389		3. 1.95	C A Butler tr Solo Aerostatics	Newbury	27. 9.09E
G-LOCH	Piper J-3C-90 Cub (L-4J-PI) (Frame No.12517)	12687	HB-OCH, 44-80391	10.12.84	J M Greenland	Blackacre Farm, Holt, Trowbridge	5.11.09P
G-LOFB	Lockheed L188CF Electra	1131	N667F, N133AJ, CF-IJW, N131US	28. 6.94	Atlantic Airlines Ltd	Coventry	8. 2.09E
G-LJFC	Lockheed L188CF Electra	1100	N665F, N289AC, N6123A	15. 6.95	Atlantic Airlines Ltd	Coventry	10. 7.09E
G-LOFD	Lockheed L188CF Electra	1143	LN-FOG, LN-MOD, N9745C, (CF-IJC), N9745C	12. 6.97	Atlantic Airlines Ltd	Coventry	15. 6.09E
G-LOFE	Lockheed L188CF Electra	1144	EI-CET, (G-FIGF), N668Q, N668F, N24AF, N138US	5. 1.99	Atlantic Airlines Ltd	Coventry	19. 3.09E
G-LOFM	Maule MX-7-180A Super Rocket	20027C	N31110	19. 7.95	Air Atlantique Ltd	Coventry	1.10.09E
G-LOFT	Cessna 500 Citation I	500-0331	LN-NAT, EC-FUM, EC-500, LN-NAT, N40AC, N96RE, N86RE, N331CC, (N5331J)	12. 1.95	Fox Tango (Jersey) Ltd	Sleap	3.11.09E
G-LOIS	Avtech Jabiru UL (Built S Walshe - pr.no.PFA 274A-0144 (sic): originally built as Irish SAAC pr.no.SAAC-68)	0144	EI-JAK	14. 9.00	D W Newman	Sackville Lodge, Riseley	29. 5.09P
G-LOKI	UltraMagic M-77C Balloon (Hot Air)	77/260		12. 4.05	L J M Muir and G D Hallett	Montgomery	26. 2.10E
G-LOKM	PZL-110 Koliber 160A	04990080	G-BYSH, SP-WGH	26.11.99	PZL International Aviation Marketing and Sales PLC	Earls Colne	1. 1.10E
G-LOKO	Cameron Locomotive 105 SS Balloon (Hot Air)	3680	HB-QBN, G-LOKO	19. 9.95	Warsteiner Brauerei Haus Cramer KG	Warstein, Germany	9. 9.09E
G-LOLA	Beech A36 Bonanza	E-2116	N67501	18. 2.02	J H and L F Strutt	Earls Colne	20. 4.09E
G-LOLL	Cameron V-77 Balloon (Hot Air)	2964		4.12.92	R K McCulloch	High Wycombe	5. 2.09E
G-LONE	Bell 206L-1 LongRanger	45729	G-CDAJ, N20AP, N3174W	5.10.04	Central Helicopters Ltd	Nottingham City-Tollerton	5.11.09E
G-LOON	Cameron C-60 Balloon (Hot-Air)	11160		2. 7.08	C Wolstenholme	Bristol	2. 7.09E
G-LOOP	Pitts S-1C (Built D Mallinson) (Lycoming O-320) (Marked as "S-1D")	850		11. 5.78	D Shutter	Leicester	12. 7.09P
G-LORC	Piper PA-28-161 Cadet	2841339	D-ESTC, N9184W, (N620FT), (SE-KMP)	12. 1.99	Sherburn Aero Club Ltd	Sherburn-in-Elmet	19. 4.09E
G-LORD	Piper PA-34-200T Seneca II	34-7970347	N2908W	6. 5.88	G-LORD Flying Club Ltd	Lee-on-Solent	8. 5.09E
G-LORN	Mudry CAP.10B	282		4. 3.99	J D Gailey	Old Sarum	25. 5.09E
G-LORR	Piper PA-28-181 Archer III	2843037	N9268X, G-LORR	19. 4.96	VA Technology Ltd	Sleap	6. 7.09E
G-LORT	Avid Speed Wing Mk.4 (Built G E Laucht - pr.no.PFA 189-12219)	1124		12. 2.92	P Mitchell	Long Marston	30. 6.09P
G-LORY	Thunder Ax4-31Z Balloon (Hot Air)	171		28.11.78	A J Moore "Glory"	Northwood	6.10.09E
G-LOSI	Cameron Z-105 Balloon (Hot Air)	10011		15. 1.01	Aeropubblicita Vicenza SRL	Caldogno, Veneto, Italy	17. 3.08A
G-LOSM	Gloster Meteor NF.11 (Built Armstrong-Whitworth Aircraft)	S4/U/2342	WM167	8. 6.84	Aviation Heritage Ltd (As "WM167" in RAF 151 Sqdn c/s: also carries "G-LOSM")	Coventry	6. 11.08P
G-LOST	Denney Kitfox Model 3 (Built R Baily and H Balfour-Paul) (Rotax 618)	PFA 172-12055		10. 8.95	J H S Booth (Noted 9.08)	Glenrothes	6. 8.01P
G-LOSY	Evektor EV-97 Eurostar (Built J A Shufflebotham)	PFA 315-14161		22.12.03	C D Reeves	(Weston Zoyland)	16. 3.09P
G-LOTA	Robinson R44 Raven	1232		8. 7.02	Rahtol Ltd	Redhill	10. 7.09E
G-LOTI	Bleriot Type XI replica (Built M L Beach) (ABC Scorpion II)	PFA 088-10410		21.12.78	Brooklands Museum Trust Ltd (On display 2008)	Brooklands	19. 7.82P
G-LOVB	British Aerospace Jetstream Series 3102	622	VH-HSW, G-31-622, G-BLCB, G-31-622	12. 8.99	Sky Aeronautical Ltd	Coventry	1. 2.09E

G-LOWS	Sky 77-24 Balloon (Hot Air)	025		19. 3.96	A J Byrne and D J Bellinger *"Dawn Treader"*		
						Thatcham	14. 7.09E
G-LOYA	Reims FR172J Rocket	FR17200352	G-BLVT	4. 8.89	K A D Mitchell	Wellesbourne Mountford	11. 7.09E
			PH-EDI/D-EEDI				
G-LOYD	Aérospatiale SA.341G Gazelle 1	1289	G-SFTC	19. 6.85	I G Lloyd	Ripley, Derbyshire	4. 7.08E
			N47298 *(Rebuilt 1990 with major components of N6957 [c/n 1060])*				
G-LOYN	Robinson R44 Raven II	11599		7. 2.07	Mandarin Aviation Ltd	Redhill	27. 2 10E
G-LPAD	Lindstrand LBL 105A Balloon (Hot Air)	632		5. 8.99	Line Packaging and Display Ltd	Gillingham, Kent	1. 7.09E
G-LPIN	P&M Aviation QuikR	8424		1.09R			
G-LROY	Piper PA-28RT-201T Turbo Arrow IV		G-BNTS	23. 3.07	R L West	Norwich	11. 2.08E
		28R-8131024	N8296R				
G-LREE	Grob G 109B	6252	D-KEKO	7. 8.07	J T Morgan tr G-LREE Group	Denham	20. 9.09E
G-LRGE	Lindstrand LBL 330A Balloon (Hot Air)	929		31. 7.03	Adventure Balloons Ltd	Hartley Wintney, Hook	2. 4.09E
					(www.Adventure Balloons.co.uk titles)		
G-LRSN	Robinson R44 Raven	0984		28. 3.01	Kidmane Developments Ltd	Bellaghy	8. 5.09E
G-LSAA	Boeing 757-236	24122	N241CV	17. 5.05	Dart Group PLC *(Operated.Jet2.com) "jet 2 Tenerife"*		
			TC-FLB, TC-ANM, EC-FFK, EC-744, G-BNSF, (D-AOEB), G-BNSF, EC-ELS, EC-203, G-BNSF			Leeds-Bradford	7.10.08E
G-LSAB	Boeing 757-27B/W	24136	N136CV	17. 5.05	Dart Group PLC *(Operated.Jet2.com) "jet 2 Menorca"*		
			TC-FLC, TC-ANN, PH-AHF, 4X-EBF, G-OAHF, OY-SHF, PH-AHF			Leeds-Bradford	2. 2.09E
G-LSAC	Boeing 757-23A	25488	N254DG	14. 3.06	Dart Group PLC *(Operated.Jet2.com) "jet 2 Lanzarote"*		
			G-LSAC, N310FV, C-GTSE, N1792B			Leeds-Bradford	22. 5.09E
G-LSAD	Boeing 757-236	24397	SX-BLW	16. 6.06	Dart Group PLC *(Operated.Jet2.com)*		
			G-OOOS, G-BRJD, EC-ESC, EC-349, G-BRJD			Leeds-Bradford	1. 8.09E
G-LSAE	Boeing 757-27B	24135	OM-SNA	28. 6.06	Dart Group PLC *(Operated.Jet2.com) "jet2 Murcia"*		
			N335FV, PH-AHE, OY-SHE, PH-AHE, OY-SHE, PH-AHE			Leeds-Bradford	11. 9.09E
G-LSAG	Boeing 757-21B	24014	B-2801	23.11.06	Dart Group PLC *(Operated.Jet2.com)*		
			N1792B			Leeds-Bradford	22. 3.09E
G-LSAH	Boeing 757-21B	24015	B-2802	23.11.06	Dart Group PLC *(Operated.Jet2.com)*		
			N5573B			Leeds-Bradford	19. 3.09E
G-LSAI	Boeing 757-21B	24016	B-2803	23.11.06	Dart Group PLC *(Operated.Jet2.com)*		
			N5573K			Leeds-Bradford	22. 4.09E
G-LSAJ	Boeing 757-236	24793	G-CDUP	6. 5.08	Jet2.com Ltd	Leeds-Bradford	16. 3.09E
			SE-DUP, G-CDUP, SE-DUP, G-OOOT, G-BRJJ, EC-490, G-BRJJ				
G-LSCM	Cessna 172S Skyhawk	172S8445	N612TG	7. 6.04	G A Luscombe	Exeter	4. 7.09E
			N165ME				
G-LSCP	Rolladen-Schneider LS6-18W	6236	BGA4814-JVK	31. 1.08	L G Blows and M F Collins	Parham Park	4. 8.08
			D-6417				
G-LSED	Rolladen-Schneider LS6-c	6260	BGA3913-HFQ	17.10.07	G McKnight tr McKnight/Baker Syndicate		
			(BGA3908-HFK)			RAF Cranwell	28. 9.08
G-LSFB	Rolladen-Schneider LS7-WI	7009	BGA5042-KEW	31. 1.08	P Thomson	Feshiebridge	28. 5.08
			F-CGYA, F-WGYA, D-1272				
G-LSFI	Gulfstream AA-5A Cheetah	AA5A-0770	G-BGSK	13. 2.84	A D Prothero tr G-LSFI Group		
						North Moor, Scunthorpe	9. 7.06T
G-LSFR	Rolladen-Schneider LS4	4260	BGA2908-ESE	30.10.07	A Mulder and M Platt *"LS4"*	Nympsfield	16. 2.08
G-LSFT	Piper PA-28-161 Warrior II	28-8516008	G-BXTX	10.11.99	Biggin Hill Flying Club Ltd	Biggin Hill	1. 4.09E
			PH-LEH, N130AV, N43682				
G-LSGB	Rolladen-Schneider LS 6b	6184	BGA3361-FMC	4.12.07	T J Brenton	Wormingford	30. 3.08
G-LSGM	Rolladen-Schneider LS3-17	3346	BGA5144-KJU	24. 1.06	P J Hampshire	(Haywards Heath)	8. 2.08
			D-6760, OO-ZLD				
G-LSHI	Colt 77A Balloon (Hot Air)	1264		20. 7.88	J H Dobson *(Lambert Smith and Hampton titles)*		
						Streatley, Berkshire	12. 7.95A
G-LSIF	Rolladen-Schneider LS1-f	383	BGA4738-JSF	24. 1.08	R C Godden	Wormingford	1. 7.08
			LN-GGE, SE-TOU				
G-LSIV	Rolladen-Schneider LS4	4189	BGA2806	28. 9.07	D M Bland tr 264 Syndicate *"264"*	Nympsfield	7. 4.08
G-LSIX	Rolladen-Schneider LS6-18W	6352	BGA4119-HQL	14. 3.08	D P Masson and A V W Nunn *"LS6"*	Lasham	
			D-0794				
G-LSJE	Reality Escapade Jabiru(3)	UK ESC 0006		19. 2.08	L S J Webb	RNAS Culdrose	13.11.09P
	(Built L S J Webb, pr no BMAA HB/486)						
G-LSKV	Rolladen-Schneider LS8-18	8095	BGA4288-HXN	16.11.07	D Pitman	Bicester	14.12.07
G-LSKY	P&M Pegasus Quik	8119		12. 8.05	G R Hall and P R Brooker		
						Harringe Court, Sellindge, Folkestone	6. 5.09P
G-LSLS	Rolladen-Schneider LS4	4191	BGA2808-ENA	22.10.07	A M Sanders tr 288 Syndicate *"288"*	Long Mynd	30. 3.08
G-LSMI	Reims Cessna F152 II	F15201710		1. 2.80	A S Bamrah t/a Falcon Flying Services	Southend	22. 9.09E
					(Operated Willowair Flying Club)		
G-LSPA	Agusta-Bell 206B-2 JetRanger II	8530	G-INVU	12. 7.06	Heliflight (UK) Ltd	Gloucestershire	12. 6.09E
			G-XXII, G-GGCC, G-BEHG				
G-LSPH	Van's RV-8	PFA 303-13733		3. 9.07	R S Partridge-Hicks		
						Little Haugh Hall, Norton, Bury St. Edmunds	24.10.08P
G-LSTR	Stoddard-Hamilton GlaStar	xxxx		20. 4.98	N M Humphries	Perrow Farm, Clewer	15. 1.09P
	(Built R Y Kendal- pr.no.PFA 295-13093) (Lycoming O-320)(Tail-wheel u/c)						
G-LSVI	Rolladen-Schneider LS6-C18	6266	BGA3910-HFM	12.10.07	F J Sheppard	Wycombe Air Park	1. 7.07
G-LSWL	Robinson R22 Beta	3671	I-JESS	28.11.05	G J Braithwaite	(Dedham, Colchester)	17.12.09E
G-LTFB	Piper PA-28-140 Cherokee	28-23343	G-AVLU	28. 2.97	S J Hall	Lydd	25. 9.09E
			N11C				
G-LTFC	Piper PA-28-140 Cherokee B	28-26259	G-AXTI	8. 6.94	Avon Aviation Ltd t/a The Bristol and Wessex Aeroplane Club		
			N11C			Bristol	4. 2.08E
G-LTMM	Aviat A-1B Husky	2436	N115AA	28. 2.08	F A de Munck	(St Emilion, France)	28. 2.09E
G-LTRF	Fournier RF7	7001	G-EHAP	10.12.97	Skyview Systems Ltd		
			(G-BGVC), D-EHAP, F-WPXV			Waits Farm, Belchamp Walter	13. 5.08P
G-LTSB	Cameron LTSB 90 SS Balloon (Hot Air)	4483		15. 1.99	ABC Flights Ltd *(Lloyds TSB titles)*		
						Clapton in Gordano, Bristol	1. 6.06A
G-LUBE	Cameron N-77 Balloon (Hot Air)	1127		25. 2.85	A C Rawson *(Cadbury titles)*	Stafford	27. 7.05A
G-LUBY	Avtech Jabiru J430	0xxx		19.12.06	K Luby	Barton	28. 5.09P
	(Built K Luby - pr.no.PFA 336-14605) (Jabiru 3300)						

G-LUCK   Reims Cessna F150M   F15001238   PH-LEO   13.12.79   Cranfield Aviation Training School Ltd   Cranfield   22. 6.09E
      D-EHRA

G-LUDM   Van's RV-8   PFA 303-14521   22. 2.06   D F Sargant   Ludham   7.12.09P
      (Built D F Sargant) (Superior XP-10)

G-LUED   Aero Designs Pulsar   PFA 202-12122   9. 3.92   J C Anderson   Sturgate   12. 5.09P
      (Built J C Anderson) (Rotax 582)

G-LUKE   Rutan LongEz   PFA 74A-10978   4. 7.84   R A Pearson   (Knowle, Solihull)   14. 8.03P
      (Built S G Busby) (Lycoming O-235)

G-LUKI   Robinson R44 Clipper   0818   G-BZLN   20.10.00   A and D Douglas   (Winchenford, Worcester)   15. 1.09E

G-LUKY   Robinson R44 Astro   0357   10. 7.97   M A Hack t/a Hack Aviation   Gloucestershire   14. 9.09E

G-LULA   Cameron C-90 Balloon (Hot Air)   10833   8. 6.06   S D Davis   Netherbury, Bridport   1. 7.09E

G-LULI   Robinson R44 Clipper II   12241   2. 5.08   Luxtronic Ltd   Wycombe Air Park   22. 5.09E

G-LULU   Grob G109   6137   6. 9.82   A P Bowden   Enstone   7. 6.09E

G-LULV   Diamond DA.42 Twin Star   42.313   29. 1.08   B A and M-L M Langevad   (London W4)   13. 2.09E

G-LUMB   Best Off Sky Ranger 912(2)   SKRxxxx435   28. 6.05   S Allcock (Noted 2007)
      (Built S Allcock - pr.no.BMAA HB/378)   Middle Bank Top Farm, Lumb, Rossendale

G-LUNA   Piper PA-32RT-300T Turbo Lance II   N2246Q   19. 3.79   Lance Aviation Ltd   Humberside   8.11.08E
      32R-7987108

G-LUND   Cessna 340 II   340-0305   G-LAST   27. 3.03   Prospect Developments (Northern) Ltd   Blackpool   17. 9.06T
      G-UNDY, G-BBNR, N69452 (Noted 10.07)

G-LUNE   Mainair Sports Pegasus Quik   8017   18.2.04   D Muir   St Michaels   31. 5.08P

G-LUNG   Rotorsport MT-03   RSUK/MT-03/018   24. 9.07   R H Sawyer and P Krysiak   Kirkbride   30.11.09P

G-LUNY   Pitts S-1S   PFA 009-14757   9. 1.08   R P Millinship tr G-LUNY Group   Leicester
      (Built C Tector)

G-LUSC   Luscombe 8E Silvaire Deluxe   3975   D-EFYR   1.11.84   M Fowler   Bruntingthorpe
      LN-PAT, (NC1248K)   (Noted Chilbolton 11.08)

G-LUSH   Piper PA-28-151 Cherokee Warrior   OH-PAB   25. 7.01   S Papi (Operated Willowair Flying Club)   Southend   9.12.09E
      28-7515201

G-LUSI   Luscombe 8F Silvaire   6770   N838B   3.10.89   J P Hunt and D M Robinson
      (Built Temco Engineering) (Continental C85)   Bourne Park, Hurstbourne Tarrant   22. 7.09P

G-LUST   Luscombe 8E Silvaire Deluxe   6492   N2065B   9.11.89   M Griffiths   Chilbolton   14. 7.05P
      (Continental C85)   NC2065B   (Noted 11.07)

G-LUVY   Aérospatiale AS.355F1 Ecureuil 2   5134   N358E   25. 2.00   DNH Helicopters Ltd   Biggin Hill   31. 8.07T
      ZS-HUA, (G-BPDP), D-HOCH (2), N358E, N5792M

G-LUXE   British Aerospace BAe 146 Series 301   E3001   G-5-300   9. 4.87   BAESystems (Operations) Ltd   Cranfield   5. 5.10S
      G-SSSH, (G-BIAD)   (Operated Directflight for FAAM [Atmospheric Research])

G-LUXY   Cessna 551 Citation II/SP   551-0421   3A-MRB   5.12.06   Mitre Aviation Ltd   Kemble   5. 3.09E
      D-IAWA, N550RD, OE-GES, SE-DEF, OO-RJE, (N421CJ), N1217V, (N64735)

G-LVBF   Lindstrand LBL 330A Balloon (Hot Air)   936   30. 1.04   Airxcite Ltd t/a Virgin Balloon Flights   Wembley   13. 2.09E

G-LVES   Cessna 182S Skylane   18280741   G-ELIE   19. 8.02   R W and A M Glaves   Nottingham-East Midlands   3.10.09E
      N23754

G-LVLV   Bombardier CL-600-2B16   5372   N314FX   27. 4.04   Gama Aviation Ltd   Farnborough   27. 4.09E
      (CL-604 Challenger)   (N413LV), N314FX, C-GLWR

G-LVPL   AirBorne XT912-B-Streak III-B   XT912-035   21.12.04   C D Connor   Mill Farm, Shifnal   23. 3.09P
      (Line number "XT912-33" also quoted) (Wing s/n S3-0016)

G-LWAY   Robinson R44 Raven   1244   N71822   22. 8.02   MFH Helicopters Ltd   Conington   12.10.09E

G-LWDC   Canadair CL600-2A12   3031   N54JC   28. 1.08   ISM Aviation Services Ltd   Humberside   28. 2.09E
      (CL-601 Challenger)

G-LWNG   Aero Designs Pulsar   PFA 202-11866   G-OMKF   14.10.02   C Moffat   Eaglescott   27. 8.09P
      (Built M K Faro) (Rotax 582) (Tri-cycle u/c)   (Noted 8.07)

G-LXRS   Bombardier BD-700-1A10 Global Express   C-FEBX   19.12.06   Profred Partners LLP   (London EC4)   19.12.09E
      9200

G-LXUS   Alpi Pioneer 300   PFA 330-14390   18. 7.05   W C Walters   Spanhoe   20. 3.09P
      (Built W C Walters)

G-LYAK   IAV Bacau Yakovlev Yak-52   822113   LY-AGN   18.12.02   Lee 52 Ltd (Poke Software titles)   Lee-on-Solent   28. 2.09P
      Ukraine AF 140 (yellow), DOSAAF 40 (yellow)

G-LYDA   Hoffmann H 36 Dimona   3515   OE-9213   5. 4.94   J W Hagley tr G-LYDA Flying Group
          Wycombe Air Park   9.10.09E

G-LYDB   Piper PA-31-350 Chieftain   31-8052107   TI-PAI   23. 1.06   Atlantic Bridge Aviation Ltd   Lydd
      C-GPAI, C-GJLR, N170PA, HI-608CA, N3583C

G-LYDC   Piper PA-31-350 Navajo Chieftain   N210PM   23. 1.06   Atlantic Bridge Aviation Ltd   Lydd   28. 2.09E
      31-7652110   N60FS, N59882, (N79JA), N59882

G-LYDF   Piper PA-31-350 Navajo Chieftain   N12CD   23. 1.06   Atlantic Bridge Aviation Ltd   Lydd   2.10.08E
      31-7952031   N27784

G-LYDS   Schempp-Hirth Nimbus 3T   4   BGA5298-KRG   2. 4.08   D H Smith "DS"   Bidford
      D-KTFP, HB-2147, D-KAPE, VH-GAA

G-LYFA   IAV Bacau Yakovlev Yak-52   822608   LY-AFA   31. 3.03   M I Boyd tr Fox Alpha Flying Group   Barton   8. 5.09P
      DOSAAF 110

G-LYNC   Robinson R22 Beta II   3069   5. 5.00   Traffic Management Services Ltd   Gamston   29. 5.09E

G-LYND   Piper PA-25-235 Pawnee D   "25-6309"   SE-IXU   8. 9.93   York Gliding Centre Ltd   Rufforth   15. 1.09E
      (Rebuild of G-ASFZ [25-2246] with new frame)   G-BSFZ, N6672Z

G-LYNI   Evektor EV-97 Eurostar   PFA 315-14409   14. 9.05   G Evans   Weston Zoyland   1. 5.09P
      (Built G Evans)

G-LYNK   CFM Shadow Series DD   303-DD   12.10.98   B J Palfreyman   Watnall   15. 4.09P

G-LYPG   Avtech Jabiru UL-450   0251   6. 7.99   A J Geary   Baxby Manor, Husthwaite   15. 6.09P
      (Built P G Gale - pr.no.PFA 274A-13466)

G-LYTB   P&M Aviation Quik GT450   8204   25. 8.06   B Light   Tarn Farm, Cockerham   5. 9.08P

G-LYTE   Thunder Ax7-77 Balloon (Hot Air)   1113   29. 9.87   G M Bulmer "Crispen"   Hereford   19. 5.91A

G-LZII   Laser Z200   PFA 123-14410   24. 4.08   K G Begley   Sywell
      (Built K G Begley)

G-LZZY   Piper PA-28RT-201T Turbo Arrow IV   G-BMHZ   8. 5.01   A C Gradidge   Popham   28. 5.09E
      28R-8031001   ZS-KII, N8096D

G-MAAA - G-MZZZ

Reg	Type	C/n	Prev id	Date	Owner/Operator	Base/Date
G-MAAN	Europa Aviation Europa XS	567		7. 1.03	P S Maan	(Desborough)
	(Built P S Maan - pr.no.PFA 247-14009) (Tri-gear u/c)					
G-MAAX	Bell 206L-1 LongRanger	45232	G-EYLE	14. 3.06	Sky Charter UK Ltd	Manston 3. 3.09E
			G-OCRP, V4-AAB, G-OCRP, G-BWCU, N2758A, C-FPET, N2758A, JA9234			
G-MABE	Reims Cessna F150L	F15001119	G-BLJP	20. 6.97	I D McClelland	Popham 26. 4.09E
			N962L			
G-MACA	Robinson R22 Beta	3836		3. 5.05	Helicentre Blackpool Ltd	Blackpool 4. 6.09E
G-MACE	Hughes 369E (Hughes 500)	0015E	HA-MSA	3. 2.05	West Country Helicopters Ltd	(Chard) 13. 3.09E
			SE-HNA			
G-MACH	SIAI-Marchetti SF.260	1-14	F-BUVY	29.10.80	Cheyne Motors Ltd	Old Sarum 16. 8.09E
			OO-AHR, OO-HAZ, (OO-RAB)			
G-MACK	Piper PA-28R-200 Cherokee Arrow II		N5213F	18. 8.78	M D Hinge (Operated Professional Air Training)	
		28R-7635449				Bournemouth 10. 8.09E
G-MACL	Cirrus SR22	2710	N926SR	3.12.07	Maclaren Asset Management Ltd	Aberdeen 10.12.09E
G-MAFA	Reims Cessna F406 Caravan II	F406-0036	G-DFLT	2. 6.98	Directflight Ltd (Operated DEFRA - Fisheries Patrol titles))	
			F-WZDZ			Exeter 7. 6.09E
G-MAFB	Reims Cessna F406 Caravan II	F406-0080	F-WWSR	27. 5.98	Directflight Ltd (Operated DEFRA - Fisheries Patrol titles)	
						Exeter 28. 9.09E
G-MAFE	Dornier 228-202K	8009	G-OALF	21.12.92	Cobham Leasing Ltd (Operated DEFRA)	
			G-MLDO, PH-SDO, D-IDON, D-CATI (2), SX-BHB, (PH-HAL), D-IDON			Bournemouth 4.11.09E
G-MAFF	Pilatus Britten-Norman BN-2T Islander	2119	G-BJED	20. 4.82	Cobham Leasing Ltd (Operated DEFRA)	
						Bournemouth 25. 9.08E
G-MAFI	Dornier 228-202K	8115	D-CAAE	16. 2.87	Cobham Leasing Ltd (Operated DEFRA)	
						Bournemouth 15. 7.09E
G-MAFT	Diamond DA.40D Star	D4.243	OE-VPU	28. 2.07	Atlantic Flight Training Ltd	Coventry 15. 3.09E
			(D-EXON)			
G-MAGC	Cameron Grand Illusion SS Balloon (Hot Air)			19. 1.95	Magical Adventures Ltd	
		4000				West Bloomfield, Michigan, US 27. 9.09E
G-MAGG	Pitts S-1SE	PFA 009-10873		17. 3.83	O T Elmer	Horsford 9. 4.08P
	(Built G C Masterton) (Lycoming O-360)					
G-MAGK	Schleicher ASW 20L	20387	BGA2740-EKE	13.11.07	A G K Mackenzie	Burn 5. 5.08
G-MAGL	Sky 77-24 Balloon (Hot Air)	164		14. 7.99	RCM SARL (Mag-Lite titles)Stuppicht, Luxembourg	10. 6.09E
G-MAGZ	Robin DR.500-200i Président	35	F-GXGC	29. 7.05	T J Thomas	Sywell 7 .2.09E
	(Officially regd as DR.400-500)					
G-MAIE	Piper PA-32R-301T Saratoga IITC	3257046	N47BK	1.12.00	B R Sennett	Shoreham 10.11.09E
			N41283			
G-MAIK	Piper PA-34-220T Seneca IV	3448078	N73BS	17.11.97	Modern Air (UK) Ltd	Fowlmere 23. 3.09E
G-MAIN	Mainair Blade 912	1202-0699-7-W1005		16. 6.99	D P Pryke	Finmere 7. 8.09P
G-MAIR	Piper PA-34-200T Seneca II	34-7970140	N3029R	15. 2.89	Bristol Flying Centre Ltd	Bristol 2. 5.09E
G-MAJA	British Aerospace Jetstream Series 4102		G-4-032	22. 4.94	Air Kilroe Ltd t/a Eastern Airways	Humberside 24. 5.09E
	(Built Jetstream Aircraft Ltd)	41032				
G-MAJB	British Aerospace Jetstream Series 4102		G-BVKT	1. 6.94	Air Kilroe Ltd t/a Eastern Airways	Humberside 8. 6.09E
	(Built Jetstream Aircraft Ltd)	41018	N140MA, G-4-018			
G-MAJC	British Aerospace Jetstream Series 4100		G-LOGJ	12. 9.94	Air Kilroe Ltd t/a Eastern Airways	Humberside 20.12.09E
		41005				
G-MAJD	British Aerospace Jetstream Series 4100		G-WAWR	27. 3.95	Air Kilroe Ltd t/a Eastern Airways	Humberside 2. 3.09E
		41006				
G-MAJE	British Aerospace Jetstream Series 4100		G-LOGK	12. 9.94	Air Kilroe Ltd t/a Eastern Airways	Humberside 24. 2.09E
		41007				
G-MAJF	British Aerospace Jetstream Series 4100		G-WAWL	6. 2.95	Air Kilroe Ltd t/a Eastern Airways	Humberside 18. 3.09E
		41008				
G-MAJG	British Aerospace Jetstream Series 4100		G-LOGL	16. 8.94	Air Kilroe Ltd t/a Eastern Airways	Humberside 30. 3.09E
		41009				
G-MAJH	British Aerospace Jetstream Series 4100		G-WAYR	4. 4.95	Air Kilroe Ltd t/a Eastern Airways	Humberside 13. 4.09E
	(Built Jetstream Aircraft Ltd)	41010				
G-MAJI	British Aerospace Jetstream Series 4100		G-WAND	20. 3.95	Air Kilroe Ltd t/a Eastern Airways	Humberside 27. 4.09E
	(Built Jetstream Aircraft Ltd)	41011				
G-MAJJ	British Aerospace Jetstream Series 4100		G-WAFT	27. 2.95	Air Kilroe Ltd t/a Eastern Airways	Humberside 28.10.09E
	(Built Jetstream Aircraft Ltd)	41024	G-4-024			
G-MAJK	British Aerospace Jetstream Series 4100		G-4-070	27. 7.95	Air Kilroe Ltd t/a Eastern Airways	Humberside 2. 9.09E
	(Built Jetstream Aircraft Ltd)	41070				
G-MAJL	British Aerospace Jetstream Series 4100		G-4-087	1. 4.96	Eastern Airways (UK) Ltd "R J Mitchell"	
	(Built Jetstream Aircraft Ltd)	41087				Humberside 16. 5.09E
G-MAJM	British Aerospace Jetstream Series 4100		G-4-096	23. 9.96	Air Kilroe Ltd t/a Eastern Airways	Humberside 29.10.09E
	(Built Jetstream Aircraft Ltd)	41096				
G-MAJP	British Aerospace Jetstream Series 4100		N550HK	14. 9.05	Air Kilroe Ltd t/a Eastern Airways	Humberside 23. 3.09E
	(Built Jetstream Aircraft Ltd)	41039	(N502TS), G-4-039			
G-MAJR	de Havilland DHC-1 Chipmunk 22	C1/0699	WP805	25. 9.96	C Adams tr Chipmunk Shareholders (As "WP805:D" in RAF c/s)	
						Lee-on-Solent 12.11.09S
G-MAJS	Airbus A300B4-605R	604	F-WWAX	26. 4.91	Monarch Airlines Ltd	Luton 25. 4.09E
G-MAJT	British Aerospace Jetstream Series 4100		N551HK	21. 9.05	Air Kilroe Ltd t/a Eastern Airways	Humberside 14. 2.10E
	(Built Jetstream Aircraft Ltd)	41040	G-4-040			
G-MAJU	British Aerospace Jetstream Series 4100		N558HK	10. 4.06	Air Kilroe Ltd t/a Eastern Airways	Humberside 26. 6.09E
	(Built Jetstream Aircraft Ltd)	41071	G-4-071			
G-MAJV	British Aerospace Jetstream Series 4100		N557HK	10. 4.06	Air Kilroe Ltd t/a Eastern Airways	Humberside 11. 5.09E
	(Built Jetstream Aircraft Ltd)	41074	G-4-074			
G-MAJW	British Aerospace Jetstream Series 4100		N303UE	8. 6.06	Air Kilroe Ltd t/a Eastern Airways	Humberside 20. 1.10E
	(Built Jetstream Aircraft Ltd)	41015	G-4-015			
G-MAJX	British Aerospace Jetstream Series 4100		N330UE	8. 6.06	Eastern Airways (Europe) Ltd	Humberside 17. 4.09E
	(Built Jetstream Aircraft Ltd)	41098	G-4-098			
G-MAJY	British Aerospace Jetstream Series 4100		N331UE	8. 6.06	Eastern Airways (Europe) Ltd	Humberside 15.10.09E
	(Built Jetstream Aircraft Ltd)	41099	G-4-099			

Reg	Type (Builder / notes)	C/n	Prev ID	Date	Owner / Operator	Location	Date
G-MAJZ	British Aerospace Jetstream Series 4100 (Built Jetstream Aircraft Ltd)	41100	N332UE G-4-100	8.6.06	Eastern Airways (Europe) Ltd	Humberside	14.1.10E
G-MAKI	Robinson R-44	1752		31.8.07	Hoe Leasing Ltd	(Hatfield)	13.9.09E
G-MAKS	Cirrus SR22	367	N800C	20.5.08	Incliner8 Ltd	(Southport)	21.5.09E
G-MALA	Piper PA-28-181 Archer II	28-8190055	G-BIIU N82748	6.3.81	D C and M E Dowell t/a M and D Aviation	Kemble	28.4.09E
G-MALC	Grumman AA-5 Traveler	AA5-0664	G-BCPM N6170A	19.11.79	B P Hogan	Turweston	7.6.09E
G-MALS	Mooney M 20K Mooney 231	25-0573	N1061T	16.8.84	P Mouterde	Neuville-les-Dames, France	28.5.09E
G-MALT	Colt Flying Hop SS Balloon (Hot Air)	1447		14.4.89	P J Stapley *"Hoppie"*	London Colney, St Albans	11.9.97A
G-MAMD	Beech B200 Super King Air	BB-1549	N1069S	16.7.99	Forest Aviation Ltd	Gamston	16.7.09E
G-MAML	Robinson R44 Raven II	12153		6.3.08	Barley Mo Ltd	Headcorn	30.3.09E
G-MAMO	Cameron V-77 Balloon (Hot Air)	1616		17.11.87	The Marble Mosaic Company Ltd *"Osprey"*	Weston-super-Mare	27.8.03A
G-MANH	British Aerospace ATP	2017	G-LOGC G-OLCC	16.11.94	Atlantic Airlines Ltd	Coventry	30.11.09E
G-MANN	Aérospatiale SA.341G Gazelle 1	1295	G-BKLW N4DQ, N4QQ, N444JJ, N47316, F-WKQH	14.4.86	MW Helicopters Ltd	Stapleford	20.6.09E
G-MANS	British Aerospace BAe 146 Series 200	E2088	G-CLHC G-MANS, G-CHSR, G-5-088	22.5.00	Flybe Ltd *(Stored 9.07)*	Exeter	25.4.08E
G-MANW	Tri-R KIS (Built M T Manwaring)	PFA 239-12628		12.9.96	M T Manwaring	(Weston Turville, Aylesbury)	
G-MANX	Clutton FRED Series II (Built P Williamson - pr.no.PFA 029-10327) (Ardem 4C02)	PW.2		31.5.78	S Styles *(Crashed near Ronaldsway 30.10.81: on rebuild Wellesbourne Mountford 7.90)*	(Birmingham)	17.8.82P
G-MANZ	Robinson R44 II	12319		2.6.08	Meadow Helicopters Ltd	(Wellingborough)	21.7.09E
G-MAPL	Robinson R44 Raven	0929	G-BZVP	7.6.02	Helicentre Lazio SRL	(Piedimonte, Italy)	6.11.09E
G-MAPP	Cessna 402B	402B0583	D-INRH N1445G	16.4.99	Blom Aerofilms Ltd	Cranfield	2.10.09E
G-MAPR	Beech A36 Bonanza	E-2713	N55916	17.9.92	M J B Cozens	RNAS Yeovilton	20.5.09E
G-MARA	Airbus A321-231	0983	D-AVZB	31.3.99	Monarch Airlines Ltd	Luton	30.3.09E
G-MARE	Schweizer 269C *(Schweizer 300)*	S-1320		12.8.88	The Earl of Caledon	Caledon Castle, County Tyrone	24.11.09E
G-MARO	Best Off Sky Ranger J2.2(2) (Built C P Whitford - pr.no.BMAA HB/348; listed as built E Daleki on G-INFO, original owner)	SKR 0305318		22.12.04	C P Whitford	Middle Pymore Farm, Bridport	3.9.08P
G-MARX	Van's RV-4 (Built T L Berry)	2394-1211	SE-XUU N42BN	16.11.04	M W Albery	Enstone	27.6.08P
G-MARZ	Thruster T 600N 450	1031-T600N-093		27.1.04	K J Underwood	(Amberley, Arundel)	14.4.09P
G-MASC	SAN Jodel D 150A Mascaret	37	F-BLDZ	1.2.91	K F and R.Richardson	Wellesbourne Mountford	5.11.07P
G-MASF	Piper PA-28-181 Cherokee Archer II	28-7790191	OY-EPT LN-NAP	24.6.97	Mid-Anglia Flight Centre Ltd t/a Mid-Anglia School of Flying	Cambridge	6.9.09E
G-MASH	Westland-Bell 47G-4A	WA/725	G-AXKU G-17-10	3.11.89	Kinetic Avionics Ltd *(US Army c/s)*	Elstree	12.3.10
G-MASI	P&M Aviation Quik GT450	8213		29.8.06	D M Merritt-Holman	(Benicolet, Spain)	3.9.08P
G-MASS	Cessna 152 II	15281605	G-BSHN N65541	6.3.95	MK Aero Support Ltd	Andrewsfield	28.4.09E
G-MATE	Moravan Zlin Z-50LX	0068		26.10.90	S A W Becker	Goodwood	22.10.09E
G-MATF	Gulfstream Aerospace Gulfstream G-IV	1109	EC-IKP, N101GA, V8-007, V8-SRI, V8-ALI, N1761D	23.10.07	Gama Aviation Ltd	Farnborough	23.10.09E
G-MATS	Colt GA-42 Gas Airship	738	JA1009 G-MATS	11.6.87	P A Lindstrand	Oswestry	23.5.90A
G-MATT	Robin R2160	97	G-BKRC F-BZAC, F-WZAC	7.5.85	V P O'Brien	(Durrow, County Laois)	22.5.09E
G-MATX	Pilatus PC-12/45	682		20.12.05	Air Matrix Ltd	Lyon-Bron, France	22.12.09E
G-MATY	Robinson R22 Beta II	3686		28.10.04	MT Aviation Ltd	Cambridge	30.11.09E
G-MATZ	Piper PA-28-140 Cherokee Cruiser	28-7325200	G-BASI N11C	11.12.90	R B Walker tr Midland Air Training School	Coventry	20.12.09E
G-MAUK	Colt 77A Balloon (Hot Air)	901		16.2.87	B Meeson *"Mondial Assistance"*	Walsall	4.6.92A
G MAUS	Europa Aviation Europa (Built A P Ringrose - pr.no.PFA 247-12651) (Rotax 912 ULS)	030		28.6.05	A P Ringrose	Dunsfold	4.11.09P
G-MAVI	Robinson R22 Beta	0960		7.2.89	Northumbria Helicopters Ltd	Carlisle	26.4.09E
G-MAVV	Aero AT-3 R100 (Operated Old Sarum Flying Club)	AT3-025		22.10.08	Cunning Plan Development Ltd	Old Sarum	20.11.09E
G-MAXG	Pitts S-1S (Built T P Jenkinson) (Lycoming IO-360)	PFA 009-13233		27.4.01	Jenks Air Ltd *"Little Stinger"*	White Waltham	8.4.09P
G-MAXI	Piper PA-34-200T Seneca II	34-7670150	N8658C	11.2.81	Draycott Seneca Syndicate Ltd	Gloucestershire	2.6.09E
G-MAXR	UltraMagic S-90 Balloon (Hot Air)	90/78		1.8.05	C F Sanger-Davies *("ReMax" titles)*	Evesham	25.3.09E
G-MAXS	Mainair Sports Pegasus Quik	8105		16.3.05	S P Maxwell	North Coates	25.3.08P
G-MAXV	Van's RV-4 (Built T P Jenkinson) (Lycoming IO-360)	PFA 181-13266		20.1.00	R S Partridge-Hicks	North Weald	12.2.09P
G-MAYB	Robinson R44 Raven	1429		7.10.04	Highmark Aviation Ltd	Sandtoft	30.10.09E
G-MAYE	Bell 407	53117	F-GLMI N14054	27.6.05	M Maye	Weston, Leixlip, County Kildare	3.9.09E
G-MAYO	Piper PA-28-161 Cherokee Warrior II	28-7716278	G-BFBG N38848	20.2.81	Air Navigation and Trading Company Ltd	Blackpool	15.7.09E
G-MAZA	Rotorsport UK MT-03	RSUK/MT-03/029		20.2.08	M Manson and N Crownshaw	Wickenby	21.2.09P
G-MBAA	Hiway Skytrike II/Excalibur (Hiro Delta 22)	01		23.4.81	M J Aubrey *(Noted 2002)*	Upper Yeld, Floodgates, Kington, Hereford	
G-MBAB	Hovey Whing-Ding II (Built R F Morton - pr.no.PFA 116-10706) (Konig SC340)	MA-59		26.5.81	M J Aubrey *(Noted SPLASH, NEC Birmingham 11.08)*	Kington, Hereford	1.2.98P
G-MBAW	Pterodactyl Ptraveller (Cuyana 430R)	017		14.7.81	J C K Scardifield	(Lymington)	31.8.86X
G-MBBB	Skycraft Scout II (Pixie 173)	0388W		3.8.81	A J and B.Chalkley	(Rhoshirwaun, Pwllheli)	

G-MBBJ (2)	Hiway Demon	80-0029	15. 2.82	M J Aubrey	Kington, Hereford	X
	(Now fitted with Trike from G-MBGA (079-16682)) (Fuji-Robin 330)			*(Noted SPLASH, NEC Birmingham 11.08)*		
G-MBBM	Eipper Quicksilver MX	10960	11. 9.81	J Brown	(Ulverscroft, Markfield)	X
	(Cuyana 430R)			*(In storage)*		
G-MBCJ	Mainair Tri-Flyer/Solar Wings Typhoon SJRN-1		30. 9.81	R A Smith	(Harwortrh, Doncaster)	30. 4.98X
	(Wing c/n T881-225) (May have replacement Sailwing c/n T382-390L)					
G-MBCK	Eipper Quicksilver MX	GWR-10962	30. 9.81	P Rowbotham	(Hathern, Loughborough)	X
	(Rotax 503)					
G-MBCL	Hiway Skytrike 160/Solar Wings Typhoon		30. 9.81	P J Callis	Halwell	X
		2332 & T1181-307				
G-MBCU	American Aerolights Eagle Amphibian	3181	5.10.81	J L May	(Drayton, Portsmouth)	9.10.07P
	(Rotax 377)					
G-MBCX	Hornet 250/Airwave Nimrod 165		12.10.81	M Maylor	(Manby, Louth)	31.12.87X
	(Built Airwave Gliders Ltd)	H090 & 0090 LJH				
G-MBDG	Eurowing Goldwing	E 20	19.10.81	B Fussell	(Llanelli)	14.12.94P
	(Konig SC 430)					
G-MBDM	Southdown Trike/Southdown Sigma	SST/001	26.10.81	A R Prentice	(Dartford)	X
	(Fuji-Robin EC-25-PS)					
G-MBET	Micro Engineering (Aviation) Mistral	MEA.103	10.11.81	B H Stephens	Old Sarum	27. 9.98P
	(Fuji-Robin EC-44-PM)			*(Noted in trailer 2002)*		
G-MBEU	Chargus T 250/Hiway Demon	T 250/06	10.11.81	R C Smith	(Clacton-on-Sea)	31. 5.86X
	(Fuji-Robin EC-25-PS)					
G-MBFK	Hiway Skytrike 250/Hiway Demon 175	LR17D	16.11.81	D W Stamp	(Kidderminster)	X
	(Fuji-Robin EC-25-PS)					
G-MBFO	Eipper Quicksilver MX	MLD-01	17.11.81	J C Larkin	(Flimby, Maryport)	20. 8.93P
	(Cuyuna 430R)					
G-MBFZ	Eurowing Goldwing	MSS-01	25.11.81	D G Palmer	Fetterangus	5. 9.00P
	(Fuji-Robin EC-34-PM)			*(Under active rebuild 2001)*		
G-MBGF	Twamley Trike/Birdman Cherokee	RWT-01	26.11.81	T B Woolley	(Narborough, Leicester)	
	(Built Birdman Enterprises Ltd)					
G-MBGS	Rotec Rally 2B	PCB-1	2.12.81	P C Bell	(Yalding, Maidstone)	
G-MBGX	Southdown Lightning DS	RBDB-1	7.12.81	T Knight	(Kingkerswell, Newton Abbot)	7. 3.92X
	(Fuji-Robin EC-44-PM) (Believed now fitted with Ultralight Aviation Systems Storm Buggy Trike ex G-MBKD)					
G-MBHE	American Aerolights Eagle 430B	4210	18.12.81	R J Osborne	Long Marston	12.10.96P
	(Cuyuna 430R)					
G-MBHK	Mainair Tri-Flyer 330/Flexiform Solo Striker		30.12.81	K T Vinning	(Stratford-upon-Avon)	11. 8.98P
	(Fuji-Robin EC-34-PM) EB-1 & 036-241181					
	(Original Tri-Flyer 250 Trike c/n 036 replaced by Tri-Flyer 330 c/n 060-382 in 1982)					
G-MBHZ	Pterodactyl Ptraveller	TD-01	6. 1.82	J C K Scardifield	(Milford on Sea, Lymington)	28. 2.86X
	(Cuyuna 430R)					
G-MBIA	Hiway Skytrike/Flexiform Sealander6172349/336		6. 1.82	I P Cook	(Royton, Oldham)	X
	(Fuji-Robin EC-34-PM)					
G-MBIO	American Aerolights Eagle 215B	E4007-Z	12. 1.82	S Montandon	(Whitbourne, Worcester)	X
	(Zenoah G25B1)					
G-MBIT	Hiway Skytrike/Demon	2501	18. 1.82	K S Hodgson	(Skutterskelfe, Yarm)	X
	(Fuji-Robin EC-25-PS)					
G-MBIY	Ultrasports Tri-Pacer/Southdown Lightning Phase II		19. 1.82	J W Burton	Tarn Farm, Cockerham	18. 4.99P
	(Fuji-Robin EC-34-PM) 330			*(Stored 2.03)*		
	(Wing c/n L170-439)					
G-MBIZ	Mainair Tri-Flyer 250/Hiway Vulcan		20. 1.82	E F Clapham, W B S Dobi, S P Slade and D M A Templeman		
	(Fuji-Robin EC-25PS) 039-251181 & SD9V				(Bristol)	----
G-MBJD	American Aerolights Eagle 215B	4169	21. 1.82	R W F Boarder	(Tring)	X
	(Zenoah G25B1)					
G-MBJF	Hiway Skytrike II/Vulcan C	80-00099	22. 1.82	C H Bestwick	(Beeston, Nottingham)	X
	(Fuji-Robin EC-25-PS) (C/n is engine serial no)					
G-MBJG	Chargus T 250/Airwave Nimrod UP					
	(Fuji-Robin EC-25-PS) CMT165045		25. 1.82	D H George	Sandown	5. 7.05P
G-MBJK	American Aerolights Eagle	2742	16. 1.82	B W Olley	(Soham, Ely)	
	(Chrysler 820)			*(Stored 2000)*		
G-MBJL	Hornet 250/Airwave Nimrod	JSRM-01	26. 1.82	A G Lowe	(Dyce, Aberdeen)	20.10.96P
	(Fuji-Robin EC-25-PS)			*(Noted at owner's home 4.02)*		
G-MBJM	Striplin Lone Ranger	LR-81-00138	26. 1.82	C K Brown	(East Leake, Loughborough)	
	(Built C K Brown) (Fuji-Robin) (C/n 81-00138 is engine serial no)					
G-MBKY	American Aerolights Eagle 215B	BF-01	12. 2.82	M J Aubrey *(Noted 2002)*		
	(Officially regd with c/n ZFE-15288 which is a corruption of engine type number [Zenoah G25B1 no.15288])					
				Upper Yeld, Floodgates, Kington, Hereford		
G-MBKZ	Hiway Skytrike/Super Scorpion	EC25P8-04	12. 2.82	S I Harding	(Mytchett, Camberley)	
	(Fuji-Robin EC-25-PS) (C/n is corruption of engine type)					
G-MBLU	Ultrasports Tri-Pacer/Southdown Lightning L195		26. 2.82	C R Franklin	(Landkey, Barnstaple)	X
	(Fuji-Robin EC-25-PS) L195/191					
G-MBMG	Rotec Rally 2B	RJP-01	3. 3.82	J R Pyper	(Craigavon, County Armagh)	
G-MBMT	Mainair Tri-Flyer/Southdown Lightning 195		8. 3.82	A G Rodenburg and T Abro *(Noted 4.04)*		
	(Fuji-Robin EC-25-PS) TRY-01 *(Wing c/n L195-195?)*				Tillicoultry, Stirling	X
G-MBOF	Pakes Jackdaw	LGP-01	26. 3.82	L G Pakes	(Ryde, Isle of Wight)	
	(Built L G Pakes)			*(Noted dismantled 6.06)*		
G-MBOH	Micro Engineering (Aviation) Mistral	008	29. 3.82	N A Bell	(Broxhill, Fordingbridge)	X
	(Fuji-Robin EC-44-PM)					
G-MBPB (2)	Pterodactyl Ptraveller	PEB-01	7. 4.82	N A Bell	(Broxhill, Fordingbridge)	
	(Built P E Bailey)			*(For rebuild 12.01)*		
G-MBPG	Mainair Tri-Flyer/Solar Wings Typhoon		13. 4.82	S D Thorpe	Otherton, Cannock	14. 6.01P
	(Fuji-Robin EC-25-PS) 189-1983 & T381-105					
	(Original Trike was c/n 067-582 and may have been used for G-MMGT)					
G-MBPJ	Centrair Moto-Delta G 11	001	14. 5.82	J B Jackson	(Mickle Trafford, Chester)	
	(Built Moto Delta)					

G-MBPU	Hiway Skytrike 250/Demon	DSS-01		21. 4.82	D Hines	(Hanklowe, Crewe)	22. 1.04P
G-MBPX	Eurowing Goldwing SP	EW-42		21. 4.82	A R Channon	(Sawston, Cambridge)	6.11.96P
	(Konig SC 430)						
G-MBPY	Ultrasports Tri-Pacer 330/Wasp Gryphon II						
	(Built Wasp) (Fuji-Robin EC-24-PM)	RKP-01		21. 4.82	D Hawkes and C Poundes	(Milton Keynes)	12. 4.03P
G-MBRB	Electraflyer Eagle Mk.I	E 2229		9.12.81	R C Bott	(Abergynolwyn, Tywyn)	
G-MBRD	American Aerolights Eagle 215B	E 2635		20. 4.82	R J Osborne	(Cove, Tiverton)	31. 8.85X
	(Fuji-Robin EC-25-PS)						
G-MBRH	Ultraflight Mirage II	83-009 & RALH-01		20. 4.82	R W F Boarder	Field Farm, Oakley	8. 1.01P
G-MBST	Mainair Gemini/Southdown Puma Sprint						
	(Fuji-Robin EC-44-PM)	141-29383		10. 4.84	G J Bowen	(Llanelli)	25. 5.03P
	(Fitted with Trike from G-MJXA)						
G-MBSX	Ultraflight Mirage II	240		14. 6.82	C J Draper t/a Medway Microlights		
						Stoke, Isle of Grain	30. 5.03P
G-MBTH	Whittaker MW4	T1081-262L	(G-MBPB (1))	6. 4.82	L Greenfield and M Whittaker tr The MW4 Flying Group		
	(Built M Whittaker - c/n 001) (Fuji-Robin EC-34-PM)					Otherton, Cannock	12. 7.04P
G-MBTJ	Ultrasports Tri-Pacer/Solar Wings Typhoon			2. 4.82	H A Comber	(Poole)	9. 8.06P
	(Fuji-Robin EC-25-PS)	CSRS-01			(Wing c/n may be T1081-286L)		
G-MBTW	Aerodyne Vector 600	1188		10. 5.82	W I Fuller	(Red Lodge, Bury St Edmunds)	X
	(Zenoah G25B1)						
G-MBUZ	Skycraft Scout II	0366		4. 5.82	A C Thorne (Noted 11.06)	(Bere Alston, Yelverton)	
G-MBWG	Huntair Pathfinder Mk.1	006		19. 5.82	T Mahmood (Noted 1.05)	Maryculter	14. 7.99P
	(Fuji-Robin EC-34-PM)						
G-MBYI	Ultraflight Lazair IIIE	A464/001		4. 6.82	C M Mackinnon	Strathaven	25. 8.06P
	(Built AMF Microflight Ltd) (Rotax 185 x 2) (Originally kit no A522 and amended during rebuild c 1982)						
G-MBYL	Huntair Pathfinder Mk.1	009		4. 6.82	S Porter	(Eglinton, Londonderry)	17. 2.02P
	(Fuji-Robin EC-44-PM)						
G-MBYM	Eipper Quicksilver MX	JW-01		4. 6.82	M P Harper and L L Perry	Priory Farm, Tibenham	21. 9.96P
	(Cuyuna 430R)						
G-MBZO	Mainair Tri-Flyer/Flexiform Medium Striker			15. 6.82	A N Burrows	(Kirk Michael, Isle of Man)	15. 4.98P
	(Fuji-Robin EC-34-PM) GRH-01 & 021-101081						
G-MBZV	American Aerolights Eagle 215B	4227-Z		16. 6.82	M J Aubrey	Kington, Hereford	X
	(Cuyana 215R)				(Noted SPLASH, NEC Birmingham 11.08)		
G-MCAB	Gardan GY-201 Minicab	PFA 056-11161		19. 5.08	P G Hooper	(Winchester)	
	(Built P G Hooper)						
G-MCAI	Robinson R44 Raven II	10423		9. 7.04	M C Allen	Denham	20. 8.09E
G-MCAP	Cameron C-80 Balloon (Hot Air)	10186		30. 7.02	L D Thurgar (Mencap titles)	Bristol	2. 1.10E
G-MCCF	Thruster T 600N Sprint	0100-T600N-048		25. 4.01	C C F Fuller	Craysmarsh Farm, Melksham	31. 5.09P
G-MCCG	Robinson R44 Raven	1758		5.10.07	Chris Ford Helicopters Ltd	Costock	21.10.09E
G-MCCY	IAV Bacau Yakovlev Yak-52	9011112	LY-AQF	11.11.04	D P McCoy	Weston, Leixlip, County Kildare	20.11.08P
			UR-BBP, Ukraine AF 129, DOSAAF 129				
G-MCDB	Vickers Supermarine 361 Spitfire LF.IX	MA764		27. 2.08	M Collenette	(Sway, Lymington)	
		CBAF IX 401			(Regd officially with fuselage no, firewall plate is CBAF 5423)		
G-MCEL	Cyclone Airsports Pegasus Quantum 15-912			10.10.01	F Hodgson	Sywell	22.10.08P
	(Rotax 912 UL)	7858					
G-MCJL	Cyclone Airsports Pegasus Quantum 15-912			16. 3.99	Lincoln Enterprises Ltd	Linley Hill, Leven	19. 5.09P
	(Rotax 912)	7497					
G-MCLY	Cessna 172P Skyhawk	17275597	N61GA	14. 6.07	McAully Flying Group Ltd	Little Snoring	21.10.09E
			SE-IXY, N64643				
G-MCMC	SOCATA TBM-700	261	N181PC	4. 4.06	Sogestao Administraca Gerencia SA	Biggin Hill	30. 9.09E
G-MCMS	Aero Designs Pulsar	PFA 202-11982		3. 2.93	B R Hunter	Sturgate	22.10.09P
	(Built M C Manning) (Rotax 582)						
G-MCOW	Lindstrand LBL 77A Balloon (Hot Air)	1142		13.12.06	S and S Villiers	Donaghadee	13. 7.09E
G-MCOX	Fuji FA.200-180AO Aero Subaru	FA200-296	(G-BIMS)	29.12.81	West Surrey Engineering Ltd	Fairoaks	19. 6.09E
G-MCOY	Flight Design CT2K	01-04-01-12		25. 7.01	D Young t/a Pegasus Flight Training (Cotswolds)		
	(Assembled Pegasus Aviation - no c/n issued)					Kemble	1. 8.07P
G-MCRO	Dyn'Aero MCR-01	LAA 301-14802		2. 9.08	M K Faro	Henstridge	
	(Built M K Faro)						
G-MCUB	Reality Escapade	UK,CKT.009?		27. 4.07	A D Janaway	Dunkeswell	18. 8.09P
	(Built A D Janaway - pr.no.PFA 345-14680) (Ulpower UL260i)						
G-MCXV	Colomban MC-15 Cri-Cri	371	F-PYVA	1. 3.00	P C Appleton	Davidstow Moor	25.10.08P
	(Built J P Lorre) (2 x JPX PUL 212)						
G-MDAC	Piper PA-28-181 Archer II	28-8290154	N8242T	6.11.87	S A Nicklen tr Alpha Charlie Flying Group		
						Henstridge	7. 7.09E
G-MDAY	Cessna 170B	26350	N2807C	2. 5.03	M Day	Bourne Park, Hurstbourne Tarrant	29. 6.11S
					(Carries "N2807C" on tail)		
G-MDBA	Dassault Falcon 2000	184	N71AX	1. 5.08	TAG Aviation (UK) Ltd	Farnborough	6. 5.09E
			XA-RET, N2261, F-WWMK				
G-MDBC	Cyclone Airsports Pegasus Quantum 15-912			4. 5.01	J H Bradbury	Arclid Green, Sandbach	26.10.08P
		7814					
G-MDBD	Airbus A330-243	266	F-WWKG	24. 6.99	Thomas Cook Airlines Ltd	Manchester	24. 6.09E
G-MDDT	Robinson R44 Raven II	11474		6.11.06	M D Tracey	Bledington, Chipping Norton	19.11.09E
G-MDGE	Robinson R22 Beta	1475	G-OGOG	25. 6.04	Mandarin AviationCLtd	Redhill	2.11.09E
			G-TILL				
G-MDJE	Cessna 208 Caravan I (Amphibian)	20800336	N208FM	13. 6.07	Loch Lomond Seaplanes Ltd		
			XA-TSV, N5263S			Pacific Quay, Glasgow	12. 6.09E
G-MDJN	Beech 95-B55 Baron	TC-1574	G-SUZI	3. 8.04	A Penner-Reinhard	Voelklingen, Germany	30.11.09E
			G-BAXR				
G-MDKD	Robinson R22 Beta	1247		18. 4.90	D Jones t/a Rotorair	Swansea	13. 3.09E
G-MDPI	Agusta A109A II	7393	G-PERI	11. 8.04	Langfast Ltd	(Nicholashayne, Wellington)	28. 9.09E
			G-EXEK, G-SLNE, G-EEVS, G-OTSL				
G-MDPY	Robinson R44 Raven II	11582		2. 2.07	McDonnell Aviation Ltd (Ashford, County Wicklow)		13 .2.09E
G-MEDE	Airbus A320-232	1194	F-WWDY	25. 4.00	British Midland Airways Ltd	London Heathrow	24. 4.09E
G-MEDF	Airbus A321-231	1690	D-AVZX	28. 2.02	British Midland Airways Ltd	London Heathrow	27. 2.09E

G-MEDG	Airbus A321-231	1711	D-AVZK	5. 4.02	British Midland Airways Ltd	London Heathrow	4. 4.09E
G-MEDH	Airbus A320-232	1922	F-WWBX	6. 3.03	British Midland Airways Ltd	London Heathrow	5. 3.09E
G-MEDJ	Airbus A321-231	2190	D-AVZD	8. 4.04	British Midland Airways Ltd	London Heathrow	7. 4.09E
G-MEDK	Airbus A320-232	2441	F-WWBQ	27. 5.05	British Midland Airways Ltd	London Heathrow	26. 5.09E
G-MEDL	Airbus A321-231	2653	D-AVZC	19. 1.06	British Midland Airways Ltd	London Heathrow	18. 1.10E
G-MEDM	Airbus A321-231	2799	D-AVZP	26. 6.06	British Midland Airways Ltd	London Heathrow	25. 6.09E
G-MEDN	Airbus A321-231	3512	D-AVZK	9. 5.08	British Midland Airways Ltd	London-Heathrow	8. 5.09E
G-MEDS	Agusta A109E Power	11679		19. 9.06	Sloane Helicopters Ltd	Sywell	18. 9.09E
G-MEDX	Agusta A109E Power	11745		5.11.08	Sloane Helicopters Ltd	Sywell	
G-MEEE	Schleicher ASW 20 L	20312	BGA2620-EEE	11. 9.07	T E Macfadyen	Nympsfield	28. 9.08
G-MEEK	Enstrom 480	5029	N485A	9. 5.06	Rocket Rentals Ltd	Gloucestershire	1. 6.09E
G-MEET	Learjet Model 40	45-2054	N50111	15. 9.06	TAG Aviation (UK) Ltd	Farnborough	19. 9.09E
G-MEGA	Piper PA-28R-201T Turbo Arrow III	28R-7803303	N999JG	13. 2.86	A W Bean	Sandtoft	17. 1.09E
G-MEGG	Europa Aviation Europa XS	358		14. 6.00	M E Mavers	Sleap	8. 6.09E
	(Built M E Mavers - pr.no.PFA 247-13202) (Rotaz 912ULS) (Monowheel u/c)						
G-MEGN	Beech B200 Super King Air	BB-1518	N65LA SU-ZBA, N3218V	30.11.06	Dragonfly Aviation Services LLP	Cardiff	2. 1.10E
G-MEGS	Cessna 172S Skyhawk	172S10723	N6245C	9. 6.08	The Cambridge Aero Club Ltd	Cambridge	30. 6.09E
G-MELL	CZAW Sportscruiser	LAA 338-14866		1.12.08	G A and J A Mellins	(Stanmore)	
	(Built G A and J A Mellins)						
G-MELS	Piper PA-28-181 Archer III	2843633	D-EASX N3139C	17. 7.07	Avicorp Ltd	Swansea	16. 7.09E
G-MELT	Cessna F172H	F172-0580	G-AWTI	23. 9.83	Falcon Aviation Ltd		
	(Built Reims Aviation SA)					Bourne Park, Hurstbourne Tarrant	20. 4.09E
G-MEME	Piper PA-28R-201 Arrow III	2837051	N9219N	17. 8.90	Henry J Clare Ltd	Bodmin	9. 4.09E
G-MENU	Robinson R44 Raven II	12664		27. 1.09	Heli Air Ltd		
					Wellesbourne Mountford/Wycombe Air Park		
G-MENY	Agusta A109 Grand	22059		19.11.07	N Menary	(Portstewart)	15.12.09E
G-MEOW	CFM Streak Shadow	K 172		23. 4.93	G J Moor	Craysmarsh Farm, Melksham	12. 4.09P
	(Built S D Hicks - pr.no.PFA 206-12025) (Rotax 582)						
G-MEPU	Rotorsport UK MT-03	RSUK/MT-03/007		20.10.06	M C Elliott	RAF Benson	19.12.08P
G-MERC	Colt 56A Balloon (Hot Air)	842		11. 6.86	A F and C.D Selby	Loughborough	9. 8.09E
G-MERE	Lindstrand LBL 77A Balloon (Hot Air)	092		7. 4.94	R D Baker	Goodnestone, Canterbury	
G-MERF	Grob G115A	8091	EI-CAB	24. 7.95	G Wylie	White Waltham	16. 6.09E
G-MERL	Piper PA-28RT-201 Arrow IV	28R-7918036	N2116N	27. 6.86	W T Jenkins	Cardiff	11.12.09E
G-MESH	CZAW Sportscruiser	LAA 338-14823		21. 7.08	M E S Heaton	(Oxenhope, Keighley)	
	(Built M E S Heaton)						
G-METH	Cameron C-90 Balloon (Hot Air)	10841		21. 4.06	A and D Methley	Marshfield, Chippenham	8. 3.09E
G-MEUP	Cameron A-120 Balloon (Hot Air)	2117		5.10.89	Innovation Ballooning Ltd *(Sopwith Aviation Company titles)*		
						Bath	25. 8.08T
G-MFAC	Cessna F172H	F172-0387	G-AVBZ	23. 8.01	Ravenair Aircraft Ltd	Liverpool	24. 7.09E
	(Built Reims Aviation SA)						
G-MFEF	Reims FR172J Rocket	FR17200426	D-EGJQ	19.10.00	M and E N Ford	Butlers Gyhll, Southwater	19. 1.10E
G-MFHI	Europa Aviation Europa	202		14.11.97	P Rees tr Hi Fliers	Rochester	25.12.07P
	(Built M F Howe - pr.no.PFA 247-12841) (Rotax 912 UL) (Tri-cycle u/c)						
G-MFLI	Cameron V-90 Balloon (Hot Air)	2650		14. 8.91	J M Percival *(Mouldform titles)* "Mayfly"		
					Bourton-on-the-Wolds, Loughborough		6. 9.09E
G-MFLJ	P&M Aviation Quik GT450	8303		29. 8.07	M F Jakeman	Deenethorpe	28. 8.09P
G-MFLY	Mainair Rapier	1359-1103-7-W1154		30. 3.04	J J Tierney	Chiltern Park, Wallingford	5.10.08P
G-MFMF	Bell 206B-3 JetRanger III	3569	G-BJNJ	4. 6.84	Western Power Distribution (South West) PLC		
						Bristol	3.12.09E
G-MFMM	Scheibe SF25C Falke	4412	(G-MBMM) D-KAEU	20. 4.82	J E Selman	(Ardagh, County Limerick)	16. 7.08E
			(Limbach SL1700)				
G-MGAA	BFC Challenger II	CH2-0297-1568		18. 8.97	J C Craddock and R J Speight		
	(Built G A Archer and J W E Pearson - pr.no.PFA 177A-13124) (Rotax 582)					(Freshwater, Isle of Wight)	21. 5.08P
G-MGAG	Aviasud Mistral 532GB	0587-045		20. 6.89	M Raj	Otherton, Cannock	27. 6.00P
	(Built Aviasud Engineering - pr.no.BMAA HB/009)						
G-MGAN	Robinson R44 Astro	0588		10. 5.99	A Taylor	Whitley, Dewsbury	2. 8.09E
G-MGCA	Avtech Jabiru UL	0130		8. 5.98	K D Pearce	Oaklands Farm, Horsham	26. 3.04P
	(Built P A James - pr.no.PFA 274-13228 although type prefix should be "274A")						
G-MGCB	Solar Wings Pegasus XL-Q	7267		16.10.96	M G Gomez	Headon Farm, Retford	5. 9.05P
	(Trike c/n SW-TE-0344) and ex G-MWUT)						
G-MGCK	Whittaker MW6-S Fatboy Flyer	PFA 164-11262		30. 3.93	M W J Whittaker and L R Orriss		
	(Built M W J Whittaker: offically regd as MW6 Merlin)					Church Farm, Askern	
					(Noted 9.07)		
G-MGDL	Cyclone Airsports Pegasus Quantum 15	7400		17. 2.98	M J Buchanan	Coldharbour Farm, Willingham	7. 6.08P
	(Rotax 582)						
G-MGEC	Rans S-6-ESD-XL Coyote II	1096.1047		13.10.97	P J Hopkins	Deenethorpe	8. 7.09E
	(Built E Carter - pr.no.PFA 204-13209) (Tri-cycle u/c)						
G-MGEF	Cyclone Airsports Pegasus Quantum 15-912	7261		18. 9.96	G D Castell	Longacre Farm, Sandy	12. 7.09P
G-MGFK	Cyclone Airsports Pegasus Quantum 15-912	7396		2. 2.98	F A A Kay	London Colney	1.10.07P
G-MGGG	Cyclone Airsports Pegasus Quantum 15-912	7377		3.11.97	R A Beauchamp Shenstone Hall Farm, Shenstone		27. 7.09P
G-MGGT	CFM Streak Shadow SA-M	K 252		3. 6.94	D R Stansfield	Heckington	25.10.08P
	(Built J W V Edmonds - pr.no.PFA 206-12723) (Rotax 618)						
G-MGGV	Cyclone Airsports Pegasus Quantum 15-912	7484		28. 4.98	G J Slater	Clench Common	1. 8.09P
G-MGMC	Cyclone Airsports Pegasus Quantum 15-912	7430		12.10.98	S M Green	(Marlborough)	14. 9.09P
G-MGMM	Piper PA-18-150 Super Cub	18-7909189	D-EBRG N9750N	1. 6.04	M J Martin	Challock	10. 7.10S

Reg	Type	C/n	Prev id	Date	Owner/Operator	Base	Date
G-MGND	Rans S-6-ESD-XL Coyote II	1096.1048		27. 6.97	P K Jenkins	Long Marston	20. 7.09P
	(Built N N Ducker - pr.no.PFA 204-13152) (Rotax 503)						
G-MGOD	Medway Raven X	MRB110/106		6. 7.93	A Wherrett, N R Andrew and D J Millward	Doynton	1. 5.00P
	(Rotax 447)				*(Noted 1.05)*		
G-MGOO	Murphy Renegade Spirit UK	301		14.11.89	P J Dale	Woodview House Farm, St Leonards	12. 7.09P
	(Built A R Max - pr.no.PFA 188-11580) (Rotax 582)						
G-MGPA	Comco Ikarus C42 FB100	0412-6635		25. 1.05	S Ashley	Dunkeswell	6. 2.08P
	(Built Fly Buy Ultralights Ltd) (Rotax 912ULS)						
G-MGPD	Solar Wings Pegasus XL-R	6905		9. 1.95	H T Mounfield	Weston Zoyland	4. 5.07P
	(Rotax 462)				*(Noted 5.07)*		
G-MGPH	CFM Streak Shadow SA-M	286	G-RSPH	27.11.97	V C Readhead	(Saxmundham)	29. 7.00P
	(Built CFM Aircraft Ltd - pr.no.PFA 206-13166) (Rotax 582)						
G-MGPX	Kolb Twinstar Mk III Xtra	PFA 205-14701		28. 1.08	S P Garton	(Althorpe, Scunthorpe)	
	(Built S P Garton)						
G-MGTG	Pegasus Quantum 15-912	7369A	G-MZIO	19.12.97	R B Milton	Plaistows Farm, St Albans	15. 2.09P
	(Original c/n 7369 amended after rebuild 11.98)						
G-MGTR	Huntwing/Experience	xxxxx		24. 7.97	A C Ryall	(Cardiff)	
	(Built A C Ryall - pr.no.BMAA HB/067) (Listed as "Huntwing Avon" in BMAA's records)						
G-MGTV	Thruster T 600N 450 Sprint	0052-T600N-070		14. 3.02	R Bingham and P A Durrans		
	(Jabiru 2200)					Mullahead, Tandragee	8.10.08P
G-MGTW	CFM Shadow Series DD	287-DD		23. 1.98	G T Webster	Easter Poldar Farm, Thornhill	24. 3.08P
G-MGUN	Cyclone AX2000	7284		18.12.96	I Lonsdale	Tarn Farm, Cockerham	11. 6.08P
G-MGUY	CFM Shadow Series CD	078		23.11.87	F J Luckhurst and R G M Proost	(Old Sarum)	16. 8.91P
					(Crashed Home Farm, Pontisbury, Shrewsbury 20. 7.91)		
G-MGWH	Thruster T 300	9013-T300-507		8.12.92	J J Hill	Baxby Manor, Husthwaite	26. 9.08P
	(Built Tempest Aviation Ltd) (Rotax 582)						
G-MGWI	Robinson R44 Astro	0663	G-BZEF	4. 5.00	Ed Murray and Sons Ltd	(Bagby)	4. 6.08E
G-MHAR	Piper PA-42-720 Cheyenne IIIA	42-5501020	N690E	1. 7.08	BAE Systems (Operations) Ltd	RAF Marham	6. 7.09E
G-MHCB	Enstrom 280C Shark	1031	N892PT	11.10.95	Springbank Aviation Ltd	Ronaldsway	10. 6.08E
G-MHCE	Enstrom F-28A	150	G-BBHD	22. 8.96	Wyke Commercial Services Ltd	Barton	8.11.07E
G-MHCG	Enstrom 280C-UK Shark	1155	G-HAYN	7. 3.97	G L Pritchard	(Capel Coch, Llangefni)	10. 2.09E
			G-BPOX, N51776				
G-MHCI	Enstrom 280C Shark	1152	N100WZ	20. 5.97	Charlie India Helicopters Ltd	Hawarden	27. 2.09E
G-MHCJ	Enstrom F-28C-UK	453	G-CTRN	30. 3.98	P E Toleman tr Paradise Helicopters	Hawarden	14. 5.08E
G-MHCK	Enstrom 280FX Shark	2006	G-BXXB	5. 6.98	D Shakespeare	(Clent, Stourbridge)	15.11.07E
			ZK-HHN, JA7702				
G-MHCL	Enstrom 280C Shark	1144	N51740	30. 6.98	J A Newton	(Knutsford)	24.11.01T
G-MHCM	Enstrom 280FX Shark	2052	G-IBWF	5. 4.06	Kingswood Bank LLP	Barton	14. 9.08E
			G-ZZWW, G-BSIE, HA-MIN, G-BSIE				
G-MHGS	Stoddard-Hamilton GlaStar	PFA 295-13473		30. 7.03	M Henderson	(Cults, Aberdeen)	27. 2.09P
	(Built M Henderson) (Lycoming O-320) (Tri-cycle u/c)						
G-MHJK	Diamond DA.42 Twin Star	42.173	OE-VPY	4. 1.07	JMS Janitorial Supplies Ltd	Redhill	31. 3.09E
			OE-VPW				
G-MHMH	Agusta-Bell 206B JetRanger II	8038	G-HOLZ	2. 9.08	Helicopter Hire LLP	Newark	26. 8.09E
			ZK-IBC, G-HOLZ, G-CDBT, 1206 R Saudi AF				
G-MHMR	Pegasus Quantum 15-912	7969	D-MHMR	19.12.05	L Zivanovic	Droitwich	3. 2.09P
G-MHRV	Van's RV-6A	PFA 181A-13422		28. 7.04	M R Harris	(Luton)	
	(Built M R Harris)						
G-MICE	Cessna 510 Mustang	510-0156		2. 2.09	Fteron Ltd	Limassol, Cyprus	
G-MICH	Robinson R22 Beta	0647	G-BNKY	3. 9.87	Tiger Helicopters Ltd	(Shobdon)	10.10.05T
				(Tail rotor struck ground Shobdon 10. 6.03, rolled onto side and substantially damaged)			
G-MICI	Cessna 182S Skylane	18280546	G-WARF	14. 6.01	S J Parrish tr Steve Parrish Racing		
			N7089F			(Douglas, Isle of Man)	26. 8.09E
G-MICK	Reims Cessna F172N Skyhawk II	F17201592	PH-JRA	9. 1.80	P W Carlton	Durham Tees Valley	5.10.09E
			PH-AXB				
G-MICY	Everett Gyroplane Series 1	018	(G-BOVF)	26. 2.90	D M Hughes	(Bartley, Southampton)	2. 5.92P
	(Volkswagen 1835)						
G-MIDC	Airbus A321-231	0835	D-AVZZ	12. 6.98	British Midland Airways Ltd	London Heathrow	11. 6.09E
G-MIDD	Piper PA-28-140 Cherokee Cruiser		G-BBDD	20. 1.97	R B Walker t/a Midland Air Training School		
		28-7325444	N11C			Coventry	5. 6.09E
G-MIDG	Bushby-Long Midget Mustang	385	N11DE	14. 3.90	C E Bellhouse	Headcorn	14. 8.09P
	(Built T Holt, rebuilt T L Owens)		N567, N2TH				
	(Lycoming O-320)						
G-MIDL	Airbus A321-231	1174	D-AVZH	22. 2.00	British Midland Airways Ltd	London Heathrow	21. 2.09E
					(Star Alliance titles)		
G-MIDO	Airbus A320-232	1987	F-WWIR	29. 4.03	British Midland Airways Ltd	London Heathrow	28. 4.09E
G-MIDP	Airbus A320-232	1732	F-WWBK	24. 5.02	British Midland Airways Ltd	London Heathrow	23. 5.09E
G-MIDR	Airbus A320-232	1697	F-WWIQ	22. 4.02	British Midland Airways Ltd	London Heathrow	21. 4.09E
G-MIDS	Airbus A320-232	1424	F-WWBO	21. 3.01	British Midland Airways Ltd	London Heathrow	20. 3.09E
G-MIDT	Airbus A320-232	1418	F-WWBI	14. 3.01	British Midland Airways Ltd	London Heathrow	13. 3.09E
G-MIDX	Airbus A320-232	1177	F-WWDP	21. 3.00	British Midland Airways Ltd	London Heathrow	20. 3.09E
					(Star Alliance titles)		
G-MIDY	Airbus A320-232	1014	F-WWDQ	28. 6.99	British Midland Airways Ltd	London Heathrow	27. 6.09E
G-MIDZ	Airbus A320-232	0934	F-WWII	19. 1.99	British Midland Airways Ltd	London Heathrow	18. 1.10E
G-MIFF	Robin DR.400-180 Régent	2076		31. 5.91	J C Harvey tr Westfield Flying Group		
						Spilstead Farm, Sedlescombe	22. 5.09E
G-MIGG	PZL-Mielec Lim-5	1C1211	G-BWUF	17. 1.03	D Miles (As "511" in Polish AF c/s)	North Weald	
			Polish AF 1211			*(Noted 1.09 for restoration)*	
G-MIII	Extra EA.300/L	013	D-EXFI	5. 9.95	Angels High Ltd	Sywell	2. 8.09E
G-MIKE	Gyroflight Brookland Hornet	MG.1		15. 5.78	M H J Goldring	(Newton Abbot)	25. 9.92P
	(Volkswagen 1830)						
G-MIKI	Rans S-6-ESA Coyote II	0996.1040		28. 2.97	S P Slade *(Active 7.08)*	The Chase, Wickwar	16. 6.07P
	(Built N R Beale - pr.no.PFA 204-13094) (Rotax 912-UL) (Tri-cycle u/c)						
G-MIKS	Robinson R44 Clipper II	10314		15. 4.04	M Glastonbury	(Leicester)	

G-MILA	Reims Cessna F172N Skyhawk II	F17201686	D-EGHC (2)	9. 6.98	P J Miller	Cuckoo Tye Farm, Long Melford	20.11.09E
			PH-AYJ				
G-MILD	Scheibe SF25C Falke	44190	D-KDET	20.12.05	The Borders (Milfield) Gliding Club Ltd	Milfield	30. 3.09E
	(Limbach SL 1700)						
G-MILE	Cameron N-90 Balloon (Hot Air)	2411		26. 9.90	Miles Air Ltd (Miles Architectural Ironmongery Ltd titles)		
	(Originally regd as N-77: new envelope c/n 10548 fitted 2004)					Bristol	9. 8.09E
G-MILI	Bell 206B-3 JetRanger III	2275	C-GGAR	5.10.94	Westflor (AG) Ltd	Damyn's Hall, Upminster	15. 4.09E
			5H-MPV				
G-MILN	Cessna 182Q Skylane	18265770	N735XQ	9. 7.99	Meon Hill Farms (Stockbridge) Ltd	Thruxton	27. 9.09E
G-MILO	Cessna T303 Crusader	T303-00211	N57MT	4. 7.08	Fortisair Ltd	Jersey	
			(N996JB), N57MT,D-IEEG, N9748C				
G-MILY	Grumman American AA-5A Cheetah AA5A-0672		G-BFXY	2. 9.96	Plane Talking Ltd	Cranfield	17.10.07E
	(C/n plate shows maufacturer as Gulfstream American)						
G-MIMA	British Aerospace BAe 146 Series 200 E2079		G-CNMF	3. 3.93	Casino Rodos Hotel, Tourism, Construction SA		
			G-5-079			Rhodes, Greece	25. 8.09E
G-MIME	Europa Aviation Europa	203		26. 9.97	N W Charles	Lydeway, Devizes	21. 9.09P
	(Built N W Charles - pr.no.PFA 247-12850) (Rotax 912 ULS)(Monowheel u/c)						
G-MIND	Cessna 404 Titan	404-0004	G-SKKC	27. 4.93	Reconnaissance Ventures Ltd	Coventry	13. 2.10E
			G-OHUB, SE-GMX, (N3932C) (Environment Agency titles + logo on tail)				
G-MINN	Lindstrand LBL 90A Balloon (Hot Air)	883		30.10.02	S M and D Johnson	Bromley	1. 7.09E
G-MINS	Nicollier HN.700 Ménestrel II PFA 217-12354			23.10.92	R Fenion	Kirkbride	16. 5.08P
	(Built R Fenion) (Volkswagen 1900)						
G-MINT	Pitts S-1S	PFA 009-10292		7. 2.83	T G Sanderson	Leicester	11.11.08P
	(Built T G Sanderson) (Lycoming AEIO-360)						
G-MIOO	Miles M.100 Student 2	M1008	G-APLK	26.10.84	Aces High Ltd	(Woking)	6. 5.86P
	(Turomeca Marbore IIF3)		G-MIOO, G-APLK, XS941, G-APLK, G-35-4				
			(On loan to Museum of Berkshire Aviation and on rebuild as "G-APLK" 2008)				
G-MIRA	Avtech Jabiru SP-430	0222	G-LUMA	29. 9.05	C P L Helsen	Balen-Keiheuvel, Belgium	9.12.09P
	(Built B Luyckx - pr.no.PFA 274-13458)						
G-MIRN	Remos GX	271		31.10.08	M Kurkic	London NW19	
	(Rotax 912 ULS)						
G-MISH	Cessna 182R Skylane II	18267888	G-RFAB	16. 6.95	Graham Churchill Plant Ltd	Finmere	15. 5.09E
			G-BIXT, N6397H				
G-MISJ	CZAW Sportscruiser	LAA 338-14862		20. 1.09	M T Dawson	Leeds-Bradford	
	(Built M T Dawson)						
G-MISS	Taylor JT.2 Titch	PFA 3234		18.12.78	D Beale	Witchford, Ely	
	(Built A Brenen)						
G-MITE	Raj Hamsa X'Air Falcon Jabiru(4)	830		3. 3.04	J T Athulathmudali	Bridport	12. 7.09P
	(Built T Jestico - pr.no.BMAA HB/296)						
G-MIWS	Cessna 310R II	310R1585	G-ODNP	1. 2.96	Wilcott Sport and Construction Ltd	Welshpool	10.12.08E
			N19TP, N2DD, N1836E				
G-MJAE	American Aerolights Eagle	1021		12. 7.82	T B Woolley	(Narborough, Leicester)	
	(C/n not confirmed)						
G-MJAJ	Eurowing Goldwing	EW-36		18. 6.82	M J Aubrey		
	(Fuji-Robin EC-44-PM)					Upper Yeld, Floodgates, Kington, Hereford	6. 8.03P
G-MJAM	Eipper Quicksilver MX	JCL-01		18. 6.82	J C Larkin	(Flimby, Maryport)	20. 8.93P
	(Cuyuna 430)						
G-MJAN	Hiway Skytrike I/Flexiform Hilander			21. 6.82	G M Sutcliffe	(Bramhall, Stockport)	4. 3.92X
	(Valmet)	RPFD-01 & 21U9					
G-MJAV	Hiway Skytrike II/Demon 175	817003		23. 6.82	J N J Roberts	(Frizlington)	X
	(Fuji-Robin 250)						
G-MJAY	Eurowing Goldwing	EW-58		23. 6.82	M Anthony	(Moreton, Alfreton)	X
	(Fuji-Robin EC-34-PM)						
G-MJAZ	Aerodyne Vector 627SR Ultravector	1251	PH-1J1	23. 6.82	B Fussell	Swansea	23. 9.93X
	(Konig SC430)		G-MJAZ		(Dismantled and stored 9.08)		
	(Originally regd as Vector 610 but converted 4.88 when PH-1J1)						
G-MJBK	Swallow AeroPlane Swallow B	582007-2		18.11.83	M A Newbould	(Markington, Harrogate)	X
	(Rotax 447)						
G-MJBL	American Aerolights Eagle 215B	2892		25. 6.82	B W Olley	(Soham, Ely)	19. 9.04P
	(Chrysler 820)						
G-MJBS	Ultralight Aviation Systems Storm Buggy/Solar Wings			29. 6.82	G I Sargeant	(Bridgwater)	
		JL814S			(BMAA records show damaged 1982)		
G-MJBV	American Aerolights Eagle 215B	RSP-001		1. 7.82	A W Johnson	(Colwall, Malvern)	11. 8.96P
	(Fuji-Robin EC-25-PS)						
G-MJBZ	Huntair Pathfinder Mk.1	PK-17		2. 7.82	J C Rose	Eastbach Farm, Coleford	28.12.93P
	(Fuji-Robin EC-34-PM)				(Noted 9.03)		
G-MJCE	Ultrasports Puma/Southdown Sprint X RGC-01			5. 7.82	L I Bateup	Clench Common	25. 8.01P
	(Fuji-Robin EC-44-PM) (Designation amended by BMAA C 1990)				(Noted 1.07)		
G-MJCU	Tarjani/Solar Wings TyphoonSCG-01 & T982-610			7. 7.82	J K Ewing	Mapperton Farm, Newton Peverill	X
	(Fuji-Robin EC-25-PS)				(Trike only noted 7.06)		
G-MJDE	Huntair Pathfinder Mk.1	020		9. 7.82	P Rayson	Cottage Farm, Norton Juxta	26.11.07P
	(Fuji-Robin EC-34-PM)						
G-MJDJ	Hiway Skytrike/Demon	VW17D		9. 7.82	A J Cowan	(Billingham)	
G-MJDP	Eurowing Goldwing	GW-001		12. 7.82	B L Keeping tr G-MJDP Flying Group		
	(Fuji-Robin EC-34-PM)					Davidstow Moor	15.11.92P
G-MJDR	Hiway Skytrike/Demon	PJB-01		14. 7.82	D R Redmile	(Markfield)	
G-MJEB	Southdown Puma Sprint	SN1231/0041		18. 4.85	R J Shelswell	(Budbrooke, Warwick)	1. 5.96P
	(Rotax 447)						
G-MJEE	Mainair Tri-Flyer 250/Solar Wings Typhoon			20. 7.82	M F Eddington	(Wincanton)	11.11.00P
	(Fuji-Robin EC-25-PS)	038-251181					
G-MJEO	American Aerolights Eagle 215B	4562		26. 7.82	A M Shaw	(Alsager, Stoke-on-Trent)	X
	(Zenoah G25B1)						
G-MJER	Ultrasports Tri-Pacer/Flexiform Solo Striker			23. 7.82	D S Simpson	(Graveley Hall Farm, Graveley)	26.12.00P
	(Rotax 447)	DSD-01					

G-MJFB	Ultrasports Tri-Pacer/Flexiform Solo Striker					
	(Fuji-Robin EC-34-PM)	AJK-01	27. 7.82	B Tetley	(Cowes)	28. 3.06P
G-MJFM	Huntair Pathfinder Mk.1	ML-0	12. 9.82	R Gillespie and S P Girr		
	(Fuji-Robin EC-34-PM)			(Killygordon and Balley Bofey, County Donegal)		23. 7.99P
G-MJFX	Skyhook TR1/Sabre	TR1/38	2. 8.82	M R Dean	(Hebden Bridge)	X
	(Hunting HS.525A)					
G-MJFZ	Hiway Skytrike/Demon	JAL-01	29. 7.82	A W Lowrie (West Rainton, Houghton Le Spring)		X
G-MJHC	Ultrasports Tri-Pacer 330/Southdown Lightning Mk II		9. 8.82	E J Allen	(Fulbourn, Cambridge)	X
	(Fuji-Robin EC-34)	82-00044	(C/n is engine serial no)			
G-MJHR	Mainair Dual Tri-Flyer/Southdown Lightning		12. 8.82	B R Barnes	(Dundrey, Bristol)	
		GNS-01				
G-MJHV	Hiway Skytrike II/Demon	AG-17	13. 8.82	A G Griffiths	(Hyde Heath, Amersham)	
G-MJIA	Ultrasports Tri-Pacer/Flexiform Solo Striker					
	(Rotax 377)	SE-007	13. 8.82	D G Ellis (Noted 1.04)	Otherton, Cannock	20. 9.96P
G-MJIC	Ultrasports Tri-Pacer/Flexiform Solo Striker					
	(Fuji-Robin EC-34-PM)	82-00043	13. 8.82	J Curran	(Newry, County Armagh)	15.10.94P
G-MJIF	Mainair Tri-Flyer/Flexiform Striker					
	(Fuji-Robin EC-34-PL)	E-1 EC25PS-04	16. 8.82	R J Payne	(Newmarket)	X
	(C/n was original engine type)					
G-MJIR	Eipper Quicksilver MXII	1392	18. 8.82	H Feeney	(Stratford-upon-Avon)	26. 1.95P
	(Rotax 503)			(Stored 8.96)		
G-MJJA	Huntair Pathfinder Mk.1	031	23. 8.82	R D Bateman and J M Watkins		
				(Swimbridge, Barnstaple and Norton, Chichester)		25. 8.02P
G-MJJK	Eipper Quicksilver MXII	3397	25. 8.82	J McCullough	Ivyville Farm, Newtownards	21. 8.06P
	(Rotax 503)					
G-MJKB	Striplin Skyranger	ST161	2. 9.82	A P Booth	(Winterbourne, Newbury)	
	(Officially quoted as c/n SRI-6-I)					
G-MJKF	Hiway Demon	WGR-01	2. 9.82	S D Hill (Peppard Common, Henley-on-Thames)		
G-MJKO	Hiway Skytrike/Gold Marque Gyr 188	90030P	7. 9.82	M J Barry	(Nether Stowey, Bridgwater)	X
	(Fuji-Robin EC-25-PS) (Assembled from spares by Windsports)					
G-MJKX	Utralight Flight Phantom	PH.82005	14. 9.82	L R Graham	Rayne Hall Farm, Braintree	1.11.09P
	(Fuji-Robin EC-50)					
G-MJMD	Hiway Skytrike II/Demon 175	OE17D	27. 9.82	T A N Brierley	Baxby Manor, Husthwaite	26. 7.06P
	(Fuji-Robin EC-34-PM)			(Noted 9.07)		
G-MJMN	Mainair Tri-Flyer/Flexiform Striker	087-04882	29. 9.82	K Medd	(Manchester)	22. 7.05P
	(Fuji-Robin EC-34-PM)					
G-MJMR	Mainair Tri-Flyer 250/Solar Wings Typhoon		30. 9.82	J C S Jones (Stored 12.97)	Greenlands, Rhuallt	
		DR-01 & 048-5182				
G-MJMS	Hiway Skytrike II/Demon 175	EEW-01	30. 9.82	D E Peace	(Rawdon, Leeds)	
G-MJNM	American Aerolights Eagle 430B	702	25.11.82	A W Johnson	(Colwall, Malvern)	19. 9.93P
	(Cuyuna 430R)			(New owner 3.06)		
G-MJNO	American Aerolights Eagle Amphibian	703	24.11.82	R S Martin	(Gosport)	9. 7.06P
	(Rotax 447)					
G-MJNU	Skyhook TR1/Cutlass	TR1/17	19.10.82	R W Taylor	(Wortley, Sheffield)	
G-MJNY	Skyhook TR1/Sabre	TR1/35	3.11.82	P Ratcliffe	(Sheffield)	
G-MJOC	Huntair Pathfinder	048	25.10.82	A J Glynn	Gerpins Lane, Upminster	31. 7.99P
	(Fuji-Robin EC-34-PM)					
G-MJOE	Eurowing Goldwing	EW-55	29.10.82	R J Osborne	(Cove, Tiverton)	X
	(Rotax 377)					
G-MJPA	Rotec Rally 2B	AT-01	5. 1.83	R Boyd	(Armagh, County Armagh)	
G-MJPE	Mainair Tri-Flyer 330/Hiway Demon 175		10.11.82	E G Astin	(Whitby)	7. 8.96P
	(Fuji-Robin EC-34-PM) 117-151282 & OG17D					
G-MJPV	Eipper Quicksilver MX	JBW-01	30.11.82	F W Ellis	Water Leisure Park, Skegness	17. 8.04P
	(Cuyuna 430R)					
G-MJRL	Eurowing Goldwing	EW-79 & SWA-5K	30.12.82	M Daniels	(Heanor)	15. 6.00P
	(Rotax 377)					
G-MJRO	Eurowing Goldwing	EW-77 & SWA-04	31.12.82	T B Smith	(Sompting, Lancing)	22. 9.99P
	(Rotax 447)					
G-MJRR	Reece SkyRanger Series 1	JR-3	26. 4.82	J R Reece	(Liverpool)	
G-MJRS	Eurowing Goldwing	EW-80 & SWA-6K	5. 1.83	R M Newlands	(East Cowes)	12.10.01P
	(Rotax 377)					
G-MJRU	MBA Tiger Cub 440	SO.86	6. 1.83	S R Davis	Kemble	31. 1.86X
G-MJSE	Skyrider Airsports Phantom	SF-101	24. 1.83	K H A Negal	Red House Farm, Preston Capes	20. 5.02P
	(Fuji-Robin EC-40-PL)			(Noted 5.04)		
G-MJSF	Skyrider Airsports Phantom	SF-105 SE-...	24. 1.83	B J Towers	Croft Farm, Defford	
	(Rotax 462)	G-MJSF				
G-MJSL	Dragon Light Aircraft Dragon Series 200	0018	24. 2.83	M J Aubrey		
	(Rotax 503)			Upper Yeld, Floodgates, Kington, Hereford		22. 9.99P
G-MJSO	Hiway Skytrike III/Demon 175	SA17D	1. 2.83	D C Read	(Bromsberrow Heath, Ledbury)	X
	(Hiro 22)					
G-MJSP	MBA Romain Super Tiger Cub Special 440		7. 2.83	A R Sunley (On rebuild 6.06)	(Chelmsford)	X
		S0.54				
G-MJST	Pterodactyl Ptraveller	GCS-01	2.12.81	B W Olley (New owner 5.06)	(Soham, Ely)	7. 5.99P
G-MJSY	Eurowing Goldwing	EW-63	8. 2.83	A J Rex	(Wrexham)	5. 1.01P
	(Rotax 377)					
G-MJSZ	Harker DH Wasp	HA.5	10. 2.83	J J Hill	(Easby, Great Ayton)	24. 3.01P
	(Built D Harker) (Rotax 447)			(On overhaul 2004)		
G-MJTC	Ultrasports Tri-Pacer/Solar Wings Typhoon Medium		14. 2.83	V C Redhead	(Saxmundham)	
		T1282-677				
G-MJTE	Skyrider Airsports Phantom	SF-106	15. 2.83	L Zivanovic	Droitwich	27. 4.05P
	(Fuji-Robin EC-44-PM)					
G-MJTM	Southdown Aerostructure Pipistrelle P2B		21. 2.83	A M Sirant	Monkswell Farm, Horrabridge	27. 4.08P
	(KFM-107ER)	019 & SAL/P2B/002				

Reg	Type	C/n	Prev id	Date	Owner/Operator	Base	Notes
G-MJTP	Mainair Tri-Flyer/Flexiform Dual Sealander (Fuji-Robin EC-44-PM)	AJDH-01 & 139-7383		25. 2.83	P Milton	(Bedford)	22. 8.00P

G-MJTP   Mainair Tri-Flyer/Flexiform Dual Sealander   25. 2.83   P Milton   (Bedford)   22. 8.00P
  (Fuji-Robin EC-44-PM)   AJDH-01 & 139-7383   *(Possibly fitted with Dual Striker Sailwing after accident 29.10.87)*

G-MJTR   Southdown Puma DS Mk.1   H362   9. 3.83   A G Rodenburg and T Abro *(Noted wrecked 4.04)*
  (Fuji-Robin EC-44-PM)   , Tillicoultry, Stirling   15. 7.96P

G-MJTX   Skyrider Aviation Phantom   SF-110   1. 3.83   P D Coppin *(Noted 9.04)*   Lee-on-Solent   22. 4.96P
  (Fuji-Robin EC-44-PM)

G-MJTZ   Skyrider Aviation Phantom   MBS-01   29. 4.83   B J Towers   (Pershore)   X
  (Fuji-Robin EC-44-PM) *(Engine No.82-00119)*

G-MJUC   MBA Tiger Cub 440   RRH-01   7. 3.83   P A Avery   Terrington St John, Wisbech   X
  (Built Micro Biplane Aviation - pr.no.PFA 140-10908)   *(Noted 4.05)*

G-MJUR   Skyrider Aviation Phantom   SF-108   5. 4.83   M J Whiteman-Haywood
  (Fuji-Robin EC-44-PM)   Pound Green, Buttonoak, Bewdley   20. 9.98P

G-MJUU   Eurowing Goldwing   EW-70   28. 3.83   E F Clapham   (Oldbury-on-Severn)   3. 5.97P
  (Fuji-Robin EC-34-PM)

G-MJUW   MBA Tiger Cub 440   SO.69   29. 3.83   D G Palmer *(Noted 2005)*   Mintlaw, Peterhead   7. 6.02P

G-MJUX   Skyrider Aviation Phantom RFF-01 & PH00094   29. 2.84   P J Glover   North Coates   2. 7.09P
  (Built Ultralight Flight Inc) (Fuji-Robin EC-44-PM)   *(Noted 8.07 fitted with wings from G-MTTN qv)*

G-MJVE   Medway Hybred 44XL/Solar Wings Typhoon XLII   19. 4.83   T A Clark   (Rheda-Wiedenbrueck, Germany)   5. 6.00P
  4483/1 & T483-761XL   *(Original Sailwing c/n T283-703XL)*

G-MJVF   CFM Shadow Series CD   002   12. 4.83   J A Cook *(Stored dismantled 1.08)*   Parham   24. 6.04P

G-MJVN   Ultrasports Tri-Pacer/Flexiform Striker   18. 4.83   R McGookin   Thirdpart Holdings, West Kilbride   5.10.93P
  (Fuji-Robin EC-44-PM)   82-00030-PR1   *(Original Trike and engine fitted in G-MJRP) (Noted 8.05)*

G-MJVP   Eipper Quicksilver MXII   1149   19. 4.83   G J Ward   (Moreton, Dorchester)   10. 7.96P
  (Rotax 503) *(Original c/n 1124 became G-MTDO)*

G-MJVU   Eipper Quicksilver MXII   1118   3. 4.84   F J Griffith   (Denbigh)   13. 7.08P
  (Rotax 503)

G-MJVX   Skyrider Aviation Phantom   JAG-01 & SF-102   27. 4.83   J R Harris   Droppingwell Farm, Bewdley   6. 2.09P
  (Fuji-Robin EC-44-PM)

G-MJVY   Dragon Light Aircraft Dragon Series 150   4. 5.83   J C Craddock   (Freshwater, Isle of Wight)   26.10.04P
  (Rotax 503)   D 150/013

G-MJWB   Eurowing Goldwing   EW-59   24. 5.83   D G Palmer   Fetterangus   25. 8.93P
  (Fuji-Robin EC-34-PM)   *(Noted 7.01)*

G-MJWF   MBA Tiger Cub 440   BRH-001 & SO.79   4. 5.83   T and R L Maycock   (Glasgow)

G-MJWK   Huntair Pathfinder 1   JWK-01   1.10.82   D Young tr Kemble Flying Club   Kemble   3. 7.05P
  (Rotax 447)

G-MJWW   MBA Super Tiger Cub 440   MU-001   11. 5.83   J J Littler and T J Gayton-Polley   (Chichester)   23. 5.98P

G-MJWZ   Solar Wings Panther XL-S   T583-781XL   9. 9.85   A L Davies   (Holywell)   27. 1.01P
  (Originally regd as XL)

G-MJXY   Hiway Skytrike 330/Demon 175   KQ17D   31. 5.83   H C Lowther   (Penrith)   25. 7.00P
  (Fuji-Robin EC-34-PM)

G-MJYD   MBA Tiger Cub 440   SO.179   1. 6.83   R A Budd   Darley Moor, Ashbourne   12.11.03P
  (Noted as engineless wreck 4.06)

G-MJYP   Mainair Gemini/Flexiform Dual Striker167-13683   7. 6.83   M S Whitehouse   (Solihull)   23. 7.02P
  (Fuji-Robin EC-44-PM)

G-MJYV   Mainair Rapier 1+1/Flexiform Solo Striker   23.11.83   L H Phillips   (Solihull)   X
  (Fuji-Robin EC-34-PM)   175-19783

G-MJYW   Lancashire Micro-Trike Dual 330/Wasp Gryphon III   28. 6.83   P D Lawrence   (Munlochy, Ross-shire)
  2/330PM/PGK/6.83/K   *(Dismantled and Trike used on G-MMPL: parts noted 7.01)*

G-MJYX   Mainair Tri-Flyer/Hiway Demon   108-251182   9. 6.83   K A Wright   North Coates   7. 9.05P
  (Fuji-Robin EC-33-PM)   *(Bagged wings only noted 6.06)*

G-MJZE   MBA Tiger Cub 440   SO.168   14. 6.83   J E D Rogerson tr Fishburn Flying Tigers
  (Morgansfield, Fishburn)   31. 1.96X

G-MJZK (2)   Southdown Puma Sprint   SN1111/0081   3. 3.86   R J Osborne   (Cove, Tiverton)   18.10.91P
  (Fuji-Robin EC-44-PM)

G-MJZU   Mainair Gemini/Flexiform Dual Striker   21. 6.83   C G Chambers   Swinford, Rugby   7. 8.04P
  (Fuji-Robin EC-44-PM)   214-41183 & JDR-02   *(Trike fitted ex G-MMVX (1))*

G-MKAA   Boeing 747-2S4F   22169   9G-MKQ   16. 8.06   MK Airlines Ltd t/a British Global   Manston   15. 8.08E
  N713BA, HL7474, LX-TAP, TU-TAP

G-MKAK   Colt 77A Balloon (Hot Air)   2039   15. 8.91   A C Ritchie   Oswestry   27. 9.09E

G-MKAS   Piper PA-28-140 Cherokee Cruiser   G-BKVR   30. 4.98   MK Aero Support Ltd   Andrewsfield   22. 1.10E
  28-7425338   OY-BGV

G-MKBA   Boeing 747-2B5F   22481   9G-MKR   29.10.07   MK Airlines Ltd t/a British Global   Manston   26.10.09E
  N778BA, HL7452

G-MKCA   Boeing 747-2B5B   22482   9K-MKM   30. 1.08   MK Airlines Ltd t/a British Global   Manston   29. 1.10E
  N207BA, HL7454

G-MKDA   Boeing 747-2B5F   22486   9G-MKS   3.10.07   MK Airlines Ltd t/a British Global   Manston   4. 1.08E
  N776BA, HL7459, N8281V

G-MKEA   Boeing 747-249F   22237   9G-MKU   24.10.07   MK Airlines Ltd t/a British Global   Manston   25.10.08E
  N920FT, VR-HKO, N633FE, (N639FE), N810FT, (N809FT)

G-MKFA   Boeing 747-245F   21841   9G-MKP   16.11.07   MK Airlines Ltd t/a British Global   Manston   19.11.08E
  N925FT, N638FE, (G-INTL), N638FE, (N635FE), N814FT, N704SW

G-MKGA   Boeing 747-2R7F   21650   9G-MKL   31.10.07   MK Airlines Ltd t/a British Global   Manston   27.10.09E
  N926FT, N639FE, N809FT, EI-BTQ, LX-DCV

G-MKHA   Boeing 747-2J6B   23071   B-2446   13.11.07   MK Airlines Ltd t/a British Global   Manston   9.12.09E
  N1781B

G-MKIA   Vickers Supermarine 300 Spitfire I   6S-30565   P9374   16.11.00   Mark One Partners Ltd *(on rebuild)*   Sandown

G-MKII   Eurocopter EC.120B Colibri   1463   F-HAAL   21. 6.07   Focus Ltd   (Cookstown, Belfast)   20. 6.09E
  F-WQDD

G-MKJA   Boeing 747-246F   22477   HS-ORB   30.10.08   MK Airlines Ltd t/a British Global   Manston   2.10.09E
  JA8937, N740SJ, JA8151, N8284V

G-MKVB   Vickers Supermarine 349 Spitfire LF.Vb   5718M   2. 5.89   Historic Aircraft Collection Ltd *(As "BM597:U-2" in RAF c/s)*
  CBAF.2461   BM597   Duxford   25. 3.09P

G-MKXI   Vickers Supermarine 365 Spitfire PR.Mk.XI   N965RF   13.11.89   P A Teichman *(As "PL965:R" RAF grey c/s with D-Day stripes)*
  6S-504719   G-MKXI, R Netherlands AF, PL965   North Weald   29. 6.09P

G-MLAL	Avtech Jabiru J400	0xxx		23.10.06	M A Scudder	Gloucestershire	9. 6.09P
	(Built M A Scudder - pr.no.PFA 325-14399)						
G-MLAW	P&M Aviation Quik GT450	8310		12. 9.07	J R Hartley	(Northampton)	11. 9.08P
G-MLFF	Piper PA-23-250 Aztec E	27-7305194	G-WEBB	31. 1.90	W C Cullinane	Waterford, County Waterford	20. 7.08E
			G-BJBU, N40476				
G-MLHI	Maule MX-7-180 Super Rocket	11073C	G-BTMJ	20. 4.04	L C Gunn tr Maulehigh	White Waltham	4. 9.09E
G-MLJL	Airbus A330-243	254	F-WWKI	15. 6.99	Thomas Cook Airlines Ltd	Manchester	14. 6.09E
G-MLLA	SOCATA TB-200 Tobago XL	1632	D-EREH	6. 6.05	C E Millar	Goodwood	9. 6.09E
G-MLLE	CEA Jodel DR.200A-B 2+2	136	OY-RVY	16.10.06	A D Evans	Sywell	26. 4.09E
			F-BRVY				
G-MLSA	Balony Kubicek BB37N Balloon (Hot-Air)	581		22. 4.08	Studio AM SAS	Padova, Italy	5. 5.09E
G-MLSN	Hughes 369E *(Hughes 500)*	0357E	G-HMAC	12.12.03	Whirlybirds Helicopters Ltd	Gloucestershire	16. 6.09E
			HB-XUO				
G-MLTY	Aérospatiale AS.365N2 Dauphin 2	6431	N365EL	4. 6.99	Crosby Enterprises Ltd	Leeds-Bradford	6. 6.09E
			JA6673				
G-MLWI	Thunder Ax7-77 Balloon (Hot Air)	1000		3. 9.86	M L and L P Willoughby *"Mr Blue Sky"*	Woodcote, Reading	12. 8.03A
G-MLZZ	Best Off S ky Ranger Swift 912S(1)			6.11.07	D M Robbins	Goodwood	1. 5.09P
	(Built D M Robbins)	SKRxxx823	*(Pr.no.BMAA HB/557)*				
G-MMAC	Dragon Light Aircraft Dragon Series 200	003	OY-...	14. 7.82	J F Ashton and J Kirwan	Ince Blundell	X
	(Fuji-Robin EC-44-PM)		G-MMAC				
G-MMAG	MBA Tiger Cub 440	SO.47		22. 6.83	M J Aubrey *(Noted 2002)*	Upper Yeld, Floodgates, Kington, Hereford	14. 9.93P
G-MMAI	Dragon Light Aircraft Dragon Series 150	0032		1. 7.83	G S Richardson	(Cleethorpes)	13. 7.97P
	(Fuji-Robin EC-44-PM)				*(Dismantled and parts split between North Coates and owner's home 11.07)*		
G-MMAR	Mainair Gemini/Southdown Puma Sprint MS						
	(Fuji-Robin EC-44-PM)	195-11083-2		23. 9.83	A R and J Fawkes	(Leckhampstead, Newbury)	17. 9.98P
G-MMBL	Ultrasports Puma/Southdown Lightning DS						
	(Fuji-Robin EC-44-PM)	80-00083		4. 7.83	B J Farrell	(Bilsborrow, Preston)	X
	(C/n is engine serial no.)						
G-MMBN	Eurowing Goldwing	EW-89		28. 6.83	E H Jenkins	(Newcastle upon Tyne)	X
	(Rotax 447)						
G-MMBT	MBA Tiger Cub 440	SO.131		19. 7.83	B Chamberlain	(Otley, Ipswich)	X
	(Built Micro Biplane Aviation - pr.no. PFA 140-10924 or 10990: c/n TR 01 reported also) (Stored 1.91)						
G-MMBU	Eipper Quicksilver MXII	CAL-222		8. 7.83	D A Norwood	Ashcroft Farm, Winsford	13. 7.08P
	(Rotax 503)						
G-MMBV	Huntair Pathfinder	044		8. 7.83	P J Bishop	Tarn Farm, Cockerham	9. 5.07P
	(Originally kit-built by M Philippe) *(Fuji-Robin EC-44-PM)*						
G-MMBY	Solar Wings Panther XL	T483-759XL		20. 7.83	R M Sheppard and P Huddleston	(Malvern and Marlborough)	3. 8.03P
G-MMBZ	Solar Wings Typhoon P	T981-5217		20. 7.83	S C Mann	(Kirkby Malzeard, Ripon)	28. 4.96P
	(Fuji-Robin EC-34-PM)				*(New owner 10.00)*		
	(Originally thought to have Sailwing c/n T781-217- 5217: possible corruption of S217 for Typhoon Small: rebuilt as c/n T981-228)						
G-MMCI	Ultrasports Puma Sprint X	P 421		28. 9.83	L A Davies	Shobdon	8. 7.06P
	(Fuji-Robin EC-44-PM) *(Also c/n DMP-01)*						
G-MMCN	Hiway Skytrike 250/Solar Wings Storm			19. 7.83	P J Ramsay	(Wrecclesham, Farnham)	X
		SMB.8069					
G-MMCV	Hiway Skytrike II/Solar Wings Typhoon			27. 7.83	G Addison	(Kinross)	8. 6.97P
	(Fuji-Robin EC-34-PM)	T583-783					
G-MMCX	MBA Super Tiger Cub 440	MU.002		8. 8.83	D Harkin	(Johnstone, Renfrew)	
G-MMCZ	Mainair Tri-Flyer/Flexiform Dual Striker	TE-01		10. 8.83	T D Adamson	Wombleton	9. 9.07P
	(Fuji-Robin EC-44-PM) *(Mainair Trike c/n 180-6883)*						
G-MMDF	Southdown Wild Cat Mk.II/Lightning Phase II			24. 8.83	J C Haigh	(Tonbridge)	4.11.03P
	(Fuji-Robin EC-34-PM)	007					
G-MMDK	Mainair Tri-Flyer/Flexiform Striker	181-16883		7. 9.83	P E Blyth	(Maltby, Rotherham)	30. 5.99P
	(Fuji-Robin EC-34-PM)						
G-MMDN	Mainair Tri-Flyer 330/Flexiform Dual Striker			30. 9.83	M G Griffiths	(Monmouth)	X
	(Mainair c/n not confirmed) 197-983 & RPO.12						
G-MMDR	Huntair Pathfinder Mk.II	137		30. 8.83	C Dolling	(Swindon)	
	(Rotax 377)						
G-MMEK	Medway Hybred 44XL	129836		16. 9.83	M G J Bridges	(Exeter)	28. 8.00P
	(Solar Wings Typhoon XLII Sailwing c/n either T883-884XL or T883-887XL)						
G-MMFD	Mainair Tri-Flyer 440	210-31082-2		20. 9.83	M E and W L Chapman	(Ashton-under-Lyne and Springhead, Oldham)	6.12.93P
	(Fuji-Robin EC-44-PM)						
	(Flexiform Dual Striker Sailwing c/n FF/LAI/83/JDR/12: Trike believed to be c/n 210-31083-2)						
G-MMFE	Mainair Tri-Flyer 440	256-784-2		20. 9.83	W Camm	(Wombwell, Barnsley)	16. 6.94P
	(Fuji-Robin EC-44-PM) *(Flexiform Striker Sailwing FF/LAI/83/JDR/13)*						
G-MMFG	Lancashire Micro-Trike 440			20. 9.83	M G Dean and M J Hadland	(Tarn Farm, Cockerham)	X
	(Fuji-Robin EC-44-PM) *(Flexiform Dual Striker Sailwing FF/LAI/83/JDR/15)*						
G-MMFS	MBA Tiger Cub 440	SO.64		1.11.83	G S Taylor *(Noted 8.07)*	Yeatsall Farm, Abbots Bromley	27. 7.01P
G-MMFV	Mainair Tri-Flyer 440/Flexiform Dual Striker			8.12.83	R A Walton	(Slough)	26. 4.97P
		83-00130 & 212-271083					
	(Fuji-Robin EC-44-PM)						
G-MMFY	Cliff Sims Aztec/Flexiform Dual Striker			14.12.83	K R M Adair and S R Browne (Bognor/Pulborough)		X
		AZT001CS					
G-MMGF	MBA Tiger Cub 440	SO.124		18.11.83	J G Boxall	Pittrichie Farm, Whiterashes	22. 8.02P
G-MMGL	MBA Tiger Cub 440	SO.148		23.11.83	H E Dunning	Baxby Manor, Husthwaite	24.10.08P
	(Built H E Dunning - pr.no.BMAA HB/050)						
G-MMGS	Solar Wings Panther XL-S	T1283-939XL		28.12.83	R J Hood	London Colney	21. 4.08P
G-MMGT	Huntwing/Pegasus Classic	JAH-7		28.11.83	H Cook	(Newport, Gwent)	24.10.08P
	(Built J A Hunt) *(BMW R100)* *(Currently with Trike c/n SW-TB-1228 ex G-MTOH)*						

G-MMGU	SMD Gazelle/Flexiform Sealander (Fuji-Robin EC-44-PM)	30-4883	1.12.83	A D Cranfield	(Marsh, Wincanton)	X
G-MMGV	Whittaker MW5 Sorcerer Series A (Built Microknight Aviation Ltd) (Fuji-Robin EC-34-M)	001	2.12.83	G N Haffey and M W J Whittaker (Noted 9.07)	Church Farm, Askern	1. 9.06P
G-MMHE	Mainair Gemini Sprint	229-184-2	8.12.83	N L Zaman	(London Colney)	27. 5.98P
G-MMHK	Hiway Skytrike/Super Scorpion (Fuji-Robin EC-25-PS)	KSC83	19.12.83	S Davison	(Newcastle upon Tyne)	X
G-MMHL	Hiway Skytrike II/Super Scorpion (Fuji-Robin EC-44)	KSC84	19.12.83	E J Blyth	(Wrelton, Pickering)	X
G-MMHN	MBA Tiger Cub 440	SO.136	19.12.83	M J Aubrey (Noted 2002) Upper Yeld, Floodgates, Kington, Hereford		
G-MMHS	SMD Gazelle/Flexiform Dual Striker	104-11283	21.12.83	C J Meadows Franklyn's Field, Chewton Mendip		
G-MMIE	MBA Tiger Cub 440	G7-7	3. 1.84	B W Olliver	(Telford)	X
G-MMIW	Southdown Puma Sprint (Fuji-Robin EC-44-PM)	590	9. 2.84	J Ryland	(Swanley)	26. 9.04P
G-MMIX	MBA Tiger Cub 440	MBCB-01	14. 2.84	N J McKain (To Dumfries and Galloway Museum 2007)	(Dumfries)	X
G-MMIZ	Southdown Lightning Mk.II	CB-01	24. 2.84	F E Hall	Prospect Farm, Wollaston	25. 4.05P
G-MMJD	Southdown Puma Sprint (Fuji-Robin EC-44-PM)	SP/1001	28. 6.83	M P Robertshaw	Wickhambrok, Newmarket	20. 7.08P
G-MMJF	Solar Wings Panther Dual XL-S	PXL842-150 & T284-988XL	27. 2.84	J Benn	RAF Scampton	22. 5.08P
G-MMJG	Mainair Tri-Flyer/Flexiform Dual Striker (Fuji-Robin EC-44-PM)	185-1983	31. 9.83	A Strang (Under repair 2004)	(Ashgill, Larkhall)	10. 9.03P
G-MMJT	Mainair Gemini/Southdown Sprint X (Fuji-Robin EC-44-PM) (No Mainair identity and probably plans-built by J B Tate)	JBT-01	20.12.83	D C de la Haye	(Elmley, Sheerness)	21. 7.07P
G-MMJV	MBA Tiger Cub 440 (Built K Bannister - pr.no.PFA 140-1090)	SO.195	25. 3.84	D G Palmer (Noted 7.01)	Fetterangus	9. 5.93P
G-MMJX	Teman Mono-Fly (Built B F J Hope) (Rotax 377)	01	6. 3.84	A Davis	Watnall	17. 7.04P
G-MMKA	Solar Wings Panther Dual XL	T284-986XL	8. 3.84	R S Wood	(Wallacestone, Falkirk)	X
G-MMKE	Birdman WT-11 Chinook (Rotax 277)	01817	2. 4.84	D M Jackson	(Belper)	X
G-MMKL	Mainair Gemini Flash (Fuji-Robin EC-44-PM)	238-384-2-W11	12. 3.84	D W Cox	(Kenilworth)	29. 9.93P
G-MMKM	Mainair Gemini/Flexiform Dual Striker (Fuji-Robin EC-44-PM)	221-01-84-0002	12. 3.84	S W Hutchinson Trenholme Farm. Ingleby, Arncliffe, Northallerton		11. 6.99P
	(Originally fitted with Mainair 440 Tri-Flyer Trike [210-1083] and part- exchanged for 440 Gemini as fitted: rebuild of Trike originally exported to US and re-imported)					
G-MMKP	MBA Tiger Cub 440	SO.203	13. 3.84	J W Beaty	(Lowick, Kettering)	X
G-MMKR	Mainair Tri-Flyer/Southdown Lightning DS (Fuji-Robin EC-44-PM) 209-171083 & CM-01		14. 3.84	C R Madden (Regd as G-MNDK in error and then restored as G-MMKR)	(Great Orton)	14. 4.07P
G-MMKX	Skyrider Aviation Phantom 330 (Fuji-Robin EC-34-PL-02)	PH-107R	18. 3.85	G J Lampitt Pound Green, Buttonoak, Bewdley		17. 6.01P
G-MMLE	Eurowing Goldwing SP	EW-81	21. 3.84	M J Aubrey	(Kington, Hereford)	
G-MMLH	Hiway Skytrike II 330/Demon	PMH-01 & DJL-01	28. 3.84	P M Hendry and D J Lukey (Geneva, Switzerland and Folkestone)		
G-MMMG	Eipper Quicksilver MXL (Rotax 447)	1383	5. 6.84	J G Campbell	Sandtoft	23. 6.09P
G-MMMH	Hadland Willow/Flexiform Striker (BMW R80/7)	MJH 383	9.12.83	M J Hadland	(Ashton-in-Makerfield, Wigan)	6.10.08P
G-MMML	Dragon Light Aircraft Dragon Series 150 OY-... (Fuji-Robin EC-44-PM) D150/002 G-MMML		28. 6.83	M J Aubrey	Kington, Hereford	6. 8.00P
G-MMMN	Solar Wings Panther Dual XL-S (Probably '1059) PXL 843-150 & T484-105?XL		4. 4.84	C Downton	(Newton Abbot)	16. 7.04P
G-MMNA	Eipper Quicksilver MXII (C/n conflicts with Quicksilver G-MMIL)	1046	30. 3.84	J W Dodson	Leicester	2. 1.05P
G-MMNB	Eipper Quicksilver MX (Cuyuna 430R)	4286	30. 3.84	J M Lindop	Long Marston	12.10.97P
G-MMNC	Eipper Quicksilver MX	4276	30. 3.84	W S Toulmin	(Great Gidding, Huntingdon)	31. 5.96P
G-MMNH	Dragon Light Aircraft Dragon Series 150 (Fuji-Robin EC-44-PM)	D150/42	27. 7.83	T J Barlow	(Dromore, County Down)	X
G-MMNN	Sherry Buzzard (Built E W Sherry - pr.no.PFA 190-10430)	1	6. 4.84	E W Sherry	(Stoke-on-Trent)	
G-MMNS	Mitchell U-2 Super Wing (Built C Baldwin)	PFA 114-10690	11. 4.84	C Baldwin and J C Lister	(Valley Farm, Winwick)	
G-MMNT	Flexiform Trike/Flexiform Solo Striker (Rotax 277)	SSL-1	16. 4.84	C R Thorne	(Lyndhurst, Hampshire)	X
G-MMOB	Mainair Gemini/Southdown Sprint (Fuji-Robin EC-44-PM) 244-584-2(K) & EM-01		11. 5.84	D Woolcock (C/n 'K' denotes kit built)	St Michaels	22. 7.09P
G-MMOH	Solar Wings Pegasus XL-R (Wing c/n SW-TB-1450)	T484-1054XL	4. 5.84	T H Scott (Trike fitted replacing one formerly on G-MBTT: new Trike now fitted ex G-MYGA)	(Coggeshall, Colchester)	
G-MMOK	Solar Wings Panther XL-S (Wing c/n PXL844-157)	T584-1066XL	9. 5.84	R F and A J Foster	(Woodbridge)	17.12.09P
G-MMOW	Mainair Gemini Flash	246-684-3-W06	21. 5.84	D P Quaintrell (Noted 10.06) Tarn Farm, Cockerham		3. 6.02P
G-MMPG	Ultrasports Tri-pacer/Lightning Mk.II (Fuji-Robin EC-34-PM)	NEA-01	8. 6.84	T J Hector	(Guilden Morden, Royston)	15. 4.01P
G-MMPH	Southdown Puma Sprint (Fuji-Robin EC-44-PM)	P 545	20. 6.84	J Siddle	(Alsager, Stoke-on-Trent)	27. 4.05P
G-MMPL	Lancashire Micro-Trike 440/Flexiform Dual Striker PDL-02 & 2/330PM/PGK/683/K		5.12.83	P D Lawrence	(Munlochy)	28. 6.07P
	(Fuji-Robin EC-44-PM) (Trike unit from G-MJYW: maybe flown with exchangeable sailwings)					

G-MMPO	Mainair Gemini Flash (Fuji-Robin EC-44-PM)	325-785-3-W65	18. 4.85	M A Feber	Ballinspittle, County Cork	9. 6.06P
G-MMPU	R J Heming Trike/Solar Wings Typhoon S4 (Fuji-Robin EC-34-PM)	RJH-01	5. 6.84	J T Halford *(Wing c/n T782-553L)*	(Langham, Holt)	22. 5.96P
G-MMPZ	Teman Mono-Fly *(Built J W Highton)* (Rotax 447)	JWH-01	2. 7.84	P B Kylo	Glassonby	20. 6.07P
G-MMRH	Hiway Skytrike/Demon	JSM-01 & 25R1	20. 6.84	A M Sirant	Monkswell Farm, Horrabridge	
G-MMRL	Solar Wings Pegasus XL-R *(Trike c/n SW-TB-1233) (Trike acquired ex G-MTOM C 2001) (Noted 7.06)*	T684-1102XL	17. 7.84	R J Hood	London Colney	3. 9.05P
G-MMRN	Southdown Puma Sprint (Fuji-Robin EC-44-PM)	P 544	16. 7.84	D C Read	(Ledbury)	18. 4.01P
G-MMRP	Mainair Gemini/Southdown Sprint (Fuji-Robin EC-44-PM)	259-884-2-P 561	7. 2.85	J C S Jones	Greenlands, Rhuallt	7 .9.08P
G-MMRW	Mainair Gemini 440/Flexiform Dual Striker	LAI/DS/25 & 216-71283	5. 1.84	M D Hinge	(Hamptworth, Salisbury)	X
G-MMSA	Solar Wings Panther XL-S *(C/n probably T784-1142XL) (Wing c/n PXL847-189)*	T184-1142XL	9. 8.84	T W Thiele and G Savage	(Radwell, Baldock)	27. 5.98P
G-MMSG	Solar Wings Panther XL-S *(Regd with c/n 8841/65XC)*	T884-1165XL	6. 9.85	R W McKee	(Mancott, Deeside)	4. 6.01P
G-MMSH	Solar Wings Panther XL-S *(Wing c/n PXL847-192)*	T884-1163XL	28. 5.85	I J Drake	(Billericay)	7. 5.90P
G-MMSO	Mainair Gemini/Southdown Sprint (Fuji-Robin EC-44-PM)	255-784-2-P 539	14. 1.86	K A Maughan *(Wing only noted 9.07)* Church Farm, Askern		26. 7.99P
G-MMSP	Mainair Gemini Flash (Fuji-Robin EC-44-PM) *(Original Sailwing c/n W03 fitted to G-MNGF 1998: current Sailwing identity not known)*	265-984-2	17. 8.84	J Whiteford	East Fortune	24. 4.01P
G-MMTA	Solar Wings Panther XL-R (Rotax 462HP) *(Sailwing c/n PXL848-194)*	T884-1164XL	25.10.84	P A McMahon	(Dun Laoghaire, County Dublin)	29. 6.03P
G-MMTC	Solar Wings Pegasus XL-R *(Sailwing c/n SW-TB-1037) (Original Trike was Ultrasports c/n PXL847-170 and later fitted to G-MNHH) (Dismantled 2.03)*	T684-1101XL	28. 9.84	T L Moses	(Uplands , Carmarthen)	8. 2.02P
G-MMTD	Mainair Tri-Flyer/Hiway Demon 175 (Fuji-Robin EC-34-PM)	150-30583 & EIA-01	16. 8.84	W E Teare *(Trike originally exported to Denmark)*	(Ramsey, Isle of Man)	10. 9.03P
G-MMTG	Mainair Gemini/Southdown Sprint	267-984-2-P577	21. 8.84	J C F Dalton *(Originally regd as Mainair Tri-Flyer with c/n RPWJ-01)*	(St Neots)	13. 8.94P
G-MMTJ	Southdown Puma Sprint (Fuji-Robin EC-44-PM)	SN1221/0006	17. 1.85	P J Kirwan *(Believed stored 2006)*	(Geashill, County Offaly)	16. 4.00P
G-MMTL	Mainair Gemini/Southdown Sprint (Fuji-Robin EC-44-PM)	268-1084-2-P576	3.10.84	K Birkett	Lee-on-Solent	3. 8.05P
G-MMTR	Solar Wings Pegasus XL-R *(Originally fitted with Ultrasports Trike/Typhoon Sailwing c/n T984-1211XL: Trike replaced by Solar Wings XL c/n SW-TB-1092 circa 8.86)*	KND-03	27. 9.84	P M Kelsey *(Noted 2.08)*	Yearby	23. 4.08P
G-MMTS	Solar Wings Panther XL	T784-1157XL	18. 9.84	T J Gayton-Polley	(Billingshurst)	30. 4.09P
G-MMTV	American Aerolights Eagle 215B Seaplane (Fuji-Robin EC-25-PS)	SGP-1	25. 9.84	L K Fowler	(Upper Sapey, Worcester)	21.11.96P
G-MMTY	Fisher FP.202U	2140	28. 9.84	B E Maggs *(Stored dismantled 6.07)* Compton Dando		
G-MMUA	Southdown Puma Sprint (Fuji-Robin EC-44-PM)	SN1221/0007	21.12.84	M R Crowhurst	(Ramsey, Isle of Man)	21. 7.05P
G-MMUH	Mainair Tri-Flyer/Sprint (Fuji-Robin EC-44-PM)	270-1084-2-P579	8.11.84	J P Nicklin	(Hayling Island)	20. 9.04P
G-MMUM	MBA Tiger Cub 440	SO.019	8. 3.83	Coulson Flying Services Ltd	(Cranfield)	
G-MMUO	Mainair Gemini Flash (Fuji-Robin EC-44-PM)	272-1084-2-W08	29.10.84	B D Bastin and D R Howells	Long Marston	3.11.09P
G-MMUR	Hiway Skytrike II/Solar Wings Storm SLI.80180 (Fuji-Robin EC-25)		28.12.84	R J Ripley *(Stored at owner's house 1998)*	Field Farm, Oakley	
G-MMUV	Southdown Puma Sprint (Fuji-Robin EC-44-PM)	SN1121/0010	7.11.84	D C Read	(Bromsberrow Heath, Ledbury)	2.11.89P
G-MMUW	Mainair Gemini Flash II (Fuji-Robin EC-44-PM)	60-784-2-W13	17. 1.85	J C K Scardifield	(Milford-on-Sea, Lymington)	23. 3.87P
G-MMUX	Mainair Gemini/Southdown Sprint (Fuji-Robin EC-44-PM)	285-185-3-P587	28.12.84	M D Howe *(Trike c/n confirmed as 284-185-3)*	Priory Farm, Tibenham	8.12.07P
G-MMVA	Southdown Puma Sprint *(Trike c/n P 588)*	SN1121/0011	7.11.84	C E Tomkins	(Orlingbury, Kettering)	26. 3.92P
G-MMVH	Southdown Raven X	SN2122/0015	10. 1.85	G, W and K Carwardine	(Hadlow Down, Uckfield and Tonbridge)	29. 4.01P
G-MMVI	Southdown Puma Sprint (Fuji-Robin EC-44-PM)	SN1121/0012	28.11.84	G R Williams	(Oakdale, Blackwood)	2.11.97P
G-MMVS	Skyhook TR1 Pixie/Zeus (Solo 210)	TR1/52	28. 2.85	B W Olley	(Soham, Ely)	X
G-MMVX	Southdown Puma Sprint (Fuji-Robin EC-44-PM) *(Wing c/n 41183)*	P452	29.11.83	M P Jones	Haverfordwest	5. 4.03P
G-MMVZ	Southdown Puma Sprint (Fuji-Robin EC-44-PM)	SN1121/0016	15. 1.85	P Whelan	(Curragh, County Kildare)	2. 8.04P
G-MMWA	Mainair Gemini Flash II (Fuji-Robin EC-44-PM) *(Trike c/n stamped as "KR271-1184-2")*	271-1184-1-W07	22.11.84	B Olson	Deenethorpe	22. 6.07P
G-MMWC	Eipper Quicksilver MXII (Rotax 503)	1041	22.10.84	J S Harris and M Holmes *(Parts used in 'Scrapheap Challenge' TV Programme, first aired 27. 5.07)*	Old Sarum	27. 7.03P
G-MMWG	P G Greenslade Trike/Flexiform Solo Striker (Rotax 377) *(Registered as Mainair Tri-Flyer Trike but now fitted with Trike from G-MJGN) (Sailwing c/n duplicates G-MMFC)*	FF/LAI/83/JDR/11	17.12.84	C R Green	(Redruth)	26. 6.99P
G-MMWL	Eurowing Goldwing (Rotax 447)	SWA-09 & EW-91	9. 4.85	A D Bales	Priory Farm, Tibenham	24. 5.05P
G-MMWS	Ultrasports Tri-Pacer/Flexiform Solo Striker (Rotax 377) *(Originally fitted with Mainair Trike)*	983.SH	21.11.84	P H Risdale	Tower Farm, Wollaston	10. 8.08P

G-MMWX	Southdown Puma Sprint	SN1121/0047	10. 4.85	G A Webb	(London SW11)	31.10.07P
	(Fuji-Robin EC-44-PM)					
G-MMXD	Mainair Gemini Flash II	282-185-3-W20	28.12.84	W A Bibby	Brook Farm, Pilling	13. 8.05P
	(Rotax 447)			(Noted 2.06)		
G-MMXJ	Mainair Gemini Flash II	289-185-3-W22	17. 1.85	R Meredith-	(Hardy Radwell, Letchworth)	6. 8.96P
	(Rotax 447)					
G-MMXL	Mainair Gemini Flash II	292-385-3-W36	17. 1.85	G W Warner (Noted 8.08)		
	(Fuji-Robin EC-44-PM)				Tarn Farm, Cockerham	16. 5.97P
G-MMXO	Southdown Puma Sprint	SN1121/0018	23. 1.85	D J Tasker	Swinford, Rugby	22. 4.09P
	(Fuji-Robin EC-44-PM)					
G-MMXU	Mainair Gemini Flash II	254-784-2-W21	29. 1.85	T J Franklin	Graveley Hall Farm, Graveley	14. 7.01P
	(Fuji-Robin EC-44-PM)			(Stored 7.03)		
G-MMXV	Mainair Gemini Flash II	298-385-3-W37	29. 1.85	D Roland	Insch	12. 5.09P
	(Rotax 503)					
G-MMXW	Mainair Gemini/Southdown Sprint	286-185-3-P597	23. 1.85	A Hodgson	(Milton Keynes)	4. 6.02P
	(Fuji-Robin EC-44-PM)					
G-MMYA	Solar Wings Pegasus XL-R/Se		30. 1.85	R G Mason	(Aylesbury)	5. 8.06P
	(Rotax 447) XL-P Proto & T784-1151XL					
	(Originally regd as XL)					
G-MMYF	Southdown Puma Sprint	SN1121/0026	28. 3.85	M Campbell	(Halifax)	14. 3.05P
	(Fuji-Robin EC-44-PM)					
G-MMYL	Cyclone 70/Aerial Arts 130SX	CH.01	8. 3.85	E W P van Zeller	(Ashford, Kent)	6. 5.07P
G-MMYN	Solar Wings Pegasus XL-R	T784-1158XL	27. 2.85	H J Long (Noted 6.07)		
				Ardenagh Great, Taghmon, County Wexford		17. 7.06P
G-MMYO	Southdown Puma Sprint	SN1121/0037	11. 4.85	P R Whitehouse	Otherton, Cannock	29. 8.00P
	(Fuji-Robin EC-44-PM) (Fitted with rainbow Medway Sailwing c3.96 after accident 20.9.95)					
G-MMYT	Southdown Puma Sprint		15. 4.85	J K Divall	(Chichester)	25. 3.94P
	SN1121/0046 & T569/P621					
	(Fuji-Robin EC-44-PM)					
G-MMYU	Southdown Puma Sprint	SN1231/0045	11. 6.85	M V Hearns	Glenrothes	21. 4.02P
	(Rotax 447)					
G-MMYV	Mainair Tri-Flyer/Flexiform Strike	JW-2	22. 3.85	S B Herbert	(Presteigne)	20.12.95P
	(Built J Webb) (Rotax 277)					
G-MMYY	Southdown Puma Sprint	SN1231/0042	18. 7.85	D J Whittle	(Liverpool)	12. 7.04P
	(Rotax 447)					
G-MMZA	Mainair Gemini Flash II	266-984-3-W60	4. 3.85	G T Johnston	(Craigavon, County Armagh)	30. 6.00P
	(Fuji-Robin EC-44-PM)					
G-MMZD	Mainair Gemini Flash	309-585-3-W49	4. 3.85	P L Dowd	Ince Blundell	24. 7.09P
	(Fuji-Robin EC-44-PM)					
G-MMZF	Mainair Gemini Flash II	299-485-3-W38	4. 3.85	J Tait	Eshott	13. 9.03P
	(Fuji-Robin EC-44-PM)			(Noted 7.05)		
G-MMZG	Solar Wings Panther XL-S		12. 8.85	P W Maddocks	Stoke, Isle of Grain	13.10.08P
	SW-TR-1008 & SW-WA-1022					
G-MMZI	Medway Half Pintrerial Arts 130SX		6. 3.85	J Messenger	(Workington)	28. 3.93X
	2385/1 & 130SX-057					
G-MMZJ	Mainair Gemini Flash	312-585-3-W51	18. 3.85	R C Bailey	Roddige	25. 4.08P
	(Rotax 462)					
G-MMZK	Mainair Gemini Flash	326-785-3-W53	18. 3.85	G Jones and B Lee	(Warrington)	3.11.99P
	(Fuji-Robin EC-44-PM) (Trike ex G-MMEZ: originally regd with Trike c/n 314-585-3 which went to G-MMIR)					
G-MMZM	Mainair Gemini Flash	304-585-3-W44	18. 3.85	H Brown	(Dunbar)	4. 1.04P
	(Fuji-Robin EC-44-PM)					
G-MMZN	Mainair Gemini Flash II	283-185-3-W23	18. 3.85	W K Dalus	(Keyworth, Nottingham)	28. 9.93P
	(Fuji-Robin EC-44-PM)					
G-MMZV	Mainair Gemini Flash	313-585-3-W52	18. 4.85	J Broome	(Boston)	28.10.09P
	(Rotax 447)					
G-MMZW	Southdown Puma Sprint		28. 3.85	M G Ashbee	(Cranbrook)	30. 9.00P
	SN1121/0043 & T566/P620			(Damaged C 8.00)		
	(Fuji-Robin EC-44-PM)		18. 4.85	I E S Cole	(Llangurig, Llanidloes)	30. 7.06P
G-MNAC	Mainair Gemini Flash	335-885-3-W72				
	(C/n now verified as 262-884-2 and W04 ex G-MMUT qv)					
G-MNAE	Mainair Gemini Flash	343-885-3-W77	18. 4.85	G C Luddington	(Bletsoe)	29. 7.00P
	(Rotax 447)					
G-MNAI	Solar Wings Panther XL-S	SW-WA-1003	15. 5.85	R G Cameron	Errol	23. 6.98P
	(Trike c/n SW-TR-1003)			(Noted stored 8.04)		
G-MNAR	Solar Wings Pegasus XL-R	SW-WA-1011	6. 8.85	D A Cansdale	(Harlow)	3. 3.03P
	(Trike c/n SW-TB-0014)					
G-MNAW	Solar Wings Pegasus XL-R	SW-WA-1014	16. 8.85	C T H Tenison	(Llanddewi Skirrid, Abergavenny)	2. 8.09P
	(Trike c/n SW-TB-1010)					
G-MNAX	Solar Wings Pegasus XL-R	SW-WA-1015	16. 8.85	B J Phillips	(Beedon, Newbury)	21. 7.96P
	(Trike c/n SW-TB-1011)					
G-MNAY	Solar Wings Pegasus XL-R	SW-WA-1016	6. 8.85	A Seaton	(Sleaford)	11. 9.99P
	(Trike c/n SW-TB-1015)					
G-MNAZ	Solar Wings Pegasus XL-R	SW-WA-1017	6. 8.85	R W Houldsworth	(Rochford)	12. 9.08P
	(Trike c/n SW-TB-1016)					
G-MNBA	Solar Wings Pegasus XL-R	SW-WA-1018	6. 9.85	J G H Featherstone	(Newton Abbot)	29. 3.09P
	(Trike c/n SW-TB-1024)					
G-MNBB	Solar Wings Pegasus XL-R	SW-WA-1019	20. 9.85	C Parkinson	Ince Blundell	3. 8.04P
	(Trike c/n SW-TB-1020)					
G-MNBC	Solar Wings Pegasus XL-R	SW-WA-1020	11.10.85	N Kelly	(Carmarthen)	9. 9.04P
	(Rotax 503) (Trike c/n SW-TB-1026)					
G-MNBD	Mainair Gemini Flash	162-683-W42 G-MMSN	6. 1.86	P Woodcock	Sittles Farm, Alrewas	30.12.03P
	(Fuji-Robin EC-44-PM) (Originally built as Mainair 440 Tri-Flyer c/n 341-585-3 and W42: unsold and.reworked by Mainair as c/n 162-683					
	and fitted to G-MMSN. This was podded to become a Gemini and used in rebuild of G-MNBD after late 1996 accident)					

G-MNBE	Southdown Puma Sprint (Rotax 447)	SN1121/0050		17. 5.85	D Newton	Hunsdon 26. 4.08P
G-MNBF	Mainair Gemini Flash (Fuji-Robin EC-44-PM)	306-585-3-W46		2. 5.85	S King and P Mokryk	(Derby) 25. 5.05P
G-MNBG	Mainair Gemini Flash (Rotax 447)	347-585-3-W66		9. 5.85	T Barnett	Baxby Manor, Husthwaite 15.11.08P
G-MNBI	Solar Wings Panther XL-R (Fuji-Robin EC-44-PM) *(Trike c/n PXL884-178)*	T884-1161XL	G-MMVF?	3. 5.85	M O'Connell	(Clonee, Dublin) 21. 6.09P
G-MNBJ	Skyhook Pixie	HLC-01		7. 5.85	G Sykes	(Holmfirth)
G-MNBM	Southdown Puma Sprint (Rotax 447)	SN1231/0058		25. 6.85	C Hall-Gardner	(Nairnside, Inverness) 7.10.01P
G-MNBN	Mainair Gemini Flash (Fuji-Robin EC-44-PM)	303-485-3-W43		11. 6.85	I H Gates	Long Marston 28. 5.05P
G-MNBP	Mainair Gemini Flash (Fuji-Robin EC-44-PM)	338-885-3-W75		15. 5.85	G A Harper	Priory Farm, Tibenham 21. 7.09P
G-MNBS	Mainair Gemini Flash (Fuji-Robin EC-44-PM)	308-585-3-W48		15. 5.85	P A Comins	(Nottingham) 20. 6.94P
G-MNBT	Mainair Gemini Flash	322-685-3-W62		15. 5.85	R R A Dean	(Chopwell, Newcastle-upon-Tyne) 16. 5.08P
G-MNBV	Mainair Gemini Flash (Rotax 447)	333-685-3-W70		15. 5.85	J Walshe	(Newtownards) 21. 8.04P
G-MNCA	Hunt Avon Sky-Trike/Hiway Demon 175 DA-01 *(Built Hiway Hang Gliders Ltd and originally regd as Adams Trike)*			28. 5.85	M A Sirant	Monkswell Farm, Horrabridge 26. 3.94X
G-MNCF	Mainair Gemini Flash (Rotax 447)	321-685-3-W61		3. 6.85	C F James	Lee-on-Solent 4. 5.08P
G-MNCG	Mainair Gemini Flash *(Rebuilt c2000)*	320-685-3-W59		3. 6.85	I D Mallinson	(Truro) 26.11.07P
G-MNCI	Southdown Puma Sprint (Rotax 447)	SN1231/0059		7. 6.85	R M Wait and N Hewitt	Mill Farm, Shifnal 25. 5.05P
G-MNCJ	Mainair Gemini Flash (Fuji-Robin EC-44) *(Original Trike stolen, new one c/n 282-1284-2 ex G-MMXF fitted c 12.89)*	351-785-3-W83		3. 6.85	R S McLeister	(Accrington) 16.11.93P
G-MNCM	CFM Shadow Series C	006		31. 5.85	K G D Macrae	Drummaird Farm, Bonnybank 19. 6.08P
G-MNCO	Eipper Quicksilver MXII	1045		3. 6.85	S Lawton	(Barnoldswick)
G-MNCP	Southdown Puma Sprint (Rotax 447)	SN1231/0071		24. 6.85	D M Lane	(Poole) 10. 4.00P
G-MNCS	Skyrider Aviation Phantom (Fuji-Robin EC-44-PM)	PH.00098		2. 1.86	S P Allen	(Kettering) 25. 7.03P
G-MNCU	Medway Hybred 44XL *(Solar Wings Typhoon Sailwing)*	26485/10		13. 6.85	J E Evans	Roddige 24. 6.05P
G-MNCV	Medway Hybred 44XL *(Pegasus XL-R Sailwing c/n SW-WA-1030)*	26485/11		13. 6.85	P D Mickleburgh	Swinford, Rugby 14. 5.08P
G-MNDC	Mainair Gemini Flash	336-885-3-W73		12. 6.85	M Medlock	Popham 21. 6.06P
G-MNDD	Mainair Scorcher *(Noted NEC, Birmingham 11.08)*	358-885-1-W85		12. 6.85	L Hurman	Enstone 4. 9.08P
G-MNDE	Medway Half Pintrerial Arts 130SX *(Wing ex G-MNBZ)* *(Noted 1.07)*	3/8685		19. 6.85	C D Wills	Chilbolton 3.10.03P
G-MNDF	Mainair Gemini Flash (Rotax 447)	327-785-3-W67		25. 6.85	W G Nicol	(Stanley, Perth) 21. 6.09P
G-MNDM	Mainair Gemini Flash	324-785-3-W64		11. 7.85	J C Birkbeck	(Appleby-in-Westmorland) 14. 5.09P
G-MNDO	Solar Wings Pegasus Flash *(Trike is c/n SW-TB-1012 and Mainair Sailwing c/n W86)*	SW-WF-0001		2. 7.85	G Carr	(Huthwaite, Sutton-in-Ashfield) 26. 7.08P
G-MNDU	Midland Ultralights Sirocco 377GB (Rotax 377)	MU-011		22. 7.85	M A Collins	Longacre Farm, Sandy 14. 2.04P
G-MNDY	Southdown Puma Sprint (Fuji-Robin EC-44-PM) *(Trike rebuilt c4.99)*	DY-01 & P 536		2. 5.84	A M Coupland	RAF Wyton 19. 6.03P
G-MNEG	Mainair Gemini Flash (Rotax 447)	360-885-3-W92		8. 7.85	A Sexton	(Nurney, County Kildare) 18.10.99P
G-MNEH	Mainair Gemini Flash	361-885-3-W90		8. 7.85	I Rawson	St Michaels 21. 7.08P
G-MNEI	Medway Hybred 44XL *(Solar Wings Typhoon XLII Sailwing c/n SW-WA-1035)* *(Damaged 28.11.92 and stored 8.96)*	8785/12		9. 7.85	L G Thompson	Long Marston 26. 7.93P
G-MNEK	Medway Half Pintrerial Arts 130S	4/8785		12. 7.85	M I Dougall *(Damaged Stoke 6. 7.93)*	(Maidstone) 25. 9.94P
G-MNER	CFM Shadow Series CD (Rotax 462)	008		15. 7.85	F C Claydon	(Wickhambrook, Newmarket) 16. 6.08P
G-MNET	Mainair Gemini Flash (Fuji-Robin EC-44-PM)	349-885-3-W81		23. 7.85	I P Stubbins	North Coates 6. 8.04P
G-MNEV	Mainair Gemini Flash (Rotax 447)	362-1085-3-W108		23. 7.85	M Gardiner	(Farnworth, Bolton) 20. 1.07P
G-MNEY	Mainair Gemini Flash (Rotax 447)	365-1085-3-W94		23. 7.85	D A Spiers	East Fortune 17. 9.04P
G-MNFB	Southdown Puma Sprint (Rotax 447)	SN1231/0077		22. 7.85	C Lawrence	Weston Zoyland 16. 8.05P
G-MNFF	Mainair Gemini Flash (Rotax 447)	371-1185-3-W110		29. 7.85	R P Cook and C H Spencer	St Michaels 24. 5.02P
G-MNFG	Southdown Puma Sprint (Rotax 447)	SN1231/0078		31. 7.85	A C Hing	Stoke, Isle of Grain 12. 6.03P
G-MNFL	AMF Microflight Chevvron 2-32A	CH.002		19. 8.85	P W Wright *(Noted 2.08)*	Saltby 13.12.00P
G-MNFM	Mainair Gemini Flash (Rotax 447)	366-1085-3-W98		10.10.85	P M Fidell	Wombleton 1. 9.05P
G-MNFN	Mainair Gemini Flash (Rotax 447)	367-1085-3-W99		6.11.85	J R Martin	(Bedale) 13. 8.04P
G-MNFP	Mainair Gemini Flash (Rotax 447)	368-1085-3-W100		23.10.85	S Farnsworth and P Howarth	Tarn Farm, Cockerham 4. 7.06P
G-MNGD	Ultrasports Tri-Pacer/Solar Wings Typhoon Medium (Fuji-Robin EC-34-PM) 012 & T681-171			13. 8.85	J E Orbell	North Connel, Oban 15. 5.05P

G-MNGG	Solar Wings Pegasus XL-R	T784-1159XL	21. 8.85	I D Mallinson	Davidstow Moor	9. 8.06P
	(Trike c/n is US.TPR.0002)			*(Noted 9.06)*		
G-MNGK	Mainair Gemini Flash	374-1085-3-W112	5. 9.85	J Pulford	Priory Farm, Tibenham	26. 4.09P
	(Rotax 447)					
G-MNGM	Mainair Gemini Flash	394-1285-3-W109	5. 9.85	R J Webb	Over Farm, Gloucester	22.10.07P
	(Rotax 447) *(Originally supplied with Mainair Trike c/n 377: However this, and Sailwing ex G-MNIO, both stolen from Popham 15/16.3.86:*					
	Subsequently, G-MNGM now comprises Trike ex G-MNIO and Sailwing ex G-MNGM)					
G-MNGT	Mainair Gemini Flash	372-1085-3-W106	30. 9.85	J W Biegus	Arclid Green, Sandbach	7. 6.02P
	(Rotax 447)					
G-MNGW	Mainair Gemini Flash	386-1185-3-W121	30. 9.85	F R Stephens	(Worthing)	23. 4.03P
	(Rotax 447)					
G-MNGX	Southdown Puma Sprint	SN1231/0088	26. 9.85	A J Morris	Sutton Meadows	3. 3.07P
	(Rotax 447)					
G-MNHD	Solar Wings Pegasus XL-R	SW-WA-1047	5.11.85	P D Stiles	(Ashley Down, Bristol)	20. 7.07P
	(Trike c/n SW-TB-1033)					
G-MNHE	Solar Wings Pegasus XL-R/Se	SW-WA-1048	11.12.85	D Stevens	Davidstow Moor	17.10.05P
	(Trike c/n SW-TB-1036)					
G-MNHF	Solar Wings Pegasus XL-R	SW-WA-1049	29.11.85	J E Cox	Shobdon	29. 9.05P
	(Trike c/n SW-TB-1038)					
G-MNHH	Solar Wings Pegasus XL-S	SW-WA-1051	22. 1.86	F J Williams	(Shefford, Bedford)	24. 6.01P
	(Trike is an Ultrasports unit c/n PXL847-170)					
G-MNHI	Solar Wings Pegasus XL-R	SW-WA-1052	8. 1.86	C Council	(Whitstable)	7. 8.07P
	(Trike c/n SW-TB-1042)					
G-MNHJ	Solar Wings Pegasus XL-R	SW-WA-1053	11. 3.86	S J Woodd	(Charlbury, Chipping Norton)	26. 6.93P
	(Trike c/n SW-TB-1056)					
G-MNHK	Solar Wings Pegasus XL-R	SW-WA-1054	9. 7.86	K Buckley	Roddige	2. 6.09P
	(Rotax 462) *(Trike c/n SW-TE-0005)*					
G-MNHL	Solar Wings Pegasus XL-R/Se	SW-WA-1055	9. 7.86	The Microlight School Ltd	Roddige	15.10.08P
	(Rotax 503) *(Trike c/n SW-TB-1077) (Noted with Sailwing (skin only or whole frame?) from G-MTRN and marked "G-MT" under wing 4.06)*					
G-MNHM	Solar Wings Pegasus XL-R	SW-WA-1056	11. 7.86	P A Howell	(Stoke-on-Trent)	12. 2.09P
	(Trike c/n SW-TB-1078)					
G-MNHN	Solar Wings Pegasus XL-R	SW-WA-1057	11. 8.86	Northwest Microlights Ltd	Rochdale	11. 4.07P
	(Trike c/n SW-TB-1079)			*(Wing stored P&M Aviation, Rochdale 6.08)*		
G-MNHR	Solar Wings Pegasus XL-R	SW-WA-1060	7. 8.86	B D Jackson	(Wincanton)	13.11.08P
	(Trike c/n SW-TB-1081)					
G-MNHS	Solar Wings Pegasus XL-R	SW-WA-1061	21. 8.86	M D Packer	Weston Zoyland	12.10.03P
	(Trike c/n SW-TB-1082)			*(Noted 7.04)*		
G-MNHT	Solar Wings Pegasus XL-R	SW-WA-1062	4. 8.86	J W Coventry	Davidstow Moor	3.11.09P
	(Trike c/n SW-TB-1084)					
G-MNIA	Mainair Gemini Flash	370-1185-3-W105	10.10.85	A E Dix	Long Marston	10. 4.89P
	(Rotax 447)			*(Noted wrecked 1990)*		
G-MNID	Mainair Gemini Flash	369-1185-3-W104	7. 2.86	G Nicholls	(Rotherham)	30. 5.07P
	(Rotax 447) *(Official c/n is incorrect as Trike and Engine no.3706877 stolen from Rufforth 10 or 11.97 so a replacement Trike is fitted.*					
	BMAA records show c/n 360-5884-W104: this is a corruption - may be c/n 360-885-3 - but this conflicts with G-MNEG (qv))					
G-MNIE	Mainair Gemini Flash	388-1185-3-W123	21.11.85	G M Hewer	(Cheltenham)	8. 7.02P
	(Rotax 447)					
G-MNIF	Mainair Gemini Flash	403-286-4-W147	7. 1.86	M Devlin	Dungannon	4. 4.08E
G-MNIG	Mainair Gemini/Flash	391-1285-3-W139	9. 1.86	A B Woods	(Halesworth)	18. 8.08P
	(Rotax 447)					
G-MNIH	Mainair Gemini Flash	379-1185-3-W116	10.12.85	N H S Insall	Dunkeswell	12. 8.08P
	(Rotax 447)					
G-MNII	Mainair Gemini Flash	390-1285-3-W128	6.11.85	R F Finnis	(Guildford)	6. 9.91P
	(Rotax 447)			*(Trike reported at St Michaels 9.96)*		
G-MNIK	Solar Wings Pegasus Photon	SW-WP-0002	29.10.85	M Belemet	Jackrell's Farm, Horsham	25. 4.07P
	(Trike c/n SW-TP-0002)					
G-MNIL	Southdown Puma Sprint	SN1231/0094	4.11.85	A Bishop	Ince Blundell	31. 8.05P
	(Rotax 447)					
G-MNIM	Maxair Hummer	PJB-01	29.10.85	K Wood	(Keyham, Leicester)	
G-MNIS	CFM Shadow Series C	014	11.11.85	R W Payne	(Langtoft, Peterborough)	25. 4.92P
G-MNIT	Aerial Arts Alpha Mk.II/130SX	130SX/176	27. 2.86	M J Edmett	(London N3)	15. 8.99
	(Originally regd as Hiway Skytrike II with same c/n)					
G-MNIZ	Mainair Gemini Flash	392-1285-3-W130	26. 2.86	A G Power	Higher Barn Farm, Houghton	25. 1.08P
	(Rotax 447)					
G-MNJB	Southdown Raven X	SN2232/0098	10.12.85	W Flood	(London SE25)	26. 5.03P
G-MNJD	Mainair Tri-Flyer 440/Sprint					
	(Fuji-Robin EC-44-PM)	243-10484-2-P 537	2. 4.84	S D Smith	Popham	7. 5.05P
G-MNJF	Dragon Light Aircraft Dragon Series 150	0068	(OY) 9-17	2. 1.86	B W Langley	South Wraxall	6. 9.06P
	(Fuji-Robin EC-44-PM)			*(Noted 9.07)*		
G-MNJG	Mainair Gemini/Southdown Puma Sprint MS		29. 9.83	T J Gayton-Polley	(Billingshurst)	20.1.10P
	SA.2030 and 251-684-2-P 593					
	(Fuji-Robin EC-44-PM)					
G-MNJH	Solar Wings Pegasus Flash	SW-WF-0004	22.10.85	C P Course	Church Farm, Wellingborough	18. 8.02P
	(Trike c/n SW-TB-102 & Mainair Sailwing c/n W89)					
G-MNJJ	Solar Wings Pegasus Flash	SW-WF-0006	22.10.85	P A Shelley	(Washbrook, Ipswich)	26.11.96P
	(Trike c/n SW-TB-1029 & Mainair Sailwing c/n W96)					
G-MNJL	Solar Wings Pegasus Flash	SW-WF-0008	21.10.85	S D Thomas	(Bilston)	11.11.94P
	(Trike c/n SW-TB-1028 & Mainair Sailwing c/n W101)					
G-MNJN	Solar Wings Pegasus Flash	SW-WF-0010	19.11.85	D Thorn	Davidstow Moor	5. 7.05P
	(Trike c/n SW-TB-1034 & Mainair Sailwing c/n W103)					
G-MNJR	Solar Wings Pegasus Flash	SW-WF-0013	30.12.85	M G Ashbee	(Cranbrook)	8.10.08P
	(Trike c/n SW-TB-1041 & Mainair Sailwing c/n W133)					
G-MNJS	Southdown Puma Sprint	SN1231/0085	18. 9.85	E A Frost	Sutton Meadows	24. 2.06P
	(Rotax 447)					

G-MNJT	Southdown Raven X	SN2232/0087	20. 9.85	P A Harris	RAF Henlow	7. 3.04P
	(Forced landed east of Exford, Devon 11. 7.03 causing substantial damage)					
G-MNJU	Mainair Gemini Flash	384-1185-3-W119	20. 9.85	H A Taylor	Finmere	28. 5.06P
	(Rotax 447)					
G-MNJX	Medway Hybred 44XL	15885/14	9.12.85	H A Stewart	(Hartlip, Sittingbourne)	23. 7.98P
G-MNKB	Solar Wings Pegasus Photon	SW-WP-0005	14. 1.86	M E Gilbert	Drummaird Farm, Bonnybank	11. 5.06P
	(Trike c/n SW-TP-0005)					
G-MNKC	Solar Wings Pegasus Photon	SW-WP-0006	14. 1.86	K B Woods	(Somersham, Huntingdon)	17. 3.04P
	(Trike c/n SW-TP-0006)			(		
G-MNKD	Solar Wings Pegasus Photon	SW-WP-0007	14. 1.86	M Sirant	Davidstow Moor	8. 4.05P
	(Originally allocated Trike c/n SW-TP-0007 but believed exported: current Trike is possibly c/n SW-TP-0016)					
G-MNKE	Solar Wings Pegasus Photon	SW-WP-0008	14. 1.86	G Forster	(Healing, Grimsby)	14. 1.09P
	(Trike c/n SW-TP-0008)					
G-MNKG	Solar Wings Pegasus Photon	SW-WP-0010	28. 1.86	T W Thompson	Eshott	11. 6.95P
	(Trike stored 9.97)					
G-MNKK	Solar Wings Pegasus Photon	SW-WP-0014	28. 1.86	M E Gilbert	(Dalgety Bay, Dunfermline)	7. 5.95P
	(Fuji-Robin EC-34-PM) *(Trike c/n SW-TP-0014)*					
G-MNKM	MBA Tiger Cub 440	SO.213	30.12.85	A R Sunley	(Chelmsford)	17. 2.04P
G-MNKO	Solar Wings Pegasus XL-Q	SW-WX-0001	2. 1.86	T A Goundry	Eshott	29. 9.06P
	(Rotax 447) *(Trike c/n SW-TB-1158)*					
G-MNKP	Solar Wings Pegasus Flash	SW-WF-0014	9. 1.86	I N Miller	Plaistows Farm, St Albans	14. 1.08P
	(Trike c/n SW-TB-1043 & Mainair Sailwing c/n W131)					
G-MNKU	Southdown Puma Sprint	SN1231/0100	29. 1.86	S P O'Hannrachain	(Coolaney, County Sligo)	30. 8.03P
	(Rotax 447)					
G-MNKV	Solar Wings Pegasus Flash	SW-WF-0017	15. 1.86	K S G Lindfield	Dunkeswell	27. 4.06P
	(Trike c/n SW-TB-1047 & Mainair Sailwing c/n W137)					
G-MNKW	Solar Wings Pegasus Flash	SW-WF-0018	28. 1.86	S P Halford	Mill Farm, Hughley, Much Wenlock	29. 7.09P
	(Trike c/n SW-TB-1049 & Mainair Sailwing c/n W140)					
G-MNKX	Solar Wings Pegasus Flash	SW-WF-0019	28. 2.86	P Samal	(Sandy)	3. 8.05P
	(Trike c/n SW-TB-1054 & Mainair Sailwing c/n W139)					
G-MNKZ	Southdown Raven X	SN2232/0102	4. 2.86	G B Gratton	Chilbolton	31. 5.07P
G-MNLH	Romain Cobra Biplane	001	23. 1.86	J W E Romain	(Welwyn)	10. 4.06P
	(Midwest AE50R)					
G-MNLI	Mainair Gemini Flash II	407-286-4-W152	28. 1.86	P M Fessi *(Noted 10.07)*	Swinford, Rugby	28.10.07P
G-MNLM	Southdown Raven X	SN2232/0110	6. 2.86	A P White	(Exmouth)	9. 6.93P
G-MNLN	Southdown Raven X	SN2232/0111	6. 2.86	A S Windley	(Matlock)	27.12.00P
G-MNLT	Southdown Raven X	SN2232/0115	6. 2.86	J L Stachini	Stoke, Isle of Grain	12. 8.01P
G-MNLY	Mainair Gemini Flash	406-386-4-W151	14. 2.86	P D Parry	(Ruthin)	25. 4.09P
G-MNLZ	Southdown Raven X	SN2232/0123	6. 2.86	R Downham	(Bacup)	12. 6.02P
G-MNMC	Mainair Gemini/Southdown Puma Sprint MS		20. 3.84	G A Davidson	(Brierfield, Nelson)	18. 6.07P
	222-284-2 & P 524					
G-MNMD	Southdown Raven X	SN2000/0121	10. 2.86	P G Overall	(Crawley)	31. 5.05P
G-MNMG	Mainair Gemini Flash II	419-386-4-W177	11. 2.86	N A M Beyer-Kay	(Southport)	20. 8.94P
	(Rotax 447)					
G-MNMI	Mainair Gemini Flash II	317-685-3-W178	11. 2.86	A D Bales	Priory Farm, Tibenham	12. 6.08P
	(Fuji-Robin EC-44) *(Trike and engine ex G-MMZL following accident 8.9.91)*					
G-MNMK	Solar Wings Pegasus XL-R	SW-WA-1038	19. 8.85	A F Smallacombe	(Okehampton)	2. 7.00P
	(Trike c/n SW-TB-1021)					
G-MNML	Southdown Puma Sprint	SN1111/0065	4. 8.83	R C Carr	(Boyton, Launceston)	14. 7.97P
	(Fuji-Robin EC-44-PM)					
G-MNMM	Aerotech MW-5(K) Sorcerer	5K-0001-02	11. 2.86	S F N Warnell	(Staines)	17. 8.99P
	(Originally regd as c/n SR101-R4008-01 - now officially regd. as c/n 5K-0001-01)					
G-MNMU	Southdown Puma Raven	SN2232/0127	17. 2.86	M J Curley	(London Colney)	26. 3.06P
G-MNMV	Mainair Gemini Flash	375-1085-3-W113	3. 3.86	S Staig	Tarn Farm, Cockerham	13. 8.06P
	(Rotax 447)					
G-MNMW	Whittaker MW6-1-1 Merlin	PFA 164-11144	16. 4.86	E F Clapham tr G-MNMW Flying Group		
	(Built E F Clapham) (Rotax 582)				Otherton, Cannock	21. 8.08P
G-MNMY	Cyclone 70/Aerial Arts 110SX	CH-02	6. 3.86	N R Beale	Deppers Bridge, Southam	15. 7.05P
G-MNNA	Southdown Raven X	SN2232/0129	4. 3.86	D and G D Palfrey	(Morebath, Tiverton)	20. 7.88P
G-MNNB	Southdown Raven	SN2122/0130	4. 3.86	J F Horn	(Yelverton)	3. 6.03P
	(Fuji-Robin EC-44-PM)					
G-MNNC	Southdown Raven X	SN2232/0131	4. 3.86	S A Sacker	Deenethorpe	5. 8.00P
G-MNNF	Mainair Gemini Flash II	402-286-4-W148	28. 2.86	W J Gunn	Long Marston	8. 4.97P
	(Rotax 447)				*(Stored 1.98)*	
G-MNNG	Squires Lightfly/Solar Wings Photon	SW-WP-0019	25. 2.86	K B Woods	Newnham, Baldock	X
	(Rotax 277) *(Trike may be Mainair Tri-Flyer c/n 032-221181 ex G-MJKY?)*					
G-MNNJ	Mainair Gemini Flash II	405-286-4-W150	28. 2.86	H D Lynch	(Fermoy, County Cork)	6. 5.05P
	(ID Plate incorrectly marked as "G-MNNZ")					
G-MNNL	Mainair Gemini Flash II	429-486-4-W186	28. 2.86	C L Rumney	(Allonby, Maryport)	21.11.05P
G-MNNM	Mainair Scorcher Solo	424-486-1-W182	(G-MNPE)	20. 3.86	S R Leeper and L L Perry	Grove Farm, Needham	9. 2.06P
G-MNNO	Southdown Raven X	SN2232/0133	26. 3.86	M J Robbins	(Tunbridge Wells)	16.12.01P
G-MNNS	Eurowing Goldwing	EW-74	8. 4.86	J S R Moodie	(Rovie Farm, Rogart)	
	(Rotax 377) *(Pr. no BMAA HB/287 allocated for rebuild but not completed)*				*(Stored 6.06)*	
G-MNNV	Mainair Gemini Flash II	431-586-4-W187	10. 3.86	A Worthington	(Chorley)	11. 4.02P
	(Believed to fly with the wing of G-MTBI)					
G-MNNY	Solar Wings Pegasus Flash	SW-WF-0023	14. 3.86	C W Payne	Croft Farm, Defford	20. 3.04P
	(Trike c/n SW-TB-1059 & Mainair Sailwing c/n W161)					
G-MNNZ	Solar Wings Pegasus Flash II	SW-WF-0101	24. 4.86	R D A Henderson	(Carnon Downs, Truro)	1. 4.98P
	(Trike c/n SW-TB-1060 & Mainair Sailwing c/n W162)					
G-MNPA	Solar Wings Pegasus Flash II	SW-WF-0102	18. 4.86	N T Murphy	(Rathangon, County Kildare)	30. 5.98P
	(Rotax 462) *(Trike c/n SW-TB-1061) (Original Mainair Sailwing c/n W174 but has now acquired W210 ex G-MNZA)*					
G-MNPC	Mainair Gemini Flash II	423-586-4-W181	17. 3.86	M S McGimpsey	Newtownards	2. 5.08P
	(Rotax 462)					

G-MNPG	Mainair Gemini Flash II	437-686-4-W204		20. 3.86	P Kirton	Easter Poldar Farm, Thornhill	4. 9.06P
	(Rotax 447)						
G-MNPY	Mainair Scorcher Solo	452-886-1-W229		25. 3.86	R N O Kingsbury	Stoke, Isle of Grain	22. 5.08P
G-MNPZ	Mainair Scorcher Solo	449-886-1-W226		25. 3.86	S Stevens	(Cornhill-on-Tweed)	4. 9.93P
	(Rotax 503) (3-Blade propeller test aircraft)						
G-MNRD	Ultraflight Lazair IIIE	81		17. 6.83	F P Welsh tr Sywell Lazair Group (Noted 10.07)		
	(Rotax 185 x 2)					Sywell	12. 4.05P
G-MNRE	Mainair Scorcher Solo	453-886-1-W230		25. 3.86	A P Pearce	Wickhambrook, Newmarket	27. 6.06P
G-MNRI	Hornet Dual Trainer/Southdown Raven			26. 3.86	R H Goll	(Llansawel, Llandeilo)	2. 8.02P
	HRWA 0051 & SN2000/0119						
G-MNRK	Hornet Dual Trainer/Southdown Raven			26. 3.86	M A H Milne	(Huntly)	30. 7.95P
	(Rotax 447) HRWA 0053 & SN2000/0183						
G-MNRM	Hornet Dual Trainer/Southdown Raven			26. 3.86	R I Cannan	(Ramsey, Isle of Man)	23. 2.09P
	(Rotax 447) HRWA 0055 & SN2000/0214						
G-MNRP	Southdown Raven X	SN2232/0135		7. 4.86	C Moore	(Haile, Egremont)	5. 7.95P
G-MNRS	Southdown Raven X	SN2232/0137		7. 4.86	M C Newman	(St Leonards-on-Sea)	29. 7.04P
G-MNRT	Midland Ultralights Sirocco 377GB	MU-016		1. 4.86	R F Hinton	(Mansfield)	18. 8.01P
G-MNRW	Mainair Gemini Flash II	411-486-4-W156		7. 4.86	D Buckthorpe (Noted 5.05)	Clench Common	12.10.04P
	(Rotax 462)						
G-MNRX	Mainair Gemini Flash II	434-686-4-W220		8. 4.86	R Downham	St Michaels	14. 8.09P
G-MNRZ	Mainair Scorcher Solo	426-586-1-W184		4. 4.86	J Lynch	Sandtoft	10. 5.07P
					(Noted at P&M Aviation 15.08, no damage)		
G-MNSA	Mainair Gemini Flash II	442-786-4-W219		18. 4.86	W F G Panayiotiou	(Llanelli)	23. 8.04P
G-MNSD	Ultrasports Tri-Pacer 250/Solar Wings Typhoon S4						
	(Hunting HS.260A)	T182-341L		23. 4.86	A Strydom	(London WC1)	X
G-MNSH	Solar Wings Pegasus Flash II	SW-WF-0104		14. 4.86	D Lee	(Newton Bank Farm, Daresbury)	14. 5.05P
	(Rotax 447) (Trike c/n SW-TB-1063 & Mainair Sailwing c/n W163)						
G-MNSI	Mainair Gemini Flash II	445-786-4-W213		9. 4.86	J-P Trouillard	(St Nazaire, France)	9. 6.03P
G-MNSJ	Mainair Gemini Flash II	443-886-4-W223		11. 4.86	G J Cadden	Smithboro, County Monaghan	14. 5.06P
G-MNSL	Southdown Raven X	SN2232/0145		17. 4.86	P B Robinson	(Ely)	11. 8.00P
G-MNSX	Southdown Raven X	SN2232/0148		30. 4.86	S F Chave	(Honiton)	18. 7.03P
G-MNSY	Southdown Raven X	SN2232/0149		30. 4.86	L A Hosegood	(Swindon)	8. 3.03P
G-MNTC	Southdown Raven X	SN2232/0150		30. 4.86	D S Bancalari	(Norwich)	12.10.92P
G-MNTD	Aerial Arts Chaser/110SX	110SX/255		24. 4.86	B Richardson	(Sunderland)	
	(C/n duplicates G-MTSF)						
G-MNTE	Southdown Raven X	SN2232/0151		30. 4.86	E Foster (Remains noted 7.07) Brook Farm, Pilling		27. 6.04P
G-MNTI	Mainair Gemini Flash II	447-886-4-W231		8. 5.86	R T Strathie Nether Huntlywood Farm, Gordon		19. 8.01P
					(Noted 2.06)		
G-MNTK	CFM Shadow Series CD	024		8. 5.86	M J Bromley	(Southport)	12. 5.08P
G-MNTM	Southdown Raven X	SN2232/0154		19. 5.86	D M Garland	(Atherstone)	24. 7.01P
G-MNTN	Southdown Raven X	SN2232/0155		2. 6.86	J Hall	(Wolverhampton)	25. 1.06P
G-MNTP	CFM Shadow Series C	K 022		19. 5.86	E G White	Landmead Farm, Garford	6. 5.07P
G-MNTT	Medway Half Pintrerial Arts 130SX	12/1486		7. 4.86	P J Burrow	(Crediton)	20. 6.03P
	(Rotax 462)						
G-MNTU	Mainair Gemini Flash II	460-886-4-W233		9. 7.86	G S Brewer	(Balderton, Newark)	24. 7.06P
	(Rotax 503)						
G-MNTV	Mainair Gemini Flash II	455-886-4-W241		9. 7.86	A M Sirant	Davidstow Moor	17.10.04P
	(Rotax 462)						
G-MNTY	Southdown Raven X	SN2232/0157		29. 5.86	S Phillips	(Snodland)	16. 5.05P
G-MNTZ	Mainair Gemini Flash II	457-886-4-W243		3. 6.86	D E Milner	(Leeds)	4. 1.06P
G-MNUA	Mainair Gemini Flash II	458-886-4-W235		29. 5.86	P Hughes and S Beggan	Newtownards	9. 5.09P
	(Rotax 462)						
G-MNUD	Solar Wings Pegasus Flash II	SW-WF-0110		10. 6.86	P G H Milbank	Sutton Meadows	20. 9.03P
	(Rotax 462) (Trike c/n SW-TE-0003 & Mainair Sailwing c/n W195)						
G-MNUE	Solar Wings Pegasus Flash II	SW-WF-0108		10. 6.86	R J Saxby	(Dorchester)	24. 7.06P
	(Rotax 462) (Trike c/n SW-TE-0002) (Original Mainair Sailwing c/n W193 but now acquired c/n W209 ex G-MNYA)						
G-MNUF	Mainair Gemini Flash II	472-786-4-W252		13. 6.86	K Jones	Hawarden	9. 7.08P
G-MNUG	Mainair Gemini Flash II	465-986-4-W245		13. 6.86	A S Nader	Ince Blundell	19.10.05P
	(Rotax 462)						
G-MNUI	Mainair Tri-Flyer/Skyhook Cutlass	MH-01		21. 5.86	M Holling	(Pollington, Goole)	28. 2.87X
	(Fuji-Robin EC-44-PM)						
G-MNUO	Mainair Gemini Flash II	421-586-4-W179		9. 7.86	P S Taylor	(Addlestone)	29. 5.06P
	(Rotax 462)						
G-MNUR	Mainair Gemini Flash II	470-986-4-W250		14. 8.86	J C Greves	(Walton-on-Thames)	30. 3.90P
G-MNUU	Southdown Raven X	SN2232/0162		26. 6.86	P N Jackson (Noted 8.05)	Davidstow Moor	10. 9.02P
G-MNUW	Southdown Raven X	SN2232/0163		17. 6.86	B A McDonald	(Cambridge)	19.12.96P
G-MNUX	Solar Wings Pegasus XL-R	SW-WA-1076		24. 6.86	A M Smith	Shotton Colliery, Peterlee	3. 5.03P
	(Trike c/n SW-TB-1072)				(Noted 2.08)		
G-MNVB	Solar Wings Pegasus XL-R	SW-WA-1077		7. 7.86	M J Melvin	(Hoddesdon)	10. 4.08P
	(Trike c/n SW-TB-1073)						
G-MNVC	Solar Wings Pegasus XL-R	SW-WA-1078		7. 7.86	M N C Ward	Shobdon	11. 6.00P
	(Trike c/n SW-TB-1074)						
G-MNVE	Solar Wings Pegasus XL-R	SW-WA-1079		19. 6.86	M P Aris	(Welwyn)	11. 8.00P
	(Trike c/n SW-TB-1075)						
G-MNVG	Solar Wings Pegasus Flash II	SW-WF-0109		11. 6.86	D J Ward	Low Farm, South Walsham	23. 8.09P
	(Rotax 447) (Trike c/n SW-TB-1069 & Mainair Sailwing c/n W194)						
G-MNVH	Solar Wings Pegasus Flash II	SW-WF-0122		23. 6.86	J A Clarke and C Hall	(London N22 and E8)	9. 4.97P
	(Rotax 462) (Trike c/n SW-TE-0001 & Mainair Sailwing c/n W260)						
G-MNVI	CFM Shadow Series C	026		17. 6.86	D R C Pugh	(Caersws, Powys)	4. 6.08P
G-MNVJ	CFM Shadow Series CD	028		17. 6.86	V C Readhead	(Saxmundham)	1. 5.08P
G-MNVK	CFM Shadow Series CD	029		17. 6.86	A K Atwell	(Newport)	5.12.09P
G-MNVL	Medway Half Pintrerial Arts 130SX		G-MNBZ	22. 9.86	A D Hutchings	(Bathford, Bath)	X
	3/21585 & 130SX-100						

G-MNVN	Southdown Puma Raven (Fuji-Robin EC-34-PM)	SN2132/0165		27. 6.86	R J Styles	(Worcester)	11. 4.08P
G-MNVO	Hovey Whing-Ding II	CW-01		14. 8.86	C Wilson	(Basildon)	
G-MNVP	Southdown Raven X	SN2232/0166	(EI- . . .)	23. 6.86	N Furlong	Kilpatrick, Stradbally, County Laois	19.12.03P
			G-MNVP, (EI- . . .), G-MNVP				
G-MNVT	Mainair Gemini Flash II	477-786-4-W258		27. 6.86	A C Barker tr ACB Hydraulics		
					(Stored 4.90)	Hinton-in-the-Hedges	28. 7.87P
G-MNVV	Mainair Gemini Flash II	467-986-4-W247		26. 6.86	T Wilbor	Bagby	20. 6.09P
G-MNVW	Mainair Gemini Flash II	466-986-4-W246		26. 6.86	J C Munro-Hunt	(Little Down Farm, Milson)	29. 9.09P
G-MNVZ	Solar Wings Pegasus Photon	SW-WP-0021		27. 6.86	J J Russ	(Washington)	27. 6.94P
	(Trike c/n SW-TP-0021)						
G-MNWD	Mainair Gemini Flash II	474-986-4-W254		27. 6.86	M B Rutherford	Swinford, Rugby	7. 7.01P
	(Rotax 462)				(Noted 11.07)		
G-MNWG	Southdown Raven X	SN2232/0170		4. 8.86	D Murray	(Clevedon)	9. 5.05P
G-MNWI	Mainair Gemini Flash II	478-986-4-W264		9. 7.86	R N Snook	Inverkip	22. 9.07P
G-MNWL	Arbiter Services Trike/Aerial Arts 130SX			23. 7.86	E H Snook	(Newport Pagnell)	
		130SX/333					
G-MNWU	Solar Wings Pegasus Flash II	SW-WF-0111		4. 8.86	S P Wass	Wing Farm, Longbridge Deverill	26. 4.05P
	(Rotax 462) (Trike c/n SW-TE-0006 & Mainair Sailwing c/n W196)				(Sailwing noted for spares use 4.07)		
G-MNWW	Solar Wings Pegasus XL Tug	SW-WA-1085		8.10.86	N P Chittytr Chiltern Flyers Aero Tow Group		
	(Rotax 462)	(Trike c/n SW-TE-0008)				Ginge, Wantage	30. 7.07P
G-MNWY	CFM Shadow Series C	K 021		28. 7.86	J Williams	Headon Farm, Retford	19. 8.03P
	(Built CFM Aircraft Ltd - pr.no.PFA 161-11130)				(Noted 8.07)		
G-MNXB	Solar Wings Photon/Mainair Tri-Flyer			29. 7.86	G W Carwardine	(Hadlow Down, Uckfield)	16. 6.98P
		SW-WP-0022 & 016-29981	(Fuji-Robin EC-34-PM)		(Noted 5.07 with Mike Phillips' Trike)		
G-MNXE	Southdown Raven X	SN2232/0202		7. 8.86	A E Silvey	Whitecross Farm, Wilburton	6.11.09P
G-MNXF	Southdown Puma Raven	SN2132/0176		2. 9.86	D E Gwenin	Holmbeck Farm, Leighton Buzzard	13. 5.99P
G-MNXG	Southdown Raven X	SN2232/0181		3. 9.86	M A Williams	(Tonbridge)	22. 7.02P
G-MNXI	Southdown Raven X	SN2232/0179		19. 8.86	P K Morley	Baxby Manor, Husthwaite	30. 9.08P
G-MNXO	Medway Hybred 44XLR	29786/19		3. 9.86	D L Turner	(Chatham)	6. 7.02P
G-MNXP	Solar Wings Pegasus Flash II	SW-WF-0117		16. 9.86	I K Priestley	(Thurleigh, Bedford)	6. 8.96P
	(Rotax 447) (Trike c/n SW-TB-1094 & Mainair Sailwing c/n W207)						
G-MNXS	Mainair Gemini Flash II	480-986-4-W267		8. 9.86	J M Macdonald	(Shrewsbury)	16. 3.89P
	(Rotax 462)						
G-MNXU	Mainair Gemini Flash II	482-1086-4-W272		18. 8.86	J M Hucker	(Abertillery)	10. 3.98P
G-MNXX	CFM Shadow Series CD	K 027		13. 8.86	R E Williams	(Margam, Port Talbot)	13. 3.08P
G-MNXZ	Whittaker MW5 Sorcerer	PFA 163-11156		13. 8.86	A J Glynn	Gerpins Farm, Upminster	29. 6.09P
	(Built P J Cheyney) (Fuji-Robin EC-34-PM)						
G-MNYA	Solar Wings Pegasus Flash II	SW-WF-0119		3. 9.86	C Trollope	Watnall	25. 3.05P
	(Rotax 447) (Trike c/n SW-TB-1098 & Mainair Sailwing c/n W259)						
G-MNYC	Solar Wings Pegasus XL-R	SW-WA-1090		3. 9.86	A N Papworth	Sutton Meadows	16. 7.08P
	(Trike c/n SW-TB-1097)						
G-MNYD	Aerial Arts Chaser/110SX	110SX/320		19. 8.86	B Richardson	(Eshott)	17.10.04P
	(Rotax 377)						
G-MNYE	Aerial Arts Chaser/110SX	110SX/321		19. 8.86	R J Ripley	(Oakley, Bedford)	18.11.99P
	(Rotax 337)						
G-MNYF	Aerial Arts Chaser/110SX	110SX/322		19. 8.86	B Richardson	(Eshott)	12. 5.06P
	(Rotax 377)						
G-MNYG	Southdown Puma Raven	SN2122/0172		19. 8.86	K Clifford	(Stanmore)	3. 7.00P
G-MNYJ	Mainair Gemini Flash II	485-1086-4-W275		8. 9.86	G B Jones	Otherton, Cannock	13. 7.03P
	(Rotax 462)						
G-MNYK	Mainair Gemini Flash II	494-1086-4-W296		11. 9.86	J J Ryan	(Enniscorthy, County Wexford)	4.10.95P
	(Rotax 582)						
G-MNYL	Southdown Raven X	SN2232/0195		2. 9.86	A D F Clifford	Broadmeadow Farm, Hereford	9. 6.98P
					(Noted 5.05)		
G-MNYM	Southdown Raven X	SN2232/0196		2. 9.86	R L Davis	Dunkeswell	11. 6.04P
G-MNYP	Southdown Raven X	SN2232/0207		3. 9.86	A G Davies	(Bristol)	14. 5.01P
G-MNYU	Solar Wings Pegasus XL-R/Se	SW-WA-1092		16. 9.86	G L Turner	Pittrichie Farm, Whitecrashes	28. 4.06P
	(Trike c/n SW-TB-1100)						
G-MNYW	Solar Wings Pegasus XL-R	SW-WA-1094		11. 9.86	M P Waldock	(Croydon)	7. 8.98P
	(Trike c/n SW-TB-1102)						
G-MNYX	Solar Wings Pegasus XL-R	SW-WA-1095		19. 9.86	P F Mayes and J P Widdowson		
	(Rotax 462)	(Trike c/n SW-TE-0009)				Pound Green, Buttonoak, Bewdley	31. 8.08P
G-MNYZ	Solar Wings Pegasus Flash II	SW-WF-0114		11. 9.86	A C Bartolozzi	(Ely)	7. 8.04P
	(Rotax 462) (Trike c/n SW-TE-0010 & Mainair Sailwing c/n W199)						
G-MNZB	Mainair Gemini Flash II	483-1086-4-W273		8. 9.86	P A Ryde	Mill Farm, Shifnal	25. 3.08P
G-MNZC	Mainair Gemini Flash II	484-1086-4-W274		6. 9.86	C J Whittaker	(Ledbury)	19. 1.89P
G-MNZD	Mainair Gemini Flash II	493-1086-4-W295		8. 9.86	N D Carter (Stored 9.96)	Little Gransden	4. 4.96P
G-MNZF	Mainair Gemini Flash II	496-1186-4-W291		8. 9.86	M Lally	Tarn Farm, Cockerham	16. 7.08P
G-MNZJ	CFM Shadow Series CD	033		19. 9.86	T E P Eves tr G-MNZJ Shadow Group	Bagby	13. 6.07P
					(Noted 2.08)		
G-MNZK	Solar Wings Pegasus XL-R/Se	SW-WA-1096		24. 9.86	P J Appleby		
					(Foxfield, Carrick-on-Shannon, County Leitrim)		29. 3.04P
G-MNZP	CFM Shadow Series BD	K 039		19. 9.86	J G Wakeford	Kittyhawk Farm, Deanland	20. 6.06P
	(Built CFM Aircraft Ltd - pr.no.PFA 161-11206)						
G-MNZR	CFM Shadow Series BD	040		19. 9.86	G Taylor (Active 7.08)	(Norwich)	20. 7.07P
G-MNZS	Aerial Arts Alpha/130SX	130SX/376		23. 9.86	N R Beale	Deppers Bridge, Southam	1. 8.00P
	(Rotax 277)						
G-MNZU	Eurowing Goldwing	EW-88		24. 9.86	P D Coppin and P R Millen		
	(Fuji-Robin EC-34-PM)					Colemore Common, Hampshire	5.11.05P
G-MNZW	Southdown Raven X	SN2232/0220		17.10.86	T A Willcox (Noted 4.06)	Doynton	7. 7.02P
G-MNZZ	CFM Shadow Series CD	036		19. 9.86	Shadow Aviation Ltd	Old Sarum	31. 8.05P
G-MOAC	Beech F33A Bonanza	CE-1349	N1563N	25. 5.89	R L Camrass	Le Touquet, France	30. 5.09E

Reg	Type	c/n	Prev id	Date	Owner	Location	Expiry
G-MOAN	Aeromot AMT-200S Super Ximango (Rotax 912-S4)	200.133	PT-PRU	29. 3.04	A E Mayhew	Rochester	1. 5.09E
G-MODE	Eurocopter EC.120B Colibri	1295	F-WQPU	19. 8.02	Cardy Construction Ltd (Compton Bassett, Calne)		17.11.09E
G-MOFB	Cameron O-120 Balloon (Hot Air)	4275		13. 1.98	D M Moffat	Alveston, Bristol	20. 8.09E
G-MOFF	Cameron O-77 Balloon (Hot Air)	2040		27. 7.89	D M Moffat "Moff"	Alveston, Bristol	7. 9.95A
G-MOFZ	Cameron O-90 Balloon (Hot Air)	3350		7. 9.94	D M Moffat	Alveston, Bristol	9. 8.09E
G-MOGI	Grumman AA-5A Cheetah	AA5A-0630	G-BFMU	1. 5.86	J G Stewart tr MOGI Flying Group	Cranfield	17. 1.09E
G-MOGY	Robinson R22 Beta	0899		23.11.88	Northumbria Helicopters Ltd	Newcastle	29. 9.09E
G-MOKE	Cameron V-77 Balloon (Hot Air)	3686		4.10.95	G Moyano tr G-MOKE ASBC Winseler Luxembourg		28. 5.09E
G-MOLE	Taylor JT.2 Titch (Buillt S R Mowle) (Continental O-200)	PFA 060-10725		20. 1.87	R Calverley	Shobdon	13. 3.08P
G-MOLI	Cameron A-250 Balloon (Hot Air) (New envelope fitted 2000 - original c/n retained)	3429 (2)		26. 1.95	J J Rudoni and A C K Rawson t/a Wickers World Hot Air Balloon Company (Stan Robertson Transport titles)	Stafford	25.10.05T
G-MOLL	Piper PA-32-301T Turbo Saratoga	32-8024040	N82535	25. 3.91	N A M and R A Brain	Gamston	11. 5.09E
G-MOLO	Pilatus PC-12/47E	1090	HB-FST	26. 1.09	Brackenridge Ltd	(Jersey)	27. 1.10E
G-MOMA	Thruster T 600N 450 Sprint	0036-T600N-088	G-CCIB	22. 8.03	Turley Farms Ltd	Wickenby	25. 8.05P
G-MONI	Monnett Moni (Built ARV Aviation Ltd) (IAME KFM.107)	PFA 142-10925		12. 1.84	R M Edworthy	(Littleover)	16. 4.02P
G-MONJ	Boeing 757-2T7	24104		26. 2.88	Monarch Airlines Ltd	Luton	7. 1.10E
G-MONK	Boeing 757-2T7	24105		26. 2.88	Monarch Airlines Ltd	Luton	31. 5.09E
G-MONR	Airbus A300B4-605R	540	VH-YMJ G-MONR, F-WWAT	15. 3.90	Monarch Airlines Ltd	Luton	2. 4.09E
G-MONS	Airbus A300B4-605R	556	VH-YMK G-MONS, F-WWAY	17. 4.90	Monarch Airlines Ltd	Luton	23. 3.09E
G-MONX	Airbus A320-212	0392	F-WWDR	19. 3.93	Monarch Airlines Ltd	Luton	17. 3.09E
G-MOOO	Learjet Model 40	45-2007	N40PX N50126	5. 8.05	LPC Aviation Ltd (Operated Northern Executive Aviation Ltd)	Manchester	9. 8.09E
G-MOOR	SOCATA TB-10 Tobago	82	G-MILK	23. 7.91	P D Kirkham	Gamston	3.12.09E
G-MOOS	Hunting Percival P 56 Provost T 1	PAC/F/335	G-BGKA 8041M/XF690	5. 4.91	H Cooke (As "XF690" in RAF c/s) RNAS Yeovilton		3. 7.09P
G-MOOV	CZAW Sportcruiser (Built S P Clifton)	LAA 338-14666		27. 5.08	S P Clifton tr G-MOOV Syndicate	(Worcester)	
G-MOPS	Best Off Sky Ranger Swift 912S (Built P Stretton pr.no.BMAA HB/547)	SKRxxxx800		4.10.07	P Stretton	(Littlestone, New Romney)	6. 7.09E
G-MOSS	Beech D55 Baron	TE-548	G-AWAD	12. 6.95	A G E Camisa	Elstree	29. 6.09E
G-MOSY	Cameron O-84 Balloon (Hot Air)	2315	EI-CAO	17. 4.96	P L Mossman (Bentley Jennison titles)	Llanishen, Chepstow	22. 7.09E
G-MOTA	Bell 206B-3 JetRanger III	4494	N81521	20.10.98	J W Sandle	Runcton Holme, King's Lynn	6.11.09E
G-MOTH	de Havilland DH.82A Tiger Moth (Built Morris Motors Ltd)	85340	7035M DE306	31. 1.78	P T Szluha (As "K-2567" in RAF c/s) (Rebuilt to DH.82 standard)	Audley End	9. 6.09S
G-MOTI	Robin DR.500-200i Président (Officially regd as DR.400-500)	0006		23.11.98	The Lord Saville of Newdigate tr The Tango India Flying Group	Biggin Hill	10. 3.09E
G-MOTO	Piper PA-24 Comanche	24-3239	G-EDHE N51867, G-ASFH, EI-AMM, N7998P	24. 3.87	L T and S Evans	Sandown	1. 1.10E
G-MOTR	Enstrom 280C Shark	1050	G-BGWS	30. 6.06	Motor Provider Ltd	Sheffield City	24. 9.08E
G-MOUL	Maule M-6-235C Super Rocket	7518C		1. 5.90	M Klinge	Prestwick	29. 6.09E
G-MOUR	Folland Gnat T 1	FL.596	8624M XS102	16. 5.90	R F Harvey and M J Gadsby tr Yellowjack Group (As "XR991" in RAF Yellowjacks c/s)	Kemble	28. 4.08P
G-MOUT	Cessna 182T Skylane	18281315	N2104H	23. 3.04	G Mountain	Leeds-Bradford	10. 7.09E
G-MOVE	Piper PA-60-601P Aerostar	61P-0593-7963263	OO-PKB G-MOVE, N8144J	5. 1.79	Airtime Aviation France Ltd (Stored engineless 12.08)	Bournemouth	6. 8.05
G-MOVI	Piper PA-32R-301 Saratoga II SP	32R-8313029	G-MARI N8248H	6. 2.89	G-BOON Ltd	Wycombe Air Park	12. 4.09E
G-MOWG	Aeroprakt A22-L Foxbat (Built J Smith)	PFA 317A-14545		21. 6.06	J Smith	East Winch	11. 2.09P
G-MOZI	Glasflügel H303 Mosquito	34	BGA3587-FWR N77RL	21. 8.07	J Christensen and P Smith	Weston-on-the-Green	31.10.07
G-MOZZ	Mudry CAP.10B	256		30.10.90	N Skipworth and J R W Luxton	Shrove Furlong Farm, Ilmer	2. 5.09E
G-MPAA	Piper PA-28-181 Archer III	2843539	N567SC	17. 6.05	MPFC Ltd	Biggin Hill	29. 6.09E
G-MPAC	Ultravia Pelican PL (Built M J Craven) (Rotax 912-UL)	PFA 165-12944		6. 4.00	J H Leigh tr The Clipgate Flying Group	Clipgate Farm, Denton	2.10.08P
G-MPBH	Reims Cessna FA152 Aerobat	FA1520374	G-FLIC G-BILV	8.12.88	The Moray Flying Club (1990)	RAF Kinloss	21. 8.09E
G-MPBI	Cessna 310R II	310R0584	F-GEBB HB-LMD, N87473	21. 7.97	M P Bolshaw	Elstree	19. 3.09E
G-MPCD	Airbus A320-212	0379	G-GZCD G-MPCD, C-FTDU, G-MPCD, C-FTDU, G-MPCD, C-FTDU, G-MPCD, C-FTDU, G-MPCD, F-WWDY	14. 3.94	Monarch Airlines Ltd	Luton	1. 5.09E
G-MPCW	Bombardier CL600-2B16 (CL-604 Challenger)	5422	G-JMMD D-ADNE, N605DC, C-GLXU	27. 2.08	MLP Aviation LLP	Biggin Hill	1. 5.09E
G-MPJM	Bombardier CL600-2B16 (CL-604 Challenger)	5403	G-JMCW D-ADNO, N604DC, C-GLWV	30. 4.08	MLP Aviation LLP	Biggin Hill	29. 4.09E
G-MPRL	Cessna 210M Centurion	21061892	EC-GKD N732YY	5. 8.02	Myriad Public Relations Ltd	Lynford House Farm, Manea	19. 8.09E
G-MPSA	Eurocopter MBB BK-117C-2 (Eurocopter EC.145)	9065		28.11.05	Metropolitan Police Authority (Metropolitan Police titles)	Lippitts Hill Camp, Chingford	12. 3.10
G-MPSB	Eurocopter MBB BK-117C-2 (Eurocopter EC.145)	9068		28.11.05	Metropolitan Police Authority (Metropolitan Police titles)	Lippitts Hill Camp, Chingford	26.11.09
G-MPSC	Eurocopter MBB BK-117C-2 (Eurocopter EC.145)	9075		19.12.05	Metropolitan Police Authority (Metropolitan Police titles)	Lippitts Hill Camp, Chingford	23. 1.12
G-MPWI	Robin HR.100-210 Safari II	163	F-GBTY F-ODFA, F-BUPD	3. 3.80	P G Clarkson and S King	Bournemouth	9. 5.09E

Reg	Type	C/n	Prev ID	Date	Owner / Notes	Location	CofA
G-MRAF	Aeroprakt A22 Foxbat (Built M Raflewski)	PFA 317-14370		7. 2.05	M Raflewski	(Dungannon)	
G-MRAJ	Hughes 369E (Hughes 500)	0010E	N51946	19. 3.98	A Jardine (stored)	Kintore Heliport	10. 6.09E
G-MRAM	Mignet HM-1000 Balerit	134		15.11.99	R A Marven	Coleman Green, Hertfordshire	21. 4.09P
G-MRDC	Robinson R44 Raven II	10851	G-ECIL	19. 9.07	Rotorcraft Ltd	(Totnes)	22.10.09E
G-MRDS	CZAW Sportcruiser (Built D I Scott)	PFA 338-14665		22. 4.08	D I Scott	Swanborough Farm, Lewes	
G-MRED	Elmwood CA-05 Christavia Mk.1 (Built E Hewett) (Continental O-200)	PFA 185-12935		2. 8.96	P H Wiltshire tr The Barton Group New Barn Farm, Barton Ashes, Crawley		9. 3.09P
G-MRJJ	Mainair Sports Pegasus Quik	7940		16. 4.03	J H Sparks	Doynton	11. 6.08P
G-MRJK	Airbus A320-214	1081	PH-BMC D-ABLA, F-WQQH, OO-SNF, F-WWIT	21. 4.05	Monarch Airlines Ltd	Luton	21. 4.09P
G-MRKI	Extra EA.300/200	05	N694M	15.12.04	Extra 200 Ltd	Wycombe Air Park	5. 3.09E
G-MRKS	Robinson R44 Raven	0771	G-RAYC	20. 5.03	TJD Trade Ltd	Cranfield	25. 6.09E
G-MRKT	Lindstrand LBL 90A Balloon (Hot Air)	037		7. 6.93	Marketplace Public Relations (London) Ltd "Kaytee"	Bristol	27. 7.08A
G-MRLL	North American P-51D-5-NA Mustang	109-27154	44-13521	22. 8.05	M Hammond (As "413521:5Q-B" in 504thFS, 339thFG c/s) "Marinell"	Airfield Farm, Hardwick	10. 9.09P
G-MRLN	Sky 240-24 Balloon (Hot Air)	161		4. 8.99	M Wady t/a Merlin Balloons "ICOM"	Hamstreet	28. 4.09E
G-MRMJ	Eurocopter AS.365N3 Dauphin 2	6713		20. 7.05	Whirligig Ltd Aldenham Grange, Letchmore Heath		2. 3.09E
G-MROC	Pegasus Quantum 15-912	7498		22. 1.99	J Waite	Tower Farm, Wollaston	24. 5.09P
G-MROD	Van's RV-7A (Built M Rhodes) (Superior XP-10)	PFA 323-14432		29.11.06	K R Emery	Otherton, Cannock	17. 5.09P
G-MROY	Comco Ikarus C42 FB100 VLA (Built R Beckham)	PFA 322-13758		9.10.01	G D Bird tr EB Flyboys Park Farm, Eaton Bray (Originally regd as FB 100 UK, amended 6. 5.08)		15. 4.09P
G-MRRR	Hughes 369E (Hughes 500)	0473E	YL-HMC D-HHMC, (F-GHTX)	3. 2.06	Estate Air Ltd	Kemble	15. 4.09E
G-MRRY	Robinson R44 Raven II	11780		11. 6.07	Celtic Motorhomes Ltd Weston, Keixlip, County Kildare		6. 8.09E
G-MRSN	Robinson R22 Beta	1654		21. 1.91	M D Thorpe t/a Yorkshire Helicopters Coney Park, Leeds		1. 7.09E
G-MRST	Piper PA-28RT-201 Arrow IV	28R-7918068	9H-AAU 5B-CEC, N3019U	27.11.86	Calverton Flying Group Ltd	Cranfield	27. 5.09E
G-MRTN	SOCATA TB-10 Tobago	62	G-BHET	9. 7.98	P A Gange and M S Colebrook	Thruxton	3.10.09E
G-MRTY	Cameron N-77 Balloon (Hot Air)	1008		24. 4.84	R A, P M G and N T M Vale "Marty"	Kidderminster	15. 2.06A
G-MRVL	Van's RV-7 (Built L W Taylor)	PFA 323-14349		28.10.05	L W Taylor	(Hadleigh, Ipswich)	
G-MSAL	Morane Saulnier MS.733 Alcyon	143	F-BLXV French.Military	16. 6.93	M Isbister tr Alcyon Flying Group (As "143" in Aéronavale c/s)	Spanhoe	2. 7.09P
G-MSCM	Denney Kitfox Model 2 (Built M Richardson - pr.no.PFA 172-11745)	638	G-BSCM	9. 8.07	D J Thomas (Noted 2007)	Narbonne, France	8. 7.03P
G-MSFC	Piper PA-38-112 Tomahawk II	38-81A0067	N25735	11. 5.90	The Sherwood Flying Club Ltd Nottingham City-Tollerton		24.11.09E
G-MSFT	Piper PA-28-161 Warrior II	28-8416093	G-MUMS N118AV	2. 4.97	Western Air (Thruxton) Ltd	Thruxton	20. 5.09E
G-MSIX	DG Flugzeugbau DG-800B (New fuselage c/n 274 fitted c 8.02)	8-156B80		21. 4.99	P Richer tr G-MSIX Group "M6"	Dunstable	5. 4.10E
G-MSJF	Boeing 737-7Q8	30710		23. 2.07	Globespan Airways Ltd t/a Flyglobespan.com	Edinburgh	27. 2.09E
G-MSKY	Comco Ikarus C42 FB UK (Built C K Jones)	PFA 322-13722		3.10.01	J S Mason and P M Yeoman Mullahead, Tandragee		9. 9.09P
G-MSON	Cameron Z-90 Balloon (Hot Air)	11036		22. 6.07	K D Peirce	Hawkhurst, Cranbrook	21. 9.09E
G-MSPT	Eurocopter EC.135 T2	0361		17. 3.05	M Sport Ltd	(Dovenby, Cockermouth)	19. 7.09E
G-MSPY	Pegasus Quantum 15-912	7625		17. 3.00	J Madhvani and R K Green Plaistows Farm, St Albans		15. 3.08P
G-MSTC	Gulfstream AA-5A Cheetah	AA5A-0833	G-BIJT N26950	30. 1.95	J Crook tr Association Of Manx Pilots	Andreas, Isle of Man	27. 4.08E
					(Attempted to land downwind Andreas 17. 6.06 and incurred substantial damage)		
G-MSTG	North American P-51D-25-NT Mustang	124-48271	45-11518	2. 9.97	M Hammond "Janie" (As "414419:LH-F" in c/s of 350th Fighter 4Sqdn-353rd Fighter Group USAAF)	Airfield Farm, Hardwick	19. 8.09P
G-MSTR	Cameron Monster 110 SS Balloon (Hot Air)	4957	G-OJOB	18. 7.01	ABC Flights Ltd (Monster.com titles) Clapton in Gordano, Bristol		20. 4.09E
G-MTAA	Solar Wings Pegasus XL-R (Trike c/n SW-TB-1108)	SW-WA-1102		15.10.86	M Skrinar	(Feltham)	13. 4.08P
G-MTAB	Mainair Gemini Flash II	492-1086-4-W290		8.10.86	J Ingle	South NormAnton, Derby	5. 6.07P
G-MTAC	Mainair Gemini Flash II	486-1086-4-W278	(YR-...) G-MTAC	15.10.86	R Massey	(Barrowford, Nelson)	7. 5.09P
G-MTAE	Mainair Gemini Flash II	500-1186-4-W302		15.10.86	C E Hannigan	Bridge of Earrn, Perth	26. 6.08P
G-MTAF	Mainair Gemini Flash II	499-1186-4-W301		5.10.86	B Eaton	(Chorley)	3. 1.09P
G-MTAG	Mainair Gemini Flash II	487-1086-4-W281		15.10.86	M J Cowie and J P Hardy	Ince Blundell	28. 5.04P
G-MTAH	Mainair Gemini Flash II	488-1086-4-W282		16.10.86	G F Atkinson	(Deighton, York)	3.11.09P
G-MTAI	Solar Wings Pegasus XL-R (Trike c/n SW-TB-1109)	SW-WA-1103		14.10.86	S T Elkington	Watnall	1. 2.08P
G-MTAJ	Solar Wings Pegasus XL-R/Se (Trike c/n SW-TB-1110)	SW-WA-1104		16.10.86	S Lyman	Deenethorpe	10. 7.09P
G-MTAL	Solar Wings Pegasus Photon (Solo 210) (Trike c/n SW-TP-0023)	SW-WP-0023		15.10.86	J W Coventry	Davidstow Moor	X
G-MTAO	Solar Wings Pegasus XL-R (Trike c/n SW-TB-1107)	SW-WA-1107		21.10.86	S P Disney	Swinford, Rugby	26. 6.01P
G-MTAP	Southdown Raven X	SN2232/0225		15.10.86	M C Newman	(St Leonards-on-Sea)	3.11.07P
G-MTAR	Mainair Gemini Flash II (Rotax 462)	504-1286-4-W307		16.10.86	J B Woolley	(Madrid, Spain)	10. 8.07P

G-MTAS	Whittaker MW5 Sorcerer	PFA 163-11166		14.10.86	R J Scott	Ashleigh Farm, Bracknell	12. 8.08P
	(Built E A Henman - may be Model MW5C?) (Rotax 503)						
G-MTAV	Solar Wings Pegasus XL-R	SW-WA-1110		21.10.86	S Fairweather and C L Harris		
						(Nottingham and Warrington)	11.10.09P
	(Trike c/n SW-TB-1115)						
G-MTAW	Solar Wings Pegasus XL-R	SW-WA-1111		21.10.86	M G Ralph	Stour Row, Sturminster Newton	23. 8.08P
	(Trike c/n SW-TB-1116)						
G-MTAX	Solar Wings Pegasus XL-R	SW-WA-1115		27.10.86	A R Lewis	Chiltern Park, Wallingford	9. 6.09P
	(Trike c/n SW-TB-1117)						
G-MTAY	Solar Wings Pegasus XL-R	SW-WA-1113		27.10.86	S A McLatchie	Enstone	16.11.05P
	(Trike c/n SW-TB-1118)						
G-MTAZ	Solar Wings Pegasus XL-R	SW-WA-1114		28.10.86	M O'Connell	(Clonee, Dublin)	25. 3.01P
	(Trike c/n SW-TB-1119)						
G-MTBB	Southdown Raven X	SN2232/0226		16.10.86	A Miller	(Woking)	15.10.02P
G-MTBD	Mainair Gemini Flash II	498-1186-4-W299		16.10.86	J Williams	Oxton	24. 8.05P
	(Wing regd as W229)						
G-MTBE	CFM Shadow Series CD	K 035		16.10.86	S K Brown	Chilbolton	24. 8.08P
	(Rotax 462HP)						
G-MTBH	Mainair Gemini Flash II	524-187-5-W327		28.10.86	T and P Sludds		
	(Rotax 462)				Glenbrien, Enniscorthy, County Wexford		19.10.08P
G-MTBJ	Mainair Gemini Flash II	509-1286-4-W312		27.10.86	R M and P J Perry *(Operated Staffordshire Aero Club)*		
						Otherton, Cannock	29.10.05P
G-MTBK	Southdown Raven X	SN2232/0230		28.10.86	G Davies *(Noted 4.06)*	Deenethorpe	27. 6.99P
G-MTBL	Solar Wings Pegasus XL-R	SW-WA-1117		6.11.86	R N Whiting Lower Mountpleasant Farm, Chatteris		16. 7.04P
	(Trike c/n SW-TB-1121)						
G-MTBN	Southdown Raven X	SN2232/0227		28.10.86	A J and S E Crosby-Jones	(Rickney, Hailsham)	9. 2.09P
G-MTBO	Southdown Raven X	SN2232/0233		28.10.86	J Liversuch	Doynton	. 2.08P
G-MTBP	Aerotech MW-5B Sorcerer	SR102-R440B-02	(EI-)	20. 1.87	L J Greenhough	Curraghroe, Ireland	
			G-MTBP				
G-MTBR	Aerotech MW-5B Sorcerer	SR102-R440B-03		20. 1.87	R Poulter	Compton Abbas	4. 8.08P
	(Fuji-Robin EC-44-PM)						
G-MTBS	Aerotech MW-5B Sorcerer	SR102-R440B-04		27.10.86	T B Fowler	(Newent)	5. 4.08P
	(Fuji-Robin EC-44-PM)						
G-MTBU	Solar Wings Pegasus XL-R	SW-WA-1118		13.11.86	R P R Staveley *(Noted 10.07)*	Watnall	29. 3.06P
	(Trike c/n SW-TB-1122)						
G-MTBV	Solar Wings Pegasus XL-R	SW-WA-1119		6.11.86	T H Scott	(Coggeshall, Colchester)	
G-MTBX	Mainair Gemini Flash II	510-1286-4-W313		6.11.86	B D Hanscomb	(Sudbury)	24. 3.05P
	(Rotax 447)						
G-MTBY	Mainair Gemini Flash II	507-1286-4-W310		6.11.86	D Pearson	(Heywood)	22. 7.05P
	(Rotax 447)						
G-MTCA	CFM Shadow Series C	K 011		6.11.86	J R L Murray	East Fortune	4. 8.04P
G-MTCE	Mainair Gemini Flash II	511-1286-4-W314		2.12.86	H Shaw	(Woodseaves, Stafford)	9. 8.04P
	(Rotax 462)						
G-MTCH	Solar Wings Pegasus XL-R	SW-WA-1124		28.11.86	M Doyle	(Tullamore, County Offaly)	11. 2.09P
	(Trike c/n SW-TB-1126)						
G-MTCK	Solar Wings Pegasus Flash II	SW-WF-0127		11.12.86	R H D C Ribeiro	(Leeds)	17. 3.08P
	(Rotax 447) *(Trike c/n SW-TB-1127 & Mainair Sailwing c/n W263)*						
G-MTCM	Southdown Raven X	SN2232/0239		11.12.86	J C Rose	Field Farm, Oakley	2. 7.97P
G-MTCN	Solar Wings Pegasus XL-R	SW-WA-1126		16.12.86	S R Hughes	Redlands, Swindon	21. 7.06P
	(Trike c/n SW-TB-1128)						
G-MTCO	Solar Wings Pegasus XL-R	SW-WA-1127		7. 1.87	R Johnson	(Bury St Edmunds)	3. 4.04P
	(Trike c/n SW-TB-1129)						
G-MTCP	Aerial Arts Chaser/110SX	110SX/476		16.12.86	B Richardson	(Eshott)	28. 6.00P
	(Rotax 377)						
G-MTCT	CFM Shadow Series CD	042		16.12.86	R Lawes	(Hayling Island)	19. 9.06P
G-MTCU	Mainair Gemini Flash IIA	451-1286-4-W228		5. 1.87	T J Philip	Ashcroft Farm, Winsford	15. 3.08P
G-MTDD	Aerial Arts Chaser/110SX	110SX/437		26. 1.87	B Richardson	(Eshott)	4. 7.00P
	(Rotax 377)						
G-MTDE	Aerial Arts Chaser/110SX	110SX/438		5. 1.87	J T Meager	(Cheltenham)	6. 7.08P
	(Rotax 377)						
G-MTDF	Mainair Gemini Flash II	515-287-5-W319		5. 1.87	P G Barnes	(Harwich)	1. 5.03P
G-MTDI	Solar Wings Pegasus XL-R/Se	SW-WA-1132		22. 1.87	R S Mott	(Redditch)	24. 3.08P
	(Trike c/n SW-TB-1134)						
	(Tipped onto nose after brake locked on after landing at Long Marston 12.11.08)						
G-MTDK	Aerotech MW-5B Sorcerer	SR102-R440B-06		22. 1.87	C C Wright	(Montrose)	10. 5.06P
	(Fuji-Robin EC-44-PM)						
G-MTDO	Eipper Quicksilver MXII	1124		27. 2.87	D L Ham	(Feniton, Honiton)	X
	(Rotax 503)						
G-MTDR	Mainair Gemini Flash II	516-287-5-W276		26. 1.87	A L S Routledge and G Bullock		
						Baxby Manor, Husthwaite	19. 6.08P
G-MTDU	CFM Shadow Series CD	K 037		26. 1.87	P G Hutchins	Rufforth	31. 8.08P
G-MTDW	Mainair Gemini Flash II	517-387-5-W212		2. 2.87	S R Leeper *(Noted dismantled 9.08)*		
						Priory Farm, Tibenham	9. 2.06P
G-MTDY	Mainair Gemini Flash II	513-187-5-W317		11. 2.87	S Penoyre	(Windlesham)	13.10.00P
	(Rotax 462)						
G-MTEC	Solar Wings Pegasus XL-R	SW-WA-1140		9. 2.87	R W Glover	Kemble	11. 6.94P
	(Trike c/n SW-TB-1142)				*(Trike only noted 2000)*		
G-MTED	Solar Wings Pegasus XL-R	SW-WA-1141		9. 2.87	A A Tollerton	(Stourbridge)	21. 4.09P
	(Trike c/n SW-TB-1143)						
G-MTEE	Solar Wings Pegasus XL-R	SW-WA-1142		13. 2.87	M Worthington	(Hinckley)	7. 8.07P
	(Trike c/n SW-TB-1144)						
	(C/n plate shows SW-WA-1144: new Sailwing fitted ? - see G-MTLG)						
G-MTEI	Mainair Gemini Flash II	440-287-5-W269		18. 2.87	P Leigh	(Purley)	19. 8.09P
G-MTEK	Mainair Gemini Flash II	523-387-5-W279		3. 3.87	M O'Hearne and G M Wrigley	Rufforth	17. 6.03P
G-MTER	Solar Wings Pegasus XL-R/Se	SW-WA-1144		19. 2.87	M Lowe *(Noted 3.07)*	Arclid Green, Sandbach	7. 4.02P
	(Trike c/n SW-TB-1146)						

G-MTES	Solar Wings Pegasus XL-R	SW-WA-1145		19. 2.87	N P Read	Davidstow Moor	29. 8.04P
	(Trike c/n SW-TB-1147)						
G-MTET	Solar Wings Pegasus XL-R	SW-WA-1146		19. 2.87	K Gilsenan	(Bedworth)	9.10.07P
	(Trike c/n SW-TB-1148)						
G-MTEU	Solar Wings Pegasus XL-R/Se	SW-WA-1147		19. 2.87	J Rudkin	(Halford, Shipston-on-Stour)	9. 4.01P
	(Trike c/n SW-TB-1149)						
G-MTEW	Solar Wings Pegasus XL-R/Se	SW-WA-1149		19. 2.87	R W and P J Holley	Mill Farm, Shifnal	4. 5.05P
	(Trike c/n SW-TB-1151)						
G-MTEX	Solar Wings Pegasus XL-R	SW-WA-1150		19. 2.87	C M and K M Bradford (Noted 11.06)		
	(Trike c/n SW-TB-1152)					Wing Farm, Longbridge Deverill	4. 5.04P
G-MTEY	Mainair Gemini Flash II	518-387-5-W217		20. 2.87	A Wells	(Boroughbridge, York)	27. 3.08P
G-MTFA	Solar Wings Pegasus XL-R	SW-WA-1156		24. 2.87	S Hindle	Tarn Farm, Cockerham	27. 7.07P
	(Rotax 462)	*(Trike c/n SW-TB-1158)*			*(Noted 8.08)*		
G-MTFB	Solar Wings Pegasus XL-R	SW-WA-1157		24. 2.87	I A Macadam	(Tunbridge Wells)	24. 9.08P
	(Rotax 462)	*(Trike c/n SW-TE-0015)*					
G-MTFC	Medway Hybred 44XLR	22087/24		23. 3.87	J K Masters	(Hartlip, Sittingbourne)	25. 7.97P
G-MTFG	AMF Microflight Chevvron 2-32C	CH.004		9. 3.87	R Gardner	(Stratford-upon-Avon)	10. 5.07P
G-MTFI	Mainair Gemini Flash II	531-487-5-W289		12. 3.87	L Parker	(Rathconrath, Mullingar)	27. 7.06P
G-MTFM	Solar Wings Pegasus XL-R	SW-WA-1158		13. 3.87	P R G Morley	Newnham, Baldock	26. 4.05P
	(Rotax 462)	*(Trike c/n SW-TE-0016)*					
G-MTFN	Whittaker MW5 Sorcerer	PFA 163-11207		13. 3.87	S M King	Errol	21. 2.05P
	(Built K Southam and D C Britton - may be Model MW5B) (Fuji-Robin EC-44-PM)						
G-MTFP	Solar Wings Pegasus XL-R	SW-WA-1160		18. 3.87	C Rickards	(Swansea)	25. 4.04P
	(Trike c/n SW-TB-1160)						
G-MTFR	Solar Wings Pegasus XL-R/Se	SW-WA-1161		18. 3.87	S Ballantyne	(Larbert)	19. 9.99P
	(Trike c/n SW-TB-1161)						
G-MTFT	Solar Wings Pegasus XL-R	SW-WA-1163		18. 3.87	A T Smith	Mill Farm, Hughley, Much Wenlock	30. 7.00P
	(Trike c/n SW-TB-1163)						
G-MTFU	CFM Shadow Series CD	K 034	EI-DDN	18. 3.87	D Plaster	(Leighton Buzzard)	12. 3.08P
			G-MTFU				
G-MTFZ	CFM Shadow Series CD	053		24. 3.87	R P Stonor	Long Marston	23. 3.08P
G-MTGA	Mainair Gemini Flash II	535-587-5-W293		26. 3.87	B S Ogden	Tarn Farm, Cockerham	25. 5.04P
G-MTGB	Thruster TST Mk.1	837-TST-011		10. 4.87	M J Aubrey		
						Upper Yeld, Floodgates, Kington, Hereford	11. 9.00P
G-MTGC	Thruster TST Mk.1	837-TST-012		10. 4.87	H Tuvey *(Noted 2.08)*	Gerpins Farm, Upminster	31. 5.04P
G-MTGD	Thruster TST Mk.1	837-TST-013		10. 4.87	J Edwards	(Ljutomer, Slovenia)	31.10.08P
G-MTGE	Thruster TST Mk.1	837-TST-014		10. 4.87	G W R Swift	(Withyham, Hartfield)	17.10.99P
G-MTGF	Thruster TST Mk.1	837-TST-015		10. 4.87	B Swindon	London Colney	1. 8.08P
						(Marked as "XH121")	
G-MTGJ	Solar Wings Pegasus XL-R	SW-WA-1165		1. 4.87	M S Taylor	(Gillingham)	17. 2.02P
	(Trike c/n SW-TB-1165)						
G-MTGK	Solar Wings Pegasus XL-R	SW-WA-1166		1. 4.87	I A Smith	(Canterbury)	1. 8.91P
	(Trike c/n SW-TB-1166)						
G-MTGL	Solar Wings Pegasus XL-R	SW-WA-1167		1. 4.87	P J and R Openshaw	Ince Blundell	9. 6.06P
	(Trike c/n SW-TB-1167)						
G-MTGM	Solar Wings Pegasus XL-R/Se	SW-WA-1168		1. 4.87	I J Steele	Roddige	1. 8.08P
	(Original Trike c/n SW-TB-1168 destroyed in gales Roddige 1.98 : now fitted with Trike c/n SW-TB-1099 ex G-MNYT)						
G-MTGN	CFM Shadow Series BD	K 041		31. 3.87	J Broome	(Boston)	15. 6.03P
G-MTGO	Mainair Gemini Flash IIA	550-587-5-W336		10. 4.87	G Evans	Arclid Green, Sandbach	16. 8.06P
	(Rotax 462)						
G-MTGR	Thruster TST Mk.1	847-TST-017		10. 4.87	M R Grunwell	Gerpins Farm, Upminster	29.11.07P
G-MTGS	Thruster TST Mk.1	847-TST-018		10. 4.87	R J Nelson	Hawksbridge Farm, Oxenhope	26. 7.09P
						(Housed in box trailer at side of hangar)	
G-MTGT	Thruster TST Mk.1	847-TST-019		10. 4.87	B J Gore	(Leeds)	2. 7.08P
G-MTGU	Thruster TST Mk.1	847-TST-020		10. 4.87	G E Norton	(Lincoln)	27. 1.06P
G-MTGV	CFM Shadow Series CD	052		8. 4.87	V R Riley	Brook Farm, Pilling	16. 5.09P
G-MTGW	CFM Shadow Series CD	054	(I-. . . .)	8. 4.87	A D Grix	(Beccles)	. 9.05P
			G-MGTW		*(Noted 9.06)*		
G-MTGX	Hornet Dual Trainer/Southdown Raven			13. 4.87	M A Pantling	Weston Zoyland	27.10.07P
	HRWA 0061 & SN2000/0270						
G-MTHB	Aerotech MW-5B Sorcerer	SR102-R440B-08		10. 4.87	K H A Negal	Red House Farm, Preston Capes	6. 4.08P
	(Fuji-Robin EC-44-PM)						
G-MTHG	Solar Wings Pegasus XL-R	SW-WA-1171		13. 4.87	R A Mott	(Redditch)	2. 2.08P
	(Trike c/n SW-TB-1170)						
G-MTHH	Solar Wings Pegasus XL-R	SW-WA-1172		13. 4.87	J Palmer	(Winkleigh)	28.12.98P
	(Trike c/n SW-TB-1171)						
G-MTHI	Solar Wings Pegasus XL-R	SW-WA-1173		13. 4.87	I E Egan	Swinford, Rugby	14.12.08P
	(Trike c/n SW-TB-1172)						
G-MTHJ	Solar Wings Pegasus XL-R	SW-WA-1174		13. 4.87	M R Harrison	(Stratford-upon-Avon)	26. 4.06P
	(Trike c/n SW-TB-1173)						
G-MTHN	Solar Wings Pegasus XL-R	SW-WA-1177		13. 4.87	M T Seal	(Cilcennin, Lampeter)	28. 3.08P
	(Trike c/n SW-TB-1177)						
G-MTHT	CFM Shadow Series CD	058		22. 4.87	J Kennedy	Mill Farm, Shifnal	10.11.09P
G-MTHV	CFM Shadow Series BD	K 049		7. 5.87	K R Bircher *(Noted 10.08)*	Over Farm, Gloucester	24. 7.00P
G-MTHW	Mainair Gemini Flash II	540-587-5-W325		14. 5.87	D Parsons	Deenethorpe	10. 6.08P
	(Rotax 462)						
G-MTHZ	Mainair Gemini Flash IIA	541-587-5-W329		14. 5.87	A I Kinnear	East Fortune	18. 7.09P
G-MTIA	Mainair Gemini Flash IIA	544-687-5-W332		14. 5.87	G W Jennings	Caernarfon	25. 5.09P
G-MTIB	Mainair Gemini Flash IIA	545-687-5-W333		14. 5.87	T H Parr	St Michaels	18. 2.09P
G-MTIE	Solar Wings Pegasus XL-R	SW-WA-1183		18. 5.87	P Wibberley	(Chesterfield)	9. 2.09P
	(Rotax 462)	*(Trike c/n SW-TE-0019)*					
G-MTIH	Solar Wings Pegasus XL-R	SW-WA-1186		18. 5.87	K N Rabey	RAF Henlow	15. 5.08P
	(Trike c/n SW-TB-118315						

Reg	Type	C/n		Owner/Operator	Location	Date
G-MTIJ	Solar Wings Pegasus XL-R/Se	SW-WA-1188		M J F Gilbody	(Urmston, Manchester)	1. 4.98P
	(Trike c/n SW-TB-1185)					
G-MTIK	Raven Aircraft Raven X	SN2232/0272		G A Oldershaw	Sutton Meadows	23. 6.08P
G-MTIL	Mainair Gemini Flash IIA	549-687-5-W338		P G Nolan	Ince Blundell	16. 7.05P
	(Rotax 462)					
G-MTIM	Mainair Gemini Flash IIA	553-687-5-W341		W M Swan	East Fortune	27. 5.09P
G-MTIN	Mainair Gemini Flash IIA	547-687-5-W335		S J Firth	(Dallerie, Crieff)	10. 6.08P
G-MTIO	Solar Wings Pegasus XL-R/Se	SW-WA-1190		A R Wade	(Basildon)	14. 4.07P
	(Trike c/n SW-TB-1187)					
G-MTIR	Solar Wings Pegasus XL-R/Se	SW-WA-1192		P Jolley	Watnall	21. 7.09P
	(Trike c/n SW-TB-1189)					
G-MTIS	Solar Wings Pegasus XL-R	SW-WA-1193		N P Power	(Eastbourne)	10. 4.09P
	(Trike c/n SW-TB-1190)					
G-MTIW	Solar Wings Pegasus XL-R	SW-WA-1196		G S Francis	Weston Zoyland	26.10.08P
	(Trike c/n SW-TB-1193)					
G-MTIX	Solar Wings Pegasus XL-R	SW-WA-1197		S Pickering	Sutton Meadows	15. 1.01P
	(Trike c/n SW-TB-1194)					
G-MTIY	Solar Wings Pegasus XL-R	SW-WA-1198		P J Tanner	Weston Zoyland	27. 5.04P
	(Trike c/n SW-TB-1195)					
G-MTIZ	Solar Wings Pegasus XL-R	SW-WA-1199		S L Blount	Sutton Meadows	22.10.03P
	(Trike c/n SW-TB-1196)					
G-MTJA	Mainair Gemini Flash IIA	551-687-5-W339		A J Holland and A McJannett-Smith	Finmere	25. 1.10P
G-MTJB	Mainair Gemini Flash IIA	554-687-5-W343		B Skidmore	Tarn Farm, Cockerham	19. 5.09P
	(Rotax 462)					
G-MTJC	Mainair Gemini Flash IIA	555-687-5-W344		T A Dockrell	(Kewstoke, Weston-super-Mare)	16. 7.07P
	(808cc Honda BF52) (Now fitted with 788-0590-7-W581 { ex-G-MWHY})					
G-MTJD	Mainair Gemini Flash IIA	552-687-5-W340		D V A M J Delage	(Prinquiau, France)	10. 3.07P
	(Rotax 462)					
G-MTJE	Mainair Gemini Flash IIA	556-687-5-W345		M P Tilzey	(Tyldesley, Manchester)	24. 1.08P
G-MTJG	Medway Hybred 44XLR	22587/25		M A Trodden	(Tupton, Chesterfield)	24. 2.99P
G-MTJH	Solar Wings Pegasus Flash	W342-687-3		C G Ludgate	(Norwich)	28. 3.04P
	(Trike c/n SW-TB-1050 previously fitted to G-MMUF)					
G-MTJL	Mainair Gemini Flash IIA	548-687-5-W337		D Allan	Eshott	25. 7.09P
G-MTJS	Solar Wings Pegasus XL-Q	SW-WX-0013		R J H Hayward	Broadmeadow Farm, Hereford	6. 4.09P
	(Trike c/n SW-TE-0022)					
G-MTJT	Mainair Gemini Flash IIA	558-787-5-W347		D F Greatbanks	(Lymm)	30.10.08P
	(Rotax 462)					
G-MTJV	Mainair Gemini Flash IIA	562-787-5-W351		A Taddeo	(Hessle)	3. 7.09P
G-MTJW	Mainair Gemini Flash IIA	563-787-5-W352		J F Ashton	(Liverpool)	4.10.95P
G-MTJX	Hornet Dual Trainer/Southdown Raven					
		HRWA 0063 & SN2000/0279		J P Kirwan	Ince Blundell	31. 3.99P
G-MTJZ	Mainair Gemini Flash IIA	561-787-5-W350		J G and J A Hamnett	(Stoke-on-Trent)	17. 6.06P
G-MTKA	Thruster TST Mk.1	867-TST-021		C M Bradford and D Marsh	Clench Common	19. 8.09P
G-MTKB	Thruster TST Mk.1	867-TST-022		M Hanna	Gransha, Rathfriland, County Down	8. 5.06P
G-MTKD	Thruster TST Mk.1	867-TST-024		Enda Spain	Kilrush, County Kildare	27. 1.06P
G-MTKE	Thruster TST Mk.1	867-TST-025		M R Jones	Wing Farm, Longbridge Deverill	27. 8.03P
G-MTKG	Solar Wings Pegasus XL-R/Se	SW-WA-1201		D J Wilkinson and D H May	Caernarfon	21.10.09P
	(Trike c/n SW-TB-1199)					
G-MTKH	Solar Wings Pegasus XL-R	SW-WA-1202		K Brooker	Jackrell's Farm, Southwater	23. 7.08P
	(Trike c/n SW-TB-1200)					
G-MTKI	Solar Wings Pegasus XL-R	SW-WA-1203		M Wady	Hamstreet, Ashford	18.10.09P
	(Trike c/n SW-TB-1201)					
G-MTKN	Mainair Gemini Flash IIA	566-887-5-W355		A J Altori	(Colne)	4. 6.03P
G-MTKR	CFM Shadow Series CD	067	9H-ABL	D P Eichhorn	(Aston Juxta Mondrum, Nantwich)	21. 6.06P
			G-MTKR			
G-MTKW	Mainair Gemini Flash IIA	569-887-5-W358		J H McIvor	Newtownards	17. 7.09P
G-MTKX	Mainair Gemini Flash IIA	568-887-5-W357		G E Jones	(Chorley)	27. 8.00P
G-MTKZ	Mainair Gemini Flash IIA	571-887-5-W360		I S McNeill	(Longniddry)	23. 8.07P
G-MTLB	Mainair Gemini Flash IIA	573-887-5-W362		M T Carr	(Warrington)	4. 9.08P
G-MTLC	Mainair Gemini Flash IIA	574-887-5-W363		R J Alston	(Cromer)	13. 7.02P
G-MTLG	Solar Wings Pegasus XL-R	SW-WA-1211		G J Simoni	Kemble	17. 8.06P
	(Trike c/n SW-TB-1207)					
G-MTLI	Solar Wings Pegasus XL-R	SW-WA-1213		M McKay	(Robertsbridge)	3. 9.04P
	(Trike c/n SW-TB-1209)					
G-MTLJ	Solar Wings Pegasus XL-R/Se	SW-WA-1214		A Brumby	Headon Farm, Retford	30. 7.06P
	(Trike c/n SW-TB-1210)					
G-MTLL	Mainair Gemini Flash IIA	578-987-5-W367		M S Lawrence	Mill Farm, Shifnal	22. 4.07P
G-MTLM	Thruster TST Mk.1	887-TST-027		R J Nelson	Leicester	24. 6.05P
G-MTLN	Thruster TST Mk.1	887-TST-028		P W Taylor	Priory Farm, Tibenham	17. 9.07P
G-MTLT	Solar Wings Pegasus XL-R	SW-WA-1216		K M Mayling	Plaistows Farm, St Albans	10.10.03P
	(Trike c/n SW-TB-1212)					
G-MTLV	Solar Wings Pegasus XL-R	SW-WA-1218		R W Keene	Over Farm, Gloucester	22. 1.04P
	(Trike c/n SW-TB-1214)					
G-MTLX	Medway Hybred 44XLR	20687/26		D A Coupland	(Ashby-de-la Launde, Lincoln)	2. 3.08P
G-MTLY	Solar Wings Pegasus XL-R	SW-WA-1220		I Johnston	(Bolton)	5. 7.92P
	(Rotax 462)	(Trike c/n SW-TE-0026)				
G-MTLZ	Whittaker MW5 Sorcerer	PFA 163-11241		J O'Keeffe	(Croom, County Limerick)	15. 8.07P
	(Built E H Gould) (Rotax 377)					
G-MTMA	Mainair Gemini Flash IIA	579-987-5-W368		R Stafford	Newtownards	16. 9.08P
G-MTMC	Mainair Gemini Flash IIA	581-987-5-W370		A R Johnson	Brenzett, Kent	1. 7.06P
G-MTME	Solar Wings Pegasus XL-R	SW-WA-1221		R J Turner	Lower Mountpleasant Farm, Chatteris	7. 9.08P
	(Trike c/n SW-TB-1216)					
G-MTMF	Solar Wings Pegasus XL-R	SW-WA-1222		H T M Smith	North Connel, Oban	23. 5.09P
	(Trike c/n SW-TB-1217)					

G-MTMG	Solar Wings Pegasus XL-R	SW-WA-1223		18. 8.87	C W and Petra E F Suckling	(Rushden)	8.11.04P
	(Trike c/n SW-TB-1218)					
G-MTML	Mainair Gemini Flash IIA	582-1087-5-W371		27. 8.87	J F Ashton (Trike only noted 5.03)	(Liverpool)	30. 7.00P
	(Rotax 462)					
G-MTMO	Raven Aircraft Raven X	SN2232/0278	(G-MTKL)	11. 9.87	H Tuvey	(South Ockendon)	3.11.07P
G-MTMP	Hornet Dual Trainer/Southdown Raven					
	(Rotax 462)	HRWA 0064 & SN2000/0288		28. 8.87	P G Owen	(York)	6. 8.99P
G-MTMR	Hornet Dual Trainer/Southdown Raven					
	(Rotax 462)	HRWA 0065 & SN2000/0297		28. 8.87	D J Smith	Hucknall	12. 1.06P
G-MTMT	Mainair Gemini Flash IIA	583-1087-5-W372		3. 9.87	C Pickvance	Tarn Farm, Cockerham	6. 9.04P
	(Rotax 462)				(Trike only 7.07)	
G-MTMV	Mainair Gemini Flash IIA	585-1087-5-W374		3. 9.87	G J Small	(Stoke-on-Trent)	23. 4.07P
G-MTMW	Mainair Gemini Flash IIA	587-1087-5-W376		9. 9.87	F Lees	(Walsall)	9. 5.09P
G-MTMX	CFM Shadow Series CD	070		4. 9.87	D R White	Plaistows Farm, St Albans	21.11.09P
G-MTMY	CFM Shadow Series CD	071		4. 9.87	A J Harpley (Noted 7.05)	Bagby	1. 2.05P
G-MTNC	Mainair Gemini Flash IIA	588-1087-5-W377		15. 9.87	M G Titmus and M E Cook	Otherton, Cannock	15. 3.08P
G-MTNE	Medway Hybred 44XLR	7987/32		12.10.87	A G Rodenburg	(Tillicoultry)	23. 9.08P
	(Fitted with new Trike as original was transferred to G-MVDC 1988)					
G-MTNF	Medway Hybred 44XLR	1987/31		12.10.87	P A Bedford	Croft Farm, Defford	7. 8.08P
G-MTNG	Mainair Gemini Flash IIA	590-1087-5-W379		21. 9.87	A N Bellis	Shobdon	8. 9.08P
G-MTNH	Mainair Gemini Flash IIA	589-1087-5-W378		17. 9.87	J R Smart	Over Farm, Gloucester	7. 9.05P
	(Rotax 462)					
G-MTNI	Mainair Gemini Flash IIA	595-1187-5-W384		18. 9.87	F J Clarehugh (Noted 9.07)	Eshott	25.11.02P
G-MTNJ	Mainair Gemini Flash IIA	593-1187-5-W382		17. 9.87	A D Rickards	Ince Blundell	28. 8.08P
	(Rotax 462)					
G-MTNL	Mainair Gemini Flash IIA	591-1187-5-W380		21. 9.87	R A Matthews (Noted 7.05)	Otherton, Cannock	14. 1.03P
G-MTNM	Mainair Gemini Flash IIA	592-1187-5-W381		22. 9.87	C J Janson	Shobdon	14.10.08P
G-MTNO	Solar Wings Pegasus XL-Q	SW-WQ-0001		23. 9.87	A F Batchelor	Rayne Hall Farm, Braintree	13. 9.08P
	(Rotax 447)	(Trike c/n SW-TB-1252)				
G-MTNP	Solar Wings Pegasus XL-Q	SW-WQ-0002		23. 9.87	G G Roberts	Rayne Hall Farm, Braintree	13. 9.08P
	(Rotax 447)	(Trike c/n SW-TB-1253)				
G-MTNR	Thruster TST Mk.1	897-TST-032		1.10.87	A M Sirant	Monkswell Farm, Horrabridge	23. 9.07P
G-MTNT	Thruster TST Mk.1	897-TST-034		1.10.87	S L Biggs tr G-MTNT Aircraft	Mendlesham	1. 6.07P
G-MTNU	Thruster TST Mk.1	897-TST-035		1.10.87	T H Brearley	Dunkeswell	10.12.09P
G-MTNV	Thruster TST Mk.1	897-TST-036		1.10.87	J B Russell (Stored 7.07)	Newry Road, Banbridge	11.10.88P
G-MTNY	Mainair Gemini Flash IIA	594-1187-5-W383		2.10.87	R C Granger	(Burnham-on-Crouch)	8. 8.03P
G-MTOA	Solar Wings Pegasus XL-R	SW-WA-1226		15. 9.87	R A Bird	East Hunsbury, Northampton	8. 8.01P
	(Trike c/n SW-TB-1221)					
G-MTOB	Solar Wings Pegasus XL-R	SW-WA-1227		15. 9.87	P S Lemm	(Otherton, Cannock)	1.10.97P
	(Trike c/n SW-TB-1222)					
G-MTOD	Solar Wings Pegasus XL-R	SW-WA-1229		15. 9.87	T A Gordon	(Liskeard)	3. 9.00P
	(Trike c/n SW-TB-1224)					
G-MTOE	Solar Wings Pegasus XL-R	SW-WA-1230		15. 9.87	K J Bright	Old Sarum	13. 7.03P
	(Trike c/n SW-TB-1225)					
G-MTOF	Solar Wings Pegasus XL-R/Se	SW-WA-1231		15. 9.87	J C Ettridge	(Hincaster, Milnthorpe)	26. 4.99P
	(Trike c/n SW-TB-1226)					
G-MTOG	Solar Wings Pegasus XL-R	SW-WA-1232		15. 9.87	J M Mclay	(Douglas, Lanark)	5. 5.06P
	(Trike c/n SW-TB-1227)					
G-MTOH	Solar Wings Pegasus XL-R	SW-WA-1233		15. 9.87	H Cook	(Pontypool)	2. 3.02P
	(Trike c/n SW-TB-1228)					
G-MTOJ	Solar Wings Pegasus XL-R/Se	SW-WA-1235		15. 9.87	B D Searle	(Hambledon, Hants)	20. 6.08P
	(Trike c/n SW-TB-1230)					
G-MTON	Solar Wings Pegasus XL-R	SW-WA-1239		2.10.87	D J Willett	(Malpas)	30. 5.08P
	(Trike c/n SW-TB-1234)					
G-MTOO	Solar Wings Pegasus XL-R	SW-WA-1240		2.10.87	G Salisbury	Kemble	29. 7.08P
	(Trike c/n SW-TB-1235)					
G-MTOP	Solar Wings Pegasus XL-R/Se	SW-WA-1241		2.10.87	D P Clarke	(Nuneaton)	30. 5.09P
	(Trike c/n SW-TB-1236)					
G-MTOR	Solar Wings Pegasus XL-R	SW-WA-1242		9.10.87	W F G Panayiotiou	(Llanelli)	28. 7.03P
	(Trike c/n SW-TB-1237)					
G-MTOT	Solar Wings Pegasus XL-R	SW-WA-1244		9.10.87	A J Lloyd (Noted 11.06)	Shobdon	25. 3.04P
	(Trike c/n SW-TB-1239)					
G-MTOU	Solar Wings Pegasus XL-R/Se	SW-WA-1245		9.10.87	D T Smith	(Thornaby)	14. 4.04P
	(Trike c/n SW-TB-1240)					
G-MTOY	Solar Wings Pegasus XL-R	SW-WA-1249		19.10.87	C M Bradford tr G-MTOY Group	Yatesbury	15. 8.06P
	(Trike c/n SW-TB-1244)					
G-MTOZ	Solar Wings Pegasus XL-R	SW-WA-1250		19.10.87	I A Macadam	Damyns Hall, Upminster	20. 1.05P
	(Trike c/n SW-TB-1245)					
G-MTPB	Mainair Gemini Flash IIA	599-1187-5-W387		15.10.87	D J Houlding and R Swan	
					(Ashton-on-Ribble, Preston)	13.11.09P
G-MTPC	Raven Aircraft Raven X	SN2232/0309		15.10.87	G W Carwardine	(Hadlow Down, Uckfield)	3.11.90P
	(Rotax 582) (Modified to "Phillips Swphift" standard 1999)					
G-MTPE	Solar Wings Pegasus XL-R	SW-WA-1260		21.10.87	J Basset	
	(Rotax 503)	(Trike c/n SW-TB-1258)			Brown Shutters Farm, Norton St Philips, Somerset	9. 6.08P
G-MTPF	Solar Wings Pegasus XL-R	SW-WA-1261		21.10.87	P M Watts and A S Mitchel	Halwell	18.11.05P
	(Trike c/n SW-TB-1259)					
G-MTPG	Solar Wings Pegasus XL-R	SW-WA-1262		21.10.87	J Sullivan	Roddige	16. 7.03P
	(Trike c/n SW-TB-1260)					
G-MTPH	Solar Wings Pegasus XL-R	SW-WA-1263		30.10.87	G Barker and L Blight	Roddige	17. 1.10P
	(Trike c/n SW-TB-1261)					
G-MTPI	Solar Wings Pegasus XL-R/Se	SW-WA-1264		30.10.87	R J Bullock	Long Marston	6. 8.06P
	(Trike c/n SW-TB-1262)					
G-MTPJ	Solar Wings Pegasus XL-R	SW-WA-1265		30.10.87	D Lockwood	Roddige	9. 6.08P
	(Trike c/n SW-TB-1263)					

G-MTPK	Solar Wings Pegasus XL-R	SW-WA-1266		30.10.87	S H James	Deenethorpe	21.10.01P
	(Trike c/n SW-TB-1264)						
G-MTPL	Solar Wings Pegasus XL-R	SW-WA-1267		30.10.87	C J Jones	(Bath)	31. 1.08P
	(Trike c/n SW-TB-1265)						
G-MTPM	Solar Wings Pegasus XL-R	SW-WA-1268		30.10.87	D K Seal	Roddige	4. 8.04P
	(Trike c/n SW-TB-1266)						
G-MTPN	Solar Wings Pegasus XL-Q	SW-WQ-0004		21.10.87	G S Stokes	Pound Green, Buttonoak, Bewdley	16. 3.09P
	(Rotax 447)	*(Trike c/n SW-TB-1267)*			*(Noted 4.07)*		
G-MTPP	Solar Wings Pegasus XL-R	SW-WA-1259		21.10.87	P Molyneux	(Southport)	8. 7.05P
	(Trike c/n SW-TB-1257)						
G-MTPR	Solar Wings Pegasus XL-R	SW-WA-1257		21.10.87	T Kenny	(Ballygar, County Galway)	16. 6.96P
	(Trike c/n SW-TB-1256)						
G-MTPS	Solar Wings Pegasus XL-Q	SW-WX-0011		23.10.87	S P Kyle	Clench Common	15. 1.09P
	(Trike c/n SW-TE-0021)			*(Heavy landing at Redlands 16. 9.08 causing substantial damage to the trike)*			
G-MTPT	Thruster TST Mk.1	8107-TST-038		23.10.87	G B Gratton tr Chilbolton Thruster Group		
						Chilbolton	8. 2.09P
G-MTPU	Thruster TST Mk.1	8107-TST-039		23.10.87	M K Ashmore	(Norwich)	20. 3.08P
G-MTPW	Thruster TST Mk.1	8107-TST-041		23.10.87	K Hawthorne	(Armagh)	18. 8.05P
G-MTPX	Thruster TST Mk.1	8107-TST-042		23.10.87	T Snook	(Newport Pagnell)	2. 5.93P
G-MTPY	Thruster TST Mk.1	8107-TST-043		23.10.87	H N Baumgartner	Withybush	2. 4.09P
G-MTRA	Mainair Gemini Flash IIA	605-1187-5-W395		28.10.87	E N Alms *"Yellow Bird"* Guy Lane Farm, Waverton		19. 2.09P
G-MTRC	Midland Ultralights Sirocco 377GB	MU-021		2.11.87	D Thorpe	Grantham	13. 4.03P
G-MTRL	Hornet Dual Trainer/Southdown Raven			4.11.87	J McAlpine	East Fortune	19. 4.09P
	HRWA 0068 & SN2000/0326						
G-MTRM	Solar Wings Pegasus XL-R	SW-WA-1276		10.11.87	R O Kibble	Deenethorpe	14. 9.08P
	(Rotax 462)	*(Trike c/n SW-TE-0030)*					
G-MTRO	Solar Wings Pegasus XL-R/Se	SW-WA-1270		2.12.87	J Hunter	Emlyn's Field, Rhuallt	1. 7.09P
	(Trike c/n SW-TB-1271)						
G-MTRS	Solar Wings Pegasus XL-R	SW-WA-1273		2.12.87	J J R Tickle	Llanerchymedd, Gwynedd	13. 6.01P
	(Trike c/n SW-TB-1274)						
G-MTRT	Raven Aircraft Raven X	SN2232/0325		12.11.87	D J Revell	Astwood, Newport Pagnell	24. 7.09P
G-MTRV	Solar Wings Pegasus XL-Q	SW-WX-0010		10.11.87	J C Field	North Coates	6. 6.06P
	(Rotax 477)	*(Trike c/n SW-TB-1276)*			*(Dumped following local undershoot 23.7 05)*		
G-MTRW	Raven Aircraft Raven X	SN2232/0328		12.11.87	P K J Chun	Rochester	20. 6.06P
G-MTRX	Whittaker MW5 Sorcerer	PFA 163-11202		11.11.87	W Turner	Otherton, Cannock	23. 7.08P
	(Built W Turner)						
G-MTRZ	Mainair Gemini Flash IIA	611-1287-5-W400		17.11.87	D F G Barlow	St Michaels	28. 3.08P
G-MTSC	Mainair Gemini Flash IIA	618-188-5-W407		17.11.87	K Wilson	(Llanddulas, Abergele)	13. 3.09P
G-MTSH	Thruster TST Mk.1	8117-TST-044		3.12.87	R R Orr	Newtownards	13. 4.07P
G-MTSJ	Thruster TST Mk.1	8117-TST-046		3.12.87	R J F Coates tr Sierra Juliet Group *(Noted 9.08)*		
						Enstone	22. 5.06P
G-MTSK	Thruster TST Mk.1	8117-TST-047		3.12.87	J S Pyke	Clipgate Farm, Denton	24.10.05P
G-MTSM	Thruster TST Mk.1	8117-TST-049		3.12.87	D J Flower	Baxby Manor, Husthwaite	27.10.08P
	(Modified to T300 standard)						
G-MTSN	Solar Wings Pegasus XL-R	SW-WA-1280		14.12.87	G P Lane	Doynton	15. 4.03P
	(Trike c/n SW-TB-1278)						
G-MTSP	Solar Wings Pegasus XL-R	SW-WA-1282		14.12.87	R J Nelson	Swinford, Rugby	11.10.05P
	(Trike c/n SW-TB-1280)				*(Noted 10.07)*		
G-MTSR	Solar Wings Pegasus XL-R	SW-WA-1283		14.12.87	J Norman	Sackville Lodge, Riseley	24. 8.07P
	(Trike c/n SW-TB-1281)						
G-MTSS	Solar Wings Pegasus XL-R	SW-WA-1284		14.12.87	P Ayres	Lower Mountpleasant Farm, Chatterris	29. 7.08P
	(Rotax 462)	*Trike c/n SW-TE-0031)*					
G-MTSY	Solar Wings Pegasus XL-R/Se	SW-WA-1289		14. 1.88	N F Waldron	(Loughborough)	24. 5.99P
	(Trike c/n SW-TB-1283)						
G-MTSZ	Solar Wings Pegasus XL-R/Se	SW-WA-1290		14. 1.88	J R Appleton	(Colne)	18. 6.07P
	(Trike c/n SW-TB-1284)						
G-MTTA	Solar Wings Pegasus XL-R	SW-WA-1291		14. 1.88	J J McMennum	Morgansfield, Fishburn	4. 9.00P
	(Rotax 462)	*(Trike c/n SW-TE-0035)*			*(Noted 7.04)*		
G-MTTB	Solar Wings Pegasus XL-R	SW-WA-1292		14. 1.88	P J Soukup	(Winkleigh)	31. 5.07P
	(Rotax 447)	*(Trike c/n SW-TB-1285)*					
G-MTTD	Solar Wings Pegasus XL-Q	SW-WQ-0011		15. 1.88	J P Dilley	Hunsdon	12.10.07P
	(Rotax 447)	*(Trike c/n SW-TB-1286)*			*(Nose gear collapsed on landing at Langstone 4. 8.07 and*		
	the aircraft tipped over onto its right side damaging nose gear, pod, wing leading edges and battens)						
G-MTTE	Solar Wings Pegasus XL-Q	SW-WQ-0012		15. 1.88	M C Mawson	Rufforth	6. 5.09P
	(Trike c/n SW-TB-1287)						
G-MTTF	Whittaker MW6 Merlin	PFA 164-11273		14.12.87	P Cotton	(Gloucester)	29. 3.95P
	(Built V E Booth) (Rotax 532)						
G-MTTI	Mainair Gemini Flash IIA	620-188-5-W409		14.12.87	P Geddes	(Cononley, Keighley)	11. 2.09P
G-MTTM	Mainair Gemini Flash IIA	609-1287-5-W398		5. 1.88	M Anderson	East Fortune	12.10.08P
G-MTTN	Skyrider Aviation Phantom	PH.00100		22. 1.88	T M Weaver	Sywell	20. 6.05P
	(Officially registered as Ultralight Flight Phantom) (Rotax 503)				*(Wings fitted to G-MJUX 8.07 (qv): noted SPLASH 11.08)*		
G-MTTP	Mainair Gemini Flash IIA	612-188-5-W401		18. 1.88	A Ormson	St Michaels	8. 5.09P
	(Rotax 462)						
G-MTTR	Mainair Gemini Flash IIA	614-188-5-W403		27. 1.88	A Westoby	Hucknall	22. 7.00P
	(Rotax 462)						
G-MTTU	Solar Wings Pegasus XL-R	SW-WA-1294		25. 2.88	A Friend *(Noted 5.07)*	Weston Zoyland	10. 2.07P
	(Trike c/n SW-TB-1332)						
G-MTTW	Mainair Gemini Flash IIA	622-188-5-W411		15. 2.88	L A Howell	(Llandudno)	10. 9.06P
	(Rotax 462)						
G-MTTX	Solar Wings Pegasus XL-Q	SW-WQ-0013		15. 2.88	B Richardson	Stanton, Morpeth	21.11.07P
	(Rotax 447)	*(Trike c/n SW-TB-1293)*					
G-MTTY	Solar Wings Pegasus XL-Q	SW-WQ-0014		21. 1.88	G A Tegg	Clench Common	23. 9.06P
G-MTTZ	Solar Wings Pegasus XL-Q	SW-WQ-0015		21. 1.88	J Haskett	(King's Lynn)	17.10.06P
	(Trike c/n SW-TE-0039)						

G-MTUA	Solar Wings Pegasus XL-R/Se	SW-WA-1295	15. 1.88	M D Reardon	(Leeds)	26. 2.09P
		(Trike c/n SW-TB-1294)				
G-MTUB	Thruster TST Mk.1	8018-TST-050	15. 1.88	M Curtin	(Clonmel, County Tipperary)	4. 9.04P
G-MTUC	Thruster TST Mk.1	8018-TST-051	15. 1.88	E J Girling	Davidstow Moor	4. 8.06P
G-MTUD	Thruster TST Mk.1	8018-TST-052	15. 1.88	M P Yeates and G de Halle	Wickenby	11.11.09P
	(Modified to T300 standard)					
G-MTUI	Solar Wings Pegasus XL-R/Se	SW-WA-1296	21. 1.88	R Green	Long Marston	21. 3.06P
		(Trike c/n SW-TB-1296)				
G-MTUJ	Solar Wings Pegasus XL-R	SW-WA-1297	21. 1.88	R W Pincombe	(Chulmleigh)	31. 5.94P
		(Trike c/n SW-TB-1297)				
G-MTUK	Solar Wings Pegasus XL-R	SW-WA-1298	21. 1.88	N Morgan	Rufforth	19..4.08P
		(Trike c/n SW-TB-1298)				
G-MTUL	Solar Wings Pegasus XL-R/Se	SW-WA-1299	21. 1.88	A D Bales	Stoke, Holy Cross	7. 4.09P
		(Trike c/n SW-TB-1299)				
G-MTUN	Solar Wings Pegasus XL-Q	SW-WQ-0016	20. 1.88	M J O'Connor	(Little Budworth, Tarporley)	26. 4.05P
	(Rotax 447) *(Trike c/n SW-TB-1301)* *(Fitted with Wing from G-MVUK?)*					
G-MTUP	Solar Wings Pegasus XL-Q	SW-WQ-0018	20. 1.88	G Davies	(Market Harborough)	26. 4.09P
	(Rotax 447)	*(Trike c/n SW-TB-1303)*				
G-MTUR	Solar Wings Pegasus XL-Q	SW-WQ-0019	20. 1.88	G Ball	(Tewkesbury)	26. 9.07P
	(Rotax 447)	*(Trike c/n SW-TB-1304)*				
G-MTUS	Solar Wings Pegasus XL-Q	SW-WQ-0020	20. 1.88	G Nicol	Pratis Farm, Leven	27.11.09P
	(Rotax 447)	*(Trike c/n SW-TB-1305)*				
G-MTUT	Solar Wings Pegasus XL-Q	SW-WQ-0021	21. 1.88	F A Dimmock	Deenethorpe	10. 5.09P
		(Trike c/n SW-TE-0040)				
G-MTUU	Mainair Gemini Flash IIA	623-288-5-W412	10. 2.88	M Harris	Eshott	7. 4.09P
G-MTUV	Mainair Gemini Flash IIA	624-288-5-W413	28. 1.88	J F Bolton	Plaistows Farm, St Albans	26. 3.08P
	(Rotax 462)					
G-MTUX	Medway Hybred 44XLR	241287/33	2. 2.88	P A R Wilson	(Cloughton, Scarborough)	29. 8.99P
G-MTUY	Solar Wings Pegasus XL-Q	SW-WQ-0022	28. 1.88	H C Lowther	Baxby Manor, Husthwaite	31. 3.08P
		(Trike c/n SW-TE-0041)				
G-MTVB	Solar Wings Pegasus XL-R	SW-WA-1302	28. 1.88	J Williams	(Worcester)	15.11.03P
		(Trike c/n SW-TB-1307)				
G-MTVG	Mainair Mercury	628-388-6-W417	12. 2.88	C Chapman	Winspurs Farm, Northrepps	14. 2.06P
	(Converted ex Gemini Flash IIA using original Sailwing from G-MTVG and Trike c/n 460-886-4 from G-MNTU)					
G-MTVH	Mainair Gemini Flash IIA	626-288-6-W415	17. 2.88	C Royle	Arclid Green, Sandbach	29. 5.09P
G-MTVI	Mainair Gemini Flash IIA	629-388-6-W416	12. 2.88	R A McDowell	(Slough)	10. 5.92P
G-MTVJ	Mainair Gemini Flash IIA	627-388-6-W418	12. 2.88	D W Buck	Watnall	27. 7.09P
G-MTVK	Solar Wings Pegasus XL-R	SW-WA-1306	15. 2.88	J D MacNamara	(Crediton)	17. 3.98P
		(Trike c/n SW-TB-1311)				
G-MTVL	Solar Wings Pegasus XL-R/Se	SW-WA-1307	15. 2.88	P A Bibby	(Lincoln)	21.10.06P
	(Original Trike c/n SW-TB-1312 but now fitted with Trike c/n SW-TB-1229 ex G-MTOI)					
G-MTVN	Solar Wings Pegasus XL-R	SW-WA-1309	15. 2.88	A I Crighton Lower Mountpleasant Farm, Chatteris		23. 4.05P
		(Trike c/n SW-TB-1314)				
G-MTVO	Solar Wings Pegasus XL-R	SW-WA-1310	15. 2.88	D A Payne	Long Marston	21. 5.09P
		(Trike c/n SW-TB-1315)				
G-MTVP	Thruster TST Mk.1	8028-TST-056	10. 2.88	J M Evans	Landmead Farm, Garford	25.10.09P
	(C/n plate marked incorrectly as 8208-TST-056)					
G-MTVR	Thruster TST Mk.1	8028-TST-057	10. 2.88	D R Lucas	(Spilsby)	30. 7.08P
G-MTVS	Thruster TST Mk.1	8028-TST-058	10. 2.88	J G McMinn	(Craigavon)	20. 6.06P
G-MTVT	Thruster TST Mk.1	8028-TST-059	10. 2.88	W H J Knowles	Yundum/Banjul, The Gambia	29. 6.07P
G-MTVV	Thruster TST Mk.1	8028-TST-061	10. 2.88	R H Y Farrer	(Newton Abbott)	9. 6.08P
G-MTVX	Solar Wings Pegasus XL-Q	SW-WQ-0025	3. 3.88	D A Foster	(Melton Mowbray)	2. 7.09P
		(Trike c/n SW-TE-0042)				
G-MTWB	Solar Wings Pegasus XL-R	SW-WA-1312	25. 2.88	R W T Gibbs	(Headington, Oxford)	12. 2.08P
		(Trike c/n SW-TB-1342)				
	(Originally fitted with Trike c/n SW-TB-1318 but damaged, repaired and resold with Sailwing c/n SW-WA-1330 as SE-YOK)					
G-MTWD	Solar Wings Pegasus XL-R	SW-WA-1314	25. 2.88	J C Rawlings	Sywell	6.12.06P
		(Trike c/n SW-TB-1320)		*(Noted 10.07)*		
G-MTWF	Mainair Gemini Flash IIA	630-388-6-W419	25. 2.88	M J J Clutterbuck		
				Broomclose Farm, Longbridge Deverill		12. 9.08P
G-MTWG	Mainair Gemini Flash IIA	631-288-6-W420	25. 2.88	N Mackenzie and P S Bunting		
				(Noted 1.06)	Greenlands, Rhuallt	28. 7.00P
G-MTWH	CFM Shadow Series CD	K 064	25. 2.88	A A Ross	Knockbain Farm, Dingwall	23. 9.08P
G-MTWK	CFM Shadow Series CD	073	25. 2.88	J P Batty and J R C Brightman		
				Sackville Lodge, Riseley		21.10.09P
G-MTWR	Mainair Gemini Flash IIA	632-388-6-W421	3. 3.88	J B Hodson	Arclid Green, Sandbach	29.10.08P
G-MTWS	Mainair Gemini Flash IIA	633-388-6-W422	3. 3.88	K W Roberts	Church Farm, Askern	22. 8.08P
G-MTWX	Mainair Gemini Flash IIA	634-488-6-W423	11. 3.88	M Rushworth	(Eccleston, Chorley)	20. 4.09P
G-MTWY	Thruster TST Mk.1	8038-TST-062	15. 3.88	J F Gardner	(Fulwood, Preston)	25. 2.06P
G-MTWZ	Thruster TST Mk.1	8038-TST-063	15. 3.88	T A Colman	Wing Farm, Longbridge Deverill	10. 2.09P
G-MTXA	Thruster TST Mk.1	8038-TST-064	15. 3.88	J Upex	Rufforth	31. 7.08E
G-MTXB	Thruster TST Mk.1	8038-TST-065	15. 3.88	J J Hill	Baxby Manor, Husthwaite	30. 8.03P
G-MTXC	Thruster TST Mk.1	8038-TST-066	15. 3.88	W Macleod	Newtownards	8. 6.04P
G-MTXD	Thruster TST Mk.1	8038-TST-067	15. 3.88	D J Flower	Baxby Manor, Husthwaite	22. 4.09P
	(Modified to T300 standard)					
G-MTXE	Hornet Dual Trainer/Southdown Raven		11. 3.88	F J Marton tr Charter Systems	Long Marston	22. 5.00P
		HRWA 0070 & SN2000/0332				
G-MTXI	Solar Wings Pegasus XL-Q	SW-WQ-0031	11. 3.88	S A Mallett	(Docking, King's Lynn)	3. 5.09P
	(Rotax 447)	*(Trike c/n SW-TB-1329)*				
G-MTXJ	Solar Wings Pegasus XL-Q	SW-WQ-0032	11. 3.88	E W Laidlaw	(Broom Loan, Kelso)	18. 3.08P
	(Rotax 447)	*(Trike c/n SW-TB-1330)*				
G-MTXK	Solar Wings Pegasus XL-Q	SW-WQ-0033	11. 3.88	J E Borril	Insch	13. 6.07P
	(Rotax 447)	*(Trike c/n SW-TB-1331)*				
G-MTXL	Noble Hardman Snowbird Mk.IV	SB-006	4. 5.88	P J Collins *(Noted 5.06)*	Kilrush, County Kildare	9. 8.05P

Reg	Type	C/n	Prev id	Date	Owner/Operator	Base	Expiry
G-MTXM	Mainair Gemini Flash IIA	636-488-6-W425		10. 5.88	C Blount, J D Penman and R Tomlinson	East Fortune	22. 8.08P
G-MTXO	Whittaker MW6 Merlin	PFA 164-11326		11. 3.88	S J Whyatt	(RAF Brize Norton)	4. 8.98P
	(Built N A Bailes) (Rotax 503)				(Noted 1.07)		
G-MTXP	Mainair Gemini Flash IIA	637-488-6-W426		23. 3.88	G S Duerden	St Michaels	27. 4.07P
G-MTXR	CFM Shadow Series CD	K 038		23. 3.88	S A O'Neill	Old Sarum	6.10.08P
G-MTXS	Mainair Gemini Flash IIA	638-488-6-W427		23. 3.88	N O'Brien	Mullinahone, County Tipperary	22. 6.07P
G-MTXU	Noble Hardman Snowbird Mk.IV	SB-007		3. 5.88	M A Oakley	Kemble	16. 5.89P
G-MTXZ	Mainair Gemini Flash IIA	641-588-6-W430		10. 5.88	P Cave	Upfield Farm, Whitson	19. 7.09P
G-MTYA	Solar Wings Pegasus XL-Q	SW-WQ-0037		29. 3.88	R Howieson	Deenethorpe	13.11.09P
	(Trike c/n SW-TE-0047)						
G-MTYC	Solar Wings Pegasus XL-Q	SW-WQ-0039		30. 3.88	C I D H Garrison	Sutton Meadows	13.10.07P
	(Trike c/n SW-TE-0049)						
G-MTYD	Solar Wings Pegasus XL-Q	SW-WQ-0040		29. 3.88	R S Colebrook	Redlands, Swindon	12. 5.09P
	(Trike c/n SW-TE-0050)						
G-MTYE	Solar Wings Pegasus XL-Q	SW-WQ-0041		29. 3.88	A J Cook	Enstone	3. 9.08P
	(Trike c/n SW-TE-0051)						
G-MTYF	Solar Wings Pegasus XL-Q	SW-WQ-0042		29. 3.88	M Quarterman	Lower Mountpleasant Farm, Chatteris	18. 5.09P
	(Trike c/n SW-TE-0052)						
G-MTYH	Solar Wings Pegasus XL-Q	SW-WQ-0044		7.11.88	I B Currer	(Barmby Moor, York)	23.12.10P
	(Trike c/n SW-TE-0054)						
G-MTYI	Solar Wings Pegasus XL-Q	SW-WQ-0045		30. 3.88	I F Hill	Roddige	30.11.09P
	(Trike c/n SW-TE-0055)						
G-MTYL	Solar Wings Pegasus XL-Q	SW-WQ-0048		30. 3.88	E T H Cox	(Church Stretton)	20.10.02P
	(Trike c/n SW-TE-0058)			(Original Sailwing now replaced by c/n 6412)			
G-MTYP	Solar Wings Pegasus XL-Q	SW-WQ-0052		30. 3.88	J Gray	(Droitwich)	12. 7.05P
	(Trike c/n SW-TE-0062)						
G-MTYR	Solar Wings Pegasus XL-Q	SW-WQ-0053		30. 3.88	D T Evans (Noted 5.05)	Broadmeadow Farm, Hereford	30. 4.99P
	(Trike c/n SW-TE-0063)						
G-MTYS	Solar Wings Pegasus XL-Q	SW-WQ-0054		30. 3.88	R G Wall	Caerleon	4.10.05P
	(Trike c/n SW-TE-0064)						
G-MTYT	Solar Wings Pegasus XL-Q	SW-WQ-0055		30. 3.88	M G Walsh	Baxby Manor, Husthwaite	13. 9.99P
	(Trike c/n SW-TE-0065)						
G-MTYU	Solar Wings Pegasus XL-Q	SW-WQ-0056		30. 3.88	S East (Noted 9.07)	Baxby Manor, Husthwaite	8. 9.05P
	(Trike c/n SW-TE-0066)						
G-MTYV	Raven Aircraft Raven X	SN2232/0341	(N) G-MTYV	8. 4.88	S R Jones	(Tonyrefail, Porth)	5. 7.07P
G-MTYW	Raven Aircraft Raven X	SN2232/0344		8. 4.88	R Solomans	Stoke, Isle of Grain	28. 7.07P
G-MTYX	Raven Aircraft Raven X	SN2232/0345		8. 4.88	C Rean	(Petersfield)	19. 9.04P
G-MTYY	Solar Wings Pegasus XL-R	SW-WA-1326		6. 5.88	L A Hosegood	(Swindon)	24. 1.05P
G-MTZA	Thruster TST Mk.1	8048-TST-068		13. 4.88	J F Gallagher	(Omagh)	13. 5.06P
G-MTZB	Thruster TST Mk.1	8048-TST-069		13. 4.88	L J and J L Eden	Long Marston	2. 6.07P
G-MTZC	Thruster TST Mk.1	8048-TST-070		13. 4.88	R W Marshall	(Armagh)	24. 8.05P
G-MTZF	Thruster TST Mk.1	8048-TST-073		13. 4.88	D C Marsh	Doynton	12. 4.09P
G-MTZG	Mainair Gemini Flash IIA	642-588-6-W431		10. 5.88	A P Fenn	Shobdon	14. 3.09P
G-MTZH	Mainair Gemini Flash IIA	643-588-6-W433		9. 6.88	D C Hughes	St Michaels	17.12.01P
	(Rotax 462)						
G-MTZJ	Solar Wings Pegasus XL-R	SW-WA-1328		6. 5.88	W G Harling	(Hedge End, Southampton)	7. 3.08P
	(Trike c/n SW-TB-1335)						
G-MTZK	Solar Wings Pegasus XL-R	SW-WA-1329		6. 5.88	G F Jones	Mill Farm, Shifnal	28. 1.07P
	(Trike c/n SW-TB-1336)						
G-MTZL	Mainair Gemini Flash IIA	645-588-6-W435		10. 5.88	N S Brayn	Popham	13. 4.06P
G-MTZM	Mainair Gemini Flash IIA	646-588-6-W436		3. 5.88	K L Smith	(Leicester)	25.10.08P
G-MTZO	Mainair Gemini Flash IIA	649-688-6-W439		6. 5.88	R C Hinds	(Newnham, Glos)	27. 8.08P
	(Rotax 462)						
G-MTZP	Solar Wings Pegasus XL-Q	SW-WQ-0059		6. 5.88	M J Newman	Sandown	23. 6.05P
	(Rotax 447) (Trike c/n SW-TB-1337)				(Noted 7.05)		
G-MTZR	Solar Wings Pegasus XL-Q	SW-WQ-0060		6. 5.88	P J Hatchett	(Rhuddlan, Rhyl)	19. 8.98P
	(Rotax 447) (Trike c/n SW-TB-1338)						
G-MTZS	Solar Wings Pegasus XL-Q	SW-WQ-0061		6. 5.88	P A Darling	(Wilmslow)	15. 7.93P
	(Rotax 447) (Trike c/n SW-TB-1339)						
G-MTZV	Mainair Gemini Flash IIA	650-688-6-W440		6. 5.88	A Robinson	Tarn Farm, Cockerham	10. 5.09P
G-MTZW	Mainair Gemini Flash IIA	651-688-6-W441		25. 5.88	J E Rourke	Ince Blundell	25. 4.09P
G-MTZX	Mainair Gemini Flash IIA	652-688-6-W442		23. 6.88	R G Cuckow and J C Thompson	Rufforth	6. 5.09P
G-MTZY	Mainair Gemini Flash IIA	653-688-6-W443		24. 5.88	S C Flower and K M Gough	Eshott	23. 2.08P
G-MTZZ	Mainair Gemini Flash IIA	654-688-6-W444		14. 6.88	G J Cadden	Smithboro, County Monaghan	3. 2.08P
G-MUCK	Lindstrand LBL 77A Balloon (Hot Air)	982		25. 1.05	C J Wootton (Poppies titles)	Ormskirk	27. 5.09E
G-MUFY	Robinson R22 Beta	1248	EI-DMS	13.12.96	Heli-Air Ltd		
			(EI-DRS (1)), G-MUFY, D-HICH		Wellesbourne Mountford/Wycombe Air Park		9.12.09E
G-MUIR	Cameron V-65 Balloon (Hot Air)	2037		23. 6.89	L J M Muir "Muriel"	East Molesey	9. 4.04A
G-MULT	Beech 76 Duchess	ME-396	N810Y	26.10.04	Folada Aero and Technical Services Ltd	Bournemouth	13. 1.09E
G-MUMM	Colt 180A Balloon (Hot Air)	1636	SE-ZES	12. 4.05	D K Hempleman-Adams	Corsham	28. 4.06A
G-MUMU	Agusta A109S Grand	22073		4. 4.08	Grand Aviation Ltd	Dunsfold	3. 4.09E
G-MUMY	Van's RV-4	PFA 181-13401		11. 1.05	S D Howes	Durham Tees Valley	14.11.09P
	(Built S D Howes) (Superior XP-10)						
G-MUNI	Mooney M 20J Mooney 201	24-3118		12. 5.89	P R Williams	Oxford	18.10.09E
G-MURG	Van's RV-6	PFA 181-12470		22. 6.05	E C Murgatroyd	Binham, Fakenham	20.12.09P
	(Built E C Murgatroyd) (Lycoming O-320)						
G-MURP	Aérospatiale AS.350B Ecureuil	2386	RP-C2388	15.12.04	M Murphy	Ravensdale, Ravensdale Park, Dundalk, County Louth	20. 4.09E
			N82632, JA6054, N49GA				
G-MURR	Whittaker MW6 Merlin	PFA 164-12502		16. 4.99	D Murray	(Charmy Down, Bath)	
	(Built M Whittaker)				(Noted 1.05)		
G-MUSH	Robinson R44 Raven II	10278		18. 2.04	Flightpath Ltd	Costock	11. 3.09E

G-MUSO	Rutan LongEz	PFA 074A-10590		11. 6.83	P A Willis	RAF Coningsby	5. 5.09P
	(Built G B Castle) (Lycoming O-235)						
G-MUTE	Colt 31A Air Chair Balloon (Hot Air)	2099		2.12.91	K Temple	(Tivetshall St Margaret, Norwich)	11.11.99A
G-MUTT	CZAW Sportcruiser	PFA 338-14667		14. 9.07	A McIvor	Rayne Hall Farm, Braintree	10.11.09P
	(Built A McIvor)						
G-MUTZ	Avtech Jabiru J430	0xxx		29.12.03	N C Dean	Little Staughton	30. 6.08P
	(Built N C Dean - pr.no.PFA 336-14171)						
G-MUZY	Titan T-51 Mustang	LAA 355-14831		18. 7.08	D Stephens	Rochester	
	(Built D Stephens)						
G-MVAB	Mainair Gemini Flash IIA	656-688-6-W446		10. 5.88	B Hindley	(Newton Bank Farm, Daresbury)	1. 7.05P
G-MVAC	CFM Shadow Series CD	K 077		12. 5.88	C A S Powell	(Heald Green, Cheadle)	22. 5.07P
G-MVAD	Mainair Gemini Flash IIA	657-688-6-W447		10. 5.88	N D Fox and C I Hemmingway		
						Tarn Farm, Cockerham	20. 7.08P
G-MVAF	Southdown Puma Sprint	P 455	G-MBAF	24. 6.87	J F Horn	Ezenridge Farm, Bere Alston, Yelverton	17. 5.05P
	(Fuji-Robin EC-44-2PM)						
G-MVAG	Thruster TST Mk.1	8058-TST-074		18. 5.88	P Higgins	(Thomastown, Enfield, County Meath)	17. 8.06P
G-MVAH	Thruster TST Mk.1	8058-TST-075		18. 5.88	M W H Henton *"Times Four"*	Popham	18. 8.05P
G-MVAI	Thruster TST Mk.1	8058-TST-076		18. 5.88	A M R Wasse	Mendlesham	7. 5.07P
G-MVAJ	Thruster TST Mk.1	8058-TST-077		18. 5.88	A J Collins	Redlands, Swindon	16. 6.02P
G-MVAL	Thruster TST Mk.1	8058-TST-079		18. 5.88	G C Brooke	(Elmstead, Colchester)	8. 8.96P
G-MVAM	CFM Shadow Series CD	082		18. 5.88	C P Barber	Brook Farm, Pilling	24. 7.06P
G-MVAN	CFM Shadow Series CD	K 048		18. 5.88	I Brewster	Longacre Farm, Sandy	17.10.08P
	(Built CFM Metal-Fax - pr.no.PFA 161-11219)						
G-MVAO	Mainair Gemini Flash IIA	658-688-6-W448		24. 5.88	S J Robson	Brook Farm, Pilling	9. 4.08P
	(Operated Brook Farm Microlight Centre)						
G-MVAP	Mainair Gemini Flash IIA	659-688-6-W449		24. 5.88	R J Miller	Long Marston	3. 9.08P
G-MVAR	Solar Wings Pegasus XL-R	SW-WA-1331		24. 5.88	A J Thomas	Deenethorpe	12. 2.09P
	(Trike c/n SW-TB-1343)						
G-MVAT	Solar Wings Pegasus XL-R	SW-WA-1333		24. 5.88	M Faulkner	(Terrington St Clement, Kings Lynn)	27.12.07P
	(Trike c/n SW-TB-1345)						
G-MVAV	Solar Wings Pegasus XL-R	SW-WA-1335		24. 5.88	D J Utting	(Bungay)	16. 2.03P
	(Trike c/n SW-TB-1347)						
G-MVAW	Solar Wings Pegasus XL-Q	SW-WQ-0064		24. 5.88	G Sharman	(East Cowes)	3. 4.08P
	(Rotax 447)	*(Trike c/n SW-TB-1348)*					
G-MVAX	Solar Wings Pegasus XL-Q	SW-WQ-0065		24. 5.88	N M Cuthbertson	(Doncaster)	20. 4.09P
	(Rotax 447)	*(Trike c/n SW-TB-1349)*					
G-MVAY	Solar Wings Pegasus XL-Q	SW-WQ-0066		24. 5.88	V O Morris	(Kidwelly)	16. 4.97P
	(Rotax 447)	*(Trike c/n SW-TB-1350)*					
G-MVBB	CFM Shadow Series BD	K 051		24. 5.88	R Garrod	(Mickfield, Stowmarket)	8.10.00P
G-MVBC	Mainair Tri-Flyer/Aerial Arts 130SX	130SX-616		24. 5.88	D Beer	(Lee, Ilfracombe)	
	(Believed to be using Mainair Tri-Flyer 250 Trike from G-MJIX)						
G-MVBE	Mainair Scorcher	661-688-6-W451		28. 7.88	A G Woodward	Heckington, Sleaford	28.12.09P
G-MVBF	Mainair Gemini Flash IIA	662-688-6-W452		14. 6.88	E McCallum	Longframlington	15. 5.08P
	(Rotax 462) *(Original Trike now fitted to G-JESA qv)*						
G-MVBG	Mainair Gemini Flash IIA	663-688-6-W453		25. 5.88	A L Cooke	Otherton, Cannock	16. 7.08P
G-MVBI	Mainair Gemini Flash IIA	665-788-6-W455		7. 6.88	S Irwin	(Morland, Penrith)	30. 9.08P
G-MVBJ	Solar Wings Pegasus XL-R	SW-WA-1338		7. 6.88	R J O Page	(Oupia, France)	4. 8.08P
	(Rotax 462)	*(Trike c/n SW-TE-0033)*					
G-MVBK	Mainair Gemini Flash IIA	666-788-6-W456		7. 6.88	B R McLoughlin	(Liverpool)	8. 8.06P
	(Rotax 462)						
G-MVBL	Mainair Gemini Flash IIA	669-788-6-W459		7. 6.88	S T Cain	Higher Barn Farm, Hoghton	3. 4.08P
G-MVBM	Mainair Gemini Flash IIA	667-788-6-W457		7. 6.88	A J Graham	Rhedyn Coch Farm, Rhuallt	22. 7.08P
	(Rotax 582) *(Trike reported stolen 8.03 but new Permit issued 5.06 and with new engine [Rotax 503] suggests replacement Trike)*						
G-MVBN	Mainair Gemini Flash IIA	668-788-6-W458		8. 6.88	M Frankcom	(Astley Park, Darwen)	2. 6.99P
G-MVBO	Mainair Gemini Flash IIA	671-788-6-W461		8. 6.88	J A Brown	(Wheaton Aston, Stafford)	20. 7.07P
G-MVBP	Thruster TST Mk.1	8068-TST-080		14. 6.88	K J Crompton	Newtownards	13. 3.08P
G-MVBT	Thruster TST Mk.1	8068-TST-083		14. 6.88	R Everitt tr TST Group Flying	Ley Farm, Chirk	19.12.07P
	(BMW R100)						
G-MVBY	Solar Wings Pegasus XL-R	SW-WA-1344		17. 6.88	J E Harman tr Pigs R Us Flying Group		
						(Napton, Southam)	9. 9.03P
	(Trike c/n SW-TB-1357)						
G-MVBZ	Solar Wings Pegasus XL-R	SW-WA-1345		17. 6.88	A G Butler	Shenstone Hall Farm, Shenstone	17. 9.05P
	(Trike c/n SW-TB-1358)						
G-MVCA	Solar Wings Pegasus XL-R	SW-WA-1346		17. 6.88	R Walker	Sutton Meadows	15. 2.09P
	(Trike c/n SW-TB-1359)						
G-MVCB	Solar Wings Pegasus XL-R	SW-WA-1347		17. 6.88	L Briscoe	Lower Mountpleasant Farm, Chatteris	7. 5.09P
	(Trike c/n SW-TB-1360)						
G-MVCC	CFM Shadow Series CD	K 045		17. 6.88	G Finney *(New owner 7.07)*	(Brighton)	5. 8.06P
G-MVCD	Medway Hybred 44XLR	MR001/34		14. 6.88	J Thompson	Longacre Farm, Sandy	27. 7.03P
	(Marked as "Raven") (Original Sailwing transferred to G-MVOS: new Sailwing c/n not known)						
G-MVCE	Mainair Gemini Flash IIA	672-788-6-W462		23. 6.88	N Ford	(Stockport)	13. 4.06P
G-MVCF	Mainair Gemini Flash IIA	673-788-6-W463		14. 7.88	J S Harris	Old Sarum	1. 6.05P
	(Rotax 462)						
G-MVCI	Noble Hardman Snowbird Mk.IV	SB-011		11.10.88	W L Chapman	(Tarn Farm, Cockerham)	13. 4.95P
G-MVCJ	Noble Hardman Snowbird Mk.IV	SB-012		11.10.88	C W Buxton *(Noted as engineless wreck 4.06)*		
	(Rotax 582) *(Officially regd with Rotax 532)*					Darley Moor, Ashbourne	14. 9.04P
G-MVCK	Cosmos Trike/La Mouette Profil 19	SDA-01		19. 7.88	S D Alsop	(Midsomer Norton, Bath)	
G-MVCL	Solar Wings Pegasus XL-Q	SW-WQ-0075		27. 6.88	T E Robinson	Insch	5.10.08P
	(Trike c/n SW-WQ-0069)						
G-MVCM	Solar Wings Pegasus XL-Q	SW-WQ-0076		27. 6.88	P J Croney	Hunsdon	25. 4.08P
	(Trike c/n SW-TE-0070)						
G-MVCN	Solar Wings Pegasus XL-Q	SW-WQ-0077		27. 6.88	S R S Evans	Rayne Hall Farm, Braintree	14. 5.08P
	(Trike c/n SW-TE-0071)				*(In own trailer)*		
G-MVCP	Solar Wings Pegasus XL-Q	SW-WQ-0079		27. 6.88	J R Fulcher	Deenethorpe	13. 6.08P
	(Trike c/n SW-TE-0073)						

G-MVCR	Solar Wings Pegasus XL-Q	SW-WQ-0080		27. 6.88	P Hoeft	(Stickney, Boston) 1.10.08P
	(Trike c/n SW-TE-0069)					
G-MVCS	Solar Wings Pegasus XL-Q	SW-WQ-0081		27. 6.88	J J Sparrow	Sywell 19. 7.02P
	(Trike c/n SW-TE-0075)					
G-MVCT	Solar Wings Pegasus XL-Q	SW-WQ-0082		27. 6.88	G J Lampitt	Pound Green, Buttonoak, Bewdley 15. 6.06P
	(Trike c/n SW-TE-0076)					
G-MVCV	Solar Wings Pegasus XL-Q	SW-WQ-0084		27. 6.88	G Stewart	Craymarsh Farm, Melksham 23.12.09P
	(Original Trike c/n SW-WQ-0078 damaged and replaced by SW-TE-0108,:later repaired and fitted with Sailwing SW-WQ-0105, regd G-MVHP)					
G-MVCW	CFM Shadow Series BD	084		28. 6.88	D A Coupland	RAF Scampton 6.10.07P
G-MVCY	Mainair Gemini Flash IIA	674-788-6-W464		14. 7.88	A M Smith	Otherton, Cannock 11.10.05P
G-MVCZ	Mainair Gemini Flash IIA	675-788-6-W465		26. 8.88	P J Devine	(Hindley, Wigan) 14. 5.08P
G-MVDA	Mainair Gemini Flash IIA	676-788-6-W466		13. 7.88	C Tweedley	(Great Orton) 8. 5.06P
	(Rotax 462)					
G-MVDD	Thruster TST Mk.1	8078-TST-086		12. 7.88	D J Love	(Witton, Norwich) 9.11.99P
G-MVDE	Thruster TST Mk.1	8078-TST-087		12. 7.88	R H Davis *(Derelict 2.03)*	Doynton 26. 8.99P
G-MVDF	Thruster TST Mk.1	8078-TST-088		12. 7.88	J Walsh and A R Sunley tr G-MVDF Syndicate	
						Wing Farm, Longbridge Deverill 12. 4.08P
	(Bounced on landing at Rayne Hall Farm 21.10.07 damaging the right landing gear and the pod and the propeller struck the ground)					
G-MVDG	Thruster TST Mk.1	8078-TST-089		12. 7.88	D G., P M and A B Smith	Popham 26. 7.00P
	(In open storage in derelict condition 8.08)					
G-MVDH	Thruster TST Mk.1	8078-TST-090		12. 7.88	P E Terrell	(Plymouth) 19. 5.09P
G-MVDJ	Medway Hybred 44XLR	MR010/38		20. 7.88	W D Hutchings	(Nottingham) 9. 2.09P
G-MVDK	Aerial Arts Chaser S	CH.702		5. 8.88	S Adams *(Noted 9.01)*	Leicester 29.11.98P
G-MVDL	Aerial Arts Chaser S	CH.701		11. 8.88	S I Deuchars "112"	(Devizes) 26. 4.09P
	(Rotax 462) *(Officially regd with Rotax 377)*					
G-MVDP	Aerial Arts Chaser S	CH.706		11. 8.88	R G Mason	(Aston Clinton) 9.11.02P
G-MVDT	Mainair Gemini Flash IIA	670-788-6-W460		20. 7.88	D C Stephens	(Coleford) 26. 5.00P
G-MVDV	Solar Wings Pegasus XL-R	SW-WA-1349		13. 7.88	D Ewing	Roddige 9. 1.08P
	(Trike c/n SW-TB-1362)					
G-MVDW	Solar Wings Pegasus XL-R	SW-WA-1350		13. 7.88	R P Brown *(Noted wrecked 7.03)*	
	(Trike c/n SW-TB-1363)					Longacre Farm, Sandy 20. 7.97P
G-MVDY	Solar Wings Pegasus XL-R	SW-WA-1352		13. 7.88	C G Murphy	(Biggin Hill, Westerham) 1. 6.92P
	(Trike c/n SW-TB-1365)					
G-MVDZ	Solar Wings Pegasus XL-R	SW-WA-1353		12. 7.88	A K Pickering	(Robertsbridge) 19. 5.00P
	(Trike c/n SW-TB-1366)					
G-MVEC	Solar Wings Pegasus XL-R	SW-WA-1356		20. 7.88	J A Jarvis	Davidstow Moor 18. 4.03P
	(Trike c/n SW-TB-1369)					
G-MVED	Solar Wings Pegasus XL-R/Se	SW-WA-1357		20. 7.88	P A Sleightholme	Baxby Manor, Husthwaite 28. 9.08P
	(Trike c/n SW-TB-1370)					
G-MVEE	Medway Hybred 44XLR	MR004/35		22. 7.88	D S L Evans	(Gravesend) 4.10.05P
	(Trike c/n same as G-MYMJ and suggests this has a replacement unit)					
G-MVEF	Solar Wings Pegasus XL-R	SW-WA-1358		19. 7.88	A W Leadley	
	(Rotax 462) *(Trike c/n SW-TE-0079)*					(Lismonaghan, Letterkenny, County Donegal) 15.11.93P
G-MVEG	Solar Wings Pegasus XL-R	SW-WA-1359		19. 7.88	A M Shaw	(Alsager, Stoke-on-Trent) 8. 8.08P
	(Rotax 462) *(Trike c/n SW-TE-0080)*					
G-MVEH	Mainair Gemini Flash IIA	677-788-6-W468		26. 8.88	K Bailey	(Oldham) 18.10.08P
G-MVEI	CFM Shadow Series CD	085		26. 7.88	I G Ferguson	North Connel, Oban 20.12.07P
G-MVEJ	Mainair Gemini Flash IIA	678-888-6-W469		27. 7.88	E Woods	(Urmston, Manchester) 30. 6.08P
	(Rotax 462)					
G-MVEK	Mainair Gemini Flash IIA	679-888-6-W470		27. 7.88	R M Rea	(Lubenham, Market Harborough) 28. 9.05P
G-MVEL	Mainair Gemini Flash IIA	680-888-6-W471		27. 7.88	M R Starling	(Swafield, North Walsham) 25. 7.03P
G-MVEN	CFM Shadow Series CD	K 047		26. 7.88	C J Johnson	Elm Farm, Wickford 15. 7.09P
G-MVEO	Mainair Gemini Flash IIA	682-888-6-W472		28. 7.88	K Donaldson	Easter Poldar Farm, Thornhill 8. 5.09P
G-MVER	Mainair Gemini Flash IIA	684-888-6-W474		28. 7.88	J R Davis	(Cheltenham) 18.12.07P
G-MVES	Mainair Gemini Flash IIA	685-888-6-W475		5. 8.88	J Helm	(East Linton) 4. 4.09P
G-MVET	Mainair Gemini Flash IIA	686-888-6-W476		19. 8.88	C Buttery	Bagby 4. 4.08P
G-MVEV	Mainair Gemini Flash IIA	687-888-6-W477		5. 8.88	C Allen	(Alderley Edge) 8. 7.01P
G-MVEX	Solar Wings Pegasus XL-Q	SW-WQ-0088		5. 8.88	D Maher	(Nenagh, CountyTipperary) 5. 3.04P
	(Trike c/n SW-WQ-0082)					
G-MVEZ	Solar Wings Pegasus XL-Q	SW-WQ-0090		9. 8.88	P W Millar	(Gorthleck, Inverness) 13. 6.99P
	(Trike c/n SW-TE-0084)					
G-MVFA	Solar Wings Pegasus XL-Q	SW-WQ-0091		9. 8.88	A Johnson	Deenethorpe 24.11.07P
	(Trike c/n SW-TE-0085)					
G-MVFB	Solar Wings Pegasus XL-Q	SW-WQ-0092		9. 8.88	M O Bloy	(King's Lynn) 15. 2.09P
	(Trike c/n SW-TE-0086)					
G-MVFC	Solar Wings Pegasus XL-Q	SW-WQ-0093		9. 8.88	D R Joint	Davidstow Moor 12. 5.09P
	(Trike c/n SW-TE-0087)					
G-MVFD	Solar Wings Pegasus XL-Q	SW-WQ-0094		9. 8.88	C D Humphries	Sywell 10. 9.07P
	(Trike c/n SW-TE-0088)					
G-MVFE	Solar Wings Pegasus XL-Q	SW-WQ-0095		9. 8.88	S J Weeks	Kemble 30. 4.00P
	(Trike c/n SW-TE-0089)					
G-MVFF	Solar Wings Pegasus XL-Q	SW-WQ-0096		9. 8.88	A Makepeace	(Guildford) 25. 8.08P
	(Trike c/n SW-TE-0090)					
G-MVFH	CFM Shadow Series CD	086		9. 8.88	G R Read and M D Goad tr G-MVFH Group	
	(Rotax 447)					Mendlesham 19. 5.08P
G-MVFJ	Thruster TST Mk.1	8088-TST-092		11. 8.88	B E Renehan tr Kestrel Flying Group	Popham 20. 4.08P
G-MVFL	Thruster TST Mk.1	8088-TST-094		11. 8.88	E J Wallington	
						Inglenook Farm, Maydensole 22. 5.02P
G-MVFM	Thruster TST Mk.1	8088-TST-095		11. 8.88	G J Boyer	Weston Zoyland 1. 9.05P
G-MVFO	Thruster TST Mk.1	8088-TST-097		11. 8.88	S R James Humberstone and A L Higgins	Sywell 7. 6.09P
G-MVFP	Solar Wings Pegasus XL-R	SW-WA-1365		9. 8.88	D J Brixton tr Shropshire Tow Group	
	(Trike c/n SW-TB-1371)					Bishops Castle, Shropshire 24. 3.03P
G-MVFT	Solar Wings Pegasus XL-R	SW-WA-1368		9. 8.88	S J Whalley	Roddige 16.12.07P
	(Trike c/n SW-TB-1374)					

G-MVFV	Solar Wings Pegasus XL-R	SW-WA-1370		9. 8.88	L R M Grigg	Deenethorpe	25. 6.05P
		(Trike c/n SW-TB-1376)					
G-MVFY	Solar Wings Pegasus XL-R	SW-WA-1373		9. 8.88	T D Bawden	Weston Zoyland	19. 6.04P
		(Trike c/n SW-TB-1379)					
G-MVFZ	Solar Wings Pegasus XL-R	SW-WA-1374		9. 8.88	R K Johnson	Popham	29. 5.05P
		(Trike c/n SW-TB-1380)					
G-MVGA	Aerial Arts Chaser S 508	CH.859		11. 8.88	N R Beale	Deppers Bridge, Southam	31. 5.06P
	(Officially regd with CH.707)						
G-MVGB	Medway Hybred 44XLR	MR011/39		1. 9.88	R Graham	(Coulsdon, Surrey)	28. 8.02P
G-MVGC	AMF Microflight Chevvron 2-32C	010		2. 9.88	W Fletcher	Broadmeadow Farm, Hereford	11. 9.08P
G-MVGD	AMF Microflight Chevvron 2-32C	011		5. 9.88	T R James	(Southam)	21. 9.08P
G-MVGF	Aerial Arts Chaser S	CH.720		2. 9.88	P J Higgins *"The Dingbat"*		
					Red House Farm, Gedney Dyke, Lutton		11.11.00P
G-MVGG	Aerial Arts Chaser S 508	CH.721		2. 9.88	P D Curtis	Rufforth	16. 9.08P
G-MVGH	Aerial Arts Chaser S 447	CH.722		2. 9.88	A Bishop	Tarn Farm, Cockerham	13. 3.09P
G-MVGK	Aerial Arts Chaser S	CH.726		2. 9.88	D J Smith	Hucknall	1. 9.99P
G-MVGM	Mainair Gemini Flash IIA	691-988-6-W481		25. 8.88	P A C R Stephens	(Rye)	7. 6.07P
G-MVGN	Solar Wings Pegasus XL-R/Se	SW-WA-1377		23. 8.88	M J Smith	(Taunton)	24. 6.05P
		(Trike c/n SW-TB-1381)					
G-MVGO	Solar Wings Pegasus XL-R	SW-WA-1378		23. 8.88	J B Peacock Lower Mountpleasant Farm, Chatteris		14. 9.09P
		(Trike c/n SW-TB-1382)					
G-MVGP	Solar Wings Pegasus XL-R	SW-WA-1379	(EC- . . .)	23. 8.88	J P Cox *(Noted 9.06)*	Deenethorpe	9. 6.00P
		(Trike c/n SW-TB-1383)	G-MVGP				
G-MVGU	Solar Wings Pegasus XL-Q	SW-WQ-0100		23. 8.88	I A Macadam	Damyns Hall, Upminster	21. 6.04P
		(Trike c/n SW-TB-0092)					
G-MVGW	Solar Wings Pegasus XL-Q	SW-WQ-0102		23. 8.88	M J L de Carvalho and V V P Pedro tr G-MVGW Group		
		(Trike c/n SW-TE-0095)				Lagos, Algarve, Portugal	8. 2.92P
G-MVGY	Medway Hybred 44XLR	MR015/41		31. 8.88	G M Griffiths *(Noted 2.07)*	Perth	16. 8.08P
G-MVGZ	Ultraflight Lazair IIIE	A338	C-?	21.10.88	D M Broom	(Towcester)	25. 3.03P
	(Rotax 185 x 2)						
G-MVHC	Powerchute Raider	80106		26. 8.88	G Martin	(Lisburn)	10..4.06P
G-MVHD	CFM Shadow Series CD	088		8. 9.88	D Raybould	(New Whittington, Chesterfield)	10. 5.08P
G-MVHE	Mainair Gemini Flash IIA	692-988-6-W482		4.10.88	B R Thomas	Oak Farm, Woodton	27. 3.08P
G-MVHF	Mainair Gemini Flash IIA	693-988-6-W483		4.10.88	M G Nicholson	St Michaels	28. 5.05P
G-MVHG	Mainair Gemini Flash IIA	694-988-6-W484		14.10.88	C A J Elder	(Reddingmuirhead, Falkirk)	10. 6.08P
G-MVHH	Mainair Gemini Flash IIA	607-1187-5-W485		24.10.88	A M Lynch	(Edinburgh)	15.11.06P
	(Original Trike c/n "695.-988-6" replaced by c/n "607-1187-5" ex G-MTSA 1995)						
G-MVHI	Thruster TST Mk.1	8098-TST-100		26. 9.88	L Hurman	Enstone	10. 3.06P
G-MVHJ	Thruster TST Mk.1	8098-TST-101		26. 9.88	S P Macdonald		
					Lower Mountpleasant Farm, Chatteris		19. 4.08P
G-MVHK	Thruster TST Mk.1	8098-TST-102		27. 9.88	D J Gordon	Woodlands Barton Farm, Roche	14. 8.07P
G-MVHL	Thruster TST Mk.1	8098-TST-103		27. 9.88	G Jones	(Llanfairfechan)	16. 7.02P
G-MVHP	Solar Wings Pegasus XL-Q	SW-WQ-0105		23. 9.88	J B Gasson Lower Mountpleasant Farm, Chatteris		15. 9.07P
		(Trike c/n SW-TE-0078)			*(Damaged Trike from G-MVCV repaired and fitted to Sailwing)*		
G-MVHR	Solar Wings Pegasus XL-Q	SW-WQ-0106		23. 9.88	J M Hucker	Broadmeadow Farm, Hereford	26. 5.04P
		(Trike c/n SW-TE-0099)				*(Noted 5.05)*	
G-MVHS	Solar Wings Pegasus XL-Q	SW-WQ-0107		23. 9.88	A P Clarke	(Glastonbury)	9. 8.06P
	(Trike c/n SW-TE-0100)						
G-MVHW	Solar Wings Pegasus XL-Q	SW-WQ-0111		23. 9.88	Ultralight Training Ltd		
		(Trike c/n SW-TE-0101)				Broadmeadow Farm. Hereford	11. 3.09P
G-MVHY	Solar Wings Pegasus XL-Q	SW-WQ-0113		23. 9.88	R P Paine	Headon Farm, Retford	17. 8.06P
		(Trike c/n SW-TE-0106)					
G-MVHZ	Hornet Dual Trainer/Southdown Raven			26. 9.88	J M Addison	Insch	11.12.05P
	HRWA 0076 & MHR-101						
G-MVIB	Mainair Gemini Flash IIA	700-1088-4-W490		14.10.88	S, A and Leslie Rosser tr LSA Systems		
						Arclid Green, Sandbach	4. 5.09P
G-MVIE	Aerial Arts Chaser S	CH.732		14.10.88	T M Stiles *(Noted 8.03)*	(Heathfield)	6. 6.97P
G-MVIF	Medway Raven X	MR020/43		4.10.88	A C Hing	Longacre Farm, Sandy	11. 6.07P
	(Originally regd as Hybred 44XLR)						
G-MVIG	CFM Shadow Series B	K 044		5.10.88	M J Green	(Waterbeach)	9.09P
	(Rotax 447)						
G-MVIH	Mainair Gemini Flash IIA	697-1088-6-W487		14.10.88	T M Gilsenan	(Eaton Bray)	24. 7.09P
G-MVIL	Noble Hardman Snowbird Mk.IV	SB-014		6. 2.89	Marine Power (Scotland) Ltd	Kirkbride	9. 8.07P
	(Rotax 582)						
G-MVIN	Noble Hardman Snowbird Mk.IV	SB-016		6. 2.89	C P Dawes	Darley Moor, Ashbourne	15. 4.09P
	(Rebuilt to Mk.V standard with Rotax 582)						
G-MVIO	Noble Hardman Snowbird Mk.IV	SB-017		12. 4.89	B Mason-Baker tr Mobility Advice Line		
					Mill Farm, Hughley, Much Wenlock		29. 7.08P
G-MVIP	AMF Microflight Chevvron 2-32C	008		11. 5.88	P C Avery Lower Mountpleasant Farm, Chatteris		19. 6.07P
G-MVIR	Thruster TST Mk.1	8108-TST-104		21.10.88	T D Gardner	Popham	9. 9.08P
	(C/n plate marked as 8118-TST-104)						
G-MVIT	Thruster TST Mk.1	8108-TST-106	(C-)	21.10.88	A C Bell	Knapthorpe Lodge, Caunton	1.11.08P
			G-MVIT				
G-MVIU	Thruster TST Mk.1	8108-TST-107		21.10.88	M D Reece	Rufforth	6. 8.09P
	(Rebuilt to part T 600 standard)						
G-MVIV	Thruster TST Mk.1	8108-TST-108		21.10.88	G Rainey	Weston Zoyland	24. 6.01P
G-MVIX	Mainair Gemini Flash IIA	702-1088-6-W492		14.10.88	R S T MacEwen	East Fortune	20.10.08P
G-MVIZ	Mainair Gemini Flash IIA	703-1088-6-W493		14.10.88	P R Hutty	(Hessle)	17. 8.08P
G-MVJA	Mainair Gemini Flash IIA	696-988-6-W486		5.12.88	J R Harrison	(Wisbech)	29. 8.06P
G-MVJC	Mainair Gemini Flash IIA	705-1088-6-W495		24.10.88	B Temple	Broadmeadow Farm, Hereford	25. 4.05P
	(Engine failure on take off Priory Farm, Tibenham 15.8.04 and substantially damaged)						
G-MVJD	Solar Wings Pegasus XL-R	SW-WA-1386		24.10.88	B L Prime	Roddige	1. 7.09P
	(Rotax 462)	*(Trike c/n SW-TE-0109)*					
G-MVJE	Mainair Gemini Flash IIA	706-1188-6-W496		21.10.88	G Zuchowski	(Wincham, Northwich)	11. 4.09P

Reg	Type	C/n	Date	Owner	Location	Code
G-MVJF	Aerial Arts Chaser S	CH.743	21.11.88	V S Rudham	Dunkeswell	2. 8.05P
G-MVJG	Aerial Arts Chaser S	CH.749	22.11.88	T H Scott	Rayne Hall Farm, Braintree	13. 6.03P
	(Noted 1.09 at P&M Aviation, Rochdale)					
G-MVJH	Aerial Arts Chaser S	CH.751	14.11.88	M van Rompaey	(Scunthorpe)	1. 9.03P
G-MVJI	Aerial Arts Chaser S	CH.752	17.11.88	T Beckham	(Newcastle upon Tyne)	1.11.03P
G-MVJJ	Aerial Arts Chaser S 508	CH.753	14.11.88	C W Potts	Stanton, Morpeth	5. 8.08P
G-MVJK	Aerial Arts Chaser S	CH.754	14.11.88	K J Samuels	(Loughton)	X
G-MVJL	Mainair Gemini Flash IIA	698-1188-6-W488	21.10.88	F Huxley	(Morpeth)	4. 5.06P
G-MVJM	Microflight Spectrum	007	21.10.88	S E Matthews tr Poppy Syndicate		
					Otherton, Cannock	2. 9.08P
G-MVJN	Solar Wings Pegasus XL-Q	SW-WQ-0116	26.10.88	R A Paintain	Chilbolton	17. 1.06P
	(Trike c/n SW-TE-0110)					
G-MVJP	Solar Wings Pegasus XL-Q	SW-WQ-0118	26.10.88	S H Bakowski	Damyn's Hall, Upminster	28. 6.09P
	(Trike c/n SW-TE-0112)					
G-MVJR	Solar Wings Pegasus XL-Q	SW-WQ-0119	26.10.88	A S Wason	Lower Upham Farm, Chiseldon	9. 8.09P
	(Trike c/n SW-TE-0113)					
G-MVJS	Solar Wings Pegasus XL-Q	SW-WQ-0120	26.10.88	S D Morley	Rayne Hall Farm, Braintree	12. 9.09P
	(Trike c/n SW-TE-0114)					
G-MVJT	Solar Wings Pegasus XL-Q	SW-WQ-0121	26.10.88	L A Hosegood	Redlands, Swindon	17. 2.08P
	(Trike c/n SW-TE-0115)					
G-MVJU	Solar Wings Pegasus XL-Q	SW-WQ-0122	26.10.88	J C Longmore	Headon Farm, Retford	8. 2.07P
	(Trike c/n SW-TE-0116)					
G-MVJW	Solar Wings Pegasus XL-Q	SW-WQ-0124	26.10.88	R Dainty and D W Stamp		
	(Trike c/n SE-TE-0118)				Pound Green, Buttonoak, Bewdley	4. 5.06P
G-MVKB	Medway Hybred 44XLR	MR023/45	11.11.88	J Newby	Sandtoft	11. 9.00P
G-MVKC	Mainair Gemini Flash IIA	709-1188-6-W499	16.11.88	K R Emery	Sittles Farm, Alrewas	2. 4.09P
G-MVKF	Solar Wings Pegasus XL-R	SW-WA-1392	14.11.88	B Shaw	(Prospect Farm, Wollaston)	12. 2.08P
	(Trike c/n SW-TB-1389)					
G-MVKH	Solar Wings Pegasus XL-R	SW-WA-1396	14.11.88	K M Elson	Roddige	15.11.07P
	(Trike c/n SW-TB-1393)					
G-MVKJ	Solar Wings Pegasus XL-R	SW-WA-1398	14.11.88	G V Warner	Croughton	7. 6.02P
	(Rotax 462) *(Trike c/n SW-TE-0132)*			*(Officially regd with Rotax 447)*		
G-MVKK	Solar Wings Pegasus XL-R	SW-WA-1397	14.11.88	G P Burns	Graveley Hall Farm, Graveley	1. 5.09P
	(Rotax 462) *(Trike c/n SW-TE-0131)*					
G-MVKL	Solar Wings Pegasus XL-R	SW-WA-1394	14.11.88	J Powell-Tuck	(Mamhilad, Pontypool)	6. 6.91P
	(Trike c/n SW-TB-1391)			*(Pod marked as "XL-Q" but is XL-R model)*		
G-MVKM	Solar Wings Pegasus XL-R	SW-WA-1399	14.11.88	A J Clarke	(Dunnington, Alcester)	12. 2.05P
	(Original Trike c/n SW-TE-0136 but now uses c/n SW-TB-1152 ex G-MVKM)					
G-MVKN	Solar Wings Pegasus XL-Q	SW-WQ-0126	14.11.88	R A and C A Allen	Siege Cross Farm, Thatcham	7. 9.08P
	(Trike c/n SW-TE-0120)					
G-MVKP	Solar Wings Pegasus XL-Q	SW-WQ-0128	14.11.88	J Williams	(Preston)	19. 9.04P
	(Trike c/n SW-TE-0122)					
G-MVKS	Solar Wings Pegasus XL-Q	SW-WQ-0130	14.11.88	K S Wright *(Stored 8.95)*	Long Marston	13. 5.94P
	(Trike c/n SW-TE-0124)					
G-MVKT	Solar Wings Pegasus XL-Q	SW-WQ-0131	14.11.88	P W Ruffle	RAF Brize Norton	21. 4.09P
	(Trike c/n SW-TE-0125)					
G-MVKU	Solar Wings Pegasus XL-Q	SW-WQ-0132	14.11.88	I K Priestley	Sackville Lodge, Riseley	21.11.08P
	(Trike c/n SW-TE-0126)					
G-MVKV	Solar Wings Pegasus XL-Q	SW-WQ-0152	14.11.88	D R Stansfield	(Sleaford)	4. 6.07P
	(Trike c/n SW-TE-0127: original Sailwing c/n SW-WQ-0133 damaged 14.8.91 and replaced)					
G-MVKW	Solar Wings Pegasus XL-Q	SW-WQ-0134	14.11.88	A T Scott	Walkeridge Farm, Overton	8. 4.08P
	(Trike c/n SW-TE-0128)					
G-MVKZ	Aerial Arts Chaser S	CH.756	5.12.88	T J Barley *(Noted 3.05)*		
					Graveley Hall Farm, Graveley	29. 7.04P
G-MVLA	Aerial Arts Chaser S	CH.762	12.12.88	K R Emery	Sittles Farm, Alrewas	23. 7.08P
G-MVLB	Aerial Arts Chaser S	CH.763	5.12.88	R P Wilkinson	Charmy Down, Bath	8. 5.06P
G-MVLC	Aerial Arts Chaser S 447	CH.764	22.11.88	B R Barnes	(Bristol)	10. 5.03P
	(Officially regd with Rotax 377)					
G-MVLD	Aerial Arts Chaser S	CH.765	22.11.88	A W Leadley	Letterkenny, County Donegal	10. 6.06P
G-MVLE	Aerial Arts Chaser S	CH.766	5.12.88	R G Hooker	Brunton	29. 1.07P
G-MVLG	Aerial Arts Chaser S	CH.768	14.11.88	A Strang	East Fortune	26.11.04P
G-MVLJ	CFM Shadow Series CD	092	11.11.88	R S Cochrane	Sutton Meadows	30. 5.07P
G-MVLL	Mainair Gemini Flash IIA	708-1188-6-W498	23.11.88	M I Deeley	(Felthorpe)	19. 5.09P
	(Sailwing c/n now W396 ex G-MTSA)					
G-MVLP	CFM Shadow Series C	095	22.11.88	D Bridgland and D T Moran	Old Sarum	25. 5.08P
	(Rotax 447) *(Officially regd with Rotax 503)*					
G-MVLR	Mainair Gemini Flash IIA	713-1288-6-W503	30.11.88	P A Louis *(Noted 8.08)*	Rusell Farm, Cockerham	18.11.00P
G-MVLS	Aerial Arts Chaser S 477	CH.773	21. 2.89	C J Meadows *(Noted 9.05)*		
					Franklyn's Field, Chewton Mendip	20. 4.05P
G-MVLT	Aerial Arts Chaser S	CH.774	5.12.88	B D Searle	(Portsmouth)	19. 7.05P
G-MVLW	Aerial Arts Chaser S	CH.778	28.12.88	E W P van Zeller	(Ashford)	5. 9.99P
G-MVLX	Solar Wings Pegasus XL-Q	SW-WQ-0114	30.11.88	J F Smith	Enstone	22. 6.08P
	(Trike c/n SW-TE-0133)					
G-MVLY	Solar Wings Pegasus XL-Q	SW-WQ-0142	5.12.88	I B Osborn	Manston	2.10.08P
	(Trike c/n SW-TE-0137)					
G-MVMA	Solar Wings Pegasus XL-Q	SW-WQ-0144	5.12.88	G C Winter-Goodwin *(Noted 9.07)*		
	(Trike c/n SW-TE-0139)				Broomclose Farm, Longbridge Deverill	3. 6.07P
G-MVMC	Solar Wings Pegasus XL-Q	SW-WQ-0146	5.12.88	P Smith and I W Barlow	(Ilkeston)	23. 3.06P
	(Trike c/n SW-TE-0141)					
G-MVMG	Thruster TST Mk.1	8128-TST-112	12.12.88	A D McCaldin	Mullahead, Tandragee	20. 7.08P
G-MVMI	Thruster TST Mk.1	8128-TST-114	12.12.88	L M Hamblyn	Old Buckenham	10. 7.09P
G-MVMK	Medway Hybred 44XLR	MR022/46	12.12.88	D J Lewis	(Grays)	5. 2.94P
G-MVML	Aerial Arts Chaser S	CH.781	28.12.88	G C Luddington	(Bolnhurst, Bedford)	29. 7.00P
G-MVMM	Aerial Arts Chaser S	CH.797	21. 2.89	D Margereson	(Chesterfield)	30. 7.04P

G-MVMO	Mainair Gemini Flash IIA	715-1288-6-W507		12.12.88	W Parker	Patna, Ayr 28. 7.08P
G-MVMR	Mainair Gemini Flash IIA	717-1288-6-W509		9. 1.89	P W Ramage	(Rufforth) 20. 9.96P
G-MVMT	Mainair Gemini Flash IIA	718-189-6-W510		22.12.88	R F Sanders	Otherton, Cannock 25. 9.98P
G-MVMU	Mainair Gemini Flash IIA	719-189-6-W511		22.12.88	P A Brunt	(Stretford, Manchester) 23. 7.07P
G-MVMV	Mainair Gemini Flash IIA	720-189-6-W512		22.12.88	J M Macdonald Mill Farm, Hughley, Much Wenlock	24. 3.06P
G-MVMW	Mainair Gemini Flash IIA	710-1188-6-W500		11.11.88	K Downes and B Nock	(Wolverhampton) 31. 7.03P
G-MVMX	Mainair Gemini Flash IIA	721-189-6-W513		23.12.88	D J Rooney	(Rathvilly, County Carlow) 27. 4.08P
	(Rotax 462) (Trike stamped incorrectly as "W512")					
G-MVMY	Mainair Gemini Flash IIA	722-189-6-W514		22.12.88	N G Leteney	(Bury) 21.12.02P
G-MVMZ	Mainair Gemini Flash IIA	723-189-6-W515		22.12.88	S Richards	Otherton, Cannock 24. 5.02P
G-MVNA	Powerchute Raider	81230		12. 7.89	J McGoldrick	Newtownards 6. 7.04P
G-MVNB	Powerchute Raider	81231		12. 7.89	A L Inwood	(Melton Mowbray) 11. 8.06P
G-MVNC	Powerchute Raider	81232		12. 7.89	W R Hanley	(Edinburgh) 25. 7.00P
G-MVNK	Powerchute Raider	90623		12. 7.89	J Lockyer	(Alsager, Stoke-on-Trent) 16. 7.95P
G-MVNL	Powerchute Raider	90624		12. 7.89	A E Askew	(Melton Mowbray) 17. 3.01P
G-MVNM	Mainair Gemini Flash IIA	725-189-6-W517		6. 1.89	C D Phillips	Dunkeswell 31. 8.08P
G-MVNN	Whittaker MW5-K Sorcerer	5K-0003-02		28. 3.90	J A T Merino	(Malaga, Spain) 9. 1.06P
	(Built K N Dando - pr.no.BMAA HB/022)					
G-MVNO	Whittaker MW5-K Sorcerer	5K-0004-02		4. 5.89	R L Wadley	Stoke, Isle of Grain 31. 5.04P
	(Built Aerotech International Ltd)					
G-MVNP	Whittaker MW5-K Sorcerer	5K-0005-02		13. 7.89	A M Edwards	(Wokingham) 30. 6.05P
	(Built Aerotech International Ltd)					
G-MVNR	Whittaker MW5-K Sorcerer	5K-0006-02		4. 5.89	E I Rowlands-Jones	(Mochdre, Newtown) 23. 8.01P
	(Built Aerotech International Ltd)					
G-MVNS	Whittaker MW5-K Sorcerer	5K-0007-02		19. 7.89	A M Sirant	Monkswell Farm, Horrabridge 30.11.07P
	(Built Aerotech International Ltd)					
G-MVNT	Whittaker MW5-K Sorcerer	5K-0008-02		28. 3.90	P E Blyth	Wombleton 5. 5.07P
	(Built Aerotech International Ltd)					
G-MVNU	Whittaker MW5-K Sorcerer	5K-0009-02		4. 5.89	J C Rose	Field Farm, Oakley 30. 6.06P
	(Built Aerotech International Ltd)					
G-MVNW	Mainair Gemini Flash IIA	726-189-6-W518		25. 1.89	D J Gregory	Ince Blundell 25. 5.08P
G-MVNX	Mainair Gemini Flash IIA	727-289-6-W519		10. 1.89	I Sidebotham	Barton 13. 5.05P
G-MVNY	Mainair Gemini Flash IIA	724-189-6-W516		11. 1.89	M K Buckland	(Daventry) 14. 8.09P
	(Rotax 462)					
G-MVNZ	Mainair Gemini Flash IIA	728-289-6-W520		11. 1.89	J Howarth	Watnall 11. 7.08P
G-MVOB	Mainair Gemini Flash IIA	729-289-6-W521		16. 1.89	G L Logan	(Great Bourton, Banbury) 23. 7.08P
G-MVOD	Aerial Arts Chaser/110SX	110SX/653		16. 1.89	N R Beale	Deppers Bridge, Southam 9. 4.05P
	(Rotax 377)				(Noted 6.06)	
G-MVOF	Mainair Gemini Flash IIA	730-289-6-W522		31. 1.89	P J Nolan	(Coventry) 13. 3.09P
G-MVOH	CFM Shadow Series CD	K 090		23. 1.89	D I Farmer	Dunkeswell 2. 9.02P
G-MVOJ	Noble Hardman Snowbird Mk.IV	SB-019		26. 7.89	C D Beetham	Bedlands Gate, Little Strickland 16. 9.08P
G-MVOL	Noble Hardman Snowbird Mk.IV	SB-021		29. 8.89	E J Lewis tr Swansea Snowbird Fliers	(Swansea) 11. 5.06P
G-MVON	Mainair Gemini Flash IIA	731-289-6-W523		30. 1.89	W R Astbury	(Stockport) 22.12.05P
G-MVOO	AMF Microflight Chevvron 2-32C	014		10. 1.89	M K Field	Sleap 10. 5.07P
G-MVOP	Aerial Arts Chaser S	CH.787		21. 2.89	D Thorpe (Noted 3.05)	Longacre Farm, Sandy 4. 5.03P
G-MVOR	Mainair Gemini Flash IIA	732-289-6-W524	(EC-)	6. 2.89	P T and R M Jenkins	Dunkeswell 5.10.03P
	(Rotax 462)		G-MVOR			
G-MVOT	Thruster TST Mk.1	8029-TST-116		17. 2.89	B L R J Keeping	Davidstow Moor 4. 4.09P
G-MVOU	Thruster TST Mk.1	8029-TST-117		17. 2.89	D W Tewson	(Marshwood, Bridport) 13. 1.08P
G-MVOV	Thruster TST Mk.1	8029-TST-118		17. 2.89	D J Seymour tr G-MVOV Group	Enstone 18. 6.08P
G-MVOW	Thruster TST Mk.1	8029-TST-119		17. 2.89	J Short and B J Merret	Dunkeswell 17. 7.00P
G-MVOX	Thruster TST Mk.1	8029-TST-120		17. 2.89	J E Davies	Haverfordwest 29. 8.07P
G-MVOY	Thruster TST Mk.1	8029-TST-121		17. 2.89	C Jones	Redlands, Swindon 22. 6.07P
G-MVPA	Mainair Gemini Flash IIA	735-289-7-W527		29. 3.89	J E Milburn	(South Shields) 30. 8.95P
G-MVPB	Mainair Gemini Flash IIA	736-389-7-W528		29. 3.89	O Carter	Baxby Manor, Husthwaite 30. 7.05P
G-MVPC	Mainair Gemini Flash IIA	737-389-7-W529		7. 2.89	W O Flannery	(Scariff, County Clare) 10. 5.09P
	(Mis-stamped with c/n inscription for "740-389-7-W532" which is identity of G-MVPI)					
G-MVPD	Mainair Gemini Flash IIA	738 380 7-W530		7. 2.89	P Thelwell (Noted 8.08)	Tarn Farm, Cockerham 16. 2.07P
G-MVPE	Mainair Gemini Flash IIA	739-389-7-W531		7. 2.89	M D Jealous and M Goodrick	(Sandbach) 3.11.08P
G-MVPF	Medway Hybred 44XLR	MR036/52		27. 2.89	G H Crick	Plaistows Farm, St Albans 13. 4.08P
G-MVPH	Whittaker MW6-S Fatboy Flyer	PFA 164-11404		7. 2.89	A K Mascord	(Dolfor, Newtown) 23. 8.99P
	(Built E A Henman) (Rotax 503)					
G-MVPI	Mainair Gemini Flash IIA	740-389-7-W532		9. 2.89	A Shand	(Banchory) 6. 7.09P
G-MVPJ	Rans S-5 Coyote	88.083		15. 2.89	M P Wiseman	Mount Airey Farm, South Cave 2. 8.99P
	(Built J Whiting - pr.no.PFA 193-11470)					
G-MVPK	CFM Shadow Series CD	K 091		15. 2.89	P Sarfas	Benson's Farm, Laindon 11. 6.08P
	(Rotax 447) (Officially regd with Rotax 503)					
G-MVPL	Medway Hybred 44XLR	MR034/50		1. 3.89	J N J Roberts	(Longacre Farm, Sandy) 30. 4.98P
G-MVPM	Whittaker MW6 Merlin	PFA 164-11272		21. 2.89	K W Curry	(Nantmel, Llandrindod Wells) 30. 4.03P
	(Built S J Field- Reported as Type MW6-T) (Rotax 503)					
G-MVPN	Whittaker MW6 Merlin	PFA 164-11280		21. 2.89	A M Field	(Glastonbury) 18. 5.93P
	(Built A M Field) (Rotax 503)					
G-MVPR	Solar Wings Pegasus XL-Q	SW-WQ-0163		14. 3.89	R S Swift	Finmere 24. 5.09P
	(Trike c/n SW-TE-0149)					
G-MVPS	Solar Wings Pegasus XL-Q	SW-WQ-0140		14. 3.89	R J Hood	London Colney 8. 6.08P
	(Trike c/n SW-TE-0143)					
G-MVPX	Solar Wings Pegasus XL-Q	SW-WQ-0158		28. 3.89	P Gregory	Clench Common 15. 7.09P
	(Trike c/n SW-TE-0144)					
G-MVPY	Solar Wings Pegasus XL-Q	SW-WQ-0188		28. 3.89	G H Dawson	Coldharbour Farm, Willingham 23. 6.08P
	(Trike c/n SW-TE-0178)					
G-MVRA	Mainair Gemini Flash IIA	743-489-7-W535		10. 4.89	F Flood	(Blackburn) 29.10.09P
G-MVRB	Mainair Gemini Flash IIA	747-489-7-W539		29. 3.89	G Callaghan	(Richhill, Armagh) 13. 5.06P
G-MVRD	Mainair Gemini Flash IIA	749-489-7-W541		9. 5.89	A R Helm	Altham West, Accrington 25. 3.08P
G-MVRF	Rotec Rally 2B	AIE-01		28. 4.89	A I Edwards	(Hixon, Stafford)

G-MVRG	Aerial Arts Chaser S	CH.798	14. 4.89	J P Kynaston	(Harlington, Dunstable)	31. 8.99P	
G-MVRH	Solar Wings Pegasus XL-Q	SW-WQ-0177	10. 4.89	K Farr	Swinford, Rugby	5. 5.09P	
	(Trike c/n SW-TE-0160)						
G-MVRI	Solar Wings Pegasus XL-Q	SW-WQ-0159	10. 4.89	P Martin	Newnham, Baldock	26. 7.09P	
	(Trike c/n SW-TE-0145)						
G-MVRJ	Solar Wings Pegasus XL-Q	SW-WQ-0154	10. 4.89	J Goldsmith-Ryan	Eaglescott	3.10.05P	
	(Trike c/n SW-TE-0172)						
G-MVRL	Aerial Arts Chaser S 447	CH.801	18. 4.89	C N Beale	Mill Farm, Shifnal	17. 4.07P	
G-MVRM	Mainair Gemini Flash IIA	752-489-7-W545	12. 4.89	J S Stevenson	East Fortune	4. 5.09P	
	(Rotax 462)						
G-MVRO	CFM Shadow Series CD	K 105	3. 4.89	K H Creed	(Langar, Nottingham)	10.11.08P	
G-MVRP	CFM Shadow Series CD	097	7. 4.89	M A Kelly	Mill Farm, Shifnal	2. 5.09P	
G-MVRR	CFM Shadow Series CD	098	7. 4.89	S P Christian	Hougham, Lincoln	14. 4.09P	
G-MVRT	CFM Shadow Series CD	104	7. 4.89	G M Teasdale	Watnall	12. 4.09P	
G-MVRU	Solar Wings Pegasus XL-Q	SW-WQ-0183	12. 4.89	I A Clark	North Coates	30. 5.09P	
	(Trike c/n SW-TE-0166)						
G-MVRV	Powerchute Kestrel	90210	28. 4.89	G M Fletcher	(Chesterfield)	3. 2.97P	
G-MVRW	Solar Wings Pegasus XL-Q	SW-WQ-0178	12. 4.89	D L Hadley	(Petham, Canterbury)	10. 8.08P	
	(Trike c/n SW-TE-0161) (Rebuilt 1999 including new factory supplied Sailwing)						
G-MVRX	Solar Wings Pegasus XL-Q	SW-WQ-0165	12. 4.89	M Everest	(Hailsham)	18. 6.05P	
	(Trike c/n SW-TE-0151)						
G-MVRY	Medway Hybred 44XLR	MR049/56	12. 4.89	K Dodman	(Stowmarket)	4. 3.99P	
G-MVRZ	Medway Hybred 44XLR	MR043/57	9. 5.89	I Oswald	(London SE9)	13.11.01P	
	(Rotax 503)						
G-MVSB	Solar Wings Pegasus XL-Q	SW-WQ-0193	18. 4.89	M Jennings and D Forde	Rufforth	23.11.02P	
	(Trike c/n SW-TE-0184)						
G-MVSD	Solar Wings Pegasus XL-Q	SW-WQ-0195	18. 4.89	D C Maxwell-Grice	Old Sarum	14. 8.08P	
	(Trike c/n SW-TE-0186)						
G-MVSE	Solar Wings Pegasus XL-Q	SW-WQ-0196	18. 4.89	L B Richardson	Bagby	17. 2.07P	
	(Trike c/n SW-TE-0187)						
G-MVSG	Aerial Arts Chaser S	CH.804	24. 4.89	M Roberts	(Melksham)	24. 7.05P	
G-MVSI	Medway Hybred 44XLR	MR040/58	18. 4.89	B E Wagenhauser	(Chew Magna, Bristol)	12. 4.09P	
G-MVSJ	Aviasud Mistral 532GB	072	18. 4.89	P R Hall and J D Hewitson	Rufforth	20. 4.08P	
	(Built Aviasud Engineering - pr.no.BMAA HB/013)						
G-MVSM	Midland Ultralights Sirocco 377GB	MU-023	21. 4.89	C G Benham	(Farthingstone, Towcester)	15. 8.04P	
G-MVSN	Mainair Gemini Flash IIA	754-589-7-W547	28. 4.89	D Kent	Eshott	31. 5.09P	
G-MVSO	Mainair Gemini Flash IIA	755-589-7-W548	27. 4.89	W R Furness	Mitchells Farm, Wilburton	25. 1.08P	
G-MVSP	Mainair Gemini Flash IIA	756-589-7-W549	27. 4.89	D R Buchanan	(Pulborough)	4. 4.04P	
G-MVST	Mainair Gemini Flash IIA	750-589-7-W543	12. 6.89	I M Watson	Tarn Farm, Cockerham	2. 6.08P	
	(Rotax 462)						
G-MVSV	Mainair Gemini Flash IIA	757-589-7-W550	11. 5.89	P Shelton	St Michaels	28. 5.09P	
G-MVSW	Solar Wings Pegasus XL-Q	SW-WQ-0198	17. 5.89	K Perratt	(Kilwinning)	10. 3.07P	
	(Trike c/n SW-TE-0189)						
G-MVSX	Solar Wings Pegasus XL-Q	SW-WQ-0199	11. 5.89	A R Law *(Noted 10.07)*	Davidstow Moor	2. 9.05P	
	(Trike c/n SW-TE-0190)						
G-MVSY	Solar Wings Pegasus XL-Q	SW-WQ-0200	11. 5.89	G P Turnbull	Weston Zoyland	12. 9.04P	
	(Trike c/n SW-TE-0191)						
G-MVSZ	Solar Wings Pegasus XL-Q	SW-WQ-0201	11. 5.89	J B Grotrian			
	(Trike c/n SW-TE-0192)				Broomclose Farm, Longbridge Deverill	17. 6.08P	
G-MVTA	Solar Wings Pegasus XL-Q	SW-WQ-0202	11. 5.89	P Hanby	(Maidstone)	16. 8.09P	
	(Trike c/n SW-TE-0193)						
G-MVTC	Mainair Gemini Flash IIA	759-689-7-W552	30. 5.89	P Hocknull	Arclid Green, Sandbach	31. 5.08P	
	(Landed heavily short of the runway threshold at Arclid Green, nosewheel dug in and aircraft cartwheeled)						
G-MVTD	Whittaker MW6 Merlin	PFA 164-11367	11. 5.89	G J Green	(Matlock)	27. 3.04P	
	(Built J S Yates) (Rotax 503)						
G-MVTF	Aerial Arts Chaser S 447	CH808	30. 5.89	P Mundy	(Prestwich, Manchester)	5. 9.08P	
G-MVTI	Solar Wings Pegasus XL-Q	SW-WQ-0206	25. 5.89	P J Taylor	(Skegness)	16. 8.09P	
	(Trike c/n SW-TE-0217)						
G-MVTJ	Solar Wings Pegasus XL-Q	SW-WQ-0207	25. 5.89	M P and R A Wells	Croft Farm, Defford	26. 1.09P	
	(Trike c/n SW-TE-0197)						
G-MVTK	Solar Wings Pegasus XL-Q	SW-WQ-0208	25. 5.89	N Musgrave	(Rhosybol, Amlwch)	21. 7.09P	
	(Trike c/n SW-TE-0198)						
G-MVTL	Aerial Arts Chaser S	CH.809	13. 6.89	N D Meer	Roddige	30. 7.06P	
G-MVTM	Aerial Arts Chaser S 447	CH.810	13. 6.89	G L Davies	Den Helder, Netherlands	13. 9.06P	
	(Officially regd with Rotax 377)						
G-MVUA	Mainair Gemini Flash IIA	760-689-7-W553	14. 6.89	E W Hughes	RAF Mona	13. 3.09P	
	(Rotax 462)						
G-MVUB	Thruster T 300	089-T300-373	13. 6.89	S Silk *(Noted 8.05)*	Rochester	26. 6.03P	
	(Rotax 532)						
G-MVUF	Solar Wings Pegasus XL-Q	SW-WQ-0213	13. 6.89	P H Flower	(Warlingham)	17. 8.07P	
	(Trike c/n SW-TE-0203)						
G-MVUG	Solar Wings Pegasus XL-Q	SW-WQ-0214	13. 6.89	I J Morgan	(Bristol)	21. 9.08P	
	(Trike c/n SW-TE-0204)						
G-MVUI	Solar Wings Pegasus XL-Q	SW-WQ-0216	13. 6.89	J K Edgecombe	Swinford, Rugby	17. 7.08P	
	(Trike c/n SW-TE-0206: Sailwing marked incorrectly as c/n SW-TE-0216)						
G-MVUJ	Solar Wings Pegasus XL-Q	SW-WQ-0217	13. 6.89	J H Cooper	Field Farm, Oakley	21 .9.09P	
	(Trike c/n SW-TE-0207)						
G-MVUK	Solar Wings Pegasus XL-Q	SW-WQ-0218	13. 6.89	D Greenslade	Redlands, Swindon	27.10.05P	
	(Trike c/n SW-TE-0208)						
G-MVUL	Solar Wings Pegasus XL-Q	SW-WQ-0219	13. 6.89	D Hamilton-Brown	(Pevensey)	23. 7.07P	
	(Trike c/n SW-TE-0209)						
G-MVUM	Solar Wings Pegasus XL-Q	SW-WQ-0220	13. 6.89	S Clay	(Falmouth)	11.10.08P	
	(Trike c/n SW-TE-0210)						
G-MVUO	AMF Microflight Chevvron 2-32C	015	14. 6.89	P Rawlinson	(Sutton, Ely)	4. 6.07P	

G-MVUP	Aviasud Mistral 532GB	1087-48	83-CQ	10. 8.89	G R Inston		Overseal, Derby	8.10.07P
	(Built Aviasud Engineering - pr.no.BMAA HB/003)							
G-MVUR	Hornet RS-ZA	HRWA0050/ZA107		3. 7.89	G R Puffett		Landmead Farm, Garford	4. 4.08P
G-MVUS	Aerial Arts Chaser S	CH.813		3. 7.89	H Poyzer		Eshott	16.12.01P
G-MVUU	Hornet R-ZA	HRWB0061 & ZA110		13. 7.89	K W Warn		(Newton Abbot)	27. 7.07P
G-MVVH	Medway Hybred 44XLR	MR047/63		11. 7.89	M S Henson		(Portsmouth)	5. 9.08P
G-MVVI	Medway Hybred 44XLR	MR050/64		12. 7.89	J L Ford		(Edlesborough, Dunstable)	12. 9.09P
G-MVVK	Solar Wings Pegasus XL-R	SW-WA-1423		11. 7.89	A J Weir		(Bath)	5. 5.09P
	(Trike c/n SW-TB-1414)							
G-MVVM	Solar Wings Pegasus XL-R	SW-WA-1425		12. 7.89	A F Cunningham		(Sandbach)	15. 7.06P
	(Trike c/n SW-TB-1416)							
G-MVVN	Solar Wings Pegasus XL-Q	SW-WQ-0226		11. 7.89	J R Butler		Watnall	28. 5.09P
	(Trike c/n SW-TE-0214)							
G-MVVO	Solar Wings Pegasus XL-Q	SW-WQ-0227		11. 7.89	A L Scarlett		Clench Common	29. 7.04P
	(Trike c/n SW-TE-0215)							
G-MVVP	Solar Wings Pegasus XL-Q	SW-WQ-0228		11. 7.89	D Ross		(Bedford)	12. 8.08P
	(Trike c/n SW-TE-0216)							
G-MVVR	Medway Hybred 44XLR	MR058/66		20. 7.89	H J Long			
	(Rotax 503)						Ardenagh Great, Taghmon, County Wexford	19.10.08P
G-MVVT	CFM Shadow Series CD	K 101		26. 7.89	W F Hayward		(Maud, Peterhead)	3.11.09P
	(Built CFM Metal-Fax - pr.no.PFA 161-11569)							
G-MVVV	AMF Microflight Chevvron 2-32C	016	PH-1W9	11. 5.89	P R Turton		Old Sarum	16. 2.09P
	(Konig SD 570)		G-MVVV					
G-MVVZ	Powerchute Raider	90628		25. 7.89	J H Cadman		(Melton Mowbray)	13. 7.02P
G-MVWJ	Powerchute Raider	90738		25. 7.89	N J Doubek		(Stanford-le-Hope)	24. 5.03P
G-MVWN	Thruster T 300	089-T300-374		26. 7.89	T B Reakes tr Whisky November Group			
	(Rotax 503)						Smalls Farm, Charterhouse	12. 7.08P
G-MVWR	Thruster T 300	089-T300-377		26. 7.89	G Rainey		Weston Zoyland	16. 3.08P
	(Rotax 503)							
G-MVWS	Thruster T 300	089-T300-378		26. 7.89	R J Humphries		Walkeridge Farm, Overton	15. 8.95P
	(Rotax 503)				(Stored for spares 3.07)			
G-MVWV	Medway Hybred 44XLR	MR060/69		24. 7.89	H Tuvey		(Aveley, South Ockendon)	8. 2.09P
	(Rotax 447)							
G-MVWW	Aviasud Mistral 532GB	0389-81		25. 7.89	P S Balmer tr Golf Whisky Whisky Group			
	(Built Aviasud Engineering - pr.no.BMAA HB/005)						Tarn Farm, Cockerham	8. 2.09P
G-MVWZ	Aviasud Mistral 532GB	1288-70		2. 8.89	G Gates tr Chilbolton Mistral Group		Chilbolton	16. 4.07P
	(Built Aviasud Engineering - pr.no.BMAA HB/008)				(Noted11.07)			
G-MVXA	Whittaker MW6 Merlin	PFA 164-11337		17. 8.89	I Brewster		Longacres Farm, Sandy	23. 4.09P
	(Built I Brewster) (Fuji-Robin EC-44-PM)							
G-MVXB	Mainair Gemini Flash IIA	762-789-7-W555		3. 8.89	M E Clennell		Longframlington	14. 8.08P
	(Rotax 462)							
G-MVXC	Mainair Gemini Flash IIA	763-889-7-W556		4. 8.89	M Dodd		(Bala)	31. 5.08P
G-MVXD	Medway Hybred 44XLR	MR061/70		3. 8.89	P R Millen		(Worthing)	9. 6.08P
	(Rotax 503) (Marked as "Raven")							
G-MVXE	Medway Hybred 44XLR	MR063/71		23. 8.89	A M Brittle		Sittles Farm, Alrewas	31. 7.00P
	(Rotax 447)							
G-MVXI	Medway Hybred 44XLR	MR064/72		9. 8.89	T de Landro		Stoke, Isle of Grain	11. 7.05P
	(Rotax 447)							
G-MVXJ	Medway Hybred 44XLR	MR065/73		25. 8.89	P J Wilks		(Edenbridge)	26. 9.90P
	(Rotax 447)							
G-MVXL	Thruster TST Mk.1	8089-TST-122		18. 8.89	A J Smith		(Cardiff)	30. 8.00P
G-MVXM	Medway Hybred 44XLR	MR055/75		17. 8.89	P J Short		(Worcester)	2. 8.04P
	(Rotax 503) (Reported as Medway Raven)							
G-MVXN	Aviasud Mistral 532GB	065		18. 8.89	P W Cade		(New York, Lincoln)	29.12.09P
	(Built Aviasud Engineering - pr.no.BMAA HB/002)							
G-MVXR	Mainair Gemini Flash IIA	764-889-7-W557		22. 8.89	D M Bayne		East Fortune	16. 8.09P
	(Rotax 462)							
G-MVXS	Mainair Gemini Flash IIA	766-889-7-W559		22. 8.89	J W Wood (Trike only 7.07)			
							Tarn Farm, Cockerham	25. 7.02P
G-MVXV	Aviasud Mistral 532GB	092		22. 8.89	M F E Chalk		Clench Common	5. 1.03P
	(Built Aviasud Engineering - pr.no.BMAA HB/004)							
G-MVXX	AMF Microflight Chevvron 2-32	018		27. 7.89	C K Brown		(Loughborough)	27. 6.05P
G-MVYC	Solar Wings Pegasus XL-Q	SW-WQ-0239		8. 9.89	P E L Street		(Lincoln)	8. 3.09P
	(Trike c/n SW-TE-0224)							
G-MVYD	Solar Wings Pegasus XL-Q	SW-WQ-0240		8. 9.89	T M Wakeley		Shobdon	29. 9.08P
	(Trike c/n SW-TE-0225)							
G-MVYE	Thruster TST Mk.1	8089-TST-123		13. 9.89	M J Aubrey		Kington, Hereford	24. 6.03P
G-MVYK	Hornet R-ZA	HRWB-0076 & ZA117		22. 9.89	P Asbridge		(Llanarmon-yn-Ial, Mold)	22. 7.99P
G-MVYL	Hornet R-ZA	HRWB-0077 & ZA115		22. 9.89	J L Thomas		(Bristol)	28. 3.04P
G-MVYN	Hornet R-ZA	HRWB-0079 & ZA136		22. 9.89	C F Janes		(Portsmouth)	12. 7.09P
G-MVYP	Medway Hybred 44XLR	MR071/77		19. 9.89	J Harmon		Stoke, Isle of Grain	12.10.08P
	(Rotax 447)							
G-MVYR	Medway Hybred 44XLR	MR068/76		19. 9.89	K J Clarke		Stoke, Isle of Grain	14. 6.09P
	(Rotax 447)							
G-MVYS	Mainair Gemini Flash IIA	770-989-7-W563		19. 9.89	J McGrath		Kirkbride	10.12.09P
G-MVYT	Noble Hardman Snowbird Mk.IV	SB-022		26. 9.89	M A Oakley		Kemble	8. 6.06P
G-MVYU	Noble Hardman Snowbird Mk.IV	SB-023		7.11.89	B Foster and P Meah		Gerpins Farm, Upminster	29. 7.08P
G-MVYV	Noble Hardman Snowbird Mk.IV	SB-024		21. 8.90	D W Hayden		Swansea	9. 4.08P
G-MVYW	Noble Hardman Snowbird Mk.IV	SB-025		22.10.90	T J Harrison		Upfield Farm, Lllanwern	25. 7.06P
G-MVYX	Noble Hardman Snowbird Mk.IV	SB-026		25.11.91	R McBlain		Kilkerran	10. 5.08P
G-MVYY	Aerial Arts Chaser S 508	CH.824		26. 9.89	C J Gordon and R H Bird		(Laurencekirk)	15. 7.07P
G-MVYZ	CFM Shadow Series BD	121		25. 9.89	C Day		(Salisbury)	15. 8.06P
G-MVZA	Thruster T 300	089-T300-379		26. 9.89	C C Belcher		Walkeridge Farm, Overton	18. 7.07P

G-MVZC	Thruster T 300 (Rotax 532)	089-T300-381	26. 9.89	R A Knight	Chilbolton	20. 6.08P
G-MVZD	Thruster T 300 (Rotax 532)	089-T300-382	26. 9.89	T Pearce tr G-MVZD Syndicate	(Twickenham)	10. 6.09P
G-MVZG	Thruster T 300 (Rotax 532)	089-T300-385	26. 9.89	R Lewis-Evans Mapperton Farm, Newton Peverill		10. 4.09P
G-MVZI	Thruster T 300 (Rotax 503)	089-T300-387	26. 9.89	R R R Whittern (Noted 9.07)	South Wraxall	19. 8.06P
G-MVZJ	Solar Wings Pegasus XL-Q	SW-WQ-0241 (Trike c/n SW-TE-0226)	26. 8.89	P Mansfield	Deenethorpe	24.11.07P
G-MVZK	Quad City Challenger II PFA 177-11498 (Built K B Tolley) (BMW R 100)		28. 9.89	G Carr (Noted Plockton 1.09)	(Isle of Lewis)	23. 9.04P
G-MVZL	Solar Wings Pegasus XL-Q	SW-WQ-0242 (Trike c/n SW-TE-0227)	4.10.89	P R Dobson	(Brentwood)	16. 6.05P
G-MVZM	Aerial Arts Chaser S 447	CH.825	2.11.89	J L Parker	(Maidstone)	20. 5.09P
G-MVZO	Medway Hybred 44XLR (Rotax 503)	MR072/78	25.10.89	G Drysdale	(Scampton, Lincoln)	30. 7.08P
G-MVZP	Murphy Renegade Spirit UK	256 (Built G S Hollingsworth - pr.no.PFA 188-11630)	17.10.89	H M Doyle Lower Mountpleasant Farm, Chatteris		21. 1.05P
G-MVZS	Mainair Gemini Flash IIA	771-1089-7-W564	17.10.89	R L Beese	(Tarporley)	10. 6.09P
G-MVZT	Solar Wings Pegasus XL-Q	SW-WQ-0243 (Trike c/n SW-TE-0228)	6.10.89	C J Meadows Franklyn's Field, Chewton Mendip		25. 8.02P
G-MVZU	Solar Wings Pegasus XL-Q	SW-WQ-0244 (Trike c/n SW-TE-0229)	6.10.89	M G McMurray	(Farcet, Peterborough)	13. 4.07P
G-MVZW	Hornet R-ZA	HRWB-0063 & ZA142	27.10.89	K W Warn	Popham	9. 8.02P
G-MVZX	Murphy Renegade Spirit UK PFA 188-11590 (Built G Holmes)		18.10.89	G Holmes	(Pickering)	16. 7.09P
G-MVZZ	AMF Microflight Chevvron 2-32	019	27. 7.89	W A L Mitchell	(Cranleigh)	3. 1.09P
G-MWAB	Mainair Gemini Flash IIA	772-1089-7-W565	24.10.89	J E Buckley	(Sandbach)	2. 1.10P
G-MWAC	Solar Wings Pegasus XL-Q	SW-WQ-0260 (Trike c/n SW-TE-0236)	25.10.89	H Lloyd-Hughes	Emlyn's Field, Rhuallt	29. 5.09P
G-MWAD	Solar Wings Pegasus XL-Q	SW-WQ-0261 (Trike c/n SW-TE-0237)	25.10.89	J K Evans	(Brixworth, Northampton)	15. 6.07P
G-MWAE	CFM Shadow Series CD	130	24.10.89	D J Adams	(Passenham, Milton Kynes)	8. 5.09P
G-MWAF	Solar Wings Pegasus XL-R	SW-WA-1441 (Trike c/n SW-TB-1422)	30.10.89	J P Bonner	Arclid Green, Sandbach	6. 7.07P
G-MWAG	Solar Wings Pegasus XL-R	SW-WA-1442 (Trike c/n SW-TB-1423)	30.10.89	X Norman	(Thame)	11. 8.08P
G-MWAJ	Murphy Renegade Spirit UK PFA 188-11438 (Built J Hall) (BMW R 100RS)		1.11.89	M Mailey (Noted 2007)	Blackhill, Draperstown	6. 4.04P
G-MWAL	Solar Wings Pegasus XL-Q	SW-WQ-0263 (Trike c/n SW-TE-0240)	2.11.89	A W Hill	(Bury, Ramsey, Huntingdon)	11. 8.06P
G-MWAN	Thruster T 300 (Rotax 532)	089-T300-389	14.11.89	E J Girling	Davidstow Moor	7. 7.08P
G-MWAP	Thruster T 300 (Rotax 503)	089-T300-391	14.11.89	S F Chave and A G Spurway "Wanda"	(Honiton)	9. 8.04P
G-MWAR	Thruster T 300 (Rotax 532)	089-T300-392	14.11.89	B Cassidy	Dunkeswell	29. 4.08P
G-MWAT	Solar Wings Pegasus XL-Q	SW-WQ-0265 (Trike c/n SW-TE-0241)	13.11.89	D G Seymour	Craymarsh Farm, Melksham	3. 5.09P
G-MWAV	Solar Wings Pegasus XL-R	SW-WA-1444 (Trike c/n SW-TB-1424 appears to have been duplicated with G-MWBL qv)	13.11.89	I J Rawlinson	(Stoke-on-Trent)	6. 4.08P
G-MWAW	Whittaker MW6 Merlin	PFA 164-11460 (Built P Palmer) (Rotax 503)	10.11.89	J K Buckingham	Insch	4. 4.08P
G-MWBJ	Medway Puma Sprint (Rotax 447)	MS003/1	21.11.89	C C Strong	(Bures, Cornwall)	14. 7.00P
G-MWBK	Solar Wings Pegasus XL-Q	SW-WQ-0271 (Trike c/n SW-TE-0248)	16.11.89	A W Jarvis	(Motcombe, Shaftesbury)	26. 4.09P
G-MWBL	Solar Wings Pegasus XL-R/Se SW-WA-1446 (Trike c/n SW-TB-1424 appears to have been duplicated with G-MWAV qv)		16.11.89	J A Valentine	Eshott (Noted 9.07)	3. 7.04P
G-MWBO	Rans S-4 Coyote	89.097 (Built L R H d'Ath - pr.no.PFA 193-11583)	29.11.89	B M Tibenham Longside, Peterhead (Crashed on take-off Hatton 9. 6.07 and substantially damaged)		28.11.07P
G-MWBP	Hornet R-ZA	HRWB-0083/ZA144	29.11.89	S Brader	Tarn Farm, Cockerham	17. 8.05P
G-MWBS	Hornet R-ZA (BMW R100)	HRWB-0085/ZA146	29.11.89	P D Jaques "Freedom Hornet"	Sandtoft	3.10.08P
G-MWBU	Hornet R-ZA	HRWB-0087/ZA148	29.11.89	J D Nelson	Plaistows Farm, St Albans	12. 9.04P
G-MWBW	Hornet R-ZA	HRWB-0089/ZA150	29.11.89	C G Bentley	(Chesterfield)	15. 5.00P
G-MWBY	Hornet R-ZA	HRWB-0091/ZA152	29.11.89	Forestair Dragoons Ltd	(London SW6)	19. 6.04P
G-MWCB	Solar Wings Pegasus XL-Q	SW-WQ-0273 (Trike c/n SW-TE-0250)	1.12.89	J C Whiting	(Lincoln)	25. 9.07P
G-MWCC	Solar Wings Pegasus XL-R/Se SW-WA-1447 (Trike c/n SW-TB-1387 ex G-MVKD when latter's Sailwing sold) (Rotax 462)		1.12.89	I K Priestley	Sackville Lodge, Riseley	26. 3.05P
G-MWCE	Mainair Gemini Flash IIA	775-1289-7-W568	19.12.89	B A Tooze	Shobdon	6. 9.05P
G-MWCF	Solar Wings Pegasus XL-Q	SW-WQ-0276 (Trike c/n SW-TE-0252)	13.12.89	R McKie	(Southampton)	29. 9.08P
G-MWCG	Microflight Spectrum	011	15.12.89	C Ricketts	Otherton, Cannock	2. 6.05P
G-MWCH	Rans S-6-ESD Coyote II	0989.067 (Built J Whiting - pr.no.PFA 204-11632 - sequence no. duplicates Kitfox G-BSFY)	15.12.89	J G Burns and T Briton tr G-MWCH Group Morgansfield, Fishburn		17.10.08P
G-MWCI	Powerchute Kestrel	91245	3. 1.90	E G Bray	Clacton	2. 7.05P
G-MWCK	Powerchute Kestrel	91247	3. 1.90	A E Askew	(Melton Mowbray)	28.12.04P
G-MWCM	Powerchute Kestrel	91249	3. 1.90	G E Lockyer	(Stoke-on-Trent)	17. 6.96P
G-MWCN	Powerchute Kestrel	91250	3. 1.90	J D McKibben (Noted 7.07)	Derryogue	16. 8.04P
G-MWCO	Powerchute Kestrel	91251	3. 1.90	J R E Gladstone	(Abingdon)	7. 6.08P

G-MWCR	Southdown Puma Sprint			24. 2.84	S R Hall	Deenethorpe	2. 8.02P
	(Fuji-Robin EC-44-PM) P 516 & SN1121/0070				(Noted 3.05)		
G-MWCS	Powerchute Kestrel	91253		3. 1.90	R S McFadyen	(Tamworth)	5. 7.07P
G-MWCU	Solar Wings Pegasus XL-R	SW-WA-1449		27.12.89	T P Noonan	(Dromcollogher, County Limerick)	5. 8.05P
	(Trike c/n SW-TB-1412)						
G-MWCW	Mainair Gemini Flash IIA	776-0190-7-W569		29.12.89	A J Thomas	(Eccleston, Chorley)	11. 8.05P
	(Rotax 462)				(Bare frame noted 11.06)		
G-MWCY	Medway Hybred 44XLR	MR077/81		15. 1.90	J K Masters	(Chigwell)	10. 9.04P
	(Rotax 503)						
G-MWCZ	Medway Hybred 44XLR	MR078/82		10. 1.90	A Titcombe	(Aylesford)	22. 6.04P
	(Rotax 503)						
G-MWDB	CFM Shadow Series CD	100		3. 7.89	M D Meade	(Shenley Brook End, Milton Keynes)	10. 7.04P
G-MWDC	Solar Wings Pegasus XL-R/Se	SW-WA-1450		5. 1.90	R Littler	(Wigan)	21. 3.08P
	(Rotax 462)	(Trike c/n SW-TE-0255)					
G-MWDD	Solar Wings Pegasus XL-Q	SW-WQ-0280		15. 1.90	M Wachowiak	(London W5)	8. 9.08P
	(Trike c/n SW-TE-0258)						
G-MWDE	Hornet RS-ZA	HRWB-0094 & ZA126		10. 1.90	H G Reid (Trike noted 4.06)	Roddige	13. 6.98P
	(Rotax 532)						
G-MWDI	Hornet RS-ZA	HRWB-0098 & ZA158		10. 1.90	R J Perrin	Brook Farm, Pilling	29. 6.05P
	(Rotax 532)						
G-MWDJ	Mainair Gemini Flash IIA	777-0190-7-W570		17. 1.90	M Gardiner	Crosland Moor	27. 6.06P
G-MWDK	Solar Wings Pegasus XL-Q	SW-WQ-0281		17. 1.90	T Wicks	(Rowde, Devizes)	13. 6.08P
	(Trike c/n SW-TE-0259)						
G-MWDL	Solar Wings Pegasus XL-Q	SW-WQ-0282		17. 1.90	G J Thomas	(Ware)	17. 6.08P
	(Trike c/n SW-TE-0260)						
G-MWDN	CFM Shadow Series CD	K 102		17. 1.90	A A Duffus	RAF Halton	16.10.09P
G-MWDS	Thruster T 300	089-T300-395		30. 1.90	A R Elliott	Siege Cross Farm, Thatcham	17. 5.08P
	(Rotax 532)						
G-MWDZ	Eipper Quicksilver MXL II	022		29. 1.90	R G Cook	Cranfield	4. 3.09P
	(Built Eipper Aircraft Inc - originally regd with pr.no.PFA 214-11869) (Rotax 503)						
G-MWEE	Solar Wings Pegasus XL-Q	SW-WQ-0147		12.12.88	S D P Bridge	Winspurs Farm, Northrepps	2. 9.01P
	(Trike c/n SW-TE-0175)						
G-MWEG	Solar Wings Pegasus XL-Q	SW-WQ-0284		30. 1.90	S P Michlig	Long Marston	5. 6.09P
	(Trike c/n SW-TE-0262)						
G-MWEH	Solar Wings Pegasus XL-Q	SW-WQ-0286		7. 2.90	K A Davidson	RAF Scampton	14. 8.07P
	(Trike c/n SW-TE-0264)						
G-MWEK	Whittaker MW5 Sorcerer	PFA 163-11284		20. 2.90	D W and M L Squire	(St Austell)	24. 9.09P
	(Built J T Francis)						
G-MWEL	Mainair Gemini Flash IIA	780-0290-7-W573		13. 2.90	E St John-Foti	Deenethorpe	12. 7.09P
G-MWEN	CFM Shadow Series CD	K 113		20. 2.90	C Dawn	(Market Rasen)	8. 8.01P
G-MWEO	Whittaker MW5 Sorcerer	PFA 163-11263		21. 2.90	J Morton (Noted 2007)	Blackhill, Draperstown	9. 9.04P
	(Built C D Wills) (Fuji-Robin EC-34-PM)						
G-MWEP	Rans S-4 Coyote	89.096		21. 2.90	E J Wallington		
	(Built K E Wedl - pr.no.PFA 193-11616)					Inglenook Farm, Maydensole	8. 1.10P
G-MWER	Solar Wings Pegasus XL-Q	SW-WQ-0287		1. 3.90	S P Tkaczyk	(Cardiff)	28. 9.08P
	(Trike c/n SW-TE-0265)						
G-MWES	Rans S-4 Coyote	89.099		1. 2.90	G Scott	Lower Mountpleasant Farm, Chatteris	18. 8.04P
	(Built I Fleming and R W Sage - pr.no.PFA 193-11737)				(Carries "N89099" on tail which matches c/n but is not a p/i) (Noted 8.06)		
G-MWEY	Hornet R-ZA	HRWB-0104/ZA135		21. 2.90	J Kidd	Tarn Farm, Cockerham	24. 9.00P
G-MWEZ	CFM Shadow Series CD	136		22. 2.90	T D Dawson tr G-MWEZ Group		
						Plaistows Farm, St Albans	2. 6.09P
G-MWFB	CFM Shadow Series CD	K 119		1. 3.90	J S Morgan	(Pershore)	
G-MWFC	TEAM Mini-MAX 88	294	G-BTXC	1. 3.90	M Bradley	North Coates	18.11.09P
	(Built M H D Soltau - pr.no.PFA 186-11648)		G-MWFC				
G-MWFD	TEAM Mini-MAX 88	293		1. 3.90	J T Blackburn	Brook Farm, Pilling	23. 8.06P
	(Built J Riley - pr.no.PFA 186-1164: sequence no. duplicates Shadow G-GORE)						
G-MWFF	Rans S-5 Coyote	89.106		10. 1.90	J S Sweetingham	(Helsby, Frodsham)	27. 1.05P
	(Built M W Holmes - pr.no.PFA 193-11639: originally built as S-4 and converted to S-5 in 2001)						
G-MWFG	Powerchute Kestrel	00358		20. 3.90	R I Simpson	Rochester	18. 5.05P
G-MWFI	Powerchute Kestrel	00360		20. 3.90	R R O'Neill	(Ballygawley, Dungannon)	28. 8.02P
G-MWFL	Powerchute Kestrel	00363		20. 3.90	A Vincent	Fenland	31. 3.02P
G-MWFT	MBA Tiger Cub 440	WFT-02		24.11.83	J R Ravenhill	Chavenage, Tetbury	31. 5.07P
G-MWFU	Quad City Challenger II UK	PFA 177-11654		16. 3.90	D A Norwood	Ashford Farm, Winsford	30.10.08P
	(Built K N Dickinson)						
G-MWFV	Quad City Challenger II UK	PFA 177-11655		16. 3.90	M Liptrop	Glassonby	26. 5.05P
	(Built E G Astin)						
G-MWFW	Rans S-4 Coyote	89.107		16. 3.90	M P Hallam	Jackrell's Farm, Southwater	12. 6.09P
	(Built G R Hillary - pr.no.PFA 193-11662)						
G-MWFX	Quad City Challenger II	CH2-1189-UK-0485		20. 3.90	I M Walton	Wellesbourne Mountford	13.11.07P
	(Rotax 462) (Built I M Walton - pr.no.PFA 177-11706)						
G-MWFY	Quad City Challenger II UK	PFA 177-11668		20. 3.90	C C B Soden	Weston Zoyland	20.10.09P
	(Built P J Ladd)						
G-MWFZ	Quad City Challenger II UK			20. 3.90	A Slade	(Enfield)	
		CH2-0190-UK-0506					
	(Built A Slade - pr.no.PFA 177-11707)						
G-MWGA	Rans S-5 Coyote	89.092		20. 3.90	A W Lowrie	Pittrichie Farm, Whiterashes	15. 5.09P
	(Built M A C Stevenson - pr.no.PFA 193-11810)						
G-MWGC	Medway Hybred 44XLR	MR087/85		26. 3.90	C Spalding	(Hatfield Peverel)	10. 6.06P
	(Rotax 503)					(Operated from Hunsdon)	
G-MWGG	Mainair Gemini Flash IIA	785-0390-7-W578		26. 3.90	D Lopez (Noted 7.05)		
	(Rotax 462)					Calton Moor Farm, Ashbourne	26. 4.05P
G-MWGI	Whittaker MW5-K Sorcerer	5K-0012-02		28. 3.90	B Barrass	Sywell	21. 7.06P
	(Built Aerotech International Ltd) (Original wings to G-MTBT by 7.96 qv)						

G-MWGJ	Whittaker MW5-K Sorcerer	5K-0014-02		6. 9.90	I Pearson	Bodmin	2.10.08P
	(Built Aerotech International Ltd)						
G-MWGK	Whittaker MW5-K Sorcerer	5K-0015-02	(G-MWLV)	19. 9.90	A A Castleton	The Chase, Wickwar	5. 5.07P
	(Built Aerotech International Ltd)						
G-MWGL	Solar Wings Pegasus XL-Q	SW-WQ-0293		28. 3.90	F McGlynn	(Newry, NI)	15. 4.08P
G-MWGM	Solar Wings Pegasus XL-Q	SW-WQ-0294		28. 3.90	G C Christopher	Longacre Farm, Sandy	2. 2.08P
	(Trike c/n SW-TE-0271)						
G-MWGN	Rans S-4 Coyote	89.113		26. 3.90	V Hallam	(Torquay)	15. 6.09P
	(Built B H Ashman - pr.no.PFA 193-11709)						
G-MWGO	Aerial Arts Chaser/110SX	110SX/566		28. 3.90	B Nicolson	(Middlesbrough)	28. 4.97P
	(Rotax 377)						
G-MWGR	Solar Wings Pegasus XL-Q	SW-WQ-0296		6. 4.90	A Maskell	Otherton, Cannock	27. 8.08P
	(Trike c/n SW-TE-0272)						
G-MWGU	Powerchute Kestrel	00368	(9H-　)	26. 4.90	M Pandolfino	(Luqa, Malta)	19. 7.91P
			G-MWGU				
G-MWGW	Powerchute Kestrel	00370		26. 4.90	S P Tomlinson	(Leominster)	23. 5.05P
G-MWGZ	Powerchute Kestrel	00373		26. 4.90	L J Lynch	(Ventnor, Isle of Wight))	27. 5.97P
G-MWHC	Solar Wings Pegasus XL-Q	SW-WQ-0304		24. 4.90	P J Lowery	Longacre Farm, Sandy	31. 5.09P
	(Trike c/n SW-TE-0274)						
G-MWHF	Solar Wings Pegasus XL-Q	SW-WQ-0305		24. 4.90	N J Trokev*(Noted 10.07)*	Swinford, Rugby	26. 3.05P
	(Trike c/n SW-TE-0275)						
G-MWHG	Solar Wings Pegasus XL-Q	SW-WQ-0306		24. 4.90	I A Lumley	(Great Orton)	4. 2.03P
	(Trike c/n SW-TE-0276)						
G-MWHH	TEAM Mini-MAX 88	326		23. 4.90	I D Worthington	(Raskelf, York)	4. 8.00P
	(Built B F Crick - pr.no.PFA 186-11814)						
G-MWHI	Mainair Gemini Flash IIA	784-0390-5-W577		26. 4.90	P Harwood	Watnall	9.10.08P
	(Rotax 503)						
G-MWHL	Solar Wings Pegasus XL-Q	SW-WQ-0308		1. 5.90	S J Reader	Roddige	7. 8.08P
	(Trike c/n SW-TE-0278)						
G-MWHM	Whittaker MW6-S Fatboy Flyer			18. 5.90	G H Davies	Otherton, Cannock	2. 8.08P
	(Built D W Squire)(Rotax 532) PFA 164-11463						
G-MWHO	Mainair Gemini Flash IIA	778-0190-5-W571		10. 5.90	B Epps	Arclid Green, Sandbach	23.10.09P
G-MWHP	Rans S-6-ESD Coyote II	1089.093		8. 5.90	J F Bickerstaffe	Higher Barn Farm, Houghton	6. 5.09P
	(Built J F Bickerstaffe - pr.no.PFA 204-11768) (Rotax 532) (Tri-cycle u/c)						
G-MWHR	Mainair Gemini Flash IIA	787-0590-7-W580		16. 5.90	B Brazier	Brook Farm, Pilling	20.11.09P
G-MWHT	Solar Wings Pegasus Quasar TC			15. 5.90	G W F J Dear and K P Byrne		
	(Trike c/n SW-TQ-0005)	SW-WQQ-0314				Mapperton Farm, Newton Peverill	6. 9.08P
G-MWHX	Solar Wings Pegasus XL-Q	SW-WQ-0318		15. 5.90	N P Kelly	Trim, County Meath	17. 7.09P
	(Trike c/n SW-TE-0280)						
G-MWIA	Mainair Gemini Flash IIA	789-0690-7-W582		21. 5.90	M Raj	Otherton, Cannock	26. 9.04P
G-MWIB	Aviasud Mistral 532GB	094		16. 5.90	N W Finn-Kelcey *"Weston Belle"*		
	(Built Aviasud Engineering - pr.no.BMAA HB/010)					Weston Underwood, Olney	14. 6.08P
G-MWIC	Whittaker MW5-C Sorcerer	PFA 163-11224		20. 2.90	A M Witt	(Bradwell Common, Milton Keynes)	29. 4.05P
	(Built I P Croft)						
G-MWIE	Solar Wings Pegasus XL-Q	SW-WQ-0325		30. 5.90	R Mercer	Long Marston	9. 9.07P
	(Trike c/n SW-TE-0282)						
G-MWIF	Rans S-6-ESD Coyote II	1089.095		30. 5.90	K Kelly	(Letterkenny, County Donegal)	8. 5.09P
	(Built M G K Prout - pr.no.PFA 204-11749) (Tri-cycle u/c)						
G-MWIG	Mainair Gemini Flash IIA	790-0690-7-W583		4. 6.90	A P Purbrick	Deenethorpe	15.11.07P
	(Rotax 462)						
G-MWIH	Mainair Gemini Flash IIA	791-0690-5-W584		4. 6.90	J P Norton	Headon Farm, Retford	27. 3.05P
G-MWIL	Medway Hybred 44XLR	MR096/90		8. 6.90	P J Bosworth	Otherton, Cannock	7.10.05P
	(Rotax 447)						
G-MWIM	Solar Wings Pegasus Quasar TC			11. 6.90	R J Styles	Mapperton Farm, Newton Peverill	6. 3.08P
	(Trike c/n SW-TQ-0008)	SW-WQQ-0326					
G-MWIO	Rans S-4 Coyote	90.117		11. 6.90	K Wales	Kemble	15.12.09P
	(Built G Ferguson - pr.no.PFA 193-11774)						
G-MWIP	Whittaker MW6 Merlin	PFA 164-11360		7. 6.90	D Beer and B J Merrett		
	(Built D Beer and B J Merrett) (Rotax 582)					Belle Vue Farm, Yarnscombe	14.10.09P
G-MWIR	Solar Wings Pegasus XL-Q	SW-WQ-0330		8. 6.90	C E Dagless	Wood Norton, Dereham	14. 7.03P
	(Trike c/n SW-TE-0283)						
G-MWIS	Solar Wings Pegasus XL-Q	SW-WQ-0331		8. 6.90	J P Quinlan	Mapperley	1. 5.09P
	(Trike c/n SW-TE-0284)						
G-MWIU	Solar Wings Pegasus Quasar TC			8. 6.90	N P Chitty	Lower Upham Farm, Chiseldon	20. 4.07P
	(Trike c/n SW-TQ-0010)	SW-WQQ-0333					
G-MWIV	Mainair Gemini Flash	792-0690-5-W585		15. 6.90	P and J Calvert	(Pickering)	14. 7.03P
G-MWIW	Solar Wings Pegasus Quasar	SW-WQ-0334		18. 6.90	M W Yaxley and S H Spring	(Grimsby)	25. 6.04P
	(Trike c/n SW-TQ-0011)						
G-MWIX	Solar Wings Pegasus Quasar TCSW-WQQ-0335			18. 6.90	G Hawes	Deenethorpe	14.10.07P
	(Trike c/n SW-TQ-0012)						
G-MWIY	Solar Wings Pegasus Quasar TCSW-WQQ-0336			22. 6.90	N S Payne	Broadmeadow Farm, Hereford	8. 4.09P
	(Trike c/n SW-TQ-0014)						
G-MWIZ	CFM Shadow Series CD	096		22.11.88	T P Ryan	Plaistows Farm, St Albans	25. 4.09P
	(Rotax 462)						
G-MWJF	CFM Shadow Series CD	K 123		26. 6.90	S N White	Chilbolton	27. 4.08P
	(Officially regd as Series "BD") (Rotax 503)						
G-MWJH	Solar Wings Pegasus Quasar	SW-WQQ-0340		29. 6.90	S W Walker	Haverfordwest	14.12.08P
	(Trike c/n SW-TQ-0017)						
G-MWJI	Solar Wings Pegasus Quasar	SW-WQQ-0341		29. 6.90	L Luscombe	Weston Zoyland	13. 7.08P
	(Trike c/n SW-TQ-0018)						
G-MWJJ	Solar Wings Pegasus Quasar	SW-WQQ-0342		29. 6.90	R Langham	Oxton	31. 7.05P
	(Trike c/n SW-TQ-0019)						
G-MWJK	Solar Wings Pegasus Quasar	SW-WQQ-0343		29. 6.90	M Richardson	(Swansea)	4.11.09P
	(Trike c/n SW-TQ-0020)						

G-MWJN	Solar Wings Pegasus XL-Q	SW-WQ-0344	29. 6.90	J C Corrall Lower Mountpleasant Farm, Chatteris	15. 1.10P
	(Trike c/n SW-TE-0288)				
G-MWJP	Medway Hybred 44XLR	MR097/91	29. 6.90	C D Simmons	(Edenbridge) 12. 5.05P
	(Rotax 503)				
G-MWJR	Medway Hybred 44XLR	MR098/92	28. 6.90	T G Almond	(Bishops Itchington, Southam) 26. 9.08P
	(Rotax 503)				
G-MWJS	Solar Wings Pegasus Quasar TC		6. 7.90	R J Milward	Sywell 14. 3.05P
	(Trike c/n SW-TQ-0021)	SW-WQQ-0349			
G-MWJT	Solar Wings Pegasus Quasar TC		16. 7.90	D L Mitchell	(Manchester) 2. 5.09P
	(Trike c/n SW-TQ-0022)	SW-WQQ-0350			
G-MWJX	Medway Puma Sprint	MS009/3	17. 7.90	K Wales	(Gloucester) 22. 9.05P
	(Rotax 447)				
G-MWKA	Murphy Renegade Spirit UK	PFA 188-11864	26. 7.90	C E Neill tr Downlands Flying Group *"Spirit of Lewes"*	
	(Built Downlands Flying Group and incorporates pr.no.PFA 188-11690)			Kittyhawk Farm, Deanland	8. 4.01P
G-MWKE	Hornet RS-ZA	HRWB-0108 & ZA167	30. 7.90	D R Stapleton	Tarn Farm, Cockerham 28. 5.09P
	(Rotax 532) *(Trike c/n overstamped on HRWB-0107)*				
G-MWKO	Solar Wings Pegasus XL-Q	SW-WQ-0357	31. 7.90	P M Golden	Clench Common 19.10.08P
	(Trike c/n SW-TE-0290)				
G-MWKX	Microflight Spectrum	016	3. 8.90	C R Ions	Eshott 14. 5.04P
G-MWKY	Solar Wings Pegasus XL-Q	SW-WQ-0362	3. 8.90	I D Edwards	Roddige 16.12.07P
	(Trike c/n SW-TE-0292)				
G-MWKZ	Solar Wings Pegasus XL-Q	SW-WQ-0363	3. 8.90	T G Burston and I A Fox-Mills	Hunsdon 22. 7.09P
	(Trike c/n SW-TE-0293)				
G-MWLA	Rans S-4 Coyote	89.114	3. 8.90	J A R Hughes	(Harwich) 29.10.09P
	(Built S H Williams - pr.no.PFA 193-11787)				
G-MWLB	Medway Hybred 44XLR	MR104/93	15. 8.90	M W Harmer	Longacre Farm, Sandy 19. 5.08P
	(Rotax 503)				
G-MWLD	CFM Shadow Series CD	106	9. 5.89	R H Cooke	(Southampton) 10.12.09P
G-MWLE	Solar Wings Pegasus XL-R	SW-WA-1474	9. 8.90	D Stevenson	Plaistows Farm, St Albans 30. 7.06P
	(Trike c/n SW-TB-1425)				
G-MWLF	Solar Wings Pegasus XL-R	SW-WA-1475	9. 8.90	G A McCann	Weston Zoyland 14. 8.09P
	(Trike c/n SW-TB-1426)				
G-MWLG	Solar Wings Pegasus XL-R	SW-WA-1476	9. 8.90	C Cohen	Roddige 10. 6.09P
	(Trike c/n SW-TB-1427)				
G-MWLH	Solar Wings Pegasus Quasar	SW-WQQ-0364	9. 8.90	B Chapman	Hunsdon 3. 8.07P
	(Trike c/n SW-TQ-0030)				
G-MWLJ	Solar Wings Pegasus Quasar	SW-WQQ-0366	9. 8.90	N Khan	(Sutton Coldfield) 21. 9.08P
	(Trike c/n SW-TQ-0032)				
G-MWLK	Solar Wings Pegasus Quasar TC		9. 8.90	D J Shippen	(Newton Bank Farm, Daresbury) 3. 1.06P
	(Trike c/n SW-TQ-0033)	SW-WQQ-0367			
G-MWLL	Solar Wings Pegasus XL-Q	SW-WQ-0338	16. 8.90	J Bacon	Felthorpe 7.10.08P
	(Trike c/n SW-TE-0287)				
G-MWLM	Solar Wings Pegasus XL-Q	SW-WQ-0322	17. 8.90	A A Judge	Hunsdon 28. 6.07P
	(Trike c/n SW-TE-0286)				
G-MWLN	Whittaker MW6-S Fatboy Flyer		16. 8.90	S J Field *"Red Lips"*	(Glastonbury) 5. 6.92P
	(Built S J Field) (Rotax 503)	PFA 164-11844			
G-MWLO	Whittaker MW6 Merlin	PFA 164-11373	21. 8.90	S P Ganecki tr G-MWLO Flying Group	
	(Built G W Peacock) (Rotax 503)			Church Farm, Askern 15.12.09P
G-MWLP	Mainair Gemini Flash	801-0990-5-W594	24. 8.90	C Moultrie and C Poziemski	East Fortune 29. 1.09P
G-MWLS	Medway Hybred 44XLR	MR081/95	29. 8.90	M A Oliver	Glassonby 4. 8.05P
	(Rotax 503)				
G-MWLT	Mainair Gemini Flash IIA	804-0990-7-W597	31. 8.90	S A Sacker *(Noted 2.08)*	
				Black Spring Farm, Castle Bytham	18. 7.03P
G-MWLU	Solar Wings Pegasus XL-R/Se	SW-WA-1478	6. 9.90	T P G Ward *(Stored 9.97)*	(Great Orton) 14.10.91P
	(Rotax 462)	*(Trike c/n SW-TE-0294)*			
G-MWLW	TEAM Mini-MAX	PFA 186-11717	14. 9.90	E J Oteng	(Brierley Hill) 15. 6.09P
	(Built W T Kirk) (Rotax 377)				
G-MWLX	Mainair Gemini Flash IIA	805-0990-7-W598	5.10.90	S D Buchanan	(Edinburgh) 8. 5.09P
G-MWLZ	Rans S-4 Coyote	90.116	8.10.90	B O McCartan *(Noted 7.07)*	
	(Built T E G Buckett - pr.no.PFA 193-11887)			Newry Road, Banbridge	11. 3.05P
G-MWMB	Powerchute Kestrel	00399	7.11.90	C A Hassell Lower Mountpleasant Farm, Chaterris	19. 5.09P
G-MWMC	Powerchute Kestrel	00400	7.11.90	R A Stewart tr Talgarreg Flying Club	(Llandysul) 3.10.05P
G-MWMD	Powerchute Kestrel	00401	7.11.90	D J Jackson	(Melton Constable) 20.11.91P
G-MWMG	Powerchute Kestrel	00404	7.11.90	M D Walton	(Tregaron) 20. 7.06P
G-MWMH	Powerchute Kestrel	00405	7.11.90	E W Potts	(Crymych, Dyfed) 12. 6.04P
G-MWMI	Solar Wings Pegasus Quasar	SW-WQQ-0383	21. 9.90	N J Hopkins	(Loughborough) 5. 9.08P
	(Trike c/n SW-TQ-0043)				
G-MWMJ	Solar Wings Pegasus Quasar	SW-WQQ-0384	21. 9.90	A S Wason	Lower Upham Farm, Chiseldon 1. 7.07P
	(Trike c/n SW-TQ-0044)				
G-MWMK	Solar Wings Pegasus Quasar	SW-WQQ-0385	21. 9.90	T M Frost	(Bristol) 26. 7.09P
	(Trike c/n SW-TQ-0045)				
G-MWML	Solar Wings Pegasus Quasar	SW-WQQ-0386	21. 9.90	S C Key	Deopham Green 18.12.07P
	(Trike c/n SW-TQ-0046)				
G-MWMM	Mainair Gemini Flash IIA	800-0890-7-W593	24. 8.90	R H Church	Croft Farm, Defford 7. 8.08P
	(Rotax 462)				
G-MWMN	Solar Wings Pegasus XL-Q	SW-WQ-0387	2.10.90	N A Rathbone and P A Arnold	Swinford, Rugby 14. 5.08P
	(Trike c/n SW-TE-0297)				
G-MWMO	Solar Wings Pegasus XL-Q	SW-WQ-0388	2.10.90	D S F McNair	(Lochgilphead) 1.12.09P
	(Trike c/n SW-TE-0298)				
G-MWMP	Solar Wings Pegasus XL-Q	SW-WQ-0389	2.10.90	L W Audwell	Trimingham, Norwich 6. 1.10P
	(Trike c/n SW-TE-0299)				
G-MWMR	Solar Wings Pegasus XL-R	SW-WA-1483	2.10.90	M I Stone	(Barnstaple) 13. 3.00P
	(Rotax 462)	*(Trike c/n SW-TE-0300)*			
G-MWMS	Mainair Gemini Flash	807-1090-5-W600	3.10.90	J Swindall	(Stoke-on-Trent) 7. 9.07P

G-MWMT	Mainair Gemini Flash IIA	808-1090-7-W601		3.10.90	R Findlay	Mill Farm, Shifnal	24. 7.08P
G-MWMU	CFM Shadow Series CD	150		2.10.90	C A Gray	Perth	1. 7.09P

(Manufacturer's records show as c/n 142 with c/n 150 sold to Namibia: plate noted 4.06 shows c/n 150CD)

G-MWMV	Solar Wings Pegasus XL-R	SW-WA-1484		5.10.90	G L Brown	Shacklewell Farm, Empingham	8. 4.09P
	(Rotax 462)						
G-MWMW	Murphy Renegade Spirit UK	254		21. 8.89	H Feeney *"Spirit of Cornwall"*		
	(Built M W Hanley -pr.no.PFA 188-11544)					Priory Farm, Tibenham	15. 5.09P
G-MWMX	Mainair Gemini Flash IIA	810-1090-7-W603		17.10.90	P G Hughes	Newtownards	4. 5.09P
	(Rotax 462)						
G-MWMY	Mainair Gemini Flash IIA	809-1090-7-W602		17.10.90	P J Harrison Lower Mountpleasant Farm, Chatteris		11.11.08P
	(Rotax 462)						
G-MWMZ	Solar Wings Pegasus XL-Q	SW-WQ-0393		8.10.90	P M Scrivener	Clench Common	14. 8.08P
	(Trike c/n SW-TE-0301)						
G-MWNA	Solar Wings Pegasus XL-Q	SW-WQ-0394		8.10.90	S N Robson	Eshott	17. 1.07P
	(Trike c/n SW-TE-0302)						
G-MWNB	Solar Wings Pegasus XL-Q	SW-WQ-0395		8.10.90	P F J Rogers	(London SW17)	21. 9.08P
	(Trike c/n SW-TE-0303)						
G-MWNC	Solar Wings Pegasus XL-Q	SW-WQ-0396		8.10.90	R G Wyatt tr G-MWNC Group	(Attleborough)	15. 8.08P
	(Trike c/n SW-TE-0304)						
G-MWND	TLAC RL5A LW Sherwood Ranger	001		9.10.90	D A Pike	Brook Farm, Pilling	13. 6.03P
	(Built D A Pike - pr.no.PFA 237-12229) (Rotax 532)						
G-MWNE	Mainair Gemini Flash IIA	803-1090-7-W596		17.10.90	T C Edwards	(Ware)	4. 5.09P
G-MWNF	Murphy Renegade Spirit UK	PFA 188-11853		15.10.90	D J White	Calton Moor Farm, Ashbourne	21. 9.04P
	(Built D J White) (BMW R100)					*(Noted 7.05)*	
G-MWNG	Solar Wings Pegasus XL-Q	SW -WQ-0399		17.10.90	H C Thomson	(Forfar)	3.11.03P
	(Trike c/n SW-TE-0305)						
G-MWNK	Solar Wings Pegasus Quasar TC						
	(Trike c/n SW-TQA-0054)	SW-WQQ-0403		1.11.90	G S Lyon	RAF Wyton	1. 8.09P
G-MWNL	Solar Wings Pegasus Quasar	SW-WQQ-0404		1.11.90	B J Lyford	Old Sarum	8. 6.08P
	(Trike c/n SW-TQA-0055)						
G-MWNO	AMF Microflight Chevvron 2-32C	025		12.11.90	I K Hogg *(Noted 7.08)*	Kirkbride	30. 4.05P
G-MWNP	AMF Microflight Chevvron 2-32C	026		31.10.90	M K Field	Sleap	13. 7.08P
G-MWNR	Murphy Renegade Spirit UK	PFA 188-11926		12.11.90	J J Lancaster	Davidstow Moor	13. 7.08P
	(Built J J Lancaster)						
G-MWNS	Mainair Gemini Flash IIA	811-1190-7-W604		6.11.90	J G Hilliard	Deenethorpe	31. 8.08P
G-MWNT	Mainair Gemini Flash IIA	812-1190-7-W605		6.11.90	C G Rodger tr November Tango Group		
	(Rotax 582)					Glenrothes	23. 7.09P
G-MWNU	Mainair Gemini Flash IIA	813-1190-5-W606		6.11.90	C C Muir	Doynton	7. 7.08P
G-MWNV	Powerchute Kestrel	00406		12.11.90	K N Byrne	(Homefield, Isle of Colonsay)	13. 3.92P
G-MWNX	Powerchute Kestrel	00408		12.11.90	J H Greenroyd	(Hebden Bridge)	24. 9.02P
G-MWOC	Powerchute Kestrel	00413		12.11.90	D M F Harvey	(Manorbier, Tenby)	28. 9.08P
G-MWOD	Powerchute Kestrel	00414		12.11.90	T Morgan	(Kidderminster)	4.10.00P
G-MWOE	Powerchute Raider	00415		12.11.90	J J Pilsworth	(Melton Mowbray)	21. 1.02P

(Originally registered as Powerchute Kestrel, type amended 27. 6.08)

G-MWOH	Solar Wings Pegasus XL-R/Se	SW-WA-1485		28.11.90	J D Buchanan	Coldharbour Farm, Willingham	7. 6.08P
	(Trike c/n SW-TB-1429)						
G-MWOI	Solar Wings Pegasus XL-R	SW-WA-1486		29.11.90	B T Geoghegan	Roddige	21. 6.07P
	(Trike c/n SW-TB-1430)						
G-MWOJ	Mainair Gemini Flash IIA	814-1290-7-W608		6.12.90	C J Pryce	Ince Blundell	15. 4.07P
G-MWOM	Solar Wings Pegasus Quasar TC			1. 3.91	M S Ahmadu	Sackville Lodge, Riseley	24. 4.09P
	(Trike c/n SW-TQ-0060)	SW-WQQ-0412					
G-MWON	CFM Shadow Series CD	K 128		18.12.90	R E M Gibson-Bevan	Wickenby	14. 7.03P
G-MWOO	Murphy Renegade Spirit UK	318		14. 9.90	R C Wood Lower Mountpleasant Farm, Chatteris		13. 8.07P
	(Built A Hipkin - pr.no.PFA 188-11811)						
G-MWOP	Solar Wings Pegasus Quasar TC			31.12.90	A Baynes	Sywell	23. 8.08P
	(Trike c/n SW-TQC-0059)	SW-WQQ-0410					
G-MWOR	Solar Wings Pegasus XL-Q	SW-WQ-0411		21.12.90	S E Smith	(North Ride, Welwyn)	1. 6.08P
	(Trike c/n SW-TE-0308)						
G-MWOV	Whittaker MW6 Merlin	PFA 164-11301		9. 1.91	L R Hodgson	Glassonby	6.10.09P
	(Built C R Melhuish) (Rotax 503)						
G-MWOY	Solar Wings Pegasus XL-Q	SW-WQ-0414		7. 1.91	S P Griffin	Sutton Meadows	6. 6.09P
	(Trike c/n SW-TE-0310)						
G-MWPB	Mainair Gemini Flash IIA	823-0191-7-W617		3. 1.91	J Fenton	St Michaels	28.10.09P
G-MWPC	Mainair Gemini Flash IIA	826-0191-7-W620		3. 1.91	S J Ware	(Woodford, Stockport)	30. 3.09P
G-MWPD	Mainair Gemini Flash IIA	824-0191-7-W618		9. 1.91	P Gazinski	East Fortune	19. 2.09P
G-MWPE	Solar Wings Pegasus XL-Q	SW-WQ-0416		9. 1.91	E C R Hudson	Upper Stow, Weedon	2. 6.08P
	(Trike c/n SW-TE-0096)					*(Trike ex G-MVGX)*	
G-MWPF	Mainair Gemini Flash IIA	825-0191-7-W619		11. 1.91	G P Taggart	Newtownards	17. 7.09P
G-MWPG	Corbett Farms Spectrum	019		9. 1.91	D Payn tr G-MWPG Group	Eshott	1. 9.08P
G-MWPH	Corbett Farms Spectrum	020		9. 1.91	A Whittaker	(Haverhill)	11. 9.07P
G-MWPJ	Solar Wings Pegasus XL-Q	SW-WQ-0418		17. 1.91	D S Parker	Carlisle	14. 5.03P
	(Trike c/n SW-TE-0312)						
G-MWPK	Solar Wings Pegasus XL-Q	SW-WQ-0419		17. 1.91	W Parker	Strathaven	12. 7.08P
	(Trike c/n SW-TE-0313)						
G-MWPN	CFM Shadow Series CD	K 147		22. 1.91	W R H Thomas	(Llethtryd, Swansea)	11. 6.99P
G-MWPO	Mainair Gemini Flash IIA	827-0191-7-W621		29. 1.91	G A Johnson	(Liverpool)	5. 1.09P
G-MWPP	CFM Streak Shadow M	K 166-SA	G-BTEM	14. 2.91	A J Price	Old Sarum	5. 9.08P
	(Built C A Mortlock - pr.no.PFA 206-11992) (Rotax 582)						
G-MWPR	Whittaker MW6 Merlin	PFA 164-11260		16.10.90	S F N Warnell	(Staines)	
	(Built P J S Ritchie)						
G-MWPS	Murphy Renegade Spirit UK	PFA 188-11931		18. 2.91	M D Stewart	(Husbands Bosworth)	1. 7.98P
	(Built A R Broughton-Tompkins)						
G-MWPW	AMF Microflight Chevvron 2-32C	027		26.11.90	E L T Westman	Broadford, Isle of Skye	26.10.09P

G-MWPX	Solar Wings Pegasus XL-R	SW-WA-1488		27. 2.91	R J Wheeler	Redlands, Swindon	1.10.08P
	(Rotax 462)	*(Trike c/n SW-TE-0315)*					
G-MWPZ	Murphy Renegade Spirit UK	PFA 188-11631		18. 3.91	J Ievers *(Noted 2.04)*	Rhosgoch	24. 2.99P
	(Built J Ievers)						
G-MWRB	Mainair Gemini Flash IIA	819-0191-7-W613		5. 2.91	R Campbell-Moore	Swansea	22. 4.09P
G-MWRC	Mainair Gemini Flash IIA	820-0191-7-W614		5. 2.91	D R Talbot	Chiltern Park, Wallingford	28. 8.08P
G-MWRD	Mainair Gemini Flash IIA	821-0191-7-W615		5. 2.91	A A Leese	(Stoke-on-Trent)	5. 8.08P
G-MWRE	Mainair Gemini Flash IIA	822-0191-7-W616		5. 2.91	A D Dias	Otherton, Cannock	4. 8.09P
G-MWRF	Mainair Gemini Flash IIA	829-0191-7-W623		4. 2.91	N Hay	London Colney	30.10.08P
G-MWRH	Mainair Gemini Flash IIA	831-0191-7-W625		5. 2.91	E G Astin	Eshott	25. 8.08P
G-MWRI	Mainair Gemini Flash IIA	828-0191-7-W622		1. 3.91	J F Booth	(Purton, Swindon)	12.12.99P
G-MWRJ	Mainair Gemini Flash IIA	832-0291-7-W626		28. 2.91	J M Breaks	(Teddington)	26. 3.08P
G-MWRL	CFM Shadow Series CD	K 152		13. 2.91	R A and C A Allen	(Midgham, Reading)	18. 8.01P
G-MWRM	Medway Hybred 44XLR	MR086/94/91/S	G-MWLC	26. 2.91	I R M Scott	East Fortune	7.10.09P
	(Rotax 503)						
G-MWRN	Solar Wings Pegasus XL-R	SW-WA-1489		5. 3.91	D T MacKenzie	Easter Poldar Farm, Thornhill	28. 3.06P
	(Rotax 462)	*(Trike c/n SW-TE-0316)*				*(Noted 8.07)*	
G-MWRP	Solar Wings Pegasus XL-R	SW-WA-1491		1. 3.91	A R Hughes	Redlands, Swindon	2.11.09P
	(Rotax 462)	*(Trike c/n SW-TE-0318)*					
G-MWRR	Mainair Gemini Flash IIA	834-0391-7-W628		7. 3.91	J Clark tr G-MWRR Group	Otherton, Cannock	7. 7.08P
G-MWRS	Ultravia Super Pelican	E001-201		9. 5.84	T B Woolley	(Narborough, Leicester)	9. 9.87P
G-MWRT	Solar Wings Pegasus XL-R	SW-WA-1492		15. 3.91	G L Gunnell	Sywell	10. 9.03P
		(Trike c/n SW-TB-1431)					
G-MWRU	Solar Wings Pegasus XL-R	SW-WA-1493		15. 3.91	A Harding	Weston Zoyland	28. 9.08P
		(Trike c/n SW-TB-1432)					
G-MWRV	Solar Wings Pegasus XL-R	SW-WA-1494		15. 3.91	M S Adams	Roddige	20. 4.05P
		(Trike c/n SW-TB-1433)					
G-MWRW	Solar Wings Pegasus XL-Q	SW-WQ-0431		25. 3.91	L B Hughes	Long Marston	31. 8.07P
		(Trike c/n SW-TE-0320)					
G-MWRX	Solar Wings Pegasus XL-Q	SW-WQ-0432		25. 3.91	W Parkes	Long Marston	17. 9.04P
		(Trike c/n SW-TE-0321)					
G-MWRY	CFM Shadow Series CD	K 162		26. 3.91	A T Armstrong	Davidstow Moor	6. 7.08P
G-MWRZ	AMF Microflight Chevvron 2-32C	028		10. 4.91	H R Bethune	(Bride, IoM)	12. 7.09P
G-MWSA	TEAM Mini-MAX 88	PFA 186-11855		8. 4.91	G J Jones	(Abington, Cambridge)	15. 4.07P
	(Built A N Baumber) (Rotax 377)						
G-MWSB	Mainair Gemini Flash IIA	837-0591-7-W631		30. 4.91	P J Bosworth	Hill Farm, Hughley, Shrewsbury	15. 8.06P
	(Rotax 582)						
G-MWSC	Rans S-6-ESD Coyote II	0191.152		13. 5.91	C J Meadows	Weston Zoyland	8. 9.09P
	(Built B E Francis - pr.no.PFA 204-12019) (Rotax 503) *(Tri-cycle u/c)*						
G-MWSD	Solar Wings Pegasus XL-Q	SW-WQ-0430		6. 3.91	A M Harley	Sutton Meadows	15. 7.09P
		(Trike c/n SW-TE-0319)					
G-MWSE	Solar Wings Pegasus XL-R	SW-WA-1496		10. 4.91	Ultra Light Training Ltd	Roddige	11. 3.07P
	(Rotax 462)	*(Trike c/n SW-TE-0323 -fitted with Trike from G-MTJR)*					
G-MWSF	Solar Wings Pegasus XL-R	SW-WA-1497		10. 4.91	N A and F W Milne (Chedburgh, Bury St Edmunds)		13. 7.08P
	(Rotax 462)	*(Trike c/n SW-TE-0324)*					
G-MWSI	Solar Wings Pegasus Quasar TCSW-WQ-0436			23. 5.91	J J C Parrish	Sywell	30. 1.10P
		(Trike c/n SW-TQC-0065)					
G-MWSJ	Solar Wings Pegasus XL-Q	SW-WQ-0437		12. 4.91	R J Collison	Little Snoring	7. 5.08P
		(Trike c/n SW-TE-0326)					
G-MWSK	Solar Wings Pegasus XL-Q	SW-WQ-0438		12. 4.91	J Doogan	(Galashiels)	26. 5.02P
		(Trike c/n SW-TE-0327)					
G-MWSL	Mainair Gemini Flash IIA	835-0491-7-W629		16. 4.91	C W Frost	(Rufforth)	11. 6.98P
G-MWSM	Mainair Gemini Flash IIA	836-0491-7-W630		16. 4.91	R M Wall	(Longacre Farm, Sandy)	19. 4.09P
G-MWSO	Solar Wings Pegasus XL-R	SW-WA-1503		25. 4.91	M A Clayton	(New Romney)	17.11.07P
	(Rotax 462)	*(Trike c/n SW-TE-0329)*					
G-MWSP	Solar Wings Pegasus XL-R	SW-WA-1504		25. 4.91	R Wilkinson *(Noted 10.06)*	Headon Farm, Retford	22. 5.06P
	(Rotax 462)	*(Trike c/n SW-TE-0330)*					
G-MWSR	Solar Wings Pegasus XL-R	SW-WA-1505		25. 4.91	G P J Davies	Broadmeadow Farm. Hereford	10. 9.08P
	(Rotax 462)	*(Trike c/n SW-TE-0331)*					
G-MWSS	Medway Hybred 44XLR	MR117/97		7. 5.91	C D Hannam and J W Taylor		
	(Rotax 503)					Over Farm, Gloucster	20. 9.03P
G-MWST	Medway Hybred 44XLR	MR118/98		8. 5.91	A Ferguson *(Noted 8.07)*	Broadford, Isle of Skye	3. 8.05P
	(Rotax 503)						
G-MWSU	Medway Hybred 44XLR	MR119/99		1. 5.92	T de Landro	Stoke, Isle of Grain	6. 10.07P
	(Rotax 503)						
G-MWSW	Whittaker MW6 Merlin	PFA 164-11328		15. 2.91	S N F Warnell	(Staines)	
	(Built S N F Warnell)						
G-MWSX	Whittaker MW5 Sorcerer	PFA 163-11549		3. 5.91	D R Drewett	Davidstow Moor	24. 4.08P
	(Built A T Armstrong)						
G-MWSY	Whittaker MW5 Sorcerer	PFA 163-11218		3. 5.91	J E Holloway *(Noted 7.05)*	Davidstow Moor	21.12.04P
	(Built J E Holloway)						
G-MWSZ	CFM Shadow Series CD	K 158	(G-MWRY)	4. 4.91	D R Drewett and P A Da Silva Turner		
					(Clapham, Worthing and Swanmore,Southampton)		26.11.09P
G-MWTB	Solar Wings Pegasus XL-Q	SW-WQ-0445		8. 5.91	G S Highley	(Corby)	17. 9.04P
		(Trike c/n SW-TE-0333)					
G-MWTC	Solar Wings Pegasus XL-Q	SW-WQ-0446		8. 5.91	M M Chittenden	Lower Road, Hockley	14. 5.09P
		(Trike c/n SW-TE-0334)				*(Operated from Rochester)*	
G-MWTD	Corbett Farms Spectrum	022		13. 5.91	J V Harris *(Noted 10.05)*	Sywell	18. 4.00P
G-MWTE	Corbett Farms Spectrum	023		13. 5.91	T H Evans	(Ammanford)	20. 6.04P
G-MWTG	Mainair Gemini Flash IIA	838-0591-7-W632		16. 5.91	M R Smith	(Oldbury)	27.10.08P
	(Rotax 582)				*(Engine failed after take-off at Otherton 30. 4.08 and collided*		
	with a boundary fence in ensuing forced landing; aircraft extensively damaged and believed beyond economic repair)						
G-MWTH	Mainair Gemini Flash IIA	839-0591-7-W633		21. 5.91	A Strang	East Fortune	1. 8.06P

G-MWTI	Solar Wings Pegasus XL-Q	SW-WQ-0274		23. 5.91	O G Johns	Field Farm, Oakley	31. 5.09P
	(Trike c/n SW-TE-0251)						
G-MWTJ	CFM Shadow Series CD	K 167		16. 5.91	T D Wolstenholme	Brook Farm, Pilling	16. 5.09P
G-MWTL	Solar Wings Pegasus XL-R	SW-WA-1508		28. 5.91	B Lindsay	(Chipping Sodbury)	13. 7.07P
	(Rotax 462)	*(Trike c/n SW-TE-0336)*					
G-MWTN	CFM Shadow Series CD	K 153		23. 5.91	M J Broom	Buttermilk Farm, Bliswell	3. 7.08P
G-MWTO	Mainair Gemini Flash IIA	840-0591-7-W634		28. 5.91	J Greenhalgh	St Michaels	22. 6.09P
G-MWTP	CFM Shadow Series CD	K 107		23. 5.91	R E M Gibson-Bevan	Wickenby	17. 7.09P
G-MWTR	Mainair Gemini Flash IIA	842-0591-7-W636		31. 5.91	M Morris	Hunsdon	10. 2.09P
	(Rotax 582)						
G-MWTT	Rans S-6-ESD Coyote II	0391.175		30. 4.91	L E Duffin *"Warrior 2"*	Insch	28 11.07P
	(Built I K Radcliffe - pr.no.PFA 204-12016) (Tri-cycle u/c)						
G-MWTU	Solar Wings Pegasus XL-Q	SW-WA-1501		21. 6.91	S Woods	(Banagher, County Offaly)	2. 9.01P
	(Trike c/n SW-TB-1435)						
G-MWTY	Mainair Gemini Flash IIA	843-0691-7-W637		12. 6.91	A McGing and J C Townsend *(Noted 8.05)*		
						Ince Blundell	28. 4.04P
G-MWTZ	Mainair Gemini Flash IIA	844-0691-7-W638		12. 6.91	C W R Felce	Riseley Lodge Farm, Bedford	14. 9.07P
G-MWUA	CFM Shadow Series CD	K 161		10. 6.91	P A James tr Cloudbase Aviation G-MWUA	Redhill	21. 6.05P
G-MWUB	Solar Wings Pegasus XL-R	SW-WA-1510		12. 6.91	T R L Bayley	(Edenbridge)	27. 8.08P
	(Rotax 462)	*(Trike c/n SW-TE-0338)*					
G-MWUC	Solar Wings Pegasus XL-R	SW-WA-1511		12. 6.91	M A Hicks	Wickenby	27. 6.05P
	(Rotax 462)	*(Trike c/n SW-TE-0339)*					
G-MWUD	Solar Wings Pegasus XL Tug	SW-WA-1512		12. 6.91	M J Taggart	Clench Common	17. 5.05P
	(Rotax 462)	*(Trike c/n SW-TE-0340)*					
G-MWUH	Murphy Renegade Spirit UK	343		12. 6.91	A I Grant	Washington, Sussex	18. 6.04P
	(Built A I Grant)						
G-MWUI	AMF Microflight Chevvron 2-32C	029		2. 7.91	N D A Graham	North Connel, Oban	12. 4.09P
G-MWUK	Rans S-6-ESD Coyote II	0491.187		1. 7.91	G K Hoult and S J C Pollock	Long Marston	7. 5.09P
	(Built G K Hoult - pr.no.PFA 204-12090) (Jabiru 2200) (Tri-cycle u/c)						
G-MWUL	Rans S-6-ESD Coyote II	0391.172		10. 6.91	K W Payne	(Ashford)	22. 9.09P
	(Built K J Lywood - pr.no.PFA 204-12054) (Rotax 503) (Tri-cycle u/c)						
G-MWUN	Rans S-6-ESD Coyote II	0391-173		10. 6.91	J Parke	Letterkenny, Ireland	15. 5.09P
	(Built S Eland - pr.no.PFA 204-12075) (Rebuilt with kit no.0695.841 (ex G-IZIT) c 1994) (Rotax 503) (Tri-cycle u/c)						
G-MWUO	Solar Wings Pegasus XL-Q	SW-WQ-0379	(ZS-...?)	26. 6.91	A P Slade	Field Farm, Oakley	18. 5.06P
	(Trike c/n SW-TE-0296)						
G-MWUR	Solar Wings Pegasus XL Tug	SW-WA-1518		21. 6.91	A W Buchan tr Nottingham Aerotow Club		
	(Rotax 462)	*(Trike c/n SW-TE-0342)*	*(Officially regd as "XL-R")*			Knapthorpe Lodge, Caunton	19. 8.09P
G-MWUS	Solar Wings Pegasus XL-R	SW-WA-1519		21. 6.91	H R Loxton	Weston Zoyland	29. 8.00P
	(Rotax 462)	*(Trike c/n SW-TE-0343)*					
G-MWUU	Solar Wings Pegasus XL-R	SW-WA-1521		28. 6.91	B R Underwood	Swinford, Rugby	13. 4.09P
	(Rotax 462)	*(Trike c/n SW-TE-0346)*					
G-MWUV	Solar Wings Pegasus XL-R	SW-WA-1522		28. 6.91	C D Baines	Arclid Green, Sandbach	2. 2.07P
	(Rotax 462)	*(Trike c/n SW-TE-0347)*					
G-MWUX	Solar Wings Pegasus XL-Q	SW-WQ-0454		28. 6.91	B D Attwell	Upfield Farm,Whitson	12. 6.08P
	(Originally supplied as a Sailwing only - Trike origin unknown)						
G-MWUY	Solar Wings Pegasus XL-Q	SW-WQ-0455		28. 6.91	M J Sharp	(Kilmarnock)	11. 1.04P
	(Trike c/n SW-TE-0345)						
G-MWUZ	Solar Wings Pegasus XL-Q	SW-WQ-0456		28. 6.91	S R Nanson	(Sittingbourne)	7. 6.06P
	(Trike c/n SW-TE-0350)						
G-MWVA	Solar Wings Pegasus XL-Q	SW-WQ-0457		28. 6.91	G Charles-Jones	Eshott	14. 4.08P
	(Trike c/n SW-TE-0351)						
G-MWVE	Solar Wings Pegasus XL-R	SW-WA-1524		18. 7.91	W A Keel-Stocker	Long Marston	7. 6.07P
	(Trike c/n SW-TB-1441)						
G-MWVF	Solar Wings Pegasus XL-R/Se	SW-WA-1525		18. 7.91	J B Wright	Roddige	8.11.07P
	(Trike c/n SW-TB-1442)						
G-MWVG	CFM Shadow Series CD	151		5. 8.91	Shadow Aviation Ltd	Old Sarum	16.10.08P
G-MWVH	CFM Shadow Series CD	181		5. 8.91	M McKenzie	Insch	25. 8.07P
G-MWVK	Mainair Mercury	849-0891-5-W643		13. 8.91	S B Walters	Swinford, Rugby	31. 7.09P
G-MWVL	Rans S-6 ESD Coyote II	0491-186		13. 8.91	A, A, J T andO D Lewis	Rufforth	25. 7.08P
	(Built J D Hall - pr.no.PFA 204-12118) (Tri-cycle u/c) (Damaged and repaired with frame.no.0892.341: original frame now fitted to G-MZAH)						
G-MWVM	Solar Wings Pegasus Quasar IITC			2. 9.91	J D Jones and A A Edmonds	Mill Farm, Shifnal	2. 6.08P
	(Trike c/n SW-TQ-0031)	SW-WX-0020	G-65-8		*(Trike c/n duplicates G-MWLI)*		
G-MWVN	Mainair Gemini Flash IIA	850-0891-7-W644		19. 8.91	J McCafferty	Rochdale	7. 3.09P
G-MWVO	Mainair Gemini Flash IIA	852-0891-7-W646		27. 8.91	P Webb	Redlands, Swindon	25. 7.05P
	(Rotax 582)						
G-MWVP	Murphy Renegade Spirit UK	345		22. 8.91	P D Mickleburgh	Swinford, Rugby	8.12.09P
	(Built I E Spencer - pr.no.PFA 188-11735)						
G-MWVR	Mainair Gemini Flash IIA	855-0991-7-W650		30. 8.91	G Cartwright	Milnathort	2. 5.09P
G-MWVS	Mainair Gemini Flash IIA	856-0991-7-W651		30. 8.91	S J J Griffiths *(Noted 11.07)*	Ash Farm, Winsford	15. 9.06P
G-MWVT	Mainair Gemini Flash IIA	860-1091-7-W655		2. 9.91	R M Wigman	Mapperley, Nottingham	7. 7.09P
G-MWVY	Mainair Gemini Flash IIA	854-0991-7-W649		4. 9.91	A Mundy	(Benfleet)	19. 5.08P
G-MWVZ	Mainair Gemini Flash IIA	863-1091-7-W658		4. 9.91	S N Pryor	(Leicester)	21. 7.09P
G-MWWB	Mainair Gemini Flash IIA	864-1091-7-W659		18. 9.91	W P Seward	(Chirk, Wrexham)	3.11.09P
G-MWWC	Mainair Gemini Flash IIA	868-1191-7-W663		23. 9.91	A and D Margereson	(Chesterfield)	30. 7.04P
	(Rotax 582)						
G-MWWD	Murphy Renegade Spirit UK	344		23. 9.91	J and A Oswald	Eshott	20.11.09P
	(Built A M Smyth and J M Walter - pr.no.PFA 188-11719)						
G-MWWE	TEAM Mini-MAX 88	PFA 186-11925		1.10.91	J Entwistle	Tarn Farm, Cockerham	23. 7.97P
	(Built J C Longmore)				*(Fuselage only 7.07: wings noted 11.06 at Eccleston, Chorley)*		
G-MWWG	Solar Wings Pegasus XL-Q	SW-WQ-0468		3.10.91	A W Guerri tr Form A Q	Rufforth	26. 1.09P
	(Trike c/n SW-TE-0355)						
G-MWWH	Solar Wings Pegasus XL-Q	SW-WQ-0469		3.10.91	A J Alexander	Watnall	5. 9.08P
	(Trike c/n SW-TE-0356)						
G-MWWI	Mainair Gemini Flash IIA	870-1291-7-W665		11.10.91	M A S Nesbitt	Strathaven	20. 5.09P

G-MWWJ	Mainair Gemini Flash IIA	865-1191-7-W660		22.10.91	I M Ferdinand and A F Glover		
					(Javea, Alicante, Spain and Woolston, Warrington)		17. 2.09P
G-MWWK	Mainair Gemini Flash IIA	866-1191-7-W661		22.10.91	J C Boyd tr JDS Group	Davidstow Moor	31. 7.09P
	(Rotax 582)						
G-MWWN	Mainair Gemini Flash IIA	872-1291-7-W667		22.10.91	F Watts	(Bournemouth)	27. 6.05P
G-MWWP	Rans S-4 Coyote	90.115		21.10.91	R P Cross	(Welton, Lincoln)	1. 8.00P
	(Built R H Braihtwaite - pr.no.PFA 193-12073)						
G-MWWR	Corbett Farms Spectrum	024		23.10.91	K A Wright	North Coates	6. 6.08P
G-MWWS	Thruster T 300	089-T300-370	EI-BYW	4.11.91	S P McCaffrey	Dunkeswell	2. 6.05P
	(Built Tempest Aviation Ltd) (Rotax 532)						
G-MWWT	Thruster T300	9012-ST300-503		25.10.91	R M Wigman	(Wantage)	
G-MWWV	Solar Wings Pegasus XL-Q	SW-WQ-0470		30.10.91	R W Livingstone	Enniskillen	7. 8.08P
	(Trike c/n SW-TE-0357)						
G-MWWZ	Cyclone Airsports Chaser S 447	CH.829		29.10.91	J F Willoughby	Shotton Colliery, Peterlee	4. 4.04P
G-MWXA	Mainair Gemini Flash IIA	873-0192-7-W668		30.10.91	M Briongo	Strathaven	29.11.09P
G-MWXB	Mainair Gemini Flash IIA	869-1191-7-W664		6.11.91	N W Barnett	Sittles Farm, Alrewas	3. 1.04P
G-MWXC	Mainair Gemini Flash IIA	874-0192-7-W669		6.11.91	N J Lindsay	Strathaven	4. 8.08P
G-MWXF	Mainair Mercury	867-1191-5-W662		12.11.91	P E Jackson	(Ruthin)	20. 4.07P
G-MWXG	Solar Wings Pegasus Quasar IITC			7.11.91	J E Moseley	Sutton Meadows	16. 9.08P
	(Trike c/n SW-TQC-0074)	SW-WQT-0471					
G-MWXH	Solar Wings Pegasus Quasar IITC			7.11.91	R P Wilkinson	Charmy Down, Bath	10. 6.06P
	(Trike c/n SW-TQC-0075)	SW-WQT-0472					
G-MWXJ	Mainair Mercury	861-1091-5-W656		15.11.91	P J Taylor	Sandtoft	31. 3.06P
G-MWXK	Mainair Mercury	862-1191-5-W657		15.11.91	M P Wilkinson	(Sandtoft)	18. 7.96P
G-MWXL	Mainair Gemini Flash IIA	859-1091-7-W654		12.12.91	S M Redding	(Ketton, Stamfod)	27. 9.08P
	(Rotax 582)						
G-MWXP	Solar Wings Pegasus XL-Q	SW-WQ-0475		26.11.91	A P Attfield	(Sutton Meadows)	18. 8.99P
	(Trike c/n SW-TE-0359)						
G-MWXR	Solar Wings Pegasus XL-Q	SW-WQ-0476		26.11.91	G W Craig	(Huntley, Aberdeen)	13. 4.08P
	(Trike c/n SW-TE-0360)						
G-MWXU	Mainair Gemini Flash IIA	882-0192-7-W677		9.12.91	C M Mackinnon (Noted dismantled 8.07)		
	(Rotax 582)					Strathaven	23. 1.03P
G-MWXV	Mainair Gemini Flash IIA	879-1291-7-W674		9.12.91	J Stones (Noted 9.07)	Eshott	3. 6.07P
	(Rotax 582)						
G-MWXW	Cyclone Airsports Chaser S	CH.830		9.12.91	K C Dodd	Roddige	7. 6.07P
	(Rotax 377)						
G-MWXX	Cyclone Airsports Chaser S 447	CH.831	(G-MWEB)	9.12.91	P I Frost	(Guilsborough, Northampton)	21. 7.05P
			(G-MWCD)				
G-MWXY	Cyclone Airsports Chaser S 447	CH.832	(G-MWEC)	19.12.91	B L Dobbs	(Dunstable)	16. 8 04P
G-MWXZ	Cyclone Airsports Chaser S 508	CH.836		31.12.91	D L Hadley	(Petham, Canterbury)	4. 6.09P
G-MWYA	Mainair Gemini Flash IIA	886-0292-7-W681		3. 1.92	R F Hunt	St Michaels	11.12.09P
	(Rotax 462)						
G-MWYB	Solar Wings Pegasus XL-Q	SW-WQ-0485		15. 1.92	A D Fowler	(Wroughton, Swindon)	7. 6.08P
	(Trike c/n SW-TE-0364)						
G-MWYC	Solar Wings Pegasus XL-Q	SW-WQ-0486		15. 1.92	M A Collins	Longacre Farm, Sandy	11. 4.07P
	(Trike c/n SW-TE-0365)						
G-MWYD	CFM Shadow Series C	K 179		8. 1.92	D W Hermiston-Hooper	Sandown	8. 8.08P
G-MWYE	Rans S-6-ESD Coyote II	0591.189		10. 1.92	G A M Moffat	(Nantwich)	11. 4.09P
	(Built G A Squires - pr.no.PFA 204-12223) (Tri-cycle u/c)						
G-MWYG	Mainair Gemini Flash IIA	884-0292-7-W679		15. 1.92	R D Saulters	Newtownards	13. 4.08P
	(Rotax 582)						
G-MWYH	Mainair Gemini Flash IIA	887-0292-7-W682		15. 1.92	R Haslam	(Ilkeston)	18.11.09P
G-MWYI	Solar Wings Pegasus Quasar IITC			30. 1.92	T S Chadfield	Graveley Hall Farm, Graveley	24.10.09P
	(Trike c/n SW-TQC-0083)	SW-WQT-0488					
G-MWYJ	Solar Wings Pegasus Quasar IITC			24. 1.92	J W Edwards	Pound Green, Buttonoak, Bewdley	19. 5.09P
	(Trike c/n SW-TQC-0084)	SW-WQT-0489					
G-MWYL	Mainair Gemini Flash IIA	877-0192-7-W672		17. 1.92	A J Hinks	East Fortune	4. 7.09P
G-MWYM	Cyclone Airsports Chaser S 1000	CH.838		21. 1.92	C J Meadows	(Shepton Mallet)	3.11.07P
	(Mosler MM-CB35) (Reported as rebuild of G-MVJI - perhaps Trike only?)						
G-MWYS	CGS Arrow Flight Hawk I Arrow H-T-470-R447			17. 2.93	D W Hermiston-Hooper tr Civilair		
	(Built Arrowflight Ltd - pr.no.BMAA HB/020) (Rotax 447)					(Ryde, Isle of Wight)	
G-MWYT	Mainair Gemini Flash IIA	881-0392-7-W676		3. 2.92	M A Hodgson	Baxby Manor, Husthwaite	24. 9.08P
G-MWYU	Solar Wings Pegasus XL-Q	SW-WQ-0491		30. 1.92	G D Barrell	(Romford)	28.10.09P
	(Trike c/n SW-TE-0364)						
G-MWYV	Mainair Gemini Flash IIA	896-0392-7-W691		3. 2.92	J N Whitworth	Oxton	10. 9.04P
	(Rotax 582)						
G-MWYY	Solar Wings Pegasus XL-Q	SW-WQ-0492		17. 2.92	R D Allard	Deenethorpe	7. 3.08P
	(Trike c/n SW-TE-0365)						
G-MWYZ	Solar Wings Pegasus XL-Q	SW-WQ-0474		20.11.91	A Boston (Noted 10.07)	Sywell	22. 6.07P
	(Trike c/n SW-TE-0358)						
G-MWZA	Mainair Mercury	888-0292-5-W683		7. 2.92	A J Malham	Rufforth	12. 3.09P
G-MWZC	Mainair Gemini Flash IIA	899-0492-7-W694		7. 2.92	R B Huyshe	Otherton, Cannock	22. 6.09P
G-MWZD	Solar Wings Pegasus Quasar IITC			2. 3.92	A R Walker	(Askern, Doncaster)	16. 5.09P
	(Trike c/n SW-TQC-0086)	SW-WQT-0494					
G-MWZE	Solar Wings Pegasus Quasar IITC			17. 2.92	H Lorimer (Noted 8.05)	Hunterston Farm, Stair	18. 7.01P
	(Trike c/n SW-TQC-0087)	SW-WQT-0495					
G-MWZF	Solar Wings Pegasus Quasar IITC			17. 2.92	R G T Corney	Clench Common	12. 7.07P
	(Rotax 582)	SW-WQT-0496		(Trike c/n SW-TQD-0108 but duplicates G-MYEK)			
G-MWZG	Mainair Gemini Flash IIA	889-0392-7-W684		7. 2.92	C J O'Sullivan	Newtownards	26. 2.07P
	(Rotax 582)						
G-MWZI	Solar Wings Pegasus XL-R	SW-WA-1533		17. 2.92	K J Slater	Roddige	4.11.07P
	(Rotax 462)	(Trike c/n SW-TE-0367)					
G-MWZJ	Solar Wings Pegasus XL-R/Se	SW-WA-1534		17. 2.92	P Kitchen (Noted 2.08)	Shotton Colliery, Peterlee	30. 8.05P
	(Rotax 462)	(Trike c/n SW-TE-0368)					

Reg	Type	c/n	Prev id	Date	Owner	Location	Expiry
G-MWZL	Mainair Gemini Flash IIA (Rotax 582)	900-0492-7-W695		17. 2.92	D Renton	East Fortune	5. 7.04P
G-MWZM	TEAM Mini-MAX 91 (Built M A J Hutt) (Mosler MM CB-40)	PFA 186-12211	G-BUDD G-MWZM	18. 2.92	C Leighton-Thomas *"My Buddy"* (Noted 1.05)	Charmy Down, Bath	29. 7.02P
G-MWZN	Mainair Gemini Flash IIA (Rotax 582)	902-0492-7-W697		25. 2.92	D F Greatbanks	(Lymm)	3. 8.07P
G-MWZO	Solar Wings Pegasus Quasar IITC (Trike c/n SW-TQC-0089)	SW-WQT-0498		26. 2.92	A Robinson	(Ashbourne)	27. 3.06P
G-MWZP	Solar Wings Pegasus Quasar IITC (Trike c/n SW-TQC-0090)	SW-WQT-0499		26. 2.92	M B Sears	(Mansfield)	17. 9.08P
G-MWZR	Solar Wings Pegasus Quasar IITC (Trike c/n SW-TQC-0091)	SW-WQT-0500		26. 2.92	R Veart	Haverfordwest	11. 6.08P
G-MWZS	Solar Wings Pegasus Quasar IITC (Trike c/n SW-TQC-0092)	SW-WQT-0501	EI-CIP G-MWZS	26. 2.92	G Bennett	Great Oakley	9. 4.08P
G-MWZT	Solar Wings Pegasus XL-R (Rotax 462) (Trike c/n SW-TE-0370)	SW-WA-1535		26. 2.92	P J Fahie	Deptford Farm, Wylye	16. 9.07P
G-MWZU	Solar Wings Pegasus XL-R (Rotax 462) (Trike c/n SW-TE-0371)	SW-WA-1536		26. 2.92	A D Winebloom	Roddige	8. 6.09P
G-MWZV	Solar Wings Pegasus XL-R (Rotax 462) (Trike c/n SW-TE-0372)	SW-WA-1537		26. 2.92	D J Newby	Clench Common	3.11.08P
G-MWZW	Solar Wings Pegasus XL-R (Rotax 462) (Trike c/n SW-TE-0373)	SW-WA-1538		26. 2.92	S N Pryor (Sailwing from cancelled G-MNHB { SW-TE-1045} transferred C 2006) (Trike stored 4.08)	Landmead Farm, Garford	14. 6.07P
G-MWZY	Solar Wings Pegasus XL-R (Rotax 462) (Trike c/n SW-TE-0375)	SW-WA-1540		26. 2.92	S J Barkworth	Rufforth	10. 9.06P
G-MWZZ	Solar Wings Pegasus XL-R (Rotax 503) (Trike c/n SW-TE-0376)	SW-WA-1541		26. 2.92	The Microlight School (Lichfield) Ltd	Roddige	8. 3.09P
G-MXMX	Piper PA-46R-350T Malibu Matrix	4692088	N61002	17.12.08	GEFA Gesellschaft fur Absatzfinanzierung mit Beschrankter Haftung	(Wuppertal, Germany)	
G-MXPH	British Aircraft Corporation 167 Strikemaster Mk.84	EEP/JP/1931	G-SARK, N2146S, Singapore AF 311, G-27-140	4. 5.07	R S Partridge-Hicks (As *"311"* in Singapore AF c/s)	North Weald	13. 8.09P
G-MXVI	Vickers Supermarine 361 Spitfire LF.XVIe	6850M CBAF.IX.4394	TE184	17. 2.89	P M Andrews tr The G2 Trust (Noted 10.08)	Wycombe Air Park	30. 5.02P
G-MYAB	Solar Wings Pegasus XL-R/Se (Rotax 462) (Trike c/n SW-TE-0377)	SW-WA-1542		26. 2.92	A N F Stewart	Long Marston	9. 5.07P
G-MYAC	Solar Wings Pegasus XL-Q (Trike c/n SW-TE-0378)	SW-WQ-0502		26. 2.92	M A Garner	(Saham Toney, Thetford)	24. 7.06P
G-MYAE	Solar Wings Pegasus XL-Q (Trike c/n SW-TE-0380)	SW-WQ-0504		26. 2.92	G P Church	Redlands, Swindon	11. 8.09P
G-MYAF	Solar Wings Pegasus XL-Q (Trike c/n SW-TE-0381)	SW-WQ-0505		26. 2.92	S P Kyle	(Wantage)	6. 1.10P
G-MYAG	Quad City Challenger II (Built F Payne)	PFA 177-12167		25. 2.92	R Shewan	Longside, Peterhead	12. 8.09P
G-MYAH	Whittaker MW5 Sorcerer (Built T Knight)	PFA 163-11233		2. 3.92	V T Betts	Otherton, Cannock	3. 5.08P
G-MYAI	Mainair Mercury	892-0392-5-W687		11. 3.92	J Ellerton	(Hazel Grove, Stockport)	6. 5.03P
G-MYAJ	Rans S-6-ESD Coyote II (Built N J Willmott - pr.no.PFA 204-12227) (Tail-wheel u/c)	1291.248		3. 3.92	R M Moulton	Weston Zoyland	27.11.09P
G-MYAK	Solar Wings Pegasus Quasar IITC (Trike c/n SW-TQC-0093)	SW-WQT-0506	D-M . . .? G-MYAK	5. 3.92	I E Brunning (Noted 8.05)	Ince Blundell	1. 9.03P
G-MYAM	Murphy Renegade Spirit UK (Built S R Groves)	PFA 188-11907		6. 3.92	A F Reid	(Ebrington, Chipping Camden)	14. 9.01P
G-MYAN	Whittaker MW5-K Sorcerer (Built Aerotech International Ltd) (Full Lotus floats)	5K-0017-02	(G-MWNI)	24. 3.92	J Hollings	Comber, County Down	1. 7.03P
G-MYAO	Mainair Gemini Flash IIA	894-0392-7-W689		11. 3.92	J H Livingstone	(Dalmeny, South Queensferry)	9. 8.09P
G-MYAR	Thruster T 300 (Built Tempest Aviation Ltd) (Rotax 503)	9022-T300-502		12. 3.92	G Hawkins	Newton Peverill Farm, Sturminster Marshall	2. 9.07P
G-MYAS	Mainair Gemini Flash IIA	895-0392-7-W690		11. 3.92	J R Davis	(Hawling, Cheltenham)	12. 6.04P
G-MYAT	TEAM Mini-MAX 88 (Built D M Couling)	PFA 186-12017		6. 3.92	T R Janaway (Forced landed 1 mile E of Ditchling Beacon 16. 6.07 with substantial damage)	(Witney)	13. 6.07P
G-MYAU	Mainair Gemini Flash IIA (Rotax 462)	890-0392-7-W685		25. 3.92	P P Allen	(Ely)	20. 6.07P
G-MYAY	Corbett Farms Spectrum	027		13. 3.92	P F Craggs (Noted 7.06)	Eshott	21.12.00P
G-MYAZ	Murphy Renegade Spirit UK (Built R Smith)	PFA 188-12027		16. 3.92	R Smith	Kilkerran	10.10.03P
G-MYBA	Rans S-6-ESD Coyote II (Built S M Vickers - pr.no.PFA 204-12210) (Tail-wheel u/c) (Now marked "1291.247.0800" and believed to be a re-date following rebuild of frame 800 - not a new one) (Stalled and crashed soon after take-off at Chilbolton 10. 5.08, extensive damage and landing gear detached, on rebuild with bigger engine)	1291.247		12. 3.92	A M Hughes	Fenland	24.10.08P
G-MYBB	Maxair Drifter (Built M Ingleton - pr.no.BMAA HB/014) (Rotax 503) (Initially imported by Medway Microlights: on rebuild 9.05 as "UK Drifter": noted 12.05)	MD.001		10. 4.92	M Ingleton	Stoke, Isle of Grain	12. 6.92P
G-MYBC	CFM Shadow Series CD (Built CFM Metal-Fax - originally pr.no.PFA 206-12221 which denotes type as Streak Shadow: now shown officially as pr.no.BMAA HB/047)	K 195		18. 3.92	M E Gilbert	Drummaird Farm, Bonnybank	20. 9.08P
G-MYBE	Solar Wings Pegasus Quasar IITCSW-WQT-0512 (Trike c/n SW-TQC-0095)			26. 3.92	N A Cook	Tarn Farm, Cockerham	23. 7.08P
G-MYBF	Solar Wings Pegasus XL-Q (Trike c/n SW-TE-0384)	SW-WQ-0513		26. 3.92	K H Pead	(Ipswich)	25. 4.08P
G-MYBI	Rans S-6-ESD Coyote II (Built G A Archer and J A Soilleux - pr.no.PFA 204-12186) (Rotax 503) (Tri-cycle u/c)	1291.249		26. 3.92	N C Tambiah	Otherton, Cannock	1 2.08P
G-MYBJ	Mainair Gemini Flash IIA (Rotax 462)	908-0593-7-W706		2. 4.92	G C Bowers	Shipmeadow, Beccles	20. 5.08P
G-MYBL	CFM Shadow Series CD	K 194		2. 4.92	R G Hicks	(Penarth)	24.11.09P
G-MYBM	TEAM Mini-MAX 91 (Built M K Dring) (Mosler MM CB-35)	PFA 186-12212		3. 4.92	B Hunter	Brook Farm, Piling	15. 8.08P

G-MYBN	Hiway Skytrike II/Demon 175	BRL-01		14. 4.92	B R Lamming	(Seaton, Hull)	
G-MYBO	Solar Wings Pegasus XL-R	SW-WA-1545		16. 4.92	D Gledhill	(London SW19)	1.11.08P
	(Trike c/n SW-TB-1445)						
G-MYBP	Solar Wings Pegasus XL-R/Se	SW-WA-1546		16. 4.92	S H Williams	(Kidderminster)	2. 8.03P
	(Trike c/n SW-TB-1446)						
G-MYBS	Solar Wings Pegasus XL-Q	SW-WQ-0518		16. 4.92	T Smith	Rochester	9. 7.08P
	(Trike c/n SW-TE-0387)						
G-MYBT	Solar Wings Pegasus Quasar IITC			16. 4.92	G A Rainbow-Ockwell	Redlands, Swindon	26. 4.09P
	(Trike c/n SW-TQC-0097)	SW-WQT-0519					
G-MYBU	Cyclone Airsports Chaser S 447	CH.837	G-69-15	28. 4.92	R L Arscott *(Noted 7.03)*	Longacre Farm, Sandy	21. 1.00P
			G-MYBU				
G-MYBV	Solar Wings Pegasus XL-Q	SW-WQ-0522		5. 5.92	P M Langdon	Glassonby	5. 6.09P
	(Trike c/n SW-TE-0393)						
G-MYBW	Solar Wings Pegasus XL-Q	SW-WQ-0523		5. 5.92	J S Chapman	(Knaresborough)	22. 7.09P
	(Trike c/n SW-TE-0394)						
G-MYBY	Solar Wings Pegasus XL-Q	SW-WQ-0525		5. 5.92	I D A Spanton *(Noted 2.08)*	Croft Farm, Defford	18. 4.05P
	(Trike c/n SW-TE-0396)						
G-MYBZ	Solar Wings Pegasus XL-Q	SW-WQ-0526		5. 5.92	A J Blackwell *(Noted 7.05)*	Long Marston	27. 9.97P
	(Trike c/n SW-TE-0397)						
G-MYCA	Whittaker MW6-T Merlin	PFA 164-11821		14. 5.92	R A L Harris	(Hove)	23. 6.06P
	(Built N B Morley and E Barfoot) (Rotax 532)						
G-MYCB	Cyclone Airsports Chaser S 447	CH.839		18. 5.92	P Sykes	Mapperton Farm, Newton Peverill	12. 5.09P
G-MYCE	Solar Wings Pegasus Quasar IITC			14. 5.92	S W Barker	(Scarborough)	23. 7.08P
	(Trike c/n SW-TQC-0098)	SW-WQT-0527					
G-MYCJ	Mainair Mercury	906-0592-5-W704		19. 5.92	J Agnew	East Fortune	28.11.04P
G-MYCK	Mainair Gemini Flash IIA	909-0592-7-W707		19. 5.92	J P Hanlon and A C McAllister	Ince Blundell	12. 6.07P
	(Rotax 462)						
G-MYCL	Mainair Mercury	910-0592-5-W708		19. 5.92	Palladium Leisure Ltd	RAF Wyton	13. 9.05P
G-MYCM	CFM Shadow Series CD	196		20. 5.92	T Jones	(London SW6)	20. 5.99P
G-MYCN	Mainair Mercury	901-0492-5-W696		22. 5.92	P Lowham *(Noted 1.07)*	Newtownards	14. 9.06P
G-MYCO	Murphy Renegade Spirit UK	PFA 188-12020		28. 5.92	S Desormes	(Exeter)	16.12.08P
	(Built C Slater)						
G-MYCP	Whittaker MW6 Merlin	PFA 164-11505		2. 6.92	A C Jones	Otherton, Cannock	7.12.09P
	(Built R M Clarke) (Rotax 532)						
G-MYCR	Mainair Gemini Flash IIA	875-0192-7-W670		10. 6.92	A P King	Long Marston	21. 7.07P
G-MYCS	Mainair Gemini Flash IIA	911-0592-7-W710		12. 6.92	G Penson tr Husthwaite Alpha Group		
						Baxby Manor, Husthwaite	25.10.07P
G-MYCT	TEAM Mini-MAX 91	PFA 186-12163		30. 3.92	D D Rayment	(Horsham)	17. 6.04P
	(Built M A Curant)						
G-MYCU	Whittaker MW6 Merlin	PFA 164-11627		9. 6.92	R D Thomasson	London Colney	11. 7.09P
	(Built P L Lonsdale and D Shackleton: sequence no.conflicts with Streak Shadow G-ORAF) (Rotax 532)						
G-MYCX	Powerchute Kestrel	00421		15. 6.92	S J Pugh-Jones *(Noted 11.07)*	Rufforth	14. 5.05P
G-MYCY	Powerchute Kestrel	00422		15. 6.92	D R M Powell	(Llandysul)	3. 6.06P
G-MYCZ	Powerchute Kestrel	00423		15. 6.92	R R O'Neill	(Ballygawley, Dungannon)	10.10.95P
G-MYDA	Powerchute Kestrel	00424		15. 6.92	K J Greatrix	(Sleaford)	2. 8.07P
G-MYDC	Mainair Mercury	916-0792-5-W715		23. 6.92	G K Thornton	(Radcliffe, Manchester)	16.10.09P
G-MYDD	CFM Shadow Series CD	K 197		22. 6.92	C H Gem	(Marbella, Malaga, Spain)	22.11.95P
G-MYDE	CFM Shadow Series CD	K 187		24. 6.92	D N L Howell	(Upper Colwall, Malvern)	19. 9.06P
G-MYDF	TEAM Mini-MAX 91	PFA 186-12129		24. 6.92	P Morrell	(Walsall)	9. 6.09P
G-MYDJ	Solar Wings Pegasus XL Tug	SW-WA-1558		1. 7.92	R C Wood and D C Richardson tr Cambridgeshire Aerotow Club		
	(Rotax 462) *(Trike c/n SW-TE-0403)* *(Officially reg as XL-R)*					Sutton Meadows	24. 4.08P
G-MYDK	Rans S-6-ESD Coyote II	0392.276		21. 4.92	R W Thompson and J W Caush	Eshott	11.10.08P
	(Built D N Kershaw - pr.no.PFA 204-12239) *(Tri-cycle u/c)*						
G-MYDM	Whittaker MW6-S Fatboy Flyer			26. 6.92	K Gregan	Kilrush, County Kildare	4. 9.09P
	(Rotax 582)	PFA 164-12105					
G-MYDN	Quad City Challenger II	CH2-1091-UK-0736		30. 6.92	T C Hooks	Newtownards	28. 9.08P
	(Built T C Hooks) *(Pr.no.PFA 177-12245)* (Rotax 462)						
G-MYDO	Rans S-5 Coyote	89.110		6. 7.92	V H Hallam	(Torquay)	4.11.09P
	(Built W A Stevens - pr.no.PFA 193-12274)						
G-MYDP	Kolb Twinstar Mk.III	K0002-1291		15. 7.92	E R Howells tr Norberts Flying Group	Leicester	11. 3.08P
	(Built P M Standen - pr.no.PFA 205-12231) (Rotax 503)						
G-MYDR	Thruster T 300	9072-T300-505		21. 7.92	H G Soper	Chiddingley, East Sussex	4.11.08P
	(Built Tempest Aviation Ltd) (Rotax 582)						
G-MYDS	Quad City Challenger II UK	CH2-1289-UK-0500		6. 3.90	M Atkinson tr G-MYDS Syndicate		
	(Built D D Smith - pr.no.PFA 177-11716)					(Bamber Bridge, Preston)	24. 5.07P
G-MYDT	Thuster T300	9072-T300-506		21. 7.92	J B Grotrian	(Warminster)	10. 1.96P
	(Built Tempest Aviation Ltd) (Rotax 582)						
G-MYDU	Thruster T 300	9072-T300-504		21. 7.92	S Collins	Killineer, Drogheda, County Louth	16.11.07P
	(Built Tempest Aviation Ltd) (Rotax 582)						
G-MYDV	Mainair Gemini Flash IIA	917-0892-7-W716		29. 7.92	S J Mazilis	(Westhoughton, Bolton)	12. 8.09P
	(Rotax 462)						
G-MYDW	Whittaker MW6 Merlin	PFA 164-12184		27. 7.92	A Chidlow *(Noted dismantled 9.07)*		
	(Built W R G West) (Rotax 503)					Church Farm, Askern	2. 9.04P
G-MYDX	Rans S-6-ESD Coyote II	0392.279		27. 7.92	K J Legg and G Cross	Redlands, Swindon	12. 6.08P
	(Built R J Goodburn - pr.no.PFA 204-12238) (Rotax 503) *(Tri-cycle u/c)*						
G-MYDZ	Mignet HM-1000 Balerit	66		3. 8.92	D S Simpson	Graveley Hall Farm, Graveley	9.12.07P
G-MYEA	Solar Wings Pegasus XL-Q	SW-WQ-0537		28. 7.92	A M Taylor	Long Marston	13. 4.08P
	(Trike c/n SW-TE-0404)						
G-MYEC	Solar Wings Pegasus XL-Q	SW-WQ-0539		28. 7.92	J I King	(Bath)	2. 6.05P
	(Trike c/n SW-TE-0406)						
G-MYED	Solar Wings Pegasus XL-R	SW-WA-1559		28. 7.92	P K Dale	Bagby	6. 8.07P
	(Rotax 462) *(Trike c/n SW-TE-0407)*						

G-MYEF	Whittaker MW6 Merlin	PFA 164-11327		28. 5.92	R D Thomasson	London Colney	
	(Built S Meadowcroft)						
G-MYEH	Solar Wings Pegasus XL-R	SW-WA-1561		4. 8.92	P G Strangward tr G-MYEH Flying Group	Roddige	18. 6.09P
	(Trike c/n SW-TB-1448)						
G-MYEI	Cyclone Airsports Chaser S 447	CH.841		18. 8.92	N S Dell	Stanton, Morpeth	17. 9.08P
G-MYEJ	Cyclone Airsports Chaser S 447	CH.842		18. 8.92	S C Reeve	Headon Farm, Retford	15. 3.08P
G-MYEK	Solar Wings Pegasus Quasar IITC			7. 8.92	M N Dando	Wolverhampton	2. 9.08P
	(Rotax 582)	SW-WQT-0540					
	(Trike c/n SW-TQD-0108 but duplicates G-MWZF)						
G-MYEM	Solar Wings Pegasus Quasar IITC			7. 8.92	D J Moore	Roddige	22. 4.08P
	(Rotax 582)	SW-WQT-0542					
	(Trike c/n SW-TQD-0101)						
G-MYEN	Solar Wings Pegasus Quasar IITC			7. 8.92	T J Feeney	(Otherton, Cannock)	25. 5.08P
	(Rotax 582)	SW-WQT-0543					
	(Trike c/n SW-TQD-0105)						
G-MYEO	Solar Wings Pegasus Quasar IITC			7. 8.92	A G Curtis	Swinford, Rugby	27.10.09P
	(Rotax 582)	SW-WQT-0544					
	(Trike c/n SW-TQD-0106)						
G-MYEP	CFM Shadow Series CD	K 205		13. 8.92	J S Seddon-Harvey	Broadmeadow Farm, Hereford	8. 6.04P
					(Noted 4.05)		
G-MYER	Cyclone AX2000	B 1052901 & CA 001	G-69-27	19. 8.92	T F Horrocks	Wick	4. 5.09P
	(Rotax 582)		G-MYER, G-69-5, 59-GF				
G-MYES	Rans S-6-ESD Coyote II	0392.283		3. 7.92	S J Matthinson	(Halifax)	14.10.08P
	(Built G R Pritchard - pr.no.PFA 204-12254) (Jabiru 2200A) (Tri-cycle u/c)						
G-MYET	Whittaker MW6 Merlin	PFA 164-12318		19. 8.92	G Campbell *(Noted 3.05)*		
	(Built M B Haine) (Rotax 503)					Newton Peverill Farm, Sturminster Marshall	8. 9.04P
G-MYEX	Powerchute Kestrel	00426		28. 8.92	R J Watkin	(Melton Mowbray)	6. 6.06P
G-MYFA	Powerchute Kestrel	00429		28. 8.92	G S Christie	(Ludlow)	
G-MYFH	Quad City Challenger II UK	CH2-0292-0798		9. 9.92	W I McMillan	RAF Mona	1.12.07P
	(Built C J and R J Lines - pr.no.PFA 177-12282)						
G-MYFI	Cyclone Airsports AX3/503	CA 002		9. 9.92	R Dilkes	Stoke, Isle of Grain	7. 8.08P
	(C/n C 3093159 also reported)						
G-MYFK	Solar Wings Pegasus Quasar IITC	SW-WQT-0553		11. 9.92	C R Cawley	(Broomfield, Chelmsford)	30. 1.08P
	(Rotax 582)	*(Trike c/n SW-TQD-0113)*					
G-MYFL	Solar Wings Pegasus Quasar IITC			11. 9.92	S B Wilkes	Roddige	29. 4.09P
	(Trike c/n SW-TQD-0103)	SW-WQT-0541/A					
	(Rotax 582) (Originally regd as c/n SW-WQT-0554: replacement Sailwing fitted to Trike G-MYFL after original Sailwing stolen 1. 1.93)						
G-MYFM	Murphy Renegade Spirit UK	PFA 188-12249		9. 9.92	A C Cale	Marley Hall, Ledbury	14. 8.09P
	(Built J M Walsh)						
G-MYFN	Rans S-5 Coyote	89.112		16. 9.92	P Doran	(Monaghan, County Monaghan)	7. 8.03P
	(Built L Kellner - pr.no.PFA 193-12273)						
G-MYFP	Mainair Gemini Flash IIA	920-0992-7-W719		2.10.92	R C Reynolds	Arclid Green, Sandbach	26. 9.08P
G-MYFR	Mainair Gemini Flash IIA	921-0992-7-W720		30. 9.92	S B Brady	Arclid Green, Sandbach	28. 8.08P
G-MYFS	Solar Wings Pegasus XL-R	SW-WA-1564		30. 9.92	B J Palfreyman	Watnall	26. 9.08P
	(Trike c/n SW-TB-1453)						
G-MYFT	Mainair Scorcher	922-0992-3-W234		30. 9.92	T Williams	(Hadfield, Glossop)	29. 4.09P
	(Rotax 503)						
G-MYFU	Mainair Gemini Flash IIA	924-1092-7-W722		7.10.92	J Payne	Deenethorpe	11.11.09P
	(Rotax 462)						
G-MYFV	Cyclone Airsports AX3/503	C 2083050		6.10.92	J K Sargent	Stoke, Isle of Grain	28.10.07P
G-MYFW	Cyclone Airsports AX3/503	C 2083051		13.10.92	The Microlight School (Lichfield) Ltd	Roddige	6. 3.09P
G-MYFX	Solar Wings Pegasus XL-Q	SW-WQ-0378		25. 6.93	J Urrutia	Clench Common	24. 8.04P
	(Trike c/n SW-TE-0295)						
G-MYFZ	Cyclone Airsports AX3/503	C 2083048		20.10.92	G Gates	Chilbolton	7. 1.08P
					(Damaged undercarriage at Chilbolton 17.10.08, permit suspended)		
G-MYGD	Cyclone Airsports AX3/503	C 2083049		21.10.92	K B Vickers	(Bamber Bridge, Preston)	28. 8.08P
G-MYGF	TEAM Mini-MAX 91	PFA 186-12175		22.10.92	R D Barnard	Ley Farm, Chirk	25. 4.09P
	(Built R D Barnard)						
G-MYGH	Rans S-6-ESD Coyote II	0692.318		30.10.92	J R Mosey	Ince Blundell	3. 9.09P
	(Built S M Hall - pr.no.PFA 204-12335)						
G-MYGJ	Mainair Mercury	923-0992-7-W721		5.10.92	J R Harnett	(Whitmore, Newcastle)	4. 4.08P
G-MYGK	Cyclone Airsports Chaser S 508	CH.846		3.11.92	P C Collins	(Llanbadoc, Usk)	14.11.95P
G-MYGM	Quad City Challenger II	CH2-0391-UK-0662		6.11.92	J White and G J Williams	Mill Farm, Shifnall	15. 7.09P
	(Built R Holt, pr.no.PFA 177-12261)						
G-MYGN	AMF Microflight Chevvron 2-32C	034		29.12.92	P J Huston	(Boston)	10. 5.08P
	(Konig SD 570)						
G-MYGO	CFM Shadow Srs CD	K114		28. 7.92	D A Crosbie	(Sudbury)	
G-MYGP	Rans S-6-ESD Coyote II	0992.349		10.11.92	D J Millin	(Newton Abbot)	2. 9.09P
	(Built J S Melville - pr.no.PFA 204-12368) (Rotax 503) (Tail-wheel u/c)						
G-MYGR	Rans S-6-ESD Coyote II	0992.348		16.11.92	D J Warren	(Knebworth)	17. 5.08P
	(Built D K Haughton - pr.no.PFA 204-12378)						
G-MYGT	Solar Wings Pegasus XL Tug	SW-WA-1569		13.11.92	J J Hoer tr Condors Aerotow Syndicate		
	(Rotax 462)	*(Trike c/n SW-TE-0413)*	*(Officially reg as XL-R)*			Dunkeswell	21. 5.09P
G-MYGU	Solar Wings Pegasus XL-R	SW-WA-1570		13.11.92	D R Western	Weston Zoyland	16. 5.05P
	(Rotax 462)	*(Trike c/n SW-TE-0414)*					
G-MYGV	Solar Wings Pegasus XL Tug	SW-WA-1571		13.11.92	D J Brixton tr Shropshire Tow Group	Leebotwood	9. 4.07P
	(Rotax 462)	*(Trike c/n SW-TE-0415)*	*(Officially reg as XL-R)*				
G-MYGZ	Mainair Gemini Flash IIA	928-1192-7-W726		18.11.92	P M Reddington	(Ormskirk)	10. 8.08P
	(Rotax 582)						
G-MYHF	Mainair Gemini Flash IIA	929-1092-7-W727		25.11.92	P J Bloor	(Knutsford)	6.10.03P
G-MYHG	Cyclone Airsports AX3/503	C 2103070		27.11.92	C Alsop and N P Thomson	Cumnock	2.12.05P
G-MYHH	Cyclone Airsports AX3/503	C 2103069		30.11.92	D J Harber	Manor Farm, Drayton St Leonard	14.11.09P
	(Also c/n CA.006)						

Reg	Type	C/n		Date	Owner	Location	Date2
G-MYHI	Rans S-6-ESD Coyote II	0692.312		8.12.92	G F Clews	Roddige	29. 1.10P
	(Built L N Anderson - pr.no.PFA 204-12279) (Tailwheel u/c)						
G-MYHJ	Cyclone Airsports AX3/503	C 2103073		11.12.92	J G Campbell	(Barnsley)	21. 9.08P
	(Reported as keel tube c/n C 3093157 - see G-MYME)						
G-MYHK	Rans S-6-ESD Coyote II	0692.311		3.12.92	M R Williamson	Sutton Meadows	18. 6.07P
	(Built J M Longley - pr.no.PFA 204-12349) (Rotax 503) (Tri-cycle u/c)						
G-MYHL	Mainair Gemini Flash IIA	932-0193-7-W730		21.12.92	B J Riley	(Barnoldswick)	28. 2.09P
G-MYHM	Cyclone Airsports AX3/503	C 2103068		18.12.92	J Walsh tr G-MYHM Group		
	(Also c/n CA.007)					Jenkin's Farm, Navestock	16. 5.09P
G-MYHN	Mainair Gemini Flash IIA	933-0193-7-W731		29.12.92	D Avery	Priory Farm, Tibenham	20. 9.07P
	(Rotax 582)						
G-MYHP	Rans S-6-ESD Coyote II (modified)	0892.343		8. 1.93	K E Gair and J G E Lane	East Barling, Essex	11. 6.09P
	(Built D A Crompton - pr.no.PFA 204-12406) (Rotax 582) (Tri-cycle u/c)						
G-MYHR	Cyclone Airsports AX3/503	C.2103071	G-68-8	15. 1.93	J K Clayton	(Norwich)	27. 6.05P
			G-MYHR				
G-MYHS	Powerchute Kestrel	00433		26. 1.93	R R O'Neill	(Ballygawley, Dungannon)	6. 4.01P
	(Frame No.00433, parachute No.931013, engine No.4104716)						
G-MYIA	Quad City Challenger II	PFA 177-12400		21. 1.93	I Pearson	Bodmin	3.10.00P
	(Built I J Arkieson)						
G-MYIE	Whittaker MW6-S Fatboy Flyer	PFA 164-11800		26. 1.93	A M Morris	(Winstanley, Wigan)	2. 2.07P
	(Built P A Mercer) (Rotax 532)						
G-MYIF	CFM Shadow Series CD	217		2. 2.93	P J Edwards	Old Sarum	10. 4.09P
G-MYIH	Mainair Gemini Flash IIA	937-0293-7-W734		9. 3.93	A N Huggart	Hunsdon	3. 7.09P
	(Rotax 582)						
G-MYII	TEAM Mini-MAX 91	PFA 186-12119		10.11.92	P A Gasson	(Three Mile Cross, Reading)	8. 3.05P
	(Built G W Peacock) (Mosler MM CB-40)						
G-MYIJ	Cyclone Airsports AX3/503	C 2103072		8. 2.93	Ultralight Training Ltd	(Coventry)	11. 3.08P
G-MYIK	Kolb Twinstar Mk.III	PFA 205-12220		13. 1.93	B A Janaway	Dunkeswell	18. 2.09P
	(Built R P Smith)						
G-MYIL	Cyclone Airsports Chaser S 508	CH.849		3. 3.93	R A Rawes *"Fricky"*	Over Farm, Gloucester	16. 6.09P
G-MYIM	Solar Wings Pegasus Quasar IITC		(EI-...)	22. 2.93	D Forde	(Clare Galway, County Galway)	16. 2.09P
	(Trike c/n SW-TQD-0122)	SW-WQT-0579	G-MYIM	*(Rotax 582)*			
G-MYIN	Solar Wings Pegasus Quasar IITC			22. 2.93	W P Hughes	RAF Henlow	7. 8.08P
	(Trike c/n SW-TQD-0123)	SW-WQT-0580					
G-MYIO	Solar Wings Pegasus Quasar IITC			22. 2.93	E Foster and J H Peet	(Eccleston, Chorley)	19. 8.05P
	(Trike c/n SW-TQD-0124)	SW-WQT-0581		*(Damaged 25. 6.05: engineless wreck noted 6.07)*			
G-MYIP	CFM Shadow Series CD	K 198		16. 3.93	T Bailey	Otherton, Cannock	16. 3.09P
G-MYIR	Rans S-6-ESD Coyote II (modified)	0892.344		17. 3.93	P Vergette	North Coates	26.10.09P
	(Built J Simpson - pr.no.PFA 204-12458) (Rotax 503) (Tri-cycle u/c)						
G-MYIS	Rans S-6-ESD Coyote II	0892 346		31.12.92	I S Everett and M Stott	Sackville Lodge, Riseley	2. 9.09P
	(Built A J Wyatt - pr.no.PFA 204-12382) (Rotax 503) (Tri-cycle u/c)						
G-MYIT	Cyclone Airsports Chaser S 508	CH.850		19. 3.93	R Barringer	(Ravensthorpe, Northampton)	28. 3.99P
G-MYIU	Cyclone Airsports AX3/503	C 3013084		22. 3.93	G R Hill	Mullaghmore, Coleraine	29. 8.06P
	(Zanzoterra Z-202) (Officially designated and regd with Rotax 503)						
G-MYIV	Mainair Gemini Flash IIA	938-0393-7-W735		30. 3.93	P S Nicholls	Finmere	9. 4.07P
	(Rotax 582)						
G-MYIX	Quad City Challenger II UK	CH2-0191-UK-0615	(Pr.no.PFA 177-12260)	5. 1.93	A Studley	Middle Pymore Farm, Bridport	25. 5.06P
	(Built I M Walton)						
G-MYIY	Mainair Gemini Flash IIA	942-0493-7-W737		1. 4.93	I C Macbeth	Arclid Green, Sandbach	2. 7.09P
G-MYIZ	TEAM Mini-MAX 91	PFA 186-12347		31. 3.93	J C Longmore	Headon Farm, Retford	22. 4.09P
	(Built J C Longmore)						
G-MYJC	Mainair Gemini Flash IIA	944-0593-7-W739		7. 4.93	M N Irven	Redlands, Swindon	14. 4.09P
	(Rotax 462)						
G-MYJD	Rans S-6-ESD Coyote II	0792.324		23. 4.93	D R Collier		
	(Built D J Dimmer and B Robins - pr.no.PFA 204-12360) (Rotax 503) (Tail-wheel u/c)			New Barn Farm, Barton Ashes, Crawley			6. 8.08P
G-MYJF	Thruster T 300	9013-T300-509		14. 4.93	P F McConville	(Dungannon)	18. 9.08P
	(Built Tempest Aviation Ltd) (Rotax 582)						
G-MYJG	Thruster Super T.300	9043-T300-510		14. 4.93	J W Rice	Redlands, Swindon	17. 9.05P
	(Built Tempest Aviation Ltd) (Rotax 582)						
G-MYJJ	Solar Wings Pegasus Quasar IITC			27. 4.93	D Murray	(Clevedon)	1. 9.04P
	(Trike c/n SW-TQD-0131)	SW-WQT-0591					
	(Rotax 582)						
G-MYJK	Solar Wings Pegasus Quasar IITC			27. 4.93	T H Parr	Bedlands Gate, Little Strickland	25. 8.08P
	(Trike c/n SW-TQD-0132)	SW-WQT-0592		*(Rotax 582) (Built with Cyclone c/n 6752)*			
G-MYJM	Mainair Gemini Flash IIA	945-0593-7-W740		29. 4.93	J T Walker		
	(Rotax 582)					Slieve Croob, Slievenamoney, Castlewellen	17. 5.09P
G-MYJO	Cyclone Airsports Chaser S 508	CH.851		30. 4.93	A W Rawlings	Croft Farm, Defford	7.10.08P
G-MYJR	Mainair Mercury	947-0593-7-W742	(EC-)	12. 5.93	D Dreux	(Child Okeford, Blandford Forum)	15. 7.06P
			G-MYJR				
G-MYJS	Solar Wings Pegasus Quasar IITC	6581		19. 5.93	J P Rooms	(Luton)	1. 1.05P
	(Rotax 582)						
G-MYJT	Solar Wings Pegasus Quasar IITC	6582		19. 5.93	S Ferguson	(Milngavie, Glasgow)	21. 6.09P
	(Rotax 582)						
G-MYJU	Solar Wings Pegasus Quasar IITC	6573		19. 5.93	P G Penhaligan	Stoke, Isle of Grain	28. 7.09P
	(Rotax 582)						
G-MYJW	Cyclone Airsports Chaser S 508	CH.856		19. 5.93	A R Mikolajczyk	Church Farm, Askern	25. 8.08P
G-MYJY	Rans S-6-ESD Coyote II	0692.317		24. 5.93	F N Pearson	Linley Hill, Leven	8. 8.06P
	(Build G A Clayton - pr.no.PFA 204-12346) (Tri-cycle u/c)						
G-MYJZ	Whittaker MW5-D Sorcerer	PFA 163-12385		22. 4.93	P A Aston tr My Jazz Group	(Torquay)	16. 4.09P
	(Built J G Beesley)						
G-MYKA	Cyclone Airsports AX3/503	C 3013086		25. 5.93	T Whittall	(Halesowen)	28. 2.09P
G-MYKB	Kolb Twinstar Mk.III (mod)	K0007-0193		31. 3.93	T Antell	(Watergore, South Petherton)	6. 4.09P
	(Built J D Holt - pr.no.PFA 205-12398)						

Reg	Type	C/n		Date	Owner	Location	Expiry
G-MYKC	Mainair Gemini Flash IIA	948-0593-7-W743		26. 5.93	R Bricknell	Headon Farm, Retford	3. 9.08P
	(Rotax 582)						
G-MYKD	Cyclone Airsports Chaser S 508	CH.857		26. 5.93	J B Allan	(Corringham, Stanford-le-Hope)	30.10.05P
G-MYKE	CFM Shadow Series BD	K 031		14. 1.88	M Hughes t/a MKH Engineering *(Noted 4.04)*		
						Greenlands, Rhuallt	26.10.96P
G-MYKF	Cyclone Airsports AX3/503	C 3013083		8. 6.93	M A Collins	Longacre Farm, Sandy	24. 7.07P
G-MYKG	Mainair Gemini Flash IIA	950-0693-7-W745		21. 6.93	B D Walker	(Sale)	2.11.07P
	(Rotax 582)						
G-MYKH	Mainair Gemini Flash IIA	951-0693-7-W746		21. 6.93	G F Atkinson	Rufforth	29. 6.09P
	(Rotax 582)						
G-MYKJ	TEAM Mini-MAX	PFA 186-12215		10. 6.93	T De Breffe Gardner	Walkeridge Farm, Overton	8. 5.06P
	(Built M Hill) (Rotax 508)						
G-MYKN	Rans S-6 Coyote II	0892.338		23. 6.93	G C Alderson		
	(Built S E Hartles - pr.no.PFA 204-12361) (Rotax 503) *(Tri-cycle u/c)*					Lower Mountpleasant Farm, Chatteris	15. 9.06P
G-MYKO	Whittaker MW6-S Fatboy Flyer						
	(Hirth 2706)	PFA 164-11919		25. 6.93	K R Challis and C S Andersson	Great Oakley	14. 9.07P
G-MYKP	Solar Wings Pegasus Quasar IITC	6627		7. 7.93	V Gledhill	(Morley)	22. 2.08P
	(Rotax 582)						
G-MYKR	Solar Wings Pegasus Quasar IITC	6635		7. 7.93	C Stallard	Chase Farm, Little Burstead	6. 8.07P
	(Rotax 582)						
G-MYKS	Solar Wings Pegasus Quasar IITC	6636		7. 7.93	D J Oskis	(Upminster)	7. 6.09P
	(Rotax 582) *(Now fitted with new Trike c/n 6780)*						
G-MYKT	Cyclone Airsports AX3/503	C 3013082		5. 7.93	J D Sanger and J E Seager	Stoke, Isle of Grain	2.10.07P
G-MYKV	Mainair Gemini Flash IIA	954-0793-7-W749		13. 7.93	P J Gulliver	Mill Farm, Shifnal	29. 9.05P
G-MYKW	Mainair Mercury	960-0893-7-W755		9. 7.93	J D Hylton	Eshott	9. 11.08P
G-MYKX	Mainair Mercury	961-0893-7-W756		3. 9.93	D T McAfee and A F Allan	(Musselburgh)	10. 7.09P
G-MYKY	Mainair Mercury	962-0893-7-W757		6. 8.93	R P Jewit	(York)	22. 7.07P
G-MYKZ	TEAM Mini-MAX 91	PFA 186-11841	G-BVAV	26. 7.93	C Libby	(Teignmouth)	29. 7.05P
	(Built P A Ellis) (Rotax 503)						
G-MYLB	TEAM Mini-MAX 91	PFA 186-12419		2. 8.93	J G Burns	Morgansfield, Fishburn	1. 2.08P
	(Built P Harvey) (Rotax 532)						
G-MYLC	Pegasus Quantum 15	6634		9. 8.93	C McKay	Perth	26. 9.08P
	(Rotax 503)						
G-MYLD	Rans S-6-ESD Coyote II	0892.350		1. 3.93	B Cartwright	Magheralin, Craigavon	27.10.05P
	(Built L R H d'Eath - pr.no.PFA 204-12394) (Rotax 503) *(Tail-wheel u/c)*						
G-MYLE	Pegasus Quantum Lite	6609		9. 8.93	S E Powell	Enstone	30. 3.09P
	(Rotax 503) *(Regd as Pegasus Quantum 15)*						
G-MYLF	Rans S-6-ESD Coyote II	0493.483		4. 8.93	A J Spencer *"Low Flyer"*	Eagle Moor, Grantham	22. 7.05P
	(Built G R and J A Pritchard - pr.no.PFA 204-12544) (Rotax 912 UL) *(Tri-cycle u/c)*						
G-MYLG	Mainair Gemini Flash IIA	959-0893-7-W754		6. 8.93	N J Axworthy and C Dunning	(Runcorn)	12. 7.09P
G-MYLH	Pegasus Quantum 15	6632		27. 8.93	G Carr	(Sutton-in-Ashfield)	2. 8.09P
	(Rotax 503)						
G-MYLI	Pegasus Quantum 15	6645		11. 8.93	A M Keyte	(Milton Keynes)	27. 5.08P
	(Rotax 503)						
G-MYLK	Pegasus Quantum 15	6602		27. 8.93	C L Minter tr G-MYLK Group	Deenethorpe	24. 9.04P
	(Rotax 503)	(Rotax 503)					
G-MYLL	Pegasus Quantum 15	6650		31. 8.93	S Hayes	Headon Farm, Retford	6. 5.09P
	(Rotax 462)						
G-MYLM	Pegasus Quantum 15	6651	(EC-)	31. 8.93	P A Ashton	(Lincoln)	26. 3.09P
	(Rotax 582)		G-MYLM				
G-MYLN	Kolb Twinstar Mk.III (mod)	K0010-0193		3. 9.93	J F Joyes	Chiltern Park, Wallingford	9. 5.08P
	(Built G E Collard - pr.no.PFA 205-12430)						
G-MYLO	Rans S-6-ESD Coyote II	0692.313		9. 9.93	P Bowers	Carlisle	14.10.09P
	(Built J G Dance and P E Lewis - pr.no.PFA 204-12334: frame no.may be 0692.315) (Tri-cycle u/c)						
G-MYLP	Kolb Twinstar Mk.III	K0005-0992	(G-BVCR)	9. 9.93	R Thompson	(Bristol)	27. 5.99P
	(Built D M Stevens - pr.no.PFA 205-12391) (Rotax 582)						
G-MYLR	Mainair Gemini Flash IIA	964-0993-7-W759		17. 9.93	M D Calder and I J Cleland	(Glasgow)	21.12.09P
	(Rotax 582)						
G-MYLS	Mainair Mercury	966-0993-7-W761		5.10.93	D Burnell-Higgs	Shobdon	6. 9.05P
G-MYLT	Mainair Blade	967-1093-7-W762		23. 9.93	T D Hall	(Long Marston, Tring)	4. 6.09P
	(Rotax 912)						
G-MYLV	CFM Shadow Series CD	220		24. 9.93	R G M-J Proost tr Aviation for Paraplegics and Tetraplegics		
					Trust	Old Sarum	24. 3.08P
G-MYLW	Rans S-6-ESD Coyote II	1292.401		4. 8.93	A D Dias	Otherton, Cannock	29. 9.05P
	(Built J R Worswick - pr.no.PFA 204-12560) (Rotax 503) *(Tri-cycle u/c)*						
	(Engine failed on take-off at Priory Farm 26. 4.08 and crashed in a field alongside the runway causing damage to nose gear and fuselage)						
G-MYLX	Medway Raven X	MRB113/109		6.10.93	T M Knight	(Lower Earley Reading)	23. 9.08P
	(Sailwing c/n also quoted for G-MYVV)						
G-MYLY	Medway Raven X	MRB001/108		23. 9.93	C R Smith	(Stanford-le-Hope)	3.10.94P
	(Sailwing c/n also quoted for G-MYVU)						
G-MYLZ	Pegasus Quantum 15	6672		6.10.93	W G McPherson	(Dunfermline)	30.11.05P
	(Rotax 462)						
G-MYMB	Pegasus Quantum 15	6674		6.10.93	D B Jones	(Bletchley, Milton Keynes)	17.11.09P
	(Rotax 582)						
G-MYMC	Pegasus Quantum 15	6675		6.10.93	D Murray	Glenrothes	26. 2.08P
	(Rotax 582)						
G-MYME	Cyclone Airsports AX3/503	C 3093157		13.10.93	M K Slaughter tr G-MYME Group	(Earley, Reading)	17. 6.09P
	(Officially regd wiith c/n as such but keel tube C 3093157 noted as fitted to G-MYHJ)						
G-MYMH	Rans S-6-ESD Coyote II	0793.520		20.10.93	A R Cattell	Lower Wasing Farm, Brimpton	6.12.07P
	(Built D J Thompsett - pr.no.PFA 204-12576) (Tri-cycle u/c)						
G-MYMI	Kolb Twinstar Mk.3	K0016-0693		21.10.93	F J Brown	(Flitwick, Bedford)	5. 9.05P
	(Built R T P Harris - pr.no.PFA 205-12537)						
G-MYMJ	Medway Raven X	MRB004/110		28.10.93	N Brigginshaw	RAF Wyton	6. 5.09P
	(Sailwing c/n also quoted for G-MYVX)						

G-MYMK	Mainair Gemini Flash IIA	968-1193-7-W763		29.10.93	A Britton	(Rickmansworth)	28. 5.06P
	(Rotax 582)						
G-MYML	Mainair Mercury	969-1193-7-W765		29.10.93	D J Dalley *(Noted 11.06)*		
						Stancombe Farm, Askerswell	7. 6.01P
G-MYMM	Air Création 503/Fun 18S GT bis	93/001		30. 9.93	W H Greenwood	Swanborough Farm, Lewes	10. 4.09P
G-MYMN	Whittaker MW6 Merlin	PFA 164-12124		29.10.93	K J Cole	(Gloucester)	25.11.03P
	(Built K J Cole) (Rotax 582)						
G-MYMO	Mainair Gemini Flash IIA	955-0793-7-W750		24. 6.93	S McCrae	(Eastham, Wirral)	24. 4.08P
G-MYMP	Rans S-6-ESD Coyote II	1291.250	(G-CHAZ)	5.11.93	R L Flowerday	Dunkeswell	11.11.08P
	(Built C H Middleton - pr.no.PFA 204-12436) (Rotax 503) *(Tri-cycle u/c)*						
G-MYMR	Rans S-6-ESD Coyote II	0893.529		17.11.93	R J Bentley		
	(Built M J Kay - pr.no.PFA 204-12580) (Rotax 503) *(Tri-cycle u/c)*					(Toomevara, Nenagh, County Tipperary)	26. 6.09P
G-MYMS	Rans S-6-ESD Coyote II	0893.526		17.11.93	M R Johnson and P G Briscoe	Long Marston	15. 3.08P
	(Built G C Moore - pr.no.PFA 204-12581) (Rotax 503) *(Tri-cycle u/c)*						
G-MYMV	Mainair Gemini Flash IIA	971-1193-7-W767		26.11.93	A J Evans	(Pembrey, Burry Port)	8.12.07P
G-MYMW	Cyclone Airsports AX3/503	C 3093156		23.11.93	L J Perring	Field Farm, Oakley	21 5.09P
G-MYMX	Pegasus Quantum 15	6705		1.12.93	N F McKenzie	Insch	7. 7.09P
	(Rotax 582)						
G-MYMY	Cyclone Airsports Chaser S 508	CH.860		7. 9.93	D L Hadley	(Canterbury)	29. 5.07P
G-MYMZ	Cyclone Airsports AX3/503	C 3093154		7.12.93	The Microlight School (Lichfield) Ltd	Roddige	26. 2.07P
G-MYNB	Pegasus Quantum 15	6719		14.12.93	S D Powell and R Maude	(Wakefield)	23. 1.10P
	(Rotax 582)						
G-MYNC	Mainair Mercury	K973-1293-7-W769		17.12.93	N L Northend	Baxby Manor, Husthwaite	22. 4.09P
G-MYND	Mainair Gemini Flash IIA	841-0591-7-W635		28. 5.91	S Wild	Headon Farm, Retford	20. 6.09P
G-MYNE	Rans S-6-ESD Coyote II	1292.408		25. 6.93	J N W Moss	Enstone	3.12.08P
	(Built G Ferguson - pr.no.PFA 204-12497) *(Tail-wheel u/c)*						
G-MYNF	Mainair Mercury	974-1293-7-W770		17. 1.94	J Anderson and M Harrowden	(Alloa / Doune)	5. 3.08P
G-MYNH	Rans S-6-ESD Coyote II	0493.487		30.12.93	E F and V M Clapham		
	(Built E F Clapham - pr.no.PFA 204-12616) (Rotax 912-UL) *(Tail-wheel u/c)*					Lower Wasing Farm, Brimpton	29. 3.01P
G-MYNI	TEAM Mini-MAX 91	PFA 186-12314		22. 2.93	I Pearson	Davidstow Moor	17.11.99P
	(Built R Barton) (Mosler MM CB-35)						
G-MYNJ	Mainair Mercury	K972-1293-7-W768		14. 1.94	S M Buchan *(Noted 9.05)*	Deenethorpe	10. 8.04P
G-MYNK	Pegasus Quantum 15	6614		17.11.93	J Britton	Redlands, Swindon	8. 2.09P
	(Rotax 582)						
G-MYNL	Pegasus Quantum 15	6648		17.11.93	S.J.Whalley	(Stoke-on-Trent)	21.12.07P
	(Rotax 582)						
G-MYNN	Pegasus Quantum 15	6679		17.11.93	V Loy	North Coates	9. 2.09P
	(Rotax 582)						
G-MYNO	Pegasus Quantum 15	6724		10. 1.94	A J Hodson	Sissinghurst, Cranbrook	1. 5.09P
	(Rotax 582)						
G-MYNP	Pegasus Quantum 15	6688		17.11.93	K A Davidson	RAF Scampton	22 .7.07P
	(Rotax 582)						
G-MYNR	Pegasus Quantum 15 Super Sport	6692		17.11.93	C A Reynolds	Lower Upham Farm, Chiseldon	15. 4.09P
	(Rotax 582)						
G-MYNS	Pegasus Quantum 15	6694		17.11.93	F J Mcvey	Insch	31.10.09P
	(Rotax 582)						
G-MYNT	Pegasus Quantum 15	6693		17.11.93	C D Arnold	Craysmarsh Farm, Melksham	8. 5.09P
	(Rotax 582)						
G-MYNV	Pegasus Quantum 15	6725		10. 1.94	J Goldsmith-Ryan	Eaglescott	31. 5.09P
	(Rotax 582)						
G-MYNX	CFM Streak Shadow SA	K 193-SA-M		15. 6.92	S P Fletcher	Old Sarum	26.10.09P
	(Built P A White - pr.no.PFA 206-12268) (Rotax 618)						
G-MYNY	Kolb Twinstar Mk.III (modified)	K0014-0693		22.11.93	B Alexander *(Noted 5.05)*	Swinford, Rugby	25. 8.98P
	(Built W R C Williams-Wynne - pr.no.PFA 205-12478) (Rotax 582)						
G-MYNZ	Pegasus Quantum 15	6709		18. 1.94	P W Rogers	(Shawforth, Rochdale)	17. 2.07P
	(Rotax 582)						
G-MYOA	Rans S-6-ESD Coyote II	0793.523		23.11.93	R W Trenholm tr Orcas Syndicate		
	(Built H Lang - pr.no.PFA 204-12578) *(Tri-cycle u/c)* (Rotax 503)					Otherton, Cannock	30. 3.08P
G-MYOG	Kolb Twinstar Mk.III (mod)	K0011-0193		19. 1.94	A P de Legh	Redhill	17. 9.09P
	(Built A P de Legh - pr.no.PFA 205-12449) (Hirth 2706)						
G-MYOH	CFM Shadow Series CD	K 201		27. 1.94	D R Sutton	Brook Farm, Pilling	13. 8.08P
G-MYOI	Rans S-6-ESD Coyote II	1292.409		3. 2.94	A W Paterson	Strathaven	12. 5.09P
	(Built P F Hill - pr.no.PFA 204-12503) (Rotax 503) *(Tailwheel u/c)*						
G-MYOL	Air Création/Fun 18S GT bis	94/001		7. 2.94	S N Bond	Sywell	29. 3.08P
	(Rotax 447)						
G-MYOM	Mainair Gemini Flash IIA	981-0294-7-W777		14. 2.94	M A Haughey	Newtownards	18. 3.07P
	(Rotax 582)						
G-MYON	CFM Shadow Series CD	240		12. 1.94	D W and S E Suttill	(Sykehouse, Goole)	20.12.05P
G-MYOO	Kolb Twinstar Mk.IIIM	K0004-0192		11. 5.92	P D Coppin	(Fareham)	3. 6.09P
	(Built P D Coppin and P Watmough - pr.no.PFA 205-12200) (Rotax 582)						
G-MYOR	Kolb Twinstar Mk.III	PFA 205-12602		16. 2.94	J J Littler	(Chichester)	30. 6.09P
	(Built O J and J H Stodhert) (Hirth 2705 RO6)						
G-MYOS	CFM Shadow Series CD	246		18. 2.94	E J and C A Bowles	Craysmarsh Farm, Melksham	25.10.08P
G-MYOT	Rans S-6-ESD Coyote II	0893.525		21. 2.94	D E Wilson	Davidstow Moor	12. 8.09P
	(Built R T Mosforth - pr.no.PFA 204-12668) (Rotax 503) *(Tail-wheel u/c)*						
G-MYOU	Pegasus Quantum 15	6726		1. 3.94	G Oliver	(Burbage, Hinkley)	22.11.08P
	(Rotax 582)						
G-MYOV	Mainair Mercury	K979-0294-7-W775		1. 3.94	P Newton	(Buxton)	14.12.03P
G-MYOW	Mainair Gemini Flash IIA	983-0294-7-W779		16. 3.94	A J A Fowler	Corn Wood Farm, Adversane	17. 9.07P
G-MYOX	Mainair Mercury	K984-0294-7-W780		23. 2.94	K Driver	Headon Farm, Retford	6.10.08P
G-MYOY	Cyclone Airsports AX3/503	C 3123191		23. 2.94	M R Smith	Otherton, Cannock	16. 7.08P
G-MYOZ	BFC Challenger II	UK CH2-1093-1045		24. 2.94	A R Thomson	Longside, Peterhead	15. 8.09P
	(Built P F Bockh - pr.no.PFA 177A-12640) (Rotax 503)						

G-MYPA	Rans S-6-ESD Coyote II	0893.527	24. 2.94	R S McLeister	Tarn Farm, Cockerham 19. 2.09P
	(Built E J Garner - pr.no.PFA 204-12678) (Tail-wheel u/c)				
G-MYPC	Kolb Twinstar Mk.III (mod)	K0012-0199	2. 3.94	J Young and S Hussain	Otherton, Cannock 3. 3.09P
	(Built R Pattrick - pr.no.PFA 205-12437)				
G-MYPE	Mainair Gemini Flash IIA	985-0394-7-W781	11. 3.94	R Cant	(Musselburgh) 10. 7.09P
	(Rotax 582)				
G-MYPG	Solar Wings Pegasus XL-Q	SW-WQ-0176	29. 3.89	R D Howie	(Grays) 29. 7.09P
G-MYPH	Pegasus Quantum 15	6764	11. 3.94	P M J White	Wombleton 8. 9.08P
	(Rotax 582)				
G-MYPI	Pegasus Quantum 15	6767	11. 3.94	P L Jarvis	Stoke, Isle of Grain 10. 9.08P
	(Rotax 582)				
G-MYPJ	Rans S-6-ESD Coyote II	1293.569	18. 3.94	K A Eden	Brook Farm, Pilling 9. 9.05P
	(Built A W Fish - pr.no.PFA 204-12692) (Rotax 503) (Tri-cycle u/c)				
G-MYPL	CFM Shadow Series CD	K 213	14. 2.94	G I Madden	(Loughton, Milton Keynes) 11. 7.07P
	(Built CFM Metal-Fax - pr.no.BMAA HB/080)				
G-MYPM	Cyclone Airsports AX3/503	C 3123188	23. 3.94	Microflight Ireland Ltd	Mullaghmore, Coleraine 26. 6.03P
				(Noted derelict 7.06)	
G-MYPN	Pegasus Quantum 15	6727	12. 4.94	P J S Albon	Sywell 19. 5.09P
	(Rotax 582)				
G-MYPP	Whittaker MW6-S Fatboy Flyer		11. 4.94	G Everett and D Smith	(Maidstone) 1. 4.08P
	(Built D S L Evans)	PFA 164-12413			
G-MYPR	Cyclone Airsports AX3/503	C 3123190	13. 4.94	W R Hibberd	Otherton, Cannock 24. 8.08P
G-MYPS	Whittaker MW6 Merlin	PFA 164-11585	19. 4.94	I S Bishop	Bicester 10. 4.06P
	(Built I S Bishop) (Rotax 503)				
G-MYPT	CFM Shadow Series CD	K 212	22. 4.94	M G and S A Collins	(Oldbury-on-Severn) 13.10.07P
G-MYPV	Mainair Mercury	986-0394-7-W782	18. 3.94	B Donnan	Swinford, Rugby 14. 3.09P
	(Rotax 582)				
G-MYPW	Mainair Gemini Flash IIA	991-0494-7-W787	3. 5.94	T C Edwards	Hunsdon 24. 5.07P
	(Rotax 582)				
G-MYPX	Pegasus Quantum 15	6785	28. 4.94	P J Callis and M Aylett	Swinford, Rugby 23. 6.08P
	(Rotax 582) (Believed to have used "B Conditions" marks "G-69-29" during trials)				
G-MYPY	Pegasus Quantum 15	6786	12. 5.94	F M Montila	Longacre Farm, Sandy 29. 8.09P
	(Rotax 582)				
G-MYPZ	BFC Challenger II UK	CH2-1093-UK-1046	2. 3.94	E G Astin	(Whitby) 14.10.05P
	(Built E G Astin - pr.no.PFA 177A-12689) (Hirth 2706) (Regd incorrectly as CH2-0194-UK-1046)				
G-MYRB	Whittaker MW5 Sorcerer	PFA 163-11543	14. 4.94	P J Careless	(Little Paxton, St Neots)
	(Built P J Careless)				
G-MYRC	Mainair Blade	988-0594-7-W784	1. 6.94	T C Brown and J Murphy	Mill Farm, Shifnal 14. 8.09P
	(Rotax 462)				
G-MYRD	Mainair Blade	989-0594-7-W785	20. 5.94	W J Walker	Tarn Farm, Cockerham 21. 2.09P
	(Rotax 582)				
G-MYRE	Cyclone Airsports Chaser S	CH863	10. 5.94	S W Barker	(Scalby, Scarborough) 3. 6.07P
	(Rotax 377)				
G-MYRF	Pegasus Quantum 15	6795	13. 5.94	C Cartwright and B Vincent	Sutton Meadows 22. 5.08P
	(Rotax 462)				
G-MYRG	TEAM Mini-Max 88	PFA 186-11891	17. 5.94	V Grayson	Stoke, Isle of Grain 28. 2.10P
	(Built D G Burrows)				
G-MYRH	BFC Challenger II UK	CH2-1093-1044	10. 3.94	C M Gray	(Fareham) 13. 4.09P
	(Built R T Hall - pr.no.PFA 177A-12690) (Rotax 582)				
G-MYRJ	BFC Challenger II UK	CH2-1093-1042	28. 3.94	C G Trow (also French regn 1.09) Clench Common 21.10.08P	
	(Built H F Breakwell and P Woodcock - pr.no.PFA 177A-12658) (Rotax 582)				
G-MYRK	Murphy Renegade Spirit UK	215	3.10.89	D J Newton	(Cropwell Bishop, Nottingham) 7. 8.08P
	(Built J Brown – pr.no. PFA 188-11425)				
G-MYRL	TEAM Mini-MAX 91	PFA 186-11967	17. 5.94	J N Hanson	Tarn Farm, Cockerham 26. 3.09P
	(Built W W Vinten) (Rotax 447)				
G-MYRM	Pegasus Quantum 15	6800	26. 5.94	B R and B Dale	(Sandwich) 30.10.09P
	(Rotax 582)				
G-MYRN	Pegasus Quantum 15	6801	26. 5.94	G Ferries	Insch 30. 3.09P
	(Rotax 582)				
G-MYRO	Cyclone Airsports AX3/503	C 4043211	6. 6.94	R I Simpson	Clipgate Farm, Denton 22. 8.08P
G-MYRP	Letov LK-2M Sluka	829409x09?	6. 6.94	R M C Hunter	Blue Tile Farm, Hindolveston 7.11.04P
	(Built R L Jones - pr.no.PFA 263-12725) (Rotax 447)				
G-MYRR	Letov LK-2M Sluka	0205	10. 6.94	M Tormey	Abbeyshrule, County Longford 18.10.08P
	(Officially regd with c/n 05)				
G-MYRS	Pegasus Quantum 15	6803	13. 6.94	R M Summers	Aberdeen 28. 7.08P
	(Rotax 582)				
G-MYRT	Pegasus Quantum 15	6732	1. 3.94	M C Taylor	Eastbach Farm, Coleford 16. 8.08P
	(Rotax 582)				
G-MYRU	Cyclone Airsports AX3/503	C 4043210	7. 6.94	W A Emmerson	(Newcastle-upon-Tyne) 6. 7.08P
G-MYRV	Cyclone Airsports AX3/503	C 4043209	8. 6.94	M Gardiner	Greenlands, Rhuallt 4. 7.08P
G-MYRW	Mainair Mercury	999-0694-7-W795	17. 6.94	G C Hobson (Operated Northern Microlight School)	
					St Michaels 5. 7.08P
G-MYRY	Pegasus Quantum Lite	6813	15. 6.94	G M Cruise-Smith	Roddige 20. 1.07P
	(Rotax 582)				
G-MYRZ	Pegasus Quantum 15	6812	15. 6.94	G D Black	(Dunblane) 31. 8.08P
	(Rotax 582)				
G-MYSA	Cyclone Airsports Chaser S 508	CH.864	15. 6.94	J R Pearce	(Oakley, Bucks) 9. 5.09P
G-MYSB	Pegasus Quantum 15	6809	22. 6.94	P H Woodward	
				Cottage Farm, Norton Juxta, Twycross 22. 6.09P	
G-MYSC	Pegasus Quantum 15	6811	22. 6.94	K R White	Dunkeswell 7. 7.08P
	(Rotax 582)				
G-MYSD	BFC Challenger II	CH2-1093-1043	23. 6.94	C E Bell	Spanhoe 11. 5.09P
	(Built C E Bell - pr.no.PFA 177A-12688)				

G-MYSG	Mainair Mercury	K993-0694-7-W790		12. 7.94	N Whitaker	(Whitchurch, Shropshire)	28.12.07P
	(Rotax 582)						
G-MYSI	Mignet HM.14/93	PFA 255-12700		18. 7.94	A R D Seaman	(Dagenham)	
	(Built A R D Seaman)						
G-MYSJ	Mainair Gemini Flash IIA	1001-0894-7-W797		2. 8.94	A Warnock	Newtownards	21. 8.08P
	(Rotax 503)						
G-MYSK	TEAM Mini-MAX 91	PFA 186-12203		25. 7.94	A D Bolshaw *(Operated Brook Farm Microlight Centre)*		
	(Built K Worthington)					Brook Farm, Pilling	1. 8.02P
G-MYSL	Aviasud Mistral 582GB	066	83-DE	27. 2.92	N W Cawley	Griffins Farm, Temple Bruer	23. 8.08P
	(Built Aviasud Engineering - pr.no..BMAA HB/007)						
G-MYSM	CFM Shadow Series CD	K 243		22. 3.94	L W Stevens Black Spring Farm, Castle Bytham		10.10.03P
	(Built CFM Metal-Fax - pr.no.BMAA HB/049)				(Noted 2.08)		
G-MYSO	Cyclone Airsports AX3/503	C 4043215		1. 8.94	N J Stoneman and S Mather	(Stoke, Kent)	22. 3.06P
G-MYSP	Rans S-6-ESD Coyote II	0392-284		26. 5.92	A J Alexander, K G Diamond and B Knight Redhill		28.11.07P
	(Built S Palmer - pr.no.PFA 204-12265) (Rotax 582) (Tri-cycle u/c)						
G-MYSR	Pegasus Quantum 15	6837		3. 8.94	W G Craig	(Dunfermline)	15. 3.09P
	(Rotax 582)						
G-MYSU	Rans S-6-ESD Coyote II	0394.600		5. 8.94	C N Nairn Nether Huntlywood Farm, Gordon		4. 9.08P
	(Built I Whyte - pr.no.PFA 204-12753)						
G-MYSV	Aerial Arts Chaser S	CH.812	(ex Korea)	24. 8.94	R J Sims and I G Reason	(Salisbury)	29. 6.09P
	(Rotax 377)						
G-MYSW	Pegasus Quantum 15	6834		13. 7.94	C T D Whipps	Thorrington, Colchester	24. 4.09P
	(Rotax 582)						
G-MYSX	Pegasus Quantum 15	6832		13. 7.94	J L Treves	Longacre Farm, Sandy	7. 6.07P
	(Rotax 503)						
G-MYSY	Pegasus Quantum 15	6864		15. 8.94	B D S Vere	Eaglescott	8. 6.08P
	(Rotax 582)						
G-MYSZ	Mainair Mercury	1006-0894-7-W802		2. 9.94	W Fletcher and S D Harvey		
	(C/n confirmed but see G-MYYY)					Broadmeadow Farm, Hereford	8.12.07P
G-MYTB	Mainair Mercury	1004-0894-7-W800		19. 8.94	P J Higgin Red House Farm, Gedney Dyke, Lutton		12. 7.09P
	(Rotax 582)						
G-MYTC	Solar Wings Pegasus XL-Q	SW-WQ-0246		28. 9.94	M J Edmett	(London N3)	
G-MYTD	Mainair Blade	1002-0894-7-W798		18. 8.94	B E Warburton and D B Meades	St Michaels	18. 4.08P
	(Rotax 582)						
G-MYTE	Rans S-6-ESD Coyote II	0394.598		22. 7.94	N D Austin	(Borehamwood)	14. 5.07P
	(Built AJ Bourner - pr.no.PFA 204-12718) (Tail-wheel u/c)						
G-MYTG	Mainair Blade	1008-0994-7-W804		16. 9.94	O P Farrell		
	(Rotax 582)					Carstown, Ballymakenny, Drogheda, County Louth	19. 6.09P
G-MYTH	CFM Shadow Series CD	089		7.11.88	H A Leek	Spanhoe	31. 8.08P
G-MYTI	Pegasus Quantum 15	6874		6.10.94	(J Madhvani)	Plaistows Farm, St Albans	26. 2.07P
	(Rotax 582)						
G-MYTJ	Pegasus Quantum 15	6877		29. 9.94	M Jones	Roddige	23. 8.08P
	(Rotax 582)						
G-MYTK	Mainair Mercury	1009-1094-7-W805		29. 9.94	D A Holroyd	Hunsdon	3. 1.10P
G-MYTL	Mainair Blade	1010-1094-7-W807		4.10.94	S Ostrowski	Davidstow Moor	26. 7.05P
	(Rotax 582)						
G-MYTM	Cyclone Airsports AX3/503	C 3123189		13. 4.94	J P Gardiner	(Farnworth)	15.10.07P
G-MYTN	Pegasus Quantum 15	6878		30. 9.94	R Nicholson	Enstone	25. 7.09P
	(Rotax 503)						
G-MYTO	Quad City Challenger II UK	PFA 177-12583		22. 7.94	R W Sage *(Noted 9.08)* Priory Farm, Tibenham		16. 4.01P
	(Built K B Tolley and D M Cottingham) (Hirth 2705.R06)						
G-MYTP	CGS Arrow Flight Hawk II	?	N215	6.10.94	R J Turner	Otherton, Cannock	12. 7.05P
	(Built M Whittaker - pr.no.PFA 266-12801: additional c/ns reported 215 & H-CGS-489-P but believed former taken from p/i) (Rotax 503)						
G-MYTT	Quad City Challenger II	PFA 177-12761		11.10.94	J Bolton	Pittrichie Farm, Whiterashes	23.10.09P
	(Built P L Fisk - c/n CH2-0394-UK-111)						
G-MYTU	Mainair Blade	1011-1094-7-W808		21.10.94	C J Barker *(Noted 10.07)*	Watnall	26. 7.07P
	(Rotax 582)						
G-MYTV	Huntwing Avon	9204010		13.10.94	M Carson	Weston Zoyland	23. 8.08P
	(Built M P Hadden - pr.no.BMAA HB/029) (Rotax 503)						
G-MYTX	Mainair Mercury	K1003-0894-7-W799		23. 9.94	R Steel	Rufforth	29. 9.08P
G-MYTY	CFM Streak Shadow M	K 242		11. 7.94	K H A Negal	Enstone	6. 6.02P
	(Built N R Beale - pr.no.PFA 206-12607) (Rotax 912-UL)						
G-MYTZ	Air Création 503/Fun 18S GT bis	94/003		7.11.94	B J Curtis	(Todmorden)	15. 9.07P
G-MYUA	Air Création 503/Fun 18S GT bis	94/002		8.11.94	J Leden	Darley Moor, Ashbourne	26. 8.08P
	(Rotax 582)						
G-MYUB	Mainair Mercury	1014-1194-7-W812		14.12.94	T A Ross *(Noted 3.06)* Arclid Green, Sandbach		7.10.05P
G-MYUC	Mainair Blade	1015-1294-7-W813		16.11.94	A D Clayton	St Michaels	4.11.08P
	(Rotax 462)						
G-MYUD	Mainair Mercury	1016-1294-7-W814		24.11.94	P W Margetson	Deenethorpe	17. 4.08P
	(Rotax 582)						
G-MYUE	Mainair Mercury	1017-1294-7-W815		22.11.94	T H R Jamin	(Marannes, France)	20. 5.08P
	(Rotax 582)						
G-MYUF	Murphy Renegade Spirit	PFA 188-12795		16.11.94	F Overall Whitehall Farm, Wethersfield		14. 2.09P
	(Built C J Dale) (Jabiru 2200A)						
G-MYUH	Solar Wings Pegasus XL-Q	6810		28.11.94	K S Daniels	(London Colney)	14. 9.08P
	(C/n 6810 refers to new Sailwing - Trike unit is ex-G-MVKR (SW-TE-0123)						
G-MYUI	Cyclone Airsports AX3/503	C 4043213		13.12.94	R and M Bailey	Plaistows Farm, St Albans	31. 7.08P
	(C/n carried is C 102822 and probably results from a changed monopole)						
G-MYUK	Mainair Mercury	1020-0195-7-W818		12.12.94	S Lear	Plaistows Farm, St Albans	6. 9.06P
	(Rotax 462)						
G-MYUL	Quad City Challenger II UK	PFA 177-12687		10. 1.95	G A Davidson *(Noted 8.08)*		
						Tarn Farm, Cockerham	24. 5.02P
G-MYUN	Mainair Blade	1019-0195-7-W817		5.12.94	G A Barratt	(Longridge, Preston)	27. 2.09P
	(Rotax 582)						

G-MYUO	Pegasus Quantum 15 (Rotax 582)	6911		23. 1.95	E J Hughes	(Diss) 14. 4.09P
G-MYUP	Letov LK-2M Sluka *(Built F Overall - pr.no.PFA 263-12785 also c/n UK.2)* (Rotax 447)	829409x24		20.12.94	J C Dawson	(Oxspring, Sheffield) 29. 8.08P
G-MYUR	Huntwing Avon *(Built S D Pain - pr.no.BMAA HB/034)* (Rotax 582)	9409030		24. 1.95	T C Saltmarsh Rayne Hall Farm, Braintree *(Noted 1.07)*	. 3.05P
G-MYUS	CFM Shadow Series CD	257		26. 1.95	R G M-J Proost tr Aviation for Paraplegics and Tetraplegics Trust Old Sarum	22. 6.09P
G-MYUU	Pegasus Quantum 15 (Rotax 462)	6917		30. 1.95	J A Slocombe	(Backfields, Rochester) 29. 7.09P
G-MYUV	Pegasus Quantum 15 (Rotax 582)	6918		6. 2.95	D W Wilson Park Hall Farm, Mapperley, Ilkeston	29.10.08P
G-MYUW	Mainair Mercury	1024-0295-7-W822		7. 2.95	G C Hobson	St Michaels 18.11.09P
G-MYUZ	Rans S-6-ESD Coyote II *(Built D K Ross and B Davies - pr.no.PFA 204-12741)* (Rotax 582) *(Tri-cycle u/c)*	1293.568		5. 1.95	J E Gattrell and A R Trace Sittles Farm, Alrewas	25. 6.09P
G-MYVA	Kolb Twinstar Mk.III (mod) *(Built S P Read)*	PFA 205-12756		13. 2.95	E Bayliss	Ince Blundell 20. 8.08P
G-MYVB	Mainair Blade (Rotax 582)	1021-0195-7-W819		15.12.94	P Mountain	St Michaels 24. 4.09P
G-MYVC	Pegasus Quantum 15 (Rotax 582)	6904		13. 2.95	I D Edwards	Roddige 13.10.07P
G-MYVE	Mainair Blade (Rotax 582)	1027-0295-7-W825		8. 2.95	S Cooke	Tarn Farm, Cockerham 16. 7.08P
G-MYVG	Letov LK-2M Sluka *(Built L W M Summers - pr.no.PFA 263-12786)* (Rotax 447)	829409x26		15. 2.95	N I Garland	Dunkeswell 28. 9.05P
G-MYVH	Mainair Blade (Rotax 582)	1028-0295-7-W826		21. 2.95	S E Wilks Knapthorpe Lodge, Caunton	23. 6.09P
G-MYVI	Air Création 503/Fun 18S GT bis	94/004		17. 2.95	P Osborne tr Northampton Aerotow Club *(Noted 10.07)* Sywell	14. 6.07P
G-MYVJ	Pegasus Quantum 15 (Rotax 582)	6974		24. 2.95	P W Davidson and A I McPherson Pratis Farm, Leven	7. 4.09P
G-MYVK	Pegasus Quantum 15 *(Rotax 582)*	6970		27. 2.95	J Thomas Weston Zoyland	1. 5.09P
G-MYVL	Mainair Mercury (Rotax 462)	1030-0395-7-W828		1. 3.95	P J Judge	Davidstow Moor 5. 8.07P
G-MYVM	Pegasus Quantum 15 (Rotax 582)	6893	G-69-17 G-MYVM	9. 3.95	G J Gibson *(Noted 10.07)*	Perth 27. 4.97P
G-MYVN	Cyclone Airsports AX3/503	C 4043212		16. 3.95	F Watt *(wings only, fuselage at Strathdon)* Insch	5.10.03P
G-MYVO	Mainair Blade (Rotax 582)	1013-1194-7-W811		8.11.94	S S Raines	Shobdon 17. 5.09P
G-MYVP	Rans S-6-ESD Coyote II *(Built J S Liming - pr.no.PFA 204-12828)* *(Tri-cycle u/c)*	0294.593		27. 3.95	K J Legg and G Cross Redlands, Swindon	22. 7.09P
G-MYVR	Pegasus Quantum 15 (Rotax 582)	6980		21. 3.95	J M Webster Park Hall Farm, Mapperley, Ilkeston *(Noted 10.07)*	29. 5.07P
G-MYVS	Mainair Mercury (Rotax 462)	1037-0495-7-W835		12. 4.95	P S Flynn	Sandtoft 25. 4.04P
G-MYVT	Letov LK-2M Sluka *(Built J Hannibal - pr.no.PFA 263-12835)* (Rotax 447)	829409x25		17. 3.95	J P Gardiner (Newton Bank Farm, Daresbury) *(Noted 11.04)*	11.11.03P
G-MYVV	Medway Hybred 44XLR (Rotax 503) *(Sailwing c/n also quoted for G-MYLX)*	MR127/109		3. 4.95	S Perity	(Wisbech) 11. 5.07P
G-MYVY	Mainair Blade (Rotax 582)	1033-0495-7-W831		29. 3.95	G Heeks	Mill Farm, Shifnal 5. 4.09P
G-MYVZ	Mainair Blade (Rotax 582)	1034-0495-7-W832		31. 3.95	R Llewellyn Landmead Farm, Garford	31. 7.08P
G-MYWA	Mainair Mercury	1035-0495-7-W833		30. 3.95	R A Atkinson Ardenagh Great, Taghmon, County Wexford	19.10.08P
G-MYWC	Huntwing Avon *(Built F J C Binks - pr.no.BMAA HB/043)* (Rotax 503)	9409038		3. 4.95	M A Coffin	(Wrotham, Sevenoaks) 24. 6.05P
G-MYWD	Thruster T 600N (Rotax 582)	9035-T600-511	(G-MYOJ)	18. 4.95	M D Kirby Chase Farm, Little Bursted *(Substantially damaged after somersaulting during take-off Seething 17. 9.05)*	16. 8.05P
G-MYWE	Thruster T 600T (Rotax 503)	9035-T600-512	(G-MYOK)	18. 4.95	W A Stephenson	(Newry, County Armagh) 1. 8.09P
G-MYWG	Pegasus Quantum 15 (Rotax 582)	6998		20. 4.95	S L Greene Plaistows Farm, St Albans	30. 5.08P
G-MYWH	Huntwing/Experience *(Built G N Hatchett - pr.no.BMAA HB/037)*	9409025		20.12.94	R S Sanby	(Eastwood, Nottingham)
G-MYWI	Pegasus Quantum 15 (Rotax 582)	7006		1. 5.95	J R Fulcher	Deenethorpe 14. 6.08P
G-MYWJ	Pegasus Quantum 15 (Rotax 582)	6919		24. 1.95	L M Sams	Long Marston 2. 9.08P
G-MYWK	Pegasus Quantum 15 (Rotax 582)	7011		1. 5.95	G McGrane	(Dunleer, County Louth) 19. 6.09P
G-MYWL	Pegasus Quantum 15 (Rotax 582)	6995		2. 5.95	E Smith	Swinford, Rugby 27. 5.09P
G-MYWM	CFM Shadow Series CD *(Built CFM Metal-Fax - pr.no.BMAA HB/056)*	K 227		9. 5.95	N J Mckinley Plaistows Farm, St Albans	18. 4.09P
G-MYWN	Cyclone Airsports Chaser S 508 *(Conceived as Aerial Arts Chaser with c/n CH865, this was built under Cyclone c/n 7016)*	CH.865		9. 5.95	R A Rawes	(Devizes) 21. 7.08P
G-MYWO	Cyclone Pegasus Quantum 15 (Rotax 582)	6932		9. 5.95	S Gill and D Hume Stanton, Morpeth	21.11.07P
G-MYWP	Kolb Twinstar Mk.III (mod) *(Built B Albiston - pr.no.PFA 205-12561)*	K0017-0993		7. 3.95	P R Day	(Southampton) 15. 6.06P
G-MYWR	Cyclone Pegasus Quantum 15 (Rotax 582)	7002		10. 5.95	R Horton *(Also carries US Ultralight marks "E032RH")* (Allestree, Derby)	16.10.09P

G-MYWS	Cyclone Airsports Chaser S 4476946 & CH.866		17. 5.95	M H Broadbent	Westfield Farm, Hailsham 6.11.07P

(Conceived as Aerial Arts Chaser with c/n CH866, this was built under Cyclone c/n 6946)

G-MYWT	Pegasus Quantum 15	6997	19. 5.95	A G Ransom	Deenethorpe 11. 7.09P
	(Rotax 582)				
G-MYWU	Pegasus Quantum 15	7024	25. 5.95	J R Buttle	Dunkeswell 20. 7.08P
	(Rotax 582)				
G-MYWV	Rans S-4C Coyote	93.212	30. 5.95	I D Daniels	Maypole Farm, Chislet 11. 5.09P
	(Built A H Trapp - pr.no.PFA 193-12826)				
G-MYWW	Pegasus Quantum 15	7021	30. 5.95	C W Bailie	Newtownards 5.12.09P
	(Rotax 503)				
G-MYWY	Pegasus Quantum 15	6982	20. 3.95	Annabel Czajka	Stoke, Isle of Grain 11. 4.09P
	(Rotax 582)				
G-MYWZ	Thruster TST Mk.1	8128-TST-115 G-MVMJ	22. 2.93	W H J KNowles	Yundum/Banjul, The Gambia 29. 9.04P
	(Rotax 503)				
G-MYXA	TEAM Mini-MAX 91	PFA 186-12266	13. 6.95	D H Clack	Tinnel, Landulph, Saltash 5.11.08P
	(Built D S Worman)				
G-MYXB	Rans S-6-ESD Coyote II	1293.567	20. 6.95	V G J Davies and D A Hall	(Waterlooville) 27. 1.10P
	(Built A Aldridge - pr.no.PFA 204-12787) (Tri-cycle u/c)				
G-MYXC	Quad City Challenger II UK		16. 5.95	K N Dickinson	Higher Barn Farm, Hoghton
	(Built K N Dickinson) CH2-0294-UK-1099 (Hirth H2706)			(Noted 6.05)	
G-MYXD	Solar Wings Pegasus Quasar IITC	7029	21. 6.95	A Cochrane	Longacre Farm, Sandy 21. 4.08P
	(Rotax 582)				
G-MYXE	Pegasus Quantum 15	7061	23. 6.95	W Bowen	Plaistows Farm, St Albans 15. 2.09P
	(Rotax 582)				
G-MYXF	Air Création 503/Fun 18S GT bis	94/005	23. 6.95	T A Morgan	Popham 15. 1.01P
G-MYXG	Rans S-6-ESD Coyote II	0394.599	29. 6.95	G H Lee (Noted 6.05) Higher Barn Farm, Houghton 20. 6.01P	
	(Built G H Lee - pr.no.PFA 204-12879) (Rotax 503) (Tri-cycle u/c)				
G-MYXH	Cyclone Airsports AX3/503	7028	3. 7.95	S C Melton	(York) 1. 4.09P
G-MYXI	Cook Aries 1	xxxx	4. 7.95	H Cook	(Newport, Gwent)
	(Built H Cook -pr.no. BMAA HB/048) (Design awaiting finalisation 10.01- planned engine fit is BMW R80)				
G-MYXJ	Mainair Blade	1048-0795-7-W846	17. 7.95	S N Robson	Eshott 14.11.08P
	(Rotax 582)				
G-MYXK	BFC Challenger II	CH2-1194-1254	11. 7.95	P J Collins	Kilrush, County Kildare 24. 9.09P
	(Built E G Astin - c/n PFA 177A-12877) (Rotax 503)				
G-MYXL	Mignet HM-1000 Balerit	112	11. 7.95	R W Hollamby	Bardown, Wadhurst 17. 7.09P
G-MYXM	Mainair Blade	1047-0795-7-W845	19. 7.95	S C Hodgson	(Chesterfield) 7. 6.09P
	(Rotax 582)				
G-MYXN	Mainair Blade	1046-0795-7-W844	27. 7.95	M R Sands	Shotton Colliery, Peterlee 10. 4.08P
	(Rotax 582)				
G-MYXO	Letov LK-2M Sluka	8295s001	27. 7.95	G W Allport	Mill Farm, Shifnal 11. 2.09P
	(Built K C Rutland - pr.no.PFA 263-12873 (Rotax 447)				
G-MYXP	Rans S-6-ESD Coyote II	0494.605	31. 7.95	R S Amor	Weston Zoyland 1. 9.09P
	(Built K J Lywood - pr.no.PFA 204-12886) (Rotax 503) (Tail-wheel u/c)				
G-MYXR	Murphy Renegade Spirit UK PFA 188-12755		2. 8.95	S Hooker	(Sellinge, Ashford)
	(Built S Hooker)				
G-MYXS	Kolb Twinstar Mk.III (modified) K0015-0693		4. 5.94	B B Boniface	St Michaels 27 9.09P
	(Built M A Smith - pr.no.PFA 205-12528) (Rotax 582)				
G-MYXT	Pegasus Quantum 15	7073	4. 8.95	P G Hill	(Southwater, Horsham) 22. 4.09P
	(Rotax 582)				
G-MYXU	Thruster T 300	9024-T300-513	16. 8.95	D W Wilson	Mullahead, Tandragee 20. 9.08P
	(Built Tempest Aviation Ltd) (Rotax 582)				
G-MYXV	Quad City Challenger II UK		19. 7.95	M L Sumner	(Market Drayton) 14.10.08P
	(Built A Hipkin) CH2-1194-UK-1243				
G-MYXW	Pegasus Quantum 15	7090	24. 8.95	P J Oakey Lower Mountpleasant Farm, Chatteris 3. 8.09P	
	(Rotax 582)				
G-MYXX	Pegasus Quantum 15	7081	25. 8.95	J H Arnold	Milverton, Taunton 3.11.08P
	(Rotax 582)				
G-MYXY	CFM Shadow Series CD	K 245	29. 8.95	A P Watkins and C W J Davis	Roddige 8.12.08P
	(Built CFM Metal-Fax - pr.no.BMAA HB/059)				
G-MYXZ	Pegasus Quantum 15	7023	21. 6.95	N I Hardstone	Roddige 1. 1.08P
	(Rotax 582)				
G-MYYA	Mainair Blade	1052-0995-7-W850	1. 9.95	K J Watt	(Northwich) 26. 4.09P
	(Rotax 462)				
G-MYYB	Pegasus Quantum 15 Lite	7079	4. 9.95	A L Johnson	Longacre Farm, Sandy 8.11.07P
	(Rotax 582)				
G-MYYC	Pegasus Quantum 15	7094	12. 9.95	A J Rowe	Rufforth 13. 6.09P
	(Rotax 582)				
G-MYYD	Cyclone Airsports Chaser S 447 CH.7099		15. 9.95	P Robshaw	Rufforth 15. 5.07P
G-MYYE	Huntwing Avon 462	9409035	21. 9.95	A J Clarke	(Dunnington, Alcester) 6. 3.08P
	(Built P J Dickinson - pr.no.BMAA HB/041) (Rotax 462)				
G-MYYF	Quad City Challenger II UK PFA 177-12811		27. 9.95	J G and J A Smith	Longside, Peterhead 9. 6.09P
	(Built G Ferries) (Rotax 503)				
G-MYYG	Mainair Blade	1054-0995-7-W852	4.10.95	S D Pryke	Felthorpe 21. 5.09P
	(Rotax 462) (Believed supplied as kit, if so c/n should be K1054-...)				
G-MYYH	Mainair Blade	1056-1095-7-W854	3.10.95	C Nicholson	(Halifax) 2. 8.08P
	(Rotax 582)				
G-MYYI	Pegasus Quantum 15	7101	28. 9.95	P J Armitage	(Grantham) 17.11.04P
	(Rotax 582)				
G-MYYJ	Huntwing Avon	9409033	29. 9.95	R M Jarvis	(Stilton, Peterborough)
	(Built M J Slatter - pr.no.BMAA HB/033) (Rotax 503)				
G-MYYK	Pegasus Quantum 15	7100	2.10.95	J D and N G Philp Lower Upham Farm, Chiseldon 3. 7.09P	
	(Rotax 582)				
G-MYYL	Cyclone Airsports AX3/503	7110	4.10.95	C A Fletcher	Priory Farm, Tibenham 13. 9.08P

G-MYYN	Pegasus Quantum 15 (Rotax 582)	7022	3.10.95	J Darby	(Stirling)	13. 2.06P
G-MYYP	AMF Microflight Chevvron 2-32C	036	31.10.95	J Cook	North Moor, Scunthorpe (Stour Row, Shaftesbury)	18.10.09P 9. 1.08P
G-MYYR	TEAM Mini-MAX 91 (Built D Palmer)	PFA 186-12724	31.10.95	K Stevens	Otherton, Cannock	4.12.06P
G-MYYS	TEAM Mini-MAX (Built J R Hopkinson	PFA 186-11989	7.11.95	J R Hopkinson	(Chesterfield)	
G-MYYU	Mainair Mercury	1062-1295-7-W862	17.11.95	J T and A C Swannick	Ince Blundell	18. 4.06P
G-MYYV	Rans S-6-ESD-XL Coyote II (Built J Whiting - pr.no.PFA 204-12943: originally kit no.0795.851) (Rotax 503) (Tri-cycle u/c)	0896.1026	17.11.95	M B Buttle	Tarn Farm, Cockerham	2. 5.08P
G-MYYW	Mainair Blade (Rotax 582)	1051-0895-7-W849	8. 8.95	M D Kirby	Chase Farm, Little Bursted	24. 5.08P
G-MYYX	Pegasus Quantum 15 (Rotax 582)	7126	17.11.95	G W Cameron	(Edinburgh)	26. 4.09P
G-MYYY	Mainair Blade (Rotax 582)	1031-0495-7-W829	15. 3.95	E D Locke	Barton	13. 4.09P
G-MYYZ	Medway Raven X (Rotax 447)	MRB135/116	10. 1.96	J W Leaper	Croft Farm, Defford	27. 6.04P
G-MYZB	Pegasus Quantum 15 (Rotax 582)	7124	22.11.95	A Gilruth tr G-MYZB Flying Group Easter Poldar Farm, Thornhill		4. 3.08P
G-MYZC	Cyclone Airsports AX3/503	7125	5.12.95	P E Owen (Noted 7.05)	Eaglescott	2. 6.04P
G-MYZE	TEAM Mini-MAX 91 (Built E H Gould) (Global GMT-35)	PFA 186-12570	28. 9.95	R B M Etherington (Noted 11.06)	Halwell	6. 6.02P
G-MYZF	Cyclone Airsports AX3/503	7133	11.12.95	Microflight (Ireland) Ltd Mullaghmore, Coleraine		9. 4.08P
G-MYZG	Cyclone Airsports AX3/503	7137	11. 1.96	D S Thomas (Bishopsteignton, Teignmouth)		27. 7.08P
G-MYZH	Chargus Titan 38	JPA-1	16. 1.96	T J Gayton-Polley	(Billingshurst)	
G-MYZJ	Pegasus Quantum 15 (Rotax 582)	7150	24. 1.96	J M Fearn	(Ripley)	6. 3.08P
G-MYZK	Pegasus Quantum 15 (Rotax 582)	7157	5. 2.96	J D G Welch	(Tweedsmuir, Biggar)	13. 2.09P
G-MYZL	Pegasus Quantum 15 (Rotax 582)	7158	5. 2.96	S Jelley	(Chichester)	28. 7.08P
G-MYZM	Pegasus Quantum 15 (Rotax 582)	7159	5. 2.96	D Hope	(Uckfield)	11. 5.09P
G-MYZO	Medway Raven X	MRB136/115	12. 2.96	M C Arnold	Rochester	26. 7.05P
G-MYZP	CFM Shadow Series DD (Built D G Cook - pr.no.PFA 161-12914: sequence no.conflicts with G-BXDY)	249	7. 2.96	R M Davies and P I Hodgson	(Amersham)	31. 5.08P
G-MYZR	Rans S-6-ESD-XL Coyote II (Built V R Leggott - pr.no.PFA 204-12958) (Rotax 503) (Tri-cycle u/c)	1295.902	9. 2.96	G J Simoni tr Rans Clan	Kemble	15. 8.08P
G-MYZV	Rans S-6-ESD-XL Coyote II (Built H Lammers - pr.no.PFA 204-12946) (Rotax 582) (Tri-cycle u/c)	0795.849	26. 2.96	B W Savory	Long Marston	2.10.08P
G-MYZY	Pegasus Quantum 15 (Rotax 582)	7156	8. 2.96	N C O Watney	Rochester	25. 6.08P
G-MZAA	Mainair Blade (Rotax 462)	1059-1195-7-W857	24.10.95	A G Butler	Shenstone Hall Farm, Shenstone	23. 6.07P
G-MZAB	Mainair Blade (Rotax 582)	1043-0695-7-W841	26. 5.95	A Meadley	Baxby Manor, Husthwaite	7. 6.05P
G-MZAC	BFC Challenger II (Built M N Calhaem - pr.no.PFA 177A-12716) (Rotax 503)	CH2-0294-1100	21. 7.95	M N Calhaem	Fradswell, Stafford	26. 3.04P
G-MZAE	Mainair Blade	1063-1295-7-W863	4.12.95	D J Guild	Great Oakley	19. 5.09P
G-MZAF	Mainair Blade (Rotax 582)	1045-0795-7-W843	1.12.95	C M Bale	Upfield Farm, Whitson	1. 4.09P
G-MZAG	Mainair Blade (Rotax 582)	1042-0695-7-W840	26. 5.95	D R G Cornwell	St Michaels	16. 5.09P
G-MZAH	Rans S-6-ESD Coyote II (Built A Hipkin- pr.no.PFA 204-12553) (Damaged and repaired with frame.0491-186 [ex G-MWVL]) (Rotax 503) (Tri-cycle u/c)	0393.470	3. 9.93	C J Collett	Long Marston	18. 8.04P
G-MZAJ	Mainair Blade (Rotax 582)	1067-0196-7-W869	20.12.95	M P Daley (Noted 5.07)	Hunsdon	24. 6.02P
G-MZAM	Mainair Blade (Rotax 582)	1044-0695-7-W842	31. 5.95	B M Marsh and P David	Shobdon	14.12.09P
G-MZAN	Pegasus Quantum 15 (Rotax 582)	7188	7. 3.96	P M Leahy	(Exeter)	24. 7.09P
G-MZAP	Mainair Blade 912	1036-0495-7-W834	31. 3.95	K D Adams	Ince Blundell	19. 4.09P
G-MZAR	Mainair Blade (Rotax 582)	1072-0296-7-W874	13. 2.96	C Bayliss	Ince Blundell	4. 4.07P
G-MZAS	Mainair Blade (Rotax 582)	1049-0895-7-W847	15. 8.95	T Carter	Pound Green, Buttonoak, Bewdley	18.10.04P
G-MZAT	Mainair Blade (Rotax 582)	1060-1195-7-W860	29.11.95	M J Moulton Cottage Farm, Norton Juxta, Twycross		21. 9.08P
G-MZAU	Mainair Blade (Stolen 1999: Sailwing located 2004: new Trike built by P&M Aviation from spare parts: original build numbers retained and replacement Rotax 582 fitted)	1064-0196-7-W864	29.11.95	A F Glover	(Woolston, Warrington)	7. 9.08P
G-MZAV	Mainair Blade (Rotax 462)	1078-0396-7-W881	11. 3.96	G Taylor	(St Helens)	6. 6.09P
G-MZAW	Pegasus Quantum 15 (Rotax 503)	7160	14. 2.96	C A Mackenzie	Sackville Lodge, Riseley	12. 7.09P
G-MZAX	Pegasus Quantum 15 (Rotax 582)	7152	11. 3.96	D W Beach (Noted 8.07)	Willingale	30. 3.05P
G-MZAY	Mainair Blade (Rotax 462)	1077-0396-7-W880	15. 3.96	E J Carass	(South Burlingham, Norwich)	15. 6.08P
G-MZAZ	Mainair Blade (Rotax 462)	1040-0595-7-W838	26. 5.95	T Porter and D Whiteley	St Michaels	27. 7.09P

G-MZBA	Mainair Blade	1068-0296-7-W870	15. 3.96	M Leyden and S Cronin	(Ennis, Ireland)	3. 8.09P
	(Rotax 912-UL)					
G-MZBB	Pegasus Quantum 15	7139	13. 3.96	T Campbell	Glenrothes	27. 8.08P
	(Rotax 582)					
G-MZBC	Pegasus Quantum 15	7077	15. 8.95	B M Quinn	Barlow, Sheffield	27 7.09P
	(Rotax 582)					
G-MZBD	Rans S-6-ESD-XL Coyote II	0795.850	15. 3.96	I C Smit	Otherton, Cannock	9. 5.09P
	(Built H W Foster - pr.no.PFA 204-12957) (Tri-cycle u/c)					
G-MZBF	Letov LK-2M Sluka	PFA 263-12881	18. 3.96	V Simpson	Mullahead, Tandragee	24. 6.09P
	(Built C R Stockdale) (Rotax 447)					
G-MZBG	Whittaker MW6-S Fatboy Flyer		20. 3.96	M W Kilvert and I Rowlands-Jones		
	(Built A W Hodder)	PFA 164-12891			(Newtown, Powys)	1. 6.01P
	(Rotax 503)					
G-MZBH	Rans S-6-ESD Coyote II	0392.277	21. 3.96	D Sutherland	Breighton	27. 4.07P
	(Built D Sutherland - pr.no.PFA 204-12244) (Tri-cycle u/c)			(Noted 12.07)		
G-MZBI	Pegasus Quantum 15	7189	21. 3.96	A B Sev, A L Bagnall and I W Barlow		
	(Rotax 582)				Park Hall Farm, Mapperley, Ilkeston	8. 8.08P
G-MZBK	Letov LK-2M Sluka	8295s002	26. 3.96	G N Holland	(Shoscombe, Bath)	24. 7.09P
	(Built R Painter - pr.no.PFA 263-12872) (Rotax 447)					
G-MZBL	Mainair Blade	1080-0496-7-W883	11. 4.96	C J Rubery	Weston Zoyland	9. 2.09P
	(Rotax 582)					
G-MZBN	CFM Shadow Series CD	K 069 G-MTWP	22. 4.96	W J Buskell (Noted 10.08)	Andrewsfield	9. 6.04P
	(Built CFM Metal-Fax - pr.no.BMAA HB/073 issued for rebuild by P James)					
G-MZBO	Pegasus Quantum 15	7218	3. 5.96	K C Beattie	(Johnstone)	15.12.07P
	(Rotax 582)					
G-MZBR	Southdown Raven X	SN2232/0082	24. 5.96	D M Lane	(Stourbridge)	
G-MZBS	CFM Shadow Series D	K 274	14. 5.96	S K Ryan	Plaistows Farm, St Albans	15. 9.06P
	(Built P A White - pr.no.PFA 161-13008)					
G-MZBT	Pegasus Quantum 15-912	7224	22. 5.96	A P Whitmarsh	Jackrell's Farm, Southwater	8. 8.09P
G-MZBU	Rans S-6-ESD-XL Coyote II	0296.938	30. 5.96	R S Marriott	Otherton, Cannock	17.11.09P
	(Built J B Marshall - pr.no.PFA 204-12992)					
G-MZBV	Rans S-6-ESD-XL Coyote II	0396.950	30. 5.96	L C Barham and R I Cannan	Andreas, Isle of Man	3. 6.09P
	(Built P F Hill - pr.no.PFA 204-13009) (Rotax 582) (Tri-cycle u/c)					
G-MZBW	Quad City Challenger II	CH2-0795-UK-1367	19. 2.96	R T L Chaloner	Dunkeswell	25. 9.07P
	(Rotax 582) (Built C Bird - pr.no.PFA 177-12971))					
G-MZBX	Whittaker MW6-S-LW Fatboy Flyer		16. 5.96	A A Comper (Noted 9.06)		
	(Built S Rose and P Tearall) PFA 164-12563				Longacre Farm, Sandy	22. 6.05P
	(Rotax 503)					
G-MZBY	Pegasus Quantum 15	7227	30. 5.96	A Hutchinson	(Scarborough)	31. 7.08P
	(Rotax 582)					
G-MZBZ	Quad City Challenger II UK					
	(Hirth 2706)	CH2 0695 UK 1360	11. 3.96	T R Gregory	Dunkeswell	22. 6.05P
	(Built J Flisher - pr.no.PFA 177-12928)					
G-MZCA	Rans S-6-ESD-XL Coyote II	0396.953	31. 5.96	W Scott	Priory Farm, Tibenham	11. 8.07P
	(Built S J Everett, K Kettles and F Williams - pr.no.PFA 204-12997) (Tri-cycle u/c) (Noted 2.08)					
G-MZCB	Cyclone Airsports Chaser S 447	7220	4. 6.96	R W Keene	Over Farm, Gloucester	2. 4.09P
G-MZCC	Mainair Blade	1086-0696-7-W889	7. 6.96	K S Rissmann	(King's Lynn)	18. 5.07P
	(Rotax 912-UL)					
G-MZCD	Mainair Blade	1087-0696-7-W890	10. 6.96	C Bayliss	Ince Blundell	29. 3.09P
	(Rotax 582)					
G-MZCE	Mainair Blade	K1088-0696-7-W891	17. 6.96	C T Halliday	Ince Blundell	29. 7.08P
	(Rotax 462)					
G-MZCF	Mainair Blade	1089-0696-7-W892	30. 8.96	C Hannaby	(Wrexham)	9. 8.04P
	(Rotax 462)					
G-MZCG	Mainair Blade	1090-0696-7-W893	17. 6.96	M R Mosley	Headon Farm, Retford	5. 8.08P
	(Rotax 462)					
G-MZCH	Whittaker MW6-S Fatboy Flyer	PFA 164-12131	7. 6.96	J T Moore	Dunkeswell	17. 7.08P
	(Built E J Blake and B G King) (Rotax 503)					
G-MZCI	Pegasus Quantum 15	7231	10. 6.96	P H Risdale	Prospect Farm, Wollaston	6.10.08P
	(Rotax 582)					
G-MZCJ	Pegasus Quantum 15	7233	14. 6.96	F E Hall	Prospect Farm, Wollaston	10. 8.08P
	(Rotax 582)					
G-MZCK	AMF Microflight Chevvron 2-32C	038	11. 7.96	T K Lane	(Symonds Yat, Ross-on-Wye)	19. 6.07P
G-MZCM	Pegasus Quantum Lite	7219	3. 5.96	S G McLachlan	(Stoke-on-Trent)	28. 5.09P
	(Rotax 582)					
G-MZCN	Mainair Blade	1079-0396-7-W882	27. 6.96	P C Williams	(Wallasey)	21. 6.04P
	(Rotax 582)					
G-MZCO	Mainair Mercury	1091-0796-7-W894	26. 6.96	E Rush	(Congleton)	13.11.06P
	(Rotax 462)					
G-MZCR	Pegasus Quantum 15	7234	28. 6.96	J E P Stubberfield	(Kenley)	23. 7.09P
	(Rotax 503)					
G-MZCS	TEAM Mini-MAX 91	PFA 186-12646	20.12.95	R F Morton	Little Rissington	11. 7.08P
	(Built C S Cox) (Rotax 377)					
G-MZCT	CFM Shadow Series CD	277	11. 7.96	W G Gill	Plaistows Farm, St Albans	21. 8.07P
G-MZCU	Mainair Blade	1082-0496-7-W885	1. 5.96	C E Pearce	Thurton	26. 6.08P
	(Rotax 462)					
G-MZCV	Pegasus Quantum 15	7235	11. 7.96	B S Toole	Guy Lane Farm, Waverton	27. 9.07P
	(Rotax 503)					
G-MZCX	Huntwing Avon Skytrike	9510055	17. 7.96	G R Coghill and W Mccarthy tr Huntwing Group		
	(Built C Harrison - pr.no.BMAA HB/072) (Rotax 503)				Wick	13. 9.06P
G-MZCY	Pegasus Quantum 15	7236	19. 7.96	J R Appleton and G A Davidson		
	(Rotax 582)				Tarn Farm, Cockerham	4. 9.08P
G-MZDA	Rans S-6-ESD-XL Coyote II	0396.951	29. 7.96	R Plummer and S Day		
	(Built J Dent and W C Lombard - pr.no.PFA 204-13019) (Rotax 582) (Tri-cycle u/c)				Waterstones Farm, Newby Wiske	25. 8.09P

G-MZDB	Pegasus Quantum 15-912	7237		31. 7.96	D T Mackenzie tr Scottish Aerotow Club		
						Easter Poldar Farm, Thornhill	10. 5.09P
G-MZDC	Pegasus Quantum 15 (Rotax 582)	7246		2. 8.96	M T Jones	Enstone	13. 6.06P
G-MZDD	Pegasus Quantum 15 (Rotax 503)	7114	G-69-23	11. 7.96	A J Todd	(Luton)	18. 2.09P
G-MZDE	Pegasus Quantum 15 (Rotax 582)	7238		12. 7.96	R G Hedley	(High Lane, Stockport)	21. 3.09P
G-MZDF	Mainair Blade (Rotax 462)	1093-0896-7-W896		15. 8.96	M Liptrot	Glassonby	31. 5.09P
G-MZDG	Rans S-6-ESD-XL Coyote II	0696.1002		7. 8.96	J M Coffin	Darley Moor, Ashbourne	30. 4.09P
	(Built R Rhodes - pr.no.PFA 204-13030) (Tri-cycle u/c)						
G-MZDH	Pegasus Quantum 15-912	7248		12. 8.96	R C Reynolds	Arclid Green, Sandbach	29. 1.10P
G-MZDJ	Medway Raven X	MRB138/119		19. 8.96	R Bryan (Noted 1.05)	Doynton	11. 8.04P
G-MZDK	Mainair Blade	1084-0596-7-W887		9. 5.96	B L Cook	Sandtoft	24. 1.08P
	(C/n reported as 1084-0696-7) (Rotax 582)						
G-MZDL	Whittaker MW6-S Fatboy Flyer			19. 8.96	J P S Ixer and M F Frost		
	(Built C D Wills) (Rotax 582) PFA 164-12412					Rayne Hall Farm, Braintree	10. 5.08P
G-MZDM	Rans S-6-ESD-XL Coyote II	0396.954		2. 9.96	M E Nicholas	Kemble	18. 9.06P
	(Built M E Nicholas - pr.no .PFA 204-13022) (Rotax 503) (Tri-cycle u/c)						
G-MZDN	Pegasus Quantum 15 (Rotax 582)	7255		5. 9.96	P G Ford	Sutton Meadows	6.11.09P
G-MZDP	AMF Microflight Chevvron 2-32C	020		3. 4.90	F Overall	Whitehall Farm, Wethersfield	16. 3.96P
					(Damaged mid 1995: stored 2001)		
G-MZDR	Rans S-6-ESD-XL Coyote II	0396.592		8. 8.96	J D Gibbons	(Newry, County Armagh)	21. 3.04P
	(Built R Pyper and P McGill - pr.no.PFA 204-13012)						
G-MZDS	Cyclone Airsports AX3/503	7253		16. 9.96	M P James	(Burton Joyce, Nottingham)	16.12.09P
G-MZDT	Mainair Blade (Rotax 582)	1096-0996-7-W899		19. 9.96	T J Williams	Barton	15. 5.09P
G-MZDU	Pegasus Quantum 15-912	7260		19. 9.96	G A Breen	Portimão, Faro, Portugal	26.10.07P
G-MZDV	Pegasus Quantum 15 (Rotax 582)	7199		9. 4.96	S A Mallett	Little Snoring	4. 6.09P
G-MZDX	Letov LK-2M Sluka	8295s004		30. 9.96	J L Barker	Priory Farm, Tibenham	3. 4.09P
	(Built T J T Dorricott - pr.no.PFA 263-12882) (Rotax 447)						
G-MZDY	Pegasus Quantum 15 (Rotax 462HP)	7263		2.10.96	R Bailey	Sutton Meadows	7.10.04P
G-MZDZ	Hunt Avon/Huntwing	9501042		23.10.96	E W Laidlaw (Under construction 2001) (Turriff)		
	(Built E W Laidlaw - pr.no.BMAA HB/045)						
G-MZEA	BFC Challenger II	CH2-0294-1101		22. 4.96	G S Cridland	Wymeswold	29. 8.08P
	(Built G S Cridland - pr.no.PFA 177A-12728) (Hirth 2706)						
G-MZEB	Mainair Blade (Rotax 462)	1074-0396-7-W876		22. 7.96	G Todd	(Clotton, Tarporley)	13. 7.05P
G-MZEC	Pegasus Quantum 15 Super Sport (Rotax 582)	7278		24.10.96	A B Godber	Bradley Ashbourne, Derby	28. 3.08P
G-MZED	Mainair Blade (Rotax 582)	1092-0796-7-W895		3. 7.96	C W Potts	Eshott	5. 6.08P
G-MZEE	Pegasus Quantum 15 (Rotax 582)	7245		9. 8.96	J L Brogan	Stoke, Isle of Grain	1. 6.09P
G-MZEG	Mainair Blade (Rotax 582)	1095-0896-7-W898		8. 8.96	R and A Soltysik	Otherton, Cannock	12.10.08P
G-MZEH	Pegasus Quantum 15 (Rotax 582)	7259		19. 9.96	P S Hall	(Rushden)	16.10.08P
G-MZEJ	Mainair Blade (Rotax 462)	1097-0996-7-W900		8.10.96	P G Thomas	St Michaels	13. 5.09P
G-MZEK	Mainair Mercury (Rotax 462)	1098-1096-7-W901		14.10.96	M Whiteman-Heywood	Arclid Green, Sandbach	6. 5.09P
G-MZEL	Cyclone Airsports AX3-503	7250		30.10.96	R I Simpson	Clipgate Farm, Denton	18. 4.04P
G-MZEM	Pegasus Quantum 15-912	7277		8.11.96	L H Black	Newtownards	9. 5.09P
G-MZEN	Rans S-6-ESD Coyote II	1294.705		9. 7.96	I Fernihough	Bradley	6. 5.09P
	(Built P Bottomley - pr.no.PFA 204-12823) (Tri-cycle u/c)						
G-MZEO	Rans S-6-ESD-XL Coyote II	0696.1001		19.11.96	R W Lenthall	Headon Farm, Retford	17. 8.06P
	(Built J A A Dungey - pr.no.PFA 204-13046)						
G-MZEP	Mainair Blade	1103-1296-7-W906		13.12.96	D C Haslam	(Newcastle-under-Lyne)	29. 4.09P
G-MZER	Cyclone AX2000	7251	G-69-28	4.12.96	J H Keep	Henstridge	16. 4.09P
			G-MZER				
G-MZES	Letov LK-2M Sluka	8296K10		5.12.96	J L Self	Priory Farm, Tibenham	27. 4.09P
	(Built C Parkinson - pr.no.PFA 263-13064) (Rotax 447)						
G-MZEU	Rans S-6-ESD-XL Coyote II	0296.939		23.12.96	N Grugan	Eshott	27. 4.09P
	(Built J E Holloway - pr.no.PFA 204-13023) (Tri-cycle u/c)						
G-MZEV	Mainair Rapier	1101-1296-7-W904		7. 1.97	W T Gardner	Tarsan Lane, Portadown	2. 1.10P
G-MZEW	Mainair Blade (Rotax 462)	1105-0197-7-W908		13. 1.97	S J Meehan	(Liss)	7. 6.08P
G-MZEX	Pegasus Quantum 15 (Rotax 582)	7292		19.11.96	J P Quinlan	Park Hall Farm, Mapperley, Ilkeston	22. 4.08P
G-MZEY	Micro Aviation B 22S Bantam	96-002	ZK-TII	7. 1.97	P F Mayes	Pound Green, Buttonoak, Bewdley	14.10.07P
G-MZEZ	Pegasus Quantum 15-912	7285		8.11.96	M J Ing	Burnwood Farm	5. 9.08P
G-MZFA	Cyclone AX2000	7301		17.12.96	R S Mcmaster	Sackville Lodge, Riseley	15. 4.09P
G-MZFB	Mainair Blade (Rotax 462)	1108-0197-7-W911		7. 1.97	A J Plant	(Manchester)	17.10.08P
G-MZFC	Letov LK-2M Sluka	8296K009		7. 1.97	R Pratt	(Eaton Socon)	31.10.07P
	(Built G Johnson - pr.no.PFA 263-13063) (Rotax 447)						
G-MZFD	Mainair Rapier (Rotax 462)	1109-0197-7-W912		24. 1.97	R Gill	Knapthorpe Lodge, Caunton	2. 9.06P

G-MZFE	Huntwing Avon	9507049	16. 1.97	G J Latham	Sittles Farm, Alrewas	15. 6.05P
	(Built G J Latham - pr.no.BMAA HB/061) (Rotax 503)					
G-MZFF	Huntwing Avon 503	9604058	22. 1.97	B J Adamson	Ince Blundell	16. 1.03P
	(Built B J Adamson - pr.no.BMAA HB/074)			(Noted 8.05)		
G-MZFG	Pegasus Quantum 15	7305	21. 1.97	A M Prentice	Yundum/Banjul, The Gambia	23. 3.05P
	(Rotax 582)					
G-MZFH	AMF Microflight Chevvron 2-32C	039	27. 3.97	A Greenwell	(Beckington, Frome)	8. 5.09P
G-MZFI	Lorimer Iolaire	xxxxx	30. 1.97	H Lorimer "Iolaire" (Stored 11.06)		
	(Built H Lorimer - pr.no.BMAA HB/035) (BMW)				Hunterston Farm, Stair	
G-MZFK	Whittaker MW6 Merlin	PFA 164-11626	10. 2.97	G J Chadwick tr G-MZFK Flying Group		
	(Built K Worthington) (Rotax 532)				Tarn Farm, Cockerham	9.12.02P
G-MZFL	Rans S-6-ESD-XL Coyote II	0696.999	12. 2.97	H Adams	Kirkbride	15. 8.08P
	(Built G A Clayton - pr.no.PFA 204-13041) (Tri-cycle u/c)					
G-MZFN	Rans S-6-ESD Coyote II	1195.894	26. 2.97	C J and W R Wallbank	Ley Farm, Chirk	16. 4.08P
	(Built C R Wallbank - pr.no.PFA 204-12977)					
G-MZFO	Thruster T 600N	9037-T600N-001	4. 3.97	J Berry	Barton	24. 8.07P
	(Rotax 503)					
G-MZFR	Thruster T 600N	9047-T600N-003	4. 3.97	P J Matthews	(Torquay)	28. 7.08P
	(Rotax 503)					
G-MZFS	Mainair Blade	1110-0297-7-W913	8. 1.97	W Russell	Easter Poldar Farm, Thornhill	16.12.09P
	(Rotax 582) (Officially regd with Trike c/n 1010-0297-7)					
G-MZFT	Pegasus Quantum 15-912	7264	2.10.96	C Childs	(Weeley)	24. 8.09P
G-MZFU	Thruster T 600N 450 Jab	9047-T600N-004	4. 3.97	G J Slater	Clench Common	13. 2.09P
G-MZFV	Pegasus Quantum 15-912	7324	13. 3.97	B Cook	Hunsdon	25. 4.09P
G-MZFX	Cyclone AX2000	7322	14. 3.97	Conair Sports Ltd	Southam	7. 6.07P
G-MZFY	Rans S-6-ESD-XL Coyote II	0696.1003	17. 3.97	L G Tserkezos	Popham	23. 3.08P
	(Built L G Tserkezos - pr.no.PFA 204-13043) (Tri-cycle u/c)					
G-MZFZ	Mainair Blade	1119-0497-7-W922	2. 4.97	D J Bateman	(Ipswich)	3. 1.10P
	(Rotax 582)					
G-MZGA	Cyclone AX2000	7303	17.12.96	N D Townend	Sackville Lodge, Riseley	1.11.08P
G-MZGB	Cyclone AX2000	7302	28. 1.97	P Hegarty	Lower Mountpleasant Farm, Chatteris	19. 5.08P
G-MZGC	Cyclone AX2000	7304	20.12.96	C E Walls	Stonewalls, Victoria Bridge, Strabane	16. 6.07P
G-MZGD	Rans S-5 Coyote	89.095	1. 4.97	M J Olsen	Wombleton	17. 8.09P
	(Built A G Headford - pr.no.PFA 193-13096))					
G-MZGF	Letov LK-2M Sluka	8296K008	8. 4.97	G Lombardi and R C Hinkins	RAF Wyton	21.10.09P
	(Built R J Cook - pr.no. PFA 263-13073) (Rotax 447)					
G-MZGH	Huntwing Avon 462	9406021	20.10.96	J H Cole	Otherton, Cannock	8.11.08P
	(Built G C Horner - pr.no.BMAA HB/070)					
G-MZGI	Mainair Blade	1117-0397-7-W920	11. 4.97	H M Roberts	Caernarfon	8. 8.08P
	(Rotax 912-UL)					
G-MZGJ	Kolb Twinstar Mk.III	K0008-0193	16. 4.97	C D Gates	(Whitstable)	16. 9.08P
	(Built P Coppock - pr.no.PFA 205-12421) (Hirth 2705 R06)					
G-MZGK	Pegasus Quantum 15	7331	30. 4.97	C D Cross and S H Moss		
	(Rotax 582)				Osbaston Lodge Farm, Nuneaton	6. 2.09P
G-MZGL	Mainair Rapier	1104-0197-7-W907	18.12.96	V J Noonan	(Wybunbury, Nantwich)	27. 7.09P
G-MZGM	Cyclone AX2000	7334	1. 5.97	W G Dunn	Dowland, Winkleigh	27.10.09P
G-MZGN	Pegasus Quantum 15	7332	2. 5.97	B J Youngs	Sutton Meadows	23. 5.08P
	(Rotax 503)					
G-MZGO	Pegasus Quantum 15	7320	20. 3.97	S F G Allen	Long Marston	12. 7.09P
	(Rotax 582)					
G-MZGP	Cyclone AX2000	7333	7. 5.97	D G Palmer tr Buchan Light Aeroplane Club		
					Mintlaw, Peterhead	14. 6.07P
G-MZGS	CFM Shadow Series DD	K 284	8. 5.97	P Bayliss	Ince Blundell	19. 2.09P
	(Built M J McChrystal - pr.no.PFA 161-13050) (Rotax 447)					
G-MZGT	Roger Hardy RH7B Tiger Light		10. 3.97	P J Fahie	Deptford Farm, Wylye	21. 1.05P
	(Built J B McNab)	PFA 230-13013		(Noted 12.06)		
G-MZGU	Arrowflight Hawk II (UK)	PFA 266-13075	8. 5.97	J N Holden (Noted 7.06)	Mullaghmore, Coleraine	3. 5.02P
	(Built Arrowflight Aviation Ltd) (Rotax 503)					
G-MZGV	Pegasus Quantum 15	7339	12. 6.97	R E Kilby tr G-MZGV Syndicate	Dunkeswell	9. 6.09P
	(Rotax 582)					
G-MZGW	Mainair Blade	1112-0297-7-W915	19. 2.97	R Almond	Wickhambrook, Newmarket	6.11.09P
	(Rotax 462)					
G-MZGY	Thruster T 600N	9057-T600N-006	28. 4.97	P E Young	Wing Farm, Longbridge Deverill	5. 2.09P
	(Rotax 503) (Type change to T600N-430)					
G-MZGZ	Thruster T.600N	9057-T600N-007	28. 4.97	J S Morgan	(Pershore)	15. 5.09P
	(Rotax 503)					
G-MZHA	Thruster T 600T	9057-T600T-008	28. 4.97	P Stark (on rebuild 9.08)	Strathaven	10. 8.05P
	(Rotax 503)					
G-MZHB	Mainair Blade	1114-0297-7-W917	19. 2.97	A Szczepanek	Guy Lane Farm, Waverton	13. 4.09P
	(Rotax 462)					
G-MZHD	Thruster T 600T	9067-T600T-010	13. 5.97	B E Foster	(Tain)	12. 6.08P
	(Rotax 503)					
G-MZHE	Thruster T 600N	9067-T600N-011	13. 5.97	R Bellew	(Collon, County Meath)	26. 6.08P
	(Rotax 503)					
G-MZHF	Thruster T 600N Sprint	9067-T600N-012	13. 5.97	R Benner and K Harmston	Watnall	4.10.08P
	(Rotax 582)					
G-MZHG	Whittaker MW6-T Merlin	PFA 164-11420	16. 6.97	R Hatton	Andreas, Isle of Man	24. 6.06P
	(Built M G Speers) (Rotax 532)					
G-MZHI	Pegasus Quantum 15	7337	27. 5.97	F P MacDonald	(Boothlands Farm, Newdigate)	12. 7.09P
	(Rotax 582)					
G-MZHJ	Mainair Rapier	1123-0697-7-W926	17. 6.97	G Standish and R Jones		
	(Rotax 462)				(Lowton, Warrington and Manchester)	22. 7.09P
G-MZHK	Pegasus Quantum 15	7352	24. 6.97	O Goodwin	(York)	16. 5.08P
	(Rotax 582)					

G-MZHM	TEAM Hi-MAX 1700R	PFA 272-12912	8. 1.97	M H McKeown	(Gorey, County Wexford) 28. 3.08P
	(Built M H McKeown) (Robin 440) (Officially regd with Rotax 447)				
G-MZHN	Pegasus Quantum 15	7351	27. 6.97	F W Frerichs	Sackville Lodge, Riseley 3. 6.08P
	(Rotax 462HP)				
G-MZHO	Quad City Challenger II	PFA 177-12936	15. 7.97	J Pavelin	East Barling, Essex 21. 8.09P
	(Built J Pavelin)				
G-MZHP	Pegasus Quantum 15	7353	15. 7.97	P C J Coidan	(Garboldisham, Diss) 10. 2.09P
	(Rotax 582)				
G-MZHR	Cyclone AX2000	7307	7. 3.97	E Shields	Darley Moor, Ashbourne 16. 8.09P
G-MZHS	Thruster T 600T	9077-T600T-013	4. 7.97	D Mahajan	Damyn's Hall, Upminster 29.10.07P
	(Rotax 582) *(Officially regd with Rotax 503)*				
G-MZHT	Whittaker MW6 Merlin	PFA 164-11244	12. 6.97	G J Chadwick	Tarn Farm, Cockerham 18. 8.05P
	(Built P Mogg) (Hirth 2706)				
G-MZHU	Thruster T 600N Sprint	9077-T600T-019	4. 7.97	E Lewis	Weston Zoyland 8.11.08P
	(Rotax 582) *(Originally built as "T 600T")*				
G-MZHV	Thruster T 600N Sprint	9077-T600T-018	4. 7.97	H G Denton	Leicester 14. 8.09P
	(Rotax 582) *(Originally built as "T 600T")*				
G-MZHW	Thruster T 600N	9077-T600N-017	4. 7.97	K H Smalley	Wickenby 26. 9.08P
	(Rotax 503)				
G-MZHY	Thruster T 600N	9077-T600N-015	4. 7.97	G Jones	Greenlands, Rhuallt 6. 4.08P
	(Rotax 503)				
G-MZIB	Pegasus Quantum 15	7354	15. 7.97	S Murphy	Trim, County Meath 12. 7.09P
	(Rotax 582)				
G-MZIC	Pegasus Quantum 15	7348	24. 6.97	H M Squire and C F Two tr Swansea Airsports Services	
	(Rotax 503)				(Clapham, Bedford) 6. 8.03P
G-MZID	Whittaker MW6 Merlin	PFA 164-11383	15. 7.97	C P F Sheppard	(Grange Mill, Matlock) 24. 8.06P
	(Built M G A Wood) (Rotax 503)				
G-MZIE	Pegasus Quantum 15	7359	6. 8.97	Flylight Airsports Ltd	Sywell 11. 2.09P
	(Rotax 582)				
G-MZIF	Pegasus Quantum 15	7355	16. 7.97	D Parsons Harringe Court, Sellindge, Folkestone 3.10.08P	
	(Rotax 582)				
G-MZIH	Mainair Blade	1128-0797-7-W931	16. 7.97	D Perry	Old Sarum 9. 8.08P
	(Rotax 462)				
G-MZII	TEAM Mini-MAX 88	PFA 186-11842	19. 3.97	M J Kirk	Weston Zoyland 10. 4.04P
	(Built G F M Garner)				
G-MZIJ	Pegasus Quantum 15	7362	14. 8.97	D L Wright	Sywell 31. 5.09P
	(Rotax 582)				
G-MZIK	Pegasus Quantum 15	7368	8. 9.97	L A Read	Eaglescott 8.10.08P
	(Rotax 582)				
G-MZIL	Mainair Rapier	1132-0897-7-W935	1. 9.97	I Lythgoe	Deenethorpe 11.11.07P
	(Rotax 462)				
G-MZIM	Mainair Rapier	1124-0697-7-W927	9. 6.97	M J McKegney	Newtownards 1. 9.08P
	(Rotax 462)				
G-MZIR	Mainair Blade	1134-0997-7-W937	18. 9.97	S Connor	Rhedyn Coch Farm, Rhuallt 29. 7.08P
	(Rotax 582)				
G-MZIS	Mainair Blade	1115-0397-7-W918	17. 2.97	M K Richings	(Scarborough) 3. 7.09P
	(Rotax 462)				
G-MZIT	Mainair Blade	1129-0897-7-W932	16. 7.97	P M Horn	Shotton Colliery, Peterlee 25. 4.08P
	(Rotax 912-UL)				
G-MZIU	Pegasus Quantum 15	7371	15.10.97	A P Douglas-Dixon	Rufforth 22. 4.09P
	(Rotax 582)				
G-MZIV	Cyclone AX2000	7372	21.10.97	C J Tomlin	Knapthorpe Lodge, Caunton 14.11.09P
G-MZIW	Mainair Blade	1127-0797-7-W930	16. 7.97	S R Pickering	(Llanbedr) 3. 2.08P
G-MZIX	Mignet HM-1000 Balerit	130	23. 9.97	P E H Scott	(Stockbridge) 10. 6.08P
G-MZIY	Rans S-6-ESD-XL Coyote II	1096.1050	29. 9.97	P A Bell	Tarn Farm, Cockerham 20.12.07P
	(Built P A Bell - pr.no.PFA 204-13184) (Tri-cycle u/c) (Rebuilt with new fuselage frame C 1998)				
G-MZIZ	Murphy Renegade Spirit UK	257 G-MWGP	21.10.92	B L R J Keeping	Davidstow Moor 26. 6.09P
	(Built B Bayley - pr.no.PFA 188-11701)				
G-MZJA	Mainair Blade	1135-0997-7-W938	30. 9.97	R C McArthur	Ince Blundell 17. 5.09P
	(Rotax 582)				
G-MZJB	Aviasud Mistral	047 (ex ?)	30. 9.97	J M Whitham (Delves Farm, Delves, Huddersfield)	
G-MZJD	Mainair Blade	1130-0897-7-W933	7. 8.97	P Barkert and R W Neal	
	(Rotax 503)				(Fulwood, Preston and Hindley, Wigan) 3.10.08P
G-MZJE	Mainair Rapier	1136-1097-7-W939	17.10.97	J E Davies	(Southport) 5. 8.04P
G-MZJF	Cyclone AX2000	7378	2.12.97	D J Lewis and V E Booth	Long Marston 21.12.04P
G-MZJG	Pegasus Quantum 15	7335	2. 5.97	P D Myer	Upfield Farm, Whitson 18. 7.09P
	(Rotax 462)				
G-MZJH	Pegasus Quantum 15	7350	25. 6.97	P Copping	Sackville Lodge, Riseley 8. 4.09P
	(Rotax 503)				
G-MZJI	Rans S-6-ESD-XL Coyote II	1096.1046	3.11.97	M A Newbould and C Topp	
	(Built J Whiting - pr.no.PFA 204-13221) (Tri-cycle u/c)				Baxby Manor, Husthwaite 22. 9.06P
G-MZJJ	Murphy Maverick 430	PFA 259-13016	5.11.97	R J Collins	Belle Vue Farm, Yarnscombe 18. 1.10P
	(Built M F Cottam) (Jabiru 2200A) (Originally regd as Maverick, amended 1.09)				
G-MZJK	Mainair Blade	1100-1196-7-W903	19.11.96	P G Angus	Higher Barn Farm, Houghton 11. 6.09P
	(Rotax 582)				
G-MZJL	Cyclone AX2000	7363	11. 8.97	M H Owen	Weston Zoyland 16. 6.09P
G-MZJM	Rans S-6-ESD-XL Coyote II	1096.1049	19.11.97	K A Hastie	Popham 25. 4.09P
	(Built R J Hopkins - pr.no.PFA 204-13215)				
G-MZJN	Pegasus Quantum 15	7376	11.11.97	J Nelson	Park Hall Farm, Mapperley, Ilkeston 24. 8.08P
	(Rotax 582)				
G-MZJO	Pegasus Quantum 15	7338	17. 6.97	D J Cook	Eaglescott 7. 6.08P
	(Rotax 582)				
G-MZJP	Whittaker MW6-S Fatboy Flyer	PFA 164-13049	21.10.97	D J Burton and C A J Funnell	(Brighton)
	(Built D J Burton and C A J Funnell)				

G-MZJR	Cyclone AX2000	7385		11.11.97	N A Martin tr Marlborough Aerotow Group		
	(HKS 700E)					Clench Common	8. 3.09P
G-MZJS	Murphy Maverick 430	PFA 259-13017		12.12.97	M F Farmer	Poplar Hall Farm, Elmsett	18. 9.09P
	(Built R D Bernard) (Jabiru 2200A)						
G-MZJT	Pegasus Quantum 15-912	7399		23.12.97	N Hammerton	(Oxted)	1. 8.09P
G-MZJV	Mainair Blade	1141-0198-7-W944		7. 1.98	M A Roberts	West Malling	13. 6.04P
G-MZJW	Pegasus Quantum 15-912	7390		27. 1.98	W H J Knowles	Yundum/Banjul, The Gambia	8.10.04P
G-MZJX	Mainair Blade	1139-0198-7-W942		9. 1.98	A D Taylor	Glassonby	31. 5.09P
	(Rotax 503)						
G-MZJY	Pegasus Quantum 15-912	7394	(EI-)	23.12.97	M F Turff	Longacre Farm, Sandy	18. 7.08P
			G-MZJY				
G-MZJZ	Mainair Blade	1121-0597-7-W924		23. 6.97	P McParlin (Noted 10.08)	Ince Blundell	29. 5.09P
G-MZKA	Pegasus Quantum 15	7380		1.12.97	A S R McSherry	(West Kilbride)	25. 4.05P
G-MZKC	Cyclone AX2000	7398		22. 1.98	D Cioffi tr Broad Farm Flyers		
						Broad Farm, Eastbourne	24. 2.09P
G-MZKD	Pegasus Quantum 15	7404		19. 3.98	S J M Morling	(Fivehead, Taunton)	20. 8.08P
G-MZKE	Rans S-6-ESD-XL Coyote II	0797.1142		19. 1.98	P A Flaherty	Honington	30. 5.07P
	(Build I Findlay - pr.no.PFA 204-13248)						
G-MZKF	Pegasus Quantum 15	7407		21. 1.98	R G Hearsey	Northiam, Rye	6. 8.09P
G-MZKG	Mainair Blade	1145-0198-7-W948		23. 1.98	N S Rigby	Ince Blundell	6. 8.09P
	(Rotax 582)						
G-MZKH	CFM Shadow Series DD	292-DD		23. 1.98	S P H Calvert	Kittyhawk Farm, Deanland	26. 9.06P
G-MZKI	Mainair Rapier	1147-0298-7-W950		12. 2.98	D L Aspinall	North Connel, Oban	30. 5.09P
G-MZKJ	Mainair Blade	1039-0595-7-W837		19. 5.95	L G M Maddick (Noted 10.07)	Leicester	1. 5.05P
	(Rotax 582)						
G-MZKK	Mainair Blade	1140-0198-7-W943		12. 2.98	D I Lee	Finmere	7. 3.08P
G-MZKL	Pegasus Quantum 15	7360		18. 8.97	G Williams	(Ilkeston)	20. 5.09P
	(Rotax 582)						
G-MZKM	Mainair Blade	1133-0897-7-W936		15. 8.97	G F J Field	Headon Farm, Retford	13.10.09P
G-MZKN	Mainair Rapier	1138-1297-7-W941		12.12.97	G Craig	Newtownards	13. 4.08P
G-MZKR	Thruster T 600N	9038-T600N-021		27. 1.98	R J Arnett	(Albufeira, Portugal)	1 .3.03P
	(Rotax 582UL)						
G-MZKS	Thruster T 600N	9038-T600N-022		27. 1.98	P J Hepburn	Stoke, Isle of Grain	21.10.09P
	(HKS 700E) (Officially regd with Rotax 582)						
G-MZKT	Thruster T 600N Sprint	9038-T600T-023		27. 1.98	A I Milne tr Great Thornes Flying Group		
	(Rotax 582UL) (Originally built as "T 600T")					Little Snoring	9. 3.09P
G-MZKU	Thruster T 600T	9038-T600T-024		27. 1.98	A S Day	RAF Wyton	25. 9.08P
	(Rotax 582UL) (Officially regd with Rotax 503)						
G-MZKV	Mainair Blade	1144-0198-7-W947		28. 1.98	J D Harriman	(Dudley)	28. 4.09P
G-MZKW	Quad City Challenger II	PFA 177-12518		22. 3.94	K W Warn	Siege Cross Farm, Thatcham	16.10.05P
	(Built K W Warn) (Hirth 2705 R06)						
G-MZKY	Pegasus Quantum 15	7403		16. 1.98	P S Constable	Redlands, Swindon	23. 2.09P
	(HKS 700E)						
G-MZKZ	Mainair Blade	K1137-0298-7-W940		18. 2.98	R P Wolstenholme (Noted 3.07)		
	(Rotax 582)					Arclid Green, Sandbach	7. 8. 04P
G-MZLA	Pegasus Quantum 15	7415		27. 2.98	D W C Beer tr G-MZLA Quantum Syndicate		
	(Rotax 582)					Trenchard Farm, Eggesford	23. 5.08P
G-MZLC	Mainair Blade	1146-0298-7-W949		26. 2.98	P A Kershaw	Ince Blundell	6. 4.08P
G-MZLD	Pegasus Quantum 15-912	7416		24. 3.98	D Hamilton	Strathaven	27. 8.08P
G-MZLE	Murphy Maverick 430	PFA 259-12955	G-BXSZ	27. 2.98	J S Hill	Castle Kennedy, Stranraer	17. 6.09P
	(Built A A Plumridge) (Jabiru 2200A)						
G-MZLF	Pegasus Quantum 15	7417		30. 3.98	S Seymour (Noted 3.05)	Deenethorpe	13. 5.04P
	(Rotax 503)						
G-MZLG	Rans S-6-ESD-XL Coyote II	0897.1143		3. 3.98	F Y Allery	(Warboys, Huntingdon)	18.11.09P
	(Built R H J Jenkins - pr.no.PFA 204-13192) (Tri-cycle u/c)						
G-MZLI	Mignet HM-1000 Balerit	133		5. 3.98	A G Barr (Noted 4.05)	Otherton, Cannock	17.10.04P
G-MZLJ	Pegasus Quantum 15	7421		20. 3.98	J H Bradbury	Arclid Green, Sandbach	26.10.09P
	(Rotax 503)						
G-MZLK	Ultrasports Tri-Pacer/Solar Wings Typhoon			9. 3.98	A Leak	(Manchester)	16.11.08P
	(Fuji-Robin EC-34-PM)	T285-1471M		(Trike unit ex G-MJEC and Sailwing is Typhoon S4+ (ex-hanglider) s/n T785-1471M)			
G-MZLL	Rans S-6-ESD-XL Coyote II	0696.998		23. 9.97	J A Willats and G W Champion		
	(Built J A Willats and G W Champion - pr.no.PFA 204-13067)					Maypole Farm, Chislet	20. 5.09P
G-MZLM	Cyclone AX2000	7425		22. 4.98	P E Hadley	Swinford, Rugby	12. 4.09P
	(Modified to tug version)						
G-MZLN	Pegasus Quantum 15	7431		14. 4.98	P A Greening	(Leighton Buzzard)	27.11.09P
	(Rotax 503)						
G-MZLP	CFM Shadow D Series SS	K 299-D		1. 4.98	D J Gordon	Woodlands Barton Farm, Roche	1.1.08P
G-MZLR	Solar Wings Pegasus XL-Q	7441		28. 5.98	B Lorraine	Eshott	4. 8.08P
	(Trike c/n SW-TB-1040 ex G-MNJP fitted with new Sailwing c/n 7441)						
G-MZLS	Cyclone AX2000	7428		6. 7.98	A C A Hayes	Otherton, Cannock	15.12.07P
	(HKS 700E V3)						
G-MZLT	Pegasus Quantum 15-912	7438		24. 4.98	M H Colin	Otherton, Cannock	1. 5.09P
G-MZLU	Cyclone AX2000	7439		28. 7.98	E Pashley	Popham	2. 5.09P
	(HKS 700E V3)						
G-MZLV	Pegasus Quantum 15	7437		29. 4.98	A Armsby	Weston Zoyland	16. 2.09P
	(Rotax 503)						
G-MZLW	Pegasus Quantum 15	7440		28. 4.98	R W R Crevel and R J Nixon	Sywell	11. 7.09P
	(Rotax 582)						
G-MZLX	Micro Aviation B 22S Bantam	97-013	ZK-JIV	9.12.97	D L Howell	Longacre Farm, Sandy	6. 1.09P
G-MZLY	Letov LK-2M Sluka	PFA 263-13065		20. 4.98	W McCarthy	Wick	22. 1.10P
	(Built B G M Chapman) (Rotax 447 1V)						
G-MZLZ	Mainair Blade	1154-0498-7-W957		21. 4.98	G A Gamblin	(Waltham Chase, Southampton)	11. 4.09P
G-MZMA	Solar Wings Pegasus Quasar IITC	6611		1. 9.93	S Dixon	Longframlington	16. 6.09P
	(Rotax 582)						

G-MZMC	Pegasus Quantum 15-912	7206		10. 5.96	J J Baker	Deenethorpe	21. 7.09P
G-MZMD	Mainair Blade	1148-0398-7-W951		5. 3.98	T Gate	(Clitheroe)	30. 4.09P
G-MZME	Medway EclipseR	151/129E	G-582	8. 4.98	T Bowles	North Connel, Oban	16. 2.09P
	(Jabiru 2200A)						
G-MZMF	Pegasus Quantum 15	7387		30. 4.98	A J Tranter	Maryculter	17.10.07P
	(HKS)						
G-MZMG	Pegasus Quantum 15 Super Sport	7446		27. 5.98	A G Kemp	Deenethorpe	22.11.09P
	(Rotax 503)						
G-MZMH	Pegasus Quantum 15-912	7402		27. 1.98	M Hurtubise	(Leamington Spa)	4. 7.07P
G-MZMJ	Mainair Blade	1155-0598-7-W958		8. 5.98	T F R Calladine	Oxton	23. 6.08P
G-MZMK	AMF Microflight Chevvron 2-32C	040		19. 5.98	P J Tyler	(Leeds)	6. 5.09P
G-MZML	Mainair Blade	1158-0698-7-W961		19. 5.98	S C Stoodley	(Diss)	14.11.08P
G-MZMM	Mainair Blade	1162-0698-7-W965		19. 5.98	J Lynch	Sturgate	3. 4.08P
	(Rotax 462)						
G-MZMN	Pegasus Quantum 15-912	7445		21. 5.98	L A Hosegood	Redlands, Swindon	12. 5.09P
G-MZMO	TEAM Mini-MAX 91	PFA 186-12951		20. 5.98	K R Mason	(Kings Heath, Birmingham)	25. 9.09P
	(Built I M Ross)						
G-MZMP	Mainair Blade	1160-0698-7-W963		20. 5.98	A M Beale	(Heybridge, Maldon)	27. 2.09P
	(Rotax 582)						
G-MZMS	Rans S-6-ES Coyote II	1298.1203		26. 5.98	L Briscoe	Lower Mountpleasant Farm, Chatteris	9.10.07P
	(Built J G Dungey - pr.no.PFA 204-13294: rebuilt with kit no 0897.1145 ex G-MZMU c9.03) (Rotax 582) (Tri-cycle u/c)						
G-MZMT	Pegasus Quantum 15	7449		18. 6.98	B J Kitson	Sutton Meadows	9. 2.09P
	(Rotax 582)						
G-MZMU	Rans S-6-ESD-XL Coyote II	0897.1145		5. 6.98	J P Lamb and J Willcox	(Wotton-under-Edge)	31 1.09P
	(Built S Cox - pr.no.PFA 204-13242: rebuilt with kit no.0298.1203 c2003) (Rotax 582)						
G-MZMV	Mainair Blade	1152-0496-7-W955		30. 3.98	J Mayer	Otherton, Cannock	22.12.07P
	(Rotax 462)						
G-MZMW	Mignet HM-1000 Balerit	125		2.10.96	M E Whapham	Corn Wood Farm, Adversane	16.11.09P
G-MZMX	Cyclone AX2000	7451		8. 9.98	L A Lacy	Roddige	9. 9.07P
	(HKS 700E V3)						
G-MZMY	Mainair Blade	1153-0498-7-W956		16. 3.98	C J Millership	St Michaels	29. 6.08P
	(Rotax 462)						
G-MZMZ	Mainair Blade	1081-0496-7-W884		22. 4.96	W A Stacey	Chase Farm, Little Burstead	2. 7.07P
G-MZNA	Quad City Challenger II UK						
	(Built M Tormey)	CH2-0894-UK-1193	EI-CLE	19. 3.98	S Hennessy	(Dublin)	14. 4.08P
G-MZNB	Pegasus Quantum 15-912	7456		17. 7.98	F Gorse	Caernarfon	10. 8.06P
G-MZNC	Mainair Blade	1161-0698-7-W964		22. 6.98	K Medd	(Manchester)	14. 7.09P
G-MZND	Mainair Rapier	1170-0898-7-W973		24. 6.98	D W Stamp	Pound Green, Buttonoak, Bewdley	24 8.07P
G-MZNE	Whittaker MW6-S Fatboy Flyer	PFA 164-13120		26. 6.98	M B Horan	(Uttoxeter)	5. 6.07P
	(Built V E Booth) (Rotax 582)						
G-MZNG	Pegasus Quantum 15-912	7457		11. 8.98	S B Wilkes	Wolverhampton	14. 4.09P
G-MZNH	CFM Shadow Series DD	K 297-DD		30. 6.98	P A James tr Cloudbase Aviation G-MZNH	Redhill	25. 6.08P
G-MZNI	Mainair Blade	1163-0698-7-W966		3. 7.98	A Joyce	(Ashbourne, County Meath)	31. 3.08P
G-MZNJ	Mainair Blade	1168-0798-7-W971		6. 7.98	S J Taft	RAF Scampton	16. 8.07P
	(Rotax 462)						
G-MZNL	Mainair Blade	1165-0798-7-W968		6. 7.98	M A Williams	Stowting Russ, Folkestone	1. 7.06P
					(Stolen from Stowting overnight 2.10.05)		
G-MZNM	TEAM Mini-MAX 91	PFA 186-12304		10. 7.98	P J Fahie	(Stour Row, Shaftesbury)	1.10.09P
	(Built N P Thomson) (Fuji-Robin EC-44) (Open cockpit)						
G-MZNN	TEAM Mini-MAX 91	PFA 186-13125		10. 7.98	P J Bishop	Tarn Farm, Cockerham	17. 6.02P
	(Built D M Dronsfield)				(Noted dismantled 7.07)		
G-MZNO	Mainair Blade	1167-0798-7-W970		9. 6.98	R C Colclough	Arclid Green, Sandbach	9. 9.08P
	(Rotax 462)						
G-MZNP	Pegasus Quantum 15-912	7466	G-69-55	22. 7.98	G J McNally	Strathaven	13. 9.08P
G-MZNR	Pegasus Quantum 15	7465		17. 8.98	E S Wills	(Paignton)	16. 4.09P
	(Rotax 503)						
G-MZNS	Pegasus Quantum 15-912 Super Sport	7473		31. 7.98	M J Robbins	Rochester	9.12.09P
G-MZNT	Pegasus Quantum 15-912 Super Sport	7470		25. 9.98	D C Maxwell	(Bracknell)	25.10.08P
G-MZNU	Mainair Rapier	174-0898-7-W977		5. 8.98	G G Wilson and R Winstanley	Eshott	10. 8.09P
G-MZNV	Rans S-6-ESD-XL Coyote II	1294.704		7. 8.98	A P Thomas		
	(Built D E Rubery - pr.no.PFA 204-12884) (Tri-cycle u/c)					New Barn Farm, Barton Ashes, Crawley	8. 5.08P
	(Suffered engine failure 23.11.07 and made forced landing 3 miles E of Popham; nose gear collapsed and aircraft overturned)						
G-MZNX	Thruster T 600N	9098-T600N-026		10. 8.98	B S Beacroft and B Rogan	(Barnetby)	7.10.08P
	(Rotax 503)						
G-MZNY	Thruster T 600N	9098-T600N-027		10. 8.98	G Price	Barton	26. 9.08P
	(Rotax 582)						
G-MZNZ	Letov LK-2M Sluka	8295s015		21. 4.98	B F Crick	Long Marston	25.11.05P
	(Built K T Vinning - pr.no.PFA 263-13274) (Rotax 447)						
G-MZOC	Mainair Blade	1172-0898-7-W975		10. 8.98	R A Carr (Noted 7.06)	Eshott	5.12.05P
G-MZOD	Pegasus Quantum 15-912	7435		28. 4.98	J W Mann	Enstone	13. 5.09P
G-MZOF	Mainair Blade	1122-0697-7-W925		5. 6.97	R M Ellis	Long Marston	15. 5.09P
	(Rotax 462)						
G-MZOG	Pegasus Quantum 15	7471		12.10.98	E Nicoliello	(Crook)	22. 6.09P
	(Rotax 503)						
G-MZOH	Whittaker MW5-D Sorcerer	PFA 163-13060		14. 8.98	M Field	Higher Barn Farm, Houghton	4. 6.09P
	(Built D M Precious) (Fuji-Robin EC-44) (Officially recorded as Rotax 377)						
G-MZOI	Letov LK-2M Sluka	8296s012		17. 8.98	B S P Finch	Kemble	29. 7.09P
	(Built K P Taylor - pr.no.PFA 263-13238) (Rotax 447 1V)						
G-MZOJ	Pegasus Quantum 15	7478		9.11.98	A C Lane	Dunkeswell	25. 6.08P
	(Rotax 582)						
G-MZOK	Whittaker MW6 Merlin	PFA 164-11568		24. 8.97	R E Arnold tr G-MZOK Syndicate		
	(Built R K Willcox) (Rotax 582)					Otherton, Cannock	22.12.09P
G-MZOM	CFM Shadow Series DD	302-DD		8. 9.98	P S Winteron and P Tidd tr Side-Stick Syndicate		
						Lower Mountpleasant Farm, Chatteris	18.11.06P

G-MZOP	Mainair Blade	1178-0998-7-W981		11. 9.98	M Gardiner	Emlyn's Farm, Rhuallt	12. 6.09P
G-MZOR	Mainair Blade	1173-0898-7-W976		21. 9.98	C Bayliss	Ince Blundell	23. 4.09P
G-MZOS	Pegasus Quantum 15-912	7458		6.10.98	R J Field	Sandown	13. 4.09P
G-MZOV	Pegasus Quantum 15	7512		9. 3.99	C S Garrett tr Pegasus XL Group	Enstone	13. 6.08P
	(Rotax 503) *(Badged as a "Quantum Super Sport")*						
G-MZOW	Pegasus Quantum 15-912	7502		9. 3.99	J C Kitchen	Stoke, Isle of Grain	10.12.09P
G-MZOX	Letov LK-2M Sluka	PFA 263-13415		15. 2.99	C M James	Maypole Farm, Chislet	1. 6.06P
	(Built C M James) (Rotax 447)						
G-MZOY	TEAM Mini-MAX 91	PFA 186-12526		29. 3.99	P R and S E Whitehouse	(Cold Norton, Stone)	
	(Built E F Smith)						
G-MZOZ	Rans S-6-ESD-XL Coyote II	1096.1052		20. 5.98	D C and S G Emmons		
	(Built D C and S G Emmons - pr.no.PFA 204-13168) (Rotax 912)					Lower Wasing Farm, Brimpton	23. 9.09P
	(Officially recorded with Rotax 503) (Tri-cycle u/c)						
G-MZPD	Pegasus Quantum 15	7013		9. 5.95	P M Dewhurst	Sywell	24. 1.08P
	(Rotax 582)						
G-MZPH	Mainair Blade	1177-0998-7-W980		26. 8.98	J D Hoyland	Chilbolton	8.12.07P
	(Rotax 582)						
G-MZPJ	TEAM Mini-MAX 91	PFA 186-12277		23.11.92	P R Jenson	Sittles Farm, Alrewas	25. 7.08P
	(Built P R Jenson) (Rotax 503)						
G-MZPW	Solar Wings Pegasus Quasar IITC	6892		26.10.94	T J Walsh	(Hereford)	30. 6.07P
	(Rotax 582)						
G-MZRC	Pegasus Quantum 15	7482		25.11.98	M Hopkins *(Noted 11.07)*	Rufforth	23. 2.03P
	(Rotax 582)						
G-MZRH	Pegasus Quantum 15	7269		11.10.96	J C Doherty	(Coalville)	25.10.09P
	(Rotax 582)						
G-MZRM	Pegasus Quantum 15-912	7455		10. 7.98	A J Coton	(Balsall Common, Coventry)	1.11.08P
G-MZRS	CFM Shadow Series CD	141		4. 4.90	P C Hancox	Croft Farm, Defford	22. 6.08P
G-MZSC	Pegasus Quantum 15-912	7370		3.10.97	J A Lockert	(Hereford)	29. 5.08P
G-MZSD	Mainair Blade	1179-0998-7-W978		21. 8.98	M D Vearncombe	Weston Zoyland	1. 4.08P
G-MZSM	Mainair Blade	1000-0794-7-W796		15. 7.94	P R Anderson	Oxton	12.11.09P
	(Rotax 582)						
G-MZTA	Mignet HM-1000 Balerit	120		14. 5.96	A Fusco tr Sky Light Group	(Burwash)	8. 5.01P
G-MZTS	Aerial Arts Chaser S 447	CH703	G-MVDM	19. 3.96	D G Ellis	(Tamworth)	7. 6.08P
G-MZUB	Rans S-6-ESD-XL Coyote II	0897.1144		30. 4.98	B O Dowsett	Little Gransden	9. 8.09P
	(Built B O Dowsett - pr.no.PFA 204-13244) (Tri-cycle u/c)						
G-MZZT	Kolb Twinstar Mk.III (modified)	K0006-0992		1. 5.98	D E Martin	Plaistows Farm, St Albans	26. 6.09P
	(Built P I Morgans - pr.no.PFA 205-12596)						
G-MZZY	Mainair Blade	1050-0895-7-W848		13.11.95	A Mucznik	Oxton	15.11.09P

G-NAAA - G-NZZZ

G-NAAA	MBB BÖ.105DBS-4	S 34/912	G-BUTN	6. 4.99	Bond Air Services Ltd *(Operated Lancashire Air Ambulance)*		
	(Rebuilt with new pod S 912 C 1993)		G-AZTI, EI-BTE, G-AZTI, EC-DRY, G-AZTI, D-HDAN				Blackpool	21. 2.09E
G-NAAB	MBB BÖ.105DBS-4	S 416	D-HDMO	23. 3.99	Bond Air Services Ltd *(Operated Hampshire Ambulance Trust)*		
			D-HSTP, D-HDMO				Thruxton	8. 4.09E
G-NACA	Norman NAC-2 Freelance 180	2001		23.11.87	A R Norman *(Stored 6.08)*	Little Rissington	
G-NACI	Norman NAC-2 Freelance 180	NAC.001	G-AXFB	20. 6.84	L J Martin and D G French	Sandown	1.10.08P
G-NADO	Titan Tornado SS	LAA 356-14780		21. 4.08	Euro Aviation Ltd	(Gravesend)	
	(Built C Firth and D G Smith)						
G-NADS	TEAM Mini-MAX 91	PFA 186-12995		8. 2.99	J P Harris	Church Farm, Askern	8. 5.09P
	(Built G Evans and P M Spencer)						
G-NADZ	Van's RV-4	3	G-BROP	21. 6.07	J K Cook	Tibenham	15. 1.09P
	(Built AE Tolle) (Lycoming O-360)		N19AT				
G-NAGG	Rotorsport UK MT-03	RSUK/MT-03/012		18. 5.07	C A Clements	Bourne Park, Hurstbourne Tarrant	28. 5.09P
G-NANI	Robinson R44 Clipper II	11537		9. 1.07	MOS GmbH	Ahrensburg, Germany	4. 2.10E
G-NANO	Avid Speed Wing	PFA 189-12094		23. 1.08	T M C Handley	(Wood Street Village, Guildford)	
	(Built T M C Handley)						
G-NAPO	Pegasus Quantum 15-912	7799		6. 4.01	A W Rodman	(West Kilbride)	26. 6.08P
G-NAPP	Van's RV-7	PFA 323-14115		3. 9.03	E Fogarty	(Tadworth)	29.10.09P
	(Built R J Napp)						
G-NARG	Air Création Tanarg 912S/iXess 15	FLT.xxx		24. 6.05	K Kirby	Sywell	1. 2.09P
	(Built P Dewhurst - pr.no.BMAA HB/450 being Flylight kit comprising Trike s/n T05020 and Wing s/n A05040-5041; G-INFO quotes Flylight Airsports Ltd as builder)						
G-NARR	Stolp SA300 Starduster Too	PFA 035-14674		16.11.07	G J D Thomson	(Blackburn, West Lothian)	
	(Built G J D Thomson)						
G-NATT	Rockwell Commander 114A	14538	N5921N	14. 1.80	Northgleam Ltd	Liverpool	16.12.09E
G-NATX	Cameron O-65 Balloon (Hot Air)	1681		3. 3.88	A G E Faulkner *(National Express Rapide titles)*		
						Willenhall	5. 5.91T
G-NATY	Folland Gnat T 1	FL.548	8642M	19. 6.90	Drilling Systems Ltd *(As "XR537" in Red Arrows c/s)*		
			XR537			Bournemouth	12. 3.09P
G-NBDD	Robin DR.400-180 Régent	1103	F-BXVN	26. 9.88	B and S E Chambers	Sibson	25. 3.09E
G-NCCI	Comco Ikarus C42 FB80	0708-6910		10.10.07	Fly42 Ltd	Yatesbury	9.10.08P
G-NCFC	Piper PA-38-112 Tomahawk II	38-81A0107	N737V	14. 1.99	A M Heynen	Shoreham	9. 7.09E
			G-BNOA, N23272				
G-NCUB	Piper J-3C-65 Cub (L-4H-PI)	11599	G-BGXV	6. 7.84	E V Moffatt and R E Nerou		
			F-BFQT, AO-GAB, 43-30308			Woodlow Farm, Bosbury	28.10.08P
G-NDAA	MBB BÖ.105DBS-4	S 914	G-WMAA	1. 2.06	Bond Air Services Ltd	Eaglescott	27. 9.09E
			G-PASB, VH-LSA, G-BDMC, D-HDEC *(Operated North Devon Air Ambulance)*				
	(Rebuilt 1994 with new airframe: original frame c/n S135 to The Helicopter Museum, Weston-super-Mare as "G-PASB" - see SECTION 4, Part 1						
G-NDOL	Europa Aviation Europa	044		30.11.93	S Longstaff	Yew Tree Farm, Lymm Dam	27. 3.09P
	(Built G K Brunwin - pr.no.PFA 247-12594) (NSI EA-81) (Monowheel u/c)						
G-NDOT	Thruster T 600N 450	0052-T600N-066		18. 6.02	P C Bailey	Hill Farm, Over, Cambridge	10. 4.09P
G-NDPA	Comco Ikarus C42 FB UK	PFA 322-14056	G-OOMW	1.12.05	P A Pilkington	North Coates	28.10.09P
	(Built R O'Malley-White)						

Reg	Type	c/n	Prev id	Date	Owner/Operator	Base	C of A
G-NEAL	Piper PA-32-260 Cherokee Six	32-1048	G-BFPY N5588J	7.11.83	V Walker tr VSD Group	Shobdon	2. 8.07
G-NEAT	Europa Aviation Europa	065		28. 6.94	M Burton	Sleap	21. 5.09P
	(Built M Burton - pr.no.PFA 247-12642) (Rotax 912) (Tri-cycle u/c)						
G-NEAU	Eurocopter EC.135 T2	0333	D-HECB	13. 9.04	Northumbria Police Authority	Durham Tees Valley	15. 3.08T
G-NEEL	RotorWay Executive 90	5002		7. 8.90	C Bedford	(Skegness)	6. 7.08P
	(Built P N Haigh) (RotorWay RI 162)						
G-NEGG	EAA Acrosport II	844	N715RJ	16. 1.04	D K Keays and R S Goodwin	Bidford	5.10.09P
	(Built R S Challis)						
G-NEGS	Thunder Ax7-77 Balloon (Hot Air)	1059		18. 3.87	M Rowlands *"Hot-Shot"*	Ashton-in-Makerfield	15 5.05A
G-NEIL	Thunder AX3/503 Maxi Sky Chariot Balloon (Hot Air)	379		2.12.81	N A Robertson *"Neil" (Operated A Moore)*	Great Missenden	6. 4.08A
G-NELI	Piper PA-28R-180 Cherokee Arrow	28R-31011	OH-PWW D-EMWE, N7693J	9. 2.01	A Jahanfar	Earls Colne	17. 4.09E
G-NELY	MD Helicopters MD.600N	RN018	N958SD	26.10.05	Eastern Atlantic Helicopters Ltd	Shoreham	11.11.09E
G-NEMO	Raj Hamsa X'Air Jabiru	602		11. 3.04	G F Allen *(Noted 8.08)*	Damyn's Hall, Upminster	
	(Built D G Smith - pr.no.BMAA HB/158)						
G-NEON	Piper PA-32-300B Cherokee Six	32-40683	D-EMKW N4246R	7. 4.00	S C A Lever	Fairoaks	24. 5.09E
G-NERC	Piper PA-31-350 Navajo Chieftain	31-7405402	G-BBXX N66869	26. 4.94	Natural Environment Research Council *(Operated Air Atlantique)*	Coventry	19. 7.09E
G-NERO	Cameron Z-105 Balloon (Hot Air)	11042		20. 9.07	Tavolera SRL *(Mondovicino titles)*	Cuneo, Italy	9. 8.09E
G-NESA	Europa Aviation Europa XS	450		17. 4.01	A M Kay	Cambridge	4. 9.09P
	(Built K G and V E Summerhill - pr.no.PFA 247-13544) (Rotax 912) (Tri-gear u/c)						
G-NESE	Tecnam P2002-JF	039		9. 6.06	N and S Easton	Perth	5. 7.09E
G-NESH	Robinson R44 Clipper II	11609		8. 2.07	M Tancock	(Hong Kong, PRC)	13. 3.09E
G-NEST	Christen Eagle II	SHAY 0001	N23MS	14. 9.06	P R Cox	Compton Abbas	18. 6.09P
	(Built M Shay) (Lycoming AEIO-360)						
G-NESV	Eurocopter EC.135 T1	0067		4. 2.99	Northumbria Police Authority *(Operated North East Police)*	Newcastle	30. 3.09E
G-NESW	Piper PA-34-220T Seneca III	34-8233072	D-GAMO N8064M	13.12.02	G C U Guida	Jersey	27.11.09E
G-NESY	Piper PA-18 Super Cub 95	18-7482	N124SA SE-CUG	18. 8.00	V Featherstone	North Side, Thorney	7. 4.11S
G-NETB	Cirrus SR22	1548	N226TS	10. 7.06	Cirrusnet Ltd	Turweston	11. 7.09E
G-NETR	Aérospatiale AS.355F1 Ecureuil 2	5164	G-JARV G-OGHL, N5796S	4.04.06	PLM Dollar Group Ltd *(Operated Network Rail)*	Cumbernauld	27. 5.09E
G-NETY	Piper PA-18-150 Super Cub	1809108	N4159K	8. 9.95	N B Mason	Rendcomb	11.12.11
G-NEWT	Beech 35 Bonanza	D-1168	G-APVW EI-BIL, G-APVW, N9866F, 4X-ACI, IDF/AF 0604, ZS-BTE	28. 2.90	J S Allison	RAF Halton	29. 7.09E
	(Continental EI-185 = C35 status)						
G-NEWZ	Bell 206B-3 JetRanger III	4475	C-GBVZ	28. 1.98	Guay Tulliemet Aviation Ltd	(Eastleigh)	17. 1.09E
G-NFLA	British Aerospace Jetstream Series 3102	637	G-BRGN G-BLHC, G-31-637	15. 2.06	Cranfield University *(Operated National Flying Laboratory Centre)*	Cranfield	16. 7.09E
G-NFLY	Tecnam P2002-EA Sierra	PFA 333-14613		28. 3.07	C N Hodgson	(London W5)	30. 7.09P
	(Built C N Hodgson) (Rotax 912ULS)						
G-NFNF	Robin DR.400-180 Régent	2047	VP-BNU VR-BNU, G-BTDU	15.11.02	N French	Lower Wasing Farm, Brimpton	10.12.09E
G-NGEL	Cessna 510 Citation Mustang	510-0076	N4085A	14. 5.08	Angel World Ltd	London Stansted	20. 5.09E
G-NGLS	Aerospool Dynamic WT9 UK	DY288		21. 1.09	Yeoman Light Aircraft Co Ltd	Manor Farm, Drayton St Leonard	
	(Built Yeoman Light Aircraft Co Ltd)						
G-NGRM	Spezio DAL-1 Tuholer	134	N6RM	14. 8.90	S H Crook New Barn Farm, Barton Ashes, Crawley		7. 2.00P
	(Built R Mitchell) (Lycoming O-290-G)			*(Crashed near Le Touquet 24. 7.99 following engine failure: noted 12.03)*				
G-NHRH	Piper PA-28-140 Cherokee	28-22807	OY-BIC SE-EZP	19. 5.82	C J Milsom	Compton Abbas	10. 9.09E
G-NHRJ	Europa Aviation Europa XS	333		30. 9.99	D A Lowe Lower Grounds Farm, Shirlowe *(Noted 3.03)*		
	(Built D A Lowe - pr.no.PFA 247-13112) (Tri-gear u/c)						
G-NICC	Evektor EV-97 teamEurostar UK	1913		1. 3.04	Pickup and Son Property Maintenance Ltd	Leicester	9. 8.08P
G-NICI	Robinson R44 Raven II	10854		31. 8.05	David Fishwick Vehicles Sales Ltd	Coal Aston	21.10.09E
G-NICS	Best Off Sky Ranger Swift 912S (1)	SKRxxxx868		11. 6.08	N G Heywood	(Staunton, Glos)	
	(Built N G Heywood - pr. no BMAA HB/576)						
G-NICY	Beech B300C Super King Air	FM-16	N816KA	21.11.07	Raytheon Systems Ltd	Hawarden	27.11.10S
	(Planned to become Beech 350C ER Shadow R.1 "ZZ417" for AAC but still flying in RAF c/s but with civilian marks 12.08)						
G-NIDG	Evektor EV-97 Eurostar	990609		29. 2.00	Skydrive Ltd	Church Farm, Shotteswell	3. 7.09E
	(Built N R Beale - pr.no.PFA 315-13580) (Also identified as Evektor 99 Eurostar)						
G-NIEN	Van's RV-9A	PFA 320-14419		19. 4.06	G R Pybus	Morgansfield, Fishburn	8. 9.09P
	(Built G R Pybus)						
G-NIFE	SNCAN Stampe SV-4A	156	F-BBBL French AF/CEV, F-BFCE, French AF/CEV	27. 5.05	C C Rollings and F J Hodson tr Tiger Airways	Gloucestershire	18. 8.11
	(Renault 4P05)			*(As "156" in French AF c/s)*			
G-NIGC	Avtech Jabiru UL-450	xxxx		3. 5.01	W D Brereton	Mill Farm, Shifnal	21. 8.09P
	(Built N Creeney - pr.no.PFA 274A-13703)						
G-NIGE	Luscombe 8E Silvaire Deluxe	3525	G-BSHG N72098, NC72098	6. 6.90	Gardan Party Ltd	Popham	7. 5.09P
	(Continental C85)						
G-NIGL	Europa Aviation Europa	147		6. 7.95	N M Graham	(Chandlers Ford, Eastleigh)	
	(Built N M Graham - pr.no.PFA 247-12775) (Conventional u/c)						
G-NIGS	Thunder Ax7-65 Balloon (Hot Air)	1663		30. 1.90	Sophie D Annett	Palestine, Andover	15. 4.06A
G-NIJM	Piper PA-28R-180 Arrow	28R-30644	D-EDTM N4923J	27. 8.04	N J Morton tr G-NIJM Syndicate	Conington	21. 2.09E
G-NIKE	Piper PA-28-181 Cherokee Archer II	28-8390086	N4315N	4. 7.89	Key Properties Ltd	White Waltham	24. 1.09E
G-NIKK	Diamond DA.20-C1 Katana	C0109	N909CT C-FDVP	5.12.05	Cubair Flight Training Ltd	Redhill	1. 1.10E

Reg	Type	C/n	Prev ID	Date	Owner/Operator	Base	Status
G-NIKO	Airbus A321-211	1250	D-AVZA	21.6.00	Thomas Cook Airlines Ltd	Manchester	20.6.09E
G-NIKX	Robinson R44 Raven II	12306	G-OMJM	17.12.08	P R Holloway	(Southam)	1.7.09E
G-NIMA	Balony Kubicek BB30Z Balloon (Hot Air)	458		16.10.06	C Williamson	Goudhurst, Cranbrook	1.4.09E
G-NIMB	Schempp-Hirth Nimbus 2C	180	BGA2495-DYZ	3.10.07	M J Slade	Eyres Field	3.4.08
G-NINA	Piper PA-28-161 Cherokee Warrior II 28-7716162		G-BEUC N3507Q	29.7.88	A P Gorrod	Tibenham	29.12.09E
G-NINB	Piper PA-28-180 Cherokee Challenger 28-7305234		SE-KHR OY-DLR, CS-AHY, N11C	16.7.99	P A Layzell	Old Buckenham	21.8.08E
	(Seriously damaged in gales at Old Buckenham 1.07)						
G-NINC	Piper PA-28-180 Cherokee G 28-7205016		SE-KVH N2166T	2.2.00	P A Layzell	Old Buckenham	12.4.09E
G-NIND	Piper PA-28-180 Cherokee Challenger 28-7305420		SE-GAT	6.6.07	P A Layzell	Old Buckenham	20.9.09E
G-NINE	Murphy Renegade 912	448		16.6.93	R F Bond	Garston Farm, Marshfield	6.6.09
	(Built R F Bond - pr.no.PFA 188-12191)						
G-NIOG	Robinson R44 Clipper II	10471		1.9.04	Alu-Fix Contracts Ltd	(Belfast)	17.10.09E
G-NIOS	Piper PA-32R-301 Saratoga II SP 32R-8513004		N4381Z N105DX, N4381Z	28.9.00	D J Everett and R R Alderslade tr Plant Aviaton	Stapleford	19.5.09E
G-NIPA	Nipper T 66 RA.45 Series 3	S 120	G-AWDD	7.6.96	R J O Walker	North Lopham, Diss	13.4.04P
	(Volkswagen 1834 (Acro)) (Built Slingsby Aircraft Co Ltd as c/n 1627 for Nipper Aircraft Ltd)						
G-NIPP	Nipper T 66 RA.45 Series 3	S 103	G-AVKJ	17.1.00	R J Porter	Insch	29.5.09P
	(Volkswagen 1834) (Originally built Avions Fairey SA as c/n T66/32: rebuilt Slingsby Aircraft Co Ltd as c/n 1587 for Nipper Aircraft Ltd)						
G-NIPR	Nipper T 66 RA.45 Series 3	S 108	G-AVXC	15.7.05	P A Gibbs	Inverness	28.10.09P
	(Ardem 4C02) (Built Slingsby Aircraft Co Ltd as c/n 1605 for Nipper Aircraft Ltd)						
G-NITA	Piper PA-28-180 Cherokee C	28-2909	G-AVVG N7517W	16.1.84	T Clifford *(Noted stored 7.08)*	Hulcote Farm, Salford, Bedford	17.11.97T
	(Used spare Frame No.28-3807S)						
G-NIVA	Eurocopter EC.155B1	6642	N84AZ	2.9.05	Lanthwaite Aviation Ltd	Cambridge	1.9.09E
G-NIVT	Schempp-Hirth Nimbus 4T	3	BGA4546-JJG D-KIXL	8.10.07	M Clarke and P G Sheard *"V1"*	Lasham	26.2.08
G-NJAG	Cessna 207 Skywagon	20700093	D-EMDN (N91152)	2.8.78	G H Nolan	Lydd	21.6.08E
G-NJBA	Rotorway Executive 162F	6927		10.3.05	BWP (TV) Ltd tr British Waterproofing	Street Farm, Takeley	16.6.09P
	(Rotorway RI 162F)						
G-NJET	Schempp-Hirth Ventus cT	161/521	BGA4461-JET RAFGSA R38	15.1.08	J Hudson	Lasham	8.3.08
G-NJIM	Piper PA-32R-301T Turbo Saratoga 32R-8229035		D-EHDL N8147H	19.9.05	J L Rivers	Coventry	6.1.09E
G-NJPW	P&M Aviation Quik GT450	8150		2.2.06	N J P West	Landmead Farm, Garford	12.2.09P
G-NJSH	Robinson R22 Beta	0780		19.4.88	A J Hawes	Sywell	10.7.09E
G-NJSP	Avtech Jabiru J430	0xxx		6.4.06	N J S Pitman	Brock Farm, Billericay	5.10.09P
	(Built N J S Pitman - pr.no.PFA 336-14514)						
G-NJTC	Aeroprakt A22-L Foxbat	PFA 317A-14565		6.9.06	B Jackson and T F Casey	Carlisle	15.2.10P
	(Built B Jackson and T F Casey)						
G-NLEE	Cessna 182Q Skylane II	18265934	G-TLTD N759EL	1.12.93	C G D Jones	Cardiff	1.7.09E
G-NLYB	Cameron N-105 Balloon (Hot Air)	10012		19.4.01	P H E van Overwalle	Nazareth, Belgium	22.6.09E
	(Pink Elephant Head Shape)						
G-NMAK	Airbus A319-115X	2550	D-AVYH	27.9.05	Twinjet Aircraft Sales Ltd *(Operated Al Kharafi Group)*	Luton	26.9.09E
G-NMBG	Avtech Jabiru J400	0xxx		15.2.06	P R Hendry-Smith and H I Smith	Little Snoring	13.4.09P
	(Built D K Shead - pr.no.PFA 325-14461)						
G-NMID	Eurocopter EC.135 T2	0300		29.9.03	Derbyshire Constabulary	(Butterley Hall, Ripley)	29.3.10S
	(Operated North Midlands Police)						
G-NMOS	Cameron C-80 Balloon (Hot Air)	4966		5.1.01	C J Thomas and M C East *(Riversoft titles)*	Farnham	17.7.09E
G-NMRM	Cessna 525A CitationJet CJ2	525A0408	N5248V	23.7.08	Il Lione Alato ARL	Jersey	22.7.09E
G-NMRV	Van's RV-6	22879	N327RV	29.9.08	M P Comley and N Horseman	Biggin Hill	
	(Built N Moon)						
G-NNAC	Piper PA-18-135 Super Cub	18-3820	PH-PSW R Neth AF R-130, 54-2420	19.5.81	PAW Flying Services Ltd	Bagby	31.5.10S
	(L-21B-PI) (Frame No.18-3820)						
G-NNON	Mainair Blade	1318-0302-7-W1113		24.4.02	D R Kennedy	Strathaven	7.6.06P
G-NOBI	Spezio HES-1 Tuholer Sport	162	N1603	28.11.90	T N J Cuypers	(Brecht, Belgium)	15.8.07P
	(Built H E Stidham) (Continental C125)						
	(Force landed at Nayland 21.4.07 due to engine problems and substantially damaged)						
G-NOCK	Reims Cessna FR182 Skylane RG II FR18200036		G-BGTK (D-EHZB)	18.1.94	F J Whidbourne Park Farm, East Worldham, Alton		15.5.09E
G-NODE	Gulfstream AA-5B Tiger	AA5B-1182	N4533L	22.5.81	Strategic Telecom Networks Ltd	Blackbushe	20.7.08T
G-NODY	American General AG-5B Tiger	10076	N1194C	3.10.91	Abraxas Aviation Ltd *(Operated Cabair)*	Denham	11.3.09E
G-NOIR	Bell 222	47031	G-OJLC G-OSEB, G-BNDA, A40-CG	9.8.91	Eastern Atlantic Helicopters Ltd	Shoreham	31.5.09E
G-NOIZ	Yakovlev Yak-55M	910104	RA-44537 HA-JAM, DOSAAF 04 (blue)	5.2.04	S C Cattlin	White Waltham	3.3.09P
G-NOMO	Cameron O-31 Balloon (Hot Air)	241		31.10.00	Tim Balloon Promotion Airships Ltd	Ceva, Piedmont, Italy	11.10.08A
G-NONE	Dyn'Aéro MCR-01 ULC	PFA 301B-14238		2.7.04	J Flisher	Dunkeswell	21.6.09P
	(Built J Flisher)						
G-NONI	Grumman AA-5 Traveler	AA5-0383	G-BBDA (EI-AYL), G-BBDA	1.8.88	P J Evans tr November India Flying Group Exeter		4.7.09E
G-NOOR	Commander Aircraft Commander 114B	14656		6.2.98	As-Al Ltd Lausanne-La Blecherette, Switzerland		13.7.09E
G-NORA	Comco Ikarus C42 FB UK	0504-6676		13.7.05	N A Rathbone	Swinford, Rugby	29.8.09P
	(Built N A Rathbone - pr.no.PFA 322-14420)						
G-NORB	Air et Aventure Saturne S11OK	SC981482		28.11.05	R N Pearce	(Halesowen)	
G-NORD	SNCAC NC.854	7	F-BFIS	20.10.78	A D Pearce	Eastbach Farm, Coleford	27.5.82P
	(Remains noted 11.01)						
G-NORT	Robinson R22 Beta	3404		7.1.03	Plane Talking Ltd	Cranfield	27.2.09E

G-NOSE	Cessna 402B	402B0823	N98AR	23. 4.96	Reconnaissance Ventures Ltd	Coventry	7. 1.10E
			G-MPCU, SE-IRL, OO-TAT, (OO-SEL), N3946C				
G-NOSS	British Aerospace Jetstream Series 3102	749	LN-FAZ	15. 7.08	Highland Airways Ltd	Inverness	
			C-GJPU, (N839JS), G-31-749				
G-NOSY	Robinson R44 Astro	0064	G-LATK	6. 3.03	R C Hields t/a Hields Aviation	Sherburn-in-Elmet	30. 5.09E
			G-BVMK				
G-NOTE	Piper PA-28-181 Archer III	2843082	D-ESPI	19. 9.97	J Beach	Elstree	5.11.09E
			N9282N				
G-NOTS	Best Off Sky Ranger 912S(1)	SKR0401433		24. 6.05	P M Dewhurst	Sywell	1. 8.09P
	(Built P M Dewhurst - pr.no.BMAA HB/352)						
G-NOTT	Nott ULD2 Balloon (Hot Air)	06		11. 6.86	J R P Nott	London NW8	
G-NOTY	Westland Scout AH.1	F9630	XT624	5.11.97	R P Coplestone	Thruxton	28. 1.09P
G-NOUS	Cessna 172S Skyhawk	172S10649	N1733L	23. 1.08	Flyglass Ltd	Wycombe Air Park	10. 2.09E
G-NOWW	Mainair Blade 912	1227-1299-7-W1020		10.12.99	C Bodill	Oxton	23. 2.06P
G-NPKJ	Van's RV-6	PFA 181-13138		12. 2.98	M R Turner	Sturgate	24. 3.09P
	(Built K Jones) (Lycoming IO-360)						
G-NPPL	Comco Ikarus C42 FB100	0306-6543	G-90-1	2. 9.03	D C Jarman tr Papa Lima Group	Old Sarum	14.10.08P
	(Officially regd as 0307-6543)						
G-NROY	Piper PA-32RT-300 Lance II	32R-7985070	G-LYNN	26.11.93	B Nedjati-Gilani	White Waltham	10. 3.09E
			G-BGNY, N3024L				
G-NRRA	SIAI-Marchetti SF.260W	116	F-GOBF	29.11.00	G Boot	Lydd	7. 5.09P
			Burkina Faso AF BF8431, OO-SMB *(As "BF8431:31" in Burkina Faso Defence Force c/s)*				
G-NRSC	Piper PA-23-250 Aztec E	27-7305142	N250MC	23. 6.00	Geminair Services Ltd	Bournemouth	11. 9.08A
			(N244AR), N250MC, EI-BXP, G-BSFL, PH-NOA, 9M-AUS, PH-NOA, N40378				
G-NRYL	Mooney M 20R Ovation	29-0303	N10391	10. 3.04	Deltamood Ltd	Kortrijk-Wevelgem, Belgium	7. 4.09E
G-NSBB	Comco Ikarus C42 FB100 VLA			15. 1.04	B Bayes and N E Sams		
	(Built B Bayes & N E Sams)	PFA 322-14162				Orlingbury Hold Farm, Orlingbury	29. 5.09P
G-NSEW	Robinson R44 Astro	0615		6. 7.99	G-NSEW Ltd	Wycombe Air Park	11. 7.09E
G-NSJS	Cessna 680 Citation Sovereign	680-0161		26. 9.07	Ferncroft Ltd	Jersey	26. 9.09E
G-NSOF	Robin HR.200-120B	334		4. 6.99	Modi Aviation Ltd	Sibson	28. 6.09E
G-NSTG	Cessna F150F	F150-0058	G-ATNI	16. 8.89	Westair Flying Services Ltd	Blackpool	26. 8.09E
	(Built Reims Aviation SA) (Wichita c/n 15063499)		*(Tail-wheel conversion)*				
G-NSUK	Piper PA-34-220T Seneca V	3449256	N126RB (2)	27. 2.03	Genus Plc	Blackbushe	27. 3.09E
G-NTWK	Aérospatiale AS.355F2 Ecureuil 2	5347	G-FTWO	16. 5.06	PLM Dollar Group Ltd *(Network Rail titles)*		
			G-OJOR, G-FTWO, G-BMUS			Inverness	17. 4.09E
G-NUFC	Best Off Sky Ranger Swift 912S(1)			22. 2.07	C R Rosby	(Belford)	
	(Built C R Rosby)	SKRxxxx768	*(Pr.no.BMAA HB/529)*				
G-NUGC	Grob G103A Twin II Acro	34040-K-271	BGA4729-JRW	17. 1.08	M G Barnes tr University of Nottingham Glidng Club		
			RAFGSA R15, RAFGGA 556			RAF Cranwell	17. 2.08
G-NUKA	Piper PA-28-181 Archer II	28-8290134	OY-CJI	9. 1.04	N Ibrahim	North Weald	15. 5.09E
			N8209A				
G-NULA	Flight Design CT2K	02-05-05-04		17.10.02	R C Skidmore tr G-NULAFlying Group		
	(Assembled Pegasus Aviation as c/n 7913)					Norton, Daventry	30. 4.08P
G-NUNI	Lindstrand LBL 77A Balloon (Hot Air)	1181		15. 1.08	J A Folkes *"University of Nottingham"*		
						Bulcote, Nottingham	21. 1.10E
G-NURA	Nicollier HN.700 Menestrel II	PFA 217-13612		6. 6.08	J D Rooney and D Smith	(Chichester)	
	(Built J D Rooney and D Smith)						
G-NUTA	Christen Eagle II	0471	D-ECCA	15. 8.06	R A Pugh tr Blue Eagle Group	Henstridge	18. 1.09P
	(Built D Sondermann) (Lycoming AEIO-360)						
G-NUTS	Cameron Mr Peanut 35 SS Balloon (Hot Air)			18. 2.81	Balloon Flights International Ltd *"Mr Peanut II" (Inflated 4.06)*		
		711				Bristol	7. 4.86A
G-NUTT	Mainair Sports Pegasus Quik	8114		29. 4.05	G P Nutter	Bagby	31. 7.08P
G-NUTY	Aérospatiale AS.350B Ecureuil	1490	G-BXKT	20. 7.98	J A Ruck	Shobdon	16.10.09E
			F-GXRT, N333FH, N5797V				
G-NVBF	Lindstrand LBL 210A Balloon (Hot Air)	249		19. 5.95	Airxcite Ltd t/a Virgin Balloon Flights	Wembley	4. 9.04T
G-NWAA	Eurocopter EC.135 T2	0427		10.10.05	Bond Air Services Ltd *"Katie"*	Blackpool	30.11.08E
					(Operated North West Ambulance Authority)		
G-NWDC	Robinson R22 Beta	3929	G-SBAR	6.11.07	J Porter	County of Derry/Eglinton	21. 9.09E
G-NWFA	Cessna 150M	15076736	C-CFBD	29. 5.08	North Weald Flying Group Ltd	North Weald	1. 5.09E
			N45103				
G-NWFC	Cessna 172P Skyhawk	17276305	N98523	4. 7.07	North Weald Flying Group Ltd	North Weald	15.11.09E
G-NWFG	Cessna 172P Skyhawk	17274192	N6396K	31. 7.07	North Weald Flying Group Ltd	North Weald	11.10.08E
G-NWPR	Cameron N-77 Balloon (Hot Air)	1181		15. 8.85	D B Court	Ormskirk	30. 6.93A
	(Rebuilt with new envelope c/n 1667)						
G-NWPS	Eurocopter EC.135 T1	0063		15.10.98	North Wales Police Authority	Boddelwydden	11. 2.08E
G-NXUS	Miller Nexus Mustang	PFA 341-14578		20. 9.06	G W Miller	(London N15)	
	(Built G W Miller)						
G-NYLE	Robinson R44 Raven II	11407		14. 9.06	N O'Farrell	Terenure, Dublin	22.10.08E
G-NYMB	Schempp-Hirth Nimbus 3dT	63	BGA4008-HKQ	9.11.07	A J Rees tr Nimbus Syndicate *"970"*	Nympsfield	15. 2.08
G-NYMF	Piper PA-25-235 Pawnee D	25-7556112	OO-PAL	8. 2.02	The Bristol Gliding Club Proprietary Ltd	Nympsfield	30. 5.09E
			N267JW, N9799P				
G-NYNA	Van's RV-9A	LAA 320-14773		15. 7.08	S Hiscox and B Greathead	Hardwick	
	(Built B Greathead and S Hiscox)						
G-NYZS	Cessna 182G Skylane	18255135	G-ASRR	8. 4.04	P Ragg	Portimão, Faro, Portugal	27.10.09E
			(G-CBIL), EI-ATF, G-ASRR, N3735U				
G-NZGL	Cameron O-105 Balloon (Hot Air)	1361		3. 9.86	R A, P M G and N T M Vale *"Nazgul"*		
						Kidderminster	19. 9.07A
G-NZSS	Boeing Stearman E75 (N2S-5) Kaydet	75-8611	N4325	31. 1.89	P R Bennett and M J Nice *(As "343251:27" in USAAC c/s)*		
	(Lycoming R-680)		Bu.43517, 42-109578			Priory Fam, Tibenham	27. 6.05T

G-OAAA - G-OZZZ

G-OAAA	Piper PA-28-161 Warrior II	2816107	N9142N	8. 9.93	Central Aircraft Leasing Ltd	Bournemouth	22. 9.09E

Reg	Type	C/n	Prev identity	Date	Owner / operator	Location	Expiry
G-OAAF	British Aerospace ATP	2029	G-JEMB N855AW, G-11-029	27. 2.07	Atlantic Airlines Ltd	Coventry	11. 7.09E
G-OABB	SAN Jodel D 150 Mascaret	01	F-BJST F-WJST	21. 1.97	K Manley	Swanborough Farm, Lewes	16. 6.09P
G-OABC	Colt 69A Balloon (Hot Air)	1159		17.11.87	P A C Stuart-Kregor	Newbury	26. 6.00A
G-OABO	Enstrom F-28A	097	G-BAIB	10. 7.98	C R Taylor	(Wacton, Norwich)	23. 7.09E
G-OABR	American General AG-5B Tiger	10124	C-GZLA N256ER	15. 4.98	Vulcan House Management UK Ltd	Biggin Hill	9. 8.07E
G-OACA	Piper PA-44-180 Seminole	44-7995202	G-GSFT EI-BYZ, N2193K	31. 7.02	D Coplowe t/a Lenham Motorsport	Panshanger	12. 2.09E
G-OACE	Valentin Taifun 17E	1017	D-KCBA	22. 1.87	I D Gumbrell t/a Dorset Flying Club	Bournemouth	31. 5.09E
G-OACF	CAB Robin DR.400-180	2534		30.10.03	A C Fletcher	Sherburn-in-Elmet	22.12.09E
G-OACI	SOCATA MS.893E Rallye 180GT	13086		5. 5.98	Full Sutton Flying Centre Ltd	Full Sutton	6. 4.08E
G-OACP	de Havilland DHC-1 Chipmunk 22 (Built OGMA) (Lycoming O-360)	35	(CS-DAO) EI-BHD, F-GBCF Portuguese AF FAP 1345	20. 8.96	Aeroclub de Portugal (Noted 9.08)	Spanhoe	10. 3.07
G-OADY	Beech 76 Duchess	ME-56	N5022M	27.10.86	Multiflight Ltd	Leeds-Bradford	3. 4.09E
G-OAER	Lindstrand LBL 105A Balloon (Hot Air)	359		4. 3.96	T M Donnelly "Aero"	Sprotbrough, Doncaster	11.10.09E
G-OAFF	Cessna 208 Caravan I	20800415	N5265N	26. 6.07	R Durie tr Army Parachute Association "Foxy Lady"	AAC Netheravon	4. 7.09E
G-OAFR	Cameron Z-105 Balloon (Hot Air)	11018		30. 5.07	PSH Skypower Ltd (Avon Fire and Rescue titles)	Woodborough, Pewsey	9. 8.09E
G-OAGI	FLS Aerospace Sprint 160 (Marketed as British Aircraft Company Redwing 160")	001	G-FLSI	30.11.06	Black Art Composites Ltd	Thruxton	10. 9.08P
G-OAGL	Bell 206B-3 JetRanger III	3035	G-CORN G-BHTR, N18098	27. 8.08	A Leslie t/a AGL Helicopters	(Crawley)	30. 4.09E
G-OAHC	Beech F33C Bonanza	CJ-133	G-BTTF PH-BND	2. 9.91	Cirrus Aviation Ltd	Clacton	5. 8.09E
G-OAJB	Cyclone AX2000	7281	G-MZFJ	16. 2.99	T A Lipinski	Sackville Lodge, Riseley	30. 5.09P
G-OAJC	Robinson R44 Raven	1381		12. 5.04	Adare International Transport Ltd	(Roscrea, County Tipperary)	29. 5.09E
G-OAJL	Comco Ikarus C42 FB100	0403-6589		18. 5.04	T Collins	Dunkeswell	20. 5.09P
G-OAJS	Piper PA-39 Twin Comanche C/R	39-15	G-BCIO N49JA, N57RG, G-BCIO, N8860Y	9. 3.94	Go-AJS Ltd	Sherburn-in-Elmet	21. 3.09E
G-OAKI	British Aerospace Jetstream Series 3102	718	SX-BSR G-OAKI, N417MX, G-31-718	5. 5.92	Jetstream Executive Travel Ltd (Noted operating with Highland Airways 2.09)	Inverness	10.2.10E
G-OAKR	Cessna 172S Skyhawk	172S9643	N21738	10. 6.04	A K Robson	Oaksey Park	12. 5.09E
G-OALD	SOCATA TB-20 Trinidad	490	N54TB F-GBLL	17. 3.88	D A Grief t/a Gold Aviation	Biggin Hill	24. 5.09E
G-OALH	Tecnam P92-EA Echo (Built L Hill)	PFA 318-13675		12. 6.01	L Hill	(Ulverston)	8. 3.09P
G-OAMF	Pegasus Quantum 15-912	7764		20.12.00	P J Kilshaw	Graveley Hall Farm, Graveley	28. 3.09P
G-OAMG	Bell 206B-3 JetRanger III	2901	G-COAL	25. 2.86	Alan Mann Helicopters Ltd	Fairoaks	19. 6.09E
G-OAMI	Bell 206B-2 JetRanger II	464	G-BAUN 5N-BAY, G-BAUN, 5N-AOU, VR-BIA, G-BAUN, N2261W	15. 3.01	Techno Solutions Ltd	Shobdon	2. 3.09E
G-OAML	Cameron AML-105 Balloon (Hot Air)	3881		4.12.96	Stratton Motor Company (Norfolk) Ltd "Aston Martin Lagonda"	Long Stratton, Norwich	9. 8.09E
G-OAMP	Reims Cessna F177RG Cardinal RG (Wichita c/n 17700098)	F177RG0006	G-AYPF	30.11.93	G D Boulger	RAF Woodvale	20.12.08E
G-OANI	Piper PA-28-161 Warrior II	28-8416091	N43570	8. 1.91	J F Mitchell (Damaged Upton Farm, Dover 16.6.96: wreck noted 9.96)	Oxford	8. 9.97
G-OANN	Zenair CH.601HDS Zodiac (Built P Noden) (Rotax 912-UL)	PFA 162-12932		2. 2.96	I J M Donnelly	Stonehaven	26. 7.06P
G-OAPE	Cessna T303 Crusader	T30300245	N303MF D-INKA, N9960C, M303HW, N9960C	3. 2.99	C Twiston-Davies and P L Drew	Jersey	27. 2.10E
G-OAPR	Brantly B 2B	446	(G-BPST) N2280U	21. 4.89	E D ap Rees t/a Helicopter International Magazine	Weston-super-Mare	1. 7.07
G-OAPW	Glaser-Dirks DG-400	4-268		17. 4.90	P L Poole	Sassuolo, Italy	27. 6.09E
G-OARA	Piper PA-28R-201 Arrow III	2837002	N802ND N9622N	28.10.98	Obmit Ltd	Shoreham	30. 5.09E
G-OARC	Piper PA-28RT-201 Arrow IV	28R-7918009	EC-HXO G-OARC, EC-JAE, EC-HXO, G-OARC, G-BMVE, N3071K	17. 8.99	Plane Talking Ltd	Denham	12.11.09E
G-OARG	Cameron C-80 Balloon (Hot Air)	3379		20.10.94	G and R Madelin "Argent"	Farnham/London SW15	14.11.06A
G-OARI	Piper PA-28R-201 Arrow III	2837005	N170ND	14.10.02	Plane Talking Ltd	Denham	17.11.09E
G-OARO	Piper PA-28R-201 Arrow III	2837006	N171ND	30.10.01	Plane Talking Ltd	Bournemouth	25.11.09E
G-OART	Piper PA-23-250 Aztec D	27-4293	G-AXKD N6936Y	26.11.93	A N and S L Palmer	Old Buckenham	3. 5.09E
G-OARU	Piper PA-28R-201 Arrow III	2837026	N174ND	24. 5.02	Plane Talking Ltd (Operated Cabair)	Bournemouth	16. 8.09E
G-OARV	ARV Aviation ARV-1 Super 2 (Built ARV Aviation Ltd - pr.no.PFA 152-11060) (Originally kit no 001 and rebuilt with kit no.008 C 1986) (Stored 1.91)	008		18. 6.84	N R Beale	(Sproughton, Ipswich)	12.10.87P
G-OASH	Robinson R22 Beta	0761	N2627Z	13. 6.88	J C Lane (Operated Heliflight (UK))	Gloucestershire	22. 6.09E
G-OASJ	Thruster T 600N 450 Sprint	0037-T600N-090		13.10.03	R C Reynolds	Arclid Green, Sandbach	8.12.09P
G-OASP	Aérospatiale AS.355F2 Ecureuil 2	5479	F-GJAJ F-WYMH	3. 8.95	Helicopter Services Ltd	Wycombe Air Park	26. 1.10E
G-OASW	Schleicher ASW 27	27227	BGA5160-KKL	10. 3.06	M P W Mee "MM" (Crashed into trees Lasham 8. 8.06 and substantially damaged)	Wycombe Air Park	14. 3.07
G-OATE	Pegasus Quantum 15-912	8064		27. 8.04	S J Goate	Sywell	26. 8.08P
G-OATV	Cameron V-77 Balloon (Hot Air)	2149		14. 2.90	A W and EP Braund-Smith	Denby Dale, Huddersfield	2.10.09E
G-OAVA	Robinson R22 Beta II	3303		8. 3.02	J Sargent	(Twentyways Farm, Ramsdean, Petersfield)	2. 4.09E
G-OAWD	Aérospatiale AS.350B Ecureuil	1790	G-IIPM G-GWIL	7. 2.06	Helicopter Ltd	Walton Wood	12. 3.09E

Reg	Type	C/n	Previous identity	Date	Owner/Operator	Location	Expiry
G-OAWS	Cameron Colt 77A Balloon (Hot Air)	4340		23. 4.98	P Lawman	Northampton	10. 9.09E
G-OBAK	Piper PA-28R-201T Turbo Arrow III	28R-7703054	D-EKOR N1146Q	27. 8.02	S P King tr G-OBAK Group Aviation	Fairoaks	14.11.08E
G-OBAL	Mooney M 20J Mooney 201	24-1601	N56569	27.11.86	Thomson Airways Ltd *(Operated Thomson Airways Flying Club)*	Cranfield	25. 4.09E
G-OBAM	Bell 206B-3 JetRanger III	4511	N6379U	25. 5.99	Cherwell Tobacco Ltd (Whitchurch, Shropshire)		13. 7.09E
G-OBAN	SAN Jodel D 140B Mousquetaire II	80	G-ATSU F-BKSA	20. 2.92	Shauna R Cameron	North Connel, Oban	18. 6.10
G-OBAX	Thruster T 600N 450 Jab Sprint	0051-T600N-053		12. 7.01	J Northage and M E Hutchinson	Baxby Manor, Husthwaite	14. 7.08P
G-OBAZ	Best Off Sky Ranger 912(2)	SKR0310391		17.11.03	B J Marsh	Plaistows Farm, St Albans	30. 6.09P
	(Built B J Marsh - pr.no.BMAA HB/322)						
G-OBBC	Colt 90A Balloon (Hot Air)	1358		11. 5.89	R A and Maxine A Riley *(BBC in the Midlands titles)* "Beeb"	Bromsgrove	23. 2.07A
G-OBBO	Cessna 182S Skylane	18280534	N7274Z	8. 6.99	A E Kedros	Oxford	29. 6.09E
G-OBBY	Robinson R44 Raven	0939		4.12.00	Holdsmart Ltd	(London E18)	29.10.09E
G-OBCC	Cessna 560 Citation Ultra	560-0497	OE-GCD N497TA, TC-MET, N5161J	8.12.06	MP Aviation LLP	Biggin Hill	28. 1.09E
G-OBDA	Diamond DA.20-A1 Katana	10260	C-FDVT	2. 7.98	Oscar Papa Ltd	Wolverhampton	30. 7.09E
G-OBDM	Europa Aviation Europa XS	572		16.12.03	B D McHugh	(Orpington)	
	(Built B D McHugh - pr.no.PFA 247-14048)						
G-OBDN	Piper PA-28-161 Warrior III	2842177	N53586	10. 7.03	R M Bennett	(Tadworth)	15. 8.09E
G-OBEE	Boeing Stearman A75N1 Kaydet	75-1174	N5580S N6734S, BuA3397	21. 2.05	P G Smith *(As "3397:174" in US Navy c/s)*	Old Buckenham	16. 6.11S
	(N2S-3 Kaydet)						
G-OBEI	SOCATA TB-200 Tobago XL	2096	F-OIUX	26. 6.02	Rapido Aviation Ltd	Weston, Leixlip, County Kildare	6. 8.09E
	(Carries Tobago GT titles)						
G-OBEN	Cessna 152 II	15281856	G-NALI, G-BHVM, N67477	16. 8.93	Flying Time Ltd *(Operated Airbase Flying Club)*	Rochester	18.12.09E
G-OBET	Sky 77-24 Balloon (Hot Air)	178		22. 2.00	P M Watkins and S M Carden	Chippenham	25. 4.09E
G-OBEV	Europa Aviation Europa	188		3. 2.98	M B Hill and N I Hill	(Dursley)	
	(Built M B Hill - pr.no.PFA 247-12813) (Monowheel u/c)						
G-OBFC	Piper PA-28-161 Warrior III	2816118	N9252X	15. 7.96	Bflying Ltd	Bournemouth	16. 8.08E
	(Went off runway landing Henstridge 15. 4.07 and badly damaged, to Ringwood for spares recovery. Noted dumped Bournemouth 4.08)						
G-OBFE	Sky 120-24 Balloon (Hot Air)	167	D-OBFE	28. 4.03	H Schmidt	Siegen, Germany	5. 9.09E
G-OBFS	Piper PA-28-161 Warrior III	2842039	N41274	4.12.98	Plane Talking Ltd	Denham	3.12.09E
G-OBGC	SOCATA TB-20 Trinidad	1898		13. 5.99	Bidford Airfield Ltd	Bidford	3. 8.09E
G-OBHD	Short SD.3-60 Variant 100	SH3714	G-BNDK, G-OBHD, G-BNDK, G-14-3714	20. 1.87	ACL Aircraft Support Ltd *(stored)*	Southend-on-Sea	5. 3.06E
G-OBIB	Colt 120A Balloon (Hot Air)	4229		9. 1.98	M W A Shemilt	Henley-on-Thames	11.10.09E
G-OBIL	Robinson R22 Beta	0792		10. 5.88	Aerolease Ltd	Conington	24. 8.09E
G-OBIO	Robinson R22 Beta	1402	N7724M	29. 6.98	Heli Air Ltd	Denham	25. 8.09E
G-OBJB	Lindstrand LBL 90A Balloon (Hot Air)	640		12.11.99	B J Bower	Pierantonio, Italy	8. 3.09E
G-OBJH	Colt 77A Balloon (Hot Air)	2569		11. 3.94	Hayrick Ltd	Cranbrook	1. 9.07
G-OBJM	Taylor JT.1 Monoplane	PFA 055-14623		2. 5.08	B J Main	Henstridge	
G-OBJP	Pegasus Quantum 15-912	7847		29. 8.01	S J Baker	Sutton Meadows	22. 8.08P
G-OBJT	Europa Aviation Europa	055	G-MUZO	16.11.00	B J Tarmar	Old Sarum	11. 9.09P
	(Built J T Grant - pr.no.PFA 247-12623) (Rotax 912ULS) (Tri-gear u/c)						
G-OBLC	Beech 76 Duchess	ME-249	N6635R	3. 6.87	Pridenote Ltd	Sturgate	29. 5.09E
G-OBLU	Cameron H-34 Balloon (Hot Air)	4914		4. 8.00	John Aimo Balloons SAS *(Blu titles)*	Mondovi, Piedmont, Italy	9. 6.09E
G-OBMI	Mainair Blade	1289-0601-7-W1084		19. 6.01	I G Webster and P Clark	Ashcroft Farm, Winsford	26. 7.09P
G-OBMP	Boeing 737-3Q8	24963		8. 1.92	British Midland Airways Ltd *(Operated bmiBaby)* "robin hood baby"	Nottingham-East Midlands	19. 3.09E
G-OBMS	Reims Cessna F172N Skyhawk II	F17201584	OO-BWA, (OO-HWA), D-EBYX	16. 4.84	A J Ransome, D Beverley and K Brown	Sherburn-in-Elmet	7. 7.09E
G-OBMW	Grumman AA-5 Traveler	AA5-0805	G-BDFV	4. 7.79	Fretcourt Ltd	Sherburn-in-Elmet	7. 7.09E
G-OBNA	Piper PA-34-220T Seneca V	3449002	N9281D, (N338DB)	25. 5.00	Palmair Ltd	Elstree	14. 8.09E
G-OBNC	Britten-Norman BN-2B-20 Islander	3000		9. 2.05	Britten-Norman Aircraft Ltd	Bembridge	
G-OBNL	Britten-Norman BN-2A-21 Islander	523	G-BDVX, Belgian Army B-07, G-BDVX	21. 5.07	B-N Group Ltd	Bembridge	13. 5.09E
G-OBPP	Schleicher ASW 27-18 E	29563	BGA5326-KSJ	23.10.08	M H Patel	Wycombe Air Park	
	(Solo 2350)						
G-OBRA	Cameron Z-315 Balloon (Hot Air)	10729		11. 8.05	Cameron Flights Southern Ltd *"Triumph"*	Woodborough, Pewsey	27. 3.09E
G-OBRY	Cameron N-180 Balloon (Hot Air)	3010		1. 3.93	A C K Rawson and J J Rudoni t/a Wickers World Hot Air Balloon Company *(Bryant Homes titles)*	Stafford	21. 8.08T
G-OBSM	Robinson R44 Raven	1030	G-CDSE, N43861, C-FAEP	15.12.05	Flight Solutions Ltd	Panshanger	28. 1.09E
G-OBTS	Cameron C-80 Balloon (Hot Air)	3589		18. 4.95	C F Cushion	Petersfield	30. 8.09E
G-OBUN	Cameron A-250 Balloon (Hot Air)	4711		29. 2.00	A C K Rawson and J J Rudoni t/a Wickers World Hot Air Balloon Company	Stafford	16.11.05T
G-OBUP	Glaser-Dirks DG-800B	8-381B280X42		31.10.07	J D Montagu	Lasham	28.11.09E
G-OBUU	Comper CLA.7 Swift replica	PFA 103-12165		25. 1.07	J A Pothecary and R H Hunt	(Old Sarum)	
	(Built J A Pothecary and R H Hunt)						
G-OBUY	Colt 69A Balloon (Hot Air)	2031		7. 8.91	A D Kent tr Balloon Preservation Flying Group *"Virgin Megastore"*	Petworth	27. 5.09E
G-OBUZ	Van's RV-6	20410	N868CM	28. 8.08	A F Hall	(Burstall, Ipswich)	
	(Built S H Martin, amended to H M Sutter 24. 1.09)						
G-OBYD	Boeing 767-304ER	28042	SE-DZG G-OBYD	4. 3.97	Thomson Airways Ltd	Luton	2. 5.09E
G-OBYE	Boeing 767-304ER	28979	D-AGYE G-OBYE	26. 2.98	Thomson Airways Ltd *"Bill Travers"*	Luton	28.10.09E

Reg	Type	C/n	Prev id	Date	Owner/Operator	Location	Status
G-OBYF	Boeing 767-304ER	28208	D-AGYF G-OBYF	8. 6.98	Thomson Airways Ltd	Luton	30. 4.09E
G-OBYG	Boeing 767-304ER	29137		13. 1.99	Thomson Airways Ltd	Luton	17.12.09E
G-OBYH	Boeing 767-304ER	28883	SE-DZO D-AGYH, G-OBYH	4. 2.99	Thomson Airways Ltd	Luton	18.11.09E
G-OBYI	Boeing 767-304ER	29138		1. 2.00	Thomson Airways Ltd	Luton	31. 1.10E
G-OBYJ	Boeing 767-304ER	29384		20. 2.00	Thomson Airways Ltd	Luton	18. 2.09E
G-OBYT	Agusta-Bell 206A JetRanger	8237	G-BNRC Oman AF 601	30. 1.95	R J Everett	(Sproughton, Ipswich)	12. 7.03T
G-OCAD	Sequoia F 8L Falco *(Built C W Garrard)* (Lycoming IO-320)	PFA 100-12114		8. 6.92	I R Court tr Falco Flying Group	Leicester	29. 1.10P
G-OCAM	Gulfstream AA-5A Cheetah	AA5A-0741	G-BLHO OO-RTJ, OO-HRN	24. 3.94	I H Seach-Allen	Wycombe Air Park	10. 9.09E
G-OCAR	Colt 77A Balloon (Hot Air)	1099		6. 8.87	S C J Derham *"Toyota"*	Bridgnorth	25. 8.00A
G-OCBI	Schweizer 269C-1 *(Schweizer 300)*	0139	N86G	14. 8.02	JWL Helicopters Ltd	Biggin Hill	11.10.08E
G-OCBT	IAV Bacau Yakovlev Yak-52 *(Officially regd with cn 1011001)*	9011011	LY-AQH HA-HUZ, LY-AMC, DOSAAF 103 (yellow)	30. 3.05	W M Burnett tr Cambridge Business Travel	Little Gransden	22. 5.09P
G-OCCD	Diamond DA.40D Star	D4.225		21. 9.06	Plane Talking Ltd *(Operated Cabair)*	Cranfield	25.10.09E
G-OCCE	Diamond DA.40D Star	D4.226	OE-VPU	22. 9.06	Plane Talking Ltd *(Operated Cabair)*	Cranfield	7. 1.10E
G-OCCF	Diamond DA.40D Star	D4.229	OE-VPU	2.10.06	Plane Talking Ltd *(Operated Cabair)*	Cranfield	31.10.09E
G-OCCG	Diamond DA.40D Star	D4.230	OE-VPU	9.10.06	Plane Talking Ltd *(Operated Cabair)*	Cranfield	7.12.09E
G-OCCH	Diamond DA.40D Star	D4.233		9.10.06	Venturi Capital Ltd *(Operated Cabair)*	Cranfield	20.11.09E
G-OCCK	Diamond DA.40D Star	D4.234	OE-VPT	23.11.06	Venturi Capital Ltd *(Operated Cabair)*	Cranfield	17. 1.10E
G-OCCL	Diamond DA.40D Star	D4.237		17.10.06	Venturi Capital Ltd *(Operated Cabair)*	Cranfield	20.11.09E
G-OCCM	Diamond DA.40D Star	D4.238		16.11.06	Plane Talking Ltd *(Operated Cabair)*	Cranfield	12.12.09E
G-OCCN	Diamond DA.40D Star	D4.241	OE-VPU (G-OCCT)	23.11.06	Venturi Capital Ltd *(Operated Cabair)*	Cranfield	29. 1.10E
G-OCCO	Diamond DA.40D Star	D4.242		29.11.06	Plane Talking Ltd *(Operated Cabair)*	Cranfield	16. 1.10E
G-OCCP	Diamond DA.40D Star	D4.245	OE-VPU (G-OCCU)	7.12.06	Plane Talking Ltd *(Operated Cabair)*	Cranfield	27. 1.10E
G-OCCR	Diamond DA.40D Star	D4.246	OE-UDV	5. 1.07	Gamich LLP *(Operated Cabair)*	Cranfield	8. 2.1E
G-OCCS	Diamond DA.40D Star	D4.249	OE-VPU	15.12.06	Plane Talking Ltd *(Operated Cabair)*	Cranfield	16. 1.10E
G-OCCT	Diamond DA.40D Star	D4.250	OE-UDP	14.12.06	Plane Talking Ltd *(Operated Cabair)*	Stapleford	28. 1.09E
G-OCCU	Diamond DA.40D Star	D4.252		18.12.06	Plane Talking Ltd *(Operated Cabair)*	Cranfield	8. 2.09E
G-OCCV	Diamond DA.42 Twin Star	42.010	F-GSIM	22.11.07	Plane Talking Ltd *(Operated Cabair)*	Cranfield	12.12.09E
G-OCCW	Diamond DA.42 Twin Star	42.154	OE-VPY	3. 8.06	Plane Talking Ltd *(Operated Cabair)*	Cranfield	6. 9.09E
G-OCCX	Diamond DA.42 Twin Star	42.155	OE-VPW	3. 8.06	Plane Talking Ltd *(Operated Cabair)*	Cranfield	10. 9.09E
G-OCCY	Diamond DA.42 Twin Star	42.158		3. 8.06	Venturi Capital Ltd *(Operated Cabair)*	Cranfield	6. 9.09E
G-OCCZ	Diamond DA.42 Twin Star	42.161		23. 8.06	Venturi Capital Ltd *(Operated Cabair)*	Cranfield	10. 9.09E
G-OCDP	Flight Design CTSW *(Assembled P&M Aviation Ltd as c/n 8226)*	06.08.22		23.10.06	M A Beadman	Armshold Farm, Kington	31.10.09P
G-OCDW	Avtech Jabiru UL-450 *(Built C D Wood - pr.no.PFA 274A-14122)*	xxxx		31. 3.04	H Burroughs	Henstridge	20. 4.09P
G-OCEG	Beech 200 Super King Air	BB-588	N578BM	11. 9.07	Cega Air Ambulance Ltd	Goodwood	13. 2.09E
G-OCFC	Robin R2160	374		21. 6.02	Cornwall Flying Club Ltd	Bodmin	24. 7.09E
G-OCFD	Bell 206B-3 JetRanger III	3165	G-WGAL G-OICS, N678TM, N678TW	10. 6.04	Rushmere Helicopters Ltd	Sywell	29. 4.09E
G-OCFM	Piper PA-34-200 Seneca	34-7350021	G-ELBC G-BANS, N15110	20. 4.04	Stapleford Flying Club Ltd *(Operated Capital Radio)*	Stapleford	27.12.09E
G-OCHM	Robinson R44 Raven	1055		4. 5.01	Westleigh Developments Ltd	(Whetstone, Leicestershire)	6. 6.09E
G-OCJK	Schweizer 269C *(Schweizer 300)*	S 1294	N69A	10.12.87	P Crawley	(Shipley)	27. 5.00
G-OCJZ	Cessna 525A CitationJet CJ2	525A0051	N4155L N6JR, N6M	4. 7.08	Go West Ltd	Bristol	20. 7.09E
G-OCLC	Aviat A-1B Husky (Floatplane)	2380	N440HY	8. 6.07	Caledonian Seaplanes Ltd	St Fillans, Loch Earn	10. 6.08E
G-OCMM	Agusta A109A II	7347	G-BXCB F-GJSH, G-ISEB, G-IADT, G-HBCA	20. 3.01	Castle Air Charters Ltd	Liskeard Heliport	13. 8.09E
G-OCMT	Evektor EV-97 teamEurostar UK *(Built Cosmik Aviation)*	1701		14. 7.03	P Crowhurst	Sywell	3. 8.09P
G-OCOK	American Champion 8KCAB Super Decathlon	825-99	N669MM	16. 6.08	J D May	White Waltham	1. 7.09E
G-OCON	Robinson R44 Raven	1608		12. 5.06	Conwell Contracts (UK) Ltd	Enniskillen	31. 5.09E
G-OCOV	Robinson R22 Beta II	3217		23. 5.01	Heli Air Ltd *(Op FlightCentre)*	Southend	15. 8.09E
G-OCPC	Reims Cessna FA152 Aerobat	FA1520343		20. 1.78	Westward Airways (Lands End) Ltd	St Just	6. 8.09E
G-OCRI	Colomban MC-15 Cri-Cri *(Built M J J Dunning - pr.no.PFA 133-12288)*	524		24. 6.92	M J J Dunning	(Bredbury, Stockport)	
G-OCRZ	CZAW Sportcruiser *(Built P Marsden)*	PFA/338-14668		3. 3.08	P Marsden	Popham	8.10.09P
G-OCSA	Bombardier BD-700-1A11 Global 5000	9241	N941TS C-FLKY	10.10.08	Global Trans Holdings Corporation	Geneva, Switzerland	9.10.09E
G-OCSD	Bombardier CL-600-2B16 *(CL-604 Challenger)*	5591	N604CD C-GLYA	4. 9.06	Ocean Sky (UK) Ltd	Manchester	5. 9.09E
G-OCSE	Bombardier CL-600-2B16 *(CL-605 Challenger)*	5710	N710TS C-GSAP, C-FMNL, C-GLXO	8. 5.08	Ocean Sky Aviation Ltd	Manchester	8. 5.09E
G-OCSF	Bombardier CL-600-2B16 *(CL-605 Challenger)*	5733	N533TS C-FPQW	11. 6.08	Ocean Sky Aviation Ltd	Manchester	10. 6.09E
G-OCST	Agusta-Bell 206B-3 JetRanger III	8694	N39AH VR-CDG, G-BMKM	14.12.94	Lift West Ltd	Liskeard Heliport	18. 2.09E
G-OCTI	Piper PA-32-260 Cherokee Six	32-288	G-BGZX 9XR-MP, 5Y-ADH, N3427W	26. 7.88	D G Williams	(Dinan, France)	2. 9.09E
G-OCTU	Piper PA-28-161 Cadet	2841280	EC-IHB G-OCTU, N91997	16.11.89	Plane Talking Ltd	Bournemouth	27. 7.09E

Regn	Type	C/n	Prev ID	Date	Owner/Operator	Location	Expiry
G-OCUB	Piper J-3C-90 Cub (L-4J-PI)	13248	OO-JOZ	21. 4.81	C A Foss and P A Brook tr Florence Flying Group "Florence"		
	(Frame No.13078)		PH-NKC, PH-UCH(1), 45-4508		(Operated Zebedee Flying Group)	Shoreham	19. 8.08P
	(Officially regd with c/n 13215, f/n 13045, but this was 45-4475/PH-UCW and rebuilt as PH-UCH(2))						
G-OCZA	CZAW Sportcruiser	LAA 338-14820		11. 7.08	S M Dawson	Eshott	
	(Built S M Dawson)						
G-ODAC	Reims Cessna F152 II	F15201824	G-BITG	19.12.96	T M and M L Jones (Operated Derby Aero Club)		
	(Rebuilt with cockpit/front fuselage of G-BITG 6.96)					Derby	14.10.09E
G-ODAD	Colt 77A Balloon (Hot Air)	2001		20. 2.91	J H Dodson "Odyssey"	Streatley, Reading	2. 4.09E
G-ODAF	Lindstrand LBL 105A Balloon (Hot Air)	1042		10. 3.05	T J Horne (LDV and Brian Currie titles)		
						North Crawley, Newport Pagnell	27. 5.09E
G-ODAG	Cessna 525A CitationJet CJ2	525A0397	N5148B	2. 5.08	Air Charter Scotland Ltd	Glasgow	1. 5.09E
G-ODAK	Piper PA-28-236 Dakota	28-7911162	D-EXMA	29. 2.00	Airways Aero Associations Ltd	Wycombe Air Park	8. 4.09E
			OH-SMO, N386WT, N22328		(Operated British Airways Flying Club)		
G-ODAT	Aero L-29 Delfin	194227	ES-YLV	28. 7.99	Graniteweb Ltd (stored 1.09)	North Weald	15. 3.06P
			Estonian AF, Soviet AF				
G-ODAY	Cameron N-56 Balloon (Hot Air)	551		16. 7.79	The British Balloon Museum and Library Ltd		
						Southampton	27. 5.09E
G-ODAZ	Robinson R44 Raven II	12167		11. 3.08	D Robson	(Doncaster)	27. 3.09E
G-ODBN	Lindstrand Flowers SS Balloon (Hot Air)	389		22. 5.96	Magical Adventures Ltd "Sainsbury's Flowers"		
						West Bloomfield, Michigan, US	30. 9.09E
G-ODCC	Bell 206L-3 LongRanger III	51070	N206LS	7. 2.07	D Chisnall t/a DCC Aviation		
						(Blackfield, Southampton)	3. 7.09E
G-ODCH	Schleicher ASW 20L	20067	BGA4860-JXH	13. 3.08	D C Heath	Shenington	
			D-7657				
G-ODCM	Cessna 525B CitationJet CJ3	525B0153	N28FR	3. 7.08	Air Charter Scotland Ltd	Glasgow	17. 7.09E
			N514SP				
G-ODCR	Robinson R44 Raven II	12168		14. 3.08	Directions 4 Business Ltd	Costock	27. 3.09E
G-ODCS	Robinson R22 Beta II	2828		19. 5.98	L Crevatin	(London NW8)	29. 9.07T
G-ODDS	Pitts S-2A	2225	N31486	31. 8.05	A C Cassidy	White Waltham	19.10.09E
	(Built Aerotek Inc) (Lycoming AEIO-360)						
G-ODDY	Lindstrand LBL 105A Balloon (Hot Air)	042		15. 7.93	P and T.Huckle	Oakwood, Derby	27. 9.09E
G-ODDZ	Schempp-Hirth Duo Discus T	49	BGA4931-KAF	22. 5.08	M R Smith	Aboyne	
G-ODEE	Van's RV-6	PFA 181A-13173	PH-RVM	14. 4.00	D Cook	Shenstone Hall Farm, Shenstone	20. 4.09P
	(Built D Powell) (Lycoming O-320)		G-ODEE				
G-ODEN	Piper PA-28-161 Cadet	2841282	N92004	22.11.89	Plane Talking Ltd	Denham	25. 3.09E
G-ODEX	Cessna 182T Skylane	18282028	N271V	25. 3.08	Friend Flying Services LLP	Conington	12. 6.09E
			G-ODEX, N280MC				
G-ODGS	Avtech Jabiru UL-450	0247		2. 8.99	D G Salt	(Ashbourne)	15. 6.09P
	(Built D G Salt - pr.no.PFA 274A-13472)						
G-ODHB	Robinson R44 Raven II	10985		5.12.05	A J Mossop (Operated Rise Helicopters)		
						Gloucestershire	17. 1.09E
G-ODIN	Mudry CAP.10B	192	F-GDTH	16.12.93	T W Harris	Wycombe Air Park	24. 9.09E
G-ODJB	Robinson R22 Beta II	3463		10. 7.03	N T Burton	Costock	30. 6.09E
G-ODJD	Raj Hamsa X'Air 582(7)	559		25. 4.01	M Bastin	Lower Upham Farm, Chiseldon	19.10.07P
	(Built D J Davis - pr.no.BMAA HB/151)						
G-ODJF	Lindstrand LBL 90B Balloon (Hot Air)	1075		11. 4.06	Helena Dos Santos SA	Corroios, Portugal	1. 7.09E
G-ODJG	Europa Aviation Europa	167		3. 5.96	C S Andersson and K R Challis	Great Oakley	9.11.07P
	(Built D J Goldsmith - pr.no.PFA 247-12889) (Rotax 912 ULS) (Monowheel u/c)						
G-ODJH	Mooney M 20C Mark 21	690083	G-BMLH	19. 1.93	A P Howells	(Pontypridd)	13. 9.08E
			N9293V				
G-ODLY	Cessna 310J	310J0077	G-TUBY	21. 3.88	R Himmelein	Fairoaks	22. 6.09E
			G-ASZZ, N3077L				
G-ODOC	Robinson R44 Astro	0372		27. 8.97	Gas and Air Ltd	Wycombe Air Park	31. 1.10E
G-ODOG	Piper PA-28R-200 Cherokee Arrow II	28R-7235197	EI-BPB	2. 8.96	Advanced Investments Ltd	Sibson	30. 6.09E
			G-BAAR, N11C				
G-ODPJ	Magni M-16 Tandem Trainer	VPM16-UK-111	G-BVWX	4. 4.03	K J Robinson and S Palmer	RAF Benson	9. 9.09P
	(Built M L Smith, pr.no PFA G/12-1251) (Arrow GT1000R)						
G-ODRY	Evektor EV-97 teamEurostar UK	2316		28. 4.05	C Prince and P Maddox	Wolverhampton	27. 4.09P
G-ODSK	Boeing 737-37Q	28537		23. 7.97	British Midland Airways Ltd (Operated bmiBaby)		
					"baby dragon fly"	Nottingham-East Midlands	27. 7.09E
G-ODTW	Europa Aviation Europa	215		7. 9.95	D T Walters	(Meopham, Gravesend)	
	(Built D T Walters - pr.no.PFA 247-12890) (Monowheel u/c)						
G-ODUD	Piper PA-28-181 Cherokee Archer II	28-7790107	G-IBBO	15. 3.04	G-ODUD Aviation Ltd	Aberdeen	6. 3.09E
			D-EPCA, N5389F				
G-ODUO	Schempp-Hirth Duo Discus	29	BGA4113-HQE	26.11.07	A J Eddie tr 3D Syndicate "3D"	Aboyne	25. 4.08
G-ODUR	Raytheon Hawker 900XP	HA-0041	N34441	2. 4.08	Hangar 8 Ltd	Oxford	1. 4.09E
G-ODVB	CFM Shadow Series DD	300-DD	G-MGDB	3.11.98	N R Henry	(Nuneaton)	18. 7.09P
G-OEAC	Mooney M 20J Mooney 201	24-1636	N57656	16. 6.88	S Lovatt	Nottingham City-Tollerton	15. 5.09E
G-OEAT	Robinson R22 Beta	0650	G-RACH	8. 1.98	C Y O Seeds Ltd	Wycombe Air Park	1. 4.09E
G-OECM	Commander Aircraft Commander 114B	14627	N6107Y	4. 3.04	ECM (Vehicle Delivery Service) Ltd	Carlisle	6. 4.09E
G-OCEO	Flylight Dragonfly	018		4. 2.09	P A and M W Aston	Exeter	
G-OEDB	Piper PA-38-112 Tomahawk	38-79A0167	G-BGGJ	9. 5.89	M A Petrie	Hawarden	24. 3.09E
			N9694N				
G-OEDP	Cameron N-77 Balloon (Hot Air)	2189		28.12.89	M J Betts "Eastern Counties Press"	Norwich	12. 6.01A
G-OEGG	Cameron Egg 65 SS Balloon (Hot Air)	2140		4.12.89	A D Kent tr Calorie Watch Balloon Team		
					"Cadbury's Chocolate Egg"	Petworth	1. 7.09E
G-OEGL	Christen Eagle II	001	N46JH	12. 1.98	R Dauncey tr The Eagle Flight Syndicate		
	(Lycoming IO-360)					Shoreham	30. 4.08P
G-OEJC	Robinson R44 Clipper (Floats)	1469		4. 4.05	Syntema Servicio y Gestion SL	Palma, Spain	21. 4.09E
G-OEKS	Comco Ikarus C42 FB80	0807-6981		17. 9.08	J D Smith	Baxby Manor, Husthwaite	
	(Built Aerosport Ltd)						
G-OELD	Pegasus Quantum 15-912	7765		20.12.00	R P Butler	Newtownards	29. 3.09P
G-OELZ	Wassmer WA.52 Europa	66	F-BTLO	10. 8.05	J A Simms tr G-OELZ Group	Breighton	22. 3.08E

Reg	Type	C/n	Prev id	Date	Owner/Operator	Location	Date
G-OEMT	Eurocopter MBB BK-117C-1	7538	D-HMEC	13. 2.06	Sterling Helicopters Ltd *(Operated East Anglia Air Ambulance)*	RAF Wyton	26. 3.09E
G-OERR	Lindstrand LBL 60A Balloon (Hot Air)	469		30. 6.97	P C Gooch	Alresford	18. 5.09E
G-OERS	Cessna 172N Skyhawk II	17268856	G-SSRS, N734HA	24. 5.94	E R Stevens	Leicester	5.10.09E
G-OERX	Cameron O-65 Balloon (Hot Air)	4004		23. 1.96	R Roehsler	(Vienna, Austria)	27. 2.97A
G-OESY	Reality Easy Raider J2.2 (1)	0005		16.11.01	J Gray	(Bookham, Leatherhead)	16. 6.09P
	(Built T F Francis - pr.no.BMAA HB/193) (Jabiru 2200)						
G-OETI	Bell 206B-3 JetRanger III	2533	G-RMIE, G-BPIE, N327WM	23. 7.02	AIM Racing Ltd	Manston	9. 3.09E
G-OETV	Piper PA-31-350 Navajo Chieftain	31-7852073	N27597	16. 6.04	Skydrift Ltd	Norwich	15. 8.09E
G-OEVA	Piper PA-32-260 Cherokee Six	32-219	G-FLJA, G-AVTJ, N3373W	13. 3.03	M G Cookson	North Weald	31. 3.09E
	(Rebuilt using spare Frame No.32-860S)						
G-OEWD	Raytheon RB390 Premier 1	RB-126	N3726G	3. 6.05	Bookajet Aircraft Management Ltd	Farnborough	9. 6.09E
G-OEZY	Europa Aviation Europa	042		8. 8.95	A W Wakefield	Conington	8.12.09P
	(Built A W Wakefield - pr.no.PFA 247-12590) (Rotax 912 UL) (Monowheel u/c)						
G-OFAA	Cameron Z-105 Balloon (Hot Air)	10886		9. 8.06	D J Constant *"Royal Navy"* Queen Camel, Yeovil		9. 4.09E
G-OFAL	Ozone Roadster/Bailey Quattro	RDL-J31E-028/0990108		18. 9.08	Malcolm Roberts Heating, Plumbing and Electrical Ltd (Pwllheli)		
	(Built Airsports Airways)						
G-OFAS	Robinson R22 Beta	0559		17. 6.86	Fast Helicopters Ltd	Thruxton	25. 4.09E
G-OFBJ	Thunder Ax7-77A Balloon (Hot Air)	2050		2. 9.91	J C Harris	Newbury	25. 9.99A
G-OFBU	Comco Ikarus C42 FB UK	0301-6328		28. 8.01	J Pearce tr Old Sarum C42 Group	Old Sarum	31. 1.08P
	(Built Fly Buy Ultralights Ltd - pr.no.PFA 322-13653)						
G-OFCH	Agusta-Bell 206B-2 JetRanger II	8337	HB-XUI, G-BKDA, LN-OQX	15. 5.00	Fleet Coast Helicopters Ltd	Shoreham	11. 7.03T
	(Rolled over, struck ground Morn Farm, Chickerell 4. 1.02 and badly damaged)						
G-OFCM	Reims Cessna F172L	F17200839	G-AZUN, (OO-FCB)	21.10.81	J R Wright	Jersey	27. 6.09E
G-OFDT	Mainair Pegasus Quik	8320		9.11.07	D Bardsley	Barton	2.12.08P
G-OFER	Piper PA-18-150 Super Cub	18-7709058	N83509	29.12.89	M S W Meagher	Shenington	20. 2.08
G-OFFA	Pietenpol AirCamper	PFA 047-13181		3.11.98	D J Street tr Offa Group *"Sweet FA"*	Bicester	21. 2.09P
	(Built Offa Group) (Lycoming O-235)						
G-OFFO	Extra EA.300/L	1226		10. 3.06	2 Excel Aviation Ltd	Sywell	23. 3.09E
	(Operated 'The Blades' display team, Barclays insignia)						
G-OFIL	Robinson R44 Astro	0555		15. 1.99	B J North t/a North Helicopters	Redhill	21. 4.09E
G-OFIT	SOCATA TB-10 Tobago	938	G-BRIU	11. 9.89	G M Richards tr GFI Aviation Group	White Waltham	7. 7.09E
G-OFIX	Grob G109B	6394	F-CJLS, HB-2111	5. 1.09	T R Dews	Wing Farm, Longbridge Deverill	
G-OFLY	Cessna 210M Centurion II	21061600	(D-EBYM), N732LQ	13.10.79	A P Mothew	Southend	30. 7.09E
G-OFMC	British Aerospace Avro 146-RJ100	E3264	G-CDUI, TC-THM, G-6-264	11. 4.07	Flightline Ltd *(Operated Ford Motor Company)* *(Ceased operations 2.12.08)*	Southend	7.12.09E
G-OFOA	British Aerospace BAe 146 Series 100	E1006	G-BKMN, EI-COF, SE-DRH, G-BKMN, G-ODAN	3. 3.98	Formula One Adminstration Ltd	Biggin Hill	14. 7.09E
G-OFOM	British Aerospace BAe 146 Series 100	E1144	N3206T, PK-DTA, G-BSLP, (PK-DTA), G-6-144, G-11-144, (G-BRLM)	16. 3.00	Formula One Management Ltd	Biggin Hill	6.10.09E
G-OFOX	Denney Kitfox	PFA 172-11523		1.11.89	P R Skeels	(Sandbach)	
	(Built P R Skeels)						
G-OFRB	Everett Gyroplane Series 2	006	(G-BLSR)	7. 8.85	T N Holcroft-Smith	(High Wycombe)	18. 2.08P
	(Rotax 582)						
G-OFRY	Cessna 152 II	15281420	G-BPHS, N49971	8. 2.93	Devon and Somerset Flight Training Ltd	Dunkeswell	14. 4.09E
G-OFST	Bell 206L-3 LongRanger III	51300	5B-CJW, G-BXIB, EC-EQQ	2.11.06	Heron Helicopters Ltd	Herne Bay	6.11.09E
G-OFTI	Piper PA-28-140 Cherokee Cruiser	28-7325201	G-BRKU, N15926	11. 6.90	M Naylor and J Webb tr G-OFTI Group	Andrewsfield	12. 2.09E
G-OGAN	Europa Aviation Europa	100		28. 7.94	J R Malpass	Henstridge	18. 9.07P
	(Built M A Jackson, M P Gogan and R S Cullum - pr.no.PFA 247-12734) (Rotax 582) (Tri-gear u/c)						
G-OGAR	PZL-Bielsko SZD-45A Ogar	B-601	SP-0004	29. 1.90	P Rasmussen tr Perranporth Ogar Flying Group	Perranporth	5. 6.09E
G-OGAY	Balony Kubicek BB26 Balloon (Hot Air)	337	OK-0337	16. 2.05	J W Soukup	Bristol	9. 7.09E
G-OGAZ	Aérospatiale SA.341G Gazelle 1	1274	G-OCJR, G-BRGS, F-GEQA, N341SG, (N341P), N341SG, N47295	12. 1.94	I M and Sheena.M Graham t/a Killochries Fold	Linlithgow	22. 6.09E
G-OGBD	Boeing 737-3L9	27833	OY-MAR, D-ADBJ, OY-MAR	16. 3.98	British Midland Airways Ltd *(Operated bmiBaby)*	Nottingham-East Midlands	12. 3.09E
G-OGBE	Boeing 737-3L9	27834	OY-MAS	24.11.98	British Midland Airways Ltd *(Operated bmiBaby)* *"derby's baby pride"*	Nottingham-East Midlands	17.12.08E
G-OGBR	Mudry CAP.232	20	N232MG	7. 2.08	G C J Cooper (Owmby-by-Spital, Market Rasen)		
G-OGCE	Bell 206L-3 LongRanger III	51206	N140JW, EI-LHD, D-HKLW, N3025J	4. 8.06	Helicopter Training and Hire Ltd	Newtownards	14.10.09E
G-OGEM	Piper PA-28-181 Archer II	28-8190226	N83816	10. 3.88	GEM Rewinds Ltd	Coventry	9.12.09E
G-OGEO	Aérospatiale SA.341G Gazelle 1	1417	G-BXJK, F-GEHC, N341AT, N49536	28. 1.02	MW Helicopters Ltd	Falkirk	17.11.09E
G-OGES	Enstrom 280FX Shark	2078	G-CBYL, HB-XAJ	15.11.02	G N Ratcliffe	Barton	24. 3.09E
G-OGET	Piper PA-39 Twin Comanche C/R	39-87	G-AYXY, N8930Y	14. 3.83	D Saxton	Lee-on-Solent	12. 9.05
					(Noted 9.07)		
G-OGGB	Grob G102 Astir CS	1072	BGA4095-HPM, D-3304	2. 4.08	M Ogbe *"HPM"*	Bicester	
G-OGGY	Aviat A-1B Husky Pup	NF0005	N144HP	27. 2.04	Chris Irvine Aviation Ltd	Perranporth	25. 9.09E
G-OGJM	Cameron C-80 Balloon (Hot Air)	4869		21.11.00	G J Madelin	Farnham	6.11.09E

Reg	Type	C/n	Prev id	Date	Owner/Operator	Base	Expiry
G-OGJP	Hughes 369E *(Hughes 500)*	0512E	N685F N5223X	23. 1.01	MJ Church Plant Ltd	Marshfield	11. 4.09E
G-OGJS	Rutan Cozy *(Built G J Stamper)* (Lycoming O-360)	PFA 159-11169		27. 1.89	G J Stamper *(Stored 2003)*	(Carlisle)	14. 9.98P
G-OGKB	Sequoia F 8L Falco *(Built A Powell and G K Brothwood)*	PFA 100-12153		3. 1.07	G K Brothwood *(Noted 1.07)*	Liverpool	
G-OGLY	Cameron Z-105 Balloon (Hot-Air)	11188		21. 7.08	H M Ogston *"The Demster"*	London SW7	24. 7.09E
G-OGOH	Robinson R22 Beta II	2738	G-IPDM G-OMSG	25.11.02	E K Richardson	Manchester	31. 5.09E
G-OGOS	Everett Gyroplane (Volkswagen 1834)	004	7Q-YES G-OGOS	30. 7.84	N A Seymour	(Norwich)	12. 9.90P
G-OGSA	Avtech Jabiru UL-450 *(Built G J Slater - pr.no.PFA 274A-13540)* (Jabiru 2200A)	0299		10. 2.00	M M Danek	Redlands, Swindon	10 1.07P
G-OGSK	Embraer EMB-135BJ Legacy	14501074	PT-SEW	14.11.08	TAG Aviation (UK) Ltd	Farnborough	13.11.09E
G-OGSS	Lindstrand LBL 120A Balloon (Hot Air)	683		19. 5.00	R Klarer	Erbach, Germany	21. 2.08A
G-OGTS	Air Command 532 Elite *(Built G E Heritage - pr.no.PFA G/104-1125)* (Rotax 532)	0432		19.12.88	GTS Engineering (Coventry) Ltd t/a GTS Cars	(Coventry)	1.10.90P
G-OHAC	Reims Cessna F182Q Skylane II	F18200048	D-ENCM	11. 7.01	The Royal Air Force Halton Aeroplane Club	RAF Halton	22. 7.09E
G-OHAL	Pietenpol AirCamper *(Built H C Danby)* (Continental C-90)	PFA 047-12840		25.11.96	J F Morris	Old Warden	12. 5.09P
G-OHAV	Hybrid Air Vehicle HAV-3 Airship (Gas) *(Built ATG Ltd)*	HAV-3/001		21. 7.08	Hybrid Air Vehicles Ltd	Cardington	
G-OHCP	Aérospatiale AS.355F1 Ecureuil 2	5249	G-BTVS G-STVE, G-TOFF, G-BKJX	14. 3.94	Staske Construction Ltd	Brooke Farm, Hulcote	21. 8.09E
G-OHGA	Hughes 369A *(Built as Hughes OH-6A Cayuse)*	301381	N357RF 69-16011	5 .1.09	MSS Holdings (UK) Ltd	Wesham House Farm, Kirkham	
G-OHGC	Scheibe SF25C Falke (Rotax 912-S)	44695	D-KBLC	26. 7.04	D J Marpole tr Heron Gliding Club	RNAS Yeovilton	24. 9.09E
G-OHHI	Bell 206L-1 LongRanger	45552	G-BWYJ D-HOBD, D-HGAD	30. 4.98	Sky Charter UK Ltd	(Whitstable)	14. 5.09E
G-OHIO	Dyn'Aéro MCR-01 *(Built P Ghiles)*	AGA4-181-20-MA0173	N3085Q	19. 1.07	J M Keane	Kittyhawk Farm, Deanland	
G-OHIY	Van's RV-10 *(Built M A Hutton)*	PFA 339-14730		8.12.07	M A Hutton	(Haxby, York)	
G-OHJE	Alpi Pioneer 300 Hawk *(Built H J Edwards)*	LAA 330A-14853		25.11.08	H J Edwards	(Y Felinheli)	
G-OHJV	Robinson R44 Raven	1722	N457R	16. 8.07	HJV Ltd	Redhill	23. 8.09E
G-OHKS	Pegasus Quantum 15(HKS) (HKS 700E s/n 99030A)	7505		24. 3.99	S J Farr	Newtownards	26. 5.08P
G-OHLI	Robinson R44 Clipper II *(Officially regd as "Raven II")*	10832		8. 8.05	K C McCarthy, D R Smith and D Keene t/a NCS Partnership	Denham	14. 9.09E
G-OHMS	Aérospatiale AS.355F1 Ecureuil 2	5194	N367E	15. 6.90	Western Power Distribution (South West) PLC	Bristol	24. 8.09E
G-OHNO	Yakovlev Yak-55	901104	OY-TLL SE-LOO, RA-07777, DOSAAF 97 (blue)	24. 4.07	R Graham, E Mason and S Whatmough	Headcorn	24. 2.09P
G-OHOV	Rotorway Executive 162F *(Built M G Bird)*	6885		14. 9.04	M G Bird	(Royston)	
G-OHPC	Cessna 208 Caravan I	20800224	N288SR N788SR, (N9820F)	4. 4.08	S Ulrich	Headcorn	10. 4.09E
G-OHSA	Cameron N-77 Balloon (Hot Air)	4269		2. 2.98	Zebedee Balloon Service Ltd *(HSA Healthcare titles)*	Hungerford	30. 7.09E
G-OHVA	Mainair Blade 912	1189-0199-7-W992		6.11.98	M C Metatidj	(La Baule, France)	27. 3.04P
G-OHVR	Robinson R44 Raven II	10212	G-STOT	15. 8.05	Transparent Film Products Ltd	Newtownards	16. 3.09E
G-OHWV	Raj Hamsa X'Air 582(4) *(Built H W Vasey, pr. no BMAA HB/121)*	474		18.11.99	B L R J and R Keeping	Davidstow Moor	8. 6.09P
G-OHYE	Thruster T 600N 450 Sprint	0042-T600N-098	G-CCRO	9. 3.04	P J Read tr G-OHYE Group	Enstone	17. 3.09P
G-OIBM	Rockwell Commander 114	14295	G-BLVZ SX-AJO, N4957W	14.10.88	E J Percival	Blackbushe	8. 8.09E
G-OIBO	Piper PA-28-180 Cherokee C	28-3794	G-AVAZ N11C	21. 1.87	Thomson Airways Ltd	White Waltham	26. 6.09E
G-OIBU	Bell 412EP	36433	N6587U C-FMQI	27. 7.07	Bristow Helicopters Ltd	Mauritania	5. 9.09E
G-OICO	Lindstrand LBL 42A Balloon (Hot Air)	566	(F-) G-OICO	3.11.98	B Esposito	London N10	12.11.99A
G-OIFM	Cameron Dude 90 SS Balloon (Hot Air) *(Radio One FM DJ's Head and Earphones)*	2841		18. 6.92	Magical Adventures Ltd *"Cool Dude"*	West Bloomfield, Michigan, US	29. 5.99A
G-OIHC	Piper PA-32R-301 Saratoga II SP	3246163	G-PUSK N237TB	6.12.06	N J Lipczynski	Biggin Hill	8.11.09E
G-OIIO	Robinson R22 Beta	2444	G-ULAB N8311Z	27. 3.02	Un Pied Sur Terre Ltd t/a Whizzard Helicopters	Welshpool	17. 7.09E
G-OIMC	Cessna 152 II	15285506	N93521	15. 5.87	East Midlands Flying School Ltd	Nottingham-East Midlands	8. 9.09E
G-OINK	Piper J-3C-65 Cub *(L-4J-PI)* *(Frame no.12443)*	12613	G-BILD G-KERK, F-BBQD, 44-80317	22. 3.83	A R Harding	Newton Farm, Sudbury	19. 7.99P
G-OINV	British Aerospace BAe 146 Series 300	E3171	VH-EWI G-6-171, VH-EWI, G-6-171	17. 2.00	Flybe Ltd *(stored 9.08)*	Exeter	15. 5.08E
G-OIOB	Mudry CAP.10B	194	N501DW	30. 1.08	A L Hall-Carpenter	Old Buckenham	5. 2.09E
G-OIOZ	Thunder AX9-120 Series 2 Balloon (Hot Air)	4434		17.11.98	M G Barlow	Skipton	27. 5.09E
G-OISO	Reims Cessna FA150 Aerobat *(Built as FRA150L)*	FRA1500213	G-BBJW	3. 4.90	L A and B A Mills	Duxford	17.10.09E
G-OITV	Enstrom 280C Shark	1038	G-HRVY G-DUGY, G-BEEL	9. 4.96	C W Brierley Jones	(Warrington)	25. 4.08E

Reg	Type	C/n	Prev id	Date	Owner	Location	Date
G-OIVN	Liberty XL-2	0008	N511XL	17. 5.07	I Shaw	Wombleton	14. 7.09P
G-OJAB	Avtech Jabiru SK	0088		19. 9.96	S D Athalye and J Berger	Elstree	22. 5.08P
	(Built K D Pearce - pr.no.PFA 274-13031)						
G-OJAC	Mooney M 20J Mooney 201	24-1490	N5767E	20. 8.90	Hornet Engineering Ltd	Biggin Hill	24. 2.09E
G-OJAE	Hughes 269C (Hughes 300)	90-0966	N1101W	12. 2.90	D P Wring	Dunkeswell	6. 3.09E
G-OJAG	Cessna 172S Skyhawk	172S9794	N66124	4. 4.05	Wycombe Air Centre Ltd	Wycombe Air Park	12. 5.09E
G-OJAJ	Dassault Falcon 2000EX	132	F-WWGN	30.11.07	BG Aviation Ltd	Farnborough	29.11.09E
G-OJAN	Robinson R22 Beta	2012	G-SANS	22. 5.01	Heliflight (UK) Ltd	Gloucestershire	5. 9.09E
			G-BUHX				
G-OJAS	Auster J/1U Workmaster	3501	F-BJAS	21. 3.00	D S Hunt (Noted in "Wings"' Museum 1.04)		
			F-WJAS, (F-OBHT)			Redhill	
G-OJAV	Fairey Britten-Norman BN-2A Mk.III-2 Trislander			6. 6.90	Lyddair Ltd (Noted 9.08)	Lydd	29. 1.07T
		1024	G-BDOS (4X-CCI), G-BDOS				
G-OJAZ	Robinson R44 Raven II	11216		2. 5.06	P C Twigg	Kemble	25. 5.09E
G-OJBB	Enstrom 280FX	2084		14. 6.99	Pendragon (Design and Build) Ltd	Gloucestershire	1. 7.09E
G-OJBM	Cameron N-90 Balloon (Hot Air)	2899		28. 9.92	P Spinlove	Chalfont St Giles	23. 9.93A
G-OJBS	Cameron N-105 Balloon (Hot Air)	4733		8. 3.00	Up and Away Ballooning Ltd	High Wycombe	8. 4.09E
G-OJBW	Lindstrand J & B Bottle SS Balloon (Hot Air)						
		436		26. 8.97	N A P Godfrey	West Leith, Tring	20. 5.02A
G-OJCH	Robinson R44 Clipper II	12323		26. 6.08	J C Hawkins	(Marksbury, Bath)	24. 7.09E
G-OJCW	Piper PA-32RT-300 Lance II	32R-7985062	N3016K	9. 1.80	P G Dobson	Blackbushe	26.10.09E
G-OJDA	EAA Acrosport II	PFA 072-11067		1. 4.98	D B Almey	Fenland	2. 6.08P
	(Built D B Almey) (Lycoming O-360-A4A) (Project type no.should be 072A)						
G-OJDC	Thunder Ax7-77 Balloon (Hot Air)	875		9. 1.89	A Heginbottom	Cheadle Hulme, Cheadle	27. 5.09E
G-OJDS	Comco Ikarus C42 FB80	0411-6633		26.11.04	J D Smith	Baxby Manor, Husthwaite	1. 2.08P
	(Built Fly Buy Ultralights Ltd)						
G-OJEG	Airbus A321-231	1015	D-AVZN	14. 5.99	Monarch Airlines Ltd	Luton	13. 5.09E
G-OJEH	Piper PA-28-181 Archer II	28-8690051	D-EDPA	17.12.02	P C and M A Greenaway	Biggin Hill	13. 2.09E
			N9125Y				
G-OJEN	Cameron V-77 Balloon (Hot Air)	3302		26. 5.94	C Westwood	Clayton West, Huddersfield	6.12.08E
G-OJGT	Maule M-5-235C Lunar Rocket	7285C	LN-AEL	30. 6.98	J G Townsend	Draycott Farm, Chiseldon	22. 7.09E
			(LN-BEK), N5635V				
G-OJHB	Colt Flying Ice Cream Cone SS Balloon (Hot Air)			23. 6.94	Stratos Ballooning Gmbh and Co KG		
		2591				Ennigerloh, Germany	16. 4.04A
G-OJHC	Cessna 182P Skylane	182-64535	N86AD	21. 8.07	Stapleford Flying Club Ltd	Stapleford	28. 8.09E
G-OJHL	Europa Aviation Europa	311		12. 5.97	J H Lace "Lady Lace"	Prestwick	16. 8.08P
	(Built J H Lace - pr.no.PFA 247-13039) (Rotax 912-UL) (Monowheel u/c)						
G-OJIB	Boeing 757-23A	24292	G-OOOG	31. 3.06	Astraeus Ltd	London Gatwick	1. 4.09E
	C-GOOG, G-OOOG, C-FOOG, G-OOOG, C-FOOG, G-OOOG, C-FOOG, G-OOOG, C-FOOG, G-OOOG						
G-OJIL	Piper PA-31-350 Navajo Chieftain		OY-BTP	28. 5.97	Redhill Aviation Ltd (Operated Redhill Charters		
		31-7652175)				Redhill	26. 6.09E
G-OJIM	Piper PA-28R-201T Turbo Arrow III		N38299	4. 8.86	G-OJIM Flyers Ltd	Biggin Hill	19. 3.09E
		28R-7703200					
G-OJJB	Mooney M 20K Mooney 231	25-1161		12. 8.88	G Italiano	Roma-Urbe, Lazio, Italy	1. 9.09E
G-OJJF	Druine D 31 Turbulent	378 & 31	OO-30	6. 1.97	J J Ferguson	Belle Vue Farm, Yarnscombe	
	(Built J J Ferguson) (Volkswagen 1300)				(Noted 4.04)		
G-OJJV	P&M Pegasus Quik	8276		7. 6.07	J J Valentine	Ince Blundell	6. 6.09P
G-OJKM	Rans S-7 Courier	1095.158		5. 3.01	M J Hasker	(Stockcross, Newbury)	22.10.08P
	(Built M Jackson - pr.no.PFA 218-12982) (Rotax 912-UL)						
G-OJLH	TEAM Mini-MAX 91	PFA 186-12164	G-MYAW	12.12.01	J L Hamer	Hartpury, Gloucester	13. 4.09P
	(Built J L Hamer)						
G-OJMB	Airbus A330-243	427	F-WWYH	8.11.01	Thomas Cook Airlines Ltd	Manchester	8.11.09E
G-OJMC	Airbus A330-243	456	F-WWKI	5. 3.02	Thomas Cook Airlines Ltd	Manchester	3.12.09E
G-OJMF	Enstrom 280FX	2086	G-DDOD	12. 6.01	JMF Ltd	Ballymoney, County Antrim	14. 9.09E
G-OJMR	Airbus A300B4-605R	605	F-WWAY	3. 5.91	Monarch Airlines Ltd	Luton	2. 5.09E
G-OJMS	Cameron Z-90 Balloon (Hot Air)	10860		28. 9.06	Joinerysoft Ltd (Joinery Soft titles)	Chipping Norton	30 .9.09E
G-OJNB	Lindstrand LBL 21A Balloon (Hot Air)	085		14. 2.94	N A P Godfrey (J & B titles)	West Leith, Tring	17. 4.04A
G-OJNE	Schempp-Hirth Nimbus 3T	22-88	BGA4344-HZW	27.11.07	J N Ellis	Sutton Bank	19. 7.08
			D-KILO				
G-OJOD	Jodel D 18	PFA 169-12774		20. 6.02	D Hawkes and C Poundes	(Milton Keynes)	
	(Built D Hawkes)						
G-OJON	Taylor JT.2 Titch	PFA 3208		6.10.78	T A Appleby	Netherthorpe	22. 3.09P
	(Built J H Fell) (Continental C90)						
G-OJPS	Bell 206B-2 JetRanger II	1484	G-UEST	30.10.06	Milford Garage Ltd t/a Milford Aviation	Cranfield	27. 7.09E
			G-ROYB, G-BLWU, ZS-PAW				
G-OJRH	Robinson R44 Astro	0321		11. 4.97	Holgate Construction Ltd		
						Emley Moor, Huddersfield	29. 7.09E
G-OJRM	Cessna T182T Turbo Skylane	T18208007	N72778	19. 7.01	Colne Airways Ltd	Earls Colne	22. 8.09E
G-OJSA	British Aerospace Jetstream Series 3102	711	OY-SVJ	20. 6.06	Diamond Air Charter Ltd	Humberside	5. 7.08E
			G-BTYG, N415MX, G-31-711				
G-OJSH	Thruster T 600N 450	0061-T600N-052		29. 5.01	P J Reed tr G-OJSH Group	Temple Cloud, Bristol	23. 9.08P
G-OJVA	Van's RV-6	PFA 181-12292		6. 9.96	J A Village	Moor Green Farm, Barlow	2. 2.10P
	(Built J A Village) (Lycoming O-320)						
G-OJVH	Cessna F150H	F150-0356	G-AWJZ	27. 3.81	A W Cairns "Blue Too"	RAF Brize Norton	14. 6.09E
	(Built Reims Aviation SA)						
G-OJVL	Van's RV-6	PFA 181-12441		28.10.02	S E Tomlinson	(Bournemouth)	
	(Built S E Tomlinson)				(Under construction at owners home 7.07)		
G-OJWB	Hawker 800XP	258674	N841WS	2.11.07	Hangar 8 Ltd	Oxford	23.12.09E
			N674XP				
G-OJWS	Piper PA-28-161 Cherokee Warrior II		N6377C	13. 7.88	P J Ward	Denham	13. 2.09E
		28-7816415					
G-OKAG	Piper PA-28R-180 Cherokee Arrow		N3764T	15. 4.88	B.R Green	North Weald	1. 6.09E
		28R-30075					

Reg	Type	C/n	Prev id	Reg date	Owner	Base	Expiry
G-OKAY	Pitts S-1E Special	12358	N35WH	27. 5.80	S R S Evans	Andrewsfield	18. 5.09P
	(Built W D Henline) (Lycoming IO-360)						
G-OKBT	Colt 25A Sky Chariot Mk.II Balloon (Hot Air)	2301		10.11.92	British Telecommunications PLC "Skypiper II"	Thatcham	18. 4.03A
G-OKCC	Cameron N-90 Balloon (Hot Air)	1741		6. 5.88	D J Head	Newbury	25. 7.00A
G-OKCP	Lindstrand LBL Battery SS Balloon (Hot Air)	621	OO-BXY G-MAXX	9. 5.05	A M Holly	Breadstone, Berkeley	28. 5.09E
G-OKED	Cessna 150L	15074250	N19223	29. 1.93	L J Pluck	Clipgate Farm, Denton	3. 4.09E
G-OKEM	Mainair Sports Pegasus Quik	8047		23. 7.04	G R F Daniel	Eaglescott	15. 7.09P
G-OKEN	Piper PA-28R-201T Turbo Arrow III	28R-7703390	N47518	20.10.87	K Woodcock	(Huddersfield)	19. 8.08E
G-OKER	Van's RV-7	PFA 323-14233		11. 5.04	R M Johnson	(Selkirk)	
	(Built R M Johnson)						
G-OKEV	Europa Aviation Europa	328		11. 6.97	K A Kedward "Freedom"	Wolverhampton	2. 3.09P
	(Built K A Pilcher - pr.no.PFA 247-13091) (Rotax 912-UL) (Tri-gear u/c)						
G-OKEY	Robinson R22 Beta	2004		14. 1.92	Fast Helicopters Ltd	Shoreham	7. 5.09E
G-OKID	Reality Escapade Kid	ESCK001		25.11.08	P M Francis	Old Sarum	
	(Built T F Francis) (Hirth F33)						
G-OKIM	Best Off Sky Ranger 912(2)	SKR0310395		23.12.03	K P Taylor	RAF Henlow	25. 9.08P
	(Built K P Taylor - pr.no.BMAA HB/333)						
G-OKIS	Tri-R KIS	PFA 239-12248		15. 6.92	M R Cleveley	Tibenham	28. 5.09P
	(Built B W Davies) (Canadian Air Motive CAM.100)						
G-OKLL	Schempp-Hirth Discus b	404	BGA3856-HDF	23. 1.08	K L Mcfarland	Bellarena	28.12.07
G-OKMA	Tri-R KIS	PFA 239-12808		22.11.95	K Miller	(Coventry)	30. 9.09P
	(Built K Miller) (Continental IO-240) (Tri-cycle u/c)						
G-OKPW	Tri-R KilS	PFA 239-12359		17. 8.93	K P Wordsworth	Lydd	20.11.07P
	(Built K P Wordsworth) (Continental O-200-A) (Tri-cycle u/c)						
G-OKTI	Aquila AT01	AT01-172		12.10.07	P H Ferdinand	North Weald	27.11.09P
	(Rotax 912 S3)						
G-OKYA	Cameron V-77 Balloon (Hot Air)	1259		4. 3.87	R J Pearce	Doagh, Ballyclare	13. 7.09E
	(Replacement envelope c/n 3331)						
G-OKYM	Piper PA-28-140 Cherokee	28-23303	G-AVLS N11C	10. 5.88	Caernarfon Airworld Ltd	Caernarfon	6. 5.09E
G-OLAA	Alpi Pioneer 300 Hawk	xxx		4.10.07	G G Hammond	Perth	2. 3.09P
	(Built G G Hammond - pr.no.PFA 330A-14719)						
G-OLAU	Robinson R22 Beta	1119		5. 9.89	Thistle Aviation Ltd	Oxford	3. 2.10E
G-OLAW	Lindstrand LBL 25A Cloudhopper Balloon (Hot Air)	170		9.12.94	George Law Plant Ltd "Law Hopper"	Kidderminster	24. 4.09E
G-OLCP	Eurocopter AS.355N Ecureuil 2	5580	G-CLIP	18. 2.02	Charterstyle Ltd	Kingswinford	11. 4.09E
G-OLCT	Cirrus SR22	3111	N948PG	18. 8.08	P Patel	Denham	20. 8.09E
G-OLDG	Cessna T182T Turbo Skylane	T18208127	G-CBTJ N5170R	17.10.02	Gold Aviation Ltd	London Stansted	22. 8.09E
G-OLDH	Aérospatiale SA.341G Gazelle 1	1307	G-UTZY G-BKLV, N341SC	10. 3.04	Gold Aviation Ltd	Biggin Hill	8. 4.09E
G-OLDK	Learjet Model 45	45-311	N40078	2.10.06	Air Partner Private Jets Ltd	Biggin Hill	1.10.09E
G-OLDM	Pegasus Quantum 15-912	7589		10.12.99	A P Watkins	Roddige	9. 4.09P
G-OLDN	Bell 206L LongRanger	45077	G-TBCA G-BFAL, N64689, A6-BCL	2.10.84	Sky Charter UK Ltd	Whitstable	30. 7.09E
G-OLDO	Eurocopter EC.120B Colibri	1489	G-HIGI	29.11.07	Gold Aviation Ltd	Biggin Hill	4. 9.09E
G-OLDP	Mainair Sports Pegasus Quik	7957		28. 5.03	M J Wilson and G Lace	Ince Blundell	30. 7.09P
G-OLDT	Learjet Model 45	45-265	N5017J	30. 6.05	Air Partner Private Jets Ltd	Biggin Hill	30. 6.09E
G-OLDW	Learjet Model 45XR	45-294	N5014E	10. 4.06	Air Partner Private Jets Ltd	Biggin Hill	10. 4.09E
G-OLEE	Reims Cessna F152 II	F15201797		11. 9.80	Redhill Air Services Ltd	Redhill	16. 4.09E
G-OLEM	Jodel D 18	PFA 169-11613	G-BSBP	11. 2.02	G E Roe	Garston Farm, Marshfield	12.12.09P
	(Built R T Pratt) (Revmaster R2100)						
G-OLEO	Thunder Ax10-210 Series 2 Balloon (Hot Air)	3974		9. 1.97	High Road Adventures Ltd t/a High Road Balloons	Studley	27. 3.09E
G-OLEZ	Piper J-3C-65 Cub	18432	G-BSAX N98260, NC98260	8. 8.01	L Powell (For restoration)	(Canterbury)	
G-OLFA	Eurocopter AS.350B3 Ecureuil	3108	N64AD	11. 5.05	Heliaviation Ltd	Blackbushe	12. 2.09E
G-OLFB	Pegasus Quantum 15-912	7767		2. 3.01	J G and P Callan	Newtownards	9. 4.08E
G-OLFC	Piper PA-38-112 Tomahawk	38-79A0995	G-BGZG N9658N	6.12.85	M W Glencross	Cranfield	21. 4.08E
G-OLFO	Robinson R44 Raven	1305		6. 6.03	Crinstown Aviation Ltd	(Cloghran, County Dublin)	25. 7.09E
G-OLFT	Rockwell Commander 114	14274	G-WJMN N4954W	28. 3.85	D A Tubby	Liverpool	16. 5.09E
G-OLFZ	P&M Aviation Quik GT450	8354		15. 2.08	A J Boyd (Noted 2.08)	Newtownards	
G-OLGA	CFM Starstreak Shadow SA-II	K 288		15.10.97	N F Smith	Halstead, Essex	1.11.08P
	(Built N F Smith - pr.no.PFA 206-13164) (Rotax 618)						
G-OLJT	Mainair Gemini Flash IIA	570-887-5-W359	G-MTKY	16. 9.98	A Wraith	Sandtoft	14. 3.04P
G-OLLI	Cameron O-31 Balloon (Hot Air)	196		11. 5.76	N A Robertson "Golly III"	Newbury	9. 1.07A
	(Golly Special shape)			*(Loaned British Balloon Museum and Library 2002)*			
G-OLLS	Cessna T206H Turbo Stationair 6	T20608401	N5361L	8. 3.04	Loch Lomond Seaplanes Ltd	Luss, Loch Lomond	9. 4.09E
	(Floatplane)						
G-OLMA	Partenavia P68B	159	G-BGBT	15. 4.85	C M Evans	Plymouth	14. 9.08E
G-OLNT	Aérospatiale SA.365N1 Dauphin 2	6309	N111EP G-POAV, G-BOPI	24. 8.06	LNT Aviation Ltd	Leeds-Bradford	25. 9.09E
G-OLOW	Robinson R44 Astro	0100		3.10.94	G-OLOW LLP	Sherburn-in-Elmet	16. 6.09E
G-OLRT	Robinson R22 Beta	1378	N4014R	21. 5.90	The Henderson Group	Gollanfield, Inverness	9.10.08E
G-OLSF	Piper PA-28-161 Cadet	2841284	G-OTYJ G-OLSF, N92008	23.11.89	Bflying Ltd (Operated Bournemouth Flying Club)	Bournemouth	18. 2.09E
G-OLTT	Pilatus PC-12/45	648	HB-FSU	27. 7.05	H Nathanson	Goodwood	1. 8.09E
G-OLUG	Cameron Z-120 Balloon (Hot Air)	10349	D-OLUG	13. 6.07	K-H Gruenauer	Schwabish Hall, Germany	27. 9.09E

G-OMAF	Dornier 228-202K	8112	D-CAAD	16. 2.87	Cobham Leasing Ltd *(Operated DEFRA (Fisheries Patrol))*	
						Bournemouth 20.11.09E
G-OMAG	Cessna 182B Skylane	52214	F-BJEC	13. 5.05	Bodmin Light Aeroplane Services Ltd Perranporth	26. 5.09E
			N7214E			
G-OMAL	Thruster T 600N 450	0061-T600N-050		16. 5.01	M Howland	Wickenby 16. 6.09P
G-OMAO	SOCATA TB-20 Trinidad	378	N37EL	14. 1.09	I R Chaplin	Stapleford
			G-GDGR			
G-OMAS	Cessna A150 Aerobat	A1500719	G-BTFS	3. 3.08	M A Segar Pittrichie Farm, Whiterashes	1. 8.09E
			N20331, HP-902, (N7332A)			
G-OMAT	Piper PA-28-140 Cherokee D	28-7125139	G-JIMY	27. 8.87	R B Walker t/a Midland Air Training School	
			G-AYUG, N11C			Leicester 16.11.09E
G-OMAX	Brantly B 2B	473	G-AVJN	7. 8.87	A Murzyn (West End Farm, Stevington, Bedford)	16.11.03
G-OMBI	Cessna 525B CitationJet CJ3	525B0179	N179CJ	30. 7.08	Ravenheat Manufacturing Ltd Leeds-Bradford	29. 7.09E
			N5211A			
G-OMCC	Aérospatiale AS.350B Ecureuil	1836	G-JTCM	26.03.03	Michael Car Centres Ltd	
		G-HLEN,G-LOLY, JA9897, N5805T, HP-1084P, HP-1084, N5805T				(Kirk Michael, Isle of Man) 29. 5.09E
G-OMCD	Robinson R44 Clipper II	10249		21. 1.04	J G M and H D McDiarmid tr McDiarmid Partnership	
						Callington, Plymouth 4. 3.09E
G-OMDB	Van's RV-6A	25735		14. 8.02	D A Roseblade (Dubai, United Arab Emirates)	
	(Built D A G Roseblade)					
G-OMDD	Thunder Ax8-90 Series 2 Balloon (Hot Air)			2. 4.98	M D Dickinson Old Sodbury, Bristol	9. 8.09E
		4345				
G-OMDG	Hoffmann H 36 Dimona	3510	OE-9215	19.11.98	D Coulson tr Ards Dimona Group *(Noted 9.06)*	
						Strandhill, Sligo, County Sligo 9. 1.05
G-OMDH	Hughes 369E *(Hughes 500)*	0293E		14.11.88	Stiltgate Ltd Wycombe Air Park	28. 4.09E
G-OMDR	Agusta-Bell 206B-3 JetRanger III	8610	G-HRAY	8.12.97	Interceptor Properties Ltd Southend	14. 1.09E
			G-VANG, G-BIZA			
G-OMEA	Cessna 560XL Citation XLS	560-5610	LX-GDX	16.11.07	The Cambridge Aero Club Ltd t/a Marshall Executive Aviation	
			N52613			Cambridge 3. 4.09E
G-OMEL	Robinson R44 Astro	0073	G-BVPB	30. 9.96	Helitrain Ltd Kemble	5. 2.10E
G-OMEN	Cameron Z-90 Balloon (Hot Air)	10614		25. 6.04	M G Howard *(Manchester Evening News titles)*	
						Dubai, UAE 5. 9.09E
G-OMEX	Zenair CH.701UL STOL	PFA 187-13556		11.12.01	S J Perry (Bucknall, Woodhall Spa)	6.11.08P
	(Built S J Perry) (Jabiru 2200A)					
G-OMEZ	Zenair CH.601HDS Zodiac	PFA 162-13552		16. 7.01	C J Gow Perth	11. 6.09P
	(Built C J Gow) (Rotax 912 ULS)					
G-OMGH	Robinson R44 Clipper II	10259		29. 1.04	Universal Energy Ltd Wycombe Air Park	13.10.09E
	(Carries R44 Raven II titles)					
G-OMGR	Cameron Z-105 Balloon (Hot-Air)	11095		14. 4.08	Omega Resource Group LLC *"Omega"*	
						Stonehouse 14. 4.09E
G-OMHC	Piper PA-28RT-201 Arrow IV	28R-7918105	N3072Y	10. 2.81	Halfpenny Green Flight Centre Ltd	
						Wolverhampton 9. 6.09E
G-OMHD	English Electric Canberra PR.Mk.9	SH.1724	XH134	15. 8.06	Midair SA *(As "XH134" in RAF c/s) (Noted 9.08)*	
	(Built Short Brothers and Harland Ltd)					Kemble
G-OMHI	Mills MH-1	MH.001		8.10.97	J P Mills *(Noted 7.05)*	(Stockport)
	(Built J P Mills)					
G-OMHP	Avtech Jabiru UL	xxxx		23. 5.00	J Livingstone (Whitburn, Bathgate)	25. 8.07P
	(Built M H Player - pr.no.PFA 274A-13584)					
G-OMIA	SOCATA MS.893A Rallye Commodore 180	D-ENME	21. 7.98	L Portelli (Coventry)	5. 1.08E
		12074	F-BUGE, (D-ENMH)			
G-OMIK	Europa Aviation Europa	270		12. 1.98	M J Clews tr Mikite Flying Group White Waltham	29. 9.09P
	(Built M J Clews - pr.no.PFA 247-12991) (Rotax 914-UL) (Monowheel u/c)					
G-OMIW	P&M Aviation Quik	8232		24. 1.07	M I Woodward Enstone	11. 2.09P
G-OMJA	Piper PA-28-181 Archer II	28-7690328	A6-DXB	26.10.07	C A Patter *(Noted 11.08)* North Coates	
			N75319			
G-OMJC	Raytheon RB390 Premier 1	RB-88	N4488F	17. 6.04	Manhattan Jet Charter Ltd Farnborough	17. 6.09E
G-OMJT	Rutan LongEz	968		14.10.92	M J Timmons Prestwick	20.12.07P
	(Built M J Timmons - pr.no.PFA 074A-10703) (Lycoming O-235)					
G-OMKA	Robinson R44 Clipper II	11533		15.12.06	MK Airlines Ltd Redhill	1. 1.10E
	(Officially regd as "Raven II")					
G-OMLC	EAA Acrosport II	PFA 072-12151		7.11.05	M A C Chapman *(Noted 1.06)* (Guildford)	
G-OMLS	Bell 206B-2 JetRanger II	1957	N80367	2. 2.04	M L Scott Bagby	7. 4.09E
			G-OMLS, D-HAFN, N9909K			
G-OMMA	Robinson R44 Raven II	12561	G-CFRU	15. 1.09	Intermedia SRL Monza, Italy	6. 1.11E
G-OMMG	Robinson R22 Beta	1041	G-BPYX	25. 2.94	Preston Associates Ltd Yearby	11. 8.09E
G-OMMM	Colt 90A Balloon (Hot Air)	2328		20. 1.93	R C & M A Trimble *(Avient Cargo titles)*	
						(Nuffield, Henley-on-Thames) 19. 4.06A
G-OMNI	Piper PA-28R-200 Cherokee Arrow II	G-BAWA	3. 1.84	Cotswold Aviation Services Ltd Gloucestershire	8. 8.09E
		28R-7335130	N11C			
G-OMOL	Maule MX-7-180C Super Rocket	28012C		15. 8.00	Highland Seaplanes Ltd North Connell, Oban	18. 7.09E
	(Floatplane)					
G-OMOO	UltraMagic T-150 Balloon (Hot Air)	150/06		4. 6.07	Robert Wiseman Dairies PLC *(Robert Wiseman titles)*	
						Skirling, Biggar 8. 5.09E
G-OMPW	Mainair Sports Pegasus Quik	8088		12. 1.05	M P Wimsey Strubby	9. 2.09P
G-OMRB	Cameron V-77 Balloon (Hot Air)	2184		29. 8.90	I J Jevons *"Harlequin"* Bristol	8. 8.09E
G-OMRH	Cessna 550 Citation Bravo	550-1086	N58HK	12.12.06	McAir Services LLP Hawarden	7.12.09E
			N52446			
G-OMRP	Flight Design CTSW	8397		3.10.08	M E Parker Sackville Lodge, Riseley	
	(Built P&M Aviation)					
G-OMSS	Best Off Sky Ranger 912(2)	SKR0409523		6. 1.05	J F Cox Strathaven	13. 3.09P
	(Built M S Schofield - pr.no.BMAA HB/425)					
G-OMST	Piper PA-28-161 Warrior III	2842121	G-BZUA	1. 8.01	Mid-Sussex Timber Co Ltd Biggin Hill	11. 6.09E
			N53363			

Reg	Type	C/n	Prev id	Date	Owner/Operator	Base	Expiry
G-OMUM	Rockwell Commander 114	14067	PH-JJJ (PH-MMM), N4737W	24. 1.97	C E Campbell	Blackbushe	18. 3.09E
G-OMWE	Zenair CH.601HD Zodiac (Built P J Roy) (Mid West AE100R)	PFA 162-12740	(N) G-OMWE, G-BVXU	21. 3.97	G Cockburn	(Hawick)	3. 9.08P
G-OMYA	Airbus A320-214	716	G-BXKB N716AW, G-BXKB, F-WWIZ	5. 3.07	Thomas Cook Airlines Ltd	Manchester	5. 5.09E
G-OMYJ	Airbus A321-211	677	G-OOAF G-UNID, G-UKLO, D-AVZO	26. 4.07	Thomas Cook Airlines Ltd	Manchester	6. 5.09E
G-OMYT	Airbus A330-243	301	G-MOJO F-WWYE	14. 5.03	Thomas Cook Airlines Ltd	Manchester	7.11.09E
G-ONAF	Naval Aircraft Factory N3N-3 (Wright Whirlwind R 760)	xxxx	N45192 Bu.4406	31. 1.89	J P Birnie tr N3N-3 Group (As "4406:12" in US Navy c/s)	Sandown	31. 8.09S
G-ONAL	Beech 200 Super King Air (modified) (Model B200 status + 4-blade propellers 1999)	BB-30	G-HAMA N244JB, N211JB, N3090C, N3030C, N200CA	16. 1.06	Northern Aviation Ltd	Durham Tees Valley	1. 2.09E
G-ONAT	Grob G102 Astir CS77	1804	BGA5296-KRE HB-1459	23.10.07	N A Toogood	RAF Weston-on-the-Green	
G-ONAV	Piper PA-31 Navajo C	31-7812004	G-IGAR D-IGAR, N27378	29. 1.93	Panther Aviation Ltd	Elstree	23. 6.09E
G-ONCB	Lindstrand LBL 31A Balloon (Hot Air)	393		4. 6.96	S J Hunphreys	Prestwood, Great Missenden	18. 5.09E
G-ONCL	Colt 77A Balloon (Hot Air)	1637		4. 4.90	T J Gouder	Thornbury, Bristol	2. 8.09E
G-ONCS	Tipsy Nipper T 66 Series 3B (Built E Shouler) (Volkswagen 1834)	PFA 1390	G-AZBA	18.12.06	N C Spooner tr Ardleigh Flying Group	Bounds Farm, Ardleigh	14. 5.08P
G-ONED	Dan Rihn DR.107 One Design (Built A Bickmore)	PFA 264-14746		26.11.07	A Bickmore	Wycombe Air Park	
G-ONEL	Agusta A109C	7630	G-JBEK VH-LUI, Malaysian AF M38-06	11. 6.07	Cheshire Helicopters Ltd	(Wilmslow)	29. 6.09E
G-ONEP	Robinson R44 Raven II	11363		4. 8.06	Neptune Property Developments Ltd	Dreemore Road, Dungannon	17. 8.09E
G-ONER	Van's RV-8 (Built J A Hawkins)	80563	N563JH	3.10.06	S L Morris	Compton Abbas	16. 4.09E
G-ONES	Slingsby T 67M-200 Firefly	2046	SE-LBB LN-TFB, G-7-122	12.11.01	Aquaman Aviation Ltd	(Banstead)	10.12.09E
G-ONET	Piper PA-28-180 Cherokee E	28-5802	G-AYAU N11C	3. 6.98	Hatfield Flying Club Ltd	Elstree	23.10.09E
G-ONEZ	Glaser-Dirks DG-200/17	2-143/1738	BGA4878-JYB D-1086	17. 1.08	R M Nuza tr One Zulu Group	Rufforth	21. 5.08
G-ONFL	Murphy Maverick 430 (Built K Godfrey and G Lockwood - pr.no.PFA 259-12750) (Rotax 503) (Originally registered as Murphy Maverick, type amended 4.12.08)	402	G-MYUJ	27.11 98	M J Whiteman-Haywood	Pound Green, Buttonoak, Bewdley	11. 9.09P
G-ONGA	Robinson R44 Raven II	10479		5.10.04	Silvergate Leisure Ltd	Sywell	6. 2.09E
G-ONGC	Robin DR.400-180R Remorqueur	1385	EI-CKA SE-GHM	11.11.98	Norfolk Gliding Club Ltd	Tibenham	25. 5.09E
G-ONHH	Forney F-1A Aircoupe	5725	G-ARHA N3030G	13.12.89	R D I Tarry "Easy Rider"	Pytchley Grange, Kettering (Derby)	12. 6.10S
G-ONIG	Murphy Elite (Built N Smith - pr.no.PFA 232-14042)	745E?		29. 4.03	N S Smith		
G-ONIX	Cameron C-80 Balloon (Hot Air)	4411		12. 8.98	D J Griffin	Bowerhill, Melksham	3. 1.10E
G-ONKA	Aeronca K (Lycoming O-145)	K283	N19780 NC19780	21.10.91	N J R Minchin "Aggnes" Hill Top Farm, Hambledon		28. 9.09P
G-ONMT	Robinson R22 Beta II	2963		20. 7.99	R C Hayward and J H Garrioch t/a Polar Helicopters	Manston	11.10.09E
G-ONON	Rotary Air Force RAF 2000 GTX-SE (Built M S R Allen)	PFA G/13-1313		13. 8.99	M P Lhermette (Marked as "RAF 2000 GTX SE Fi")	(Faversham)	22. 8.08P
G-ONPA (2)	Piper PA-31-350 Navajo Chieftain	31-7952110	N89PA N35225	6. 5.98	Synergy Aircraft Leasing Ltd	Fairoaks	15.10.09E
G-ONSO	Pitts S-1S (Built T D McNamara) (Lycoming O-360)	TM-1	G-BRRS N18TM	24. 7.06	A P S Maynard	(Pulborough)	25. 6.93P
G-ONTV	Agusta-Bell 206B-3 JetRanger III	8733	D-HUNT TC-HKJ, (D-HSAV), I-GPFP, I-PIEF	1. 4.98	Castle Air Charters Ltd	Liskeard Heliport	27. 4.09E
G-ONUN	Van's RV-6A (Built R E Nunn) (Lycoming O-360)	PFA 181-12976		20. 2.96	R E Nunn	Clipgate Farm, Denton	27. 5.09P
G-ONUP	Enstrom F-28C	348	G-MHCA G-SHWW, G-SMUJ, G-BHTF	18. 1.00	M A Petrie	Hawarden	20. 6.02S
G-ONYX	Bell 206B-3 JetRanger III	4160	G-BXPN N18EA, D-HOBA, (D-HOBE)	22. 1.98	Kenrye Developments Ltd	Belfast International	30. 7.08E
G-ONZO	Cameron N-77 Balloon (Hot Air)	1089		13.11.84	K Temple "Gonzo" Tivetshall St Margaret, Norwich		19. 7.99A
G-OOAN	Boeing 767-39H	26256	G-UKLH	26. 1.99	Thomson Airways Ltd "Caribbean Star"	Manchester	4. 4.09E
G-OOAR	Airbus A320-214	1320	F-WWDT	3.11.00	Thomson Airways Ltd	Manchester	2.11.09E
G-OOAV	Airbus A321-211	1720	D-AVXA	29. 4.02	Thomson Airways Ltd	Manchester	28. 4.09E
G-OOBC	Boeing 757-28A	33098		28. 3.03	Thomson Airways Ltd	Manchester	27. 3.09E
G-OOBD	Boeing 757-28A	33099		31. 3.03	Thomson Airways Ltd	Manchester	30. 3.09E
G-OOBE	Boeing 757-28A	33100		19. 5.03	Thomson Airways Ltd	Manchester	18. 5.09E
G-OOBF	Boeing 757-28A	33101		19. 4.04	Northern Aviation Ltd	Manchester	18. 4.09E
G-OOBI	Boeing 757-2B7	27146	N615AU	29. 6.04	Thomson Airways Ltd	Manchester	9.10.09E
G-OOBJ	Boeing 757-2B7	27147	N616AU	21. 5.04	Thomson Airways Ltd	Manchester	5.12.09E
G-OOBK	Boeing 767-324	27392	VN-A762 S7-RGV, EI-CMD, N1785B, (N48901)	18.11.04	Thomson Airways Ltd	Manchester	17. 2.09E
G-OOBL	Boeing 767-324	27393	VN-A764 S7-RGW, EI-CME, N1794B, (N58902)	4. 4.05	Thomson Airways Ltd	Manchester	30. 5.09E
G-OOBM	Boeing 767-324ER	27568	VN-A765 S7-RGU, EI-CMH, N47904	10.11.05	Thomson Airways Ltd	Manchester	15. 1.10E
G-OOCH	UltraMagic H-42 Balloon (Hot Air)	42-03		6. 9.07	P C Gooch	Alresford	4. 8.09E

G-OODE	SNCAN Stampe SV-4C	500	G-AZNN	9. 5.77	A R Radford	(Dulverton) 17.11.08S
	(Gipsy Major 10)		F-BDGI, French AF			
G-OODI	Pitts S-1D	KH.1	G-BBBU	23.12.80	C Hutson and R S Wood "Little Bumble"	Hucknall 24. 3.09P
	(Built Etheridge and Lincs Aerial Spraying) (Lycoming IO-360)					
G-OODM	Cessna 525A CitationJet CJ2	525A0190	N680JB	8.12.06	Hangar 8 Ltd	Oxford 3. 1.10E
			N5141F			
G-OODW	Piper PA-28-181 Archer II	28-8490031	N4332C	14. 7.87	Goodwood Road Racing Company Ltd	Goodwood 19.12.09E
					(Operated Goodwood Flying Club)	
G-OOER	Lindstrand LBL 25A Cloudhopper Balloon (Hot Air)			15. 8.94	Airborne Adventures Ltd	Skipton 26. 5.09E
		125				
G-OOFE	Thruster T 600N 450 Sprint	0036-T600N-087		8. 7.03	G Cousins	Damyn's Hall, Upminster 27. 7.08P
G-OOFR	Robinson R44 Raven II	11928		9.10.07	Beechview Aviation Ltd	(Ballyclare) 11.12.09E
G-OOFT	Piper PA-28-161 Warrior III	2842083	N170FT	25. 5.00	Plane Talking Ltd	Elstree 22. 6.09E
G-OOGA	Gulfstream GA-7 Cougar	GA7-0111	SE-IEA	3. 2.86	B Robinson	Denham 20.12.08E
	(C/n correct but duplicates that for YV-1334P)		N758G			
G-OOGI	Gulfstream GA-7 Cougar	GA7-0077	G-PLAS	16. 1.95	Plane Talking Ltd (Operated Cabair)	Cranfield 13.10.07E
			G-BGHL, N789GA			
G-OOGL	Hughes 369E (Hughes 500)	0234E	ZS-HVH	21.11.06	Trans Holding Ltd	Shoreham 8.12.09E
			N1603S			
G-OOGO	Grumman American GA-7 Cougar	GA7-0049	N762GA	12.11.97	M M Naviede	Elstree 23. 1.09E
G-OOGS	Gulfstream GA-7 Cougar	GA7-0105	G-BGJW	19. 6.98	Cloud 9 Aviation (Leasing) Ltd	Full Sutton 27. 3.08E
			N737G			
G-OOIO	Eurocopter AS.350B3 Ecureuil	3463		17.10.01	Hovering Ltd	Elstree 19.11.08E
G-OOJC	Bensen B 8MR	PFA G/101-1303		4.12.98	J R Cooper (Noted 8.05)	Little Rissington
	(Built J R Cooper) (Converted ex Air Command)					
G-OOJP	Commander Aircraft Commander 114B	14567	N92JT	24.12.99	R J Rother	Kirknewton 1. 6.09E
			D-EYCA			
G-OOLE	Cessna 172M Skyhawk II	17266712	G-BOSI	25. 8.89	P S Eccersley	Humberside 22. 4.09E
			N80714			
G-OOLL	Air Création Tanarg 912S/iXess 15	FLT.xxx		27. 4.06	T D Erskine	Strathaven 21. 8.08P
	(Built J W McCarthy - pr.no.BMAA HB/487 being Flylight kit comprising Trike s/n T05083 and Wing s/n A05151-5142)					
G-OOMF	Piper PA-18-150 Super Cub	18-8560	N45554	13. 4.06	R C and C G Bell	Enstone 14. 5.11S
			Israeli DF 020			
G-OONA	Robinson R44 Clipper II	10907		18.10.05	Honeybee Aviation Ltd	Elstree 8.11.09E
G-OONE	Mooney M 20J Mooney 201	24-3039		31. 7.87	Go One Aviation Ltd	Welshpool 25. 9.09E
G-OONK	Cirrus SR22	1230	N202NK	3.11.06	Heathfield Rentals Ltd	Exeter 16.11.09E
G-OONY	Piper PA-28-161 Warrior II	28-8316015	N83071	26. 7.89	D A Field	Compton Abbas 18.11.09E
G-OOON	Piper PA-34-220T Seneca III	34-8533024	N822CB	8. 1.03	Pelican Air Ltd	Cambridge 10. 3.09E
			ZS-LWI, N2431Q, N9513N			
G-OOPE	Airbus A321-211	0852	G-OOAE	14. 4.08	Thomson Airways Ltd	Manchester 13. 7.09E
			(G-UNIF), D-AVZG			
G-OOPH	Airbus A321-211	0781	G-OOAH	4. 2.08	Thomson Airways Ltd	Manchester 2. 3.09E
			G-UNIE, D-AVZK			
G-OOPU	Airbus A320-214	1637	G-OOAU	6. 3.08	Thomson Airways Ltd	Manchester 9. 1.10E
			F-WWDM			
G-OOPW	Airbus A320-214	1777	G-OOAW	11. 3.08	Thomson Airways Ltd	Manchester 8. 5.09E
			F-WWDM			
G-OOPX	Airbus A320-214	2180	G-OOAX	24. 1.08	Thomson Airways Ltd	Manchester 6. 4.09E
			F-WWDY			
G-OORV	Van's RV-6	24319	N120XK	21.12.06	T I Williams	Shoreham 26. 5.09P
	(Built C and D Henwood) (Lycoming O-320)					
G-OOSE	Rutan VariEze	1536		7.12.78	B O Smith and J A Towers (Stored dismantled 2.08)	
	(Built J A Towers - pr.no.PFA 074-10326)					Yearby
G-OOSH	Zenair CH.601UL Zodiac	PFA 162A-14022		18.11.05	D J Paget	Dunkeswell 22. 7.08P
G-OOSI	Cessna 404 Titan	404-0855	VT-DAT	31. 1.03	Reconnaissance Ventures Ltd	Coventry 7. 5.09E
			N404N, F-WQFV, F-ZBDB, F-BRGN, N68104			
G-OOSY	de Havilland DH.82A Tiger Moth	85831	F-BGFI	6. 9.94	M Goosey tr Flying Tigers (Frame noted Woburn 8.03)	
	(Composite rebuild)		French AF, DE971		(Top Farm, Eccleshall, Stafford)	
G-OOTC	Piper PA-28R-201T Turbo Arrow III		G-CLIV	18. 1.94	D G and C M King	Turweston 22. 7.09E
		28R-7703086	N3011Q			
G-OOTT	Eurocopter AS.350B3 Ecureuil	3953		20. 7.05	Libertas (UK) Ltd	Southend 16. 3.09E
G-OOTW	Cameron Z-275 Balloon (Hot Air)	10380		6. 6.03	Airborne Balloon Management Ltd	Tonbridge 5. 9.09E
G-OOWS	Eurocopter AS.350B3 Ecureuil	4386		18. 3.08	Millburn World Travel Services Ltd	Monaco 8. 7.09E
G-OOXP	Aero Designs Pulsar XP	PFA 202-11915		25.10.90	K A O'Neill	Plaistows Farm, St Albans 1.11.08P
	(Built G W Associates Ltd)					
G-OPAG	Piper PA-34-200 Seneca	34-7250348	N506DM	16.10.90	A H Lavender	Biggin Hill 11. 5.09E
			G-BNGB, F-BTQT, F-BTMT			
G-OPAM	Reims Cessna F152 II	F15201536	G-BFZS	5. 9.86	PJC (Leasing) Ltd "Little Red Rooster"	Stapleford 26. 6.09E
G-OPAT	Beech 76 Duchess	ME-304	G-BHAO	6.12.82	R D J Axford	Wycombe Air Park 8. 8.09E
G-OPAZ	Pazmany PL-2	PFA 069-10673		20. 3.98	K Morris "Y Myddryg Bach Melyn"	Haverfordwest 15. 8.08P
	(Built K Morris) (Lycoming O-235)					
G-OPCG	Cessna 182T Skylane	18280948	N2451Y	18. 2.02	P L Nolan	Fairoaks 26. 3.09E
G-OPCS	Hughes 369E (Hughes 500)	0333E	CS-HBN	31. 1.01	Eastern Atlantic Helicopters Ltd	Shoreham 14. 7.09E
			N500AH			
G-OPDG	Robinson R44 Raven II	11815		27. 7.07	Wirral Leisure (North West) Ltd	(Prenton) 21. 8.09E
G-OPDS	Denney Kitfox Model 4	PFA 172A-12259		8. 1.93	P Madden	Strathaven 5. 9.09P
	(Built P D Sparling)					
G-OPEJ	TEAM Mini-Max 91	PFA 186-14388		5. 1.07	P E Jackson	(Ruthin) 14.10.09P
	(Built P E Jackson)					
G-OPEN	Bell 206B-3 JetRanger III	4300	N743BT	20. 1.05	Gazelle Aviation LLP	(Wetherby) 31. 1.09E
			N206AJ, N2155K, C-GFNP			
G-OPEP	Piper PA-28RT-201T Turbo Arrow IV		OY-PEP	3.12.97	SAM Ltd	Cranfield 13.10.09E
		28R-7931070	N2217Q			

Reg	Type	C/n	Prev Ident	Date	Owner/Operator	Location	Expiry
G-OPET	Piper PA-28-181 Cherokee Archer II	28-7690067	OH-PET OY-BLC	3. 1.02	Cambrian Flying Group Ltd	Cardiff	24. 3.09E
G-OPFA	Alpi Pioneer 300	6		23.11.04	S Eddison and R Minett	Gloucestershire	5.10.07P
	(Built S Eddison and R Minett - pr.no.PFA 330-14298)						
G-OPFR	Diamond DA.42 Twin Star	42.077	OE-VPI	5.12.05	P F Rothwell	Cranfield	23. 1.09E
G-OPFT	Cessna 172R Skyhawk	17280316	N9491F	11. 3.98	Cleveland Flying School Ltd	Durham Tees Valley	4. 3.09E
G-OPFW	Hawker Siddeley HS.748 Series 2A/266	1714	G-BMFT VP-BFT, VR-BFT, G-BMFT, 5W-FAO, G11-10	1. 7.98	PTB (Emerald) Proprietary Ltd (Stored 11.08)	Blackpool	16. 2.07T
G-OPHA	Robinson R44 Astro	0359	PH-WBW G-OPHA, CS-HDW, G-OPHA	17. 7.97	H W Euridge	(Redlynch, Salisbury)	29. 6.09E
G-OPHT	Schleicher ASH 26E	26105		6. 2.97	P Turner "T1"	Nympsfield	21. 9.08E
G-OPIC	Reims Cessna FRA150L Aerobat	FRA1500234	G-BGNZ PH-GAB, D-EIQE	20. 6.95	A V Harmer	(Shotesham All Saints, Norwich)	6. 3.09E
G-OPIK	Eiriavion PIK-20E	20233	PH-651	27. 1.82	A J McWilliam tr G-OPIK Group	Aston Down	30. 3.09E
G-OPIT	CFM Streak Shadow	K 126-SA		22.11.89	C Hannan (Noted stored 6.08) AAC Middle Wallop		8. 7.03P
	(Built L W Opit - pr.no.PFA 161A-11624) (Rotax 532)						
G-OPJB	Boeing 757-23A	24924	N924AW TJ-CAH, N924AW, C-FXOK, (5Y-BHG)	19. 3.05	Astraeus Ltd	London Gatwick	24. 3.09E
G-OPJD	Piper PA-28RT-201T Turbo Arrow IV	28R-8231028	N8097V	2.10.89	J M McMillan	Thruxton	6. 4.09E
G-OPJK	Europa Aviation Europa	017		29. 4.93	F D Hollinshead	Sleap	1. 9.09P
	(Built P J Kember - pr.no.PFA 247-12487) (Rotax 912-UL) (Monowheel u/c)						
G-OPJS	Pietenpol AirCamper	PFA 047-12834		10.11.00	P J Shenton	Sywell	
	(Built P J and J W Shenton)				(Noted 1.05)		
G-OPKF	Cameron Bowler 90 SS Balloon (Hot Air)	2314		12. 6.90	D K Fish	Manchester	2. 8.03A
G-OPLC	de Havilland DH.104 Dove 8	04212	G-BLRB VP962	10. 1.91	W G T Pritchard (Operated Mayfair Dove)	Biggin Hill	9. 9.11
G-OPME	Piper PA-23-250 Aztec D	27-4099	G-AZGB, N878SH, N9...N	31. 3.94	Portway Aviation Ltd	Shobdon	3.11.09E
G-OPMT	Lindstrand LBL 105A Balloon (Hot Air)	052		30. 9.93	K R Karlstrom	Northwood	30. 9.09E
G-OPNH	Stoddard-Hamilton Glasair Super II-SRG	2364	G-CINY	14.10.98	J L Mangelschots	Balen-Keiheuvel, Belgium	28. 5.09P
	(Built P N Haigh - pr.no.PFA 149-13011) (Lycoming IO-360)						
G-OPPL	Gulfstream AA-5A Cheetah	AA5A-0867	G-BGNN	11.10.85	Plane Talking Ltd	Blackbushe	8. 8.09E
G-OPRC	Europa Aviation Europa XS	378		6. 6.01	M J Ashby-Arnold	Wombleton	16. 3.09P
	(Built I Chaplin - pr.no.PFA 247-13281) (Rotax 912 ULS) (Tri-gear u/c)						
G-OPSF	Piper PA-38-112 Tomahawk	38-79A0998	EI-BLT G-BGZI, N9664N	13.10.82	P I Higham	High Cross, Ware	5. 2.09E
G-OPSL	Piper PA-32R-301 Saratoga II SP	32R-8013085	G-IMPW N8186A	4. 1.99	P R Tomkins	Biggin Hill	11. 7.09E
G-OPSS	Cirrus SR20-G2	1458	N410CD	28.10.04	Cumulus Aircraft Rentals Ltd	Wellesbourne Mountford	13.12.09E
G-OPST	Cessna 182R Skylane II	18267932	OO-HFF N9317H	16. 6.88	M J G Wellings and Welmacs Ltd	Shoreham	21. 5.09E
G-OPTF	Robinson R44 Raven II	10235		9. 1.04	Franks Helicopter Leasing Ltd	Wycombe Air Park	17. 2.10E
G-OPTI	Piper PA-28-161 Warrior II	28-7716210	N5888V	29. 9.06	A K Hulme	Andrewsfield	20.12.08E
G-OPUB	Slingsby T 67M-160 Firefly	2002	G-DLTA G-SFTX	18.10.96	P M Barker	Sherburn-in-Elmet	3.10.09E
G-OPUK	Piper PA-28-161 Warrior III	2842288	N30904	29.08.07	Haydan Aviation Ltd	Stapleford	30.10.09E
G-OPUP	Beagle B 121 Pup Series 2	B121-062	G-AXEU (5N-AJC)	31.10.84	F A Zubiel	White Waltham	12. 6.09E
G-OPUS	Avtech Jabiru SK	0194		16. 7.98	K W Whistance (Much Dewchurch, Hereford)		13.10.09P
	(Built S Percy - pr.no.PFA 274-13343)						
G-OPVM	Van's RV-9A	PFA 320-14351		8. 8.05	P Mather	Andrewsfield	17.12.09P
	(Built P Mather) (Lycoming IO-320)						
G-OPWK	Grumman AA-5A Cheetah	AA5A-0663	G-OAEL N26706	26. 5.92	J H Sandham t/a Sandham Aviation	Carlisle	6. 9.02E
G-OPWS	Mooney M 20K Mooney 231	25-0663	N1162W	12. 4.91	A R Mills	Fowlmere	12.12.08E
G-OPYE	Cessna 172S Skyhawk SP	172S8059	N653SP	19. 2.99	Far North Aviation	Wick	25. 1.09E
G-ORAC	Cameron Van 110 SS Balloon (Hot Air)	4577		22. 6.99	A G Kennedy (RAC titles)	Nelson	20. 8.09E
G-ORAE	Van's RV-7	PFA 323-14016		20. 3.03	R W Eaton tr G-ORAE Group	Netherthorpe	22. 9.09P
	(Built R W Eaton) (Lycoming O-320)						
G-ORAF	CFM Streak Shadow	K 134-SA		18. 5.90	P A Hunn (George Town, Cayman Islands)		1.11.00P
	(Built G A Taylor - pr.no.PFA 161A-11627: sequence no.conflicts with MW6 G-MYCU) (Rotax 532) (Dismantled 5.00)						
G-ORAL	Hawker Siddeley HS.748 Series 2A/334	1756	G-BPDA G-GLAS, 9Y-TFS, G-11-8	8. 3.99	PTB (Emerald) Proprietary Ltd (Stored 11.08)	Blackpool	12.11.07E
G-ORAM	Thruster T600N 450	0071-T600N-117		13. 6.07	J A Ward (Greetwell, Lincoln)		12. 6.08P
G-ORAN	Cessna 525 CitationJet	525-0423	G-OEBJ N292SG, N62SH, N5201J	8. 8.06	CJIJets Syndicate LLP	(London EC4)	23. 8.09E
G-ORAR	Piper PA-28-181 Archer III	2890224	N9255G	6. 6.95	P N and S M Thornton	Goodwood	8. 7.09E
G-ORAS	Clutton FRED Series II	PFA 029-11002		14. 6.01	A I Sutherland	Fearn	8.12.09P
	(Built A I Sutherland) (Volkswagen 1834)						
G-ORAU	Evektor EV-97A Eurostar	PFA 315A-14655		4. 6.07	W R C Williams-Wynne	Talybont, Gwynedd	19.12.08P
	(Built W R C Williams-Wynne)						
G-ORAY	Reims Cessna F182Q Skylane II	F18200132	G-BHDN	18. 3.94	Unicorn Consultants Ltd	Gamston	6.11.09E
G-ORBK	Robinson R44 Raven II	10213	G-CCNO	28.11.03	GTC (UK) Ltd	Wycombe Air Park	22.12.08E
G-ORBS	Mainair Blade	1336-0802-7-W1131		19. 8.02	J W Dodson	Leicester	11.10.07P
	(Rotax 582)						
G-ORCA	Van's RV-4	PFA 181-12924		25.11.04	M R H Wishart	Tingwall	29. 7.08P
	(Built M R H Wishart) (Superior XP-IO)						
G-ORCW	Schempp-Hirth Ventus 2cT	134/...	BGA5108-KHQ	21.11.05	R C Wilson "A39"	Aboyne	7.12.07
G-ORDH	Eurocopter AS.355N Ecureuil 2	5744	F-WWXS	11. 7.06	Harpin Ltd	Leeds-Bradford	5.10.09E
G-ORDS	Thruster T 600N 450	0042-T600N-100		14. 1.04	Thruster Air Services Ltd	Ginge, Wantage	25. 4.09P
G-ORED	Pilatus Britten-Norman BN-2T Islander	2142	G-BJYW	10. 1.85	Fly BN Ltd	Bembridge	21. 5.09E
G-OREV	Revolution Helicopters Mini-500	0112		8. 8.96	R H Everett	(Lee-on-Solent)	

G-ORGY	Cameron Z-210 Balloon (Hot Air)	10320		9. 7.02	Cameron Flights Southern Ltd *("GoBallooning" titles)*		
						Woodborough, Pewsey	10. 3.09E
G-ORHE	Cessna 500 Citation I	500-0220	(N619EA)	25. 3.96	EASSDA Ireland Ltd	Belfast International	24. 7.08E
			G-OBEL, G-BOGA, N932HA, N93WD, N5220J				
G-ORIG	Glaser-Dirks DG-800A	8-39-A29	BGA4972	5. 4.94	I Godfrey	Lasham	13. 4.10E
			G-ORIG				
G-ORIX	ARV K1 Super 2	034	G-BUXH	16. 9.93	T M Lyons	(Newcastle)	9. 4.07P
	(Built P M Harrison-pr.noPFA 152-12424)		(G-BNVK)				
	(Mid West AE.100R)						
G-ORJA	Beech B200 Super King Air	BB-1570	N1120Z	5.06.03	Airwest Ltd	Bristol	4. 6.09E
			N50PM, N1120Z				
G-ORJW	Laverda F 8L Falco Series 4	403	(PH-...)	2.12.85	Viking BV	Standalone Farm, Meppershall	13. 9.10S
			G-ORJW, D-ELDV, D-ELDY				
G-ORKY	Aérospatiale AS.350B2 Ecureuil	2153	N66NN	3. 1.08	MCJ Helicopters Ltd	Redhill	3. 3.09E
			JA9791				
G-ORLA	P&M Pegasus Quik	8268		21. 5.07	J Summers	Redlands, Swindon	21. 5.09P
G-ORLE	Agusta A109A	7163	G-USTB	22. 6.07	Oracle Aviation LLP	Redhill	18. 8.09E
			D-HEEG, D-HEEF, VR-CKN, HB-XKM				
G-ORMA	Aérospatiale AS.355F1 Ecureuil 2	5192	G-SITE	9.11.98	MW Helicopters Ltd *(Sky News titles)*	Stapleford	13. 10.09E
			G-BPHC, N365E				
G-ORMB	Robinson R22 Beta	1607		14.12.90	Scotia Helicopters Ltd	Cumbernauld	19. 4.09E
G-ORMG	Cessna 172R Skyhawk	17280344	N9518F	25. 9.98	J R T Royle	Andrewsfield	19. 10.09E
G-ORMW	Comco Ikarus C42 FB100	0501-6653		11. 4.05	A Boswell tr C42 Dodo Syndicate	Old Sarum	5. 4.09P
	(Built Aerosport Ltd)						
G-OROD	Piper PA-18-150 Super Cub	18-7856	SE-CRD	27. 6.89	B W Faulkner	(Petersfield)	13. 3.11
G-OROO	Cessna 560XL Citation XLS	560-5724		30. 8.07	Rooney Air Ltd	Edinburgh	29. 8.09E
G-OROS	Comco Ikarus C42 FB80	0509-6759		7.10.05	R I Simpson	Clipgate Farm, Denton	29.10.08P
	(Built Aerosport Ltd)						
G-ORPC	Europa Aviation Europa XS	443		5. 2.04	P W Churms	(Farnborough)	
	(Built P W Churms - pr.no.PFA 247-13521)				*(Noted unmarked at Kemble 7.05)*		
G-ORPR	Cameron O-77 Balloon (Hot Air)	2341		26. 6.90	S R Vining	Puxey, Sturminster Newton	18. 5.09E
G-ORRG	Robin DR.400-180 Régent	1216	OO-VPI	6. 2.08	P G Folland tr Radley Robin Group		
						Chilton Foliat, Hungerford	1. 8.09E
G-ORTH	Beech E90 King Air	LW-136	G-DEXY	12.11.03	P A and C J Crowther	Biggin Hill	18. 2.09E
			N750DC, N30CW, N84GA, N328TB, TR-LTT				
G-ORUG	Thruster T 600N 450 Sprint	0033-T600N-080		2. 9.03	Lincoln Enterprises Ltd	Linley Hill, Leven	18. 9.08P
G-ORVE	Van's RV-6	21710	N2084J	16. 7.07	F M Sperryn and R J F Swain	(Ellenhall, Stafford)	22. 9.09P
	(Built M R Spiller) (Lycoming O-320)						
G-ORVG	Van's RV-6	PFA 181A-13509		2. 1.01	J T M Ball tr RV Group	Biggin Hill	15. 3.09P
	(Built R J Fry) (Lycoming O-360)						
G-ORVI	Van's RV-6	20036	N1021	16. 6.08	J D N Cooke	Shenstone Hall Farm, Shenstone	
	(Built L B Porter)						
G-ORVR	Partenavia P68	115	G-BFBD	2.10.95	Ravenair Aircraft Ltd	Liverpool	24. 4.09E
	(Officially regd as "P68B")						
G-ORVS	Van's RV-9	PFA 320-13999		10. 9.07	C J Marsh	Binstead, Isle of Wight	
	(Built C J Marsh)						
G-ORZA	Diamond DA.42 Twin Star	42.062	G-FCAC	4. 8.06	M J Hill	Bournemouth	6. 3.09E
			OE-VPI				
G-OSAT	Cameron Z-105 Balloon (Hot Air)	10564		18. 6.04	Lotus Balloons Ltd *"Astra"* Broughton, Stockbridge		5. 1.10E
G-OSAW	QAC Quickie Q.2	2443	G-BVYT	17. 9.04	S A Wilson	RNAS Yeovilton	2. 9.00P
	(Built N A Evans) (Revmaster R2100)		N3797S		*(Noted 3.06)*		
G-OSCC	Piper PA-32-300 Cherokee Six	32-7540020	G-BGFD	27.11.84	BG and G Airlines Ltd	Jersey	17. 4.09E
			D-EOSH, N32186				
G-OSCO	TEAM Mini-MAX 91	PFA 186-12878		24.12.96	M A Perry	Benson's Farm, Laindon	13. 6.08P
	(Built PJ Schofield)						
G-OSDF	Schempp-Hirth Ventus a	17	BGA3878-HED	20. 5.08	S D Foster	RAF Keevil	
			D-2524				
G-OSDI	Beech 58 Baron	TH-1111	G-BHFY	27. 7.84	A W Eldridge and J A Heard	Guernsey	18.12.08E
G-OSEA	Pilatus Britten-Norman BN-2B-26 Islander		G-BKOL	27. 8.85	W T Johnson and Sons (Huddersfield) Ltd		
		2175				Crosland Moor	23. 3.09E
G-OSEP	Mainair Blade 912	1340-0902-7-W1135		29.10.02	J D Smith	Baxby Manor, Husthwaite	23.10.09P
G-OSFA	Diamond HK 36 TC Super Dimona	36.649		15. 6.99	Oxfordshire Sportflying Ltd	Enstone	8. 8.09E
G-OSFS	Reims Cessna F177RG Cardinal RG		F-BUMP	26. 1.04	Cardinal Sin Ltd t/a Staverton Flying School		
		F177RG0082				Gloucestershire	4. 6.09E
G-OSHK	Schempp-Hirth SHK-1	V1	BGA1467-CDU	28. 3.08	P B Hibbard	Wormingford	
			D-8441				
G-OSHL	Robinson R22 Beta	1000		19. 4.89	Sloane Helicopters Ltd	Sywell	22. 5.09E
G-OSIC	Pitts S-1C	1921-77	G-BUAW	7.10.02	J A Dodd	White Waltham	29. 8.08P
	(Built R Hendry) (Lycoming O-320)		N29DH				
G-OSII	Cessna 172N Skyhawk II	17267768	G-BIVY	17.10.95	M J Crack tr India India Flying Group		
			N73973			Andrewsfield	7. 4.09E
G-OSIS	Pitts S-1S	PFA 009-12043		19. 9.94	C Butler	(Stanfree, Chesterfield)	
	(Built C Butler)						
G-OSIT	Pitts S-1T	1023	N96JD	7.12.01	C Butler	Netherthorpe	26. 2.09E
	(Built Pitts Aerobatics) (Lycoming AEIO-360)						
G-OSIX	Piper PA-32-260 Cherokee Six	32-499	G-AZMO	5. 8.86	J T Le Bon	Lee-on-Solent	2. 6.09E
			SE-EYN				
G-OSJF	Piper PA-23-250 Aztec F	27-8054041	G-SFHR	25. 7.05	S J Fawley and C Seville	Blackpool	13. 2.10E
			G-BHSO, N2527Z				
G-OSJL	Robinson R44 Raven II	11452		23.10.06	Darlo Air Ltd	(Maynooth, County Kildare)	6.12.09E
G-OSJN	Europa Aviation Europa XS	495		3. 6.03	N Landell-Mills	Geneva	27. 5.09P
	(Built S J Nash - pr.no.PFA 247-13687) (Rotax 914-UL)						
G-OSKP	Enstrom 480	5002	F-GSOT	6. 6.94	C C Butt	Hawarden	18. 3.09E
			G-OSKP, N480EN				

Reg	Type	C/n	Prev id	Date	Owner	Base	Date
G-OSKR	Best Off Sky Ranger 912(2)	SKR0201162		14. 1.03	Sky Ranger UK Ltd	Sywell	15. 6.09P
	(Built Sky Ranger UK Ltd - pr.no.BMAA HB/249)						
G-OSKY	Cessna 172M Skyhawk II	17267389	A6-KCB N73343	27. 2.79	Skyhawk Leasing Ltd	Wellesbourne Mountford	9. 7.09E
G-OSLD	Europa Aviation Europa XS	485		23. 8.00	S Percy and C Davies	(Grantham)	10. 3.09P
	(Built S C Percy - pr.no.PFA 247-13641) (Rotax 914-UL) (Tri-gear u/c)						
G-OSLO	Schweizer 269C *(Schweizer 300)*	S 1360	N7507L	15. 3.89	AH Helicopter Services Ltd	Dunkeswell	25. 3.09E
G-OSMD	Bell 206B-2 JetRanger II	2034	G-LTEK G-BMIB, ZS-HGH	12. 2.99	Stuart Aviation Ltd	White Waltham	17. 5.09E
G-OSND	Reims Cessna FRA150M Aerobat	FRA1500272	G-BDOU	16.10.84	Wilkins and Wilkins (Special Auctions) Ltd t/a Henlow Flying Club	RAF Henlow	2. 3.09E
G-OSOE	Hawker Siddeley HS.748 Series 2A/275	1697	G-AYYG, ZK-MCF, C-GRCU, ZK-MCF, G-AYYG, ZK-MCF, G-AYYG, ZK-MCF, G-AYYG, G-11-9	17.11.97	PTB (Emerald) Proprietary Ltd *(stored11 .08)*	Blackpool	12.12.08E
G-OSOH	Cessna 525 CitationJet	525-0271	HB-VNK N860DB, N860DD	11. 2.08	Hangar 8 Ltd	Oxford	26. 2.09E
G-OSPD	Evektor EV-97 teamEurostar UK	1708		3. 9.03	I Nicholls	Rochester	14. 9.08P
G-OSPK	Cessna 172S Skyhawk II	172S10261	N6069D	22. 9.06	Kenward Orthopaedic Ltd	Leeds-Bradford	18.10.09E
G-OSPS	Piper PA-18 Super Cub 95 (L-18C-PI)	18-1555	OO-SPS G-AWRH, OO-HMI, French Army 51-15555	9. 7.92	J P Morrissey Weston, Leixlip, County Kildare		27. 6.10
	(Frame No.18-1527)						
G-OSPY	Cirrus SR20 GTS	1546	N81706	9. 9.05	Cumulus Aircraft Rentals Ltd	Blackbushe	28. 4.09E
G-OSSA	Cessna TU206B Super Skywagon B	U2060824	4X-CHT C-GDTO, N139LA, (N3824G)	17.11.03	Skydive St Andrews Ltd	Sorbie Farm, Kingsmuir	28. 1.09E
G-OSSF	Gulfstream AA-5A Cheetah	AA5A-0863	G-MELD G-BHCB	1. 2.00	The Burnett Group Ltd	Kemble	6. 4.07T
G-OSST	Colt 77A Balloon (Hot Air)	737		28.10.85	A A Brown *"Concorde II" (Noted 9.05)*	Guildford	10.10.96A
G-OSTC	Gulfstream AA-5A Cheetah	AA5A-0848	N26967	22. 4.91	5th Generation Designs Ltd	White Waltham	10. 2.09E
G-OSTL	Comco Ikarus C42 FB100	0503-6661		30. 3.05	S T Ling	Dunkeswell	3. 4.07P
G-OSTU	Gulfstream AA-5A Cheetah	AA5A-0807	G-BGCL	18. 4.95	The Burnett Group Ltd	Kemble	31. 7.08E
G-OSTY	Cessna F150G	F150-0129	G-AVCU	21. 3.97	R F Newman	Stapleford	4. 6.09E
	(Built Reims Aviation SA)						
G-OSUP	Lindstrand LBL 90A Balloon (Hot Air)	098		17. 3.94	T J Orchard *(British Airways Clubs titles)*	Aylesbury	27. 8.09E
G-OSUS	Mooney M 20K Mooney 231	25-0429	OY-SUS (N3597H)	7.11.94	J B and M O King	Goodwood	17. 2.09E
G-OSUT	Scheibe SF25C Rotax-Falke	44588	D-KTIK	24. 4.06	Yorkshire Gliding Club (Proprietary) Ltd	Sutton Bank	18. 5.09E
G-OSVM	Cessna 560XL Citation XLS	560-5770	N5030U	28. 3.08	SVM Aviation Ltd	Belfast International	27. 3.09E
G-OSZA	Pitts S-2A	2134	N60CP N80058	22. 7.05	P J Heilbron	(Guildford)	10. 9.09E
	(Built Aerotek Inc) (Lycoming AEIO-360)						
G-OSZB	Pitts S-2B	5200	G-OGEE OH-SKY	10. 2.04	P M Ambrose	Popham	25. 4.09E
	(Built Christen Industries Inc) (Lycoming AEIO-540)						
G-OTAL	ARV Aviation ARV-1 Super 2	024	G-BNGZ	10. 9.87	N R Beale	Church Farm, Shotteswell	2. 5.08P
	(Rotax 914-UL)						
G-OTAM	Cessna 172M Skyhawk II	17264098	N29060	13. 2.89	G V White	Shipdham	16. 6.09E
G-OTAN	Piper PA-18-135 Super Cub	18-3845	OO-TAN (OO-DPD), R Neth AF R-155, 54-2445	28.10.96	S D Turner and C G Dodds *(As "54-2445:A-445" in US Army c/s)*	Andrewsfield	25. 6.09E
	(L-21B-PI) *(Frame No.18-3850)*						
G-OTBA	Hawker Siddeley HS.748 Series 2A/242	1712	A3-MCA ZK-MCA, G-11-7	14. 3.01	PTB (Emerald) Proprietary Ltd *(Stored 11.08)*	Blackpool	3. 5.07T
G-OTBY	Piper PA-32-300 Six	32-7940219	N2932G	14. 2.91	M J Willing	Jersey	5. 4.09E
G-OTCH	CFM Streak Shadow	K207		28.10.93	D Goodman and I N Drury	(Newark)	3. 9.02P
	(Built H E Gotch, pr no PFA 206-12401)						
G-OTCS	Beech B300C Super King Air	FM-18	N818KA	9. 4.08	Raytheon Systems Ltd	Hawarden	27. 4.11
	(Planned to become Beech 350C ER Shadow R.1 "ZZ419" for AAC but still flying in RAF c/s but with civilian marks 12.08)						
G-OTCV	Best Off Sky Ranger 912S(1)	SKR0407511		13.12.04	T C Viner *"Terry Viner"*	Wolvey	27. 4.09P
	(Built T C Viner - pr.no.BMAA HB/436)						
G-OTCZ	Schempp-Hirth Ventus 2cT	137/352	BGA5147-KJX D-KAAQ	7.12.05	D H Conway tr CZ Group *"CZ"*	Nympsfield	31.12.07
G-OTDA	Boeing 737-31S	29266	D-ADBV N1786B	5. 2.04	Globespan Airways Ltd t/a Flyglobespan.com	Edinburgh	8. 4.09E
G-OTDI	Diamond DA.40D Star	D4.031		10. 9.03	Atrium Ltd	Denham	4.12.09E
G-OTFL	Eurocopter EC.120B Colibri	1073	G-IBRI LX-HCR	6. 7.05	Tyrone Farbrication Ltd	(Dungannon)	13.12.09E
G-OTFT	Piper PA-38-112 Tomahawk	38-78A0311	G-BNKW N9274T	14. 3.97	P Tribble	RAF Henlow	15. 1.09E
G-OTGA	Piper PA-28R-201 Arrow III	28R-7837281	ZS-KFI	21. 2.01	TG Aviation Ltd	Manston	10. 4.09E
G-OTHE	Enstrom 280C-UK Shark	1226	G-OPJT G-BKCO	22. 9.87	G E Heritage	(Breach Oak Farm, Corley, Coventry)	12. 2.09E
G-OTIB	Robin DR.400-180R Remorqueur	1545	D-EGIA	26. 4.00	The Windrushers Gliding Club Ltd	Bicester	29. 5.09E
G-OTIG	Gulfstream AA-5B Tiger	AA5B-0996	G-PENN (I-TIGR), N3756L	28. 7.00	D H Green	Elstree	14.10.09E
G-OTIM	Bensen B 8MV	PFA G/101-1084		5. 6.90	T J Deane	(Tilehurst, Reading)	
	(Built T J Deane)						
G-OTIV	Aerospool Dynamic WT9 UK	DY194/2007		6.11.07	D N E d'Ath	Sackville Lodge, Riseley	5.11.08P
	(Official c/n is "DY194")						
G-OTJB	Robinson R44 Raven	0813		4. 8.00	D N and J Farrell	Liverpool	21. 9.09E
G-OTJH	Pegasus Quantum 15-912	7791		20. 3.01	L R Gartside	Newnham, Baldock	12. 4.08P
G-OTJS	Robinson R44 Raven II	12305		9. 7.08	TJS Hire (Humberside) Ltd t/a TJS Self Drive	(Scunthorpe)	29. 7.09E
G-OTNA	Robinson R44 Raven II	11092		7. 2.06	Abel Developments Ltd	(Little Cressingham, Thetford)	9. 4.09E
G-OTOE	Aeronca 7AC Champion	7AC-4621	G-BRWW N1070E, NC1070E	2. 4.90	J M Gale *(Damaged Coombe Farm 31.5.95)*	Coombe Farm, Spreyton, Crediton	10. 5.95V
	(Continental C65)						
G-OTOO	Stolp SA.300 Starduster Too	PFA 035-13352		26. 8.98	I M Castle	Spanhoe	
	(Built I M Castle)						

Reg	Type	C/n	Prev ID	Date	Owner	Location	Date
G-OTOY	Robinson R22 Beta	0888	G-BPEW	5. 9.97	Heli Air Ltd		
						Wellesbourne Mountford/Wycombe Air Park	19.10.08E
G-OTRV	Van's RV-6	PFA 181-13302		27. 5.98	A Burani	North Weald	27. 3.08P
	(Built W R C Williams-Wynne) (Lycoming O-360) *(Tailwheel u/c)*						
G-OTRY	Schleicher ASW 24	24023	BGA3372-FMP	18. 1.08	A R Harrison and G Pursey	Dunstable	8. 7.08
G-OTSP	Aérospatiale AS.355F1 Ecureuil 2	5177	G-XPOL	31. 3.98	MW Helicopters Ltd	Stapleford	6. 5.09E
			G-BPRF, N363E				
G-OTTI	Cameron OTTI 34 SS Balloon (Hot Air)	3490		23. 3.95	Ballonwerbung Hamburg GmbH	Kiel, Germany	30. 4.05A
G-OTTO	Cameron Katalog 82 SS Balloon (Hot Air)			15. 6.92	Ballonwerbung Hamburg GmbH 3A *"Otto Versand Katalog"*		
	(New envelope 1999 - c/n 4382)	2843				Kiel, Germany	6. 7.03A
G-OTTZ	Robinson R44 Raven II	11779		22. 6.07	Glenmore Helicopters Ltd		
						Ballybofey, County Donegal	20. 7.09E
G-OTUG	Piper PA-18-150 Super Cub	18-5352	(G-BKNM)	17. 2.83	A J Lewis	Gloucestershire	18. 5.11
	(Frame No.18-5424)		PH-MBA, French Army 18-5352, N10F				
G-OTUI	SOCATA TB-20 Trinidad	1096	G-KKDL	7. 3.03	D J Taylor and J T Flint *(TUI colours)*	Bourn	7. 2.09E
			G-BSHU				
G-OTUN	Evektor EV-97 Eurostar	PFA 315-13865		15. 5.02	S P Slater	Bodmin	24. 7.09P
	(Built E O Otun)						
G-OTUP	Lindstrand LBL 180A Balloon (Hot Air)	111		28. 3.94	A M Sharp	Hereford	9. 4.09E
G-OTVI	Robinson R44 Raven II	10833		9. 9.05	R C Hields tr Hields Aviation	Sherburn-in-Elmet	30.10.09E
G-OTVR	Piper PA-34-220T Seneca V	3449279	N53497	25. 7.05	Bladerunner Aviation Ltd	Barton	28. 8.09E
G-OTWO	Rutan Defiant	114		24. 6.87	B Wronski	Gloucestershire	27. 8.08P
	(Built D G Foreman) (Lycoming O-320)						
G-OTYE	Evektor EV-97 Eurostar	PFA 315-13858		15. 4.02	A B Godber and J Tye *"Ali Minimum"*		
	(Built A B Godber and J Tye)					Bradley, Ashbourne	29. 5.08P
G-OTYP	Piper PA-28-180 Cherokee Challenger		F-BTYP	13. 1.04	T C Lewis	Cambridge	31. 5.09E
		28-7305166	N11C				
G-OUCH	Cameron N-105 Balloon (Hot Air)	4830		3. 5.00	Flying Pictures Ltd *(Elastoplast titles)*	Chilbolton	26. 3.03A
G-OUHI	Europa Aviation Europa XS	488		7. 6.01	Airplan Flight Equipment Ltd	Barton	
	(Built D R Philpott - pr.no.PFA 247-13684) (Tri-gear u/c)						
G-OUIK	Mainair Sports Pegasus Quik	7983		22. 8.03	M A Scholes	Broadmeadow Farm, Hereford	23. 8.09P
G-OUMC	Lindstrand LBL 105A Balloon (Hot Air)	724		14. 9.00	A M Holly tr Executive Ballooning *(Uphill Motor Company titles)*		
						Breadstone, Berkeley	18. 5.09E
G-OUNI	Cirrus SR20	1705	G-TABI	18. 8.08	Unique Helicopters (NI) Ltd	Enniskillen	7. 9.09E
			N950SR				
G-OURO	Europa Aviation Europa	016		13.12.93	M Crunden	Damyn's Hall, Upminster	10. 7.07P
	(Buillt D Dufton - pr.no.PFA 247-12522) (NSI EA-81/100) *(Tri-gear u/c)*				*(Noted 9.07)*		
G-OUVI	Cameron O-105 Balloon (Hot Air)	1766		4. 5.89	P Spellward tr Bristol University Hot Air Ballooning Society		
					"Uvistat II"	Bristol	27. 9.09E
G-OVAA	Colt Jumbo SS Balloon (Hot Air)	1426		11. 5.89	I Chadwick tr Balloon Preservation Flying Group		
	(Conventional Balloon (Hot Air) with nose/wings and tail of Virgin Boeing 747)				*(Inflated 4.06)*	Partridge Green, Horsham	5. 5.08A
G-OVAG	Tipsy Nipper T 66 Series 1	T66/15	OO-VAG	7. 4.04	L D Johnston	Perth	30. 6.09P
	(Built Avions Fairey SA) (Jabiru 2200A)		OO-LYS				
G-OVAL	Comco Ikarus C42 FB100	0407-6608		18. 8.04	N G Tomes	Dunkeswell	14. 8.09P
	(Built Fly Buy Ultralights Ltd)						
G-OVBF	Cameron A-250 Balloon (Hot Air)	3494		1. 3.95	Airxcite Ltd t/a Virgin Balloon Flights *"Virgin Oscar"*		
						Wembley	18. 3.07E
G-OVET	Cameron O-56 Balloon (Hot Air)	3939		25. 6.96	A R Hardwick and E Fearon	Bristol	1. 7.09E
G-OVFM	Cessna 120	14720	N2119V	29. 4.88	A Sutherland and A P Bacon	Wick	6. 5.09P
	(Continental O-200-A)		NC2119V				
G-OVFR	Reims Cessna F172N Skyhawk II	F17201892		23. 5.79	Marine and Aviation Ltd	Lee-on-Solent	13. 7.09E
G-OVIA	Lindstrand LBL 105A Balloon (Hot Air)	1002		9. 7.04	N C Lindsay *"Southern Railways"*	Pulborough	21. 4.09E
G-OVIC	Cameron A-250 Balloon (Hot Air)	4409	SE-ZKA	29.10.04	M E White	Templeogue, Dublin	13. 7.08E
G-OVID	Avid Flyer	NMFC 11760	N879UP	31. 5.91	W J Lister	Strathaven	7. 5.08P
	(Built J Pelafigue) (Rotax 532)						
G-OVII	Van's RV-7	PFA 323-14100		30. 9.04	T J Richardson	Thruxton	25. 2.09P
	(Built T J Richardson) (Superior XP-10)						
G-OVIN	Rockwell Commander 112TC	13090	OY-DVN	19.11.04	G-OVIN Aviation Ltd	Sibson	26. 2.10E
			D-EIXN, N4585W				
G-OVLA	Comco Ikarus C42 FB UK	0303-6550		4. 2.03	B C and P A Webb t/a Webb Plant Sales		
	(Built N Sams and B Bayes - pr.no.PFA 322-14028)					Dunkeswell	20.11.09P
G-OVMC	Reims Cessna F152 II	F15201667		29. 5.79	Atlantic Flight Training Ltd	Coventry	8.10.09E
G-OVNR	Robinson R22 Beta	1634		24.12.90	Helicopter Training and Hire Ltd	Newtownards	10. 9.09E
G-OVOL	Best Off Sky Ranger 912S(1)	SP012		2. 6.05	A S Docherty	Graveley Hall Farm, Graveley	21. 6.08P
	(Built P Dewhurst - pr.no.BMAA HB/447; Sky Ranger UK Ltd listed as builder on G-INFO)						
G-OVON	Piper PA-18-95 Super Cub	18-1596	OY-ELG	1. 6.05	Veronica F A Stanley	Gloucestershire	14. 8.11
			D-ECXO, French Army 51-15596				
G-OWAC	Reims Cessna F152 II	F15201678	G-BHEB	25. 2.80	Aviation South West Ltd	Exeter	10. 4.08E
			(OO-HNW)				
G-OWAI	Schleicher ASK 21	21675	BGA4487-JFV	16. 6.08	Scottish Gliding Union – Walking on Air	Portmoak	
G-OWAK	Reims Cessna F152 II	F15201677	G-BHEA	25. 2.80	A S Bamrah t/a Falcon Flying Services	Rochester	10. 1.10E
G-OWAL	Piper PA-34-220T Seneca III	3448030	D-GAPN	7. 7.98	R G and W Allison	Gamston	20.12.08E
			N9163K				
G-OWAN	Cessna 210D Centurion	21058321	N672P	11.06.07	G Owen	Leeds-Bradford	26. 7.09E
			HB-CII, D-EDEG, OE-DEG, N3821Y				
G-OWAP	Piper PA-28-161 Cherokee Warrior II		G-BXNH	13. 6.05	Airways Aero Association Ltd	Wycombe Air Park	21.12.08E
		28-7816314	N2828M		*(Operated British Airways Flying Club)*		
G-OWAR	Piper PA-28-161 Warrior II	28-8616054	TF-OBO	18. 2.88	Bickertons Aerodromes Ltd *(Operated The Pilot Centre)*		
			N9521N			Denham	19. 2.09E
G-OWAZ	Pitts S-1C	43JM	G-BRPI	22.11.94	P E S Latham *"Tiny Dancer"*	Sleap	20. 3.09P
	(Built J Magueri) (Lycoming O-320)		N199M				
G-OWCS	Cessna 182J Skylane	18257009	D-EFSA	25.11.02	P Ragg *(Operates in Africa)*	(Weerberg, Austria)	15. 1.06
			N2909F				
G-OWEL	Colt 105A Balloon (Hot Air)	1773		18. 5.90	S R Seager	Aylesbury	16. 3.98T

G-OWEN	K & S Jungster 1	PFA 044-10124			13.11.78	R C Owen	(Danehill, Haywards Heath)
	(Built R C Owen) (Continental C90)						
G-OWET	Thurston TSC-1A2 Teal	037	C-FNOR		28. 9.94	J Reddington	Denham 13.11.08E
			(N1342W)				
G-OWFS	Cessna A152 Aerobat	A1520805	G-DESY		21. 5.02	Westair Flying Services Ltd	Blackpool 19.11.09E
			G-BNJE, N7386L				
G-OWGC	Slingsby T 61F Venture T 2	1875	XZ555		14. 8.91	Wolds Gliding Club Ltd	Pocklington 23. 1.09E
G-OWLC	Piper PA-31 Turbo Navajo	31-679	G-AYFZ		13. 6.91	Channel Airways Ltd	Guernsey 31. 7.09E
			N6771L				
G-OWMC	Thruster T 600N 450	0122-T600N-076			5. 3.03	A R Hughes tr Wiltshire Microlight Centre	
							Yatesbury 8. 5.09P
G-OWND	Robinson R44 Astro	0644			26. 8.99	R E Todd	Sandtoft 15. 9.09E
G-OWOW	Cessna 152 II	15283199	G-BMSZ		10. 5.95	Plane Talking Ltd *(Operated Wycombe Flying Centre)*	
			N47254				Wycombe Air Park 22.12.09E
G-OWRD	Agusta A109C	7649	G-USTC		21. 2.05	Wickford Development Company Ltd	
			JA6695, (G-LAXO)				Wickford House, Hatfield Peverel 24. 6.09E
G-OWRT	Cessna 182G Skylane	18255077	G-ASUL		24. 8.00	Blackpool and Fylde Aero Club Ltd	Blackpool 6. 7.09E
			N3677U				
G-OWST	Cessna 172S Skyhawk	172S8163	G-WABH		17. 6.05	Manx Aero Marine Management Ltd)	Blackpool 3. 7.09E
			N961SP				
G-OWWW	Europa Aviation Europa XS	051			9. 6.94	R F W Holder tr Whisky Group	High Cross, Ware 16. 5.09P
	(Built W R C Williams-Wynne and R F W Holder - pr.no.PFA 247-12683) (Rotax 912 ULS) (Tri-gear u/c)							
G-OWYE	Lindstrand LBL 240A Balloon (Hot Air)	645			27. 4.00	Wye Valley Aviation Ltd	Bridstow, Ross-on-Wye 10. 9.09E
G-OWYN	Aviamilano F 14 Nibbio	208	HB-EVZ		2. 2.87	R Nash	Shoreham 3. 9.08P
			I-SERE				
G-OXBA	Cameron Z-160 Balloon (Hot-Air)	11129			16. 6.08	J E Rose *"Oxford Balloon Company"*	Abingdon 17.6.09E
G-OXBC	Cameron A-140 Balloon (Hot Air)	4981			2. 2.01	J E Rose *"Oxford Balloon Company"*	Abingdon 13.12.08E
G-OXBY	Cameron N-90 Balloon (Hot Air)	1993	PH-DUM		9. 6.94	C A Oxby *"The Zit"*	(Doncaster)
G-OXKB	Cameron Jaguar XK8 Sports Car 110 SS Balloon (Hot Air)				9. 7.96	D M Moffat *"Jaguar XK8"*	Bristol 12. 8.09E
		3941					
G-OXLS	Cessna 560XL Citation XLS	560-5675	N5266F		18. 1.07	Go XLS Ltd	Guernsey 18.1.10E
G-OXOM	Piper PA-28-161 Cadet	2841285	G-BRSG (2)		9.12.03	S J Skilton t/a Aviation Rentals	Elstree 23. 1.10E
			N92011				
G-OXTC	Piper PA-23-250 Aztec D	27-4344	G-AZOD		31. 5.89	A S Bamrah t/a Falcon Flying Services *(Noted 6.05)*	
			N697RC, N6976Y				Biggin Hill 15. 6.98T
G-OXVI	Vickers Supermarine 361 Spitfire LF.XVIe	7246M			22. 8.89	Spitfire Ltd *(As "TD248:CR-S" in RAF 74 Sqdn c/s)*	
		CBAF.IX.4262	TD248				Duxford 7. 7.09P
G-OYAK	SPP Yakovlev Yak C-11	171205	EAF 705		25. 2.88	A H Soper *(As "9" (white) in Russian AF c/s)*	
	(C/n quoted as 1701139 and or 690120 also)		OK-KIH				Little Gransden 22.12.07P
G-OYES	Mainair Blade 912	1186-1198-7-W989			12.11.98	B Mcadam and A Hatton (Dalkeith and Loanhead) 21. 5.09P	
G-OYIO	Robin DR.400-120 Dauphin 2+2	2038	OO-YIO		16. 2.07	Bustard Flying Club Ltd	Boscombe Down 17. 5.09E
	(Officially regd as DR.400-120 Petit Prince)						
G-OYST	Agusta-Bell 206B-2 JetRanger II	8440	G-JIMW		9.10.02	Adroit Services Corporation	(Guernsey) 14. 5.09E
			G-UNIK, G-TPPH, G-BCYP				
G-OYTE	Rans S-6-ES Coyote II	0404 1563			21. 7.04	I M Vass	Morgansfield, Fishburn 24. 3.09P
	(Built I M Vass - pr.no.PFA 204-14263) (Tri-cycle u/c)						
G-OZAC	Bell 407	53062	OY-HMM		8. 5.07	Narragansett LLP t/a Helilux (Pontprenn, Cardiff) 4. 6.09E	
			OE-XWG, D-HASI, C-GFNM				
G-OZAR	Enstrom 480	5007	G-BWFF		31. 7.95	Benham Helicopters Ltd	Gloucestershire 10. 1.09E
G-OZBB	Airbus A320-212	0389	C-GZUM		21. 3.94	Monarch Airlines Ltd	Luton 29. 4.09E
			G-OZBB, C-GZUM, G-OZBB, C-GXBB, G-OZBB, C-FTDW, G-OZBB, C-FTDW, G-OZBB,				
			C-FTDW, G-OZBB, C-FTDW, G-OZBB, C-FTDW, G-OZBB, F-WWDI				
G-OZBE	Airbus A321-231	1707	D-AVZH		27. 3.02	Monarch Airlines Ltd	Luton 26. 3.09E
G-OZBF	Airbus A321-231	1763	D-AVZB		20. 6.02	Monarch Airlines Ltd	Luton 19. 6.09E
G-OZBG	Airbus A321-231	1941	D-AVXC		20. 3.03	Monarch Airlines Ltd	Luton 19. 3.09E
G-OZBH	Airbus A321-231	2105	D-AVXB		17. 3.04	Monarch Airlines Ltd	Luton 16. 3.09E
G-OZBI	Airbus A321-231	2234	D-AVZV		4. 6.04	Monarch Airlines Ltd	Luton 3. 6.09E
G-OZBK	Airbus A320-214	1370	PH-BMD		28. 4.05	Monarch Airlines Ltd	Luton 27. 4.09E
			D-ABLB, F-WQQI, OO-SNG, F-WWIL.				
G-OZBL	Airbus A321-231	0864	G-MIDE		12. 5.06	Monarch Airlines Ltd	Luton 13. 8.09E
			D-AVZB				
G-OZBM	Airbus A321-231	1045	G-MIDJ		14. 3.07	Monarch Airlines Ltd	Luton 15. 7.09E
			D-AVZO				
G-OZBN	Airbus A321-231	1153	G-MIDK		2. 4.07	Monarch Airlines Ltd	Luton 27.11.09E
			D-AVZF				
G-OZBO	Airbus A321-231	1207	G-MIDM		14. 5.07	Monarch Airlines Ltd	Luton 17. 4.09E
			D-AVZR				
G-OZBP	Airbus A321-231	1433	G-TTIB		6. 2.08	Monarch Airlines Ltd	Luton 26. 2.09E
			D-AVZC				
G-OZBR	Airbus A321-231	1794	N586NK		2. 4.08	Monarch Airlines Ltd	Luton 3. 4.09E
			(C-FZVF), D-AVZF				
G-OZBS	Airbus A321-231	1428	G-TTIA		15. 8.08	Monarch Airlines Ltd	Luton 18. 2.09E
			D-AVZA				
G-OZEE	Avid Speed Wing Mk.4	PFA 189-12308			18. 4.94	G D Bailey	Old Sarum 7. 1.10P
	(Built S C Goozee)						
G-OZEF	Europa Aviation Europa XS	538			23.12.03	Z M Ahmad	(Southall)
	(Built Z M Ahmad - pr.no.PFA 247-14041)						
G-OZIE	Avtech Jabiru J400	0xxx			30. 6.05	S A Bowkett	Sleap 4. 2.10P
	(Built S A Bowkett - pr.no.PFA 325-14284)						
G-OZOI	Cessna R182 Skylane RG II	R18201950	G-ROBK		31. 5.85	J R and F.L Gibson Fleming tr Ranston Farms	
							Ranston Farm, Iwerne Courtney 30. 7.09E
G-OZOO	Cessna 172N Skyhawk II	17267663	G-BWEI		17.11.99	R A Brown	(Clowne, Chesterfield) 17. 8.09E
			N73767				

G-OZOZ	Schempp-Hirth Nimbus 3dT	6	BGA4458-JEQ	27.11.07	C M Hawkes tr OZ Syndicate	Ringmer	22. 9.08
			OO-ZOZ, HB-1921, D-7695				
G-OZRH	British Aerospace BAe 146 Series 200	E2047	(EI-DDF)	29. 1.96	Flightline Ltd (Stored 2.09)	Southend	1. 2.09E
			N188US, N364PS		(Ceased operations 3.12.08)		
G-OZZI	Avtech Jabiru SK	0157		15. 8.97	A H Godfrey	(Weston-super-Mare)	22. 6.09P
	(Built A H Godfrey and E J Stradling - pr.no.PFA 274-13176)						
G-OZZO	Mudry CAP.231	08	F-GOZO	9. 1.09	R M Buchan	North Weald	
G-OZZY	Robinson R22 Beta II	2982	EI-RZZ	2. 9.03	London Helicopter Centres Ltd	Redhill	2. 9.09E
			G-PWEL				

G-PAAA - G-PZZZ

G-PACE	Robin R1180T Aiglon	218		16.10.78	T C Wise and M T Fitzpatrick	RAF Henlow	18. 4.09E
G-PACL	Robinson R22 Beta	1893	N2314S	17.12.91	J N Plange	(Scunthorpe)	2.10.09E
G-PACT	Piper PA-28-181 Archer III	2843546	N5368F	25. 3.03	A Parsons	(London SW6)	9. 4.09E
G-PADD	Gulfstream AA-5A Cheetah	AA5A-0780	G-ESTE	27.10.03	Caseright Ltd (Noted 1.09)	Turweston	8.12.04T
			G-GHNC, N26877				
G-PADE	Reality Escapade Jabiru(3)	JAESC 0027		2. 6.04	C L G Innocent	(Worthing)	27. 6.08P
	(Built C L G Innocent - pr.no.BMAA HB/369) (Tailwheel u/c)						
G-PADI	Cameron V-77 Balloon (Hot Air)	1809		18. 8.88	M E J Whitewood "Padiwac"	Bovingdon	9. 8.09E
G-PAFR	DG Flugzeugbau DG-300 Elan	3E344	BGA3500-FSX	5.10.07	P Morgan "405"	Parham Park	17. 1.08
G-PAIZ	Piper PA-12 Super Cruiser	12-2018	N3215M	11. 4.94	B R Pearson (Carries "NC3215M" on tail)		
			NC3215M			Eaglescott	16. 8.07T
G-PALY	Piper PA-28-181 Archer III	2843039	PH-AEC	8. 8.07	Innovative Aviation Ltd	(Ripon)	28. 9.09E
G-PAMY	Robinson R44 Clipper II	11641		6. 3.07	Batchelor Aviation Ltd	Redhill	15. 3.09E
G-PARG	Pitts S-1S	19528-1	N18FW	30. 6.03	R C Pargeter	(Worcester)	15. 4.09P
	(Built F G Weaver) (Lycoming O-360)						
G-PARI	Cessna 172RG Cutlass II	172RG0010	N4685R	19.11.79	Applied Signs Ltd	Tatenhill	30. 5.09E
G-PART	Partenavia P68	62	F-GMPT	19.12.84	Ravenair Aircraft Ltd	Liverpool	10. 2.09E
	(Officially regd as "P68B")		G-PART, OY-CEY, D-GATE, PH-EEO, (N718R)				
G-PASH	Aérospatiale AS.355F1 Ecureuil 2	5040	F-GHLI	17. 5.96	Diamond Aviation Ltd	South Duffield, Selby	23. 5.09E
			LX-HUG, F-GHLI, N356E				
G-PASN	Enstrom F-28F	427	G-BSHZ	19. 4.05	Passion 4 Health International Ltd	(Chertsey)	4. 3.09E
			N51702				
G-PASX	MBB BÖ.105DBS-4	S 814	D-HDZX	20.12.89	Police Aviation Services Ltd	Gloucestershire	13. 2.09E
G-PATF	Europa Aviation Europa	107		5. 1.99	E P Farrell	(Beaconsfield)	
	(Built E P Farrell - pr.no.PFA 247-12757) (Monowheel u/c)						
G-PATG	Cameron O-90 Balloon (Hot Air)	3856		13. 3.96	P Mackley	Bradley Stoke, Bristol	21. 9.09E
G-PATM	Eurocopter AS.350B2 Ecureuil	4474	SE-HJL	14. 8.08	Mealey Construction Ltd	(Carlow, Ireland)	14. 8.09E
G-PATN	SOCATA TB-10 Tobago	307	G-LUAR	25. 3.97	M D Booth tr G-PATN Owners Group	Humberside	6. 4.09E
G-PATO	Zenair CH.601UL Zodiac	PFA 162A-14328		2. 3.05	N D Townend	Sackville Lodge, Riseley	16. 8.08P
	(Built D L Walker) (Rotax 912 UL) (Tri-cycle u/c)						
G-PATP	Lindstrand LBL 77A Balloon (Hot Air)	471		8. 7.97	P Pruchnickyj	Weston Turville, Buckingham	19. 7.09E
G-PATS	Europa Aviation Europa	216		19. 7.95	D J G Kesterton tr G-PATS Flying Group		
	(Built N Surman - pr.no.PFA 247-12888) (Monowheel u/c)					(Milton Keynes)	
G-PATX	Lindstrand LBL 90A Balloon (Hot Air)	778		19. 6.01	P C Gooch	Alresford	22. 7.09E
G-PATZ	Europa Aviation Europa	069		2. 6.98	H P H Griffin tr G-PATZ Group	Denham	18. 6.09P
	(Built H P H Griffin - pr.no.PFA 247-12625) (Rotax 912 UL) (Monowheel u/c)						
G-PAVL	Robin R3000/120	170		22.11.96	Autogas Worldwide Ltd	(Newport)	20. 3.09T
G-PAWL	Piper PA-28-140 Cherokee	28-24456	G-AWEU	8. 9.82	A E Davies tr G-PAWL Group	Barton	5.11.09E
			N11C				
G-PAWN	Piper PA-25-260 Pawnee C	25-5207	G-BEHS	12. 3.01	A P Meredith	Lasham	25. 6.93A
			OE-AFX, N8755L				
G-PAWS	Gulfstream AA-5A Cheetah	AA5A-0806	N2623Q	8. 2.82	M J Patrick	Goodwood	16.10.09E
G-PAWZ	Best Off Sky Ranger Swift 912S(1)			23. 7.07	S D McMurran	Norton, Daventry	19. 5.09P
		SKRxxxx758					
	(Built S D McMurran - pr.no.BMAA HB/528)						
G-PAXX	Piper PA-20-135 Pacer	20-1107	N135XX	20. 5.83	D W Grace	Landmead Farm, Garford	4.10.10SE
			G-PAXX, (G-ARCE), F-BLLA, CN-TDJ, F-DADR				
G-PAYD	Robin DR.400-180 Régent	847	D-EAYD	14. 1.03	A Head	Bicester	30. 4.09E
G-PAZY	Pazmany PL-4A	PFA 017-10378	G-BLAJ	20.11.89	M Richardson	(Durrington, Salisbury)	3.10.95P
	(Built J D Le Pine) (Continental A65)						
G-PBEC	Van's RV-7	72125		21. 8.07	P G Reid	Derby	16.12.08P
	(Built P G Reid- pr.no.PFA 323-14382) (Superior XP-10)						
G-PBEE	Robinson R44 Clipper	0829		11. 9.00	P Barnard	Guernsey	21. 9.09E
G-PBEK	Agusta A109A	7135	G-BXIV	20.12.04	Castle Air Charters Ltd	Liskeard Heliport	2. 4.09E
			F-GERU, HB-XOK, D-HFZF				
G-PBEL	CFM Shadow Series DD	305-DD		27.10.98	P Richardson	Graveley Hall Farm, Graveley	20.10.09P
G-PBIX	Vickers Supermarine 361 Spitfire LF.XVIe		N382RW	15.10.08	Pemberton-Billing LLP (on rebuild)	Sandown	
		CBAF.IX 4640	G-XVIA, 8075M, 7245M, RW382				
	(Officially regd with c/n CBAF IX 11581)						
G-PBRL	Robinson R22 Beta	4053		15. 6.06	Cardy Construction Ltd	Headcorn	6. 7.09E
G-PBUS	Avtech Jabiru SK	0164		18. 8.98	J F Heath	Carlisle	8. 7.09E
	(Built G R Pybus - pr.no.PFA 274-13269)						
G-PBYA	Consolidated PBY-5A Catalina	CV-283	C-FNJF	19.11.04	Catalina Aircraft Ltd (As "433915" in USAAF c/s)		
	(Built Canadian Vickers Ltd)		CF-NJF, F-ZBBD, CF-NJF, F-ZBAY, CF-NJF, RCAF 11005			Duxford	26. 4.09S
	(Originally built for RCAF as Canso A: new c/s represents OA-10A Catalina 44-33915 of 5th Emergency Rescue Squadron, 8th Air Force)						
G-PBYY	Enstrom 280FX Shark	2077	G-BXKV	15. 8.97	B Morgan	Gloucestershire	31. 5.09E
			D-HHML				
G-PCAF	Pietenpol AirCamper	PFA 047-12433		1. 6.94	C C and F M Barley	Manor Farm, Tongham	10. 9.08P
	(Built C C and F M Barley)						
G-PCAM	Fairey Britten-Norman BN-2A Mk.III-2 Trislander	G-BEPH	26. 9.01	Aurigny Air Services Ltd	Guernsey	14. 6.04T
		1052	S7-AAG, G-BEPH		(ABN AMRO Bank titles) (Stored 1.06)		

G-PCAT	SOCATA TB-10 Tobago	60	G-BHER	17. 7.03	R White	Oxford	13. 6.09E
			4X-AKK, G-BHER				
G-PCCC	Alpi Pioneer 300	112		31. 3.04	R Pidcock	White Fen Farm, Benwick	24. 5.09P
	(Built F A Civaciuti - pr.no.PFA 330-14220)						
G-PCDP	Moravan Zlin Z-526F Trener	1163	SP-CDP	24.10.94	J Mann *"Ticker"*	Brock Farm, Billericay	23. 4.09E
	(Walter M137A)						
G-PCOP	Beech B200 Super King Air	BB-1860	N6200G	7.10.05	Albert Bartlett and Sons (Airdrie) Ltd	Glasgow	22.11.09E
G-PDGE	Eurocopter EC.120B Colibri	1211	F-WQPD	20. 7.01	A J Wicklow	Cumbernauld	10. 9.09E
G-PDGF	Eurocopter AS.350B2 Ecureuil	9024	G-FROH	25. 5.07	PLM Dollar Group Ltd	Inverness	24. 1.10E
G-PDGG	Aeromere F 8L Falco Series 3	208	OO-TOS	6. 1.98	P D G Grist	Sibson	31. 5.10S
			I-BLIZ				
G-PDGN	Aérospatiale SA.365N Dauphin 2	6074	PH-SSU	5. 4.01	PLM Dollar Group Ltd	Inverness	19. 7.09E
			5N-ATX, PH-SSU, (G-BLDR), G-TRAF, G-BLDR				
G-PDGR	Aérospatiale AS.350B2 Ecureuil	2559	G-RICC	26. 1.07	PLM Dollar Group Ltd	Inverness	23. 3.09E
			G-BTXA				
G-PDGT	Aérospatiale AS.355F2 Ecureuil 2	5374	N325SC	27.11.07	PLM Dollar Group Ltd t/a PDG Helicopters		
			G-BOOV			Inverness	26.11.09E
G-PDHJ	Cessna T182R Turbo Skylane II	T18268092	N6888H	3. 1.85	P G Vallance Ltd	Redhill	22. 8.09E
G-PDOC	Piper PA-44-180 Seminole	44-7995090	G-PVAF	17.12.85	T White t/a Medicare	Newcastle	20.10.09E
			N2242A				
G-PDOG	Cessna O-1E Bird Dog	24550	F-GKGP	25. 9.98	J D Needham *(As "24550:GP" in USAF c/s)*		
	(Regd as Cessna 305C)		French Army			Old Manor Farm, Anwick	27. 5.11S
G-PDSI	Cessna 172N Skyhawk II	17270420	N739BU	4. 1.88	A J Clements and C I Bateman tr DA Flying Group		
						Blackbushe	19. 4.09E
G-PEAK	Agusta-Bell 206B-2 JetRanger II	8242	G-BLJE	7. 3.94	Total Digital Solutions Ltd	(Bolton)	5. 6.09E
			SE-HBW				
G-PEAR	P&M Pegasus Quik	8309		20. 9.07	C D Hayle	(Balby, Doncaster)	15.11.09P
G-PECK	Piper PA-32-300 Cherokee Six D	32-7140008	G-ETAV	22. 4.03	H Peck	Gamston	29. 4.09E
			G-MCAR, G-LADA, G-AYWK, N8616N				
G-PEGA	Pegasus Quantum 15-912	7700		14. 8.00	B A Showell	Maypole Farm, Chislet	21. 8.07P
G-PEGE	Best Off Sky Ranger 912(2)	SKR 0511640		31. 1.06	A N Hughes	Weston Zoyland	26.10.08P
	(Built A N Hughes - pr.no.BMAA HB/479) (C/n possibly SKR0508640)						
G-PEGG	Colt 90A Balloon (Hot Air)	1550		28. 6.89	Ballon Vole Association Fontaine les Dijon, France		19. 2.09E
G-PEGI	Piper PA-34-200T Seneca II	34-7970339	N2907A	27.11.89	ACS Aviation Ltd	Perth	27. 1.10E
G-PEGY	Europa Aviation Europa	096		16. 5.00	M T Dawson	Leeds-Bradford	5. 4.09P
	(Built M T Dawson - pr.no.PFA 247-12713) (Rotax 914-UL) (Tri-gear u/c)						
G-PEGZ	Centrair 101A Pégase	101A0179	BGA3871-HDW	16.10.07	J A P Eldem	Walney Island	3. 5.06
			F-CGEE				
G-PEJM	Piper PA-28-181 Archer III	2843355	N41860	28. 6.00	I Harris	Dunkeswell	9. 7.09E
G-PEKT	SOCATA TB-20 Trinidad	532	N24AS	28. 7.89	A J Dales	Mount Airey Farm, South Cave	20. 4.09E
G-PELS	Agusta-Bell 206A JetRanger	8185	G-DNCN	6.11.06	M P May	(Ossett)	15. 6.09E
			9H-AAJ, Libyan Arab Rep AF 8185, 5A-BAM				
G-PENH	UltraMagic M-90 Balloon (Hot Air)	90-98		10.12.07	G Holtham	Heage, Belper	3. 2.09E
G-PEPA	Cessna 206H Stationair	20608181	G-MGMG	15. 6.04	R D Lygo	Goodwood	25.11.09E
			N5076D				
G-PEPS	Robinson R44 Astro	0722	G-LFBW	13. 9.06	Hopkinsons Fair Deals Ltd		
			G-ODES			(East Hardwick, Pontefract)	17. 3.09E
G-PERC	Cameron N-90 Balloon (Hot Air)	10127		29. 8.01	P A Foot and I R Warrington *(Stanton Percival titles)*		
						Stamford	17. 2.09E
G-PERE	Robinson R22 Beta II	3382	N70881	24. 2.03	Aero Maintenance Ltd	Walton Wood	6. 3.09E
G-PERZ	Bell 206B-3 JetRanger III	4411	N6272T	7. 1.97	Alpha Air Ltd	(Gravesend)	5. 4.09E
G-PEST	Hawker Tempest II	12202	HA604	9.10.89	Tempest Two Ltd *(On rebuild 2008)*	Hemswell	
	(Built Bristol Aeroplane Co Ltd)		Indian AF, MW401				
	(Regd with c/n "1181")						
G-PETH	Piper PA-24-260 Comanche C	24-4979	N9469P	15.10.04	J V Hutchinson	(Frangy, France)	29. 1.09E
G-PETR	Piper PA-28-140 Cherokee Cruiser		G-BCJL	23. 9.85	A A Gardner	Ronaldsway	5. 2.10E
		28-7425320	N9591N				
G-PETS	Diamond DA.42 Twin Star	42.169		2.10.06	Airways Aircraft Leasing Ltd	Newcastle	14.12.09E
G-PEYO	Gefa-Flug AS 105 GD Airship (Hot Air)	0047		12.12.07	International Merchandising Promotion and Services SA		
	(Rotax 582)					Genval, Belgium	11.12.09E
G-PFAA	EAA Biplane Model P2	PEB/03		19. 9.78	T A Fulcher	(Rochford)	9. 4.09P
	(Built P E Barker pr.no.PFA 1338) (Continental PC90)						
G-PFAF	Clutton FRED Series II	PFA 029-10310		30.10.78	M S Perkins	Stoke Golding	13.11.08P
	(Built K Fern and M S Perkins) (Volkswagen 1834)						
G-PFAG	Evans VP-1	PFA 7022		13.11.78	D Pope	(Attleborough)	30. 6.89P
	(Built N S Giles-Townsend) (Volkswagen 1600)			*(Stored 1.06)*			
G-PFAH	Evans VP-1	PFA 7004		23.11.78	J A Scott	Chestnut Farm, Tipps End, Welney	26. 5.09P
	(Built J A Scott) (Volkswagen 1834)						
G-PFAL	Clutton FRED Series II	PFA 029-10243		7.12.78	J M Robinson	Derrytrasna Glen, Bannfoot	27. 7.88P
	(Built H Pugh) (Volkswagen 1600)			*(Noted 8.07)*			
G-PFAP	Phoenix Currie Wot	PFA 058-10315		12.12.78	J H Seed *(As "C1904:Z" in RFC c/s)*		
	(Built P G Abbey as an SE.5a replica) (Continental O-200-A)					Black Spring Farm, Castle Bytham	22. 6.09P
G-PFAR	Isaacs Fury II	PFA 011-10220		18.12.78	G Edwards	Roughay Farm, Bishops Waltham	9. 6.07P
	(Built C J Repik) (Continental O-200-A)				*(As "K2059" in RAF 25 Sqdn c/s)*		
G-PFAT	Monnett Sonerai II	PFA 015-10312		26.10.78	H B Carter	(St Clement, Jersey)	24.10.92P
	(Built H B Carter) (Volkswagen 1834)				*(Stored Newcastle 5.93)*		
G-PFAW	Evans VP-1	PFA 062-10183		18.12.78	R F Shingler	Forest Farm, Welshpool	28. 6.07P
	(Built R F Shingler) (Volkswagen 1834)						
G-PFAY	EAA Biplane	1525		18.12.78	A K Lang and A L Young		
	(Built A K Lang and A L Young - pr.no.PFA 1525)					(Ilton, Ilminster and Henstridge)	
G-PFCI	Piper PA-34-220T Seneca IV	3447014	N401JC	17. 5.06	MYG (Jersey) Ltd	Jersey	22. 7.09E
			G-PFCI, N35AL, D-GLPE, N9267L				
G-PFCL	Cessna 172S Skyhawk SP	172S9330	N53287	19. 3.03	Critical Simulations Ltd	Elstree	10. 4.09E

Reg	Type	C/n	Prev ID	Date	Owner	Location	Expiry
G-PFFN	Beech 200 Super King Air	BB-456	N456CD	7. 4.00	The Puffin Club Ltd	Kemble	17. 4.09E
	N861D, N124BB, C6-BFP, C6-CAA, N80NF, N80NE, N100FB						
G-PFOX	Robinson R44 Raven	1480	G-CDKU	14.11.08	Fox Brothers (North West) Ltd	(Thornton Cleveleys)	23. 5.09E
G-PFSL	Reims Cessna F152	F15201746	PH-TWF	30. 8.00	P A Simon	Headcorn	6. 4.09E
			D-ENAX				
G-PGAC	Dyn'Aéro MCR-01 Club	48		27. 1.99	D T S Walsh and G A Coatesworth	Cambridge	26. 7.09P
	(Built G A Coatesworth - pr.no.PFA 301-13186) (Rotax 912 UL)						
G-PGFG	Tecnam P92-EM Echo	PFA 318-13772		30.10.01	P G Fitzgerald *"Charlie's Angel"*		
	(Built P G Fitzgerald) (Rotax 912S)					Franklyn's Field, Chewton Mendip	26. 6.09P
G-PGGY	Robinson R44 Clipper II	11115		3. 4.06	Linic Consultants Ltd	Redhill	27. 4.09E
G-PGHM	Air Création 582(1)/Kiss 450	FL024		4. 2.04	P G H Millbank	Sutton Meadows	22. 7.09P
	(Built P G H Millbank - pr.no.BMAA HB/341 being Flylight kit comprising Trike s/n T03111 and Wing s/n A04004-xxxx)						
G-PGSI	Robin R2160 Alpha Sport	309	F-GSAF	9. 3.00	M A Spencer	North Weald	20. 7.09E
G-PGUY	Sky 70-16 Balloon (Hot Air)	131		13.12.99	J L Guy *"Marie Curie Cancer Care"*	Skipton	28. 5.09E
G-PHAA	Reims Cessna F150M	F15001159		19. 6.97	P H Archard t/a PHA Aviation	Elstree	21. 7.09E
G-PHEW	Cirrus SR22-G3 GTS	2915	N107CT	20. 3.08	G3 Aviation Ltd	Fairoaks	25. 3.09E
G-PHIL	Gyroflight Brookland Hornet	17		7. 7.78	A J Philpotts	St Merryn	11. 8.89P
	(Volkswagen 1600)				*(Stored 5.90)*		
G-PHLB	Rotary Air Force RAF 2000 GTX-SE			11. 3.04	P R Bell	(Lower Apperley, Gloucester)	23. 5.05P
	(Built P R Bell)	PFA G/13-1359					
G-PHLY	Reims Cessna FRA150L Aerobat	FRA1500214	G-BBKU	24. 3.06	M Bonsall	Netherthorpe	25. 6.09E
G-PHMG	Van's RV-8	PFA 303-13639		27. 4.07	M Gibson and P R Hall	(Goole and Doncaster)	13. 4.09P
	(Built M Gibson and P R Hall)						
G-PHNX	Schempp-Hirth Duo Discus xT	157	BGA5248-KOG	14. 3.07	J L Birch and R Maskell *"72"*	Gransden Lodge	4. 3.08
G-PHOR	Reims Cessna FRA150L Aerobat	FRA1500157	G-BACC	19.10.06	M Bonsall	Netherthorpe	28. 2.10E
G-PHOX	Aeroprakt A22-L Foxbat	PFA 317A-14635		8. 5.07	J D Webb	Rhosgoch	2. 6.09P
	(Built J D Webb)						
G-PHSI	Colt 90A Balloon (Hot Air)	2181		12. 5.92	P H Strickland	Bedford	21. 7.01A
G-PHTG	SOCATA TB-10 Tobago	1008		15.11.89	A J Baggarley	Shoreham	14.10.09E
G-PHTO	Beech 390 Premier 1	RB-125	N312SL	26. 4.06	Bookajet Aircraft Management Ltd	Farnborough	16. 5.09E
			N3725F				
G-PHUN	Reims Cessna FRA150L Aerobat	FRA1500177	G-BAIN	27. 6.06	M Bonsall	Netherthorpe	4. 8.09E
G-PHVM	Van's RV-8	PFA 303-14609		16.10.07	G Howes and V Millard	Crowfield	
	(Built G Howes and V Millard)						
G-PHXS	Europa Aviation Europa XS	523		22. 7.02	P Handford	(Wellingborough)	21.12.09P
	(Built P Handford - pr.no.PFA 247-13876) (Rotax 912 ULS) (Tri-gear u/c)						
G-PHYL	Denney Kitfox Model 4	PFA 172A-12189		14. 9.98	J Dunn	Siege Cross Farm, Thatcham	28. 6.09P
	(Built J Dunn)						
G-PHYS	Avtech Jabiru SP-470	xxxx		19. 2.03	C Mayer tr G-PHYS Group	Plymouth	8.10.09P
	(Built P C Knight - pr.no.PFA 274B-13926)						
G-PHYZ	Jabiru J430	PFA 336-14617		9. 6.08	P C Knight	Wolverhampton	11.12.09P
	(Built P C Knight) (Jabiru 3300A)						
G-PIAF	Thunder Ax7-65 Balloon (Hot Air)	1885		19.11.90	L Battersey *"No Regrets/La Vie en Rose"*	Newbury	29.11.09E
G-PICX	P&M Aviation Quik R	8411		5. 1.09	R J Cook	Cumbernauld	4. 1.10P
G-PIDG	Robinson R44 Astro	0678		23.11.99	P J Rogers	Sywell	23. 1.09E
G-PIEL	Menavia Piel CP.301A Emeraude	218	G-BARY	17.11.88	P R Thorne	Cublington	8. 1.10P
			F-BIJR				
G-PIES	Thunder Ax7-77Z Balloon (Hot Air)	263		13. 2.80	S J Hollingsworth and M K Bellamy *(Pork Farms titles)*		
						Bleasby and Ironville, Nottngham	21. 9.09E
G-PIET	Pietenpol AirCamper	PFA 047-12267		1. 4.93	A R Wyatt	Panshanger	15.12.09P
	(Built N D Marshall) (Continental C90)						
G-PIGG	Lindstrand Flying Pig SS Balloon (Hot Air)	473		18. 8.97	I Heidenreich	Remscheid, Germany	18. 3.09E
G-PIGI	Evektor EV-97 teamEurostar UK	2315		23. 2.05	P A Aston tr Pigs Might Fly Group	Exeter	22. 2.08P
	(Built Cosmik Aviation Ltd)						
G-PIGS	SOCATA Rallye 150ST	2696	G-BDWB	13. 6.88	D Hodgson tr Boonhill Flying Group	Wombleton	25. 9.09E
G-PIGY	Short SC.7 Skyvan 3A Variant 100	SH1943	LX-JUL	21.12.95	Invicta Aviation Ltd		
			5T-MAM, (G-14-111)			Langar/RAF Weston-on-the-Green	15. 4.09E
G-PIIT	Pitts S-2AE	1984	N3QQ	14. 2.07	Mansfield Property Consultancy Ltd	Leicester	27. 8.08P
	(Built R S McGlashon) (Lycoming AEIO-360)						
G-PIIX	Cessna P210N Pressurized Centurion II	P21000130	G-KATH	12. 6.95	D L Harrisberg and R Dennis	Elstree	26. 3.09E
			(N4898P)				
G-PIKB	Eiriavion PIK-20B	20144C	BGA2164-DJZ	21. 5.08	P H Collin	Shipdham	
G-PIKD	Eiriavion PIK-20D	20638	BGA2412-DVJ	21. 5.07	M C Hayes *"DVJ" and "869"*	Shobdon	22. 3.08
G-PIKK	Piper PA-28-140 Cherokee	28-22932	G-AVLA	19. 8.88	T Manning tr Coventry Aviators Flying Group		
			N11C, (N9509W)			Coventry	24.11.09E
G-PILE	RotorWay Executive 90	5143		27. 7.93	J B Russell	Magheramorne, County Antrim	5.11.98P
	(Built J B Russell) (RotorWay RI 162)						
G-PILL	Avid Flyer Mk.4	PFA 189-12333		12. 8.97	D R Meston	Old Sarum	8. 8.08P
	(Built D R Meston) (Rotax 912-UL)						
G-PILY	Pilatus B4-PC-11	138	BGA2296-DQM	12.11.07	N Frost	(Buxton)	11. 2.08
			RAFGSA 506				
G-PILZ	Rotorsport UK MT-03	RSUK/MT-03/013		21. 6.07	Specialsalvia Ltd	Kirkbride	12. 7.08P
G-PIMM	UltraMagic M-77 Balloon (Hot Air)	77/263		1. 3.05	G Everett	Sandway, Maidstone	26. 9.09E
G-PIMP	Robinson R44 Raven	12123		5. 2.08	Helitech Charter Ltd	Denham	27. 2.09E
G-PINC	Cameron Z-90 Balloon (Hot Air)	10441		23. 9.03	M Cowling	Dubai, United Arab Emirates	17. 8.09E
G-PING	Gulfstream AA-5A Cheetah	AA5A-0878	G-OCWC	6.12.95	P J Kirkpatrick tr Kirks Flying Group		
			G-WULL, N27153			Standalone Farm, Meppershall	3. 7.09E
G-PINT	Cameron Barrel 60 SS Balloon (Hot Air)	794		4. 1.82	D K Fish *"Charles Wells, BBM&L"*	Manchester	23. 8.09E
	(Wells Brewery Beer Barrel shape)						

G-PINX	Lindstrand Pink Panther SS Balloon (Hot Air)	032		23. 4.93	Magical Adventures Ltd	West Bloomfield, Michigan, US	30. 9.09E
G-PION	Alpi Pioneer 300	xxx		7. 6.05	P F J Burton	Henstridge	27. 7.08P
	(Built F A Cavaciuti - pr.no.PFA 330-14294)						
G-PIPI	Mainair Pegasus Quik	8109		30. 3.05	N R Williams	Long Marston	8. 4.09P
G-PIPP	Piper PA-32R-301T Saratoga II TC	3257454	D-ETEP	18. 4.08	Poores Travel Consultants Ltd	Fairoaks	27. 4.09E
			N1021S				
G-PIPR	Piper PA-18 Super Cub 95	18-826	G-BCDC	11.10.96	D S Sweet	Dunkeswell	19.10.07
	(Frame No.18-832)		4X-ANQ, IDF/AF, 4X-ADE				
G-PIPS	Van's RV-4	PFA 181-11836		3. 8.90	F W Hardiman	Fowle Hall Farm, Laddingford	20. 5.08P
	(Built C J Marsh) (Lycoming O-320-D1A)						
G-PIPY	Cameron Scottish Piper 105 SS Balloon (Hot Air)	3815		30. 1.96	D M Moffat *"Pipy"*	Alveston, Bristol	12. 8.09E
G-PIRO	Cameron TR-70 Balloon (Hot Air)	10789		28. 4.05	A C Booth	Bristol	9. 8.09E
G-PITS	Pitts S-2AE	PFA 009-11001		4. 7.85	P N A and S N Whitehead	Leicester	5. 8.04P
	(Built B Bray) (Lycoming IO-360)						
G-PITZ	Pitts S-2A	100ER	N183ER	2.10.87	J A Coutts	Nut Tree Farm, Redenhall	22. 3.09P
	(Built Razorback Air Services) (Lycoming AEIO-360)						
G-PIXE	Colt 31A Balloon (Hot Air)	4883		11. 7.00	N D Eliot	London SW19	9. 8.09E
G-PIXI	Pegasus Quantum 15-912	7557		27. 8.99	K J Rexter	Cumbernauld	19. 9.08P
G-PIXL	Robinson R44 Clipper II	11221		28. 6.06	Flying TV Ltd	Denham	6. 7.09E
G-PIXX	Robinson R44 Raven II	10263		16. 4.04	Flying TV Ltd	Denham	10. 5.09E
G-PIXY	Super Marine Spitfire Mk.26	PFA 324-14477		13. 2.06	R Collenette	(Boldre, Lymington)	
	(Built R Collenette)						
G-PIZZ	Lindstrand LBL 105A Balloon (Hot Air)	629		27. 7.99	HD Bargain SRL *(Runner Pizza titles)*Florence, Italy		27. 8.06A
G-PJCC	Piper PA-28-161 Warrior II	2816043	OY-ODN	30. 3.04	PJC (Leasing) Ltd	Stapleford	20. 4.09E
			SE-IUI				
G-PJLO	Boeing 767-35EER	26064	B-16605	7. 8.06	Thomson Airways Ltd	Manchester	1. 4.09E
G-PJMT	Neico Lancair 320	PFA 191-12348		8. 5.98	V Hatton and P Gilroy	(Churston Ferrers,	
	(Built P J and M T Holland) (Lycoming IO-320-D) *(Tri-cycle u/c)*					Brixham and Lindridge, Teignmouth)	14. 6.09P
G-PJNZ	Commander Aircraft Commander 114B	14618	N6033Z	7. 9.04	M A Perry	Dunkeswell	21. 9.09E
G-PJSY	Van's RV-6	PFA 181-13107		19. 7.04	P J York	Leicester	7. 4.09P
	(Built P J York) (Lycoming O-320)						
G-PJTM	Reims FR172K Hawk XP	FR17200611	EI-CHJ	13.10.98	P J McNamara t/a Jane Air	Haverfordwest	23.11.09E
			G-BFIF				
G-PKPK	Schweizer 269C *(Schweizer 300)*	S 1454	EI-CAR	3. 8.93	C H Dobson	(South Elkington, Louth)	26. 9.09E
			N69A				
G-PKRG	Cessna 560XL Citation XLS	560-5613	N613XL	22. 9.06	Parkridge (Aviation) Ltd	(Shirley, Solihull)	21. 9.09E
			N5265B				
G-PLAC	Piper PA-31-350 Chieftain	31-8052038	G-OLDA	23.12.98	Y Leysen	Biggin Hill	10. 3.09E
			G-BNDS, N131PP, N3550N				
G-PLAD	Kolb Twinstar Mk.III Xtra	PFA 205-14350		25. 1.05	P J Ladd	Craymarsh Farm, Melksham	16. 5.07P
	(Built P J Ladd) (Jabiru 2200A)						
G-PLAJ	British Aerospace Jetstream Series 3102	738	N2274C	30. 3.00	Jetstream Executive Travel Ltd	Inverness	30.11.09E
			C-GJPH, N331QB, G-31-738				
G-PLAL	Eurocopter EC.135 T2	0407		26. 6.06	Pure Leisure Air Ltd	(Yealand Redmayne, Carnforth)	1.10.09E
G-PLAN	Reims Cessna F150L	F15001066	PH-SPR	11. 8.78	D A Johnson tr G-PLAN Flying Group	Barton	11. 2.09E
G-PLAY	Robin R2112	170	F-ODIT	1. 8.79	A M and Gay F Granger tr Alpha Flying Group	Cranfield	10. 8.08E
G-PLAZ	Rockwell Commander 112A	345	G-RDCI	15. 4.04	I Hunt	Cardiff	16.10.09E
			G-BFWG, ZS-JRX, N1345J				
G-PLEE	Cessna 182Q Skylane II	18266570	N95538	4.12.87	Sunderland Parachute Centre Ltd t/a Peterlee Parachute Centre	Shotton Colliery, Peterlee	3. 6.09E
G-PLIV	Pazmany PL-4A	PFA 017-10155		19.12.78	B P North	RAF Halton	31 7.08P
	(Built B P North) (Continental A65-8)						
G-PLMB	Aérospatiale AS.350B Ecureuil	1207	G-BMMB	26. 3.86	PLM Dollar Group Ltd	Inverness	15. 1.10E
			C-GBEW, (N36033)				
G-PLMH	Eurocopter AS.350B2 Ecureuil	2156	F-WQDJ	9. 1.95	PLM Dollar Group Ltd	Inverness	25. 2.09E
			G-PLMH, HB-XTE, F-WQPK, HB-XTE				
G-PLMI	Aérospatiale SA.365C1 Dauphin 2	5001	F-GFYH	19. 6.95	PLM Dollar Group Ltd	Cumbernauld	8. 7.09E
			F-WZAE				
G-PLOD	Tecnam P92-EM Echo	PFA 318-14152		23. 6.04	G M and J Jupp	Conington	18. 8.09P
	(Built S P Pearson) (Jabiru 2200A)						
G-PLOW	Hughes 269B *(Hughes 300)*	67-0317	G-AVUM	13. 9.83	C Walton Ltd t/a Sulby Aerial Surveys	Sibbertoft	29.11.92
G-PLPC	Schweizer 269C *(Schweizer 300)*	S 1558	G-JMAT	14. 4.97	A R Baker	(Selby)	28. 8.09E
G-PLPL	Agusta A109E Power	11168	G-TMWC	4. 6.07	Iceland Foods Ltd	Fairoaks	27. 4.09E
			VH-BQR, VH-FOX				
G-PLPM	Europa Aviation Europa XS	383		17. 5.00	P L P Mansfield	(Hartley Wintney)	
	(Built P L P Mansfield - pr.no.PFA 247-13287) *(Monowheel u/c)*						
G-PLSA	Aero Designs Pulsar XP	PFA 202-12283	G-NEVS	20.12.04	C A Yardley	Gamston	2 .8.09P
	(Built N Warrener)						
G-PLXI	British Aerospace ATP	2001	G-MATP	26. 8.94	BAE Systems (Operations) Ltd	Millom	2.12.92P
	(Development a/c with PW 127D engines)		(G-OATP)		*(Forward fuselage exhibited at Millom Museum))*		
G-PMAM	Cameron V-65 Balloon (Hot Air)	1155		29. 5.85	P A Meecham *"Tempus Fugit"*	Milton-under-Wychwood, Chipping Norton	4. 1.10E
G-PMHT	SOCATA TBM-850	440		29. 2.08	Ewan Ltd	Gloucestershire	1. 4.09E
	(Officially regd as TBM-700N)						
G-PMNF	Vickers Supermarine 361 Spitfire HF.IX	CBAF.10372	SAAF?? TA805	29. 4.96	P R Monk *(As "TA805/FX-M" in 234 Sqn RAF c/s)*	Biggin Hill	6. 2.09P
G-PNEU	Colt Bibendum 110 SS Balloon (Hot Air)	4223		5. 1.98	A M Holly *(Michelin titles)*	Breadstone, Berkeley	26. 6.02A
	(Built Cameron Balloons Ltd)						
G-PNGC	Schleicher ASK 21	21770	BGA5078-KGJ	24. 1.06	T World tr Portsmouth Naval Gliding Centre *"N3"*	Lee-on-Solent	

Reg	Type	c/n	Prev id	Date	Owner/Operator	Location	Date
G-PNIX	Reims Cessna FRA150L Aerobat	FRA1500205	G-BBEO	2.11.04	D C Bonsall tr Dukeries Aviation	Netherthorpe	2.7.09E
	(Operated Phoenix Flying Club)						
G-POCO	Cessna 152	15283956	N6592B	8.10.04	K M Watts	Shobdon	17.3.09E
			G-POCO, N6592B				
G-POGO	Flight Design CT2K	01-06-02-12		30.7.01	L I Bailey	Norton, Daventry	16.8.08P
	(Assembled Pegasus Aviation - no c/n issued)						
G-POLL	Best Off Sky Ranger 912S(1)	SKR0305313?		26.2.04	D L Pollitt	Tarn Farm, Cockerham	7.8.09P
	(Built D L Pollitt - pr.no.BMAA HB/290)						
G-POLY	Cameron N-77 Balloon (Hot Air)	428		13.7.78	D M Barnes, N.F Biggs, D J Thornley, J L Hinton and M A C Life		
					tr The Empty Wallets Balloon Group *"Polywallets"*	Bristol	27.9.09E
G-POND	Oldfield Baby Lakes	01	N87ED	2.10.90	U Reichert	(Fehrbellin, Germany)	30.7.08P
	(Built G E Davis) (Continental A80)						
G-POOH	Piper J-3C-65 Cub	6932	F-BEGY	17.10.79	P Robinson		
	(Frame No.7015)		NC38324		Upper Harford Farm, Bourton-on-the-Water		9.8.10S
G-POOL	ARV Aviation ARV-1 Super 2	025	G-BNHA	28.8.87	P A Dawson	(St Denis du Pin, France)	9.9.90T
G-POOP	Dyn'Aéro MCR-01 Club	81		5.11.97	E and K Nicholson tr Eurodata Computer Supplies		
	(Built P Bondar - pr.no.PFA 301-13190)					Leicester	15.12.09P
G-POPA	Beech A36 Bonanza	E-2177	N7007F	20.5.92	C J O'Sullivan	North Weald	18.1.10E
			N7204R				
G-POPE	Eiriavion PIK-20E	20257		5.3.80	E P Lambert tr G-POPE Syndicate	Aston Down	25.8.09E
G-POPI	SOCATA TB-10 Tobago	315	G-BKEN	20.4.90	C J Earle tr G-POPI Flying Group	Little Snoring	18.3.09E
			(G-BKEL)				
G-POPP	Colt 105A Balloon (Hot Air)	1776		1.3.91	R Ashford *"Mercier"*	Petworth	31.7.08A
G-POPW	Cessna 182S Skylane	18280204		10.7.98	D L Price	Conington	21.8.09E
G-POPY	Best Off Sky Ranger Swift 912S(1)	SKRxxxx737		6.3.07	C D and L J Church		
	(Built C D and L J Church - pr.no.BMAA HB/519)				Newton Peverill Farm, Sturminster Marshall		25.6.09P
G-PORK	Grumman AA-5B Tiger	AA5B-0625	EI-BMT	28.2.84	D Thomas and C M M Grange tr Tiger Touring Group		
			G-BFHS			Bournemouth	3.2.10E
G-PORT	Bell 206B-3 JetRanger III	2784	N37AH	23.8.89	J Poole	East Wellow, Romsey	19.8.09E
			N39TV, N397TV, N2774R				
G-POSH	Colt 56A Balloon (Hot Air)	822	G-BMPT	10.6.86	B K Rippon	Didcot	9.9.09E
G-POUX	Pou du Ciel-Bifly	JBMD-01	59-ABT	29.6.07	G D Priest	(Redditch)	
	(Built J Bierinx and M Dugourd)						
G-POWB	Beech B300 Super King Air	FL-506	N7106L	8.2.07	Hagondale Ltd *(Operated Titan Airways)*		
						London Stansted	8.2.09E
G-POWC	Boeing 737-33AQC	25402	SE-DPB	3.4.07	Titan Airways Ltd	London Stansted	2.4.09E
			N33AW				
G-POWL	Cessna 182R Skylane II	18267813	N9070G	11.11.82	Powell Print Ltd	Manston	5.6.09E
			D-EOMF, N6265N				
G-POZA	Reality Escapde Jabiru ULP(1)	JAESC 0014		5.2.04	M R Jones	Wing Farm, Longbridge Deverill	
	(Built M R Jones - pr.no.BMAA HB/347) (UL260i)						
G-PPLC	Cessna 560 Citation V	560-0059	F-GKHL	18.2.05	Sterling Helicopters Ltd t/a Sterling Aviation		
			N2687L			Biggin Hill	5.3.10E
G-PPLG	Rotorsport UK MT-03	RSUK/MT-03/010		9.1.07	J E Butler	Chipping Campden	17.2.09P
G-PPLL	Van's RV-7A	PFA 323-14240		28.6.04	P G Leonard	Damyn's Hall, Upminster	20.3.09P
	(Built P G Leonard) (Lycoming O-360)						
G-PPOD	Europa Aviation Europa XS	PFA 247-13745		26.3.08	S Easom	(Kimberley, Notts)	
	(Built S Easom)						
G-PPPP	Denney Kitfox Model 3	771		9.1.91	R Powers	Otherton, Cannock	23.7.09P
	(Built P Eastwood - pr.no.PFA 172-11830)						
G-PPTS	Robinson R44 Clipper	0664		14.10.99	J and L Prowse	(Coleshill, Birmingham)	22.12.09E
G-PRAG	Brügger MB.2 Colibri	PFA 043-10362		29.11.78	D Frankland tr Colibri Flying Group	RAF Mona	26.2.04P
	(Built P Russell) (Volkswagen 1835)						
G-PRAH	Flight Design CT2K	01-06-01-12		31.7.01	G N S Farrant	Manor Farm, Drayton St Leonard	4.5.07P
	(Assembled Pegasus Aviation - no c/n issued)						
G-PRDH	Aérospatiale AS355F2 Ecureuil 2	5367	G-DOOZ	30.4.08	EZ-Int Ltd	Gloucestershire	13.4.09E
			G-BNSX				
G-PREI	Raytheon RB390 Premier 1	RB-60	LX-PRE	13.10.05	Craft Air SA	Farnborough	13.10.09E
			N6160D				
G-PRET	Robinson R44 Astro	0381		8.10.97	J A Wilson		
					Folly Farm, Cop Hill, Slaithwaite, Huddersfield		10.12.08E
G-PREY	Pereira Osprey 2	88		28.9.99	N S Dalrymple	(Dunoon)	8.6.98P
	(Built J J and A J C Zwetsloot - pr.no.PFA 070-10193) (Lycoming IO-320)						
G-PREZ	Robin DR.500-200i Président	0038		26.7.02	C Morris tr Régent Group	Bidford	25.8.09E
	(Officially regd as DR.400-500)						
G-PRII	Hawker Hunter PR.11	41H-670690	N723WT	14.7.99	Deep Cleavage Ltd	Exeter	11.6.09P
			A2616, WT723		*(As "XG194/N" in 111 Sqdn 'Black Arrows' RAF c/s)*		
G-PRIM	Piper PA-38-112 Tomahawk	38-78A0669	N2398A	28.1.87	Braddock Ltd *(Noted derelict 11.07)*	Chilbolton	25.12.01T
G-PRKR	Bombardier CL-600-2B16	5617	C-FEYU	10.1.06	TAG Aviation (UK) Ltd	Farnborough	9.1.10E
	(CL-604 Challenger)		C-GLXB				
G-PRLY	Avtech Jabiru SK	0219	G-BYKY	11.3.02	N C Cowell	City of Derry	22.4.09P
	(Built N J Bond - pr.no.PFA 274-13385)						
G-PRNT	Cameron V-90 Balloon (Hot Air)	2819		23.3.92	Shaun Bradley Project Services Ltd	Stockbridge	30.9.09E
G-PROB	Eurocopter AS.350B2 Ecureuil	2825	G-PROD	25.6.01	Irvine Aviation Ltd	Denham	26.4.09E
G-PROF	Lindstrand LBL 90A Balloon (Hot Air)	740		14.2.01	S J Wardle	Thrapston, Kettering	31.8.08A
	(Professional Financial Services titles)						
G-PROJ	Robinson R44 Raven II	11695		24.4.07	Project Racing Team Ltd	Bournemouth	24.5.09E
G-PROM	Aérospatiale AS.350B Ecureuil	1486	G-MAGY	11.10.96	P Hughes t/a General Cabins and Engineering		
			G-BIYC		*(Noted 1.07)*	Newtownards	23.10.05T
G-PROS	Van's RV-7A	PFA 323-14146		27.4.06	S A Jarrett	(Clevedon)	
	(Built S A Jarret)						

Reg	Type	C/n	Prev id	Date	Owner / Operator	Location	Expiry
G-PROV	Hunting Percival P 84 Jet Provost T 52A (T 4) PAC/W/23905		Singapore AF 352, SAAF (S Yemen) AF 104, G-27-7, XS228 (As "104" in SAAF (S Yemen) AF c/s)	13.12.83	Hollytree Management Ltd tr Provost Group	North Weald	12. 7.09P
G-PROW	Evektor EV-97 Eurostar PFA 315-13968 (Built G M Prowling)			30.10.02	S Hoyle	Baxby Manor, Husthwaite	7. 4.09P
G-PRSI	Pegasus Quantum 15-912	7492		17.12.98	R J Matthews	Damyn's Hall, Upminster	8. 2.09P
G-PRTT	Cameron N-31 Balloon (Hot Air)	1374		6.11.86	J M Albury "Baby Pritt"	Cirencester	13.11.00A
G-PRXI	Vickers Supermarine 365 Spitfire PR.XI 6S/583003		PL983 G-15-109, N74138, PL983	6. 6.83	Propshop Ltd (As "PL983:JV-F" in RAF 4 Sqdn, 2 TAF c/s) (On rebuild 6.06)	Sandown	11. 6.01P
G-PSAX	Lindstrand LBL 77B Balloon (Hot Air)	960		8.10.03	M V Farrant	Loxwood, Billingshurst	1. 7.09E
G-PSFG	Robin R2160i	337	G-COVD G-BYOF	5.12.07	Mardenair Ltd	Goodwood	29. 1.09E
G-PSGC	Piper PA-25-260 Pawnee C	25-5324	G-BDDT CS-AIX, N8820L	29. 4.04	Peterborough and Spalding Gliding Club Ltd	Crowland	23. 1.10E
G-PSHK	Schempp-Hirth SHK-1	40	BGA1392-CAR	18. 3.08	P Gentil "422"	Aston Down	
G-PSHR	Agusta-Bell 206B-3 JetRanger III	8690	G-HSLB F-GUJR, SX-HEN, F-GRCY, I-ELEP	22. 8.05	Sky Select Ltd	Gloucestershire	2. 6.09E
G-PSKY	Best Off Sky Ranger 912S(1) SKR0409524 (Built S Ivell - pr.no.BMAA HB/430)			3. 2.05	G Mills tr Sky Ranger Flying Group G-PSKY	Crosland Moor	5. 9.08P
G-PSNI	Eurocopter EC.135 T2	0337		26. 7.04	Police Service of Northern Ireland	Belfast International	20. 4.11T
G-PSON	Colt Cylinder One SS Balloon (Hot Air) 1780 (Panasonic Battery shape)		PH-SON	14. 3.95	R S and A D Kent tr Balloon Preservation Group (Panasonic Battery titles)	Petworth	9. 9.09E
G-PSRT	Piper PA-28-151 Cherokee Warrior 28-7615225		G-BSGN N9657K	18. 3.99	P A S Dyke	RAF Waddington	4.10.09E
G-PSST	Hawker Hunter F 58A	HABL-003115	Swiss AF J-4104 G-9-317, A2568, XF947	12. 2.97	Heritage Aviation Developments Ltd "Miss Demeanour"	Exeter	30.11.09P
G-PSTR	Beech 200 Super King Air	BB-209	G-FPAS D-IACS, ZP-TTC, ZP-PTC, EB-001 Bolivian AF, N5450M, N545GM	12.12.08	Red Air LLP	Manchester	
G-PSUE	CFM Shadow Series CD	K 139	G-MYAA	1. 4.99	D A Crosbie	(Sudbury)	19. 5.03P
G-PSUK	Thruster T 600N 450	0044-T600N-101		26. 5.04	A J Dunlop	RAF Wyton	29.12.09P
G-PTAG	Europa Aviation Europa 337 (Built R C Harrison - pr.no.PFA 247-13121) (Rotax 914) (Tri-gear u/c)			14.12.98	R C Harrison	Wickenby	8. 4.09P
G-PTAR	Best Off Sky Ranger 912S(1) SKRxxxx687 (Built A C Aiken - pr.no.BMAA HB/509)			6. 7.06	T W Lorimer	Strathaven	9. 2.09P
G-PTDP	Bücker Bü.133C Jungmeister	1018	G-AEZX (2) N5A, PP-TDP	31. 8.05	T J Reeve	North Lopham, Diss	27. 7.00P
G-PTRE	SOCATA TB-20 Trinidad	762	G-BNKU	14. 6.88	Trantshore Ltd	Rochester	14. 6.09E
G-PTRI	Cessna 182T Skylane	18282059	N61910	28.11.08	Patriot Aviation Ltd	Cranfield	
G-PTTS	Pitts S-2A 2179 (Built Aerotek Inc) (Lycoming AEIO-360)		N555JR N32TP, N31450	9. 5.03	N D Voce	Leicester	19. 3.09E
G-PTWO	Pilatus P 2-05	600-30	Swiss AF U-110 Swiss AF A-110	26. 2.81	R G Meredith (As "U-110" in Swiss AF c/s)	Rochester	13. 5.09P
G-PUDL	Piper PA-18-150 Super Cub	18-7292	SE-CSE	24. 2.98	C M Edwards	North Weald	16. 6.07
G-PUDS	Europa Aviation Europa 253 (Built I Milner - pr.no.PFA 247-12999) (Rotax 914-UL) (Tri-gear u/c)			9.10.97	M J Riley	Wycombe Air Park	2. 7.09P
G-PUFF	Thunder Ax7-77 Bolt Balloon (Hot Air)	165		17.11.78	C A Gould tr Intervarsity Balloon Club "Puffin II"	Ipswich	26. 7.09E
G-PUGS	Cessna 182H Skylane	18256480	SE-ESM N8380S	15. 5.00	N C and M F Shaw	Great Massingham	23. 6.09E
G-PUKA	Avtech Jabiru J400 0130 (Built D P Harris - pr.no.PFA 325-14120)			11. 9.03	D P Harris	Franklyn's Field, Chewton Mendip	19. 1.10P
G-PUMA	Aérospatiale AS.332L Super Puma	2038	F-WMHB	31. 1.83	CHC Scotia Ltd	Aberdeen	12. 4.09E
G-PUMB	Aérospatiale AS.332L Super Puma	2075		31. 1.83	CHC Scotia Ltd	Aberdeen	15. 5.09E
G-PUME	Aérospatiale AS.332L Super Puma	2091		3. 8.83	CHC Scotia Ltd	Aberdeen	6. 9.09E
G-PUMN	Eurocopter AS.332L2 Super Puma	2484	LN-OHF	16. 7.99	CHC Scotia Ltd	Aberdeen	26. 7.09E
G-PUMO	Eurocopter AS.332L2 Super Puma	2467		30. 9.98	CHC Scotia Ltd	Aberdeen	24.10.09E
G-PUMS	Eurocopter AS.332L2 Super Puma	2504		18. 8.00	CHC Scotia Ltd	Aberdeen	30. 1.10E
G-PUNK	Thunder AX8-105 Balloon (Hot Air)	1719		28. 3.90	S C Kinsey	Amersham	15. 5.99T
G-PUPP	Beagle B 121 Pup Series 2	B121-174	G-BASD (SE-FOG), G-BASD	23.11.93	A D Wood and B R Hunter	Sturgate	27. 5.09E
G-PUPY	Europa Aviation Europa XS 499 (Built P G Johnson - pr.no.PFA 247-13694) (Monowheel u/c)			10. 9.02	V F Flett	(Lhanbryde, Elgin)	
G-PURL	Piper PA-32R-301 Saratoga II HP 3213078		N620PL N92434	30.11.05	I Blamire	Lee-on-Solent	16.12.09E
G-PURR	Gulfstream AA-5A Cheetah	AA5A-0794	G-BJDN N26893	22. 2.82	N Bass t/a Nabco Retail Display	Elstree	1. 9.09E
G-PURS	RotorWay Executive 3827 (Built J E Houseman) (RotorWay RW 152)			19. 1.90	J E Houseman Headlinks Farm, Clitheroe (Noted 2007)		5. 6.96P
G-PUSH	Rutan LongEz PFA 074A-10740 (Built E G Peterson)			11. 7.83	E G Peterson	(Woodthorpe, Nottingham)	
G-PUSI	Cessna T303 Crusader	T30300273	N3479V	26. 7.88	A J Beck t/a Crusader Craft	Henstridge	9. 7.09E
G-PUSS	Cameron N-77 Balloon (Hot Air)	1577		6.10.87	L D Thurgar "Dick Whittington"	Bristol	18. 6.01A
G-PUSY	TLAC RL5A LW Sherwood Ranger xxxx (Built B J Chester-Master - pr.no.PFA 237-12964) (Rotax 582)		G-MZNF	25. 6.99	S C Briggs	(Santa Luce, Pisa, Italy)	13. 7.06P
G-PUTT	Cameron Golfball 76 SS Balloon (Hot Air) 2060		LX-KIK	8. 8.95	D P Hopkins t/a Lakeside Lodge Golf Centre	Pidley, Huntingdon	
G-PVBF	Lindstrand LBL 260S Balloon (Hot Air)	504		7. 4.98	Virgin Balloon Flights Ltd	London SE16	15. 2.07E
G-PVCV	Robin DR.400-140 Major	919	F-BVCV	19.10.06	Leonie M Poor and P N Bevan	(Perth)	1.12.09E
G-PVET	de Havilland DHC-1 Chipmunk 22	C1/0017	WB565	23. 5.97	Connect Properties Ltd (As "WB565:X" in AAC c/s)	Kemble	7. 2.010S
G-PVIP	Cessna 421C Golden Eagle	421C0118	G-RLMC PH-SBI, D-IMAZ, I-CCNN, N3849C	30. 6.04	Passion 4 Health International Ltd	(Chertsey)	22. 1.07E
G-PVML	Robin DR.400-140B Major	972	F-BVML	28. 2.06	Weald Air Services Ltd	Headcorn	7. 8.09E

G-PVPC	Pilatus PC-12/45	632	HB-FPV	27. 6.05	GE Capital Corporation (Leasing) Ltd		
						Bournemouth	7. 7.09E
G-PVSS	P&M Aviation Quik GT450	8302		8. 8.07	P V Stevens	Field Farm, Oakley	7. 8.09P
	(Permit suspended 4.10.08)						
G-PVST	Thruster T 600N 450 Sprint	0122-T600N-074		29.10.02	R J Davey	Anwick	15. 5.09P
G-PWBE	de Havilland DH.82A Tiger Moth	LES.1	VH-KRW	23. 7.99	P W Beales	Swansea	8. 1.07P
	(Built Lawrence Engineering and Sales Proprietary Ltd., Camden, NSW, Australia ex-RAAF spares)						
G-PWIT	Bell 206L-1 LongRanger	45193	D-HHSW	18. 5.00	A R King	Gloucestershire	19. 7.09E
			G-DWMI, N18092				
G-PWNS	Cessna 525 CitationJet	525-0153	VP-CNF	30. 3.07	Hangar 8 Ltd	Oxford	15. 4.09E
			N551Q, N551G, N5090V				
G-PWUL	Van's RV-6	PFA 181-12773		3. 7.02	D Stephens and S King	Damyn's Hall, Upminster	31. 7.08P
	(Built P C Woolley) (Superior XP-10)						
G-PXII	Pitts S-12	170	N6212	4. 3.08	Pitts 12 Ltd	Wycombe Air Park	20. 4.09P
	(Built R Briegleband and H Hutchinson) (Ivchenko Vedeneyev M-14P)						
G-PYNE	Thruster T 600N 450	0072-T600N-067		27. 8.02	R Dereham	Shipmeadow, Beccles	2. 4.09P
G-PYPA	Robinson R44 Raven II	11668		30. 3.07	E P Arditti	Alderney	3. 5.09E
G-PYPE	Van's RV-7	PFA 323-14398		12. 9.06	R and L Pyper	Newtownards	16. 4.09P
	(Built R Pyper) (Superior XP-10)						
G-PYRO	Cameron N-65 Balloon (Hot Air)	567		8. 1.80	A C Booth *"Pyromania"*	Bristol	22. 6.09E
G-PZAZ	Piper PA-31-350 Navajo Chieftain		G-VTAX	18. 1.95	Air Medical Fleet Ltd	Oxford	24. 5.09E
		31-7405214	(G-UTAX), N54266				
G-PZIZ	Piper PA-31-350 Navajo Chieftain	31-7405429	G-CAFZ	30.10.98	Air Medical Fleet Ltd	Oxford	24. 4.09E
			G-BPPT, N54297, N9655N				

G-RAAA - G-RZZZ

G-RABA	Reims FR172H Rocket	FR17200292	D-ECSE	14.12.04	Air Ads Ltd	Blackpool	25. 2.09E
G-RABS	Alpi Pioneer 300	xxx		31. 8.06	J Mullen	(Lanark)	8.10.09P
	(Built J Mullen - pr.no.PFA 330-14563)						
G-RACI	Beech C90 King Air	LJ-819	G-SHAM	10. 4.03	E Flight SRL	(Milan, Italy)	1. 8.08E
			N2063A				
G-RACO	Piper PA-28R-200 Cherokee Arrow II		N1498X	12. 9.91	Graco Group Ltd	Barton	23. 7.09E
		28R-7535300					
G-RACR	UltraMagic M-65C Balloon (Hot Air)	65/143		8. 4.05	R A Vale	Kidderminster	21. 4.09E
G-RACY	Cessna 182S Skylane	18280588	N7273Y	19.10.99	N J and P.D Fuller	Cambridge	17. 1.09E
G-RADA	Soko P-2 Kraguj	024	Yugoslav AF	25. 9.96	M G Roberts tr Flight Consultancy Services		
			30140			Biggin Hill	5. 9.05P
G-RADI	Piper PA-28-181 Archer II	28-8690002	N2582X	6. 5.98	M Ruter	White Waltham	5. 7.09E
			N9608N				
G-RADR	Douglas AD-4NA Skyraider	7722	G-RAID	30.10.03	T J Manna (As "26922:AK 402" of USN VA-176 Sqdn)		
		(SFERMA c/n 42)	F-AZED, TR-K.., French AF 42, Bu.126922	(USS Intrepid c/s) North Weald				31. 5.09P
G-RAEF	Schempp-Hirth SHK-1	39	BGA1544-CGZ	20. 6.08	R A Earnshaw-Fretwell	RAF Keevil	
G-RAEM	Rutan LongEz	557		15. 3.82	G F H Singleton tr Easy Group	(Matlock)	18. 6.93P
	(Built G F H Singleton - pr.no.PFA 074A-10638) (Lycoming O-235)						
G-RAES	Boeing 777-236	27491	(G-ZZZN)	10. 6.97	British Airways PLC	London Heathrow	9. 6.09E
G-RAFA	Grob G115A	8081	D-EGVV	2. 3.89	RAF College Flying Club Ltd	RAF Cranwell	3. 7.09E
G-RAFB	Grob G115A	8079	D-EGVV	2. 3.89	RAF College Flying Club Ltd	RAF Cranwell	25.11.09E
G-RAFC	Robin R2112 Alpha	192		19. 5.80	J E Churchill tr RAF Charlie Group	Conington	5. 8.09E
G-RAFD	Beech B200GT Super King Air	BY-32	N32EU	23. 6.08	Serco Ltd	RAF Cranwell	25. 6.09E
G-RAFE	Thunder Ax7-77 Bolt Balloon (Hot Air)	176		18.12.78	L P Hooper tr Giraffe Balloon Syndicate *"Giraffe"*		
						Bristol	9. 7.09E
G-RAFG	Slingsby T 67C Firefly	2076		2.11.89	Arrow Flying Ltd	Popham	3. 6.09E
G-RAFH	Thruster T 600N 450	0032-T600N-063		10. 4.02	M E Howard tr RAF Microlight Flying Association (FH)		
						RAF Halton	20. 4.08P
G-RAFI	Hunting Percival P 84 Jet Provost T 4	8458M	18.12.92	R J Everett (As "XP672:03" in RAF c/s)			
		PAC/W/17641	XP672			(Spoughton, Ipswich)	11. 3.00P
G-RAFO	Beech B200 Super King Air	BB-1836	N60476	11. 3.04	Serco Ltd *(Allocated "ZK455")*	RAF Cranwell	18. 3.09E
G-RAFP	Beech B200 Super King Air	BB-1837	N61037	11. 3.04	Serco Ltd *(Allocated "ZK456")*	RAF Cranwell	18. 3.09E
G-RAFR	Best Off Sky Ranger J2.2(1)	SKR0404487		8.10.04	M E Howard tr RAF Microlight Flying Association (FR)		
	(Built P Waters - pr.no.BMAA HB/410)					RAF Halton	4. 9.09P
G-RAFS	Thruster T 600N 450	0041-T600N-097		5. 4.04	M E Howard tr RAF Microlight Flying Association (FS)		
						RAF Halton	19. 4.09P
G-RAFT	Rutan LongEz	PFA 074A-10734		9. 8.82	B Wronski *"A Craft of Graft"*	Gloucestershire	16. 7.07P
	(Built D G Foreman) (Continental O-240-A)						
G-RAFV	Avid Speed Wing	PFA 189-11738	G-MOTT	28. 7.04	A F Vizoso	RAF Halton	30. 4.09P
	(Built M D Ott)						
G-RAFW	Mooney M 20E Super 21	805	G-ATHW	14.11.84	Vinola (Knitwear) Manufacturing Co Ltd	Leicester	15. 9.09E
			N5881Q				
G-RAFX	Beech B200GT Super King Air	BY-36	N3196N	12. 5.08	Serco Ltd	RAF Cranwell	15. 5.09E
G-RAFY	Best Off Sky Ranger Swift 912S(1)			7. 3.07	M E Howard tr RAF Microlight Flying Association		
		SKRxxxx757				RAF Halton	23 .8.09P
	(Built J Kumela and P Waters - pr no.BMAA HB/523, listed as M Howard)						
G-RAFZ	Rotary Air Force RAF 2000 GTX-SE			7. 5.02	John Pavitt (Engineers) Ltd	(Torrington)	
	(Built J W Pavitt)	PFA G/13-1295					
G-RAGE	Wilson Cassutt IIIM	PFA 034-10241	G-BEUN	17.10.06	R S Grace	Duxford	7. 7.97P
	(Built M S Crossley) (Continental C90)						
G-RAGS	Pietenpol AirCamper	PFA 047-11551		8. 6.94	R F Billington	(Kenilworth)	
	(Built R F Billington)						
G-RAGT	Piper PA-32-301FT 6x	3232038	N3116F	3. 6.05	Oxhill Aviation	Wellesbourne Mountford	5. 6.09E
G-RAIG	Scottish Aviation Bulldog Series 100/101		SE-LLI	12. 9.03	Power Aerobatics Ltd	Kemble	12. 7 10T
		BH100/146	Fv61037, G-AZMR				
G-RAIL	Colt 105A Balloon (Hot Air)	1434		31. 3.89	Ballooning World Ltd *"Railfreight"*	London NW1	4. 1.04A
G-RAIR	Schleicher ASH 25	25095	BGA3623-FYD	31.10.07	P T Reading and Viscount Cobham	Lasham	30. 1.08

G-RAIX	CCF Harvard 4 (T-6J-CCF Texan)	CCF4...	G-BIWX	16. 2.98	M R Paul (As "KF584:RAI-X" in RAF c/s)		
	(Possibly c/n CCF4-409 ex 51-17227)		MM53-846, RM-22/51-17			Dunsfold	25. 9.08P
G-RAJA	Raj Hamsa X'Air 582(2)	456		13. 9.99	M D Gregory	Belle Vue Farm, Yarnscombe	14. 4.09P
	(Built S R Roberts - pr.no.BMAA HB/118)						
G-RALA	Robinson R44 Clipper II	10788		12. 7.05	Rala Aviation Ltd	Cambridge	11. 8.09E
G-RALD	Robinson R22HP	0218	G-CHIL	25. 1.96	Heli Air Ltd		
			(G-BMXI), N9074K		Wellesbourne Mountford/Wycombe Air Park		15. 1.10E
G-RAMA	Cameron C-70 Balloon (Hot Air)	10939		23.11.06	Poppies (UK) Ltd	Wootton Fitzpaine, Bridport	25. 8.09E
G-RAMI	Bell 206B-3 JetRanger III	2955	N1080N	18.10.90	M D Thorpe t/a Yorkshire Helicopters		
						Coney Park, Leeds	4.10.07E
G-RAMP	Piper J-3C-65 Cub	6658	N35941	5. 7.90	J A Holman and T A Hinton	Doynton	31. 8.01P
			NC35941				
G-RAMS	Piper PA-32R-301 Saratoga II SP		N8271Z	17.10.80	Mike Sierra LLP	Gamston	28. 7.09E
		32R-8013134					
G-RAMY	Bell 206B-2 JetRanger II	1401	N59554	22. 9.95	Lincair Ltd	Humberside	10. 2.09E
G-RANS	Rans S-10 Sakota	0489.049		17. 8.89	J D Weller	(Sutton Coldfield)	23. 6.00P
	(Built J D Weller - pr.no.PFA 194-11537) (Rotax 532)						
G-RAPH	Cameron O-77 Balloon (Hot Air)	1673		21. 3.88	P A Sweatman "Walsall Litho"	Coventry	13. 7.09E
G-RAPI	Lindstrand LBL 105A Balloon (Hot Air)	998		16. 7.04	M White t/a Rapido Balloons (Rapido titles)		
						Cirencester	16. 8.09E
G-RARB	Cessna 172N Skyhawk II	17272334	G-BOII	4. 6.96	Prior Group Holdings Ltd	North Weald	16. 7.09E
			N4702D				
G-RASA	Diamond DA.42 Twin Star	42.144	OE-VPY	30. 6.06	C D Hill	North Weald	13. 8.09E
G-RASC	Evans VP-2	V2-1178		14.12.78	R F Powell	(Llanrwst)	14.12.06P
	(Built R A Codling - pr.no.PFA 063-10422) (Continental A65)						
G-RASH	Grob G109B	6217	OH-686	24. 6.04	C Kaminski tr G-RASH Syndicate	Eaglescott	2. 9.09E
G-RATA	Robinson R22 Beta	3875		24. 6.05	T Puhl	Wiehl, Germany	14. 7.09E
G-RATC	Van's RV-4	PFA 181-13996		30. 5.06	A F Ratcliffe	(Whaston, Richmond)	
	(Built A F Ratcliffe)						
G-RATE	Gulfstream AA-5A Cheetah	AA5A-0781	G-BIFF	11. 6.84	A M Chester tr G-RATE Flying Group	Cranfield	14.12.09E
			(G-BIBR), N26879				
G-RATH	Rotorway Executive 162F	6886		12.10.04	M S Cole	Street Farm, Takeley	5. 1.10P
	(Built M S Cole)						
G-RATI	Reims Cessna F172M Skyhawk II	F17201311	G-PATI	22.12.05	D Daniel	Cranfield	7. 7.09E
			G-WACZ, G-BCUK				
G-RATV	Piper PA-28RT-201T Turbo Arrow IV		G-WILS	20. 6.05	Tango Victor Ltd	Fairoaks	22. 5.09E
		28R-8431005	PH-DPD, N4330W				
G-RATZ	Europa Aviation Europa	037		16. 6.95	W Goldsmith	Morgansfield, Fishburn	23. 8.08P
	(Built R Muller - pr.no.PFA 247-12582) (Monowheel u/c)						
G-RAVE	Mainair Mercury 582/Southdown Raven X		G-MNZV	22.12.98	M J Robbins	Rochester	20. 3.04P
	538-0487 & SN2232/0219		(Sailwing is ex G-MNCV [SN2000/0219])				
G-RAVN	Robinson R44 Raven	1022		23. 3.01	A and L Smith t/a Brambledown Aircraft Hire		
						(Bradley Green, Redditch)	23. 4.09E
G-RAWS	RotorWay Executive 162F	6492/6978		14.11.00	Raw Sports Ltd	Street Farm, Takeley	16. 6.09P
	(Built B W Grindle)						
G-RAYA	Denney Kitfox Model 4	PFA 172A-12403		14.12.92	R M Cornwell	Redlands, Swindon	20. 3.09P
	(Built A K Ray)						
G-RAYB	P&M Aviation Quik GT450	8237		19. 2.07	R Blatchford	Dunkeswell	18. 2.08P
G-RAYH	Zenair CH.701UL STOL	PFA 187-13583		7. 7.03	R Horner	Baxby Manor, Husthwaite	16.11.09P
	(Built R Horner) (Jabiru 2200A)						
G-RAYO	Lindstrand LBL 90A Balloon (Hot Air)	949		13.10.03	R Owen	Standish, Wigan	28. 4.09E
G-RAYS	Zenair CH.250 Zenith	RED.001		26.10.78	M J Malbon	Derby	30. 3.09P
	(Built R E Delves - originally pr.no.PFA 024-10460 - completed MJ Malbon as pr.no.PFA 113-10460) (Lycoming O-320)						
G-RAYY	Cirrus SR22	2921	N924SR	18. 4.08	Cumulus Aircraft Rentals Ltd	(Spain)	21.12.09E
G-RAYZ	Tecnam P2002-EA Sierra	190		5. 2.07	R Wells	Morgansfield, Fishburn	4. 4.09P
	(Built R Wells, pr. no PFA 333-14567)						
G-RAZY	Piper PA-28-181 Archer II	28-8090102	G-REXS	11. 2.04	T H Pemberton	Hawarden	19. 6.09E
			N8093Y				
G-RAZZ	Maule MX-7-180 Super Rocket	11050C	N266MM	10.11.04	C D Baird	(Lower Froyle, Alton)	24.11.07E
			D-EOLW, N6118L				
G-RBBB	Europa Aviation Europa	073		6. 5.94	T J Hartwell	Sackville Lodge, Riseley	12. 8.05P
	(Built W M Goodman and I H McCleod - pr.no.PFA 247-12664) (Rotax 912 UL) (Monowheel u/c)						
G-RBCI	Fairey Britten-Norman BN-2A Mk.III-2 Trislander	G-BDWV	16. 3.01	Aurigny Air Services Ltd	Guernsey	6. 7.09E
		1035	8P-ASF, G-BDWV				
G-RBCT	Schempp-Hirth Ventus 2cT	03/10	BGA4505-JGP	27. 7.07	M J Weston and J D Huband	Aston Down	2. 4.08
			N200EE, D-KHIA				
G-RBJW	Europa Aviation Europa XS	473		15. 7.04	J Worthington and R J Bull		
	(Built J Worthington and R J Bull - pr.no.PFA 247-13600)					(Kinloss, Foress and Nairn)	
G-RBMS	Cirrus SR22	2781	N837SR	19.12.07	D J Bowie	Sleap	3. 1.09P
G-RBMV	Cameron O-31 Balloon (Hot Air)	4658		27. 7.99	P D Griffiths	Totton, Southanpton	1. 7.09E
G-RBOW	Thunder Ax7-65 Balloon (Hot Air)	1439		24. 4.89	R S Mcdonald "Rain-Beau-Lune"		
						Burcott, Leighton Buzzard	2. 8.09E
G-RBSN	Comco Ikarus C42 FB80	0407-6610		23. 8.04	P B and M Robinson	Sutton Meadows	25. 8.08P
	(Built Fly Buy Ultralights Ltd)						
G-RCED	Rockwell Commander 114	14241	VR-CED	19. 6.92	D J and D Pitman	Bournemouth	16. 5.09E
			N4917W				
G-RCHY	Evektor EV-97 Eurostar	PFA 315-14187		30. 3.04	N McKenzie	Kirkbride	6. 7.09E
	(Built N McKenzie)						
G-RCKT	Harmon Rocket II	PFA 314-13536		10.10.03	K E Armstrong	Armshold Farm, Kington	24. 9.08P
	(Built K E Armstrong: type is a modified Van's RV-4 taildragger) (Lycoming O-540)						
G-RCMC	Murphy Renegade 912	485		1. 2.93	R C M Collisson	Bicester	. 6.05P
	(Built B D Godden - pr.no.PFA 188-12483)					(Noted 1.07)	
G-RCMF	Cameron V-77 Balloon (Hot Air)	1618		23.11.87	J M Percival Bourton-on-the-Wolds, Loughborough		2.10.09E
G-RCML	Sky 77-24 Balloon (Hot Air)	148		9. 3.99	RCM SARL	Stuppicht, Luxembourg	29. 5.07

G-RCNB	Eurocopter EC.120B Colibri	1333	F-WQPX	20. 3.03	D N Brown t/a Furbs Pension Fund	Deenethorpe	28. 4.09E
G-RCOM	Bell 206L-3 LongRanger III	51599	TC-HZT	24.10.02	3GRComm Ltd	Gloucestershire	5. 3.09E
G-RCRC	P&M Pegasus Quik	8252		9. 3.07	R M Brown	Perth	22. 3.09P
G-RCST	Avtech Jabiru J430	0xxx		18. 4.06	G R Cotterell	White House Farm, Southery	27. 6.08P
	(Built G R Cotterell - pr.no.PFA 336-14513)						
G-RCWK	Cessna 182T Skylane	18281982	N11603	2.11.07	R C W King	Gloucestershire	4.11.09E
G-RDCO	Avtech Jabiru J400	0xxx		15. 4.03	RDCO (International) LLP	Sleap	20.12.05P
	(Built J M Record - pr.no.PFA 325-14052)						
G-RDDT	Schempp-Hirth Duo Discus T	116/448	BGA5150-KKA	5. 4.06	R Witter *"DDT"*	Lleweni Parc	12. 4.08
G-RDEL	Robinson R44 Raven	1071		5. 6.01	Isaonas SL	(Palma de Mallorca, Spain)	27. 6.09E
G-RDHS	Europa Aviation Europa XS	549		31. 5.02	R D H Spencer	Earls Colne	24. 9.09P
	(Built R D H Spencer - pr.no.PFA 247-13887) (Tri-gear u/c)						
G-RDNS	Rans S-6-S Super Six Coyote	xxxx		2.11.04	P G Cowling and J S Crofts	Wombleton	24. 5.09P
	(Built G J McDill - pr.no.PFA 204-14307) (Tailwheel u/c)						
G-READ	Colt 77A Balloon (Hot Air)	1158	EI-BYI, G-READ	16.11.87	C A Gould tr Intervarsity Balloon Club *(Also carries EI-BYI)* *"Sunday Express / Daily Express"*	Ipswich	23. 7.09E
G-REAL	Eurocopter AS.350B2 Ecureuil	3032	G-DRHL	26. 8.04	Imagine Leisure Ltd	Dunsfold	29. 4.09E
G-REAP	Pitts S-1S	PFA 009-11557		7. 2.90	R Dixon *"The Grim Reaper"*	Netherthorpe	10.11.09P
	(Built S D Howes) (Lycoming O-360)						
G-REAR (2)	Lindstrand LBL 69X Balloon (Hot Air)	977		12. 2.04	A M Holly *(Sloggi titles)*	Breadstone, Berkeley	28. 5.09E
	(Second envelope with c/n 977)						
G-REAS	Van's RV-6A	PFA 181-12188		16. 8.94	T J Smith	Sleap	17. 8.09P
	(Built D W Reast) (Lycoming O-320)						
G-REBB	Murphy Rebel	376R	N13BN	23. 8.05	M Stow	(Blaydon-on-Tyne)	
	(Built W W Newkirk)						
G-RECE	Cameron C-80 Balloon (Hot Air)	10435		16. 6.03	M Kotsageridis	Thessaloniki, Greece	16. 6.04A
G-RECK	Piper PA-28-140 Cherokee B	28-25656	G-AXJW, N11C	17. 3.88	R J Grantham	Clutton Hill Farm, Clutton	27.11.09E
G-RECO	Jurca MJ.5-L2 Sirocco	96	F-PYYD, F-WYYD	30. 9.91	J D Tseliki	(Douglas, Isle of Man)	
	(Built J Y Guillou)				(Stored 11.07)		
G-RECS	Piper PA-38-112 Tomahawk II	38-81A0118	N5824H, D-EFFX, N23138	23. 4.02	S H and C L Maynard	(Middlesbrough)	2. 5.05T
G-REDB	Cessna 310Q	310Q0811	G-BBIC, N69600	17. 6.93	Red Baron Haulage Ltd	Full Sutton	11. 9.09E
G-REDC	Pegasus Quantum 15-912	7572		30. 9.99	R F Richardson	Winspurs Farm, Northrepps	10. 8.09P
G-REDD	Cessna 310R II	310R1833	G-BMGT, ZS-KSY, (N2738X)	2.10.96	G Wightman	Blackpool	25. 3.05
					(Noted 10.07)		
G-REDI	Robinson R44 Clipper	0817		2. 8.00	Redeye.com Ltd	Sheffield City	15. 9.09E
G-REDJ	Eurocopter AS.332L2 Super Puma II	2608	F-WWOJ	19. 5.04	International Aviation Leasing Ltd	Aberdeen	20. 5.09E
					(Operated Bond Offshore Helicopters Ltd)		
G-REDK	Eurocopter AS.332L2 Super Puma II	2610	F-WWOM	2. 6.04	International Aviation Leasing Ltd	Aberdeen	6. 6.09E
					(Operated Bond Offshore Helicopters Ltd)		
G-REDL	Eurocopter AS.332L2 Super Puma II	2612	F-WWOD	30. 6.04	International Aviation Leasing Ltd	Aberdeen	5. 7.09E
					(Operated Bond Offshore Helicopters Ltd)		
G-REDM	Eurocopter AS.332L2 Super Puma II	2614	F-WWOF	26. 7.04	International Aviation Leasing Ltd	Aberdeen	29.7.09E
					(Operated Bond Offshore Helicopters Ltd)		
G-REDN	Eurocopter AS.332L2 Super Puma II	2616	F-WQDH	20. 8.04	International Aviation Leasing Ltd	Aberdeen	22. 8.09E
					(Operated Bond Offshore Helicopters Ltd)		
G-REDO	Eurocopter AS.332L2 Super Puma II	2622	F-WWOH	12. 9.05	International Aviation Leasing Ltd	Sumburgh	15. 9.09E
					(Operated Bond Offshore Helicopters Ltd, Offshore SAR role)		
G-REDP	Eurocopter AS.332L2 Super Puma II	2634	F-WWOB	17.11.05	International Aviation Leasing Ltd	Sumburgh	14.11.09E
					(Operated Bond Offshore Helicopters Ltd, Offshore SAR role)		
G-REDR	Eurocopter EC.225LP Super Puma II	2699		27. 6.08	International Aviation Leasing Ltd	Aberdeen	23. 6.09E
					(Operated Bond Offshore Helicopters Ltd)		
G-REDS	Cessna 560XL Citation Excel	560-5167	N250SM, N5188N	10.10.02	Bridge Aviation Ltd	Hawarden	9.10.09E
G-REDT	Eurocopter EC.225LP Super Puma II	2701		4. 9.08	International Aviation Leasing Ltd	Aberdeen	3. 9.09E
					(Operated Bond Offshore Helicopters Ltd)		
G-REDU	Eurocopter EC.225LP Super Puma	2690		23. 5.08	Bond Offshore Helicopters Ltd	Aberdeen	22. 5.09E
G-REDX	Experimental Aviation Berkut	002		27. 1.95	G V Waters	(Attleborough)	14. 6.09P
	(Built G V Waters - pr.no.PFA 252-12481) (Lycoming O-360)						
G-REDY	Robinson R22 Beta II	3402	G-CBXO, N71909	28. 7.03	Fly Executive Ltd	Cranfield	1. 4.09E
G-REDZ	Thruster T 600N 450 Sprint	0037-T600N-091		5. 8.03	M R Jones	Wing Farm, Longbridge Deverill	4. 8.07P
	(While practising simulated engine-failure on take-off Redlands, Swindon 15. 7.07 failed to respond to corrective actions and impacted nose-down, insurance wreck bought by Galaxy Microlights: new owner 11.07)						
G-REEC	Sequoia F 8L Falco	654	LN-LCA	2. 7.96	J D Tseliki	Kittyhawk Farm, Deanland	22. 7.09P
	(Built B Eriksen) (Lycoming IO-320)						
G-REED	Mainair Blade 912S	1282-0501-7-W1077		11. 6.01	I C Macbeth	Arclid Green, Sandbach	12. 4.08P
G-REEF	Mainair Blade 912S	1285-0501-7-W1080		15. 6.01	G Mowll	Caernarfon	2. 7.09P
G-REEK	Grumman AA-5A Cheetah	AA5A-0429	N7129L	12. 9.77	J and A Pearson	(Dundee)	10.12.01
G-REEM	Aérospatiale AS.355F1 Ecureuil 2	5175	G-EMAN, G-WEKR, G-CHLA, N818RL, C-FLXH, N818RL, N818R, N5798U	9. 3.98	Heliking Ltd	Denham	24. 6.09E
G-REER	Centrair 101A Pégase	101A033	BGA3593-FWX, F-CFRZ	15.10.07	P M Greer	Nympsfield	11. 4.08
G-REES	SAN Jodel D 140C Mousquetaire III	156	F-BMFR	23. 4.80	C C Rea tr G-REES Flying Group	Sheepcote Farm, Stourbridge	5. 9.10P
G-REET	Grumman American AA-5B Tiger	AA5B-0706	G-BFPB	2. 9.05	Tiger AA-5B Ltd	(Leamington Spa)	1.11.09E
G-REGC	Zenair CH.601XL Zodiac	LAA 162B-14784		3. 9.08	G P Couttie *(wings only, under construction)*	Perth	
	(Built GP Couttie)						
G-REGE	Robinson R44 Raven	1517		20.10.05	Rege Aviation LLP	(Hull)	3.11.09E
G-REGS	Thunder Ax7-77 Balloon (Hot Air)	1812		4. 7.90	D R Rawlings	Haverhill	15. 4.09E
G-REJP	Europa Aviation Europa XS	xxxx		31. 8.06	A Milner	(Hauxton, Cambridge)	19 .8.09P
	(Built A Milner - pr.no.PFA 247-14086)						

Reg	Type	C/n	Prev ID	Date	Owner/Operator	Location	Expiry
G-REKO	Solar Wings Pegasus Quasar IITC (Trike c/n SW-TQC-0073)	SW-WQT-0467	G-MWWA	14.11.01	M Sims	Haverfordwest	12. 7.07P
G-RELL	Druine D 62B Condor (Built Rollason Aircraft and Engines)	RAE 619	G-OPJH G-AVDW	14. 8.07	P S Grellier	New Barn Farm, Barton Ashes, Crawley	29. 9.09P
G-REMH	Bell 206B-3 JetRanger III	4626	N65560 C-FMQK, (N65560)	16. 9.08	Nottinghamshire Helicopters (2008) Ltd	Costock	6.11.09E
G-RENO	SOCATA TB-10 Tobago	249		10.12.81	Lamond Ltd	Coventry	24. 5.09E
G-REPH	Pegasus Quantum 15-912	7785		6. 2.01	R S Partridge-Hicks	(Bury St Edmunds)	3. 5.03P
G-RESC	Eurocopter MBB BK-117C-1C	7504	D-HELW I-BKBS, D-HOTZ, X-..., D-HOTZ, D-HECA, D-HMBF	6. 7.07	Sterling Helicopters Ltd	RAF Wyton	2. 8.09E
G-RESG	Dyn'Aéro MCR-01 Club (Built R E S Greenwood - pr.no.PFA 301A-13994)	237		10. 4.03	R E S Greenwood	Newmarket	22.12.09P
G-REST	Beech P35 Bonanza	D-7171	G-ASFJ	14.12.82	C R E S Taylor	Biggin Hill	27.11.09E
G-RETA	CASA 1-131E Jungmann Series 2000 (Enma Tigre G-IV-B)	2197	Spanish AF E3B-305	24. 3.80	Richard Shuttleworth Trustees (As "4477:GD+EG" in Luftwaffe WW2 c/s)	Old Warden	10. 4.09P
G-REVE	Van's RV-6 (Built R C Dyer)	PFA 181-12945		29. 8.07	R C Dyer	(Felixstowe)	
G-REVO	Best Off Sky Ranger 912(2) (Built R T Henry - pr.no.BMAA HB/346)	SKRxxxx408		2. 2.04	H Murray	(Castlewellan)	14. 8.09P
G-REYG	Dassault Falcon 900EX	193	F-WWFU	18. 4.08	Spanacre Ltd	London City	20. 4.09E
G-REYS	Bombardier CL-600-2B16 (CL-604 Challenger)	5467	N467RD C-GLWX	17. 9.01	Greyscape Ltd	Farnborough	16. 9.09E
G-RFIO	Aeromot AMT-200 Super Ximango (Rotax 912 UL)	200048		6. 3.95	M D Evens	Kirkbride	30. 6.09E
G-RFLY	Extra EA.300/L	1284		22. 7.08	Firefly Aero Services Ltd	(Acaster Malbis, York)	22. 7.09E
G-RFOX	Denney Kitfox Model 3 (Built L G G Faulkner and R Nicklin)	PFA 172-12029		5. 9.05	L G G Faulkner	Otherton, Cannock	
G-RFSB	Sportavia-Pützer RF5B Sperber (Limbach 1700)	51045	N55HC D-KEAO	2.12.88	J F McAulay tr G-RFSB Group	RAF Cranwell	1.12.09E
G-RFUN	Robinson R44 Raven	1239		17. 7.02	Brooklands Developments Ltd	(Sheffield)	20. 8.09E
G-RGAP	Cessna 172S Skyhawk	172S10421	N1216Z	18. 1.07	Certain Ltd	Wycombe Air Park	8. 2.09E
G-RGEN	Cessna T337D Super Skymaster	3371062	G-EDOT G-BJIY, 9Q-CPF, PH-JWL, N86056 (Noted 9.07)	24. 5.96	Lego SPA	Vicenza, Italy	11. 6.06
G-RGNT	Robinson R44 Raven II	10514	G-DMCG	26. 1.05	P R Nott tr Regent Aviation	(Frating)	2.11.09E
G-RGTS	Schempp-Hirth Discus b	140	BGA4301-HYB D-4684	29.11.07	G R Green "T5"	Wormingford	28. 2.08
G-RGUS	Fairchild 24R-46A Argus III (UC-61K-FA)	1145	(PH-) G-RGUS, ZS-UJZ, ZS-BAY, KK527, 44-83184	16. 9.86	P J and J L Bryan (As "44-83184:7" in USAAF c/s)	Sibson	28. 5.11S
G-RGZT	Cirrus SR20	1915	N195PG	30. 4.08	D Whalley	Guernsey	
G-RHAM	Best Off Sky Ranger 582(1) (Built G Eden - pr.no.BMAA HB/482)	SKR0509647		9. 1.06	L Smart and T Driffield	Baxby Manor, Husthwaite	25. 9.08P
G-RHCB	Schweizer 269C-1 (Schweizer 300)	0036	N201WL	20. 3.98	Helicopter One Ltd	Bournemouth	5. 4.09T
G-RHHT	Piper PA-32RT-300 Lance II	32R-7885190	N36476	3. 7.78	M R Boutel	Sywell	23. 5.09E
G-RHMS	Embraer EMB.135BJ Legacy	14501072	PT-SEV	6.11.08	Astra Fire Ltd	(Jersey)	5.11.09E
G-RHYM	Piper PA-31 Turbo Navajo B	31-815	G-BJLO F-BTQG, (F-BTDV), N7428L	24. 4.02	ATC Trading Ltd	Lasham	30. 1.10E
G-RHYS	RotorWay Executive 90 (Built B Williams) (RotorWay RI 162)	5140		8.11.93	A K Voase	(Hornsea)	21. 7.04P
G-RIAM	SOCATA TB-10 Tobago	85	F-GFLA F-ZVLA	31. 1.07	H Varia	Leicester	2. 8.09E
G-RIBA	P&M Aviation Quik GT450	8217		21.11.06	R J Murphy	East Fortune	20.11.09P
G-RICK	Beech 95-B55 Baron	TC-1472	G-BAAG	23. 5.84	J Jack	Inverness	10.11.09E
G-RICO	American General AG-5B Tiger	10162	N130U	14. 5.99	I J Ward	Blackbushe	12. 7.09E
G-RICS	Europa Aviation Europa (Built R G Allen - pr.no.PFA 247-12747) (NSI EA81) (Conventional u/c)	125		19. 3.96	R G Allen t/a The Flying Property Doctor	Wellcross Grange, Slinfold	29. 5.08P
G-RIDA	Eurocopter AS.355NP Ecureuil 2	5754	F-WQDE	7.12.07	Eurocopter UK Ltd	Oxford	23.10.09E
G-RIDE	Stephens Akro (Built N Mardis) (Lycoming AIO-360)	111	N81AC N55NM	10. 8.78	R Mitchell tr Mitchell Aviation (Noted 10.06)	Sleap	13. 8.92P
G-RIDG	Van's RV-7A (Built B A Ridgway)	PFA 323-14449		4. 1.06	B A Ridgway	Rhigos	
G-RIDL	Robinson R22 Beta II	3194		30. 3.01	Corserve International Ltd	(Stockport)	16. 7.09E
G-RIEF	DG Flugzeugbau DG-1000T	10-85T23	BGA5239-KNC	19. 7.06	J T Hitchcock "EF"	Parham Park	17. 7.08
G-RIET	Hoffmann H 36 Dimona	36224	I-RIET	6. 8.02	L J McKelvie tr Dimona Gliding Group	Bellarena	24.1.09E
G-RIEV	Rolladen-Schneider LS8-18	8039	BGA4192-HTP D-3175	4..1.08	R D Grieve	(North Lopham, Diss)	9. 5.08
G-RIFB	Hughes 269C (Hughes 300)	116-0562	N7428F	17. 5.90	R A Roberts t/a Puddleduck Plane Partnership	Shoreham	6. 4.09E
G-RIFN	Mudry CAP.10B	276		6. 6.96	D E Starkey and R A J Spurrell	White Waltham	19. 8.09E
G-RIFS	Rotorsport UK MT-03	RSUK/MT-03/020		18.10.07	B Griffiths	Charity Farm, Baxterley	23.11.09P
G-RIFY	Christen Eagle II (Built G Nelson)	GN-1	N961GN	10. 9.08	C J Gow	Dundee	25. 1.10P
G-RIGB	Thunder Ax7-77 Balloon (Hot Air)	1201		16. 3.88	N J Bettin	Farnham	13. 7.09E
G-RIGH	Piper PA-32R-301 Saratoga IIHP	3246123	N41272 G-RIGH, N41272	23.12.98	G M R Graham	Fowlmere	27.1.09E
G-RIGS	Piper PA-60-601P Aerostar	61P-0621-7963281	N8220J	18. 5.79	G G Caravatti and P G Penati "Marilyn"	Milan-Bresso, Italy	18. 5.09E
G-RIHN	Dan Rihn DR.107 One Design (Built J P Brown)	PFA 264-14201		18. 5.04	J P Brown	White Waltham	26. 9.08P
G-RIII	Van's RV-3B (Built R S Grace)	PFA 099-14341		19.12.08	R S Grace and D H Bruce	Bentwaters	
G-RIIN	PZL-104M Wilga 2000	00010010	SP-WEI	27. 6.01	E A M Austin (stored with Sealand Aviation)	Campbell River, BC, Canada	22. 7.07E
G-RIIV	Van's RV-4 (Built E C Lorr)	1340	N24EL	20. 2.08	C Baldwin	(Timperley, Altrincham)	

G-RIKI	Mainair Blade 912	1280-0401-7-W1075			29. 8.01	R Cook	Easter Poldar Farm, Thornhill 17.12.09P
G-RIKS	Europa Aviation Europa XS	393			18.10.01	R Morris	Benington 4.11.09P
	(Built R Morris - pr.no.PFA 247-13329) (Tri-gear u/c)						
G-RIKY	Mainair Sports Pegasus Quik	8007			17.12.03	P J Bent	Swinford, Rugby 14. 3.09P
G-RILA	Flight Design CTSW	06.08.11			29. 9.06	P A Mahony	RNAS Yeovilton 5. 1.09P
	(Assembled P&M Aviation Ltd as c/n 8182)						
G-RILY	Monnett Sonerai 2L	PFA 015-10353			20.12.78	P C Avery (stored) Lower Moutpleasant, Chatteris 5.10.89P
	(Built K D Riley)						
G-RIMB	Lindstrand LBL 105A Balloon (Hot Air)	827			15. 3.02	D Grimshaw (Parkinson's of Leyland titles) Leyland 23. 3.09E
G-RIME	Lindstrand LBL 25A Cloudhopper Balloon (Hot Air)				9.12.03	N Ivison	Barton Seagrave, Kettering 9. 7.09E
		954					
G-RIMM	Westland Wasp HAS.1	F9605	NZ Navy		11. 3.99	G P Hinkley (As "XT435:430" in RN c/s)	
			NZ3907, XT435				Green Barn Farm, Badwell Green 24. 9.08P
G-RINN	Mainair Blade	1261-1000-7-W1055			2. 1.01	J P Lang	Guy Lane Farm, Waverton 9. 2.08P
	(Rotax 582)						
G-RINO	Thunder Ax7-77 Balloon (Hot Air)	975			24. 6.87	D J Head "Cerous"	Newbury 5. 3.94T
G-RINS	Rans S-6-ESD Coyote II	0498.1220			15. 3.99	D Watt	Ladthwaite Farm, Kirkby Steven 18. 5.09P
	(Built D G Watts - pr.no.PFA 204-13361) (Rotax 582)						
G-RINT	CFM Streak Shadow	K 199-SA			7.12.93	D and J S Grint	Shoreham 8. 1.10P
	(Built D Grint- pr.no.PFA 206-12251) (Rotax 582)						
G-RINZ	Van's RV-7	70950	G-UZZL		8. 1.09	P Chaplin	(Ridgmont, Beds)
	(Built P Chaplin, pr.no. PFA 323-13982)						
G-RIOT	Silence Twister	PFA 329-14700			11.10.07	Zulu Glasstek Ltd	Baileys Farm, Long Crendon
	(Built P M Wells)						
G-RISE	Cameron V-90 Balloon (Hot Air)	2395			21. 9.90	D L Smith "Rise N' Shine"	Newbury 18. 9.05T
G-RISH	Rotorway Executive 162F	6926			15. 3.05	C S Rische	(Felmingham, North Walsham)
	(Built C S Rische)						
G-RISK	Hughes 369E (Hughes 500)	0157E	SE-HNZ		28. 6.06	Wavendon Social Housing Ltd	Sywell 15. 9.09E
			LN-OMV				
G-RISY	Van's RV-7	PFA 323-14320			10. 2.05	A J A Weal	(Worthing) 31. 7.09P
	(Built A J A Weal)(Superior XP-10)						
G-RITT	P&M Aviation Quik GT450	8230			8.12.06	M A Lewis	(Lydbrook) 8. 2.09P
G-RIVE	Jodel D 153	PFA 235-12856			14. 7.04	P Fines	Strubby 4. 1.10P
	(Built P Fines) (Wiksch WAM-120)						
G-RIVR	Thruster T 600F	9029-T600N-031			3.12.99	Thruster Air Services Ltd	Ginge, Wantage 7.12.00P
	(Hirth H2706) (Officially regd as "T 600N" with Rotax 582 and noted 1.05 in float configuration)						
G-RIVT	Van's RV-6	PFA 181-12743			31. 7.95	N Reddish	Netherthorpe 1. 5.09P
	(Built N Reddish) (Lycoming O-320)						
G-RIXA	Piper J-3C Cub	18711	7Q-YDF		19. 1.07	A J Rix	(Pent Farm, Postling)
			5Y-KEV, VP-KEV, VP-NAE, ZS-AZT				
G-RIXS	Europa Aviation Europa XS	533			2. 7.02	R Iddon	Blackpool 14. 7.09P
	(Built R Iddon - pr.no.PFA 247-13822) (Tri-gear u/c)						
G-RIXY	Cameron Z-77 Balloon (Hot Air)	10788			23. 1.06	Rix Petroleum Ltd "Rix"	Hull 9. 2.09E
G-RIZE	Cameron O-90 Balloon (Hot Air)	3163			13.12.93	S F Burden	Noordwijk, Netherlands 25. 4.09E
G-RIZI	Cameron N-90 Balloon (Hot Air)	3080	(F-GXIL)		12. 5.93	R Wiles	Durgates, Wadhurst 25. 5.04A
			G-RIZI				
G-RIZZ	Piper PA-28-161 Cherokee Warrior II		D-EMFW		11. 2.99	Modi Aviation Ltd	Sibson 10. 4.09E
		28-7816494	N9563N				
G-RJAH	Boeing Stearman D75N1 (PT-27BW) Kaydet		N75957		6. 4.90	R J Horne (As "44" in US Army Air Corps c/s: noted 1.08)	
	(Continental W670)	75-4041	RCAF FJ991, 42-15852				Little Rissington 14. 5.10S
G-RJAM	Sequoia F 8L Falco	PFA 100-11665			26. 7.00	R J Marks (Noted 11.04)	Dunkeswell
	(Built R J Marks)						
G-RJCC	Cessna 172S Skyhawk	172S10525	OE-DAN		21.12.07	R J Chapman	North Weald 23.12.08E
G-RJMS	Piper PA-28R-201 Arrow III	28R-7837059	N6223H		19. 1.88	M G Hill	Crosland Moor 6. 7.09E
G-RJRJ	Aerotechnik EV-97A Eurostar		29. 1.08			D P Myatt tr G-RJRJ Flying Group	
		LAA 315A-14763					(Old Marston, Oxford)
	(Built D P Myatt and J Patterson)						
G-RJWW	Maule M-5-235C Lunar Rocket	7250C	G-BRWG		6.10.87	PAW Flying Services Ltd	Full Sutton 2. 4.09E
			N5632H				
G-RJWX	Europa Aviation Europa XS	359			11. 9.00	J R Jones	Sleap 29. 1.10P
	(Built J R Jones - pr.no.PFA 247-13197) (Monowheel u/c)						
G-RJXA	Embraer EMB-145EP	145136	PT-SDN		18. 6.99	British Midland Airways Ltd (Operated bmi Regional)	
							Nottingham-East Midlands 17. 6.09E
G-RJXB	Embraer EMB-145EP	145142	PT-SDS		23. 6.99	British Midland Airways Ltd (Operated bmi Regional)	
							Nottingham-East Midlands 27. 6.09E
G-RJXC	Embraer EMB-145EP	145153	PT-SEE		15. 7.99	British Midland Airways Ltd (Operated bmi Regional)	
							Nottingham-East Midlands 14. 7.09E
G-RJXD	Embraer EMB-145EP	145207	PT-SGX		4. 2.00	British Midland Airways Ltd (Operated bmi Regional)	
							Nottingham-East Midlands 3. 2.10E
G-RJXE	Embraer EMB-145EP	145245	PT-SIJ		10. 4.00	British Midland Airways Ltd (Operated bmi Regional)	
							Nottingham-East Midlands 9. 4.09E
G-RJXF	Embraer EMB-145EP	145280	PT-SJW		29. 6.00	British Midland Airways Ltd (Operated bmi Regional)	
							Nottingham-East Midlands 28. 6.09E
G-RJXG	Embraer EMB-145EP	145390	PT-SQO		20. 2.01	British Midland Airways Ltd (Operated bmi Regional)	
							Nottingham-East Midlands 19. 2.08E
G-RJXH	Embraer EMB-145EP	145442	PT-SVD		1. 6.01	British Midland Airways Ltd (Operated bmi Regional)	
							Nottingham-East Midlands 31. 5.09E
G-RJXI	Embraer EMB-145EP	145454	PT-SUZ		22. 6.01	British Midland Airways Ltd (Operated bmi Regional)	
							(Star Alliance titles) Nottingham-East Midlands 21. 6.09E
G-RJXJ	Embraer EMB-135ER	145473	PT-SVS		23. 7.01	British Midland Airways Ltd (Operated bmi Regional)	
							Nottingham-East Midlands 22. 7.09E
G-RJXK	Embraer EMB-135ER	145494	PT-SXN		14. 9.01	British Midland Airways Ltd (Operated bmi Regional)	
							(Star Alliance titles) Nottingham-East Midlands 13. 9.09E

Reg	Type	c/n	Prev id	Date	Owner	Location	
G-RJXL	Embraer EMB-135ER	145376	PT-SQA	20.12.04	British Midland Airways Ltd *(Operated bmi Regional)*		
			(EI-LCY), PT-SQA, (CN-RLF), PT-SQA			Nottingham-East Midlands	19.12.09E
G-RJXM	Embraer EMB-145MP	145216	PH-RXA	23.12.05	British Midland Airways Ltd *(Operated bmi Regional)*		
			PT-SHC			Nottingham-East Midlands	22.12.09E
G-RJXN	Embraer EMB-145MP	145336	SP-LGI	19.10.06	British Midland Regional Ltd *(Operated bmi Regional)*		
			PT-SNC			Aberdeen	18.10.09E
G-RJXO	Embraer EMB-145MP	145339	SP-LGK	31.10.06	British Midland Regional Ltd *(Operated bmi Regional)*		
			PT-SNF			Aberdeen	30.10.09E
G-RJXP	Embraer EMB-135ER	145431	G-CDFS	22. 9.08	British Midland Airways Ltd *(Operated bmi Regional)*		
			EI-ORK, PT-SUC, (CN-RLG), PT-SUC			Nottingham-East Midlands	13.1.10E
G-RJXR	Embraer EMB-145EP	145070	G-CCYH	25. 4.08	British Midland Regional Ltd *(Operated bmi Regional)*		
			SE-DZA, PT-SAO			Aberdeen	22. 9.09E
G-RKEL	Agusta-Bell 206B-3 JetRanger III	8617	HB-XPR	2. 8.01	Nunkeeling Ltd	(Brough)	12. 6.09E
			F-GCVE				
G-RKET	Taylor JT.2 Titch	PFA 3223	G-BIBK	25. 8.99	P A Dunley	(Castle Donington, Derby)	
	(Built P A Dunley)						
G-RKKT	Reims FR172G Rocket	FR17200225	G-AYJW	15. 1.09	K L Irvine	Aberdeen	19 .4.09E
G-RLEF	Hawker Hurricane XII	42020	RCAF 5385	5. 3.07	P J Lawton	Thruxton	
	(Built Canadian Car and Foundry Co)						
G-RLMW	Tecnam P2002-EA Sierra	162		1. 6.06	R O'Malley-White	Weston Zoyland	20. 2.09P
	(Built J S Melville and R O'Malley-White - pr.no.PFA 333-14536)						
G-RLON	Fairey Britten-Norman BN-2A Mk.III-2 Trislander	G-ITEX	26. 4.02	Aurigny Air Services Ltd *(Royal London Asset Management*		
		1008	G-OCTA, VR-CAA, (G-OLPL), VR-CAA, DQ-FCF, G-BCXW		*titles)* Guernsey	16 12.08E
G-RLWG	Ryan ST3-KR	1716	N58612	20.10.08	R A Fleming	Breighton	
G-RMAC	Europa Aviation Europa	109		3. 7.97	P J Lawless	Kemble	16. 6.09P
	(Built P J Lawless - pr.no.PFA 247-12717) (Monowheel u/c)						
G-RMAN	Aero Designs Pulsar	PFA 202-13071		6. 6.97	M B Redman	Old Sarum	26. 8.09P
	(Built M B Redman)						
G-RMAX	Cameron C-80 Balloon (Hot-Air)	4705		6.12.99	RE/MAX Ireland Ltd	Dublin	1. 7.09E
G-RMBM	Robinson R44 Raven II	11049		8. 2.06	R and B Moseley t/a Bramble Developments		
						Hannington, Rushden	22. 2.09E
G-RMHE	Aerospool Dynamic WT9 UK	DY155/2006		2.10.06	R M Hughes-Ellis	Welshpool	24. 5.09P
	(Built Yeoman Light Aircraft Co Ltd) (Official c/n is "DY155")						
G-RMIT	Van's RV-4	PFA 181-12207		4. 9.96	J P Kloos	Truleigh Manor Farm, Edburton	13. 6.09P
	(Built J P Kloos) (Lycoming O-320)						
G-RMMT	Europa Aviation Europa XS	A260	N929N	28. 1.05	N Schmitt *"Grommit"*	Nottingham City-Tollerton	15. 8.09P
	(Built N Schmitt) (Tri-cycle u/c)		(N29N reported)				
G-RMPY	Evektor EV-97 Eurostar	PFA 315-14139		4. 2.04	N R Beale	Church Farm, Shotteswell	2. 8.09P
	(Built N R Beale)						
G-RMRV	Van's RV-7A	PFA 323-14434		25. 5.07	R Morris	Cambridge	26. 8.09E
	(Built R Morris)						
G-RMSM	American Champion 8KCAB Super Decathlon	1064-2008		7. 3.08	R P Jones	(Trumpington, Cambs)	27. 5.09E
G-RMSY	Cameron TR-70 Balloon (Hot-Air)	11159		6. 5.08	A M Holly *"Gordon Ramsey/Healthy Appetite"*		
						Berkeley	3. 6.09E
G-RNAC	IAV Bacau Yakovlev Yak-52	888912	RA-44463	25. 7.03	M Hynett tr RNAEC Group *"23"*	Bembridge	22.11.08P
			DOSAAF 99				
G-RNBW	Bell 206B-2 JetRanger II	2270	F-GQFH	9. 1.98	Rainbow Helicopters Ltd	Whimple	24. 3.09E
			F-WQFH, HB-XUF, F-GFBP, N900JJ, N16UC				
G-RNCH	Piper PA-28-181 Archer II	28-8190141	HB-PHR	19. 4.06	Carlisle Flight Training Ltd	Carlisle	11. 5.09E
			D-EIFP, N83235				
G-RNDD	Robin DR.500-200i Président	0037		2. 5.03	Witham (Specialist Vehicles) Ltd		
	(Officially regd as DR.400-500)					(Colsterworth, Grantham)	28. 7.09E
G-RNGO	Robinson R22 Beta II	3035		19. 1.00	Janabeck Investments Ltd	Kemble	16. 3.09E
G-RNHF	Hawker Sea Fury T 20	"ES.3615"	N281L	1. 6.07	Royal Navy Historic Flight	Yeovilton	23. 6.80F
			N8476W, G-BCOW, D-CACO, G-9-64, VX281				
	(In "Royal Navy" c/s coded "281": dismantled.6.07 and fuselage returned Yeovilton 12.08 – to be remarried later in 2009)						
G-RNIE	Cameron Ball 70 SS Balloon (Hot Air)	2333		3. 8.90	N J Bland *"Schwarzenegger" (Inflated 6.08)* Didcot		8. 6.06A
G-RNLI	Vickers Supermarine 236 Walrus 1	S2/5591	W2718	13.12.90	Solent Sky Ltd *(As "W2718/AA5Y" in 751 Sqdn RN c/s)*		
						Southampton	
G-RNRM	Cessna A185F Skywagon	185-02541	N1826R	20. 1.87	Skydive St Andrews Ltd *"Thunderchild"*		
						Sorbie Farm, Kingsmuir	11. 3.09E
G-RNRS	Scottish Aviation Bulldog Series 100/101		SE-LLF	12. 9.03	Power Aerobatics Ltd	Kemble	3. 6.10T
		BH100/132	Fv61026, G-AZIT				
G-ROAD	Robinson R44 Raven II	11589		29. 1.07	Ainscough Ltd	(Ince, Wigan)	26. 2.09E
G-ROBD	Europa Aviation Europa	078		23. 2.94	R D Davies	(Cowbridge)	
	(Built R D Davies - pr.no.PFA 247-12671) (Monowheel u/c)						
G-ROBJ	Robin DR.500-200i Président	45		2. 9.08	D R L Jones	Oaksey Park	18. 9.08E
	(Built Apex Aircraft)						
G-ROBN	Robin R1180T Aiglon	220		16. 8.78	N D Anderson	Old Sarum	26.11.07T
G-ROBT	Hawker Hurricane I	---	P2902	19. 9.94	R A Roberts	Moat Farm, Milden	
	(Built Gloster Aircraft Co Ltd)	*(On rebuild by Hawker Restorations Ltd from remains salvaged 1988 at Dunkirk Beach: to be "P2902/DX-X")*					
G-ROBZ	Grob G109B	6442	I-BREM	19. 6.07	J D Huband tr Bravo Zulu Group		
						Sandhill Farm, Shrivenham	16. 9.09E
G-ROCH	Cessna T303 Crusader	T30300129	N4962C	29. 3.90	R S Bentley	Cambridge	7. 6.09E
G-ROCK	Thunder Ax7-77 Balloon (Hot Air)	781		25. 2.86	M A Green *"Rocky"*	Rednal	13. 7.09E
G-ROCR	Schweizer 269C *(Schweizer 300)*	S 1336	N219MS	14. 6.90	C Hayles t/a Hayles Aviation	(Newbury)	4. 6.09E
G-ROCT	Robinson R44 Raven II	11854		10. 8.07	C R Turton tr Marketwatch	Headcorn	30. 8.09E
G-RODC	Steen Skybolt	4568	N10624	20. 2.02	J S Firth and A P Ransome	Sherburn-in-Elmet	30. 3.09P
	(Built R H Williams) (Lycoming IO-360)						
G-RODD	Cessna 310R II	310R0544	G-TEDD	2.10.89	R J Herbert Engineering Ltd	Marshland, Wisbech	30. 7.09E
			G-MADI, N87396, G-MADI, N87396				
G-RODG	Avtech Jabiru UL	xxxx		14. 4.99	P C Appleton and J Barker *(Noted 7.05)*		
	(Built I M Donnelly - pr.no.PFA 274A-13379)					Davidstow Moor	9. 5.04P

Reg	Type	C/n	Prev id	Date	Owner	Location	Date
G-RODI	Isaacs Fury	PFA 011-10130		22.12.78	M R Jones (As "K3731" in RAF 43 Sqdn c/s)	Little Rissington	5. 3.09P
	(Built D C J Summerfield) (Lycoming O-290)						
G-RODJ	Comco Ikarus C42 FB80	0709-6912		2.10.07	R K Jenkins tr Swansea Sport Flying	Swansea	28.10.09P
G-RODZ	Van's RV-3A	10622	N68AR	4. 7.07	R M Laver	Shoreham	2. 6.09P
	(Built T F Hinckley) (Lycoming O-320)						
G-ROEI	Avro Roe 1 replica	PFA 344-14629		6. 2.08	Brooklands Museum Trust Ltd	Brooklands	
	(Built Brooklands Museum)						
G-ROGE	Robinson R44 Raven II	11462		1.11.06	Phil Rogerson Ltd Yeoland Conyers, Carnforth		16.11.08E
G-ROGY	Cameron Concept 60 Balloon (Hot Air)	3055		11. 5.93	S A Laing	Banchory	21. 9.09E
G-ROKT	Reims FR172E Rocket	FR1720046	N261SA	1.05.03	Sylmar Aviation and Services Ltd		8. 5.09E
			D-ECLY			Lower Wasing Farm, Brimpton	
G-ROLF	Piper PA-32R-301 Saratoga II SP		N83052	7. 1.81	P F Larkins	High Cross, Ware	19. 5.09E
		32R-8113018					
G-ROLL	Pitts S-2A	2175	N31444	20. 2.80	Aerobatic Displays Ltd "Breitling Angels" (yellow) c/s		
	(Built Aerotek Inc) (Lycoming AEIO-360)					Wycombe Air Park	8. 6.09E
G-ROLY	Reims Cessna F172N Skyhawk II	F17201945	G-BHIH	1.12.04	R B A Stones tr G-ROLY Group	Gamston	4.10.09E
G-ROME	III Sky Arrow 650 TC	C011		26. 5.99	Sky Arrow (Kits) UK Ltd	Old Sarum	26. 6.09E
	(Built Iniziative Industriali Italiane)						
G-ROMP	Extra EA.230H	001	S5-MBP	13. 1.05	G G Ferriman	Jericho Farm, Lambley	18. 5.09E
	(Built W Hawickhorst)		OO-JVD, D-EIWH				
G-ROMS	Lindstrand LBL 105G Balloon (Hot Air)	401		13. 9.96	T D Donnelly tr Gromit Balloon Group "Gromit"		
						Sprotbrough, Doncaster	13. 9.00A
G-ROMW	Cyclone AX2000	7486		4. 2.99	K V Falvey	Sackville Lodge, Riseley	7. 8.09P
	(HKS 700E V3)						
G-RONA	Europa Aviation Europa	043		17. 1.95	C M Noakes "Mr Jake"		
	(Built C M Noakes - pr.no.PFA 247-12588) (Monowheel u/c)					Shenstone Hall Farm, Shenstone	22.10.08P
G-RONG	Piper PA-28R-200 Cherokee Arrow II		N16451	14. 6.90	E Tang	Elstree	18.11.08E
		28R-7335148					
G-RONI	Cameron V-77 Balloon (Hot Air)	2349		27. 7.90	R E Simpson "Roni"	Great Missenden	15. 8.02A
G-RONS	Robin DR.400-180 Régent	2088		17. 7.91	R and K Baker	Swansea	24.10.08E
G-RONW	Clutton FRED Series II	PFA 029-10121		18.12.78	F J Keitch	(Clayhidon, Cullompton)	29. 3.04P
	(Built P Gronow)						
G-ROOK	Reims Cessna F172P Skyhawk II	F17202081	PH-TGY	12. 1.81	Rolim Ltd (Operated Bon Accord Flying Group)		
			G-ROOK			Aberdeen	23. 1.09E
G-ROOV	Europa Aviation Europa XS	354		16. 7.98	P W Hawkins and K Siggery	Biggin Hill	20. 6.09P
	(Built D Richardson - pr.no.PFA 247-13214) (Rotax 914-UL) (Tri-gear u/c)						
G-RORI	Folland Gnat T 1	FL.549	8621M	18.10.93	Swept Wing Ltd (As "XR538:01" in RAF c/s)		
			XR538			North Weald	18. 6.09P
G-RORY	Focke-Wulf Piaggio FWP.149D	014	G-TOWN	2. 8.88	M Edwards	Barton	7. 1.08
	(Piaggio c/n 338)		D-EFFY, 90+06, BB+394 7				
G-ROSI	Thunder Ax7-77 Balloon (Hot Air)	1284		29. 6.88	J E Rose "Rosi" (Inflated 6.08)	Abingdon	21. 9.96A
G-ROSS	Practavia Pilot Sprite	132		28. 2.80	A D Janaway	Exeter	
	(Built F M T Ross - pr.no.PFA 005-10404)						
G-ROTF	Robinson R22 Beta	3928	EI-DKO	27.11.06	Rotorflight Ltd	Bristol	27.11.09E
G-ROTG	Robinson R44 Raven II	11573		30. 1.07	Rotorflight Ltd	Bristol	16. 3.09E
G-ROTI	Luscombe 8A Silvaire	2117	N45590	18. 4.89	R Ludgate and A L Chapman (Stored 7.05)		
	(Continental A65)		NC45590			Old Hay, Paddock Wood	9.10.97P
G-ROTR	Brantly B 2B	403	N2192U	9.12.91	P G R Brown	(Crediton)	17.11.02
G-ROTS	CFM Streak Shadow	K 120-SA		21.12.89	A G Vallis and C J Kendal	Barton	10. 7.09P
	(Buillt H R Cayzer - pr.no.PFA 161A-11603) (Rotax 582)						
G-ROUP	Reims Cessna F172M Skyhawk II	F17201451	G-BDPH	23. 5.84	Perranporth Flying School Ltd	Perranporth	16. 4.09E
G-ROUS	Piper PA-34-200T Seneca II	34-7870187	(G-BFTB)	26. 4.78	Oxford Aviation Training Ltd	Oxford	18. 5.09E
			N9412C				
G-ROUT	Robinson R22 Beta	1241	N8068U	23. 1.90	Preston Associates Ltd	(Guisborough)	19. 8.07T
G-ROVE	Piper PA-18-135 Super Cub	18-3846	PH-VLO	6. 5.82	S J Gaveston (As "R-156" in R Netherlands AF c/s)		
	(L-21B-PI) (Frame No.18-3853)		(PH-DKF), R Neth AF R-156, 54-2446 (also carries '54-2446')			Headcorn	1. 6.11S
G-ROVY	Robinson R22 Beta II	2957		9. 7.99	Plane Talking Ltd	Blackbushe	17.11.09E
G-ROWA	Aquila AT01	AT01-174		31.10.07	Chicory Crops Ltd	Gloucestershire	14.11.08E
G-ROWE	Reims Cessna F182P Skylane II	F18200007	OO-CNG	18.12.95	D Rowe	St Just	10. 6.09E
G-ROWI	Europa Aviation Europa XS	435		16. 6.99	R M Carson	(Cheltenham)	
	(Built R M Carson - pr.no.PFA 247-13482) (Wilksch WAM-120) (Monowheel u/c)						
G-ROWL	Grumman AA-5B Tiger	AA5B-0595	(N28410)	26.10.77	T A Timms	Standalone Farm, Meppershall	26. 6.09E
G-ROWR	Robinson R44 Raven	1036		17. 4.01	R A Oldworth	(Petworth)	27. 4.09E
G-ROWS	Piper PA-28-151 Cherokee Warrior		N8949F	15. 9.78	S Goodchild		
		28-7715296				Eddsfield, Octon Lodge Farm, Thwing	27. 3.09E
G-ROXI	Cameron C-80 Balloon (Hot-Air)	11106		7. 7.08	A Murphy	Dunshaughlin, Ireland	3. 8.09E
G-ROYC	Avtech Jabiru UL-450	xxxx		24. 4.03	M Daleki	Field Farm, Oakley	3. 3.09P
	(Built R Clark - pr.no.PFA 274A-13990)						
G-ROYM	Robinson R44 Raven II	12295		2. 6.08	Business Agility Ltd	Wycombe Air Park	11. 6.09E
G-ROZI	Robinson R44 Astro	0252		26. 3.96	Rotormotive Ltd	(Sproughton, Ipswich)	29. 4.09E
G-ROZY	Cameron R-36 Gas/Balloon (Hot Air)	1141		20. 5.85	J W Soukup	Bristol	18. 9.96A
G-ROZZ	Comco Ikarus C42 FB80	0407-6607		19. 8.04	A J Blackwell	Long Marston	19.10.08P
	(Built Fly Buy Ultralights Ltd)						
G-RPAF	Europa Aviation Europa XS	605		26. 1.05	R P Frost	Sherburn-in-Elmet	7. 8.09P
	(Built R P Frost - pr.no.PFA 247-14202, tricycle undercarriage)						
G-RPBM	Cameron Z-210 Balloon (Hot Air)	10230		6. 3.02	The Balloon Company Ltd t/a First Flight		
					(Robert Price Builders Merchants titles) Langford, Bristol		2.10.09E
G-RPCC	Europa Aviation Europa XS	PFA 247-14615		10. 1.07	R P Churchill-Colman	(Curdridge, Southampton)	
	(Built R P Churchill-Colman)						
G-RPEZ	Rutan LongEz	PFA 074A-10746		3. 4.84	D G Foreman	(Swanley)	
	(Built B A Fairston and D Richardson)						
G-RPRV	Van's RV-9A	PFA 320-13936		17.10.03	C B Amery	Nottingham City-Tollerton	16. 6.09P
	(Built G R Pybus) (Lycoming O-320)						
G-RRAK	Enstrom 480B	5055	G-RIBZ	31. 7.08	R A Kingston	(Hythe)	17. 9.09E

Reg	Type	C/n	Prev id	Date	Owner	Location	Date
G-RRAT	CZAW Sportcruiser *(Built G Sipson)*	LAA 338-14821		22. 9.08	G Sipson	(Lutterworth)	
G-RRAZ	Embraer EMB-135BJ Legacy	14500954	G-RUBN PT-SFC	26. 9.07	Raz Air Ltd	London Stansted	12.12.08E
G-RRCU	CEA Jodel DR.221B Dauphin	129	F-BRCU	9.12.99	Merlin Flying Club Ltd	Hucknall	3. 4.09E
G-RRED	Piper PA-28-182 Archer II	2843673	N6048L	4. 9.08	J P Reddington	Denham	18. 9.09E
G-RRFC	SOCATA TB-20 Trinidad GT	2053	F-OILV	9. 5.01	C A Hawkins	Blackbushe	27. 7.09E
G-RRGN	Vickers Supermarine 390 Spitfire PR.XIX	6S/594677	PS853	23.12.96	Rolls-Royce PLC *(As "PS853:C" in RAF 2nd TAF/PRU c/s)* Filton		3. 9.09P
G-RROB	Robinson R44 Raven II	10011		6.12.02	Something Different Charters LLP	Stapleford	3. 3.09E
G-RROD	Piper PA-30 Twin Comanche B	30-1221	G-SHAW LN-BWS, N10F	20. 6.00	R McFadyen	Henstridge	25. 8.09E
G-RROW	Lindstrand LBL 105A Balloon (Hot Air)	1118		30. 6.06	Lindstrand Hot Air Balloons Ltd *(Redrow titles)* Oswestry		16. 8.09E
G-RRRT	Beech F33A Bonanza	CE-1292	HB-KAM OY-BVO	10.12.08	P R S Earl	Little Rissington	
G-RRSR	Piper J-3C-65 Cub	12905	N1315V 44-80609	7. 9.05	R W Roberts *(As "480173:H-57" in USAAC c/s) "Special Delivery"* Duxford		7. 3.09S
G-RRVX	Van's RV-10 *(Built R E Garforth)*	PFA 339-14601		5.12.06	R E Garforth *(Under construction 1.08)*	(Hockley)	
G-RSAF	British Aircraft Corporation 167 Strikemaster Mk.80A	EEP/JP/3687	R Saudi AF 1120, G-27-231	8. 4.05	M A Petrie *(As "417" in RAF of Oman c/s)* Hawarden		
G-RSHI	Piper PA-34-220T Seneca V	3449077	D-GMGM N9265Q	4. 2.08	A G Hill tr R S Hill and Sons	Bournemouth	4. 3.09E
G-RSKR	Piper PA-28-161 Warrior II	28-7916181	G-BOJY N3030G	27. 4.95	Transport Command Ltd	Shoreham	4.12.07E
G-RSKY	Best Off Sky Ranger 912(2) *(Built C G Benham - pr.no.BMAA HB/382)*	SKR0403452		12.10.04	C G Benham Red House Farm, Preston Capes		20. 9.08P
G-RSMC	Medway SLA 100 Executive	131106		24. 8.07	Nene Valley Microlights Ltd	Conington	10. 9.08P
G-RSMT	Rotorsport UK MT-03	RSUK/MT-03/015		1. 5.07	Rotorsport UK Ltd Poplar Farm, Prolly Moor, Wentor, Bishops Castle		29. 6.09P
G-RSSF	Denney Kitfox Model 2 *(Built R W Somerville)*	PFA 172-12125		9.10.92	R W Somerville Comber, County Down *(Noted 10.03)*		15. 5.97P
G-RSVP	Robinson R22 Beta II	2788		5. 2.98	Fly Executve Ltd	Blackbushe	24. 3.09E
G-RSWO	Cessna 172R Skyhawk	17280206	N9401F	25. 2.98	AC Management Associates Ltd	Kemble	3. 4.09E
G-RSWW	Robinson R22 Beta	1775	N40815	16. 5.91	R S Weston-Woods t/a Woodstock Enterprises Rochester		8. 8.09E
G-RSXL	Cessna 560XL Citation XLS	56-5699	N5148M	16. 5.07	Aircraft Leasing Overseas Ltd	Farnborough	16 .5.09E
G-RTBI	Thunder Ax6-56 Balloon (Hot Air)	2584		19. 4.94	P J Waller	Wymondham	8. 7.02A
G-RTFM	Avtech Jabiru J400 *(Built I A Macphee - pr.no.PFA 325-14463)*	xxxx		28. 2.08	I A Macphee	(Norwich)	
G-RTHS	Rans S-6-ES Coyote II *(Built T Harrison-Smith - pr/no.PFA 204-14753) (Rotax 912-UL)*	1107.1841		17. 1.08	T Harrison-Smith Brock Farm, Billericay		23.10.09P
G-RTIN	Rotorsport UK MT-03	RS-UK/MT-03/047		21. 7.08	P McCrory	(Omagh, NI)	12. 8.09P
G-RTMS	Rans S-6-ES Coyote II *(Built C J Arthur - pr.no.PFA 204-14149) (Tri-cycle u/c)*	1202.1470		19. 8.04	C J Arthur	Eshott	8. 7.09P
G-RTMY	Comco Ikarus C42 FB100 *(Built Aerosport Ltd)*	0502-6655		11. 4.05	R F Learney tr Mike Yankee Group	Redhill	10. 4.09P
G-RTRT	PZL-104MA Wilga 2000	00060021	SP-WHO	8. 6.06	Erica A M Austin	Oaksey Park	26. 7.09E
G-RTWW	Robinson R44 Astro	0438		20. 3.98	R Woods t/a Rotorvation Helicopters (Fawkham, Longfield)		7. 5.09E
G-RUBB	Gulfstream AA-5B Tiger	AA5B-0928	(G-BKVI) OO-NAS, (OO-HRC)	20. 9.83	D E Gee	Blackbushe	12.12.09E
G-RUBY	Piper PA-28RT-201T Turbo Arrow IV	28R-8331037	G-BROU N4306K	5. 1.90	R Harman t/a Arrow Aircraft Group	Tatenhill	30. 6.09E
G-RUES	Robin HR.100-210 Safari II	185	F-BVCH	31. 7.02	R H R Rue	Turweston	23. 9.09E
G-RUFF	Mainair Blade 912	1203-0799-7-W1006		18. 6.99	S L Walker	Ince Blundell	17. 6.08P
G-RUFS	Avtech Jabiru UL *(Built J W Holland - pr.no.PFA 274A-13359)*	0200		19.11.99	S Richens Lower Upham Farm, Chiseldon		9. 7.09P
G-RUGS	Campbell Cricket Mk.4 *(Built J L G Mclane)*	PFA G/103-1307		11. 2.99	J L G Mclane	(Gilling East, York)	
G-RUIA	Reims Cessna F172N Skyhawk II	F17201856	PH-AXA (3)	4.10.79	Knockin Flying Club Ltd Sandford Hall, Knockin		17. 9.09E
G-RULE	Robinson R44 Raven II	11039		3. 2.06	M Wallis and P W Brown t/a Huckair	Cranfield	11. 2.10E
G-RUMI	Noble Hardman Snowbird Mk.IV	SB-018	G-MVOI	9. 9.02	G Crossley *(Noted 8.04)*	(Anglesey)	13. 6.02P
G-RUMM	Grumman F8F-2P Bearcat	D 1088	NX700HL NX700H, N1YY, N4995V, Bu.121714	20. 3.98	Patina Ltd *(As "121714:201B" in USN c/s)* Duxford *(Operated The Fighter Collection)*		5. 7.09P
G-RUMN	American AA-1A Trainer	AA1A-0086	N87599 D-EAFB, (N9386L)	30. 5.80	M T Manwaring	Fenland	26. 5.09E
G-RUMW	Grumman FM-2 Wildcat	5765	N4845V BuA.86711	15. 4.98	Patina Ltd *(As "F" in FAA c/s) (Operated The Fighter Collection)* Duxford		1. 7.09P
G-RUNT	Cassutt Racer IIIM *(Built N A Brendish - pr.no.PFA 034-10860) (Lycoming O-235)*	161149		12. 4.83	R S Grace *"Nemesis" & "1"*	Bentwaters	16. 7.08P
G-RUSL	Van's RV-6A *(Built G Russell)*	PFA 181-13522		22.10.01	G R Russell Middle Pymore Farm, Bridport *(Noted 10.05)*		
G-RUVE	Van's RV-8 *(Built J P Brady and D J Taylor, pr.no. PFA 303-14716)*	82747		6. 1.09	J P Brady and D J Taylor	RAF Benson	
G-RUVI	Zenair CH.601UL Zodiac *(Built P G Depper) (Rotax 912 S) (Tri-cycle u/c)*	PFA 162A-13933		8.11.02	P G Depper *"Indulgence"*	Shobdon	10. 9.09P
G-RUVY	Van's RV-9A *(Built R D Taylor) (Lycoming O-320)*	PFA 320-13807		4. 1.02	R Taylor	Henstridge	21. 5.09P
G-RUZZ	Robinson R44 Raven II	10082		20. 5.03	Russell Harrison PLC Wellesbourne Mountford		20. 6.09T
G-RVAB	Van's RV-7 *(Built I M Belmore)*	PFA 323-14005		20. 9.04	I M Belmore and A T Banks	(Horsham)	

Reg	Type	PFA/No	Extra	Date	Owner	Location	Date2
G-RVAC	Van's RV-7	PFA 323-14445		7. 9.05	A F S and B Caldecourt	Popham	10. 3.09P
	(Built A F S and B Caldecourt) (Lycoming O-320)						
G-RVAL	Van's RV-8	PFA 303-13532		23. 7.01	R N York	Dunsfold	18.11.08P
	(Built R N York) (Lycoming O-360)						
G-RVAN	Van's RV-6	PFA 181-12657		25. 4.97	D Broom	Benington	22. 4.07P
	(Built D Broom) (Lycoming IO-320)						
G-RVAW	Van's RV-6	PFA 181-13234		24.11.97	P E Bates tr High Flatts RV Group		
	(Built A A Wordsworth) (Lycoming IO-320-A1A)					High Flatts Farm, Chester-le-Street	16. 8.08P
G-RVBA	Van's RV-8A	PFA 303-13309		26.10.99	D P Richard	(London SW16)	
	(Built S Hawksworth)						
G-RVBC	Van's RV-6A	PFA 181-12618		16. 2.00	T G Gibbs	(Faukland, Radstock)	19. 8.09P
	(Built T G Gibbs) (Superior XP-10-360)						
G-RVBF	Cameron A-340 Balloon (Hot Air)	10493		23. 2.04	Airxcite Ltd t/a Virgin Balloon Flights	Wembley	10. 9.09E
G-RVCE	Van's RV-6A	PFA 181-13372		28. 6.01	M D Barnard and C Voelger	Glebe Farm, Southam	23. 7.08E
	(Built M D Barnard and C Voelger) (Lycoming O-320)						
G-RVCG	Van's RV-6A	PFA 181A-13602		26. 4.01	G C Calder	Shoreham	29. 5.09P
	(Built C J Griffin) (Lycoming O-320)						
G-RVCH	Van's RV-8A	PFA 303-14116		9.11.07	C R Harrison	Dunkeswell	
	(Built C R Harrison)						
G-RVCL	Van's RV-6	PFA 181A-13439		18. 2.99	R Manning	Netherthorpe	23 .8.08P
	(Built C Lamb) (Lycoming O-360)						
G-RVDG	Van's RV-9	PFA 320-14310		6. 1.05	D M Gill	Bicester	24. 4.09P
	(Built D M Gill) (Lycoming IO-320) (Originally regd as RV-9A, amended 12. 5.08)						
G-RVDJ	Van's RV-6	PFA 181-12938		8. 2.99	J D Jewitt	Cliffe, Selby	3.10.09P
	(Built J D Hewitt) (Lycoming O-360)						
G-RVDP	Van's RV-4	PFA 181-13416		10. 5.00	P White	(Fethard, County Tipperary)	17. 4.09P
	(Built D H Pattison) (Lycoming O-320)						
G-RVDR	Van's RV-6A	PFA 181-13098		15. 5.00	P R Redfern	Breighton	31. 7.09P
	(Built D E Reast) (Lycoming IO-320)						
G-RVDX	Van's RV-4	926	G-FTUO	31.10.08	M R Tingle	Cantley, Norwich	1. 6.09P
	(Built T Martin) (Lycoming IO-360-B4A)		C-FTUQ				
G-RVEE	Van's RV-6A	PFA 181-12262		16. 2.93	J C A Wheeler	Perth	28. 5.09P
	(Built J C A Wheeler) (Lycoming O-360) (Tri-cycle u/c)						
G-RVET	Van's RV-6	PFA 181-12852		9. 3.98	D R Coleman	Rochester	11. 2.09P
	(Built D R Coleman) (Lycoming O-320)						
G-RVGA	Van's RV-6A	PFA 181-13079		11. 5.98	D P Dawson	RAF Henlow	20. 4.09P
	(Built D P Dawson) (Lycoming IO-320)						
G-RVIA	Van's RV-6A	PFA 181-12289		13. 8.97	K R W Scull and J Watkins	Upfield Farm, Whitson	11.11.09P
	(Built A J Rose) (Lycoming O-320)						
G-RVIB	Van's RV-6	PFA 181-13220		22. 6.99	K Martin and P Gorman	Kilrush, County Kildare	2. 5.09P
	(Built I M Belmore) (Lycoming O-320)						
G-RVIC	Van's RV-6A	PFA 181-13319		11. 6.04	I T Corse	(Laurencekirk)	
	(Built I T Corse)						
G-RVII	Van's RV-7	PFA 181A-13576		13. 9.01	P H C Hall	Popham	
	(Built P H Hall) (Project conceived originally as a RV-6, hence the '181A type prefix) (Noted 5.07)						
G-RVIN	Van's RV-6	PFA 181-13236		28.11.97	R G Jones	Rednal	13. 4.09P
	(Built N Reddish) (Lycoming O-320)						
G-RVIO	Van's RV-10	PFA 339-14548		14. 7.06	R C Hopkinson	Turweston	18.12.09P
	(Built R C Hopkinson, originally reg'd as PFA 339-14547, amended 27.12.08) (Lycoming IO-540)						
G-RVIS	Van's RV-8	PFA 303-14031		17. 6.03	I V Sharman	(Horley)	
	(Built I V Sharman)						
G-RVIT	Van's RV-6	PFA 181-12422		1. 5.95	P J Shotbolt	Ingthorpe Farm, Great Casterton	1. 4.09P
	(Built K F Crumplin) (Lycoming O-360)						
G-RVIV	Van's RV-4	PFA 181-12366		31.12.97	G S Scott	Truleigh Manor Farm, Edburton	21. 4.09P
	(Built G S Scott) (Lycoming O-320)						
G-RVIX	Van's RV-9A	90243		11. 9.01	R E Garforth	Southend	19.11.08P
	(Built R E Garforth - pr.no.PFA 320-13779) (Lycoming O-320)						
G-RVJM	Van's RV-6	PFA 181A-13861		4.12.02	M D Challoner	(Stalbridge, Sturminster Newton)	
	(Built M D Challoner)						
G-RVJO	Van's RV-9A	PFA 320-13778		5. 1.07	J E Singleton	Hinton-in-the-Hedges	21. 1.10P
	(Built J E Singleton) (Superior XP-10-360)						
G-RVJP	Van's RV-9A	PFA 320-14364		28.10.05	R M Palmer	White Fen Farm, Benwick	27. 3.09P
	(Built R M Palmer) (Lycoming O-320)						
G-RVJW	Van's RV-4	PFA 181-12987		26. 8.05	J M Williams	(Winsford)	5. 8.09P
	(Built J M Williams) (Lycoming O-320)						
G-RVLC	Van's RV-9A	PFA 320-13780		27. 4.07	L J Clark	(Broom, Alcester)	
	(Built L J Clark)						
G-RVMB	Van's RV-9A	PFA 320-14324		16. 6.06	M James and R W Littledale	Enstone	22. 9.09P
	(Built M James and R W Littledale) (Lycoming O-320)						
G-RVMC	Van's RV-7	PFA 323-13897		9. 5.03	M R McNeil	Redmoor Farm, North Duffield	22. 9.09P
	(Built M R McNeil) (Lycoming O-360)						
G-RVMJ	Van's RV-4	PFA 181-13433		16. 2.99	M J de Ruiter	(Aghalee, Craigavon)	
	(Built M J de Ruiter)						
G-RVMT	Van's RV-6	PFA 181A-13644		30. 1.01	M J Aldridge	Rougham	7. 5.09P
	(Built M R Tingle) (Lycoming O-360)						
G-RVMZ	Van's RV-8	PFA 303-13395		12.11.99	A E Kay		
	(Built M W Zipfell) (Lycoming O-360)					Parsons Farm, Waterperry Common, Oakley	4. 1.09P
G-RVNH	Van's RV-9A	PFA 320-13952		20. 7.06	N R Haines	(Lea, Malmesbury)	29. 7.09P
	(Built N R Haines) (Lycoming O-320)						
G-RVNS	Van's RV-4	PFA 181-12443	G-CBGN	12.10.07	N P D Smith	(Upper Caldecote, Biggleswade)	26. 3.08P
	(Built G A Nash) (Lycoming O-320)						
G-RVPH	Van's RV-8	PFA 303-13906		25. 5.04	J C P Herbert	(Saffron Walden)	
	(Built J C P Herbert)						

Reg	Type	C/n	Prev ID	Date	Owner	Location	CofA
G-RVPL	Van's RV-8 (Built A P Lawton) (Lycoming AEIO-360)	PFA 303-13885		6. 8.04	A P Lawton	Great Massingham	11. 1.10P
G-RVPM	Van's RV-4 (Built D F Sargant) (Lycoming O-320)	PFA 181-12270	G-RVDS	20. 2.06	P J McMahon	Ludham	22. 4.09P
G-RVPW	Van's RV-6A (Built P Waldron) (Lycoming O-320)	PFA 181A-13481		9. 6.03	P Waldron	Netherthorpe	8.11.08P
	(Nosewheel collapsed and tipped onto nose landing at Netherthorpe 7. 6.08)						
G-RVRA	Piper PA-28-140 Cherokee Cruiser	28-7625038	G-OWVA N4459X	14. 1.97	Par Contractors Ltd	RAF Mona	22. 5.09E
G-RVRB	Piper PA-34-200T Seneca II	34-7970440	G-BTAJ N22MJ, N45113	24. 2.97	Ravenair Aircraft Ltd	Liverpool	21.10.09E
G-RVRC	Piper PA-23-250 Aztec E	27-7405336	G-BNPD N101VH, N40591	14.10.97	West-Tec Ltd	Wellesbourne Mountford	27.10.09E
G-RVRD	Piper PA-23-250 Aztec E	27-4634	G-BRAV G-BBCM, N14021	16. 3.98	Ravenair Aircraft Ltd	Liverpool	13. 4.09E
G-RVRE	Partenavia P68B	57	D-GIFR (N4412H), D-GIFR, LN-LMS	8.12.03	Ravenair Aircraft Ltd	Liverpool	18. 3.09E
G-RVRF	Piper PA-38-112 Tomahawk	38-78A0714	G-BGEL N9723N	21.11.97	Ravenair Aircraft Ltdr	Liverpool	13.10.09E
G-RVRG	Piper PA-38-112 Tomahawk	38-79A1092	G-BHAF N9703N	3. 8.98	Ravenair Aircraft Ltd	Liverpoo	15. 8.08E
G-RVRH	Van's RV-3B (Built R Hodgson)	PFA 099-10821		17. 2.03	R Hodgson	(Bramley, Guildford)	
G-RVRI	Cessna 172H Skyhawk	17255822	G-CCCC SE-ELU, N2622L	26. 9.05	Ravenair Aircraft Ltd	Liverpoo	5. 7.09E
G-RVRJ	Piper PA-E23-250 Aztec E	27-7305004	G-BBGB N40206	12.10.04	Ravenair Aircraft Ltd	Liverpool	27. 7.09E
G-RVRK	Piper PA-38-112 Tomahawk	38-79A1068	G-BGZW N9674N	9. 8.05	Ravenair Aircraft Ltd	Liverpool	11. 2.09E
G-RVRL	Piper PA-38-112 Tomahawk	38-78A0711	G-BGBY N9689N	9.8.05	Ravenair Aircraft Ltd	Liverpool	8. 5.09E
G-RVRM	Piper PA-38-112 Tomahawk	38-78A0525	G-BGEK N9662N	20.10.05	Ravenair Aircraft Ltd	Liverpool	24. 7.09E
G-RVRN	Piper PA-28-161 Warrior II	28-7916325	G-BPID N2137V	12.12.05	Ravenair Aircraft Ltd	Liverpool	10. 8.09E
G-RVRO	Piper PA-38-112 Tomahawk II	38-82A0017	G-BOUD N91365	14. 6.06	Ravenair Aircraft Ltd	Barton	4. 9.09E
G-RVRP	Van's RV-7 (Built R C Parris)	PFA 323-14085		16. 7.03	R C Parris	(Leighton Buzzard)	
G-RVRR	Piper PA-38-112 Tomahawk	38-79A0199	G-BRHT N2474C	20. 8.07	Ravenair Aircraft Ltd	Barton	8. 5.09E
G-RVRT	Piper PA-28-140 Cherokee C	28-26933	G-AYKX N11C	13. 9.06	Ravenair Aircraft Ltd	Liverpool	17. 6.09E
G-RVRU	Piper PA-38-112 Tomahawk	38-80A0081	G-NCFE G-BKMK, OO-GME, (OO-HKD), N9676N	1. 7.99	Ravenair Aircraft Ltd	Liverpool	30.11.09E
G-RVRV	Van's RV-4 (Built P Jenkins)	PFA 181-13024		29. 9.98	P Jenkins	(Inverness)	
G-RVRW	Piper PA-23-250 Aztec E	27-7305045	G-BAVZ N40241	17.12.04	Ravenair Aircraft Ltd	Liverpool	1. 9.09E
G-RVSA	Van's RV-6A (Buil W H Knott) (Lycoming O-360)	PFA 181A-12574		19. 5.99	W H Knott	Dornoch	10. 4.09P
	(Overturned on landing at Morgansfield, Fishburn 30.8.08)						
G-RVSD	Van's RV-9A (Built S W Damarell)	PFA 320-14092		23. 5.06	S W Damarell	(Peatmor, Swindon)	
G-RVSG	Van's RV-9A (Built S Gerrish)	PFA 320-14265		10.11.04	S Gerrish	Lasham	
G-RVSH	Van's RV-6A (Built S J D Hall)	PFA 181A-13026		20. 9.02	S J D Hall	Blackbushe	11. 8.06P
G-RVSR	Van's RV-8 (Built S W and R K Elders)	PFA 303-14470		4. 6.07	S W and R K Elders	(Branston, Lincoln)	
G-RVSX	Van's RV-6 (Built R L West) (Lycoming O-320)	PFA 181-13090		18. 9.97	R L and V A West	Tavira, Portugal	25. 7.08P
G-RVTE	Van's RV-6 (Buit E McShane and T Feeny)	PFA 181A-13523		23. 1.08	E McShane and T Feeny	Strabane and Eglinton, Londonderry	
G-RVTN	Van's RV-10 (Built C I Law)	PFA 339-14602		15. 5.07	C I Law	Wickenby	
G-RVTT	Van's RV-7 (Built A Phillips)	PFA 323-13852		9.11.07	A Phillips	Boarhunt Farm, Fareham	
G-RVUK	Van's RV-7 (Built R J Fray) (Lycoming O-360)	PFA 323-14441		8. 6.06	R J Fray	Furze Farm, Haddon, Peterborough	15.11.08P
G-RVVI	Van's RV-6 (Built J E Alsford and J N Parr) (Lycoming AEIO-360)	PFA 181-12418		26. 1.93	J Reynolds Racing Ltd	Nottingham City-Tollerton	9. 7.08P
G-RVVY	Van's RV-10 (Built P R Marskell)	PFA 339-14599		16. 3.07	P R Marskell	(Chippenham)	
G-RWAY	Rotorway Executive 162F (Built D L Urch and S Andrews) (RotorWay RI 162F)	6414	G-URCH	18.11.04	A G Rackstraw	Nottingham City-Tollerton	
G-RWEW	Robinson R44 Clipper II	11148		5. 4.06	R Williamson t/a Northern Heli Charters	Leeds-Bradford	7. 5.09E
G-RWGS	Robinson R-44 II	11963		29.10.07	R W G Simpson	(Peterborough)	8.11.08E
G-RWGW	Learjet Model 45	45-213	G-MUTD D-CEWR, N50126	1. 2.07	Woodlands Air LLP	Manchester	18.11.08E
G-RWHC	Cameron A-180 Balloon (Hot Air)	2700		16. 4.92	J J Rudoni and A C K Rawson t/a Wickers World Hot Air Balloon Company	Stafford	13. 4.00T
G-RWIA	Robinson R22 Beta	0753	G-BOEZ	26.11.07	R W I'Anson	(Wilmslow)	26. 3.06T
G-RWIN	Rearwin 175 Skyranger (Continental A75)	1522	N32391 NC32391	12. 9.90	A B Bourne and N D Battye	RAF Henlow	18. 7.05P

G-RWLA	Eurocopter EC.135 T2+	635		11. 2.08	Oxford Air Services Ltd	Oxford	16. 7.09E
G-RWLY	Europa Aviation Europa XS	469		22. 3.01	C R Arkle	(Ascot)	
	(Built C R Arkle - pr.no.PFA 247-13701) (Tri-gear u/c)						
G-RWMW	Zenair CH.601XL Zodiac	PFA 162B-14231	G-DROO	16. 8.06	R W H Watson and M Whyte	Maybole	15. 8.08P
	(Built A G Campbell) (Rotax 912 ULS)						
G-RWRW	UltraMagic M-77 Balloon (Hot Air)	77/221		11.11.02	Flying Pictures Ltd	Chilbolton	
G-RWSS	Denney Kitfox Model 2	PFA 172-12008		16. 4.91	R W Somerville	(Larne)	14. 6.93P
	(Built R W Somerville)				(Under rebuild 2006?)		
G-RXUK	Lindstrand LBL 105A Balloon (Hot Air)	232		29. 3.95	Zebedee Balloon Service Ltd Newtown, Hungerford		22.10.09E
G-RYAL	Avtech Jabiru UL	0212		6. 7.99	A C Ryall	Upfield Farm, Whitson	15. 8.08P
	(Built A C Ryall - pr.no.PFA 274A-13365)						
G-RYDR	Rotorsport UK MT-03	RSUK/MT-03/033		4. 3.08	P M Ryder	Kirkbride	16. 3.09P
G-RYNS	Piper PA-32-301FT 6x	3232071	N30970	14. 9.07	D A Earle	Dunkeswell	17. 9.09E
G-RYPE	DG Flugzeugbau DG-1000T	10-113T35	BGA5292-KRA	20. 3.08	R Abbott and S Ancsey tr DG-1000T Partners		
						Dunstable	
G-RYPH	Mainair Blade 912	1248-0500-7-W1041		8. 6.00	I A Cunningham	Easter Poldar Farm, Thornhill	10. 4.08P
G-RYZZ	Robinson R44 Raven II	11418	N31448	15.11.06	Rivermead Aviation Ltd (Operated Rise Helicopters)		
						Gloucestershire	4. 2.10E
G-RZEE	Schleicher ASW 19B	19126	BGA2282-DPX	7. 4.08	R Johnson	Long Mynd	
G-RZLY	Flight Design CTSW	06-11-15	N102RK	13. 6.08	J D Macnamara	(Crediton)	

G-SAAA - G-SZZZ

G-SAAA	Flight Design CTSW	05.12.09		17. 2.06	D J Collier tr Sunfun Group		
	(Assembled P&M Aviation Ltd as c/n 8161)				Lower Mountpleasant Farm, Chatteris		15. 7.08P
G-SAAB	Rockwell Commander 112TC	13002	G-BEFS	5.12.79	Zytech Ltd	Earls Colne	2. 4.09E
			N1502J				
G-SAAL	Piper PA-34-220T Seneca V	3449273	N123NN	18. 9.08	F Saal t/a Saal Aviation		
			G-MDCA, N53643			Les Milles, France	13.10.09E
G-SAAM	Cessna T182R Turbo Skylane II	T18268200	G-TAGL	23. 5.84	Sound Power Ltd	(Newcastle upon Tyne)	10. 2.10E
			G-SAAM, N2399E				
G-SAAW	Boeing 737-8Q8	32841		16. 5.05	Globespan Airways Ltd t/a Flyglobespan.com		
						Edinburgh	11. 5.09E
G-SABA	Piper PA-28R-201T Turbo Arrow III		G-BFEN	22. 8.79	C A Burton	Sherburn-in-Elmet	9. 6.09E
		28R-7703268	N38745				
G-SABI	Dassault Falcon 900EX	150	N900NS	29. 9.08	London Executive Aviation Ltd	London Stansted	12.10.09E
			F-WWFI				
G-SABR	North American F-86A-5NA Sabre	151-43547	N178	6.11.91	Golden Apple Operations Ltd	Duxford	20. 6.09P
	(Regd with c/n 151-083)		N68388, 48-178		(As "8178:FU-178"in 4th Fighter Wing USAF c/s)		
					(Operated The Old Flying Machine Company)		
G-SACB	Reims Cessna F152 II	F15201501	G-BFRB	7. 3.84	P Wilson	Haverfordwest	20. 5.09E
G-SACD	Cessna F172H	F172-0385	G-AVCD	13. 6.83	Northbrook College (Sussex)	Shoreham	27. 7.00T
	(Built Reims Aviation SA)				(Noted as instructional airframe 11.05)		
G-SACH	Stoddard-Hamilton GlaStar	PFA 295-13088		27. 8.99	R S Holt	Croft Farm, Defford	2.11.09P
	(Built R S Holt) (Tailwheel u/c) (Lycoming IO-320)						
G-SACI	Piper PA-28-161 Warrior II	28-8216123	N81535	26. 7.89	PJC (Leasing) Ltd	Stapleford	2. 5.09E
G-SACK	Robin R2160	316		2. 5.97	Sherburn Aero Club Ltd	Sherburn-in-Elmet	19. 6.08E
G-SACM	TL 2000 Sting Carbon	LAA 347-14798		30. 4.08	M Clare		
	(Built M Clare)				Orlingbury Hold Farm, Hannington, Northants		
G-SACO	Piper PA-28-161 Warrior II	28-8416085	N4358Z	1. 6.89	Stapleford Flying Club Ltd	Stapleford	7. 9.09E
G-SACR	Piper PA-28-161 Cadet	2841046	N91618	6. 2.89	Sherburn Aero Club Ltd	Sherburn-in-Elmet	3. 4.09E
G-SACS	Piper PA-28-161 Cadet	2841047	N91619	6. 2.89	Sherburn Aero Club Ltd	Sherburn-in-Elmet	3. 4.09E
G-SACT	Piper PA-28-161 Cadet	2841048	N9162D	6. 2.89	Sherburn Aero Club Ltd	Sherburn-in-Elmet	24. 3.09E
G-SACX	Aero AT-3 R100	AT3-028		7.11.07	Sherburn Aero Club Ltd	Sherburn-in-Elmet	13.11.09E
G-SACY	Aero AT-3 R100	AT3-029		12.12.07	Sherburn Aero Club Ltd	Sherburn-in-Elmet	15.12.09E
G-SAFE	Cameron N-77 Balloon (Hot Air)	511		14. 2.79	P J Waller "The High Flyer"	Wymondham	21. 4.91A
G-SAFI	Piel CP.1320	PFA 183-12103		23. 7.01	C S Carleton-Smith	(Great Missenden)	
	(Built C S Carleton-Smith)						
G-SAFR	SAAB 91D Safir	91-382	PH-RLR	10.10.95	Sylmar Aviation and Services Ltd (on rebuild) (Noted 5.08)		
						Lower Wasing Farm, Brimpton	
G-SAGA	Grob G109B	6364	OE-9254	28. 6.90	G-GROB Ltd	Wycombe Air Park	16. 7.09E
G-SAGE	Luscombe 8A Silvaire	2581	G-AKTL	15. 8.90	C D Howell	Higherlands Farm, Branscombe	14. 7.09P
	(Continental A65)		N71154, NC71154				
G-SAHI	FLS Aerospace Sprint 160	001		21.10.80	M J A Trughill	Iron Pear Tree Farm, Kirdford	13. 7.07P
	(Lycoming O-235) (Built Trago Mills Ltd as type SAH-1)						
G-SAIG	Robinson R44 Raven II	11364		4. 8.06	Torfield Aviation Ltd	Headcorn	21. 9.09E
G-SAIX	Cameron N-77 Balloon (Hot Air)	626	N386CB	14. 1.99	B Sevenich, Benedikt, S Harren and C Walther		
						Aachen and Bonn, Germany	21. 2.00A
G-SAJA	Schempp-Hirth Discus 2c	22	BGA5243-KOB	22..1.07	J Arnold "JA"	RAF Keevil	25. 1.08
G-SALA	Piper PA-32-300 Six	32-7940106	(G-BHEJ)	17.10.79	Stonebold Ltd	White Waltham	20. 2.09E
			N2184Z				
G-SALE	Cameron Z-90 Balloon (Hot Air)	10944		15.12.06	R D Baker Rowling, Goodnestone, Canterbury		19.12.09E
G-SALL	Reims Cessna F150L	F15000682	PH-LTY	19. 1.79	D and P A Hailey Lower Wasing Farm, Brimpton		20. 9.09E
			D-ECPH				
G-SAMG	Grob G109B	6278		16. 5.84	T M Holloway tr RAF Gliding and Soaring Association		
						RAF Halton	4. 3.10E
G-SAMJ	Partenavia P68B	101	D-GERA	27. 4.01	Ravenair Aircraft Ltd	Liverpool	6. 8.09E
	(C/n indicates P68 model)		CS-AYB, D-GERA				
G-SAMM	Cessna 340A II	340A0742	N37TJ	7. 3.88	D M Harbottle	Fairoaks	8. 9.09E
	(RAM-conversion)		N2671A				
G-SAMP	Agusta A109E Power	11673		30. 6.06	Deans Foods Ltd	(Tring)	29. 6.09E
G-SAMY	Europa Aviation Europa	221		17. 8.95	P Vallis	(Alfreton)	
	(Built K R Tallent and P Vallis - pr.no.PFA 247-12901) (Tri-gear u/c)						

G-SAMZ	Cessna 150D	15060536	G-ASSO N4536U	19. 4.84	F A Bakir	Yew Tree Farm, Lymm Dam	10. 7.09E
G-SAOC	Schempp-Hirth Discus 2cT	54		29. 6.07	T M Holloway tr RAF Gliding and Soaring Association *"R6"* (Operated Chilterns Gliding Centre)	RAF Halton	4. 7.08
G-SAPM	SOCATA TB-20 Trinidad	1009	G-EWFN G-BRTY	8.12.04	G-SAPM Ltd	Filton	7. 4.09E
G-SARA	Piper PA-28-181 Archer II	28-7990039		6. 4.81	Apollo Aviation Advisory Ltd	Shoreham	23. 5.09E
G-SARB	Sikorsky S-92A	920045	N80562	18. 9.07	CHC Scotia Ltd *(Operated Marine and Coastguard Agency)*	(Aberdeen)	18. 9.09E
G-SARC	Sikorsky S-92A	920052	N45168	30.11.07	CHC Scotia Ltd *(Operated Marine and Coastguard Agency)*	(Aberdeen)	2.12.09E
G-SARD	Agusta AW139	31208		19. 3.08	CHC Scotia Ltd *(Operated Marine and Coastguard Agency)*	Lee-on-Solent	26. 3.09E
G-SARH	Piper PA-28-161 Warrior II	28-8216173	N8232Q	18. 2.91	Solo Services Ltd and Tempora Ltd	Shoreham	18. 2.09E
G-SARM	Comco Ikarus C42 FB100	0504-6674		13. 5.05	J Green tr G-SARM Group	Old Sarum	18. 5.08E
G-SARO	Saro Skeeter AOP.12	S2/5097	XL812	17. 7.78	B Chamberlain *(As "XL812" in AAC c/s) (Noted 8.08)*	AAC Middle Wallop	30.10.06
G-SARV	Van's RV-4 *(Built S N Aston) (Lycoming O-320)*	PFA 181-12606		2.10.00	J E Singleton tr Hinton Flying Group	Hinton-in-the-Hedges	28. 5.09P
G-SASA	Eurocopter EC.135 T2+ *(Originally regd as EC.135 T1, amended 29. 3.08)*	0147		12.10.00	Bond Air Services Ltd *(Operated Scottish Air Ambulance)*	Inverness	21.10.09E
G-SASB	Eurocopter EC.135 T2+	0151		29. 9.00	Bond Air Services Ltd *(Operated Scottish Air Ambulance)*	Glasgow City Heliport	5.10.08E
G-SASC	Beech B200C Super King Air	BL-150	N6178D	30.12.05	Gama Aviation Ltd *(Operated Scottish Air Ambulance)*	Glasgow	4. 1.10E
G-SASD	Beech B200C Super King Air	BL-151	N6178F	4. 1.06	Gama Aviation Ltd *(Operated Scottish Air Ambulance)*	Aberdeen	29. 1.09E
G-SASG	Schleicher ASW 27-18E	29530		16.11.07	F B Jeynes	Bidford	
G-SASH	MD Helicopters MD.900 Explorer	900-00080	PH-SHF N7008Q	10. 6.05	Yorkshire Air Ambulance Ltd	Leeds-Bradford	21. 6.09E
G-SASI	CZAW Sportcruiser *(Built F Sayyah and J C Simpson)*	PFA 338-14651		9. 7.07	F Sayyah and J C Simpson *(Noted 9.08)*	Chilsford Farm, Kirdford	
G-SATL	Cameron Sphere 105 SS Balloon (Hot Air)	2696		5.12.91	Ballonverbung Hamburg GmbH	Kiel, Germany	29. 4.97A
G-SATN	Piper PA-25-260 Pawnee C	25-5179	N8722L	10. 8.05	T M Holloway tr RAF Gliding and Soaring Association	RAF Halton	
G-SAUF	Colt 90A Balloon (Hot Air) *(New envelope c/n 2492 c1990/1)*	1497		25. 5.89	K H Medau	Baden, Germany	21. 6.04A
G-SAUK	Rans S-6-ES Coyote II *(Built D A Smith and E Robshaw - pr.no.PFA 204-14346) (Tri-cycle u/c)*	0904.1611		5. 1.05	M D Tulloch	Pittrichie Farm, Whiterashes	26. 4.09P
G-SAVY	ICP MXP-740 Savannah VG Jabiru (2) *(Built C S Hollingowrth and SP Yardley-pr.no. BMAA HB/499)*	06-03-51-469		2. 1.09	C S Hollingworth and SP Yardley	Sywnnerton, Staffs	
G-SAWI	Piper PA-32RT-300T Turbo Lance II	32R-7887069	OY-CJJ N36719	23. 6.99	Regularity Ltd	Exeter	15. 6.09E
G-SAXC	Cameron N-105 Balloon (Hot Air)	3864	G-SAXO	6. 1.06	The Altitude Balloon Company Ltd	Thame	1. 7.09E
G-SAXN	Beech 200 Super King Air	BB-108	G-OMNH N108BM, RP-C1979, TR-LWC	23. 5.06	Saxonair Ltd	Norwich	20. 8.09E
G-SAXT	Schempp-Hirth Duo Discus xT	158	BGA5242-KOA D-KIIH	15. 3.07	T M Holloway tr RAF Gliding and Soaring Association *"26"* (Operated Chilterns Gliding Centre)	RAF Halton	13. 3.08
G-SAYS	Rotary Air Force RAF 2000 GTX-SE *(Built K Aziz)*	PFA G/13-1322		4. 9.00	D Beevers	Melrose Farm, Melbourne	10. 7.07P
G-SAZY	Avtech Jabiru J400 *(Built N J Bond)*	PFA 325-14057		16. 4.03	J E Howe	Henstridge	6. 3.09P
G-SAZZ	Piel CP.328 Super Emeraude *(Built D J Long)*	PFA 216-11940		4. 7.01	D J Long	Gloucestershire	11.12.08P
G-SBAE	Reims Cessna F172P Skyhawk II	F17202200	D-EOCD (3)	3. 6.98	BAE Systems (Operations) Ltd	Blackpool	7. 8.09E
G-SBHH	Schweizer 269C *(Schweizer 300)*	S 1314	G-XALP N41S	7. 5.02	C S, H C S and J W Padield tr S and J Padfield and Partners *(Left by road 7. 1.09)*	Biggin Hill	29. 1.10E
G-SBIZ	Cameron Z-90 Balloon (Hot Air)	10348		12.12.02	Snow Business International Ltd *(Snow Business titles)*	Stroud	30. 7.09E
G-SBKR	SOCATA TB-10 Tobago	1077	D-EAGG	10. 3.04	S C M Bagley	Duxford	29. 4.09E
G-SBKS	Cessna 206H Stationair	20608290	N22188	21. 6.07	Alard Properties Ltd	Sleap	1. 7.09E
G-SBLT	Steen Skybolt *(Built M A McCallum and N Workman)*	MH-01		14. 4.92	S D Arnold tr Skybolt Group	(Coventry)	
G-SBMM	Piper PA-28R-180 Cherokee Arrow	28R-30877	G-BBEL SE-FDX	8. 2.02	K S Kalsi	Cambridge	20.10.09E
G-SBMO	Robin R2160i	116	EI-BMO SE-GSZ	12. 2.99	D Henderson, U Simpson and M Mannion	Weston, Leixlip, County Kildare	24. 3.06T
G-SBOL	Steen Skybolt *(Built K R H Wingate, originally started by W Penaluna)*	PFA 064-14453		6.12.07	K R H Wingate	Halwell	
G-SBRA	Robinson R44 Raven II	10233		17.12.03	Airpoint Aviation Ltd	(Dublin)	28. 5.09E
G-SBRK	Aero AT-3 R100	AT3-021	(F-GURH)	14. 3.07	Sywell Aerodrome Ltd	Sywell	26. 2.09P
G-SBUS	Britten-Norman BN-2A-26 Islander *(Built PADC)*	3013	G-BMMH RP-C578	31.10.86	Isles of Scilly Skybus Ltd	St Just	17. 4.09E
G-SBUT	Robinson R22 Beta II	2739	G-BXMT	18. 5.98	Fast Helicopters Ltd *(Damaged Shoreham 17.10.08)*	Shoreham	31. 1.09E
G-SCAN	Vinten Wallis WA-116 Series 100/R *(Rotax 532)*	001		5. 7.82	K H Wallis	Reymerston Hall, Norfolk	14. 2.06P
G-SCBI	SOCATA TB-20 Trinidad	1908	F-OIGV	10. 8.99	S C Brown t/a Ace Services	Enstone	18. 8.09E
G-SCCZ	CZAW Sportcruiser *(Built J W Ellis)*	LAA 338-14845		29.10.08	J W Ellis	(Kidderminster)	
G-SCFO	Cameron O-77 Balloon (Hot Air)	1131		3. 5.85	M K Grigson *"Southern Counties" (Operated Balloon Preservation Group)*	Petworth	24. 5.95A

G-SCHI	Eurocopter AS.350B2 Ecureuil	3337	F-WQOQ	5. 2.01	Patriot Aviation Ltd	Cranfield	2. 4.09E
G-SCHO	Robinson R22 Beta	3833		3. 5.05	Blades Aviation (UK) LLP	Costock	23. 5.09E
G-SCII	Agusta A109C	7628	G-JONA	18. 8.06	C and M Coldstores		
			VP-CWA, JA6610			(Carrickmacross, County Monaghan)	6. 4.09E
G-SCIP	SOCATA TB-20 Trinidad GT	2014	F-OILO	19. 9.00	The Studio People Ltd	Welshpool	5.11.09E
G-SCLX	FLS Aerospace Sprint 160	002	G-PLYM	14. 7.94	E J F McEntee	Kirdford	1. 6.09E
G-SCNN	Schempp-Hirth Standard Cirrus	173	BGA1677-CNN	22.12.07	G C Short	Keiheuvel, Belgium	13. 4.08
G-SCOI	Agusta A109E Power	11051	G-HPWH	16. 8.02	Trustair Ltd	Euxton, Chorley	23. 6.09E
			G-HWPH				
G-SCOL	Gippsland GA-8 Airvan	GA8-05-088	VH-FNG	28. 3.06	Sunderland Parachute Centre Ltd		
						Shotton Colliery, Peterlee	4. 5.09E
G-SCPD	Reality Escapade 912(1)	JAESC 0015		30. 1.04	R W L Breckell	Ince Blundell	23.10.08P
	(Built R Gibson - pr.no.BMAA HB/319)						
G-SCPI	CZAW Sportcruiser	LAA 338-14855		9.12.08	I M Speight and P R W Goslin	Henstridge	
	(Built I M Speight and P R W Goslin)						
G-SCPL	Piper PA-28-140 Cherokee Cruiser		G-BPVL	4. 5.89	Aeros Leasing Ltd	Gloucestershire	17.12.09E
		28-7725160	N1785H				
G-SCRZ	CZAW Sportcruiser	PFA 338-14684		29. 8.07	P M Grant	Wickenby	2. 6.09P
	(Built P M Grant)						
G-SCSC	CZAW Sportcruiser	LAA 338-14852		3.10.08	A Daltry-Cooke	(Bury St Edmunds)	
	(Built A Daltry-Cooke)						
G-SCTA	Westland Scout AH.1	F9701	XV126	18.12.95	G R Harrison	Shoreham	26. 4.09P
G-SCUB	Piper PA-18-135 Super Cub	18-3847	PH-GAX	13.12.78	M E Needham (As "54-2447" in US Army c/s)		
	(L-21B-PI) (Frame No.18-3849)		R Neth AF R-157, 54-2447			Old Manor Farm, Anwick	31. 5.10S
		(Collided with power cables landing Old Manor Farm, Anwick 6.10.07, struck the ground and extensively damaged)					
G-SCUD	Montgomerie-Bensen B 8MR PFA G/101-1294			18. 8.97	D Taylor	(Fritchley, Belper)	
	(Built D Taylor)						
G-SCUL	Rutan Cozy	PFA 159-13212		28. 5.98	K R W Scull	(Trostrey, Usk)	
	(Built K R W Scull)						
G-SCZR	CZAW Sportcruiser	PFA 338-14647		7. 5.08	D L Walker	(Lewes)	
	(Built D L Walker)						
G-SDAT	Flight Design CTSW	07.03.21		23. 7.07	A R Wade	Damyn's Hall, Upminster	22. 7.09P
	(Assembled P&M Aviation Ltd with c/n 8312)						
G-SDAY	Aérospatiale AS.355F2 Ecureuil 2	5193	G-SYPA	15.12.08	London Helicopter Centres Ltd	Redhill	2. 4.09E
			LV-WHC, F-WYMS, G-BPRE, N366E				
G-SDCI	Bell 206B-2 JetRanger II	925	G-GHCL	24. 2.00	S D Coomes	Auldhouse, East Kilbride	29. 6.09E
			G-SHVV, N72GM, N83106				
G-SDEV	de Havilland DH.104 Sea Devon C 20	04472	XK895	29. 3.90	Aviation Heritage Ltd (As "XK895:CU-19" in RN 771 Sqdn c/s)		
					(Noted 9.08)	Kemble	17. 9.01
G-SDFM	Evektor EV-97 Eurostar	PFA 315-13884		23. 8.02	M J Miles tr G-SDFM Eurostar Group		
	(Built A K Paterson)					Priory Farm, Tibenham	15. 4.09P
G-SDLW	Cameron O-105 Balloon (Hot Air)	2460		11. 3.91	S P Watkins	Bristol	4. 6.05A
G-SDOB	Tecnam P2002-EA Sierra	PFA 333-14529		26. 4.06	S P S Dornan	Kirknewton	15. 2.10P
	(Built G E Collard and S P S Dornan)						
G-SDOI	Aeroprakt A22 Foxbat	PFA 317-14064		26. 6.03	S A Owen	Kirknewton	30. 8.08P
	(Built S P S Dornan)						
G-SDOZ	Tecnam P92-EA Echo-Super			9. 9.04	D M Stewart tr Cumbernauld Flyers G-SDOZ		
	(Built S P S Dornan) PFA 318A-14287					Cumbernauld	5. 5.09P
G-SEAI	Cessna U206G Stationair II	U20604059	N756FQ	20. 3.92	K O'Connor	Weston, Leixlip, County Kildare	12. 6.08T
	(Amphibian)						
G-SEAJ	Cessna 525 CitationJet	525-0113	N111AM	13. 2.08	CJ 525 Ltd	Bristol	21. 2.09E
			N5214K				
G-SEAT	Colt 42A Balloon (Hot Air)	817		28. 5.86	D G Such and M Tomlin	Barkway, Royston	7. 4.09E
G-SEBY	UltraMagic M-105 Balloon (Hot Air)	105/144		19. 3.07	Prestige Milano Group SRL	Ferrara, Italy	17. 8.09E
G-SEDO	Cameron N-105 Balloon (Hot Air)	10388		28. 3.03	Wye Valley Aviation Ltd	Bridstow Ross-on-Wye	9. 7.09E
G-SEED	Piper J-3C-90 Cub (L-4H-PI)	11098	EI-BAP	28. 1.80	J H Seed	Black Spring Farm, Castle Bytham	15. 8.08P
	(Frame No.10932)		F-BFBZ, 44-80203, 43-29807				
	(Official identity is c/n 12499/44-80203 and probably rebuilt 1945)						
G-SEEE	P&M Aviation Quik GT450	8235		22. 1.07	R Meredith-Hardy	(Baldock)	11. 2.09P
G-SEEK	Cessna T210N Turbo Centurion II	21064579	N9721Y	14.10.83	A Hopper	Little Shelford	30.11.09E
G-SEFC	Boeing 737-7Q8	30687	N1787B	1. 5.07	Globespan Airways Ltd t/a Flyglobespan.com		
						Edinburgh	1. 5.09E
G-SEFI	Robinson R44 Raven II	10147	N75271	2.10.03	Kermann Avionics Sales Ltd	Denham	27.11.09E
G-SEGA	Cameron Sonic 90 SS Balloon (Hot Air)	2896		16. 9.92	A D Kent tr Balloon Preservation Flying Group		
	(Sonic The Hedgehog shape)				"Sonic"	Petworth	29. 6.00A
G-SEIL	Pilatus Britten-Norman BN-2B-26 Islander		G-BIIP	7.12.07	Highland Airways Ltd	North Connel, Oban	26. 3.09E
		2103	6Y-JQJ, 6Y-JKJ, N411JA, G-BIIP				
G-SEJW	Piper PA-28-161 Cherokee Warrior II		N9557N	19. 4.78	Keen Leasing (IOM) Ltd (Operated Leading Edge)		
		28-7816469				Perth	18. 6.09E
G-SELC	Diamond DA.42 Twin Star	42.032		30. 6.05	Stapleford Flying Club Ltd	Stapleford	17. 9.09E
G-SELF	Europa Aviation Europa	279		10. 8.01	N D Crisp, A H Lames and E J Hatcher	Rochester	12. 5.09P
	(Built N D Crisp, A H Lames and E J Hatcher - pr.no.PFA 247-12996) (Jabiru 3300) (Monowheel u/c)						
G-SELL	Robin DR.400-180 Régent	1153	D-EEMT	7. 3.85	C R Beard Farmers Ltd		
						Grange Farm, Sutton-on-Trent	17. 3.09E
G-SELY	Agusta-Bell 206B-3 JetRanger III	8740		26. 7.96	DSC North Ltd	Inverness	21. 9.09E
G-SEMI	Piper PA-44-180 Seminole	44-7995052	G-DENW	23. 2.99	M Djukic and J Benfell "Lady Gabriella II"		
			N21439			Wolverhampton	23. 3.08E
G-SEMR	Cessna T206H Turbo Stationair	T20608669	N11347	6. 2.07	Semer LLP	Poplar Hall Farm, Elmsett	18. 2.09E
G-SENA	Rutan LongEz	1325	F-PZSQ	11.11.96	G Bennett	(Caister-on-Sea, Great Yarmouth)	
	(Built R Bazin)		F-WZSQ				
G-SEND	Colt 90A Balloon (Hot Air)	2100		2.12.91	Air du Vent	Paris, France	27. 7.08T
G-SENE	Piper PA-34-200T Seneca II	34-8170069	N797WA	20.11.03	M O'Hara (Noted 10.07) (centralaviation.co.uk titles)		
			N8314P			Wolverhampton	26.11.06T

Reg	Type	C/n	Prev ids	Date	Owner/Operator	Location	Date
G-SENX	Piper PA-34-200T Seneca II	34-7870356	G-DARE G-WOTS, G-SEVL, N36742	15. 5.95	First Air Ltd	Cardiff	5.12.08E
G-SEPT	Cameron N-105 Balloon (Hot Air)	1880		22.11.88	P Gooch *(Septodont - Dentist`s Supplies titles)*	Alresford	26. 8.07A
G-SERE	Diamond DA.42 Twin Star	42.314		19.12.07	Sere Ltd	Gamston	20. 1.09E
G-SERL	SOCATA TB-10 Tobago	109	G-LANA EI-BIH	28. 5.92	R J Searle	Rochester	18. 7.09E
G-SERV	Cameron N-105 Balloon (Hot Air)	10382		16. 4.03	PSH Skypower Ltd *(Servo Connectors titles)*	Woodborough, Pewsey	15. 3.09E
G-SETI	Cameron Sky 80-16 Balloon (Hot Air)	4853		25. 9.00	R P Allan	Aston Rowant, Watlington	9. 7.09E
G-SEVA	Replica Plans SE.5a	PFA 020-10955		19. 6.85	I D Gregory *(As "F-141:G" in RFC 141 Sqdn c/s)*	Boscombe Down	19. 2.09P
	(Built I D Gregory) (Continental C90)						
G-SEVE	Cessna 172N Skyhawk II	17269970	N738GR	10. 1.90	MK Aero Support Ltd *(Operated Sheffield Aero Club)*	Netherthorpe	15. 6.09E
G-SEVN	Van's RV-7	PFA 323-13795		13. 9.01	N Reddish	Netherthorpe	28. 8.09P
	(Built N Reddish) (Lycoming O-360)						
G-SEWP	Aérospatiale AS.355F2 Ecureuil 2	5480	G-OFIN G-DANS, G-BTNM	14. 8.00	Gryphon Aviation LLP *(Operated South East Wales Police)*	Cardiff Heliport	15. 7.09E
G-SEXE	Scheibe SF25C-2000 Falke	44396	N716SF (D-KNII)	31. 7.03	Repulor Ltd	Saltby	10. 4.09E
	(Limbach L 2000)						
G-SEXI	Cessna 172M Skyhawk II	17263806	N1964V	21. 4.92	Willowair Flying Club (1996) Ltd	(Southend)	5. 9.04T
	(Bounced landing Nayland 2. 2.02 and overran, struck hedge and substantially damaged)						
G-SEXX	Piper PA-28-161 Cherokee Warrior II	28-7816196	SE-GVD	12.05.03	Weald Air Services Ltd	Headcorn	14. 1.10E
G-SFAR	Comco Ikarus C42 FB100	0704-6883		27. 3.07	S Farrow	Barton	21. 5.09P
G-SFCJ	Cessna 525 CitationJet	525-0245	N33CJ N5124J	21. 7.04	Sureflight Aviation Ltd	Oxford	30. 7.09E
G-SFLA	Comco Ikarus C42 FB80	0701-6867		15. 6.07	Solent Flight Ltd	Phoenix Farm, Lower Upham	17. 6.08P
G-SFLB	Comco Ikarus C42 FB80	0709-6914		13.11.07	Solent Flight Ltd	Phoenix Farm, Lower Upham	12.11.09P
G-SFLY	Diamond DA.40 Star	40362		31. 3.04	L and Nathalie.P L Turner	Sleap	24. 6.09E
G-SFOX	RotorWay Executive 90	5059	G-BUAH	11.10.93	Magpie Technology Ltd	Crabtree Farm, Crowborough	19.12.07P
	(Built I L Griffith) (RotorWay RI 162)						
G-SFPB	Reims Cessna F406 Caravan II	F406-0065		11.11.91	Reims Aviation Industries SA	Reims-Prunay, France	26. 4.09E
G-SFRY	Thunder Ax7-77 Balloon (Hot Air)	1667		23. 1.90	M Rowlands	Wigan	8. 9.09E
G-SFSL	Cameron Z-105 Balloon (Hot Air)	10308		31. 7.02	B A Benjamin tr Somerfield Staff Lottery Fund *(Somerfield Supermarkets titles)*	Bristol	14. 2.09E
G-SFTZ	Slingsby T 67M-160 Firefly	2000		7. 2.83	Western Air (Thruxton) Ltd	Thruxton	12. 3.09E
G-SGEC	Beech B200 Super King Air	BB-1747	N214FW	19. 8.03	Keypoint Aviation LLP	Gamston	26. 8.09E
G-SGEN	Comco Ikarus C42 FB80	0407-6611		27. 8.04	G A Arturi	Old Sarum	10. 1.08P
	(Built Fly Buy Ultralights Ltd)						
G-SGSE	Piper PA-28-181 Cherokee Archer II	28-7890332	G-BOJX N3774M	2.12.96	U Patel	Barton	7. 6.09E
G-SHAA	Enstrom 280C-UK Shark	1011	N280Q	8. 7.88	C J and D Whitehead t/a ELT Radio Telephones	(Read, Burnley)	20. 5.09E
G-SHAF	Robinson R44 Raven II	10892		20.10.05	Tresillian Leisure Ltd	Denham	10.11.09E
G-SHAK	Cameron Cabin SS Balloon (Hot Air)	2820	SE-ZHO G-ODIS	23. 8.07	Magical Adventures Ltd	Oswestry	27. 9.09E
G-SHAN	Robinson R44 Clipper II	10617		28. 1.05	D Mollenhauer and T Eschner	Cranfield	18. 3.09E
G-SHAR	Cessna 182T Skylane	18281636	N1968L	11.11.05	S Harding	Denham	4.12.09E
G-SHAY	Piper PA-28R-201T Turbo Arrow III	28R-7703365	G-JEFS G-BFDG, N47381	17. 9.01	R Rudderham tr Alpha Yankee	Earls Colne	19.11.09E
G-SHED	Piper PA-28-181 Cherokee Archer II	28-7890068	G-BRAU N47411	12. 6.89	D R Allard tr G-SHED Flying Group	Gloucestershire	28. 6.09E
G-SHEE	P&M Aviation Quik GT450	8284		31. 7.07	L Cottle	Baxby Manor, Husthwaite	12. 8.09P
G-SHEZ	Mainair Sports Pegasus Quik	7993		28.10.03	R Wells	Old Sarum	8.11.09P
G-SHHH	Glaser-Dirks DG-100G Elan	E71G46	BGA2749-EKP	13. 3.08	P J Masson	Lasham	
G-SHIM	CFM Streak Shadow	K 228-SA		19. 5.93	J A Weston	Shobdon	5. 3.09P
	(Built E G Shimmin - pr.no.PFA 206-12501) (Rotax 582)						
G-SHMI	Evektor EV-97 teamEurostar UK	3013		3.10.07	Poet Pilot (UK) Ltd *(Operated Skytime Flight Training)*	Gloucestershire	2.10.08P
	(Built Cosmik Aviation Ltd)						
G-SHMS	Agusta Bell 206B-2 JetRanger II	8739	EI-GWT G-CORT	29.10.07	S H Moore and Sons Ltd	(Pomeroy, Dungannon)	4.12.08E
G-SHOG	Colomban MC-15 Cri-Cri	001	G-PFAB F-PYPU	3.10.96	K D and C S Rhodes	Henstridge	31. 3.09P
	(Built G Nappez) (JPX PUL-212)						
G-SHRK	Enstrom 280C-UK Shark	1173	N373SA G-SHRK, G-BGMX, EI-CCS, G-SHXX, G-BGMX, EI-BHR, G-BGMX, (F-GBOS)	6. 1.97	Flighthire Ltd	Henstridge	30. 6.09E
G-SHRN	Schweizer 269C-1 *(Schweizer 300)*	0336	N86G	30. 6.08	CSL International Ltd	Doncaster-Robin Hood	29. 7.09E
G-SHSH	Europa Aviation Europa	113		7. 4.98	S G Hayman and J Price	Rochester	8. 8.09P
	(Built D G Hillam - pr.no.PFA 247-12722) (Monowheel u/c)						
G-SHSP	Cessna 172S Skyhawk SP	172S8078	N9552Q	25. 3.99	Shropshire Aero Club Ltd	Sleap	1. 5.09E
G-SHUF	Mainair Blade	1241-0200-7-W1034		10. 3.00	R G Bradley	(Newton Bank Farm, Daresbury)	27. 3.07P
	(Rotax 582)						
G-SHUG	Piper PA-28R-201T Turbo Arrow III		N1026Q	17. 5.88	G-SHUG Ltd	Wycombe Air Park	10. 7.09E
G-SHUU	Enstrom 280C-UK-2 Shark	1221	G-OMCP G-KENY, G-BJFG, N8617N	16.10.89	D Ellis	Hawarden	6. 8.09E
G-SHUV	Aerosport Woody Pusher	PFA 007A-13960		20. 9.02	J R Wraight	(Chatham)	
	(Built J R Wraight)						
G-SHWK	Cessna 172S Skyhawk	172S9642	N21733	2. 6.04	The Cambridge Aero Club Ltd	Cambridge	19. 6.09E
G-SIAI	SIAI-Marchetti SF.260W	361/31-005	F-GVAB (2) OO-XCP, FAB-184	15. 1.01	D Gage *(As "FAB-184" in Bolivian AF c/s)*	Wycombe Air Park	29. 3.09P
G-SIAM	Cameron V-90 Balloon (Hot Air)	4096	G-BXBS	7. 3.01	S Steffensen	Skien, Norway	27. 9.09E
G-SICA	Britten-Norman BN-2B-20 Islander	2304	G-SLAP	19. 7.06	Shetland Leasing and Property Development Ltd *(www.shetland.gov.uk titles)*	Tingwall	17.12.09E

G-SICB	Pilatus Britten-Norman BN-2B-20 Islander	2260	G-NESU	12. 6.06	Shetland Islands Council (www.shetland.gov.uk titles)	Tingwall	2. 4.09E
G-SIGN	Piper PA-39 Twin Comanche C/R	39-8	G-BTVN OY-TOO N8853Y	9. 2.78	D Buttle	Blackbushe	26. 5.09E
G-SIIB	Pitts S-2B (Built Aviat Inc) (Lycoming AEIO-540)	5218	G-BUVY N6073U	24. 3.93	M Zikes (Prague, Czech Republic) (Noted damaged Oloumuc, Czech Republic 9.07)		30. 4.08E
G-SIIE	Pitts S-2B (Built Christen Industries Inc) (Lycoming AEIO-540)	5057	G-SKYD N5331N	6. 2.04	J and T J Bennett (Hareby, Spilsby)		5. 8.09E
G-SIII	Extra EA.300	058	D-ETYE	10. 1.95	Fun Flight Ltd "61"	White Waltham	21.12.09E
G-SIIS	Pitts S-1S (Built J A Harris) (Lycoming O-360)	PFA 009-13485	G-RIPE	3. 7.02	I H Searson	Leicester	9.12.09P
G-SIJJ	North American P-51D-20-NA Mustang	122-31894	F-AZMU N5306M, HK-2812P, HK-2812X, N5411V, 44-72035	20.03.03	P A Teichman "Jumpin' Jacques" (As "472035" in USAF c/s)	North Weald	15. 7.09P
G-SIJW	Scottish Aviation Bulldog Series 120/121	BH120/295	XX630	31. 3.00	M Miles (As "XX630:25" in RAF c/s)	Shenington	15. 3.08S
G-SILS	Pietenpol AirCamper (Built D Silsbury -single-seat version of Aircamper designated Pietenpol Skyscout) (On build 3.07)	PFA 047-13331		29. 6.98	D Silsbury	Dunkeswell	
G-SILY	Pegasus Quantum 15	8074		17.12.04	N J Brownlow	(Nottingham)	15. 1.10P
G-SIMI	Cameron A-315 Balloon (Hot Air)	3391		10. 3.95	Balloon School (International) Ltd t/a Balloon Safaris	Colhook Common, Petworth	11. 7.09E
G-SIMM	Comco Ikarus C42 FB100 VLA (Built D Simmons)	PFA 322-14286		6. 9.04	D Simmons	(Newmarket)	21. 9.08P
G-SIMP	Avtech Jabiru UL-450 (Built J C Simpson - pr.no.PFA 274B-13794)	xxxx		4. 1.02	L J Field	Kittyhawk Farm, Deanland	18. 2.09P
G-SIMS	Robinson R22 Beta	1596	N7800R LV-RBZ	14. 6.04	HS (Holdings) Ltd t/a Heli-One	Durham Tees Valley	24. 7.09E
G-SIMY	Piper PA-32-300 Cherokee Six	32-7640082	G-OCPF G-BOCH, N9292K	22. 3.04	I Simpson	Carlisle	26. 9.09E
G-SINK	Schleicher ASH 25	25139	BGA5009-KDM F-CHAY	17. 9.07	A F W Watson tr G-SINK Group "RC"	Cranwell	25. 3.08
G-SIPA	SIPA 903	63	G-BGBM F-BGBM	31. 5.83	A C Leak and J H Dilland (On restoration 2007)	(Southampton)	14. 2.89P
G-SIRA	Embraer EMB-135BJ Legacy	14500832	OE-IAS (N832SG), PT-SIL	19.10.05	Amsair Aircraft Ltd	London Stansted	27.10.09E
G-SIRD	Robinson R44 Raven II	11745		21. 5.07	Peglington Productions Ltd	Wycombe Air Park	31. 5.09E
G-SIRE	Best Off Sky Ranger Swift 912S(1) (Built P Rigby)	SKR0608740	(Project no.BMAA HB/531)	26. 3.07	P Rigby	Flint Farm, Norfolk	18.12.09P
G-SIRJ	Cessna 680 Citation Sovereign	680-0216		26. 6.08	Bookajet Ltd	Farnborough	25. 6.09E
G-SIRO	Dassault Falcon 900EX	172	F-WWFL	16. 5.07	Condor Aviation LLP	Leeds-Bradford	16. 5.09E
G-SIRS	Cessna 560XL Citation Excel	560-5185	N51042	1. 8.01	London Executive Aviation Ltd	London Stansted	1. 8.09E
G-SISI	Schempp-Hirth Duo Discus	193	BGA5002-KDE PH-1141	17. 8.07	R N John tr Glider Sierra India	Dunstable	19.11.07
G-SISU	P&M Aviation Quik GT450	6215		29. 8.06	Executive and Business Aviation Support Ltd	Woodstock, Oxford	22. 5.09P
G-SITA	Pegasus Quantum 15-912	7797		18. 6.01	A D Curtin	Newnham, Baldock	15. 6.09P
G-SIVJ	Westland SA.341C Gazelle HT.2	2012	G-CBSG ZB649	26. 6.02	Skytrace (UK) Ltd	Wolverhampton	25. 3.09P
G-SIVR	MD Helicopters MD.900 Explorer	900-00102	N7002S	20. 8.02	Mandarin Aviation Ltd	Redhill	5. 9.09E
G-SIVW	Lake LA-250 Renegade (Built Aerofab Inc)	233	N8553T	6. 2.03	C J Siva-Jothy	Redhill	24. 5.08E
G-SIXC	Douglas DC-6B	45550	N93459 N90645, B-1006, XW-PFZ, B-1006	20. 3.87	Air Atlantique Ltd	Coventry	4. 4.05T
G-SIXD	Piper PA-32-300 Cherokee Six D	32-7140007	HB-OMH N8615N	25. 3.98	M B Payne and I Gordon	King's Farm, Thurrock	16. 1.10E
G-SIXS	Whittaker MW6-S Fatboy Flyer (Built R H Braithwaite)	PFA 164-12521		27. 8.03	P E Young	(Morpeth)	27. 3.09P
G-SIXT	Piper PA-28-161 Warrior II	2816056	G-BSSX N9141H	22. 2.08	Airways Aero Associations Ltd Wycombe Air Park (Operated British Airways Flying Club) (Hybrid BEA / BOAC c/s to celebrate 60th Anniversary)		14.11.09E
G-SIXX	Colt 77A Balloon (Hot Air)	1327		21.10.88	M Dear and M Taylor "6X"	Marlow and Aylesbury	27. 4.09E
G-SIXY	Van's RV-6 (Built C J Hall and C R P Hamlett)	PFA 181-13368		9. 3.99	C J Hall and C R P Hamlett	(Cambridge)	
G-SIZZ	Avtech Jabiru J400 (Built K J Betterley - pr.no.PFA 325-14483)	0xxx		13. 2. 06	K J Betterley	Sandown	16. 4.09P
G-SJBI	Pitts S-2C (Built Aviat Aircraft) (Lycoming AEIO-540)	6082	N10UK	11. 6.08	S L Walton	(London WC2)	6. 8.09P
G-SJCH	Pilatus Britten-Norman BN-2T-4S Islander	4006	G-BWPK	18.11.99	Hampshire Police Authority "Sir John Charles Hoddinott"	Lee-on-Solent	26. 2.08E
G-SJEN	Comco Ikarus C42 FB80 (Built M C Henry)	0405-6602		1. 7.04	C M Mackinnon	Strathaven	9. 4.09P
G-SJES	Evektor EV-97 teamEurostar UK (Built Cosmik Aviation Ltd)	2918		15. 6.07	Purple Aviation Ltd	Eshott	14. 6.08P
G-SJKR	Lindstrand LBL 90A Balloon (Hot Air)	756		26. 1.01	S J Roake "Smarthouse"	Frimley, Camberley	15. 2.09E
G-SJMH	Robin DR.400-140B (Thielert TAE 125)	2637		10. 7.08	C S and J A Bailey	(London NW3)	19. 8.09E
G-SJPI	Aerospool Dynamic WT9 UK (Built Yeoman Light Aircraft Co)(Originally regd as DY257, amended 1.09)	DY281		29. 4.08	Yeoman Light Aircraft Co Ltd	Manor Farm, Drayton St Leonard	
G-SJSS	Bombardier CL600-2B16 (CL-604 Challenger)	5760	C-FTRQ	18.11.08	TAG Aviation (UK) Ltd	Farnborough	
G-SKAN	Reims Cessna F172M Skyhawk II	F17201120	G-BFKT F-BVBJ	8. 7.85	J Williams and M Richardson	Boscombe Down	16. 4.09E
G-SKCI	Rutan VariEze (Built S K Cockburn)	PFA 074-12081		30. 3.01	A Levitt	(Blackshaw Edge, Hebden Bridge)	

Reg	Type	C/n	Previous ID	Date	Owner/Operator	Location	Date
G-SKEW	Mudry CAP.232	11	F-GXRB, F-GRRG, F-GCKK, French Army	28.11.03	J H Askew	Wickenby	28. 2.09E
G-SKIE	Steen Skybolt *(Built D Axe)* (Lycoming IO-540)	AACA-357	ZK-DEN	29. 8.97	K G G Howe and M J Coles	Barton	27. 3.09P
G-SKII	Agusta-Bell 206B-3 JetRanger III	8562	EI-BKT, D-HAFD, HB-XIC	22. 4.03	K Toner t/a K P Toner (Developments) Kilmaddy, Dungannon, County Tyrone		13. 5.09E
G-SKKY	Cessna 172S Skyhawk	172S9850	N14897	30. 6.05	Skyquest Ltd	White Waltham	1. 8.09E
G-SKNT	Pitts S-2A *(Built Aerotek Inc)* (Lycoming AEIO-540)	2048	G-PEAL, N81LF, N48KA	31. 3.03	First Light Aviation Ltd	(Bucknell)	9.11.09E
G-SKOT	Cameron V-42 Balloon (Hot Air)	4813		27. 6.00	S A Laing	Banchory	21. 9.09E
G-SKPG	Best Off Sky Ranger 912(2) *(Built P Gibbs - pr.no.BMAA HB/400)*	SKR0404483		11.11.04	P Gibbs	Plaistows Farm, St Albans	19. 7.09P
G-SKPH	Yakovlev Yak-50	853010	G-BWWH, LY-ABL, LY-XNI, DOSAAF	15. 3.05	R S Partridge-Hicks and I C Austin (As "853010") Little Haugh Hall, Norton, Bury St Edmunds		9. 1.09P
G-SKRA	Best Off Sky Ranger 912(2) *(Built P A Banks- pr.no.BMAA HB/458)*	SKR0504599		21.11.05	P A Banks	Finmere	10. 7.09P
G-SKRG	Best Off Sky Ranger 912(2) *(Built R W Goddin - pr.no.BMAA HB/298)*	SKR0307352		2. 9.03	I D Town and R W Goddin White Hill Fam, Melbourn		13.12.09P
G-SKSW	Best Off Sky Ranger Swift 912S(1) *(Built M D and S M North - pr.no.BMAA HB/553)*	SKR0707804		3.10.07	M D and S M North	(Milton Keynes)	6. 7.09P
G-SKUA	Stoddard-Hamilton GlaStar *(Built L A James)* (Lycoming O-320) *(Tri-cycle u/c)*	PFA 295-13241	G-LEZZ	30. 8.07	F P Smiddy	Rochester	27. 6.08P
G-SKYC	Slingsby T 67M Firefly	2009	G-BLDP	13. 6.97	T W Cassells	Bagby	26.10.09E
G-SKYE	Cessna TU206G Turbo Stationair 6 II	U20604568	(G-DROP), N9783M	1. 8.79	S M C Harvey	Hinton-in-the-Hedges	20. 7.09E
G-SKYF	SOCATA TB-10 Tobago	1589	VH-YHG	1. 5.01	W L McNeil	Enstone	21. 6.09E
G-SKYJ	Cameron Z-315 Balloon (Hot Air)	10964		14. 6.07	Cameron Flights Southern Ltd *(Cameron Balloons titles)* Woodborough, Pewsey		28. 5.09E
G-SKYK	Cameron A-275 Balloon (Hot Air)	4879		31. 7.00	Cameron Flights Southern Ltd *(Cameron Balloons titles)* Woodborough, Pewsey		6. 4.09E
G-SKYL	Cessna 182S Skylane	18280176	N4104D	19. 6.98	Skylane Aviation Ltd	Sherburn-in-Elmet	5.10.09E
G-SKYN	Aérospatiale AS.355F1 Ecureuil 2	5185	G-OGRK, G-BWZC, (G-MOBZ), N107KF, N5799R	21.11.03	Arena Aviation Ltd *(Operated Sky News)*	Redhill	24. 4.09E
G-SKYO	Slingsby T 67M-200 Firefly	2264		20. 9.00	R H Evelyn	White Waltham	10. 4.09E
G-SKYR	Cameron A-180 Balloon (Hot Air)	2826		31. 3.92	Cameron Flights Southern Ltd *"Candy Floss"* Woodborough, Pewsey		29. 4.00T
G-SKYT	III Sky Arrow 650 TC *(Built Iniziative Industriali Italian)*	C004		6. 9.96	W M Bell and S J Brooks	Bicester	11. 6.09P
G-SKYU	Cameron A-210 Balloon (Hot Air)	10129		28. 8.01	Cameron Flights Southern Ltd *(Evening Advertiser titles)* Woodborough, Pewsey		5. 3.09E
G-SKYV	Piper PA-28RT-201T Turbo Arrow IV	28R-8031132	G-BNZG, N82376	20. 9.04	North Yorks Properties Ltd	(Port Soderick, IoM)	18. 3.02
G-SKYW	Aérospatiale AS.355F1 Ecureuil 2	5261	G-BTIS, G-TALI	17. 1.05	Skywalker Aviation Ltd	Elstree	8. 7.09E
G-SKYX	Cameron A-210 Balloon (Hot Air)	4613		22. 6.99	Cameron Flights Southern Ltd *(Whitely Village titles)* Woodborough, Pewsey		7. 8.08T
G-SKYY	Cameron A-250 Balloon (Hot Air)	3402		9. 3.95	Cameron Flights Southern Ltd *"City of Southampton"* Woodborough, Pewsey		9. 3.01T
G-SLAC	Cameron N-77 Balloon (Hot Air)	2295		7. 6.90	B L Alderson *"Scottish Life"*	Southport	23. 3.09E
G-SLAK	Thruster T.600N 450	0122-T600N-075	G-CBXH	24. 9.08	M P Williams	Craysmarsh Farm, Melksham	28. 4.09P
G-SLCE	Cameron C-80 Balloon (Hot Air)	4022		24. 2.97	A M Holly	Breadstone, Berkeley	20. 5.09E
G-SLCT	Diamond DA.42 Twin Star	42.031		30. 6.05	Stapleford Flying Club Ltd	Stapleford	20. 7.09E
G-SLEA	Mudry CAP.10B	124		19.12.80	M J M Jenkins	RAF Wittering	14. 8.09E
G-SLII	Cameron O-90 Balloon (Hot Air)	2388		20. 9.90	R B and A M Harris *"Mad Dash"* Buckden, St Neots		17. 8.03A
G-SLIP	Reality Easy Raider BMW R100 *(Built J S Harris - pr.no.BMAA HB/215)*	0004		21. 5.02	D R Squires	(Wokingham)	
G-SLMG	Diamond HK 36 TTC Super Dimona	36.727	N267JP	5. 8.04	P R Thody and A R Morley tr G-SLMG Syndicate Kemble		11. 3.10E
G-SLNT	Flight Design CTSW *(Assembled P&M Aviation Ltd with c/n 8254)*	06.10.02		28. 2.07	S Munday	Longacre Farm, Sandy	5. 3.09E
G-SLNW	Robinson R22 Beta II	3524	G-LNIC	7. 4.06	Heli-4-Charter LLP	Barton	10. 2.09E
G-SLOK	Robinson R44 Raven II	10752		23. 5.05	Heli-4-Charter LLP	Manchester	24. 6.09E
G-SLTN	SOCATA TB-20 Trinidad	763	HB-KBR	6. 8.99	Oceana Air Ltd	Elstree	27. 9.09E
G-SLYN	Piper PA-28-161 Warrior II *(Thielert TAE 125-02)*	28-8116204	N161WA, N8373K	12. 4.89	Airtime Aviation France Ltd	Compton Abbas	27. 4.09E
G-SMAC	MD Helicopters MD.500N Notar	LN020	N8330F, N5200R	21.12.05	R A Roberts t/a Puddleduck Plane Partnership West Molesey		16. 3.09E
G-SMAN	Airbus A330-243	261	F-WWKR	26. 3.99	Monarch Airlines Ltd	Luton	25. 3.09E
G-SMAS	British Aircraft Corporation 167 Strikemaster Mk.80A	EEP/JP/149	R Saudi AF 1104, G-27-23	25. 4.05	M A Petrie (As ""1104" in Royal Saudi AF c/s) *(Noted 3.06)*	Hawarden	
G-SMBM	Pegasus Quantum 15-912 Super Sport	7602		24. 1.00	N Charles and P A Henretty	Swinford, Rugby	20. 3.09P
G-SMCL	Cessna 150M	15077385	N63546	17. 9.07	A A McLellan	North Weald	31. 1.09E
G-SMDH	Europa Aviation Europa XS *(Built S W Pitt - pr.no.PFA 247-13367)* *(Tri-gear u/c)*	403		8.10.98	S W Pitt	Popham	21.11.08P
G-SMDJ	Eurocopter AS.350B2 Ecureuil	3187		21. 4.99	M Ziani de Ferranti	(Llanfairfechan)	12. 8.09E
G-SMIG	Cameron O-65 Balloon (Hot Air)	922		6. 6.83	R D Parry *(San Miguel titles) (Active 5.05)* Stroud		28. 7.87A
G-SMKM	Cirrus SR20	1662	N50910	27. 7.06	K Mallet	Jersey	15. 5.09E
G-SMMA	Reims Cessna F406 Caravan II	F406-0094		24. 4.08	Secretary of State for Scotland per Environmental and Rural Affairs Department	Edinburgh	7. 5.09E
G-SMMB	Reims Cessna F406 Caravan II	F406-0095		6. 1.09	Secretary of State for Scotland per Environmental and Rural Affairs Department	Edinburgh	
G-SMRS	Cessna 172F Skyhawk	17252558	N8656U	17. 3.06	M R Sarlin *"The Missus"*	Andrewsfield	3. 7.09E

G-SMRT	Lindstrand LBL 260A Balloon (Hot Air)	1034		2. 6.05	M E White	Templeogue, Dublin	13. 7.09E
G-SMTH	Piper PA-28-140 Cherokee C	28-26916	G-AYJS	28. 9.90	R W Harris and A Jahanfar	Southend	17.12.08E
			N11C		*(Operated Flywatch Ltd)*		
G-SMTJ	Airbus A321-211	1972	D-AVXG	15. 5.03	Thomas Cook Airlines Ltd	Manchester	14. 5.09E
G-SMYK	PZL-Swidnik PW-5 Smyk	17.06.020	BGA4311-HYM	28. 4.08	P Webber tr PW-5 Syndicate *"PW5"*	Lasham	
G-SNAK	Lindstrand LBL 105A Balloon (Hot Air)	404		23. 9.96	Ballooning Adventures Ltd	(Hexham)	3. 4.07T
G-SNAL	Cessna 182T Skylane	18282123	N6310X	12. 9.08	N S Lyndhurst	Goodwood	21.10.09E
G-SNAP	Cameron V-77 Balloon (Hot Air)	1217		29.11.85	C J S Limon *"Snapshot"*	Great Missenden	19. 9.04A
G-SNEV	CFM Streak Shadow SA	K 283		17. 9.96	J D Reed	Henstridge	25. 7.08P
	(Built N G Smart - pr.no.PFA 206-13042) (Rotax 582)						
G-SNIF	Cameron A-300 Balloon (Hot Air)	10658		14. 4.05	A C K Rawson and J J Rudoni *"Stan Robinson"*		
						Stafford	19. 3.09E
G-SNOG	Air Création 582(1)/Kiss 400	FL011		2. 5.02	P S Wesley	Sywell	4. 4.08P
	(Built B H Ashman - pr.no.BMAA HB/219 being Flylight kit comprising Trike s/n T02033 and Wing s/n A02048-2045)						
G-SNOP	Europa Aviation Europa	040	G-DESL	3. 1.07	Bob Crowe Aircraft Sales Ltd	Cranfield	10.11.98P
			G-WWWG , "G-DSEL", G-WWWG				
	(Built W R C Williams-Wynne - pr.no.PFA 247-12597) *(Monowheel u/c)*						
G-SNOW (2)	Cameron V-77 Balloon (Hot Air)	2050		21. 6.79	G G Cannon and P Haworth	Foulridge, Colne	27. 5.09E
	(Officially regd with c/n 541 but fitted with replacement envelope 1989)						
G-SNOZ	Europa Aviation Europa	032	G-DONZ	7.10.04	P O Bayliss	(Porthcawl)	
	(Built D J Smith and D McNicholl - pr.no.PFA 247-12545)						
G-SNUZ	Piper PA-28-161 Warrior II	28-8416021	G-PSFT	19.12.01	JCOA Ltd	Fairoaks	29. 1.09E
			G-BPDS, N4328P				
G-SNZY	Learjet 45	45-375	N4003L	28.10.08	TAG Aviation (UK) Ltd	Farnborough	27.10.09E
G-SOAF	British Aircraft Corporation 167 Strikemaster Mk.82A		Omani AF 425	21. 2.05	Strikemaster Flying Club *(As "425" in RAF of Oman c/s)*		
		PS.376				Hawarden	30. 9.09P
G-SOAR	Eiriavion PIK-20E	20214		21. 6.79	R I Huttlestone	Bidford	2. 9.09E
G-SOBI	Piper PA-28-181 Cherokee Archer II		D-EAQL	3. 5.00	Northern Aviation Ltd	Durham Tees Valley	17. 8.09E
		28-7690212					
G-SOCK	Mainair Sports Pegasus Quik	8041		25. 5.04	J F Shaw and K R McCartney		
						Baxby Manor, Husthwaite	31. 7.09P
G-SOCT	Yakovlev Yak-50	842804	LY-XCD	17. 3.04	C R Turton	Headcorn	5. 6.09P
			DOSAAF 32		*(Also carries "CT304:RB-A" in pseudo-RAF scheme)*		
G-SOEI	Hawker Siddeley HS.748 Series 2A/242	1689	ZK-DES	25. 2.98	PTB (Emerald) Proprietary Ltd *(Stored 11.08)*		
						Blackpool	17. 4.07T
G-SOFT	Thunder Ax7-77 Balloon (Hot Air)	1339		5.12.88	A J Bowen	Aberdour, Burntisland	11. 9.99A
					"Enterprise Software" (Noted 8.06)		
G-SOHO	Diamond DA.40D Star	D4.079		12. 2.04	Soho Aviation Ltd	Biggin Hill	11. 5.09E
G-SOKO	Solo P-2 Kraguj	033	G-BRXK	31. 7.07	A L Tuttle *(As "30149:149" in Yugoslav AF c/s)*		
			Yugoslav AF 30149			Spanhoe	9. 7.09P
G-SONX	Sonex Sonex	LAA 337-14776		13.11.08	M Chambers	Crosland Moor	
	(Built M Chambers)						
G-SOOC	Hughes 369HS *(Hughes 500)*	111-0354S	G-BRRX	6.10.93	R J H Strong	Vagg Hill, Yeovil	23. 2.06
			N9083F		*(Noted 12.07)*		
G-SOOM	Glaser-Dirks DG-500M	5E42M20	BGA4907	14. 5.92	G W Kirton	(Lamassara, Andorra)	5.10.06
			G-SOOM				
G-SOOS	Colt 21A Cloudhopper Balloon (Hot Air)	1263		7. 6.88	P J Stapley	Redcar	25. 3.95A
G-SOOT	Piper PA-28-180 Cherokee C	28-4033	G-AVNM	19. 8.88	A G Branch	Exeter	23. 9.09E
			N11C				
G-SOOZ	Rans S-6-ESN Coyote II	0899.1335		27. 4.01	S N Lawrence	Rufforth	27.11.09P
	(Built A Batters - pr.no.PFA 204-13543) *(Tri-cycle u/c)*						
G-SOPH	Best Off Sky Ranger 912(2)	SKR0212286		25. 2.03	G E Reynolds	Sackville Lodge, Riseley	1. 9.08P
	(Built N A Reed - pr.no.BMAA HB/259)						
G-SOPP	Enstrom 280FX	2024	G-OSAB	23.10.97	F P M Sopp and L A Moore		
			N86259			Jefferies Farm, Billingshurst	17. 6.09E
G-SORA	DG Flugzeugbau DG-500/22 Elan	5E35S7	BGA5269-KPC	23. 2.07	C A Boyle, C P Arthur, B Douglas and R Jackson *"KPC"*		
			PH-1082, D-5219			Rufforth	19. 3.08
G-SORT	Cameron N-90 Balloon (Hot Air)	2878		13. 7.92	A Brown *"Streamline"*	Bristol	8. 7.04A
G-SOUL	Cessna 310R II	310R0140	N5020J	27. 6.88	Reconnaissance Ventures Ltd	Coventry	27. 6.09E
					(Atlantic Reconnaissance & OSRL titles, red/white c/s)		
G-SOVA	Cessna 550 Citation II	550-0649	N649DA	11.12.06	Mitre Aviation Ltd	Biggin Hill	18.12.08E
			HB-VMH, N44LQ, N44LC, N4320P, I-ATSE, (N1310Z)				
G-SOVB	Learjet Model 45	45-138	N138AX	12. 9.06	Murray Air Ltd	Biggin Hill	11. 9.09E
			G-OLDJ, N5018G				
G-SOVC	Learjet Model 45	45-161	N161AV	25. 9.07	Cumulus Investment Holdings Ltd	Biggin Hill	15.10.09E
G-SPAM	Avid Aerobat	829		9. 5.91	R A Hirst	Shobdon	18. 8.09P
	(Built C M Hicks - pr.no.PFA 189-12074)						
G-SPAO	Eurocopter EC.135 T2+	0546		19. 4.07	Bond Air Services Ltd *(Operated Strathclyde Police)*		
						Glasgow City Heliport	4. 9.09E
G-SPAT	Aero AT-3 R100	AT3.008	SP-EAR	20.10.04	S2T Aero Ltd	North Weald	21.11.08E
			(SP-ERM)				
G-SPCZ	CZAW Sporcruiser	LAA 338-14842		22. 9.08	R J Robinson	Hemel Hempstead	
	(Built R J Robinson)						
G-SPDR	de Havilland DH.115 Sea Vampire T 35	15641	VH-RAN	19. 5.00	M J Cobb *(As "N6-766": for overhaul 2007)*		
			Royal Australian Navy N6-766, XG766			Gyor-Per, Hungary	
G-SPDY	Raj Hamsa X'Air Hawk	xxxx		27. 4.07	G H Gilmour-White	(Thorverton, Exeter)	
	(Builder G H Gilmour-White, actually built by Scout groups in Exeter area - pr.no.PFA 340-14678) *(Noted NEC Birmingham 11.08)*						
G-SPED	Alpi Pioneer 300	LAA 330-14797		16. 7.08	M Taylor	(Withensea)	
	(Built M Taylor)						
G-SPEE	Robinson R22 Beta	0939	G-BPJC	20. 7.94	Verve Systems Ltd	Shobdon	28. 2.09E
G-SPEL	Sky 220-24 Balloon (Hot Air)	045		26. 7.96	T G Church t/a Pendle Balloon Company *(Pendle titles)*		
						Clayton le Dale, Blackburn	19. 9.09E
G-SPEY	Agusta-Bell 206B-3 JetRanger III	8608	G-BIGO	1. 4.81	Castle Air Charters Ltd	Liskeard-Heliport	12.12.08E

Reg	Type	C/n	Prev id	Date	Owner/Operator	Location	Expiry
G-SPFX	Rutan Cozy *(Built B D Tutty)*	PFA 159-13113		30. 4.97	B D Tutty	(Gillingham)	
G-SPHU	Eurocopter EC.135 T2	0245	D-HKBA	12.11.02	Bond Air Services Ltd *(Operated Great Western Air Ambulance)* Filton		27. 2.09E
G-SPIN	Pitts S-2A *(Built Aerotek Inc)* (Lycoming AEIO-540)	2110	N5CQ	13. 3.80	S D Judd *(Breitling Angels c/s, navy blue colours)* Wycombe Air Park		11. 5.09E
G-SPIT	Vickers Supermarine 379 Spitfire FR.XIVe	6S/649205	(G-BGHB) Indian AF T-20, MV293	2. 3.79	Patina Ltd *(As "MV268:JE-J")* *(Operated The Fighter Collection)*	Duxford	20. 4.09P
G-SPJE	Robinson R44 Raven II	12026		4.12.07	Abel Alarm Co Ltd	Leicester	13.12.09E
G-SPMM	Best Off Sky Ranger Swift 912S(1) *(Built S M Pink and M J Milne)*	SKRxxxx773		1. 6.07	S M Pink and M J Milne *(Pr.no.BMAA HB/539)*	Titsey, Oxted	
G-SPOG	SAN Jodel DR.1050 Ambassadeur	155	G-AXVS F-BJNL	25. 9.95	P D Thomas and T J Bates	Dairy House Farm, Worlston	13. 6.77S
	(Damaged Stoneacre Farm, Bredhurst 17. 2.91: on rebuild 1995)						
G-SPOR	Beech B200 Super King Air	BB-1557	N57TL N57TS	3. 9.99	Select Plant Hire Company Ltd	Southend	19. 9.09E
G-SPUR	Cessna 550 Citation II	550-0714	N593EM N12035	27.10.98	London Executive Aviation Ltd	London Stansted	15.11.09E
G-SPVK	Eurocopter AS.350B3 Ecureuil	4301	G-CERU F-WWXL	24. 9.07	GBL Aviation LLP	(Chesterfield)	3. 2.10E
G-SPYS	Robinson R44 Raven II	11274		14. 6.06	SKP Partnerships LLP	Wycombe Air Park	6. 7.09E
G-SRAH	Schempp-Hirth Mini-Nimbus C	96	BGA2446-DXQ	25. 3.08	P Hawkins	RAF Weston-on-the-Green	
G-SRAW	Alpi Pioneer 300 *(Built B W Grindle - pr.no.PFA 330-14292)*	xxx		3. 6.05	A R Lloyd and M Clare	Orlingbury Hold Farm, Hannington, Northampton	1.11.08P
G-SRDG	Dassault Falcon 7X	36	F-WWZX	19. 1.09	Triair (Bermuda) Ltd	Farnborough	28. 1.10E
G-SRII	Reality Easy Raider 503	10		2. 3.01	R J Creasey tr Sierra Romeo India India Group	Maypole Farm, Chislet	12.11.04P
	(Built T F Francis - pr.no.BMAA HB/163: originally regd as Sky Raider II 503 until 8.01)						
G-SROE	Westland Scout AH.1	F9508	XP907	26.10.95	Bolenda Engineering Ltd *(As "XP907" in AAC c/s)*	Ipswich	20. 3.06P
G-SRPH	Robinson R44 Raven	1849		2. 4.08	S Rooney t/a Rooney Helicopter Hire	(Dundalk, Ireland)	7. 5.09E
G-SRUM	Aero AT-3 100	AT3-044		10.11.08	Cunning Plan Development Ltd *(Operated Old Sarum Flying Club)*	Old Sarum	30.11.09E
G-SRVA	Cirrus SR20	1513	N60986	31. 8.05	Aero GB Ltd	Gloucestershire	7. 7.09E
G-SRVO	Cameron N-90 Balloon (Hot Air)	3551		10. 4.95	Servo and Electronic Sales Ltd *(Servo titles)*	Lydd	29. 7.04A
G-SRWN	Piper PA-28-161 Warrior II	28-8116284	G-MAND G-BRKT, N8082Z	30. 7.02	S Smith	Henstridge	3.12.01T
G-SRYY	Europa Aviation Europa XS *(Built S R Young - pr.no.PFA 247-13806)* (Jabiru 3300A) (Tri-gear u/c)	530		19. 9.02	S R Young	Nortom Malreward	16. 5.09P
G-SSBS	Colt 77A Balloon (Hot-Air)	010		2. 5.78	D G Such and M Tomlin	Royston	6. 4.09E
G-SSCL	Hughes 369E *(Hughes 500)*	0491E	N684F	25. 4.98	Stevens Construction Ltd	Rochester	12. 3.09E
G-SSEA	Aérospatiale-Alenia ATR 42-300	196	OY-CIT C-FZVZ, C-GITI, F-WWEK	29. 8.03	NAC Nordic Aviation Contractor A/S	Guernsey	20. 8.09E
G-SSEX	Rotorway Executive 162F *(Built J Donnon)*	6809		21. 3.06	M Middleby	(Killyleagh, Downpatrick)	
G-SSIX	Rans S-6-116 Coyote II	0394.602		5. 9.94	R I Kelly	Wellesbourne Mountford	14. 7.05P
	(Built J V Squires - pr.no.PFA 204A-12749) (Frame rebuilt and remarked as "0899.1335.800ES") (Rotax 582) (Tailwheel u/c)						
G-SSKY	Pilatus Britten-Norman BN-2B-26 Islander	2247	G-BSWT	11. 5.92	Isles of Scilly Skybus Ltd	St Just	31. 3.09E
G-SSLF	Lindstrand LBL 210A Balloon (Hot Air)	649		29. 2.00	High On Adventure Balloons Ltd *(Somerfield titles)*	West Clandon, Guildford	9. 6.09E
G-SSSC	Sikorsky S-76C	760408		26.10.93	CHC Scotia Ltd	Aberdeen	13. 1.10E
G-SSSD	Sikorsky S-76C	760415		26.10.93	CHC Scotia Ltd	Aberdeen	3. 1.10E
G-SSSE	Sikorsky S-76C	760417		23.11.93	CHC Scotia Ltd	Aberdeen	2. 2.10E
G-SSTI	Cameron N-105 Balloon (Hot Air)	3238		30. 3.94	A A Brown *"Concorde"*	Guildford	4. 9.09E
G-SSWV	Sportavia-Pützer RF5B Sperber	51032	N55WV D-KEAI	31. 5.90	N Fisher and D Athey tr The G-SSWV Flying Group	Camphill	23. 1.09P
G-SSXX	Eurocopter EC.135 T2	0270	G-SSSX	31. 3.03	Bond Air Services Ltd *(Operated Essex Air Ambulance)*	Boreham	27. 5.09E
G-STAA	Robinson R44 Astro	0492	G-HALE	11. 4.06	Walker Plant Services Ltd	Gamston	24. 9.09E
G-STAT	Cessna U206F Stationair II	U20603485	A6-MAM N8732Q	20. 2.79	K Brady tr Scottish Parachute Club	East Leys Farm, Grindale	17.10.05
	(Forced landed 8.03; fuselage noted 8.07)						
G-STAV	Cameron O-84 Balloon (Hot Air)	2913		29. 9.92	F Horsfall	Chipping Camden	1. 7.07A
G-STAY	Reims FR172K Hawk XP	FR17200620	D-EOVX OE-DVX	15.12.00	J M Wilkins	Swansea	25. 3.09E
G-STCC	Bombardier CL-600-2B16 *(CL-604 Challenger)*	5623	N623HA	9. 1.08	Private Jet Holding Ltd	London Stansted & Biggin Hill	14. 1.09E
G-STCH	Fieseler Fi 156A-1 Storch *(Argus AS10C)*	2088	Luftwaffe 2088	21. 5.03	P R Holloway	Old Warden	
G-STDL	Phillips ST2 Speedtwin *(2 x 140hp Walter LOM M332B) (Noted 5.07)*	PFA 207-12674	G-DPST	21. 6.06	Speedtwin Developments Ltd	Poplar Hall Farm, Elmsett	4. 8.09P
	(Developed from original Speedtwin Developments design by late P Phillips: assets and company acquired by M Ducker)						
G-STEA	Piper PA-28R-200 Cherokee Arrow II	28R-7235096	HB-OIH N4569T	18. 6.02	P J Alderton	Shoreham	3.12.08E
G-STEM	Stemme S 10-V	14-027	D-KSTE	2. 7.97	J Abbess tr G-STEM Group	Tibenham	19. 5.09E
G-STEN	Stemme S 10	10-32	D-KGCH	9. 1.92	J P Lyell tr G-STEN Syndicate *"4"*	Lasham	18. 5.09E
G-STEP	Schweizer 269C *(Schweizer 300)*	S 1494		1.10.90	M Johnson	Neath	28. 4.09E
G-STER	Bell 206B-3 JetRanger III	4116	OO-EGA	23. 3.94	Maintopic Ltd	Sherburn-in-Elmet	23. 6.09E
G-STEU	Rolladen-Schneider LS6-18W	6362	BGA4153-HRY	24. 1.08	F K Russell	Dunstable	4. 4.08
G-STEV	CEA Jodel DR.221 Dauphin	61	F-BOZD	9. 3.82	S W Talbot	Croft Farm, Defford	26. 5.09E
G-STGR	Agusta A109S Grand	22027	ZS-BAX	24.10.07	WA Developments International Ltd	Carlisle	20.11.09E
G-STHA	Piper PA-31-350 Chieftain	31-8052077	G-GLUG N2287J, G-BLOE, G-NITE, N3559A	29. 5.07	Skydrift Ltd *(SkySouth.co.uk titles)*	Shoreham	13. 4.09E

Reg	Type	c/n	Prev id	Date	Owner/Operator	Location	Expiry
G-STIG	Focke-Wulf FW.44J Stieglitz	183	OO-JKT (2), D-EHDH (2), LV-YYX	16. 2.04	P R Holloway (As "D2692" in Luftwaffe c/s)	Old Warden	26. 7.10S
G-STME	Stemme S 10-VT	11-115		17. 1.08	R A Roberts	Lasham	25. 1.09E
G-STMP	SAN Stampe SV-4A	241	F-BCKB	11. 3.83	A C Thorne	Bere Alston, Yelverton	
					(Noted dismantled 11.06)		
G-STNG	TL 2000 Sting Carbon	LAA 347-14789		2. 4.08	A G Rackstraw tr Geesting 3 Syndicate	Nottingham City-Tollerton	
	(Built A G Rackstraw, D L Hill and J V Bradbury)						
G-STNS	Agusta A109A II	7324	N716HA, N4RP, N109WS, D-HOOC, N1YB, N109KA	26. 4.06	Heliflight (UK) Ltd	Gloucestershire	14. 6.09E
G-STOB	Raytheon Hawker 400XP	RK-502	N502XP	20. 2.07	STA (2006) LLP	Carlisle	2. 4.09E
G-STOK	Cameron Colt 77B Balloon (Hot Air)	4791		4. 5.00	J.E Wetters and M H Read "Hollybush"	Timperley, Altrincham	13. 4.09E
G-STON	Eurocopter AS.355N Ecureuil 2	5663	VP-BCE	1.12.05	Gryphon Aviation LLP	Cardiff Heliport	26. 2.09E
G-STOO	Stolp SA.300 Starduster Too	PFA 035-13870		30. 1.03	K F Crumplin	Henstridge	7. 5.09P
	(Built K F Crumplin) (Lycoming IO-540)						
G-STOP	Robinson R44 Raven II	10852		5. 9.05	Cartis Ltd H O'Kelly and L Denning	(Dublin)	15. 9.09E
G-STOW	Cameron Wine Box 90 SS Balloon (Hot Air)	4420		2.10.98	I Martin and D Groombridge t/a Flying Enterprises Partnership (Stowells of Chelsea titles)	Bristol	23. 7.09E
G-STPH	Robinson R44 Raven	1613		14. 6.06	Westrock Aviation Ltd	Enniskillen	3. 7.09E
G-STPI	Cameron A-250 Balloon (Hot Air)	4102		26. 2.97	The Ballooning Business Ltd	Walcote, Alcester	20. 2.09E
G-STRF	Boeing 737-76N	29885	EI-CXD	1. 4.04	Astraeus Ltd	London Gatwick	31. 3.09E
G-STRG	Cyclone AX2000	7837		24. 7.01	D Young tr Pegasus Flight Training (Cotswolds)	Kemble	10.10.08P
	(HKS 700E V3)						
G-STRH	Boeing 737-76N	32737	EI-CXE	17. 5.04	Astraeus Ltd	London Gatwick	16. 5.09E
G-STRL	Eurocopter AS.355N Ecureuil 2	5733		14.12.04	Harrier Enterprises Ltd	(Douglas, Isle of Man)	3. 7.09E
G-STRM	Cameron N-90 Balloon (Hot Air)	3568		3. 7.95	A Brown	Winscombe	6. 9.06E
G-STRX	Boeing 757-28A	25621	N459AX, N551NA, N25621, C-FXOO	5. 2.08	Astraeus Ltd (Operated for bmi)	London Heathrow	4. 2.09E
G-STRY	Boeing 757-28A	28161	N369AX, N543NA, N161KB, C-FOON	16.12.07	Astraeus Ltd (Operated for bmi)	London Heathrow	15.12.09E
G-STRZ	Boeing 757-258	27622	4X-EBI	1. 4.07	Astraeus Ltd	London Gatwick	4. 4.09E
G-STUA	Pitts S-2A	2164	N13GT	6. 3.91	P J G Margetson-Rushmore tr G-STUA Group	Stapleford	21. 3.09E
	(Built Aerotek Inc) (Lycoming AEIO-540)						
G-STUB	Pitts S-2B (Lycoming AEIO-540)	5163	N260Y	5. 5.94	A F D Kingdon	(Banbury)	13. 8.09E
	(Built Christen Industries Inc) (Lycoming AEIO-540)						
G-STUE	Europa Aviation Europa	xxxx		20.11.06	S Philp	(Worcester)	
	(Built S Philp) - pr.no.PFA 247-12869)						
G-STUF	Learjet Model 40	45-2074	N40012	27. 4.07	Air Partner Private Jets Ltd	Biggin Hill	26. 4.09E
G-STUY	Robinson R44 Raven II	10508		8.10.04	S Mayers	Redhill	19.11.09E
G-STVT	CZAW Sportcruiser	PFA 338-14676		14. 3.08	S Taylor	(Worksop)	
	(Built S Taylor)						
G-STWO	ARV Aviation ARV-1 Super 2	002		24. 4.85	P M Paul	Draycott Farm, Chiseldon	4. 9.09P
	(Built ARV Aviation Ltd - pr.no.PFA 152-11048)						
G-STYL	Pitts S-1S	GJSN-1P	N665JG	26. 1.88	A P Durston	Cawston	31. 3.09P
	(Built G Harben and G Smith) (Lycoming-O-320)						
G-SUCH	Cameron N-77 Balloon (Hot Air)	676	G-BIGD	3. 9.01	D G Such	Barkway, Royston	8. 3.09E
G-SUCK	Cameron Z-105 Balloon (Hot Air)	10280		16. 5.02	R P Wade	Shevington, Wigan	2. 5.09E
G-SUCT	Robinson R22 Beta	4078		29. 9.06	P Irwin tr Irwin Plant Sales	Enniskillen	23.10.09E
G-SUEA	Diamond DA.42 Twin Star	42.256		26. 6.07	S D Coxen t/a Sue Air	Stapleford	11. 7.09E
G-SUEB	Piper PA-28-181 Archer III	2843466	N495AF, G-SUEB, N5330M	18. 7.01	ACS Aviation Ltd (Operated Leading Edge)	Perth	28.10.09E
G-SUED	Thunder Ax8-90 Balloon (Hot Air)	1546	G-PINE	22.10.02	E C Lubbock and S A Kidd	Billericay	3. 4.09E
G-SUEL	P&M Aviation Quik GT450	8301		23. 7.07	J M Ingram	Over Farm, Gloucester	19. 7.08P
G-SUEY	Bell 206L-1 LongRanger	45612	C-GCET, N300CS, N3901Q	5. 3.04	Aerospeed Ltd	Manston	26. 9.09E
G-SUEZ	Agusta-Bell 206B-2 JetRanger II	8319	SU-YAE, YU-HAZ	16. 9.98	Aerospeed Ltd	Manston	5. 7.08E
G-SUFF	Eurocopter EC.135 T1	0118		1. 2.00	Suffolk Constabulary Air Support Unit	Ellough, Beccles	23. 8.09S
G-SUFK	Eurocopter EC.135 P2+	0730		31.10.08	Eurocopter UK Ltd	Oxford	
G-SUKI	Piper PA-38-112 Tomahawk	38-79A0260	G-BPNV, N2313D	22. 5.91	Ravenair Aircraft Ltd	Liverpool	17. 9.09E
G-SULI	Diamond DA.40 Star	40.617	N670DS	22. 9.08	E A Sullivan	Stapleford	13.11.09E
G-SUMX	Robinson R22 Beta II	3274		1.11.01	J A Bickerstaffe	Higher Barn Farm, Hoghton	29. 1.10E
G-SUMZ	Robinson R44 Raven II	10490		11.11.04	Frankham Brothers Ltd	Bruntingthorpe	1.12.09E
G-SUNN	Robinson R44 Clipper	1367	N7531L	16. 7.04	C Wilkins	(Thruxton)	19. 2.09E
G-SUPA	Piper PA-18-150 Super Cub	18-5395	PH-BAJ, PH-MBF, French Army 18-5395), N10F	13.12.78	D Sutton tr G-SUPA Owners Group	Headcorn	29. 1.11S
	(Frame no.18-5512)						
G-SURG	Piper PA-30 Twin Comanche B	30-1424	G-VIST, G-AVHZ, N8287Y	18. 6.90	A R Taylor	Turweston	5. 6.09E
G-SURY	Eurocopter EC.135 T2	0283		17. 6.03	Surrey Police Authority	Fairoaks	12. 2.10T
G-SUSE	Europa Aviation Europa XS	554		25. 6.02	P R Tunney	(Sale)	
	(Built P R Tunney - pr.no.PFA 247-13905) (BMW1100RS)						
G-SUSI	Cameron V-77 Balloon (Hot Air)	1133		22. 7.85	J H Dyden "Susi"	Okehampton	9. 8.04A
G-SUSX	MD Helicopters MD.900 Explorer	900-00065	N3065W	19. 1.00	Sussex Police Authority	Shoreham	18. 2.10S
G-SUTD	Avtech Jabiru UL-D	662		14. 8.06	E Bentley	(Stockton-on-Tees)	13.12.07P
	(On start up Wickenby 18. 2.07 moved off, collided with portacabin and weighbridge and incurred substantial damage)						
G-SUTN	III Sky Arrow 650 TC	C007		27. 8.98	D J Goldsmith	Headcorn	2. 6.09P
	(Built Iniziative Industriali Italian)						
G-SUZN	Piper PA-28-161 Warrior II	28-8016187	N3573C, N9540N	16. 1.91	E Reed t/a St George Flight Training	Durham Tees Valley	12. 6.09E
G-SUZY	Taylor JT.1 Monoplane	PFA 055-10395		1.12.78	N Gregson	Ashcroft Farm, Winsford	27. 1.04P
	(Built S A Kaniok) (Volkswagen 1600)						

Reg	Type	C/n	Prev id	Date	Owner/Operator	Location	Date
G-SVDG	Avtech Jabiru SK *(Built R Tellegen - pr.no.PFA 274-13442)*	xxxx		5.12.05	R Tellegen	Old Sarum	14. 1.08P
G-SVEA	Piper PA-28-161 Warrior II	28-7916082	N30299	16.12.98	E-C V Dunning tr G-SVEA Group	RAF Brize Norton	26. 3.09E
G-SVEN	Centrair 101A Pégase	101A0262	BGA4329-HZF, PH-796	15. 1.08	A J Cronshaw	Gransden Lodge	13. 2.08
G-SVET	Yakovlev Yak-50	822210	RA-44459, LY-AGG, DOSAAF 107	16. 9.03	Yak-52 Ltd *"Svetlana"*	Compton Abbas	18.12.09P
G-SVGN	Cessna 680 Citation Sovereign	680-0198	N51072	25. 4.08	Prestige JF Ltd	Belfast International	24. 4.09E
G-SVIP	Cessna 421B Golden Eagle	421B0820	N4686Q, D-IMVB, N1590G, N6BNYJ	12. 3.97	T Stone-Brown	(Henfield)	26.12.03T
G-SVIV	SNCAN Stampe SV-4C *(Gipsy Major 10)*	475	N65214, F-BDBL	7. 8.90	R Taylor	Perranporth	15.10.09
G-SVNC	Rolladen-Schneider LS4	4190	BGA3552-FVE, RAFGSA 232, RAFGSA R30, D-4542	13.11.07	M C Jenkins *"7C"*	Dunstable	15. 3.08
G-SVPN	Piper PA-32R-301T Saratoga II TC	3257310	N48HB, N164MA, N9529N	24. 8.05	Caspian Air Services Ltd	Oxford	22. 9.09E
G-SVSB	Cessna 680 Citation Sovereign	680-0094	N5263D	27. 9.06	Ferron Trading Ltd	Jersey	27. 9.09E
G-SWAK	Oldfield Baby Lakes *(Built R W Hunt)*	88	N4287X	2.11.07	J P Nash	(Brighton)	
G-SWAT	Robinson R44 Raven II	10041	N75097	24. 2.03	J S Corr	Weston, Leixlip, County Kildare	28. 5.09E
G-SWAY	Piper PA-18-95 Super Cub *(Originally regd as -150, amended 16.11.08)*	18-6039	OY-EFY, D-EJEQ, SE-CLH, N7879D	3. 6.08	R Lillywhite	(Haywards Heath)	23.11.09
G-SWCT	Flight Design CTSW *(Assembled P&M Aviation Ltd with c/n 8364)*	07.11.05		31. 1.08	J A Shufflebotham	(Marton, Macclesfield)	30. 1.09P
G-SWEE	Beech 95-B55 Baron	TC-1406	G-AZDK	16. 4.03	Orman (Carrolls Farm) Ltd	Great Massingham	6. 2.09E
G-SWEL	Hughes 369HS *(Hughes 500)*	61-0328S	G-RBUT, C-FTXZ, CF-TXZ	18. 7.96	M A Crook and A E Wright	Barton	27. 7.09E
G-SWLL	Aero AT-3 R100	AT3.012	SP-KAC	24.10.05	Sywell Aerodrome Ltd	Sywell	24.11.09P
G-SWON	Pitts S-1S *(Built J Heverling)* (Lycoming AEIO-540)	093	N522H	14. 7.05	S L Goldspink	(Northill, Biggleswade)	15.11.08P
G-SWOT	Phoenix Currie Super Wot *(Built G Chittenden)* (Continental O-200-A)	PFA 3011		10. 9.80	D A Porter *(As "C3011:S" in RAF c/s [SE.5a guise])*	Griffins Farm, Temple Bruer	6.11.08P
G-SWPR	Cameron N-56 Balloon (Hot Air)	829		16. 3.82	A Brown *"Post Code"*	Bristol	5. 7.95A
G-SWSW	Schempp-Hirth Ventus bT	61/273	BGA4562-JJY, PH-981, D-KMIH	17. 8.07	S R Way	Parham Park	19. 1.08
G-SWWM	Westland SA.341C Gazelle HT.2	1033	XW853	6. 5.03	M S Beaton	Deer Park Farm, Babcary	7. 5.09P
G-SXIX	Rans S-19 *(Built J L Almey)*	LAA 361-14851		7. 1.09	J L Almey	(Spalding)	
G-SXTY	Bombardier Learjet Model 60	60-280	OE-GKP, N50127	21. 6.07	TAG Aviation (UK) Ltd	Farnborough	26. 6.09E
G-SYCO	Europa Aviation Europa *(Built J W E de Frayssinet - pr.no.PFA 247-12540) (NSI EA-81/118) (Conventional u/c)*	031		27.11.95	P J Tiller	(Northampton)	23. 1.06P
G-SYEL	Aero AT-3 R100	AT3.019		21. 8.06	Sywell Aerodrome Ltd	Sywell	13. 9.09E
G-SYFW	WAR Focke-Wulf FW190 replica *(Built M R Parr - pr.no.PFA 081-10584) (Continental O-200-A)*	269		28. 2.83	R P Cross *(As W/Nr "7334/2+1" in Luftwaffe c/s)*	Wickenby	10.11.05P
G-SYGA	Beech B200 Super King Air	BB-1044	G-BPPM, N7061T, C-GJJT, N815CE, (N815CE), N815CE, N62895	15.11.07	Synergy Aircraft Leasing Ltd	Falroaks	14.11.09E
G-SYLJ	Embraer EMB-135BJ Legacy	14500937	(PT-SCI), G-SYLJ, PT-SCI	12.12.05	TAG Aviation (UK) Ltd	Farnborough	18.12.09E
G-SYPS	MD Helicopters MD.900 Explorer	900-00104	G-76-104, N7034X, (PH-PXF)	3. 7.03	South Yorkshire Police Authority	Sheffield City	3. 7.10S
G-SYWL	Aero AT-3 R100	AT3.011	SP-KOT	24.10.05	Sywell Aerodrome Ltd	Sywell	24.11.09P

G-TAAA - G-TZZZ

Reg	Type	C/n	Prev id	Date	Owner/Operator	Location	Date
G-TAAB	Cirrus SR22	1769	N944CD	10. 7.06	TAA UK Ltd	Denham	11. 7.09E
G-TAAC	Cirrus SR20	1694	N997SR	14. 9.06	TAA UK Ltd	Denham	21. 9.09E
G-TABS	Embraer EMB-110P1 Bandeirante	110212	G-PBAC, F-GCLA, F-OGME, F-GCLA, PT-GME	18. 8.98	Skydrift Ltd	Norwich	4. 6.09E
G-TABY	Cirrus SR20	2000	N200CD	27. 8.08	N Carter	Jersey	
G-TACK	Grob G109B	6279		30. 5.84	A P Mayne	Exeter	23. 5.09E
G-TADC	Aeroprakt A22 Foxbat *(Built R J Sharp)*	PFA 317-13883		16. 4.02	R J Sharp	Rochester	7. 8.08P
G-TAFC	Maule M-7-235B Super Rocket *(Floatplane)*	23062C	N210SA, G-TAFC, N210SA, N9164M, C-GFVX	11. 1.05	The Amphibious Flying Club Ltd	Enniskillen	7. 8.09E
G-TAFF	CASA 1-131E Jungmann *(Enma Tigre G-IV-B)*	1129	G-BFNE, Spanish AF E3B-148	7. 9.84	A J E Smith *(On rebuild 12.07)*	Breighton	22. 7.05P
G-TAFI	Bücker Bü.133C Jungmeister *(Built Dornier-Werke AG) (Siemens Bramo)*	24	N2210, HB-MIF, Swiss AF U-77	27. 1.93	R J Lamplough	Manor Farm, East Garston	5. 7.01P
G-TAGA	Bombardier CL-600-2B16 *(CL604 Challenger)*	5659	C-FJCB, C-GLYK	30. 4.07	TAG Aviation (UK) Ltd	Farnborough	30. 4.09E
G-TAGG	Eurocopter EC.135 T2	0341		3. 9.04	Taggart Homes Ltd	(Londonderry)	1.12.08E
G-TAGH	Beech B200 Super King Air	BB-1720	N208CW, N608TA	13. 3.06	Taggart Aviation Ltd	Shoreham	23. 3.08E
G-TAGR	Europa Aviation Europa *(Built A G Rackstraw - pr.no.PFA 247-13061)*	317		23. 8.02	C G Sutton	(Kenilworth)	5. 4.07P
G-TAGT	Robinson R22 Beta	4015		6.04.06	Aerial Helicopters Ltd *(Operated The FlightCentre Ltd)*	Southend	28. 4.09E
G-TAIL	Cessna 150J	15070152	N60220	21. 4.89	T N Ashworth	Blackpool	14. 7.09E
G-TAJF	Lindstrand LBL 77A Balloon (Hot Air)	905		28. 4.03	T A J Fowles	Chester	14. 8.09E
G-TAKE	Aérospatiale AS.355F1 Ecureuil 2	5088	G-OITN, N400HH, N5788B	18. 8.05	Arena Aviation Ltd	Redhill	20. 2.10E

Reg	Type	C/n	Prev id	Date	Owner/Operator	Location	Expiry
G-TALA	Cessna 152 II	15285134	G-BNPZ N6109Q	6. 3.07	Tatenhill Aviation Ltd	Tatenhill	3. 3.09E
G-TALB	Cessna 152 II	15283767	G-BORO N5130B	6. 3.07	Tatenhill Aviation Ltd	Tatenhill	3. 4.09E
G-TALC	Cessna 152 II	15284941	G-BPBG N5418P	24. 4.07	Tatenhill Aviation Ltd	Tatenhill	22. 7.09E
G-TALD	Reims Cessna F152 II	F15201718	G-BHRM F-GCHR	5. 4.07	Tatenhill Aviation Ltd	Tatenhill	25. 4.09E
G-TALE	Piper PA-28-181 Archer II	28-8290048	G-BJOA N8453H	30.10.07	Tatenhill Aviation Ltd	Tatenhill	27.11.09E
G-TALF	Piper PA-24-250 Comanche	24-1094	G-APUZ N6000P	27.11.07	Tatenhill Aviation Ltd	Tatenhill	14.10.09E
G-TALG	Piper PA-28-151 Cherokee Warrior	28-7715219	G-BELP N9543N	14. 2.08	Tatenhill Aviation Ltd	Tatenhill	16. 9.09E
G-TALH	Piper PA-28-181 Archer II	28-7790208	G-CIFR PH-MIT, OO-HBB, N7654F	21.10.08	Tatenhill Aviation Ltd	Tatenhill	4. 9.08E
G-TALN	RotorWay A600 Talon	8022		19. 8.08	Southern Helicopters Ltd	Street Farm, Takeley	
G-TAMB	Schweizer 269D (Schweizer 333)	0052A	N86G	6. 6.05	Total Air Management Services Ltd	Sheffield City	21. 7.09E
G-TAMC	Schweizer 269D (Schweizer 333)	0054A	N86G	2. 8.05	Total Air Management Services Ltd	Sheffield City	13. 9.09E
G-TAMD	Schweizer 269D (Schweizer 333)	0056A	N86G	1.12.05	Total Air Management Services Ltd	Sheffield City	13. 6.09E
G-TAME	Schweizer 269D (Schweizer 333)	0035A	N2119S	10. 1.05	Total Air Management Services Ltd	Sheffield City	16. 6.09E
G-TAMF	Bell 206B-3 JetRanger III	2734	G-BXDS G-OVBJ. G-BXDS, OY-HDK, N661PS	15. 2.07	Total Air Management Services Ltd	Sheffield City	24. 7.09E
G-TAMR	Cessna 172S Skyhawk SP	172S8480	N2458J	7. 6.00	Apem Ltd	(Manchester)	3. 8.09E
G-TAMS	Beech A23-24 Musketeer Super	MA-190	OY-DKF	30. 6.00	Aerograde Ltd	Old Buckenham	28. 4.09E
G-TANA	Air Création Tanarg 912S(2)/iXess 15 FLT.xxx			17. 1.06	A P Marks	Naseby, Northampton	12. 9.08P
	(Built A Marks - pr.no.BMAA HB/485 being Flylight kit comprisiing Trike s/n T05099 and Wing s/n A05187-5194)						
G-TAND	Robinson R44 Astro	0478		12. 6.98	Global Air Charter Ltd	Blackbushe	1.10.09E
G-TANJ	Raj Hamsa X'Air 582(5)	629		21. 6.01	R Thorman	Perth	22. 5.08P
	(Built R Thorman - pr.no.BMAA HB/171)						
G-TANK	Cameron N-90 Balloon (Hot Air)	3625		20. 6.95	A M, A H and D J Mercer "Hoyer"	Belfast	7. 9.09E
G-TANS	SOCATA TB-20 Trinidad	1870	F-GRBX	25. 9.98	K P Threlfall	Wolverhampton	5. 3.09E
G-TANY	EAA Acrosport II	PFA 072A-13821		19. 2.04	P J Tanulak	Sleap	17.12.09P
	(Built P J Tanulak) (Lycoming O-360)						
G-TAPE	Piper PA-23-250 Aztec D	27-4054	G-AWVW OY-RPF, G-AWVW, N6799Y, N9654N	7.10.83	D J Hare (Operated Merlix Air)	Fairoaks	10. 5.09E
G-TAPS	Piper PA-28RT-201T Turbo Arrow IV	28R-8131080	HB-PLV N83423	2. 6.04	P G Doble	Fairoaks	5. 7.09E
G-TARN	Pietenpol AirCamper	PFA 047-13349		3. 8.98	P J Heilbron New Barn Farm, Barton Ashes, Crawley		
	(Built P J Heilbron)						
G-TARR	P&M Pegasus Quik	8264		27. 4.07	M J Tarrant	(Devizes)	26. 4.09P
G-TART	Piper PA-28-236 Dakota	28-7911261	N2945C	18.12.90	Prescot Planes Ltd	Goodwood	18. 6.09E
G-TASH	Cessna 172N	17270531	PH-KOS N739GL	4.11.98	Flight Academy (Gyrocopters) Ltd	Barton	20.12.08E
G-TASK	Cessna 404 Titan	404-0829	PH-MPC SE-IHL, N6806Q	10. 3.93	Reconnaissance Ventures Ltd (Red and white Coastguard c/s, operates for MCA)	Coventry	8. 7.09E
G-TATA	Rotorsport UK MT-03	RSUK/MT-03/041		12. 5.08	D J Watson (Crashed Irlam, Manchester 9.10.08)	Barton	21. 5.09P
G-TATO	Robinson R22 Beta	3418	EI-OBJ	8. 5.07	Mullahead Property Company Ltd	Mullahead, Tandragee	15. 5.09E
G-TATS	Aérospatiale AS.350BA Ecureuil	1905	F-GHSN N37AW	14. 5.01	T J Hoare	(Hollycombe, Liphook)	7. 6.09E
G-TATT	Gardan GY-20 Minicab	PFA 056-10347		30.11.78	P W Tattershall tr Tatt's Group (Noted 2007) Smelthwaites Farm , Newton in Bowland, Clitheroe		
	(Built L Tattershall)						
G-TAXI	Piper PA-23-250 Aztec E	27-7305085	N40270	6. 4.78	M Roberts	Bagby	17. 7.09E
G-TAYC	Gulfstream Aerospace Gulfstream IV-X	4060	N460GA	18. 1.07	TAG Aviation (UK) Ltd	Farnborough	17. 1.10E
G-TAYI	Grob G115	8008	(D-ENFT) G-TAYI, G-DODO, D-ENFT	12. 9.90	K P Widdowson and K Hackshall	Sandtoft	9. 9.09E
G-TAYS	Reims Cessna F152 II	F15201697	G-LFCA	28.10.91	Tayside Aviation Ltd	Glenrothes	8. 7.09E
G-TAZZ	Dan Rihn DR.107 One Design	PFA 264-14038		20. 2.06	C J Gow	(Broughty Ferry, Dundee)	
	(Built C J Gow)						
G-TBAE	British Aerospace BAe 146 Series 200	E2018	G-JEAR G-HWPB, G-6-018, G-BSRU, G-OSKI, N603AW	6. 1.03	BAE Systems (Corporate Air Travel) Ltd	Warton	7. 4.09E
G-TBAG	Murphy Renegade 912	PFA 188-11912		11.12.90	M R Tetley	Newton-on-Rawcliffe, Yorkshire	24.10.09P
	(Built M Tetley)						
G-TBAH	Bell 206B-2 JetRanger II	2051	G-OMJB N315JP, N712WG, N712WC, N9989K	10.12.01	RB Helicopters Ltd Kilmaddy, Dungannon, County Tyrone		6. 2.09E
G-TBBC	Pegasus Quantum 15-912	7583		6.12.99	J Horn	Eshott	25. 4.08P
G-TBEA	Cessna 525A CitationJet CJ2	525A-0191	N776LB	19. 5.06	Xclusive Jet Charter Ltd	Bournemouth	31. 5.09E
G-TBGL	Agusta A109A II	7412	G-VJCB G-BOUA	6. 1.99	Bulford Holdings Ltd (Noted 12.07)	Fairoaks	22.10.08E
G-TBGT	SOCATA TB-20 Trinidad GT	2027	F-OILF	1.12.00	A J Maitland-Robinson	(St Lawrence, Jersey)	11. 2.09E
G-TBHH	Aérospatiale AS.355F2 Ecureuil 2	5346	G-HOOT G-SCOW, ZS-HSW, G-POON, G-MCAL	1.12.06	Hughes Helicopters Ltd t/a Biggin Hill Helicopters	Biggin Hill	11. 2.09E
G-TBIC	British Aerospace BAe 146 Series 200	E2025	N167US N349PS	15. 1.97	NEX Aviation Aircrafts Ltd (stored 2.09) (All- white colours)	Southend	16. 1.09E
G-TBIO	SOCATA TB-10 Tobago	340	F-BNGZ	10. 2.83	R G L Solomon and J S Ritchie St Andre de Cognac, France / Oxted		30. 5.09E
G-TBJP	Mainair Sports Pegasus Quik	8071		29. 9.04	R Rajkowski	Long Marston	6.10.08P
G-TBLB	P&M Aviation Quik GT450	8188		1. 6.06	B L Benson	(Egerton, Malpas)	23. 7.09P
G-TBLY	Eurocopter EC.120B Colibri	1192	F-WQOV	12. 3.01	A D Bly Aircraft Leasing Ltd	Panshanger	28. 2.08E
G-TBMR	P&M Aviation Quik GT450	8407		19. 9.08	B Robertson	Culloden Moor, Inverness	
G-TBMW	Murphy Renegade Spirit UK	PFA 188A-11725	(G-MYIG)	20.10.98	S J and M J Spavins	Longacre Farm, Sandy	8. 2.07P
	(Built J R Peters and S J Spavins)			(Stalled and spun in Brooklands Farm, Alconbury 2. 7.06 and substantially damaged)				

G-TBOK	SOCATA TB-10 Tobago	1111	SX-ABF	26. 6.02	TB10 Ltd	Dunkeswell 10.11.09E
			F-GKUA			
G-TBSV	SOCATA TB-20 Trinidad GT	2169	N403MS	10.10.06	Condron Concrete Ltd	
			F-HKJT, F-WWRB			Ballyduff, Tullamore, County Offaly 20. 8.09E
G-TBTB	Robinson R44 Raven	1559	G-CDUN	24. 3.06	A R Banks t/a ARB Helicopters "Balhousie Care Group"	
						Forfar 18. 3.09E
G-TBTN	SOCATA TB-10 Tobago	322	G-BKIA	7. 8.03	Airways International Ltd	Perth 4. 5.09E
G-TBXX	SOCATA TB-20 Trinidad	276		16. 3.82	Aeroplane Ltd	Headcorn 9. 6.09E
G-TBZI	SOCATA TB-21 Trinidad TC	871	N21HR	25. 7.96	PMM Management Ltd	Biggin Hill 6. 3.09E
G-TBZO	SOCATA TB-20 Trinidad	444		8. 8.84	R P Lewis and D L Clarke	Shoreham 27. 4.09E
G-TCAL	Robinson R44 Raven II	11628		13. 3.07	C M Gough-Cooper	Barton 31. 3.09E
G-TCAN	Colt 69A Balloon (Hot Air)	1996		19. 7.91	H C J Williams "Toucan"	Bristol 9. 9.09E
G-TCAS	Cameron Z-275 Balloon (Hot Air)	10343		28. 2.03	The Ballooning Business Ltd (Central Auto Supplies titles)	
						Walcote, Alcester 20. 2.09E
G-TCBA	Boeing 757-28A	28203	G-OOOY	22. 5.06	Thomas Cook Airlines Ltd	Manchester 20. 5.09E
G-TCCA	Boeing 767-31K	27205	G-SJMC	11. 2.08	Thomas Cook Airlines Ltd	Manchester 22.11.09E
			C-GLMC, G-SJMC, N6038E			
G-TCEE	Hughes 369HS (Hughes 500)	61-0326S	G-AZVM	6.09.05	Aviation Styling Ltd Phoenix Farm, Lower Upham 22. 5.09E
			N9091F			
G-TCHI	Vickers Supermarine 509 Spitfire Tr.9		BS410	19.11.08	M B Phillips (On rebuild at Sandown)	(Exeter)
	(Originally a Mk.IX)	6S-200618				
G-TCHO	Vickers Supermarine 361 Spitfire IX		EN179	12.12.08	M B Phillips	(Exeter)
G-TCMM	Agusta-Bell 206B-3 JetRanger III	8560	EI-BXX	24. 3.04	R and M Crane Hire (Bunclody, County Wexford) 30. 4.09E
			G-JMVB, G-OIML			
G-TCNM	Tecnam P92-EA Echo PFA 318-13922			12. 8.02	F G Walker	(Hawarden) 21.10.08P
	(Built J Quaife)					
G-TCNY	Mainair Sports Pegasus Quik	8037		13. 5.04	T Butler	Enstone 22. 5.09P
G-TCOM	Piper PA-30 Twin Comanche C	30-1967	N555JC	29. 1.96	Commair Ltd	Jersey 24. 5.09E
			N8810Y			
G-TCSM	Bell 206B-3 JetRanger III	3881	G-CDYS	17. 7.08	Aerial Helicopters Ltd	Southend 19. 8.09E
			G-BOTM, N31940			
G-TCTC	Piper PA-28RT-201T Turbo Arrow IV	2831001	N9130B	1.12.89	M-D Lopez	(Brussels, Belgium) 12. 4.09E
	(Originally built as N9524N [28R-8631006])					
G-TCUB	Piper J-3C-65 Cub	13970	N9039Q	31. 7.87	C Kirk Whaley Farm, New York, Lincoln 8. 7.11S
	(Frame No.13805)		N67666, NC67666, Bu.29684, 45-55204			
G-TCXA	Airbus A330-243	795	F-WWKR	16.11.06	Thomas Cook Airlines Ltd	Manchester 15.11.08E
G-TDOG	Scottish Aviation Bulldog Series 120/121		XX538	17. 9.01	G S Taylor (As "XX538:O" in RAF c/s)	Shobdon 7. 9.11
		BH120/230				
G-TDRA	Cessna 172S Skyhawk	172S9848	N1539T	26. 7.05	TDR Aviation Ltd	Newtownards 17. 8.09E
G-TDSA	Reims Cessna F406 Caravan II	F406-0096		4.12.08	W Johnston and M Evans t/a Nor Leasing	
						Farnborough
G-TDVB	Dyn'Aéro MCR-01 ULC	242		23. 1.03	D V Brunt Plaistows Farm, St Albans 26. 9.09P
	(Built D Brunt - pr.no.PFA 301B-14015) (Overran the runway on landing at Willingale 12. 1.08 and overturned causing substantial damage)					
G-TDYN	Aerospool Dynamic WT9 UK	DY147/2006		2.10.06	L J and A A Rice Quebec Farm, Knook, Warminster 15. 7.09P
	(Official c/n is "DY147")					
G-TEAS	Air Création Tanarg 912S/iXess 15	FLT.xxx		30. 1.06	G C Teasdale	Old Sarum 27 .6.08P
	(Built G C Teasdale - pr.no.BMAA HB/489 being Flylight kit comprising Trike s/n T05081 and Wing s/n A05149-5143)					
G-TEBZ	Piper PA-28R-201 Cherokee Arrow III		N105CC	7. 1.00	Bowen-Air Ltd	(Stretton, Burton-on-Trent) 24. 9.09E
		28R-7737050				
G-TECC	Aeronca 7AC Champion	7AC-5269	N1704E	26. 6.91	N J Orchard-Armitage	Waldershare Park 14. 8.08P
			NC1704E			
	(Made a forced landing in a field on the east side of Coningsby, Lincs 16. 7.08 due to engine failure, substantial damage)					
G-TECH	Rockwell Commander 114	14074	G-BEDH	8. 8.85	P A Reed and S Rae	Elstree 14. 8.09E
			N4744W			
G-TECK	Cameron V-77 Balloon (Hot Air)	625		21. 3.86	M W A Shemilt	Henley-on-Thames 5. 8.02A
G-TECM	Tecnam P92-EM Echo PFA 318-13667			1.12.00	N G H Staunton Draycott Farm, Chiseldon 28.10.09P
	(Built D A Lawrence)					
G-TECO	Tecnam P92-EA Echo PFA 318-13830			16. 2.05	A N Buchan (Calton Moor Farm, Ashbourne) 16. 5.09P
	(Built A N Buchan)					
G-TECS	Tecnam P2002-EA Sierra PFA 333-14325			16. 6.04	D A Lawrence Draycott Farm, Chiseldon 5. 6.09P
	(Built D A Lawrence) (Originally regd as pr.no.PFA 318A-14250)					
G-TEDB	Reims Cessna F150L	F15000772	G-AZLZ	20. 1.05	E L Bamford	Haverfordwest 18. 5.09E
G-TEDF	Cameron N-90 Balloon (Hot Air)	2634		8. 8.91	Fort Vale Engineering Ltd	Nelson 10. 7.05A
G-TEDI	Best Off Sky Ranger J2.2(1)	SKR0207217		1. 5.03	A Bradfield	Stoke, Isle of Grain 25.12.09P
	(Built D A Smith and E Robshaw - pr.no.BMAA HB/243)					
G-TEDW	Air Création 582(2)/Kiss 450	FL026		21. 1.04	K Buckley (permit suspended)	Roddige 28. 5.08P
	(Built D J Wood - pr.no.BMAA HB/343 being Flylight kit comprising Trike s/n T03103 and Wing s/n A03184-3179)					
G-TEDY	Evans VP-1 PFA 062-10383		G-BHGN	4.10.90	N K Marston "The Plank"	(Harrow) 1. 7.97P
	(Built A Cameron) (Volkswagen 1834)					
G-TEEE	P&M Aviation Quik GT450	8386		21. 5.08	S E Bettley	Arclid Green, Sandbach 20. 5.09P
G-TEFC	Piper PA-28-140 Cherokee F	28-7325088	OY-PRC	18. 6.80	I A P Harper and C J Watson tr Foxtrot Charlie Flyers	
			N15530			Wolverhampton 11. 5.09E
G-TEGS	Bell 206B-3 JetRanger III	4622	C-FLZN	17. 4.07	E Drinkwater	(Barton) 31. 5.09E
G-TEHL	CFM Streak Shadow M	185	G-MYJE	20.11.98	J Anderson	Plaistows Farm, St Albans 18. 7.07P
	(Built A K Paterson - pr.no.PFA 206-13412) (Rotax 503)					
G-TELC	Rotorsport UK MT-03	RSUK/MT-03/028		23. 1.08	A J Turner	Writtle, Chelmsford 30. 1.09P
G-TELY	Agusta A109A II	7326	N1HQ	10. 3.89	Castle Air Charters Ltd	Liskeard Heliport 8. 9.09E
			N200SH			
G-TEMB	Tecnam P2002-EA Sierra PFA 333-14593			29.11.06	M B Hill	Nympsfield 8.12.09P
	(Built M B Hill)					
G-TEMP	Piper PA-28-180 Cherokee E	28-5806	G-AYBK	15. 5.89	F Busch International Ltd	Andrewsfield 21. 9.09E
			N11C			
G-TEMT	Hawker Tempest II	420	Indian AF	9.10.89	Tempest Two Ltd (To be "MW763:HF-A" in RAF 183 Sqdn c/s)	
			HA586, MW763			Wickenby

Reg	Type	Construction no.	Prev ident	Date	Owner/Operator	Base	Expiry
G-TENG	Extra EA.300/L	172		8.12.03	D McGinn	North Weald	1. 1.10E
G-TENS	HOAC DV.20 Katana	20148	G-BXBW D-ESHM	28. 2.01	D C Wellard	Croft Farm, Defford	26. 7.09E
G-TENT	Auster J/1N Alpha	2058	G-AKJU TW513	1. 2.90	R C Callaway-Lewis North Honer Farm, South Mundham, Chichester		21.10.09P
G-TERN	Europa Aviation Europa	106		18. 7.97	J Smith	(York)	13. 5.08P
	(Built J E G Lundesjo - pr.no.PFA 247-12780) (NSI EA-81/100) (Monowheel u/c)						
G-TERR	Cyclone Airsports Pegasus Quik	7925		6. 1.03	T R Thomas	Kemble	13. 1.08P
G-TERY	Piper PA-28-181 Archer II	28-7990078	G-BOXZ N22402	13. 1.89	J R Bratherton	Bagby	3. 6.09E
G-TESI	Tecnam P2002-EA Sierra	PFA 333-14481		23.11.05	C C Burgess	White Waltham	6. 6.09P
	(Built P J Mitchell)						
G-TESR	Tecnam P2002-RG Sierra	PFA 333A-14758		4. 1.08	Tecnam UK Ltd	Hinton-in-the-Hedges	18. 8.09P
	(Built P J Mitchell)						
G-TEST	Piper PA-34-200 Seneca	34-7450116	OO-RPW G-BLCD, PH-PLZ, N41409	28. 7.89	Stapleford Flying Club Ltd	Stapleford	23.12.09E
G-TETI	Cameron N-90 Balloon (Hot Air)	2877	D-OBMW	9. 2.00	Teti SpA	Firenze, Italy	
G-TEWS	Piper PA-28-140 Cherokee B	28-25128	G-KEAN G-AWTM, N11C	23. 5.88	P M Ireland	South Lodge Farm, Widmerpool	4.11.09E
G-TEXA	British Aerospace Jetstream Srs 4100	41041	N318UE G-4-041	2. 4.08	Highland Airways Ltd	Inverness	
G-TEXN	North American T-6G-NT Texan	168-176	G-BHTH N2807G, 49-3072	22. 6.05	Thunderprop Ltd (As "3072:72 in US Navy c/s) Shoreham		5 12.08E
G-TEXS	Van's RV-6	23830	N996SF	28.10.04	D McCann	(Clonaslee, County Laois)	1. 3.08P
	(Built S Formhals)						
G-TEZZ	CZAW Sportcruiser	LAA 338-14863		11.11.08	T D Baker	Bakersfield	
	(Built T D Baker)						
G-TFIN	Piper PA-32RT-300T Turbo Lance II	32R-7887012	N221RT D-ELAL	23.4.03	M D Parker	Bourn	9. 5.09E
G-TFIX	Pegasus Quantum 15-912	8048		21. 7.04	T G Jones	Caernarfon	8. 7.09P
G-TFLX	P&M Aviation Quik GT450	8379		16. 4.08	L A Wood	(Southampton)	23. 4.09P
G-TFLY	Air Création 582(2)/Kiss 450	FL029		28. 6.05	A J Ladell	Sutton Meadows	12.11.09P
	(Built A J Ladell - pr.no.BMAA HB/438 being Flylight kit [actually FL030 as FL027 duplicated] comprising Trike s/n T040843 &Wing s/n D065015)						
G-TFOG	Best Off Sky Ranger 912(2)	SKR0511661		2. 3.06	T J Fogg	Tarn Farm, Cockerham	12. 7.09P
	(Built T J Fogg - pr.no.BMAA HB/494)						
G-TFOX	Denney Kitfox Model 2	PFA 172-11817		3. 6.91	S J Perkins	Little Staughton	14. 9.09P
	(Built F A Roberts)						
G-TFUN	Valentin Taifun 17E	1011	D-KIHP	28.12.83	G F Wynn tr North West Taifun Group	Blackpool	23. 1.08E
	(Hangared in Container)						
G-TFYN	Piper PA-32RT-300 Lance II	32R-7885128	N5HG D-ELAE, N31740	28. 4.00	R C Poolman	Gloucestershire	5. 7.03T
	(Noted 1.06)						
G-TGDL	Robinson R44 Raven II	11746		21. 5.07	Enable International Ltd	Wellesbourne Mountford	21. 6.09E
G-TGER	Gulfstream AA-5B Tiger	AA5B-0952	G-BFZP	20. 2.86	L J Haldenby	Rochester	3. 9.08E
G-TGGR	Eurocopter EC.120B Colibri	1224	SE-JMF	22. 7.04	Winterburn and Son Ltd (Gomersal, Cleckheaton)		1. 8.09E
G-TGRA	Agusta A109A	7201	D-HEED N3983N, HB-XNF, I-PATZ	15. 2.01	Tiger Helicopters Ltd	Shobdon	14. 5.09E
G-TGRD	Robinson R22 Beta II	2712	G-OPTS	16. 6.04	Tiger Helicopters Ltd	Shobdon	25. 8.09E
G-TGRE	Robinson R22 Alpha	0471	G-SOLD N8559X	11. 9.03	Tiger Helicopters Ltd	Shobdon	28. 1.10E
G-TGRS	Robinson R22 Beta	1069	G-DELL N80466	5.11.97	Tiger Helicopters Ltd	Shobdon	23. 8.09E
G-TGRZ	Bell 206B-2 JetRanger II	2288	G-BXZX N27EA, N286CA, N93AT, N16873	15. 6.00	Tiger Helicopters Ltd	Shobdon	21.11.09E
G-TGTT	Robinson R44 Raven II	10023	G-STUS N369SB, G-STUS	8. 1.08	London Helicopter Centres Ltd	Redhill	6.12.09E
G-TGUN	Aero AT-3 R100	AT3-045		10.11.08	Cunning Plan Development Ltd	Old Sarum	30.11.09E
	(Operated Old Sarum Flying Club)						
G-THAT	Raj Hamsa X'Air Falcon 912(1)	613		27. 5.02	A N Green	Stoke, Isle of Grain	5. 7.08P
	(Built M G Thatcher - pr.no.BMAA HB/221)						
G-THEA	Boeing Stearman E75 (N2S-5) Kaydet	75-5736A	(EI-RYR) N1733B, USN Bu.38122	18. 3.81	C M Ryan "Spirit of Tipperary'" Weston, Leixlip, County Kildare		18.12.08E
	(Lycoming R-680)						
G-THEO	TEAM Mini-MAX 91	PFA 186-13099		9. 2.99	D W Melville	Dunkeswell	18. 8.09P
	(Built T Willford) (Built up rear fuselage)						
G-THIN	Reims FR172E Rocket	FR17200016	G-BXYY OY-AHO, F-WLIP	4.12.02	C A Ussher	New Laithe Farm, Harewood	24. 6.09E
G-THLA	Robinson R22 Beta II	3462		18. 7.03	Thurston Helicopters Ltd	Headcorn	8. 8.09E
G-THMB	Van's RV-9A	PFA 320-14266		26. 6.06	C H P Bell Eddsfield, Octon Lodge Farm, Thwing		25. 6.09P
	(Built C H P Bell) (Lycoming O-320)						
G-THOE	Boeing 737-3Q8	26313	G-BZZH N14384	9.12.04	Thomson Airways Ltd	Luton	6.12.09E
G-THOF	Boeing 737-3Q8	26314	G-BZZI N73385	9.12.04	Thomson Airways Ltd	Luton	27. 3.09E
G-THOG	Boeing 737-31S	29057	D-ADBM	1. 4.05	Thomson Airways Ltd	Luton	7. 4.09E
G-THOH	Boeing 737-31S	29058	D-ADBN	22. 4.05	Thomson Airways Ltd	Luton	21. 4.09E
G-THOI	Boeing 737-36Q	29327	G-OFRA	27. 5.05	Thomson Airways Ltd	Luton	17. 5.09E
G-THOK	Boeing 737-36Q	28660	G-IGOB EC-GNU	20. 4.06	Thomson Airways Ltd	Luton	24. 1.10E
G-THOL	Boeing 737-36N	28594	G-IGOK N1786B	27. 4.06	Thomson Airways Ltd	Luton	23. 4.09E
G-THOM	Thunder Ax6-56 Balloon (Hot Air)	366		14. 7.81	T H Wilson "Macavity"	Shieldaig, Strathcarron	14. 8.07A
G-THON	Boeing 737-36N	28596	G-IGOL N1015X	27. 6.06	Thomson Airways Ltd	Luton	25. 6.09E
G-THOO	Boeing 737-33V	29335	HA-LKT G-EZYK	30. 1.07	Thomson Airways Ltd	Luton	29. 1.10E

Reg	Type	C/n	Prev ID	Date	Owner/Operator	Location	Date
G-THOP	Boeing 737-3U3	28740	N335AW	28. 2.07	Thomson Airways Ltd	Luton	22. 5.09E
			N1790B, N1787B, (PK-GGM), (PK-GGK)				
G-THOS	Thunder Ax7-77 Balloon (Hot Air)	769		20. 2.86	C E A Breton *"Tohskcub"*	Saltford, Bristol	14. 3.01A
G-THOT	Avtech Jabiru SK	xxxx		16. 9.97	S G Holton	Poplar Hall Farm, Elmsett	26.11.08P
	(Built N V Cook - pr.no.PFA 274-13159)						
G-THRE	Cessna 182S Skylane	18280454	N2391A	6. 5.99	C Malet	Roques sur Garonne, France	22. 2.08E
G-THRM	Schleicher ASW 27	27142	G-CJWC	26.10.07	C G Starkey *"900"*	Lasham	28.12.07
			BGA4831-JWC				
G-THSL	Piper PA-28R-201 Arrow III	28R-7837278	N36396	11. 9.78	D M Markscheffel	Southend	3. 4.09E
G-THZL	SOCATA TB-20 Trinidad	534	F-GJDR	9. 5.96	Thistle Aviation Ltd	Oxford	15. 5.09E
			N65TB				
G-TICH	Taylor JT.2 Titch	PFA 060-3213		12. 2.01	R Davitt	Lower Wasing Farm, Brimpton	
	(Built A J House, C J Wheeler and R Davitt - pr.no.originally allocated as PFA 3213)						
G-TIDS	SAN Jodel D 150 Mascaret	44	OO-GAN	15. 4.86	M R Parker	Sywell	26.11.09P
G-TIGA	de Havilland DH.82A Tiger Moth	83547	G-AOEG	5. 6.85	D E Leatherland *(Operated Truman Aviation)*		
	(Built Morris Motors Ltd)		T7120			Nottingham City-Tollerton	2. 5.10S
G-TIGC	Aérospatiale AS.332L Super Puma	2024	G-BJYH	14. 4.82	Bristow Helicopters Ltd *"Royal Burgh of Montrose"*		
			F-WTNJ			Aberdeen	17. 5.09E
G-TIGE	Aérospatiale AS.332L Super Puma	2028	G-BJYJ	15. 4.82	Bristow Helicopters Ltd *"City of Dundee"* Aberdeen		7. 6.09E
			F-WTNM				
G-TIGF	Aérospatiale AS.332L Super Puma	2030	F-WKQJ	15. 4.82	Bristow Helicopters Ltd *"Peterhead"*	Aberdeen	27. 6.09E
G-TIGG	Aérospatiale AS.332L Super Puma	2032	F-WXFT	15. 4.82	Bristow Helicopters Ltd *"Macduff"*	Aberdeen	1. 8.09E
G-TIGJ	Aérospatiale AS.332L Super Puma	2042	VH-BHT	15. 4.82	Bristow Helicopters Ltd *"Rosehearty"*	Norwich	29. 6.09E
			G-TIGJ				
G-TIGS	Aérospatiale AS.332L Super Puma	2086		6. 5.83	Bristow Helicopters Ltd *"Findochty"*	Aberdeen	27. 6.09E
G-TIGV	Aérospatiale AS.332L Super Puma	2099	LN-ONC	12. 1.84	Bristow Helicopters Ltd *"Burghead"*	Aberdeen	25. 6.09E
			G-TIGV, LN-ONC, G-TIGV, LN-OPF, G-TIGV				
G-TIII	Pitts S-2A	2196	G-BGSE	27. 2.89	B G McCartney tr Treble India Group	Redhill	18.12.09E
	(Built Aerotek Inc) (Lycoming AEIO-360)		N947				
G-TILE	Robinson R22 Beta	1100		4. 8.89	Fenland Helicopters Ltd	Cranfield	9. 7.09E
G-TILI	Bell 206B-2 JetRanger II	2061	F-GHFN	6. 3.96	TLC Handling Ltd	Cranfield	30. 3.09E
			N7037A, XC-BOQ				
G-TIMB	Rutan VariEze	PFA 074-10795	G-BKXJ	11. 6.85	P G Kavanagh *"Kitty"*	Sleap	15. 8.07P
	(Built B Wronski) (Continental O-200-A)						
G-TIMC	Robinson R44 Raven II	11102	G-CDUR	30. 3.06	T Clark Aviation LLP	Wycombe Air Park	6. 4.09E
G-TIMG	Beagle Terrier 2	"PFA 00-318"		7. 3.01	T J Goodwin	(Manningtree)	
	(Built T J Goodwin to comprise Auster 6 fuselage frame and wing of VF505 unused in rebuild of Terrier G-ASOM - noted 8.03)						
G-TIMH	Robinson R22	4108	N3158D	19. 2.07	Central Helicopters Ltd	Nottingham City-Tollerton	27. 2.09E
G-TIMK	Piper PA-28-181 Archer II	28-8090214	OO-TRT	25. 8.81	T Baker	Wolverhampton	1. 9.09E
			PH-EAS, OO-HLN, N8142H				
G-TIML	Cessna 172S Skyhawk	172S10187	N6031F	31. 7.06	Tim Leacock Aircraft Sales Ltd	Compton Abbas	2. 9.09E
G-TIMM	Folland Gnat T 1	FL.519	8618M	19. 2.92	Swept Wing Ltd *(As "XS111" in RAF c/s)*		
			XP504				North Weald	20. 5.08P
G-TIMP	Aeronca 7BCM Champion	7AC-3392	N84681	14. 8.92	R B Valler	Goodwood	19. 9.07P
	(Continental C85)		NC84681				
G-TIMS	Falconar F-12A Cruiser	PFA 022-12134		1.10.91	T Sheridan	Wellingborough	
	(Built T Sheridan)						
G-TIMY	Sud-Aviation Gardan GY-80-160 Horizon	36	I-TIKI	17. 1.00	R G Whyte	Sywell	28. 7.09E
G-TIMZ	Robinson R44 Raven	1872		14. 5.08	D E Burt	(Pontefract)	29. 5.09E
G-TINA	SOCATA TB-10 Tobago	67		30.10.79	A Lister	Shipdham	14. 5.09E
G-TING	Cameron O-120 Balloon (Hot Air)	4007		4.10.96	Floating Sensations Ltd	Thatcham	11. 8.06T
G-TINK	Robinson R22 Beta	0937	G-NICH	22. 5.01	Helicentre Liverpool Ltd	Walton Wood	8. 1.10E
G-TINS	Cameron N-90 Balloon (Hot Air)	1626		27. 1.88	J R Clifton *(Carling Black Label titles)*		
						Nelson, New Zealand	11.10.03A
G-TINT	Evektor EV-97A Eurostar	PFA 315-14394		8. 8.05	I A Cunningham	Perth	11. 1.08P
	(Built I A Cunningham)						
G-TINY	Moravan Zlin Z-526F Trener	1257	OK-CMD	10. 5.95	D Evans	North Weald	1. 4.09E
	(Walter M137A)		G-TINY, YR-ZAD				
G-TIPS	Nipper T 66 Series 3	T66/50	OO-VAL	27. 3.95	F L Cuypers and F V Neefs	Denham	10. 8.06P
			9Q-CYJ, 9O-CYJ, (OO-CYJ), (OO-CCD)				
	(Built Avions Fairey SA: rebuilt R F L Cuypers - pr.no.PFA 025-12696) (Jabiru 2200A)						
G-TIVS	S-6-ES Coyote II	1203.1536		10. 5.04	D Kay	Little Gransden	29.10.08P
	(Built S Hoyle - pr.no.PFA 204-14236) (Tri-cycle u/c)						
G-TIVV	Evektor EV-97 Eurostar	PFA 315-14435		4. 8.05	I Shulver	Baxby Manor, Husthwaite	13.11.09P
	(Built S Hoyle)						
G-TJAL	Jabiru SPL-430	0210		21. 2.03	D W Cross	Wickenby	3. 3.09P
	(Built T J Adams-Lewis - pr.no.PFA 274A-13360)						
G-TJAV	Mainair Sports Pegasus Quik	8070		23. 9.04	D S Croney	Retreat Farm, Little Baddow	23.12.07P
G-TJAY	Piper PA-22-135 Tri-Pacer	22-730	N730TJ	11. 5.93	D Pegley	(Wisborough Green, Billingshurst)	2.11.11
			N2353A				
G-TJDM	Van's RV-6A	PFA 181A-13370		21. 9.07	J D Michie	White Waltham	23.12.09E
	(Built J D Michie)						
G-TKAY	Europa Aviation Europa	179		2. 6.99	A M Kay	Nuthampstead	14. 8.07P
	(Built A M Kay - pr.no.PFA 247-12804) (Monowheel u/c)						
G-TKGR	Lindstrand Racing Car SS Balloon (Hot Air)			28. 8.96	Brown and Williamson Tobacco Corporation (Export) Ltd		
		380			*"Team Green"*	Louisville, Kentucky, US	20. 8.99A
G-TKIS	Tri-R KIS	029		23.12.93	J L Bone	Biggin Hill	28. 4.06P
	(Built J L Bone - pr.no.FA 239-12358) (Lycoming O-290-D2) (Tail-wheel u/c)						
G-TKPZ	Cessna 310R II	310R1225	G-BRAH	19. 3.90	Aircraft Engineers Ltd	Prestwick	1. 4.08E
			N1909G				
G-TLDK	Piper PA-22-150 Caribbean	22-4726	N6072D	27. 1.97	A M Thomson *(Noted 2006)*	(Cheriton, Alresford)	
	(Tailwheel u/c)						
G-TLDL	Medway SLA 100 Executive	290906		29. 3.07	D T Lucas	Stoke, Isle of Grain	28. 3.08E

Reg	Type	C/n	Previous identity	Date	Owner/Operator	Location	Date
G-TLEL	American Blimp Corp A-60+ Airship	003	I-TIRE N2017A	17. 5.02	Lightship Europe Ltd	(Chilbolton)	26. 5.05T
G-TLET	Piper PA-28-161 Cadet (Thielert TAE 125-01)	2841259	G-GFCF G-RHBH, N9193Z	25. 8.04	A D and C Realff t/a ADR Aviation	Headcorn	27. 3.09E
G-TLFK	Cessna 680 Citation Sovereign	680-0213	N52397	27. 6.08	TAG Aviation (UK) Ltd	Farnborough	30. 6.09E
G-TLTL	Schempp-Hirth Discus CS	257CS	BGA4679-JPU	11. 1.08	E K.Armitage "TL2"	Camphill	27. 2.08
G-TMAN	Ozone/Adventure Roadster-Funflyer Quattro MAG-J-03B100/1070108			22. 2.08	P A Mahony	(Derriford, Plymouth)	
G-TMCB	Best Off Sky Ranger 912(2) (Built A H McBreen - pr.no.BMAA HB/310)	SKR0309378		23.10.03	P R Hanman	Over Farm, Gloucester	3.12.08P
G-TMCC	Cameron N-90 Balloon (Hot Air)	4327		30. 3.98	M S Jennings (The Mall-Cribbs Causeway titles)	Bristol	16. 7.09E
G-TMKI	Percival P 56 Provost T 1	PAC/F/268	WW453	1. 7.92	B L Robinson	(Barrington, Ilminster)	
G-TMOL	SOCATA TB-20 Trinidad	2103	F-OJBQ	24.12.01	Blackbrooks LLP	Belfast International	11. 3.09E
G-TMRA	Short SD.3-60 Variant 100	SH3686	G-SSWC SE-LBA, G-BMHX, G-14-3686	5.11.06	HD Air Ltd (Operated Highland Airways)	Inverness	12.11.09E
G-TMRB	Short SD.3-60 Variant 100	SH3690	G-SSWB C6-BFT, N690PC, G-BMLE, G-14-3690	14.12.06	HD Air Ltd (Operated Highland Airways) (Hdair.com titles, noted 9.08)	Inverness	17. 2.09E
G-TMRO	Short SD.3-60 Variant 100	SH3712	EI-SMA G-OBLK, G-BNDI, G-OBLK, G-BNDI, G-14-3172	15. 7.05	ACL Aircraft Trading Ltd (Noted stored 10.06)	Rennes, France	21. 7.06E
G-TMUR	Agusta A109A II	7289	G-CEPO RP-C2400, I-MIIT, N109BB	14. 5.07	Castle Air Charters Ltd	Liskeard Heliport	2.11.09E
G-TNGO	Van's RV-6 (Built H R Schweitzer) (Lycoming O-320)	21897	N97HS	27. 3.08	R Marsden "23"	(Grendon, Atherstone)	7. 5.09E
G-TNRG	Air Création Tanarg 912S(2)/iXess 15 (Built C M Saysell - pr.no.BMAA HB/468 being Flylight kit comprising Trike s/n T05070 and Wing s/n A05147-5129)	FLT002		2.11.05	C M Saysell	Plaistows Farm, St Albans	14.11.09P
G-TNTN	Thunder Ax6-56 Balloon (Hot Air)	1991		25. 4.91	H M Savage and J F Trehern "Tintin"	Edinburgh	3. 8.09E
G-TOAD	SAN Jodel D 140 Mousquetaire	27	F-BIZG	27. 9.88	J H Stevens	Headcorn	8. 9.09E
G-TOAK	SOCATA TB-20 Trinidad	468	N83AV	5.12.89	K Kane and A Marshall tr Phoenix Group	Enniskillen	16. 4.09E
G-TOBA	SOCATA TB-10 Tobago	625	N600N	4. 4.91	E J Downing	Lee-on-Solent	15. 5.08E
G-TOBI	Reims Cessna F172K	F17200792	G-AYVB	5. 1.84	A P Brisley tr The TOBI Group	Leicester	14. 7.09E
G-TODG	Flight Design CTSW (Assembled P&M Aviation Ltd with c/n 8288)	07.04.06		26. 4.07	M G Titmus	Otherton, Cannock	26. 4.09P
G-TOFT	Thunder and Colt 90A Balloon (Hot Air)	1693		8. 3.90	C S Perceval "Bumble"	Great Missenden	1. 7.09E
G-TOGO	Van's RV-6A (Built G Schwetz) (Lycoming IO-320)	PFA 181A-13447		6. 4.99	I R Thomas "Gernot"	Shoreham	15. 5.09P
G-TOHS	Cameron V-31 Balloon (Hot Air)	10267		4.11.02	J P Moore	Great Missenden	30.10.09E
G-TOIL	Enstrom 480B	5082		4. 7.05	M Wade	(Clare, Ireland)	10. 8.09E
G-TOLI	Robinson R44 Raven II	12009		17.11.07	JNK 2000 Ltd	(Thornbury, Bromyard)	6.12.08E
G-TOLL	Piper PA-28R-201 Arrow III	28R-7837025	N52HV D-ECIW, N9007K	12.10.00	Arrow Aircraft Ltd	Tatenhill	24. 1.09E
G-TOLY	Robinson R22 Beta II	2809	G-NSHR	8. 2.01	HelicopterServices Ltd	Wycombe Air Park	13. 3.09E
G-TOMC	North American AT-6D Texan	88-14602	French AF 114700, 42-44514	22. 4.02	A A Marshall tr Texan Restoration (On rebuild 5.05)	Bruntingthorpe	
G-TOMJ	Flight Design CT2K (Assembled Mainair Sports Ltd with c/n 7975)	03-04-01-14		28. 7.03	J Fleming	(Grantown-on-Spey)	21. 8.07P
G-TOMM	Robinson R22 Beta II	3384		5.11.02	EBG (Helicopters) Ltd	Redhill	2.12.08E
G-TOMS	Piper PA-38-112 Tomahawk	38-79A0453	N9658N	22. 1.79	A J Hutchinson tr G-TOMS Group	Swansea	3.11.09E
G-TOMX	Dyn'Aero MCR-01 Club (Built P T Knight, pr.no. PFA 301-14624)	345		6. 1.09	P T Knight	Sittles Farm, Alrewas	
G-TOMZ	Denney Kitfox Model 2 (Built P T Knight and L James) (Rotax 912)	PFA 172-11977		15.11.00	G G Ansell	Kimbolton	20. 7.09P
G-TONN	Mainair Sports Pegasus Quik	7954		28. 5.03	J C Boyd	Davidstow Moor	21. 6.08P
G-TONS	Slingsby T 67M-200 Firefly	2045	LN-TFA SE-LBA, LN-TFA, G-7-121	22. 7.03	D I Stanbridge	Norwich	13. 2.09E
G-TOOB	Schempp-Hirth Discus 2b	72	BGA4820/JVR	30. 4.08	M F Evans and P Davis	Lasham	
G-TOOL	Thunder Ax8-105 Balloon (Hot Air)	1670		29. 3.90	D V Howard (Toolmaster Hire titles)	Bath	21. 9.09E
G-TOOT	Dyn'Aéro MCR-01 Club (Built E K Griffin)	PFA 301-13542		1. 3.01	S W Hosking	Mapperton Farm, Newton Peverill	28. 9.09P
G-TOPC	Aérospatiale AS.355F1 Ecureuil 2	5313	I-LGOG 3A-MCS, D-HOSY, OE-BXV, D-HOSY	29. 7.97	Kinetic Avionics Ltd	Elstree	6.11.09E
G-TOPK	Europa Aviation Europa XS (Built P J Kember - pr.no.PFA 247-14193) (Tri-Gear u/c)	1000		16. 3.04	P J Kember	Fowle Hall Farm, Laddingford	20.6.09P
G-TOPO	Piper PA-23-250 Turbo Aztec E	27-4587	G-BGWW OO-ABH, N13971	23. 1.07	Keen Leasing (IoM) Ltd	Ronaldsway	7. 6.09E
G-TOPS	Aérospatiale AS.355F1 Ecureuil 2	5151	G-BPRH N360E, N5794F	7. 5.91	Sterling Helicopters Ltd	Conington	23. 1.10E
G-TOPZ	Aérospatiale SA.342J Gazelle	1473	F-GGTJ C-GVWC, F-WXFX	20.12.06	Top Yachts Ltd	(Exeter)	28. 5.09E
G-TORC	Piper PA-28R-200 Cherokee Arrow II	28R-7535036	OE-DIU N32236	18. 7.03	Solo Leisure Ltd	Old Sarum	25. 9.09E
G-TORI	Zenair CH.701SP STOL (Built S J Thomas) (Heavy landing Netherthorpe 2.8.07: nose under-carriage collapsed:, damage to propeller and engine shock-loaded)	7-9496	G-CCSK	10. 9.08	M J Maddock	(Coleford)	23. 4.08P
G-TORK	Cameron Z-105 Balloon (Hot Air)	10968		5. 1.07	M E Dunstan-Sewell (Rotork titles)	St Andrews, Bristol	15. 1.10E
G-TORN	Flight Design CTSW (Assembled P&M Aviation Ltd with c/n 8189)	06.05.04		1. 2.07	D J Haygreen	(Rhos-on-Sea, Colwyn Bay)	31. 1.08P
G-TOSH	Robinson R22 Beta	0933	N2629S LV-RBD, N8012T	14. 3.97	J T Helicopters Ltd	Thruxton	5.10.09E
G-TOTN	Cessna 210M Centurion II	21061674	G-BVZM OO-CNJ, N732PV	15. 7.04	K Bettoney	(Laxey, Isle of Man)	21. 6.09E
G-TOTO	Reims Cessna F177RG Cardinal RG	F177RG0049	G-OADE G-AZKH	29. 8.89	A S C Richardson	White Waltham	17. 8.09E

Reg	Type	C/n	Prev ID	Date	Owner/Operator	Base	Date
G-TOUR	Robin R2112	187		9.10.79	A Carnegie	Goodwood	8. 4.09E
G-TOWS	Piper PA-25-260 Pawnee C	25-4853	PH-VBT	17. 7.91	Lasham Gliding Society Ltd	Lasham	3. 4.08E
	(Hoffman 4 -blade propeller)		D-EAVI, N4370Y, N9722N				
G-TOYA	Boeing 737-3Q8	26310	G-BZZE	13.12.04	British Midland Airways Ltd *(Operated bmiBaby)*		
			N14381		*"brummie baby"*	Nottingham-East Midlands	17.12.08E
G-TOYB	Boeing 737-3Q8	26311	G-BZZF	24.11.04	British Midland Airways Ltd *(Operated bmiBaby)*		
			N19382			Nottingham-East Midlands	27. 1.10E
G-TOYC	Boeing 737-3Q8	26312	G-BZZG	13.12.04	British Midland Airways Ltd *(Operated bmiBaby)*		
			N14383			Nottingham-East Midlands	3. 3.09E
G-TOYD	Boeing 737-3Q8	26307	G-EZYT	13. 6.05	British Midland Airways Ltd *(Operated bmiBaby)*		
			HB-IIE, N721LF, (HB-IIE)			Nottingham-East Midlands	27. 6.09E
G-TOYE	Boeing 737-33A	27455	OO-LTU	4. 5.05	British Midland Airways Ltd *(Operated bmiBaby)*		
						Nottingham-East Midlands	12. 5.09E
G-TOYF	Boeing 737-36N	28557	G-IGOO	28.11.05	British Midland Airways Ltd *(Operated bmiBaby)*		
			G-SMDB		*"rainbow baby"*	Nottingham-East Midlands	20. 3.09E
G-TOYG	Boeing 737-36N	28872	G-IGOJ	13. 1.06	British Midland Airways Ltd *(Operated bmiBaby)*		
			N1795B, (N968WP)		*"butterfly baby"*	Nottingham-East Midlands	20.11.09E
G-TOYH	Boeing 737-36N	28570	G-IGOY	22.12.05	British Midland Airways Ltd *(Operated bmiBaby)*		
			CS-TGQ		*"baby of the north"*	Nottingham-East Midlands	10. 4.09E
G-TOYI	Boeing 737-3Q8	28054	YJ-AV18	25. 7.08	British Midland Airways Ltd *(Operated bmiBaby)*		
					"geordie baby"	Nottingham-East Midlands	24. 7.09E
G-TOYJ	Boeing 737-36M	28332	PK-GGW	10. 4.07	British Midland Airways Ltd *(Operated bmiBaby)*		
			YR-BGY, OO-VEA, (OO-EBZ)			Nottingham-East Midlands	10. 4.09E
G-TOYK	Boeing 737-33R	28870	N870GX	31. 5.07	British Midland Airways Ltd *(Operated bmiBaby)*		
			PP-VPX, N965WP			Nottingham-East Midlands	31. 5.09E
G-TOYM	Boeing 737-36Q	29141	VT-SJD	15. 8.08	British Midland Airways Ltd *(Operated bmiBaby)*		
					"Groovy Baby"	Nottingham-East Midlands	18. 8.09E
G-TOYZ	Bell 206B-3 JetRanger III	3949	G-RGER	21.11.96	Potter Aviation Ltd	Welshpool	4. 3.09E
			N75EA, JA9452, N32018				
G-TPAL	P&M Aviation Quik GT450	8363		28. 3.08	R Robertson	East Fortune	2. 4.09P
G-TPSL	Cessna 182S Skylane	18280398	N23700	11.12.98	A N Purslow	Popham	24. 3.09E
G-TPWL	P&M Aviation Quik GT450	8187		16. 5.06	P W Lupton	Arclid Green, Sandbach	9. 5.09E
G-TRAC	Robinson R44 Astro	0598		10. 5.99	C Sharples	Thruxton	24. 5.09E
G-TRAM	Pegasus Quantum 15-912 Super Sport	7552		29. 7.99	P J May tr G-TRAM Group	Mapperley, Ilkeston	28.10.09P
G-TRAN	Beech 76 Duchess	ME-408	G-NIFR	15. 3.93	Multiflight Ltd	Leeds-Bradford	20.10.09E
			N1808A				
G-TRAT	Pilatus PC-12/47	710	HB-FQX	18. 4.06	D J Trathen *"14"*	Bournemouth	18. 4.09E
G-TRAX	Reims Cessna F172M Skyhawk	F17201081	D-EIQU	22.11.06	Skytrax Aviation Ltd	Manor Farm, Glatton	6. 3.09E
	(Thielert TAE 125-01)						
G-TRBO	Schleicher ASW 28-18E	28743	BGA5238-KNW	18. 7.06	C J Davison and A Closkey	Saltby	22. 1.08
G-TRCY	Robinson R44 Astro	0668		22.10.99	Sugarfree Air Ltd	Nicosia, Cyprus	16. 4.09E
G-TREC	Cessna 421C Golden Eagle	421C0838	G-TLOL	2. 7.96	Sovereign Business Integration PLC	Cranfield	6. 3.09E
			(N2659K)				
G-TREE	Bell 206B-3 JetRanger III	2826	N2779U	15. 6.87	R B Eaton t/a Bush Woodlands	Wolverhampton	12. 3.09E
G-TREK	Jodel D 18	182		1. 5.92	R H Mole	Leicester	7. 9.09P
	(Built R H Mole - pr.no.PFA 169-11265) (JPX 4TX 65hp)						
G-TREX	Alpi Pioneer 300	9		6. 1.05	S R Winter	Wilingale	1. 2.08P
	(Built R K King - pr.no.PFA 330-14305)						
G-TRIB	Lindstrand HS-110 Airship (Hot Air)	174	(N....)	23. 1.95	J Addison	Melton Mowbray	17. 8.05A
G-TRIC	de Havilland DHC-1 Chipmunk 22A	C1/0080	G-AOSZ	18.12.89	A A Fernandez *(As "18013:013" in RCAF c/s)*		
			WB635			Ocana, Castilla, La Mancha, Spain	2.11.09S
G-TRIG	Cameron Z-90 Balloon (Hot Air)	10446		28. 7.03	Trigger Concepts Ltd *(Intel Inside/Centrino titles)*		
						Swallowfield, Reading	21. 9.09E
G-TRIM	Monnett Moni	00258T		16. 2.84	E A Brotherton-Ratcliffe	*(London SW6)*	
	(Built Monnett Aircraft- pr.no.PFA 142-11012)						
G-TRIN	SOCATA TB-20 Trinidad	1131		25. 6.90	D P Boyle	Leeds-Bradford	20. 5.09E
G-TRNT	Robinson R44 Raven II	10293	OE-XHW	17. 9.04	Charles Trent Ltd	Bournemouth	1.10.09E
G-TROP	Cessna T310R II	310R1381	N4250C	31.12.86	D E Carpenter	Shoreham	19. 5.09E
G-TROY	North American T-28A Trojan	142/174-545	F-AZFV	21. 4.99	S G Howell and S Tilling *(As "517692:142" in French AF c/s)*		
			French AF 142, 51-7692			Duxford	12.12.08P
G-TRTM	DG Flugzeugbau DG-808C	8-378B277X39		23. 8.07	ATSI Ltd	*(Chalfont St Giles)*	24. 9.09E
G-TRUD	Enstrom 480	5022	XT-BOK	27. 2.01	Sussex Aviation Ltd	Shoreham	1. 4.09E
G-TRUE	Hughes 369E *(Hughes 500)*	0490E	N6TK	12. 9.94	N E Bailey *(Ogbourne Maizey, Marlborough)*		22. 6.09E
			ZK-HFP				
G-TRUK	Stoddard-Hamilton Glasair RG	575R		23. 7.84	M P Jackson	Fairoaks	26. 6.09P
	(Built M P Jackson - pr.no.PFA 149-11015) (Lycoming O-320)						
G-TRUX	Colt 77A Balloon (Hot Air)	1860		13.11.90	J B R Elliot	Gorleston, Great Yarmouth	10. 2.06E
G-TRYK	Air Création 582(2)/Kiss 450	FL004		31.10.01	M A Pantling *(Noted 9.07)*	Weston Zoyland	19. 6.09P
	(Built S Elsbury - pr.no.BMAA HB/191 being Flylight kit comprising Trike s/n T01098 and Wing s/n A01157-1163)						
G-TRYX	Enstrom 480B	5083		15. 7.05	Atryx Aviation LLP	North Weald	10. 8.09E
G-TSAC	Tecnam P2002-EA Sierra	PFA 333-14611		19.12.07	A G Cozens	Goodwood	19. 6.09P
	(Built A G Cozens)						
G-TSDS	Piper PA-32R-301 Saratoga II SP		N145AV	3.10.05	I R Jones	Liverpool	17.11.09E
		32R-8013132	EC-HHM, G-TRIP, G-HOSK, PH-WET, OO-HKN, N8261X				
G-TSGA	Piper PA-28R-201 Cherokee Arrow III		G-ONSF	3. 7.07	TSG Aviation Ltd	Conington	4. 4.09E
		28R-7737082	G-EMAK, D-EMAK, N38180				
G-TSGE	Cirrus SR20	1899	N621DA	16.12.08	Caseright Ltd *(Operated Airways Flying Club)*	~	
						Wycombe Air Park	
G-TSGJ	Piper PA-28-181 Archer II	28-8090109	N8097W	12. 9.88	J O Elliott and G White tr Golf Juliet Flying Group		
						Durham Tees Valley	12. 2.09E
G-TSIX	North American AT-6C-1-NT Harvard IIA		FAP1535	19. 3.79	S J Davies *(As "111836/JZ:6" in USN c/s)*	Sandtoft	22.12.09P
		88-9725	SAAF7183, EX289, 41-33262				
G-TSJF	Cessna 525B CitationJet CJ3	525B0231	OE-GJF	19.11.08	Lunar Jet Ltd	Luton	23.11.09E
			N5247U				

G-TSKD	Raj Hamsa X'Air Falcon Jabiru(2)	633		8. 5.01	T Sexton and K B Dupuy	Southend	17.11.09P
	(Built T Sexton and K B Dupuy - pr.no.BMAA HB/165)						
G-TSKY	Beagle B 121 Pup Series 2	B121-010	OE-CFM	6. 4.98	R G Hayes	North Weald & Elstree	31. 5.09E
			HB-NAA, G-AWDY, HB-NAA, G-AWDY				
G-TSLC	Schweizer 269C-1 *(Schweizer 300)*	0246	(G-CDYV (1))	22. 6.06	TSL Contractors Ltd	Glenforsa, Isle of Mull	25. 7.09E
			N86G				
G-TSOB	Rans S-6-ES Coyote II	1202.1471		28. 6.04	S Luck *"The Spirit of Brooklands"*	Audley End	13. 3.09P
	(Built S C Luck - pr.no.PFA 204-14066)(Tri-cycle u/c)						
G-TSOL	EAA Acrosport	PFA 072-11391	G-BPKI	18. 7.00	A G Fowles	(Shrewsbury)	31. 3.00P
	(Built J Sykes) (Lycoming O-320)						
G-TSUE	Europa Aviation Europa	048		15. 8.05	A L and S Thorne	White Waltham	12. 5.09P
	(Built A L Thorne - pr.no.PFA 247-12612) (Tri-gear u/c)						
G-TSWI	Lindstrand LBL 90A Balloon (Hot Air)	1149		5. 2.07	Dylan Harvey Group Ltd	Burnley	22. 4.09E
					(Dylan Harvey Property Investments titles)		
G-TTDD	Zenair CH.701 STOL	PFA 187-13106		1. 9.97	D B Dainton and V D Asque	Little Staughton	12. 3.08P
	(Built B E Trinder and D B Dainton) (Jabiru 2200A)						
G-TTFG	Colt 77B Balloon (Hot Air)	1993	G-BUZF	5. 2.08	M J and T J Turner *"Patricia"*		
						Wellingborough and Southampton	3. 9.09E
G-TTHC	Robinson R22 Beta	1196		21.12.89	Multiflight Ltd	Leeds-Bradford	29. 6.09E
G-TTIC	Airbus A321-231	1869	D-AVZZ	12.12.02	EasyJet Airline Co Ltd *(stored 9.08)*	Shannon, Eire	11.12.09E
G-TTID	Airbus A321-231	2462	D-AVZB	12. 5.05	EasyJet Airline Co Ltd	London Gatwick	11. 5.09E
			(G-EUXI)				
G-TTIE	Airbus A321-231	2682	D-AVZD	23. 5.06	EasyJet Airline Co Ltd	London Gatwick	22. 5.09E
			(G-EUXJ)				
G-TTIF	Airbus A321-231	3106	D-AVZC	25. 5.07	EasyJet Airline Co Ltd	London Gatwick	24. 5.09E
			(G-EUXL)				
G-TTIG	Airbus A321-231	3382	D-AVZL	21. 2.08	EasyJet Airline Co Ltd	London Gatwick	20. 2.09E
G-TTIH	Airbus A321-231	3546	D-AVZO	6. 6.08	EasyJet Airline Co Ltd	London Gatwick	5. 6.09E
G-TTII	Airbus A321-231	3575	D-AVZD	2. 7.08	EasyJet Airline Co Ltd	London Gatwick	1. 7.09E
G-TTMB	Bell 206B-3 JetRanger III	947	G-RNME	26. 6.03	Sky Charter UK Ltd	Biggin Hill	23. 8.09E
			G-CBDF, N211KR, JA9119, N58064				
G-TTOB	Airbus A320-232	1687	F-WWIM	11. 2.02	EasyJet Airline Co Ltd	London Gatwick	13. 210E
					(for British Airways 09)		
G-TTOC	Airbus A320-232	1715	F-WWDB	6. 3.02	EasyJet Airline Co Ltd	London Gatwick	5. 3.09E
G-TTOD	Airbus A320-232	1723	F-WWBH	14. 3.02	EasyJet Airline Co Ltd	London Gatwick	18. 9.09E
G-TTOE	Airbus A320-232	1754	F-WWDH	11. 4.02	EasyJet Airline Co Ltd	London Gatwick	10. 4.09E
					(for British Airways 09)		
G-TTOF	Airbus A320-232	1918	F-WWIS	13. 2.03	EasyJet Airline Co Ltd	London Gatwick	15. 8.09E
G-TTOG	Airbus A320-232	1969	F-WWDZ	10. 4.03	EasyJet Airline Co Ltd	London Gatwick	9. 4.09E
G-TTOH	Airbus A320-232	1993	F-WWDO	2. 5.03	EasyJet Airline Co Ltd	London Gatwick	1. 5.09E
G-TTOI	Airbus A320-232	2137	F-WWBN	11.12.03	EasyJet Airline Co Ltd	London Gatwick	10.12.09E
G-TTOJ	Airbus A320-232	2157	F-WWDE	30. 3.04	EasyJet Airline Co Ltd	London Gatwick	29. 3.09E
G-TTOY	CFM Streak Shadow SA	K 233		15. 4.96	J Softley	Brimpton	11.12.07P
	(Built D A Payne - pr.no.PFA 206-12805) (Rotax 618)						
	(Struck the ground heavily in the undershoot area short of the runway on landing at Brimpton and extensively damaged)						
G-TTRL	Van's RV-9A	PFA 320-14248		11.12.07	J E Gattrell	Sittles Farm, Alrewas	2. 6.09P
	(Built J E Gattrell) (Lycoming O-320)						
G-TUBB	Avtech Jabiru UL-450	0256		1.10.99	A H Bower	Chavenage, Tetbury	17. 2.08P
	(Built A H Bower and A Silvester - pr.no.PFA 274A-13484)						
G-TUCK	Van's RV-8	81534		25. 9.03	M A Tuck	Oxford	18. 8.08P
	(Built M A Tuck - pr.no.PFA 303-13706) (Superior XP-10-360)						
G-TUDR	Cameron V-77 Balloon (Hot Air)	1135		20. 5.85	J W Soukup *"Tudor Rose and HVIIIR"*	Bristol	29. 9.04A
G-TUGG	Piper PA-18-150 Super Cub	18-8274	PH-MAH	10. 1.83	Ulster Gliding Club Ltd	Bellarena	2. 9.10S
	(Lycoming O-360-A3) (Frame No.18-8497)		N5451Y				
G-TUGI	CZAW Sportcruiser	LAA 338-14786		28. 3.08	T J Wilson	Plymouth	
	(Built T J Wilson)						
G-TUGS	Piper PA-25-235 Pawnee D	25-7756062	G-BFEW	31. 7.06	J A Stephen	Aboyne	26. 4.07E
			N82553				
G-TUGY	Robin DR.400-180 Régent	2052	D-EPAR	27. 4.98	J M Airey tr Buckminster Gliding Club Group	Saltby	19. 5.09E
G-TULP	Lindstrand LBL Tulips SS Balloon (Hot Air)	662	(PH-AJT)	16.10.00	Oxford Promotions (UK) Ltd *(Operated F Prell)*		
			(PH-TLP), PH-ORA)			(Kentucky, US)	3. 4.03A
G-TUNE	Robinson R22 Beta	0818	N60661	12. 1.99	D T Carslaw t/a HR Helicopters	Kintore	6. 2.09E
			G-OJVI, (G-OJVJ)				
G-TURF	Reims Cessna F406 Caravan II	F406-0020	PH-FWF	17.10.96	Reconnaisance Ventures Ltd	Coventry	20. 1.10C
			(EI-CND), PH-FWF, F-WZDS *(Coastguard titles, red/white c/s with MCA logo on tail)*				
G-TUSA	Pegasus Quantum 15-912	7841		9. 8.01	N J Holt	Weston Zoyland	27. 4.08P
	(Veered to right on take-off Weston Zoyland 31. 7.07, struck fence and susbstantially damaged)						
G-TUTU	Cameron O-105 Balloon (Hot Air)	10659		17. 1.05	A C K Rawson and J J Rudoni	Stafford	18.12.08E
G-TVAM	MBB BÖ.105DBS-4	S 392	G-SPOL	26. 6.03	Bond Air Services Ltd *(Operated Thames Valley Air Ambulance)*		
			VR-BGV, D-HDLH			White Waltham	5. 6.09E
G-TVBF	Lindstrand LBL 310A Balloon (Hot Air)	439		2. 4.97	Airxcite Ltd t/a Virgin Balloon Flights	Wembley	7. 7.08E
G-TVCO	Gippsland GA-8 Airvan	GA8-06-101		1.11.06	Zyox Ltd	Oxford	19. 3.09E
G-TVEE	Hughes 369HS *(Hughes 500)*	14-0557S	N45457	26. 1.05	M Webb	Elstree	21. 5.09E
			ZK-HCM, N22352, C-GCXK, N500AH, N500WH				
G-TVHD	Aérospatiale AS.355F2 Ecureuil 2	5449	ZK-ILN	7. 2.08	Arena Aviation Ltd	Redhill	4. 3.09E
			JA6638				
G-TVII	Hawker Hunter T 7	41H-693834	XX467	8.12.97	G R Montgomery tr G-TVII Group *(As "XX467:86")*		
			R Jordanian AF 836, RSAF 70-617, G-9-214, XL605			Exeter	
G-TVIJ	CCF Harvard 4 (T-6J-CCF Texan)	CCF4-442	G-BSBE	10.12.93	R W Davies *(As "28521:TA-521" in USAF yellow c/s)*		
			Moz PLAF 1730, FAP 1730, WGAF AA+652, 52-8521				
						Little Engeham Farm, Woodchurch	23. 7.07P
G-TVTV	Cameron TV 90SS Balloon (Hot Air)	2357		14. 9.90	J Krebs	Erfstadt, Germany	19. 8.02A
G-TWAZ	Rolladen-Schneider LS7-WL	7074	BGA4452-JEJ	25. 4.08	S Derwin and M Boulton *"WA2"*	Rufforth	
			OE-5477				

G-TWEL	Piper PA-28-181 Archer II	28-8090290	N81963	12. 6.80	IAE Ltd	Cranfield	17. 6.09E
G-TWEY	Colt 69A Balloon (Hot Air)	700		24. 7.85	N Bland	Didcot	30.10.09E
G-TWIN	Piper PA-44-180 Seminole	44-7995072	N30267	6.11.78	Bonus Aviation Ltd	Cranfield	21. 5.09E
G-TWIZ	Rockwell Commander 114	14375	SE-GSP	9. 5.90	B C and P M Cox	Biggin Hill	23. 6.09E
			N5808N				
G-TWNN	Beech 76 Duchess	ME-329	N127MR	25. 3.08	Folada Aero and Technical Services Ltd		
			N127MB, N67161		*(Operated Professional Air Training)* Bournemouth		20. 5.09E
G-TWOA	Schempp-Hirth Discus 2a	82	BGA4843-JWQ	31.10.07	A J McNamara *"TC"*	Wycombe Air Park	22.11.07
G-TWOC	Schempp-Hirth Ventus 2cT	141/369	BGA5165-KKS	6. 3.06	D Heslop *"2C"*	Wormingford	27. 3.08
G-TWOT	Schempp-Hirth Discus 2T	14/127	BGA5156-KKG	31. 8.06	S G Lapworth *"2T"*	Lasham	4. 4.08
			OY-XSY, D-KKAH				
G-TWSR	Silence Twister	PFA 329-14385		24. 3.05	J A Hallam	Gloucestershire	5. 4.08P
	(Built J A Hallam)						
G-TWSS	Silence Twister	PFA 329-14608		9. 9.08	A P Hatton	(Newark)	
	(Built A P Hatton)						
G-TWST	Silence Twister	PFA 329-14211		7. 9.04	Zulu Glasstek Ltd	Grange Farm, Boughton South	15.11.08P
	(Built P M Wells)						
G-TWTW	Denney Kitfox Model 2	PFA 172-11730		24. 3.04	T Willford	Spetisbury, Blandford Forum	22.10.09P
	(Built T Willford)						
G-TYAK	IAV Bacau Yakovlev Yak-52	899907	RA-01038	23.12.02	S J Ducker	Breighton	17.11.09P
			LY-AIE, DOSAAF 94 (yellow)				
G-TYCN	Agusta A109E Power	11123	G-VMCO	30. 7.03	A J Walter (Aviation) Ltd	(Horsham)	30. 7.09E
G-TYER	Robin DR.500-200i Président	0021	F-GTZB	25. 4.00	Chartfleet Ltd	Northorpe, Bourne, Lincoln	22. 6.09E
	(Officially regd as DR.400-500)						
G-TYGA	Gulfstream AA-5B Tiger	AA5B-1161	G-BHNZ	22. 2.82	D H and R J Carman	Rochester	13. 2.10E
			(D-EGDS), N4547L				
G-TYGR	Best Off Sky Ranger 912S(1)	SKRxxxx498		8.11.04	M J Poole	(Barnsley)	4. 7.08P
	(Built M J Poole - pr.no.BMAA HB/420)						
G-TYKE	Avtech Jabiru UL-450	xxxx		8. 6.01	K W Allan	Balgrummo Steading, Bonnybank	9.12.09P
	(Built A Parker - pr.no.PFA 274A-13739)						
G-TYMO	de Havilland DH.82A Tiger Moth	195	A17-194	8. 9.08	N Rose	(Bournemouth)	
	(Built de Havilland Aircraft Pty Ltd)				*(To be painted in yellow training c/s with blue/white WW2 RAAF roundels)*		
G-TYMS	Cessna 172P Skyhawk	17275815	N65674	9. 2.07	ESS Land Management	(Hailsham)	19. 6.09E
G-TYNE	SOCATA TB-20 Trinidad	1523	F-GRBM	6.11.97	N V Price	Newcastle	22.12.09E
			F-WWRW, CS-AZH, F-OHDE				
G-TYRE	Reims Cessna F172M Skyhawk II	F17201222	OY-BIA	16. 2.79	J S C English	Nottingham-East Midlands	31. 8.09E
G-TZEE	SOCATA TB-10 Tobago	727	F-GFQG	9. 1.03	Zytech Ltd	Earls Colne	16. 3.09E
G-TZII	Thorp T-211B	PFA 305-13285		2. 6.99	M J Newton Frandley	Cranfield	29. 8.08P
	(Built AD Aerospace Ltd) (Wilksch WAM-120)						

G-UAAA - G-UZZZ

G-UACA	Best Off Sky Ranger R100(2)	SKRxxxx384		25. 6.04	R G Openshaw *(Noted 1.07)*		
	(Built R Openshaw - pr.no.BMAA HB/324)				Harringe Court, Sellindge, Folkestone		
G-UAKE	North American P-51D-5-NA Mustang		44-13954	17. 2.04	P S Warner	(Dumbleton, Evesham)	
		109-27587					
G-UANO	de Havilland DHC-1 Chipmunk Mk.20	57	G-BYYW	18.10.06	N Rhind tr Gooney Bird Group *(As "1367" in Portuguese AF c/s)*		
	(Built OGMA)		CS-DAQ, Portuguese AF FAP 1367			White Waltham	
G-UANT	Piper PA-28-140 Cherokee F	28-7325568	OO-MYR	12. 4.02	Air Navigation and Trading Company Ltd		
			N56084			Blackpool	24.11.09E
G-UAPA	Robin DR.400-140B Major	2213	F-GMXC	11. 1.95	Carlos Saraiva Lda	(Alges, Portugal)	21.10.08E
G-UAPO	Ruschmeyer R90-230RG	019	D-EECT	2. 3.95	P Randall	Sturgate	23. 7.09E
G-UAVA	Piper PA-30 Twin Comanche B	30-1413	D-GLDU	16. 6.03	M D Northwood	Enstone	15. 4.09E
			HB-LDU, N8279Y				
G-UCCC	Cameron Sign 90 SS Balloon (Hot Air)	3918		5. 7.96	B Conway	Wheatley, Oxford	6. 9.99A
G-UCLU	Schleicher ASK 21	21010	BGA2612-EDW	11. 7.08	J Wellman tr University College London Union		
						RAF Halton	
G-UDGE	Thruster T600N Sprint	9099-T600N-037	G-BYPI	17. 9.99	A P Scott tr G-UDGE Syndicate	Shobdon	16.12.09P
	(Rotax 582)						
G-UDMS	Piper PA-46R-350T Malibu Mirage	4692068	N6077F	27.10.08	Underground Digital Media Ltd	Earls Colne	26.10.09E
G-UDOG	Scottish Aviation Bulldog Series 120/121		XX518	24. 1.02	Gamit Ltd *(As "XX518:S" in RAF c/s)*	North Weald	15. 8.10S
		BH.120/204					
G-UFAW	Raj Hamsa X'Air 582(5)	582		24. 7.01	P Batchelor	(Sedgewick Park, Horsham)	12. 9.10P
	(Built J H Goddard - pr.no.BMAA HB/167)						
G-UFCB	Cessna 172S Skyhawk SP	172S8318	N455SP	25. 1.00	The Cambridge Aero Club Ltd	Cambridge	1. 4.09E
G-UFCC	Cessna 172S Skyhawk SP	172S8611	N2466X	8. 1.01	Skypix Aviation Ltd	Kemble	30. 4.09E
G-UFCD	Cessna 172S Skyhawk SP	172S8443	G-OYZK	4. 1.01	Iolar Ltd	Cambridge	7.12.09E
			N7262C				
G-UFCE	Cessna 172S Skyhawk SP	172S9305	N5318Y	20. 2.03	Ulster Flying Club (1961) Ltd	Newtownards	21 3.09E
G-UFCF	Cessna 172S Skyhawk SP	172S9306	N5320F	20. 2.03	Global Traffic Network UK Ltd	(London WC1)	4. 3.09E
G-UFCG	Cessna 172S Skyhawk SP	172S9450	N2154T	28. 7.03	Ulster Flying Club (1961) Ltd	Newtownards	7. 8.09E
G-UFCH	Cessna 172S Skyhawk SP	172S9507	N5320F	4.11.03	Global Traffic Network UK Ltd	(London WC1)	12.11.08E
G-UFCI	Cessna 172S Skyhawk	172S10508	N21946	12. 2.08	Ulster Flying Club (1961) Ltd	Newtownards	17. 2.09E
G-UFCJ	Cessna 172S Skyhawk	172S10485	G-RMIN	25. 2.08	Ulster Flying Club (1961) Ltd	Newtownards	13. 3.09E
			N2246T				
G-UFLY	Cessna F150H	F150-0264	G-AVVY	29. 9.89	Westair Flying Services Ltd	Blackpool	6. 5.09E
	(Built Reims Aviation SA)						
G-UHIH	Bell UH-1H Iroquois	13208	NX41574	14.12.05	MSS Holdings (UK) Ltd *(As "72-21509:129" in US Army c/s)*		
			72-21509		*"Miss Jo"*	Wesham House Farm, Kirkham	12. 3.08P
G-UILA	Aquila AT01	AT01-165		18. 4.07	Aquila Sport Aeroplanes LLP	North Weald	28. 5.09E
G-UILD	Grob G109B	6419		28. 1.86	M H Player	Wing Farm, Longbridge Deverill	26. 5.09E
G-UILE	Neico Lancair 320	PFA 191-12538		17. 1.94	R J Martin	(Alresford)	19. 1.10P
	(Built R J Martin) (Lycoming IO-320)						

G-UILT	Cessna T303 Crusader	T30300280	G-EDRY	3. 7.00	W J Forrest tr G-UILT Group	Blackpool	1. 6.09E
			N4817V				
G-UINN	Stolp SA.300 Starduster Too	HB.1980-1	EI-CDQ	16. 3.98	J D H Gordon	Charterhall	29 1.10P
	(Built Haakon Baaken) (Lycoming O-360)		C-GTLJ				
G-UIST	British Aerospace Jetstream Series 3102	750	N190PC	15. 3.02	Highland Airways Ltd	Inverness	27. 5.09E
			(N331QH), N840JS, G-31-750				
G-UJAB	Avtech Jabiru UL	0193		27. 1.99	C A Thomas	Top Farm, Croydon, Royston	1. 9.09P
	(Built C A Thomas - pr.no.PFA 274A-13373)						
G-UJGK	Avtech Jabiru UL-450	0329		17. 4.00	W G Upton and J G Kosak	RNAS Culdrose	11. 6.09P
	(Built W G Upton and J G Kosak - pr.no.PFA 274A-13558)						
G-UKAT	Aero AT-3	PFA 327-14107		14. 4.04	T Archer tr G-UKAT Group	North Weald	22.12.09P
	(Built T Archer) (Rotax 912 ULS)						
G-UKAW	Agusta A109E	11003	I-VRGT	21.12.07	Westland Helicopters Ltd	Yeovil	30. 1.10E
G-UKOZ	Avtech Jabiru SK	0190		16. 6.99	D J Burnett	White House Farm, Southery	6.11.09P
	(Built D J Burnett - pr.no.PFA 274-13310)						
G-UKPS	Cessna 208 Caravan I	20800423	N5148N	29. 4.08	UK Parachute Services Ltd	Old Buckenham	8. 5.09E
G-UKUK	Head Ax8-105 Balloon (Hot Air)	248	N8303U	1. 9.97	P A George "Union Jack"	Princes Risborough	14. 8.09E
G-ULAS	de Havilland DHC-1 Chipmunk 22	C1/0554	WK517	14. 6.96	ULAS Flying Club Ltd (As "WK517" in RAF c/s)		
						RAF Benson	2.10.11
G-ULES	Aérospatiale AS.355F2 Ecureuil 2	5364	G-OBHL	6. 3.03	Select Plant Hire Company Ltd	Southend	6. 2.09E
			G-HARO, G-DAFT, G-BNNN				
G-ULHI	Scottish Aviation Bulldog Series 100/101		G-OPOD	30. 9.03	Power Aerobatics Ltd	Kemble	28.1.11T
		BH100/148	SE-LLK, Fv61038, G-AZMS				
G-ULIA	Cameron V-77 Balloon (Hot Air)	2860		20. 5.92	J M Dean	High Littleton, Bath	24. 9.09E
G-ULPS	Everett Gyroplane Series 1	007	G-BMNY	13. 7.93	C J Watkinson	(Goole)	10. 7.01P
	(Volkswagen 1835)						
G-ULSY	Comco Ikarus C42 FB80	0405-6603		26. 7.04	P J Fahie tr Ikarus 1 Flying Group (Operated Swallow Aviation)		25. 7.08P
	(Built Fly Buy Ultralights Ltd)					Deptford Farm, Wylye	
G-ULTR	Cameron A-105 Balloon (Hot Air)	4100		24. 2.97	P Glydon (Ultrafilter titles)	Bristol	9. 6.09E
G-UMAS	Rotorsport UK MT-03	RSUK/MT/03/024		12.11.07	BAE Systems (Operations) Ltd	Warton	8. 1.09P
G-UMMI	Piper PA-31 Navajo C	31-7912060	G-BGSO	11. 8.92	J A, G M, D T A and J A Rees t/a Messrs Rees of Poynston		14. 8.09E
			N3519F			West	Haverfordwest
G-UMMY	Best Off Sky Ranger J2.2(1)	SKR0409521		25. 7.05	A R Williams	Damyn's Hall, Upminster	8. 4.09P
	(Built A R Williams - pr.no.BMAA HB/437; BMAA have J Watkins as builder but never owned this aircraft)						
G-UNDD	Piper PA-23-250 Aztec E	27-4832	G-BATX	22. 3.00	G J and D P Deadman	Goodwood	4. 2.09E
			N14271				
G-UNER	Lindstrand LBL 90A Balloon (Hot Air)	895		16. 4.03	St Dunstans (St Dunstans titles)	London W1	1. 7.09E
G-UNGE	Lindstrand LBL 90A Balloon (Hot Air)	122	G-BVPJ	6.12.96	M T Stevens tr Silver Ghost Balloon Club	Warwick	13. 7.09E
G-UNGO	Pietenpol AirCamper	PFA 047-13951		16. 9.02	A R Wyatt	(Buntingford)	
	(Built A R Wyatt and P Thody)						
G-UNIN	Schempp-Hirth Ventus b	135	BGA4378-JBG	8.11.07	W R Longstaff tr U9 Syndicate	Feshie Bridge	
			OE-5315				
G-UNIV	Montgomerie-Parsons Two-Place Gyroplane		G-BWTP	3. 8.99	Department of Aerospace Engineering, University of Glasgow		
	(Built J M Montgomerie)	PFA G/8-1276				(Glasgow)	18. 1.05P
	(Rotax 618)						
G-UNIX	VPM M16 Tandem Trainer	PFA G/12-1349	ZU-AHX	10. 3.06	A P Wilkinson	Melrose Farm, Melbourne	28. 8.09P
	(Built A P Wilkinson) (Rotax 912 ULS)						
G-UNNA	Jabiru UL-450WW	xxxx		13. 4.07	N D A Graham	North Connel, Oban	10.11.09P
	(Built N D A Graham - pr.no.PFA 274A-14442) (Type amended to UL-450WW 11.12.08)						
G-UPFS	Waco UPF-7	5660	N32029	27. 8.04	D N Peters and N R Finlayson	Little Gransden	11.11.07
G-UPHI	Best Off Sky Ranger Swift 912S(1)			2.10.06	Flylight Airsports Ltd	Sywell	5. 2.09P
	(Built P M Dewhurst)	SKR0507629		(Pr.no.BMAA HB/480; marked as SKR0507647 which is G-RHAM)			
G-UPHL	Cameron Concept 80 Balloon (Hot Air)	3002		23. 2.93	N Edmunds (Uphill Motors titles)	Usk	20. 4.06T
G-UPPI	British Aircraft Corporation 167 Strikemaster Mk.80A			23. 1.04	G P Williams	(Swansea)	19. 5.04P
		EEP/JP/159	ZU-JAK, G-UPPI, G-CBPB, 1108 RSaudi AF				
G-UPPP	Colt 77A Balloon (Hot Air)	852		4. 8.86	D Michel		
						Neuves Maisons, Meurthe-et-Moselle, France	17. 2.05A
G-UNRL	Lindstrand RR21 Balloon (Hot-Air)	260		25. 5.95	Alton Aviation Ltd	Hawarden	21.10.09E
G-UPTA	Best Off Sky Ranger 912(1)	SKR0508645		15. 2.06	D Minnock	(Navan)	20. 8.08P
	(Built P E Tait - pr.no.BMAA HB/488, officially marked as SKR0508629)						
G-UPUP	Cameron V-77 Balloon (Hot Air)	1828		21. 7.89	S R Burden "Fantasia"	Noordwijk, Netherlands	9. 8.09E
G-UPUZ	Lindstrand LBL 120A Balloon (Hot Air)	969		26. 1.04	C J Sanger-Davies	Hawarden	23. 8.09E
G-UROP	Beech 95-B55 Baron	TC-2452	N64311	17. 9.90	Pooler International Ltd	Sleap	12.10.07E
G-URRR	Air Command 582 Sport	0630		13. 6.90	L Armes	(Basildon)	
	(Built L Armes - pr.no.PFA G/4-1200)						
G-URUS	Maule MX-7-180B Super Rocket	22014C	N611BH	28. 6.04	Broomco Ltd	Thruxton	11. 3.09E
G-USAA	Cessna F150G	F150-0188	G-OIDW	13. 8.08	A Naish (As "00195700" in pseudo-USAF c/s)		
			N70163, D-EGTI		"Lil' Baby Doll"	Wolverhampton	6. 8.09E
G-USAM (2)	Cameron Uncle Sam SS Balloon (Hot Air)			20. 5.85	Corn Palace Balloon Club Ltd	(US)	27. 6.00A
	(New envelope c/n 4526 C 3.99)	1120			(Active Albuquerque, New Mexico, US 10.06)		
G-USAR	Cessna 441 Conquest II	441-0355	D-ILYS	3. 7.08	I Anneskiy	Sandtoft	22. 9.09E
			N355VR, AP-BCW, N1213S				
G-USIL	Thunder Ax7-77 Balloon (Hot Air)	1587		22. 8.89	Window on the World Ltd "Mantis"	London SE1	22. 4.09E
G-USKY	Aviat A-1B Husky	2261		8. 4.04	B Walker and Co (Dursley) Ltd	Gloucestershire	2. 7.09E
G-USMC	Cameron Chestie 90 SS Balloon (Hot Air)			24. 4.86	J W Soukup	Bristol	15. 6.00A
	(US Marine Corps Bulldog shape)	1251			(Active Albuquerque, New Mexico, US 10.06)		
G-USRV	Van's RV-6	23771	N200HC	9. 7.04	M P Comley and N Horseman		
	(Built F M Carter) (Lycoming O-320)					(Bromley and Oxted)	11.10.07P
G-USSI	Stoddard-Hamilton Glasair III	3380		30.12.03	Lord Rotherwick	Oxford	
	(Built H R Rotherwick) (Lycoming IO-540)						
G-USSR	Cameron Doll 90SS Balloon (Hot Air)	2273		29. 3.90	Corn Palace Balloon Club Ltd "Matrioshka"	(US)	9. 6.00A
	(Russian Doll shape)				(Active Albuquerque, New Mexico, US 10.06)		
G-USSY	Piper PA-28-181 Archer II	28-8290011	N8439R	7.11.88	Western Air (Thruxton) Ltd	Thruxton	25. 2.09E

G-USTH	Agusta A109A II		7304	N109UK	12. 9.05	Stratton Motor Company (Norfolk) Ltd	
	F-GKGV, (F-GUHS), F-GKGV, N109PS, N109FM					Long Stratton, Norwich	1.12.08E
G-USTS	Agusta A109A II		7275	G-MKSF	24.11.03	MB Air Ltd t/a Eagle Helicopters	
				N18SF, F-GDPR		Newcastle City Heliport	21. 2.09E
G-USTY	Clutton FRED Series III	PFA 029-10390			11.10.78	N D Dykes tr GUSTY Group	Netherthorpe 8.12.05P
	(Built S Styles) (Volkswagen 1834)						
G-UTSI	Rand Robinson KR-2	KBG-01			2.10.89	K B Gutridge	Biggin Hill 21. 8.08P
	(Built K B Gutridge - pr.no.PFA 129-10966) (Revmaster R2100)						
G-UTSY	Piper PA-28R-201 Cherokee Arrow III		N3346Q	29. 8.86	Arrow Aviation Ltd	Southend 14. 3.09E
		28R-7737052					
G-UTTS	Robinson R44 Raven		0865	G-ROAP	20.10.00	The Premiair Club Ltd	(London SE22) 21.12.08E
G-UTZI	Robinson R44 Raven II		10590		24.12.04	S K Miles	(Sant Feliu Guixols, Girona, Spain) 26. 2.09E
G-UURO	Evektor EV-97 Eurostar	2005.25.27			4. 1.06	S A Lewis tr Romeo Oscar Syndicate	
	(Built E M Middleton, pr no PFA 315-14480)					Broadmeadow Farm, Hereford	20. 2.09P
G-UVBF	Lindstrand LBL 400A Balloon (Hot Air)		1051		19. 8.05	Airxcite Ltd t/a Virgin Balloon Flights	Wembley 18. 6.09E
G-UVIP	Cessna 421C Golden Eagle	421C0603		G-BSKH	23.11.98	MMAir Ltd	North Weald 18. 9.08E
				N88600			
G-UVNR	British Aircraft Corporation 167 Strikemaster Mk.87				4. 5.01	Global Aviation Services Ltd	Hawarden 24. 5.08P
	EEP/JP/2876 & PS.168 (or PS.174?)			G-BXFS, Botswana DF OJ10, Kenyan AF 605, G-27-195			
G-UYAD	Bombardier CL-600-2B16		5307	LX-FAZ	28. 4.08	Coldstream SARL	Luxembourg
	(Challenger 604)			C-GIDG, VP-BHA, VR-BHA, C-FXUQ, C-GLXH			
G-UZEL	Aérospatiale SA.341G Gazelle 1		1413	G-BRNH	21.11.89	Fairalls of Godstone Ltd	Redhill 9. 6.09E
				YU-HBO			
G-UZLE	Colt 77A Balloon (Hot Air)		2021		1. 8.91	Flying Pictures Ltd "John Courage"	Chilbolton 25. 5.00A
G-UZUP	Evektor EV-97A Eurostar	PFA 315A-14528			21. 6.06	S A Woodhams "Serenity"	Netherthorpe 22.11.07P
	(Built S A Woodhams)						
G-UZZY	Enstrom 480		5013	G-BWMD	29.10.04	Shoreham Helicopters Ltds.	Shoreham 1. 1.10E
				(F-GOTA), G-BWMD			

G-VAAA - G-VZZZ

G-VAAC	Piper PA-28-181 Archer III		2843398	G-CCDN	11. 9.07	A J Catzelfis	Cranfield 8. 5.09E
				HB-PQA, N4176W			
G-VAIR	Airbus A340-313		164	F-WWJA	21. 4.97	Virgin Atlantic Airways Ltd "Maiden Tokyo"	
						London Gatwick	20. 4.09E
G-VALI	Cessna 182S Skylane		18280757	N238ME	2. 3.07	Valley Flying Company Ltd	Valley Farm, Stafford 24. 5.09E
G-VALS	Pietenpol AirCamper	PFA 047-13157			30. 7.97	J R D Bygraves	Little Gransden
	(Built J R D Bygraves)					(Noted 10.05)	
G-VALV	Robinson R44 Raven		1421		9. 9.04	Valve Train Components Ltd	(Matlock) 4.10.09E
G-VALY	SOCATA TB-21 Trinidad		2081	N246SS	30. 3.04	R J Thwaites and Westflight Aviation Ltd	
				(N717TB)			Gloucestershire 22.10.09E
G-VALZ	Cameron N-120 Balloon (Hot Air)		4998		9. 1.01	Ladybird Balloons Ltd	Bingham, Nottingham 14.12.09E
G-VANA	Gippsland GA-8 Airvan	GA8-04-046		VH-KLN	20.12.05	P Marsden	Old Buckenham 22. 1.10E
G-VAND	Gippsland GA-8 Airvan	GA8-07-114			19. 9.07	Go Adventure Ireland Ltd	(Feathard, Ireland) 6. 7.09E
G-VANN	Van's RV-7A	PFA 323-14034			5. 7.04	D N and J A Carnegie	Kirkbride 23. 5.09P
	(Built D N and J A Carnegie) (Lycoming O-320)						
G-VANS	Van's RV-4		355	N16TS	7. 9.92	M J Wells and R J Marshall	
	(Built T Saylor) (Lycoming O-320)					Watchford Farm, Yarcombe 12.12.08P
G-VANX	Gippsland GA-8 Airvan	GA8-07-115		VH-AUM	31. 3.08	Airkix Aircraft Ltd	Tilstock 17. 4.09E
G-VANZ	Van's RV-6A	PFA 181-12531			15. 7.93	S J Baxter	(Macclesfield)
	(Built S J Baxter)						
G-VARG	Varga 2150A Kachina	VAC 157-80		OO-RTY	14. 5.84	J Denton	RAF Scampton 22. 9.08E
				N80716			
G-VART	Rotorway Executive 90		5003	G-BSUR	11. 8.03	I R Brown and K E Parker	(Sittingbourne) 1. 8.08P
	(Built N J Bethell) (RotorWay RI 162)						
G-VAST	Boeing 747-41R		28757		17. 6.97	Virgin Atlantic Airways Ltd "Ladybird"	
						London Heathrow	16. 6.09E
G-VATL	Airbus A340-642		376	F-WWCC	31.10.03	Virgin Atlantic Airways Ltd "Miss Kitty"	
						London Heathrow	30.10.09E
G-VBCA	Cirrus SR22		2656	N967SR	11.10.07	C A S Atha	Bagby 17.10.09E
G-VBFA	UltraMagic N-250 Balloon (Hot Air)	250/44			6. 4.06	Airxcite Ltd t/a Virgin Balloon Flights	Wembley 9. 2.09E
G-VBFB	UltraMagic N-355 Balloon (Hot Air)	355/09			5. 5.06	Airxcite Ltd t/a Virgin Balloon Flights	
						(Virgin / MK News)	Wembley 2. 4.09E
G-VBFC	UltraMagic N-250 Balloon (Hot Air)	250/45			5. 5.06	Airxcite Ltd t/a Virgin Balloon Flights	Wembley 13. 3.09E
G-VBFD	UltraMagic N-250 Balloon (Hot Air)	250/46			20. 6.06	Airxcite Ltd t/a Virgin Balloon Flights	Wembley 16. 3.09E
G-VBFE	UltraMagic N-355 Balloon (Hot Air)	355/10			7. 7.06	Airxcite Ltd t/a Virgin Balloon Flights	
						(Virgin / Gazette titles)	Wembley 8. 7.09E
G-VBFF	Lindstrand LBL 360A Balloon (Hot Air)	1116			8. 8.06	Airxcite Ltd t/a Virgin Balloon Flights	Wembley 20. 8.09E
G-VBFG	Cameron Z-350 Balloon (Hot Air)	10984			8. 3.07	Airxcite Ltd t/a Virgin Balloon Flights	Wembley 30. 8.09E
G-VBFH	Cameron Z-350 Balloon (Hot Air)	10985			8. 3.07	Airxcite Ltd t/a Virgin Balloon Flights	Wembley 27. 2.09E
G-VBFI	Cameron Z-350 Balloon (Hot Air)	10986			8. 3.07	Airxcite Ltd t/a Virgin Balloon Flights	Wembley 17.9.09E
G-VBFJ	Cameron Z-350 Balloon (Hot Air)	11006			8. 3.07	Airxcite Ltd t/a Virgin Balloon Flights	Wembley 24.10.09E
G-VBFK	Cameron Z-350 Balloon (Hot Air)	11007			8. 3.07	Airxcite Ltd t/a Virgin Balloon Flights	Wembley 23. 4.09E
G-VBFM	Cameron Z-375 Balloon (Hot-Air)	11133			18. 4.08	Airxcite Ltd t/a Virgin Balloon Flights	Wembley 21. 4.09E
G-VBFN	Cameron Z-375 Balloon (Hot-Air)	11134			25. 4.08	Airxcite Ltd t/a Virgin Balloon Flights	Wembley 29. 5.09E
G-VBFO	Cameron Z-375 Balloon (Hot-Air)	11135			6. 5.08	Airxcite Ltd t/a Virgin Balloon Flights	Wembley 3. 6.09E
G-VBFP	UltraMagic N-425 Balloon (Hot-Air)	425/26			28. 7.08	Airxcite Ltd t/a Virgin Balloon Flights	Wembley 19. 8.09E
G-VBIG	Boeing 747-4Q8		26255		10. 6.96	Virgin Atlantic Airways Ltd "Tinker Belle"	
						London Gatwick	9. 6.09E
G-VBLU	Airbus A340-642		723	F-WWCS	30. 1.06	Virgin Atlantic Airways Ltd "Soul Sister"	
						London Heathrow	29. 1.10E
G-VBUG	Airbus A340-642		804	F-WWCV	28. 2.07	Virgin Atlantic Airways Ltd "Lady Bird"	
						London Heathrow	27. 2.09E

Reg	Type	C/n	Prev ID	Date	Owner/Operator	Location	Date
G-VCED	Airbus A320-231	0193	OY-CNI F-WWIX	21. 1.97	Thomas Cook Airlines Ltd	Manchester	19.11.09E
G-VCIO	EAA Acrosport II	PFA 072A-12388		9.10.97	C M Knight	Batwell Farm, Gillingham	22. 9.09P
	(Built F Sharples, V Millard and R F Bond) (Lycoming O-360)						
G-VCJH	Robinson R22 Beta	1569		26.10.90	Just Plane Trading Ltd	Top Farm, Croydon, Royston	24. 6.09E
G-VCML	Beech 58 Baron	TH-1346	N2289R	31.10.97	St Angelo Aviation Ltd	Lydd	16. 4.09E
G-VCXT	Schempp-Hirth Ventus 2cT	144/..	BGA5158-KKJ D-KOZZ	4.11.05	R F Aldous "RA"	Kirchheim-Hahnwide, Germany	30. 4.08
G-VDOG	Cessna 305C Bird Dog (L-19E)	24582	F-BIFB French Army	18. 8.06	E P Morrow (As "24582" in US Army c/s)	Newtownards	31. 5.10
G-VECD	Robin R1180T Aiglon II	234	F-GCAD	22. 6.00	B Lee Eddsfield, Octon Lodge Farm, Thwing		5. 8.09E
G-VECG	Robin R2160 Alpha Sport	322	F-GSRD	6. 2.02	I A Anderson	Little Snoring	1. 3.09E
G-VECT	Cessna 560XL Citation Excel	560-5161	N405MM N404MM	31.10.08	Bookajet Aircraft Management Ltd	Farnborough	30.10.09E
G-VEGA	Slingsby T.65A Vega	1889	BGA2729-EJT G-VEGA, (G-BFZN)	20.10.78	W A M Sanderson	Wormingford	16. 2.08
G-VEIL	Airbus A340-642	575	F-WWCK	8. 4.04	Virgin Atlantic Airways Ltd "Queen of the Skies"	London Heathrow	7. 4.09E
G-VEIT	Robinson R44 Raven II	10091		11. 6.03	Field Marshall Helicopters Ltd	Wycombe Air Park	3. 8.09E
G-VELA	SIAI-Marchetti S 208	4-149	N949W	30.10.89	Broadland Flyers Ltd	Norwich	18. 7.08E
	(Officially regd as "S 205-22R")						
G-VELD	Airbus A340-313	214	F-WWJY	16. 3.98	Virgin Atlantic Airways Ltd "African Queen"	London Gatwick	15. 3.09E
G-VENC	Schempp-Hirth Ventus 2c	9/21	BGA4249-HVY	17. 9.07	J B Giddins "584"	Hinton-in-the-Hedges	9. 3.08
G-VENI	de Havilland DH.112 Venom FB.50 (FB.1)	733	Swiss AF J-1523	8. 6.84	Aviation and Computer Consultancy Ltd		
	(Built F + W)			(In open store as "VV612" in RAF silver c/s 1.09)		(Bournemouth)	25. 7.01P
G-VENM	de Havilland DH.112 Venom FB.50 (FB.1)	824	G-BLIE	16. 6.99	Aviation Heritage Ltd (As "WK436" in RAF 11 Sqdn c/s)		
	(Built F + W)		Swiss AF J-1614			Coventry	11. 6.09P
G-VENT	Schempp-Hirth Ventus 2cM	3/17	BGA4918 D-KBTL	25. 9.01	P D Barker tr G-VENT Syndicate	(Haywards Heath)	28. 4.09E
G-VERA	Gardan GY-201 Minicab	PFA 056-12236		7. 6.94	D K Shipton	(Peterborough)	
	(Built D K Shipton)						
G-VERN	Piper PA-32R-300 Cherokee Lance	32R-7680151	G-BVBG N19BP, N8363C	16. 4.03	D J Whitcombe	Cardiff	30.11.09E
G-VETA	Hawker Hunter T Mk.7	41H-693751	G-BVWN A2729, XL600		Classic Jet Heritage Ltd	(Ludlow)	27. 6.09P
G-VETS	Enstrom 280C-UK Shark	1015	G-FSDC G-BKTG, OY-HBP	11. 9.95	B G Rhodes (Noted 4.06)	(Macclesfield)	28. 7.02
G-VEYE	Robinson R22	0140	G-BPTP N9056H	8. 2.00	Manor PC's Ltd	Tatenhill	31. 3.09E
G-VEZE	Rutan VariEze	PFA 074-10285		2. 9.77	S D Brown, S Evans and M Roper	Biggin Hill	30. 5.08P
	(Built S D Brown, S Evans and M Roper)						
G-VFAB	Boeing 747-4Q8	24958		28. 4.94	Virgin Atlantic Airways Ltd "Lady Penelope"	London Gatwick	27. 4.09E
G-VFAR	Airbus A340-313X	225	(G-VPOW) F-WWJ	12. 6.98	Virgin Atlantic Airways Ltd "Diana"	London Gatwick	11. 6.09E
G-VFAS	Piper PA-28R-200 Cherokee Arrow II	28R-7435104	G-MEAH G-BSNM, N46PR, G-BSNM, N46PR, N54439	15. 1.08	P Wood	Duxford	14. 9.09E
G-VFIT	Airbus A340-642	753	F-WWCG	24. 5.06	Virgin Atlantic Airways Ltd "Dancing Queen"	London Heathrow	23. 5.09E
G-VFIZ	Airbus A340-642	764	F-WWCB	19. 7.06	Virgin Atlantic Airways Ltd "Bubbles"	London Heathrow	18. 7.09E
G-VFOX	Airbus A340-642	449	F-WWCM	23.12.02	Virgin Atlantic Airways Ltd "Silver Lady"	London Heathrow	22.12.09E
G-VGAG	Cirrus SR20 GTS	1572	N54149	25.10.05	Alfred Graham Ltd	Southend	16.11.09E
G-VGAL	Boeing 747-443	32337	(EI-CVH)	26. 4.01	Virgin Atlantic Airways Ltd "Jersey Girl"	London Gatwick	25. 4.09E
G-VGAS	Airbus A340-642	639	F-WWCI	9. 5.05	Virgin Atlantic Airways Ltd "Varga Girl"	London Heathrow	8. 5.09E
G-VGMB	Eurocopter EC.135 P2+	0550	N643LH	8. 6.07	Finlay (Holdings) Ltd	Enniskillen	19. 7.09E
G-VGMC	Eurocopter AS.355N Ecureuil 2	5693	G-HEMH F-WQPV	2. 3.04	E A and A Jackson t/a Eassda Aviation	Redhill	5. 2.09E
G-VGOA	Airbus A340-642	371	F-WWCB	30. 8.03	Virgin Atlantic Airways Ltd "Indian Princess"	London Heathrow	29. 8.09E
G-VGVG	ICP MXP-740 Savannah VG Jabiru(1)	xx.07-51-588		22. 6.07	M A Jones	RAF Scampton	2. 6.09P
	(Built M F Cottam - pr.no.BMAA HB/542)						
G-VHOL	Airbus A340-311	002	F-WWAS	30. 5.97	Virgin Atlantic Airways Ltd "Jetstreamer"	London Gatwick	29. 5.08E
G-VHOT	Boeing 747-4Q8	26326		12.10.94	Virgin Atlantic Airways Ltd "Tubular Belle"	London Gatwick	11.10. 09E
G-VIBA	Cameron DP-80 Airship (Hot Air)	1729		28. 5.91	J W Soukup	Bristol	3. 2.99A
G-VICC	Piper PA-28-161 Warrior II	28-7916317	G-JFHL N2249U	3. 3.92	Freedom Aviation Ltd	RAF Lyneham	13. 8.09E
G-VICE	Hughes 369E (Hughes 500)	0365E	D-HLIS	16. 5.95	M W A Dunn	(Longdown, Exeter)	18.12.09E
G-VICI	de Havilland DH.112 Venom FB.50 (FB.1)	783	HB-RVB (G-BMOB), Swiss AF J-1573	6. 2.95	Aviation and Computer Consultancy Ltd (In open store as "J-1573" in Swiss AF c/s 1.09)	Bournemouth	24.11.99P
	(Built F + W)						
G-VICM	Beech F33C Bonanza	CJ-136	PH-BNG	3. 7.91	Velocity Engineering Ltd	Elstree	20. 5.09E
G-VICS	Commander Aircraft Commander 114B	14655	N655V	3. 2.98	Millennium Aviation Ltd	Guernsey	17. 4.09E
G-VICT	Piper PA-31 Turbo Navajo B	31-7401211	G-BBZI N7590L	10. 9.99	Aircraft Leasing APS	Bournemouth	13. 8.09E

Reg	Type	c/n	Prev id	Date	Owner	Location	Date
G-VIEW	Vinten Wallis WA-116/L (Limbach L2000)	002		5. 7.82	K H Wallis (Stored 8.01)	Reymerston Hall, Norfolk	6.10.85P
G-VIIA	Boeing 777-236	27483	N5022E (G-ZZZF)	3. 7.97	British Airways PLC	London Gatwick	2. 7.09E
G-VIIB	Boeing 777-236	27484	N5023Q (G-ZZZG)	23. 5.97	British Airways PLC	London Gatwick	30. 1.10E
G-VIIC	Boeing 777-236	27485	N5016R (G-ZZZH)	6. 2.97	British Airways PLC	London Gatwick	20. 8.09E
G-VIID	Boeing 777-236	27486	(G-ZZZI)	18. 2.97	British Airways PLC	London Gatwick	15. 9.09E
G-VIIE	Boeing 777-236	27487	(G-ZZZJ)	27. 2.97	British Airways PLC	London Gatwick	23. 9.09E
G-VIIF	Boeing 777-236	27488	(G-ZZZK)	19. 3.97	British Airways PLC	London Gatwick	1.11.09E
G-VIIG	Boeing 777-236	27489	(G-ZZZL)	9. 4.97	British Airways PLC	London Gatwick	8. 4.09E
G-VIIH	Boeing 777-236	27490	(G-ZZZM)	7. 5.97	British Airways PLC	London Gatwick	6. 5.09E
G-VIIJ	Boeing 777-236	27492	(G-ZZZP)	29.12.97	British Airways PLC	London Gatwick	21. 8.09E
G-VIIK	Boeing 777-236	28840		3. 2.98	British Airways PLC	London Gatwick	2. 2.10E
G-VIIL	Boeing 777-236	27493		13. 3.98	British Airways PLC	London Gatwick	13. 3.09E
G-VIIM	Boeing 777-236	28841		26. 3.98	British Airways PLC	London Heathrow	15. 9.09E
G-VIIN	Boeing 777-236	29319		21. 8.98	British Airways PLC	London Heathrow	20. 8.09E
G-VIIO	Boeing 777-236	29320		26. 1.99	British Airways PLC	London Gatwick	25. 1.10E
G-VIIP	Boeing 777-236	29321		9. 2.99	British Airways PLC	London Gatwick	8. 2.10E
G-VIIR	Boeing 777-236	29322		18. 3.99	British Airways PLC	London Gatwick	17. 3.09E
G-VIIS	Boeing 777-236	29323		1. 4.99	British Airways PLC	London Heathrow	31. 3.09E
G-VIIT	Boeing 777-236	29962		26. 5.99	British Airways PLC	London Heathrow	25. 5.09E
G-VIIU	Boeing 777-236	29963		28. 5.99	British Airways PLC	London Heathrow	27. 5.09E
G-VIIV	Boeing 777-236	29964		29. 6.99	British Airways PLC	London Gatwick	28. 6.09E
G-VIIW	Boeing 777-236	29965		30. 7.99	British Airways PLC	London Gatwick	29. 7.09E
G-VIIX	Boeing 777-236	29966		11. 8.99	British Airways PLC	London Gatwick	10. 8.09E
G-VIIY	Boeing 777-236	29967		22.10.99	British Airways PLC	London Gatwick	21.10.09E
G-VIIZ	CZAW Sportcruiser (Built N I G Hart)	PFA 338-14672		4. 9.07	Skyview Systems Ltd	Waits Farm, Belchamp Water	2. 4.09P
G-VIKE	Bellanca 17-30A Super Viking 300A	79-30911	N302CB	8. 7.80	S J Doughty	Wolverhampton	21. 7.09E
G-VIKY	Cameron A-120 Balloon (Hot Air)	3068		27. 4.93	P J Stapley	London Colney	12.12.08E
G-VILA	Avtech Jabiru UL (Built D Cassidy - pr.no.PFA 274A-13364)	0213	G-BYIF	18. 7.02	G T Clipstone	(Ipswich)	10. 8.09P
G-VILL	Laser Lazer Z200 (Built M G Jefferies) (Lycoming AEIO-360)	10	G-BOYZ	10. 6.96	J Owczarek	(Hochdahl, Germany)	11. 8.09P
G-VINH	Flight Design CTSW (Assembled P&M Aviation Ltd with c/n 8190)	06.05.16		28. 7.06	Aardbus Ltd	Damyn's Hall, Upminster	10. 7.09P
G-VINO	Sky 90-24 Balloon (Hot Air)	102		25. 2.98	Fivedata Ltd (Lambrini Bianco titles)	Todmorden	4. 6.06A
G-VIPA	Cessna 182S Skylane	18280720	N148ME	13. 9.00	Rollright Aviation Ltd	Oxford	23.11.09E
G-VIPH	Agusta A109C	7643	EI-CUV G-BVNH, G-LAXO	21. 9.01	Cheqair Ltd	Tharston Industrial Estate, Long Stratton	26. 7.09E
G-VIPI	British Aerospace BAe 125 Series 800B (Built Corporate Jets Ltd)	258222	G-5-745	27. 7.92	Yeates of Leicester Ltd	Farnborough	28. 9.09E
G-VIPP	Piper PA-31-350 Navajo Chieftain	31-7952244	G-OGRV G-BMPZ, N3543D	6. 8.93	Capital Air Charter Ltd	Exeter	28. 8.09E
G-VIPR	Eurocopter EC.120B Colibri	1049	F-GRAE	8.12.05	Amey Aviation LLP	(Milton Keynes)	7. 1.10E
G-VIPU	Piper PA-31-350 Navajo Chieftain	31-8152115	G-MOHS G-BWOC,N40898,(CP-1665)	8.11.07	Capital Air Charter Ltd	Exeter	21.11.09E
G-VIPV	Piper PA-31-350 Navajo Chieftain	31-7952092	G-MRMR OH-PRE, G-WROX, G-BNZI, N3517T	13.11.07	Capital Air Charter Ltd	Exeter	6. 2.10E
G-VIPW	Piper PA-31-350 Navajo Chieftain	31-7952129	G-NEWR N35251	28. 7.08	Capital Air Charter Ltd	Exeter	6. 7.09E
G-VIPX	Piper PA-31-350 Navajo Chieftain	31-7305006	G-PMAX G-GRAM, G-BRHF, N7679L	3. 9.07	Capital Air Charter Ltd	Exeter	19. 9.09E
G-VIPY	Piper PA-31-350 Navajo Chieftain	31-7852143	EI-JTC G-POLO, (EI-...), G-POLO, N27750	10.10.97	Capital Air Charter Ltd	Exeter	12.10.09E
G-VIPZ	Sikorsky S-61N Mk.II	61-824	G-DAWS G-LAWS G-BHOF, LN-ONK, G-BHOF, LN-ONK, G-BHOF	3. 5.06	British International Helicopter Services Ltd t/a British International	Penzance Heliport	10. 7.09E
G-VITE	Robin R1180T Aiglon	219		16.10.78	D T Scrutton and N B Rolfe tr G-VITE Flying Group	Stapleford	22.10.09E
G-VITL	Lindstrand LBL 105A Balloon (Hot Air)	720		24. 8.00	Vital Services Group Ltd t/a Vital Resources (Vital Resources titles)	Salford	21. 8.09E
G-VIVA	Thunder Ax7-65 Bolt Balloon (Hot Air)	190		28.11.78	R J Mitchener (Inflated 4.02)	Andover	18. 3.99A
G-VIVI	Taylor JT.2 Titch (Built D G Tucker)	PFA 060-12405		4.11.96	D G Tucker	Great Oakley	21. 2.06P
	(Departed from runway on take-off New Farm House, Great Oakley 2. 7.05 and badly damaged: stored 9.08)						
G-VIVM	Hunting Percival P 84 Jet Provost T 5	PAC/W/23907	G-BVWF XS230	25. 3.96	The Skys The Ltd (International Test Pilots School titles)	North Weald	10.12.08P
G-VIVO	Nicollier HN.700 Ménestrel II (Built D G Tucker)	PFA 217-14039		5. 7.05	D G Tucker	Great Oakley	
G-VIVS	Piper PA-28-151 Cherokee Warrior	28-7615377	LN-NAL	31. 3.06	S J Harrison and V A Donnelly	Carlisle	18.11.09P
G-VIXN	de Havilland DH.110 Sea Vixen FAW.2 (TT)	10145	8828M XS587	5. 8.85	P G Vallance Ltd	Charlwood, Surrey	
	(In Gatwick Aviation Museum 2007 as "XS587" in RN c/s)						
G-VIXX	Alpi Pioneer 300 (Built K P O'Sullivan - pr.no.PFA 330-14465)	xxx	G-CESE G-CERJ	20. 7.07	K P O'Sullivan	(Gilcombe, Bruton)	
G-VIZA	Lindstrand LBL 260A Balloon (Hot Air)	792	A6-XEV	8.12.06	A Nimmo	Dubai, United Arab Emirates	11.12.09E
G-VIZZ	Sportavia RS.180 Sportsman	6018	D-EFBK	25.10.79	J D Howard and S J Morris tr Exeter Fournier Group	Exeter	31. 5.09E
G-VJAB	Avtech Jabiru UL	0142		25. 6.98	A Thornton	Ince Blundell	31. 8.09P
	(Built S T Aviation Ltd - pr.no.PFA 274-13322 although type prefix should be "274A")						
G-VJET	Avro 698 Vulcan B 2	Not known	XL426	7. 7.87	R J Clarkson tr The Vulcan Restoration Trust	Southend	
	(Noted as "XL426" and "G-VJET" 2.09)						

G-VJIM	Thunder and Colt Jumbo SS Balloon (Hot Air)	(G-BPJI)	7. 8.89	Magical Adventures Ltd (Virgin Atlantic titles) "Jumbo Jim"
	(Registered as Colt Jumbo-2)	1298		West Bloomfield, Michigan, US 14.10.02A
G-VKIT	Europa Aviation Europa	163	11. 6.01	T H Crow	Bicester	11. 5.09P
	(Built T H Crow - pr.no.PFA 247-12783) (Monowheel u/c)				
G-VKUP	Cameron Z-90 Balloon (Hot Air)	10803	10. 5.06	Global Brands Ltd (VK Vodka Kick titles)
				Clay Cross, Chesterfield	22. 7.09E
G-VLCC	Schleicher ASG 29E	29511	BGA5270-KPD	30. 4.08	Viscount Cobham and K M H Wilson "CC"
			D-KLCC			Lasham	28. 2.09
G-VLCN	Avro 698 Vulcan B 2	-	XH558	6. 2.95	Vulcan to the Sky Trust Ltd (As "XH558" in RAF c/s)
						Bruntingthorpe	2. 7.09P
G-VLIP	Boeing 747-443	32338	(EI-CVI)	15. 5.01	Virgin Atlantic Airways Ltd "Hot Lips"
						London Gatwick	14. 5.09E
G-VMCG	Piper PA-38-112 Tomahawk	38-79A0950	G-BSVX	12. 9.03	W G E James	Withybush	29. 6.09E
			N2336P				
G-VMDE (2)	Cessna P210N Pressurized Centurion II		(N4717P)	20. 7.78	S J Davies	(Sandtoft)	3. 7.09E
		P21000088					
G-VMEG	Airbus A340-642	391	F-WWCK	5.10.02	Virgin Atlantic Airways Ltd "Mystic Maiden"
						London Heathrow	3.10.09E
G-VMJM	SOCATA TB-10 Tobago	1361	G-BTOK	21. 4.92	Cardonstar Ltd	Enstone	7. 6.09E
G-VMSL	Robinson R22 Alpha	0483	G-KILY	5. 2.98	L L F Smith	Wycombe Air Park	26.12.03T
			N8561M				
					(Forced landed and rolled over near Turweston 4. 6.01)
G-VNAP	Airbus A340-642	622	F-WWCE	24. 2.05	Virgin Atlantic Airways Ltd "Sleeping Beauty"
						London Heathrow	23. 2.09E
G-VNOM	de Havilland DH.112 Venom FB.50 (FB.1)	842	Swiss AF J-1632	13. 7.84	T J Manna	Salisbury Hall, London Colney
	(Built F + W)				(Unmarked pod only 5.04) (On loan to de Havilland Heritage Museum)
G-VNON	Reality Escapade Jabiru(3)	JAESC 0008		4.10.05	P A Vernon	Craysmarsh Farm, Melksham	19. 8.09P
	(Built P A Vernon -pr.no.BMAA HB/325)						
G-VNTS	Schempp-Hirth Ventus bT	46/240	BGA4400-JCE	14. 8.07	A G Reid tr 911 Syndicate "911"	Bidford	28. 1.08
			D-KFMS				
G-VNUS	Hughes 269C	122-0175	G-BATT	20. 9.00	Enable International Ltd	Wellesbourne Mountford	2.10.08E
	(Hughes 300)						
G-VOAR	Piper PA-28-181 Archer III	2843011	N9256Q	3.11.95	Solent Flight Ltd	Fairoaks	10. 1.10E
G-VOCE	Robinson R22 Beta	1249	G-BSCL	30. 7.07	J J Voce	(Guiseley, Leeds)	11. 8.02P
G-VODA (1)	Cameron N-77 Balloon (Hot Air)	2208		8. 2.90	I Harris	Bishops Cannings, Devizes	9. 9.09E
	(Crown ring removed and fitted to new envelope G-VODA (2) c/n 4164 12.97 by Cameron Balloons: original envelope rebuilt by
	Zebedee Balloon Service with new crown ring 1.07 and registered G-CEJC as c/n 4164 qv)
G-VOGE	Airbus A340-642	416	F-WWCF	29.11.02	Virgin Atlantic Airways Ltd "Cover Girl"
						London Heathrow	28.11.09E
G-VOID	Piper PA-28RT-201 Arrow IV	28R-8118049	ZS-KTM	17. 8.87	B R Green	Stapleford	18. 9.09E
			(G-GCAA), ZS-KTM, N83232				
G-VOIP	Westland SA.341G Gazelle HT.3	1792	G-HOBZ	15.11.05	Q.Milne	(Echt, Westhill, Aberdeen)	5. 6.08P
			G-CBSJ, ZA802				
G-VOLO	Alpi Pioneer 300	xxx		21. 6.05	J W Clark and J Buglass	Sleap
	(Built J W Clark and J Buglass - pr.no.PFA 330-14389)			(Noted 8.05)		
G-VOLP	Lindstrand LBL 150A Balloon (Hot-Air)	1199		20. 5.08	Idea Balloon SAS	Firenze, Italy	3. 6.09E
G-VONA	Sikorsky S-76A	760086	G-BUXB	15. 4.03	Von Essen Aviation Ltd	Blackbushe	17. 8.09E
			(F-GSJG), G-BUXB, VR-CCZ, N399BB, N39RP				
G-VONB	Sikorsky S-76B	760399	G-POAH	8.10.03	Von Essen Aviation Ltd	Blackbushe	17. 5.09E
G-VONC	Sikorsky S-76B	760354	N966PR	29.11.06	Von Essen Aviation Ltd	Blackbushe	2. 5.09E
			N24PL, N421MK				
G-VOND	Bell 222	47041	G-OWCG	17.11.03	Von Essen Aviation Ltd	Denham	12. 3.09E
			G-VERT, G-JLBZ, G-BNDB, A4O-CH				
G-VONE	Eurocopter AS.355N Ecureuil 2	5572	G-LCON	11. 3.04	Von Essen Aviation Ltd	Denham	27. 6.09E
G-VONG	Aérospatiale AS.355F1 Ecureuil 2	5327	G-OILX	4. 5.06	Von Essen Aviation Ltd	Denham	19. 2.09E
			ZH141, G-OILX, ZH141, G-OILX, G-RMGN, G-BMCY				
G-VONH	Aérospatiale AS.355F1 Ecureuil 2	5303	G-BKUL	12. 5.06	Von Essen Aviation Ltd	Blackbushe	12. 4.09E
			ZJ140, G-FFHI, G-GWHH, G-BKUL				
G-VONJ	Raytheon RB390 Premier 1	RB-66	N931BR	4.11.05	Von Essen Aviation Ltd	Farnborough	8.11.09E
			VP-BAE, N50586				
G-VONK	Aérospatiale AS.355F1 Ecureuil 2	5325	G-BLRI (2)	15. 1.07	Von Essen Aviation Ltd	Denham	18. 4.09E
			ZJ139, G-NUTZ, G-BLRI				
G-VONS	Piper PA-32R-301T Saratoga IITC	3257155	N602MA	28. 7.03	W S Stanley	Gloucestershire	20. 1.09E
G-VOOM	Pitts S-1S	PFA 009-12989		8. 4.03	P G Roberts	(Maidenhead)
	(Built P G Roberts)						
G-VORN	Evektor EV-97 Eurostar	20042126	G-ODAV	2. 5.07	J Parker	Fenland	13. 1.10P
	(Built B R Davies - pr.no.PFA 315-14299)						
G-VPAT	Evans VP-1 Series 2	PFA 062-13907		11. 2.04	A P Twort	Kittyhawk Farm, Deanland
	(Built A P Twort)				(Under construction 2004)	
G-VPCB	Evans VP-1 Series 2	PFA 062-13901		28. 2.03	C I A Bloom	Kittyhawk Farm, Deanland
	(Built C Bloom)				(Under construction 2004)	
G-VPPL	SOCATA TB-20 Trinidad	283	G-BPAS	12.12.08	P Murer, L Printie and P J Wood
			A2-ADR, F-GDBO			(Bishops Stortford)	5. 7.09E
G-VPSJ	Europa Aviation Europa	023		29. 7.93	J D Bean	Enstone
	(Built J D Bean - pr.no.PFA 247-12520) (Monowheel u/c)					
G-VRED	Airbus A340-642	768	F-WWCH	19.10.06	Virgin Atlantic Airways Ltd "Scarlet Lady"
						London Heathrow	18.10.09E
G-VROC	Boeing 747-41R	32746		22.10.03	Virgin Atlantic Airways Ltd "Mustang Sally"
						London Heathrow	21.10.09E
G-VROD	Aeroprakt A22 Foxbat	PFA 317-13991		18. 3.03	S E Kearney	Derryogue	17. 7.08P
	(Bullt P A Sanders)						
G-VROE	Avro 652A Anson T 21	3634	G-BFIR	3. 3.98	Air Atlantique Ltd (As "WD413" in RAF c/s)
			7881M, WD413			Coventry	31.10.08P

G-VROM	Boeing 747-443	32339	(EI-CVJ)	29. 5.01	Virgin Atlantic Airways Ltd "Barbarella"		
						London Gatwick	28. 5.09E
G-VROS	Boeing 747-443	30885	(EI-CVG)	22. 3.01	Virgin Atlantic Airways Ltd "English Rose"		
						London Heathrow	21. 3.09E
G-VROY	Boeing 747-443	32340	(EI-CVK)	18. 6.01	Virgin Atlantic Airways Ltd "Pretty Woman"		
						London Gatwick	17. 6.09E
G-VRTX	Enstrom 280FX Shark	2044	G-CBNH	8. 7.02	Bladerunner Aviation Ltd	Barton	19. 6.09E
			Chilean Army H-180				
G-VRVI	Cameron O-90 Balloon (Hot Air)	2522		27. 2.91	SNT Property Ltd	Bristol	5. 8.05A
G-VSEA	Airbus A340-311	003	F-WWDA	7. 7.97	Virgin Atlantic Airways Ltd "Plane Sailing"		
						London Gatwick	6. 7.09E
G-VSGE	Cameron O-105 Balloon (Hot Air)	2382	I-VSGE	14. 8.02	G Sbocchelli	Rome, Italy	17. 8.09E
			G-BSSD				
G-VSHY	Airbus A340-642	383	F-WWCD	26. 7.02	Virgin Atlantic Airways Ltd "Madam Butterfly"		
						London Heathrow	25. 7.09E
G-VSIX	Schempp-Hirth Ventus 2cT	102/293	BGA5006-KDJ	13.11.07	M Nash-Wortham tr V6 Group	Lasham	11. 2.08
G-VSSH	Airbus A340-642	615	F-WWCZ.	31. 1.05	Virgin Atlantic Airways Ltd "Sweet Dreamer"		
						London Heathrow	30. 1.10E
G-VSUN	Airbus A340-313	114	F-WWJI	30. 4.96	Virgin Atlantic Airways Ltd "Rainbow Lady"		
			(F-GLZJ)			London Heathrow	29. 4.09E
G-VTAL	Beech V35 Bonanza	D-7978	HB-EJB	27. 2.03	R Chamberlain tr Wellesbourne Bonanza Group		
			D-EFTH			Wellesbourne Mountford	27. 4.09E
G-VTCT	Schempp-Hirth Ventus 2cT	90/266	BGA4976-KCC	9. 1.08	J B Hoolahan tr V26 Syndicate	Challock	9. 5.08
G-VTII	de Havilland DH.115 Vampire T 11	15127	WZ507	9. 1.80	M B Hooton tr Vampire Preservation Group		
					(As "WZ507:74" in RAF c/s)	North Weald	19.11.09P
G-VTOP	Boeing 747-4Q8	28194		28. 1.97	Virgin Atlantic Airways Ltd "Virginia Plain"		
						London Gatwick	17. 3.09E
G-VTUS	Schempp-Hirth Ventus 2cT	64/199	BGA4886-JYJ	19.10.07	P G Myers tr Ventus 02 Syndicate	Chipping	2. 4.08
G-VTWO	Schempp-Hirth Ventus 2c	28/75	BGA5084-KGQ	13. 4.06	F and B Birlison "565"	Aston Down	3.12.07
			D-0602				
G-VUEA	Cessna 550 Citation II	550-0671	G-BWOM	20. 6.02	AD Aviation Ltd	Liverpool	21. 5.09E
			N671EA, 9M-TAA, (N6761L)				
G-VUEM	Cessna 501 Citation I	501-0178	G-FLVU	24. 4.06	Frandley Aviation Partnership LLP	Liverpool	12. 7.09E
			N83ND, N4246A, LV-PML, N67749				
G-VUEZ	Cessna 550 Citation II	550-0008	N70XA	21. 4.05	AD Aviation Ltd	Liverpool	12. 6.09E
			N70X, N550JF, (N108AJ), OE-GIW, N575W, N98840				
G-VVBF	Colt 315A Balloon (Hot Air)	4058		3. 3.97	Airxcite Ltd t/a Virgin Balloon Flights	Wembley	17. 8.05T
G-VVBK	Piper PA-34-200T Seneca II	34-7570303	G-BSBS	26. 1.89	Ravenair Aircraft Ltd	Liverpool	19.11.09E
			G-BDRI, SE-GLG				
G-VVBL	Robinson R44 Raven II	11606		31. 1.07	Valley View Building and Engineering Services Ltd		
						Ramsden Bellhouse	6. 3.09E
G-VVIP	Cessna 421C Golden Eagle	421C0699	G-BMWB	7. 7.92	My Sky Air Charter Ltd	Cranfield	9. 9.09E
			N2655L				
G-VVPA	Bombardier CL600-2B16	5612	OE-IPK	29. 2.08	TAG Aviation (UK) Ltd	Farnborough	5. 3.09E
	(CL-604 Challenger)		C-FEPN, C-GLXY				
G-VVTV	Diamond DA.42 Twin Star	42.170	OE-VPY	18. 9.06	A D R R Northeast and S A Cook	Oxford	1.12.09E
G-VVVV	Best Off Sky Ranger 912(2)	SKR0407510		15.12.04	J Thomas	Weston Zoyland	20. 3.09P
	(Built J Thomas and J B Hobbs - pr.no.BMAA HB/427)						
G-VVWW	Enstrom 280C Shark	2056	N7802J	22.10.03	P J Odendaal	Southend	21. 1.09E
			JA7822				
G-VWEB	Airbus A340-642	787	F-WWCZ	20.12.06	Virgin Atlantic Airways Ltd "Surfer Girl"		
						London Gatwick	19.12.08E
G-VWIN	Airbus A340-642	736	F-WWCL	28. 2.06	Virgin Atlantic Airways Ltd "Lady Luck"		
						London Heathrow	27. 2.09E
G-VWKD	Airbus A340-642	706	F-WWCQ	28.11.05	Virgin Atlantic Airways Ltd "Miss Behavin"		
						London Heathrow	27.11.09E
G-VWOW	Boeing 747-41R	32745		31.10.01	Virgin Atlantic Airways Ltd "Cosmic Girl"		
						London Heathrow	12.12.09E
G-VXLG	Boeing 747-41R	29406		30. 9.98	Virgin Atlantic Airways Ltd "Ruby Tuesday"		
						London Heathrow	29. 9.09E
G-VYGR	Colt 120A Balloon (Hot Air)	2479		24. 9.93	H van Hoesel	S'Hertogenbosch, Netherlands	20. 5.08E
G-VYOU	Airbus A340-642	765	F-WWCK	23. 8.06	Virgin Atlantic Airways Ltd "Emmeline Heansy"		
						London Heathrow	22. 8.09E

G-WAAA - G-WZZZ

G-WAAC	Cameron N-56 Balloon (Hot Air)	492		14. 2.79	N P Hemsley tr Whacko Balloon Group "Whacko"		
						Crawley	26. 6.97A
G-WAAN	MBB BÖ.105DB	S 20	G-AZOR	14.11.03	PLM Dollar Group Ltd "Pride of Cumbria"		
			EC-DOE, G-AZOR, D-HDAC			(Penrith)	26. 7.09E
G-WAAS	MBB BÖ.105DBS-4	S 138/911	G-ESAM	26. 6.03	Bond Air Services Ltd (Operated Welsh Air Ambulance)		
	(Remanufactured with new pod c/n S 911 c1992)		G-BUIB, G-BDYZ, D-HDEF			Swansea	24. 6.09E
G-WACB	Reims Cessna F152 II	F15201972		16. 9.86	Wycombe Air Centre Ltd	Wycombe Air Park	2. 3.09E
G-WACE	Reims Cessna F152 II	F15201978		16. 9.86	Wycombe Air Centre Ltd	Wycombe Air Park	2. 5.09E
G-WACF	Cessna 152 II	15284852	N628GH	20. 1.87	Wycombe Air Centre Ltd	Wycombe Air Park	24.11.09E
			(LV-PMB), N628GH				
G-WACG	Cessna 152 II	15285536	ZS-KXY	4.11.86	Wycombe Air Centre Ltd	Wycombe Air Park	10. 4.09E
			(N93699)				
G-WACH	Reims Cessna FA152 Aerobat	FA1520425		18. 6.87	Wycombe Air Centre Ltd	Wycombe Air Park	7. 8.09E
G-WACI	Beech 76 Duchess	ME-289	N6703Y	26. 7.88	Wycombe Air Centre Ltd	Wycombe Air Park	22.11.09E
G-WACJ	Beech 76 Duchess	ME-278	N6700Y	3. 1.89	Wycombe Air Centre Ltd	Wycombe Air Park	7. 5.09E
G-WACL	Reims Cessna F172N Skyhawk II	F17201912	G-BHGG	19. 6.89	A G Arthur	Perranporth	22. 4.09E
G-WACO	Waco UPF-7	5400	N29903	28. 1.87	R F L Cuypers	Antwerp, Belgium	13. 5.90P
			NC29903			(Damaged Liverpool 15. 4.89: under restoration 2006)		

Reg	Type	C/n	Prev ID	Date	Owner	Location	Expiry
G-WACT	Reims Cessna F152 II	F15201908	G-BKFT	24. 6.86	Northumbria Flying School Ltd	Newcastle	5. 8.09E
G-WACU	Reims Cessna FA152 Aerobat	FA1520380	G-BJZU	10. 7.86	Wycombe Air Centre Ltd	Wycombe Air Park	9. 6.09E
G-WACW	Cessna 172P Skyhawk II	17274057	N5307K	16. 5.88	The Exeter Flying Club Ltd	Exeter	28. 6.09E
G-WACY	Reims Cessna F172P Skyhawk II	F17202217	F-GDOZ	3.10.86	Wycombe Air Centre Ltd	Wycombe Air Park	7. 1.10E
G-WADI	Piper PA-46-350P Malibu Mirage	4636205		8. 5.99	Air Malibu AG	(Triesen, Liechtenstein)	2. 6.09E
G-WADS	Robinson R22 Beta	1224	G-NICO	25. 4.96	Un Pied Sur Terre Ltd t/a Whizzard Helicopters	Welshpool	14. 4.09E
G-WAGG	Robinson R22 Beta II	2960		7. 7.99	J B Wagstaff t/a N J Wagstaff Leasing	Costock	17. 9.09E
G-WAGN	Stinson 108-3 Voyager	108-4216	N6216M NC6216M	22. 6.05	S E H Ellcome	Cumbernauld	25. 4.10S
	(Built Consolidated Vultee Aircraft)						
G-WAGS	Robinson R44 Raven II	10891		7.10.05	Wagstaff Homes Ltd	Gamston	12.11.09E
G-WAHL	QAC Quickie	PFA 094-10619		20. 9.00	A A M Wahlberg *(Noted 9.04)*	Lee-on-Solent	
	(Built A A M Wahlberg)						
G-WAIN	Cessna 550 Citation Bravo	550-1100	N110BR N5203S	24. 3.06	Ferron Trading Ltd	Jersey	23. 3.09E
G-WAIR	Piper PA-32-301 Saratoga	32-8506010	N2607X N9577N	14. 1.91	P J Hopkins t/a Finningley Aviation	Ninescores Farm, Finningley	16. 1.09E
G-WAIT	Cameron V-77 Balloon (Hot Air)	2390		20.11.90	C P Brown	Ely	24. 7.99A
G-WAKE	Mainair Blade 912	1244-0300-7-W1037		6. 3.00	B W Webster	Rochdale	4. 5.09P
G-WAKY	Cyclone AX2000	7890		5. 4.02	York Microlight Centre Ltd	Rufforth	18. 8.08P
	(HKS700E V3)						
G-WALI	Robinson R44 Raven II	10849		30. 8.05	Casdron Enterprises Ltd	Phoenix Farm, Lower Upham	29. 9.08E
G-WALY	Maule MX-7-180 Star Rocket	11028C	N5668H	23. 1.03	J R Colthurst	Radley Farm, Hungerford	20. 8.09E
G-WAMS	Piper PA-28R-201 Arrow	2844050	N491A N5328Q	29. 4.04	Stapleford Flying Club Ltd	Stapleford	20. 5.09E
G-WANT	Robinson R22 Beta	4125	N138SH	3. 9.08	Rotormotive Ltd	Little Blakenham	21. 9.09E
G-WARA	Piper PA-28-161 Warrior III	2842021	EC-HXU	3. 9.97	S J Skilton t/a Aviation Rentals	White Waltham	6. 4.09E
			G-WARA, N9289N, (G-WARA), N9289N				
G-WARB	Piper PA-28-161 Warrior III	2842034	N41286	4. 9.98	OSF Ltd	Wolverhampton	9. 9.09E
			(G-WARB), N41286				
G-WARD	Taylor JT.1 Monoplane	WB.VI		1.12.80	R P J Hunter	Redhill	22. 2.00P
	(Built G Ward - pr.no.PFA 1407) (Volkswagen 1834)				*(Damaged Redhill 17. 9.99)*		
G-WARE	Piper PA-28-161 Warrior II	28-8416080	N4357L ("N4354Z")	21. 7.89	W B Ware	Filton	25. 6.09E
G-WARH	Piper PA-28-161 Warrior III	2842063	N4177Y G-WARH	4. 2.00	Central Aircraft Leasing Ltd	Fairoaks	18. 3.09E
G-WARO	Piper PA-28-161 Warrior III	2842015	EC-HVT	24.10.97	S J Skilton t/a Aviation Rentals	Exeter	17. 3.09E
			G-WARO, N92946, (G-WARO), N92946		*(Operated Exeter Flying School)*		
G-WARP	Cessna 182F	18254633	G-ASHB N3233U	6. 6.95	R D Fowden	Haverfordwest	17. 4.09E
G-WARR	Piper PA-28-161 Warrior II	28-7916321	N3074U	15. 9.88	B Huda	Jersey	27. 4.09E
G-WARS	Piper PA-28-161 Warrior III	2842022	N9281X	7.11.97	Blaneby Ltd	Biggin Hill	12.11.09E
			(G-WARS), N9281X				
G-WARU	Piper PA-28-161 Warrior III	2842023	EC-HVU	6.11.97	S J Skilton t/a Aviation Rentals	Fairoaks	1. 6.09E
			G-WARU, N92880				
G-WARV	Piper PA-28-161 Warrior III	2842036	N41247	9.10.98	Plane Talking Ltd	Denham	21.10.09E
			(G-WARV), N41247				
G-WARW	Piper PA-28-161 Warrior III	2842037	N41254	17.11.98	Lomac Aviators Ltd	Liverpool	27. 4.09E
			(G-WARW), N41254				
G-WARX	Piper PA-28-161 Warrior III	2842038	N4126D	15.12.98	C M A Clark	Shobdon	17. 4.09E
			(G-WARX), N4126D				
G-WARY	Piper PA-28-161 Warrior III	2842024	N9287X	13.11.97	Transport Command Ltd	Shoreham	12. 1.10E
			(G-WARY), N9287X				
G-WARZ	Piper PA-28-161 Warrior III	2842025	EC-IBI	26.11.97	S J Skilton tr Aviation Rentals	Blackpool	27. 2.09E
			G-WARZ, N92944		*(Operated Flight Academy)*		
G-WASN	Eurocopter EC135 T2+	0746		16.12.08	Eurocopter UK Ltd	Oxford	
G-WATJ	Beech B200GT Super King Air	BY-14	N43004	3. 1.08	Saxonhenge Ltd	Caernarfon	10. 1.10E
G-WATR	Christen A-1 Husky (Floatplane)	1040	N2941W	2. 4.03	S N Gregory	Lochearnhead	17. 6.09E
G-WAVA	Robin HR.200-120B	352		10. 7.00	Plane Talking Ltd	Elstree	11. 1.10E
G-WAVE (2)	Grob G109B	6381		1. 8.85	C G Wray	Park Farm, Eaton Bray	14. 5.09E
G-WAVI	Robin HR.200-120B	346	G-BZDG	8. 5.01	Plane Talking Ltd	Elstree	12. 4.09E
G-WAVN	Robin HR.200-120B	344	G-VECA	2. 5.02	Plane Talking Ltd	Elstree	20. 3.09E
G-WAVS	Piper PA-28-161 Warrior III	2842035	G-WARC	1.11.05	Abraxas Aviation Ltd	Elstree	17. 9.09E
			N41244, (G-WARC), N41244				
G-WAVT	Robin R2160I	375	G-CBLG	7.12.04	Plane Talking Ltd	Elstree	25. 5.09E
G-WAVV	Robin HR.200-120B	291	G-GORF F-GORF	6. 3.06	Abraxas Aviation Ltd	(Poole)	12. 3.09E
G-WAVY	Grob G109B	6374	F-CAQP F-WAQP	5. 5.05	G M Brightman and T Donovan tr G-WAVY Group	Shenington	26. 5.09E
G-WAZP	Best Off Sky Ranger 912(2)	SKR0212288		10. 6.04	L V McClune	Hunsdon	23.10.09P
	(Built K H A Negal - pr.no.BMAA HB/273)						
G-WBAT	Wombat Gyrocopter	CJ-001	G-BSID	31. 5.90	M R Harrison	(Guernsey)	
	(Built C D Julian) (Rotax 532)						
G-WBEV	Cameron N-77 Balloon (Hot Air)	4376	G-PVCU	15.12.04	T J and M Turner *"Beverley's"*	Southampton and Wellingborough	19. 8.09E
G-WBHH	Bell 206B-3 JetRanger III	2410	N5001N	16. 4.07	Hughes Helicopter Co Ltd t/a Biggin Hill Helicopters	Biggin Hill	
G-WBLY	Mainair Sports Pegasus Quik	8057		30. 7.04	A J Lindsay *"Coastbuster"*	Newtownards	29. 7.09P
G-WBMG	Cameron N Ele 90SS Balloon (Hot Air)	3086	(G-BUYV)	5. 7.93	P H E van Overwalle	Nazareth, Belgium	22. 6.02A
G-WBTS	Falconar F-11W-200	PFA 32-10070	G-BDPL	22.10.90	W C Brown	Chilbolton	28.7.09P
	(Built A J Watson) (Continental O-200-A)						
G-WBVS	Diamond DA.40D Star	D4.060		23.10.03	G W Beavis	Durham Tees Valley	11. 5.09E

G-WCAO	Eurocopter EC.135 T2		0204	D-HECU	8. 4.02	Avon and Somerset Constabulary and Gloucestershire Constabulary (Operated Western Counties Police)		
							Filton	13. 6 11
G-WCAT	Colt Flying Mitt SS Balloon (Hot Air)		1744		30. 5.90	I Chadwick tr Balloon Preservation Flying Group		
						"Washcat"	Petworth	28.11.03A
G-WCCI	Embraer EMB-135BJ Legacy		145505	G-REUB	7. 8.07	Altarello Ltd	London Stansted	7.12.09E
				PT-SAF				
G-WCCP	Beech B200 Super King Air		BB-1295	N295CP	16.10.06	William Cook Aviation Ltd	(Sheffield)	20.12.09E
				N95MW, N3079S				
G-WCEI	SOCATA MS.894E Rallye 220GT		12141	G-BAOC	28. 5.85	R A L Lucas	Bagby	14.11.08E
G-WCOM	Robinson R44 Raven		1917		15. 8.08	CDS Aviation Ltd	(Kettering)	15. 9.09E
G-WCRD	Aérospatiale SA.341G Gazelle		1390	F-GEHD	25.10.02	Wickford Development Company Ltd		
				N6KT, N49527			Wickford House, Hatfield Peverel	29. 1.09E
G-WCUB	Piper PA-18-150 Super Cub		18-8278	HB-OLR	11. 5.01	P A Walley	Croft Farm, Defford	13.11.10
				N5514Y				
G-WDEB	Thunder Ax7-77 Balloon (Hot Air)		1606		26. 9.89	A Heginbottom	Cheadle	19. 8.09E
G-WDEV	Westland SA.341G Gazelle 1		1098	G-IZEL	30. 9.98	Mentorvale Construction Ltd	(Balgriffin, Dublin)	16. 7.09E
				G-BBHW				
G-WDGC	Rolladen-Schneider LS8-18		8395	G-CEWJ	8. 2.08	W D G Chappel "M9"	(Pewsey)	21. 3.08
				BGA4904-JZC				
G-WDKR	Aérospatiale AS.355F2 Ecureuil 2		5115	ZJ635	24. 7.95	Cheshire Helicopters Ltd	(Sharcott, Wilmslow)	19. 3.09E
				G-NEXT, G-WDKR, G-NEXT, I-NEXT, G-NEXT, G-OMAV, G-NEXT				
G-WEBS	American Champion 7ECA Citabria Aurora				30. 1.06	P J Webb	Andrewsfield	14. 5.09E
			1395-2005					
G-WEEK	Best Off Sky Ranger 912(2)		SKRxxxx628		19. 1.06	D J Prothero and R J Brown	RNAS Culdrose	28. 9.08P
	(Built D J Prothero and R J Brown - pr.no.BMAA HB/476)							
G-WEGO	Robinson R44 Raven II		10325		28. 4.04	A and E Fire Equipment Ltd	Gloucestershire	13. 5.09E
G-WELI	Cameron N-77 Balloon (Hot Air)		1078		26. 9.84	M A Shannon "Wellie"	Southampton	5. 7.04A
G-WELS	Cameron N-65 Balloon (Hot Air)		1297		7. 4.86	K J Vickery "Talisman"	Billingshurst	26. 6.92A
G-WELY	Agusta A109E Power		11710		9. 8.07	Titan Airways Ltd	London Stansted	8. 8.09E
G-WEMS	Robinson R44 Astro		730	G-HMPF	3. 6.08	J and E Tatham	Basingstoke	20. 3.09E
G-WENA	Aérospatiale AS.355F2 Ecureuil 2		5260	G-MOBI	19. 4.04	Multiflight Ltd	Leeds-Bradford	3. 5.09E
				G-MUFF, G-CORR				
G-WEND	Piper PA-28RT-201 Arrow IV	28R-8118026		PH-SYL	8.11.82	Tayside Aviation Ltd	Glenrothes	14. 6.09E
				N8296L				
G-WERY	SOCATA TB-20 Trinidad		305		2. 4.82	G L Appleyard and C Hawkesworth tr WERY Flying Group		
							Sherburn-in-Elmet	15. 6.09E
G-WESX	CFM Streak Shadow		K 116-SA		2. 2.90	M Catania	(Mold)	22. 5.08P
	(Built N Ramsey - pr.no.PFA 161A-11561) (Rotax 582)							
G-WETI	Cameron N-31 Balloon (Hot Air)		449		27.11.78	C A Butter and J J T Cooke	Marsh Benham	11. 9.00A
G-WFFW	Piper PA-28-161 Warrior II	28-8116161		N8342A	26.10.93	S Letheren and D Jelly		
						(Sutton Benger, Chippenham)		12. 2.10E
G-WFLY	Mainair Sports Pegasus Quik		8073		8.10.04	D E Lord	Crosland Moor	17.10.08P
G-WFOX	Robinson R22 Beta II		2826		2. 6.98	G Kenna	Tatenhill	28. 7.09E
G-WGCS	Piper PA-18 Super Cub 95		18-1528	(G-BLSV)	21.12.84	S C Thompson	Newells Farm, Bolney	14. 8.09P
	(L-18C-PI) (Frame No.18-1500)			French Army F-MBCH, French Army 51-15528				
G-WGHB	Canadair CL-30 (T-33AN) Silver Star Mk.3			CF-EHB	9. 5.74	R H and G C Cooper	Mendlesham	13. 6.77P
			T33-640	CAF 133640, RCAF 21640	(On rebuild 8.06)			
G-WGSC	Pilatus PC-6/B2-H4 Turbo-Porter		848	(G-BRVM)	2. 1.90	D M Penny	Coleraine	29. 3.09E
				OE-EC				
G-WGSI	Air Creation Tanarg 912S/iXess 13				16.12.08	J A Ganderton	(Buckingham)	
	(Built JA Ganderton)	BMAA HB/585						
G-WHAM	Eurocopter AS.350B3 Ecureuil		3494		18. 1.02	B M Christie t/a Horizon Helicopter Hire Goodwood		21. 4.09E
G-WHAT	Colt 77A Balloon (Hot Air)		1911		15. 3.91	M A Scholes "Chad"	London SE25	15..5.08T
G-WHEE	Pegasus Quantum 15-912		7510		26. 3.99	Airways Airsports Ltd	Darley Moor, Ashbourne	8. 3.09P
G-WHEN	Tecnam P92-EM Echo	PFA 318-13679			7. 2.01	E Windle	Popham	30. 9.09P
	(Built C D Marsh)							
G-WHIM	Colt 77A Balloon (Hot Air)		1476		10. 4.89	D L Morgan	Ilford	28. 7.04A
G-WHOA	Evektor EV-97 Eurostar	PFA 315-13967		G-DATH	8.10.02	E Stokes and S Connah tr Eurostar Flying Group		
	(Built D N E D'Ath)						Barton	17. 4.09P
G-WHOG	CFM Streak Shadow		K 253-SA		21. 9.94	B R Cannell "Wart Hog"	Old Sarum	20. 7.09P
	(Built B R Cannell - pr.no.PFA 206-12776) (Rotax 618)							
G-WHOO	RotorWay Executive 162F		6495		5. 6.01	C A Saul	Street Farm, Takeley	11. 5.09P
	(Built C A Saull) (RotorWay RI 162F)							
G-WHRL	Schweizer 269C (Schweizer 300)		S 1453	EC-GGX	19. 4.90	M Gardiner	Henstridge	11. 9.09E
				CS-HDG, G-WHRL, N41S				
G-WHST	Eurocopter AS.350B2 Ecureuil		2915	G-BWYA	9. 8.96	Keltruck Ltd	(West Bromwich)	26. 9.09E
G-WIBB	Jodel D 18	PFA 169-11640			18. 6.96	C J Bragg	Hill Farm, Nayland	2.11.09P
	(Built J Wibberley) (Subaru EA81)							
G-WIBS	CASA 1-131E Jungmann Series 2000		2005	Spanish AF		C Willoughby	(Ashford)	
				E3B-401	25. 3.99			
G-WICH	Clutton FRED Srs II	PFA 029-10331			16.10.08	L A Tomlinson	(Billericay)	
	(Built R H Hearn and rebuilt L A Tomlinson)							
G-WIDZ	Staaken Z-21 Flitzer	PFA 223-14314			26. 8.05	T F Crossman	(Loddon, Norwich)	
	(Built T F Crossman)							
G-WIEZ	Cameron C-80 Balloon (Hot Air)		3265	PH-WIE	5. 4.07	M B Young	Bristol	3. 4.09E
G-WIFE	Cessna R182 Skylane RG II		R18200244	G-BGVT	11.12.01	A L Brown tr Wife 182 Group	Glenrothes	9. 5.09E
				N3162C				
G-WIFI	Cameron Z-90 Balloon (Hot Air)		10624		9. 9.04	Trigger Concepts Ltd	Swallowfield, Reading	11.10.09E
						(Centrino titles)		
G-WIGY	Pitts S-1S		7-0115	G-ITTI	31. 5.07	M J Wright	Leicester	12. 3.09P
	(Built S Eisenberger) (Lycoming AEIO-360)			N91VA				
G-WIII	Schempp-Hirth Ventus bT		49/247	BGA4862-JXK	8. 7.08	P Turner and B Goodyer "W3"	Haleshead	
				D-KLOE				

G-WIIZ	Agusta-Bell 206B-2 JetRanger II	8111	G-DBHH	28.10.03	B J Green tr Helicopters R Go		
	G-AWVO, VH-BHI, PK-HCA, G-AWVO, 9Y-TDN, PK-HBG, G-AWVO					Draycott Farm, Chiseldon	9. 7.09E
G-WILB	UltraMagic M-105 Balloon (Hot-Air)	105/161		11. 4.08	A S Davidson, B N Trowbridge and W C Bailey		
					"William Bailey"	Swadlincote	15. 4.09E
G-WILD	Pitts S-1T	1017	ZS-LMM	6.12.85	N J Wakefield	Shobdon	26.11.09E
	(Built Pitts Aerobatics) (Lycoming AEIO-360)						
G-WILG	PZL-104 Wilga 35A	62153	G-AZYJ	15. 4.97	M H Bletsoe-Brown	Sywell	19. 8.09E
G-WILT	Comco Ikarus C42 FB100	0506-6687		14. 7.05	M A Curtis	(Witcombe, Martock)	30. 8.09P
	(Built Aerosport Ltd)						
G-WIMP	Colt 56A Balloon (Hot Air)	755		13. 2.86	T and B Chamberlain	Melbourne, York	19. 8.09E
G-WINA	Cessna 560XL Citation Excel	560-5343	N5145V	17.12.03	Inclination 1 LLP	Stapleford	21.12.09E
G-WINH	Evektor EV-97 teamEurostar UK	3216		9. 7.08	H M Wooldridge	(Jedburgh)	10. 7.09P
	(Built Cosmik Aviation)						
G-WINI	Scottish Aviation Bulldog Series 120/121		G-CBCO	23. 9.03	A Bole (As "XX546:03" in RAF c/s)	Conington	15. 6.09S
		BH120/238	XX546				
G-WINK	Grumman AA-5B Tiger	AA5B-0327	N74658	14.12.90	B S Cooke tr Wink Group	Elstree	1. 5.09E
G-WINN	Stolp SA.200 Starduster Too	615	N6275	15. 1.08	J C and R D P Cadle	Bidford	
	(Built B Scofield)						
G-WINS	Piper PA-32-300 Cherokee Six	32-7640065	N8476C	24. 4.91	Cheyenne Ltd	Jersey	13.11.09E
G-WINT	Pilatus PC-12/47	830		12. 7.07	Air Winton Ltd	Oxford	18. 7.09E
G-WIRE	Aérospatiale AS.355F1 Ecureuil 2	5312	G-CEGB	22. 1.90	National Grid Electricity Transmission PLC	Oxford	18. 6.09E
			G-BLJL				
G-WIRL	Robinson R22 Beta	0671		27. 7.87	Rivermead Aviation Ltd (Operated Rise Helicopters)		
						Gloucestershire	2. 8.09E
G-WISE	Piper PA-28-181 Archer III	2843658	N30910	17. 8.07	M Arnold (Operated Old Sarum Flying Club)		
						Old Sarum	23. 9.09E
G-WISZ	Steen Skybolt	PFA 064-13961		8. 7.08	G S Reid	(Attleborough)	
	(Built G S Reid)						
G-WIWI	Sikorsky S-76C	760684	N2584V	25. 6.08	Air Harrods Ltd	London Stansted	24. 6.09E
G-WIXI	Akrotech Europe CAP.10B	279		27. 1.98	A R Harris	(Chester)	16. 6.09E
G-WIZA	Robinson R22 Beta	0861	G-PERL	16.11.94	Patriot Aviation Ltd	Cranfield	7. 2.09E
			N90815				
G-WIZI	Enstrom 280FX Shark	2040	Chilean Army	8. 7.02	K G Ward	Hawarden	10. 2.09E
			H-177				
G-WIZR	Robinson R22 Beta II	2799		9. 3.98	Aerolease Ltd	Conington	13. 5.09E
G-WIZS	Mainair Sports Pegasus Quik	8019		17. 3.04	G R Barker	Bourn	26. 4.08P
G-WIZY	Robinson R22 Beta	0566	G-BMWX	26. 8.97	Fancy Plates Ltd	Enniskillen	22. 6.09E
			N24196				
G-WIZZ	Agusta-Bell 206B-2 JetRanger II	8540		7.12.77	Rivermead Aviation Ltd (Operated Rise Helicopters)		
						Gloucestershire	27. 5.09E
G-WJAC	Cameron TR-70 Balloon (Hot Air)	10694		29. 4.05	S J and J A Bellaby	Nottingham	26. 5.09E
G-WJCJ	Eurocopter EC.155 B1	6748	F-WWOO	31.10.06	Starspeed Ltd	Blackbushe	6.11.09E
G-WLAC	Piper PA-18-150 Super Cub	18-8899	G-HAHA	2. 6.98	White Waltham Airfield Ltd	White Waltham	12. 8.08E
			G-BSWE, N9194P				
G-WLDN	Robinson R44 Raven	1507		16. 9.05	Fly Executive Ltd	Cranfield	21.10.09E
G-WLGC	Piper PA-28-181 Archer III	2843484	G-FLUX	16. 4.07	Staircase 8 Ltd	Goodwood	27. 4.09E
			N5339U				
G-WLKI	Lindstrand LBL 150A Balloon (Hot Air)	1140		27. 3.07	C Wilkinson	Cornhill-on-Tweed	5. 4.09E
G-WLLM	Beech C90GTI King Air	LJ-1902	N3202A	11.12.08	Wilpot Ltd	Ronaldsway	
G-WLLS	Rolladen-Schneider LS8-18	8038	BGA4189-HTL	6.11.07	A and L Wells "LS"	Nympsfield	22.11.07
G-WLMS	Mainair Blade 912	1223-0999-7-W1016		23. 9.99	L W Jones	Finmere	7 12.08P
G-WLSN	Best Off Sky Ranger 912S(1)	SKRxxxx639		24.11.05	A, A R and A R Wilson	Darley Moor, Ashbourne	26. 7.09P
	(Built A., A R and A R Wilson - pr.no.BMAA HB/474)						
G-WLVS	Dassault Falcon 2000EX	141	F-WWGK	2. 4.08	Trinity Aviation Ltd (Wolves logo)	Manchester	1. 4.09E
G-WMAO	Eurocopter EC.135 P2+	0501		22. 8.06	West Midlands Police Authority	Birmingham	17. 7.11S
G-WMAS	Eurocopter EC.135 T2	0174		18. 6.01	Bond Air Services Ltd	RAF Cosford	26. 6.09E
					(Operated County Air Ambulance)		
G-WMLT	Cessna 182Q Skylane II	18266689	G-BOPG	23. 4.02	G Wimlett	Blackpool	1. 7.09E
			N95962				
G-WMTM	Gulfstream AA-5B Tiger	AA5B-1035	N4517V	8. 1.91	G Hance tr Falcon Flying Group	Aberdeen	25. 8.09E
G-WMWM	Robinson R44 Raven	0767		27. 4.00	MMAIR Ltd		
					Yew Tree Farm, Ford End, Clavering, Saffron Walden		3. 8.08E
	(Failed to gain height on take-off from Courcheval, France 15.3.08, the left skid struck the ground and helicopter rolled over & destroyed)						
G-WNAA	Agusta A109E Power	11090	G-TVAC	28. 5.03	Sloane Helicopters Ltd	Coventry	10. 4.09E
					(Operated Warwickshire and Northampton Air Ambulance)		
G-WNCH	Beech B200 Super King Air	BB-1259	G-OMGI	19. 6.06	Winch Air Ltd	Fairoaks	18. 7.09E
			N800MG, D-IDSM, N734P				
G-WNGS	Cameron N-105 Balloon (Hot Air)	4385		15. 7.98	R M Horn	Chelmsford	27. 2.09E
G-WNTR	Piper PA-28-161 Cherokee Warrior II		G-BFNJ	13. 1.06	D M Jarman tr Fleetlands Flying Group		
		28-7816281	N9520N			Lee-on-Solent	6. 6.09E
G-WOCO	Waco YMF-5C	F5C091	N770MM	10. 1.05	Classic Aviation Ltd	Gloucestershire	12. 5.09E
	(Built Waco Classic Aircraft Corporation 2000)						
G-WOFM	Agusta A109E Power	11678	G-NWRR	29. 8.06	Quinnasette Ltd	Oxford	8. 8.09E
G-WOLF	Piper PA-28-140 Cherokee Cruiser						
		28-7425439	OY-TOD	20. 3.80	M W Fitch t/a The Yak Group	Elstree	23. 6.09E
G-WONE	Schempp-Hirth Ventus 2cT	55/179	BGA4795-JUQ	11. 9.07	J P Wright	Lasham	26. 4.08
G-WONN	Eurocopter EC.135 T2+	0597		30. 8.07	Bond Air Services Ltd	Gloucestershire	28. 2.09E
G-WOOD	Beech 95-B55A Baron	TC-1283	SE-GRC	17. 9.79	M A Rooney	Sturgate	9. 3.09E
			G-AYID, SE-EXK				
G-WOOF	Enstrom 480	5027		3. 3.98	Netcopter.co.uk Ltd and Curvature Ltd	Hawarden	23. 7.09E
G-WOOL	Colt 77A Balloon (Hot Air)	2044		23. 2.93	T G, C L Pembrey and N P Helmsley	Steyning	21. 9.09E
					tr Whacko Balloon Group		
G-WORM	Thruster T 600N 450 Sprint	9109-T600N-039		5.10.99	C Childs	(Thorrington, Colchester)	12. 4.08P
	(Rotax 582 UL)						

Reg	Type	C/n	Prev id	Date	Owner/Operator	Base	Date
G-WOWA	de Havilland DHC-8-311	296	C-GZOF	23.10.03	Air South West Ltd	Plymouth	22.10.09E
			G-BRYS, PH-SDG, D-BKIS, C-GFQL				
G-WOWB	de Havilland DHC-8-311	334	C-GZOU	29.10.03	Air South West Ltd	Plymouth	28.10.09E
			G-BRYT, D-BKIR, C-GFEN				
G-WOWC	de Havilland DHC-8-311	311	N784BC	29.10.04	Air South West Ltd	Plymouth	11.11.09E
			G-BRYO, N434AW, C-GEVP				
G-WOWD	de Havilland DHC-8-311	286	C-FDIY	6. 5.05	Air South West Ltd	Plymouth	5. 5.09E
			N547DS, JY-RWA, C-FXGF, N432AW, C-GFCF, N432AW, C-GFCF				
G-WOWE	de Havilland DHC-8-311	256	C-FFBG	3. 3.06	Air South West Ltd	Plymouth	3. 3.09E
			G-BRYI, C-GEOA		*"Cloud Surfer"*		
G-WPAS	MD Helicopters MD.900 Explorer	900-00053		1. 7.98	Police Aviation Services Ltd *(Operated Wiltshire Police)*		
						Devizes	9.11.10S
G-WRBI	Agusta A109E Power	11017	G-CRST	22.11.07	Fuel The Jet LLP	(Dukinfield)	24. 7.09E
			N709AT, HB-XQM				
G-WREN	Pitts S-2A	2229	N947	8. 1.81	Modi Aviation Ltd	Sibson	27. 4.09E
	(Built Aerotek Inc) (Lycoming AEIO-360)						
G-WRFM	Enstrom 280C-UK Shark	1202	G-CTSI	21. 4.89	A J Clark	(Codnor, Ripley)	25. 6.09E
			G-BKIO, (G-BKHN), SE-HLB				
G-WRIT	Colt 77A Balloon (Hot Air)	1328		15. 9.88	G Pusey *"Legal Eagle"*	Seville, Spain	22. 7.09E
G-WRSY	Enstrom 480B	5077		19. 4.05	Pietas Ltd	Denham	7. 5.09E
G-WRWR	Robinson R22 Beta II	2964		20. 7.99	MFH Helicopters Ltd	Conington	22. 8.09E
G-WSKY	Enstrom 280C-UK-2 Shark	1037	G-BEEK	25. 7.83	M I Edwards	Brandon, Suffolk	15. 7.09E
G-WSSX	Comco Ikarus C42 FB100	0608-6837		31.10.06	R P Connell	Old Sarum	1.11.08P
	(Built Aerosport Ltd)						
G-WTAV	Robinson R44 Raven II	11449		29. 9.06	William Taylor Aviation Ltd *(Operated The Flight Centre)*		
						Southend	28.10.09E
G-WTEC	Cirrus SR22	2627	N819SR	29. 8.07	B J White	Goodwood	2. 9.09E
G-WTOR	Dassault Falcon 900EX	211	F-WWFN	21. 1.09	Executive Jet Charter Ltd	Farnborough	
G-WTWO	Aquila AT01	AT01-176		9. 1.08	J P Wright	(Ellisfield, Basingstoke)	14 2.09E
G-WUFF	Europa Aviation Europa	235		19. 1.99	M A Barker	Breighton	20. 5.09P
	(Built M A Barker - pr.no.PFA 247-12942) (Monowheel u/c)						
G-WULF	WAR Focke-Wulf FW190 replica	204		24. 2.78	A Howe *(As "8+-" in Luftwaffe c/s)*	(Birmingham)	22. 6.01P
	(Built SBV Aeroservices Ltd - pr.no.PFA 081-10328) (Continental O-200-A)						
G-WUSH	Eurocopter EC.120B Colibri	1290		15. 5.02	Bridgestock Ltd	(Ballyhaunis, County Mayo)	18. 8.09E
G-WVBF	Lindstrand LBL 210A Balloon (Hot Air)	312		6.12.95	Airxcite Ltd t/a Virgin Balloon Flights	Wembley	22. 4.04T
G-WVIP	Beech B200 Super King Air	BB-625	N869AM	18.08.04	Capital Air Charter Ltd	Exeter	19. 8.09E
			N8SZ, N8SP, N18BH, N302EC, N6682U				
G-WWAL	Piper PA-28R-180 Cherokee Arrow		G-AZSH	23.10.98	White Waltham Airfield Ltd	White Waltham	2. 1.09E
		28R-30461	N4612J				
G-WWAY	Piper PA-28-181 Archer II	28-8690031	D-ELCX	30. 3.04	R A Witchell	Andrewsfield	24. 3.09E
			N165AV, N9643N				
G-WWBB	Airbus A330-243	404	F-WWKP	30. 5.01	British Midland Airways Ltd	London Heathrow	29. 5.09E
G-WWBD	Airbus A330-243	401	F-WWKN	9. 5.01	British Midland Airways Ltd *(Star Alliance titles)*		
						London Heathrow	8. 5.09E
G-WWBM	Airbus A330-243	398	F-WWKL	27. 4.01	British Midland Airways Ltd	London Heathrow	26. 4.09E
G-WWIZ	Beech 58 Baron	TH-429	G-GAMA	18.10.96	F R M Harding *(stored 11.08)*	Bournemouth	5. 7.08E
			G-BBSD				
G-WWOW	Robinson R44 Raven I	1724		11. 6.07	Capital Helicopters Ltd	Perth	10. 7.09E
G-WWZZ	CZAW Sportcruiser	LAA 338-14877		7. 1.09	L Hogan and D M Hepworth	Glenrothes	
	(Built L Hogan and D M Hepworth)						
G-WYAT	CFM Streak Shadow SA	K 279		9. 6.97	J C Carter	Cambridge	21.11.04P
	(Built M G Whyatt - pr.no.PFA 206-12993) (Rotax 618)						
G-WYCH	Cameron Witch 90SS Balloon (Hot Air)	1330		30. 9.86	Corn Palace Balloon Club Ltd *"Hilda"*	(US)	13. 7.99A
	(Active Albuquerque, New Mexico, US 10.06)						
G-WYDE	Schleicher ASW 22BL	22053	BGA3388-FNF	4. 3.08	D M Byass tr 461 Syndicate *"461"*		
						Wycombe Air Park	
G-WYKD	Air Création Tanarg 912S(2)/iXess 15 FLT.xxx			4. 1.08	D C Dewey Lower Mountpleasant Farm, Chatteris		6. 6.09P
	(Built D C Dewey - pr.no.BMAA HB/559 being Flylight kit comprising Trike s/n T07095 and Wing s/n A07060-7185 [possibly A7160-7185])						
G-WYLE	Rans S-6-ES Coyote II	0904.1610		26.11.04	A and R W Osborne	Priory Farm, Tibenham	12. 6.09P
	(Built A and R W Osborne - pr.no.PFA 204-14330)						
G-WYND	Wittman W.8 Tailwind	PFA 031-12407		2. 8.99	R S Marriott	(Scunthorpe)	
	(Built R S Marriott and C Clark)						
G-WYNE	British Aerospace BAe 125 Series 800B		G-CJAA	17.10.06	Club 328 Ltd	Biggin Hill	13. 2.09E
	(Built Corporate Jets Ltd)	258240	G-HCFR, HB-VLT, G-SHEA, G-BUWC, G-5-772				
G-WYNT	Cameron N-56 Balloon (Hot Air)	1038		3. 4.84	S L G Williams	Bristol	25. 6.09E
					"Gwyntoedd Dros Cymru" and "Winds over Wales"		
G-WYPA	MBB BÖ.105DBS-4	S 815	D-HDZY	27.10.89	Police Aviation Services Ltd	Gloucestershire	27. 1.10E
G-WYSP	Robinson R44 Astro	0657		17. 9.99	Clear Aviation Ltd	Sherburn-in-Elmet	2.10.09E
G-WYSZ	Robin DR.400-100 Cadet	1829	G-FTIM	6. 5.88	R S M Fendt	Little Rissington	15. 1.09E
G-WYVN	DG Flugzeugbau DG-1000T	10-63T5	BGA5179-KLH	10. 2.06	J W Sage tr Army Gliding Association *"12" (Operated Wyvern		
					Army) Gliding Club)* Trenchard Lines, Upavon		17. 3.08
G-WZOL	TLAC RL5B LWS Sherwood Ranger		G-MZOL	20. 1.99	S J Spavins	Longacre Farm, Sandy	16. 4.09P
	(Built G W F Webb)	PFA 237-12887	(Jabiru 2200A)				
G-WZOY	Rans S-6-ES Coyote II	0707.1821		29.11.07	M H Wise and S P Read	(Weston Zoyland)	24. 4.09P
	(Built S P Read - pr.no.PFA 204-14735, tailwheel variant)						
G-WZRD	Eurocopter EC.120B Colibri	1455		3.11.06	Conductia Enterprises Ltd	(Nicosia, Cyprus)	13. 3.09E

G-XAAA - G-XZZZ

Reg	Type	C/n	Prev id	Date	Owner/Operator	Base	Date
G-XALT	Piper PA-38-112 Tomahawk	38-79A0801	PH-ALT	9.10.06	D Shew	Thruxton	13. 1.09E
			OO-TLT, N9651N				
G-XARV	ARV Aviation ARV-1 Super 2	010	G-OPIG	8.11.95	D J Burton	Kittyhawk Farm, Deanland	6. 6.08P
	(Rotax 912-S)		G-BMSJ				

Reg	Type	Serial	Prev ids	Date	Owner/Operator	Base	Expiry
G-XATS	Pitts S-2A	2147	CS-AZE	29. 3.01	Air Training Services Ltd *(Operated "Black Formation")*		
	(Built Pitts Aerobatics) (Lycoming AEIO-360)		N338BD			Wycombe Air Park	3.12.09E
G-XAVI	Piper PA-28-161 Warrior II	28-7916258	G-SACZ	12. 6.06	J R Santamaria	Guernsey	10. 7.09E
			N2098N				
G-XAXA	Fairey Britten-Norman BN-2A-26 Islander	530	G-LOTO	22. 8.00	AirX Ltd t/a Blue Islands	Jersey	28.11.09E
			G-BDWG, (N90255), (C-GYUF), G-BDWG				
G-XAYR	Raj Hamsa X'Air 582(2)	471		4. 1.00	C Cartwright and B Vincent	(Eaton Socon)	30. 4.09P
	(Built M J Kaye - pr.no.BMAA HB/122)						
G-XBCI	Bell 206B-3 JetRanger III	4466	N206EE	17. 6.04	BCI Helicopter Charters Ltd	(Thruxton)	15. 7.09E
			RP-C1778, N80706, C-GAJH				
G-XBEL	Cessna 560XL Citation XLS	560-5698	N5091J	2. 5.07	Aviation Beauport Ltd	Jersey	27. 6.09E
G-XBGA	Glaser-Dirks DG-500-22 Elan	5E71S12	BGA3955-HHJ	13. 2.08	N Kelly	Bicester	27. 5.08
G-XBLU	Cessna 680 Citation Sovereign	680-0143	N1318X	15. 8.07	Datel Holdings Ltd	(Stone)	14. 8.09E
G-XBOX	Bell 206B-3 JetRanger III	3370	G-OOHO	31. 1.05	Mainstream Digital Ltd	Kemble	24. 8.09E
			G-OCHC, G-KLEE, G-SIZL, G-BOSW, N2063T				
G-XCBI	Schweizer 269C-1 *(Schweizer 300)*	0301		7. 8.07	B Durkan	Enniskillen	1. 9.09E
G-XCCC	Extra EA.300/L	142		20. 8.01	P T Fellows	Rochester	18. 9.09E
G-XCIT	Alpi Pioneer 300	4		16. 9.04	A Thomas	Shobdon	15. 8.08P
	(Built A Thomas - pr.no.PFA 330-14296)						
G-XCIV	Rolladen-Schneider LS4-a	4355	BGA3709-GBT	6.11.07	S M Platt tr IV Group *"IV"*	Long Mynd	21. 3.08
			N220BB				
G-XCUB	Piper PA-18-150 Super Cub	18-8109036	N9348T	1. 5.81	M C Barraclough	(East Tisted, Alton)	23. 5.11S
G-XDUO	Schempp-Hirth Duo Discus xT	162	BGA5247-KOF	8. 3.07	F B Jeynes tr G-XDUO Group *"DUO"*	Bidford	6. 3.08
G-XDWE	P&M Aviation Quik GT450	8242		15. 2.07	D Ewing	Enstone	14. 2.08P
G-XELA	Robinson R44 Raven II	11378		26. 8.06	A Yew	Shoreham	21. 9.09E
G-XELL	Schleicher ASW 27-18E	29532	BGA5307-KRP	12. 3.08	S R Ell *"E11"*	Sutton Bank	
G-XENA	Piper PA-28-161 Cherokee Warrior II	28-7716158					
G-XERO	CZAW Sportcruiser	PFA 338-14658	N3486Q	29. 6.98	P Brewer	Shoreham	16. 5.09E
	(Built M R Mosley)			15. 5.08	M R Mosley	Headon Farm, Retford	
G-XFLY	Lambert Aircraft Mission M212-100	PFA 306-13380		3. 2.00	Lambert Aircraft Engineering BVBA	Kortrijk-Wevelgem, Belgium	4. 6.08P
G-XHOT	Cameron Z-105 Balloon (Hot Air)	10999		5. 1.07	S F Burden	Noordwijk ,Netherlands	25. 4.09E
G-XIII	Van's RV-7	PFA 323-14165		20. 2.04	G Wright tr G-XIIIGroup	Sherburn-in-Elmet	17. 8.09P
	(Built G Wright) (Lycoming O-360)						
G-XIIX	Robinson R22 Beta	0736		8. 2.88		Blackbushe	
G-XINE	Piper PA-28-161 Cherokee Warrior II	28-7716112	G-BPAC	14.10.03	P Tee	Denham	22. 5.09E
			N2567Q				
G-XIOO	Raj Hamsa X'Air 133(1)	681		27. 1.03	B J Fallows	Haverfordwest	5.11.08P
	(Built R Paton and A Start - pr.no.BMAA HB/247)						
G-XIXI	Evektor EV-97 teamEurostar UK	2938		12. 7.07	J A C Cockfield	RNAS Culdrose	30. 6.08P
	(Built Cosmik Aviation Ltd)						
G-XIXX	Elan DG-300 Elan	3E9	BGA3124-FBF	1. 9.08	S D Black	Saltby	
			BGA2952-EUA				
G-XJCB	Sikorsky S-76C+	760616	N8093J	29. 1.07	J C Bamford Excavations Ltd	Nottingham-East Midlands	14. 2.09E
G-XJJM	P&M Pegasus Quik	8306		23. 8.07	J J Murtagh	Barton	22. 8.08P
G-XJON	Schempp-Hirth Ventus 2b	114	BGA4895-JYT	17. 9.07	J C Bastin	Lasham	1. 3.08
			(BGA4885)				
G-XKEN	Piper PA-34-200T Seneca II	34-7970003	N3036A	5. 9.01	Beresford Pumps Ltd	Coventry	30.10.08E
G-XKKA	Diamond HK 36 TTC Super Dimona	36.677	S5-KKA	16. 2.07	S M Godleman tr G-XKKA Group	Headcorn	17. 3.09E
G-XLAG	Boeing 737-86N	33003	C-FEAG	29. 4.02	GECAS *(stored 9.08)*	Lasham	22. 5.09E
			G-XLAG				
G-XLAM	Best Off Sky Ranger 912S(1)	SKR0504609		19.12.05	D A Archer tr XLAM SkyRanger Syndicate	Sywell	25. 9.08P
	(Built D M Broom - pr.no.BMAA HB/460)						
G-XLAO	Boeing 737-86N/W	32690		2. 5.07	Celestial Aviation Trading 54 Ltd *(stored*	Lasham	1. 5.09E
G-XLGB	Cessna 560XL Citation Excel	560-5259	G-XLMB	30. 6.08	Tosh Air Ltd	London Stansted	25. 6.09E
			N52526				
G-XLII	Schleicher ASW 27-18E (ASG-29E)	29554	BGA5325-KSI	10. 7.08	N Hoare and G Smith *"42"*	Dunstable	15. 7.09
G-XLLL	Aérospatiale AS.355F1 Ecureuil 2	5033	G-PASF	14. 2.06	Sharpness Dock Ltd	(Victoria Wharf, Plymouth)	8. 4.09E
			G-SCHU, N915EG, N5777H				
G-XLNT	Zenair CH.601XL Zodiac	PFA 162B-14182		27. 1.04	P H Ronfell tr Zenair G-XLNT Group		
	(Built P H and S J Ronfell)					Tarn Farm, Cockerham	8. 9.09P
G-XLTG	Cessna 182S Skylane	18280234	N9571L	17. 7.98	D H Morgan	Denham	5. 8.09E
G-XLXL	Robin DR.400-160 Knight	813	G-BAUD	3. 1.92	L R Marchant	Rochester	3. 8.09E
G-XMGO	Aeromot AMT-200S Super Ximango	200127		18. 4.01	R P Beck and G McLean	Rufforth	11. 6.09E
	(Rotax 912 S4)						
G-XMII	Eurocopter EC.135 T2	0215		15. 4.02	Merseyside Police Authority	RAF Woodvale	6. 8.09E
G-XOAR	Schleicher ASG 29E	29518	BGA5285-KPT	18. 4.08	R Browne *"XS"*	RAF Cranwell	
			D-KPRB				
G-XOIL	Eurocopter AS.355N Ecureuil 2	5627	G-LOUN	5. 3.03	Firstearl Marine and Aviation Ltd	Denham	15. 6.09E
G-XONE	Bombardier CL600-2B16	5426	N51VR	10. 6.08	Gama Aviation Ltd	Farnborough	10. 6.09E
	(Challenger 604)		JY-ONE, N604JA, C-GLYC				
G-XPBI	Letov LK-2M Sluka	PFA 263-13341		4.12.98	K H A Negal	Red House Farm, Preston Capes	14. 8.06P
	(Built P Bishop) (Rotax 447)						
G-XPDA	Cameron Z-120 Balloon (Hot Air)	11038		6. 8.07	ABC Flights Ltd *(Expedia.co.uk titles)*		
						Clapton in Gordano, Bristol	30. 7.09E
G-XPII	Cessna R172K Hawk XP	R1723071	G-DIVA	6.11.06	A M Deacon tr The Hawk Flying Group	Leicester	17.10.09E
			N758FX				
G-XPWW	Cameron TR-77 Balloon (Hot-Air)	11063		8. 4.08	Chalmers Ballong Corps *"Blaklader"*		
						Goteburg, Sweden	14. 4.09E
G-XPXP	Aero Designs Pulsar XP	218		30. 3.92	B J Edwards	Belle Vue Farm, Yarnscombe	20. 7.08P
	(Built B J Edwards - pr.no.PFA 202-11958) (Tail-wheel u/c)						

Reg	Type	C/n	Prev id	Date	Owner/Operator	Location	Date
G-XRAF	Raj Hamsa X'Air 582(2)	513		7. 4.00	S Marathe	Sackville Lodge, Riseley	21.11.08P
	(Built M E Howard, S Jennings and S Stockill - pr.no.BMAA HB/132)						
G-XRAY	Rand Robinson KR-2	PFA 129-11227		30. 4.87	R S Smith	Barthol Chapel	
	(Built R S Smith)				*(Under construction 2001)*		
G-XRED	Pitts S-1C	338H	G-SWUN	28.11.05	J E Rands	Wickenby	8. 7.09P
	(Built R Merrick) (Lycoming O-320)		G-BSXH, N14RM				
G-XRLD	Cameron A-250 Balloon (Hot Air)	4820		25. 4.00	J A B Gray *(Red Letter Days titles)*		
						Daglingworth, Cirencester	27. 2.09E
G-XRVB	Van's RV-8	82057		22. 9.08	P G Winters	(Coventry)	
	(Built PG Winters, pr no PFA 303-14190)						
G-XRXR	Raj Hamsa X'Air 582(5)	431		13. 9.99	R J Philpotts	Pound Green, Buttonoak, Bewdley	19. 5.08P
	(Built I S Walsh - pr.no.BMAA HB/102)						
G-XRVX	Van's RV-10	PFA 339-14592		24.11.06	N K Lamping	(Weaverham, Northwich)	
	(Built N K Lamping)						
G-XSAM	Van's RV-9A	PFA 320-13797		18. 9.02	D G Lucas	Bodmin	12. 3.09E
	(Built D G Lucas) (Wilksch WAM-120)						
G-XSDJ	Europa Aviation Europa XS	402		3. 2.99	D N Joyce	Gloucestershire	21. 6.09P
	(Built D N Joyce - pr.no.PFA 247-13378) (Rotax 914-UL) (Monowheel u/c)						
G-XSEA	Van's RV-8	PFA 303-14228		15. 8.05	H M Darlington	Bury Farm, High Easter	20. 5.09P
	(Built N I Hart) (Superior XP-10-360)						
G-XSEL	Silence Twister	PFA 329-14594		3.10.07	Skyview Systems Ltd	Lavenham	16. 9.09P
	(Built NI G Hart) (Jabiru 2200A)						
G-XSFT	Piper PA-23-250 Aztec F	27-7754103	G-CPPC	18. 6.86	Yager International SPA	Madrid, Spain	16. 6.09E
			G-BGBH, N63773				
G-XSKY	Cameron N-77 Balloon (Hot Air)	2508		26. 3.91	T M C Smith and J R Rivers-Scott tr Phoenix Ballooning		
						Congleton	12. 8.09E
G-XTEE	AirBorne XT912-B-Streak III-B	XT912-026	T2-2252	25. 8.04	G J Webster t/a Airborne Australia In UK		
	(Wing s/n S3B-051)					Mill Farm, Shifnal	17. 3.09P
G-XTEK	Robinson R44 Astro	0647		11. 8.99	R C Hields t/a Hields Aviation	Sherburn-in-Elmet	22.10.09E
G-XTHT	AirBorne XT912-B-Streak III-B	XT912-200		4.12.07	H A Taylor	Bicester	16.12.08P
	(Wing s/n SB3-212)						
G-XTNI	AirBorne XT912-B-Streak III-B	XT912-067		10. 5.05	A J Parry	Tarsan Lane, Portadown	9. 5.07P
	(Wing s/n ST3-043)				*(Noted 7.07)*		
G-XTNR	AirBorne XT912-B-Streak III-B	XT912-050	T2-2283	21. 7.06	N Rose	Old Sarum	2. 7.07P
	(Wing s/n ST3-26-XT)						
G-XTOR	Fairey Britten-Norman BN-2A Mk.III-2 Trislander	G-BAXD		1. 4.96	Aurigny Air Services Ltd	Guernsey	5. 7.09E
	(Fuselage ex N3266G [1065] fitted 2.96)	359					
G-XTRA	Extra EA.230	12A	SE-XVB	21. 1.87	Xtra Aerobatics Ltd	Sherburn-in-Elmet	17. 6.09P
			G-XTRA, D-EDLF				
G-XTRM	Robinson R44 Raven II	11923		3.10.07	Anglian Helicopters Ltd	Norwich	16. 1.10E
G-XTUN	Westland-Bell 47G-3B1	WA/382	G-BGZK	11. 5.99	P A Rogers *(As "XT223" in AAC c/s)*		
			XT223			(Betws yn Rhos, Abergele)	10. 1.11S
G-XVBF	Lindstrand LBL 330A Balloon (Hot Air)	966		30. 1.04	Airxcite Ltd t/a Virgin Balloon Flights	Wembley	9.11.09E
G-XVOM	Van's RV-6	PFA 181-12894		6. 4.01	A Baker-Munton	Leicester	3. 7.09P
	(Built A Baker-Munton) (Lycoming O-320)						
G-XWEB	Best Off Sky Ranger 912(2)	SKR0411539		13. 4.05	K B Woods	Newnham, Baldock	3. 4.09P
	(Built K B Woods and T J Hector - pr.no.BMAA HB/443)						
G-XWON	Rolladen-Schneider LS8-18	8305	BGA4783-JUC	7. 1.08	P K Carpenter and S M Godleman	Challock	1. 4.08
G-XXBH	Agusta-Bell 206B JetRanger III	8596	G-BYBA	7. 5.08	Barnsely House Aviation Ltd	(Cirencester)	9.12.09E
			G-BHXV, G-OWJM, G-BHXV				
G-XXEA	Sikorsky S-76C	760492		21.12.98	T C Hewlett, Director of Royal Travel	Blackbushe	4. 1.10E
					(Operated Queen's Flight)		
G-XXIV	Agusta-Bell 206B-3 JetRanger III	8717		27. 4.89	Bart Fifty Nine Ltd	(Portbury, Bristol)	5. 7.09E
G-XXIX	Schleicher ASG 29E	29514	BGA5319-KSC	28. 4.08	P R and A H Pentecost *"630"*	Lasham	24. 4.09
			D-KPRA				
G-XXRS	Bombardier BD-700-1A10 Global Express	C-FCSR		24. 1.06	TAG Aviation (UK) Ltd	Farnborough	23. 1.10E
		9169					
G-XXRV	Van's RV-9	90645	N2667T	9. 1.09	D R Gilbert and D Slabbert	(Haywards Heath)	
	(Built B Wilson)						
G-XXTR	Extra EA.300/L	126	G-ECCC	13. 8.02	Extreme Aerobatics Ltd	Shoreham	7. 4.09E
			D-EDGE				
G-XXVB	Schempp-Hirth Ventus B	32	BGA2743-EKH	28.11.07	R Johnson	Parham Park	29.11.07
G-XXVI	Sukhoi Su-26M	04-10	RA-0410	2. 4.93	A N Onn *"39"*	Headcorn	23. 4.09P
G-XYAK	IAV Bacau Yakovlev Yak-52	899413	RA-44469	6. 3.03	R Davies *"69"*	Denham	19. 7.09P
			LY-AFX, DOSAAF 69 (blue)				
G-XYJY	Best Off Sky Ranger 912(2)	SKRxxxxxxx		20.10.03	A V Francis	Little Gransden	21. 6.09P
	(Built A V Francis - pr.no.BMAA HB/309)						
G-XYZT	Aeromot AMT-200S Super Ximango	200.176	PR-AOC	19. 6.08	B Chalabi and M Zacharia	Wycombe Air Park	19. 6.09E
	(Rotax 912 SA)		(PR-LFC)				
G-XZXZ	Robinson R44 Raven II	12567		26.11.08	Ashley Martin Ltd	(Inishowen, Ireland)	6. 1.10E

G-YAAA - G-YZZZ

Reg	Type	C/n	Prev id	Date	Owner/Operator	Location	Date
G-YAAK	Yakovlev Yak-50	812003	G-BWJT	23. 3.05	R J Luke	Lee-on-Solent	20.11.08P
			RA-01385, DOSAAF50				
G-YACB	Robinson R22 Beta II	3092	G-VOSL	24. 1.02	J Chapman t/a Property Network		
						(Inchmarlo, Banchory)	27. 6.09E
G-YADA	Comco Ikarus C42 FB100	0707-6901		29. 6.07	D F Hughes	Stoke, Isle of Grain	19. 9.08P
G-YAKA	Yakovlev Yak-50	822303	LY-ANJ	10.11.94	M Chapman	Stewton, Louth	1.10.08P
			DOSAAF 80				
G-YAKB	Aerostar Yakovlev Yak-52	9211517	RA-44491	25.11.02	Kemble Air Services Ltd	Kemble	21. 6.07P
			LY-AOB				
G-YAKC	IAV Bacau Yakovlev Yak-52	867212	LY-AKC	25. 6.02	T J Wilson	Andrewsfield	7. 8.09P
			DOSAAF 153 (yellow)?				

G-YAKD	IAV Bacau Yakovlev Yak-52	845002	LY-AQQ 18.10.07	P Doggett	Andrewsfield	5.11.09P
			DOSAAF 152 (red) ?			
G-YAKF	Aerostar Yakovlev Yak-52	9111205	ZU-IAK 25.10.07	B Gwynett	Haverfordwest	29. 6.09P
			RA02090, DOSAAF10			
G-YAKH	IAV Bacau Yakovlev Yak-52	899915	RA-01948 24.12.02	Plus 7 Minus 5 Ltd (As "33" (white) in Soviet AF c/s)		
			LY-AFV, DOSAAF 102 (yellow)		White Waltham	8. 5.09P
G-YAKI	IAV Bacau Yakovlev Yak-52	866904	LY-ANM 20. 9.94	Yak One Ltd (As "100" in DOSAAF c/s)		
			DOSAAF 100		Popham	7. 8.09P
G-YAKK	Yakovlev Yak-50	853104	RA-01293 5.11.02	Whisky UK Ltd	North Weald	16. 7.09P
G-YAKM	Yakovlev Yak-50	842710	RA-44461 6. 2.04	Airborne Services Ltd (As "61" (red) in Soviet AF c/s)		
			Ukraine 28 (blue)		Compton Abbas	11. 4.08P
G-YAKN	IAV Bacau Yakovlev Yak-52	855905	RA-44466 6. 2.04	Airborne Services Ltd (As "66" (red) in Soviet AF c/s)		
			DOSAAF 105 (blue)		Compton Abbas	23. 5.08P
G-YAKO	IAV Bacau Yakovlev Yak-52	822203	RA-01493 (1) 8. 5.99	M K Shaw	Norwich	30. 4.08P
G-YAKP	Yakovlev Yak-9	01-35	DOSAAF 3. 1.08	M V Rijkse and N M R Richards Gyor-Pet, Hungary		
G-YAKR	IAV Bacau Yakovlev Yak-52	899803	LY-AOV 15.11.02	R A Alexander tr G-YAKR Group (As "03" (yellow))		
			Ukraine AF 75 (yellow), DOSAAF 75		North Weald	13. 1.09P
G-YAKT	IAV Bacau Yakovlev Yak-52	8910302	RA-01564 21. 1.03	S Wilkinson tr G-YAKT Group (As '01564')		
			DOSAAF 149 (yellow)		White Waltham	15. 6.09P
G-YAKU	Yakovlev Yak-50	822305	RA-44549 6.11.03	D J Hopkinson (As "49" (red) in Soviet AF c/s)		
			G-BXNO, LY-ASD, DOSAAF 82		Compton Abbas	18.12.09P
G-YAKV	Aerostar Yakovlev Yak-52	9111311	RA-02209 8. 7.03	P D Scandrett (As "31" in Soviet AF c/s)		
			RA-9111311, DOSAAF 31		Rendcomb	25. 9.09P
G-YAKX	Aerostar Yakovlev Yak-52	9111307	RA-44473 13. 3.96	The X-Fliers Ltd (As "27" (red) in Soviet AF c/s)		
			G-YAKX, RA-9111307, DOSAAF 27		Popham	8. 1.09P
G-YAKY	IAV Bacau Yakovlev Yak-52	844109	LY-AKX 26. 2.96	W T Marriott (On rebuild 2005)	(Wickenby)	7. 3.02P
			DOSAAF 24 (red)			
G-YAKZ	Yakovlev Yak-50	853206	RA-44533 7.11.03	Airborne Services Ltd (As "33" (red) in Soviet AF c/s)		
					Compton Abbas	10. 5.09P
G-YANK	Piper PA-28-181 Archer II	28-8090163	N81314 19. 3.93	J A Millar-Craig tr G-YANK Flying Group	Tatenhill	20. 7.09E
G-YARR	Mainair Rapier	1255-0700-7-W1049	14. 8.00	D Yarr	St Michaels	30. 3.09P
G-YARV	ARV Aviation ARV-1 Super 2	K 004	G-BMDO 15.10.01	A M Oliver	(Market Lavington, Devizes)	18. 8.09P
	(Built Hornet Aviation Ltd - pr.no.PFA 152-11127)		(Rotax 914)			
G-YAWW	Piper PA-28RT-201T Turbo Arrow IV	28R-8031024	N2929Y 15.11.90	Barton Aviation Ltd	Liverpool	9. 7.09E
G-YBAA	Reims FR172J Rocket	FR17200579	5Y-BAA 15.11.84	A Evans	Bourn	21. 6.09E
G-YCII	LET Yakovlev C-11	25III/08	F-AZPA 13. 1.00	R W Davies (As "11" (yellow) in Soviet AF c/s)		
			Egyptian AF		Little Engeham Farm, Woodchurch	14. 6.05P
				(Clipped tree on final approach North Weald 1. 6.05 and damaged)		
G-YCUB	Piper PA-18-150 Super Cub	1809077	N4993X 23. 8.96	F W Rogers Garage (Saltash) Ltd		
			N4157T		Bealbury, Plymouth	29. 5.11S
G-YCUE	Agusta A109A	7149	EI-CHV 4. 4.08	Q Aviation Ltd	Shobdon	
			VR-BMM, HB-XTJ, D-HASV			
G-YEAH	Robinson R44 Raven II	10453	3. 8.04	Turboprop Leasing LLP (Manor Park, Runcorn)		30. 9.09E
G-YEHA	Schleicher ASW 27	27136	BGA4819-JVQ 9. 4.08	B L Cooper "68"	Wycombe Air Park	
G-YELL	Murphy Rebel	PFA 232-12381	1. 5.95	A H Godfrey (Lympsham, Weston-super-Mare)		
	(Built A D Keen)					
G-YELO	Rotorsport UK MT-03	RSUK/MT-03/050	22. 8.08	M Black	(Luton)	
G-YEOM	Piper PA-31-350 Chieftain	31-8352022	N41108 3. 1.89	Foster Yeoman Ltd	Bristol	8. 6.09E
G-YEWS	RotorWay Executive	3850	22. 6.89	R Turrell and P Mason	(Wickford)	17. 6.93P
	(Built D G Pollard - c/n DGP-1) (RotorWay RW 152)					
G-YFLY	Magni M-16 Tandem Trainer	VPM16-UK114	G-BWGI 14.10.96	A J Unwin	Kemble	13.10.06P
	(Built Arrow Engines UK) (Subaru EA81)					
G-YFUT	IAV Bacau Yakovlev Yak-52	888410	LY-FUT 6. 2.03	R Oliver	Swansea	7. 8.09P
			Ukraine AF 22 (yellow), DOSAAF 22			
G-YFZT	Cessna 172S Skyhawk	172S9587	N20974 24. 2.04	AB Integro Aviation Ltd	Wycombe Air Park	10. 4.09E
G-YHPV	Cessna 310N	310N0054	N510PS 1.12.04	P O Hayes and V E Young		
			G-YHPV, N510PS, G-AWTA, EI-ATB, N4154Q	Waterford, County Waterford		17. 8.09E
G-YIII	Reims Cessna F150L	F15000827	PH-CEX 5. 6.80	Merlin Flying Club Ltd	Hucknall	30.10.09E
G-YIPI	Reims FR172K Hawk XP	FR1720616	OY-IPI 9. 1.03	A J G Davis	St Mary's, Isles of Scilly	4. 3.09E
			D-EIPI			
G-YJET	Montgomerie-Bensen B 8MR	PFA G/01-1072	G-BMUH 25. 9.96	A Shuttleworth	Barton	7. 5.07P
	(Built J M Montgomerie) (Rotax 582)					
G-YKCT	Aerostar Yakovlev Yak-52	9010307	LY-ATI 29. 5.02	A Fergusson tr G-YKCT Group	Maybole	13. 6.09P
			Ukraine AF 04, DOSAAF 04			
G-YKSO	Yakovlev Yak-50	791506	LY-APT 8. 4.02	Classic Displays Ltd	North Weald	1. 6.09P
				(Landed with undercarriage retracted at White Waltham 16.6.08)		
G-YKSS	Yakovlev Yak-55	901103	RA-44525 1. 7.03	I D Trask	Headcorn	2. 8.09P
			DOSAAF 96 (blue)			
G-YKSZ	Aerostar Yakovlev Yak-52	9311709	16.12.93	N Rhind tr Tzarina Group (As "01" (yellow) in Soviet AF c/s)		
					White Waltham	25. 9.09P
G-YKYK	Aerostar Yakovlev Yak-52	9812106	LY-AHB 16. 6.03	K J Pilling	North Weald	31. 8.09P
G-YLYB	Cameron N-105 Balloon (Hot Air)	4482	15. 1.99	P L N Dowlen tr Blackhorse Balloon Club		
				(Lloyds TSB titles)	High Wycombe	16. 7.09E
G-YMBO	Robinson R22 Mariner	2054M	OY-HFR 21. 8.95	S A Storey	(Chorley)	18. 9.09E
G-YMFC	Waco YMF	F5033	N90B 6. 4.04	S J Brenchley	Coventry	8. 9.09E
	(Built Classic Aircraft Corporation, 1990)					
G-YMMA	Boeing 777-236	30302	N5017Q 7. 1.00	British Airways PLC	London Heathrow	6. 1.10E
G-YMMB	Boeing 777-236	30303	18. 1.00	British Airways PLC	London Heathrow	17. 1.10E
G-YMMC	Boeing 777-236	30304	4. 2.00	British Airways PLC	London Heathrow	3. 2.10E
G-YMMD	Boeing 777-236	30305	19. 2.00	British Airways PLC	London Heathrow	17. 2.09E
G-YMME	Boeing 777-236	30306	16. 4.00	British Airways PLC	London Heathrow	14. 4.09E
G-YMMF	Boeing 777-236	30307	17. 5.00	British Airways PLC	London Heathrow	16. 5.09E
G-YMMG	Boeing 777-236	30308	28. 9.00	British Airways PLC	London Heathrow	28. 7.09E

G-YMMH	Boeing 777-236	30309		14.10.00	British Airways PLC	London Heathrow	13.10.09E
G-YMMI	Boeing 777-236	30310		2.11.00	British Airways PLC	London Heathrow	1.11.09E
G-YMMJ	Boeing 777-236	30311		8.12.00	British Airways PLC	London Heathrow	7.12.09E
G-YMMK	Boeing 777-236	30312		8.12.00	British Airways PLC	London Heathrow	2.10.09E
G-YMML	Boeing 777-236	30313		10. 4.01	British Airways PLC	London Heathrow	13. 4.09E
G-YMMN	Boeing 777-236	30316		15. 6.01	British Airways PLC	London Heathrow	14. 6.09E
G-YMMO	Boeing 777-236	30317		17. 9.01	British Airways PLC	London Heathrow	13. 9.09E
G-YMMP	Boeing 777-236	30315		30.10.01	British Airways PLC	London Heathrow	29.10.09E
G-YMMR	Boeing 777-236	36516		1.09R	British Airways PLC	London Heathrow	
G-YMMS	Boeing 777-236	36517		3.09R	British Airways PLC	London Heathrow	
G-YMMT	Boeing 777-236	36518		3.09R	British Airways PLC	London Heathrow	
G-YMMU	Boeing 777-236	36519		4.09R	British Airways PLC	London Heathrow	
G-YNOT	Druine D 62B Condor	RAE 649	G-AYFH	10.11.83	A Littlefair (Noted 6.05)	Thruxton	4. 9.03P
	(Built Rollason Aircraft and Engines)						
G-YNYS	Cessna 172S Skyhawk	172S8725	N835SP	23.11.05	T V Hughes	Caernarfon	30. 4.09E
G-YOBI	Schleicher ASH 25	25088	BGA3606-FXL	4. 4.08	J Kangurs "108"	Husbands Bosworth	
G-YODA	Schempp-Hirth Ventus 2cT	82/249	BGA4943-KAT	6.11.07	P C Naegeli "520"	Lasham	15. 3.08
G-YOGI	Robin DR.400-140B Major	1090	G-BDME	1.10.86	M M Pepper	Spanhoe	30. 4.09E
G-YOHO	Glasflügel H201B Standard Libelle	597	BGA3750-GDM	27.11.07	M P Theo	Waldershare Park	23. 1.08
			D-6666				
G-YOLK	P&M Aviation Quik GT450	8398		14. 7.08	P N Sherratt	(Taynton, Glos)	13. 7.09P
G-YORK	Reims Cessna F172M Skyhawk II	F17201354	PH-LUY	14.12.78	H-R A E Waetjen	(Athboy, County Meath)	2. 9.09E
			F-WLIT				
G-YOTS	Aerostar Yakovlev Yak-52	9010308	LY-AOW	4. 5.03	G S Jones tr YOTS Group		
			Ukraine AF 105, DOSAAF 05 (yellow)			Wellcross Grange, Slinfold	15. 6.09P
G-YOYO	Pitts S-1E	PFA 009-10885	G-OTSW	22. 5.96	J D L Richardson	Exeter	13.10.09P
	(Built W R Penaluna) (Lycoming IO-360)		G-BLHE				
G-YPDN	Rotorsport UK MT-03	RSUK/MT-03/045		18. 6.08	T M Jones	(Leeds)	8. 7.09P
G-YPOL	MD Helicopters MD.900 Explorer	900-00078	N7038S	4.10.00	West Yorkshire Police Authority	Wakefield	25. 1.10S
G-YPRS	Cessna 550 Citation Bravo	550-0935	G-IPAC	11. 6.08	Executive Aviation Services Ltd	Gloucestershire	21. 1.10E
			G-IPAL, EI-PAL , N5264A				
G-YPSY	Andreasson BA-4B	PFA 038-10352		7. 6.78	D J Howell "65"	Wolverhampton	30. 3.09P
	(Built H P Burrill) (Continental O-200-A)						
G-YRAF	Rotary Air Force RAF 2000 GTX-SE			1. 6.01	J R Cooper	Rhigos	22. 5.08P
	(Built C V King & J R Cooper) PFA G/13-1289						
G-YRIL	Luscombe 8E Silvaire Deluxe	5945	N1318B	3. 2.92	C Potter	North Weald	7.12.08P
	(Continental O-200-A)		NC1318B				
G-YROC	Rotorsport UK MT-03	RSUK/MT-03/044		14. 5.08	C V Catherall	Chiltern Park, Wallingford	21. 5.09E
G-YROE	ELA Aviacion ELA 07R	01050510712		26. 3.07	J P R MacLaren	(Glasgow)	
G-YROI	Air Command 532 Elite	0002	N532CG	3. 9.87	W B Lumb	(Manchester)	17.12.90P
	(Built Air Command Manufacturing Inc)						
G-YROJ	Rotary Air Force RAF 2000 GTX-SE			26.11.04	J R Mercer	(Formby, Liverpool)	
	(Built J R Mercer) PFA G/13-1343						
G-YROM	Rotorsport UK MT-03	RSUK-MT-03-019		21. 9.07	M W King	(Etchingham)	23.11.09P
G-YROO	Rotary Air Force RAF 2000 GTX-SE			27.11.01	K D and C S Rhodes	Henstridge	24. 4.09P
	PFA G/13-1341						
	(Built K D Rhodes and C S Oakes)						
G-YROX	Rotorsport UK MT-03	RSUK/MT-03/005		21. 8.06	C A M Holmes-Surplus and N F Surplus	(Larne)	23.10.09P
G-YROY	Montgomerie-Bensen B 8MR			12. 9.89	S S Wilson	Melrose Farm, Melbourne	14.11.07P
	(Built R D Armishaw) PFA G/101A-1145				(Rotax 532)		
G-YRUS	Jodel D 140E	PFA 251-14090	G-YRNS	8. 9.03	W E Massam	(Blagdon, Bristol)	
	(Built W E Massam)						
G-YSMO	Mainair Sports Pegasus Quik	8049		12. 7.04	I G Harban	Long Marston	12. 7.09P
G-YSPY	Cessna 172Q Cutlass II	17275932	N917AT	4. 2.03	J Henderson	Kittyhawk Farm, Deanland	2. 7.06T
			N917ER, (N65957)				
G-YSTT	Piper PA-32R-301 Saratoga IIHP	3246056	N848T	4. 8.97	A W Kendrick	Wolverhampton	27. 4.09E
			N9282D				
G-YULL	Piper PA-28-180 Cherokee E	28-5603	G-BEAJ	30. 3.79	ASG Leasing Ltd	Guernsey	18.11.09E
			9H-AAC, N2390R				
G-YUMM	Cameron N-90 Balloon (Hot Air)	2723		12.12.91	H Stringer	Scalby, Scarborough	23. 8.09E
G-YUPI	Cameron N-90 Balloon (Hot Air)	1602		12. 1.88	MCVH SA	Brussels, Belgium	22.11.98A
G-YVES	Alpi Pioneer 300	2		7.12.04	M C Birchall	Upfield Farm, Whitson	20. 7.08P
	(Built M C Birchall - pr.no.PFA 330-14290)						
G-YVET	Cameron V-90 Balloon (Hot Air)	3182		11.10.93	J A Hibberd	Rotterdam, Netherlands	12. 8.09E
G-YYAK	IAV Bacau Yakovlev Yak-52	878101	LY-AOM	18. 4.02	J Armstrong and D W Lamb	Durham Tees Valley	27. 9.09P
			DOSAAF 118				
G-YYYY	Max Holste MH.1521C1 Broussard	208	F-GDPZ	10. 3.00	P F Burrow tr Eggesford Heritage Flight (As "208: IR" in		
			French Air Force		French A/F c/s)	Trenchard Farm, Eggesford	8. 8.09S
G-YZYZ	Mainair Blade 912	1357-0803-7-W1152		14. 8.03	P G Eastlake	Hunsdon	16. 8.08P

G-ZAAA - G-ZZZZ

G-ZAAP	CZAW Sportcruiser	PFA 338-14663		31. 1.08	L A Seers	Rochester	30. 6.09P
	(Built L A Seers)						
G-ZAAZ	Van's RV-8	PFA 303-13279		2. 7.02	P A Soper	(Layham, Ipswich)	21. 7.09P
	(Built P A Soper)						
G-ZABC	Sky 90-24 Balloon (Hot Air)	062		10. 4.97	P Donnelly	Maghera	23. 8.09E
G-ZACE	Cessna 172S Skyhawk SP	172S8808	F-HAMC	3. 9.02	Sywell Aerodrome Ltd	Sywell	9. 9.09E
			N3527P				
G-ZACH	Robin DR.400-100 Cadet	1831	G-FTIO	20.10.92	A P Wellings	Sandown	29.10.09E
G-ZADA	Best Off Sky Ranger 912S(1)	SKRxxxx547		11.10.06	B Bisley	Stoke, Isle of Grain	20. 8.08P
	(Built D F Hughes - pr.no.BMAA HB/446)						

Reg	Type	C/n	Prev. identities	Reg. date	Owner/Operator	Base	CofA/Permit
G-ZADY	Eurocopter EC.120B Colibri	1316	N127DF, F-WQDZ	6. 6.05	MCJ Helicopters Ltd	Redhill	20. 9.09E
G-ZAIR	Zenair CH.601HD Zodiac *(Built B E Shaw) (Rotax 912 UL) (Tri-cycle u/c)*	PFA 162-12194		21. 2.92	J R Standring	Crosland Moor	2. 9.09P
G-ZANG	Piper PA-28-140 Cherokee E	28-7225178	SE-FYT	29. 7.04	W J Hockenhull t/a Gauntlet Holdings	RAF Waddington	26. 2.10E
G-ZANY	Diamond DA.40D Star	D4.040		23.10.03	Altair Aviation Ltd	Stapleford	19.12.09E
G-ZAPH	Bell 206B-3 JetRanger III	4401	G-DBMW, C-GAJH	6. 2.01	Northern Flights Ltd	Fairoaks	30. 5.09E
G-ZAPK	British Aerospace BAe 146 Series 200QC	E2148	G-BTIA, ZS-NCB, G-BTIA, G-6-148, G-PRIN	25. 4.96	Titan Airways Ltd	London Stansted	17. 4.09E
G-ZAPN	British Aerospace BAe 146 Series 200QC	E2119	ZK-NZC, G-BPBT	20. 9.99	Titan Airways Ltd	London Stansted	15.11.08E
G-ZAPO	British Aerospace BAe 146 Series 200QC	E2176	F-GMMP, G-BWLG, VH-NJQ, G-PRCS	28. 7.00	Titan Airways Ltd	London Stansted	3. 8.09E
G-ZAPR	British Aerospace BAe 146 Series 200QT	E2114	VH-JJZ, G-BOXE	19.12.03	Titan Airways Ltd	London Stansted	15. 1.09E
G-ZAPU	Boeing 757-2Y0	26151	EI-MON, 4X-BAY, SE-DUL, SX-BBY, XA-KWK, XA-SCB	22. 4.03	Titan Airways Ltd	London Stansted	29. 4.09E
G-ZAPV	Boeing 737-3Y0	24546	G-IGOC, EI-BZH	27. 2.04	Hagondale Ltd *(Operated Titan Airways in Royal Mail c/s)*	Exeter	9. 5.09E
G-ZAPW	Boeing 737-3L9	24219	G-IGOX, N219TY, PH-TSW, OY-MMO, G-BOZB, OY-MMO, N1786B	11. 2.05	Titan Airways Ltd	Bournemouth	20. 3.09E
G-ZAPX	Boeing 757-256	29309	EC-HIS	17. 5.06	Titan Airways Ltd	London Stansted	16. 5.09E
G-ZAPY	Robinson R22 Beta	0788	G-INGB	8. 7.98	Heli Air Ltd	Wellesbourne Mountford/Wycombe Air Park	12. 2.09E
G-ZAPZ	Boeing 737-33A(QC)	25401	SE-DPA, TF-ELA, SE-DPA, N1786B	22.12.06	Hagondale Ltd *(Operated Titan Airways)*	Leeds-Bradford	16.1.09E
G-ZARI	Grumman AA-5B Tiger	AA5B-0845	G-BHVY, N28835	7. 3.86	ZARI Aviation Ltd	Biggin Hill	3. 3.09E
G-ZARV	ARV Aviation ARV-1 Super 2 *(Built P R Snowden) (Rotax 914-UL)*	PFA 152-13035		26. 2.97	P R Snowden	Higham, Bury St Edmunds	21. 6.08P
G-ZAVI	Comco Ikarus C42 FB100	0601-6777		25. 1.06	J King	Damyn's Hall, Upminster	14. 3.09P
G-ZAZA	Piper PA-18 Super Cub 95 *(L-18C-PI)*	18-2041	D-ENAS, R Neth AF R-66, 52-2441	1. 5.84	Airborne Taxi Services Ltd *(Operated A Swire)*	(Lambourn Gallops, Lambourne)	11. 5.09P
G-ZAZZ	Lindstrand LBL 120A Balloon (Hot-Air)	1200		21. 1.09	Idea Balloon SAS Di Stefano Travaglia and Co	Firenze, Italy	
G-ZBED	Robinson R22 Beta	1684	N63993, F-GHHM	18.11.99	P D Spinks	Stream Farm, Sherburn-in-Elmet	3. 1.10E
G-ZBLT	Cessna 182S Skylane	18280910	N72764, G-ZBLT, N72764	6. 7.01	K Dardis tr Cessna 182S Group	Abbeyshrule, County Longford	23. 9.09E
G-ZBOP	PZL-Bielsko SZD-36A Cobra 15	W-168	BGA1886-CXJ	16. 7.08	S Bruce *"791"*	Feshiebridge	
G-ZEBO	Thunder Ax8-105 Series 2 Balloon (Hot Air)	2197		22. 5.92	S M Waterton *"Gazebo"*	Borehamwood	12. 3.09E
G-ZEBY	Piper PA-28-140 Cherokee F	28-7325240	G-BFBF, EI-BMG, G-BFBF, PH-SRF	7.04.04	G Gee	Full Sutton	12. 6.09E
G-ZECH	CZAW Sportcruiser *(Built P J Reilly)*	PFA 338-14685		11. 1.08	P J Reilly	Old Sarum	
G-ZEIN	Slingsby T 67M-260 Firefly	2234		19. 7.95	R C P Brookhouse	Manston	9. 6.09E
G-ZELE	Westland SA.341C Gazelle HT.2	1007	G-CBSA, XW845	27. 5.03	A Cook t/a C3 Consulting *(As "47" in RAF c/s)*	Crookfoot Farm, Elwick	11.11.09P
G-ZENA	Zenair CH.701UL STOL *(Built A N Aston)*	PFA 187-13637		16.10.00	A N Aston	(Wolverhampton)	
G-ZENI	Zenair CH.601HD Zodiac *(Built P P Plumley)*	PFA 162-14366		17. 8.06	P P Plumley	(Newport Pagnell)	
G-ZENN	Schempp-Hirth Ventus 2cT	136/348	BGA5148-KJY, D-KOZX	11.11.05	Z Marczynski *"304"*	Lasham	22. 2.08
G-ZENR	Zenair CH.601HD Zodiac *(Built D Collinson) (Rotax 912 ULS)*	6-1203	G-BRJB	9. 4.08	J M Pipping	Weston Zoyland	19. 3.09P
G-ZENY	Zenair CH.601HD Zodiac *(Built T R Pugh, pr. no PFA 162-13668)*	6-9167		7. 7.08	T R and B K Pugh	(Fordingbridge)	
G-ZEPI	Colt GA-42 Gas Airship *(RR Continental O-200B)*	878	G-ISPY, (G-BPRB)	9. 4.92	P A Lindstrand	Oswestry	12. 5.93A
G-ZERO	Grumman AA-5B Tiger	AA5B-0051	OO-PEC	3. 9.80	Emery-Little Insurance Brokers Ltd	Compton Abbas	26. 3.09E
G-ZETA	Lindstrand LBL 105A Balloon (Hot Air)	952		27. 1.04	S Travaglia *(Lindstrand titles)*	Tavarnelle Val di Pesa, Florence, Italy	17. 8.09E
G-ZEXL	Extra EA.300/L	1225		10. 3.06	2 Excel Aviation Ltd *(Operated 'The Blades' display team, Barclays insignia)*	Sywell	23. 3.09E
G-ZGZG	Cessna 182T Skylane	18282036	N12722	20.12.07	J Noble	Shoreham	12. 1.10E
G-ZHKF	Reality Escapade 912(1) *(Built C D Wills - pr.no.BMAA HB/415)*	JAESC 0045		26.11.04	C D and C M Wills	Chilbolton	14.12.09P
G-ZHWH	RotorWay Executive 162F *(Built B Alexander) (RotorWay RI 162F)*	6596		19.11.01	B Alexander	(Canterbury)	
G-ZIGI	Robin DR.400-180 Régent	2107		19.11.91	D C R Writer	Rochester	9. 7.09E
G-ZIGY	Europa Aviation Europa XS *(Built K D Weston - pr.no.PFA 247-13693)*	497		25. 2.05	K D Weston	(Gosport)	
G-ZIII	Pitts S-2B *(Built Christen Industries Inc) (Lycoming AEIO-540)*	5151	G-CDBH, SE-LVI, F-GMOV, OO-MOV, N10ZX, (N71ZX), N10ZX	3. 5.05	A N R Houghton t/a Nick Houghton Aerobatics	Sibson	13. 4.09E
G-ZINT	Cameron Z-77 Balloon (Hot Air)	10488		17. 9.03	Film Production Consultants SRL	Rome, Italy	31. 3.07A
G-ZIPA	Rockwell Commander 114A *(Originally laid down as c/n 14436)*	14505	G-BHRA, N5891N	3. 9.98	Northern Aviation Ltd	Durham Tees Valley	19. 6.09E
G-ZIPI	Robin DR.400-180 Régent	1557		22. 2.82	A J Cooper	Rochester	23. 9.09E

G-ZIPY	Wittman W.8 Tailwind	PFA 031-11339		29. 5.91	K J Nurcombe	Spanhoe	20. 2.08P
	(Built M J Butler) (Lycoming O-235)						
G-ZIRA	Staaken Z-1RA Stummelflitzer	094		26. 6.08	D H Pattison	Lower Upham Farm, Chiseldon	
	(Built D H Pattison, pr. no PFA 342-14596)						
G-ZITZ	Aérospatiale AS.355F2 Ecureuil 2	5135	N596SJ	26. 4.04	Heli Aviation Ltd	Redhill	4.12.09E
			9M-BDA, F-GIFR, F-WIFR, F-GIFR, F-WZKZ				
G-ZIZI	Cessna 525 CitationJet	525-0345	N5185V	10.11.99	Ortac Air Ltd	Guernsey	17.11.09E
G-ZIZZ	Agusta A109A II	7390	N109AR	16.11.07	Fortis Property Investment LLP	Southend	
			8P-BHA, (N), G-BXPX, I-DVRE				
G-ZJET	Cessna 510 Mustang	510-0161		3. 2.09	C J Reeston	La Massana, Andorra	
G-ZLLE	Aérospatiale SA.341G Gazelle 1	1012	N504KH	4.10.01	MW Helicopters Ltd	Stapleford	6.11.07E
			JA9098				
G-ZLOJ	Beech A36 Bonanza	E-1677	ZS-LOJ	11. 9.98	W D Gray *(Operated Bournemouth Flying Club)*		
			N6748J			Bournemouth	5. 2.09E
G-ZMAM	Piper PA-28-181 Cherokee Archer II		G-BNPN	3.11.00	Z Mahmood	Elstree	28.10.08E
		28-7890059	N47379				
G-ZODY	Zenair CH.601UL Zodiac	6-2354?		26. 5.04	B H Stephens tr Sarum AX2000 Group	Old Sarum	21.11.07P
	(Built B H Stephens and Partners - pr.no.PFA 162A-14239) (Tri-cycle u/c)						
G-ZOGT	Cirrus SR20	2010	N556PG	12. 8.08	Caseright Ltd	Turweston	3. 9.09E
G-ZONX	Sonex Aircraft Sonex	PFA 337-14689		15. 5.07	A Carter	(Holmfirth)	
	(Built A Carter)						
G-ZOOL	Reims Cessna FA152 Aerobat	FA1520357	G-BGXZ	11.11.94	W J D Tollett	Turweston	9. 5.09E
G-ZOOS	Balony Kubicek BB20XR Balloon (Hot-Air)						
		631		29. 8.08	Balony Kubicek Spol Sro	Brno, Czech Republic	3. 9.09E
G-ZOOT	Robinson R44 Clipper II	11924		9. 1.08	C Evans	Shoreham	16. 1.10E
G-ZORO	Europa Aviation Europa	074		20. 6.95	N T Read	(Gillingham)	
	(Built N T Read - pr.no.PFA 247-12672) (Monowheel u/c)						
G-ZOSA	American Champion 7GCAA Citabria	509-2006		30.11.06	R McQueen	(Mauchline)	12. 7.10S
G-ZRZZ	Cirrus SR22	2020	N634SR	30. 3.07	Computerised Training Systems Ltd	Humberside	21. 5.09E
G-ZSKD	Cameron Z-90 Balloon (Hot Air)	10749		16. 2.06	J E Lipinski	Hunsdon	21. 8.08E
G-ZSKY	Best Off Sky Ranger Swift 912S(1)						
		SKR0703771		20. 6.07	N R Henry and J J C Scott		
	(Built N R Henry and J J C Scott - pr.no.BMAA HB/543)					(Nuneaton and Coalville)	20. 9.08P
G-ZTED	Europa Aviation Europa	015		30. 4.96	J J Kennedy	Perth	19. 2.09P
	(Built J J Kennedy and E W Gladstone - pr.no.PFA 247-12492) (Monowheel u/c)						
G-ZUMI	Van's RV-8	PFA 303-13527		6. 3.02	S E Leach	Perth	15.12.09E
	(Built P M Wells) (Lycoming IO-360)						
G-ZUMO	Pilatus PC-12/47	732	HB-FRQ	20. 7.06	CCH Way Ltd	Monaco, France	3. 9.09E
G-ZVKO	Edge 360	1	N360CH	14. 2.06	P J Tomlinson	Little Rissington	19. 6.09P
	(Built C Huey) (Lycoming IO-360)						
G-ZXCL	Extra EA.300/L	1223		27. 2.06	2 Excel Aviation Ltd	Sywell	15. 3.09E
					(Operated 'The Blades' display team, Barclays insignia)		
G-ZXEL	Extra EA.300/L	1224		27. 2.06	2 Excel Aviation Ltd	Sywell	15. 3.09E
					(Operated 'The Blades' display team, Barclays insignia)		
G-ZXZX	Learjet Model 45	45-005	N455LJ	16. 1.04	Gama Aviation Ltd	Farnborough	18. 1.09E
G-ZYAK	IAV Bacau Yakovlev Yak-52	877415	LY-AFK	14. 2.03	J A H van Rossom	(Brussels, Belgium)	10. 7.09P
			DOSAAF 27				
G-ZZAC	Evektor EV-97 Eurostar	2006.29.28		10. 5.07	S A Ivell	Crosland Moor	8. 7.09P
	(Built S A Ivell, pr. no PFA 315-14642- plate details above also shown on G-CEHL)						
G-ZZAJ	Schleicher ASH 26E	26232		15. 7.05	A T Johnstone	Wycombe Air Park	12. 3.10E
G-ZZAP	American Champion 8KCAB Super Decathlon		N900JF	28. 7.04	L Maikowski, E Mason, S Hipwell and J Pothecary		
		871-2000				Shoreham	16.10.08E
G-ZZDG	Cirrus SR20	1733	N985SR	19.12.06	Little Mouse Productions Ltd	Thruxton	19.12.10E
G-ZZEL	Westland SA.341B Gazelle AH.1	1152	G-BZYJ	25.11.02	Tregenna Castle Hotel Ltd	RAF Shawbury	12. 2.08E
			XW885				
G-ZZLE	Westland SA.341C Gazelle HT.2	1402	G-CBSE	29. 4.05	Estates (UK) Management Ltd *(As "XX436:CU-39" in RN c/s)*		
			XX436				(Hull)	13. 8.09P
G-ZZOE	Eurocopter EC.120B Colibri	1196	F-WQOX	21. 3.01	J F H James	Banbury	9. 7.09E
G-ZZOW	Medway EclipseR	178/156		31. 8.06	T J F Jones	Caernarfon	30. 8.08P
G-ZZSA	Eurocopter EC.225LP Super Puma	2603	F-WWOJ	21. 7.05	Bristow Helicopters Ltd	Aberdeen	27. 7.09E
G-ZZSB	Eurocopter EC.225LP Super Puma	2615	F-WWOG	11. 8.05	Bristow Helicopters Ltd	Aberdeen	15. 8.09E
G-ZZSC	Eurocopter EC.225LP Super Puma	2654	F-WWOG	13. 9.06	Bristow Helicopters Ltd	Aberdeen	14.10.09E
G-ZZSD	Eurocopter EC.225LP Super Puma	2658	F-WWOQ	5.12.06	Bristow Helicopters Ltd	Aberdeen	18.12.08E
G-ZZSE	Eurocopter EC.225LP Super Puma	2660	F-WWOT	14. 2.07	Bristow Helicopters Ltd	Aberdeen	25. 2.09E
G-ZZSF	Eurocopter EC.225LP Super Puma	2662	F-WWOR	5. 4.07	Bristow Helicopters Ltd	Aberdeen	15. 4.09E
G-ZZSG	Eurocopter EC.225LP Super Puma	2714		17.12.08	Bristow Helicopters Ltd	Aberdeen	
G-ZZTT	Schweizer 269C *(Schweizer 300)*	S1884	C-FFZZ	20. 6.08	M V Chadwick	Gloucestershire	17. 7.09E
			N86G				
G-ZZXX	P&M Aviation Quik GT450	8177		19. 4.06	Nature First Ltd	Gloucestershire	7. 7.09P
G-ZZZA	Boeing 777-236	27105	N77779	20. 5.96	British Airways PLC	London Heathrow	19. 5.09E
G-ZZZB	Boeing 777-236	27106	N77771	28. 3.97	British Airways PLC	London Heathrow	3.12.09E
G-ZZZC	Boeing 777-236	27107	N5014K	11.11.95	British Airways PLC	London Heathrow	10.11.09E
G-ZZZG	Alpi Pioneer 300	xxx		9. 3.05	J D Clabon and J Reed	Hardwick, Abergavenny	16. 3.09P
	(Built C K Parsons - pr.no.PFA 330-14373)				*(Stored dismantled after accident damage)*		
G-ZZZS	Eurocopter EC.120B Colibri	1321	OO-WER	26.11.07	R E S and D Medway	Redhill	20.12.09E
			F-WQDI				

PART 3 – DE-REGISTERED EXTANT AIRCRAFT

The following have been noted since 2005 and are still considered to be extant.

Registration	Type	Serial No	Previous Identity	Reg.date	Registered Owner (Operator)	(Unconfirmed) Base	CofA Validity
G-ABTC	Comper CLA.7 Swift	S 32/1		1. 1.32	P Channon	Porthtowan	18. 7.84P
					(Cancelled 22. 2.99 by CAA: noted 6.04)		
G-ACGT	Avro 594B Avian IIIA	R3/CN/171	EI-AAB	8. 5.33	Yorkshire Light Aircraft	(Yorkshire)	21. 7.39
	(Originally regd as Avro 594A)				*(Cancelled xx.xx.xx by CAA: under restoration 11.04)*		
G-ADXS	Mignet HM.14 Pou-Du-Ciel	CLS.1		18.11.35	C L Storey. *"The Fleeing Fly"*	Breighton	
	(Built C L Storey)				*(Cancelled 1.12.36 as WFU: on display 12.07)*		
G-AFGD	BA L 25c Swallow II	469	BK897	4. 4.38	A T Williams, B Arden, C A Cook, J Hughes and M Barmby		
	(Pobjoy Cataract 3)		G-AFGD		tr South Wales Swallow Group	Shobdon	9. 4.01P
					(Cancelled 6. 4.01 by CAA: noted 11.06 for restoration)		
G-AFIU	Parker CA-4 Parasol	CA-4		19.10.82	S P Connatty	Barton	
	(Built C F Parker) (Luton Minor components with registration reserved in 1938)				*(Cancelled 31. 3.99 by CAA: stored 4.06)*		
G-AFLW	Miles M.17 Monarch	792		2.11.38	N I Dalziel	White Waltham	30. 7.98
					(Cancelled 3. 5.01 by CAA: noted 6.06)		
G-AFVN	Tipsy Trainer 1	12		15. 7.39	D F Lingard	Fenland	2. 1.03P
	(Walter Mikron 2)				*(Cancelled 20.11.06 as WFU)*		
G-AGOY	Miles M.38 Messenger 3	4690	EI-AGE	5. 6.45	P A Brook	(West Chiltington, Pulborough)	25.11.53
			G-AGOY, HB-EIP, G-AGOY, U-0247				
					(On rebuild 4.92: as "U-0247" :cancelled 20.12.06 by CAA)		
G-AHHK	Auster J/1 Autocrat	2014		11. 5.46	C J Baker	Carr Farm, Thorney, Newark	22. 3.70
					(Cancelled 3. 4.89 as WFU: derelict frame noted 1.05)		
G-AHUJ	Miles M.14A Hawk Trainer 3	1900	R1914	6. 6.46	W J D Roberts tr Strathallan Aircraft Collection		
						Strathallan	9. 7.98P
					(Cancelled 19.11.99 as WFU: stored as "R1914" 6.07)		
G-AIJI	Auster J/1N Alpha	2307		15. 4.47	C J Baker	Carr Farm, Thorney, Newark	
	(Originally regd as J/1 Autocrat)				*(Damaged in gales Humberside 12. 1.75: cancelled 12. 3.75 as WFU: dismantled frame noted1.05)*		
G-AIJS	Auster V J/4 Archer	2074		13.11.46	Not known	Not known	14.12.71
					(Cancelled 1. 9.81 as WFU: fuselage noted 22.5.08 Northbound on M3)		
G-AIRI	de Havilland DH.82A Tiger Moth	3761	N5488	22.10.46	E R Goodwin	Little Gransden	9.11.81
					(Cancelled 3. 4.89 as WFU: stored 10.05)		
G-AJBJ	de Havilland DH.89A Dragon Rapide	6765	NF894	20. 1.47	John Pierce Aviation Ltd	Ley Farm, Chirk	14. 9.61T
					(Cancelled 16.12.91 by CAA: noted 5.05 without marks)		
G-AJCL (2)	de Havilland DH.89A Dragon Rapide	6722	NF851	7. 9.48	John Pierce Aviation Ltd	Ley Farm, Chirk	
					(WFU Shobdon 1.71: cancelled 24. 5.71: noted 5.05 without marks)		
G-AJVH	Fairey Swordfish II	?	LS326	28. 5.47	Royal Navy Historic Flight	RNAS Yeovilton	
					(Cancelled 30. 4.59 as restored to RN as "LS326:L2" in RN 836 Sqdn c/s -"City of Liverpool")		
G-AKBO	Miles M.38 Messenger 2A	6378		15. 7.47	P R Holloway	Enstone	3. 8.03
					(Cancelled 24. 8.04 by CAA: under restoration 5.06)		
G-AKOE	de Havilland DH.89A Dragon Rapide 4	6601	X7484	3.12.47	J E Pierce	Ley Farm, Chirk	25. 7.82
					(Cancelled 18. 6.02 by CAA: noted 5.05 in BEA c/s)		
G-AKUG (2)	Luscombe 8A Silvaire	3689	N77962	21. 7.88	(R S Bird)	Glebe Farm, Stockton	16. 3.05P
	(Continental A65)		NC77962				
					(Damaged on take off Stockton, Wiltshire 17. 7.04: cancelled 18. 2.05 by CAA: under repair 2007)		
G-AKWT	Taylorcraft J Auster 5	998	MT360	1. 4.48	C J Baker	Carr Farm, Thorney, Newark	22. 7.49
					(Crashed Tollerton 7.8.48: derelict frame stored 1.05)		
G-AKZN	Percival Proctor III	K 386	8380M	24. 5.48	Royal Air Force Museum Reserve Collection		
			Z7197			MoD Stafford	29.11.63
					(Cancelled 27 .9.63 as WFU and reverted to "Z7197": noted 2.04)		
G-ALNV	Taylorcraft J Auster 5	1216	RT578	21. 4.49	C J Baker	Carr Farm, Thorney, Newark	4. 7.50
					(WFU and silver frame stored 1.05)		
G-AMKL	Auster B 4	2983	XA177	3. 7.51	C J Baker	Carr Farm, Thorney, Newark	
			G-AMKL, G-25-2		*(Dismantled Rearsby 1956: cancelled 24. 9.58: new fuselage 1.05)*		
G-AMLZ	Percival P.50 Prince 6E	P.46	(VR-TBN)	23.11.51	Cancelled 9.10.84 as PWFU		18. 6.71
					(Displayed at Liverpool Airport)		
G-AMTD	Auster J/5F Aiglet Trainer	2783	EI-AVL	24. 5.52	The Leicestershire Aero Club Ltd	Leicester	8.12.93
			G-AMTD				
					(Damaged landing Hayrish Farm, Okehampton 7. 8.93: cancelled 15. 1.99 as WFU: wings noted 10.07)		
G-ANHW	Taylorcraft J Auster 5D	1396	TJ320	5.12.53	D J Baker	Carr Farm, Thorney, Newark	9. 3.70
	(Originally regd as Auster 5)				*(Forced landed Carlton Manor, Norfolk 1970: WFU 15.12.71: derelict fuselage stored 1.05)*		
G-ANWX	Auster J/5L Aiglet Trainer	3131		25.11.54	M F Frost tr Nayland Aiglet Group		
						Maypole Farm, Chislet	2. 5.94
					(Overturned landing Fenland 1. 8.93 and substantially damaged: cancelled 24. 9.93 as WFU: noted dismantled 8.05)		
G-AOAI	Blackburn Beverley C 1	1002	XB259	15. 3.55	Fort Paull Armouries (As "XB259") Paull, Yorkshire		
					(Cancelled 30.3.55, still present 1.09)		
G-AOCP (2)	Taylorcraft J Auster 5	1800	W462	25. 5.56	C J Baker	Carr Farm, Thorney, Newark	
	(Composite using G-AKOT)				*(WFU 22. 6.68: fuselage frame noted 1.05)*		
G-APKM	Auster J/1N Alpha	3385		27. 1.58	C J Baker	Carr Farm, Thorney, Newark	9. 1.89
					(Cancelled 9.10.91 as temporary WFU: noted dismantled 1.05)		
G-APRF	Auster Alpha 5	3412	VR-LAF	8.12.58	W B Bateson	Blackpool	14.11.00
			G-APRF		*(Cancelled 14. 6.05 by CAA: stored 10.07)*		
G-APRJ	Avro 694 Lincoln B 2	-	RF342	29.12.58	?	Martham, Great Yarmouth	
			G-36-3, G-29-1, G-APRJ, RF342				
					(Cancelled 22. 2.05 by CAA: airframe noted 12.05: nose, as "G-29-1", stored 2.06)		
G-APSO	de Havilland DH.104 Dove 5	04505	(N1046T)	16. 2.59	(Devonair Ltd)	Little Rissington	8. 7.78T
			G-APSO				
					(Cancelled 2. 5.01 as WFU: wings fitted to G-BWWC: forward fuselage only fitted with stub wings as engine test-bed 1.08)		

G-APSZ	Cessna 172	46472	N6372E	21. 5.59	Not known	Ronaldsway	4. 6.84
	(Damaged Barton 2. 3.84 and cancelled: stored 10.06)						
G-APYW	Piper PA-22-150 Caribbean	22-4994	N7131D	3. 3.60	?	Midden Zeeland, Netherlands	6. 7.88
	(Cancelled 12. 7.93 by CAA: frame noted 10.05)						
G-ARAP	Champion 7FC Tri-Traveler	7FC-394		12. 9.60	(J McGonagal)	Bellarena	26. 6.82P
	(Originally regd as a 7EC))			*(Damaged in crash 22. 9.81 Eglington: cancelled 30.5.84: fuselage noted 9.07)*			
G-ARCI	Cessna 310D	39266	N6966T	21.10.60	Sandtoft Air Services Ltd	Blackpool	25. 4.84
	(Damaged Sandtoft 22. 8.86: cancelled 3. 1.89 by CAA: in open store less tail 11.05)						
G-ARDG	Lancashire Aircraft EP-9 Prospector 2	47		14. 7.60	G Pearce	Redhill	
	(Cancelled 28. 5.82 as WFU: noted 6.05)						
G-ARDZ	SAN Jodel D 140A Mousquetaire	49		10.11.60	M J Wright	Cherry Tree Farm, Monewden	29.11.91
	(Cancelled 26. 2.99 by CAA: noted 4.08)						
G-ARGB	Auster 6A Tugmaster	2593	VF635	12.10.60	C J Baker	Carr Farm, Thorney, Newark	21. 6.74
	(Cancelled 21. 6.74(?): dismantled fuselage noted 1.05)						
G-AROJ	Beagle A 109 Airedale	B 508	HB-EUC G-AROJ	17. 5.61	C J Baker	Carr Farm, Thorney, Newark	8. 1.76
	(Originally regd with c/n A 109-1)			*(Cancelled 21. 1.80: noted dismantled 1.05)*			
G-ARPO (2)	de Havilland DH.121 Trident 1C	2116	(G-ARPP)	23. 3.64	International Fire Training Centre		
					(WFU 12.12.83: noted 2.08)	Durham Tees Valley	12. 1.86T
G-ARTM	Beagle A 61 Terrier 1	3723	WE536	9.10.61	C J Baker	Carr Farm, Thorney, Newark	13.11.71
	(Crashed Priory Farm, Turvey, Bedford 28. 5.70 and cancelled 12. 9.73 as WFU: fuselage, part rebuilt. noted 1.05)						
G-ARUO	Piper PA-24 Comanche	24-2427	N7251P	16. 1.62	Not known	Farley Farm, Romsey	22. 8.00
	(Cancelled 18. 7.00 by CAA: stored derelict 10.07)						
G-ARXC	Beagle A 109 Airedale	B 510	EI-ATD G-ARXC	9. 4.62	C J Baker	Carr Farm, Thorney, Newark	27. 6.76
	(Originally regd with c/n A 109-3)			*(Cancelled 12. 4.89 as WFU: fuselage on rebuild 1.05)*			
G-ARXN	Tipsy Nipper T 66 Series 3	T66/77		3. 7.62	C E Pickton and I Wood tr The Griffon Flying Group	Hucknall	19. 8.90P
	(Built Cobelavia SA) (Volkswagen 1800)			*(Cancelled 12. 4.89 by CAA: on rebuild 6.06)*			
G-ASER	Piper PA-23-250 Aztec B	27-2283		28. 1.63	(424Sqdn ATC)	Southampton	17. 8.74
	(Crashed into Nigg Bay, Cromarty, Aberdeen 14. 9.72: cancelled 24.11.72 as WFU: stored Aviation Museum 12.07)						
G-ASJZ	SAN Jodel D 117A	826	F-BITD	5. 7.63	W J Siertsema	Chilbolton	12. 7.06P
	(Swung to left landing Old Buckenham 10. 6.06, undercarriage collapsed and substantially damaged: cancelled 10.10.06 as TWFU)						
G-ASLP	Bensen B 7	11		3. 9.63	R Light and T Smith	(Stockport)	
	(Cancelled 4. 9.73 as WFU: parts only stored 8.06)						
G-ASNY	Campbell Bensen B8	RCA203		15. 1.64	(D L Wallis)	(Stockport)	16. 3.70P
	(Built Campbell Aircraft Ltd) (McCulloch O-100-1)			*(Cancelled 17.12.91 by CAA) (With R Light complete 8.06)*			
G-ASWF	Beagle A 109 Airedale	B 537		26. 8.64	(C J Baker)	Spanhoe	24. 7.83
	(Cancelled 3. 2.89 by CAA: noted dismantled 10.07)						
G-ASXF	Brantly 305	1014		7.10.64	?	Amen Corner, Binfield, Bracknell	16 .2.79
	(Cancelled 24. 5.82 as WFU: in open storage 6.08)						
G-ATIG	Handley Page HPR.7 Dart Herald	214 177	PP-SDI G-ATIG	25. 8.65	Nordic Oil Services Ltd	Norwich	14.10.97T
					(Cancelled 29.10.96 as WFU: instructional use 2.06)		
G-ATKG	Hiller UH-12B	496	RThai.AF103	21.10.65	?	Eshott	28.11.89T
	(Cancelled 21.1.80 as WFU: noted 2005)						
G-ATLH	Fewsdale Tigercraft Gyroplane	F T5		6.12.65	R Light	(Stockport)	
	(Cancelled 10. 2.82 as WFU: reported complete 8.06)						
G-ATMN (2)	Cessna F150F	F150-0060	(G-ATNE)	6. 1.66	C R Hardiman	(Blaenannarch, Cardigan)	2. 7.84T
	(Built Reims Aviation SA) (Wichita c/n 15063526)			*Cancelled 21.10.04 as WFU: noted roadrunning on M1 north of Luton 30. 8.07)*			
G-ATMW	Piper PA-28-140 Cherokee	28-21486		11. 1.66	Bencray Ltd *(Operated Blackpool Air Centre)*	Blackpool	6. 8.08E
	(Cancelled 16.11.07 as PWFU)						
G-ATPD	Hawker Siddeley HS.125 Series 1B/522	25085	5N-AGU G-ATPD	11. 2.66	Wessex Air (Holdings) Ltd	Bournemouth	14.10.98T
					(WFU 1997 and cancelled 2.12.03 as WFU: noted with Fire Section 1.09)		
G-ATRP	Piper PA-28-140 Cherokee	28-21885	N11C	4. 3.66	JRB Aviation Ltd	Southend	20. 9.84
	(Damaged Boughton Monchelsea 16.10.81: cancelled 10.11.86 as WFU: wreck stored dismantled 1.09)						
G-ATWE	Morane-Saulnier MS.892A Rallye Commodore 150 10634			13. 6.66	(D I Murray)	Upfield Farm, Whitson	15. 2.82
	(Badly damaged in forced landing west of Taunton 29. 3.81: cancelled 3. 4.89 by CAA, restored 24. 4.89: cancelled 17. 2.99 by CAA: noted 9.08)						
G-ATWT	Bensen B 8M	21102	G-29-3	5. 7.66	Not known	Bere Alston, Yelverton	
	(Buit Napier Aircraft Co)			*(WFU 10.70 and cancelled 31. 1.77 as WFU: noted dismantled 11.06)*			
G-AVEZ	Handley Page HPR.7 Dart Herald 210	169	PP-ASW G-AVEZ, HB-AAH	31. 1.67	?	Norwich	
					(WFU on 5. 1.81 and cancelled 4. 1.83: on fire dump 2.06)		
G-AVFJ	Hawker Siddeley HS.121 Trident 2E	2149		1. 2.67	International Fire Training Centre		
						Durham Tees Valley	18. 9.83T
	(WFU 6.82: cancelled 9. 7.82: front fuselage noted 2,08)						
G-AVGJ	SAN Jodel DR.1050 Ambassadeur	265	F-BJYJ	31. 1.67	(D J Kirkwood and S T Gilbert)	Enstone	22. 4.85P
	(WFU 1985 with glue failure cancelled 10. 6.93 by CAA: noted 5.05)						
G-AVJH	Druine D 62 Condor	PFA 603		31. 3.67	R Chapman	London Gatwick	4.11.83P
	(Built J Norton)			*(Crashed Nefyn, Gwynedd 31. 7.83: cancelled 5. 1.89: as spares 5.05 for rebuild of G-AXGU qv)*			
G-AVKL	Piper PA-30 Twin Comanche B	30-1418	OY-DHL G-AVKL, N8284Y	25. 4.67	Northbrook College (Sussex)	Shoreham	27. 6.08E
					(Cancelled 28.9.07 as WFU, stored)		
G-AVKT	Tipsy Nipper T 66 Series 3	T66/70	OO-HEL OO-DEL	1. 5.67	?	Yearby	
	(Built Cobelavia SA)						
	(Crashed Constable Burton, Paull, Yorkshire 19. 9.72: cancelled 14. 2.73 as destroyed: frame possibly noted 12.06)						
G-AVLH	Piper PA-28-140 Cherokee	28-23368		8. 5.67	(M B Rothschild)	(Kent)	18. 8.00
	(Cancelled 23. 4.02 by CAA: for possible rebuild 1.05)						
G-AVMJ	British Aircraft Corporation One-Eleven 510ED BAC.138			11. 5.67	(Not known	Horton, Wimborne	17.11.94T
	(WFU 6.94 and cancelled 11. 5.01 by CAA: noted 2007)						
G-AVMT	British Aircraft Corporation One-Eleven 510ED BAC.147			11. 5.67	European Aviation Air Charter Ltd	Cardiff	5.12.03T
	(Cancelled 17.12.04 as WFU: fuselage with Fire Section 9.08)						
G-AVNP	Piper PA-28-180 Cherokee C	28-4113	N11C	26. 5.67	(Southend Airport Fire Services)	Southend	21.10.01T
	(Force landed near Nayland 28. 4.01: cancelled 27.11.01 as destroyed: wreck used for rescue training 1.07)						
G-AVPH	Cessna F150G	F150-0197		20. 6.67	The Zero 9 Flight Academy Ltd	Ellough, Beccles	9. 4.86T
	(Built Reims Aviation SA)			*(Cancelled 26. 3.02 by CAA: fuselage stored 10.08)*			
G-AVPS	Piper PA-30-160 Twin Comanche B	30-1548	N8393Y	27. 6.67	(J M Bisco)	Farley Farm, Romsey	11.11.05
	(Damaged 2004: cancelled 6. 7.05 by CAA: stored derelict 10.07)						

G-AVTT	Ercoupe 415D	4399	SE-BFZ	21. 8.67	Wright Farm Eggs Ltd	Monewden	20. 1.86
	(Continental C85)		NC3774H		*(Cancelled 12. 4.02 as temporarily WFU: stored 5.08)*		
G-AVWE	Piper PA-28-140 Cherokee	28-23720	N11C	19.10.67	W C C Never	Blackpool	22. 4.82T
					(WFU and cancelled 8. 6.89 by CAA: fuselage stored 10.07)		
G-AWBT	Piper PA-30 Twin Comanche B	30-1668	N8508Y	22. 1.68	Cranfield University	Cranfield	25. 3.89
					(Damaged Humberside 10. 3.88: cancelled 15. 7.88 as WFU: derelict airframe 1.07)		
G-AWKM	Beagle B 121 Pup Series 1	B121-017		11. 6.68	(D M G Jenkins) Bourne Park, Hurstbourne Tarrant		29. 6.84
					(Damaged Swansea 7.91: cancelled 28. 5.02 by CAA: fuselage stored 5.06)		
G-AWKP	CEA Jodel DR.253 Régent	130		14. 6.68	G R W Wright	Blackpool	1.10.98
					(Forced landed SE Waterford 8. 6.98: cancelled 13.10.98 by CAA: fuselage noted 10.07)		
G-AWKX	Beech A65 Queen Air	LC-303		21. 6.68	(Northbrook College)	Shoreham	25.10.89T
					(Cancelled 19 12 90 as PWFU: as instructional airframe 3.06)		
G-AWMZ	Cessna F172H	F172-0554		2. 8.68	?	Cark-in-Cartmel	22. 4.77
	(Built Reims Aviation SA) (Hit ground Bucknarrowbridge, Bootle 18. 1.76: cancelled 1. 9.81 as WFU: used as parachute club training aid 4.05)							
G-AWOX	Westland Wessex 60 Series 1	WA/686	G-17-2	28. 8.68	Paintball Adventure West	Bristol	13. 1.83
	G-AWOX, 5N-AJO, G-AWOX, 9Y-TFB, G-AWOX, VH-BHE (3), G-AWOX, VR-BCV, G-AWOX, G-17-1							
					(Cancelled 23.11.82 as TWFU: noted 2.06)		
G-AWUA	Cessna P206D Super Skylane	P206-0550	N8750Z	21.11.68	J E Ball and R W F Marsh	Blackpool	4.12.87
					(Damaged Thruxton 16.10.87: cancelled 11. 8.88 as destroyed: wreck stored 10.07)		
G-AWUH	Cessna F150H	F150-0307		25.11.68	H D Hounsell	Phoenix Farm, Lower Upham	16. 7.94
	(Built Reims Aviation SA)				*(Cancelled 8. 7.97 as WFU: fuselage dumped 8.06)*		
G-AWWO	CEA Jodel DR.1050 Ambassadeur	552	F-BLOI	8. 1.69	A R Grimshaw and A A Macleod	(Spalding)	15. 5.06
					(Cancelled 29 .3.05 as PWFU: noted 10.05)		
G-AWZS	Hawker Siddeley HS.121 Trident 3B Series 101	2319		14. 1.69	International Fire Training Centre	Durham Tees Valley	9. 9.86T
					(WFU 5.12.85 and cancelled 18. 3.86 as WFU: noted 2.08)		
G-AXAU	Piper PA-30 Twin Comanche	30-1753	N8613Y	15. 3.99	Bartcourt Ltd	Bournemouth	8. 3.86T
					(Cancelled 2. 5.02 by CAA: noted minus tail 6.05)		
G-AXEI	Ward P 45 Gnome	P 45		25. 4.69	A J E Smith and N H Ponsford	Breighton	
	(Built M Ward)				*(Cancelled 30. 5.84 as WFU: noted 12.07)*		
G-AXGU	Druine D 62B Condor	RAE 640		3. 6.69	R Chapman	London Gatwick	22. 5.76
	(Built Rollason Aircraft and Engines)				*(Crashed near Godalming, Surrey 31. 3.75: cancelled 8. 3.88 as WFU: stored 5.05)*		
G-AXIY	Bird Gyrocopter	GB.001		3. 7.69	G Bird	(Stockport)	
	(Built G Bird)				*(Cancelled 9 8.91 by CAA: with R Light dismantled 8.06)*		
G-AXMD	Omega O-20 Balloon (Hot Air)	06		7. 8.69	(P F Smart) "Nimble"	Oakley, Basingstoke	
	(Acquired second envelope c/n 07 c 1969 or 1970)				*(Cancelled 7.12.89 as WFU: inflated 1.09)*		
G-AXTH	Piper PA-28-140 Cherokee B	28-26283	N11C	26.11.69	West London Aero Services Ltd	Blackpool	27.10.90T
	(Damaged in forced landing near Compton Abbas 28. 2.88: .cancelled by CAA 13. 7.95) (Wreck stored 10.07)							
G-AXYZ	WHE Airbuggy	1005		10. 3.70	(R Light)	Stockport	22.12.92P
	(Volkswagen 1600) (Originally regd as McCandless M 4)				*(Complete 8.06: cancelled 8. 9.06 by CAA)*		
G-AXZB	WHE Airbuggy	1007		10. 3.70	(R Light)	Stockport	18.11.86P
	(Volkswagen 1834) (Originally regd as McCandless M 4)				*(Complete 8.06: cancelled 8. 9.06 by CAA)*		
G-AYDW	Beagle A 61 Terrier 2	B 646	G-ARLM (1)	20. 5.70	Stick & Rudder Associates Trenchard Farm, Eggesford		1. 7.73
	(Conversion of Auster 6 c/n 1936)		TW568		*(Cancelled 1. 7.85 by CAA: noted 2.06)*		
G-AYGB	Cessna 310Q	310Q0111	N7611Q	2. 7.70	Perth College	Perth	23.10.87T
					(Cancelled 23. 6.94 by CAA: instructional airframe 1.06)		
G-AYNS	Airmaster H2-B1	1		21.12.70	D J Fry	Amen Corner, Binfield, Bracknell	
					(Cancelled 30. 5.84 by CAA: extant 6.08)		
G-AYSK	Phoenix Luton LA-4A Minor	PFA 832		17. 2.71	S R Smith tr Luton Minor Group	Barton	24. 5.05P
	(Built L Plant) (Continental A65)						
	(After being hand-swung Barton 8. 9.06 moved off unmanned & crashed inverted with severe damage: noted 12.06: canx 16. 1.07 as PWFU)							
G-AZDF (2)	Cameron O-84 Balloon (Hot Air)	24		18. 8.71	K L C M Busemeyer	London W2	
					(Cancelled 22. 4.88 as WFU: noted 2006)		
G-AZGC	SNCAN Stampe SV-4C	120	F-BCGE	4.10.71	V Lindsay	Folly Farm, Hungerford	22. 2.91
	(Damaged taxiing Folly Farm, Hungerford 28. 5.90: cancelled 19. 9.00 by CAA: fuselage stored 1.09)							
G-AZHE	Slingsby T.61B Falke	1755	N61TB	18.10.71		Abbots Bromley	
					(Cancelled by CAA14. 3.99, stored 11.08)		
G-AZLP	Vickers 813 Viscount	346	ZS CDT	4. 1.72	International Fire Training Centre	Durham Tees Valley	3. 4.82T
			(ZS-SBT), ZS-CDT		*(Cancelled 19.12.86 as WFU) (Fire services fuselage only 2.08)*		
G-AZLS	Vickers 813 Viscount	348	ZS-CDV	4. 1.72	International Fire Training Centre	Durham Tees Valley	9. 6.83T
			(ZS-SBV), ZS-CDV		*(Cancelled 19.12.86 as WFU) (Fire services fuselage only 2.08)*		
G-AZMX	Piper PA-28-140 Cherokee D	28-24777	SE-FLL	7. 2.72	Mooney Aviation Ltd	Ley Farm, Chirk	24.10.83
			LN-LMK (3)		*(Cancelled 9. 1.84 as PWFU: airframe noted 8.07)*		
G-AZNC	Vickers 813 Viscount	352	(G-AZLW) (1)	8. 2.72	British Aerospace PLC	Durham Tees Valley	18. 5.83T
			ZS-CDZ, (ZS-SBZ), ZS-CDZ		*(Cancelled 27.10.88 as WFU).(Used by Fire Services 2.08)*		
G-AZRV	Piper PA-28R-200 Cherokee Arrow II	28R-7135191	N2309T	4. 4.72	General Airline Ltd	Compton Abbas	25. 8.02T
	(Crashed on take-off Compton Abbas 30.12.00: cancelled 20. 6.01 as destroyed: fuselage for training 1.06)							
G-AZRX	Sud-Aviation Gardan GY-80-160 Horizon	14	F-BLIJ	4. 4.72	Adventure Island Pleasure Ground	Southend-on-Sea	20. 2.92
	(Damaged Sandtoft 14. 8.91: cancelled 21.10.91 by CAA: on display Crazy Golf Course, Marine Parade 1.09)							
G-AZXG	Piper PA-23-250 Aztec D	27-4328	N6963Y	23. 6.72	Cranfield University	Cranfield	18. 9.94
					(Crashed Little Snoring 25.10.91: cancelled 6. 5.93 by CAA: airframe dumped 9.08)		
G-BAAX	Cameron O-84 Balloon (Hot Air)	50		8. 8.72	The New Holker Estates Company Ltd	Cark-in-Cartmel, Grange-over-Sands	31. 5.85A
					(Cancelled 11. 5.93 as WFU: stored 2006)		
G-BADZ	Pitts S-2A	2038		21. 9.72	(D Richardson)	Exeter	5. 6.00
	(Built Aerotek Inc)				*(Cancelled 4. 4.02 by CAA: noted in hangar roof 12.05)*		
G-BAEW	Reims Cessna F.172M	F1720914		27. 9.72	Northampton School of Flying	Hulcote Farm, Salford, Bedford	
					(Cancelled 22. 3.08 by CAA, noted stored 7.08)		

G-BAGO	Cessna 421B Golden Eagle	421B0356	N7613Q	24.10.72	(M S Choksey)		Coventry	7. 3.07

(Cancelled 15. 4.05 as sold to US: noted 6.05 as "G-BAGO")

G-BAIL	Reims FR.172J Rocket	FR17200370		22.11.72	R H Blair tr Gloucestershire Flying ClubBournemouth			7. 7.00

(Overturned on landing 6. 3.99 Farley Farm, Romsey: cancelled 6. 7.99 by CAA)

G-BAOM	SOCATA MS.880B Rallye Club	2255		6. 2.73	P J D Feehan		Exeter	17. 4.03

(Cancelled 27.11.03 as PWFU: noted 12.05)

G-BAPF	Vickers 814 Viscount	338	SE-FOY G-BAPF, D-ANUN	12. 2.73	The Fire Service College		Moreton-in-Marsh	13. 6.90

"Marilyn Monroe"
(Cancelled 17. 6.92 by CAA: airframe extant 9.07 in Hot Air c/s)

G-BAPM	Fuji FA.200-160 Aero Subaru	FA200-172		13. 2.73	Oakfleet Ltd		Glebe Farm, Stockton	28. 5.01

(Cancelled 6.11.98 by CAA: noted 9.06)

G-BASL	Piper PA-28-140 Cherokee F	28-7325195	N11C	13. 3.73	Justgold Ltd		Blackpool	11. 5.08E

(Cancelled 25. 2.08 by CAA)

G-BASU	Piper PA-31-350 Navajo Chieftain	31-7305023	N7693L	15. 3.73	Keystart Ltd t/a Streamline Aviation			
							Trenchard Farm, Eggesford	3.11.87T

(Crashed on take-off Duonreay 12. 5.87 and badly damaged: cancelled 24. 7.89 as destroyed: fuselage noted 2.06)

G-BAUA	Piper PA-23-250 Aztec D	27-4048	N6718Y	26. 3.73	David Parr & Associates Ltd		Shoreham	27. 7.92

(Cancelled 15. 9.00 by CAA: stored dismantled 3.06)

G-BAUI	Piper PA-23-250 Aztec D	27-4335	LN-RTS	29. 3.73	(Gloucester University)		Gloucestershire	5.12.88

(Cancelled 26. 1.89 by CAA: noted as Instructional airframe 1.06)

G-BAUJ	Piper PA-23-250 Aztec E	27-7304986	N14390	29. 3.73	(S Bramwell)		Cranfield	25. 7.94T

(Cancelled 31.10.02 by CAA: noted dumped 9.08)

G-BAUR	Fokker F-27 Friendship 200	10225	PH-FEP 9V-BAP, 9M-AMI, (VR-RCZ), PH-FEP	5. 4.73	(Jersey European Airways Ltd)		Exeter	

(Cancelled 25. 1.96 as WFU: fuselage on fire dump 12.05)

G-BAVS	Grumman AA-5 Traveler	AA5-0349		12. 4.73	(V J Peake)		Bournemouth	8.11.94

(Cancelled 31.10.96 by CAA: noted 6.05)

G-BAYL	SNCAN Nord 1203 Norecrin VI	161	F-BEQV	18. 5.73	J E Pierce		Ley Farm, Chirk	

(Cancelled 14.11.91 by CAA: fuselage outside 5.05)

G-BBBX	Cessna 310L	310L0134	OY-EGW N3284X	28. 6.73	Atlantic Air Transport Ltd		Coventry	30.10.07E

(Cancelled 18. 4.07 as PWFU)

G-BBEV	Piper PA-28-140 Cherokee D	28-7125340	LN-MTM	8. 8.73	(Comed Schedule Services Ltd)		Blackpool	9. 9.01T

(Cancelled as PWFU 16. 5.07: noted 6.07)

G-BBFC	Grumman AA-1B Trainer	AA1B-0245	(N9945L)	14. 8.73	(I J Hiatt tr G-BBFC Flying Club)		Bournemouth	25.12.96

(Damaged Perranporth 9. 6.96: cancelled as temporarily unregd 14.10.96: fuselage noted 6.05)

G-BBHE	Enstrom F-28A	153	EI-BSD G-BBHE	3. 9.73	Clarke Aviation Ltd	Waterford, County Waterford		24. 4.08E

(Cancelled 22. 2.06 as PWFU: noted 8.08)

G-BBNO	Piper PA-23-250 Aztec	27-4656	N964PA	22.10.73	A S Bamrah t/a Falcon Flying Services		Biggin Hill	18. 1.92

(Cancelled 13. 3.01 as PWFU: noted 6.07)

G-BBRZ	Grumman AA-5 Traveler	AA5-0471	(EI-AYV) G-BBRZ	15.11.73	C P Osborne		Movenis, Coleraine	30. 4.99

(Cancelled 10. 2.05 by CAA: fuselage only noted 4.05)

G-BCEO	Grumman AA-5 Traveler	7. 5.74	AA5-0575			W Bateson		Blackpool

(Crashed near Selby Farm, Stanton, Morpeth 28. 4.02: cancelled 11. 7.02 as destroyed: wreck noted 10.07)

G-BCGA	Piper PA-34-200-2 Seneca	34-7450166	N41975	4. 6.74	Not known		Ronaldsway	15. 7.78

(Crashed and DBR landing RAF Waddington 18.12.77: fuselage stored 10.06)

G-BCGX	Bede BD-5	4916		18. 6.74	R Hodgson		(Cumbernauld)	

(Built R Hodgson - pr.no.PFA 014-10063)
(No Permit issued and cancelled 4.12.96 as WFU: noted road-running 9.05)

G-BCIE	Piper PA-28-151 Cherokee Warrior	28-7415405	N9588N	3. 7.74	Perth College		Perth	19.12.99T

(Extensively damaged Perth 27. 5.99: cancelled 15. 9.99 as destroyed: dumped 1.06)

G-BCJH	Mooney M 20F Executive	670126	N9549M	11. 7.74	P J Bossard		Bourn	30. 6.91

(Cancelled 26. 9.00 by CAA: derelict 10.05)

G-BCMF	Levi Go-Plane RL.6 Series 1	EAA.3678		5. 9.74	R Levi		(Porchfield, Isle of Wight)	

(Built R Levi)
(DBR on first flight Bembridge 16.11.74: cancelled 5.12.83 by CAA: stored 6.06)

G-BCTU	Reims Cessna FRA150M AerobatFRA1500268			30.12.74	J S Rees		Willey Park Farm, Caterham	11. 1.00

(Cancelled 17. 1.00 as WFU: noted 3.06)

G-BCUW	Reims Cessna F177RG Cardinal RG F177RG0119		SE-GKL	10.1.75	S J Westley		Cranfield	12. 5.00T

(Cancelled 18. 8.04 by CAA: noted 1.07)

G-BCVE	Evans VP-2	V2-1015		16. 1.75	Staffordshire Wing HQ, Air Training Corps Stafford			

(Built G Bentley - pr.no.PFA 7210)
(Cancelled 9. 6.93 as TWFU: used as Ground Instructor 12.08)

G-BDCC	de Havilland DHC.1 Chipmunk 22	C1/0258	WD321	25. 4.75	Coventry Gliding Club Ltd	Husbands Bosworth		24. 3.02

(Written off 29. 8.99 and cancelled 8. 4.04 as WFU: fuselage dumped 5.05: wings only noted 10.07)

G-BDCE	Cessna F172H	F172-0704	PH-EHB	5. 5.75	Copperplane Ltd		Bournemouth	26. 4.01T

(Built Reims Aviation SA)
(Damaged by gales Bournemouth: cancelled 12.11.02 by CAA: stored 11.06)

G-BDGY	Piper PA-28-140 Cherokee	28-23613	N3536K	5. 8.75	S J Willcox		Compton Dando	

(Cancelled 4. 1.05 as PWFU: stored dismantled 6.07)

G-BDIN	Scottish Aviation Bulldog Series 100/125 BH120/377		R Jordan AF 40820. 8.75 JY-BAI, G-BDIN		R D Dickson tr British Disabled Flying Association			
							Lasham	4. 7.76S

(Noted less engine 2006: cancelled 1.8.07 as WFU)

G-BDKV	Piper PA-28R-200 Cherokee Arrow II 28R-7335297		EI-AYE (G-BBEH), N55837	29.10.75	(Bravo Juliet Whiskey Flying Ltd)		Fairoaks	8. 4.95

(Canx 25. 5.94 as destroyed : dumped as "G-OOAT" 5.06)

G-BDNZ	Cameron O-77 Balloon (Hot Air)	203		8. 1.76	D G Such		Barkway, Royston	15. 6.96A

(Tethered 9.05: cancelled 24. 5.06 by CAA)

G-BDRB	Grumman AA-5B Tiger	AA5B-0175		6. 2.76	Dorset Air Ltd		Bournemouth	23. 8.96

(Crashed on take-off Wing Farm, Longbridge Deverill 16. 5.94: cancelled 3.10.94 as WFU: fuselage noted 1.07)

G-BDXH	Boeing 747-236B	21635		23. 2.79	European Skybus Ltd		Bournemouth	2. 5.04T

(Cancelled 7. 3.06 as WFU: fuselage stored 11.08)

G-BECC	Socata Rallye 150ST	2748		14. 7.76	G R E Tapper		Swansea	15. 5.00

(Cancelled by CAA 30. 1.06, noted 9.08)

G-BEDB	SNCAN Nord 1203 Norecrin II	117	F-BEOB	5. 8.76	(B F G Lister)		Ley Farm, Chirk	11. 6.80P

(Cancelled 14.11.91 by CAA: noted stripped 5.05)

G-BENF	Cessna T210L Turbo Centurion II	21061356	N732AE D-EIPY/N732AE	17. 2.77	?		Cherry Tree Farm, Monewden	24. 5.82

(Crashed Ipswich 29. 5.81: cancelled 25. 3.85 as destroyed: in open storage 2.06)

G-BERW   Rockwell Commander 114   14214   N4884W   6. 5.77   Romeo Whiskey Ltd   Lee-on-Solent   5. 5.07
(Cancelled 27. 7.07 as PWFU: noted 9.07)

G-BETO   Morane-Saulnier MS.885 Super Rallye   34   F-BKED   18. 5.77   (A J and A Hawley)   Farley Farm, Romsey   11.12.04
(Cancelled 27.10.06 as PWFU: stored derelict 10.07)

G-BEUK   Fuji FA.200-160 Aero Subaru   FA200-284   24. 5.77   C B Mellor ta BM Aviation   Glebe Farm, Stockton   2.11.00T
(Overran runway on take-off Glebe Farm 8. 1.99 and badly damaged: cancelled 25. 6.02 by CAA) (Noted 9.06)

G-BEWP   Reims Cessna F150M   F15001426   13. 6.77   Perth College   Perth   12. 8.85
(Crashed Aboyne 4.10.83 and cancelled 5.12.83 as destroyed:instructional use 1.06)

G-BEYN   Evans VP-2   V2-3167   1. 8.77   C D Denham tr East Fortune Flying Group
(Built C D Denham - pr.no.PFA 063-10271)   *(Cancelled 2. 9.91 by CAA: noted 2006)*   (Musselborough)

G-BEZS   Reims FR172J Rocket   FR17200562   (I-CCAJ)   11. 8.77   B A Wallace   Bourn   22. 9.79
(Damaged near Stapleford 15. 6.79: front fuselage stored 2.02)

G-BFDV   Westland WG.13 Lynx HC.28   WA/028   TAD.013   3.10.77   School of Electrical and Aeronautical Engineering
(Originally regd as "Lynx 02F")   Qatar AF 1, G-17-20   Princess Marina College, Arborfield
(Cancelled 6.78: as Instructional airframe "QP-30" 9.05)

G-BFHX   Evans VP-1   PFA 062-10283   2.12.77   A D Bohanna and D I Trussler   Popham   7. 4.99P
(Built D F Gibson) (Volkswagen 1600)   *(Cancelled 21. 4.05 by CAA: stored 10.05)*

G-BFKG   Reims Cessna F152 II   F15201463   26. 1. 78   Luton Flight Training Ltd   Biggin Hill   25.11.90T
(Blown over by jet blast Luton 11.11.89: cancelled 16. 3.92 as WFU: fuselage noted 6.07)

G-BFNU   Britten-Norman BN-2B-21 Islander   877   16. 3.78   Isles of Scilly Skybus Ltd   St Just   18. 89T
(Built IRMA)   *(Cancelled 28. 1.94 as WFU: fuselage only 3.07)*

G-BFWK   Piper PA-28-161 Cherokee Warrior II   N9589N   23. 6.78   Marham Investments Ltd   Belfast International   8.12.99T
   28-7816610   *(Cancelled 26. 5.98 as WFU: wrecked fuselage stored 1.06)*

G-BFWL   Reims Cessna F150L   F15000971   PH-KDC   4.10.78   P Maher tr G-BFWL Flying Group   Barton   27. 3.00
(Cancelled 21. 2.00 as WFU: fuselage noted 1.04)

G-BFZR   Gulfstream American AA-5B Tiger   AA5B-0979   EI-BJS   3.11.78   P C Morrissey   Oxford   24. 5.07
   G-BFZR
(Forced-landed after take-off Oxford 15.10.04: cancelled 3.11.05 by CAA: remnants noted 8.07)

G-BGAY   Cameron O-77 Balloon (Hot Air)   446   4.12.78   P C A and S W C Hall   Uxbridge   16.12.91A
(Cancelled 4. 8.98 by CAA: extant 2007)

G-BGBF   Druine D 31A Turbulent   PFA 1658   24.10.78   K Pullen tr Eaglescott Turbulent Group   Eaglescott   25. 3.04P
(Built L Davies) (Volkswagen 1600)   *(Noted in hangar roof 3.06: cancelled 10. 9.07 by CAA)*

G-BGCX   Taylor JT.2 Titch   PFA 3221   23.11.78   (G M R Walters)   Lower Wasing Farm, Brimpton
(Built G M R Walters)   *(No Permit issued and cancelled 27. 3.99 as PWFU: noted 6.05)*

G-BGEA   Reims Cessna F150M   F15001396   OY-BJK   22. 3.79   C J Hopewell   Sibson   8 .7.06T
(Cancelled 4. 2.05 as PWFU: fuselage stored externally 7.07)

G-BGFK   Evans VP-1   PFA 062-10343   20.12.78   Not known   Waterstones Farm, Newby Wiske
(Built I N M Cameron)   *(Cancelled 7. 4.99: stored 2.08)*

G-BGGG   Piper PA-38-112 Tomahawk   38-79A0163   N9675N   10. 1.79   CMV Ltd   Bagby   28. 6.04T
(Cancelled 6.10.05 by CAA: stored 2.08)

G-BGHW   Thunder Ax8-90 Balloon (Hot Air)   175   30. 1.79   W G Johnston   Edinburgh
(Cancelled 19. 5.93 by CAA: stored 2001)

G-BGRN   Piper PA-38-112 Tomahawk   38-79A0897   N9684N   25. 4.79   Goodwood Road Racing Company Ltd   Goodwood   12. 2.00T
(Cancelled 30. 8.01 as WFU: noted derelict 6.06)

G-BGZS   Keirs Heated Air Tube Balloon (Minimum Lift)   7. 8.79   M N J Kirby   Manchester
(Built K J Faulkner)   01   *(Cancelled 2.12.93 by CAA: extant 5.07)*

G-BHEH   Cessna 310G   310G-0016   N1720   14. 4.80   F J Shevill   Shoreham   9.12.96
   N8916Z   *(Cancelled 24. 8.00 as WFU: fuselage dumped 1.06)*

G-BHGP   SOCATA TB-10 Tobago   100   17. 1.80   D Suleyman   Stapleford   29. 5.05
(Cancelled 21. 3.07 as temporarily wfu)

G-BHIC   Reims Cessna F182Q Skylane II   F18200135   18.12.79   Oxford Aviation Services Ltd   Alton   3. 8.08E
(SMA SR305-230-diesel)   *(Cancelled 4. 5.07 as destroyed: noted Air Salvage International 8.07)*

G-BHJA   Cessna A152 Aerobat   A1520835   N4954A   11. 3.80   Cornwall Flying Club Ltd   Biggin Hill   9. 4.92T
(Damaged in heavy landing Bodmin 21. 7.90: cancelled 8.4.02 by CAA: fuselage noted 6.07)

G-BHKE   Bensen B 8MS   VW.1   7. 1.80   N B Gray   Kirkbride
(Built V C Whitehead - pr.no.G/01-1009)   *(Cancelled 3. 2.04 by CAA: noted 7.08)*

G-BHMH   Reims Cessna FA152 Aerobat   FA1520367   16. 5.80   Flairhire Ltd t/a Redhill Flying Club   Biggin Hill   13. 8.89T
(Damaged when wing struck tree Hale Farm, Chiddingstone 22. 9.86: cancelled as WFU 9. 8.89: fuselage noted 6.07)

G-BHMM   Avenger T 200-2112 Balloon (Minimum Lift)   29. 1.80   M Murphy   Herne Bay
(Built M Murphy)   MM2   *(Cancelled 4. 8.98 by CAA: extant 5.07)*

G-BHPN   Colt 14A Cloudhopper Balloon (Hot Air)   081   (SE-..)   6. 3.80   Lindtstrand Technologies Ltd   Oswestry   29. 1.06E
   G-BHPN   *(Cancelled 24. 8.06 by CAA: active 1.07)*

G-BHSA   Cessna 152 II   152-83693   (N4889B)   1. 5.80   D Copley   Sturgate
(Cancelled 18. 5.04 as PWFU: noted 8.05 in bare metal)

G-BHSL   CASA 1131E Jungmann   1117   E3B-236   18. 6.80   H I Taylor   Gloucestershire   19. 7.96P
   Spanish AF
(Damaged on take off Cranfield 6. 7.96. cancelled 23. 8.00 by CAA: stored dismantled 1.06)

G-BHUP   Reims Cessna F152 II   F15201773   2. 5.80   Stapleford Flying Club Ltd   Stapleford   9.10.89T
(Damaged near Barton 17. 5.89 and cancelled 15. 2.95 by CAA) (Gutted fuselage noted 11.06)

G-BICY   Piper PA-23-160 Apache   23-1640   OO-AOL   26. 9.80   A M Lynn c/o Busy Bee Engineering   Sibson   15. 7.07
   5N-ACL, VR-NDF, PH-ACL, N4010P
(Cancelled 1. 8.06 as PWFU: noted 9.08 in external storage)

G-BIFN   Bensen B 8MR   KW.1   7.10.80   (R Light)   Stockport
(Built K Willows - pr.no.PFA G/01-1010)   *(Dismantled 8.06: cancelled 8. 9.06 by CAA)*

G-BIGM   Avenger T 200-2112 Balloon (Minimum Lift)   6.10.80   M Murphy   Herne Bay
(Built M Murphy)   MM3   *(Cancelled 4. 8.98 by CAA: extant 5.07)*

G-BIIF   Fournier RF4D   4047   25.11.80   J A Taylor and J A Bridges   Biggin Hill   18. 3.93A
(Cancelled 24. 9.92 by CAA: fuselage noted 6.05)

G-BIJX   Reims Cessna F152 II   F15201829   29.12.80   A S Bamrah t/a Falcon Flying Services   Biggin Hill   3 .6.05
(Cancelled 28.11.03 as PWFU: fuselage noted 6.07)

G-BILK   Reims Cessna FA.152 Aerobat   FA1520372   9. 1.81   Exeter Flying Club Ltd   Exeter   13. 5.02T
(Forced landed and overturned in field near Exeter 18.4.01 and substantially damaged: cancelled 10.8.01 as destroyed: noted 12.05)

G-BINZ	Rango NA-8 Balloon (Minimum Lift)	SBG-14		9. 2.81	M O Davies and T J Sweeting t/a Stansted Balloon Group
						Bishops Stortford
					(Cancelled 2.12.93 by CAA: extant 5.07)	
G-BIOS	Morris Scruggs BL2B Balloon (Minimum Lift)			5. 2.81	D Eaves	Southampton
		81220			*(Cancelled 27.10.88 as PWFU: extant 5.07)*	
G-BIRB	SOCATA MS.880B Rallye 100T	2460	F-BVAQ	30. 3.81	(E Smith) *(Cancelled 13. 7.92 by CAA: noted 6.06)*	
					Jungle Jim's adventure playground, Shanklin, Isle of Wight	16. 6.90
G-BIRY	Cameron V-77 Balloon (Hot Air)	715		12. 3.81	(P G Bish)	Hungerford 15. 5.99A
					(Cancelled 10.12.02 by CAA: noted 1.05)	
G-BIUL	Cameron Bellows 60SS Balloon (Hot Air)	703		27. 3.81	(J Haydon)	Abingdon 12. 5.91A
	(Expansion Joint Shape)				*(Cancelled 26. 6.98 by PWFU: stored intact 2007)*	
G-BIVL	Bensen B 8M	TED-01		10. 4.81	R Gardiner	Bere Alston, Yelverton 29. 4.87P
	(Built T E Davies - pr.no.PFA G/01-1011)				*(Cancelled 3. 4.97 by CAA: noted 11.06)*	
G-BIVS	Stansted Featherlight Mk.2 Balloon (Minimum Lift)			15. 4.81	J M J Roberts and S R Rushton	
		002			Rayne, Braintreee and Castle Donington, Derby	
					(Cancelled 13.12.88 by CAA: extant 5.07)	
G-BIWD	Morris Scruggs RS.5000 Balloon (Minimum Lift)			26. 6.81	D Eaves	Southampton
		81545			*(Cancelled 30.11.01 as PWFU: extant 5.07)*	
G-BJAA	Unicorn UE-1A Balloon (Minimum Lift)	81007		2. 6.81	K H Turner t/a Hot Air Cold Ash Cold Ash, Newbury	
					(Cancelled 30.11.88 by CAA: extant 5.07)	
G-BJDV	Kingram 01 Balloon (Minimum Lift)	TS-01		4. 8.81	S Ingram and T J King Eastleigh and Southampton	
	(Bullt T King)				*(Cancelled 12.12.88 by CAA: extant 5.07)*	
G-BJDY	Unicorn UE-4A Balloon (Minimum Lift)	81012		28. 7.81	I Chadwick tr Unicorn Group	
					Partridge Green, Horsham	
					(Cancelled 19. 7.82 as WFU: extant 5.07)	
G-BJEN	Morris Scruggs RS.5000 Balloon (Minimum Lift)			5. 8.81	N J Richardson	Eastleigh
		81548			*(Cancelled 14.1.02 as PWFU: extant 5.07)*	
G-BJES	Morris Scruggs RS.5000 Balloon (Minimum Lift)			5. 8.81	J E Christopher	Eastleigh
		81551			*(Cancelled 2.12.93 by CAA: extant 5.07)*	
G-BJFW	Windsor Mk V Balloon (Minimum Lift)	402		11. 8.81	S E Meagher tr The Windsor Balloon Group	
						London SW15
					(Cancelled 18.10.88 as PWFU: extant 5.07)	
G-BJGF	Eaves Dodo Mk.1 Balloon (Minimum Lift) DD.1			19. 8.81	D and D Eaves	Southampton
					(Cancelled 30.11.01 as PWFU: extant 5.07)	
G-BJGG	Eaves Dodo Mk.2 Balloon (Minimum Lift) DD.2			19. 8.81	D and D Eaves	Southampton
					(Cancelled 30.11.01 as PWFU: extant 5.07)	
G-BJGN	Morris Scruggs RS.5000 Balloon (Minimum Lift)			21. 8.81	K H Turner t/a Hot Air Cold Ash Cold Ash, Newbury	
		81554			*(Cancelled 30.11.88 by CAA; extant 5.07)*	
G-BJHI	Chown Osprey Lizzieliner Mk.1B Balloon (Minimum Lift)			9. 9.81	A P and K E Chown	Southampton
		04			*(Cancelled 10. 1.83 by CAA: extant 5.07)*	
G-BJHJ	Chown Osprey Lizzieliner Mk.1C Balloon (Minimum Lift)			9. 9.81	D Eaves	Southampton
		07			*(Cancelled 27.10.88 as PWFU: extant 5.07)*	
G-BJHN	Chown Osprey Lizzieliner Mk.1B Balloon (Minimum Lift)			9. 9.81	J E Christopher	Eastleigh
		14			*(Cancelled 2.12.93 by CAA: extant 5.07)*	
G-BJHO	Chown Osprey Lizzieliner Mk.1C Balloon (Minimum Lift)			9. 9.81	G G Kneller	Southampton
		15			*(Cancelled 2.12.93 by CAA: extant 5.07)*	
G-BJHP	Chown Osprey Lizzieliner Mk.1C Balloon (Minimum Lift)			9. 9.81	N J Richardson	Eastleigh
		16			*(Cancelled 14.1.02 as PWFU: extant 5.07)*	
G-BJHR	Chown Osprey Lizzieliner Mk.1B Balloon (Minimum Lift)			9. 9.81	M Christopher	Eastleigh
		17			*(Cancelled 8.12.88 by CAA: extant 5.07)*	
G-BJHW	Chown Osprey Lizzieliner Mk.1C Balloon (Minimum Lift)			9. 9.81	N J Richardson	Eastleigh
		19			*(Cancelled 14.1.02 as PWFU: extant 5.07)*	
G-BJHY	Chown Osprey Lizzieliner Mk.1B Balloon (Minimum Lift)			9. 9.81	S Ingram and T J King Eastleigh and Southampton	
		21			*(Cancelled 12.12.88 by CAA: extant 5.07)*	
G-BJHZ	Chown Osprey Lizzieliner Mk.1B Balloon (Minimum Lift)			9. 9.81	M Christopher	Eastleigh
		27			*(Cancelled 8.12.88 by CAA: extant 5.07)*	
G-BJIK	Chown Osprey Lizzieliner Mk.1B Balloon (Minimum Lift)			9. 9.81	A P and K E Chown	Southampton
		23			*(Cancelled 2. 6.83 as WFU: extant 5.07)*	
G-BJJD	Eaves Dodo Mk 1 Balloon (Minimum Lift) DD.6			9. 9.81	A P Chown and K R Bundy	Southampton
					(Cancelled 2. 6.83 as WFU: extant 5.07)	
G-BJJE	Eaves Dodo Mk 3 Balloon (Minimum Lift) DD.7			9. 9.81	D Eaves	Southampton
					(Cancelled 30.11.01 as PWFU: extant 5.07)	
G-BJJF	Eaves Dodo Mk 4 Balloon (Minimum Lift) DD.8			9. 9.81	D Eaves	Southampton
					(Cancelled 27.10.88 as PWFU: extant 5.07)	
G-BJJG	Eaves Dodo Mk 5 Balloon (Minimum Lift) DD.9			9. 9.81	D Eaves	Southampton
					(Cancelled 27.10.88 as PWFU: extant 5.07)	
G-BJJM	Rooke & Hounsell Bitterne Mk.1 Balloon (Minimum Lift)			9. 9.81	A P and K E Chown	Southampton
		RH.06			*(Cancelled 10. 1.83 by CAA: extant 5.07)*	
G-BJKV	Chown Osprey Mk.1F Balloon (Minimum Lift)30			17. 9.81	B Diggle	Cheadle
					(Cancelled 8.12.88 by CAA: extant 5.07)	
G-BJKZ	Chown Osprey Mk.1F Balloon (Minimum Lift)31			17. 9.81	M N J Kirby	Manchester
					(Cancelled 17.11.88 as PWFU: extant 5.07)	
G-BJLE	Chown Osprey Lizzieliner Mk.1B Balloon (Minimum Lift)			21. 9.81	I Chadwick	Partridge Green, Horsham
		32			*(Cancelled 21. 4.98 as PWFU: extant 5.07)*	
G-BJLN	Stansted Mk.3 Balloon (Minimum Lift)	301		23. 9.81	A P Newman and T J Sweeeting t/a Stansted	
					Balloon Group Braintree and Bishops Stortford	
					(Cancelled 29.11.88 by CAA: extant 5.07)	
G-BJLP	Stansted Mk.3 Balloon (Minimum Lift)	302		23. 9.81	M O Davies and N P Kemp t/a Stansted Balloon Group	
					Little Hallingbury, Bishops Stortford and Braintree	
					(Cancelled 12.12.88 by CAA: extant 5.07)	
G-BJMG	Eaves European E 26C Balloon (Minimum Lift)			25. 9.81	A P Chown and D Eaves	Southampton
		S 4			*(Cancelled 15.10.98 by CAA: extant 5.07)*	
G-BJMH	Chown Osprey Mk.3A Balloon (Minimum Lift)37			9. 9.81	D Eaves	Southampton
					(Cancelled 27.10.88 as PWFU: extant 5.07)	

G-BJMT	Chown Osprey Mk.1E Balloon (Minimum Lift)			2.10.81	M J Sheather	Southampton
	AKC-45				*(Cancelled 29.11.88 by CAA: extant 5.07)*	
G-BJNB	WAR Vought F-4U Corsair replicaPFA 118-10711			13.10.81	A V Francis	Beeches Farm, South Scarle
	(Built A V Francis)				*(Cancelled 8.11.89 by CAA: under slow rebuild 8.05)*	
G-BJNI	Chown Osprey Mk.1C Balloon (Minimum Lift)			9.10.81	M J Sheather	Southampton
	AKC-49				*(Cancelled 29.11.88 by CAA: extant 5.07)*	
G-BJOD	Hollman Sportster HA-2M Gyroplane HP81-01			26.10.81	W O'Riordan	Amen Corner, Binfield, Bracknell
	(Built HJ Goddard and W O'Riordan)				*(Cancelled 19. 6.91 by CAA, extant 6.08)*	
G-BJPT	Chown Osprey Mk.3G Balloon (Minimum Lift)			16.10.81	A P Chown	Southampton
	AKC-79				*(Cancelled 2. 6. 83 by CAA: extant 5.07)*	
G-BJRB	Eaves European E 254 Balloon (Minimum Lift)			23.10.81	D Eaves	Southampton
	S 5				*(Cancelled 30.11.01 by CAA: extant 5.07)*	
G-BJRC	Eaves European E 84R Balloon (Minimum Lift)			23.10.81	D Eaves	Southampton
	S 7				*(Cancelled 30.11.01 by CAA: extant 5.07)*	
G-BJRD	Eaves European E 84R Balloon (Minimum Lift)			23.10.81	D Eaves	Southampton
	S 8				*(Cancelled 30.11.01 by CAA: extant 5.07)*	
G-BJRL	Chown Osprey Mk.4B Balloon (Minimum Lift)			28.10.81	G G Kneller	Southampton
	AKC-67				*(Cancelled 2.12.93 by CAA: extant 5.07)*	
G-BJRO	Chown Osprey Mk.4D Balloon (Minimum Lift)			28.10.81	M Christopher	Eastleigh
	AKC-82				*(Cancelled 8.12.88 by CAA: extant 5.07)*	
G-BJSC	Chown Osprey Mk.4D Balloon (Minimum Lift)			12.11.81	N J Richardson	Eastleigh
	AKC-84				*(Cancelled 14. 1.02 as PWFU: extant 5.07)*	
G-BJSD	Chown Osprey Mk.4D Balloon (Minimum Lift)			12.11.81	N J Richardson	Eastleigh
	AKC-83				*(Cancelled 14. 1.02 as PWFU: extant 5.07)*	
G-BJSF	Chown Osprey Mk.4B Balloon (Minimum Lift)			9.11.81	J E Christopher	Eastleigh
	AKC-66				*(Cancelled 2.12.93 by CAA: extant 5.07)*	
G-BJSI	Chown Osprey Mk.1E Balloon (Minimum Lift)			9.11.81	N J Richardson	Eastleigh
	AKC-43				*(Cancelled 14. 1.02 as PWFU: extant 5.07)*	
G-BJSK	Chown Osprey Mk.1E Balloon (Minimum Lift)			9.11.81	J E Christopher	Eastleigh
	AKC-65				*(Cancelled 2.12.93 by CAA: extant 5.07)*	
G-BJSX	Unicorn UE-1C Balloon (Minimum Lift)	82023		10.11.81	N J Richardson	Eastleigh
					(Cancelled 14. 1.02 as PWFU: extant 5.07)	
G-BJTZ	Chown Osprey Mk.4A Balloon (Minimum Lift)			27.11.81	M J Sheather	Southampton
	AKC-38				*(Cancelled 29.11.88 by CAA: extant 5.07)*	
G-BJUO	Unicorn UE-4B Balloon (Minimum Lift)	81022		2.11.81	I Chadwick tr Unicorn Group	
						Partridge Green, Horsham
					(DBF 12.4.82 Alton Towers: cancelled 19.7.82 as WFU: extant 5.07)	
G-BJVM	Cessna 172N Skyhawk II	17269374	N737FA	14.12.81	I C Maclennan	Gunton Hall, Somerton 1. 8.08E
					(Cancelled 18.12.07 by CAA)	
G-BJZX	Grob G109	6109	(D-KGRO)	3. 9.82	Oxfordshire Sport Flying Ltd	Blackpool 4. 9.00
					(Cancelled 18. 3.02 as WFU: fuselage noted 10.07)	
G-BKIE	Short SD.3-30 Variant100	SH3005	G-SLUG	15. 9.82	International Fire Training Centre	
			G-BKIE, G-METP, G-METO, G-BKIE, C-GTAS, G-14-3005 Durham Tees Valley 22. 8.93T				
					(Cancelled 16.9.97 as PWFU).(Fire services use 2.08)	
G-BKRU	Crossley Racer	PFA 131-10797			(M S Crossley)	(Peterborough) 24. 1.90P
	(Built M S Crossley) (Continental C90-14F)				*(Cancelled 2. 3.99 by CAA: noted 5.05)*	
G-BKRV	Hovey Beta Bird	PFA 135-10875		30. 3.83	M J Aubrey	Kington, Hereford 25.6.97P
	(Built A V Francis) (Rotax 503)				*(Cancelled 18. 6.98 by CAA: noted 2002)*	
G-BLDC	K & S Jungster 1	PFA 044-10701		29.12.83	(A W Brown)	Longside, Peterhead 6. 3.90P
	(Built C A Laycock)				*(No Permit issued - cancelled 6. 3.99 by CAA: on build 2007)*	
G-BLLM	Piper PA-23-250 Aztec E	27-4619	G-BBNM	18. 1.84	C and M Thomas t/a Ammanford Trade Sales Alton 21. 8.98
			OY-POR, G-BBNM, N14001			
					(Cancelled 8. 4.02 by CAA: noted Air Salvage International 8.07)	
G-BLPK	Cameron V-65 Balloon (Hot Air)	1069		24. 9.84	A J and C P Nicholls t/a Bernard Hunter and Bristol Cine Sales
						Ashton, Bristol 9. 8.96A
					(Cancelled 19. 1.99 by CAA: noted 5.07)	
G-BLRJ	CEA Jodel DR.1051 Sicile	502	F-BLRJ	8. 2.78	M P Hallam	Deenethorpe 17. 7.00
					(Cancelled 6. 3.02 as WFU: noted 6.03)	
G-BLSD	de Havilland DH.112 Venom FB.54	928	N203DM	20. 5.85	Aces High Ltd	Grove Technology Park, Wantage
	(Built F + W)		G-BLSD, Swiss AF J-1758		*(Cancelled 5.. 6.96 as WFU: as gate guardian 10.07)*	
G-BLTT	Slingsby T.67B Firefly	2023		16. 1.85	C W Ward *(noted 9.08)*	Haverfordwest 5. 8.00
G-BLTU	Slingsby T 67B Firefly	2024		16. 1.85	(RAF Wyton Flying Club Ltd)	
						Chiltern Park, Wallingford 4. 4.07T
					(Cancelled 26. 6.06 as PWFU: noted 6.07)	
G-BLWW	Aerocar Taylor Mini-Imp Model CPFA 136-10880			1. 3.85	M K Field tr The Brize Group	Sleap 4. 6.87P
	(Built W E Wilks) (Continental O-200-A)				*(Cancelled 13.10.00 by CAA: noted 8.07)*	
G-BLYJ	Cameron V-77 Balloon (Hot Air)	408		1. 5.85	E E Clark and J A Lomas	Melton Mowbray 15. 6.89A
					(Cancelled 7. 5.93 as destroyed: inflated 4.06)	
G-BMFN	QAC Quickie Tri-Q 200	EMK 017		27. 9.85	A H Hartog	Thruxton 1. 5.02P
	(Built EMK Aeroplane Ltd - pr.no.PFA 094A1-11062) (Continental O-200-A)				*(Cancelled 30. 3.05 by CAA: noted 8.06)*	
G-BMGC	Fairey Swordfish II	?-	RCan Navy W5856	23.10.85	Royal Navy Historic Flight	RNAS Yeovilton
			W5856		*(As "W5856:A2A" in RN 810 Sqdn c/s-"City of Leeds")*	
	(Built Blackburn Aeroplane and Motor Company Ltd)				*(Cancelled 2. 9.91 by CAA)*	
G-BMIR (2)	Westland Wasp HAS.1	F9670	XT788	24. 1.86	Park Aviation Supply	
						(Little Glovers Farm, Charlwood, Surrey)
	(Cancelled 22.12.95 by CAA) (Exhibited in Flightaid's travelling roadshow as "XT788/474" in Royal Navy c/s 9.07)					
G-BMJB	Cessna 152 II	15280030	N757VD	3. 2.86	Bobbington Air Training School Ltd	Lee-on-Solent 16. 6.00
					(Cancelled 12. 6.00 as WFU: fuselage noted 9.07 - wings stored Halfpenny Green 10.07)	
G-BMJG	Piper PA-28R-200 Cherokee Arrow 28R-35046		ZS-TNS	23.12.85	Western Air (Thruxton) Ltd	Blackpool 4. 2.99T
			ZS-FYC, N9345N			
	(Damaged Thruxton 11.10.98: cancelled 15. 4.99 by CAA: fuselage noted 10.07)					
G-BMKW	Cameron V-77 Balloon (Hot Air)	608		29. 1.86	M H Redman	Stalbridge, Sturminster Newton 21. 9.00A
					(Noted 8.06: cancelled 1. 2.08 by CAA)	
G-BMLC	Short SD.3-60 Variant 100	SH3688	SE-LDA	18. 2.86	BAC Leasing Ltd	(Coventry) 24. 5.05T
			G-BMLC, G-14-3688		*(Cancelled 6. 6.07 as WFU)*	

G-BMOO   Clutton FRED SeriesII   PFA 029-10770   11. 4.86   (N Purllant)   Saltby   8. 8.91P
         (Built N Purllant) (Webster Whirlwind radial)   (Cancelled 22. 2.99 by CAA: noted 6.07 less wings or tailplane in pseudo-RAF c/s)
G-BMYA   Colt 56A Balloon (Hot Air)   864   13. 8.86   (J Haydon)   Abingdon 2.12.92A
                                                                                 (Cancelled 29. 4.97 as PWFU: stored intact 2007)
G-BNCX   Hawker Hunter T 7   41H/695454   XL621   9. 1.87   FLS Aerospace (Lovaux) Ltd   Dunsfold 28. 3.87P
                                                                                 (Cancelled 1. 3.93 as PWFU) (As Gate guardian "XL621")
G-BNJA   Wag Aero Wag-a-Bond   PFA 137-10886   3. 4.87   B E Maggs   Willey Park Farm, Caterham   3. 8.03P
         (Built R A Yates) (Continental O-200-A)   (Cancelled 17. 2.04 by CAA: noted 3.06)
G-BNKF   Colt AS-56 Airship (Hot Air)   899   20. 5.87   Formtrack Ltd   London SE16 14. 9.98A
                                                                                 (Cancelled 20.10.00 by CAA: noted 5.07)
G-BNNC   Cameron N-77 Balloon (Hot Air)   1523   16. 6.87   T M C McCoy   Peasedown St John, Bath   9.10.96
                                                                                 (Cancelled 2. 6.98 as WFU: stored 2007)
G-BNPL   Piper PA-38-112 Tomahawk   38-79A0524   N2420G   28. 7.87   Cardiff-Wales Flying Club   Gloucestershire 30. 1.03T
                                                                                 (Cancelled 24. 3.05 by CAA: fuselage noted 7.05 in outside storage)
G-BNXG   Cameron DP-70 Airship (Hot Air)   1558   23. 9.87   Rexstyle Ltd   (US) 23.10.88A
                                                                                 (Cancelled 18. 6.93 by CAA: noted 8.06)
G-BOAM   Robinson R22 Beta   0717   10.12.87   Plane Talking Ltd   Quatro Vientos, Madrild 27. 1.08E
                                                                                 (Cancelled 17. 2.07 by CAA: noted 5.07)
G-BOBZ   Piper PA-28-181 Archer II   28-8090257   N81671   21.12.87   Trustcomms International Ltd   Biggin Hill   9. 3.98
                                                                                 (Cancelled 29. 4.05 by CAA: noted 6.07)
G-BODH   Slingsby Cadet III Motor Glider   BGA 474   5. 1.88   M M Bain "Fochinell"   Wick 13. 8.02P
                                     PFA 042-10108
         (Re-built C D Denham believed from Slingsby T 8 Tutor G-ALNK {MHL/RT.13}) (Volkswagen 1834)   (Cancelled 1. 3.05 by CAA: stored 6.07)
G-BOJD   Cameron N-77 Balloon (Hot Air)   1653   11. 3.88   P A Sweatman "Bluebird"   Birmingham   3. 9.05
                                                                                 (Cancelled 29. 6.06 as WFU: extant 5.07)
G-BOKK   Piper PA-28-161 Warrior II   28-8116300   N8427L   6. 4.88   Gosky Aviation Ltd   Blackpool   7. 6.97T
                                                   (Damaged Hamgreen, Redditch 18. 5.95: cancelled 8. 9.95 as WFU: wreck noted 10.07)
G-BORM   Hawker Siddeley HS.748 Series 2B/217 1670   RP-C1043   29. 7.88   (Parkhouse Aviation)   Wycombe Air Park
                                                   V2-LAA, VP-LAA, 9Y-TDH   (Cancelled 18. 6.92 by CAA: cockpit only 12.05)
G-BOVG   Cessna F172H   F172-0627   OO-ANN   2. 8.88   No.1476 Squadron, ATC   RAF Halton 14. 9.91
         (Built Reims Aviation SA)   D-ELTR
                                                   (Damaged Southend 1991: cancelled 26. 9.95 as WFU: instructional fuselage 9.07)
G-BOWK   Cameron N-90 Balloon (Hot Air)   1764   1. 8.88   S R Bridge (Cavendish Loans titles)   Grantham
                                                                                 (Cancelled 8.11.01 as WFU: inflated 4.06)
G-BOXH   Pitts S-1S   MP4   N8LA   29. 7.88   E Mason and R Graham   Not known 16. 5.07P
         (Built B Halstock and J Mills)
         (Damaged in accident Oving near Chichester 10.12.06: cancelled 17. 3.07: wreck noted 9. 3.07 northbound on M40 between Junctions 9 &10)
G-BPAD   Piper PA-34-200T Seneca II   34-7870431   N21208   23. 8.88   Liverpool Flying School Ltd   Cranfield
                                                   (Destroyed in crash Saddle Hill, Bowland, Lancashire 15. 7.92: cancelled 20. 2.97 as destroyed: wreck noted 1.06)
G-BPAV   Clutton FRED series 2   PFA 029-12074   21.11.78   P A Valentine   Wycombe Air Park
         (Built P A Valentine)   (Cancelled 12. 8.03 by CAA: unfinished fuselage noted 5.06)
G-BPCJ   Cessna 150J   15070797   N61096   26. 9.88   B E Simpson and C R Hughes
                                                                                 Amen Corner, Binfield, Bracknell
                                                   (Badly damaged in gales Compton Abbas 25. 1.90: cancelled 4. 7.90 by CAA: in open storage 6.08)
G-BPDK   Sorrell SNS-7 Hyperbipe   242   N85BL   6.10.88   A J Cable   Barton 23. 6.95P
                                                                                 (Cancelled 17. 2.99 by CAA: wings only noted 10.06)
G-BPEL   Piper PA-28-151 Cherokee Warrior 28-7415172 C-FEYM   10.10.88   R W Harris and A Jahanfar   Southend   8. 2.92T
                                                                                 (Cancelled 28. 2.02 as WFU: dismantled wreck stored 1.09)
G-BPGM   Cessna 152   15284932   N5380P   14.11.88   J D Peace and Co   Glenrothes 14. 4.05T
                                                                                 (Cancelled 5.10.04 as PWFU: noted dumped 6.06)
G-BPLF   Cameron V-77 Balloon (Hot Air)   1903   16. 1.89   I R Warrington and R Macmillan   Stamford
                                                                                 (Cancelled 22. 9.04 by CAA: inflated 4.06)
G-BPMM   Champion 7ECA Citabria   498   N5132T   22. 3.89   J Murray   (Ballymena, County Antrim) 25. 2.97P
                                                                                 (Noted 1.04: cancelled 29. 4.05 by CAA)
G-BPOA   Gloster Meteor T 7   ?-   WF877   16. 3.89   (Aces High Ltd)   Duxford
                                                                                 (Cancelled 5. 6.96 as WFU: noted 4.06)
G-BPYI   Cameron O-77 Balloon (Hot Air)   1988   9. 5.89   N J Logue   Pembroke Dock   9. 7.05A
                                                                                 (Cancelled 10. 5.05 by CAA: inflated 4.06)
G-BRBF   Cessna 152 II   15281993   N67748   8. 6.89   G Jackson t/a Jacksons Tool and Plant Hire Bagby   5. 7.98T
                                                                                 (Cancelled 17. 5.01 by CAA: noted stored 2.08)
G-BRCI   Pitts S-1C   4668   N351S   6. 7.89   G L A Vandormael   Sint-Truiden, Belgium   2. 8.08P
         (Built J Ballentyne) (Lycoming O-320)   (Cancelled 25. 2.08 by CAA)
G-BREA   Bensen B 8MR   PFA G/01-1006   6. 7.89   P Robichaud   Little Rissington   6. 9.06P
         (Built R Firth) (Rotax 503)   (Cancelled 25. 9.06 as TWFU)
G-BREZ   Cessna 172M Skyhawk II   17266742   N80775   14. 7.89   Not known   Fenland
                                                                                 (Cancelled 16. 4.93 - to EI-CHS: under restoration 2.08)
G-BRFN   Piper PA-38-112 Tomahawk   38-79A0397   N2326F   23.10.89   Light Aircraft Leasing (UK) Ltd   Exeter 10.12.03T
                                                                                 (Cancelled 25. 9.03 by CAA: noted 12.05)
G-BRGP   Colt Flying Stork SS Balloon (Hot Air) 1409   25. 7.89   T and C Realisations Ltd "Great Eggspectations"
                                                                                                                         (US) 11.10.94A
                                                   (Cancelled 10. 3.95 by CAA: active Albuquerque, New Mexico, US 10.06 as "G-BRGP")
G-BRHB   Boeing Stearman B75N1 (N2S-3) Kaydet   EC-AID   10. 8.89   P R Bennett and R Sage   Priory Farm, Tibenham
                                     75-6508   N67955, Bu.05334   (Noted 3.05: cancelled 3. 8.05 as WFU)
G-BRKX   Air Command 532 Elite   0619   8. 9.89   K Davis   Church Farm, Askern 10.12.90
         (Built K Davis - pr.no PFA G/04-1150)   (Cancelled 28. 2.02 by CAA: noted stored 9.07)
G-BRML   Piper PA-38-112 Tomahawk   38-79A1017   N2510P   3.10.89   P H Rogers   Wellesbourne Mountford   3. 6.02T
                                                                                 (Cancelled 5. 4.05 by CAA: dumped 8.05)
G-BRTC   Cessna 150G   15065996   N3296J   1. 3.90   Thorpe Air Ltd   Kirknewton
                                                   (Blown over by gales Bournemouth 23.12.91 and badly damaged: cancelled 3. 2.99 as PWFU: wreck noted 3.06)
G-BRUA   Cessna 152 II   15281212   N49267   11. 1.90   BBC Air Ltd   Exeter   5. 11.05T
                                                                                 (Cancelled 21.11.05 as PWFU: fuselage noted 1.07)
G-BRUE   Cameron V-77 Balloon (Hot Air)   2183   15.12.89   B J Newman and P L Harrison   Rushden 26. 7.99A
                                                                                 (Cancelled 13. 3.01 as PWFU: noted 8.05)

G-BRVH	Smyth Model S Sidewinder	PFA 092-11251			19.12.89	I C White	Abbeville, France 10. 5.02P
	(Built I Bellamy) (Lycoming O-290)					*(Cancelled 24. 7.02 by CAA: noted 6.07)*	
G-BSET	Beagle B 206 Basset CC.1	B 006	XS765		3.12.86	IAE Ltd	Cranfield 28. 7.98
						(Cancelled 25. 3.04 as WFU: spares source as "XS765" 7.05)	
G-BSGR	Boeing Stearman E75 (PT-17) Kaydet 75-4721		N75864		19. 6.90	A G Dunkerley	Kemble
			EC-ATY, N55050, 42-16558			*(Cancelled 10. 3.99 by CAA: noted unmarked 2.04)*	
	(Composite rebuild of EC-AMD {75-4721} and EC-ATY {75-6714} and also reported as (ex?) N126SE)						
G-BSHR	Reims Cessna F 172N Skyhawk II	F17201616	G-BFGE		23.10.84	Deep Cleavage Ltd	Exeter 24. 4.03T
						(Cancelled 21. 2.02 as WFU: on fire dump 2.06)	
G-BSOV	PIper PA-38-112 Tomahawk II	38-81A0031	N25637		20. 8.90	A Dodd	Cranfield 1. 3.98T
					(Damaged Panshanger 7.10.95: cancelled 5. 6.01 by CAA: noted dismantled 1.06)		
G-BSPC	SAN Jodel D 140C Mousquetaire III	150	F-BMFN		2.11.81	B E Cotton	Rufforth 31.10.85
						(Cancelled 15. 8.94 by CAA: noted derelict 9.07)	
G-BSPF	Cessna T303 Crusader	T30300100	OY-SVH		31. 7.90	K P Gibben tr G-BSPF Crusader Group	Blackpool 28.10.99
			N3116C				
	(Crashed Burton Joyce, Nottingham 16. 7.98: cancelled 25. 8.98 as WFU: wreck noted 10.07)						
G-BSUH	Cessna 140	8092	N89088		15.10.90	K J O'Brien	Abbeyshrule, County Longford 2. 5.94
	(Continental C85)		NC89088				
	(Damaged Gowran Grange 6.93: cancelled 28. 4.95 by CAA: airframe stored 5.06)						
G-BSUT	Rans S-6-ESA Coyote II	0990.138			2.10.90	N J Hancock and S J Mathison	Barton 8. 2.07P
	(Built P Clegg - pr.no.PFA 204-11897) (Rotax 582) *(Tri-cycle u/c)*					*(Cancelled 21. 1.08 by CAA)*	
	(Had accident 7. 8.06 Warrington (Cheshire) strip: noted in workshops near Leyland 12.07 on rebuild with Jabiru 2200B)						
G-BSXP	Air Command 532 Elite	0633			5.11.90	(R Light)	Stockport
	(Built B J West)					*(Cancelled 8.12.00 as PWFU: reported dismantled 8.06)*	
G-BSYK	Piper PA-38-112 Tomahawk II	38-81A0143	N23449		23. 1.91	Flychoice Ltd	Halfpenny Green
						(No CofA issued: cancelled 10. 3.99 by CAA: stored 10.07)	
G-BSYL	Piper PA-38-112 Tomahawk II	38-81A0172	N91333		23. 1.91	Flychoice Ltd	Halfpenny Green
						(No CofA issued: cancelled 10. 3.99 by CAA: stored 10.07)	
G-BSYM	Piper PA-38-112 Tomahawk II	38-82A0072	N2507V		30. 1.91	Flychoice Ltd	Wellesbourne Mountford 4. 9.94T
						(Damaged 27. 7.94: cancelled 26.10.00 by CAA: dumped 5.05)	
G-BTAR	Piper PA-38-112 Tomahawk	38-79A0383	N2584D		13. 2.91	Aerohire Ltd	Blackpool 12. 3.00T
						(Damaged Liverpool 19. 6.98: cancelled 9. 4.02 by CAA: noted 10.07)	
G-BTBN	Denney Kitfox Model 2	686			31.12.90	R C Bowley	Croft Farm, Defford 19. 8.04P
	(Built Valley Avon Flying Group - pr.no.PFA 172-11859)					*(Cancelled 21. 7.05 as WFU)*	
G-BTFP	Piper PA-38-112 Tomahawk	38-78A0340	N6201A		17. 4.91	CMV Ltd	Bagby 6. 8.00T
						(Cancelled 10.10.05 by CAA: stored 2.08)	
G-BTIG	Montgomerie-Bensen B 8MR	PFA G/01-1093			21. 3.91	K Jarvis	Kirkbride 10. 4.04P
	(Built N Beale and D Beevers) (Rotax 532)					*(Cancelled 13. 4.04 by CAA: noted 7.08)*	
G-BTIN	Cessna 150C	15059905	N7805Z		26. 3.91	Perth Technical College	Perth 17. 4.00
					(Overturned by gales Edinburgh 23.12.99 and cancelled 10. 5.01 as WFU: as instructional airframe 1.06)		
G-BTLL	Pilatus P 3-03	323-5	A-806		18. 4.91	D L Masters	Headcorn 23. 6.94P
						(Cancelled 27.10.95 by CAA: stored as "A-806" c/s 6.05)	
G-BTRE	Reims Cessna F172H	F17200657	N10657		3. 7.91	S Clark	(London SW4) 18.10.07E
					(Cancelled 24. 1.05 as Destroyed: noted 3.05 on trailer Northbound on M20 near Aylesford, Kent)		
G-BTRX	Cameron V-77 Balloon (Hot Air)	1143	VH-HIH		12. 7.91	R P Jones and N P Hemsley	Horsham and Crawley 16. 4.97A
						(Cancelled 2. 5.97 as WFU: inflated 6.02)	
G-BTSC	Evans VP-2	PFA 063-10342			20.10.78	G B O'Neill	Hulcote Farm, Salford, Bedford 13. 2.96P
	(Built D J Keam- Truro School) (Arrow GT500)					*(Cancelled 20. 1.03 by CAA, noted stored 7.08)*	
G-BTUD	CFM Image	IM-01	G-MWPV		21. 8.91	D G Cook	(Aldringham, Leiston) 21. 1.95P
	(Built D G Cook - pr.no.PFA 222-12012)					*(Cancelled 5. 2.99 as PWFU: noted 2007)*	
G-BTVG	Cessna 140	12350	N2114N		30. 8.91	V C Gover	Kirknewton 15. 4.99P
						(Cancelled 18. 5.01 by CAA: noted 3.06)	
G-BTYX	Cessna 140	11004	N76568		27.11.91	J R H Willis and A Coulson tr G-BTYX Group	
			NC76568			*(Cancelled 10. 4.01 by CAA: stored 6.05)*	Rochester 23. 2.98T
G-BUDY	Colt 17A Cloudhopper Balloon (Hot Air)	413			28. 6. 82	Bondbaste Ltd	(France) 19. 1.94A
						(Cancelled 19. 5.93 by CAA: active 1.07)	
G-BUEZ	Hawker Hunter F 6A	S4/U/3275	8736M		3. 4.92	The Old Flying Machine (Air Museum) Company Ltd	
	(Built Armstrong-Whitworth Aircraft Ltd)		XF375			*(Cancelled 28. 8.01 as WFU: noted 10.07)* Spanhoe	
G-BUFF	Wassmer Jodel D 112	1302	F-BMYD		9. 8.78	(M Mold)	Watchford Farm, Yarcombe
					(Cancelled 29. 8.91 by CAA - no CofA or Permit issued: fuselage noted 8.07)		
G-BUGI	Evans VP-2	PFA 7201			16. 4.92	J A Rees	Long Marston 12. 1.04P
	(Built D Silsbury) (Continental A65-8)					*(Cancelled 24. 7.06 by CAA: noted 12.06)*	
G-BUOC	Cameron A-210 Balloon (Hot Air)	2924			5.10.92	(C Bailey)	Not known 12. 6.03T
						(Cancelled 7. 1.05 by CAA: extant 1.07)	
G-BUWJ	Pitts S-1C	2002	N110R		25. 3.93	G Breen tr G-BUWJ Flying Group *(Cancelled 8.12.05 by CAA)*	
	(Built J T Griffins) (Lycoming O-320)					Portimão, Faro, Portugal 14. 4.06P	
G-BUZL	Magni M-16 Tandem Trainer	VPM16-UK-105			18. 6.93	C M Jones	Kirkbride 22. 4.08P
	(Rotax 914)					*(Cancelled 20.11.07 by CAA)*	
G-BVBF	Piper PA-28-151 Cherokee Warrior	28-7515206	N31JM		22. 7.93	R K Spence	Cardiff
			N32633			*(No UK CofA issued: cancelled 18. 3.99 by CAA: noted 1.06)*	
G-BVKV	Cameron N-90 Balloon (Hot Air)	3236			24. 3.94	Pringle of Scotland Ltd	Hawick 3. 2.97A
						(Cancelled 24. 9.01 as PWFU: stored 2006)	
G-BVOD	Montgomerie-Parsons Two-Place Gyroplane				8. 6.94	J M Montgomerie	Crosshill
		G/08-1238				*(Cancelled 23.11.00 as WFU - no PtoF issued: noted hung in rafters 8.05)*	
G-BVXC	English Electric Canberra B(I).8	6649	WT333		9. 1.95	Classic Aviation Projects Ltd	Bruntingthorpe
						(Cancelled 22. 4.03 as PWFU: as "WT333" 3.06)	
G-BWAE	Rotary Air Force RAF 2000	PFA G/13-1252			27. 2.95	D P Kearns	(Lichfield) 23. 7.03P
	(Built B J Crockett)				*(Damaged Kemble 30. 7.96: cancelled 1. 9.03 as WFU: noted on M25 Westbound 1.06)*		
G-BWBC	Cameron N-90AS Balloon (Hot Air)	3574			12. 6.95	Wetterauer Montgolfieren EV "Zeppelin"	
						(Cancelled 31. 1.06 by CAA) Budingen, Germany 16. 3.06A	
G-BWCW	Barnett Rotorcraft J4B	PFA G/14-1256			5. 5.95	S H Kirkby	Farley Farm, Romsey
	(Built S H Kirkby)					*(Cancelled 2. 3.05 as PWFU: stored 10.07)*	
G-BWLX	Westland Scout AH.1	F9709	XV134		29.12.95	JM Helicopters Ltd	Oaksey Park 13. 8.04P
						(As "XV134:P" in AAC c/s: cancelled 7. 9.04 by CAA: stored 6.05)	

G-BWNX	Thunder Ax10-180 Series2 Balloon (Hot Air)		G-OWBC	2. 1.96	MJN Balloon Management Ltd	London SW1	2. 4.01T
		2352			*(Cancelled 26. 2.02 by CAA: noted 3.05)*		
G-BWOL	Hawker Sea Fury FB.11	ES.3617 & 61631	D-CACY (2)	18. 3.96	The Old Flying Machine (Air Museum) Company Ltd		
			G-9-66, WG599			Catfield, Norfolk	
					(Cancelled 4. 1.01 by CAA: on restoration)		
G-BWTF	Lindstrand Bear SS Balloon (Hot Air)	375		3. 6.96	Free Enterprise Balloons Ltd	London SE16	31.10.06A
					(Cancelled 9.10.06 by CAA: active Albuquerque, New Mexico, US 10.06 as "G-BWTF")		
G-BWTU	Lindstrand LBL 77A Balloon (Hot Air)	376		17. 6.96	Virgin Airship and Balloon Company Ltd	Telford	14. 1.02A
					(Cancelled 31. 1.03 as PWFU: noted active Tavistock 8.06)		
G-BWUW	British Aircraft Corporation BAC 145 Jet Provost T 5A			18. 7.96	North East Wales Institute		
		EEP/JP/1045	XW423			Deeside College, Connah's Quay, Deeside	14. 2.02P
					(Cancelled 29. 6.06 as PWFU: to Instructional airframe.as "XW423:14" in RAF c/s)		
G-BWVL	Cessna 150M	15077229	N50NA	13. 8.96	A D Shaw	Kemble	18. 1.03T
			N63286		*(Cancelled 26. 4.05 by CAA: stored 8.06)*		
G-BWWJ	Hughes 269C	113-0256	G-BMYZ	25. 2.87	Dave Nieman Models Ltd	Ashley Farm	26.10.96
	(Hughes 300C)		N8996F		*(Cancelled 25. 6.02 by CAA: stored 6.08)*		
G-BXBB	Piper PA-20 Pacer	20-959	EC-AOZ	24. 1.97	M.E.R.Coghlan	Farley Farm, Romsey	
			N1133C		*(Cancelled 22. 4.03 by CAA: stored as "EC-AOZ")*		
G-BXBH	Hunting Percival P 84 Jet Provost T 3A		XM365	29. 1.97	G-BXBH Provost Ltd	North Weald	31. 8.01P
		PAC/W/9241			*(Cancelled 10.10.02 by CAA: noted as "XM365" 1.09)*		
G-BXDD	Rotary Air Force RAF 2000 GTX-SE			9. 1.97	A Wane	Kirkbride	4. 7.00P
	(Built R M Savage)	PFA G/13-1284			*(Noted 5.07: cancelled 25. 9.07 by CAA)*		
G-BXMW	Cameron A-275 Balloon (Hot Air)	4247		19. 2.98	Ballooning Network Ltd	Bristol	23. 9.04T
					(Cancelled 23. 9.04 as PWFU: noted 2006)		
G-BXSB	Cameron PM-80 Balloon (Hot Air)	4298		11. 3.98	Flying Pictures Ltd	(US)	13.10.02A
	(Coca Cola bottle)				*(Cancelled 31. 1.02 by CAA: active 2006)*		
G-BXYU	Reims Cessna F152 II	F15201804	OH-CKD	31. 7.98	Exeter Flying Club Ltd	Exeter	24. 8.01T
			SE-IFY				
					(Cancelled 16.10.99 as destroyed Whiddon Down, Okehampton 2. 8.99, unmarked fuselage noted 12.05)		
G-BYDX	American General AG-5B Tiger	10051	N374SA	6. 1.99	A J Watson tr Bibit Group	Farley Farm, Romsey	5. 5.08
			G-BYDX, F-GKBH, N1191Y				
					(Damaged 2005: cancelled 29.11.05 as destroyed: on rebuild 10.07)		
G-BYED	British Aircraft Corporation BAC 145 Jet Provost T 5A			23.11.98	M A Petrie and J E Rowley	Hawarden	23. 5.01P
		EEP/JP/966	N166A, XW302		*(Cancelled 30.12.04 as WFU: noted 5.05)*		
G-BYFK	Cameron Printer 105 SS Balloon (Hot Air) 4522			4. 3.99	Flying Pictures Ltd	Chilbolton, Stockbridge	26. 5.03A
					(Samsung Printers titles) (Cancelled 29. 9.03 as WFU)		
G-BYIW	Cameron PM-80 Balloon (Hot Air)	4596		14. 5.99	A Schneider	Borken, Germany	27. 4.05A
	(Coca Cola bottle)				*(Cancelled 28. 1.05 by CAA)*		
G-BYKR	Piper PA-28-161 Warrior II	2816061	HB-PLM	22. 6.99	Oxford Aviation Services Ltd	Oxford	11. 8.08E
					(Engine failed on take off Oxford 30. 8.06 and substantially damaged: cancelled 22. 8.07 as destroyed: noted 8.07)		
G-BYKX	Cameron N-90 Balloon (Hot Air)	4657		10. 8.99	G Davis "Knowledgepool"	Reading	9. 6.08A
					(Cancelled 1.8.07 by CAA)		
G-BYOV	Cyclone Airsports Pegasus Quantum 15-912			17. 8.99	Microlight Hire Ltd	Wickenby	14.11.07P
		7554			*(Cancelled 3. 1.08 by CAA)*		
G-BYOY	Canadair CL-30 (T-33AN) Silver Star Mk.3		N36TH	8. 2.00	K K Gerstorfer	North Weald	
		T33-231	N333DV, N134AT, N10018, N134AT, RCAF 21231				
					(Cancelled 8. 6.05 by CAA: noted as "N36TH" in USAF c/s 1.09)		
G-BZAJ	WSK PZL-110 Koliber 160A	04990082	SP-WGK	10. 2.00	Koliber (No1) Ltd	North Weald	
					(Crashed Clayton 26.10.05 with extensive damage: cancelled 9. 5.06 as destroyed: fuselage dumped 6.07 as "AJ")		
G-BZBD	Westland Scout AH.1	F 9638	XT632	7. 3.00	Military Helicopters Ltd	North Weald	10. 7.01P
					(Cancelled 5.10.00 as PWFU: to Kennet Aviation for spares or restoration 1.06)		
G-BZDT	Maule MXT-7-180 Super Rocket	14099C		11. 8.00	Strongcrew Ltd	East Winch	2 .8.06
					(Cancelled 1.12.05 as destroyed: noted wrecked 10.08)		
G-BZFG	Sky 105-24 Balloon (Hot Air)	4842		27. 4.00	Virgin Airship and Balloon CompanyLtd	Telford	28. 4.03A
					(Cancelled 12.11.03 as PWFU: inflated 4.06)		
G-BZRC	de Havilland DH.115 Vampire T 11	15143	WZ584	26. 3.01	(D Copley)	Armthorpe, Doncaster	
					(Cancelled 22. 2.05 by CAA: dismantled as "WZ584:K" 12.05)		
G-BZRD	de Havilland DH.115 Vampire T 11	15687	XH313	27. 3.01	(D Copley)	Tangmere, Sussex	
					(Dismantled as "XH313:E" 1.05: cancelled 22. 2.05 by CAA)		
G-BZRE	Hunting Percival P 56 Provost T 1 PAC/F/265		7689M?	15. 5.01	(Parkhouse Aviation)	Bournemouth	
			WW450		*(Cancelled 22. 2.05 by CAA: fuselage stored as "WW421:P-B" 11.08)*		
	(Officially regd with c/n PAC/F/234 as fitted with wings from 7688M? ex WW421)						
G-BZRF	Hunting Percival P 56 Provost T 1 PAC/F/062		7698M	15. 5.01	(Parkhouse Aviation)	Exeter	
			WV499		*(Cancelled 22. 2.05 by CAA: dismantled as "WV499:P-G" 1.07)*		
G-BZTU	Mainair Blade 912	1272-0201-7-W1066		8. 2.01	I Johnson	Ellough, Beccles	24. 3.05P
					(Had accident Waldringfield, Suffolk 31. 5.04 and cancelled 25.11.04 as destroyed: noted 12.04)		
G-BZVL	Aero-Vodochody L-39C Albatros	730932	ES-YLB	22. 4.02	Rocket Seat Ltd	Alton	25. 4.03P
			Soviet AF		*(Cancelled 8. 1.03 as PWFU: noted Air Salvage International 8.07)*		
G-BZWR	Mainair Rapier	1275-0301-7-W1070		7. 3.01	R J Swann	Carlisle	24. 8.04P
					(Cancelled 22. 9.04 by CAA: noted 2.07)		
G-CBCU	BAe.Harrier GR.3	FL/41H-0250295	ZD668	9.11.01	Y DumortierHannants Model Warehouse, Oulton Broad		
	(C/n officially quoted as 41H-0250295)				*(Cancelled 14. 3.05 as sold to USA: noted 2.07)*		
G-CBFD	Westland Gazelle HT.Mk.2	1158	XW887	24.10.01	Aerocars Ltd	Deer Park Farm, Babcary	20.12.04P
					(Cancelled 4. 8.04 by CAA: cab and frame noted 12.07)		
G-CBGK	BAe.Harrier GR.3	FL/41H-0150252	9220M	13.12.01	Y DumortierHannants Model Warehouse, Oulton Broad		
	(C/n officially quoted as 41H-712218)		XZ995		*(Cancelled 14. 3.05 as sold to USA: noted 2.07)*		
G-CCBI	Raj Hamsa X'Air R100(2)	600		4. 2.03	H Adams	Kirkbride	14. 9.06P
	(Built H Adams - pr.no.BMAA/HB/192)				*(Cancelled 6. 3.06 by CAA)*		
G-CCIC	Thruster T 600N 450 Sprint 0036-T600N-086			25. 7.03	M L Smith	Popham	6.10.05P
					(Cancelled 26. 3.07 as PWFU: noted 5.07)		
G-CCJS	Reality Easy Raider	0002		2. 9.03	K Wright	Andreas, Isle of Man	
	(Built K Wright - pr.no.BMAA/HB/293)				*(Noted 10.07: cancelled 7. 1.08 by CAA)*		
G-CCNL	Raj Hamsa X'Air Falcon 133(1)	909		24.12.03	G A J Salter	Longacre Farm, Sandy	20. 7.06P
	(Built S Rance and A Davis - pr.no.BMAA/HB/326)				*(Cancelled 31. 7.06 by CAA) (Noted 9.06)*		

G-CCOA Scottish Aviation Bulldog Series 120/122   Ghana AF G-111 4. 9.96 Cranfield University   (Isle of Wight)
                                    BH120/375 G-BCUU   (Damaged Cranfield 22. 8.01: cancelled 11. 6.02 as WFU)
                        (Fuselage noted 2004 as "G-AXEH" to represent prototype Bulldog for proposed Beagle museum)
G-CDCZ Mainair Pegasus Quantum 15-912   8072   1.10.04 Light Flight LtdLower Mountpleasant Farm, Chatteris 3.10.06P
                                                                (Cancelled - sold as ZU- ECB 26. 1.06: noted as "G-CDCZ" 3.06)
G-CEXP Handley Page HPR.7 Dart Herald 209   195 I-ZERC   29.10.87 British Airports Authority   London Gatwick 7.11.96T
                                            G-BFRJ, 4X-AHO   (WFU 8.3.96: cancelled 22. 3.96 by CAA: stored 10.05)
G-CFLY Cessna 172F   17252635 PH-SNO   25. 8.78 I Hughes and B T Williams tr Cee-Fly   Blackpool   13. 7.95
                                            N8731U   (Cancelled 5. 6.95 by CAA: stored 10.07)
G-CHTT Varga 2150A Kachina   VAC-162-80   7. 9.84 H W Hall   Southend   6. 9.87
                    (Damaged near Hatherleigh, Devon 27. 4.86 and cancelled 9. 8.94 by CAA: wreck stored dismantled 2.08)
G-CONV Convair 440-54 Metropolitan   484 CS-TML   19. 7.01 Atlantic Air Transport Ltd   Coventry
        (Built General Dynamics Corporation)   N357SA, N28KE, N28KA, N4402
                            (Atlantic c/s with Air Atlantique titles - minus engines - in open store 6.06: cancelled 20.12.06 as WFU)
G-DADS Hughes 369HS (Hughes 500)   22-0369S N888SS   11. 6.90 Executive Aviation Services Ltd   Sywell   2. 8.02T
                                            N9101F   (Cancelled 31.10.02 as destroyed : noted stored 7.07)
G-DAJW K & S Jungster I   PFA 1517   20.11.78 A J Walters   (Tranent)
                                                                (Cancelled 2. 9.91 by CAA: reported as stored 2004)
G-DESS Mooney M 20J Model 201   24-1272 N11598   20.10.87 R M Hitchin   Stock   18. 5.06
                    (Badly damaged landing 14.11.04 Wadswick Manor Farm, Corsham : cancelled 17. 3.05 as destroyed: wreckage noted 1.07)
G-DKGF Viking Dragonfly Mk.1   PFA 139-10898   16.10.86 P C Dowbor   Enstone
        (Built K G Fathers) (Volkswagen 1834)   (Cancelled 29. 3.01 by CAA: derelict 5.05)
G-DRCI Avtech Jabiru UL   xxxx   20. 9.04 D R Calo   (Chipperfield, Kings Langley)
        (Built D R Calo - pr.no.PFA 274A-14301)   (Cancelled 19. 1.05 by CAA no PtoF yet issued)
G-ECAT Fokker F-27 Friendship 500   10672 G-JEAI   14. 4.00 Euroceltic Airways Ltd
                                            VH-EWZ, PH-EXS   Strandhill, Sligo, County Sligo 16.12.02T
                    (Skidded off end of runway in heavy rain Sligo 3.11.02, badly damaged and cancelled 12. 8.03 by CAA: fuselage with Fire Service 6.07)
G-EGGG Lindstrand LBL 90A Balloon (Hot Air)   269   14. 6.95 S M Edwards (Humpty Dumpty shape)
                                                                                Houston. Texas, US
                            (Cancelled 26.2.97 by CAA: to N912HD 5.97: active Albuquerque, NM, US 10.03 as "G-EGGG")
G-EIIR Cameron N-77 Balloon (Hot Air)   358   16.11.77 D V Howard   Bath   14. 5.93A
                                                                (Cancelled by CAA 23.10.01: stored 1.07)
G-EMIL Messerschmitt Bf109E-3   1983 Luftwaffe 1983? 11.12.03 G R Lacey   Fairoaks
                        (Fuselage complete with wings and engine work under way 2007: cancelled 11.1.07 by CAA)
G-FANC Fairchild 24R-46 Argus   R46-347 N77647   16.10.89 A T Fines   Priory Farm, Tibenham 26. 5.03T
                                            NC77647
                        (Cancelled 30. 7.03 by CAA after arson attack Felthorpe 18. 2.03: fuselage noted 2007)
G-FAYE Reims Cessna F150M   F15001252 PH-VSK   24. 1.80 Cheshire Air Training Services Ltd   Sibson   29. 7.07T
                        (Withdrawn for spares 8.06: cancelled 8.1.07 by CAA: noted 9.08)
G-FBIX de Havilland DH.100 Vampire FB.9   22100 7705M   24. 7.91 D G Jones   Bournemouth
                                            WL505   (Cancelled 17. 5.05 by CAA: stored unmarked 1.07)
G-FISK Pazmany PL-4A   PFA 017-10129   14.12.88 K S Woodard   Little Snoring 11. 4.96P
        (Built K S Woodard) (Volkswagen 1834)   (Cancelled 8.11.00 by CAA: noted stored 8.05)
G-FLAP Cessna A152 Aerobat   A1520856 G-BHJB   14. 6.02 JN Leasing Ltd   Sandtoft   18. 9.08E
                                            N4662A   (Cancelled 20.10.06 by CAA)
G-FLTY Embraer EMB-110P1 Bandeirante   110215 G-ZUSS   28. 8.92 Skydrift Ltd   Southend   5. 8.05T
                                    G-REGA, N711NH, PT-GMH (Cancelled 11. 4.06 by CAA: in open store, engineless 10.08)
G-FTAX Cessna 421C Golden Eagle   421C0308 N8363G   23. 8.84 Gold Air International Ltd   Cambridge 16. 5.01T
                                            G-BFFM, N8363G
                                                                (Cancelled 8. 7.03 as WFU: noted in open store minus various parts 9.03)
G-FUJI Fuji FA.200-180 Aero Subaru   FA200-156 D-EMMI   14. 9.79 R Gizzi   Glebe Farm, Stockton 29. 6.92
                        (Damaged landing in field Newton, Powys 5. 5.92: cancelled 1.3.94 as WFU: noted 9.06)
G-FXII Vickers Supermarine 366 Spitfire F XIIE   EN224   4.12.89 (P R Arnold)   Not known
                                    6S/197707   (Cancelled 9. 5.02 as temporarily WFU: in store 2006)
G-FYAP Williams Mk.2 Balloon (Minimum Lift) MDW-03   6. 1.82 G E Clarke   Luton
                                                                (Cancelled 8.12.88 by CAA: extant 5.07)
G-FYBB Chown Portswood Mk.16 Balloon (Minimum Lift)   15. 1.82 A P Chown   Southampton
                                    ASK-151   (Cancelled 15.10.84 as PWFU: extant 5.07)
G-FYBO Chown Osprey Mk.4B Balloon (Minimum Lift)   29. 1.82 D Eaves   Southampton
                                    AKC-94   (Cancelled 27.10.88 as PWFU: extant 5.07)
G-FYBP Eaves European E 84PW Balloon (Minimum Lift)   29. 1.82 D Eaves   Southampton
                                    S 20   (Cancelled 30.11.01 as PWFU: extant 5.07)
G-FYBX Chown Portswood Mk.16 Balloon (Minimum Lift)   1. 2.82 I Chadwick   Partridge Green, Horsham
                                    ASK-161   (Cancelled 21. 4.98 as PWFU: extant 5.07)
G-FYCT Solent Osprey Mk.4D Balloon (Minimum Lift)   18. 2.82 S T Wallbank   Luton
                                    ASK-277   (Cancelled 2.12.93 by CAA: extant 5.07)
G-FYDB Eaves European E 84EL Euroliner Balloon (Minimum Lift) 17. 3.82 D Eaves   Southampton
                                    S 23   (Cancelled 27.10.88 as PWFU: extant 5.07)
G-FYDC Eaves European EDH.1 Balloon (Minimum Lift)   17. 3.82 D Eaves and H W Davies   Southampton
                                    S 24   (Cancelled 2. 1.02 as PWFU: extant 5.07)
G-FYDG Solent Osprey Mk.4D Balloon (Minimum Lift)   29. 3.82 M D Williams   Houghton Regis, Dunstable
                                    ASK-270   (Cancelled 8.11.88 as PWFU: extant 5.07)
G-FYDU Solent Osprey Mk.4D Balloon (Minimum Lift)   23. 4.82 J R Moody   Sandown, Isle of Wight
                                    ASK-267   (Cancelled 18.10.88 as PWFU: extant 5.07)
G-FYFA Eaves European E 84LD Balloon (Minimum Lift)   12.10.82 D Goddard and D Eaves   Southampton
                                    S 26   (Cancelled 2. 1.02 as PWFU: extant 5.07)
G-FYFG Eaves European E 84DE Balloon (Minimum Lift)   26.11.82 D Eaves   Southampton
                                    S 28   (Cancelled 30.11.01 as PWFU: extant 5.07)
G-FYFH Eaves European E 84DS Balloon (Minimum Lift)   26.11.82 D Eaves   Southampton
                                    S 30   (Cancelled 30.11.01 as PWFU: extant 5.07)
G-FYGH Busby Buz-B20N Balloon (Minimum Lift)   8. 6.89 D P Busby   Southampton
                                    DSD-01N   (Cancelled 18.10.95 by CAA: extant 5.07)
G-GCJL British Aerospace Jetstream Series 410041001   5. 2.91 BAE Systems (Operations) Ltd   Humberside 29. 4.95S
                                                                (Cancelled 15.11.02 as WFU: stored 6.05)

G-GRAY   Cessna 172N Skyhawk II   17272375   N4859D   3.12.79   Truman Aviation Ltd   Tollerton   13. 2.95
         (Damaged ditching Firth of Forth, Musslelurgh 2. 4.93: cancelled 27. 9.00 as WFU: stored 10.05)
G-GREG   CEA Jodel DR.220 2+2   47   F-BOKR   3.10.84   J T Wilson   Crosland Moor   19. 2.91
         (Cancelled 1. 4.97 by CAA: noted 9.07)
G-HAPR   Bristol 171 Sycamore HC.14   13387   8010M   15. 6.78   E D ap Rees t/a Helicopters Unlimited
                                                   XG547   *(As "XG547:T-S" in RAF CFS c/s)*
                                                                         (Cancelled 24. 6.08 on transfer to Royal Army Museum, Brussels)
G-HEAD   Colt Flying Head Balloon (Hot Air) 304   18. 8.81   E K Nyberg   (Stockholm, Sweden)
                                                                         (Cancelled 4.12.01 by CAA: extant 5.07)
G-HEKY   McCulloch J-2   039   G-ORVB,   14. 9.07   C J Watkinson   (Great Heck, Goole)
                                                   (G-BLGI), (G-BKKL), Bahrain Public Security BPS-3, N4329G
                                                                         (Wfu 30. 1.09, preserved Weston-Super-Mare 21.12.08)
G-HMES   Piper PA-28-161 Warrior II   28-8126070 OY-CSN   21. 4.89   Cleveland Flying Scholl Ltd   Bagby   20. 8.01T
                                                   N8471N   *(Cancelled. 5.5.04 as wfu: noted dismantled 2.08)*
G-HOST   Cameron N-77 Balloon (Hot-Air)   434   4. 9.78   D Grimshaw   (Preston)   18. 5.93A
                                                                         (Cancelled 13.11.01 as PWFU, inflated 7.08)
G-IBRO   Reims Cessna F152   F15201957 EI-BRO   11.10.95   East Midlands Aircraft Hire Ltd   Leicester   14. 3.05T
         (Engine failed during landing 1 m N Leicester 3. 3.05 and substantially damaged: canx 29. 6.05 as destroyed: bare fuselage & wings noted 10.07)
G-IJMI   Extra EA.300/L   1193   16. 2.05   Aerobatiques LLP   Hawarden   31. 3.08E
                                                                         (Cancelled 21. 1.08 by CAA)
G-IXTI   Extra EA.300/L   121   15. 9.00   J C Merry   (East Coker, Yeovil)   22.10.06T
                                                                         (Cancelled 12. 9.05 by CAA)
G-JABO   WAR Focke-Wulf FW190-A3 replica   23. 8.01   S P Taylor   Clench Common
         (Built S P Taylor)   PFA 081-11786   *(Cancelled 19. 7.07 by CAA: noted 1.08)*
G-JEAT   British Aerospace BAe 146 Series 100 E1071 N171TR   11.10.96   Jersey European Airways (UK) Ltd   Exeter   23.10.05T
                                              J8-VBB, G-BVUY, B-2706, G-5-071   *(Cancelled 4. 8.04 as WFU: on fire dump 1.07)*
G-JSCL   Rans S-10 Sakota   1289.075   12. 4.90   D L Davies   Emlyns Field, Rhuallt
         (Built J D Bedford - pr.no PFA 194-11781)   *(Crashed Emlyns Field 16. 7.91: cancelled 16.12.97 as WFU: remains noted 4.04)*
G-KNOT   Hunting Percival P 84 Jet Provost T 3A   9. 6.99   R S Partridge-Hicks   North Weald   10.10.07P
                                     PAC/W/13893 G-BVEG
                                                   XN629   *(Cancelled 21. 6.07 as WFU: noted as "XN629:49" in RAF c/s 1.09)*
G-LEZE   Rutan LongEz   PFA 074A-10702   31. 3.82   K G M Loyal, A J Draper, J R J Giesler and C McGeachy
         (Built K G M Loyal) (Wilksch Diesel)   *(Cancelled 22. 5.03 by CAA: on rebuild 2006)* Nympsfield   5.11.01P
G-LOFG   Lockheed L188C Electra   1116   LN-FOL (2) 21. 6.00   Atlantic Air Transport Ltd   Coventry
                                                   N669F, N404GN, N6126A
         (Cancelled 16.6.04 as destroyed; airframe, minus starboard outer wing, on fire dump as "LN-FOL" 6.06)
G-LOWE   Monnett Sonerai I   367   16.11.78   R M Kinch   Shenington   12. 8.97P
         (Built J A Lowe - pr.no.PFA 15-10344) (Volkswagen 1834)   *(Cancelled 16. 9.97 as Temporarily WFU: noted 5.08)*
G-LYDD   Piper PA-31 Turbo Navajo   31-537   G-BBDU   8. 5.89   Janes Aviation Ltd   Blackpool   12. 5.89T
                                                   N6796L
                                              (Damaged Lydd 17. 7.91, cancelled 30. 3.93 as WFU: fuselage on fire dump 11.05)
G-MALK   Reims Cessna F172N Skyhawk II F17201886 PH-SVS   1. 7.81   Edinburgh Airport Fire Service   Edinburgh
                                                   PH-AXF (3)
                                     (Crashed near Lochgilphead 23. 7.97: cancelled 23.12.97 as destroyed: fuselage for instructional use 2.06)
G-MANT   Cessna 210L Centurion II   21060970   G-MAXY   22. 5.85   Sea-Front Crazee Golf   Great Yarmouth   2.10.94
                                                   N550SV   *(Damaged near Oxford 16. 2.92, cancelled 3. 4.92 by CAA: noted 9.05)*
G-MAPS   Sky Flying Map SS Balloon (Hot Air) 105   20. 7.98   The Balloon Advertising Company Ltd "OS Map"
                                                                                                        Petworth   28. 2.01A
                                                                         (Cancelled 31. 7.01 as WFU: on loan to Balloon Preservation Group)
G-MBTG   Mainair Gemini/Southdown Sprint   26. 4.82   D M Pearson   Roddige   15.10.94P
                                     064-19482 & P 431
         (Originally regd as Mainair Tri-Flyer Dual)   *(Cancelled 31. 3.00 by CAA: noted 4.06)*
G-MBWH   Jordan Duet Series 1   D82001   20. 5.82   Designability Ltd   Kemble
                                                                         (Cancelled 22. 3.02 as WFU: noted 9.08)
G-MESS   SNCAN 1101 Noralpha   87   F-BEEV   21. 5.03   G Spooner   Earls Colne
                                                   F-WZBI, French AF 87 *(Cancelled 25. 1.07 as WFU: noted dismantled 2007)*
G-MGFO   Pegasus Quantum 15   7410   24. 3.98   A Gulliver   Clench Common   19. 3.00P
                                                                         (Cancelled 10. 5.99 by CAA: stored 5.06)
G-MHBD   Cameron O-105 Balloon (Hot Air)   1021   23. 2.84   P A Sweatman (Dawsons Toys titles) Birmingham   25. 7.90A
                                                                         (Cancelled as WFU 17. 4.98: extant 5.07)
G-MJBN   American Aerolights Eagle Rainbow 3132   (A Smith)   Sibsey
                                                                         (Cancelled 6. 9.94 by CAA: stored 1.07)
G-MJDH   Huntair Pathfinder Mk.1   015   9. 7.82   T Mahmood   Insch   12. 8.01P
         (Fuji-Robin EC-44-PM)   *(Cancelled 10. 6.02 as WFU: noted wrecked 3.07)*
G-MJLK   Squires Dragonfly 250-II   D 105   10. 9.82   G Carter   Breighton
         (Built G A Squires)   *(Cancelled 18. 4.90 as WFU: wreck stored 12.07)*
G-MJOI   Ultrasports Tri-Pacer/Hiway Demon 817003   1.11.82   S J Walker   Biggin Hill
                                                                         (Cancelled 1.11.89 as WFU: noted 6.05)
G-MJXD   MBA Tiger Cub 440   011/061   16. 5.83   (W L Rogers)   Halwell
                                                                         (Cancelled 3. 4.02 as WFU: noted 5.05)
G-MJYE   Popplewell Trike/Southdown Lightning GP-02   1. 6.83   J A Hindley   Lower Mountpleasant Farm, Chatteris   X
         (Fuji-Robin EC-44-PM)   *(Cancelled 4. 4.02 as WFU: wreck noted 5.05)*
G-MMAE   Dragon Light Aircraft Dragon Series 200 005   7. 9.82   P J Sheehy and K S Matcham   Lee-on-Solent   1. 5.08P
         (Fuji-Robin EC-44-PM)   *(Cancelled 27.10.07 by CAA)*
G-MMBE   MBA Tiger Cub 440   SO.74   30. 6.83   R W Pearce and R J B Jordan
                                                                                           Sheardale Strip, Coals Naughton
                                                                         (Cancelled 4. 2.92 by CAA: noted 9.08)
G-MMDP   Mainair Gemini Sprint X   183-22883   10. 9.84   G V Cowle   Kirkbride
                                                                         (Cancelled 18. 2.08 by CAA: noted 5.08)
G-MMIH   MBA Tiger Cub 440   SO.130   25. 4.84   R A Davis   Kemble   19. 8.93P
                                                                         (Cancelled 3. 3.05 by CAA: noted 3.06)
G-MMKY   Jordan Duet Series 1   CHS-01   19. 3.84   C H Smith   Field Farm, Oakley
         (Rotax 503)   *(Cancelled 1. 9.95 by CAA: fuselage stored 1.06)*

G-MMLV	Southdown Puma 330/Lightning	P3-84-164		29.11.84	C L Newcombe	RNAS Yeovilton 31. 5.97P

(Officially regd as Southdown Lightning/Tri-Pacer) (Fuji-Robin EC-34-PM)   *(Cancelled 30. 4.01 by CAA as PWFU: noted 3.06)*
(C/n also quoted as NOP 3-84-164)

| G-MMNV | Weedhopper JC-24 | NLR-01 | | 17. 4.84 | N L Rice | Strathaven |

(Cancelled 4. 6.90 as WFU: noted 6.06)

| G-MMUL | Ward Elf | E-47 | | 16.10.84 | N H Ponsford | Breighton |

(Built M Ward)   *(Cancelled 12. 4.89 by CAA: noted 12.07)*

| G-MMUT | Mainair Gemini Flash II | 235-484-2 -W04 | | 5.10.84 | S C Briggs | Rochdale 5. 7.01P |

(Fuji-Robin EC-44-PM) *(Original c/n 62-884-2-W04)*   *(Cancelled as PWFU 14. 1.05: noted 11.06 for trials)*
(Fitted with new Trike first used on G-MMFC (3) and Sailwing c/n W73 6.98 - also see G-MNAC)

| G-MMVP | Mainair Gemini Flash II | 76-1284-2-W12 | | 17.12.84 | S C McGowan | Longacre Farm, Sandy 24. 1.05P |

(Fuji-Robin EC-44-PM)   *(Cancelled 7. 9.04 by CAA: noted 7.05)*

| G-MMYZ | Southdown Puma Sprint | SN1231/0034 | | 28. 2.85 | M Bodill | Roddige 19. 2.99P |

(Rotax 447)   *(Damaged in gales Roddige 1.98 cancelled 31. 5.01 by CAA: Trike noted in poor state 1.04)*

| G-MMZB | Mainair Gemini Flash | 319-685-3-W58 | | 4. 3.85 | M A Nolan | (Eccleston, Chorley) 23. 5.02P |

(Fuji-Robin EC-44-PM)   *(Cancelled 24. 2.05 by CAA: engineless wreck noted 6.07)*

| G-MNBR | Mainair Gemini Flash | 345-985-3-W79 | | 15. 5.85 | N A P Gregory | Long Marston 5. 2.94P |

(Rotax 447)   *(Cancelled 31. 5.00 by CAA: stored 7.05)*

| G-MNFX | Southdown Puma Sprint | SN1231/0079 | | 14. 8.85 | A M Shaw | (Eccleston, Chorley) 6. 9.04P |

(Rotax 447)   *(Cancelled 15. 2.05 as PWFU: engineless wreck noted 6.07)*

| G-MNGO | Hiway Skytrike/Solar Wings Storm | 21U8 | | 5. 9.85 | S Adams | (Gaddesbry) |

(Cancelled 20. 3.89 by CAA: stored 2005)

| G-MNMO | Mainair Gemini Flash II | 398-186-4-W141 | | 27. 2.86 | P D Hawkesworth and G Wigglesworth | |
| | | | | | | Bere Alston, Yelverton 28. 5.99P |

(Rotax 447)   *(Cancelled 10. 3.00 by CAA: Trike noted 11.06)*

| G-MNNL | Mainair Gemini Flash II | 429-486-4-W186 | | 28. 2.86 | D Wilson | Oxton, Nottingham 21.11.05P |

(Noted 9.07: cancelled 13.11.07 by CAA)

| G-MNTS | Mainair Gemini Flash II | 450-886-4-W227 | | 3. 4.86 | C G Lomas | (Brotherton, Boston) 16. 1.02P |

(Rotax 462)   *(New owner 3.07: cancelled 18. 9.07 by CAA)*

| G-MNYV | Solar Wings Pegasus XL-R/Se | SW-WA-1093 | | 11. 9.86 | (B J Green) | Sywell 30.11.99P |

(Trike c/n SW-TB-1101)   *(Cancelled 23. 8.02 by CAA: noted 2.07)*

| G-MTBA | Solar Wings Pegasus XL-R | SW-WA-1115 | | 27.10.86 | R J W Franklin and M C Buffery | Redlands, Swindon 24. 6.93P |

(Trike c/n SW-TB-1120)   *(Cancelled 19. 4.05 by CAA: noted as wreck 8.05)*

| G-MTBT | Aerotech MW.5B Sorcerer | SR102-R440B-05 | | 10. 4.87 | N W Finn-Kelcey | Weston Underwood, Olney 19. 5.92P |

(Fuji-Robin EC-44-PM) *(pr.no BMAA/HB/027 allocated for rebuild after accident 12.10.91 using wings of G-MWGI (qv))*
(Cancelled 7. 8.96 by CAA: noted 9.07)

| G-MTBW | Mainair Gemini Flash II | 520-187-5-W322 | | 6.11.86 | J Sharman | Otherton, Cannock 21. 9.97P |

(Cancelled 23. 2.98 by CAA: noted 7.05)

| G-MTCW | Mainair Gemini Flash II | 502-1186-4-W304 | | 5. 1.87 | E W Hughes | (Eccleston, Chorley) 21. 4.07P |

(Rotax 462)   *(Cancelled 19.12.06 by CAA: noted 6.07)*

| G-MTDH | Solar Wings Pegasus XL-R | SW-WA-1131 | | 22. 1.87 | J Packman | Long Marston 23. 1.07P |

(Trike c/n SW-TB-1133) *(Rebuilt 5.04 with Sailwing c/n SW-WA-1005 ex G-MNAK)*   *(Cancelled 29.10.06 by CAA)*

| G-MTDV | Solar Wings Pegasus XL-R | SW-WA-1136 | | 3. 2.87 | S J Adcock | Rufforth 28. 8.94P |

(Cancelled 8. 6.00 by CAA: noted 11.07)

| G-MTEI | Mainair Gemini Flash II | 440-287-5-W269 | | 18. 2.87 | B F Levy and R E Symonds | |
| | | | | | | (Guildford and Send, Woking) 26. 1.08P |

(Cancelled 25. 2.08 by CAA)

| G-MTEJ | Mainair Gemini Flash II | 522-387-5-W277 | | 18. 2.87 | M Atkinson | Tarn Farm, Cockerham 17. 3.06P |

(Rotax 462)   *(Noted 11.06: cancelled 21. 2.07 as wfu)*

| G-MTXH | Solar Wings Pegasus XL-Q | SW-WQ-0030 | | 11. 3.88 | J Rhodes | Church Farm, Askern 21. 7.97P |

(Rotax 447) *(Trike c/n SW-TB-1328)*   *(Cancelled 12. 5.05 by CAA: wing only noted 9.07)*

| G-MVDS | Hiway Skytrike/Demon 175 | PB-01 | | 30. 6.88 | P Butler | Broadmeadow Farm, Hereford |

(Cancelled 24. 1.95 by CAA: stored 11.06)

| G-MVFW | Solar Wings Pegasus XL-Q | SW-WA-1371 | | 9. 8.98 | S F Chaplin *(stored 9.08)* | Haverfordwest 28. 8.00P |
| G-MVHN | Aerial Arts Chaser S | CH.728 | | 9. 8.88 | J E Sweetingham | Benson's Farm, Laindon 10. 6.01P |

(Cancelled 4. 2.05 as PWFU: noted 1.08)

| G-MVME | Thruster TST Mk.1 | 8128-TST-110 | | 12.12.88 | S J Payne | Wing Farm, Longbridge Deverill 10. 4.06P |

(Cancelled 21. 8.06 as WFU: noted for spares 4.07)

| G-MVSU | Microflight Spectrum | 008 | | 4. 5.89 | M W Shepherd | Otherton, Cannock 21. 5.04P |

(Cancelled 22. 4.04 as destroyed: noted 5.07)

| G-MVYF | Hornet R-ZA | HRWB0066/ZA112 | | 22. 9.89 | Hornet Microlights Ltd | Kirkbride |

(Cancelled 08. 1.91 by CAA: noted 5.08)

| G-MVZR | Aviasud Mistral 532GB | 090 | | 9.10.89 | S E and J A Robinson | Crosland Moor 7. 6.01P |

(Built Aviasud Engineering - pr.no.BMAA/HB/011)   *(Cancelled 14. 3.05 by CAA: noted 9.07)*

| G-MWBR | Hornet RS-ZA | HRWB-0084/ZA145 | | 29.11.89 | I A Clark | Longacre Farm, Sandy 4. 9.06P |

(Cancelled 18. 6.07 by CAA: noted 7.07)

| G-MWCP | Powerchute Kestrel | 91252 | | 3. 1.90 | Iris Fraser | Insch 20.10.01P |

(Cancelled 10. 5.05 by CAA: stored 11.05)

| G-MWHS | AMF Chevvron 2-32C | 021 | | 18. 5.90 | Airshare Flying Club Ltd | Kirkbride |

(Cancelled 22.11.00 by CAA: noted 5.08)

| G-MWJZ | CFM Shadow Series CD | K 132 | | 19. 7.90 | D Mahajan | Lower Mountpleasant Farm, Chatteris 23. 7.99P |

(Severely damaged Chatteris during 1999: cancelled 24.12.01 as WFU: engine and wings removed and stored 5.05)

| G-MYBG | Solar Wings Pegasus XL-Q | SW-WQ-0514 | | 26. 3.92 | M Aylett and P A Henretty | Swinford, Rugby 9. 7.03P |

(Trike c/n SW-TE-0385)   *(Cancelled 2..6.06 by CAA: noted damaged 10.07)*

| G-MYUL | Quad City Challenger II UKCH2-1293-UK-1063 | | | 10. 1.95 | P Knott | Crosland Moor 24. 5.02P |

(Built A G Easson - pr.no.PFA 177-12687)   *(Cancelled 24. 5.05 by CAA: noted 9.07)*

| G-MYWB | Edel Corniche-Scorpion | 004 | | 31. 3.95 | P F Funnell | Rufforth |

(Built Edel - pr.no.BMAA/HB/071)   *(Cancelled 7. 8.98 by CAA: noted 11.07)*

| G-MZAK | Mainair Mercury | 1070-0296-7-W872 | | 15. 1.96 | M J Taylor | Rochdale 16. 5.05P |

(Cancelled 30. 6.05 as transferred to South Africa: trike & wings stored at P&M Avn 12.08)

| G-NAAT | Folland Gnat T 1 | FL.507 | XM697 | 27.11.89 | Hunter Flying Club | Exeter |

(Cancelled 10..4.95 as WFU: noted 12.05)

Reg	Type	C/n	Prev id	Date	Owner/Operator	Location	
G-NBSI	Cameron N-77 Balloon (Hot Air)	427		3. 8.78	D S Dunlop and A J Matthews tr Nottingham Hot Air Balloon Club	Nottingham	21. 4.91A
					(Cancelled 14. 6.93 as WFU: active 9.05)		
G-NFLC	Handley Page HP137 Jetstream 1	222	G-AXUI G-8-9	12.12.95	Air Service Training	Perth	3. 6.04T
					(Cancelled 3.8.04 as WFU: used as instructional airframe 1.06)		
G-NRDC	NDN Aircraft NDN-6 Fieldmaster	004		8. 6.81	EPA Aircraft Company Ltd Sandown, Isle of Wight		17.10.87P
					(Cancelled 3. 2.95 by CAA: wreck noted 4.06)		
G-OEWA	de Havilland DH.104 Dove 8	04528	G-DDCD G-ARUM	10. 6.98	D.C.Hunter	Little Rissington	
					(Cancelled 24. 5.05 by CAA: stored 1.08 as "G-DDCD")		
G-OFMB	Rand-Robinson KR-2	7808	N5337X	29. 4.97	F M and S I Burden	Gloucestershire	
	(Built M A Shepard)				*(Cancelled 10. 1.06 as PWFU: on fire dump 2.08)*		
G-OHEA	Hawker Siddeley HS 125 Series 3B/RA	25144	G-AVRG G-5-12	25.11.86	Cranfield University	Cranfield	7. 8.92T
					(Cancelled 23. 6.94 as WFU: fuselage dumped 2.08)		
G-OICV	Robinson R22 Beta	0991	G-BPWH	11. 2.93	Helicentre Ltd	Blackpool	18. 3.01
					(Damaged Blackpool 18. 7.99: cancelled 19.11.99 as WFU: shell only 10.07)		
G-OLPG	Colt 77A Balloon (Hot Air)	2568		11. 3.94	D J Farrar	Collingham, Wetherby	16. 2.03
					(Cancelled 9. 3.04 by CAA)		
G-OMOG	Gulfstream AA-5A Cheetah	AA5A-0793	G-BHWR N26892	4. 3.88	Solent Flight Aircraft Ltd Phoenix Farm, Lower Upham		15. 4.02T
					(Cancelled 23. 7.01 by CAA: fuselage noted 10.05)		
G-ONOW	Bell 206A JetRanger	605	G-AYMX	8. 8.88	J Lucketti	Walton Wood	27. 4.00T
					(Cancelled 24. 5.05 by CAA: noted 11.06)		
G-OPDM	Enstrom 280FX Shark	2021	N8627Q PH-GBL, N650PG	7. 1.98	(Lamindene Ltd)	Seething	15. 5.04T
					(Crashed County Kerry 7. 6.03: cancelled 12.. 2.04 by CAA: cockpit noted 5.05)		
G-ORJX	BAE Systems Avro 146-RJX85	E2376		16. 2.00	BAE Systems (Operations) Ltd	Woodford	
					(Cancelled 12.12.02 as WFU: stored 3.06)		
G-OVNE	Cessna 401A	401A-0036	N401XX (N171SF), N71SF, N6236Q	11. 3.88	M A Billings	Norwich	8.10.92
					(Cancelled 8.. 2.94 by CAA: noted 10.05)		
G-RACA	Percival P 57 Sea Prince T 1	P57/49	WM735	2. 9.80	D A Cotton "Gods Kitchen"	Long Marston	4.11.80P
					(Cancelled 28.11.95 by CAA: derelict 7.05)		
G-RANZ	Rans S-10 Sakota	0589.050		2.11.89	O M C Dismore	Popham	27. 6.03P
	(Built B A Philips - pr.no.PFA 194-11536) (Rotax 532)				*(Cancelled 22. 9.05 by CAA: stored 10.05)*		
G-RAVL	Handley Page 137 Jetstream 200	208	G-AWVK N1035S, G-AWVK	2.12.86	Cranfield University	Cranfield	26. 2.94
					(Cancelled 30. 1.01 as WFU: for Instructional use 1.07)		
G-REID	Rotorway Scorpion 133	1147	G-BGAW	7.12.81	Not known	?	18.3.91P
					(Cancelled 19. 4.99 by CAA: noted 8.06 southbound on A34 near Winchester)		
G-SADE	Reims Cessna F150L	F15000752	G-AZJW	28. 5.91	N E Sams	Hulcote Farm, Salford, Bedford	21. 9.97T
					(Cancelled 24. 5.05 by CAA: stored 1.06)		
G-SHIV	Gulfstream GA-7 Cougar	GA7-0092	N713G	22.11.84	Wesley Aircraft Ltd	Cranfield	18.1.98T
					(Cancelled 16. 9.04 by CAA: dumped 9.08)		
G-SION	Piper PA-38-112 Tomahawk II	38-81A0146	N23661	30. 1.91	F D Dunstan t/a Naiad Air Services	Enstone	
					(Cancelled 9. 9.02 by CAA: noted 9.08)		
G-SMHK	Cameron D-38 Airship (Hot Air)	697		5. 1.81	San Miguel Brewery Ltd	Hong Kong	
					(Cancelled 14. 7.93 as PWFU: active 4.06)		
G-SSWE	Short SD.3-60 Variant 100	SH3705	SE-IXE (G-BNBA), G-14-3705	15. 7.02	BAC Leasing Ltd	Coventry	22. 8.05T
					(Cancelled 6. 6.07 as PWFU)		
G-SSWM	Short SD.3-60 Variant 100	SH3648	SE-KCI G-OAAS, OY-MMB, G-BLIL, G-14-3648	28. 9.01	BAC Leasing Ltd	Coventry	14.10.06E
					(Cancelled 6. 6.07 as PWFU)		
G-SSWO	Short SD.3-60 Variant 100	SH3609	SE-KLO N343MV, (G-BKMY), G-14-3609	8.10.01	BAC Leasing Ltd	Blackpool	4.12.04T
					(Cancelled 6. 6.07 as PWFU: stored externally 10.07)		
G-SSWR	Short SD.3-60 Variant 100	SH3670	SE-KGV HR-IAQ, N108PS, B-3603, G-BLWJ, G-14-3670	2.10.01	BAC Leasing Ltd	Coventry	13.11.06E
					(Cancelled 6. 6.07 as PWFU)		
G-STOR	Fieseler Fi 156D-0 Storch	110451	Luftwaffe 11045121. 5.03		G R Lacey	Fairoaks	
					(Cancelled 25. 1.07 as WFU: to Robert Blanchard, Miami, Florida for completion 9.07)		
G-STUK	Junkers Ju 87/R4	6234	Luftwaffe 6234 19.12.03		G R Lacey	Fairoaks	
					(Scheduled rebuild to start 2006 and be complete by 2009/2010: cancelled 11. 1.07 by CAA)		
G-THUG	MD Helicopters MD.600N	RN026	G-RHUG N92088	4. 7.00	Helidirect UK Ltd	Shoreham	17.11.00
					(Substantially damaged landing Peplow Hall, Shropshire 27. 8.00: .cancelled 22.11.00 as destroyed: wreck stored 11.05)		
G-TIGH	Aérospatiale AS.332L Super Puma	2034	F-WXFL	15. 4.82	Bristow Helicopters Ltd	Aberdeen	24. 8.92T
					(Damaged 100m NE of Shetland Isles 14. 3.92: cancelled 3. 8.92 as destroyed: for instruction use 3.06)		
G-TOBY	Cessna 172B	47852	G-ARCM N6952X	8. 4.81	J A Kelman	Shoreham	28. 4.85
					(Damaged Sandown, IoW 15.10.83: cancelled 27. 2.90 by CAA: instructional airframe 11.05)		
G-UPPY	Cameron DP-80 Airship (Hot Air)	2274		29. 3.90	Jacques W Soukup Enterprises Ltd	Bristol	27. 8.94A
					(Cancelled 15. 9.05 by CAA: active 9.05)		
G-VDIR	Cessna 310R II	310R0211	N5091J	31. 1.91	J Driver	North Weald	21. 6.07T
					(Landed on grass North Weald 4. 9.05 and severely damaged: cancelled 3. 3.06 as destroyed: noted damaged 1.09)		
G-VIBA	Cameron DP-80 Airship (Hot Air)	1729		28. 5.91	Jacques W Soukup Enterprises Ltd	Bristol	3. 2.99A
					(Cancelled 15. 9.05 by CAA: active 9.05)		
G-VULC	Avro 698 Vulcan B 2A	?	N655AV G-VULC, XM655	27. 2.84	Radarmoor Ltd	Wellesbourne Mountford	
					(Cancelled 25. 3.02 as WFU: noted 3.06 as "XM655")		
G-YROS	Bensen B 8M PFA G/101-1004			29. 1.81	Flight Academy (Gyrocopters) Ltd	Kirkbride	6. 6.97P
	(Built J M Montgomerie) (HAPI 60-6M)				*(Noted 7.08) (Cancelled 15. 5.07 by CAA)*		
G-YUGO	Hawker Siddeley HS.125 Series 1B/R-52225094			25. 8.88	RCR Aviation Ltd	Biggin Hill	19. 4.91
					(Cancelled 29. 3.93 as PWFU: noted 6.05)		
G-YURO	Europa Aviation Europa	001		6. 4.92	Europa Management (International) Ltd Wombleton		9. 6.95P
	(Built Europa Aviation Ltd - pr.no.PFA 220-11981)				*(Cancelled 22. 4.98 as WFU: noted incomplete 4.05)*		

The following preserved balloons and airships are held in the **British Balloon Museum and Library** collection based in Newbury.

Registration	Type	Construction No	Previous Identity	Reg.Date	Remarks	CofA Expy
G-ATGN	Thorn K-800 Coal Gas Balloon (Gas Filled) (Built J Thorn)	2		12. 7.65	*"Eccles"Cancelled 23. 6.81 as WFU*	
G-ATXR	Abingdon Spherical Free Balloon (Hot Air) (Built RAF Abingdon Free Balloon Club)	AFB-1		22. 7.66	*(Basket only) Cancelled 14. 7.86 by CAA*	1. 9.76
G-AVTL	Brighton Ax7-65 Balloon (Hot Air) (Built Hot-Air Group and originally regd as Hot-Air Group ¼ Free Balloon with c/n 1)	01		17. 8.67	*Cancelled 11. 9.81 as WFU*	
G-AWCR	Piccard Ax6 Balloon (Hot Air)	6204		29. 1.68	*"London Pride 1"Cancelled 24. 5.78 as WFU*	
G-AWJB	Brighton MAB-65 Balloon (Hot Air)	MAB-3		3. 5.68	*Cancelled 4.12.70 on sale to Italy (ntu) (Regd HB-BOU (1) 2.73) (As "HB-BOU")*	
G-AWMO	Omega O-84 Balloon (Hot Air) (Built Omega Aerostatics Ltd)	01		31. 7.68	*"Blue Strike" Cancelled 13. 5.69 to OY-BOB*	
G-AWOK	Sussex Gas Balloon (Gas Filled (Built University of Sussex Ballooning Society)	SARD.1		7. 8.68	*"Sardinia" Cancelled 29. 2.84 as WFU (Withdrawn 1970)*	
G-AXVU	Omega 84 Balloon (Hot Air)	09		7. 1.70	*"Henry VIII" Cancelled 22. 8.89 as WFU*	28. 4.77S
G-AXXP	Bradshaw 76 (Ax7) Balloon (Hot Air) (Built R F D Bradshaw)	RB.001		20. 2.70	*"Ignis Volens" Cancelled 9. 9.81 (WFU 2.77)*	
G-AYAJ	Cameron O-84 Balloon (Hot Air) (Built D A Cameron)	11		31. 3.70	*"Flaming Pearl"Cancelled 1. 2.90 as PWFU*	
G-AYAL	Omega 56 Balloon (Hot Air)	10		2. 4.70	*"Nimble II" Cancelled 18.10.84 by CAA*	25. 8.76S
G-AZBH	Cameron O-84 Balloon (Hot Air)	23		8. 7.71	*"Serendipity" Cancelled 30. 8.85 as WFU*	31. 3.85A
G-AZER	Cameron O-42 (Ax5) Balloon (Hot Air)	26		9. 9.71	*"Shy Tot" Cancelled 25. 3.92 by CAA*	15. 5.81A
G-AZJI	Western O-65 Balloon (Hot Air)	007		2.12.71	*"Peek-A-Boo"Cancelled 19. 5.93 by CAA*	
G-AZSP	Cameron O-84 Balloon (Hot Air)	43		18. 4.72	*"Esso" Cancelled 11. 1.82 as WFU*	22. 3.82A
G-AZUV	Cameron O-65 Balloon (Hot Air)	41		12. 5.72	*"Icarus" Cancelled 6. 1.82 by CAA (Damaged Rendham Green, Suffolk xx.xx.xx)*	23. 6.83A
G-AZUW	Cameron A-140 Balloon (Hot Air)	45		12. 5.72	*"Cumulonimbus" Cancelled 7. 6.73 - to F-WTVO 6.73, to F-BTVO and 5Y-SIL*	
G-AZYL	Portslade Free Balloon (Hot Air) (Built Portslade School)	MK 17		10. 7.72	*Cancelled 25. 4.85 as PWFU*	
G-BAMK	Cameron D-96 Airship (Hot Air)	72		11. 1.73	*"Isibidbi" Cancelled 16. 8.00 by CAA*	24. 4.90A
G-BAXF	Cameron O-77 Balloon (Hot Air)	74		3. 5.73	*"Granna" Cancelled 5. 9.95 by CAA*	20. 7.86A
G-BAXK	Thunder Ax7-77 Balloon (Hot Air)	005		9. 5.73	*"Jack O'Newbury" Cancelled 7. 9.01 as WFU*	2. 7.91A
G-BAVU	Cameron A-105 Balloon (Hot Air)	66		11. 4.73	*Cancelled 6.12.01 by CAA*	5.10.84A
G-BBFS	Vandem-Bemden K-460 (Gasfilled) Balloon (Built F Vandem-Bemden - pr/no.VDB-16)	75	OO-BGX	10. 8.73	*"Le Tomate" Cancelled 19. 5.93 by CAA*	
G-BBLL	Cameron O-84 Balloon (Hot Air)	84		2.10.73	*"Boadicea" Cancelled 19. 5.93 by CAA*	25. 5.81A
G-BBYU	Cameron O-56 Balloon (Hot Air)	96		19. 2.74	*"Chieftain" Cancelled 9. 8.89 as WFU*	28. 2.82A
G-BCAR	Thunder Ax7-77 Balloon (Hot Air)	019		5. 3.74	*"Marie Antoinette" Cancelled 2. 4.92 by CAA*	
G-BCFD	West Ax3-15 Balloon (Hot Air) (Built J West)	JW.1		16. 5.74	*"Hellfire" Cancelled 30. 1.87 by CAA*	
G-BCFE	Byrne Odyssey 4000 Balloon (Minimum Lift) (Built A J Byrne)	AJB-2		20. 5.74	*"Odyssey" Cancelled 19. 9.85 as WFU*	
G-BDVG	Thunder Ax6-56A Balloon (Hot Air)	067		2. 4.76	*"Argonaut" Cancelled 3. 4.92 by CAA*	26. 5.95A
G-BEEE	Thunder Ax6-56A Balloon (Hot Air)	070		20. 8.76	*"Avia" Cancelled 19. 5.93 by CAA*	11. 5.84A
G-BEPO	Cameron N-77 Balloon (Hot Air)	279		1. 4.77	*"Sungas" Cancelled 14. 5.98 as WFU*	27. 6.94A
G-BEPZ	Cameron D-96 Airship (Hot Air)	300		13. 4.77	*"Zanussi" Cancelled 28. 4.94 as WFU (Damaged Warren Farm, Savernake Forest 8. 1.94 and DBR during recovery)*	12. 2.90A
G-BETF	Cameron Champion 35 SS Balloon (Hot Air) (Champion Spark Plug shape)	280		17. 5.77	*"Champion" Cancelled 24. 1.92 as WFU*	6. 4.84A
G-BETH	Thunder Ax6-56A Balloon (Hot Air)	113		27. 5.77	*"Debenhams" Cancelled 11. 5.93 as WFU*	31. 5.78
G-BEVI (3)	Thunder Ax7-77A Balloon (Hot Air)	125		30. 5.77	*"Prime Bang" Cancelled 8. 1.92 as WFU*	
G-BFAB	Cameron N-56 Balloon (Hot Air)	297		15. 8.77	*"Phonogram" Cancelled 21. 4.92 by CAA*	10. 8.92A
G-BFOZ	Thunder Ax6-56 Plug Balloon (Hot Air)	144		20. 3.78	*"Motorway" Cancelled 16. 4.92 by CAA*	10. 9.89A
G-BGAS	Colting Ax8-105A Balloon (Hot Air)	001		27. 6.78	*Cancelled 23.12.81 as destroyed (Destroyed Flims, Switzerland 20. 9.80:: basket only)*	12. 9.82A
G-BGOO	Colt Flame 56SS Balloon (Hot Air) (Smiling Flame shape)	039		27. 4.79	*"Mr Gas" Cancelled 19. 5.93 by CAA*	
G-BGPF	Thunder Ax6-56Z Balloon (Hot Air)	206		13. 7.79	*"Pepsi" Cancelled 21.11.89 as WFU*	27. 6.82A
G-BHKN	Colt 14A Cloudhopper Balloon (Hot Air) (Officially regd as Colt 12A)	068		17. 1.80	*"Green Ice 2" Cancelled 5.12.89 as WFU*	
G-BHKR	Colt 14A Cloudhopper Balloon (Hot Air) (Officially regd as Colt 12A)	071		17. 1.80	*"Green Ice 5" Cancelled 5.12.89 as WFU*	
G-BIAZ	Cameron AT-165 Balloon (Hot-Air)	400		7. 2.78	*"Zanussi" Cancelled 27. 5.80 as destroyed (Used for 1978 Atlantic attempt: hot air envelope destroyed Trubenbuch, Austria 14. 1.80: inner helium cell envelope only)*	3. 4.80
G-BIDV	Colt 17A Cloudhopper Balloon (Hot Air) (Originally was Colt 14A c/n 034)	789		29. 1.79	*"Smirnoff" Cancelled 20. 5.93 by CAA*	19.12.89A
G-BIGT	Colt 77A Balloon (Hot Air)	078		28. 2.80	*"Big T" Cancelled 4. 2.87 by CAA (Damaged Belton Hall, Grantham 23. 8.81?)*	20. 2.83A
G-BKES	Cameron Bottle 57 SS Balloon (Hot Air) (Robinsons Barley Water Bottle)	846		25. 6.82	*"Robinsons Barley Water" Cancelled 1. 5.90 by CAA*	13. 5.87A
G-BKMR	Thunder Ax3 Maxi Sky Chariot Balloon (Hot Air)	497		12. 1.83	*"The Weasel "Cancelled 23. 4.98 as WFU*	31. 8.90A
G-BLIO	Cameron R-42 Balloon (Gas & Hot Air)	1015		17. 4.84	*Cancelled 24. 1.90 as destroyed*	17. 5.84P
G-BMEZ	Cameron DP-70 Airship (Hot Air) (Originally regd as D-50)	1130		18. 9.85	*Cancelled 20. 6.91 as sold as EC-FUS (Envelope only)*	4. 5.89A
G-BNHN	Colt Ariel Bottle SS Balloon (Hot Air)	1045		30. 3.87	*"Ariel" Cancelled 24. 1.92 as WFU*	5. 5.89A
G-BOGR	Colt 180A Balloon (Hot Air)	1183		11. 5.88	*"Britannia"Cancelled 28. 4.97 as WFU*	13. 3.92T

G-BOTL	Colt 42A SS Balloon (Hot Air)	466		23.11.82	"Bottle" Cancelled 21.11.89 as WFU	
G-BPKN	Colt AS-80 Mk.II Airship (Hot Air)	1297		11. 1.89	"Fuji" Cancelled 7. 1.91 by CAA	14. 3.91A
G-BPLD	Thunder and Colt AS-261 Airship (Hot Air)	1380		25. 1.89	Cancelled 13. 6.89 - to F-WGGM, F-GHRI 5.91, to F-WGGM	
G-BRZC	Cameron N-90 Balloon (Hot Air)	2227		8. 2.90	"Unipart II" Cancelled 29. 4.97 as WFU	2.12.92A
G-BUBL	Thunder Ax8-105 Balloon (Hot Air)	1147		10.12.87	"Mercier" and "L'Espit d'Adventure"Cancelled 16. 6.98 as WFU	
						16. 9.91T
G-BUUU	Cameron Bottle 77 SS Balloon (Hot Air)	2980		11. 2.93	"Bells Whiskey" Cancelled 22.10.01 by CAA	4. 3.94A
	(Bells Whiskey Bottle shape)					
G-BVBJ	Colt Flying Coffee Jar 1 SS Balloon (Hot Air)			27. 7.93	"Maxwell House I" Cancelled 29. 4.97 as WFU	21.11.96A
	(Maxwell House Jar)	2427				
G-BVBK	Colt Flying Coffee Jar 2 SS Balloon (Hot Air)			27. 7.93	"Maxwell House II" Cancelled 29. 4.97 as WFU	14. 2.97A
	(Maxwell House Jar)	2428				
G-BVBX	Cameron N-90M Balloon (Hot Air)	3102		10. 8.93	"Mercury" Cancelled 10. 2.97 as temporarily WFU	27. 9.95A
G-BVFY	Colt 210A Balloon (Hot Air)	2493	DQ-BVF	30. 9.93	"Scotair" Cancelled 14. 3.06 by CAA	11. 5.00T
			G-BVFY			
G-BVIO	Colt Flying Drinks Can SS Balloon (Hot Air)			4. 2.94	"Budweiser Can II" Cancelled 6.11.01 as WFU	9. 6.00A
	(Budweiser Can shape)	2538				
G-BVWH	Cameron N-90 Lightbulb SS Balloon (Hot Air)			8.12.94	"Phillips Light Bulb" Cancelled 17.12.01 as WFU	2. 9.98A
		3404				
G-CHUB	Colt Cylinder Two N-51 Balloon (Hot Air)	1720		11. 4.90	"Chubb Fire Extinguisher" Cancelled 12.12.01 as WFU	
	(Fire Extinguisher shape)					19.12.95A
G-FTFT	Colt Financial Times 90 SS Balloon (Hot Air)			14. 1.88	"Financial Times" Cancelled 13. 5.98 as WFU	5. 6.95A
		1163				
G-FZZZ	Colt 56A Balloon (Hot Air)	507		23. 2.83	"Alka Seltzer 1" Cancelled 29. 4.97 as WFU	
G-LCIO	Colt 240A Balloon (Hot Air)	1381		23. 1.89	"Star Flyer 2" Cancelled 25 .5.94 as WFU	7. 3.91A
					(Damaged landing after first overflight Mt Everest by hot air balloon 21.10.91)	
G-LOAG	Cameron N-77 Balloon (Hot Air)	359		10.11.77	"Famous Grouse" Cancelled 31. 3.93 as destroyed	6. 4.84A
					(Envelope only)	
G-OBUD	Colt 69A Balloon (Hot Air)	698		26. 6.85	"Budweiser" Cancelled 29. 4.97 as WFU	1. 2.90A
G-OFIZ	Cameron Can 80 SS Balloon (Hot Air)	2106		30.10.89	"Andrews Can" Cancelled 10. 2.97 as temporarily WFU	
						2.12.91A
G-PARR	Colt Bottle 90 SS Balloon (Hot Air)	1953		15. 3.91	"Old Parr" Cancelled 10. 2.97 as temporarily WFU	29. 9.94A
	(Old Parr Whisky bottle shape)					
G-PERR	Cameron Bottle 60 SS Balloon (Hot Air)	699		28. 1.81	"Perrier" Cancelled 24. 1.92 as WFU	3. 6.84A
G-PLUG	Colt 105A Balloon (Hot Air)	1958		17. 4.91	Cancelled 23. 7.96 by CAA	14. 8.95T
G-PUBS	Colt Beer Glass 56 SS Balloon (Hot Air)	037		7. 6.79	Cancelled 1.12.95 by CAA	30.11.90A

The following preserved, balloons and airships are held in the **Balloon Preservation Group** collection based in Petworth.

Registration	Type	Construction No	Previous Identity	Reg.Date	Remarks	CofA Expy
G-AYVA	Cameron O-84 Balloon (Hot Air)	17		30. 3.71	"April Fool" Cancelled 19. 5.93 by CAA	6. 9.76
G-BAKO	Cameron O-84 Balloon (Hot Air)	57		18.12.72	"Pied Piper" Cancelled 19. 5.93 by CAA	12. 7.76
G-BAND	Cameron O-84 Balloon (Hot Air)	52		22. 1.73	"Clover" Cancelled 17. 4.98 as PWFU	
G-BAOW	Cameron O-65 Balloon (Hot Air)	59		6. 2.73	"Winslow Boy" Cancelled 15.10.01 by CAA	9. 5.74S
G-BAST	Cameron O-84 Balloon (Hot Air)	70		15. 3.73	"Honey" Cancelled 19. 5.93 by CAA	2. 5.84A
G-BAYC	Cameron O-65 Balloon (Hot Air)	68	(HB-BOU) G-BAYC	17. 5.73	"Viva Verdi""Cancelled 15. 5.98 as WFU	25. 5.78S
G-BBYL	Cameron O-77 Balloon (Hot Air)	89		8. 2.74	"Jammy" Cancelled 19. 5.93 by CAA	19. 6.77S
G-BBYR	Cameron O-65 Balloon (Hot Air)	97		14. 2.74	"Phoenix" Cancelled 30. 1.87 by CAA	15. 7.81
G-BCAP	Cameron O-56 Balloon (Hot Air)	92		5. 3.74	"Honey Child" Cancelled 30. 3.93 as WFU	1. 5.88A
G-BCAS	Thunder Ax7-77 Balloon (Hot Air)	018		5. 3.74	"Drifter" Cancelled 30.11.01 by CAA	9. 4.91A
G-BCCH	Thunder Ax6-56A Balloon (Hot Air)	024		4. 4.74	"Wrangler" Cancelled 15.11.82 as sold Belgium - NTU	
						11. 4.81A
G-BCNR	Thunder Ax7-77A Balloon (Hot Air)	028		13. 9.74	"Howdy" Cancelled 19. 5.93 by CAA	15. 5.81A
G-BCRE	Cameron O-77 Balloon (Hot Air)	128		30.10.74	"Snapdragon" Cancelled 19. 5.93 by CAA	6.10.83A
G-BDGO	Thunder Ax7-77 Balloon (Hot Air)	048		16. 7.75	"J & B" Cancelled 12. 6.02 by CAA	2. 2.82A
G-BDMO	Thunder Ax7-77A Balloon (Hot Air)	053	(EC-...) G-BDMO	25.11.75	"Flash Harry" Cancelled 8. 3.95 as WFU	16. 8.86A
G-BEJB	Thunder Ax6-56A Balloon (Hot Air)	096		31.12.76	"Baby J & B" Cancelled 10. 5.02 by CAA	21. 5.87A
					(Original canopy destroyed by fire Latimer 4. 9.77: replacement c/n not known)	
G-BGST	Thunder Ax7-65 Bolt Balloon (Hot Air)	217		14. 5.79	"Black Fred" Cancelled 7.12.01 by CAA	23. 3.91A
G-BHAT	Thunder Ax7-77 Bolt Balloon (Hot Air)	250		17. 3.80	"Witter" Cancelled 29. 4.93 as WFU	14. 6.92A
G-BHYO	Cameron N-77 Balloon (Hot Air)	659		30. 6.80	"Alcock and Sissons" Cancelled 3. 1.08 by CAA	8. 5.97A
G-BJZC	Thunder Ax7-65Z Balloon (Hot Air)	416		5. 3.82	"Greenpeace Trinity" Cancelled 8. 7.98 as WFU	17. 6.94A
G-BKIY	Thunder Ax3 Sky Chariot Balloon (Hot Air)	464		7.10.82	"Michaelangelo" Cancelled 15.11.01 as WFU	
G-BKOW	Colt 77A Balloon (Hot Air)	505		6. 9.84	"Lady Di" Cancelled 29. 4.97 as WFU (Elle titles)	14. 2.88A
G-BKIK	Cameron DG-19 Airship (Gas Filled)	776		23. 8.82	"B & Q" Cancelled 5. 9.00 as WFU	4. 9.88A
	(Rotax 400)					
G-BLDL	Cameron Truck 56 SS Balloon (Hot Air)	990		10. 1.84	"Europa" Cancelled 21.10.96 by CAA	
G-BLGX	Thunder Ax7-65 Balloon (Hot Air)	551		16. 4.84	Cancelled 19. 5.93 by CAA	23. 9.05A
G-BLIP	Cameron N-77 Balloon (Hot Air)	1031		17. 4.84	"Systems 80" Cancelled 23. 6.98 as WFU	26. 3.94A
G-BLJF	Cameron O-65 Balloon (Hot Air)	1041		14 .5.84	Cancelled 17.11.05 as PWFU	16. 8.00A
G-BLKJ	Thunder Ax7-65 Balloon (Hot Air)	580		18. 7.84	"Up & Coming" Cancelled 22. 5.97 as PWFU	3. 2.96A
G-BLSH	Cameron V-77 Balloon (Hot Air)	1085		7.12.84	"Compass Rose" Cancelled 30. 3.98 as WFU	14. 1.95A
G-BLUE	Colting Ax7-77A Balloon (Hot Air)	77A-011		2. 5.78	Cancelled 30.11.01 by CAA	20. 9.99A
	(Officially regd as Colt 77A c/n 11)					
G-BLZB	Cameron N-65 Balloon (Hot Air)	1164		21. 5.85	"Pro-Sport" Cancelled 22.11.01 as WFU	25. 4.90A
G-BMKX	Cameron Elephant 77 SS Balloon (Hot Air)	1196		6. 2.86	"Benjamin I" Cancelled 21.10.96 as WFU	19. 2.89A
G-BMST	Cameron N-31 Balloon (Hot Air)	1317		4. 6.86	"B&Q" Cancelled 1. 5.92 as WFU	16. 2.90A
					(Badly damaged and for spares 12.01)	

Reg	Type	c/n	Prev	Date	Remarks	
G-BMUR	Cameron Zero 25 Airship (Gas Filled)	1169		11. 6.86	"Zero 25" Cancelled 21.10.96 as WFU	
G-BNCH	Cameron V-77 Balloon (Hot Air)	1398		11.12.86	"Sapper II" Cancelled 25. 6.02 as WFU	19. 6.92A
G-BNHL	Colt Beer Glass 90 SS Balloon (Hot Air)	1042		24 .3.87	"Gatzweiler" Cancelled 22. 6.98 as WFU	4. 3.97A
G-BOCF	Colt 77A Balloon (Hot Air)	1178		4. 1.88	Cancelled 6.10.03 as WFU	25. 7.94T
G-BOGT	Colt 77A Balloon (Hot Air)	1212		21. 3.88	"British Gas" Cancelled 9. 5.97 as WFU	2.12.94A
G-BONK	Colt 180A Balloon (Hot Air)	1167		14.12.87	"Bonkette" Cancelled 28.11.01 as WFU	2.11.94T
G-BONV	Colt 17A Cloudhopper Balloon (Hot Air)	1238		3. 5.88	"Bryant Group" Cancelled 22.11.01 as WFU	1. 4.93A
G-BOOP	Cameron N-90 Balloon (Hot Air)	1702	(G-BOMX)	11. 5.88	"Betty Boop" Cancelled 31.10.95 by CAA (Unipart titles)	28. 9.95A
G-BORA	Colt 77A Balloon (Hot Air)	1233		19. 5.88	"Carla" Cancelled 17. 9.98 as WFU	24. 8.94A
G-BOTE	Thunder Ax8-90 Balloon (Hot Air)	555		14. 6.88	"Barge Fox" Cancelled 12.12.95 as WFU	16. 2.95T
G-BPAH	Colt 69A Balloon (Hot Air)	512		2. 6.83	"J & B Phil" Cancelled 13. 5.02 by CAA	15. 8.88A
G-BPDF	Cameron V-77 Balloon (Hot Air)	1806		6.10.88	Cancelled 17. 3.05 by CAA	31. 7.00A
G-BPFJ	Cameron Can 90 SS Balloon (Hot Air) (Budweiser Beer Can shape)	1834		14.11.88	"Budweiser Can I" Cancelled 9. 5.97 as WFU	10.12.93A
G-BPFX	Colt 21A Cloudhopper Balloon (Hot Air)	1348		7.11.88	"Budweiser Hopper"Cancelled 23.12.98 as WFU	21.11.96T
G-BPSZ	Cameron N-180 Balloon (Hot Air)	1911		14. 3.89	"Park Furnishers"Cancelled 9. 5.01 as WFU	30. 4.01T
G-BRFR	Cameron N-105 Balloon (Hot Air)	2042		14. 7.89	"Rover" Cancelled 9. 5.97 as WFU (Badly damaged, spares use only)	6.12.93A
G-BRLX	Cameron N-77 Balloon (Hot Air)	2095		13. 9.89	"National Power" Cancelled 23.10.01 by CAA	1. 6.96A
G-BSBM	Cameron N-77 Balloon (Hot Air)	2229		8. 3.90	"Nuclear Electric 1" Cancelled 15. 7.98 as WFU	21.11.96A
G-BTML	Cameron Rupert Bear 90 SS Balloon (Hot Air)	2533		16. 5.91	"Rupert Bear" Cancelled 29. 4.97 as WFU	31.12.94A
G-BTJF	Thunder Ax10-180 Series 2 Balloon (Hot Air)	1952		28. 3.91	"Yorkshire Lad" Cancelled 4. 8.03 as destroyed	4. 5.01T
G-BUET	Colt Flying Drinks Can SS Balloon (Hot Air) (Budweiser Can shape)	2162		30. 3.92	"Bud King Can" Cancelled 29. 4.97 as WFU	10.12.93A
G-BUEU	Colt 21A Cloudhopper Balloon (Hot Air)	2163		30. 3.92	"Bud King Hopper" Cancelled 29. 4.97 as WFU	2.12.94A
G-BUKC	Cameron A-180 Balloon (Hot Air)	2870		3. 7.92	"Cloud Nine" Cancelled 11.10.99 as WFU	2. 3.00T
G-BUXA	Colt 210A Balloon (Hot Air)	2400		28. 4.93	"Buxam" Cancelled 20.12.01 as WFU	7. 4.99T
G-BWPL	Airtour AH-56 Balloon (Hot Air)	011	G-OAFC	19. 3.96	"Paul J Donnellan" Cancelled 17. 9.01 as WFU (As "G-OAFC")	
G-BWUR	Thunder Ax10-210 Series 2 Balloon (Hot Air)	3910		11. 7.96	"Kinetic" Cancelled 14. 3.06 by CAA	7. 4.01T
G-BWZP	Cameron Home Special 105 SS Balloon (Hot Air)	4051		6.12.96	"Barclays Mortgages titles" Cancelled 15. 1.04 as WFU	10. 4.02A
G-BXAX	Cameron O-77 Balloon (Hot Air)	2010		25. 5.89	"Citroën" Cancelled 31. 1.02 as WFU	21.11.96A
G-BXHM	Lindstrand LBL 25A Cloudhopper Balloon (Hot Air)	466		30. 5.97	"Bud Ice and Michelob" Cancelled 6.11.01 as WFU	7. 5.00A
G-BXND	Cameron Thomas the Tank Engine 110 SS Balloon (Hot Air)	4254		23. 2.00	"Thomas" Cancelled 19.11.02 by CAA	25. 6.02A
G-COLR	Colt 69A Balloon (Hot Air)	780		8. 4.86	"Bubble" Cancelled 21. 5.93 as WFU	1. 4.93A
G-COMP	Cameron N-90 Balloon (Hot Air)	1564		24. 9.87	"Computacentre I" Cancelled 18.12.01 by CAA	20. 5.97A
G-CURE	Colt 77A Balloon (Hot Air) (Standard shape plus Tablet blisters)	1424		3. 7.89	"Alka Seltzer III" Cancelled 29. 4.97 as WFU	21.11.96A
G-DHLZ	Colt 31A Air Chair Balloon (Hot Air)	2604		2. 6.94	"DHL Parcel" Cancelled 9. 4.99 as WFU	23. 7.99A
G-ETFT	Colt Financial Times SS Balloon (Hot Air)	1792	G-BSGZ	11. 1.91	"Financial Time II" Cancelled 10.12.02 by CAA	14.10.00A
G-FZZY	Colt 69A Balloon (Hot Air)	779		19. 2.86	"Alka Seltzer II" Cancelled 29. 4.97 as WFU	16. 2.90A
G-GEUP	Cameron N-77 Balloon (Hot Air)	880		8.12.82	"Gee-Up" Cancelled 9. 5.01 as WFU	19. 7.96
G-GRIP	Cameron Colt Bibendum 110 SS Balloon (Hot Air)	4224		5. 1.98	(Michelin titles) Cancelled 7. 9.05 as WFU	25. 1.02A
G-GURL	Cameron A-210 Balloon (Hot Air)	2387		3. 9.90	"Hot Airlines" Cancelled 2.12.98 as WFU	9. 8.96T
G-HENS	Cameron N-65 Balloon (Hot Air)	740		8. 7.81	"Free Range" Cancelled 8. 4.93 by CAA	16. 7.90A
G-HLIX	Cameron Helix Oilcan 61 SS Balloon (Hot Air) (Originally regd as 80 SS)	1192		20. 9.85	"Helix Oil Can" Cancelled 29. 4.97 as WFU	25. 4.90A
G-IGEL	Cameron N-90 Balloon (Hot Air)	2726		7. 4.92	"Computacentre II" Cancelled 18.12.01 by CAA	12. 5.97A
G-IMAG	Cameron O-77 Balloon (Hot Air) (Second envelope c/n 2254 as original DBF 6.92)	1718		9. 3.90	"Agfa" Cancelled 31. 1.02 as WFU (Noted 8.08)	19. 1.00A
"G-OAFC"	Airtour AH-56 Balloon (Hot Air)	011		23. 5.90	Cancelled 17. 1.96 as PWFU - re-regd as G-BWPL qv	
G-OCND	Cameron O-77 Balloon (Hot Air)	1020		6. 2.84	"CND Airborne" Cancelled 19. 5.95 by CAA	6.11.93A
G-OHDC	Colt Film Cassette SS Balloon (Hot Air) (Agfa Film Can shape)	2633		8. 8.94	"Agfa HDC Can" Cancelled 31.1.02 as WFU	26. 8.99A
G-JANB	Colt Flying Bottle SS Balloon (Hot Air) (J & B Whisky Bottle shape)	1643		16. 2.90	"J & B Bottle" Cancelled 20.12.01 by CAA	30. 9.96A
G-LLAI	Colt 21A Cloudhopper Balloon (Hot Air) (Lowndes Laing Insurance titles)	519	(G-BKTX)	18. 7.83	"Llama" Cancelled 16. 7.90 by CAA	
G-MAAC	Advanced Airship Corporation ANR-1 Airship (Gas Filled)	01		16. 1.89	"ANR-1" Cancelled 15.11.00 by CAA	
G-NPWR	Cameron RX-100 Balloon (Hot Air)	2849		13. 7.92	"Nuclear Rozier" Cancelled 15. 7.98 as WFU	21.11.96A
G-NWPB	Thunder Ax7-77Z Balloon (Hot Air)	278		13. 5.80	"Post Office" Cancelled 27. 4.90 by CAA	17.10.89A
G-OLDV	Colt 90A Balloon (Hot Air)	2592		5. 5.94	"LDV" Cancelled 29. 6.99 as WFU	10.11.98A
G-OSVY	Sky 31-24 Balloon (Hot Air)	104		28. 5.98	"OS Hopper" Cancelled 31. 7.01 as WFU	11. 3.00A
G-OXRG	Colt Film Can SS Balloon (Hot Air) (Agfacolor Film Can shape)	2138		17. 1.92	"Agfa XRG Can" Cancelled 29. 4.97 as WFU	21.11.96A
G-PONY	Colt 31A Air Chair Balloon (Hot Air)	434		23. 8.82	"Neddie" Cancelled 19. 5.95 by CAA	
G-PURE	Cameron Can 70 SS Balloon (Hot Air) (Guinness Can)	1913		18. 1.89	"Guinness Can" Cancelled 29. 4.97 as WFU	10.12.93A
G-PYLN	Cameron Pylon 80 SS Balloon (Hot Air) (Electricity Pylon shape)	2958	G-BUSO	18. 1.93	"Essex Girl" Cancelled 6.11.01 as WFU	25. 4.97A
G-RARE	Thunder Ax5-42 SS Balloon (Hot Air) (J & B Rare Whisky Bottle shape)	266		20. 2.80	"J & B Hamish" Cancelled 14. 5.02 by CAA	7. 4.95A
G-RIPS	Cameron Action Man-Parachutist 110 SS Balloon (Hot Air)	4092		29. 4.97	"Action Man" Cancelled 23. 7.02 as WFU	25. 5.00A
G-SCAH	Cameron V-77 Balloon (Hot Air)	788		18. 1.82	"Orpheus" Cancelled 30.11.01 by CAA	24. 7.87A

G-SEUK	Cameron TV 80 SS Balloon (Hot Air)	3810		12. 4.96	*"Samsung Monitor"* Cancelled 31. 1.02 as WFU	24. 3.00A
	(Samsung Computer shape)					
G-SGAS	Colt 77A Balloon (Hot Air)	2073		31.10.91	*(Shell Gas titles)* Cancelled 23. 6.07 as destroyed	26. 4.01A
G-TTWO	Colt 56A Balloon (Hot Air)	087		14. 5.80	*"Tea 4 Two"* Cancelled 14.11.95 as WFU	1. 9.87A
G-UNIP	Cameron Oil Container SS Balloon (Hot Air)			15. 3.91	*"Unipart Can"* Cancelled 31.1.02 as WFU	7.11.96A
	(Unipart Sureflow Oil Can)	2532				
G-VOLT	Cameron N-77 Balloon (Hot Air)	2157		8.11.89	*"National Power II"* Cancelled 23.10.01 as WFU	25. 4.97A
G-WATT	Cameron Cooling Tower SS Balloon (Hot Air)			8.11.89	*"Cooling Tower"* Cancelled 23.10.01 as WFU	22. 8.96A
		2158				
G-WINE	Thunder AX7-77Z Balloon (Hot Air)	472		25.11.82	*"Gemini"* Cancelled 10. 4.02 by CAA	17. 6.97A
G-WORK	Thunder Ax10-180 Series 2 Balloon (Hot Air)		DQ-PBF	12. 5.93	Cancelled 3.11.97 - sold as DQ-PBF *(As "DQ-PBF")*	26. 5.97A
		2396	G-WORK		*(Paradise Balloon Flights titles)*	
G-ZUMP	Cameron N-77 Balloon (Hot Air)	377		18. 1.78	*"Gazump"* Cancelled 8. 4.98 as WFU	3. 5.91A
	(Rebuilt 1985 with new canopy c/n 1107)					

The following are preserved in Museums and available private collections. Full details are shown in SECTION 4, Part 1.

Registration	Type	Location
G-EACN	BAT FK.23 Bantam 1	Schiphol, Netherlands
G-EACQ	Avro 534 Baby	Brisbane, Australia
G-EAML	Airco DH.6	Pretoria, South Africa
G-EAOU	Vickers FB.27A Vimy IV	Adelaide, South Australia
G-EAQM	Airco DH.9	Canberra, ACT, Australia
G-EBIB	Royal Aircraft Factory SE.5a	South Kensington, London
G-EBIC	Royal Aircraft Factory SE.5a	Hendon, London
G-EBJE	Avro 504K	Hendon, London
G-EBJG	Parnall Pixie III	Coventry, Warwickshire
G-EBMB	Hawker Cygnet I	RAF Cosford, Shropshire
G-EBNO	de Havilland DH.60 Moth	Halmstad, Sweden
G-EBNU	Avro 504K	Jyväskylä, Finland
G-EBOV	Avro 581E Avian	South Brisbane, Queensland, Australia
G-EBUB	Westland Widgeon III	Wangaratta, Victoria, Australia
G-EBYY	Cierva C 8L Mk.2	Paris Le Bourget, France
G-EBZM	Avro 594A Avian IIIA	Manchester
G-AAAH	de Havilland DH.60G Moth	Santa Paula, California, US
G-AACN	Handley Page HP.39 Gugnunc	Wroughton, Wiltshire
G-AAHD	Avro 594 Avian IV	Stockholm, Sweden
G-AAMX (2)	American Moth Corporation DH.60GM Moth	Hendon, London
G-AAMZ (2)	de Havilland DH.60G Moth	Santa Paula, California, US
G-AANJ (2)	Luft-Verkehrs Gesellschaft C VI	Hendon, London
G-AARO (2)	Arrow Sport A2-60	Chantilly, Virginia, US
G-ABAA	Avro 504K	Manchester
G-ABBB	Bristol 105A Bulldog IIA	Hendon, London
G-ABDW	de Havilland DH.80A Puss Moth	East Fortune, Scotland
G-ABIH	de Havilland DH.80A Puss Moth	Rhinebeck, New York, US
G-ABLF	Avro 616 Avian Sport	Salisbury, South Australia
G-ABLK	Avro 616 Avian V	South Brisbane, Queensland, Australia
G-ABLM	Cierva C 24	Salisbury Hall, London Colney, Hertfordshire
G-ABMR	Hawker Hart	Hendon, London
G-ABOI	Wheeler Slymph	Coventry, Warwickshire
G-ABUU	Comper CLA.7 Swift	Madrid, Spain
G-ABXH	Cierva C 19 Mk.IVP	Madrid, Spain
G-ACGO	Saunders-Roe A 19 Cloud	Prague, Czech Republic
G-ACGR	Percival Type D Gull Four IIA	Brussels, Belgium
G-ACIT	de Havilland DH84 Dragon 1	Wroughton, Wiltshire
G-ACPP	de Havilland DH.89 Dragon Rapide	Wetaskiwin, Alberta, Canada
G-ACUP	Percival Type D Gull Six	Wangaratta, Victoria, Australia
G-ACUU	Cierva C 30A	Duxford, Cambridgeshire
G-ACUX	Short S 16 Scion 1	Belfast, Northern Ireland
G-ACVA	Kay Gyroplane 33/1	East Fortune, Scotland
G-ACWM	Cierva C 30A	Weston-super-Mare, Somerset
G-ACWP	Cierva C 30A	South Kensington, London
G-ACXA	Cierva C 30A	Milan, Italy
G-ACXK	de Havilland DH.60G-III Moth Major	Madrid, Spain
G-ACYK	Spartan Cruiser III	East Fortune, Scotland
G-ACYR	de Havilland DH.89 Dragon Rapide	Madrid, Spain
G-ADAH	de Havilland DH.89 Dragon Rapide	Manchester
G-ADLS	Miles M.3C Falcon Six	Madrid, Spain
G-ADMW	Miles M.2H Hawk Major	RAF Stafford, Staffordhire
G-ADOT	de Havilland DH.87B Hornet Moth	Salisbury Hall, London Colney, Hertfordshire
G-ADPR	Percival Type D Gull Six	Auckland, New Zealand
G-ADWO	de Havilland DH.82A Tiger Moth	Southampton, Hampshire
G-AEEH	Mignet HM.14 Pou-Du-Ciel	RAF Cosford, Shropshire
G-AEGV	Mignet HM.14 Pou-Du-Ciel	Coventry, Warwickshire
G-AEHM	Mignet HM.14 Pou-Du-Ciel	Wroughton, Wiltshire
G-AEJZ	Mignet HM.14 Pou-Du-Ciel	Hemswell, Lincolnshire
G-AEKR	Mignet HM.14 Pou-Du-Ciel	Doncaster, Yorkshire
G-AEKV	Kronfeld (BAC) Drone de luxe	Brooklands, Surrey
G-AEKW	Miles M.12 Mohawk	RAF Cosford, Shropshire
G-AERD	Percival Type D Gull Six	Canberra, ACT, Australia
G-AERN	de Havilland DH.89A Dragon Rapide	Madrid, Spain
G-AETA	Caudron G III	Hendon, London
G-AEVZ	BA L 25c Swallow II	Madrid, Spain
G-AEYF	General Aircraft Monospar St 25 Ambulance	Egeskov, Denmark
G-AFBS	Miles M.14A Hawk Trainer 3	Duxford, Cambridgeshire
G-AFDX	Hanriot HD.1	Hendon, London
G-AFGK	Miles M.11A Whitney Straight	Wetaskiwin, Alberta, Canada
G-AFJR	Tipsy Trainer 1	Brussels, Belgium
G-AFNJ	de Havilland DH.94 Moth Minor	La Ferté-Alais, Essonne, France
G-AFOR	de Havilland DH.94 Moth Minor	Caboolture, Queensland, Australia
G-AFOW	de Havilland DH.94 Moth Minor	Albury, New South Wales, Australia
G-AFRV	Tipsy Trainer I	Brussels, Belgium
G-AFTN	Taylorcraft Plus C2	Coalville, Leicestershire
G-AFVH	Tipsy S 2	Brussels, Belgium
G-AFWN	Auster J/1 Autocrat	Stauning, Denmark
G-AGBN	General Aircraft GAL.42 Cygnet 2	East Fortune, Scotland

G-AGCN	Lockheed 18-56 Lodestar II (C-56D-LO)	Auckland, New Zealand
G-AGIJ	Lockheed 18-56 Lodestar II (C-60A-5-LO)	Stockholm, Sweden
G-AGNV	Avro 685 York C 1	RAF Cosford, Shropshire
G-AGOS	Reid and Sigrist RS.4 Desford Trainer	Coalville. Leicestershire
G-AGPG	Avro 652A Anson 19 Series 2	Hooton Park, Cheshire
G-AGRU	Vickers 657 Viking 1	Brooklands, Surrey
G-AGRW	Vickers 639 Viking 1	Vienna, Austria
G-AGTB	Percival Proctor V	Kogarah, New South Wales, Australia
G-AGXS	Auster V J/1 Autocrat	Sils-Girona, Spain
G-AGYX	Douglas C-47A-10-DK Dakota 3	Hendon, London
G-AGZI	Consolidated-Vultee CV.32-3 (LB-30) Liberator II	Anchorage, Alaska, US
G-AHAT	Auster J/1N Alpha	Dumfries, Scotland
G-AHAY	Auster V J/1 Autocrat	Beersheba, Israel
G-AHDI	Percival Proctor I	Melbourne, Victoria, Australia
G-AHED	de Havilland DH.89A Dragon Rapide 6	RAF Stafford, Staffordshire
G-AHHE	Auster V J/1 Autocrat	Hamilton East, New Zealand
G-AHJR (2)	Short S 25 Sunderland MR.5	Auckland, New Zealand
G-AHKO	Taylorcraft Plus D	Stauning, Denmark
G-AHKY	Miles M.18 Series 2	East Fortune, Scotland
G-AHLO	de Havilland DH.80A Puss Moth	Rockcliffe, Ottawa, Ontario, Canada
G-AHLX	Douglas C-47A-30-DK Dakota	Belgrade, Serbia
G-AHMJ	Cierva C 30A	Polk City, Florida ,US
G-AHOT	Vickers 498 Viking 1A	Johannesburg, South Africa
G-AHRI	de Havilland DH.104 Dove 1B	Newark, Nottinghamshire
G-AHTW	Airspeed AS.40 Oxford 1	Duxford, Cambridgeshire
G-AHVG	Percival Proctor II	Alice Springs, Northern Territory, Australia
G-AHZY	Percival Proctor V	Brussels, Belgium
G-AIBE	Fairey Fulmar 2	RNAS Yeovilton, Somerset
G-AICH	Bristol 170 Freighter Mk.1A	Buenos Aires, Argentina
G-AIJK	Auster V J/4 Archer	Coalville. Leicestershire
G-AIKR	Airspeed AS.65 Consul	Rockcliffe, Ottawa, Ontario, Canada
G-AIMI	Bristol 170 Freighter 21E	Point Cook, Victoria, Australia
G-AINT	Bristol 170 Freighter 31MNZ	Christchurch, New Zealand
G-AIPE	Taylorcraft J Auster 5	Rosendaal, Netherlands
G-AIPW	Taylorcraft Auster 5A Series 160	Amman, Jordan
G-AISU	Vickers Supermarine 349 Spitfire LF.VB	RAF Coningsby, Lincolnshire
G-AITB	Airspeed AS.40 Oxford 1	Hendon, London
G-AITF	Airspeed AS.40 Oxford 1	Pretoria, South Africa
G-AIWY	de Havilland DH.89A Dragon Rapide	Helsingør, Denmark
G-AIXA	Taylorcraft Plus D	Hendon, London
G-AIYT	Douglas C-47A-10-DK Dakota	Beersheba, Israel
G-AIZE	Fairchild F 24W-41A Argus II	RAF Cosford, Shropshire
G-AIZG	Vickers Supermarine 236 Walrus 1	RNAS Yeovilton, Somerset
G-AIZW	Auster V J/1 Autocrat	Halmstad, Sweden
G-AJAV	Douglas C-47A-5-DK Dakota	Aragua, Maracay, Venezuela
G-AJEB	Auster J/1N Alpha	Hooton Park, Cheshire
G-AJEC	Auster V J/1 Autocrat	Wanaka, New Zealand
G-AJHW	Sikorsky S-51	Point Cook, Victoria, Australia
G-AJJP	Fairey FB.2 Jet Gyrodyne	Woodley, Berkshire
G-AJKF (2)	de Havilland DH.84 Dragon III	Point Cook, Victoria, Australia
G-AJKG (2)	Miles M.38 Messenger 2A	Melbourne, Victoria, Australia
G-AJLR	Airspeed AS.65 Consul	Singapore
G-AJMC	Bristol 156 Beaufighter TF.X	Beersheba, Israel
G-AJOC	Miles M.38 Messenger 2A	Belfast, Northern Ireland
G-AJOZ	Fairchild 24W-41A Argus 1	Elvington, Yorkshire
G-AJPC	Fairchild F 24W-41A Argus II	Helsinki, Finland
G-AJRH	Auster J/1N Alpha	Loughborough, Leicestershire
G-AJTI	Miles M.65 Gemini 1A	Pretoria, South Africa
G-AJVL	Miles M.38 Messenger 2A	Caboolture, Queensland, Australia
G-AKAA	Piper J-3C-65 Cub (L-4H-PI)	Madrid, Spain
G-AKAO	Miles M.38 Messenger 2A	Halmstad, Sweden
G-AKCO	Short S 25 Sandringham 7	Paris Le Bourget, France
G-AKDK	Miles M.65 Gemini 1A	Helsingør, Denmark
G-AKEE	de Havilland DH.82A Tiger Moth	Ratamalana, Sri Lanka
G-AKEL	Miles M.65 Gemini 1A	Belfast, Northern Ireland
G-AKGE	Miles M.65 Gemini 3C	Belfast, Northern Ireland
G-AKGV	de Havilland DH.89A Dragon Rapide	Sault Sainte Marie, Ontario, Canada
G-AKIS	Miles M.38 Messenger 2A	Brussels, Belgium
G-AKIZ	Fairchild F 24R-41A Argus II	Helsinki, Finland
G-AKKA	Miles M 65 Gemini 1A	Stavangar, Norway
G-AKKR	Miles M.14A Hawk Trainer 3	AAC Middle Wallop, Hampshire
G-AKKY	Miles M.14A Hawk Trainer 3	Woodley, Berkshire
G-AKLL	Douglas C-47A-30-DK Dakota	Sinsheim, Germany
G-AKLS	Short SA.6 Sealand 1	Belgrade, Serbia
G-AKLW	Short SA.6 Sealand 1	Belfast, Northern Ireland
G-AKNP	Short S.45 Solent 3	Oakland, California, US
G-AKNV	de Havilland DH.89A Dragon Rapide	Brussels, Belgium
G-AKOW	Taylorcraft J Auster 5	AAC Middle Wallop, Hampshire
G-AKRS	de Havilland DH.89A Dragon Rapide	Beersheba, Israel
G-AKVD	Chrislea CH.3 Series 2 Super Ace	Tokyo, Japan
G-AKZY	Messerschmitt Bf.108D-1 Taifun	Albuquerque, New Mexico, US
G-ALBN	Bristol 173 Mk.1	Kemble, Gloucestershire
G-ALBP	Miles M.38 Messenger 4A	Wangaratta, Victoria, Australia
G-ALCK	Percival Proctor III	Duxford, Cambridgeshire

G-ALCS (2)	Miles M.65 Gemini 3C	Leitrim, County Leitrim, Ireland
G-ALCU	de Havilland DH.104 Dove 2B	Coventry, Warwickshire
G-ALDG	Handley Page HP.81 Hermes IV	Duxford, Cambridgeshire
G-ALFO	Douglas C-47A-90-DL Dakota	Addison, Dallas, Texas, US
G-ALFT	de Havilland DH.104 Dove 6	Caernarfon, Wales
G-ALFU	de Havilland DH.104 Dove 6	Duxford, Cambridgeshire
G-ALGB	de Havilland DH.89A Dragon Rapide	Paris Le Bourget, France
G-ALIS	Percival Proctor III	Bull Creek, Western Australia
G-ALJZ	EoN AP.5 Olympia 2B	Woodley, Berkshire
G-ALMB	Westland-Sikorsky S-51 Dragonfly Mk.1A	Vigna di Valle. Italy
G-ALMN	EoN AP.7 Primary	Woodley, Berkshire
G-ALNH	Slingsby T 6 Kite 1	AAC Middle Wallop, Hampshire
G-ALRX	Bristol 175 Britannia Series 101	Kemble, Gloucestershire
(G-ALSP)	Bristol 171 Sycamore 3	Rochester, Kent
G-ALSX	Bristol 171 Sycamore 3	Weston-super-Mare, Somerset
G-ALUA	Winter LF-1 Zaunkönig	Munich, Germany
G-ALWC	Douglas C-47A-25-DK Dakota	Toulouse, France
G-ALWF	Vickers 701 Viscount	Duxford, Cambridgeshire
G-ALXT	de Havilland DH.89A Dragon Rapide	Wroughton, Wiltshire
G-ALYB	Taylorcraft J Auster 5	Doncaster, Yorkshire
G-ALZE	Britten-Norman BN-1F	Southampton, Hampshire
G-ALZF	de Havilland DH.89A Dragon Rapide	La Ferté-Alais, Essonne, France
G-ALZL	de Havilland DH.114 Heron Series 1	Bull Creek, Western Australia
G-ALZO (2)	Airspeed AS.57 Ambassador 2	Duxford, Cambridgeshire
G-AMAU	Hawker Hurricane IIc	RAF Coningsby, Lincolnshire
G-AMCA	Douglas C-47B-30-DK Dakota 3	Lelystad, Netherlands
G-AMDA	Avro 652A Anson 1	Duxford, Cambridgeshire
G-AMDD	de Havilland DH.104 Dove 6	Leitrim, County Leitrim, Ireland
G-AMFU	de Havilland DH.104 Dove 6	Lelystad, Netherlands
G-AMHB	Westland-Sikorsky S-51 Dragonfly Mk.1B	Bebeduoro, Brazil
G-AMHJ	Douglas C-47A-25-DK Dakota 6	RAF Shawbury, Shropshire
G-AMJD	de Havilland DH.82A Tiger Moth	Brussels, Belgium
G-AMJR	de Havilland DH.82A Tiger Moth	Jyväskylä, Finland
G-AMJT	Westland-Sikorsky S-55 Whirlwind HAR.1	Elvington, Yorkshire
G-AMJW	Westland-Sikorsky S-51 Mk.1A	Bangkok, Thailand
G-AMJY	Douglas C-47B-40-DK Dakota	Ratamalana, Sri Lanka
G-AMLF	de Havilland DH.82A Tiger Moth	Santa Paula, California, US
G-AMLZ	Percival P 50 Prince 6E	Liverpool-John Lennon, Merseyside
G-AMMA	de Havilland DHC-1 Chipmunk 21	Stauning, Denmark
G-AMMC	Miles M.14A Hawk Trainer 3	Auckland, New Zealand
G-AMNL	Douglas C-47B-35-DK Dakota	Montevideo, Uruguay
G-AMOG (2)	Vickers 701 Viscount	East Fortune, Scotland
G-AMOI	Vickers 701 Viscount	Bebeduoro, Brazil
G-AMOU	de Havilland DH.82A Tiger Moth	Bangkok, Thailand
G-AMPM	de Havilland DH.82A Tiger Moth	Mackay, Queensland, Australia
G-AMPO	Douglas C-47B-30-DK Dakota 3	RAF Lyneham, Wiltshire
G-AMRM	de Havilland DH.82A Tiger Moth	Auckland, New Zealand
G-AMSM	Douglas C-47B-20-DK Dakota	Brenzett, Kent
G-AMTL	de Havilland DH.82A Tiger Moth	Zaventem, Belgium
G-AMWI	Bristol 171 Sycamore 4	Kogarah, New South Wales, Australia
G-AMXR	de Havilland DH.104 Dove 6	Salisbury Hall, London Colney, Hertfordshire
G-AMXS	de Havilland DH.104 Dove 2A	Maracay, Venezuela
G-AMXX	de Havilland DH.104 Dove 2A	Hermeskeil, Trier, Germany
G-AMYA (2)	Zlin Z.381 Bestmann	Polk City, Florida, US
G-AMYJ	Douglas C-47B-25-DK Dakota 6	Elvington, Yorkshire
G-AMZH	Douglas C-47B-20-DK Dakota	Port Moresby, Papua-New Guinea
G-AMZO	de Havilland DH.87B Hornet Moth	Stauning, Denmark
G-AMZW	Douglas C-47B-20-DK Dakota	Johannesburg, South Africa
G-ANAV	de Havilland DH.106 Comet 1A	Wroughton, Wiltshire
G-ANBY	de Havilland DH.82A Tiger Moth	Shawbury, Shropshire
G-ANCF	Bristol 175 Britannia Series 308F	Liverpool, Merseyside
G-ANCN	de Havilland DH.82A Tiger Moth	Dayton, Ohio, US
G-ANCY	de Havilland DH.82A Tiger Moth	Stauning, Denmark
G-ANEJ	de Havilland DH.82A Tiger Moth	Kuala Lumpur, Malaysia
G-ANFH	Westland WS.55 Whirlwind 1	Weston-super-Mare, Somerset
G-ANFU	Taylorcraft J Auster 5	Newcastle upon Tyne, Northumberland & Tyneside
G-ANFW	de Havilland DH.82A Tiger Moth	Ta'Qali, Malta
G-ANGV	Auster V J/1B Aiglet	Queenstown, New Zealand
G-ANHD	Vickers 701C Viscount	Bebeduoro, Brazil
G-ANHM	Taylorcraft G Auster 4	Murwillumbah, New South Wales, Australia
G-ANIU	Taylorcraft J Auster 5	Stockholm, Sweden
G-ANIZ	de Havilland DH.82A Tiger Moth	Galveston, New Mexico, US
G-ANJG	de Havilland DH.82A Tiger Moth	La Ferté-Alais, Essonne, France
G-ANJV	Westland WS-55 Whirlwind 3	Weston-super-Mare, Somerset
G-ANKV	de Havilland DH.82A Tiger Moth	Croydon, London
G-ANLW	Westland WS-51 Series 2 Widgeon	Flixton, Bungay, Suffolk
G-ANNC	de Havilland DH.82A Tiger Moth	Santa Teresa, New Mexico, US
G-ANNW	Auster J/5F Aiglet Trainer	Kuwait City, Kuwait
G-ANOS	de Havilland DH.82A Tiger Moth	Brandon, Manitoba, Canada
G-ANOV	de Havilland DH.104 Dove 6	East Fortune, Scotland
G-ANPV (2)	de Havilland DH.114 Heron 2D	Melbourne, Victoria, Australia
G-ANRX	de Havilland DH.82A Tiger Moth	Salisbury Hall, London Colney, Hertfordshire
G-ANSG	de Havilland DH.82A Tiger Moth	La Ferté-Alais, Essonne, France
G-ANSO	Gloster Meteor T 7	Halmstad, Sweden

G-ANTK	Avro 685 York C 1	Duxford, Cambridgeshire
G-ANUO	de Havilland DH.114 Heron 2D	Croydon, London
G-ANVU	de Havilland DH.104 Dove 1B	Linköping, Sweden
G-ANXB	de Havilland DH.114 Heron 1B	Newark, Nottinghamshire
G-ANXP	Piper J-3C-65 Cub (L-4H-PI)	Liorac-sur-Louyre, Dordogne, France
G-ANZS	de Havilland DH.82A Tiger Moth	Yering, Victoria, Australia
G-AODA	Westland WS-55 Whirlwind 3	Weston-super-Mare, Somerset
G-AOEL	de Havilland DH.82A Tiger Moth	East Fortune, Scotland
G-AOFR	de Havilland DH.82A Tiger Moth	Egeskov, Denmark
G-AOFX (2)	Vickers 701C Viscount	Sao Paulo, Brazil
G-AOGA	Miles M.75 Aries 1	Leitrim, County Leitrim, Republic of Ireland
G-AOGJ	de Havilland DH.82A Tiger Moth	La Ferté-Alais, Essonne, France
G-AOGW	de Havilland DH.114 Heron 2E	Sault Sainte Marie, Ontario, Canada
G-AOHD (2)	Hunting Percival P 84 Jet Provost T 2	Point Cook, Victoria,Australia
G-AOIE	Douglas DC-7C	Leitrim, County Leitrim, Republic of Ireland
G-AOJG	Hunting-Percival P 66 President 1	Helsingør, Denmark
G-AOJT	de Havilland DH.106 Comet IXB	Salisbury Hall, London Colney, Hertfordshire
G-AOJX	de Havilland DH.82A Tiger Moth	Brussels, Belgium
G-AOKO	Percival P 40 Prentice 1	Doncaster, Yorkshire
G-AOKZ	Percival P 40 Prentice 1	Coventry, Warwickshire
G-AOMF	Percival P 40 Prentice 1	Wanaka, New Zealand
G-AOPL	Percival P 40 Prentice 1	Pretoria, South Africa
G-AOPO	Percival P 40 Prentice 1	Brussels, Belgium
G-AOSP	de Havilland DHC-1 Chipmunk 22	Scone, New South Wales, Australia
G-AOTI	de Havilland DH.114 Heron 2D	Salisbury Hall, London Colney, Hertfordshire
G-AOUF	de Havilland DH.104 Dove 6	Helsingør, Denmark
G-AOUJ	Fairey Ultralight Helicopter	Weston-super-Mare, Somerset
G-AOUR	de Havilland DH.82A Tiger Moth	Belfast, Northern Ireland
G-AOVF	Bristol 175 Britannia Series 312F	RAF Cosford, Shropshire
G-AOVT	Bristol 175 Britannia Series 312	Duxford, Cambridgeshire
G-AOXG	de Havilland DH.82A Tiger Moth	RNAS Yeovilton, Somerset
G-AOVU	de Havilland DH.106 Comet 4C	Seattle, Washington, US
G-AOXL	de Havilland DH.114 Heron 1B	Stavangar, Norway
G-AOYU	de Havilland DH.82A Tiger Moth	Wetaskiwin, Alberta, Canada
G-AOZE	Westland WS-51/2 Widgeon	Weston-super-Mare, Somerset
G-AOZZ	Armstrong-Whitworth 650 Argosy Series 100	Belleville, Michigan, US
G-APAD	Edgar Percival EP.9	Greenock, South Australia
G-APAS	de Havilland DH.106 Comet 1A	RAF Cosford, Shropshire
G-APCN	Boulton Paul P 108 Balliol T 2	Negombo, Sri Lanka
G-APDB	de Havilland DH.106 Comet 4	Duxford, Cambridgeshire
G-APEJ	Vickers 953C Vanguard Merchantman	Brooklands, Surrey
G-APEP	Vickers 953C Vanguard Merchantman	Brooklands, Surrey
G-APES	Vickers 953C Vanguard Merchantman	East Midlands
G-APFJ	Boeing 707-436	East Fortune, Scotland
G-APHV	Avro 652A Anson C 19 Series 2	East Fortune, Scotland
G-APHY	Scottish Aviation Twin Pioneer Series 1	Quesnel, British Columbia, Canada
G-APIM	Vickers 806 Viscount	Brooklands, Surrey
G-APIT	Percival P 40 Prentice 1	Lasham, Hampshire
G-APIY	Percival P 40 Prentice 1	Newark, Nottinghamshire
G-APJJ (2)	Fairey Ultralight Helicopter	Coventry, Warwickshire
G-APJP	de Havilland DH.82A Tiger Moth	Helsingør, Denmark
G-APJT	Scottish Aviation Twin Pioneer Series 1	Kuala Lumpur, Malaysia
G-APLG	Auster J/5L Aiglet Trainer	Carlisle, Cumbria
G-APMY	Piper PA-23-160 Apache	Doncaster, Yorkshire
G-APNJ	Cessna 310	Newark, Nottinghamshire
G-APNV	Saunders-Roe P 531-1	RNAS Yeovilton, Somerset
G-APPT	de Havilland DH.82A Tiger Moth	Brussels, Belgium
G-APRL	Armstrong-Whitworth 650 Argosy Series 101	Coventry, Warwickshire
G-APTS	de Havilland DHC-1 Chipmunk 22A	Adelaide, South Australia
G-APTW	Westland WS-51/2 Widgeon	Sunderland, Northumberland and Tyneside
G-APUD	Bensen B-7MC	Manchester
G-APUP	Sopwith Pup replica	Hendon, London
G-APVV	Mooney M 20A	Newark, Nottinghamshire
G-APWA	Handley Page HPR.7 Dart Herald 100	Woodley, Berkshire
G-APWJ	Handley Page HPR.7 Dart Herald 201	Duxford, Cambridgeshire
G-APWN	Westland WS-55 Whirlwind 3	Coventry, Warwickshire
G-APWY	Piaggio P 166	Wroughton, Wiltshire
G-APXA	Westland-Sikorsky S-55 Whirlwind Series 2	Kuwait City, Kuwaitt
G-APXB	Westland-Sikorsky S-55 Whirlwind Series 2	Kuwait City, Kuwait
G-APXG	de Havilland DH.114 Heron 2D	Winnipeg, Manitoba, Canada
G-APXW	Lancashire Aircraft EP-9 Prospector	AAC Middle Wallop, Hampshire
G-APXX	de Havilland DHA.3 Drover 2	Lasham, Hampshire
G-APYD	de Havilland DH.106 Comet 4B	Wroughton, Wiltshire
G-ARAD	Phoenix Luton LA-5A Major	Sunderland, Northumberland & Tyneside
G-ARCX	Gloster Meteor NF.14	East Fortune, Scotland
G-ARDE	de Havilland DH.104 Dove 6	Sharjah, United Arab Emirates
G-AREA	de Havilland DH.104 Dove 8	Salisbury Hall, London Colney, Hertfordshire
G-ARGI (2)	Auster 6A Tugmaster	Doncaster, Yorkshire
G-ARHX	de Havilland DH.104 Dove 8	Doncaster, Yorkshire
G-ARLU (2)	Cessna 172B	Baldonnel, Northern Ireland
G-ARPH	de Havilland DH.121 Trident 1C	East Fortune, Scotland
G-ARRM	Beagle B 206X	Shoreham, West Sussex
G-ARTZ (1)	McCandless M 2 Gyroplane	Belfast, Northern Ireland
G-ARUE (2)	de Havilland DH.104 Dove 7	Sinsheim, Germany

G-ARVF	Vickers VC-10 Series 1101	Hermeskeil, Trier, Germany
G-ARVM (2)	Vickers VC-10 Series 1101	Brooklands, Surrey
G-ARVN (2)	Servotec CR LTH 1 Grasshopper 1	Weston-super-Mare, Somerset
G-ARYB	de Havilland DH.125 Series 1	Coventry, Warwickshire
G-ARYC	de Havilland DH.125 Series 1	Salisbury Hall, London Colney, Hertfordshire
G-ARYD	Auster AOP.6	AAC Middle Wallop, Hampshire
G-ASCB	Beagle A 109 Airedale	Alverca, Portugal
G-ASCD	Beagle A 61 Terrier 2	Elvington, Yorkshire
G-ASCF	Beagle A 61 Terrier 2	Gardermoen, Norway
G-ASCT	Bensen B 7MC	Weston-super-Mare, Somerset
G-ASCX	de Havilland DH.114 Heron 2D	Launceston, Tasmania, Australia
G-ASCY	Phoenix Luton LA-4A Minor	Miami, Florida, US
G-ASDS	Vickers 843 Viscount	Beijing, China
G-ASFI	de Havilland DH.114 Heron 2D	Bankstown, New South Wales, Australia
G-ASGC	Vickers Super VC-10 Series 1151	Duxford, Cambridgeshire
G-ASHD	Brantly B 2A	Weston-super-Mare, Somerset
G-ASIX	Vickers VC-10 Series 1103	Brooklands, Surrey
G-ASJD	British Aircraft Corporation One-Eleven 201AC	Boscombe Down, Wiltshire
G-ASKB	de Havilland DH.98 Mosquito TT.35	Miami, Florida, US
G-ASKC	de Havilland DH.98 Mosquito TT.35	Duxford, Cambridgeshire
G-ASKK	Handley Page HPR.7 Dart Herald 211	Norwich, Norfolk
G-ASOF	Beagle B.206 Series.1	Birmingham, Alabama, US
G-ASOL	Bell 47D-1	Sunderland, Northumberland & Tyneside
G-ASRF	Gowland GWG.2 Jenny Wren	Flixton, Bungay, Suffolk
G-ASRL	Beagle A 61 Terrier 2	Krugersdorp, South Africa
G-ASSM	Hawker Siddeley HS.125 Series 1/522	South Kensington, London
G-ASSZ	Cessna 310A	Helsingør, Denmark
G-ASTL	Fairey Firefly 1	RNAS Yeovilton, Somerset
G-ASTP	Hiller UH-12C	Weston-super-Mare, Somerset
G-ASUG	Beech E18S-9700	East Fortune, Scotland
G-ASVC	de Havilland DH.114 Heron 2D	Caloundra, Queensland, Australia
G-ASVO	Handley Page HPR.7 Dart Herald 214	Inverness, Scotland
G-ASWJ	Beagle B 206C Series 1	(Coventry, Warwickshire)
G-ASXM	Armstrong-Whitworth 650 Argosy Series 222	Marlborough, New Zealand
G-ASXN	Armstrong-Whitworth 650 Argosy Series 222	Marlborough, New Zealand
G-ASXX	Avro 683 Lancaster B VII	East Kirkby, Lincolnshire
G-ASYD	British Aircraft Corporation One-Eleven 475AM	Brooklands, Surrey
G-ATBZ	Westland WS-58 Wessex 60 Series 1	Weston-super-Mare, Somerset
G-ATDD	Beagle B 206 Series 1	Kemble, Gloucestershire
G-ATFG	Brantly B 2B	Weston-super-Mare, Somerset
G-ATGJ	de Havilland DH.104 Riley Dove 5	Ballarat, Victoria, Australia
G-ATGK	de Havilland DH.104 Riley Dove 400	Amman, Jordan
G-ATJJ	de Havilland DHC.1 Chipmunk 22	Brooklands, Surrey
G-ATKV	Westland WS-55 Whirlwind 3	Weston-super-Mare, Somerset
G-ATOY	Piper PA-24-260 Comanche B	East Fortune, Scotland
G-ATTN	Piccard Balloon (Hot Air) (62,000 cu ft)	Wroughton, Wiltshire
G-ATVP	Vickers FB.5 Gunbus replica	Hendon, London
G-ATXL	Avro 504K replica	Rhinebeck, New York, US
G-ATXX	McCandless M 4	Belfast, Northern Ireland
G-AVAA	Cessna F150G	Doncaster, Yorkshire
G-AVAV	Vickers Supermarine 509 Spitfire Tr.9	Oshkosh, Wisconsin, US
G-AVFH	Hawker Siddeley HS.121 Trident 2E	Salisbury Hall, London Colney, Hertfordshire
G-AVFB	Hawker Siddeley HS.121 Trident 2E	Duxford, Cambridgeshire
G-AVHE	Vickers 812 Viscount	Stuttgart, Germany
G-AVJB	Vickers 815 Viscount	Hillerstorp, Sweden
G-AVKE	Gadfly HDW-1	Weston-super-Mare, Somerset
G-AVLP	Beagle B.206 Series.2	Birmingham, Alabama, US
G-AVMO	British Aircraft Corporation One-Eleven 510ED	East Fortune, Scotland
G-AVMU	British Aircraft Corporation One-Eleven 510ED	Duxford, Cambridgeshire
G-AVNE	Westland WS-58 Wessex 60 Series 1	Weston-super-Mare, Somerset
G-AVPC	Druine D 31 Turbulent	East Fortune, Scotland
G-AVPN	Handley Page HPR.7 Dart Herald 213	Elvington, Yorkshire
G-AVVO	Avro 652A Anson 19 Series 2	Newark, Nottinghamshire
G-AVVR	Avro 652A Anson 19 Series 2	Pendeford, Wolverhampton, West Midlands
G-AVXV	Bleriot XI	La Baule, Loire-Atlantique, France
G-AVZB	LET Z-37 Cmelak	Wroughton, Wiltshire
G-AWAU	Vickers FB.27A Vimy replica	Hendon, London
G-AWAW	Cessna F150F	South Kensington, London
G-AWFM	de Havilland DH.104 Dove 6	Johannesburg, South Africa
G-AWHA	CASA 2111D	Munich, Germany
G-AWHB	CASA 2111D	Seattle, Washington, US
G-AWHE	Hispano HA.1112-MIL Buchon	Midland, Texas, US
G-AWHJ	Hispano HA.1112-MIL Buchon	Kalamazoo, Michigan, US
G-AWHL	Hispano HA.1112-MIL Buchon	Seattle, Washington, US
G-AWHN	Hispano HA.1112-MIL Buchon	Tillamook, Oregon, US
G-AWHO	Hispano HA.1112-MIL Buchon	Oshkosh, Wisconsin, US
G-AWHS	Hispano HA.1112-MIL Buchon	Sinsheim, Germany
G-AWID	Britten-Norman BN-2A Islander	Khlong Luang, Thailand
G-AWIJ	Vickers Supermarine 329 Spitfire IIA	RAF Coningsby, Lincolnshire
G-AWJV	de Havilland DH.98 Mosquito TT.35	Salisbury Hall, London Colney, Hertfordshire
G-AWON	English Electric Lightning F 53	Norwich, Norfolk
G-AWRP	Servotech CR.LTH.1 Grasshopper II	Weston-super-Mare, Somerset
G-AWRS	Avro 652A Anson C 19 Series 2	Sunderland, Northumberland & Tyneside
G-AWSA	Avro 652A Anson C 19/2	Flixton, Bungay, Suffolk

G-AWTD	Percival P 56 Provost T 1	Gweru, Zimbabwe
G-AWYY	Slingsby T 57 Sopwith Camel F 1 replica	RNAS Yeovilton, Somerset
G-AWZI	Hawker Siddeley HS.121 Trident 3B Series 101	Farnborough, Hampshire
G-AWZJ	Hawker Siddeley HS.121 Trident 3B Series 101	Dumfries, Scotland
G-AWZK	Hawker Siddeley HS.121 Trident 3B Series 101	Manchester
G-AWZM	Hawker Siddeley HS.121 Trident 3B Series 101	Wroughton, Wiltshire
G-AWZP	Hawker Siddeley HS.121 Trident 3B Series 101	Manchester
G-AXDN	British Aircraft Corporation Concorde	Duxford, Cambridgeshire
G-AXEE	English Electric Lightning F 53	Kuwait City, Kuwait
G-AXEF	British Aircraft Corporation 167 Strikemaster Mk.81	Santa Rosa, California , US
G-AXEH	Beagle B 125 Bulldog 1	East Fortune, Scotland (See G-CCOA below)
G-AXFM	Servotec CR.LTH.1 Grasshopper II	Weston-super-Mare, Somerset
G-AXKS	Westland-Bell 47G-4A	AAC Middle Wallop, Hampshire
G-AXOM	Penn-Smith Gyroplane	Lower Stondon, Bedfordshire
G-AYAG	Boeing 707-321	Leitrim, County Leitrim, Republic of Ireland
G-AYAZ	Britten-Norman BN-2A-7 Islander	Hong Kong, China
G-AYBX	Campbell Cricket	Alexandria, Egypt
G-AYFA	Scottish Aviation Twin Pioneer Mk.3	Carlisle, Cumbria
G-AYFO	Bücker Bü.133 Jungmeister	Polk City, Florida, US
G-AYHS	British Aircraft Corporation 167 Strikemaster Mk.84	Olympia, Washington, US
G-AYTA	SOCATA MS.880B Rallye Club	Manchester
G-AYUK	Western-Brighton M-B65 Balloon (Hot Air)	Munich, Germany
G-AYXT	Westland WS-55 Whirlwind HAS.7 (Series 2)	Weston-super-Mare, Somerset
G-AYZJ	Westland WS-55 Whirlwind HAS.7	Newark, Nottinghamshire
G-AYZM	Scottish Aviation Bulldog Series 101	Halmstad, Sweden
G-AZAK	Scottish Aviation Bulldog Series 101 (SK-61)	Linköping, Sweden
G-AZAU	Servotec CR.LTH.1 Grasshopper II	Weston-super-Mare, Somerset
G-AZAZ	Bensen B 8M	RNAS Yeovilton, Somerset
G-AZBV	Britten-Norman BN-2A-2 Islander	Beersheba, Israel
G-AZCM	Beagle B 121 Pup Series 150	Manston
G-AZFW	Hawker Siddeley HS.121 Trident 2E Series 102	Guangzou, China
G-AZJO	Scottish Aviation Bulldog Series 101 (SK-61)	Linköping, Sweden
G-AZLM	Reims Cessna F172L	Flixton, Bungay, Suffolk
G-AZPH	Pitts S 1S	South Kensington, London
G-AZWO	Scottish Aviation Bulldog Series 101 (SK-61)	Linköping, Sweden
G-AZYB	Bell 47H-1	Weston-super-Mare, Somerset
G-BACK	de Havilland DH.82A Tiger Moth	Santiago, Chile
G-BAGJ	Westland SA.341G Gazelle 1	Sunderland, Northumberland & Tyneside
G-BAHB	de Havilland DH.104 Dove 5	Port Adelaide, South Australia
G-BAMH	Westland S-55 Whirlwind Series 3	East Midlands
G-BAJJ	Hawker Siddeley HS.121 Trident 2E Series 108	Beijing, China
G-BAPS	Campbell Cougar Gyroplane	Weston-super-Mare, Somerset
G-BAVN	Boeing Stearman A75N-1 Kaydet	Västerås, Sweden
G-BBBV	Handley Page HP.137 Jetstream	East Fortune, Scotland
G-BBDG	British Aircraft Corporation Concorde Type 1 Variant 100	Brooklands, Surrey
G-BBGN	Cameron A-375 Balloon (Hot Air)	Wroughton, Wiltshire
G-BBMI	Dewoitine D 26	Polk City, Florida, US
G-BBNC	de Havilland DHC-1 Chipmunk T 10	Salisbury Hall, London Colney, Hertfordshire
G-BBVF	Scottish Aviation Twin Pioneer 3	East Fortune, Scotland
G-BBVU	Hawker Siddeley HS.121 Trident 2E Series 109	Guangzou, China
G-BBVV	Hawker Siddeley HS.121 Trident 2E Series 109	Nanjing, China
G-BBVW	Hawker Siddeley HS.121 Trident 2E Series 109	Guangzou, China
G-BBVZ	Hawker Siddeley HS.121 Trident 2E Series 109	Beijing, China
G-BBWG	Hawker Siddeley HS.121 Trident 2E Series 109	Beijing, China
G-BBZL	Westland-Bell 47G-3B1	Stavangar, Norway
G-BBYM	Handley Page HP.137 Jetstream 200	RAF Cosford, Shropshire
G-BCOH	Avro 683 Lancaster Mk.10 AR	Polk City, Florida, US
G-BCWL	Westland Lysander IIIA	Polk City, Florida, US
G-BCXO	MBB BÖ.105DD	Land's End, Cornwall
G-BCYK	Avro (Canada) CF-100 Canuck Mk.IV	Duxford, Cambridgeshire
G-BCZS	Fairey Britten-Norman BN-2A-21 Islander	Stavangar, Norway
G-BDBS	Short SD.3-30 UTT	Langford Lodge, Belfast, Northern Ireland
G-BDBZ	Westland WS-55 Whirlwind 2 (HAR.10)	Elvington, Yorkshire
G-BDDX	Whittaker MW2B Excalibur	Trago Mills, Newton Abbot, Devon
G-BDFU	PMPS Dragonfly MPA Mk.1	East Fortune, Scotland
G-BDIW	de Havilland DH.106 Comet 4C	Hermeskeil, Trier, Germany
G-BDIX	de Havilland DH.106 Comet 4C	East Fortune, Scotland
G-BDVO	Short SC.7 Skyvan 3 Variant 100	Caracas, Venezuela
G-BDPU	Fairey Britten-Norman BN-2A-21 Islander	Brussels, Belgium
G-BDUP	Bristol 175 Britannia Series 253	Kemble, Gloucestershire
G-BDVS	Fokker F 27 Friendship 200	Flixton, Bungay, Suffolk
G-BDYG	Percival P 56 Provost T 1	East Fortune, Scotland
G-BEBC	Westland WS-55 Whirlwind HAR.10	Norwich, Norfolk
G-BECL	CASA 352L	La Ferté-Alais, Essonne, France
G-BECE	Aerospace Developments AD500 Series B.1 Airship	Doncaster, Yorkshire
G-BEDV	Vickers 668 Varsity T 1	Duxford, Cambridgeshire
G-BEED	Fairey Britten-Norman BN-2A-21 Islander	Grace Hollogne, Belgium
G-BEEX	de Havilland DH.106 Comet 4C	Sunderland, Northumberland & Tyneside
G-BEOX	Lockheed 414 Hudson IIIA	Hendon, London
G-BEOZ	Armstrong-Whitworth AW.650 Argosy 101	East Midlands
G-BESY	British Aircraft Corporation 167 Strikemaster Mk.80A	Duxford, Cambridgeshire
G-BEWT	Short SD.3-30 Variant 100	Millville, New Jersey, US
G-BEYB	Fairey Flycatcher replica	RNAS Yeovilton, Somerset
G-BEYF	Handley Page HPR.7 Dart Herald 401 (nose only)	Wycombe Air Park, Buckinghamshire

G-BFBP	Piper PA-25-235 Pawnee D	Wainfleet, Lincolnshire
G-BFCZ	Sopwith Camel F 1 replica	Brooklands, Surrey
G-BFDE	Sopwith Tabloid Scout replica	Hendon, London
G-BFEY	Piper PA-25-235 Pawnee D	Wainfleet, Lincolnshire
G-BFHD	CASA 352L	Washington, US
G-BFHE	CASA 352L	Johannesburg, South Africa
G-BFHG	CASA 352L	Polk City, Florida, US
G-BFIP	Wallbro Monoplane replica	Flixton, Bungay, Suffolk
G-BFOO	British Aircraft Corporation 167 Strikemaster Mk.80A	Dhahran, Saudi Arabia
G-BFTZ	SOCATA MS.880B Rallye Club	Newark, Nottinghamshire
G-BFXL	Williams Albatross D Va replica	RNAS Yeovilton, Somerset
G-BFYO	SPAD XIII replica	Duxford, Cambridgeshire
G-BGCF	Douglas C-47A-90-DL Dakota	Barksdale AFB, Louisiana, US
G-BGGR	North American AT-6A Harvard	Stuttgart, Germany
G-BGHF	Westland WG.30 Series 100-60	Weston-super-Mare, Somerset
G-BGLB	Bede BD.5B	Wroughton, Wiltshire
G-BGSB	Hunting-Percival P 56 Provost T 1	Bait al Falaj, Muscat, Oman
G-BGWZ	Eclipse Super Eagle	RNAS Yeovilton, Somerset
G-BHDK	Boeing TB-29A-45-BN Superfortress	Duxford, Cambridgeshire
G-BHMY	Fokker F 27 Friendship 600	Norwich, Norfolk
G-BHNG	Piper PA-23-250 Aztec E	Filching Manor, Wannock, Sussex
G-BHUB	Douglas C-47A-85-DL Dakota	Duxford, Cambridgeshire
G-BHUW	Boeing Stearman A75N1 (N2S-5) Kaydet	Munich, Germany
G-BIAT	Sopwith Pup replica	Christchurch, New Zealand
G-BIAU	Sopwith Pup replica	RNAS Yeovilton, Somerset
G-BIDN	Percival P.57 Sea Prince T.1	New York, Ontario, Canada
G-BIDW	Sopwith 1½ Strutter replica	Hendon, London
G-BIHN	Airship Industries Skyship 500	Millom, Cumbria
G-BIRW	Morane Saulnier MS.505 Criquet	East Fortune, Scotland
G-BJAD	Clutton FRED Series II	Newark, Nottinghamshire
G-BJCL	Morane Saulnier MS.230 Parasol	Polk City, Florida, US
G-BJHS	Short S 25 Sandringham	Polk City, Florida, US
G-BJHV	Voisin Scale replica	Brooklands, Surrey
G-BJSG	Vickers Supermarine 361 Spitfire LF.IXc	Chino, California, US
G-BJWY	Sikorsky S-55 (HRS-2) Whirlwind HAR.21	Carlisle, Cumbria
G-BKBR (2)	Cameron Chateau 84SS Balloon (Hot Air)	Balleroy, Calvados, France
G-BKDT	Royal Aircraft Factory SE.5a replica	Elvington, Yorkshire
G-BKFD	Westland WG.30 Series 100	Weston-super-Mare, Somerset
G-BKFF	Westland WG.30 Series 100	Weston-super-Mare, Somerset
G-BKGD	Westland WG.30 Series 100	Weston-super-Mare, Somerset
G-BKLZ	Vinten Wallis WA-116MC	Hermeskeil, Trier, Germany
G-BKMW	Short SD.3-30 Sherpa Variant 100	Belfast, Ireland
G-BKNN	Cameron Minar-E-Pakistan Balloon (Hot Air)	Balleroy, Calvados, France
G-BKPG	Luscombe P3 Rattler Strike	Newark, Nottinghamshire
G-BKPY	SAAB 91B/2 Safir	Newark, Nottinghamshire
G-BKRG	Beech C-45G-BH	Lelystad, Netherlands
G-BKRL	Chichester-Miles Leopard	Bournemouth, Dorset
G-BLFE	Cameron Sphinx 72 SS Balloon (Hot Air)	Balleroy, Calvados, France
G-BLFL	Douglas C-47B-45-DK Dakota	Berlin, Germany
G-BLKA	de Havilland DH.112 Venom FB.Mk.54	Salisbury Hall, London Colney, Hertfordshire
G-BLKU	Colt Flame 56 SS Balloon (Hot Air)	Manchester
(G-BLMC)	Avro 698 Vulcan B 2A	East Midlands
G-BLRW	Cameron Elephant 77 SS Balloon (Hot Air)	Balleroy, Calvados, France
G-BLWM	Bristol 20 M 1C replica	Hendon, London
(G-BLXI (1))	Bleriot Type XI replica	Cannes, France
G-BLZW	Republic P-47D-30-RA Thunderbolt	Palm Springs, California, US
G-BMEW	Lockheed 18-56 Lodestar	Gardermoen, Norway
G-BMFB	Douglas Skyraider AEW.1 (AD-4W)	Tillamook, Oregon, US
G-BMUN	Cameron Harley 78 SS Balloon (Hot Air)	Balleroy, Calvados, France
G-BMWN	Cameron Temple 80 SS Balloon (Hot Air)	Balleroy, Calvados, France
G-BMYP	Fairey Gannet AEW.3	Elvington, Yorkshire
G-BMZF	Aero-Vodochody SBLim-2A	RNAS Yeovilton, Somerset
G-BNFK	Cameron Egg 89 SS Balloon (Hot Air)	Balleroy, Calvados, France
G-BNPG	Percival P 66 Pembroke C 1	Västerås, Sweden
G-BNJU	Cameron Bust 80 SS Balloon (Hot Air)	Balleroy, Calvados, France
G-BOAA	British Aircraft Corporation Concorde Type 1 Variant 102	East Fortune, Scotland
G-BOAB	British Aircraft Corporation Concorde Type 1 Variant 102	London Heathrow
G-BOAC	British Aircraft Corporation Concorde Type 1 Variant 102	Manchester
G-BOAD	British Aircraft Corporation Concorde Type 1 Variant 102	New York, US
G-BOAE	British Aircraft Corporation Concorde Type 1 Variant 102	Barbados Grantley Adams
G-BOAF	British Aircraft Corporation Concorde Type 1 Variant 102	Filton, Bristol
G-BOAG	British Aircraft Corporation Concorde Type 1 Variant 102	Seattle, Washington, US
G-BOCB	Hawker Siddeley HS.125 Series 1B/522	Doncaster, Yorkshire
G-BOOM	Hawker Hunter T 7 (T 53)	Amman, Jordan
G-BPLT	Bristol 20 M 1C replica	Los Cerillos, Santiago, Chile
G-BPOV	Cameron Magazine 90 SS Balloon (Hot Air)	Balleroy, Calvados, France
G-BPSP	Cameron Ship 90 SS Balloon (Hot Air)	Balleroy, Calvados, France
G-BRAM	Mikoyan MiG-21PF	RAF Cosford, Shropshire
G-BRDV	Replica Viking Spitfire prototype	Southampton, Hampshire
G-BRMA	Westland-Sikorsky S-51 Dragonfly HR.5	Weston-super-Mare, Somerset
G-BRMB	Bristol 192 Belvedere HC.1	Weston-super-Mare, Somerset
G-BRMC	Stampe et Renard SV-4B	Antwerp, Belgium
G-BRNM	Chichester-Miles Leopard	Bournemouth, Dorset
G-BRXM	Colt GA-42 Gas Airship.	Helsinki, Finland

G-BSKS	Nieuport 28C-1	Fort Rucker, Alabama, US
G-BSST	British Aircraft Corporation Concorde 002	RNAS Yeovilton, Somerset
G-BSSY	CSS-13 Aeroklubowy	Old Warden, Bedfordshire
G-BTHD	Yakovlev Yak-3U	Chino, California, US
G-BTSY	English Electric Lightning F 6	Binbrook, Lincolnshire
G-BTUC	Embraer EMB-312 Tucano	Langford Lodge, Belfast, Northern Ireland
G-BUCF	Grumman F8F-1B Bearcat	Chino, California, US
G-BURM	English Electric Canberra TT.18	Temora, New South Wales, Australia
G-BUWA	Vickers Supermarine 349 Spitfire F Vc	Seattle, Washington, US
G-BVLM	de Havilland DH.115 Vampire T 55	Amman, Jordan
G-BVOL	Douglas C-47B-40-DL Dakota	Lelystad, Netherlands
G-BVPO	de Havilland DH.100 Vampire FB.6	Amman, Jordan
G-BVWG	Hawker Hunter T 8C	Cape Town, South Africa
G-BVWV	Hawker Hunter F 6A	Cape Town, South Africa
G-BWGR	North American TB-25N-NC Mitchell	Brussels, Belgium
G-BWJZ	de Havilland DHC-1 Chipmunk 22	Manston, Kent
G-BWKA	Hawker Hunter F 58	Amman, Jordan
G-BWKC	Hawker Hunter F 58	Amman, Jordan
G-BXSL	Westland Scout AH.Mk.1	Hermeskeil, Trier, Germany
G-BXYA	Lotnicze Zaklady Naprawcz CSS-13	Polk City, Florida, US
G-BYDR	North American B-25D Mitchell	Seattle, Washington, US
G-BYDS	Messerschmitt Bf.109E-3	Seattle, Washington, US
G-BYKV	Avro 504K replica	Point Cook, Victoria, Australia
G-BZNL	North American F-86A Sabre	Seattle, Washington, US
G-CBEP	British Aerospace Jetstream Series 3200	Bankstown, New South Wales, Australia
G-CCMV	Vought FG-1D Corsair	Addison, Dallas, Texas, US
G-CCVV	Vickers Supermarine 379 Spitfire FR.XIVe	Polk City, Florida, US
G-CONI	Lockheed 749A-79 Constellation	Wroughton, Wiltshire
G-DELB	Robinson R22 Beta	Doncaster, Yorkshire
G-DUCK	Grumman G 44 Widgeon (OA-14)	Biscarrosse, Landes, France
G-DEVN	de Havilland DH.104 Devon C 2/2	Merseburg, Germany
G-DMCA	McDonnell Douglas DC-10-30	Manchester International
G-EHIL	EH Industries EH-101	Weston-super-Mare, Somerset
G-ELEC	Westland WG.30 Series 200	Weston-super-Mare, Somerset
G-EFIS	Westland WG.30 Series 100	Weston-super- Mare
G-FIST	Fieseler Fi.156C-3 Storch	Vigna di Valle, Italy
G-FIRE	Vickers Supermarine 379 Spitfire FR.XIVc	Palm Springs, California, US
G-FOKW	Focke-Wulf Fw.190A-5	Seattle, Washington, US
G-FORT	Boeing 299-O (B-17G-95-DL) Fortress	Galveston, New Mexico, US
G-FRJB	Aircraft Designs Sheriff SA-1	East Midlands
G-FSIX	English Electric Lightning F 6	Cape Town, South Africa
G-FXIV	Vickers Supermarine 379 Spitfire FR.XIVc	Hannover, Germany
G-HAUL	Westland WG.30-300	Weston-super-Mare, Somerset
G-HELI	Saro Skeeter AOP.12	Gatow, Berlin, Germany
G-HNTR	Hawker Hunter T 7	Elvington, Yorkshire
G-HUNN	Hispano HA.1112-M1L Buchon	Addison, Dallas, Texas, US
G-HUNT	Hawker Hunter F 51	Oshkosh, Wisconsin, US
G-IRJX	BAE Systems Avro 146-RJX100	Manchester
G-JMAC	British Aerospace Jetstream Series 4100	Liverpool, Merseyside
G-JSSD	Handley Page HP.137 Jetstream 1	East Fortune, Scotland
G-LANC	Avro 683 Lancaster B X	Duxford, Cambridgeshire
G-LIOA	Lockheed 10A Electra	South Kensington, London
G-LIZY	Westland Lysander III	Duxford, Cambridgeshire
G-LTNG	English Electric Lightning T 5	Cape Town, South Africa
G-LYNX	Westland WG.13 Lynx 800	Weston-super-Mare, Somerset
G-MBBZ	Volmer VJ.24W	Newark, Nottinghamshire
G-MBDL	Striplin (AES) Lone Ranger	Sunderland, Northumberland & Tyneside
G-MBEP	American Aerolights Eagle 215B	Caernarfon, Wales
G-MJDW	Eipper Quicksilver MXII	Newark, Nottinghamshire
G-MJKP	Hiway Skystrike/Super Scorpion	Doncaster, Yorkshire
G-MJPB	Manuel Ladybird	Brooklands, Surrey
G-MJRA	Mainair Tri-Flyer 250/Hiway Demon	Elvington, Yorkshire
G-MJSU	MBA Tiger Cub 440	Flixton, Bungay, Suffolk
(G-MJWH)	Chargus Vortex 120	Coventry, Warwickshire
G-MJWS	Eurowing Goldwing	Langford Lodge, Belfast, Northern Ireland
G-MJXE	Mainair Tri-Flyer 330/Hiway Demon 175	Manchester
G-MMCB	Huntair Pathfinder II	Wroughton, Wiltshire
G-MMLI	Mainair Tri-Flyer 250/Solar Wings Typhoon S	East Fortune, Scotland
G-MTFK	Moult Trike/Flexiform Striker	Flixton, Bungay, Suffolk
G-MURY	Robinson R44 Astro	Chantilly, Virginia, US
G-OGIL	Short SD.3-30 Variant.100	Sunderland, Northumberland & Tyneside
G-OIOI	EH Industries EH-101 Heliliner	Hendon, London
G-OMIG	Aero-Vodochody SBLim-2A	San Carlos, Brazil
G-OTED	Robinson R22HP	Weston-super-Mare, Somerset
G-OTHL	Robinson R22 Beta	Hendon, London
G-OPAS	Vickers 806 Viscount	Bournemouth, Dorset
G-OPIB	English Electric Lightning F 6	Cape Town, South Africa
G-PASB	MBB BÖ.105D	Weston-super-Mare, Somerset
G-RBOS	Colt AS 105 Airship (Hot Air)	Wroughton, Wiltshire
G-RENT	Robinson R22 Beta	Langford Lodge, Belfast, Northern Ireland
G-RWWW	Westland WS-55 Whirlwind HCC.12	Weston-super-Mare, Somerset
G-SALY	Hawker Sea Fury FB.X	Midland, Texas, US
G-SEXY	American AA-1 Yankee	Liverpool, Merseyside
G-SFTA	Westland SA.341G Gazelle 1	Sunderland, Northumberland & Tyneside

G-SWIF	Vickers Supermarine 552 Swift F 7	Southampton, Hampshire
G-SXVI	Vickers Supermarine 361 Spitfire LF.XVIe	McMinnville, Oregon, US
G-TFRB	Air Command 532 Elite Sport	Elvington, Yorkshire
G-THUN	Republic P-47D-40RA Thunderbolt	Millville, New Jersey, US
G-TURK	Cameron Sultan 80 SS Balloon (Hot Air)	Balleroy, Calvados, France
G-TURP	Aérospatiale SA341G Gazelle 1	Charlwood, Surrey
G-USTV	Messerschmitt Bf.109G-2/Trop	Hendon, London
G-USUK	Colt 2500A Balloon (Hot Air)	Duxford, Cambridgeshire
G-VIII	Vickers Supermarine 359 Spitfire LF.VIII	Addison, Dallas, Texas, US
G-VTOL	Hawker Siddeley Harrier T 52	Brooklands, Surrey
G-WWII	Vickers-Supermarine 379 Spitfire F.XIVe	Chino, California, US
G-XVIB	Vickers Supermarine 361 Spitfire LF.XVIe	Polk City, Florida, US

PART 4 – AIRCRAFT REGISTERED and CANCELLED in 2008 and 2009

Registration	Type	Construction Number	Previous Identity	Date	Registered Owner (Operator)	Cancellation details	Date
G-BABH	Reims Cessna F150L	F1500820	(OD-) G-BABH	27. 2.08	S Ghoussub (Cancelled 26.2.08 then restored 27.2.08)	To OD-	27.2.08
G-BHBI	Mooney M.20J (Mooney 201)	24-0842	N4764H	24. 9.79	D Caron (Restored 7. 2.08 after cancelled by CAA 3. 1.08)	To F-	25.4.08
G-CDUP	Boeing 757-236	24793	SE-DUP G-CDUP, SE-DUP, G-OOOT, G-BRJJ, EC-490, G-BRJJ	29. 6.90	Thomsonfly.com	To G-LSAJ	6. 5.08
G-CEUI	Rotorsport UK MT-03	RSUK/MT-03/021		10. 3.08	C M Jones (Destroyed in crash 9. 5.08 at Kirkbride)	Cancelled by CAA	23. 9.08
G-CEXT	Eurocopter AS.365N3 Dauphin 2	6808		4. 6.08	Eurocopter UK Ltd	To ZJ780	7. 1.09
G-CEXU	Eurocopter AS.365N3 Dauphin 2	6813		21. 5.08	Eurocopter UK Ltd	To ZJ781	7. 1.09
G-CEXV	Eurocopter AS.365N3 Dauphin 2	6818		1. 7.08	Eurocopter UK Ltd	To ZJ782	19. 1.09
G-CEXW	Eurocopter AS.365N3 Dauphin 2	6822		30. 7.08	Eurocopter UK Ltd	To ZJ783	24.10.08
G-CEXZ	Eurocopter EC.155B1	6789	F-WQDF	1. 2.08	Eurocopter UK Ltd	To G-HOTB	22. 4.08
G-CEYT	Fuji FA.200-180AO	FA200-249	PH-PDZ	7. 2.08	T R Cooper	To 5H-	8. 5.08
G-CEYV	British Aerospace Jetstream 4100	41075	N559HK G-4-075	25. 3.08	Trident Turboprop (Dublin) Ltd	To SX-	17. 6.08
G-CEYW	British Aerospace Jetstream 4100	41076	N560HK G-4-076	25. 3.08	Trident Turboprop (Dublin) Ltd	To SX-ROD	24. 7.08
G-CFBD	Cessna 150M	150-76736	N45103	29. 5.08	J S Willcocks	To G-NWFA	29. 5.08
G-CFBU	Fokker F.28-0100	11498	EC-JOM HB-JVD, N1466A, PH-EZK	4. 8.08	Eskglen Shipping Company Ltd	To 5N-HIR	16. 1.09
G-CFDW	Piaggio P.180 Avanti	1086	YV-1676 I-BPAF	2. 4.08	International Trade Holding Co SA	To N108GF	3. 4.08
G-CFHE	Eurocopter AS.350B3 Ecureuil	4536		1. 9.08	Helicopters Worldwide Ltd (Canx 2. 1.09 as reregd in New Zealand)	Jersey 13.10.09E	
G-CFHH	Eurocopter EC.130B4	4537		16. 7.08	Eurocopter UK Ltd (Cancelled by CAA)	Cancelled	13.11.08
G-CFIR	Grob G.109B	6205	D-KGFM	29. 5.08	D A Smith		
G-CFIV	Cameron TR-70 Balloon (Hot-Air)	11093		7. 7.08	Cameron Balloons Ltd	To OE-	29. 9.08
G-CFIX	Van's RV-9 (Built S Shannon)	90121	N211TX	10. 4.08	W H Greenwood	To G-IOSL	22. 1.09
G-CFJC	Sikorsky S-76C	760708	N415Y	13. 8.08	Bristow Helicopters Ltd	To N415Y	15. 8.08
G-CFJT	Centrair 101A Pegase	101A0284	BGA304-FJT	31. 3.08	D M Smith and A Marlow	To PH-	4. 9.08
G-CFOD	Boeing 737-329	23774	EC-JQX	31.10.08	CIT Capital Aviation (UK) Ltd	To N473CT	5.11.08
G-CFPK	Parajet Powered Parachute	100		26.11.08	Parajet Automotive Ltd (Cancelled as temporarily withdrawn from use)	Cancelled	15. 1.09
G-CFRO	Parajet Powered Parachute Skybuggy	200		12. 1.09	Parajet Automotive Ltd (Cancelled as temporarily withdrawn from use)	Cancelled	15. 1.09
G-CFRU	Robinson R44 Raven II	12561		10.12.08	Heli Air Ltd	To G-OMMA	15. 1.09
G-CHPC	Schleicher ASW 20CL	20787	BGA4087-HPC D-3424	4. 1.08	P J Williams and B L Liddiard (Cancelled as destroyed)	Cancelled	23.10.08
G-CKCA	Rolladen-Schneider LS8-18	8424	BGA4974-KCA		M K Ganszauge, I Haikonen and I Tourola (Restored 2. 6.08)	To OH-	8. 9.08
G-CPEU	Boeing 757-236	29941	C-FLEU G-CPEU, C-FLEU, G-CPEU, G-CPEU, N1795B	1. 5.99	Thomson Airways Ltd	To Canada 16.12.08E	
G-CPEV	Boeing 757-236	29943	C-GOEV G-CPEV, C-GOEV, G-CPEV, N1795B, (G-CPEW)	11. 6.99	Thomson Airways Ltd	To Canada 19.12.08E	
G-DCVT	PZL-Bielsko SZD-36A Cobra 15	W-609	BGA1847-CVT	23. 1.08	P Q Benn	To SP	3. 3.08
G-DHJZ	Airbus A320-214	1965	C-FOJZ G-DHJZ, C-FOJZ, G-DHJZ, C-FOJZ, G-DHJZ, C-FOJZ, G-DHJZ, F-WWDY	9. 4.03	Thomas Cook Airlines Ltd	To Canada 18.12.08E	
G-DHRG	Airbus A320-214	1942	C-GHRG G-DHRG, C-GHRG, G-DHRG, OY-VKR, G-DHRG, F-WWIY	12. 3.03	Thomas Cook Airlines Ltd	To Canada 15.12.08E	
G-DOSA	Diamond DA.42MPP Twin Star	42.319	OE-VDK OE-FHG	14. 7.08	DO Systems Ltd	To ZA179	7.11.08
G-DOSB	Diamond DA.42MPP Twin Star	42.328		14. 7.08	DO Systems Ltd	To ZA180	7.11.08
G-ECOB	de Havilland DHC-8-402	4185	C-FNEN	18. 1.08	Flybe Ltd	To LN-WDT	1. 8.08
G-ECOC	de Havilland DHC-8-402	4197	C-FOKA	20. 3.08	Flybe Ltd	To LN-WDU	6.11.08
G-ECOE	de Havilland DHC-8-402	4212	C-FQXJ	30. 7.08	Flybe Ltd	To LN-WDV	9.10.08
G-ECOF	de Havilland DHC-8-402	4216	C-GRJU	21. 8.08	Flybe Ltd	To LN-WDW	3. 9.08
G-HOIL	Learjet 60	60-313	N613H N4003L	7. 3.08	Direct Air Executive Ltd	To M-	9. 1.09
G-IPAC	Cessna 550 Citation Bravo	550-0935	G-IPAL EI-PAL, N5264A	21. 4.08	Executive Aviation Services Ltd	To G-YPRS	11. 6.08
G-JMCW	Bombardier CL600-2B16 (CL-604 Challenger)	5403	D-ADND N604DC, C-GLWV	27. 2.08	MP Aviation LLP	To G-MPJM	30. 4.08
G-JMMD	Bombardier CL600-2B16 (CL-604 Challenger)	5422	D-ADNE N605DC, C-GLXU	27. 2.08	MP Aviation LLP	To G-MPCW	30. 4.08
G-KAZD	Sikorsky S-76C	760664	N4508N	31. 1.08	Caledonian Helicopters Ltd	To 9M-SPW	3. 4.08
G-KKAZ	Airbus A320-214	2003	C-FZAZ G-KKAZ, C-FZAZ, G-KKAZ, C-FZAZ, G-KKAZ, C-FZAZ, G-KKAZ, C-FZAZ, G-KKAZ, F-WWBN	23. 5.03	Thomas Cook Airways Ltd	To C-FZAZ	5.11.08
G-LAVH	Robinson R.22			7. 4.08	Lakeside Collection Ltd (Crashed Bury 15. 5.08 and cancelled as destroyed)	Cancelled	4.11.08
G-NAVA	Bell 430	49123	N4324X	3. 4.08	V Kpnstantakopoulus	To SX-	1. 7.08
G-OASG	Schleicher ASW 27-18	29015	13. 2.08		P F Brice	To D-	23. 9.08
G-OOBA	Boeing 757-28A	32446	C-GUBA G-OOBA, N446GE, (N558NA)	9. 2.01	Thomson Airways Ltd	To C-	19.12.08
G-OOBG	Boeing 757-236	29942	C-FUBG G-OOBG, C-FUBG, G-OOBG, C-FUBG, G-OOBG, C-FUBG, G-OOBG, N544NA, N1795B, (G-CPEV)	11. 3.04	Thomson Airways Ltd	To C-FUBG	24.11.08

G-OOBH	Boeing 757-236	29944	C-FOBH	11. 3.04	Thomson Airways Ltd	To C-FOBH	21.10.08
			G-OOBH, C-FOBH, G-OOBH, C-FOBH, G-OOBH, C-FOBH, G-OOBH, N545NA				
G-OOOX	Boeing 757-2Y0	26158		24. 2.93	Thomson Airways Ltd	To C-	22. 3.09E
G-OOPP	Airbus A320-214	1571				To C-GTDG	19.11.08
G-OXLD	Boeing 737-81Q	30618	N732MA	19. 5.08	XL Airways Ltd	To N732MA	17. 9.08
G-PASG	MBB BÖ.105DBS-4	S 819	(AP-BHR)	7.12.92	Trelawny Ltd	To AP-BHR	27. 3.08
			G-PASG, G-MHSL, D-HFCC (Restored 6. 3.08)				
G-PUKB	Piper PA-28-181 Acher III	283660				To D-	7.10.08
G-SUEW	Airbus A320-214	1961	C-GUEW	3. 4.03	Thomas Cook Airlines Ltd	Manchester	6. 5.09E
			G-SUEW, C-GUEW, G-SUEW, C-GUEW, G-SUEW, F-WWIX				
G-SWIZ	Schweizer 269C-1	0337	N31144	23. 4.08	MLG Aviation Ltd	To EC-	7. 1.09
G-TCAC	Airbus A320-232	1411	C-FRAA	1.11.08	Thomas Cook Airlines Ltd	To C-FRAA	21.10.08
G-VRST	Piper PA-46-350P Malibu Mirage	4636189	(T7-FBB)	4. 3.08	Avialec International Ltd	To T7-FBB	10. 3.08
			G-VRST				
G-XLFR	Boeing 737-8Q8	35279	N86G	3. 7.08	Caseright Ltd	To F-HAXL	12. 9.08
G-ZZSO	Eurocopter EC.225LP Super Puma			11. 6.08	Bristow Southeast Asia Ltd	To VH-ZFB	8. 8.08
G-ZZSP	Eurocopter EC.225LP Super Puma	2709		4.12.08	Bristow Helicopters Ltd	To VH-ZFC	22.12.08

SECTION 2

PART 1 – REPUBLIC OF IRELAND REGISTER

No official C of A data is available and it is difficult to determine the status of aircraft. We are grateful, therefore, for the few reports, which find their way into the "Round and About" section of Air-Britain News. This year we are indebted to the excellent monthly Irish Air Letter - journal of Current and Historical Irish Aviation - and the Editors and Publishers Paul Cunniffe, Karl E Hayes and Eamon C Powers - email: ial.magazine@upcmail.ie.

Other information has come from Ian Burnett's monthly Overseas Register section published in Air-Britain News and additional important data has been supplied by Richard Cawsey, Ken Parfitt and Barrie Womersley. Those aircraft still listed on the official Irish Aviation Authority's website Register are retained even if there have not been any recent positive sightings. In fact several aircraft known to have been broken up remain on the current register. A reminder that the Status decode indicates that N = paperwork change date or non-active specimen sighted and A = indicates some activity, hopefully! Official cancellations which are still noted as extant are contained in Part 2 below.

Just a remnder, the Aer Lingus names are in English on the port side and Gaelic on the starboard side. Many thanks to all contributors this year.

Registration	Type	Construction No	Previous Identity	Date	Registered Owner (Operator)	(Unconfirmed) Base	Status
EI-ABI (2)	de Havilland DH.84 Dragon 2	6105	EI-AFK G-AECZ, AV982, G-AECZ	12. 8.85	Aer Lingus Ltd *"Iolar'"*	Dublin	A2005
EI-ADV	Piper PA-12 Super Cruiser (Lycoming O-235)	12-3459	NC4031H	11. 5.48	R E Levis	Not known	N2006
					(Badly damaged in force landing Maynooth, Weston 8. 7.99: on rebuild)		
EI-AED	Cessna 120	11783	N77342 NC77342	11. 3.08	E McNeill and P O'Reilly	Birr	
EI-AFE	Piper J-3C-90 Cub	16687	OO-COR D-ELAB, N9954F, EI-AFE, NC79076	11. 3.49	J Conlan	Whiteisland House, Kildare	A2006
EI-AFF	BA L.25C Swallow II (Pobjoy Cataract II)	406	G-ADMF	18. 5.49	J Molloy, J J Sullivan and B Donoghue Ardenagh Great, Taghmon		N 6.07
EI-AGD	Taylorcraft Plus D	108	G-AFUB HL534, G-AFUB	26. 5.53	B and K O'Sullivan *(Current status unknown)* (Abbeyshrule)		N 4.96
EI-AGJ	Auster V J/1 Autocrat	2208	G-AIPZ	3.11.53	T G Rafter	Seven Parks Farm, Balbriggan	N2005
					(Suffered damage as result of hangar collapse Ballyboghil)		
EI-AHI (2)	de Havilland DH.82A Tiger Moth	85347	G-APRA DE313	17. 9.93	High Fidelity Flyers	Monasterevin	A 4.06
EI-AKM	Piper J-3C-65 Cub	15810	N88194 NC88194	17.11.58	J A Kent	Kilmoon, Ashbourne	N11.07
EI-ALH	Taylorcraft Plus D (Built Auster Aircraft Ltd)	106	G-AHLJ HH987, G-AFTZ	5. 5.60	N Reilly	Ballyjamesduff	N 9.05
EI-ALP	Avro 643 Cadet (Genet Major)	848	G-ADIE	12. 9.60	J C O'Loughlin	Seven Parks Farm, Balbriggan	N2006
					(Engine seizure 12. 6.77; stored)		
EI-AMK	Auster V J/1 Autocrat	1838	G-AGTV	19. 9.62	J J O'Sullivan	(Newcastle, Dublin)	N1998
					(WFU after engine failure 5.79: sold 4.95: stored for Irish Air Corps Museum, current status unknown)		
EI-AMY	Auster J/1N Alpha	2634	G-AJUW	9. 4.63	T Lennon *(Current status unknown)*	(Maynooth)	N 4.92
EI-ANT	Champion 7ECA Citabria	7ECA-38		13. 1.65	T Croke, H Sydner, D Foley and E Lennon	Gorey	A 4.06
EI-ANY	Piper PA-18 Super Cub 95	18-7152	G-AREU N3096Z	18.11.64	The Bogavia Group	Kilrush	A 4.08
EI-AOB	Piper PA-28-140 Cherokee	28-20667		28. 4.65	Knock Flying Group	Waterford	A 9.04
EI-AOS	Cessna 310B	35578	G-ARIG EI-AOS, G-ARIG, N5378A	1.11.65	Southair Ltd *(WFU and completely scrapped 1992)*		
EI-APS (2)	Schleicher ASK14	14008	(EI-114) G-AWVV, D-KOBB	24.11.69	E Shiel, P Ward and P Finlay (Gowran Grange, Naas)		N10.04
EI-ARH (2)	Slingsby T.56 SE5 rep (Lycoming O-235)	1590	G-AVOT	22. 6.67	L Garrison *(Current status unknown)* (Flabob, California, US)		N 5.96
EI-ARM	Slingsby T.56 SE5 rep (Lycoming O-235) *(Regd with c/n 1595 ex G-AVOY)*	1594	G-AVOX	22. 6.67	M L Putman Sanger, Texas. US *(Registered in US as N912AC)*		N10.99
EI-ARW	Jodel DR.1050	118		14. 8.67	J Davy	Moyne	N 2.03
EI-ASR (2)	McCandless M.4 Gyroplane (Built R and W McCandless) (Volkswagen)	M.4-5	G-AXHZ	29. 9.69	G J J Fasenfeld Sion Mills, Strabane *(Reported as sold to R.McGregor: current status unknown)*		N 4.96
EI-AST	Cessna F150H (Built Reims Aviation SA)	F150-0273		30. 1.68	Ormand Flying Club Ltd	Birr	A 5.06
EI-ATJ	Beagle B.121 Pup Series 2	B121-029	G-35-029	10. 2.69	L.O'Leary	Waterford	A 4.06
EI-ATK	Piper PA-28-140 Cherokee	28-24120	G-AVUP N11C	18.10.68	Mayo Flying Club	Abbeyshrule	N 5.06
					(Damaged Connaught 14. 2.87: noted wrecked)		
EI-ATL	Aeronca 7AC Champion	7AC-4674	N1119E	22. 9.69	Kildare Flying Club	(Abbeyshrule)	
					(Damaged Weston 26.11.75; used for spares in restoration of EI-AVB, current status unknown)		
EI-ATS	SOCATA MS.880B Rallye Club	1582		20. 4.70	ATS Group *(Stored: current status unknown)* (Abbeyshrule)		N 4.96
EI-AUB	de Havilland DH.82A Tiger Moth				*See SECTION 4, Part 1* Stayner, Ontario, Canada		
EI-AUG	SOCATA MS.894A Rallye Minerva 220	11080		17. 6.70	K O'Leary *(Fuselage only)*	Haverfordwest	N 6.06
EI-AUM	Auster V J/1 Autocrat	2612	G-AJRN	11. 9.70	T G Rafter Seven Parks Farm, Balbriggan *(Wings noted Monastervin 4.06)*		N2005
EI-AUO	Reims Cessna FA150K Aerobat	FA1500074		2. 3.70	S Burke	Spanish Point	N 9.06
EI-AUS	Auster J/5F Aiglet Trainer	2779	G-AMRL N2002	17.11.70	T Stevens and T Lennon *(Current status unknown)* (Powerscourt)		
EI-AUT	Forney F-1A Aircoupe	5731	G-ARXS D-EBSA, N3037G	21.12.70	Southair Ltd *(Current status unknown)*	(Cork)	N8.97
EI-AUY	Morane-Saulnier MS.502 Criquet (Argus AS.10)	338	F-BCDG French Military	30.11.70	Historical Aircraft Preservation Group Duxford *(As "CF+HF" in Luftwaffe c/s)*		A9.08
EI-AVB	Aeronca 7AC Champion (Continental A65)	7AC-1790	7P-AXK ZS-AXK	14. 6.71	T Brett	Thonotosassa, Florida, US	N10.99

Reg	Type	c/n	Prev id	Date	Owner	Location	Code
EI-AVE (2)	Piper PA-18-95 Super Cub	18-7375	G-ARCT EI-AVE, G-ARCT, N10F	9. 1.73	P.J.Gallagher	Strandhill, Sligo	
EI-AVM	Reims Cessna F150L	F15000745		3. 3.72	Tojo Air Leasing Ltd	Abbeyshrule	A10.08
EI-AWD	Piper PA-22-160 Tri-Pacer	22-6411	G-APXV N9437D	17. 1.73	J P Montcalm	Clonkeen, Emyvale	N2005
					(Blown over in gales Cork 12.81; stored)		
EI-AWH	Cessna 210J Centurion	21059067	G-AZCC (EI-AWH), G-AZCC, 5N-AIE, N1734C, (N6167F)	19. 1.73	Rathcoole Flying Club	Rathcoole	A4.05
EI-AWP	de Havilland DH.82A Tiger Moth	85931	F-BGCL French AF, DF195	4. 7.72	A P Bruton	Abbeyshrule	A10.08
	(Regd with c/n 19577)						
EI-AWR	Malmö MFI-9 Junior	010	LN-HAG (SE-EBW)	12. 6.73	A Szorfy	Abbeyshrule	A5.06
EI-AYB	Gardan GY-80-180 Horizon	156	F-BNQP	5.10.73	J B Smith	Abbeyshrule	A8.06
EI-AYD	Grumman-American AA-5 Traveler	0380	G-BAZE N5480L	9. 7.73	V O'Rourke, P Howick and H Martini		
					(Written off after forced landing Castlehayestown, Taghmon 21. 8.94)		
EI-AYF	Reims Cessna FRA150L Aerobat	FRA1500218		26. 3.74	S Bruton	Abbeyshrule	A 10.08
EI-AYI	Morane MS.880B Rallye Club	189	F-OBXE	21.11.73	J McNamara	Cloncarmeel	A2006
EI-AYK	Reims Cessna F172M Skyhawk II	F17201092		25. 3.74	D Gallagher	Abbeyshrule	A10.08
EI-AYN	Britten-Norman BN-2A-8 Islander	704	G-BBFJ	26. 3.74	Galway Aviation Services Ltd *(Operated Aer Arann Islands)*		
	(Built IRMA)				"Inis-Mor"	Connemara	A7.05
					(Stored Bembridge?)		3.08
EI-AYR	Schleicher ASK 16	16022	(EI-119)	5. 4.74	B O'Broin	Kilrush	A5.06
EI-AYT (2)	SOCATA MS.894A Rallye Minerva 220	11065	G-AXIU	6. 8.74	K A O'Connor	Abbeyshrule	N5.00
					(Damaged Palklasmore 12.11.89: wreck only)		
EI-AYY	Evans VP-1	MD01		18. 8.75	R Dowd	Thurles	A 5.06
	(Built M Donoghue as SAAC pr.no.003)						
EI-BAJ	SNCAN Stampe SV-4C	171	F-BBPN	17.10.74	Dublin Tiger Group *(On rebuild)*	Trim	N 4.06
EI-BAR	Thunder Ax8-105 Balloon (Hot Air)	014	G-BCAM	26. 2.75	J Burke and V Hourihane *"Rockwell"*	Cahir	
					(WFU: current status unknown)		
EI-BAT	Reims Cessna F150M	F15001196		2. 5.75	K Kacprzak	Weston, Dublin	A 9.08
EI-BAV	Piper PA-22-108 Colt	22-8347	G-ARKO	30. 4.75	E Finnamore and J Deegen	Birr	A 1.03
EI-BAY (1)	Cameron (Ax8) O-84 Balloon (Hot Air)				See G-AYJZ in SECTION 1, Part 2		
EI-BBC	Piper PA-28-180 Cherokee B	28-1049	G-ASEJ	18. 6.75	Vero Beach Ltd	Strandhill, Sligo	A 4.06
EI-BBD	Evans VP-1	VP-1-No.2		13. 8.76	Volksplane Group	Celbridge	N2006
	(Built B Feeley and D Goss as SAAC pr.no.002)		(Volkswagen 1600)		*(Damaged 12. 9.81: on rebuild)*		
EI-BBE	Champion 7FC Tri-Traveller	7FC-393	G-APZW	7. 9.75	R McNally and C Carey	Abbeyshrule	A 8.06
	(Tail-wheel conversion to 7EC Traveller status)						
EI-BBG	SOCATA Rallye 100ST	2592		27.10.75	Weston Ltd *(Believed probably scrapped)*		
EI-BBI	Reims Cessna 150ST	2663		13.10.75	Kilkenny Airport Ltd	Kilkenny	N 6.07
EI-BBJ	SOCATA MS.880B Rallye 100S	2361	F-BUVX	7.11.75	Weston Ltd *(Derelict)*	Weston, Dublin	N 5.06
EI-BBO	SOCATA MS.893E Rallye 180GT	12522	F-BVNM	8. 3.76	G P Moorhead	Hacketstown	A 1.03
EI-BBV	Piper J-3C-65 Cub (L-4J-PI)	13058	D-ELWY F-BEGB, 44-80762	14. 6.76	F Cronin	Kilrush	A 4.08
	(Frame No.12888)				*(As "480762" in USAAF c/s)*		
EI-BCE	Britten Norman BN-2A-26 Islander	519	G-BDUV	14. 9.76	Galway Aviation Services Ltd *(Operated Aer Arann Islands)*		
					"Inis-Meain"	Connemara	A 7.05
EI-BCF	Bensen B-8M Gyrocopter	47941	N....	24. 8.76	P Flanagan	(Kilrush)	N1997
	(McCulloch.AF O-100)				*(Stored; current status unknown)*		
EI-BCJ (2)	Aeromere F.8L Falco 3	204	G-ATAK D-ENYB	19. 1.77	M P McLoughlin	(Naas)	N 1.03
					(On rebuild)		
EI-BCK	Reims Cessna F172N Skyhawk II	F17201543		22.11.76	K A O'Connor	Weston, Dublin	A 5.06
EI-BCL	Cessna 182P Skylane II	18264300	N1366M	22.11.76	L Burke	Carnmore, Galway	A 7.06
	(Reims assembled with c/n F1820045)						
EI-BCM	Piper J-3C-65 Cub (L-4H-PI)	11983	F-BNAV N9857F, 44-79687 ??	26.11.76	Kilmoon Flying Group	Abbeyshrule	A 5.06
EI-BCN	Piper J-3C-65 Cub (L-4H-PI)	12335	F-BFQE OO-PIE, 44-80039	26.11.76	H Diver	Kilrush	A4.08
EI-BCO	Piper J-3C-65 Cub	"1"	F-BBIV	26.11.76	J Molloy	Kilmoon, Ashbourne	
					(Believed still stored as unconverted "F-BBIV")		
EI-BCP	Druine D.62B Condor	RAE 618	G-AVCZ	27. 1.77	A Delaney	Dolla	A 7.02
	(Built Rollason Aircraft and Engines)						
EI-BCS	SOCATA MS.880B Rallye 100T	2550	F-BVZV	4. 2.77	Organic Fruit and Vegetables of Ireland Ltd	Kilkenny	A 8.04
EI-BCU	SOCATA MS.880B Rallye 100T	2595	F-BXTH	10. 2.77	Weston Ltd *(Derelict)*	Weston, Dublin	N 5.06
EI-BCW	SOCATA MS.880B Rallye Club	1783	G-AYKE	18. 4.77	Kilkenny Flying Club		
					(Believed probably scrapped during 1998)		
EI-BDH	SOCATA MS.880B Rallye Club	1270	G-AWOB	18. 7.77	Munster Wings Ltd		
					(Damaged Cork 5.12.78: stored for repair but used as spares source and scrapped during late 1980s)		
EI-BDL	Evans VP-2	V2-2101		7. 9.77	P Buggle	Kilrush	A 5.06
	(Built J Duggan as PFA 7213 and then SAAC pr.no.004)		(Volkswagen)				
EI-BDM	Piper PA-23-250 Aztec D	27-4166	G-AXIV N6826Y	10.10.77	G A Costello *(Dismantled)*	Dromod	N 4.06
EI-BDR	Piper PA-28-180 Cherokee C	28-3980	G-BAAO LN-AEL, SE-FAG	8.12.77	Cherokee Group	Waterford	N 8.06
EI-BEA	SOCATA Rallye 100ST	3007		28. 2.78	Weston Ltd	Weston, Dublin	N 4.01
					(Dismantled fuselage hangared)		
EI-BEN	Piper J-3C-65 Cub (L-4J-PI)	12546	G-BCUC F-BFMN, 44-80250	28. 4.78	J J O'Sullivan	Weston, Dublin	A 7.03
	(Frame No.12376)						
EI-BEP	SOCATA MS.892A Rallye Commodore 150	11947	F-BTJT	14. 4.78	H Lynch and J O'Leary *(Stripped hulk noted)*	Abbeyshrule	N 1.03
EI-BFE	Cessna F150G	F150-0158	G-AVGM	3. 8.78	Southair Ltd *(Current status unknown)*	(Cork)	N 1.02
	(Built Reims Aviation SA)						
EI-BFF	Beech A23-24 Musketeer Super III	MA-352	G-AXCJ	20. 8.78	J Lankfer	Fenland	A 11.08
EI-BFI	SOCATA Rallye 100ST	2618		10. 8.78	J O'Neill *(Crashed 14.12.85 and wrecked)*		
						Abbeyshrule	N 5.06

EI-BFO	Piper J-3C-90 Cub (L-4J-PI)	12701	F-BFQJ	11. 9.78	D Gordon *(Frame stored)*	Trim	N 4.06
	(Frame No.12531) (Regd as c/n 8911)		N79856, NC79856, 44-80405				
EI-BFP	SOCATA Rallye 100ST	2942	F-GARR	6.10.78	Limerick Flying Club (Coonagh) Ltd	Coonagh	N10.06
EI-BFR	SOCATA Rallye 100ST	2429	F-OCVK	9.11.78	Wexford Flying Group	Ardenagh Great, Taghmon	A 6.07
EI-BGA	SOCATA Rallye 100ST	2549	G-BCXC	23.11.78	J F Frew	Mullaghmore	A 6.06
					(Believed scrapped 1998 but remnant seen as garden ornament!)		
EI-BGC	SOCATA MS.880B Rallye Club	1265	F-BRDC	22.12.78	P Moran	Roscommon	
					(WFU and cannibalised; current status unknown)		
EI-BGD	SOCATA MS.880B Rallye Club	2287	F-BUJI	18.12.78	N Kavanagh	Abbeyshrule	N 1.03
					(Stripped hulk; current status unknown)		
EI-BGJ	Reims Cessna F152 II	F15201664		14. 5.79	Sligo Aeronautical Club Ltd	Strandhill, Sligo	A 5.06
EI-BGS	SOCATA MS.893E Rallye 180GT	12675	F-BXTY	25. 4.79	M Farrelly		
					(Badly damaged in gales Millicent, Clane 3.91 and stored as spares source; believed probably scrapped)		
EI-BGT	Colt 77A Balloon (Hot Air)	041		14. 5.79	M J Mills "Spirit of Ireland" (Ryan Air titles)	Navan	N 9.01
	(New envelope c/n 1092 - original fitted to EI-BBM)						
EI-BGU	SOCATA MS.880B Rallye Club	875	F-BONM	9. 5.79	M F Neary	Abbeyshrule	N 9.99
					(Wreck stored: current status unknown)		
EI-BHC	Reims Cessna F177RG Cardinal RG	G-AYTG		11. 7.79	L Gavin "Hot Chocolate"	Weston, Dublin	A 10.08
	(Wichita c/n F177RG0010)	F177RG0010					
EI-BHF	SOCATA MS.892A Rallye Commodore 150	10742	F-BPBP	10. 7.79	B Mullen		
					(WFU Strandhill 1987: engine to EI-BYL; scrapped c.1989)		
EI-BHI	Bell 206B-2 JetRanger II	906	G-BAKX	14. 8.79	G Tracey	Tallaght, Dublin	A 8.06
EI-BHM	Reims Cessna F337E Super Skymaster	OO-PDC	1.11.79	City of Dublin VEC	Bolton St, Dublin	N 9.01
	(Wichita c/n 33701217)	F33700004	OO-PDG		*(With College of Technology as instructional airframe)*		
EI-BHN	SOCATA MS.893A Rallye Commodore 180	11422	F-BRRO	11.10.79	T Garvan *(On overhaul)*	Hacketstown	N 1.03
EI-BHP	SOCATA MS.893A Rallye Commodore 180	11459	F-BSAA	12.10.79	Spanish Point Flying Club *(Current status unknown)*	(Spanish Point)	
EI-BHT	Beech 77 Skipper	WA-77		17.10.79	M Casey	Galway	N5.08
					(Crashed 8kms from Ballaghaderreen 11.5.08 and substantially damaged)		
EI-BHV	Aeronca 7EC Traveler	7EC-739	G-AVDU	30.10.79	P O'Donnell and Partners	Ballyboe, Kilsheelan	A3.08
			N9837Y				
EI-BHW	Cessna F150F	F150-0013	G-ATMK	22.11.79	R Sharpe *(Current status unknown)*		
	(Built Reims Aviation SA) (Wichita c/n 15062671)					(Weston, Dublin)	
EI-BIB	Reims Cessna F152 II	F15201724		30.11.79	Galway Flying Club Ltd	Carnmore, Galway	A 7.06
EI-BID	Piper PA-18 Super Cub 95 (L-18C-PI)	18-1524	D-EAES	30.11.79	S Coghlan and P Ryan	Carnmore, Galway	A 4.06
			French Army 18-1524, 51-15524				
EI-BIG	Moravan Zlin 526 Trener Master	1086	D-EBUP	7.12.79	P V Lonkhuyzen *(Damaged 9.91 and acquired for spares?)*		
			OO-BUT			Luxters Farm, Hambleden, Henley-on-Thames	N2002
EI-BIJ	Agusta-Bell 206B-2 JetRanger II	8432	G-BCVZ	29. 1.80	Medavia Properties Ltd *(Operated Celtic Helicopters Ltd)*	Dublin Heliport	A 6.06
EI-BIK	Piper PA-18-150 Super Cub	18-7909088	N82276	1. 2.80	Dublin Gliding Club Ltd	Kilrush	A 4.08
	(Modified to 180hp)						
EI-BIM	Morane MS.880B Rallye Club	305	F-BKYJ	28. 3.80	D Millar	Abbeyshrule	N 6.97
					(Stored: current status unknown)		
EI-BIO	Piper J-3C-65 Cub (L-4J-PI)	12657	F-BGXP	27. 5.80	H Duggan	Kilrush	A 6.06
			OO-GAE, 44-80361				
EI-BIR	Reims Cessna F172M Skyhawk II	F17201225	F-BVXI	24. 3.80	Figile Flying Group	Abbeyshrule	N 10.08
EI-BIS	Robin R1180TD Aiglon	268		14. 5.80	The Robin Aiglon Group	Abbeyshrule	N 10.08
EI-BIT	SOCATA MS.887 Rallye 125	2169	F-BULQ	18. 3.80	Spanish Point Flying Club *(Derelict)*	Kilrush	N 8.04
EI-BIV	Bellanca 8KCAB Super Decathlon	464-79	N5032Q	3. 6.80	Aerocrat Pilots Ltd	Weston, Dublin	A 5.06
EI-BIW	SOCATA MS.880B Rallye Club	1144	F-BPGB	19. 5.80	E J Barr		
	(Crashed on take off Rosnakil, Fanad 10. 8.86 , substantially damaged and scrapped although rear section of fuselage used as display item in nightclub at Intercounty Hotel, Lifford from 1988 until fire destroyed the hotel about 1991)						
EI-BJB	Aeronca 7DC Champion	7AC-925	G-BKKM	16. 4.80	W Kennedy *(Stored incomplete)*	Killenaule	N12.00
	(Continental C85)		EI-BJB, N82296, NC82296				
EI-BJC	Aeronca 7AC Champion	7AC-4927	N1366E	2. 4.80	E Griffin	Blackwater	N 8.04
	(Continental A65)		NC1366E, SE-FBW, OY-DKN				
EI-BJI	Reims FR172E Rocket	FR17200040	G-BAAS	23. 5.80	Irish Parachute Club Ltd		
			SE-FBW, OY-DKN		*(Crashed Edenderry 9.82: probably scrapped pre 1990)*		
EI-BJJ	Aeronca 15AC Sedan	15AC-226	(G-BHXP)	6. 6.80	O Bruton *(Stored: current status unknown)*		
			EI-BJJ, N1214H			Abbeyshrule	N 3.98
EI-BJK	SOCATA Rallye 110ST	3226	F-GBKY	8. 7.80	M Keenan	Kilrush	A 4.06
EI-BJM	Cessna A152 Aerobat	A1520936	N761CC	18. 9.80	K A O'Connor	Weston, Dublin	A 5.06
EI-BJO	Cessna R172K Hawk XP II	R1723340	N758TD	6. 8.80	The XP Group	Carnmore, Galway	A 7.06
EI-BJT	Piper PA-38-112 Tomahawk	38-78A0818	G-BGEU	16.10.80	S Corrigan and W Lennon	Abbeyshrule	A 5.06
			N9650N				
EI-BKC	Aeronca 15AC Sedan	15AC-467	N1394H	5.11.80	G Hendrick, M Farrell and J Keating	Birr	A 1.03
EI-BKF	Cessna F172H	F172-0476	G-AVUX	4.12.80	D Darby	Haverfordwest	N 9.08
	(Built Reims Aviation SA)						
EI-BKK	Taylor JT.1 Monoplane	PFA 1421	G-AYYC	2. 2.81	J Sullivan	Waterford	N 1.06
	(Built S B Sharp) (Volkswagen 1500)						
EI-BKN	SOCATA Rallye 100ST	3035	F-GBCK	18. 2.81	Weston Ltd *(Stored)*	Weston, Dublin	N 8.02
EI-BLB	SNCAN Stampe SV-4C	323	F-BCTE	27. 7.81	J E Hutchinson and R A Stafford	(Dolla)	N2006
	(Hit overhead cables and crashed Albert Lock Jamestown Canal 1. 6.97 and substantially damaged: remains stored)						
EI-BLD	MBB BÖ.105DB	S.381	D-HDLQ	21. 7.81	Irish Helicopters Ltd		
						Trevet Airfield, Dunshaughlin, County Meath	A 5.06
EI-BLE	Eipper Quicksilver	IMA-003		20. 8.81	R P St.George-Smith		
	(Yamaha KT100SP)				*(Severely damaged in accident near Kilkenny (airfield?), 8.81: believed scrapped)*		
EI-BLN	Eipper Quicksilver MX	MX.01		26. 8.81	O J Conway and B Daffy *(Believed scrapped)*		
	(Cuyana 340)					(Ennis)	
EI-BMA	SOCATA MS.880B Rallye Club	1965	F-BTJR	26. 1.82	W Rankin and M Kelleher	Abbeyshrule	N 1.03
					(Wings only noted)		

EI-BMB	SOCATA MS.880B Rallye 100T	2505	G-BJCO F-BVLB	5. 1.82	Glyde Court Developments Ltd	Weston, Dublin	N 5.06
EI-BMF	Laverda F.8L Super Falco Series IV	416	G-AWSU	28. 1.82	M Slazenger	Powerscourt	A 8.05
EI-BMH	SOCATA MS.880B Rallye Club	1277	(G-BIDS) F-BSTJ	19. 2.82	N J Bracken		

(To Abbeyshrule 1982 with "EI-BMH" chalked on tail: found to have severe corrosion, removed to private house in Lifford and scrapped in early 1990s. Did not carry Irish marks officially and remained as "G-BIDS")

EI-BMI	SOCATA TB-9 Tampico	203	F-GCOV	12. 5.82	D Pratt	Weston, Dublin	A 10.08
EI-BMJ	SOCATA MS.880B Rallye 100T	2594	F-BXTG	10. 3.82	Limerick Flying Club (Coonagh)Ltd	Coonagh	A10.06
EI-BMM	Reims Cessna F152 II	F15201899		10. 3.82	P Redmond	Weston, Dublin	A 5.06
EI-BMN	Reims Cessna F152 II	F15201912		10. 3.82	K A.O'Connor	Weston, Dublin	A 4.06
EI-BMU	Monnett Sonerai IIL	01224		19. 5.82	A Fenton *(noted stored 9.08)*	Strandhill, Sligo	N 9.08

(Built D Connaire and P Ford as SAAC pr.no.014) (Volkswagen 2100)

EI-BMV	American Aviation AA-5 Traveler	AA5-0200	G-BAEJ	28. 7.82	K A H E Tierney	Abbeyshrule	N 1.03

(Damaged Brittas Bay 3.93: stripped hulk noted)

EI-BMW	Skytrike/Hiway Vulcan	LM-100		1. 6.82	L Maddock *(Current status unknown)*	(Carlow)	

(Built L Maddock) (Fuji-Robin)

EI-BNF	Eurowing Goldwing	xxxx		22. 9.82	T Morelli *(Scrapped 1985)*		

(Fuji-Robin)

EI-BNH	Hiway Skytrike	AS.09		18.10.82	M Martin *(Current status unknown)*	Tullamore	

(Fuji-Robin EC-25-PS)

EI-BNJ	Evans VP-2	xxxx		24. 1.83	G A Cashman *(Believed scrapped 1996)*		

(Volkswagen 2000)

EI-BNK	Cessna U206F Stationair	U20601706	G-HILL PH-ADN, D-EEXY, N9506G	23.12.82	Irish Parachute Club Ltd	Clonbullogue	A 4.06
EI-BNL	Rand Robinson KR-2	xxxx		13. 1.83	K Hayes		

(Volkswagen 2000)   *(Reported construction abandoned and destroyed pre 2006)*

EI-BNP	Rotorway Executive 145	xxxx		1. 3.83	R L Renfroe *(Not completed 1989)*		

(Rotorway 145)

EI-BNT	Cvjetkovic CA-65	xxxx		23. 3.83	B Tobin and P G Ryan	(Tallagh)	N 1.03

(Lycoming O-290)   *(Under construction)*

EI-BNU	SOCATA MS.880B Rallye Club	1204	F-BPQV	7. 4.83	P A Doyle	Coonagh	N 1.03
EI-BOA	Pterodactyl	xxxx		3. 5.83	A Murphy		

(Cuyana 430)   *(Believed dismantled and probably scrapped 1985)*

EI-BOE	SOCATA TB-10 Tobago	301	F-GDBL	12. 9.83	Tobago Group	Weston, Dublin	A 10.08
EI-BOH	Eipper Quicksilver	xxxx		8. 9.83	J Leech		

(Yamaha 970cc)   *(Believed dismantled and probably scrapped 1980s)*

EI-BOV	Rand Robinson KR-2	xxxx		7. 5.84	G O'Hara and G Callan "Kitty Hawk"		

(Built G O'Hara and G Callan as SAAC pr.no.011) (Volkswagen 1835)   (Strandhill, Sligo)

(Damaged Carnmore 3.91 on re-build 1999: current status unknown)

EI-BOX	Box Duet	xxxx		12.10.84	K Riccius *(Current status unknown)*	(Newcastle)	

(Rotax 503)

EI-BPE	Viking Dragonfly	xxxx		15.10.84	G G Bracken *(Not completed and stored)*		

(Built G G Bracken as SAAC pr.no.016) (HAPI Volkswagen 1835)   (Westport)   N 1.01

EI-BPL	Reims Cessna F172K	F17200758	G-AYSG	28. 3.85	Phoenix Flying Ltd	Shannon	A 5.08
EI-BPN	Flexiform Striker	xxxx		12. 3.85	P H Collins *(Current status unknown)*		

(Fuji Robin 50cc)   (Dunlaoghaire)

EI-BPO	Southdown Puma	1923		12. 3.85	A Channing	Millicent Farm, Clane	A2006

(Fuji-Robin EC-44-PM) (C/n also reported as 1924)

EI-BPP	Eipper Quicksilver MX	3207		12. 3.85	J A Smith	Abbeyshrule	N 1.03

(Cuyana 430)   *(Stored)*

EI-BPT	Skyhook Sabre	xxxx		26. 3.85	T M McGrath	(Glounthane)	

(Rowena Solo 210)   *(Believed dismantled)*

EI-BPU	Hiway Demon	xxxx		26. 3.85	A Channing	Abbeyshrule	A 5.00

(Fuji-Robin EC-25-PS)

EI-BRK	Flexiform Trike	LM.102		17. 6.85	L Maddock		

(Built L Maddock) (Fuji Robin)   *(Damage to propeller taxiing Clonmore pre 1994: WFU and scrapped during 1994)*

EI-BRS	Cessna P172D	P17257173	G-WPUI G-AXPI, 9M-AMR, N11B, (N8573X)	2. 9.85	P Mathews *(In poor condition)*	Waterford	N 8.06
EI-BRU	Evans VP-1	V-12-84-CQ		5.11.85	Home Bru Flying Group	Weston, Dublin	A 6.02

(Built C Quinn as SAAC pr.no.018) (Volkswagen 1600)

EI-BRV	Hiway Demon Skytrike	xxxx		5.11.85	M Garvey and C Tully	Rockfield, Kells	A2006

(Fuji-Robin EC-25-PS)

EI-BRW	Hovey Delta Bird	xxxx		5.11.85	A & E Aerosport		

(Built A & E Aerosport) (Volkswagen 1300)

(Originally regd as Ultra-Lite Deltabird but is a Bimax Osprey; dismantled after crash near Fermoy 1986 and scrapped)

EI-BSB	Wassmer Jodel D.112	1067	G-AWIG F-BKAA	23. 6.87	Estartit Ltd	Ardenagh Great, Taghmon	A 7.06

(Re-built W Kennedy as SAAC pr.no.025)

EI-BSC	Reims Cessna F172N Skyhawk II	F17201651	G-NIUS	10.12.85	S Phelan	Weston, Dublin	A 10.08
EI-BSG	Bensen B-80 Gyrocopter	HB		30. 1.86	J Todd *(Stored: current status unknown)*		

(McCullough 4318)   (Riverstick)   N 3.90

EI-BSK	SOCATA TB-9 Tampico	618		9. 4.86	T Drury	Weston, Dublin	A 5.06
EI-BSL	Piper PA-34-220T Seneca III	34-8233041	N8468X	27. 6.86	P Greenan	Weston, Dublin	A 5.06
EI-BSN	Cameron O-65 Balloon (Hot Air)	1278		14. 4.86	C O'Neill and T Hooper "Erin-Go-Bragh"	Cavan	A 6.06
EI-BSO	Piper PA-28-140 Cherokee B	28-25449	C-GOBL N8241N	16. 4.86	H M Hanley	Waterford	A 4.06
EI-BSW	Solar Wings Pegasus XL-R	SW-WA-1122		22. 6.87	E Fitzgerald	(Ballycashin)	A2006

(Rotax 447) (Trike c/n SW-TB-1124)

EI-BSX	Piper J-3C-65 Cub	8912	G-ICUB F-BEGT, NC79805, 45-4515, 42-36788	25. 3.86	J and T O'Dwyer *(Current status unknown)*	(Gowran Grange, Naas)	

(Frame No.8999)

(Official c/n 13255 is incorrect as a/c probably rebuilt c.1945)

EI-BUA	Cessna 172M Skyhawk II	17265451	N5458H	8. 8.86	K A O'Connor	Weston, Dublin	A 10.08
EI-BUC	Jodel D.9 Bébé	PFA 929	G-BASY	20. 1.87	B Lyons and M Blake	Thurles, Moyne	A 4.06

(Built R L Sambell) (Volkswagen 1500)

Reg	Type	C/n	Prev id	Date	Owner/Operator	Location	Code
EI-BUF	Cessna 210N Centurion II	21063070	G-MCDS G-BHNB, N6496N	18.12.86	210 Group	Abbeyshrule	A 10.08
EI-BUG	SOCATA ST-10 Diplomate	125	G-STIO OH-SAB	4. 2.87	J Cooke *(Derelict)*	Weston, Dublin	N 1.03
EI-BUH	Lake LA-4-200 Buccaneer	543	G-PARK G-BBGK, N39779	27. 5.87	P Redden	Weston, Dublin	A.6.04
EI-BUJ	SOCATA MS.892A Rallye Commodore 150	10737	G-FOAM G-AVPL	27. 2.87	T Cunniffe *(Damaged pre 1992: stored and probably scrapped)*		
EI-BUL	Whittaker MW.5 Sorcerer *(Built Aerotech and J Greene) (Citröen 602cc)*	1		4. 3.87	J Culleton *Current status unknown)*	(Mountmellick)	
EI-BUN	Beech 76 Duchess	ME-371	(EI-BUO) N37001	26. 6.87	K A O'Connor *(Operated National Flight Centre)*	Weston, Dublin	A 5.07
EI-BUT	GEMS MS.893A Rallye Commodore 18010559		SE-IMV F-BNBU	30. 7.87	T Keating *(Galerien c/s)*	Weston, Dublin	A 4.06
EI-BVB	Whittaker MW.6 Merlin *(Built R England as SAAC pr.no.051) (Rotax 503)*	1		14. 9.87	R England *(Current status unknown)*	(Watergrasshill)	N 9.00
EI-BVJ (2)	AMF Microflight Chevvron 2-32 *(Konig SD570)*	009		16. 2.88	S.J.Dunne *(Current status unknown)*	(Bolybeg, Ballymore Eustace)	
EI-BVK	Piper PA-38-112 Tomahawk	38-79A0966	OO-FLG OO-HLG, N9705N	2. 3.88	M Martin	Abbeyshrule	A 10.08
EI-BVT	Evans VP-2	V2-2129	G-BEIE	29. 4.88	P Morrison *(Under construction: current status unknown)*	(Cobh)	N 1.01
	(Regd F G Morris as PFA 7221 and then J J O'Sullivan as SAAC pr.no.020) (Volkswagen 1834)						
EI-BVY	Heintz Zenith CH.200AA-RW	2-582		7. 6.88	J Matthews and M Skelly *(Current status unknown)*	(Abbeyshrule)	A 7.01
	(Built M Skellly and J Mathews as SAAC pr.no.026) (Lycoming O-320)						
EI-BWH	Partenavia P.68C	212	G-BHJP	11.12.87	K Buckley	Cork	A 3.08
EI-BXL	Polaris FIB (Flying Inflatable Boat) *(Rotax 503)*	M.561628		27. 6.91	M McKeon *(Presumed stored at owner's home)*	(Roslevan, Ennis)	
EI-BXO	Fouga (Valmet) CM-170 Magister	213	N18FM Finnish AF FM-28	21.11.88	G W Connolly *(Stored: current status unknown)*	(Swords)	N 4.96
EI-BXT	Druine D.62B Condor *(Built Rollason Aircraft and Engines)*	RAE 626	G-AVZE	24. 8.88	The Condor Group	Abbeyshrule	A 5.06
EI-BYA	Thruster TST Mk.1 *(Rotax 503)*	8504	G-MNDA	1. 2.89	E Fagan *(Current status unknown)*	(Killykeen, Kilnaleck)	
EI-BYF	Cessna 150M Commuter	15076654	N3924V	20.11.89	The High Kings Flying Group Ltd	Abbeyshrule	A 8.06
EI-BYG	SOCATA TB-9 Tampico Club	928		23. 8.89	M McGinn	Weston, Dublin	A 10.08
EI-BYJ	Bell 206B-2 JetRanger II	1897	N49725	23. 6.89	Medeva Properties Ltd	Dublin Heliport	A 1.03
EI-BYL (1)	Heintz Zenith CH-250	2866	(EI-BYD (1))	14. 6.89	M McLoughlin	Kilrush	A 5.06
	(Built A Corcoran as SAAC pr.no.020) (Lycoming O-320)						
EI-BYO	Aérospatiale-Alenia ATR 42-310	161	OY-CIS EI-BYO, F-WWEH	20.12.02	Nordic Aviation Contractors (Ireland) Ltd *(Operated Aer Arann Express)*	Dublin	A 6.06
EI-BYR	Bell 206L-3 LongRanger III	51284	(EI-LMG) EI-BYR, D-HBAD	15. 8.89	H.S.S	Dublin	N 9.07
EI-BYX	Champion 7GCAA Citabria	7GCAA-40	N546DS	4. 4.90	P J Gallagher	Coonagh	A10.06
EI-BYY	Piper J-3C-85 Cub	12494	EC-AQZ HB-OSG, 44-80198	12. 4.90	The Cub Club	Galway	A12.01
	(Frame No.12322)						
	(Regd with c/n 22288 and officially ex G-AKTJ, N3595K, NC3595K)						
EI-CAC	Grob G-115A	8092		22.10.89	G Tracey	Weston, Dublin	A 10.08
EI-CAD	Grob G-115A	8104	G-WIZB EI-CAD	22. 8.03	C Phillips	Kilrush	N 10.08
EI-CAE	Grob G-115A	8105		5. 4.90	O O'Reilly	Cork	N 9.08
EI-CAN	Aerotech MW.5(K) Sorcerer *(Rotax 447)*	5K-0011-02	(G-MWGH)	15. 6.90	V Vaughan	Glountha, Kilkenny	N 6.07
EI-CAP	Cessna R182 Skylane RGII	R18200056	G-BMUF N7342W	27. 4.90	M J Hanlon	Weston, Dublin	A 8.02
EI-CAU	AMF Microflight Chevvron 2-32C *(Konig SD32)*	022		14.11.90	J Tarrant	Rathcoole	A 7.05
EI-CAW	Bell 206B-2 JetRanger II	780	N2947W	11. 7.90	Medeva Properties Ltd	Dublin Heliport	A 5.00
EI-CAX	Cessna P210N Pressurized Centurion II P21000215		(EI-CAS) G-OPMB, N4553K	9. 7.90	K A O'Connor *(Stored)*	Weston, Dublin	N 5.06
EI-CAY	Mooney M.20C Ranger	690074	N9272V	14.11.90	Ranger Flights Ltd *(Stored dismantled)*	Hacketstown	N 1.03
EI-CBK	Aérospatiale-Alenia ATR 42-310	199	F-WWEM	25. 7.90	Nordic Aviation Contractors (Ireland) Ltd *(Operated Aer Arann Express)*	Dublin	A 9.08
EI-CBQ	Boeing 737-3YO	24907	9M-AAA UR-GAE, EI-CBQ	19. 3.91	Airplanes Holdings Ltd *(Operated Kras Air)* *(stored Dinard)*	Krasnoyarsk-Yemilianovo	A2008
EI-CBR	McDonnell-Douglas MD-83	49939		3.12.90	Airplanes 111 Ltd *(Operated Avianca)* *"Ciudad de Bucaramanga"*	Bogota-Eldorado	
EI-CBS	McDonnell-Douglas MD-83	49942		10.12.90	GECAS Technical Services Ltd *(Operated SAM)* *"Ciudad de Cucuta"*	Medellin-Olaya Herrara	A2008
EI-CBY	McDonnell-Douglas MD-83	49944		30. 7.91	GE Transportation Finance (Ireland) Ltd *(Operated Avianca)* *"Ciudad de Barranquilla"*	Bogota-Eldorado	A2008
EI-CBZ	McDonnell-Douglas MD-83	49945		13. 8.91	GE Transportation Finance (Ireland) Ltd *(Operated Avianca)* *"Ciudad de Santiago de Cali"*	Bogota-Eldorado	A2008
EI-CCC	McDonnell-Douglas MD-83	49946		27. 9.91	Airplanes 111 Ltd *(Operated Avianca)* *"Ciudad de Pereira"*	Bogota-Eldorado	A2008
EI-CCD	Grob G-115A	8108	D-EIUD (P/i may be D-EIWD)	15. 8.90	Kal Aviation Ltd	Weston, Dublin	A 5.06
EI-CCE (2)	McDonnell-Douglas MD-83	49947		19. 9.91	GE Transportation Finance (Ireland) Ltd *(Operated Avianca)* *"Ciudad de Medelin"*	Bogota-Eldorado	A2008
EI-CCF	Aeronca 11AC Chief *(Continental A65)*	11AC-S-40	N3826E NC3826E	10. 1.91	G McGuinness	Trim	N 3.07
EI-CCJ	Cessna 152 II	15280174	N24251	9.10.90	M P Cahill *(Stored: current status unknown)*	Dublin	N 2.95

EI-CCK	Cessna 152 II	15279610	N757BM	9.10.90	M P Cahill (Newcastle, Dublin)
					(Damaged pre 1995: current status unknown)
EI-CCL	Cessna 152 II	15280382	N24791	9.10.90	M P Cahill Dublin
					(Damaged Bray Head 4. 5.93: current status unknown)
EI-CCM	Cessna 152 II	15282320	N68679	9.10.90	E Hopkins Newcastle, Dublin A 5.07
EI-CDD	Boeing 737-548	24989	EI-BXH	3. 7.91	Castle 2003-2 Ireland Ltd *(Operated Rossiya Russian Airlines)*
					St Petersburg-Pulkovo A2008
EI-CDE	Boeing 737-548	25115	PT-SLM	21. 5.91	Castle 2003-2 Ireland Ltd *(Operated Rossiya Russian Airlines)*
			EI-CDE, (EI-BXJ)		St Petersburg-Pulkovo A2008
EI-CDF	Boeing 737-548	25737		23. 3.92	Jetscape Aviation Ireland Ltd
					(Operated Rossiya Russian Airlines)
					St Petersburg-Pulkovo A2008
EI-CDG	Boeing 737-548	25738		7. 4.92	Nordic Aviation Contractors (Ireland) Ltd
					(Operated Rossiya Russian Airlines)
					St Petersburg-Pulkovo A2008
EI-CDH	Boeing 737-548	25739		14. 4.92	Jetscape Aviation Ireland Ltd
					(Operated Rossiya Russian Airlines)
					St Petersburg-Pulkovo A2008
EI-CDP	Cessna 182L	18258955	G-FALL	20. 5.91	Irish Parachute Club Ltd Clonbullogue A 4.06
			OY-AHS, N4230S		
EI-CDV	Cessna 150G	15066677	N2777S	17. 7.91	K A O'Connor Weston, Dublin A 5.06
EI-CDX	Cessna 210K Centurion	21059329	G-AYGN	14. 8.91	Falcon Aviation Ltd Waterford A 4.06
			N9429M		
EI-CDY	McDonnell-Douglas MD-83	49948		27. 9.91	GE Transportation Finance (Ireland) Ltd *(Operated SAM)*
					"Ciudad de Santa Maria" Medellin-Olaya Herrara A2008
EI-CEG	SOCATA MS.893E Rallye 180GT	13083	SE-GTS	31.10.91	M Jarrett Powerscourt A3.07
EI-CEN	Thruster T.300	9012-T300-500		2. 3.92	P J Murphy *(Current status unknown)*
	(Rotax 582)				(Antville, Macroom)
EI-CEP	McDonnell-Douglas MD-83	53122		14. 4.92	GE Transportation Finance (Ireland) Ltd *(Operated Avianca)*
					"San Andres Isla" Bogota-Eldorado A2008
EI-CEQ	McDonnell-Douglas MD-83	53123		14. 4.92	GE Transportation Finance (Ireland) Ltd *(Operated Avianca)*
					"Ciudad de Leticia" Bogota-Eldorado A2008
EI-CER	McDonnell-Douglas MD-83	53125	N9017P	20. 5.92	Airplanes 111 Ltd *(Operated Avianca)*
					"Ciudad de Monteria" Bogota-Eldorado A2008
EI-CES	Taylorcraft BC-65	2231	G-BTEG	25. 3.92	B J Douglas (Thomastown) A 7.06
			N27590, NC27590		
EI-CEY	Boeing 757-2Y0ER	26152		10. 8.92	Aero Ireland Ltd *(Operated Avianca)*
					Bogota-Eldorado A2008
EI-CEZ	Boeing 757-2Y0ER	26154		18. 9.92	Airplanes Holdings Ltd *(Operated Avianca)*
					Bogota-Eldorado A2008
EI-CFE	Robinson R22 Beta	1709	G-BTHG	15. 5.91	Millicent Golf and Country Club Clane A 9.02
EI-CFF	Piper PA-12 Super Cruiser	12-3928	N78544	23. 5.91	J and T O'Dwyer Kilrush A 4.08
	(Lycoming O-235)		NC78544		
EI-CFG	Rousseau Piel CP.301B Emeraude	112	G-ARIW	1. 6.91	F Doyle *(Stored as "G-ARIW")* Murntown, Taghmon N 1.02
			F-BIRQ		
EI-CFH	Piper PA-12 Super Cruiser	12-3110	(EI-CCE)	1. 6.91	G Treacy Shinrone A 6.06
	(Lycoming O-320)		N4214M, NC4214M		
EI-CFO	Piper J-3C-65 Cub (L-4H-PI)	11947	OO-RAZ	13. 5.92	J Mathews and Partners *(As "479651" in USAAF c/s)*
			OO-RAF, 44-79651		Derrytrasna Glen, Bannfoot N 8.07
EI-CFP	Cessna 172P Skyhawk II	17274428	N52178	15. 7.91	K A O'Connor *(Operated National Flight Centre)*
					Weston, Dublin A 10.08
EI-CFX	Robinson R22 Beta	0793	G-OSPI	16. 6.92	B O'Sullivan Thurles A 8.02
EI-CFY	Cessna 172N Skyhawk II	17268902	N734JZ	18. 6.92	K A O'Connor Weston, Dublin A 4.06
EI-CFZ	McDonnell-Douglas MD-83	53120	N6206F	29. 7.92	Airplanes 111 Ltd *(Operated Avianca)*
					"Ciudad de San Juan de Pasto" Bogota-Eldorado A2008
EI-CGB	TEAM Mini-MAX	xxxx		20. 8.92	M Garvey *(Current status unknown)*
	(Built M Garvey as SAAC pr.no.036)				(Abbeyshrule)
EI-CGC	Stlnson 108-3 Station Wagon	108-5243	OO-IAC	17. 7.92	D A Weldon (Dublin) A 1.03
			OO-JAC, N3B		
EI-CGD	Cessna 172M Skyhawk II	17262309	OO-BMT	30. 7.92	G Cashman Weston, Dublin A 5.07
			N12846		
EI-CGF	Phoenix Luton LA-5 Major	PAL-1124	G-BENH	31. 7.92	J Duggan Ardenagh Great, Taghmon N 6.07
	(Regd C D McCartney as PFA 1208 then F Doyle as SAAC pr.no.019)				
EI-CGG	Ercoupe 415C	3147	N2522H	10. 9.92	Irish Ercoupe Group *(Derelict)* Weston, Dublin N 5.06
	(Continental C75)		NC2522H		
EI-CGH	Cessna 210N Centurion II	21063524	N6374A	16.11.92	J Smith Abbeyshrule A 4.08
EI-CGJ	Solar Wings Pegasus XL-R	SW-WA-1506	G-MWTV	5. 4.93	P Hearty *(Crashed Portarlington late 1995 and scrapped)*
	(Rotax 447)				
EI-CGM	Solar Wings Pegasus XL-R	SW-WA-1502	G-MWVC	14.11.92	Microflight Ltd *(Current status unknown)*
	(Rotax 447)				(Ballyfore, Daingean)
EI-CGN	Solar Wings Pegasus XL-R	SW-WA-1529	G-MWXM	14.11.92	V Power Donamore, New Ross A 8.00
	(Rotax 447)				
EI-CGP	Piper PA-28-140 Cherokee C	28-26928	G-MLUA	25.11.92	L A Tattan *(Operated Euroair Training)* Cork A 5.07
			G-AYJT, N11C		
EI-CGT	Cessna 152 II	15282331	G-BPBL	10.12.92	J Rafter *(Current status unknown)* (Naul)
			N16SU, N68715		
EI-CGV	Piper J-5A Cub Cruiser	5-624	G-BPKT	11.12.92	B Reilly Trim N12.07
			N35372, NC35372		
EI-CHH (2)	Boeing 737-317	23177	(N302AL)	15. 1.93	Airplanes Finance Ltd *(Operated KD Avia)*
			EI-CHH, (EI-CGX), PT-WBG, PP-SNU, C-FCPL		Kaliningrad-Khrabovo A2008
EI-CHK	Piper J-3C-65 Cub Special	23019	C-FHNS	10. 3.93	N Higgins *(Current status unknown)* (Longwood) A 7.99
			CF-HNS, N1492N, NC1492N		
EI-CHM	Cessna 150M Commuter	15079288	G-BSZX	2. 3.93	K A O'Connor *(Operated National Flight Centre)*
			N714MU		*(Crashed 25. 5.06 near Mullingar)* Weston, Dublin A 5.06

Reg	Type	C/n	Prev id	Date	Owner/Operator	Location	
EI-CHR	CFM Shadow Series BD (Rotax 447)	063	G-MTKT	20. 5.93	B Kelly	Ardclough, Straffan	N 5.04
EI-CHT	Solar Wings Pegasus XL-R	SW-WA-1568	G-BZXU	27. 3.02	J Grattan	Hawkfield, Newbridge	N 5.04
EI-CIA	SOCATA MS.880B Rallye Club	1218	G-MONA G-AWJK	26. 4.93	G Hackett and C Mason	Thurles, Moyne	N 6.07
EI-CIF	Piper PA-28-180 Cherokee C (Rebuilt 1967 with spare frame c/n 28-3808S)	28-2853	G-AVVV N8880J	12. 6.93	AA Flying Group	Waterford	A 8.06
EI-CIG	Piper PA-18-150 Super Cub (Frame No.18-7360)	18-7203	G-BGWF ST-AFJ, ST-ABN	12. 6.93	K A O'Connor	Weston, Dublin	A 5.06
EI-CIJ	Cessna 340	3400304	G-BBVE N69451	2. 7.93	Airlink Airways Ltd	Liverpool	A 7.06
EI-CIM	Avid Flyer Model IV (Built P Swan as SAAC pr.no.041)	1125D		17. 8.93	P Swan	Weston, Dublin	A 6.04
EI-CIN	Cessna 150K	15071728	G-OCIN EI-CIN, G-BSXG, N6228G	6. 9.93	K A.O'Connor	Weston, Dublin	A 5.07
EI-CIR	Cessna 551 Citation II (Built as Cessna 550 c/n 550-0128)	551-0174	N60AR EI-CIR, F-WLEF, 9A-BPU, RC-BPU, YU-BPU, N220LA, N536M, N2631V	29.11.93	Aircraft International Renting Ltd	Dinard, France	N 3.08
EI-CIV	Piper PA-28-140 Cherokee Cruiser	28-7725232	G-BEXY N9648N	20.11.93	L A Tatton	Abbeysrule	N 6.07
EI-CIW	McDonnell-Douglas MD-83	49785	HL-7271	30.12.93	Aergo Leasing 113 Ltd (Operated Meridiana) "Isola Tremiti"	Olbia	A2008
EI-CIZ	Steen Skybolt (Built B J Counts) (Lycoming IO-360)	001	G-BSAO N303BC	12.12.93	J Keane (Crashed near Ard Fert, County Kerry 29. 7.07 and substantially damaged)	Coonagh	
EI-CJJ	Slingsby T-31M Motor Tutor (Built J J Sullivan as SAAC pr.no.40?) (Volkswagen VW1600)	907	XE794	19. 1.06	J J Sullivan	Gorey	
EI-CJR	SNCAN Stampe SV-4∧	318	G-BKBK OO-BLCR, F-BCLR	28. 2.94	P McKenna	Carnmore, Galway	A 4.06
EI-CJS	Jodel Wassmer D.120A Paris-Nice	339	F-BOYF	28. 2.94	A Flood	Birr	A 1.03
EI-CJT	Slingsby T.31 Cadet III (Built P C Williams - c/n PCW-001) (Volkswagen 1835)	830	G-BPCW XA288	25. 2.94	J Tarrant (Stored)	Rathcoole	N2006
EI-CJV	Konsuprod Moskito 2 (Rotax 582)	004	D-MBGM	12. 3.94	Messrs Peril, Kingston, Hanly and Fitzgerald (Dismantled)	Coonagh	N 8.04
EI-CJZ	Whittaker MW-6S Fatboy Flyer (Built D M Precious) (Rotax 503)	PFA 164-11493	G-MWTW	24. 3.94	M McCarthy	Watergrasshill	A 9.00
EI-CKF	Hunt Avon/Hunt Wing (Built J Hunt- pr.no. BMAA/HB/015)	JAH-8	G-MWPT EI-CKF, G-MWPT	3. 6.94	M Leyden	(Ennis)	
EI-CKG	Hunt Avon (Built J Hunt) (Rotax 447)	92009013		2. 7.94	B Kenny (Current status unknown)	(Clara)	
EI-CKH	Piper PA-18 Super Cub 95	18-7248	G-APZK N10F	3. 6.94	G Brady	Kilrush	A 5.06
EI-CKI	Thruster TST Mk.1 (Rotax 503)	8078-TST-091	G-MVDI	3. 6.94	D.Baker	(Brannockstown)	N 9.07
EI-CKJ	Cameron N-77 Balloon (Hot Air)	3305		6. 7.94	F Meldon "Goodfellas"	Blackrock	A 9.06
EI-CKM	McDonnell-Douglas MD-83	49792	TC-INC EC-CKM, (D-ALLW), EI-CKM, XA-RPH, EC-FFP, EC-733, XA-RPH	10. 8.94	Airplanes Finance Ltd (Operated Meridiana) "Isola dell'Asinara"	Olbia	A2008
EI-CKN	Whittaker MW-6S Fatboy Flyer (Built Aero-Tech International) (Rotax 462)	BCA.8942		29. 7.94	F Byrne and M O'Carroll (Current status unknown) (Kilrush)		
EI-CKT	Mainair Gemini/Flash (Fuji-Robin EC-44-PM)	307-585-3- W47	G-MNCB	27. 9.94	C Burke (Current status unknown) (Darrary, Clonakilty)		
EI-CKU	Solar Wings Pegasus XL-R (Rotax 447) (Trike c/n SW-TB-1434)	SW-WA-1500	G-MWVB	14.10.94	M O'Regan (Current status unknown) (Edenderry)		
EI-CKZ	Jodel D.18 (Volkswagen 1834)	229		5. 4.95	J O'Brien (Under construction?) (Glen of Imal)		
EI-CLA	HOAC DV-20 Katana	20106		24. 3.95	Weston Ltd	Weston, Dublin	A 5.06
EI-CLL	Whittaker MW-6S Fatboy Flyer (Built Aero-Tech International) (Rotax 503)	1069		2. 4.95	F Stack (Stored?)	(Midleton)	
EI-CLQ	Reims Cessna F172N Skyhawk II	F17201653	G-BFLV	26. 5.95	Just Having Fun 172 Group	Limetree, Portarlington	A 10.08
EI-CLW	Boeing 737-3Y0	25187	XA-SAB	10. 6.95	Airplanes Finance Ltd (Operated Kras Air) (Stored DNR)	Krasnoyarsk-Yemilianovo	A2008
EI-CLZ	Boeing 737-3Y0	25179	XA-RJR N3521N	27. 7.95	Airplanes Finance Ltd (Operated Kras Air) (Stored DNR)	Krasnoyarsk-Yemilianovo	A2008
EI-CMB	Piper PA-28-140 Cherokee Cruiser	28-7725094	G-BELR N9541N	5. 9.95	Dublin Flyers Ltd	Dublin	A 10.08
EI-CMK	Eurowing Goldwing ST (Built M Garrigan as SAAC pr.no.57) (Fuji-Robin EC-PM-34)	76		22.12.95	M Garrigan (Current status uncertain) (Clondara)		
EI-CML	Cessna 150M	15076786	G-BNSS N45207	5. 1.96	K A O'Connor	Weston, Dublin	A 5.06
EI-CMN	Piper PA-12 Super Cruiser (Lycoming O-235)	12-1617	N2363M NC2363M	26. 1.96	A McNamee and Partners	Birr	A 5.06
EI-CMR	Rutan LongEz (Built F O'Caoimh as SAAC pr.no.028) (Lycoming O-235)	1716		2. 5.96	F and C.O'Caoimh	Waterford	A 4.06
EI-CMT	Piper PA-34-200T Seneca II	34-7870088	G-BNER N2590M	23. 4.96	Atlantic Flight Training Ltd	Cork	A 3.08
EI-CMU	Mainair Mercury (Rotax 462)	1071-0296-7 and W873		3. 5.96	M Mannion	(Athy, Co Kildare)	N 8.01
EI-CMV	Cessna 150L	150-72747	G-MSES N1447Q	17. 5.96	K A O'Connor	Weston, Dublin	A 5.06
EI-CMW	Rotorway Executive (Rotorway RW 162D)	3550		13. 5.96	B McNamee (Current status unknown) (Dunboyne)		
EI-CNA	Letov LK-2M Sluka (Built G Doody as SAAC pr.no.059) (Rotax 447)	8295S005		28. 6.96	G Doody	(Portlaoise)	A 7.00

EI-CNC	Team Mini-Max 1600	514		10. 9.96	A M S Allen	Enniskillen	A 7.01
	(Built A M S Allen as SAAC pr.no.042) (Rotax 447)						
EI-CNF	Boeing 737-4Y0	25180	EC-KUI EI-CNF	20.10.08	Airplanes Finance Ltd	Shannon	
EI-CNG	Air and Space 18-A Gyroplane	18-75	G-BALB N6170S	10. 9.96	P Joyce	Waterford	A 8.06
EI-CNL	Sikorsky S-61N Mk.II	61746	G-BDDA ZS-RBU, G-BDDA, N91201, G-BDDA	19.12.96	CHC Ireland Ltd (stored Aberdeen)	Aberdeen	9.08
EI-CNQ	British Aerospace BAe 146 Series 200	E2031	G-OWLD N173US, N353PS	2. 7.97	CityJet Ltd (Operated Aer Arran)	Galway	A 2008
EI-CNR	McDonnell-Douglas MD-83	53199	N531LS PK-FED, N531LS, SU-BMF, EI-CNR, SE-DLU, N13627	10. 4.97	Aircraft Finance Trust Ireland Ltd (Operated Meridiana)	Olbia	A2008
EI-CNU	Pegasus Quantum 15-912	7326		10. 4.97	M Ffrench	Donamore, New Ross,	A 6.01
EI-COE	Europa Aviation Europa	286		29. 5.97	F Flynn (Under construction)	(Urlanmore)	N 1.01
	(Built F Flynn as SAAC pr.no.060) (Jabiru 2200) (Monowheel u/c)						
EI-COG	Gyroscopic Rotorcraft Gyroplane	G.120		11. 3.98	R C Fidler and D D Bracken(Current status unknown)		
	(Subaru AE81) (Official c/n G.120 may be type designation)				(Letterkenny)		A 8.98
EI-COH	Boeing 737-430	27001	D-ABKB (VT-S..), D-ABKB	6. 6.97	ACS Aircraft Leasing (Ireland) Ltd (Operated Air One) Rome -Fiumicino		A2008
EI-COI	Boeing 737-430	27002	D-ABKC	13.11.97	Challey Ltd (Operated Air One)	Rome -Fiumicino	A2008
EI-COJ	Boeing 737-430	27005	D-ABKK (D-ABKF)	13.11.97	Challey Ltd (Operated Air One)	Rome -Fiumicino	A2008
EI-COK	Boeing 737-430	27003	F-GRNZ EI-COK, D-ABKD	22. 4.02	ACS Aircraft Leasing (Ireland) Ltd (Operated Air One) Rome -Fiumicino		A2008
EI-COM	Whittaker MW-6S Fatboy Flyer	1		10.10.97	M Watson (Under construction)	Clonbullogue	N 1.01
	(Built M Watson as SAAC pr.no.064) (Rotax 582)						
EI-COO	Carlson Sparrow II	302		13. 8.97	D Logue (Current status unknown)		
	(Rotax 532)					(Weston, Dublin)	
EI-COT	Reims Cessna F172N Skyhawk II	F17201884	D-EIEF	24.11.97	Tojo Air Leasing Ltd	Abbeyshrule	A10.08
EI-COY	Piper J-3C-65 Cub Special (Floatplane). 22519		N3319N NC3319N	5.11.97	W Flood	Abbeyshrule	N 1.07
	(Continental A65-8)						
EI-COZ	Piper PA-28-140 Cherokee C	28-26796	G-AYMZ N11C	5.11.97	L A Tattan	Cork	N 5.07
EI-CPC	Airbus A321-211	815	D-AVZT	8. 5.98	Aer Lingus Ltd "St.Fergus/Feargus"	Dublin	A2008
EI-CPD	Airbus A321-211	841	D-AVZA	19. 6.98	Aer Lingus Ltd "St.Davnet/Damhnat"	Dublin	A2008
EI-CPE	Airbus A321-211	926	D-AVZQ	11.12.98	Aer Lingus Ltd "St.Enda/Eanna"	Dublin	A2008
EI-CPF	Airbus A321-211	991	D-AVZE	9. 4.99	Aer Lingus Ltd "St.Ida/Ide"	Dublin	A2008
EI-CPG	Airbus A321-211	1023	D-AVZR	28. 5.99	Aer Lingus Ltd "St.Aidan/Aodhan"	Dublin	A2008
EI-CPH	Airbus A321-211	1094	F-WWDD D-AVZA	22.11.99	Aer Lingus Ltd "St.Dervilla/Dearbhile"	Dublin	A2008
EI-CPI	Rutan LongEz	17		18.12.97	D J Ryan "Lady Elizabeth"	Waterford	A 4.06
	(Lycoming O-235)						
EI-CPN	Auster J/4	2073	G-AIJR	1. 4.98	E Fagan	Abbeyshrule	A12.00
EI-CPO	Robinson R.22B2 Beta	2775	G-BXUJ	23. 9.98	D Byrne	Weston, Dublin	N 1.07
EI-CPP	Piper J-3C-65 Cub (L-4H-PI)	12052	G-BIGH F-BFQV, OO-GAS, OO-GAZ, 44-79756	23. 3.98	E Fitzgerald Ardenagh Great, Taghmon		A 8.06
	(Rebuilt Glasthule, Dublin 1994/1998)						
EI-CPT	Aérospatiale-Alenia ATR 42-300	191	C-GIQS (ZS-NYP), C-GIQS, F-WWEA (Operated Aer Arann Express)	12. 6.98	Nordic Aviation Contractors (Ireland) Ltd Dublin		A 6.06
EI-CPX	III Sky Arrow 650T	K.122		24. 6.98	M McCarthy	Watergrasshill	A.8.00
	(Built M McCarthy as SAAC pr.no.67)						
EI-CRB	Lindstrand LBL 90A Balloon (Hot Air)	550		23. 9.98	J and C Concannon (Current status unknown)	(Tuam)	
EI-CRD	Boeing 767-31BER	26259	B-2565	29.10.98	ILFC Ireland Ltd (Operated Alitalia) Rome-Fiumicino		A2008
EI-CRE	McDonnell-Douglas MD-83	49854	D-ALLL	11.12.98	AAR Ireland Ltd (Operated Meridiana) Olbia "Tavolara-Punta Coda Cavallo"		A2008
EI-CRF	Boeing 767-31B	25170	B-2566	4.12.98	ILFC Ireland Ltd (Operated Alitalia) Rome-Fiumicino		A2008
EI-CRG	Robin DR400/180 Régent	2021	D-EHEC	11.12.98	D and B Lodge	Waterford	A 4.06
EI-CRH	McDonnell-Douglas MD-83	49935	HB-IKM G-DCAC, N3004C	10. 2.99	Airplanes 111 Ltd (Operated Meridiana) Olbia "Torre Guaceto"		A2008
EI-CRK	Airbus A330-301	070	(EI-NYC) F-WWKV	18.11.94	Aer Lingus Ltd "St Brigid/Brighid"	Dublin	A2008
EI-CRL	Boeing 767-343ER	30008	(I-DEIB)	22. 3.99	GECAS Technical Services Ltd (Operated Alitalia) "Leonardo da Vinci" Rome-Fiumicino		A2008
EI-CRM	Boeing 767-343	30009		8. 4.99	GECAS Technical Services Ltd (Operated Alitalia) "Amerigo Vespucci" Rome-Fiumicino		A2008
EI-CRO	Boeing 767-3Q8ER	29383		16. 4.99	ILFC Ireland Ltd (Operated Alitalia) "Francesco de Pinedo" Rome-Fiumicino		A2008
EI-CRR	Aeronca 11AC Chief	11AC-1605	OO-ESM (OO-DEL), OO-ESM	13. 4.99	L Maddock and Partners	Killamaster	A 1.03
EI-CRU	Cessna 152	15285621	G-BNSW N94213	21. 9.99	W Reilly	Inis Mor	A 5.04
EI-CRV	Hoffman H.36 Dimona	3674	OE-9319 HB-2081	2. 6.99	The Dimona Group	Waterford	A 4.06
EI-CRW	McDonnell-Douglas MD-83	49951	HB-IKN G-GMJM, N13627	8. 4.99	Airplanes IAL Ltd (Operated Meridiana) Olbia "Portofino"		A2008
EI-CRX	SOCATA TB-9 Tampico	1170	F-GKUL	21. 5.99	The Hotel Bravo Flying Club Ltd	Weston, Dublin	A 10.08
EI-CRY	Medway EclipseR	160/138		2. 6.99	G A Murphy (Current status unknown)	(Rathcoole)	
EI-CSG	Boeing 737-8AS	29922	N1786B	31. 5.00	CIT Aerospace International Ltd (Operated MIAT Mongolian Airlines) Ulan Bator		A 2008
EI-CSN	Boeing 737-8AS	29927	N1784B	11.12.00	Ryanair Ltd	Dublin	A2008
EI-CSO	Boeing 737-8AS	29928	N1784B	11. 1.01	Ryanair Ltd	Dublin	A2008

Reg	Type	c/n	Prev id	Date	Owner/Operator	Location	Ref
EI-CSP	Boeing 737-8AS	29929	N1786B	25. 1.01	Ryanair Ltd	Dublin	A2008
EI-CSQ	Boeing 737-8AS	29930	N1786B	26. 1.01	Ryanair Ltd (for Norwegian)	Dublin	A2008
EI-CSR	Boeing 737-8AS	29931	N1787B	5.12.01	Ryanair Ltd	Dublin	A2008
EI-CSS	Boeing 737-8AS	29932	N1787B	14.12.01	Ryanair Ltd (to VQ- 1.09)	Dublin	A2008
EI-CST	Boeing 737-8AS	29933		19.12.01	Ryanair Ltd	Dublin	A2008
EI-CSV	Boeing 737-8AS	29934		18. 1.02	Ryanair Ltd	Dublin	A2008
EI-CSW	Boeing 737-8AS	29935		4. 2.02	Ryanair Ltd	Dublin	A2008
EI-CTA	Boeing 737-8AS	29936		19.11.02	Ryanair Ltd	Dublin	A2008
EI-CTB	Boeing 737-8AS	29937		19.11.02	Ryanair Ltd	Dublin	A2008
EI-CTC	Medway EclipseR	158/137		2. 6.99	P A McMahon	Dunlaoghaire	A 1.03
EI-CTG	Stoddard-Hamilton SH-2R Glasair RG	721R	N721WR	3. 6.99	K Higgins	Carnmore, Galway	A 10.08
EI-CTI	Reims Cessna FRA150L	FRA1500261	G-BCRN	29. 4.99	J Logan and T Bradford	Ballynacarigy	A 1.03
					(Wings only noted Clonbullogue 4.06)		
EI-CTL	Aerotech MW-5B Sorcerer	SR102-R440B-07	G-MTFH	21. 5.99	M Wade	Kilrush	A 1.03
	(Fuji-Robin EC-44-PM)						
EI-CUA	Boeing 737-4K5	24901	D-AHLR	29. 9.99	Aerco Ireland Ltd (Operated Blu Express)		
						Rome-Fiumicino	A2008
EI-CUD	Boeing 737-4Q8	26298	TC-JEI	13. 3.00	Castle 2003-2 Ireland Ltd (Operated Blu Express)		
						Rome-Fiumicino	A2008
EI-CUE	Cameron N-105 Balloon (Hot Air)	4683		16. 9.99	Eircom Ltd "Eircom"	Celbridge	A12.03
EI-CUJ	Cessna 172N Skyhawk II	17271985	G-BJGO	19.11.99	M Nally	Abbeyshrule	A 10.08
			N6038E				
EI-CUM	Airbus A320-232	542	N721LF	24. 3.05	ILFC Ireland Ltd (Operated Windjet)	Catania	A2008
			S7-RGL, PK-AWE, N542LF, EI-CUM, OO-COF. F-WWIH				
EI-CUN	Boeing 737-4K5	27074	D-AHLS	13. 4.00	Aerco Ireland Ltd (Operated Blu Express)		
			(D-AHLG)			Rome-Fiumicino	A2008
EI-CUP	Cessna 335	335-0018	N2706X	5. 5.00	J Greany	Kerry	A 6.04
EI-CUS	Agusta-Bell 206B-3 JetRanger III	8721		24. 8.00	Doherty Quarries and Waste Management.		
			(EI-...), G-OONS, G-LIND, G-OONS			Carryduff	A 7.01
EI-CUT	Maule MX 7-180A	21080C		6. 4.01	Cosair Ltd	Trim	A 4.06
	(Nosewheel u/c)						
EI-CUW	Pilatus Britten-Norman BN-2B-20 Islander	2293	G-BWYW	8.11.00	Galway Aviation Services Ltd	Galway	A 5.07
					(Operated Aer Arann Islands)		
EI-CVA	Airbus A320-214	1242	F-WWIT	22. 6.00	Aer Lingus Ltd "St Schira/Scire"	Dublin	A2008
EI-CVB	Airbus A320-214	1394	F-WWIV	8. 2.01	Aer Lingus Ltd "St Mobhi/Mobhi"	Dublin	A2008
EI-CVC	Airbus A320-214	1443	F-WWBG	6. 4.01	Aer Lingus Ltd "St Kealin/Caoilfhionn"	Dublin	A2008
EI-CVD	Airbus A320-214	1467	F-WWDK	10. 5.01	Aer Lingus Ltd "St Kevin/Caoimhin"	Dublin	A2008
EI-CVL	Ercoupe 415CD	4754	G-ASNF	15. 3.01	B Lyons and J Hackett	Thurles, Moyne	N 6.07
			PH-NCF, NC94647				
EI-CVM	Schweizer 269C (Schweizer 300)	S1328	G-GIRO	7.11.00	B Moloney	Tralee	A 1.03
			N41S				
EI-CVR	Aérospatiale-Alenia ATR 42-310	022	F-GGLK	17. 1.01	Nordic Aviation Contractor (Ireland) Ltd	Dublin	A2008
			OH-LTB, F-WWEI		(Operated Aer Arann Express)		
EI-CVW	Bensen B8M Gyrocopter	FK-199801		26. 5.05	F Kavanagh	Kilrush	A 5.06
	(Built F Kavanagh)						
EI-CVY	Brock KB-2 Gyrocopter	074		7. 8.03	G Smyth	(Swords)	
EI-CWE	Boeing 737-42C	24232	N941PG	18. 5.01	Rockshaw Ltd (Operated Air One)		
			PH-BPE, G-UKLD			Rome -Fiumicino	A2008
EI-CWF	Boeing 737-42C	24814	PH-BPG	16. 5.01	Rockshaw Ltd (Operated Air One)		
			G-UKLG			Rome -Fiumicino	A2008
EI-CWR	Robinson R22 Beta II	3234	G-CBDB	2.11.01	Eirecopter Helicopters Ltd	Weston, Dublin	A10.08
EI-CWW	Boeing 737-4YO	24906	EC-GAZ	19.12.01	Airplanes Holdings Ltd (Operated Air One)		
			EC-850, 9M-MJO			Rome -Fiumicino	A2008
EI-CWX	Boeing 737-4YO	24912	EC-GBN	6.12.01	Airplanes Holdings Ltd (Operated Air One)		
			EC-851, 9M-MJQ			Rome -Fiumicino	A2008
EI-CXC	Raj Hamsa X'Air 502T	333	(44 SU)	6. 9.02	R Dunleavy	(Barnesmore, Co Donegal)	A 5.08
EI-CXK	Boeing 737-4S3	25596	G-OGBA	9. 4.02	Bravo Aircraft Management Ltd (Operated Transaero Airlines)		
			G-OBMK			Moscow-Domodedovo	A2008
EI-CXN	Boeing 737-329	23772	OO-SDW	1. 5.02	Embarcadero Aircraft Securitization Trust Ireland Ltd		
			N506GX, OO-SDW		(Operated Transaero Airlines)	Moscow-Domodedovo	A2008
EI-CXO	Boeing 767-3GS	28111	N581LF	12. 4.02	ILFC Ireland Ltd (Operated Blue Panorama Airlines)		
			D-AMUJ			Rome-Fiumicino	A2008
EI-CXR	Boeing 737-329	24355	OO-SYA	31. 5.02	Embarcadero Aircraft Securitization Trust Ireland Ltd		
			(OO-SQA)		(Operated Transaero Airlines)	Moscow-Domodedovo	A2008
EI-CXS	Sikorsky S.61N	61816	IAC257	14.10.04	CHC Ireland Ltd (IMES Rescue titles)		
			EI-CXS, C-GBKZ, LN-OQU			Strandhill, Sligo	A2008
EI-CXV	Boeing 737-8CX	32364		3. 7.02	MASL Ireland (14) Ltd Ulan Bator, Mongolia		A2
					(Operated MIAT Mongolian Airlines) "Khubelai Khaan"		008
EI-CXY	Evektor EV-97 Eurostar	2000-0701	OK-FUR	31. 10.02	G Doody, E McEvoy and S Pallister	Portlaoise	A 7.05
EI-CXZ	Boeing 767-216ER	24973	N502GX	25. 7.02	Embarcadero Aircraft Securitization Trust Ireland Ltd		
		VH-RMM, N483GX, CC-CEF			(Operated Transaero Airlines)	Moscow-Domodedovo	A2008
EI-CZA	ATEC Zephyr 2000	Z580602A		17. 7.03	P Whitehouse-Tedd	(Carnmore, Galway)	N 8.06
	(Built M Higgins)						
EI-CZC	CFM Streak Shadow	K269SA11	G-BWHJ	16. 7.02	M Culhane and D Burrows	(Rathcoole)	
					(Current status unknown)		
EI-CZD	Boeing 767-216ER	23623	N762TA	2. 9.02	Capablue Ltd (Operated Transaero Airlines)		
			CC-CJU, N4529T			Moscow-Domodedovo	A2008
EI-CZH	Boeing 767-3G5ER	29435	D-AMUO	9. 8.02	ILFC Ireland Ltd (Operated Blue Panorama Airlines)		
						Rome-Fiumicino	A2008
EI-CZK	Boeing 737-4YO	24519	N519AP	10. 1.03	Aergo Leasing 113 Ltd (Operated Transaero Airlines)		
			TC-ACA, VR-CAB			Moscow-Domodedovo	A2008
EI-CZL	Schweizer 269C-1	0147	G-CDTW	19.12.02	Cahir Oil Ltd	Weston, Dublin	N10.08
	(Schweizer 300)		EI-CZL, N86G				
EI-CZM	Robinson R.44 Raven II	10054		24. 4.03	M I C A D Developments Ltd	Oranmore, Galway	A 6.07

EI-CZN	Sikorsky S.61N	61740	G-CBWC	15. 4.03	CHC Ireland Ltd *(IMES Rescue titles)*		
			OY-HDO, LN-OSU			Dublin	A2008
EI-CZP	Schweizer 269C-1	0149		2. 5.03	NG Kam Tim	Weston, Dublin	A 5.06
	(Schweizer 300)				*(Operated European Helicopter Academy)*		
EI-DAA	Airbus A330-202	397	F-WWKX	17. 4.01	Aer Lingus Ltd *"St Keeva/Caoimhe"*	Dublin	A2008
EI-DAC	Boeing 737-8AS	29938		2.12.02	Ryanair Ltd	Dublin	A2008
EI-DAD	Boeing 737-8AS	33544		3.12.02	Ryanair Ltd	Dublin	A2008
EI-DAE	Boeing 737-8AS	33545		9.12.02	Ryanair Ltd	Dublin	A2008
EI-DAF	Boeing 737-8AS	29939		9. 1.03	Ryanair Ltd	Dublin	A2008
EI-DAG	Boeing 737-8AS	29940		17. 1.03	Ryanair Ltd	Dublin	A2008
EI-DAH	Boeing 737-8AS	33546		22. 1.03	Ryanair Ltd	Dublin	A2008
EI-DAI	Boeing 737-8AS	33547		3. 2.03	Ryanair Ltd	Dublin	A2008
EI-DAJ	Boeing 737-8AS	33548		4. 2.03	Ryanair Ltd	Dublin	A2008
EI-DAK	Boeing 737-8AS	33717		17. 4.03	Ryanair Ltd	Dublin	A2008
EI-DAL	Boeing 737-8AS	33718		22. 4.03	Ryanair Ltd	Dublin	A2008
EI-DAM	Boeing 737-8AS	33719		23. 4.03	Ryanair Ltd	Dublin	A2008
EI-DAN	Boeing 737-8AS	33549		2. 9.03	Ryanair Ltd	Dublin	A2008
EI-DAO	Boeing 737-8AS	33550	N1800B	5. 9.03	Ryanair Ltd	Dublin	A2008
EI-DAP	Boeing 737-8AS	33551	N6066U	18. 9.03	Ryanair Ltd	Dublin	A2008
EI-DAR	Boeing 737-8AS	33552	(EI-DAQ)	11. 9.03	Ryanair Ltd	Dublin	A2008
EI-DAS	Boeing 737-8AS	33553	(EI-DAR)	12. 9.03	Ryanair Ltd	Dublin	A2008
EI-DAT	Boeing 737-8AS	33554		5.12.03	Ryanair Ltd	Dublin	A2008
EI-DAV	Boeing 737-8AS	33555		9. 1.04	Ryanair Ltd	Dublin	A2008
EI-DAW	Boeing 737-8AS	33556		8. 1.04	Ryanair Ltd	Dublin	A2008
EI-DAX	Boeing 737-8AS	33557		23. 1.04	Ryanair Ltd	Dublin	A2008
EI-DAY	Boeing 737-8AS	33558		2. 2.04	Ryanair Ltd	Dublin	A2008
EI-DAZ	Boeing 737-8AS	33559		3. 2.04	Ryanair Ltd	Dublin	A2008
EI-DBF	Boeing 767-3Q8	24745	F-GHGF	23. 4.03	ACG Acquisition Ireland Ltd *(Operated Transaero Airlines)*		
						Moscow-Domodedovo	A2008
EI-DBG	Boeing 767-3Q8	24746	F-GHGG	14 .5.03	Transalpine Lesing Ltd *(Operated Transaero Airlines)*		
						Moscow-Domodedovo	A2008
EI-DBH	CFM Streak Shadow SA-11	K.278		14. 4.03	M O'Mahony *(Stored?)*		
						(Ballyskerdane, Carrignavar)	
EI-DBI	Raj Hamsa X'Air Mk.2 Falcon	671		16. 4.03	E Hamilton	Kilrush	A 5.06
	(Jabiru 2200)						
EI-DBJ	Huntwing Pegasus XL Classic	xxxxx	G-MZCZ	19. 5.03	P A McMahon	Clonbullogue	A 5.06
	(Built C Kiernan - pr.no.BMAA/HB/039)						
EI-DBK	Boeing 777-243ER	32783		10.10.03	GECAS Technical Services Ltd *(Operated.Alitalia)*		
					"Ostuni"	Rome-Fiumicino	A2008
EI-DBL	Boeing 777-243ER	32781		14. 11.03	GECAS Technical Services Ltd *(Operated.Alitalia)*		
					"Sestriere"	Rome-Fiumicino	A2008
EI-DBM	Boeing 777-243ER	32782		12.12.03	GECAS Technical Services Ltd *(Operated.Alitalia)*		
					"Argentario"	Rome-Fiumicino	A2008
EI-DBO	Air Création 582(1)/Kiss 400	xxxx		13. 5.03	E Spain	(Monasterevin)	A 6.07
	(Wing s/n A03034-3033)						
EI-DBP	Boeing 767-35H	26389	C-GGBJ	23. 5.03	Centennial Aviation (Ireland) Ltd *(Operated.Alitalia)*		
			(VH-BZN),		*"Duca degli Abruzzi"*	Rome-Fiumicino	A2008
			ZK-NCM, N800CZ, N60659				
EI-DBU	Boeing 767-37E	25077	F-GHGH	8. 7.03	Pegasus Aviation Ireland Ltd *(Operated Transaero Airlines)*		
						Moscow-Domodedovo	A2008
EI-DBV	Rand Kar X'Air 602T	516	44-AEE	13. 8.03	S Scanlon	Emlagh, Lispole	A2006
	(Rotax 582)						
EI-DBW	Boeing 767-201	23899	N647US	10. 9.03	Orix Aircraft Management Ltd *(Operated Transaero Airlines)*		
			N607P			Moscow-Domodedovo	A2008
EI-DBX	Magni M-18 Spartan	18-032181		3. 7.03	M Concannon	Abbeyshrule	A 8.06
EI-DCA	Raj Hamsa X'Air	742		18. 7.03	S Cahill	Ferskill, Granard	A2006
	(Jabiru 2200)						
EI-DCB	Boeing 737-8AS	33560		10. 2.04	Ryanair Ltd	Dublin	A2008
EI-DCC	Boeing 737-8AS	33561		11. 3.04	Ryanair Ltd	Dublin	A2008
EI-DCD	Boeing 737-8AS	33562		12. 3.04	Ryanair Ltd	Dublin	A2008
EI-DCE	Boeing 737-8AS	33563		25. 3.04	Ryanair Ltd	Dublin	A2008
EI-DCF	Boeing 737-8AS	33804		1. 7.04	Ryanair Ltd	Dublin	A2008
EI-DCG	Boeing 737-8AS	33805		2. 7.04	Ryanair Ltd	Dublin	A2008
EI-DCH	Boeing 737-8AS	33566		3. 8.04	Ryaniar Ltd	Dublin	A2008
EI-DCI	Boeing 737-8AS	33567		3. 8.04	Ryanair Ltd	Dublin	A2008
EI-DCJ	Boeing 737-8AS	33564		1. 9.04	Ryanair Ltd	Dublin	A2008
EI-DCK	Boeing 737-8AS	33565		1. 9.04	Ryanair Ltd	Dublin	A2008
EI-DCL	Boeing 737-8AS	33806	ex N1786B	1.10.04	Ryanair Ltd	Dublin	A2008
EI-DCM	Boeing 737-8AS	33807		1.10.04	Ryanair Ltd	Dublin	A2008
EI-DCN	Boeing 737-8AS	33808	N60436	1.11.04	Ryanair Ltd	Dublin	A2008
EI-DCO	Boeing 737-8AS	33809		1.11.04	Ryanair Ltd	Dublin	A2008
EI-DCP	Boeing 737-8AS	33810		1.11.04	Ryanair Ltd	Dublin	A2008
EI-DCR	Boeing 737-8AS	33811		2.12.04	Ryanair Ltd	Dublin	A2008
EI-DCS	Boeing 737-8AS	33812		3.12.04	Ryanair Ltd	Dublin	A2008
EI-DCT	Boeing 737-8AS	33813		11.12.04	Ryanair Ltd	Dublin	A2008
EI-DCV	Boeing 737-8AS	33814		14.12.04	Ryanair Ltd	Dublin	A2008
EI-DCW	Boeing 737-8AS	33568		13. 1.05	Ryanair Ltd	Dublin	A2008
EI-DCX	Boeing 737-8AS	33569		21. 1.05	Ryanair Ltd	Dublin	A2008
EI-DCY	Boeing 737-8AS	33570		25. 1.05	Ryanair Ltd	Dublin	A2008
EI-DCZ	Boeing 737-8AS	33815		26. 1.05	Ryanair Ltd	Dublin	A2008
EI-DDA	Robinson R44 Raven II	10105	G-CCIP	26. 9.03	Eirecopter Helicopters Ltd	Weston, Dublin	A 8.08
EI-DDB	Eurocopter EC.120B Colibri	1341	G-CCIL	30.12.03	J Cuddy	Weston, Dublin	A 10.08
EI-DDC	Reims Cessna F.172M	1082	G-BCEC	15.10.03	Trim Flying Club Ltd	Trim	A 10.08

Reg	Type	C/n	Prev id	Date	Owner/Operator	Location	Code
EI-DDD	Aeronca 7AC Champion	7AC-2895	G-BTRH N84204, NC84204	27. 4.04	J Sullivan and M Quinn	Coonagh	A10.06
EI-DDH	Boeing 777-243ER	32784		15. 5.04	GECAS Technical Services Ltd *(Operated.Alitalia)* *"Tropea"*	Rome-Fiumicino	A2008
EI-DDI	Schweizer S.269C-1 *(Schweizer 300CBi)*	0156	OO-SAC N86G	6.11.03	B Hade *(Operated European Helicopter Academy)*	Weston, Dublin	A 5.06
EI-DDJ	Raj Hamsa X'Air 582	863		24. 9.03	P J McHugh	Haugh, Donegal Town	A2006
EI-DDK	Boeing 737-4S3	24165	N758BC VT-SIH, VT-JAI, N690MA, G-BPKC	3.12.03	Boeing Capital Leasing Ltd *(Operated Transaero Airlines)*	Moscow-Domodedovo	A2008
EI-DDO	Montgomerie Merlin	0072		21. 5.04	C Condell *(Current status unknown)*	(Celbridge)	
EI-DDP	Southdown Puma Sprint	1121/0031	G-MMYJ	27. 5.04	M Mannion	Kilrush	N 4.07
EI-DDR	Bensen B.8V Gyrocopter	xxxx		2. 6.05	P MacCabe and K Reynolds	Kilrush	A 5.06
	(Built P MaccCabe and K Reynolds as SAAC pr.no.037) (Limbach SL1700)						
EI-DDW	Boeing 767-3S1ER	26608	N979PG C-GGBI, (N769TA)	9. 1.04	Pegasus Aviation Ireland Ltd *(Operated.Alitalia)* *"Sebastiano Caboto"*	Rome-Fiumicino, Italy	A2008
EI-DDX	Cessna 172S	172S8313	G-UFCA N2461P	19. 2.04	Flight Training Ltd	Cork	A 3.08
EI-DDY	Boeing 737-4YO	24904	HA-LEV TC-JDE	6. 5.04	Aerco Ireland Ltd *(Operated Transaero Airlines)*	Moscow-Domodedovo	A2008
EI-DDZ	Piper PA-28-181Cherokee Archer II	28-7690211	PH-PDW OO-HAT, N8882E	4. 6.04	Ardnari Ltd	Weston, Dublin	A 8.05
EI-DEA	Airbus A320-214	2191	F-WWBX	30. 4.04	Aer Lingus Ltd *"St Fidelma/Fiedeilme"*	Dublin	A2008
EI-DEB	Airbus A320-214	2206	F-WWBP	19. 5.04	Aer Lingus Ltd *"St Nathy/Nathi"*	Dublin	A2008
EI-DEC	Airbus A320-214	2217	F-WWBH	4. 6.04	Aer Lingus Ltd *"St Fergal/Fearghal"*	Dublin	A2008
EI-DEE	Airbus A320-214	2250	F-WWBE	27. 8.04	Aer Lingus Ltd *"St Ultan/Ultan"*	Dublin	A2008
EI-DEF	Airbus A320-214	2256	F-WWBK	2. 9.04	Aer Lingus Ltd *"St Declan/Deaglan"*	Dublin	A2008
EI-DEG	Airbus A320-214	2272	F-WWIB	10. 9.04	Aer Lingus Ltd *"St Fachtna/Fachtna"*	Dublin	A2008
EI-DEH	Airbus A320-214	2294	F-WWDF	20.10.04	Aer Lingus Ltd *"St Conleth/Connlaodh"*	Dublin	A2008
EI-DEI	Airbus A320-214	2374	F-WWDU	14.2.05	Aer Lingus Ltd *"St Oliver Plunkett/Oilibhear Pluinceid"*	Dublin	A2008
EI-DEJ	Airbus A320-214	2364	F-WWDI	3.2.05	Aer Lingus Ltd *"St Kilian/Cillian"*	Dublin	A2008
EI-DEK	Airbus A320-214	2399	F-WWIZ	24 3.05	Aer Lingus Ltd *"St Eunan/Eunan"*	Dublin	A2008
EI-DEL	Airbus A320-214	2409	F-WWDE	13.4 05	Aer Lingus Ltd *"St Ibar/Ibhar"*	Dublin	A2008
EI-DEM	Airbus A320-214	2411	F-WWDG	7.4.05	Aer Lingus Ltd *"St Canice/Cainneach"*	Dublin	A2008
EI-DEN	Airbus A320-214	2432	F-WWBK	13. 5.05	Aer Lingus Ltd *"St Kieran/Ciaran"*	Dublin	A2008
EI-DEO	Airbus A320-214	2486	F-WWIV	6. 7.05	Aer Lingus Ltd *"St Senan/Seanan"*	Dublin	A2008
EI-DEP	Airbus A320-214	2542	F-WWIU	7. 10.05	Aer Lingus Ltd *"St Eugene/Eoghan"*	Dublin	A2008
EI-DER	Airbus A320-214	2583	F-WWDE	3. 11.05	Aer Lingus Ltd *"St Mel/Mel"*	Dublin	A2008
EI-DES	Airbus A320-214	2635	F-WWDZ	22.12.05	Aer Lingus Ltd *"St Pappin/Paipan"*	Dublin	A2008
EI-DET	Airbus A320-214	2810	F-WWIP	28. 6.06	Aer Lingus Ltd *"St Brendan/Breandan"*	Dublin	A2008
EI-DEW	British Aerospace BAe 146 Series 300	E3142	G-UKAC G-5-142	20 5.04	CityJet Ltd *(Operated Air France Regional)*	Paris CDG	A2008
EI-DEX	British Aerospace BAe 146 Series 300	E3157	G-UKID G-6-157	11. 6.04	CityJet Ltd *(stored)* *(D-AMAX reserved for WDL)*	Norwich	N2008
EI-DEY	Airbus A319-112	1102	D-ANDA F-WQQE, OO-SSD, D-AVYI	6. 5.04	Olbia Ltd *(Operated Meridiana)* *"Capo Rizzuto"*	Olbia	A2008
EI-DEZ	Airbus A319-112	1283	D-ANDE F-WQQF, OO-SSI, D-AVYI	25. 2.04	Olbia Ltd *(Operated Meridiana)* *"Capo Gallo"*	Olbia	A2008
EI-DFA	Airbus A319-112	1305	D-ANDI F-WQQG, OO-SSJ, D-AVWX	30. 3.04	Olbia Ltd *(Operated Meridiana)* *"Capo Carbonara"*	Olbia	A2008
EI-DFG	Embraer EMB-170-100LR *(Embraer 170)*	17000008	(I-EMCX) PT-SKA	24. 3.04	GECAS Technical Services Ltd *(Operated Alitalia Express)* *"Via Appia"*	Rome-Fiumicino	A2008
EI-DFH	Embraer EMB-170-100LR *(Embraer 170)*	17000009	PT-SKB	20. 4.04	Aldus Portfolio Leasing Ltd *(Operated Alitalia Express)* *"Via Aurélia"*	Rome-Fiumicino	A2008
EI-DFI	Embraer EMB-170-100LR *(Embraer 170)*	17000010	PT-SKC	20. 5.04	Aldus Portfolio Leasing Ltd *(Operated Alitalia Express)* *"Via Cassia"*	Rome-Fiumicino	A2008
EI-DFJ	Embraer EMB-170-100LR *(Embraer 170)*	17000011	PT-SKD	30. 6.04	Aldus Portfolio Leasing Ltd *(Operated Alitalia Express)* *"Via Flaminia"*	Rome-Fiumicino	A2008
EI-DFK	Embraer EMB-170-100LR *(Embraer 170)*	17000032	PT-SUA	30. 6.04	GECAS Technical Services Ltd *(Operated Alitalia Express)* *"Via Salaria"*	Rome-Fiumicino	A2008
EI-DFL	Embraer EMB-170-100LR *(Embraer 170)*	17000036	PT-SUF	16. 7.04	GECAS Technical Services Ltd *(Operated Alitalia Express)* *"Via Tiburtina Valeria"*	Rome-Fiumicino	A2008
EI-DFM	Evektor EV-97 Eurostar	2003-1706		8. 3.04	M O'Connell	Enniskillen,	N8.08
EI-DFN	Airbus A.320-211	0204	F-GJVC	3.08R	AerCap *(Operated Windjet)*	Catania	
EI-DFO	Airbus A.320-211	0371	A6-ABX C-FTDD, SU-LBA, TC-OND, N531LF, C-FLSJ, F-WWIQ	20. 4.04	Triton Aviation Ireland Ltd *(Operated Windjet)*	Catania	A2008
EI-DFP	Airbus A.319-112	1048	F-OHJV F-WIHE, OO-SSA, D-AVYT	11. 5.04	Wilmington Trust SP Services (Dublin) Ltd *(Operated Meridiana) "Capo Caccia"*	Olbia	A2008
EI-DFS	Boeing 767-33A	25346	ET-AKW V8-RBE	31. 5.04	Transalpine Leasing Ltd *(Operated Transaero Airlines)*	Moscow-Domodedovo	A2008
EI-DFW	Robinson R44 Raven	1377	G-CCUM N7536G	3. 6.04	Blue Star Helicopters Ltd	Cork	A 3.08
EI-DFX	Air Création 582(1)/Kiss 400 *(Wing s/n A04007-4007)*	xxxx		13. 5.04	H Eoghan	Tullamore	A 9.06
EI-DFY	Raj Hamsa X'Air R100(2) *(Built P McGirr and R Gillespie – pr. no BMAA/HB/096)*	430	G-BYLN	13. 5.04	P McGirr and R Gillespie	Drumavish Killygordon	A2006
EI-DGA	Urban Air UFM-11UK Lambada	16/11		16. 4.04	P and D Dunkin	Abbeyshrule	A 10.08
EI-DGG	Raj Hamsa X'Air 133	899		9. 6.04	P A Weldon	Granard	A 708
EI-DGH	Raj Hamsa X'Air 582	861		9. 6.04	M Garvey and T McGowan	Clonmellon, Devlin	A2006
EI-DGI	ICP MXP740 Savannah Jabiru 03-10-51-2365 *(Built N Farrell - pr.no.BMAA/HB/34)*		G-CCPR	7. 9.04	N Farrell *(Crashed and destroyed Ferskill 2. 4.05)*	(Ferskill, Granard)	
EI-DGJ	Raj Hamsa X'Air 582(11) *(Built R Morelli - pr.no.BMAA/HB/210)*	707	G-CCEV	9. 6.04	N Brereton	Granard	A12.06
EI-DGK	Raj Hamsa X'Air 133	856		9. 6.04	B Chambers	(Castlefinn)	

Reg	Type	c/n	Prev id	Date	Owner/Operator	Location	Status
EI-DGP	Urban Air UFM-11UK Lambada	15/11	OK-IUA-68	24.11.04	M Tormey	Abbeyshrule	A 10.08
EI-DGR	Urban Air UFM-11UK Lambada	17/11		21. 7.04	M Tormey	Abbeyshrule	N 1.05
EI-DGS	ATEC Zephyr 2000	861003A		20.10.04	P Jones	(Galway)	N12.06
EI-DGT	Urban Air UFM-11UK Lambada	14/11	OK-FUA-09	12. 8.04	A and P Aviation Ltd	Carnmore, Galway	A 7.06
EI-DGV	ATEC Zephyr 2000	Z509702A		8. 9.05	M Donoghue	Carnmore, Galway	A 8.04
EI-DGW	Cameron Z-90 Balloon (Hot Air)	10607		15. 9.04	J Leahy	Navan	N 1.07
EI-DGX	Cessna 152	15281296	G-BPJL N49473	19.10.04	K A O'Connor	Weston, Dublin	A 10.08
EI-DGY	Urban Air UFM-11 Lambada	10/11	OK-EUU-55	15.10.04	D McMorrow	Abbeyshrule	N10.08
EI-DGZ	Boeing 737-86N/W	28624	EC-HMK N1786B	27.10.04	Celestial Aviation Trading 18 Ltd (stored 10.08) Lasham		A2008
EI-DHA	Boeing 737-8AS	33571		1. 2.05	Ryanair Ltd	Dublin	A2008
EI-DHB	Boeing 737-8AS	33572		23. 2.05	Ryanair Ltd	Dublin	A2008
EI-DHC	Boeing 737-8AS	33573		17. 2.05	Ryanair Ltd	Dublin	A2008
EI-DHD	Boeing 737-8AS	33816	N1784B	25. 2.05	Ryanair Ltd	Dublin	A2008
EI-DHE	Boeing 737-8AS	33574	N1786B	2. 3.05	Ryanair Ltd	Dublin	A2008
EI-DHF	Boeing 737-8AS	33575	N1782B	3. 3.05	Ryanair Ltd	Dublin	A2008
EI-DHG	Boeing 737-8AS	33576	N1787B	18. 3.05	Ryanair Ltd	Dublin	A2008
EI-DHH	Boeing 737-8AS	33817		29. 3.05	Ryanair Ltd	Dublin	A2008
EI-DHI	Boeing 737-8AS	33818		11. 4.05	Ryanair Ltd	Dublin	A2008
EI-DHJ	Boeing 737-8AS	33819		20. 4.05	Ryanair Ltd	Dublin	A2008
EI-DHK	Boeing 737-8AS	33820		28. 4.05	Ryanair Ltd	Dublin	A2008
EI-DHM	Boeing 737-8AS	33821		28. 4.05	Ryanair Ltd	Dublin	A2008
EI-DHN	Boeing 737-8AS	33577		1. 9.05	Ryanair Ltd	Dublin	A2008
EI-DHO	Boeing 737-8AS	33578	N1786B	14.10.05	Ryanair Ltd	Dublin	A2008
EI-DHP	Boeing 737-8AS	33579		21.10.05	Ryanair Ltd	Dublin	A2008
EI-DHR	Boeing 737-8AS	33822		24.10.05	Ryanair Ltd	Dublin	A2008
EI-DHS	Boeing 737-8AS	33580		7.11.05	Ryanair Ltd	Dublin	A2008
EI-DHT	Boeing 737-8AS	33581		14.11.05	Ryanair Ltd	Dublin	A2008
EI-DHV	Boeing 737-8AS	33582		14.11.05	Ryanair Ltd	Dublin	A2008
EI-DHW	Boeing 737-8AS	33823	N1786B	23.11.05	Ryanair Ltd	Dublin	A2008
EI-DHX	Boeing 737-8AS	33585	N60436	5.12.05	Ryanair Ltd	Dublin	A2008
EI-DHY	Boeing 737-8AS	33824	N1781B	6.12.05	Ryanair Ltd	Dublin	A2008
EI-DHZ	Boeing 737-8AS	33583		19.12.05	Ryanair Ltd	Dublin	A2008
EI-DIA	Solar Wings Pegasus XL-Q (Trike c/n SW-TE-0379)	SW-WQ-0503	G-MYAD	15. 9.04	P Byrne (Current status unknown)	(Hacketstown)	
EI-DIB	Air Création 582(1)/Kiss 400 (Wing s/n A04117-4123)	xxxx		10. 9.04	E Redmond (Current status unknown)	(Ferns)	
EI-DIF	Piper PA.31-350 Navajo Chieftain	31-7752105	G-OAMT G-BXKS, N350RC, EC-EBN, N27230	4. 2.05	Wrenair Ltd (Visionair)	Weston, Dublin	N 10.08
EI-DIP	Airbus A330-202	339	A6-EYW EI-DIP, I-VLEF, C-GGWD, F-WWYZ	10. 3.08	Calliope Ltd (Operated Air One)	Rome-Fiumicino	A2008
EI-DIR	Airbus A330-202	272	A6-EYV EI-DIR, I-VLEE, F-WQQL, C-GGWC, F-WWKE	22. 5.08	Calliope Ltd (Operated Air One)	Rome-Fiumicino	A2008
EI-DIY	Van's RV-4 (Built J A Kent)	3254		16. 3.05	J A Kent (Under construction?)	(Pinecroft, Dunshaughlin)	
EI-DJH	Airbus A.320-232	814	I-PEKW N471LF, SU-LBB, F-WWII	20.12.04	ILFC Ireland Ltd (Operated Myway)	Bergamo-Orio al Serio	A2008
EI-DJK	Boeing 737-382	24365	9H-ADM CS-TIB	9. 1.05	Triton Aviation Ireland Ltd (Operated KD Avia) "Yuri Ternirkanov"	Kaliningrad-Khrabovo	A2008
EI-DJM	Piper PA-28-161 Warrior II	28-8316106	HB-POV N4314K	21. 2.05	Waterford Aero Club	Waterford	A 4.06
EI-DJO	Agusta A109E	11158	D-HIRL N32GH, D-HOME	14. 2.05	Tandrelle Ltd	Dublin	A 5.08
EI-DJR	Boeing 737-3YO	23927	G-IGOG F-GLLE, PT-TEK	7. 7.05	Larrett Ltd (Operated KD Avia) "Alexander Marinesko"	Kaliningrad-Khrabovo	A2008
EI-DJS	Boeing 737-3YO	23926	G-IGOH F-GLLD, PT-TEJ	13. 7.05	Wodell Ltd (Operated KD Avia) "Viktor Geraschchenko"	Kaliningrad-Khrabovo	A2008
EI-DJT	Boeing 737-86N/W	28592	N975RY EC-IEN, CN-RNN, N1779B, N1768B	16. 4.05	Lift Ireland Leasing Ltd (stored 10.08)	Lasham	A2008
EI-DJU	Boeing 737-86N/W	28619	N255RY EC-HLN. N1786B	28. 4.05	Celestial Aviation Trading 17 Ltd (stored 9.08)	Dublin	A2008
EI-DJW	Robinson R44 Raven	1498		14. 6.05	Horizon Helicopters Ltd	Weston, Dublin	
EI-DJX	Farrington Twinstarr (Built S Howell)	98016	N234MJ	22. 6.05	F Kavanagh	Shipdham	A 8..06
EI-DJY	Grob G.115	8048	D-EFFX (2)	29. 4.05	Atlantic Flight Training Ltd	Cork	A 5.07
EI-DJZ	Lindstrand LBL-31A Cloudhopper	1035		7. 7.05	M E White	Dublin	N 1.07
EI-DKB	ICP MXP740 Savannah Jabiru (Built N Farrell)	04-11-51-343		6. 5.05	B Gurnett and Partners	(Ardfert)	N 10.06
EI-DKC	Pegasus Quasar	SVV-WQQ-0351	G-MWJU	22. 4.05	K Daly	Abbeyshrule	A 8.06
EI-DKD	Boeing 737-86N/W	28617	N974RY EC-HJJ, N1787B	27. 4.05	OH Aircraft III (Ireland) Ltd (stored 9.08)	Lasham	A2008
EI-DKE	Air Création 582(1)/Kiss 400 (Wing s/n AO4172-4187)	xxxx		12. 5.05	J Bennett	Kilrush	A 4.06
EI-DKI	Robinson R22 Beta II	3882	N74703	29. 7.05	P Gilboy	Weston, Dublin	N 4.07
EI-DKJ	Thruster T600N	0047-T600N-105	G-CDBN	11. 5.05	C Brogan	Kilrush	A 4.06
EI-DKK	Raj Hamsa X'Air Jabiru 3(5) (Built M Tolan)	857		11. 5.05	M Tolan	Tandragee	A 5.06
EI-DKL	Boeing 757-231	28482	N714P	21. 6.05	Pegasus Palls 99 Ireland Ltd Rome-Fiumicino, Italy (Operated Blue Panorama Airlines)		A2008
EI-DKM	Agusta Bell 206B Jetranger	8623	F-GCVY	7. 7.05	Stelbury Ltd	Weston, Dublin	A 6.07
EI-DKN	ELA Aviacion ELA-07	00045		31. 5.05	S Brennan	Kilrush	A 5.06
EI-DKT	Raj Hamsa X'Air 582(11)	798		22. 6.05	I Brereton	Clonbullogue	A 5.06

EI-DKU	Air Création 582(1)/Kiss 400	xxxx		22. 6.05	J Doran	Shinglis, Ballymore	A2006
	(Wing s/n A05036-5040						
EI-DKW	Evektor EV-97 Eurostar	2005-2513		28. 6.05	Ormond Flying Club Ltd	Birr	A 5.06
EI-DKY	Raj Hamsa X'Air 582	720	G-CBTY	27. 7.05	M Clarke	(Clonsilla, Dublin)	N11.07
	(Built K Quigley - pr.no.BMAA/HB/222)						
EI-DKZ	Reality Escapade 912(1)	JAESC0040	G-CDFH	29. 7.05	J Deegan	Limetree, Portarlington	A 4.06
	(Built J Deegan - pr.no.BMAA/HB/423)						
EI-DLB	Boeing 737-8AS	33584	N5573L	19.12.05	Ryanair Ltd	Dublin	A2008
EI-DLC	Boeing 737-8AS	33586	N1786B	13. 1.06	Ryanair Ltd	Dublin	A2008
EI-DLD	Boeing 737-8AS	33825		13. 1.06	Ryanair Ltd	Dublin	A2008
EI-DLE	Boeing 737-8AS	33587		9 .2.06	Ryanair Ltd	Dublin	A2008
EI-DLF	Boeing 737-8AS	33588		13..2.06	Ryanair Ltd	Dublin	A2008
EI-DLG	Boeing 737-8AS	33589	N1786B	14 .2.06	Ryanair Ltd	Dublin	A2008
EI-DLH	Boeing 737-8AS	33590		6. 3.06	Ryanair Ltd	Dublin	A2008
EI-DLI	Boeing 737-8AS	33591	N1786B	22. 3.06	Ryanair Ltd	Dublin	A2008
EI-DLJ	Boeing 737-8AS	34177		28. 3.06	Ryanair Ltd	Dublin	A2008
EI-DLK	Boeing 737-8AS	33592	N1786B	29. 3.06	Ryanair Ltd	Dublin	A2008
EI-DLL	Boeing 737-8AS	33593		10. 4.06	Ryanair Ltd	Dublin	A2008
EI-DLM	Boeing 737-8AS	33594		20. 4.06	Ryanair Ltd	Dublin	A2008
EI-DLN	Boeing 737-8AS	33595		24. 4.06	Ryanair Ltd	Dublin	A2008
EI-DLO	Boeing 737-8AS	34178		25. 4.06	Ryanair Ltd	Dublin	A2008
EI-DLR	Boeing 737-8AS	33596		25. 9.06	Ryanair Ltd	Dublin	A2008
EI-DLS	Boeing 737-8AS	33621		26. 9.06	Ryanair Ltd	Dublin	A2008
EI-DLT	Boeing 737-8AS	33597		27. 9.06	Ryanair Ltd	Dublin	A2008
EI-DLV	Boeing 737-8AS	33598		28. 9.06	Ryanair Ltd	Dublin	A2008
EI-DLW	Boeing 737-8AS	33599		17.10.06	Ryanair Ltd	Dublin	A2008
EI-DLX	Boeing 737-8AS	33600		18.10.06	Ryanair Ltd	Dublin	A2008
EI-DLY	Boeing 737-8AS	33601		26.10.06	Ryanair Ltd	Dublin	A2008
EI-DLZ	Boeing 737-8AS	33622		8.11.06	Ryanair Ltd	Dublin	A2008
EI-DMA	SOCATA MS892E-150	12376	G-BVAN	22.12.05	J Lynn, C Bates and C Dungan	Kerry	N 5.08
			F-BVAN				
EI-DMB	Best Off Sky Ranger 912S(1)	SKR0503588		19. 8.05	Fun 2 Fly Ltd	Kilpatrick, Stradbally	A 8.06
	(Built N Furlong amd E Spain)						
EI-DMC	Schweizer S.269C-1	0205	N86G	18. 8.05	B Hade	Weston, Dublin	A 5.06
	(Schweizer 300CBi)						
EI-DMG	Cessna 441 Conquest	441-0165	N140MP	4. 7.01	Dawn Meats Group Ltd	Waterford	A 10.08
			N27214				
EI-DMJ	Boeing 767-306ER	27958	PH-BZB	7. 10.05	ILFC Ireland Ltd *(Operated NEOS)*		
						Milan-Malpensa	A2008
EI-DMM	Boeing 737-33A	24092	G-IGOI	30.11.05	GAIF II Ireland Two Ltd *(Operated KD Avia)*		
			G-OBMD			"Valery Gergiev"	Kaliningrad-Khrabovo	A2008
EI-DMN	Boeing 737-3K2	23411	N550FA	2. 12.05	Pegasus Palls.99 Ireland Ltd *(Operated KD Avia)*		
			TC-ESA,			"Lidor Samiev"	Kaliningrad-Khrabovo	A2008
	N943PG, PH-HVF, XA-STM, PH-HVF, XA-STM, PH-HVF, XA-STM, PH-HVF, XA-STM, PH-HVF, XA-STM, PH-HVF, PH-HVF, CS-TIR, PH-HVF						
EI-DMP	Boeing 767-2Q8ER	24448	N330LF	22.12.06	ILFC Ireland Ltd	Krasnoyarsk-Yemilianovo	A2008
			OB-1765-P, OB-1765, CC-CJR, N201LF, N264MT, S7-AAS, (S7-1HM) *(Operated Kras Air)*				
EI-DMR	Boeing 737-436	25851	G-DOCR	27.10.05	Dillondell Ltd	Rome -Fiumicino, Italy	A2008
					(Operated Air One)		
EI-DMU	Whittaker MW6S	PFA 164-12235		13.12.05	G Maher *(Stored?)*	(Loughlinstown)	
	(Built G Maher)						
EI-DNA	Boeing 757-231	28483	N715TW	8. 12.05	Rockshaw Ltd 2008 *(Operated Blue Panorama Airlines)*		
						Rome-Fiumicino	A2008
EI-DND	Boeing 737-86N/W	28612	EC-IUC	3. 1.06	Celestial Aviation Trading 18 Ltd *(stored 10.08)*		
			TC-SUA, N1786B				Lasham	A2008
EI-DNH	Boeing 737-3Y5	25614	9H-ABS	21.12.05	Boeing Capital Leasing Ltd *(Operated Kras Air) (stored DME)*		
						Krasnoyarsk-Yemilianovo	A2008
EI-DNL	Bensen B.8M Gyrocopter	B8M-073		10. 1.06	J Henry and H O'Driscoll	(Blessington)	
	(Built J Henry and H O'Driscoll)				*(Under construction?)*		
EI-DNM	Boeing 737-4S3	24166	EC-JHX	1. 3.06	Boeing Capital Leasing Ltd *(Operated Transaero Airlines)*		
			VT-SIY, N768BC, VT-SII, VT-JAJ, N691MA, G-BPKD			Moscow-Domodedovo	A2008
EI-DNN	Bede BD-5G	HJC.4523	G-BCOX	7. 2.07	H J and E.M Cox	(Waterford)	N2007
	(Built H J Cox) (Midwest AE110RA)						
EI-DNO	Bede BD-5A	4885	G-BCLV	14. 2.07	R A Gardiner	(Waterford)	N2007
	(Built R A Gardiner - pr.no.PFA 14-10074) (Hirth 2706E)						
EI-DNP	Airbus A320-212	421	A40-EF	1. 4.05	Ovenstone Ltd *(Operated Windjet)*	Catania, Italy	A2008
			F-WWIO				
EI-DNR	Raj Hamsa X'Air 582(5)	791	G-CCAX	27. 2.06	N Furlong and J Grattan	Kilpatrick, Stradbally	A2008
	(Built N Farrell - pr.no.BMAA/HB/251)						
EI-DNS	Boeing 737-329	23771	F-GUYH	4. 4.06	Embarcadero Aircraft Securitization Trust Ireland Ltd		
			F-WQUE, CN-RDB, OO-SDV			*(Operated Kras Air)* Krasnoyarsk-Yemilianovo	A2008
EI-DNT	Boeing 737-329	24356	F-GRNV	14. 6.06	Embarcadero Aircraft Securitization Trust Ireland Ltd		
			F-WQUE, CN-RDA, OO-SYB, (OO-SQB)			Krasnoyarsk-Yemilianovo	A2008
					(Operated.Kras Air) (stored DME)		
EI-DNU	Schweizer 269C-1	0233	N86G	12. 5.06	NG Kam Tim	Weston, Dublin	A 5.06
	(Schweizer 300CBi)						
EI-DNV	Urban Air UFM-11 Lambada	12/11	OK-EUU 56	27. 2.06	F Maughan	(Ardclogh, Straffan)	A7.08
EI-DNW	Best Off Sky Ranger J2.2(1)	SKRxxxx453	G-CCUC	31. 3.06	M Kerrisson	Coonagh	A10.06
	(Built M Kerrisson - pr.no.BMAA/HB/373)						
EI-DNX	Boeing 737-31S	29055	VT-SAW	13. 4.06	Osprey Aviation Ireland Ltd	Pisa	A2008
			VT-SIX, D-ADBK			*(Operated Air One) (stored 10.08)*		
EI-DNY	Boeing 737-3TO	23360	N17309	4. 4.06	BCI Aircraft Leasing Ireland Ltd	Tijuana	A2008
					(Operated Aerovolar)		
EI-DNZ	Boeing 737-3TO	23363	N60312	4. 4.06	BCI Aircraft Leasing Ireland Ltd	Tijuana	A2008
					(Operated Aerovolar)		

EI-DOB	Zenair CH.701 STOL	7-9272		13. 2.07	D O'Brien	(Mullagh)	N2007
EI-DOD	Airbus A320-231	0444	G-FHAJ	11. 4.06	Hannover Leasing Aircraft Ireland Ltd *(Operated Myair)*		
			D-ACAF, N444RX, TC-ONF, N444RX, F-WWBY			Bergamo-Orio al Serio	A2008
EI-DOE	Airbus A320-211	215	F-GJVE	9. 6.06	ALS Irish Aircraft Leasing MSN 215 Ltd *(Operated Windjet)*		
						Catania	A2008
EI-DOF	Boeing 767-306ER	27610	PH-BZD	24. 4.06	ILFC Ireland Ltd *(Operated Israir)*		
						Tel Aviv-Ben Gurion	A2008
EI-DOH	Boeing 737-31S	29056	VT-SAX	30. 6.06	Challey Ltd *(Operated Air One)*	Rome-Fiumicino	A2008
			VT-SIW, D-ADBL				
EI-DOI	Evektor EV-97 Eurostar	20062708		30. 3.06	E.McEvoy	Eyne	
EI-DOM	Boeing 737-3G7	24011	N370WL	4. 8.06	CIT Capital Finance Ireland Ltd *(Operated KD Avia)*		
			N304AW		"Sergey Prisekin"	Kaliningrad-Khrabovo	A2008
EI-DON	Boeing 737-3Y0	23812	N375PA	28.12.06	CIT Capital Finance Ireland Ltd *(Operated KD Avia)*		
			N238CT, PT-TEI			Kaliningrad-Khrabovo	A2008
EI-DOO	Boeing 737-35B	23971	N222DZ	28.12.06	CIT Capital Finance Ireland Ltd *(Operated KD Avia)*		
			D-AGEB		"Yuriy Antonov"	Kaliningrad-Khrabovo	A2008
EI-DOP	Airbus A320-232	816	B-HSF	22. 6.06	ILFC Ireland Ltd *(Operated Windjet)*	Catania	A2008
			F-WWIT				
EI-DOS	Boeing 737-49R	28881	PK-GWZ	21. 4.06	Celestial Aviation Trading 37 Ltd *(Operated Air One)*		
			N460PR, N1790B			Rome-Fiumicino	A2008
EI-DOT	Bombardier CL-600-2D24	15066		23. 5.06	Challey Ltd *(Operated Air One Cityliner)*		
	(CRJ 900 Regional Jet)					Rome-Fiumicino	A2008
EI-DOU	Bombardier CL-600-2D24	15068		23. 5.06	Challey Ltd *(Operated Air One Cityliner)*		
	(CRJ 900 Regional Jet)				*(Operated Air One Cityliner)*	Rome-Fiumicino	A2008
EI-DOV	Boeing 737-48E	27632	HL-7512	21. 6.06	ILFC Ireland Ltd *(Operated Air One)*		
						Rome-Fiumicino	A2008
EI-DOW	Mainair Blade 912	1361-0104-7-W1156	G-CCPB	1. 6.06	D G Fortune	Kilrush	A 5.06
EI-DOX	Solar Wings Pegasus XL-R	SW-WA-1089	G-MNYB	12. 5.06	T Noonan	Fermoy	
	(Trike c/n SW-TB-1096)						
EI-DOY	PZL Koliber			3.08R	Limerick Flying Club (Coonagh) Ltd	Coonagh	N10.08
EI-DPA	Boeing 737-8AS	33602		16.11.06	Ryanair Ltd	Dublin	A2008
EI-DPB	Boeing 737-8AS	33603	N1787B	20.11.06	Ryanair Ltd	Dublin	A2008
EI-DPC	Boeing 737-8AS	33604	N1786B	6.12.06	Ryanair Ltd	Dublin	A2008
EI-DPD	Boeing 737-8AS	33623	N1786B	6.12.06	Ryanair Ltd	Dublin	A2008
EI-DPE	Boeing 737-8AS	33605		21.12.06	Ryanair Ltd	Dublin	A2008
EI-DPF	Boeing 737-8AS	33606		23. 1.07	Ryanair Ltd	Dublin	A2008
EI-DPG	Boeing 737-8AS	33607		26. 1.07	Ryanair Ltd	Dublin	A2008
EI-DPH	Boeing 737-8AS	33624		1. 2.07	Ryanair Ltd	Dublin	A2008
EI-DPI	Boeing 737-8AS	33608		7. 2.07	Ryanair Ltd	Dublin	A2008
EI-DPJ	Boeing 737-8AS	33609		13. 2.07	Ryanair Ltd	Dublin	A2008
EI-DPK	Boeing 737-8AS	33610		16. 2.07	Ryanair Ltd	Dublin	A2008
EI-DPL	Boeing 737-8AS	33611		23. 2.07	Ryanair Ltd	Coonagh	A2008
EI-DPM	Boeing 737-8AS	33640	N1786B	5. 3.07	Ryanair Ltd	Dublin	A2008
EI-DPN	Boeing 737-8AS	35549	N1787B	7. 3.07	Ryanair Ltd	Dublin	A2008
EI-DPO	Boeing 737-8AS	33612		14. 3.07	Ryanair Ltd	Dublin	A2008
EI-DPP	Boeing 737-8AS	33613		20. 3.07	Ryanair Ltd	Dublin	A2008
EI-DPR	Boeing 737-8AS	33614	N1786B	28. 3.07	Ryanair Ltd	Dublin	A2008
EI-DPS	Boeing 737-8AS	33641		29. 3.07	Ryanair Ltd	Dublin	A2008
EI-DPT	Boeing 737-8AS	35550	N1787B	4. 4.07	Ryanair Ltd	Dublin	A2008
EI-DPV	Boeing 737-8AS	35551	N1779B	13. 4.07	Ryanair Ltd	Dublin	A2008
EI-DPW	Boeing 737-8AS	35552		15. 5.07	Ryanair Ltd	Dublin	A2008
EI-DPX	Boeing 737-8AS	35553		30. 5.07	Ryanair Ltd	Dublin	A2008
EI-DPY	Boeing 737-8AS	33615		11. 9.07	Ryanair Ltd	Dublin	A2008
EI-DPZ	Boeing 737-8AS	33616		12. 9.07	Ryanair Ltd	Dublin	A2008
EI-DRA	Boeing 737-852/W	35114	N1779B	6. 9.06	Mexican Aircraft Leasing II Ltd *(Operated AeroMexico)*		
						Mexico City-Benito Juarez	A2008
EI-DRB	Boeing 737-852/W	35115		10.10.06	Mexican Aircraft Leasing II Ltd *(Operated AeroMexico)*		
						Mexico City-Benito Juarez	A2008
EI-DRC	Boeing 737-852/W	35116		19.10.06	Mexican Aircraft Leasing II Ltd *(Operated AeroMexico)*		
						Mexico City-Benito Juarez	A2008
EI-DRD	Boeing 737-752/W	35117	N1786B	5.12.06	Mexican Aircraft Leasing II Ltd *(Operated AeroMexico)*		
						Mexico City-Benito Juarez	A2008
EI-DRE	Boeing 737-752/W	35787	N1786B	21.11.06	Mexican Aircraft Leasing II Ltd) *(Operated AeroMexico)*		
						Mexico City-Benito Juarez	A2008
EI-DRH	Mainair Blade	1320-0402-7-W1115	G-CBOL	8. 6.06	J McErlain	Newtownards	A 4.06
EI-DRI	Bombardier CL-600-2D24	15075		19. 6.06	Challey Ltd *(Operated Air One Cityliner)*		
	(CRJ 900 Regional Jet)					Rome-Fiumicino	A2008
EI-DRJ	Bombardier CL-600-2D24	15077		21. 7.06	Challey Ltd *(Operated Air One Cityliner)*		
	(CRJ 900 Regional Jet)					Rome-Fiumicino	A2008
EI-DRK	Bombardier CL-600-2D24	15076		22. 6.06	Challey Ltd *(Operated Air One Cityliner)*Rome-FiumicinoA2008		
	(CRJ 900 Regional Jet)					Rome-Fiumicino	A2008
EI-DRL	Raj Hamsa X'Air Jabiru	1005		23. 6.06	C Kiernan	Granard	
EI-DRM	Urban Air UFM-10 Samba	3/10	OK-FUU-31	7. 7.06	M Tormey	Abbeyshrule	A 10.08
EI-DRN	Robinson R44 Raven	1607		19. 7.06	Blue Star Helicopters Ltd	Cork	A 6.07
EI-DRO	Tecnam P20021-JF	044		3. 8.06	Ossory Flying and Gliding Club Ltd	Kilkenny	N 6.07
EI-DRT	Air Création Tanarg 912S/iXess 15A						
		060826078		1. 8.06	L Daly	Tullamore	
EI-DRU	Tecnam P92/EM Echo	543	I-6351	29.12.06	P Gallogly	Abbeyshrule	A9.08
EI-DRW	Evektor EV-97R Eurostar	20062709		31. 7.06	Eurostar Flying Club Ltd	Coonagh	A10.06
EI-DRX	Raj Hamsa X'Air 582(5)	1048		21 .8.06	M Sheelan and D McShane	Granard	
EI-DSA	Airbus A320-216	2869	F-WWBE	14. 9.06	Aircraft Purchase Company No.1 Ltd *(Operated Air One)*		
						Rome-Fiumicino	A2008

EI-DSB	Airbus A320-216	2932	F-WWBX	9.11.06	BF Best Aviation Alpha *(Operated Air One)*	Rome-Fiumicino	A2008
EI-DSC	Airbus A320-216	2995	F-WWIY	18. 1.07	BF Best Aviation Alpha *(Operated Air One)*	Rome-Fiumicino	A2008
EI-DSD	Airbus A320-216	3076	F-WWIP	22. 3.07	BF Best Aviation Alpha *(Operated Air One)*	Rome-Fiumicino	A2008
EI-DSE	Airbus A320-216	3079	F-WWIL	29. 3.07	BF Best Aviation Alpha *(Operated Air One)*	Rome-Fiumicino	A2008
EI-DSF	Airbus A320-216	3080	F-WWIV	4. 4.07	Aircraft Purchase Company No.4 Ltd *(Operated Air One)*	Rome-Fiumicino	A2008
EI-DSG	Airbus A320-216	3115	F-WWIZ	26. 4.07	Aircraft Purchase Company No 4 Ltd *(Operated Air One)*	Rome-Fiumicino	A2008
EI-DSH	Airbus A320-216	3178	F-WWDS	12. 7.07	Aircraft Purchase Company No 5 Ltd *(Operated Air One)*	Rome-Fiumicino	A2008
EI-DSI	Airbus A320-216	3213	F-WWIU	27. 9.07	Aircraft Purchase Company No 6 Ltd *(Operated Air One)*	Rome-Fiumicino	A2008
EI-DSJ	Airbus A320-216	3295	F-WWDV	9.11.07	Aircraft Purchase Company No 6 Ltd *(Operated Air One)*	Rome-Fiumicino	A2008
EI-DSK	Airbus A320-216	3328	F-WWIX	4.12.07	Aircraft Purchase Company No 6 Ltd *(Operated Air One)*	Rome-Fiumicino	A2008
EI-DSL	Airbus A320-216	3343	F-WWBO	18.12.07	Aircraft Purchase Company No 6 Ltd *(Operated Air One)*	Rome-Fiumicino	A2008
EI-DSM	Airbus A320-216	3362	F-WWIR	22. 1.08	Aircraft Purchase Company No 7 Ltd *(Operated Air One)*	Rome-Fiumicino	A2008
EI-DSN	Airbus A320-216	3412	F-WWIL	28. 2.08	Aircraft Purchase Company No 8 Ltd *(Operated Air One)*	Rome-Fiumicino	A2008
EI-DSO	Airbus A320-216	3464	F-WWBM	10. 4.08	Aircraft Purchase Company No 8 Ltd *(Operated Air One)*	Rome-Fiumicino	A2008
EI-DSP	Airbus A320-216	3482	F-WWDM	30. 4.08	Aircraft Purchase Company No 9 Ltd *(Operated Air One)*	Rome-Fiumicino	A2008
EI-DSR	Airbus A320-216	3502	F-WWBR	5. 6.08	Aircraft Purchase Company No 10 Ltd *(Operated Air One)*	Rome-Fiumicino	A2008
EI-DSS	Airbus A320-216	3515	F-WWDP	12. 6.08	Aircraft Purchase Company No 10 Ltd *(Operated Air One)*	Rome-Fiumicino	A2008
EI-DST	Airbus A320-216	3532	F-WWBR	26. 6.08	Aircraft Purchase Company No 10 Ltd *(Operated Air One)*	Rome-Fiumicino	A2008
EI-DSU	Airbus A320-216	3563	F-WWBI	25. 7.08	Aircraft Purchase Company No 10 Ltd *(Operated Air One)*	Rome-Fiumicino	A2008
EI-DSV	Airbus A320-216	3598	F-WW		Sunflower Aircraft Leasing Ltd *(Operated Air One)*	Rome-Fiumicino	
EI-DSW	Airbus A320-216	3609	F-WWIE		Sunflower Aircraft Leasing Ltd *(Operated Air One)*	Rome-Fiumicino	A2008
EI-DSX	Airbus A320-216	3643	F-WWBT		Sunflower Aircraft Leasing Ltd *(Operated Air One)*	Rome-Fiumicino	A2008
EI-DSY	Airbus A320-216	3666	F-WWDY		Purchase Fleet Fleet Ltd *(Operated Air One)*	Rome-Fiumicino	A2008
EI-DSZ	Airbus A320-216	3695	F-WWBI		Purchase Fleet Fleet Ltd *(Operated Air One)*	Rome-Fiumicino	A2008
EI-DTA	Airbus A320-216	3732	F-WWDM		Purchase Fleet Fleet Ltd *(Operated Air One)*	Rome-Fiumicino	A2008
EI-DTB	Airbus A320-216	3815	F-WW		*(Operated Air One)*	Rome-Fiumicino	A2008
EI-DTC	Airbus A320-216	3831	F-WW		*(Operated Air One)*	Rome-Fiumicino	A2008
EI-DTD	Airbus A320-216	3846	F-WW		*(Operated Air One)*	Rome-Fiumicino	A2008
EI-DTE	Airbus A320-216	3885	F-WW		*(Operated Air One)*	Rome-Fiumicino	A2008
EI-DTF	Airbus A320-216	3906	F-WW		*(Operated Air One)*	Rome-Fiumicino	A2008
EI-DTG	Airbus A320-216	3921	F-WW		*(Operated Air One)*	Rome-Fiumicino	A2008
EI-DTI	Airbus A320-216	3956	F-WW		*(Operated Air One)*	Rome-Fiumicino	A2008
EI-DTJ	Airbus A320-216	3976	F-WW		*(Operated Air One)*	Rome-Fiumicino	A2008
EI-DTK	Airbus A320-216	3978	F-WW		*(Operated Air One)*	Rome-Fiumicino	A2008
EI-DTL	Airbus A320-216	4075	F-WW		*(Operated Air One)*	Rome-Fiumicino	A2008
EI-DTM	Airbus A320-216	4092	F-WW		*(Operated Air One)*	Rome-Fiumicino	A2008
EI-DTN	Airbus A320-216	4124	F-WW		*(Operated Air One)*	Rome-Fiumicino	A2008
EI-DTO	Airbus A320-216	4143	F-WW		*(Operated Air One)*	Rome-Fiumicino	A2008
EI-DTP	Airbus A320-216	4158	F-WW		*(Operated Air One)*	Rome-Fiumicino	A2008
EI-DTR	Robinson R44 Raven	1652		20.12.06	Loughoran Properties Ltd	Galway	
EI-DTS	Piper PA18-95 Super Cub	18-5822	OO-VIK N7484D	4.10.06	P.Dunne, K Synott and M Murphy	(Drogheda, County Louth)	N11.07
EI-DTT	ELA Aviacion ELA 07 R100	04061050722		6.10.06	N Steele	Kilrush	
EI-DTU	Boeing 737-5Y0	25175	B-2546	24.10.06	Celestial Aviation Trading Ltd *(Operated Transaero Airlines)*	Moscow-Domodedovo	A2008
EI-DTV	Boeing 737-5Y0	25183	B-2549	10.11.06	Airplanes Holdings Ltd *(Operated Transaero Airlines)*	Moscow-Domodedovo	A2008
EI-DTW	Boeing 737-5Y0	25188	B-2550	6.12.06	Airplanes Holdings Ltd *(Operated Transaero Airlines)*	Moscow-Domodedovo	A2008
EI-DTX	Boeing 737-5Y8	28052	LY-AZX PT-SSE	5.10.06	ILFC Ireland Ltd *(Operated Transaero Airlines)*	Moscow-Domodedovo	A2008
EI-DTY	Boeing 737-3M8	25017	G-IGOV	8.12.06	Celestial Aviation Trading 36 Ltd *(Operated KD Avia)*	Kaliningrad-Khrabovo	A2008
	N250GE, LZ-BOF, N250GE, 9V-TRD, N760BE, N35030, (OO-LTH)						
EI-DUA	Boeing 757-256	26247	N241LF PP-VTQ, EC-GZY, N1795B	16.11.06	ILFC Ireland Ltd *(Operated Kras Air)*	Krasnoyarsk-Yemilianovo	A2008
EI-DUB	Airbus A330-301ER	055	F-WWKP	6. 5.94	Aer Lingus Ltd *"St.Patrick/Padraig"*	Dublin	A2008
EI-DUC	Boeing 757-256	26248	N263LF PP-VTR, EC-GZZ	16.11.06	ILFC Ireland Ltd *(Operated Kras Air)*	Krasnoyarsk-Yemilianovo	A2008

EI-DUD	Boeing 757-256	26249	N271LF	20.12.06	ILFC Ireland Ltd *(Operated Kras Air)*	
			PP-VTS, EC-HAA, N1786B		Krasnoyarsk-Yemilianovo	A2008
EI-DUE	Boeing 757-256	26250	N272LF	18. 1.07	ILFC Ireland Ltd *(Operated Kras Air) (stored DME)*	
			PP-VTT, EC-HDM		Krasnoyarsk-Yemilianovo	A2008
EI-DUF	Aérospatiale SA.365N Dauphin 2	6315	PR-YOF	13.11.07	Dauphin 2 Aviation Ltd	Trevet	A 5.08
			F-WQEX, JA9932, F-WQAZ			
EI-DUH	Scintex CP.1310-C3 Super Emeraude	921	F-BJMR	12.12.06	W Kennedy	Killenaule	A 5.07
EI-DUI	Gulfstream-American GA-7 Cougar	GA7-0114	G-GENN	11. 5.07	D O'Toole	Kilkenny	A 3.08
			G-BNAB, G-BGYP			
EI-DUJ	Evektor EV-97 Eurostar	20062814		9. 3.07	E Fitzpatrick	(Ballyliffin)	
EI-DUK	Bombardier CL-600-2D24	15104		28.11.06	Challey Ltd *(Operated Air One Cityliner)*	
	(CRJ 900 Regional Jet)				Rome-Fiumicino, Italy	A2008
EI-DUL	Alpi Aviation Pioneer	181-UK		21. 5.07	J Hackett	Shobdon	N5.08
	(Built J Hackett)					
EI-DUM	Bombardier CL.600-2D24	15103		24. 1.07	Al Waha Lease (Ireland No 2) Ltd *(Operated Myair)*	
	(CRJ 900 Regional Jet)				Bergamo-Orio al Serio	A2008
EI-DUO	Airbus A330-203	0841	F-WWYT	25 .5.07	Aer Lingus Ltd *"St.Columba/Column"*	Dublin	A2008
EI-DUS	Boeing 737-3M8	24021	TF-ELM	12. 1.07	Aerco Ireland Ltd *(Operated Mistral Air) "Maestrale"*	A2008
	F-GIXP, 9V-SQZ, N40495, OO-LTB, (F-GKTE), OO-ITB, (F-ODSU), (OO-BTB)				Rome-Ciampino	
EI-DUT	Bell 206B-3 JetRanger III	4551	G-CRLH	23. 3.07	AV-8 Helicopters Ireland Ltd	(Craugwell)	A 4.08
			G-RJTT, C-GRJE			
EI-DUU	Bombardier CL.600-2D24	15102		24. 1.07	Al Waha Lease (Ireland No 2) Ltd *(Operated Myair)*	
	(CRJ 900 Regional Jet)				Bergamo-Orio al Serio	A2008
EI-DUV	Beech 95 B55 Baron	TC-1618	N3045W	13. 3.07	J Given	Weston, Dublin	
EI-DUX	Bombardier CL-600-2D24	15110		31. 1.07	Al Waha Lease (Ireland No 2) Ltd *(Operated Myair)*	
	(CRJ 900 Regional Jet)				Bergamo-Orio al Serio	A2008
EI-DUY	Bombardier CL-600-2D24	15112		31. 1.07	Al Waha Lease (Ireland No 2) Ltd *(Operated Myair)*	
	(CRJ 900 Regional Jet)				Bergamo-Orio al Serio	A2008
EI-DUZ	Airbus A330-203	0847	F-WWKM	26. 6.07	Aer Lingus Ltd *"St.Aoife/Aoife"*	Dublin	A2008
EI-DVA	Boeing 737-36E	25159	F-GIXM	9. 2.07	Celestial Aviation Trading 19 Ltd *(Operated Mistral Air)*	
	F-WIXM, (F-GLXO), N315FL, EC-FFN, EC-703)				Rome-Ciampino	A2008
EI-DVC	Boeing 737-33A	25426	SE-DPC	9. 2.07	Ansett Worldwide Aviation Ireland Ltd *(Operated Mistral Air)*	
			N34AW		*"Libeccio"*	Rome-Ciampino	A2008
EI-DVD	Airbus A319-113	0647	F-GPMH	7. 2.07	Castle 2003-1 Ireland Ltd *(Operated Windjet)*	
			D-AVYD			Catania	A2008
EI-DVE	Airbus A320-214	3129	F-WWBJ	18. 5.07	Aer Lingus Ltd *"St.Aideen/Etaion"*	Dublin	A2008
EI-DVF	Airbus A320-214	3136	F-WWDF	17. 5.07	Aer Lingus Ltd *"St.Jarlath/Iarflaith"*	Dublin	A2008
EI-DVG	Airbus A320-214	3318	F-WWIV	28.11.07	Aer Lingus Ltd *"St.Flannan/Flannan"*	Dublin	A2008
EI-DVH	Airbus A320-214	3345	F-WWBP	14.12.07	Aer Lingus Ltd *"St.Clare/Ciara"*	Dublin	A2008
EI-DVI	Airbus A320-214	3501	F-WWBQ	3. 6.08	Aer Lingus Ltd *"St Emer/Eimear"*	Dublin	A2008
EI-DVO	Barnett J4B2	227	C-FRKB	9. 3.07	T Brennan	(Castleconnell)	
EI-DVP	Bombardier CL-600-2D24	15116		9. 3.07	Aircraft Purchase Co No.2 Ltd *(Operated Air One Cityliner)*	
	(CRJ 900 Regional Jet)				Rome-Fiumicino	A2008
EI-DVR	Bombardier CL-600-2D24	15118		16. 4.07	Aircraft Purchase Co No.3 Ltd *(Operated Air One Cityliner)*	
	(CRJ 900 Regional Jet)				Rome-Fiumicino	A2008
EI-DVS	Bombardier CL-600-2D24	15119		30. 4.07	Aircraft Purchase Co No.3 Ltd *(Operated Air One Cityliner)*	
	(CRJ 900 Regional Jet)				Rome-Fiumicino	A2008
EI-DVT	Bombardier CL-600-2D24	15123		30. 4.07	Aircraft Purchase Co No.4 Ltd *(Operated Air One Cityliner)*	
	(CRJ 900 Regional Jet)				Rome-Fiumicino	A2008
EI-DVU	Airbus A319-113	660	F-GPMI	9. 3.07	Castle 2003-2 Ireland Ltd *(Operated WindJet)*	
			D-AVYC			Catania	A2008
EI-DVX	Robinson R44 Raven II	11600	G-CEKN	20. 3.07	Aceville Developments Ltd	
					Clogheen Business Park, Cork	A 6.07
EI-DVY	Boeing 737-31S	29059	LZ-BOM	10. 7.07	DSF Aircraft Leasing (Ireland) Ltd *(Operated Blu-Express)*	
			D-ADBO		*"Città di Palermo"*	Rome -Fiumicino	A2008
EI-DVZ	Robinson R44 Raven II	11629		7. 3.07	D.Mcauliffe	Cork	A 6.07
EI-DWA	Boeing 737-8AS	33617		12. 9.07	Ryanair Ltd	Dublin	A2008
EI-DWB	Boeing 737-8AS	36075		18. 9.07	Ryanair Ltd	Dublin	A2008
EI-DWC	Boeing 737-8AS	36076		20. 9.07	Ryanair Ltd	Dublin	A2008
EI-DWD	Boeing 737-8AS	33642		25. 9.07	Ryanair Ltd	Dublin	A2008
EI-DWE	Boeing 737-8AS	36074		27. 9.07	Ryanair Ltd	Dublin	A2008
EI-DWF	Boeing 737-8AS	33619		3.10.07	Ryanair Ltd	Dublin	A2008
EI-DWG	Boeing 737-8AS	33620		3.10.07	Ryanair Ltd	Dublin	A2008
EI-DWH	Boeing 737-8AS	33637		19.10.07	Ryanair Ltd	Dublin	A2008
EI-DWI	Boeing 737-8AS	33643		19.10.07	Ryanair Ltd	Dublin	A2008
EI-DWJ	Boeing 737-8AS	36077		.22.10.07	Ryanair Ltd	Dublin	A2008
EI-DWK	Boeing 737-8AS	36078		27.10.07	Ryanair Ltd	Dublin	A2008
EI-DWL	Boeing 737-8AS	33618		26.10.07	Ryanair Ltd	Dublin	A2008
EI-DWM	Boeing 737-8AS	36080		7.11.07	Ryanair Ltd	Dublin	A2008
EI-DWO	Boeing 737-8AS	36079		19.11.07	Ryanair Ltd	Dublin	A2008
EI-DWP	Boeing 737-8AS	36082		21.11.07	Ryanair Ltd	Dublin	A2008
EI-DWR	Boeing 737-8AS	36081	N1786B	29.11.07	Ryanair Ltd	Dublin	A2008
EI-DWS	Boeing 737-8AS	33625	N1786B	7. 1.08	Ryanair Ltd	Dublin	A2008
EI-DWT	Boeing 737-8AS	33626		18. 1.08	Ryanair Ltd	Dublin	A2008
EI-DWV	Boeing 737-8AS	33627		22. 1.08	Ryanair Ltd	Dublin	A2008
EI-DWW	Boeing 737-8AS	33629	N1781B	5. 2.08	Ryanair Ltd	Dublin	A2008
EI-DWX	Boeing 737-8AS	33630		5. 2.08	Ryanair Ltd	Dublin	A2008
EI-DWY	Boeing 737-8AS	33638	N1781B	14. 2.08	Ryanair Ltd	Dublin	A2008
EI-DWZ	Boeing 737-8AS	33628	N1796B	14. 2.08	Ryanair Ltd	Dublin	A2008
EI-DXA	Comco Ikarus C42	0604-6809		26. 1.07	M.Kirrane	(County Galway)	
EI-DXB	Boeing 737-31S	29060	LZ-BON	20. 6.07	DSF Aircraft Leasing (Ireland) Ltd *(Operated Blu Express)*	
			D-ADBP, N1786B		*"Città di Roma"*	Rome-Fiumicino	A2008
EI-DXC	Boeing 737-4Q8	26300	TC-JKA	22. 6.07	Castle 2003-1 Ireland Ltd *(Operated Air One)*	
			SX-BFA, TC-JEL			Rome-Fiumicino	A2008

EI-DXG	Boeing 737-4Q8	25376	TC-JEN	9. 5.07	ILFC Ireland Ltd (Operated Air One)		
						Rome-Fiumicino	A2008
EI-DXH	Robinson R44 Raven	1699		2. 5.07	Gannon Brothers (Keelogues) Ltd	Oranmore	A 6.07
EI-DXI	Robinson R22 Beta II	4117	N3013G	19. 4.07	CNW Helicopters Ltd	Cork	N 7.07
EI-DXJ	Robinson R22 Beta II	4120	N3015F	19. 4.07	Montague Aviation (Sales and Leasing) Ltd (Gorey)		
EI-DXK	Robinson R44 Raven II	11621		19. 4.07	Ashdown Park Hotel Ltd	(Gorey)	
EI-DXL	CFM Shadow Series CD	K.232	PH-2S5	15.10.07	F Lynch	Fermoy	
EI-DXM	Raj Hansa X'Air 582(4)	402	G-BYTT	11. 5.07	B P Nugent	(Tallaght, Dublin)	
	(Built R P Reeves - pr.no.BMAA/HB/100)						
EI-DXN	Zenair CH.601HD Zodiac	9-9095		30. 5.07	N Gallagher	Wexford	
EI-DXP	Cyclone AX3/503	7252	G-MZDO	29. 6.07	J McCann	Limetree	
EI-DXS	CFM Shadow Series C	K.023	G-MYNA	4.10.07	R.W.Frost	Mallow, County.Cork	
EI-DXT	Urban Air UFM-10 Samba	10/10	OK-GUA 19	14.12.07	N Irwin	(Femoy, County Cork)	
EI-DXU	ELA Aviacion ELA 07 R115	100612307		11.12.07	R.Savage	(Kildare)	A4.08
EI-DXW	Bombardier Learjet 60	60-300	G-CJMC	24.12.07	Airlink Airways Ltd	Shannon	A2008
			OH-AEM, N40081				
EI-DXX	Raj Hamsa X'Air 582(6)	685	G-CBFT	20.12.07	S.J.MacSweeney	Birr	
	(Built T Collins - pr.no.BMAA/HB/190)						
EI-DXY	Airbus A320-212	0525	D-AKNX	4.08R	ILFC Ireland Ltd (Operated Rossiya Russian Airlines)		
			N601LF, PH-VAD, C-GTDB, F-GJVV, N451LF, F-WWIK			St Petersburg	A2008
EI-DXZ	Urban Air UFM-10 Samba	20/10	OK-GUA 27	14.12.07	D.O'Leary	Kilrush	
EI-DYA	Boeing 737-8AS	33631	N1786B	4. 3.08	Ryanair Ltd	Dublin	A2008
EI-DYB	Boeing 737-8AS	33633		10. 3.08	Ryanair Ltd	Dublin	A2008
EI-DYC	Boeing 737-8AS	36567	N1787B	10. 3.08	Ryanair Ltd	Dublin	A2008
EI-DYD	Boeing 737-8AS	33632	N1786B	10. 3.08	Ryanair Ltd	Dublin	A2008
EI-DYE	Boeing 737-8AS	36568		14. 3.08	Ryanair Ltd	Dublin	A2008
EI-DYF	Boeing 737-8AS	36569	N1786B	14. 3.08	Ryanair Ltd	Dublin	A2008
EI-DYG	Boeing 737-8AS	33639		25. 3.08	Ryanair Ltd	Dublin	A2008
EI-DYH	Boeing 737-8AS	36570		8. 4.08	Ryanair Ltd	Dublin	A2008
EI-DYI	Boeing 737-8AS	36571		8. 4.08	Ryanair Ltd	Dublin	A2008
EI-DYJ	Boeing 737-8AS	36572		15. 4.08	Ryanair Ltd	Dublin	A2008
EI-DYK	Boeing 737-8AS	36573		15. 4.08	Ryanair Ltd	Dublin	A2008
EI-DYL	Boeing 737-8AS	36574		11. 6.08	Ryanair Ltd	Dublin	A2008
EI-DYM	Boeing 737-8AS	36575		11. 6.08	Ryanair Ltd	Dublin	A2008
EI-DYN	Boeing 737-8AS	36576		12. 6.08	Ryanair Ltd	Dublin	A2008
EI-DYO	Boeing 737-8AS	33636		12.9.08	Ryanair Ltd	Dublin	A2008
EI-DYP	Boeing 737-8AS	37515		19.9.08	Ryanair Ltd	Dublin	A2008
EI-DYR	Boeing 737-8AS	37513		5.12.08	Ryanair Ltd	Dublin	
EI-DYS	Boeing 737-8AS	37514		5.12.08	Ryanair Ltd	Dublin	
EI-DYT	Boeing 737-8AS	33634		15.12.08	Ryanair Ltd	Dublin	
EI-DYV	Boeing 737-8AS	37512		15.12.08	Ryanair Ltd	Dublin	
EI-DYW	Boeing 737-8AS	33635		5. 1.09	Ryanair Ltd	Dublin	
EI-DYX	Boeing 737-8AS	37517		5. 1.09	Ryanair Ltd	Dublin	
EI-DYY	Boeing 737-8AS	37521	N1787B	14. 1.09	Ryanair Ltd	Dublin	
EI-DYZ	Boeing 737-8AS	37518		14. 1.09	Ryanair Ltd	Dublin	
EI-DZB	Colt 14A Cloudhopper Balloon (Hot Air)	2580	G-BVKX	11.12.07	P Baker	Abbeyview, Trim	
EI-DZE	Urban Air UFM-10 Samba	14/10	OK-GUA 24	18.12.07	P Keane	Abbeyshrule	A10.08
EI-DZF	Pipistrel Sinus 912	254		26. 2.08	Light Sport Aviation Ltd	Birr	
EI-DZG	Robinson R44 Raven II	12148		11. 3.08	Suir Shipping	Kilkenny	3.08
EI-DZH	Boeing 767-3Q8ER	29390	N101LF	5. 3.08	ILFC Ireland Ltd (Operated Rossiya Russian Airlines)		
			JA767C, N6009F			St Petersburg-Polkovo	A2008
EI-DZI	Robinson R44 Raven	1522	G-CDLX	25. 1.08	P.Reynolds and T.Kelly	Letterkenny	A 5.08
EI-DZJ	Robinson R44 Raven II	10551	G-CDCA	5. 2.08	L Behan and Sons Ltd	Weston, Dublin	
EI-DZK	Robinson R22B Beta	3179	G-FEBY	12. 2.08	Eirecopter Helicopters Ltd	Weston, Dublin	A10.08
EI-DZM	Robinson R44 Raven II	12207		29. 4.08	Tercoy Ltd	Kilkenny	A10.08
EI-DZO	Dominator Gyroplane Ultrawhite	SAAC 112		8. 4.08	P O'Reilly	(Robertstown, Co Kildare)	
	(Built P O'Reilly)						
EI-DZR	Airbus A320-212	0427	N265AV	28. 5.08	ILFC Ireland Ltd (Operated Rossiya Russian Airlines)		
			C-GJUL, C-GVXC, F-WWIH			St Petersburg-Pulkovo	A2008
EI-DZS	BRM Land Africa	4/08		28. 4.08	Alfrom Engineering Ltd	(Enfield, Co Meath)	
EI-DZU	Boeing 737-3M8	24020			Celestial Aviation Trading 2 Ltd	()	
EI-EAG	Pipistrel Virus 912	265V912		14. 7.08	R Armstrong	(Virginia, Co Cavan)	
EI-EAI	Sukhoi Su-26M2	01-04	G-SIID	13. 6.08	D Bruton	Abbeyshrule	
			RA-44531, PK-SDM				
EI-EAK	AirBorne Windsports Edge XT	E-619	N30192	28. 7.08	M O'Brien	Whitegate, Co Clare	
EI-EAM	Cessna 172R	17280781	G-TAIT	5. 2.08	Atlantic Flight Training Ltd	Cork	
			G-DREY, N23726				
EI-EAR	Boeing 767-3Q8ER	27616	N364LF	14. 8.08	(Operated Rossiya Russian Airlines)		
			JA767A			St Petersburg-Pulkovo	A2008
EI-EAP	Mainair Blade	1327-0502-7-W1122	G-CBOV	25. 6.08	H D Lynch	(Knock, Fermoy, County Cork)	
EI-EAR	Boeing 767-3Q8ER	27616	N364LF	14. 8.08	ILFC Ireland Ltd (Operated Rossiya Russian Airlines)		
			JA767A			St Petersburg-Pulovo	
EI-EAS	Robinson R22 Beta	2605	N318JR	31.12.08	Mildand Helicopters Ltd	Dublin	
			C-FYGJ				
EI-EAW	AirBorne Windsports Edge XT582 Cruze						
		XT582B-011		22. 8.08	F Heary	Navan, County Meath	
EI-EAX	Raj Hamsa X'Air 582(2)	676	G-CBII	25. 8.08	A Bray	Kilrush	
	(Built A Worthington - pr.no.BMAA/HB/185)						
EI-EAY	Raj Hamsa X'Air 582(5)	525	G-CBHV	12.12.01	R Smith	Birr	
	(Built J D Buchanan - pr.no.BMAA/HB/139)						
EI-EAZ	Cessna 172R	17281146	N74LU	9. 8.07	Atlantic Flight Training Ltd	Cork	A 3.08
EI-EBA	Boeing 737-8AS	37516		20. 1.09	Ryanair Ltd	Dublin	A1.09
EI-EBB	Boeing 737-8AS	37519	N1787B	20. 1.09	Ryanair Ltd	Dublin	A1.09
EI-EBC	Boeing 737-8AS	37520		09	Ryanair Ltd	Dublin	A2.09

EI-EBD	Boeing 737-8AS	37522		09	Ryanair Ltd	Dublin	A2.09
EI-EBE	Boeing 737-8AS	37523		09	Ryanair Ltd	Dublin	A2.09
EI-EBF	Boeing 737-8AS	37524	N60697 N1786B	09	Ryanair Ltd	Dublin	A2.09
EI-EBG	Boeing 737-8AS	37525		09	Ryanair Ltd	Dublin	A2.09
EI-EBH	Boeing 737-8AS	37526		09R	Ryanair Ltd	Dublin	
EI-EBI	Boeing 737-8AS	37527		09R	Ryanair Ltd	Dublin	
EI-EBJ	Robinson R44 Raven	1358		18. 5.04	Gibbons Developments Ltd	Oranmore	N 3.07
EI-EBK	Boeing 737-8AS	37528		09R	Ryanair Ltd	Dublin	
EI-EBL	Boeing 737-8AS	37529		09R	Ryanair Ltd	Dublin	
EI-EBM	Boeing 737-8AS	37002		09R	Ryanair Ltd	Dublin	
EI-EBN	Boeing 737-8AS	37003		09R	Ryanair Ltd	Dublin	
EI-EBO	Boeing 737-8AS	37004		09R	Ryanair Ltd	Dublin	
EI-EBP	Boeing 737-8AS	37531		09R	Ryanair Ltd	Dublin	
EI-EBR	Boeing 737-8AS	37530		09R	Ryanair Ltd	Dublin	
EI-EBS	Boeing 737-8AS	37002		09R	Ryanair Ltd	Dublin	
EI-EBT	Boeing 737-8AS	37001		09R	Ryanair Ltd	Dublin	
EI-EBV	Boeing 737-8AS	37009		09R	Ryanair Ltd	Dublin	
EI-EBW	Boeing 737-8AS	37010		09R	Ryanair Ltd	Dublin	
EI-EBX	Boeing 737-8AS	37007		09R	Ryanair Ltd	Dublin	
EI-EBY	Boeing 737-8AS	37006		09R	Ryanair Ltd	Dublin	
EI-EBZ	Boeing 737-8AS	37008		09R	Ryanair Ltd	Dublin	
EI-ECA	Agusta A109A II	7387	N109RP JA9662	28. 2.97	Blue Star Helicopters Ltd *(Operated Premier Helicopters)*	Cork	A2008
EI-ECB	Boeing 767-3Q8ER	27617	N151LF JA767B	23.10.08	ILFC Ireland Ltd *(Operated Rossiya Russian Airlines)* St Petersburg-Pulkovo		A2008
EI-ECE	Hawker 800XP	258496	G-RDMV N175TM, N125TM	30.10.08	Airlink Airways Ltd	Shannon	A2008
EI-ECG	BRM Land Africa	114/912/K4/08		23.10.08	J McGuiness	Wexford	
EI-ECK	Raj Hamsa X'Air Hawk	1158		28.10.08	N Geh	(Gort, Co Galway)	
EI-ECL	Boeing 737-86N/W	32655	EC-JDU	24.10.08	Celestial Aviation Trading 26 Ltd *(stored)* Budapest		2008
EI-ECM	Boeing 737-86N/W	32658	EC-KKU D-ALIG, EC-JFB	24.10.08	Celestial Aviation Trading 26 Ltd *(stored)* Budapest		2008
EI-ECN	Boeing 737-86N/W	28591	EC-KFB TC-APY, TC-IAH, N1786B	24.10.08	LIFT Ireland Leasing Ltd *(stored)*		2008
EI-ECO	Raj Hamsa X'Air Hawk	1104		23.10.08	J McLoughlin	Lifford, Co Donegal	
EI-ECP	Raj Hamsa X'Air Hawk	934	44-ALU	23.10.08	R Gillispie and Partners	Killygordon, Co Donegal	
EI-ECR	Cessna 525A CitationJet	525A-0438	N438TA N5026Q	19.12.08	Aircraft International Renting	Shannon	
EI-ECS	Pipistrel Taunus 503	039		27.11.08	Light Sports Aviation Ltd	Birr	
EI-ECU	Agusta A.109S	22094		23. 1.09	Emerald Acquistions Ltd	Weston	
EI-ECV	Raj Hamsa X'Air Hawk		G-BYCL	27.11.08	D P Myers	Cork	
EI-ECX	Airbus A319-132	2698	N515NK D-AVXF	11.1.2.08	ILFC *(Operated Windjet)*	Catania	
EI-ECY	Airbus A319-132	2723	N519NK D-AVWE	11.12.08	ILFC *(Operated Windjet)*	Catania	
EI-ECZ	Raj Hamsa X'Air Hawk	1163		26.11.08	M Tolan	Crossmolina, Co Mayo	
EI-EDA	Raj Hamsa X'Air Hawk	1161		26.11.08	M Bowden	Letterkenny	
EI-EDC	Reims Cessna FA152	FA1520376	G-BILJ	28. 1.09	K O'Connor	Weston, Dublin	
EI-EDD	Airbus A320-232	0496	EC-JIB C-GTDC, F-WWBV	15.12.08	Castle 2003-1 Ireland Ltd	Dublin	
EI-EDI	Comco Ikarus C42 FB	0009-6272	I-7501	26.11.08	M Owens	Granard	
EI-EDL	Boeing 737-8BK/W	33018	OY-SEL	15.12.08	CIT Aerospace Intenational *(for Titan Airways 5.09)* (Southend)		
EI-EDM	Airbus A319-132	2424	N501NK D-AVYT	22. 1.09	ILFC Ireland Ltd *(Operated WindJet)*	Catania	
EI-EDN	Boeing 737-76N	24757	OM-NGL				
EI-EDR	Piper PA-28R-200 Cherokee Arrow II	28R-7435265	G-BCGD N9628N	19.11.87	Dublin Flyers Ltd	Dublin	A 4.06
EI-EDS	Airbus A320-214	3755	F-WWBU		Aer Lingus *(delivered all-white)*	Dublin	
EI-EGG	Robinson R44 Raven	1344	G-CCLI	10.12.03	B Haugh	Weston, Dublin	A 5.06
EI-EHB	Robinson R22 Beta II	3569		18. 5.04	Blue Star Helicopters Ltd	Cork	A 4.06
EI-EHE	Robinson R22 Beta II	3654		1.10.04	Blue Star Helicopters Ltd	Cork	A 4.06
EI-EHG	Robinson R22 Beta	3509	N75302	16. 4.04	G Jordan	(Legan, Killglass)	A 8.06
EI-EJR	Robinson R44 Raven	1504		8. 9.05	Gerair Ltd	(Edenderry)	
EI-ELL	Medway EclipseR	157/136		2. 6.99	Microflex Ltd	Kilrush	A 1.03
EI-ESK	Robinson R44 Raven II	11484	G-CEFR	6.11.07	Esker Bus and & Coach Ltd (Kilbeggan, Co Westmeath)		
EI-EUR	Eurocopter EC.120B Colibri	1138	G-BZMK F-WQOE	14.12.00	Atlantic Helicopters Ltd	Dublin	A 6.07
EI-EWR	Airbus A330-202	330	F-WWKV	9. 5.00	Aer Lingus Ltd "St Laurence O'Toole/Lorcan O Tuathail" Dublin		A2008
EI-EXC	Robinson R44 Raven	1312		24. 6.03	S Keaney	(Carrigtwohill)	N 2.05
EI-EXG	Robinson R22 Beta II	3698	N7337F	18.11.04	21st Century Aviation Ltd Oranmore Heliport, Galway		A 4.06
EI-EXH	Robinson R44 Raven	1730		9.10.07	Executive Helicopter Maintenance Ltd	Oranmore	A8.08
EI-EXM	Robinson R44 Raven	1700	N30607	27. 7.07	Dunbarra Aviation Ltd	Galway	N 5.08
EI-FAB	Eurocopter EC.120B Colibri	1155	F-HIAN VP-BRD, F-WQDK	10. 7.07	Billy Jet Ltd	(Rathangane)	A 4.08
EI-FAC	Aérospatiale AS.350B1 Ecureil	1991	G-BVJE SE-HRS	14. 4.08	Irish Helicopters Ltd	Dublin	
EI-FAR	Robinson R44 Raven II	11305		23. 8.06	Fardolan Ltd	(Corrofin, Tuam, Galway)	A 8.08

Reg	Type	C/n	Prev id	Date	Owner/Operator	Location	
EI-FBG	Reims Cessna F182Q Skylane	F18200032	D-EFBG (F-GAGU)	4. 7.00	J Paxton	Weston, Dublin	A 10.08
EI-FGL	Eurocopter EC.120B Colibri	1492	PH-ECM F-WWXM	5.12.07	Fanning Machine Rentals Ltd	(Arklow)	
EI-FII	Cessna 172RG Cutlass II	172RG0550	G-BHVC N9048K, G-BHVC, N372SA, G-BHVC, N5515V	28.11.08	K O'Connor	Weston, Dublin	
EI-FOX	Robinson R44 Raven	1693		17. 4.07	Trotfox Ltd	Farranfore, Kerry	
EI-FXA	Aérospatiale-Alenia ATR 42-300F	282	N282AT (N281AE), N282AT, F-WWLI	22. 4.05	Air Contractors (Ireland) Ltd *(Operated Fedex)*	Dublin	A2008
EI-FXB	Aérospatiale-Alenia ATR 42-300F	243	(N927FX) N246AE, N243AT, F-WWEQ	12. 5.05	Air Contractors (Ireland) Ltd *(Operated Fedex)*	Dublin	A2008
EI-FXC	Aérospatiale-Alenia ATR 42-300F	310	N310DK (N925FX), N271AT, N273AT, F-WWEC	25. 8.05	Air Contractors (Ireland) Ltd *(Operated Fedex)*	Dublin	A2008
EI-FXD	Aérospatiale-Alenia ATR 42-320F	273	N271AT N273AT, F-WWEQ	29. 6.05	Air Contractors (Ireland) Ltd *(Operated Fedex)*	Dublin	A2008
EI-FXE	Aérospatiale-Alenia ATR 42-320F	327	N327AT (N926FX), N327AT, F-WWLM	21.10.05	Air Contractors (Ireland) Ltd *(Operated Fedex)*	Dublin	A2008
EI-FXG	Aérospatiale-Alenia ATR 72-202F	224	(N814FX) D-ANFA, F-WWEQ	9. 8.05	Air Contractors (Ireland) Ltd *(Operated Fedex)*	Dublin	A2008
EI-FXH	Aérospatiale-Alenia ATR 72-202F	229	N815FX D-ANFB, F-WWEX	2. 2.06	Air Contractors (Ireland) Ltd *(Operated Fedex)*	Dublin	A2008
EI-FXI	Aérospatiale-Alenia ATR 72-202F	294	N818FX D-ANFE, F-WWLS	18.10.06	Air Contractors (Ireland) Ltd *(Operated Fedex)*	Dublin	A2008
EI-FXJ	Aérospatiale-Alenia ATR 72-202F	292	N813FX D-ANFF, F-WWLT	17. 5.07	Air Contractors (Ireland) Ltd *(Operated Fedex)*	Dublin	A2008
EI-FXK	Aérospatiale-Alenia ATR 72-202F	256	N817FX D-ANFD, F-WWEE	10. 8.07	Air Contractors (Ireland) Ltd *(Operated Fedex)*	Dublin	A2008
EI-GAN	Bell 407	53551	N20446 C-GFNR	13. 6.03	Robswall Property Ltd	Dublin	A 6.04
EI-GAV	Robinson R22 Beta II	3485	N75264	17.10.03	Weston Davinci Services Ltd	Weston, Dublin	A 5.07
EI-GBA	Boeing 767-266ER	23180	N573JW ZS-SRC, N575SW, SU-GAJ, N1789B	25. 5.04	Arbor Finance Ltd *(Operated.Kras Air)*	Krasnoyarsk-Yemilianovo	A2008
EI-GCE	Sikorsky S-61N	61817	LN-ORC (4) (LN-OQU)	30. 4.07	CHC Ireland Ltd *(IMES Rescue titles)*	Shannon	A2008
EI-GDL	Gulfstream Aerospace Gulfstream V-SP (Gulfstream 550)	5068	N968GA	10. 8.05	Westair Aviation Ltd	Shannon	
EI-GEM	Hawker 850XP *(900XP)*	258901	N3201T	258901	Airlink Airways Ltd	Belfast International	A 7.08
EI-GER	Maule MX-7-180A Star Rocket (Tail-wheel u/c)	20006C		7. 1.94	P J L.Ryan	Trim	A 4.06
EI-GFC	SOCATA TB-9 Tampico	141	G-BIAA	9.10.93	B McGrath, J Ryan and D O'Neill	Waterford	A 4.06
EI-GHT	Bell 206B JetRanger III	3565	G-JAHL N666ST	14. 3.06	Dunican High Reach Equipment Ltd	(Garristown)	A 4.06
EI-GJL	Eurocopter AS.365N3 Dauphin 2	6785	G-CEUK F-WWOZ	27. 5.08	AIBP	(Airdee, Co Louth)	
EI-GKL	Robinson R22 Beta II	3570		19. 5.04	Eamon Duffy (Rosemount) Ltd	Oranmore	N 6.07
EI-GLA	Schleicher ASK 21	21002	EI-150 D-6957	28. 3.07	Dublin Gliding Club Ltd *"ICS"*	Kilkenny	N 6.07
EI-GLB	Schleicher ASK 21	21060	EI-164 D-4089	28. 3.07	Dublin Gliding Club Ltd	Bellarena	N 7.07
EI-GLC	Centrair 101A Pégase	101-102	EI-163 PH-738	28. 3.07	Dublin Gliding Club Ltd *"ZC"*	Gowran Grange, Naas	
EI-GLD	Schleicher ASK 13	13131	EI-112	28. 3.07	Dublin Gliding Club Ltd	Gowran Grange, Naas	
EI-GLF	Schleicher K 8B	8468	EI-108	28. 3.07	Dublin Gliding Club Ltd *"08"*	Gowran Grange, Naas	
EI-GLG	Schleicher Ka 6CR	662	EI-127 PH-259	3.08R			
EI-GLH	Sportine Aviacija LAK-17A	136	EI-169 HA-4511	28. 3.07	S Kinnear *"T8"*	Gowran Grange, Naas	
EI-GLI	Schempp-Hirth Duo Discus T	106/435	EI-159	28. 3.07	B Ramseyer *"BR"*	Gowran Grange, Naas	
EI-GLJ	Glaser-Dirks DG-200	2-88	EI-145 PH-930, D-7610	28. 3.07	M A Kelly	Gowran Grange, Naas	
EI-GLK	Schempp-Hirth Standard Cirrus	304	EI-148 BGA 4334, D-2060	28. 3.07	P Conran and D McKenna *"HZL"*	Gowran Grange, Naas	
EI-GLL	Glaser-Dirks DG-200	2-22	EI-147 D-6780	28. 3.07	P Denman and C Craig *"DS"*	Gowran Grange, Naas	
EI-GLM	Schleicher Ka 6CR	6565	EI-111 IGA 9	28. 3.07	P Denman and C Craig *"11"*	Gowran Grange, Naas	
EI-GLN	Glasflügel H201 Standard Libelle	267	EI-165 BGA 1693-CPF	28. 3.07	D McMahon *"T15"*	Gowran Grange, Naas	
EI-GLO	Scheibe Zugvogel IIIB	1085	EI-146 D-4096	28. 3.07	M J Walsh, J Murphey and N Shortt *"TK"*	Gowran Grange, Naas	
EI-GLP	EoN AP.5 Olympia 2B	EoN/O/155	EI-115 BGA 1097	28. 3.07	J Cashin	Kilkenny	
EI-GLR	Schleicher ASW 20L	20054	EI-167 BGA 2371	28. 3.07	K Commins *"189"*	Gowran Grange, Naas	
EI-GLT	Schempp-Hirth Discus b	219	EI-149 BGA 3320-FKK	4. 5.07	D Thomas	Gowran Grange, Naas	
EI-GLS	Rolladen-Schneider LS7-WL	7135	EI-177 3A-MCD (2)	28. 3.07	M McHugo	Gowran Grange, Naas	
EI-GLU	Schleicher Ka 6CR	808	EI-161 BGA 3536-FUM, D-6289	28. 3.07	K Commins, R Woods and S Kinnear	Kilkenny	N 6.07
EI-GLV	Schleicher ASW 19B	19316	EI-153 BGA 4274-HWZ, HB-1524	28. 3.07	C Sinclair and B O'Neill *"53"*	Gowran Grange, Naas	
EI-GLW	Schleicher Ka 6CR	6649	EI-128 D-1393	28. 3.07	J Murphy and Partners	Bellarena	N 7.07

Reg	Type	C/n	Prev id	Date	Owner/Operator	Location	
EI-GMB	Schleicher ASW 17	17031	EI-132 D-2365	28. 3.07	ASW-17 Group "TK"	Gowran Grange, Naas	N 7.08
EI-GMC	Schleicher ASK 18	18007	EI-136 BGA 2945-ETT, D-6868	20. 9.07	The Eighteen Group	Gowran Grange, Naas	N 7.08
EI-GMD	Bölkow Phoebus C	908	EI-158 BGA 4202-HTZ, OO-ZDJ, BGA 1573	28. 3.07	F McDonnell and partners	Gowran Grange, Naas	
EI-GME	Eiriavion PIK-20D	20603	OH-562	18. 5.07	P McKenzie-Brown	Kilkenny	N 6.07
EI-GMF	Schleicher ASK 13	13189	EI-113	28. 3.07	Ossory Flying and Gliding Club Ltd	Kilkenny	N 6.07
EI-GPT	Robinson R22 Beta II	3317	N70637	8.11.04	Treaty Plant and Tool (Hire and Sales) Ltd	(Limerick)	A 6.04
EI-GPZ	Robinson R44 Raven	1388		5. 8.04	G and P Transport Ltd	Castlebar	A 6.07
EI-GSE	Reims Cessna F.172M	F17201105	D-EDXO	12. 4.02	K A O'Connor (Operated National Flight Centre)	Weston, Dublin	A 10.08
EI-GSM	Cessna 182S	18280188	N9541Q	17. 6.98	Westpoint Flying Group Ltd	Weston, Dublin	A 10.08
EI-GTY	Robinson R22 Beta II	3808		17. 6.05	Executive Helicopter Maintenance Ltd	Oranmore	A 6.07
EI-GWY	Cessna 172R Skyhawk	17280162	N9497F	31.12.97	Atlantic Flight Training Ltd	Cork	A 5.07
EI-HAM	Light-Aero Avid Flyer	1072-90		18.11.96	J Duggan and partners	(Bray)	
	(Built H Goulding as SAAC pr.no.034) (Rotax 582)						
EI-HAZ	Robinson R44 Raven	1558		3. 5.06	Forestbrook Developments Ltd	Cork	
EI-HCS	Grob G-109B	6414	G-BMHR	18. 8.95	H Sydner	Gorey	A 4.06
EI-HER	Bell 206B-3 JetRanger III	3408	G-HIER G-BRFD, N2069N	1. 7.94	S L Ryan	Thurles	A 6.07
EI-HHH	Agusta A109E Power	11208	D-HPWR	8. 5.06	F Gormley and Partners	Weston, Dublin	A 3.08
EI-HOK.	Eurocopter EC.130B4 Ecureuil	4034	G-CDVW F-WQVY, F-WQDA	30. 5.06	Heli Leasing Partnership (L O' Kane and J Hegarty)	Weston, Dublin	A 5.08
EI-HUM	Van's RV-7	70588-1		8. 2.07	G Humphreys	Coonagh	A 6.08
	(Built G Humphreys)						
EI-HXM	Bell 206B-2 JetRanger II	4105	ZS-HXM N7131J	28. 7.00	Premier Star Equipment Ltd	Manston	A5.08
EI-IAN	Pilatus PC-6/B2-H4 Turbo Porter	810	HB-FGI	30. 8.05	Irish Parachute Club Ltd	Clonbullogue	A 4.06
EI-IGA	Boeing 757-230	24748	I-AIGA D-ABJW, N298BA, PH-DBH, D-ABND	20.10.06	Constitution Aircraft Leasing (Ireland) 3 Ltd (Operated Air Italy)	Milan-Malpensa	A2008
EI-IGB	Boeing 757-230	24738	I-AIGB N248BA, PH-DBB, D-ABNB	21.11.06	Constitution Aircraft Leasing (Ireland) 3 Ltd (Operated Air Italy) "Citta de Somma Lombardo"	Milan-Malpensa	A2008
EI-IGC	Boeing 757-230	24747	I-AIGC D-ABSG, N723BA, (SP-FVK), N723BA, PH-DBA, D-ANBC	20. 9.06	Constitution Aircraft Leasing (Ireland) 3 Ltd (Operated Air Italy Polska)	Warsaw-Okecie	A2008
EI-ILS	Eurocopter EC.135T2+	0712	G-CFFR D-HTSF	28.10.08	Irish Helicopters Ltd	Westpoint Heliport	A2008
EI-ING	Reims Cessna F172P	F17202084	G-BING	19. 8.05	21st Century Flyers Ltd	Weston, Dublin	A 10.08
EI-IRE	Bombardier CL-600-2B16 (CL-604 Challenger)	5515	N515DM C-GLXF	20. 8.02	Starair (Ireland) Ltd	Dublin	A 1.03
EI-IRV	Aérospatiale AS.350B Ecureuil	1713	D-HENY	14.10.03	S Harries	Weston, Dublin	A 6.07
EI-JAC	Bell 206B JetRanger	3594	G-CCLY G-TILT, G-BRJO, N2295Z	26. 5.05	Aerial Explorations	Weston, Dublin	A 6.07
EI-JAL	Robinson R44 Raven II	10329	N7530N	5. 8.04	D Doherty	City of Derry	A 7.07
EI-JAR	Robinson R44 Raven	1523		8.12.05	J Coleman	Cork	A 6.07
EI-JFC	Agusta A109S	22021	N84RE	21.11.06	J J Fleming Contstruction Co	(Bandon, Cork)	A 5.08
EI-JFD	Robinson R44 Raven	0969		13. 3.01	New World Plant Ltd	Galway	A 6.04
EI-JFK	Airbus A330-301	086	F-GMDE	11. 7.95	Aer Lingus Ltd "St.Colmcille/Colmcille"	Dublin	A2008
EI-JIM	Urban Air UFM-10 Samba XLA	43		21.12.06	J Smith	(Laytown)	A5.08
EI-JIV	Lockheed L.382G Hercules	4673	ZS-JIV D2-THE, ZS-JIV	15.11.02	Air Contractors (Ireland) Ltd (ORSL titles)	Dublin	A2008
EI-JPK	Tecnam P.2002-JF Sierra	079		8. 4.08	Limerick Flying Club (Coonagh) Ltd	Coonagh	
EI-JWP	Robnson R44 Raven II	11653		11. 6.07	Joyce Walker Aviation Ltd	Enniskillen	A.7.07
EI-KDH	Piper PA-28-181 Archer III	2843422	N301PA N41870	1. 6.05	K O'Driscoll and D Harris	Weston, Dublin	A 5.06
EI-KEO	Agusta A109S	22004	G-DACN	10. 9.07	Clear Skies Aviation Ltd (Operated Premier Helicopters)	Lifford, County.Donegal	A 3.08
EI-KEV	Raj Hamsa X'Air 133(1)	567	G-BZLD	21. 5.04	K Glynn	Birr	A 5.06
	(Built C Blackburn)						
EI-KEY	Robinson R44 Raven	1649		20.12.06	Gerry Keyes Ltd	(Limerick)	
EI-KHR	Robinson R22 Beta II	3849	N74572	8. 6.05	Billy Jet Ltd (Operated Kildare Helicopters)	Weston, Dublin	A 5.06
EI-KJC	Hawker 850XP	258805	N71025	24. 1.07	Skypro Executive Jets Ltd (Operated Airlink Airways)	(Dublin)	A 5.08
EI-LAF	Bell 206B-3 JetRanger III	4090	N47LM N62AJ, G-DPPA, C-FHPA	13. 4.04	Shamrock Helicopters Ltd	Weston, Dublin	A 5.06
EI-LAX	Airbus A330-202	269	F-WWKV	29. 4.99	Aer Lingus Ltd "St.Mella/Mella"	Dublin	A2008
EI-LCM	Socata TB-850	436	N850JS	13. 6.08	G Power	Weston, Dublin	A 6.08
	(Registered as TB-700N)						
EI-LEM	SOCATA TB-9 Tampico Club	1384	G-INIT I-IAFS	15. 8.08	M Fleming	Waterford	
EI-LFC	Tecnam P.2002-JF Sierra	63		10. 7.07	Limerick Flying Club (Coonagh) Ltd	Coonagh	
EI-LIT	MBB BÖ.105S	S.434	A6-DBH Dubai 105, D-HDMH	20. 2.96	Irish Helicopters Ltd	Trevet Airfield, Dunshaughlin, County Meath	A 5.06
EI-LKS	Eurocopter EC.130B4 Ecureuil	3643	F-WQDQ	20. 1.03	WIGAF Leasing Co Ltd (Operated Premier Helicopters	Dublin	A 6.07
EI-LMK	Agusta A109S	22061		29.11.07	Skyheli Ltd	Dublin	A7.08
EI-LNX	Eurocopter EC.130B4 Ecureuil	3498	N460AE	10. 6.02	WIGAF Leasing Co Ltd (Operated Premier Helicopters)	Dublin	A2008
EI-LOC	Robinson R44 Raven	1620		26. 7.06	Donville Heli's Ltd	Galway	A 6.07
EI-LVA	Airbus A321-231	1950	I-LIVA D-AVXE]	2.10.07	AWAS Aviation Trading Ltd (Operated Livingston)	Milan-Malpensa	A2008

Reg	Type	Serial	Prev ids	Date	Owner/Operator	Location	Code
EI-LVB	Airbus A321-231	1970	I-LIVB, D-AVZK	10. 5.07	AWAS Aviation Trading Ltd (Operated Livingston)	Milan-Malpensa	A2008
EI-LVD	Airbus A321-231	792	I-LIVD, F-WQST, D-ALAH, D-AVZM	10. 5.07	GAIF 11 Ireland Four Ltd (Operated Livingston)	Milan-Malpensa	A2008
EI-MAG	Robinson R22 Beta	2592	G-DHGS	3. 8.01	J Smyth and Sons Ltd	Oranmore	N12.06
EI-MAX	Gates Learjet 31A	31A-233	N233BX, LX-PAT, N5005X	26. 4.04	Airlink Airways	Westport	A3.08
EI-MCF	Cessna 172R Skyhawk	17280799	N2469D	20. 1.00	Galway Flying Club Ltd	Carnmore, Galway	A 6.06
EI-MCG	Cessna 172R Skyhawk	17281539	N6311Y	18.11.08	Galway Flying Club Ltd	Galway	
EI-MCP	Agusta A109C	7634	VH-NBX, VH-XNB, N109CW, N7LQ, VP-CHJ, VP-CEC, VR-CEC, 3A-MSG	13. 7.06	Quarry and Mining Equipment Ltd	Belfast City	A 4.08
EI-MEJ	Bell 206B-3 JetRanger III	4582	N909WB	6. 4.05	Gaelic Helicopters Ltd	Mallow	A 5.08
EI-MEL	Agusta A109C	7672	LV-WXA, N27ET, LV-WXA, N4NM	20. 6.00	M.Walsh	Celtic Heliport, Knocksedan, Dublin	N 8.07
EI-MEN	Agusta A109S	22017		5. 7.06	Men-Entirl Ltd	Weston, Dublin	A 7.07
EI-MER	Bell 206B JetRanger	4513	N60507	28. 9.99	Gaelic Helicopters Ltd	Westpoint	A 5.07
EI-MES	Sikorsky S-61N	61776	G-BXAE, LN-OQO	27. 3.97	CHC Ireland Ltd (IMES Rescue titles)	Dublin	A2008
EI-MIK	Eurocopter EC.120B Colibri	1104	G-BZIU	22. 6.01	Executive Helicopter Maintenance Ltd	Oranmore	N 7.07
EI-MIP	Aérospatiale SA.365N Dauphin 2	6119	G-BLEY, F-WTNM	20. 3.96	CHC Ireland Ltd	Cork	A 5.07
EI-MIT	Agusta A109E Power Elite	11162		17. 1.03	Fernwavw Ireland Ltd	Dublin	A 7.08
EI-MJR	Robinson R44 Raven	1391	N72603	5. 8.04	M Melville	Oranmore	A 3.08
EI-MLY	Agusta AW139	31123		7. 5.08	Arkiva Ltd	Weston, Dublin	A10.08
EI-MMO	Robinson R44 Raven	1389	G-CDRE, EI-MMO, (EI-EHF)	9. 1.08	Tallis Windfield Construction Ltd	Kilkenny	
EI-MOR	Robinson R44 Raven	1392		5. 8.04	Blue Star Helicopters Ltd	Cork	A 5.07
EI-MPW	Robinson R44 Raven	1554		14. 2.06	Connacht Helicopters Ltd	Ballina	A 4.06
EI-MSG	Agusta A109E	11692		27. 2.07	Beckdrive Ltd	Dublin	A 7.08
EI-MTZ	Urban Air Samba XXL	SAXL68		16. 6.08	M Motz	(Tullamore)	A10.08
EI-MUL	Robinson R44 Clipper	1074		29. 8.01	Cotton Box Design Group Ltd	Galway	A 6.07
EI-NBD	Robinson R44 Raven	1571		10. 3.06	N B Property Developments Ltd	Oranmore Heliport	A 6.07
EI-NBG	Agusta A109S	22047		30. 8.07	A Logue and W Moffet	Ballinderry	A 3.08
EI-NBP	Robinson R44 Raven	1728		10. 8.07	N.B.Property Developments Ltd	Oranmore	A 3.08
EI-NFW	Cessna 172S Skyhawk	172S9861	G-CDOU, N1538W	28. 2.06	Galway Flying Club Ltd	Carnmore, Galway	A 7.06
EI-NJA	Robinson R44 Raven II	11945	N155N.	21.12.07	Nojo Aviation Ltd	Weston	A 1.08
EI-NVL	Jora Jora	C129		25 7.03	N Van Lonkhuyzen	Abbeyshrule	A 5.08
EI-ODD	Bell 206B-3 JetRanger III	3627	G-CDES, N22751	25.11.05	Zero Altitude Ltd	Dublin	A7.08
EI-OFM	Reims Cessna F172N	F17201988	G-EOFM, D-EDFM	6. 5.05	C Phillips	Kilrush	A10.08
EI-OLI	Robinson R44 Raven	1698		20. 6.07	Alcock and Brown Aviation Ltd	Oranmore	A 3.08
EI-OOR	Cessna 172S Skyhawk	172S10374	N11688	23.12.08	Sligo Flying School Ltd	Sligo	
EI-ORD	Airbus A330-301	059	(EI-USA), F-GMDD	6. 6.97	Aer Lingus PLC "St.Maeve/Maedbh"	Dublin	A2008
EI-PAT	British Aerospace BAe.146 Series 200	E2030	G-ZAPL, G-WLCY, N172US, N352US	11. 9.99	Brimstage Ltd	Dublin	
EI-PCI	Bell 206B-3 JetRanger III	4072	N208M, JA9850, C-GAJN	6. 2.03	Malcove Ltd	Dublin	A 6.07
EI-PDG	Aérospatiale AS.350B Ecureuil	1089	G-BMAV	19.10.07	Irish Helicopters Ltd	Trevet Airfield, Dunshaughlin, County Meath	A 3.08
EI-PEC	Robinson R44 Raven II	10354		2. 6.04	P Sexton	Carrickwood, Lough Ennel, Mullingar	A2006
EI-PII	Robinson R44 Raven II	0822	G-RDWD, G-EUGN	18. 3.08	P Barrow and Partners	Weston, Dublin	
EI-PJD	Aérospatiale AS.350B Ecureuil	3594	SE-JGY	15.10.03	New World Plant Ltd	Weston, Dublin	A 5.07
EI-PKS	Bell 206B-3 JetRanger III	4480	OE-XAC, D-HFIS	7.11.03	Hawk Springs Ltd (Operated Premier Helicopters)	Dublin	N11.07
EI-PMI	Agusta-Bell 206B-3 JetRanger III	8614	EI-BLG, G-BIGS	19. 9.96	Ping Golf Equipment Ltd (Current status unknown)	Dublin	A 8.99
EI-POD	Cessna 177B	17702729	N1444C	3. 8.95	Trim Flying Club Ltd	Trim	A 10.08
EI-POP	Cameron Z-90 Balloon (Hot Air)	10753		23. 9.05	The Travel Department Ltd	Dublin	A 1.07
EI-PRI	Bell 206B-3 JetRanger III	4523	N6389V, C-GLZM	29. 2.00	Brentwood Properties Ltd	Castleknock	A10.02
EI-RAV	Robinson R44 Raven	1581		31. 5.06	Executive Helicopters Maintenance Ltd	Oranmore	
EI-RCG	Sikorsky S-61N	61807	G-87-1, G-BZSN, LN-OQB	25. 9.01	CHC Ireland Ltd (IMES Rescue titles)	Shannon	A2008
EI-REA	Aérospatiale-Alenia ATR 72-201	441	F-WQNC, F-WQOF, G-BWTL, F-WWLG	30. 5.02	Comhfhorbairt (Gaillimh) (Operated Aer Arann Express)	Dublin	A2008
EI-REB	Aérospatiale-Alenia ATR 72-201	470	F-WQNH, F-WQOL, F-WQOF, G-BWTM, F-WWED	17. 5.02	Comhfhorbairt (Gaillimh) (Operated Aer Arann Express)	Dublin	A2008
EI-REH	Aérospatiale-Alenia ATR 72-202	260	OY-RTA, F-WQNF, EC-FIV, EC-873, F-WWEH	14. 2.06	Comhfhorbairt (Gaillimh) (Operated Aer Arann Express)	Galway	A2008
EI-REI	Aérospatiale-Alenia ATR 72-201	267	OY-RTB, F-WQNI, EC-JFX, EC-874, F-WWEM	19.11.05	Comhfhorbairt (Gaillimh) (Operated Aer Arann Express)	Galway	A2008
EI-REJ	Aérospatiale-Alenia ATR 72-201	126	ES-KRA, OH-KRA, F-WWEM	18. 5.06	Comhfhorbairt (Gaillimh) (Operated Aer Arann Express)	Galway	A2008
EI-REL	Aérospatiale-Alenia ATR 72-212A	748	F-WWEI	25. 5.07	Comhfhorbairt (Gaillimh) (Operated Aer Arann Express)	Galway	A2008
EI-REM	Aérospatiale-Alenia ATR 72-212A	760	F-WWEW	25.10.07	Comhfhorbairt (Gaillimh) (Operated Aer Arann Express)	Galway	A2008
EI-REO	Aérospatiale-Alenia ATR 72-212A	787	F-WWEF	12.8.08	Comhfhorbairt (Gaillimh) (Operated Aer Arann Express)	Galway	A2008

Reg	Type	c/n	Prev id	Date	Owner/Operator	Location	Status
EI-REP	Aérospatiale-Alenia ATR 72-212A	797	F-WWEZ	12.8.08	Comhfhorbairt (Gaillimh) (Operated Aer Arann Express)		
						Galway	A2008
EI-RER	Aérospatiale-Alenia ATR 72-212A	822	F-WWEL	9.08R	Comhfhorbairt (Gaillimh) (Operated Aer Arann Express)		
						Galway	A2008
EI-RES	Aérospatiale-Alenia ATR 72-2xx			12.08R	Comhfhorbairt (Gaillimh) (Operated Aer Arann Express)		
						Galway	A2008
EI-RET	Aérospatiale-Alenia ATR 72-2xx			1.09R	Comhfhorbairt (Gaillimh) (Operated Aer Arann Express)		
						Galway	A2008
EI-REU	Aérospatiale-Alenia ATR 72-2xx			2.09R	Comhfhorbairt (Gaillimh) (Operated Aer Arann Express)		
						Galway	A2008
EI-REW	Aérospatiale-Alenia ATR 72-500			4.09R	Comhfhorbairt (Gaillimh) (Operated Aer Arann Express)		
						Galway	A200)
EI-REX	Bombardier Learjet 60	60-149	N260CA	25.11.05	Airlink Airways Ltd	Dublin	A 5.08
			VP-BEZ, SU-EZI, SU-BNI, (ZS-JRM), N149LY				
EI-RHM	Bell 407	53137	G-DCDB	19. 1.06	Euro Jet Ireland Ltd	Dublin	A 5.08
			C-FCDB				
EI-RJA	British Aerospace Avro 146-RJ85	E2329	G-CDYK	23.10.07	CityJet Ltd "Rathlin Island"	Paris CDG	A2008
			N513XJ, G-6-329		(Operated Air France)		
EI-RJB	British Aerospace Avro 146-RJ85	E2330	G-CEBS	8. 6.07	CityJet Ltd "Bere Island"	Paris CDG	A2008
			N514XJ, G-6-330		(Operated Air France)		
EI-RJC	British Aerospace Avro 146-RJ85	E2333	G-CEHA	6.12.07	CityJet Ltd "Achill Island"	Paris CDG	A2008
			N515XJ, G-6-333		(Operated Air France)		
EI-RJD	British Aerospace Avro 146-RJ85	E2334	G-CEFL	10. 8.07	CityJet Ltd "Valentia Island"	Paris CDG	A2008
			N516XJ, G-6-334		(Operated Air France)		
EI-RJE	British Aerospace Avro 146-RJ85	E2335	G-CEBU	9. 3.07	CityJet Ltd "St MacDara's Island"	Paris CDG	A2008
			N517XJ, G-6-335		(Operated Air France)		
EI-RJF	British Aerospace Avro 146-RJ85	E2337	G-CEFN	24. 8.07	CityJet Ltd "Great Blasket island"	Paris CDG	A2008
			N518XJ, G-6-337		(Operated Air France)		
EI-RJG	British Aerospace Avro 146-RJ85	E2344	G-CEHB	18.12.07	CityJet Ltd "Sherkin Island"	Paris CDG	A2008
			N519XJ, G-6-344		(Operated Air France)		
EI-RJH	British Aerospace Avro 146-RJ85	E2345	N520XJ	1 .4.08	CityJet Ltd "Inishturk"	Paris CDG	A2008
			G-6-345		(Operated Air France)		
EI-RJI	British Aerospace Avro 146-RJ85	E2346	G-CDZP	2. 5.07	CityJet Ltd "Skellig Michael"	Paris CDG	A2008
			N521XJ, G-6-346		(Operated Air France)		
EI-RJJ	British Aerospace Avro 146-RJ85	E2347	G-CEIF	1. 2.08	CityJet Ltd "Hare Island"	Paris CDG	A2008
			N522XJ, G-6-347		(Operated Air France)		
EI-RJK	British Aerospace Avro 146-RJ85	E2348	N523XJ	20. 9.07	CityJet Ltd "Collanmore Island"	Paris CDG	A2008
			G-6-348		(Operated Air France)		
EI-RJL	British Aerospace Avro 146-RJ85	E2349	N524XJ	20. 9.07	CityJet Ltd "Inishmurray"	Norwich	N11.07
			G-6-349		(Operated Air France) [Reserved as OH-SAQ 1.09]		
EI-RJM	British Aerospace Avro 146-RJ85	E2350	N525XJ	13. 7.07	CityJet Ltd "Caher Island"	Norwich	N11.07
			G-6-350		(Operated Air France)		
EI-RJN	British Aerospace Avro 146-RJ85	E2351	N526XJ	11. 1.07	CityJet Ltd "Lake Isle of Inisheer"	Paris CDG	A2008
			G-6-351		(Operated Air France)		
EI-RJO	British Aerospace Avro 146-RJ85	E2352	N527XJ	11. 1.07	CityJet Ltd "Inis Mor"	Paris CDG	A2008
			G-6-352		(Operated Air France)		
EI-RJP	British Aerospace Avro 146-RJ85	E2363	N529XJ	18. 8.06	CityJet Ltd "Clare Island"	Paris CDG	A2008
			G-6-363		(Operated Air France)		
EI-RJR	British Aerospace Avro 146-RJ85	E2364	N530XJ	27.11.06	CityJet Ltd "Tory Island"	Paris CDG	A2008
			G-6-364		(Operated Air France)		
EI-RJS	British Aerospace Avro 146-RJ85	E2365	N531XJ	16. 4.07	CityJet Ltd "Dursey Island"	Paris CDG	A2008
			G-6-365		(Operated Air France)		
EI-RJT	British Aerospace Avro 146-RJ85	E2366	N532XJ	.16. 4.07	CityJet Ltd) "Inishbofin"	Paris CDG	A2008
			G-6-366		(Operated Air France		
EI-RJU	British Aerospace Avro 146-RJ85	E2367	N533XJ	.24. 5 07	CityJet Ltd "Cape Clear"	Paris CDG	A2008
			G-6-367		(Operated Air France)		
EI-RJV	British Aerospace Avro 146-RJ85	F2370	N534XJ	24. 5.07	CityJet Ltd "Lambay Island"	Paris CDG	A2008
			G-6-370		(Operated Air France)		
EI-RJW	British Aerospace Avro 146-RJ85	E2371	N535XJ	13. 7.07	CityJet Ltd "Garinish Island"	Paris CDG	A2008
			G-6-371		(Operated Air France)		
EI-RJX	British Aerospace Avro 146-RJ85	E2372	N536XJ	20. 9.07	CityJet Ltd "Scattery Island"	Paris CDG	A2008
			G-6-372		(Operated Air France)		
EI-RJY	British Aerospace Avro 146-RJ85	E2307	N502XJ	14.11.08	CityJet Ltd "Inis Meain"	Paris CDG	A2008
			G-6-307		(Operated Air France)		
EI-RJZ	British Aerospace Avro 146-RJ85	E2326	N512XJ	15. 5.08	CityJet Ltd	Paris CDG	A2008
			G-6-326		(Operated Air France)		
EI-RMC	Bell 206B-3 JetRanger III	488	G-BWLO	16.12.99	Westair Aviation Ltd	Shannon	A 7.01
			N2290W				
EI-ROB	Robin R.1180TD	270	PH-AIG	30. 3.05	Extras Ltd	Waterford	A 10.08
EI-RON	Robinson R44 Raven	1606		19. 7.06	Atlantic Distributors Ltd	Galway	
EI-SAC	Cessna 172P Skyhawk	17276263	N98149	22. 9.00	Sligo Aeronautical Club Ltd	Strandhill, Sligo	A 5.08
EI-SAR	Sikorsky S-61N	61-143	G-AYOM	26. 6.98	CHC Ireland Ltd (IMES Rescue titles)	Waterford	A2008
	(Mitsubishi c/n M61-001)		N4585, JA9506, N94565				
EI-SAT	Steen Skybolt	1	N52DH	22.10.99	B O'Sullivan	Abbeyshrule	A 10.08
	(Built D Hall)						
EI-SEA	Progressive Aerodyne Searey Amphibian			19. 4.06	J Brennan	Strandhill, Sligo	A 9.08
	(Built J Brennan)	1DK359C					
EI-SGF	Robinson R44 Raven	1401		1.10.04	M Reilly and S Filan	Carraroe	
EI-SGN	Robinson R44 Raven	1648		18.10.06	M Reilly and S Filan	Carraroe	A 9.08
EI-SKB	Piper PA-44-180 Seminole	44-7995112	G-BGJB	17.12.07	Shemburn Ltd	Waterford	
			G-ISFT, EI-CHF, G-BGJB, N3046B				
EI-SKC	Piper PA-44-180 Seminole	44-8095021	G-BHRP	23. 5.08	Shemburn Ltd	Waterford	
			N81602				

EI-SKE	Robin DR.400-140B Earl	2630	D-ERAA	20.12.07	Shemburn Ltd	Weston, Dublin	A10.08
			(PH-ASG), (PH-NEW), (PH-NFW)				
EI-SKG	Robin DR.400-135CDi	2610		30.11.06	Shemburn Ltd	Weston, Dublin	
EI-SKL	Robin DR.400-135CDi	2611		30.11.06	Shemburn Ltd	Weston, Dublin	
EI-SKP	Reims Cessna F172P	F17202101	PH-VSZ	16. 2.06	Shemburn Ltd	Waterford	A 4.06
			D-EOFR				
EI-SKR	Piper PA-44-180 Seminole	44-7995008	G-BOHX	3.08R	Shemburn Ltd	Waterford	
			N36814				
EI-SKS	Robin R.2160	307	OO-OBC	13. 7.04	Shemburn Ltd	Weston, Dublin	A 5.06
EI-SKT	Piper PA-44-180 Seminole	44-7995004	G-BGSG	27.11.02	Shemburn Ltd	Weston, Dublin	A 5.06
			N36538				
EI-SKU	Piper PA28RT-201 Arrow IV	28R-7918145	G-BXYS	14. 2.03	Shemburn Ltd	Waterford	A 4.06
			PH-SBS, N29561				
EI-SKV	Robin R.2160D	171	PH-BLO	28. 3.03	Shemburn Ltd	Weston, Dublin	A10.08
EI-SKW	Piper PA-28-161 Warrior II	28-8216115	D-EIBV	18. 2.04	Shemburn Ltd	Weston, Dublin	A 10.08
			N9630N]				
EI-SLA	Aérospatiale-Alenia ATR 42-300	149	SE-LST	4. 3.05	Air Contractors (Ireland) Ltd	Dublin	A2008
			F-WQNP, G-WFEP, N4210G, F-WWEV				
EI-SLC	Aérospatiale-Alenia ATR 42-300	082	OY-CIE	27. 8.04	Air Contractors (Ireland) Ltd	Dublin	A2008
			D-BATB, F-WWEH				
EI-SLF	Aérospatiale-Alenia ATR 72-202	210	OY-RUA	26.11.02	Air Contractors (Ireland) Ltd	Dublin	A2008
			B-22703, F-WWEH				
EI-SLG	Aérospatiale-Alenia ATR 72-201	183	F-WQNI	18. 4.05	Air Contractors (Ireland) Ltd	Dublin	A2008
			EC-EYK, EC-515, F-WWES				
EI-SLH	Aérospatiale-Alenia ATR 72-202	157	OY-RTG	12. 8.05	Air Contractors (Ireland) Ltd	Dublin	A2008
			F-WQNH, EC-EUJ, EC-384, F-WWEL				
EI-SMD	Robinson R44 Clipper	1848		19. 8.08	New World Plant Ltd	Carnmore	
EI-SMK	Zenair CH.701 STOL	7-3551		15.10.03	S King	(County Kildare)	
	(Built S King)						
EI-SNJ	Bell 407	53442	N407J	17.12.03	Moriam Ltd	Dublin	A 6.07
			PP-MSJ, N6096D, C-GFNR				
EI-SPB	Cessna T206H Stationair TC	T20608753	N2321V	4.10.07	P Morrissey	Dublin	
EI-SQG	Agusta A109E Power	11084		1. 8.00	Quinn Group Ltd	Dublin	A 5.08
					(Operated Premier Helicopters)		
EI-STR	Bell 407	53282	N44504	19. 5.00	G and H Homes Ltd	(Listowel)	N 1.03
EI-STT	Cessna 172M	17266228	D-EVBB	30 .8.00	Trim Flying Club Ltd	Trim	A 10.08
			N9557H				
EI-SUB	Robinson R44 Raven	1535		17. 1.06	EI-SUB Ltd	Killarney	A 6.07
EI-SWD	Robinson R44 Raven	1633		30. 8.06	New World Plant Ltd	Galway	A 3.08
EI-TAB	Airbus A320-233	1624	(N485TA)	27. 6.02	Wilmington Trust SP Services (Dublin) Ltd (Operated TACA)		
			F-WWIZ		"Mensajero de Esperanza"		
						San Salvador-Comalapa	A2008
EI-TAD	Airbus A320-233	2301	F-WWDF	6.12.05	Alvi Leasing Ltd (Operated TACA)		
						San Salvador-Comalapa	A2008
EI-TAG	Airbus A320-233	2791	(N495TA)	1. 6.06	Wilmington Trust SP Services (Dublin) Ltd (Operated TACA)		
			F-WWBY			San Salvador-Comalapa	A2008
EI-TGF	Robinson R22 Beta II	3855		1. 7.05	Skyexpress Ltd	Oranmore Heliport, Galway	A 4.06
EI-TIM	Piper J-5A Cub Cruiser	5-36	N27151	1. 2.08	N and P Murphy	Trim	
			NC27151				
EI-TIP	Bell 430	49074	N430MK	12. 6.02	Starair (Ireland) Ltd	Dublin	A 5.08
			N9151Z, C-GAHJ				
EI-TKI	Robinson R22 Beta	1195	G-OBIP	22. 8.91	J McDaid	(Slavary, Buncrana)	A10.00
EI-TMH	Robinson R44 Raven	1402		26. 8.04	Architectural Construction Ltd	Weston, Dublin	A 6.07
EI-TOM	Bell 407	53744	N5080N	31. 7.07	Tougher's Oil Distributors Ltd		
			C-FLVT			(Newhall, County Clare)	A 3.08
EI-TON	Raj Hamsa X'Air 582(5)	718	G-CCCZ	9. 2.06	R A Merrigan	Birr	
	(Built M B Cooke - pr.no.BMAA/HB/200)						
EI-TOY	Robinson R44 Raven	1294		2. 4.03	Metroheli Ltd	Weston, Dublin	A 5.08
EI-TWO	Agusta A109E	11131	D-HARY (3)	17. 2.05	Alburn Transport Ltd	Dublin	A 5.08
			B-7770				
EI-UFO	Piper PA-22-150 Tri-Pacer	22-4942	G-BRZR	12. 2.94	W Treacy	Trim	A 4.06
	(Tail-wheel conversion)		N7045D				
EI-UNA	Boeing 767-3P6ER	26233	A4O-GU	27.3.08	Capablue Ltd	Moscow-Domodedovo	A2008
					(Operated Transaero Airlines)		
EI-UNB	Boeing 767-3P6ER	26234	A4O-GY	16. 1.08	Capablue Ltd	Moscow-Domodedovo	A2008
					(Operated Transaero Airlines)		
EI-UND	Boeing 767-3P6ER	26236	A4O-GS	12. 2.08	Capablue Ltd	Moscow-Domodedovo	A2008
					(Operated Transaero Airlines)		
EI-UNF	Boeing 767-3P6ER	26238	A4O-GT	27. 3.08	Capablue Ltd	Moscow-Domodedovo	A2008
					(Operated Transaero Airlines)		
EI-UNI	Robinson R-44 Raven II	11498		8.12.06	Unipipe (Ireland) Ltd	Weston, Dublin	A 6.07
EI-UNW	Boeing 777-222	30214	N208UA		Capablus Ltd	Moscow-Domodedovo	A2009
					(Operated Transaero Airlines)		
EI-UNX	Boeing 777-222	30213	N207UA	7.08	Capablue Ltd	Moscow-Domodedovo	A2008
					(Operated Transaero Airlines)		
EI-UNY	Boeing 777-222	26918	N767UA	7.08	Capablue Ltd	Moscow-Domodedovo	A2008
					(Operated Transaero Airlines)		
EI-UNZ	Boeing 777-222	26925	N770UA	7.08	Capablue Ltd	Moscow-Domodedovo	A2008
					(Operated Transaero Airlines)		
EI-UPA	McDonnell-Douglas MD-11F	48426	I-DUPA	11. 7.05	Pegasus Aviation MD-11-1 Ltd	Rome-Fiumicino	A2008
			N9020Z		(Operated Alitalia Cargo)	"Gioacchino Rossini"	
EI-UPE	McDonnell-Douglas MD-11F	48427	I-DUPE	27.10.05	Pegasus Aviation MD-11-3 Ltd	Rome-Fiumicino	A2008
					(Operated Alitalia Cargo) "Giuseppe Verdi"		

Reg	Type	C/n	Prev ID	Date	Owner/Operator	Location	Notes
EI-UPI	McDonnell-Douglas MD-11F	48428	I-DUPI N9020U	31. 8.05	Pegasus Aviation MD-11-2 Ltd Rome-Fiumicino		A2008
					(Operated Alitalia Cargo) "Giacomo Puccini"		
EI-UPO	McDonnell-Douglas MD-11F	48429	I-DUPO	28. 9.05	Pegasus Aviation MD-11-4 Ltd Rome-Fiumicino		A2008
					(Operated Alitalia Cargo)"Nicolo Paganini"		
EI-UPU	McDonnell-Douglas MD-11C	48430	I-DUPU	25. 7.06	Pegasus Aviation MD-11-5 Ltd Rome-Fiumicino		A2008
					(Operated Alitalia Cargo)"Antonio Vivaldi"		
	(Above aircraft returned to lessor from 8. 1.09 and stored)						
EI-VIC	Robinson R44 Raven II	11644		3. 4.07	Aeroglen Ltd	Dublin	A 6.07
EI-VIV	Bombardier Learjet 60	60-305	OH-VIV N40050	18. 7.07	Airlink Airways Ltd	Shannon	A 7.07
EI-VLN	Piper PA-18A-150 Super Cub	18-6797	G-ASCU VP-JBL	17.10.07	D O'Mahoney	(Kilrush)	
EI-WAC	Piper PA-23-250 Aztec E	27-4683	G-AZBK N14077	26. 5.95	Westair Aviation Ltd	Shannon	A 7.01
EI-WAT	Tecnam P.2002-JF Sierra	086		2. 9.08	Waterford Aero Club Ltd	Waterford	
EI-WAV	Bell 430	49028	N4213V	24.12.97	Westair Aviation Ltd	Shannon	A 5.07
EI-WFD	Tecnam P.2002-JF Sierra	080		15. 5.08	Waterford Aero Club Ltd	Waterford	
EI-WFO	Bombardier Learjet 45	45-368	N4003W	3. 7.08	Midwest Atlantic Ltd *"Wind Force One"*	Shannon	A 8.08
EI-WIG	Best Off Sky Ranger 912(2)	SKR0504608		29. 6.07	M Brereton	Limetree	
	(Built M Brereton)						
EI-WJN	Hawker Siddeley HS.125 Series 700A	257062	N416RD	30. 5.00	Westair Aviation Ltd	Shannon	A 3.08
	N26EA, RA02809, G-5-708, RA02809, (G-BWJX), G-5-708, N7062B, HB-VGF, G-5-708, HB-VGF, G-5-16						
EI-WMN	Piper PA-23-250 Aztec F	27-7954063	G-ZSFT	12.10.00	Westair Aviation Ltd	Shannon	A 5.07
	G-SALT, G-BGTH, N2551M, N9731N						
EI-WRN	Piper PA-28-151 Cherokee Warrior						
		28-7615212	G-BDZX N9559N	5.10.99	P and M Corrigan	Weston, Dublin	A 4.06
EI-WWI	Robinson R44 Raven	11799		17. 7.07	Talger Developments Ltd		
						(Baltinglass, County Wicklow)	
EI-WXA	British Aerospace Avro 146-RJ85	E2310	N503XJ G-6-310	9.09R	CityJet Ltd	Paris CDG	A2008
					(Operated Air France)		
EI-WXB	British Aerospace Avro 146-RJ85	E2311	N504XJ G-6-311	14.11.08	CityJet Ltd	Paris CDG	A2008
					(Operated Air France)		
EI-WXP	Hawker 800XP	258382	SE-DYE N23451	9.11.07	Westair Aviation Ltd	Shannon	A 5.08
EI-XLA	Urban Air UFM-10 Samba XLA	XXLA 35		28. 3.06	K.Dardis	Abbeyshrule	N 1.08
EI-XLS	Cessna 560XL Citation Excel	560-5666	LN-EXL N51780	13. 5.08	Skylink Airways Ltd	Shannon	10.08
EI-YBZ	Robinson R44 Raven	1468		15. 4.05	ILH Enterprises Ltd	Limerick	
EI-YLG	Robin HR200/120B	336	G-BYLG	28.11.05	The Leinster Aero Club Ltd	Weston, Dublin	A 9.07
EI-ZZZ	Bell 222	47061	(EI-MED)	28. 4.08	Executive Helicopter Maintenance Ltd Carnmore		
	N40EA, SE-HTN, G-DMAF, G-BLSZ, D-HCHS, (D-HAAD)						

REGISTRATIONS AWAITED 2009:

EI-...	Aerial Arts Chaser S	CH.723	G-MVGI	3.08R	Not known	Mill Farm, Hughley, Much Wenlock
		(Officially transferred from UK to Republic of Ireland 6.1.03 but noted stored as "G-MVGI" 9.04)				
EI-...	Bensen B.8M	PFA G/01-1196	G-BTAH	3.08R	Not known	
	(Built T B Johnson)				*(Officially transferred from UK to Republic of Ireland 25. 4.06)*	
EI-...	Raven Aircraft Raven X	SN2232/0257	G-MTHC	3.08R	*(Officially transferred from UK to Republic of Ireland 25. 4.06)*	
EI-...	Rotary Air Force RAF 2000 GTX-SE					
	(Built M T Byrne)	PFA G/13-1302	G-BYDW	3.08R	(R.I.Young)	(Kilrush)
					(Officially transferred from UK to Republic of Ireland 15. 5.06)	
EI-...	Rans S-4 Coyote	89.098	G-MVXW	3.08R	Not known	
	(Built D Hedley-Goddard - pr.no.PFA 193-11545)				*(Officially transferred from UK to Republic of Ireland 6. 2.07)*	
EI-...	Thruster T.600NT	9067-T600T-009	G-MZHC	3.08R	*(Officially transferred from UK to Republic of Ireland 25.10.07)*	
EI-...	Robinson R44	0822	G-RDWD	3.08R	Redwood Properties Ltd	Weston
			G-EUGN		*(Officially transferred from UK to Republic of Ireland 6.12.07)*	
EI-...	Robinson R44 Raven II	10551	G-CDCA	3.08R	L Behan and Sons Ltd (Rathcoole, County Dublin)	
					(Officially transferred from UK to Republic of Ireland 17. 1.08)	
EI-..	Aérospatiale SA.315B Lama	2489	I-LOGI	3.08R		
			(F-GEEK), N49521			
EI-...	Aérospatiale SA.315B Lama	2568	I-ELPA	3.08R		
			F-GCFO			
EI-...	Aérospatiale SA.315B Lama	2661	I-EPEP	3.08R		
EI-...	Boeing 737-3Q8	23507	N327AW	3.08R	Not known	Kaliningrad-Khrabovo
			N398US, N348AU, N751L		*(Operated KD Avia)*	
EI-...	Boeing 737-301	23260	N325AW	3.08R	Not known	Kaliningrad-Khrabovo
			N582US, N309P		*(Operated KD Avia)*	
EI-...	Boeing 737-301	23261	N324AW	3.08R	Not known	Kaliningrad-Khrabovo
			N583US, N312P		*(Operated KD Avia)*	
EI-...	MBB BK.117B-2	7164	I-HBHG	3.08R		
			D-HBHG, Abu Dhabi Police S-716, D-HBHG			
EI-...	McDonnell Douglas MD-82	49112	9A-CDC	3.08R	Eir Jet Ltd	Shannon
			PK-ALI, PK-IMD, N14814, N814NY, N480AC			
EI-...	Piper J-5A Cub Cruiser	5-36	N27151	3.08R		
			NC27151			
EI-...	Wassmer WA.81 Piranha	804	F-GAIF	3.08R	Not known	Abbeyshrule A 6.07
EI-	Cessna 120	11783	N77342	2.08		
			NC77342			
EI-	Cessna U206G Stationair II	U20605475	N566N	2.08		
			N5429X			
EI-	Robinson R22 Beta	2605	C-FYGJ	2.08		
EI-	Robinson R22B2 Beta	3179	G-FEBY	2.08		
EI-	Raj Hamsa X'Air Jabiru(1)	331	G-BYCL	15.10.98	D O'Keefe, K Rutter and A J Clarke London Colney 31. 7.08P	
	(Built G A J Salter - pr.no.BMAA/HB/088)					
EI-	Bell 407	53828	N328BL	8.08		
			C-FTMY, C-GFNY			
EI-	Robinson R44 Raven II	10779	G-CDMI	10.08	Helicopter Support Ireland Ltd	
						(Midleton, Co Cork) 15. 7.09E
EI-	ELA Aviacion ELA 07S	06071650722	G-CETW	1.10.07	C Hewer *(Noted 7.08)*	Kirkbride
EI-	Cessna 172RG Cutlass II	172RG0550	G-BHVC	30. 5.80	K O'Connor Weston, Leixlip, County Kildare 13. 5.09E	
			N9048K, G-BHVC, N372SA, G-BHVC, N5515V			
EI	Reims Cessna FA152 Aerobat	FA1520376	G-BILJ	31.12.80	K O'Connor	Weston, Dublin 25. 8.09E
EI-	Cessna 172S Skyhawk SP	172S8561	G-BZPM	11. 1.01	R Carey	Weston, Dublin 27. 3.09E
			N72760			

PART 2 – DE-REGISTERED EXTANT AIRCRAFT

The following have been reported since 2005 and are believed to be extant.

Registration	Type	Construction No	Previous Reg Identity	Date	Registered Owner (Operator)	(Unconfirmed) Base	CofA Validity
EI-ACY	Auster V J/1 Autocrat	2146	G-AIBK	20. 5.47	Not known	(Dublin)	N 11.07
	(Crashed Oughterard 5. 4.67 and cancelled xx.xx.xx?: noted 11.07 en route Dromore, County.Down to Dublin for rebuild)						
EI-AMF	Taylorcraft Plus D	157	G-ARRK	26. 4.62	C J Baker	Carr Farm,Thorney, Newark	N 1.05
	(Built Auster Aircraft Ltd)		G-AHUM, LB286		*(Cancelled 3.4.70 as WFU: fuselage partly restored)*		
EI-ANA	Taylorcraft Plus D	206	G-AHCG	29.8 .63	N Reilly	Ballyjamesduff	N 9.05
	(Built Auster Aircraft Ltd)		LB347		*(Cancelled as WFU c.1972)*		
EI-APF	Cessna F150G	F150-0112		6. 3.66	Sligo Aero Club Ltd		N 3.06
					(Cancelled 16.1.06: noted wrecked Kirknewton)		
EI-AVC	Reims Cessna F.337F Super Skymaster	0032	N4757	26. 8.71	Not known	Castlerock	N 7.07
	(Wichita c/n 33701355)				*(Cancelled)*		
EI-AYL (2)	Beagle A.109 Airedale				Details in SECTION 1, Part 2	Spanhoe	N 4.07
EI-BAS	Reims Cessna F172M	F17201262		2. 5.75	(Iona National Airways)	Bournemouth	N 6.05
					(Cancelled 6.3.03 as beyond repair: dismantled)		
EI-BBK	Beagle A.109 Airedale				Details in SECTION 1, Part 2	Spanhoe	N 4.07
EI-BHK	SOCATA MS.880B Rallye Club	1307	F-BRJE	20. 8.79	Not known	Kilkenny	N 6.06
					(Cancelled 8.9.00 as WFU: derelict)		
EI-BKE	Morane MS.885 Super Rallye	278	F-BKUN	9. 2.81	Not known	Abbeyshrule	N 5.06
			F-WKUN		*(Crashed Ballyclumack, Wexford 5.4.81: stripped hulk stored)*		
EI-BNR	American Aviation AA-5 Traveler	AA5-0203	N9992Q	1. 3.83	Not known	Abbeyshrule	N 5.06
	(Regd with c/n 202 in error)		CS-AHJ		*(DBR on 21.2.88: cancelled 22.7.88: noted wrecked)*		
EI-CAA	Reims FR172J Rocket	FR17200486	G-BHTW	17. 8.89	O.Bruton	Abbeyshrule	N 5.06
			5Y-ATO		*(Damaged 1993/94: cancelled 27.11.98 as WFU: noted wrecked)*		
EI-CAZ	Fairchild-Hiller FH-227D	519	SE-KBR	23. 9.91	Norwich Airport Fire Service	Norwich	N 2.06
			C-FNAK, CF-NAK, (N701U, N2735R		*(Cancelled 15.12.94: dumped)*		
EI-CFV	SOCATA MS.880B Rallye Club	1850	G-OLFS	13. 5.92	Not known	Abbeyshrule	N.5.06
			G-AYYZ		*(Cancelled 15.11.00 as scrapped: noted wrecked)*		
EI-CHN	SOCATA MS.880B Rallye Club	901	G-AVIO	22. 2.93	Limerick Flying Club (Coonagh) Ltd	Abbeyshrule	N 5.06
					(Cancelled 3.7.03 as scrapped: noted wrecked)		
EI-CJD	Boeing 737-204ADV	22966	G-BKHE	18. 2.94	Dublin Airport Authority	Dublin	N 1.05
			(G-BKGU)		*(Cancelled 29.10.04 as WFU: used for tug practice and other duties)*		

The following are preserved in Museums and available private collections. Full details are shown in SECTION 4, Part 1.

Registration	Type	Base
("EI-ABH")	HM.14 Pou-du-Ciel replica	Meath
EI-AKA	Fokker F-27 Friendship 100	Lelystad, Netherlands
EI-ALR	Douglas C-47-DL Dakota	Nimes-Garons, Gard, France
EI-ALT	Douglas C-47A-10-DK Dakota	Paris Le Bourget, France
EI-APT (2)	Fokker D.VII/65 replica	Antwerp, Belgium
EI-APU (2)	Fokker D.VII/65 replica	Marlborough, New Zealand
EI-APV	Fokker D.VII/65 replica	Birmingham, Alabama, US
EI-ARC	Pfalz D.III replica	Marlborough, New Zealand
EI-ARD	Pfalz D.III replica	Marlborough, New Zealand
EI-ARS (2)	Douglas C-54E-5-DO Skymaster	Rhein-Main Air Force Base, Frankfurt, Germany
EI-ATP	Phoenix Luton LA-4A Minor	Concourse E, Miami International Airport
EI-AYO (2)	Douglas DC-3A-197	Wroughton, Wiltshire
EI-BAG	Cessna 172A	Langford Lodge, Belfast, Northern Ireland
EI-BUO	Aero Composites Sea Hawker	Langford Lodge, Belfast, Northern Ireland

PART 3 – AIRCRAFT REGISTERED and CANCELLED in 2008 and 2009

Registration	Type	Construction No	Previous Reg Identity	Date	Registered Owner (Operator)	Fate	Date
EI-DZU	Boeing 737-3M8	24020	N103KH G-EZYB, N797BB, I-TEAA, OO-LTA	13. 6.08	Celestial Aviation Trading 2 Ltd	To VT-QQP	20. 6.08
EI-DZW	Airbus A319-112	3309	N554SX D-AVYQ	6. 5.08	Aircraft Portfolio Holding Company Ltd	To LX-HBB	31. 7.08
EI-DZX	Airbus A319-112	3331	N501SX D-AVYL	6. 5.08	Aircraft Portfolio Holding Company Ltd	To 6Y-	28. 7.08
EI-DZY	Airbus A319-112	3385	N502SX D-AVWF	6. 5.08	Aircraft Portfolio Holding Company Ltd	To AP-BJE	8.08
EI-DZY	Airbus A319-112	3338	N504SX D-AVWG	7. 5.08	Aircraft Portfolio Holding Company Ltd	To AP-BJF	8.08
EI-EAF	Airbus A319-112	3171	N553SX D-AVXF	6. 5.08	ALS Irish Leasing MSN 3171 Ltd	To SU-BBB	28. 7.08
EI-EAN	Airbus A320-232	3050	VT-INH F-WWDS	5. 6.08	Nollaig Aviation Leasing Ltd	To A6-EIG	19. 6.08
EI-EAO	Airbus A320-232	3004	VT-ING F-WWBE	18. 4.08	Nollaig Aviation Leasing LtD	To A6-	15. 5.08
EI-ECD	Boeing 737-8FH	30826	EC-JHV (N3775)	30.9.08	Airspeed Ireland Leasing 18 Ltd	To TC-SNH	23.12.08

SECTION 3

PART 1 – ISLE OF MAN IRELAND REGISTER

The Isle of Man civil aircraft register came into existence on 1st May.2007. The Isle of Man is a self-governing British Crown Dependency and not part of the UK or the European Union. Unlike the UK register it is possible to transfer existing registrations to other aircraft.   At present there are no plans to include public commercial transport aircraft on this register. Our thanks go to Alan Johnson and Paul Hewins.

Registration	Type	Construction No	Previous Identity	Date	Registered Owner (Operator)	(Unconfirmed) Base	Status
M-ABUS	Airbus A340-313	955	F-WWJM	8.10.08	Klaret Aviation Ltd	Luxembourg	1.09
					(Stored Copenhagen until 4.09 then to Basle for VIP fitment)		
M-ACPT	British Aerospace BAe125 Series 1000B	259004	VP-CPT VR-CPT, G-5-779, G-LRBJ	22. 2.08	Remo Investments Ltd	Biggin Hill	2.09
M-AGIC	Cessna 680 Citation Sovereign	680-0138	N51984	20. 6.07	Trustair Ltd	Blackpool	1.09
M-AJDM	Cessna 525A CitationJet CJ2	525A-0009	F-HAPP N525LC, N5235G	22. 1.08	Mazia Investments Ltd	(Tortola, BVI)	9.08
M-AJOR	Hawker 900XP *(Fuselage no 258933)*	HA-0058	N3088A	30. 6.08	INEOS Aviation LLP	Bournemouth	1.09
M-ALAN	Piper PA-30 Twin Comanche C	30-1982	G-BKCL G-AXSP, N8824Y	18.12.07	A Burrows	Ronaldsway	9.08
M-ALUN	British Aerospace BAe125 Series 700A	257075	N125XX N124AR, N125TR, N125AM, (G-BHKF), G-5-13	19. 6.08	Briarwood Products Ltd	Filton	6.08
M-AMND	Dassault Falcon 2000EX	114	F-GVNG	3.12.08	Doha Capital Ltd	(Tortola, BVI)	1.09
M-ANIN	SOCATA TB-20 Trindad GT	2161	N882 F-OIMA	3. 8.07	Harland Aviation Ltd	Ronaldsway	9.08
M-AXIM	Cessna T206H Turbo Stationair 8	T20608513	N357TR N357TM	24. 7.08	C D B Cope	Ronaldsway	12.08
M-BIGG	Bombardier CL-600-2B16 Challenger	5722	C-FOGE	24. 1.08	Signal Aviation Ltd	(St Helier, Jersey)	2.09
M-BIRD	Cessna 525B Citation Jet CJ3	525B-0255	N5181U	30. 7.08	Scorpion Aviation Ltd	Not known	12.08
M-BOAT	Eurocopter EC.130B4 Ecureuil	3998	VP-BLL F-GSYE	28. 8.08	Highland Helicopter (Isle of Man) Ltd *(Based on MV 'Lady Christine')*		10.08
M-BONO	Cessna 172N Skyhawk II	17270299	G-BONO C-GSMF, N738WS	19.11.07	J D McCandless	Newtownards	9.08
M-BWFC	Cessna 560 Citation XLS+	560-5690	N560FC (VP-BWC), N5130J	1. 5.07	Bakewell Industries Ltd	Ronaldsway	12.08
M-CHEM	Dassault Falcon 2000EX EASy	128	N628SA (VP-BOE), F-WWGS	1.11.07	INEOS Aviation LLP	Bournemouth	1.09
M-CVRS	Bombardier BD-700-1A10 Global Express	9294					
M-DASO	Dassault Falcon 50	268	G-DASO G-ITIH, F-WQBL, N268FJ, F-WQBL, PH-JNL, CS-TMS, EC-GTR, F-WWHS	15. 1.08	Bramptonia Ltd	Coventry	1.09
M-DBOY	Agusta A109C	7622	G-DBOY N621MM, HB-ZEE, OE-XSG, N67SH, 9M-SJI, M38-03, 9M-TDJ	20. 5.08	Heriair Ltd	Ronaldsway	12.08
M-DSCL	Embraer EMB.135BJ Legacy	14500851	OE-ISN PT-SIO	xx. 1.09			
M-DKDI	Cessna 750 Citation X	750-0227	P4-LJG N5267J	2.10.08	Dikad International Establishment	Vaduz	1.09
M-EDIA	Piper PA-34-200T Seneca	34-7970055	G-TAIR N3059H	18.12.07	Nigel Kenny Aviation Ltd	Ronaldsway	9.08
M-EGGA	Beech 200 Super King Air	BB-1933	N3103L	8. 5.08	Langley Aviation	Gamston	1.09
M-EIRE	Bombardier CL-600-2B16 *(Challenger 604)*	5562	N562ME N562BA, C-GLXM	8. 8.08	Mercury Engineering Ltd	Dublin	2.09
M-ELON	Cessna 525B CitationJet CJ3	525B-0148	N148CJ N52397	1. 5.07	Sleepwell Aviation Ltd	Ronaldsway	1.09
M-EOCV	Bombardier Learjet 45	45-306	OY-OCV N5009T	24. 6.08	Aviation Partnership Denmark ApS	(Swords, Ireland)	10.08
M-ERIT	Agusta-Westland AW139	31102		13.12.07	Merit Engineering Ltd	Enniskillen	12.08
M-ERRY	Sikorsky S-76B	760356	M-ONTY [(1)] G-BWDO, VR-CPN, N9HM	14. 4.08	Trustair Ltd	Blackpool	10.08
M-FALC	Dassault Falcon 900EX	31	HZ-OFC4 F-GSAI, F-WWFC	31.10.07	Noclaf Ltd	Luton	9.08
M-FIVE	Beech B300 Super King Air 350	FL-580	N34010	11. 6.08	Larvotto LP	Kemble	12.08
M-FMHG	Gulfstream Aviation Gulfstream IVSP	1305	N305GA [(2)] N888SQ, (N913SC), N439GA	22. 7.07	Future Aviation LLP	(George Town, CI)	1.09
M-FOUR	Beech A36 Bonanza	E-3541	N68MR N5111Y, (N566C), N5111Y	13.12.07	Larvotto LP	Kemble	12.08
M-FSRE	Beech B200 Super King Air	BB-1202	N5NV G-REBK, D-IHAP, N44VM, N2707M	3. 7.08	IAL King Air Ltd	(Tortola, BVI)	1.09
M-FZMH	Bombardier CL600-2B19 *(Challenger 850)*	8068	C-FLOA C-FMMQ	10.10.08	AK VI Limited		11.08
M-GBAL	Bombardier BD-700-1A10 Global Express	9210	N190H C-FIOT	8. 8.08	Noclaf Ltd	Luton	1.09
M-GINZ	SOCATA TB-20 Trinidad GT	2140	N565G	18. 7.07	Whitesand Investments Ltd	Blackpool	10.08
M-GLAS	Beech C90A King Air	LJ-1734	N59GG N36634	6. 8.08	Glasdon Group Ltd	Blackpool	12.08
M-GLRS	Bombardier Learjet 45	45-249	C-GLRS N40075	8. 4.08	Bombardier Transportation GmbH Berlin, Germany		12.08
M-GOLF	Cessna FR182RG Skylane RG	FR18200046	N409SA N400SA, G-BJDI, N8062H	8. 4.08	P R Piggin and C J Harding	(Baldrine, Isle of Man)	11.08

Reg	Type	C/n	Prev id	Date	Owner	Location	Date
M-GPIK	Dassault Falcon 50EX	289	N315DV	10.10.08	Dassault Falcon Leasing Ltd		1.09
			(N589FJ), N315DV, N214DV, F-WWHQ				
M-GULF	Gulfstream Aerospace Gulfstream IV	1082	N1082A	17.8.07	Earth One Ltd	Ronaldsway	12.08
			(N82BR), N1082A				
M-HAWK	Hawker 800XP	258494	VP-BXP	15.11.07	INEOS Aviation LLP	Bournemouth	12.08
			N808TA				
M-HDAM	British Aerospace BAe 125 Series 800B	258037	7O-ADC	3.8.07	ABG Air Ltd	Farnborough	12.08
			4W-ACN, G-5-501, G-5-15				
M-HOIL	Bombardier Learjet 60	60-313	G-HOIL	9.1.09			1.09
			N613H, N4003L				
M-ICKY	Pilatus PC-12/45	508	N508DL	19.10.07	Saxon Logistics Ltd	Goodwood	12.08
			(N118CD), N508DL, ZS-KAL				
M-ICRO	Cessna 525A CitationJet CJ2+	525A-0347	N5262X	2.5.07	Pektron Group Ltd	Gamston	12.08
M-IDAS	Agusta A109E Power	11112	N555GS	16.10.07	Trustair Ltd	Blackpool	9.08
			N109LF				
M-IFES	Bombardier CL-600-1A11 *(Challenger 600)*	1067	N240AK	6.3.08	Inflite Aviation (IoM) Ltd	Douglas, IoM	9.08
			N205EL, N800AB, N50928, C-GZBE, C-GLXH, (VR-CBP), C-GLXH				
M-IFLY	Pilatus PC-12/47E	1022	HB-FRN	23.6.08	N J Vetch	Goodwood	12.08
M-INOR	Hawker 900XP *(Fuselage no 258935)*	HA-0059	N3400D	30.6.08	INEOS Aviation LLP	Bournemouth	12.08
M-JANP	Bombardier BD-700-1A10 Global Express XRS	9253	C-FQPI	xx.1.09			1.09
			(HZ-BJP), (HZ-SJP), C-FQPI				
M-JETI	British Aerospace BAe 125 Series 800B	258056	G-JETI	25.2.08	Cassel Invest Ltd	(Tortola, BVI)	1.09
			G-5-509				
M-JETT	Dassault Falcon 200	490	N490SJ		Piraeus Leasing Chrimatodotikes Mishoseie	Athens, Greece	2.09
			PH-APV				
			N917JG, N917JC, HC-BVH, N200RT (N208RT), N200RT, N95JT, N2TF, N806F, N14EN, N204FJ, F-WPUY				
M-JMMM	Dassault Falcon 900B	159	CS-DPE	2.5.08	3M Executive Aviation (SPV) Ltd	(Tortola, BVI)	1.09
			LX-COS, LX-NAN, F-WQBL, LX-NAN, N263PW, P4-NAN, F-WWFD				
M-KOGO	Eurocopter EC135 T2+	0661	D-HTSF	16.5.08	Rotorflying Ltd	Douglas, IoM	9.08
M-LCJP	Hawker 900XP	HA-0072	N33612	20.11.08	Yolenal Ltd	Nicosia, Cyprus	1.09
M-LEAR	Gates Learjet 31	31-011	D-CTWO	9.1.09	TNT Airways SA	Brussels, Belgium	1.09
			HB-VJI, N3803G				
M-LEFB	Cessna 550 Citation II	550-0172	SE-RCZ	1.7.08	Patagonia Assets Ltd	(Tortola, BVI)	1.09
			N800TV, N412P, N78CS, N88JJ, N72MM, (N28MM), N88795				
M-LEKT	Robin DR.400/180 Régent	1181	G-LEKT	7.4.08	T D Allan, P and J P Bromley	Ronaldsway	11.08
			D-EEKT				
M-LJGI	Dassault Falcon 2000Easy	143	(P4-LGM)	30.10.08	Ven Air	Dublin	1.09
			F-WWGR				
M-LNDN	Eurocopter EC155B1	6834		xx.1.09			1.09
M-MANX	Cessna 425 Conquest	425-0044	N425HS	16.8.07	Mastercraft Ltd	Wycombe Air Park	1.09
			N555BE, VH-PTH, N6774L				
M-MIKE	Cessna 525B CitationJet 2	525B-0280	N150MJ	31.10.08	M F Jacobson	Luton	1.09
			N5197A				
M-MUFC	Piper PA-44-180 Seminole	44-8207005	N629RS	2.6.08	629 Aviation Ltd	Bournemouth	1.09
			4X-CCU, G-BNUU, N8012U				
M-NATH	Embraer EMB-135BJ Legacy	14501021	N915LX	16.6.08	Pheebe Ltd	Douglas, IoM	11.08
			PT-SVX				
M-NEWT	Bombardier BD-100-1A10 Challenger 300	20151	C-FLQX	13.11.07	Sterling Aviation Properties LLP	Luton	1.09
M-NINE	Beech G58 Baron	TH-2203	N220Q	13.12.07	Larvotto LP	Kemble	11.08
M-NOEL	Bombadier BD-100-1A10 Challenger 300	20206	(C-FSNQ)	7.8.08	ABS Service Ltd	Not known	9.08
M-OLTT	Pilatus PA-12/47E	1063	HB-FRR	20.10.08	One Luxury Travel LP		12.08
M-ONAV	Hawker 900XP	HA-0073	N3283V	20.11.08	Monavia Limited	Guernsey	1.09
M-ONTY [2]	Sikorsky S-76C	760696	N2580E	20.10.08	Trustair Ltd	Blackpool	1.09
M-OODY	Cessna 525B CitationJet 2	525B-0238		19.12.08	Futures Aviation Services Ltd	Grand Cayman	12.08
M-OORE	Beech 350 Super King Air	FL-569	N569KA	14.1.08	Byecross (IOM) Ltd	Ronaldsway	2.09
M-OPED	Piper PA-32-301XTC Saratoga	3255029	G-SUEC	21.2.08	H L Cham	Ronaldsway	A 2.08
			D-EGTC, N30908				
M-OSPB	Gulfstream Aerospace Gulfstream 200	205		26.11.08	G200 Limited	Hamilton, Bermuda	1.09
M-OTOR	Beech C90A King Air	LJ-1733	N590PS	29.11.07	Pektron Group Ltd	Gamston	1.09
M-PARK	Cessna 525 CitationJet	525-0358	G-HMMV	3.7.08	Parkridge (Aviation) Ltd	(Solihull)	10.08
			N51564				
M-PHML	American General AG-5B Tiger	10141	G-PHML	19.12.07	J R Shannon	Ronaldsway	4.08
			PH-MLB				
M-PRVT	Cessna 750 Citation X	750-0291	N2068G	21.11.08	Unifox Holdings Ltd	Belize City	1.09
			N5125J				
M-PSAC	Cessna 525A CitationJet CJ2+	525A0389	N5153K	11.3.08	T H Scott	Jersey	1.09
M-RAVA	LET L.200D Morava	171402	OK-RHJ	24.1.08	R H Jowett	(Derbyhaven, Isle of Man)	6.08
			(OK-MAL), SP-NXY, SP-NAC				
M-RLIV	Bombardier CL-600-2B16 *(Challenger 605)*	5731	C-FPQT	28.3.08	Mobyhold Ltd	(London E1)	2.09
M-RURU	Dassault Falcon 900B	140	N900UT	31.10.07	Opus Nominees Ltd	Luton	2.09
			N70HS, VR-CES, F-WWFL				
M-SAIR	Dassault Falcon 900B	141	C-GHML	21.9.07	W A Developments International Ltd	Carlisle	1.09
			XA-OVA, XA-OVR, N141FJ, F-WWFK *(Operated Stobart Air)*				
M-SHEP	Socata TBM-700N (TBM-850)	467		27.8.08	L W and J K Shephard	Lydd	1.09
M-SKSM	Bombadier BD-700-1A11 Global 5000	9227	M-LLGC	22.12.08	Tesker Management Ltd	Douglas	
			C-FJNZ				
M-SKZL	Bombardier CL-600-2B16 *(Challenger 604)*	5404	VP-BGO	4.9.08	Kerzner Investment Management Ltd	(Tortola, BVI)	2.09
			C-GLYO				

M-SMJJ	Cessna 414A	414A0425	G-SMJJ N2694H	17. 6.08	Gull Air Ltd	Guernsey	10.08
M-SSSV	Bombardier Learjet 60	60-325	P4-SSV N5013Y	21.11.08	Distant Horizon Ltd	Douglas	
M-STCO	Dassault Falcon F2000EX	110	VP-BAK F-WWMG	23. 7.08	STC (Bermuda) Ltd	(Hamilton, Bermuda)	10.08
M-TEAM	Cessna 525 CitationJet CJ1+	525-0609	N50VC N5161J	22.10.08	Mistral Aviation Ltd	Guernsey	1.09
M-TSRI	Beech C90GT King Air	LJ-1795	N90GE N90GP, N7295T	27. 6.08	Timpson Ltd	Manchester	1.09
M-URUS	Boeing 737-7GC (BBJ)	34622	P4-RUS N357BJ	17. 7.08	Ingram Services Ltd	(Tortola, BVI)	1.09
M-USCA	SOCATA TBM-850	456		19. 6.08	Sterna Aviation Ltd	(Santon, IoM)	11.08
M-USHY	Cessna 441 Conquest	441-0209	N711GE N2728G	7. 5.08	Flying Dogs Ltd	Guernsey	1.09
M-VRNY	Gulfstream Aerospace Gulfstream V-SP (Gulfstream 550)	5225					
M-WMWM	Cessna 525A CitationJet CJ2	525A0113	G-OJCT N525VV	16. 4.08	Standard Aviation Ltd	Farnborough	2.09
M-WOOD	Cessna 550 Citation Bravo	550-1042	G-OJMW G-ORDB, N51869	3.12.08	Horizon Air Charter LLP	Gloucestershie	1.09
M-XONE	Cessna 525A CitationJet CJ2	525A-0031	VP-BFC N312CJ, N5204D	20. 6.07	Newshore Ltd	Biggin Hill	12.08
M-YAIR	Hawker 390 Premier 1A	RB-146	N1CR N6146J	16. 4.08	RB209 IOM Ltd	Blackpool	1.09
M-YAKW	Cessna 208B Grand Caravan	208B1059	G-OAKW N4024W, N5075K	1.11.07	A K Webb	Wellesbourne Mountford	11.08
M-YCHT	Eurocopter EC.135T2+	0630		20. 3.08	Longbay Ltd	Blackbushe	12.08
M-YEDT	Gulfstream Aviation Gulfstream 100	141	N223GA CC-CWK, N106GX, 4X-CVI	10. 3.08	Opal Consulting LLC	(Ramsey, IoM)	11.08
M-YGTS	Cirrus SR20 GTS	1972	N496PG	28. 8.08	Stamp Aviation Ltd	Shoreham	9.08
M-YJET	Dassault Falcon 2000LX	148	F-WWGE	30. 7.08	My Jet Ltd	Biggin Hill	10.08
M-YNJC	Embraer EMB-135BJ Legacy	14500961	G-ONJC PT-SFI	31. 8.07	Newjetco (Europe) Ltd	London Stansted	12.08
M-YSKY	Raytheon 390 Premier 1A	RB-209	N209BP	6.11.07	RB209 IOM Ltd	Blackpool	1.09
M-YWAY	Agusta A109F	22098		28.10.08	Trustair Ltd	Blackpool	1.09

PART 2 – AIRCRAFT CANCELLED IN 2008 AND 2009

Registration	Type	Construction No	Previous Identity	Date	Registered Owner (Operator)	Cancellation Details	Date
M-ISSY	British Aerospace BAe 125 Series 800B	258043	N937BC N313CQ, N313CC, N319AT,	11. 8.08	Total Aero Service (UK) Ltd (D-CAZH), G-5-12	To HA-YFI	18.11.08
M-LLGC	Bombardier BD-700-1A11 Global 5000	9227	C-FJNZ	31.10.07	LL Avia Management SA	To M-SKSM	22.12.08
M-SVNX	Dassault Falcon 7X	20	F-WW	30. 9.08	Transcontinental Wings SA	To OH-FFD	30.10.08
M-TAGB	Bombardier BD-100-1A10 (Challenger 300)	20172	C-	3. 7.08	Execujet Europe GmbH	To D-BAVA	31.10.08

SECTION 4

PART 1 – UK & EIRE CIVIL REGISTERED AIRCRAFT IN MUSEUMS AND PRIVATE COLLECTIONS

Publication by Air-Britain in 2008 of Bob Ogden's third *"Aviation Museums and Collections"* series book covering *"The Rest of the World (excluding Europe and North America)"* has enabled Barrie Womersley to update many of the entries below. Details are only shown for those individual aircraft and replicas, formerly with a UK registration provenance, which are readily accessible to public viewing. Some Museums and collections also hold aircraft with current UK Certificates of Registration and these entries are cross-referenced to their relevant Sections. Full access details to these museums, and a great deal more information, can be found in Bob Ogden's three books. (Note 'fsm' is a Full Scale Model)

Also many thanks to Ken Ellis' 21st edition of "Wrecks and Relics", published in 2008, for numerous UK updates.

Registration	Type	Construction No	Previous Id	Date	Remarks	CofA Expy
ENGLAND						
BEDFORDSHIRE						
Stondon Transport Museum, Lower Stondon (www.transportmuseum.co.uk)						
G-AXOM	Penn-Smith Gyroplane	DJPS.1		26. 9.69	Cancelled 11.10.74 as WFU	24. 2.71P
	(Volkswagen 1600)					
BAPC.77	Mignet HM.14 Pou-Du-Ciel				*(As "G-ADRG")*	
	(Citroen 425cc) *(Modern reproduction)*					
Richard Shuttleworth Trustees, Shuttleworth Airfield, Shuttleworth-Old Warden (www.shuttleworth.org)						
G-BSSY	Polikarpov Po-2	xxxx	YU-CLJ	6.11.90	Cancelled 23. 6.94 by CAA - sold as N588NB 7.94	
			Yugoslav JRV 0094		*(As fictitious "ZK-POZ")*	
BAPC.1	Avro Triplane Type IV replica				Retrospectively G-ARSG as per SECTION 1, Part 2	
BAPC.2	Bristol Boxkite replica				Retrospectively G-ASPP as per SECTION 1, Part 2	
BAPC.3	Bleriot Type XI				Retrospectively G-AANG (2) as per SECTION 1, Part 2	
BAPC.4	Deperdussin Monoplane				Retrospectively G-AANH (2) as per SECTION 1, Part 2	
BAPC.5	Blackburn Single Seat Monoplane				Retrospectively G-AANI (2) as per SECTION 1, Part 2	
BAPC.8	Dixon Ornithopter reconstruction					
BAPC.11	English Electric S.1 Wren composite				Originally G-EBNV as per SECTION 1, Part 2	
BAPC.271	Messerschmitt Me 163B Komet fsm				*(As "191454")*	
	(Walter HWK 509A-2 rocket motor) *(Wingless)*					
BGA.580	EoN AP.7 Primary				Details in SECTION 6, Part 1	
BGA.2932	Fauvel AV.36C				Details in SECTION 6, Part 1	
BERKSHIRE						
Museum of Berkshire Aviation, Royal Berkshire Aviation Society and The Herald Society (+) ,Woodley						
G-AJJP	Fairey FB.2 Jet Gyrodyne	F.9420 & FB.2		1. 3.47	Cancelled 9.11.50 - to RAF as XD759 *(As "XJ389")*	
G-AKKY	Miles M.14A Hawk Trainer 3	2078	T9841	23. 6.48	Cancelled 12. 4.73 as WFU *(As "L6906")*	6.11.64
	(Also allocated BAPC.44 to reflect rebuild status from various parts)				*(WFU 11.60)*	
G-APWA	Handley Page HPR.7 Dart Herald 100 (+) 149		PP-SDM	28. 9.59	Cancelled 29. 1.87 as WFU	6. 4.82T
			G-APWA, PP-SDM, PP-ASV, G-APWA *(BEA titles)*			
BAPC.233	Broburn Wanderlust sailplane	---			*Built 1946*	
BAPC.248	McBroom Hang Glider	---			*Built 1974*	
BGA.529	EoN AP.5 Olympia 1	EoN/O/017	RAFGSA.103		*Crashed 31.10.57*	
			BGA.529			
BGA 562	EoN AP.5 Olympia 2B	EoN/O/037	G-ALJZ			
			G-ALMN			
BGA 589	EoN AP.7 Primary	EoN/P/012	BGA 589			
BRISTOL						
City Museum and Art Gallery, Clifton (www.bristol-city.gov.uk/museums)						
BAPC.40	Bristol Boxkite reconstruction				*(Built for "Those Magnificent Men in Their Flying Machines"*	
	(Gnome)	BOX 3 & BM.7281			*1965 film)*	
Bristol Aero Collection, Filton *(also see Gloucestershire and Kemble)*						
G-BOAF	British Aircraft Corporation Concorde Type 1 Variant 102			12. 6.80	Cancelled 4. 5.04 as WFU	11. 6.04T
		216 & 100-016	G-N94AF, G-BFKX			
BUCKINGHAMSHIRE						
Royal Air Force High Wyconbe						
BAPC.223	Hawker Hurricane I fsm				*(As "V7467:LE-D" in RAF 242 Sqdn c/s)*	
CAMBRIDGESHIRE						
Imperial War Museum, Duxford (www.iwm.org.uk)						
EI-AUY	Morane-Saulnier MS.502 Criquet	338	F-BCDG	30.11.70	Cancellation details not known	
	(Argus AS.10)		French Military		*(On loan from G Warner) (As "CF+HF" in Luftwaffe c/s)*	
G-ACUU	Cierva C.30A	726	(G-AIXE)	26. 6.34	Cancelled 14.11.88 as WFU *(As "HM580:KX-K")*	30. 4.60
	(Avro 671) (AS Civet)		HM580, G-ACUU		*(WFU 4.60)*	
G-AFBS	Miles M.14A Hawk Trainer 3	539	(G-AKKU)	17. 9.37	Cancelled 22.12.95 by CAA	25. 2.63
			BB661, G-AFBS		*(Dismantled and unmarked 4.08)*	
G-AHTW	Airspeed AS.40 Oxford 1	3083	V3388	6. 6.46	Cancelled 3. 4.89 by CAA *(As "V3388")*	15.12.60
G-ALCK	Percival Proctor III	H.536	LZ766	18. 6.48	WFU *(As "LZ766")*	19. 6.63
G-AMDA	Avro 652A Anson 1	xxxx	N4877	20. 7.50	Cancelled 9. 9.81 by CAA *(As "N4877:MK-V")*	14.12.62
G-ASKC	de Havilland DH.98 Mosquito TT.35	xxxx	TA719	8. 7.63	Crashed 27. 7.64 *(As "TA719:6 T")*	18. 1.64
G-BCYK	Avro (Canada) CF-100 Canuck Mk.IV	xxxx	RCAF 18393	18. 3.75	Cancelled 15. 9.81 as WFU *(As "18393" in RCAF c/s)*	
G-BEDV	Vickers 668 Varsity T.1	xxxx	WJ945	26. 7.76	Cancelled 15. 6.89 by CAA *(As "WJ945:21")*	15.10.87P
G-BESY	British Aircraft Corporation 167 Strikemaster Mk.80A			26. 4.77	Cancelled 7.77 *(As "1133" in Saudi c/s)*	
	(Officially registered as Mk.88)	PS.364	G-27-299, Saudi AF 1133, G-27-299			

G-LANC	Avro 683 Lancaster B.X	xxxx	RCAF KB889	31. 1.85	Cancelled 2. 9.91 by CAA	
	(Built Victory Aircraft, Canada)				(As "KB889:NA-I" in RAF 428 Sqdn c/s)	
G-LIZY	Westland Lysander III	"504/39"	RCAF 1558	20. 6.86	Cancelled 18. 4.89 as WFU	
	(C/n also quoted as "Y1351")		V9300		(As "V9673:MA-J" in RAF 161 Sqdn c/s)	
G-USUK	Colt 2500A Balloon (Hot Air)	1100		1. 6.87	Cancelled 21. 8.90 as WFU "Virgin Atlantic Flyer"	19. 8.87P
	(On loan from Virgin Atlantic Airways Ltd) (Gondola displayed - remainder stored)					
BAPC.93	Fieseler Fi 103 (V-1)					
BAPC.267	Hawker Hurricane fsm				(As "P2954:WX-E" in RAF c/s)	

American Air Museum, Duxford

G-BFYO	SPAD XIII replica	0035	D-EOWM	16.11.78	Cancelled 14.10.86 as WFU	21. 6.82P
	(Built Williams Flugzeugbau) (Lycoming AIO-360)				(As "1 4513 S" in 3rd Escadrille French AF c/s)	
G-BHDK	Boeing TB-29A-45-BN Superfortress	11225	44-61748	27. 9.79	Cancelled 29. 2.84 as WFU	
					"Hawg Wild" (As "461748:Y" in USAF c/s)	
G-BHUB	Douglas C-47A-85DL Dakota	19975	"G-AGIV"	30. 4.80	Cancelled 19.10.81 as WFU	
			Spanish AF T3-29, N51V, N9985F, SE-BBH, 43-15509 (As "315509:W7-S" in USAAF c/s)			
BAPC.255	North American P-51D Mustang fsm				(As "463209:WZ-S" in 78th FG c/s)	
	(Built Rialto, CA, US 1990)					

Duxford Aviation Society, Duxford

G-ALDG	Handley Page HP.81 Hermes IV	HP.81/8		27.10.49	Cancelled 12.10.62 as PWFU	9. 1.63
					"Horsa" (BOAC c/s) (Fuselage only)	
G-ALFU	de Havilland DH.104 Dove 6	04234		14.12.48	Cancelled 14.11.72 as PWFU	4. 6.71
G-ALWF	Vickers 701 Viscount	5		2. 1.50	Cancelled 18. 4.72 as PWFU (BEA c/s)	16. 4.72
G-ALZO (2)	Airspeed AS.57 Ambassador 2	5226	R Jordan AF 108	5. 4.50	Cancelled 10. 9.81 as PWFU (Dan-Air c/s)	14. 5.71
			G-ALZO, (G-AMAD)			
G-ANTK	Avro 685 York C.1	xxxx		MW232	23. 7.54 Cancelled 27.10.64 as PWFU (Dan Air c/s)	29.10.64T
G-AOVT	Bristol 175 Britannia 312	13427		23. 6.58	Cancelled 21. 9.81 as PWFU (Monarch c/s)	11. 3.75T
G-APDB	de Havilland DH.106 Comet 4	6403	9M-AOB	2. 5.57	Cancelled 18. 2.74 as PWFU (Dan-Air c/s)	7.10.74
			G-APDB			
G-APWJ	Handley Page HPR.7 Dart Herald 201	158		28. 9.59	Cancelled 10. 7.85 as PWFU (Air UK c/s)	21.12.85
G-ASGC	Vickers Super VC-10 Series 1151	853		11. 4.63	Cancelled 22. 4.80 as PWFU (BOAC-Cunard c/s)	20. 4.80
G-AVFB	Hawker Siddeley HS.121 Trident 2E	2141	5B-DAC	1. 2.67	Cancelled 9. 7.82 as PWFU (BEA c/s)	30. 9.82
			G-AVFB			
G-AVMU	British Aircraft Corporation One-Eleven 510ED			11. 5.67	Cancelled 12. 7.93 as PWFU (British Airways c/s)	8. 1.95T
			BAC.148		"County of Dorset"	
G-AXDN	British Aircraft Corporation Concorde	01		16. 4.69	Cancelled 10.11.86 as PWFU	30. 9.77
	(Officially registered with Bristol c/n 13522)					

CHESHIRE
Hooton Park Trust and Griffin Trust (+), Hooton Park

G-AGPG	Avro 652A Anson 19 Series 2	1212		15. 6.45	Cancelled 5.11.75 as PWFU	13. 2.71
	(Originally registered as Anson XII, to Anson XIX in 1.47 and to Avro 19 Series.2 in 5.52) (On loan from The Aeroplane Collection)					
BAPC.68	Hawker Hurricane fsm (+)		"P3975"		(Built for "Battle of Britain" film) (As "P2725:TM-B")	
BGA.791	Slingsby T.8 Tutor	xxxx	VM684		(On loan from P Storrar) (As "VM684")	

CORNWALL
Land's End Theme Park, Land's End (www.landsend-landmark.co.uk)

| G-BCXO | MBB Bö.105DD | S.80 | D-HDCE | 27. 2.75 | Cancelled 4. 3.92 as PWFU | |
| | (C/n S.80 is the original pod, replaced 1992 and subsequently rebuilt as display piece with fictitious marks "G-CDBS") | | | | | |

CUMBRIA
Solway Aviation Museum, Carlisle (www.solway-aviation-museum.org.uk)

G-APLG	Auster J/5L Aiglet Trainer	3148		4. 3.58	Cancelled 11. 2.99 by CAA	26.10.68
G-BJWY	Sikorsky S-55 (HRS-2) Whirlwind HAR.21		A2576	25. 1.82	Cancelled 23. 2.94 by CAA (As "WV198:K")	
		55xxx	WV198, Bu.130191		(On loan from D.Charles)	

RAF Millom and Militaria Museum, Haverigg (www.rafmillom.co.uk)

G-AMLZ	Percival P.50 Prince 6E	P.46	(VR-TBN)	23.11.51	Cancelled 9.10.84 as PWFU	18. 6.71
G-BIHN	Airship Industries Skyship 500 Airship (Gas Filled)			2.11.80	Cancelled 31. 1.91 by CAA	1. 4.79
		1214/02			(Destroyed San Francisco, Ca, US 1985: gondola only)	
G-PLAH	British Aerospace Jetstream Series 3102	640	G-LOVA	1.11.99	Cancelled 22. 1.08 by CAA	26. 7.02T
			G-OAKA, G-BUFM, G-LAKH, G-BUFM, N410MX, G-31-640 (Nose only)			
BAPC.231	Mignet HM.14 Pou-Du-Ciel				(On loan from South Copeland Aviation Group)	
	(Thought originally built Ulverston 1936 with Anzani engine)				(As "G-ADRX")	
BAPC.260	Mignet HM.280					

DEVON
Trago Mills Shopping Mall, Newton Abbot (www.trago.co.uk)

| G-BDDX | Whittaker MW2B Excalibur | 001 | | 28. 5.75 | Cancelled 23. 6.83 as PWFU | |
| | (Built M W Whittaker - pr.no PFA 041-10106) (Volkswagen 1500) | | | | | |

DORSET
BournemouthAviation Museum, Wonderland Family Adventure Park, Bournemouth Airport (www.aviation-museum.co.uk)

G-ASER	Piper PA-23-250 Aztec B	27-2283		28. 1.63	Cancelled 24.11.72 as PWFU	17. 8.74
					(Crashed into Nigg Bay, Cromarty, Aberdeen 14. 9.72)	
G-BKRL	Chichester-Miles Leopard	001		21. 3.83	Cancelled 25.1.99 as PWFU	14.12.91P
	(Built Designability Ltd) (Noel Penny 301)					
G-DUSK	de Havilland DH.115 Vampire T.11	15596	XE856	1.12.99	Details in SECTION 1, Part 2	
G-OPAS	Vickers 806 Viscount	263	G-AOYN	5.10.94	Cancelled 28. 7.97 as destroyed (nose only)	26. 3.97T
					(Wfu at Southend 6.96 and broken up), (Parcelforce colours)	

GLOUCESTERSHIRE
Bristol Aero Collection, Kemble (www.bristolaero.com)

G-ALBN	Bristol 173 Mk.1	12871	7648M	22. 7.48	Cancelled 21. 7.60 - to RAF as XF785 in 1953 (*As "XF785"*)
			XF785		
G-ALRX	Bristol 175 Britannia Series 101	12874	(WB473)	25. 6.51	Cancelled 5. 4.54 as PWFU
			(VX447)		(*DBR landing Littleton-upon-Severn 4. 2.54*)
					(*Nose only - on loan from Britannia Aircraft Preservation Trust*)
G-ATDD	Beagle B.206 Series 1	B.013	(VH-85)	27. 4.65	Cancelled 9. 4.74 as PWFU (*Nose only*)
	(*Originally a Beagle B.206R - to Series 1 1966*)		G-ATDD		(*Undercarriage collapsed Sherburn 6.73*)
BAPC.87	Bristol 30/46 Babe III reconstruction	1			(*As "G-EASQ"*)
	(*Built W.Sneesby*)				

Britannia Aircraft Preservation Trust, Kemble

G-BDUP	Bristol 175 Britannia Series .253	13508	EL-WXA	31. 3.76	Cancelled 9. 8.84 to CU-T120 (*As "XM496" in RAF c/s*)
			CU-T120, G-BDUP, XM496		

HAMPSHIRE
Farnborough Air Sciences Trust (FAST Museum) Farnborough

G-AWZI	Hawker Siddeley HS.121 Trident 3B Series 101			14. 1.69	Cancelled 9. 7.87 as destroyed	5. 8.85T
	2310				(*WFU 1. 5.85: cockpit only*)	

Whittle Memorial, Ively, Farnborough

BAPC.285	Gloster E28/39 fsm	
	(*Built Sir Frank Whittle Commemorative Trust*)	

Prince's Mead Shopping Centre, Farnborough

BAPC.208	Royal Aircraft Factory SE.5A	(*As "D276:A"*)
	(*Built AJD Engineering*)	

Second World War Aircraft Preservation Society, Lasham

G-APIT	Percival P.40 Prentice 1	PAC-016	VR192	28.11.57	Cancelled 8.11.79 as PWFU (*As "VR192"*)	7. 9.67
G-APXX	de Havilland DHA.3 Drover 2	5014	VH-EAS	15.12.59	Cancelled 26.11.73 as PWFU - registration not taken up	
			VH-EAZ		(*As "VH-FDT"*)	

Museum of Army Flying, AAC Middle Wallop (www.flying-museum.org.uk)

G-ABOX (2)	Sopwith Pup				Details in SECTION 1, Part 2	
G-AKKR	Miles M.14A Hawk Trainer 3	1995	"T9967"	23. 6.48	Cancelled 16. 7.69 as PWFU (*As "T9707"*)	10. 4.65
	(*May be T9967 [2160] from 1943 rebuild*)		8378M, G-AKKR, T9708			
G-AKOW	Taylorcraft J Auster 5	1579	PH-NAD (2)	23.12.47	Cancelled 5. 8.87 as PWFU (*As "TJ569"*)	26. 6.82
	(*Regd as c/n TJ569A after rebuild in Holland*)		PH-NEG, G-AKOW, TJ569			
G-APOI	Saunders-Roe Skeeter Series 8				Details in SECTION 1, Part 2	
G-APXW	Lancashire Aircraft EP-9 Prospector	43		22.12.59	Cancelled 20. 5.82 as PWFU	22. 5.76
					(*Composite rebuild ex G-APWZ and others*) (*As "XM819" in Army c/s*)	
G-ARYD	Auster AOP.6	xxxx	WJ358	8. 3.62	Cancelled 5. 8.87 as PWFU (*As "WJ358"*)	
					(*Conversion abandoned 9.63*)	
G-AXKS	Westland-Bell 47G-4A	WA.723	G-17-8	22. 7.69	Cancelled 22. 4.82 as PWFU	21. 9.82
G-SARO	Saro Skeeter AOP.12				Details in SECTION 1, Part 2	
BAPC.80	Airspeed AS.58 Horsa II				(*Composite from LH208, TL659 and 8569M*) (*As "KJ351"*)	
BAPC.163	AFEE 10/42 Rotachute Rotabuggy reconstruction				(*On loan from Wessex Aviation Society*) (*As "B-415"*)	
BAPC.185	WACO CG-4A Hadrian Glider				(*Fuselage only*) (*As "243809"*)	
BAPC.261	General Aircraft Hotspur replica				(*As "HH379"*)	
	(*Composite from anonymous cockpit of Mk.1 and rear of Mk.II, HH379*)					
BGA 285	Slingsby T.6 Kite 1	247A	G-ALNH		(*As "G-2-4" in 1 GTS RAF c/s*)	
			BGA 285			

Solent Sky, Southampton (www.spitfireonline.co.uk)

G-ADWO	de Havilland DH.82A Tiger Moth	3455	BB807	9.12.35	Cancelled 15. 9.58 as destroyed (*As "BB807"*)	
			G-ADWO			
	(*Restored 3.51 and overhauled with fuselage of BB860 (ex G-ADXT); damaged landing Christchurch 31. 7.58 and WFU:*					
	fuselage/parts ex G-AOAC and parts ex G-AOJJ used in composite rebuild 1987/90: completed to static condition 1990)					
G-ALZE	Britten-Norman BN-1F	1		16. 3.50	Cancelled 8. 6.89 as PWFU	
G-BRDV	Replica Viking Spitfire prototype			3. 7.89	Cancelled 19.5.00 as PWFU	18. 2.95P
		PFA 130-10796			(*As "K5054" in RAF c/s*)	
	(*Built Viking Wood Products - c/n HD36/001*) (*Jaguar V-12 350hp*)				(*On loan from Replica Spitfire Ltd*)	
G-RNLI	Vickers Supermarine 236 Walrus 1				Details in SECTION1, Part 2	
G-SWIF	Vickers Supermarine 552 Swift F.7	VA.9597	XF114	1. 6.90	Cancelled 19. 7.04 as PWFU	
BAPC.7	Southampton University Man Powered Aircraft (SUMPAC)					
BAPC.164	Wight Quadraplane Type 1 fsm				(*As "N248"*)	
BAPC.210	Avro 504J				(*As "C4451"*)	
	(*Built AJD Engineering*) (*Gnome Monosoupape 100hp*)					
BAPC.215	Airwave Hang Glider					
BAPC.253	Mignet HM.14 Pou-Du-Ciel replica				(*Built 1990s*) (*As "G-ADZW"*) (*On loan from H.Shore*)	

HERTFORDSHIRE
de Havilland Aircraft Heritage Centre, Salisbury Hall, London Colney (www.dehavillandmuseum.co.uk)

G-ABLM	Cierva C.24	710		22. 4.31	Cancelled as PWFU 12.34	16. 1.35
	(*DH Gipsy III*)				(*On loan from Science Museum*)	
G-ADOT	de Havilland DH.87B Hornet Moth	8027	X9326	?.11.35	Cancelled as PWFU	15.10.59
					G-ADOT	
G-AFOJ	de Havilland DH.94 Moth Minor				Details in SECTION1 Part 2	
G-AKDW	de Havilland DH.89A Dragon Rapide				Details in SECTION1 Part 2	
G-AMXR	de Havilland DH.104 Dove 6	04379	D-CFSB	21. 1.53	Cancelled 22. 7.54 - to D-CFSB 7.54	
			G-AMXR, N4280V		(*Subsequently to and displayed as D-IFSB*)	
G-ANRX	de Havilland DH.82A Tiger Moth	3863	N6550	25. 5.54	PWFU 20. 6.61 *"Border City"*	20. 6.61

G-AOJT	de Havilland DH.106 Comet IXB	06020	F-BGNX	11. 5.56	Cancelled 9. 7.56 as PWFU	5. 7.56
					(Fuselage only) (As "F-BGNX" in Air France titles)	
G-AOTI	de Havilland DH.114 Heron 2D	14107	G-5-19	25. 7.56	Cancelled 17.10.95 as PWFU *(Unmarked)*	24. 6.87T
G-AREA	de Havilland DH.104 Dove 8	04520		3. 8.60	Cancelled 19. 9.00 by CAA	18. 9.87
G-ARYC	de Havilland DH.125 Series 1	25003		1. 3.62	Cancelled 31. 3.76 as PWFU *(WFU 1.8.73)*	1. 8.73
G-AVFH	Hawker Siddeley HS.121 Trident 2E	2147		1. 2.67	Cancelled 12. 5.82 *(Forward fuselage only)*	18. 5.83T
					(WFU 24.10.81)	
G-AWJV	de Havilland DH.98 Mosquito TT.35	xxxx	TA634	21. 5.68	Cancelled 19.10.70 as PWFU	
					(As "TA634:8K-K" in RAF 571 Sqdn c/s)	
G-BBNC	de Havilland DHC-1 Chipmunk T.10	C1/0682	WP790	12.10.73	Cancelled 23. 9.74 as PWFU *(As "WP790:T")*	
G-BLKA	de Havilland DH.112 Venom FB.Mk.54 (FB.4)		(G-VENM (1))	13. 7.84	Cancelled 13.10.00 by CAA	14. 7.95P
	(Built F + W) (Officially regd as c/n 431)	960	Swiss AF J-1790		*(Unmarked pod only)*	
G-VNOM	de Havilland DH.112 Venom FB.50 (FB.1)				Details in SECTION1 Part 2	
BAPC.186	de Havilland DH.82B Queen Bee composite		"K3584"		*(As "LF789:R2-K")*	
			(Original p/i not known)			
BAPC.216	de Havilland DH.88 Comet fsm				*(As "G-ACSS")*	
BAPC.232	Airspeed AS.58 Horsa I/II Glider composite				*(Composite airframe from unidentified components)*	

KENT

Brenzett Aeronautical Museum Trust, Brenzett, Romney Marsh (www.brenzettaero.co.uk)

G-AMSM	Douglas C-47B-20-DK Dakota	15764/27209	KN274	28. 4.52	Cancelled 11. 9.78 as PWFU	
			43-49948		*(Ground-looped on take-off Lydd 17. 8.78) (Nose only)*	

Dover Museum, Dover (www.dovermuseum.co.uk)

BAPC.290   Fieseler Fi.104 flying-bomb fsm

National Battle of Britain Memorial, Capel Le Ferne, Folkestone (www.battleofbritainmemorial.org)

BAPC.291	Hawker Hurricane I fsm			*(As "P2970:US-X" in RAF 56 Sqdn c/s)*
	(Built GB Replicas)			"Little Willie"
BAPC.299	Supermarine Spitfire I fsm			*(As "R6775:YT-J" in RAF 72 Sqdn c/s)'*
	(Built GB Replicas)			

Kent Battle of Britain Museum, Hawkinge (www.kbobm.org)

BAPC.36	Fieseler Fi 103 (V-1) fsm			*(Built for "Operation Crossbow" film)*
BAPC.63	Hawker Hurricane fsm		"L1592"	*(As "P3208:SD-T" in RAF 501 Sqdn c/s)*
				(Built for "Battle of Britain" film)
BAPC.64	Hawker Hurricane fsm			*(As "P3059:SD-N" in RAF 501 Sqdn c/s)*
				(Built for "Battle of Britain" film)
BAPC.65	Supermarine Spitfire fsm			*(As "N3289:DW-K" in RAF 610 Sqdn c/s)*
				(Built for "Battle of Britain" film)
BAPC.66	Messerschmitt Bf109 fsm	1480		*(As "480:6") (Built for "Battle of Britain" film)*
BAPC.67	Messerschmitt Bf109 fsm			*(As "14" in JG52 c/s) (Built for "Battle of Britain" film)*
BAPC.69	Supermarine Spitfire fsm			*(As "N3313:KL-B" in RAF 54 Sqdn c/s)*
				(Built for "Battle of Britain" film)
BAPC.74	Messerschmitt Bf109 fsm	6357		*(As "6357:6") (Built for "Battle of Britain" film)*
BAPC.133	Fokker Dr.1 fsm			*(As "425/17")*
BAPC.272	Hawker Hurricane fsm			*(As "N2532:GZ-H" in RAF 32 Sqdn c/s)*
BAPC.273	Hawker Hurricane fsm			*(As "P2921:GZ-L" in RAF 32 Sqdn c/s)*
BAPC.278	Hawker Hurricane fsm			*(As "P3679:GZ-K" in RAF 32 Sqdn c/s)*
BAPC.297	Supermarine Spitfire reproduction			*(As "K5054")*

LEICESTERSHIRE

Aeropark, Nottingham East Midlands Airport *(www.eastmidlandsairport.com)*

G-APES	Vickers 953C Vanguard Merchantman	721		9. 9.57	Cancelled 28. 2.97 as WFU *(Nose only)* "Swiftsure"	2.10.95T
G-BAMH	Westland S-55 Whirlwind Series 3	WA.83	VR-BEP	10. 1.73	Cancelled 31.10.73 - to VR-BEP *(As "XG588 in SAR c/s)*	
			G-BAMH, XG588			
G-BEOZ	Armstrong-Whitworth AW.650 Argosy	1016660	N895U	28. 3.77	Cancelled 19.11.87 as WFU "Fat Albert"	28. 5.86T
			N6502R, G-1-7		*(Elan titles)*	
G-BHDD	Vickers 668 Varsity T.1	xxxx	WL626	18.10.79	Details in SECTION 1, Part 2	
(G-BLMC)	Avro 698 Vulcan B.2A		XM575	R	Reservation 8.84 not taken up *(As "XM575")*	
G-FRJB	Aircraft Designs Sheriff SA-1	0001		18. 5.81	Cancelled 6. 2.87 by CAA	
					(Not completed: unfinished airframe without marks)	

Snibston Discovery Park, Coalville

G-AFTN	Taylorcraft Plus C2	102	HL535	2. 5.39	Cancelled 13. 1.99 by CAA	1.11.57
			G-AFTN			
G-AGOS	Reid and Sigrist RS.4 Desford Trainer	3	VZ728	?. 5.45	Cancelled 9.11.81 as PWFU *(As "VZ728")*	28.11.80P
			G-AGOS			
G-AIJK	Auster V J/4 Archer	2067		13.11.46	Cancelled 8. 8.68 as PWFU	24. 8.68

Charnwood Museum, Loughborough

G-AJRH	Auster J/1N Alpha	2606		12. 5.47	Cancelled 18. 1.99 by CAA	5. 6.69

Whittle Memorial, A426 Lutterworth

BAPC.284	Gloster E28/39 fsm	xxxx				
	(Built Sir Frank Whittle Commemorative Trust)					

Cold War Jets Collection, Bruntingthorpe, Lutterworth

G-CPDA	de Havilland DH.106 Comet 4C	6473	XS235	10. 8.00	Cancelled 27. 3.08 as PWFU "Canopus"	

Stanford Hall and Percy Pilcher Museum, Stanford Hall, Stanford (www.stanfordhall.co.uk)

BAPC.45	Pilcher Hawk Glider reconstruction	xxxx				
	(Built Armstrong-Whitworth Aviation apprentices 1957/58)					

LINCOLNSHIRE
Lightning Association, Binbrook (www.lightning association.org.uk)
G-BTSY   English Electric Lightning F.6   95207   XR724   25. 7.91   Cancelled 26. 5.92 as TWFU - no Permit issued
                                                                              (As "XR724")

Battle of Britain Memorial Flight, RAF Coningsby (www.bbmf.co.uk)
G-AISU   Vickers Supermarine 349 Spitfire LF.VB   AB910   25.10.46   Cancelled 22. 8.55 as transferred to Military Marks
                                            CBAF.1061   *(As "AB910:IR-G" in RAF 222 Sqdn c/s)*
G-AMAU   Hawker Hurricane IIc   xxxx   PZ865   1. 5.50   Cancelled 19.12.72 as transferred to Military Marks
         (12,780th and final Hurricane built)   *(As "PZ865:JX-E" in RAFSEAC c/s)*
G-AWIJ   Vickers Supermarine 329 Spitfire IIA CBAF.14   P7350   25. 4.68   Cancelled 29. 2.84 to MOD
                                                                              (As "P7350:XT-D" in RAF 603 Sqdn c/s) "Blue Peter"

Royal Air Force Digby
BAPC.229   Supermarine Spitfire IX fsm   xxxx   "L1096"   *(As "MJ832:DN-Y" in RAF 416 Sqdn c/s) "City of Oshawa"*

Lincolnshire Aviation Heritage Centre, East Kirkby (www.lincsaviation.co.uk)
G-ASXX   Avro 683 Lancaster B.VII   xxxx   (8375M)   22.10.64   Cancelled 16.2.79 as WFU
                                                   French Navy WU-15, NX611
         (As "NX611:LE-C" in RAF 630 Sqdn c/s "City of Sheffield" [starboard] and "NX611:DX-C" in RAF 57 Sqdn c/s "Just Jane" [port])

Thorpe Camp Visitor Centre, Woodhall Spa (www.thorpecamp.org.uk)
G-ANNN   de Havilland DH.82A Tiger Moth   84073   T5968   2. 2.54   Cancelled 6.11.00 as PWFU
BAPC.294   Fairchild Argus fsm

LONDON
Croydon Airport Visitor Centre, Croydon (www.croydon.gov.uk/airport-soc/)
G-ANKV   de Havilland DH.82A Tiger Moth   84166   T7793   30.12.53   Cancelled 9.56 - not converted
         (Provenance uncertain)   *(As "T7793" in RAF c/s)*
G-ANUO   de Havilland DH.114 Heron 2D   14062   27. 9.54   Cancelled 9. 8.96 as WFU   12. 9.86T
                                                                              (As "G-AOXL" in Morton Air Services c/s)

Royal Air Force Memorial Chapel, Biggin Hill
BAPC.219   Hawker Hurricane I fsm   xxxx   *(As "L1710:AL-D" in RAF 79 Sqdn c/s)*
BAPC.220   Supermarine Spitfire I fsm   xxxx   *(As "N3194:GR-Z" in RAF 92 Sqdn c/s)*

Royal Air Force Museum, Hendon (www.rafmuseum.org.uk)
G-EBIC   Royal Aircraft Factory.SE.5A   688/2404   "B4563"   26. 9.23   Cancelled 31.12.38   3. 9.30
         (Wolseley Viper 200hp) (Regd with c/n 687/2404) 9208M, G-EBIC, F937   *(WFU 9.30) (As "F938")*
G-EBJE   Avro 504K   927   (9205M)   16. 7.24   Cancelled 9.12.34 (As "E449")   29. 9.34
         (Includes components of Avro 548A G-EBKN ex E449)
G-AAMX (2)   American Moth Corporation DH.60GM Moth   NC926M   11. 9.86   Cancelled 19. 8.95 as WFU   7. 5.94P
         (DH Gipsy II)   125
G-AANJ (2)   Luft-Verkehrs Gesellschaft C.VI   4503   9239M   29.10.81   Cancelled 11.12.03 as WFU   16. 5.03P
         (Benz 230hp)   C7198, 18, "1594", C7198, 18   *(As "7198/18" in German Air Force c/s)*
         (Composite aircraft including parts from LVG 1594: captured 1916/17 and allotted RFC serial "XG7")
G-ABBB   Bristol 105A Bulldog IIA   7446   "K2227"   12. 6.30   Cancelled 22. 9.61 as PWFU
                                                   G-ABBB, R-11, G-ABBB   *(As "K2227")*
G-ABMR   Hawker Hart   H.H-1   "J9933"   28. 5.31   Cancelled 2. 2.59 - to "J9933" and later "J9941")
                                                   G-ABMR   *(As "J9941" in RAF 57 Sqdn c/s)*   11. 6.57
G-AETA   Caudron G.III   7487   OO-ELA   29. 1.37   Sold to RAF 1972
         (Anzani 90hp) (Also reported as c/n 5019 or 5021) O-BELA, (9203M)   *(As "3066" in RNAS c/s)*
G-AFDX   Hanriot HD.1   "HD.1"   OO-APJ   4. 5.38   Cancellation details not known
                                                   Belgian AF H-1, Belgian AF N75 *(As "HD-75")*
         (DBR landing Old Warden 17.6.39: wings destroyed in air raid Brooklands 1940, fuselage survived and rebuilt 1968)
G-AGYX   Douglas C-47A-10DK Dakota 3   12472   5N-ATA   15. 1.46   Cancelled 1.7.65 - to PH-MAG 7.65 *(Nose only)*
                                                   PH-MAG, G-AGYX, (OD-...), G-AGYX, KG437, 42-9264 *(Subsequently N9050T)*
G-AITB   Airspeed AS.40 Oxford 1   xxxx   MP425   1.11.46   WFU *(As "MP425" in RAF 1536 BATF c/s)*   24. 5.61
G-AIXA   Taylorcraft Plus D   134   LB264   13. 1.47   Cancelled 13.12.02 by CAA (As "LB264")   21. 2.02P
G-APUP   Sopwith Pup replica   B.5292 & PFA 1582   9213M   13. 2.59   Cancelled 4.10.84 by CAA (As "N5182")   28. 6.78
         (Built K C D St Cyrien) Le Rhone)   G-APUP, N5182
G-ATVP   Vickers FB.5 Gunbus replica VAFA-01 & FB.5   31. 5.66   Cancelled 27. 2.69 as WFU   6. 5.69
         (Built Vintage Aircraft and Flying Association) (Gnome Monosoupape 100 hp) *(As "2345" in RFC c/s)*
G-AWAU   Vickers FB.27A Vimy replica   VAFA-02   "H651"   8. 1.68   Cancelled 19. 7.73 as WFU   4.8.69
                                                                              (As "F8614") "Triple First"
G-BEOX   Lockheed 414 Hudson IIIA   414-6464   VH-AGJ   25. 3.77   Cancelled 22.12.81 as WFU
         (A-29A-LO)   VH-SMM, R.Australian AF A16-199, FH174, 41-36975 *(As "A16-199: SF-R")*
G-BFDE   Sopwith Tabloid Scout replica   168   22. 9.77   Cancelled 8.12.86 as WFU   4. 6.83P
         (Built D M Cashmore - pr.no.PFA 067-10186) (Continental PC.60)   *(As "168" in RNAS c/s)*
G-BIDW   Sopwith "1BD" Strutter replica   WA/5   "9382"   24. 9.80   Cancelled 4. 2.87 by CAA   29.12.80P
         (Built Westward Airways (Lands End) Ltd) (Le Clerget)   *(As "A8226" in RFC 45 Sqdn c/s)*
G-BLWM   Bristol 20 M.1C replica   -------   "C4912"   12. 3.85   Cancelled 12. 5.88 by CAA   12. 8.87P
         (Built D M Cashmore - pr.no.PFA 112-10862) (110 hp Gnome)   *(As "C4994" in RFC c/s)*
G-OIOI   EH Industries EH-101 Heliliner   50008   23.11.88   Cancelled 1. 4.96 - to MOD   5. 5.94P
         (Airframe No.PP8)   *(As "ZJ116")*
G-OTHL   Robinson R22 Beta   0738   G-DSGN   28.11.94   Cancelled 8. 2.00 as WFU (As "G-RAFM")   27. 4.03T
G-USTV   Messerschmitt Bf.109G-2/Trop   xxxx   8478M   26.10.90   Cancelled as PWFU 24. 9.98   30. 5.98P
         (Built Erla Maschinenwerk GmbH)   10639   RN228, Luftwaffe   *(As "10639:6" in Luftwaffe III/JG77 c/s)*
BAPC.83   Kawasaki Type 5 Model 1b (Ki 100)   8476M   *(As "24")*
BAPC.92   Fieseler Fi 103 (V-1)
BAPC.100   Clarke TWK   *(On loan from Science Museum)*
BAPC.106   Bleriot Type XI *(1910 original)*   9209M   *(As "164")*
           (Anzani 40hp)

BAPC.107   Bleriot Type XXVII (1911 original)   9202M
BAPC.165   Bristol F.2b Fighter   (As "E2466" in RAF 22 Sqdn c/s)
            (RR Falcon replica)
BAPC.181   Royal Aircraft Factory BE.2b reconstruction   (As "687")
            (Renault V8) (Restoration from original components)
BAPC.205   Hawker Hurricane IIc fsm   (As "BE421:XP-G" in RAF 174 Sqdn c/s)
BAPC.206   Supermarine Spitfire IX fsm   (As "MH486:FF-A" in RAF 132 Sqdn c/s)
BAPC.292   Eurofighter Typhoon fsm
BAPC.293   Supermarine Spitfire fsm
            (Built Concepts and Innovations)
BAPC.296   Army Balloon Factory Nulli reproduction

Royal Air Force, Bentley Priory, HQ 11/18 Groups
BAPC.217   Supermarine Spitfire I fsm   (As "K9926:JH-C" in RAF 317 Sqdn c/s)
BAPC.218   Hawker Hurricane IIc fsm   "P3386"   (As "BN230:FT-A"in RAF 43 Sqdn c/s)

Royal Air Force, Northolt
BAPC.221   Supermarine Spitfire LF.IX fsm   (As "EN526:SZ-G" in RAF 316 Sqdn c/s)

Royal Air Force, Uxbridge
BAPC.222   Supermarine Spitfire IX fsm   (As "BR600:SH-V" in RAF 64 Sqdn c/s)

Science Museum, South Kensington, London (www.sciencemuseum.org.uk)
G-EBIB   Royal Aircraft Factory SE.5A   687/2404   "F939"   26. 9.23   Cancelled 1.12.46   8. 8.35
            (Regd with c/n 688/2404)   G-EBIB, F937   (WFU)
G-AAAH   de Havilland DH.60G Moth   804   30. 8.28   Cancelled 12.31   23.12.30
            (Original but note two BAPC.reproductions depicted as "G-AAAH" exist –see below) "Jason"
G-ACWP   Cierva C.30A   728   AP507   24. 7.34   Cancelled 1. 6.40 on sale (Impressment)   6. 3.41
            (Avro 671)   G-ACWP   (As "AP507:KX-P" in RAF 529 Sqdn c/s)
G-ASSM   Hawker Siddeley HS.125 Series 1/522 25010   5N-AMK   5. 5.64   Cancelled 28. 5.80 as sold in Nigeria
                                                              G-ASSM
G-AWAW   Cessna F150F   F150-0037   OY-DKJ   5. 1.68   Cancelled 16. 5.90 as WFU   8. 6.92T
            (Built Reims Aviation SA) (Wichita c/n 15063167)
G-AZPH   Pitts S.1S   S1S-001-C   N11CB   13. 3.72   Cancelled 8. 1.97 as WFU   4. 9.91P
            (Lycoming IO-360)   "Neil Williams" (Ground-looped landing Little Snoring 10.5.91)
G-LIOA   Lockheed 10A Electra   1037   N5171N   6. 5.83   Cancelled 26. 4.02 as WFU
                                                              NC243, NC14959   (As "NC5171N")
BAPC.50   Roe Triplane Type I
            (1909 original) (JAP 9hp)
BAPC.51   Vickers FB.27 Vimy IV   13
            (Rebuild of 1919 original) (RR Eagle VIII 360hp)
BAPC.53   Wright Flyer reconstruction
            (Built Hatfield)
BAPC.54   JAP/Harding Monoplane
            (Built J.A.Prestwich & Co 1910) (Modified Bleriot XI) (JAP Anzani 45hp)
BAPC.55   Levasseur-Antoinette Developed Type VII Monoplane
            (1909 original) (Antoinette V8 50hp)
BAPC.56   Fokker E.III   (Captured at Somme, France 4.1916)
            (Oberusal 100hp)   (As "210/16") (Skeletal airframe)
BAPC.62   Cody Type V Biplane
            (1912 original) (Austro-Daimler 120hp)   (As "304")
BAPC.124   Lilienthal Glider Type XI reconstruction   (Display reproduction of BAPC.52 qv)

BAPC.199   Fieseler Fi 103 (V-1)   (As "442795")
BGA 2091   Schempp-Hirth HS.4 Standard Cirrus   396   AGA...   (As "DFY")   9. 5.02

Imperial War Museum, South Lambeth, London (www.iwm.org.uk)
BAPC.90   Colditz Cock replica   xxxx   (Built for BBC "The Colditz Story" film)
BAPC.198   Fieseler Fi 103 (V-1)   xxxx

MANCHESTER
Museum of Science and Industry in Manchester, Castlefield, Manchester (www.msim.org.uk)
G-EBZM   Avro 594A Avian IIIA   R3/CN/160   ?.7.28   Cancelled 1.12.46 by Secretary of State   20. 1.38
            (ADC Cirrus) (Fitted with parts from G-ABEE)   (On loan from The Aeroplane Collection)
G-ABAA   Avro 504K   xxxx   9244M   11. 9.30   Cancelled 1. 1.39   11. 4.39
                                                              "H2311", G-ABAA
G-ADAH   de Havilland DH.89 Dragon Rapide   6278   30. 1.35   Cancelled 18. 2.59 as PWFU "Pioneer"   9. 6.47
                                                                (Allied Airways (Gandar Dower) titles) (On loan from The Aeroplane Collection)
G-APUD   Bensen B-7Mc   1   11. 5.59   Cancelled 27. 2.70 as WFU   27. 9.60
                                                                                          (On loan from The Aeroplane Collection)
G-AWZP   Hawker Siddeley HS.121 Trident 3B Series 101   14. 1.69   Cancelled 27. 6.86 as destroyed
            14. 3.86T
                                                 2317   (Nose section only)
G-AYTA   SOCATA MS.880B Rallye Club   1789   19. 2.71   Cancelled 12. 5.93 as PWFU   7.11.88
G-BLKU   Colt Flame 56 SS Balloon (Hot Air)   572   17. 7.84   Cancelled 1. 5.92 as PWFU "Mr.Wonderfuel II"
G-MJXE   Mainair Tri-Flyer 330/Hiway Demon 175   17. 5.83   Cancelled 19.10.00 as TWFU   21. 3.95P
                                102-131082 & HS-001   (On loan from The Aeroplane Collection)
BAPC.6   Roe Triplane Type I   (As "14") "Bullseye Avroplane"
            (JAP 9hp)
BAPC.12   Mignet HM.14 Pou-Du-Ciel
            (Scott A2S)
BAPC.98   Yokosuka MXY-7 Ohka II   8485M   (As "997")
BAPC.175   Volmer VJ-23 Swingwing Powered Hang Glider ---
            (McCulloch 9hp)

BAPC.182	Wood Ornithopter					*(Stored 4.08)*	
BAPC.251	Hiway Spectrum Hang-Glider					*(Stored 4.08)*	
	(Built 1980)						
BAPC.252	Flexiform Wing Hang-Glider					*(Stored 4.08)*	
	(Built 1982)						
BGA 1156	EoN AP.10 460 Series 1	EoN/S/007	BGA 2666	26. 1.64		*(On loan from J.H.May) (As "BQT")*	18. 4.97
			AGA.6, BGA 1156				

Aviation Viewing Park, Manchester International Airport

G-AWZK	Hawker Siddeley HS.121 Trident 3B Series 101			14. 1.69		Cancelled 29. 5.90 as WFU	
	14.10.86T						
		2312				*(BEA Quarter Union Jack titles)*	
G-BOAC	British Aircraft Corporation Concorde Type 1 Variant 102		G-N81AC	3.4.74		Cancelled 4. 5.04 as WFU	16. 5.05T
		204 & 100-004	G-BOAC				
G-DMCA	McDonnell Douglas DC-10-30	48266	N3016Z	12. 3.96		Cancelled 3.11.03 as destroyed	11. 3.03T
	(Forward 60 feet of fuselage, including flight deck and 70 seats, retained for use an education classroom)						
G-IRJX	BAE Systems Avro 146-RJX100	E3378		24. 5.00		Cancelled 20. 2.03 as PWFU	

MERSEYSIDE
Wirral Aviation Society, Liverpool Marriott Hotel South, Liverpool-John Lennon Airport (www.jetstream-club.org)

G-ANCF	Bristol 175 Britannia Series 308F	12922	5Y-AZP	3. 1.58		Cancelled 21. 2.84 as WFU	12. 1.81
	(Originally regd as Series 305)		G-ANCF, LV-GJB, LV-PPJ, (G-ANCF), G-14-1, G-18-4, G-ANCF, (N6597C)				
						(On loan from Britannia Aircraft Preservation Trust) (Fuselage only)	
G-JMAC	British Aerospace Jetstream Series 4100		G-JAMD	12. 6.92		Cancelled 21. 5.03 by CAA	6.10.97A
		41004	G-JXLI				
G-SEXY	American AA-1 Yankee	AA1-0442	G-AYLM	30. 6.81		Cancelled 15.11.00 by CAA	17. 3.95
	(Regd incorrectly as c/n AA1-0042)					*(Badly damaged in forced landing Burscough, Lancashire 11.2.94)*	
BAPC.280	de Havilland DH.89 Dragon Rapide fsm					*"Neptune" (As "G-ANZP" in Federated Air Transport c/s)*	

WEST MIDLANDS
Boulton Paul Aircraft Heritage Project, Pendeford, Wolverhampton (www.boultonpaul.com)

G-AVVR	Avro 652A Anson 19 Series 2	"34530"	VP519	6.10.67		Cancelled by CAA 16. 9.72 - not converted	
						(On loan from The Aeroplane Collection) (Cockpit only as "VP519")	
G-FBPI	Air Navigation and Engineering Co ANEC IV Missel Thrush					Details in SECTION1, Part 2	
BAPC.274	Boulton & Paul P.6 fsm					*(As "X-25")*	
BAPC.281	Boulton Paul Defiant recreation					*(As "L7005:PS-B" in RAF 264 Sqdn c/s)*	
BGA 1759	Slingsby T.8 Tutor		RAFGSA.178	10.72			

NORFOLK
City of Norwich Aviation Museum, Norwich Airport (www.cnam.co.uk)

G-ASKK	Handley Page HPR.7 Dart Herald 211	161	PP-ASU	17. 7.63		Cancelled 29. 4.85 as WFU	19. 5.85T
			G-ASKK, PI-C910, CF-MCK				
G-AWON	English Electric Lightning F.53	95291	G-27-56	9. 8.68		Cancelled 24. 9.68 to R.Saudi AF as 53-686	
						(Subsequently RSAF 201, 203 and 1305) (As "ZF592")	
G-BEBC	Westland WS-55 Whirlwind HAR.10	WA.371	8463M	25. 6.76		Cancelled 5.12.83 as WFU *(As "XP355:A")*	
			XP355			*(Not converted)*	
G-BHMY	Fokker F.27 Friendship 600	10196	F-GBDK (2)	6. 5.80		Cancelled 22. 3.03 as PWFU	22. 5.99T
			(F-GBRV), PK-PFS, JA8606, PH-FDL *(Donated by KLM (UK) Ltd - less engines)*				
G-BTAZ	Evans VP-2					Details in SECTION1, Part 2	
G-OVNE	Cessna 401A	401A-0036	N401XX	11. 3.88		Cancelled 8. 2.94 by CAA.	8.10.92
			(N171SF), N71SF, N6236Q				

NORTHAMPTONSHIRE
"Carpetbagger" Aviation Museum, Harrington, Market Harborough (www.harringtonmuseum.org.uk)

G-APWK	Westland-Sikorsky S-51 Widgeon Series.2			26. 8.59		Cancelled 10.9.73 as PWFU.	
		WA/H/152				*(Forward fuselage only)*	

Sywell Aviation Museum, Sywell, Northampton (www.sywellaerodrome.co.uk/history)

BAPC.234	Vickers FB.5 Gunbus fsm	xxxx				*(As "GBH-7") (Built 1985 for "Gunbus" film)*	
BAPC.257	de Havilland DH.88 Comet fsm	xxxx				*(As "G-ACSS") "Grosvenor House"*	

NORTHUMBERLAND and TYNESIDE
North East Aircraft Museum, Usworth, Sunderland (www.neam.org.uk)

G-APTW	Westland WS-51/2 Widgeon	WA/H/150		27. 4.59		Cancelled 24. 8.77 as WFU	26. 9.75
G-ARAD	Phoenix Luton LA-5A Major	PAL/1204		29. 4.60		Cancelled 16.10.02 as WFU - completed but not flown	
	(Built W T Sproat - pr/no PFA 836)						
G-ARHX	de Havilland DH.104 Dove 8	04513		11. 1.61		Cancelled 6.12.78 as PWFU	8. 9.78
G-ASOL	Bell 47D-1	4	N146B	31. 1.64		Cancelled 5.12.83 as WFU	6. 9.71
G-AWRS	Avro 652A Anson C.19 Series 2	"33785"	TX213	14.10.68		Cancelled 30. 5.84 as PWFU	10. 8.73
G-BEEX	de Havilland DH.106 Comet 4C	6458	SU-ALM	10. 9.76		Cancelled 19. 5.83	
						(Not converted and broken up Lasham 8.77: nose section only)	
G-MBDL	Striplin (AES) Lone Ranger	109		21.10.81		Cancelled 13. 6.90 by CAA	
G-OGIL	Short SD.3-30 Var.100	SH.3068	G-BITV	23. 1.89		Cancelled 12.11.92 as WFU	21. 4.93T
			G-14-3068			*(Damaged Newcastle 1. 7.92)*	
G-SFTA	Westland SA.341G Gazelle 1	1039	G-SFTA	10. 9.82		Cancelled 21. 5.86 as WFU	24. 2.86
			HB-XIL, G-BAGJ, (XW858)			*(Crashed near Alston, Cumbria 7. 3.84) (As "G-BAGJ")*	
BAPC.96	Brown Helicopter						
BAPC.97	Luton LA.4 Minor					*(As "G-AFUG")*	
	(JAP J99)						
BAPC.119	Bensen B.7 Gyroglider						
BAPC.211	Mignet HM.14 Pou-Du-Ciel replica					*(As "G-ADVU")*	
	(Built Ken Fern/Vintage and Rotary Wing Collection 1993)						
BAPC.228	Olympus Hang Glider						

NOTTINGHAMSHIRE
Wonderland Pleasure Park, Farnsfield, Mansfield
BAPC.288   Hawker Hurricane fsm   *(As "V7467:LE-D" in RAF 242 Sqdn c/s)*

Newark Air Museum, Winthorpe, Newark (www.newarkairmuseum.co.uk)

G-AHRI	de Havilland DH.104 Dove 1B	04008	4X-ARI G-AHRI	11. 7.46	Cancelled 18. 5.72 as WFU
G-ANXB	de Havilland DH.114 Heron 1B	14048	G-5-14	3.12.54	Cancelled 2.11.81 as PWFU 25. 3.79 *(BEA Scottish Airways titles) "Sir James Young Simpson"*
G-APIY	Percival P.40 Prentice 1	PAC-075	VR249	28.11.57	Cancelled 19. 4.73 18. 3.67 *(WFU 18.3.67) (As "VR249:FA-EL" in RAFC c/s)*
G-APNJ	Cessna 310	35335	EI-AJY N3635D	2. 6.58	Cancelled 5.12.83 as WFU Newark 28.11.74
G-APVV	Mooney M.20A	1474	N8164E	30. 7.59	Cancelled 3. 4.89 by CAA *(Crashed at Barton 11.1.81)* 19. 9.81
G-AVVO	Avro 652A Anson 19 Series 2	34219	VL348		Cancelled 16. 9.72 by CAA (As "VL348") 6.10.67
G-AXMB	Slingsby T.7 Motor Cadet Mk.2 *(Originally regd as Mk.1)*	xxxx	BGA.805 VM590	5. 8.69	Cancelled 9.1.92 by CAA 9. 7.82 *(Dismantled)*
G-AYZJ	Westland WS-55 Whirlwind HAS.7	WA.263 *(Also c/n WAG/34)*	XM685	24. 5.71	Cancelled 29.12.80 as WFU *(As "XM685/PO-513")*
G-BFTZ	SOCATA MS.880B Rallye Club	1269	F-BPAX	2. 6.78	Cancelled 14.11.91 by CAA 19. 9.81 *(On loan from The Aeroplane Collection)*
G-BJAD	Clutton FRED Series II				Details in SECTION 1, Part 2
G-BKPG	Luscombe P3 Rattler Strike	003		7. 3.83	Cancelled 31. 7.91 by CAA *(No Permit issued)*
G-BKPY	SAAB 91B/2 Safir	91321	R NorAF 56321	23. 3.83	Cancelled 8. 2.02 as WFU (As "56321" in R.NorAF c/s)
G-MBBZ	Volmer VJ-24W	7		23. 9.81	Cancelled 29.11.95 as WFU
G-MBUE	MBA Tiger Cub 440	MBA-001		29. 4.82	Cancelled 6. 9.94 by CAA *(Originally regd as Micro-Bipe c/n 001)*
G-MJDW	Eipper Quicksilver MXII *(Cuyuna 430)*	RI-01 *(C/n noted as 3506)*		15. 7.82	Cancelled 13. 2.08 as PWFU 5. 5.07P
G-MNRT	Midland Ultralights Sirocco 377GB				Details in SECTION 1, Part 2
BAPC.20	Lee-Richards Annular				*(Built for "Those Magnificent Men in Their Flying Machines" 1965 film)*
BAPC.43	Mignet HM.14 Pou-Du-Ciel replica *(Scott A2S)*				
BAPC.101	Mignet HM.14 Pou-Du-Ciel replica				
BAPC.183	Zurowski ZP-1 Helicopter *(Panhard 850cc)*				*(Polish AF c/s)*

OXFORDSHIRE
Royal Air Force Benson
BAPC.226   Supermarine Spitfire XI fsm   xxxx   *(As "EN343" in PRU c/s)*

SHROPSHIRE
Royal Air Force Cosford Museum including Michael Beetham Conservation Centre ($) and National 'Cold War' Exhibition %, Cosford (www.rafmuseum.com)

G-EBMB	Hawker Cygnet I ($) *(Bristol Cherub III)*	1	No.14 *(Lympne 1924)*	29. 7.25	Cancelled 30.11.61 30.11.61
G-AEEH	Mignet HM.14 Pou-Du-Ciel *(Built E G Davis)*	EGD.1		13. 3.36	Cancelled 8.46 in census - WFU 15. 5.38 15. 5.38
G-AEKW	Miles M.12 Mohawk ($)	298	HM503 G-AEKW, "G-AEKN"	14. 7.36	Crashed Spain 1. 1.50 1. 3.50
"G-AFAP"	CASA 352L *(Junkers Ju 52/3m)*	163	Spanish AF T2B-272		*(Original British Airways titles) (Not original G-AFAP)*
G-AGNV	Avro 685 York C.1 (%)	1223	"MW100" "LV633", G-AGNV, TS798	20. 8.45	WFU 9.10.64 6. 3.65 *(As "TS798")*
G-AIZE	Fairchild F.24W-41A Argus II *(UC-61A-FA)*	565	N9996F G-AIZE, 43-14601	18.12.46	Cancelled 6. 3.73as WFU (As "FS628") 6. 8.66
"G-AJOV"	Westland WS-51 Dragonfly HR.3	WA/H/80	WP495		*(BEA titles) (Not original G-AJOV)*
G-APAS	de Havilland DH.106 Comet 1A	06022	8351M XM823, G-APAS, G-5-23, F-BGNZ	23. 5.57	Cancelled 22.10.58 (BOAC titles)
G-BBYM	Handley Page HP.137 Jetstream 200	243	G-AYWR G-8-13	13. 2.74	Cancelled 7. 6.00 as WFU 20. 9.98A
G-BRAM	Mikoyan MiG-21PF (%)	xxxx	Hungarian AF 503	22. 5.89	Cancelled 16. 4.99 by CAA (As "503" in Russian AF c/s)
BAPC.82	Hawker Afghan Hind *(RR Kestrel)*	41H/81899			*(R.Afghan AF c/s)*
BAPC.84	Mitsubishi Ki 46 III (Dinah)		8484M		*(As "5439")*
BAPC.94	Fieseler Fi 103 (V-1)		8483M		
BAPC.99	Yokosuka MXY-7 Ohka II		8486M		
BGA 572	Slingsby T.21B Sedbergh TX.1 ($)	539	8884M VX275, BGA 572		*(As "VX275")*

Assault Glider Trust, RAF Shawbury (www.assaultglidertrust.co.uk)

G-AMHJ	Douglas C-47A-25DK Dakota 6	13468	SU-AZI G-AMHJ, ZS-BRW, KG651, 42-108962	6. 2.51	Cancelled 23. 1.03 as wfu (As "KG651") 5.12.00A
G-ANBY	de Havilland DH.82A Tiger Moth	86042	EM840	2. 9.53	Cancelled as PWFU 30. 4.59 *(Not converted and scrapped 4.60 - on rebuild as "EM840" 8.08)*
BAPC.279	Airspeed AS.58 Horsa reconstruction				*(As "LH291")*

Wartime Aircraft Recovery Group Aviation Museum, Sleap (www.wargroup.homestead.com)
BAPC.148   Hawker Fury II fsm   *(As "K7271" in RAF 1 Sqdn c/s)*

SOMERSET
The Helicopter Museum, Weston-super-Mare (www.helicoptermuseum.co.uk)

Reg	Type	c/n	Prev id / date	Notes	Date
G-ACWM	Cierva C.30A	715	(G-AHMK) 24. 7.34	Cancelled 17. 3.59 as WFU (No external marks)	13. 7.40
	(Avro 671)		AP506, G-ACWM	(On loan from E.D.ap Rees)	
G-ALSX	Bristol 171 Sycamore 3	12892	G-48-1 17.11.50	Cancelled as WFU	24. 9.65
			G-ALSX, VR-TBS, G-ALSX	(On loan from E.D.ap Rees)	
G-ANFH	Westland WS.55 Whirlwind Series 1	WA.15	27.10.53	Cancelled 2. 9.77 as WFU (No external marks)	17. 7.71
				(On loan from E.D.ap Rees)	
G-ANJV	Westland WS-55 Whirlwind Series 3	WA.24	VR-BET 14.12.53	Cancelled 8. 1.74 on sale in Bermuda (No external marks)	
			G-ANJV	(On loan from E.D.ap Rees) (Stored 2.08)	
G-AODA	Westland WS-55 Whirlwind Series 3	WA.113	9Y-TDA 13. 5.55	Cancelled 23. 9.93 by CAA "Dorado"	23. 8.91A
			EP-HAC, G-AODA	(Bristow Helicopters c/s)	
G-AOZE	Westland WS-51/2 Widgeon	WA/H/141	5N-ABW 11. 1.57	Cancelled 20. 6.62 on sale in Nigeria	
			G-AOZE	(On loan from E.D.ap Rees) (Stored 2.08)	
G-ARVN (2)	Servotec CR LTH1 Grasshopper 1	1	16. 2.63	Cancelled 14. 3.77 as WFU	18. 5.63
				(On loan from E.D.ap Rees) (Stored 2.08)	
G-ASCT	Bensen B.7Mc	DC.3	14. 8.62	Cancelled 20. 9.73 as PWFU (Stored 2.08	11.11.66P
	(McCulloch 4318E)			(Built D.Campbell))	
G-ASHD	Brantly B.2A	314	2. 4.63	Cancelled 22. 6.67 as Destroyed	5. 6.67
				(Crashed into River Colne, Brightlingsea, Essex 19. 2.67) (Stored 2.08)	
G-ASTP	Hiller UH-12C	1045	N9750C 4. 6.64	Cancelled 24.1.90 by CAA	3. 7.82
G-ATBZ	Westland WS-58 Wessex 60 Series 1	WA/461	22. 3.65	Cancelled as TWFU 23.11.82 (As "G-ATBZ")	15.12.81
				(WFU 5.12.81 - to G-17-4) (Stored 2.08)	
G-ATFG	Brantly B.2B	448	16. 6.65	Cancelled 25. 9.87 as WFU	25. 3.85
	(Composite with parts from G-ASLO and G-AXSR)				
G-ATKV	Westland WS-55 Whirlwind 3	WA/493	VR-BEU 11.11.65	Cancelled 8. 1.74 (To and "as VR-BEU") (Stored 2.08)	
			G-ATKV, EP-HAN (1), G-ATKV		
G-AVKE	Gadfly HDW-1	HDW-1	19. 4.67	Cancelled 12.10.81 as WFU	
	(Continental IO-340A)			(On loan from E.D.ap Rees)	
G-AVNE	Westland WS-58 Wessex 60 Series 1	WA.561	G-17-3 15. 5.67	Cancelled 23.11.82 as TWFU	7. 2.83
			G-AVNE, 5N-AJL, G-AVNE, 9M-ASS, VH-BHC, PK-HBQ, G-AVNE, (G-AVMC)		
				(As "G-AVNE" and "G-17-3")	
G-AWRP	Servotec CR.LTH.1 Grasshopper II	GB.1	14.10.68	Cancelled 5.12.83 as WFU	12. 5.72P
G-AXFM	Servotec CR.LTH.1 Grasshopper II	GB.2	19. 5.69	Cancelled 5.12.83 as WFU	
				(Completed as Ground-Running Rig) (Stored 2.08)	
G-AYXT	Westland WS-55 Whirlwind HAS.7 (Series .2	WA.167	XK940 28. 4.71	Cancelled 8. 8.00 by CAA (As "XK940")	4. 2.99P
G-AZAU	Servotec CR.LTH.1 Grasshopper II	GB.3	21. 6.71	Cancelled 5.12.83 as WFU (Incomplete Rig) (Stored 2.08)	
G-AZYB	Bell 47H-1	1538	LN-OQG 4. 7.72	Cancelled 22. 4.85 as destroyed (As "OO-SHW")	8. 9.84
			SE-HBE, OO-SHW	(Crashed St.Mary Bourne, Thruxton 21. 4.84)	
				(On loan from E.D.ap Rees)	
G-BAPS	Campbell Cougar Gyroplane	CA/6000	14. 2.73	Cancelled 21. 1.87 by CAA	20. 5.74
	(Continental O-240-A)			(On loan from A.M.W.Curzon-Howe-Herrick)	
G-BGHF	Westland WG.30 Series 100-60	WA.001.P	4. 1.79	Cancelled 29. 3.89 as WFU	1. 8.86
G-BKFD	Westland WG.30 Series.100	004	G-17-28 22. 6.82	Cancelled 6.12.82 (To and "as N5820T") (Stored 2.08)	
G-BKFF	Westland WG.30 Series.100	006	G-17-30 22. 6.82	Cancelled 6.12.82 (To and "as N5840T") (Stored 2.08)	
G-BKGD	Westland WG.30 Series.100	002	(G-BKBJ) 15. 7.82	Cancelled 15. 4.93 as WFU	6. 7.93
G-BRMA	Westland-Sikorsky S-51 Dragonfly HR.5	WA/H/50	WG719 15. 6.78	Cancelled 30. 3.89 as WFU (As "WG719")	
				(On loan from E.D.ap Rees)	
G-BRMB	Bristol 192 Belvedere HC.1	13347	7997M 15. 6.78	Cancelled 3. 7.96 as WFU (As "XG452")	
			XG452	(On loan from E.D.ap Rees)	
G-EFIS	Westland WG.30 Series 100	014	G-17-18 24. 6.84	Cancelled 27.11.84 (To N114WG 11.84) (As "N114WG")	
G-EHIL	EH Industries EH-101	50003	ZH647 9. 7.87	Cancelled 28.4.99 as PWFU (To MoD as ZH647)	9. 7.87
	(Airframe No.PP3)				
G-ELEC	Westland WG.30 Series 200	007	G-BKNV 17. 6.83	Cancelled 27. 2.98 as WFU	28. 6.95P
G-HAUL	Westland WG.30 Series 300	020	G-17-22 3. 7.86	Cancelled 22. 4.92 as WFU	27.10.86P
G-HEKY	McCulloch J-2	039	G-ORVB 14. 9.07	Cancelled 30. 1.97 as WFU	
			(G-BLGI), (G-BKKL), Bahrain Public Security BPS-3, N4329G		
G-OTED	Robinson R-22 HP	0209	G-BMYR 17. 1.96	Cancelled 26. 3.02 as PWFU	17. 2.02
			ZS-HLG		
G-PASB	MBB BD6.105D	S.135	VH-LSA 2. 3.89	Cancelled 9. 8.94 as WFU	
			G-BDMC, D-HDEC	(Original pod from 1994 rebuild)	
G-RWWW	Westland WS-55 Whirlwind HCC.12	WA/418	8727M 21. 6.90	Cancelled 10. 7.00 as WFU	25. 8.96P
			XR486	(As "XR486" in Queens Flight c/s)	
BAPC.10	Hafner R-11 Revoplane				
	(Salmson 45hp)				
BAPC.60	Murray M.1 Helicopter				
	(JAPJ99 36hp)				
BAPC.128	Watkinson CG-4 Cyclogyroplane Man Powered Gyroplane Mark IV				
BAPC.153	Westland WG-33 Mock-up			(Engineering mock-up)	
BAPC.212	Bensen B.6 Gyrocopter			(Stored 2.08)	
BAPC.213	Cranfield Vertigo Man Powered Helicopter			(Stored 2.08)	
BAPC.264	Bensen B.8M			(Built 1984)	
BAPC.289	Gyro-Boat				

Fleet Air Arm Museum/FAAM Cobham Hall ($), RNAS Yeovilton (www.fleetairarm.com)

Reg	Type	c/n	Prev id / date	Notes	Date
G-AIBE	Fairey Fulmar 2	F.3707	N1854 29. 7.46	Cancelled 30. 4.59 - to N1854 (As "N1854")	6. 7.59
			G-AIBE, N1854		
G-AIZG	Vickers Supermarine 236 Walrus 1	6S/21840	EI-ACC 20.12.46	Cancelled 1963 (As "L2301")	
			IAC N-18, L2301		
G-AOXG	de Havilland DH.82A Tiger Moth ($)	83805	XL717 3.10.56	Cancelled as sold as XL717 10.56 (As "G-ABUL")	
			G-AOXG, T7291		
G-APNV	Saunders-Roe P.531-1	S2/5268	24. 6.58	Cancelled 1.10.59 - to XN332 10.59 (As "XN332: 759")	

G-ASTL	Fairey Firefly 1	F.5607	SE-BRD	1. 6.64	WFU 3. 2.82 (As "Z2033: 275 N" in RN 1771 Sqdn c/s)	
			Z2033			
G-AWYY	Slingsby T.57 Sopwith Camel F.1 replica 1701		"C1701"	14. 2.69	Cancelled 25.11.91 as WFU (As "B6401")	1. 9.85P
	(Clerget)		N1917H, G-AWYY			
G-AZAZ	Bensen B.8M ($)	RNEC.1		2. 7.71	Cancelled 19. 9.75 as WFU	
	(Built T E Davies)					
G-BEYB	Fairey Flycatcher replica	WA/3		11. 7.77	Cancelled 12. 7.96 as WFU (As "S1287:5" in FAA c/s)	
	(Built Westward Airways (Lands End) Ltd)					
G-BFXL	Albatros D.Va replica	0034	D-EGKO	24. 8.78	Cancelled 10. 3.97 as WFU	5.11.91P
	(Built Williams Flugzeugbau) (Ranger 6-440-C5)				(As "D5397/17" in German c/s and "D-EGKO" on lower fuselage)	
G-BGWZ	Eclipse Super Eagle ($)	ESE.007		29. 6.79	Cancelled 5.12.83 as WFU (No external marks)	
G-BIAU	Sopwith Pup replica	EMK 002		4. 1.83	Cancelled 10. 3.97 as WFU	13. 9.89P
	(Built Skysport Engineering) (Le Rhone 80hp)				(As "N6452" in RNAS c/s)	
G-BMZF	WSK-Mielec LIM-2	1B-01420	Polish AF 01420	18.12.86	Cancelled 23. 2.90 as WFU (As "01420" in North Korean c/s)	
	(MiG-15bis)					
G-BSST	British Aircraft Corporation Concorde 002	002		6. 5.68	Cancelled 21. 1.87 as WFU (WFU 4. 3.76)	31.10.74P
	(Officially regd with Bristol c/n 13520)				(On loan from Science Museum)	
BAPC.58	Yokosuka MXY-7 Ohka II	xxxx			(As "15-1585") (On loan from Science Museum)	
BAPC.88	Fokker Dr.1 5/8th scale model	xxxx			(As "102/17")	
	(Modified Lawrence Parasol airframe)					
BAPC.111	Sopwith Triplane fsm	xxxx			(As "N5492:B" in Royal Navy Air Service c/s) "Black Maria"	
BAPC.149	Short S.27 replica ($)	xxxx				

SUFFOLK

Norfolk and Suffolk Aviation Museum, Flixton, Bungay (www.aviationmuseum.net)

G-ANLW	Westland WS-51 Series 2 Widgeon WA/H/133		"MD497"	23. 3.54	Cancelled 15.11.02 as WFU	27. 5.81A
			G-ANLW		(On loan from Sloane Helicopters Ltd)	
G-ASRF	Gowland GWG.2 Jenny Wren	PFA 1300		18. 3.64	Cancelled 11.12.96 by CAA	4. 6.71P
	(Built G W Gowland - c/n GWG.2 using modified Luton Minor wings once fitted to G-AGEP)					
G-AWSA	Avro 652A Anson C.19/2	"293483"	(N5054)	21.10.68	Cancelled 18. 8.69 as sold in US (As "VL349:V7-Q")	
			G-AWSA, VL349		(Not delivered)	
G-AZLM	Cessna F172L	F17200842		31.12.71	Cancelled 15. 4.91 as destroyed	
	(Built Reims Aviation SA)				(Crashed on take off Badminton 23.3.91) (Fuselage only)	
G-BABY	Taylor JT.2 Titch	JRB-2		21. 8.72	Cancelled 4.12.96 by CAA.	10.10.91
	(Built J Bygraves - pr/noPFA 3204)					
G-BDVS	Fokker F.27 Friendship 200	10232	S2-ABK	20. 4.76	Cancelled 19.12.96 as WFU	
			PH-FEX, PH-EXC, 9M-AMM, PH-FEX (Scrapped 12.96 - nose only) "Eric Gandar Dower"			
G-BFIP	Wallbro Monoplane replica	WA-1		16.12.77	Cancelled 28. 3.01 as TWFU	22. 4.82P
	(McCulloch/Wallis)				(On loan from K.H.Wallis) (No external marks)	
G-MJSU	MBA Tiger Cub 440	SO.75/1		2. 2.83	Cancelled 23. 6.93 by CAA	31. 1.86E
G-MBUD	Wheeler (Skycraft) Scout Mk.III/R/3	0432/R/3		12. 5.82	Cancelled 6.9.94 by CAA	
	(Modified to Super Scout) (Note same c/n as G-MBOU)					
G-MTFK	Moult Trike/Flexiform Striker	DIM-01		23. 3.87	Cancelled 13. 6.90 by CAA	
	(Officially regd with c/n SO.175)					
G-MMWL	Eurowing Goldwing				Details in SECTION 1, Part 2	
BAPC.71	Supermarine Spitfire fsm		"P9390"		(As "P8140:ZP-K" in RAF 74 Sqdn c/s)	
			"N3317"		"Nuflier" (Built for "Battle of Britain" film)	
BAPC.115	Mignet HM.14 Pou-Du-Ciel replica				(On loan from I Hancock)	
	(Douglas 500cc)					
BAPC.147	Bensen B.7 Gyroglider				(As "LHS-1")	
BAPC.239	Fokker D.VIII 5/8th scale model				(As "694")	
BGA 1461	EoN AP.7 Primary		(CDN)		(As "CDN")	5.69*
BGA 2384	Grunau Baby III		BGA 2074	7. 6.78	(As "DUD")	29. 3.92
			RAFGSA.374, D-9142			
BGA 4002	Penrose Pegasus 2 replica	001	HKJ	7.93	(As "HKJ")	15. 9.98
BGA 4757	Colditz Cock replica	xxxx	"JTA"	1.00	(As "JTA")	20. 2.00
	(Built Southdown Aero Services and J.Lee)				"Spirit of Colditz"	

SURREY

Brooklands Museum, Brooklands, Weybridge (www.motor-software.co.uk/brooklands)

G-AEKV	Kronfeld (BAC) Drone de luxe	30		13. 1.37	Cancelled 14. 1.99 as WFU	6.10.60P
					(On loan from M.L.Beach) (Allocated BGA 2510 5.79)	
G-AGRU	Vickers 657 Viking 1	112	VP-TAX	8. 5.46	WFU 9.63 "Vagrant" (BEA titles)	9. 1.64
			G-AGRU			
G-APEJ	Vickers 953C Vanguard Merchantman	713		9. 9.57	Cancelled 15.11.96 as WFU "Ajax"	
					(WFU 24.12.92: broken up 1. 6.95: nose section only)	
G-APEP	Vickers 953C Vanguard Merchantman	719		9. 9.57	Cancelled 28. 2.97 as WFU "Superb"	1.10.98T
					(Hunting Cargo Airlines titles)	
G-APIM	Vickers 806 Viscount	412		19.11.57	Cancelled "Viscount Stephen Piercey"	19. 7.88T
					(DBR struck by Short SD.3-30 G-BHWT on 11. 1.88) (British Air Ferries titles)	
G-ARRM	Beagle B.206X	B.001		23. 6.61	WFU 1965? and cancelled 9. 4.74 as PWFU	23.12.64
	(Originally regd as Beagle B.206 Series 1 [B2/1010]: re-designated 9.61)				(On loan to Shoreham Airport Historical Association, noted 5.05)	
G-ARVM (2)	Vickers VC-10 Series 1101	815	(G-ARVJ)	16. 1.63	WFU 22.10.79 (Nose only)	5. 8.80
G-ASIX	Vickers VC-10 Series 1103	820		29. 5.63	Cancelled 10.10.74 - to A4O-AB 10.74) (As "A4O-AB")	
G-ASYD	British Aircraft Corporation One-Eleven 475AM			9.11.64	Cancelled 25. 7.94 as WFU	13. 7.94
		BAC.053				
	(Originally regd as Series 400AM: converted to prototype Serie 500 1967: to Series 475EM 1970)					
G-ATJJ	de Havilland DHC.1 Chipmunk 22	C1/0797	WP921	21. 9.65	Cancelled 19.1.68 - restored to RAF as WP921 (As "WP921')	
					(Cockpit section only)	
G-BBDG	British Aircraft Corporation Concorde Type 1 Variant 100			7. 8.73	Cancelled 12.81 as WFU	. 3.82P
		13523 & 100-02				
G-BFCZ	Sopwith Camel F.1 replica	WA/2		12.10.77	Cancelled 23. 1.03 as WFU (As "B7270")	23. 2.89P
	(Built Westward Airways (Lands End) Ltd) (Clerget 9B)					

G-BJHV	Voisin Scale replica	MPS-1		1. 9.81	Cancelled 4. 7.91 by CAA	
	(Built M P Sayer)				(On loan from M.P.Sayer)	
G-LOTI	Bleriot Type XI replica				Details in SECTION 1, Part 2	
G-MJPB	Manuel Ladybird	WLM-14		9.11.82	Cancelled 13. 6.90 by CAA	
					(On loan from Estate of W.L.Manuel)	
G-ROEI	Avro Roe 1 replica				Details in SECTION 1, Part 2	
G-VTOL	Hawker Siddeley Harrier T.52 B3/41H/735795		ZA250	27. 7.70	Cancelled 3.90 by CAA	2.11.86S
			G-VTOL, (XW273)			
BAPC.29	Mignet HM.14 Pou-Du-Ciel replica	---			(As "G-ADRY")	
	(Built P.D.Roberts, Swansea 1960/78) (Anzani "V")					
BAPC.114	Vickers Type 60 Viking IV reconstruction	-	"R4"		(As "G-EBED") (Built for "The Land Time Forgot" film)	
BAPC.177	Avro 504K fsm		"G1381"		(As "G-AACA" in Brooklands School of Flying c/s)	
	(Clerget 130hp)					
BAPC.187	Roe Type I Biplane reconstruction					
	(Built M.L.Beach) (ABC 24hp)					
BAPC.249	Hawker Fury I fsm				(As "K5673" in RAF 1 Sqdn 'A' Flight c/s)	
	(Built Brooklands 1990s)					
BAPC.250	Royal Aircraft Factory SE.5a replica		(As "F5475:A") "1st Battalion Honourable Artillery Company")			
	(Built Brooklands 1990s)					
BAPC.256	Santos Dumont Type 20 Demoiselle reconstruction					
	(Built J Aubot 1996/97)					
BGA 162	Manuel Willow Wren			9.34	"The Willow Wren"	
BGA 643	Slingsby T.15 Gull III	364A	TJ711	11.49	(As "ATH") (On loan from M L Beach)	20. 6.04
BGA 3922	Abbott-Baynes Scud I replica	001		R	(As "HFZ")	

Gatwick Aviation Museum, Charlwood (www.gatwick-aviation-museum.co.uk)

G-BLID	de Havilland DH.112 Venom FB.50 (FB.1)				Details in SECTION1, Part 2	
G-DACA	Percival P.57 Sea Prince T.1				Details in SECTION1, Part 2	
G-GACA	Percival P.57 Sea Prince T.1				Details in SECTION1, Part 2	
G-JETH	Hawker Sea Hawk FGA.6				Details in SECTION1, Part 2	
G-JETM	Gloster Meteor T.7				Details in SECTION1, Part 2	
G-VIXN	de Havilland DH.110 Sea Vixen FAW.2 (TT)				Details in SECTION1, Part 2	

Wings Museum, Redhill (www.wingsmuseum.co.uk)

| G-KOOL | de Havilland DH.104 Sea Devon C.2/2 | | | | Details in SECTION1 Part 2 | |

SUSSEX
Shoreham Airport Historical Association, Shoreham Airport (www.thearchiveshoreham.co.uk)

G-ARRM	Beagle B.206				On loan from Brooklands Museum, Surrey (qv)	
BAPC.277	Mignet HM.14 Pou-Du-Ciel replica				"L'Autre Aviation" on tail	
BAPC.300	Piffard Hummingbird reproduction					
BGA.628	EoN AP.8 Baby				Details is SECTION 5 Part 1	

Tangmere Military Aviation Museum, Tangmere (www.tangmere-museum.org.uk)

BAPC.214	Supermarine Spitfire prototype fsm				(As "K5054")	
BAPC.241	Hawker Hurricane I fsm				(As "L1679:JX-G" in RAF 1 Sqdn c/s)	
	(Built Aerofab 1994)					
BAPC.242	Supermarine Spitfire VB replica				(As "BL924:AZ-G" in RAF 234 Sqdn c/s)	
	(Built TDL Reps 1994)				"Valde Maar Atterdag"	

WARWICKSHIRE
Midland Air Museum, Coventry (www.midlandairmuseum.org.uk)

G-EBJG	Parnall Pixie III	xxxx	No.17/18*	. 9.24	Cancelled 1.12.46 by Sec of State	2.10.36
			(*Lympne 1924?)		(Components only 2.05)	
G-ABOI	Wheeler Slymph	AHW.1		17. 7.31	Cancelled 1.12.46 by Sec of State	
					(On loan from A.H.Wheeler) (Dismantled components only 2.05)	
G-AEGV	Mignet HM.14 Pou-Du-Ciel	EMAC.1		22. 4.36	Cancelled 12.37 (WFU 26.5.37)	26. 5.37
	(Built East Midlands Aviation Company)					
G-ALCU	de Havilland DH.104 Dove 2B	04022	VT-CEH	3. 8.48	Cancelled 8. 9.78 as WFU	16. 3.73
					(Displayed as "G-ALVD" in 'Dunlop Aviation Division' c/s)	
G-AOKZ	Percival P.40 Prentice 1	PAC-238	VS623	20. 4.56	Not converted (Became instructional airframe)	
					(As "VS623" with wings from G-AONB - No wheel spats)	
G-APJJ (2)	Fairey Ultralight Helicopter	F.9428		4.12.57	Cancelled 2. 3.73 as WFU (Royal Navy' c/s)	1. 4.59
G-APRL	Armstrong-Whitworth 650 Argosy Series 101	AW.6652	N890U	2. 1.59	Cancelled 19.11.87 as WFU (Elan titles) "Edna"	23. 3.87T
			N602Z, N6507R, G-APRL			
G-APWN	Westland WS-55 Whirlwind 3	WA.298	VR-BER	8. 9.59	Cancelled 25. 6.81 as WFU "Skerries"	17. 5.78
			G-APWN, 5N-AGI, G-APWN		(Bristow Helicopters titles)	
G-ARYB	de Havilland DH.125 Series.1	25002		1. 3.62	Cancelled 4. 3.69 (Mounted wingless on plinths)	22. 1.68
G-ASWJ	Beagle B.206C Series 1	B.009		9. 9.64	Cancelled 9. 9.75 as WFU	
	(To RAF Halton as 8449M in 1976: on loan to City of Bristol College, Ashley Down, Bristol as "8449M")					
(G-MJWH)	Chargus Vortex 120			R		
	(Regn reserved 1983 for Chargus T.250 and engine: fitted to 1974 Vortex hang glider: abandoned and only wing on display)					
BAPC.9	Humber-Bleriot XI Monoplane reconstruction				(No markings)	
	(Humber)					
BAPC.32	Crossley Tom Thumb				(Not completed Banbury 1937) (Stored 4.08)	
BAPC.126	Rollason-Druine D.31 Turbulent				(Static airframe) (Yellow c/s, no markings)	
BAPC.179	Sopwith Pup fsm				(As "A7317")	
"BGA 804"	Slingsby Cadet TX.1				(As "BAA") (Also see SECTION 5, Part 1)	

WILTSHIRE

Royal Air Force, Lyneham

| G-AMPO | Douglas C-47B-30DK Dakota 3 | 16437/33185 | LN-RTO | 25. 2.52 | Cancelled 18.10.01 as WFU (As "FZ625") | 29. 3.97 |
| | (Regd as c/n 16438/33186) | | G-AMPO, KN566, 44-76853 | | | |

National Museum of Science & Industry, Wroughton (www.sciencemuseum.org.uk/wroughton)

Reg	Type	c/n	Prev id	Date	Remarks	Date
G-AACN	Handley Page HP.39 Gugnunc	1	K1908 G-AACN	2.11.28	Cancelled 12.30 on transfer to RAF	19.9.30
G-ACIT	de Havilland DH84 Dragon 1	6039		24. 7.33	Cancelled 26. 4.02 as WFU	25. 5.74
G-AEHM	Mignet HM.14 Pou-Du-Ciel	HJD.1		30. 4.36	Cancelled in 3.39 census "Blue Finch"	
	(Built H J Dolman) (ABC Scorpion 35 hp)					
G-ALXT	de Havilland DH.89A Dragon Rapide	6736	4R-AAI CY-AAI, G-ALXT, NF865	24. 1.50	Cancelled 5. 7.51 - to CY-AAI "Star of Scotia" *(Railway Air Service titles)*	
G-ANAV	de Havilland DH.106 Comet 1A	06013	CF-CUM	15. 8.53	Cancelled 1. 7.55 as WFU *(Broken up RAE Farnborough 1955: nose section)*	
G-APWY	Piaggio P.166	362		16.12.59	Cancelled 20.10.00 by CAA	14. 3.81
G-APYD	de Havilland DH.106 Comet 4B	6438	SX-DAL G-APYD	21. 1.60	Cancelled 23.11.79 as WFU *(Dan-Air titles)*	3. 8.79
G-ATTN	Piccard Balloon (Hot Air) (62,000 cu ft) 15 & 1352			27. 4.66	Cancelled 5.12.77 as PWFU *(Envelope and basket stored 4.08) "The Red Dragon"*	
G-AVZB	LET Z-37 Cmelak	04-08	OK-WKQ	30.11.67	Cancelled 21.12.88 as WFU	5. 4.84A
G-AWZM	Hawker Siddeley HS.121 Trident 3B Series 101	2314		14. 1.69	Cancelled 18. 3.86 as WFU *(WFU 13.12.85) (British Airways titles)*	13.12.85T
G-BBGN	Cameron A-375 Balloon (Hot Air)	90		23. 8.73	Cancelled 22. 8.89 as WFU	
G-BGLB	Bede BD.5B	3796 & PFA 14-10085		2. 3.79	Cancelled 21.11.91 by CAA	4.8.81
	(Hirth 230R)					
G-CONI	Lockheed 749A-79 Constellation	2553	N7777G (N173X), N7777G, TI-1045P, PH-LDT, PH-TET	12. 5.82	Cancelled 13. 6.84 as WFU *(As "N7777G" in TWA c/s)*	
G-MMCB	Huntair Pathfinder II	136		13. 7.83	Cancelled 23.11.88 as WFU	
G-RBOS	Colt AS-105 HA Airship	390		9. 2.82	Cancelled 3. 4.97 by CAA	6. 3.87
EI-AYO (2)	Douglas DC-3A-197	1911	N655GP N65556, N255JB, N8695E, N333H, NC16071	5.3.76	Cancelled 28.11.78 as sold to UK Science Museum	
BAPC.52	Lilienthal Glider Type XI					
	(1895 original)					
BAPC.162	Goodhart Man Powered Aircraft Newbury Manflier					
BAPC.172	Chargus Midas Super E Hang Glider					
BAPC.173	Birdman Promotions Grasshopper					
BAPC.174	Bensen B.7 Gyroglider					
BAPC.188	McBroom Cobra 88 Hang Glider					
BAPC.276	Hartman Ornithopter					

YORKSHIRE

AeroVenture, Doncaster *(www.aeroventure.org.uk)*

Reg	Type	c/n	Prev id	Date	Remarks	Date
G-AJUD	Auster V J/1 Autocrat	2614		5. 6.47	Cancelled 31. 3.99 by CAA	18. 5.74
G-ALYB	Taylorcraft J Auster 5	1173	RT520	3. 2.50	Cancelled 29. 2.84 by CAA *(Fuselage only)*	26. 5.63
G-AOKO	Percival P.40 Prentice 1	PAC-234	VS621	13. 4.56	Cancelled 9.10.84 as WFU *(On loan from Atlantic Air Transport Ltd)*	23.10.72
G-APMY	Piper PA-23-160 Apache	23-1258	EI-AJT	15. 5.58	WFU 1.11.81 *(On loan from W.Fern)*	1.11.81
G-ARGI (2)	Auster 6A Tugmaster	2299	VF530	8.12.60	WFU at Heathfield in 7.73 *(Fuselage stored 4.08)*	4.7.76
G-AVAA	Cessna F150G	F150-0164		14.10.66	Cancelled 16. 4.96 by CAA *(Fuselage only)*	5. 7.96
	(Built Reims Aviation SA)					
G-AWCL	Cessna F.150H	F150-0276		25. 1.68	Cancelled as destroyed 2. 2.88	10. 7.88
	(Built Reims Aviation SA)					
G-BECE	Aerospace Developments AD500 Series B.1 Airship (Hot Air) (2 x Porsche 930/03/AD11)	1214/1		14. 7.76	Cancelled 30. 5.84 as destroyed *(Badly damaged in gales Cardington 9.3.79: gondola only)*	1. 4.79
G-BOCB	Hawker Siddeley HS.125 Series 1B/522	25106	G-OMCA G-DJMJ, G-AWUF, 5N-ALY, G-AWUF, HZ-BIN	14. 9.87	Cancelled as WFU 22. 2.95 *(Cockpit only)* *(WFU Luton 1994 for spares)*	16.10.90
G-DELB	Robinson R22 Beta	0799	N26461	18. 5.88	Cancelled 20. 4.95 by CAA *(DBR Sherburn-in-Elmet 27.12.94)*	
G-MJKP	Hiway Skystrike-Super Scorpion	PEB-01		7. 9.82	Cancelled 9.12.94 as WFU	
	(Fuji-Robin EC-25)					
G-MJPO	Eurowing Goldwing	018		16.11.82	Cancelled 9. 4.02 as PWFU	
G-MVRS	CFM Shadow Series BD	099		7. 4.89	Cancelled 5. 7.90 as destroyed *(Engineless fuselage shell in Storage Shed 4.04)*	4. 6.90
G-MYJX	Whittaker MW.8	001		24. 5.93	Cancelled 31.7.01 by CAA	
	(Built M Whittaker - pr no.PFA 243-12345)					
G-VOCE	Robinson R22				See SECTION 1, Part 2	
EI-JWM	Robinson R22 Beta	1386	G-BSLB	21.11.92	Cancelled 28. 5.07	
BAPC.207	Austin Whippet fsm				*(As "K-158") (On loan from D Charles)*	
	(Built Ken Fern/Vintage and Rotary Wing Collection c.1993)					
BGA .2036	Slingsby T.21B	630	RAFGSA 247	3.75	WB969	
BGA 2517	Slingsby T.30B Prefect TX.1	577	WE987	6.79	*(As "WE987")*	
BGA 3239	Slingsby T.31B	708	WT913	26.10.86	*(On loan from J.M.Brookes and Partners)* *(As "WT913")*	21. 7.96

Eden Camp Modern History Theme Museum, Malton (www.edencamp.co.uk)

Reg	Type	Prev id	Remarks
BAPC.230	Supermarine Spitfire fsm	"AA908"	*(As "AB550:GE-P" in RAF 349 Sqdn c/s)*
	(Built TDL Replicas 1993)		
BAPC.235	Fieseler Fi 103 (V-1) fsm		
	(Built TDL Replicas 1993)		
BAPC.236	Hawker Hurricane fsm		*(As "P2793:SD-M" in RAF 501 Sqdn c/s)*
	(Built G B Moulders, Norfolk 1993)		

Fort Paull Armouries, Paull, Hedon (www.fortpaull.com)

Reg	Type	c/n	Prev id	Date	Remarks
G-AOAI	Blackburn Beverley C.1	1002	XB259	15. 3.55	Cancelled 30. 3.55 as transferred to military marks *(As XB259)*

Museum and Art Gallery, Doncaster (www.doncaster.gov.uk)

G-AEKR	Mignet HM.14 Pou-Du-Ciel	CAC.1		26. 6.36	WFU and cancelled 31. 7.38	22. 6.37
	(Buit E Claybourne & Co)		(Stored Doncaster 1938/1960: dbf RAF Finningley 4.9.70: rebuilt and and allocated "G-AEKR" (BAPC.121)			
BAPC.275	Bensen B.7					
	(Built S J R Wood, Warmsworth) (Volkswagen 1600)					

Street Life Museum, High Street, Hull (www.hullcc.gov.uk)

BAPC.287	Blackburn Lincock fsm		(As "G-EBVO")			
	(Built BAE, Brough c 2002)					

Yorkshire Air Museum, Elvington (www.yorkshireairmuseum.co.uk)

G-AJOZ	Fairchild 24W-41A Argus 1	347	FK338	21. 4.47	Cancelled	15.12.63
	(UC-61-FA)		42-32142		(Crashed Rennes, France 16. 8.62)	
G-AMJT	Westland-Sikorsky S-55 Whirlwind HAR.1WA/1		G-17-1	25. 5.51	Cancelled 13. 3.53 - to RN as XA862 (Front fuselage)	
G-AMYJ	Douglas C-47B-25DK Dakota 6 15968/32716		SU-AZF	23. 2.53	Cancelled 12.12.01 as WFU	4. 4.97A
			G-AMYJ, XF747, G-AMYJ, KN353, 44-76384			
G-ASCD	Beagle A.61 Terrier 2	B.615	PH-SFT	23. 7.62	Cancelled 5.10.89 as WFU (As "TJ704:JA")	26. 9.71
			(PH-SCD), G-ASCD, VW993			
G-AVPN	Handley Page HPR.7 Dart Herald 213	176	I-TIVB	22. 6.67	Cancelled 8.12.97 as WFU	14.12.99T
			G-AVPN, D-BIBI, (HB-AAK)		(Channel Express titles	
G-BDBZ	Westland WS-55 Whirlwind 2 (HAR.10) WA.62		XJ398	23. 4.75	Cancelled 28. 3.85 by CAA (Not converted) (As "XJ398")	
	(Regd with c/n WA.386)		(XD768)		(On loan from Yorkshire Helicopter Preservation Group)	
G-BKDT	Royal Aircraft Factory SE.5A replica	278		26. 5.82	Cancelled 11. 7.91 by CAA (No Permit issued)	
	(Built J A Tetley - pr.no.PFA 080-10325)				(As "F943" - these marks carried by G-BIHF also)	
G-BMYP	Fairey Gannet AEW.3	F.9461	8610M	19. 9.86	Cancelled 22. 2.05 by CAA)	
	(Built Westland Aircraft Ltd)		XL502		(As "XL502" in 849 Sqdn:B" Flight RN c/s)	
G-HNTR	Hawker Hunter T.7	HABL-003311	8834M	7. 7.89	Cancelled 11.10.91 as WFU	
			XL572		(As "XL571:V" in "Blue Diamonds" c/s)	
G-MJRA	Mainair Tri-Flyer 250/Hiway Demon PRJM-01			21.12.82	Cancelled 24. 1.95 by CAA	28. 6.91
G-TFRB	Air Command 532 Elite Sport PFA G/04-1167			26. 4.90	Cancelled 7. 6.01 by CAA	6. 8.98P
	(Built F R Blennerhasset - kit no.0628)					
BAPC.28	Wright Flyer fsm					
BAPC.41	Royal Aircraft Factory BE.2c replica		(As "6232")			
	(Built RAF Halton apprentices)					
BAPC.42	Avro 504K fsm		(As "H1968")			
BAPC.76	Mignet HM.14 Pou-Du-Ciel replica		(As "G-AFFI")			
	(Modern reproduction) (Scott)					
BAPC.89	Cayley Glider fsm					
BAPC.130	Blackburn (1911) Monoplane fsm		"Mercury" (Built for TV Series."The Flambards")			
BAPC.157	WACO CG-4A Hadrian Glider		(As "237123") (Fuselage frame section only and tail pieces ex 456476)			
BAPC.240	Messerschmitt Bf.109G fsm					
	(Built D.Thorton 1994)					
BAPC.254	Supermarine Spitfire 1 fsm		(As "R6690:PR-A" in RAF 609 Sqdn c/s)			
BAPC.265	Hawker Hurricane fsm		(As "P3873:YO-H" in RCAF 1 Sqdn c/s)			
BAPC.270	de Havilland DH.60 Moth fsm		(As "G-AAAH") "Jason"			

SCOTLAND

Dumfries and Galloway Aviation Museum, Dumfries (www.members.xoom.com/dgamuseum)

G-AHAT	Auster J/1N Alpha	1849	(HB-EOK)	11. 2.46	Cancelled 7. 7.75 as WFU	6. 2.75
					(Crashed 31. 8.74) (Frame only)	
G-AWZJ	Hawker Siddeley HS.121 Trident 3B Series 101			14. 1.69	Cancelled 7. 3.86 as WFU	12. 9.86T
		2311			(Forward fuselage only)	

National Museum of Flight, East Fortune (www.nms.ac.uk/flight)

G-ABDW	de Havilland DH.80A Puss Moth	2051	VH-UQB	23. 8.30	Cancelled 12.33 WFU and 21. 1.82 PWFU	
			G-ABDW		(To VH-UQB 27. 5.31 and restored 25. 3.77) (As "VH-UQB")	
G-ACVA	Kay Gyroplane 33/1	1002		26. 6.34	Cancelled 9.58	
	(Built Oddie Bradbury and Cull Ltd) (Pobjoy R 75hp)				(On loan from Glasgow Museum of Transport)	
G-ACYK	Spartan Cruiser III	101		2. 5.35	Crashed Largs, Ayrshire 14.1.38 (Fuselage only)	2. 6.38
G-AGBN	General Aircraft GAL.42 Cygnet 2	111	ES915	4.10.40	Cancelled 15.11.88 as WFU	28.11.80P
			G-AGBN			
G-AHKY	Miles M.18 Series 2	4426	HM545	26. 4.46	Cancelled 19. 3.92 as WFU	20. 9.89P
			U-0224, U-8			
G-AMOG (2)	Vickers 701 Viscount	7	(G-AMNZ)	23. 5.52	Cancelled 17. 5.76 as WFU"RMA Robert Falcon Scott"	
					(BEA titles)	14. 6.77
G-ANOV	de Havilland DH.104 Dove 6	04445	G-5-16	11. 3.54	Cancelled 6. 7.81 as WFU	31. 5.75
					(Civil Aviation Authority titles	
G-AOEL	de Havilland DH.82A Tiger Moth	82537	N9510	27. 9.55	WFU 18. 7.72	18. 7.72
G-APFJ	Boeing 707-436	17711		7. 8.59	WFU 12. 6.81 (Nose only)	16. 2.82T
G-APHV	Avro 652A Anson C.19 Series 2	xxxx	VM360	19. 9.57	Cancelled 21. 1.82 as PWFU (As "VM360")15. 6.73	
G-ARCX	Gloster Meteor NF.14	AW.2163	WM261	8. 9.60	Cancelled 25.10.73 as WFU (WFU 2.69)	20. 2.69S
	(Built Armstrong-Whitworth Aircraft)					
G-ARPH	de Havilland DH.121 Trident 1C	2108		13. 4.61	WFU 26. 3.82 (Nose only)	8. 9.82T
G-ASUG	Beech E18S-9700	BA-111	N575C	3. 7.64	WFU 12. 5.75 (Loganair c/s)	23. 7.75
			N555CB, N24R			
G-ATOY	Piper PA-24-260 Comanche B	24-4346	N8893P	7. 2.66	Crashed near Elstree 6. 3.79 "Myth Too" (Fuselage only)	
G-AVMO	British Aircraft Corporation One-Eleven 510ED			11. 5.67	Cancelled 12. 7.93 as WFU (British Airways titles) 3. 2.95T	
		BAC.143			"Lothian Region"	
G-AVPC	Druine D.31 Turbulent	PFA 544		15. 6.67	Cancelled 13. 9.02 as PWFU	28. 9.99P
	(Built J Sharp)					
G-AXEH	Beagle B.125 Bulldog 1	B.125-001		25. 4.69	Cancelled 15. 1.77 as WFU	15. 1.77
G-BBVF	Scottish Aviation Twin Pioneer 3	558	7978M	17.12.73	Cancelled 8. 8.83 as PWFU	14. 5.82
			XM961			

G-BDFU	PMPS Dragonfly MPA Mk.1	01		14. 7.75	Cancelled 12.83 as WFU	
	(Built Prestwick MPA Group)				(On loan from R.J.Hardy and R.Churcher)	
G-BDIX	de Havilland DH.106 Comet 4C	6471	XR399	1. 9.75	Cancelled 2. 9.91 by CAA (Dan-Air titles)	11.10.81T
G-BDYG	Percival P.56 Provost T.1	PAC/F/056	7696M	25. 5.76	Cancelled 4.11.91 by CAA (As "WV493:29 A-P")	28.11.80P
			WV493			
G-BIRW	Morane-Saulnier MS.505 Criquet	695/28	OO-FIS	10. 4.81	Cancelled 15.11.88 as WFU	3. 6.83P
			F-BDQS, French AF 695		(As "FI+S" in Luftwaffe c/s)	
G-BOAA	British Aircraft Corporation Concorde Type 1 Variant 102			3. 4.74	Cancelled 4. 5.04 as WFU	24. 2.01T
		206 & 100-006	G-N94AA , G-BOAA			
G-BVWK	Air & Space 18-A Gyroplane	18-14	SE-HID	19.12.94	Cancelled 18.10.00 as TWFU	
			N6108S			
G-JSSD	Handley Page HP.137 Jetstream 1	227	N510F	14. 6.79	Cancelled 4. 1.96 by CAA	9.10.90
			N510E, N12227, G-AXJZ			
	(Converted to BAe Jetstream Series 3001 prototype.1979/80)					
G-MBJX	Hiway Skytrike I/Hiway Super Scorpion MM-01			2. 2.82	Cancelled 13. 6.90 by CAA	
	(Valmet SM160 s/n 15108)					
G-MBPM	Eurowing Goldwing	EW-21		14. 4.82	Cancelled 30. 8.00 as WFU	21. 8.98P
	(Fuji-Robin EC-34-PM)					
G-MMLI	Mainair Tri-Flyer 250/Solar Wings Typhoon S	BAPC.244		26. 3.84	Cancelled 7. 9.94 by CAA	
	RPAT-01 & T484-423L				(Originally regd as Hiway Skytrike Mk.II 250)	
BAPC.49	Pilcher Hawk Glider					
	(1896 original) (Rebuilt after fatal crash Stanford Hall, Leicester 30.9.1899)					
BAPC.160	Chargus 18/50 Hang Glider					
BAPC.195	Birdman Sports Moonraker 77 Hang Glider				(Built c.1977)	
BAPC.196	Southdown Sailwings Sigma 2m Hang Glider				(Built c.1980)	
BAPC.197	Scotkites Cirrus III Hang Glider				(Built 1977)	
BAPC.245	Electraflyer Floater Hang Glider				(Wing only)	
	(Built 1979)					
BAPC.246	Hiway Cloudbase Hang Glider				(Built 1978)	
BAPC.247	Albatros ASG.21 Hang Glider				(Built 1977)	
BAPC.262	Catto CP-16					
BGA 852	Slingsby T.8 Tutor		TS291	2. 7.58	(As "TS291")	
BGA 902	Slingsby T.12 Gull I			15. 5.59	(As "BED" & "G-ALPHA")	
BGA 1014	Slingsby T.21B	556	SE-SHK	1.62	(As "BJV")	

Royal Museum of Scotland, Edinburgh (www.rnms.ac.uk)

BAPC.85	Weir W-2	xxxx			(As "W-2") (On loan)	
	(Weir Dryad II 50hp)					

603 (City of Edinburgh) Squadron Association, Edinburgh Airport

BAPC.227	Supermarine Spitfire IA fsm				(As "L1070:XT-A" in RAF 603 Sqdn c/s)	

Museum of Transport, Kelvin Hall, Glasgow

BAPC.48	Pilcher Hawk glider replica				(Stored 12.07)	
	(Built No.2175 Sqdn ATC, Glasgow 1966)					

Highland Aviation Museum, Dalcross, Inverness (www.highlandaviationmuseum.co.uk)

G-ASVO	Handley Page HPR.7 Dart Herald 214	185	PP-SDG	13. 8.64	Cancelled 25. 9.01 by CAA	14. 1.00T
			G-ASVO, G-8-3		(WFU after collision Hurn 8.4.97: front fuselage only)	

Montrose Air Station Heritage Centre, Montrose (wwwrafmontrose.org.uk)

BAPC.59	Sopwith Camel				(As "B5577:W")	

WALES
Caernarfon Air Museum, Caernarfon, Gwynedd (www.caeairparc.com)

G-MBEP	American Aerolights Eagle 215B	2877		9.11.81	Cancelled 16. 5.96 as WFU	8. 4.96E
	(Chrysler 820)					
BAPC.201	Mignet HM.14 Pou-Du-Ciel replica					
BAPC.286	Mignet HM.14 Flea					
	(Scott A2S)					

National Waterfront Museum, Swansea

BAPC.47	Watkins CHW Monoplane					
	(Watkins 40hp)					

IRELAND
Irish Aer Corps Museum and Heritage Centre, Baldonnel, Dublin

G-ARLU (2)	Cessna 172B	17248502	N8002X	14. 6.61	Cancelled 6. 8.80 as WFU	6.10.78
					(Dbr Biggin Hill 30.10.77)(As "IAC 98") (Fuselage only)	

Nutgrove Shopping Centre, Churchtown, Dublin

EI-124	Grob G102 Astir Standard CS 77	1761	D-85	.80		

South East Aviation Enthusiasts Group c/o Cavan and Leitrim Railway, Dromod, Leitrim, County Leitrim

G-ALCS (2)	Miles M.65 Gemini 3C	WAL/C/1001		7.11.49	Cancelled 30. 5.84 by CAA	
	(Originally regd as Series 3A with c/n 6534)				(WFU 1983)	
	(Cockpit only remains and the provenance was suspect but now thought to be from Miles M.65 Gemini 1A G-AKEL when transferred to					
	Ulster Folk & Transport Museum: components only noted 4.96 and was for rebuild with G-AKGE)					
G-AMDD	de Havilland DH.104 Dove 6	04292		8. 8.50	Cancelled 26. 9.68 (As "IAC 176")	
	(Originally regd as Series.2, then Series 2B)				(To VQ-ZJC 9.68, 3D-AAI, VP-YKF and IAC 176)	
G-AOGA	Miles M.75 Aries 1	75/1007	EI-ANB	9.11.55	Cancelled 30. 5.84	10.10.69
			G-AOGA		(To EI-ANB 18. 5.63, restored 10. 9.65: damaged Cork 8. 8.69)	
G-AOIE	Douglas DC-7C	45115	PH-SAX	27. 8.56	Cancelled 31. 3.70 as WFU	
			G-AOIE		(To PH-SAX 10. 4.67, restored 18.11.69: scrapped 10.97: fuselage only)	

G-AYAG	Boeing 707-321	18085	N759PA	26. 3.70	Cancelled 8.12.72	
					(To G-41-2-72, (CS-BDG) (N435MA) and VP-BDF 12.72) (As "VP-BDF") (Nose only)	
IAHC.1	Mignet HM.14 Pou-Du-Ciel	xxxx			"St.Patrick" (Noted 4.04)	
BGA 1410	Grunau Baby III		RAFGSA 378	5. 9.67	(As "CBK")	
	(Built Sfg.Schaffin)		D-4676			
BGA 1424	Slingsby T.8 Tutor	SSK/FF27	RAFGSA 214	10.67	(As "CBZ")	

Ulster Folk and Transport Museum, Holywood, Belfast (www.nidex.com/uftm)

G-ACUX	Short S.16 Scion 1	S.776	VH-UUP	26. 6.34	Cancelled 2.38 and 7.81	
			G-ACUX		(To VH-UUP 2.10.35 and restored 25.3.77) (Stripped frame)	
G-AJOC	Miles M.38 Messenger 2A	6370		23. 4.47	Cancelled 5. 1.82 as WFU	18. 5.72
					(Rear fuselage)	
G-AKEL	Miles M.65 Gemini 1A	6484		8. 9.47	Cancelled 30. 5.84 as WFU	29. 4.72
					(Centre section) (But see entry for South East Aviation Enthusiasts Group above)	
G-AKGE	Miles M.65 Gemini 3C	6488	EI-ALM	18.10.47	Cancelled 30. 5.84	7. 6.74
			G-AKGE			
G-AKLW	Short SA.6 Sealand 1	SH.1571	(USA)	26.11.47	Sold abroad 8.51 (On display dismantled 6.05)	
			R Saudi AF, SU-AHY, G-AKLW			
G-AOUR	de Havilland DH.82A Tiger Moth	86341	NL898	14. 8.56	Crashed Newtownards 6. 6.65	19.11.66
G-ARTZ (1)	McCandless M.2	M2/1		24. 6.61	Replaced by G-ARTZ (2) – see SECTION 1, Part 2	
	(Triumph 650cc)					
G-ATXX	McCandless M.4	M4/3		27. 7.66	Cancelled 9. 9.70 as WFU	
	(Volkswagen 1600)					
G-BKMW	Short SD.3-30 Sherpa Variant 100	SH3094	G-14-3094	13.12.82	Cancelled 14.11.96 as WFU (Broken up 3.96) (Cockpit only)	
	14. 9.90					
BGA 470	Short Nimbus	S.1312		.47	(Stored 1.08)	8.75
IAHC.6	Ferguson monoplane replica					
	(Built Capt J.Kelly Rogers 1974) (Original engine)					
IAHC.9	Ferguson monoplane replica				(Stored 1.08)	
	(Built L.Hannah 1980)					

Ulster Aviation Heritage, Langford Lodge, Belfast (www.ulsteraviationsociety.co.uk)

EI-BAG	Cessna 172A	47571	G-ARAV	7. 8.74	(Damaged 3.10.76)	26. 6.79
			N9771T			
EI-BUO	Aero Composites Sea Hawker	80		25. 8.87		
	(Aka Glass S.005E)					
G-BDBS	Short SD.3-30 UTT SH.1935 & SH.3001		G-14-3001	21. 4.75	Cancelled 1. 7.93 as WFU	28. 9.92S
	(Airframe originally laid down as SC.7 Skyvan c/n SH.1935)					
G-BTUC	Embraer EMB-312 Tucano	312007	G-14-007	19. 6.86	Cancelled 20.12.96 as WFU	11. 9.93
			PP-ZTC			
G-MJWS	Eurowing Goldwing	EW-22		16. 5.83	Cancelled 23. 6.97 by CAA	
	(Fuji-Robin EC-34-PM)					
G-RENT	Robinson R22 Beta	0758	N2635M	17. 3.88	Cancelled 11.12.03 as WFU	12. 6.94T
					(Damaged Newtownards 30.9.92)	
BAPC.263	Chargus Cyclone					
	(Built 1979)					
BAPC.266	Rogallo Hang Glider					

ARGENTINA

Monumento de Aeroclub Colon, Colon

| G-AGAS | General Aircraft GAL.42 Cygnet II GAL/42/117 | | | 2. 4.40 | Cancelled 8.8.41. to LV-KGA (As "LV-FAH") | |

Museo Nacional de Aerónautica, Buenos Aires

G-AICH	Bristol 170 Freighter Mk.1A	12751		26. 8.46	Cancelled 19.12.46 - to LV-XIM	
					(Subsequently LV-AEY, Argentine AF T-30 and as "TC-330")	
G-AZPY	BAC One-Eleven Srs.515FB	BAC.187	D-ALAT	21. 3.72	Cancelled 1. 5.72 - to D-AMAS (As "LV-MHT")	
					(Subsequently LV-PEW and LV-MZM)	

Museo Nacional Malvinas, Oliva (www.museomalvinas.com.ar)

| G-AYHP | English Electric Canberra B.62 | 71234 | G-27-112 | 22. 7.70 | Cancelled 28. 9.70 - to Argentina AF and as "B102" | |
| | | | WJ714 | | | |

AUSTRALIA

Australian War Memorial, Canberra, Australian Capital Territory (www.awm.gov.au)

| G-EAQM | Airco DH.9 | --- | F1278 | 31.12.19 | Cancelled 8. 1.20 | 1. 1.21 |
| | (AS Puma) | | | | (NTU and to Australia 1920 as "G-EAQM") | |

National Museum of Australia, Canberra, Australian Capital Territory (www.nma.gov.au)

G-AERD	Percival Type D Gull Six	D.65	HB-OFU	16. 9.77	Cancelled 28.11.86 on sale to Australia	
G-AHTN	Percival P.28 Proctor I	K.279	P6245	29. 5.46	Cancelled 22.6.48 - to Australia as VH-BLC	
					(Subsequently VH-FEP)	

Australian Aviation Museum, Bankstown, New South Wales (www.aamb.com.au)

G-ASFI	de Havilland DH.114 Heron 2D	14108	(N4661T)	4. 3.63	Cancelled 15. 9.64. - to CR-GAT	
	(Converted to Riley Heron)		G-ASFI, West German AF CA+001, G-5-15			
					(Subsequently VH-CLW, T3-ATA, DQ-FDY, VH-CLW and DQ-FDY) (As "DQ-FDY")	

Camden Museum of Aviation, Kogarah, New South Wales (www.camdenmuseumofaviation.com.au)

G-AGTB	Percival Proctor V	Ae.8		8.12.45	Cancelled 5.11.47 - to VH-BCM 11.47	
	(C/n reported as changed to Ae.9)				(Subsequently VH-SST and VH-BCM) (As "NP336")	
G-AMWI	Bristol 171 Sycamore HC.51	13070		1.12.52	Cancelled 1958 - to RN as "XN635"	
					(Subsequently VH-BAW) (As "XR592")	

Temora Aviation Museum, Temora, New South Wales (www.aviationmuseum.com.au)

G-BURM	English Electric Canberra TT.18	xxxx	WJ680	11.12.92	Cancelled 3. 7.02 - *to VH-ZQN*	2.12.02P
	(Built Handley Page Ltd)				*(As "A84-234" in RAAF 77 Sqdn c/s)*	
G-METE	Gloster Meteor F.8	G5/361641	VZ467	5.11.91	Cancelled 26.10.01 - *to VH-MBX*	20.6.02P
					"Halestorm" (As "A77-851" in RAAF 77 Sqdn c/s)	
G-CDAN	Vickers-Supermarine 361 Spitfire LF.XVIe		TB863	30.11.82	Cancelled 16. 1.89 - *to ZK-XVI*	
		CBAF/10895			*(Subsequently VH-XVI)*	

Central Australian Aviation Museum, Alice Springs, Northern Territory

G-AHVG	Percival Proctor II	H.224	BV658	17. 6.46	Cancelled 25. 3.57 - *to VH-AVG*
					(As "VH-ACM")

Mackay Tiger Moth Museum, Mackay, Queensland

G-AMPM	de Havilland DH.82A Tiger Moth	86128	EM945	23. 2.52	Cancelled 31. 3.52 - *to ZK-BBF*
					(Subsequently VH-IVN)

Queensland Museum, South Brisbane, Queensland

G-EACQ	Avro 534 Baby	534/1	VH-UCQ	29. 5.19	Sold 6.21 - *to G-AUCQ 12.7.21 (As "G-EACQ")*
			G-AUCQ, G-EACQ, K-131		*(Subsequently VH-UCQ 10.30)*
G-EBOV	Avro 581E Avian	5116	No 9	7. 7.26	Cancelled 14. 1.30 as sold in Australia 30. 1.29
			(Lympne 1926)		
	(Originally regd as Avro 581, to 581A in 1927 and modified to 581E)				
G-ABLK	Avro 616 Avian V	R3/CN/523	VH-UQG	4.31	Cancelled - *to VH-UQG 16.9.31*
			G-ABLK		*(Restored 16. 8.32 and crashed South Reggane, Sahara 12.4.33)*

Queensland Air Museum, Caloundra Airfield, Queensland (www.qam.com.au)

G-ASVC	de Havilland DH.114 Heron 2D	14123	EC-AOF	31. 7.64	Cancelled 1.10.64 - *to VQ-FAF*
	(Converted to Riley Heron)				*(Subsequently VH-KAM)*
G-ATZR	Beagle B.206 Srs.2	B.047		28. 9.66	Cancelled 21.12.68 - *to VH-UNL*

Sir Charles Kingsford Smith Memorial, Brisbane , Queensland

G-AUSU	Fokker F.VIIa/3m	4954	N1985	4. 7.28	Cancelled - *re-regd 11. 6.29 as VH-USU*
					"Southern Cross"

Captain Harry Butler Memorial, Minlaton, South Australia

G-AUCH	Bristol Monoplane M.1c	2819	C5001	12. 7.21	Cancelled - *re-regd 15.10.31 as VH-UQI* 27. 6.22
			G-AUCH, VH-UCH		*(As "C5001")*

Classic Jets Fighter Museum, Parafield Airport, Adelaide, South Australia (www.classicjets.com)

G-APTS	de Havilland DHC-1 Chipmunk 22A	C1/0683	WP791	21. 4.59	Cancelled 1. 7.93 - *to VH-ZIZ*
	(Originally registered as Mk.22)				*(As "WP971" and "VH-ZIZ")*

Lincoln Nitschke's Military and Historical Aircraft Collection, Greenock, South Australia

G-APAD	Edgar Percival EP.9	27	(VH-SSW)	18. 3.57	Cancelled 1. 8.58 - *to VH-SSX 8.9.58*
			G-43-6		

Sir Ross and Sir Keith Smith War Memorial, Adelaide,South Australia

G-EAOU	Vickers FB.27A Vimy IV	---	(A5-1)	23.10.19	Cancelled 1920 *(As "G-EAOU")* 31.10.20
			G-EAOU/F8630		

Queen Victoria Museum and Art Gallery, Launceston, Tasmania (www.qvmag.tas.gov.au)

G-ABOM	Desoutter II	D.30	EI-AAD	11. 11.31	Cancelled as PWFU 12.32 - regd 11. 3.32 as VH-UEE
G-ASCX	de Havilland DH.114 Heron 2D	14124	West German AF 30. 8.62		Cancelled 7.5.70 *-to VH-CLV*
	(Converted to Riley Heron)		CA+002		

Australian National Aviation Museum, Moorabbin, Melbourne, Victoria (www.aarg.com.au)

G-AHDI	Percival Proctor I	K.253	P6194	26. 2.46	Cancelled 1. 6.51 - *to VH-AUC 6.51*
					(As "VH-AUC" and "A75-1")
G-AJKG (2)	Miles M.38 Messenger 2A	6373		30. 5.47	Cancelled 17. 8.53 - *to VH-AVQ (Stored)*
G-ANPV(2)	de Havilland DH.114 Heron 2D	14098	G-5-24	20.11.56	Cancelled 5. 1.71 - *to VH-CLX (As "VH-CLX")*
	(Converted to Riley Heron)		(G-ANPV)		
G-APRJ	Avro 694 Lincoln B.2	xxxx	RF342	29.12.58	Cancelled 22.2.05 by CAA *(As "RF342")*
			G-36-3,, G-29-1, G-APRJ, RF342		

Ballarat Aviation Museum, Ballarat, Victoria (www.ballarat.com/aviation_museum.htm)

G-ATGJ	de Havilland DH.104 Riley Dove 5	04113	R.Jordanian AF D-101 12. 7.65		Cancelled 1.11.65 as TWFU
	(Originally registered as DH.104 Dove 5B)		TJ-ACB, YI-ABL		*(Restored 9.10.69: cancelled 20.3.74 - sold as VH-ABK)*

Royal Australian Air Force Museum, Point Cook, Victoria (www.defence.gov.au/RAAF/raafmuseum)

G-AIMI	Bristol 170 Freighter 21E	12799		3.12.46	Cancelled 24. 1.49 - *to RAF as WB482 30. 3.49*
					(Subsequently R.Australian AF A81-1 on 14. 4.49 and VH-SJG) (As "A81-1")
G-AJHW	Sikorsky S-51	51-17	WB220	27. 2.47	Cancelled 22. 5.57 - *to CF-JTO 6.57*
			G-AJHW		*(Subsequently R.Australian AF A80-374)*
G-AJKF (2)	de Havilland DH.84 Dragon III	2081	RAAF A34-92	28. 3.47	Cancelled 19. 8.48 as NTU - *to VH-BDS 28. 4.48*
	(Built de Havilland Aircraft Pty Ltd, Australia)				*(Subsequently VH-AML) (As "VH-AML" and "A34-92")*
G-AOHD (2)	Hunting Percival P.84 Jet Provost T.2	P.84/12	RAAF A99-001	26. 3.56	Cancelled - *to RAAF as A99-001 11.8.61*
			G-AOHD		*(Restored to UK but subsequently A99-001)*
G-AVZD	Hawker Siddeley HS.748 Series.2/228	1601	A10-601	6.12.67	Cancelled 9. 8.68 - *to R Australian AF as A10-601*
G-BYKV	Avro 504K replica	0015		27. 5.99	Cancelled 16. 8.02 as transferred to VH- *(As "E3747")*
	(Built Hawker Restorations Ltd)				*(Subsequently "A3-17")*

Royal Australian Air Force Association Aviation Heritage Museum of Western Australia, Bull Creek, Western Australia (www.raafawa.org.au/wa/museum)

G-ALIS	Percival Proctor III	K.392	Z7203	21. 2.49	Cancelled 21. 2.52 - to VH-BQR 2.52
					(Subsequently VH-GAS) (As "VH-BQR")
G-ALZL	de Havilland DH.114 Heron Series 1	10903	LN-BDH	30. 3.50	Cancelled 25. 4.54 - to LN-BDH
			G-ALZL		

(Restored 21.5.54: cancelled 2.12.66 - to OY-DGS and subsequently to,and displayed as, "VH-CJS")

G-BJSH	Sindlinger HH-1 Hawker Hurricane	W-140		5.11.81	Cancelled 19. 8.86 - to VH-AFW
	(Built A F Winstanley - pr.no.PFA/26-10663)				
BGA 334	Slingsby T.12 Gull I	293A		4.38	Cancelled - to VH-GHL (As "VH-GHL")

AUSTRIA
McDonald's Restaurant, Vienna-Schwechat Airport, Vienna

G-AGRW	Vickers 639 Viking 1	115	XF640	8. 5.46	WFU 8.64	9. 7.68
	(Originally registered as 498 Viking 1A)		G-AGRW		(No markings)	

BARBADOS
Concored Experience, Grantly Adams Airport, Christ Church, Bridgetown

G-BOAE	British Aircraft Corporation Concorde Type 1 Variant 102			9. 5.75	Cancelled 4. 5.04 as WFU (As "G-BOAE")	18. 7.05T
		212 & 100-012	G-N94AE, G-BOAE			

BELGIUM
Stampe and Vertongen Museum, Antwerp

G-BRMC	Stampe et Renard SV-4B	1160	SLN-03	17. 3.78	Cancelled 2. 9.93 - to OO-GWD
			Belgium AF V-18		(As "OO-GWD")
EI-APT (2)	Fokker D.VII/65 replica	02	EI-APU	2. 6.67	Cancelled 28. 5.85 - to N903AC
	(Built Rousseau Aviation)		F-BNDG-		(As "O-BOBE")

Koninklijk Leger Museum/Musée Royal de l'Armée, Brussels (www.klm-mra.be)

G-ACGR	Percival Tyoe D Gull Four IIA	D.29		11. 5.33	Cancelled 12.34 - crashed Waterloo, Belgium 12.34	20. 6.35
	(DH Gipsy Major I) (Originally regd as P.1B)				(As "G-ACGR")	
G-AFJR	Tipsy Trainer 1	2		20. 8.38	Cancelled 12. 4.89 as TWFU	10. 9.64
	(Converted to Belfair)				(As "G-AFJR")	
G-AFRV	Tipsy Trainer I	10		15. 7.39	Cancelled 10. 2.87 by CAA (As "G-AFRV")	
G-AFVH	Tipsy S.2	29	OO-ASB	7. 6.39	Cancelled 27. 7.49 - to OO-TIP (As "OO-TIP")	
G-AHZY	Percival Proctor V	Ae.84		14. 8.46	Cancelled 25. 7.57 - to OO-ARM (As "OO-ARM")	
G-AKIS	Miles M.38 Messenger 2A	6725		19. 9.47	Cancelled 24. 2.70 as WFU (As "G-AKIS")	5. 8.70
G-AKNV	de Havilland DH.89A Dragon Rapide	6458	G-AKNV	2.12.47	Cancelled 27. 9.55 - to OO-AFG	
			EI-AGK, G-AKNV, R5922		(Subsequently OO-CNP) (As OO-CNP)	
G-AMJD	de Havilland DH.82A Tiger Moth	83728	T7238	9. 4.51	Cancelled 11.11.52 - to OO-SOI (As "T-24:UR-!")	
G-AMTP	de Havilland DH.82A Tiger Moth	84875	T6534	17. 7.52	Cancelled 29. 8.52 - to OO-ETP (As "OO-ETP")	
G-AOJX	de Havilland DH.82A Tiger Moth	3272	K4276	18. 4.56	Cancelled 5. 6.56 - to OO-EVS (As "OO-EVS")	
G-AOPO	Percival P.40 Prentice 1	PAC-215	VS613	30. 5.56	Cancelled 11. 9.58 - to OO-OPO (As "OO-OPO")	
G-APPT	de Havilland DH.82A Tiger Moth	84567	T6100	24.10.58	Cancelled 2. 1.59 - to OO-SOK	
					(Subsequently OO-SOW) (As "OO-SOW")	
G-BDPU	Fairey Britten-Norman BN-2A-21 Islander	510		5. 2.76	Cancelled 19.11.76 - to Belgium Army as B-06:OTA-LF 8.76	
	(Originally regd as BN-2A-26)				(As "B-06")	
G-BWGR	North American TB-25N-NC Mitchell		N9494Z	18. 8.95	Cancelled 22. 2.05 by CAA - no UK CofA issued:	
		108-34200	44-30925		(As "151632")	
	(Official c/n 108-30925 - corruption of USAAF serial)					
G-HAPR	Bristol 171 Sycamore HC.14				See SECTION 1 ,Part 2 (As "66")	
BAPC.19	Bristol F2b Fighter fuselage frame	---				
	(Rebuilt to static condition by Skysport Engineering 6.89 with parts from J8264)					

Musée de la Base de Bierset, Grace Hollogne

G-BEED	Fairey Britten-Norman BN-2B-21 Islander	549	25. 8.76	Cancelled 25. 8.77 - to Belgium Army as B-11:OTA-LK
				(As "B-11")

BRAZIL
Museu Aeroespacial, Campo do Afonos, Rio De Janeiro (www.musal.aer.mil.br)

G-AVHB	HS.125 Srs.3A/RA	25136 and NA701	15. 2.67	Cancelled 7. 5.68 - to N501W (As "C93-2113")
	(Originally regd as Srs.3A) Subsequently N506N, N505W, N605W, N700RG, N700RD, N700RG, N125HS, 12HI-105, 02, MT0014			

Museu de Armas, Veiculos Motorizados e Avioes Antigos "Eduardo Andreia Matarazzo", Bebeduoro (www.shaolincuritiba.com.br/museu)

G-AMHB	Westland-Sikorsky S-51 Dragonfly Mk.1B		18. 1.51	Cancelled 12. 5.51 - to OO-CWA
		WA/H/030		(Subsequently XB-JUQ and as "PT-HAL")
G-ANHD	Vickers 701C Viscount	64		12.12.53 Cancelled 23. 4.63 - to and as "PP-SRO")

Museu Asas de um Sonho, Centroe Tecnológico, San Carlos (www.museutam.com.br)

G-ADAS	Miles M.2H Hawk Major	138			19.12.34 Cancelled 1.37 – to Spanish Republicans in 8/36..
.	(Built Phillips & Powis Aircraft Ltd)				Subsequently CX-AAW (As "G-ADAS")
G-OMIG	WSK SBLim-2A	622047	PLW-6247	10.11.92	Cancelled 1. 8.00 by CAA as sold to Brazil (As "6247")
	(MiG-15UTI)		(Polish AF)		
	(Built Aero Vodochody as S.103/MiG 15bis; later rebuilt in Poland)				

CANADA
Reynolds-Alberta Museum, Wetaskiwin, Alberta (http://machinemuseum.net)

G-ACPP	de Havilland DH.89 Dragon Rapide	6254		20. 2.35	Cancelled - sold as CF-PTK (As "CF-PTK")
G-AFGK	Miles M.11A Whitney Straight	509	U-1	6. 4.38	Cancelled 13. 9.77 - to N72511
					(Subsequently to, and displayed as, "CF-FGK")
G-AOYU	de Havilland DH.82A Tiger Moth	82270	N9151	27.12.56	Cancelled 14. 7.71 on sale to US
					(Subsequently to, and displayed as, "C-GABB")

Quesnel Heritage Aircraft Museum, Richbar Store, Quesnel, British Columbia

G-APHY	Scottish Aviation Twin Pioneer Series.1	508	9K-ACC	2.10.57	Cancelled 16. 8.74 - to C-FSTX (Front fuselage only)	
			G-APHY, VR-OAF		(Subsequently to, and displayed as, "C-GSTX")	

Commonwealth Air Training Plan Museum, Brandon Municipal Airport, Brandon, Manitoba

G-ANOS	de Havilland DH.82A Tiger Moth	85461	DE465	4. 3.54	Cancelled 31. 8.72 - to CF-JNF (As "4188")	
					(Subsequently C-FNJF)	

Western Canada Aviation Museum, Winnipeg, Manitoba (www.wcam.mb.ca)

G-APXG	de Havilland DH.114 Heron 2D	14137		20.11.59	Cancelled 25. 6.60 - to Kuwait AF 303 (As "C-FCNX")	
	(Converted to Saunders ST-27 [008])				(Subsequently 9K-BAA and CF-CNX)	

National Air Force Museum of Canada, CFB Trenton, Astra, Ontario (www.airforcemuseum.ca)

BAPC.224	Supermarine Spitfire V fsm		(As "ML380")
	(Built TDL Replicas)		

Canada Aviation Museum, Rockcliffe, Ottawa, Ontario

G-AANM (2)	Bristol F 2b Fighter composite				Details at SECTION 1, Part 2 (As "D7889")	
G-AHLO	de Havilland DH.80A Puss Moth	2187	HM534	1. 5.46	Cancelled 26. 9.69 - to CF-PEI 10.69 (As "CF-PEI")	
			(DR630), Bu.A8877			
G-AIKR	Airspeed AS.65 Consul	4338	PK286	25. 9.46	WFU (As "G-AIKR")	14. 5.65

Canadian Bushplane Heritage Centre, Sault Sainte Marie, Ontario (www.bushplane.com)

G-AKGV	de Havilland DH.89A Dragon Rapide	6796	F-BFPU	9.10.47	Cancelled 25. 7.50 - sold as F-BFPU	
			G-AKGV, NR697		(Restored 7.11.75: cancelled 21. 6.76 - sold as (C-GXFJ)	
					(Subsequently to, and displayed as, "C-FAYE")	
G-AOGW	de Havilland DH.114 Heron 2E	14095		2. 2.56	Cancelled 14. 2.73 – to, and displayed as, "C-GCML"	
	(Converted to Saunders ST-27 [009]					

Collingwood Clasic Aircraft Foundation Stayner, Ontario (www.classicaircraft.ca)

EI-AUB	de Havilland DH.82A Tiger Moth	86509	F-BGCP	26. 8.69	Cancelled 7.10.75 - sold as N82JS	
	Registered as c/n 86508 (ex NM200))		French AF, NM201		(Subsequently to, and displayed as, "C-GSTP" -	

Toronto Aerospace Museum, North York, Ontario (http://torontoaerospacemuseum.com/indexh.htm)

G-BIDN	Percival P.57 Sea Prince T.1	P57/31	WF133	22. 9.80	Cancelled 13.11.84 - to N57AW	19. 2.98P
	(Originally registered with c/n P57/27)				(Subsequently to, and displayed as, "C-GJIE")	

CHILE

Museo Nacional de Aēronautica de Chile, Los Cerillos, Santiago

G-ATTP	BAC One-Eleven Series.207AJ	039	9J-RCH	28. 4.66	Cancelled 19.11.91 - to and displayed as "CC-CYM"
					7Q-YKE, 9J-RCH, G-ATTP, VP-YXA
G-BACK	de Havilland DH.82A Tiger Moth	85879	F-BDOB	4. 9.72	Cancelled 25. 1.89 as sold to Chilean AF Museum in 12.87
			French AF, DF130		(Subsequently to, and displayed as, "CC-DMC")
G-BPLT	Bristol 20 M.1C replica	AJD-1		18. 1.89	Cancelled 22. 6.89 - to CC-DMA (As "C4988")
	(Built AJD Engineering Ltd)				

CHINA (PEOPLES REPUBLIC)

China Aviation Museum, Chiangping, Beijing (www.china.org.cn)

G-ASDS	Vickers 843 Viscount	453		8.11.62	Cancelled 19. 9.63 - to China as 84303
					(Subsequently 406 and B-406) (As "50258")
G-ATNA	de Havilland DH.121 Trident 1E Series 103		AP-ATK	14. 1.66	Cancelled 2. 3.66: restored as AP-ATK 3.66
		2130	G-ATNA, AP-ATK		(Subsequently to China as 232) (As "50051?")
G-AZFU	Hawker Siddeley HS.121 Trident 2E Series 107			29. 9.71	Cancelled 16. 3.73 - to China as 242
		2158			(Subsequently B-2202)
G-BBWG	Hawker Siddeley HS.121 Trident 2E Series 109			3. 1.74	Cancelled 22. 5.78 - to China as 269
		2188			(Subsequently B-269) (As "50055")

China Civil Aviation Museum, Chiangping, Beijing (www.china.org.cn)

G-XIAN	British Aerospace BAe 146 Series 100	E1019	G-5-019	22. 8.86	Cancelled 8. 9.86 - to B-2701
			G-5-523, G-5-019		

CZECH REPUBLIC

Historicky Ustav Armady Ceske Republicky - Letecke Muzeum Kbely, Prague

G-ACGO	Saunders-Roe A.19 Cloud	A.19/5		8. 5.33	Cancelled - to OK-BAK (As "OK-BAK")

DENMARK

Danmarks Flyvemuseum, HelsingF8r

G-AIWY	de Havilland DH.89A Dragon Rapide	6775	NR676	22.11.46	Cancelled 7. 1.47 - to OY-AAO (As "OY-AAO")
G-AKDK	Miles M.65 Gemini 1A	6469		22. 8.47	Cancelled 5.11.73 as WFU (As "G-AKGE")
				27. 3.70	
G-AOJG	Hunting-Percival P.66 President IHPAL/PEM/79			27. 3.56	Cancelled 4. 7.59 - to Danish AF as 69-697 (As "OY-AVA")
	(Originally regd as Prince 5) (Also c/n P66/79)				(Subeqently Danish AF M-697 and OY-AVA)
G-AOUF	de Havilland DH.104 Dove 6	04476		19. 7.56	Cancelled 23. 4.68 - to D-IBYW (As "OY-DHZ")
					(Subsequently OY-DHZ)
G-APJP	de Havilland DH.82A Tiger Moth	82869	(G-AOCV)	30. 7.57	Cancelled 30.10.79 - to SE-GXO (As "S-16")
			R4961		
G-ASSZ	Cessna 310A	35407	N5207A	12. 5.64	Cancelled 2. 2.69 - to OY-DRH (As "OY-DRH")
	(Riley 65 conversion)				

Egeskov Veteranmuseum, Egeskov

G-AEYF	General Aircraft Monospar ST.25 Ambulance			31. 5.37	Cancelled - to Denmark as OY-DAZ (As "OY-DAZ")
		GAL/ST25/95			
G-AOFR	de Havilland DH.82A Tiger Moth	86425	NL913	27.10.55	Cancelled 20.11.60 - to SE-COX (As "NL913")
					(Subsequently OY-BAK and "S-11")

Dansk Veteranflysamlung, Stauning

G-AFWN	Auster J/1 Autocrat	124		1. 8.39	Cancelled 23. 7.56 - to D-EKOM (As "OY-...")
	(Originally regd as Taylorcraft Plus D, converted in 1945)				
G-AHKO	Taylorcraft Plus D	228	LB381	24. 4.46	Cancelled 10. 3.56 - to D-ECOD (As "LB381")
					(Subsequently OY-DSH)
G-AMMA	de Havilland DHC-1 Chipmunk 21	C1/0470		21. 9.51	Cancelled 23. 4.69 - to OY-DHJ (As "OY-AHJ")
G-AMZO	de Havilland DH.87B Hornet Moth	8040	SE-ALD	15. 5.53	Cancelled 14. 2.74 - restored as OY-DEZ
			OY-DEZ, VR-RAI		*(As "OY-DEZ")*
G-ANCY	de Havilland DH.82A Tiger Moth	85234	DE164	12. 9.53	Cancelled 1. 3.55 - to OO-DLA (As "OY-ECH")

EGYPT
Military Museum, Alexandria

| G-AYBX | Campbell Cricket | CA/331 | | 20. 4.70 | Cancelled 1. 9.70 - to Kuwait (As "G-AYBX") |

EL SALVADOR
Museo Nacional de Aviación, Aeropuerto Internacional de Ilopango, San Salvador (www.fas.gob.sv/museo)

| G-ARZO | Douglas DC-6A/B | 45078 | CF-CZQ | 25. 5.62 | Cancelled 31.12.62 –to CF-CZQ (As "301") |
| | | | OD-ADP, CF-CZQ | | subsequently N122M |

FALKLAND ISLANDS
Falkland Islands Museum and National Trust (www.falklands-museum.com)

| G-BOVC | Everett Autogyro Series 2 | 014 | | 22.11.88 | Cancelled 17.8.92 by CAA | 29. 3.91P |
| | | | | | *(Subsequently to, and displayed as "VP-FBS")* | |

FINLAND
Aviation Museum of Central Finland (Keski-Suomen Ilmailumuseo, Tikkakoski (www.k-silmailumuseo.fi)

G-EBNU	Avro 504K	xxxx---	E448	19. 3.26	Cancelled 9.26 - to Finnish AF as 1H49 (As "AV-57")
G-AMJR	de Havilland DH.82A Tiger Moth	85167	T6958	23. 5.51	Cancelled 20. 9.51 - to OH-ELA (As "OH-XLA")
GN-101	Folland Fo.141 Gnat F.1	FL-8	G-39-6		*(As "G-39-6")*

Suomen Ilmailumuseo, Tietotie, Helsinki (www.ilmailumuseo.fi)

G-AJPC	Fairchild F.24W-41A Argus II	324	FK315	21. 4.47	Cancelled 11. 1.52 - to OH-FCJ (As "OH-FCJ")
	(UC-61-FA)		42-32119		
G-AKIZ	Fairchild F.24R-41A Argus II	287	EV779	23. 9.47	Cancelled 10. 1.52 - to OH-FCK. (As "OH-FCK")
	(UC-61-FA)		41-38843		
G-BRXM	Colt GA-42 Gas Airship	1152		31. 1.90	Cancelled 14. 9.90 - to OH-ITA (As "OH-KTA")
					(Gondola only)

FRANCE
Musée des Ballons, Chateau de Balleroy, Balleroy, 14 Calvados

G-BKBR (2)	Cameron Chateau 84SS Balloon (Hot Air) 743			11. 5.82	Cancelled 29. 4.93 as WFU	
	(Forbes Chateau de Balleroy shape)					
G-BKNN	Cameron Minar-E-Pakistan Balloon (Hot Air)			7. 2.82	Cancelled 29. 4.93 as WFU	
	(240ft Moslem National Monument shape) 900					
G-BLFE	Cameron Sphinx 72SS Balloon (Hot Air) 1011			22. 2.84	Cancelled 29. 4.93 as WFU	
	(Egyptian Sphinx shape)					
G-BLRW	Cameron Elephant 77SS Balloon (Hot Air)			14.12.84	"Great Sky Elephant" Cancelled 14.11.02 by CAA	1.10.00A
		1074				
G-BMUN	Cameron Harley 78SS Balloon (Hot Air) 1188			10. 6.86	Cancelled 12.11.01 as WFU	23. 5.99
	(Harley Davidson Motorcycle shape)					
G-BMWN	Cameron Temple 80SS Balloon (Hot Air) 1211			9. 7.86	*Temple"* Cancelled 14.11.02 by CAA "	17. 6.96A
G-BNFK	Cameron Egg 89SS Balloon (Hot Air)	1436		20. 2.87	"Faberge Easter Egg" Cancelled 14.11.02 by CAA	15. 7.02A
	(Faberge Rosebud Egg shape)					
G-BNJU	Cameron Bust 80SS Balloon (Hot Air)	1324		13. 5.87	"Ludwig von Beethoven" Cancelled 1.5.03 as WFU	19. 1.03A
G-BPOV	Cameron Magazine 90SS Balloon (Hot Air)			10. 3.89	"Forbes Capitalist Tool" Cancelled 14.11.02 by CAA	5. 7.01A
	(Forbes Magazine shape)	1890				
G-BPSP	Cameron Ship 90SS Balloon (Hot Air)	1848		10. 3.89	"Santa Maria" Cancelled 14.11.02 by CAA	17. 6.94
	(Columbus Santa Maria shape)					
G-BRWZ	Cameron Macaw 90SS Balloon (Hot Air)				Details in SECTION 1, Part 2	
G-BTCZ	Cameron Chateau-84SS Balloon (Hot Air)				Details in SECTION 1, Part 2	
G-TURK	Cameron Sultan 80SS Balloon (Hot Air) 1711			12. 4.88	Cancelled 28. 8.02 by CAA	18. 6.00A

Musée -Aeronautique Presq'EEle CF4te D'Amour, La Baule-Escoublac Aerodrome, La Baule 44 Loire-Atlantique

| G-AVXV | Bleriot XI | 225 | | 2.11.67 | Cancelled 16. 7.92 - to F-AZIN (As "F-AZIN") |

Musée Historique de l'Hydraviation, Biscarrosse, 40 Landes

| G-DUCK | Grumman G.44 Widgeon (OA-14) | 1218 | N3103Q | 15.11.88 | Cancelled 24. 3.93 on transfer to France |
| | | | N58337, 42-38217, NC28679 | | *(As "G-DUCK")* |

Amicale Jean-Baptiste Salis, La Ferté-Alais, 91 Essonne

G-AFNJ	de Havilland DH.94 Moth Minor	94038	AW113	15. 5.39	Cancelled 9. 6.40 as impressed as AW113, restored 6.4.46
			G-AFNJ		cancelled 17. 7.54 - sold as F-BAOG
					(Subsequently F-PAOG) (As "F-PAOG")
G-ALZF	de Havilland DH.89A Dragon Rapide	6541	X7381	24. 3.50	Cancelled - sold as F-BGON
					(Subsequently F-AZCA) (As "F-AZCA")
G-ANJG	de Havilland DH.82A Tiger Moth	83875	T7349	12.12.53	Cancelled 26. 5.54 - sold as F-BGZT (As "F-BGZT")
G-ANSG	de Havilland DH.82A Tiger Moth	85569	DE615	2. 6.54	Cancelled: crashed near Caen, France 15.6.57
					(As "G-ANSG")
G-AOGJ	de Havilland DH.82A Tiger Moth	83283	T7025	15.12.55	Cancelled 16. 1.56 - to OO-SOB 3.56. .
	(C/n 83285 also quoted)				*(As "OO-SOB")*
G-BECL	CASA 352L	24	Spanish AF T2B-212	27. 7.76	Cancelled 19. 6.90 - sold as F-AZJU
	(Junkers Ju.52/3M) (C/n also reported as 103)				*(As "N9+AA")*

Association des Cages à Poules d'Acquitaine, Liorac-sur-Louyre, 24 Dordogne
G-ANXP   Piper J3C-65 Cub (L-4H-PI)   12192   N79819   13.12.54   Cancelled 14.10.55 - *sold as D-EGUL 10.55.*
                                                                              44-79896   *(Subsequently PH-CMS, (OO-LSD), OO-GMS*
                                                                                                          - to F-GLMS 12.91) (As "F-GLMS")-

Collection de la Base Aéronavale de Nimes-Garons, 30 Gard
EI-ALR   Douglas C-47-DL Dakota   4579   EI-ACG   2. 1.61   Cancelled 14. 1.61 - *sold to French Navy as 8487/87*
                                                                              41-18487   *(Call sign F-YFGC later F-YGGB) (As "87")*

Musée de l'Air et de l'Espace, Le Bourget, 93 Seine-Saint-Denis, Paris (www.mae.org)
G-EBYY   Cierva C.8L Mk.2   ---   21. 6.28   Sold 4.30 abroad? *(As "G-EBYY")*   13. 7.29
          (Avro 617) (AS Lynx @ 180hp)
G-AKCO   Short S.25 Sandringham 7   SH57C   JM719   29. 7.47   Cancelled 10. 5.55
          (Sunderland GR.3 c/n SB2022 conversion)   *(To VH-APG 10.54 subsequently F-OBIP) (As "F-OBIP")*
G-ALGB   de Havilland DH.89A Dragon Rapide   6706   HG721   17.12.48   Cancelled - *sold as F-BHCD 10.54 (As "F-BHCD")*
EI-ALT   Douglas C-47A-10-DK Dakota   12471   EI-ACT   2. 1.61   Cancelled in 2. 1.61 - *to French Navy as 12471:71*
                                                                              KG436, 42-92647   *(As "12471:71")*

Musée de L'Automoiliste, Aire de Breguieres, Mougins, Cannes, 06 Alpes-Maritimes
(G-BLXI (1)) Bleriot Type XI replica   EMK 010   3.85R   NTU - to BAPC.132 *(No markings)*
              (Anzani 25hp)
          (Built L.D.Goldsmith - pr.no PFA 88-10864 built 1976 from original components; rebuilt Skysport Engineering 1982 - possibly same a/c as BAPC.189)

Ailes Anciennes Toulouse, Blagnac, Toulouse, 31 Haute-Garonne
G-ALWC   Douglas C-47A-25-DK Dakota   13590   KG723   10. 1.50   Cancelled 19.11. 82 - *to F-GBOL, NTU; (As "G-ALWC")* 6. 2.83
                                                                              42-93654   Cancelled 29. 2.84 by CAA, restored 1. 5.84, cancelled 3. 4.89 by CAA

GERMANY
Deutches Tecknikmuseum, Berlin
G-BLFL   Douglas C-47B-45-DK Dakota   16954, 34214   N951CA   14. 3.84   Cancelled 12. 8.85 to N951CA: restored 5.11.85
                                                        G-BLFL, Spanish AF T3-54, N73856, 45-951
                                                                                            Cancelled 27. 8.86 - to N951CA, *(As "45-0951")*
BAPC.194 Santos Dumont Type 20 Demoiselle   24 bis   *(Built for "Those Magnificent Men in Their Flying Machines"*
          (Built Personal Plane Services)   PPS/DEM/1   *1965 film) (As "BAPC.194")*
          (ABC Scorpion 30hp)

Luftwaffen Museum, Gatow, Berlin
G-HELI   Saro Skeeter AOP.12   S2/5110?   15. 6.78   Cancelled 22. 3.95 on sale to Germany. *(As "XM556")*
          (Composite of cabin 7870M/XM556 and boom 7979M/XM529 [S2/5105])

Luftbrückengedenkanlage, Rhein-Main Air Base, Frankfurt
EI-ARS (2) Douglas C-54E-5-DO Skymaster   27289   N88887   9.12.69   Cancelled 22. 6.77 - restored as N88887 *(As "44-9063")*
                        EL-ALP, N88887, ZS-LMH, N88887, FAR-91, N88887, EI-ARS, LN-TUR, EI-ARS, HB-ILU, N88887, NC88887, 44-9063

Luftfahrt Museum, Laatzen- Hannover, Hannover
G-FXIV   Vickers Supermarine 379 Spitfire FR.XIVc xxx   Indian AF T44   11. 4.80   Cancelled 5. 2.85 as WFU *(As "MV370")*
                                                          Indian AF HS..., MV370

Flugausstellung Junior, Hermeskeil, Trier (www.flugaustellung.de)
G-AMXX   de Havilland DH.104 Dove 2A   04406   22. 1.53   Cancelled 21.10.54 - *to RN as Sea Devon C.20 XJ348:*
                                                                                            Restored as G-NAVY 6. 1.82: cancelled 2. 7.91 as WFU.
                                                                                            (As "XJ348")
G-ARVF   Vickers VC-10-1101   808   16. 1.63   Cancelled as WFU 11. 4.83   23. 7.81
                                                                                            (As "G-ARVF" in UAE titles)
G-BDIW   de Havilland DH.106 Comet 4C   6470   XR398   1. 9.75   Cancelled 23. 2.81 to Germany   8.6.81
                                                                                            (As "G-BDIW" in Dan-Air titles)
G-BKLZ   Vinten Wallis WA-116MC   UMA-01   8.12.82   Cancelled as destroyed 8. 6.89   16.12.83P
          (Aka Vinten VJ-22 Autogyro)   *(As "G-55-2")*
G-BXSL   Westland Scout AH.Mk.1   F.9762   XW799   17. 2.98   Cancelled 7. 5.02 by CAA *(As "G-BXSL")*   19. 8.02P

Luftfahrt Museum Merseburg, Merseburg Sud
G-DEVN   de Havilland DH.104 Devon C.2/2   04269   WB533   26.10.84   Cancelled 16.11.90 by CAA *(As "WB533")*   4.2.85P

Deutsches Museum, Oberschleisseim, Munich (www.deutsches-museum.de)
G-ALUA   Winter LF-1 ZaunkF6nig   V-2   VX190   28. 6.49   Cancelled 16. 4.74 - to EI-AYU
                                                      D-YBAR   *(Subsequently D-EBCQ) (As "D-EBCQ")*
G-AWHA   CASA 2111D   025   Spanish AF   14. 5.68   Cancelled 15. 8.70 - to D-CAG
          (He.111H-16)   B2I-77   *(As "B2I-77")*
G-AYUK   Western-Brighton M-B65 Balloon (Hot Air) 003   17. 3.71   Cancelled 10.12.73 - to D-Westfalen II
                                                                                            (As "D-Westfalen II")
G-BHUW   Boeing-Stearman A75N1 (N2S-5) Kaydet   N474   16. 5.80   Cancelled 7.12.83 - to D-EFTX
                                                      75-3475 N64639, BuA.30038   *(As "D-EFTX")*

Auto und Technik Museum, Sinsheim (www.tecknik.museum.de)
G-AKLL   Douglas C-47A-30-DK Dakota   14005/25450   KG773   18.11.47   Cancelled 6. 6.50 - to EC-AEU *(As "D-CADE")*
                                                      43-48189   *(Subsequently Spanish AF T.3-62, N8041A and "D-CORA")*
G-ARUE (2) de Havilland DH.104 Dove 7   04530   IAC 194   7.10.80   Sold as D-IKER 10.83 and cancelled 17.7.86 by CAA
                                                      (G-ARUE)   *(No markings)*
G-AWHS   Hispano HA.1112-MIL Buchon   228   Spanish AF   14. 5.68   Cancelled 17. 2.69 on sale to Spain
          (Messerschmitt Bf.109G) (Daimler-Benz.605D) C4K-170   *(Subsequently N170BG) (As "4+-" in Luftwaffe c/s)*

Albatros Flugmuseum, Stuttgart Airport, Stuttgart

G-AVHE	Vickers 812 Viscount	363	(G-AVGY)	20. 2.67	Cancelled 14. 2.73 as destroyed (As "G-AVHE")	
			N251V		(WFU 30. 3.70 and b/u 8.72) (Forward fuselage only	
G-BGGR	North American AT-6A Harvard	77-4176	Portuguese AF	17. 1.79	Cancelled 20. 4.79 - D-FOBY reserved 4.79)	
			1608, 41-217		(As "D-FOBY")	

Deutsches Segelfligzeugmuseum, Wassererkuppe

BGA 1711	Aachen FVA.10B Rheinland	xxxx	CPZ	4.72	(As "D-12-354")
			RAFGGA521		
BGA 3277	Lippisch Hols-der-Teufel replica	xxxx-	FHQ	6.87	(As "BGA 3277")

ISRAEL
Israeli Air Force Museum, Hatzerim Air Force Base, Beersheba

G-AHAY	Auster V J/1 Autocrat	1956		12. 3.46	Cancelled - to Israel 10. 3.83 for preservation
					(Subsequently "VQ-PAS" and "1948") (As "13")
G-AIYT	Douglas C-47A-10-DK Dakota	12486	KG451	20.12.46	Cancelled 12. 3.47 - to ZS-BCJ
			42-92661		
G-AJMC	Bristol 156 Beaufighter TF.X	---	RD448	10. 4.47	Cancelled 28. 5.49 - to Israeli DF/AF
					(As "171")
G-AZBV	Britten-Norman BN-2A-2 Islander	285	(EI-AVO)	16. 7.71	Cancelled 16. 3.72 - to 4X-AYK 5.72 (As "004:4X-FMD")
			G-AZBV, G-51-285		(Subsequently 4X-FNP)
G-BCBB	Boeing 720-023B	18013	4R-ACS	9. 4.74	Cancelled 26.10.81 - to 4X-BMB subsequently 4X-JYG
			G-BCBB, C9-ARG, G-BCBB, 6O-SAU, G-BCBB, N7527A		(As "010")
G-BDZZ	North American T-6G Texan	182-720	French AF	15. 6.76	Cancelled 20.12.76 - to Israel (As "001")
			51-15033		
G-BPFY	Consolidated-Vultee 28-5ACF (PBY-5A) Catalina	N212DM		25.10.88	Cancelled 19. 8.98 - to N285RA
		2087	G-BPFY, N212DM, G-BPFY, C-FHNH, CF-HNH, F-ZBAV, N5555H, N2846D, Bu.64017		

ITALY
Museo Nazionale della Scienza e della Tecnica, Milan

G-ACXA	Cierva C.30A	753		4. 4.35	Cancelled - to I-CIER 8.35 (As "I-CIER")
	(Avro 671)				

Museo Storico dell'Aeronautica Militare Italiana, Vigna di Valle

G-ALMB	Westland-Sikorsky S-51 Dragonfly Mk.1A			29. 3.49	Cancelled 13. 4.51 - to I-MCOM (As "MM80118")
	WA/H/006				
G-FIST	Fieseler Fi.156C-3 Storch	156-5802	D-EDEC	23.11.83	Cancelled 4.12.90 by CAA: restored 25.2.91:
			I-FAGG, MM12822		Cancelled 24. 4.95 on sale to Italy) (As "MM12822/20")

JAPAN
Misawa Aviation and Science Museum, Misawa

G-ANAM	Westland-Sikorsky S-51 Mk.1A	WA/H/091		29. 6.53	Cancelled 17. 7.53 - to JA7014

Tokyo Metropolitan College of Industrial Technology, Arakakawa, Tokyo

G-AKVD	Chrislea CH.3 Series 2 Super Ace	112	(VH-BRP)	8. 3.48	Cancelled 10. 2.53 - to JA3062
			G-AKVD		

JORDAN
Royal Jordanian Air Force Historic Flight, King Abdulla Air Base, Amman

G-AIPW	Taylorcraft Auster 5A Series 160	2204		9. 1.47	Cancelled 13.11.95 on sale to Jordan
	(Originally regd as J/1 Autocrat)				(As "A-410" in Arab Legion AF c/s)
G-ATGK	de Havilland DH.104 Riley Dove 400	04288	F-BORJ	12. 7.65	Cancelled 7. 3.67 - sold as F-BORJ (As "JY-AEU")
	(Originally regd as DH.104 Dove 5B)		G-ATGK, R.Jordanian AF D-102, TJ-ACC, (TJ-ABG)		(Restored 21. 2.75: cancelled 19.12.75 - sold as JY-AEU)
G-BOOM	Hawker Hunter T.7 (T.53)	41H/693749	G-9-432	6.10.80	Cancelled 23.6.97 on sale to Jordan. (As Jordan AF "800")
			R.Danish AF ET-274, R.Netherlands AF N-307		
G-BVLM	de Havilland DH.115 Vampire T.55	976	ZH563	6. 4.94	Cancelled 23. 6.97 on sale to Jordan (As Jordan AF "209")
	(Built F + W)		Swiss AF U-1216		
G-BVPO	de Havilland DH.100 Vampire FB.6	615	HB-RVO	11. 7.94	Cancelled 23. 6.97 on sale to Jordan. (As Jordan AF "109")
	(Built F + W)		Swiss AF J-1106		
G-BWKA	Hawker Hunter F.58	41H-697442	Swiss AF J-4075	12.10.95	Cancelled 23. 6.97 on sale to Jordan. (As Jordan AF "843")
G-BWKC	Hawker Hunter F.58	41H-697394	Swiss AF J-4025	12.10.95	Cancelled 29. 9.99 on sale to Jordan (As Jordan AF "712:E")

KUWAIT
Educational Science Museum, Safat

G-ANXY	Auster J/5L Aiglet Trainer	3134		30.12.54	Cancelled 25.6.60 - to K-AAAI (As "K-AAAI")
					(Subsequently 9K-AAI)
G-AXEE	English Electric Lightning F.53	95311	G-27-86	24. 4.69	Cancelled 10. 6.69 - to Kuwaiti AF as 418
					(As "53-418")

Kuwait Air Force Collection, Kuwait International Airport

G-ANNW	Auster J/5F Aiglet Trainer	3120		15. 2.54	Cancelled 25. 6.60 - to K-AAAE (As "K-AAAE")
					(Subsequently 9K-AAE)

G-APXA or G-APXB ?? No positive identification; either

G-APXA	Westland-Sikorsky S-55 Whirlwind Series.2			28.10.59	Cancelled 25. 6.60 - to 9K-BHA
	(Originally regd as Series 1)	WA/318			(Subsequently Kuwait AF 312)

or

G-APXB	Westland-Sikorsky S-55 Whirlwind Series.2			28.10.59	Cancelled 25. 6.60 - to 9K-BHB
	(Originally regd as Series 1)	WA/319			(Subsequently Kuwait AF 313)

MALTA
Malta Aviation Museum Foundation, Ta'Qali

G-ANFW	de Havilland DH.82A Tiger Moth	85660	DE730	5.11.53	Cancelled 10. 3.00 by CAA (As G-"ANFW")	21. 7.01
	(Built Morris Motors) (Regd with Fuselage No.3737)					

MALAYSIA
Muzium Tentera Udara Diraja Malaysia, Sungai Besi Airfield, Kuala Lumpur

G-AMZM	Percival P.56 Provost T.51	P56/20	G-23-6	23. 5.53	Cancelled 27. 4.61 - *to FM1036*
	(Also c/n PAC/F/20)		(WV437)		
G-ANEJ	de Havilland DH.82A Tiger Moth	85592	DE638	1.10.53	Cancelled as WFU 10. 9.73 *(As "T7245")*
					Dbr landing Owstwich, Yorkshire 15. 5.65
					(Sold R.Malaysian AF 2.89)
G-APJT	Scottish Aviation Twin Pioneer Series.1	529		18.12.57	Cancelled 18. 4.58 - *to Malaysian AF as FM1001 4.58*

NETHERLANDS
Aviodrome Museum, Lelystad Airfield, Lelystad

G-EACN	BAT FK.23 Bantam	FK23/15	K-123	22. 7.19	Cancelled .7.19 - NTU and no CofA issued *(As "K-123")*	
	(ABC Wasp)		F1654		*(Originally regd as K-123 29. 5.19)*	
G-AMCA	Douglas C-47B-30DK Dakota 3	16218/32966	KN487	1. 6.50	Cancelled 16.10.03 as WFU	10.12.00A
			44-76634		*(As "PH-ALR" in KLM orange prewar c/s Holland titles)*	
G-AMFU	de Havilland DH.104 Dove 6	04117	VP-KDE	30.10.50	Cancelled 7. 8.69 - *to OO-SCD. (As "OO-SCD")*	
	(Originally regd as a Dove 1)				*(Front fuselage only)*	
G-BKRG	Beech C-45G-BH	AF-222	N75WB	5. 5.83	Cancelled 27. 4.98 as WFU *(As "G-BKRG")*	
	(Regd as C-45H)		N9072Z, 51-11665			
G-BVOL	Douglas C-47B-40-DL Dakota	9836	ZS-NJE (2)	14. 6.94	Cancelled 16. 5.96 on sale to the Netherlands for spares	
			SAAF 6867, FD938, 42-23974		*(As "PH-TCB" in postwar KLM c/s)*	
EI-AKA	Fokker F-27 Friendship 100	10105	PH-FAA	10. 9.57	Cancelled 6.66 - *to PH-FSF.*	
					(Subsequently ZK-NAH, VH-NLS) (As "PH-FHF")	
BAPC.22	Mignet HM.14 Pou-Du-Ciel replica	WM.1			*(As "G-AEOF")*	
	(Scott A2S)					
BAPC.105	Bleriot Type XI	54				
	(Composite from original components including c/n 54: built L.D.Goldsmith 1976 at RAF Colerne) (Anzani "V" 25hp)					

Vliegend Museum Seppe, Seppe Airfield, Rosendaal

G-AIPE	Taylorcraft J Auster 5	1416	TJ347	17.12.46	Cancelled 22. 5.52 - *to PH-NET (2) (As "PH-NET")*

NEW ZEALAND
Classic Flyers Museum, Mount Maungaiui, Bay of Plenty (www.classicflyersnz.com)

G-AMFN	de Havilland DH.82A Tiger Moth	83454	T5819	20.10.50	Cancelled 18.8.54 - *to ZK-BJQ*

Jean Batten Memorial, Terminal Building, Auckland International Airport, Auckland

G-ADPR	Percival Type D Gull Six	D.55	AX866	29. 8.35	Cancelled 14. 3.95 - *to ZK-DPR (As "G-ADPR")*	1. 8.95P
			G-ADPR			

Museum of Transport, Technology and Social History, Point Chevalier, Auckland www.motat.org.nz)

G-AGCN	Lockheed 18-56 Lodestar II (C-56D-LO)	2020	AX756	29. 9.41	Cancelled 19.11.47 - *to AX756*
			42-53504, NC25630		
	(Originally regd as 18-08 Lodestar I; converted 1944)		*(Subsequently EC-Axx 12.48, Spanish AF T.4-? 1.49, N9933F and displayed as "ZK-BVE")*		
G-AHJR (2)	Short S.25 Sunderland MR.5	SH1552	SZ584	27. 6.46	Cancelled 15. 5.48 - restored as SZ584 4.48 *(As "NZ4115")*
G-AMNF	de Havilland DH.82A Tiger Moth	84648	T6200	13.11.51	Cancelled 25. 2.52 - *to ZK-BAD (As "ZK-AIN")*
G-AMMC	Miles M.14A Hawk Trainer 3	779	L8353	15. 9.51	Cancelled 1.10.53 - *to ZK-AYW (As "L8353")*

Air Force World - Royal New Zealand Air Force Museum, RNZAF Wigram, Christchurch (www.airforcemuseum.co.nz)

G-AINT	Bristol 170 Freighter 31MNZ	12834	G-18-100	27. 1.47	Cancelled 17. 4.52 - *to R.New Zealand AF as NZ5903*
G-BIAT	Sopwith Pup replica	001		3.12.82	Cancelled 9. 8.89 - *to Australia - NTU - to New Zealand*
	(Built Skysport Engineering Ltd)				*(As "N6160")*

Ashburton Aviation Museum, Ashburton (www.ashburton.co.nz/aviation)

G-ALAD (2)	de Havilland DH.82A Tiger Moth	-------	"T6296"	14. 6.51	Cancelled 21.2.52 - *to ZK-BAW- subsequently to, and*	
					displayed as "ZK-CDU"	
G-ALKI	Taylorcraft Auster 5C	1272	TJ187	13. 5.49		Cancelled 22.10.51 - *to ZK-AZF*
G-ALKG	DFS 68 Weihe	535	BGA.433	18. 3.49		Cancelled 10 1.64 - *to ZK-GAE 10.52*
	(Built by Jacobs-Schweyer, rebuilt by Slingsby)					

Croydon Aviation Heritage Trust, Mandeville, Gore (www.croydonaircraft.com)

G-ABHC	de Havilland DH 80A Puss Moth	2125		27. 1.31	Cancelled x.12.32 - *to New Zealand Permanent Air Force 8.31*
					as 2125, subsequently ZK-AEV, NZ590 and displayed as "ZK-AEV"
G-ADRH	de Havilland DH.87B Hornet Moth				Details in SECTION 1, Part 2
G-AEDT	de Havilland DH.90 Dragonfly	7508	N2034	9. 5.36	Cancelled 23. 3.98 - *to and displayed as "ZK-AYR"*
			G-AEDT, VH-AAD, G-AEDT, (VH-ABM), G-AEDT		
G-AFPR	de Havilland DH.94 Moth Minor	94031	X5122	16. 5.39	Cancelled 19. 3.99 - *to and displayed as "ZK-AJN"*
			G-AFPR		
G-AHTV	Percival P.28 Proctor I	K.305	P6271	5. 6.46	Cancelled 3.12.53 - *to VH-BCX, subsequently to, and*
					displayed as "ZK-DPP"
G-ALZA	de Havilland DH.82A Tiger Moth	83589	ZK-BAH	19. 1.53	Cancelled 19. 8.53 – *to and displayed as "ZK-BAH".*
					T5853
G-ALZI	de Havilland DH.82A Tiger Moth	84013	T7611	24. 3.50	Cancelled 9.11.51 - *to and displayed as "ZK-AZO"*
G-AMMK	de Havilland DH.82A Tiger Moth	82521	N9494	2.10.51	Cancelled 12.10.51 – *to and displayed as "ZK-AYY"*
G-ANDB	de Havilland DH.82A Tiger Moth	83343	T7035	28.11.53	Cancelled 1.3.54 - *to and displayed as "ZK-BFH"*
G-ATFU	de Havilland DH.85 Leopard Moth	7007	HB-OTA	30. 6.65	Cancelled 7.11.96 - *to and displayed as "ZK-ARG"*
			CH-366		

Ferrymead Aeronautical Society, Christchurch (www.ferrymead.org.nz/societies/aeronautical)

G-AINK	Bristol 170 Freighter Mk.31	12826	WH575	27. 1.47	Cancelled 6. 4.51.- *to and displayed as "ZK-AYG"*	
	(Originally regd as Mk.21)		G-AINK, G-18-92, G-AINK		*(Front fuselage only)*	
G-AZBY	Westland S-58 Wessex 60 Series 1	WA/740	G-17-5	21. 7.71	Cancelled 23.11.82 as TWFU *(As "ZK-IDL")*	14.12.82
			G-AZBY, 5N-ALR, G-AZBY			

New Zealand Fighter Pilots Museum and Alpine Fighter Collection, Wanaka Airport Wanaka (www.nzfpm.co.nz and www.alpinefighter.co.nz)
G-AMUH   de Havilland DHC.1 Chipmunk 21   C1/0834   2. 9.52   Cancelled 9. 1.87 - *to ZK-MUH (As "WB588")*

Omaka Aviation Heritage Centre, Blenheim (www.omaka.org.nz)
G-AJSG   Fairchild F.24W-41A Argus II   837   HB600   15. 5.47   Cancelled 27. 9.54. - to VH-DDG, subsequently VH-EMF
       (UC-61-FA)   43-14873   *(As "VH-EMP")*
G-ATIJ   Pfalz D.III replica   PT.16   EI-ARD   29. 5.67   Cancelled 28. 5.85 *to N905AC, subsequently to, and*
       (Built Hampshire Aeroplane Club)   *displayed as " ZK-JPI"*
G-AMMV   de Havilland DH.82A Tiger Moth   3985   N6712   17.10.51   Cancelled 8. 1.52. - to and displayed as *"ZK-AZQ"*

Wanaka Transport and Toy Museum, Wanaka Airport, Wanaka (www.wanakatransportandtoymuseum.com)
G-AJEC   Auster V J/1 Autocrat   2327   14. 3.47   Cancelled 18.11.54 - *to and displayed as "ZK-BJL"*
G-AOMF   Percival P.40 Prentice 1   PAC-252   (VH-...)   3. 5.56   Cancelled - *to and displayed as "ZK-DJC"*
       (Officially regd with c/n 5820/1)   G-AOMF, VS316

NORWAY
Forsvarsmuseet Flysamlingen, Gardemoen
G-ASCF   Beagle A.61 Terrier 2   B.617   WE548   23. 7.62   Cancelled 10. 4.67 - *to SE-ELO (As "RT514")*
G-BMEW   Lockheed 18-56 Lodestar   18-2444   OH-SIR   30. 9.85   Cancelled 15. 7.86 on sale to "Canada" *(As "G-AGIH")*
       (C-60A-5-LO) *(Gulfstar conversion c.4.59)*   (N283M), OH-MAP, N283M, N9223R, N105G, N69898 ,NC69898, 42-55983

Flyhistorick Museum Sola, Stavangar-Lufthavn
G-AKKA   Miles M.65 Gemini 1A   6528   21.10.47   Cancelled 27. 4.48 - *to LN-TAH (As "LN-TAH")*
G-AOXL   de Havilland DH.114 Heron 1B   14015   (LN-BFY)   5. 4.57   Cancelled 13. 9.71 - *to LN-BFY*: NTU, and restored 21.9.71
                                     G-AOXL, PK-GHB   Cancelled 11.10.71 - *to LN-BFY*
                                                    (As "LN-PSG" in Braathens- SAFE c/s)
G-BBZL   Westland-Bell 47G-3B1   WA/583   S Yemen AF 404 26. 2.74   Cancelled 2. 6.82- *to SE-HME (As "LN-ORB")*
                                                         (Subsequently "LN-ORB")
G-BCZS   Fairey Britten-Norman BN-2A-21 Islander 441   1. 4.75   Cancelled 19. 8.77 - *to LN-MAF (As "LN-MAF")*

Sultanate of OMAN
Sultanate of Oman Armed Forces Museum, Bait al Falaj Airfield, Muscat
G-BGSB   Hunting-Percival P.56 Provost T.1   PAC/F/057   7922M   21. 5.79   Cancelled 11.12.87 by CAA - *to Oman AF*
       (C/n officially quoted as 886391) (Also c/n P56/57) WV494   *(As "XF868")*

PAPUA - NEW GUINEA
Air Nuigini Collection, Jackson Airport, Port Moresby
G-AMZH   Douglas C-47B-20-DK Dakota   15665/27110   KN421   2. 5.53   Cancelled 20. 5.65 - *to VH-SBW*
                                             43-49849   *(Subsequently P2-SBW and displayed as "P2-ANQ")*

Papua New Guinea Gallery National Museum and Art Gallery
G-ABHO   Ford 5-AT-C   5-AT-60   NC401H   .12.30   Cancelled - to VH-UBI 26.10.35
                                                     (Fuselage only)

PORTUGAL
Museu do Ar, Alverca (www.emfa.pt/museu)
G-ASCB   Beagle A.109 Airedale   B.527   23. 7.62   Crashed into River Douro, Barqueiros do Douro, Portugal
                                                       26. 7.64: rebuilt *as CS-AIB* 6.68 and cancelled *(As "CS-AIB")*
BGA 619   Slingsby T.21B   551   10.48   Sold as CS-PAI *(As "CS-PAI")*

SAUDI ARABIA
Dhahran Air Force Base Collection, King Abdul-al-Azix Air Base, Dhahran
G-BFOO   British Aircraft Corporation 167 Strikemaster Mk.80A   22..3.78   Cancelled xx 5.78 - *to R.Saudi AF as 1135*
                                     PS.366   G-27-312

SERBIA and MONTENEGRO
Muzej Yugoslovenskog Vazduhplovsta, Surcin Airport, Belgrade
G-AHLX   Douglas C-47A-30-DK Dakota   14035/25480   KG803   8. 5.46   Cancelled 23.12.47 - *to YU-ABG (As "YU-ABG")*
                                             43-48219
G-AKLS   Short SA.6 Sealand 1   SH1567   G-14-2   26.11.47   Cancelled 7. 3.51 - *to YU-CFK (As "0662")*
                                             G-AKLS, (VP-TBC), G-AKLS
11601   Folland Fo.141 Gnat F.1   FL-14   G-39-8   *(As "11601")*

SINGAPORE
Singapore Science Centre, Singapore
G-AJLR   Airspeed AS.65 Consul   5136   R6029   25. 5.47   Cancelled 26. 2.73 as WFU *(As "VR-SCO")*   23. 4.63
                                                 (On rebuild New Zealand 2009)

REPUBLIC of SOUTH AFRICA
Thunder City, Cape Town International Airport, Cape Town
G-BPFE   English Electric Lightning T.5   B1/95013   XS452   26.10.88   Cancelled 15.7.96 - *to ZU-BBD*
G-BVWG   Hawker Hunter T.8C   41H-693836   XL598   8.12.94   Cancelled 12. 6.95 - *to ZU-ATH "880"*
       (Officially regd with c/n 41H-695320)
G-BVWV   Hawker Hunter F.6A   41H-679991   8829M   22.12.94   Cancelled 30. 8.95 - *to ZU-AUJ (All yellow - no marks carried)*
       (Officially regd with c/n 41H-674112)   XE653
G-BXFW   British Aircraft Corporation 167 Strikemaster Mk.83   29. 4.97   Cancelled 20. 2.98 - *to ZU-PER*
                             EEP/JP/???? and PS.161   Botswana OJ6, ZG808, Kuwait AF 113, G-27-154
G-FSIX   English Electric Lightning F.6   95116   XP693   31.12.92   Cancelled 13. 2.97 - *to ZU-BEY (As "XP693")*
G-LTNG   English Electric Lightning T.5   B1/95011   8503M   8.11.89   Cancelled 13. 2.97 - *to ZU-BEX (As "XS451")*
                                            XS451
G-OPIB   English Electric Lightning F.6   95238   XR773   31.12.92   Cancelled 13. 2.97 - *to ZU-BEW (As "XR773")*

SPAIN

Col-Lecccio d'Automobils de Salvador Claret, Sils-Girona

G-AGXS	Auster V J/1 Autocrat	1967		24. 1.46	Cancelled 12. 5.55 – *to and displayed as "EC-ALD"*

FundaciF3n Infante de Orleans, Cuatro-Vientos, Madrid

G-ABUU	Comper CLA.7 Swift	S.32/5		7. 3.32	Cancelled 18.1.99 - *to EC-HAM (As "EC-AAT")*
G-ACXK	de Havilland DH.60G-III Moth Major	5095		18. 8.34	Cancelled 11.45 *(As "EC-INK")*
					(Abandoned Bucharest, Romania on German invasion 9.39)
G-ADLS	Miles M.3C Falcon Six	231		15. 7.35	Cancelled 8.36 - *to EC-ACB (As "EC-ACB")*
	(Provenance not confirmed)				
G-AEVZ	BA L.25c Swallow II	475		19. 3.37	Cancelled 7.9.01 *as sold to Spain as EC-IMP* 15. 6.01P
	(Blackburn Cirrus Minor)				*(As "EC-IMP")*
G-AFAX	BA Eagle 2				Cancelled 10. 6.08 *as sold to Spain* 15. 5.08P
G-AKAA	Piper J3C-65 Cub (L-4H-PI)	10780	43-29489	23. 6.47	Cancelled 31.10.96 - *to EC-GQE* 23. 5.96P
					(As "EC-GQE")

Museo del Aire, Cuatro-Vientos, Madrid

G-ABXH	Cierva C.19 Mk.IVP	5158		1. 6.32	Cancelled - *to EC-W13 and EC-ATT 12.32*
	(Avro 620)				*(Subsequently Spanish AF 30-62, EC-CAB and EC-AIM)*
					(As "EC-AIM")
G-ACYR	de Havilland DH.89 Dragon Rapide	6261		15.10.34	Cancelled 18. 3.59 by CAA 23. 8.47
					(As "G-ACYR in Olley Air Services titles)
G-AERN	de Havilland DH.89A Dragon Rapide	6345		13. 1.37	Cancelled 18. 1.54 *sold as EC-AKO (As "40-1")*
BGA 1402	Slingsby HP-14C	1637			Sold 5.68 *as EC-BOL (As "EC-BOL")*

SRI LANKA

Katunayake-Negombe Base Collection, Negombo

G-APCN	Boulton Paul P.108 Balliol T.2	BPA.10C	WG224	12. 5.57	Cancelled 13. 8.57 - *to Ceylon AF as CA310 8.57*
	(Second issue of c/n)				

Sri Lanka Air Force Musem, Ratamalana Air Force Base, Ratamalana

G-AKEE	de Havilland DH.82A Tiger Moth	---	"T7179"	18. 8.47	Cancelled 25. 9.47 - *to VP-CAW*
					(Subsequently CY-AAW) (As "CX-123")
G-AMJY	Douglas C-47B-40-DK Dakota	16808/33556	KP254	2. 6.51	Cancelled 11.11.59 - *to 4R-ACI*
			44-77224		*(As "CR-822")*

SWEDEN

Svedinos Bil Och Flygmuseum, Slöinge, Halmstad

G-EBNO	de Havilland DH.60 Moth	261		19. 2.26	Cancelled 26. 7.28 - *to S-AABS*
	(Cirrus I)				*(Subsequently SE-ABS) (As "Fv5555")*
G-AIZW	Auster V J/1 Autocrat	2230		31. 1.47	Cancelled 14. 8.58 - *to SE-CGR*
					(As "SE-CGR")
G-AKAO	Miles M.38 Messenger 2A	6703		27. 6.47	Cancelled 7. 9.53 - *to SE-BYY*
					(As "SE-BYY")
G-ANSO	Gloster Meteor T.7	G5/1525	G-7-1	12. 6.54	Cancelled 11. 8.59 - *to SE-DCC*
					(As "WS774:4")
	(Originally built & regd 19. 6.50 as Meteor F.8 G-AMCJ [G5/1210]: to R.Danish AF as 490, then Egyptian AF as 1424, rebuilt as G-ANSO)				
G-AYZM	Scottish Aviation Bulldog Serie 101	BH.100-105		25. 5.71	Cancelled 2. 9.71 - *to Swedish Army as Fv61005 8.71.*
					(As "Fv61005")

High Chapperal Park, Hillerstorp

G-AVJB	Vickers 815 Viscount	375	(LX-LGD)	21. 3.67	Cancelled 28.10.86 - *to SE-IVY*
			G-AVJB, AP-AJF		*"Big Airland" (As "SE-IVY")*

Flyvapenmuseum, Malmslatt, Linköping

G-ANVU	de Havilland DH.104 Dove 1B	04082	VR-NAP	12.11.54	Cancelled 20. 6.85 by CAA 14. 9.77T
	(Originally regd as Series.1)				restored 15.4.86: cancelled 16. 9.86 *on sale to Sweden)*
					(As "G-ANVU")
G-AZAK	Scottish Aviation Bulldog Series 101 (SK-61)			18. 6.71	Cancelled 17. 9.71 - *to Swedish Army as Fv61006*
		BH.100/106			*(As "Fv61006")*
G-AZJO	Scottish Aviation Bulldog Series 101 (SK-61)			8.12.71	Cancelled 7. 2.72 - *to Swedish Army as Fv61030*
		BH.100/137			*(As "Fv61030")*
G-AZWO	Scottish Aviation Bulldog Series 101 (SK-61)			8. 6.72	Cancelled 19.10.72 - *to Swedish Army as Fv61068*
		BH.100/186			*(As "Fv61068")*

Arlanda Flygmuseum, Arlanda Airport, Stockholm

G-AAHD	Avro 594 Avian IV	R3/CN/318		5.29	Cancelled - *to Sweden as SE-ADT 8.33*
					(As "SE-ADT" in nearby shopping complex)
G-AGIJ	Lockheed 18-56 Lodestar II	2593	43-16433	4. 3.44	Cancelled 9. 7.45 - *to R.Norwegian AF as 2593:T-AE*
	(C-60A-5-LO)				*(Subsequently OH-VKP and SE-BZE) (As "SE-BZE")*
G-ANIU	Taylorcraft J Auster 5	841	MS977	5.12.53	Cancelled 12.10.55 - *to LN-BDU.(Subsequently SE-CBT)*
					(As "SE-CBT")

Västerås Flygmuseum, Hässlo Airfield, Västerås

G-BAVN	Boeing-Stearman A75N-1 Kaydet	75-5659	4X-AMT	13. 4.73	Cancelled 22.10.84 - *to SE-AMT 8.84*
	(Regd with c/n "3250-2606", which is a part number)		N5367N, 42-17496		*(As "SE-AMT")*
G-BNPG	Percival P.66 Pembroke C.1	PAC/66/082	XK884	30. 6.87	Cancelled 4. 5.88 - *to SE-BKH*
	(Also c/n K66/045)				*(As "SE-BKH")*

THAILAND

Foundation for the Preservation and the Development of Thai Aircraft, Don Muang Air Force Base, Don Muang, Bangkok

G-AMOU	de Havilland DH.82A Tiger Moth	84695	N200D	5. 2.52	Cancelled 18.11.93 *on sale to Thailand.*
			9M-ALJ, VR-RBZ, G-AMOU, T6269 *(As "21")*		

Golden Jubillee Museum of Agriculture, Kaset Heliport, Khlong Luang
G-AWID   Britten-Norman BN-2A Islander   26   17. 4.68   Cancelled 7.10.68 - *to R.Thailand AF as 501*

Jesada Technical Museum, Nakhon Pathom, Bangkok
G-AODD   Douglas C-47A-60-DL Dakota   10239   OD-AAO   27. 5.55   Cancelled 5. 9.55 - *to Burmese AF as UBT-715*
                                              LR-AAO, NC36412, 42-24377 *(Subsequently "N2270M")*

Royal Thai Air Force Museum, Don Muang Air Force Base, Don Muang, Bangkok
G-AMJW   Westland-Sikorsky S-51 Mk.1A   WA/H/120   G-17-2   9. 1.52   Cancelled 22. 5.53 - *to R.Thailand AF as 305-53*
                                              (Subsequently to and displayed as "H1-4/96")
G-AMNT   Percival P.50 Prince 3A   P50/41   18. 2.52   Cancelled 4. 4.52 - *to R.Thailand AF as T1-1/98.*
                                              (Subsequently to and displayed as "T1-1/9_6_")

TURKEY
Rahmi M KoE7 Museum, Sutluce, Istanbul (www.rmk-museum.org.tr)
G-MKVI   de Havilland DH.100 Vampire FB.6   676   Swiss AF J-1167 2. 6.92   Cancelled 2. 1.09 by CAA *(As "WL505")*
    (Built FFW)

UNITED ARAB EMIRATES
Al-Mahata Museum, The Sharjah Aviation Museum, Sharjah
G-AMXA   de Havilland DH.106 Comet 2   06023   8. 1.53   Cancelled 2. 3.55. - *to RAF as XK655*
                                              (Front fuselage only)
G-ARDE   de Havilland DH.104 Dove 6   04469   I-TONY   15.11.60   Cancelled 30. 5.01 by CAA*)*   25. 8.91
                                              (As "G-AJPR" in Gulf Air c/s)
G-ARKU   de Havilland DH.114 Heron 2   14072   VR-NAQ   17. 3.61   Cancelled 28.3.61 - *to RN as XR445*
            Restored 20. 4.90 as G-ODLG (2), to (VH-NJP) 23.8.93; restored again 31.8.93, cancelled 8. 9.93 - *to VH-NJP (As "G-ANFE")*
G-BSMF   Avro 652A Anson C.19   ????   TX183   5. 9.90   Cancelled 23. 4.01 as sold to UAE
                                              (As "G-AKVW")

UNITED STATES
Southern Museum of Flight, Birmingham, Alabama (www.southernmuseumofflight.org/
G-ASOF   Beagle B.206 Series.1   B.007   28. 1.64   Cancelled 29.12.80 - *to N163 (As "N163")*
G-AVLK   Beagle B.206 Series 2   B.059   8. 5.67   Cancelled 16. 4.74 - *to N15JP (As "N15JP")*
EI-APV   Fokker D.VII/65 replica   03   F-BNDH   2. 6.67   Cancelled 28. 5.85 - *to N904AC (As "N904AC")*
    (Built Rousseau Aviation)

United States Army Aviation Museum, Fort Rucker, Alabama (www.armyavnmuseum.org)
G-BSKS   Nieuport 28C-1   6531   "N5246"   27. 6.90   Cancelled 1. 4.93 on sale to US
                                        US Navy   *(As "17-6531:5" in 94 Aero Sqn AEF c/s)*

Alaska Aviation Heritage Museum, Anchorage, Alaska (www.alaskaairmuseum.org)
G-AGZI   Consolidated-Vultee CV.32-3 (LB-30) Liberator II 55   AL557   11. 1.46   Cancelled 24. 2.48 - *to SX-DAA*
                                              (Subsequently N9981F, N68735 and N92MK) (As "N92MK")

Planes of Fame Air Museum, Chino, California (www.planesoffame.org)
G-BJSG   Vickers Supermarine 361 Spitfire LF.IXc   HS543   29. 1.81   Cancelled 3.12.01 - *to NX2TF*
    (Also firewall No.6S/730116)   6S/735188   Indian AF, G-15-11, ML417 *(As "NX2TF")*
G-BTHD   Yakovlev Yak-3U   170101   (France)   7. 3.91   Cancelled 14. 3.05 - *to N.....*
    (Conversion of LET Yak C.11)   Egypt AF 533   *(As "30")*
G-WWII   Vickers-Supermarine 379 Spitfire F.XIVe   F-AZSJ   9. 7.79   Cancelled 6. 2.98 - *to F-AZSJ, restored 19. 3.92 -*
                                    6S/663452   G-WWII, F-AZSJ, Indian AF, SM832   *cancelled 16. 2.04 -*
                                                      to N54SF (As "NX54SF")   5. 6 04P
BAPC.110   Fokker D.VIIF fsm   *(As "5125:18")*
BAPC.136   Deperdussin 1913 Monoplane fsm   *(As "19")*
BAPC.140   Curtiss 42A (R3C2) fsm   *(As "3" in US Army c/s)*
BAPC.141   Macchi M.39 fsm (Gipsy Queen)   *(As "5")*
BAPC.156   Supermarine S.6B fsm   *(As "S1595")*

Yanks Air Museum, Chino, California (www.yanksair.com)
G-BUCF   Grumman F8F-1B Bearcat   D.779   R.Thai AF 12209518. 2.92   Cancelled 12.11.92 - *to N2209*
                                    BuA.122095   *(As "N2209")*

Palm Springs Air Museum, Palm Springs, California (www.palmspringsairmuseum.org)
G-BLZW   Republic P-47D-30-RA Thunderbolt399-55744   N47DE   15. 7.85   Cancelled 4.11.85 - *to NX47RP.*
                                    Peruvian AF 122, Peruvian AF 547, 45-49205 *(Subsequently N47DE 6.86) (As "228473")*
G-FIRE   Vickers Supermarine 379 Spitfire FR.XIVc   Belgium AF SG12821. 3.79   Cancelled 13. 2.89 -*to N8118J 2.89*
                                    6S/648206   G-15-1, NH904   *(Subsequently "N114BP")*

Western Aerospace Museum, Oakland, California (www.westernaerospacemuseum.org/
G-AKNP   Short S.45 Solent 3   S.1295   NJ203   2.12.47   Cancelled 20. 3.51 - *to VH-TOB*
                                              (Subsequently N9946F) (As "NJ203")

Aviation Museum of Santa Paula, Santa Paula, California (www.amszp.org/
G-AAMZ (2)   de Havilland DH.60G Moth   1293   EC-ABX   13. 7.87   Cancelled 4. 9.98 - *to N60MZ*
                                    EC-BAU, Spanish AF 30-52, EC-NAN, M-CNAN, MW-134 *(As "G-AAMZ")*
G-AMLF   de Havilland DH.82A Tiger Moth   86572   PG675   18. 8.51   Cancelled 21. 7.71 - *to N675LF (As "G-ADGV").*

Pacific Coast Air Museum, Santa Rosa, California (pacificcoastairmuseum.org)
G-AXEF   British Aircraft Corporation 167 Strikemaster Mk.81   G-27-35   24. 4.69Cancelled 10. 6.69 - *to South Yemen AF as 503*
                  EEP/JP/165 & PS.128   *(Subsequently Singapore AF 322 and N167SM (As "N167M")*

Miami International Airport, Miami, Florida
EI-ATP   Phoenix Luton LA-4A Minor   PAL 1124   G-ASCY   29. 8.69   Cancelled as sold USA 7.73 - *subsequently N924GB*
    (Built Cornelius Bros)   *(Preserved hanging from roof in Concourse E 2008)*

Church Street Collection, Orlando, Florida
BAPC.139   Fokker Dr.1 Triplane fsm   *(As "102/17")*

Fantasy of Flight, Polk City, Florida (www.fantasyofflight.com)
G-AHMJ   Cierva C.30A   R3/CA/43   K4235   8. 5.46   Cancelled 9. 2.50 as WFU
           (Avro 671) (Rota I) *(Official c/n quoted incorrectly as 774 - which was a Danish Avro 621)*
                                                                                  (Restored 8. 4.93: cancelled 12.11.98 - to US) (As "K4235")
G-AMYA(2) Zlin Z.381 Bestmann   461   OO-AVC   17. 6.87   Cancelled by CAA 31.10.96 - to NX181BU   21. 2.96P
           (Czech-built BFCcker BFC.181 Bestmann)   OK-AVC   *(As "AM+YA")*
G-ASKB   de Havilland DH.98 Mosquito TT.35   xxxx   N35MK   8. 7.63   Cancelled 17. 6.83 - to N35MK and restored 16.3.87:
                                                                                  G-ASKB, N35MK, G-ASKB, RS712 cancelled 20.10.87 - to N35MK 3.88 (As "NX35MK")
                                                                                  (Used in "Mosquito Squadron" 1968 film as "HJ690: HT-N")
                                        (On loan to Experimental Aircraft Association Air Venture Museum, Witttman Field, Oshkosh, Wisconsin)
G-AYFO   Bücker BFC.133 Jungmeister   4   HB-MIO   24. 6.70   Cancelled 28. 4.71 - to N40BJ (As "YR-PAX")
           (Built Dornier)   Swiss AF U-57
G-BBMI   Dewoitine D.26   10853   HB-RAA   11.10.73   Cancelled 30. 5.84 - to N282DW
           (Built EKW)   Swiss AF 282   *(As "N282DW")*
G-BCOH   Avro 683 Lancaster Mk.10 AR   277   CF-TQC   24. 9.74   Cancelled 23. 2.93
           (Built Victory Aircraft, Canada)   RCAF KB976   *(As "G-BCOH")*
G-BCWL   Westland Lysander IIIA   1244   RCAF   9. 9.75   Cancelled 3. 6.99 - to N.....(As "V9281").
           (Built National Steel Car Corporation Ltd.) (Composite - main airframe possibly RCAF 2403, parts from RCAF 2341, 2349, 2391)
G-BFHG   CASA 352L   153   Spanish AF   23.11.77   Cancelled 27. 9.94 - to US
           (Junkers Ju 52/3m) (C/n reported as 155)   T2B-262   *(Subsequently "D2+60" and "D-TABX") (As "VK-NZ")*
G-BJCL   Morane Saulnier MS.230 Parasol   1049   EI-ARG   22. 7.81   Cancelled 27. 1.88 - to N230MS
                                                        F-BGMR, French Military   *(As "N230MS")*
G-BJHS   Short S.25 Sandringham   SH.55C   (EI-BYI)   11. 9.81   Cancelled 12. 8.93 - to N814ML
           (Sunderland GR.3 c/n SH974 conversion)   G-BJHS, N158J, VH-BRF, R.NZ AF NZ4108, ML814
                                                                                  (Carries "N814ML, G-BJHS and ML814")
G-BXYA   CSS-13 Aeroklubowy   0365   SP-ACP (3)   3. 7.98   Cancelled 13.11.98 - to US (As "N50074")
           (Licence built Polikarpov Po-2)   (SP-FCN), SP-ACN (3), PLW-..
G-CCVV   Vickers Supermarine 379 Spitfire FR.XIVe   Indian AF "42" 18. 5.88   Cancelled 6. 1.93 as TWFU (As "G-CCVV")
                                         6S/649186   MV262
G-XVIB   Vickers Supermarine 361 Spitfire LF.XVIe   N476TE   3. 7.89   Cancelled 1. 2.90 - to N476TE: restored 3.5.94:
                                         CBAF.IX.4610   G-XVIB, 8071M, 7451M, TE476 cancelled 21. 9.95 and restored 1.96 as N476TE)

Eighth Air Force Museum, Barksdale Air Force Base, Louisiana (www.mightyeighth.org)
G-BGCF   Douglas C-47A-90-DL Dakota   20596   Spanish AF   20.11.78   Cancelled 30. 1.80 - to N3753C (As "43-16130")
                                                        T3-33, N86453, 43-16130

Air Zoo, Kalamazoo, Michigan (www.airzoo.org)
G-AWHJ   Hispano HA.1112-MIL Buchon   171   Spanish AF   14. 5.68   Cancelled 20. 2.69 - to N90605, subsequently N76GE
           (Messerschmitt Bf.109G)   C4K-100   *(As C4.K-19")*

Yankee Air Museum, Belleville, Michigan (www.yankeeairmuseum.org)
G-AOZZ   Armstrong-Whitworth 650 ArgosySeries.100   12. 3.57   Cancelled 1.10.68 - to G-11-1, subsequently N896U
                                         AW.6651   *(As "N896U")*

Millville Army Airfield Museum, Millville, New Jersey (www.p47millville.org)
G-BEWT   Short SD.3-30 Variant 100   SH3011   G-14-3011   20. 6.77   Cancelled 28.10.77 - to N331GW (As "82-25343")
G-THUN   Republic P-47D-40RA Thunderbolt   N47DD   18. 6.99   Cancelled 21. 7.06 - to NX47DD (As "226671")   7. 7.07P
                                         399-55731   Peruvian AF 119, Peruvian AF 545, 45-49192
                                                        (Composite rebuild from wreck of original N47DD plus an unidentified P-47N fuselage)

Southwest Soaring Museum, Moriaty, New Mexico (www.swsoaringmuseum.org)
BGA.3219   Slingsby T.21B Seburgh TX.1   606   WB941   7.87   To N941B (As "N941B")

War Eagles Museum, Santa Teresa, New Mexico (www.war-eagles-air-museum.com)
G-ANNC   de Havilland DH.82A Tiger Moth   84569   T6102   22. 1.54   Cancelled 9. 4.58 - to OO-SOM (2) 4.58
                                                                                  (Subsequently N7158N)

Lone Star Flight Museum, Galveston Airport, New Mexico (www.lsfm.org)
G-FORT   Boeing 299-O (B-17G-95-DL) Fortress 8627   F-BEEC   11. 4.84   Cancelled 2. 7.87 - to N900RW (As "238050")
                                                        ZS-EEC, F-BEEC, 44-85718
G-ANIZ   de Havilland DH.82A Tiger Moth   83896   T7467   7.12.53   Cancelled 6.12.67 - to N9714. (As "N9714")

Intrepid Air and Space Museum, Manhattan, New York (www.intrepidmuseum.org/pages/concorde)
G-BOAD   British Aircraft Corporation Concorde Type 1 Variant 102   9. 5.75   Cancelled 4. 5.04 as WFU (As "G-BOAD")   3.12.04T
                                     210 & 100-010   G-N94AD, G-BOAD

Rhinebeck Aerodrome Museum, Rhinebeck, New York (www.oldrhinebeck.org)
G-ABIH   de Havilland DH.80A Puss Moth   2140   17. 2.31   Cancelled 11.31 - to NC770N
                                                                                  (Subsequently N770N and NC770N) (As "N770N")
G-ATXL   Avro 504K replica   HAC-1   19. 7.66   Cancelled 6. 8.71 - to N2929
           (Built Hampshire Aero Club)   *(As "E2939")*

National Museum of United States Air Force, Wright-Patterson Air Force Base, Dayton, Ohio (www.nationalmuseum.af.mil)
G-ANCN   de Havilland DH.82A Tiger Moth   85674   DE744   4. 9.53   Cancelled 4..55 - to OO-NCN subsequently N39DH.   21. 6.55
           (Officially regd with c/n 85521)   *(As "N39DH")*
G-MOSI   de Havilland DH.98 Mosquito TT.35   xxxx   N98DH   10.11.81   Cancelled 21. 1.87 by CAA   17.12.84P
                                                        N9797, G-ASKA, RS709   *(Sold to USA) (As "NS519")*

Evergreen Aviation Museum, McMinnville, Oregon (www.sprucegoose.org)
G-SXVI   Vickers Supermarine 361 Spitfire LF.XVIe   7001M   25. 2.87   Cancelled 15. 1.90 - to N356V - subsequently N356TE
                                         CBAF-11470   6709M, TE356   *(As "N356TE")*

Tillamook Naval Air Station Museum, Tillamook, Oregon (www.tillamookair.com)

G-AWHN	Hispano HA.1112-MIL Buchon	193	Spanish AF	14. 5.68	Cancelled 20. 2.69 - to N90602 (As "N90602")
	(Messerschmitt Bf.109G)		C4K-130		
G-BMFB	Douglas Skyraider AEW.1 (AD-4W)	7850	SE-EBK	24. 9.85	Cancelled 1.5.90 - to N4277N (As "NX4277N")
			G-31-12, WV181, BuA.126867		

Cavanaugh Flight Museum, Addison Airport, Dallas, Texas (www.cavanaughflightmuseum.com)

G-ALFO	Douglas C-47A-90-DL Dakota	20401	N20DH	30.12.48	Cancelled 22.12.50 - to N94529. (As "32585")	
			N700E, N300A, N94529, VH-BHC, 43-15935			
G-HUNN	Hispano HA.1112-M1L Buchon	235	G-BJZZ	29. 4.87	Cancelled 9.10.91 - to N109GU (As "N100GU")	31. 5.92P
	(Messerschmitt Bf.109G)		N48157, Spanish AF C4K-172			
G-VIII	Vickers Supermarine 359 Spitfire LF.VIII		I-SPIT	27. 4.89	Cancelled 9. 7.93 - to N719MT	18. 6.93A
		6S/479770	Indian AF T17, MT719		(As *NX719MT")	
G-CCMV	Vought FG-1D Corsair	3660	N448AG	21.11.00	Cancelled 5. 9.02 - to N451FG	13. 5.03P
	(Built Goodyear Aircraft Corporation)		N4717C, Bu.92399		(As "N451FG")	

Commemorative Air Force American Airpower Heritage Museum, Midland, Texas (www.commemorativeairforce.org)

G-SALY	Hawker Sea Fury FB.XI	41H-696792	WJ288	12. 7.83	Cancelled 2.1.91 - to N15S (As "WJ288:153:P in RN c/s)	
					(On loan from Memphis, Tennessee)	
G-AWHE	Hispano HA.1112-MIL Buchon	67	Spanish AF	14. 5.68	Cancelled 20. 2.69 - to N109ME (As "N109ME")	
	(Messerschmitt Bf.109G)		C4K-31		(Regd incorrectly as c/n 64)	
G-AKZY	Messerschmitt Bf.108D-1 Taifun	3059	Luftwaffe	7. 6.48	Cancelled 9. 1.50 - to HB-DUB - subsequently N2231)	
			D-ERPN		(As "N2231") (On loan from Hobbs, New Mexico)	
G-MXIV	Vickers Supermarine 379 Spitfire FR.XIVc		Indian AF T3	11. 4.80	Cancelled 15. 5.85 - to NX749DP	19. 7.85P
		6S/583887	NH749		(As "NX749DP") (On loan from Camarillo, California)	

National Air and Space Museum, Steven F.Udvar-Hazy Centre, Chantilly, Virginia (www.nasm.si.edu)

G-AARO (2)	Arrow Sport A2-60	341	N932S	17. 9.79	Cancelled 15. 6.83 - to N280AS	18. 2.83P
			NC932S		(Subsequently N9325) (As "G-AARO")	
G-BFHD	CASA 352L	146	Spanish AF	23.11.77	Cancelled 21. 1.88 on sale to West Germany	
	(Junkers Ju 52/3m)		T2B-255, "721-8"		(Subsequently to NASM) (As "N8+AA" in Lufthansa c/s)	
G-MURY	Robinson R44 Astro	0201		19. 7.95	Cancelled 9.10.03 as sold to US (As "G-MURY")	17. 5.04T

Museum of Flight, Boeing Field, Seattle, Washington (www.museumofflight.org)

G-AOVU	de Havilland DH.106 Comet 4C	6424	(G-APMD)	22.10.59	Cancelled 25. 3.60 - to XA-NAR, subsequently N888WA
			(G-APDN)		(As "N888WA")
G-AVAV	Vickers Supermarine 509 Spitfire Tr.9		Irish Air Corps 1598.11.66		Cancelled 18. 5.75 - to N8R. subsequently N8R
		CBAF/7269	G-15-172, MJ772		(As "N8R") (On loan from Museum of Flight)
G-AWHL	Hispano HA.1112-MIL Buchon	186	Spanish AF C4K-122	14. 5.68	Cancelled 17. 2.69 on sale to Spain, subsequently NX109J
	(Messerschmitt Bf.109G)				(As "N109J")
G-BOAG	British Aircraft Corporation Concorde Type 1 Variant 102			9. 2.81	Cancelled 4. 5.04 as WFU	3. 4.05T
		214 & 100-014	G-BFKW		(As "G-BOAG")	

Olympic Flight Museum, Olympia, Washington (www.olympicflightmuseum.com)

| G-AYHS | British Aircraft Corporation 167 Strikemaster Mk.84 | | G-27-143 | | 22. 7.70 Cancelled 28. 9.70.- to Singapore AF as 314 |
| | | EEP/JP/1934 & PS.151 | | | - subsequently N121463 and N72445 (As "XR366") |

Flying Heritage Collection, Seattle, Washington (www.flyingheritage.com)

G-AWHB	CASA 2111D	049	Spanish AF	14. 5.68	Cancelled as WFU 11. 9.74, restored 16.10.89,
	(Heinkel 111H-16)		B2I-57		cancelled 27. 4.01 as sold US: (As "G-AWHB")
	(Officially quoted as c/n 167 ex Spanish AF B2I-37)				
G-BUWA	Vickers-Supermarine 349 Spitfire F.Vc		C-FDUY	19. 3.93	Cancelled 12.1 .00 as PWFU	1. 7.00
	(Built Westland Aircraft Ltd 1942)	WASP/20/288	7555M, 5378M, AR614		(To N614VC 2.00)	
G-BYDS	Messerschmitt Bf.109E-3	1342	Luftwaffe	24.11.98	Cancelled 16.11.04 as transferred to US (To N342FH 11.04)
G-BYDR	North American B-25D Mitchell	100-20644	N25644		Cancelled 15. 4.04 - to N25644
			N88972, CF-OGQ, KL161, 43-3318 (As "N25644")		
G-BZNL	North American F-86A Sabre	161-211	49-1211	14.11.00	Cancelled 20.12.01 to N4912 (As "N4912")
G-FOKW	Focke-Wulf Fw.190A-5	0151227)	Luftwaffe DG+HO 6. 3.96		Cancelled 8. 2.01 - to N19027 (As "N19027")

Experimental Aircraft Association Air Venture Museum, Witttman Field, Oshkosh, Wisconsin (www.eaa.org)

G-ASKB	de Havilland DH.98 Mosquito TT.35				Cancelled 17. 6.63 as sold to USA
					(On loan from Fantasy of Flight, Polk City, Florida qv)
G-AVAV	Vickers Supermarine 509 Spitfire Tr.				Cancelled 16. 5.75 as sold to USA
					(On loan from Museum of Flight, Seattle, Washington)
G-AWHO	Hispano HA.1112-MIL Buchon	199	Spanish AF	14. 5.68	Cancelled 20. 2.69 - to N90601, subsequently N109BF
	(Messerschmitt Bf.109G)		C4K-127		(As "N109BF")
G-HUNT	Hawker Hunter F.51	41H-680277	G-9-440	5. 7.78	Cancelled 10.12.87 - to N50972, subsequently N611JR
			Danish AF E-418, Danish AF 35-418 (As "WB188")		

URUGUAY

Museo Aeronãutico, San Gabriel, Montevideo

G-AMNL	Douglas C-47B-35-DK Dakota	16644/33392	XF767	30.11.51	Cancelled 23.11.61 - to I-TAVO
			G-AMNL, KN682, 44-77060 (Subsequently to and displayed as "CX-BDB")		
G-ANOW	de Havilland DHC.1 Chipmunk 21	C1/0972		8. 3.54	Cancelled 19. 7.68 - to CX-BGH (As "G-ANOW").

VENEZUELA

Museo Aeronautica de la Fuerza Aerea Venezolana, Maracay

| G-AMXS | de Havilland DH.104 Dove 2A | 04382 | (N4281C) | 21. 1.53 | Cancelled 28. 8.53 - to YV-T-FTQ |
| | | | | | (Subsequently 3C-R1) (As "2531") |

ZIMBABWE

Zimbabwe Military Museum, Gweru

| G-AWTD | Percival P.56 Provost T.1 | P56/285 | (D-....) | 8.11.68 | Cancelled 24. 3.69 as sold to Germany |
| | | (Also c/n PAC/F/285) | XF554 | | - to Rhodesian AF by 1973 as 3614 |

PART 2 – BRITISH AVIATION PRESERVATION COUNCIL REGISTER

The British Aviation Preservation Council (BAPC) was formed in 1967 and is the national body for the preservation of aviation related items. It is a voluntary staffed body which undertakes a representation, co-ordination and enabling role. BAPC membership includes national, local authority, independent and service museums, private collections, voluntary groups and other organisations involved in the advancement of aviation preservation in the UK. A number of overseas aircraft preservation organisations have affiliated membership.

The BAPC Register of Anonymous Airframes was started in the 1980s as a way of flagging up aircraft which had not managed to be given a formal method of identification, for example a civilian registration, a military serial or a construction number for one reason or another. Such examples include "pioneer" aircraft built and flown before registration systems were devised, unfinished projects, deliberate omissions and Hang gliders and similar devices. Additionally, the register allows other airframes and similar items which would not normally need an formal identity such as man-powered aircraft, full scale models for use as "gate guardians" or other display purposes and non flying reproductions intended only for display purposes. Most exhibits held in Museums are usually on display.

Register No	Type	Construction No	Previous Identity	Remarks	Location
BAPC.1	Avro Triplane Type IV replica			Details in SECTION 4, Part 1	Shuttleworth
BAPC.2	Bristol Boxkite replica			Details in SECTION 4, Part 1	Shuttleworth
BAPC.3	Bleriot Type XI			Details in SECTION 4, Part 1	Shuttleworth
BAPC.4	Deperdussin Monoplane			Details in SECTION 4, Part 1	Shuttleworth
BAPC.5	Blackburn Single Seat Monoplane			Details in SECTION 4, Part 1	Shuttleworth
BAPC.6	Roe Triplane Type I			Details in SECTION 4, Part 1	Manchester
BAPC.7	Southampton University Man Powered Aircraft (SUMPAC)			Details in SECTION 4, Part 1	Southampton
BAPC.8	Dixon Ornithopter reconstruction			Details in SECTION 4, Part 1	Shuttleworth
BAPC.9	Humber-Bleriot XI Monoplane reconstruction			Details in SECTION 4, Part 1	Coventry
BAPC.10	Hafner R-11 Revoplane			Details in SECTION 4, Part 1	Weston-super-Mare
BAPC.11	English Electric S.1 Wren composite			Details in SECTION 4, Part 1	Shuttleworth
BAPC.12	Mignet HM.14 Pou-Du-Ciel			Details in SECTION 4, Part 1	Manchester
BAPC.13	Mignet HM.14 Pou-Du-Ciel (Douglas 600cc)			Brimpex Metal Treatments Ltd (Was under restoration 3.98)	Sheffield
BAPC.14	Addyman Standard Training Glider			Ponsford Collection	Selby
BAPC.15	Addyman Standard Training Glider (Rebuilt Yorkshire Aeroplanes)	YA2		Ponsford Collection	Leeds
BAPC.16	Addyman Ultralight			Ponsford Collection	Selby
BAPC.17	Woodhams Sprite			BB Aviation	Bossingham, Canterbury
BAPC.18	Killick Man Powered Gyroplane			Ponsford Collection	Selby
BAPC.19	Bristol F2b Fighter fuselage frame			Details in SECTION 4, Part 1	Brussels, Belgium
BAPC.20	Lee-Richards Annular Bi-plane reconstruction			Details in SECTION 4, Part 1	Newark
BAPC.21	Thruxton Jackaroo (Used as spares in rebuild of G-APAL)			M.J.Brett (Conversion abandoned)	-----
BAPC.22	Mignet HM.14 Pou-Du-Ciel			Details in SECTION 4, Part 1	Schiphol, Netherlands
BAPC.23	Allocated in error – originally used by 1/2th scale SE.5 replica at Newark Air Museum				
BAPC.24	Allocated in error – originally used by 2/3rd scale Currie Wot replica at Newark Air Museum				
BAPC.25	Nyborg TGN.III Sailplane			P Williams	Warwick
BAPC.26	Auster AOP.9			Fuselage frame only - scrapped Swansea	
BAPC.27	Mignet HM.14 Pou-Du-Ciel reconstruction (Under construction 1988 - presumably abandoned)			M J Abbey	-----
BAPC.28	Wright Flyer fsm			Details in SECTION 4, Part 1	Elvington
BAPC.29	Mignet HM.14 Pou-Du-Ciel			Details in SECTION 4, Part 1	Brooklands
BAPC.30	DFS Grunau Baby			Destroyed by fire Swansea 1969	
BAPC.31	Slingsby T.7 Tutor			Believed scrapped Swansea	
BAPC.32	Crossley Tom Thumb			Details in SECTION 4, Part 1	Coventry
BAPC.33	DFS 108-49 Grunau Baby IIB		BGA 2400 VN148, LN+ST	(To Denmark for rebuild 2003)	
BAPC.34	DFS 108-49 Grunau Baby IIB	030892	RAFGSA.281 RAFGGA GK.4/LZ+AR	D.Elsdon (Originally on rebuild as BGA 2362: possibly used for spares)	Hazlemere, Buckingham
BAPC.35	EoN AP.7 Primary	EoN/P/063		ex Russavia Collection (On rebuild as BGA 2493: current status unknown)	Pocklington
BAPC.36	Fieseler Fi 103 V1 fsm			Details in SECTION 4, Part 1	Hawkinge
BAPC.37	Blake Bluetit			See G-BXIY - details in SECTION 1, Part 2	
BAPC.38	Bristol Scout D fsm (Gnome 80 hp)			K Williams and M Thorn (As "A1742")	Solihull
BAPC.39	Addyman Zephyr Sailplane			Ponsford Collection (Parts held for eventual rebuild)	Selby
BAPC.40	Bristol Boxkite reconstructionBOX 3 & BM.7281			Details in SECTION 4, Part 1	Bristol
BAPC.41	Royal Aircraft Factory BE.2c replica			Details in SECTION 4, Part 1	Elvington
BAPC.42	Avro 504K fsm			Details in SECTION 4, Part 1	Elvington
BAPC.43	Mignet HM.14 Pou-Du-Ciel			Details in SECTION 4, Part 1	Newark
BAPC.44	Miles M.14A Magister			Details in SECTION 4, Part 1	Woodley
BAPC.45	Pilcher Hawk Glider reconstruction			Details in SECTION 4, Part 1	Stanford Hall
BAPC.46	Mignet HM.14 Pou-Du-Ciel			Probably scrapped	
BAPC.47	Watkins CHW monoplane			Details in SECTION 4, Part 1	Swansea
BAPC.48	Pilcher Hawk Glider reconstruction			Details in SECTION 4, Part 1	Glasgow
BAPC.49	Pilcher Hawk Glider			Details in SECTION 4, Part 1	East Fortune
BAPC.50	Roe Triplane Type I			Details in SECTION 4, Part 1	South Kensington, London
BAPC.51	Vickers FB.27 Vimy IV			Details in SECTION 4, Part 1	South Kensington, London
BAPC.52	Lilienthal Glider Type XI			Details in SECTION 4, Part 1	Wroughton
BAPC.53	Wright Flyer reconstruction			Details in SECTION 4, Part 1	South Kensington, London
BAPC.54	JAP/Harding Monoplane			Details in SECTION 4, Part 1	South Kensington, London
BAPC.55	Levasseur-Antoinette Developed Type VII Monoplane			Details in SECTION 4, Part 1	South Kensington, London
BAPC.56	Fokker E.III			Details in SECTION 4, Part 1	South Kensington, London
BAPC.57	Pilcher Hawk Glider reconstruction (Built Martin and Miller, Edinburgh 1930)			E Littledike	St Albans

BAPC.58	Yokosuka MXY-7 Ohka II			Details in SECTION 4, Part 1	RNAS Yeovilton
BAPC.59	Sopwith F1 Camel fsm			Details in SECTION 4, Part 1	Montrose
BAPC.60	Murray M.1 Helicopter			Details in SECTION 4, Part 1	Weston-super-Mare
BAPC.61	Stewart Man Powered Ornithopter			A Smith *"Bellbird II"*	Sibsey
BAPC.62	Cody Type V Biplane			Details in SECTION 4, Part 1	South Kensington, London
BAPC.63	Hawker Hurricane fsm			Details in SECTION 4, Part 1	Hawkinge
BAPC.64	Hawker Hurricane fsm			Details in SECTION 4, Part 1	Hawkinge
BAPC.65	Supermarine Spitfire fsm			Details in SECTION 4, Part 1	Hawkinge
BAPC.66	Messerschmitt Bf109 fsm			Details in SECTION 4, Part 1	Hawkinge
BAPC.67	Messerschmitt Bf109 fsm			Details in SECTION 4, Part 1	Hawkinge
BAPC.68	Hawker Hurricane fsm			Details in SECTION 4, Part 1	Hooton Park
BAPC.69	Supermarine Spitfire fsm			Details in SECTION 4, Part 1	Hawkinge
BAPC.70	Auster AOP.5			Details in SECTION 4, Part 1	East Fortune
BAPC.71	Supermarine Spitfire fsm			Details in SECTION 4, Part 1	Flixton
BAPC.72	Hawker Hurricane fsm			Details in SECTION 4, Part 1	Gloucestershire
BAPC.73	Hawker Hurricane fsm			Not known *(Current status unknown)*	
				(Was displayed "Queens Head" Public House, Bishops Stortford)	
BAPC.74	Messerschmitt Bf109 fsm			Details in SECTION 4, Part 1	Hawkinge
BAPC.75	Mignet HM.14 Pou-Du-Ciel			See G-AEFG - details in SECTION 1, Part 2	Selby
BAPC.76	Mignet HM.14 Pou-Du-Ciel			Details in SECTION 4, Part 1	Elvington
BAPC.77	Mignet HM.14 Pou-Du-Ciel			Details in SECTION 4, Part 1	Lower Stondon
BAPC.78	Hawker Afghan Hind			See G-AENP - details in SECTION 1, Part 2	
BAPC.79	Fiat G.46-4b	71	FHE MM53211	Not known	La Ferte Alais, France
				(Was stored "as MM53211:ZI-4")	
BAPC.80	Airspeed AS.58 Horsa II			Details in SECTION 4, Part 1	AAC Middle Wallop
BAPC.81	Hawkridge Nacelle Dagling	10471	BGA 493	Russavia Collection	Hemel Hempstead
				(On rebuild)	
BAPC.82	Hawker Afghan Hind			Details in SECTION 4, Part 1	RAF Cosford
BAPC.83	Kawasaki Type 5 Model 1b (Ki 100)			Details in SECTION 4, Part 1	Hendon
BAPC.84	Mitsubishi Ki 46 III (Dinah)			Details in SECTION 4, Part 1	RAF Cosford
BAPC.85	Weir W-2			Details in SECTION 4, Part 1	Edinburgh
BAPC.86	DH.82A Tiger Moth			Current status unknown	------
BAPC.87	Bristol 30/46 Babe III reconstruction			Details in SECTION 4, Part 1	Kemble
BAPC.88	Fokker Dr.1 5/8th scale model			Details in SECTION 4, Part 1	RNAS Yeovilton
BAPC.89	Cayley Glider fsm			Details in SECTION 4, Part 1	Elvington
BAPC.90	Colditz Cock Glider reconstruction			Details in SECTION 4, Part 1	South Lambeth, London
BAPC.91	Fieseler Fi 103R-IV (V-1)			Details in SECTION 4, Part 1	Headcorn
BAPC.92	Fieseler Fi 103 (V-1)			Details in SECTION 4, Part 1	Hendon
BAPC.93	Fieseler Fi 103 (V-1)			Details in SECTION 4, Part 1	Duxford
BAPC.94	Fieseler Fi 103 (V-1)			Details in SECTION 4, Part 1	RAF Cosford
BAPC.95	Gizmer Autogyro			F.Fewsdale *(Current status unknown)*	Darlington
BAPC.96	Brown Helicopter			Details in SECTION 4, Part 1	Sunderland
BAPC.97	Luton LA.4 Minor			Details in SECTION 4, Part 1	Sunderland
BAPC.98	Yokosuka MXY-7 Ohka II			Details in SECTION 4, Part 1	Manchester
BAPC.99	Yokosuka MXY-7 Ohka II			Details in SECTION 4, Part 1	RAF Cosford
BAPC.100	Clarke TWK			Details in SECTION 4, Part 1	Hendon
BAPC.101	Mignet HM.14 Pou-Du-Ciel			Details in SECTION 4, Part 1	Newark
BAPC.102	Mignet HM.14 Pou-Du-Ciel			Not constructed - parts to BAPC.75	
BAPC.103	Pilcher Hawk Hang-Glider reconstruction			Personal Plane Services Ltd	Wycombe Air Park
	(Built E.A.S.Hulton, London 1969)				
BAPC.104	Bleriot Type XI		G-AVXV	Not known *(Sold as F-AZIN 1992)*	
BAPC.105	Bleriot Type XI		54	Details in SECTION 4, Part 1	Lelystad, Netherlands
BAPC.106	Bleriot Type XI			Details in SECTION 4, Part 1	RAF Cosford
BAPC.107	Bleriot Type XXVII			Details in SECTION 4, Part 1	Hendon
BAPC.108	Fairey Swordfish IV			Details in SECTION 4, Part 1	RAF Stafford
BAPC.109	Slingsby T.7 Cadet TX.1	28	8599M BGA 679	Not known	
				(Current status unknown)	
BAPC.110	Fokker D.VIIF fsm			Details in SECTION 4, Part 1	Chino, California, US
BAPC.111	Sopwith Triplane fsm			Details in SECTION 4, Part 1	RNAS Yeovilton
BAPC.112	AirCo DH.2 fsm			See G-BFVH - details in SECTION 1, Part 2	
BAPC.113	Royal Aircraft Factory SE.5A fsm			Ex Leisure Sport *(As "B4863": current status unknown)*	
BAPC.114	Vickers Type 60 Viking IV reconstruction			Details in SECTION 4, Part 1	Brooklands
BAPC.115	Mignet HM.14 Pou-Du-Ciel			Details in SECTION 4, Part 1	Flixton
BAPC.116	Santos-Dumont Demoiselle XX reconstruction			Current status unknown	------
	(JAP J99)			*(Ex Flambards Theme Park)*	
BAPC.117	Royal Aircraft Factory BE.2c fsm			P Smith	Hawkinge
	(Built Ackland and Shaw 1976) (Gipsy Major)			*(Built for "Wings" BBC TV 1976 series)*	
BAPC.118	Albatros D.Va fsm			Not known *(As "C19/15": current status unknown)*	
BAPC.119	Bensen B.7 Gyroglider			Details in SECTION 4, Part 1	Sunderland
BAPC.120	Mignet HM.14 Pou-Du-Ciel			Details in SECTION 4, Part 1 *(As G-AEJZ)*	Hemswell
BAPC.121	Mignet HM.14 Pou-Du-Ciel			Details in SECTION 4, Part 1	Doncaster
				(As "G-AEKR")	
BAPC.122	Avro 504 fsm			Not known *(As "1881": current status unknown)*	
	(Built Personal Plane Services 1976) (Ford 1300)			*(Built for "Wings" BBC TV 1976 series)*	
BAPC.123	Vickers FB.5 Gunbus fsm	1186/2	ZS-UHN	A.Topen *(As "P641")*	Cranfield
	(Built IES Projects Ltd 1975 for "Shout at the Devil" 1976 film)			*(Small components only)*	
BAPC.124	Lilienthal Glider Type XI reconstruction			Details in SECTION 4, Part 1	South Kensington, London
BAPC.125	Clay Cherub ground trainer			Not known	(Coventry)
BAPC.126	Rollason-Druine D.31 Turbulent			Details in SECTION 4, Part 1	Coventry
BAPC.127	Halton Man Powered Aircraft Group Jupiter			Details in SECTION 4, Part 1	Filching Manor, Wannock
BAPC.128	Watkinson CG-4 Cyclogyroplane Man Powered Gyroplane Mark IV			Details in SECTION 4, Part 1	Weston-super-Mare

BAPC.129	Blackburn (1911) Monoplane fsm		Not known *(Built 1975? for "The Flambards" TV Series)*	
			"Mercury" (Sold 1993: current status unknown)	
BAPC.130	Blackburn (1911) Monoplane fsm		Details in SECTION 4, Part 1	Elvington
BAPC.131	Pilcher Hawk Glider reconstruction		C.Paton	London E
	(Built C.Paton 1972 for film)		*(Current status unknown - probably stored)*	
BAPC.132	Bleriot Type XI	PFA 88- 10864	Details in SECTION 4, Part 1	Mougins, Cannes, France
BAPC.133	Fokker Dr.1 fsm		Details in SECTION 4, Part 1	Hawkinge
BAPC.134	Aerotek Pitts S.2A	"G-RKSF"	Toyota Cars	(Northampton)
BAPC.135	Bristol 20 M.1C Monoplane fsm		Current status unknown	
			(Ex Leisure Sport - as "C4912": sold 10.87:)	
BAPC.136	Deperdussin 1913 Monoplane fsm		Details in SECTION 4, Part 1	Chino, California, US
BAPC.137	Sopwith Baby Floatplane fsm		Current status unknown	--------
	(Built FEM Displays Ltd 1978)			*(Ex Leisure Sport)*
BAPC.138	Hansa Brandenberg W.29 fsm		Current status unknown	--------
	(Ford 1300)		*(Ex Leisure Sport - as "2292": sold prior to 10.87)*	
BAPC.139	Fokker Dr.1 Triplane fsm		Details in SECTION 4, Part 1	Orlando, Florida, US
BAPC.140	Curtiss 42A R3C2 fsm		Details in SECTION 4, Part 1	Chino, California, US
BAPC.141	Macchi M.39 fsm		Details in SECTION 4, Part 1	Chino, California, US
BAPC.142	Royal Aircraft Factory SE.5A fsm		Not known	Switzerland
			(As "F5459:Y") (Sold 1.5.93: current status unknown)	
BAPC.143	Paxton Man Powered Aircraft		R.A.Paxton	Gloucestershire
			(Current status unknown: presumed stored)	
BAPC.144	Weybridge Man Powered Aircraft Group Mercury		Not known	RAF Cranwell
	(Previously "Dumbo" rebuilt)		*"Mercury" (Current status unknown)*	
BAPC.145	Oliver Man Powered Aircraft		Not known	Warton
			(Current status unknown: possibly scrapped)	
BAPC.146	Pedals Aeronauts Man Powered Aircraft Toucan		Not known *(Current status unknown)*	
			"Toucan" (Centre section/power train only)	
BAPC.147	Bensen B.7 Gyroglider		Details in SECTION 4, Part 1	Flixton
BAPC.148	Hawker Fury II fsm		Details in SECTION 4, Part 1	Sleap
BAPC.149	Short S.27 fsm		Details in SECTION 4, Part 1	RNAS Yeovilton
BAPC.150	Sepecat Jaguar GR.1 fsm	"XX718"	RAF Exhibition Production and Transportation Team	
		"XX732"	*(As "XX725:GU" in RAF 54 Sqdn c/s)*	Oman
BAPC.151	Sepecat Jaguar GR.1A fsm	"XX824"	RAF Exhibition Production and Transportation Team	
			(As"XZ363:A")	RAF Cranwell
BAPC.152	BAe Hawk T.1A fsm	"XX262"	RAF Exhibition Production and Transportation Team	
		"XX162"	*(As "XX226:74" in RAF 74 Sqdn c/s)*	RAF Cranwell
BAPC.153	Westland WG-33 Mock-up		Details in SECTION 4, Part 1	Weston-super-Mare
BAPC.154	Druine D.31 Turbulent	PFA 1654	Lincolnshire Aviation Society	
			(Unfinished: was stored 3.96)	
BAPC.155	Panavia Tornado GR.1 fsm	"ZA368"	RAF Exhibition Production and Transportation Team	
		"ZA446","ZA600", "ZA322"	*As "ZA556")*	RAF Cranwell
BAPC.156	Supermarine S.6B fsm		National Air Race Museum	Chino, California, US
			(As "S1595")	
BAPC.157	WACO CG-4A Hadrian Glider		Details in SECTION 4, Part 1	Elvington
BAPC.158	Fieseler Fi 103 (V1)		Defence Explosives Ordnance Disposal School	Chattenden
BAPC.159	Yokosuka MXY-7 Ohka II		Defence Explosives Ordnance Disposal School	Chattenden
BAPC.160	Chargus 18/50 Hang Glider		Details in SECTION 4, Part 1	East Fortune
BAPC.161	Stewart Man Powered Ornithopter		Not known	(Louth)
	(Built A Stewart)		*"Coppelia" (Was stored 8.98: current status unknown)*	
BAPC.162	Goodhart Man Powered Aircraft Newbury Manflier		Details in SECTION 4, Part 1	Wroughton
BAPC.163	AFEE 10/42 Rotachute Rotabuggy reconstruction		Details in SECTION 4, Part 1	AAC Middle Wallop
BAPC.164	Wight Quadraplane Type 1 fsm		Details in SECTION 4, Part 1	Southampton
BAPC.165	Bristol F.2b Fighter		Details in SECTION 4, Part 1	Hendon
BAPC.166	Bristol F.2b Fighter composite		See G-AANM - details in SECTION 1, Part 2	
BAPC.167	Royal Aircraft Factory SE.5A fsm		Exported 12.97	(US)
	(Built TDL Replicas Ltd)			
BAPC.168	DH.60G Moth reconstruction	8058	Details in SECTION 4, Part 1	Croydon
BAPC.169	Sepecat Jaguar GR.1 fsm		RAF (No.1 School of Technical Training)	
	(Engine systems static demonstration airframe)		*(As "XX110")*	RAF Cosford
BAPC.170	Pilcher Hawk Glider reconstruction		A Gourlay	Strathallan
	(Built A.Gourlay 1983)		*(Built for "Kings Royal" BBC film)*	
BAPC.171	BAe Hawk T.1 fsm	"XX297"	RAF Exhibition Production and Transportation Team	
		"XX262"	*(As "XX253")*	RAF Cranwell
BAPC.172	Chargus Midas Super E Hang Glider		Details in SECTION 4, Part 1	Wroughton
BAPC.173	Birdman Promotions Grasshopper		Details in SECTION 4, Part 1	Wroughton
BAPC.174	Bensen B.7 Gyroglider		Details in SECTION 4, Part 1	Wroughton
BAPC.175	Volmer VJ-23 Swingwing Powered Hang Glider		Details in SECTION 4, Part 1	Manchester
BAPC.176	Royal Aircraft Factory SE.5A scale model		Details in SECTION 4, Part 1	Not known
BAPC.177	Avro 504K fsm		Details in SECTION 4, Part 1	Brooklands
BAPC.178	Avro 504K fsm	"E373"	By-gone Times Antique Warehouse *(German c/s)*	
			(Current status unknown)	Eccleston, Leyland
BAPC.179	Sopwith Pup fsm		Details in SECTION 4, Part 1	Coventry
BAPC.180	McCurdy Silver Dart reconstruction		Reynolds Pioneer Museum (?)	
				Wetaskiwin, Alberta, Canada
BAPC.181	Royal Aircraft Factory BE.2b reconstruction		Details in SECTION 4, Part 1	Hendon
BAPC.182	Wood Ornithopter		Details in SECTION 4, Part 1	Manchester
BAPC.183	Zurowski ZP-1 Helicopter		Details in SECTION 4, Part 1	Newark
BAPC.184	Supermarine Spitfire IX fsm		Rolls Royce Heritage Trust	Derby
	(Built Specialised Mouldings Ltd 1985)		*(As "EN398)*	
BAPC.185	WACO CG-4A Hadrian Glider		Details in SECTION 4, Part 1	AAC Middle Wallop
BAPC.186	de Havilland DH.82B Queen Bee composite		Details in SECTION 4, Part 1	London Colney
BAPC.187	Roe Type I Biplane reconstruction		Details in SECTION 4, Part 1	Brooklands
BAPC.188	McBroom Cobra 88 Hang Glider		Details in SECTION 4, Part 1	Wroughton

BAPC.189	Bleriot Type XI replica		See BAPC.132 (*Current status unknown*)
	(Anzani) (*Some original parts ex Goldsmith Trust*)		(*Sold Christies 31.10.86, probably to France*)
BAPC.190	Supermarine Spitfire fsm		P Smith (*As "K5054"*)	Hawkinge
BAPC.191	BAe Harrier GR.7 fsm	"ZD472"	RAF Exhibition Production and Transportation Team
			(*As "ZH139:01"*)	RAF Cranwell
BAPC.192	Weedhopper JC24		M J Aubrey	Kington, Hertford
BAPC.193	Hovey WDII Whing Ding		M J Aubrey	Kington, Hertford
BAPC.194	Santos Dumont Type 20 Demoiselle		Details in SECTION 4, Part 1	Berlin, Germany
BAPC.195	Birdman Sports Moonraker 77 Hang Glider		Details in SECTION 4, Part 1	East Fortune
BAPC.196	Southdown Sailwings Sigma 2m Hang Glider		Details in SECTION 4, Part 1	East Fortune
BAPC.197	Scotkites Cirrus III Hang Glider		Details in SECTION 4, Part 1	East Fortune
BAPC.198	Fieseler Fi 103 (V-1)		Details in SECTION 4, Part 1	South Lambeth, London
BAPC.199	Fieseler Fi 103 (V-1)		Details in SECTION 4, Part 1	South Kensington, London
BAPC.200	Bensen B.7 Gyroglider		Not known	Leeds
	(*Composite of three airframes*)		(*Current status unknown*)
BAPC.201	Mignet HM.14 Pou-Du-Ciel		Scrapped 2006
BAPC.202	Supermarine Spitfire V fsm		Not known
BAPC.203	Chrislea LC.1 Airguard replica		The Aeroplane Collection	Wigan
			(*Current status unknown: burnt 1998?*)
BAPC.204	McBroom Hang Glider		Details in SECTION 4, Part 1	Hooton Park
BAPC.205	Hawker Hurricane IIc fsm		Details in SECTION 4, Part 1	Hendon
BAPC.206	Supermarine Spitfire IX fsm		Details in SECTION 4, Part 1	Hendon
BAPC.207	Austin Whippet fsm		Details in SECTION 4, Part 1	Doncaster
BAPC.208	Royal Aircraft Factory SE.5A		Details in SECTION 4, Part 1	Farnborough
BAPC.209	Supermarine Spitfire LF.IXC fsm		Details in SECTION 4, Part 1	Niagara Falls, Ontario, Canada
BAPC.210	Avro 504J		Details in SECTION 4, Part 1	Southampton
	(*Built AJD Engineering*)		
BAPC.211	Mignet HM.14 Pou-Du-Ciel		Details in SECTION 4, Part 1	Sunderland
BAPC.212	Bensen B.6 Gyrocopter		Details in SECTION 4, Part 1	Weston-super-Mare
BAPC.213	Cranfield Vertigo Man Powered Helicopter		Details in SECTION 4, Part 1	Weston-super-Mare
BAPC.214	Supermarine Spitfire Prototype fsm		Details in SECTION 4, Part 1	Tangmere
BAPC.215	Airwave Hang Glider		Details in SECTION 4, Part 1	Southampton
BAPC.216	de Havilland DH.88 Comet fsm		Details in SECTION 4, Part 1	London Colney
BAPC.217	Supermarine Spitfire I fsm		Details in SECTION 4, Part 1	RAF Bentley Priory
BAPC.218	Hawker Hurricane IIc fsm		Details in SECTION 4, Part 1	RAF Bentley Priory
BAPC.219	Hawker Hurricane I fsm		Details in SECTION 4, Part 1	Biggin Hill
BAPC.220	Supermarine Spitfire I fsm		Details in SECTION 4, Part 1	Biggin Hill
BAPC.221	Supermarine Spitfire LF.IX fsm		Details in SECTION 4, Part 1	RAF Northolt
BAPC.222	Supermarine Spitfire IX fsm		Details in SECTION 4, Part 1	RAF Uxbridge
BAPC.223	Hawker Hurricane I fsm		Details in SECTION 4, Part 1	RAF High Wycombe
BAPC.224	Supermarine Spitfire V fsm		Details in SECTION 4, Part 1	Trenton, Ontario, Canada
BAPC.225	Supermarine Spitfire IX fsm		Details in SECTION 4, Part 1	RAF Cranwell
BAPC.226	Supermarine Spitfire XI fsm		Details in SECTION 4, Part 1	RAF Benson
BAPC.227	Supermarine Spitfire IA fsm		Details in SECTION 4, Part 1	Edinburgh
BAPC.228	Olympus Hang Glider		Details in SECTION 4, Part 1	Sunderland
BAPC.229	Supermarine Spitfire IX fsm		Details in SECTION 4, Part 1	RAF Digby
BAPC.230	Supermarine Spitfire fsm		Details in SECTION 4, Part 1	Malton
BAPC.231	Mignet HM.14 Pou-Du-Ciel		Details in SECTION 4, Part 1	RAF Millom
BAPC.232	Airspeed AS.58 Horsa I/II Glider composite		Details in SECTION 4, Part 1	London Colney
BAPC.233	Broburn Wanderlust sailplane		Details in SECTION 4, Part 1	Woodley
BAPC.234	Vickers FB.5 Gunbus fsm		Details in SECTION 4, Part 1	Sywell
BAPC.235	Fieseler Fi 103 (V-1) fsm		Details in SECTION 4, Part 1	Malton
BAPC.236	Hawker Hurricane fsm		Details in SECTION 4, Part 1	Malton
BAPC.237	Fieseler Fi 103 (V-1)		Details in SECTION 4, Part 1	RAF Stafford
BAPC.238	Waxflatter Ornithopter replica		Personal Plane Services Ltd	Wycombe Air Park
	(*Built Personal Plane Services*)		(*Built for "Young Sherlock Holmes" film*)
BAPC.239	Fokker D.VIII 5/8th scale model		Details in SECTION 4, Part 1	Flixton
BAPC.240	Messerschmitt Bf.109G fsm		Details in SECTION 4, Part 1	Elvington
BAPC.241	Hawker Hurricane I fsm		Details in SECTION 4, Part 1	Tangmere
BAPC.242	Supermarine Spitfire VB fsm		Details in SECTION 4, Part 1	Tangmere
BAPC.243	Mignet HM.14 Pou-Du-Ciel	"A-FLEA"	P.Ward	Malvern Wells
	(*Built Bill Francis*) (Scott A2S)		(*As "G-ADYV"*)
BAPC.244	Mainair Tri-Flyer 250/Solar Wings Typhoon S		Not known	--------
BAPC.245	Electraflyer Floater Hang Glider		Details in SECTION 4, Part 1	East Fortune
BAPC.246	Hiway Cloudbase Hang Glider		Details in SECTION 4, Part 1	East Fortune
BAPC.247	Albatros ASG.21 Hang Glider		Details in SECTION 4, Part 1	East Fortune
BAPC.248	McBroom Hang Glider		Details in SECTION 4, Part 1	Woodley
BAPC.249	Hawker Fury I fsm		Details in SECTION 4, Part 1	Brooklands
BAPC.250	Royal Aircraft Factory SE.5A replica		Details in SECTION 4, Part 1	Brooklands
BAPC.251	Hiway Spectrum Hang Glider		Details in SECTION 4, Part 1	Manchester
BAPC.252	Flexiform Wing Hang Glider		Details in SECTION 4, Part 1	Manchester
BAPC.253	Mignet HM.14 Pou-Du-Ciel replica		Details in SECTION 4, Part 1	Southampton
BAPC.254	Supermarine Spitfire 1 fsm		Details in SECTION 4, Part 1	Elvington
BAPC.255	North American P-51D Mustang fsm		Details in SECTION 4, Part 1	Duxford
BAPC.256	Santos Dumont Type 20 Demoiselle reconstruction		Details in SECTION 4, Part 1	Brooklands
BAPC.257	de Havilland DH.88 Comet model		Details in SECTION 4, Part 1	Sywell
BAPC.258	Adams RFD-GQ Balloon (5,000 cu.ft) xxxx		British Balloon Museum and Library	Newbury
	(*Built RFD-GQ Parachutes*)		
BAPC.259	Gloster Gamecock		Details in SECTION 4, Part 1	Gloucestershire
BAPC.260	Mignet HM.280		Details in SECTION 4, Part 1	RAF Millom
BAPC.261	General Aircraft Hotspur replica		Details in SECTION 4, Part 1	AAC Middle Wallop
BAPC.262	Catto CP-16		Details in SECTION 4, Part 1	East Fortune
BAPC.263	Chargus Cyclone		Details in SECTION 4, Part 1	Langford Lodge, Belfast
BAPC.264	Bensen B8M		Details in SECTION 4, Part 1	Weston-super-Mare

BAPC.265	Hawker Hurricane fsm	Details in SECTION 4, Part 1	Elvington
BAPC.266	Rogallo Hang Glider	Details in SECTION 4, Part 1	Langford Lodge, Belfast
BAPC.267	Hawker Hurricane fsm	Details in SECTION 4, Part 1	Duxford
BAPC.268	Supermarine Spitfire fsm	B Wallond	St Mawgan
		(As "OU-Z") (Built for "Dark Blue World" film 2001)	
BAPC.269	Supermarine Spitfire V fsm	Details in SECTION 4, Part 1	USAF Lakenheath
BAPC.270	de Havilland DH.60 Moth fsm	Details in SECTION 4, Part 1	Elvington
BAPC.271	Messerschmitt Me 163B Komet fsm	Details in SECTION 4, Part 1	Shuttleworth
BAPC.272	Hawker Hurricane fsm	Details in SECTION 4, Part 1	Hawkinge
BAPC.273	Hawker Hurricane fsm	Details in SECTION 4, Part 1	Hawkinge
BAPC.274	Boulton & Paul P.6 fsm	Details in SECTION 4, Part 1	Wolverhampton
BAPC.275	Bensen B.7	Details in SECTION 4, Part 1	Doncaster
BAPC.276	Hartman Ornithopter	Details in SECTION 4, Part 1	Wroughton
BAPC.277	Mignet HM.14 Pou-Du-Ciel	Details in SECTION 4, Part 1	Shoreham
BAPC.278	Hawker Hurricane fsm	Details in SECTION 4, Part 1	Hawkinge
BAPC.279	Airspeed AS.58 Horsa reconstruction	Details in SECTION 4, Part 1	RAF Shawbury
BAPC.280	de Havilland DH.89 Dragon Rapide fsm	Details in SECTION 4, Part 1	Liverpool
BAPC.281	Boulton Paul Defiant fsm	Details in SECTION 4, Part 1	Wolverhampton
BAPC.282	Manx Eider Duck	Not known	Ronaldsway
BAPC.283	Supermarine Spitfire fsm	A Saunders	Jurby
	(Built F Brown)	(Built for "Piece of Cake" TV series 1988)	
BAPC.284	Gloster E28/39 fsm	Details in SECTION 4, Part 1	Lutterworth
BAPC.285	Gloster E28/39 fsm	Details in SECTION 4, Part 1	Farnborough
BAPC.286	Mignet HM.14 Flea	Details in SECTION 4, Part 1	Caernarfon
	(Scott A2S)		
BAPC.287	Blackburn F2 Lincock fsm	Details in SECTION 4, Part 1	Hull
BAPC.288	Hawker Hurricane fsm	Details in SECTION 4, Part 1	Farnsfield, Mansfield
BAPC.289	Gyro-Boat	Details in SECTION 4, Part 1	Weston-super-Mare
BAPC.290	Fieseler Fi.104 flying-bomb fsm	Details in SECTION 4, Part 1	Dover
BAPC.291	Hawker Hurricane I fsm	Details in SECTION 4, Part 1	Capel Le Ferne, Folkestone
BAPC.292	Eurofighter Typhoon fsm	Details in SECTION 4, Part 1	Hendon
BAPC.293	Supermarine Spitfire fsm	Details in SECTION 4, Part 1	Hendon
BAPC.294	Fairchild Argus	Details in SECTION 4, Part 1	Woodhall Spa
BAPC.295	Leonardo Da Vinci hang-glider reproduction	Skysport Engineering	Hatch
	(Built Skysport Engineering)	(Built for Channel 4 TV documentary "Leonardo's Dream Machines")	
BAPC.296	Army Balloon Factory Nulli reproduction		Hendon
BAPC.297	Supermarine Spitfire reproduction	Details in SECTION 4, Part 1	Hawkinge
BAPC.298	Supermarine Spitfire IX fsm	Details in SECTION 4, Part 1	Hawkinge
BAPC.299	Supermarine Spitfire I fsm	Details in SECTION 4, Part 1	Capel le Ferne .Folkestone
BAPC.300	Piffard Hummingbird reproduction	Details in SECTION 4, Part 1	Shoreham

PART 3 – IRISH AVIATION HISTORICAL COUNCIL REGISTER

The IAHC Register came into existence with similar objectives to the BAPC.

Register No.	Type	Construction No	Previous Identity	Remarks	Location
IAHC.1	Mignet HM.14 Pou-Du-Ciel			Details in SECTION 4, Part 1	
					Dromod, County Leitrim
IAHC.2	Aldritt Monoplane replica			Details in SECTION 4, Part 1	
					Filching Manor, Wannock
IAHC.3	Mignet HM.14 Pou-Du-Ciel			M.Donohoe	Delgany
	(Built 1937 but unflown)				
IAHC.4	Hawker Hector		IAAC85.	D.McCarthy	Not known
				(Believed components on rebuild Florida, USA)	
IAHC.5	Not known			Not known	
IAHC.6.	Ferguson Monoplane replica			Details in SECTION 4, Part 1	Belfast
IAHC.7	Sligo Concept			G.O'Hara	Sligo
				(Was stored incomplete 8.91: current status unknown)	
IAHC.8	O'Hara Autogyro			G.O'Hara	Sligo
				(Was stored incomplete 8.91: current status unknown)	
IAHC.9	Ferguson Monoplane replica			Details in SECTION 4, Part 1	Belfast

SECTION 5

PART 1 – OVERSEAS CIVIL REGISTERED AIRCRAFT LOCATED IN UK AND IRELAND

A further batch of aircraft has been removed from this edition where no recent sightings have been recorded. Several others are in danger of suffering a similar fate and your contributions are invited if you can provide an update on their current status either to the Editor or to paul.hewins@virgin.net.

As in previous editions leased and stored airliners are omitted unless there is a reasonable likelihood they will still be present when this reaches the reader. Unless the current economic situation improves, some of the increasing number of stored airliners may become of a long term nature and will be considered for inclusion in the next edition.   A few airliner types have also been removed as their UK presence is more accurately rotational or as regular visitors. Underlining indicates a significant change to previously published information while an asterisk in Part 1 denotes the registration no longer appears on the relevant country register.

This Section could not have been produced without the assistance of the following to whom due credit is acknowledged: Jeff Bell (Sywell), Peter Budden (Bournemouth, mainly), Nigel Burch (Biggin Hill), Mike Cain, Jim Brazier and Kevin Dupuy (Southend), Terry Dann, Dave Haines (Gloucestershire), Dave Hughes, Phil and Nigel Kemp (North Weald), Andy Mac (Stapleford), Bernard Martin, Nigel Ponsford (Breighton), Bob Sauvary (Jersey), Martin Steggalls (Crowfield), Bill Teasdale and Barrie Womersley plus the numerous contributors to the AB-Sightings, Airfields, Civil Spotters and Helicopters mailing lists and the invaluable Wrecks & Relics 21.

Registration Type		Construction No	Previous Identity	Owner (Operator)	(Unconfirmed) Base	Last noted
CANADA						
C-FQIP	Lake LA-4-200 Buccaneer	679	N1068L	P J Molloy	Elstree	1.09
C-GWJO*	Boeing 737-2A3	20299	HR-SHO	Newcastle Aviation Academy	Newcastle	11.07
			HR-TNR, CX-BHM, N1797B, N1787B (For instructional use)			
PORTUGAL						
CS-ARI	Robin HR.100-210 Safari	159	F-BUHV	Not known (To be G-CEGD)	Cranfield	8.08
GERMANY						
D-ASDB	VFW-Fokker VFW-614	G-019	OY-RRW	Luthansa Resource Technical Training	MoD St Athan	12.08
			D-ASDB, German AF 17+03		(Instructional Airframe)	
D-CALM	Dornier Do 228-101	7051		Deutschen Zentrum fur Luft und Raumfahrt	Oxford	1.09
D-EAAW	Bölkow BÖ.209 Monsun 160RV	181		Not known	Farley Farm, Romsey	6.08
D-EAGC	Cessna F172H	F172-0637	(D-EBEB)	Not known	Liverpool	9.08
D-EAMB	Bölkow BÖ.208C Junior	597	OE-AMB	Not known	Wolverhampton	12.08
			D-ECGE			
D-EANS	Mooney M.20G Statesman	680008	N586MA	Not known	Lee-on-Solent	1.08
D-EAOB	Piper PA-28-181 Archer II	2890082	N9147X	Not known	Cavan, County Meath	7.08
D-EAPF	Robin DR.400-180R Remorqueur	1630		P Fink	Lasham	9.07
D-EAWW	Piper PA-28R-201 Arrow III	28R-7837199	N9469C	Not known	Oxford	7.08
D-EBLI	Bölkow BÖ.207	223		Not known	Farley Farm, Romsey	6.08
D-EBLO	Bölkow BÖ.207	224		Not known	Lane Farm, Builth Wells	7.08
D-EBWE*	Piper PA-28-235 Cherokee	28-10431	N8874W	Not known	Manston	7.08
D-EBXR	Reims FR172K Hawk XP	FR17200597	HB-CXO	Not known	Waterford	7.08
D-ECFE	Oberlerchner JOB 15-150	060	OE-CAO	Not known	Barton	1.09
D-ECGI	Bölkow BÖ.208C Junior	598		Not known	Bidford	4.08
D-ECOX	Dornier Do.27Q-1	2018		Not known	Nether Wallop	11.08
D-EDEL	Piper PA-32-300 Cherokee Six D	32-7140009	N8617N	Not known	Blackbushe	1.09
D-EDEQ	Beech B24R Sierra 200	MC-239		C Jones	Shoreham	12.08
D-EDFD	Piper PA-28-181 Archer II	2890145	N649CT	Winged Bull Aviation	Fairoaks	1.09
			N9203D			
D-EDNA	Bölkow BÖ.208C Junior	578		C Hampson	Dunkeswell	10.08
D-EEAH	Bölkow BÖ.208C Junior	658	(D-EJMH)	J Webb	Bourne Park, Hurstbourne Tarrant	6.08
D-EEHW	Cessna P210N Pressurized Centurion II		N731FX	Not known	Exeter	1.08
		P21000455				
D-EEPI	Wassmer WA.54 Atlantic	151		R Hunter	Stapleford	8.08
D-EEVY	Cessna 170A	19537	D-ELYC	Not known	Andrewsfield	1.09
			N5503C			
D-EFDL	Grumman AA-5 Traveler	AA5-0645		Not known	Kilkenny	10.08
D-EFFA	Ruschmeyer R90-230RG	018	D-ELVY (2)	K Cropp	Southend	10.08
			(D-EEBY (2))			
D-EFJG	Bölkow BÖ.209 Monsun 160RV	129		R.Truesdale	Newtownards	8.08
D-EFQE	Bölkow BÖ.207	266		J Webb	Popham	9.08
D-EFTI	Bölkow BÖ.207	219		M Hayles	Turweston	1.09
D-EFVS	Wassmer WA.52 Europa	22		M Hales	Sandown, Isle of Wight	1.09
D-EFZC	SIAI-Marchetti S.208	2-18		Not known	Brimpton	7.08
D-EFZO	Cessna F172F	F172-0156		Not known	Stapleford	6.07
D-EGDC	Grumman AA-5B Tiger	AA5B-0728		Not known	Guernsey	1.09
D-EGEC	Piaggio FWP.149D	153	91+31	Not known	Standalone Farm	1.09
			ND+104, KB+130		Meppershall	
D-EGEU*	Piper PA-22-108 Colt	22-9055	EL-AEU	Not known	Derby	12.08
			5N-AEH	(Badly damaged by storms 27.10.02 Farley Farm, Romsey)		
D-EGHW	Bölkow BÖ.209 Monsun 150FV	170	HB-UER	Not known	(Thruxton)	1.09
			D-EAAJ			
D-EGLW*	Piper PA-38-112 Tomahawk	38-80A0105	N9694N	Not known (Fire and Rescue trainer)	Old Warden	8.07
D-EGVA	Piper PA-28R-200 Cherokee Arrow II		N9255K	M Williams	Wellesbourne Mountford	1.09
		28R-7635229				
D-EHAY	CEA DR.253B Régent	190		Not known	Wolverhampton	12.08
D-EHJL	Piaggio FWP.149	045	90+31	C A Tyers (Windmill Aviation)	Spanhoe	1.09
			AC+441, AS+441, GA+394, D-EGEW, GA+394			
D-EHKY	Bölkow BÖ.207	272		Not known	Haverfordwest	4.07

D-EHLA	Bölkow BÖ.207	273		J Webb	Lodge Farm, St Osyth	11.08
D-EHOP	Bölkow BÖ.207	206		Not known	Hill Farm, Nayland	9.07
D-EHUQ*	Bölkow BÖ.207	207		J Kempton	Landmead Farm, Garford	8.07
				(Spares source for G-EFTE)		
D-EHYX*	Bölkow BÖ.207	209		Not known	Spalding	6.05
		(Crashed landing 27. 8.04 Coetir Bach Farm, Maesybont: damaged fuselage for sale with Skycraft)				
D-EIAR	CEA DR.250-160 Capitaine	98		D G Holmann	Leicester	3.08
D-EIKR	Robin DR.400-180 Regent	1839	F-ODSI	Not known	(Cambridge)	4.07
D-EIVF	PZL-110 Koliber 150	03930051		Not known	Kilrush	11.08
D-EJBI	Bölkow BÖ.207	242	G-EJBI	J O'Donnell	Biggin Hill	12.08
			D-EJBI			
D-EJLY	Cessna 182K Skylane	18257879	N2679Q	Not known	Stoodleigh	4.08
D-EKHW	Piper PA-28RT-201T Turbo Arrow IV			Not known	Hawarden	9.08
		28R-8031094				
D-EKJD	Reims FR172J Rocket	FR17200582		T Paravicni	Bourn	7.08
D-EKUR	Mooney M.20K Model231	25-0437	(N3655H)	Not known	Garston Farm, Marshfield	7.08
				(Damaged frame stored after stalling on takeoff 25.7.08)		
D-ELRN	Extra EA.400	20		Not known	Old Buckenham	1.09
D-ELSR	Robin DR.400-180R Remo 180	2012		Not known	Wolverhampton	12.08
D-EMZC*	Reims FR172G Rocket	FR17200154		Not known *(Current status unknown)*	Cork	3.05
D-ENBW	Robin DR.400/180R Remorqueur	1715		Windrushers Gliding Club	Bicester	12.08
D-ENTO	American General AG-5B Tiger	10166	N1198T	Not known	Elstree	1.09
D-EOAJ	Piaggio FWP.149D	028	90+18	Not known	Goodwood	7.08
			AC+409, DE+394			
D-EQXD	Klemm Kl.35D	1979	(G-KLEM)	P Holloway	Old Warden	8.08
			N5050, N505Q, SE-BGD, Fv5050 *(As "NQ+NR" in Luftwaffe c/s)*			
D-ETRE	Tecnam P2002-JF Sierra	003	LX-TRE	Not known	Kilrush	11.08
D-ETTO	Extra EA.300/L	1174		Not known	Panshanger	10.08
D-EWAT	Commander Aircraft Commander 114B	14564		Not known	Blackbushe	1.09
D-FBPS	Cessna 208B Grand Caravan	208B0494	LV-YJC	Not known	Langar	9.08
			N208BA, N1219G	*(Operated British Parachute School)*		
D-FLOH	Cessna 208B Grand Caravan	208B0576	N1041F	Not known	Langar	9.08
				(Operated British Parachute School)		
D-GACR	Piper PA-34-220T Seneca III	34-8133215	N8429L	Not known	Oxford	8.08
D-GPEZ	Piper PA-30 Twin Comanche C	30-1871	N8798Y	Not known	RAF Wittering	12.08
			N9703N			
D-HCKV	Agusta A109A-II	7345	N109HC	University Technical School	Gloucestershire	8.08
			N2GN	*(Damaged near Newby Bridge, Cumbria 2.1.00: hulk marked "G-OPAS")*		
D-IBPN	Beech 58P Baron	TJ-424	N6526S	Small World Aviation	North Weald	9.08
D-KIFF	SFS-31 Milan	6604		N Grayson	Boscombe Down	7.06
D-KIOJ	Schempp-Hirth Nimbus 4M	3	G-IIOJ	S G Jones *"110"*	Lasham	8.08
			D-KLXX			
D-KMDP	Fournier RF-3	37	F-BMDP	Not known	Carnmore, Galway	10.08
D-MBRG	Aerostyle Breezer	046		Not known *(Also carries "G-90-2")*	Wolverhampton	5.06
D-MDMM	Impulse 100	Not known		Not known	Damyns Hall, Upminster	12.08
D-MPGB	Remos GX	not known		Remos Aircraft UK	Shobdon	10.08
D-0606	Lange E1 Antares 18S	46ST05		T J Wills *"1"*	Bidford	7.08
D-1091	Schempp-Hirth Discus b	227		S Roberts *"WD"*	Wycombe Air Park	.07
D-1155 *	Schleicher K.8B	8589		Not known *(Stored)*	Edgehill	.08
D-2782 *	Schempp-Hirth Cirrus VTC	163Y		M Cuming *"PC" (Derelict)*	Edgehill	8.07
D-4670	Schempp-Hirth Ventus 2cxaj	121/520		D Francis *"F2"*	Bicester	7.08
D-5410	Schempp-Hirth Ventus 2cxa	116/513		Southern Sailplanes *"210"*	Membury	.08

SPAIN

EC-CFA*	Boeing 727-256	20811	N907RF	Not known	Shannon	9.08
			EC-AFA	*(Stored)*		
EC-DDX*	Boeing 727-256A	21779		Directions Finningley	Sheffield-Doncaster	11.07
				(Fuselage used as training aid)		
EC-EP6	ELA Aviacion ELA-07	03060940724		Not known	Kirkbride	7.08

FRANCE

F-BBSO*	Taylorcraft Auster 5	1792	G-AMJM	D.J.Baker	Carr Farm, Thorney, Newark	1.08
			TW452	*(Dismantled frame)*		
F-BMCY*	Potez 840	02	N840HP	Not known *(Stored dismantled)*	North Roe, Shetland	4.06
			F-BJSU, F-WJSU	*(Damaged Sumburgh 29. 3.81)*		
F-BMHM	Piper J-3C-65 Cub	11907	Fr Military	A R Capel	Barton Ashes	1.09
			44-79611			
F-BPFP *	Sud-Aviation SA.315B Lama	2006/15		I Clark	(Sandy)	2.07
F-BRHN*	Bölkow BÖ.208C Junior	688	D-EEAK	B Parant *(Stored)*	Farley Farm, Romsey	4.07
F-BRIC	SEEMS MS.885 Super Rallye	5277	PH-MSC	B Girollet	Guernsey	10.08
F-BROC	CEA DR.360 Chevalier	379		M Hales	(Northern Ireland)	11.08
F-BSPQ	Robin DR.300-120 Petit Prince	621		E J Horsfall	Blackpool	5.08
F-BTKO*	Robin HR.100-210 Safari	142		Fly Ltd *(Stored dismantled)*	Turweston	1.09
F-BXCP	Max Holste MH.1521M Broussard	149	ALAT	Bremont Watch Co Ltd	White Waltham	1.09
F-GAIF *	Wassmer WA.81 Pirana	804		Not known *(Canx 6.07)*	Abbeyshrule	10.08
F-GAOE	Robin HR.200/100S Club	104		*(Fuselage stored)*	Great Eversden	11.08
F-GCTU*	Piper PA-38-112 Tomahawk	38-80A0085	N9694N	Not known	Sandford Holiday Park, Dorset	1.08
				(Stripped fuselage)		
F-GFGH	SOCATA Rallye 235E Gabier	13337	F-ODNQ	I Watts	Bagby	8.08
F-GFOR	Robin ATL	42		M Godsell	Haverfordwest	9.08
F-GGHH	Robin ATL	118		M Hurtrez	Wing Farm, Longbridge Deverill	9.08
F-GIBU	Aérospatiale SA.342J Gazelle	1470	HB-XMU	Global Aviation Services Ltd	(Ruabon, Wrexham)	10.08
			N9000A			
F-GJPB *	SOCATA TB-9 Tampico	896		Northbrook College *(Instructional airframe)*	Shoreham	12.06

Reg	Type	c/n
F-GJQI	Robin ATL L	133
F-GKGN	Grumman-American AA-5B Tiger	AA5B-0089
F-GKMZ	Mudry CAP.232	09
F-GLAO	SOCATA TB-9 Tampico Club	1106
F-GLTR	Cessna 172R	17280833
F-GMHH*	Robin HR.100-210 Safari	155
F-GODZ	Pilatus PC-6/340 Porter	340
F-GOTC	Mudry CAP.232	15
F-GOXD	Robin DR.400-180RP Remorquer	1817
F-GPBF	Piper PA-31T Cheyenne II	31T-7920094
F-GXDB	Mudry CAP.232	33
F-GXFP	Sud-Aviation SA.318C Alouette Astazou	2152
F-GXHD	Robin ATL	110
F-HOLF	Aérospatiale AS355NP Ecureuil 2	5751
F-JITM	Funk FK-14 Polaris	Not known
F-PURU	Dyn'Aéro MCR-01 Sportster	218
F-PYOY	Heintz Zenith 100	52
F-WUTH	Progressor Pou Gyrocopter	01
44ADC	Aeroprakt A20 Vista	Not known
95MR	Power Assist Swift	Not known

HUNGARY

Reg	Type	c/n
HA-ACO	Dornier Do.28D-2 Skyservant (Walter M-601 turbo conversion)	4335
HA-ANG	Antonov An-2P	1G132-53
HA-CBG	Yakovlev Yak-18T	22202034044
HA-HUA	Yakovlev Yak-18T	01-32
HA-HUB	Yakovlev Yak-12M	210999
HA-HUD	Sukhoi Su-29	"76021"
HA-HUE	Yakovlev Yak-18T	12-33
HA-IDL	Sud Aviation Alouette II	1388
HA-JAB	Yakovlev Yak-18T	22202023842
HA-LAQ	LET L-410UVP-E4	841332
HA-LFB	Aérospatiale SA.341G Gazelle	1074
HA-LFH	Aérospatiale SA.342J Gazelle	1775
HA-LFM	Aérospatiale SA.342J Gazelle	1301
HA-LFQ	Aérospatiale SA.342L Gazelle	1854
HA-LFZ	Sud-Aviation SA318C Alouette II	2043
HA-MKF	Antonov An-2	1G233-43
HA-NAH	Technoavia SMG-92 Finist	00-003
HA-PPC	Sud Aviation SE.3130 Alouette II	1500
HA-PPY	SOKO SO341 Gazelle (Aerospatiale c/n 1118)	021
HA-SEU *	PZL-104 Wilga 35A	CF15810606
HA-SMD	Yakovlev Yak-18T	13-35
HA-VOC	Dornier Do.28D-2 Skyservant (Walter M-601 turbo conversion?)	4331
HA-YAB	Yakovlev Yak-18T	12-35
HA-YAD	Yakovlev Yak-18T	22202054812
HA-YAE	Yakovlev Yak-18T	11-35
HA-YAF	Yakovlev Yak-18T	08-34
HA-YAG	Yakovlev Yak-18T	05-36
HA-YAJ	Yakovlev Yak-18T	01-33
HA-YAK	Yakovlev Yak-18T	22202044785
HA-YAM	Yakovlev Yak-18T	22202047812
HA-YAN	Yakovlev Yak-18T	10-34
HA-YAO	Sukhoi Su-29	N1001.001
HA-YAP	Yakovlev Yak-18T	22202034023

Reg (prev ids)	Owner/Operator	Location	Date
	L van Dam (Current status unknown)	Weston Zoyland	8.05
G-BGDN, N6147A	B Moran	Kilrush	10.07
	FCP Ltd	Headcorn	12.08
	Aero Club de Bigorre (Dismantled)	Bournemouth	8.05
	(Current status unknown)		
	Citicapital Societe par Actions Simplifiee	Andrewsfield	5.08
	(Crashed Sainte-Hélène-sur-Isère 3. 1.03: stored)		
3A-MUZ, F-BUHH	Fly Ltd	Turweston	1.09
	(Stored dismantled)		
(N340N), ST-AFR, HB-FAR	SARL Fly High Icarius	Bank End Farm, Cockerham	9.08
	(Operated Black Knights Parachute Club)		
	T Cassells	Bagby	10.08
OO-CXD, HB-KBU, D-EAJD	G Richardson	Little Staughton	8.08
OH-PYE, SE-ICS	F Michienzi	Elstree	11.08
	D Britten "Diana"	Fairoaks	10.08
French Army	F Cilliers	(Bury St Edmunds)	6.06
F-GGHD	E Watson	Duxford	8.08
	Fin Air Trade SAS	Denham	12.08
	Not known (Current status unknown)	Lasham	8.06
	Fire Defence PLC	Dunkeswell	5.08
	B L Featherstone (In open store)	Southend	10.08
	Not known	Gowran, Kilkenny	10.08
	Not known	Abbeyshrule	9.08
	Not known	Easter Poldar Farm, Thornhill	2.07
	(Current status unknown)		
G-BWCN	Trener Kft	RAF Weston-on-the-Green	8.08
5N-AYE, D-ILID, 9V-BKL, D-ILID (Operated Wingglider Ltd)			
	Not known	Hinton in the Hedges	12.08
LZ-524, RA-44490	Not known	White Waltham	1.09
N7818T	Kobo-Coop 96 Kft	Popham	1.09
LY-AQG	Kobo-Coop 96 Kft	North Weald	8.08
G-PFKD, LY-FKD, SP-FKD, SP-AAD, PLW85 (Operated R Bade)			
	Kobo-Coop 96 Kft	North Weald	8.08
	Kobo-Coop 96 Kft	Rochester	10.08
75+48	Kobo-Coop 96 Kft	Spilstead Farm, Sedlescombe	9.08
QW+233, QW+738, PA+139, PG+137			
FLARF-02160, CCCP-44420	Kobo-Coop 96 Kft	Spilstead Farm, Sedlescombe	1.09
HAF-332, HA-YFB	Farnair Hungary Kft	Sibson	10.08
N223DP, N90778	Not known	(Mosser, Cumbria)	2.09
RP-C5131	Not known	Breighton	12.08
G-OCMJ	Hidroplan Nord Kft	Breighton	12.08
G-HTPS, G-BRNI, YU-HBI		(Operated A Parker)	
IAC241	Not known	Breighton	12.08
French Army	Hidroplan Nord Kft	Brierley	7.08
OM-248, OM-UIN, OK-UIN	Trener Kft	Popham	1.09
RA-44484	Not known (Op Wingglider Ltd)	Hibaldstow	10.08
G-UGLY, G-BSFN, XP967, F-WIEQ	Not known	(Hull)	10.08
HA-LFR, HA-VLA, YU-HDN, JRV12653	J R Saul (Current status unknown)	Brierley	7.05
YU-DHU	Not known (spares use)	Husbands Bosworth	7.08
LZ-TCC	Not known	Elstree	1.09
TC-FBC, D-IDWM, CN-85, D-IDWM	Trener Kft	Langar	9.08
	(Operated Wingglider Ltd)		
RA-44777	Kobo-Coop 96 Kft	Rendcomb	6.08
RA-81584	Kobo-Coop 96 Kft	Elstree	1.09
RA-44000	Kobo-Coop 96 Kft	Shobdon	12.07
RA-44480	Kobo-Coop 96 Kft	North Weald	10.08
RA-01555	Kobo-Coop 96 Kft	Compton Abbas	1.09
	(Operated R McGuire)		
LY-APP, LY-AOG	Kobo-Coop 96 Kft	Wycombe Air Park	11.08
LY-AFS, DOSAAF	Kobo-Coop 96 Kft	Stoke Golding	8.08
RA-44504	Kobo-Coop 96 Kft	Great Oakley	8.05
LY-AMJ , DOSAAF, CCCP-81558		(Current status unknown)	
RA-44465, LY-AOL	Kobo-Coop 96 Kft	Oxford	10.08
RA-44479	Kobo-Coop 96 Kft (Operated D Barke)	Southend	2.09
RA-44545, LY-AIH, ES-FYE	Kobo-Coop 96 Kft	White Waltham	12.08

HA-YAR	Sukhoi Su-29	75-03	RA-01609	Kobo-Coop 96 Kft	White Waltham	1.09
			RA-7503			
HA-YAU	Yakovlev Yak-18T	15-35	RA-44527	Kobo-Coop 96 Kft	White Waltham	1.09
HA-YAV	Yakovlev Yak-18T	22202047817	RA-01153	Kobo-Coop 96 Kft	Eggesford	10.08
				(Operated M Robinson)		
HA-YAW	Sukhoi Su-29	74-05	N229JD	Kobo-Coop 96 Kft	Fairoaks	1.09
HA-YAZ	Yakovlev Yak-18T	7201413	CCCP44311	Kobo-Coop 96 Kft	Goodwood	1.09
HA-YDF	Technoavia SMG-92 Finist	01-0005		G-92 Kereskedelmi.Kft	South Cerney	10.08
				(Operated Wingglider Ltd)		
HA-YFC	LET L-410-FG	851528		Farnair Hungary	Sibson	10.08

SWITZERLAND

HB-CIU	Reims FR172J Rocket	FR17200437	D-EJXX	Bonanza Viaggi SA	Eddsfield	10.08
HB-DFT	Mooney M.20J	24-0837		Air Link AG	Andrewsfield	5.08
HB-OBP *	Piper J-3C-65 Cub	11709	43-30418	Not known	Dunsfold	4.07
HB-OLP	Piper PA-28-140 Cherokee	28-20495	N6425W	A Krapf	Seething	5.08

SAUDI ARABIA

HZ-ARK	Gulfstream Aerospace Gulfstream V-SP (Gulfstream 550)	5074	N574GA	Mawarid Ltd	Farnborough	1.09
HZ-OFC5	Dassault Falcon 900EASy	180	F-WWFD	Olayan Finance Co	Luton	2.09
HZ-SJP3	Bombardier CL-600-2B-16 (CL-604 Challenger)	5346	N604JP C-GLXS	Jouannou and Parskevaides	Farnborough and Larnaca	12.08

ITALY

I-EIXM*	Piper PA-18-135 Super Cub	18-3572	MM54-2372 54-2372	Not known (In open store as "EI-184")	Kesgrave, Ipswich	2.08
I-TOMI*	Nardi FN.305D	Not known		Not known (Stored)	Wycombe Air Park	5.05
I-6570	Aeropro Eurofox	not known		Not known	Eyne, Ireland	10.08
I-6929	Aeropro Eurofox	Not known		Not known	Kilrush	5.08
I-6943	Pegasus Quantum 914	Not known	G-59-7	R Meredith-Hardy	Barton	10.07
I-9266	Aeroprakt A22 Foxbat	not known		Not known	Birr	7.08

NORWAY

LN-AMY	North American AT-6D Harvard	88-16849	(LN-LCS)	T Manna	North Weald	10.08
			(LN-LCN), N10595, 42-85068 "Amy" (As "8084" in Breitling Fighter Team titles)			
LN-GDA	Brdritschka HB-21	21013	PH-947 D-KIDU, HB-2046	Ståle Lien	Shenington	8.08
LN-KKA*	Fokker F.27-050	20117	PH-DLT	Air Salvage International	Alton	5.06
			D-AFKY, PH-DLT, OE-LFZ, (VH-FNL), PH-EXA (Fuselage only)			

ARGENTINA

LV-AZF	Boeing 747-267B	23048	N230AL	Southern Winds (Stored)	Manston	1.09
			LV-AZF, N230AL, G-VRUM, (ZS-PJI), (G-CCMB), G-VRUM, TF-ATV, G-VRUM, B-HIF, VR-HIF, N6066U			
LV-RIE	Nord 1002 Pingouin	240		R.J.Lamplough (Stored)	East Garston	12.05
LV-WTY	McDonnell-Douglas MD-81	48011	LV-PMJ N532MD, HB-INM	Not known (Stored unmarked)	Shannon	10.06

LUXEMBOURG

LX-FTA	Dassault Falcon 900C	201	N210FJ F-WWFA	Northgate SARL (Operated Global Jet Luxembourg SA)	Farnborough	1.09

LITHUANIA

LY-BIG	Antonov An-2T	1G236-23	Ukraine AF 48 (red)	Air Unique "Baltic Bear"	Tatenhill	8.08
LY-CCP	Yakovlev Yak-18T	22202044623	LY-EMI CCCP81366	Not known	Cherry Tree Farm, Monewden	8.08

UNITED STATES

N1FD	SOCATA TB-200 XL Tobago	1614		Siek Aviation Inc	Blackbushe	1.09
N1FY	Cessna 421C Golden Eagle I	421C1067	N345TG	LME Aviation (Operated Estate Air)	Kemble	1.09
N2CL	Piper PA-28RT-201T Turbo Arrow IV	28R-8131054	N8333S N9649N	Southern Aircraft Consultancy Inc (Under repair Stapleford)	Frensham	10.07
N2FU	Learjet Model 31	31-027	N30LJ N91201	Wilmington Trust Company (Operated Formula One Administration)	Biggin Hill	11.08
N2NR	Agusta A109A-II	7350	N800AH	N2NR Inc	(Oxford)	1.09
N2RK	Lockheed L.188PF Electra	2010	N178RV	Electra Aero Inc	Coventry	8.08
			C-GNWC, N178RV, N63AJ, CF-NAX, N33506, ZK-TEB, (ZK-BMQ) (Stored)			
N3HK	Cessna 340 II	340-0538	G-VAUN D-IOFW, N5148J	Southern Aircraft Consultancy Inc	North Weald	1.09
N4HG	Lockheed L.188PF Electra	1140	G-LOFH N9744C	Electra Airways (Stored unmarked)	Coventry	8.08
N4VQ	Beech A36 Bonanza	E-3014	SP-FNK N3263W	VIP Transport Inc	Not known	11.06
			(Overran runway Fenland 30.10.06) (Current status unknown)			
N5LL	Piper PA-31 Navajo C	31-7812041	N27495	Southern Aircraft Consultancy Inc	Cardiff	12.08
N6NE	Lockheed Jetstar 731	5006/40	(VR-CCC)	Aerospace Finance Leasing Inc	Southampton	7.07
			N6NE, N222Y, N731JS, N227K, N12R, N9280R (Damaged Southampton 27.11.92: on fire dump)			
N7EX	Extra EA300/L	073		Southern Aircraft Consultancy Inc	Membury	1.09
N7EY	Piper PA-30 Twin Comanche	30-571	F-BNFH F-OCDS, N7508Y	Charnwood Aviation	White Waltham	1.09
N8MZ	Piper PA-30 Twin Comanche B	30-1648	G-ORDO N8485Y	Francis Aviation	Lee-on-Solent	1.09
N9AY	Cessna 421C Golden Eagle III	421C0844	G-NSGI	Sooty Aviation Inc	Jersey	1.09
			N421EL, XA-RAE, N421EB, (N21MW), N421EB, N2659Z			

Registration	Type	c/n	Previous identities	Owner/Operator	Base	Date
N9FJ	Aérospatiale AS.350B-2 Ecureuil	3148		Boultbee Aviation	Denham	12.08
N9SZ	Cirrus Design SR22-GTS	1232		Belle-Ile Inc	Weston, Dublin	11.08
N10MC	Cirrus Design SR22	1084		K R Baldwin Inc	Jersey	12.08
N11FV	Cessna T303 Crusader	T30300133	G-BXRI, HB-LNI, (N5143C)	Auster Aviation	Guernsey	10.08
N12AB	Ruschmeyer R90-230RG	027		Cremair Inc	Elstree	8.07
N12AG	Pilatus PC-12/47	854	HB-FSK	Aircraft Guaranty Corporation	(Fairoaks)	2.09
N12SJ	Cirrus Design SR22–G3-GTS Turbo	2740		Johnson Airways	Turweston	1.09
N12ZX	Mooney M.20J	24-3227		S Ames	Oxford	7.08
N13DT	Robinson R44 Raven I	1651		MCR Aviation	(Republic of Ireland)	5.08
N14AF	Rockwell Commander 112TC-A	13258	G-GRIF, G-BHXC, N1005C	Southern Aircraft Consultancy	Burnham on Crouch	1.09
N14HF	Maule MT-7-235 Star Rocket	18084C		Hamilton-Fairley Aviation	Bramshill	5.08
N14MT	Cessna TR182 Skylane RG	R18201227		Southern Aircraft Consultancy Inc	North Weald	7.08
N17GL	Beech D17S (UC-43-BH)	4885	G-LAJT, ZS-AJT, ZS-CLM, N1591V, NC60004, CR-LBF, 43-10837	International Air Services (Operated G W Lynch)	Great Oakley	
N17UK	Cirrus Design SR22	0200	N7UK	Southern Aircraft Consultancy Inc	Rochester	1.09
N18GH	McDonnell Douglas MD.520N	LN014	N317PC, N16113	Adrian Raymond Aviation	(Radstock)	2.08
N18V	Beech UC-43-BH Traveler	6869	NC18, Bu 32898, FT507, 44-67761	R.J.Lamplough (As "DR828:PB1")	East Garston	8.04
N19F	Cessna 337A Super Skymaster (Robertson STOL conversion)	33700289	N6289F	Southern Aircraft Consultancy Inc	Wadswick Manor Farm, Corsham	8.07
N19ET	Liberty Aerospace XL-2	0091		E A Terris	Wycombe Air Park	6.08
N19GL	Brantly B.2B	2004		Southern Aircraft Consultancy Inc	Hill Top Farm, Hambledon	5.07
N20AG	SOCATA TB-20 Trinidad	2003	N29KF	Archway International Inc	Jersey	10.08
N20UK	Mooney M.20F Executive	22-1380	N9155J, G-BDVU	E-Plane Inc	Biggin Hill	10.08
N21UH	United Helicopter Corp UH-12C	UH2001		Southern Aircraft Consultancy Inc	Shipmeadow, Beccles	3.07
N22CG	Cessna 441 Conquest II	441-0119		Jubilee Airways Inc (Operated M.Klinge)	Prestwick	6.08
N22NN	Cessna 182P Skylane	18263497	OE-DGU, N5717J	Southern Aircraft Consultancy Inc	Elstree	8.08
N23KY	Cessna P210N Centurion	P21000447	N731ER	Southern Aircraft Consultancy Inc (Operated Pacnet Europe)	Fairoaks	11.08
N25KB	Piper PA-24-250 Comanche	24-3034	F-BKRK, N7814P	Southern Aircraft Consultancy Inc (Operated K Bettoney)	Farley Farm, Romsey	6.08
N25PR	Piper PA-30-160 Twin Comanche B	30-1511	G-AVPR, N8395Y	PSL Aviation	Gloucestershire	8.08
N25XZ	Cessna 182G	18255388	HB-CST, OE-DDM , N2188R	Southern Aircraft Consultancy Inc	Bodmin	10.08
N26HE	Cessna 421C Golden Eagle II (Winglets)	421C0687		Wells Fargo Bank Northwest NA (Operated Springhurst Ltd)	Biggin Hill	1.09
N27BG	Cessna 340A	340A0656		Traca Inc (Operated B Gregory)	Cranfield	8.08
N27HK	Beech 200 Super King Air	BB-1350	A7-AHK, N1570F, N147VC, N1570F	Aircraft Guaranty Trust LLC	Weston, Dublin	11.08
N27MW	Beech B58 Baron	TH-995	ZS-MTG	B58 Aviation Inc	Fairoaks	1.09
N27UB	Cessna 525B CitationJet CJ3	525B0225		Fegotila Inc	Gloucestershire	1.09
N28TE	Raytheon 58 Baron	TH-1951		Ecosse Aviation Inc	Blackbushe	1.09
N30FL	Beech C90 King Air	LJ-741	(N90FL), F-GFLD, HB-GGW, I-AZIO	Keep Holdings Inc	Southend	2.09
N30MD	Agusta A.109A-II	7308	N212AT	Murtagh Aviation	Liskeard	8.08
N30NW	Piper PA-30-160 Twin Comanche	30-312	G-ASON, N7273Y	Centreline Aerospace Inc	Norwich	9.08
N31GN	Cessna 310R II	310R-1541	N410RS, G-BTGN, N410RS, N5331C	J A Keim	Kirknewton	8.08
N31RB	Grumman-American AA-5B Tiger	AA5B-0156		Southern Aircraft Consultancy Inc (Operated T Cromber t/a Echo Echo Group)	Bournemouth	1.09
N32LE	Piper PA-32R-301T Turbo Saratoga SP	32R-8329016		Southern Aircraft Consultancy (Operated Light into Europe)	Great Oakley	10.08
N33EW	Mitsubishi MU-2B-60	1519SA	N331W, N33TW, N434MA	Florida Express Corp (Operated King Aviation)	Southend	10.08
N33NW	SOCATA TB-20 Trinidad	1073	N666HM, OO-PDV, F-GLAC	Southern Aircraft Consultancy Inc	Nottingham	1.09
N34FA	SOCATA TB-20 Trinidad	866	G-BPFG	Southern Aircraft Consultancy Inc	Elstree	1.09
N34RF	Beech C90B King Air	LJ-1371	VT-PPC, N696WW, C-FSGZ	Roflec Inc	Guernsey	12.08
N35AD	Piper PA-30 Twin Comanche B	30-1121	HB-LDE, N8014Y	Southern Aircraft Consultancy Inc	Jersey	10.08
N35AG	Agusta A109S Grand	22050		Aircraft Guaranty Management LLC (Operated Fiat Group)	Fairoaks	1.09
N35AL	Diamond DA 42 Twin Star	42.147	OE-VPY	Able Liston Aviation	Jersey	11.08
N35SN	Beech 35-33 Debonair	CD-207	D-EKOW	Plane Fun Inc	Old Sarum	1.09
N36NB	Beech A36 Bonanza	E-2274	F-GKTZ, N7249H	Minute Aviation Inc	Biggin Hill	3.07
N36SU	Beech A36 Bonanza	E-3034	OY-TFE, N1096Y	Zoomair Inc	Fairoaks	12.08
N36TH*	Canadair CL-30 (T-33AN) Silver Star Mk.3			See G-BYOY in SECTION 1, Part 3	North Weald	
N37LP	Bell 407	53049		Aircraft Guaranty Title LLC	Weston, Dublin	10.08
N37LW	Piper PA-23-250 Aztec	27-134	G-EEVA, G-ASND, N4800P	Southern Aircraft Consultancy Inc	Morgansfield, Fishburn	4.08
N37US	Piper PA-34-200T Seneca II	34-8070111	G-PLUS, N81406	Southern Aircraft Consultancy Inc (Operated Skycabs)	Jersey	10.08

Reg	Type	Serial
N37VB	Cessna 421C	421C-0418
N39SE	Diamond DA.40 Star	40.299
N39TA	Beech B24R Sierra 200	MC-230
N40AU	Mooney M.20TN Acclaim	31-0038
N40GD	Cirrus Design SR22	0473
N40XR	Bombardier Learjet 40	45-2028
N41AK	Beech F90 King Air	LA-188
N41FT	Piper PA-39 Twin Comanche C/R	39-59
N42FW*	Beech E33 Bonanza	CD-1199
N43GG*	Piper PA-34-200T Seneca II	34-7670066
N44NE	Cessna 414	414-0070
N45PJ	Piper PA-46-500TP Malibu Meridian	4697031
N46BM	Beech E90 King Air	LW-198
N46PJ	Cessna 551 Citation II/SP	551-0027
N46PL	Piper PA-46-500TP Malibu Meridian	4697054
N46WK	Piper PA-46-500TP Malibu Meridian	4697090
N48CA	Piper PA-32R-301 Saratoga II HP	3246232
N48NS	Cessna 550 Citation Bravo	550-0939
N49BH	Aviat A-1B Husky	2315
N50AY	Rockwell Commander 114	14527
N51AH	Piper PA-32R-301 Saratoga SP	32R-8413017
N51ER	American Champion 7GCAA	484-2004
N51WF	Rockwell 690C Turbo Commander	11684
N53SB	Reims FR172H Rocket	FR172H0265
N55BN	Beech 95-B55 Baron	TC-1572
N55EN	Beech E55 Baron	TE-942
N56GH	Bell 206B-3 JetRanger III	4281
N57CR	Hiller UH-12C	909
N58AM	Piper PA-31T1 Cheyenne 1A	31-1104005
N58GT	Beech B58 Baron (Winglets)	TH-1090
N58YD	Beech 58 Baron	TH-1427
N59SD	McDonnell Douglas MD.369E	0019E
N59VT	Beech K35 Bonanza	D-5897
N60BM	Rockwell 690A Turbo Commander	11172
N60GM	Cessna 421C Golden Eagle III	421C0828
N60LW	Cessna 550 Citation Bravo	550-1129
N60NZ	Beech 60 Duke	P-339
N61DE	Piper PA-32-300 Six	32-7940030
N61FD	SIAI-Marchetti SF.260C	719
N61HB	Piper PA-34-220T Seneca V	3449217
N61MF *	Mooney M.20J	24-0847
N61PS	Pitts S-2B	5230
N63EN	Cessna 340	340-0063
N64GG	Beech B300 King Air	FL-274
N64JG	Bell 206B-2 Jet Ranger	1507
N64LA	Cessna 421C Golden Eagle	421C1064
N64VB	Beech 58 Baron	TH-305
N65JF	Piper PA-28-181 Archer II	28-7990140
N65MJ	Beech 58P Baron	TJ-487
N65PF	Piper PA-30 Twin Comanche B	30-1515
N65TG	Agusta A119	14529
N66MS	Piper PA-28RT-201T Turbo Arrow IV	28R-8431021
N66SG	Bombardier Learjet 45	45-073
N66SW*	Cessna 340	340-0011

Reg / previous ids	Operator	Location	Date
EC-IFT G-FWRP, N3919C	Lowndes Aviation	Bournemouth	1.09
	Southern Aircraft Consultancy Inc	Bodmin	11.08
G-BBVJ	Southern Aircraft Consultancy Inc	Sturgate	10.08
	BKF Aviation	Welshpool	5.08
	Aircraft Guaranty Trust LLC	Sherburn-in-Elmet	9.08
	Wells Fargo Bank Northwest NA	Bournemouth	1.09
(Operated Jet-Care International)			
N41CK N6429M	N41AK Inc	Glasgow	8.08
G-BZLW ZS-NLF, ZS-MRH, ZS-IKG, N8904Y	Southern Aircraft Consultancy Inc	Farley Farm, Romsey	6.08
N7682N	Southern Aircraft Consultancy Inc	Kirknewton	3.06
(Operated Feroz Wadia) (Cx 1.07) (Current status unknown)			
G-ROLA N4537X, G-ROLA, N4537X	Southern Aircraft Consultancy Inc *(Damaged Humberside 27.9.05) (Cx 6.08)*	Shoreham	12.08
G-DYNE N8170Q	J & G Aviation	Tollerton	11.08
	Billings Flying Service	Weston, Dublin	10.08
G-WELL N202CC, (N7PB), N202CC	Sherborne Aviation	Bournemouth	1.09
N522CC N552CC, N44GT, N552CC, N98753	Aircraft Guaranty Trust LLC	Abbeyshrule	12.08
D-FKAI N53263, (D-FKAI), N53263, (PH-EPS) *(Current status unknown)*	AvCorp Leasing	Gloucestershire and Jersey	8.05
SE-LTM N189DB, N46WK, N46WE, N5343C	Skypark Holding	Gloucestershire	1.09
	Southern Aircraft Consultancy Inc	Panshanger	8.08
VP-BNS (N939BB), N5076K	Tower House Investments	Jersey	1.09
G-USKI	Southern Aircraft Consultancy Inc	Hunts Green	1.09
(Operated B Hill)			
HB-NCZ G-BGTE, N5910N	Stronghold Aviation	Rochester	8.08
G-REAH G-CELL, (G-BLRI), N4361D	Southern Aircraft Consultancy Inc	Panshanger	2.09
	Southern Aircraft Consultancy Inc	Abbeyshrule	8.08
N5936K	Aviation Air Services	Fairoaks	1.08
G-CCSB OO-RTC, F-BSHK	Southern Aircraft Consultancy Inc	Ashley Farm Warfield	10.08
G-KCAS G-KCEA, N2840W	Snowadam Inc *(Operated C.Butler)*	Tatenhill	1.09
	Monckton Byng Inc	Elstree	12.07
	Aircraft Guaranty Trust LLC	Dublin	7.08
(Operated Hennessy Aviation)			
	Pulse Helicopter Corp	(Liverpool)	11.08
N2427W	Gardiner Aircraft	North Weald	11.08
HB-GIK	Swiftair Inc	Finmere	8.08
G-OLYD N7255H, ZS-LYC, N7255H	Southern Aircraft Consultancy Inc	Gamston	8.08
	Sky Dock Helicopter Holdings	(Faldingworth)	5.08
D-EMEF	Southern Aircraft Consultancy Inc	White Waltham	1.09
N60B TF-ERR, (D-IIGI), TF-ERR, C-GERR, TF-ERR, N9164N	Get Mapping Aircraft Inc *(Operated Cooper Aerial Surveys)*	Wickenby	9.08
	Southern Aircraft Consultancy Inc	Gamston	10.08
N52029	PIHL Delaware Inc	Luton	12.08
	International Air Services	Haverfordwest	9.08
(Operated D F Keedy)			
G-LADE N3008L	Southern Aircraft Consultancy Inc	Andrewsfield	1.09
	Aerial Obsessions Inc "35"	North Weald	8.08
G-CBAA N53445	HBC Aviation Inc	Thurrock and Guernsey	1.09
G-BYDD	M Flynn *(Current status unknown)*	Bournemouth	9.05
D-EIWM *(Overran runway landing Fairoaks 8. 5.05: cancelled 6.06 by FAA: wreck stored)*			
	D J Swartz	Wickenby	10.06
G-REEN G-AZYR, N5893M	Echo November Inc	North Weald	1.09
	Specsavers Aviation	Guernsey	2.09
N589LB	San Juan Aviation *(Stored)*	Hawarden	5.07
G-MUVG N421DD, N6865P	N64LA Inc	Fairoaks	12.08
N273TB	Galv-Aero Flight Center	Sleap	1.09
N2087C	Southern Aircraft Consultancy Inc	Nottingham	9.08
	Grange Aviation	Donegal, County Donegal	10.08
G-AVUD N8422Y	Southern Aircraft Consultancy Inc	Biggin Hill	10.08
	Milltown Helicopter Inc	(Ireland)	7.08
G-BRRJ N4353T	International Air Services *(Operated M Stower)*	Elstree	1.09
N65U	Woolsington Wunderbus Inc	Newcastle	1.09
(Operated Sagesoft)			
N5035Q	Not known *(Cancelled 5.03 by FAA as sold in UK)*	Gamston	4.06

Reg	Type	c/n	Owner	Location	Date
N67DP	Cirrus Design SR22-G3-GTS	2933	N67DP Inc	Blackbushe	12.08
N69LJ	Bombardier Learjet 60	60-027	Wilmington Trust Co	Biggin Hill	12.08
N69LP	Piper PA-61P Aerostar 601P	61P-0541-230	G-TIME　Southern Aircraft Consultancy Inc	Bournemouth	2.09
			N8058J		
N70AA	Beech 70 Queen Air	LB-35	G-REXP　ST Aviation	Wellesbourne Mountford	12.08
			N70AA, G-KEAA, G-REXP, G-AYPC		
N70QJ	Sikorsky S-76A	760284	N700J　Shannon Helicopters	Shannon	9.08
N70VB	Ted Smith Aerostar 600A	60-0446-150	C-GVHQ　Southern Aircraft Consultancy Inc	Blackbushe	1.09
			N9805Q		
N71VE	Rockwell Commander 690A	11043	N71VT　Airbourne Inc	Wickenby	1.09
			N2VQ, N2VA　(Operated Cooper Aerial Surveys)		
N71WZ	Piper PA-46-350P Malibu Mirage	4636275	C-FLER　Arlington Aviation	Bournemouth	1.09
N72GD	Raytheon RB390 Premier 1A	RB-163	N7163E　Stallion Enterprises (N59RK reserved)	Bournemouth	1.09
N73AE	Mudry CAP.10B	278	Cole Aviation　Spilstead Farm, Sedlescombe		11.07
N73GR	Piper PA-28-181 Archer III	2843586	Southern Aircraft Consultancy Inc	Kirknewton	12.08
N74DC	Pitts S-2A Special	2228	I-ALAT　H J Seery (Operated D.Cockburn)	Rush Green	10.08
N74PM	Agusta A109C	7636	D-HOFP　Ortac Inc	(Whitegate)	10.08
			I-SEIN　(Operated Huktra UK Ltd)		
N75FW	Cessna 421C Golden Eagle	421C0706	G-OSCH　Forward Aviation	Leeds/Bradford	11.08
			G-SALI, N26552		
N75TC	Cessna 172N	17268913	Aircraft Guaranty Title & Trust LLC	Tibenham	6.08
N75TQ	Boeing Stearman B75N1(N2S-3)	75-1180	G-BRSK　Southern Aircraft Consultancy Inc	Priory Farm	9.08
			N5565N, Bu.3403　(USN marks as "3403/180")	Tibenham	
N76AF	Sikorsky S.76C	760533	Vulcan Aircraft	Blackbushe	10.08
N77YY	Piper PA-32R-301T Saratoga II TC	3257120	G-LLYY　Flying Start Aviation Inc	Guernsey	1.08
			N4165C　(Operated M J Start)		
N78GG	Beech F33A Bonanza	CE-699	G-ENSI　Southern Aircraft Consultancy Inc	Blackbushe	1.09
			D-ENSI　(Operated G Garnett)		
N78HB	Aviat A-1B Husky	2066	N115BB　HBC Aviation Inc	King's Farm, Thurrock	1.06
			G-FOFF, N115BB　(Operated T Holding)		
N78XP	Reims FR172K Hawk XP II	FR17200603	G-BFFZ　Blackburn Aeroplane Co	Bodmin	1.09
			F-WZDU		
N79AP	Beech 58P Baron	TJ-206	VH-ORP　Aircraft Guaranty Title LLC	Enstone	12.07
			ZK-TML, N6648Z　(Operated R & B Services Ltd)		
N79EL	Beech 400A Beechjet	RK-214	Edra Lauren Leasing Corporation	East Midlands	3.08
			(Operated DFS Furniture)		
N79HR	Lancair Columbia LC41-550FG	41017	Rotherwick Inc	Oxford	10.08
N80BA	Pitts S-1A	648-4	Thomas D Stronge	(Belfast)	1.06
			(Crashed 7.11.99 - stored)		
N80HB	Cessna 525B CitationJet CJ3	525B0163	N5267K　HBC Aviation	Guernsey	1.09
N80HQ	Cessna 510 Citation Mustang	510-0021	Jane Air Inc	Southampton	1.09
N80JN*	Mitsubishi MU-2J	626	EC-GLU　Aircraft Guaranty Title Corp	Waterford	7.08
			OY-ATZ, SE-GHY, N476MA　(Cancelled 6.07 by FAA: derelict)		
N80MC	Mudry CAP.10B	221	Cole Aviation　Spilstead Farm, Sedlescombe		11.07
N80N	Cessna T337G Super Skymaster	P3370197	Marks Parks Inc	Wolverhampton	8.07
N80NS	Cirrus Design SR22-G3	2839	Bonus Aviation	Newcastle	8.08
N81AW	Piper PA-34-220T Seneca III	34-8133107	Southern Aircraft Consultancy Inc	East Midlands	12.08
N84VK	Piper PA-24-180 Comanche	24-1492	N84VK Inc	Tatenhill	1.09
			D-EINS		
N85LB	Cessna 340A II	340A0486	N6382P		
			G-OPLB　Southern Aircraft Consultancy Inc (Operated A Ruff)		
			G-FCHJ, G-BJLS, (N6315X)　Newcastle and Eshott		5.08
N85WS	Pitts S-1T	1028	Southern Aircraft Consultancy Inc	Great Oakley	10.08
N88NA	Piper PA-32R-301T Turbo Saratoga SP	32R-8529005	G-PAPS　Southern Aircraft Consultancy Inc	Gamston	10.08
			F-GELX, N4385D　(Operated Nicol Aviation)		
N88SU	Sukhoi Su-29	90-03	Bahamair LLC	Abbeyshrule	10.08
N89GH	Cirrus Design SR22	1178	Aircraft Guaranty Title Corp	Denham	11.08
N89SS	Bell 206B-2 JetRanger II	1010	G-HMSS　Aircraft Guaranty Corp	Kilrush	10.08
			ZS-HMS, C-GXOI, N58008		
N90DJ	Reims/Cessna F182Q Skylane	F18200091	D-EIIP　Deejay Aviation	Jersey	10.08
N90YA	Cessna 425 Corsair	425-0090	N90GA　Southern Aircraft Consultancy Inc	Donegal	9.08
			G-BHNY, (N68476)		
N91ME	SOCATA TB-20 Trinidad	2152	Carr Aviation	Wellesbourne Mountford	12.08
N91TH	Agusta A109E Power	11651	Agusta Holding Inc	(Republic of Ireland)	2.09
			(Operated Blue Star Helicopters)		
N92RW	Beech F33A Bonanza	CE-972	D M Lara	Cork	4.08
N94SA	Champion 7ECA Citabria	227	OY-AUG　International Air Services　Blockmoor Farm, Soham		7.08
			D-EFLO　(Operated J Surbey)		
N95D	Piper PA-34-220T Seneca V	3449060	N9506N　Zeta Aviation Inc	Welshpool	12.08
N95GT	Cirrus Design SR22-GTS	1758	N588CD　Southern Aircraft Consultancy Inc	Rochester	1.09
N95TA	Piper PA-31 Turbo Navajo B	31-7300971	N7576L　High Flyers Aviation	Newcastle	1.09
N96HC	Bell 206L-1 Long Ranger II	45285	Southern Aircraft Consultancy Inc　Cork, County Cork		1.09
N96JL	Cessna 421C Golden Eagle	421C-0627	Lespa Aviation	Kemble	9.08
N96XW *	Farrington Twinstarr Gyrocopter	TS-008	Not known	Shipdham	7.08
			(Cancelled 8.04 by FAA: noted as "96XW")		
N97GP	SOCATA TB-20 Trinidad	1837	G-WASI　Air Touring Inc	Goodwood	10.08
			D-EVHV		
N98AG	Partenavia AP.68TP-300 Spartacus	8011	I-VULE　Aircraft Guaranty Trust LLC	Alscot	10.08
N99ET	SOCATA TB-10 Tobago	226	G-BJDG　Southern Aircraft Consultancy Inc	Cardiff	12.08
			F-BNGR		
N99XT	Piper PA-32-301xtc	3255024	Fletcher Aviation	Guernsey	11.08
N100JS	Cessna 525B CitationJet CJ3	525B-0095	N5214K　Jato Aviation	Luton	1.09
N100LH	Rotorway Exec 90	5249	R J Whitney	Street Farm	10.08
			(Built by Larry L Henderson as c/n 001)	Takeley	
N100VA	Eclipse Aviation EA500	000138	Victor Alpha Inc	Oxford	10.08

Reg	Type	Serial	Previous identities	Owner/Operator	Location	Date
N100YY	Cirrus Design SR20	1183		Southern Aircraft Consultancy Inc	Deenthorpe	10.08
N101DW	Piper PA-32R-300 Cherokee Lance	32R-7680399		Southern Aircraft Consultancy Inc	Panshanger	7.08
N101UK	Mooney M.20K	25-0631		Southern Aircraft Consultancy Inc	Newcastle	10.08
N104PF	Cessna 172R	17280313		P Johal	Leicester	11.08
N105SK	Reims Cessna F150L	F15000877	G-IAWE, EI-AWE	Aerospace Trust Management LLC	Sleap	7.07
N106ML	Beech C90GT King Air	LJ-1757		Coppercrest Inc	(Shoreham)	12.08
N108SR	Cirrus Design SR22	1868		Gardiner Aircraft Inc	North Weald	1.09
N109AG	Agusta A109A-II	7260	N20RQ, N20RG	JLC Aviation	(Shoreham)	12.08
N109AN	Agusta A109A-II	7348		MW Helicopters Inc	Stapleford	12.08
N109GR	Agusta A109S Grand	22090		Wells Fargo Bank Northwest NA (Operated Prodrive)	Banbury	12.08
N109MJ	Agusta A109E Power	11617	N606SR	Newshore Holding Inc	Ronaldsway	11.08
N109TD	Agusta A109E Power	11011	5N-BGX, N108WP, N27BV, N27BD, N1ZL	N109TD Inc	(Bournemouth)	11.08
N109TF	Agusta A109A-II	7328	VH-NWD, VH-DMR, (VH-MRS)	Chestham Park Inc (Operated Castle Helicopters Inc)	(Liskeard)	12.08
N109TK	Agusta A109C	7650	N109TW, D-HCKM	Botany Aviation	(Botany Bay)	1.09
N109WF	Agusta A109A-II	7298	N109BC	Agusta 109 LLC (Operated Lenham Racing)	Stapleford	7.08
N112JA	Rockwell Commander 112TC-A	13182	5Y-MBK	Southern Aircraft Consultancy Inc	Sandown, Isle of Wight	1.09
N112SR	Cirrus Design SR22-GTS	1869		Saratoga Facilities Inc	Redhill	12.08
N112WM	Piper PA-32-300 Cherokee Six D	32-7140001	G-AZTD, N8611N	Southern Aircraft Consultancy Inc	Full Sutton	8.08
N113AC	SOCATA TB-20 Trinidad GT	2121	G-TTAC, F-OIMD, (N212GT)	Southern Aircraft Consultancy Inc	Shoreham	12.08
N114ED	Commander Aircraft Commander 114B	14637	G-PADS, N60987	Southern Aircraft Consultancy Inc	Guernsey	11.08
N115MD	Commander Aircraft Commander 114TC	20039		Southern Aircraft Consultancy Inc	Fairoaks	1.09
N115TB	Commander Aircraft Commander 114TC	20031		Aircraft Guaranty Corporation (Current status unknown)	Oxford	9.06
N116HS	Bell UH-1L	6171	Bu154949	Yorkshire Helicopters USA Inc (Stored dismantled)	Coney Park, Leeds	5.08
N116WG	Westland WG-30-100	016	(G-BLLG)	Cogent PLC (Operated Robert Gordon Institute of Technology)	Montrose	4.07
N117EA	Eclipse Aviation EA500	000104		Cordite Inc	Ronaldsway	12.08
N119BM	Agusta A119 Koala	14016		HSS (USA) Ltd (Operated The Mansfield Group)	Dublin	12.08
N120CS	Cessna 525 CitationJet CJ1	525-0490	N130CS, N52141	York House Real Estate Kft Inc	Weston, Dublin	1.09
N120HH	Bell 407	53661		407 Holding Inc (Operated Oyster Leasing Ltd)	Peldon, Colchester	1.09
N121EL*	Gates Learjet 25	25-010	(N121GL), (N82UH), (N10BF), N102PS, N671WM, N846HC, N846GA (For instructional use)	Kingston University	Roehampton, Surrey	10.06
N121JF	Beech F33A Bonanza	CE-1578	OO-PMK, F-GJGA, N81701	Aero Algarve Ltd	Elstree	1.09
N121MT	Britten-Norman BN-2T Turbine Islander (Build IRMA)	880	N200LQ, USAF 88-0916, N5097R, N73413, (YV-2173P), N413JA, G-BFNX	Swiftair Inc	Finmere	10.08
N122MG	Cirrus Design SR22-GTS	1250		122MG Inc	Turweston	1.09
N123AX	Piper PA-32R-301 Saratoga II HP	3246060	G-LLTT, N9283P	Axis Aircraft Leasing Inc	Gloucestershire	8.08
N123DU	Piper PA-28-161 Cherokee Warrior II	28-7716195	G-BPDU	Fletcher Aviation (Southern Flight Centre titles)	Guernsey	11.08
N123DV	Cirrus Design SR22-GTS	1313	N5672V	Fletcher Aviation	Guernsey	1.09
N123SA	Piper PA-18-150 Super Cub	18-1372	French Army 51-15372	Southern Aircraft Consultancy Inc (Operated B Walsh)	Glenforsa	8.08
N123UK	Mooney M.20J	24-3167	G-ZZIP, N1086N	Southern Aircraft Consultancy Inc (Operated H T El-Kasaby)	Southend	2.09
N124CP	Cirrus Design SR22-G3-GTSX Turbo	3040		Amsair Executive Aviation	Stapleford	1.09
N125AV	Beech 58 Baron	TH-1341	5B-CJV, N6342U	Sav Air Inc	Tatenhill	8.08
N125XP	Hawker 800XP	258486	N485LT, A7-AAL, (HZ-KSRD), N4515	N125XP Inc	Luton	2.09
N126ZZ	Hawker 4000	RC-10	(N810HH)	Meir Aviation	Luton	1.09
N127BU	Cessna 551 Citation II/SP	551-0179	N203BE, HZ-ZTC, HZ-AAI, N2635D	Dolphin Express	Biggin Hill	9.08
N129SC	Piper PA-32-300 Cherokee Six	32-7440057		Manx Orthopaedic Services	Ronaldsway	10.08
N131CD	Cirrus Design SR20	1031		N131CD Inc	Elstree	12.08
N132CK	Cessna 421A	421A0038	EI-TCK, G-AXAW, (EI-TCK), G-AXAW, N2238Q	Southern Aircraft Consultancy Inc	Leeds/Bradford	1.09
N132LE	Piper PA-32-300 Cherokee Six	32-40038	G-AVFS	Southern Aircraft Consultancy (Operated Light into Europe)	New Farm House, Great Oakley	6.08
N134TT	Cessna 305C Bird Dog	24541	F-GFVE, F-WFVE, French Army (US Marines c/s)	Southern Aircraft Consultancy Inc	Belle Vue Farm, Yarnscombe	2.08
N136SA	American General AG-5B	10164	G-RICA	Southern Aircraft Consultancy Inc	(Dunkeswell)	9.08
N139PG	Cirrus Design SR20	1910		Cirrus Group Inc	Galway	10.08
N141HT	Cirrus Design SR22 Turbo	2219		Aircraft Guaranty Management LLC	Gloucestershire	8.08
N142TW	Beech 58 Baron		TH-1841	Specialized Aircraft Services Inc	Fairoaks	1.09

Reg	Type	Serial
N145DF	Cessna S550 Citation II	S550-0018
N145DR	Piper PA-34-220T Seneca V	3449240
N146FL	Beech F90 King Air	LA-59
N147CD	Cirrus Design SR20	1043
N147DC	Douglas C-47A-75-DL Dakota	19347
N147GT	Cirrus Design SR22-G2	1069
N147KA	Cirrus Design SR22-GTS	1944
N147LD	Cirrus Design SR22	0937
N147LK	Cirrus Design SR22-GTS	1687
N147RJ	Cessna 310R-II	310R1294
N147VC	Cirrus Design SR22	0689
N150JC	Beech A35 Bonanza	D-2084
N150ZZ	Cirrus Design SR22-G3	2609
N151CG	Cirrus Design SR22	0344
N153H	Bell 222B	47138
N154DJ	Cessna T303 Crusader	T30300230
N160SR	Cirrus Design SR22-GTS	2161
N161FF	Piper PA-28-161 Cherokee Warrior II	28-7716097
N164SR	Cirrus Design SR20-G2	1763
N170AZ	Cessna 170A	19674
N171JB	Piper PA-28R-180 Cherokee Arrow	28R-30756
N171JJ	Bombardier BD-700 Global 5000	9209
N171WM	Piper PA-23-250 Aztec C	27-3498
N172AM	Cessna 172M Skyhawk II	17264993
N173RG	Velocity 173RG	3RE052
N174ST	Agusta A.109E Power	11115
N177SA	Reims Cessna F177RG Cardinal RG	F177RG0171
N180BB	Cessna 180K	18053103
N180FN	Cessna 180K	18053201
N180LK	Piper PA-28-180 Cherokee F	28-7105121
N181WW	Beagle B.206 Series 1	B.018
N182GC	Reims Cessna F182Q Skylane II	F18200068
N184BK	Bombardier BD-100 Challenger 300	20209
N184VB	Cessna 441 Conquest II	441-0184
N186CB	Piper PA-46-350P Malibu Mirage	4622085
N187SA	Piper PA-28R-200 Cherokee Arrow II	28R-7235139
N188S	Agusta A109A-II	7349
N188WS	Cessna 560XL Citation XL	560-5179
N189SA	Piper PA-31-325 Navajo C/R	31-7512045
N191ME	Cessna T206H Turbo Stationair	T20608188
N192JM	Mooney M.20R Ovation	29-0337
N192SR	Cirrus Design SR22-GTS G3 Turbo	2467
N195NJ	Agusta A109E Power	11043
N196PG	Cirrus Design SR20-G3-GTS	1968
N198JH	Cessna 525 CitationJet	525-0265
N199PS	Piper PA-34-220T Seneca V	3449108
N199ZZ	Cirrus Design SR22-GTS-G3	2542
N200GK	Piper PA-28R-200 Cherokee Arrow II	28R-7335287
N200RE	Beech E90 King Air	LW-164
N200UP	Dassault Falcon 50	55
N201W	Bell 47D-1	83
N201YK	Mooney M.20J	24-0518
N202AA	Cessna 421C Golden Eagle	421C1015
N203CD	Cirrus Design SR20-G2	1451
N203SA	Piper AE-1 Cub Cruiser	5-1477
N206CF	Cessna TU206G Turbo Stationair 6	U20605128
N206HE	Bell 206B JetRanger	2880
N206MF	Bell 206B-3 JetRanger III	4488
N208B	Cessna 208B Grand Caravan	208B1023

Reg	Operator	Location	Date
N1AF	Wells Fargo Bank Northwest NA	Luton	5.07
N814CC, N501NB, (N1259K) *(Operated Star Aviation)*			
	Cleevewood Aviation Inc	Gloucestershire	11.08
G-FLTI	Keep Holdings	Guernsey	2.08
	Free Flight Aviation	Blackbushe	1.09
G-DAKS	Aces High US Inc	Dunsfold	6.08
TS423, "108841, "KG374", "G-AGHY", TS423, 42-100884 *(As "2100884:L4" in US AF c/s)*			
	Free Flight Aviation	Denham	1.09
N174SR	Free Flight Aviation	Shoreham	1.09
N23AM	Free Flight Aviation	Denham	1.09
N745CD	Free Flight Aviation	Blackbushe	1.09
G-RIST	Justin Developments Aviation	Bournemouth	1.09
G-DATS, (N6128X)			
	Free Flight Aviation	Wycombe Air Park	7.08
N8674A	R.M.Hornblower *(Unmarked on trailer)*	Southend	1.09
	Alexander Fitzgibbons	Denham	8.08
	N151CG Inc	Old Sarum	9.08
	Kea Lew Inc	Castleknock, County Dublin	10.08
F-GGLJ	N154DJ Inc	Denham	1.09
N9891C			
	Southern Aircraft Consultancy Inc	Weston, Dublin	11.08
G-BYXU	Southern Aircraft Consultancy Inc	Waterford	7.08
EI-BXU, G-BNUP, N2282Q	*(Operated F McGovern & F O'Sullivan)*		
	Lisa Hall	Cambridge	10.08
HB-CAZ	Southern Aircraft Consultancy Inc	Strathallan	6.08
N5720C	*(Operated A Gregori)*		
N7414J	J A Keim	Kirknewton	5.08
C-FIIG	Aircraft Guaranty Corp	Luton	1.09
	(Operated MBI International)		
G-BXPS	International Air Services	Biggin Hill	6.08
G-AYLY, N6258Y	*(Operated W Moore marked "G-BXPS")*		
G-BXHG	Southern Aircraft Consultancy Inc		
N64057		Coonagh, Co Limerick	10.08
	Aircraft Guaranty Title & Trust LLC	North Weald	10.08
	Jet Finance Group	(Private site)	8.08
F-GBFI	Southern Aircraft Consultancy Inc	Southend	1.09
	(Operated A Jahanfar)		
	Southern Aircraft Consultancy Inc	(Baldonnel)	1.09
	Rivet Inc	Fordham, Newmarket	7.08
	Boston Commercial Corporation	Tatenhill	5.08
G-BCJF	International Air Services	North Weald	11.08
N181WW, G-BCJF, XS773	*(Operated G Nolan)*		
G-BFOD	Southern Aircraft Consultancy Inc	Alderney	1.09
	(Operated G Clarke)		
C-FSLR	Latium 3 Inc	Hawarden	1.09
	Diplomat Freight Services	East Midlands	10.08
D-EXCC	Aircraft Guaranty Holdings & Trust LLC	Liverpool	10.08
N9188D			
G-BOJH	Southern Aircraft Consultancy Inc	Cumbernauld	8.08
N2821T	"Knight of the Thistle"		
	JSJ Aviation	Leeds-Bradford	8.08
N86TW	Beacon Eire Inc	Weston, Dublin	1.09
N512DR, N51984	*(Reserved as "N186WS")*		
G-BMGH	Southern Aircraft Consultancy Inc	Southend	2.09
ZS-LEU, N8493, A2-CAT *(Operated J Jacques)*			
	Low Desert Aviation	Bagby	10.08
	Southern Aircraft Consultancy Inc	Plymouth	12.08
	Hazelhurst Aircraft Inc	Goodwood	10.08
	Beacon Helicopters Inc	Weston, Dublin	8.08
	Cirrus Design Corp	Turweston	1.09
	Aircraft Guaranty Management LLC	(Bournemouth)	5.08
	(Operated Enex Aviation)		
	Veryord Inc	Elstree	1.09
	November Zulu Ltd	Stapleford	1.09
G-BBIA	Southern Aircraft Consultancy Inc	Stapleford	1.09
N11C	*(Operated G H Kilby)*		
	Gray Aviation	Cranfield	1.09
N96UH	Wells Fargo Bank Northwest NA	Farnborough	2.09
N300CR, N625CR, N332MQ, N332MC, N1CN, (N30N), N839F, N73FJ, F-WZHU			
48-0803	Southern Aircraft Consultancy Inc		1.09
	(Stored dismantled)	Phoenix Farm, Lower Upham	
	J McTaggart	Dirleton, Archerfield	4.08
	Simply Living Ltd	Biggin Hill	11.07
	Mustarrow Inc	Liverpool	11.08
G-BWUG	Southern Aircraft Consultancy Inc	Eggesford	6.08
(ZK-USN), N62073, NC62073, Bu30274 *(As "Bu30274" in US Navy c/s)*			
	Southern Aircraft Consultancy Inc		
		Navan, County Meath	6.07
N316JP	Southern Aircraft Consultancy Inc	(Weymouth)	9.08
	Morrissey Fencing Inc	Republic of Ireland	1.09
N208ST	Aircraft Guaranty Title & Trust LLC	Strathallan	10.08
	(Operated B Munro)		

Reg	Type	C/n	Prev id	Owner	Location	Date
N208ER	Bell 206B Jet Ranger	4527		Aircraft Guaranty Holdings & Trust LLC		
					Weston, Dublin	10.08
N209DW	Lancair Columbia LC41-550FG	41504		White Columbia Inc	Oxford	1.09
N209SA	Piper PA-22-108 Colt	22-8448	EI-AYS	Southern Aircraft Consultancy Inc	Abbeyshrule	9.08
			G-ARKT			
N210AD	Cessna 210G Centurion	21058835	OE-DES	Uniplane Inc	Guernsey	1.08
N210CP	Cessna 210M Centurion	21062034		Robert Helmstetter	Sligo	12.08
N210EU	Cessna T210L Turbo Centurion	21061152	SP-FWK	International Air Services	Elstree	1.09
	(N103AG), D-EAWO, N2191S			*(Operated A Miller)*		
N210NM	Cessna 210K Centurion	21059255	D-ECAL	Alpine Air Leasing	Biggin Hill	9.08
			N8255M			
N212W	Hiller UH-12A	237	51-4015	Southern Aircraft Consultancy Inc	Henstridge	8.07
N214AE	Aérospatiale AS.350B2 Ecureuil	4019		Axle Heli Inc	(Republic of Ireland)	7.08
N216GC	Piper PA-28R-200 Cherokee Arrow B	28R-7135151	G-EVVA	American Flight Academy	Elstree	1.09
			G-BAZU, EI-AVH, N11C			
N216HK *	CGS Hawk IIA	HT468R447		CGS Aviation Inc	Castlerock, County Londonderry	7.07
	(C/n on plate H-CGS-490P)			*(Cancelled 11.91 by FAA: stored)*		
N218BA	Boeing 747-245F	20827	G-GAFX	Wilmington Trust Co	Manston	11.08
	N641FE, VP-BXP, N641FE, (N632FE), N812FT, N702SW *(Being scrapped 11.08)*					
N218SA	Piper PA-24-250 Comanche	24-1877	G-OJOK	Southern Aircraft Consultancy Inc		
			PH-DZE, D-EIEI, N6749P		Boonhill Farm, Fadmoor	6.08
N219DW	Cirrus Design SR22-G3-GTSX Turbo	3148		DMW Aviation	Fairoaks	1.09
N219PM	Cirrus Design SR22-G3-GTSX Turbo	2756		PMM Aviation	(East Midlands)	10.08
N220RJ	Cirrus Design SR22-GTS	1775		CD Aero	Fairoaks	1.09
N221CH	Cirrus Design SR22-GTS-G3 Turbo	2672		Rift Valley Flying Co	Elstree	1.09
N221LD	Cirrus Design SR22-G3-GTS	2929		N221LD Inc	Turweston	9.08
N222ED	Cirrus Design SR22-G2	1103		Engdev Inc	Coventry	8.08
N222LB	Bell 407	53229	N222BX	N222LB Inc	Shannon	9.08
N222SW	Cirrus Design SR22-G2	0977		Staywhite Inc	Cork	7.08
N222WX	Bell 222A	47021	EI-BOR	Newtown Aviation		
			LN-OSB	Ashgrove House, Newtown, Tramore, County Waterford		10.08
N223JG	SOCATA TBM-850	406		Jag Aviation	Guernsey	12.08
N224CJ	Cessna 525 CitationJet	525-0224	N52038	Janabeck Aviation	Gloucestershire	1.09
N224RC	Cirrus Design SR22-G3-GTS Turbo	2919	N917PG	N499AG Inc	Bournemouth	1.09
N226CA	Cessna 172S Skyhawk	172S9793		International Air Services	Newcastle	10.08
				(Operated Peter Walton)		
N228CX	SOCATA TBM-700	84		Turbine Aviation Inc *(Operated B.Holmes)*	Southend	1.09
N228TM	Raytheon Hawker 800XP	258458		Bellatin Aviation	Cork, County Cork	10.08
N230MJ	Piper PA-30 Twin Comanche B	30-1302	G-AVCX	Cabledraw Inc	Lydd	7.08
			N8185Y			
N234RG	Pilatus PC-12/45	520		Wells Fargo Bank Northwest NA	Belfast City	2.09
N235PF	Piper PA-28-235 Cherokee Pathfinder	28-7410083	OO-DDC	Southern Aircraft Consultancy Inc	Southend	2.09
				(Operated Pathfinder Group)		
N239AX	Dassault Falcon 900B	39	N573J	Bank of Utah	Biggin Hill	1.09
			N5733, N181BS, N1818S, (N900BF), N428FJ, F-WWFF			
N239MY	Hughes OH-6A	49-1132	N910GD	Southern Aircraft Consultancy Inc	Kilrush	11.08
			68-17172			
N242ML	Cessna 525 CitationJet	525-0506		Branksome Aviation	Bournemouth	1.09
N243SA	Piper PA-22-108 Colt	22-8376	G-ARKR	Southern Aircraft Consultancy Inc	Henstridge	8.08
N245CB	Piper PA-34-220T Seneca III	34-8333007		Waka Inc	Biggin Hill	6.08
N249SP	Cessna 210L Centurion	21060990	4X-CGU	Alpine Air Leasing	Standalone Farm, Meppershall	1.09
N249SR	British Aerospace BAe125 Series 800A	258249	N500HF	N800SR Aviation	Dublin	9.08
			(N826SU), N326SU, N933H, G-5-786			
N250AC	Piper PA-31 Navajo C	31-7612040	N-NWAC	North West Air Inc	Liverpool	1.09
			G-BDUJ, N59814			
N250BL	Cessna 525A CitationJet CJ2+	525A0403	N5103J	Bravo Lima Aviation	Cranfield	1.09
N250BW	Piper PA-23-250 Aztec C	27-3799	N6602W	Southern Aircraft Consultancy Inc	Seething	8.08
			G-AYSA, N6509Y			
N250CC	Piper PA-24-250 Comanche	24-1931	N957JK	Aerodynamics Worldwide	Gloucestershire	2.08
			OE-DEU, N6798P			
N250MD	Piper PA-31 Turbo Navajo B	31-742	D-ICHY	Oilsearch Aviation	Gloucestershire	8.08
			F-BTCK, N7222L			
N250TB	Piper PA-23-250 Aztec D	27-4577	G-VHFA	Motor City Aviation LLC	Prestwick	8.07
			G-BZFE, G-AZFE, EI-BPA, G-AZFE, N13962 *(Stored)*			
N250TM	Beech 200 Super King Air	BB-822	F-GIND	Richard Lewis Aviation	Cranfield	12.08
			N3FH, N3844E			
NX251RJ	North American TP-51 Mustang	124-44703	44-84847	S Hinton	Duxford	9.08
			(As "44-84847:CY-D in USAAF c/s) "Miss Velma")			
N257JM	SOCATA TBM-850	356		Blackbrook Aviation	Filton	1.09
N257SA	Piper PA-32-300 Cherokee Six B	32-40755	OY-PCF	Southern Aircraft Consultancy Inc	Wadswick	11.08
			OH-PCF			
N258RP	Beech 58 Baron	TH-1737	G-BWRP	Aradian Aviation	Guernsey	10.08
			VR-BVB, N3217H			
N259BK	Hughes OH-6A	30-1376	69-16006	Aircraft Guaranty Management LLC		
				(Operated Ocean Helicopters)	(Republic of Ireland)	12.07
N259SA	Cessna F172G	F172-0278	EI-BAO	Southern Aircraft Consultancy Inc	North Coates	7.08
	(Built Reims Aviation SA)		G-ATNH	*(On rebuild for Humberside Flying Club)*		
N260AP	SIAI-Marchetti SF.260D	839	I-ISAK	Pauls Airplane Inc	Old Sarum	6.08
N262BM	Cirrus Design SR20	1143		Southern Aircraft Consultancy Inc	Eglinton	10.08
N262J	SOCATA TBM-700	292		Sales Force Management Inc	Southend	1.09
N266EA	Beech 58 Baron	TH-2031		Baron 58 Inc	Guernsey	11.08
N276SA	Brantly B.2B	474	G-AXSR	Southern Aircraft Consultancy Inc	(Stevenage)	10.07
			G-ROOF, G-AXSR, N2237U	*(Damaged landing Flixton 17.10.07)*		

Reg	Type	Serial
N277CD	Cessna 210L Centurion	21059663
N277DS	Cessna R182	R18201871
N277SA	Piper PA-28-140 Cherokee	28-21661
N278DB	Mooney M.20R Ovation	29-0301
N278SA	Cessna 177RG Cardinal RG	177RG0571
N280SA	Maule MX-7-180 Star Rocket	11070C
N286MD	Cirrus Design SR22-G3-GTS-Turbo	3173
N288GS	Beech 200 Super King Air	BB-1555
N289CW	Cessna T303 Crusader	T30300032
N297CJ	SNCASE SE.313B Alouette II	1847
N297GT	SOCATA TB-21 Trinidad	2197
N300AQ	Bombardier Learjet 45	45-211
N305RD	Mooney M20K	25-0844
N305SE	Mooney M20K	25-0377
N308CJ	Cessna 208B Grand Caravan	208B1116
N309CJ	Cessna 525A CitationJet CJ2+	525A-0309
N309LJ*	Learjet Inc Learjet 25	25-034
N310QQ	Cessna 310Q	310Q0695
N310WT	Cessna 310R II	310R1257
N320MR	Piper PA-30 Twin Comanche C *(Modified to PA-39 C/R status)*	30-1917
N321KL	Mooney M.20J (201)	24-1102
N322MC	MD Helicopters MD 369E	0224E
N322RJ	Beech 60 Duke	P-322
N324JC	Cessna 500 Citation I	500-0324
N324JS	SOCATA TBM-700	230
N327BM	Cirrus Design SR22-GTS Turbo	2355
N337UK	Reims/Cessns F337G Skymaster	F33700084
N338DB	Piper PA-46-500TP Malibu Meridian	4697155
N340AJ	Bell 206L-4 Long Ranger	52132
N340DW	Cessna 340A-II	340A0497
N340GJ	Cessna 340A	340A0637
N340SC	Cessna 340	340-0363
N340YP	Cessna 340A II	340A0990
N343RR	Piper PA-46-500TP Malibu Meridian	4697197
N345TB	SOCATA TB-20 Trinidad	1914
N346X	Maule M5-210C Strata Rocket	6156C
N347DK	Douglas C-47B-25-DK Dakota 3	16072/32820
N350AY	Aérospatiale AS.350B3 Ecureuil	4267
N350DG	Lancair Columbia LC42-550FG	42074
N350PB	Piper PA-31-350 Chieftain *(Panther II conversion and winglets)*	31-8252028
N350UK	Aérospatiale AS.350B Ecureuil	1244
N352CD	Cirrus Design SR22-GTS	1367
N352CM	Piper PA-46-350P Malibu Mirage	4636019
N352F	Farnborough F1C3 Kestrel	0001
N355GW	Cessna 172S Skyhawk SP	172S9355
N357PS	Dassault Falcon 20F-5	357
N359DW	Piper PA-30 Twin Comanche	30-770
N364AB	Beech B36TC Bonanza	EA-519
N364UZ	Beech C90 King Air	LJ-805
N365LL	Aérospatiale AS.365N2 Dauphin 2	6492
N365WA	Cessna 550 Citation II	550-0333
N369AL	Cirrus Design SR20	1552
N369AN	Cessna 182S Skylane	18280696
N369HL	Hughes 369D *(Hughes 500)*	117-0220D
N370SA	Piper PA-23-250 Aztec F	27-8054005

Reg	Owner	Location	Date
SE-IGY	Bonner-Davies Flying Inc	Headcorn	5.08
N1163Q			
PH-HJR	Schuybroek Aviation	Fairoaks	10.08
D-ELSH, N5457T			
SE-EYG	C M McCoole	Coonagh, County Limerick	10.08
	Aircraft Guaranty Management & Trust LLC	Blackpool	12.08
OO-ALT	Southern Aircraft Consultancy Inc	Gloucestershire	11.08
N2171Q			
G-BSKT	P J Coyne	Galway	9.08
	Silver Go Inc	Southend	2.09
	(Operated M di Prima)		
N98DA	Avtrade Inc	Shoreham	12.08
F-GJDP	T303 Holding Inc	Perranporth	10.08
N19HK, N45526, C-GNTK, (N9636T)			
F-GLPI	Southern Aircraft Consultancy Inc	Redhill	10.08
(FAP9214), 77+00			
	Fab Aircraft Inc	Jersey	10.08
	Boultbee Aviation 2 Inc	Luton	1.09
N50490, N50145			
	Southern Aircraft Consultancy Inc	Dunkeswell	6.08
N231RH	Navajo Aviation	Deenethorpe	10.08
G-JCIT	CJ Airways Inc	Jersey	1.09
N5096S			
	CJ Airways Inc	Guernsey	12.08
N309AJ	City of Bristol College	Gloucestershire	8.08
N19FN, N17AR, N3UC, N6GC, N242WT, N954FA, N954GA *(For ground instructional use)*			
G-BAUE	Veryord Inc *(Current status unknown)*	Elstree	5.06
N8048Q	*(Operated H Gold)*		
G-BGXK	Southern Aircraft Consultancy Inc	Perth	12.08
N6070X	*(Stored marked "G-BGXK")*		
G-CALV (2)	N320MR Inc	Elstree	1.09
G-AZFO, N8761Y			
G-BPKL	International Air Services	Stapleford	8.08
N1008K	*(Operated London Link Flying Ltd)*		
	AAA Flight Inc *(Operated Jepar Rotorcraft)*	Blackpool	2.08
	Southern Aircraft Consultancy Inc	Old Buckenham	1.09
N52TC	Foxdale Aviation	Biggin Hill	12.08
N324C, (N5324J)			
	Sunlit Beacon Inc	Lydd	1.09
	SR Turbo Air Inc	Coventry	4.08
G-BOWD	E-Plane Inc	Biggin Hill	10.08
N337BC, G-BLSB, EI-BET, D-INAI, (N53697)			
N53677	Oakfield Aviation	Jersey	11.07
N98867	Yorkshire Helicopters (USA) Inc	Coney Park, Leeds	1.09
5Y-BKR, N98867			
G-BISJ	Southern Aircraft Consultancy Inc	Coventry	9.08
OO-LFK, N6328X			
	Bee Bee Aviation	Elstree	12.08
	Hastingwood Management Inc	North Weald	8.08
VR-CHR	ILEA Inc	Biggin Hill	1.09
G-OCAN, D-ICIC, (N3970C)			
	Herb Aviation *(Reserved as N268DS)*	Leeds-Bradford	7.08
	Monty 345TB LLC	Biggin Hill	7.08
	E S Miserey	Biggin Hill	9.06
G-AMSV	DC3 Holding Inc	Coventry	8.08
(F-BSGV), KN397, 44-76488			
	Glenkerrin Aviation	(Republic of Ireland)	9.08
	Skypartners Worldwide Inc	Blackpool	8.08
HP-1309	PFB Self Drive Inc	Coventry	10.08
N3548S			
F-GJYG	M W Helicopters Inc	(Canterbury)	12.08
	Fundamental Flying Inc	Bournemouth	1.09
G-DODI	Continental Capital Markets Aviation	(Bournemouth)	12.08
	Farnborough Aircraft Inc	Redhill	9.08
	Southern Aircraft Consultancy Inc	Rochester	11.08
N342KF	Falcon Acquisitions LLC	Farnborough	2.09
N342K, N435TP, N435T, N4469F, F-WMKI			
G-ATET	L W Durrell	Jersey	3.08
N230ET			
	Andair Inc	Gloucestershire	11.08
VP-BKW	Shoreline Consultancy Services	Farnborough	2.09
VR-BKW, G-BJSY, ZS-KGO, N2068W			
G-BUL	Wells Fargo Bank Northwest NA	London Stansted	11.08
N914K			
N123GM	Wrenair Inc	Weston, Dublin	12.08
N313CE, PT-LCW, N67990	*(Operated Visionair)*		
	C Barnett	Jersey	8.08
	Air View Ltd	Jersey	10.08
G-CCUN	Southern Aircraft Consultancy Inc	Redhill	10.08
N644WA, N58169			
G-BKVN	Southern Aircraft Consultancy Inc	Southend and Guernsey	10.08
N6959A			

Registration	Type	c/n	Previous identities	Owner/Operator	Location	Date
N373DJ	Cessna 650 Citation III	650-0038	N366GE, N366G	MacBeth Aviation	Kemble	10.08
N375SA	Piper PA-34-200T Seneca II	34-7670002	G-BMWP, N3946X	Southern Aircraft Consultancy Inc	Gamston	8.08
N376SR	Cirrus Design SR22-G3-GTSX Turbo	2736		Caseright Inc (for Czech Republic)	Jersey	1.09
N377GM	Dassault Falcon 2000EASy	32	N999BE, N666BE, F-WWGK	Wilmington Trust Co (Operated Propinvest Asset Management)	Biggin Hill	1.09
N380CR	Cessna 525 CitationJet CJ1+	525-0643	N5228Z	50 North Aviation	Leeds-Bradford	1.09
N382AS	Reims Cessna F182Q Skylane	F1820049	D-EAAF	Southern Aircraft Consultancy Inc	Bagby	8.08
N382EA	Eclipse Aviation EA500	000082		Aircraft Guaranty Management LLC	Leeds-Bradford	11.08
N393N	Robinson R44 Raven I	1467	G-CDHV	Pelmont Aviation	(Gamston)	9.08
N395TC	Commander Aircraft Commander 114TC	20003		AQZ Aviation Inc	Bembridge	1.09
N400HF	Lancair Columbia LC41-550FG	41577		Feggair Inc	Biggin Hill	1.09
N400UK	Lancair Columbia LC41-550FG	41062		Lucy in the Sky Corp	Denham	1.09
N400YY	Extra EA400	019		Bas Aviation	Leeds-Bradford	7.08
N401JN	Cessna 401	401-0166	G-ROAR, G-BZFL, G-AWSF, N4066Q	Special Scope Inc	Blackpool	8.08
N402BL	Beech F90 King Air	LA-130	N81SD	Hastingwood Management	North Weald	1.09
N403HP	Piper PA-46-350P Malibu Mirage	4636312		Vector Sky Service	Shoreham and Hilversuim	10.08
N407AG	Bell 407	53559		N407AG Inc	Weston, Dublin	5.08
N407CG	Bell 407	53731	N3009Y	Relar Inc	(Galway)	5.08
N407CL	Bell 407	53597		N407CL Inc	Dublin	1.09
N407WD	Bell 407	53694	HP-1609	Newtown Aviation	(Waterford, County Waterford)	6.08
N411BC	Piper PA-28-181 Archer III	2843339		Southern Aircraft Consultancy Inc	Elstree	11.08
N411DP	Commander Aircraft Commander 114A	14517	D-EGGB	International Air Services	(Hadleigh, Suffolk)	9.07
N414AK	Cessna 414A Chancellor II	414A-0321	D-IAAU (N2686Y)	N414AK Aviation	Southend	2.09
N414FZ	Cessna 414RAM	414-0175	G-AZFZ, N8245Q	Lizard Aviation Inc	Jersey	1.09
N414MB	Pitts S-2A	2236		LME Aviation	Kemble	7.08
N418WS	Beech 58 Baron	TH-1967	N4467N	Millburn World Travel Services Two Inc (Operated W Scott & Partners Ltd)	Edinburgh	11.08
N421CA*	Cessna 421C Golden Eagle III	421C0153	XA-RYC, N115JH, N5263J	Golden Eagle Haulage Inc (Cancelled 2.07 by FAA) (Current status unknown)	Wycombe Air Park	10.05
N421DD	Cessna 421C Golden Eagle	421C0315		Fidair Corporation	Fairoaks	1.09
N421EA	Cessna 421C Golden Eagle	421C1079		Nielaster Inc	Biggin Hill	9.08
N423RS	Consolidated-Vultee PBY-5A Catalina	1785	C-FJJG, CF-JJG, N4002A, BuAer48423	Wells Fargo Bank Northwest NA (Operated Super Catalina Restoration as "JV828" in RAF 210 Sqdn c/s)	Lee-on-Solent	12.07
N425DR	Cessna 425 Conquest I	425-0199	VP-BDR	Intercity Co Inc	Wycombe Air Park	5.08
N425SL	Cessna 425 Corsair	425-0236	G-BNDY, N1262T	Aircraft Guaranty Title & Trust LLC (Operated Standard Aviation Ltd)	Leeds-Bradford	12.08
N434A	Cirrus Design SR22-GTS	1382		Cirrus Design Corp	Turweston	1.09
N438DD	Cessna 310D	39278		C Koscso	Bourn	9.08
N440GC	Piper PA-44-180T Turbo Seminole	44-8107065	G-GISO, D-GISO, N82112, N9602N	Lucon Chasnais Flying Inc	Coventry	10.08
N441GS	Robinson R44 Raven II	11764		MacAdam Air	Weston, Dublin	5.08
N442BJ	Reims Cessna F177RG Cardinal RG	F177RG0094	F-BVBC	Southern Aircraft Consultancy Inc	Derby	12.08
N446SE	Piper PA-32R-301T Saratoga II	3257446		PTS Aviation	Liverpool	11.08
N449J (2)	Agusta A.109S Grand	22094	EI-ECU	Jay Industries Inc	Weston	12.08
N449TA	Piper PA-31 Turbo Navajo	31-480	G-CCRY, F-BTMM, N449TA	William L Shoufler	Elstree	8.08
N454CC	Bell UH-1E	6199	Bu155344	Southern Aircraft Consultancy Inc (Operated Independent Helicopters Ltd)	Howth, County Dublin	7.05
N456PP	Beech C90A King Air	LJ-1699		Air Montgomery Inc	Guernsey	11.08
N456TL	Reims Cessna FT337GP Super Skymaster	FP3370019	SX-PBA, F-ODFY, F-BUDU	CCC Aviation	Coventry	10.07
N458BG	de Havilland DHC.1 Chipmunk 22	C1/0508	WG458	BG Chipmunks Inc (As "WG458:2")	Breighton	12.08
N463RD	SOCATA TBM850	463		Flanes Ltd	Biggin Hill	1.09
N470RD	Cirrus Design SRV-G2	1636		CD1636 Inc	Weston, Dublin	11.08
N473DC	Douglas C-47A Dakota III	19345	N5831B, C-FKAZ, CF-KAZ, TS422, 42-100882	Dakota Heritage Inc (As "2100882/P-3X" in USAF c/s)	Liverpool	11.08
N480BB	Enstrom 480B	5056		Aircraft Guaranty Title Corp	Shoreham	7.07
N480DD	Enstrom 480	5017	G-HADA	DWM International	Redhill	10.08
N480JB	Enstrom 480B	5108		Eastern Atlantic Helicopters	Shoreham	6.07
N480KP	Enstrom 480B	5053		Eastern Atlantic Helicopters	North Weald	8.07
N480LR	Enstrom 480B	5103		Southern Aircraft Consultancy Inc	Galway	7.08
N480PP	Enstrom 480B	5120		Eastern Atlantic Helicopters	Shoreham	10.08
N482CD	Cirrus Design SR22-GTS	1482		Heritage Aviation	Sleap	1.09
N485ED	Piper PA-23-250 Aztec C	27-3864	G-BAED, N6567Y	Southern Aircraft Consultancy Inc	Waterford	8.08
N497XP	Hawker 400XP	RK-497		Aircraft Guaranty Management & Trust LLC (Operated V & P Midlands Ltd)	East Midlands	12.08
N498YY	Cessna 525 CitationJet	525-0498	N498YY, N5223K, N5201J	John Mills Aviation	Luton	1.09
N499AG	Piper PA-30 Twin Comanche	30-1415	F-GALF, G-AVJT, N8281Y	N499AG Inc	Bournemouth	1.09
N499MS	Piper PA-28-181 Archer III	2843166	G-EPJM, N41268	MS Aviation	Jersey	10.08
N500AV	Piper PA-24-260 Comanche C	24-4805	OO-SAP	Southern Aircraft Consultancy Inc	Welshpool	12.08

Registration	Type	c/n	Previous identities	Owner/Operator	Base	Date
N500CS	Beech B200 Super King Air	BB-773	N83JE, N3913U, OY-BEH	FML Beech Inc	Filton	12.08
N500LN	Howard 500 (Lockheed PV-1 Ventura [5560] conversion)	500-113	N381RD, N206G, N200G, N539N, SAAF 6417, FP579, Bu.34670	Western Aviation Leasing Inc (Operated Baker Petroleum)	Exeter	12.05
N500RK	Hughes 369HS (Hughes 500)	73-0502S	N901WJ, XC-UHF	Southern Aircraft Consultancy Inc	(Somerton)	10.08
N500SY	McDonnell Douglas MD.369E	0007E		0454E Inc (Operated Hitachi Capital)	Shoreham	11.08
N500TY	McDonnell Douglas MD.369E	0086E	C-GRVV	Eastern Atlantic Helicopters	Shoreham	10.08
N500UK	Eclipse Aviation EA500	000051		N500UK Inc	Blackpool	8.08
N500XV	Hughes 369D (Hughes 500)	120-0881D	OO-LVK, OE-XBB, N190CA, N5293E, C-GHVK	Southern Aircraft Consultancy Inc	Blackpool	9.08
N503DW	Mudry CAP.10B	202		Kennard Aviation	Lydd	8.08
N505HA	Aérospatiale SA.341G Gazelle	1022	JA9164	Southern Aircraft Consultancy Inc	Breighton	12.08
N510W	Bell 222B	47133	N7040Z	Wells Fargo Bank Northwest NA	Naas, County Kildare	4.08
N511TC	Cessna 525 CitationJet	525-0074	N26581	Eagle III LLC	Cambridge	12.08
N515SC	Piper PA-32R-301T Saratoga II TC	3257315		Southern Aircraft Consultancy Inc	Cardiff	4.07
N518XL	Liberty Aerospace XL-2	0013		W Roberts	Biggin Hill	1.09
N519MC	Piper PA-28-140 Cherokee Cruiser	28-7325519	G-BBID	R Lobell	Elstree	1.09
N521CD	Cirrus Design SR22-G3-GTS Turbo	2441		Assegai Aviation	Denham	1.09
N521LB	Beech E90 King Air	LW-249	N68CC, (N28CC), N30KC	Monckton Byng Inc	Elstree	9.08
N524SF	Cessna 525 CitationJet	525-0240	N525GM	C P Lockyer Inc	Coventry	10.08
N525DB	Reims Cessna F172H	F172-0484	G-AWGR, N525DB, G-AWGR	Southern Aircraft Consultancy Inc	Sleap	5.07
N525DT	Cessna 525A CitatiopJet CJ2	525A0003	N132CJ, N5148N	Cleevewood Holdings Inc	Gloucestershire	11.08
N525PM	Cessna 525A CitationJet CJ2	525A-0067	N5141F	Wells Fargo Bank Northwest NA	Oxford	10.08
N526AG	Eurocopter EC.120B Colibri	1397		Southern Aircraft Consultancy Inc (Operated P Mealy)(N313PM reserved)	(Weston, Dublin)	5.08
N527EW	Cessna 501 Citation 1	501-0322	(N769EW), (N669DM), N314GS, N374GS, N2663J	Rockville Aero Inc	Jersey	11.08
N531RM	Pitts S.2C (Built Aviat)	6018		Southern Aircraft Consultancy Inc	Panshanger	8.08
N535CE	Cessna 560 Citation Ultra	560-0635		Latium Jet Services (IOM)	Gloucestershire	12.08
N535TK	Maule MXT-7-180	14025C		Centreline Aerospace	Shipmeadow, Beccles	9.08
N536K	Beech A36 Bonanza	E-3220		Aircraft Guaranty Management LLC	Lydd	8.08
N542CD	Cirrus Design SR22-GTS	1186		Siek Aviation	Fairoaks	12.08
N550LD	Cessna 550 Citation II	550-0323	VP-CLD, N323AM, TC-YZB, TC-FMB, TC-FAL, OE-GCP, (N5703C)	Castleton Inc	Filton	1.09
N551TT	Piper PA-32R-301T Saratoga II TC	3257026	G-GOTO, N92965, G-GOTO, N92965	Southern Aircraft Consultancy Inc	Blackbushe	12.08
N554CF	Beech E90 King Air	LW-66	N3166W	Sky Clad Inc	Weston, Dublin	1.09
N554RB	Beech E55 Baron	TE-1141	G-BNRH, N7855E	E Hilvert	Coventry	9.08
N555WA	MD Helicopters MD.900	900-00010	N9208V	N555WA Inc (Operated Stobart Air)	(Crick)	11.08
N556MA *	Beagle B.121 Pup 1	B121-013	G-AWEB	G V Crowe	Shipdham	11.08
	(Forced landed short of Thurrock 14. 7.05 due to engine failure: cancelled 7.06 by FAA: outside storage)					
N559C	Piper PA-34-220T Seneca V	3449238		Chiswell Aviation Inc	Guernsey and Alderney	9.08
N560TH	Cessna 560XL Citation Excel	560-5215	VP-CPC, N5091J, N560TH	N560TH Inc	Blackpool	1.09
N562RR	Piper PA-32-301FT 6x	3232021	N30614	Countrywide Aviation (N116KY reserved)	Full Sutton	8.08
N565F	Aérospatiale SA.341G Gazelle	1182		Skyrunner Aviation	Manor Farm, Beccles	11.08
N566N *	Cessna U206G Turbo Stationair	U20605745		American King Air Ferries Inc (Operated Irish Parachute Club) (Canx 2.08)	Clonbullogue	12.07
N569DM	Cessna 525A CitationJet CJ2	525A0088		Euro Exec Aviation	Cranfield	1.09
N573VE	Cirrus Design SR22-G2	1078		Aircraft Guaranty Corp	Biggin Hill	9.08
N575GM	SOCATA TB-20 Trinidad	1872		Wedd Aviation	Cambridge	12.08
N575NR	Cessna 560XLS Citation Excel	560-5759		Cross Jet Inc	Kerry, Co Kerry	1.09
N577PA	Cessna 425 Conquest I	425-0194	N12214	Brocken Inc	Jersey	12.08
N581AF	Beech 58 Baron	TH-2063		N581AF Inc	Sleap	11.08
N582C	SOCATA TBM-700C2	274		Air Touring Inc	Ronaldsway	11.08
N591JM	Agusta A109C	7609	N109KH, N133H, N1NQ	Gateway Aviation	Manston	9.08
N593CD	Cirrus Design SR22-GTS	1809		Hannah Aviation	Manchester	10.08
N601AR	Piper Aerostar 601P	61P-0569-7963247	N3839H, F-GKCL, N3839H, G-RACE, N8083J	Southern Aircraft Consultancy Inc (Operated The Fabric Factory)	Jersey and Southend	10.08
N604FD	Eurocopter EC.155B	6580		Wells Fargo Bank Northwest NA	Denham	12.08
N606AT	Cessna 650 Citation VI	650-0225	(N225CV), N1301Z	Longborough Aviation (Operated CityWest Hotel)	Weston, Dublin	12.08
N613F	Piper PA-39 Twin Comanche C/R	39-45	N8887Y	Southern Aircraft Consultancy Inc	Stapleford	12.08
N642P	Piper PA-31 Turbo Navajo B	31-761	N500UD, G-EEAC, G-SKKA, G-FOAL, G-RMAE, N7239L	Corporate Air (Ireland) Inc	Belfast	1.09
N646CD	Cessna T210M Turbo Centurion	21063402		210 Air Lift Corp	Biggin Hill	11.08
N646JR	Piper PA-32RT-300T Turbo Lance II	32R-7987019	PH-LFD, N3032A	Southern Aircraft Consultancy Inc	Thruxton	11.08
N652P	Piper PA-18-150 Super Cub	18-7809098	G-BTDX, N62595	Southern Aircraft Consultancy Inc	(Ireland)	6.07
N656JM	Reims Cessna FR182 Skylane RGII	FR1820049	G-BHEO	JM Aviation (Europe) Inc	Old Sarum	10.08
N661KK	Piper PA-28-181 Archer II	2890028	HB-PKN, N9104F	Southern Aircraft Consultancy Inc	Fairoaks	1.09

Registration	Type	c/n	Previous identities	Owner	Base	Date
N662KK	Piper PA-18-150 Super Cub	18-8209023	N45490, IDF/AF112	Southern Aircraft Consultancy Inc	Fairoaks	10.08
N663CD	Cirrus Design SR22-GTS	1847		Phantom Air	Sleap	1.09
N663KK	Cirrus Design SR22-G3-GTS-Turbo	3064		Southern Aircraft Consultancy Inc	Fairoaks	12.08
N663TB	Beech H18	BA-663	F-BVEB, 9Q-CSP, G-ASNX	P H McMillan	North Weald	1.09
N665CH	Cessna 525 CitationJet	525-0504		Volante Aviation	Coventry	1.09
N666AW	Piper PA-31 Navajo C	31-7612061		Atlantic International Air Charter Inc	Biggin Hill	9.08
N666BM	Pitts S-1T (Built Aviat)	1057		International Air Services *"Devil Poo" (Operated S P Johnson)*	Enstone	7.08
N666GA	Gulfstream AA-5B Tiger	AA5B-1136		Southern Aircraft Consultancy Inc	Thruxton	12.08
N666VK	Cessna 340A II	340A-0345	G-FEBE, N405LS, (N37320)	Triple Six VK Inc	Denham	1.09
N667DL	Mooney M 20R	29-0455		M E Zuccaro	Biggin Hill	1.09
N671B	Raytheon A36 Bonanza	E-3409		N671B Inc	Leeds-Bradford	10.08
N672LE	Eurocopter EC.155B1	6652	F-WQEP	HEC01 LLC *(Operated TAG Aviation)*	Fairoaks	1.09
N673SA	Piper PA-24-250 Comanche	24-2240	G-ARFH, N7087P	Southern Aircraft Consultancy Inc	East Winch	8.08
N674BW	Grumman AA-5A Cheetah	AA5A-0674	G-BXOO, N26721	Go Aviation UK Inc	Lydd	5.08
N675BW	Beech V35B Bonanza	D-10134	D-ENCA	Southern Aircraft Consultancy Inc	Denham	1.09
N681EW	Reims Cessna F182Q Skylane II	F18200039	G-BLEW, F-GAQD	Southern Aircraft Consultancy Inc	Henstridge	1.09
N683GW	Beech C90A King Air	LJ-1683		N683GW Inc	Cranfield	1.09
N690CL	Rockwell 690A Turbo Commander	11153	N46663, N53RF, N57074	Centerline Aerospace Inc	Norwich	1.08
N691J	Piper PA-28RT-201T Turbo Arrow IV	28R-8631003	N473BS, G-BNYY, N25WA, N77860, G-BNYY, N9129X, N9517N	Piper Arrow Inc *(Operated I Jacobs t/a Chatham Glyn Fabrics)*	Southend	2.09
N694LM	Cessna 500 Citation I	500-0354	N354RC, G-TJHI, G-CCCL, N51GA, G-BEIZ, (N5363J)	Kando Jet *"Patricia V"*	Kemble	10.08
N696DA	Diamond DA 20-A1 Katana	10218		Southern Aircraft Consultancy Inc	Truleigh Manor Fam, Edburton	9.08
N696XX	McDonnell Douglas MD.369E	0544E	N90DE	696 Heli Inc *(Operated Kuki Helicopters)*	Gamston	10.08
N697RB	Pitts S-1T	1042		Aerospace Trust Management	Breighton	7.08
N700AZ	SOCATA TBM700	254		Elvaston Inc	Weston, Dublin	1.09
N700EL	SOCATA TBM-700	209	N701AR	Air Twinlite Inc	Dolly's Grove, Dublin	1.09
N700GY	SOCATA TBM-700C2	302	D-FBFT	N700VB Inc	Guernsey	1.09
N700KV	SOCATA TBM-700C2	296		Dumont HPA Inc	Lydd	7.08
N700S	SOCATA TBM-700	193		N700S Inc	Blackbushe	1.09
N700VA	SOCATA TBM-700	233	F-OIKI	Wells Fargo Bank Northwest NA *(Overran runway into River Tay, Dundee 24.10.03: fuselage with Recovair)*	Fairoaks	11.08
N700VB	SOCATA TBM-700	237	F-OIKJ	Aircraft Guaranty Title Corp	Biggin Hill	6.08
N702MB	SOCATA TBM-700	314		TBM 700 Inc	Bournemouth	1.09
N707BM	Bell 206L-1 Long Ranger	45533		Billy Moloney Inc	Cork	7.08
N707QJ	Boeing 707-368C	21261	A20-261, N7486B, HZ-ACI	T M Vaughan	Manston	1.09
N707TJ	Boeing-Stearman A75N1 (N2S-1) Kaydet (Pratt & Whitney R-985 450hp)	75-950	N9PK, N50057, Bu.3173	M G Plaskett (Team Guinot) *(Operated V.S.E.Norman t/a Aerosuperbatics Ltd)*	Rendcomb	8.08
N707XJ	Cessna 177A Cardinal	17701340	SE-FKO, (LN-FAK), (OY-AGM), N30579	Southern Aircraft Consultancy Inc *(Operated I A Quereshi)*	Shoreham	4.08
N708SP	Bombardier Learjet 45	45-014		Tappetto Magico Inc	Biggin Hill	1.09
N709AM	SOCATA TB-21 Trinidad	2101		AMC Aviation	Sherburn-in-Elmet	10.08
N709EL	Beech 400A Beechjet	RK-52	(N709EW), N709JB	GAL Air Inc *(Operated DFS Furniture)*	East Midlands	1.09
N711TL	Piper PA-60 Aerostar 700P	60-8423017	N700SX, N15GK, XB-EXQ, N6906Y	Southern Aircraft Consultancy Inc	Biggin Hill	12.08
N712DB	Beech 65-A90 King Air	LJ-311	F-GNBA, HB-GIN, F-GIGP, N114SV, N10XL, N909K	Metro Air Inc *(Operated Skyclad)*	Weston, Dublin	7.07
N715BC	Beech A36 Bonanza	E-782	F-BXOZ	N715BC Inc	Denham	1.09
N717HL	Beech 58P Baron	TJ-160		Dawson Lion Inc	Abbeyshrule	10.08
N719CD	Cirrus Design SR22	0051		Southern Aircraft Consultancy Inc	Plymouth	11.08
N719EL	Hawker 400XP	RK-488		Edra Lauren Leasing Corp *(Operated DFS Furniture)*	East Midlands	1.09
N720B	Bell 206L-1 LongRanger II	45452	G-DALE, G-HBUS	Omega Air Inc	Dublin	4.08
N722DR	Cirrus Design SR22-G3-GTSX	2705		N120SR Aviation	North Weald	9.08
N722P	Beech A36 Bonanza	E-2219		Southern Aircraft Consultancy Inc	Sandown, IOW	1.09
N730WF	Cirrus Design SR22	1147		R & R Flying Inc	Abbeyshrule	10.08
N731	Boeing Stearman A75N-1	75-045		Wings Venture Ltd *"352"*	Oxford	8.08
N735CX	Cessna 182Q Skylane II (Modified to Advanced Lift 260 STOL)	18265329		Wilmington Trust Company *(Operated B.Holmes)*	Barnard's Farm, Thurrock	1.09
N737M	Boeing 737-8EQ	33361	N737SP, N737M	Wells Fargo Bank Northwest NA *(Operated EIE Eagle Inc Establishment)*	Luton	4.08
N741CD	Cirrus Design SR22	0137		Staveley Aviation	Blackpool	9.08
N741D	Beech 76 Duchess	ME-398	D-GEWU	Southern Aircraft Consultancy Inc	Perranporth	10.08
N742TJ	Rutan Long Ez	2268		Southern Aircraft Consultancy Inc	Gloucestershire	12.08
N745HA	Agusta A109A-II	7413	G-CBDR	Heli Holding Inc	Liskeard Heliport	1.09
N747MM	Piper PA-28R-200 Cherokee Arrow II	28R-7335445	PH-MLP, N56489	N747MM Aviation	Denham	1.09
N747WW	Piper PA-23-250 Aztec D	27-4330	G-AXOG, N6965Y	International Air Services *(Operated A Mattacks)*	Biggin Hill	6.08
N747YK	Cessna 310R II	310R0138	G-BTYK, N200VC, N5018J	YK Inc	Jersey	12.08

Reg	Type	Serial
N748D	Avro 748 Series 1	1559
N750GF	Cessna 750 Citation X	750-0244
N750NS	Cessna 750 Citation X	750-0172
N750PP	Cessna 501 Citation I/SP	501-0686
N752DS	Diamond DA 40 Star	40.752
N753TW	Cirrus Design SR22-GTS	1413
N761JU	Cessna T210M Centurion	21062300
N766AM	Aérospatiale AS.355N Ecureuil 2	5601
N767CM	Beech A36 Bonanza	E-2723
N770RM	SOCATA TB-9 Tampico	131
N771SR	Cirrus Design SR22-GTS G3 Turbo	2771
N775RG	Maule M5-210C Strata Rocket	6048C
N780ND	World Helicopters Hiller UH-12C	WH6003
N781CD	Cirrus Design SR20-G2	1423
N784F	Bell 206B-3 JetRanger III	2508
N789MC	Cessna T310Q II	310Q0914
N790BH	Cirrus Design SR22-G3	2964
N790JC	Dassault Falcon 900B	17
N799CD	Cirrus Design SR22-GTS	1543
N799JH	Piper PA-28RT-201T Turbo Arrow IV	28R-8231051
N800BN	Bombardier CL-600-2B19 (CL-604 Challenger)	5600
N800FR	Raytheon RB390 Premier 1A	RB-165
N800HL	Bell 222	47054
N800UK	Raytheon Hawker 800XP	258577
N800VM	Beech 76 Duchess	ME-318
N800WK	Agusta A109A-II	7341
N808CA	Piper PA-32R-301 Saratoga II HP	3246240
N808RW	Cirrus Design SR22-G3-GTS	3039
N808VT	Piper PA-28R-201 Cherokee Arrow III	28R-7737051
N814BP	Raytheon RB390 Premier 1A	RB-214
N814WS	Cessna 510 Citation Mustang	510-0032
N816RL	Beech E90 King Air	LW-187
N818MJ	Piper PA-23-250 Aztec B	27-2486
N818Y	Piper PA-30 Twin Comanche B	30-1458
N820CD	Cirrus Design SR22	0180
N821CC	Cirrus Design SR22	1427
N831M	Hiller UH-12B	330
N834CD	Cirrus Design SR22	0168
N836TP	Beech A36TP Bonanza	E-2124
N840CD	Cirrus Design SR20-GTS	1535
N840PN	Rockwell 690C Turbo Commander	11679
N840TC	Rockwell 690C Turbo Commander	11688
N841WS	Gulfstream Aerospace Gulfstream G450	4099
N843SR	Cirrus Design SR22-G3-GTSX	2790
N850KF	Cessna 310Q	310Q0041
N850LH	SOCATA TBM-850	374
N851WA	SOCATA TBM-850	394
N852CD	Cirrus Design SR22	0219
N852FT*	Boeing 747-122F	19757
N866C	Cirrus Design SR22	0397
N866LP	Piper PA-46-350P Malibu Mirage	4636130
N868AT	SOCATA TBM700	232
N877SW	Agusta A109A-II	7283
N882JH	Maule M.7-235B	23056C
N883DP	Cessna R182 Skylane RGII	R18201883
N888DM	Piper PA-30 Turbo Twin Comanche C	30-1833
N888MY	Cessna 182T Skylane	18281957

Reg	Owner	Location	Date
G-ASJT XW750, G-ASJT	Aerospace Trust Management (Operated Aerowings SA)	Southend	2.09
N52655	S'porter Air Inc	Gloucestershire	11.08
N5066U	Aircraft Guaranty Holdings & Trust LLC (Operated Aviation Beauport)	Jersey	12.08
N6763M	M J Woods	Enniskillen	12.08
	Coutale Inc	Wycombe Air Park	1.09
	N753TW Inc	Denham	1.09
	International Air Services (Operated A W Chesters) (Had wheels up landing 7. 8.07)	Wycombe Air Park	8.07
	Beacon Aviation (Operated Beacon Energy (Aviation) Ltd)	Beacon Farm, Leicestershire	11.08
G-ORSP N56037	Makins Aviation	Leeds/Bradford	1.09
PH-CAG	M P Sandell (Roaded out 1.09)	(Bournemouth)	1.09
	H K DeCarlucci	Denham	1.09
G-CBVW A2-WNP, ZS-LVB	Southern Aircraft Consultancy Inc	Great Massingham	9.08
	Southern Aircraft Consultancy Inc	Rochester	7.08
	Southern Aircraft Consultancy Inc	Carnmore, Galway	11.08
N16LT	Southern Aircraft Consultancy Inc	Oaksey Park	1.09
G-LLMC G-BKSB, VR-CEM, G-BKSB, HB-LMO, OE-FYL, (N69680)	Aerospace Trust Management	Jersey	10.08
N127PG	Aircraft Guaranty Management & Trust LLC	Manston	1.09
N944AD N411FJ, F-WWFO	Minnesota Choice Aviation III	Biggin Hill	1.09
	GPA Inc	Kilrush	11.08
HB-PNE PH-HJM, N8206B	Southern Aircraft Consultancy Inc (Operated J Havers)	North Weald	7.08
C-GLWZ	Wilmington Trust Co	Luton	1.09
N7165X	Wells Fargo Bank Northwest NA (Operated White and Cope Aviation)	Luton	12.08
N800HH N8140A, N37VA	Yorkshire Helicopters USA Inc	Coney Park, Leeds	1.09
N51027	Wells Fargo Bank Northwest NA (Operated Liberty Aviation)	Leeds-Bradford	10.08
G-BHGM	Southern Aircraft Consultancy Inc	Gloucestershire	11.08
N500WK	Ottoman Empire Inc	Shoreham	1.09
	Buchanan Aviation	Dundee	5.08
	Redwood Air Services	White Waltham	12.08
	Southern Aircraft Consultancy Inc	Panshanger	1.09
	Clark 1207 Inc	Hawarden	9.08
N4107D	Millburn World Travel Services Four Inc (Operated Walter Scott & Partners Ltd)	Edinburgh	2.09
N66BP N816EP, N900MH, N2187L	Springair Inc (Operated English Braids Ltd)	Gloucestershire	8.08
G-ASNH	Retail Management Associates	Gloucestershire	11.08
ZS-CAO ZS-EYB, A2-ZFE, ZS-EYB, VQ-ZIY, ZS-EYB, N8318Y	One Eighty Yankee Aviation Inc	Guernsey	11.08
	Southern Aircraft Consultancy Inc	Guernsey	10.08
	Cirrus N821CC Inc	Cambridge	12.08
51-16170	Southern Aircraft Consultancy Inc	Shipmeadow, Beccles	4.08
	Southern Aircraft Consultancy Inc	Seething	10.08
N6770M	Hastingwood Aviation Inc (Operated Velcourt East PLC)	Tatenhill	9.08
	Weston Flyers	Weston, Dublin	11.08
ZS-SLL N840VB, (N5931K), N840VB, N5931K	Southern Aircraft Consultancy Inc	Fairoaks	1.09
XC-HAB (N5940K)	Aircraft Guaranty Title Corp (Operated Select Interiors)	North Weald	1.09
N199GA	Milburn World Travel Services Five Inc (Operated Walter Scott & Partners Ltd)	Edinburgh	12.08
	XYZ Aviation	Denham	1.09
G-XLKF G-BMMC, YU-BGY, N7541Q	Southern Aircraft Consultancy Inc	Jersey	10.08
F-WWRR	Liton Services	Biggin Hill	12.08
	WA Aviation	Cambridge	11.08
	Southern Aircraft Consultancy Inc	Guernsey	1.09
N4712U	PIK Ltd (Unmarked in fire service use)	Prestwick	12.08
	Aircraft Guaranty Trust LLC	Turweston	1.09
N666LP N92928	TLP Aviation Inc	(Fairoaks)	8.08
	Air Touring Inc	Biggin Hill	10.08
N8772W N877SW	N877SW Inc	Shoreham	10.08
	Everbright Aviation Inc	Exeter	11.06
G-GOZO G-BJZO, (G-BJYE), N5521T	Southern Aircraft Consultancy Inc (Operated D Pelling)	Mount Airey Farm, Hull	10.08
N968BC (N968P), N968PC	Southern Aircraft Consultancy Inc (Operated D Keith)	Enniskillen	12.08
	Jet Force Inc	Panshanger	2.09

Reg	Type	C/N	Previous ids	Owner/Operator	Base	Date
N889VF	Cessna T303 Crusader	T30300102	D-ILEI, N3141C	Southern Aircraft Consultancy Inc	Liverpool	9.08
N897US	Fokker F.28-0100	11392	PH-EZD	Aircraft Finance Services Inc *(Fuselage stored)*	Norwich	3.08
N900CB	Cessna 421C Golden Eagle III	421C0837	VP-CPR, VR-CPR, N2659F	Lancaster Aviation *(Operated Gold Arrow Aircraft Ltd)*	Leeds-Bradford	1.09
N900RK	Mooney M.20J	24-3402		Romeo Kilo Flying Group	Cranfield	1.09
N900UK	Cirrus Design SR22	1463		Annas Flight Services	Turweston	1.09
N901RL	Bell 430	49078		Aircraft Guaranty Holdings & Trust LLC	Dublin	1.09
N902JW	MD Helicopters MD.902	9000086	N7006X	Blue Anchor Leisure *(Operated John Woodward Property Developments)*	Gamston	12.08
N902SR	Cirrus Design SR22-GTS	2356		Lucy Lu Inc	Liverpool	1.09
N903LF	MD Helicopters MD900	900-00030		Hirecopter Inc *(Operated Gardner Books)*	(Eastbourne)	12.08
N908W	Sikorsky S-92	920007		Laws Helicopter LLC *(Operated Air Harrods)*	London Stansted	11.08
N911CS	Beech U-8F Seminole	LF-21		Orchtrans Inc	Orchardleigh, Frome	1.09
N911DN	Bell UH-1H Iroquois	9624	67-17426	Yorkshire Helicopters USA Inc	Sparkford	7.08
N916CD	Cirrus Design SR22	0318		Farnborough Aircraft Inc	Redhill	9.08
N918Y	Piper PA-30 Twin Comanche	30-736	ZS-NLH, N31RK, ZS-NLH, ZS-FZR, CR-AJR, ZS-EIU, VQ-ZIS, N7658Y	Southern Aircraft Consultancy Inc	Sturgate	1.09
N922CE	Cirrus Design SR22-G3	2521		Eden Aviation	Coventry	11.08
N928HW	Commander Aircraft Commander 114B	14672		Southern Aircraft Consultancy Inc	Stapleford	12.08
N930Z	Piper PA-46-350P Malibu Mirage	4622188	D-ERBU, (D-ERUU), G-DODY	Go Aviation UK	Lydd	12.08
N937BP	Mooney M.20J	24-3046	G-OOOO, N205EE	Southern Aircraft Consultancy Inc	Wycombe Air Park	6.08
N937DR	Cessna 172R	17280217		Southern Aircraft Consultancy Inc	Donegal	6.07
N950H	Dassault Falcon 50EX	307		Island Aviation Inc	Farnborough	2.09
N955SH	Piper PA-46-350P Malibu Mirage *(DLX conversion)*	4636339		Southern Aircraft Consultancy Inc	North Weald	6.08
N957T	Piper PA-32R-301 Saratoga II HP	3246176		Severn Valley Aviation	Shobdon	10.08
N958MD	Cessna 340A	340A0734		My Spartacus Inc *(Operated D Clarkson)* *(Mabil Airline gmbh titles)*	Southend	2.09
N967LV	Piper PA-32R-301T Saratoga II TC	3257481		N967LV Inc	Cranfield	12.08
N970SR	Cirrus Design SE22 Turbo	2285		Cirrus Design Corp	Turweston	12.08
N971RJ	Piper PA-39 Twin Comanche C/R	39-111	G-AZBC, N8951Y	Aircraft Guaranty Corporation	Biggin Hill	1.09
N973BB	Mitsubishi MU-2B-60 Marquise	1509SA		Romeo Aviation Inc	Jersey	2.09
N980HB	Rockwell Commander 695	95006	N171CT, N171CP, N4468F, YV-366CP, N9759S	HBC Aviation Inc	Guernsey	1.09
N982CD	Cirrus Design SR22-GTS	1853		November CD Inc	Denham	1.09
N987AL	Dassault Falcon 900EASy	194	F-WWFK	Aircraft Trust & Finance Corp	Biggin Hill	12.08
N988SR	Cirrus Design SR22-GTS	2038		Aircraft Guaranty Management LLC	Jersey	10.08
N989Y	Piper PA-24-260 Comanche B	24-4306	G-UVNA, G-BAHG, 5Y-AFX, N8831P	Southern Aircraft Consultancy Inc	Great Oakley	9.08
N994K	Hughes 269A (TH-55A)	0840	67-16733	Southern Aircraft Consultancy Inc	Perranporth	10.08
N994SR	Cirrus Design SR20-G2	1669		Ashpitel Aviation	Thruxton	12.08
N997JM	SOCATA TBM-700	244	LX-JFG, F-GLBQ	Sunwave Aviation	Dunkeswell	8.06
N999AM	Cessna 500 Citation I *(Citation Stallion conversion)*	500-0232	N126R, N500PB, N5232J	Xentrapharm Aviation	Weston, Dublin	1.09
N999BE	Dassault Falcon 7X	8	F-WWUE	Wilmington Trust Co *(Operated B Eccleston)*	Biggin Hill	1.09
N999F	Beech F33A Bonanza	CE-1282	OO-OVB	N T N Fox Systems Inc	Newcastle	10.08
N999MH	Cessna 195B	7168	OH-CSE	E Detiger	Compton Abbas	9.08
N999PD	Waco YMF-F5C	F5C108		Airpark Aviators	Coventry	10.07
N999RL	Robinson R44 Raven II	10614	G-CDEZ	Heli Twinlite	Dolly's Grove, Dublin	4.08
N1024L	Beech 60 Duke	P-78	C-FOPH, CF-OPH, N1024L, CF-OPH	Southern Aircraft Consultancy Inc *(Operated R.Ogden)*	North Weald	5.08
N1027G	Maule M.7-235B	23032C		Southern Aircraft Consultancy Inc *(Operated T Clark)*	Elstree	1.09
N1092H	Beech C90A King Air	LJ-1454		Park Close Aviation Inc	Blackbushe	8.08
N1125Y	Piper PA-46-310P Malibu	46-8408073		Go Aviation UK Inc	Lydd	5.08
N1196R	Raven S-40A Balloon (Hot Air)	S40A-141		P Sweatman "Froggy"	Birmingham	4.07
N1262K	Cessna 425 Corsair	425-0234		Goldsteel Inc	Jersey	12.08
N1320S	Cessna 182P Skylane II	18264884		Hamilton-Fairley Avn	Hatch Gate Farm, Bramshill	12.08
N1325M	Boeing Stearman E75(N2S-5) Kaydet	75-8484	Bu43390	Eastern Stearman Inc *(Operated Blackbarn Aviation) (Frame only)*	Priory Farm, Tibenham	8.08
NC1328	Fairchild F24R-46KS Argus	3310		Eastern Stearman Inc *(Operated Blackbarn Aviation) (Frame only)*	Priory Farm, Tibenham	3.07
N1329T	Cessna T182T Turbo Skylane	T18208667		Denston Hall Inc *(Reserved as N148RM)*	Appleacre Farm, Stradishall	12.08
N1344	Ryan PT-22-RY Recruit	2086	41-20877	Flying Heritage Inc *(Operated Mrs.H.Mitchell t/a PT Flight)*	Sleap	1.09
N1350J	Rockwell Commander 112B	516		Fish Associates Inc	Tatenhill	10.08
N1376C	Lancair Columbia LC41-550FG	41656		GP Aviation Inc	Blackbushe	8.08
N1407J	Rockwell Commander 112A	407		Blue Lake Aviation Inc	Blackbushe	12.08
N1417W	Lancair Columbia LC42-550FG	42523		My Columbia Inc	Biggin Hill	7.07
N1424C	Cessna 182T Skylane	18281610		Glendoe Inc	(Bowldown)	11.08
N1551D	Cessna 190	7773		Southern Aircraft Consultancy Inc	Old Buckenham	1.09
N1554E	Cessna 172N	17271044		International Air Services *(Operated S Turton)*	(Barnstaple)	5.05
N1569C	Cirrus Design SR22	0581		A E Balogh	Coventry	12.08

Reg	Type	Serial	Prev Ident	Owner/Operator	Location	Date
N1604K*	Luscombe 8A Silvaire			See G-BSOE - details in SECTION 1, Part 2	Sturgate	
N1711G	Cessna 340	340-0516		Air Touring Inc	(Biggin Hill)	11.06
N1731B	Boeing A75N-1 Stearman	75-5716	42-17553	Eastern Stearman Inc (As "42-17553:716")	Bidford	1.09
N1745M	Cessna 182P Skylane II	18264424		D Thomas	Cardiff	11.08
N1757H	Cessna 310C	35857		Southern Aircraft Consultancy Inc	Panshanger	6.08
N1778X	Cessna 210L Centurion	21060798		Southern Aircraft Consultancy Inc	Denham	1.09
N1937Z	Cessna 172RG Cutlass RG	172RG0908	EI-BVS	Air Twinlite Inc	Ronaldsway	6.07
N1944A	Douglas DC-3C-47A-80-DL	19677	(N5211A)	Wings Venture Ltd	Oxford	9.08
			N3239W, RDanAF K-683, RNorAF 43-15211	(As "315211:J8-Z")		
N2061K	Beech 58P Pressurised Baron	TJ-161		R Wagstaff	Oxford	1.09
N2086P	Piper PA-23 Apache	23-674	N286GB	Southern Aircraft Consultancy Inc	Blackpool	9.08
			N2086P			
N2105J*	Bell 222	47066		Anglo Services Inc	Galway	10.08
				(Damaged in hangar fire 9.4.06: cancelled 8.06 by FAA)		
N2121T	Gulfstream AA-5B Tiger	AA5B-1031		J.Siebols	Southend	2.09
N2136E	Piper PA-28RT-201 Arrow IV	28R-7918002		Southern Aircraft Consultancy Inc	Doncaster/Sheffield	1.09
N2216X	Cessna 337 Super Skymaster	3370116		Southern Aircraft Consultancy Inc	Belfast	8.08
N2231F	Cessna 182T Skylane	18281925		Southern Aircraft Consultancy Inc	Perth	12.08
N2273Q	Piper PA-28-181 Cherokee Archer II			Southern Aircraft Consultancy Inc	Panshanger	2.09
		28-7790389				
N2299L	Beech F33A Bonanza	CE-677		Stafford W Freeborn	Thruxton	10.08
N2341S	Beech B300 King Air	FL-241		Specsavers Aviation Inc	Guernsey	11.08
N2366D	Cessna 170B	20518		Southern Aircraft Consultancy Inc	Turweston	1.09
N2379C	Cessna R182 Skylane RG	R18200170		West Country Aviation Inc	(Bromsberrow)	10.08
N2401Z	Piper PA-23-250 Aztec F	27-8054034		Pan Maritime US Inc	Filton	3.07
N2405Y	Piper PA-28-181 Archer II	28-8590070		Southern Aircraft Consultancy Inc	Panshanger	2.09
N2445V	Cessna 182S Skylane	18280699		N2445V Inc	Gloucestershire	8.08
N2454Y	Cessna 182S Skylane	18280918		Seima Aviation	Great Massingham	5.07
N2536Y	Britten-Norman BN-2T Islander	2303	G-CDCJ	Wells Fargo Bank Northwest NA	Ronaldsway	1.09
N2548T	Navion Model H Rangemaster	NAV-4-2548		Navion Airways Inc	Guernsey	10.08
NC2612	Stinson Junior R	8754		A.L.Young (Stored)	Henstridge	8.07
N2652P	Piper PA-22-135 Tri-Pacer	22-2992		Southern Aircraft Consultancy Inc		
	(Tailwheel conversion)			"Lil Red"	Taghmon, County Wexford	9.06
N2711H	Eclipse Aviation EA500	000142		Simply Group Jets Inc	North Weald	1.09
N2742Y	Hughes 369HS	62-0389S		Crestband Inc	(Trewen)	1.09
N2923N	Piper PA-32-300 Cherokee Six	32-7940207		Southern Aircraft Consultancy Inc	Jersey	10.08
N2929W	Piper PA-28-151 Cherokee Warrior		OO-GPE	Funair Inc	Elstree	1.09
		28-7415457	N9619N	(Operated M Gorlow)		
N2943D	Piper PA-28RT-201 Arrow IV	28R-7918231	G-BSLD	Southern Aircraft Consultancy Inc	Barton	1.09
			N2943D	(Operated E.Gawronek)		
N2967N	Piper PA-32-300 Six	32-7940242		Aerotechnics Aviation Inc	Guernsey	11.08
N2989M	Piper PA-32-300 Six	32-7840062		International Air Services	Bagby	12.08
				(Operated Mark Johnston Racing)		
N3023W	Beech V35B Bonanza	D-9517		M A Sargent	Guernsey	11.08
N3084F	Reims Cessna F150L	F1500670		MRC Aviation	Lower Mountpleasant, Chatteris	9.08
N3109X	Cessna 150F	15064509		Southern Aircraft Consultancy Inc	Kilrush	11.08
				(Operated The Lucy Flying Group)		
N3400W	Piper PA-32-260 Cherokee Six	32-261		L R Harville (Current status unknown)	Coventry	7.05
N3586D	Piper PA-31-325 Navajo C/R	31-8012065		L. W.Durrell	Jersey	10.08
N3596T	Aero Commander 500	500-752	N359CT	Centreline Aerospace	Norwich	12.08
			N8437C, (N3821C)			
N3669D	Beech 60 Duke	P-544	G-CBYK	Vetch Aviation	Goodwood	12.08
			N3669D			
N3864	Ryan Navion B	NAV-4-2285B		International Air Services	Earls Colne	2.08
				(Operated G Spooner)		
N3922B	Boeing-Stearman E75 (PT-17) Kaydet		42-17642	Eastern Stearman Inc	Priory Farm, Tibenham	8.08
	(Continental W670)	75-5805		(Operated P Hoffmann)		
N4085E	Piper PA-18-150 Super Cub	18-7809059		R N Hall	Goodwood	3.06
N4102D	Reims Cessna FR182 Skylane RG		PH-CTM	Schuybroek Aviation	Seething	7.08
		FR18200029	SE-IBB			
N4168D	Piper PA-34-220T Seneca V	3449158		AAL Inc	Shoreham	12.08
N4173T	Cessna 320D Skyknight	320D0073		N4173T Inc (Operated J.Irwin)	Cranfield	8.08
N4178W	Piper PA-32R-301T Saratoga IITC	3257178		Mistress Two Inc	Blackbushe	1.09
N4238C	Mudry CAP.10B	155		Southern Aircraft Consultancy Inc		
				(As "52" in Mexican AF c/s)	Rotary Farm, Hatch	10.08
N4297A	Piper PA-39 Twin Comanche C/R	39-114	G-AZBW	Southern Aircraft Consultancy Inc	Kirkwall	11.08
			N8954Y	(Operated T Norman)		
N4305H	Mooney M.20J	24-0788		Southern Aircraft Consultancy Inc	Elmsett	6.08
N4337K	Cessna 150K	15071583	G-BTSA	T L Crook	Coleman Green	1.08
			N6083G			
N4422P	Piper PA-23-160 Geronimo	23-1936		W J Armstrong Inc	Thruxton	9.08
N4446	Lancair Columbia LC41-550FG	41756	N1571C	A Bauermeister	Biggin Hill	12.08
N4514X	Piper PA-28-181 Cherokee Archer II			Baxter 4514X Holdings Inc	Cambridge	9.08
		28-7690022				
N4519U (1)	Head AX9-118 Balloon (Hot Air)	184		P Sweatman "Ground Hog"	Birmingham	4.07
	(Original envelope- replacement in use with Northern Light Balloon Expeditions)					
NC4531H	Piper PA-15 Vagabond	15-305		E A Terris	Wycombe Air Park	7.08
N4575C	Grumman G.21A Goose	B-120		Aerofloat G21A Inc	Weston, Dublin	9.08
N4596N	Boeing-Stearman E75 (PT-13D) Kaydet		42-17782	Phil Dacy Aviation	North Weald	10.08
	(Lycoming R680-7)	75-5945		(US Mail c/s)		
N4599W	Rockwell Commander 112TC	13089		N4599W Inc	Conington	11.08
N4698W	Rockwell Commander 112TC-A	13274		Southern Aircraft Consultancy Inc	Bournemouth	8.08
N4712V	Boeing Stearman PT-13D Kaydet	75-5094	42-16931	Southern Aircraft Consultancy Inc	Hardwick	9.08
				(As "W:104" in USAAC c/s)		

Reg	Type	Serial	Prev id	Owner/Operator	Location	Date
N4770B	Cessna 152	15283626		N R Coplowe	Panshanger	2.09
N4779B*	Cessna 152	15283630		Not known *(Cancelled 9.04 by FAA)*	Shobdon	10.07
N4806E	Douglas B-26C Invader	27451	44-34172	A26 Europe Inc *(Stored)*	(Canterbury, Kent)	2.06
N5020A	Cessna T182T Skylane	T18208097		Tancred Aviation	Sherburn-in-Elmet	8.07
N5025J	Hiller UH-12B	726		Hiller Inc *(Stored)*	Henstridge	8.07
N5043X	Cessna 172C	17249424	G-BWJP	International Air Services	(Ipswich)	7.06
				(Operated C Evans)		
N5052P	Piper PA-24-180 Comanche	24-56	G-ATFS	T A G Randell	Farley Farm, Romsey	8.05
			N5052P	*(Under restoration)*		
N5057V	Boeing-Stearman PT-13D Kaydet	75-5598	42-17435	M G Plaskett	Rendcomb	8.08
				(Team Guinot) (Operated V.S.E.Norman)		
N5084V	Cirrus Design SR22-G2	0831		SR22 Holding Inc	North Weald	1.09
N5106Y	Hughes 369D	81-1057D		Trafficopters Inc	Weston, Dublin	6.08
	(Hughes 500)					
N5120	Bell 430	49095		Wells Fargo Bank Northwest NA	Blackpool	1.09
				(Operated JJB Sports)		
N5240H	Piper PA-16 Clipper	16-44		Southern Aircraft Consultancy Inc		
				(Operated D.Hillier)	Wellcross Grange, Slinfold	7.08
N5264Q	MD Helicopters MD.369E	0126E		Southern Aircraft Consultancy Inc		
					Donegal, County Donegal	4.08
N5277T	Piper PA-32-260 Cherokee Six E	32-7200031		K R Denman	Goodwood	4.08
N5315V	Hiller UH-12C	757		Southern Aircraft Consultancy Inc	Lower Upham	4.08
N5317V	Hiller UH-12C	768		Canaan Helicopters	(Sherbourne)	2.06
				(Operated Pulse Helicopters)		
N5336Z	Cirrus Design SR20	1413		Southern Aircraft Consultancy Inc	Perth	8.08
N5428C	Cessna 170A	19462		Southern Aircraft Consultancy Inc	Audley End	9.08
				(Operated P.Norman)		
N5632R	Maule M-5-235C Lunar Rocket	7244C		Southern Aircraft Consultancy Inc		
				(Operated RD Group)	Stowes Farm, Tillingham	4.06
N5647S	Maule M-5-235C Rocket	7345C		Virginia Aircraft Trust Corp		
					Yeatsall Farm, Abbotts Bromley	8.08
N5730H	Piper PA-16 Clipper	16-342		Southern Aircraft Consultancy Inc		
					Yeatsall Farm, Abbotts Bromley	8.08
N5736	Raytheon Hawker 800XP2	258471	N43642	Hawker Partnership Inc	Cork and Luton	12.08
				(Operated Howard Holdings plc)		
N5834N*	Rockwell Commander 114	14383		W F Chmura	Peterstone, Cardiff	11.04
				(Crashed 23.10.98 - cancelled 7.99 by FAA - hulk only)		
N5839P	Piper PA-24-180 Comanche	24-920		Aircraft Guaranty Management LLC	Blackbushe	1.09
N5880T	Westland WG-30-100	009	G-17-31	Offshore Fire & Survival Training Centre	Norwich	12.08
N5900H	Piper PA-16 Clipper	16-520		Southern Aircraft Consultancy Inc	Shenstone	11.08
N5915V	Piper PA-28-161Cherokee Warrior II	28-7716215		Southern Aircraft Consultancy Inc	North Weald	10.08
N6010Y	Commander Aircraft Commander 114B	14589		Camrose Inc	Biggin Hill	1.09
N6024V	Commander Aircraft Commander 114B	14609		Hinsby Inc	Guernsey	12.08
N6039X	Commander Aircraft Commander 114B	14639		Little Beetle Inc	Guernsey	10.08
N6048B	Commander Aircraft Commander 114B	14676		Hinsby Inc	Guernsey	10.08
N6078T	Cessna T182T Skylane	T18208621		Aircraft Guaranty Title Corp LLC	Shobdon	5.07
N6081F	Commander Aircraft Commander 114B	14681		DSS Inc	Kemble	9.08
N6088F	Commander Aircraft Commander 114TC	20043	N948PW	Turnberry Holdings Inc	Blackbushe	1.09
N6088Z	Commander Aircraft Commander 114B	14662	N6088F	88 Zulu Inc	Guernsey	11.08
N6095A	Commander Aircraft Commander 114B	14635		Bonbois Aviation	Guernsey	10.08
N6130X	Maule M6-235C Super Rocket	7497C		Pelmont Aviation	Chilbolton	8.08
N6182G	Cessna 172N Skyhawk II	17273576		Southern Aircraft Consultancy Inc	Cambridge	12.08
N6302W	Government Aircraft Factory N22B Nomad	F-159	VH-HWB	Chatteris Aviation Inc *(Operated London Parachute Centre)*		
					Lower Mountpleasant Farm, Chatteris	9.08
N6339U	Piper PA-28-236 Dakota	28-8011089	OO-JFD F-GCMU, OO-HLM, N8152S)	Southern Aircraft Consultancy Inc	Wickenby	10.07
N6438C	Stinson L-5C Sentinel	1428		Eastern Stearman Inc	Priory Farm, Tibenham	10.08
				(Operated P Bennett and N Nice as "298177:R-8")		
N6498V	Cessna T303 Crusader	T30300313	G-CRUS N6498V	Southern Aircraft Consultancy Inc	Guernsey	10.08
N6593W	Cessna P210N Centurion	P210-00801		Southern Aircraft Consultancy Inc		
	(Silver Eagle Allison turboprop conversion)			"Rose Anne"	Brittas House, Limerick	6.08
				(Operated Pacific Network Air)		
N6601Y	Piper PA-23-250 Aztec C	27-3905	XC-DAZ N6601Y	3 Greens Aviation	Blackpool	11.05
				(Current status unknown)		
N6602Y	Piper PA-28-140 Cherokee	28-21943	G-ATTG N11C	Southern Aircraft Consultancy Inc	Seething	10.08
N6620W	Alon A-2 Aircoupe	A-110		Southern Aircraft Consultancy Inc	Plymouth	10.07
N6632L	Beech C23 Musketeer	M-2188		W J Forrest	Ventfield Farm, Oxford	8.06
N6819F	Cessna 150F	15063419		W J Davis *(On fire dump)*	Shoreham	7.07
N6830B	Piper PA-22-150 Tri-Pacer	22-4128		Southern Aircraft Consultancy Inc	Compton Abbas	8.08
N6907E	Cessna 175A Skylark	56407		Southern Aircraft Consultancy Inc	Popham	10.08
				(Operated C Webb)		
N6920B	Piper PA-34-220T Seneca III	34-8533025		Southern Aircraft Consultancy Inc	Thruxton	12.08
N6954J	Piper PA-32R-300 Cherokee Lance	32R-7680394		Matrix Aviation Inc	Norwich	1.09
N7027E	Hawker Tempest V	Not known	EJ693	K Weeks *(Stored)*	Wycombe Air Park	7.08
N7070A	Cessna S550 Citation II	S550-0068	N4049 N404G, N1272Z	Omega Air Inc	Dublin	9.08
N7148R	Beech B55 Baron	TC-2028	N2198L C-GWFD, N2198L, D-IGRW, N2198L	Air Services Holdings Corp	Exeter	1.09
N7172Z	Hughes 369C	122-0438S		Southern Aircraft Consultancy Inc	(Reading)	11.08

Reg	Type	Serial	Prev ident	Operator	Location	Date
N7205T	Beech A36 Bonanza	E-2182		Minster Enterprises	Tatenhill	1.09
N7219L	Beech B55 Baron	TC-717	HB-GBX	Southern Aircraft Consultancy Inc	Elstree	1.09
			OE-FDF, HB-GBX			
N7223Y	Beech 58 Baron	TH-1456		Southern Aircraft Consultancy Inc	Elstree	1.09
N7238X	Piper PA-18-95 Super Cub	18-1629	G-BWUO	International Air Services	Wymeswold	10.08
			OO-MEU, OO-HNG, French Army, 51-15629 *(Operated A W Myers)*			
N7242N	Agusta A109A-II	7355	ZK-HJC	Cannon Air	Liskeard Heliport	10.08
N7251Y	Beech A36 Bonanza	E-2277		Turbo Arrow Inc	Elstree	1.09
N7263S	Cessna 150H	15067963		Cesna Inc *(Stored)*	Plaistows Farm, St Albans	5.08
N7348P	Piper PA-24-250 Comanche	24-2526		Southern Aircraft Consultancy Inc	Netherthorpe	8.08
				(Operated J.Bown)		
N7374A	Cessna A150M Aerobat 135 *(Tail-wheel conversion)*	A1500726		Southern Aircraft Consultancy Inc "Turnin' Tricks" *(Current status unknown)*	Branscombe	10.05
N7423V	Mooney M.20E Chapparal	21-1163		International Air Services *(Operated J Holme)*	Old Sarum	1.09
N7456P	Piper PA-24-250 Comanche	24-2646		Southern Aircraft Consultancy Inc	Gamston	8.08
N7600E	Bellanca 14-19-2 Cruisemaster	4102		Egmond Aircraft LLC *(Operated H Cox)*	Westover Farm, Sheepwash	9.08
N7640F	Piper PA-32R-300 Cherokee Lance	32R-7780069	ZS-OGX N7640F	Southern Aircraft Consultancy Inc	Wellesbourne Mountford	3.08
N7801R	Bell 47G-5	7801		Skyman Logistics	Beckley, Oxford	8.04
N7832P	Piper PA-24-250 Comanche	24-3052		Three Two Papa Inc	Enstone	11.08
N7976Y	Piper PA-30 Twin Comanche B	30-1075		Southern Aircraft Consultancy Inc	Guernsey	10.08
N8040T	Bell 206B-3 JetRanger	3615	N2271V	Company Publishing Inc	(Stevenage)	9.08
N8105Z	Piper PA-28RT-201T Turbo Arrow IV	28R-8031007		Southern Aircraft Consultancy Inc	Elstree	4.08
N8153E	Piper PA-28RT-201T Turbo Arrow IV	28R-8131185	N9561N N84205	P B Payne	RAF Mona	4.07
N8159Q	Cirrus Design SR20	1388		DSL Corporation *(to be G-CRLA)*	Swansea	11.08
N8225Y	Cessna 177RG Cardinal RG	177RG1247		International Air Services *(Operated D J Knight Cardinal Group)*	Upper Hill Farm, Hughley	1.09
N8241Z	Piper PA-28-161 Warrior II	28-8316079		Pett Air Inc	Henstridge	5.08
N8258F	Beech B36TC Bonanza	EA-513		Millfore Aviation Inc	(Filton)	12.08
N8412B	Piper PA-28RT-201T Turbo Arrow IV	28R-8131164		Sweepline Inc	Bourne Park, Hurstbourne Tarrant	1.08
N8523Y	Piper PA-30 Twin Comanche	30-1684		Leadbolt Inc	Gloucestershire	5.07
N8702K	Cessna 340A	340A0623		Southern Aircraft Consultancy Inc	Goodwood	9.08
N8754J	Aviat A-1 Husky *(Built Christen Industries)*	1160		Southern Aircraft Consultancy Inc *(Operated A.Febrache)*	Guernsey	8.08
N8829P	Piper PA-24-260 Comanche	24-4285		J Melville	Avon Farm, Saltford	1.09
N8862V	Bellanca 17-31ATC Turbo Super Viking	31022		S B Barber	Popham	10.08
N8911Y	Piper PA-39 Twin Comanche C/R	39-66	G-AYFT N8911Y	Southern Aircraft Consultancy Inc *(Stored)*	Farley Farm, Romsey	6.08
N8990F	Hughes 269C	64-0313		Southern Aircraft Consultancy Inc	Kilrush	11.08
N9057F	Hughes 369HS	129-0230S		Southern Aircraft Consultancy Inc	Kilrush	11.08
N9070L	British Aerospace BAe 146 Series 300	E3147	ZK-NZJ G-6-147, G-5-147, G-11-147	T S Whetter *(Stored)*	Bournemouth	1.09
N9086L	British Aerospace BAe 146 Series 300	E3135	ZK-NZG G-5-135	T S Whetter *(Stored)*	Bournemouth	1.09
N9089Z	North American TB-25N Mitchell	108-35186	(G-BKXW) N9089Z, 44-30861	Aero Associates Inc *(Stored dismantled with Parkhouse Aviation)*	Wycombe Air Park	4.08
N9122N	Piper PA-46-310P Malibu	4608097		Air Libra Inc	Oxford	1.09
N9123X	Piper PA-32R-301T Turbo Saratoga SP	3229003		Vector Sky Service Inc	Shoreham and Hilversum	10.07
N9133D	Bell 407	53648		Duignan & McCarthy Inc	Knocksedan, Dublin	9.08
N9146N	Cessna 401B *(RAM conversion)*	401B0010		A J Air Ltd Inc *(In derelict condition)*	Weston, Dublin	4.08
N9275Y	Piper PA-46-310P Malibu	46-8608026		International Air Services *(Operated D F Keedy)*	Haverfordwest	1.09
N9305M	Mooney M.20E	1238		Overseas Real Estate Finance & Investment Corp	St Just	10.08
N9325N	Piper PA-28R-200 Cherokee Arrow *(Lopresti version)*	28R-35025		Southern Aircraft Consultancy Inc *(Operated H Mercado)*	Fowlmere	1.09
N9362	Sud-Aviation SA316B Alouette III	1739		Southern Aircraft Consultancy Inc	Halton Moor, Leeds	8.08
N9381P	Piper PA-24-260 Comanche C	24-4882		Southern Aircraft Consultancy Inc	Elstree	1.09
N9405H	Beech D.17S	4803	(D-EJVW) C-FJVW, N9405H, Bu33004	International Air Services *(Operated G W Lynch)*	Great Oakley	9.08
N9533Y	Cessna T.210N Centurion	21064539		Simply Living Ltd	Liverpool	7.05
N9680Q	Cessna 172M	17265764		Aircraft Guaranty Holdings & Trust LLC *(Operated Jersey Aero Club)*	Jersey	10.08
N9838Z	Beech B90 King Air	LJ-435	D-IHCH D-ILVW	Skydive Midwest Aviation	Dunkeswell	10.08
N9861M	Maule M.4-210C	1058C		Southern Aircraft Consultancy Inc	Fairoaks	1.09
N9870C	Cessna T303 Crusader	T30300227		Aircraft Guaranty Holdings & Trust LLC	Liverpool	12.08
N9950	Curtiss P-40N Warhawk	33723	44-7983	Sky Fire Corp *(Stored in container)*	(Greenham Common)	2.04
N10053	Boeing Stearman A75N1	75-4986	XB-XIH	Eastern Stearman *(Under restoration for R Knights)*	Felixkirk	7.08
N10522	Piper PA-46-350P Malibu Mirage	4636398		Aircraft Guaranty Title & Trust LLC	Blackpool	1.09
N11824	Cessna 150L	15075652		Southern Aircraft Consultancy Inc	Turweston	1.09
N13253	Cessna 172M Skyhawk	17262613		Anglia Aviation Inc *(Stored)*	Plaistows Farm, St Albans	5.08

Reg	Type	c/n	Prev id	Operator	Location	Date
N14113	North American T-28B Trojan	174-398	Haiti AF 1236	Radial Revelations Ltd	Duxford	10.08
			N14113, FrAF 119, 51-7545 "Little Rascal" (As "51-7545:119" in French AF c/s)			
NC16403*	Cessna C.34 Airmaster	322		Alan House	Lower Wasing Farm, Brimpton	9.08
			(Cancelled 5.99 by FAA and stored)			
N17596	Schweizer S269C-1	0300		Magell Aviation USA Inc	(Ballymena)	1.08
NC17633	Spartan 7W Executive	21		Aircraft Preservation Inc	Little Gransden	9.08
NC18028	Beech D17S	147	NC18028	P.H.McConnell	Popham	10.08
N19753	Cessna 172L	17260723		Aircraft Guaranty Title & Trust Llc	Elstree	1.09
N20981	Cessna 172M	17263885		Aircraft Guaranty Title & Trust LLC	Abbeyshrule	10.08
N21381	Piper PA-34-200 Seneca	34-7350274	F-BUTM	Tickton Inc	Dunkeswell	10.08
			F-ETAL			
N21419	British Aircraft Corporation 167 Strikemaster Mk.81	EEP/JP/168	R Singapore AF 323	NW MAS Ltd	Hawarden	10.07
			South Yemen AF 504, G-AXFX (Stored at Hawarden Air Services)			
N21927	Cessna 172S Skyhawk SP	172S10505		Coppersmith Inc	Oxford	1.09
N23659	Beech B58 Baron	TH-893		International Air Services	Guernsey	1.08
			(Operated M G Williams)			
N24136	Beech A36 Bonanza	E-1233		Dickens Aviation Inc	North Weald	8.07
N24730*	Piper PA-38-112 Tomahawk			See G-BTIL - detail in SECTION 1, Part 2	Eaglescott	
N25644	North American B-25D Mitchell	100-20644	G-BYDR	Vulcan Warbirds Inc	Duxford	7.08
			N88972, CF-OGQ, KL161, 43-3318 "Grumpy" (As "KL161/VO-B" in RAF 98 Sqn c/s)			
N26634	Piper PA-24-250 Comanche	24-3551	G-BFKR	Atlanticair Inc	Slinfold	7.08
			PH-BUS, D-ELPY, N8306P			
N28141	Bellanca 17-30A	80-30982		Viking Air	Cranfield	10.08
N29566	Piper PA-28RT-201 Arrow IV	28R-7918146	D-EJLH	Southern Aircraft Consultancy Inc	Denham	5.08
N30562	Bell 407	53750		Air Move Partnership	Weston, Dublin	1.09
N30593	Cessna 210L Centurion	21059938		Southern Aircraft Consultancy Inc	Cranfield	1.09
N31008	Piper PA-32R-301 Saratoga IIHP	3246229		China Saratoga Airline	Elstree	1.09
N31356	Douglas DC-4-1009	42914	C-FTAW	Aces High US Inc	North Weald	10.08
			EL-ADR, N6404 (As "44-42914" in USAF c/s)			
N32625 *	Piper PA-34-200T Seneca II	34-7570039	G-PALM	(Fire Section) (Cx 5.99)	Guernsey	1.08
			SE-LAN, N32625			
N33514	Hiller UH-12B	661	51-16408	Pulse Helicopter Corporation	(Sherbourne)	2.06
			(Damaged 18.11.04 - stored)			
N33870	Fairchild M62A (PT-19-FA) Cornell	T40-237	G-BTNY	Aerospace Trust Management LLC	Mendlesham	9.08
			N33870, US Army (As "02538" in US Army c/s) (Operated P Earthey)			
NC33884	Aeronca 65CA Chief	CA.14101		P W & J M Brewer	Bodmin	10.08
N36362	Cessna 180 Skywagon	31691	G-BHVZ	Southern Aircraft Consultancy Inc (Operated W Burgess)		
			F-BHMU, N4739B		Bourne Park, Hurstbourne Tarrant	1.09
N36665	Beech A36 Bonanza	E-1696		M Flynn	Fairoaks	1.09
N37172	Beech B300 King Air	FL-472		Wells Fargo Bank Northwest NA	Biggin Hill	2.09
N37379	Cessna 421C Golden Eagle	421C0654	G-DJEA	Bettany Aircraft	Jersey	10.08
			TC-AAA, N37379, (N24BS), N37379 (Reserved as N339TB)			
N38273	Piper PA-28R-201 Cherokee Arrow III	28R-7737086		S W Freeborn	Blackbushe	12.08
			(Operated L.Slater)			
N38763	Hiller UH-12B	497	G-ATZB	M Elkins	Elstree	5.08
			102 R Thai AF			
N38940	Boeing-Stearman A75N1 (PT-17) Kaydet (Continental R670)	75-1822	(G-BSNK)	Eastern Stearman Inc	Priory Farm, Tibenham	9.08
			N38940, N55300, 41-8263 (Operated P Bennett as "18263/822" in US Army c/s)			
N38945	Piper PA-32R-300 Cherokee Lance	32R-7780490		Southern Aircraft Consultancy Inc	Stapleford	7.08
N39605	Piper PA-34-200T Seneca II	34-7870397		Fly Horizon US Inc	Swansea	9.08
N41098	Cessna 421B Golden Eagle	421B0448		MC 1 Inc	Elstree	1.09
N41702	Supermarine Spitfire XVIII	6S-676390	TP298	Military Aircraft Restoration Corp	Sandown	1.08
			Indian AF HS649	(Stored)		
N42527	Bell 407	53384		Aircraft Guaranty Title & Trust LLC	Shannon	10.08
			(Operated Rollico Aviation)			
N44914	Douglas C-54D Skymaster	10630	Bu56498	Aces High US Inc	North Weald	10.08
			42-72525 (As "56498" in US Air Transport Command c/s)			
N45458	Piper PA-18-150 Super Cub	18-8553	IDF/AF012	Palace Aviation Investment (Stored)	Steventon	4.07
N45507	Piper PA-18-150 Super Cub	18-8566	IDF/AF024	Palace Aviation Investment (Stored)	Steventon	4.07
N47351*	Cessna 152	15283219	Not known		Hill Farm, Nayland	3.05
			(Cancelled 4.91 by FAA as destroyed: derelict fuselage stored) (Current status unknown)			
N47494	Piper PA-28R-201 Cherokee Arrow III	28R-7737166		M R Horwitz Inc	Panshanger	2.09
N49272	Fairchild M.62C/PT-23A-HO Cornell (Continental W670)	437HO	42-49413	Flying Heritage Inc	Sleap	1.09
			(Operated R.E.Mitchell t/a PT Flight as "23" in USAAC c/s)			
N49337	Pitts S-1T	1046		Southern Aircraft Consultancy Inc	Shoreham	9.08
N50029	Cessna 172	28807	LX-AIB	Southern Aircraft Consultancy Inc	Exeter	1.09
			N6707A	(Operated E.Byrd)		
N52485	Boeing-Stearman A75N1 (PT-17) Kaydet	75-4494		Roland Stearman Aviation (As "169" in US Navy c/s)	Cherry Tree Farm, Monewden	5.08
N53103	Cessna 177RG Cardinal RG	177RG1347		Vectis Aircraft	Sandown, Isle of Wight	1.09
N53517	Piper PA-46-350P Malibu Mirage	4636330		Aircraft Guaranty Management LLC	Coventry	9.08
N54105	Cirrus Design SR22-G2	1139		Gopub Aviation	Leeds-Bradford	1.09
N54211*	Piper PA-23-250 Aztec E	27-7554006	G-ITTU	Southern Aircraft Consultancy Inc	(Elstree)	8.07
			D-IKLW, G-BCSW, N54211 (Noted road running on M25 (S) 6. 8.07) (Cx 6.08)			
N54922	Boeing-Stearman A75N1 (PT-17) Kaydet (Pratt & Witney 985-14B)	75-3491	Bu.30054	M G Plaskett	Rendcomb	7.08
			(Team Guinot) (Operated V.S.E.Norman)			
N56421	Ryan PT-22-RY Recruit	1539	41-15510	Flying Heritage Inc	Sleap	1.09
			(Operated R.E.Mitchell t/a PT Flight as "855" in US Army c/s)			
N56462	Maule M.6-235 Rocket	7409C		Southern Aircraft Consultancy Inc	East Winch	8.07
N56643	Maule M.5-180C	8086C		Southern Aircraft Consultancy Inc	(Reading)	1.09
			(Operated C Schofield)			

Reg	Type	c/n	Prev reg	Owner	Location	Date
N57783	Stinson L-5 Sentinel	76-511	42-98270 ?	J F Tillman	Priory Farm, Tibenham	8.08
				(Frame - spares for N6438C)		
N58283	Aerospatiale SA.341G Gazelle	1015		D B Pearce	Bourne Park	2.09
N58566	Consolidated-Vultee BT-15-VN Valiant	10670	42-41882	Flying Heritage Inc	Sleap	11.06
				(Operated R.E.Mitchell t/a PT Flight in US Army c/s)		
N60256	Beech C35 Bonanza	D-3346	OO-DOL	R.M.Hornblower	Southend	2.09
			OO-JAN	*(Nosewheel collapsed landing 28. 1.05 - in open store with no propeller)*		
N60526	Beech E55 Baron	TE-1159		E Walsh	Elstree	8.08
N61787	Piper J-3C-65 Cub	13624	45-4884	Gypsy Fliers	Draycott Farm, Chiseldon	8.06
				(As "54884/57-D")		
N61970	Piper PA-24-250 Comanche	24-3364	OO-GOE	Southern Aircraft Consultancy Inc	Gamston	8.08
			F-OCBM, 5R-MVA, N8198P, N10F	*(Operated Nunn & Green)*		
N62171	Hiller Felt UH-12C	GF-2		P J Coyne	Tuam, Galway	12.04
N62842	Boeing-Stearman PT-17 Kaydet	75-3851		Eastern Stearman Inc	Priory Farm, Tibenham	8.08
				(Frame stored)		
N63590	Boeing-Stearman N2S-3 Kaydet	75-7143	Bu.07539	Eastern Stearman Inc	Brock Farm, Brentwood	8.08
				(Operated I Stockwell as "07539/143" in US Navy c/s)		
N65200	Boeing-Stearman D75N1 Kaydet	75-3817	FJ767	Eastern Stearman Inc	Goodwood	7.08
N65565	Boeing Stearman B75N1 Kaydet	75-7463		Ortac Inc	Sywell	11.07
N68427	Boeing-Stearman A75N1 (N2S-4) Kaydet	75-5000	Bu 55771	Eastern Stearman Inc	Priory Farm, Tibenham	8.08
				(Operated Blackbarn Aviation) (Frame only)		
N70457*	MD Helicopters MD.600N	RN-057		Aces High	Pinewood Studios	1.08
				(Cancelled 10.01: stored as "511" for film)		
N70844	Piper PA-23-250 Aztec D	27-4194	G-AZSZ	International Air Services	Biggin Hill	4.08
			N6851Y	*(Operated A A Mattacks)*		
N71763	Cessna 180K	18053191		China Pilot Inc	Franklins Field, Chew Mendip	7.08
N74189	Boeing Stearman PT-17	75-717		M G Plaskett	Rendcomb	9.08
				(Team Guinot) (Operated Aerosuperbatics Ltd)		
N75048	Piper PA-28-181 Cherokee Archer II	28-7690286		Southern Aircraft Consultancy Inc		
				(Operated I Sibley)	St Marys, Isle of Scilly	1.09
N75822	Cessna 172N	17267979		Hercmar Inc *(Operated C.Murgatroyd)*	Crowfield	12.08
N76402*	Cessna 140	10828	NC76402		Blackpool	11.05
				(Crashed near Meppershall 9.8.98 : cancelled 4.99 by FAA) (Wreck stored)		
N80035	Pitts S-2A	2070		Southern Aircraft Consultancy Inc	Panshanger	9.08
N80056	Cessna 421B Golden Eagle	421B0654	G-HASI	CB Aviation Inc	Hawarden	2.09
			G-BTDK, OY-BFA, N1558G			
N80364	Cessna 500 Citation I	500-0299	OY-TKI	Wells Fargo Bank Northwest NA	Weston, Dublin	8.08
		N80364, (OY-EBD), N80364, PT-OZX, YV-940CP, N5133K, ZS-MGH, N55AK, N66TR, N3JJ, HB-VEO, N5299J				
				(Operated National Flight Centre)		
N80533	Cessna 172M Skyhawk	17266640		Southern Aircraft Consultancy Inc	Alderney	11.07
N81188	Piper PA-28-236 Dakota	28-8211026		Retail Management Associates		
					Charlton Park, Malmesbury	8.07
N84718	Piper PA-28RT-201T Turbo Arrow IV	28R-8231013		Southern Aircraft Consultancy Inc	East Midlands	10.08
N90011	MD Helicopters MD.902	900-00115		Latium Helicopter Charters UK Inc	Swettenham)	1.09
N91384	Rockwell Commander 690A	11118	SE-FLN	Airbourne Inc	Wickenby	6.08
N92562	Piper PA-46-350P Malibu Mirage	4636010		Trevair Inc	Blackpool	1.09
N93938	Erco 415C	1261		Merkado Holdings	Panshanger	6.08
N95590	Rockwell 690B Turbo Commander	11482	G-CECN	Finmap International Inc	Wickenby	10.08
		HS-TFG, N745T, N4224U, YV-212CP, (N81805)		*(Operated Cooper Aerial Surveys)*		
N96240	Beech D18S (3TM)	CA-159	G-AYAH	Edwards Worldwide Aviation	North Weald	10.08
			N6123, RCAF 1559			
N97121*	Embraer EMB-110P1 Bandeirante	110.334	PT-SDK	Guernsey Airport Fire Service *(Hulk only)*	Guernsey	10.08
N97821	Mooney M.20J	24-1080		Southern Aircraft Consultancy Inc	Panshanger	7.08
			OO-LFK, N6328X			

AUSTRIA

Reg	Type	c/n	Prev reg	Owner	Location	Date
OE-IFB	Bombardier CL-600-2B16	5704	(D-AFIB)	Vista Jet Gmbh	Oxford	1.09
	(CL-605 Challenger)		C-FLKC			
OE-FYA	Diamond DA 42 Twin Star	42.361	OE-VPY	Diamond Finance Services	Bournemouth	1.09
				(Operated CTC Aviation)		
OE-FYB	Diamond DA 42 Twin Star	42.365	OE-VPI	Diamond Finance Services	Bournemouth	1.09
				(Operated CTC Aviation)		
OE-KKC	Diamond DA 40D Star	D4.036	(OM-HLH)	Diamond Aircraft Industries GmbH	Gamston	10.07
			OE-DDC			
OE-LRE*	Bombardier CL-600-2B19	7059	(JA02J)	Air Salvage International	Alton	2.07
	(CL-600 Regional Jet)		OE-LRE, C-FMND	*(Fuselage stored)*		
OE-XBA	Agusta-Bell AB206B-3 JetRanger III	8557	HB-XPW	Belair-Helicopter Luftverkehrs	(Strathallan)	8.06
			G-TKHM, G-MKAN, G-DOUG *(Operated B Munro)*			

CZECH REPUBLIC

Reg	Type	c/n	Prev reg	Owner	Location	Date
OK-DUA 14	Jora sro Jora	Not known		Not known	Abbeyshrule	10.06
OK-DUU 15	Urban Air UFM-11 Lambada	3/11		P Kearney	Kilkenny	7.06
OK-FUA 05	Urban Air UFM-11 Lambada	13/11	OK-EUU-02	S Walsh	Waterford	7.08
OK-GUA 16	Urban Air UFM-10 Samba	Not known		J Smith	Minnistown, County Mear	10.08
OK-GUA 28	Urban Air UFM-10 Samba	21/10		S Coyne *(Current status unknown)*	Abbeyshrule	8.04
OK-IUA 69	TL Ultralight TL 2000 Sting RG	Not known		Not known	Tarn Farm, Cockerham	9.06
OK-JUA 03	Urban Air Samba XXL	Not known		Not known	Willingale	9.08
OK-KUA 16	Urban Air Samba XXL	Not known		Not known	Abbeyshrule	9.08
OK-KUA 26	Urban Air Samba XXL	Not known		Not known	Kilkenny	10.08
OK-LUA 36	Urban Air Samba XXL	Not known		Not known	Abbeyshrule	10.08
OK-MUA 78	Urban Air Samba XXL	Not known		Not known	Abbeyshrule	10.08
OK-NUA 18	Urban Air Samba XXL	Not known		Not known	Abbeyshrule	10.08
OK-NUA 19	Urban Air Samba XXL	Not known		Not known	Abbeyshrule	10.08

BELGIUM

Reg	Type	c/n
OO-AJK*	Nord 1203 Norecrin	261
OO-DHN*	Boeing 727-31	20113
OO-DHR*	Boeing 727-35F	19834
OO-EII	Bücker Bü.133C Jungmeister	51
OO-GCO	Grumman-American AA-5A Cheetah	AA5A-0526
OO-MEL*	Focke-Wulf Piaggio FWP.149D	113
OO-MHB*	Piper PA-28-236 Dakota	28-8011143
OO-NAT	SOCATA MS.880B Rallye Club	2253
OO-TND*	Boeing 737-301F	23515
OO-WIO*	Reims Cessna FRA150L Aerobat	FRA1500183
OO-A95	CFM Shadow C-D	200CD

DENMARK

Reg	Type	c/n
OY-BTZ	Piper PA-31-350 Navajo Chieftain	31-7752031
OY-CKR	Piper PA-31-350 Navajo Chieftain	31-7652124
OY-DFD	Mooney M.20F Executive	670327
OY-DRS	Reims Cessna F172K	F17200786
OY-EGZ	Cessna F172H	F172-0324
OY-FAA	Taylor J-2 Cub	964
OY-HGB*	Hughes 369D (Hughes 500)	1146D
OY-ILG	Bombardier BD-700 Global Express	9163
OY-MUB*	Short SD.3-30 Variant 200	SH.3069

NETHERLANDS

Reg	Type	c/n
PH-DUC	Stoddard-Hamilton Glasair IIRG-S	2069
PH-HEW	Robinson R44 Astro	0785
PH-IRL	CZAW Sportcruiser	07SC053
PH-KRC	Cessna 180K	18052799
PH-NLK*	Piper PA-23-160 Apache	23-1694
PH-PAB*	Neico Lancair 360	766
PH-PIM	Cessna R172K Hawk XP	R1722376
PH-PWA	Van's RV-8	80836
PH-TMH	Piper PA-38-112 Tomahawk	38-79A0261
PH-TWR	Ken Brock KB-2 Gyroplane	1006
PH-WRF	Robinson R44 Astro	0816
PH-ZZY	SOCATA MS893E Rallye 180GT	12074
PH-3P3 *	WDL Fascination D4BK	106
PH-3W6	CZAW CH-601XL Zodiac	6-9666

ARUBA

Reg	Type	c/n
P4-HEC	Eurocopter EC.155B	6600
P4-MMG	Boeing 727-30	18368

RUSSIA

Reg	Type	c/n
FLARF01035	Yakovlev Yak-52	8910106
RA-01274	Yakovlev Yak-55	910103
RA3350K	Sukhoi Su-26MZ	900305

THE PHILIPPINES

Reg	Type	c/n
RP-C2900	Agusta A109A	7228
RP-C8023*	Conroy CL-44-O	16

SWEDEN

Reg	Type	c/n
SE-BOG	Boeing Stearman B75N1	75-7128
SE-BRG*	Fairey Firefly TT.1	F.6071
SE-EOS	Piper PA-28-180 Cherokee C	28-2533
SE-GVH	Piper PA-38-112 Tomahawk	38-78A0053
SE-HXF*	Rotorway Scorpion	SE-1

Reg	Operator	Location	Date
F-BFJE	Not known *(Stored unmarked)*	Exeter	1.07
N260NE	European Air Transport-DHL	Lasham	11.08
N97891	*(Stored: acquired false marks "N9748C" for film 6.06)*		
N932FT	European Air Transport-DHL	Lasham	10.08
(N526FE), N932FT, N1958		*(Stored)*	
D-EIII (2)	RLM Aviation *(Current status unknown)*	Fairoaks	8.05
Spanish. AF		*(Stored)*	
OO-HGB	N Foden	Broughton	12.07
	(Converted to flight simulator)		
90+93	Not known	Draycott Farm, Chiseldon	5.07
AC+470, JC+394, AS+428		*(Stored dismantled)*	
G-BMHB	R W H Watson	Blackpool	12.05
D6-PAD, N81321, N9593N	*(Damaged Southend 20.10.90 : wreck stored:)*		
G-BAOK	R W H Watson	Grimmet Farm, Maybole	7.05
	(Fuselage stored) (Current status unknown)		
N346US	Air Salvage International	Lasham	6.07
N325P	*(Fuselage stored)*		
F-BUMG	Department of Engineering, Salford University	Salford	8.03
	(Used as instructional airframe)		
	Euro Shadow NV *(Current status unknown)*	Old Sarum	1.06
SE-GPM	Company Flight K/S	East Midlands	1.09
ZS-NWV	COWI Air Services	Gloucestershire	9.08
G-BFDN, N59899			
N2968L	M Hales	Fairoaks	1.09
LN-LJY	U Odlund *(N453BG reserved)*	Old Buckenham	1.09
N17013	P and C Bak	Alderney	1.07
LN-EAP	J Hansen	Croft Farm, Defford	7.08
CS-HCI	Biggin Hill Helicopters	Biggin Hill	6.07
G-ONTA	*(Cabin in outside storage)*		
C-FCPH	Graff Aviation Ltd	Luton	12.08
G-BITX	Wolds Gliding Club	Pocklington	7.08
G-14-3069	*(Fuselage used as mobile briefing room)*		
N51DA	R S van Dijk	Little Gransden	2.08
	Q Aviation Ltd	(Leominster)	8.08
	A V Grant	(Waterford)	7.08
SE-KRC	S J Beaty	Wold Lodge, Finedon	9.08
N61790			
OY-DCG	Not known	Water Leisure Park, Skegness	8.08
	(Wreck stored for spares)		
SE-CKW, N10F	D C Ratcliffe *(Current status unknown)*	Shoreham	6.05
G-EPIM	A H Creaser	(Heckington, Lincs)	1.09
PH-PIM, N736AQ			
	W Moore	Membury	7.08
N2314D	A Breslin	Kilrush	11.08
	A G W Davis	Shipdham	7.06
	Helicon BV *(For sale)*	Shobdon	12.08
OO-AON	M L B Warriner	Trevethoe Farm, Lelant	10.07
F-GACN			
	R Simpson	(Longhope, Gloucestershire)	7.06
	O C D Masters	Kilrush	11.08
LX-HEC	Not known	Blackbushe	1.09
F-WQPX			
VP-CMM	ATC (Lasham)	Southend	2.09
VR-CMM, N841MM, N728JE, N72700, N9234Z, D-ABIM *(Stored with no markings)*			
LY-AIG	Not known	Haverfordwest	7.07
Ukraine AF 23 (yellow)		(Spares use)	
DOSAAF 03	Not known *"03"*	Wolverhampton	12.08
I-SKIP	J Askew	Wickenby	4.08
RA-44528			
I-DEKO	Castle Helicopters	Liskeard Heliport	3.07
N9047C	*(Stored)*		
9G-LCA	Transglobal Airways Corporation	Bournemouth	1.09
(P4-GUP), 4K-GUP, EI-BND, N447T			
N59085	V S Norman *(Team Guinot)*	Rendcomb	8.08
BuA07524			
DT989	ARCO *(Under restoration)*	Duxford	4.08
	G Nichols	Phoenix Farm, Lower Upham	1.09
	Not known *(In open store)*	Little Staughton	12.07
	Not known *(Stored)*	Earls Colne	4.06

SE-IIV	Piper PA-24-260 Comanche C	24-4970	HB-OHZ	Not known	Gamston	6.08
			N9462P			
SE-KBU	Christen A-1 Husky	1038		A Allan	Lochearnhead	8.06
SE-LTE	Cessna P337H Pressurized Skymaster		N73S	Not known	Sleap	1.09
		P337-0352	N6MQ			
SE-UCF	Slingsby T.61F Venture	1983	ZA664	Goteborgs Segelflygklubb	Shenington	8.08

POLAND

SP-CHD*	PZL-101A Gawron	74134		(T Wood) (Stored in container)	North Weald	5.07

SUDAN

ST-AHZ	Piper PA-31 Turbo Navajo	31-473	G-AXMR	Not known	Elstree	8.04
			N6558L	(Fire practice use: burnt-out fuselage noted)		

GREECE

SX-BFM*	Piper PA-31-350 Chieftain	31-8052204	N4504J	Not known	(St Leonards, Ringwood)	3.07
				(Fuselage stored unmarked and derelict)		
SX-BNL*	Embraer EMB.110P2 Bandeirante	110224	N614KC	Not known	Kemble	7.07
			PT-GMQ	(EuroAir titles) (Fire dump as "G-FIRE")		
SX-HCF	Agusta A109A-II	7207	N71PT	Castle Air Charters Ltd	Liskeard Heliport	4.08
			N4263A	(Cabin stored)		
SX-122*	Glasflügel H303 Mosquito	94		Skycraft (Crashed 8. 6.79: stored)	Spalding	6.05
				(Current status unknown)		

SLOVENIA

S5-HPC*	Agusta A109A	7129	SL-HPC	Castle Helicopters	Liskeard Heliport	4.08
			YU-HBN	(Slovenian Police titles) (Stored)		

TURKEY

TC-ALM*	Boeing 727-230	20431	TC-IKO	Fire Services	East Midlands	12.07
			TC-JUH, TC-ALB, N878UM, D-ABDI	(Used as trainer)		
TC-MBG	Fokker F.27 Friendship 600	10459	G-CEXG	MNG	Edinburgh	11.08
			G-JEAP, 9Q-CBI, OY-APF, 9Q-CBI, PH-RUA, VH-EWR			
				(Fuselage stored following ground collision 1.2.08)		

ICELAND

TF-ELL	Boeing 737-210C	20138	N41026	Ardennes Epsilon Ltd	Southend	2.09
			F-GGFI, N4906	(ATA Brasil c/s: was to become PR-CMA)		

AUSTRALIA

VH-AHL*	Hawker Siddeley HS.748 Series 2/228	1606	A10-606	Clewer Aviation (In open store)	Southend	2.09
VH-AMQ*	Hawker Siddeley HS.748 Series 2/228	1603	A10-603	Clewer Aviation "Wg.Cdr.Grant 'Bing' Kelly"		
				(In open store)	Southend	2.09
VH-AYS*	Hawker Siddeley HS.748 Series 2/228	1608	A10-608	Clewer Aviation (In open store)	Southend	2.09
VH-IJH	Super Marine Spitfire Mk26	036		I Hutchison	Perth	12.08
VH-PSR	Agusta A119 Koala	14037		Silver Rook Ltd	(Douglas, Isle of Man)	6.07

BERMUDA (Current series)

VP-BAM	Bombardier BD-700 Global 5000	9157	C-FBQD	Theberton Inc	London Stansted	12.08
VP-BAT	Boeing 747SP-21	21648	VR-BAT	Worldwide Aircraft Holding (Bermuda)	Bournemouth	12.08
			N148UA, N539PA			
VP-BBW	Boeing 737-7BJ	30076	N737BF	Altitude 41 Ltd	Farnborough and Moscow	12.08
			P4-CZT, VP-CZT, N737MC, D-AXXL, N374MC, N1784B, N1786B			
				(Operated GAMA Aviation)		
VP-BBX	Gulfstream Aerospace Gulfstream V-SP	622	N806AC	Altitude 50 Ltd	Farnborough and Moscow	1.09
	(Gulfstream 550)		N304K, N622GA	(Operated GAMA Aviation)		
VP-BBZ	Bombardier Learjet 60	60-328	N5000E	GAMA Aviation	Farnborough	8.08
VP-BCC	Bombardier CL-600-2B19	7717	C-GZSQ	CCC (Bermuda) Inc	Farnborough and Athens	12.08
	(CL-600 Regional Jet)		C-FMNX			
VP-BCL	Bombardier CL-600-2C10	10247	N710TS	Global Jet Charters	Farnborough and Athens	2.09
	(CRJ-700 Regional Jet)		C-FHMG	(Operated Consolidated Contracters)		
VP-BCT	Rockwell 695B Turbo Commander	96208	N695BE	Control Techniques (Bermuda) Ltd	Welshpool	8.08
			VH-PJC, VH-LTM, N230GA			
VP-BDL	Dassault Falcon 2000	111	F-WWVF	Sioux Corporation	Luton	11.08
VP-BGN	Gulfstream Aerospace Gulfstream V-SP	5011	N991GA	Rockfield Holdings	Luton	11.08
	(Gulfstream 550)		(N522QS)			
VP-BJA	Bombardier CL-600-2B19	5639	C-FGYI	Jetsteff Aviation	Biggin Hill	1.09
	(CL-604 Challenger)					
VP-BJK	Gulfstream Aerospace Gulfstream V-SP	5200	N990GA	AC Executive Aircraft Bermuda Ltd	Dublin	1.09
	(Gulfstream 550)					
VP-BKI	Gulfstream Aerospace Gulfstream IVSP	1255	N934DF	Picton Ltd (Operated GAMA Aviation)		
			VP-BNN, N600PM, N437GA		Farnborough and Moscow	2.09
VP-BKK	Hawker Siddeley HS.125 Series.400A/731		VR-BKK	Jetsteff Aviation	Bournemouth	12.08
		25238	N808V, N125GC, G-TOPF, G-AYER, 9K-ACR, G-AYER			
VP-BKQ	Bell 430	49008	N62833	Arkesden Aviation	Blackbushe	11.08
VP-BKZ	Gulfstream Aerospace Gulfstream V	602	N602GV	Dennis Vanguard International (Switchgear)		
			N538GA		Birmingham	2.09
VP-BLA	Gulfstream Aerospace Gulfstream V-SP	5024	N924GA	ISPAT Aviation	Luton	2.09
	(Gulfstream 550)					
VP-BLS	Pilatus PC-XII	176	N176BS	B.L.Schroeder	Fairoaks	1.09
			VP-BLS, HB-FSL			
VP-BLW	Gulfstream Aerospace Gulfstream V-SP	5129	N529GA	Specialised Transportation Bermuda Ltd	Biggin Hill	12.08
	(Gulfstream 550)					

Reg	Type	Serial
VP-BMP	Dassault Falcon 50EX	345
VP-BMZ	Rockwell Turbo Commander 690D	15033
	(Built Gulfstream Aerospace)	
VP-BNI	Sikorsky S76C	760506
VP-BNK	Hawker 800XP	258625
VP-BNL	Gulfstream Aerospace Gulfstream V	607
VP-BNM	Sikorsky S-76B	760333
VP-BNO	Gulfstream Aerospace Gulfstream V-SP	5050
	(Gulfstream 550)	
VP-BNZ	Boeing 737-7HD	35959
VP-BOO	Hawker 800XP	258477
VP-BOW	Bombardier BD-700 Global Express	9141
VP-BPS*	Consolidated 28-5ACF (PBY-5A) Catalina	1997
VP-BTC	Gulfstream Aerospace Gulfstream V-SP	5176
	(Gulfstream 550)	
VP-BUS	Gulfstream Aerospace Gulfstream IV	1127
VP-BVS	Embraer EMB.135BJ Legacy	14500979
VP-BWR	Boeing 737-79T	29317
VP-BZE	Dassault Falcon 7X	14

CAYMAN ISLANDS

Reg	Type	Serial
VP-CAP	Bombardier CL-600-2B19	5415
	(CL-604 Challenger)	
VP-CBD	Sikorsky S76C	760514
VP-CBG	North American Rockwell Sabre 65	465-33
VP-CBX	Gulfstream Aerospace Gulfstream V	511
VP-CBY	Airbus A320-212	0313
VP-CEB	Bombardier BD.700 Global Express	9083
VP-CED	Cessna 550 Citation Bravo	550-0870
VP-CEO	Bombardier CL-600-2B19	5539
	(CL-604 Challenger)	
VP-CFB	Gulfstream Aerospace Gulfstream G450	4137
VP-CFS	Hawker 800XP	258582
VP-CFT	Bombardier CL-600-2B16	5067
	(CL-601-3A Challenger)	
VP-CGN	Gulfstream Aerospace Gulfstream V-SP	5149
	(Gulfstream 550)	
VP-CGS	Bombardier BD-700 Global Express	9102
VP-CHH	Bombardier CL-600-2B16	5716
	(CL-605 Challenger)	
VP-CHU	Bombardier CL-600-2B19	5510
	(CL-604 Challenger)	
VP-CIC	Bombardier CL-600-2B16	5011
	(CL-601-3A Challenger)	
VP-CJI	Cessna 525 CitationJet	525-0526
VP-CLA	Gulfstream Aerospace Gulfstream IV	1402
VP-CLV	Bombardier BD-100 Challenger 300	20041
VP-CMR	Gulfstream Aerospace Gulfstream IV	1117
VP-COD	Hawker 850XP	258816
VP-COK	British Aerospace BAe125 -700A	257028
VP-COM	Cessna 500 Citation I	500-318
VP-COP	Bombardier CL-600-2B19	5552
	(CL-604 Challenger)	
VP-CRB	Bombardier Learjet 60	60-125
VP-CSF	Gulfstream Aerospace Gulfstream IV	1390
VP-CSP	British Aerospace BAe 125 Series 800B	258210
VP-CVU	Bombardier BD-700 Global 5000	9257
VP-CVV	Bombardier BD-700 Global Express XRS	9272
VP-CXP	Hawker 800XPi	258728

Reg	Operator	Location	Date
F-WWHA	Tower House Consultants Ltd		
		Jersey and Southampton	10.08
VR-BMZ	Aviatica Trading Co Ltd - Marlborough Fine Art Ltd		
G-MFAL, N49GA, (N5925N)		Fairoaks	12.08
N7686S	Not known	(Weybridge)	1.09
TC-HRT, N728TP			
N305JA	Nebula III Ltd	Farnborough and Moscow	6.07
N625XP	*(Operated GAMA Aviation)*		
N303K	Nebula Ltd	Farnborough	9.08
N559GA	*(Operated GAMA Aviation)*		
N595JS	Nebula II Ltd	Blackbushe	6.08
N595ST, N5AY			
N950GA	Cloud Air Services	Farnborough	5.08
	Dennis Vanguard International (Switchgear)		
		Birmingham	7.08
OE-GEO	Not known	Bournemouth	1.09
N44767			
C-GAGS	Express Aviation	Luton	1.09
VR-BPS	PS (Bermuda) Ltd	Weston, Dublin	11.08
G-BLSC, C-FMIR, N608FF, CF-MIR, N10023, Bu.46633 *(Stored)*			
N476GA	Altaviation Ltd	Farnborough	12.08
VR-BUS	A E C International Ltd	Farnborough	2.09
VR-BLR, N427GA	*(Op U Schwarzenbach)*		
	Not known	Luton	2.09
N1787B	Bel Air Ltd	London Stansted	12.08
F-WWUK	Flying Lion/Stork Ltd	Luton	1.09
N318FX	Thunder Air	Farnborough	1.09
C-GLWT			
N764PB	Not known	Fairoaks	12.08
N265C	Not known	Dublin	10.08
N465SR, (N271MB), (N869EG), N869KC, N994			
N511GA	Aravco	Farnborough	1.09
TC-OAC	Not known *(Stored)*	Southend	2.09
TC-ABG, A6-EGD, A4O-EA, F-WWIZ			
C-GKLF	Silver Arrows SA	Luton	2.09
N700AU, C-GHYT			
N50612	Myair	Manchester	2.09
VP-BDY	Not known	Farnborough	2.09
PP-BIA, N539AB, C-GLXK			
N337GA	Meral Holdings	Farnborough	12.08
XA-JMS	Not known	Farnborough	12.08
(N170SK), N50182			
HB-IUF	Not known	(Manchester)	1.09
N220TW, 9A-CRT, 9A-CRO, N603CC, C-GLXF			
N649GA	Adams Trust Appointed Fund/Millican Trustees SARL		
		Luton	12.08
HB-IGS	PJS – Jet Aviation Business Jets	Farnborough	2.09
N700CY, C-GIXM			
N605JM	Aviamax Aviation	Farnborough	1.09
C-FNIN, C-GLYA			
N610SA	Avijet Ltd	Farnborough	2.08
B-7696, N511SC, C-GLWV			
VR-CIC	TGC Aviation Ltd - Fakhar Ltd	Farnborough	2.09
N602UK, N611MH, JA8283, N603CC, C-GLXD			
SP-KCL	Not known	Biggin Hill	12.08
N526LC			
N602PL	International Jet Club	Farnborough	1.09
N602PM, N479GA			
N141LJ	Czar Aviation	London Stansted	1.09
C-GZED			
N105BH	Fitzwilton PLC	Luton	2.09
G-HARF, N1761J			
(N850ZH)	Iceland Foods Ltd	Hawarden	1.09
N74166			
N899DM	Joli Ltd	Farnborough	2.09
N7728, N603GY, N700TL, G-5-534, G-BFSO			
VR-COM	Rapid 3864 Ltd	Biggin Hill	2.09
N944B, N518CC, N5318J			
N552TS	Not known	Farnborough	4.08
ZS-ALT, N552CC, C-GLWR			
N60LR	Lisane Ltd *"La Petite Souris"*	Guernsey	11.08
N1874M	MSF Aviation	Luton	1.09
N490GA			
HB-VMI	Not known	Hawarden	4.08
G-RAAR, G-5-705			
C-FMLT	Global Jet Concept	Luton	2.09
C-FNSV	Global Jet Luxemburg	Luton	1.09
N110DD	Scottish & Newcastle Breweries PLC	Hawarden	1.09
N728XP			

BERMUDA (Old series)

VR-BEB*	British Aircraft Corporation One-Eleven 527FK		RP-C1181	European Aviation Ltd	Bournemouth	1.09
		BAC.226	PI-C1181	*(Fire Compound - all white and no marks)*		

INDIA

VT-EKE *	Westland WG.30-160	021	G-BLPR	Turbine World	Honeycrock Farm, Redhill	12.07
			G-17-17			
VT-EKK *	Westland WG.30-160	025	G-17-13	Turbine World	Honeycrock Farm, Redhill	
VT-EKL *	Westland WG.30-160	028	G-17-14	Turbine World	Honeycrock Farm, Redhill	
VT-EKM *	Westland WG.30-160	027	G-17-15	Turbine World	Honeycrock Farm, Redhill	
VT-EKT *	Westland WG.30-160	035	G-17-23	Turbine World	Honeycrock Farm, Redhill	
VT-EKW *	Westland WG.30-160	038	G-17-26	Turbine World	Honeycrock Farm, Redhill	
VT-EKX *	Westland WG.30-160	039	G-17-27	Turbine World	Honeycrock Farm, Redhill	
	("Nine" WG.30s reported as "under secure lock and key" 12.07 but not sighted - probably including VT-EKK to VT-EKX reported earlier)					
VT-UBG	Hawker Siddeley HS.125 Series F400B	25254	G-5-624	United Breweries (Holdings) Ltd	Hawarden	1.09
			VT-UBG, G-VJAY, G-5-624, G-AYLG, 3D-AVL, G-AYLG *(Stored stripped)*			

MEXICO

XB-RIY	Boeing- Stearman N2S-3 Kaydet	75-7275	N52093	Not known *(Current status unknown)*	Rendcomb	4.04
			BuA 07671	*(Stored - composite)*		

LATVIA

YL-LEU*	WSK-PZL Antonov An-2R	1G-165-45	CCCP19731	Hawarden Air Services	Hawarden	10.07
			SP-ZFP, CCCP19731	*(As "CCCP-19731") (Dismantled)*		
YL-LEV*	WSK-PZL Antonov An-2R	1G-148-29	CCCP07268	Hawarden Air Services	Hawarden	10.07
				(As "CCCP07268")		
YL-LEW*	WSK-PZL Antonov An-2R	1G-182-28	CCCP56471	Hawarden Air Services	Hawarden	10.07
				(As "CCCP56471")		
YL-LEX*	WSK-PZL Antonov An-2R	1G-187-58	CCCP54949	Hawarden Air Services	Hawarden	10.07
				(As "CCCP54949")		
YL-LEY*	WSK-PZL Antonov An-2R	1G-173-11	CCCP40784	Hawarden Air Services	Hawarden	10.07
				(As "CCCP40784")		
YL-LEZ*	WSK-PZL Antonov An-2R	1G-165-47	CCCP19733	Hawarden Air Services	Hawarden	5.08
				(As "CCCP19733")		
YL-LFA*	WSK-PZL Antonov An-2R	1G-172-20	CCCP40748	Hawarden Air Services	Hawarden	10.07
				(As "CCCP40748")		
YL-LFB*	WSK-PZL Antonov An-2R	1G-173-12	CCCP40785	Hawarden Air Services	Hawarden	10.07
				(As "CCCP40785")		
YL-LFC*	WSK-PZL Antonov An-2R	1G-206-44	CCCP17939	Hawarden Air Services	Hawarden	10.07
				(As "CCCP17939")		
YL-LFD*	WSK-PZL Antonov An-2R	1G-172-21	CCCP40749	Hawarden Air Services	Hawarden	10.07
				(As "CCCP40749")		
YL-LHN*	Mil Mi-2	524006025	CCCP20320	Hawarden Air Services	Hawarden	10.07
				(As "CCCP20320")		
YL-LHO*	Mil Mi-2	535025126	CCCP20619	Hawarden Air Services	Hawarden	10.07
				(As "CCCP20619")		
YL-MIG*	Aviatika MAI-890	037		Hawarden Air Services *("37 yellow")*	Hawarden	11.08
YL-PAF*	Aero Vodochody L-29S Delfin	591771	Soviet AF 18 red	Hawarden Air Services	Hawarden	10.07
				(Stored dismantled)		
YL-PAG*	Aero Vodochody L-29 Delfin	491273	Soviet AF 51 red	Not known *(Stored unmarked)*	Breighton	12.08

SERBIA and MONTENEGRO

YU-DLG	UTVA 66	0812 ?	JRV51109	Shuttle Air	Biggin Hill	6.08
YU-FCS	Cessna 550 Citation II	550-0321	VP-CCO	Not known	Biggin Hill	12.08
			N321GN, TC-COY, N321SE, N5430G			
YU-HDL	Soko/Aérospatiale SA.341G Gazelle	031	JRV12804	Not known	Weston, Dublin	9.08
YU-HEH	Soko Aérospatiale SA.341G Gazelle	011	JRV12619	Kestrel Shipping	(Bickerstaffe)	5.08
YU-HEI	Soko Aérospatiale SA.341G Gazelle	012	JRV12620	Not known *(Honister.com titles)*	(Mosser, Cumbria)	10.07
YU-HES	Aérospatiale SA.342J Gazelle	1057	F-GOSO	Not known	(Brookmans Park)	12.08
			EC-EQU, C-GEJE, (N341NA), N9042U, C-FGCE, CF-GCE			
YU-HET	Aérospatiale SA.342 Gazelle	1204	F-GFDG	Not known	Darwen	10.08
			TG-KOV			
YU-HEV	Aérospatiale SA.342J Gazelle	1393	F-GCCZ	Not known	(Republic of Ireland)	8.08
			(KAF-401)			
YU-HEY	Aérospatiale SA.341G Gazelle	1320	F-GEHF	Not known	Stapleford	4.08
			N905XX, N905X, N49508			
YU-MAN	Aérospatiale SA.341G Gazelle	1277	G-WMAN	J Wightman	(Ballyclare, County Antrim)	9.07
			ZS-HUR, N4491L, YV-54CP			
YU-PJB	Aérospatiale SA.341G Gazelle	1392	G-BZLA	P J Brown	Redhill	10.08
			N2TV, N49534			
YU-YAB	SOKO G-2A Galeb	Not known	JRV23170	Shuttle Air	Biggin Hill	5.07

NEW ZEALAND

ZK-BMI*	Auster B.8 Agricola Series 1	B.101	(G-ANYG)	D.J.Baker	Carr Farm, Thorney, Newark	1.05
			G-25-3	*(Rear fuselage frame - new fin constructed 2004)*		
ZK-CCU*	Auster B.8 Agricola	B.105	ZK-BMM	D J Baker	Carr Farm, Thorney, Newark	1.05
	(Composite rebuild by Airepair as c/n AIRP/850 after crash)			*(Centre section stored in container)*		
ZK-GIL	Schempp Hirth Discus 2a	41		B J Flewett *"2a"*	Wycombe Air Park	8.08
ZK-IGM	Eurocopter EC.130B4	3770		North Shore Helicopters Ltd	Redhill	11.08
ZK-JQK	Pacific Aerospace PAC 750XL	118		Pacific Aerospace Corporation	Hinton in the Hedges	9.08
				(Operated Hinton Skydiving Centre)		
ZK-KAY	Pacific Aerospace PAC 750XL	107		Pacific Aerospace Corporation	Cark	1.09
				(Operated North West Parachute Centre)		

| ZK-PCI | Pilatus PC-6/B1-H2 | 523 | HB-FBA | | Highland Air Ltd *(Operated Skydive)* | Grindale | 9.08 |
| | | | | | *(Noted road running 22.9.08 Hessel)* | | |

REPUBLIC of SOUTH AFRICA

ZS-MBI	Rockwell Commander 114	14361			F W A Engelbrecht	Oxford	1.09
ZS-MRU*	Douglas DC-3	4363	N234Z		Nationwide Charter Pty Ltd	Dunsfold	8.08
			HZ-TA3, N234Z, N1699M, N69D, N1699M, BuAe4703 *(Canx 1.08)*				
					"Spirit of Adventure" (Reserved as TF-AVN)		
ZS-ODJ	Hawker Siddeley HS.748 Series 2A/263				See G-BPNJ - details in SECTION 1, Part 2		
						Blackpool	
ZU-DCX *	Chayair Sycamore Mk 1	SYCA0043			Not known	Kilrush	2.08

NIGERIA

5N-AAN*	British Aerospace BAe 125 Series.F3B/RA		F-GFMP		Newcastle Aviation Academy	Newcastle	11.07
		25125	G-AVAI, LN-NPA, G-AVAI		*(For instructional use)*		
5N BET	Aérospatiale AS365N Dauphin 2	6087	TJ-DEM		Not known	*(Longside, Peterhead)*	10.07
			5N-ATP, PH-SSR, F-ODQG, F-WXFB *(Stored)*				
5N-BGV	Grumman G-1159 Gulfstream II	177	5N-AGV		Federal Republic of Nigeria *(Stored)*	Luton	1.09
			N17587				
5N-HHH*	British Aircraft Corporation One-Eleven 401AK		HZ-NB2		Airport Fire Service	Southend	2.09
		BAC.064	N5024		*(For rescue training as "G-FIRE")*		

GHANA

9G-BOB	Westland Wessex HC.2	WA/624	G-HANA		Not known	Honeycrock Farm,Redhill	12.07
			XV729		*(Africa Gateway titles)*		
9G-MKA	Douglas DC-8F-55	45804	N855BC		MK Airlines	Manston	1.09
			CX-BLN, C-GMXP, N855BC, HP-927, PH-DCZ, OY-KTC *(Stored)*				
9G-MKH	Douglas DC-8-62AF	46153	TF-MKH		MK Airlines	Filton	6.08
			N735PL, JA8052		*(Stored)*		

ZAMBIA

| 9J-RBC | Piper PA-28-140 Cherokee | 28-20693 | N11C | | N Livni | North Weald | 7.08 |
| | | | N6602W | | *"Namakau"* | | |

SIERRA LEONE

9L-LSA	Sud Aviation SA330L Puma	1506	Chilean Army H261		Not known	Not known	8.06
					"301" (Road running SW at Horsham 14.8.06)		
9L-LSG	Sud Aviation SA330F Puma	1242	Chilean Army H259		Parkhouse Aviation ?	Not known	10.08
					(Road running M40(S) 1.10.08)		

MALAYSIA

| 9M-BCR | Dassault Falcon 20C | 35 | N809P | | Everett Aero | Sproughton | 3.06 |
| | | | (N1777R), N809F, F-WMKG | | | | |

PART 2 – OVERSEAS CIVIL REGISTERED AIRCRAFT LOCATED IN MUSEUMS & PRIVATE COLLECTIONS.

Registration Type		Construction No	Previous IdentityOwner(Operator)		Location

MUSCAT and OMAN

A40-AB	Vickers VC-10 Series 1103			See G-ASIX - details in SECTION 4, Part 1	
					Brooklands

CANADA

CF-BXO	Vickers-Supermarine 304 Stranraer	CV-209	RCAF 920	RAF Museum *(As "920:QN-" in RCAF c/s)*	Hendon
CF-EPV	Aviation Traders ATL.98 Carvair	10448/8	EI-AMR	56th Fighter Group Museum	Halesworth
			N88819, 42-72343	*(Cockpit section only)*	
CF-EQS	Boeing-Stearman A75N1 (PT-17-BW) Kaydet		75-1728	American Air Museum	Duxford
		41-8169		*(As "217786:25" in USAAF c/s)*	
CF-KCG	Grumman TBM-3E Avenger AS.3	2066	RCN326	American Air Museum	Duxford
			Bu.69327	*(As "46214::X-3" in USN c/s)*	
C-GYZI	Cameron O-77 Balloon (Hot Air)	269		Balloon Preservation Group *"Aeolus"*	Petworth

GERMANY

D-CATA	Hawker Sea Fury T.20S	ES.8503	D-FATA	Royal Naval Historic Flight	RNAS Yeovilton
			G-9-30, VZ345	*(As "VZ345": crashed 19.4.85 and stored)(For sale)*	
D-HMQV	Bolkow Bö.102 Helitrainer		6216	The Helicopter Museum	Weston-super-Mare
				(Development aircraft)	
D-HOAY	Kamov Ka.26	7001309	DDR-SPY	The Helicopter Museum	Weston-super-Mare
			DM-SPY	*(As "DDR-SPY")*	
D-HZYR	Bölkow Bö.105M	5100	81+00	The Helicopter Museum	Weston-super-Mare
D-IFSB	de Havilland DH.104 Dove 6			See G-AMXR - details in SECTION 4, Part 1	
					Salisbury Hall, London Colney
D-Opha	Fire Balloons 3000 Balloon (Hot Air)	057	D-TALCID	Balloon Preservation Group *"Talcid"*	Petworth
D-Pamgas	Cameron N-90 Balloon (Hot Air)	1288		Balloon Preservation Group *"Pamgas"*	Petworth
DDR-SPY	Kamov Ka.26			See D-HOAY above	Weston-super-Mare

FRANCE

F-BDRS	Boeing B-17G-95DL Flying Fortress	--	N68269	American Air Museum *"Mary Alice"*	Duxford
			32376, NL68269, 44-83735(As "231983:IY-G" in 401st BG/615th BS USAAF c/s)		
F-BGEQ	de Havilland DH.82A Tiger Moth	86305	French AF	Brooklands Museum	Denford Manor, Hungerford
			NL846	*(Stored two-thirds restored)*	
F-BGNR	Vickers 708 Viscount	35	(OY-AFO)	Midland Air Museum	Coventry
			(OY-AFN), F-BGNR		
F-BGNX	de Havilland DH.106 Comet 1XB			See G-AOJT - details in SECTION 4, Part 1	
					Salisbury Hall, London Colney
F-BTGV	Aero Spacelines 377SGT Super Guppy	201001	N211AS	British Aviation Heritage-Cold War Jets Collection	
				(As "1")	Bruntingthorpe
F-BTRP	Sud-Aviation SA.321F Super Frelon	01	F-WMHC	The Helicopter Museum	Weston-super-Mare
	(Converted from SA.321 c/n 116)		F-BTRP, F-WKQC, F-OCZV, F-RAFR, F-OCMF, F-BMHC, F-WMHC		
				(As "F-OCMF" in Olympic Airways c/s)	
F-WGGM	Thunder & Colt AS-261 HA Airship			See G-BPLD - details in SECTION 1, Part 3 Newbury	
F-WQAP	Aérospatiale SA365N Dauphin 2	6001	F-WZJJ	The Helicopter Museum	Weston-super-Mare
F-HMFI	Farman F.40	6799	9204M	RAF Museum	RAF Cosford
	(Modified to F141 Status)			*(At Conservation Centre: no markings)*	

SWITZERLAND

HB-BOU	Brighton MAB-65 Balloon (Hot Air)			See G-AWJB - details in SECTION 1 Part 3 Newbury	
HB-NAV	Beagle B.121 Pup Series 150			See G-AZCM - details in SECTION 4, Part 1 Dover	

NORWAY

LN-BNM	Noorduyn AT-16-ND Harvard IIB	14-639	31-329	RAF Museum	Hendon
			R.Dan AF, FE905, 42-12392	*(As "FE905" in RAF/RCAF c/s)*	

ARGENTINA

LQ-BLT	MBB BÖ.105-CBS	S.863		North East Aircraft Museum	Usworth, Sunderland
	(Non-airworthy pod is original airframe which crashed 13.6.96: shipped to UK and rebuilt with airframe c/n S.915)				

UNITED STATES

N7SY	Hunting Percival P.57 Sea Prince			See G-BRFC - details in SECTION 4, Part 1	
					Bournemouth
N18E	Boeing 247D	1722	NC18E	National Museum of Science & Industry Wroughton	
			NC18, NC13340		
N46EA	Percival P.66 Pembroke C.1	P66/83	8452M	P.G.Vallance Ltd	Charlwood, Surrey
	(Regd with c/n K66-046)		XK885	*(Gatwick Aviation Museum)*	
N47DD	Republic P47D-30-RA Thunderbolt	399-55731	N47DD	Imperial War Museum Collection-American Air Museum	
			Peru AF FAP119, 45-49192 "Oregon's Britannia" (As "226413:ZU-N") Duxford		
N51RT	North American F-51D Mustang	122-40949	N555BM	R C Tullius *(Loaned to RAF Museum)*	Hendon
			YV-508CP, N555BM, N4409, N6319T, RCAF9235, 44-74409		
				"The Duck" *(As "413317:VF-B in 336FS-4th FG c/s)*	
NX71MY	Vimy 19/94 Inc Vimy FB-27	01		Brooklands Museum *(Stored)*	Meppershall
N112WG	Westland WG-30-100	012		The Helicopter Museum	Weston-super-Mare
N114WG	Westland WG-30-100			See G-EFIS - details in SECTION 4, Part 1	
					Weston-super-Mare
N118WG	Westland WG-30-100	018		The Helicopter Museum	Weston-super-Mare
N196B	North American F-86A-5-NA Sabre		48-0242	Midland Air Museum	Coventry
		151-43611		*(As "8242:FU-242" in USAF c/s)*	

Reg	Type	c/n	Prev id	Owner / Location
NC285RS	North American Navion	NAV-4-119		South East Aviation Enthusiasts Group
				"My Way" Dromod,County.Leitrim
				(Crashed 11. 6.79: cockpit section and tailplane only)
N413JB	Cameron O-84 Balloon (Hot Air)	723		Balloon Preservation Group *"Autumn Fall"* Petworth
N588NB	Polikarpov Po-2			See G-BSSY - details in SECTION 4 Part 1
				Old Warden
N2138J	English Electric Canberra TT.18		WK126	S D Picatti Gloucestershire
	(Built A V Roe & Co)	EEA/R3/EA3/6640		*(Stored: loaned to Gloucestershire Aviation Collection as "WK126:843")*
N2700	Fairchild C-119G-FA	10689	3C-ABA	Wings Museum Redhill
			Belgian AF CP-9, 51-2700	*(Nose only)*
N3188H	ERCO 415C Ercoupe	3813	NC3188H	AeroVenture Doncaster
				(Damaged c7.89: fuselage suspended from roof)
N4565L	Douglas DC-3-201A	2108	(N3TV)	Aero Venture Doncaster
			LV-GYP, LV-PCV, N129H, N512, N51D, N80C, NC21744	
N4990T	Thunder Ax7-65B Balloon (Hot Air)	123		British Balloon Museum & Library *"Stormy Weather"*
				Newbury
N5023U	Avian Magnum IX Balloon (Hot Air)	169		Balloon Preservation Group *"Tumbleweed"* Petworth
NC5171N	Lockheed 10A Electra			See details in SECTION 4, Part 1 South Kensington
N5237V	Boeing B-17G-95-DL Flying Fortress	32509	(N6466D)	RAF Museum Hendon
			N5237V, Bu.77233, 44-83868 *(As "44-83868:N" in 94th BG USAAF c/s)*	
N5419	Bristol Scout D replica	01		FAA Museum RNAS Yeovilton
	(Built Leo Opdycke 1983)			*(Frame only)*
N5820T	Westland WG-30-100			See G-BKFD - details in SECTION 4, Part 1
				Weston-super-Mare
N5840T	Westland WG-30-100			See G-BKFF - details in SECTION 4, Part 1
				Weston-super-Mare
N6526D	North American P-51D-25NA Mustang		RCAF 9289	RAF Museum *"Little Friend"* RAF Cosford
	(Composite)	122-39874	44-73415	*(As "413573:B6-K" in 361st FS-357th FG USAAF c/s)*
N6699D	Piasecki HUP-3 Retriever	51	RCN 622	Not known Weston-super-Mare
			USN/51-16622	*(Loaned to The Helicopter Museum as "622" in RCN c/s)*
N7614C	North American B-25J/PBJ-1J Mitchell		44-31171	Imperial War Museum/American Air Museum Duxford
		108-37246		*(As "31171" in US Marines c/s)*
N7777G	Lockheed L.749A-79 Constellation			See G-CONI - details in SECTION 4, Part 1
				Wroughton
N9050T	Douglas C-47A-10DK Dakota 3			See G-AGYX - details in SECTION 4, Part 1 Hendon
N9115Z	North American TB-25N-20NC Mitchell		(8838M)	RAF Museum Hendon
		108-32641	44-29366	*"Hanover Street"* and *"Catch 22"* (As "34037" in USAAF c/s)
N12006	Raven S.50A Balloon (Hot Air)	111		R Higbie *"Cheers"* Newbury
				(On loan to British Balloon Museum & Library)
N14234	Handley Page HP.137 Jetstream			See G-BBBV - details in SECTION 4, Part 1
				East Fortune
N16676	Fairchild F.24CR-C8F Argus	3101	NC16676	A Langendal *(Frame only)* Flixton
				(On loan to Norfolk & Suffolk Aviation Museum)
N33600	Cessna L-19A-CE Bird Dog	22303	51-11989	Museum of Army Flying AAC Middle Wallop
				(As "111989" in US Army c/s)
N66630	Schweizer TG-3A	63	42-52983	Imperial War Museum Duxford
			(P/i not confirmed)	*(As "252983" in USAAC c/s)*
N99153	North American T-28C Trojan	252-52	Zaire AF FG-289	W R Montague Flixton
	(FAA quote c/n 226-93)		Congo AF FA-289, Bu.146289	*(Crashed Limoges, France 14.12.77)*
				(On loan to Norfolk & Suffolk Aviation Museum: fuselage only as "146289:2W")

BELGIUM

Reg	Type	c/n	Prev id	Owner / Location
OO-BFH	Piccard Gas Balloon	xxxx		National Museum of Science & Industry Wroughton
				(Gondola only)
OO-BRM	Thunder Ax7-77 Balloon (Hot Air)	1111		Balloon Preservation Group Petworth
OO-JAT	Cameron Zero 25 Airship	1407		Balloon Preservation Group Petworth
OO-SHW	Bell 47H-1			See G-AZYB - details in SECTION 4, Part 1
				Weston-super-Mare

DENMARK

Reg	Type	c/n	Prev id	Owner / Location
OY-BOB	Omega O-80 Balloon (Hot Air)			See G-AWMO - details in SECTION 1, Part 3 Newbury
OY-BOW	Colting 77A Balloon (Hot Air)	77A-014	SE-ZVB	British Balloon Museum & Library *"Circus"* Newbury

RUSSIA

Reg	Type	c/n	Prev id	Owner / Location
RA-01378	Yakovlev Yak-52	833004	DOSAAF 14	Wellesbourne Wartime Museum
	(Composite with c/n 833805/DOSAAF 134 which is now N54GT)			Wellesbourne Mountford
RA-01641	Antonov An-2R	1G-190-47		Staffordshire Aircraft Restoration Team *"3"* Sleap
				(Crashed Milton 2.11.99: forward fuselage preserved)

SWEDEN

Reg	Type	c/n	Prev id	Owner / Location
SE-AZB	Cierva C.30A Autogiro	R3/CA.954	K4232	RAF Museum Hendon
	(Avro 671)			*(As "K4232")*

POLAND

Reg	Type	c/n	Prev id	Owner / Location
SP-SAY	Mil Mi-2	529538125		The Helicopter Museum Weston-super-Mare

GREECE

Reg	Type	c/n	Prev id	Owner / Location
SX-OAD	Boeing 747-212B	21684	9V-SQI	Cold War Jets Collection *"Olympic Flame"*
				Bruntingthorpe
				(Carried false marks "G-ASDA" 8.06 for ASDA promotion)

ICELAND

TF-ABP	Lockheed L.1011-385-100 Tristar	1045	VR-HOG	Aces High Flying Museum	(North Weald)
			N323EA	*(Nose only)(Left North Weald by 2008)*	
TF-SHC	Miles M.25 Martinet TT.1	xxxx	MS902	Museum of Berkshire Aviation	Woodley
				(Crashed 18.7.51: on rebuild with Master components)	

AUSTRALIA

VH-ALB	Vickers-Supermarine 228 Seagull V	xxxx	A2-4	RAF Museum *(As "A2-4")*	Hendon
VH-ASM	Avro 652A Anson I	72960	W2068	RAF Museum *(As "W2068::68" in RAF c/s)*	Hendon
VH-AYY	Kavanagh D-77 Balloon (Hot Air)	KB136		Balloon Preservation Group *"Carlsberg"*	Petworth
VH-BRC	Short S.24 Sandringham IV	SH.55C	N158C	Science Museum *"Beachcomber"*	Southampton
				VP-LVE, N158C, VH-BRC, ZK-AMH, JM715 *(On loan to Hall of Aviation) (Ansett c/s)*	
"VH-FDT"	de Havilland DHA.3 Drover			See G-APXX –details in SECTION 4, Part 1	Lasham
VH-SNB	de Havilland DH.84A Dragon	2002	VH-ASK	National Museums of Scotland/Museum of Flight	
			A34-13		East Fortune
VH-UQB	de Havilland DH.80A Puss Moth			See G-ABDW - details in SECTION 4, Part 1	
					East Fortune
VH-UTH	General Aircraft Monospar ST-12	ST12/36		Newark Air Museum	Winthorpe
VH-UUP	Short S.16 Scion 1			See G-ACUX - details in SECTION 4, Part 1	Belfast

BERMUDA (New series)

VP-BDF	Boeing 707-312			See G-AYAG - details in SECTION 4, Part 1	
					Dromond, County Leitrim

FALKLAND ISLANDS

VP-FAK	de Havilland Canada DHC-3 Otter	294	(VP-FAI)	de Havilland Aircraft Heritage Centre	
				(As '294')	Salisbury Hall, London Colney

BERMUDA (Old series)

VR-BEU	Westland WS-55 Whirlwind 3			See G-ATKV - details in SECTION 4, Part 1	
					Weston-super-Mare

KENYA

5Y-SIL	Cameron A-140 Balloon (Hot Air)			See G-AZUW - details in SECTION 1, Part 3 Newbury	

SENEGAL

6W-SAF	Douglas C-47A-65-DL	19074	F-GEFU	Wings Museum	Redhill
			42-100611	*(As "42-100766") "Lilly Belle" (Nose section only)*	

PART 3 – OVERSEAS-REGISTERED ENTRIES REMOVED FROM 2008 EDITION

Registration Type		C/n	Reason for removal

UNITED ARAB EMIRATES

A6-ESH	Airbus A319-133X	910	Regular visitor only
A6-HEH	Boeing 737-8AJ	32825	Regular visitor only
A6-HRS	Boeing 737-7EO	29251	Regular visitor only
A6-MRM	Boeing 737-8EC	32450	Regular visitor only

GERMANY

D-EAAH	Bölkow BÖ.209 Monsun 160RV	168	To ZK-MON 8.08
D-EBWS	Cessna T210N Turbo Centurion II	21064341	To G-EEWS 5.08
D-EGKE	SOCATA Rallye 180TS Galerien	3325	To G-EGKE 6.08
D-EIIP	Reims Cessna F182Q Skylane	F18200091	To N90DJ 2.08 – see SECTION 5 Part 1
D-EKDN	Beech A36 Bonanza	E-2353	To G-KSHI 11.08
D-EMUH	Bölkow BÖ.208C Junior	623	To Belgium by 5.08
D-EXGC	Extra EA.200	027	To G-EXGC 6.08
D-GEWU	Beech 76 Duchess	ME-398	To N741D 4.08- see SECTION 5 Part 1
D-HGBX	Enstrom F.280	1189	Pod gone from North Weald by 2008
D-KAAD	Schleicher ASG 29E	29519	To G-CKOO 5.08
D-KBJG	Schleicher ASG 29E	29512	To G-CKON 5.08
D-KEEJ	Schleicher ASG 29E	29513	To G-CKOZ 4.08
D-KGLM	Grob G.109B	6237	To G-CEVO 3.08
D-KKAM	Schleicher ASW 22BLE	22065	To G-KKAM 6.08
D-KLCC	Schleicher ASG 29E	29511	To G-VLCC 4.08
D-KNZG	Schleicher ASG 29E	29510	To G-CKOY 5.08
D-KPRA	Schleicher ASG 29E	29514	To G-XXIX 4.08
D-KPRB	Schleicher ASG 29E	29518	To G-XOAR 4.08
D-KPRC	Schleicher ASG 29E	29501	To G-CKNU 3.08
D-7429	Schleicher ASG 29	29015	To G-OASG 2.08
D-9729	Schleicher ASG 29	29024	To G-CKOE 2.08

FRANCE

F-GOZO	Mudry CAP.231	8	To G-OZZO 1.09
F-GYRO	Mudry CAP.232	25	No UK reports since 9.04 – at Dijon, France 9.06
21YV	Dyn'Aéro MCR-01	314	Crashed Highclere 11.4.08
31WI	Farrington Twinstarr Gyrocopter	TS97013	No reports since 8.06

HUNGARY

HA-ACL	Dornier Do.28D-2 Skyservant	4125	To EC-KTC 7.08
HA-JAC	Yakovlev Yak-18T	22202034139	No UK reports since 6.04. At Nogaro, France 9.08
HA-MKE	WSK-PZL Antonov An-2R	1G158-34	No reports since roaded out from Popham 4.05
HA-TVA	Scottish Aviation Bulldog Series 100 BH100/134		Returned to Hungary by 9.08
HA-YAH	Technoavia Yak-18T	18-33	To VH-YKV 7.08

SWITZERLAND

HB-ITF	Gulfstream Aerospace Gulfstream IV	1202	To G-CFOH 11.08
HB-IVR	Bombardier CL-600-2B-16	5318	To ZS-LEO 3.08

SAUDI ARABIA

HZ-AB3	Boeing 727-2U5AR	22362	Maintenance visitor only

ITALY

I-LELF	SIAI-Marchetti SF.260C	568/41-004	To Breightling Devils Aerobatic Team by 7.08
I-TERB	British Aerospace BAe.146 Series 200	E2012	Scrapped Southend 4.08
I-TERV	British Aerospace BAe.146 Series 200	E-2014	Scrapped Southend by 11.7.08

LUXEMBOURG

LX-TRE	Tecnam P2002JF Sierra	003	To D-ETRE 10.08 - see SECTION 5 Part 1

LITHUANIA

LY-AHD	Yakovlev Yak-12	30119	No reports since 12.04
LY-ALT	Yakovlev Yak-52	822704	No reports since 8.04
LY-MHC	Antonov An-2R	1G215-33	To Switzerland by 7.08

BULGARIA

LZ-TIM	British Aerospace BAe 146 Series 100	E1258	Returned to Bulgaria 5.12.08

UNITED STATES

N8UF	Agusta A109A-II	7268	Sold in Texas, USA 5.08
N8YG	Piper PA-32R-301T Saratoga II TC	3257151	To SP-KRO 5.08
N31NB	Piper PA-31 Turbo Navajo B	31-7401239	To 5T-...12.08
N37EL	SOCATA TB-20 Trinidad	378	To G-OMAO 1.09
N40EA	Bell 222A	47061	To EI-ZZZ 4.08
N43SV	Boeing-Stearman PT-13D Kaydet	75-5541	No reports since 5.04 – returned to USA?
N50VC	Cessna 525 CitationJet CJ1+	525-0609	To M-TEAM 10.08
N54EW	Britten-Norman BN-2T Islander	2145	To VH-YVH 12.08
N57MT	Cessna T303 Crusader	T30300211	To G-MILO 7.08
N59GG	Beech C90A King Air	LJ-1734	To M-GLAS 8.08

N61FM	Agusta A.109A	7197	Sold in Texas, USA 5.08
N73MW	Beech B200 Super King Air	BB-22	Crashed Kaduna, Nigeria 28.11.05
N75CY	Partenavia AP.68TP300 Spartacus	8001	To USA 2.5.08
N90BE	Mooney M.20K	25-1143	To ZS-SGR 10.08
N96MR	Cessna 525B CitationJet CJ3	525B0067	To OM-LBG 10.08
N109AB	Agusta A109E Power	11015	To F-GXDF 5.08
N109NL	Agusta A109A-II	7415	Sold in Texas, USA 5.08
N121HT	Cirrus Design SR22	0794	To Teuge, Netherlands by 3.08
N122SM	Cessna 525A CitationJet CJ2	525A-0151	To D-ISCO 3.08
N123NN	Piper PA-34-220T Seneca V	3449273	To G-SAAL 9.08
N125MM	Rockwell Turbo Commander 690C	11605	Sold in Texas, USA 10.08
N177MA	Piper PA-46-350P Malibu Mirage	4622177	No UK reports since 7.04 – seen mainland Europe 2006/7
N184CD	Cirrus Design SR20	1087	To G-JOEW 10.08
N208NJ	Cessna 208B Grand Caravan	208B1051	To Lanseria, RSA by 9.08
N212MZ	Mooney M.20F	22-1332	Sold in France 6.08
N218Y	Cessna 310Q	310Q0507	To Ostend, Belgium 27.10.06
N250TP	Beech A36TP Bonanza	E-2408	Wreck at Dodson's, Rantoul KS by 10.07
N252JP	Hughes 369E	0346E	To D-HHHM 3.08
N295S	Piper PA-46-350P Malibu Mirage	4636174	To USA by 1.08
N297SR	Cirrus Design SR22-GTS	2058	To D-ETRM 10.08
N380CA	Piper PA-32R-301T Saratoga IITC	3257080	No UK reports since 6.05 – possibly to Switzerland
N382RW*	Vickers-Supermarine 361 Spitfire LFXVIe		
		CBAF.IX4640	To G-PBIX 10.08
N399BH	Sikorsky S.76B	760311	Crashed Bettystown, Co Meath 18.9.08
N409SA	Reims Cessna FR182 Skylane RG		
		FR18200046	To M-GOLF 4.08
N449J (1)	Agusta A109E Power	11056	To G-BZEI 11.08
N456MS	Bombardier BD-700 Global 5000	9149	To VT-BAJ 12.08
N468DB	Beech G58 Baron	TH-2161	Sold in Virginia USA 3.08
N477KA	Bell 407	53579	To Sabadell, Spain by 12.06
N485LT	Hawker 800XP	258485	To N125XP 11.08 – see SECTION 5 Part 1
N501DW	Mudry CAP.10B	194	To G-OIOB 1.08
N502TC	Piper PA-30 Twin Comanche	30-881	No reports since11.03
N517TS	Agusta A109E Power	11057	To Brasil 8.08
N520DR	Cirrus Design SR20	1491	To F-GZPN 11.08
N550PD	Cessna 550 Citation Bravo	550-0995	To 5Y-SIR 10.08
N588CD	Cirrus Design SR22-GTS	1758	To N95GT – see SECTION 5 Part 1
N590CD	Cirrus Design SR22-G2	0957	Sold in Florida, USA 12.08
N629RS	Piper PA-44-180T Turbo Seminole		
		44-8207005	To M-MUFC 6.08
N638DB	Piper PA-46-350P Malibu Mirage	4636248	To Innsbruck, Austria by 9.08
N652NR	Cessna 560 Citation Encore	560-0652	To YR-ELV 9.08
N660WB	Pilatus PC-12/47	760	Sold in USA 10.08
N669MM	Bellanca 8KCAB-180 Super Decathlon	825-99	To G-OCOK 6.08
N680GG	Cessna 680 Sovereign	680-0104	Traded in to Cessna 6.08
N686RH	Bell 407	53714	Sold in Kentucky, USA 8.08
N702SR	Cirrus Design SR22-GTS	2198	Crashed near Liege, Belgium 17.12.08
N735BZ	Cessna 182Q Skylane	18265307	Returned to Texas, USA by 8.06
N775SB	Bell 407	53705	To N409TD10.08
N800C	Cirrus Design SR22	0367	To G-MAKS 5.08
N808NC	Gulfstream 695B Commander 1200	96085	To Canada by 6.08
N846MA	Cessna 560 Citation V	560-0046	Sold in Maine, USA 10.08
N898US	Fokker F.28-0100	11398	To VH-NHF 6.08
N900NS	Dassault Falcon 900EASy	150	To G-SABI 9.08
N909PS	Cessna 501 Citation I/SP	501-0008	Returned to USA 2.10.08
N951SF	Beech 56TC Baron	TG-83	To 5H-…8.08
N956CD	Cirrus Design SR22	1844	To Groningen- Eelde, Netherlands by 10.08
N983AJ	Beech B200 Super King Air	BB-983	To G-JASS 6.08
N1835W	Beech 95-B55 Baron	TC-1513	To I-…. 6.08
N2480X	Piper PA-31T1 Cheyenne I	31T-8104026	Sold in Texas, USA 3.08
N2500	Beech D.18S	A-558	To Australia 10.08
N3044B	Piper PA-34-200T Seneca II	34-7970012	Sold in Spain 9.08
N3103L	Beech 200 Super King Air	BB-1933	To M-EGGA 5.08
N5113S	Cessna 750 Citation X	750-0013	To LV-… 6.08
N5320N	Piper PA-46-500TP Malibu Meridian	4697153	Sold in USA 9.08 – Operating in USA & Canada
N7098V	North American TF-51D Mustang	122-40411	To D-FTSI 9.08
N8010M	Bell 407	53728	To N407MD 2008
N45462	Piper PA-18-150 Super Cub	18-8309015	To Antwerp for restoration 1.08
N45477	Piper PA-18-150 Super Cub	18-8309003	To Antwerp for restoration 1.08
N45526	Piper PA-18-150 Super Cub	18-8309014	To Antwerp for restoration 1.08
N45531	Piper PA-18-150 Super Cub	18-8209022	To G-ECMK 7.08
N45543	Piper PA-18-150 Super Cub	18-8109034	To Antwerp for restoration 1.08
N45552	Piper PA-18-150 Super Cub	18-8563	To Midden Zeeland, Netherlands 1.08
N59269	Boeing Stearman A75L3	75-3867	Returned to USA by 9.06
N77342	Cessna 120	11783	To EI-AED 3.08
N84142	Lake LA-250 Buccaneer	69	Left UK 16.4.07 – In Germany 9.08
N90724	Hiller UH-12C	810	No reports since 11.03
N92001	MD Helicopters MD.900	900-00040	To VT-…6.08
N95409	Cessna 172R	17280424	To Kefalonia by 6.08

BELGIUM

OO-DFS	Piper PA-18 Super Cub 95	18-1637	To Michigan, USA by 11.07
OO-SDK	Boeing 737-229C	20916	Scrapped Bournemouth 5.08

DENMARK
OY-NMH	Government Aircraft Factory N-24A Nomad74FA		To Herning, Denmark by 6.08 Replaced by G-UKPS
OY-OCV	Bombardier Learjet 45	45-306	To M-EOCV 6.08
OY-PBH	LET L-410UVP-E20	972736	Rotationally based on a temporary basis with other aircraft

INDONESIA
PK-MTV	British Aerospace ATP	2046	Scrapped Woodford by 12.8.08

ARUBA
P4-LJG	Cessna 750 Citation X	750-0228	To M-DKDI 10.08

RUSSIA
FLARF02089	Polikarpov I-15bis	4439	Exported in container 3.08
RA01370	Yakovlev Yak-18T	22202032912	Scrapped White Waltham by 11.7.08

SWEDEN
SE-DRB	British Aerospace BAe 146 Series 200	E2057	Scrapped Exeter 24.6.08
SE-GPU	Piper PA-28-161 Cherokee Warrior II		Returned to Sweden by 5.07
		28-7716200	
SE-IFB	Reims/Cessna F172N	F17202005	To G-CFCI 4.08

GREECE
SX-AJM	Piper PA-28R-200 Cherokee Arrow II		To SP-AIM 9.08
		28R-7435174I	
SX-BLX	Airbus A320-211	029	To N290SE 6.08

TURKEY
TC-MBE	Fokker F.27 Friendship 500	10639	Dismantled and removed from Coventry 14.7.08

UKRAINE
UR-VTV	LET L-410UVP Turbolet	810705	Replaced by Cessna 208 G-OHPC by 5.08

AUSTRALIA
VH-JRQ	Jabiru Aircraft Pty J160-C	069	To RAAus register 4.07
VH-JVL	Piper PA-18-150 Super Cub	18-6615	To G-CFSV 1.09

BERMUDA
VP-BAA	Boeing 727-51	19123	Maintenance visitor only
VP-BAB	Boeing 727-76	19254	Maintenance visitor only
VP-BCI	Bombardier CL-600-2B19	7351	To N387AA 10.08
VP-BEP	Gulfstream Aerospace Gulfstream V	636	To N886DT 3.08
VP-BGE	Cessna 500 Citation I	500-0287	Crashed Farnborough, Kent 30.3.08
VP-BGO	Bombardier CL-600-2B19	5404	To M-SKZL 9.08
VP-BLR	Gulfstream Aerospace Gulfstream V-SP	5059	To N659GA 10.08
VP-BUL	Aérospatiale AS.365N2 Dauphin 2	6492	To N365LL 2.08 – see SECTION 5 Part 1

CAYMAN ISLANDS
VP-CAT	Cessna 501 Citation I	501-0232	To Vodochody, Russia by 6.08
VP-CFF	Gulfstream Aerospace Gulfstream IVSP	1265	To N165GD 12.08
VP-CKA	Boeing 727-82	20489	Scrapped Southend by 1.8.08
VP-CMD	Dassault Falcon 2000EX/EASy	82	To C-GSEC 4.08
VP-CPT	British Aerospace BAe 125 Series 1000B		
		259004	To M-ACPT 2.08
VP-CRC	Bombardier BD-700 Global Express	9196	To G-CEYL 10.08
VP-CSN	Cessna 560 Citation Ultra	560-0401	To OY-KLG 9.08

LATVIA
YL-CBJ	Yakovlev Yak-52	790404	To VH-XTD 7.08

NEW ZEALAND
ZK-AGM*	de Havilland DH.83 Fox Moth	"4085"	No reports since 12.03

NIGERIA
5N-AGV	Grumman G-1159 Gulfstream II	177	To 5N-BGV 11.08 – see SECTION 5 Part 1
5N-AJT*	Bell 212	30636	No reports since1.04
5N-AJU*	Bell 212	30632	No reports since1.04
5N-AJV*	Bell 212	30868	No reports since1.04
5N-AJW*	Bell 212	30601	No reports since1.04
5N BDA	Aérospatiale AS365N Dauphin 2	6077	To N607AV 11.08
5N-BHN*	Bell 212	32135	No reports since1.04

SECTION 6

PART 1 – BRITISH GLIDING ASSOCIATION

The BGA glider register follows a similar format to the main aircraft registers in this book.
Column 1 shows the three-letter Trigraph issued by the BGA.
Column 2 shows the BGA number - the Certificate of Airworthiness (CofA) number issued by the British Gliding Association. This is the primary reference and can usually be found on the fin or rear fuselage in small characters.
Column 3 shows the markings actually carried on the glider, which is usually either the trigraph or a BGA-allocated competition number. Occasionally ex-military or civil markings are carried. - an index to these marks is in Part 2 below and a dash indicates that no code is worn.

The official BGA list is extended by including non-current gliders and those with recently lapsed CofAs for which no cancellation details are known but which may survive. We include the complete expiry dates for CofA and the complete date for the first issue where known. Where a BGA CofA number has been reserved for future use, the reservation date is shown prefixed by the letter 'R'. Most entries with a CofA expiry before the year 2004 have been deleted if there is no news on their fate or continued existence. The non-current gliders include examples known to be in storage or under restoration in the ownership of members of the Vintage Glider Club (www.vintagegliderclub.org). Similar entries, where a reason for the non-renewal of CofA is known, that is accident details or sale abroad, have been retained but these will be removed in the next edition. There is no official record held of bases, so information in the "(Unconfirmed) Base" column is largely related to owners' addresses and feedback we receive from readers, as well as information given on gliding club websites and in the BGA magazine "Sailplane & Gliding".

With the completion of transition to European Aviation Safety Agency (EASA) rules following the deadline of 28th September 2008, the majority of active gliders are now G- registered, the only exceptions being a number of vintage and one-off designs which are exempted under the EASA Regulation 1592/2002 "New Annex II" list and which will remain unregistered and under BGA control. BGA numbers are still allocated to newly-registered gliders, but EASA CofAs are issued, normally on the recommendation of BGA-authorized inspectors.

The list below **only** includes gliders which remain under BGA control and have not received a CAA registration. All G- registered giders can be found in section 1.

The BGA register has been updated by Richard Cawsey. Special thanks are due to the staff at the British Gliding Association offices in Leicester for their assistance. Information is current to January 2009.

Trigraph	BGA	Code	Type	Constructor's No	Previous Identity	Date	Owner(Operator)	(Unconfirmed) Base	CofA Expy
-	162	-	Manuel Willow Wren	-		9.34	Brooklands Museum	Brooklands	*
AAA	231	-	Abbott-Baynes Scud II	215B	G-ALOT	8.35	L P Woodage	Dunstable	1. 6.06
			(Completed by Slingsby)		BGA 231				
-	236	-	Slingsby T.6 Kirby Kite	27A	G-ALUD	14.11.35	P Underwood	Eaton Bray	*
					BGA 236, BGA 222		(Remains only, for possible rebuild 2007)		
AAX	251	-	Slingsby T.6 Kirby Kite	227A	(ex RAF)	30. 3.36	R Boyd	Rivar Hill	28. 5.09
					BGA 251				
ABG	260	-	Schweyer Rhönsperber	35/22		4. 5.36	F K Russell tr Rhönsperber Syndicate	Dunstable	3. 9.09
-	266	-	Slingsby T.1 Falcon I Waterglider	237A		29. 5.36	Windermere Steamboats & Museum	Windermere	*
ABZ	277	-	Grunau Baby II	-	RAFGSA 270	25. 8.36	J R Furnell	Portmoak	27. 7.09
			(Built F Coleman)		BGA 277, G-ALKU, BGA 277				
ACF	283	ACF	Abbott-Baynes Scud III	2	G-ALJR	18.12.36	L P Woodage	Dunstable	4. 3.06
					BGA 283		(Registered as G-ALJR)		
ACH	285	E	Slingsby T.6 Kirby Kite	247A	G-ALNH	30.12.36	Museum of Army Flying	AAC Middle Wallop	5.99*
					BGA 285		(As "G 285" in 1 GTS RAF c/s)		
ADJ	310	-	Slingsby T.6 Kirby Kite	258B	RAFGSA 182	9. 2.37	A M Maufe	Tibenham	26. 8.09
					VD218, BGA 310		(Rebuilt 1982 with components ex BGA 327 c/n 285A)		
AEM	337	-	Schleicher Rhönbussard	620	RAFGSA 265	25. 4.38	C Wills and S White	Lasham	14. 9.08
					BGA 337, G-ALME, BGA 337, TK710, BGA 337				
-	370		Grunau Baby II	1		11.10.38	N Scully	Saltby	8. 6.77*
			(Built S Hobson)				(Stored 2003)		
AGE	378	-	Slingsby T.12 Gull	312A	G-ALPJ	14. 9.38	M L Beach	Halton	16. 8.04
					BGA 378				
AHC	400	F	Slingsby T.6 Kirby Kite	336A	VD165	6. 5.39	D Bramwell	Thame	4. 5.09
			(Uses wings from Special T.6 c/n 355A)		BGA 400		(In 1 GTS RAF c/s)		
AHU	416	-	Scott Viking I	114	G-ALRD	19. 6.39	W den Baars	Haamstede, Netherlands	28. 5.07
					BGA 416				
-	448	-	Jacobs Schweyer Weihe	000348	G-ALJW	6.47	D Phillips	(Snitterfield)	*
					BGA 448, LO+WQ		(Damaged Thun, Switzerland 20.7.79: current status unknown)		
AKD	449		DFS Olympia-Meise	227	LF+VO	7.47	T Bolt (For restoration)	(Plymouth)	31. 5.85*
-	470	-	Short Nimbus	S.1312		.47	Ulster Folk & Transport Museum	Holywood, Belfast	8.75*
							(Stored 2008)		
ALR	485	-	Slingsby T.8 Tutor	513	G-ALPE, BGA 485	11.46	R van Aalst	Asperden, Germany	5. 8.09
ALW	490	G-ALRK	Hütter H.17	-	G-ALRK	13. 8.48	N I Newton	Wycombe Air Park	25. 4.09
			(Built D Campbell)		BGA 490				
-	491		Hawkridge Dagling	08471		2.47	N H Ponsford (Stored 2008)	(Selby)	*
-	493	-	Hawkridge Nacelle Dagling	10471		7.47	P J Underwood	Eaton Bray	*
			(Also allotted BAPC 81)				(On rebuild 2008)		
AMK	503	AMK	EoN AP.5 Olympia 2	EoN/O/003	G-ALJP, BGA 503	5.47	R Maxfield (Under restoration 2008)	Liversedge	28. 5.95
AMM	505	AMM	EoN AP.5 Olympia 2	EoN/O/006	G-ALJV, BGA 505	5.47	J R Furnell	Portmoak	26. 7.09
AMR	509	AMR	EoN AP.5 Olympia 2	EoN/O/011	G-ALLA, BGA 509	5.47	K J Nurcombe	Husbands Bosworth	26. 8.09
AMV	513		EoN AP.5 Olympia 2	EoN/O/014	G-ALNB, BGA 513	5.47	P J Teagle (Stored 2008)	(Sutton Bank)	8.90*
AMW	514	AMW	EoN AP.5 Olympia 2	EoN/O/015	G-ALKM, BGA 514	5.47	Not known (Noted 7.07)	Husbands Bosworth	16. 4.03
AND	521		Slingsby T.26 Kite 2	MHL/RK.5		.	Not known (Stored)	Chalfont St.Giles	20. 6.80
ANW	538	ANW	EoN AP.5 Olympia 2	EoN/O/040	G-ALNE, BGA 538	7.47	Midland Air Museum	Baginton	9. 3.04
ANZ	541	215	EoN AP.5 Olympia 2	EoN/O/043		9.47	Not known (Noted 6.08)	RAF Halton	5.92*
APC	544	APC	EoN AP.5 Olympia 2	EoN/O/046	G-ALMJ, BGA 544	9.47	R D Bryce-Smith	Gransden Lodge	7. 3.09
-	562	-	EoN AP.5 Olympia 2	EoN/O/037	G-ALJZ	7.47	Museum of Berkshire Aviation	Woodley	*
					BGA 562		(Crashed 20.7.58; wreck on display 2008)		

APZ	565	-	Slingsby T.25 Gull IV	505	G-ALPB, BGA 565	.	A Fidler	Crowland	27. 6.08
			(Rebuilt with Kite 2 fuselage no. MHL/210)						
AQN	578	AQN	Grunau Baby IIB	G.3348	G-ALSO	27. 7.48	G D Pullen	Lasham	15. 6.09
			(Built by Hawkridge)		BGA 578				
AQQ	580	AQQ	EoN AP.7 Primary	EoN/P/003	G-ALPS	.	The Shuttleworth Collection	Old Warden	16. 3.09
					BGA 580				
-	588		EoN AP.7 Primary	EoN/P/011		.	N H Ponsford *(Stored 2008)*	(Selby)	*
-	589	G-ALMN	EoN AP.7 Primary	EoN/P/012	G-ALMN	19. 5.48	Museum of Berkshire Aviation	Woodley	4.51*
					BGA 589		*(Stored 2008)*		
ARK	599	ARK /	Slingsby T.30A Prefect	548	PH-1	.	K M Fresson	Parham	15. 8.04
		G-ALLF			BGA 599, G-ALLF, BGA 599		*(Registered as G-ALLF)*		
ARM	601	ARM	Slingsby T.21B	543	G-ALKX, BGA 601	8.48	South London Gliding Centre	Kenley	28. 4.09
			(Rebuilt 1974 with wings and tail from BGA 900)						
ASB	614	ASB	Slingsby T.21B	549	RNGSA	9.48	R A Robertson and partners	Talgarth	4. 8.09
					BGA 614, G-ALLT, BGA 614				
ASC	615		Grunau Baby IIB	G-4848		2.49	M Diller	Burgheim, Germany	13. 8.94
			(Built by Hawkridge)				*(Under restoration 2006)*		
ASN	625		Slingsby T.30B Prefect	567	G-ALPC, BGA 625	1.49	J Kosak	Culdrose	12. 5.09
-	628	-	EoN AP.8 Baby	EoN/B/004	(BGA 645)	3.49	R Kent	Shoreham	*
					G-ALRU, BGA 628		*(Crashed Bardney 28.5.71; on rebuild 4.08)*		
AST	629	G-ALRH	EoN AP.8 Baby	EoN/B/005	G-ALRH	3.49	EoN Baby Syndicate	Chipping	1. 9.96
					BGA 629		*"Liver Bird" (Last known extant 2000)*		
ATH	643	-	Slingsby T.15 Gull III	364A	TJ711	7.11.49	Brooklands Museum	Brooklands	20. 6.04
ATL	646	-	Slingsby T.21B	536	G-ALKS	6.50	G Markham *(Stored 3.07)*	Enstone	12. 7.96
ATR	651	-	Slingsby T.13 Petrel	361A	EI-101	7.50	G P Saw	Wycombe Air Park	15. 3.09
					IGA 101, IAC 101, BGA 651, G-ALPP				
ATV	655	OK-8592	Zlin 24 Krajanek	101	G-ALMP, OK-8592	4.50	J M Dredge	Wycombe Air Park	5. 5.07
AUD	663	663	Slingsby T.26 Kite 2B	727		1.52	F G Bradney and E Mason	Lasham	22. 4.08
AUF	665	-	Slingsby T.21B	653		4.51	R Harvey *(Stored at Delta Jets 9.08)*	Kemble	4.86*
AUG	666	-	Slingsby T.21B	643		15. 6.51	Cambridge Gliding Club	Gransden Lodge	13. 4.09
AUP	673	N21	Slingsby T.21B	636		26. 7.51	T21 Group	Lee-on-Solent	3.12.08
AUU	678	AUU	EoN AP.5 Olympia 2	EoN/O/076		10. 4.52	Mrs B Lee	Parham	15. 7.04
AVA	684	-	Abbott-Baynes Scud III	3		10. 1.53	E A Hull	Dunstable	7. 6.09
AVB	685	AVB	Slingsby T.34A Sky	644	G-644	10. 2.53	D C Phillips	Snitterfield	9. 4.09
AVC	686	AVC	Slingsby T.34A Sky	670		3.53	P J Teagle *"Kinder Scout II"*	Camphill	5. 8.07
AVF	689	AVF	Slingsby T.26 Kite 2A	728	RAFGSA 294	8. 4.53	C P Raine *"Percy"*	Thame	29. 8.09
					BGA 689				
AVL	694		Slingsby T.34A Sky	671	G-671	15. 5.53	M P Wakem	Long Mynd	5. 9.09
AVQ	698	G46	Slingsby T.34A Sky	645	G-645	9. 9.53	L M Middleton *"Gertie"*	Easterton	25.10.09
AVT	701	AVT	Slingsby T.30B Prefect	857		14. 2.54	K Schickling	Aschaffenburg, Germany	14. 5.09
AWD	711	AWD	Slingsby T.21B	950		30. 9.54	D B Brown tr T.21 Syndicate	Chipping	19. 9.04
AWS	724	AWS	Slingsby T.41 Skylark 2S	997		31. 7.56	D M Cornelius	Dunstable	29. 8.06
AWT	725		Slingsby T.37 Skylark	879		23. 6.55	P F Woodcock	(South Yorkshire)	25. 6.89
							(For restoration 2006)		
AWU	726	AWU	EoN AP.5 Olympia 2	EoN/O/082		20. 5.55	M J Riley	Sackville Lodge, Riseley	11. 5.08
AWX	729	-	Slingsby T.41 Skylark 2	946		27. 1.56	A G Leach	Bembridge	19. 7.09
AWZ	731	AWZ	Slingsby T.7 Cadet	SSK/FF169	RA847	8. 1.57	R Moyse	Lasham	27. 4.08
AXB	733	AXB	Slingsby T.41 Skylark 2	926		24. 2.56	A L Shaw	Lyveden	30. 6.02
AXD	735	AXD	Slingsby T.43 Skylark 3	1014		.	A P Stacey	RAF Keevil	5. 6.04
							(Badly damaged Aston Down 11.7.03; new owner 2.08)		
AXJ	740	AXJ	Slingsby T.42A Eagle 2	994		.56	A Kendall	Pocklington	11. 2.09
AXL	742	AXL	Slingsby T.43 Skylark 3	1030		7. 6.56	J D Leber	Kingston Deverill	15. 6.09
AXP	745	AXP	Slingsby T.41 Skylark 2	949		5. 4.56	I McHardy	Drumshade	2. 6.09
AXV	751	-	Slingsby T.26 Kite 2A	-		16. 4.56	R Wilgoss	Wycombe Air Park	25. 8.08
AYD	759	AYD	Slingsby T.41 Skylark 2	1048		21. 7.56	R Milligan	Falgunzeon	30. 8.09
AYF	761	AYF	Slingsby T.43 Skylark 3B	1058		8. 9.56	D Chisholm *(Noted 9.07)*	Rufforth	28. 8.05
AYH	763	AYH	Slingsby T.43 Skylark 3B	1066		11.10.56	A D Griffiths	Upwood	22. 6.09
-	765	-	Slingsby T.21B	1080		31.10.56	Not known	AAC Wattisham	4.70*
							(Fuselage for use in repair of BGA 3324 8.04)		
AYY	778	33	Slingsby T.41 Skylark 2C	1073		1. 2.57	A C Cummins	Llantisilio	8. 6.09
AZC	782	782	Slingsby T.21B	1096		27. 5.57	L Starkl Wiener Neustadt West, Austria		30. 5.09
-	791	VM684	Slingsby T.8 Tutor	-	VM684	20. 1.57	Hooton Park Trust	Hooton Park	2.71*
							(On loan from P Storrar)		
AZP	793		Slingsby T.41 Skylark 2	999		13. 1.57	R Milligan *(Under restoration 6.07)*	Falgunzeon	13. 8.97
AZQ	794	VM687	Slingsby T.8 Tutor		VM687	.57	D Gibbs	Lee-on-Solent	22. 4.06
AZR	795	AZR	EoN AP.5 Olympia 2	EoN/O/101		3. 6.58	Not known *(Under restoration)*	Syerston	28. 7.95
AZX	801	AZX	Slingsby T.41 Skylark 2	995	BGA 1909	9. 4.57	B J Griffin	Saltby	11. 5.09
					AGA 4, BGA 801				
AZY	802		Slingsby T.41 Skylark 2 (Mod.)	963		16. 4.57	A J Jackson *(Stored 2006)*	(Burn)	29. 6.97
BAA	804	BAA	Slingsby T.8 Tutor	931	XE761, VM589	10. 5.57	A P Stacey *(Under restoration 5.06)*	RAF Keevil	9. 3.97
							(Note also Cadet TX.1 "BGA 804 ex VM589" at Midland Air Museum, Coventry)		
BAC	806	BAC	Slingsby T.43 Skylark 3B	1101	RNGSA CU19	17. 7.57	F K Hutchinson	Husbands Bosworth	24. 4.04
					BGA 806				
BAL	813	BAL	Slingsby T.43 Skylark 3B	1111		12.11.57	D A Wilson	Milfield	13. 5.06
BAM	814	BAM	Slingsby T.41 Skylark 2	1108		1. 2.58	R G Boyton	Wormingford	2. 6.02
BAN	815	BAN	Slingsby T.30B Prefect	1120		3. 1.58	J S Allison *(Stored 8.08)*	Bicester	3. 7.07
BAV	822	BAV	Slingsby T.41 Skylark 2B	1113		22. 2.58	M H Simms	Shipdham	16. 4.02
BAW	823	BAW	Slingsby T.43 Skylark 3B	1126		14. 2.58	R Joy and Partner	Halesland	15. 6.09
BAY	825	BAY	Slingsby T.42B Eagle 3	1116		28. 3.58	M Lodge *(Under restoration 7.08)*	Ringmer	15. 8.00
BAZ	826	BAZ	Slingsby T.41 Skylark 2	1112		26. 3.58	A Wilson	Sutton Bank	27. 6.09
-	830		Slingsby T.42B Eagle 3	1119		21. 6.58	A P Stacey *(New owner 11.08)*	RAF Keevil	7.79*
BBG	833	BBG	Slingsby T.8 Tutor	-	VW535	3. 9.57	J Bennett	Upwood	26. 7.07
BBH	834	BBH	EoN Olympia 2	EoN/O/041	(BGA 539)	22. 8.57	L P Woodage	Dunstable	10. 5.09
BBQ	841	BBQ	Slingsby T.42B Eagle 3	1115		14. 5.58	L Adamson and partners	Milfield	3.10.05

Reg	No	Comp	Type	C/n	Prev ID	Date	Owner	Location	Last
BBT	844	BBT	Slingsby T.43 Skylark 3B	1134	RAFGSA 234 BGA 844	6. 6.58	J P Gilbert	Wormingford	27. 4.09
BBU	845	BBU	Slingsby T.41 Skylark 2B	1135		13. 6.58	D A Bullock	Bicester	12.10.08
-	852	TS291	Slingsby T.8 Tutor	SSK/FF250	TS291	2. 7.58	Museum of Flight	East Fortune	12.66*
BCF	856		Slingsby T.21B (Built Leighton Park School)	1		10.10.58	P.Underwood *(Blown over Haddenham 14.6.80: to Poland 10.05)*	Eaton Bray	5. 81*
BCH	858	BCH	Slingsby T.8 Tutor	SSK/FF489	VM547	30. 9.58	K van Rooy	Weelde, Belgium	24. 1.05
BCP	864	BCP	Slingsby T.43 Skylark 3B	1140		1.11.58	C Barrett *(New owner 2008)*	Shipdham	13. 4.02
BCS	867	549	Slingsby T.43 Skylark 3B	1144		5.12.58	A P Benbow and J Farnell *(New owners 8.08)*	Portmoak	16. 4.05
BCU	869	2	Slingsby T.21B	1148		1.59	M Kopplow & partners *(Under restoration 5.08)*	Delmenhorst, Germany	21. 5.86
BCV	870	155	Slingsby T.43 Skylark 3B	1195		6. 4.59	J Turner (Kent Vintage Glider Group)	Challock	25. 3.09
BCW	871	BCW	Slingsby T.43 Skylark 3B	1147		12. 3.59	G Walker	Parham	28. 2.07
BCY	873	T45	Slingsby T.45 Swallow	1198		10. 4.59	T Wilkinson *(Stored 7.06)*	Sackville Lodge, Riseley	19. 5.05
BDA	875	BDA	Slingsby T.21B	1205	AGA 7 BGA 875	22. 6.59	J M Van Dijk	Venlo, Netherlands	26.10.08
BDF	880	BDF	Slingsby T.42B Eagle 3	1213		28. 9.59	D C Phillips	Snitterfield	14. 8.04
BDR	890	BDR	Slingsby T.45 Swallow	1243		11. 6.60	M King *"Sarah"*	Waldershare Park	19. 6.08
BDW	895		Slingsby T.8 Tutor	-	VM637	30. 4.59	Newark Air Museum	Winthorpe	6.93
BDX	896	BDX	Slingsby T.41 Skylark 2 (Built C Hurst)	CH.095/1		10. 6.59	H D Maddams	Ridgewell	7. 8.09
BEA	899	BEA	Slingsby T.41 Skylark 2	1194		1. 7.59	P Q Benn	Aston Down	17. 5.09
-	902	-	Slingsby T.12 Gull	?		15. 5.59	Museum of Flight	East Fortune	*
BEF	904	-	Slingsby T.8 Tutor	SSK/FF934		29.10.59	J Szladowski *(Stored 6.06)*	Camphill	2. 5.96
BEL	909	BEL	EoN AP.5 Olympia 2B	EoN/O/126		21.12.59	J G Gilbert and partners	Wormingford	11. 5.05
BEM	910	BEM	Slingsby T.45 Swallow	1221		5. 2.60	J M Muir	Aston Down	11. 5.08
BET	916		Slingsby T.43 Skylark 3B	1227		9. 3.60	A C Robertson and partners *(Stored 7.05)*	Feshiebridge	31. 5.98
BEX	920	91	Slingsby T.43 Skylark 3F	1229		8. 4.60	A J Pettitt	Rivar Hill	2. 8.09
BEY	921	BEY	Slingsby T.45 Swallow	1230		14. 4.60	G P Hayes	Kenley	4. 7.09
BEZ	922	BEZ	Slingsby T.43 Skylark 3F	1232		29. 4.60	T L Cook	Feshiebridge	13. 5.09
BFE	927	BFE	Slingsby T.43 Skylark 3F	1244		24. 6.60	I Dunkley	New Zealand	13. 3.09
BFG	929	BFG	Slingsby T.43 Skylark 3F	1245		8. 7.60	T J Wilkinson	Sackville Lodge, Riseley	14. 6.06
BFP	936	D1	Schleicher K 7	702		30. 5.60	Dartmoor Gliding Society *(Stored 2007)* Brentor		28. 4.96
BFY	945	BFY	Slingsby T.21B	1251	RAFGGA 515 RAFGSA 286, BGA 945	9.60	M Wood	Sutton Bank	10. 6.09
BGB	948	-	Slingsby T.21B (Robin EC-44PM)	1274	RAFGSA 282 BGA 948	11.60	J Elliott and H Bosworth	Strubby	25. 8.05
BGD	950	BGD	Slingsby T.43 Skylark 3F	1276		26.11.60	Essex University Gliding Club AAC Wattisham		21. 5.05
BGL	957	BGL	Slingsby T.43 Skylark 3F			1. 3.61	P A Rose	Walney Island	9. 3.08
BGR	962	BGR	EoN AP.5 Olympia 2B	EoN/O/124		4. 6.60	M H Gagg	RAF Cosford	5. 1.05
BHC	973	BHC	EoN AP.5 Olympia 2B	EoN/O/138		9. 1.61	M Pedwell	Bidford	1. 5.06
BHQ	985	BHQ	Slingsby T.43 Skylark 3F	1304		15. 4.61	T Wiseman	Andreas	25.10.09
BHT	988	BHT	Slingsby T.43 Skylark 3F	1306		19. 4.61	A P Stacey *(Stored 1.09)*	RAF Keevil	17. 8.07
BJB	996	BJB	Slingsby T.43 Skylark 3F (Built Jones, Pentelow and Saint)	SSK/JPS/1		19. 4.61	C J Ferrier	Falgunzeon	20. 1.09
BJC	997	BJC	EoN AP.5 Olympia 2B	EoN/O/135		15. 4.61	P J Devey	Lyveden	29. 9.04
BJF	1000	BJF	Slingsby T.21B	1309		16. 6.61	Sedbergh Syndicate	Wormingford	3. 6.09
BJJ	1003	-	Slingsby T.45 Swallow	1310		23. 6.61	A P Stacey *(Stored 1.09)*	RAF Keevil	30. 8.82
BJK	1004	BJK	Slingsby T.43 Skylark 3F	1311		14. 7.61	R Skinner	Wormingford	7. 8.08
BJP	1008	BJP	Slingsby T.45 Swallow	1316		4. 9.61	G Williams	Seighford	5. 6.07
BJQ	1009	BJQ	Slingsby T.49A Capstan	1314		23. 2.62	Bidford Gliding Centre	Bidford	1. 6.08
-	1013	113	Slingsby T.43 Skylark 3G	1320		12.61	J McIver *(Under restoration 2008)*	(Dumfries)	7.77*
BJV	1014	-	Slingsby T.21B	556	SE-SHK	1.62	Museum of Flight *(Stored)*	East Fortune	*
BJY	1017	BJY	Slingsby T.45 Swallow	1324		1. 3.62	D A Wiseman	Andreas	13. 6.09
BJZ	1018		Slingsby T.45 Swallow	1325		17. 3.62	J P Marshall *(Stored 2006)*	North Connel	20.11.96
BKA	1019	BKA	Slingsby T.50 Skylark 4	1326	EI-117 BGA 1019	28. 5.62	Mendip Gliding Club	Halesland	5.11.09
BKC	1021	BKC	Jacobs Schweyer Weihe (Built AB Flygindustri)	231	SE-SNE Fv.8312	15. 4.61	B Briggs	RAF Cranwell	27. 6.09
BKE	1023	BKE	Slingsby T.43 Skylark 3F (Built C Ross)	1715/CR/1		13. 7.61	G Ballantyne	Portmoak	6. 6.09
BKH	1026	BKH	Schleicher Ka 2B	1028		26. 7.61	T J Wilkinson Sackville Lodge, Riseley *(Hit tree on approach, Sackville Lodge 29.6.08)*		7. 4.09
BKJ	1027	BKJ/270	Schleicher Ka 6CR	565	9G-AAR	7.61	Vale of White Horse Gliding Centre Sandhill Farm, Shrivenham		24. 3.06
BKL	1029	BKL	EoN AP.5 Olympia 2B	EoN/O/134		18. 6.61	J E Herring	Lasham	6. 6.09
BKN	1031	BKN	Schleicher K 7	1091		23. 9.61	P Hibbard	Wormingford	4. 8.04
BKS	1035	BKS	EoN AP.5 Olympia 2B	EoN/O/146		11.11.61	N W Woodward	Wycombe Air Park	8. 4.09
BKU	1037	BKU	EoN AP.5 Olympia 2B	EoN/O/153		1.62	D N MacKay	Aboyne	14. 5.08
BKW	1039	BKW	Schleicher Ka 6 Rhönsegler	295	OH-RSA	10. 9.62	P J Montgomery *(Under restoration)* (W.Sussex)		2. 5.01
BKX	1040	BKX	EoN AP.5 Olympia 2B	EoN/O/148		19. 3.62	D J Allibone	Eyres Field	5.11.06
BLA	1043	BLA	Slingsby T.50 Skylark 4	1331		5. 5.62	I Russell	Milfield	9. 2.09
BLC	1045		Slingsby T.50 Skylark 4	1333		28. 5.62	V W Allison	(Charlbury)	15. 9.09
BLE	1047	BLE	Slingsby T.50 Skylark 4	1335	RNGSA 1-228 BGA 1047	28. 6.62	S Frank	Easterton	4. 5.09
BLH	1050	BLH	Slingsby T.50 Skylark 4	1338	RAFGSA BGA 1050	10. 7.62	D Wakefield	Rufforth	15. 7.09
BLJ	1051	BLJ	EoN AP.6 Olympia 419X	EoN/4/009		10. 1.62	I D Walton and Syndicate *"Big Bird"* Long Mynd		25. 9.07
BLK	1052	67	EoN AP.6 Olympia 419X	EoN/4/007	G-APSX	13. 3.62	G T Bowes *"Wild Goose"*	Seighford	16. 9.08
BLL	1053	BLL	Slingsby T.34A Sky	821	PH-203	6. 4.62	H Stubbe	Lemelerveld, Netherlands	16. 7.07
BLN	1055	BLN	EoN AP.5 Olympia 2B	EoN/O/152		7. 3.62	M R Derwent	RAF Cranwell	22. 2.09

BLP	1056	BLP	EoN AP.5 Olympia 2B	EoN/O/149		7. 3.62	R E Wooller and partners	Chipping	24. 4.09
BLQ	1057	BLQ	EoN AP.5 Olympia 2 Special	EoN/O/042	RAFGSA 145 (BGA 540)	27. 7.62	K Wood and partners	Winthorpe	12. 7.06
BLS	1059		EoN AP.5 Olympia 2B *(EoN rebuild of BGA 897 [EoN/O/128])*	EoN/O/151		14. 7.62	R Andrews	Long Mynd	7. 7.07
BLU	1061	BLU	Slingsby T.45 Swallow	1340		27. 7.62	J M Brookes	Strubby	4. 6.09
BLW	1063	BLW	Slingsby T.50 Skylark 4	1342		30. 8.62	S R A Trusler	RAF Weston-on-the-Green	25. 9.09
BLZ	1066	1066	Slingsby T.50 Skylark 4	1346		26.11.62	M S Radice	Kingston Deverill	30. 3.09
BMM	1078	BMM	SZD-9bis Bocian 1D	P-397		10.62	E W Burgess *(Stored 4.07)*	Currock Hill	19. 6.05
BMQ	1081	BMQ	Slingsby T.21B	1351		16.11.62	W E Masterton	Blenheim, Jamaica	25. 1.04
BMU	1085		Slingsby T.21B (T) *(Rotax 503)*	1355	9G-ABD BGA 1085	9.11.62	D Woolerton and partners *"Spruce Goose" (Fuselage stored 8.08)*	North Coates	27. 9.97
BMW	1087	BMW	Slingsby T.50 Skylark 4	1357		1. 1.63	M Williams	Lasham	14. 1.10
BMX	1088	739	Slingsby T.50 Skylark 4	1358	RAFGSA 308 BGA 1088	4. 1.63	S Stanwix *(739 Syndicate)*	Eyres Field	18. 6.09
BMY	1089	163	Slingsby T.50 Skylark 4	1361		26. 1.63	M H Simms *(Stored 2006)*	Shipdham	7. 4.98
BNA	1091	-	Shenstone Harbinger Mk.2	1		12.12.62	S Edyvean *(Noted 7.07)*	Bicester	7. 5.04
BNC	1093	BNC	Jacobs Schweyer Weihe *(Built AB Kockums Flygindustri)*	1	SE-SHU	11. 3.63	K S Green	Lasham	22. 9.08
BNE	1095	BNE	Slingsby T.50 Skylark 4	1375		7. 4.63	D Kershaw	Lasham	1. 3.09
BNK	1100	BNK	Slingsby T.50 Skylark 4	1362		2. 2.63	E D Weekes and partners	RAF Weston-on-the-Green	10. 3.09
BNM	1102	"BMN"	Slingsby T.50 Skylark 4	1367		28. 2.63	D Hertzberg	Ridgewell	27. 7.09
BNN	1103	BNN	Slingsby T.50 Skylark 4	1366		22. 2.63	A A Jenkins	Bicester	19. 6.09
BNQ	1105	BNQ	Slingsby T.50 Skylark 4	1369		30. 3.63	Not known *(Stored 5.08)*	North Connel	29. 4.00
BNR	1106	BNR	Slingsby T.49B Capstan	1370		1. 8.63	A Walford	Gransden Lodge	20. 4.08
BNS	1107	XS652	Slingsby T.45 Swallow	1373	XS652 BGA 1107	20. 3.63	P N Ling and Partner	Rufforth	2. 8.09
BPA	1115	BPA	Slingsby T.50 Skylark 4	1383		21. 5.63	A P Stacey	RAF Keevil	3. 1.06
						(Overshot field landing 9.6.05 Halesland; under restoration 2007)			
BPC	1117	BPC	Slingsby T.50 Skylark 4	1389		19. 7.63	J L Grayer and partner	Ringmer	27. 9.09
BPD	1118	N55	Slingsby T.49B Capstan	1390		22. 7.63	H Newbery	(Wimborne)	8. 9.09
BPE	1119	BPE	Slingsby T.50 Skylark 4	1391		28. 6.63	M H Simms	Shipdham	24. 2.09
BPG	1121	741	Slingsby T.50 Skylark 4	1393		18. 7.63	P Orchard	Long Mynd	20. 7.09
BPK	1124	BPK	Slingsby T.50 Skylark 4	1381		22. 6.63	Y Marom	Crowland	10.11.06
BPN	1127	BPN	Standard Austria	003	OE-0496	13. 4.63	R K Avery and partners	Eaglescott	19. 7.09
BPS	1131	BPS	Slingsby T.49B Capstan	1399		13. 9.63	Deeside Capstan Group	Aboyne	12. 6.09
BPT	1132		Slingsby T.49B Capstan	1400		21.10.63	Not known *(Fuselage stored 2004)*	Bicester	11. 2.95
BPU	1133		Slingsby T.49B Capstan	1402		15.11.63	J Hailey tr Capstan Syndicate *(Under repair 2004)*	Dunstable	17. 3.98
BPV	1134	BPV	Slingsby T.49B Capstan	1404		20.12.63	G L Barrett	RAF Weston-on-the-Green	16. 4.09
BPW	1135	BPW	Slingsby T.49B Capstan	1408		17. 1.64	Ulster Gliding Club	Bellarena	26. 1.06
BPX	1136	859	Slingsby T.45 Swallow	1397	XS859 BGA 1136	1. 1.64	N R Antcliffe	Pocklington	14. 1.08
BPZ	1138	BPZ	Slingsby T.50 Skylark 4	1406		6. 3.64	T Smith *(Stored 2006)*	Swindon	10. 7.00
BQE	1143	RA905	Slingsby T.7 Cadet	-	RAFGSA 273 RA905	11. 8.63	Trenchard Museum	RAF Halton	14. 3.00
BQF	1144	1	Slingsby T.21B	1168	XN189	14.10.63	C Mioni *(Under restoration 10.07)*	Thionville-Yutz, France	13. 4.02
-	1147		DFS Kranich II *(Built Schleicher)*	821	RAFGSA 215	11.63	M C Russell	Bishops Stortford	11.66*
						(To Bad Tolz Vintage Gliding Club, Germany for restoration 7.02)			
BQP	1152	BQP	Slingsby T.30B Prefect	646	RAFGSA 159	14. 2.64	R J Brimfield	Dunstable	2. 8.09
BQQ	1153	-	EoN AP.5 Olympia 2B *(Rebuilt 1993 using wings from BGA 678)*	EoN/O/121	RAFGSA 244	8. 2.64	I D Smith *"Dopey"*	Nympsfield	23. 8.08
BQT	1156	BQT	EoN AP.10 460 Srs.1	EoN/S/007	BGA 2666 AGA 6, BGA 1156	26. 1.64	Museum of Science & Industry	Manchester	18. 4.97
BQU	1157	BQU	Schleicher K 7	7141	RNGSA AR66 BGA 1157	15. 4.64	W Hoekstra	Haamstede, Netherlands	31. 3.04
BRA	1163	BRA	Slingsby T.49B Capstan	1417		24. 4.64	I Pattingale	RAF Odiham	29. 5.04
BRB	1164	T51	Slingsby T.51 Dart 15	1423	RAFGSA 334 BGA 1164	27. 4.64	M Sansom	North Hill	16. 6.08
BRC	1165	BRC	Slingsby T.45 Swallow 1	1407		1. 5.64	J R Smalley	Kirton in Lindsey	20. 4.06
BRD	1166	BRD	Slingsby T.51 Dart 15	1425	RAFGSA 335 BGA 1166	9. 5.64	T.J.Wilkinson *(Crashed on approach Sutton Bank 30.8.06; stored 9.08)*	Sackville Lodge, Riseley	5. 6.07
BRE	1167	BRE	Slingsby T.45 Swallow 2	1415		8. 5.64	P Flack	Shipdham	1. 4.09
BRG	1169	-	Slingsby T.45 Swallow	1410		23. 5.64	A W F Edwards	Gransden Lodge	7. 2.09
BRJ	1171	426	EoN AP.10 460 Srs.1	EoN/S/011		18. 3.64	T J Wilkinson	Sackville Lodge, Riseley	24. 5.08
BRK	1172	243	EoN AP.10 460 Srs.1A *(Registered as G-APWL)*	EoN/S/001	G-APWL BGA 1172, G-APWL, RAFGSA 268, G-APWL	26. 4.64	J W Williams	Eaglescott	26. 4.00
BRL	1173		EoN Olympia 2B	EoN/O/132		12. 5.64	R J Lockett	(Colchester)	27. 3.99
BRM	1174	BRM	Schleicher K 7	776	D-4635	16. 5.64	D S Driver *(Cancelled 16.9.08)*	Lleweni Parc	21.10.07
BRQ	1177	BRQ	EoN AP.10 460 Srs.1C	EoN/S/003	G-ARFU	10. 6.64	J Steel and partners *(Stored 2007)*	Falgunzeon	4. 8.96
BRT	1180	BRT	Slingsby T.51 Dart 15	1430		19. 6.64	C Logue	RAF Marham	8. 7.07
BRU	1181	BRU	Slingsby T.51 Dart 15	1429		11. 6.64	M H Simms	Shipdham	3. 4.07
BRW	1183	BRW	Slingsby T.49B Capstan	1413		25. 6.64	D A Sinclair	Lasham	3. 2.09
BSC	1189	H23	Slingsby T.50 Skylark 4	1422		25. 8.64	A P Stacey	Keevil	22. 4.09
BSE	1191	BSE	Slingsby T.49B Capstan	1414		11. 9.64	Windrushers Gliding Club	Bicester	20. 1.10
BSG	1193	BSG	Slingsby T.50 Skylark 4	1436		17. 9.64	North Wales Gliding Club	Llantisilio	25. 8.09
BSH	1194	BSH	Slingsby T.50 Skylark 4	1444		3.11.64	J M Verrill	Lee-on-Solent	19. 9.07
BSK	1196	BSK	Slingsby T.49B Capstan	1418		21.10.64	S Whitaker	Parham	21.11.09
BSM	1198	597	Slingsby T.51 Dart 15	1439		30.10.64	D Tait	Cross Hayes	29. 5.06
BSQ	1201	463	EoN AP.10 460 Srs.1	EoN/S/014		1. 5.64	K G Ashford	Husbands Bosworth	10. 5.05
BSR	1202	BSR	Slingsby T.50 Skylark 4	1443		17.12.64	A J Young	Challock	15.10.08

BSS	1203	T49	Slingsby T.49B Capstan	1449		12.64	M Tomlinson	Talgarth	20. 8.08
			(Crashed on field landing near Talgarth 26.1.08)						
BSW	1207	BSW	Slingsby T.51 Dart 15	1459		19. 2.65	B L Owen	Tibenham	25. 9.08
BSZ	1210	BSZ	Slingsby T.50 Skylark 4	1460		26. 4.65	G P Hayes	Kenley	16. 8.09
BTA	1211	BTA	Slingsby T.45 Swallow	1473		6.65	A P Stacey *(Stored 1.09)*	RAF Keevil	7. 5.06
BTE	1215	BTE	Slingsby T.21B	557	OH-KSA SE-SHL	1.65	J Assmann *"Buttercup"*	Borkenberge, Germany	1. 5.09
BTG	1217	BTG	EoN AP.10 460 Srs.1	EoN/S/024		25. 2.65	C Shepherd	Weston-on-the-Green	17. 5.08
BTH	1218	BTH	Slingsby T.21B	JHB/2		3.65	P Gilmore	Aston Down	14. 9.08
			(Built J Hulme; restored 1995 with wings from BGA 3238)						
BTK	1220		Slingsby T.50 Skylark 4	1364	SE-SZW	3.65	S Foster	(Kingswinford)	28. 7.09
BTM	1222	211	Schleicher Ka 6CR	6174		25. 3.65	G A Childs	Strubby	24. 3.07
BTN	1223	BTN	EoN AP.10 460 Srs.1	EoN/S/022	AGA 15 BGA 1223	21. 3.65	S C Thompson	Parham	21. 8.08
BTQ	1225	BTQ	EoN AP.10 460 Srs.1	EoN/S/029		4. 4.65	D Street	Burn	28. 7.09
BTV	1230	BTV	Jacobs Schweyer Weihe	000358	RAFGGA	7. 5.65	I Dunkley	New Zealand	11. 8.07
BUC	1237	A23	Slingsby T.49B Capstan	1472		27. 6.65	P R Redshaw	Walney Island	11. 5.09
BUE	1239	BUE	Slingsby T.50 Skylark 4	1468		7.65	G J Jones	Seighford	1. 5.09
BUR	1249	BUR	Slingsby T.49B Capstan	1482		11.65	R J Playle	Edgehill	18. 7.09
BUT	1251	BUT	Slingsby T.43 Skylark 3F	VRT.1		7.65	I Bannister tr Sky Syndicate	Chipping	9. 5.09
			(Built V and R Tull)						
BUU	1252	BUU	EoN Baby	EoN/B/047	RAFGSA 255	9. 4.65	R H Short	Lyveden	21. 7.08
BUV	1253	BUV	EoN AP.10 460 Srs.1	EoN/S/030		10. 7.65	T Edwards	Camphill	3. 2.09
BUW	1254	BUW	Slingsby T.21B	?	RAFGSA 242	8.65	J N Wardle *"Lucy"*	Lasham	9. 8.06
BVF	1263	BVF	Slingsby T.45 Swallow	1481		12.11.65	J S Morgan *(Stored 1.08)*	Pershore	13. 8.03
BVJ	1266	BVJ	Slingsby T.51 Dart 17R	1486		1.66	A P Stacey	RAF Keevil	14. 6.07
			(Hit hedge on field landing, Chedworth, Glos. 5.5.07; for rebuild)						
BVL	1268	404	Slingsby T.51 Dart 15	1487		1.66	D Stabler *(Noted 2007)*	Shipdham	16. 8.99
BVM	1269	150	Slingsby T.51 Dart 17R	1492		1.66	N H Ponsford *(Stored 2008)*	(Selby)	5.89*
BVN	1270	BVN	EoN AP.10 460 Srs.1	EoN/S/023		6. 3.65	C Heide	North Hill	19. 8.08
BVW	1278		EoN AP.6 Olympia 403	EoN/4/001	RAFGSA 306 G-APEW	20. 8.65	F G Bradney	Lasham	29. 5.01
			(Under restoration 2008)						
BWE	1286	BWE	EoN AP.10 460 Srs.1	EoN/S/035		30.12.65	C Hughes	Talgarth	14. 9.08
BWG	1288	465	EoN AP.10 465 Srs.2	EoN/S/038		7.12.65	R Kent *(Preserved 2006)*	Shoreham	27. 4.97
BWT	1299	163	Slingsby T.51 Dart 15R	1508		4.66	D White	Aboyne	23. 9.08
BWU	1300	BWU	EoN AP.10 460 Srs.1	EoN/S/034		21. 1.66	S H Gibson	Skirwith	16. 4.09
BWX	1303	BWX	EoN AP.5 Olympia 2B	101		2. 2.66	P Bendrey and M Deittert	Aston Down	19. 7.05
			(Built from spares)						
BXB	1307		EoN AP.10 460 Srs.1	EoN/S/040		28. 3.66	I Pattingale *(Stored 2007)*	(Odiham)	30.10.02
BXK	1315		Slingsby T.21B	1510		6.66	Not known	Rufforth	18. 7.80*
			(Damaged Falgunzeon 18.5.80: current status unknown)						
BXM	1317	9A	Slingsby T.51 Dart 17R	1521		6. 7.66	P R Davie	Dunstable	20. 7.08
BXP	1319		Slingsby T.45 Swallow 2	1522		19. 7.66	Carlton Moor Gliding Club	Carlton Moor	17.10
BXR	1321		LET L-13 Blanik	173301	G-ATPX	6. 5.66	Not known *(Stored 6.08)*	Shipdham	1.12.92
BXT	1323	BXT	Schleicher Ka 6CR	6492		30. 4.66	C Knowles	Gransden Lodge	6. 7.08
BXY	1328	BXY	EoN AP.10 460 Srs.1	EoN/S/042		20. 6.66	G K Stanford *(Stored 2007)*	Brentor	26. 7.03
BYA	1330	BYA	Slingsby T.51 Dart 17R	1518		23. 7.66	Not known *(Fuselage stored 8.08)*	Keevil	18. 5.05
			(Damaged Easterton 15.8.04)						
BYE	1334	643	EoN AP.10 460 Srs.1	EoN/S/044		22. 9.66	G Bartle	Ringmer	20. 7.09
BYG	1336	225	Slingsby T.51 Dart 17R	1535	RAFGSA BGA 1336	28.11.66	W T Emery	Rufforth	13. 6.05
BYJ	1338	478	Slingsby T.45 Swallow	1568		24. 2.67	N C Stone *(For rebuild 5.08)*	(Morpeth)	18.11.96
-	1346		Slingsby T.31B	?	RAFGSA 297	8. 8.66	Not known *(Noted 6.07)*	Halfpenny Green	24. 1.79*
BZA	1354	BZA	Slingsby T.21B	1162	RAFGSA 318 XN183	28.11.66	Bicester T21 Syndicate	Bicester	15. 8.09
BZB	1355	BZB	EoN AP.10 460 Srs.1	EoN/S/047		26.10.66	D C Ratcliffe Syndicate	Parham	21. 5.04
BZC	1356	BZC	Slingsby T.51 Dart 17R	1563		17. 2.67	A N Ely	Strubby	28. 3.04
BZG	1360	BZG	Slingsby T.49B Capstan	1581		29. 4.67	Dorset Gliding Club	Eyres Field	5.10.09
BZH	1361	406	Slingsby T.51 Dart 17R	1580		20. 4.67	M Ladley *(New owner 3.08)*	Shipdham	19.12.00
BZL	1364	BZL	Slingsby T.45 Swallow	1596		12. 7.67	Cairngorm Swallow Syndicate	Feshiebridge	14. 8.00
							(Stored 10.08)		
BZM	1365	BZM	Slingsby T.45 Swallow	1597		12. 7.67	F Webster *(Stored 6.08)*	Easterton	4. 6.05
BZP	1367	F4	SZD-24-4A Foka 4	W-301		24. 1.67	J H Atherton	Edgehill	3. 6.06
BZQ	1368		Schleicher Ka 6CR	6551		3. 2.67	Dartmoor Gliding Society *(Stored 2007)*	Brentor	24. 8.99
BZV	1373	BZV	EoN AP.10 460 Srs.1	EoN/S/046		15. 2.67	P J Chaisty	Usk	11. 8.09
BZY	1376	BZY	Slingsby T.31B	SSK/FF1817	BGA 1175	16. 3.67	D Bramwell tr The Blue Brick Syndicate	Thame	4. 5.09
			(Rebuild of BGA 1175)						
CAF	1382	CAF	EoN AP.5 Olympia 2B	EoN/O/131	RAFGSA 254	5. 4.67	B Kozuh	Ljubljana, Slovenia	17. 7.05
CAN	1389	CAN	EoN AP.10 460 Srs.1	EoN/S/050		26. 3.67	B Kozuh	Grobnik, Croatia	14. 8.08
CAT	1394	CAT	EoN AP.10 460 Srs.1	EoN/S/051		13. 5.67	D C Phillips and partners	Snitterfield	8. 7.09
CAX	1398	CAX	Slingsby T.45 Swallow	1598		7.67	G M Hicks *(Stored 2005)*	Waldershare Park	17. 8.02
CBK	1410	-	Grunau Baby III	-	RAFGSA 378 D-4676	5. 9.67	P Bedford	Dromod, County Leitrim	4.83*
			(Built Sfg.Schaffin)				*(Preserved at Cavan and Leitrim Railway 6.07)*		
CBM	1412	CBM	Schleicher Ka 6CR	6607		7.67	C G T Huck *(Stored 12.08)*	Aston Down	9. 6.05
CBR	1416	CBR	Avionautica Rio M-100S	044		8. 7.67	G Viglione	Rattlesden	28. 7.06
-	1424	-	Slingsby T.8 Tutor	SSK/FF27	RAFGSA 214 RA877	10.67	P Bedford	Dromod, County Leitrim	4.78*
							(Preserved at Cavan and Leitrim Railway 6.07)		
CCD	1428	373	Schleicher Ka 6E	4127		12.67	M H Phelps	Edgehill	18. 9.06
CCS	1441	CCS	Slingsby T.41 Skylark 2	1008	PH-230	3.68	Nottingham University Gliding Club	Cranwell	10. 3.09
CDK	1458	CDK	Schleicher K 8B	8747		5.68	Burn Gliding Club	Burn	5. 2.07
-	1461	-	EoN AP.7 Primary	?		30. 5.68	Norfolk & Suffolk Aviation Museum	Flixton	29. 5.69
CDR	1464	CDR	Scheibe Bergfalke III	5625		8.68	N M Neil	Eaglescott	2. 4.04
CDX	1470	CDX	SZD-30 Pirat	W-392		4. 6.68	Newark Air Museum	Darlton	6. 1.07
CEH	1480	CEH	Wassmer WA-22 Super Javelot	68	F-OTAN-C6	7.68	N A Mills	Wycombe Air Park	19. 8.08

ID	BGA No	Code	Type	c/n	Prev identity	Date	Owner	Location	CofA
CEK	1482		Slingsby T.21B (T) *(Fuji-Robin EC-34PM s/n 82-00391)*	1151	F-CCLU, RAFGSA 369, XN147	19. 7.68	D Woolerton *(Stored 8.08)*	North Coates	7. 5.05
CEN	1485	CEN	SZD-30 Pirat	W-393	SP-2520	7.68	A Spencer	Kirton in Lindsey	19. 4.08
CFC	1499	CFC	Schleicher K 7	470	RAFGSA 387, F-OTAN-C1	11.68	P Barnes	Dunstable	10. 9.07
CFT	1514	62	Slingsby T59A Kestrel 17	1729		29. 3.73	J A Kane	Sutton Bank	30. 6.05
CGJ	1529	CGJ	Schleicher K 8B	8773		2.69	Nene Valley Gliding Club	Upwood	2. 5.08
CGN	1533	309	Schleicher Ka 6E	4173		3.69	R H Targett	Nympsfield	18. 4.01
CGU	1539		EoN Olympia 2B	EoN/O/115	RAFGSA 228	4.69	A Levitt	Chipping	6. 5.09
CGV	1540	CGV	PIK-16C Vasama	48		4.69	D J Osborne and partners	Currock Hill	29. 8.08
CGX	1542	CGX	Bölkow Phoebus C	869		4.69	T Coldwell	Sackville Lodge, Riseley	3. 7.08
CHE	1549	CHE	Slingsby T.41 Skylark 2 *(Built Doncaster Sailplane Services)*	DSS.002		6.69	M S Howey	Burn	30. 5.05
CHF	1550	CHF	SZD-9bis Bocian 1E	P-432		5.69	T J Wilkinson *(Blown over, Sackville Lodge 27.8.95; stored 9.08)*	Sackville Lodge, Riseley	2. 8.96
CHG	1551	N52	SZD-30 Pirat	B-294		27. 6.69	Seahawk Gliding Club	RNAS Culdrose	1. 9.08
CHK	1554	CHK	EoN AP.5 Olympia 2B	EoN/O/130	RAFGSA 253	3. 6.69	R W Sheffield	Halesland	17. 9.08
CHQ	1559		Slingsby T.31B	1186	RAFGSA 316, XN247	6.69	N H Ponsford *(Stored 2006)*	Wigan	7.82*
CJF	1574	474	Schleicher K 8B	8803		29.11.69	G R Smith	(Surrey)	20.11.06
CJG	1575	CJG	Wassmer WA-21 Javelot II	38	F-OTAN-C4, F-CCEZ	7. 1.70	R S Hanslip	Burn	11. 5.04
CJJ	1577	CJJ	Bölkow Phoebus C	913		15. 1.70	P Maddocks	Portmoak	10. 4.07
CJL	1579	222	Schempp-Hirth SHK-1	42	OO-ZLG	2.70	M F Brook	RAF Wittering	29. 6.06
CJM	1580	CJM	Schleicher K 8B	8814		8. 3.70	G R Smith	(Surrey)	28. 4.06
CJP	1582	CJP	Schleicher ASW 15	15041		3.70	C Paine	Ridgewell	20. 7.07
-	1588		Slingsby T.21B	1167		3.70	V Meers *(Stored 2008)*	(Wolverhampton)	*
CKC	1595	595	Bölkow Phoebus C	936	XN188	21. 4.70	S W Bennett	Milfield	27. 1.07
CKF	1598	961	Glasflügel Standard Libelle	101	(BGA 1590)	4.70	S M Turner	Crowland	20. 5.06
-	1599		Slingsby T.8 Tutor	JHB5 / SSK/FF918		5.70	M H Simms *(Under restoration 6.07)*	Shipdham	17. 5.79
CKJ	1601		Slingsby T.30B Prefect	740	VW506	4.71	Not known *(Stored 2006)*	Crosshill	14. 4.90
-	1625	-	EoN AP.7 Primary	EoN/P/035	WP267	8. 2.71	T Akerman *(Last known on rebuild 2004)*	Poitiers, France	7. 2.72
CLK	1626	CLK	Schleicher K 7 *(Partly modified to ASK 13 standard)*	607	D-5714	1. 2.71	Cornish Gliding Club	Perranporth	20. 8.08
CLR	1632	284	Glasflügel Standard Libelle 201B	173		15. 4.71	R A Christie	Easterton	27. 4.07
CLY	1639	"CYL"	Schempp-Hirth Gö 3 Minimoa	378	PH-390, D-5076	20. 3.72	F K Russell	Dunstable	1.10.09
CMY	1663	-	Grunau Baby IIIC *(Built by LSV Füssen)*	1	RAFGSA 373, D-1090	22. 1.72	Not known *(New owners 6.08; under restoration)*	Füssen, Germany	13. 7.81*
CMZ	1664	CMZ	Schleicher K 7 *(Partly modified to ASK 13 standard)*	323	D-5589	11. 6.72	Cornish Gliding Club	Perranporth	28. 7.06
CNK	1674	CNK	SZD-30 Pirat	B-459		16. 3.72	D L Hyde	Portmoak	26. 4.08
CNV	1683	229	Slingsby T59F Kestrel 19	1790		22. 6.72	R Birch *(Ground-looped on field landing near Kintbury 30.5.06; awaiting repair 2008)*	Aston Down	25. 3.07
CPB	1689	858	Slingsby T59D Kestrel 19	1796		28.10.72	A T Vidion	Tibenham	26. 5.07
CPG	1694	CPG	Schleicher K 7	7036	D-4029	15. 4.72	S R Watson	Aboyne	28. 7.08
CPL	1698	CPL	Slingsby T.8 Tutor	SSK/FF477	RAFGSA 183	26. 4.72	A P Stacey *"Mistress Tutor"*	RAF Keevil	17. 3.08
CPX	1709	CPX	SZD-30 Pirat	B-460		7. 4.72	M Codd	Talgarth	26. 6.08
CPZ	1711	*	Aachen FVA.10B Rheinland	?	RAFGGA 521	12. 4.72	Deutsches Segelflugmuseum *(On display as " D-12-354" 2006)*	Wasserkuppe, Germany	24. 8.96
CQC	1714	CQC	SZD-30 Pirat	B-472		15. 4.72	N White	Crowland	20. 4.08
CQG	1718	CQG	EoN AP.5 Olympia 2B	EoN/O/044	(BGA 542)	24. 4.72	A Wilson and C Jakuba	Sutton Bank	10.11.07
CQN	1724	CQN	Schempp-Hirth Standard Cirrus 204G			19. 5.72	M G Sankey and partners	Lasham	5. 6.06
COO	1726	139	Schempp-Hirth Nimbus-2	5		4.72	I R Duncan	Portmoak	22. 3.08
CQW	1732	342	SZD-36A Cobra 15	W-572		8. 6.72	P Zelazowski	Edgehill	3.11.07
CRF	1741	351	Birmingham Guild BG-135	001		28. 2.72	C D Stevens	Lee-on-Solent	24. 8.08
CRJ	1744	KT	Slingsby T59A Kestrel 17	1728		7.72	H Otten *(To D-8156 2008)*	Germany	19. 5.08
CRK	1745	-	Slingsby T.8 Tutor	930	XE760, VM539	25. 7.72	R Birch *(Stored 2008)*	(Aston Down)	8.82*
CRL	1746	CRL	Schleicher ASK 13	13013	D-1846	4. 8.72	Midland Gliding Club	Long Mynd	9. 4.07
CRM	1747	-	Grunau Baby III	1	RAFGSA 361, D-8061	27. 7.72	R Wasey *(Stored 1.07)*	(Gloucestershire)	26.11.96
-	1759	-	Slingsby T.8 Tutor	-	RAFGSA 178	15.10.72	Boulton Paul Association	Wolverhampton	7.77*
CSB	1761	CSB	Slingsby T59F Kestrel 19	1798		17.11.72	W Fischer	Eyres Field	13. 9.08
CSL	1770		Slingsby T.8 Tutor	928	XE758, VF181	15.10.72	W den Baars	Haamstede, Netherlands	19. 9.00
CSV	1779	CSV	SZD-30 Pirat	B-515		3.12.72	M P Flanagan	Darlton	20. 3.06
CTF	1789		Schleicher Rhönlerche II *(Built LSC Wermelskirchen; owner quotes p/i D-4346, but unconfirmed)*	1	D-3574	26. 1.73	M Goodman *(Stored 2005)*	Lleweni Parc	24. 1.04
CTS	1800	CTS	EoN AP.5 Olympia 2B	EoN/O/157	RNGSA	13. 1.73	J R Rolfe	Upwood	21. 5.08
CTZ	1807	CTZ	Schleicher K 8B	8035/B5	D-KOCU, D-5203	3. 4.73	Scottish Gliding Union Ltd	Portmoak	12. 9.07
CUM	1819	CUM	SZD-30 Pirat	B-534		24. 2.73	E Hughes	Pocklington	4. 4.06
CVC	1832	CVC	SZD-30 Pirat	B-535		3.73	T Wilkinson	Sackville Lodge, Riseley	20. 7.08
CVH	1837	CVH	Schempp-Hirth SHK	34	N6524A	30. 3.73	J C Fletcher *(Stored 7.07)*	Bicester	27. 7.06
CVP	1843	CVP	SZD-9bis Bocian 1E	P-597		17. 3.73	Not known *(Stored 4.07)*	Aboyne	3. 8.04
CVQ	1844	428	Glasflügel Standard Libelle 201B	374		23. 3.73	C J Taunton and partners	Dunstable	29. 4.04
CVR	1845	CVR	SZD-30 Pirat	B-538		27. 3.73	J R Hornby	Darlton	26. 6.04
-	1872	D-5627	Schleicher Rhönlerche II	390	D-5627	22. 4.73	Sailplane Preservation Group *(Stored 9.07)*	Shoreham	11.76*

CWV	1873	Z	Schleicher Rhönlerche II	123	D-8226	22. 4.73	Not known	Aston Down	26. 5.94
							(Departed for restoration 10.08)		
CXH	1885	CXH	SZD-36A Cobra 15	W-619		10. 6.73	C D Street	Parham	11. 9.04
CXL	1888	CXL	SZD-30 Pirat	B-548		6.73	A K Holden	Rivar Hill	1. 6.07
CXP	1891		Yorkshire Sailplanes YS-55 Consort						
				07	BGA 1892	10. 5.76	A D Coles	North Hill	23. 4.06
CYC	1904	CYC	Pilatus B4-PC11	029	N47247	7.73	D F Barley	Ringmer	24.10.07
CYJ	1910	CYJ	Grunau Baby IIB	031000	D-6021	11. 8.73	C Bird	Dunstable	1.90*
			(Built Petera 1943)				*(Last known under restoration during 2000)*		
CYK	1911	248	Pilatus B4-PC11	078		8.73	I M Trotter tr Pilatus Soaring Syndicate	Portmoak	31. 3.07
CYN	1914	N4	Slingsby T59D Kestrel 19	JP/054		10.74	S J Cooke and partners	Gransden Lodge	29.12.08
			(Built D Jones and T Pentelow)						
CYV	1921	CYV	Birmingham Guild BG-135	5		9.73	E J Gunner	Kingston Deverill	2.12.09
CZM	1937	CZM	München Mü 13D III	10/52	D-1488	9.74	H Chapple	Bicester	30. 4.09
CZW	1946	A3	Slingsby T59D Kestrel 20	1846		17.10.76	C D Berry	Bidford	21. 4.04
DAL	1960	DAL	EoN AP.6 Olympia 419	EoN/4/010		4.74	B Kozuh	Ljubljana, Slovenia	11. 6.09
DAM	1961	676	ICA-Brasov IS-29D	27		4.74	M Barnard *(Extant 2008)*	(Lanarkshire)	24. 9.00
DAR	1965	DAR	Slingsby T.21B	SSK/FF1200	RAFGSA 404	1. 6.74	P T Nash	Crowland	25. 7.09
DBA	1974	207	EoN AP.5 Olympia 2B	EoN/O/156	RNGSA 208	25. 5.74	W R Williams *(Noted 6.08)*	RAF Halton	20. 6.04
DBB	1975	DBB	Slingsby T.51 Dart 17R	DG/51/01		5. 2.76	M Ladley	Shipdham	28. 9.08
			(Built from parts by Greenfly Aviation)						
DBD	1977	DBD	SZD-30 Pirat	S-02.02		6.74	E W Burgess	Lyveden	9. 6.08
DBJ	1982	691	Slingsby T59D Kestrel 19	1856	BGA 1892	19.10.74	T Barr-Smith	Kenley	10. 4.06
					BGA 1982				
DBU	1992	-	Schempp-Hirth Gö 4 Goevier II	557	D-5233	13. 7.74	R Arnold *(Noted 8.08)*	Abbots Bromley	19. 7.87
DBW	1994	DBW	SZD-9bis Bocian 1E	P-641		12. 7.74	Sackville Gliding Club Sackville Lodge, Riseley		3. 4.99
							(Stored 9.08)		
DCE	2002	DCE	Slingsby T.41 Skylark 2B	1003	RAFGGA 540	25.10.74	J Salvin	Darlton	1. 4.09
					PH-225				
DCN	2010		Slingsby T.21B	1250	RAFGGA 501	31.12.74	M R Dawson	(Vinax, France)	16. 7.95
					RAFGSA 287, BGA 943		*(New owner 1.07)*		
DCZ	2021	DCZ	King-Elliott-Street Osprey 2	1470		10.75	G R Thurston	(Halesworth)	6.11.07
			(Built using Dart fuselage (c/n 1457) from unregistered Chard Osprey; Dart c/n 1470 was BGA 1245)						
DDC	2024	DDC	Slingsby T.21B	1157	RAFGSA 313	3.75	J S Shaw and partners	Perranporth	29. 3.09
					XN153				
DDK	2031	DDK	SZD-30 Pirat	S-04.08		4.75	P Jennings	Bembridge	15.10.05
DDQ	2036	-	Slingsby T.21B	630	RAFGSA 247	3.75	AeroVenture	Doncaster	*
					WB969		*(Damaged 24.8.80; frame on display 2007)*		
DEB	2047	DEB	Slingsby T59D Kestrel 19	1866		24.10.75	J L Smoker	RAF Weston-on-the-Green	19. 6.05
DEF	2050	DEF	ICA-Brasov IS-28B2	49		8.77	Not known *(Stored 2007)*	Shipdham	*
DEP	2058	DEP	Schleicher Ka 6CR	6452	AGA .	4.75	M D Brooks	Saltby	9.11.08
					BGA 2058, RAFGSA 350				
DEY	2067	DEY	LET L-13 Blanik	026352	RAFGSA R12	10. 7.75	Eight Ball Soaring Association	Shipdham	9. 9.03
					BGA 2067		*(Fuselage stored 6.08)*		
DFY	2091	DFY	Schempp-Hirth Standard Cirrus	396	AGA .	5.11.75	Science Museum *(On display)*	South Kensington	3. 3.92
DGH	2100	DGH	SZD-30 Pirat	B-533	RNGSA	12.75	T Bell and V Turner	Kingston Deverill	10. 3.07
DGP	2106	DGP	LET L-13 Blanik	026560		26. 5.76	B Kozuh	Ljubljana, Slovenia	30. 6.06
DGV	2112	-	Breguet 905S Fauvette	2	HB-632	6. 7.76	P Oldfield	(N.Yorkshire)	27. 9.08
DHY	2139	DHY	Schleicher K 7	1137	RAFGSA 266	14. 4.76	G Whittaker	Chipping	21. 1.07
					D-5162				
DJF	2146	500	Halford JSH Scorpion	001		7.77	R G Greenslade	(Doncaster)	30.12.80*
							(Previously at South Yorkshire Air Museum - for restoration)		
DJP	2154	DJP	Schleicher K 8B	8588	RAFGSA 335	21. 7.76	Sackville Vintage Gliding Club *(Stored 9.08)*		
								Sackville Lodge, Riseley	17. 6.03
DJS	2157	DJS	Schempp-Hirth SHK-1	51	SE-TNF	16. 7.76	J S S Selman	Limerick, Ireland	3. 8.05
					OY-MFX, HB-898				
DJT	2158	DJT	Schleicher K 7 (Mod.)	?	RAFGSA	7.76	Denbigh Gliding Club	Lleweni Parc	3. 6.06
							(Note: BGA 4271 is marked "DJT" also)		
DJW	2161	-	Manuel Condor	1		7.76	C V and R C Inwood *(Stored 2005)*	Lasham	18. 5.98
DKY	2187	DKY	Schleicher K 7	7187	RAFGSA 342	4.11.76	Defford Aero Club *(Stored 2005)*	Challock	14. 8.02
DLD	2192	DLD	Schleicher K 8B	8766	RAFGSA 383	17.11.76	Shalbourne Soaring Society	Rivar Hill	7. 8.06
							(Stored 4.08)		
DLG	2195	DLG	Schempp-Hirth Standard Cirrus	579	AGA 2	16.10.76	S Naylor	Burn	24. 9.08
DLQ	2203	609	Glasflügel Club Libelle 205	112	RAFGSA 773	11.76	Not known *(Wreck noted 9.08)*	Rattlesden	21. 6.94
DLW	2209	DLW	SZD-30 Pirat	B-467	PH-433	2. 6.77	G F Bryce and partners	North Connel	29. 4.96
							(Stored 5.08)		
DLZ	2212	456	Swales SD3-15T	03		12.76	R E Harris	Rivar Hill	25. 5.05
DMF	2218	DMF	Schleicher K 7	7073	D-4313	2. 3.77	J S Morgan	Bidford	22. 9.08
DMJ	2221	DMJ	Schleicher K 8B	8077	PH-290	19. 3.77	Not known *(Stored 10.04)*	Strathaven	23. 9.93
DNB	2238		Grunau Baby IIB	2	RAFGSA 380	2.77R	P Underwood	Eaton Bray	
			(Built Flg.u.Arbeitsg.Hall)		D-5766		*(On rebuild 2008)*		
DPG	2267	DPG	München Mü 13D III	005	D-1327	14. 6.77	G J Moore	Dunstable	24. 5.09
DPJ	2269	DPJ	Grob G102 Astir CS77	1641		8. 7.77	G Chaplin	Lasham	26. 4.05
DPP	2274	DPP	Schleicher Ka 2B Rhönschwalbe	105	D-1880	1. 7.77	B G Hoekstra	Breda, Netherlands	8. 7.02
DPR	2276	D-1265	Scheibe L-Spatz	05	D-1265	7. 7.77	C P Raine *"Sparrowfahrt"*	Thame	25. 7.01
DPT	2278	DPT	Scheibe L-Spatz 55	01	RAFGSA	25. 8.77	B V Smith *(Stored 6.08)*	Rufforth	12. 7.98
DPU	2279	DPU	EoN AP.5 Olympia 2B	EoN/O/142	RAFGSA 274	5. 9.77	J M Turner	Challock	12. 5.07
DPZ	2284	HB-561	Slingsby T.34A Sky	822	HB-561	9. 8.77	J S Morgan *(Under restoration 2007)*	Pershore	3. 7.00
DQP	2298	DQP	Schleicher K 8B	1181	?	15.11.77	P Hardman	Dunstable	1.10.06
DRK	2318	NT	Grob G102 Astir CS77	1686		31. 1.78	N Toogood	Weston-on-the-Green	27. 4.07
DRR	2324	DRR	Schleicher Ka 2 Rhönschwalbe	49	D-8108	11. 1.78	Dumfries and District Gliding Club	Falgunzeon	4. 8.09
DSA	2333	DSA	Slingsby T.30B Prefect	575	WE985	10. 2.78	J M Turner	Challock	13. 6.09
DSE	2337	227	Schempp-Hirth Mini Nimbus	36		2.78	G J Binnie	Bicester	4. 8.08
DSG	2339		Schleicher Ka 6CR	6393	D-5696	13. 4.78	R N Boddy	Wycombe Air Park	29. 8.07

Reg	BGA No	Comp	Type	c/n	Previous identities	Date	Owner	Location	Last date
DSM	2344	-	Fauvel AV.22S	3	F-CCGM	4.78	I Dunkley (Under restoration 2008)	Jezow, Poland	1. 8.95
DTR	2372	DTR	EoN AP.6 Olympia 401	EoN/4/005	NEJSGSA 7, RAFGSA 252, G-APSI	31. 5.78	P Blackman (Stored 2006)	(Ringmer)	15. 5.02
DTZ	2380	S30	Slingsby T.30B Prefect	573	WE983	21. 6.78	D Gibbs	Lee-on-Solent	31.10.09
DUC	2383	-	CARMAM M-100S Mésange	012	F-CCSA	6. 6.78	Not known (Stored 2006)	Carlton Moor	5.88*
DUD	2384	-	Grunau Baby III	?	BGA 2074, RAFGSA 374, D-9142	7. 6.78	Norfolk & Suffolk Aviation Museum	Flixton	29. 3.92
DUS	2396	638	Schleicher Ka 6E	4263	OY-XCB, HB-948	8.78	R Bartlett	Tibenham	10.11.05
DUY	2402	652	Glaser-Dirks DG-100	24	PH-525	13.10.78	A C Saxton and partners (Stored 6.08)	Rufforth	26. 7.05
DWE	2432	DWE	Schleicher K 7	7132	D-5427	3.11.78	N T Large	Lleweni Parc	5. 1.04
DWF	2433	-	Grunau Baby IIB (Built RNAY Fleetlands)	-	AGA 16, RNGSA 1-13, VW743	19. 4.80	Not known	Bicester	9. 1.02
DWP	2441	447	Glasflügel Mosquito B	136		15.12.78	R H Yarney	Lasham	23. 8.08
DXM	2463	DXM	Schleicher K 7 (Partly modified to ASK 13 standard)	626	RAFGGA 551, D-5707	20. 3.79	Vale of Neath Gliding Club	Shipdham	26. 4.04
DXY	2474	HB-474	Müller Moswey III	-	HB-474	20. 4.79	B Pearson	Eaglescott	9. 8.04
DYB	2477	"DYN"	Schleicher K 7	167/59	D-5775	29. 3.79	South London Gliding Centre	Kenley	9. 5.04
DYN	2486	DYN	Schleicher Ka 6CR	6129Si	D-8458	1. 5.79	J Hunneman (See BGA 2477)	Rivar Hill	24. 4.03
DZC	2498		Scheibe L-Spatz 55	642	RAFGGA 502, D-5629	4. 5.79	G A Ford (Stored 2006)	(Aston Down)	23.10.98
DZN	2508	990	Slingsby T65A Vega 17L	1910		13. 7.79	D A White	Aboyne	30. 7.07
DZS	2512	DZS	SZD-8bis-0 Jaskolka	183	HB-583	30. 5.79	R A Wilgoss	Wycombe Air Park	28. 8.08
DZV	2515	839	Scheibe SF 27A Zugvogel V	6065	D-5839	17. 7.79	N Newham	Usk	8. 5.05
DZW	2516	DZW	Schleicher Ka 6CR	6628	D-1045	11. 7.79	Not known (Stored 9.08)	Feshiebridge	18. 7.03
DZX	2517	-	Slingsby T.30B Prefect	577	WE987	8. 6.79	AeroVenture (On loan)	Doncaster	17. 7.89
EAC	2522	367	Grob G102 Astir CS77	1803		14. 6.79	I Pickering	Aston Down	27. 7.06
EAU	2538	EAU	Schleicher K 7 (Partly modified to ASK 13 standard)	7092	PH-304	29. 1.80	Welland Gliding Club	Lyveden	8. 9.07
EAV	2539	360	Schempp-Hirth Mini Nimbus C	136		31. 7.79	G D Crawford	RAF Weston-on-the-Green	22. 4.06
EBC	2546	EBC	Slingsby T.30B Prefect	1060	RAFGSA 33, BGA 1618, BGA 808	1. 8.79	K R Reeves (Noted 11.06) "Jonathan Livingstone Prefect"	RAF Syerston	16. 5.04
EBG	2550	EBG	Eiriavion PIK-20D-78	20662		4. 9.79	P F Woodcock	Camphill	23.11.07
EBP	2557	EBP	Allgaier Geier I	3/4	D-9025	4. 9.79	R A Earnshaw-Fretwell (Stored 1.09)	Keevil	21. 7.01
ECR	2583	WE990	Slingsby T.30B Prefect	580	WE990	7.11.79	D Ladley (Under restoration 2007)	Norfolk	7.84*
ECT	2585	604	Glasflügel 604	2	I-FEVG, D-0279	4.10.79	P T Nash (To D-0279 2008)	Crowland	1. 6.08
EDC	2594	-	Schleicher K 7	244	D-8527	13. 2.80	J C Shipley (Stored 8.07)	Camphill	8. 7.04
EDD	2595	W17	Schleicher ASW 17	17043	D-6865	23. 4.80	M D Etherington	Saltby	14.12.05
EDH	2599	EDH	Glasflügel Mosquito B	184		25. 3.80	D G Cooper	Tibenham	24. 7.05
EDL	2602	-	Focke-Wulf Weihe 50	4	D-0893, HB-555	26. 1.80	F K Russell (Last known being restored during 2000)	Dunstable	14.10.96
EED	2619	EED	Schleicher K 8B	590	RAFGSA R91, NEJSGSA, BGA 2619, D-5703	1. 3.80	A Twigg	Bicester	9. 8.08
EEV	2635	BW	Centrair ASW 20FL	20145		15. 5.80	R Baez	Wittstock-Berlinchen, Germany	2. 9.08
EFC	2642	EFC	Siebert Sie 3	3018	D-0811	3. 4.80	M S A Skinner	Cross Hayes	6. 6.09
EFJ	2648	EFJ	Centrair ASW 20F	20127		12. 4.80	D E Ball	Wycombe Air Park	26. 5.06
EFN	2652	EFN	Scheibe L-Spatz 55	635	D-1617	17. 5.80	J A Halliday	Aston Down	6. 7.08
EFS	2656	LS3	Rolladen-Schneider LS3	3022	HB-1356	14. 5.80	S Carmichael	Dunstable	29. 8.07
EGF	2669	EGF	Slingsby T65C Sport Vega	1936		28. 6.80	P Aitken	Lee-on-Solent	24. 2.08
EGG	2670	JH	Slingsby T65C Sport Vega	1939		23. 9.80	R Robbins	Usk	22.12.05
EGP	2677	BS1	Schleicher ASW 20L	20336		17. 9.80	B K Scaysbrook	Husbands Bosworth	25. 7.08
EHA	2688	D-5084	Schleicher K 8B	136/59	D-5084	2. 9.80	Not known (Stored 6.04)	Fairwood Common	2. 9.81
EHB	2689	K3	Schleicher Ka 3	3	RAFGGA 559	23.10.80	L S Hood	RAF Cranwell	28. 5.05
EHC	2690	EHC	Akaflieg Braunschweig SB-5B	5017	D-9310	14. 8.80	R I Davidson	Husbands Bosworth	12. 5.05
EHE	2692	WE992	Slingsby T.30B Prefect	582	WE992	29. 9.80	A P Stacey	RAF Keevil	26. 4.09
EHS	2704	EHS	ICA-Brasov IS-28B2	89		3.12.80	M Terry	Darlton	24. 3.08
EHX	2709	EHX	Grunau Baby IIB	134	D-1128	12.80	W R Williams	RAF Halton	4. 5.09
EJD	2715	261	Slingsby T65D Vega 17L	1930	BGA 2715	29. 6.81	A J French (Damaged Dunstable 28.3.97; wreck noted 2006)	Rufforth	28. 5.97
EJJ	2720	"WJ306"	Slingsby T.21B (See BGA 3240 for the real WJ306)	618	RAFGSA 120, BGA 662, WB957	1. 3.81	A C Jarvis	Parham	11. 5.09
EJM	2723	385	Schempp-Hirth Janus C	112	BGA 4168, RAFGSA R1, BGA 2723, D-7013	2.81	H A Torode	Lasham	16. 4.08
EJS	2728	319	Slingsby T65C Sport Vega	1948		20. 3.81	A D McLeman	Portmoak	19. 9.08
EJY	2734	EJY	SZD-9bis Bocian 1D	P-351	D-1587	13. 4.81	J A Stephen	Aboyne	29. 3.08
EKM	2747	-	Schleicher K 8B	657	PH-258	28. 5.81	Not known (Wreck stored 11.08)	Aston Down	2.89
EKX	2757	EKX	Schleicher Ka 6E	4027	D-1221	20. 6.81	A Coatsworth	Eyres Field	25. 8.08
ELC	2762	ELC	Slingsby T.45 Swallow	1474	AGA, RAFGSA 346	25. 5.81	J Povall	AAC Dishforth	25.11.09
ELE	2764	ELE	Schleicher ASK 21	21065		1. 7.81	Midland Gliding Club	Long Mynd	29. 6.07
ELH	2767	ELH	Slingsby T.21B (Possibly ex WB966 [627])	?	RAFGSA 314, RAF	16. 9.81	Not known (Stored 2005)	Enstone	10. 7.91
ELL	2770	-	Vogt Lo 100 Zwergreiher	25	HB-591	27. 7.81	LO100 Syndicate ("Total Excellium" titles)	RAF Halton	2.12.09
ELS	2776	ELS	EoN AP.10 460 Srs.1	EoN/S/020	RAFGGA 530	7. 2.82	D G Shepherd	Easterton	4. 5.09
ELU	2778	696	Schleicher ASW 20L	20462		15. 4.82	G Fryer	Aston Down	30. 4.06
ELV	2779	ELV	Scheibe Zugvogel IIIB	1088	F-CCPX	5. 9.81	C R W Hill	Upwood	18. 4.09
EMK	2793	EMK	Slingsby T.45 Swallow	?	RAFGGA 545	14. 4.82	P T Pollard-Wilkins	Ringmer	1. 9.09
EMW	2804	17	Grunau Baby III	?	D-1373	5. 7.89	M T Sands	Santo Tome del Puerto, Spain	2. 7.08
ENY	2830	ENY	Schleicher ASK 13	13606	RAFGSA R17	22. 7.82	Aquila Gliding Club (Stored 8.07)	Hinton-in-the-Hedges	2. 6.04

BGA	No	Code	Type	c/n	Prev id	Date	Owner	Location	Date
EPJ	2840	EPJ	Nord 2000	10399/69	F-CACX	26. 8.92	S Dijkstra and partners	Woensdrecht, Netherlands	9. 6.07
EPM	2843	EPM	Scheibe SF 34	5115		22.10.82	Angus Gliding Club	Drumshade	29. 8.05
EPR	2847	EPR	Hütter H.17	-	(Kenya) PH-269	30. 9.82	A C Jarvis	Parham	14. 5.09
EPV	2851	EPV	Schleicher K 7	7148	D-5468	8.10.82	South London Gliding Centre	Kenley	11. 5.08
EPW	2852	EPW	Schleicher Ka 6CR	6537	(Kenya)	21. 3.83	J Kitchen	Kirton in Lindsey	7. 2.05
EPZ	2855	D-4012	Scheibe Bergfalke II/55	370	D-4012	15. 1.83	A P Stacey and R Fretwell *(Noted 11.08)*	Keevil	11. 8.96
EOK	2865	EOK	Centrair 101A Pégase	101054		30. 5.83	L J Desmet	Pocklington	7. 6.08
EQM	2867	EQM	CARMAM M-100S Mésange	81	F-CDKQ	20. 3.83	S C Renfrew	Usk	4.11.07
EQP	2869	-	Glaser-Dirks DG-202/17	2-187/1761		10. 3.83	Not known	Aston Down	22.10.92
			(Cockpit under conversion to simulator 12.08)						
EOX	2877	EQX	CARMAM M-200 Foehn	54	F-CDKR	11. 4.83	R Pettifer and partners	Chipping	12. 7.08
EQY	2878	-	BAC.VII rep	01		8. 9.91	D Rogers	(Middlesex)	21. 5.96P
			(Rebuild of BAC Drone using wings of G-AEJR and new fuselage)				*(Being refurbished as powered aircraft)*		
ERB	2881	ERB	Slingsby T.50 Skylark 4 Special	001		25. 4.83	B V Smith	Sutton Bank	31.10.09
			(Built C Almack)						
ERU	2898	NX	Schempp-Hirth Nimbus-3/25.5	13	RAFGSA R26 D-6330	4. 5.83	L Urbani	Roitzschjora, Germany	11. 4.08
							(To RA-3484K 2008)		
ERW	2900	ERW	Slingsby T.21B	1130	RAFGSA 237 BGA 842	24. 5.83	N Jardine	Sebring, Florida	11. 6.05
							"The Spruce Goose"		
ERX	2901	180	Centrair 101A Pégase	101058		3. 8.83	C N Harder	Rivar Hill	14. 4.08
ERZ	2903	-	Oberlerchner Mg 19a Steinadler	015	OE-0324	1. 6.83	C Wills	Wycombe Air Park	6. 4.06
ESK	2913	ESK	Schleicher Ka 2B	697	RAFGGA 594 D-5947	23. 7.83	W R Williams *(Noted 6.08)*	RAF Halton	20. 5.00
ESM	2915	ESM	Breguet 905SA Fauvette	30	F-CCJA	14.10.83	J Doppelbauer	Gunzenhausen, Germany	20. 8.08
ESX	2925	ESX	Schleicher K 8B	8805	RAFGGA 553	10. 9.83	Not known	Aston Down	31.12.96
							(W/o Pocklington 2. 2.96; stored dismantled 12.08)		
ETB	2929	ETB	Schleicher Ka 6E	4365	HB-1021	20.11.83	A J Padgett	RAF Marham	27. 9.08
ETE	2932	-	Fauvel AV.36CR	214	RAFGSA R53 D-5353, D-8259	8.87	J S Allison	Bicester	7. 6.98
							"The Budgie" (Noted 8.08)		
ETP	2941	WB943	Slingsby T.21B	610	WB943	16. 6.84	P Hepworth tr Ouse T.21 Syndicate	Rufforth	19. 1.09
ETR	2943	S7	Schleicher K 7	3	D-8339	21. 2.84	Shenington Gliding Club	Edgehill	26. 7.04
ETU	2946	ETU	Schleicher K 7	?	RAFGSA R8 BGA 2607	24. 3.84	M J Libell	Strubby	25. 5.04
EUE	2956	EUE	Scheibe SF 27A Zugvogel V	6106	D-5342	6. 4.84	Newark & Notts Gliding Club	Darlton	8. 4.07
EUN	2964	-	Slingsby T.21B	588	RAFGSA R92 20. 4.84 RAFGSA 212, WB925		N I Newton	Wycombe Air Park	20. 6.08
EUQ	2966	EUQ	Schleicher K 7	863	D-4639	8. 5.84	J Marsden	Wormingford	1. 3.07
EUZ	2975		Slingsby T.21B	620	WB959	24. 6.84	Dartmoor Gliding Association	Brentor	31. 8.04
EVB	2977	EVB	Schleicher K 7	7004	D-5109	12. 6.84	Channel Gliding Club	Waldershare Park	11. 5.05
EVC	2978	EVC	CARMAM M-200 Foehn	55	F-CDKT	20. 6.84	W S Van Beek	Netherlands	6. 4.08
EVG	2982	EVG	Schleicher K 7	396	D-0018	17. 7.84	Derbyshire & Lancashire Gliding Club Camphill		16. 4.08
EVN	2988		Monnett Monerai	312	BGA 3190 (BGA 2988)	7.11.87	Not known	Bellarena	6.11.88
							(Noted 5.07)		
EVR	2991	EVR	LET L-13 Blanik	172604	G-ASVS OK-3840	30. 8.84	N A Mills	Hinton-in-the-Hedges	3. 7.07
FBR	3134	773	Grob G102 Astir CS77	1701	SE-TSV	5. 3.89	R Robinson	Wormingford	23. 4.08
FCC	3145	XN243	Slingsby T.31B	1182	XN243	6. 5.85	R Linde	Emmerich, Germany	30. 4.09
FCF	3148	993	Slingsby T.21B	MHL.017	WB990	12. 5.85	G Pullen	Lasham	29. 5.09
FCG	3149	WT871	Slingsby T.31B	681	WT871	5. 5.85	C Wevers	Amersfoort, Netherlands	21. 2.04
FCK	3152	671	Schempp-Hirth Ventus b/16.6	241		6. 5.85	L J Scott	Sleap	21. 6.05
FCT	3160	WB944	Slingsby T.21B	611	WB944	16.12.86	D C Perkins	Bicester	8. 5.09
FCZ	3166	-	Slingsby T.1 Falcon 1 replica	-		9. 7.85	D D Knight	RAF Halton	9. 4.09
			(Built Southdown Aero Services)						
FDC	3169	FDC	Pottier JP 15-34 Kit Club	TAH.50/60		10. 3.87	T A Hollings	Rufforth	18. 9.08
FDD	3170	FDD	Schleicher K 8B	8972	AGA 5	11. 7.85	Shalbourne Soaring Society	Rivar Hill	3. 3.07
							(Stored 4.08)		
FDF	3172	FDF	Grob G102 Astir CS	1321	D-7338	2. 9.85	R H Davies	Nympsfield	27. 8.08
FDQ	3181	FDQ	Slingsby T.31B	710	WT915	19. 9.85	J F Forster *"Chris Wills"*	Brüggen, Germany	17. 5.09
FDV	3186	D-5826	LET L-13 Blanik	173333	D-5826 D-KOEB, D-5826	4.86	T Wiltshire	Shipdham	4. 7.98
							(Stored 4.08)		
FDW	3187	438	Glaser-Dirks DG-300 Elan	3E143		26. 1.86	C Hadley	Brentor	16. 8.08
FDY	3189	FDY	Slingsby T.21B	MHL.005	WB978	26. 1.86	R Lloyd	Challock	11. 9.08
FED	3194	WT914	Slingsby T.31B	709	WT914	8. 2.86	Not known *(Stored 2007)*	Tibenham	7. 2.87
FEE	3195	-	Slingsby T.21B	MHL.016	WB989	20. 1.86	K Schickling	Aschaffenburg, Germany	8. 8.09
FEL	3201	FEL	Schleicher K 7	7231	RAFGGA 575 D-5. . .	22. 9.86	Dukeries Gliding Club	Darlton	19.11.05
FEZ	3214	-	EoN AP.7 Primary	EoN/P/037	RAFGSA R13 19. 9.86 RAFGSA 113, WP269		A P Stacey	RAF Keevil	3. 6.01
							(Stored 1.09)		
FFA	3215	FFA	Schleicher ASK 13	13651AB		15. 5.86	Staffordshire Gliding Club	Seighford	13. 2.07
FFG	3221	WB920	Slingsby T.21B	559	WB920	2. 6.86	J H Wisselink	Woensdrecht, Netherlands	5. 9.09
FFL	3225	FFL	Slingsby T.21B	MHL.020	WB993	28. 6.87	B van Aalst	Asperden, Germany	30. 4.09
FFQ	3229	FFQ	Slingsby T.31B	913	XE800	18. 8.86	W J Storey	(Surrey)	1. 7.09
FFW	3235	FFW	Slingsby T.21B	1155	XN151	2.10.87	R Schmid	Aalen-Elchingen, Germany	18. 6.09
FFZ	3238	WB981	Slingsby T.21B	MHL.008	WB981	21. 8.86	A P Stacey	RAF Keevil	19. 5.09
FGA	3239	WT913	Slingsby T.31B	708	WT913	26.10.86	AeroVenture *(On loan)*	Doncaster	21. 7.96
FGB	3240	WJ306	Slingsby T.21B	654	WJ306	23. 8.86	Oxford Gliding Club RAF Weston-on-the-Green		29. 8.09
							"Daisy" (BGA 2720 also carries "WJ306")		
FGC	3241	WT918	Slingsby T.31B	713	WT918	24. 8.86	K Litek	Jena, Germany	4. 8.09
FGE	3243	-	Slingsby T.21B	619	WB958	9.87	Not known *(Stored 11.06)*	Edgehill	21. 4.93
FGG	3245	WG498	Slingsby T.21B	665	WG498	29. 9.86	A Flewelling and partners	Aston Down	26. 4.09
FGM	3250	FGM	Slingsby T.21B	1160	XN156	19. 7.87	R B Petrie	Portmoak	22. 2.09
FGS	3255	XN157	Slingsby T.21B	1161	XN157	11.10.86	D W Cole	Long Mynd	21. 8.09

FGZ	3262	FGZ	Schleicher K 7	7238	D-5376	1.87	Dartmoor Gliding Society *(Stored 2007)*Brentor	9.10.99
FHB	3264		Slingsby T.21B (T)	MHL.018	WB991	17. 2.87	G Traves	East Kirkby	12. 9.04
			(Fuji-Robin EC-34PM)					
FHK	3272	WT900	Slingsby T.31B	695	WT900	22. 4.87	A Hepburn and partners	Lee-on-Solent	6. 5.06
FHQ	3277	-	Hols der Teufel rep	001		21. 3.90	Deutsches Segelflugmuseum		
			(Built M L Beach)				*(On display 2006)*	Wasserkuppe, Germany	N/E
FHU	3281	FHU	Schleicher K 7	629	RAFGSA R15	17. 6.87	Dartmoor Gliding Society	Brentor	4. 3.05
			(Modified to ASK 13 standard)		RAFGGA, D-5722		*(Stored 2007)*		
FHY	3285	H5	Scheibe SF 27A Zugvogel V	6045	D-1868	28. 6.87	J M Pursey	North Hill	27. 9.08
FJA	3287	FJA	Slingsby T.21B	1152	XN148	8. 7.87	G Follmann	Lachen-Speyerdorf, Germany	16. 5.09
FJB	3288	FJB	Slingsby T.21B	MHL.002	WB975	8. 7.87	Angus Gliding Club *(As "WB975")* Drumshade	16. 6.07
FJD	3290	T21	Slingsby T.21B	MHL.007	WB980	29. 8.87	K W Payne and partners Husbands Bosworth	14. 5.08
FJF	3292	FJF	Slingsby T.21B	586	WB923	7. 9.87	R L Horsnell	Snitterfield	14. 5.08
FJG	3293		Slingsby T.31B	1180	XN241	8. 9.87	M H Simms *(Under restoration 11.08)*Shipdham	7. 9.88
FJN	3299	903	Slingsby T.31B	698	WT903	17. 2.88	B Kozuh	Ljubljana, Slovenia	19. 7.06
FJQ	3301	FJQ	Schempp-Hirth Ventus cT	104/365		24. 3.88	B Rood	Hinton-in-the-Hedges	29. 8.06
FKA	3311	FKA	Schleicher Ka 6CR	6239	D-7037, D-5435	21. 2.88	E Drake	Kingston Deverill	15. 6.06
FKP	3324	WB971	Slingsby T.21B	632	WB971	28. 2.88	M Powell	AAC Wattisham	13. 6.05
							(Damaged Camphill 1. 7.04; for rebuild with fuselage of BGA 765)	
FKX	3332	FKX	Schleicher Ka 6CR	6433	D-4316	30. 4.88	J Bates and partners	Lasham	1. 7.05
FLB	3336	XA295/D	Slingsby T.31B	837	XA295	23. 8.88	R Birch	Aston Down	19. 4.08
FLK	3344	FLK	Schleicher K 7	985	D-5047	12. 1.89	Darlton Gliding Club *(Cancelled 21.1.08)*Darlton	14. 9.08
FLL	3345	FLL	SZD-9bis Bocian 1D	F-877	OH-336	30. 7.88	Bath, Wilts and North Dorset Gliding Club	
					OH-KBP			Kingston Deverill	21. 5.08
FLQ	3349	FLQ	Schleicher K 8B	8195A	D-8887	15. 8.88	F J Glanville	Long Mynd	26. 5.07
FMA	3359	-	Slingsby T.38 Grasshopper	793	WZ797	8. 8.88	Not known *(Stored 2006)*	Upwood	7. 8.89
FME	3363	927	Schleicher ASW 15	15164	D-0825	1. 8.88	T J Stanley	Sutton Bank	3. 1.07
FMM	3370	FMM	Schleicher Ka 6CR	6328	D-1260	20.10.88	D Hall	Burn	21. 5.05
FMR	3374	FMR	Neukom Standard Elfe S-2	05	HB-801	8.11.88	M A Braddock and partners	Camphill	10. 4.09
FMZ	3382	FMZ	Schleicher K 7	7018	D-6035	22.11.88	Nene Valley Gliding Club	Upwood	17. 7.04
FNC	3385	-	Slingsby T.21B	601	WB934	5.11.88	G Follmann	Oberschleissheim, Germany	2. 5.09
FNX	3404	FNX	Wassmer WA-30 Bijave	84	F-CCTJ	2. 1.89	8 Ball Soaring Association	Shipdham	17. 1.05
FPQ	3421	FPQ	Schleicher K 7	EB180/61	D-5184	15. 2.89	East Sussex Gliding Club	Ringmer	24. 2.05
FPS	3423	FPS	Slingsby T.21B	MHL.001	OH-914X	3. 2.89	J Holland Brandenburg-Mühlenfeld, Germany	14. 6.09
					LN-GAO, BGA 3423, WB974				
FPU	3425	FPU	Schleicher Ka 2B Rhönschwalbe	-	HB-698	17. 2.89	T J Wilkinson	Sackville Lodge, Riseley	4. 4.06
			(Built Segelfluggruppe Zwingen)						
FQD	3434	FQD	Schleicher K 8B	8289	D-1908	6. 3.89	Kent Gliding Club	Challock	7. 1.05
FQE	3435	FQE	Schleicher K 8B	3	D-6329	3. 4.89	Cotswold Gliding Club *(Stored 12.08)*Aston Down	9. 4.01
FRG	3461	FRG	Siebert Sie 3	3009	D-0739	7. 4.89	A Cridge	Talgarth	11. 1.09
FRQ	3469	XT653	Slingsby T.45 Swallow	1420	XT653	27. 4.89	D Shrimpton	RAF Keevil	21. 5.09
FSB	3480	-	Slingsby T.38 Grasshopper	1269	XP492	R	Not known *(Stored 2005)*	Eyres Field	
FSC	3481	WZ755	Slingsby T.38 Grasshopper	751	WZ755	27. 4.90	Boulton Paul Heritage Project Wolverhampton	30. 4.93
							(On display 5.08)		
FSE	3483	FSE	Schleicher Ka 6CR	6021	D-1946	19. 8.89	G W Lobb	North Hill	28. 7.04
FSJ	3487	WT908	Slingsby T.31B	703	WT908	22. 5.89	R J Brimfield	Dunstable	24. 9.09
FSK	3488	WZ795	Slingsby T.38 Grasshopper	791	WZ795	26. 6.89	E Janssen	Lemelerveld, Netherlands	27. 5.09
FSV	3498	WZ819	Slingsby T.38 Grasshopper	800	WZ819	26. 6.89	P D Mann *(Noted 6.08)*	RAF Halton	6. 6.04
FTF	3508	FTF	Schleicher Ka 6CR	6294	D-6081	5. 9.89	T Delap	Ridgewell	12. 6.06
FTM	3514	-	Schleicher K 8B	513	D-5708	30. 8.89	Vale of Neath Gliding Club	Rhigos	9. 4.06
FTU	3521	FTU	Schleicher K 7	302	HB-599	25. 9.89	Dartmoor Gliding Society *(Scrapped .06)*Brentor	25. 3.03
FUD	3529	2	SZD-9bis Bocian 1E	P-689	SP-2807	2.11.89	Mendip Gliding Club *(Stored 7.08)* Halesland	16. 4.04
FUF	3531	FUF	Scheibe SF 27A Zugvogel V	6089	D-6068	30. 9.89	East Sussex Gliding Club	Ringmer	22. 4.04
FUW	3545	XE807	Slingsby T.31B Cadet TX.3	920	XE807	20.11.89	G Tischler	Germany	12. 7.09
FVA	3548	N15	Schleicher K 8B	1051	D-5117	13. 4.90	Portsmouth Naval Gliding Club Lee-on-Solent	18.10.06
FWJ	3580	S3	Rolladen-Schneider LS7-WL	7078		22. 3.90	J P Popika	Gransden Lodge	1. 8.08
FXE	3600	35	Rolladen-Schneider LS7	7090		23. 3.90	J C Kingerlee	RAF Weston-on-the-Green	28. 9.05
FXF	3601	FXF	Slingsby T.50 Skylark 4	1455	HB-812	7. 5.90	A J Hewitt	Shipdham	5. 5.08
FXN	3608	FXN	CARMAM M-200 Foehn	4	OO-ZNI	14. 4.90	R Idle *(Under restoration 2007)*	Burn	9. 9.01
					(OO-ZXS), F-CCXS				
FXP	3609	FXP	LET L-23 Super Blanik	907609		17. 7.90	Cambridge University GC	Gransden Lodge	28. 6.07
FXR	3611	L12	Sportine Aviacija LAK-12	6162		4. 9.90	S R Blackmore	Hinton-in-the-Hedges	23. 4.05
FXT	3613		Centrair 101A Pégase	101056	F-CFQV	4.90	K Ludlow	Viterbo, Italy	4. 8.02
FZG	3650	FZG	SZD-9bis Bocian 1D	F-859	SP-2450	24. 9.90	J H Nash *(Stored 9.08)*Sackville Lodge, Riseley	14.10.06
FZM	3655	FZM	Scheibe SF 27A Zugvogel V	6103	D-1772	7. 8.90	N Dickenson	Chipping	31. 8.08
FZU	3662		Slingsby T.38 Grasshopper	761	WZ765	8. 8.91	Luftwaffenmuseum	Berlin-Gatow	26.12.96
							(On display 2006)		
GAC	3670	GAC	Schleicher Ka 6CR	6301	(BGA 3647)	11.90	McLean Aviation	Rufforth	2. 2.99
					RAFGGA 557, D-5572		*(W/o 25.11.98; stored 2006)*		
GAJ	3676	GAJ	Glaser-Dirks DG-300 Club Elan			10.12.90	S M Lewis	Long Mynd	9. 6.08
				3E385C56					
GAK	3677	GAK	LET L-13 Blanik	174522	2-84 (Lithuania)	5. 7.97	North Wales Gliding Club	Llantisilio	27. 1.07
GAQ	3682	GAQ	Schleicher K 7	3	PH-788	19. 4.91	Channel Gliding Club	Waldershare Park	24. 7.06
					D-5550		*(Wfu 2006)*		
GBE	3696	-	Schleicher Ka 6CR-Pe	6133A	D-4085	23.12.90	S Simpson	Darlton	9. 9.08
GBM	3703	GBM	Scheibe SF 27A Zugvogel V	6060	RAFGGA	2. 1.91	G Cook tr BFMT Syndicate	North Hill	12.12.07
					D-5409				
GCG	3722	S81	Schleicher K 8B	8186	D-5227	5. 2.91	Shenington Gliding Club *(Stored 4.08)* Edgehill	24.10.04
GCJ	3724	GCJ	Sportine Aviacija LAK-12	626	?	30. 3.91	P Crowhurst	Crowland	27. 5.05
			(New wings with reconditioned 1982-built fuselage)						
GCS	3732	H12	Glasflügel Club Libelle 205	159	F-CEQL	7. 7.91	D G Coats	Portmoak	31. 8.08
GDH	3746	GDH	Glasflügel Club Libelle 205	63	OO-ZKH	29. 4.91	Not known *(Wreck noted 9.08)*	Rattlesden	28. 4.92
GDN	3751	294	Rolladen-Schneider LS3-17	3291	D-6932	28. 4.91	S J Pepler	Sandhill Farm, Shrivenham	15. 5.08
GDW	3759	GDW	Scheibe SF 27A Zugvogel V	6116	D-1997	16. 5.91	M W Hands	Saltby	26. 7.06

GEA	3763	GEA	Schleicher Ka 6CR	849	(BGA 3605) D-5801	7. 6.91	C Deane	Rufforth	7. 6.08
GEN	3774	GEN	Slingsby T.21B	1154	RAFGGA 550 XN150	16. 5.92	A Harris *(Blown over 30.6.07; under restoration)*	Germany	11. 6.08
GEQ	3776	2001	SZD-12A Mucha 100A	462	SP-2001	6. 6.91	R A Earnshaw-Fretwell	Upavon	11. 7.09
HAE	3781	HAE	Glasflügel Club Libelle 205	75	D-8687	5. 7.91	S R Morgan	Lee-on-Solent	11. 9.08
HAG	3783	HAG	Schleicher K 7	834	RAFGGA 557 D-5795	21. 5.92	Denbigh Gliding Club	Lleweni Parc	24. 3.07
HAK	3786	XA302	Slingsby T.31B	844	XA302	17. 8.91	RAF Museum *(On display 4.08)*	Hendon	24. 5.96
HAN	3789	278	Schempp-Hirth Standard Cirrus	130	D-0326	14. 8.91	I Ashdown	Parham	8. 4.05
HAS	3793	HAS	SZD-50-3 Puchacz	B-2043		17. 8.91	The Gliding Centre	Husbands Bosworth	19. 2.08
HBX	3823	HBX	Slingsby T.45 Swallow	1386	8801M, XS650	16. 5.93	J P Ben David	Lasham	20. 7.09
HBZ	3825	HBZ	Slingsby T.15 Gull III rep	-		28. 6.92	P R Philpot	Chipping	15. 7.09
HCG	3833	HCG	Maupin Woodstock One *(Built R Harvey)*	-		7.10.92	R Harvey	Tibenham	27. 1.09
HCK	3836	WB962	Slingsby T.21B	623	RAFGGA WB962	2. 1.92	V Mallon Kleve-Wisseler Dünen, Germany		1. 5.09
HCM	3838	HCM	Schleicher K 7	498	D-5669	4. 3.92	M P Barnard *(Stored 4.08)*	Edgehill	29. 8.02
HCN	3839	HCN	CARMAM M-200 Foehn	24	F-CDDR	21.12.92	8 Ball Soaring Association	Shipdham	28. 6.05
HCP	3840	HCP	Avialsa A.60 Fauconnet	123K	F-CDLA	19. 2.93	C Kaminski *(Being refurbished)*	Eaglescott	31. 7.95
HCY	3849	HCY	Glaser-Dirks DG-300 Club Elan	3E413C67		10. 5.94	S T Dry	RAF Keevil	28. 8.05
HDM	3862	"HDH"	SZD-12A Mucha 100A	448	SP-1987	15. 4.92	T J Wilkinson	Sackville Lodge, Riseley	19. 5.05
HFC	3901	WB924	Slingsby T.21B	587	WB924	25. 7.92	P Hardman	Dunstable	27. 8.09
HFE	3903	XN187	Slingsby T.21B	1166	XN187	23. 6.92	A Hill and partners	RAF Halton	6. 1.10
HFG	3905	HFG	Slingsby T.21B	1165	XN186	28. 6.92	M H Simms *(Wears XN186)*	RAF Watton	21. 7.09
HFZ	3922	-	Abbott-Baynes Scud replica *(Built by Mike Beach)*	001		R	Brooklands Museum	Brooklands	
HGA	3923	HGA	Wassmer WA-26P Squale	43	F-CDUH	30. 3.93	E C Murgatroyd Sackville Lodge, Riseley		15. 5.04
HCH	3930	HGH	Schleicher ASW 19B	19351	D-1199	26. 8.92	A Wood	North Hill	19. 1.04
HGY	3945		SZD-24C Foka	W-180	SP-2385	16.12.92	Peterborough & Spalding Gliding Club	Crowland	27. 6.07
HHG	3953	WT910	Slingsby T.31B	705	WT910	9. 1.93	N J Jardine	Sebring, Florida	5. 8.06
HJD	3974	HJD	Schleicher Ka 6E	4141	D-.... OH-505, SE-TFM	4. 2.94	J P Stafford	Edgehill	30. 8.07
HJJ	3979		Slingsby T.38 Grasshopper	797	WZ816	R	J Wilkins *(Stored 2008)*	Redhill	
HJM	3982	HJM	Hütter H.28 III replica *(Built E R Duffin)*	ED.02		25. 5.93	B Pearson *(Being refurbished)*	Eaglescott	12. 6.99
HJN	3983	HJN	Schempp-Hirth Standard Cirrus	440G	HB-1206	2. 6.93	A Fidler	Crowland	13. 9.08
HJZ	3993	865	Schleicher ASW 15B	15190	OH-408	15. 5.94	R R Beezer	Camphill	29. 9.05
HKJ	4002	-	Penrose Pegasus 2 *(Built J M Lee)*	001		14. 7.93	Norfolk & Suffolk Aviation Museum	Flixton	15. 9.98
HKP	4007	HKP	Schleicher ASK 23B	23100	D-2935 HB-1935	9. 8.93	Midland Gliding Club *(To Denmark as OY-CXL 9.08)*	Long Mynd	30. 1.07
HKT	4011	HKT	Schleicher ASW 19 *(C/n conflicts with OE-5174 but believed correct)*	19168	D-7958	4.10.93	P Clayton	Burn	26. 8.06
HKW	4014	HKW	Marco J 5 *(Built D Austin - regd with c/n 001)*	009	G-BSBO	2. 6.94	G K Owen "Flying Penguin II"	Bidford	19. 3.04
HLR	4033	XE786	Slingsby T.31B	899	XE786	18.12.93	D Thomson *(Stored 2006)*	Arbroath	15. 4.04
HLU	4036	HLU	Scheibe SF 27A Zugvogel V	6101	SE-TGP	22. 2.94	.. King	(Solihull)	8. 5.08
HMH	4045	HMH	Schleicher K 8B *(Built by Bayer; officially regd as c/n 2330)*	5	D-5735	15. 4.94	Shenington Gliding Club	Edgehill	31. 3.08
HND	4064	HND	Scheibe Zugvogel IIIA	1044	HB-735 D-9119	23. 5.94	M Y Kiteley	Sackville Lodge, Riseley	13. 7.08
HNJ	4069	HNJ	Schleicher K 7	7031	D-1667 RAFGGA ??, D-6233	6. 5.94	N J Orchard-Armitage	Waldershare Park	5. 4.05
HNS	4077	XN185	Slingsby T.21B	1164	8942M XN185	21. 6.94	RAF Museum *(Stored 2007)*	RAF Stafford	12. 4.04
HPF	4090	"HPH"	SZD-9bis Bocian 1E *(Overshot landing 24.4.00; stored 6.08)*	P-740	OH-508	3. 8.94	Bath, Wilts and North Dorset Gliding Club	Kingston Deverill	23. 2.01
HPG	4091	HPG	Maupin Woodstock *(Built J M Stockwell)*	551	VR-HKI	14. 7.96	J M Stockwell	Boonah, Australia	10. 9.08
HPJ	4093	HPJ	Edgley EA9 Optimist	EA9/001		22.11.94	J K Edgley	Tibenham	25. 8.09
HPP	4098		Slingsby T.38 Grasshopper	863	XA230	5. 2.95	E Fowkes	Henlow	3. 9.08
HQB	4110	WB935	Slingsby T.21B *(Officially regd with c/n 1099 which is a corruption of fuselage no. SSK/FF1099)*	602	WB935	1.10.94	C E Anson	Hahnweide, Germany	4. 4.09
HQC	4111	HQC	Scheibe Bergfalke II/55	322	D-9004	20.12.94	S H Gibson	Gransden Lodge	5.10.06
HQG	4115	HQG	Sportine Aviacija LAK-12	6222		30. 4.95	J M Pursey	North Hill	11. 9.08
HQN	4121	D64	Schempp-Hirth Nimbus-2B	139	D-6494	29. 1.95	A J Nurse	Nympsfield	10. 3.05
HQT	4125	A77	Grob G102 Astir CS77	1678	RAFGGA 561	12. 2.95	E Beckmann	Lasham	10. 3.06
HRD	4135	-	Slingsby T.21B	634	WB973	18. 3.95	C Langenau	Aukrug, Germany	14. 6.09
HRQ	4145	169	Schempp-Hirth Mini Nimbus C	123	(BGA 4122) SE-TVB	17. 4.95	C Buzzard	Husbands Bosworth	4. 4.07
HRT	4148	HRT	Schleicher K 8B	8390A	D-5599	9. 3.96	Heron Gliding Club	RNAS Yeovilton	20. 6.04
HSH	4162	HSH	Scheibe Zugvogel IIIB	7/1041	D-6558	12. 7.95	K S Smith	Wormingford	18.12.05
HSU	4173		Schleicher ASK 18	18025	AGA 16	R	Booker Gliding Club *(Being refurbished)*	Wycombe Air Park	
HUP	4216	WK	Schempp-Hirth Ventus-2cT	4/11		16. 2.96	W Kos *(To SP-0069 5.08)*	Bielsko-Biala, Poland	6. 4.08
HVB	4228	HVB	Slingsby T.31B	850	(BGA 3249) XA308	27. 4.96	M Hoogenbosch	Hilversum, Netherlands	1. 5.09
HVC	4229	HVC	Slingsby T.38 Grasshopper	765	WZ769	4. 5.01	J F Forster	Hilversum, Netherlands	21. 9.05
HVD	4230	KO	SZD-55-1	551193052		23. 4.96	K Ostromecki *(To C-FSVQ 5.08)*	Poland	4. 3.08
HVJ	4235	962	Scheibe SF 27A Zugvogel V	6012	OE-0762	1. 6.96	C P Bleaden	Kirton in Lindsey	27. 7.04
HWD	4254	HWD	Schempp-Hirth Standard Cirrus	97	HB-987	3. 6.96	M R Hoskins	Rivar Hill	8. 5.06
HWE	4255	HWE	Schleicher K 8B	1151	HB-700	31. 5.96	G Smith *(Fuselage stored 2008)*	(Surrey)	9. 2.04
HWG	4257	HWG	Glasflügel Standard Libelle 201B	259	HB-1051	19. 6.96	M Kalweit	Dunstable	28. 8.08

HWN	4263	598	Schempp-Hirth Nimbus-3T	8/60	D-KHIF	5. 7.96	H Hampel *(To D-KHIF 4.08)*Michelbach,Germany		4. 7.08
HWQ	4265	HWQ	Scheibe L-Spatz 55	607	D-6195	12. 7.96	A Gruber *"Heisse Kartoffel"*	Usk	6. 8.08
HWT	4268	S83	Schleicher K 8B	8780	HB-958	13. 7.96	A K Bailey	Edgehill	31. 5.08
HWY	4273	168	Jastreb Standard Cirrus G/81	359	LN-GAL	6. 9.96	D D Copeland	Lasham	7. 5.08
HXA	4275	Z33	Scheibe Zugvogel IIIB	1107	D-2005	17. 3.97	P Kent	Saltby	29. 5.08
HXL	4286	OK-0927	Letov LF-107 Lunak	39	OK-0927 OK-0827	1.11.96	G P Saw *"Czech Mate"*	Wycombe Air Park	24. 3.09
HYN	4312	HYN/1018	Schleicher K 8B	8310A	D-1018	9.11.97	G Brook	Upwood	9. 4.05
HZC	4326	216	Grob G102 Astir CS	1092	D-6991	24. 3.97	K G Laws	Lasham	15.12.05
HZN	4336	D-6173	Schleicher Ka 2B Rhönschwalbe	195	D-6173	28. 3.97	R A Willgoss	Wycombe Air Park	26. 8.08
HZP	4337	56	Rolladen-Schneider LS8-18	8117		12. 3.97	S J Redman	Gransden Lodge	25. 4.05
HZT	4341	X50	Centrair ASW 20F	20150	F-CFLL	19. 8.97	T J Banks	Ringmer	24. 3.08
JAK	4357		Schleicher Ka 6E	4301	F-CDRJ	R	Not known		
JAM	4359	777	Schleicher ASW 15B	15353	D-2360	29. 5.97	T J Beckwith	Sackville Lodge, Riseley	23. 7.06
JAP	4361	-	Slingsby T.38 Grasshopper *(Believed to be ex WZ818 [799])*	779	WZ783	R	R H Targett	Nympsfield	
JAU	4366	WB922	Slingsby T.21B	585	WB922	27. 5.97	A Clarke	RAF Hullavington	28. 8.09
JBA	4372	JBA / XP463	Slingsby T.38 Grasshopper *(Assembled from components; p/i is starboard wing only)*	1262	XP463	8. 6.98	P A Wheatcroft	Lasham	5. 9.09
JBE	4376	LX	ISF Mistral-C	MC020/79	OY-XLX PH-667	4. 7.97	R R Penman	RNAS Yeovilton	13. 8.08
JBP	4385	B2	Rolladen-Schneider LS6-18W	6378		25. 7.97	L E Garcia-Castillo *(Cancelled 22.1.08; to D-8561)*	Ocana, Spain	2. 6.08
JBZ	4395	JBZ	Grob G102 Astir CS	1492	D-4794	30. 8.97	S J Harris	(Welshpool)	17. 9.08
JCR	4411	JCR	Grob G102 Astir CS	1181	OE-5188	28.10.97	B Harrison	Kingston Deverill	11.11.05
JCS	4412	WT898	Slingsby T.31B	693	BGA 3284 WT898	23.10.97	G Schwab	Graz, Austria	28. 6.04
JDA	4420	GR	Schempp-Hirth Nimbus-3/24.5	8	D-1788	9.11.97	G R Ross	Lasham	7. 3.06
JDB	4421	WZ828	Slingsby T.38 Grasshopper	809	WZ828	6.11.97	A Clarke	RAF Hullavington	28. 9.09
JDW	4440	JDW	PZL-Swidnik PW-5 Smyk	17.09.018		23.12.97	Burn Gliding Club *(Stored for spares 2.08)*Burn		14.12.00
JFW	4488	JFW	Sportine Aviacija LAK-12	6192	LX-CDM	4. 4.98	E W Burgess	Lyveden	5. 3.09
JGA	4492	JGA	Fedorov Me7b Mechta	M010		16.10.98	N Wilkinson	Challock	14. 8.08
JGF	4497	JGF	Neukom Elfe S4D	416	BGA 3316 D-4820	13. 5.98	C V Inwood	Lasham	29. 4.06
JHA	4516	EU	Schempp-Hirth Std. Cirrus 75	645	D-4240	9. 5.98	G Carruthers *(To Slovakia as OM-7516 2007)*	Pocklington	2. 4.07
JHB	4517	JHB	Scheibe L-Spatz 55	552	D-1618	15. 8.98	A Gruber	Usk	6. 8.08
JHE	4520	JHE	Grob G102 Astir CS Jeans	2189	CS-PBI BGA 3977, D-7764	17. 5.98	Aero Club de Portugal	Sintra	17. 4.08
JHH	4523	986	Schempp-Hirth Standard Cirrus 349G		D-3006	20. 5.98	R J Lodge	Dunstable	13. 2.08
JJM	4551	JJM	Schempp-Hirth Standard Cirrus 403G		D-2933	17. 7.98	Skycraft	Spalding	12. 7.05
JJN	4552	JJN	Slingsby T.38 Grasshopper *(Regd as '2067', from Frame no.SSK/FF/2067)*	1267	XP490	22. 7.98	611 VGS	RAF Watton	21. 7.99
JJS	4556	XA240	Slingsby T.38 Grasshopper	873	XA240	8.12.08	A P Benbow and J Farnell	Portmoak	7.12.09
JJU	4558	H2	Rolladen-Schneider LS8-a	8200		24. 8.98	A J French	Dunstable	13. 8.07
JKH	4571	P30	Schempp-Hirth Ventus cT	174/566	RAFGSA R30	22.10.98	J F Fitzgerald *(To VH-PEO 4.08)*	Usk	11. 4.08
JLE	4592	JLE	Schleicher ASK 13	13245	RAFGSA R90 NEJSGSA 1	21.10.98	British Army (Germany) Gliding Centre Javelin Barracks, Elmpt Station, Germany		17. 3.07
JLF	4593	JLF	Schleicher ASK 13	13150	AGA 14	13.12.98	Wyvern Gliding Club Trenchard Lines, Upavon		7. 7.07
JLU	4606	11	Schempp-Hirth Ventus-2cT	37/126		3.99	R L Fox and P M Kirschner *(To Australia as VH-IIK 10.08)*	Bicester	21. 4.08
JLX	4609	JLX	Schempp-Hirth Standard Cirrus 279G		OO-ZGL, D-1985	11.98	M W Fisher	Talgarth	30. 3.07
JME	4616	JME	Schleicher K 7	5	D-8867	12.98	W E Masterton	Blenheim, Jamaica	25. 1.04
JPK	4670	-	Slingsby T.34A Sky	672	RAFGSA 876 XA876, G-672	5.99	J Tournier	Wycombe Air Park	2. 6.07
JQY	4707	R92	Slingsby T.21B Sedbergh	666	RAFGSA R92 NEJSGSA 4, WG499	6.99	RAFGSA Crusaders Gliding Club Kingsfield, Cyprus		26.12.09
JRM	4720	212	Grob G102 Astir CS	1332	(BGA 4314) AGA 6	21. 9.99	Anglia Gliding Club *(Collision with motor glider on take-off, Honington 11.8.07)*	AAC Wattisham	6. 4.08
JRN	4721	PT	Glaser-Dirks DG-202/17C	2-118CL04	D-7267	1.10.99	T G Roberts *(Cancelled 22.1.08)*	Lasham	6. 9.08
JRP	4722	JRP	Grob G102 Astir CS Jeans	2244	D-5951	9.99	Borders Gliding Club *(Stored 6.08)*	Rufforth	30.10.07
JRQ	4723	PM3	Pfenninger-Markwalder Elfe PM3	001	N6351U N63514, HB-526	11.99	G McLean	Lleweni Parc	23. 8.08
JRZ	4732		Colditz Cock rep *(Under construction by M Francis)*	-		R	R M Francis	Camphill	
JSB	4734	UWE	Rolladen-Schneider LS4	4424	D-4541	2.00	H Vare *(To D-9114 .08)*	Speyer, Germany	16. 2.08
JSP	4746	JSP	Slingsby T.31B *(Restoration using wings of XE798)*	1189	BGA 2724 XN250	4. 7.04	R Wulfers	Deelen, Netherlands	4. 5.08
JSO	4747	F1	Rolladen-Schneider LS8-b	8301	D-KKAF	5.00	I Mountain *(Carries "BGA 4756" which is now G-CJSZ)*	RAF Cranwell	19.11.08
JTA	4757	-	Colditz Cock rep *(Built by Southdown Aero Services and John Lee)*	SA3		1.00	Norfolk & Suffolk Aviation Museum	Flixton	20. 2.00
JTC	4759	JTC	Glaser-Dirks DG-100G	84G5	(BGA 4744) HB-1335	25. 5.00	A Burger	(Neustadt, Germany)	5. 7.05
JTE	4761	JTE	Schempp-Hirth Standard Cirrus 470G		D-3718	2.00	P W Symonds	Ringmer	6. 4.08
JTX	4778	JTX	Start+Flug H101 Salto	47	D-9260	3.00	C Schneeberger *(To D-9260 2008)*	La Motte du Caire, France	4. 1.08
JVY	4827	F6	Schempp-Hirth Discus b	175	RAFGSA R6	8.00	M R Garwood	Husbands Bosworth	23. 9.08
JWE	4833	JWE	Slingsby T.21B	1159	XN155	1. 7.00	M Selss	Bad Tolz, Germany	18. 6.09
JWN	4841	UY	Rolladen-Schneider LS4-a	4728	D-7008	24. 2.01	D Bartek *(To D-1103 4.08)*Dannstadt, Germany		16. 2.08
JXD	4856	WB961	Slingsby T.21B	622	WB961	20. 1.01	F Brune	Eudenbach, Germany	26. 6.06
JXE	4857	JXE	SZD-22C Mucha Standard	F-717	SP-2330	12. 8.01	C E Harwood	Wormingford	11. 6.05
JXJ	4861	W7	Schleicher ASW 28	28012		29. 1.01	E W Johnston	Dunstable	26. 3.07
JXS	4869	JXS	Schleicher K 8B	8778	RAFGSA R95 RAFGSA 395	7. 3.04	Stratford on Avon Gliding Club *(Stored 6.08)*	Snitterfield	20. 3.08

JYA	4877	WB988	Slingsby T.21B	MHL.015	WB988	31. 3.01	C Bravo	Santo Tome del Puerto, Spain	4. 3.09
JYG	4884	OK-0833	Letov LF-107 Lunak	49	OK-0833	21. 9.02	M Launer	Rossfeld, Germany	16. 8.09
JYQ	4892	485	Glaser-Dirks DG-101G Elan	E181G147	D-1485	15. 6.02	A M Booth	Wormingford	26. 8.08
JYV	4897	JYV	Schleicher K 8B	133	D-8395	18. 6.01	European Soaring Club	Le Blanc, France	4. 7.04
JYW	4898	JYW	Schleicher K 8B	8432A	D-5682	18. 6.01	European Soaring Club	Le Blanc, France	4. 7.04
JZD	4905	JZD	Dittmar Condor IV	018	(D-0125) LV-DHV	7. 3.02	J Kruse	Uetersen, Germany	16. 7.06
KAA	4926	XE790/KAA	Slingsby T.31B	903	XE790	14. 9.02	N Stalpers	Castricum, Netherlands	2.10.09
KAG	4932	EE	Schempp-Hirth Nimbus-3T	23/89	D-KMHF	15.11.01	K Engelhardt *(To D-KMHF 4.08)* Lüsse, Germany		8. 9.08
KAZ	4949	J2	Glaser-Dirks DG-600/18	6-5	VH-GHS D-1666	19. 3.02	M Geisen	Mönchsheide, Germany *(To D-6615 .08)*	11. 2.08
KBB	4951	KBB	Schempp-Hirth Mini Nimbus C	147	HB-1508	12. 2.02	K E Ballington	Cross Hayes	13. 7.04
KBP	4963	XA310	Slingsby T.31B	852	XA310	20. 4.02	A P Stacey *(Stored 1.09)*	RAF Keevil	17. 6.07
KBW	4970	OM-0973	Letov LF-107 Lunak	22	OM-0973 OK-0973	9. 6.02	P Walsh	Saltby	24. 8.09
KBZ	4973		Rolladen-Schneider LS8-b	8425	D-3229	12. 5.02	P G Crabb *(Cancelled 14.10.08)*	Husbands Bosworth	9. 2.09
KCG	4980	T99	Schleicher ASW 27B	27182		31. 5.02	T N McGee	Dunstable	15.12.06
KCL	4984	KCL	Rolladen-Schneider LS4	4123	D-4239	12. 7.02	R L Fox *(To Australia as VH-XCL 3.08)*	Pocklington	2. 5.08
KDG	5004	6S	Glasflügel Club Libelle 205	119	OO-YHL D-2473	22.10.02	Not known *(Wreck removed from fire dump Summer 2007)*	Perth	21.10.03
KDR	5013	KDR	SZD-48-3 Jantar-Standard 3	B-1642	DOSAAF	22.10.03	S J Kochanowski	Gamston	11.12.05
KDT	5015		Letov LF-107 Lunak	12	OK-0975	29. 9.02	D Poll *(Wears OK-0975)*	Switzerland	13. 7.09
KFW	5066	KFW	Grunau Baby IIB	5	D-6932, D-1932	9. 9.07	R Slade	Kingston Deverill	12.10.09
KFX	5067	T11	Centrair 101AP Pégase	101029	HB-1664	18.11.03	A McNicholas	Sandhill Farm, Shrivenham	28. 1.08
KFZ	5069		Grob G103A Twin II Acro	34012-K-245	ZE659 BGA 3089	8. 9.03R	T Dews *(Stored 2005)*	Longbridge Deverill	
KGE	5074		Slingsby T.38 Grasshopper	'785'	WZ789 ?	11. 9.03R	W den Baars	Haamstede, Netherlands	
			[Possibly c/n 778 ex WZ782 reported with W den Baars]						
KHL	5104		Rolladen-Schneider LS1-f	452	F-CEKZ	17. 5.04R	K Sleigh	Rattlesden	
KKW	5168	KKW	Allstar PZL SZD-51-1 Junior	511.A.05.010		27.7.05	Scottish Gliding Union *(Hit power cable 17.5.06 landing near Glenrothes; stored 6.08)*	Portmoak	26. 7.06
KLE	5176	KLE	SZD-22B Mucha Standard	524	OO-ZIS	30.8.07	B Stephenson	Saltby	29. 8.08
KMR	5208	-	Letov LF-107 Lunak	54	OK-0838	13.4.06	W Seitz *(Registered as G-CKMR)*	Pohlheim, Germany	19. 3.09
KNI	5225	W9	Glasflügel Club Libelle 205	150	F-CEQG	7.3.06R	K Sleigh *(Marked as "G-CKNI")*	Rattlesden	
KNN	5230	-	Slingsby T.21B	MHL.012	OY-XSI SE-SMA, WB985	4.06	R Wassermann *(Registered as G-CKNN)*	Donzdorf, Germany	19. 4.09
KOS	5258		Letov LF-107 Lunak	45	G-CKOS OK-0829	21.4.07	J Rehousek	Germany	7. 3.09
KPF	5272		DG Flugzeugbau DG-808C8-377	B276	D-KBTM	8.3.07R	T Meaker	Lasham	
			(Badly damaged in heavy field landing as D-KBTM 11.9.07)						
KPR	5283	XE802	Slingsby T.31B	915	XE802	8.5.07R	M H Simms *(New owner 12.08)*	Shipdham	
KRA	5292		DG Flugzeugbau DG-1000T	10-113T35		26.07.07R	K McLean *(Not taken up; to BGA 5315 / G-RYPE)*	Rufforth	
KRL	5303		Schleicher ASG 29E	29562		21.12.07R	J Clarke *(Not taken up; to BGA 5339)*		.
KSF	5322		Lange E1 Antares 18T	?		30.6.08R	N G G Hackett	Husbands Bosworth	
KSP	5332		Schempp-Hirth Duo Discus XLT	193		8.8.08R	G J Basey	Pocklington	
KSS	5334		Lange E1 Antares	54...		27.8.08R	J Inglis		
KST	5335		Schleicher ASG 29E	29569		28.8.08R	R Ellis	Husbands Bosworth	
KSU	5336	MC	Schleicher ASG 29E	29573		27.10.08R	M Clarke	Lasham	
KSV	5337	W	Lange E1 Antares 18T	..T04	(BGA 5334) ?	3.11.08R	W Inglis	Bidford	
KSW	5338		Edgley EA9 Optimist	1	(BGA 4916) ?	3.11.08R	T Henderson	(East Grinstead)	
KSX	5339	F3	Schleicher ASG 29E	29562	(BGA 5303)	18.11.08R	M Foreman	Lasham	

PART 2 (i) – BGA COMPETITION NUMBER INDEX

BGA Competition Numbers are issued to pilots and not to individual gliders, and hence may change when the glider changes hands. There is no formal tie-up of Competition Numbers against BGA numbers, and gliders may be found wearing lapsed numbers or other markings. Therefore, this listing is a composite one based on BGA information and reported sightings. Identities marked with an asterisk indicate where gliders have been observed with the numbers shown although not listed in the current BGA record. In some cases because joint (syndicate) ownership is common this means that the Competition Number belongs to a member of a syndicate other than the one whose name appears as owner in the BGA's records. The member's name is shown where the glider concerned is not identified or the number is reserved for future use. The missing numbers are not allocated.

No.	BGA No.	No.	BGA No.	No.	BGA No.	No.	BGA No.
1	1144*, D-0606	74	G-DCTE*	153	G-DCGH	232	G-CJDT
2	869*, 3529*, 4886	76	G-DDMM	154	G-DFHS*	233	G-CKGF
3	G-EXPD	77	G-DBZZ	155	870	234	G-FCOM
4	G-STEN	78	G-DHCU	156	J B Clarke	236	G-GLAK
5	G D A Green	79	G-DFRA	157	G-ILBO	237	G-CHHW
6	G-HOJO	80	A J Davis	158	G-CFMO	238	G-CFPE*
7	G-CKOO	81	J R Upton, G-DDXB*	159	G-CFKL	239	G-CEXY
8	G-CWLC	82	G-CHFX	160	G-DDXK	240	G-HDAV*
08	G-CKLF	83	G-CGAN	161	G-CJPR	241	G-DCRB*
9	R C Ellis	84	G-CHWL	163	1089*, 1299*, G-CFNG	242	G-CFPL
10	L G Watts	85	D J Robertson	165	G-DCMH	243	1172*, G-CJKY
11	4606*	86	G-DDRB	166	G-DEEH	244	S G Olender
12	G-WYVN	87	G-CJLW	167	G-CGBR	245	G-CHJF
13	D-KOOL	88	G-DEUY	168	4273	246	G-CFVH
14	G-DDAJ	89	J A Millar	169	4145*	247	G-CFXJ
15	G-CJJZ	90	R A Foot	170	G-CKOI	248	1911*
16	G-CJFE	91	920	171	G-CFYZ	250	W J Murray
17	2804	92	G-DCVK	172	G-CKDS	251	G-DDMD
18	G-DCEC	93	G-DFFP	173	G-CFXM*	253	G-CJRA
19	M P Roberts	94	G-BZYG	174	M Clarke	254	G-DCTM*
20	G-DETZ	95	G-CJSU	175	G-XIXX	256	G-CFUR
21	G-CJLZ	96	G-CHBG	176	G-CJCT*	257	G-CFJS
22	J Zealley	98	G-DUOX	177	G-CFBH	258	G-DDRO
23	G-BYEC	99	B.G.A.	178	G-CFBA	259	G-DDMS
24	G-CKCE	100	G-CHHR	180	2901	260	G-CDPX
25	G-CHJC	101	L Hepworth	181	G-DENV	261	2715*, G-LIVS
26	G-SAXT	102	G-DGCL	182	G-DBWM	262	D W Allison
27	G-CJGL	104	G-CKBU	183	G-CJUP*	263	G-DHAA
28	D S McKay	105	G-CHNT	184	G-DCMV	264	G-LSIV*
29	G-CFWK*	106	G-DDZT	185	G-CJOO	265	G-DDNG
31	G-CHWA	107	G-DEAE	187	G-CFHG	266	G-DDLM
33	778	108	G-YOBI*	188	G-DELR	267	G-DDXN
34	T J Murphy	109	G-CFNN	190	G-CFNU	268	G-CFRW*
35	3600	110	R Jones	191	G-DDWJ	270	1027*, G-DDSP
36	G-CJSG	111	G-KPLG	192	M A Gale	271	G-DFAF
37	G-EEBN	112	G-OJNE	193	G-DEJR	272	G-DDVY
38	G-CHML	113	1013*, G-CFCR	194	G-CFUV	273	G-DCNC
39	W S Stephen	114	G-CHAO	195	G-DDGY	274	G-CJEZ
40	B Fitchett	115	G-BZEM*	196	R C Sharman, G-CFHD*	276	G-DENX
41	R F Aldous, G-CKGT*	116	G-DDHH	198	G-CJNJ	277	G-MOZI
42	G-XLII	117	G-DEON	199	G-JULL	278	3789*
44	M J Aldridge	118	G-DESH	200	G-CHUZ	279	G-DEOA
45	G-CKOH	119	E W Richards	201	G-CFOC	281	G-EENE
46	G-CJUF	120	G-CFEG	202	J Matthews	282	G-CUMU
47	G-DCCL	121	G-DRAT	203	G-CHJX*	283	G-DERA
48	G-CHNU	122	G-CHMK	205	G-CKLP	284	1632*
49	G-DCTP	123	G-AXZH	206	G-CGBS	285	G-CFXD
50	G-DEES	124	G-CKFP	207	1974*, G-CKMC	286	G-DDXT
51	G-CFLW	125	G-CFKG	208	G-CJOC	287	G-DDPH
52	G-CGBX*, G-CHXB*	126	G-LSED	209	G-CKNG	288	G-LSLS
53	G-DCSD	128	G-CFFK	210	D-5410	290	G-CKOE
54	R Jones	129	G-DDFC	211	1222	292	G-CHJT*, G-CKDW
55	G-CFSU*, G-CHNM	130	R Lemin	212	4720*	293	G-CKPU
56	4337	131	G-CKSD	213	G-DHSL	294	3751
57	M J Young	132	G-DDXD	214	G-CEWP	296	G-CJSE
59	G-CHVU	134	G-CKFH*	215	541*, G-DETK	300	G-CKCD, G-DEKW
60	G-HJSM	136	G-CFHL	216	4326	301	G-CJMT
61	G-CKFE, G-IKAH*	137	G-CHDL*	217	G-DEUJ	302	G-CGAX*
62	1514, G-CHPD*	138	R Theil	218	G-CKKH	303	S G Olender
63	G-CJWX	139	1726*	219	G-CGEH	304	G-ZENN
64	G-CKGC	140	R D Payne	220	G-CHNW	306	G-CKKF
65	G-CHFA	141	G-CFGF	221	G-CJFR	307	G-CEVV
66	J Delafield	143	G-CFJM	222	1579*	308	G-CHEC
066	G-CKBC*	144	G-CJFX	223	G-DETJ	310	P G Sheard
67	1052*	146	G-DCWY*	224	G-CFYH	311	G-DBZF
68	G-YEHA	147	G-SRAH	225	1336*	313	G-DHSR*
69	E C Wright	148	S Burton	226	G-DENO	314	G-CFLE
70	G-CKHP	149	G-CKFM	227	A T Farmer, 2337*	315	G-CHNF
71	G-CKBG	150	1269*, G-CKDN	229	1683	317	G-DBWJ
72	G-PHNX	151	G-DCNY	230	G-CFTW	318	G-CFEH
73	G-CKBM	152	G-DDZF	231	G-DESO	319	2728

320	G-INCA	428	1844*	538	G-CFEJ*	646	G-GCJA
321	G-CKJE	429	G-DHAD	540	G-TOOB	648	G-DDSH
322	G-DCWG*	431	G-DEHO	541	G-BGCU*	651	G-CENK
323	G-DEPF	432	G-CHYR	542	G-DDOK	652	2402*
324	G-DDCC	433	G-DDLE	543	G-CJDE	656	M B Jefferyes
325	G-CHXW	434	G-CJDJ	546	G-CGDA	660	G-CHYF
326	G-CFYM	435	G-DEHL*, G-DENU	547	G-CJOA	661	G-CJNY
328	G-OTRY	437	W A Coates, G-DDPL*	549	867*	662	G-CFWS
330	G-CFNR*	438	3187	550	L G Watts	663	663
332	G-CFTP	440	G-CKKY	551	G-DDBP	665	J B Dalton
333	G-DFAW	441	G-CJNO	552	G-EEBK	666	G-DUOT
334	G-DDRU	443	G-DEUS	554	G-CJUK	667	G-CHBV*
335	G-DHET	444	G-DDKL	555	R S Maxwell-Fendt	668	G-YOHO
337	G-DEEA	445	G-CHHU	556	G-DDOR	669	G-CFZB*
339	G-ECOL	446	G-DEUH	558	G-DBYM	671	3152
341	I R Willows	447	2441	560	G-CHXR	672	G-DEGJ
342	1732*	449	G-DCGT*, G-CKKX	563	G-JNUS	674	G-CFNT
346	G-DHCE	450	G-DGDJ*	564	G-CFES	676	1961*, G-CJNK
347	G-CGCM	451	G-CEVK	565	G-DCVG*, G-VTWO	677	G-DCWB
350	G-DBYU	452	G-DEMF	566	G-DCRN	678	G-DCUC
351	1741	453	G-DEHG*	567	G-CFXA*	679	G-DCBA
352	G-CJTL	456	2212*, G-CKET	569	G-DEGK	680	G-DDDR
353	G-DDKX	458	G-DCEO	570	G-HKAA	683	G-DCDF
354	G-DDXW	460	G-DGIK	571	G-CFCJ	685	J R Luxton
355	G-DCVY*, G-DHCH	461	G-WYDE	572	G-CJEM*	686	G-DBXG
356	G-CHBE*	463	1201*	574	G-CFPT	687	G-CHEJ
357	M P Brooks	464	G-DFBO	575	G-DDBN	688	G-DDRT
360	2539	465	1288*	576	G-DDZJ	690	G-CKGU
363	D K Gardiner	466	G-ECPA	577	G-DCHB	691	1982*
364	G-CHMO	467	G-CHDR*	579	G-DCTB	692	G-CHNV
365	G-CHLB	468	G-DCWE	580	G-DDXX	693	G-CHPX*
366	G-DBUF	470	G-DEFA*	581	P S Worth	695	G-EDDD
367	2522*	473	G-DHEM	583	G-DHGL	696	2778
368	G-CFLC	474	1574	584	G-VENC	698	G-CFHW
369	G-CFVM	475	G-DCBY	585	G-DHNX	699	G-DDTA
370	G-CFER*, G-CKGA	476	G-CHZX*	586	G-DEFE	700	G-CKCN
371	G-CFMY	477	G-DCYO	588	G-DDNC	701	G-CFGW
372	G-DCAS	478	1338*	590	G-DESW	703	G-DCOR*
373	1428*	480	G-DDOE*, G-CFZV	591	G-CHDD	704	G-DDTV
374	G-CHZA	481	G-DEHV	592	G-BDZG*	705	G-CFNL
375	G-DDPY	483	G-DDXA*	593	G-DDMK	706	G-DCUJ
376	C J Short	484	G-CFOT*	594	G-DEAK*	707	G-DCRS
378	G-DDLH	485	4892	595	1595	708	G-CHNE
379	G-DESC	486	G-CHEW	597	1198*	709	G-DCNF*
380	G-CHMT	488	G-CFBT*	598	4263*	710	J D Atkinson, G-CJBW*
381	G-CEWZ	490	G-DEHK	601	G-CKRT	711	G-CHXO*
382	G-CEVD*	491	G-CEVE	602	M N Bishop, G-DCMS*	712	G-CHWH
383	G-DEOW	493	G-CHSO	603	G-DJAN	714	G-XXVB
385	2723*	494	G-CJJP	604	2585*	715	G-DCAG
386	G-ORIG	495	G-CFRR	605	G-CHBU*	716	G-DDEO*
387	G-DCSK	496	G-CHBH	606	G-CFPW	719	G-DELZ
388	G-CJPP	497	G-CHSZ	607	G-CKRV, G-DHEZ	720	G-CGBL
390	G-CHRC	498	G-DFSA	609	2203*, G-CFWC	721	G-CFCP
391	G-CJGF	499	G-KKAM	610	G-DDGX	722	G-CJWK
392	G-DDMU*	500	G-DCAZ, 2146*	611	G-CHEO*	723	G-DBWO
393	G-CHVM	501	G-DCTU	612	G-CFUT	724	G-DCKZ
394	G-DHCR	502	G-CHGZ	615	G-CJJB	725	G-CGAU
395	G-CFBW*	503	G-CKDY	616	G-DEMU*	727	G-DFBM*
400	G-BLRM	505	G-CKNB	617	G-CKJC	728	G-DDWS
401	G-DCPD	506	G-CEUN	618	G-FLUZ	729	G-CHBA
402	G-DCTR	507	G-CGCD*	619	G-DCDH	730	P J Bramley
403	G-BSOM*	509	G-CHGB	620	G-JIFI	732	G-DDVK
404	1268*	510	G-CFDE	621	G-LIDY	733	G-DDWB*
405	G-PAFR*	511	G-DDMR*	622	G-DCNG	734	F G Bradney
406	1361*, G-CKDA	513	G-CJHG*	624	G-CHUL*	735	G-CHEN
407	G-DDJN	515	G-DEME	625	G-DCNW	737	G-DEFF*
408	G-DEKU	516	G-CHJL	626	G-BZSP*	739	1088
409	G-CKBK	517	G-DBWS	627	G-CFFX	741	1121
410	G-IICX	518	G-CFTK*	628	G-CJMR	742	G-DDYU*
411	G-DFCM	519	G-CFMS	629	G-OASG	743	G-DCKY*
413	G-DEHZ*	520	G-YODA	630	G-XXIX	744	G-CFJE
415	V F Tull	521	G-CGBG	631	G-CFAO	745	G-DDNK
417	G-DCRW	522	G-CHBP, G-CJDF	633	G-CKBT	747	G-LSVI
418	G-CJTM	523	G-DDBK*	634	G-CFRH*	748	G-CGCR
419	M L Boxall	524	G-CGDZ	636	G-CJMN	750	G-EEDE
420	G-CJVG	525	G-DCNE	637	G-CHGO*	751	G-CHSK
421	G-CKBX	527	G-LDER	638	2396	753	G-CFTY
422	G-PSHK	530	A A Maitland, G-HAUT*	639	G-DDZB*	755	G-CHBM*
423	G-DCVW	532	G-DCXM	641	G-DFCD	757	G-DDZY
424	G-CKHT	533	G-DDMP	642	G-DDUL	758	J Nash
425	G-CGBY	535	G-DCLM*, G-CKAV	643	1334*, G-EEFK	759	G-DDKD*
426	1171*	537	G-CJBH	644	G-DEBX	760	G-DDTK

761	G-DCPU	818	G-DCNX	878	G-DCCJ*, G-CJYS*	951	G-DDHW*
762	G-CFCA	819	G-CHLM	880	G-CJWG	952	G-DFOG
765	G-DEPS*	820	G-DEDN	881	G-FEBB	954	G-CFZO
766	G-DDTY	821	G-DDRN	882	G-CHDV*	959	G-DDDM, G-DDFN*
767	G-DDFX	822	G-CFBB	886	G-DDWT*	960	G-CKKK
768	G-CFWU	823	G-CJAO*	888	G-IFWD	961	1598*
770	G-GSST	824	G-DDHN	891	G-IUMB	962	4235*
771	G-DENJ	826	G-DCZU	894	G-CJUB	963	G-CHHH
772	G-CFDG	827	G-DEGD	895	J A Inglis	968	G-DEOJ
773	3134*	828	G-DDYE	899	G-CJJH	969	G-DFMG*
775	G-CHWB	831	G-DDMB*	900	G-THRM	970	G-NYMB
776	G-CKKV	832	G-DCWX	901	G-CKJG	971	G-DDVP
777	4359*	837	D S Carter	902	G-EENT	972	G-DDST
778	G-CGAF	838	G-CHHK	903	3299*	973	G-CFPD
779	C Villa	839	2515*	906	G-CKFD	977	G-CKAR
780	G-DFBY	840	G-OSDF	909	G-DDZG	978	G-DCWT
781	G-CJMO	841	G-CJDK	910	G-OKLL*	979	G-CHHN
782	782*	842	G-DCUS	911	G-VNTS	980	G-CFWP
783	G-CHGX	843	G-CGBN*	912	G-DDUB	983	G-KESY
785	G-CFOY	844	A M Smith	913	G-CHYE	985	G-CHKR
786	G-DEAT	846	G-DCHT*	914	G-CGDY	986	4523*
787	C J Pollard	849	G-DEHU	915	G-DDTP	987	G-CFHJ
788	G-DDKS	850	G-DDYF*	917	G-DCWR	988	G-CJVX
790	G-CJKN	851	G-DDBC	918	G-CEWE	989	G-PIKB
791	G-ZBOP	853	G-CFTN*	919	G-DHKL	990	2508*
795	G-CHEH	854	G-FERV	920	G-KOBH	991	G-DHDH*
797	G-CKLD	855	G-CHHT	921	G-DJAH	992	G-DEUK
798	G-DDRW	857	G-DCHZ	922	G-CGBU*	993	3148
799	G-DCLZ	858	1689*	927	3363	994	G-HCAC
800	G-LEES	859	1136*	928	G-CGEE*	996	G-DEEK
801	G-CGDU	860	G-CHKA	930	G-CHVP	997	D M Smith
802	G-CHRW	862	G-DCFY	933	G-CJJT	998	G-CFRC
803	G-CFUL*	865	3993*	937	G-ECLW	1018	4312*
805	G-CHLN	867	G-CJGN	940	G-CHFY	1066	1066*
806	G-CFGU	868	G-CJHU	942	G-RAIR	2001	3776*
808	G-DCSR*, G-CKDO	869	G-PIKD	943	G-NIMB		
810	G-DDVV*	870	G-CHFF*	944	G-CFTV		
811	G-DDHC	871	G-CJXW	948	G-DCLP		
812	G-DCAO	873	G-DCTT	949	G-GBPP		
813	G-CJNZ	877	G-DDSX	950	G-CFJR*		

PART 2 (ii) – BGA ALPHA/NUMERIC COMPETITION NUMBER INDEX

Code	Reg.	Code	Reg.	Code	Reg.	Code	Reg.
0Z	G-OZOZ	AW	G-CGAR	DP	G-CHUO	HE	G-HEBB
1F	G-LSIF	B	G-CFMH	DS	G-LYDS	HL	J P Gorringe
1UP	G-CKOU	B2	4385*	DS2	G-CKFN	HPH	4090*
1Z	G-ONEZ	B3	G-CKKM*, G-CKRD	DUO	G-XDUO	HS	G-CJCD
2C	G-TWOC	B4	G-DCUT	DV8	G-DCRH	IM	G-CJCV*
2CK	J A Clark	B8	G-CHVF	DVM	G-EDMV*	IS28	G-DDLT*
2CS	G-DEGS	B9	G-CHJR	DW	G-CJEX	IS30	G-DFDP*
2R	G-CFCS	B11	G-CHZU	DYN	2477*	IV	G-XCIV
2S	G-CKPE	B12	G-CJYP*	DZ	G-DZDZ	J1	G-CJUH
2T	G-TWOT*	B19	G-CJRV	E	285*	J2	4949
2UP	G-CJUM	B20	G-CJYR	E1	G-CKNU*	J3	G-CFYN
2W	G-CKFK	B33	G-CHRS	E3	G-GLID	J5	G-CKMZ
2ZC	G-CHWF	B55	G-CKGM*	E4	G-XJON	J7	G-PEGZ
3D	G-ODUO	BB	G-GBBB	E5	G-CJTN	J8	G-CKCM*
4A	G-FORA	BD	J F Beringer	E6	G-RYPE	J15	G-CFAM
4T	G-CJUW	BF1	G-CKKP	E7	G-CKDF	J34	G-EHAV*
5GC	G-CEYC	BJ	G-BMBJ	E8	G-CFUH	J50	G-CJVV*
5K	G-CKDC	BMN	1102*	E11	G-XELL	JA	G-SAJA
6B	G-LSGB	BS	G-CJZL	E17	G-CKJZ	JA9	G-CJCN
6S	5004*	BS1	2677	E60	G-CFVT*	JB	G-CJSS
6X	G-CKHX	BT	G-CJGR	EA	G-CKCH	JD	G-DCEL
7A	G-CKJM	BW	2635*	EB	G-CJOP	JED	G-CJED*
7C	G-SVNC	BZ	G-DCVE	EC	G-CFXY	JF	G-DDJF
7D	G-CFDA*	C	G-DDLC	ED	G-GCMW*	JG	J P Gorringe
7Q	G-CJAS	C1	G-CTAG	EE	4932*	JH	2670*
7R	G-CFYK	C2	G-CTWO	EF	G-CJNP*, G-RIEF	JH1	G-CJVF
7V	G-DDHX	C3	G-CJGY	EN	G-CHZY	JO1	G-CJJE
7X	G-CJSJ	C4	G-JNSC	EU	4516*	JS	G-CJVJ
8T	G-CKOR	C6	G-CJWA	EW	G-CJMV*	JW	G-CKJS
9A	1317	C7	G-CJCJ	EW2	G-EWEW*	K	G-DEVP
9E	G-CKJN	C29	G-CHKU*	EZ	G-CKEZ	K1	A E Kay
15A	G-CJVW	C30	G-CGBO	F	400*	K3	2689*
17K	G-DCOJ	C34	G-CHKD*	F1	4747	K4	G-DHYL
17R	G-DBWP	C64	G-CJZM, 4973*	F2	G-CJCP*, D-4670	K5	G-CKHG
19X	S Black	C66	G-CKJK	F3	G-CJCY*, 5339	K8	G-CJJK
20L	G-MAGK	C74	G-CJVU	F4	1367	K9	G-DHPR
26E	G-CCLR	C75	G-CKDZ*	F6	4827*	K13	G-CFZN
27B	G-CJXZ	CB	G-CJPH	F20	G-CHVX	K18	G-CKNM
28E	G-CKJA	CC	G-VLCC	F21	G-CHFV	K19	G-DCZO
28T	G-TRBO	CD1	G-CJUX	F94	G-CKKE	K21	G-CJGE
29E	G-SASG	CH	G-DKEN	FB	G-LSFB	KA	G-CKML*
34Z	G-DCSF*	CJ	G-CFRJ	FE	G-CJUG*	KC	G-CFYW
97Z	G-CHHO	CL	G-CJPS	FGT	G-DDJR*	KE	G-CJEH*
A1	G-CHSA	CP	G-LSCP	G1	G-CJJF	KL	G-CHHP
A2	G-CHDX	CS	C D Sterritt	G2	G-GTWO*	KM	G-CDDB
A3	1946*	CT	G-CJXT	G7	G-SVEN*	KO	4230*, G-CKHS
A5	A P C Sampson	CU	G-CJGB	G9	G-CKOZ	KR	4627
A7	G-CJKK	CYL	1639*	G41	G-CJHZ	KT	1744*
A8	G-CJLJ	CZ	G-OTCZ	G46	698	KV	G-LSKV
A9	G-CHVT*	D	G-DDRJ	G81	G-CJBJ*	KW	G-CJDG
A11	G-DDUE*	D1	936*, 4638	GA	G-CJWU	L	G-DFCW
A14	G-CHYS*	D4	G-CJEA	GAZ	G-FGAZ*	L2	G-CJGS
A19	G-CFNH	D5	G-CHPH	GB1	G-CKKN	L3	G-CJBK
A20	G-CHOD*	D6	G-CKLY	GB2	G-CFPH	L4	G-LLLL
A23	1237	D7	G-DSVN	GM	G-LSGM	L5	G-CGAD
A26	G-CHYY	D8	G-CJVP	GO	G-CKRM	L7	G-CJBO, G-CKMO*
A27	G-CJDC	D9	G-IRLE	GP	G-CJVM	L8	G-STEU
A28	G-CKAL	D11	G-CKNJ	GR	4420*	L10	G-CEUP
A30	G-DDHK*	D15	G-CHSD	GR8	G-CKMA*	L12	3611*
A34	G-CJHR	D19	G-CHMM*	GT	G-CKLT	L18	G-CHWC
A39	G-ORCW	D31	S A Young, G-CHUH*	GW	G-CKJF	L19	G-CKPA
A61	G-CHYU	D53	G-CJTR*	GX	G-CKJD*	L24	G-CJTH
A77	4125*	D54	G-DHSJ	H	G-DEVJ	L51	G-CFOZ
A98	G-CEVN	D64	4121*	H1	G-CKBH	L53	G-CKHB
AA	G-CTAA*	D70	G-DHRR	H2	4558	L57	G-CFWF*
AC	G-CJBR	DA	G-DAWZ	H4	G-CJSW*, G-CKBV	L58	G-RIEV
AD	G-CKMG*	DB	G-CKME	H5	3285*	L99	G-DCCP
AG	A L Green	DC	G-CJCK	H8	G-CHTS	LA	G-CJRR
AG1	G-CKBF*	DD	G-CHYA	H11	G-FEBJ	LC	G-CFEJ
AH	G-CHEE	DD2	G-ODDZ	H12	3732	LD	G-CHZZ
AJ	G-ZZAJ*	DDT	G-RDDT*	H17	2847	LE	G-CKOM
AP	G-CKJV	DF	G-CJVB	H20	G-CFDM	LGC	G-CLGC*
AP1	G-CKKD	DG	G-CFYU	H23	1189	LL	G-DTWO
AS	G-VEGA	DG1	P Smith	HB1	G-CJPA	LM	G-KHCC
AT	A Towse	DG3	D N Mackay	HB2	G-CGDX	LS	G-WLLS
AV	G-CKCY*	DH2	G-ODCH*	HD	G-CFPN	LS3	2656
AV8	G-CJTW	DM	G-CJXR	HDH	3862*	LS4	G-CHXT*, G-LSFR

Code	Registration	Code	Registration	Code	Registration	Code	Registration
LS6	G-LSIX	P50	G-CJOG	RY	G-CHNZ	V7	G-DEHH
LS7	G-CJLK	P61	G-CHZV	RZ	G-RZEE	V8	G-CKCJ
LS8	G-CHVL	P70	G-DEWR	S	G-CFYY	V9	G-CKGD
LT	G-CJHY	PE	G-KEPE	S1	G-CKAK	V10	G-CFYC*
LW	G-CKJB*	PF	G-CJPF, G-CKEC*	S2	G-DHOK	V11	G-EVII
LX	4376*	PG	G-DEPE*	S3	3580	V12	G-CKMD
LY	G-EFLY	PH	G-OSHK*	S5	G-CHXZ	V17	G-CJTB
LZ	G-CHZO*	PH1	G-CJKP	S6	G-DFBE	V26	G-VTCT
M	G-DFEO	PH2	G-CKFB	S7	2943*	V66	G-HAAH
M2	G-CKFC	PK	G-JAPK	S8	G-CHUW	V2C	G-IICT
M4	G-CJAW	PM3	4723	S9	S S Turner, G-CKOY*	V2T	G-CVZT
M5	G-DDYX	PN	P C Naegeli	S10	G-BXGZ*	VE	G-DEWG*
M6	G-MSIX	PP	I W Paterson	S13	G-DDVX*	VS	G-DDVS*
M7	G-DETM	PS	G-CFVZ	S19	G-CJKS	W	5337
M8	G-CHXC	PS1	G-CKRN	S22	G-CHTN	W1	G-WONE
M9	G-WDGC	PT	4721	S27	G-CJWF	W2	G-CKOJ*
M11	G-CKLN*	PV	G-CKPV*	S30	2380	W3	G-WIII
M19	G-CJUN*	PW5	G-SMYK*	S33	G-CJRB	W4	G-IDER
M25	G-DRCS*	PZ	G-CHMX	S60	G-CJWV*	W5	G-CJXG
M80	G-CJUZ	Q5	G-CFHR	S75	G-CKFA*	W6	G-CRJW
MB	G-CKED	R1	G-CJFH	S81	3722*	W7	4861*
MC	5336	R2	G-CKEV	S83	4268*	W8	G-CJKL
MF	G-DEMT*	R3	G-CJOD	SA1	G-EEVL*	W9	5225*
ML	G-DERP	R4	G-CJLN	SC	G-CJNT	W10	G-CJNE
MM	G-CKBV, G-OASW*	R6	G-SAOC	SH	G-BXSH*	W17	2595
MP	G-OBPP	R7	G-CJKT*	SH1	Surrey & Hants GC	W19	G-CEWI
MW	M S F Wood	R9	G-CFFB	SH2	G-CJUV	W20	D C Heath
MY	G-CKCB	R10	G-CJLC	SH3	G-CFKM	W27	G-CJCM*
N	G-CKEB	R11	G-CJYU	SH4	G-CFUP	W54	G-CHVE*
N1	G-CJDZ*	R12	G-CKJP*	SH6	Surrey & Hants GC	W81	G-CKMY*
N2	G-CFPP	R17	RAFGSA	SH7	G-CJZY	WA1	G-OWAI
N3	G-PNGC	R18	G-CKMW	SH8	G-DFEB	WA2	G-TWAZ
N4	1914	R19	G-CKRW	SH9	G-CJSH	WE	G-CJDM
N5	G-CHUE*	R20	G-CJKO	SI	G-SISI	WE4	G-CKCV*
N6	G-CGCX	R21	G-CJKJ	SK	G-CJRU	WK	4216*
N8	G-EJAE*	R22	G-DJMC	SK1	G-CKEL*	X1	G-IXXI, G-XWON*
N11	G-DDJB	R23	G-CJMS*	SM	S D Minson	X4	G-CKGL
N12	G-CKBL	R25	G-CJKZ	SO1	G-CJXL	X5	G-CJST*
N15	3548	R28	G-CKGK*	SP	P G Scott	X7	N G Hackett
N16	G-CFZP	R30	(ASK 13, Odiham)*	SR	G-GRSR	X8	G-CHZG
N19	G-CHRA	R32	G-CJPO*	SW	G-SWSW	X9	G-CKOK
N21	673	R33	G-CJKU*	T	G-LIBL	X11	G-DKFU
N25	G-DJLL	R35	G-DERJ	T1	G-OPHT	X15	G-CJUE
N28	G-CFSD	R36	G-CJMA	T2	T W Slater	X17	G-CKHE*
N29	G-CFGR	R37	G-CJMZ*	T3	G-CKGB	X19	G-DHCV
N36	G-CHDP*	R38	G-CJWJ*	T4	G-CKHD	X27	P T Healy
N51	G-DEVM	R39	G-CJLP	T5	G-RGTS	X50	4341*
N52	1551*	R41	G-CJRX*	T6	G-CJYD*	X70	G-CHUJ*
N53	Seahawk GC	R43	G-CJHO*	T9	G-CKPZ	X96	G-DDVL
N55	1118*, G-CJYF*	R46	G-CJMJ*	T10	G-DCKV	X97	G-XBGA
N56	G-CFTC	R48	G-CJKG*	T11	5067	XD2	G-CKHF
N57	Seahawk GC	R49	G-CJMK*	T12	G-CJWM	XE	G-CKON
NC	G-CKNC	R53	G-CJGM	T19	G-CHOR	XS	G-XOAR
NG1	G-CKCP	R55	G-CJFC	T21	K J Scott, 3290*	Y4	G-CHXE
NH	G-CKBN	R56	G-CJPZ*	T27	G-CJRH	Y7	G-KOYY
NJ1	G-CJWR*	R57	G-CJLR	T34	G-DDUT	Y11	G-CKFL*
NT	2318	R59	G-CJPY*	T40	G-CFHO	Y44	G-CJXA
NU	Notts Uni GC	R61	G-CJMW*	T42	D E Williams	YG	G-DCYG*
NU2	G-NUGC	R63	G-CJML	T45	873*	Z	1873*, G-CFMK*
NW	G-DETG	R67	G-CJON	T49	1203	Z1	G-CJUJ
NX	2898*	R69	RAFGSA	T4C	T Forsey	Z3	G-CJTF*
OD	G-CKOD*	R71	G-DEYS*	T50	M H Simms	Z4	G-CFLF
OL	G-CKOL	R73	G-CJUR	T51	1164	Z5	G-CHWS
OV	D V Wilson	R75	G-CJLS*	T54	G-CGDT	Z6	C Curtis, G-CFZL*
P	G-CFHM	R77	G-CJSD	T65	G-BGBV	Z7	G-DCDC
P1	G-CJKD	R80	G-CJSV*	T99	4980*	Z8	G-CHTM
P2	G-CJDY	R88	G-CJPV*	TB2	G-CGCT	Z9	G-CEUG
P3	G-CJAR	R92	4707	TC	G-TWOA	Z10	G-CJKM
P4	G-CJNM	R93	G-DJNC*	TL2	G-TLTL	Z12	G-CJOV
P5	G-CHRX	RA	G-VCXT	U1	G-CHZM	Z19	G-GZIP*
P6	P J Pengilly, G-CEUR*	RB	G-CKCR*, G-RBCT	U2	G-DDNU*, G-CHOZ*	Z25	G-DDVZ*
P7	G-CKPY	RB1	G-CJYN*	U9	G-UNIN	Z27	G-CKLB
P8	G-CJBB*	RC	G-SINK	UP2	G-CKFT	Z33	4275
P9	G-DDWR	RH	G-DEMB	UWE	4734*	Z35	G-CJXN
P10	G-CJZX	RM	G-CKMM*	UY	4841*	Z45	G-CHLY
P19	G-DCPV*	RNT	G-EENZ*	V	A C Broadbridge	Z55	G-CKLR
P20	G-DDHV*	RP1	G-CHVG	V1	G-NIVT	Z99	G-CHNH
P23	G-DJMD*	RS	G-CJRE	V2	R Jones	ZZ	G-CJZZ*
P30	4571*	RT	G-DEUD	V5	G-CHLS		
P31	G-CHKZ*	RW	G-CJPL	V6	G-VSIX		

Note: Codes "SY" to "ZZ" are allocated to the Air Cadets Central Gliding School

PART 2 (iii) – CIVIL REGISTRATION and MILITARY SERIAL DECODE INDEX

Several former British military gliders carry their former service serials for authenticity. A few imported vintage specimens also carry their previous UK and overseas civil registrations. Whilst details of marks carried are included in Part 1, Column 3 this specific decode Index is including for ease of reference. Examples known are shown below.

Country	Regn or Serial	BGA No.
UK		
	G-ALRH	629
	G-ALRK	490
	RA905	1143
	TS291	852
	VM684	791
	VM687	794
	WB920	3221
	WB922	4366
	WB924	3901
	WB935	4110
	WB943	2941
	WB944	3160
	WB961	4856
	WB962	3836
	WB971	3324
	WB975	3288
	WB981	3238
	WB988	4877
	WE990	2583
	WE992	2692
	WG498	3245
	WJ306	2720*, 3240
	WT871	3149
	WT898	4412
	WT900	3272
	WT908	3487
	WT910	3953
	WT913	3239
	WT914	3194
	WT918	3241
	WZ795	3488
	WZ819	3498
	WZ828	4421
	XA240	4556
	XA295	3336
	XA302	3786
	XA310	4963
	XE786	4033
	XE790	4926
	XE802	5283
	XE807	3545
	XN157	3255
	XN185	4077
	XN186	3905
	XN187	3903
	XN243	3145
	XP463	4372
	XS652	1107
	XT653	3469
GERMANY		
	D-12-354	1711
	D-1265	2276
	D-4012	2855
	D-5084	2688
	D-5627	1872
	D-5826	3186
	D-6173	4336
SWITZERLAND		
	HB-474	2474
	HB-561	2284
CZECH REPUBLIC		
	OK-0833	4884
	OK-0927	4286
	OK-0975	5015
	OK-8592	655
SLOVAKIA		
	OM-0973	4970

PART 3 - BGA NUMBER / CAA REGISTRATION INDEX

This section provides a cross-reference of former BGA numbers to current CAA Registrations for EASA Aircraft under Regulation (EC) No. 216/2008.

BGA No.	CAA Reg	BGA No.	CAA Reg	BGA No.	CAA Reg	BGA No.	CAA Reg.	BGA No.	CAA Reg.
283	G-ALJR	1469	G-DCDW	1669	G-DCNE	1859	G-DCWF	2089	G-DDFW
599	G-ALLF	1472	G-DCDZ	1670	G-DCNF	1860	G-DCWG	2090	G-DDFX
998	G-DBJD	1473	G-ECEA	1671	G-DCNG	1861	G-DCWH	2093	G-DDGA
1094	G-DBND	1474	G-DCEB	1673	G-DCNJ	1862	G-DCWJ	2097	G-DDGE
1098	G-DBNH	1475	G-DCEC	1676	G-DCNM	1869	G-DCWR	2099	G-DDGG
1149	G-DBOL	1483	G-DCEL	1677	G-SCNN	1870	G-DCWS	2102	G-DDGK
1172	G-APWL	1484	G-DCEM	1678	G-DCNP	1871	G-DCWT	2114	G-DDGX
1185	G-DBRY	1487	G-DCEO	1681	G-DCNS	1875	G-DCWX	2115	G-DDGY
1187	G-DBSA	1493	G-DCEW	1684	G-DCNW	1876	G-DCWY	2117	G-DDHA
1197	G-DBSL	1494	G-DCEX	1685	G-DCNX	1877	G-DCWZ	2119	G-DDHC
1219	G-DBTJ	1495	G-DCEY	1686	G-DCNY	1886	G-ZBOP	2123	G-DDHG
1240	G-DBUF	1497	G-DCFA	1688	G-ECPA	1887	G-DCXK	2124	G-DDHH
1257	G-DBUZ	1501	G-DCFE	1691	G-DCPD	1889	G-DCXM	2125	G-DDHJ
1259	G-DBVB	1502	G-DCFF	1696	G-DCPJ	1897	G-DCXV	2126	G-DDHK
1262	G-IKAH	1503	G-DCFG	1699	G-DCPM	1902	G-DCYA	2127	G-DDHL
1265	G-DBVH	1506	G-DCFK	1706	G-DCPU	1905	G-DCYD	2128	G-DDHM
1273	G-DBVR	1507	G-DCFL	1707	G-DCPV	1908	G-DCYG	2129	G-DDHN
1279	G-DBVX	1513	G-DCFS	1720	G-DCOJ	1913	G-DCYM	2132	G-DDHE
1280	G-DBVY	1517	G-DCFW	1722	G-ECOL	1916	G-DCYO	2134	G-DDHT
1281	G-DBVZ	1518	G-DCFX	1723	G-FCOM	1919	G-DCYT	2136	G-DDHV
1284	G-DBWC	1519	G-DCFY	1725	G-CEWE	1925	G-DCYZ	2137	G-DDHW
1290	G-DBWJ	1522	G-DCGB	1727	G-DCOR	1929	G-DCZD	2138	G-DDHX
1293	G-DBWM	1524	G-DCGD	1734	G-DCOY	1930	G-DCZE	2140	G-DDHZ
1295	G-DBWP	1525	G-DCGE	1737	G-DCRB	1932	G-DCZG	2142	G-DDJB
1296	G-DBWO	1528	G-DCGH	1743	G-DCRH	1934	G-DCZJ	2144	G-DDJD
1298	G-DBWS	1532	G-DCGM	1748	G-DCRN	1938	G-DCZN	2145	G-DDJE
1310	G-DBXE	1535	G-DCGO	1750	G-DCRO	1940	G-DCZO	2150	G-DDJK
1312	G-DBXG	1537	G-DCGS	1752	G-DCRS	1941	G-DCZR	2151	G-DDJL
1313	G-DBXH	1538	G-DCGT	1753	G-DCRT	1944	G-DCZU	2152	G-DDJM
1316	G-DRAT	1543	G-DCGY	1755	G-DCRV	1949	G-DCZZ	2153	G-DDJN
1326	G-ATRB	1544	G-RAEF	1756	G-DCRW	1952	G-DDAC	2155	G-CEWP
1332	G-DBYC	1546	G-DCHB	1763	G-DCSD	1958	G-DDAJ	2156	G-DDJR
1340	G-DBYL	1547	G-DCHC	1765	G-DCSF	1959	G-DDAK	2162	G-DDJX
1341	G-DBYM	1553	G-DCHJ	1768	G-DCSJ	1962	G-DDAN	2164	G-PIKB
1348	G-DBYU	1555	G-DCHL	1769	G-DCSK	1963	G-DDAP	2167	G-DDKC
1351	G-DBYX	1562	G-DCHT	1772	G-DCSN	1966	G-DDAS	2168	G-DDKD
1359	G-DBZF	1563	G-DCHU	1773	G-DCSP	1968	G-DDAU	2169	G-DDKE
1375	G-DBZX	1565	G-DCHW	1775	G-DCSR	1969	G-HDAV	2171	G-DDKG
1377	G-DBZZ	1568	G-DCHZ	1780	G-ECSW	1970	G-DDAW	2175	G-DDKL
1380	G-HCAC	1570	G-DCJB	1785	G-DCTB	1976	G-DDBC	2176	G-DDKM
1381	G-DCAE	1578	G-DCJK	1788	G-DCTE	1980	G-DDBG	2177	G-DDKN
1383	G-DCAG	1581	G-DCJN	1792	G-DCTJ	1983	G-DDBK	2180	G-DDKR
1391	G-DCAO	1584	G-DCJR	1794	G-DCTL	1986	G-DDBN	2181	G-DDKS
1392	G-PSHK	1591	G-DCJY	1795	G-DCTM	1987	G-DDBP	2182	G-DDKT
1393	G-DCAS	1596	G-DCKD	1797	G-DCTP	1988	G-CETJ	2183	G-DDKU
1396	G-FCAV	1603	G-DCKL	1798	G-DCTO	1990	G-DDBS	2185	G-DDKW
1400	G-DCAZ	1605	G-DCKN	1799	G-DCTR	1993	G-DDBV	2186	G-DDKX
1401	G-DCBA	1606	G-DCKP	1801	G-DCTT	1995	G-DDBX	2189	G-DDLA
1421	G-DCBW	1608	G-DCKR	1802	G-DCTU	1998	G-DDCA	2190	G-DDLB
1423	G-DCBY	1611	G-DCKU	1803	G-DCTV	2000	G-DDCC	2191	G-DDLC
1425	G-DCCA	1612	G-DCKV	1805	G-DCTX	2018	G-DDCW	2193	G-DDLE
1426	G-DCCB	1615	G-DCKY	1809	G-DCUB	2022	G-DDDA	2196	G-DDLH
1427	G-FCCC	1616	G-DCKZ	1810	G-DCUC	2023	G-DDDB	2197	G-DDLJ
1429	G-DCCE	1617	G-DCLA	1811	G-DCUD	2025	G-EDDD	2200	G-DDLM
1430	G-DCCF	1628	G-DCLM	1816	G-DCUJ	2026	G-DDDE	2202	G-DDLP
1431	G-DCCG	1629	G-LIBY	1818	G-DCUL	2032	G-DDDL	2205	G-DDLS
1433	G-DCCJ	1630	G-DCLP	1821	G-DCUO	2033	G-DDDM	2206	G-DDLT
1435	G-DCCL	1631	G-DCLO	1822	G-DCUS	2034	G-DDDN	2207	G-DJNC
1436	G-DCCM	1634	G-DCLT	1823	G-DCUT	2037	G-DDDR	2211	G-DDLY
1438	G-DCCP	1636	G-DCLV	1830	G-DCVA	2041	G-EDDV	2214	G-DDMB
1440	G-DCCR	1637	G-ECLW	1831	G-DCVB	2042	G-DDDW	2216	G-DDMD
1442	G-DCCT	1640	G-DCLZ	1834	G-DCVE	2044	G-FDDY	2219	G-DDMG
1443	G-DCCU	1646	G-DCMF	1836	G-DCVG	2046	G-DDEA	2220	G-DDMH
1444	G-DCCV	1647	G-DCMG	1839	G-DCVK	2051	G-DDEG	2222	G-DDMK
1445	G-DCCW	1648	G-DCMH	1840	G-DCVL	2059	G-DDEO	2223	G-DDML
1446	G-DCCX	1650	G-DCMK	1841	G-DCVM	2064	G-DDEV	2224	G-DDMM
1447	G-DCCY	1653	G-DCMN	1846	G-DCVS	2065	G-DDEW	2226	G-DDMP
1448	G-DCCZ	1655	G-DCMO	1847	G-DCVT	2066	G-DDEX	2227	G-DDMO
1449	G-DCDA	1656	G-DCMR	1849	G-DCVV	2071	G-DDFC	2228	G-DDMR
1450	G-ECDB	1657	G-DCMS	1850	G-DCVW	2073	G-DDFE	2229	G-DDMS
1452	G-KSIX	1660	G-DCMV	1852	G-DCVY	2078	G-DDFK	2231	G-DDMU
1454	G-DCDF	1661	G-DCMW	1854	G-DCWA	2079	G-DDFL	2232	G-EDMV
1455	G-DCDG	1662	G-DENO	1855	G-DCWB	2081	G-DDFN	2234	G-DDMX
1456	G-DCDH	1667	G-DCNC	1857	G-DCWD	2084	G-DDFR	2239	G-DDNC
1467	G-OSHK	1668	G-DCND	1858	G-DCWE	2088	G-DDFV	2240	G-DDND

No.	Reg.	No.	Reg.	No.	Reg.	No.	Reg.	No.	Reg.
2241	G-DDNE	2397	G-DDUT	2548	G-EEBE	2694	G-DEHG	2857	G-DEOB
2242	G-DDNF	2401	G-DDUX	2549	G-EEBF	2695	G-DEHH	2859	G-DEOD
2243	G-DDNG	2405	G-DDVB	2552	G-FEBJ	2697	G-DEHK	2860	G-DEOE
2245	G-DDNJ	2406	G-DDVC	2553	G-EEBK	2698	G-DEHL	2861	G-DEOF
2246	G-DDNK	2407	G-DDVD	2554	G-EEBL	2699	G-DEHM	2862	G-CEXY
2247	G-AXZH	2410	G-DDVG	2555	G-EEBM	2700	G-BILH	2864	G-DEOJ
2251	G-CEVV	2411	G-DDVH	2556	G-EEBN	2701	G-DEHP	2868	G-DEON
2254	G-DDNT	2412	G-PIKD	2559	G-EEBR	2702	G-DEHO	2870	G-CEVK
2255	G-DDNU	2413	G-DDVK	2560	G-EEBS	2705	G-DEHT	2871	G-CEWC
2256	G-DDNV	2414	G-DDVL	2565	G-DEBX	2706	G-DEHU	2873	G-DEOT
2257	G-DDNW	2415	G-DDVM	2567	G-EEBZ	2707	G-DEHV	2874	G-DEOU
2258	G-DDNX	2416	G-DDVN	2570	G-DECC	2708	G-DEHW	2875	G-DEOV
2260	G-DDNZ	2417	G-DDVP	2573	G-DECF	2710	G-DEHY	2876	G-DEOW
2261	G-DDPA	2420	G-DDVS	2574	G-DECG	2711	G-DEHZ	2879	G-DEOZ
2268	G-DDPH	2423	G-DDVV	2575	G-DECH	2712	G-DEJA	2880	G-DERA
2270	G-DDPK	2425	G-DDVX	2576	G-DECJ	2713	G-DEJB	2887	G-DERH
2271	G-DDPL	2426	G-DDVY	2577	G-EECK	2714	G-DEJC	2888	G-DERJ
2275	G-DDPO	2427	G-DDVZ	2578	G-DECL	2716	G-DEJE	2893	G-DERP
2282	G-RZEE	2429	G-DDWB	2579	G-DECM	2717	G-DEJF	2895	G-DERR
2283	G-DDPY	2430	G-DDWC	2581	G-DECP	2719	G-DEJH	2896	G-DERS
2285	G-DDOA	2434	G-DDWG	2582	G-FECO	2726	G-CEVZ	2899	G-FERV
2286	G-DDOB	2436	G-DDWJ	2584	G-DECS	2727	G-DEJR	2902	G-KESY
2287	G-DDOC	2438	G-DDWL	2588	G-DECW	2729	G-VEGA	2905	G-DESB
2289	G-DDOE	2440	G-DDWN	2591	G-DECZ	2735	G-DEJZ	2906	G-DESC
2290	G-DDOF	2442	G-CEWW	2592	G-BFYW	2736	G-EEKA	2908	G-LSFR
2291	G-GSST	2443	G-DDWR	2593	G-DEDB	2738	G-DEKC	2911	G-DESH
2294	G-DDOK	2444	G-DDWS	2596	G-EEDE	2739	G-DEKD	2912	G-DESJ
2296	G-PILY	2445	G-DDWT	2597	G-HAUT	2740	G-MAGK	2918	G-DESO
2300	G-DDOR	2446	G-DDWU	2598	G-DEDG	2741	G-DEKF	2922	G-DESU
2301	G-CEWO	2448	G-DDWW	2600	G-DEDJ	2742	G-DEKG	2924	G-DESW
2303	G-DDOU	2452	G-DDXA	2601	G-DEDK	2743	G-XXVB	2926	G-EESY
2306	G-DDOX	2453	G-DDXB	2603	G-DEDM	2744	G-DEKJ	2928	G-DETA
2307	G-DDOY	2455	G-DDXD	2604	G-DEDN	2749	G-SHHH	2931	G-DETD
2309	G-DDRA	2456	G-DDXE	2605	G-DGIO	2752	G-DEKS	2934	G-DETG
2310	G-DDRB	2457	G-DDXF	2610	G-DEDU	2753	G-DEKT	2936	G-DETJ
2312	G-DDRD	2458	G-DDXG	2611	G-BGCU	2754	G-DEKU	2937	G-DETK
2313	G-DDRE	2459	G-DDXH	2612	G-UCLU	2755	G-DEKV	2939	G-DETM
2317	G-DDRJ	2460	G-DDXJ	2613	G-DEDX	2756	G-DEKW	2944	G-DETS
2319	G-DDRL	2461	G-DDXK	2614	G-DEDY	2760	G-DELA	2947	G-DETV
2320	G-DDRM	2462	G-DDXL	2615	G-DEDZ	2763	G-DELD	2950	G-DETY
2321	G-DDRN	2464	G-DDXN	2616	G-DEEA	2766	G-DELG	2951	G-DETZ
2322	G-DDRP	2466	G-SRAH	2618	G-DEEC	2772	G-DELN	2954	G-DEUC
2323	G-DDRO	2469	G-DDXT	2620	G-MEEE	2774	G-DELO	2955	G-DEUD
2326	G-DDRT	2470	G-BDWZ	2621	G-DEEF	2775	G-DELR	2957	G-DEUF
2327	G-DDRU	2472	G-DDXW	2622	G-DEEG	2777	G-EELT	2959	G-DEUH
2328	G-DDRV	2473	G-DDXX	2623	G-DEEH	2781	G-DELX	2960	G-DEUJ
2329	G-DDRW	2478	G-DDYC	2624	G-DEEJ	2782	G-EELY	2961	G-DEUK
2331	G-DDRY	2479	G-DDYE	2625	G-DEEK	2783	G-DELZ	2968	G-DEUS
2332	G-DDRZ	2480	G-DDYF	2627	G-DEEM	2785	G-DEMB	2971	G-DEUV
2334	G-DDSB	2481	G-BDZG	2628	G-DEEN	2788	G-DEME	2973	G-EEUX
2338	G-DDSF	2482	G-DDYH	2629	G-DEEP	2789	G-DEMF	2974	G-DEUY
2340	G-DDSH	2483	G-DDYJ	2630	G-DEEO	2790	G-DEMG	2979	G-CEVD
2341	G-DDSJ	2485	G-DDYL	2631	G-EEER	2792	G-DEMJ	2980	G-CEVE
2343	G-DDSL	2489	G-DDYR	2632	G-DEES	2794	G-BGCB	2981	G-DEVF
2346	G-DDSP	2491	G-DDYU	2636	G-DEEW	2796	G-DEMN	2983	G-DEVH
2350	G-DDST	2494	G-DDYX	2637	G-DEEX	2797	G-DEMP	2984	G-DEVJ
2351	G-DDSU	2495	G-NIMB	2639	G-ILBO	2799	G-DEMR	2985	G-DEVK
2352	G-DDSV	2496	G-DDZA	2640	G-DEFA	2800	G-BGBV	2986	G-EEVL
2354	G-DDSX	2497	G-DDZB	2641	G-DEFB	2801	G-DEMT	2987	G-DEVM
2355	G-DDSY	2501	G-DDZF	2644	G-DEFE	2802	G-DEMU	2989	G-DEVP
2357	G-DDTA	2502	G-DDZG	2645	G-DEFF	2806	G-LSIV	2990	G-DEVO
2359	G-DDTC	2504	G-DDZJ	2646	G-DEFG	2807	G-DEMZ	2992	G-FEVS
2361	G-DDTE	2507	G-DDZM	2649	G-EEFK	2808	G-LSLS	2995	G-DEVV
2363	G-DDTG	2509	G-DDZP	2650	G-EFLY	2812	G-EENE	2996	G-DEVW
2366	G-DDTK	2511	G-DDZR	2651	G-FGAZ	2816	G-DENJ	2997	G-DEVX
2368	G-DDTM	2513	G-DDZT	2657	G-EEFT	2817	G-EENK	2998	G-DEVY
2369	G-DDTN	2514	G-DDZU	2659	G-DEFV	2820	G-EENN	3006	G-DEWG
2370	G-DDTP	2518	G-DDZY	2660	G-DEFW	2825	G-EENT	3013	G-DEWP
2373	G-DDTS	2523	G-EEAD	2663	G-DEFZ	2826	G-DENU	3015	G-DEWR
2375	G-DDTU	2524	G-DEAE	2667	G-DEGD	2827	G-DENV	3024	G-DEXA
2376	G-DDTV	2525	G-DEAF	2668	G-DEGE	2828	G-EENW	3064	G-DEYS
2377	G-DDTW	2526	G-DEAG	2671	G-DEGH	2829	G-DENX	3076	G-DEWZ
2378	G-DDTX	2527	G-DEAH	2672	G-DEGJ	2831	G-EENZ	3101	G-DFAF
2379	G-DDTY	2528	G-DEAJ	2673	G-DEGK	2835	G-DEPD	3103	G-CFAJ
2382	G-DDUB	2529	G-DEAK	2676	G-DEGN	2836	G-DEPE	3106	G-CFAM
2385	G-DDUE	2531	G-DEAM	2679	G-DEGR	2837	G-DEPF	3109	G-CFAO
2386	G-DDUF	2535	G-DEAR	2680	G-DEGS	2845	G-DEPP	3110	G-DFAR
2388	G-DDUH	2537	G-DEAT	2681	G-DEGT	2848	G-DEPS	3112	G-DFAT
2390	G-DDUK	2540	G-DEAW	2684	G-DEGW	2849	G-DEPT	3114	G-DFAV
2391	G-DDUL	2544	G-EEBA	2685	G-DEGX	2850	G-DEPU	3115	G-DFAW
2394	G-DADJ	2545	G-FEBB	2687	G-DEGZ	2853	G-DEPX	3119	G-CFBA
2395	G-DDUR	2547	G-EEBD	2691	G-IUMB	2856	G-DEOA	3120	G-CFBB

3121	G-CFBC	3307	G-CFJW	3470	G-CFRR	3606	G-YOBI	3727	G-CGCM
3122	G-DFBD	3308	G-CFJX	3471	G-CFRS	3607	G-CFXM	3729	G-CGCP
3123	G-DFBE	3310	G-CFJZ	3474	G-CFRV	3610	G-CFZO	3730	G-CGCO
3124	G-XIXX	3312	G-DFKB	3475	G-CFRW	3612	G-CFXS	3731	G-CGCR
3126	G-CFBH	3315	G-GTWO	3476	G-CFRX	3614	G-CFXU	3733	G-CGCT
3127	G-DFBJ	3317	G-CFKG	3478	G-CFRZ	3616	G-CFXW	3734	G-CGCU
3130	G-DFBM	3318	G-DFKH	3479	G-DFSA	3618	G-CFXY	3736	G-CGCX
3131	G-CFBN	3321	G-CFKL	3482	G-CFSD	3620	G-CFYA	3737	G-CGCY
3133	G-DFBO	3322	G-CFKM	3486	G-CFSH	3621	G-CFYB	3739	G-CGDA
3136	G-CFBT	3328	G-CFKT	3494	G-CFSR	3622	G-CFYC	3740	G-CGDB
3138	G-CFBV	3329	G-CFKY	3495	G-CFSS	3623	G-RAIR	3742	G-CGDD
3139	G-CFBW	3337	G-CFLC	3496	G-CFST	3624	G-CFYE	3743	G-CGDE
3141	G-DFBY	3339	G-CFLE	3497	G-CFSU	3625	G-CFYF	3744	G-CGDF
3142	G-CFBZ	3340	G-CFLF	3500	G-PAFR	3626	G-CFYG	3747	G-DGDJ
3144	G-CFCB	3342	G-CFLH	3502	G-CFSZ	3627	G-CFYH	3748	G-CGDK
3146	G-DFCD	3351	G-CFLS	3504	G-CFTB	3628	G-CFYJ	3750	G-YOHO
3151	G-CFCJ	3352	G-EFLT	3505	G-CFTC	3629	G-CFYK	3753	G-CGDO
3154	G-DFCM	3355	G-CFLW	3506	G-CFTD	3630	G-CFYL	3754	G-CGDR
3155	G-CFCN	3356	G-CFLX	3510	G-CFTH	3631	G-CFYM	3755	G-CGDS
3156	G-CFCP	3358	G-CFLZ	3511	G-DFTJ	3632	G-CFYN	3756	G-CGDT
3158	G-CFCR	3361	G-LSGB	3512	G-CFTK	3635	G-CFYR	3757	G-CGDU
3159	G-CFCS	3365	G-DFMG	3513	G-CFTL	3638	G-CFYU	3758	G-GGDV
3162	G-CFCV	3366	G-CFMH	3515	G-CFTN	3639	G-CFYV	3760	G-CGDX
3163	G-DFCW	3368	G-CFMK	3516	G-CFTP	3640	G-CFYW	3761	G-CGDY
3165	G-DFCY	3369	G-CFML	3518	G-CFTR	3641	G-CFYX	3762	G-CGDZ
3167	G-CFDA	3371	G-CFMN	3519	G-CFTS	3642	G-CFYY	3764	G-CGEB
3171	G-CFDE	3372	G-OTRY	3522	G-CFTV	3643	G-CFYZ	3767	G-CGEE
3176	G-DFDK	3373	G-CFMO	3523	G-CFTW	3644	G-CFZA	3769	G-CGEG
3180	G-DFDP	3375	G-CFMS	3525	G-CFTY	3645	G-CFZB	3770	G-CGEH
3182	G-CFDR	3376	G-CFMT	3528	G-CFUB	3646	G-CFJF	3772	G-CGEL
3185	G-CFDM	3377	G-CFMU	3532	G-GBBB	3649	G-CFZF	3773	G-CGEM
3188	G-CFDX	3381	G-CFMY	3533	G-CFUH	3651	G-CFZH	3775	G-CGEP
3191	G-DFEA	3386	G-CFND	3534	G-CFUJ	3653	G-CFZK	3777	G-DHAA
3192	G-DFEB	3387	G-CFNE	3535	G-CFUL	3654	G-CFZL	3778	G-CHAB
3196	G-CFEF	3388	G-WYDE	3537	G-CFUN	3656	G-CFZN	3779	G-CHAC
3197	G-CFEG	3389	G-CFNG	3538	G-CFUP	3657	G-CFZP	3780	G-DHAD
3198	G-CFEH	3390	G-CFNH	3540	G-CFUR	3658	G-CFXO	3782	G-CHAF
3199	G-CFEJ	3392	G-CFNK	3541	G-CFUS	3659	G-CFZR	3785	G-CJGF
3203	G-CFEN	3393	G-CFNL	3542	G-CFUT	3663	G-CFZV	3787	G-DHAL
3205	G-DFEO	3394	G-CFNM	3543	G-CFUU	3664	G-CFZW	3790	G-DHAP
3206	G-CFER	3395	G-CFNN	3544	G-CFUV	3667	G-CFZZ	3791	G-CHAO
3207	G-CFES	3396	G-CFNP	3546	G-CFUY	3669	G-CGAB	3794	G-DHAT
3212	G-DFEX	3397	G-CUMU	3550	G-CFVC	3671	G-CGAD	3796	G-EHAV
3216	G-CFFB	3398	G-CFNR	3552	G-SVNC	3673	G-CGAF	3798	G-CHAX
3217	G-CFFC	3399	G-CFNS	3553	G-CFVE	3674	G-CGAG	3799	G-CHAY
3224	G-CFFK	3400	G-CFNT	3555	G-CFVH	3675	G-CGAH	3801	G-CHBA
3228	G-DFFP	3401	G-CFNU	3558	G-CFVL	3679	G-CGAM	3802	G-CHBB
3231	G-CFFS	3408	G-CFPB	3559	G-CFVM	3680	G-CGAN	3803	G-CHBC
3232	G-CFFT	3410	G-CFPD	3560	G-CFVN	3681	G-CGAP	3804	G-CHBD
3233	G-CFFU	3411	G-CFPE	3561	G-CFVP	3683	G-CGAR	3805	G-CHBE
3234	G-CFFV	3412	G-CFPF	3562	G-EUFO	3684	G-CGAS	3806	G-CHBF
3236	G-CFFX	3414	G-CFPH	3564	G-CFVS	3685	G-CGAT	3807	G-CHBG
3237	G-CFFY	3417	G-CFPL	3565	G-CFVT	3686	G-CGAU	3808	G-CHBH
3244	G-CFGF	3418	G-CFPM	3566	G-CFVU	3687	G-CGAV	3809	G-GBPP
3247	G-DFGJ	3419	G-CFPN	3567	G-CFVV	3688	G-DGAW	3810	G-CHBK
3248	G-CFGK	3420	G-CFPP	3568	G-CFVW	3689	G-CGAX	3811	G-CHBL
3252	G-CFGP	3424	G-CFPT	3571	G-CFVZ	3692	G-CGBA	3812	G-CHBM
3254	G-CFGR	3426	G-AWTP	3572	G-CFWA	3693	G-CGBB	3814	G-CHBP
3256	G-DFGT	3427	G-CFPW	3573	G-CFWB	3695	G-CGBD	3815	G-CHBO
3257	G-CFGU	3428	G-CFPX	3574	G-CFWC	3697	G-CGBF	3817	G-CHBS
3259	G-CFGW	3432	G-CFOB	3575	G-IFWD	3698	G-CGBG	3819	G-CHBT
3261	G-LDER	3433	G-CFOC	3576	G-CFWE	3700	G-CGBJ	3820	G-CHBU
3266	G-CFHD	3436	G-CFOF	3577	G-CFWF	3701	G-CGBK	3821	G-CHBV
3268	G-CFHF	3437	G-DFOG	3579	G-CFWH	3702	G-CGBL	3826	G-DHCA
3269	G-CFHG	3438	G-CEVN	3581	G-CFWK	3704	G-CGBN	3827	G-EHCB
3271	G-CFHJ	3440	G-CFOK	3582	G-CFWL	3706	G-CGBO	3829	G-EHCC
3273	G-CFHL	3441	G-CFDG	3583	G-CFWM	3707	G-CGBR	3831	G-DHCE
3274	G-CFHM	3442	G-CFOM	3585	G-CFWP	3708	G-CGBS	3832	G-DHCF
3275	G-CFHN	3446	G-CFOR	3587	G-MOZI	3709	G-XCIV	3834	G-DHCH
3278	G-CFHR	3448	G-CFOT	3588	G-CFWS	3710	G-CGBU	3835	G-DHCJ
3279	G-DFHS	3449	G-CFOU	3589	G-CFWT	3711	G-CGBV	3837	G-DHCL
3280	G-CFHT	3453	G-CFOY	3590	G-CFWU	3713	G-CGBX	3841	G-DHCO
3282	G-CFHV	3454	G-CFOZ	3592	G-CFWW	3714	G-CGBY	3842	G-DHCR
3283	G-CFHW	3455	G-DFRA	3593	G-REER	3715	G-CGBZ	3845	G-DHCU
3286	G-CFHZ	3456	G-CFRB	3594	G-CFWY	3716	G-CGCA	3846	G-DHCV
3291	G-CFJE	3457	G-CFRC	3595	G-CFWZ	3717	G-GLAK	3847	G-DHCW
3294	G-CFJH	3458	G-CFRP	3596	G-CFXA	3718	G-CGCC	3848	G-DHCX
3296	G-CFJK	3459	G-CFRE	3597	G-CFXB	3719	G-CGCD	3850	G-EHCZ
3298	G-CFJM	3462	G-CFRH	3598	G-CFXC	3720	G-CWLC	3851	G-CHDA
3302	G-CFJR	3463	G-CFRJ	3599	G-CFXD	3721	G-CGCF	3852	G-CHDB
3303	G-CFJS	3464	G-CFRK	3603	G-CFXH	3725	G-CGCK	3853	G-CHDC
3306	G-CFJV	3465	G-CFRL	3604	G-CFXJ	3726	G-CGCL	3854	G-CHDD

3855	G-CHDE	3988	G-CHJT	4120	G-CHOM	4244	G-CHVT	4364	G-CJAS
3856	G-OKLL	3990	G-CHJV	4123	G-CHOR	4245	G-CHVU	4365	G-CJAT
3858	G-DHDH	3991	G-CHJX	4124	G-CHOS	4246	G-CHVV	4367	G-CJAV
3859	G-CHDJ	3992	G-CHJY	4127	G-CHOV	4247	G-CHVW	4368	G-CJAW
3861	G-CHDL	3994	G-CHKA	4128	G-CHOW	4248	G-CHVX	4369	G-CJAX
3863	G-CHDN	3995	G-CHKB	4129	G-DHOX	4249	G-VENC	4371	G-CJAZ
3864	G-CHDP	3996	G-CHKC	4130	G-CHOY	4250	G-CHVZ	4373	G-CJBB
3866	G-CHDR	3997	G-CHKD	4131	G-CHOZ	4251	G-CHWA	4377	G-CJBF
3869	G-CHDU	4003	G-CHKK	4132	G-CHRA	4252	G-CHWB	4378	G-UNIN
3870	G-CHDV	4004	G-DHKL	4133	G-CHRB	4253	G-CHWC	4379	G-CJBH
3871	G-PEGZ	4005	G-CHKM	4134	G-CHRC	4256	G-CHWF	4380	G-CJBJ
3872	G-CHDX	4008	G-NYMB	4138	G-CHRG	4258	G-CHWH	4381	G-CJBK
3873	G-CHDY	4009	G-CHKR	4139	G-CHRJ	4261	G-CHWL	4383	G-CJBM
3874	G-IDER	4010	G-CHKS	4140	G-CHRK	4262	G-DSVN	4386	G-CJBO
3876	G-DHEB	4012	G-CHKU	4141	G-CHRL	4264	G-CHWP	4387	G-CJBR
3877	G-CHEC	4013	G-CHKV	4143	G-CHRN	4267	G-CHWS	4388	G-CJBS
3878	G-OSDF	4015	G-CHKX	4146	G-DHRR	4271	G-CHWW	4389	G-CJBT
3879	G-CHEE	4016	G-CHKY	4147	G-CHRS	4272	G-CHWX	4392	G-CJBW
3880	G-CHEF	4017	G-CHKZ	4151	G-CHRW	4276	G-CHXB	4393	G-CJBX
3881	G-CHEG	4019	G-CHLB	4152	G-CHRX	4278	G-CHXC	4394	G-CJBY
3882	G-CHEH	4020	G-CHLC	4153	G-STEU	4279	G-CHXD	4396	G-CJCA
3883	G-CHEJ	4025	G-CHLH	4155	G-CHSA	4280	G-CHXE	4399	G-CJCD
3884	G-CHEK	4027	G-CHLK	4156	G-CHSB	4283	G-CHXH	4400	G-VNTS
3885	G-DZDZ	4029	G-CHLM	4158	G-CHSD	4284	G-CHXJ	4401	G-CJCF
3886	G-DHEM	4030	G-CHLN	4159	G-CHSE	4287	G-CHXM	4402	G-CJCG
3887	G-CHEN	4031	G-CHLP	4161	G-CHSG	4288	G-LSKV	4404	G-CJCJ
3888	G-CHEP	4032	G-CEWZ	4163	G-DHSJ	4289	G-CHXP	4405	G-CJCK
3889	G-CHEO	4034	G-CHLS	4164	G-CHSK	4290	G-CHXO	4407	G-CJCM
3890	G-DHER	4038	G-CHLV	4165	G-DHSL	4291	G-CHXR	4408	G-CJCN
3891	G-DHES	4039	G-CHLX	4166	G-CHSM	4292	G-EVII	4409	G-CJCP
3892	G-DHET	4040	G-CHLY	4167	G-CHSN	4293	G-CHXT	4410	G-CEWI
3894	G-DHEV	4042	G-CHMA	4169	G-CHSO	4294	G-CHXU	4413	G-CJCT
3895	G-CHEW	4043	G-CHMB	4170	G-DHSR	4295	G-CHXV	4414	G-CJCU
3898	G-DHEZ	4044	G-CHMG	4174	G-CHSV	4296	G-CHXW	4415	G-CJCV
3899	G-CHFA	4046	G-CHMK	4176	G-CHSX	4297	G-CHXX	4416	G-CJCW
3900	G-CHFB	4047	G-CHML	4178	G-CHSZ	4298	G-CHXY	4417	G-CJCX
3904	G-CHFF	4048	G-CHMM	4180	G-CHTB	4299	G-CHXZ	4418	G-CJCY
3906	G-CHFH	4050	G-DHMP	4181	G-CHTC	4300	G-CHYA	4419	G-CJCZ
3910	G-LSVI	4051	G-CHMO	4182	G-CHTD	4301	G-RGTS	4422	G-CJDC
3913	G-LSED	4053	G-CHMS	4183	G-CHTE	4303	G-CHYD	4423	G-CJDD
3918	G-CHFV	4054	G-CHMT	4184	G-CHTF	4304	G-CHYE	4424	G-CJDE
3919	G-CHFW	4055	G-CHMU	4185	G-DHTG	4305	G-CHYF	4425	G-CJDF
3920	G-CHFX	4056	G-CHMV	4186	G-JNSC	4307	G-CHYH	4426	G-CJDG
3921	G-CHFY	4058	G-CHMX	4187	G-CHTJ	4308	G-CHYJ	4428	G-CJDJ
3924	G-CHGB	4059	G-CHMY	4189	G-WLLS	4309	G-CHYK	4429	G-CJDK
3928	G-CHGF	4060	G-CHMZ	4190	G-CHTM	4310	G-DHYL	4430	G-GRSR
3929	G-CHGG	4061	G-CHNA	4191	G-CHTN	4311	G-SMYK	4431	G-CJDM
3932	G-CHGK	4062	G-JNUS	4192	G-RIEV	4313	G-CHYP	4433	G-CJDP
3933	G-DHGL	4063	G-CHNC	4194	G-CHTR	4315	G-CHYR	4435	G-CJDR
3935	G-IRLE	4065	G-CHNE	4195	G-CHTS	4316	G-CHYS	4436	G-CJDS
3936	G-CHGP	4066	G-CHNF	4196	G-EHTT	4317	G-CHYT	4437	G-CJDT
3937	G-CHGO	4067	G-CHNG	4197	G-CHTU	4318	G-CHYU	4438	G-CJDU
3938	G-CHGR	4068	G-CHNH	4198	G-CHTV	4320	G-CHYW	4439	G-CJDV
3939	G-CHGS	4070	G-CHNK	4201	G-CHTY	4321	G-CHYX	4441	G-CJDX
3940	G-CHGT	4072	G-CHNM	4203	G-CHUA	4322	G-CHYY	4442	G-CJDY
3942	G-CHGV	4073	G-CHNN	4204	G-DHUB	4324	G-CHZA	4443	G-CJDZ
3943	G-CHGW	4078	G-CHNT	4206	G-CHUD	4325	G-CHZB	4444	G-CJEA
3944	G-CHGX	4079	G-CHNU	4207	G-CHUE	4327	G-CHZG	4445	G-CJEB
3946	G-CHGZ	4080	G-CHNV	4208	G-CHUF	4328	G-CHZE	4446	G-CJEC
3951	G-CHHE	4081	G-CHNW	4210	G-CHUH	4329	G-SVEN	4447	G-DJED
3954	G-CHHH	4082	G-DHNX	4211	G-CHUJ	4330	G-CHZG	4448	G-CJEE
3955	G-XBGA	4083	G-CHNY	4212	G-DHUK	4331	G-CHZH	4449	G-FORA
3956	G-CHHK	4084	G-CHNZ	4213	G-CHUL	4332	G-CHZJ	4450	G-CTAG
3958	G-CHHM	4085	G-DHPA	4215	G-CHUN	4335	G-CHZM	4451	G-CJEH
3959	G-CHHN	4087	G-CHPC	4217	G-CHUO	4338	G-CHZO	4452	G-TWAZ
3960	G-CHHP	4088	G-CHPD	4218	G-CHUR	4339	G-CHZR	4454	G-CJEL
3961	G-CHHO	4089	G-CHPE	4219	G-CHUS	4342	G-CHZU	4455	G-CJEM
3962	G-CHHR	4092	G-CHPH	4220	G-CHUT	4343	G-CHZV	4457	G-CJEP
3963	G-CHHS	4095	G-CHPL	4221	G-CHUU	4344	G-OJNE	4458	G-OZOZ
3964	G-CHHT	4096	G-OGGB	4223	G-CHUW	4345	G-CHZX	4459	G-CJER
3965	G-CHHU	4099	G-CHPO	4225	G-CHUY	4346	G-CHZY	4461	G-NJET
3967	G-CHHW	4100	G-DHPR	4226	G-CHUZ	4347	G-CHZZ	4462	G-CJEU
3968	G-CHHX	4102	G-CHPT	4231	G-CHVE	4348	G-DJAA	4463	G-CJEV
3969	G-LIBL	4104	G-CHPV	4232	G-CHVF	4349	G-DJAB	4464	G-CJEW
3971	G-CHJA	4105	G-CHPW	4233	G-CHVG	4350	G-DJAC	4465	G-CJEX
3973	G-CHJC	4106	G-CHPX	4234	G-CHVH	4351	G-DJAD	4467	G-CJEZ
3975	G-CHJE	4112	G-CHOD	4236	G-CHVK	4352	G-EJAE	4468	G-CJFA
3976	G-CHJF	4113	G-ODUO	4237	G-CHVL	4355	G-DJAH	4470	G-CJFC
3978	G-CHJH	4114	G-CHOF	4238	G-CHVM	4358	G-CJAL	4472	G-CJFE
3981	G-CHJL	4117	G-CFCA	4240	G-CHVP	4360	G-DJAN	4473	G-CJFF
3985	G-CHJP	4118	G-DHOK	4241	G-CHVO	4362	G-CJAO	4475	G-CJFH
3986	G-CHJR	4119	G-LSIX	4242	G-CHVR	4363	G-CJAR	4476	G-CJFJ

4477	G-CJFK	4584	G-CJKW	4691	G-CJOG	4800	G-CJUV	4915	G-EIER
4478	G-CJFL	4585	G-CJKX	4692	G-CJOH	4801	G-CJUW	4921	G-IICT
4479	G-CJFM	4586	G-CJKY	4693	G-CJOJ	4802	G-CJUX	4923	G-CJZX
4480	G-DRCS	4587	G-CJKZ	4694	G-CEUN	4804	G-CJUZ	4924	G-CJZY
4482	G-CENK	4588	G-CJLA	4696	G-CEUG	4805	G-CJVA	4925	G-CJZZ
4483	G-CJFR	4590	G-CJLC	4697	G-CJON	4806	G-CJVB	4928	G-CKAC
4485	G-CJFT	4594	G-CJLG	4698	G-CJOP	4807	G-CJVC	4930	G-CKAE
4486	G-CJFU	4595	G-CJLH	4699	G-CJOO	4809	G-CJVE	4931	G-ODDZ
4487	G-OWAI	4596	G-CJLJ	4700	G-CJOR	4810	G-CJVF	4933	G-CKAH
4489	G-CJFX	4597	G-CJLK	4701	G-CJOS	4811	G-CJVG	4934	G-CKAJ
4490	G-CJFY	4598	G-DJLL	4703	G-CJOU	4813	G-CJVJ	4935	G-CKAK
4491	G-CJFZ	4600	G-CJLN	4704	G-CJOV	4814	G-LSCP	4936	G-CKAL
4493	G-CJGB	4601	G-CJLP	4705	G-CJOW	4815	G-CJVL	4937	G-CKAM
4495	G-CJGD	4602	G-CJLO	4706	G-CJOX	4816	G-CJVM	4938	G-CKAN
4496	G-CJGE	4603	G-CJLR	4708	G-CJOZ	4818	G-CJVP	4939	G-CKAP
4498	G-DJGG	4604	G-CJLS	4709	G-CJRA	4819	G-YEHA	4941	G-CKAR
4499	G-CJGH	4607	G-CJLV	4710	G-CJRB	4820	G-TOOB	4942	G-CKAS
4500	G-CJGJ	4608	G-CJLW	4711	G-CJRC	4821	G-CJVS	4943	G-YODA
4501	G-CJGK	4610	G-CJLY	4712	G-CJRD	4822	G-CJED	4944	G-CKAU
4502	G-CJGL	4611	G-CJLZ	4713	G-CJRE	4823	G-CJVU	4945	G-CKAV
4503	G-CJGM	4612	G-CJMA	4714	G-CJRF	4824	G-CJVV	4946	G-CKAW
4504	G-CJGN	4614	G-DJMC	4715	G-CJRG	4825	G-CJVW	4947	G-CKAX
4505	G-RBCT	4615	G-DJMD	4716	G-CJRH	4826	G-CJVX	4948	G-CKAY
4507	G-CJGR	4618	G-CJMG	4717	G-CJRJ	4828	G-CJVZ	4950	G-CKBA
4508	G-CJGS	4619	G-CJMH	4718	G-FLUZ	4829	G-CJWA	4952	G-CKBC
4510	G-CJGU	4620	G-CJMJ	4719	G-CJRL	4830	G-CJWB	4953	G-CKBD
4511	G-CLGC	4621	G-CJMK	4724	G-CJRR	4831	G-THRM	4955	G-CKBF
4512	G-CJGW	4622	G-CJML	4725	G-DKBW	4832	G-CJWD	4956	G-CKBG
4513	G-CJGX	4624	G-CJMN	4726	G-CJRT	4834	G-CJWF	4957	G-CKBH
4514	G-CJGY	4625	G-CJMO	4727	G-CJRU	4835	G-CJWG	4959	G-CKBK
4515	G-CJGZ	4626	G-CJMP	4728	G-CJRV	4836	G-CTWO	4960	G-CKBL
4519	G-CJHD	4628	G-CJMR	4729	G-NUGC	4837	G-CJWJ	4961	G-CKBM
4522	G-CJHG	4629	G-CJMS	4730	G-CJRX	4838	G-CJWK	4962	G-CKBN
4524	G-CJHJ	4630	G-CJMT	4736	G-CJSD	4840	G-CJWM	4966	G-CKBS
4525	G-CJHK	4631	G-CJMU	4737	G-CJSE	4842	G-CJWP	4967	G-CKBT
4526	G-CJHL	4632	G-CJMV	4738	G-LSIF	4843	G-TWOA	4968	G-CKBU
4527	G-CJHM	4633	G-CJMW	4739	G-CJSG	4844	G-CJWR	4969	G-CKBV
4528	G-CJHN	4634	G-CJMX	4740	G-CJSH	4845	G-DJWS	4971	G-CKBX
4529	G-DJHP	4635	G-CJMY	4741	G-CJSJ	4846	G-CJWT	4975	G-CKCB
4530	G-CJHO	4636	G-CJMZ	4742	G-CJSK	4847	G-CJWU	4976	G-VTCT
4531	G-CJHR	4637	G-CJNA	4743	G-CJSL	4848	G-CJWV	4977	G-CKCD
4532	G-CJHS	4638	G-CJNB	4745	G-CJSN	4850	G-CJWX	4978	G-CKCE
4533	G-HOJO	4641	G-CJNE	4749	G-CJSS	4853	G-CJXA	4981	G-CKCH
4534	G-CJHU	4642	G-CJNF	4750	G-CJST	4854	G-CJXB	4982	G-CKCJ
4536	G-CJHW	4643	G-CJNG	4751	G-CJSU	4855	G-CJXC	4985	G-CKCM
4537	G-CJHX	4645	G-CJNJ	4752	G-CJSV	4859	G-CJXG	4986	G-CKCN
4538	G-CJHY	4646	G-CJNK	4753	G-CJSW	4860	G-ODCH	4987	G-CKCP
4539	G-CJHZ	4648	G-CJNM	4754	G-CJSX	4862	G-WIII	4988	G-CEUP
4541	G-CJJB	4649	G-CJNN	4756	G-CJSZ	4863	G-CJXL	4989	G-CKCR
4543	G-CJJD	4650	G-CJNP	4758	G-CJTB	4864	G-CJXM	4990	G-JAPK
4544	G-CJJE	4651	G-CJNO	4762	G-CJTF	4865	G-CJXN	4991	G-CKCT
4545	G-CJJF	4652	G-CJNR	4764	G-CJTH	4866	G-CJXP	4993	G-CKCV
4546	G-NIVT	4654	G-CJNT	4765	G-CJTJ	4868	G-CJXR	4994	G-CKCW
4547	G-CJJH	4657	G-LLLL	4766	G-CJTK	4870	G-CJXT	4996	G-CKCY
4548	G-CJJJ	4658	G-CJNX	4767	G-CJTL	4871	G-GCJA	4997	G-CKCZ
4549	G-CJJK	4659	G-CJNY	4768	G-CJTM	4873	G-CJXW	4998	G-CKDA
4550	G-CJJL	4660	G-CJNZ	4769	G-CJTN	4874	G-CJXX	4999	G-CKDB
4553	G-CJJP	4661	G-CJPA	4770	G-CJTP	4875	G-CJXY	5000	G-CKDC
4555	G-CJJR	4663	G-CJPC	4771	G-CJTO	4876	G-CJXZ	5002	G-SISI
4557	G-CJJT	4664	G-CVZT	4772	G-CJTR	4878	G-ONEZ	5003	G-CKDF
4561	G-CJJX	4666	G-CJPF	4773	G-CJTS	4880	G-CJYC	5005	G-CKDH
4562	G-SWSW	4668	G-CJPH	4775	G-CJTU	4881	G-CJYD	5006	G-VSIX
4563	G-CJJZ	4669	G-CJPJ	4776	G-HAAH	4882	G-CJYE	5007	G-CKDK
4564	G-CJKA	4671	G-CJPL	4777	G-CJTW	4883	G-CJYF	5009	G-SINK
4565	G-CJKB	4672	G-CJPM	4779	G-CJTY	4886	G-VTUS	5010	G-CKDN
4566	G-CFOX	4674	G-CJPP	4782	G-CJUB	4888	G-CJYL	5011	G-CKDP
4567	G-CJKD	4675	G-CJPO	4783	G-XWON	4890	G-CJYN	5012	G-CKDO
4568	G-CJKE	4676	G-CJPR	4784	G-GZIP	4891	G-CJYP	5014	G-CKDS
4569	G-CJKF	4677	G-CJPS	4785	G-CJUE	4893	G-CJYR	5016	G-CKDU
4570	G-CJKG	4678	G-CJPT	4786	G-CJUF	4894	G-CJYS	5017	G-CKDV
4572	G-CJKJ	4679	G-TLTL	4787	G-CJUG	4895	G-XJON	5018	G-CKDW
4573	G-CJKK	4680	G-CJPV	4788	G-CJUH	4896	G-CJYU	5019	G-CKDX
4574	G-CJKL	4681	G-CJPW	4789	G-CJUJ	4899	G-CJYX	5020	G-CKDY
4575	G-CJKM	4682	G-CJPX	4790	G-CJUK	4903	G-CJZB	5021	G-CKDZ
4576	G-CJKN	4683	G-CJPY	4791	G-LIDY	4904	G-WDGC	5022	G-CKEA
4577	G-CJKP	4684	G-CJPZ	4792	G-CJUM	4906	G-CJZE	5023	G-CKEB
4578	G-CJKO	4685	G-CJOA	4793	G-CJUN	4908	G-CJZG	5024	G-CKEC
4579	G-CJKR	4686	G-CJOB	4794	G-CJUP	4909	G-CJZH	5025	G-CKED
4580	G-CJKS	4687	G-CJOC	4795	G-WONE	4911	G-CJZK	5026	G-CKEE
4581	G-CJKT	4688	G-CJOD	4796	G-CJUR	4912	G-CJZL	5030	G-CKEJ
4582	G-CJKU	4689	G-CJOE	4797	G-CJUS	4913	G-CJZM	5031	G-CKEK
4583	G-CJKV	4690	G-CEYC	4799	G-CJUU	4914	G-CJZN	5032	G-CKEL

5033	G-HKAA	5098	G-CKHE	5161	G-CKKM	5219	G-CKNC	5278	G-CKPL
5034	G-DKEN	5099	G-CKHF	5162	G-CKKN	5220	G-CKND	5279	G-CKPM
5035	G-CKEP	5100	G-CKHG	5163	G-CKKP	5221	G-CKNE	5280	G-CKPN
5037	G-CKER	5101	G-CKHH	5164	G-CKKR	5222	G-CKNF	5281	G-CKPO
5038	G-CKES	5102	G-CDDB	5165	G-TWOC	5223	G-CKNG	5282	G-CKPP
5039	G-CKET	5103	G-CKHK	5167	G-CKKV	5224	G-KHCC	5284	G-EWEW
5040	G-GCMW	5105	G-CKHM	5169	G-CKKX	5226	G-CKNJ	5285	G-XOAR
5041	G-CKEV	5106	G-CKHN	5170	G-CKKY	5227	G-CKNK	5286	G-CKPU
5042	G-LSFB	5107	G-CKHP	5171	G-DAVS	5228	G-CKNL	5287	G-CKPV
5043	G-CKEX	5108	G-ORCW	5172	G-CKLA	5229	G-CKNM	5288	G-SAOC
5044	G-EKEY	5109	G-CKHR	5173	G-CKLB	5230	G-CKNN	5289	G-CKPX
5045	G-CKEZ	5110	G-CKHS	5174	G-CKLC	5231	G-CKNO	5290	G-CKPY
5046	G-CKFA	5111	G-CKHT	5175	G-CKLD	5232	G-DAWZ	5291	G-CKPZ
5047	G-CKFB	5112	G-CKHV	5177	G-CKLF	5233	G-CKNR	5293	G-CKRB
5048	G-CKFC	5113	G-CKHW	5178	G-CKLG	5234	G-CKNS	5294	G-CKRC
5049	G-CKFD	5114	G-CKHX	5179	G-WYVN	5235	G-OASG	5295	G-CKRD
5050	G-CKFE	5115	G-JIFI	5180	G-DUOT	5236	G-CKNU	5296	G-ONAT
5052	G-CKFG	5116	G-KEPE	5182	G-DDJF	5237	G-CKNV	5297	G-CKRF
5053	G-CKFH	5117	G-CKJA	5183	G-CKLN	5238	G-TRBO	5298	G-LYDS
5054	G-CKFJ	5118	G-CKJB	5184	G-CKLP	5239	G-RIEF	5299	G-CKRH
5055	G-CKFK	5119	G-CKJC	5185	G-CKLR	5240	G-IZII	5300	G-CKRI
5056	G-CKFL	5120	G-CKJD	5186	G-CKLS	5243	G-SAJA	5301	G-CKRJ
5057	G-CKFM	5121	G-CKJE	5187	G-CKLT	5245	G-CKOD	5302	G-KPLG
5058	G-CKFN	5122	G-CKJF	5188	G-CKLV	5246	G-CKOE	5304	G-CKRM
5059	G-CKFP	5123	G-CKJG	5189	G-CKLW	5247	G-XDUO	5305	G-CKRN
5060	G-CEUR	5124	G-CKJH	5190	G-CKLX	5248	G-PHNX	5306	G-CKRO
5061	G-CKFR	5125	G-CKJJ	5191	G-CKLY	5249	G-CKOH	5307	G-XELL
5063	G-CKFT	5126	G-CKJK	5192	G-CKMA	5250	G-CKOI	5308	G-CKRR
5064	G-DKFU	5127	G-CKJL	5193	G-CKMB	5251	G-CKOJ	5309	G-CKRS
5065	G-CKFV	5128	G-CKJM	5194	G-CKMC	5252	G-CKOK	5310	G-CKRT
5068	G-CKFY	5129	G-CKJN	5195	G-CKMD	5253	G-CKOL	5311	G-CKRU
5070	G-CKGA	5130	G-CKJP	5196	G-CKME	5254	G-CKOM	5312	G-CKRV
5071	G-CKGB	5131	G-GLID	5197	G-CKMF	5255	G-CKON	5313	G-CKRW
5072	G-CKGC	5132	G-CKJS	5198	G-CKMG	5256	G-CKOO	5314	G-CKRX
5073	G-CKGD	5133	G-CTAA	5199	G-IICX	5257	G-KOBH	5315	G-RYPE
5075	G-CKGF	5144	G-LSGM	5200	G-CKMI	5259	G-CKOR	5316	G-SASG
5077	G-CKGH	5145	G-CKJV	5201	G-CKMJ	5260	G-CKOT	5317	G-HEBB
5078	G-PNGC	5146	G-KCHG	5203	G-CKML	5261	G-CKOU	5318	G-IXXI
5079	G-CKGK	5147	G-OTCZ	5204	G-CKMM	5262	G-CKOV	5319	G-XXIX
5080	G-CKGL	5148	G-KOYY	5205	G-CKMN	5263	G-CKOW	5320	G-CKSD
5081	G-CKGM	5149	G-CKJZ	5206	G-CKMO	5264	G-CKOX	5321	G-KKAM
5082	G-CKGN	5150	G-RDDT	5207	G-CKMP	5265	G-CKOY	5323	G-CHRH
5084	G-VTWO	5151	G-CKKB	5208	G-CKMR	5266	G-CKOZ	5324	G-CKSH
5087	G-CKGT	5152	G-CKKC	5209	G-DUOX	5267	G-CKPA	5325	G-XLII
5088	G-CKGU	5153	G-CKKD	5210	G-CKMT	5269	G-SORA	5326	G-OBPP
5089	G-CKGV	5154	G-CKKE	5211	G-DGIK	5270	G-VLCC	5327	G-CKSK
5091	G-CKGX	5155	G-CKKF	5212	G-CKMV	5271	G-CKPE	5328	G-CKSL
5092	G-CKGY	5156	G-TWOT	5213	G-CKMW	5273	G-CKPG	5329	G-CKSM
5094	G-CKHA	5157	G-ZENN	5215	G-CKMY	5274	G-SAXT	5330	G-CMWK
5095	G-CKHB	5158	G-VCXT	5216	G-CKMZ	5275	G-CFHO	5331	G-CKSO
5096	G-CKHC	5159	G-CKKK	5217	G-DTWO	5276	G-CKPJ	5333	G-CRJW
5097	G-CKHD	5160	G-OASW	5218	G-CKNB	5277	G-CKPK	5340	G-CKSY

PART 4 – IRISH GLIDING AND SOARING ASSOCIATION REGISTER

The system was similar to the British Gliding Association and until 2007 the register was maintained by the Irish Gliding & Soaring Association. Originally this was kept by the Irish Aviation Club using the prefix "IAC". From 1960 until 1967 gliders were allocated with a number prefixed "IGA". The IGSA listing is updated from Air-Britain sources. In March 2007 responsibility for glider registration was taken over by the Irish Aviation Authority, and all active gliders were re-registered in the sequence from EI-GLA. Remaining aircraft are shown below.

No	Code	Type	Constructor's No	Previous Identity	Date	Owner(Operator)	(Unconfirmed) Base	Status
IGA 6		Slingsby T.8 Tutor	-	IAC 6 VM657	.56	Meath Aero Museum	Ashbourne, County.Meath	N 3.01
EI-100		SZD-12A Mucha 100A	494	OY-XAN	.95	P Bedford *(Preserved at Cavan & Leitrim Railway)*	Dromod	N 6.07
EI-102		Slingsby T.26 Kite 2	?	IGA 102 IAC 102, BGA ..	.54	J J Sullivan and partners *(Reserved as EI-GMG)*	Gowran Grange	N 5.03
EI-105		Schleicher K 7	775	IGA 7	.60	Dublin Gliding Club *(Sold to private syndicate)*	(Roscommon)	N 6.03
EI-118		EoN AP.8 Baby	EoN/B/001	BGA 608 RAFGSA 217, BGA 608, G-ALLU, BGA 608 *(Reserved as EI-GMK)*	.73	W Tracey	Gowran Grange	
EI-120		LET L-13 Blanik	175205	RAFGSA BGA 1730	.75	Private Syndicate *(Reserved as EI-GMM)*	Gowran Grange	N 4.06
EI-124	124	Grob G102 Astir CS 77 (Astir Standard)	1761		.80	Dublin Gliding Club *(New owner 2.08)*Gowran Grange		N 9.08
EI-127		Schleicher Ka 6CR	662	PH-259	?	N van Kuyk *(Reserved as EI-GLG)*	Not known	
EI-130		Scheibe L-Spatz	200	BGA 2199 D-4707	?	J J Sullivan *"White Cloud" (Reserved as EI-GMI)*	Gowran Grange	
EI-133	33	Schleicher K 8B	8557	D-8517 D-9367	.91	Dublin Gliding Club *(Reserved as EI-GLE)*	Gowran Grange	A10.01
EI-134	34	Schleicher ASW 15B	15249	D-1087	.91	J & C O'Brien *(Reserved as EI-GLX)*Gowran Grange		
EI-135		Slingsby T.38 Grasshopper *(Wings from WZ756 or WZ768)*	758	WZ762	.91	(Syndicate) *(Stored as "WZ762")*	Gowran Grange	N 4.06
EI-139		Slingsby T.31B	902	BGA 3485 G-BOKG, XE789	.93	P Bedford	Dromod	N 6.07
						(Preserved at Cavan & Leitrim Railway; reserved as EI-GMH)		
EI-140		SZD-12A Mucha 100A	491	HB-647	.93	D Mongey *(Reserved as EI-GMJ)*	Gowran Grange	
EI-144		Scheibe SF 27A Zugvogel V	6049	(EI-142) D-1444	.94	R Staeps *(Reserved as EI-GLY)*	Gowran Grange	
EI-154		LET L-13 Blanik	173214	BGA 1500 G-ATCG	6.02	J Selman	Ardagh	
EI-157		Slingsby T.21B	1158	BGA 1465 RAFGSA 333, XN154	.02	C Sinclair *(Reserved as EI-GLZ)*	Gowran Grange	

SECTION 7

PART 1 – OVERSEAS REGISTRATION PREFIX INDEX

The previous identity origins of many of the current UK and Irish registered aircraft are many and varied. Therefore, we include both current and historical lists of ICAO national country allocations so the reader can deduce, in brief, the aircraft's provenance. Thanks to Mike Cain for an update this year

Current Prefixes:

Prefix	Country	Commenced	Historical Prefix	Prefix	Country	Commenced	Historical Prefix
AP-	Pakistan	1947		LX-	Luxembourg	1935	UL-
A2-	Botswana	1972	VQ-ZE -VQ-Z	LY-	Lithuania	1936	LY-, RY-, CCCP-
A3-	Tonga	1971	VQ-F	LZ-	Bulgaria	1929	
A4O-	Oman	1974		M-	Isle of Man	2007	G-
A5-	Bhutan	1983		N	United States	1921	
A6-	United Arab Emirates-	1977	A6-	OB-	Peru	1940	OA-
A7-	Qatar	1975		OD-	Lebanon	1951	F-, LR-
A8-	Liberia	2003	LI-, EL-	OE-	Austria	1936	A-
A9C-	Bahrain	1977		OH-	Finland	1931	K-S
B-	China (Peoples' Republic of)	1975	XT	OK-	Czech Republic	1929	L-B
B-	China (Republic of)	1949	XT	OM-	Slovakia	19xx	OK-
B-H, -K, -L-	Hong Kong	1997	VR-H	OO-	Belgium	1929	O-B
B-M-	Macau	1999	CR-M	OY-	Denmark	1929	T-D
C-	Canada	1974	G-C, CF-	P-	Korea (North)	1953	
CC-	Chile	1929		PH-	Netherlands	1929	H-N
CN-	Morocco	1952	F-D	PJ-	Netherlands Antilles	1929	
CP-	Bolivia	1954	CB	PK-	Indonesia	1929	
CS-	Portugal	1929	C-P	PP-	Brazil	1932	P-B
CU-	Cuba	1947	NM-	PR-	Brazil	1950	
CX-	Uruguay	1929		PT-	Brazil	1950	
C2-	Nauru	1971	VH-	PU-	Brazil (ultralights)	1950	
C3-	Andorra	1993		PZ-	Suriname	1929	
C5-	Gambia	1978	VP-X	P2-	Papua New Guinea	1974	VH-
C6-	Bahamas	1975	VP-B	P4-	Aruba	1986	PJ-
C9-	Mozambique	1975	CR-A, CR-B	RA-	Russia	1991	RR-, CCCP-
D-	Germany	1929		RDPL-	Laos	1975	F-L, XW-
DQ-	Fiji	1971	VQ-F	RP-	Philippines	1975	PI-
D2-	Angola	1975	CR-L	SE-	Sweden	1929	S-A
D4-	Cape Verde Islands	1975	CR-C	SP-	Poland	1929	P-P
D6-	Comoros	1975	F-O	ST-	Sudan	1959	SN-
EC-	Spain	1929	M-	SU-	Egypt	1931	
EI-, EJ-	Ireland	1928		SU-Y	Palestine	1995	VQ-P (1930-48)
EK-	Armenia	1991	CCCP-	SX-	Greece	1929	
EP-	Iran	1944	RV-	S2-	Bangladesh	1972	AP-
ER-	Moldova	1991	CCCP-		(Formerly East Pakistan)		
ES-	Estonia	1929	ES-, CCCP-	S5-	Slovenia	1993	YU-, SL-
ET-	Ethiopia	1945		S7-	Seychelles	1976	VQ-S
EW-	Belarus	1991	CCCP-	S9-	Sao Tome	1977	CR-S
EX-	Kyrgyzstan	1991	CCCP-	TC-	Turkey	1929	
EY-	Tajikistan	1991	CCCP-	TF-	Iceland	1937	
EZ-	Turkmenistan	1993	CCCP-	TG-	Guatemala	1948	LG-
E3-	Eritrea	1994	ET-	TI-	Costa Rica	1927	
E7-	Bosnia Herzegovina	2009	YU-, T9-	TJ-	Cameroon	1960	F-O, VR-N
F-	France	1919		TL-	Central African Republic	1961	F-O
F-O	French Overseas Territories	1929		TN-	Congo (Peoples' Republic of)	1960	F-O
G-	United Kingdom	1919		TR-	Gabon	1960	F-O
HA-	Hungary	1935	H-M	TS-	Tunisia	1956	F-O
HB-	Switzerland	1935	CH-	TT-	Chad	1960	F-O
HC-	Ecuador	1929		TU-	Ivory Coast	1960	F-O
HH-	Haiti	1929		TY-	Benin	1960	F-O
HI-	Dominican Republic	1929		TZ-	Mali	1960	F-O
HK-	Colombia	1946	C-	T3-	Kiribati	1983	VP-P
HL-	Korea (South)	1948		T7-	San Marino	1997	
HP-	Panama	1952	R-, RX-	T8A-	Palau	2004	V6-
HR-	Honduras	1961	XH-		(Formerly part of Micronesia)		
HS-	Thailand	1929	H-S	UK-	Uzbekistan	1991	CCCP-
HV-	Vatican state	1929		UN-	Kazakhstan	1991	CCCP-
HZ-	Saudi Arabia	1945	UH-	UR-	Ukraine	1991	CCCP-
H4-	Solomon Islands	1978	VP-P	VH-	Australia	1929	G-AU
I-	Italy	1929		VN-	Vietnam	1975	F-VN, XV-
JA-	Japan	1948	J-	VP-A	Anguilla	1997	
JU-	Mongolia	1998	MT-, HMAY-	VP-B	Bermuda	1997	VR-B
JY-	Jordan	1954	TJ- ,VQ-P	VP-C	Cayman Islands	1997	VR-C
J2-	Djibouti	1977	F-O	VP-F	Falkland Islands	1929	
J3-	Grenada	1974	VQ-G	VP-G	Gibraltar	1997	VR-G
J5-	Guinea Bissau	1979	CR-G	VP-LVA	British Virgin Islands	1971	
J6-	St. Lucia	1981	VQ-L	to VP-LZZ			
J7-	Dominica	1978	VP-L	VQ-H	St. Helena	1929	
J8-	St. Vincent	1979	VP-V	VQ-T	Turks and Caicos Islands	1980	VP-J
LN-	Norway	1931	N-	VT-	India	1930	G-IA, CR-I
LQ-	Argentina (Government)	1932		V2-	Antigua	1981	VP-L, VP-A
LV-	Argentina	1932	R-	V3-	Belize	1983	VP-H

Prefix	Country	Commenced	Historical Prefix
V4--	St.Kitts and Nevis	1983	VP-LKA-LLZ
V5-	Namibia	1990	ZS-
V6--	Micronesia	1990	
V7--	Marshall Islands	1991	MI-
V8-	Brunei	1984	VR-U-
XA-	Mexico (Commercial)	1929	X-
XB-	Mexico (Private)	1929	X-
XC-	Mexico (Government)	1929	X-
XT-	Burkina Faso	1984	F-O
	(Formerly Upper Volta)		
XU-	Cambodia	1954	F-KH, KW-
XY-	Myanmar	1938	VT-
	(Formerly Burma)		
YA-	Afghanistan	1929	
YI-	Iraq	1931	
YJ-	Vanuatu	1980	F-O or VP-P
	(Formerly New Hebrides)		
YK-	Syria	1949	F-, SR-
YL-	Latvia	1929	YL-, CCCP
YN-	Nicaragua	1981	YN-, AN-
YR-	Romania	1936	CV-
YS-	El Salvador	1939	
YU-	Serbia	1933	X-S, UN
	(Formerly part of Yugoslavia until 1992)		
YV-	Venezuela	1929	
Z-	Zimbabwe	1980	VP-W, VP-Y
ZA-	Albania	1946	
ZK-, ZM-	New Zealand	1929	G-NZ
ZP-	Paraguay	1929	
ZS-, ZU-	South Africa	1929	G-U
Z3-	Macedonia	1992	YU
3A-	Monaco	1959	CZ, MC
3B-	Mauritius	1959	VQ-M
3C-	Equatorial Guinea	1970	EC-
3D-	Swaziland	1971	VQ-ZIA - ZLZ
3X-	Guinea	1958	F-O
4K-	Azerbaijan	1991	CCCP-
4L-	Georgia	1991	CCCP-
4O-	Montenegro	2008	X-S, UN-, YU-
	(Used YU- with Serbia until 2008)		

Prefix	Country	Commenced	Historical Prefix
4R-	Sri Lanka	1954	VP-C, CY-
4X	Israel	1948	
5A-	Libya	1959	I-
5B-	Cyprus	1960	VQ-C
5H	Tanzania	1964	
	(Formerly Zanzibar (VP-Z) and Tanganyika (VR-T))		
5N-	Nigeria	1960	VR-N
5R-	Madagascar	1960	F-O
5T-	Mauritania	1960	F-O
5U-	Niger	1960	F-O
5V-	Togo	1976	F-O
5W-	Western Samoa	1962	ZK-
5X--	Uganda	1962	VP-U
5Y-	Kenya	1963	VP-K
6O-	Somalia	1969	I-, 6OS-
6V-	Senegal	1960	F-O
6Y-	Jamaica	1964	VP-J
7O-	Yemen	1974	YE-, 4W-
7P-	Lesotho	1967	VQ-ZAA-ZDZ
7Q-	Malawi	1962	F-O
7T-	Algeria	1962	F-O
8P-	Barbados	1968	VQ-B
8Q-	Maldive Republic	1976	(VP-)
8R-	Guyana	1967	VQ-G
9A-	Croatia	1991	YU-, RC-
9G-	Ghana	1957	VP-A
9H-	Malta	1968	VP-M
9J-	Zambia	1964	VP-Y
9K-	Kuwait	1960	K
9L-	Sierra Leone	1961	VR-L
9M-	Malaysia	1963	VR-J/-O/-R/-S/-W
9N	Nepal	1960	
9Q	Congo (Democratic Republic)	1962	OO-C, 9O-
	(Formerly Belgian Congo and Zaire)		
9U-	Burundi	1966	OO-C, BR-
9V-	Singapore	1966	VR-S, 9M-
9XR	Rwanda	1966	OO-C
9Y-	Trinidad and Tobago	1965	VP-T

Historical Prefixes:

Prefix	Country	Period	Current Prefix
A-	Austria	1929-1939	OE-
AN-	Nicaragua	1936-1981	YN-
BR-	Burundi	1962-1965	9U-
C-	Colombia	1929-1946	HK-
CB-	Bolivia	1929-1954	CP-
CCCP-	Soviet Union	1929-1991	RA- (Russia)
CF-	Canada	1929-1974	C
CH--	Switzerland	1929-1936	HB-
CR-A, -M	Mozambique	1929-1975	C9-
CR-B, -H	Mozambique	1971-1975	C9-
CR-C	Cape Verde Islands	1929-1975	D4-
CR-G	Portuguese Guinea (Guinea Bissau)		
		1929-1975	J5-
CR-I	Portuguese India	1929-1961	VT-
CR-L	Angola	1929-1975	D2-
CR-S	Sao Tome and Principe	1929-1977	S9-
CR-T	Timor	1929-1976	PK-
CV-	Romania	1929-1936	YR-
CY-	Ceylon	1948-1954	4R-
CZ-	Monaco	1929-1949	MC
DDR-	East Germany	1981-1990	D
DM-	East Germany	1955-1981	DDR-
EL-	Liberia	1952-2003	A8-.
ES-	Estonia	1929-1939	Merged into Soviet Union CCCP-
EZ-	Saarland	1929-1933	SL-
F-D	French Morocco	1929-1952	CN-
F-KH	Cambodia	1953-1960	XU-
F-LA	Laos	1955-1959	XW-
F-O	Algeria	1929-1962	7T-
F-O	Benin	1929-1960	TY-
F-O	Cameroon	1929-1960	TJ-

Prefix	Country	Period	Current Prefix
F-O	Chad	1929-1960	TT-
F-O	Congo	1929-1960	TN-
F-O	Djibouti	1929-1977	J2-.
F-O	Gabon	1929-1960	TR-
F-O	Guinea	1929-1958	3X-
F-O	Indo-China	1948-1950s	see Cambodia, Laos, Vietnam
F-O	Ivory Coast	1929-1960	TU-
F-O	Madagascar	1929-1960	5R-
F-O	Mali	1929-1960	TZ-
F-O	Mauritania	1929-1960	5T-
F-O	Niger	1929-1960	5U-
F-O	Senegal	1929-1960	6V-
F-O	Togo	1929-1976	5V-.
F-O	Tunisia	1929-1956	TS-
F-O	Ubangi-Shari	1929-1960	TL-
F-O	Upper Volta	1929-1960	XT-
F-VN	French Indo-China	1949-1959	XV- Vietnam
FC-	Free French	1940-1944	F-
G-AU	Australia	1921-1928	VH-
G-C	Canada	1920-1928	CF-
G-IA	India	1919-1928	VT-
G-K	Kenya	1928-1928	VP-K
G-NZ	New Zealand	1921-1928	ZK-
G-U	Union of South Africa	1927-1928	ZS-
H-M	Hungary	19xx-1935	HA-.
HMAY	Mongolia	19xx-1998	MT- (or JU-?)
H-S	Siam	1919-1929	HS-.
J-	Japan	1929-1945	JA
JZ-	Dutch East Indies	1954-1963	PK-
K-	Kuwait	1967-1968	Interim - 9K
K-S	Finland	19xx-1931	OH-

Prefix	Country	Period	Current Prefix
KA-	Katanga	1961-1963	Unofficial - 9O
KW-	Cambodia	1954-1954	XU-
L-B	Czechoslovakia	1919-1929	OK-.
LG	Guatemala	1936-1948	TG
LI-	Liberia	1929-1952	EL-, now A8-
LR-	Lebanon	1944-1954	OD-
LY-	Lithuania	1929-1939	Merged into Soviet Union CCCP-
M-	Spain	1929-1933	EC-
MC-	Monaco	1949-1959	3A-
MT-	Mongolia	1948-1998	JU
N-	Norway	1919-1931	LN-.
O-B	Belgium,	1919-1929	OO-.
OA-	Peru	1929-1938	OB-
OO-C	Belgian Congo	1929-1960	9O-
OK-	Czechoslovakia	1929-1993	OK- (Czech Rep) OM- (Slovakia)
P-B	Brazil	1927-1932	PP-
P-P	Poland	1919-1929	SP-
PI-	Philippines	1945-1973	RP-
R-	Argentina (three digits)	1928-1937	LV-
R-	Argentina (four letters)	1927-1931	
R-	Panama (two digits)	1929-1943	RX-
RR	Russia	1922-1929	CCCP-
RV-	Persia (Iran)	1929-1944	EP-
RX-	Panama	1943-1952	HP-
RY-	Lithuania	1929-1939	Merged into Soviet Union CCCP-
S-A	Sweden	1929-1929	SE-.
SA-	Saudi Arabia	1946 1952	HZ-
SL-	Saarland	1953-1957	D-
SL-	Slovenia	1991-1991	Unofficial, to S5-.
SN-	Sudan	1929-1955	ST-
SR-	Syria	1946-1951	YK-
T-D	Denmark	1919-1929	OY-.
TJ-	Transjordan	1946-1954	JY-
TS-	Saar Territory	1930-1931	Unofficial, to EZ-
T9-	Bosnia Herzegovina	1992-2009	E7-
UL-	Luxembourg	1929-1935	LX-
UN-	Yugoslavia	1928-1933	YU-
VO-	Newfoundland	1934-1949	Merged into Canada CF-
VP-A	Gold Coast	1929-1957	9G- (Ghana)
VP-B	Bahamas	1929-1973	C6-
VP-C	Ceylon	1929-1948	CY-
VP-G	British Guiana	1929-1967	8R-
VP-H	British Honduras (Belize)	1947-1983	V3-
VP-J	Jamaica	1930-1962	6Y-(Jamaica) & VQ-T (Turks & Caicos Islands)
VP-K	Kenya	1929-1963	5Y-
VP-LAA to –LIZ Leeward Is (Antigua)		1929-1981	V2-
VP-LKA to –LLZ Leeward Is (St. Kitts, Nevis)		1929-1983	V4-
VP-LLA to –LLZ Leeward Is (Anguila)		1929-1997	VP-A
VP-LMA to –LMZ Leeward Is (Dominica)		1929-1978	J7-
	(Montserrat)	1929-1997	VP-M
VP-LVA to –LZZ Leeward Is (BVI)		1929-1997	VP-L
VP-M	Malta	1929-1968	9H-
VP-N	Nyasaland	1929-1953	VP-Y
VP-P	Western Pacific Islands	1929- 1978	H4- (Solomon Islands) &
		1929-1981	T3- (Kiribati)
VP-VP-R	Northern Rhodesia	1929-1953	VP-Y (Central African Federation)
VP-S	Somaliland	1929-1960	6OS-
VP-T	Trinidad and Tobago	1931-1965	9Y-
VP-U	Uganda	1929-1962	5X-
VP-V	St. Vincent & Grenadines	1959-1979	J8-
VP-W	Wei-Hai-Wei (Shantung, China)	1929-1930	XT-
VP-W, VP-Y	(Southern) Rhodesia	1965-1980	Z- (Zimbabwe)
VP-X	The Gambia	1929-1945	C5-.
VP-Y	Central African Federation	1953-1965	became VP-W (Rhodesia), 7Q- (Malawi) & 9J- (Zambia)

Prefix	Country	Period	Current Prefix
VP-Z	Zanzibar	1929-1963	5H- (Tanzania)
VQ-B	Barbados	1952-1968	8P-
VQ-C	Cyprus	1952-1960	5B-
VQ-F	Fiji, Tonga and Friendly Isles	1929-1971	DQ- (Fiji), A3- (Tonga)
VQ-G	Grenada	1962-1974	J3-
VQ-L	St. Lucia	1965-1981	J6-
VQ-M	Mauritius	1929-1968	3B-
VQ-P	Palestine	1930-1948	either TJ-/JY- (Transjordan) or 4X- (Israel)
VQ-S	Seychelles	1929-1977	S7-
VQ-ZAA to -ZDZ	Basutoland	1929-1967	7P- (Lesotho)
VQ-ZEA to -ZHZ	Bechuanaland	1929-1968	A2- (Botswana)
VQ-ZIA to -ZLZ	Swaziland	1929-1975	3D-
VR-A	Aden	1939-1969	4W (Yemen)
VR-B	Bermuda	1931-1997	VP-B
VR-C	Cayman Islands	1968-1997	VP-C
VR-G	Gibraltar	1929-1997	VP-G
VR-H	Hong Kong	1929-1997	B-H
VR-J	Johore	1929-1957	9M-
VR-L	Sierra Leone	1929-1961	9L-
VR-N	British Cameroons	1929-1960	either TJ- or 5N
VR-O	Sabah (North Borneo)	1929-1963	9M-
VR-R	Malaya	1929-1959	9M-
VR-S	Singapore	1929-1963	9M- , then 9V- 1965
VR-T	Tanganyika	1930-1963	5H- (Tanzania)
VR-U	Brunei	1929-1984	V8-
VR-W	Sarawak	1929-1963	9M-
X-	Mexico	1929-1934	XA-, XB- & XC-.
X-S	Yugoslavia	1927-1928	UN-.
XH-	Honduras	1929-1960	HR-
XT	China	1929-1949	B-
XV-	South Vietnam	1959-1975	VN-
XW-	Laos	1959-1975	RDPL-
YE-	Yemen	1955-1969	4W-
YL-	Latvia	1929-1939	Merged into Soviet Union CCCP-
YN-	Nicaragua	1929-1936	AN-
4W-	Yemen	1969-1990	Merged into 7O-
6OS	Somalia	1960-1969	6O-
9O-	Zaïre	1960-1966	9Q-

PART 2 – MILITARY SERIALS DECODE

In certain circumstances the Civil Aviation Authority may permit the operation of aircraft without the need to carry regulation size national registration letters. These conditions are referred to as "exemptions". The CAA issues to operators Exemption Certificates which are usually valid for two years. The basic requirements are that the owner undertakes to notify the CAA of the markings carried and may not fly overseas, without specific permission of the overseas country. In the case of aircraft wearing military marks the authority of the relevant department at the Ministry of Defence is required for UK markings whilst an equivalent establishment must sanction any overseas markings to be carried.

Below are current details of aircraft which are known to be wearing military and, in a very few cases, other markings. The information is compiled from members' observations and includes any BAPC and "B" Conditions identities known to be located in the UK and Ireland. Full details of BAPC markings are carried in SECTION 3 and c/ns for the others can be found in their respective Sections. We should point out that some of the serials used are spurious. The Glider de-code is at SECTION 6, Part 2 (iii)

Serial	Code	Regn	Type		Serial	Code	Regn	Type
					F-943		G-BIHF	Royal Aircraft Factory SE.5a replica (RFC)
					F943		G-BKDT	Royal Aircraft Factory SE.5a replica (RFC)
UNITED KINGDOM (RAF unless otherwise shown)					F5447	N	G-BKER	Royal Aircraft Factory SE.5a replica (RFC)
01		G-BPVE	Bleriot Type XI 1909 replica		F5459	Y	G-INNY	Royal Aircraft Factory SE.5a replica (RFC)
4		BAPC.11	English Electric Wren composite		F5459	Y	BAPC.142	Royal Aircraft Factory SE.5a replica (RFC)
12A		BAPC.2	Bristol Boxkite reconstruction		F5475	A	BAPC.250	Royal Aircraft Factory SE.5a replica (RFC)
14		BAPC.6	Roe Triplane Type I		F8010	Z	G-BDWJ	Royal Aircraft Factory SE.5a replica (RFC)
168		G-BFDE	Sopwith Tabloid Scout replica (RNAS)					
304		BAPC.62	Cody Type V Biplane (RFC)		F8614		G-AWAU	Vickers FB.27A Vimy replica
687		BAPC.181	Royal Aircraft Factory BE.2b replica (RFC)		H1968		BAPC.42	Avro 504K replica
1881		BAPC.122	Avro 504 fsm		H3426		BAPC.68	Hawker Hurricane replica
2345		G-ATVP	Vickers FB.5 Gunbus replica (RFC)		H5199		G-ADEV	Avro 504K (Royal Air Force)
2882		BAPC.234	Vickers FB.5 Gunbus replica (RFC)		J7326		G-EBQP	de Havilland DH.53 Humming Bird (Intended marks)
3066		G-AETA	Caudron G.III (RNAS)		J9941		G-ABMR	Hawker Hart II
5964		BAPC.112	AirCo DH.2 fsm (RFC)		K-123		G-EACN	BAT FK.23 Bantam
5964		G-BFVH	AirCo DH.2 (RFC)		K1786		G-AFTA	Hawker Tomtit (Royal Air Force)
6232		BAPC.41	Royal Aircraft Factory BE.2c replica (RFC)		K1930		G-BKBB	Hawker Fury II replica
9917		G-EBKY	Sopwith Pup (RFC)		K20546		G-AYJY	Hawker (Isaacs) Fury II
A485		BAPC.176	Royal Aircraft Factory SE.5a replica (RFC)		K2048		G-BZNW	Hawker (Isaacs) Fury II
A1742		BAPC.38	Bristol Scout D fsm (RFC)		K2050		G-ASCM	Hawker (Isaacs) Fury II
A7317		BAPC.179	Sopwith Pup fsm (RFC)		K2059		G-PFAR	Hawker (Isaacs) Fury II
A8226		G-BIDW	Sopwith "1½" Strutter replica (RFC)		K2075		G-BEER	Hawker (Isaacs) Fury II
B-415		BAPC.163	AFEE 10/42 Rotachute Rotabuggy reconstruction		K2227		G-ABBB	Bristol Bulldog IIA
					K-2567		G-MOTH	de Havilland DH.82A Tiger Moth
B595	W	G-BUOD	SE.5A replica (RFC)		K2572		G-AOZH	de Havilland DH.82A Tiger Moth
B1807	A7	G-EAVX	Sopwith Pup (RFC) – intended marks		K-2585		G-ANKT	de Havilland DH.82A Tiger Moth
B2458	R	G-BPOB	Sopwith F1 Camel replica (RFC)		K2587		G-BJAP	de Havilland DH.82A Tiger Moth
B4863		BAPC.113	Royal Aircraft Factory SE.5a fsm		K3241		G-AHSA	Avro Tutor
B5577	W	BAPC.59	Sopwith Camel fsm (RFC)		K3661	562	G-BURZ	Hawker Nimrod I
B6401		G-AWYY	Sopwith F1 Camel replica (RFC)		K3731		G-RODI	Hawker (Isaacs) Fury
B7270		G-BFCZ	Sopwith F1 Camel replica (RFC)		K4232		SE-AZB	Cierva C.30A
C1904	Z	G-PFAP	Royal Aircraft Factory SE.5a (Currie Wot) (RFC)		K4235		G-AHMJ	Cierva C.30A
C3009	B	G-BFWD	Royal Aircraft Factory SE.5a (Currie Wot) (RFC)		K-4259	71	G-ANMO	de Havilland DH.82A Tiger Moth
					K5054		G-BRDV	Supermarine Spitfire Prototype replica
C3011	S	G-SWOT	Royal Aircraft Factory SE.5a (Currie Wot) (RFC)		K5054		BAPC.190	Supermarine Spitfire Prototype fsm
C4451		BAPC.210	Avro 504J (RFC)		K5054		BAPC.214	Supermarine Spitfire Prototype fsm
C4912		BAPC.135	Bristol 20 M.1C Monoplane fsm		K5414	XV	G-AENP	Hawker Afghan Hind
C4918		G-BWJM	Bristol 20 M.1C Monoplane replica		K5673		BAPC.249	Hawker Fury I fsm
C4988		G-BPLT	Bristol 20 M.1C Monoplane replica		K5673		G-BZAS	Hawker (Isaacs) Fury I
C4994		G-BLWM	Bristol 20 M.1C Monoplane replica		K7271		BAPC.148	Hawker Fury II fsm
C5430	V	G-CCXG	Royal Aircraft Factory SE.5a replica (RFC)		K7271		G-CCKV	Hawker (Isaacs) Fury II
C6468	A	G-CEKL	Royal Aircraft Factory SE.5a replica (RFC))		K7985		G-AMRK	Gloster Gladiator I
					K8203		G-BTVE	Hawker Demon I
C9533	M	G-BUWE	Royal Aircraft Factory SE.5a replica (RFC)		K8303	D	G-BWWN	Hawker (Isaacs) Fury
D276	A	BAPC.208	Royal Aircraft Factory SE.5a replica (RFC)		K9926	JH-C	BAPC.217	Supermarine Spitfire fsm
					L1070	XT-A	BAPC.227	Supermarine Spitfire fsm
D7889		G-AANM	Bristol F.2b Fighter		L1679	JX-G	BAPC.241	Hawker Hurricane 1 fsm
D8096	D	G-AEPH	Bristol F.2b Fighter (Royal Air Force)		L1710	AL-D	BAPC.219	Hawker Hurricane fsm
E449		G-EBJE	Avro 504K		L2301		G-AIZG	Supermarine Walrus 1 (Royal Navy)
E2466		BAPC.165	Bristol F.2b Fighter		L6906		G-AKKY	Miles Magister
E2939		G-ATXL	Avro 504K replica		L7005	PS-B	BAPC.281	Boulton Paul Defiant fsm
E3747		G-BYKV	Avro 504K replica		L8353		G-AMMC	Miles M.14A Hawk Trainer 3
E8894		G-CDLI	Airco DH.9		N248		BAPC.164	Wight Quadraplane Type 1 fsm
F-141	G	G-SEVA	Royal Aircraft Factory SE.5a replica (RFC)		N500		G-BWRA	Sopwith Triplane replica
					N1854		G-AIBE	Fairey Fulmar 2 (Royal Navy)
F235	B	G-BMDB	Royal Aircraft Factory SE.5a replica (RFC)		N2532	GZ-H	BAPC.272	Hawker Hurricane fsm
					N3194	GR-Z	BAPC.220	Supermarine Spitfire fsm
F904		G-EBIA	Royal Aircraft Factory SE.5a replica (RFC)		N3289	DW-K	BAPC.65	Supermarine Spitfire fsm
					N3313	KL-B	BAPC.69	Supermarine Spitfire fsm
F938		G-EBIC	Royal Aircraft Factory SE.5a replica (RFC)		N3317	AI-A	BAPC.268	Supermarine Spitfire fsm
					N3788		G-AKPF	Miles M.14A Hawk Trainer
					N4877	MK-V	G-AMDA	Avro 652A Anson 1

Serial	Code	Registration	Type
N5182		G-APUP	Sopwith Pup replica (RNAS)
N5195		G-ABOX	Sopwith Pup (RNAS)
N5199		G-BZND	Sopwith Pup replica
N5492	B	BAPC.111	Sopwith Triplane fsm (RNAS)
N5903		G-GLAD	Gloster Gladiator II
N6290		G-BOCK	Sopwith Triplane replica (RNAS)
N6452		G-BIAU	Sopwith Pup replica (RNAS)
N-6466		G-ANKZ	de Havilland DH.82A Tiger Moth
N-6473		G-AOBO	de Havilland DH.82A Tiger Moth
N6720	VX	G-BYTN	de Havilland DH.82A Tiger Moth
N-6797		G-ANEH	de Havilland DH.82A Tiger Moth
N6847		G-APAL	de Havilland DH.82A Tiger Moth
N6965	FL-J	G-AJTW	de Havilland DH.82A Tiger Moth
N-9192	RCO-N	G-DHZF	de Havilland DH.82A Tiger Moth
N9389		G-ANJA	de Havilland DH.82A Tiger Moth
P641		BAPC.123	Vickers FB.5 Gunbus fsm
P2790		G-ORGI	Hawker Hurricane IIB
P2793	SD-M	BAPC.236	Hawker Hurricane fsm
P2902	DX-X	G-ROBT	Hawker Hurricane I
P2921	GZ-L	BAPC.273	Hawker Hurricane fsm
P2954	WX-E	BAPC.267	Hawker Hurricane fsm
P2970	US-X	BAPC.291	Hawker Hurricane fsm
P3059	SD-N	BAPC.64	Hawker Hurricane fsm
P3208	SD-T	BAPC.63	Hawker Hurricane fsm
P3679	GZ-K	BAPC.278	Hawker Hurricane fsm
P3873	YO-H	BAPC.265	Hawker Hurricane fsm
P6382	C	G-AJRS	Miles Magister
P6775	YT-J	BAPC.299	Vickers-Supermarine Spitfire fsm
P7350	XT-D	G-AWIJ	Vickers-Supermarine Spitfire F.IIA
P8140	ZP-K	BAPC.71	Vickers-Supermarine Spitfire fsm
P8448	UM-D	BAPC.225	Vickers-Supermarine Spitfire replica
R1914		G-AHUJ	Miles Magister
R3821	UX-N	G-BPIV	Bristol Blenheim IV
R4118	UP-W	G-HUPW	Hawker Hurricane I
R-5136		G-APAP	de Havilland DH.82A Tiger Moth
R5172	FIJE	G-AOIS	de Havilland DH.82A Tiger Moth
R6690	PR-A	BAPC.254	Vickers-Supermarine Spitfire 1 fsm
S1287	5	G-BEYB	Fairey Flycatcher replica (FAA)
S1595		BAPC.156	Supermarine S.6B fsm
S1579	571	G-BBVO	Hawker Nimrod (Isaacs Fury) (Royal Navy)
S1581	573	G-BWWK	Hawker Nimrod 1 (FAA)
T5672		G-ALRI	de Havilland DH.82A Tiger Moth
T-585		G-ANKK	de Havilland DH.82A Tiger Moth
T-587	RUC-W	G-AXBW	de Havilland DH.82A Tiger Moth
T6313		G-AHVU	de Havilland DH.82A Tiger Moth
T-6953		G-ANNI	de Havilland DH.82A Tiger Moth
T-7230		G-AFVE	de Havilland DH.82A Tiger Moth
T7245		G-ANEJ	de Havilland DH.82A Tiger Moth
T7281		G-ARTL	de Havilland DH.82A Tiger Moth
T7328		G-APPN	de Havilland DH.82A Tiger Moth
T7793		G-ANKV	de Havilland DH.82A Tiger Moth
T-7842		G-AMTF	de Havilland DH.82A Tiger Moth
T9707		G-AKKR	Miles M.14A Hawk Trainer
T9738		G-AKAT	Miles M.14A Hawk Trainer
T7909		G-ANON	de Havilland DH.82A Tiger Moth
T-7997		G-AHUF	de Havilland DH.82A Tiger Moth
V3388		G-AHTW	Airspeed Oxford 1V
V6799	SD-X	BAPC.72	Hawker Hurricane fsm
V7467	LE-D	BAPC.223	Hawker Hurricane fsm {1}
V7467	LE-D	BAPC.288	Hawker Hurricane fsm {2}
V9367	MA-B	G-AZWT	Westland Lysander IIIA
V9673	MA-J	G-LIZY	Westland Lysander III
W2068	68	VH-ASM	Avro 652A Anson I
W2718	AA5Y	G-RNLI	Vickers-Supermarine Walrus (Royal Navy)
W5856	A2A	G-BMGC	Fairey Swordfish II
W9385	YG-L	G-ADND	de Havilland DH.87B Hornet Moth
X4683	EB-N	G-CDPM	Jurca MJ.100 Spitfire (80% scale replica Spitfire)
Z2033	N/275	G-ASTL	Fairey Firefly TT.1
Z5140	HA-C	G-HURI	Hawker Hurricane IIB
Z5252	GO-B	G-BWHA	Hawker Hurricane IIB
Z7015	7-L	G-BKTH	Hawker Sea Hurricane IB (Royal Navy)
Z7197		G-AKZN	Percival Proctor III
AB196		G-CCGH	Super Marine Spitfire Mk.26
AB550	GE-P	BAPC.230	Vickers-Supermarine Spitfire fsm
AB910	IR-G	G-AISU	Vickers-Supermarine Spitfire LF.Vb
AP507	KX-P	G-ACWP	Cierva C.30A
AR213	JZ-E	G-AIST	Vickers-Supermarine Spitfire IA
AR501	NN-A	G-AWII	Vickers-Supermarine Spitfire Vc
AR614	DU-Z	G-BUWA	Vickers-Supermarine Spitfire Vc
BB807		G-ADWO	de Havilland DH.82A Tiger Moth
BE421	XP-G	BAPC.205	Hawker Hurricane IIc fsm
BL924	AZ-G	BAPC.242	Vickers-Supermarine Spitfire Vb fsm
BM597	U-2	G-MKVB	Vickers-Supermarine Spitfire Vb
BM631	XR-C	BAPC.269	Vickers-Supermarine Spitfire V fsm
BN230	FT-A	BAPC.218	Hawker Hurricane fsm
BR600	SH-V	BAPC.222	Vickers-Supermarine Spitfire fsm
BR600		BAPC.224	Vickers-Supermarine Spitfire fsm
DE-208		G-AGYU	de Havilland DH.82A Tiger Moth
DE470	16	G-ANMY	de Havilland DH.82A Tiger Moth
DE623		G-ANFI	de Havilland DH.82A Tiger Moth
DE673		G-ADNZ	de Havilland DH.82A Tiger Moth
DE730		G-ANFW	de Havilland DH.82A Tiger Moth
DE992		G-AXXV	de Havilland DH.82A Tiger Moth
DF112		G-ANRM	de Havilland DH.82A Tiger Moth
DF128	RCO-U	G-AOJJ	de Havilland DH.82A Tiger Moth
DF155		G-ANFV	de Havilland DH.82A Tiger Moth
DR828	PB-1	N18V	Beech Traveler
EM720		G-AXAN	de Havilland DH.82A Tiger Moth
EM840		G-ANBY	de Havilland DH.82A Tiger Moth
EN343		BAPC.226	Vickers-Supermarine Spitfire fsm
EN398		BAPC.184	Vickers-Supermarine Spitfire IX fsm
EN526	SZ-G	BAPC.221	Vickers-Supermarine Spitfire replica
EP120	AE-A	G-LFVB	Supermarine Spitfire Vb
FB226	MT-A	G-BDWM	North American Mustang (Bonsall Mustang)
FE695	94	G-BTXI	North American Harvard IIB
FE788		G-CTKL	Noorduyn AT-16 Harvard IIB
FE905		LN-BNM	North American Harvard IIB
FH153	58	G-BBHK	Noorduyn AT-16-ND Harvard IIB (RCAF c/s)
FR886		G-BDMS	Piper Cub
FS628		G-AIZE	Fairchild Argus
FT375		G-BWUL	North American Harvard IIB
FT391		G-AZBN	North American Harvard IIB
FX301	FD-NQ	G-JUDI	North American Harvard III
FZ625		G-AMPO	Douglas Dakota 3
HB275		G-BKGM	Beech Expeditor
HG691		G-AIYR	de Havilland DH.89A Dragon Rapide
HH268		BAPC.261	General Aircraft Hotspur replica
HM580	KX-K	G-ACUU	Cierva C.30A
HS503		BAPC.108	Fairey Swordfish IV
JF343*	JW-P	G-CCZP	Super Marine Spitfire Mk.26
JG891	T-B	G-LFVC	Vickers Supermarine 349 Spitfire L.Vc
JV828		N423RS	Consolidated-Vultee PBY-5A Catalina
KB889	NA-I	G-LANC	Avro Lancaster X
KD345	130	G-FGID	Vought FG-1D Corsair (Royal Navy)
KF584	RAI-X	G-RAIX	North American Harvard IV
KF729		G-BJST	CCF Harvard 4
KJ351		BAPC.80	Airspeed AS.58 Horsa II
KK116		G-AMPY	Douglas C-47B-15-DK Dakota 3
KZ321	JV-N	G-HURY	Hawker Hurricane IV
LB264		G-AIXA	Taylorcraft Plus D (Auster I)
LB312		G-AHXE	Taylorcraft Plus D (Auster I)
LB367		G-AHGZ	Taylorcraft Plus D (Auster I)
LB375		G-AHGW	Taylorcraft Plus D (Auster I)
LB381		G-AHKO	Taylorcraft Plus D (Auster I)
LF789	R2-K	BAPC.186	de Havilland DH.82B Queen Bee composite
LF858		G-BLUZ	de Havilland DH.82B Queen Bee
LH291		BAPC 279	Airspeed AS51 Horsa I
LS326	L 2	G-AJVH	Fairey Swordfish II
LZ766		G-ALCK	Percival Proctor III
MAV467	R-O	BAPC.202	Vickers-Supermarine Spitfire V fsm
MH415	FU-N	BAPC.209	Vickers-SupermarineSpitfire LF.IXC fsm
MH434	ZD-B	G-ASJV	Vickers-Supermarine Spitfire IXB
MH486	FF-A	BAPC.206	Vickers-Supermarine Spitfire IX fsm
MJ627	9G-P	G-BMSB	Vickers-Supermarine Spitfire IX
MJ832	DN-Y	BAPC.229	Vickers-Supermarine Spitfire fsm
MK732	3W-17	G-HVDM	Vickers-Supermarine Spitfire IXc
MK805	SH-B	----------	Vickers-Supermarine Spitfire IX replica
ML407	OU-V	G-LFIX	Vickers-Supermarine Spitfire IX
MP425		G-AITB	Airspeed Oxford I
MT197		G-ANHS	Auster 4
MT438		G-AREI	Auster III
MT928	ZX-M	G-BKMI	Vickers-Supermarine Spitfire VIIIc
MV268	JE-J	G-SPIT	Vickers-Supermarine Spitfire XIVe
MV370		G-FXIV	Vickers-Supermarine Spitfire XIVc
MW763	HF-A	G-TEMT	Hawker Tempest II
NJ203		G-AKNP	Short S.45 Solent 3
NJ633		G-AKXP	Auster 5

Serial	Code	Reg	Type
NJ673		G-AOCR	Auster 5
NJ695		G-AJXV	Auster 4
NJ719		G-ANFU	Auster 5 - intended marks
NL750		G-AOBH	de Havilland DH.82A Tiger Moth
NL913		G-AOFR	de Havilland DH.82A Tiger Moth
NL985		G-BWIK	de Havilland DH.82A Tiger Moth
NM181		G-AZGZ	de Havilland DH.82A Tiger Moth
NP336		G-AGTB	Percival Proctor V
NS519		G-MOSI	de Havilland DH.98 Mosquito TT.35
NX534		G-BUDL	Taylorcraft E Auster III
NX611	LE-C:DX-C	G-ASXX	Avro Lancaster B.VII
PL344	TL-B	G-IXCC	Vickers-Supermarine Spitfire IX
PL965	R	G-MKXI	Vickers-Supermarine Spitfire PR.XI
PL983	JV-F	G-PRXI	Vickers-Supermarine Spitfire XI
PS853	C	G-RRGN	Vickers-Supermarine Spitfire PR.XIX
PT462	SW-A	G-CTIX	Vickers-Supermarine Spitfire IX
PV303	ON-B	G-CCJL	Super Marine Spitfire Mk.26
PZ865	JX-E	G-AMAU	Hawker Hurricane IIc
RB412	DW-B	G-CEFC	Super Marine Spitfire Mk.26
RG333		G-AIEK	Miles Messenger
RM221		G-ANXR	Percival Proctor IV
RR232		G-BRSF	Vickers-Supermarine Spitfire IXc
RT486	PF-A	G-AJGJ	Auster 5
RT610		G-AKWS	Auster 5A
SM845	GZ-J	G-BUOS	Vickers-Supermarine Spitfire XVIIIe
SX336	VL-105	G-KASX	Vickers Supermarine Seafire F.XVII (Royal Navy)
TA634	8K-K	G-AWJV	de Havilland DH.98 Mosquito TT.35
TA719	6 T	G-ASKC	de Havilland DH.98 Mosquito TT.35
TA805	FX-M	G-PMNF	Vickers-Supermarine Spitfire IX
TB252	GW-H	G-XVIE	Vickers-Supermarine Spitfire XVIe
TD248	CR-S	G-OXVI	Vickers-Supermarine Spitfire XVIe
TJ398		BAPC.70	Auster AOP.5
TJ534		G-AKSY	Auster 5
TJ565		G-AMVD	Auster 5
TJ569		G-AKOW	Auster 5
TJ672	DT-S	G-ANIJ	Auster 5
TJ704	JA	G-ASCD	Beagle A.61 Terrier 2 (Auster AOP.6)
TS423		N147DC	Douglas C-47A-75-DL Dakota (Army Air Force)
TS798		G-AGNV	Avro 685 York C.1
TW439		G-ANRP	Auster 5
TW467		G-ANIE	Auster 5
TW511		G-APAF	Auster 5 (Army Air Corps)
TW536	T-SV	G-BNGE	Auster AOP.6
TW591		G-ARIH	Auster AOP.6 (Army Air Corps)
TW641		G-ATDN	Auster AOP.6 (Army Air Corps)
TX310		G-AIDL	de Havilland DH.89A Dragon Rapide 6
VF512	PF-M	G-ARRX	Auster AOP.6
VF516		G-ASMZ	Auster AOP.6
VF526	T	G-ARXU	Auster AOP.6 (Army Air Corps)
VF581	G	G-ARSL	Auster AOP.6 (Army Air Corps)
VL348		G-AVVO	Avro Anson C.19 Series 2
VL349	V7-Q	G-AWSA	Avro Anson C.19 Series 2
VM286		G-BPUR	Piper J-3L-65 Cub
VM360		G-APHV	Avro Anson C.19 Series 2
VN799		G-CDSX	English Electric Canberra T.Mk.4 (Prototype)
VP519		G-AVVR	Avro 652A Anson 19 Series.2 (Cockpit only)
VP955		G-DVON	de Havilland DH.104 Devon C.2/2
VP981		G-DHDV	de Havilland DH.104 Devon C.2/2
VR192		G-APIT	Percival Prentice T.1
VR249	FA-EL	G-APIY	Percival Prentice T.1
VR259	M	G-APJB	Percival Prentice T.1
VS623		G-AOKZ	Percival Prentice T.1
VT871		G-DHXX	de Havilland DH.100 Vampire FB.6
VV612		G-VENI	de Havilland DH.112 Venom FB.1
VX113	36	G-ARNO	Auster AOP.6 (Army Air Corps)
VX147		G-AVIL	Ercoupe 415
VX927		G-ASYG	Beagle A 61 Terrier 2 (Army Air Corps)
VZ345		D-CATA	Hawker Sea Fury T.20 (Royal Navy)
VZ638		G-JETM	Gloster Meteor T.7 (RN and FRU)
VZ728		G-AGOS	Reid and Sigrist Bobsleigh
WB188		G-HUNT	Hawker Hunter F.51
WB188		G-BZPB	Hawker Hunter GA.Mk.11
WB188		G-BZPC	Hawker Hunter GA.Mk.11
WB533		G-DEVN	de Havilland DH.104 Devon C.2/2
WB565	X	G-PVET	de Havilland DHC-1 Chipmunk T.10 (Army Air Corps)
WB569	R	G-BYSJ	de Havilland DHC-1 Chipmunk T.10
WB571	34	G-AOSF	de Havilland DHC-1 Chipmunk T.10
WB585	M	G-AOSY	de Havilland DHC-1 Chipmunk T.10
WB588	D	G-AOTD	de Havilland DHC-1 Chipmunk T.10
WB615	E	G-BXIA	de Havilland DHC-1 Chipmunk T.10 (Army Air Corps)
WB654	U	G-BXGO	de Havilland DHC-1 Chipmunk T.10 (Army Air Corps)
WB671	910	G-BWTG	de Havilland DHC-1 Chipmunk T.10 (Royal Navy)
WB697	95	G-BXCT	de Havilland DHC-1 Chipmunk T.10
WB702		G-AOFE	de Havilland DHC-1 Chipmunk T.10
WB703		G-ARMC	de Havilland DHC-1 Chipmunk T.10
WB711		G-APPM	de Havilland DHC-1 Chipmunk T.10
WB726	E	G-AOSK	de Havilland DHC-1 Chipmunk T.10
WD286		G-BBND	de Havilland DHC-1 Chipmunk T.10
WD292		G-BCRX	de Havilland DHC-1 Chipmunk T.10
WD310	B	G-BWUN	de Havilland DHC-1 Chipmunk T.10
WD331		G-BXDH	de Havilland DHC-1 Chipmunk T.10
WD347		G-BBRV	de Havilland DHC-1 Chipmunk T.10
WD363		G-BCIH	de Havilland DHC-1 Chipmunk T.10
WD373	12	G-BXDI	de Havilland DHC-1 Chipmunk T.10
WD379	K	G-APLO	de Havilland DHC-1 Chipmunk T.10
WD390	68	G-BWNK	de Havilland DHC-1 Chipmunk T.10
WD413		G-VROE	Avro 652A Anson T.21
WE569		G-ASAJ	Beagle Terrier (Auster T.7) (Army Air Corps)
WF118		G-DACA	Percival P.57 Sea Prince T.1
WG288	153:P	G-SALY	Hawker Sea Fury FB.XI (Royal Navy)
WG308	8	G-BYHL	de Havilland DHC-1 Chipmunk T.10
WG316		G-BCAH	de Havilland DHC-1 Chipmunk T.10
WG321	G	G-DHCC	de Havilland DHC-1 Chipmunk T.10 (Army Air Corps)
WG348		G-BBMV	de Havilland DHC-1 Chipmunk T.10
WG350		G-BPAL	de Havilland DHC-1 Chipmunk T.10
WG407	67	G-BWMX	de Havilland DHC-1 Chipmunk T.10
WG422	16	G-BFAX	de Havilland DHC-1 Chipmunk T.10
WG458	G	N458BG	de Havilland DHC.1 Chipmunk T.10
WG465		G-BCEY	de Havilland DHC-1 Chipmunk T.10
WG469	72	G-BWJY	de Havilland DHC-1 Chipmunk T.10
WG472		G-AOTY	de Havilland DHC-1 Chipmunk T.10
WG719		G-BRMA	Westland Dragonfly HR.5
WJ358		G-ARYD	Auster AOP.6 (Army Air Corps)
WJ945	21	G-BEDV	Vickers Varsity T.1
WK126	843	N2138J	English Electric Canberra TT.18
WK163		G-BVWC	English Electric Canberra B.2
WK436		G-VENM	de Havilland DH.112 Venom FB.50 (FB.1)
WK512	A	G-BXIM	de Havilland DHC-1 Chipmunk T.10 (Army Air Corps)
WK514		G-BBMO	de Havilland DHC-1 Chipmunk T.10
WK517		G-ULAS	de Havilland DHC-1 Chipmunk T.10
WK522		G-BCOU	de Havilland DHC-1 Chipmunk T.10
WK549		G-BTWF	de Havilland DHC-1 Chipmunk T.10
WK577		G-BCYM	de Havilland DHC-1 Chipmunk T.10
WK585		G-BZGA	de Havilland DHC-1 Chipmunk T.10
WK586	V	G-BXGX	de Havilland DHC-1 Chipmunk T.10 (Army Air Corps)
WK590	69	G-BWVZ	de Havilland DHC-1 Chipmunk T.10
WK609	93	G-BXDN	de Havilland DHC-1 Chipmunk T.10
WK611		G-ARWB	de Havilland DHC-1 Chipmunk T.10
WK622		G-BCZH	de Havilland DHC-1 Chipmunk T.10
WK624	M	G-BWHI	de Havilland DHC-1 Chipmunk T.10
WK628		G-BBMW	de Havilland DHC-1 Chipmunk T.10
WK630		G-BXDG	de Havilland DHC-1 Chipmunk T.10
WK633	B	G-BXEC	de Havilland DHC-1 Chipmunk T.10
WK640	C	G-BWUV	de Havilland DHC-1 Chipmunk T.10
WK642		G-BXDP	de Havilland DHC-1 Chipmunk T.10
WL626	P	G-BHDD	Vickers Varsity T.1
WM167		G-LOSM	Armstrong-Whitworth Meteor NF.11
WP308	572	G-GACA	Hunting Percival P.57 Sea Prince T.1
WP788		G-BCHL	de Havilland DHC-1 Chipmunk T.10
WP790	T	G-BBNC	de Havilland DHC-1 Chipmunk T.10
WP795	901	G-BVZZ	de Havilland DHC-1 Chipmunk T.10 (Royal Navy)
WP800	2	G-BCXN	de Havilland DHC-1 Chipmunk T.10
WP803		G-HAPY	de Havilland DHC-1 Chipmunk T.10
WP805		G-MAJR	de Havilland DHC-1 Chipmunk T.10
WP808		G-BDEU	de Havilland DHC-1 Chipmunk T.10
WP809	78	G-BVTX	de Havilland DHC-1 Chipmunk T.10 (Royal Navy)
WP833		G-BZDU	de Havilland DHC-1 Chipmunk T.10
WP840	9	G-BXDM	de Havilland DHC-1 Chipmunk T.10
WP844		G-BWOX	de Havilland DHC-1 Chipmunk T.10
WP857	24	G-BDRJ	de Havilland DHC-1 Chipmunk T.10

WP859	E	G-BXCP	de Havilland DHC-1 Chipmunk T.10
WP860	6	G-BXDA	de Havilland DHC-1 Chipmunk T.10
WP870	12	G-BCOI	de Havilland DHC-1 Chipmunk T.10
WP896		G-BWVY	de Havilland DHC-1 Chipmunk T.10
WP901	B	G-BWNT	de Havilland DHC-1 Chipmunk T.10
WP903	B	G-BCGC	de Havilland DHC-1 Chipmunk T.10 (Queens Flight)
WP925	C	G-BXHA	de Havilland DHC-1 Chipmunk T.10 (Army Air Corps)
WP928	D	G-BXGM	de Havilland DHC-1 Chipmunk T.10 (Army Air Corps)
WP929		G-BXCV	de Havilland DHC-1 Chipmunk T.10
WP930	J	G-BXHF	de Havilland DHC-1 Chipmunk T.10 (Army Air Corps)
WP971		G-ATHD	de Havilland DHC-1 Chipmunk T.10
WP983	B	G-BXNN	de Havilland DHC-1 Chipmunk T.10 (Army Air Corps)
WP984	H	G-BWTO	de Havilland DHC-1 Chipmunk T.10
WR360	K	G-DHSS	de Havilland DH.112 Venom FB.1
WR410		G-DHUU	de Havilland DH.112 Venom FB.1
WR421		G-DHTT	de Havilland DH.112 Venom FB.1
WR470		G-DHVM	de Havilland DH.112 Venom FB.1
WS774	4	G-ANSO	Gloster Meteor T.7
WT333		G-BVXC	English Electric Canberra B(I).8
WT722	878:VL	G-BWGN	Hawker Hunter T.8C (Royal Navy)
WV198	K	G-BJWY	Sikorsky Whirlwind HAR.21
WV318	D	G-FFOX	Hawker Hunter T.7B
WV322	Y	G-BZSE	Hawker Hunter T.11
WV372	R	G-BXFI	Hawker Hunter T.7
WV499	G	G-BZRF	Hunting Percival P.56 Provost T.1
WV493	29:A-P	G-BDYG	Percival Provost T.1
WV740		G-BNPH	Hunting Percival Pembroke C.1
WV783		(G-ALSP)	Bristol 171 Sycamore 3
WW421	P	G-BZRE	Hunting Percival Provost T.1
WZ507	74	G-VTII	de Havilland DH.115 Vampire T.11
WZ584	K	G-BZRC	de Havilland DH.115 Vampire T.11
WZ662		G-BKVK	Auster AOP.9 (Army Air Corps)
WZ706		G-BURR	Auster AOP.9 (Army Air Corps)
WZ847	F	G-CPMK	de Havilland DHC-1 Chipmunk T.10
WZ868	H	G-ARMF	de Havilland DHC-1 Chipmunk T.10
WZ872	E	G-BZGB	de Havilland DHC-1 Chipmunk T.10
WZ879	X	G-BWUT	de Havilland DHC-1 Chipmunk T.10
WZ882	K	G-BXGP	de Havilland DHC-1 Chipmunk T.10 (Army Air Corps)
XA880		G-BVXR	de Havilland DH.104 Devon C.2 (RAE)
XB259		G-AOAI	Blackburn Beverley C.1
XD693	Z-Q	G-AOBU	Percival Jet Provost T.1
XE489		G-JETH	Armstrong-Whitworth Sea Hawk FGA.6
XE601		G-ETPS	Hawker Hunter FGA.Mk.9 (ETPS)
XE665	876:VL	G-BWGM	Hawker Hunter T.8C (Royal Navy)
XE685	871:VL	G-GAII	Hawker Hunter T.8C (Royal Navy)
XE689	864:VL	G-BWGK	Hawker Hunter GA.11 (Royal Navy)
XE897		G-DHVV	de Havilland DH.115 Vampire T.55
XE956		G-OBLN	de Havilland DH.115 Vampire T.11
XF597	AH	G-BKFW	Percival Provost T.1
XF603		G-KAPW	Percival Provost T.1
XF690		G-MOOS	Percival Provost T.1
XF785		G-ALBN	Bristol 173 Mk.1
XF836		G-AWRY	Percival Provost T.1
XF868		G-BGSB	Hunting-Percival P.56 Provost T.1
XF877	JX	G-AWVF	Percival Provost T.1
XG160	U	G-BWAF	Hawker Hunter F.6A
XG194	N	G-PRII	Hawker Hunter PR.11 (Royal Navy)
XG452		G-BRMB	Bristol Belvedere HC.1
XG547	T-S	G-HAPR	Bristol Sycamore HC.14
XG588		G-BAMH	Westland S-55 Whirlwind Series.3
XG775		G-DHWW	de Havilland DH.115 Vampire T.11 (Royal Navy)
XH313	E	G-BZRD	de Havilland DH.115 Vampire T.11
XH558		G-VLCN	Avro Vulcan B.2
XJ348		G-AMXX	de Havilland DH.104 Dove 2A
XJ389		G-AJJP	Fairey Jet Gyrodyne
XJ398		G-BDBZ	Westland WS-55 Whirlwind 2
XJ729		G-BVGE	Westland Whirlwind HAR.10
XJ771		G-HELV	de Havilland DH.115 Vampire T.55
XK895	CU-19	G-SDEV	de Havilland DH.104 Sea Devon C.20 (Royal Navy)
XK940		G-AYXT	Westland Whirlwind HAS.7
XL426		G-VJET	Avro Vulcan B.2
XL502		G-BMYP	Fairey Gannet AEW.3 (Royal Navy)
XL571	V	G-HNTR	Hawker Hunter T.7 (Blue Diamonds c/s)
XL573		G-BVGH	Hawker Hunter T.7
XL577	V	G-BXKF	Hawker Hunter T.7 (Blue Diamonds c/s)
XL587	Z	G-HPUX	Hawker Hunter T.7
XL602		G-BWFT	Hawker Hunter T.8M
XL621		G-BNCX	Hawker Hunter T.7
XL714		G-AOGR	de Havilland DH.82A Tiger Moth
XL-716		G-AOIL	de Havilland DH.82A Tiger Moth
XL809		G-BLIX	Saro Skeeter AOP.12 (Army Air Corps)
XL812		G-SARO	Saro Skeeter AOP.12
XL954		G-BXES	Percival Pembroke C.1
XM223		G-BWWC	de Havilland DH.104 Devon C.2
XM365		G-BXBH	Hunting Jet Provost T.3A
XM424		G-BWDS	Hunting Jet Provost T.3A
XM478		G-BXDL	Hunting Jet Provost T.3A
XM479	54	G-BVEZ	Hunting Jet Provost T.3A
XM496		G-BDUP	Bristol 175 Britannia Series 253
XM556		G-HELI	Saro Skeeter AOP.12
XM575		(G-BLMC)	Avro Vulcan B.2A
XM655		G-VULC	Avro Vulcan B.2A
XM685	PO:513	G-AYZJ	Westland Whirlwind HAS.7
XM819		G-APXW	Lancashire Aircraft EP.9 (Army Air Corps)
XN332	759	G-APNV	Saunders-Roe P.531-1
XN441		G-BGKT	Auster AOP.9 (Army Air Corps)
XN459		G-BWOT	Hunting Jet Provost T.3A
XN629	49	G-KNOT	Hunting Jet Provost T.3A
XP254		G-ASCC	Auster AOP.11 (Army Air Corps)
XP279		G-BWKK	Auster AOP.9 (Army Air Corps)
XP355	A	G-BEBC	Westland Whirlwind HAR.10
XP672	03	G-RAFI	Hunting Jet Provost T.4
XP693		G-FSIX	English Electric Lightning F.6
XP772		G-DHCZ	de Havilland DHC.2 Beaver AL.1 (Army Air Corps)
XP907		G-SROE	Westland Scout AH.1
XP924	134	G-CVIX	de Havilland DH.110 Sea Vixen D.3 (Royal Navy)
XR240		G-BDFH	Auster AOP.9 (Army Air Corps)
XR241		G-AXRR	Auster AOP.9 (Army Air Corps)
XR246		G-AZBU	Auster AOP.9 (RAE Radio Flight)
XR486		G-RWWW	Westland Whirlwind HCC.12 (Queens Flight)
XR537		G-NATY	Folland Gnat T.1
XR538	01	G-RORI	Folland Gnat T.1 (Training c/s)
XR592		G-AMWI	Bristol 171 Sycamore 4
XR595	M	G-BWHU	Westland Scout AH.1 (Army Air Corps)
XR673		G-BXLO	Hunting Jet Provost T.4
XR724		G-BTSY	English Electric Lightning F.6
XR773		G-OPIB	English Electric Lightning F.6
XR944		G-ATTB	Wallis WA.116
XR991		G-MOUR	Folland Gnat T.1 (Yellowjacks c/s)
XR993		G-BVPP	Folland Gnat T.1 (Red Arrows c/s)
XS111		G-TIMM	Folland Gnat T.1
XS165	37	G-ASAZ	Hiller UH-12E-4 (Royal Navy)
XS235		G-CPDA	de Havilland DH.106 Comet 4C
XS451		G-LTNG	English Electric Lightning T.5
XS587		G-VIXN	de Havilland DH.110 Sea Vixen FAW.2 (Royal Navy)
XS765		G-BSET	Beagle Basset CC.1
XS770		G-HRHI	Beagle Basset CC.1 (Queens Flight)
XT223		G-XTUN	Westland Sioux AH.1 (Army Air Corps)
XT420	606	G-CBUI	Westland Wasp HAS.1 (Royal Navy)
XT435	430	G-RIMM	Westland Wasp HAS.1 (Royal Navy)
XT634		G-BYRX	Westland Scout AH.1 (Army Air Corps)
XT787		G-KAXT	Westland Wasp HAS.1 (Royal Navy)
XT788	474	G-BMIR	Westland Wasp HAS.1 (Royal Navy)
XT793	456	G-BZPP	Westland Wasp HAS.1 (Royal Navy)
XV130	R	G-BWJW	Westland Scout AH.1 (Army Air Corps)
XV134	P	G-BWLX	Westland Scout AH.1 (Army Air Corps)
XV137		G-CRUM	Westland Scout AH.1 (Army Air Corps)
XV140	K	G-KAXL	Westland Scout AH.1 (Army Air Corps)
XV268		G-BVER	de Havilland DHC.2 Beaver (Army Air Corps)
XW289	73	G-JPVA	BAC Jet Provost T.5A

XW293	Z	G-BWCS	BAC Jet Provost T.5
XW324	K	G-BWSG	BAC Jet Provost T.5
XW325	E	G-BWGF	BAC Jet Provost T.5A
XW333		G-BVTC	BAC Jet Provost T.5A
XW354		G-JPTV	BAC Jet Provost T.5A
XW422		G-BWEB	BAC Jet Provost T.5A
XW423	14	G-BWUW	BAC Jet Provost T.5A
XW433		G-JPRO	BAC Jet Provost T.5A (CFS)
XW635		G-AWSW	Beagle Husky
XW784	VL	G-BBRN	Mitchell-Procter Kittiwake (Royal Navy)
XW799		G-BXSL	Westland Scout AH.Mk.1
XW854		G-CBSD	Westland Gazelle HT.2 (Royal Navy)
XW858	C	G-DMSS	Westland Gazelle HT.3
XW861	CU-52	G-BZFJ	Westland Gazelle HT.2 (Royal Navy)
XW898	G	G-CBXT	Westland Gazelle HT.3 (Royal Navy)
XX110		BAPC.169	Sepecat Jaguar GR.1 fsm
XX226	74	BAPC.152	BAe Hawk T.1A fsm
XX253		BAPC.171	BAe Hawk T.1 (Red Arrows c/s)
XX406	P	G-CBSH	Westland SA.341D Gazelle HT.3
XX436	CU-39	G-ZZLE	Westland SA.341C Gazelle HT.2 (Royal Navy)
XX467	86	G-TVII	Hawker Hunter T.7 (TWU)
XX513	10	G-CCMI	Scottish Aviation Bulldog
XX514		G-BWIB	Scottish Aviation Bulldog
XX515	4	G-CBBC	Scottish Aviation Bulldog
XX518	S	G-UDOG	Scottish Aviation Bulldog
XX521	H	G-CBEH	Scottish Aviation Bulldog
XX522	06	G-DAWG	Scottish Aviation Bulldog
XX524	04	G-DDOG	Scottish Aviation Bulldog
XX525	8	G-CBJJ	Scottish Aviation Bulldog
XX528	D	G-BZON	Scottish Aviation Bulldog
XX534	B	G-EDAV	Scottish Aviation Bulldog
XX537	C	G-CBCB	Scottish Aviation Bulldog
XX538	O	G-TDOG	Scottish Aviation Bulldog
XX543	F	G-CBAB	Scottish Aviation Bulldog
XX546	03	G-WINI	Scottish Aviation Bulldog
XX549	6	G-CBID	Scottish Aviation Bulldog
XX551	E	G-BZDP	Scottish Aviation Bulldog
XX554	09	G-BZMD	Scottish Aviation Bulldog
XX561	7	G-BZEP	Scottish Aviation Bulldog
XX611	7	G-CBDK	Scottish Aviation Bulldog
XX612	A03	G-BZXC	Scottish Aviation Bulldog
XX614	V	G-GGRR	Scottish Aviation Bulldog
XX619	T	G-CBBW	Scottish Aviation Bulldog
XX621	H	G-CBEF	Scottish Aviation Bulldog
XX622	B	G-CBGX	Scottish Aviation Bulldog
XX624	E	G-KDOG	Scottish Aviation Bulldog
XX625	01	G-CBBR	Scottish Aviation Bulldog
XX626	W:02	G-CDVV	Scottish Aviation Bulldog
XX628	9	G-CBFU	Scottish Aviation Bulldog
XX629	V	G-BZXZ	Scottish Aviation Bulldog
XX630	25	G-SIJW	Scottish Aviation Bulldog
XX631	W	G-BZXS	Scottish Aviation Bulldog
XX636	Y	G-CBFP	Scottish Aviation Bulldog
XX638		G-DOGG	Scottish Aviation Bulldog
XX658	03	G-BZPS	Scottish Aviation Bulldog
XX667	16	G-BZFN	Scottish Aviation Bulldog
XX668	I	G-CBAN	Scottish Aviation Bulldog
XX692	A	G-BZMH	Scottish Aviation Bulldog
XX693	07	G-BZML	Scottish Aviation Bulldog
XX694	E	G-CBBS	Scottish Aviation Bulldog
XX695	3	G-CBBT	Scottish Aviation Bulldog
XX698	9	G-BZME	Scottish Aviation Bulldog
XX699	F	G-CBCV	Scottish Aviation Bulldog
XX700	17	G-CBEK	Scottish Aviation Bulldog
XX702		G-CBCR	Scottish Aviation Bulldog
XX704		G-BCUV	Scottish Aviation Bulldog
XX707	4	G-CBDS	Scottish Aviation Bulldog
XX711	X	G-CBBU	Scottish Aviation Bulldog
XX713	2	G-CBJK	Scottish Aviation Bulldog
XX725	GU	BAPC.150	Sepecat Jaguar GR.1
XX885		G-HHAA	Hawker Siddeley Buccaneer S.2B
XZ329		G-BZYD	Westland Gazelle AH.1 (Army Air Corps)
XZ363	A	BAPC.151	Sepecat Jaguar GR.1A
XZ934	U	G-CBSI	Westland SA.341C Gazelle HT.2 (Royal Navy)
ZA556		BAPC.155	Panavia Tornado GR.1 fsm
ZA634	C	G-BUHA	Slingsby T.61F Venture T.2
ZA652		G-BUDC	Slingsby T.61F Venture T.2
ZB500		G-LYNX	Westland Lynx 800 (Army Air Corps)
ZB627	A	G-CBSK	Westland SA.314G Gazelle HT.3

ZB629		G-CBZL	Westland SA.314G Gazelle HT.3
ZB647	40	G-CBSF	Westland SA.314G Gazelle HT.2
ZF592		G-AWON	English Electric Lightning F.53
ZH139	01	BAPC.191	BAe Harrier GR.7
ZJ116		G-OIOI	EH Industries EH-101 Heliliner
8449M		G-ASWJ	Beagle B.206
-	F	G-RUMW	Grumman FM-2 Wildcat (FAA)
-	12	G-ARSG	Roe Triplane IV replica

"B" Conditions markings

G-17-3		G-AVNE	Westland Wessex 60
G-29-1		G-APRJ	Avro Lincoln B.2 (Fuselage only)
U-0247		G-AGOY	Miles M.38 Messenger (intended marks)
W-2		BAPC.85	Weir W-2
X-25		BAPC.274	Boulton and Paul P.6 fsm

Other markings

| SR-XP020 | | G-BZUG | TLAC RL7A XP Sherwood Ranger |

OTHER ARMED FORCES:

AUSTRALIA

A2-4		VH-ALB	Supermarine Seagull
A16-199	SF-R	G-BEOX	Lockheed Hudson IIIA
A17-48		G-BPHR	DH.82A Tiger Moth
A21-14		G-AFOR	de Havilland DH.94 Moth Minor
A77-851		G-METE	Gloster Meteor F.8
A81-17		G-AIMI	Bristol 170 Freighter 21E
A84-234		G-BURM	English Electric Canberra TT.18
N6-766		G-SPDR	DH.115 Sea Vampire T.55 (Navy)

BELGIUM

66		BAPC.19	Bristol F2b Fighter fuselage frame
B-06		G-BDPU	Britten-Norman BN-2A-21 Islander
B-11		G-BEED	Britten-Norman BN-2A-21 Islander
HD-75		G-AFDX	Hanriot HD.1
T-24	UR-1	G-AMJD	de Havilland DH.82A Tiger Moth

BOLIVIA

| FAB-184 | | G-SIAI | SIAI-Marchetti SF.260W |

BURKINA FASO

| BF8431 | 31 | G-NRRA | SIAI-Marchetti SF.260W |

CANADA

622		N6699D	Piasecki HUP-3 Retriever (RCN)
RCAF 671		G-BNZC	de Havilland DHC-1 Chipmunk
920	QN-	CF-BXO	Supermarine Stranraer
3349		G-BYNF	North American NA-64 Yale I
4188		G-ANOS	de Havilland DH.82A Tiger Moth
5403	XP-L	G-HHII	Hawker Hurricane X
5429	Z	G-KAMM	Hawker Hurricane XIIA
16693	693	G-BLPG	Auster J/1N (AOP.6 c/s)
18013	013	G-TRIC	de Havilland DHC-1 Chipmunk
18393		G-BCYK	Avro Canada CF.100 Canuck IV
20310	310	G-BSBG	North American Harvard IV

PEOPLES' REPUBLIC OF CHINA (including HONG KONG*)

68		G-BVVG	Nanchang CJ-6A (Chinese AF)
50051		G-BAJJ	Hawker Siddeley HS.121 Trident 2E Series 108
50055		G-BBWG	Hawker Siddeley HS.121 Trident 2E Series 109
50258		G-ASDS	Vickers 843 Viscount
HKG-6*		G-BPCL	Scottish Aviation Bulldog
HKG-11*		G-BYRY	Slingsby T.67M-200 Firefly
HKG-13*		G-BXKW	Slingsby T.67M-200 Firefly

FINLAND

| AV-57 | | G-EBNU | Avro 504K |

FRANCE

1 4513	S	G-BFYO	SPAD XIIr replica
19		BAPC.136	Deperdussin 1913 Monoplane fsm
20	315-SQ	G-BWGG	Max Holste Broussard (ALAT)
78		G-BIZK	Nord 3202 (Air Force)
82	8	G-CCVH	Curtiss H75A-1
124		G-BOSJ	Nord 3400
143		G-MSAL	Morane-Saulnier MS.733 (Aéronavale)
156		G-NIFE	Stampe SV-4A (Air Force)

157	01	G-AVEB	Morane Saulnier MS.230 (Air Force)
185	44-CA	G-BWLR	Max Holste Broussard
208	IR	G-YYYY	Max Holste Broussard
394		G-BIMO	Stampe SV-4C (Air Force)
18-5395	CDG	G-CUBJ	Piper L-18C Super Cub (ALAT)
51-7545	119	N14113	North American T-28B Trojan (Air Force)
517692	142	G-TROY	North American T-28A Trojan
MS.824		G-AWBU	Morane-Saulnier N replica (Air Force)
N1977	8	G-BWMJ	Nieuport Scout 17/23 replica (French AF)

GERMANY

1		G-BWUE	Hispano HA.1112-MIL Buchon
1+4		G-BSLX	WAR FW190 scale replica
2+1	7334	G-SYFW	WAR FW190 scale replica
4+--		G-AWHS	Hispano HA.1112-MIL Buchon
8+--		G-WULF	WAR FW190 scale replica
- + 9		G-CCFW	WAR FW190 scale replica
14		BAPC.67	Messerschmitt Bf.109 fsm
+14		G-BSMD	Nord 1101 (Messerschmitt guise)
17+TF		G-BZTJ	Bücker Bü.133C Jungmeister
50 483	CW+BG	G-BXBD	CASA 1131 Jungmann
97+04		G-APVF	Putzer Elster B
99+32		G-BZGK	North American OV-10B Bronco
102/17		BAPC.88	Fokker Dr.1 5/8th scale model
152/17		G-ATJM	Fokker Dr.1 replica
210/16		BAPC.56	Fokker E.III replica
403/17		G-CDXR	Fokker Dr.1 Triplane replica (German Army Air Service)
422/15		G-AVJO	Fokker E-III replica
425/17		BAPC.133	Fokker Dr.1 Triplane replica
450/17		G-BVGZ	Fokker Dr.1 Triplane replica (German Army Air Service)
477/17		G-FOKK	Fokker Dr.1 Triplane replica
694		BAPC.239	Fokker D.VIII 5/8th scale model
1480	6	BAPC.66	Messerschmitt Bf.109 replica
C.L.1.1801/18		G-BNPV	Bowers Fly Baby (German Army Air Service)
C.L.1.1803/18		G-BUYU	Bowers Fly Baby (German Army Air Service)
2292		BAPC.138	Hansa Brandenberg W.29 fsm
4477	GD+EG	G-RETA	CASA 1131E Jungmann Series 2000
5125/18		BAPC.110	Fokker D.VIIF fsm
6357	6	BAPC.74	Messerschmitt Bf.109 replica
7198/18		G-AANJ	LVG C.VI
10639	6 (Black)	G-USTV	Messerschmitt Bf.109G-2
191454		BAPC.271	Messerschmitt Me 163B Komet fsm
C19/15		BAPC.118	Albatros D.Va fsm
D692		G-BVAW	Staaken Flitzer
D-2692		G-STIG	Focke-Wulf FW.44J Stieglit
D5397/17		G-BFXL	Albatros D.VA replica
DR1/17		BAPC.139	Fokker Dr.1 Triplane fsm
-	6G+ED	G-BZOB	Slepcev Storch
-	BU+CC	G-BUCC	CASA 1131E Jungmann
-	BU+CK	G-BUCK	CASA 1131E Jungmann
-	CC+43	G-CJCI	Pilatus P.2 (Arado Ar.96B guise)
-	CF+HF	EI-AUY	Morane-Saulnier MS.502 Criquet
-	DM+BK	G-BPHZ	Morane-Saulnier MS.505 Criquet
-	FI+S	G-BIRW	Morane-Saulnier MS.505 Criquet
-	GL+SU	G-GLSU	Bucker Bu.181B-1 Bestmann
-	KG+EM	G-ETME	Nord 1002 Pingouin
-	N8+AA	G-BFHD	CASA 352L
-	N9+AA	G-BECL	CASA.352L
-	NJ+C11	G-ATBG	Messerschmitt Bf.108 (Nord 1002)
-	S4+A01	G-BWHP	CASA 1131E Jungmann
-	S5+B06	G-BSFB	CASA 1131E Jungmann
-	VK-NZ	G-BFHG	CASA 352L

HUNGARY

503		G-BRAM	MiG 21PF (Russian c/s)

IRELAND

176		G-AMDD	de Havilland DH.104 Dove 6
177		G-BLIW	Percival Provost T.51

ISRAEL

13		G-AHAY	Auster V J/1 Autocrat
171		G-AJMC	Bristol 156 Beaufighter TF.X

ITALY

	W7	G-AGFT	Avia FL.3
mm12822	20	G-FIST	Fiesler Fi.156C-3 Storch
mm53211	ZI-4	BAPC.79	Fiat G.46-4B
44mm52801	97-4	G-BBII	Fiat G.46-3B

JAPAN

15-1585		BAPC.58	Yokosuka MXY-7 Ohka II
24		BAPC.83	Kawasaki Ki 100-1b
997		BAPC.98	Yokosuka MXY-7 Ohka II

JORDAN

A-410		G-AIPW	Taylorcraft Auster 5A Series 160 (Arab Legion AF c/s)
109		G-BVPO	de Havilland DH.100 Vampire FB.6
209		G-BVLM	de Havilland DH.115 Vampire T.55
712	E	G-BWKC	Hawker Hunter F.58
800		G-BOOM	Hawker Hunter T.7 (T.53)
843		G-BWKC	Hawker Hunter F.58

KUWAIT

53-418		G-AXEE	English Electric Lightning F.53

MEXICO

52		N4238C	Mudry CAP.10B (Air Force)

NETHERLANDS

174	K	G-BEPV	Fokker S.11 Instructor (Navy)
BI-005		G-BUVN	CASA 1131E Jungmann
E-15		G-BIYU	Fokker S.11 Instructor
H-98		G-CCCA	Vickers Supermarine 509 Spitfire Tr.IX (Air Force)
H-99		G-ILDA	Vickers Supermarine 509 Spitfire Tr.IX (Air Force)
N-294		G-KAXF	Hawker Hunter F.6A
N-321		G-BWGL	Hawker Hunter T.8C
R-55		G-BLMI	Piper L-18C Super Cub (Air Force)
(Also carries 52-2466)			
R-151		G-BIYR	Piper L-21B Super Cub (Air Force)
R-156		G-ROVE	Piper L-21B Super Cub (Air Force)
R-163		G-BIRH	Piper L-21B Super Cub (Air Force)
(Also carries 54-2453)			
R-167		G-LION	Piper L-21B Super Cub (Air Force)

NEW ZEALAND

NZ4115		G-AHJR (2)	Short S.25 Sunderland MR.5
NZ6001		G-ARTR	de Havilland DHC-2 Beaver 1

NORTH KOREA

No marks		G-BMZF	MiG-15

NORWAY

56321		G-BKPY	Saab Safir

OMAN

417		G-RSAF	BAC 167 Strikemaster Mk.82A
425		G-SOAF	BAC 167 Strikemaster Mk.82A

POLAND

1018		G-ISKA	WSK-PZL Mielec TS-11 Iskra
PLW-6247		G-OMIG	WSK SBLim-2A

PORTUGAL

1365		G-DHPM	de Havilland DHC-1 Chipmunk
1373		G-CBJG	de Havilland DHC-1 Chipmunk
1377		G-BARS	de Havilland DHC-1 Chipmunk
1747		G-BGPB	CCF Harvard 4

RUSSIA

1 (White)		G-BZMY	Yakovlev Yak C-11 (Soviet AF)
01 (Yellow)		G-YKSZ	Yakovlev Yak-52 (Soviet AF)
07 (Yellow)		G-BMJY	Yakovlev Yak-18 (Soviet AF)
9 (White)		G-OYAK	Yakovlev Yak-11(Soviet AF)
09 (Yellow)		G-BVMU	Yakovlev Yak-52 (DOSAAF)
10 (Yellow)		G-BTZB	Yakovlev Yak-50 (DOSAAF)
11 (Yellow)		G-YCII	Yakovlev Yak C-11 (Soviet AF)
21 (White)		G-CDBJ	Yakovlev Yak-3 (Russian AF c/s)
26 (Grey)		G-BVXK	Yakovlev Yak-52 (DOSAAF)
27 (Red)		G-YAKX	Yakovlev Yak-52 (DOSAAF)
31 (Black)		G-YAKV	Yakovlev Yak-52 (DOSAAF)
33 (White)		G-YAKH	Yakovlev Yak-52 (Soviet AF)
33 (Red)		G-YAKZ	Yakovlev Yak-50 (Soviet AF)
36 (White)		G-IYAK	Yakovlev Yak C-11 (DOSAAF)
36 (White)		G-KYAK	Yakovlev Yak C-11 (DOSAAF)
39		G-XXVI	Sukhoi Su-26M
42 (White)		G-CBRU	Yakovlev Yak-52 (DOSAAF)

48 (Grey)		G-CBSN	Yakovlev Yak-52 (DOSAAF)
49 (Red)		G-YAKU	Yakovlev Yak-50 (Soviet AF)
50 (Grey)		G-CBRW	Yakovlev Yak-52 (DOSAAF)
55 (Grey)		G-BVOK	Yakovlev Yak-52 (DOSAAF)
61(Red)		G-YAKM	Yakovlev Yak-50 (Soviet AF)
66 (Red)		G-YAKN	Yakovlev Yak-50 (Soviet AF)
139 (Yellow)		G-BWOD	Yakovlev Yak-52 (DOSAAF)
503		G-BRAM	See HUNGARY above

SAUDI ARABIA

1104		G-SMAS	BAC 167 Strikemaster Mk.80A
1133		G-AMZW	Douglas C-47B-20-DK Dakota

SOUTH AFRICA

92		G-BYCX	Westland Wasp HAS.Mk.1 (Navy)

SOUTH ARABIA (South Yemen)

104		G-PROV	Hunting Percival P.84 Jet Provost T.52A (T.4)

SPAIN

E3B-153	781-75	G-BPTS	CASA 1131 Jungmann
E3B-350	05-97	G-BHPL	CASA 1131 Jungmann
E3B-369	781-32	G-BPDM	CASA 1131 Jungmann
E3B-494	81-47	G-CDLC	CASA 1131 Jungmann

SRI LANKA

CR-822		G-AMJY	Douglas C-47B-40-DK Dakota
CX-123		G-AKEE	de Havilland DH.82A Tiger Moth

SWEDEN

Fv5555		G-EBNO	de Havilland DH.60 Moth

SWITZERLAND

A-10		G-BECW	CASA 1131E Jungmann
A-12		G-CCHY	Bücker Bü.131 Jungmann
A-50		G-CBCE	CASA 1131E Jungmann replica
A-57		G-BECT	CASA 1131E Jungmann
A-125		G-BLKZ	Pilatus P.2-05
A-806		G-BTLL	Pilatus P.3
C-552		G-DORN	EKW C-3605
J-1167		G-MKVI	de Havilland DH.100 Vampire FB.6
J-1573		G-VICI	de Havilland DH.112 Venom FB.50
J-1605		G-BLID	de Havilland DH.112 Venom FB.50
J-1758		G-BLSD	de Havilland DH.112 Venom FB.50
J-4021		G-HHAC	Hawker Hunter F.58
J-4031		G-BWFR	Hawker Hunter F.58
J-4058		G-HHAD	Hawker Hunter F.58
J-4072		G-HHAB	Hawker Hunter F.58
J-4081		G-HHAF	Hawker Hunter F.58
J-4090		G-SIAL	Hawker Hunter F.58
U-80		G-BUKK	Bücker Bü.133 Jungmeister
U-95		G-BVGP	Bücker Bü.133 Jungmeister
U-99		G-AXMT	Bücker Bü.133 Jungmeister
U-110		G-PTWO	Pilatus P.2
V-54		G-BVSD	SE.3130 Alouette II

UNITED STATES

001		G-BYPY	Ryan ST3-KR (Army)
00195700		G-OIDW	Cessna F150G (Pseudo Air Force)
02538		N33870	Fairchild PT-19 Cornell (Army Air Corps)
07539	143	N63590	Boeing Stearman Kaydet (Navy)
14		G-ISDN	Boeing Stearman Kaydet (Army)
17-6532	15	G-BSKS	Nieuport 28C-1
18-0012		G-BLXT	Royal Aircraft Factory SE.5A
18-2001		G-BIZV	Piper L-18C Super Cub (Army)
112		G-BSWC	Boeing Stearman Kaydet (Army Air Corps)
118		G-BSDS	Boeing Stearman Kaydet (Army Air Corps)
169		N52485	Boeing Stearman Kaydet (Navy))
1102	102	G-AZLE	Boeing Stearman Kaydet (Navy)
1164		G-BKGL	Beech C-45 (Army)
14863		G-BGOR	North American AT-6D Texan (Army Air Force)
16037		G-BSFD	Piper J-3C-65 Cub (Army)
16136	205	G-BRUJ	Boeing Stearman Kaydet (Navy)
18263	822	N38940	Boeing Stearman Kaydet (Army Air Corps)
111836	JZ-6	G-TSIX	North American AT-6C Texan (Navy)
111989		N33600	Cessna L-19A Bird Dog (Army)

115042	TA-042	G-BGHU	North American T-6G Texan (Air Force)
115227		G-BKRA	North American T-6G Texan (Navy)
115302	TP	G-BJTP	Piper L-18C Super Cub (Marin
115373	A-373	G-AYPM	Piper L-21A Super Cub (Army)
115684	VM	G-BKVM	Piper L-21A Super Cub (Army)
124485	DF-A	G-BEDF	Boeing B-17G Flying Fortress (Army Air Corps)
126603		G-BHWH	Weedhopper JC-24C (Navy)
146289	2W	N99153	North American T-28C Trojan
151632		G-BWGR	North American TB-25N Mitchell (Air Force)
23		N49272	Fairchild PT-23 Cornell (Army Air Corps)
26		G-BAVO	Boeing Stearman Kaydet (Army)
27		G-AGYY	Ryan PT-21 (Army Air Corps)
21714	201B	G-RUMM	Grumman F8F-2P Bearcat (Navy)
24550	GP	G-PDOG	Cessna O-1E Bird Dog (Air Force)
24582		G-VDOG	Cessna L-1E Bird Dog (Army)
26922	AK 402	G-RADR	Douglas AD-4NA Skyraider (Navy)
28521	TA-521	G-TVIJ	North American T-6J Harvard (Air Force)
29261		G-CDET	Culver Cadet (Army Air Force)
212540	RD 40	G-BBHK	Noorduyn AT-16-ND Harvard IIB (Navy)
217786	25	CF-EQS	Boeing Stearman Kaydet (Army Air Force)
219993		G-CEJU	Bell P-39Q Airacobra
226413	ZU-N	N47DD	Republic P-47D Thunderbolt (Army Air Force)
228473		G-BLZW	Republic P-47D-30-RA Thunderbolt
231983	IY-G	F-BDRS	Boeing B-17G Flying Fortress (Army Air Force)
236657	D-72	G-BGSJ	Piper L-4A-PI (Army Air Corps)
237123		BAPC.157	Waco CG-4A Hadrian
238410	A-44	G-BHPK	Piper L-4A (Army Air Corps)
243809		BAPC.185	WACO CG-4A Hadrian Glider
252983		N66630	Schweizer TG-3A (Army Air Corps)
298177	R-8	N6438C	Stinson L-5C Sentinel
3		BAPC.140	Curtiss 42A R3C2 fsm (Army)
3-1923		G-BRHP	Aeronca O-58B Grasshopper (Army)
379		G-ILLE	Boeing Stearman Kaydet (Army Air Corps)
3072	72	G-TEXN	North American T-6G-NT Texan (Navy)
3397	174	G-OBEE	Boeing Stearman A75N-1 (Navy)
3583	44-D	G-FINT	Piper L-4B Cub
30274		N203SA	Piper AE-1 Cub Cruiser (Navy)
31145	G-26	G-BBLH	Piper L-4B (Army)
31171		N7614C	North American B-25J Mitchell (Marines)
31430		G-BHVV	Piper J-3C-65 Cub (Army Air Force)
31952		G-BRPR	Aeronca L-3C Grasshopper (Army)
314887		G-AJPI	Fairchild UC-61 Forwarder (Army Air Force)
315211	JB-Z	N1944A	Douglas C-47A
315509	W7-S	G-BHUB	Douglas C-47A Dakota (Army Air Force)
329405	A-23	G-BCOB	Piper L-4H (Army Air Corps)
329417		G-BDHK	Piper L-4A (Army Air Corps)
329471	F-44	G-BGXA	Piper L-4H (Army Air Corps)
329601	D-44	G-AXHR	Piper L-4H (Army Air Corps)
329854	R-44	G-BMKC	Piper L-4H (Army Air Corps)
329934	B-72	G-BCPH	Piper L-4H (Army Air Corps)
330238	A-24	G-LIVH	Piper L-4H (Army Air Corps)
330485	C-44	G-AJES	Piper L-4H (Army Air Corps)
343251	27	G-NZSS	Boeing Stearman Kaydet (Army Air Corps)
41-33275	CE	G-BICE	North American AT-6C Texan (Army Air Corps)
42-17553	716	N1731B	Boeing A75N-1 Stearman
42-35870	129	G-BWLJ	Taylorcraft DCO-65 O (Navy)
42-58678	IY	G-BRIY	Taylorcraft L-2A (Army Air Corps)
42-78044		G-BRXL	Aeronca L-3F (Army)
42-84555	EP-H	G-ELMH	North American AT-6D Harvard (Army Air Corps)
42-100766	6W-SAF		Douglas C-47A-65-DL (Nose section only)
43	SC	G-AZSC	North American AT-16 Texan (Army Air Force)
44		G-RJAH	Boeing Stearman Kaydet (Army Air Corps)
44-9063		EI-ARS (2)	Douglas C-54E-5-DO Skymaster

44-30861		N9089Z	North American B-25J Mitchell (Army Air Corps)
44-42914		N31356	Douglas DC-4-1009
44-79609	S-44	G-BHXY	Piper L-4H (Army Air Force)
44-83184	7	G-RGUS	Fairchild UC-61K Forwarder (Army)
44-83868	N	N5237V	Boeing B-17G Flying Fortress (Army Air Corps)
45-0951		G-BLFL	Douglas C-47B-45-DK Dakota
46-16130		G-BGCF	Douglas C-47A-90-DL Dakota
49		G-KITT	Curtiss TP-40M Kittyhawk (Air Force)
441		G-BTFG	Boeing Stearman Kaydet (Navy)
4406	12	G-ONAF	Naval Aircraft Factory N3N-3 (Navy)
40467	19	G-BTCC	Grumman F6F Hellcat (Navy)
46214	X-3	CF-KCG	Grumman TBM-3E Avenger (Navy)
413317	VF-B	N51RT	North American P-51D Mustang (Army Air Corps)
413521	5Q-B	G-MRLL	North American P-51D Mustang (Army Air Corps)
413573	B6-K	N6526D	North American P-51D Mustang (Army Air Corps)
413704	B7-H	G-BTCD	North American P-51D Mustang (Army Air Force)
414419	LH-F	G-MSTG	North American P-51D Mustang (Army Air Force)
433915		G-PBYA	Consolidated PBY-5A Catalina (USAAF)
436021		G-BWEZ	Piper L-4 (Army Air Corps)
454467	J-44	G-BILI	Piper L-4J (Army Air Corps)
454537	J-04	G-BFDL	Piper L-4J (Army Air Corps)
461748	Y	G-BHDK	Boeing B-29A Superfortress (Air Force)
463209	WZ-S	BAPC.255	North American P-51D Mustang (Army Air Corps)
472035		G-SIJJ	North American P-51D Mustang (Army Air Force)
472216	HO-M	G-BIXL	North American P-51D Mustang (Army Air Corps)
472218	WZ-I	G-HAEC	North American P-51D Mustang (Army Air Force)
479651		EI-CFO	Piper L-4H (Army Air Corps)
479744	49-M	G-BGPD	Piper L-4H (Army Air Corps)
479766	63-D	G-BKHG	Piper L-4H (Army Air Corps)
479897	JD	G-BOXJ	Piper L-4H (Army Air Corps)
480015	M-44	G-AKIB	Piper L-4H (Army Air Corps)
480133	B-44	G-BDCD	Piper L-4J (Army Air Corps)
480173	H-57	G-RRSR	Piper L-4J (Army Air Corps)
480321	H-44	G-FRAN	Piper L-4J (Army Air Corps)
480480	E-44	G-BECN	Piper L-4J (Army Air Corps)
480636	A-58	G-AXHP	Piper L-4J (Army Air Corps)
480723	E5-J	G-BFZB	Piper L-4J (Army Air Corps)
480752	E-39	G-BCXJ	Piper L-4J (Army Air Corps)
480762		EI-BBV	Piper L-4J (Army Air Corps)
493209	ANG	G-DDMV	North American T-6G Texan (California Air National Guard)
5 : 146-11083		G-BNAI	SPAD replica (Wolf W.II) (Army Air Corps)
51-11701A :			
	AF258	G-BSZC	Beech C-45H (Air Force)
51-15319	A-319	G-FUZZ	Piper L-18C Super Cub (Army)
54-2445	A-445	G-OTAN	Piper L-21B Super Cub (Army)
54-2447		G-SCUB	Piper L-21B Super Cub (Army)
54884	D-57-	N61787	Piper J-3C-65 Cub
56498		N44914	Douglas C-54D Skymaster
6-1042	7	G-BMZX	SPAD replica (Wolf W.II) (Army Air Corps)
624	D-39	G-BVMH	Piper L-4 (Wag-Aero Cuby) (Army Air Corps)
669		G-CCXA	Boeing Stearman A75N1 (Army Air Corps)
699		G-CCXB	Boeing Stearman A75N1 (Army Air Corps)
72-21509	129	G-UHIH	Bell UH-1H Iroquois (Army)
7797		G-BFAF	Aeronca L-16A (Army)
85		G-BTBI	Republic P-47 Thunderbolt scale replica (Air Force)
854		G-BTBH	Ryan PT-22 (Army Air Corps)
855		N56421	Ryan PT-22 (Army Air Corps)
897	E	G-BJEV	Aeronca Chief (Navy)
8178	FU-178	G-SABR	North American F-86A Sabre (Air Force)
8242	FU-242	N196B	North American F-86A Sabre (Air Force)
80105	19	G-CCBN	Replica SE5A (US Air Service)

90678	27	G-BRVG	North American SNJ-7 Texan (Navy)
92844	8	G-BXUL	Vought FG-1D Corsair (Navy)
93542	LTA-542	G-BRLV	North American T-6 Texan (Air Force)
C1661-TA		G-BTUV	Aeronca 65TAC Defender (Air Force)
-	G-57	G-AKAZ (2)	Piper L-4A (Army Air Corps)

VENUEZULA

2531		G-AMXS	de Havilland DH.104 Dove 2A

YUGOSLAVIA

146		G-BSXD	Soko P-2 Kraguj
30149	149	G-SOKO	Soko P-2 Kraguj

UNATTRIBUTED

164	BAPC.106	Bleriot Type XI
5439	BAPC.84	Mitsubishi Ki 46 III (Dinah)
442795	BAPC.199	Fieseler Fi 103 (V-1)
GBH-7	BAPC.234	Vickers FB.5 Gunbus fsm
LHS-1	BAPC.147	Bensen B.7 Gyroglider
QP-30	G-BFDV	Westland WG.13 Lynx HC.28 (SEAE)

PART 3 – "B CONDITIONS" MARKINGS

Air Navigation Order (ANO2000) promulgates the specific circumstances under which aerospace manufacturers can pursue the conduct of aircraft trials without the need for valid Certificates of Airworthiness. ANO2000 establishes both "A" and "B" conditions but we are only concerned here with the latter requirements which stipulate the use of identity marks as approved by the CAA for the purposes of "B Conditions" flight.

In brief, under "B Conditions" an aircraft must fly only for the purpose of:
(a) experimenting with or testing the aircraft (including any engines installed thereon) or any equipment installed or carried in the aircraft;
(b) enabling it to qualify for the issue of a certificate of airworthiness or the validation thereof or the approval of a modification of the aircraft or the issue of a permit to fly;
(c) demonstrating and displaying the aircraft, any engines installed thereon or any equipment installed or carried in the aircraft with a view to the sale thereof or of other similar aircraft, engines or equipment;
(d) demonstrating and displaying the aircraft to employees of the operator;
(e) the giving of flying training to or the testing of flight crew employed by the operator or the training or testing of other persons employed by the operator; or
(f) proceeding to or from a place at which any experiment, inspection, repair, modification, maintenance, approval, test or weighing of the aircraft, the installation of equipment in the aircraft, demonstration, display or training is to take place or at which installation of furnishings in, or the painting of, the aircraft is to be undertaken.

The flight must be operated by a person approved by the CAA for the purposes of these Conditions and subject to any additional conditions which may be specified in such an approval. If not registered in the United Kingdom the aircraft must be marked in a manner approved by the CAA for the purposes of these Conditions. The aircraft must carry such flight crew as may be necessary to ensure the safety of the aircraft. No person can act as pilot in command of the aircraft except a person approved for the purpose by the CAA.

Prompted by the SBAC a radically new system was introduced in 1948. In essence, this remains in existence today. Whilst deemed "current" many Companies included have long since merged or ceased to trade and so, by coincidence, the table below enscapsulates in miniature the absorbing changes within the UK aircraft industry which have occurred during the period 1948 to date. The same can also be said for the original series covering the period from 1929 to 1948.

CURRENT SERIES

Prefix	Company	Period	Issued	Remarks
G-1-	Sir W G Armstrong-Whitworth Aircraft Ltd	1948-1967	1.1.48	Cancelled
G-1-	Rolls-Royce Ltd (Bristol Engines Division)	1949-19xx	9.4.69	Cancelled
G-2-	Blackburn Aircraft Ltd	1949-1967	1.1.48	Cancelled
G-3-	Boulton Paul Aircraft Ltd	1948-1973	1.1.48	Cancelled 31.12.73
G-03	BAE Systems (Operating) Ltd	19xx-		Current
G-4-	Portsmouth Aviation Ltd	1948-1949	1.1.48	Cancelled 23.5.49
G-4-	Miles Aviation and Transport (R & D) Ltd	1969-19xx	1.5.69	Cancelled
G-04	BAe Systems (Operating) Ltd	19xx-		Current
G-5-	The de Havilland Aircraft Co Ltd	1948-	1.1.48	Current
	(became Raytheon Services Ltd)			
G-6-	Fairey Aviation Ltd	1948-1969	1.1.48	Cancelled 17.1.69
G-7-	Gloster Aircraft Ltd	1948-1961	1.1.48	Cancelled
G-7-	Slingsby Sailplanes Ltd	1971-	21.10.71	Current
	(became Slingsby Aviation Ltd)			
G-8-	Handley Page Ltd	1948-1970	1.1.48	Cancelled 28.2.70
G-08	BAE Systems (Operating) Ltd	19xx-		Current
G-9-	Hawker Aircraft Ltd	1948-1996	1.1.48	Cancelled
	(became British Aerospace Defence Ltd)			
G-10-	Reid and Sigrist Ltd	1948-1953	1.1.48	Cancelled 1.4.53
G-11-	A.V.Roe and Co. Ltd	1948-	1.1.48	Current
	(became BAe Systems (Operations) Ltd)			
G-12-	Saunders-Roe Ltd	1948-1967	1.1.48	Cancelled 9.6.67
G-13-	Not allocated			
G-14-	Short Brothers and Harland Ltd	1948-	1.1.48	Current
	(became Short Brothers plc)			
G-15-	Vickers Armstrong Ltd, Supermarine Division	1948-1968	1.1.48	Cancelled 17.10.68
G-16-	Vickers Armstrong Ltd, Weybridge Division	1948-1999	1.1.48	Cancelled
	(became British Aerospace Airbus Ltd)			
G-17-	Westland Aircraft Ltd	1948-	1.1.48	Current
	(became GKN Westland Helicopters Ltd)			
G-18-	The Bristol Aeroplane Co.Ltd	1948-1975	1.1.48	Cancelled 31.7.75
G-19-	Heston Aircraft Ltd	1948-1960	1.1.48	Cancelled 4.2.60
G-20-	General Aircraft Ltd	1948-1949	1.1.48	Cancelled 23.5.49
G-21-	Miles Aircraft Ltd (H P Reading Ltd)	1948-1963	1.1.48	Cancelled 11.2.63
G-22-	de Havilland Aircraft Co Ltd, Airspeed Division	1948-1952	1.1.48	Cancelled 23.5.52
G-23-	Percival Aircraft Ltd	1948-1966	1.1.48	Cancelled 31.5.66
G-24-	Cunliffe-Owen Aircraft Ltd	1948-1949	1.1.48	Cancelled 23.5.49
G-25-	Auster Aircraft Ltd	1948-1962	1.1.48	Cancelled
G-26-	Slingsby Sailplanes Ltd	1948-1949	1.1.48	Cancelled 19.12.49
G-27-	English Electric Co Ltd Aircraft Division	1948-1991	1.1.48	Cancelled
	(became British Aerospace Military Aircraft Division Ltd)			
G-28-	British European Airways Corporation (Helicopters)	1948-	1.1.48	Current
	(became Brintel Helicopters Ltd)			
G-29-	D Napier and Son Ltd	1948-1962	1.1.48	Cancelled 9.11.62
G-30-	Pest Control Ltd	1952-1957	1.1.48	Cancelled 4.3.57
G-31-	Scottish Aviation Ltd	1948-	1.1.48	Current
	(became BAe Systems (Operations) Ltd)			
G-32-	Cierva Autogiro Co. Ltd	1948-1951	1.1.48	Cancelled 9.3.51
G-33-	Flight Refuelling Ltd	Not known		

G-34-	Chrislea Aircraft Ltd	1948-1952	1.1.48	Cancelled
G-35-	F.G.Miles Ltd (became Beagle Aircraft Ltd)	1951-1970	9.8.54	Cancelled 29.6.70
G-36-	College of Aeronautics	1954-	9.8.54	Current
	(became Cranfield Aerospace Ltd)			
G-37-	Rolls-Royce Ltd	1954-1971	9.8.54	Cancelled 17.9.71
G-38-	de Havilland Propellers Ltd	1954-1975	9.8.54	Cancelled 22.10.75
	(became Hawker Siddeley Dynamics)			
G-39-	Folland Aircraft Ltd	1954-1965	9.8.54	Cancelled 2.4.65
G-40-	Wiltshire School of Flying Ltd	Not known		Not taken up
G-41-	Aviation Traders (Engineering) Ltd	1956-1976	3.10.56	Cancelled 27.2.76
G-42-	Armstrong Siddeley Motors Ltd	1956-1959	13.11.56	Cancelled 28.8.59
G-43-	Edgar Percival Aircraft Ltd	1956-1959	21.11.56	Cancelled 26.6.59
G-44-	Agricultural Aviation Ltd	1959-1959	17.4.59	Cancelled 14.12.59
G-45-	Bristol Siddeley Engines Ltd	1959-1969	27.5.59	Cancelled 8.4.69
G-46-	Saunders-Roe Ltd, Helicopter Division	1959-1962	15.6.59	Cancelled 3.5.62
G-47-	Lancashire Aircraft Co. Ltd	1960-19xx	8.2.60	Cancelled
G-48-	Westland Aircraft Ltd, Bristol Division	1960-1969	7.7.60	Cancelled 28.2.69
G-49-	F.G.Miles Engineering Ltd	1965-1969	23.7.65	Cancelled c.1969
G-50-	Alvis Ltd	1967-1975	16.2.67	Cancelled
G-51-	Britten-Norman Ltd (became BN Group Ltd)	1967-	20.9.67	Current
G-52-	Marshalls of Cambridge (Engineering) Ltd	1968-	18.1.68	Current
	(became Marshalls of Cambridge Aerospace Ltd)			
G-53-	Norman Aeroplane Co. Ltd	1977-19xx	23.5.77	Cancelled
G-54-	Cameron Balloons Ltd	197x-	Not known	Current
G-55-	W.Vinten Ltd	19xx-19xx	Not known	Cancelled
G-56-	Edgley Aircraft Ltd	19xx-19xx	Not known	Cancelled
G-57-	Airship Industries (UK) Ltd	19xx-19xx	Not known	Cancelled
G-58-	ARV Aviation (became Island Aircraft)	19xx-19xx	Not known	Cancelled
G-59-	Mainair Sports Ltd	19xx	7.05	Cancelle
G-60-	FR Aviation Ltd	19xx-	Not known	(Current together with G-71)
G-61-	Aviation Enterprises Ltd	19xx-	Not known	Current
G-62-	Curtiss and Green Ltd	19xx-19xx	Not known	Cancelled
G-63-	Thunder and Colt Balloons Ltd	1994-19xx	c.1994	Cancelled
G-64-	Brooklands Aerospace Group plc	19xx-19xx	Not known	Cancelled
G-65-	Solar Wings Aviation Ltd	19xx-1995	Not known	Cancelled
G-66-	Aerial Arts Ltd	19xx-19xx	Not known	Cancelled
G-67-	Atlantic Aerengineering Ltd	19xx	Not known	Current
G-68-	Medway Microlights Ltd	19xx	Not known	Current
G-69-	Cyclone Airsports Ltd (formerly Aerial Arts)	19xx	7.05	Cancelled
G-70-	FLS Aerospace (Lovaux) Ltd	19xx	1997	Cancelled
G-71-	FR Aviation Ltd	19xx	Not known	Current
G-72-	Lindstrand Balloons Ltd	19xx	Not known	Current
G-73-	Aviation (Scotland) Ltd	19xx	1995	Cancelled
G-74-	Fleaplanes UK Ltd	19xx	2001	Cancelled
G-75-	Chichester Miles Consultants Ltd	19xx	Not known	Current
G-76-	Police Aviation Services Ltd	19xx	Not known	Current
G-77-	Thruster Air Services Ltd	19xx	Not known	Current
G-78-	Bristow Helicopters Ltd	19xx	Not known	Current
G-79-	McAlpine Helicopters Ltd	19xx	Not known	Current
G-80-	British Microlight Aircraft Association	19xx	Not known	Current
G-81-	Cooper Aerial Services	19xx	Not known	Cancelled
G-82-	European Helicopters Ltd	19xx	1999	Cancelled
G-83-	Mann Aviation Group (Engineering) Ltd	19xx	Not known	Current
G-84-	Intora-Firebird plc	19xx	Not known	Cancelled
G-85-	CFM Aircraft Ltd	19xx	2004	
G-86-	Advanced Technologies Group Ltd	19xx	Not known	Current
G-87-	CHC Scotia Ltd	19xx	Not known	Current
G-88-	Air Hanson Engineering	19xx	Not known	Current
G-89	Not known			
G-90	Not known			
G-91	Bella Aviation	2004-2005		
G-92	Not known			
G-93	P&M Aviation Ltd	7.2005		
G-94	Rotorsport UK Ltd	2006		

ORIGINAL SERIES

Prefix	Company	Period	Issued	Remarks
A	The Sir W G Armstrong Whitworth Aircraft Ltd	1929-1948	23.12.29	
B	Blackburn Aeroplane and Motor Co.Ltd	1929-1948	23.12.29	
C	Boulton and Paul Ltd	1929-1948	23.12.29	
D	Bristol Aeroplane Co.	Not taken up		
D	Cunliffe Owen Aircraft Ltd	Not taken up		
D	Portmouth Aviation Ltd	1947-1948	1947	
E	de Havilland Aircraft Co Ltd	1929-1948	23.12.29	
F	The Fairey Aviation Co Ltd	1929-1948	23.12.29	
G	Gloster Aircraft Ltd	1929-1948	23.12.29	
H	Handley Page Ltd	1929-1948	23.12.29	
I	H G Hawker Engineering Co Ltd	1929-1948	23.12.29	
J	George Parnall and Co (became Parnall Aircraft Ltd)	1929-1946	23.12.29	Cancelled 1946
J	Reid and Sigrist Ltd	1947-1948	1947	
K	A V Roe and Co Ltd	1929-1948	23.12.29	
L	Saunders-Roe Ltd	1929-1948	23.12.29	
M	Short Bros (Rochester & Bedford) Ltd	1929-1948	23.12.29	
N	Supermarine Aviation Works (Vickers) Ltd	1929-1948	23.12.29	
O	Vickers (Aviation) Ltd	1929-1948	23.12.29	
P	Westland Aircraft Works	1929-1948	23.12.29	
R	The Bristol Aeroplane Co.Ltd	1929-1948	23.12.29	
S	Spartan Aircraft Ltd	1930-1936	30. 8.30	Cancelled 29. 2.36
S	Heston Aircraft Ltd	1936-1948	15. 5.36	
S	Comper Aircraft Co. Ltd	Not taken up		
T	General Aircraft Ltd	1933-1948	8. 5.33	
U	Phillips & Powis Aircraft Ltd	1934-1948	5. 2.34	
V	Airspeed (1934) Ltd	1934-1948	27. 6.34	
W	G & J Weir Ltd	1933-1948	8. 5.33	Cancelled 1946
X	Percival Aircraft Ltd	1936-1948	21.1.36	
Y	The British Aircraft Manufacturing Co.Ltd	1936-1938	1936	Cancelled 1938
Y	Cunliffe Owen Aircraft Ltd	1940-1948	28.10.40	
Z	Taylorcraft Aeroplanes (England) Ltd	1946-1948	12.1.46	
AA	Believed not allocated			
AB	Slingsby Sailplanes Ltd	1947-1948	1947	

PART 4 – FICTITIOUS MARKINGS

Registration	Type	Rematks	Location
"K.158"	Austin Whippet replica	See BAPC.207 - (a)	Doncaster
"EI-ABH"	Mignet HM.14 Pou-Du-Ciel replica	(b)	Meath, Ireland
"F-OCMF"	Sud SA.321F Super Frelon	See F-BTRP - (a)	Weston-super-Mare
"G-EASQ"	Bristol 30/46 Babe III replica	See BAPC.87 - (a)	Kemble
"G-EBED"	Vickers 60 Viking IV replica	See BAPC.114 - (a)	Brooklands
"G-EBVO"	Blackburn Lincock fsm	See BAPC.287 - (a)	Brooklands
"G-AAAH"	de Havilland DH.60 Moth replica	See BAPC.270 - (a)	Elvington
"G-AAAH"	de Havilland DH.60G Moth replica	See BAPC.168 - (a)	Croydon
"G-AACA"	Avro 504K replica	See BAPC.177 - (a)	Brooklands
"G-ABUL"	de Havilland DH.82A Tiger Moth	See G-AOXG - (b)	RNAS Yeovilton
"G-ACSS"	de Havilland DH.88 Comet	See BAPC.216 - (a)	London Colney
"G-ACSS"	de Havilland DH.88 Comet model	See BAPC.257 - (a)	Hatfield
"G-ADNV"	de Havilland DH.82A Tiger Moth	See G-AMLF - (b)	Santa Paula, California, US
"G-ADRG"	Mignet HM.14 Pou-Du-Ciel replica	See BAPC.77 - (b)	Stondon
"G-ADRX"	Mignet HM.14 Pou-Du-Ciel replica	See BAPC.231 - (a)	Haverigg
"G-ADRY"	Mignet HM.14 Pou-Du-Ciel replica	See BAPC.29 - (a)	Dover
"G-ADVU"	Mignet HM.14 Pou-Du-Ciel replica	See BAPC.211 - (a)	Sunderland
"G-ADYV"	Mignet HM.14 Pou-Du-Ciel replica	See BAPC.243 - (a)	Malvern Wells
"G-ADZW"	Mignet HM.14 Pou-Du-Ciel replica	See BAPC.253 - (a)	Southampton
"G-AEAJ"	de Havilland DH.89 Dragon Rapide replica	See BAPC.280 - (a)	Liverpool
"G-AEOF"	Mignet HM.14 Pou-Du-Ciel replica	See BAPC.22 - (a)	Schipol, Netherlands
"G-AFAP"	CASA 352L	(c)	Cosford
"G-AFFI"	Mignet HM.14 Pou-Du-Ciel	See BAPC.76 - (a)	Elvington
"G-AFUG"	Luton LA.4 Minor	See BAPC 97 - (a)	Sunderland
"G-AGIH"	Lockheed 18-56 Lodestar	See G-BMEW - (b)	Gardermoen, Norway
"G-AJOV"	Westland WS-51 Dragonfly HR.3	(c)	Cosford
"G-AJOZ"	Fairchild F.24W-41A Argus 1	(c)	Woodhall Spa
"G-AJPR"	de Havilland DH.104 Dove 6	See G-ARDE - (b)	
		Al Mahata Museum, The Sharjah Aviation Museum,, Sharjah,UAE	
"G-ALVD"	de Havilland DH.104 Dove 2B	See G-ALCU (c)	Coventry
"G-AMZZ" (2)	Douglas C-47A-DK Dakota [12254,]	Al Mahata Museum, The Sharjah Aviation Museum, Sharjah,UAE	
	(ex 42-92452 - to RCAF FZ669, CAF12943, C-GCXE, HI-502, N688EA),		
"G-AOXL"	de Havilland DH.114 Heron 2D	See G-ANUO - (b)	Croydon
"G-BMAF"	Cessna 150J	See G-BOWC - (a)	Croft Farm, Defford
"G-CARS"	Pitts S-2A Special	See BAPC.134 - (a)	(Northampton)
"G-CDBS"	MBB Bö.105DD	See G-BCXO - (b)	Land's End Cornwall
"G-ESKY"	Piper PA-23-250 Aztec D	See G-BADI - (c)	North Weald
"G-FIRE"	British Aircraft Corporation One-Eleven 401AK	See 5N-HHH - (b) (Note authentic G-FIRE (e)	Southend
"G-FIRE"	Embraer EMB.110P2 Bandeirante	See SX-BNL - (b) (Note authentic G-FIRE (e)	Southend
"G-MAZY"	de Havilland DH.82A Tiger Moth	H.Hodgson "Maisie"	Newark
	(On loan from Cotswold Aircraft Restoration Group: rebuilt for static display as composite ex Newark components		
	and G-AMBB/T6801; also reported as ex DE561 [lost at sea 1942])		
"G-OOAT"	Piper PA-28-151 Cherokee Warrior	See G-BCTA - (c)	Fairoaks
"G-OOAT"	Piper PA-28R-200 Cherokee Arrow II	See G-BDKV - (c)	Fairoaks
"G-OPAS"	Agusta A109A-II	See D-HCKV - (b)	Gloucestershire
"G-PRAT"	Gulfstream AA-5A Cheetah	See G-BIVV - (c)	North Weald
"G-RAFM"	Robinson R22 Beta	See G-OTHL - (b)	Hendon
"G-SHOG"	Colomban MC-15 Cri-Cri	V.S.E.Norman (Static model 1999)	Rendcomb
"G-SMOKE"	Hawker Siddeley HS.121 Trident 2E	See G-AVFG - (c)	Manchester
"VH-FDT"	de Havilland DHA.3 Drover 2	See G-APXX - (b)	Lasham
"ZK-POZ"	CSS-13 Aeroklubowy	See G-BSSY - (b)	Old Warden

PART 5 – NO EXTERNAL MARKINGS

These are listed by Type to ease identification.

Registration	Type	Comments
G-AANI	Blackburn Monoplane	(c)
G-AANG	Bleriot XI	(c)
G-AANH	Deperdussin Monoplane	(c)
G-EBNV	English Electric Wren	(d)
G-BAAF	Manning-Flanders MF.1	(c)
G-BFIP	Wallbro Monoplane	(b)
G-TURP	Aérospatiale SA341G Gazelle 1	(b)

PART 4 and PART 5 Notes:

(a) Details at SECTION 5, Part 2
(b) Details at SECTION 5, Part 1
(c) Details at SECTION 1, Part 2
(d) Details at SECTION 1, Part 1
(e) Details at SECTION 1, Part 3

PART 6 – GLIDER TYPE INDEX (UK AND IRELAND)

Below is a summary of BGA and IGSA numbers. All BGA certified gliders are now referenced below under their BGA numbers rather than Trigraph reference. Those allocated G- registrations are shown in the relevant Index at Section 7, Part 10.

FLUGWISSENSCHAFTLICHEN VEREINIGUNG AACHEN
FVA-10B RHEINLAND
    BGA 1711

ABBOTT-BAYNES
SCUD I replica
    BGA 3922
SCUD II
    BGA 231
SCUD III
    BGA 283 684

AEROMERE see **CARMAM**

AKAFLIEG BRAUNSCHWEIG
SB.5
    BGA 2690

ALLGAIER
GEIER
    BGA 2557

AMS-FLIGHT see **GLASER-DIRKS**

AVIALSA see **SCHEIBE**

AVIONAUTICA RIO see **CARMAM**

BAC
VII replica
    BGA 2878

BIRMINGHAM GUILD LTD including **SWALES** and **YORKSHIRE SAILPLANES**
BG.135, SD.3 and YS-55 CONSORT
    BGA 1741 1891 1921 2212

BÖLKOW
PHOEBUS
    BGA 1542 1577 1595

BREGUET
905 FAUVETTE
    BGA 2112 2915

SOCIÉTÉ CARMAM see **AEROMERE** and **AVIONAUTICA RIO**
M-100S MESANGE
    BGA 1416 2383 2867
M-200 FOEHN
    BGA 2877 2978 3839
JP 15-34 KIT-CLUB and JP 15-36A AIGLON
    BGA 3169

SOCIÉTÉ NOUVELLE CENTRAIR see **SCHLEICHER**
101 PÉGASE
    BGA 2865 2901 3613 5067 EI-162

CHARD see **KING-ELLIOTT-STREET**

COLDITZ
COCK replica- designs unrelated
    BGA 4732 4757

DFS also see **GRUNAU, EoN, NORD, FOCKE-WULF, WEIHE** and **SCHLEICHER** production
KRANICH
    BGA 1147
OLYMPIA-MEISE
    BGA 449
WEIHE
    BGA 448 1021 1093 1230 2602

DG FLUGZEUGBAU see **GLASER-DIRKS** and **ROLLADEN-SCHNEIDER**
DG-1000
    BGA 5292

DITTMAR
CONDOR IV
    BGA 4905

EDGLEY AERONAUTICS
EA9 OPTIMIST
    BGA 4093 5338

EIRI
PIK-20
    BGA 2550

ELLIOTTS of NEWBURY see **DFS** and **NORD**
AP.5 OLYMPIA
    BGA 503 505 509 513 514 538 541 544 562 678 726 795 834 909
    962 973 997 1029 1035 1037 1040 1055 1056 1057 1059 1153
    1173 1303 1382 1539 1554 1718 1800 1974 2279
AP.6 OLYMPIA 401, 403 and 419 variants
    BGA 1051 1052 1278 1960 2372
AP.7 PRIMARY and ETON TX.1
    BGA 580 588 589 1461 1625 3214
AP.8 BABY
    BGA 628 629 1252 EI-118
AP.10 460, 463 and 465 variants
    BGA 1156 1171 1172 1177 1201 1217 1223 1225 1253 1270 1286
    1288 1300 1307 1328 1334 1355 1373 1389 1394 2776

FAUVEL
AV.22S
    BGA 2344
AV.36
    BGA 2932

FEDOROV see **AVIASTROITEL**
Me7 MECHTA
    BGA 4492

GLASER-DIRKS
DG-100 and DG-101
    BGA 4660 4759 4892
DG-200 and DG-202
    BGA 2869 4721
DG-300 and DG-303 ELAN
    BGA 3187 3676 3849 4156
DG-600
    BGA 4949
DG-800 and DG-808
    BGA 5272
DG-1000 see DG FLUGZEUGBAU

GLASFLÜGEL ING EUGEN HANLE
H.201 STANDARD LIBELLE
    BGA 1598 1632 1844 4257
H.205 CLUB LIBELLE
    BGA 2203 3732 3746 3781 5004 5225
H.303 MOSQUITO
    BGA 2441 2599

GROB (BURKHART GROB LUFT und RAUMFAHRT GmbH) see **SCHEMPP-HIRTH**
G102 ASTIR VARIANTS
    BGA 2269 2318 2522 3134 3172 4125 4326 4395 4411 4520 4720
    4722 EI-124
G103 TWIN ASTIR VARIANTS
    BGA 5069 EI-160

GRUNAU including **DFS** and **HAWKRIDGE** production
BABY
    BGA 277 370 578 615 1410 1663 1747 1910 2238 2384 2433 2709
    2804 5066

HALFORD
JSH SCORPION
    BGA 2146

HAWKRIDGE
DAGLING
   BGA 491 493

HOLS DER TEUFEL
REPLICA
   BGA 3277

HÜTTER
H.17
   BGA 490 2847
H.28 rep
   BGA 3982

ICA-BRASOV
IS-28B2
   BGA 2050 2704
IS-29D
   BGA 1961

ISF including **VALENTIN** production
MISTRAL C
   BGA 4376

JASTREB see **GLASFLÜGEL, SCHEMPP-HIRTH**

KING-ELLIOTT-STREET
OSPREY
   BGA 2021

LAK
LAK-12 LIETUVA
   BGA 3611 3724 4115 4388 4488

LANGE FLUGZEUGBAU
E1 ANTARES
   BGA 5322 5334 5337

LET
L-13 BLANIK
   BGA 1321 2067 2106 2991 3186 3677 EI-120 EI-154
L-23 SUPER BLANIK
   BGA 3609

LETOV (VOJENSKÁ továrna na letadla LETOV)
LF-107 LUNAK
   BGA 4286 4884 4970 5015 5208 5258

MANUEL
CONDOR
   BGA 2161
WILLOW WREN
   BGA 162

MARCO
J-5
   BGA 4014

MAUPIN
WOODSTOCK
   BGA 3833 4091

MONNETT
MONERAI
   BGA 2988

MÜLLER
MOSWEY III
   BGA 2474

MÜNCHEN
MÜ 13D
   BGA 1937 2267

NEUKOM
STANDARD ELFE S-2
   BGA 3374
ELFE S4
   BGA 4497

NORD see **EoN**
2000
   BGA 2840

OBERLERCHNER
Mg19a STEINADLER
   BGA 2903

PENROSE
PEGASUS
   BGA 4002

PFENNINGER-MARKWALDER
ELFE PM3
   BGA 4723

PIK see **EIRI**
PIK-16C VASAMA
   BGA 1540

PILATUS FLUGZEUGWERKE
B4-PC11
   BGA 1904 1911

POTTIER see **CARMAM**

PZL-BIELSKO see **SZD**

PZL-SWIDNIK
PW-5 SMYK
   BGA 4440

ROLLADEN-SCHNEIDER FLUGZEUGBAU GmbH
LS1
   BGA 5104
LS3
   BGA 2656 3751
LS4
   BGA 4734 4841 4984
LS6
   BGA 4385
LS7
   BGA 3580 3600
LS8
   BGA 4337 4558 4747 4973

SCHEIBE-FLUGZEUGBAU GmbH including **AVIALSA/ROCHETEAU** production
BERGFALKE
   BGA 1464 2855 4111
L-SPATZ and A60 FAUCONNET
   BGA 2276 2278 2498 2652 3840 4265 4517 EI-130
ZUGVOGEL III
   BGA 2779 4064 4162 4275
SF 27A ZUGVOGEL V
   BGA 2515 2956 3285 3531 3655 3703 3759 4036 4235 EI-144
SF 34
   BGA 2843

SCHEMPP-HIRTH FLUGZEUGBAU GmbH including **GROB, JASTREB** and **LANAVERRE** production
GÖ 3 MINIMOA
   BGA 1639
GÖ 4 GOEVIER
   BGA 1992
STANDARD AUSTRIA
   BGA 1127
SHK
   BGA 1579 1837 2157
HS.4 STANDARD CIRRUS
   BGA 1724 2091 2195 3789 3983 4254 4273 4516 4523 4551 4609 4761
HS.5 NIMBUS 2
   BGA 1726 4121
HS.6 JANUS
   BGA 2723
HS.7 MINI NIMBUS
   BGA 2337 2539 4145 4951
NIMBUS 3
   BGA 2898 4263 4420 4932
NIMBUS 3D
   BGA 3581 3610 3827 4008 4322 4458 4835 4853 5116
DISCUS A, B and CS variants
   BGA 4827
DUO DISCUS
   BGA 5332

VENTUS A, B and C variants
BGA 3152 3301 4571
VENTUS 2
BGA 4216 4606

ALEXANDER SCHLEICHER SEGELFLUGZEUGBAU including
CENTRAIR production
RHÖNBUSSARD
BGA 337
Ka 2 RHÖNSCHWALBE
BGA 1026 2274 2324 2913 3425 4336
Ka 3
BGA 2689
RHÖNLERCHE II
BGA 1789 1872 1873
Ka 6, BR, CR RHÖNSEGLER
BGA 1027 1039 1222 1323 1412 2058 2339 2486 2516 2852 3311
3332 3370 3483 3508 3670 3696 3763 EI-127
Ka 6E
BGA 1428 1533 2396 2757 2929 3974 4357
Ka 7 RHÖNADLER
BGA 936 1031 1157 1174 1499 1626 1664 1694 2139 2158 2187
2218 2432 2463 2477 2538 2594 2851 2943 2946 2966 2977 2982
3201 3262 3281 3307 3344 3382 3421 3521 3682 3783 3838 4069
4616 EI-105
K 8
BGA 1458 1529 1574 1580 1807 2154 2192 2221 2298 2619 2688
2747 2925 3170 3349 3434 3435 3514 3548 3722 4045 4148 4255
4268 4312 4869 4897 4898 EI-133
ASK 13
BGA 1746 2830 3215 4592 4593
ASW 15
BGA 1582 3363 3993 4359 EI-134
ASW 17
BGA 2595
ASK 18
BGA 4173
ASW 19
BGA 3930 4011
ASW 20
BGA 2635 2644 2648 2677 2778 4341
ASK 21
BGA 2764
ASK 23
BGA 4007
ASW 27
BGA 4980
ASW 28
BGA 4861
ASG 29
BGA 5303 5333 5335 5336 5339

SCHWEYER
RHÖNSPERBER
BGA 260

SCOTT
VIKING
BGA 416

SHENSTONE
HARBINGER
BGA 1091

SHORT
NIMBUS
BGA 470

SIEBERT
SIE 3
BGA 2642 3461

SLINGSBY SAILPLANES LTD including **YORKSHIRE SAILPLANES**
production
T.1 FALCON I
BGA 266 3166
T.6 KIRBY KITE
BGA 236 251 285 310 400
T.7 CADET
BGA 731 1143
T.8 TUTOR
BGA 485 791 794 804 833 852 858 895 904 1424 1599 1698 1745
1759 1770 IGA 6

T.12 GULL
BGA 378 902
T.13 PETREL
BGA 651
T.15 GULL III
BGA 643 3825
T.21
BGA 570 601 614 646 665 666 673 711 765 782 856 869 875 945
948 1000 1014 1081 1085 1144 1215 1218 1254 1315 1354 1482
1588 1965 2010 2024 2036 2720 2767 2900 2941 2964 2975 3148
3160 3189 3195 3221 3225 3235 3238 3240 3243 3245 3250 3255
3264 3287 3288 3290 3292 3324 3385 3423 3774 3836 3901 3903
3905 4077 4110 4135 4366 4707 4833 4856 4877 5230 EI-157
T.25 GULL IV
BGA 565
T.26 KITE 2
BGA 521 663 689 751 EI-102
T.30 PREFECT
BGA 599 625 701 815 1152 1601 2333 2380 2517 2546 2583 2692
T.31B
BGA 1346 1376 1559 3145 3149 3181 3185 3194 3229 3239 3241
3272 3293 3299 3336 3487 3545 3786 3953 4033 4228 4412 4746
4926 4963 5283 EI-139
T.34 SKY
BGA 685 686 694 698 1053 2284 4670
T.37 SKYLARK 1
BGA 725
T.38 GRASSHOPPER
BGA 3359 3480 3481 3488 3498 3979 4098 4229 4361 4372 4421
4552 4556 5074 EI-135
T.41 SKYLARK 2
BGA 724 729 733 745 759 778 793 801 802 814 822 826 845 896
899 1441 1549 2002
T.42 EAGLE
BGA 740 825 830 841 880
T.43 SKYLARK 3
BGA 735 742 761 763 806 813 823 844 864 867 870 871 916 920
922 927 929 950 957 985 988 996 1004 1013 1023 1251
T.45 SWALLOW
BGA 873 890 910 921 1003 1008 1017 1018 1061 1107 1136 1165
1167 1169 1211 1263 1319 1338 1364 1365 1398 2762 2793 3469
3823
T.49 CAPSTAN
BGA 1009 1106 1118 1131 1132 1133 1134 1135 1163 1183 1191
1196 1203 1237 1249 1360
T.50 SKYLARK 4
BGA 1019 1043 1045 1047 1050 1063 1066 1087 1088 1089 1095
1100 1102 1103 1105 1115 1117 1115 1117 1119 1121 1124 1138
1189 1193 1194 1202 1210 1220 1239 2881 3601
T.51 DART
BGA 1164 1166 1180 1181 1198 1207 1266 1268 1269 1296 1299
1317 1330 1336 1356 1361 1975
T.59 KESTREL
BGA 1514 1683 1689 1723 1744 1761 1914 1946 1949 1982 2047
T.65 VEGA
BGA 2508 2669 2670 2715 2728

STANDARD AUSTRIA see **SCHEMPP-HIRTH**

START+FLUG
H101 SALTO
BGA 4778

SWALES see **BIRMINGHAM GUILD**

SZD
SZD-8 JASKOLKA
BGA 2512
SZD-9bis BOCIAN
BGA 1078 1550 1843 1994 2734 3345
SZD-12A MUCHA
BGA 3776 3862 EI-100 EI-140
SZD-22 MUCHA STANDARD
BGA 4857 5176
SZD-24 and SZD-32 FOKA
BGA 1367 1646 3945
SZD-30 PIRAT
BGA 1470 1485 1551 1674 1709 1714 1779 1819 1832 1845 1888
1977 2031 2100 2209
SZD-36A COBRA 15
BGA 1732 1885
SZD-41A and SZD-48 JANTAR-STANDARD
BGA 5013

SZD-50-3 PUCHACZ
    BGA 3793
SZD-51-1 JUNIOR
    BGA 5168
SZD-55-1
    BGA 4230

VALENTIN see **ISF**

VOGT
LO-100 ZWERGREIHER
    BGA 2770

VTC (VAZDUHOPLOVNO TEHNICKI CENTAR) see **SCHEMPP-HIRTH**

SOCIÉTÉ DES ETABLISSMENTS BENJAMIN WASSMER
WA21 JAVELOT II
    BGA 1575
WA22 SUPER JAVELOT
    BGA 1480
WA26P SQUALE
    BGA 3923
WA30 BIJAVE
    BGA 3404

YORKSHIRE SAILPLANES see **BIRMINGHAM GUILD, SLINGSBY**

ZLIN (ZLINSKA LETECKNA AKCIOVA)
24 KRAJANEK
    BGA 655

PART 7 - AIRCRAFT TYPE INDEX (OVERSEAS)

This Index covers entries in SECTION 5, Part 1 and 2.

AERO VODOCHODY NÁRODNÍ PODNIK see **LET**
L-29 DELFIN
    YL-PAF YL-PAG

AERONCA AIRCRAFT CORPORATION
A65A CHIEF
    NC33884

AEROPRO
EUROFOX
    I-6570 I-6929

AEROPRAKT
A-20
    44ADC
A-22
    I-9266

AEROSPACELINES
377SGT SUPER GUPPY
    F-BTGV

AÉROSPATIALE including **EUROCOPTER** production and see
SUD-AVIATION
AS.350B ECUREUIL/ ASTAR
    N9FJ N214AE N350AY N350UK
AS.355 ECUREUIL 2/ TWINSTAR
    F-HOLF N766AM
EC.155 DAUPHIN
    N604FD N672LE P4-HEC
SA.365 DAUPHIN 2
    F-WQAP N365LL 5N-BET

AEROSTYLE GmbH
BREEZER
    D-MBRG

COSTRUZIONI AERONAUTICHE GIOVANNI AGUSTA SpA
A109 variants
    D-HCKV N2NR N30MD N35AG N74PM N91TH N109AG
    N109AN N109GR N109MJ N109TD N109TF N109TK N109WF
    N174ST N188S N195NJ N449J N591JM N745HA N800WK
    N877SW N7242N RP-C2900 SX-HCF S5-HPC
A119
    N65TG N119BM VH-PSR

AIRBUS INDUSTRIE
A320
    VP-CBY

AMERICAN AVIATION CORPORATION see **GRUMMAN-AMERICAN**

ANTONOV
AN-2
    HA-ANG HA-MKF LY-BIG RA-01641 YL-LEU YL-LEV YL-LEW
    YL-LEX YL-LEY YL-LEZ YL-LFA YL-LFB YL-LFC YL-LFD

AUSTER AIRCRAFT LTD
Model H AUSTER 5
    F-BBSO
B.8 AGRICOLA
    ZK-BMI ZK-CCU

AVIATIKA JOINT STOCK COMPANY
MAI-890
    YL-MIG

AVIATION TRADERS ENGINEERING LIMITED
ATL98 CARVAIR
    CF-EPV

A V ROE and CO LTD including **BAe** and **HAWKER SIDDELEY
AVIATION** design and production
652A ANSON
    VH-ASM
671 - see **CIERVA**

748
    N748D VH-AHL VH-AMQ VH-AYS ZS-ODJ

BAE SYSTEMS (OPERATIONS) LTD including **BRITISH
AEROSPACE** plc, **BRITISH AEROSPACE (REGIONAL AIRCRAFT)
Ltd, HANDLEY-PAGE** and **SCOTTISH AVIATION** production
JETSTREAM variants to Series 32
    N14234
146 including Avro variants
    N9070L N9086L

BEAGLE AIRCRAFT LTD
B.121 PUP
    HB-NAV N556MA
B.206
    N181WW

BEECH AIRCRAFT CORPORATION Including **HAWKER
BEECHCRAFTCORPORATION**
17 TRAVELER
    N17GL N18V N9405H NC18028
18/3NM, 3TM and C-45
    N663TB N96240
C23 MUSKETEER
    N6632L
B24R SIERRA 200
    D-EDEQ N39TA
33 DEBONAIR and BONANZA
    N35SN N42FW
F33A BONANZA
    N78GG N92RW N121JF N999F N2299L
A35, C35, K35, and V35B BONANZA models
    N59VT N150JC N675BW N3023W N60256
36 BONANZA
    N4VQ N36NB N36SU N364AB N536K N671B N715BC N722P
    N767CM N836TP N7205T N7251Y N8258F N24136 N36665
50 TWIN BONANZA
    N911CS
56, and 58 BARON models
    D-IBPN N27MW N28TE N55BN N55EN N58GT N58YD N64VB
    N65MJ N79AP N125AV N142TW N258RP N266EA N418WS
    N554RB N581AF N717HL N2061K N7148R N7219L N7223Y
    N23659 N60526
60 DUKE
    N60NZ N322RJ N1024L N3669D
65, 70 and 80 QUEEN AIR models
    N70AA
76 DUCHESS
    N741D N800VM
90 KING AIR
    N30FL N34RF N41AK N46BM N106ML N146FL N200RE
    N364UZ N402BL N456PP N521LB N554CF N683GW N712DB
    N816RL N1092H N9838Z
200, 300 and 350 SUPER KING AIR models
    N27HK N64GG N250TM N288GS N500CS N2341S N37172
400 BEECHJET
    N79EL N497XP N709EL N719EL

BELL HELICOPTER TEXTRON CANADA INC including **AGUSTA
BELL HELICOPTER** and **WESTLAND HELICOPTERS LTD**
    production
47 variants
    N201W N7801R OO-SHW
206A and 206B JETRANGER variants
    N56GH N64JG N89SS N206HE N206MF N208ER N784F
    N8040T OE-XBA
206L LONG RANGER
    N96HC N340AJ N707BM N720B
222
    N153H N222WX N510W N800HL N2105J
407
    N37LP N120HH N222LB N407AG N407CG N407CL N407WD
    N9133D N30562 N42527
430
    N901RL N5120 VP-BKQ
UH-1 IROQUOIS
    N116HS N454CC N911DN

BELLANCA-AIRCRAFT CORPORATION
14 CRUISEMASTER
    N7600E
17-30A
    N28141
31ATC SUPER VIKING
    N8862V

BOEING AIRCRAFT CO including **BOEING COMPANY**
B-17G FORTRESS
    F-BDRS N5237V
247
    N18E
707
    N707QJ VP-BDF
727-100 series
    OO-DHN OO-DHR P4-MMG
727-200 series
    EC-CFA EC-DDX TC-ALM
737-200 series
    C-GWJO TF-ELL
737-700 series
    VP-BBW VP-BNZ VP-BWR
737-800 series
    N737M
747-100 series
    N852FT
747-200 series
    N218BA SX-OAD
747SP
    VP-BAT

BOEING AIRPLANE CO
STEARMAN 75 KAYDET, N2S, PT-13, PT-17: variants
    CF-EQS N75TQ N707TJ N731 N1325M N1731B N3922B
    N4596N N4712V N5057V N10053 N38940 N52485 N54922
    N62842 N63590 N65200 N65565 N68427 N74189 SE-BOG
    XB-RIY

BÖLKOW APPARATEBAU GmbH including **MALMO** and **MBB**
production
BÖ.102 HELITRAINER
    D-HMQV
BÖ.105
    D-HZYR LQ-BLT
BÖ.207
    D-EBLI D-EBLO D-EFQE D-EFTI D-EHKY D-EHLA D-EHOP
    D-EHUQ D-EHYX D-EJBI
BÖ.208 JUNIOR
    D-EAMB D-ECGI D-EDNA D-EEAH F-BRHN
BÖ.209 MONSUN
    D-EAAW D-EFJG D-EGHW

BOMBARDIER INC see also **LEAR**
CANADAIR CL-600 CHALLENGER variants
    HZ-SJP3 N800BN OE-IFB VP-CAP VP-CEO VP-CFT VP-CHH
    VP-CHU VP-CIC VP-CJA VP-COP
CANADAIR CRJ 200 REGIONAL JET
    OE-LRE VP-BCC
BD-100 CHALLENGER 300
    N184BK VP-CLV
BD-700 GLOBAL variants
    N171JJ OY-ILG VP-BAM VP-BOW VP-CEB VP-CGS VP-CVU
    VP-CVV

BRANTLY HELICOPTER CORPORATION
B.2
    N19GL N276SA

BRDITSCHKA
HB-21
    LN-GDA

BRIGHTON MA AND COMPANY LTD
Balloon (Hot Air)
MAB-65
    HB-BOU

BRISTOL AEROPLANE CO LTD
SCOUT D replica
    N5419
175 BRITANNIA
    EL-WXA

BRITISH AIRCRAFT CORPORATION (BAC)
ONE-ELEVEN
    VR-BEB 5N-HHH
BAC167 STRIKEMASTER
    N21419

BRITTEN-NORMAN LTD
BN 2 ISLANDER
    N121MT N2536Y

BROCK MANUFACTURING
KB2 GYROCOPTER
    PH-TWR

BÜCKER
Bü.133 JUNGMEISTER
    OO-EII

CAMERON BALLOONS LTD see **CAMERON-COLT** and
CAMERON-THUNDER
Airship (Hot Air)
Zero 25
    OO-JAT
Balloon (Hot Air)
77 variants
    C-GYZI
84 series
    N413JB
140 variants
    5Y-SIL

CESSNA AIRCRAFT COMPANY including **REIMS AVIATION SA**
Production (F.prefix)
C.34 AIRMASTER
    NC16403
140
    N76402
150
    N105SK N3084F N3109X N4337K N6819F N7263S N11824
A150 AEROBAT
    N7374A OO-WIO
152
    N4770B N4779B N47351
170
    D-EEVY N170AZ N2366D N5428C
172 SKYHAWK
    D-EAGC D-EFZO F-GLTR N75TC N104PF N172AM N226CA
    N259SA N355GW N525DB N937DR N1554E N5043X N6182G
    N9680Q N13253 N19753 N20981 N21927 N50029 N75822
    N80533 OY-DRS OY-EGZ
172RG CUTLASS
    N1937Z
R172K HAWK XP
    D-EBXR N78XP PH-PIM
REIMS FR172 ROCKET variants
    D-EKJD D-EMZC HB-CIU N53SB
175A SKYLARK
    N6907E
177(RG) CARDINAL
    N177SA N278SA N442BJ N707XJ N8225Y N53103
180 and SKYWAGON
    N180BB N180FN N36362 N71763 PH-KRC
182 SKYLANE
    D-EJLY N14MT N22NN N25XZ N90DJ N182GC N277DS
    N369AN N382AS N656JM N681EW N735CX N883DP N888MY
    N1320S N1329T N1424C N1745M N2231F N2379C N2445V
    N2454Y N4102D N5020A N6078T
190 and 195 models
    N999MH N1551D
206 SUPER SKYLANE, SUPER SKYWAGON and STATIONAIR
    models
    N191ME N206CF N566N
208 and 208B (GRAND) CARAVAN I
    D-FBPS D-FLOH N208B N308CJ
210 CENTURION
    D-EEHW N23KY N210AD N210CP N210EU N210NM N249SP
    N277CD N646CD N761JU N1778X N6593W N9533Y N30593
T303 CRUSADER
    N11FV N154DJ N289CW N889VF N6498V N9870C
305 BIRD DOG (L-19)
    N134TT N33600
310
    N31GN N147RJ N310QQ N310WT N438DD N747YK N789MC

N850KF N1757H
320 SKYKNIGHT
   N4173T
337 SUPER SKYMASTER
   N19F N80N N337UK N2216X N456TL SE-LTE
340
   N3HK N27BG N63EN N66SW N85LB N340DW N340GJ
   N340SC N340YP N666VK N958MD N1711G N8702K
401
   N401JN N9146N
414
   N44NE N414AK N414FZ
421 GOLDEN EAGLE variants
   N1FY N9AY N26HE N37VB N60GM N64LA N75FW N96JL
   N132CK N202AA N421CA N421DD N421EA N900CB N37379
   N41098 N80056
425 CORSAIR and 425 CONQUEST II
   N90YA N425DR N425SL N577PA N1262K
441 CONQUEST II
   N22CG N184VB
500 and 501 CITATION 1
   N324JC N527EW N694LM N750PP N999AM N80364 VP-COM
510 CITATION MUSTANG
   N80HQ N814WS
525 CITATIONJET
   N198JH N224CJ N242ML N380CR N498YY N511TC N524SF
   N665CH VP-CJI
525A CITATIONJET 2
   N120CS N250BL N309CJ N525DT N525PM N569DM
525B CITATIONJET 3
   N27UB N80HB N100JS
550, S550 CITATION BRAVO and 551 CITATION II models
   N46PJ N48NS N60LW N127BU N145DF N365WA N550LD
   N7070A VP-CED YU-FCS
560 CITATION ULTRA and ENCORE
   N535CE
560XL CITATION EXCEL
   N188WS N560TH N575NR
650 CITATION III and CITATION VI
   N373DJ N606AT
750 CITATION X
   N750GF N750NS

CFM METAL-FAX
SHADOW
   OO-A95

CGS
HAWK
   N216HK

CHAMPION AIRCRAFT CORPORATION see also **BELLANCA**
CITABRIA,SKYTRAC
   N51ER N94SA

CHAYAIR MANUFACTURING AND AVIATION (PTY) LTD
SYCAMORE
   ZU-DCX

CHRISTEN INDUSTRIES INC including **AVIAT** and see **PITTS**
A-1 and A-1B HUSKY vriants
   N49BH N78HB N8754J SE-KBU

CIERVA
C.30A (AVRO 671)
   SE-AZB

CIRRUS DESIGN CORPORATION
SR20
   N100YY N131CD N139PG N147CD N164SR N196PG N203CD
   N262BM N369AL N470RD N781CD N840CD N994SR N5336Z
   N8159Q
SR22
   N9SZ N10MC N12SJ N17UK N40GD N69DP N80NS N89GH
   N95GT N108SR N112SR N122MG N123DV N124CP N141HT
   N147GT N147KA N147LD N147LK N147VC N150ZZ N151CG
   N160SR N192SR N199ZZ N219DW N219PM N220RJ N221CH
   N221LD N222ED N222SW N224RC N286MD N327BM N352CD
   N376SR N434A N482CD N521CD N542CD N573VE N593CD
   N663CD N663KK N719CD N722DR N730WF N741CD N753TW
   N771SR N790BH N799CD N808RW N820CD N821CC N834CD
   N843SR N852CD N866C N900UK N902SR N916CD N922CE
   N970SR N982CD N986SR N1569C N5084V N54105

COLT BALLOONS LTD including **CAMERON BALLOONS LTD**,
THUNDER and **COLT LTD BALLOONS** production and see
COLTING BALLOONS
Balloon (Hot Air)
77 variants
   OY-BOW
90 series
   D-Pamgas

COMMANDER AIRCRAFT COMPANY see **ROCKWELL**

CONSOLIDATED VULTEE AIRCRAFT see **STINSON AIRCRAFT
CORPORATION**
BT-15 VALIANT
   N58566
PBY CATALINA
   N423RS VP-BPS

CURTISS-WRIGHT CORPORATION
P-40N WARHAWK
   N9950

CZECH AIRCRAFT WORKS (CZAW)
SPORTCRUISER
   PH-IRL

DALLACH
FASCINATION D4 BK
   PH-3P3

AVIONS MARCEL DASSAULT
FALCON 7X
   N999BE VP-BZE
FALCON 20 and 200 models
   N357PS 9M-BCR
FALCON 50
   N200UP N950H VP-BMP
FALCON 900 and 900EX models
   HZ-OFC5 LX-FTA N239AX N790JC N987AL
FALCON 2000 and 2000EX models
   N377GM VP-BDL

DE HAVILLAND AIRCRAFT LTD
DH.80A PUSS MOTH
   VH-UQB
DH.82A TIGER MOTH
   F-BGEQ
DH.84 DRAGON
   VH-SNB
DH.104 DOVE
   D-IFSB VP-YKF
DH.106 COMET
   F-BGNX
DH.125 see **HAWKER SIDDELEY**

DE HAVILLAND (AUSTRALIA)
DHA-3 DROVER
   VH-FDT

DE HAVILLAND (CANADA) including **BOMBARDIER INC** and
OGMA production
DHC-1 CHIPMUNK
   N458BG
DHC-2 BEAVER
   OY-JRR
DHC-3 OTTER
   VP-FAK

DIAMOND AIRCRAFT INDUSTRIES GmbH
DA.20 KATANA
   N696DA
DA.40(D) STAR
   N39SE N752DS OE-KKC
DA.42 TWIN STAR
   N35AL OE-FYA OE-FYB

DORNIER
DO.27
   D-ECOX
DO.28 SKYSERVANT
   HA-ACO HA-VOC

228
D-CALM

DOUGLAS AIRCRAFT COMPANY INC
A-26 INVADER
N4806E
DC-3, C-47 DAKOTA and SKYTRAIN variants
N147DC N347DK N473DC N1944A N4565L N9050T ZS-MRU
6W-SAF
DC-4
N31356 N44914
DC-8
9G-MKA 9G-MKH

DYN'AÉRO SA
MCR-01
F-PURU

ECLIPSE AVIATION CORPORATION
ECLIPSE 500
N100VA N117EA N382EA N500UK N2711H

ELA AVIACIÓN S.L
ELA 07
EC-EP6

EMBRAER
110 BANDEIRANTE
N97121 SX-BNL
EMB135BJ LEGACY
VP-BVS

ENGLISH ELECTRIC CO LTD (AVRO production)
CANBERRA
N2138J

ENSTROM HELICOPTER CORPORATION
480
N480BB N480DD N480JB N480KP N480LR N480PP

ERCO including **ALON** and **FORNEY** production
ERCOUPE 415
N3188H N6620W N93938

EUROCOPTER see also **AÉROSPATIALE**
EC.120 COLIBRI
N526AG
EC.130 ECUREUIL
ZK-IGM

EXTRA FLUGZEUGBAU GmbH
EA.300
D-ETTO N7EX
EA.400
D-ELRN N400YY

FAIRCHILD ENGINE and AIRPLANE
24 ARGUS
NC1328 N16676
CORNELL
N33870 N49272
C-119
N2700

FAIREY AVIATION CO LTD
FIREFLY
SE-BRG

FARMAN
F.40
F-HMFI

FARNBOROUGH AIRCRAFT CORPORATION LTD
F1C3 KESTREL
N352F

FARRINGTON AIRCRAFT CORP
TWINSTARR GYROCOPTER
N96XW

FOKKER BV
F.27 FRIENDSHIP
TC-MBG

F.27-050 (FOKKER 50)
LN-KKA
F.28-010 (FOKKER 100)
N897US

AVIONS FOURNIER
RF-3
D-KMDP

GENERAL AIRCRAFT LTD
MONOSPAR ST.12
VH-UTH

GLASFLÜGEL ING EUGEN HANLE
H303 MOSQUITO
SX-122

GOVERNMENT AIRCRAFT FACTORY
N22 NOMAD
N6302W

GRUMMAN AIRCRAFT ENGINEERING
G.21 GOOSE
N4575C
TBM-3 AVENGER
CF-KCG

**GRUMMAN AMERICAN AVIATION CORPORATION (1),
AMERICAN GENERAL AVIATION (2)** and **GULFSTREAM
AMERICAN CORPORATION (3)** production
GRUMMAN AA-5 TRAVELLER (1)
D-EFDL
GRUMMAN AA-5A CHEETAH (1)
N674BW OO-GCO
GRUMMAN AA-5B TIGER (1)
D-EGDC D-ENTO F-GKGN
GULFSTREAM AA-5B TIGER (3)
N31RB N666GA N2121T
AMERICAN GENERAL AG-5B TIGER (2)
N136SA

GULFSTREAM AEROSPACE CORPORATION
G1159 GULFSTREAM II
5N-BGV
GULFSTREAM IV and V variants
HZ-ARK N841WS VP-BBX VP-BGN VP-BJK VP-BKI VP-BKZ
VP-BLA VP-BLW VP-BNL VP-BNO VP-BTC VP-BUS VP-CBX
VP-CFB VP-CGN VP-CLA VP-CMR VP-CSF

HAWKER AIRCRAFT LTD
TEMPEST
N7027E
SEA FURY
D-CATA

HAWKER SIDDELEY AVIATION including **BAe, CORPORATE JETS
LTD, DE HAVILLAND** and **RAYTHEON-HAWKER** production
HS.125
N125XP N228TM N249SR N800UK N5736 VP-BKK VP-BNK
VP-BOO VP-CFS VP-COD VP-COK VP-CSP VP-CXP VT-UBG
5N-AAN

HILLER HELICOPTERS INC
UH-12 (360)
N21UH N57CR N212W N780ND N831M N5025J N5315V
N5317V N33514 N38763 N62171

HOWARD
500
N500LN

HUGHES TOOL CO and **HUGHES HELICOPTERS INC** including
SCHWEIZER AIRCRAFT CORPORATION (269 wef 1986) and
McDONNELL- DOUGLAS (369 wef 1983) production
269
N994K N8990F N17596
369
N59SD N239MY N259BK N322MC N369HL N500RK N500SY
N500TY N500XV N696XX N2742Y N5106Y N5264Q N7172Z
N9057F OY-HGB

IMPULSE AIRCRAFT
IMPULSE
    D-MDMM

JODEL including **CEA, SAN** and **WASSMER** production and see
ROBIN
DR.250/160
    D-EIAR
DR253
    D-EHAY
DR.300/120
    F-BSPQ
DR.360
    F-BROC

JORA spol sro
JORA
    OK-DUA 14

KAMOV COMPANY
Ka.26
    D-HOAY DDR-SPY

KAVANAGH BALLOONS PTY LIMITED
Balloon (Hot Air)
D-77
    VH-AYY

LEIGHTFLUGZEUGBAU KLEMM GMBH - see **BA**
KL.35
    D-EQXD

LAKE AIRCRAFT CORPORATION INC
LA-4 BUCCANEER
    C-FQIP

LEARJET INC including **BOMBARDIER AEROSPACE** production
LEARJET Model 25
    N121EL N309LJ
LEARJET Model 31
    N2FU
LEARJET Model 40
    N40XR
LEARJET Model 45
    N66DN N66SG N708SP
LEARJET Model 60
    N69LJ VP-BBZ VP-CRB

LET NARODNI PODNIK KUNOVICE
L-410 TURBOLET
    HA-LAQ HA-YFC

LIBERTY AEROSPACE INC
XL-2
    N19ET N518XL

LOCKHEED AIRCRAFT CORPORATION including **LOCKHEED-CALIFORNIA CO** and **CANADAIR** production
10 ELECTRA
    NC5171N
L.188 ELECTRA
    N2RK N4HG
L.749 CONSTELLATION
    N7777G
L.1011 TRISTAR
    TF-ABP
JETSTAR
    N6NE
T-33A
    N36TH

LUSCOMBE AIRPLANE CORPORATION
8 SILVAIRE
    N1604K

McDONNELL DOUGLAS CORPORATION
MD-80
    LV-WTY

McDONNELL DOUGLAS HELICOPTER CO see **HUGHES** and
MD HELICOPTERS

AVIONS MAX HOLSTE
MH.1521 BROUSSARD
    F-BXCP

MAULE AIRCRAFT CORPORATION
M-4
    N9861M
M-5 LUNAR ROCKET
    N346X N775RG N5632R N5647S N56643
M-6 SUPER ROCKET
    N6130X N56462
M(XT)-7 SUPER, STAR ROCKET and STARCRAFT models
    N14HF N280SA N535TK N882JH N1027G

MD HELICOPTERS INC
MD.520N
    N18GH
MD.600N
    N70457
MD.900
    N555WA N902JW N903LF N90011

MIL
Mil-2
    SP-SAY YL-LHN YL-LHO

MILES AIRCRAFT LTD
M.25 MARTINET
    TF-SHC

MITSUBISHI
MU-2
    N33EW N80JN N973BB

MOONEY AIRCRAFT CORPORATION
M.20 and M.252 variants
    D-EANS D-EKUR HB-DFT N12ZX N20UK N40AU N61MF
    N101UK N123UK N192JM N201YK N278DB N305RD N305SE
    N321KL N667DL N900RK N937BP N4305H N7423V N9305M
    N97821 OY-DFD

MORANE-SAULNIER including **GEMS, MORANE, SEEMS** and
SOCATA production
MS.880, MS.885, MS.887, MS.892 and MS.894 variants
    F-BRIC F-GFGH OO-NAT PH-ZZY

AVIONS MUDRY AND CIE including **AKROTECH EUROPE** and
CONSTRUCTIONS AÉRONAUTIQUES DE BOURGOGNE
CAP.10
    N73AE N80MC N503DW N4238C
CAP.222, CAP.231 and CAP.232 variants
    F-GKMZ F-GOTC F-GXDB

NARDI
FN.305
    I-TOMI

NEICO
LANCAIR 360
    N250JF PH-PAB
LANCAIR COLUMBIA variants
    N79HR N209DW N350DG N400HF N400UK N1376C N1417W
    N4446

NOORDUYN AVIATION LTD see **NORTH AMERICAN**

NORD
1002 PINGOUIN
    LV-RIE
1203 NORECRIN
    OO-AJK

NORTH AMERICAN AVIATION INC and including **CAC, CCF,
NOORDUYN AVIATION LTD** and **NORTH AMERICAN ROCKWELL**
production
B-25 MITCHELL
    N7614C N9089Z N9115Z N25644
F-86 SABRE
    N196B
P-51 MUSTANG
    N51RT NX251RJ N6526D
AT-16 HARVARD
    LN-AMY LN-BNM

T-28 TROJAN
  N14113 N99153

JOSEF OBERLERCHNER HOLZINDUSTRIE
JOB 15
  D-ECFE

OMEGA BALLOONS
Balloon (Hot Air)
80
  OY-BOB

PACIFIC AEROSPACE CORPORATION
PAC 750
  ZK-JQK ZK-KAY

PARTENAVIA COSTRUZIONI AERONAUTICHE SpA
P.68
  N98AG

PEGASUS AVIATION
QUANTUM
  I-6943

PERCIVAL AIRCRAFT CO LTD
P.66 PEMBROKE
  N46EA

PIAGGIO AERO INDUSTRIES including **FOCKE WULF** production
P.149
  D-EGEC D-EHJL D-EOAJ OO-MEL

PIASECKI HELICOPTER CORPORATION
HUP-3 RETRIEVER
  N6699D

PICCARD BALLOONS
Balloon (Hot Air)
  OO-BFH

PILATUS AIRCRAFT LTD
PC.6 PORTER
  F-GODZ ZK-PCI
PC.12
  N12AG N234RG VP-BLS

PIPER AIRCRAFT CORPORATION including **TAYLOR AIRCRAFT
CO LTD** *and **THE NEW PIPER AIRCRAFT INC** production
J-2 CUB *
  OY-FAA
J-3C CUB (L-4 and O-59 versions)
  F-BMHM HB-OBP N61787
J-5A CUB CRUISER
  N203SA
PA-15 VAGABOND
  NC4531H
PA-16 CLIPPER
  N5240H N5730H N5900H
PA-18 SUPER CUB variants
  I-EIXM N123SA N652P N662KK N4085E N7238X N45458
  N45507
PA-22-108 COLT
  D-EGEU N209SA N243SA
PA-22 TRI-PACER
  N2652P N6830B
PA-23 APACHE variants,
  N2086P PH-NLK
PA-23-250 AZTEC variants
  N37LW N171WM N250BW N250TB N370SA N485ED N747WW
  N818MJ N989Y N2401Z N4422P N6601Y N54211 N70844
PA-24 COMANCHE variants
  N25KB N84VK N218SA N250CC N500AV N673SA N5052P
  N5839P N7348P N7456P N7832P N8829P N9381P N26634
  N61970 SE-IIV
PA-28-140 CHEROKEE (CRUISER)
  HB-OLP N277SA N519MC N6602Y 9J-RBC
PA-28-161 (CHEROKEE) WARRIOR
  N123DU N161FF N2929W N5915V N8241Z
PA-28-180 CHEROKEE
  N180LK SE-EOS
PA-28-181 (CHEROKEE) ARCHER
  D-EAOB D-EDFD N65JF N73GR N411BC N499MS N661KK
  N2273Q N2405Y N4514X N75048

PA-28-235 CHEROKEE
  D-EBWE N235PF
PA-28-236 DAKOTA
  N6339U N81188 OO-MHB
PA-28R (CHEROKEE) ARROW variants
  D-EAWW D-EGVA N171JB N187SA N200GK N216GC N747MM
  N808VT N9325N N38273 N47494
PA-28RT ARROW variants
  D-EKHW N2CL N66MS N691J N799JH N2136E N2943D
  N8105Z N8153E N8412B N29566 N84718
PA-30 TWIN COMANCHE - also see PA-39
  D-GPEZ N7EY N8MZ N25PR N30NW N35AD N41FT N65PF
  N230MJ N359DW N499AG N818Y N888DM N918Y N7976Y
  N8523Y
PA-31 NAVAJO (CHIEFTAIN) variants
  N5LL N95TA N189SA N250AC N250MD N350PB N449TA
  N642P N666AW N3586D OY-BTZ OY-CKR ST-AHZ SX-BFM
PA-31T CHEYENNE
  F-GPBF N58AM
PA-32 CHEROKEE SIX variants
  D-EDEL N61DE N99XT N112WM N129SC N132LE N257SA
  N562RR N2923N N2967N N2989M N3400W N5277T
PA-32R-300 (CHEROKEE) LANCE
  N101DW N6954J N7640F N38945
PA-32R-301 SARATOGA variants
  N32LE N48CA N51AH N67SP N77YY N88NA N123AX N446SE
  N515SC N551TT N808CA N957T N987LV N4178W N9123X
  N30614 N31008
PA-32RT LANCE
  N646JR
PA-34 SENECA variants
  D-GACR N37US N43GG N61HB N81AW N95D N145DR
  N199PS N245CB N375SA N559C N4168D N6920B N21381
  N32625 N39605
PA-38 TOMAHAWK
  D-EGLW F-GCTU N24730 PH-TMH SE-GVH
PA-39 TWIN COMANCHE C/R - also see PA-30
  N320MR N613F N971RJ N4297A N8911Y
PA-44-180 SEMINOLE
  N440GC
PA-46 MALIBU variants
  N45PJ N46PL N46WK N71WZ N186CB N338DB N343RR
  N352CM N403HP N866LP N930Z N955SH N1125Y N9122N
  N9275Y N10522 N53597 N92562
PA-60-601P AEROSTAR 601 (**TED SMITH** production)
  N69LP N70VB N711TL

PITTS
S-1
  N80BA N85WS N666BM N697RB N49337
S-2
  N61PS N74DC N414MB N531RM N80035

POLIKARPOV
PO-2
  N588NB

AVIONS POTEZ
840
  F-BMCY

POWER ASSIST
SWIFT
  95MR

PROGRESSOR
POU GYRO
F-WUTH

PZL WARSZAWA-OKECIE SA
PZL-101 GAWRON
SP-CHD
PZL-104 WILGA
  HA-SEU
PZL-110 KOLIBER
  D-EIVF

RAVEN INDUSTRIES
Balloon (Hot Air)
S.40
  N1196R
S.50
  N12006

RAYTHEON HAWKER see **HAWKER SIDDELEY AVIATION**
RB390 PREMIER
    N72GD N800FR N814BP
HAWKER 4000
    N126ZZ

REMOS
GX
    D-MPGB

REPUBLIC AVIATION CORPORATION
P-47 THUNDERBOLT
    N47DD

AVIONS PIERRE ROBIN including **CONSTRUCTIONS AÉRONAUTIQUES DE BOURGOGNE**
DR.400 and DR..500 variants
    D-EAPF D-EIKR D-ELSR D-ENBW F-GOXD
HR.100
    CS-ARI F-BTKO F-GMHH
HR.200
    F-GAOE
ATL
    F-GFOR F-GGHH F-GJQI F-GXHD

ROBINSON HELICOPTER CO INC
R.44 RAVEN I, II
    N13DT N393N N441GS N999RL PH-HEW PH-WRF

ROCKWELL INTERNATIONAL CORPORATION including **GULFSTREAM** and **COMMANDER AIRCRAFT COMPANY (114)** production
500, 680, 685 and 690 COMMANDER variants
    N51WF N60BM N71VE N690CL N840PN N840TC N980HB
    N3596T N91384 N95590 VP-BCT VP-BMZ
COMMANDER 112 and 114
    D-EWAT N14AF N50AY N112JA N114ED N115MD N115TB
    N395TC N411DP N928HW N1350J N1407J N4599W N4698W
    N5834N N6010Y N6024V N6039X N6048B N6081F N6088F
    N6088Z N6095A ZS-MBI
SABRE 65
    VP-CBG

ROTORWAY HELICOPTERS INTERNATIONAL
SCORPION
    SE-HXF
EXECUTIVE
    N100LH

RUSCHMEYER LUFTFAHRTTECHNIK GmbH
RUSHMEYER R90
    D-EFFA N12AB

RUTAN
LONG EZ
    N742TJ

RYAN AERONAUTICAL CORPORATION
ST3KR, PT-22
    N1344 N56421
NAVION
    D-ECDL NC285RS N2548T N3864

SCHEIBE-FLUGZEUGBAU GmbH
SFS-31 MILAN
    D-KIFF
SF-25 FALKE (inc SLINGSBY T.61)
    SE-UCF

SCHEMPP-HIRTH FLUGZEUBAU GmbH
CIRRUS
    D-2782
DISCUS
    ZK-GIL
NIMBUS
    D-KIOJ

ALEXANDER SCHLEICHER GmbH and CO
K.8B
    D-1155
ASW 28
    D-9004

SCHROEDER FIRE BALLOONS
Balloon (Hot Air)
3000
    D-Opha

SCHWEIZER AIRCRAFT CORPORATION
TG-3
    N66630

SHORT BROTHERS LTD
S.16 SCION
    VH-UUP
S.24 SANDRINGHAM
    VH-BRC
SD.3-30
    OY-MUB

SIAI-MARCHETTI SpA
S.205/208
    D-EFZC
SF.260
    N61FD N260AP

SIKORSKY AIRCRAFT see **WESTLAND**
S-76
    N70QJ N76AF VP-BNI VP-BNM VP-CBD
S-92
    N908W

SOCATA see **MORANE-SAULNIER**
TB-9 TAMPICO and TB-10 TOBAGO
    F-GJPB F-GLAO I-IAFS N99ET N770RM
TB-20, TB-21 TRINIDAD and TB-200 TOBAGO GT/XL
    N1FD N20AG N33NW N34FA N91ME N97GP N113AC N297GT
    N345TB N575GM N709AM
TBM-700 and TBM-850
    N181PC N223JG N228CX N257JM N262J N324JS N463RD
    N582C N700AZ N700EL N700GY N700KV N700S N700VA
    N700VB N702MB N850LH N851WA N868AT N997JM

SOKO
G-2 GALEB
    YU-YAB

SPARTAN
7W EXECUTIVE
    NC17633

STEARMAN see **BOEING-STEARMAN**

STINSON AIRCRAFT CORPORATION
JUNIOR R
    NC2612
L-5 SENTINEL
    N6438C N57783

STODDARD-HAMILTON
GLASAIR
    PH-DUC

SUD-AVIATION and including **AÉROSPATIALE, SOKO** and **WESTLAND HELICOPTERS** production
SE.313 and SE318 ALOUETTE II
    F-GXFP HA-IDL HA-LFZ HA-PPC N297CJ
SA.315 LAMA
    F-BPFP
SA.321 SUPER FRELON
    F-BTRP
SA.330 PUMA
    9L-LSA 9L-LSG
SA.341 and SA.342 GAZELLE
    F-GIBU HA-LFB HA-LFH HA-LFM HA-LFQ HA-PPY N505HA
    N565F N58283 YU-HDL YU-HEH YU-HEI YU-HES YU-HET
    YU-HEV YU-HEY YU-MAN YU-PJB

SUKHOI
Su-26
    RA3350K
Su-29
    HA-HUD HA-YAO HA-YAR HA-YAW N88SU

SUPER MARINE AIRCRAFT (PTY)
SPITFIRE Mk26
　　VH-IJH

COSTRUZIONI AERONAUTICHE TECNAM Srl
P.2002 SIERRA
　　D-ETRE

SCF TECHNOAVIA
SMG-92 FINIST
　　HA-NAH HA-YDF

THUNDER BALLOONS LTD including **THUNDER and COLT LTD**
Balloon (Hot Air)
Ax7 series
　　N4990T OO-BRM
Ax10 series
　　DQ-PBF

TL ULTRALIGHT Sro
TL-2000 STING
　　OK-IUA 69

URBAN AIR
UFM-10 SAMBA
　　OK-GUA 16 OK-GUA 28 OK-JUA 03 OK-KUA 16 OK-KUA 26
　　OK-LUA 36 OK-MUA 78 OK-NUA 18 OK-NUA 19
UFM-11/13 LAMBADA
　　OK-DUU 15 OK-FUA 05

UTVA AIRCRAFT FACTORY
UTVA 56
　　YU-DLG

VAN'S AIRCRAFT INC
RV-8
　　PH-PWA

VELOCITY INC
VELOCITY
　　N173RG

VFW-FOKKER GmbH
VFW-614
　　D-ASDB

VICKERS
VIMY FB-27
　　NX71MY
700 series VISCOUNT
　　F-BGNR

(SUPER) VC-10
　　A40-AB

VICKERS SUPERMARINE Ltd
228 SEAGULL
　　VH-ALB
304 STRANRAER
　　CF-BXO
361 SPITFIRE
　　N41702

WACO AIRCRAFT CORPORATION
YMF
　　N999PD

SOCIÉTÉ WASSMER
WA.52 EUROPA
　　D-EFVS
WA.54 ATLANTIC
　　D-EEPI
WA.81 PIRANA
　　F-GAIF

WESTLAND HELICOPTERS LTD see also **SIKORSKY**
WESTLAND-SIKORSKY S-55 WHIRLWIND
　　VR-BEP VR-BEU
WESTLAND-SIKORSKY S-58 WESSEX
　　9G-BOB
WG.30
　　N112WG N114WG N116WG N118WG N5820T N5840T N5880T
　　VT-EKE VT-EKK VT-EKL VT-EKM VT-EKT VT-EKW VT-EKX

YAKOVLEV including **ACROSTAR, IAV-BACHAU, LET,**
NANCHANG, SPP and **WSK** production
Yak-12
　　HA-HUB
Yak-18T
　　HA-CBG HA-HUA HA-HUE HA-JAB HA-SMD HA-YAB HA-YAD
　　HA-YAE HA-YAF HA-YAG HA-YAJ HA-YAK HA-YAM HA-YAN
　　HA-YAP HA-YAU HA-YAV HA-YAZ LY-CCP
Yak-52
　　FLARF01035 RA-01378
Yak-55
　　RA-01274

ZENAIR
ZENITH 100
　　F-PYOY
CH-600 ZODIAC variants
　　PH-3W6

PART 8 – AIRCRAFT TYPE INDEX (IRELAND)

This Index covers entries in SECTION 2, Part 1 and SECTION 4

AERONCA AIRCRAFT CORPORATION
7AC CHAMPION
  EI-ATL AVB BJC DDD
7DC CHAMPION
  EI-BJB
11AC CHIEF
  EI-CCF CRR
15AC SEDAN
  EI-BJJ BKC

AÉROSPATIALE including EUROCOPTER production
AS.350B ECUREUIL models
  EI-FAC IRV PJD
AS.365N and SA.365 DAUPHIN 2 models
  EI-DUF GJL MIP

AÉROSPATIALE-ALENIA
ATR-42
  EI-BYO CBK CPT CVR FXA FXB FXC FXD FXE FXH FXI FXJ
  FXK SLA SLC
ATR-72
  EI-FXG REA REB REH REI REJ REL REM REO REP RER RES
  RET REU REW SLF SLG SLH

AERO COMPOSITES
SEA HAWKER
  EI-BUO

COSTRUZIONI AERONAUTICHE GIOVANNI AGUSTA SpA
A109 variants
  EI-ECA HHH JFC LMK MCP MEL MEN MIT MSG NBG SQG
  TWO
AW 139
  EI-MLY

AIR and SPACE
18A
  EI-CNG

AIRBORNE WINDSPORTS
EDGE XT
  EI-EAK EAW

AIRBUS SAS including AIRBUS INDUSTRIE
A300
  EI-OZB
A319
  EI-DEY DEZ DFA DFP DVD DVU ECY EDM
A320
  EI-CUM CVA CVB CVC CVD DEA DEB DEC DEE DEF DEG
  DEH DEI DEJ DEK DEL DEM DEN DEO DEP DER DES
  DET DFO DIR DJH DNP DOD DOE DOP DOZ DSA DSB DSC
  DSD DSE DSF DSG DSH DSI DSJ DSK DSL DSM DSN DSO
  DSP DSR DSS DST DSV DSW DSX DSY DSZ DTA DTB DTC
  DTD DTE DTF DTG DTH DTI DTJ DTK DTL DTM DTN DTO
  DTP DVB DVE DVF DVG DVH DVI DXY DZR EDD EDS TAB
  TAD TAF TAG
A321
  EI-CPC CPD CPE CPF CPG CPH LVA LVB LVD
A330
  EI-CRK DAA DUB DUO DUZ EWR JFK LAX ORD

AIR CRÉATION
KISS 400
  EI-DBO DFX DIB DKE DKU
IXESS (TANARG) 912
  EI-DRT

ALPI AVIATION SRL
PIONEER 300 (HAWK)
  EI-DUL

AMF MICROFLIGHT LTD
CHEVVRON
  EI-BVJ

ATEC
2000 ZEPHYR
  EI-CZA DGS DGV

AUSTER AIRCRAFT LTD
V J/1 AUTOCRAT
  EI-ACY AGJ AMK AUM
J/1N ALPHA
  EI-AMY
V J/4
  EI-CPN
J/5F AIGLET TRAINER
  EI-AUS

AVIAMILANO SRL
F.8L FALCO including LAVERDA variant
  EI-BCJ BMF

AVID AIRCRAFT INC
AVID FLYER
  EI-CIM HAM

A V ROE and CO LTD
643 CADET
  EI-ALP ALU
748
  EI-BSF

BAE SYSTEMS (OPERATIONS) LTD
146 including Avro variants
  EI-CNQ CPL DEW DEX RJA RJB RJC RJD RJE RJF RJG RJH
  RJI RJK RJL RJM RJN RJO RJP RJR RJS RJU RJV RJW RJX
  RJY RJZ WXA WXB

BARNETT ROTORCRAFT
BARNETT J4B-2
  EI-DVO

BEAGLE AIRCRAFT LTD
A.109 AIREDALE
  (EI-AYL) (EI-BBK)
B.121 PUP
  EI-ATJ

BEAGLE-AUSTER AIRCRAFT LTD
A.61 TERRIER
  EI-ASU

BEDE AVIATION
BD-5G
  EI-DNN DNO

BEECH AIRCRAFT CORPORATION
23 MUSKETEER
  EI-BFF
B55 BARON
  EI-DUV
76 DUCHESS
  EI-BUN
77 SKIPPER
  EI-BHT

BELL HELICOPTER TEXTRON INC including AGUSTA BELL HELICOPTER CO,
206A and 206B JETRANGER variants
  EI-BHI BIJ BYJ CAW CUS DKM DUT GHT HER HXM JAC LAF
  MER ODD PCI PKS PMI PRI RMC
206L LONG RANGER
  EI-BYR
222
  EI-DZN MED ZZZ
407
  EI-GAN RHM SNJ STR TOM
430
  EI-TIP WAV

BELLANCA AIRCRAFT CORPORATION
8KCAB SUPER DECATHLON
  EI-BIV

BENSEN AIRCRAFT CORPORATION including **MONTGOMERIE**
variants
B.8 GYROCOPTER
    EI-BCF BSG DDR DNL
MERLIN
    EI-DDO

BEST OFF
SKYRANGER
    EI-DMB WIG

BOEING AIRCRAFT CO including **THE BOEING COMPANY**
737-300 series
    EI-CBQ CHH CLW CLZ CSU CXN CXR DJK DJR DJS DMM
    DMN DNH DNS DNT DNX DNY DNZ DOH DOM DON DOO
    DOU DTY DUS DVA DVC DVY DXB DXO DZU
737-400 series
    EI-CNF COH COI COJ COK CUA CUD CUN CWE CWF CWW
    CWX CXI CXK CZK DDK DDY DFD DGM DNM DOS DOV DXC
    DXG
737-500 series
    EI-CDD CDE CDF CDG CDH DTU DTV DTW DTX DUD DUE
737-700 series
    EI- DRD DRE DZC
737-800 series
    EI- CSG CSN CSO CSP CSQ CSR CSS CST CSV CSW CTA
    CTB CXV DAC DAD DAE DAF DAG DAH DAI DAJ DAK DAL
    DAM DAN DAO DAP DAR DAS DAT DAV DAW DAX DAY DAZ
    DCB DCC DCD DCE DCF DCG DCH DCI DCJ DCK DCL DCM
    DCN DCO DCP DCR DCS DCT DCV DCW DCX DCY DCZ DGZ
    DHA DHB DHC DHD DHE DHF DHG DHI DHJ DHK DHM DHN
    DHS DHT DHV DHW DHX DHY DHZ DJR DJU DKD DLB DLC
    DLD DLE DLF DLG DLH DLI DLJ DLK DLL DLM DLN DLO DLR
    DLS DLT DLV DLW DLX DLY DLZ DND DPA DPB DPC DPD
    DPE DPF DPG DPH DPI DPJ DPK DPL DPM DPN DPO DPP
    DPR DPS DPT DPV DPW DPX DPY DPZ DRA DRB DRC DRE
    DWA DWB DWC DWD DWE DWF DWG DWH DWI DWJ DWK
    DWL DWM DWO DWP DWR DWS DWT DWV DWW DWX DWY
    DWZ DYA DYB DYC DYD DYE DYF DYG DYH DYI DYJ DYK
    DYL DYM DYN DTO DYP DYR DYS DYT DYV DYW DYX DYY
    DYZ EBA EBB EBC EBD EBE EBF EBG EBH EBI EBK EBL
    EBM EBN EBO EBP EBR EBS EBT EBV EBW EBX EBY EBZ
    ECL ECM ECN EDL
757-200 series
    EI-CEY CEZ DKL DNA DUA DUC IGA IGB IGC
767-200 series
    EI-CXZ CZD DBW DMP GBA UND
767-300 series
    EI-CRD CRF CRL CRM CRO CXO CZH DBF DBG DBP DBU
    DDW DFS DMJ DOF EAR ECB UNA UNB UNE UNF
777-200 series
    EI-DBK DBL DBM DDH UNW UNX UNY UNZ

BÖLKOW
PHOEBUS
    EI-GMD

BOMBARDIER INC see also **LEARJET**
CANADAIR CL-600 REGIONAL JET
    EI-DOT DOU DRI DRJ DRK DUK DUM DUU DUX DUY DVP
    DVR DVS DVT
CANADAIR CL604 CHALLENGER
    EI-IRE

BOX
DUET
    EI-BOX

BRITISH AIRCRAFT MANUFACTURING COMPANY LTD (BA)
L 25C SWALLOW 2
    EI-AFF

BRITTEN-NORMAN LTD
BN.2A ISLANDER
    EI-AYN BCE CUW

BRM CONSTRUCOES AERONAUTICAS
LAND AFRICA
    EI-DZS ECG

BROCK MANUFACTURING
KB2 GYROCOPTER
    EI-CVY

CAMERON BALLOONS LTD
Balloon (Hot Air)
65 variants
    EI-BSN
77 variant
    EI-CKJ
84 variant
    (EI-BAY)
90 variant
    EI-DGW ECC POP
105 variant
    EI-CUE

CARLSON
SPARROW
    EI-COO

SOCIÉTÉ NOUVELLE CENTRAIR
101A PÉGASE
    EI-GLC

CESSNA AIRCRAFT COMPANY including **REIMS AVIATION SA**
Production (F.prefix)
150
    EI-APF AST AVM BAT BFE BHW BYF CDV CHM CIN CML
    CMV
A150 AEROBAT
    EI-AUC AYF CTI
152
    EI-BGJ BIB BMM BMN CCJ CCK CCL CCM CGT CRU DGX
A152 AEROBAT
    EI-BJM EDC
172 SKYHAWK
    EI-AOK AYK BAG BAS BCK BIC BIR BKF BPL BRS BSC BUA
    CAA CFP CFY CGD CHS CLQ COT CUJ DDC DDX EAZ GSE
    GWY ING MCF MCG NFW OFM OOS SAC SKP STT
172RG
    EI-FII
R172 HAWK XP
    EI-BJO
REIMS FR172 ROCKET
    EI-BJI
177(RG) CARDINAL
    EI-BHC POD
(R)182 SKYLANE (RG)
    EI-BCL CAP CDP FBG GSM
206 SUPER SKYLANE, STATIONAIR
    EI-BNK SPB
210 CENTURION
    EI-AWH BUF CAX CDX CGH
310
    EI-AOS
335
    EI-CUP
337 SUPER SKYMASTER
    EI-AVC BHM
340
    EI-CIJ
441 CONQUEST
    EI-DMG
525 CITATIONJET variants
    EI-ECR MJC
551 CITATION II
    EI-CIR
560XL
    EI-XLS

CFM METAL-FAX
(STREAK) SHADOW
    EI-CHR CZC DBH DXL DXS

CHAMPION AIRCRAFT CORPORATION see **AERONCA** and
BELLANCA
7EC TRAVELLER
    EI-BHV
7ECA CITABRIA
    EI-ANT
7FC TRI-TRAVELLER
    EI-BBE
7GCAA CITABRIA
    EI-BYX

COLT BALLOONS LTD
Balloon (Hot Air)
14A CLOUDHOPPER
    EI-DZB
21A
    EI-DZA
77A
    EI-BGT

COMCO IKARUS GmbH
IKARUS C42
    EI-DXA EDI

CVJETKOVIC
CA-65
    EI-BNT

CYCLONE AIRSPORTS LTD
AX3
    EI-DXP

DE HAVILLAND AIRCRAFT CO LTD
DH.82A TIGER MOTH
    EI-AHI AUB AWP
DH.84 DRAGON
    EI-ABI

DOMINATOR GYROPLANE ULTRAWHITE
    EI-DZO

DOUGLAS
DC-3A and C-47 variants
    EI-ALR ALT AYO
C-54E-5-DO SKYMASTER
    EI-ARS

DRUINE
D.62 CONDOR
    EI-BCP BXT

EIPPER
QUICKSILVER
    EI-BLE BLN BOH BPP

EIRI-AVION O/Y
PIK-20D
    EI-GME

ELA AVIACIÓN S.L
ELA 07
    EI-DKN DTT DXU

ELLIOTTS OF NEWBURY see also **DFS** and **NORD**
EoN AP.5 OLYMPIA 2B
    EI-GLP

EMBRAER
EMB-170
    EI-DFG DFH DFI DFJ DFK DFL

ERCO
ERCOUPE 415
    EI-CGG CIH CVL

EUROCOPTER
EC120 COLIBRI
    EI-DDB EUR FAB FGL MIK
EC130B ECUREUIL
    EI-HOK LKS LNX
EC135T2+
    EI-ILS

EUROPA AVIATION
EUROPA
    EI-COE

EUROWING
GOLDWING
    EI-BNF CMK

EVANS
VP-1
    EI-AYY BBD BRU

VP-2
    EI-BDL BNJ BVT

EVEKTOR
EV-97 EUROSTAR
    EI-CXY DFM DKW DOI DRW DUJ

FLEXIFORM
STRIKER
    EI-BPN
TRIKE
    EI-BRK

FOKKER BV including **FAIRCHILD-HILLER (1)** and **FOKKER-VFW NV (2)** production
D.VII/65 replica
    EI-APT APU APV
F.27
    EI-AKA
FH.227 (1)
    EI-CAZ
F.28-100 (2)
    EI-DGE

FORNEY
F-1A AIRCOUPE
    EI-AUT

FOUGA
CM-170 MAGISTER
    EI-BXO

GARDAN
GY-80 HORIZON
    EI-AYB

GLASER-DIRKS FLUGZEUGBAU GmbH
DG-200 series
    EI-GLJ GLL

GLASFLÜGEL ING EUGEN HANLE
H.201 STANDARD LIBELLE
    EI-GLN

GROB-WERKE GmbH and Co KG
G.103 TWIN ASTIR
    EI-GML
G.109
    EI-HCS
G.115
    EI-CAC CAD CAE CCD DJY

GRUMMAN AMERICAN AVIATION CORPORATION (1) including **AMERICAN AVIATION CORPORATION (2)** and **GULFSTREAM AMERICAN CORPORATION (4)** production
AMERICAN AA-5 TRAVELER (2)
    EI-BMV BNR
GRUMMAN AA-5 TRAVELLER (1)
    EI-AYD
GULFSTREAM GA-7 COUGAR (3)
    EI-DUI

GULFSTREAM AEROSPACE CORPORATION
GULFSTREAM V SP
    EI-GDL

GYROSCOPIC ROTORCRAFT
GYROPLANE
    EI-COG

HAWKER SIDDELEY AVIATION incl. **BRITISH AEROSPACE PLC**, **CORPORATE JETS LTD** and **RAYTHEON-HAWKER** production
HS.125 Series 700
    EI-WJN
800XP
    EI-ECE WXP
850XP
    EI-GEM KJC

HIWAY HANG GLIDERS LTD
SKYTRIKE with Demon & Vulcan wings
    EI-BMW BNH BPU BRV

HOAC FLUGZEUGWERKE (HOFFMANN FLUGZEUGBAU FRIESACH)
DV-20 KATANA
    EI-CLA
H-36 DIMONA
    EI-CRV

HOVEY
DELTA BIRD
    EI-BRW

HOWELL SIDNEY
TWINSTARR
    EI-DJX

HUGHES TOOL CO and **HUGHES HELICOPTERS INC** including **SCHWEIZER AIRCRAFT CORPORATION** (269 wef 1986)
269 (Srs 300)
    EI-CVM CZL CZP DDI DMC DNU

HUNT
AVON trike
    EI-CKF CKG
PEGASUS XL
    EI-DBJ

ICP SRL
MXP-740 SAVANNAH
    EI-DGI DKB

III (INIZIATIVE INDUSTRIALI ITALIANE) SpA
SKY ARROW
    EI-CPX

JODEL including **CEA, SAN** and **WASSMER** production
D.9 BÉBÉ
    EI-BUC
D.112
    EI-BSB
D.120 PARIS-NICE
    EI-CJS
D.18
    EI-CKZ
DR.1050
    EI-ARW

JORA SPOL SRO
JORA
    EI-NVL

LAK including **AB SPORTINE AVIAICIJA** production
LAK-17A
    EI-GLH

LAKE AIRCRAFT CORPORATION
LA-4 BUCCANEER
    EI-BUH

LEARJET INC including **BOMBARDIER AEROSPACE** production
LEARJET 31
    EI-MAX
LEARJET 60
    EI-DXW REX VIV

LETOV AIR
LK-2M SLUKA
    EI-CNA

LINDSTRAND BALLOONS LTD
Balloon (Hot Air)
LBL 31
    EI-DJZ
LBL 90A
    EI-CRB

LOCKHEED-CALIFORNIA CO
L.382 HERCULES
    EI-JIV

McCANDLESS
M.4 GYROPLANE
    EI-ASR

McDONNELL DOUGLAS CORPORATION
DC-9-82 and DC-9-83
    EI-CBR CBS CBY CBZ CCC CCE CDY CEP CEQ CER CFZ CIW CKM CNR CRE CRH CRW
MD-11
    EI-UPA UPE UPI UPO UPU

MAGNI GYRO of ITALY
M-18 SPARTAN
    EI-DBX

MAINAIR SPORTS LTD
BLADE
    EI-DOW DRH EAP
GEMINI FLASH
    EI-CKT
MERCURY
    EI-CMU

MALMÖ
MFI-9 JUNIOR
    EI-AWR

MAULE AIRCRAFT CORPORATION
MX-7
    EI-CUT GER

MEDWAY MICROLIGHTS LTD
ECLIPSE R
    EI-CRY CTC ELL

MESSERSCHMITT-BÖLKOW-BLOHM GmbH including **EUROCOPTER DEUTSCHLAND GmbH** production
BÖ.105 varriants
    EI-BLD LIT

MIGNET
HM.14 POU-DU-CIEL replica
    ("EI-ABH"")

MONNETT
MONI
    EI-BMU

MOONEY AIRCRAFT CORPORATION
M.20
    EI-CAY

MORANE-SAULNIER
MS.502 CRIQUET
    EI-AUY

MOSKITO
MOSKITO 2
    EI-CJV

PARTENAVIA COSTRUZIONI AERONAUTICHE SpA
P.68
    EI-BWH

PEGASUS AVIATION
QUANTUM
    EI-CNU
QUASAR
    EI-DKC

PFALZ
D.III replica
    EI-ARC

PHOENIX
LUTON LA-4 MINOR
    EI-ATP
LUTON LA-5A MAJOR
    EI-CGF

PIEL AVIATION including **SCINTEX** production
CP.301 EMERAUDE
    EI-CFG
CP.1310-C3 SUPER EMERAUDE
    EI-DUK

PILATUS AIRCRAFT LTD
PC.12
    EI-IAN

PIPER AIRCRAFT CORPORATION
J-3C CUB
    EI-AFE AKM BBV BCM BCN BCO BEN BFO BIO BSX BYY
    CFO CHK COY CPP
J-5A CUB CRUISER
    EI-CGV
PA-12 SUPER CRUISER
    EI-ADV CFF CFH CMN
PA-18 SUPER CUB
    EI-ANY AVE BID BIK CIG CKH DTS
PA-22-108 COLT
    EI-BAV
PA-22-150 TRI-PACER
    EI-UFO
PA-22-160 TRI-PACER
    EI-AWD
PA-23-250 AZTEC
    EI-BDM WAC WMN
PA-28-140 CHEROKEE (CRUISER)
    EI-AOB ATK BSO CGP CIV CMB COZ
PA-28-151 CHEROKEE WARRIOR
    EI-WRN
PA-28-161 (CHEROKEE) WARRIOR
    EI-DJM SKW
PA-28-180 CHEROKEE
    EI-BBC BDR CIF
PA-28-181 (CHEROKEE) ARCHER
    EI-DDZ KDH
PA-28R-200 CHEROKEE ARROW II
    EI-EDR
PA-28RT-201 ARROW IV
    EI-SKU
PA-31-350 NAVAJO CHIEFTAIN
    EI-DIF
PA-34-200T SENECA II
    EI-CMT
PA-34-220T SENECA III
    EI-BSL
PA-38-112 TOMAHAWK
    EI-BJT BVK
PA-44-180 SEMINOLE
    EI-SKB SKC SKR SKT

PIPISTRELLE
TAUNUS 503
    EI-ECS

PROGRESSIVE AERODYNE INC
SEAREY AMPHIBIAN
    EI-SEA

PTERODACTYL LTD
MICROLIGHT
    EI-BOA

PZL WARSZAWA-OKECIE SA
PZL-110 KOLIBER
    EI-DOY

RAJ HAMSA
X'AIR
    EI-CXC DBI DBV DCA DDJ DFY DGG DGH DGJ DGK DKT
    DKY DNR DRL DRX DXM DXX DZP EAX EAY ECK ECO ECP
    ECV ECZ EDA KEV TON

RAND-ROBINSON
KR-2
    EI-BNL BOV

REALITY AIRCRAFT
ESCAPADE
    EI-DKZ

AVIONS PIERRE ROBIN
HR.200/120B
    EI-YLG
DR.400 variants
    EI-CRG SKE SKG SKL

R.1180T AIGLON
    EI-BIS ROB
R.2160D
    EI-SKS SKV

ROBINSON HELICOPTER CO INC
R22 variants
    EI-CFE CFX CPO CWR DKI DXI DXJ EHG EMG EXG GAV GKL
    GPT GTY JWM KHR MAG TGF TKI
R44 variants
    EI-CZM DDA DFW DJW DRN DTR DVX DVZ DXH DXK DZI
    DZM EAS EBJ EGG EJR ESK EXC EXH EXM FAR FOX GPZ
    HAZ JAL JAR JFD JOR JWP KEY LAD LOC MJR MMO MOR
    MPW MUL NBD NBP NJA OLI PEC PII RAV RON SGF SGN
    SMD SUB TMH TOY UNI VIC WWI

ROLLADEN-SCHNEIDER FLUGZEUGBAU GmbH
LS7-WL
    EI-GLS

ROTORWAY
EXECUTIVE
    EI-BNP CMW

RUTAN
LONG-EZE
    EI-CMR CPI

SCHEIBE-FLUGZEUGBAU GmbH including **AVIALSA/ROCHETAU**
    production
ZUGVOGEL III
    EI-GLO

ALEXANDER SCHLEICHER GmbH and Co
Ka 6CR
    EI-GLG GLM GLU GLW
K 8B
    EI-GLF
ASK 13
    EI-GLD GMF
ASK 14
    EI-APS
ASK 16
    EI-AYR
ASW 17
    EI-GMB
ASW 18
    EI-GMC
ASW 20L
    EI-GLR
ASK 21
    EI-GLA GLB]

SCHEMPP-HIRTH FLUGZEUBAU GmbH
CIRRUS
    EI-GLk
DISCUS B
    EI-GLT
DUO DISCUS T
    EI-GLI

SIKORSKY AIRCRAFT
S-61N
    EI-CNL CXS CZN GCE MES RCG SAR

SKYHOOK
SABRE
    EI-BPT

SLINGSBY SAILPLANES LTD
T.21 CADET
    EI-CJT
T.31 MOTOR TUTOR
    EI-CKJ
T.56 SE.5 replica
    EI-ARH ARM

SNCAN STAMPE including **AIA** production
STAMPE SV.4A/C
    EI-BAJ BLB CJR

SOCATA including **MORANE-SAULNIER, SEEMS** (wef 1962) and
GEMS (wef 1965) production
MS.880B RALLYE CLUB
    EI-ATS AWU AYI BCW BDH BGC BGD BGU BHK BIM BIW
    BMA BMH BNU CFV CHN CIA
(MS.880B) RALLYE 100, 110 and 150 series
    EI-BBG BBI BBJ BCS BCU BDK BEA BFI BFP BFR BGA BJK
    BKN BMB BMJ
MS.885 SUPER RALLYE
    EI-BKE
MS.892A RALLYE COMMODORE 150
    EI-BEP BHF BUJ
MS.892E RALLYE 150GT and 180GT
    EI-BGG BBO BGS CEG
MS.893A RALLYE COMMODORE 180
    EI-BHN BHP BUT
MS.894A RALLYE MINERVA 220
    EI-AUG AYT
MS.887 RALLYE 125
    EI-BIT
ST.10 DIPLOMATE
    EI-BUG
TB-9 TAMPICO
    EI-BMI BSK BYG CRX GFC LEM
TB-10 TOBAGO
    EI-BOE
TBM 700
    EI-LCM

SOLAR WINGS LTD
PEGASUS XL-Q and XL-R
    EI-BSW CGJ CGM CGN CHT CKU DIA DNW DOX

SOUTHDOWN SAILWINGS LTD
PUMA and SPRINT
    EI-BPO DDP

SPARTAN AIRCRAFT LTD
3-SEATER II
    (EI-ABU)

STEEN AERO LAB.INC
SKYBOLT
    EI-CIZ SAT

STINSON AIRCRAFT CORPORATION
108 STATION WAGON
    EI-CGC

STODDARD-HAMILTON
GLASAIR
    EI-CTG

SUKHOI
SU-26M2
    EI-EAI

TAYLOR
JT.1 MONOPLANE
    EI-BKK

TAYLORCRAFT AIRCRAFT CORPORATION
PLUS D
    EI-AGD ALH AMF
BC-65
    EI-CES

TEAM
MINI-MAX
    EI-CNC CGB

CONSTRUZIONI AERONAUTICHE TECNAM SRL
P92/EM ECHO
    EI-DRU
P2002 SIERRA
    EI-DRO JPK LFC WAT WFD

THRUSTER AIR SERVICES LTD
TST
    EI-BYA CKI
T.300/T600
    EI-CEN DKJ DXV

THUNDER BALLOONS LTD
Balloon (Hot Air)
AX8
    EI-BAR

URBAN AIR SRO
UFM-10 SAMBA variants
    EI-DRM DXT DXZ DZE JIM XLA
UFM-11 LAMBADA
    EI-DGA DGP DGR DGT DGY DNV

VAN'S AIRCRAFT INC
RV-7
    EI-HUM

VIKING
DRAGONFLY
    EI-BPE

WHITTAKER
MW5
    EI-BUL CAN CTL
MW6
    EI-BVB CJZ CKN CLL COM DMU

ZENAIR see **HEINTZ** and **COLOMBAN**
CH.200 and 250 ZENITH variants
    EI-BKM BVY BYL
CH.601 ZODIAC
    EI-DXN
CH.701 STOL
    EI-DOB SMK

ZLIN
526 TRENER MASTER
    EI-BIG

PART 9 – AIRCRAFT TYPE INDEX (ISLE OF MAN) This Index covers entries in SECTION 3.

COSTRUZIONI AERONAUTICHE GIOVANNI AGUSTA SpA
A109C
    M-DBOY
A109E POWER
    M-IDAS
A109S GRAND
    M-YWAY
AW139
    M-ERIT

AIRBUS
A340-313
    M-ABUS

AMERCAN-GENERAL AVIATION
AG-5B TIGER
    M-PHML

BEECH AIRCRAFT CORPORATION including **RAYTHEON AIRCRAFT COMPANY** production
A36 BONANZA
    M-FOUR
G58 BARON
    M-NINE
C90A KING AIR
    M-GLAS
B200 SUPER KING AIR
    M-EGGA
350 SUPERKING AIR
    M-FIVE OORE

BOMBARDIER INC see also **LEARJET**
BD-100 CHALLENGER 300
    M-NEWT NOEL
BD-600 CHALLENGER
    M-EIRE IFES RLIV SKZL
BD-700 GLOBAL variants
    M-GBAL JANP SKSM
CL-600 CHALLENGER variants
    M-BIGG FZMH

BRITISH AEROSPACE PLC
BAe 125 Series 700A
    M-ALUN
BAe 125 Series 800B
    M-HDAM JETI
BAe 125 Series 1000
    M-ACPT

CESSNA AIRCRAFT COMPANY
172N SKYHAWK
    M-BONO
182RG SKYLANE RG
    M-GOLF
208B GRAND CARAVAN
    M-YAKW
T206H TURBO STATIONAIR
    M-AXIM
414A
    M-SMJJ
425 CONQUEST
    M-MANX
441 CONQUEST
    M-USHY
525 CITATIONJET variants
    M-AJDM BIRD ELON ICRO MIKE OODY PSAC TEAM WMWM
    XONE
550 CITATION BRAVO
    M-WOOD
560 (XL) CITATION variants
    M-ANSL BWFC
680 CITATION SOVEREIGN
    M-AGIC
750 CITATION X
    M-DKDI PRVT

CIRRUS DESIGN CORPORATION
SR 20 GTS
    M-YGTS

DASSAULT AVIATION
FALCON 200
    M-JETT
FALCON 50 variants
    M-DASO GPIK
FALCON 900
    M-FALC JMMM RURU SAIR
FALCON 2000 variants
    M-AMND CHEM LJGI YJET

EMBRAER
EMB-135BJ LEGACY
    M-DSCL NATH YNJC

EUROCOPTER
EC 130B4 ECUREUIL
    M-BOAT
EC 135T2+
    M-KOGO YCHT
EC 155B1 DAUPHIN
    M-LNDN

GULFSTREAM AEROSPACE CORPORATION
GULFSTREAM 100
    M-YEDT
GULFSTREAM 200
    M-OSPB
GULFSTREAM IV
    M-GULF

HAWKER
900XP
    M-LCJP ONAV

LEARJET including **BOMBARDIER AEROSPACE** production
31
    M-LEAR
45
    M-EOCV GLRS
60 variants
    M-HOIL SSSV

LET KUNOVICE
L-200A MORAVA
    M-RAVA

PILATUS AIRCRAFT LTD
PC.12 variants
    M-ICKY IFLI OLTT

PIPER AIRCRAFT CORPORATION
PA-28 variants
    M-AZDA
PA-30 TWIN COMANCHE
    M-ALAN
PA-32-301XTC SARATOGA
    M-OPED
PA-34-200T SENECA
    M-EDIA
PA-44-180 SEMINOLE
    M-MUFC

RAYTHEON AIRCRAFT COMPANY
RB390 PREMIER (Including HAWKER)
    M-YAIR YSKY

ROBIN
DR400/180 REGENT
M-LEKT

SIKORSKY AIRCRAFT
S-76B
    M-ERRY ONTY [2]

SOCATA
TB-20 TRINIDAD
    M-ANIN GINZ
TBM-850
    M-SHEP USCA

PART 10 – AIRCRAFT TYPE INDEX (UK)

This Index covers all entries in SECTION 1, Parts 1 to 3, and entries in SECTION 4 Part 1, plus selected default engine details for which see also note under 'Type' page viii.

ABBOTT-BAYNES SAILPLANES LTD
SCUD III
    G-ALJR

ABINGDON
Balloon (Hot Air)
SPHERICAL FREE
    G-ATXR

ACE AVIATION
MAGIC LASER
    G-CENP CFTA

ACRO
ADVANCED
    G-BPAA

ETABLISSEMENTS AERONAUTIQUES R ADAM
RA.14 LOISIR
    G-BHIK

ADVANCED AIRSHIP CORPORATION
Airship (Gas-Filled)
ANR-1
    G-MAAC

ADVANCED TECHNOLOGIES INC
FIREBIRD CH1 ATI
    G-BXZN

AERIAL ARTS (LTD)
ALPHA (Rotax 277)
    G-MNIT MNZS
CHASER (Rotax 377) with 110SX and 130SX wings
    G-MNTD MNYD MNYE MNYF MTCP MTDD MTDE MVOD MWGO
CHASER S (Rotax 377)
    G-MVDK MVDL MVDP MVDR MVGA MVGF MVGG MVGH (MVGI)
    MVIE MVJF MVJG MVJH MVJI MVJJ MVJK MVKZ MVLA MVLB
    MVLC MVLD MVLE MVLG MVLS MVLT MVLW MVML MVMM
    MVOP MVRG MVRL MVSG MVTF MVTL MVTM MVUS MVYY
    MVZM MWWZ MWXW MWXX MWXY MWXZ MWYM MYBU MYCB
    MYEI MYEJ MYGK MYIL MYIT MYJO MYJW MYKD MYMY MYRE
    MYSA MYSV MYWN MYWS MYYD MZCB MZTS

AÉRIANE SA
SWIFT'LIGHT PAS
    G-CEVX CFIB

AERO SP ZOO
AT-3 variants
    G-DPEP MAVV SACX SACY SPAT SRUM SWLL SYEL SYWL
    TGUN UKAT

AERO COMMANDER INC
680 COMMANDER
    G-AWOE

AERO DESIGNS
PULSAR X (Rotax 582)
    G-BSFA BTDR BTRF BTWY BUDI BUJL BUSR BUYB BVLN BVSF
    BVTW BXDU CCBZ CCIG IIAN LUED LWNG MCMS RMAN
PULSAR XP (Rotax 912 and 912-UL)
    G-BUOW BUZB CBLA CEDJ EPOX LEEN OOXP PLSA XPXP
PULSAR 3 (Rotax 912-ULS)
    G-BYJL CDNF

AERO DYNAMICS LTD
SPARROW HAWK
    G-BOZU

AERO VODOCHODY NÁRODNÍ PODNIK see CZL and LET
C-104
    G-CCOB
L-29 DELFIN
    G-BYCT DELF ODAT
L-39 ALBATROS
    G-BZDI BZVL CCWB CFPO

SB Lim-2A
    G-BMZF OMIG
Lim-5
    G-MIGG

AEROCAR
TAYLOR COOT A
    G-COOT
TAYLOR MINI IMP
    G-BLWW

AEROCHUTE INDUSTRIES PTY LTD
DUAL
    G-CEZH CFCF CFFG HUTE

AERODYNE SYSTEMS INC
VECTOR
    G-MBTW MJAZ

AEROFAB INC see LAKE

AEROLA LTD
ALATUS-M
    G-CEWG CFDT, CFEY CFMV CFSI CFSN

AEROMERE SpA see AVIAMILANO

AEROMOT INDUSTRIA MECANICO METALURGICA LTDA
AMT-200 SUPER XIMANGO
    G-BWNY CECJ JTPC KHOM LLEW MOAN RFIO XMGO XYZT

AERONAUTICAL CORPORATION OF AMERICA
AERONCA C.2
    G-ABHE
AERONCA C.3
    G-ADRR ADYS AEFT AESB CDUW

AERONAUTICAL CORPORATION OF GB LTD
AERONCA 100
    G-AETG AEVS AEWU AEXD

AERONCA AIRCRAFT CORPORATION
AERONCA K
    G-ONKA
7AC CHAMPION
    G-AJON AKTR AOEH ATHK AVDT AWVN BGWV BPFM BPGK
    BRAR BRCV BRER BRWA BRXG BTGM BTNO BVCS LEVI OTOE
    TECC
7ACA CHAMP
    G-HAMP
7BCM CHAMPION (L-16)
    G-AKTO BFAF TIMP
7BM CHAMPION
    G-DHAH
7DC CHAMPION
    G-BRFI
11AC CHIEF,
    G-AKUO AKVN BJEV BPRA BPRX BPXY BRCW BRFJ BRWR
    BRXF BRXL BSTC BTFL BTSR BUAB BUTF IIAC IVOR
11CC SUPER CHIEF
    G-BBJNY BTRI
15AC SEDAN
    G-AREX
65C(TAC) SUPER CHIEF
    G-BTRG BTUV
O-58B (L-3) GRASSHOPPER
    G-BRHP BRPR

AEROPHILE SA
Balloon (Gas-Filled)
AEROPHILE 5500
    G-CCYF

AEROPRAKT
A22 FOXBAT (Rotax 912-ULS)
    G-CFHK CBGJ CBJH CBYH CCCE CCJV CDDW CDTZ CEOP
    CESI CEWR CHAD COXS CWTD EOID FBAT FBTT FJTH FOXB
    FXBT GFOX MOWG MRAF NJTC PHOX SDOI TADC VROD

AEROS COMPANY
DISCUS c/w Delta Trikes Aviation ALIZE trike
    G-CENZ
DISCUS/DRAGONFLY
    G-CFFH

AÉROSPATIALE including **EUROCOPTER production;** also see
AÉROSPATIALE-ALENIA, ATR and **SOCATA**
AS.332L SUPER PUMA including EC.225LP variant
    G-BKZE BKZG BLXR BMCW BMCX BUZD BWWI BWZX CDSV
    CHCF CHCG CHCH CHCI CHCL CHCM JSAR PUMA PUMB
    PUME PUMN PUMO PUMS REDJ REDK REDL REDM REDN
    REDO REDP REDR REDT REDU TIGC TIGE TIGF TIGG TIGH
    TIGJ TIGS TIGV TIGZ ZZSA ZZSB ZZSC ZZSD ZZSE ZZSF ZZSG
AS.350B ECUREUIL variants
    G-BRVO BVXM BXGA BZVG CBHL CDTD CEYO CFHU CORL
    DEMM DOIT ECOU EFTF EJOC FIBS HELM IANW IFBP IHDC
    JBBZ JCOP JESI KELY LARR MURP NUTY OAWD OLFA OMCC
    OOIO OOTT ORKY PATM PDGF PDGR PLMB PLMH PROB
    PROM REAL SCHI SMDJ SPVK TATS WHAM WHST
AS.355 ECUREUIL 2 variants
    G-BOSN BPRI BPRJ BPRL BSTE BSYI BUFW BVLG BYPA BYZA
    CAMB CCWK CPOL DANZ DBOK DEUX DFOX EMHH FFRI ICSG
    HBRO HEAN JEMH JETU JPAL LECA LENI LHEL LINE LNTY
    LUVY NETR NTWK OASP OHCP OHMS OLCP ORDH ORMA
    OTSP PASH PDGT PRDH REEM RIDA SDAY SEWP SKYN SKYW
    STON STRL TAKE TBHH TOPC TOPS TVHD ULES VGMC VONE
    VONG VONH VONK WENA WIRE XLLL XOIL ZITZ
AS.365 (and SA.365) DAUPHIN variants
    G-BKXD BLEZ BLUM BTEU BTNC BTUX CHCO CHCR CEYU
    CFFW DAUF DORF DPHN HEMS LCPL MLTY MRMJ OLNT PDGN
    PLMI

AÉROSPATIALE-ALENIA
ATR.-42
    G-CDFF DRFC IONA RHUM SSEA
ATR -72
    G-BWDA BWDB BXTN

AEROSPOOL SPOL S.R.O.
WT9 UK DYNAMIC
    G-CENO DYMC DYNA DYNM EECC FRDY GRMN JFDI JFLO
    NGLS OTIV RMHE SJPI TDYN

AEROSPORT
SCAMP
    G-BKFL BKPB BOOW
WOODY PUSHER including **WOODS** production
    G-AWWP AYVP BSFV SHUV

AEROSTAR SA see **YAKOVELEV**

AEROTECH INTERNATIONAL LTD see **WHITTAKER**

AEROTEK INC see **PITTS**

AESL see **VICTA**

AQUILA TECHNISCHE ENTWICKLUNGEN GmbH
AT01
    G-DCHO OKTI ROWA UILA WTWO

COSTRUZIONI AERONAUTICHE GIOVANNI AGUSTA SpA
A.109 variants
    G-BWNZ BZEI CCUK CDWY CERO CFMZ CGRI DNHI DPPF ELTE
    EMHB EMHC ETOU FUFU GDSG GRND HBEK HDTV IFRH IMAR
    IWRB JJJL JMON JMXA JODI JONW MDPI MEDS MEDX MENY
    MOMO MUMU OCMM ONEL "OPAS" ORLE PBEK PLPL SAMP
    SCII SCOI STGR STNS TBGL TELY TGRA TMUR TYCN UKAW
    USTC USTH USTS VIPH WELY WNAA WOFM WRBI YCUE ZIZZ
AW139
    G-CGIJ CGWB CHCP CHCT CHCV SARD

AHERNE
BARRACUDA
    G-BZSV

AIR AND SPACE MANUFACTURING INC
AIR AND SPACE 18A GYROPLANE
    G-BVWK BVWL

AIR COMMAND MANUFACTURING INC
503 (COMMANDER)
    G-BOAS BOIK BPAO BRSP KENB
532 ELITE
    G-BOGV BOKF BPPU BPUE BPUG BRGO BRKX BRLB BSND
    BSXP OGTS TFRB YROI
582 SPORT
    G-BTCB URRR

AIR CRÉATION
503 FUN 18 GT
    G-MYMM MYOL MYTZ MYUA MYVI MYXF
582, KISS
    G-BZXP CBEB CBJL CBKE CBKS CBLX CBMX CBNY CBRZ
    CCEK CCFA CCGM CCHJ CCHM CCPA CHKN COXY KIZZ PGHM
    SNOG TEDW TFLY TRYK
IXESS (TANARG) 912
    G-CDRJ CEBH CEBY CEDT CEIV CFID CFNX DJST ELSI FWKS
    IMUP IXES NARG OOLL SYUT TANA TEAS TNRG WGSI WYKD

AIR ET ADVENTURE
SATURNE S11OK
    G-NORB

AIR NAVIGATION AND ENGINEERING CO
ANEC II
    G-EBJO
ANEC IV MISSEL THRUSH
    G-FBPI

AIRBORNE WINDSPORTS PTY LTD
XT912/STREAK
    G-CDGE CDRD CEHH CEHZ CFNI CFNZ EDLY LVPL XTEE XTHT
    XTNI XTNR

AIRBUS SAS including **AIRBUS INDUSTRIE**
A300 variants
    G-MAJS MONR MONS OJMR
A319 variants
    G-DBCA DBCB DBCC DBCD DBCE DBCF DBCG DBCH DBCI
    DBCJ DBCK EJAR EJJB EUOA EUOB EUOC EUOD EUOE EUOF
    EUOG EUOH EUOI EUPA EUPB EUPC EUPB EUPC EUPD EUPE
    EUPF EUPG EUPH EUPJ EUPK EUPL EUPM EUPN EUPO EUPP
    EUPR EUPS EUPT EUPU EUPV EUPW EUPX EUPY EUPZ EZAA
    EZAB EZAC EZAD EZAE EZAF EZAG EZAH EZAI EZAJ EZAK
    EZAL EZAM EZAN EZAO EZAP EZAS EZAT EZAU EZAV EZAW
    EZAX EZAY EZAZ EZBA EZBB EZBC EZBD EZBE EZBF ZEZG
    EZBH EZBI EZBJ EZBK EZBL EZBM EZBN EZBO EZBP EZBR
    EZBT EZBU EZBV EZBW EZBX EZBY EZBZ EZDA EZDB EZDC
    EZDD EZDE EZDF EZDH EZDI EZDJ EZDK EZDL EZDM EZDN
    EZDO EZDP EZDR EZDS EZDT EZDU EZDV EZDW EZDX EZDY
    EZDZ EZEA EZEB EZEC EZED EZEF EZEG EZEJ EZEK EZEO
    EZEP EZET EZEU EZEV EZEW EZEZ EZFA EZIA EZIC EZID EZIE
    EZIG EZIH EZIJ EZIK EZIL EZIM EZIN EZIO EZIP EZIR EZIS
    EZIT EZIU EZIV EZIW EZIX EZIY EZIZ EZMH EZMS EZNC EZNM
    EZPG EZSM NMAK
A320 variants
    G-BUSD BUSG BUSH BUSI BUSJ BUSK BYTH CRPH EUKA
    EUKB EUKC EUKD EUKE EUKF EUKG EUKH EUKI EUKJ EUKK
    EUKL EUUA EUUB EUUC EUUD EUUE EUUF EUUG EUUH EUUI
    EUUJ EUUK EUUL EUUM EUUN EUUO EUUP EUUR EUUS EUUT
    EUUU EUUV EUUW EUUX EUUY EUUZ EUYA EUYB EUYC EUYD
    EUYE EUYF EUYG EUYH EUYI EUYJ EUYK EUYL FTDF GTDL
    MEDE MEDH MEDK MEDL MIDO MIDP MIDR MIDS MIDT MIDV
    MIDX MIDY MIDZ MONX MPCD MRCK OOAR OOAU OOAW
    OOPU OOPW OOPX OZBB OZBR TTOB TTOC TTOD TTOE TTOF
    TTOG TTOH TTOI TTOJ TTOK VCED
A321 variants
    G-DHJH EUXC EUXD EUXE EUXF EUXG EUXH EUXI EUXJ EUXK
    EUXL EUXM MEDF MEDG MEDJ MEDL MEDM MEDN MIDC MIDJ
    MIDL MIDO MARA NIKO OJEG OMYJ OOAV OOPE OOPH OOPH
    OZBE OZBF OZBG OZBH OZBI OZBL OZBN OZBO OZBP OZBR
    OZBS SMTJ TTIC TTID TTIE TTIF TTIG TTIH TTII
A330 variants
    G-EOMA MDBD MLJL OJMB OJMC OMYT SMAN TCXA WWBB
    WWBC WWBD WWBM
A340 variants
    G-VAIR VATL VBLU VBUG VBUS VEIL VELD VFAR VFIT VFIZ
    VFOX VFUN VGAS VGOA VHOL VMEG VNAP VOGE VRED VSEA
    VSHY VSSH VSUN VWEB VWIN VWKD VYOU

AIRCRAFT DESIGNS LTD
SHERIFF SA-1
    G-FRJB

AIRCRAFT MANUFACTURING CO (AIRCO)
DH.2 replica
    G-BFVH
DH.6
    G-EAML
DH.9
    G-EAQM CDLI

AIRSHIP INDUSTRIES (UK) LTD including **AEROSPACE DEVELOPMENTS**
Airship (Hot Air)
AD 500
    G-BECE
Airship (Gas Filled)
SKYSHIP 500
    G-BIHN

AIRSPEED LTD
AS.40 OXFORD
    G-AHTW AITB AITF
AS.57 AMBASSADOR
    G-ALZO
AS.65 CONSUL
    G-AIKR AJLR

AIRTOUR BALLOON CO LTD
Balloon (Hot Air)
31 series
    G-BLVA
56 series
    "G-OAFC" G-BKVW BKVX BLVB BSGH BWPL
77 series
    G-BLYT BOBH IVAC

ALLPORT
Balloon (Minimum Lift)
HOT AIR FREE
    G-BJIA BJSS

ALON INC see **ERCOUPE**

SOCIÉTÉ ALPAVIA see **FOURNIER**

ALPI AVIATION SRL
PIONEER 200
    G-CDSB CEVJ CEWL CFKW
PIONEER 300 (HAWK)
    G-CDPA CDSD CDYY CDZA CEAR CEEG CEIX CEMY CEPW
    CETX DEBT EKIM EWES FAJC GBOB GTOM HORK IPKA ITBT
    JVJK KITH LEAH LLOY LXUS OHJE OLAA OPFA PCCC PION
    RABS SPED SRAW TREX XCIT VIXX VOLO YVES ZZZG

AMERICAN AEROLIGHTS INC
EAGLE
    G-MBCU MBEP MBFS MBHE MBIO MBJD MBJK MBKY MBRD
    MBWE MBZV MJAE MJBL MJBV MJEO MJNM MJNO MMTV

AMERICAN AIRCRAFT
FALCON
    G-BUYF

AMERICAN AVIATION CORPORATION see **GRUMMAN-AMERICAN**

AMERICAN BLIMP CORPORATION
Airship (Gas-Filled)
A-60+
    G-TLEL

AMERICAN CHAMPION AIRCRAFT CORPORATION
7ECA CITABRIA AURORA
    G-BPMM CIDD EGWN IRGJ WEBS
7GCBC EXPLORER
    G-EXPL GCBC
8KCAB SUPER DECATHLON
    G-CEOE DDGJ EEEZ IGLZ IZZZ OCOK ZZAP

AMERICAN MOTH CORPORATION see **DE HAVILLAND**

AMF MICROFLIGHT LTD including **AMF AVIATION ENTERPRISES LTD**
CHEVVRON (Konig SD570)
    G-MNFL MTFG MVGC MVGD MVGE MVIP MVOO MVUO MVVV
    MVXX MVZZ MWHS MWNO MWPW MWRZ MWUI MYGN MYYP
    MZCK MZDP MZFH MZMK

ANDERSON
EA-1 KINGFISHER AMPHIBIAN
    G-BUTE BXBC

ANDREASSON including **CROSBY**
BA.4B
    G-AWPZ AYFV BEBS BFXF JEDS YPSY

ANONIMA POIAZIONARA VERCELLESE IND. AERONAUTICHE
AVIA FL.3
    G-AGFT

ARBITER SERVICES
Trike with Aerial Arts 130SX wing
    G-MNWL

ARKLE see **MITCHELL**

ARMSTRONG-WHITWORTH AIRCRAFT see **GLOSTER** and **HAWKER**
AW.650 ARGOSY
    G-AOZZ APRL ASXM ASXN BEOZ

ARROW AIRCRAFT (LEEDS) LTD
ACTIVE
    G-ABVE

ARROW AIRCRAFT AND MOTORS CORPORATION
ARROW SPORT A2-60
    G-AARO

ARROWFLIGHT LTD see **CGS**

ARV AVIATION LTD
ARV-1 variants (Hewland AE75)
    G-BMOK BMWF BNGV BNGW BNGY BNHB BOGK BPMX BSRK
    BWBZ DEXP ERMO OARV ORIX OTAL POOL STWO XARV
    YARV ZARV

AUSTER AIRCRAFT LTD see also **BEAGLE-AUSTER AIRCRAFT LTD** and **BEAGLE AIRCRAFT LTD**
PLUS C.2
    G-AFTN
PLUS D
    G-AHCR AHGW AHGZ AHKO AHSD AHUG AHWJ AHXE AIXA
Model E AUSTER III
    G-AHLK AREI BUDL
Model G AUSTER, 4
    G-A JXV AJXY ANHS ANHU
Model H AUSTER 5 and AUSTER 5D ALPHA 5 variants
    G-AGLK AIKE AIPE AJGJ AJXC AKOW AKSY AKSZ AKWS AKWT
    AKXP ALBK ALBK ALFA ALNV ALXZ ALYB ALYG AMVD ANFU
    ANHM ANHR ANHW ANHX ANIE ANIJ ANIU ANRP AOCP AOCR
    AOCU AOFJ AOVW APAF APAH APBE APBW APRF APTU BDFX
    BICD BXKX
V J/1 AUTOCRAT and variants
    G-AFWN AGTO AGTT AGVG AGVN AGXS AGXV AGYK AHAM
    AHAP AHAT AHAU AHAY AHHE AHHK AHSP AIBM AIBX AIBY
    AIGD AIJI AIPV AIPW AIRC AIZU AIZW AIZY AJEB AJEC AJEE
    AJEM AJIH AJIT AJIU AJRB AJRE AJRHN AJUD AJUE AJYB
    AMTM APKM AXUJ BRKC BVGT CDPG JAYI
J/1N ALPHA
    G-AGXN AGXU AGYD AGYH AGYT AHAL AHAV AHCL AHCN
    AHHH AHHT AHSO AHSS AIBH AIBR AIBW AIFZ AIGF AIGT AJAE
    AJAJ AJAS AJEH AJEI AJIS AJIW AJUL AJYB APIK APJZ APKN
    APTR ARRL ARUY BLPG TENT
V J/1B AIGLET
    G-AMKU ANGV ARBM
J/1U WORKMASTER
    G-APMH APSR OJAS
V J/2 ARROW
    G-AJAM AWLX BEAH
V J/4 ARCHER
    G-AIJK AIJM AIJS AIJT AIPR
J/5B, J/5G, J/5P, and J/5V AUTOCAR variants
    G-AOHZ AOIY APUW ARKG ARLY ARNB ARUG ASFK AXMN

J/5F, J/5K and J/5/L AIGLET TRAINER variants
G-AMMS AMRF AMTA AMTD AMUI AMYD AMZI AMZT AMZU
ANNW ANWX AOFS APLG APVG BGKZ
J/5Q and J/5R ALPINE variants
G-ANXC AOGV AOZL APCB
6A, AOP.6 and TUGMASTER variants
G-ARGB ARGI ARHM ARIH ARRX ARXU ARYD ASEF ASIP ASOC
ASTI BKXP BNGE
AOP.9, AOP.11 and BEAGLE E.3 variants
G-ASCC AVHT AVXY AXRR AXWA AYUA AZBU BDFH BGKT
BGTC BJXR BKVK BURR BWKK BXON CEHR
B.4
G-AMKL
B.8 AGRICOLA
G-CBOA

AUSTIN
WHIPPET replica
"K.158"

AUTOMOBILOVE ZAVODY MRAZ
M.1 SOKOL
G-AIXN

AVENGER
Balloon (Minimum Lift)
T.200-2112
G-BHMJ BHMK BHMM BIGM BIGR BIPW BIRL

AVIAMILANO SRL including **AEROMERE, LAVERDA** and **SEQUOIA**
production
F.8L FALCO
G-BVDP BWYO BYLL CCOR CWAG CYLL FALC FALO FATE
GANE LMAX OCAD OGKB ORJW PDGG REEC RJAM
F.14 NIBBIO
G-OWYN

AVIASUD ENGINEERING SA
MISTRAL
G-MGAG MVSJ MVUP MVWW MVWZ MVXN MVXV MVZR MWIB
MYSL MZJB

AVIASTROITEL LTD
AC-4C
G-CJUX
FEDEROV ME7 MECHTA
G-CJFZ

AVIAT AIRCRAFT INC see **CHRISTEN**

AVIATION COMPOSITES CO LTD see **EUROPA AVIATION**

AVIATION ENTERPRISES LTD
MAGNUM
G-CDBC

AVID AIRCRAFT INC
AVID FLYER (Rotax 582) including Aerobat, Hauler and Speedwing
variants
G-BSPW BTGL BTKG BTMS BTRC BUFV BUIR BUJJ BUJV BULC
BULY BUON BUZE BUZM-BVBR BVBV BVFO BVHT BVIV BVLW
BVSN BVYX BWRC BXNA CURV ELKS IJAC IMPY LAPN LORT
NANO OVID OZEE PILL RAFV SPAM

AVRO AIRCRAFT LTD see **ENGLISH ELECTRIC** and **HAWKER**
CF-100 CANUCK
G-BCYK

A V ROE and CO LTD including **BAe** and **HAWKER SIDDELEY**
AVIATION design and production
AVRO ROE 1 replica
G-ROEI
TRIPLANE replica
G-ARSG
504K, 504L and replicas
G-EASD EBJE EBNU
"G-AACA" G-ABAA ADEV ATXL BYKV
534 BABY
G-EACQ
581, 594 and 616 AVIAN
G-EBOV EBZM
G-AAHD ABLF ABLK ACGT EUJG
620 - see **CIERVA**

621 TUTOR
G-AHSA
652A ANSON and AVRO NINETEEN
G-AGPG AHKX AMDA APHV AVVO AVVR AWRS AWSA AYWA
VROE
671 - see **CIERVA**
683 LANCASTER
G-ASXX BCOH BVBP LANC
685 YORK
G-AGNV ANTK
694 LINCOLN
G-APRJ
698 VULCAN
G-BLMC VJET VLCN VULC
748
G-ATMI ATMJ AVXI AYIM BEJD BGMO BIUV BORM BPNJ BURJ
BVOU BVOV OPFW ORAL OSOE OTBA SOEI

AVTECH PTY LTD including **JABIRU AIRCRAFT COMPANY PTY LTD**
JABIRU SK, SPL and UL variants (Jabiru 2200A)
G-BXAO BXSI BYBM BYBZ BYCZ BYFC BYIA BYIM BYJD BYNR
BYNS BYSF BYTK BYTV BYYL BYYT BYZS BZAP BZDZ BZEN
BZFI BZGT BZHR BZIV BZLV BZMC BZST BZSZ BZTY BZUL
BZWK BZXN BZYK CBFZ CBGR CBIF CBJM CBJY CBKY CBOP
CBPP CBPR CBSU CBZM CCAE CCBY CCEL CCMC CCRX
CCVN CDFK CDNY CDZX CECE CECG CEKM CNAB CEOM CFIS
CFTX COVE CSDJ DANY DJAY DMAC DRCI DWMS ENRE EPIC
EPOC EUAN EWBC GPAS HINZ IKEV IPAT JAAB JABA JABB
JABE JABS JABY JABZ JACO JAJP JAXS JBSP JMAL JPMA JSPL
JUDD KKER LEEE LOIS LUMA LYPG MGCA MIRA NIGC OCDW
ODGS OGSA OJAB OMHP OPUS OZZI PBUS PHYS PRLY RODG
ROYC RUFS RYAL SIMP SUTD SVDG THOT TJAL TUBB TYKE
UJAB UJGK UKOZ UNNA VILA VJAB
JABIRU J160
G-CFSJ
JABIRU J400 and J430 variants (Jabiru 3300A)
G-CCGG CCID CCPV CCYA CDCP CDBD CDJL CDLS CDSI CDTL
CDUT CDXJ CEFP CEKW CEPM CFGH ESGJ GPSF JABI JABJ
JABU JJAB KEVI KIDD LUBY MLAL MUTZ NJSP NMBG OZIE
PHYZ PUKA RCST RDCO SAZY SIZZ

BAC (1935) LTD including **KRONFELD LTD**
DRONE
G-ADPJ AEDB AEKV

BAE SYSTEMS (OPERATIONS) LTD including **BRITISH AEROSPACE**
plc, BRITISH AEROSPACE (REGIONAL AIRCRAFT) Ltd, HANDLEY-
PAGE and **SCOTTISH AVIATION** production
HARRIER
G-CBCU CBGK
JETSTREAM variants to Series 32
G-BBBV BBYM BLKP BTXG BWWW CBEP CCPW EIGG FARA
ISLB ISLC ISLD IJYS JSSD JURA JXTA JXTC LOVB NFLA NOSS
OAKI OJSA PLAJ RAVL UIST
JETSTREAM Series 41 variants
G-CDYI GCJL ISAY JMAC MAJA MAJB MAJC MAJD MAJE MAJF
MAJG MAJH MAJI MAJJ MAJK MAJL MAJM MAJP MAJT MAJU
MAJV MAJW MAJX MAJY MAJZ TEXA
ATP and JETSTREAM Series 61
G-BTPA BTPC BTPE BTPF BTPG BTPH BTPJ BTPL BTTO BTUE
BTZG BUKJ BUUP BUUR JEMA JEMC JEMD JEME MANH MANL
OAAF PLXI
146 including Avro variants
G-BLRA BPNT BXAR BXAS BZAT BZAU BZAV BZAW BZAX BZAY
BZAZ CCJC CCJP CDCN CDXH CDZP CEBN CEBU CEIH CFAA
CFDH DEFM FLTA FLTB FLTC FLTD GNTZ IRJX JEAJ JEAM
JEAO JEAS JEAT JEAX JEAY JEBA JEBB JEBF JEBG LCYB
LCYC LUXE MANS MIMA OFMC OFOA OFOM OINV ORJX OZRH
TBAE TBIC ZAPK ZAPN ZAPO ZAPR

BAILEY AVIATION
QUATTRO 175 (DUDEK REACTION SPORT Wing)
G-CEOT CEVT

BALONY-KUBICEK Spol SrO
Balloon (Hot Air)
BB20
G-CCWT CEBL CFIW DNGA ZOOS
BB22 variants
G-CDRZ CERM
BB26
G-CEBG CRBV DBSR

BB30
G-NIMA
BB37 variants
G-CDWA MLSA

THE BALLOON WORKS
Balloon (Hot Air)
FIREFLY 7
G-CBPG

BARKER
CHARADE
G-CBUN

BARNETT ROTORCRAFT
BARNETT J4B-2
G-BRVR BRVS BWCW

BARON
Balloon (Minimum Lift)
TIGER T.200
G-BIMK

BB MICROLIGHT
BB03 TRYA
G-CFMA

BEAGLE AIRCRAFT LTD
A.109 AIREDALE
G-ARNP AROJ ARRO ARXB ARXC ARXD ARYZ ARZS ASAI
ASBH ASBY ASCB ASRK ASWF ATCC AVKP AWGA
B.121 PUP
G-AVDF AVLM AVLN AVZN AVZP AWKM AWKO AWVC AWWE
AWYJ AWYO AXCX AXDU AXDV AXDW AXEV AXHO AXIA AXIE
AXIF AXJH AXJI AXJJ AXJO AXMW AXMX AXNN AXNP AXNR
AXNS AXOJ AXOZ AXPA AXPB AXPC AXPM AXPN AXSC AXSD
AXUA AZCK AZCL AZCM AZCN AZCP AZCT AZCU AZCV AZCZ
AZDA AZDG AZEV AZEW AZEY AZFA AZGF AZSW BAKW BASP
BDCO IPUP JIMB OPUP PUPP TSKY
B.206 / BASSET
G-ARRM ASOF ASWJ ATDD AVLK BSET FLYP HRHI

BEAGLE-AUSTER AIRCRAFT LTD
A.61 TERRIER
G-ARLP ARLR ARNO ARSL ARTM ARUI ASAJ ASAK ASAX ASCD
ASCF ASDK ASMZ ASOI ASOM ASRL ASUI ASYG ASZE ASZX
ATBU ATDN ATHU AVYK AYDW AYDX TIMG
D.4
G-ARLG
D.5 HUSKY
G-ASNC ATCD ATMH AVSR AWSW AXBF
D.6
G-ARCS ARDJ

BEDE see **BROOKMOOR BEDE AIRCRAFT**

BEECH AIRCRAFT CORPORATION including **RAYTHEON AIRCRAFT COMPANY** production
17 TRAVELER
G-BRVE
18/3NM, 3TM and C-45
G-ASUG BKGL BKGM BKRG BKRN BSZC
19A MUSKETEER SPORT III,
G-AWFZ AWTS AWTV
A23 MUSKETEER II
G-ATBI
A23-24 MUSKETEER SUPER III
G-TAMS
B24R SIERRA 200
G-BBSC
C23 SUNDOWNER 180
G-AYYU BAHO BARH BASN BBSB BBTY BUXN GUCK
C24R MUSKETEER SUPER R
G-BYDG BZPG CBCY
F33, F33A and F33C BONANZA
G-BGSW BTHW BTZA COLA GRYZ HOPE HOSS JUST KSHI
MOAC OAHC RRRT VICM
35, G35, H35, N35, P35 S35 and V35B BONANZA
G-APTY ARKJ ARZN ASJL ATSR BBTS BONZ EHMJ NEWT REST
VTAL
A36 BONANZA
G-BMYD BSEY CDJV EISG FOZZ JLHS LOLA MAPR POPA ZLOJ

95-A55A and 95-B55A BARON
G-ASOH BFLZ BLJM BNBY BXDF BZIT FABM MDJN RICK SWEE
UROP WOOD
55 BARON variants
G-AWAJ FLAK MOSS
58 BARON variants
G-BLKY BMLM BNUN BTFT BXPM BYDY CIZZ CCVP DAFY FLTZ
IOCO OSDI VCML WWIZ
60 DUKE
G-IASL
65 QUEENAIR variants
G-AVDS AWKX
76 DUCHESS
G-BGHP BGRG BGVH BIMZ BNTT BNUO BNYO BODX BOFC
BRPU BXHD BXWA BXXT BYNY BZNN BZOY BZPJ BZRT CBBF
GBSL GCCL GDMW JLRW MULT OADY OBLC OPAT TRAN WACI
WACJ
90 KING AIR variants
G-BMKD CFBX OJRO ORTH RACI WLLM
95 TRAVELAIR variants
G-ASMF ASYJ
200 and 300 SUPER KING AIR variants
G-BGRE BPPM BVMA BYCP BZNE CDFY CDZT CEGP CEGR
CGAW CLOW FPLB FPLD FPLE FRYI FSEU GBMR IMEA JASS
JENC JIMG JOAL KLYN KVIP MAMD MEGN NICY OCEG ONAL
ORJA OTCS PCOP PFFN POWB PSTR RAFD RAFO RAFP RAFX
SASC SASD SAXN SGEC SPOR SYGA TAGH WATJ WCCP
WNCH WVIP

BELL
Balloon (Minimum Lift)
FD 31T
G-BITY

BELL AIRCRAFT CORPORATION
P-39Q AIRACOBRA
G-CEJU

BELL HELICOPTER TEXTRON INC including **AGUSTA BELL HELICOPTER CO, BELL HELICOPTER, TEXTRON CANADA, IPTN (412)** and **WESTLAND HELICOPTERS LTD** production
47D and 47G (WESTLAND)
G-ARXH ASOL AXKO AXKS AXKX AXKY BAXS BBRI BBZL BFEF
BFYI BHAR BHBE BHNV BPAI CHOP CIGY GGTT LHCI MASH
XTUN
47H and 47J (AGUSTA-BELL)
G-ASLR AZYB BFPP
206A and 206B JETRANGER
G-AVII AVSZ BARP BBCA BBOR BEWY BKEW BKZI BLGV BLZN
BNYD BOLO BPWI BSBW BTFX BTHY BUZZ BVGA BXAY BXKL
BXNS BXNT BXRY BXUF BYBC BYBI BYSE BZEE BZNI CBYX
CCBL CCVO CDGV CFFM CHGL CLAY COIN CPTS CRDY CRLH
DNCN DOFY ELLI ENES EWAW FEZZ FOXM GAND GEZZ GSJH
GUST HANY HEBE HELE HMPH HMPT HOLZ HPAD IBIG ISPH
JAES JBDB JBHH JETX JLEE JWBI KETH LBDC LILY LSPA
MFMF MILI MOTA NEWZ OAGL OAMG OAMI OBAM OBYT OCFD
OCST OETI OFCH OFST OJPS OMDR ONOW ONYX OPEN
OSMD OYST PEAK PERZ PORT PSHR RAMI RAMY REMH RKEL
RNBW SDCI SELY SHMS SKII SPEY STER SUEZ TAMF TBAH
TCMM TCSM TEGS TGRZ TILI TOYZ TREE TTMB WBHH WIIZ
WIZZ WLLY XBCI XBOX XXBH XXIV ZAPH
206L LONGRANGER
G-CBXD CDYR CSWL CYRS ELIT EYRE FANY GANG JGBI LEEZ
LILA LIMO LONE MAAX ODCC OGCE OHHI OLDN PWIT RCOM
SUEY
212
G-BALZ BIXV
222
G-NOIR VOND
407
G-CEOA MAYE OZAC
412
G-CCYX CDAF OIBU
UH-1H IROQUOIS
G-HUEY UHIH

BELLANCA AIRCRAFT CORPORATION including **AERONCA, CHAMPION** and **AMERICAN CHAMPION** production
7ECA CITABRIA
G-BLHS BOID BOTO BPMM BSLW IDD
7GCAA CITABRIA
G-BFHP BUGE JOIE ZOSA

7GCBC CITABRIA
G-BBEN BBXY BDBH BGGA BGGB BGGC BIZW BKBP BVLT
CONR HUNI
7KCAB CITABRIA
G-AYXU BOLG
8GCBC SCOUT
G-BCSM BGGD
8KCAB DECATHLON
G-BTXX
17-30A SUPER VIKING
G-VIKE

BENSEN AIRCRAFT CORPORATION including **CAMPBELL-BENSEN** and **MONTGOMERIE-BENSEN** production
B.7 GYROPLANE variants
G-APSY APUD ARBF ASCT ASLP ASNY
B.8 GYROPLANE variants
G-ARTJ ASME ASWN ATLP ATOZ ATWT AWDW AWPY AXBG
AZAZ BCGB BHEM BHKE BIFN BIGU BIHX BIPY BIVK BIVL BJAO
BKBS BLLA BLLB BMBW BMOT BMYF BMZW BNJL BOUV BOWZ
BOZW BPCV BPNN BPOO BPSK BPTV BRBS BRCF BREA BREU
BRHL BRXN BSBX BSJB BSMG BSMX BSNL BSNY BSZM BTBL
BTFW BTIG BTJN BTJS BTTD BUJK BUPF BVAZ BVIF BVJF
BVMG BVPX BWAH BWEY BWJN BWSZ BXCL BYTS BZID BZIP
BZOF CBFW CBNX CBSV CCXS CDBE CDMK CDVJ FGSI IPFM
JOEL OOJC OTIM SCUD YJET YROS YROY

BENSEN-PARSONS see PARSONS

BEST OFF
SKY RANGER (SWIFT) variants
G-CBIV CBVR CBVS CBWW CBXS CCAF CCBA CCBG CCBJ
CCCK CCCM CCCR CCCY CCDG CCDH CCDW CCDY CCEH
CCIK CCIO CCIY CCJA CCJT CCJW CCKF CCKG CCLF CCLU
CCMX CCMZ CCNJ CCNR CCNS CCNU CCPF CCPL CCRR
CCRV CCSX CCTR CCUD CCUF CCVR CCWC CCWU CCXH
CCXL CCXM CCXN CCYM CCZM CDAY CDBA CDBO CDBV
CDCH CDDR CDDU CDFJ CDFP CDHA CDHE CDIJ CDIP CDIU
CDJC CDJP CDKH CDKI CDKX CDLG CDLK CDMP CDMV CDNE
CDOV CDPE CDPV CDTP CDUL CDUS CDVA CDWB CDWM
CDYJ CECP CEDI CEDZ CEHD CEKK CENG CENS CERB CESD
CETO CETU CETV CEUJ CEXM CEZE CFBL CFBS CFBY CFCD
CFCK CFDN CFGO CFIA CFJG CFJJ CFLN CFMI CFNO CFOW
CFRM CFSW CFVK CFWR CRAB CUBE CZMI DOIN DOZZ ERTE
EVAJ FLDG FONZ FRNK GLHI HABI HIYA HULK INCE ISEL JAYS
JEZZ JPWM KLYE KULA LASN LDAH LUMB MARO MLZZ MOPS
NICS NOTS NUFC OBAZ OKIM OMSS OSKR OTCV OVOL PAWS
POLL PSKY PTAR RAFR REVO RHAM RSKY SKPG SKRA SKRG
SKSW SOPH SPMM TEDI TFOG TMCB TYGR UACA UMMY UPHI
UPTA VVVV WAZP WEEK WLSN XLAM XWEB XYJY ZADA ZSKY

BETTS
TB.1
G-BVUG

BIERINX and DUGOURD
POU du CIEL BI-FLY
G-POUX

BILSAM ENTERPRISES POLSKA SP ZOO
SKY CRUISER
G-CECR

BINDER AVIATIK GmbH see PIEL

BIRDMAN ENTERPRISES LTD
WT-11 CHINOOK
G-MMKE

BLACKBURN AEROPLANE AND MOTOR CO LTD
LINCOCK fsm
"G-EBVO"
MONOPLANE
G-AANI
B.2
G-AEBJ

BLACKBURN AND GENERAL AIRCRAFT LTD
BEVERLEY
G-AOAI

BLAKE
BLUETIT
G-BXIY

BLERIOT CIE
XI
G-AANG AVXV BLXI BPVE LOTI

BOEING AIRCRAFT CO including BOEING COMPANY
B-17G FORTRESS
G-BEDF FORT
B-29 SUPERFORTRESS
G-BHDK
707-300 series
G-AYAG
707-400 series
G-APFG APFJ
737-200 series
G-BYYK CEAE CEAF CEAH FIGP GPFI
737-300 series
G-BYZJ CELA CELB CELC CELD CELE CELF CELG CELH CELI
CELJ CELK CELO CELP CELR CELS CELU CELV CELW CELX
CELY CELZ GSPN JMCL LGTE LGTF LGTG LGTH LGTI OBMP
ODSK OFRA OGBD OGBE OTDA POWC STRA THOE THOF
THOG THOH THOI THOK THOL THON THOO THOP TOYA TOYB
TOYC TOYD TOYE TOYF TOYG TOYH TOYI TOYJ TOYK TOYM
ZAPV ZAPW ZAPZ
737-400 series
G-DOCA DOCB DOCE DOCF DOCG DOCH DOCL DOCN DOCO
DOCS DOCT DOCU DOCV DOCW DOCX DOCY DOCZ GBTA
GBTB
737-500 series
G-BVKB BVKD BVZE BVZG GFFD GFFH GFFI GFFJ
737-600 series
G- CDKT
737-700 series
G-EZJA EZJB EZJC EZJF EZJJ EZJK EZJL EZJM EZJN EZJO
EZJP EZJS EZJT EZJU EZJV EZJW EZJX EZJY EZJZ EZKA EZKB
EZKC EZKD EZKE EZKF EZKG MSJF SEFC STRF STRH
737-800 series
G-CDEG CDZH CDZI CDZL CDZM CEJO CEJP DLCH FDZA FDZB
FDZD FDZE FDZF FDZG FDZJ FDZO FZDP SAAW THOK XLAG
XLAH XLAM XLAO
747-200 series
G-BDXG BDXH BDXJ MKAA MKBA MKCA MKDA MKEA MKFA
MKGA MKHA MKJA
747-400 series
G-BNLA BNLB BNLC BNLD BNLE BNLF BNLG BNLH BNLI BNLJ
BNLK BNLL BNLM BNLN BNLO BNLP BNLR BNLS BNLT BNLU
BNLV BNLW BNLX BNLY BNLZ BYGA BYGB BYGC BYGD BYGE
BYGF BYGG CIVA CIVB CIVC CIVD CIVE CIVF CIVG CIVH CIVI
CIVJ CIVK CIVL CIVM CIVN CIVO CIVP CIVR CIVS CIVT CIVU
CIVV CIVW CIVX CIVY CIVZ GSSA GSSB GSSC VAST VBIG
VFAB VGAL VHOT VLIP VROC VROM VROS VROY VTOP VWOW
VXLG
757-200 series
G-BIKC BIKF BIKG BIKI BIKJ BIKK BIKM BIKN BIKO BIKP BIKS
BIKU BIKV BIKZ BMRA BMRB BMRC BMRD BMRE BMRF BMRH
BMRJ BPEC BPED BPEE BPEI BPEJ BPEK BYAD BYAE BYAH
BYAI BYAJ BYAK BYAL BYAO BYAP BYAR BYAS BYAT BYAU
BYAW BYAX BYAY CEJM CPEL CPEM CPEN CPEO CPEP CPER
CPES CPET DAJB FCLB FCLC FCLE FCLF FCLG FCLH FCLI
FCLJ FCLK JMCD JMCE JMCF JMCG LSAA LSAB LSAC LSAD
LSAE LSAG LSAH LSAI LSAJ MONJ MONK OJIB OOBC OOBD
OOBE OOBF OOBI OOBJ OOPK OPJB STRX STRY STRZ TCBA
ZAPU ZAPX
757-300 series
G-JMAA JMAB
767-200 series
G-CECU CEMK
767-300 series
G-BNWA BNWB BNWC BNWD BNWH BNWI BNWM BNWN BNWO
BNWR BNWS BNWT BNWU BNWV BNWW BNWX BNWY BNWZ
BZHA BZHB BZHC CDPT CEFG CEOD DAJC DBLA DIMB OOBM
OBYD OBYE OBYF OBYG OBYH OBYI OBYJ OOAN OOBK OOBL
OOPN PJLO TCCA VKNI
777-200 series
G-RAES VIIA VIIB VIIC VIID VIIE VIIF VIIG VIIH VIIJ VIIK VIIL VIIM
VIIN VIIO VIIP VIIR VIIS VIIT VIIU VIIV VIIW VIIX VIIY YMMA
YMMB YMMC YMMD YMME YMMF YMMG YMMH YMMI YMMJ
YMMK YMML YMMN YMMO YMMP YMMR YMMS YMMT YMMU
ZZZA ZZZB ZZZC

BOEING AIRPLANE CO
STEARMAN 75 KAYDET, N2S, PT-13, PT-17
G-AROY AWLO AZLE BAVN BAVO BHUW BIXN BNIW BRHB
BRSK BRUJ BSDS BSGR BSWC BTFG CCXA CCXB IIIG ILLE
ISDN NZSS RJAH THEA

BOLAND
Balloon (Hot Air)
52-12
G-BYMW

BÖLKOW APPARATEBAU GmbH including **MALMO, MBB** and **WAGGON-U MASCHINENBAU AG** production
PHOEBUS variants
G-CGDD CJWP CKLX DCHJ DCJB
BÖ.207
G-EFTE
BÖ 208 JUNIOR
G-ASFR ASZD ATDO ATRI ATSI ATSX ATTR ATUI ATVX ATXZ
AVKR AVLO AVZI BIJD BJEX BOKW BSME CLEM ECGO
BÖ 209 MONSUN
G-AYPE AZBB AZDD AZOA AZOB AZRA AZTA AZVA AZVB EFJD
EMHK

BOMBARDIER INC
CANADAIR CL-600 series CHALLENGER
G-CHAI CJMB CMBL DGET EMLI FTSL HARK IMAC JMMP LGKO
LVLV LWDC MPCW MPJM OCSD OCSE OCSF PRKR REYS SJSS
STCC TAGA UYAD VVPA XONE
CANADAIR REGIONAL JET series
G-DUOD
BD-100 CHALLENGER 300/3000
G-KALS KSFR
BD-700 GLOBAL EXPRESS
G-CEYL LXRS OCSA XXRS

BONSALL
DB-1 MUSTANG
G-BDWM

BOULTON PAUL AIRCRAFT LTD
P.108 BALLIOL
G-APCN

BOWERS
FLY BABY
G-BFRD BNPV BUYU

BRADSHAW
Balloon (Hot Air)
HAB-76
G-AXXP

BRANDLI
BX-2 CHERRY
G-BXUX

BRANTLY HELICOPTER CORPORATION
B.2
G-ASHD ASXD ATFG AVIP AWDU BPIJ OAPR OMAX ROTR
305
G-ASXF

SOCITE ANOYME DES ATELIERS D'AVIATION LOUIS BREGUET
905A FAUVETTE
G-DEGR

BREMNER see **MITCHELL** wing

BRIGHTON MA AND COMPANY LTD
Balloon (Hot Air)
Ax7-65
G-AVTL AWJB

BRISTOL AEROPLANE CO LTD
BOXKITE
G-ASPP
F.2B FIGHTER
G-AANM AEPH
20 M.1C replica
G-BLWM BPLT BWJM
30/46 BABE III replica
"G-EASQ"

105 BULLDOG
G-ABBB
149 BOLINGBROKE (BLENHEIM)
G-BPIV
156 BEAUFIGHTER
G-AJMC DINT
170 FREIGHTER
G-AICH AIMI AINT
171 SYCAMORE
G-ALSP ALSX AMWI
173
G-ALBN
175 BRITANNIA
G-ALRX ANCF AOVF AOVT BDUP
192 BELVEDERE
G-BRMB

BRITISH AERIAL TRANSPORT COMPANY LTD
FK-23 BANTAM
G-EACN

BRITISH AIRCRAFT CORPORATION (BAC) see **HUNTING**
ONE-ELEVEN
"G-FIRE" G-ASJD ASYD AVMJ AVMO AVMT AVMU AWYV
CONCORDE
G-AXDN BBDG BOAA BOAB BOAC BOAD BOAE BOAF BOAG
SSST

BRITISH AIRCRAFT MANUFACTURING COMPANY LTD see **BRITISH KLEMM** and **KLEMM**
SWALLOW 2
G-ADPS AEVZ AFCL AFGC AFGD AFGE

BRITISH KLEMM AEROPLANE CO see **KLEMM**
L.25 SWALLOW
G-ACXE

BRITTEN-NORMAN LTD including **BRITTEN-NORMAN (BEMBRIDGE) LTD, FAIREY BRITTEN-NORMAN LTD, IRMA** and **PILATUS (BN-2)** production
BN.1F
G-ALZE
BN.2A, BN2B, BN2T ISLANDER, and DEFENDER
G-AVCN AWID AWNT AXUB AXZK AYAZ AYRU AZBV BCEN
BCWR BCZS BDJV BDPN BDPU BDZI BEDW BEED BEEG BEFI
BELF BFNU BJEE BJEF BJEJ BJOP BJWO BKOK BLDV BLNJ
BPCA BSPT BSWR BUBN BVHY CEIR CEUB CEUC CEUD CEUE
CHES CHEZ CIAS CZNE GMPB HEBS JSAT LEAP MAFF OBNC
OBNL ORED OSEA SBUS SEIL SICA SICB SJCH SSKY XAXA
BN.2A III TRISLANDER
G-BBYO BDOT BDTN BDTO BEDP BEVR BEVT BEVV FTSE
JOEY LCOC OJAV PCAM RBCI RLON XTOR

CONSTRUCTIONS AERONAUTIQUE MAURICE BROCHET
MB.50 PIPISTRELLE
G-AVKB BADV

BROOKLANDS AERO LTD
MOSQUITO
G-AWIF

BROOKLANDS AIRCRAFT CO see **OPTICA**

BROOKMOOR BEDE AIRCRAFT
BD-4
G-BEKL BKZV BOPD BYLS
BD-5
G-BGLB BJPI

BRÜGGER
MB.2 COLIBRI
G-BKCI BKRH BNDP BNDT BPBP BRWV BUDW BUTY BVIS
BVVN BXVS HRLM KARA PRAG

BÜCKER including **CASA** and **DORNIER-WERKE AG** production
Bü.131 JUNGMANN (CASA 1-131)
G-BECT BECW BHPL BHSL BIRI BJAL BPDM BPTS BPVW BSAJ
BSFB BSLH BTDT BTDZ BUCC BUCK BUOR BUVN BVPO BWHP
BYIJ BZJV CCHY CDJU CDLC CDRU DUDS EHBJ EMJA JGMN
JUNG JWJW RETA TAFF WIBS
Bü.133 JUNGMEISTER
G-AEZX AXMT AYFO BUKK BUTX BVJP BVXJ BZTJ PTDP TAFI

Bü 181 BESTMANN
G-AMYA CBKB GLSU

BUSBY
Balloon (Minimum Lift)
BUZ B20N
G-FYGH

BUSHBY-LONG see LOEHLE
MIDGET MUSTANG
G-AWIR BXHT IIJC IIMT MIDG

BYRNE
Balloon (Minimum Lift)
ODYSSEY 4000
G-BCFE

CAB see MINICAB

CALL AIRCRAFT CO see IMCO

CAMBRIDGE HOT-AIR BALLOONING ASSOCIATION
Balloon (Hot Air)
CHABA 42
G-BBGZ

CAMERON BALLOONS LTD see also CAMERON-COLT and
CAMERON-THUNDER
Airship (Gas-Filled)
DG-19
G-BKIK
Zero 25
G-BMUR
Airship (Hot Air)
D-38
G-SMHK
DP-70
G-BMEZ BNXG-BPFF BRDT
DP-80
G-UPPY VIBA
D-96
G-BAMK BEPZ
Balloon (Gas/Hot Air)
R-15
G-CICI
R-36
G-ROZY
R-42
G-BLIO
R-77
G-BUFA BUFC BUFE
Balloon (Hot Air)
20 variants
G-BIBS BJUV BOYO BRCJ BRCO
21 series
G-BTXM
24 series
G-BSCK BVCY
31 variants
G-BEJK BEUY BGHS BKIX BKIZ BMST BPUB BRMT BVFB BZYR
CBIH CBLN CCHP CDFI CEJT CESX CESY CEYD IHOP LEAU
NOMO PRTT RBMV TOHS WETI
34 variants
G-BRKL BUCB BVZX BYNW BZBT EROS EZER FZZI IAMP OBLU
RAPP
42 variants
G-AZER BCDL BCEU BMWU BPHD BPXG BUPP BWEE BXJH
BXTG BYRK CCAY CCJY CCSI HOPI SKOT
56 variants
G-AZKK BBYU BCOJ BCXZ BDPK BDSF BDUI BDUZ BDYH BECK
BEEH BEND BENN BERT BEXX BEXZ BFAB BFFT BFKL BGOI
BHGF BHSN BICU BKRS BKZF BMYA BNZN BOWM BRIR BRSA
BTHZ BZKK CDJZ CFJP HOFM HOOV LENN ODAY OVET SWPR
WAAC WYNT
60 series
G-BTZU BVDM BVDY BWRT BXJZ CBJS CBVD CENN CEOI IFIF
LOON ROGY
65 variants
G-AZIP AZUP AZUV AZXB BAOW BAYC BBYR BCAP BCFN BCRI
BDRK BDSK BEIF BGJU BHKH BHNC BHND BHOT BIBO BIGL
BISH BIWK BIWU BIYI BJAW BJWJ BJZA BKGR BKWR BLEP
BLJF BLPK BLZB BMCD BMJN BMKY BMPD BMVW BMYJ BNAN
BNAU BNAW BOAL BOOB BOWV BPGD BPPA BPXF BREH BRMI

BROE BROG BSAS BSGP BTUH BWBA BWHG BXGY BXUU
BZPD BYZL CEVH GLUE HENS KAFE MUIR NATX OERX PMAM
PYRO SMIG WELS
70 variants
G-BXOT BYJX BZEK CCPP CFNB PIRO RAMA RMSY WJAC
77 variants
G-BAXF BBOC BBYL BCNP BCRE BCZO BDBI BDNZ BDSE BEEI
BEPO BFUZ BFYK BGAY BGAZ BHDV BHHB BHHK BHHN BHII
BHYO BIEF BIET BIRY BJGK BKNP BKPN BKTR BKWW BKZB
BLFY BLIP BLJH BLLD BLPP BLSH BLYJ BLZS BMAD BMKJ
BMKP BMKW BMLJ BMLW BMOH BMPP BMTN BMTX BMZB
BNCB BNCH BNCJ BNDN BNDV BNEO BNFG BNFO BNGJ BNGN
BNIN BNIU BNJG BNKT BNMA BNMG BNNC BNNE BNPE BNTW
BNTZ BNUC BOAU BOBR BOEK BOFF BOGP BOGY BOJB BOJD
BOJU BOOZ BORB BORN BOTW BOVV BOWB BOWL BOXG
BOYS BOZN BPBV BPBY BPDF BPDG BPHH BPHJ BPLF BPLV
BPPP BPSH BPSR BPTD BPVC BPVM BPWC BPYI BPYS BPYT
BPYV BRBO BRFE BRFO BRIE BRKW BRLX BRMU BRMV BRNW
BRRF BRRR BRSD BRTV BRUE BRUV BRZA BRZT BSBI BSBM
BSBR BSDX BSEV BSHO BSIC BSIJ BSLI BSKD BSMS BSUV
BSWV BSWY BSXM BTAG BTJH BTKZ BTOP BTPT BTRX BTWJ
BTWM BTXW BTZV BUAF BUAM BUDU BUEV BUGD BUGP
BUGS BUHM BUNG BUPI BUTJ BUWU BUZK BVBS BVBU BVDR
BVFF BVHK BVUK BVXB BWAJ BWAN BWKV BWPC BWTJ
BWYN BXAX BXSX BXTJ BXVT BYBN BYHY BYLY BYNJ BZBI
BZPW CBHX CBKV CCAR CCHW CCPO CCSP CEJA CEJC CEPU
CEPV CGOD CHUK CTGR CXHK DRYI EIIR ENNY EPDI ERIK
FABB FELT FUZY GEES GEEZ GEUP GPPN GUNS HARE HENY
IDDI JINI JLMW KEYY KODA KTEE LAZR LEGO LEXI LIBB LIOT
LOAG LOAN LOLL LUBE MAMO MOFF MOKE MRTY NBSI NWPR
OATV OCND OEDP OHSA OJEN OKYA OMRB ONZO ORPR PADI
POLY PUSS RAPH RCMF RONI SAFE SAIX SCAH SCFO SLAC
SNAP SNOW SUCH SUSI TECK TUDR ULIA UPUP VODA VOLT
WAIT WBEV WELI XPWW XSKY ZINT ZUMP
80 series
G-BUYC BVEN BVGJ BVUU BVZN BWAO BWGP BXJP BXLG
BXSC BXSJ BYER BYJJ BYTJ BZMV BZPK CBEY CDJY CEEB
CELM CEMF CEMU CFEB CFTM EVET HOTM LIMP MCAP NMOS
OARG OBTS OGJM ONIX RECE RMAX SLCE UPHL WIEZ
84 series
G-AYAJ AYJZ AYVA AZBH AZDF AZNT AZRN AZSP BAAX BAGY
BAKO BALD BAND BAST BBLL BNFP BNXR BOWU BOYM BREX
BRGD BSKE BSKU BSMK BVXD MOSY STAV
90 variants
G-BMFU BMJZ BNII BOOP BOWK BPSO BROY BRPJ BRZC
BSCA BSNJ BSWX BTBP BTCM BTFU BTHF BTJU BTTB BTTL
BTWV BTXF BUAJ BUFJ BUFX BUGY BUIE BUIU BUIZ BUOE
BUUO BUVW BVBX BVDX BVFP BVHO BVHR BVKV BVMR BVOC
BVOP BVPK BVTN BWAU BWBC BWDU BWIP BWJI BWNO
BWNS BWPT BWUU BWVU BXAM BXJO BXVV BYDT BYHC BYIU
BYJC BYKX BYMY BYNN BYOK BYOX BYTW BYZX BZEY BZFD
BZIX BZJH BZKX BZOX BZRU BZTK BZUU BZXR BZYW BZYY
CBAT CBED CBKI CBKJ CBLU CBRV CBUO CCBB CCBT CCJF
CCMN CCNN CCPT CCUJ CCXF CDHS CDHY CDIO CDOB CDOI
CDPC CDRF CECD CEES CEJZ CEOS CEPR CERH CESH CEUV
CFEA CFLK COMP CONC CPSF CTEL CXCX DEKA DIAL DRYS
EEFA ELLE FBMW FOGG FVEL GLAW GOCX GOGW HBUG IBEV
IBLU IGEL IGLE INSR ITOI IWON JMJR JULU KAYI LAAC LAGR
LTSB LULA MFLI MILE MOFZ MSON OJBM OJMS OKCC OMEN
OXBY PATG PERC PINC PRNT RISE RIXY RIZE RIZI ROXI SALE
SBIZ SIAM SLII SORT SRVO STRM TANK TEDF TETI TINS TMCC
TRIG VKUP VRVI WIFI YUMM YUPI YVET ZSKD
100 series
G-CEFS NPWR
105 variants
G-BAVU BMEE BMOV BNFN BOTD BOTK BPBW BPJE BRFR
BRLL BSNZ BSRD BTEA BTFM BTIZ BTKW BTPB BTRL BUAV
BUHU BULD BURX BUWF BVCA BVEU BVHV BVNR BVUA BVXA
BWDH BWEW BWKF BWOW BWPZ BWRY BWSU BXBM BXBY
BXEN BXOW BXXG BXXL BYFJ BYHU BYIL BYKI BYMX BYNX
BYPD BZDJ BZDN BZKU BZVU BZXO CAMP CBEC CBHW CBMC
CBNW CCFN CCGY CCIU CCOT CCVD CCYI CDIT CDMC CDWD
CDYG CDZW CEDA CEDF CEEK CEGC CEHU CEIN CEJR CEKS
CESC CFAU CFEK CITR CLIC DOOM DRGN ELEE ENRY FFAB
FOWS FUSE GFAB HONK JOSH JSON KSKS LOSI METH MHBD
NLYB NZGL OAFR OAML OFAA OGLY OJBS OSAT OUCH OUVI
POPP SAXC SDLW SEDO SEPT SERV SFSL SSTI SUCK TORK
TUTU ULTR VSGE WNGS XHOT YLYB
120 variants
G-BNEX BOHL BOZY BPSS BPTX BPZK BRXA BSYB BTEE BTKN
BTOU BTUU BTXS BUFT BURN BVSO BVXF BWAG BWKD BWLD
BWYS BXBR BXVJ BXWI BYSV CBFF CBMK CBOW CBVV CCEN
CCTS CCVZ CCXE CDIK CDLB CDRI CEXN CFKI ENZO FLOA

GHIA HOTT LOBO MEUP MOFB NERO OLUG TING VALZ VIKY XPDA
133 series
G-BWAA BZVE CBUW
140 variants
G-AZUW BVYU BWTE DSPK FLTG OXBC
145 series
G-CETK DENT HIBM
160 variants
G-CBHD OXBA
165 series
G-BIAZ
180 variants
G-BRZI BTYE BUJR BUKC BVKL BXMM OBRY RWHC SKYR
200 series
G-BXOS BZJU CCJG
210 series
G-BUOC BVBN BXBA BXJC BXRM BYMG BYSM BZBE BZXF CCNV CFKF CFOE CVBF GURL JHNY JOJO ORGY RPBM SKYU SKYX
225 series
G-CCBV CCPZ CDRN
250 series
G-BUBR BVIG BWKU BWKX BWZJ BXPK BYHX BYYD BZIK CBFY CCGZ CDDV HIUP MOLI OBUN OVBF OVIC SKYY STPI XRLD
275 series
G-BWML BXIC BXMW BYSK BYZG BZTT CBYC CBZZ CCNC CCSG CCSJ CCZI CDDC CDIH CDRZ CFCC OOTW SKYK TCAS
300 series
G-BZNU CBAW SNIF
315 series
G-BZSU CCRH KNIX OBRA SIMI SKYJ
340 series
G-BZUO KVBF RVBF
350 series
G-CCOS CCSA CDDL CDIB CERC EVBF VBFG VBFH VBFI VBFJ VBFK
375 series
G-BBGN VBFM VBFN VBFO
425 series
G-CCGT

Special Shapes

SHAPE	REGISTRATION(S)
ACTION MAN PARACHUTIST	G-RIPS
APPLE	G-BWSO
BALL	G-RNIE
BEER BARREL	G-PINT
BEER CAN	G-IBET
BEER CRATE	G-FGSK
BEETHOVEN BUST	G-BNJU
BELLOWS	G-BIUL
BELLS WHISKY BOTTLE	G-BUUU
BENIHANA	G-BMVS
BERENTZEN BOTTLE	G-KORN
BERTIE BASSETT	G-BXAL BZTS
BIBENDUM	G-GRIP
BOWLER	G-OPKF
BRADFORD AND BINGLEY	G-BWMY
BUDDY	G-WLVE
BUDWEISER CAN	G-BPFJ
BULB	G-BVWI
BULL	G-CBON
BUS	G-BUSS
CABIN	G-SHAK
CAN	G-BXPR CDMO OFIZ PURE
CARROTS	G-BWSP HUCH
CHAMPION SPARK PLUG	G-BETF
CHATEAU DE BALLEROY	G-BKBR BTCZ
CHESTIE	G-USMC
CHICK	G-BYEI
CLOWN	G-CLWN
CLUB	G-BWNP
COCA COLA BOTTLE	G-BXSB BYIV BYIW BYIX
COOLING TOWER	G-WATT
COTTAGE	G-COTT
DRAGON	G-GBGF
DUDE	G-OIFM
EAGLE	G-BVMJ
FABERGE EGG	G-BNFK
ELEPHANT	G-BLRW BMKX BPRC
EGG	G-OEGG
FIRE EXTINGUISHER	G-BZJA

FLAME	G-CBIU
FORKLIFT	G-BZVE
FORBES' MAGAZINE	G-BPOV
FURNESS BUILDING	G-BSIO
GOLFBALL	G-PUTT
GOLLY	G-OLLI
GRAND ILLUSION	G-MAGC
HARLEY	G-BMUN
HELIX OILCAN	G-HLIX
HOFMEISTER LAGER BEAR	G-HEYY
HOME SPECIAL	G-BWZP
IKEA	G-IKEA
JAGUAR XK8 SPORTS CAR	G-OXKB
KATALOG	G-OTTO
KP CHOC DIPS TUB	G-DIPI
LIGHTBULB	G-BVWI LAMP
LIPS	G-LIPS
LOCOMOTION	G-LOKO
MACAW	G-BRWZ
MINAR E PAKISTAN	G-BKNN
MONSTER	G-MSTR
MONSTER TRUCK	G-BWMU
MR PEANUT	G-NUTS
N ELE	G-WBMG
OIL CAN	G-UNIP
ORANGE	G-CDXW
OTTI	G-OTTI
PERRIER BOTTLE	G-PERR
PIG	G-HOGS
POT	G-CHAM
PRINTER	G-BYFK
PYLON	G-PYLN
ROBINSON'S BARLEY WATER	G-BKES
RUPERT BEAR	G-BTML
RUSSIAN DOLL	G-USSR
SAMSUNG COMPUTER	G-SEUK
SANTA MARIA SHIP	G-BPSP
SATURN	G-DREX
SAUCER	G-GUFO
SCOTTISH PIPER	G-PIPY
SHOPPING TROLLEY	G-CFOP
SIGN	G-UCCC
SONIC THE HEDGEHOG	G-SEGA
SPHERE	G-BVFU BYJW IBBC SATL
SPHINX	G-BLFE
STRAWBERRY	G-BXTF
SUGAR BOX	G-BZDX BZDY
SULTAN	G-TURK
TEMPLE	G-BMWN
TENNENT'S LAGER GLASS	G-BTSL
TRAIN	G-BTMY
TRAINER'S SHOE	G-BUDN
TRUCK	G-BLDL DERV
TV	G-TVTV
UNCLE SAM	G-USAM
VAN	G-ORAC
WITCH	G-WYCH
WINE BOX	G-STOW

CAMPBELL AIRCRAFT LTD including **BENSEN** and **EVERETT GYROPLANES LTD** production
COUGAR
G-BAPS
CRICKET
G-AXPZ AXRC AXVK AXVM AYBX AYCC AYHI AYPZ BHBA BKVS BORG BRLF BSPJ BSRL BTEI BTMP BUIG BVDJ BVIT BVLD BVOH BWSD BWUA BWUZ BXCJ BXHU BXUA BYMO BYMP BZKN CBWN CCPD CDXV CFCH CFJD GYRO KGED RUGS

CANADIAN HOME ROTORS
SAFARI
G-CCKJ

CAPRONI VIZZOLA COSTRUZIONI AERONAUTICHE SpA
CALIF A-21
G-CKNC

CARLSON
SPARROW
G-BSUX VVB

SOCIÉTÉ CARMAM
JP-15/36A AIGLON
    G-CHKZ CHMU DDYL DEDB
M100S MÉSANGE
    G-CHOF

CASA see **BUCKER (1131)**, **HEINKEL (2111)** and **JUNKERS (352L)**

CASSUTT including **MUSSO SPECIAL**, **SPEED TWO** and **WILSON** variants
RACER
    G-BFMF BNJZ BOMB BOXW BPVO BXMF CXDZ FRAY RAGE
    RUNT

AVIONS CAUDRON
G.III
    G-AETA

CCF see **HAWKER** and **NORTH AMERICAN**

CEA see **JODEL** and **ROBIN**

SOCIÉTÉ NOUVELLE CENTRAIR
MOTO-DELTA
    G-MBPJ
101 PÉGASE variants
    G-CEVE CFCB CFEH CFFC CFFS CFGW CFJK CFMK CFNM
    CFRP CFRR CFRV CFRX CFVM CFVN CFVP CFVV CFWY CFXD
    CGBU CGCY CHDD CHNY CHNZ CKBA CKGM CKHM CKKB
    CKMF DESH DESW DETJ DETM DEVM DEVO DFCD DHES PEGZ
    REER SVEN
201 MARIANNE
    G-CJXB CJXN
SNC-34 ALLIANCE
    G-CJHR

CESSNA AIRCRAFT COMPANY including **REIMS AVIATION SA** production **(F.prefix)**
C.165 AIRMASTER
    G-BTDE
120
    G-AJJS AJJT AKTS AKVM BHLW BJML BPWD BPZB BRJC BRPE
    BRPF BRPG BRPH BRUN BRXH BSUH BTBW BTEW BTVG
    BTYW BTYX BUHZ BUJM BUKO BVUZ JOLY OVFM
140 variants
    G-AKUR ALOD ALTO ANGK BOCI BPHW BPHX BPKO BPUU
    BTYX BUHO BYCD HALJ
150 variants
    "G-BMAF" G-APXY ARFI ARFO ASMS ASMW ASST ASUE ASYP
    ASZB ASZU ATEF ATHV ATHZ ATKF ATMC ATML ATMM ATMN
    ATMY ATNE ATNL ATOD ATRK ATRM ATUF ATYM ATZY AVAA
    AVAR AVEM AVEN AVER AVGU AVHM AVIA AVIB AVIT AVMD
    AVMF AVNC AVPH AVUG AVUH AVZU AWAW AWAX AWBX
    AWCP AWES AWFF AWGK AWLA AWMT AWOT AWPJ AWPU
    AWRK AWTJ AWTX AWUG AWUH AWUJ AWUK AWUL AWUN
    AWUO AWUT AWUU AXGG AXPF AYBD AYGC AYRF AZLH AZLY
    AZZR AZXC BABC BAEU BAHI BAIK BAIP BAMC BAXU BAXV
    BAYO BAYP BAZS BBBC BBCI BBDT BBJX BBKA BBKB BBKE
    BBKY BBNJ BCBX BCCC BCRT BCUH BCUJ BDBU BDFJ BDFZ
    BDOD BDSL BDTX BDUM BDUO BDZC BEIG BELT BEOK BEWP
    BFIY BFOG BFSR BFVU BFWL BGBI BGEA BGOJ BHIY BIFY
    BIOC BJOV BLVS BMBB BMLX BMXJ BNFI BOBV BOIV BOMN
    BORY BOTP BOUJ BOUZ BOVT BOWC BPAB BPAW BPAX BPCJ
    BPEM BPGZ BPNA BPOS BPRP BPWG BPWM BPWN BRBH
    BRJT BRLR BRNC BRTC BRTJ BSBZ BSEJ BSJU BSKA BSSB
    BSYV BSYW BSZU BSZV BTES BTGP BTHE BTIN BTSN BTTE
    BTYC BUCS BUCT BUGG BURH BUTT BWII BWVL BZJW CDIS
    CEOK SBM CSFC DENA DENB DENC DEND ECBH EJMG FAYE
    FFEN FINA GBLR GCNZ GFLY GLED GOLY HFCB HIVE HULL
    IANJ JWDS LUCK KMCL MABE NSTG NWFA OJVH OKED OSTY
    PHAA PLAN SADE SALL SAMZ SMCL TAIL TEDB UFLY USAA YIII
A150 AEROBAT variants
    G-AXRT AXSW AXUF AYCF AYOZ AYRO AZID AZJY AZOZ AZUZ
    AZZX BABD BACN BACO BACP BAEP BAEV BAEZ BAII BAOP
    BAPI BAPJ BBTB BBXB BCDY BCFR BCKU BCKV BCTU BCUY
    BCVG BCVH BDAI BDEX BDOW BDRD BEIA BEMY BEOE BEOY
    BFGG BFGX BFGZ BFIE BFRR BHRH BIBN BJTB BLPH BMEX
    BOFW BOYU BPJW BTFS BUCA BUTT CLUB FMSG HFCA JAGS
    JHAC OISO OPIC OSND PHLY PHOR PHUN PNIX
152
    G-BFEK BFFC BFFE BFFW BFHU BFHV BFKG BFLU BFOE BFOF
    BGAA BGAB BGAE BGFX BGGO BGGP BGHI BGIB BGLG BGNT
    BHAA BHAI BHAV BHCP BHDM BHDR BHDS BHDW BHEC BHFC

BHFI BHHG BHIN BHPY BHRB BHRN BHSA BHUI BHUP BHWA
BHWB BHYX BHZH BICG BIDH BIJV BIJW BIJX BILR BILS BIOK
BITF BITH BIUM BIXH BIZG BJKY BJNF BJVJ BJVT BJWH BJYD
BKAZ BKFC BKGW BKTV BKWY BLJO BLWV BLZE BLZH BLZP
BMCV BMFZ BMGG BMJB BMJC BMJD BMMM BMSU BMTA
BMTB BMTJ BMVB BMXA BMXB BMXC BMXX BNAJ BNDO BNFR
BNFS BNHJ BNHK BNID BNJB BNJC BNJD BNJH BNKC BNKI
BNKP BNKR BNKS BNKV BNMD BNME BNMF BNNR BNOZ BNPY
BNRK BNRL BNSI BNSM BNSN BNSU BNSV BNUL BNUS BNUT
BNYL BOAI BODO BOFL BOFM BOHI BOHJ BOIO BOIR BOKY
BOLV BOLW BONW BOOI BOTG BOYL BOZR BPBJ BPBK BPEO
BPFZ BPGM BPHT BPIY BPME BPTU BRBF BRBP BRND BRNE
BRNK BRNN BRPV BRTD BRTP BRUA BSCP BSCZ BSDO BSDP
BSFP BSFR BSTO BSTP BSWH BSZI BSZO BSZW BTAL BTCE
BTDW BTFC BTGH BTGR BTGW BTGX BTIK BTVW BTVX BTYT
BUEF BUEG BVTM BWEU BWEV BWNB BWNC BWND BXJM
BXTB BXVB BXVY BXWC BXYU BYFA BYMH BYMJ BZAE BZEB
BZEC BZHE BZHF BZWH CCHT CCTW CDTX CEFM CEPX CEUS
CEZM CHIK CPFC DACF ENTT ENTW FIFO FIGA FIGB FLOP
GFIA GFIB GFIC GFID HART HFCL HFCT IBRO JIMH KATT LAMS
LSMI MASS OBEN ODAC OFRY OIMC OLEE OPAM OVMC
OWAC OWAK OWOW PFSL POCO SACB TALA TALB TALC TALD
TAYS WACB WACE WACF WACG WACT
A152 AEROBAT
    G-BFGL BFKF BFMK BFRV BFZN BFZU BGAF BGLN BHAD BHED
    BHEN BHJA BHMG BHMH BILK BIMT BLAC BLAX BMUO BMYG
    BOPX BOSO BOYB BRUM BZEA ECAD FIFE FLAP FLIP JONI
    LEIC MPBH OCPC OWFS WACH WACU ZOOL
170
    G-AORB APVS AWOU BCLS MDAY
172 SKYHAWK and CUTLASS variants
    G-APSZ ARID ARLU ARMO ARMR AROA ARWO ARWR ARYI
    ARYK ARYS ASIB ASMJ ASNW ASOK ASSS ASUP ASVM ASWL
    ATAF ATFY ATKT ATLM ATSL ATWJ AVEC AVHH AVIC AVIS
    AVJF AVKG AVPI AVTP AVVC AVZV AWGD AWLF AWMP AWMZ
    AWUX AWUZ AWVA AXBH AXBJ AXDI AXSI AXVB AYCT AYRG
    AYRT AYUV AZDZ AZJV AZKW AZKZ AZLM AZLV AZTK AZTS
    AZUM AZXD AZZV BAEO BAEY BAIW BAIX BANX BAOB BAOS
    BAVB BAXY BAZT BBDH BBJY BBJZ BBKI BBKZ BBNZ BBOA
    BBTG BBTH BCHK BCOL BCPK BCRB BCUF BCVJ BCYR BCZM
    BDCE BDNU BDZD BEHV BEMB BENK BEUX BEWR BEZK BEZO
    BEZR BEZV BFGD BFKB BFMX BFOV BFPH BFRS BFTH BFZV
    BGAG BGBR BGHJ BGIU BGIY BGLO BGMP BGND BGRO BGSV
    BGVS BHAW BHCC BHCM BHDX BHDZ BHMI BHPZ BHSB BHUG
    BHUJ BHVR BHYP BHYR BIBW BIDF BIGJ BIHI BIIB BIIE BIOB
    BITM BIZF BJDE BJDW BJGY BJVM BJWI BJWW BJXZ BKCE
    BKEP BKEV BKII BKIJ BKLO BLHJ BLVW BMCI BMHS BMIG
    BNKD BNKE BNRR BNST BNTP BNXD BNYM BOEN BOHH BOIL
    BOIX BOIY BOJR BOJS BOLI BOLY BOMS BONR BONS BOOL
    BORW BOUE BOUF BOVG BOYP BPML BPRM BPTL BPVA
    BPVY BPWS BRAK BRBI BRBJ BRCM BRWX BRZS BSEP BSHR
    BSNG BSOG BSOO BSPE BSTM BTMA BTMR BTRE BUJN BULH
    BURD BUZN BXGV BXOI BXSD BXSE BXSR BXXK BYBD BYEA
    BYES BYNA BZBF BZGH BZZD CBFO CBME CBOR CBXJ CCTT
    CDDK CDMM CEKI CEMH CESS CFCI CFIO CFLY CFMM CFOI
    CFSM CLUX CMBR COCO CSCS CXSM DCKK DEMH DODD
    DRBG DUNK DUVL ECGC ECON EETG EGEG EICK ENII ENNK
    ENOA EOLX ETAT ETDC FACE FLOW FNLD FNLY GBFF GBLP
    GBTL GEHL GFEA GFMT GFSA GRAY GWYN GYAV GZDO
    HERC HILS ICOM ILPY IMAD IZZS IZZY JFWI JMKE JONZ LACI
    LANE LAVE LENX LICK LSCM LLCH MALK MCLY MELT MFAC
    MICK MILA NOUS NWFC NWFG OAKR OBMS OERS OFCM
    OJAG OOLE OPFT OPYE ORMG OSII OSPK OSKY OTAM OVFR
    OWST OZOO PDSI PFCL RATI RARB RGAP RJCC ROLY ROOK
    ROUP RSNO RUIA RVRI SACD SBAE SEVE SEXI SHSP SHWK
    SKAN SKKY SMRS TAMR TASH TDRA TIML TOBI TOBY TRAX
    TRIO TYMS TYRE UFCB UFCC UFCD UFCE UFCF UFCG UFCH
    UFCI UFCJ WACL WACW WACY YFZT YNYS YORK YSPY ZACE
172RG CUTLASS
    G-BHYC BILU PARI
R172K HAWK XP
    G-BHYD BPCI BPWR BTMK FANL XPII
REIMS FR172 ROCKET variants
    G-AWCN AWDR AWWU AWYB AYGX BAIL BARC BBKG BCTK
    BDOE BFSS BLPF BZVB DRAM DRID EDTO JANS LOYA MFEF
    RABA YBAA ROKT RKKT THIN
REIMS FR172K HAWK XP
    G-BFIU BFIU DAVD EFBP PJTM STAY YIPI
175 SKYLARK
    G-ARCV ARFG ARML ARMN AROC ARRI ARUZ ARWS
177(RG) CARDINAL
    G-AYPG AYPH AYSX AYSY AZTF AZTW AZVP BAGN BAIS BAJA
    BAJB BAJE BBHI BBJV BCUW BEBN BFIV BFMH BFPZ BPSL

BRDO BRPS BTSZ BUJE FIJJ FNEY GBFR LNYS OAMP OSFS
TOTO

180 including 180K SKYWAGON
G-ARAT ASIT AXZO BEOD BETG BNCS BOIA BUPG CIBO DAPH

(T) 182 SKYLANE variants
G-ARAW ASLH ASSF ASXZ ATCX ATLA ATPT ATTD AVCV AVDA
AVGY AVID AWJA AXNX AXZU AYOW AYWD AZNO BAAT BAFL
BAHD BAHX BAMJ BBGX BBYH BBYS BCWB BDBJ BDIG BEKO
BFSA BFZD BGAJ BGPA BHDP BHIB BHIC BHVP BHYA BJVH
BKHJ BKKN BKKO BMMK BMUD BNMO BNRY BOPH BOTH
BOWO BPUM BRKR BRRK BSDW BSRR BTHA BUVO BWMC
BWRR BXEZ BXZM BYEM BZVO CBIL CBMP CBVX CCAN CCYS
CDRC CDXI CEFV DATG DAVZ DOVE DRGS DTFF EEZS EFAM
EIRE EIWT EKOS ENRM EOHL ESME ESSL FAUX GBUN GCYC
GHOW GUMS HHDR HRND HRNT HUFF IATU IBZS IFAB IJAG
IOPT IRPC ISEH IZZI JBRN JENI JHPC JOBS JOON KEMY KTWO
KWAX LANS LEGG LVES MICI MILN MISH MOUT NLEE NOCK
NYZS OBBO ODEX OHAC OJHC OJRM OLDG OMAG OPCG
OPST ORAY OWCS OWRT OZOI PDHJ PLEE POPW POWL PTRI
PUGS RACY RCWK ROWE SAAM SHAR SKYL SNAL THRE TPSL
VALI VIPA WARP WHDP WIFE WMLT XLTG ZBLT ZGZG

185 SKYWAGON
G-AYNN BBEX BDKC BKPC BLOS BWWF BXRH BYBP RNRM

190
G-BTBJ

195A
G-BSPK

205(A)
G-ASNK ASOX

(T)P206D SUPER SKYLANE
G-AWUA AYCJ

(U)206 SUPER SKYWAGON variants
G-ASVN ATCE ATLT BGWR BMHC BPGE DROP LEMO

(U)206 STATIONAIR variants
G-AZRZ BAGV BMOF BOFD BSUE BXDB BXRO CCSN LEMO
PEPA SBKS SEAI STAT

(U)206 TURBO STATIONAIR variants
G-BFCT CCRC OLLS OSSA SEMR SKYE

207 SKYWAGON
G-NJAG

208 CARAVAN and 208B GRAND CARAVAN
G-BZAH EELS ETHY GOTF MDJE OAFF OHPC UKPS

210 CENTURION variants
G-ASXR BENF BEYV BNZM BSGT CDMH DECK EEWS EMLS
MANT MPRL OFLY OWAN PIIX SEEK TOTN VMDE

T303 CRUSADER
G-BSPF CMOS CRUZ CYLS DOLY GAME IKAP INDC JUIN MILO
OAPE PUSI ROCH UILT

305 BIRD DOG (L-19)
G-PDOG VDOG

310 variants
G-APNJ ARCI ASSZ AXLG AYGB AYND AZUY BALN BARG BARV
BBXL BGTT BHEH BIFA BJMR BODY BPIL BRIA BTFF BWYE
BWYG BXUY BXYG EGEE EGLT FFWD FISH IMLI MIWS MPBI
ODLY REDB REDD RIST RODD SOUL TKPZ TROP VDIR XLKF
YHPV

(T)337 SUPER SKYMASTER variants
G-AXHA BCBZ BMJR HIVA RGEN

REIMS F337 SUPER SKYMASTER variants
G-AZKO BFGH BFJR BOYR BTVV

340
G-BVES CCXJ HAFG LIZA LUND SAMM

401 variants
G-AVKN AZFR AZRD DACC OVNE

402 variants
BXJA MAPP NOSE

404 TITAN,
G-BWLF EXEX FIFA MIND OOSI TASK

REIMS F406 CARAVAN II
G-BVJT CVXN FIND LEAF MAFA MAFB SFPB SMMA SMMB
TDSA TURF

421 GOLDEN EAGLE variants
G-BAGO BFTT BHKJ FTAX HIJK JACK KWLI PVIP SVIP TAMY
TREC UVIP VVIP

425 CORSAIR,
G-KRMA

441 CONQUEST
G-USAR

500 CITATION
G-DJAE JTNC LOFT ORHE

501 CITATION 1
G-VUEM

510 CITATION MUSTANG
G-FBLK FBNK KLNW LEAA LEAB LEAC LEAI MICE NGEL ZJET

525 CITATIONJET variants
G-BVCM CITJ CJAD CJDB EDCJ EDCK EDCL EEBJ FBLI FBLK
FLBK GEBJ HCSA HGRC IUAN NMRM OCJZ ODAG ODCM OMBI
OODM ORAN OSOH PWNS SEAJ SFCJ TBEA TSJF ZIZI

550 CITATION II
G-CEUO DWJM EJEL ESTA FCDB FIRM FJET GHPG IDAB IKOS
JBIS JBIZ JETC JETJ JETO JMDW ORDB RDBS SOVA SPUR
VUEA VUEZ

550 CITATION BRAVO
G-OMRH WAIN YPRS

551 CITATION variants
G-FLVU LUXY

560 CITATION V
G-JOPT PPLC

560 CITATION ULTRA variants
G-KDMA OBCC

560 XL CITATION EXCEL
G-CBRG CIEL ELOA FCAP IPAX KPEI LDFM REDS SIRS VECT
WINA XLGB

560 XL CITATION XLS
G-NSJS OMEA OROO OXLS PKRG RSXL XBEL

680 CITATION SOVEREIGN
G-GEVO CFGB SIRJ SVGN SVSB TLFK XBLU

750 Citation X
G-CDCX CEDK

CFM METAL-FAX including **CFM AIRCRAFT LTD**
IMAGE
G-BTUD

SHADOW Series B and BD (Rotax 447)
G-MNZP MNZR MTFU MTGN MTHV MVBB MVCW MVIG MVRS
MVRT MVYZ MYKE

SHADOW Series C and CD (Rotax 503)
G-BZLF MGUY MJVF MNCM MNER MNIS MNTK MNTP MNVI
MNVJ MNVK MNWY MNXX MNZJ MNZZ MTBE MTCA MTCT
MTDU MTFU MTGV MTGW MTHT MTKR MTMX MTMY MTWH
MTWK MTXR MVAC MVAM MVAN MVCC MVEI MVEN MVFH
MVHD MVLJ MVLP MVOH MVPK MVRO MVRP MVRR MVVT
MWAE MWDB MWDN MWEN MWEZ MWFB MWIZ MWJF MWLD
MWMU MWON MWPN MWRL MWSY MWSZ MWTJ MWTN MWTP
MWUA MWVG MWVH MWYD MYBC MYBL MYCM MYDD MYDE
MYEP MYGO MYIF MYIP MYLV MYOH MYON MYOS MYPL MYPT
MYSM MYTH MYUS MYWF MYWM MYXY MZBN MZCT MZRS
PSUE

SHADOW Series DD (Rotax 582)
G-BXZY BYCJ CCMW DARK DMWW LYNK MGTW MYZP MZBS
MZGS MZKH MZNH MZOM ODVB PBEL

SHADOW D Series SS (Rotax 912)
G-MZLP

STREAK SHADOW and STARSTREAK SHADOW
G-BONP BROI BRSO BRWP BRZZ BSMN BSOR BSPL BSRX
BSSV BTDD BTEL BTGT BTKP BTZZ BUGM BUIL BULJ BUOB
BUTB BUVX BUWR BUXC BVDT BVFR BVLF BVOR BVPY BVTD
BWAI BWCA BWOZ BWPS BXFK BXVD BXWR BYAZ BYFI BYOO
BZEZ BZMZ BZWJ BZWY CBCZ CBNO CEZU DOTT ENEE FAME
GORE HLCF MEOW MGGT MGPH MWPP MYNX MYTY OLGA
OPIT ORAF OTCH RINT ROTS SHIM SNEV TEHL TTOY WESX
WHOG WYAT

CGS including **ARROWFLIGHT AVIATION LTD**
HAWK
G-MWYS MYTP MZGU

CHAMPION AIRCRAFT CORPORATION see also **AERONCA** and
BELLANCA
7FC TRI-TRAVELER
G-APYT ARAP ARAS

CHANCE-VOUGHT see **VOUGHT**

CHARGUS GLIDING CO LTD see also **HIWAY**
T.250
G-MBEU MBJG
VORTEX 120
G-MJWH

CHICHESTER-MILES CONSULTANTS LTD including
DESIGNABILITY LTD
LEOPARD
G-BKRL BRNM

CHILTON AIRCRAFT
DW.1 and 2 variants
    G-AESZ AFGH AFGI AFSV BWGJ CDXU DWIA DWIB

CHOWN
Balloon (Minimum Lift)
OSPREY variants
    G-BBJHI BJHJ BJHN BJHO BJHP BJHR BJHW BJHY BJHZ BJIC
    BJID BJIK BJKV BJKZ BJLE BJMH BJMT BJND BJNH BJHI BJPL
    BJPT BJRA BJRG BJRL BJRO BJSC BJSD BJSF BJSI BJSK BJTZ
    FYBO
PORTSWOOD variants
    G-FYBB FYBX

CHRISLEA AIRCRAFT CO LTD
LC.1 AIRGUARD
    G-AFIN
CH.3 SUPER ACE
    G-AKUW AKVD AKVF
CH.3 Series 4 SKYJEEP
    G-AKVR

CHRISTEN INDUSTRIES INC including **AVIAT AIRCRAFT INC**
and homebuilt, also see **PITTS**
EAGLE
    G-CCYO CENC CFIF CFIJ EEGL EGAL EGEL EGIL EGLE EGUL
    ELKA IXII NEST NUTA OEGL RIFY
A-1 HUSKY variants
    G-BUVR CDOD DBLX DOGY HAIB HSKE HSKI HUND HUSK JJDC
    LTMM OCLC OGGY USKY WATR

CHRIS TENA
MINI COUPE
    G-BPDJ

CIERVA AUTOGYRO COMPANY including **DE HAVILLAND**
AIRCRAFT CO LTD and **A V ROE** and **CO LTD** variants
C.8
    G-EBYY
C.19 (AVRO 620)
    G-ABXH
C.24
    G-ABLM
C.30A (AVRO 671)
    G-ACUU ACWM ACWP ACXA AHMJ

CIRRUS DESIGN CORPORATION
SR20
    G-CDLY CIRI CIRS DOLI EDHO GEMM JOEW OPSS OSPY OUNI
    RGZT SMKM SRVA SRZO TAAC TABI TABY VGAG ZOGT ZZDG
SR22
    G-CGRD CYPM ETFL HEJB MACL MAKS NETB OLCT OONK
    RAYY RBMS TAAB VBCA WTEC ZRZZ

CIVILIAN AIRCRAFT CO
CAC.1 COUPE
    G-ABNT

CLIFF SIMS
AZTEC trike
    G-MMFY

CLUTTON
FRED (Volkswagen 1834)
    G-BBBW BDBF BGFF BGHZ BISG BITK BJAD BKAF BKDP BKEY
    BKVF BKZT BLNO BMAX BMMF BMOO BMSL BNZR BOLS BPAV
    BVCO BWAP MANX ORAS PFAF PFAL RONW USTY WICH

COATES
SWALESONG
    G-AYDV

COLOMBAN
MC-12 and MC-15 CRI-CRI variants
    "G-SHOG" G-BOUT BWFO CDNJ CRIC CRIK MCXV OCRI SHOG

COLT BALLOONS LTD including **THUNDER and COLT LTD** and
CAMERON BALLOONS LTD (2) production
Airship (Gas-Filled)
GA-42
    G-BKXM MATS ZEPI

Airship (Hot Air)
AS-56
    G-BNKF BTXH NOVO
AS-80 (Rotax 462)
    G-BPCG BPGT BPKN
AS-105 (Rotax 462)
    G-BTSW BWKE BWMV BXEY BXNV BXYF RBOS
AS-120 (Rotax 582)
    G-BXKU
AS-261
    G-BPLD
Balloon (Hot Air)
12A Cloudhopper
    G-BHOJ
14A Cloudhopper
    G-BHKN BHKR BHPN
17A Cloudhopper
    G-BIDV BIYT BJWV BKBO BKDS BKIU BKXM BLHI BONV BPXH
    BUDY HELP HEXE
21 series
    G-BLVY BLXG BMKI BNFM BOLN BOLP BOLR BPFX BSAK BSIG
    BTXM BUEU LLAI SOOS
H-24
    G-BZUV
25 series
    G-BSOF BUPH BVAO OKBT
31 series
    G-BHIG BROJ BSDV BSMM BVTL BXXU DNGR DHLZ DOWN
    HOUS IMAN MUTE PIXE PONY
42 series
    G-BJZR SEAT
56 series
    G-BHEX BICM BISX BIXW BJXP BJYF BKSD BLLW BLOT BTZY
    BVCN BVOZ BVUC CCYP CFBI EZXO FZZZ ILEE MERC POSH
    TTWO WIMP
65D
    G-BLCH
69 series
    G-BLEB BOVW BPAH BSHC BSHD BTMO COLR FZZY JBJB
    OABC OBUD TCAN TWEY
77 series
    G-BGOD BIGT BKOW BLTA BLUE BMYN BOCF BOGT BOHD
    BORA BORE BORT BPEZ BPFB BRLT BRVF BRVU BSCI BSUB
    BSUK BTDS BTTS BTZS BUJH BUKS BULF BURG BUVE BUVS
    BUVT BUYO BVAX BXFN BXIE BYFX CDUY CHEL CURE DING
    DRAW DURX EZVS FLAG GGOW GOBT HOME HOTI HOTZ IMAG
    JONO LSHI MAUK MKAK OAWS OBJH OCAR ODAD OLPG ONCL
    OSST READ SGAS SIXX SSBS STOK TTFG TRUX UPPP UZLE
    WHAT WHIM WOOL WRIT
90 series
    G-BPUW BRHG BRRU BSIU BTCS BTPVI BXUW FOWL IRLY
    JNNB OBBC OLDV OMMM PEGG PHSI SAUF SEND TOFT
105 series
    G-BLMZ BMBS BNAG BPZS BRUH BSCC BSHS BSNU BTHX
    BURL BUSV BWMA BWRM BYIO FVRY OMGR OWEL PLUG
    POPP RAIL
120 series
    G-BXCO BYDJ BZIL BZNF CBEJ CFNJ OBIB VYGR
160 series
    G-CFKX
180 series
    G-BMXM BOGR BONK CUCU MUMM
210 series
    G-BULN BUXA BVFY BZYO
240 series
    G-IGLA LCIO
260 series
    G-HUGO
315 series
    G-CCIE VVBF
2500 series
    G-USUK

Special Shapes

SHAPE	REGISTRATION(S)
AGFA FILM CASSETTE	G-OHDC
ARIEL BOTTLE	G-BNHN
BEER GLASS	G-BNHL PUBS
BIBENDUM	G-PNEU
BLACK KNIGHT	G-BNMI
BOTTLE	G-BOTL
BUDWEISER CAN	G-BUET BVIO
CLOWN	G-GWIZ

CYLINDER	G-CHUB
DRACHENFISCH	G-BMUJ
EGG	G-BWWL
FILM CAN	G-OXRG
FINANCIAL TIMES	G-ETFT FTFT
FLAME	G-BLKU
FLYING HEAD	G-HEAD
FLYING JEANS	G-JCJC
FLYING MITT	G-WCAT
FLYING YACHT	G-BXXJ
GAS FLAME	G-BGOO
HEAD	G-HEAD
HOP	G-MALT
ICE CREAM CONE	G-BWBE BWBF OJHB
J and B WHISKY BOTTLE	G-JANB
JUMBO	G-OVAA
KINDERMOND	G-BMUL
MAXWELL HOUSE COFFEE JAR	G-BVBJ BVBK
MICKEY MOUSE	G-BTRB
OLD PARR WHISKY BOTTLE	G-PARR
PANASONIC BATTERY	G-PSON
PIG	G-BUZS
PIGGY BANK	G-BXVW
SATZENBRAU BOTTLE	G-BIRE
STORK	G-BRGP
TANK	G-BXND
UFO	G-BMUK
WORLD	G-DHLI

COLTING BALLOONS LTD
Balloon (Hot Air)
AX8-105A
G-BGAS

COMCO IKARUS GmbH including **AEROSPORT LTD** (formerly **FLYBUY ULTRALIGHTS LTD**) production
IKARUS C42 variants
G-CBFV CBGP CBIJ CBJW CBKU CBPD CBRF CBTG CBVY CBXC CCCT CCFZ CCLS CCNT CCPS CCYR CCZL CDBU CDCG CDCM CDCO CDIX CDJK CDMS CDNR CDOK CDOT CDPP CDRO CDRP CDRY CDSW CDUK CDVI CDWI CDYD CDYO CDYT CDZG CEAK CEAN CECC CECL CEDC CEDR CEEW CEFA CEGL CEGZ CEHG CEHV CEJW CEPY CETR CETZ CEVA CEWY CEZA CFBE CFGM CFHP CFIT CFIY CFLD CFOG CLIF CFTO CVAL CWAY DASS DJBC DMCI DNKS DOZI DTOY DUGE EDEE EGGI FBII FIFT FLYB FLYC FLYM FROM GNJW GRPA GSCV HBBH HIJN HNGE IBAZ IAJS ICRS IKRS INJA JADW JENK JWDB MGPA MROY MSKY NCCI NDPA NORA NPPL NSBB OAJL OEKS OFBU OJDS ORMW OROS OSTL OVAL OVLA RBSN RODJ ROZZ RTMY SARM SFLA SFLB SGEN SIMM SJEN ULSY WILT WOLV WSSX YADA ZAVI

COMMANDER AIRCRAFT COMPANY see **ROCKWELL**

COMMONWEALTH AIRCRAFT CORPORATION PTY LTD see **NORTH AMERICAN**

COMPER AIRCRAFT CO
CLA.7 SWIFT
G-ABTC ABUS ABUU ACTF ECTF LCGL OBUU

CONSOLIDATED VULTEE AIRCRAFT CORPORATION see **STINSON AIRCRAFT CORPORATION**
CV.32-3 LIBERATOR
G-AGZI
PBY-5A CATALINA
G-PBYA

CONVAIR see **GENERAL DYNAMICS CORPORATION**

COOK
ARIES P
G-MYXI

COPE
BUG
G-BXTV

CORBEN
BABY ACE
G-BTSB BUAA
JUNIOR ACE
G-BSDI

CORBETT FARMS LTD see **MICROFLIGHT AIRCRAFT LTD**

CORBY
CJ-1 STARLET
G-BVVZ CBHP CCHN CCXO ILSE

CORVUS AIRCRAFT KFT
CA22 CRUSADER
G-CSDR

COSMIK AVIATION LTD
SUPERCHASER
G-DREG

COSMOS
TRIKE with La Mouette wing
G-MVCK

ETABLISSEMENT COUESNON - see JODEL

CRANFIELD INSTITUTE OF TECHNOLOGY
A.1-400 EAGLE
G-COAI

CREMER
Balloon (Minimum Lift)
HOT AIR FREE
G-BJLX BJLY BJRP BJRR BJRV

CROSBY see **ANDREASSON**

CROSSLEY
RACER
G-BKRU

CSS see **POLIKARPOV**

CUB PROSPECTOR see **PIPER**

CULVER
LCA CADET
G-CDET

CURRIE
WOT variants
G-APNT ARZW ASBA AVEY AYMP AYNA BANV BDFB BFAH BFWD BKCN BLPB BXMX CWBM CWOT PFAP SWOT

CURTISS-WRIGHT AIRCRAFT CORPORATION
TRAVEL AIR 12Q TRAVELAIR
G-AAOK

CURTISS-WRIGHT CORPORATION
H-75A
G-CCVH
P-40B TOMAHAWK
G-CDWH
P-40N KITTYHAWK
G-KITT

CURTISS ROBERTSON
ROBIN C.2
G-BTYY HFBM

CUSTOMCRAFT BALLOON SERVICES
Balloon (Hot Air)
A25
G-CCKZ DUMP

CVJETKOVIC AIRCRAFT
CA-65 SKYFLY
G-CFVJ

CYCLONE AIRSPORTS LTD see also **PEGASUS AVIATION** and **SOLAR WINGS (AVIATION)**
70 trike (Rotax 377/277) with Aerial Arts 110SX &130SX wings
G-MMYL MNMY
AX3
G-BVJG MYFI MYFV MYFW MYFZ MYGD MYHG MYHH MYHJ MYHM MYHR MYIJ MYIU MYKA MYKT MYME MYMW MYMZ MYOY MYPM MYPR MYRO MYRU MYRV MYSO MYTM MYUI MYVN MYXH MYYL MYZC MYZF MYZG MZDS MZEL

AX2000
G-BYJM CBGS CBMB CBUX JONY MGUN MYER MZER MZFA
MZFX MZGA MZGB MZGC MZGM MZGP MZHR MZIV MZJF MZJL
MZJR MZKC MZLM MZLS MZLU MZMX OAJB ROMW STRG
WAKY

CZECH AIRCRAFT WORKS (CZAW)
SPORTCRUISER
G-CESZ CFEZ CFIU CFKB CFLG CFNV CFOV CFPA CFPJ CFUZ
CRAR CRUI CRWZ CRZA CZAW CZSC DADZ DOIG EDDS ENST
EWZZ FELX IBUZ JAYZ KRUZ MELL MESH MISJ MOOV MRDS
MUTT OCZA RRAT SASI SCCZ SCPI SCRZ SCSC SCZR SPCZ
TEZZ VIIZ XERO ZAAP ZECH

DAN RIHN
DR.107 ONE DESIGN
G-CEPZ CVII IDII IIID IIPB LOAD ONED RIHN TAZZ

DART AIRCRAFT LTD
KITTEN
G-AEXT

DASSAULT AVIATION including **AVIONS MARCEL DASSAULT** and
AVIONS MARCEL DASSAULT-BREGUET AVIATION production
FALCON 7X
G-SRDG
FALCON 10
G-ECJI
FALCON 20
G-FFRA FRAD FRAF FRAH FRAI FRAJ FRAK FRAL FRAO FRAP
FRAR FRAS FRAT FRAU FRAW FRBA
FALCON 900 variants
G-CBHT FFFG FNES GALX HMEI HMEV JMMX JPSX REYG SABI
SIRO WTOR
FALCON 2000 variants
G-GEDY JETF KWIN MDBA OJAJ WLVS

DAVIS
DA-2A
G-BPFL

DE HAVILLAND AIRCRAFT LTD including **AMERICAN MOTH
CORPORATION, DE HAVILLAND AIRCRAFT PTY LTD, F + W,
MORANE-SAULNIER, MORRIS MOTORS** and **OGMA** production –
also see **AIRCO** and **HAWKER SIDDELEY AVIATION**
DH.51
G-EBIR
DH.53 HUMMING BIRD
G-EBHX EBQP
DH.60G and DH.60M MOTH variants including replicas*
G-EBLV EBWD
"G-AAAH" x 2* G-AAAH AADR AAEG AAHI AAHY AAJT AALY
AAMX AAMY AAMZ AANL AANO AANV AAOR AAWO AAYT AAZG
ABAG ABDA ABDX ABEV ABSD ABYA ABZB ACGZ ACNS ACXB
ACXK ADHD ATBL EBNO EBZN BVNG
DH.71 TIGER MOTH
G-ECDX
DH.80A PUSS MOTH
G-AAZP ABDW ABIH ABLS AEOA AHLO FAVC
DH.82 TIGER MOTH variants and replicas*
"G-ABUL"* "G-ACDR"* "G-MAZY" G-ACDA ACDC ACDI ACMD
ADGT ADGV ADGZ ADIA ADJJ ADNZ ADPC ADWJ ADWO ADXT
AFGZ AFVE AFWI AGEG AGHY AGNJ AGPK AGYU AGZZ AHAN
AHIZ AHLT AHOO AHPZ AHUF AHUV AHVU AHVV AIDS AIRI
AIRK AIXJ AJHS AJOA AJTW AJVE AKEE AKUE AKUS ALBD
ALIW ALJL ALNA ALND ALRI ALUC ALVP ALWS ALWW AMBB
AMCK AMCM AMHF AMIV AMJD AMLF AMJR AMNN AMOU
AMPM AMRM AMTF AMTK AMTP AMTV AMVS ANCN ANCS
ANCX ANCY ANDE ANDM ANDP ANEH ANEJ ANEL ANEM ANEN
ANEW ANEZ ANFC ANFI ANFL ANFM ANFP ANFV ANFW ANHK
ANJD ANJG ANKK ANKT ANKV ANKZ ANLD ANLS ANM ANMY
ANNB ANNC ANNE ANNG ANNI ANNK ANOH ANOM ANON
ANOO ANOS ANPE ANPK ANRF ANRM ANRN ANRX ANSG
ANSM ANTE ANZS ANZU ANZZ AOAA AOBH AOBX AODR AODT
AOEI AOEL AOES AOET AOFR AOGI AOGJ AOGR AOHY AOIL
AOIM AOIS AOJJ AOJK AOJX AOUR AOYU AOXG AOXN AOZH
APAL APAM APAO APAP APBI APCC APFU APGL APIH APJP
APLU APMX APPT ARAZ AREH ARTL ASKP ASPV AVPJ AXAN
AXBW AXBZ AXXV AYDI AYIT AZDY AZGZ AZZZ BACK BAFG
BBRB BYLB BEWN BFHH BHLT BHUM BJAP BJZF BMPY BNDW
BPAJ BPHR BRHW BTOG BWIK BWMK BWMS BWVT BYTN
CDJO CFII DHTM DHZF ECDS EMSY ERDS MOTH OOSY PWBE
TIGA TYMO

DH.82B QUEEN BEE
G-BLUZ
DH.83 FOX MOTH variants
G-ACCB ACEJ AOJH
DH.84 DRAGON
G-ACET ACIT AJKF ECAN
DH.85 LEOPARD MOTH
G-ACLL ACMA ACMN ACOJ ACUS AIYS
DH.87B HORNET MOTH
G-ADKC ADKK ADKL ADKM ADLY ADMT ADND ADNE ADOT
ADRH ADUR AELO AESE AHBL AHBM AMZO
DH.88 COMET including reps*
"G-ACSS" x 2* G-ACSP ACSS
DH.89 DRAGON RAPIDE variants including replica*
"G-AEAJ"* G-ACPP ACYR ACZE ADAH AEML AERN AGJG AGSH
AGTM AHAG AHED AHGD AIDL AIWY AIYR AJBJ AJCL AKDW
AKGV AKIF AKNV AKOE AKRP AKRS ALGB ALXT ALZF
DH.90 DRAGONFLY
G-AEDU
DH.94 MOTH MINOR
G-AFNG AFNI AFNJ AFOB AFOJ AFOR AFOW AFPN
DH.98 MOSQUITO
G-ASKB ASKC AWJV MOSI
DH.100 VAMPIRE
G-BVPD DHXX FBIX
DH.104 DOVE and (SEA) DEVON including Riley conversions
"G-ALVD" G-AHRI ALCU ALFT ALFU AMDD AMFU AMXR AMXS
AMXX ANOV ANUW ANVU AOUF APSO ARBE ARDE AREA
ARHW ARHX ARJB ARUE ATGJ ATGK AWFM BAHB BVXR
BWWC DEVN DHDV DVON HBBC KOOL OEWA OPLC SDEV
DH.106 COMET
G-ANAV AOJT AOVU APAS APDB APDF APYD BDIW BDIX BEEX
CPDA
DH.110 SEA VIXEN
G-CVIX VIXN
DH.112 VENOM
G-BLID BLKA BLSD DHSS DHTT DHUU DHVM VENI VENM VICI
VNOM
DH.114 HERON and SEA HERON
"G-AOXL" G-ALZL ANPV ANUO ANXB AOGW AORG AOTI AOXL
APXG ASCX ASFI ASVC
DH.115 VAMPIRE and SEA VAMPIRE
G-BVLM BZRC BZRD DHVV DHWW DUSK HELV OBLN SPDR
VTII
DH.121 TRIDENT see HAWKER SIDDELEY
DH.125 see HAWKER SIDDELEY

DE HAVILLAND AIRCRAFT PTY LTD
DHA.3 DROVER
G-APXX

DE HAVILLAND CANADA including **DE HAVILLAND INC,
BOMBARDIER INC** *and **OGMA** production
DHC-1 CHIPMUNK
G-AKDN ALWB AMMA AMUF ANWB AOFE AOJR AORW AOSF
AOSK AOSP AOSY AOTD AOTF AOTR AOTY AOUO AOUP AOZP
APLO APPA APPM APTS APYG ARGG ARMC ARMD ARMF
ARWB ATHD ATVF BAPB BARS BAVH BBMN BBMO BBMR BBMT
BBMV BBMW BBMX BBMZ BBNA BBNC BBND BBRV BBSS
BCAH BCCX BCEY BCGC BCHL BCHV BCIH BCKN BCOI BCOO
BCOU BCOY BCPU BCRX BCSA BCSL BCXN BCYM BCZH BDCC
BDDD BDEU BDRJ BFAW BFAX BFDC BNZC BPAL BTWF BVTX
BVZZ BWHI BWJY BWJZ BWMX BWNK BWNT BWOX BWTG
BWTO BWUN BWUT BWUV BWVY BWVZ BXCP BXCT BXCV
BXDA BXDG BXDH BXDI BXDM BXDN BXDP BXEC BXGL BXGM
BXGO BXGP BXGX BXHA BXHF BXIA BXIM BXNN BYHL BYSJ
BZDU BZGA BZGB CBJG CERD CHPY CPMK DHCC DHPM HAPY
HDAE ITWB MAJR OACP PVET TRIC UANO ULAS
DHC-2 BEAVER
G-BVER DHCZ
DHC-6 TWIN OTTER
G-BIHO BVVK BZFP CBML
DHC-8 DASH EIGHT variants*
G-ECOA ECOD ECOG ECOH ECOI ECOJ ECOK ECOM ECOO
ECOV ECOW ECOY ECOZ JECE JECF JECG JECH JECI JECJ
JECK JECL JECM JECN JECO JECP JECR JECS JECT JECU
JECV JECW JECX JECY JEDI JEDJ JEDK JEDL JEDM JEDN
JEDO JEDP JEDR JEDT JEDU JEDV JEDW KKEV WOWA WOWB
WOWC WOWD WOWE

DEMOISELLE
G-CFGC

DEMON see **HIWAY**

DENNEY AEROCRAFT COMPANY including **SKYSTAR**
KITFOX (Rotax 582)
> G-BNYX BONY BPII BPKK BRCT BSAZ BSCG BSCH BSFX BSFY
> BSGG BSHK BSIF BSIK BSRT BSSF BSUZ BSVK BTAT BTBG
> BTBN BTDC BTDN BTIF BTIR BTKD BTMT BTNR BTOL BTSV
> BTTY BTVC BTWB BUDR BUIP BUKF BUKP BULZ BUNM BUOL
> BUPW BUWS BUYK BUZA BVAH BVCT BVEY BVGO BWAR
> BWHV BWSJ BWSN BWYI BXBP BXCW BXWH BZAR CBDI CBTX
> CDXY CJUD CRES CTOY DJNH ELIZ EYAS FBOY FOXC FOXD
> FOXF FOXG FOXI FOXS FOXX FOXZ FSHA HOBO HUTT KAWA
> KFOX KITF KITY KTTY LACR LEED LESJ LESZ LOST MSCM
> OFOX OPDS PHYL PPPP RAYA RFOX RSSF RWSS TFOX TOMZ
> TWTW

DEPERDUSSIN CIE
MONOPLANE
> G-AANH

DESIGNABILITY LTD see **CHICHESTER-MILES**

DESOUTTER AIRCRAFT COMPANY
DESOUTTER 1
> G-AAPZ

CONSTRUCTIONS AÉRONAUTIQUES EMILE DEWOITINE
D.26
> G-BBMI

DG FLUGZEUGBAU GmbH see **GLASER-DIRKS FLUGZEUGBAU GmbH**

DIAMOND AIRCRAFT INDUSTRIES GmbH
DA.20 KATANA
> G-BXGH BXJV BXJW BXMZ BXOF BXPC BXPD BXTS BYMB NIKK
> OBDA
DA.40(D) STAR
> G-CBFA CCFR CCFS CCFU CCHA CCHB CCHC CCHD CCHE
> CCHF CCHG CCHK CCKH CCKI CCLB CCLC CCLV CCLW CCMF
> CCPX CCUS CCXU CCZU CDEJ CDEK CDEL CDSF CDSZ CFJN
> CFJO DAKM DIAM DSPL EMDM EMMM HASO JKMG KAFT LAFT
> MAFT MOPB OCCD OCCE OCCF OCCG OCCH OCCK OCCL
> OCCM OCCN OCCO OCCP OCCR OCCS OCCT OCCU OCCV
> OTDI SFLY SOHO SULI WBVS ZANY
DA.42 TWIN STAR
> G-CDKR CDSZ CDTG CEWN CTCD CTCE CDTF CDXK CEFX
> CTCH DJET DMND DOSC ELSE ENGA FCAB GSYJ HAFT HANG
> IANV ITFL JKMH JKMJ KELV LLMW LULV MHJK OCCW OCCX
> OCCY OCCZ OPFR ORZA PETS RASA SELC SERE SLCT SUEA
> VVTV

DOLGOPRUDNENSKOGO DESIGN BUREAU OF AUTOMATION
Balloon (Hot Air)
DKBA AT 0301-0
> G-DKBA

DORNIER including **AG** fur **DORNIER-FLUGZEUGE, DORNIER GmbH, DORNIER WERKE AG, DORNIER LUFTFAHRT GmbH** and see **BUCKER**
DO.27
> G-BMFG
DO.28 SKYSERVANT
> G-ASUR
228
> G-MAFE MAFI OMAF
328
> G-BWIR BWWT BYHG BYMK BYML BZOG CCGS CJAB

DOUGLAS AIRCRAFT COMPANY INC including **DOUGLAS AIRCRAFT CORPORATION** and see **McDONNELL DOUGLAS**
AD-4 SKYRAIDER
> G-BMFB RADR
C-47 DAKOTA, and C-53 STORMTROOPER
> "G-AMSU" "G-AMZZ" G-AGYX AHLX AIYT AJAV AKLL ALFO
> ALWC AMCA AMHJ AMJY AMNL AMPO AMPY AMRA AMSM
> AMYJ AMZH AMZW ANAF BGCF BHUB BLFL DAKK
DC-6
> G-APSA SIXC
DC-7C
> G-AOIE

DRAGON BALLOONS
Balloon (Hot Air)
G77
> G-BKRZ

DRAGON LIGHT AIRCRAFT CO LTD
DRAGON 150 and 200
> G-MJSL MJVY MMAC MMAE MMAI MMML MMNH MMPR MNJF

DRAYTON BALLOONS
Balloon (Hot Air)
B-56
> G-BITS

DRUINE including **ROLLASON AIRCRAFT** and **ENGINES LTD** (D.31/D.62) production
D.31 TURBULENT
> G-AJCP APIZ APNZ APOL APTZ APUY APVN APVZ APWP ARBZ
> ARGZ ARIM ARLZ ARMZ ARNZ ARRU ARRZ ASFX ASHT ASMM
> ASSY ASTA ATBS AVPC AWBM AWDO AWMR AWWT BFXG
> BGBF BKUI BKXR BLTC BUKH BVLU BWID CFLP OJJF
D.53 TURBI, D.54 TURBI
> G-AOTK APBO APFA
D.62 CONDOR (Continental O-200-A)
> G-ARHZ ARVZ ASEU ASRB ASRC ATAU ATAV ATOH ATUG
> ATVW AVAW AVEX AVJH AVMB AVOH AVXW AWAT AWEI
> AWFN AWFO AWFP AWSN AWSP AWSS AWST AXGS AXGU
> AXGV AXGZ AYFC AYFD AYFE AYFF AYFG AYZS BADM BUOF
> RELL YNOT

DUDEK PARAGLIDING - see **BAILEY AVIATION**

DYKE
DELTA
> G-DYKE

SOCIÉTÉ DYN'AÉRO
CR100
> G-BZGY
MCR-01 variants (Rotax 912)
> G-BYEZ BYTM BZXG CBNL CBZX CCFG CCMM CCPN CCTE
> CCUI CCWH CDBY CDGG CDLL CDWG CENA CUTE CWMT
> DECO DGHI HARD KARK LMLV MHMH NONE OHIO PGAC POOP
> RESG TDVB TOOT

E-PLANE (Bishop & Castelli)
> G-EFUN

EAA
ACROSPORT
> G-BJHK BKCV BLCI BPGH BSHY BTAK BTWI BVVL CCFX NEGG
> OJDA OMLC TANY TSOL VCIO
BIPLANE
> G-ATEP AVZW BBMH BPUA PFAA PFAY

EAGLE see **AMERICAN AEROLIGHTS**

EAVES
Balloon (Minimum Lift)
DODO variants
> G-BJGF BJGG BJIC BJJD BJJE BJJF BJJG
EUROPEAN variants
> G-BJMG BJRB BJRC BJRD FYBP FYDB FYDC FYDN FYFA FYFG
> FYFH FYFI

ECLIPSE GLIDERS
SUPER EAGLE
> G-BGWZ

EDGAR PERCIVAL including **LANCASHIRE AIRCRAFT COMPANY** production
EP.9 PROSPECTOR
> G-APAD APXW ARDG

EDGE
360
> G-ZVKO

EDWARDS
GYROCOPTER
> G-ASDF

FLUGZEUGBAU EICHELSDORFER
SB.5
    G-DEJH

EH INDUSTRIES LTD
EH-101
    G-EHIL OIOI

EIPPER AIRCRAFT INC
QUICKSILVER MX
    G-MBBM MBCK MBFO MBYM MJAM MJBT MJDW MJIR MJJK
    MJPV MJVP MJVU MMBU MMMG MMNA MMNB MMNC MMWC
    MNCO MTDO MWDZ

EIRIAVION O/Y including **MOLINO**
PIK-20 series
    G-BHNP CJBH CJDK CJVE CJXG CKFE DDFE DDFK DDHH
    DDHN DDHV DDJN DDKT DDLJ DDLY DDMU DDOU DDPL DDRT
    DDVN DDWS DDZT DEAR DEAT EDMV OPIK PIKB PIKD POPE
    SOAR

EKW see also **DORNIER-WERKE AG**
C-3605
    G-CCYZ DORN

ELA AVIACIÓN S.L
ELA 07
    G-CECB CEEA CEEF CEER CEGY CEHO CENFCENR

ELECTRA FLYING CORPORATION
EAGLE
MBRB

ELLIOTTS OF NEWBURY
EoN AP.5 OLYMPIA 2B
    G-ALJZ
EoN AP.7 PRIMARY
    G-ALMN
EoN AP.10 460
    G-APWL

ELMWOOD
CA-05 CHRISTAVIA
    G-MRED

EMBRAER
EMB-110 BANDEIRANTE
    "G-FIRE" G-FLTY TABS
EMB-135BJ LEGACY
    G-CFJA CJMD CMAF IRSH OGSK RHMS RRAZ SIRA SYLJ WCCI
EMB-135ER
    G- RJXJ RJXK RJXL RJXP
EMB-145 variants
    G-EMBC EMBI EMBJ EMBK EMBL EMBM EMBN EMBP EMBU
    EMBV EMBW EMBX EMBY ERJA ERJC RJXA RJXB RJXC RJXD
    RJXE RJXF RJXG RJXH RJXI RJXM RJXN RJXO RJXR SYLJ
EMB-312 TUCANO
    G-BTUC CEHJ
ERJ190-200LR (Embraer 195)
    G-FBEA FBEB FBEC FBED FBEE FBEF FBEG FBEH FBEI FBEJ
    FBEK FBEL FBEM FBEN

ENGLISH ELECTRIC CO LTD including **AVRO (CANBERRA)**
production
WREN
    G-EBNV
CANBERRA
    G-BURM BVWC BVXC CDSX OMHD
LIGHTNING
    G-AWON AXEE BTSY FSIX LTNG OPIB

ENSTROM HELICOPTER CORPORATION
F-28
    G-BBHE BBIH BBPN BBPO BDKD BHAX BONG BRZG BURI
    BWOV BXLW BXXW BYKF BZHI EGAN MHCE MHCJ OABO
    ONUP PASN WSEC
280 SHARK
    G-BEYA BIBJ BPXE BSDZ BSLV BXFD BXRD BYSW CKCK COLL
    GKAT HDIX HKCF HYST IDUP MHCB MHCG MHCI MHCK MHCL
    MHCM MOTR OGES OITV OJBB OJMF OPDM OTHE PBYY SHAA
    SHRK SHUU SOPP VETS VRTX VVWW WIZI WRFM WRSY
    WSKY

480
    G-CUDY ENHP GUAY IGHH IJBB JPTT LADD LADZ MEEK OSKP
    OZAR RRAK TOIL TRUD TRYX UZZY WOOF

ENGINEERING AND RESEARCH CORPORATION including
AIR PRODUCTS LTD (FORNEY) and ALON INC (A-2) production
ALON A-2
    G-AVIL HARY
ERCOUPE 415 variants
    G-AVTT COUP EGHB ERCO
FORNEY F-1A
G-ARHB ARHC AROO ONHH

EUROCOPTER see also **AÉROSPATIALE, SUD-AVIATION** and **MBB**
EC.120 COLIBRI
    G-BXYD CBNB CFFP CFOA COML DEVL DRLH EIZO ETIM FCKD
    FEDA GTJM HEHE HVRZ IGPW ISSY JJFB LHCC LHMS MKII
    MODE OLDO OTFL PDGE RCNB TBLY TGGR VIPR WUSH WZRD
    ZADY ZZOE ZZZS
EC.130 ECUREUIL
    G- ECBO VFBR
EC.155 DAUPHIN 2
    G-CEOJ EURT EWAT HBJT HOTB ISST ISSV ISSW NIVA WJCJ
EC.225LP SUPER PUMA - see **AÉROSPATIALE**

EUROCOPTER DEUTSCHLAND GmbH
EC.135 variants
    G-BZRS CCAU CHSU CPSH DAAT DORS EMAA EMID ESEX
    EWRT HBOB IWRC KRNW LASU MSPT NEAU NESV NMID NWAA
    NWPS PLAL PSNI RWLA SASA SASB SPAO SPHU SSXX SUFF
    SUFK SURY TAGG VGMB WASN WCAO WMAO WMAS WONN
    XMII

EUROPA AVIATION including **AVIATION COMPOSITES CO LTD**
EUROPA variants (Rotax 912 variants)
    G-BVGF BVIZ BVJN BVKF BVLV BVOS BVOW BVRA BVUV BVVH
    BVVP BVWM BWCV BWDP BWDX BWEG BWFH BWFX BWIJ
    BWIV BWJH BWNL BWON BWRO BWUP BWVS BWWB BWYD
    BWZA BXCH BXDY BXFG BXGG BXHY BXII BXIJ BXLK BXNC
    BXTD BXUM BYFG BYIK BYJI BYPM BYSA BZAM BZHS BZNY
    BZTH BZTI BZTN CBES CBHI CBOF CBWP CBXW CBYN CCEF
    CCFK CCGW CCJX CCOV CCRJ CCUL CCUY CDBX CDEX CDPY
    CDVS CEBV CEMI CEOW CERI CEYK CFKZ CFMP CHAH CHEB
    CHET CHOX CHUG CEIW CFLI CLAV CORA CROB CROY CUTY
    DAMY DAYS DDBD DEBR DLCB DRMM DURO EENI EESA EIKY
    EMIN EMSI EOFS EORJ EUAB EURX EXES EZZA FELL FIZY
    FLOR FLOX FLYT FOGI GBXS GCAC GIDY GIWT HOLM HUEW
    IANI IBBS IGII IKRK ILUM IMAB IOWE IRON IRPW IVER IVET
    JAMY JERO JHKP JHYS JIMM JOST JULZ KDCC KIMM KIRB
    KITS LABS LACE LAMM LDVO LEBE LILP LINN MAAN MAUS
    MEGG MFHI MIME NDOL NEAT NESA NHRJ NIGL OBDM OBEV
    OBJT ODJG ODTW OEZY OGAN OIZI OJHL OKEV OMIK OPJK
    OPRC ORPC OSJN OSLD OUHI OURO OWWW OZEF PATF
    PATS PATZ PEGY PHXS PLPM PTAG PUDS PUPY RATZ RBBB
    RBJW RDHS REJP RICS RIKS RIXS RJWX RMAC RMMT ROBD
    RONA ROOV ROWI RPAF RPCC RWLY SAMY SELF SHSH
    SMDH SNOP SNOZ SRYY STUE SUSE SYCO TAGR TERN TKAY
    TOPK TSUE VKIT VPSJ WUFF WWWG XSDJ YURO ZORO ZTED

EUROWING LTD
GOLDWING
    G-MBDG MBFZ MBPM MBPX MJAJ MJAY MJDP MJOE MJRL
    MJRO MJRS MJSY MJUU MJWB MJWS MMBN MMLE MMWL
    MNNS MNZU

EVANS
VP-1
    G-AYUJ AYXW BAAD BAJC BAPP BBXZ BCTT BDAR BDTB BDTL
    BDUL BEIS BEKM BFAS BFHX BFJJ BGFK BGLF BHMT BHYV
    BIDD BIFO BKFI BLCW BLWT BMJM BVAM BVEL BVJU BVUT
    BWFJ EVPI GVPI PFAG PFAH PFAW TEDY VPAT VPCB
VP-2
    G-BCVE BEYN BFYL BGFC BGPM BJVC BJZB BMSC BPBB BTAZ
    BTHJ BTSC BUGI BUKZ BVPM BXOC CCEI RASC

EVEKTOR including **COSMIK AVIATION LTD** production
EV-97(A) (TEAM) EUROSTAR (Rotax 912-UL)
    G-CBIY CBJR CBMZ CBNK CBRR CBVM CBWE CBWG CCAC
    CCBK CCBM CCCO CCDX CCEJ CCEM CCKL CCMO CCMP
    CCPH CCPJ CCSR CCTH CCTI CCTO CCTP CCUT CCVA CCVK
    CCWP CCZZ CDAC CDAP CDAZ CDCC CDCT CDEP CDIY CDJR
    CDNG CDNI CDNM CDNP CDOA CDOZ CDPL CDTA CDTU CDVD
    CDVU CDXM CDYP CEAM CEBF CEBP CECY CEDV CEDX CEFK

CEFZ CEHL CEGO CEKJ CEME CENB CEND CERE CESF CESV
CETT CEVS CEYY CEZD CEZF CFDJ CFEE CFEO CFLL
CFNW CFTJ CFGX CFRT CSMK CTAV DATH DODG DOMS DSKI
DTSM EMLE EVRO EZZY GHEE HOTA ICMT IDOL IFLE IHOT
JEEP JLAT JUGE JVBP KEJY LBUZ LOSY LYNI NICC NIDG
OCMT ODRY OSPD OTUN OTYE PROW RCHY RJRJ RMPY
SDFM SHMI SJES TINT TIVV UURO UZUP VORN WHOA WINH
XIXI ZZAC

EVERETT GYROPLANES LTD including R J EVERETT ENGINEERING and see CAMPBELL
GYROPLANE variants
    G-BIPI BMZN BMZP BMZS BTMV BTVB BUAI BULT BUZC BWCK
    LAXY MICY OFRB OGOS ULPS

EXPERIMENTAL AVIATION
BERKUT
    G-REDX

EXTRA FLUGZEUGBAU GmbH
EA.230/260
    G-CBUA EXTR ROMP XTRA
EA.300
    G-BZFR BZII DUKK EEEK EXEA EXGC FIII IIDI IIEX IIHI IIMI IIUI
    IIXI IIZI IJMI IXTI JJIL JOKR KAYH KIII MIII MRKI OFFO RFLY SIII
    TENG XCCC XXTR ZEXL ZXCL ZXEL

EXTREME SARL
SILEX
    G-BZKG

F + W see DE HAVILLAND

FAIRCHILD ENGINE and AIRPLANE CORPORATION
24R ARGUS including replica*
    "G-AJOZ"* G-AIZE AJOZ AJPC AJPI AKIZ BCBH BCBL FANC
    RGUS
M-62 CORNELL
    G-CEVL

FAIREY AVIATION CO LTD
FLYCATCHER
    G-BEYB
FIREFLY
    G-ASTL
FULMAR
    G-AIBE
GANNET
    G-BMYP KAEW
FB.2 JET GYRODYNE
    G-AJJP
SWORDFISH
    G-AJVH BMGC
ULTRA-LIGHT HELICOPTER
    G-APJJ

FAIRTRAVEL LTD
LINNET 2
    G-ASMT ASZR

FALCONAR
F-9
    G-AYEG
F-11
    G-AWHY WBTS
F-12
    G-BGHT CBWV TIMS

FEDOROV
Me-7 MECHTA
    G-CHMZ CHPT CHUO

FEWSDALE TIGERCRAFT LTD
GYROPLANE
    G-ATLH

FFA FLUGZEUGWERKE AG
DIAMANT series
    G-CHGT CKRS DCDG DCDW DCGM DCGS

FIAT AERONAUTICA D'ITALIA
FIAT CR.42
    G-CBLS

FIAT-SEZIONE AERITALIA
FIAT G.46
    G-BBII

FIESELER WERKE GmbH
Fi/156c-3 STORCH
    G-FIST STCH STOR

FISHER FLYING PRODUCTS INC
SUPER KOALA variants
    G-BTBF BUVL MMTY

FLAGLOR
SKY SCOOTER
    G-BDWE

FLEET AIRCRAFT OF CANADA LTD
80 CANUCK
    G-FLCA

FLEXIFORM SKY SAILS see also GARLAND, HIWAY and MAINAIR
TRIKE
    G MMNT

FLIGHT DESIGN GmbH
CT2K (Rotax 912-ULS)
    G-CBAI CBDH CBDJ CBEW CBEX CBIB CBIE CBLV CBNA CBUF
    CBVZ CBWA CCNG CCNP CDJF CDPZ COMU CTDH DMCT
    GGCT IDSL KKCW MCOY NULA POGO PRAH TOMJ
CTSW
    G-CDWJ CDWS CDXL CEDE CEDM CEEO CEIE CEKT CENE
    CERA CESW CETF CETH CEWT CEZZ CFAZ CFDO CFDP CFFJ
    CFGZ CFKS CJHP CLEG CTDW CTSW DEFT FICS IROE KBOX
    KFLY KUPP LCKY OCDP OMRP RILA RZLY SAAA SDAT SWCT
    TODG TORN VINH
CTLS
    G-CTLS
EXXTACY/ALIZE
    CFDZ

FLYLIGHT AIRPORTS LTD
DOODLE BUG-TARGET
    G-BZKH BZKI BZKJ CBZY
DRAGONFLY
    G-CFKK CFNC CFNY CFOS CFSO IWIZ OECO
LIGHTLY-DISCUS
    G-CEOL

FLS AEROSPACE (LOVAUX) LTD
SPRINT
    G-BVNU BXWU BXWV OAGI SAHI SCLX

FOCKE-WULF FLUGZEUGBAU GmbH see PIAGGIO
FW 44J STIEGLITZ
    G-STIG
FW 190 variants
    G-DORA FOKW FWAB

FOKKER BV including FOKKER VFW NV, ROYAL NETHERLANDS AIRCRAFT FACTORY production and replicas.
Dr.1
    G-ATJM BVGZ CDXR FOKK
E.III replica
    G-AVJO CFHY GSAL
S.11 INSTRUCTOR
    G-BEPV BIYU
F.27 FRIENDSHIP
    G-BAUR BDVS BHMY BNIZ BVOB ECAT JEAI
F.27-050 (Fokker 50)
    G-UKTA
100
    G-CFDD

FOLLAND AIRCRAFT LTD
GNAT
    G-BVPP MOUR NAAT NATY RORI TIMM

FORNEY see ERCOUPE

FOSTER WIKNER AIRCRAFT CO LTD
GM.1 WICKO
    G-AFJB

AVIONS FOURNIER including **ALPAVIA** and **SPORTAVIA-PÜTZER**
RF3
    G-ATBP AYJD BCWK BFZA BHLU BIIA BIPN BLXH BNHT
RF4D
    G-AVHY AVKD AVNZ AVWY AWBJ AWEK AWEL AWEM AWGN
    AWLZ BHJN BIIF BUPJ BXLN IVEL
RF5 and RF5B SPERBER
    G-AYME AZJC AZPF AZRK AZRM BACE BEVO BJXK BPWK
    CBPC KCIG RFSB SSWV
RF6B-100
    G-BKIF BLWH BOLC
RF7
    G-LTRF

FRED see **CLUTTON**

FRESH BREEZE MÜLLER & WERNER GBR
FLYKE trike and SILEX L sailwing & Monster paramotor
    G-CESL

FUJI HEAVY INDUSTRIES LTD
FA.200
    G-BAPM BBGI BBRC BBZN BCFF BCKS BCKT BCNZ BDFR BEUK
    BFGO FEWG FUJI HAMI HECB KARI MCOX

GADFLY AIRCRAFT CO LTD
HDW-1
    G-AVKE

GAERTNER
Balloon (Hot Air)
AX4 SKYRANGER
    G-BSGB

GARDAN see **MINICAB**

GARDAN see **SUD-AVIATION GARDAN**

GAZEBO BALLOONS
Balloon (Hot Air)
AX6-65
    G-BCGP

GAZELLE see **SOUTHERN MICROLIGHT**

GEFA-FLUG GmbH
Airship (Hot Air)
AS 105 GD
    G-PEYO

GENERAL AIRCRAFT LTD
MONOSPAR ST.25 AMBULANCE
    G-AEYF
GAL.42 CYGNET
    G-AGBN

GENERAL AVIA
F22
    G-FZZA

GENERAL DYNAMICS CORPORATION
CONVAIR CV-440-54
    G-CONV

GIPPSLAND AERONAUTICS PTY LTD
GA-8 AIRVAN
    G-CDYA SCOL TVCO VANA VAND

GLASER-DIRKS FLUGZEUGBAU GmbH including **DG FLUGZEUGBAU GmbH, AMS-FLIGHT DOO, ELAN OVARNA SPORTNEGA ORODJA N.SOL.O** production
DG-100 ELAN series
    G-CFBH CFBW CFFU CFYU CHMS CHWP CJNZ CJPF CJRL
    CJXP CKDY CKHV CKMG DDFN DDHJ DDHK DDHL DDMD DDRB
    DEPU DGIO
DG-200 series
    G-CFOC CHBD CJAE CJAW CJDD CJDP CJHW CJKF CJKM
    CJPW CJVP CJWT CKAC CKDU CKDX DADJ DDTA DDTM DDXN
    DDYH DEDM DEME DHDH DEMU EEBR EEKA ONEZ
DG-300 (CLUB) ELAN and ELAN ACRO series
    G-CFAJ CFJR CFJS CFJX CFLC CFLX CFNS CFSR CFTS CFUJ
    CFUT CFUU CFWM CFZW CGBS CHBE CHDR CHMB CHSB
    CHVM CJDV CJNO CJRC CJTK CJTN CJVL CKAU CKBC CKBF

    CKRF CKJH CKOR DESO DFGT DHCU DJAB PAFR XIXX
DG-400
    G-BLRM BNXL BPIN BPXB BRTW BYTG CKCC DGSM DIRK HAJJ
    INCA KESS LEES OAPW
DG-500 ELAN series
    G-BRRG BZYG CGBZ CHBP CHEF CHGV CHNA CHYE CHRC
    CJSX CJZB CJZK CKAW CKAX CKHC CKJJ CKNK CKOW CKOX
    SOOM SORA XBGA
DG-600
    G-CFNT CKBS DFKB KOFM
DG-800 variants
    G-BVJK BXSH BXUI BYEC CCRA CJJH DGCL DGIV EEZO IANB
    MSIX OBUP ORIG TRTM
DG-1000 variants
    G-CKFN CKLY CKKV CKND CKNF CKOH DGIK RIEF WYVN

GLASFLÜGEL ING EUGEN HANLE
H201 STANDARD LIBELLE
    G-AXZH CFZB CHJR CHWC CJAS CJBF CJEU CJGZ CJHJ CJNG
    CJWV CKCM DCFS DCFW DCFX DCFY DCKY DCLM DCLP DCLV
    DCMH DCMO DCMS DCMV DCMW DCNE DCNF DCNG DCNJ
    DCNP DCNY DCPM DCRB DCRO DCRV DCRW DCSJ DCSR
    DCTU DCUJ DCVL DCWE DCWG DCWT DCWX DCWY DCWZ
    DCYG DDBP DDCC DDMS DENO DFAR DHAA DHAD DHCO
    ECLW ECPA EFLT EHAV LIBL LIBY YOHO
H205 CLUB LIBELLE
    G-CFYG CKAM CKNI DDEO
H206 HORNET
    G-CKLC DDKD DDKM
H301 LIBELLE
    G-CGAN CHLK
H303 MOSQUITO
    G-CFBN CHMT CJEH CJNR CJTO CJTW DDTK DDTV DDTX
    DDTY DDVZ DDWL DDWR DDXW DEAK DECS DEDJ MOZI
304
    G-CHMM DAWZ DEHU

GLASFLUGEL DEUTSCHE- BRASILIANISCHE FLUGZEUG GMBH
GLASFLUGEL 304
    G-EDNT

GLOBE AIRCRAFT CORPORATION
GC-1B SWIFT
    G-AHUN ARNN BFNM

GLOSTER AIRCRAFT CO LTD including **ARMSTRONG-WHITWORTH** production
GAMECOCK replica
    G-CBTS
GLADIATOR
    G-AMRK CBHO GLAD
METEOR variants
    G-ANSO ARCX BPOA BWMF JETM LOSM METE

GOULD-TAYLORCRAFT see **TAYLORCRAFT**

GOWLAND
GWG.2 JENNY WREN
    G-ASRF

GRANGER
ARCHAEOPTERYX
    G-ABXL

GREAT LAKES AIRCRAFT INC see **OLDFIELD**
2T-1A SPORT TRAINER
    G-BIIZ BUPV GLII GLST

GREEN
Balloon (Hot Air)
S-25
    G-BSON

GREENSLADE
TRIKE with Flexiform wing
    G-MMWG

GRIFFITHS
GH.4
    G-ATGZ

GROB-WERKE GMB & CO KG including **GROB FLUGZEUGBAU GmbH &CO KG** and **BURKHART GROB LUFT-UND RAUMFAHRT GMBH & CO KG**
G102 ASTIR
 G-CEWP CEWW CFCJ CFEF CFFB CFGK CFHT CFHW CFRL
 CFSH CFSZ CFTK CFTR CGAT CGBJ CGBK CGCL CGDO CGEB
 CHBM CHBT CHGB CHJV CHKB CHKM CHRA CHSE CHTD
 CHTE CHTR CHUN CHVK CHXB CHXM CHXY CJAZ CJCF CJCW
 CFJH CJHG CJHN CJLR CJML CJMV CJNA CJON CJPJ CJPM
 CJRD CJSD CJSH CJSK CJUS CJWR CJYC CJYP CKAY CKBD
 CKBL CKCP CKEE CKGH CKMC CKRN CMWK DDJD DDJX
 DDKR DDKS DDKU DDKW DDKX DDLH DDLM DDMH DDMP
 DDMR DDNC DDNE DDNK DDOB DDOE DDOR DDPO DDPY
 DDRU DDRW DDSH DDSU DDUL DDUX DDWU DDXJ DDYF
 DDZJ DDZU DEAF DEAW DEKF DELN DEOD DEVK DFEB DFEX
 DFSA DHTG EEBM EEVL FECO GCMW GSST OGGB ONAT
G103 TWIN ASTIR
 G-CFHO CHOS CJLZ CJWM CKRH DDRO DDSJ DDSL DEGN
 DEWZ DFEA DHCA
G103 TWIN ACRO variants
 G-CFWC CHBH CHOS CHWW CJKV CJOG CKFG CKMT DEOT
 DEWG DEWP DEWR DEXA DEYS DHCJ NUGC
G104 SPEED ASTIR
 G-CFXA FEBB
G109
 G-BIXZ BJVK BJZX BLMG BLUV BMCG BMFY BMGR BMLK BMLL
 BMMP BXSP BXXI BYJH BZLY CBLY CDNA CEYN CHAR DKDP
 IPSI KEMC KNEK LLAN LREE LULU RASH ROBZ SAGA SAMG
 TACK UILD WAVE WAVY
G115 variants
 G-BOPT BOPU BPKF BVHC BVHD BVHE BVHF BVHG BYDB
 BYFD BYUA BYUB BYUC BYUD BYUE BYUF BYUG BYUH BYUI
 BYUJ BYUK BYUL BYUM BYUN BYUO BYUP BYUR BYUS BYUT
 BYUU BYUV BYUW BYUX BYUY BYUZ BYVA BYVB BYVC BYVD
 BYVE BYVF BYVG BYVH BYVI BYVJ BYVK BYVL BYVM BYVN
 BYVO BYVP BYVR BYVS BYVT BYVU BYVV BYVW BYVX BYVY
 BYVZ BYWA BYWB BYWC BYWD BYWE BYWF BYWG BYWH
 BYWI BYWJ BYWK BYWL BYWM BYWN BYWO BYWP BYWR
 BYWS BYWT BYWU BYWV BYWW BYWX BYWY BYWZ BYXA
 BYXB BYXC BYXD BYXE BYXF BYXG BYXH BYXI BYXJ BYXK
 BYXL BYXM BYXN BYXO BYXP BYXR BYXS BYXT BYXX BYXY
 BYXZ BYYA BYYB GROE MERF RAFA RAFB TAYI

GRUMMAN AIRCRAFT ENGINEERING
G.44 WIDGEON
 G-DUCK
F-6F HELLCAT
 G-BTCC
F-8F BEARCAT
 G-BUCF RUMM
FM-2 WILDCAT
 G-RUMW

GRUMMAN AMERICAN AVIATION CORPORATION (3) including **AMERICAN AVIATION CORPORATION (1), AMERICAN GENERAL AVIATION (2)** and **GULFSTREAM AMERICAN CORPORATION (4)** production
AMERICAN AA-1 YANKEE (1)
 G-AYLP BFOJ SEXY
AMERICAN AA-1A TRAINER (1)
 G-AYHA AZKS RUMN
GRUMMAN AA-1B TRAINER (3)
 G-BBFC BBWZ BCLW BDNW BDNX BERY
GRUMMAN AA-1C LYNX (3)
 G-BEXN BTLP
AMERICAN AA-5 TRAVELLER (1)
 G-AZMJ AZVG BAFA BAJN BAJO BIWW
GRUMMAN AA-5 TRAVELLER (3)
 G-BAOU BASH BAVR BAVS BBBI BBCZ BBDL BBDM BBLS BBRZ
 BBSA BBUE BBUFCCCJ BCCK BCEE BCEF BCEO BCEP BCIJ
 BCLI BCPN BDFY BEZC BEZF BEZG BEZH BEZI BIAY BLFW
 BMYI BSTR MALC NONI OBMW
GRUMMAN AA-5A CHEETAH (3)
 G-BDLO BEBE BFIJ BFIN BFLX BFZO BNVB BXHH CHTA
 JAJB JNAS JUDY MILY MOGI OPWK PURR REEK
GULFSTREAM AA-5A CHEETAH (4)
 G-BGCM BGFG BGFI BGVV BHZO CCAT DOEA IFLI KINE LSFI
 MSTC OCAM OMOG OPPL OSSF OSTC OSTU PADD PAWS
 PING RATE
GRUMMAN AA-5B TIGER (3)
 G-BCRR BDRB BFTF BFTG BFVS BFXW BFZP BHLX BIPA BKPS
 BOXU BXTT ERRY PORK REET ROWL RUBB WINK ZARI ZERO

GULFSTREAM AA-5B TIGER (4)
 G-BFXX BGPH BGVY BHZK BIBT BIPV BJAJ BOZO BOZZ BPIZ
 BTII CFPC DAVO DINA DONI GAJB IRIS NODE OTIG TGER TYGA
 WMTM
AMERICAN GENERAL AG-5B TIGER (2)
 G-BTUZ BYDX CCXX CDGS GIRY NODY OABR RICO
GA-7 COUGAR (3)
 G-BOOE BOXR OOGO
GA-7 COUGAR (4)
 G-BGNV BGON BGSY BLHR CDND CYMA EENY GOTC HIRE
 OOGA OOGI OOGS

GULFSTREAM AEROSPACE CORPORATION
G159 GULFSTREAM I
 G-BNCE
GULFSTREAM G-IV
 G-CFOH EVLN MATF TAYC
GULFSTREAM GV-SP (Gulfstream 550)
 G-EGNS GSSO HRDS JCBB JCBC

GULFSTREAM-AMERICAN CORPORATION see **GRUMMAN AMERICAN**

GYROFLIGHT
BROOKLAND HORNET
 G-BRPP MIKE PHIL

HADLAND
WILLOW
 G-MMMH

HALLAM
FLECHE
 G-FLCT

HANDLEY PAGE LTD
O/400 replica
 G-BKMG
HP.39 GUGNUNC
 G-AACN
HP.81 HERMES
 G-ALDG

HANDLEY PAGE (READING) LTD
HPR.7 DART HERALD
 G-APWA APWJ ASKK ASVO ATIG AVEZ AVPN BAZJ BEYF CEXP

HANRIOT ET CIE
HD.1
 G-AFDX

HAPI
CYGNET SF-2A
 G-BRZD BWFN BXCA BXHJ BYYC CCKT

HARKER
DH WASP
 G-MJSZ

HARMON
ROCKET
 G-RCKT

HASELDINE
HUMMELBIRD
 G-CETN

HATZ
CB-1
 G-BRSY BXXH CBYW HATZ TIKO

AÉRONAUTIQUE HAVRAISE see **MINICAB**

HAWKER AIRCRAFT LTD including **AVRO** and **CCF** production and see **ARMSTRONG WHITWORTH** and **W.A.R**
AUDAX
 G-BVVI
CYGNET
 G-CAMM EBJI EBMB
DEMON
 G-BTVE
FURY (Biplane)
 G-BKBB

FURY
    G-BWOL CBEL CBZP
HART
    G-ABMR
HIND
    G-AENP CBLK
HUNTER
    G-BNCX BOOM BUEZ BVGH BVWG BVWV BWAF BWFR BWFT
    BWGK BWGL BWGM BWGN BWKA BWKC BWOU BXFI BXKF
    BZPB BZPC BZSE BZSR EGHH ETPS FFOX GAII HHAB HHAC
    HHAF HNTR HPUX HUNT HVIP KAXF PRII PSST SIAL TVII VETA
HURRICANE
    G-AMAU BYDL CBOE HHII HITT HRLI HUPW HURI HURR ROBT
NIMROD
    G-BURZ BWWK
SEA FURY
    G-BUCM RNHF SALY
SEA HAWK see **ARMSTRONG WHITWORTH**
SEA HURRICANE
    G-BKTH
TEMPEST
    G-PEST TEMT
TOMTIT
    G-AFTA

HAWKER SIDDELEY AVIATION including **BRITISH AEROSPACE PLC,
CORPORATE JETS LTD** and **RAYTHEON-HAWKER** production
DH.121 TRIDENT, HS.121 TRIDENT
    G-ARPH ARPO AVFB AVFE AVFG AVFH AVFJ AWZI AWZJ
    AWZM AWZP AWZR AWZS AWZU AZFW BAJJ BBVU BBVV
    BBVW BBVZ BBWG
DH 125, HS.125, BAe and HAWKER 800/900 variants
    G-ARYB ARYC ASSM ATPD BOCB BYHM BZNR CDLT CFBP
    DCTA FINK GMAB IFTE IFTF JETI JJSI JMAX LAOR ODUR OHEA
    OJWB VIPI WYNE YUGO
BUCCANEER
    G-HHAA
HARRIER
    G-VTOL

HEAD BALLOONS INC
Balloon (Hot Air)
Ax8-105
    G-ENGR UKUK

HEINKEL
CASA 2111 (He.111H-16)
    G-AWHA AWHB

HEINTZ see **ZENAIR**

HELIO
H295 SUPER COURIER
    G-BAGT BGIX

HELTON AIRCRAFT CORPORATION
LARK 95
    G-LARK

R J HEMMING
TRIKE with Solar Wings Typhoon wing
    G-MMPU

HILL see **MAXAIR**

HILLER HELICOPTERS INC
UH-12 (360)
    G-ASAZ ASTP ATKG

HINDUSTAN AERONAUTICS LTD
PUSHPAK
    G-AVPO BXTO

HISPANO see **MESSERSCHMITT**

HIWAY HANG GLIDERS LTD
SKYTRIKE with Demon, Excalibur, Flexiform, Gold Marque, Hiway,
Solar Wings, Super Scorpion & Vulcan wings
    G-MBAA MBBJ MBCL MBEU MBFK MBIA MBIT MBJF MBJX MBKZ
    MBPU   MJAN MJAV MJDJ MJDR MJFZ MJHV MJKF MJKO MJKP
    MJMD MJMS MJPE MJSO MJXY MMCN MMCV MMHG MMHK
    MMHL MMLH MMRH MMUR MNGO MNME MVDS MYBN

HOAC FLUGZEUGWERKE (HOFFMANN FLUGZEUGBAU FRIESACH)
including **DIAMOND AIRCRAFT INDUSTRIES GmbH** production
DV.20 KATANA
    G-BWFI BWGY KEHO TENS
H 36 DIMONA/
    G-BKPA BLCV BNUX CEUT KOKL LYDA OMDG RIET
HK 36 SUPER DIMONA variants
    G- BYFL FMKA GEOS HKSD IMOK LIDA OSFA SLMG XKKA

HOLMAN
BRISTOL TYPE 2000
    G-CCGP

HORNET MICROLIGHTS LTD
HORNET 250 with Airwave Nimrod wing (Fuji-Robin EC-25-PS)
    G-MBCX MBJL
HORNET DUAL TRAINER with Southdown Raven wing (Rotax462)
    G-MNRI MNRK MNRM MTGX MTJX MTMP MTMR MTRL MTXE
    MVHZ
HORNET R variants (Combi) (Rotax 462)
    G-MVUR MVUU MVYK MVYL MVYN MVZW MWBP MWBR MWBS
    MWBU MWBW MWBY MWDE MWDI MWEU MWEY MWKE

HOVEY
BETA BIRD
    G-BKRV
WD-II/III WHING DING
    G-MBAB MNVO

HOWARD
SPECIAL T-MINUS
    G-BRXS

HOWES
Balloon (Hot Air)
AX6
    G-BDWO

HUGHES TOOL CO and **HUGHES HELICOPTERS INC** including
SCHWEIZER AIRCRAFT CORPORATION (269 wef 1986**)** and
McDONNELL- DOUGLAS (369 wef 1983**)** production
269 (Series 300)
    G-BAXE BMWA BOVX BOXT BPJB BPPY BRTT BSML BSVR
    BWAV BWDV BWNJ BWWJ BWZY BXMY BXRP BZXJ CBCN
    CCVG CDOJ CDTW CDYW CEAW CEBE CECO CEOY DASY
    DCBI ECBI FCBI HCBI IBHH IRYC JAMA JMDI LINX MARE OCBI
    OCJK OJAE OOGL OSLO PKPK PLOW PLPC RHCB RIFB ROCR
    SBHH SHRN STEP TAMB TAMC TAMD TAME TASS TSLC VNUS
    WHRL XCBI ZZTT
369 (Series 500)
    G-AYIA BIOA BPLZ BRTL BTRP CCPY CCUO DADS DIZZ ERIS
    GSOO GSPG HAUS HKHM HSOO HUES HUKA IDWR JETZ JIVE
    KSWI LIBS LINC LOGO MACE MLSN MRAJ MRRR OGJP OMDH
    OPCS ORRR RISK SOOC SSCL SWEL TCEE TRUE TVEE VICE

HUNT
AVON Trike variants with HIWAY & HUNT wings
    G-BZRG BZTW BZUZ MNCA MGTR MMGT MNCA MYTV MYUR
    MYWC MYWH MYYE MYYJ MZCX MZDZ MZFE MZGH

HUNTAIR LTD
PATHFINDER
    G-MBWG MBYK MBYL MJBZ MJDE MJDH MJFM MJJA MJOC
    MJUV MJWK MMBV MMCB MMDR MMOG

HUNTING PERCIVAL AIRCRAFT LTD including **BRITISH AIRCRAFT
CORPORATION (BAC)** and see **PERCIVAL**
P.66 PEMBROKE
    G-BNPG BNPH BXES
P.66 PRESIDENT
    G-AOJG
P.84 JET PROVOST variants
    G-AOBU AOHD BKOU BVEZ BVSP BWDR BWDS BWGT BWOT
    BWSG BWSH BXBH BXLO KNOT PROV RAFI TORE VIVM
BAC.145 JET PROVOST variants
    G-BVTC BWCS BWEB BWGF BWGS BWOF BYED BWUU JPRO
    JPTV JPVA
BAC.167 STRIKEMASTER variants
    G-AXEF AYHS BESY BFOO CDHB CFBK FLYY MXPH RSAF
    SMAS UPPI UVNR

HYBRED see **MEDWAY**

HYBRID AIR VEHICLES
HAV-3
    G-OHAV

IAV-BACHAU see YAKOVLEV

ICA (INTREPRINDEREA DE CONSTRUCTII AERONAUTICE-BRASOV)
IS-28A
    G-DDEG DDLT DDZR DEHW DEJA DJNC
IS-28M
    G-BKXN BMMV BMOM
IS-29D
    G-DDBG DDEW
IS-30
    G-DFDP
IS-32A
    DFAV

ICP SRL
MXP-740 SAVANNAH variants
    G-CBBM CCII CCJO CCJU CCLP CCSV CCXP CDAT CDCR
    CDEH CDJD CDKN CDKO CDLR CDSH CDTT CDTY CDUV CDVK
    CDZU CEBC CECK CEED CEEX CEFY CEGK CENU CEVU CEZB
    CFKV CFSX CSUE DOTW VGVG

III (INIZIATIVE INDUSTRIALI ITALIANE) SpA
SKY ARROW (Rotax 912)
    G-BXGT BYCY BYZR BZVT CBTB CIAO FINZ GULP IOIA ROME
    SKYT SUTN

ILYUSHIN
Il-2
    G-BZVW BZVX

INTERAVIA
Balloon (Hot Air)
70TA
    G-BUUT
80TA
    G-BZYT

INTERPLANE AIRCRAFT INC
ZJ-VIERA
    G-CFAP FLEE

ISAACS
FURY
    G-ASCM AYJY BBVO BCMT BEER BIYK BKZM BMEU BWWN
    BZAS BZNW CCKV EHMF FURI PFAR RODI
SPITFIRE
    G-BBJI BXOM

ISSOIRE AVIATION
SILENE series
    G-CJUG DHPA

JACKAROO AIRCRAFT see THRUXTON

JACOBS
Balloon (Hot Air)
V35 AIRCHAIR
    G-CEWF

JASTREB see SCHEMPP-HIRTH

JODEL including CEA, SAN and WASSMER production and see
FALCONAR and ROBIN
D.9 and D.92 variants
    G-AVPD AWFT AXKJ AXYU AZBL BAGF BDEI BDNT BGFJ BURE
    BZBZ KDIX
D.11, D.112, D.117 and, D.119 variants
    G-ARDO ARNY ASIS ASJZ ASXY ATIN ATIZ ATJN ATWB AVPM
    AWFW AWMD AWVB AWVZ AWWI AXAT AXCG AXCY AXFN
    AXHV AXWT AXXW AXZT AYBP AYBR AYCP AYEB AYGA AYHX
    AYKJ AYKK AYKT AYMU AYWH AYXP AZFF AZHC AZII AZKP
    AZVL BAAW BAKR BAPR BARF BATJ BAUH BAZM BBPS BCGW
    BCLU BDBV BDDG BDIH BDJD BDMM BEDD BEZZ BFEH BFGK
    BFNG BFXR BGTX BGWO BHCE BHEL BHFF BHHX BHKT BHNL
    BHNX BIAH BIDX BIEO BIOU BIPT BITO BIVB BIVC BIWN BIYW
    BIZY BJOT BKAO BKIR BMIP BOOH BPFD BRCA BRVZ BUFF
    BVEH BVPS BVVE BWMB DAVE INNI
D.18
    G-BODT BSYA BTRZ BUAG BUPR BWVC BWVV BXFC CBRC

    CBRD JRKD OJOD OLEM TREK WIBB
D.120 PARIS-NICE
    G-ASPF ASXU ATLV AVLY AVYV AXNJ AYGG AYLV AYRS AZEF
    AZGA AZLF BACJ BANU BCGM BDDF BDEH BDWX BFOP BHGJ
    BHNK BHPS BHXD BHXS BHZV BICR BIEN BJFM BJOE BJYK
    BKAE BKCW BKCZ BKGB BKJS BKPX BMDS BMID BMLB BMYU
    BOWP BYBE CCBR DIZO
D.140 MOUSQUETAIRE
    G-ARDZ ARLX AROW ARRY ATKX BJOB BSPC BWAB CVST
    DCXL EGUR EHIC JRME OBAN REES TOAD YRUS
D.150 MASCARET variants
    G-ASKL ASRT AVEF AZBI BACL BFEB BHEG BHEZ BHVF BIDG
    BLAT BLXO BMEH BVSS BVST CECH CEZW DISO EDGE FARR
    IEJH JDEL LDWS MASC OABB TIDS
DR.1050, and DR.1051 variants
    G-ARFT ARRD ARRE ARUH ARXT ASXS ATAG ATEV ATFD
    ATGE ATIC ATJA ATLB ATWA AVGJ AVGZ AVHL AVJK AVOA
    AWUE AWVE AWWN AWWO AXLS AXSM AXUK AYEH AYEJ
    AYEV AYEW AYGD AYJA AYKD AYLC AYLF AYLL AYUT AYYO
    AYYT AYZK AZOU AZWF BAEE BDMW BEAB BEYZ BFBA BGBE
    BGRI BHHE BHOL BHSY BHTC BHUE BIOI BKDX BLKM BLRJ
    BPLH BTHH BXIO BXYJ BYCS BYFM CCNA CEIS CESA CFIC
    DANA IOSI IOSO JEJH JODL JWIV LAKI RIVE SPOG
DR.200, DR.220 and DR.221 variants
    G-AVOC AVOM AYDZ BANA BFHR BHRW BLCT BLLH BMKF
    BUTH CPCD GREG MLLE RRCU STEV
DR.250 and DR.253 variants
    G-ATTM AWKP AWYL AXWV AYUB BJBO BKPE BOSM BSZF
    BUVM BXCG BYEH BYHP
DR.300, DR.315, DR.340 and DR.360 variants
    G-AXDK AYCO AZIJ AZJN BGVB BICP BLAM BLGH BLHH BOEH
    BOZV BVYG BVYM BXOU DRSV DRZF KIMB

JORDAN AVIATION
DUET
    G-MBWH MMKY

JUNKERS FLUGZEUG UND MOTORENWERKE AG including CASA
production
Ju 87/R4
    G-STUK
CASA 352L
    "G-AFAP" G- BECL BFHD BFHE BFHG

JURCA
MJ.2 TEMPETE
    G-ASUS AYTV
MJ.5 SIROCCO
    G-CEAO CLAX RECO
MJ.100 SPITFIRE
    G-CDPM

K & S
JUNGSTER
    G-BLDC DAJW OWEN
SA.102.5 CAVALIER
    G-AZHH BCKF BCMJ BCRK BDKJ BDLY BUNJ BWSI

KAY
GYROPLANE
    G-ACVA

KEIRS
HEATED AIR TUBE BALLOON (Minimum Lift)
    G-BGZS

KEN BROCK
KB-2 (Rotax 582)
    G-BSEG BUZV BVMN

KENSINGER
KF
    G-ASSV

KING
Balloon (Minimum Lift)
KINGRAM 01
    G-BJDV

KIRK
Balloon (Minimum Lift)
SKYRIDER
    G-BJTF

LEIGHTFLUGZEUGBAU KLEMM GMBH - see BA
L.25-1A
    G-AAUP
KL.35
    G-KLEM

KNIGHT see PAYNE

KOLB
TWINSTAR (Rotax 582)
    G-BUZT BYTA CCFJ CCRB CDFA CDZS CODY CEBI CYRA IANN
    KOLB MGPX MWWM MYDP MYIK MYKB MYLN MYLP MYMI
    MYNY MYOG MYOO MYOR MYPC MYVA MYWP MYXS MZGJ
    MZZT PLAD

KRONFELD LTD see BAC (1935) LTD

LA MOUETTE
PROFIL (Wing)
    G-MVCK

LAFAYETTE
HI-NUSKI Mk.1
    G-MBWI

LAK including AB SPORTINE AVIAICIJA production
LAK-12 LIETUVA
    G-CGAB CHGO CHGR CHGX CHHM CHHW CHRB CHTF CJBS
    CJBY CJOH CJYL DHSR GLAK
LAK-17 series
    G-CJOU CJVJ CKCR CKHE CKKK CKMP CKOI DAVS
LAK-19T
    G-CKOU CKPA EWEW

LAKE AIRCRAFT CORPORATION including AEROFAB INC and CONSOLIDATED AERONAUTIC INC)
LA-4
    G-BASO BOLL
LA-250 RENEGADE
    G-LAKE SIVW

LAMBERT AIRCRAFT ENGINEERING BVBA
MISSION M212-100
    G-XFLY

LANCAIR see NEICO

LANCASHIRE
MICRO-TRIKE with Flexiiform & Wasp wings
    G-MJYW MMFG MMPL

LANCASHIRE AIRCRAFT see EDGAR PERCIVAL

LANGE FLUGZEUGBAU GmbH
E1 ANTARES
    G-DCDC

LASER
LAZER Z200, Z230
G-BWKT CBHR CDDP LAZA LZII VILL

LAVERDA see AVIAMILANO

LAZAIR see ULTRAFLIGHT

TONY LE VIER ASSOCIATES INC
COSMIC WIND
    G-ARUL BAER

LEARJET INC including BOMBARDIER AEROSPACE production
LEARJET Model 40
    G-HPPY MEET MOOO STUF
LEARJET Model 45
    G-CDNK CDSR CPRI GMAA GOMO JANV LLOD OLDK OLDT
    OLDW RWGW SNZY SOVB SOVC ZXZX
LEARJET Model 60
    G-HCGD LGAR SXTY

LEDERLIN
38OL LADYBUG
    G-AYMR

SOCIÉTÉ DES AVIONS LEOPOLDOFF
L-6
    G-BYKS
L-7
    G-AYKS

LET NARODNI PODNIK KUNOVICE
L-13 BLANIK
    G-CHTY CJDU CJNX DCVB DDEX DDVD
ZLIN Z.37 CMELAK (Bumble Bee)
    G-AVZB

LETOV LTD
LF-107 LUNAK
    G-CKMR
LK-2M SLUKA
    G-BYLJ MYRP MYRR MYUP MYVG MYVT MYXO MZBF MZBK
    MZDX MZES MZFC MZGF MZLY MZNZ MZOI MZOX XPBI

LEVI
LEVI GO-PLANE RL6 Srs 1
    G-BCMF

LIBERTY AEROSPACE INC
XL-2
    G-OIVN

LIGHTNING see SOUTHDOWN

LILLIPUT BALLOONS UK
Balloon (Minimum Lift)
TYPE 1
    G-HONY
TYPE 4
    G-GRWL

LINDSTRAND (HOT AIR) BALLOONS LTD
Airship (Hot Air)
GA 42
    G-CFKN
HS 110
    G-BZFU HSTH TRIB
Balloon (Gas)
LBL 14A
    G-BWBB BXAJ
Balloon (Hot Air)
LBL 9A
    G-CEHX
LBL 21 series
    G-BVRL BYEY CBYS OJNB UNRL
LBL 25 CLOUDHOPPER
    G-BVUI BXHM BYYJ CBZJ CDAD CEGG EECO HOPR OLAW
    OOER RIME
LBL 31A
    G-BWHD BXIZ BXUH BZIH BZNV BZUK CDUJ CDXF CEOU CFRF
    FFFT LELE ONCB
LBL 35A CLOUDHOPPER
    G-CDIW CFAW HOPA
LBL 42A
    G-BWCG CBLO
LBL 56 series
    G-COSY DBAT
LBL 60 series
    G-CCBP CFIK IRLZ OERR CDZO
LBL 69 series
    G-BVDS BVGG BVIR BWLA BYKA CBBX HSBC LBLI REAR
LBL 77 series
    G-BUBS BUWI BUZR BVPV BVRR BWAW BWBO BWFK BWKZ
    BWMH BWTU BXDR BYJG BYJR BYKW BYLW BYRZ BYYE BZBJ
    BZGV BZKE CCFV CDWX CDYL CDYX ERRI HERD ICKY LBUK
    MCOW MERE MUCK NUNI PATP PSAX TAJF
LBL 90 series
    G-VWW BVZT BWBT BWTN BWWE BWZU BXLF BXXO BXZF
    BXZI BZLU BZPV CBIM CBNI CCJH CCSS CDDM CDDN CDEU
    CDHJ CDIV CHLL DUGI EDRE FLEW FWAY GOGB JEMI MINN
    MRKT OBJB ODJF OSUP PATX PROF RAYO SJKR TSWI UNER
    UNGE
LBL 105 series
    G-BUYJ BUZJ BVDO BVON BVRU BWGA BWOK BWRZ BWSB
    BWTB BWWY BXDZ BXHE BXJG BXUO BYFU BYIY BYJN BYJZ
    BYLX BZAG BZUD CBPH CBPW CCIA CCSM CCVF CCXD CDLV
    CDMW CECS CEJI CEMV ENRI FLGT FRIL GOAL HAPI ICOI
    IOFR ITVM JENO LPAD OAER ODAF ODDY OPMT OUMC OVIA

PIZZ RAPI RIMB ROMS RROW RXUK SNAK VITL ZETA
LBL 120 series
    G-BVLZ BWDM BWEA BZBL CBTR CBVH CFSY DUBI ENBD
    OGSS UPUZ ZAZZ
LBL 150A
    G-BVEW BXCM CDHP CEOV IRTH VOLP
LBL 180A
    G-CBZU OTUP
LBL 210A
    G-BVLL BVML BXNX BZDE CCKX CCRS DVBF FBVF HVBF JVBF
    NVBF SSLF WVBF
LBL 240A
    G-BXBL BXMK CCKY OWYE
LBL 260 series
    G-PVBF SMRT VIZA
LBL 310A
    G-BZPE CBIW TVBF
LBL 317 series
    G-CDHN CFFL
LBL 330A
    G-BXVE CCWE CDHK CDHL LRGE LVBF XVBF
LBL 360A
    G-CENX VBFF
LBL 400A
    G-UVBF

Special Shapes

SHAPE	REGISTRATION(S)
BABY BEL	G-BXUG
BATTERY	G-OKCP
BANANAS	G-CEMW
BEAR	G-BWTF
CAKE	G-BZNZ
DOG	G-CDOG
FLOWERS	G-ODBN
FOUR	G-BVVU
HOUSE	G-CDWV
HUMPTY DUMPTY	G-EGGG
J & B BOTTLE	G-OJBW
NEWSPAPER	G-BVGK FFTT
PIG	G-PIGG
PINK PANTHER	G-PINX
POP CAN	G-BXHN
RACING CAR	G-TKGR
SUN	G-BZIC
TELEWEST SPHERE	G-BXHO
TULIPS	G-TULP

LINDSTRAND TECHNOLOGIES LTD
Balloon (Gas)
LTL 203T
    G-CFBF G-CFMF LAPS

LOCKHEED AIRCRAFT CORPORATION including **LOCKHEED-CALIFORNIA CO** and **CANADAIR** production
10 ELECTRA
    G-LIOA
18 LODESTAR
    G-AGCN AGIJ BMEW
414 HUDSON
    G-BEOX
L.188 ELECTRA
    G-FIJR FIJV FIZU LOFA LOFB LOFC LOFD LOFE LOFG OFRT
L.749 CONSTELLATION
    G-CONI
T-33A
    G-BYOY WGHB

LORIMER
IOLAIRE
    G-MZFI

LOVEGROVE see **BENSEN**
AV-8 GYROPLANE
    G-BXXR
SHEFFY GYROPLANE
    G-CDFW

LUSCOMBE AIRCRAFT COMPANY
RATTLER
    G-BKPG

LUSCOMBE AIRPLANE CORPORATION
8 / SILVAIRE variants
    G-AFUP AFYD AFZK AFZN AGMI AHEC AICX AJAP AJJU AJKB
    AKTI AKTN AKTT AKUF AKUG AKUH AKUJ AKUK AKUL AKUM
    AKUP AKVP BNIO BNIP BPOU BPPO BPVZ BPZA BPZC BPZE
    BRDJ BRGF BRGG BRHX BRHY BRJA BRJK BROO BRPZ BRRB
    BRSW BRUG BSHH BSHI BSNE BSNT BSOE BSOX BSSA BSTX
    BSUD BSYF BSYH BTCH BTCJ BTDF BTIJ BTJA BTJB BTJC
    BUAO BUKU BULO BVEP BVGW BVGY BWOB CCRK DAIR EITE
    KENM LUSC LUSI LUST NIGE ROTI SAGE YRIL

LVG
C.VI
    G-AANJ

LYNDEN
AURORA
    G-CBZS

R and W McCANDLESS
M.2 GYROPLANE
    G-ARTZ (1)
M.4 GYROPLANE
    G-ARTZ (2) ATXX AXVN BVLE

McDONNELL-DOUGLAS CORPORATION
MD-82
    G-CEPA CEPB CEPC CEPD CEPE CEPI CEPJ CEPK
MD-83
    G-FLTL
DC-10-30
    G-DCMA

McDONNELL DOUGLAS HELICOPTER CO see **HUGHES** and **MD HELICOPTERS**

MACAIR
MERLIN
    G-BWEN

MAGNI GYRO of ITALY - see **VPM**

MAINAIR SPORTS LTD see **PEGASUS/FLASH** and **SOUTHDOWN INTERNATIONAL**
BLADE (Rotax 912)
    G-BYCW BYHN BYHO BYHS BYJB BYKC BYKD BYNM BYON
    BYOW BYRO BYRP BYRR BYTL BYTU BYZB BZAA BZAL BZDC
    BZDD BZEG BZEL BZFO BZFS BZGM BZGS BZGW BZJL BZJN
    BZMS BZNS BZPA BZPN BZPZ BZRB BZRW BZTM BZTR BZTU
    BZTV BZTX BZUB BZUN BZWB BZXM BZXT CBAD CBBG CBDD
    CBDL CBDN CBDP CBEM CBET CBGT CBHG CBHJ CBHM CBJT
    CBKM CBKN CBKO CBLD CBLM CBLT CBMM CBNC CBOG
    CBOM CBOO CBRE CBRJ CBRM CBSM CBSZ CBTE CBTM
    CBTW CBVG CBWM CBXM CBXV CBYF CBYM CBZA CBZB
    CBZD CCAB CCAG CCAM CCAW CCDM CCGK CCIF CCPM
    CCTM CCWL CCXR CCZW CDAG CDCU CDOR CEMR CLFC
    EEYE ENVY FERN FLYF JAIR JBEN JMAN JOOL LENF MAIN
    MYLT MYRC MYRD MYTD MYTG MYTL MYTU MYUC MYUN
    MYVB MYVE MYVH MYVO MYVY MYVZ MYXJ MYXM MYXN
    MYYA MYYG MYYH MYYW MYYY MZAA MZAB MZAE MZAF
    MZAG MZAJ MZAM MZAP MZAR MZAS MZAT MZAU MZAV MZAY
    MZAZ MZBA MZBL MZCC MZCD MZCE MZCG MZCN MZCU
    MZDF MZDK MZDT MZEB MZED MZEG MZEJ MZEW MZFB
    MZFS MZFZ MZGI MZGW MZHB MZIH MZIR MZIS MZIT MZIW
    MZJA MZJD MZJK MZJV MZJX MZJZ MZKG MZKJ MZKK MZKM
    MZKV MZKZ MZLC MZLZ MZMD MZMJ MZML MZMM MZMP
    MZMV MZMY MZMZ MZNC MZNI MZNJ MZNL MZNO MZOC
    MZOF MZOP MZOR MZPH MZSD MZSM MZZY NNON NOOK
    NOWW OBMI OHVA ORBS OSEP OYES REED REEF RIKI RINN
    RUFF RYPH SHUF WAKE WLMS YZYZ
GEMINI wih Flexiform and Southdown wings
    G-JESA MBST MBTG MJYP MJZU MMAR MMDP MMHE MMJT
    MMKM MMOB MMPJ MMRP MMRW MMSO MMTG MMTL MMUX
    MMXW MNJG MNMC
GEMINI FLASH variants (Rotax 503)
    G-MMDP MMKL MMPO MMSP MMTG MMUO MMUT MMUW
    MMVP MMWA MMXD MMXJ MMXL MMXU MMXV MMZA MMZB
    MMZF MMZJ MMZK MMZM MMZN MMZV MNAC MNAE MNBD
    MNBF MNBG MNBN MNBP MNBR MNBS MNBT MNBV MNBW
    MNCF MNCG MNCJ MNDC MNDF MNDM MNEF MNEG MNEH
    MNET MNEV MNEY MNFF MNFM MNFN MNFP MNGK MNGM
    MNGT MNGW MNIA MNID MNIE MNIF MNIG MNIH MNII MNIZ
    MNJU MNLI MNLY MNMG MNMI MNMO MNMV MNNF MNNJ

MNNL MNNV MNPC MNPG MNRW MNRX MNSA MNSI MNSJ
MNTI MNTS MNTU MNTV MNTZ MNUA MNUF MNUG MNUO
MNUR MNVT MNVV MNVW MNWD MNWI MNXS MNXU MNYJ
MNYK MNZB MNZC MNZD MNZF MTAB MTAC MTAE MTAF
MTAG MTAH MTAR MTBD MTBH MTBJ MTBW MTBX MTBY
MTCE MTCU MTCW MTDF MTDR MTDW MTDY MTEI MTEJ
MTEK MTEY MTFI MTGA MTGO MTHW MTHZ MTIA MTIB MTIL
MTIM MTIN MTJA MTJB MTJC MTJD MTJE MTJL MTJT MTJV
MTJW MTJZ MTKN MTKW MTKX MTKZ MTLB MTLC MTLL MTMA
MTMC MTML MTMT MTMV MTMW MTNC MTNG MTNH MTNI
MTNJ MTNL MTNM MTNY MTPB MTRA MTRZ MTSC MTTI MTTM
MTTP MTTR MTTW MTUU MTUV MTVH MTVI MTVJ MTWF
MTWG MTWR MTWS MTWX MTXM MTXP MTXS MTXZ MTZG
MTZH MTZL MTZM MTZO MTZV MTZW MTZX MTZY MTZZ MVAB
MVAD MVAO MVAP MVBF MVBG MVBI MVBK MVBL MVBM
MVBN MVBO MVCE MVCF MVCY MVCZ MVDA MVDT MVEH
MVEJ MVEK MVEL MVEO MVER MVES MVET MVEV MVGM
MVHE MVHF MVHG MVHH MVIB MVIH MVIX MVIZ MVJA MVJC
MVJE MVJL MVKC MVLL MVLR MVMO MVMR MVMT MVMU
MVMV MVMW MVMX MVMY MVMZ MVNM MVNW MVNX MVNY
MVNZ MVOB MVOF MVON MVOR MVPA MVPB MVPC MVPD
MVPE MVPI MVRA MVRB MVRD MVRM MVSN MVSO MVSP
MVST MVSV MVUA MVXB MVXC MVXR MVXS MVYS MVZS
MWAB MWCE MWCW MWDJ MWEL MWGG MWHI MWHO
MWHR MWIA MWIG MWIH MWIV MWLP MWLT MWLX MWMM
MWMS MWMT MWMX MWMY MWNE MWNS MWNT MWNU
MWOJ MWPB MWPC MWPD MWPF MWPO MWRB MWRC
MWRD MWRE MWRF MWRH MWRI MWRJ MWRR MWSB MWSL
MWSM MWTG MWTH MWTO MWTR MWTY MWTZ MWVN
MWVO MWVR MWVS MWVT MWVY MWVZ MWWB MWWC
MWWI MWWJ MWWK MWWN MWXA MWXB MWXC MWXL
MWXN MWXU MWXV MWYA MWYG MWYH MWYL MWYT MWYV
MWZC MWZG MWZL MWZN MYAO MYAS MYAU MYBJ MYCK
MYCR MYCS MYDV MYFP MYFR MYFU MYGZ MYHF MYHL
MYHN MYIH MYIV MYIY MYJC MYJM MYKC MYKG MYKH MYKV
MYLG MYLR MYMK MYMO MYMV MYND MYOM MYOW MYPE
MYPW MYSJ MZCF OLJT

MERCURY (Rotax 503)
G-MTVG MWVK MWXF MWXJ MWXK MWZA MYAI MYCJ MYCL
MYCN MYDC MYGJ MYJR MYKX MYKY MYLS MYML MYNC
MYNF MYNJ MYOV MYOX MYPV MYRW MYSG MYSZ MYTB
MYTK MYTX MYUB MYUD MYUE MYUK MYUW MYVL MYVS
MYWA MYYU MZAK MZCO MZEK RAVE

RAPIER (Rotax 503)
G-BYBV BYOZ BZAB BZUF BZWR CCHV MFLY MJYV MZEP
MZEV MZFD MZGL MZHJ MZIL MZIM MZJE MZKN MZND MZNU
MZON YARR

SCORCHER SOLO (Rotax 447)
G-MNDD MNNM MNPY MNPZ MNRE MNRZ MVBE MYFT MZKI
MZKN

(DUAL) TRI-FLYER trike with Flexiform, Solar Wings & Southdown wings
G-CCVX MBCJ MBHK MBIZ MBMT MBPG MBZO MJEE MJHR
MJIF MJMN MJMR MJPE MJRA MJTP MJXE MJYX MMCZ MMDK
MMDN MMEJ MMFD MMFE MMFV MMJG MMKR MMLI MMTD
MMUH MMYV MNFA MNJD MNUI MVBC

MALMO see **BÖLKOW**

MANNING-FLANDERS
MF.1 replica
G-BAAF

MANUEL
LADYBIRD
G-MJPB

MARGAN'SKI & MYSLOWSKI ZAKLADY LOTNICZE Sp.z.o.o.
MDM-1 FOX
G-CFOX
SWIFT S-1
G-EIER IZII

MARQUART
MA.5 CHARGER
G-BHBT BVJX

MAULE AIRCRAFT CORPORATION
M-5-180C LUNAR ROCKET
G-BVFZ
M-5-235C LUNAR ROCKET
G-BHJK BICX BIES BPMB BVFT CCBF FMGG OJGT RJWW
M-6-235 SUPER ROCKET
G-BKGC MOUL

M-7-235 SUPER ROCKET
G-TAFC
MT-7-235 SUPER ROCKET
G-HIND
MX-7-180 SUPER ROCKET variants
G-BSKG JREE LOFM MLHI OMOL RAZZ URUS WALY
MXT-7-160 SUPER, ROCKET
G-BUXD
MXT-7-180 SUPER, ROCKET
G-BTXT BUEP BVIK BVIL CROL GROL

AVIONS MAX HOLSTE
MH.1521 BROUSSARD variants
G-BWGG BWLR CBGL YYYY

MAXAIR
DRIFTER
G-MYBB
HUMMER
G-MBYH MJCF MMZZ MNIM

MD HELICOPTERS INC
MD.500N NOTAR
G SMAC
MD.600N
G-NELY THUG
MD.900 EXPLORER
G-BXZK CMBS EHMS GMPX GNAA HAAT HPOL KAAT KSSH
LNAA SASH SIVR SUSX SYPS WPAS YPOL

MEDWAY MICROLIGHTS LTD see **RAVEN** and **SOUTHDOWN**
AV8R
G-CCGO
ECLIPSER (Rotax 912-UL)
G-BYBO BYSS BYXV BYXW BZWI CBMR CBMS CCCI CCZR
ZZOW
HALF PINT trike (JPX PUL 425) with Aerial Arts 130SX wing
G-MMZI MNDE MNEK MNTT MNVL
HYBRED 44XL (Fuji-Robin EC-44)
G-MJVE MMEK MMKH MNCU MNCV MNEI MNJX
HYBRED 44XLR (Rotax 447)
G-BYBJ BYRH MNMN MNXO MTFC MTJG MTLX MTNE MTNF
MTUX MVCD MVDJ MVEE MVGB MVGY MVKB MVMK MVPF
MVPL MVRY MVRZ MVSI MVVH MVVI MVVR MVWV MVXD MVXE
MVXI MVXJ MVXM MVYP MVYR MVZO MWCY MWCZ MWGC
MWIL MWJP MWJR MWLB MWLS MWRM MWSS MWST MWSU
MWVU MYVV MYVX
SLA 80 Executive
G-CCJJ CDZY CEII DBIN
SLA 95I
G-CENJ
SLA 100 Executive
G-CDXD CEHE RSMC

SOCIÉTÉ MENAVIA see **PIEL**

MESSERSCHMITT AG including **HISPANO HA.1112** * versions
Bf.108D-1 TAIFUN
G-AKZY
Bf.109
G-AWHE* AWHJ* AWHL* AWHN* AWHO* AWHS* BWUE* AYDS
CDTI EMIL HUNN* USTV

MESSERSCHMITT-BÖLKOW-BLOHM GmbH including **EUROCOPTER
DEUTSCHLAND GmbH** production
BÖ.105 variants
"G-CDBS" G-BATC BCXO BFYA BTHV BTKL BUXS CDBS EYNL
NAAA NAAB NDAA ENVO PASB PASG PASX TVAM WAAN WAAS
WYPA
BK-117C-1
G-DCPA OEMT RESC
BK-117C-2 (EC145)
G-MPSA MPSB MPSC

MICKLEBURGH
L107 SPARROW
G-BZVC

MICRO AVIATION
B-22 BANTAM (Rotax 582)
G-BXZU BZYS CFHB CFHC MZEY MZLX

MICRO BIPLANE AVIATION
TIGER CUB 440 (Fuji-Robin EC-44)
    G-MJRU MJSP MJSU MJUC MJUW MJWF MJWJ MJWW MJXD
    MJXF MJYD MJZE MMAG MMBE MMBH MMBT MMCX MMFS
    MMGF MMGL MMHN MMIE MMIH MMIX MMJV MMKP MMLB
    MMUM MNJC MNKM MWFT

MICRO ENIGINEERING (AVIATON) LTD (MEA)
MISTRAL
    G-MBET MBOH

MICROFLIGHT AIRCRAFT LTD including **CORBETT FARMS**
production
SPECTRUM (Rotax 503)
    G-MVJM MVSU MWCG MWKX MWPG MWPH MWTD MWTE
    MWWR MYAY

MIDLAND ULTRALIGHTS LTD
SIROCCO
    G-MNDU MNRT MTRC MVSM

MIGNET
HM.14 POU-DU-CIEL replicas
    "G-ADRG" "G-ADRX" "G-ADRY" "G-ADVU" "G-ADYV" "G-ADZW"
    "G-AEOF" "G-AFFI"
HM.14 POU-DU-CIEL
    G-ADXS AEBB AEEH AEFG AEGV AEHM AEJZ AEKR MYSI
HM.293
    G-AXPG

SOCIÉTÉ D'EXPLOITATION DES AERONEFS HENRI MIGNET
HM-1000 BALERIT (Rotax 582)
    G-MRAM MYDZ MYXL MZIX MZLI MZMW MZTA

MOSKOVSKII MASHINOSTROITELNYY ZAVOD IMIENI AI MIKOYANA
MiG-21
    G-BRAM

MILES AIRCRAFT LTD including **PHILLIPS AND POWIS AIRCRAFT LTD**
M.2L HAWK SPEED SIX
    G-ADGP
M.2W HAWK TRAINER
    G-ADWT
M.3 FALCON
    G-ADLS AEEG
M.5 SPARROWHAWK
    G-ADNL
M.11A WHITNEY STRAIGHT
    G-AERV AEUJ AFGK
M.12 MOHAWK
    G-AEKW
M.14A HAWK TRAINER 3
    G-AFBS AHUJ AIUA AJRS AKAT AKKR AKKY AKPF AMMC
    ANWO
M.17 MONARCH
    G-AFJU AFLW AFRZ
M.18
    G-AHKY
M.38 MESSENGER variants
    G-AGOY AIEK AJKG AJOC AJOE AJVL AJWB AKAO AKBO AKIN
    AKIS AKVZ ALBP
M.65 GEMINI variants
    G-AJTI AKDK AKEL AKEN AKGE AKHP AKHU AKKA AKKB AKKH
    ALCS
M.75 ARIES
    G-AOGA
M.100 STUDENT
    G-MIOO

MILLER
NEXUS MUSTANG
    G-NXUS

MILLS
MH-1
    G-OMHI

MINICAB including **AÉRONAUTIQUE Havraise, CONSTRUCTIONS
AERONAUTIQUE DE BEARN, GARDAN, NOUVELLE SOC COMETAL**
and **SRCM** production
GY-20 and GY-201 MINICAB
    G-ATPV AVRW AWEP AWUB AWWM AZJE BANC BBFL BCER
    BCNC BCPD BDGB BEBR BGKO BGMJ BGMR MCAB

MIRAGE see **ULTRAFLIGHT**

MITCHELL
U-2 SUPER WING
    G-MMNS

MITCHELL-PROCTER see **PROCTER**
KITTIWAKE
    G-ATXN BBRN

MONNETT see **SONEX**
MONI
    G-BMVU CBTL INOW MONI TRIM
SONERAI
    G-BGEH BGLK BICJ BJBM BJLC BKDC BKFA BKNO BLAI BMIS
    BOBY BSGJ BVCC CCOZ LOWE PFAT RILY

MONOCOUPE CORPORATION
90A
    G-AFEL

MONTGOMERIE-BENSEN see **BENSEN**

MOONEY AIRCRAFT CORPORATION
M.20 variants
    G-APVV ASUB ATOU AWLP BCJH BDTV BHJI BIBB BIWR BJHB
    BKMA BKMB BPCR BPFC BSXI BWJG BWTW BXML BYEE CEJN
    CERT DBYE DESS DEST FLYA GCKI JAKI JAST JDIX JENA
    MALS MUNI NRYL OBAL ODJH OEAC OJAC OJJB OONE OPWS
    OSUS RAFW

MORANE-SAULNIER including **GEMS, SOCIÉTÉ LEVASSEUR,
MORANE, SEEMS,and SOCATA** production and see **DE HAVILLAND**
and **FIESELER**
TYPE N
    G-AWBU
MS.230 PARASOL
    G-AVEB BJCL
MS.315
    G-BZNK
MS.502 CRIQUET
    G-BIRW BPHZ
MS.733 ALCYON
    G-MSAL
MS.800 series RALLYE variants
    G-ARXW ASAT ASAU ATWE AVIN AVTV AVVJ AWKT AWOA
    AWYX AXCM AXGE AXHS AXHT AXOH AXOS AXOT AYRH
    AYTA AYYX AZEE AZGL AZKC AZKE AZMZ AZUT AZVF AZVH
    AZVI AZYD BAAI BAOH BAOJ BAOM BBED BBGC BBLM BCLT
    BCOR BCVC BCXB BDEC BDWA BDWH BECA BECB BEIL BERA
    BERC BETO BEVB BEVC BEVW BFAK BFDF BFGS BFTZ BGKC
    BGMT BGSA BHWK BIAC BIIK BIRB BJDF BKBF BKGA BKGT
    BKJF BKOA BKVA BKVB BLGS BLIY BPJD BRDN BTIU BTOW
    BTUG BUKR BWWG BXZT BYPN BZNX CCZA EGKE EISO EXIT
    FOSY GIGI HENT HHAV KHRE MELV OACI OMIA PIGS WCEI

MORAVA see **LET NARODNI PODNIK KUNOVICE**

MORAVAN NARODNI PODNIK
ZLIN Z-226T TRENER SPEZIAL
    G-EJGO
ZLIN Z-242L
    G-BWTC BWTD EKMN
ZLIN Z-326 TRENER MASTER
    G-BEWO BKOB
ZLIN Z-50LX
    G-MATE
ZLIN Z-526 TRENER MASTER variants (Walter Minor 6-3)
    G-AWJX AWJY AWSH BLMA BPNO PCDP TINY

MORETON
Balloon (Minimum Lift)
ORIENTAL
    G-BINY

MORRIS
Balloon (Minimum Lift)
SCRUGGS BL2 series
    G-BILE BILG BINL BINM BINX BIOS BIPH BISL BISM BISS BIST
SCRUGGS RS5000
    G-BIWB BIWC BIWD BJEN BJES BJGN

MORRIS MOTORS LTD see **DE HAVILLAND**

MOSS BROS AIRCRAFT LTD
MOSS MA.1
    G-AFHA
MOSS MA.2
    G-AFJV

MOTO-DELTA see CENTRAIR

MOULT
TRIKE with Flexiform wing
    G-MTFK

AVIONS MUDRY ET CIE including AKROTECH EUROPE and CONSTRUCTIONS AÉRONAUTIQUES DE BOURGOGNE
CAP.10
    G-BECZ BKCX BLVK BRDD BXBK BXBU BXFE BXRA BXRB
    BXRC BYFY CAPI CAPX CCNX CCXC CDCE CDIF CPDW CPXC
    CZCZ GDTU IVAL LORN MOZZ ODIN OIOB RIFN SLEA WIXI
CAP.20 and CAP.21
    G-BIPO BPPS
CAP.231 and CAP.232
    G-GKKI IIAI IIVI OGBR SKEW

MURPHY
QUICKSILVER GT500
    G-CEWY

MURPHY AIRCRAFT MANUFACTURING LTD
ELITE
    G-CBRT ONIG
MAVERICK
    G-BYCV CBGO CBVF CDYM MZJJ MZJS MZLE ONFL
REBEL (Lycoming O-235)
    G-BUTK BVHS BWCY BWFZ BWLL BYBK BYPP BZFT CBFK
    CCPK DIKY LJCC YELL
RENEGADE SPIRIT UK (Rotax 582)
    G-BYBU MGOO MVZP MVZX MWAJ MWKA MWMW MWNF
    MWNR MWOO MWPS MWPZ MWUH MWVP MWWD MYAM
    MYAZ MYCO MYFM MYRK MYUF MYXR MZIZ REBB TBMW
RENEGADE 912
    G-BTHN BTKB BWPE FIRZ NINE RCMC TBAG

NANCHANG see YAKOVLEV

NASH see PROCTER

NAVAL AIRCRAFT FACTORY
N3N-3
    G-ONAF

NDN AIRCRAFT LTD
NDN-6 FIELDMASTER
    G-NRDC

NEICO
LANCAIR 200, 235, 320
    G-BSRI BUNO BVLA CBAF FOPP JBAS PJMT UILE

NEUKOM
ELFE
    G-CJXY

THE NEW KOLB AIRCRAFT COMPANY
FIREFLY
    G-CEPN

NICOLLIER
HN.700 MENESTREL
    G-BVHL CCCJ CCDS CCKN CCVW CDHZ CDZR MINS NURA
    VIVO

NIEUPORT
SCOUT 17/23
    G-BWMJ
28C-1
    G-BSKS

NOBLE HARDMAN AVIATION LTD including THE SNOWBIRD AEROPLANE CO LTD
SNOWBIRD (Rotax 532)
    G-BZYV MTXL MTXU MVCI MVCJ MVIL MVIN MVIO MVOJ MVOL
    MVYT MVYU MVYV MVYW MVYX RUMI

NOORDUYN AVIATION LTD see NORTH AMERICAN

SOCIÉTÉ NATIONALE DE CONSTRUCTIONS AÉRONAUTIQUES DU NORD (SNCAN)
1002 PINGOUIN
    G-ASTG ATBG ETME
1101 NORALPHA
    G-ATDB ATHN BSMD MESS
1203 NORECRIN
    G-BAYL BEDB
3202
    G-BIZK BIZM BPMU
3400
    G-BOSJ

THE NORMAN AEROPLANE CO LTD
NAC-2 FREELANCE
    G-NACA NACI

NORTH AMERICAN AVIATION INC including CAC, CCF, NOORDUYN AVIATION LTD and see NORTH AMERICAN ROCKWELL production
B-25 MITCHELL
    G-BWGR BYDS
F-86 SABRE
    G-BZNL SABR
P-51 MUSTANG
    G-BIXL BTCD CEBW HAEC MRLL MSTG SIJJ UAKE
NA-64 YALE
    G-BYNF
OV-10B BRONCO
    G-BZGK BZGL
(A) T-6 TEXAN, AT-16 HARVARD variants
    G-AZBN AZSC BBHK BGGR BGHU BGOR BGPB BICE BJST
    BKRA BRBC BRLV BRVG BSBG BTXI BUKY BWUL BZHL CCOY
    CTKL DDMV ELMH HRVD JUDI RAIX TEXN TOMC TSIX TVIJ
T-28/A TROJAN
    G-TROY

NORTH WING DESIGN
STRATUS-ATF
    G-CEYP

NOSTALGAIR
N.3 PUP
    G-BVEA

NOTT
Balloon (Hot Air)
Various
    G-CCSW NOTT

NOTT-CAMERON
Balloon (Hot Air)
NCA ULD- 2
    G-BNXK

NOVA VERTRIEBSGESELLSCHAFT GmbH
Paragliders
VERTEX
    G-BYLI BYZT BZVI CCET
PHOCUS
    G-BZYI
PHILOU
    G-BZXI
X LARGE 37
    G-BZJI

OLDFIELD
BABY LAKES
    G-BBGL BGEI BGLS BKHD BMIY BWMO POND SWAK

OMEGA BALLOONS
Balloon (Hot Air)
O-20
    G-AXMD
56
    G-AYAL
84
    G-AWMO AXJB AXVU

OPTICA INDUSTRIES LTD including FLS production
OA.7 OPTICA
    G-BMPL BOPO BOPR

ORLICAN
L-40 META-SOKOL
    G-APUE APVU

OZONE/ADVENTURE SA
ROADSTER-ADVENTURE FUNFLYER QUATTRO
    G-TMAN

ROADSTER-ADVENTURE BAILEY QUATTRO
    G-OFAL

PACIFIC AIRWAVE
PULSE 2 - SKYCYLE Trike)
    G-CEZN

PAKES
JACKDAW
    G-MBOF

PARAMANIA -see **PASSION'ALLES**

G PARNALL and COMPANY
PARNALL ELF
    G-AAIN
PARNALL PIXIE
    G-EBJG

PARATOYS
28/LOWBOY 313
    G-CFLB

PARSONS including **BENSEN-PARSONS** and **MONTGOMERIE-PARSONS**
TWO PLACE GYROPLANE
    G-BPIF BTFE BUWH BVOD CBOU CDGT IIXX IVYS UNIV

PARTENAVIA COSTRUZIONI AERONAUTICHE SpA
P.64B OSCAR
    G-BMDP
P.68B and C
    G-BCDK BFBU BHBZ BHJS BMOI ENCE FJMS HUBB KIMK OLMA
    ORVR PART RVRE SAMJ

PASSION'ALLES
CHARIOT Z trike- PARAMANIA ACTION GT26 sailwing
    G-CEOZ

PAYNE
Balloon (Hot Air)
FREE
    G-AZRI
AX7-62
    G-BFMZ

PAYNE
KNIGHT TWISTER
    G-BRAX

PAZMANY
PL-1
    G-BDHJ
PL-2
    G-OPAZ
PL-4A
    G-BMMI BRFX FISK PAZY PLIV

PEARSON
Balloon (Minimum Lift)
Series 2
    G-BIXX

PEGASUS AVIATION including **CYCLONEAIRSPORTS LTD, MAINAIR SPORTS LTD** and **P&M Ltd** production
QUANTUM series (Rotax 912)
    G-BYDZ BYEW BYFF BYFF BYHR BYIS BYIZ BYJK BYKT BYLC
    BYMF BYMI BYMT BYND BYOG BYOV BYPB BYPJ BYPL BYRJ
    BYRU BYSX BYTC BYYN BYYP BYYY BZAI BZBR BZDL BZDS
    BZED BZFC BZFH BZGZ BZHN BZHO BZIM BZIW BZJO BZJZ
    BZLL BZLX BZLZ BZMI BZMW BZNB BZNC BZNM BZOD BZOE
    BZOO BZOU BZOV BZRJ BZRP BZRR BZSA BZSG BZSI BZSM
    BZSS BZSX BZUC BZUE BZUI BZUX BZVJ BZVV BZWS BZWU
    BZXV BZXX BZYN CBBB CBBN CBBP CBCD CBCF CBCX CBDX
    CBDZ CBEN CBEU CBEV CBGG CBHK CBHN CBHY CBIZ CBJO

    CBKW CBLL CBMV CBNT CBOY CBSP CBTD CBTZ CBUD CBUS
    CBUU CBUZ CBYI CBYV CCCD CCDK CCDZ CCFT CCIH CCJD
    CCNE CCNW CCOC CCRF CCRT CCUR CCWN CCWO CCWW
    CCYL CCZB CDAA CDAO CDCY CDCZ CDDF CDEN CDFR CDGX
    CDIL CDIR CDLZ CDOD CDPW CDRR CDTB CDTC CDVH CDXG
    CFBM DINO DSLL EDMC EMLY EOFW FESS FFUN GBJP ICWT
    ISEW JAWC JGSI KAZI KICK MCEL MCJL MDBC MGDL MGEF
    MGFK MGFO MGGG MGGV MGMC MGTG MHMR MROC MSPY
    MYLC MYLE MYLH MYLI MYLK MYLL MYLM MYLZ MYMB MYMC
    MYMX MYNB MYNK MYNL MYNN MYNO MYNP MYNR MYNS
    MYNT MYNV MYNZ MYOU MYPH MYPI MYPN MYPX MYPY
    MYRF MYRM MYRN MYRS MYRT MYRY MYRZ MYSB MYSC
    MYSR MYSW MYSX MYSY MYTI MYTJ MYTN MYUO MYUU
    MYUV MYVC MYVJ MYVK MYVM MYVR MYWG MYWI MYWJ
    MYWK MYWL MYWO MYWR MYWT MYWU MYWW MYWY MYXE
    MYXT MYXW MYXX MYXZ MYYB MYYC MYYI MYYK MYYN
    MYYX MYZB MYZJ MYZK MYZL MYZM MYZY MZAN MZAW
    MZAX MZBB MZBC MZBI MZBO MZBT MZBY MZCI MZCJ MZCM
    MZCR MZCV MZCY MZDB MZDC MZDD MZDE MZDH MZDN
    MZDU MZDV MZDY MZEC MZEE MZEH MZEM MZEX MZEZ
    MZFG MZFM MZFT MZFV MZGK MZGN MZGO MZGV MZHI
    MZHK MZHN MZHP MZIB MZIC MZIE MZIF MZIJ MZIK MZIU
    MZJG MZJH MZJN MZJO MZJT MZJW MZJY MZKA MZKD MZKF
    MZKL MZKY MZLA MZLD MZLF MZLJ MZLN MZLT MZLV MZLW
    MZMC MZMF MZMG MZMH MZMN MZMT MZNB MZNG MZNP
    MZNR MZNS MZNT MZOD MZOG MZOJ MZOS MZOV MZOW
    MZPD MZRC MZRH MZRM MZSC NAPO OAMF OATE OBJP
    OELD OLDM OHKS OLFB OTJH PEGA PIXI PRSI REDC REPH
    RUSA SILY SITA SMBM TBBC TFIX TRAM TUSA WHEE ZZXX
QUIK variants (Rotax 912-UL(S))
    G-CBRY CBVN CBYE CBYO CBZH CBZT CCAD CCAS CCAZ
    CCCG CCDB CCDD CCDF CCDO CCEA CCEW CCFB CCFL
    CCGC CCGI CCHH CCHI CCHO CCIV CCJM CCKM CCKO CCLM
    CCLX CCMD CCME CCML CCMS CCNM CCOG CCOK CCOU
    CCOW CCPC CCPG CCRW CCSD CCSF CCSH CCSL CCSY
    CCTC CCTD CCTU CCTZ CCUA CCVB CCWR CCWV CCXT
    CCXZ CCYE CCYJ CCZO CDAR CDAX CDBB CDCF CDCI CDCK
    CDEC CDEW CDFG CDFO CDGC CDGD CDGO CDKK CDKM
    CDLA CDLD CDLJ CDMJ CDMU CDMZ CDNH CDOC
    CDOM CDOP CDPD CDRG CDRT CDRW CDSA CDSM CDSS
    CDTO CDTR CDUH CDUU CDVG CDVN CDVO CDVR CDVZ
    CDWO CDWP CDWR CDWS CDWW CDWZ CDXM CDXN CEBD
    CEBM CEBT CECA CECM CEDN CEEI CEEM CEGJ CEGT CEGV
    CEGW CEHC CEHI CEHW CEJJ CEJX CEKG CEMB CEML CEMM
    CEMO CEMT CEMX CEMZ CENL CENV CEPP CERN CERP
    CERV CERW CESG CESR CETL CETM CEUF CEUH CEUZ CEVB
    CEVG CEVP CEVW CEWD CEWH CEZT CEZX CFAT CFCZ CFDL
    CFDY CFEM CFEV CFEX CFFN CFFO CFGD CFGT CFGV CFIG
    CFIL CFIM CFKJ CFKO CFKR CFKU CFLA CFLM CFLR CFMB
    CFMD CFOO CFPI CFPR CFSF CFTG CJAI CJAY CJGG CWEB
    CWIC CWIK CWMC CWVY DCMI DECX DDDY DTAR EEWZ
    EJMM ERYR EZAR FEET FLEX FFIT FRGT GAZN GBEE GCEA
    GEMX GTFC GTEE GTGT GTJD GTSO GTTP HAMS HALT HOFF
    IGLY JOBA JULE KEVS KUIK KWIC KWKR LSKY LUNE LYTB
    MASI MAXS MFLJ MLAW MRJJ NJPW NUTT OFDT OJJV OKEM
    OLDP OLFZ OMIW OMPW ORLA OUIK PEAR PIPI PVSS RAYB
    RCRC RIBA RIKY RITT SEEE SHEE SHEZ SISU SOCK SUEL
    TARR TBJP TBLB TBMR TCNY TEEE TERR TFLX TJAV TONN
    TPWL WBLY WFLY WIZS XDWE XJJM YOLK YSMO

PENN-SMITH
GYROPLANE
    G-AXOM

PERCIVAL AIRCRAFT CO LTD including **HUNTING PERCIVAL AIRCRAFT LTD** production
Type D GULL FOUR
    G-ACGR
Type D GULL SIX
    G-ACUP ADPR AERD
Type E MEW GULL including REPLICA*
    G-AEXF HEKL*
Type K VEGA GULL
    G-AEZJ
Type Q SIX
    G-AFFD
PROCTOR variants
    G-AGTB AHDI AHTE AHVG AHZY AKEX AKIU AKZN ALCK ALIS
    ALJF ANXR AOGE
P.40 PRENTICE
    G-AOKL AOKO AOKZ AOLK AOLU AOMF AOPL AOPO APIT APIY
    APJB APPL

P.50 PRINCE
G-AMLZ
P.56 PROVOST
G-AWPH AWRY AWTD AWVF BDYG BGSB BKFW BLIW BZRE
BZRF KAPW MOOS TMKI
P.57 SEA PRINCE
G-BIDN BRFC DACA GACA RACA

PEREIRA
OSPREY
G-BVGI CCCW GEOF PREY

PERFORMANCE DEIGNS INC
BARNSTORMER/VOYAGER
G-CFKP

PHANTOM see **SKYRIDER**

PHILLIPS
ST.2 SPEEDTWIN
G-STDL

PHILLIPS AND POWIS AIRCRAFT LTD - see **MILES AIRCRAFT LTD**

PHOENIX
LUTON LA-4, LA-4A MINOR including ORD-HUME O-H7, PARKER CA-4
and PHOENIX DUET versions and including replica
G-AFIR AFIU "AFUG"* AMAW ARIF ARXP ASAA ASCY ASEA
ASEB ASML ASXJ ATCJ ATFW ATKH ATWS AVDY AVUO AWIP
AWMN AXGR AXKH AYDY AYSK AYTT AZHU AZPV BANF BBCY
BBEA BCFY BDJG BIJS BKHR BRWU
LA-5A MAJOR
G-ARAD

INDUSTRIE AERONAUTICHE E MECCANICHE RINALDO PIAGGIO
SpA including **PIAGGIO AERO INDUSTRIES SpA** and **FOCKE-WULF**
FLUGZEUGBAU GMBH production
P.149
G-RORY
P.166
G-APWY

DON PICCARD BALLOONS INC
Balloon (Hot Air)
Piccard Balloon
G-ATTN
AX6
G-AWCR AZHR

PIEL AVIATION including **COOPAVIA, ROUSSEAU, SOCIÉTÉ**
MENAVIA and **SOCIÉTÉ SCINTEX** production
CP.301 EMERAUDE
G-ARDD ARRS ARUV ASCZ ASLX ASVG AXXC AYCE AYEC
AYTR AZGY AZYS BBKL BCCR BDCI BDDZ BDKH BHRR BIDO
BIJU BIVF BKFR BKNZ BKUR BLRL BPRT BSVE BXAH BXYE
DENS PIEL
CP.328 SUPER EMERAUDE
G-SAZZ
CP.1310-C3 SUPER EMERAUDE
G-ASMV ASNI BCHP BGVE BJCF BJVS BLXI BXRF
CP.1315-C3 SUPER EMERAUDE
G-BHEK
CP.1320
G-CFIH SAFI
CP.1330 SUPER EMERAUDE
G-BANW

PIETENPOL
AIRCAMPER
G-ADRA BBSW BKVO BMDE BMLT BNMH BRXY BUCO BUXK
BUZO BVYY BWAT BWVB BXZO BYFT BYKG BYLD BYZY CCKR
DAYZ ECOX ECVB EDFS IMBY KIRC LEOD OFFA OHAL OPJS
PCAF PIET RAGS SILS TARN UNGO VALS

PIK see **EIRI** and **SIREN**

PILATUS AIRCRAFT LTD
P.2
G-PTWO
P.3
G-BTLL
PC.6 TURBO PORTER
G-BYNE CECI WGSC

PC.12 variants
G-INTO MATX OCLE OLTT PVPC TRAT WINT ZUMO

PILATUS FLUGZEUGWERKE AG
B4-PC11 variants
G-CHDA CHDE CHLC CHVH CJXX CKSK CKSO DCSN DCSP
DCUB DCUODCUT DCVG DCVK DCVM DCVV DCYA DCZD
DDBC DDLA DDND DDSV DEOU ECSW PILY

PIPER AIRCRAFT CORPORATION including **TAYLOR AIRCRAFT CO**
LTD, and **THE NEW PIPER AIRCRAFT INC** production
J-2 CUB
G-AEXZ AFFH JTWO
J-3 CUB variants
G-AFDO AGAT AGIV AGVV AHIP AIIH AISS AISX AJAD AJES
AKAA AKAZ AKIB AKRA AKTH AKUN ASPS ATKI ATZM AXGP
AXHP AXHR AYCN AYEN BAET BBHJ BBLH BBUU BBXS BCNX
BCOB BCOM BCPH BCPJ BCUB BCXJ BDCD BDEY BDEZ BDHK
BDJP BDMS BDOL BECN BEDJ BEUI BFBY BFDL BFHI BFZB
BGPD BGSJ BGTI BGXA BHPK BHVV BHXY BHZU BIJE BILI
BJAF BJAY BJSZ BKHG BLPA BMKC ANXP BOTU BOXJ BPCF
BPUR BPVH BPYN BREB BROR BSBT BSFD BSNF BSTI BSVH
BSYO BTBX BTET BTSP BTUM BTZX BVAF BVPN BWEZ CCOX
CCUB COPS CUBS CUBY FRAN HEWI KIRK KURK KUUI LFOR
LIVH LOCH NCUB OCUB OINK OLEZ POOH RAMP RIXA RRSR
SEED TCUB
J-4 CUB COUPÉ variants
G-AFGM AFWH AFZA BRBV BSDJ BUWL
J-5A CUB CRUISER
G-BRIL BRLI BSDK BSXT BTKA
L-4BCUB
G-FINT
PA-12 SUPER CRUISER
G-AMPG ARTH AWPW AXUC BCAZ BOWN BSYG CDCS PAIZ
PA-15 VAGABOND
G-ALGA ASHU AWOF BDVB BOVB BRJL BRPY BRSX BSFW
BTFJ BTOT BUKN CCEE FKNH
PA-16 CLIPPER
G-BAMR BBUG BIAP BSVI BSWF
PA-17 VAGABOND
G-AKTP ALEH ALIJ AMYL AWKD AWOH BCVB BDVA BDVC BIHT
BLMP BSMV BSWG BTBY BTCI BUXX
PA-18 SUPER CUB variants
G-AMEN APZJ ARAM ARAN ARAO AREO ARGV ARVO ATRG
AVOO AWMF AXLZ AYPM AYPO AYPS AYPT AZRL BAFT BAFV
BAKV BBOL BBYB BCFO BCMD BEOI BEUA BEUU BFFP BGPN
BGWH BGYN BHGC BHOM BIDJ BIDK BIID BIJB BIMM BIRH BITA
BIYJ BIYR BIYY BIZV BJBK BJCI BJEI BJFE BJIV BJTP BJWX
BJWZ BKET BKJB BKRF BKTA BKVM BLHM BLLN BLLO BLMI
BLMR BLMT BLPE BLRC BMAY BMEA BMKB BNXM BOOC BPJG
BPJH BPUL BROZ BRRL BSHV BTBU BTUR BVIE BVIW BVMI
BVRZ BWOR BWUB BZHT CCKW CDPR CFSV CUBB CUBI CUBJ
CUBN CUBP CVMI DADG ECMK ECUB EGPG FUZZ HACK HELN
JCUB KAMP LCUB LION MGMM NESY NETY NNAC OFER OOMF
OROD OSPS OTAN OTUG OVON PIPR PUDL ROVE SCUB SUPA
SWAY TUGG WCUB WGCS WLAC XCUB YCUB ZAZA
PA-20 PACER (Conversions ex PA-22 standard*)
G-APXT* APYI* APZX" ARBS" ARGY* ATBX ATXA* AVDV* BFMR
BIYP ARBS BSED* BTLM* BUDE* BUOI BUXV* BWWU* BXBB
PAXX
PA-22-108 COLT
G-ARGO ARJE ARJF ARJH ARKK ARKM ARKN ARKP ARKS
ARND ARNE ARNG ARNJ ARNK ARNL ARON ARSU CBEI GGLE
PA-22-135 TRI-PACER
G-BMCS BUVA TJAY
PA-22-150 TRI-PACER
G-APXU
PA-22-150 CARIBBEAN,
G-APYW ARAX ARCC ARCF ARDS AREL ARFB ARHN ARHR
ARIK ARIL AWLI AZRS BRNX TLDK
PA-22-160 TRI-PACER
G-APUR APXR APYN APZL ARAI ARBV ARET AREV ARFD ARHP
ARYH AVDV BTKV EMSB HALL
PA-23-160 APACHE
G-APFV APMY ARCW ARJS ARJT ARJU ARMA ASMY BICY
PA-(E)23-250 AZTEC
"G-ESKY" G-ASEP ASER ASHH ATFF AXDC AYBO AYMO AZXG
AZYU BADI BADJ BAPL BATN BAUA BAUI BAUJ BAVL BBCC
BBDO BBHF BBIF BBMJ BBNO BBRA BBTJ BCBG BCCE BCEX
BFBB BGTG BGWW BHNG BJNZ BJXX BKJW BKVT BLLM BMFD
BNUV BSVP CALL ESKY KEYS LIZZ MLFF NRSC OART OPME
OSJF OXTC RVRC RVRD RVRJ RVRW TAPE TAXI TOPO UNDD
XSFT

PA-24 COMANCHE (-180)
G-ARHI ARUO AXMA AZKR BRDW BWNI MOTO
PA-24-250 COMANCHE
G-APXJ ARBO ARDB ARLB ARLK ARXG ARYV ASCJ ASEO BAHJ
BYTI DISK TALF
PA-24-260 COMANCHE
G-ATJL ATNV ATOY AVCM AVGA AXTO AZWY BRXW KSVB
PETH
PA-25 PAWNEE
G-ATFR
PA-25-235 PAWNEE
G-ASIY ASVP AVPY AVXA AXED AZPA BAUC BCBJ BDDS BDPJ
BEII BETL BETM BFBP BFEV BFEY BFPR BFPS BFSC BFSD BILL
BNZV BPWL BSTH BUXY BVYP BXST CMGC CTUG LYND NYMF
TUGS
PA-25-260 PAWNEE
G-BFRY BHUU BLDG CCUV DSGC PAWN PSGC SATN TOWS
PA-28-140 CHEROKEE, CRUISER and FLITELINER
G-ASSW ASVZ ATEZ ATJG ATMW ATOI ATOJ ATOK ATOL ATOM
ATON ATOO ATOP ATOR ATPN ATRO ATRP ATRR ATTI ATTK
ATTV ATUB ATUD ATVK ATVO AVFR AVFX AVFZ AVGC AVGD
AVGE AVGI AVLB AVLC AVLE AVLF AVLG AVLH AVLI AVLJ
AVLT AVRP AVSI AVUS AVUT AVUU AVWA AVWD AVWE AVWG
AVWI AVWJ AVWL AVWM AVYP AVYR AWBE AWBG AWBH
AWBS AWEV AWEX AWPS AXAB AXIO AXIR AXJV AXJX AXSZ
AXTA AXTC AXTH AXTJ AXTL AYIG AYJP AYJR AYKW AYNF
AYNJ AYPV AYRM AYWE AZEG AZFC AZMX AZRH AZWB AZWD
BAFU BAFW BAGX BAHE BAHF BAKH BASL BATW BAWK BAXZ
BBBY BBDC BBEF BBEV BBIL BBIX BBYP BBZF BCDJ BCGI
BCGJ BCGN BCJM BCJN BCJP BDGY BDSH BDWY BEAC BEEU
BEFF BEYT BFXK BGAX BGRC BHXK BIYX BOFY BOSR BRBW
BRPK BRPL BRWO BSLU BSSE BSTZ BTEX BTGO BTON BULR
BXPL BYCA BZWG CCLJ CGHM COLH DENE DIAT EEKY FIAT
GCAT JDJM KATS LFSC LFSI LTFB LTFC MATZ MIDD MKAS
NHRH OFTI OKYM OMAT PAWL PETR PIKK RECK RVRA RVRT
SCPL SMTH TEFC TEWS UANT WOLF ZANG ZEBY
PA-28-150 CHEROKEE
G-BIFB
PA-28-151 CHEROKEE WARRIOR
G-BBXW BCIE BCIR BCRL BCTF BCTA BDGM BDPA BEBZ BEFA
BHFK BIEY BNMB BNNT BOHR BOTF BPEL BPKR BPMF BPPK
BRBD BRTX BTNT BTUW BVBF BXLY CCZV CDMA CEGU CPTM
FMAM FPIG GUSS JAMP LUSH PSRT ROWS TALG VIVS
PA-28-160 CHEROKEE
G-ARVT ARVU ARVV ATDA ATIS BSER BSLM BWYB JAKS LIZI
PA-28-161 (CHEROKEE) WARRIOR II
G-BFBR BFDK BFMG BFNI BFNK BFTA BFWB BFWK BFYM
BGKS BGOG BGPJ BGPL BGVK BGYH BHJO BHOR BHRC BHVB
BICW BIIT BIUW BJBW BJBX BJCA BJSV BLVL BMFP BMKR
BMTR BMUZ BNCR BNEL BNJT BNNO BNNS BNNY BNNZ BNOE
BNOF BNOH BNOJ BNOM BNON BNOP BNRG BNSY BNSZ
BNTD BNXE BNXT BNXU BNZB BNZZ BOAH BODB BODC BODD
BODE BODR BOER BOFZ BOHA BOHO BOIG BOJW BOJZ BOKB
BOKK BOKX BOMY BOPC BORK BORL BOTI BOTN BOUP BOVK
BOXA BOXB BOXC BOYH BOYI BOZI BPBM BPCK BPDT BPFH
BPHL BPIU BPKM BPMR BPOM BPRN BPRY BPWE BRBA BRBB
BRBE BRDF BRDG BRDM BRFM BRSE BRUB BSAW BSBA BSCV
BSCY BSGL BSHP BSJX BSLK BSLT BSOK BSOZ BSPI BSPM
BSSC BSSW BSSX BSVG BSVM BSXA BSXB BSXC BSYY BSYZ
BSZT BTAW BTBC BTDV BTFO BTGY BTID BTIV BTKT BTNE
BTNH BTNV BTRK BTRS BTRY BTSJ BUFH BUFY BUIF BUIJ
BUIK BUJO BUJP BUKX BURT BVJZ BXAB BXVU BYHI BYKP
BZLH CBAL CCYY CDDG CDER CDMX CDMY CDON CEGS CEIZ
CEJF CEMD CETD CETE CEXO CEXR CFMX CGDJ CKEY CLAC
CLEA CSGT DKEY EDGA EDGI EEGU EGLL EGTB EKKL ELZN
ELZY EMSL EOLD ERFS ESFT EVIE EVTO EXXO FIZZ FLAV
FPSA GALB GBAB GHKX GRRC GURU HAMR HMES IKBP ISDB
JASE JAVO KART KBPI KNAP KYTE LACA LACB LAZL LBMM
LFSJ LFSK LSFT MAYO MSFT NINA OAAA OANI OJWS OONY
OPTI OPUK OWAP OWAR PJCC RIZZ RSKR RVRN SACI SACO
SARH SEJW SEXX SLYN SNUZ SRWN SUZN SVEA VICC WARE
WARR WFFW WNTR XAVI XENA XINE
PA-28-161 WARRIOR III
G-BXOJ BYHH BZBS BZDA BZIO BZMT CBKR CBWD CBYU
CEEV CEEY CEEZ CEJD COVA COVB DOME FNPT GFTA GFTB
GOTH GYTO HMED ISHA JACA OBDN OBFC OBFS OMST OOFT
WARA WARB WARH WARO WARS WARU WARV WARW WARX
WARY WARZ WAVS
PA-28-161 CADET
G-BPJO BPJP BPJR BPJS BPJU BRJV BTIM BWOH BWOI BWOJ
BXJJ BXTY BXTZ CDEF CEEN CEEU CEJV CEZI CEZL CEZO
EGTR EJRS EKIR EXON EXXO FOXA GFCA GFCB JLIN KCIN
KDET LORC OCTU ODEN OLSF OXOM SACR SACS SACT TLET

PA-28-180 CHEROKEE, CHALLENGER and ARCHER
G-ARYR ASFL ASHX ASII ASIJ ASIL ASKT ASRW ASUD ASWX
ATAS ATEM ATHR ATNB ATOT ATTX ATUL ATVS ATYS ATZK
AVAX AVBG AVBH AVBS AVBT AVGK AVNN AVNO AVNP AVNS
AVNU AVNW AVOZ AVPV AVRK AVRU AVRZ AVSA AVSB AVSC
AVSD AVSE AVSF AVSP AVYL AVYM AVZR AWDP AWIT AWSL
AWTL AWXR AWXS AXSG AXTP AXZD AXZF AYAB AYAR AYAT
AYAW AYEE AYEF AYPJ AYUH AZDX AZLN AZYF BABG BAJR
BASJ BATV BBBN BBEC BBHY BBKX BBPP BBPY BCCF BCLL
BEYL BGTJ BKCC BODM BOHM BRBG BRGI BSEF BSGD BUTZ
BUUX BUYY BXJD CBMO CDEO CJBC DEVS DLTR EFCM GALA
GBRB HOCK HRYZ ITUG KEES LFSG NINB NINC NIND NITA
OIBO ONET OTYP SOOT TEMP WACP YULL
PA-28-181 (CHEROKEE) ARCHER II
G-BDSB BEIP BEMW BEXW BFDI BFSY BFVG BGBG BGVZ
BGWM BHNO BHWZ BHZE BIIV BIUY BJAG BLFI BMIW BMPC
BMSD BNGT BNPO BNRP BNVE BNYP BOBZ BOEE BOJM BOMP
BOMU BOOF BOPA BORS BOSE BPAY BPFI BPGU BPOT BPTE
BPXA BPYO BRBX BRME BRNV BRUD BRXD BSCS BSEU BSIM
BSIZ BSKW BSNX BSVB BSXS BSZJ BTAM BTGZ BTKX BTYI
BUMP BVNS BWPH BXEX BXIF BXOZ BXRG BXWO BYKL BYSP
CBSO CBTT CCAV CDGW CHAS CHIP DJJA EFIR EHGF EHLX
ERNI FBRN GASP HARN ILLY JANA JANT JCAS JJAN JJEN
JOYT KAIR MALA MASF MDAC MELS NIKE NUKA ODUD OGEM
OJEH OMJA OODW OPET PALY RADI RAZY RNCH RRED SARA
SGSE SHED SOBI TALE TALH TERY TIMK TSGJ TWEL USSY
WISE WWAY YANK ZMAM
PA-28-181 ARCHER III
G-BWUH BXTW BYHK BZHK BZHV CCHL DIXY EGLS FEAB
FORR GFPA GFPB GFPC ISAX JACB JACC JACH JACS JADJ
JONM JOYZ KEMI KEVB LACD LKTB LORR MPAA NOTE ORAR
PACT PEJM SUEB VAAC VOAR WLGC
PA-28-201T TURBO DAKOTA
G-BNYB BOKA BXCC
PA-28-235 CHEROKEE and PATHFINDER)
G-ASLV AWSM BXYM BZEH CCBH EWME
PA-28-236 DAKOTA
G-BGXS BHTA BPCX BRKH CSBD DAKO FRGN FWPW KOTA
LEAM ODAK TART
PA-28R-180 CHEROKEE ARROW
G-AVWN AVWO AVWR AVWT AVWU AVWV AVXF AVYS AVYT
AWAZ AWBA AWBB AWBC AWEZ AWFB AWFC AWFD AWFJ
AZWS BAPW BWNM CCIJ CSWH FBWH NELI NIJM OKAG SBMM
WWAL
PA-28R-200 CHEROKEE ARROW
G-AXCA AXWZ AYAC AYII AYPU AYRI AZAJ AZDE AZFI AZFM
AZRV   BCPG BFZH BMJG BTLG CBVU GYMM
PA-28R-200 CHEROKEE ARROW II
G-AZNL AZOG AZSF BAHS BAIH BAMY BAWG BBDE BBEB
BBFD BBZH BBZV BCGS BCJO BDKV BHEV BHGY BHWY BIKE
BIZO BKXF BLXP BMGB BMKK BMNL BMOE BTRT BZDH CBEE
DMCS DSFT EDVL ELUT EPTR FULL GDOG HALC MACK ODOG
OMNI RACO RONG STEA TORC VFAS
PA-28R-201 (CHEROKEE) ARROW III
G-BEWX BGKU BGKV BIDI BMLS BMPR BNEE BNSG BOBA
BYHJ BYYO BZKL BZMB CBPI CBZR CEOF CEOG FROS HERB
IBFW IRKB MEME OARA OARI OARO OARU OTGA RJMS TEBZ
THSL TOLL TSGA UTSY WAMS
PA-28R-201T TURBO (CHEROKEE) ARROW III
G-BEOH BFDO BFTC BGOL BMIV BNNX BNVT BOIC BOYV BSNP
BSPN DDAY DIZY ECJM JDPB JESS MEGA OBAK OJIM OKEN
OOTC SABA SHAY SHUG
PA-28RT-201 ARROW IV
G-BGVN BHAY BOET BOJI BONC BPZM BREP BUUM BVDH
BXYO BXYP BXYR BXYT CDYC CEDD GEHP GHRW ISCA JANO
LAOL LBRC MERL MRST OARC OMHC VOID WEND
PA-28RT-201T TURBO ARROW IV
G-BHFJ BMHT BNJR BNTC BNTS BOGM BOOG BOWY BPBO
BPXJ BRLG BUND BUNH BWMI BYKP DAAH DAAZ DONS EXAM
GPMW IJOE LZZY OPEP OPJD RATV RUBY SKYV TAPS TCTC
YAWW
PA-30 TWIN COMANCHE - also see PA-39
G-ASRO ASSB ASSP ASWW ASYK ATEW ATFK ATMT ATSZ
ATWR ATXD AVCY AVJJ AVKL AVPS AVVI AWBN AWBT AXAU
AYSB AZAB BAKJ BAWN BLOR BZRO CDHF COMB ELAM RROD
SURG TCOM UAVA
PA-31 TURBO NAVAJO
G-BBDS BEZL BFIB BLFZ BPYR CBTN EEJE EGLG FILL GURN
IMEC ISFC LYDD ONAV OWLC RHYM UMMI VICT
PA-31-325 NAVAJO C/R
G-BWHF
PA-31-350 (NAVAJO) CHIEFTAIN
G-BASU BBNT BVYF CEBK CITY EMAX FCSL GLTT HVRD IFIT

JAJK LIDE LYDB LYDC LYDF NERC OETV OJIL ONPA PLAC
PZAZ PZIZ STHA VIPP VIPU VIPV VIPW VIPY VIPX YEOM
PA-31T2 CHEYENNE IIXL
   G-CHEY FCED
PA-32-260 CHEROKEE SIX
   G-ATJV ATRW ATRX BBFV BHGO BRGT CCFI ELDR ETBY NEAL
   OCTI OEVA OSIX
PA-32-300 CHEROKEE SIX
   G-AVFU AVUZ AZDJ BAGG BBSM BEZP BGUB BRNZ BSTV
   BXWP CDUX CSIX DENI DIGI DIWY FAVS FRAG IFFR ILTS KFRA
   KNOW NEON OSCC OTBY PECK SALA SIMY SIXD WINS
PA-32-301FT 6x
   G-RAGT RYNS
PA-32-301 SARATOGA
   G-BMDC BVWZ WAIR
PA-32-301T TURBO SARATOGA
   G-MOLL
PA-32R-300 (CHEROKEE) LANCE
   G-BDWP BEHH BHBG BTCA CEYE DTCP VERN
PA-32R-301 SARATOGA variants
   G-BJCW BKMT BMJA BPVI BYFR BYPU CCST EENA ELLA GOBD
   HDEW HYLT JPOT MOVI NIOS OIHC OPSL PIPP PURL RAMS
   RIGH ROLF TSDS YSTT
PA-32R-301T TURBO SARATOGA variants
   G-BOGO BPVN CLOP GOTO MAIE NJIM SVPN VONS
PA-32RT-300 LANCE II
   G-BFUB BFYC BOTV BRHA BSUF JUPP NROY OJCW RHHT
   TFYN
PA-32RT-300T TURBO LANCE II
   G-LUNA SAWI TFIN
PA-34-200 SENECA
   G-AZOL BABK BACB BADL BAIG BAKD BASM BATR BBLU BBNH
   BBNI BBPX BBXK BCGA BCID BPAD BRHO BVEV EMER EXEC
   EZYU FLYI OCFM OPAG TEST
PA-34-200T SENECA II
   G-BCVY BDUN BEAG BEHU BEJV BEVG BFLH BGFT BHFH
   BHYG BLWD BMUT BNEN BNRX BOCG BOFE BOIZ BORH BOSD
   BOUK BOUL BOUM BOWE BPON BPXX BSDN BSGK BSHA BSII
   BSPG BSUW BTGV BYBH CAHA CBWB CDPV CHEM CLOS
   CLUE CTWW CVLH DAZY ELIS FILE GAFA GFEY GOAC GOGS
   GUYS IEIO IFLP JDBC JLCA LORD MAIR MAXI PEGI ROUS RSHI
   RVRB SENE SENX VVBK XKEN
PA-34-220T SENECA III
   G-BLYK BMDK BMJO BOJK BUBU BWDT GFCD HCSL HMJB
   HTRL JANN NESW OOON OWAL
PA-34-220T SENECA IV
   G-DISD MAIK PFCI
PA-34-220T SENECA V
   G-BZTG GSYS JMOS NSUK OBNA OTVR SAAL
PA-38-112 TOMAHAWK
   G-BGBK BGBN BGBW BGGE BGGG BGGI BGGL BGGM BGGN
   BGIG BGKY BGLA BGRM BGRN BGRR BGRX BGSH BGWN
   BGXB BGXO BGZF BHCZ BJNN BJUR BJUS BJYN BKAS BLWP
   BMKG BMSF BMTO BMVL BMVM BNCO BNDE BNEK BNGR
   BNHG BNIM BNKH BNNU BNPL BNPM BNSL BNUY BNVD BNXV
   BNYK BODP BODS BOHS BOHT BOHU BOLD BOLE BOLF BOMO
   BOMZ BPES BPHI BPIK BPPE BPPF BRFL BRFN BRHR BRLO
   BRLP BRML BRSJ BSFE BSKL BSOT BSOU BSOV BSYK BSYL
   BSYM BTAP BTAR BTAS BTFP BTIL BTJK BTJL BTND BVHM
   BVLP BWNU BWSC BXET BXZA BYMC BYMD CHER CWFA
   CWFB DFLY DTOO EDNA EMMS EORG GALL GTHM LFSA LFSB
   LFSD LFSH LFSM LFSN MSFC NCFC OEDB OLFC OPSF OTFT
   PRIM RECS RVRF RVRG RVRK RVRL RVRM RVRO RVRR RVRU
   SION SUKI TOMS VMCG XALT
PA-39 TWIN COMANCHE C/R - also see PA-30
   G-ASMA AYZE LARE OAJS OGET SIGN
PA-42-720 CHEYENNE IIIA
   G-GMED GZRP MHAR
PA-44-180 SEMINOLE
   G-BGCO BGTF BHFE BRUI BRUX CFSA DENZ GAFT OACA
   PDOC SEMI TWIN
PA-46-350P MALIBU MIRAGE
   G-DIPM DNOP EODE GREY JCAR VRST WADI
PA-46-350T MALIBU MATRIX
   G-MXMX UDMS
PA-46-500TP MALIBU MERIDIAN
   G-CEJB DERI DERK
PA-60-601P AEROSTAR 601 (TED SMITH production)
   G-MOVE RIGS

PIPER, C W R
CP.1 METISSE
   G-BVCP

PITTS AVIATION ENTERPRISES INC including AEROTEK INC, AVIAT INC and CHRISTEN INDUSTRIES INC
S-1 variants
   G-AXNZ AZCE AZPH BADZ BBOH BETI BHSS BIRD BKDR BKKZ
   BKPZ BKVP BLAG BMTU BOXH BOXV BOZS BPDV BPRD BPZY
   BRAA BRBN BRCE BRCI BRJN BRVL BRZL BRZX BSRH BTEF
   BTOO BUWJ BVSZ BXAF BXAU BXFB BXTI BYIR BYJP BZSB
   CCFO CCXK CEOB FARL FCUK FLIK FORZ IIIL IIIR IIIX IIIV JAWZ
   LITZ LOOP LUNY MAGG MAXG MINT OKAY ONSO OODI OSIC
   OSIS OSIT OWAZ PARG REAP SIIS SKNT STYL SWON VOOM
   WAZZ WIGY WILD XRED YOYO
S-2 variants
   G-BADW BOEM BPLY BTTR BTUK BTUL BYIP CCTF ENIO EWIZ
   FDPS FOLY HISS ICAS IICI IIDY IIIE IIII IIIT ITII KITI ODDS OSZA
   OSZB PIIT PITS PITZ PTTS ROLL SIIB SIIE SJBI SKNT SPIN
   STUA STUB TIII WREN XATS ZIII

PLUMB
BGP.1 BIPLANE
   G-BGPI FUNN

POBER
P-9 PIXIE
   G-BUXO

POLIKARPOV
Po-2 (CSS-13)
   G-BXYA

PORTERFIELD AIRPLANE CO
CP-50
   G-AFZL
CP-65
   G-BVWY

PORTSLADE SCHOOL
Balloon (Hot Air)
FREE BALLOON
   G-AZYL

AVIONS POTTIER
P.80S
   G-BTYH

POWERCHUTE SYSTEMS INTERNATIONAL LTD
KESTREL (Rotax 503
   G-MVRV MWCI MWCK MWCM MWCN MWCO MWCP MWCS
   MWFG MWFI MWFL MWGU MWGW MWGZ MWMB MWMC
   MWMD MWMG MWMH MWNV MWNX MWOD MWOE
   MYCX MYCY MYCZ MYDA MYEX MYFA MYHS
RAIDER (Rotax 447)
   G-MVHC MVNA MVNB MVNC MVNK MVNL MVVZ MVWJ

PRACTAVIA
PILOT SPRITE
   G-AZZH BALY BCVF BCWH ROSS

PRESTWICK MPA GROUP
DRAGONFLY MPA Mk 1
   G-BDFU

PRICE
Balloon (Hot Air)
AX7-77
   G-BMDJ

PRIVATEER see SLINGSBY

PROCTER see MITCHELL
PETREL
   G-AXSF

PROGRESSIVE AERODYNE INC
SEAREY AMPHIBIAN
   G-CREY

PROTECH
PT-2C
   G-EWAN

PTERODACTYL LTD see also SOLEAIR
PFLEDGLING, PTRAVELER
   G-MBAW MBHZ MBPB MJST MMPI

ALFONS PUTZER KG
ELSTER B
G-APVF BMWV

PZL-BIELSKO including SZYBOWCOWY ZAKLAD DOSWIADCZALNY (SZD)
SZD-9bis BOCIAN
G-DBJD DCEB DCKN DCNB DCNM DDBX DDDN DDNF
SZD-24-4 FOKA
G-DBZZ
SZD-30 PIRAT
G-CKSH DCHL DCKD DCPV DCTX DCYD DCZE DCZG DCZJ
DDAN DDAP DDAU DDBV DDDW DDFW DDHZ DDNT DDTW
DEOB
SZD-32A FOKA
G-DCMF
SZD-36A COBRA
G-DDAC DDCA DCVS DCVT DDAC IMEC ZBOP
SZD-38A JANTAR-1
G-CFNE DDDE DDFL DDFV EDDV HDAV
SZD-41A JANTAR STANDARD 1
G-CHBS DDFX DDHC DDJL DDJM
SZD-42-1 JANTAR 2
G-DDNU DEUV
SZD-45A OGAR
G-BEBG BKTM BMFI OGAR
SZD-48 JANTAR STANDARD 2 & 3
G-CFHV CFOT DDVK DESP DFTJ DHUB
SZD-50-3 PUCHACZ
G-CFEN CFTH CFUY CFWE CFWT CFXO CFYA CFYL CGBD
CGCK CGCU CGEL CHAC CHAF CHDP CHEP CHFH CJEC CJRF
CJRJ CKAN CKHW DEUF DHCF FEVS
SZD-51-1 JUNIOR
G-CFFV CFFY CFHF CFPM CFTC CFUS CFZA CFZF CFZP CGCC
CHDB CHDU CHEK CHMA CHNK CHOV CHRG CJLG CJMG
CJMY CJVC CKHA CKHN CKHR CKPN DHCR DHCW
SZD-55-1 PROMYK
G-CGAX CHEC CHHR CKBN CKLR
SZD-59 ACRO
G-CHWX

PZL-SWIDNIK (including ZAKLAD SZYBOWCOWY JEZOW)
PW-5 SMYK
G-CEUP CHZB CJCG CJKE CKPX CKRU SMYK
PW-6U
G-CKRX

PZL WARSZAWA-OKECIE SA
PZL-104 WILGA variants
G-BUNC BWDF BXBZ RIIN RTRT WILG
PZL-110 KOLIBER variants
G-BUDO BVAI BXLR BXLS BYSI BZAJ BZLC CBGA CDDE CCIZ
KOLI LOKM

QAC
QUICKIE,
G-BKFM BKSE BMFN BMVG BNJO BPMW BSPA BSSK BWIZ
BXOY CUIK IMBI KUTU KWKI OSAW WAHL
TRI-Q
G-BWIZ FARY

QUAD CITY including BFC kits
CHALLENGER (Rotax 503)
G-BYKU BZHP CAMR CBDU CCFD IBFC MGAA MVZK MWFU
MWFX MWFY MWFZ MYAG MYDN MYDS MYFH MYGM MYIA
MYIX MYOZ MYPZ MYRH MYRJ MYSD MYTO MYTT MYUL MYXC
MYXK MYXV MYYF MZAC MZBW MZBZ MZEA MZHO MZKW
MZNA

RAJ HAMSA
X'AIR (FALCON and HAWK) variants
G-BYHV BYJU BYLT BYMR BYNT BYOH BYOJ BYOR BYPO
BYPW BYRV BYSY BYTR BYTZ BYYM BYYR BYZF BYZW BZAF
BZAK BZBP BZDK BZEJ BZER BZEU BZEX BZGN BZGU BZGX
BZHJ ZIA BZIS BZIY BZKC BZLT BZMR BZNG BZVH BZVK BZVR
BZWC BZYM BZYX BZXA CBAH CBAV CBBH CBCI CBCM CBDO
CBDV CBDW CBDY CBFE CBHB CBIC CBIS CBJX CBKL CBLF
CBLH CBLP CBLW CBMA CBNJ CBOC CBPU CBTK CBUC CBUJ
CBVC CBVE CBVO CBWY CBXA CBXR CCBI CCBU CCBX CCCV
CCCZ CCDJ CCDL CCDP CCDR CCEP CCES CCEY CCGJ CCGR
CCHS CCIW CCKJ CCMK CCNF CCNL CCNZ CCOH CCOO CCRI
CCSO CCVJ CCWF CCWZ CCZJ CCZS CDDH CDDO CDEM
CDFM CDHO CDKC CDPS CDSN CDWL CEDO CEEC CEOH

CEON CESJ CFCE CFIP CFJL CFJU CFKD CFKE CWAL DNBH
HARI HITM IWIN MITE NEMO ODJD OHWV RAJA SPDY TANJ
THAT TSKD UFAW XAYR XIOO ZRAF XRXR

RAND-ROBINSON
KR-2
G-BLDN BNML BOUN BPRR BRJX BRJY BRSN BSTL BTGD
BUDF BUDS BURF BUWT BVIA BVZJ BYLP CBAU CEHT DGWW
JCMW KISS KRII OFMB UTSI XRAY

RANGO BALLOON AND KITE COMPANY
Balloon (Minimum Lift)
NA variants
G-BINZ BJAS BJRH FYFW FYFY FYGI

RANS
S-4 COYOTE (Rotax 447)
G-BZKO MWBO MWEP MWES MWFW MWGN MWIO MWLA
MWLZ MWWP MYWV
S-5 COYOTE (Rotax 447)
G-MVPJ MWFF MWGA MYDO MYFN MZGD
S-6 COYOTE variants (Rotax 503)
G-BSMU BSSI BSTT BSUA BSUT BTNW BTXD BUEW BUOK
BUTM BUWK BVCL BVFM BVIN BVOI BVPW BVUM BVZO BVZV
BWHK BWWP BWYR BXCU BXRZ BXWK BYBR BYCM BYCN
BYIB BYID BYJO BYMN BYMU BYMV BYNP BYOT BYOU BYPT
BYPZ BYRG BYRS BYSN BYZO BZBC BZBX BZEW BZGF BZGR
BZKF BZLE BZMJ BZNH BZNJ BZRA BZRY BZUH BZVM BZYA
BZYL CBAS CBAZ CBFX CBNV CBOK CBOS CBTO CBUY CBXZ
CBYD CBZG CBZN CCDC CCEG CCJN CCLH CCNB CCNH
CCOF CCTV CCTX CCZN CDGB CDGH CDKE CDVF CDYB
CETY CLEE HTWE IZIT KEPP MGEC MGND MIKI MWCH MWHP
MWIF MWSC MWTT MWUK MWUL MWUN MWVL MWWL MWYE
MYAJ MYBA MYBI MYDK MYDX MYES MYGH MYGP MYGR
MYHI MYHK MYHP MYIR MYIS MYJD MYJY MYKN MYLD MYLF
MYLO MYLW MYMH MYMP MYMR MYMS MYNE MYNH MYOA
MYOI MYOT MYPA MYPJ MYSP MYSU MYTE MYUZ MYVP MYXB
MYXG MYXP MYYV MYZR MYZV MZAH MZBD MZBH MZBU
MZBV MZCA MZDA MZDG MZDM MZDR MZEN MZEO MZEU
MZFL MZFN MZIY MZJI MZJM MZKE MZLG MZLL MZMS
MZMU MZNV MZOZ MZUB OYTE RDNS RINS RTHS RTMS
SAUK SOOZ SSIX TIVS TSOB WYLE WZOY
S-7 COURIER
G-BVNY BWKJ BWMN CBNF CEEJ KATI OJKM
S-9 CHAOS
G-BPUS BSEE
S-10 SAKOTA (Rotax 532)
G-BRPT BRZW BSBV BSGS BSMT BSWB BTCR BTGG BTJX
BTWZ BUAX BUKB BVFA BVHI BWIA BWIL JSCL RANS RANZ
S-12 AIRAILE
G-BZAO

RAYTHEON AIRCRAFT COMPANY including HAWKER 400A
RB390 PREMIER
G-CJAG FRYL OEWD OMJC PHTO PREI VONJ
400A
G-EDCS KLNR STOB
850A
G-CERX

REALITY AIRCRAFT LTD
EASY RAIDER
G-CBKF CBXE CBXF CCEZ CCHR CCJS CCMJ OESY SLIP SRII
ESCAPADE
G-CCYB CDCW CDEV CDIZ CDKL CDLE CDSK CDTJ CECF
CEDB CEIL CFAS CFBO DIZI DRPK ECKB ESCA ESCC ESCP
ESGA ESKA IMNY LEEK LSJE MCUB OKID PADE POZA SCPD
VNON ZHKF

REARWIN AIRCRAFT and ENGINES INC
175 SKYRANGER
G-BTGI RWIN
8125 CLOUDSTER
G-EVLE
8500 SPORTSTER
G-AEOF

REECE
SKY RANGER
G-MJRR

REID and SIGRIST
RS.4 DESFORD
G-AGOS

REIMS AVIATION SA see **CESSNA**

REMOS
GX
G-MIRN

RENEGADE see **MURPHY**

REPLICA PLANS
SE.5a
G-BDWJ BIHF BKER BMDB BUOD BUWE CCBN CCXG CEKL
INNY SEVA

REPUBLIC AVIATION CORPORATION
P-47 THUNDERBOLT
G-BLZW CDVX THUN

REVOLUTION HELICOPTERS
MINI-500
G-BWCZ OREV PDWI

RIDOUT
Balloon (Minimum Lift)
ARENA
G-BIRP BJNA
EUROPEAN
G-BJDK BJFC BJMZ
JARRE
G-BJMX
STEVENDON SKYREACHER
G-BIWA
WARREN
G-BIWF
ZELENSKI
G-BIWG

RIGG
Balloon (Minimum Lift)
SKYLINER II
G-BIAR

AVIONS PIERRE ROBIN including **ALPHA AVIATION
MANUFACTURING LTD** (R2160), **CONSTRUCTIONS
AÉRONAUTIQUES DE BOURGOGNE** and **ROBIN AVIATION**
production
DR.400 variants
G-BAEB BAEM BAEN BAFP BAFX BAGC BAGR BAGS BAHL
BAJZ BAKM BALF BALG BALH BALI BALJ BAMS BAMT BAMU
BAMV BANB BAPV BAPX BAZC BBAX BBAY BBCH BBCS BBDP
BBJU BBMB BCXE BDUY BEUP BFJZ BGRH BGWC BHAJ BHJU
BHLE BHLH BHOA BIHD BIZI BJUD BKDH BKDI BKDJ BKVL
BNFV BOGI BPHG BPZP BRBK BRBL BRBM BRNT BRNU BSDH
BSFF BSLA BSSP BSVS BSYU BSZD BTRU BUGJ BUYS BXRT
BYHT BZMM CBBA CBEZ CBMT CBZK CCKP CCWM CCZX CDAI
CDBM CDIM CDOY CEKE CETB CONB DIGN DUDZ EGGS EHMM
ELEN ELUN EOMK ETIV EUSO EYCO FCSP FTIL FTIN FUEL
GAOH GAOM GBUE GBVX GCIY GCUF GDEF GDKR GGJK GLKE
GOSL HAIR HANS HXTD IEYE IOOI JBDH JBUZ JEDH JMTS
JUDE KIMY LARA LEOS LGCA LGCB LGCC MAGZ MIFF NBDD
NFNF OACF ONGC ORRG OTIB OYIO PAYD PVCV PVML RONS
SELL SJMH TUGY UAPA WYSZ XLXL YOGI ZACH ZIGI ZIPI
DR.500-200i PRÉSIDENT
G-BYIT BZIJ CDMD CHIX DPYE GMIB GSRV IYCO KENW MOTI
PREZ RNDD ROBJ TYER
HR.100-200B ROYAL
G-AZHB AZHK BBCN BXWB CBFN
HR.100-210 SAFARI II
G-BAPY BAWR BAYR BBAW BBCN BBIO BLWF HRIO MPWI
RUES
HR.100-285 TIARA
G-BEUD BLHN
HR.200 variants
G-BBOE BCCY BETD BFBE BGXR BLTM BNIK BVMM BWFG
BXDT BXGW BXOR BXVK BYLH BYNK BYSG BZET BZLG BZXK
GBJS GBXF GMKD GMKE HHUK HRCC JPAT NSOF WAVA WAVI
WAVN WAVV
R.1180T(D) AIGLON
G-BGHM BIRT BJVV GBAO GDER GEEP PACE ROBN VECD
VITE

R.2100 SUPER CLUB,
G-BKXA
R.2100A,
G-BGBA BICS
R.2112 ALPHA
G-BIVA BZFB CBNG EWHT PLAY RAFC TOUR
R.2120
G-CBLECBVB ECAC
R.2160 (ALPHA SPORT)
G-BLWY BVYO BWZG BYBF CETG ILUA MATT OCFC PGSI
PSFG SACK SBMO VECG WAVT
R.3000 variants
G-BLYP BOLU BZOL CCCN ENNI PAVL
ATL variants
G-GFNO GFRD GFRO GGHZ

ROBINSON AIRCRAFT CO
REDWING
G-ABNX

ROBINSON HELICOPTER CO INC
R22 variants
"G-RAFM" G-BJUC BLDK BLME BLTF BMIZ BOAM BOCN BODZ
BOVR BOYC BOYX BPGV BPIT BPNI BPTZ BRBY BROX BRRY
BRVI BRWD BRXV BSCE BSEK BSGF BTBA BTDI BTHI BTNA
BTOC BUBW BVPR BWHY BWTH BXOA BXSG BXSY BXUC
BXXN BXYK BYCF BYIE BYZP BYZZ BZBU BZJJ BZMO BZYE
CBBK CBVL CBWZ CBXK CBXN CBZF CCAP CCDE CCGE CCGF
CCMR CCVU CDAW CDED CDBG CDDD CDMG CDSU CESN
CESU CFHU CHAN CHIS CHPA CHPR CHYL CHZN CMSN CRAY
CTRL DAAM DABS DEER DEFY DELB DERB DGOD DLDL DMCD
DODB EFGH EFOF EIBM EPAR ERBL EROM ETIN FIRS FLYH
FOGY FOLI GEGE GJCD GOUP HARR HBMW HIEL HIPO HIZZ
HONI HRBS HRHE HSLA HUGS HURN IAGD IBED ICCL IIFR IIPT
INKY IORG ISMO JARA JATD JBII JCAP JERS JHEW JONB JONH
JOYD JSAK JWFT KNIB KUKI LAIN LHCA LHCB LIPE LSWL LYNC
MACA MATY MAVI MDGE MDKD MICH MOGY MRSN MUFY
NJSH NORT NWDC OASH OAVA OBIL OBIO OCOV ODCS ODJB
OEAT OFAS OGOH OICV OIIO OJAN OKEY OLAU OLRT OMMG
ONMT ORMB OSHL OTED OTHL OTOY OVNR OZZY PACL PBRL
PERE RALD RATA REDY RENT RIDL RNGO ROTF ROUT ROVY
RSVP RSWW RWIA SBUT SCHO SIMS SLNW SPEE SUCT SUMX
TAGT TATO TGRD TGRE TGRS THLA TILE TIMH TINK TOLY
TOMM TOSH TTHC TUNE VCJH VEYE VMSL VOCE WADS
WAGG WANT WFOX WIRL WIZA WIZR WIZY WRWR YACB
YMBO ZAPY ZFLY
R44 variants
G-BWVH BYCE BYKK BZGO BZLP BZMG BZOP BZPL BZTA
BZXY CBAK CBFJ CBOT CBRO CBVI CBYY CBZE CCFC CCNY
CCRD CCTL CCWD CCWJ CCYC CCYG CCYT CCZH CDCB
CDCV CDHH CDKY CDSE CDXX CDJZ CDSY CDUE CDWK
CDXA CDXB CEAU CECW CECX CEDG CEEE CEHK CEHY CEIM
CEKF CEKX CEMC CERS CESB CESO CEST CEUU CEUX CEVI
CEWV CEYA CFAN CFCM CFFD CFKC CFNF CGGG CHAP
CHUM CIDA CJLL CKEM CLOT CMCC CMXX CPHA CRIB CROW
CULF DAVG DAVV DBUG DCON DCSE DCSG DIGG DKMK
DMRA DMRS DORM DOVS DRIV DSPI DSPZ DWCE DYCE EDES
EECH EEZA EGTC EJRC EJTC EKKO EKYD ELMO EMEL EMMI
ESSY ETFF ETNT EVEV EWAD EZZR FABI FAJM FARE FCUM
FLBI FLYS FLYX FOFO FUNY GACB GATE GATT GBEN GDAV
GDJF GDOV GENI GERS GEST GGNG GGRH GIBB GILI GLIB
GOES GRWW GSPY HAGL HDEF HFLY HGRB HHOG HOCA
HRHS HRPN HTEL HVER IAJJ ICAB IFDM IFTS IGJC IGZZ IJNK
ILET ILLG IMBS IMMY INDX ITPH IVEN IVIV JAJA JAKF JANI
JBKA JCWM JEFA JILY JKAY JORD JPJR JRED JTSA JWEB KEIF
KELI KIDG KLAS KNYT KPAO KRIB KYDD LARY LEVO LHXL LLIZ
LMBO LMCG LNAD LOTA LOYN LRSN LUKI LUKY LULI LWAY
MAKI MAPL MAYB MCAI MCCG MDDT MDPY MEGS MENU
MGAN MGWI MIKS MRDC MRKS MRRY MURY MUSH NANI
NESH NICI NIKX NIOG NOSY NSEW NYLE OAJC OBBY OBSM
OCHM OCON ODHB ODOC OEJC OFIL OHLI OHJV OHVR OJAZ
OJCH OJRH OLFO OLOW OMCD OMEL OMGH OMKA OMMA
ONEP ONGA OOFR OONA OPDG OPHA OPTF ORBK OSJL OSSI
OTJB OTJS OTNA OTTZ OTVI OWND PBEE PEPS PFOX PGGY
PIDG PIMP PIXL PIXX PPTS PRET PROJ RALA RAVN RDEL
REDI REGE RFUN RGNT RMBM ROAD ROCT ROGE ROTG
ROWR ROYM ROZI RROB RTWW RULE RUZZ RWEW RWGS
RYZZ SAIG SBRA SEFI SHAF SHAN SIRD SLOK SPJE SPYS
STAA STOP STPH STUY SUMZ SUNN SWAT TAND TBTB TGDL
TGDT TIMC TIMZ TOLI TRAC TRCY TRNT UTTS UTZI VALV VEIT
VVBL WAGS WALI WCOM WEGO WEMS WLDN WMWM WTAV
WWOW WYSP XELA XTEK XTRM XZXZ YEAH ZBED ZOOT

ROCKWELL INTERNATIONAL CORPORATION including
COMMANDER AIRCRAFT COMPANY (COMMANDER 114B)
production
COMMANDER 112 variants
    G-BDAK BDFW BDIE BDKW BDLT BEBU BEDG BENJ BEPY
    BFPO BFZM BHRO BIOJ BLTK BMWR BPTG CNCN CRIL DASH
    EHXP ERIC FLPI HROI IMPX JILL LITE OVIN PLAZ SAAB
COMMANDER 114 and 114A variants
    G-BDYD BERI BERW BFAI BFXS BGBZ BHSE BKAY BMJL BOLT
    BUSW BYKB DANT DDIG DIME HILO JURG LADS NATT OIBM
    OLFT OMUM RCED TECH TWIZ ZIPA
COMMANDER 114B
    G-EMCA FATB HMBJ HPSB HPSF HPSL JFER KEEF NOOR
    OECM OOJP PJNZ VICS
COMMANDER 690
    G-CECN

ROGER HARDY
RH7B TIGER LIGHT
    G-MZGT

ROGERSON
HORIZON 1
    G-DOGZ

ROLLADEN-SCHNEIDER FLUGZEUGBAU GmBH including
DG FLUGZEUGBAU GmBH production
LS1 variants
    G-CFOZ CJST LSIF
LS3 variants
    G-CEVD CEVV CGAD CGDA CHYH CJDJ CJYX CKHB CKMV
    DECP DEEF DEES DEEX DEGE LSGM ILBO
LS4 variants
    G-CFAO CFHL CFJM CFKG CFNU CFYH CHKX CHMX CHNV
    CHPL CHVV CHXT CHXZ CHZM CHZY CJEP CJKP CJLC CJLH
    CJSW CJUB CKAV CKCB CKDK CKEC CKFL CKKX CKLG CKLN
    CKLS CKNS DEHK DEHL DEKV DEMB DEMF DEMG DEMT DEOA
    DETG DETV DETY DEUH DGDJ DHNX DKEN EELT EENE EESY
    FERV GBPP LSED LSFR LSLS SVNC XCIV
LS6 variants
    G-CFCP CGAR CGBG CGBO CGBR CGCM CHAO CHBC CHHH
    CHHT CHHU CHJC CHJF CHJX CHMK CHOZ CHPD CHSA CHYA
    CJDG CJNP CKBH CKEP DFRA DHET DHEZ DFBE LSCP LSED
    LSGB LSVI STEU
LS7 variants
    G-CEVN CFMY CFTV CFTY CFUV CFVH CFWF CFWU CFYB
    CFYK CFYW CFZV CGBL CHAY CHBA CHDX CHEH CJLK CJSJ
    CJTR CJZZ CKHS CKMO CKSY DFOG EUFO LSFB TWAZ
LS8 variants
    G- CHTM CHTS CHUW CHVF CHVL CHVU CHWL CHWS CHXC
    CHXW CHYF CHZG CJBB CJBO CJCP CJCY CJDE CJDK CJDT
    CJDY CJEA CJFX CJGS CJHU CJHY CJJK CJKD CJKN CJLN
    CJMO CJMT CJMU CJNB CJNJ CJNK CJNM CJOD CJPH CJPL
    CJPR CJRA CJSU CJTL CJTM CJTY CJUE CKEL CKET
    CKEZ CKFM CKFV CKHP CKJE CKMA CKME CKPM CKSD CTAG
    DSVN FLUZ GCJA GZIP LLLL LSKV RIEV WDGC WLLS XWON

ROLLASON AIRCRAFT and ENGINES LTD see also **DRUINE**
BETA
    G-AWHX BADC BETE BUPC

ROMAIN
COBRA BIPLANE
    G-MNLH

ROOKE & HOUNSELL
Balloon (Minimum Lift)
BITTERNE MK.1
    G-BJJM

ROOSTER see **LIGHTWING**

ROTARY AIR FORCE INC
RAF 2000 variants (Subaru EJ22)
    G-BUYL BVSM BWAD BWAE BWHS BWTK BWWS BXAC BXDD
    BXDE BXEA BXEB BXGS BXKM BXMG BYIN BYJA CBCJ CBHC
    CBHZ CBIT CBJE CBJN CCEU CCUH CDJN CFEI HEKK HOWL
    IMEL IRAF JEJE ONON PHLB RAFZ SAYS YRAF YROJ YROO

ROTEC ENGINEERING INC
RALLY 2B
    G-MBGS MBMG MJPA MVRF

ROTORSPORT (UK) LTD
UK CALIDUS
    G-CLDS
UK MT-03
    G-CDYF CDZZ CEHM CEHN CEIA CEOX CERF CEVY CEXX
    CEYR CFAI CFAK CFAR CFCG CFCL CFGG CFGY CFIE CFJB
    CFKA CFLO COLI GSMT JBRE JYRO KENG KEVG LUNG MAZA
    MEPU NAGG PILZ PPLG RIFS RSMT RTIN TATA TELC UMAS
    YELO YPDN YROC YROM YROX

ROTORWAY
(SCORPION) EXECUTIVE
    G-BNZL BNZO BPCM BRGX BSRP BUJZ BURP BUSN BVOY
    BVTV BWLY BWUJ BYNH BYNI BZBW BZES BZOM BZXD CBIK
    CBJV CBWO CBWU CBYB CBZI CCFY CCMU CDBK CDRS DADA
    EFFI ESUS FLIT JONG KENI NEEL NJBA OHOV PILE PURS
    RATH RAWS REID RHYS RISH RWAY SFOX SSEX VART WHOO
    YEWS ZHWH
A600 TALON
    G-TALN

ATELIERS AÉRONAUTIQUE ROUSSEAU see **PIEL**

ROYAL AIRCRAFT FACTORY see **REPLICA PLANS** and **SLINGSBY**
BE.2C
    G-AWYI
SE.5, SE.5A
    G-EBIA
    G--EBIB EBIC BKDT

RUSCHMEYER LUFTFAHRTTECHNIK GmbH
RUSHMEYER R90
    G-EERH UAPO

RUTAN
COZY
    G-BXDO BXVX BYLZ CESP COZI OGJS SCUL SPFX
DEFIANT
    G-OTWO
LONG-EZ
    G-BKXO BLLZ BLMN BLTS BMHA BMIM BMUG BOOX BPWP
    BRFB BSIH BUPA BZMF CBLZ HAIG ICON LEZE LGEZ LUKE
    MUSO OMJT PUSH RAEM RAFT RPEZ SENA
VARIEZE
    G-BEZE BEZY BIMX BKST BVAY BVKM EZDG EMMY IPSY KENZ
    LASS OOSE SKCI TIMB VEZE

RYAN AERONAUTICAL CORPORATION
ST3KR, PT-22
    G-AGYY BTBH BYPY RLWG

SAAB-SCANIA AB including **SVENSKA AEROPLAN AB (SAAB)**
32 LANSEN
    G-BMSG
91 SAFIR
    G-BCFW HRLK SAFR
SF.340 variants
    G-GNTB GNTF LGNA LGNB LGNC LGND LGNE LGNF LGNG
    LGNH LGNI LGNJ LGNK LGNL LGNM LGNN
2000
    G-CDEA CDEB CDKA CDKB CERY CERZ CFLU CFLV

SAFFERY MODEL BALLOONS including **CUPRO SAPHIRE LTD**
Balloon (Minimum Lift)
S.200
    G-BIHU
S.200 RIGG SKYLINER
    G-BHLJ
S.330
    G-BERN BFBM
SMITH PRINCESS
    G-FYGM

SAN see **JODEL**

SAUNDERS-ROE LTD
A.19 CLOUD
    G-ACGO
P.531-2
    G-APNV APVL
SKEETER
    G-APOI BLIX HELI SARO

SCALLAN
Balloon (Minimum Lift)
EAGLE
    G-FYEO
FIREFLY
    G-FYEZ

SCHEIBE-FLUGZEUGBAU GmbH
BERGFALKE
    G-CKGY EEBD
L-SPATZ
    G-CFPF DDUH
ZUGVOGEL
    G-CFLL CFRS CFSU CFVL CFYE CHKV CHVA EEBS
SF24 MOTORSPATZ
    G-BZPF
SF25 FALKE variants including SLINGSBY T.61* derivatives
    G-AVIZ AXEO AXIW AXJR AYBG AYSD* AYUM* AYUN* AYUP*
    AYUR* AYYL* AYZU* AYZW* AZHD* AZIL* AZMC* AZMD* AZPC*
    AZYY* BADH* BAIZ* BAKY* BAMB* BDZA BECF BEGG BFPA
    BFUD BGMV BHSD BIGZ BKVG BLCU BLTR BLZA BMBZ BMVA
    BODU BPIR BPZU BRRD BRWT BSEL* BSUO BSWL* BSWM*
    BTDA* BTRW* BTTZ* BTUA* BTWC* BTWD* BTWE* BUDA*
    BUDB* BUDC* BUDT* BUED* BUEK* BUFG* BUFN* BUFR*
    BUGL* BUGT* BUGV* BUGW* BUGZ* BUHA* BUHR* BUIH*
    BUJA* BUJB* BUJI* BUJX* BUNB* BVKK* BVKU* BVLX* BWTR*
    BXAN BXMV CCHX CDFD CDSC CFMW CKNN* FEFE FHAS
    FLKE FLKS GBGA HBOS KAOM KDEY KFAN KGAO KWAK
    MFMM MILD OHGC OSUT OWGC* SEXE
SF26A
    G-DDRL DEJZ
SF27A
    G-CFOF CFWV CGAV CHSX CHUS DEKS
SF28A TANDEM FALKE
    G-BARZ BYEJ CCIS

SCHEMPP-HIRTH FLUGZEUGBAU GmbH including **SCHEMPP-HIRTH KG** and **SCHEMPP-HIRTH GMBH & CO KG**
SHK-1
    G-CFJF CFJZ DCAO DCCB DCGT DCJK DCJN DDMK DDTG
    RAEF
(STANDARD) CIRRUS variants including BURKHART GROB FLUGZEUGBAU,JASTREB FABRIKA AVIONAI JEDRILICA, LANAVERRE INDUSTRIE, and VAZDUHOPLOVNO TEHNICKI CENTAR (VTC) production
    G-CDDB CFBB CFCN CFLW CFMT CFMU CFRJ CFRZ CFVS
    CFYJ CFZK CGAH CGCD CGCO CGEP CHAX CHFF CHGG
    CHHP CHJY CHKC CHKD CHKR CHKS CHKU CHMY CHNM
    CHTU CHUL CHUR CHVZ CHXX CHZJ CHZU CJCJ CJCJ
    CJCN CJCU CJDS CJER CJEV CJFA CJGN CJGY CJJJ CJMH
    CJOS CJOW CJRG CJRT CJUU CJVU CKDZ CKEA CKEB CKES
    CKFA CKJF CKHT CKJG CKJT CKFK CKMD CKMD CKNB CKNE
    CTWO DCDH DCFK DCGY DCJR DCKZ DCLA DCLO DCNC
    DCOR DCOY DCPU DCRH DCTB DCTT DCVE DCWR DCWS
    DCYM DCYT DDAS DDDA DDDM DDDR DDGE DDGX DDHX
    DDVS DDVY DDXL DDZF DEEN DEHK DHEV ECEA KCHG SCNN
DISCUS variants including ORLICAN AKCIOVA, SPOLECNOST production
    G-CEUN CEWZ CFCA CFDM CFEJ CFES CFFT CFFX CFHR
    CFKM CFLE CFMO CFNL CFNR CFOY CFTW CFUL CFUP CFXM
    CFYM CFYN CGCT CGDX CHDZ CHEE CHEN CHGK CHGS
    CHHO CHJH CHJL CHKA CHKY CHLN CHLS CHLY CHML CHMO
    CHOM CHOR CHOW CHPH CHPX CHRH CHRS CHRX CHSD
    CHSO CHUZ CHXH CHYU CHZE CJAO CJBR CJBW CJCK CJFC
    CJGL CJGM CJGR CJGU CJHM CJJE CJJZ CJKR CJKX CJLC
    CJLP CJLW CJNE CJOA CJOC CJPP CJRR CJSE CJUB CJUP
    CJUV CJVB CJVF CJVX CJWK CJXL CJXR CJYF CJYN CJZG
    CKAH CKAP CKFB CKFT CKJZ CKLD CKLV CKOD CKOK CKPB
    CKPG CKRO CKSM CLGC CUMU DFBY DHCL DHEM DHGL
    DHKL DHMP DHPR DHSJ DJAH DJAN DJMD DTWO HOJO IDER
    KOBH ODDZ RGTS SAJA SAOC TOOB TWOA TWOT
DUO DISCUS T
    G-CHNF CHNN CHNW CHRW CHSW CJCX CJEM CJFF CJFH
    CJJP CJOO CJPA CJTU CJUM CJXW CKCV CKEV CKGF CKHK
    CKKE CKKN CKKY CKML CKNJ CKOJ CKOL CKPE CKPO CKPY
    DDJF DJAC DUOT DUOX HKAA JIFI ODUO OKLL PHNX RDDT
    SAXT SISI TLTL XDUO
JANUS variants
    G-BMBJ BXJS CHTB CHUH CJFE CJVV CKLF CTAA DDTC DEOV
    DEOW DJAA JNSC JNUS
(MINI) NIMBUS variants
    G-CDTH CENK CEWE CFAM CFCS CFGF CFHG CFPP CFVT
    CFWK CFZO CHBF CHBV CHFX CHNH CHNU CHOY CHYY

    CHZA CJCT CJDZ CJED CJGH CJGU CJMN CJMV CJTJ CJWG
    CJXA CJYS CJZL CKBG CKFH CKJC CKLT CKPV DDAJ DDGY
    DDHW DDKL DDMM DDNG DDPH DDTU DDXT DDYU DEAJ
    DEAM DEEK DEFB DEFF DEGS DEGW DEHP DEON DEVF
    DFBM ECOL EDDD EEBF EEBK EEER EENN EHCB HAUT HJSM
    IVDM KEPE KOYY LYDS NIMB NYMB NIVT OJNE OZOZ
VENTUS variants
    G-CEUR CFBT CFDE CFEG CFFK CFMN CFNN CFPE CFPL
    CFRB CFUH CFVW CFYC CFZH CGAP CGAS CHFA CHFV CHFY
    CHHN CHUY CHVE CHVT CHWA CHWH CHXR CJEX CJFR CJGF
    CJKY CJOR CJSL CJTS CJUF CJVA CJWU CJWX CJYU CJZM
    CKAJ CKAS CKBK CKCD CKCH CKDA CKDO CKDV CKFC CKFP
    CKFU CKGA CKGB CKGC CKGD CKGL CKJB CKJM CKKF CKNO
    CKNR CKPK CVZT DEHH DEKJ DELG DELR DENJ DEPX DEUJ
    DEUS DFAW DFHS DHSL DHYL DKFU EVII FORA IFWD HAAH
    IICT IICX IIIO IRLE KHCC KPLG KTCC NJET ORCW OSDF OTCZ
    RBCT SWSW TWOC UNIN VCXT VENC VENT VNTS VSIX VTCT
    VTUS VTWO WIII WONE XJON XXVB YODA ZENN

ALEXANDER SCHLEICHER SEGELFLUGZEUGBAU GmbH and Co
including **SA CENTRAIR** and **JUBI GMBH SPORTFLUGZEUGBAU** production *
Ka 6 variants
    G-AWTP CEVK CEWO CFBZ CFCR CFDR CFKY CFLS CFND
    CFNP CFSS CFTB CFUB CFVZ CFWA CFXC CFXS CFXU CFZR
    CGCP CGDE CGDF CGEM CHAB CHFB CHJP CHPO CHSN
    CHZH CJAL CJCZ CJEW CJHD CJHL CJLV CJSG CKDB CKMJ
    DBNB DBNH DBOL DBTJ DBUZ DBVR DBVX DBVZ DBYL DBYM
    DBYU DBYX DBZX DCAE DCAG DCAS DCCA DCCG DCCJ DCCL
    DCCR DCCU DCCV DCDA DCDF DCDZ DCEL DCEM DCEO
    DCEY DCFL DCGB DCGD DCGE DCHB DCHZ DCJY DCKL DCLZ
    DCPJ DDAW DDCW DDEV DDGG DDGK DDHG DDHM DDSY
    DDHT DDJE DDJR DDKN DDLE DDLP DDMO DDNW DDNX
    DDOC DDOF DDOK DDRA DDRD DDRE DDRY DDSB DDSY
    DDUR DDVG DDVH DDWC DDXH DDYC DDYJ DEAH DECF
    DEDG DEEW DEKC DFGJ DFKH DGAW DHAL DHEB DHUK
    ECDB EELY FGAZ HCAC KSIX
K 7 variants
    G-CFJW CFOU CFXH DBVB DCLT DCMG DCWJ DDAK DDML
    DDOX DDRM DDWN DDYR DEDK DELX
K 8 variants
    G-CFHN CFLH CFOR CFTN CFWL CFXB CFXW CGDB CGDK
    CGEG CHDN CHDY CHJE CHKK CHLH CHNG CHRJ CHYW
    CHYX CHZX CJAT CJFT CJGD CJHK CJLS CJNN CJOJ CJOZ
    CJSN CKDH CKMI DCFF DCGH DCHU DCMN DCYZ DDDL DDGA
    DDHA DDJB DDKG DDLS DDMB DDMG DDNZ DDOY DDRV
    DDRZ DDSF DDTN DDUF DDUK DDWG DEEM DEFG DEJF
    DEOZ DEPT DESJ DETD DFBJ EHCZ
Ka 10
    G-DEVH
ASK 13
    G-CFGR CFHM CFMH CFPX CFSD CFVC CFVU CFWB CFZN
    CGBA CHDC CHFW CHMV CHPE CHSM CHTJ CHUD CHUF
    CHUU CHVO CHVW CHXJ CHXV CJFM CJGW CJKT CJLO JMJ
    CJMP CJMW CJMZ CJPC CJPV CJPY CJRX CJSV CJWB CJWJ
    CJXM CJYE CJZE CKFJ CKFR CKHH CHXP CKJL CKKR CKLA
    CKRB DCBW DCCE DCCF DCCM DCCT DCCW DCCX DCCX
    DCCY DCCZ DCEX DCFA DCFE DCFG DCGO DCHW DCKR
    DCKU DCKV DCMK DCRT DCWH DDDB DDKE DDLC DDMX
    DDNV DDOA DDRJ DDUE DDVB DDVC DDVX DEDU DEKD
    DEOE DEOF DEPP DETS DEUC DEVJ DEVP DFAT DFCW DHAL
    DFEO DJLL EEBL EEBZ FCAV FCCC
ASK 14
    G-BKSP BSIY KOHF
ASW 15 variants
    G-CFBC CFDA CFKB CFML CFMS CFOB CFPB CFRK CFTD
    CGCR CGDS CGDY CGEH CHEJ CHNT CHTC CHZD CJCA CJDM
    CJDR CJJX CJPX CJRE CJVW CKRR CKSL DCHT DCKP DCZN
    DFCY DHOX DJED DJGG DJWS GTWO
ASK 16
    G-BCHT BCTI
ASW 17
    G-DCPD DCTE DEGD
ASK 18
    G-CHRN CJHO CJKG CJMA CJMK CJPO CJPZ CJSZ CKNM
    DDJK DDLB DDNJ DDPA EEUX
ASW 19
    G-CEWI CEXY CFGP CFNH CFWP CFWZ CGCA CHHK CHLM
    CHLV CHNC CHUA CHXE CHXU CJBK CJBT CJFU CJHS CJKS
    CJNT CJRB CJRV CJUN CJUW CJUZ CKEX CKGU DDHX DDSX
    DDTE DDVL DDVP DDXX DDZG DEEH DEJR DELA DEPE DERP
    DERR DERS DFFP DHCE DHER DHCV FEBJ RZEE

ASW 20
G-BUCG CEVZ CFBA CFHD CFJE CFKL CFPH CFPN CFRW
CFTL CFTP CFUN CFWS CFZL CHBU CHDJ CHDL CHEO CHGW
CHHS CHJT CHOD CHUJ CHUT CHVP CHVX CHYK CHZZ CJEE
CJFJ CJFK CJHZ CJTP CJZH CKCY CKDC CKER CKHF CKJN
CKMY CKPZ DDST DDTP DDUT DDVV DDXB DDXK DDYE DDYX
DEAE DEBX DECC DEEC DEEJ DEFA DEFE DEFV DEHV DEHZ
DEKU DELZ DENV DEOJ DEPF DEPS DERA DERH DETZ DEUD
DEUK DEUY DFAF DHCH DHOK EEBN EEDE EEFK EENW EFLY
EHTT EKEY IUMB KKAM MAGK MEEE

ASK 21
G-CEWC CFBV CFYF CFYV CGAF CGAG CGAM CGBB CGBF
CGBN CGBV CHLP CHPV CHPW CHTV CHVG CHYS CHYT
CHZR CJAV CJAX CJBM CJGJ CJJR CJKA CJKJ CJKK CJKO
CJKU CJKZ CJMS CJOX CJTR CJVZ CJWD CKCT CKCZ CKDF
CKDP, CKEJ, CKEK CKGX CKFY CKJP CKKP CKGK CKLW
CKMW CKNL CKOT CKPP CKRI CKRW DECW DECZ DEGZ
DEHO DEKG DERH DERJ DESB DESU DHCX DHRR DJAD DJMC
EENK KXXI OWAI PNGC UCLU

ASW 22
G-CGBX CHTN LDER

ASK 23
G-CGCF DEVW DEVX DEVY DEYV

ASW 24
G-CFNG CGDT CGDU CGDZ CHBB CHBG CHYD CJCD CJEB
CJEL CJRU CJTB CJTH CJXT OTRY

ASH 25 variants
G-CFST CFWW CFYZ CHLX CHXO CJCV CJDF CWLC DRCS
GBBB RAIR SINK YOBI

ASH 26E
G-BWBY CCLR CDPX KEAM OPHT ZZAJ

ASW 27
G-CEUG CHUE CHXD CHYR CHZO CJCM CJDC CJJF CJJT CJLY
CJOV CJPS CJPT CJRH CJSS CJUH CJUJ CJVM CJWE CJYD
CJZX CKCN CKDN CKDS CKDW CKED CKFD CKHD CKHG
CKKH CKLB CKOM CKON CKOO CKOY CKOZ CKRJ CKRM
CKRT CKRV HEBB IXXI LIDY OASW SASG THRM VLCC XLII
XOAR XXIX YEHA

ASW 28
G-CJVS CJWA CJZN CKAL CKBM CKBU CKBV CKCJ CKGN
CKGV CKJA CKKD CKJN CKJS CKJV CKKD CKLP CKMM CKMZ
CKNG CKNV CKRC GLID TRBO

ASG 29
G-CKOE CKON CKOO CKOY CKOZ CRJW OBPP VLCC XOAR
XXIX

SCHROEDER FIRE BALLOONS GmbH
Balloon (Hot Air)
G
G-CBVK CFHX

SCHWEIZER AIRCRAFT CORPORATION see HUGHES

SOCIÉTÉ SCINTEX see PIEL

SCOTTISH AVIATION
TWIN PIONEER
G-APHY APJT APRS AYFA BBVF
BULLDOG variants
G-ASAL AXEH AXIG AYZM AZAK AZJO AZWO BCUO BCUP
BCUS BCUV BDIN BDOG BHXA BHZR BHZS BHZT BPCL BULL
BWIB BZDP BZEP BZFN BZMD BZME BZMH BZML BZON BZPS
BZXS BZXZ CBAB CBAN CBBC CBBL CBBR CBBS CBBT CBBU
CBBW CBCB CBCR CBCV CBDK CBDS CBEF CBEH CBEK CBFP
CBFU CBGX CBID CBJJ CCMI CCOA CDVV DAWG DDOG DISA
DOGE DOGG EDAV GGRR GRRR JWCM KDOG RAIG RNRS
SIJW TDOG UDOG ULHI WINI

SE see ROYAL AIRCRAFT FACTORY, SLINGSBY and REPLICA PLANS

SEEMS see MORANE-SAULNIER

SERVOTECH LTD
GRASSHOPPER
G-ARVN AWRP AXFM AZAU

SHAW
TWIN-EZE
G-IVAN

SHERRY
BUZZARD
G-MMNN

SHERWOOD RANGER see TLAC

SHIELD
XYLA
G-AWPN

SHORT BROTHERS LTD see EMBRAER
S.16 SCION
G-ACUX
S.25 SANDRINGHAM/SUNDERLAND
G-AHJR AKCO BJHS
S.45 SOLENT
G-AKNP
SA.6 SEALAND
G-AKLS AKLW
SC.5 BELFAST
G-BEPS
SC.7 SKYVAN
G-BDVO BEOL PIGY
SD.3-30
G-BDBS BEWT BKIE BKMW OGIL SSWA
SD.3-60
G-BKMX BMLC BOEG CEAL CLAS EXPS GPBV JEMX OBHD
SSWE SSWM SSWO SSWR TMRA TMRB TMRO

SIAI-MARCHETTI SpA
S.205
G-AVEH AYXS BBRX BFAP VELA
SF.260
G-BAGB IGIE ITAF MACH NRRA SIAI
SM.1019
G-LISO

SIKORSKY AIRCRAFT see also VERTICAL AVIATION TECHNOLOGIES (S-52) and WESTLAND
S-51
"G-AJOV" G-AJHW
S-61 variants
G-ATBJ ATFM AYOY BCEA BCEB BCLD BDIJ BDOC BFFJ BFRI
BGWK BHOG BHOH BIMU BPWB
S-76 variants
G-BHBF BIBG BIEJ BISZ BJFL BJGX BMAL BOYF BURS BVCX
BYDF BYOM CEYZ CFDV CFJC CFPU CFPY CHCD DRNT EEBB
FULM JCBA JCBJ KAZA KAZB LJRM SSSC SSSD SSSE VIPZ
VONA VONB VONC WIWI XJCB XXEA
S-92
G-CGMU CGOD CHCK IACA IACB IACC IACD IACE IACF SARB
SARC

SILENCE
TWISTER
G-CDKJ RIOT TWSR TWSS TWST XSEL

SIPA
903, S91
G-AMSG ATXO AWLG BBBO BBDV BDAO BDKM BGME BHMA
DWEL SIPA

SKANDINAVISK AERO INDUSTRI
KRAMME KZ.VIII
G-AYKZ

SKY BALLOONS LTD including CAMERON BALLOONS
Balloon (Hot Air)
16 series
G-BWVP
21 series
G-BYCB
25 series
G-BXWX BZSL CFPS
31 series
G-BWOY BXVP OSVY
56 series
G-BWYP
65 series
G-BWUS BXKO BXUS DUNG
70 series
G-PGUY

77 series
G-BWSL BXHL BXVG BXXP BZLS CLRK KSKY LOWS MAGL OBET RCML
80 series
G-BYBS BYOI SETI
90 series
G-BWKR BXGD BXJT BXLP BXPP BXVR BXWL BYZV BZKV CLOE CZAG GPEG LEAS VINO ZABC
105 series
G-BWDZ BWOA BWPP BXCN BXDV BXIW BXXS BYNV BZFG CROP
120 series
G-BWIX BWPF BWYU BXLC BXWG BYEX CFAY OBFE
140 series
G-BYKZ
160 series
G-BWUK
180 series
G-BWIW BXVL
200 series
G-BWST BXIH
220 series
G-SPEL
240 series
G-BXUE MRLN
260 series
G-KTKT

Special Shape

SHAPE	REGISTRATION
FLYING MAP	G-MAPS

SKYCRAFT (UK) LTD
SCOUT
G-MBBB MBUZ

SKYFOX
CA-25N GAZELLE
G-IDAY

SKYHOOK SAILWINGS LTD
TR1 Trike with Cutlass, Pixie and Zeus wings
G-MJFX MNBJ MJNU MJNY MMVS

SKYRIDER AVIATION
AIRSPORTS PHANTOM
G-MJSE MJSF MJTE MJTX MJTZ MJUR MJUX MJVX MMKX MNCS MTTN

SKYSTAR see **DENNEY**

SLEPCEV
STORCH
G-BZOB

SLINGSBY AIRCRAFT CO LTD see **TIPSY**

SLINGSBY SAILPLANES LTD including **SLINGSBY ENGINEERING LTD** and see **FOURNIER, SCHEIBE** and **SOPWITH**
T.6 KITE 1
G-ALNH
T.30 KIRKBY PREFECT
G-ALLF
T.31 MOTOR CADET derivatives
G-AYAN BCYH BDSM BEMM BNPF BODH BOOD BPIP BRVJ BUAC BVFS BZLK
T.51 DART
G-DBRY DBSA DBSL DBUF DBVH DBWJ DBWM DBWO DBWP DBWS DBXE DBXG DBXH DCAZ DCBA DRAT IKAH
T.53
G-DDHE
T.59 KESTREL
G-BDWZ BDXG BDZG CETJ CFNK DCAZ DCNS DCNW DCOJ DCSD DCSF DCSK DCTJ DCTL DCTM DCTO DCTR DCVW DCVY DCWA DCWB DCWD DCWF DCXM DCZO DCZR DDBK DDBN DDEA DFDK FCOM KESY
T.61 see **SCHEIBE**
T.65 (SPORT) VEGA variants
G-BFYW BGBV BGCB BGCU BILH DCZU DDBS DDWT DDXD DDXE DDZA DDZP DECJ DECL DECM DEDX DEDY DEDZ DEEA DEEG DEFW DEGH DEGJ DEGT DEGX DEHG DEHY DEJC DEJE DELD DEMB DEMJ DEMN DEMP DEMZ EEAD EEBA EECK VEGA

T.67A and T.67M FIREFLY
G-BIOW BJIG BJNG BJXB BJZN BKAM BKTZ BLLP BLLR BLLS BLPI BLRF BLTU BLTW BLUX BLVI BNSO BNSP BNSR BOCL BOCM BONT BONU BUUA BUUB BUUC BUUD BUUE BUUF BUUI BUUJ BUUK BWGO BWXA BWXB BWXC BWXD BWXE BWXF BWXG BWXH BWXI BWXJ BWXK BWXL BWXM BWXN BWXO BWXP BWXR BWXS BWXT BWXU BWXV BWXW BWXX BWXY BWXZ BWXW BYBX BYOB BYOD BYRY BYYG CDHC EFSM FLYG GFAA HONG KONG ONES OPUB RAFG SFTZ SKYC SKYO TONS ZEIN

SMD
GAZELLE with FlexiformSealander sailwing
G-MMGU MMHS

SMITH
DSA-1 MINIPLANE
G-BTGJ
SMYTH
MODEL S SIDEWINDER
G-BRVH

SNCAN including **AIA DE MAISON-BLANCHE(1), SAN(3)** and **SOCIÉTÉ STAMPE ET RENAULT(2) (SV-4)** production
NC854
G-BCGH BGEW BIUP BJEL BJLB NORD
NC856 NORVEGIE
G-CDWE
NC858
G-BDJR BDXX BPZD
SV-4A (DH Gipsy Major 10)
G-AZNK BLOL
SV-4A (Renault 4P)
G-BHYI BZSY(3) NIFE STMP(3)
SV-4B (DH Gipsy Major 10)
G-AIYG AWIW AYIJ AZSA(2) BRMC2)
SV-4C (DH Gipsy Major 10)
G-AXRP BEPC BIMO BPLM(1) BRXP OODE
SV-4C (Lycoming IO-360)
G-BMNV
SV-4C (Renault 4P)
G-AMPI ATIR(1) AWXZ AXCZ AXHC AXNW AYCG AYDR AYGE AYZI AZGC AZGE BAKN BEPF BHFG BKRK BKSX BTIO BWRS BXSV BYDK EEUP FORC GMAX HJSS(1)
SV-4C(G) (DH Gipsy Major 1C)
G-ASHS
SV-4C(G) (DH Gipsy Major 10)
G-AWEF AYCK(1) AYJB AYWT(1) AZCB BWEF FORD SVIV
SV-4E (Lycoming O-360)
G-BNYZ

SNIAS see **SUD** and **AÉROSPATIALE**

SOCATA see **MORANE-SAULNIER**
ST.10 DIPLOMATE
G-AYKG AZIB HOLY
TB-9 TAMPICO
G-BHIT BHOZ BIBA BIXA BIXB BIZE BIZR BJKF BKCR BKIB BKIT BKUE BKVC BLCM BRIV BTWX BTZP CMED DLEE GHZJ GMSI
TB-10 TOBAGO
G-BGXC BGXD BGXT BHDE BHGP BHJF BITE BKBN BKBV BKBW BKIS BLCG BLYE BMYC BNDR BNRA BOIT BSDL BTIE CBGC CBHA CBPE CFME CONL CTCL DAND EDEN FAIR FLEA FSZY GBHI GKUE GOLF HALP HELA HILT IANC IANH IGGL JURE MOOR MRTN OFIT PATN PCAT PHTG POPI RENO RIAM SBKR SERL SKYF SONA TBIO TBOK TBTN TEDS TINA TOBA TZEE VMJM
TB-200 TOBAGO GT
G-BXLT BXVA EGAG HEVN MLLA OBEI
TB-20 TRINIDAD
G-BLXA BLYD BMIX BNXX BPTI BSCN BTZO BYJS BYTB BZPI CCGL CDDA CDDT CEPT CORB CPMS CTIO CTZO DLOM DMAH EGJA FFTI FIFI GOOD HGPI HOOD JDEE KPTT OALD OBGC OTUI PEKT PTRE RRFC SAPM SCBI SCIP SLTN TANS TBGT TBSV TBXX TBZO THZL TMOL TOAK TRIN TYNE VPPL WERY
TB-21 TRINIDAD GT TURBO
G-BZLI CBFM TBZI VALY
TBM-700
G-KEMW MCMC PMHT

FABRIKA VAZDUHOPLOVA SOKA
SOKO P-2 KRAGUJ
G-BSXD RADA SOKO

SOLAR WINGS LTD and **SOLAR WINGS AVIATION LTD** including **HOLD CONTROL PLC** and see **CYCLONE AIRSPORTS LTD** and **PEGASUS AVIATION**

PANTHER XL (Fuji-Robin EC-44-PM)
G-MMBY MMKA MMTS

PANTHER XL-R (Rotax 447)
G-MNBI

PANTHER XL-S (Fuji-Robin EC-44-PM)
G-MJWZ MMGS MMJF MMMN MMOK MMSA MMSG MMSH MMZG MNAH MNAI MNAK MNHH

PEGASUS XL-Q (Rotax 462)
G-BZWM DEAN MGCB MNKO MTJS MTNO MTNP MTPN MTPS MTRV MTTD MTTE MTTX MTTY MTTZ MTUN MTUP MTUR MTUS MTUT MTUY MTVX MTXI MTXJ MTXH MTXK MTYA MTYC MTYD MTYE MTYF MTYH MTYI MTYL MTYP MTYR MTYS MTYT MTYU MTZP MTZR MTZS MVAW MVAX MVAY MVCL MVCM MVCN MVCP MVCR MVCS MVCT MVCV MVEX MVEZ MVFA MVFB MVFC MVFD MVFE MVFF MVGU MVGW MVHP MVHR MVHS MVHW MVHY MVJN MVJP MVJR MVJS MVJT MVJU MVJW MVKN MVKO MVKP MVKS MVKT MVKU MVKV MVKW MVLX MVLY MVMA MVMC MVPR MVPS MVPX MVPY MVRH MVRI MVRJ MVRU MVRW MVRX MVSB MVSD MVSE MVSW MVSX MVSY MVSZ MVTA MVTI MVTJ MVTK MVUF MVUG MVUI MVUJ MVUK MVUL MVUM MVVN MVVO MVVP MVYC MVYD MVZJ MVZL MVZT MVZU MVZV MWAC MWAD MWAL MWAT MWBK MWCB MWCF MWDD MWDK MWDL MWEE MWEG MWEH MWER MWFS MWGL MWGM MWGR MWHC MWHF MWHG MWHL MWHX MWIE MWIR MWIS MWJN MWKO MWKY MWKZ MWLL MWLM MWMN MWMO MWMP MWMZ MWNA MWNB MWNC MWNG MWOR MWOY MWPE MWPJ MWPK MWRW MWRX MWSD MWSJ MWSK MWTB MWTC MWTI MWTL MWUO MWUX MWUY MWUZ MWVA MWWG MWWH MWWV MWXP MWXR MWYB MWYC MWYU MWYY MWYZ MYAC MYAE MYAF MYBF MYBS MYBV MYBW MYBY MYBZ MYEA MYEC MYFX MYPG MYTC MYUH MZLR

PEGASUS XL-R variants (Rotax 447)
G-MGPD MMOH MMRL MMTA MMTC MMTR MMYA MMYN MNAR MNAW MNAX MNAY MNAZ MNBA MNBB MNBC MNGG MNHC MNHD MNHE MNHF MNHI MNHJ MNHK MNHL MNHM MNHN MNHR MNHS MNHT MNMK MNUX MNVB MNVC MNVE MNWW MNYC MNYU MNYV MNYW MNYX MNZK MTAA MTAI MTAJ MTAO MTAV MTAW MTAX MTAY MTAZ MTBA MTBL MTBR MTBU MTBV MTCH MTCN MTCO MTDG MTDH MTDI MTDV MTEC MTED MTEE MTES MTET MTEU MTEW MTEX MTFA MTFB MTFM MTFO MTFP MTFR MTFT MTGJ MTGK MTGL MTGM MTHG MTHH MTHI MTHJ MTHN MTIE MTIH MTIJ MTIO MTIP MTIR MTIS MTIW MTIX MTIY MTIZ MTKG MTKH MTKI MTLG MTLI MTLJ MTLT MTLV MTLY MTME MTMF MTMG MTMH MTOA MTOB MTOD MTOE MTOF MTOG MTOH MTOJ MTON MTOO MTOP MTOR MTOS MTOT MTOU MTOY MTOZ MTPE MTPF MTPG MTPH MTPI MTPJ MTPK MTPL MTPM MTPR MTRM MTRO MTRS MTSN MTSO MTSP MTSR MTSS MTSY MTSZ MTTA MTTB MTTU MTUA MTUI MTUK MTUL MTVB MTVK MTVL MTVN MTVO MTWB MTWD MTYY MTZJ MTZK MVAR MVAT MVAV MBVJ MVBY MVBZ MVCA MVCB MVDV MVDW MVDY MVDZ MVEC MVED MVEF MVEG MVFP MVFT MVFV MVFY MVFZ MVGN MVGO MVGP MVJD MVKF MVKH MVKJ MVKK MVKL MVKM MVVK MVVM MWAF MWAG MWAV MWBL MWCC MWCU MWDC MWLE MWLF MWLG MWLU MWMR MWMV MWOH MWOI MWPX MWRN MWRP MWRT MWRU MWRV MWSE MWSF MWSO MWSP MWSR MWTU MWUB MWUC MWUD MWUF MWUP MWUR MWUS MWUU MWUV MWVE MWVF MWZI MWZJ MWZT MWZU MWZV MWZW MWZY MWZZ MYAB MYBG MYBO MYBP MYDJ MYED MYEG MYEH MYFS MYGT MYGU MYGV

PEGASUS FLASH (Rotax 447)
G-MNDO MNJH MNJJ MNJL MNJN MNJR MNKP MNKV MNKW MNKX MNNY MNNZ MNPA MNSH MNSN MNUD MNUE MNVG MNVH MNWU MNXP MNYA MNYZ MTCK MTJH

PEGASUS QUASAR (Rotax 503)
G-MWHT MWIM MWIU MWIW MWIX MWIY MWJH MWJI MWJJ MWJK MWJS MWJT MWLH MWLJ MWLK MWMI MWMJ MWMK MWML MWNK MWNL MWOM MWOP MWSI MWVM MWXG MWXH MWYI MWYJ MWZD MWZE MWZF MWZO MWZP MWZR MWZS MYAK MYBE MYBT MYCE MYEK MYEM MYEN MYEO MYFK MYFL MYIM MYIN MYIO MYJJ MYJK MYJS MYJT MYJU MYKP MYKR MYKS MYTR MYXD MZMA MZPW REKO

PEGASUS PHOTON (Solo 210)
G-MNIK MNKB MNKC MNKD MNKE MNKG MNKK MNVZ MNXB MTAL

TRIKE with Typhoon wing
G-MMBZ

SOLENT BALLOON GROUP
Balloon (Minimum Lift)
OSPREY variants
G-BJTN BJTY BJUE BJUU FYAV FYBD FYBE FYBF FYBG FYBH FYBI FYCL FYCT FYCV FYCZ FYDF FYDG FYDO FYDS FYDU FYEV FYFN

SOMERS-KENDAL
SK.1
G-AOBG

SONEX AIRCRAFT see also **MONNETT**
SONEX
G-CEFJ SONX ZONX

SOPWITH AVIATION CO LTD
CAMEL including replicas
G-AWYY BFCZ BPOB BZSC
DOVE including replicas
G-EAGA
PUP including replicas
G-EBKY
G-ABOX APUP BIAT BIAU BZND EAVX
1½ STRUTTER replica
G-BIDW
TABLOID SCOUT
G-BFDE
TRIPLANE including replicas
G-BOCK BWRA

SORRELL AVIATION
SNS-7 HYPERBIPE (Lycoming IO-360)
G-BPDK HIPE

SOUTHDOWN AEROSTRUCTURE LTD
PIPISTRELLE
G-MJTM

SOUTHDOWN INTERNATIONAL LTD/SOUTHDOWN SAILWINGS LTD including **MEDWAY MICROLIGHTS LTD** and **RAVEN AIRCRAFT INTERNATIONAL** production
PUMA SPRINT
G-MJEB MJTR MJZK MMAO MMIW MMJD MMLW MMPH MMRN MMTJ MMUA MMUV MMVA MMVI MMVX MMVZ MMWX MMXO MMYF MMYO MMYT MMYU MMYY MMYZ MMZW MNAV MNBE MNBM MNCI MNCP MNDY MNFB MNFG MNFX MNGX MNIL MNJS MNKU MNML MVAF MWBJ MWCR MWJX
PUMA RAVEN (Fuji-Robin EC-44-PM)
G-MNMU MNVN MNXF MNYG
RAVEN variants (Rotax 447)
G-MGOD MMVH MNJB MNJT MNKZ MNLM MNLN MNLT MNLZ MNMD MNNA MNNB MNNC MNNO MNRP MNRS MNSL MNSX MNSY MNTC MNTE MNTM MNTN MNTY MNUU MNUW MNVP MNWG MNXE MNXG MNXI MNYL MNYM MNYP MNZW MNZX MTAP MTBB MTBK MTBN MTBO MTCM MTIK MTMO MTPC MTRT MTRW MTYV MTYW MTYX MVIF MYLX MYLY MYMJ MYYZ MYZO MZBR MZDJ
WILD CAT Mk.II
G-MMDF
TRIKE with SIGMA wing
G-MBDM
TRIKE with LIGHTNING wing
G-MMIZ MYJE

SOUTHERN AIRCRAFT LTD
MARTLET
G-AAYX

SPAD
XIII
G-BFYO

SPARTAN AIRCRAFT LTD
ARROW
G-ABWP
CRUISER
G-ACYK

SPEICH
AIR COMMAND GYROPLANE
G-BPGC

SPEZIO
DAL-1 TUHOLER
    G-NGRM NOBI

SPORTAVIA-PÜTZER GmbH see also **FOURNIER**
RS.180 SPORTSMAN
    G-VIZZ

SPP see also **YAKOVLEV**
AERO 45
    G-APRR AYLZ
SUPER AERO 145
    G-ATBH
MORAVA L-200A
    G-ASFD

SQUIRES
DRAGONFLY 250-II
    G-MJLK
LIGHTFLY Trike with Solar Wings wing
    G-MNNG

SRCM see **MINICAB**

STAAKEN
Z-1 FLITZER, Z-21(A) FLITZER
    G-BVAW BYYZ ENIA ERDA ERIW ERTI FLIZ FLZR FZIS WIDZ
A-1A STUMMELFLITZER
    G-ZIRA

STANSTED BALLOON GROUP
Balloon (Minimum Lift)
All variants
    G-BIVS BJLN BJLP

STARCK
AS.80
    G-BJAE

STAR-LITE
SL-1
    G-BUZH FARO SOLA

STEARMAN see **BOEING-STEARMAN**

STEEN AERO LAB INC
SKYBOLT (Lycoming O-360)
    G-BGRT BIMN BRIS BUXI BVXE BZWV ENGO BWPJ CBYJ CCPE
    KEST RODC SBLT SBOL SKIE WISZ

STEMME GmbH and Co KG
S 10 variants (Limbach L2400)
    G-BVYZ BXGZ BXHR BZSP EXPD JCKT JULL STEM STEN STME

STEPHENS
AKRO
    G-RIDE

STERN
ST.80 BALADE
    G-BWVI

STINSON AIRCRAFT CORPORATION
HW-75
    G-AFYO BMSA
V-77 RELIANT
    G-BUCH
108 VOYAGER (Consolidated Vultee Aircraft production)
    G-BHMR BPTA BRZK CFGE WAGN

STITS
SA.3A PLAYBOY
    G-BDRL BGLZ BVVR

STODDARD-HAMILTON
GLASAIR
    G-BKHW BMIO BODI BOVU BSAI BUBT BUHS BZBO CDAB ICBM
    IIRG KRES KSIR LAIR LASR OPNH TRUK USSI
GLASTAR (Lycoming 320)
    G-BYEK BZDM CBAR CBCL CBJD CTEC ETCW GERY IARC IKES
    LAZZ LSTR MHGS SACH SKUA

STOLP AIRCRAFT CORPORATION
SA.100 STARDUSTER
    G-BSZG IIIM
SA.200 STARDUSTER TOO
    G-WINN
SA.300 STARDUSTER TOO
    G-BNNA BOBT BRVB BSZB BTGS BUPB BZKD CDBR CEZK
    DUST JIII KEEN NARR OTOO STOO UINN
SA.500 STARLET
    G-AZTV
SA.750 ACRODUSTER TOO
    G-BLES BUGB
SA.900 V-STAR
    G-BLAF

STOREY
TSR.3
    G-AWIV

STRIPLIN
LONE RANGER
    G-MBDL MBJM
SKY RANGER
    G-MJKB MMFZ

STROJIRNY PRVNI PETILESKY (SPP) (see MORAVA)

STROJNIK
S-2A
    G-BMPS

SUD-AVIATION including **AÉROSPATIALE, ICA-BRASOV** and
WESTLAND HELICOPTERS LTD (GAZELLE) production
SE.313 ALOUETTE II variants
    G-BVSD BZGG UGLY
SE.316 ALOUETTE III
    G-CDSG CDSJ
SA.315B LAMA
    G-LAMA
SA.341 and SA.342 GAZELLE
    G-BXTH BZDV BZYD CBGZ CBJZ CBKA CBKC CBKD CBSD
    CBSF CBSH CBSI CBSK CBZL CDJT CDNO CDNS CDXE DFKI
    DMSS EHUP EROL EZEL FUKM GAZA GAZZ KANE LEDR LOYD
    MANN OGAZ OGEO OLDH SFTA SIVJ SWWM TOPZ TURP UZEL
    VOIP WCRD WDEV ZELE ZLLE ZZEL ZZLE

SUD-AVIATION GARDAN
HORIZON
    ASJY, ASZS, ATGY, ATJT, AVMA, AVRS, AWAC, AZAW, AZYA,
    BFAA, BJAV, BKNI, BYBL, BYME, BYPE, GYAT, GYBO, TIMY

SUKHOI
Su-26M
    G-IIIS IIIZ XXVI

SUPER SCORPION see **HIWAY**

SUPER MARINE AIRCRAFT (PTY)
SPITFIRE Mk.26
    G-CCGH CCJL CCZP CEFC CENI CEPL HABT PIXY

SWALLOW AEROPLANE CO
SWALLOW B
    G-MJBK

SWEARINGEN AIRCRAFT CORPN
SA.226TC METRO II
    G-CEGE

SZD see **PZL**

TARJANI
Trike wih Solar Wings Typhoon wing
    G-MJCU

TAYLOR
JT.1 MONOPLANE (Volkswagen 1600)
    G-APRT AWGZ AXYK AYSH AYUS BBBB BDAD BDAG BDNC
    BDNG BDNO BEUM BEVS BEYW BFBC BFOU BGCY BGHY BILZ
    BJMO BKEU BKHY BLDB BMAO BMET BRUO BUXL BYAV CDGA
    CRIS DRAY OBJM SUZY WARD

JT.2 TITCH
G-AYZH BABE BARN BDRG BFID BGCX BGMS BIAX BKWD BVNI
EOFF MISS MOLE OJON RKET TICH VIVI

TAYLOR see **AEROCAR**

TAYLOR-WATKINSON
DINGBAT
G-AFJA

TAYLOR AIRCRAFT CO INC see **PIPER**

TAYLORCRAFT see **AUSTER**

TAYLORCRAFT AIRCRAFT CORPORATION
BC-12D
G-AHNR AKVO BIGK BOLB BPHO BPHP BPPZ BREY BRIH BRPX
BRXE BSDA BTFK BVDZ BVXS
BC-65
G-BSCW
BL-65
G-BVRH
DCO-65
G-BWLJ
DF-65
G-BRIY
F-19
G-BRIJ
F-21
G-BPJV
F-22 varants
G-BVOX BWBI

TCHEMMA
Balloon (Hot-Air)
T01/77
G-CFHS

TEAM
HI-MAX (Rotax 447)
G-CBNZ MZHM
MINI-MAX (Rotax 447)
G-BVSB BVSX BVYK BXCD BXSU BYFV BYII BYJE BYYX BZFK
BZOR BZTC CBIN CBPL CBXU CCGB CEDL CEDW MWFC
MWFD MWHH MWLW MWSA MWWE MWZM MYAT MYBM MYCT
MYDF MYGF MYII MYIZ MYKJ MYKZ MYLB MYNI MYRG MYRL
MYSK MYXA MYYR MYYS MYZE MZCS MZII MZMO MZNM MZNN
MZOY MZPJ NADS OJLH OPEJ OSCO THEO

CONSTRUZIONI AERONAUTICHE TECNAM SRL
P92 ECHO variants (Jabiru 2200)
G-BZHG BZWT CBAX CBDM CBGE CBLB CBUG CBYZ CCAL
CCDU CDSJ CDZK DWPF OALH PGFG PLOD SDOZ TCNM TECM
WHEN
P2002 SIERRA variants
G-CDTE CDTV CENH CEOC CEVM CFSB NESE RAYZ RLMW
SDOB TECS TESI TESR TEMB TSAC

TEMAN
MONO-FLY
G-MMJX MMPZ

TEVERSON
BISPORT
G-CBGH

THE LIGHT AIRCRAFT COMPANY (TLAC)
SHERWOOD RANGER variants
G-BZUG CBHU CCBW CDPH GKFC HVAN MWND PUSY WZOL

THORN
Balloon (Gas-Filled)
COAL GAS BALLOON
G-ATGN

THORP AERO INC including **AD AEROSPACE LTD** and **VENTURE LIGHT AIRCRAFT RESOURCES** production
T.18
G-BLIT BSVN BYBY HATF
T.211
G-BTHP BYJF CCXI TZII

THRUSTER AIR SERVICES LTD including **THRUSTER AIRCRAFT (UK) LTD**
TST Mk.1 (Rotax 503)
G-MTGB MTGC MTGD MTGE MTGF MTGR MTGS MTGT MTGU
MTKA MTKB MTKD MTKE MTLM MTLN MTNR MTNT MTNU
MTNV MTPT MTPU MTPW MTPX MTPY MTSH MTSJ MTSK
MTSM MTUB MTUC MTUD MTUE MTVP MTVR MTVS MTVT
MTVV MTWY MTWZ MTXA MTXB MTXC MTXD MTZA MTZB
MTZC MTZF MVAG MVAH MVAI MVAJ MVAL MVBP MVBT MVDD
MVDE MVDF MVDG MVDH MVFJ MVFL MVFM MVFO MVHI
MVHJ MVHK MVHL MVIR MVIT MVIU MVIV MVIW MVME MVMG
MVMI MVOT MVOV MVOW MVOX MVOY MVXL MVYE MWIU
MYWZ
T.300 variants
G-MGWH MVUB MVWN MVWR MVWS MVZA MVZC MVZD MVZG
MVZI MWAN MWAP MWAR MWDS MWWS MYAR MYDR MYDT
MYDU MYJF MYJG MYXU
T.600 (Jabiru 2200A)
G-BYPF BYPG BYPH BZDB BZGP BZIG BZJC BZJD BZNP BZTD
CBDC CBGU CBGV CBGW CBIO CBIP CBIR CBKG CBPN CBVA
CBWI CBWJ CBXG CBYT CCBC CCCB CCCF CCCU CCDV CCEB
CCIC CCMT CCRN CCRP CCUZ CCXV CCXW CDBZ CDDI CDDX
CDGI CDIA CDJE CDRH CDSO CSAV CXIP DIDY EVEY FJCE
INGE IRAL KDCD KIPP KYLE MARZ MCCF MGTV MOMA MYWD
MYWE MZFO MZFR MZFU MZGX MZGY MZGZ MZHA MZHD
MZHE MZHF MZHS MZHU MZHV MZHW MZHY MZKR MZKS
MZKT MZKU MZNX MZNY NDOT OASJ OBAX OHYE OJSH OMAL
OOFE ORDS ORUG OWMC PSUK PVST PYNE RAFH RAFS
REDZ RIVR SLAK UDGE ULLY WORM

THRUXTON see **JACKAROO AIRCRAFT**
JACKAROO
G-ANZT AOEX AOIR APAJ

THUNDER BALLOONS LTD including **CAMERON BALLOONS LTD** and **THUNDER and COLT LTD**
Airship (Hot Air)
AS-33
G-ERMS
Balloon (Hot Air)
O.5
G-BBOD
Ax3 SKY CHARIOT
G-BHUR BKBD BKIY BKMR NEIL
Ax4 series
G-LORY
Ax5 series
G-BDAY BEMU BLOV
Ax6 series
G-BBDJ BBOO BCCH BDVG BECS BEEE BEJB BERD BETH BFIT
BFOZ BGPF BHTG BIIL BJVU BLWB BPSJ BPUF DICK LDYS LIFE
RTBI THOM TNTN
Ax7 series
G-BAXK BBOX BCAR BCAS BCCG BCIN BCNR BCSX BDGH
BDGO BDMO BEVI BFIX BGRS BGST BHAT BHEU BHHH BHIS
BHSP BHZX BJSW BJZC BKDK BKUU BLAH BLCC BLCY BLET
BLGX BLKJ BLTN BLUI BLZF BMCC BMHJ BMMW BMOG BMUU
BMVT BMYS BNBL BNBV BNBW BNCC BNCU BNGO BNMX
BNXZ BNZK BOIJ BORD BOSB BPGF BPHU BPNU BPVU BPYZ
BRDE BRLS BRVN BRXB BRZE BSAV BSCF BSCO BSOJ BSZH
BTAN BTAU BTHK BTRR BTSX BTTW BTVA BTXK BUDK BUIN
BUKI BULB BUNV BUPU BVDB BVUH BYNU BZBH CDFN FUND
GASS GGGG GHIN HOWE LENS LYTE MLWI NEGS NIGS NWPB
OFBJ OJDC PIAF PIES PUFF RAFE RBOW REGS RIGB RINO
ROCK ROSI SFRY SOFT THOS USIL VIVA WDEB WINE
Ax8 series
G-BGHW BJMW BOHF BORR BOTE BPZZ BRVY BSCX BSPB
BSTK BSTY BTBB BTHM BTJD BTPX BTRO BUBL BUBY BUEI
BUJW BUXW BUYD BVDW BVGB BVKH BVPA BVWB BWKW
BYLV CBFH GEMS HAZE INGA OMDD PUNK SUED TOOL ZEBO
Ax9 series
G-BTJO BTOZ BTRN BUAT BULK BVKZ BZBN FABS OIOZ
Ax10 series
G-BTJF BTYF BUNZ BUOZ BUVZ BWNX BZGJ CCEO CDKZ
OLEO WORK
Ax11 series
G-BXAD BZHX BZRZ

Special Shapes

SHAPE	REGISTRATION(S)
ICE CREAM	G-ICES
JUMBO JET	G-VJIM
WHISKY BOTTLE	G-RARE

THURSTON
TEAL
G-OWET

TIPSY AIRCRAFT CO LTD including AVIONS FAIREY SA, COBELAVIA SA and SLINGSBY (for NIPPER AIRCRAFT LTD*)
production
S2
G-AFVH
BELFAIR
G-APIE APOD
JUNIOR
G-AMVP
NIPPER variants
G-APYB ARBG ARDY ARFV ARXN ASXI ASZV ATBW ATUH AVKI* AVKK* AVKT AVTC* AVXD* AWDA* BWHR AWJE* AWJF* AWLR* AWLS* AXLI* AXZM* BLMW BRIK BRPM BWCT BYLO CBCK CCFE CORD* ENIE NIPA* NIPP* NIPR* ONCS OVAG TIPS
TRAINER I
G-AFJR AFRV AFSC AFVN AFWT AISA AISC

TITAN
T-51 MUSTANG
G-MUZY

TITAN
TORNADO SS
G-NADO

TLAC see THE LIGHT AIRCRAFT COMPANY previously THE LITTLE AIRCRAFT COMPANY

TL ULTRALIGHT COMPANY
TL-2000 STING
G-CEPS CESM CFDS LCMW SACM STNG

TRAGO MILLS see FLS

TRI-R TECHNOLOGIES
KIS
G-BVTA BVZD BZDR MANW OKIS OKMA OKPW TKIS

TROTTER
Balloon (Hot Air)
AX3-20
G-BRBT

TURNER
SUPER T-40A
G-BRIO

TWAMLEY
TRIKE
G-MBGF MJWI

ULTRAFLIGHT LTD including AMF MICROFLIGHT LTD production
LAZAIR
G-MBYI MNRD MTFL MVGZ

ULTRALIGHT AVIATION SYSTEMS
STORM BUGGY trike with Lightning & Solar Wings wings
G-MBGX MJBS

ULTRAMAGIC SA
Balloon (Hot Air)
V-14
G-CFMR
H-31
G-BZIZ BZPY CEFB CEJL
H-42
G-CEAY OOCH
M-56
G-CEJG
M-65C
G-CEBO RACR

77 variants
G-BXPT BZKW BZSH BZSO CBRK CBWK CCLO CCRG CERL DAIV DWPH DXCC HOLI KNEE LOKI PIMM RWRW
90 variants
G-CCYU CEEL CEIK CFDF CFFA CFOL CSFD GBBT KEWT LEEH LEMM MAXR PENH
105 variants
G-BZPX BZRX CBRB CCOP CDGF CDPN CEAV CEKH CELN CEMG CEUL CFJI EPSN GBGB WILB
M-120
G-CDJI CDNZ CEUM
S-130
G-CBKK CBZV CEAX CEMN
M-145
G-BZGI
T-150
G-OMOO
S-160
G-CDFC
T-180
G-CCTN CCUE
210 variants
G-BZPR BZPT CDWN
N-250
G-BZJX CBUE CDST VBFA VBFC VBFD
N-300
G-CBPZ
N-355
G-VBFB VBFE
N-425
G-VBFP

ULTRASPORTS
PANTHER trike with Flexiform wing
G-MJVR
PUMA trike with Southdown wing
G-MJCE MMBL MMCI
TRI-PACER trike with Excalibur, Flexiform, Hiway, Solar Wings, Southdown & Wasp wings
G-MBIY MBLK MBLU MBPY MBTJ MJER MJFB MJHC MJIA MJIC MJOI MJTC MJVN MMPG MMRK MMWS MNGD MNSD MTTL MZLK

ULTRAVIA
PELICAN variants
G-BWWA MPAC MWRS

UNICORN GROUP
Balloon (Minimum Lift)
UE variants
G-BINR BINS BINT BIWJ BJAA BJDY BJGM BJLF BJLG BJSX BJUO FYEK

UNIVERSITY OF SUSSEX BALLOONING SOCIETY
Balloon (Gas -Filled)
GAS BALLOON
G-AWOK

VAHDAT-HAGH
SEMICOPTER
G-BZEV
SHIRAZ
G-CCUU

VALENTIN FLUGZEUGBAU GMBH
MISTRAL C
G-CJUR DJHP DKBW
TAIFUN 17E
G-BMSE OACE TFUN

VAN'S AIRCRAFT INC
RV-3 variants
G-BVDC CCTG RIII RODZ RVRH
RV-4
G-BOHW BULG BVDI BVLR BVRV BVUN BVVS BXPI BXRV BZPH CDJB CEID CEVC IIGI IKON INTS MARX MAXV MUMY NADZ ORCA PIPS RATC RIIV RMIT RVDP RVDX RVIV RVJW RVMJ RVNS RVPM RVRV SARV VANS
RV-6 variants
G-BUEC BUTD BVCG BXJY BXVM BXVO BXWT BXYX BYDV BYEL BZOZ BZRV BZUY BZVN BZWZ BZXB CBCP CBUK CCJI CCVS CDAE CDVT CEYM CSPR DFUN EDRV EERV ESTR EYOR GDRV GLUC GPAG GRIN GRVE HACE HAMY HOPY JAEE JIMZ

JSRV KELL MURG NPKJ NMRV OBUZ OJVA OJVL OMDB ONUN
OORV ORVE ORVG ORVI OTRV PJSY PWUL REAS REVE RIVT
RRVX RUSL RVAN RVAW RVBC RVCE RVCG RVCL RVDJ RVDR
RVEE RVET RVGA RVIA RVIB RVIC RVIN RVIT RVJM RVMT
RVPW RVSA RVSH RVSX RVTE RVVI SIXY TEXS TJDM TOGO
USRV VANZ XVOM

RV-7 variants
G-CBJU CCVM CCZD CDJW CDME CDRM CDYZ CECV CEIG
CEIT CETS CFET COLS COPZ CTED DIDG DOTY FIXX GERT
HUTY IMCD ISMA IVII JFRV JMRV JTEM KAOS KELS MROD
MRVL NAPP OKER ORAE OVII PBEC PPLL PROS PYPE RIDG
RISY RMRV RVAB RVAC RVII RVMC RVTT RVUK RVRP SEVN
STAF UZZL VANN XIII

RV-8 variants
G-BZWN CCIR CDDY CDPJ CEGI CETI CHPK DAZZ DUDE EGBS
GIGZ GORV GUNZ HILZ HRVS IGHT IIRW JBTR JILS KELZ LEXX
LEXY LSPH LUDM MHRV PHMG PHVM RVAL RVBA RVCH RVIS
RVLC RVMZ RVPH RVPL RVSR TUCK XRVB XSEA ZAAZ ZUMI

RV-9 variants
G-CCGU CCND CCZT CCZY CDCD CDMF CDMN CDRV CDXT
CDZD CEEP CEGH CERK CETP CFED CFHI CFMC DHOP ENTS
GNRV HOXN HUMH IINI IOSL JBRS KMRV NIEN NYNA ONER
OPVM ORVS RPRV RUVY RVDG RVIX RVJO RVJP RVMB RVNH
RVSD RVSG THMB TTRL XSAM

RV-10
G-OHIY RVIO RVTN XRVX

VAN DEN BEMDEN
Balloon (Gas-Filled)
FREE
G-BBFS BIHP BWCC
OMEGA III
G-BDTU

VARGA
2150A KACHINA
G-BLHW BPVK CHTT DJCR VARG

VENTURE LIGHT AIRCRAFT RESOURCES see THORP

VFW-FOKKER GmbH
FK-3
G-CHJA

VICKERS-ARMSTRONGS (AIRCRAFT) LTD
FB.5 GUNBUS replica
G-ATVP
FB.27 VIMY (including replica*)
G-EAOU
G-AWAU*
60 VIKING IV replica
"G-EBED"
600 series VIKING
G-AGRU AGRW AHOT
668 VARSITY
G-BEDV BHDD
700 series VISCOUNT
G-ALWF AMOG AMOI ANHD AOFX
800 series VISCOUNT
G-APIM ASDS AVHE AVJB AZLC AZLP AZLS BAPF OPAS
953 VANGUARD MERCHANTMAN
G-APEJ APEP APES
VC-10
G-ARVF ARVM ASIX
SUPER VC-10
G-ASGC

VICKERS SUPERMARINE LTD including WESTLAND AIRCRAFT LTD
Production
236 WALRUS
G-AIZG RNLI
SPITFIRE variants including replica*
G-AIDN AIST AISU ALGT ASJV AVAV AWII AWIJ BJSG BKMI
BMSB BRDV* BRSF BUOS BUWA BYDE CBNU CCCA CCVV
CDGU CDGY CFGJ CFGN CTIX CZAF FIRE FXII FXIV ILDA IXCC
LFIX LFVB MCDB MKIA MKVB MXVI MKXI OXVI PBIX PMNF PRXI
RRGN SPIT SXVI TCHI TCHO VIII WWII XVIB
SEAFIRE variants
G-BWEM CDTM CFGI KASX
552 SWIFT
G-SWIF

VICTA including **AESL** production
AIRTOURER
G-ATCL ATEX ATHT ATJC AWMI AWVG AXIX AYLA AYWM AZBE
AZHI AZHT AZMN AZOE AZOF AZRP AZTM

VIKING
DRAGONFLY
G-BKPD BNEV BRKY DKGF

VOISIN
Replica
G-BJHV

VOLMER
VJ.22 SPORTSMAN
G-BAHP
VJ.24W
G-MBBZ

VOUGHT
F4U CORSAIR
G-CCMV FGID

VPM SNC and SRL including Magni Gyro
M-14 SCOUT
G-BUEN
M-16 TANDEM TRAINER
G-BUPM BUZL BXEJ BXIX BZJM BZXW CBUP CCAH CERG
CVPM DBDB IBFP IJMC ODPJ UNIX YFLY

WACO
UPF-7
G-UPFS WACO
YKS-7
G-BWAC
YMF
G-WOCO YMFC

WAG-AERO INC
CUBY SPORT TRAINER
G-BTWL BVMH BZHU
SUPER SPORT
G-DTUG
WAG-A-BOND
G-BNJA

WALLBRO
MONOPLANE
G-BFIP

WALLINGFORD MODEL BALLOONS
Balloon (Minimum Lift)
WMB.2 WINDTRACKER
G-BIAI BIBX BILB

WALLIS AUTOGYROS LTD including BEAGLE-MILES AIRCRAFT
LTD, BEAGLE- WALLIS LTD and VINTEN-WALLIS LTD production
WA.116
G-ARRT ARZB ASDY ATHM ATTB AVDG AXAS BGGU BLIK BMJX
SCAN VIEW
WA.117
G-AVJV VTEN
WA.118
G-AVJW
WA.120
G-AYVO BGGV
WA.121
G-BAHH
WA.122
G-BGGW
WA.201
G-BNDG

W.A.R.
FOCKE-WULF FW190 replicas
G-BSLX CCFW JABO SYFW WULF
VOUGHT F-4U CORSAIR replica
G-BJNB

WARD
ELF
G-MMUL

GNOME
  G-AXEI

SOCIÉTÉ DES ETABLISSMENTS BENJAMIN WASSMER see **JODEL**
WA26P SQUALE
  G-CHHX DEEP
WA28F ESPADON
  G-CJDX CJXC
WA30 BIJAVE
  G-DEKT
WA.41 SUPER BALADOU
  G-ATSY ATZS AVEU
WA.51 PACIFIC
  G-AZYZ
WA.52 EUROPA
  G-BTLB OELZ
WA.81 PIRANHA
  G-BKOT

WATKINSON see **TAYLOR-WATKINSON**

JOHN WEBB
TRIKE with Flexiform wing
  G-MMYV

WEEDHOPPER OF UTAH INC
JC-24
  G-BHWH MJMB MMNV

WELLS
Balloon (Minimum Lift)
AIRSPEED 300
  G-FYGJ

WEST
Balloon (Hot Air)
AX3-15
  G-BCFD

WESTERN
Balloon (Hot Air)
20
  G-AYMV
O-31
  G-AZPX
65 series
  G-AYUK AZJI AZOO BBCB BBUT

WESTLAND AIRCRAFT LTD see **FAIREY** and **SUPERMARINE**
WIDGEON
  G-EBUB
LYSANDER
  G-AZWT BCWL CCOM LIZY

WESTLAND HELICOPTERS LTD also see **SIKORSKY** and **SUD AVIATION**
WESTLAND-SIKORSKY S-51 DRAGONFLY
  G-ALMB AMHB AMJW BRMA
WESTLAND-SIKORSKY S-51/2 WIDGEON
  G-ANLW AOZE APTW
WESTLAND-SIKORSKY S-55 WHIRLWIND
  G-AMJT ANFH ANJV AODA APWN APXA APXB ATKV AYXT AYZJ
  BAMH BDBZ BEBC BJWY BVGE RWWW
WESTLAND-SIKORSKY S-58 WESSEX
  G-ATBZ AVNE AWOX AWXX BYRC CCUP
WG.13 LYNX
  G- BFDV LYNX
WG.30
  G-BGHF BKFD BKFF BKGD BLTY EFIS ELEC HAUL
SCOUT
  G-BWHU BWJW BWLX BXRR BXRS BXSL BYKJ BYRX BZBD
  CBUH CRUM NOTY SCTA SROE
WASP
  G-BMIR BYCX BZPP CBUI KANZ KAXT RIMM

WESTLAND-AGUSTA see **EH INDUSTRIES**

WESTLAND-BELL see **BELL**

W H EKIN (ENGINEERING) CO LTD
WHE AIRBUGGY
  G-AXYZ AXZB

WHEELER
SCOUT
  G-MJAL MNKN

RON WHEELER AIRCRAFT SALES PTY
SLYMPH
  G-ABOI

WHITTAKER including **AEROTECH INTERNATIONAL LTD**
MW2B EXCALIBUR
  G-BDDX
MW4
  G-MBTH
MW5 SORCERER series (Rotax 447)
  G-BZWX BZXL CBBO CEFT MMGV MNMM MNXZ MTAS MTBP
  MTBR MTBS MTBT MTDK MTFN MTHB MTLZ MTRX MVNN
  MVNO MVNP MVNR MVNS MVNT MVNU MWEK MWEO MWGI
  MWGJ MWGK MWIC MWJW MWSX MWSY MYAH MYAN MYJZ
  MYRB MZOH
MW6 MERLIN, MW6-S FATBOY FLYER and MW6-T
  G-BUOA BYTX BZYU CBMU CBWS CBYP CCWG MGCK MNMW
  MTTF MTXO MURR MVPH MVPM MVPN MVTD MVXA MWAW
  MWHM MWIP MWLN MWLO MWOV MWPR MWSW MYCA MYCP
  MYCU MYDM MYDW MYEF MYET MYIE MYKO MYMN MYPP
  MYPS MYZN MZBG MZBX MZCH MZDL MZFK MZHG MZHT MZID
  MZJP MZNE MZOK SIXS
MW7 (Rotax 532)
  G-BOKH BPHK BPUP BREE BRMW BSXX BTFV BTUS BWVN
  BZOW

WILD
Balloon (Minimum Lift)
BVS SPECIAL
  G-BJUB

WILLIAMS
KFZ-1 TIGERFALCK
  G-KFZI

WILLIAMS
Balloon (Minimum Lift)
All variants
  G-FYAN FYAO FYAP FYAU FYDI FYDP FYFJ

WILLIAMS FLUGZEUGBAU
ALBATROSS D.Va replica
  G-BFXL

WILLS
AERA 2
  G-BJKW

WINDSOR BALLOON GROUP
Balloon (Minimum Lift)
WINDSOR MK,4 MLB
  G-BJFW

WINTER
LF-1 ZAUNKÖNIG
  G-ALUA

WITTMAN
W.8 and W.10 TAILWIND (Continental O-200-A)
  G-BCBR BDAP BDBD BJWT BMHL BNOB BOHV BOIB BPYJ
  CEJE CFON WYND ZIPY

WOLF
W-II BOREDOM FIGHTER
  G-BMZX BNAI

WOMBAT
GYROCOPTER
  G-BWLZ WBAT

WOODS see **AEROSPORT**

WSK see **YAKOVLEV**

WSK PZL MIELEC
TS-11 ISKRA
  G-BXVZ ISKA

YAKOVLEV including **ACROSTAR, IAV-BACHAU, LET, NANCHANG AIRCRAFT MANUFACTURING COMPANY (NAMC CJ-6A*)** and **SPP +** production
Yak-1
    G-BTZD
Yak-3
    G-BTHD CDBJ
Yak-9
    G-YAKP
Yak-11 (C-11)
    G-BTUB BTZE BZMY KYAK OYAK YCII
Yak-18 variants
    G-BMJY+ BVVG* BXZB* CEIB
Yak-50
    G-BTZB BWFM BWWX BWYK CBPM EYAK FUNK GYAK HAMM
    IIYK IVAR JYAK SKPH SOCT SVET VLAD YAAK YAKA YAKK
    YAKM YAKU YAKZ YKSO
Yak-52
    G-BVMU BVOK BVVA BVVW BVXK BWFP BWOD BWSV BWVR
    BXAK BXAV BXJB BZJB BZTF CBLJ CBMD CBMI CBOZ CBRH
    CBRP CBRU CBRW CBSL CBSR CBSS CBVT CCCP CCJK CCSU
    CDFE CDJJ CUPS FLSH HOGZ HYAK IMIC IUII LAOK LENA LYAK
    LYFA MCCY OCBT RNAC TYAK XYAK YAKB YAKC YAKD YAKF
    YAKH YAKI YAKN YAKO YAKR YAKT YAKV YAKX YAKY YFUT
    YKCT YKSZ YKYK YOTS YYAK ZYAK
Yak-55
    G-OHNO NOIZ YKSS

YORKSHIRE
Balloon (Hot Air)
A66
    G-BHOO

YORKSHIRE SAILPLANES
YS-53 SOVEREIGN
    G-DCUD DCXV

ZEBEDEE BALLOON SERVICE
Balloon (Hot Air)
V-31 HAB
    G-BXIT

ZENAIR see **HEINTZ AND /COLOMBAN**
CH.250 ZENITH variants
    G-BIRZ BTXZ GFKY RAYS
CH.601 ZODIAC variants (Rotax 912)
    G-BRII BUTG BUZG BVAB BVAC BVVM BVZR BYEO BYJT BYLF
    BYPR BZFV CBAP CBDG CBDT CBGB CBIX CBJP CBPV CBRX
    CBUR CCAK CCED CCLL CCTA CCVL CCVT CCZK CDAK CDAL
    CDDS CDFL CDGP CDJG CDJM CDLW CDMT CDNT CDPI CDWU
    CDXO CDZB CEAT CEBA CEBZ CECZ CEUW CEZS CEZV CFKH
    CFRY CLEO CSZM CZAC DAGJ DONT DROO EEZZ EXLL EZUB
    FOXL JAME KHOP KIMA OANN OMEZ OMWE OOSH PATO
    REGC RUVI RWMW XLNT YOXI ZAIR ZENI ZENR ZENY ZODY
CH.701 variants (Rotax 912)
    G-BRDB BTMW BXIG BZJP BZVA CBCH CBGD CBMW CBZW
    CCIT CCJB CCVI CDGR CDYU CEWS EOIN FAMH IMME JFMK
    OMEX RAYH TTDD TORI ZENA

ZIVKO AERONAUTICS INC
EDGE 540
    G-EDGY

ZLIN see **LET NARODNI PODNIK KUNOVICE** and **MORAVAN ARODNI PODNIK**

NOTES

<u>**NOTES**</u>

AIR-BRITAIN SALES

Companion volumes to this publication are also available by post-free mail order from

Air-Britain Sales Department (Dept UKI09)
41 Penshurst Road, Leigh,
Tonbridge, Kent TN11 8HL

For a full list of current titles and details of how to order, visit our secure e-commerce site at www.air-britain.co.uk
Visa / Mastercard / Solo / Maestro accepted - please give full details of card number and expiry date.

ANNUAL PUBLICATIONS - 2009 - NOW AVAILABLE

UK and IRELAND QUICK REFERENCE 2009 £6.95 (Members) £7.95 (Non-members)
Basic easy-to-carry current registration and type listing, foreign aircraft based in UK, IoM and Ireland, current military serials UK and Ireland, aircraft museums and expanded base index. A5 size, 176 pages.

BUSINESS JETS & TURBOPROPS QUICK REFERENCE 2009 £6.95 (Members) £7.95 (Non-members)
Now expanded to include all purpose-built business jets and business turboprops, in both civil and military use, in registration or serial order by country. Easy-to-carry A5 size, 160 pages.

AIRLINE FLEETS QUICK REFERENCE 2009 £6.95 (Members) £7.95 (Non-members)
Pocket guide now includes airliners of over 19 seats of 1700 major operators likely to be seen worldwide; regn, type, c/n, fleet numbers. Listed by country and airline. A5 size, 240 pages.

BUSINESS JETS INTERNATIONAL 2009 £18.00 (Members) £23.00 (Non-members)
The 24th annual edition of the complete production listings of all business jet types in c/n order, giving full identities, fates and a comprehensive cross-reference index containing over 50,000 registrations. Hardback, 576 pages.

AIRLINE FLEETS 2009 £19.95 (Members) £26.00 (Non-members)
Listing over 2,800 operators'fleets by country with registrations, c/ns, line numbers, fleet numbers and names, plus numerous appendices including airliners in non-airline service, IATA and ICAO airline and base codes, operator index, etc. Now 720 pages A5 size hardback.

EUROPEAN REGISTERS HANDBOOK 2009 Available May - £17.50 (Members) £26.25 (Non-members)
Current civil registers of 44 European countries between the Atlantic and Russia, all powered aircraft, balloons, gliders, microlights. Full previous identities and many extra permit and reservation details. Now in new dual format A5 softback easy-carry book combined with CD containing all the usual data.

BALLOONS AND AIRSHIPS OF THE WORLD 2009 £16.50 (Members) £24.75 (Non-members)
New A5 softback with 544 pages listing all known full-size lighter-than-air registrations since 1920. Contains over 32,000 registrations from almost 100 countries and comes with a free DVD with over 6,000 images of balloons and airships.

Also for publication during 2009: **BUSINESS TURBOPROPS 2009** *and* **TURBOPROP AIRLINERS OF THE WORLD** - *look out for announcements of availability and price.*

For details of other Air-Britain civil aviation titles including type histories, airline histories and complete civil registers, please check our sales website for current availability. Air-Britain also publishes a comprehensive range of military titles, please check for latest details of RAF Serial Registers, detailed RAF aircraft type "Files", Squadron Histories and Royal Navy Aircraft Histories.

IMPORTANT NOTE – Members receive substantial discounts on prices of all Air-Britain publications. For details of membership see the following page or visit our website at http://www.air-britain.co.uk

AIR-BRITAIN MEMBERSHIP

Join on-line at www.air-britain.co.uk

If you are not currently a member of Air-Britain, the publishers of this book, you may be interested in what we have on offer to provide for your interest in aviation.

About Air-Britain
Formed 61years ago, we are the world's most progressive aviation society, and exist to bring together aviation enthusiasts with every type of interest. Our members include aircraft historians, aviation writers, spotters and pilots – and those who just have a fascination with aircraft and aviation. Air-Britain is a non-profit organisation, which is independently audited, and any financial surpluses are used to provide services to the world-wide membership which currently stands at around 4,000, some 700 of whom live overseas.

Membership of Air-Britain
Membership is open to all. A basic membership fee is charged and every member receives a copy of the quarterly house magazine, Air-Britain Aviation World, and is entitled to use all the Air-Britain specialist services and buy **Air-Britain publications at discounted prices**. A membership subscription includes the choice to add any or all of our other 3 magazines, News and/or Archive and/or Aeromilitaria. Air-Britain also publishes 10-20 books per annum (around 70 titles in stock at any one time). Membership runs January – December each year, but new members have a choice of options periods to get their initial subscription started.

Air-Britain Aviation World is the quarterly 48-page house magazine containing not only news of Air-Britain activities, but also a wealth of features, often illustrated in colour, on many different aviation subjects, contemporary and historical, contributed by our members.

Air-Britain News is the world aviation news monthly, containing data on aircraft registrations worldwide and news of Airlines and Airliners, Business Jets, Local Airfield News, Civil and Military Air Show Reports, and International Military Aviation News. An average 160 pages of lavishly–illustrated information for the dedicated enthusiast.

Air-Britain Archive is the quarterly 48-page specialist journal of civil aviation history. Packed with the results of historical research by Air-Britain specialists into aircraft types, overseas registers and previously unpublished facts about the rich heritage of civil aviation. Up to 100 photographs per issue, some in colour.

Air-Britain Aeromilitaria is the quarterly 48-page unique source for meticulously researched details of military aviation history edited by the acclaimed authors of Air-Britain's military monographs featuring British, Commonwealth, European and U.S. Military aviation articles. Illustrated in colour and black & white.

Other Benefits
Additional to the above, members have exclusive access to the Air-Britain e-mail Information Exchange Service (ab-ix) where they can exchange information and solve each other's queries, and to an on-line UK airfield residents database. Other benefits include numerous Branches, use of the Specialists Information Service; Air-Britain trips; and access to black & white and colour photograph libraries. During the summer we also host our own popular FLY-IN. Each autumn, we host an Aircraft Recognition Contest.

Membership Subscription Rates – from £20 per annum.
Membership subscription rates start from as little as £20 per annum (2009), and this amount provides a copy of 'Air-Britain Aviation World' quarterly as well as all the other benefits covered above. Subscriptions to include any or all of our other three magazines vary between £25 and £62 per annum (slightly higher to overseas).

** *Join now for two years 2009-2010 and save £5.00 off the total***

Join on-line at www.air-britain.co.uk or, write to 'Air-Britain' at 1 Rose Cottages, 179 Penn Road, Hazlemere, High Wycombe, Bucks HP15 7NE, UK.
Alternatively telephone on 01394 450767 (+44 1394 450767 from outside UK) or e-mail: membenquiry@air-britain.co.uk and ask for a membership pack containing the full details of subscription rates, samples of our magazines and a book list.